ISBN 978-0-282-91002-0
PIBN 10872888

1 MONTH OF
FREE
READING

at
www.ForgottenBooks.com

---◆---

By purchasing this book you are
eligible for one month membership to
ForgottenBooks.com, giving you
unlimited access to our entire
collection of over 1,000,000 titles via
our web site and mobile apps.

To claim your free month visit:

www.forgottenbooks.com/free872888

WILLIAM A.BRADY,
Director –General·
WORLD -PICTURES
present

JUNE ELVIDGE
MONTAGU LOVE
in
"The Guardian"
Story by W.D.M.Ferguson
Directed by ARTHUR ASHLEY

Not a Special Price Picture
But
A SPECIAL *Fair-Priced Picture*
on the Dependable Program

The hit pictures of 1917 are being produced by Essanay. Any K. E. S. E. office. Are you getting them?

Geo. K. Spoor.

The One Best Bet of the Week

Harry Carey in "The Texas Sphinx"

HARRY CAREY'S millions of admirers will say that is some title for a Carey picture—because with all the dash and go that they find in his work, they know he is a master of the "quiet" method of getting his big stuff over on the screen. They'll enjoy every foot of this picture. It's great and thrilling, tense and absorbing, with a walloping

Harry Carey—"The Texas Sphinx"

punch at the end. There's a stage robbery and Harry is suspected. There's a pretty love story and for a time it seems that Harry is to lose out, but the punch climax comes with a satisfactory surprise that will bring the fans to the edges of their seats.

A MERRY L-KO

"Cactus and Kale" — Mile-a-Minute Comedy

OUT in the L-KO studios there's a big two-reeler made every week. There are a lot of people working, and the L-KO is some busy place. No comedy company in the country is equipped to the point of production that can equal the L-KO. That's why you can COUNT on the big two-reel L-KO every week as a humdinger. In "Cactus and Kale" there is about the swiftest action— brilliant comedy action—you've ever seen. As usual there are funny stunts and daring stunts, and pretty girls and screamingly funny situations and titles, too. Produced under the personal supervision of J. G. Blystone. The featured players are Walter Stephens, Gladys Varden, Bert Roach and Catherine Young.

The Kale

Mary Fuller Feature

Beautiful Star in "To the Highest Bidder"—Romantic Drama

MARY in this strong two-reel drama, falls heir to five thousand dollars, and leaves her home in the country and a faithful lover "to see life." She sees it with a fast crowd, and when her money is nearly gone she offers herself unconditionally to the highest bidder. The highest bid comes from an anonymous source, and while Mary is hesitating a chap offers to double it. Before Mary can decide she is handed a letter, a bid that causes her to say that all bids are off. Returning home she finds the country lover, and the fans find a climax too big to be told in words. A big picture that will go everywhere.

UNIVE Advance

Released Week of Sept. 10, Book Thru

UNIVERSAL FILM MFG. CO.,

"The Boulevard Speedhound"

EDDIE is a speedhound and takes Lee for a ride in a powerful racing car. They are followed to Eddie's

Lee Poses As Eddie's Wife

house by a cycle cop. Eddie's wife, Edith, is away, but to avoid arrest the cop is told that Mrs. Eddie's wife is sick and they have been for the doctor. The cop has to be shown, and so Lee dashes upstairs, puts on a nighty and gets into bed, where he poses as Eddie's wife. The cop leaves and Lee ducks, too. Outside he meets his best girl and sees the cop returning, still suspicious. The girl takes Lee's place and then Eddie's wife returns and finds the strange girl in her room. Lively, funny and clever, this Nestor will tickle them all.

WILLIAM FRANEY

"Short Skirts and Deep Water" Corking One-Reel Joker

BILL FRANEY and Gale Henry are re-united in this grouch assassinator, "Short

Bill Prefers Land Dangers

Skirts and Deep Water," and they will give your fans the ride of their lives. They are members of the Anti-Sin League, and Bill is sent to the beach to see that the girls wear skirts of proper length. Gale follows to see what he does, loses her own bathing skirt and is arrested, while Bill is marooned at high tide. It is a bang-up Joker— one continuous laugh from start to finish.

GALE HENRY

"Nearly a Queen," One-Reel Joker Has Melodramatic Plot

CAST up by the sea as a baby, Gale is brought up in a humble fisherman's cottage. She is engaged to Milton Sims, and the opening is full of big laughs. The cottage is visited by

"Queen" Gale and Her Prime Minister

a guy in a gorgeous uniform, who tells them that Gale is a lost princess, and takes her away with him in a boat. In the middle of the bay he ties her up in a bag and throws her overboard. She is rescued by Milt, captured again, tied in a shack which is set on fire. Then comes the punch, and it is as funny as it is surprising.

Helen Gibson in "The Perilous Leap"

Three Reel Gold Seal Offers Many Thrilling Situations and Much Exciting Action--Strong Story and Cast

HELEN GIBSON does stunts in this picture that will fairly take your breath away. How she does them and comes up smiling after, is a mystery that only Helen herself could solve. In this Gold Seal she is the daughter of a prosperous rancher on the Border, who is visited by some strangers, who ask permission to store some property in his barn. This is granted, when it is learned that there are smugglers in the neighborhood. The news comes from Helen's

A Flying Leap from Train to Bridge

sweetheart, Val Paul, a Secret Service operative. It develops that the stored goods is opium, and Val lays for the gang. He is bested in a tremendous fight, put aboard a freight train, and the gang think they have won. But they haven't counted on Helen, who, at a mad gallop, overtakes the train, jumps aboard from her horse, and after a perilous leap to and from a bridge and the fast train, rescues her lover. Book this thriller and please your fans.

Two-a-Week News Service

Predominant Popularity Due to Overwhelming Merit

HERE'S big news, Exhibitors! You can now book the Universal Animated Weekly from week to week. You won't be asked to sign up a long-time contract to be able to show all the world's great news events first on the screen in your town. This is a big move in your favor. It is a great opportunity. For fifteen straight weeks, and many, many times before that, the U. A. W. has scored a BIG scoop. It was the first and only News Weekly to show completely and exclusively "Pershing in France." These were the official French Government pictures, and were

Holland Ships in Hudson River

shown in leading Broadway theatres by the Animated the SAME DAY THE NEGATIVE WAS RECEIVED FROM FRANCE. That is typical of the progressive methods that are at your service. You can't get this service elsewhere. Write your nearest Universal Exchange for full particulars now. You need this class of service every week.

RSAL Notices

any Universal Exchange, or

CARL LAEMMLE, President
"The Largest Film Manufacturing Concern in the Universe"

1600 Broadway, New York

BETTER THAN EVER

Universal Screen Magazine Shows Fascinating Subjects

EVERY week sees a broadening in interest of the subjects shown on this fascinating one-reel feature. It is a veritable mine of information and entertainment. There are shown on the current release sea birds by the million on an inland lake; making butter on the farm; the most fascinating pictures of physical culture for babies, posed by a husky 18-months-old baby girl; making shrapnel and other ammunition, an unusual glimpse of war preparations in America; and the unique and exclusive Miracles in Mud, this week's subject being "Swat the Fly." A release that captures them all--young and old--and gets them on the dullest day.

Max Asher

"In the Clutches of Milk," a Clever Victor Stunt Comedy

SOME of the funniest stunts you ever saw are pulled in this one-reel Victor comedy in which Max Asher is a hotel keeper. Max has a chronic thirst, and so he draws a drink from the bath tub, from the gas jet, from his bootleg and various other queer places. He gets hold of a bottle of poison, and to save his life is ordered to drink milk. He is chased by an irate milkman through several hundred feet of the liveliest action you ever saw, trying all the time to drink from the milk bottle. Good fun.

Teaching Wireless to Women

Universal Current Events Shows World News First

YOUR patrons read many varied accounts of world happenings in the newspapers. They never knew just what did happen until they see the actual scene, just as it occurred, in UNIVERSAL CURRENT EVENTS—the news weekly that is showing EVERY WEEK the world events that are

Building Steel Ships, Pittsburgh
Universal Current Events

making HISTORY. It is to the movie patron the same as being there. There is nothing hidden from the camera. And Universal camera correspondents have privileges that are rarely accorded. The magnitude of the organization they represent; the fact that their work is shown to millions every week, gets them IN RIGHT wherever they go. If you aren't showing this and the Animated—this two-a-week news service—you are not getting the best to be had. Get it now.

Exhibitors-

You Can Book the Popular UNIVERSAL Twice-a-Week News Service WITHOUT A CONTRACT

Here's big news, Exhibitors! You can now book the Universal Animated Weekly from week to week. You won't be asked to sign up a long-time contract to be able to show all the world's great news events first on the screen in your town. This is your big opportunity. For fifteen straight weeks, and many, many times before that, the

Universal Animated Weekly

has scored BIG scoops. It was the first and only News Weekly to show completely and exclusively "Pershing in France." These were shown in leading Broadway theatres the SAME DAY THE NEGATIVE WAS RECEIVED FROM FRANCE. That is typical of the progressive methods that are at your service. You can't get it elsewhere.

Universal Current Events

Your patrons read different accounts of world happenings in the newspapers. They never know just what did happen until they see the actual scene, just as it occurred, in UNIVERSAL CURRENT EVENTS—the news weekly that is showing EVERY WEEK the world events that are making HISTORY. It is to the movie patron the same as being there. If you aren't showing this and the Animated—this two-a-week news service— you are not getting the best to be had. Get this service now thru any Universal Exchange.

It's Service Not Advertising that Makes these Two Incomparable Releases First on the Screen and First in Popularity...

"As Refreshing as an Ocean Breeze."

Butterfly Pictures present

BEN WILSON and NEVA GERBER

in a fascinating Comedy Drama:

"The Spindle of Life"

The Romance of "Mr. Sandman" and "Girl from the Sea."

Directed by George Cochrane

Book thru any Butterfly Exchange or from Universal Film Mfg Co-Carl Laemmle, President ~~~ 1600 Broadway   New York

greater
run
than
"War
Brides"

Wonderful
EMILY STEVENS

The Slacker

Wm. Christy Cabanne's master piece that thrilled the nation

NO

STANDARD PICTURES

WILLIAM FOX

PRESENTS
TO EXHIBITORS FOR OPEN BOOKING
AS AN INDIVIDUAL ATTRACTION
FOR RELEASE **NOW**

WILLIAM FARNUM

IN

THE CONQUEROR

A RED-BLOODED ACTOR IN A RED-BLOODED STORY

INDEFINITE ENGAGEMENT
AT THE
GLOBE THEATRE, N.Y.

SEE THE PICTURE AT YOUR
NEAREST FOX EXCHANGE AND
BOOK IT NOW

FOX INVARIABLE POLICY :-
YOU MUST SEE THIS PICTURE
BEFORE YOU CAN BOOK IT.

FOX FILM CORPORATION

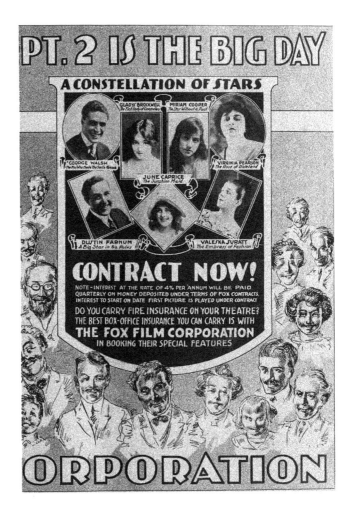

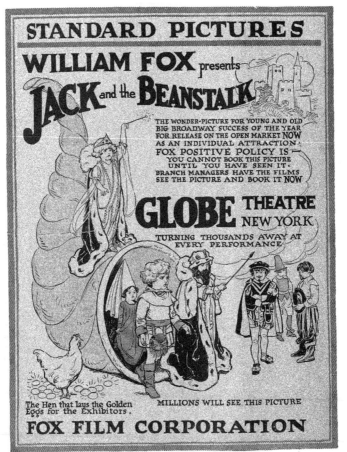

STANDARD PICTURES

WILLIAM FOX presents

JACK and the BEANSTALK

THE WONDER-PICTURE FOR YOUNG AND OLD
BIG BROADWAY SUCCESS OF THE YEAR
FOR RELEASE ON THE OPEN MARKET NOW
AS AN INDIVIDUAL ATTRACTION:
FOX POSITIVE POLICY IS —
YOU CANNOT BOOK THIS PICTURE
UNTIL YOU HAVE SEEN IT.
BRANCH MANAGERS HAVE THE FILMS
SEE THE PICTURE AND BOOK IT NOW

GLOBE THEATRE
NEW YORK

TURNING THOUSANDS AWAY AT
EVERY PERFORMANCE

The Hen that lays the Golden
Eggs for the Exhibitors.

MILLIONS WILL SEE THIS PICTURE

FOX FILM CORPORATION

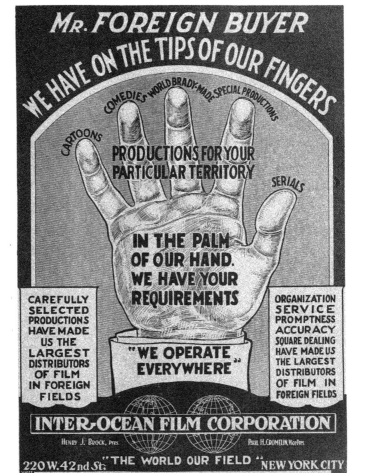

8 Big Star Features For September

Beginning September 3rd, the Mutual Film Corporation will offer Exhibitors *Two New Features—"BIG STARS ONLY"—EVERY WEEK.* 8 Big Star Productions will be released each month. Big productions in five and six reels, featuring famous stars, directed by America's leading directors. Such stars as Mary Miles Minter, Ann Murdock, Gail Kane, Olive Tell, Marjorie Rambeau, Julia Sanderson, William Russell, Margarita Fischer, Jackie Saunders, Juliette Day, William Gillette, Nance O'Neil, Edna Goodrich, Helen Holmes and Charlie Chaplin. Other stars will be announced soon.

Here Is the Mutual's September Release Schedule:

Week of Sept. 3rd
MARY MILES MINTER in "Charity Castle"
EDNA GOODRICH in "Reputation"

Week of Sept. 10th
GAIL KANE in "The Specter of Suspicion"
ANN MURDOCK in "Outcast"

Week of Sept. 17th
JULIETTE DAY in "The Rainbow Girl"
MARGARITA FISCHER in "The Girl Who Couldn't Grow Up"

Week of Sept. 24th
WILLIAM RUSSELL in "Sands of Sacrifice"
JULIA SANDERSON in "The Runaway"

Book Mutual Pictures on a service contract of one to seven days each week, thus providing a change of five to ten reels daily, including such featured stars as Mary Miles Minter, Charlie Chaplin, the Charles Frohman Successes in Motion Pictures and all other big subjects. Mutual Pictures may also be booked in series of stars, on open booking, or exhibitors can arrange for two or more Mutual Pictures— "BIG STARS ONLY"—each week regularly.

Get in touch with your nearest Mutual Exchange at once for futher details of New Fall Policy

MUTUAL FILM CORPORATION
JOHN R. FREULER, President
Exchanges Everywhere

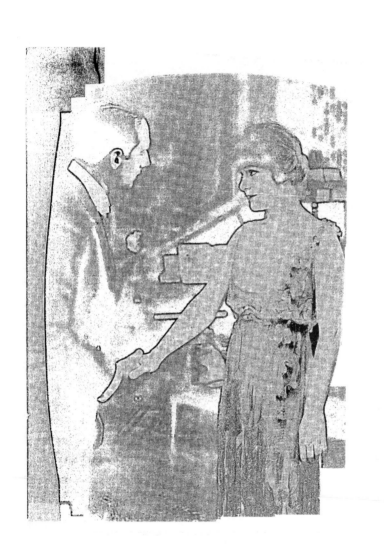

Very Sincerely Yours,
—, with kind personal
Manager Peoples Amusement Co.

Letters Like This
Prove The Value of
MUTUAL PICTURES
"Big Stars Only"

Letters like this from influential
exhibitors indicate clearly the class of high
grade attractions available at Mutual Exchanges.
Boost the receipts of YOUR box-office by arranging to present
Mutual Pictures—"Big Stars Only"—with such favorites as:

MARY MILES MINTER	ANN MURDOCK
JULIA SANDERSON	GAIL KANE
EDNA GOODRICH	JULIETTE DAY
CHARLIE CHAPLIN	JACKIE SAUNDERS
WILLIAM RUSSELL	WILLIAM GILLETTE
OLIVE TELL	HELEN HOLMES
MARGARITA FISCHER	MARJORIE RAMBEAU

NANCE O'NEIL

Wire, write or call at your nearest Mutual Exchange for full details regarding
Mutual's New Fall Policy—Two Mutual Pictures—*"Big Stars Only"*—EachWeek.

MUTUAL FILM CORPORATION
JOHN R. FREULER, *President*
Exchanges Everywhere

CUB　　　　　　　　　　　　　　　　　**CUB**

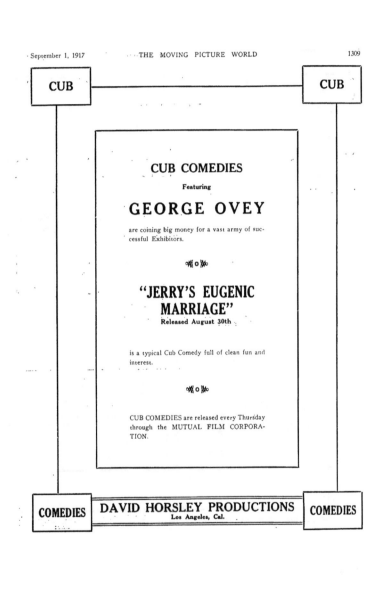

CUB COMEDIES

Featuring

·GEORGE OVEY

are coining big money for a vast army of successful Exhibitors.

"JERRY'S EUGENIC MARRIAGE"
Released August 30th

is a typical Cub Comedy full of clean fun and
interest.

CUB COMEDIES are released every Thursday
through the MUTUAL FILM CORPORA-
TION.

COMEDIES　**DAVID HORSLEY PRODUCTIONS**　**COMEDIES**
Los Angeles, Cal.

But, at this moment, America will unconsciously say, "Here is one of the greatest motion pictures we have ever seen."

The story has to do with GOLD—the fight for wealth —the hunger for that power which comes through great possessions. it has to do with that latent appetite which resides in every human breast for MONEY.

For the

STATE RIGHTS

Surely, no elemental quality is so dominant in modern society, and this powerful story of Aaron Hoffman's, built on this theme, touches "home" in every home.

The "girl with the dimple" has again proven herself to· possess superior dramatic qualifications, and there is no actress on the screen to-day who can point to a single performance greater than this one of Miss Walker's.

Ogden Pictures Corporation
Studios and Laboratories, Ogden, Utah
Address All Communications to
Executive Offices
729 7th Avenue, New York, N. Y.

WALKER
the Screen" in

the AGES"

n Hoffman

n ～ ～ ～ *Directed by Harry Revier.*

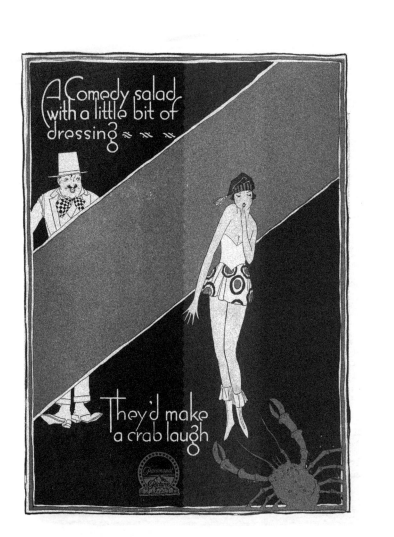

FIRST  SERIAL

will be distinguished
by the quality
that has made PARAMOUNT PICTURES *supreme*

Exhibitors know
the significance of that statement

READY IN OCTOBER

Paramount Pictures Corporation
FOUR EIGHTY-FIVE FIFTH AVENUE, at FORTY-FIRST STREET
NEW YORK
Controlled by FAMOUS PLAYERS-LASKY CORPORATION
ADOLPH ZUKOR, Pres.   JESSE L. LASKY, Vice-Pres.   CECIL B. DEMILLE, Director General

FIRST  SERIAL

BEHIND THE FIRST SERIAL

-will be put the same genius, ability and keen appreciation of exhibitors' needs as have marked all PARAMOUNT productions in the past. *Ready in* OCTOBER.

Paramount Pictures Corporation

FOUR EIGHTY-FIVE FIFTH AVENUE, *at* FORTY-FIRST STREET
NEW YORK

Controlled by FAMOUS PLAYERS-LASKY CORPORATION
ADOLPH ZUKOR, *Pres.*   JESSE L. LASKY, *Vice-Pres.*   CECIL B. DEMILLE, *Director General*

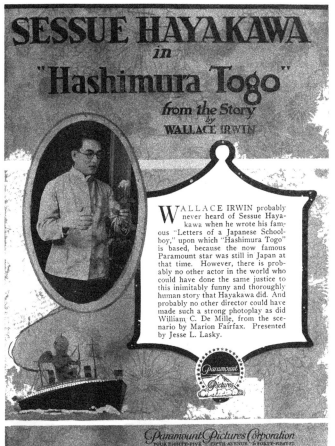

WALLACE IRWIN probably
never heard of Sessue Hayakawa when he wrote his famous "Letters of a Japanese School-
boy," upon which "Hashimura Togo"
is based, because the now famous
Paramount star was still in Japan at
that time. However, there is probably no other actor in the world who
could have done the same justice to
this inimitably funny and thoroughly
human story that Hayakawa did. And
probably no other director could have
made such a strong photoplay as did
William C. De Mille, from the scenario by Marion Fairfax. Presented
by Jesse L. Lasky.

VIVIAN MARTIN in **"Little Miss Optimist"**

AN excellent story for Vivian Martin—which with her winsomeness and personal charm—a certain success.

The adventures of a poor mountain girl who wants something better and gets it in spite of all obstacles.

You won't know what the finish is until the fade-out.

Presented by Oliver Morosco
Scenario by Gardner Hunting
Directed by Robert Thornby

A Paramount Picture

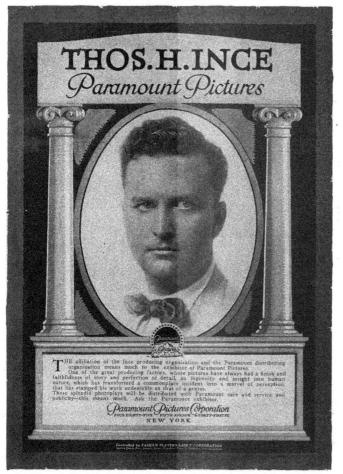

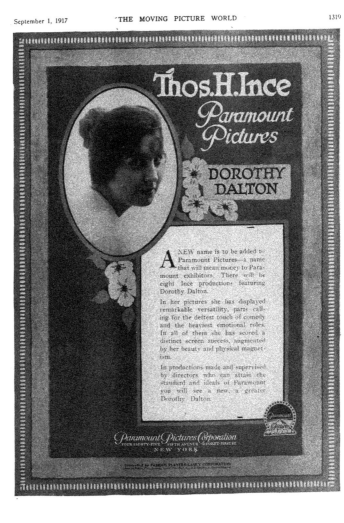

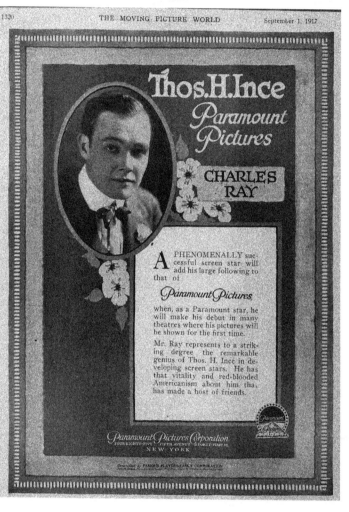

Thos. H. Ince

Paramount Pictures

CHARLES RAY

A PHENOMENALLY successful screen star will add his large following to that of

Paramount Pictures

when, as a Paramount star, he will make his debut in many theatres where his pictures will be shown for the first time.

Mr. Ray represents to a striking degree the remarkable genius of Thos. H. Ince in developing screen stars. He has that vitality and red-blooded Americanism about him that has made a host of friends.

Paramount Pictures Corporation
FOUR EIGHTY-FIVE   FIFTH AVENUE   AT FORTY-FIRST ST.
NEW YORK

Controlled by FAMOUS PLAYERS-LASKY CORPORATION

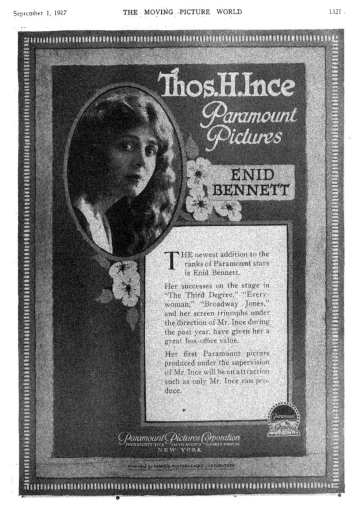

THE PROFIT-WINNERS
FOR THE WEEK OF AUGUST 26th

The Star of "THE SAWDUST RING"

Bessie Love

in

"WEE LADY BETTY"

SHE KNEW THE GHOST THAT
HAUNTED THE ARMOR IN
HER IRISH CASTLE OF KILCRONY

It pays to be swindled
by Crooks like these—

"GRAFTERS"

with
Anna Lehr
and
Jack Devereaux

Produced under the
supervision of
ALLAN DWAN

A Few of the coming Triangle
your theatre and

Julian Johnson says in the Photoplay
Magazine,"She's the screen's most
credible vampire"

Louise Glaum
in
"IDOLATERS"

This play will smash even the
record of "The Wolf Woman"—
one of the greatest money-makers
ever produced.

RELEASED SEPTEMBER 9

"The girl with the eyes that speak"

Bessie Love
in
"POLLY ANN"

She will bring happiness to your
patrons and prosperity to you.

RELEASED SEPTEMBER 9

roductions that will sell out
ve *you* the *profits*.

'RE a busy man, like all Exhibitors. Are you making the common mistake of being too busy—of keeping your nose too near the grindstone—of paying too close attention to petty details?

This cuts off your foresight and blinds you to the importance of new ideas which may have a direct and lasting influence on your business—progressive ideas of great value which you should study and apply.

Have you been too busy to send for the Paralta Plan book? If you have, it's time for you to look up and see what's going on in the world. Don't let anything relating to your business get by you without knowing all about it. If you are wise you will consider the Paralta Plan.

It will cost you nothing. It will put money in your pocket. Send for the book and read it. It will take but half an hour and you will progress five years.

"ASK ANY TRIANGLE EXCHANGE."

CARL ANDERSON, President   ROBERT T. KANE, Vice-Prest.
HERMAN FICHTENBERG, Chairman Directors   HERMAN KATZ, Treas.
NAT. I. BROWN; Secretary and Gen'l Manager.

729 SEVENTH AVENUE
NEW YORK CITY -

The *Only Official* Motion Pictures

OF

The Great Russian Revolution

AND

Behind the Battle Line in Russia

Shown the Entire Week of August 19-26, at

RIALTO THEATER

NEW YORK

STATE RIGHT BUYERS

are invited to this presentation all week

Presented by

The Skobeleff Committee

For the Relief of Russian
Wounded and Disabled Soldiers

UNDER THE AUSPICES OF

The Provisional Russian Government

The proceeds of these pictures to be donated to the relief of wounded Russian soldiers and prisoners of war.

The Skobeleff Committee

IVAN D. DORED
Special Envoy

**Imperial Hotel
New York City**

THE RIALTO
"The Temple of the Motion Picture"
TIMES SQUARE
NEW YORK

Aug. 13, 1917.

The Skobeleff Committee,
Imperial Hotel,
Broadway & 31st St.,
Manhattan.

Gentlemen :-

My opinion as to the
importance and merit of your pictures of
The Revolution in Russia and Scenes at
the Russian Battle-Front is best demonstrated
by the fact that I have set aside my entire
regular programme for the week of Aug. 19
in order to give them the sort of presentation they deserve.

Yours Very Truly

Managing Director.

Goldwyn Pictures

Start With Goldwyn at the Beginning

WHEN the eyes of the nation are on this new organization's splendid productions, when artists and critics everywhere are saying: "Here are the most beautiful pictures we have ever seen."

When billboard campaigns and skilled exploitation have made American audiences eager to come into your theatres. In other words, when the stage is all set for *an immediate profit for your box-office.*

This is the time for every exhibitor to sign a Goldwyn Pictures contract. You benefit by everything Goldwyn has done for its productions and its stars. You have to do less yourself—if you sign now—than for any other productions ever made.

Goldwyn Pictures are letter-perfect, scenically beautiful and dramatically powerful. And in the words of a score of great critics they are "better than Goldwyn ever promised they would be."

Advisory Board:
SAMUEL GOLDFISH
Chairman
EDGAR SELWYN
IRVIN S. COBB
ARTHUR HOPKINS
MARGARET MAYO
ROI COOPER MEGRUE
ARCHIBALD SELWYN
CROSBY GAIGE
PORTER EMERSON BROWNE

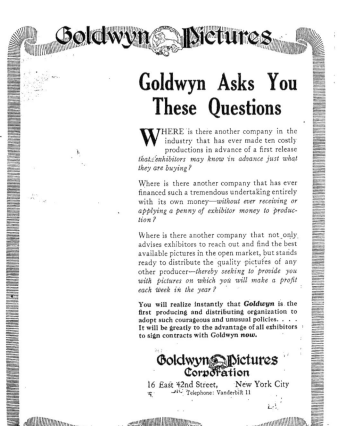

Goldwyn Pictures

Goldwyn
presents

Mae Marsh
in

Polly of the Circus

A tremendous photo-spectacle
from the celebrated play
by Margaret Mayo

"A Remarkable Production of Greater Beauty,
More Charm and Pathos Than Any Film Achievement
of This Generation " — Victor Watson, New York American

In Answering Advertisements, Please Mention the MOVING PICTURE WORLD.

Goldwyn Pictures

=== Goldwyn ===
presents

Madge Kennedy
in

Baby Mine

From The World-Famed
Farce Comedy

by Margaret Mayo

Proclaimed By The Pittsburg Press as "The
Picture That Goes Down In Film History as
The Greatest Comedy Ever Screened"

Dressler Producing
Corporation
presents

Marie
Dressler
in

The
Scrublady

First of Eight Laugh-
making Comedies
Starring one of the
Favorite Comediennes
of the American Stage

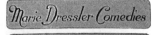

Exhibitors Everywhere Should Book These
Splendid Comedies, Released Exclusively Through

Goldwyn Distributing Corporation

Goldwyn

announces
a powerfull and vital

Rex Beach
Picture

From the most popular
American author's tremendous
novel

The
Auction
Block

"The greatest Rex Beach
Picture ever produced"

REX BEACH PICTURES

This and All Future Rex Beach Productions
To Be Released Exclusively Through
Goldwyn Distributing Corporation

Pathé

MOLLIE
KING
and
CREIGHTON HALE
are popular with
your patrons. They
are real box-office
attractions

Pathé

MOLLIE KING
and
CREIGHTON HALE
are popular with your patrons. They are real box-office attractions

Pathé

Out of 26 theatres now open in Omaha 15 are showing

THE FATAL RING
with
PEARL WHITE

¶ Every theatre showing this serial reports good business despite the hot weather. Miss White in a Pathe serial again proves to be a life saver in the "off season."

¶ The man who hasn't tried Pathé serials and who is waiting for the fall season in order to get a profit owes it to himself to book "The Fatal Ring." The business he will get will surprise him.

A big box office star in a big box office serial - Book "The Fatal Ring."

Produced by Astra
Directed by Geo. B. Seitz

Written by Fred Jackson
Scenarios by B. Millhauser

In Answering Advertisements, Please Mention the MOVING PICTURE WORLD.

In Answering Advertisements, Please Mention the MOVING PICTURE WORLD.

But One Other·
has ever Scored such

As the First and Only Official Italian War Pictures

The ITALIAN

Here is the Proof

Sworn box office statement of "The Italian Battlefront,"
Forty-fourth Street Theatre, New York. Two performances
daily. Prices, 25c. to $2.00. Seating capacity, 1,430.
Average daily temperature, 76°:

Wednesday, August 8:—	
(Opening Night)	$839.25
Thursday, August 9:—	
Matinee	783.75
Night	1,002.25
Friday, August 10:—	
Matinee	639.75
Night	888.75
Saturday, August 11:—	
Matinee	773.75
Night	937.00
Sunday, August 12:—	
Matinee	794.00
Night	1,010.25
Monday, August 13:—	
Matinee	735.25
Night	880.50
Tuesday, August 14:—	
Matinee	601.50
Night	896.00
Total for Week	**$10,782.00**

Pictures which Challenge the Box-Office

FOR STATES
THE FORT PITT
OF PITT
JOS. M. GAITES, Gen. Mgr., New
TELEPHONE,

Moving Picture Sweeping Success...
BATTLE FRONT"

Here is the Reason

These are the kind of the so-called "war pictures" for which the public—and the trade—have been seeking.

Which means that they are "different"—

Different, in that heroism is supplanted for horror. Romance, beauty, drama, art, action, suspense take the place of a deadly round of deadliness.

In other words, these art records of the Italian battlefront contain that quality so essential to entertainment and successful screen presentations:

A GREAT, HUMAN DRAMATIC, NOTE—

Plus—

The most marvelous natural scenery that has ever been shown in any picture.

It is because of this that up to the date of the release of this advertisement, standing room has been at a premium in every theatre at which these pictures have been presented, and scalpers have been reaping a harvest.

Brandon Studio

of every Representative Exhibitor in America

RIGHTS, Address

CORPORATION
SBURGH
York Offices, 19th Floor, Times Bldg.
BRYANT 3282.

GENERAL FILM COMPANY,

GEORGE ADE

NEW FABLES IN SLANG

photoplays written by America's most
famous humorist exclusively for Essanay

FIT FOR EVERY PROGRAM

One every week beginning Sept. 1

"The Fable of the Twelve-Cylinder Speed of the Leisure Class"

Screen time 25 minutes

GEORGE K. SPOOR, PRESIDENT

TRADEMARK
Reg. U. S. Pat. 1907

1333 Argyle St., Chicago

TRADEMARK
Reg. U. S. Pat. 1907

Distributed exclusively by General Film Company

GENERAL FILM COMPANY

A drama of picturesque fortunes--- of lurking echoes from the past--- of a young, wistful heart and the soul of chivalry--- and of unconscious love triumphant.

FALCON
FEATURES

Such a drama is

The Martinache Marriage

featuring

MARGARET LANDIS
and Philo McCullough

a Four-Part Production of
the Story by

Beatrix Demarest Lloyd

Supervised by
H. M. & E. D. Horkheimer

Book It Now

" The Martinache Marriage "
Second of the
FALCON FEATURES
following
" The Mainspring "
by Louis Joseph Vance

Distributed Exclusively by General Film Company

GENERAL FILM COMPANY,

The 4-Reel "O. Henry ' Pictures are Here!!!

Book no
other Film
until you
Reserve
for your
Audiences
these
Gilt-edged
VALUES!

From photo; Courtesy Doubleday, Page & Co.

Beginning
Sept. 1 with that
Charming Classic

**"THE DEFEAT OF
THE CITY"**

A drama of exquisite suspense, a patrician wife, and a
hero husband with blessed
old home ties.

MORE GOOD NEWS—The two-reel O. Henry
releases continue, alternating with the four-reel
subjects. First will be a "Jeff Peters" story—"The
Atavism of John Tom Little Bear."

BROADWAY STAR FEATURES

Distributed Exclusively by General Film Company

Entered at the General Post Office, New York City, as Second Class Matter

Founded by J. P. CHALMERS in 1907.

Published Weekly by the

CHALMERS PUBLISHING COMPANY

17 MADISON AVENUE, NEW YORK CITY

(Telephone, 3510-3511 Madison Square)

J. P. Chalmers, Sr.................................President
J. F. Chalmers.............................Vice-President
E. J. Chalmers..................Secretary and Treasurer
John Wylie..................................General Manager

The office of the company is the address of the officers.

CHICAGO OFFICE—Suite 917-919 Schiller Building, 64 West Randolph St., Chicago, Ill. Telephone, Central 5099.

PACIFIC COAST OFFICE—610-611 Wright and Callender Building, Los Angeles, Cal. Telephone, Broadway 4640.

SUBSCRIPTION RATES.

United States, Cuba, Mexico, Hawaii, Porto
  Rico and Philippine Islands...............$3.00 per year
Canada .... 3.50 per year
Foreign Countries (Postpaid)................. 4.00 per year

Changes of address should give both old and new addresses in full and be clearly written. Two weeks' time should be allowed for change.

ADVERTISING RATES.

CLASSIFIED ADVERTISING—One dollar for twenty words or less; over twenty words, five cents per word.
DISPLAY ADVERTISING RATES made known on application.

NOTE—Address all correspondence, remittances and subscriptions to MOVING PICTURE WORLD, P. O. Box 226, Madison Square Station, New York, and not to individuals.

"CINE-MUNDIAL," the monthly Spanish edition of the Moving Picture World, is published at 17 Madison Ave. by the Chalmers Publishing Company. It reaches the South American and Spanish-speaking market. Yearly subscription, $1.50. Advertising rates on application.

(The INDEX to this issue is on page 1436.)

Saturday, September 1, 1917

Facts and Comments

THE exhibitor with a touch of advertising is a curious minded man. His interest in his neighbors and in life is so fresh that he is said to be original, which merely means that his ideas and actions are not faked. He isn't half-hearted nor half alive, but is genuinely there. He doesn't "get there," but is there all the time. The kernel in the nut is his desire to be friendly. This is the real difference between exhibitors—one can't help being friendly because it is in him naturally; the other wants to be a success, perhaps, but he wants it for himself. He merely tries to be friendly. To the latter success is quite possible, but hardly in the amusement business. The other—well, the people like to talk about

him and the more freshly curious his mind is the more they delight to tell each other about him. There's exhibitor Harry Pomeroy of the Photodrome in Toronto. He got the small boys hunting through the long grass for snakes for him. We don't know why he wanted them. But he made us write this and that's the personal advertising touch of genius that pays in the exhibiting of pictures.

* * *

THERE have been from time to time suggestions that the number of denominations of our smaller coins be increased. Cashiers in our picture theaters would have their work greatly simplified by the introduction of a 15-cent piece, while we have often believed that a 20-cent piece would be used in greater number than our old standby, the quarter. Possibly there are banking and other reasons why it might be inadvisable to have too many different small coins, but we would welcome consideration of the question by the powers that be and believe an addition or two would facilitate the transaction of business in many lines outside the moving picture theaters. The daily change passing the little ticket window of our theaters is of such volume that if the 6-cent and 11-cent admissions talked of a short time ago had become effective the Government would have been justified in striking new coins for those exact amounts.

* * *

THE greatly increased demand for good, serviceable programs at reasonable prices for family group and children's matinees, church, school and similar entertainment is emphasizing the need of a Central Bureau or Exchange or Film Library in all the larger centers where such programs may be secured. The present exchange system of handling moving picture productions is ignoring altogether this very important end of the business and the film industry will have to take cognizance of this increasing demand sooner or later if it is to be taken full advantage of. When one requires a book on any subject whatever nowadays they naturally go to the library. They do not have to find out who published the book and go to the publisher nor do they have to visit a half dozen different booksellers before they secure the particular book they may desire. Why not so with film?

* * *

INDICATIONS continue to multiply justifying the belief that the whole industry will enjoy a season of excellent business during the coming fall and winter. Business in general is booming, good wages are being paid over the whole country and theaters every state in the Union. The anxiety and worry and increased strain under which the people are at present laboring make short periods of respite and entertainment more imperative than ever and nothing that we know of at present quite equals the moving picture in providing these short and necessarily frequent moments of relaxation.

* * *

BE SURE you are right, then go ahead, is an old motto and a mighty good one in business. Any enterprise that is begun on a wrong foundation starts with a handicap that will usually prove, sooner or later, insurmountable. When, to a faulty foundation, is added improper business methods, the situation becomes correspondingly worse. Submission to "big stick" methods in the slightest degree will result in a greater use of the big stick.

Presentation, Not Exhibition ▣ ▣ ▣ ▣ By Louis Reeves Harrison

THERE is no great difference between the two words in ordinary use. Exhibition is probably more general, sometimes expressing a section of the other, and presentation has come to be regarded as more ceremonious, characterized by more elaborate form. Such is the distinction here intended. The manager of the Rialto, S. L. Rothapfel, for instance, has made the showing of moving pictures very imposing and impressive. Finding the Rialto packed with an enthusiastic audience at a very early hour in the afternoon, I made some inquiries and learned that five representations were being given daily.

The success of an exhibitor, quite as well as that of a producer or an actor, is something to be studied as an example and even utilized as one, provided it is due to some definite policy carried out consistently, or to exceptional taste and full appreciation of what an audience needs, or, above all, to a sincere desire to make moving pictures a big factor in our daily lives. A careful study of the effects which have led to Rialto popularity brought to light an almost unsuspected artistry in offering moving pictures before a mixed audience for acceptance.

The Rothapfel idea seems to be to make a whole impression of the visual kind, with a delightful appeal to the ear besides, the latter not intrusive while a picture is being shown, but appropriate and harmonious. Then aside from this charm, the music alone is decidedly worth while, a delight in itself, and it affords in sole performance a refreshing relief from possible eye strain. The eye is also given no decorative distraction. The theater interior is one of very dignified beauty. It might not even attract attention because of its noble simplicity of design.

Here we have a form of exhibition so elevated that it can consistently be called "presentation." It starts with a house design full of meaning, one of its subtlest charms. Good taste is pleased, and common taste, very rarely pure, is not offended. There is nothing incongruous, nothing inappropriate, though the ordinary exhibition room may confound and jar the ears in many ways, wrong in shape, wrong in color, wrong in proportion, so many points of unconscious irritation for the audience. After visiting a harmonious theater one can sincerely say, "I am very pleased to have met you, and I hope to have the pleasure of calling again." Such is the effect of artistic design.

It is often next to impossible for the really ambitious exhibitor to get the right sort of house, so much depends on opportunity, and his opportunity may be limited by the inexorable laws of supply and demand, but he can sometimes compensate by making his patrons comfortable, placing them in chairs meant to give the spectators a sense of ease while they are his guests.

An interesting experiment would be that of having each audience vote on the question of time versus comfort. "Would you prefer a two-hour performance in easier chairs, or three hours in those you are using?" This new art is violating many old conventions, sweeping time-honored traditions into the dust heap—we may yet provide chairs for the spectator which he can call his own, which do not compel him to dig his elbows in his sides to keep them from jabbing his neighbor's, with people directly in front of him far enough apart for him to see the whole screen between their heads, instead of twisting himself with cat-like contortions to get a glimpse of the pictured story.

Before the average exhibitor can go to any large ex-

pense in such matters as house beauty and comfort, he may feel that he should be playing on velvet in the game. The quality of his projection, dealt with elsewhere in the MOVING PICTURE WORLD, becomes highly important. But, after he has done all in his power to be fair with his patrons, his thoughts turn to how he can set the tide of victory flowing in his favor. The ordinary attendance may pay expenses with a dangerously narrow profit besides—by what magic can he find out the secret of filling his house to overflowing? How can he lay hands on the big money?

The "flash" has been tried. It works in some places, especially in large city locations, where new people are constantly passing. The billboard gets them in—sometimes it keep them out—but the neighborhood house can only be built up on steady patronage, and that means steady, high quality of performance. Let us suppose that an ambitious exhibitor, anxious to reach a state of high-class presentation, willing to take a chance and in dead earnest, is getting 20 per cent. of the possible patronage in his neighborhood. How can he get a line on the other 80 per cent. of them?

Get away from biased viewpoint. Certain beaming women will exclaim "How cute!" every time a baby is shown on the screen; even little animals may temporarily stir their maternal instincts. But the constant introduction of babies and little animals would soon empty the house. Little Jimmie wants an exciting chase, in which the heroine arrives at the very last minute to save the hero from the villain's clutches. But Little Jimmie would empty the house of all but his own kind. The man who selects his own program must broaden the scope of his selective taste until he can rise to a point of discriminating among all screen stories.

Have a definite policy and carry it out consistently, try to learn what an audience needs in order to arrive at that policy. What are you looking for when you turn over the leaves of a story magazine? Something new? Something refreshing? Do you prefer fresh fruit to dried apples? The evaporated kind may do for the people who are attending your theater—how about those who are not? Your surplus profits must come from them. Demand at least some originality. Let us suppose you find a good magazine story with a definite aim which bears on subjects uppermost in the minds of people today. To every friend you meet you are going to say, "You ought to read so and so—it is great."

Your patrons ought to leave your theater as so many publicity agents, speaking to all their friends of the consistently fine presentation you are making of stories entirely new and of a kind which leaves a strong after impression. If a story starts out to show where tenderness, sentiment and consideration may be better than harsh justice, the introduction of extraneous matter is wrong, so much padding and destroys both the pleasurable illusion and the strength of impression to be made. The moment a story is no longer consistent it becomes self-destructive. The people may enjoy a few scenes but the whole effect is boredom.

To attain presentation means an effort on your part to make moving pictures a big factor in our lives. Your audience goes to the theater in a receptive mood, very much as a woman goes shopping—she is willing to buy something good. It is for you to supply the vision. People are there to be impressed. It is for you to make the impression. It is not a case of this or that actor or director, but of a great, big composite artistry in all the leading factors of production.

Summer Musings 🎬 🎬 🎬 🎬 🎬 🎬 🎬 🎬 🎬 🎬 🎬 By Sam Spedon

THIS is our vacation time and we are not supposed to be bothering our heads about anything but doing the "dolce far niente" act at some summer resort with our wife, to show the rest of the guests that we are the real things, even if we don't own an automobile. No use, you can't teach an old dog new tricks. We stood it for three days, then we had to get back on the job among the reel people before we got too lazy to work at all. We don't have to write this and you don't have to read it. You may find it different and it may give you something to think about and help relieve your minds.

Green Fields of Virginia and Canada.

We are going to the convention to be held at Ocean View, Norfolk, Va., the latter part of this month by the Exhibitors of the Virginias, Carolinas, District of Columbia and adjacent territory. We are looking forward to meeting our old friends in that section; they are arranging for a real business session of much interest. Jake Wells, president of the American Exhibitors' Association, will be there. H. B, Varner of Charlctte, N. C.; Percy Wells of Wilmington, N. C.; Harry Crandall of Washington, D. C., and we are informed Lee Ochs, president of the National Exhibitors' Association, will be there; C. C. Pettijohn, general manager of the A. E. A., is expected. We ought to hear a whole lot of worth while news and get a big ear full. Besides it will give us another chance of sizing up the Southern situation, which we consider one of the most prolific on the motion picture map. Nothing like getting a broad view of things outside the confines of our little six by eight. September 9 and 10 we will jump to St. Johns, New Brunswick, to mix with the exhibitors of the Maritime provinces of Canada. They tell us there is a live "bunch" up there and we want to get better acquainted with them. They are keen for organization and we may learn a whole lot that is new touching upon a territory the industry should cultivate.

Never Too Old to Learn.

The other day we called a film man's attention to an article on motion pictures, published in one of the national magazines. He said: "I know. It's an old story." We agree with him. Motion pictures grow stale to us and so do we. That's the reason we lose business keenness and do not keep up with the procession. The heart and the mind must ever keep young in this business. It presents new phases every day, it changes over night. If we are alert we can always learn something new from the other fellow's experience. We should not give up the student habit; listen, read and learn all the time. It is a mistake to conclude we know it all. Just as soon as we do we lag backward. The world doesn't stand still; neither does the film business. When we get too old and wise to learn it is time to take off our shoes, turn ourselves loose and await the end.

Identity.

When an individual player becomes identified with any make of pictures and becomes recognized as part of them it is an assurance of their character and it is mighty hard to make people believe differently. As soon as those pictures lose the personnel of their players they lose in popularity. We believe the picture should be the thing. "The play's the thing" applied to the stage as the special medium of entertainment, but just the same the play is considered better if it has the popular and capable actors to put it over and properly interpret it.

When a public individual loses his identity in the public eye he is soon forgotten and the asset for which he was valued is lost. It would have been a wise move on the part of some producing companies who have lost much of their indentity to have followed the co-operative method by making those who contributed to their prosperity sharers in it instead of believing they themselves were the alpha and omega of the whole business. This could have been done for a year or term of years instead of considering them mere employees. The more progressive producers recognize that they must retain personnel and identity as that which counts for success.

There are some newcomers into the producing of motion pictures who had a false idea that they could conduct it as they would manufacturing, and some old timers believed it, gradually they learned their mistake and they are now willing to leave it to those who know and from present indications the man who knows how isn't looking for a job.

No Such an Animal as Monopoly

By Sam Spedon.

AT the present time all sorts of questions and rumors are ripe about an amalgamation of star feature productions. Will it lead to monopoly of all that is worth showing and seeing? Will it develop into a merger of producers and exhibitors who will control all the best theaters? Will the best star features be vested in one exchange?

A Dream.

Many a thinking man has dreamed of such an amalgamation and looked forward to its realization. It has never come to pass, and it is the belief of many it never will. As we see it, concentration of productions does not necessarily mean monopoly. It means co-operation. Each star or unit of stars produces its own pictures at its own expense and has a monetary interest and guarantee in the profits of its products leased through one distributing source. In this way each star being a partner or part of the whole receives his profit from the success of his own products and the exchange handles them just as a department store handles different products on consignment. Nor does concentration necessarily mean that any one exchange can secure and hold everything of the best no matter how much it might desire it. The co-operative system does not destroy the individual identity of each unit, who will naturally look out for its own interests. Therefore if results or profits from the amalgamation do not measure up to its expectations that unit will withdraw from the amalgamation and release through some other channel.

Many to Select From.

There are not less than ten producing companies provided with stars of first magnitude well equipped to supply the varied demands for high grade pictures and there always will be a plenty to furnish all the other grades. It is well to remember that no matter how long or short a picture may be or who the players may be, no picture will be acceptable to the public and survive unless it meets a certain standard of perfection and tells a story worth while picturizing.

Nothing Less Than Good.

We may have good, better and best pictures, valued accordingly, but nothing less than good will satisfy. Therefore there is no need of apprehending a monopoly of production by one concern. We will always find a supply equal to the demand and our circumstances. Anything less than good means failure.

Control of Theaters.

It may be that the key-note of organization was struck by an exhibitors' circuit in protecting the exhibitors against the invasion of the theater field by large moneyed interests, a report of which was circulated two or three years ago when such an invasion was likened to the United Cigar Store intersts. There always will be in human affairs an effort for control, hence the cause and need for union or organization in the regulation of them.

N. A. M. P. I. By-Laws

THE recent first Members' Annual Meeting of the National Association of the Motion Picture Industry shed some light on the by-laws governing the organization that would seem to call for careful and immediate consideration if the Association is intended to be representative of the whole industry and all branches of it impartially. It is not an easy task to draft a set of by-laws that will meet all the requirements of such an organization and the defects that developed in the present by-laws were doubtless unforeseen. It was also propitious that these defects should be brought into the limelight thus early in the life of the Association, as this makes possible an early correction, which, in turn, will result in unhampered development of this very necessary trade organization.

Undoubtedly the gravest error uncovered in the by-laws in the short discussion at the annual meeting was the limiting of membership for exhibitors to Class Two, or rather making membership in this Class contingent to or dependent on membership in another and outside organization. Class Two limits membership in the N. A. M. P. I. to exhibitors who are members of the Motion Picture Exhibitors' League of America. It was further developed in the discussion that no further provision was made for membership of exhibitors except through Class Five, which already includes publishers, authors, actors, directors, agencies and all others not included in the first four classes.

Producers and importers are admitted as a class, not as a separate organization and altogether independent of any other affiliation, and the same is true of the manufacturers and dealers in equipment in Class Three and distributors of motion pictures in Class Four. Exhibitors are by far the most numerous of any class or group in the industry and this fact was evidently in mind when Class Two was given double the representation of any of the other classes on the Board of Directors. Why then should exhibitor representation in the N. A. M. P. I. be limited to exhibitors only who are members of another organization?

The president of the N. A. M. P. I. is making strenuous and laudable efforts to keep petty politics out of the deliberations of his Association. All unwittingly or otherwise, however, the Association is hereby saddled with a fundamental bit of trouble making—a discriminating and unfair regulation that is bound to be a canker until it is corrected.

Surely it would not be a hard matter to adjust some method of prorating representation of the different Classes on a basis of membership, if that is necessary. As pointed out by a member at the annual meeting, membership in the Association should be on broad, demo-

cratic principles of equal representation. If not, and if the organization is to be made the catspaw of any clique or group, no matter of what class in the industry, the end of its usefulness will not be far distant.

There is no politics behind our motive in bringing this forward for consideration at this time, however much some may try to make it appear that there is. A storm of protest may result on the ground that this discourages unity of organization and fosters the idea of several antagonistic groups. This we deny. It is no part of the work of the N. A. M. P. I. to bring exhibitors or any other class together in an outside organization of their own, but it is the duty of the Association to open its classes of membership to each branch of the industry on an equal basis for all, without fear or favor. The N. A. M. P. I. should become a strong organization, representative of this great industry and any flaws in its by-laws or anything else that stands in the way of its progress should be eliminated and corrected with all possible despatch.

A Triumph for Decency

By EDWARD WEITZEL.

THE day of the salacious moving picture has evidently come to an end. Unscrupulous adventurers who still labor under the delusion that there is considerable profit to be made by manufacturing screen dramas that pander to the lowest instincts of humanity, will do well to heed the fate of the first release of a company that sought to place on the market a photoplay of this description. The claim to an ethical purpose put forth in behalf of the picture deceived neither the National Board of Review nor the better class of trade journals, the real nature of the play being unmistakable. Everything was done to "put the picture over." The author of the scenario was a playwright of experience and reputation, the director was equally distinguished and the members of the cast were high salaried players chosen for their fitness for their respective characters. An expensive advertising campaign, to which the MOVING PICTURE WORLD refused to open its columns, absorbed still more of the company's funds; but the failure of the picture to pass the censorship and the frank exposure of its true character by a number of the reviewers of the moving picture press proved too great a handicap, and the original version was withdrawn from the market. Last week the National Board of Review and representatives of the trade papers were asked to pass judgment upon a second and much chastened edition of the offending picture. Practically all the obnoxious material had been eliminated, the "cleaning up" process resulting in a screen drama that no longer presents scenes of depravity under the cloak of exposing the dangers of driving lewd women from their accustomed haunts.

The family moving picture theater is not the proper forum for discussions on such a subject.

A gratifying indication of the success attending the efforts to put a stop to the making of undesirable pictures is revealed by the remark of a speculative gentleman, after reading the reviews of the release in question.

"Six months ago such a bunch of 'roasts' would have been worth all kinds of money to that picture. The talk about it being offcolor would have boomed it in great shape, but you can't get away with that stuff now."

Correct, Mr. Speculator! And the bars are up for good in every sense of the word!

Activities of War Committees

OF THE MOTION PICTURE INDUSTRY

Have You Any Films to Give to the Soldiers in France?

THROUGH the MOVING PICTURE WORLD one of the veteran chaplains of the United States Army appeals to the manufacturers and exchangemen of the country on behalf of the soldiers on service in France. The chaplain, who has been many years in the service, must be nameless on account of the War Department prohibition against the publication of the identity of persons or organizations destined for foreign service. Suffice it to say he has, since pictures became a public amusement, been using them for the entertainment of the men under his care. He states that in time to come, perhaps within a year, the Young Men's Christian Association will be in a position to exhibit motion pictures to the men in France. In the meantime that organization will have its hands full taking care of the entertainment of the men in the camps of the regular army, the National Guard and the national army in the United States.

Until such time as the Y. M. C. A. can extend its work to France the only motion pictures the soldiers in camp will be able to see are those which may be provided by the manufacturers and exchangemen here and exhibited under the direction of the chaplains of the different organizations. The visitor to the WORLD office, who expects soon to join his regiment on the other side, said he would take up with his brother chaplains the work of organizing the distribution and exhibiting of the pictures in the several camps. What is necessary first are the films—and those of comedies, especially.

It is not stipulated that the films shall be new or even nearly new. Old films will be welcomed by the soldiers. There must be many such subjects available in the vaults of the exchanges in this country, subjects the owners of which would be glad to give to such a high purpose—it would be difficult to conceive of a higher. It need not be pointed out that the class of pictures should be of the best in theme—the cleanest—only such as a man would show in his own home and surrounded by his own family. This is vital.

The Moving Picture World will be glad to forward to the proper army official for shipment to the soldiers in France any such film as may be sent to this office and to acknowledge in its columns the receipt of all such. In case of New York contributions we will arrange for their collection.

Who will be the first to contribute films for the entertainment of the men who are giving their all representing the United States abroad?

Brady Praises Friend

WILLIAM A. BRADY, chairman of the war committee for the motion picture industry, which is working in conjunction with the officials in Washington, uttered strong words of praise last week for Arthur S. Friend, chairman of the industry's delegation to the Food Commission. Mr. Brady said also that Herbert C. Hoover, head of the commission, seemed to be the first of the Washington officials to appraise at its full value the aid that may be given by the motion picture industry in the work of prosecuting the war.

The president of the National Association said no end of credit should be given to Mr. Friend, who was entering heart and soul into his work in the capital city. "He is Johnny on the Spot," he said. "He is spending his own money and is getting results."

The treasurer of the Famous Players-Lasky Company, in order to facilitate his work in Washington has opened offices in that city. There he will attend various conferences with Mr. Hoover and the other authorities interested in the food situation. Mr. Friend is a lawyer as well as a man of marked executive ability.

William L. Sherrill, vice-chairman of the general committee, and also chairman of the committee to the shipping board, will go to Washington this week to confer with Edward Hurley, chairman of the shipping board. Mr. Sherrill will present to Mr. Hurley some well defined ideas as to how the picture industry can aid the board in its work of creating a large merchant marine and equipping it with man power. Already several applications have been made for the making of pictures on this division of the government's work.

Mr. Brady was gratified last week to receive the following letter from William G. McAdoo, Secretary of the Treasury. It is self-explanatory:

The Secretary of the Treasury,
                    Washington, August 8, 1917.
My Dear Mr. Brady: I have your letter of the 1st of August advising me of the appointment of Messrs. Zukor, Loew, Irwin, Brulatour and Spoor as a committee representing the motion picture industry to co-operate with the Treasury Department in placing its activities before the public of the country, especially in connection with the Liberty Loan. I deeply appreciate your interest in the matter, and shall be glad to write to each of the gentlemen named in accordance with your suggestion. I am sure that the film can perform a great patriotic service to the country at this time, and I am indeed pleased to have your co-operation.

I am taking the liberty of expressing the hope that you will submit some concrete suggestions in the near future. I shall be glad to have them, and shall give them my careful consideration in connection with the campaign for the next loan.

I am advising Mr. Oscar Price, who has just been appointed Director of Publicity for the loan, of the committee you have selected to co-operate with the Treasury Department. May I suggest that you keep in touch with him as to assistance which may be rendered by the motion picture industry in carrying the message of the next loan, when it is announced, to the people of the United States?

With best wishes I am
                    Cordially yours,
                    W. G. McADOO.
William A. Brady, Esq., Times Building, New York, N. Y.

War Work Under Way in Boston

Louis B. Mayer, in Charge of the New England Campaign. Addresses Massachusetts Exhibitors.

President Louis B. Mayer of the New England Metro and the American Feature Film Company of Boston has started a vigorous campaign in New England to aid the National Government in its war campaign of publicity. Mr. Mayer was given the assignment of taking full charge of the New

England campaign by William A. Brady; chairman of the motion-picture committee.

One of Mr. Mayer's first acts was to address the members of the Massachusetts branch of the Motion Picture Exhibitors' League of America at a special session on Tuesday, August 13, at the league headquarters, 127 Pleasant street, Boston. A large gathering was in attendance.

Mr. Mayer was introduced by President Ernest H. Horstmann. His address was full of instructive points on how the exhibitors could play an important part in aiding the Government in war times. He told them of the great service which President Wilson expected of them and stated that by their sincere co-operation the motion picture industry should be able to help the Government materially in the vigorous prosecution and conduct of the war.

"The motion picture," Mr. Mayer said, "has become the great intermediary between the public and the Government at Washington. By throwing instructive reading matter up on the screen in every motion picture house invaluable aid to the government in its various propagandas such as food conservation and liberty bond sales may be given."

Mr. Mayer, with Mrs. Alice Rice Carroll, a prominent Massachusetts exhibitor and well known lecturer, is mapping out a program, which will be put into operation in the near future. Mr. Mayer announces he will be glad to receive suggestions of any sort from New England exhibitors in regard to this new movement.

The first publicity matter to be thrown on New England screens will be literature regarding the movement for shoppers to carry home their own bundles, rather than have them delivered. It is expected this movement will meet with success.

The Massachusetts Branch of the Motion Picture Exhibitors' League of America went on record at the session as supporting the Government in its work by co-operating in every way possible with Mr. Mayer and Mrs. Carroll.

Mrs. Carroll is one of the few women exhibitors in Massachusetts, or in fact New England. She controls the Home theater in Everett and the Regent theater in Arlington, both of which houses are doing a big business, owing to her unceasing efforts to make her patrons happy and give them the show they want. She has also been an active worker in women's club circles and led the movement against motion picture censorship in New England. It was Mrs. Carroll's work and lectures which she gave before the women's clubs in several New Hampshire cities that killed censorship in that State.

The Roll of Honor

CARL METCALFE, one of the oldest of the screen players, has been commissioned second lieutenant in the national army, having been graduated last week from the Plattsburg training camp. Lieutenant Metcalfe has been receiving the congratulations of his fellow-members of the Screen Club, among whom there is a firm belief that promotion will quickly come to him when he gets into real work.

* * *

Paul McAllister, author and screen player, has been commissioned a captain of infantry following the recent graduation exercises at the Plattsburg camp.

* * *

Victor Smith, known to his friends as "Vic," long time studio manager and general manager of the Vitagraph, has been commissioned a second lieutenant in the Quartermasters Department.

* * *

Bud Fisher, creator of Mutt and Jeff, is off for Plattsburg training camp this week. W. A. Brook, manager of the Bud Fisher Company, has been ordered to Governors Island for a course of training for the Quartermasters' Department.

* * *

Kent Watson, correspondent of the Moving Picture World at Dallas, has left for the army training camp at Fort Worth.

* * *

Robert Warwick, screen player, leaves this week for Plattsburg to enter the officers' training corps.

* * *

Alan J. Bachrach, late of the V-L-S-E sales force, is being showered with congratulations upon having won his shoulder straps following the three months' course of training which he has been undergoing at Fort Myer, Va. Mr. Bachrach is a second lieutenant of the new National Army, and has been assigned to the Quartermaster Corps for active duty. The new lieutenant has had experience from both sides of the business, having been manager of the Casino theater when that house was operated as a picture and

vaudeville theater by the Brylawski interests, and with other houses owned and operated by them.

* * *

Noman M. Dickson, traveling representative for K-E-S-E out of the Indianapolis office, who joined the officers' reserve training corps at Fort Benjamin Harrison, has received a commission as first lieutenant, and expects to see active service soon.

* * *

Victor A. Nulty, for many years associated with Kessel & Bauman—The New York Motion Picture Company—has been promoted to the rank of corporal in the Second Machine Gun Troop of the First Texas Cavalry, at present stationed at Hillsboro, Texas. Corporal McNulty writes: "I don' know how or where I am going, but it makes no difference, because my companions are rattle-snake eaters and German killers."

Asta Nielsen, Danish Actress in America

A FEW years ago, when pictures made in Europe were common on the American screens, Asta Nielsen's abilities as a vampire and comedy lead were recognised by most patrons. She has appeared in Nordisk and other Continental brands and is of the black-haired, black-eyed type and rather slender. A story is told of a patron new to pictures who asked, "Who is that holding a stick up in front of the screen?" "That isn't any stick," he was admonished, "that's Asta Nielsen." She does give that up-and-down effect with a tight fitting silk dress on and has the ability to make excellent comedy use of it. But her mobility of countenance and the power of registering with dramatic effectiveness all kinds of emotions has given her high standing as an artist. She may make use of tears, but they are not needed to show her grief. Among so many impressions as a screen critic gets, it is hard to remember more than a general impression of work seen three years ago; but the writer has enjoyed many of her pictures and terror and laughter are equally convincing in her.

Asta Nielsen.

She was born in Copenhagen not many years ago and began her theatrical career at the Royal theater playing Ibsen characters. Then at the New theater, also in Copenhagen, she made a distinct hit as "Trilby." Her first film appearance was in a picture made for the Nordisk in 1912 and has worked under several brands since. She arrived in America this week on the "United States," a Danish steamer, and is at the Biltmore at present. The war has, of course, given the death blow to artistic activity in Europe. Miss Nielsen probably finds it a good time to take a vacation. She intends to visit the Pacific Coast and may go on to Japan. It is affirmed that she has not come here under contract and is not connected with any film maker on this side of the water.

"THE SPY" AT THE GLOBE.

William Fox will present "The Spy," George Bronson-Howard's sensational expose of the nation-wide workings of the German spy system in this country, in which Dustin Farnum appears in the stellar role, at the Globe theater, beginning Monday night, August 27. "Jack and the Beanstalk" will close there on August 26. "The Conqueror," which was announced to follow "Jack and the Beanstalk" will be seen later on Broadway.

"The Spy" is released as a special production, under a separate contract, by William Fox, and bookings can be fixed now with any branch manager of the Fox Film Corporation.

Association's All-Star Picture a Winner ▨ ▨ ▨ ▨ ▨

Manufacturers' Review of Great Scenes from Screen Productions Is a Most Interesting Novelty

A WHALE of a subject is the all-star composite production assembled by the National Association of the Motion Picture Industry and shown to the trade at the Strand theater on the morning of Thursday, August 16. There was a large gathering of film men present, and they all were enthusiastic over the remarkable entertaining qualities of the great scenes from great screen plays. Never but once before had anything similar been attempted, and that was by a single company. Here were scenes taken from the works of a number of manufacturers. President William A. Brady of the association announced in a short address before the pictures were shown that there would be exhibited but three of the five reels it is intended to release. The two others were not yet ready.

The three reels shown were "Love Scenes from Great Screen Plays," "Great Fights in Motion Pictures" and "Daredevil Deeds of Motion Picture Artists." The two remaining reels are "Great Acting Moments" and "Funny Moments of Funny Stars."

Mr. Brady stated in his preliminary talk that the picture had been contributed by all the manufacturers, but that by no means did the present showing represent all that were to come. Independent of the matter contained in the two reels that were not to be shown there were to be contributions from Goldwyn, which company would present one scene from each of its earlier subjects. Paramount, too, with a rich store of productions, would add its bit to the whole.

"In assembling these pictures," said the head of the National Association, "our object is to raise a fund for the legitimate legislative work of the association. In the past year we have had to combat adverse legislation in forty-eight states, and we were successful. We will probably meet more of the same sort in the coming year, but it is also probable we will have more friends than we have had in the past.

"At the present moment there are over a dozen committees of your industry working in Washington in co-operation with the Army and Navy departments, with the Food Commission, with all the factors of war activity. Our men are giving up their time and money without recompense, making daily and weekly trips to Washington.

"The picture you are to see is to be issued, say, one reel a month for a period of five months, or oftener if it should be the wish of those who purchase it." Mr. Brady then described how the subject would be strengthened by the addition of the productions of other manufacturers. "These pictures," he went on, "which will comprise the work of every star of real prominence in the United States, will be sold for the benefit of the association."

Tender Moments in the Love Scenes.

In the first reel, "Love Scenes From Great Screen Plays," there were fourteen subjects. It is purely a matter of individual opinion as to which of these was the greatest, but there can be no question that the scenes from Vitagraph's "The Christian" stood out. Earle Williams and Edith Storey were the players, and truly it was a great moment from a great story. Then, too, there was a real touch in the flash from Mutual's "Youth's Endearing Young Charms," in which Mary Miles Minter shone. Context was unnecessary to establish the situation. It spoke for itself; it all was eloquent of life, of the persistence, the determination of a woman not to be scorned by the man she loved.

There was more than a reminiscent interest in the scene showing Mary Pickford and Henry Walthall in Biograph's "Ramona." Not only was this an extract from a picture, the making of which was the occasion and the reason of Biograph journeying to the Pacific Coast for the first time; not only was it taken from a subject conceded up to that time, 1910, to be the most expensive single reel ever made, but it showed us Miss Walthall in her teens—not so long ago at that—and Mr. Walthall at the beginning of a screen career destined to be notable.

Other scenes in the opening reel, and every last one of them of interest, were Rupert Julian and Ella Hall, in Bluebird's "The Bugler of Algiers"; Carlyle Blackwell and Ethel Clayton, in World Film's "A Woman's Way"; Donald Cameron and Lillian Walker, in Vitagraph's "Kitty Mackay";

Franklyn Farnum, in Universal's "The Woman He Feared"; Anita Stewart and Evart Overton, in Vitagraph's "The Glory of Yolanda"; Francis X. Bushman and Beverly Bayne, in "Romeo and Juliet"; Clara Kimball Young, in World Film's "The Dark Silence"; Madame Petrova, in Metro's "The Black Butterfly"; Alice Brady, in World Film's "La Vie de Boheme," and Harold Lockwood and May Allison, in Metro's "Pidgin Island."

Some Hot Scraps With Real Thrills.

Real thrills there were in the series of great fights. One of the shorter but decidedly picturesque was that of Neal Hart in Universal's "The Raid." Douglas Fairbanks was shown in a red-hot muss from Triangle's "Reggie Mixes In." It was one gem out of a rather wide choice in the same subject. It was enough—enough to show what the robust player can put over when he sets out to do things; and it demonstrated his ability to pick opponents who can take as well as give punishment. Jack Sherrill in World Film's "Then I'll Come Back to You" staged a mill that held attention tight. Then there were William S. Hart and House Peters in Triangle's "Between Men"; E. H. Sothern in Vitagraph's "An Enemy to the King"; Robert Warwick, in World Film's "Alias Jimmy Valentine"; Mr. Bushman, in Metro's "Pennington's Choice"; Alice Brady, in World Film's "Tangled Fates." Last and by no means least, there was Charles Chaplin and his robust associate in the escalator scene from Mutual's "The Floor Walker." It is good to see as when it was released and displays Chaplin at his best. It is a situation to make even an exhibitor laugh.

Regret was expressed by some of those present that the battle between William Farnum and Tom Santschi in Selig's "The Spoilers" had not been included. Executive Secretary Elliott of the association said he had written Mr. Selig asking for the excerpt. Also on Mr. Elliott's list was the fight between William S. Hart and Robert Edeson in Triangle's "On the Night Stage."

When the Players Take Risks.

The final reel shown was devoted to "Daredevil Deeds of Motion Pictures." There was an even dozen extracts shown, and the incidents were of a universal subject. Helen Holmes put over a train thriller in a Universal subject. Then there were Alice Brady, in World Film's "Miss Petticoats"; Mr. Bushman and Miss Bayne, in Metro's "The Great Secret"; Mr. Lockwood and Miss Allison, in Metro's "The River of Romance"; Miss Bayne, in Metro's "Pennington's Choice"; Joseph Kilgour and Virginia Pearson, in Fox's "The Turn of the Road"; Charles Richman, in Vitagraph's "The Secret Kingdom" and the same company's "A Goat Without Horns"; Mary Anderson, in Vitagraph's "The Dangers of Doris" and "The Gang"; Edith Storey, in "Aladdin from Broadway," and a scene from the storm on shipboard from Triangle's "Aloha Oe"—a finely staged spectacle.

It will be noted that some companies have supplied a large number of extracts. With the expansion of the list, as outlined by Mr. Brady in his introductory address, the series is bound to be of even greater interest. The inevitable result of the showing of these "bits" from so many subjects is to arouse curiosity among picturegoers to see the story surrounding these "punches," which, in spite of being separated from their context, are able so strongly to grip the interest.

Perhaps it was this phase of the showing that was uppermost in the mind of one feminine observer who remarked at the conclusion: "But it is all so tantalizing!" Then, again, she made have had in mind those tenderer moments revealed in the first thousand feet.

WALT WHITMAN AS SOUTHERN PLANTER.

Walt Whitman, veteran character actor, will soon make his appearance as a Southern planter, wearing long coat, checkered trousers and wide black hat, in a Triangle production, "The Tar-Heel Warrior," directed by E. Mason Hopper. A company of colored players has been engaged

NEW JEWEL FOR BROADWAY THEATER.

Jewels Productions, Inc., will put into the Broadway Theatre, starting August 28, a super-feature in five reels, titled "Sirens of the Sea." Allen Hollbar produced the offering after the scenario by Grace Helen Bailey. Louise Lovely and Jack Mulhall will be seen in the leading roles.

Nicholas Power Company Wins Suit

Action in United States Court for Infringement of Fire Shutter Brought by LeRoy and Baird Finally Disposed of by Judge Manton—Power Company Wins on All Contentions.

THE opinion in the case of Jean A. LeRoy and Chester R. Baird against Nicholas Power Company, handed down last week by Judge Manton in the United States District Court for the Southern District of New York, terminated litigation which has been virtually pending for the last three and one-half years. The suit was based on a patent for fire shutter granted to LeRoy on October 7, 1913, No. 1,075,215, and which was claimed by LeRoy to be infringed by the fire shutter known as the Nicholas Power Style "B" shutter used on all the Power Cameragraphs in recent years.

The litigation was started by two suits instituted shortly after the grant of the patent in the fall of 1913, against two exhibitors using Power No. 6 Cameragraphs in theaters, in the city of Buffalo. These suits were brought without knowledge of the Nicholas Power Company, but as soon as the company received notice of them, they took over the entire defense.

After it became known that the defense of these suits had been undertaken by the Nicholas Power Company, the plaintiffs dismissed the Buffalo suits of their own motion and instituted proceedings in the Federal Court in this city against the Nicholas Power Company directly. The suit came to trial in the latter part of April and the decision handed down is a complete victory for the Nicholas Power Company on every point which they urged against the patent.

The Nicholas Power Company rested their defense on three principal grounds; first, that Nicholas Power was the first and original inventor of the shutter and not LeRoy; second, that the shutter had been used publicly for more than two years before the LeRoy application for patent; and third, that the LeRoy patent was invalid in view of numerous prior patents on fire shutters, principal among them the patents of the Edison Company.

Mr. Power testified as to his invention of the shutter more than eleven years ago and was corroborated as to his early work by witnesses from the Power factory, also by Mr. Timothy of the Department of Gas, Water Supply and Electricity, Mr. Cecil of the New York Herald, and others, Mr. Timothy stating that the first fire shutter ever presented to his department was one invented by Mr. Power. The rebuttal of the plaintiff to this evidence is summed up by the Court in the decision in the following language:

The only contradiction of this is the testimony of Bogdanffy, a former employee of Power, who claimed that he made the drawing for this shutter and showed it to Mr. Power and directed its construction. The record of the City Water Department shows that Shutter "B," which Bogdanffy says he suggested to Mr. Power is April, 1907, was submitted to the Department for approval or disapproval in December, 1906, and the witness (Mr. Timothy) called from that Department, is therefore confirmatory of the claim that it was made prior to March 12, 1908. I regard Bogdanffy's claim that he made a drawing of the parts in co-operation with Mr. Power (indeed it is even claimed that he was the real inventor of the Power Shutter "B") as not well founded. His testimony is in direct conflict with many circumstances portrayed by the evidence which cannot be erroneous and point with unerring certainty to the untruthfulness of his claim.

The Court's opinion that the patent was invalid in view of the various patents prior to LeRoy is summed up in the following clause:

The cases are uniform in holding that there is no invention merely selecting and fitting together the most desirable parts of different machines in the same art, if each operates the same in the new machine as it did in the old and effects the same result. In view of this condition of the prior art, I am of the opinion that the claim of the defendant, that LeRoy's patent is anticipated by the art, and is, therefore, void of invention, is well founded.

NEW COMEDY PLAYERS IN UNIVERSAL FILMS.

Among the new players recently engaged to work at Universal City are Mattie Cummont and Henry Murdock, well-known laugh-makers, who will be under the direction of F. F. Beaudine. Mattie is the short, roly-poly woman who has been working recently with the Fox company and with Max Linder. Henry Murdock has been working with the Kalem company for a year or more, first with its Florida company and more recently with Ham and Bud in California.

King Vidor, formerly scenario editor of the LaSalle company, has been engaged to write for the oddly assorted pair.

Another new comedy man to join the Universal is Al Santell, who has been added to the directing staff to alternate with Craig Hutchison in staging comedies in which Dave Morris and Gladys Tennison are the principal players.

At Leading Picture Theaters

Programs for the Week of Aug. 19 at New York's Best Motion Picture Houses—The Revolution in Russia at the Rialto.

FOR the first time in the history of the Rialto all photoplays were eliminated from the program the week of Aug 19 and the dramatic spectacle, The Revolution in Russia, was given the place of honor, supplemented by scenes from the Russian battle fronts in the Caucasus, along the Black Sea, and on the southwest frontier. The films are owned by the Skobeleff Committee for the Relief of Russian Wounded and Prisoners of War and the proceeds from their exhibition will go to the committee's relief fund. The pictures are official and bear the endorsement of the Russian Commission now in Washington. The soloists were Greek Evans and Alberto Bachmann.

British War Pictures at the Strand.

The Strand Theater presented motion pictures of the Germans retreating at the Battle of Arras. They are official and authentic British War pictures and are shown through special arrangements with the Official Government Pictures, Inc. All branches of the service are seen in actual operation in this great drive, which proved so disastrous to the Germans. Another feature was Billie Burke in her first Paramount picture, "The Mysterious Miss Terry," an adaptation from a story by Gelett Burgess. Miss Burke's impersonation of Mavis Terry demonstrates a novel method of finding both happiness and a husband. The cast includes Thomas Meighan, Walter Heirs, Gerald Smith, George Wright and Bessie Learn. An animated cartoon entitled "Colonel Heeza Liar's Temperance Lecture," and the Strand Topical Review, were also shown.

On the musical program were Grace Hoffman and Antone Lescault.

"Pay Me" at the Broadway.

This second week of the engagement of "Pay Me," the Jewel five-part western melodrama with Dorothy Phillips at the head of the cast, indicates that it has caught on at the Broadway theater.

Eighty-First St. Theater Bill.

At the Eighty-First St. theater the following pictures were shown.

On Monday, Tuesday and Wednesday, Wm. Desmond was seen in "Master of His Home," a Triangle Komedy, "His Cool Nerve" being on the program. On Thursday, Friday, Saturday and Sunday, Enid Bennett, in "They're Off," and the Keystone Comedy, "Thirst," were the picture features.

GAUMONT-MUTUAL WEEKLY.

Spectators who see the Gaumont-Mutual Weekly No. 138, the current issue, will have an opportunity of seeing President and Mrs. Wilson at close range—with Secretary of War Baker thrown in for good measure. The occasion is the graduating exercises of the student officers at the training camp at Fort Myers, Va. Major General Scott, who recently returned from Russia, is also with the President. War pictures again predominate in Mutual Weekly No. 138. See lane guards march in at an Atlantic port are shown in their drab war paint. Government officials investigate a new aero propeller, which meets all atmospheric conditions and also lifts an aeroplane 2,000 feet a minute. At Washington, D. C., Mrs. Lansing, wife of the Secretary of State, gives a luncheon to the ladies of the Cabinet, where only dried foods are served.

At least one cantonment will not suffer from a lack of lumber. This issue of the Mutual Weekly shows a huge raft containing eight million feet of lumber on an ocean voyage of 1,500 miles to San Diego, Cal. Another California picture shows Uncle Sam in the hog raising business, an undertaking necessary to assure food for the National Army. Miss Edna Goodrich, the beautiful Mutual star who will soon appear in "Reputation," finds time between the taking of scenes to make bandages for the Red Cross. A Gaumont cameraman took the picture at the Empire studio at Glendale, L. I.

On the same reel are some authoritative styles in footwear, showing the latest wrinkles in shoes.

Margery Wilson's Play Completed.

"Mountain Dew," the first starring vehicle of Margery Wilson, has been completed and will be released on the Triangle program early in September. The star appears as a girl of the Kentucky Cumberlands where feudists thrive. Charlie Gunn, the most popular of Triangle leading men, has the chief masculine role that of a schoolmaster.

The Motion Picture Exhibitor

WRITE US EARLY AND OFTEN

THE MOVING PICTURE WORLD carries the most complete record of Exhibitors' News. This department aims at being the fullest and fairest chronicle of all the important doings in the ranks of organized exhibitors. To keep the department as complete and as useful as it is now we request the secretaries of all organizations to favor us with reports of all the news. Coming events in the ranks of the organized exhibitors are best advertised in this department of the Moving Picture World.

Big Round-Up at Ocean City

Many Southern Exhibitors Will Be There—Prominent Men in Trade to Attend.

AMONG the prominent men in the film industry who will attend the joint convention and exposition to be held by the State Exhibitors' Association of North and South Carolina, Virginia, Maryland and District of Columbia to start on August 30th and end the night of September the 1st, are President Lee A. Ochs, of the M. P. E. L. A.; Samuel Trigger, prominent exhibitor of New York City; Charles C. Pettijohn, general manager of the American Exhibitors' Association; I. E. Mosher, prominent theater owner of Buffalo, New York; Frank J. Rembusch, of Shelbyville, Indiana; Harry Crandall, of the Washington syndicate of theaters, and Guy Wonders, of Baltimore. Governor Stuart, of Virginia, has also accepted an invitation to attend and deliver an address before the convention.

The idea of the joint convention and exposition originated with Jake Wells, of the great Wells chain of theaters, and now president of the American Exhibitors' Association. Mr. Wells' idea is to discuss at this convention only matters which are more of a local nature than national, and to come to certain agreement between the different states as to taking action on various matters affecting the theater owners of the territory embraced, so that concerted action can be obtained through strong committees selected from the different states, when necessary to present matters before legislative bodies, manufacturers, distributors

Jake Wells

or other interests. Mr. Wells is largely interested in each of the states which is to be represented and is exerting every effort to make the convention the greatest gathering of theater owners ever held in the South. Harry Bernstein, of Richmond, Va., is in active charge of arrangements.

The idea of an exposition in connection with the convention is not with an idea of making money, but simply to help clear up certain items of heavy expense incident to the convention, and also to make the convention more attractive and tend to largely increase the attendance. Exhibits have been contracted for by every exchange serving the territory covered and the various trade papers will also be represented and have booths. Attendance of a dozen or more picture stars has been insured, and they will be guests of honor at the banquet and movie ball to take place on the last night.

American Association Men Meet

Affairs of New Exhibitors' Organization Discussed and Attitude Toward National Association of Industry Defined—Will Meet at Ocean City, Va.

AN IMPORTANT meeting of several of the officials of the newly formed American Exhibitors' Association was held at the offices of the association, Times building, New York, on Thursday, August 16. Those present were President Jake Wells, Vice-president Guy Wonders, Treasurer William Fait, Jr., General Manager Charles C. Pettijohn and Harry Crandall. Among other things it was decided to call a meeting of the association to be held at Ocean City, Va., at the same time as the convention of the Virginia League, when exhibitors from many southern states will be present. The date of this meeting is August 30.

Arrangements were also made to take a lease on a suite of rooms on the 20th floor of the Times Building, which will be the national headquarters of the association. General Manager Charles C. Pettijohn will have charge of this office and will establish at once a bureau for the adjustment of such complaints as may be referred to him by members of the association. Mr. Pettijohn's wide experience as a lawyer will enable him to be of invaluable assistance to members.

Regarding the matter of affiliation with the National Association of the Motion Picture Industry General Manager Pettijohn was instructed to define the attitude of the American Exhibitors' Association toward the N. A. M. P. I. In accordance with those instructions the following letter was written:

To the President and Directors of the National Association of Motion Picture Industry.

Gentlemen: In order that the attitude of the American Exhibitors' Association toward the National Association of Motion Picture Industry may be clearly understood, and that the directors may have definitely in mind our position with reference to what has been termed "our application to affiliate with the National Association of Motion Picture Industry," I am instructed by our directors to write you the following:

First—The American Exhibitors' Association, on July 20, 1917, tendered, through Wm. A. Brady, not as the president of the National Association of Motion Picture Industry, but as the designated official, by reason of his selection by President Wilson, our hearty co-operation and services to help carry on the work set aside for our government for the motion picture industry during the present crisis. We are building a business organization of exhibitors to the end that this may be effectively done and results obtained.

Second—We care not whether we have one or fifty votes, either as directors or members of the National Association of the Motion Picture Industry, because voting inside the industry can not interest us.

Third—We are asking nothing of you, and are offering only our affiliation and assistance in a stand with the other branches of the industry for what is healthful, and against that which unjustly attacks.

Coming League and Other Exhibitors' Conventions
(Secretaries Are Requested to Send Dates and Particulars Promptly)

Fourth—On the other hand, we will not, at any time, by any unit, vote or combination of votes, permit ourselves to be bound to support any act, measure or effort that is not for the best interests of real exhibitors of America, who comprise our membership, nor for or against any faction in any other branch of the industry that may hereafter develop.

Fifth—We desire to have it clearly understood that our services are tendered, and that no application is made at this time for votes, or for any change in the by-laws of your organization.

Sixth—We ask that the directors at the Meeting August 27, 1917, either promptly reject or accept our proffer of affiliation, assistance and co-operation in such manner as our position may be clearly and definitely interpreted by our officers and entire membership.

Ochs Statements Refuted.

Percy Wells of North Carolina Takes Issue With Maligners of American Association.

INDIGNATION is expressed in strong terms by Percy W. Wells, North Carolina State President of the American Exhibitors' Association at the length to which Lee A. Ochs is using the Trade Review since the convention in an endeavor to belittle his "enemies" at the convention, which he insists on characterizing as "bolters." Mr. Wells is of the opinion that the Exhibitors' Trade Review had best leave off the monopolization of its columns as a medium for the personal laudation of Lee A. Ochs if it expects to exist and be accepted as a bona fide trade publication of the industry.

"It is passing strange," stated Mr. Wells to a representative of the Moving Picture World, "that Mr. Ochs' paper cannot obtain statements for publication denouncing the 'deplorable tactics of the minority' except from those who have been fixed with offices in the Ochs League. This week's issue of the Ochs mouthpiece has a certain article purporting to come from Nebraska, but which bears certain earmarks of phraseology which savor strongly of a certain member of the Trade Review staff, which starts off with a eulogy of Mr. Ochs and ends with a denunciation of the members of the American Exhibitors' Association. Mr. Thomas, who is supposed to have spoken the words, it will be noted, was made third vice-president by the Ochs machine. It is to laugh at his statement that 'not meaning to boost myself, but the new organization looks good to me!'

"I would like to submit to Messrs. Thomas, Eager and the other gentlemen, who are blindly following a leader whom they have fallen in with, a few figures that have been obtained by Martin Quigley, of Chicago, relative to that 178 to 40 majority which they have grasped as their only chance for an argument. The city of Chicago voted 20 delegates on the convention floor, which would represent 488 theaters, whereas the City License Bureau of Chicago, where the theater owners have to pay their amusement tax, shows that there are only 378 theaters in the city of Chicago, this including theaters which offer only stage attractions. According to the Chicago representation on the floor of the convention there must be 488 bona fide theater owners in Chicago—and every one of them members of the Ochs organization!"

Furthermore the records show that up to July 1st the exhibitors' organization's roster in Chicago showed an inclusive membership of 122 men. Of the 122 men listed 55 are merely managers—not owners—exchange attaches and several men who formerly owned theaters and at present are not actively engaged in any branch of the industry. And only 80 of the 122 have paid dues. Of the Illinois state branch of the Ochs organization there are twelve members, six of whom have never paid dues.

"Another instance of the steam roller scandal is found in the Boston delegation which voted 30 delegates when the Boston license report shows them only entitled to 9. Mr. Ochs, however, had apparently visited Boston before the convention and had acknowledged through the Trade Review that he had promised to give the next convention to Boston, notwithstanding the fact that the convention is supposed to have the privilege of voting on its convention city from the floor. What do you call that but gag rule?

"When 87 men walked out of the convention hall at the Coliseum," concluded Mr. Wells, "and left 74 delegates there, we absolutely had a majority of that convention with us, and I defy anyone to prove otherwise."

Mr. Wells states that he has been in correspondence with many representative exhibitors in the States of North Carolina, South Carolina, Virginia and Georgia, and that almost unanimously every theater owner who has been approached has come out strongly for the A. E. A., which, to use Mr. Wells' words, "is an organization with no commercial alliance, nor any kind of the exhibitor, first, last and always."

MARYLAND EXHIBITORS MEET.

On Sunday night, August 12, a special meeting was called and held by the Maryland Exhibitors' League at their headquarters, in the New Theater Building, 210 West Lexington street, at which reports were submitted by the delegates to

the Chicago convention, including Thos. D. Goldberg, J. Louis Rome and Guy L. Wonders and the committee which was working on the projected moving of the film exchanges from Washington to Baltimore, including F. A. Hornig, Louis Schlichter and L. A. DeHoff. Owing to the arrangements for a premiere screening of the Fox feature, "Jack and the Beanstalk," which was held immediately after this meeting, being in charge of Mr. DeHoff, the manager of the New theater, he was not able to attend and act in his official capacity as secretary of the League, so E. B. McCurdy was appointed secretary in his place for the evening. The well arranged private presentation of "Jack and the Beanstalk" took place after the meeting of the League. Among those who attended the meeting and the screening were: Guy L. Wonders, Louis Schlichter, L. A. DeHoff, William M. Tyler, Nick Burns, W. Albers, B. Rosenbauer, M. E. Berger, Joseph Brodie, W. E. Stumpf, E. B. McCurdy, Paul Emmert, Thomas D. Goldberg, Miss T. Marks, Messrs. Cook, Emerick and Volbreck, Harry Lewy, Harry Woods, L. Benesch.

New Exhibitors' Organization.

Associated Theaters, Incorporated, Formed at Minneapolis for Booking Purposes.

WITH two hundred theaters enrolled and determined not to start its actual business activities until one thousand theaters are stockholding members, "Associated Theaters, Incorporated," was formed at the Hôtel Dyckman, Minneapolis, Minnesota, Tuesday, August 14. The following officers were elected, each of whom is also a member of the board of directors: President, H. L. Hartman, Mandan, North Dakota; vice-president, Forest Secor, Forest City, Iowa; treasurer, Henry P. Greene, Minneapolis, Minnesota; secretary, William S. Smith, Menominee, Wisconsin; chairman board of directors, Chas. W. Gates, Aberdeen, South Dakota; general manager, Thomas J. Hamlin, Minneapolis, Minnesota.

The "Hamlin Plan" of booking was adopted, which is intended to conduct the booking of film, supplies and equipment at a minimum expense and solve the present high cost of marketing and distributing by co-operative collective merchandising.

Fiscal offices were opened at once in the Lumber Exchange building, Minneapolis, but the actual opening of the proposed large central Minneapolis exchange and various sub-stations for inspection and shipping may not take place until December, according to Mr. Hamlin.

President Hartman is also president of the North Dakota State Branch of the Motion Picture Exhibitors' League of America. Vice-President Secor is secretary-treasurer of the Iowa Organization of Exhibitors and Exchangemen. Treasurer Greene, of Minnesota, is a director of the Motion Picture Exhibitors' Corporation of the Northwest. Secretary Smith is a prominent Wisconsin exhibitor and his brother-partner was a secretary of the early Wisconsin exhibitors' organization. Chairman Chas. W. Gates is vice-president of the Motion Picture Exhibitors' Corporation of the Northwest. General Manager Hamlin was the founder of Amusements, a territorial theater trade weekly of Minneapolis.

"We have incorporated for $100,000 under the laws of South Dakota, as "Associated Theaters Incorporated," declared Mr. Hamlin. "We have no connection either directly or indirectly with any other organisation or group in the motion picture industry.

"No exhibitor is expected to subscribe for more stock than what he would ordinarily pay for ten days' film rental, and no theatre can hold more than $1,500 worth of stock.

"Neither myself nor any member of the board are drawing a cent of salary and the entire expense of organising will not equal ten per cent.

"We expect to do a film rental business alone of fully $50,000 a week," continued General Manager Hamlin, 'and are incorporated to produce, buy, sell, lease and rent film, equipment and supplies, to buy, sell and operate theaters and to book films, vaudeville, tabloids and road attractions."

OKLAHOMA MEETING CALLED.

Members of the Motion Picture Exhibitors' League of America, Oklahoma Branch, will meet at the Lee-Huckins Hotel, Oklahoma City, on August 21, Tuesday. All theater owners and managers in the state are invited to attend, as there is business of vital importance to the industry to be discussed.

This meeting is of more than ordinary importance, as it will in all probability determine whether Oklahoma will remain in the League or join the newly organised American

Exhibitors' Association. For this reason it is hoped that every exhibitor in the state will be present to voice his views on this matter. L. W. BROPHY, Secretary.

Composers' Society Moves Against Brooklynites

Three Exhibitors Haled to Court—League to Co-operate With Musicians and to Appeal to Congress.

THE American Society of Authors, Composers and Publishers is pushing its campaign against those exhibitors who are using the music copyrighted by its members. Just at present its legal hand is being laid on Brooklyn men. Last week William Brandt, executive secretary of the Motion Picture Exhibitors' League of America, was served with a summons complaining of an alleged violation of the copyright act and asking damages in the sum of $3,000. The specific offense cited is that his musician played the music of "Naughty, Naughty, Naughty." The latter allegation pained Mr. Brandt at least as much as did the general charge. The executive secretary is the staid head of a family, the father of three children, and his New Albany theater is a family house. He will enter a denial.

Two other Brooklyn prominent exhibitors were summoned similarly to Mr. Brandt. Warde & Glynn, owners of the Century and the Alhambra, in widely separated parts of Brooklyn, both large houses, and Charles Cranides, one of the directors of the Brooklyn league, were served with papers. The alleged damages in each of the latter instances also was $3,000 and counsel fees. The actions are brought in the Eastern District of the Circuit Court of the United States before Judge Chatfield. The defendants are given twenty days in which to make answer. Goldsmith & Rosenthal is representing the exhibitors. They will be paid from the music fund created by the New York exhibitors through the $3 tax levied on the picture men of the state.

On Thursday of last week Mr. Brandt and Sam Grant, of Boston, who has been active in his city in combating the American Society, called on President Weber of the International Musicians. The Boston idea was explained to Mr. Weber and his co-operation was asked to the end that the same methods may be adopted throughout the country.

In Boston, Mr. Grant explained, a hundred theaters have agreed not to use taxable music. An agreement also was sought with the Musicians' Union whereby the members of the latter organization will refrain from using any music on which a tax is charged unless they are specifically instructed by the managers of the houses. The Boston organization took formal action in line with the suggestion and adopted a resolution declaring any member who did to the contrary should be subject to discipline. The Boston organization notified its members that lack of knowledge of the law would serve as no excuse, that they must be on their guard. It is expected the action of the Boston local will be adopted by all the New England organizations and that there will be full co-operation with the league.

Mr. Weber assured Messrs. Brandt and Grant he would be glad to co-operate with the league in having musicians throughout the country adopt the Boston view—that no licensed music be played except on the instructions of the house manager.

There is in preparation a bill for presentation to Congress amending the present copyright law. It is Mr. Weber's opinion the national legislature never intended to make possible the present situation in the music business.

It is reported there is a measure of dissension among the members of the American Society over the apportionment of the money collected from amusement purveyors. It is said one of the most successful of the publishers is asking why those members of the organization whose product is not particularly profitable should be permitted to share and share alike with him.

LEAGUE'S EXECUTIVE COMMITTEE TO MEET.

William Brandt, executive secretary of the Motion Picture Exhibitors' League of America, has received word from all of the national officers of the organization as well as the members of the executive committee that they will be in New York for the coming meeting to be held on August 25. Eugene M. Clarke of the executive committee will come from Mississippi and Frank D. Eager will make the trip from Nebraska. From Chicago will come First Vice-president Joseph Hopp, Financial Secretary William J. Sweeney, Executive Committeeman Alfred Hamburger and Robert Levy.

After settling several important matters to come before the committee the exhibitor members of the Board of Directors of the National Association of the Motion Picture Industry will attend a stated meeting of that organization.

Trigger Resigns

Formally Relinquishes the Office of President of Manhattan Local Exhibitors' Organization.

THE special meeting of Manhattan Local No. 1 of the Exhibitors' League to receive the resignation of Sam H. Trigger from its presidency was held at its rooms on Tuesday, August 14. Mr. Trigger called the meeting to order and immediately proceeded to business with the following address:

"Gentlemen: It is a most unpleasant task to be asked by gentlemen purporting to be my friends to explain my conduct. This is the first time in my life that friends have questioned my God-given right to exercise my conscience and my judgment.

"As your president, I entered the hall at the Chicago convention. I was not permitted to take part in the deliberations of the convention, refused the right to voice your sentiments on any of your desires or to vote on any measure. I realized I was not a delegate and left the convention. For this act I have no apologies to offer. That I have aligned myself with the American Exhibitors' Association needs no explanation except that I am glad to do my bit in this organization of business men that really stands for something, and that I believe will accomplish something for you and for me as exhibitors.

"I now hand to our secretary my resignation as president of this local. This act I will also explain. I should not continue as president of a local that is affiliated with a national organization that I do not believe in. A few of you have indicated that you prefer a new president. You should have one. This resignation I owe you, but my personal liberty to exercise my best judgment at all times I do not.

"Now, boys, that my unpleasant task is over, let me just say this in conclusion: Forget our political differences, and let's be the same old friends and pals we have always been.

"I care not for presidencies, but my friends I love. As fellow exhibitors, continue to do as you have done for fifteen years—call on your old daddy day or night—and even if I have turned my sixty-fifth milestone, you will find me so full of enthusiasm for my friends that you can still call me 'Pal.'

"To those of you who join me in the American Exhibitors' Association, I say, 'God bless you.' To those of you who do not, I say, 'God bless you, too.'"

Several of the members expressed their regrets at the action of Mr. Trigger and assured him they would never hold him their friend. It was made clear while Mr. Trigger has resigned as president of the local he had not resigned from membership in it. Nothing was said on that point. The meeting then adjourned to meet again at the call of the first vice-president, C. R. Martineau, to whom Mr. Trigger handed the gavel.

Mr. Trigger's formal resignation was as follows:

To Manhattan Local No. 1:
M. P. E. L. of America:
Gentlemen—I herewith tender to you my resignation as President of Manhattan Local No. 1, Motion Picture Exhibitors' League of America, same to take effect at once.
(Signed) S. H. TRIGGER, President.

PRESIDENT MARTINEAU'S ACCEPTANCE.

Editor Moving Picture World:

Dear Sir: In assuming the presidency of Manhattan Local No. 1 of the Motion Picture Exhibitors' League of America, I take this opportunity to pledge my support to the National League and all its officials and will use my best efforts to promote a closer bond of friendship between all local exhibitors whether in the organization or not.

It will be my greatest desire to protect the individual members from unfair trade methods and abuse and at the same time to work for the best interest of the entire industry.

I will endeavor to see that all differences between branches of the industry and exhibitors are properly arbitrated. I will be at the service of the exhibitors at all times and will do my utmost to assist them in protecting their interests.

MOTION PICTURE EXHIBITORS' LEAGUE OF A.
Manhattan Local No. 1.
C. R. Martineau, President.

BOSTON MOVING AHEAD ON CONVENTION PLANS

Samuel Grant, head of the committee of arrangements for the Boston convention and exposition next year, in a visit to New York last week stated that the municipal authorities were co-operating with the Massachusetts exhibitors in plans for the entertainment of visiting motion picture men. The city officials make no attempt to conceal their satisfaction that the League decided on the Hub for the next gathering place. Mayor James M. Curley has notified Mr. Grant that the city of Boston will give an official entertainment to the visiting exhibitors and film men. It will take the form of an outing down the Bay on one of the big excursion steamers, with stops at some of the picturesque spots. Prominent officials will go along to assist in the entertainment. Also being arranged is a demonstration by some of the municipality's fireboats.

Joseph Girard, Butterfly Player

JOSEPH GIRARD, who fills important roles in "The Double Standard" and "The Lair of the Wolf," two of the latest Butterfly features, dates his connection with motion pictures away back to the almost "prehistoric" period of 1895. At that time, just a stripling of a boy, Girard was doing "heavy" parts on a tour of New England and the Canadian provinces with the Sawtelle Dramatic Company.

The show was not going very well, so the management secured from Chicago what was called an "anamatagraph" as an added attraction. Having secured the machine, their next trouble was to get an operator, for no one seemed able to penetrate its secrets. However, young Girard said that he had been brought up in a print shop and he thought that he could run the thing. So it was turned over to him, with ten dollars a week extra for running it in addition to playing "heavy." There was not much that Joe would not have done in those lean days for ten dollars, but he soon discovered that the "anamatagraph" was a real gold mine. In every town where it was set up it became at once the biggest riot the place had

Joseph Girard.

ever seen. For this was the first moving picture which had ever been projected in that part of the country, and just to see them move was enough for the fans. Everywhere the manager was approached by scientific men, doctors, lawyers, mechanics, etc., all of them anxious to study the principle of the new wonder. The manager, not knowing even which end of the thing was turned toward the screen, passed them all over to Girard, who explained what little he knew about the wonderful invention. It was something on the order of a graft, however, for every one dropped something into Joe's hand after the demonstration was over.

Girard continued in the "legitimate" for many years, and it was not until 1913 that he entered the picture field as an actor. At this time he left the stage to join Edison, and shortly afterward he became a member of the permanent stock company at Universal City, where he has remained ever since. One of Girard's most successful parts was the mysterious "Voice" in the big serial, "The Voice on the Wire."

VAN DYKE COMPANY RETURNS.

The Van Dyke Company, headed by Jean Sothern, which has been at Atlantic Highlands for some weeks making exteriors for "Peg O' the Sea," a coming Art Drama, returned to the studio this week to put the finishing touches on the production, which is being directed by Eugene Nowland. The trip was highly successful, according to the actors, both from results obtained and for recreation, for the visit was something of a vacation for the players.

Little Picture Actress Saves Mother

AN interesting story appeared in the local papers recently which gave little Anna Mead a place among the heroines of the day. Anna, though not a screen star of note, has appeared in a sufficient number of small parts to say that she belongs, and presence of mind on the occasion mentioned proves that she has the qualifications.

Here's the story:

"What was declared to be the most remarkable rescue from drowning in the waters around New York so far this summer was performed yesterday by Anna Mead, eleven years old, of No. 745 Amsterdam avenue. She succeeded in raising her mother to the surface of the waters at the Steeplechase Park bathing pavilion, Coney Island, and thereby saved Mrs. Mead's life.

Anna Mead.

"Mother and daughter had been in the water together for some time. Mrs. Mead was holding to the ropes, and her daughter was swimming some distance away. The tide was coming in so fast that Mrs. Mead lost her hold of the ropes, toppled backward and disappeared under the surface. The water at that point was over Mrs. Mead's head, and there being no bathers in the immediate vicinity no person noticed her sink.

"It was not until Mrs. Mead had come to the surface for the second time that her feeble cries were heard by her daughter, who went to her mother's assistance. Anna dived several times, as her mother again disappeared before she could get hold of her. When she finally did she came to the surface with her arms around her mother's waist.

"Anna's feat was highly praised by the guards, who declared her a plucky girl.

"Mr. Mead wished to reward the guards for their work, but they refused to accept, saying that if any rewards were to be given the daughter was the one deserving of them."

NEW DIRECTOR FOR EACH PRODUCTION.

M. A. Schlesinger, president of the Mayfair Film Corporation, has announced that he has made tentative arrangements with four of the leading directors of the trade to direct the sparkling Mayfair star, Peggy Hyland, in her forthcoming releases. Mr. Schlesinger proposes to have a new director for each Peggy Hyland-Mayfair production, so that they will lack the sameness so often prevalent.

It is a physical impossibility for any man to conceive new touches and novel effects in production after production, and in this way some degree of variety is certain to be attained. The names of the men engaged will not be announced until they begin their work on the production, but each one has a number of successful pictures to his credit. They will all enter the Mayfair employ, however, with the understanding that their engagement is ended when the production is completed.

Then also each new director will naturally seek to bring out the charm in Miss Hyland which makes the strongest appeal to him and in this way the greatest possible percentage of the public will be pleased. The name of the director engaged to produce the second Peggy Hyland picture, soon to go under way, will be announced later.

BILL DESMOND, DETECTIVE.

William Desmond, Triangle star, who made a record as a Sherlock Holmes in "Time Lock and Diamonds," has been cast for another detective role in a forthcoming production entitled "Flying Colors." Frank Borzage is directing the company.

Big Possibilities for Pictures in the Orient.

Charles Margelis, Back from a Seven Months' Trip from Yokohama to Java, Believes There Is Great Chance for Picture Promoters in the East.

By Hanford C. Judson.

AFTER a seven months' sales tour with the Ince picture "Civilization," Charles Margelis is back in New York and talked interestingly to a World representative of his trip and of business conditions in the East. He was able to place seven copies of the Ince picture for the Harper Film Corporation, but he had to hustle to do it. The chief need of hustling, and he wants to make this point clear to any who may contemplate following with other pictures, is that the East lack laws to protect the film man from "dupers." Let us say that the salesman disposes of one print in Yokohama. If he lets a ship or two go by, he'll find that his picture is in Shanghai before he is and there'll be no need of his going any further. All the prints that are needed will be ahead of him. His advice is, "Don't sell a single copy till there is a man who can go to the East with six or seven copies, all the paper, cuts and advertising needed, who can be on the job and cover the whole East at once."

At Yokohama Mr. Margelis sold his picture to a Japanese theater man, who opened with it at the Imperial theater, where it played for a week with admissions from $2.25, the highest, to five cents, the lowest. With the print went a trunk of paper, including 250 one sheets, 50 three sheets, 35 six sheets, 10 twenty-four sheets, 2,000 post cards with a set of cuts, as they do not do as good photoengraving in the Orient as we turn out. All the printed matter they need is a set of samples they can follow, for that will fill the bill. Mr. Margelis showed me specimens of the publicity. Some of it was in English to attract Americans in the East, but most of it merely looked interesting. Mr. Margelis didn't "have time" to translate what it told.

From Yokohama he went to Peking, where he disposed of a print, and from there to Shanghai, to Manila, to the Strait Settlements and to Java. He was enthusiastic at the way he was treated by merchants in the East and the reception he got—after war was declared—by the English clubs and the like. In China, he says, a business man's word is his bond. If he tells you he will be in his office at any time with money to pay for a print, he is there without fail and has real money, not checks. He says that "Civilization" made good in the East and that there is a demand for pictures. It is a fresh field, we understand from him. Pictures particularly true of picture production with native players. It hasn't been done—or hadn't when he left—and he believes there is a great future for that particular branch of the industry. He showed me a request from an acquaintance in the Orient to lead him whatever picture equipment he thought would be good there. He is contemplating making a second trip as a representative of producers and manufacturers in this country. He expects to take a photographer with him with a view to establishing a production plant in the East.

Mr. Margelis was born in Ohio and graduated from the Starling Medical College, but the peculiarities of the practice of that profession were not found to be wholly agreeable to him so he became a showman. He has traveled with many celebrated boxers and pugilists, among them Billy Papke, the

Chas. Margelis

Australian champion. He has had experience in the film business even before this recent successful trip to the Orient. He says in closing, "Tell them all to beware of 'dupers' in the East. Move quick if you want to make sales." He also says that in the East it is absolutely necessary to be a man of your word. If you fake once, you won't get a second chance.

A K-E-S-E MUSIC CUE SHEET.

Believing that a music cue sheet would help the picture theater musician, to give a little extra punch to Essanay's "Skinner's Baby," the services of George W. Bergnon were engaged and this is the result:

1. At Screening...........'Time 1.45)..Pastel Menuet-Paradis
   (¾ Allegro)
2. T. William Manning Skinner.. (2.00)..Theme
   Souvenir ....German
   (Andante con moto)
3. T. McLaughlin, The Senior—... (2.30)..Serenade ....Drdla
   (Tranquillo)
4. T. Skinner was Still— ..... (1.00)..Theme
5. T. The Next Day at the Office.. (4.00)..Little Concert Waltz.Frontini
6. T. Thee Honey Received a
   Visit ....(3.00)..Mother ....Romberg
   (Andante)
7. T. Hope—As a Boy—......... (4.15)..A Doll Scene.........Nicode
   (Waltz)
8. D. Skinner Kisses Honey—.... (2.00)..Theme
9. T. When the Colbys Left—.. (4.20)..Meditation ....Williams
   (Slow Andante)
10. T. The Following Sunday—... (2.20)..Canzonetta ....Godard
    (Allegretto)
11. One Day Several Weeks—.... (3.20)..Intermezzo ....Arensky
    (Presto)
12. D. Skinner Sits on Steps..... (1.15)..Agitato No. 4........Andino
13. D. Skinner Enters House...... (2.45)..Dream of the Flowers..Cohen
    (Andante)
14. T. Then Because He Did Not— (1.30)..Bob ....Kaplan
    (One Step)
15. T. Then Happiness Carried—.. (3.30)..He Will Understand...Frimi
    (Fox Trot)
16. T. Skinner Could Hardly Wait. (3.30)..Theme
17. T. What's the Matter With—".. (1.15)..Tete-a-Tete........De Koven
    (Moderato)
18. T. Then Came a Day......... (2.00)..Theme
19. T. A Sweet Blossom of Humanity .... (1.00)..Dreaming of You......Lehar
    (Waltz)
20. T. Skinner Discovers He Is Too
    Late .... (2.30)..Allegro No. 1........Minot
    (Galop)
21. D. Skinner Enters Home..... (3.30)..Theme
22. D. Skinner Enters Back Door.. (3.30)..Intermezzo ....Huerter
    (Moderato)
23. D. Doctor Summons Skinner.. (2.00)..Somebody is Coming to My
    House
    (Song)
24. T. McLaughlin and Perkins... ("",0)..Theme
   T—stands for TITLE. D—stands for DESCRIPTION OF ACTION.
   NOTE—This music is synchronized on a basis of 15 minutes to the
   1,000 feet of perfect film.

ANNA CASE TO ENTER PICTURES.

Announcement that Anna Case, the beautiful young American soprano of the Metropolitan Opera Company, is to enter motion pictures for a limited period is made by Julius Steger, under whose direction the prima donna's photoplays will be produced.

Miss Case's first picture will be begun in February next immediately after she completes her concert engagements, for which she has been booked ever since the end of her last record-breaking tournee. The story, based upon real life experiences, will relate the struggles against great odds of a poor, but gifted, American girl, who, through force of her character and talents alone, rises to a position of dominance in the world's greatest opera company.

Miss Case has no idea of retiring from concert and opera. She will have ample time for music and pictures, devoting half the year to the one and half to the other. Mr. Steger already has arranged for her first scenario. The picture, seven reels, will be shown first as a special attraction at a leading Broadway theater. Joseph M. Schenck will be Mr. Steger's partner in the enterprise.

JOE FISHER ESCAPES U-BOAT ATTACK.

Among the passengers of the steamship City of Athens, which was torpedoed recently by a U-boat, was Joe Fisher, who was representing Fisher's Bioscope, Limited, of South Africa, in this country. Fisher was on his way home with a consignment of pictures for a circuit of theaters. He was accompanied by a fellow townsman, Charles Moore. Upon arriving at Cape Town Fisher cabled to Henry J. Brock in answer to an inquiry: "Ship sunk; Moore and self rescued; terrible experience; lost everything."

Fisher's friends in New York will be glad to learn of his escape from the U-boat.

Grinding the Crank

With Thornton Fisher

O. Henry Picture Releases in Story Form.

It was "past one at Rooney's" when "The Guilty Party" came out of "The Green Door." His pocket contained "The Gold That Glittered." When the cop on the beat asked him why he was sneaking out so stealthily he replied, "Strictly Business." But the cop pinched him and said that's "No Story" and took him to headquarters realizing that this was "A Departmental Case."

THE FILM FOOLOSOFER

SAYS" DEVELOPING A PLOT IS A BLAMED SIGHT HARDER SOME- TIMES THAN DEVELOPING THE FILM AFTER YOU'VE GOT THE PLOT."

"Be careful of that stone sidewalk," said the director as the new extra struck it head first, "because stone sidewalks are expensive."

* * *

We're going to recommend moving picture policemen for our local force. You can get a bunch of reserves from the picture police station to the heroine's home in fifty seconds flat.

* * *

And the way the little ninety-pound leading lady pulls open the door of a two-ton office safe so easily makes us think sometimes that maybe the safe door isn't a regular iron thing after all.

* * *

F. Canby Pork, who is writing the subtitles for a new feature, has not been informed concerning what the story is to be. At present it is the plan of the producers to make the story fit the subtitles.

* * *

"Moving picture actors are born, not made," said an actor the other day. "That's all right," returned the cynic, "I'm not blaming you!"

Words from the publicity man's note book:
dashing   superb   epochal   star
sensational   mystery   tremendous   stupendous
spectacle   gripping   scream   moral
thrilling   suspense   supe la ive   triumph

* * *

Gather around the piano and let's sing:
Humpty Dumpty sat on a wall,
Humpty Dumpty had a great fall,
For Dumpty, poor guy, a "double" was he,
Who's getting good money for falling, you see.

THE GUY IN THE ROW BEHIND US WHO KNOWS EVERY BODY IN THE BUSINESS. (?)

Picture magnates travel from New York to California and hack like a man going around the corner to the delicatessen for a bottle of milk.

* * *

"This is a great old world," said the dyed-in-the-wool film man as he reached for his favorite trade paper.

* * *

"How much do you weigh?" inquired a director of a heavy man he was interrogating.
"Two hundred and twenty pounds," replied the heavy one.
"I mean from the neck down," shot back the boss.

* * *

We've seen a piano player in a movie theater play the piano, talk to his girl back in the first row, read a copy of a movie magazine, count the change in his pocket, and scratch the back of his neck all in the space of two minutes—and the music sounded like it.

* * *

From Daylight to Darkness.

It's cruel, we know, but don't it tickle your funny bone (when after having been in the moving picture theater long enough to adapt your eyes to the darkness until you can discern everything perfectly) to watch the other customers come in from the broad daylight and grope for a seat like a blind-folded man.

* * *

So long!

(IN THE STUDIO DRESSING ROOM) PANNING THE BUNCH.

Strand to Give Daily Concerts

Beginning September 16 One Hour's Entertainment by Symphony Orchestra Will Be Feature at Big House.

HAROLD EDEL, managing director of the Strand theater, announces that the Strand concert orchestra, which now numbers forty musicians, will be enlarged to full symphonic strength and be known in the future as the Strand Symphony Orchestra.

Daily symphonic concerts of one hour's duration will be inaugurated Sunday, September 16, and will become a part of the regular Strand program from that date. The concerts will commence daily at 2:15 and at 2:30 on Sundays, and will precede the usual presentation of motion pictures and vocal and instrumental soloists.

The owners of the Strand theater attribute the success of that institution largely to the excellent musical program presented in conjunction with the projecting of motion pictures and the orchestra has been gradually enlarged and special efforts have been made to secure the best vocal and instrumental talent obtainable. When the Strand was first opened, in April, 1914, the orchestra was composed of sixteen members. This number was doubled in less than two years. and when Mr. Edel took charge of the theater a year ago the orchestra was enlarged to forty pieces, including the organists.

Mr. Edel was one of the first to put a large orchestra in a moving picture theater. In 1910, when he was given charge of the Alhambra Theater, in Cleveland, Ohio, he had an orchestra of fifteen pieces. He has always been a firm believer in good music as a means of entertainment. Regarding his latest introduction he said:

"I am not inaugurating the presentation of daily symphony concerts in order to increase attendance to our performances. Everyone who visits the Strand must realise that one of our greatest problems is to take care of our patrons. We play to a daily average of 12,000 people. My greatest desire is to give the public the best entertainment at the lowest prices possible, and I think that by giving daily symphony concerts, as fine as the most discriminating music lover could wish, we are presenting the ideal form of entertainment, pleasing those who are familiar with symphonic music and cultivating and educating the ones who are not. I have met very few persons who do not love music, and on the other hand I know that there are thousands of people in New York who seldom have an opportunity to hear real good music on account of prohibitive prices. In this connection let me say that although the symphony concerts will increase the expenses of the Strand Theater over $35,000 a year our prices will remain the same, 15, 25 and 50 cents, and the patrons who come to hear the concerts are entitled to stay as long as they please and attend the regular Strand show which follows immediately after the concert. I have engaged Signor Adriano Ariani, the famous Italian conductor, to direct the concerts."

As a conductor Signor Ariani obtained his experience under Mancinelli and Mascagni. He was Mascagni's substitute director for four years. Since the Augustenm was inaugurated at Rome Signor Ariani contributed with his own work the marvelous development of that great symphonic institution. He also has been conductor of operas and symphonic music at Rome, Pesaro, Senigallia, Bari, Naples, Macerata, Venice. Tolentino, Genoa, Florence, Monte Carlo (Monaco), Oporto, New York, Philadelphia and Boston.

ROY STEWART IN "DEVIL DODGER."

Roy Stewart will make his appearance as a fearless young man of the west in a forthcoming Triangle release. "Devil Dodger," directed by Cliff Smith, who assisted in the production of a number of Triangle plays featuring William S. Hart.

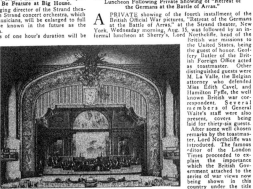

The Strand Symphony Orchestra.

The Moving Picture's Part in the War

Lord Northcliffe Emphasizes It in Speech at Informal Luncheon Following Private Showing of "Retreat of the Germans at the Battle of Arras."

A PRIVATE showing of the fourth installment of the British Official War pictures, "Retreat of the Germans at the Battle of Arras," at the Strand theater, New York, Wednesday morning, Aug. 15, was followed by an informal luncheon at Sherry's. Lord Northcliffe, head of the British war missions to the United States, being the guest of honor. Geoffery Butler of the British Foreign Office acted as toastmaster. Other distinguished guests were M. La Valle, the Belgian attorney who defended Miss Edith Cavel, and Hamilton Fyffe, the well known British war correspondent. Several members of General Waite's staff were also present, covers being laid for thirty-six guests.

After some well chosen remarks by the toastmaster, Lord Northcliffe was introduced. The famous editor of the London Times proceeded to explain the importance which the British Government attached to the series of war views now being shown in this country under the title of "British Official War Pictures," and to voice the opinion that the series is of the greatest value in showing the people of the United States the conditions our soldiers must face while helping to crush the common foe of humanity. M. La Valle followed with a short speech expressing the gratitude and brotherly feeling of the Belgians for this country, and his appreciation of the merits of the pictures shown that morning. M. La Valle is a magnetic speaker and it was easy to understand the passionate earnestness with which he sought to save the life of the brave English woman. Hamilton Fyffe spoke briefly of the immense amount of good he had seen the moving pictures do among the soldiers of Russia, many of whom were not able to read, but were forcibly impressed with the efforts being made by their Allies for the common cause.

The motion picture trade papers were represented by Joseph L. Kelley, Motion Picture News; T. O. Eltonhead, Exhibitors' Trade Review; Dickson G. Watts, Morning Telegraph, and Edward Weitzel, Moving Picture World.

PREPARING FOR ST. JOHN'S MEETING.

A preliminary meeting of local managers and theater men was held last week to appoint a committee to look after the entertainment side of the convention. On the committee were appointed W. H. Golding, president of the League; S. C. Hurley, secretary; F. G. Spencer, of the Lyric and Unique, and vice-president for Prince Edward Island; W. C. McKay, of the St. John opera house; A. B. Farmer, of the Star theater; G. A. Margetts, of the Canadian Universal Film Exchange; Reg. March, of the Pathe; Miss Kathleen Golding and Miss Alice Fairweather, motion picture editor of the St. John Standard. Among the plans are a reception at the Manor House. a favorite place for entertainments situated four miles out of St. John, and a sail on the St. John River.

The president and officers of the Canadian Motion Picture Association of Montreal have been invited to attend. L. B. Ouimet, of Pathe, general manager for Canada, and E. Auger, of the Vitagraph, are to be present as well as other managers who have accepted the invitation of the League.

NEW SOUTHERN PRODUCING COMPANY.

The Diamond Film Company is the title of a new film manufacturing concern. just incorporated in New Orleans. R. M. Chisholm is president of the company and with him are associated a number of southern business men. The company is capitalised for $100,000 and has taken over the plant and studio in New Orleans formerly operated by the Nola Film Company.

Kenean Buel

Selected to Direct the Lee Children for Fox—Has Had Wide Experience.

K ENEAN BUEL, one of the veteran directors of the Fox Film Corporation, yet one of the youngest in point of age, has been selected by William Fox, personally, to direct the future activities of the famous Lee children—Jane and Katherine.

These two youngsters, probably the best known children in the films, made an instantaneous and universal success in their first picture, "Two Little Imps," which was directed by

Kenean Buel.

Mr. Buel. There was immediate d e m a n d from exhibitors and the public for similar pictures by the Fox "baby grands."

The p r o b l e m of selecting the future director for these children was a most serious one, and Mr. Fox had repeated conferences with his aids and advisers. The most capable directors, not only of the Fox Company, but other producers, were considered. After looking over the lists submitted to him, Mr. Fox said:

"There is no necessity of going outside of our own organisation for a director for the Lee children. Kenean Buel is the man. He has already produced a marvelous picture with them, and for years I have watched his work with children. Children like and work with him, and I have the greatest confidence in his ability."

This decision of Mr. Fox places Mr. Buel in charge of one of the most unique and important features of the program of the Fox Film Corporation. He will direct Jane and Katherine Lee in future productions. Already their first picture under Mr. Buel's direction has created a furore throughout the country, and their future pictures may be looked forward to with confidence under the capable direction of Mr. Buel.

Kenean Buel is only thirty-four years old, and graduated from college at the age of eighteen, two years later being admitted to the bar as a practicing lawyer.

Born in the Blue Grass region of Kentucky, it was the hope of his parents that he would follow the law, as had his ancestors. The law, however, was too prosaic and dull for the young Kentuckian, who had an imagination, and wanted to create rather than follow precedents.

The stage lured him away from his Blackstone, and he joined a stock company as its business manager. Owing to the illness of one of his players, he was suddenly called upon to play a part. He next began playing juvenile leads, and made a success. Naturally from this he drifted into playwriting and stage direction and thence to pictures.

Mr. Buel is one of the most modest and retiring men in the motion picture business, and is exceptionally well liked by his players. Together with his wife, he lives on his estate in the Ramapo mountains in New Jersey, and is one of the best known breeders of prize winning live stock.

ROSEMARY THEBY RETURNS TO UNIVERSAL.

Rosemary Theby has recently signed a contract with Universal to appear in a series of comedies with Eddie Lyons and Lee Moran. This will be the second time that Miss Theby has appeared under the big "U" banner. Previous to her present connection she appeared in a series of comedies under the direction of Harry Myers which gained wide popularity. Miss Theby may also be featured in dramatic roles after she has completed the work already laid out.

E. B. Hatrick Promoted

Becomes Secretary of the International Film Service— Organized News Film Service.

A NNOUNCEMENT is made of the selection of E. B. Hatrick as secretary of the International Film Service. Mr. Hatrick's experience covers a wide range of newspaper and film activities. For several years he was employed as a reporter, telegraph editor and bureau manager on the United Press Association. In 1909, he left that organization to accept a position as editor of the Hearst Syndicate and in that capacity he took charge of the news

E. B. Hatrick

photograph d e p a r tments of the various Hearst newspapers and welded them into one organisation for the gathering and distribution of photograph illustrations for newspapers and magazines. This organisation secured some of the most notable beats in the history of the newspaper world, including such famous pictures as the Scott South Pole expedition, sinking of the battleship Audacious, the destruction of the German battleship Bluecher in the battle of the North Sea, first pictures of German invasion of Belgium, etc.

After the establishment of the news picture organisation, Mr. Hatrick conceived the idea of utilising this institution for the gathering of an up-to-the-minute news film. His theory was that good trained news photographers were better adapted for this work than studio motion picture operators and with the close alliance with the Hearst system of gathering news he would be in a better position to get material more quickly than any film organisation. A combination was made with the Selig Polyscope Company of Chicago and in February, 1914, the Hearst-Selig News Pictorial made its appearance on the screen. This reel was issued through the General Film Company and met with instant success.

For two years Mr. Hatrick had editorial charge of this film and later on when the International Film Service established its own system of exchanges, he organized and issued the Hearst International News Reel. He also, at this time, took charge of the organisation of the laboratory work for the International, and the scenic, educational and cartoon reels. When the amalgamation was made between the International Film Service and the Pathe Exchange, Mr. Hatrick took charge of the work of combining the two staffs of field operators and of the gathering of all negative for the Hearst-Pathe News.

NORMA TALMADGE WANTS BOOK PLAYS.

Following the phenomenal success of her recent screen adaptation of Cynthia Stockley's novel "Poppy" Miss Norma Talmage has announced that in the future all of her scenarios will be written from books. The avowed intention of the young screen favorite is carried out in "The Moth," her newest photoplay, taken from the novel by William Dana Orcutt which has been announced to follow "Poppy" among the Norma Talmage releases, and in "The Secret of the Storm Country," on which Miss Talmage will begin work next week in Ithaca, N. Y. "The Secret of the Storm Country" was written by Grace Miller White as a sequel to "Tess of the Storm Country," which is also familiar to the film public.

BESSIE LOVE IN "POLLY ANN."

Bessie Love is working on "Polly Ann," in which she appears in the role of an orphan compelled to earn her living as a slavey in a small town hotel. Later she is adopted by a wealthy man, who takes her into his home to replace a dissolute son.

Yankee Plays for the World

Is the Slogan of General Manager H. O. Davis, Who Inaugurates Big Campaign for Foreign Markets.

Y ANKEE plays for the World" is the new slogan soon to be adopted and carried out in policy by the Triangle Film Corporation as the result of the determination of General Manager and Vice-President H. O. Davis to invade the foreign exhibiting market on a larger scale and along different lines than ever before undertaken in the industry.

Decidedly an aggressive one, the campaign will be based upon Mr. Davis' personal investigations of the field and his belief that the war has stimulated rather than retarded the European and Oriental amusement demand. Distinctive Americanism will be so outstanding in the product that the stamp will be as recognizable as the brand.

"One of the chief reasons why American producers have partially failed in their efforts to get safe and sane export business," said Mr. Davis, "is that they have persisted in giving foreign exhibitors and foreign cinema patrons a product which they can obtain of better quality and more cheaply at home. We have been trying to make French plays and Japanese plays and East Indian plays in the United States when we knew nothing of the customs, likes and dislikes of these peoples. Even if this were not true, we have been offering the foreign consumer nothing that he could not obtain from the producers of his own country, and every nationality prefers to patronize home industry.

"It would be just as logical for American exhibitors to go to France, Japan and India for their American pictures as for foreign exhibitors to buy from us something they can get from their own producers.

"However, it is not reasonable to believe that American producers can compete with foreign producers in their own fields and the Triangle Film Corporation does not propose longer to try. We will endeavor to lead the industry in supplying the already brisk demand for a distinctly Yankee, if I may use the term, film play that does not encroach upon the foreign producer but fills a well established place of its own.

"The American business drama, the so-called Western plays, the comedy drama and the good old "melodrama" are four types of screen productions that the foreign producer cannot make as well as we can, and these forms of drama never fail to attract and retain the interest of the masses in almost every country under the sun.

"Foreign producers have been smarter than we in that they long have realized their failings and have not attempted to invade America with cowboy thrillers or other forms of cinema entertainment, which, they recognized, we were far more proficient in making than they. On the other hand they borrowed freely of American ideas and introduced them to their public when they were keen enough to take advantage of a demand that we did not appreciate.

"They appropriated our custard pies, our chases and our dare-devil automobile and train wreck stunts and let us struggle with vampires and problem plays and spectacles in which we were trying to interpret the Southern European and Oriental nature without knowing how. American producers have not failed utterly, but they have made themselves ridiculous in many instances.

"These principles," continued Mr. Davis, "are applicable to the exhibiting situation throughout the United States for the simple reason that Americans are loyal to their own customs and peculiarities and would rather see American life depicted upon the screen than anything else.

"The vein of humor that streaks every genuine Yankee gives him a keen appreciation of the comedy and comedy drama, his love of adventure and zest for the rough and ragged whets his appetite for the Western 'thriller' and melodrama, and his native ambition and enterprise stir him to enthusiastic enjoyment of the play that shows zeal and devotion to duty attaining success and reward."

J. WARREN KERRIGAN'S CONDITION.

J. Warren Kerrigan whose leg was broken as the result of the falling of his horse at Santa Barbara on Friday, the 10th inst., is now in the Cottage hospital of that city under the care of Dr. C. H. Stevens. Dr. Stevens, who set Mr. Kerrigan's leg, said that he found him in splendid physical condition, which, with his rugged constitution, would make his recovery very rapid and he felt confident that the star would be able to resume his work by the middle of September.

Sherrill Talks of His Coming Picture

Enthusiastic Over "The Man Without a Country," Featuring Arnold Daly and Directed by Jack Noble.

O NE cannot talk two minutes with William L. Sherrill, president of the Frohman Amusement Company, and listen to his description of "The Man Without a Country," a coming Frohman production, without partaking of the enthusiasm of the manufacturer. The subject is to be in seven or eight reels and will be ready for showing about the first week in September. Anthony P. Kelly is the author of the script, and in the preparation of it he spent much time and study. He has built upon the basis of Edward Everett Hale's dramatic story a structure which comprises many events in United States history. It will interest exhibitors and the photoplay public to know that Mr. Sherrill has obtained from Secretary Daniels, of the Navy Department, permission for the full use of the old frigate, "Constitution," now in the Charlestown Navy Yard. The rights accorded by the Secretary extend to the taking of pictures on or off the historic ship.

Arnold Daly will play Philip Nolan, the Man Without a Country. Mr. Daly has told Mr. Sherrill three reasons why he is anxious his interpretation shall be the best thing he has done in a screen way. You may take our word for it, the reasons seem to be sufficient—Mr. Daly has a real incentive.

"I think one of the wonderfully attractive things about this business is that a man can bring himself to such a pitch of enthusiasm that he sincerely, honestly believes he is going to have the best picture ever made," said Mr. Sherrill. "I can say deliberately that this story makes one of the most unusual scenarios I have ever seen. I believe there is no other player who can portray Philip Nolan as Arnold Daly is now portraying that character. The picture is being directed by John Noble. In the cast supporting Mr. Daly are Duncan McRae, Sydney Bracy, Frederick Truesdell, Charles J. Graham, Jack Sherrill and Anna Lehr and Mrs. Carr.

"We are putting everything into the picture that is absolutely authentic and perfect as to type, period and history. We are spending $15,000 on costumes alone—these are being made especially for the production. We believe we are going to have a great picture, one worthy of the subject and of the times in which it will be released."

SAM E. MORRIS, CONTROLS OHIO TERRITORY.

Sam E. Morris, who has been a member of the Selznick executive staff ever since the formation of the Lewis J. Selznick Enterprises, Inc., has been placed in entire charge of Selznick branches in the large Cleveland territory. This is one of the richest districts in the United States for Selznick contracts, and congratulations are due to Mr. Morris from his many friends in the industry.

Under the Cleveland branch is included the entire state of Ohio and the eastern half of the state of Kentucky. A sub-office is located at Cincinnati. Mr. Morris is well known throughout Ohio, and has previously made a great record through his sales of pictures in this state. His family and relatives reside in Cleveland, and taking charge of the Cleveland office is like going home to Sam Morris.

ACTIVITIES AT GLENDALE.

The Empire All Star Corporation Studios at Glendale, L. I., are in full swing now, with three companies busily at work. Dell Henderson is at work on "My Wife," the great Frohman stage success in which Ann Murdock is starring, supported by a cast whose names include those of Rex McDougal, Hubert Druce, Ferdinand Gottschalk and many others equally well known.

Albert Capellani is directing Edna Goodrich in "American Maid," which it is unanimously agreed is the best story Miss Goodrich has yet been provided with. And John B. O'Brien, who is enthusiastic over his new star, Olive Tell, who, supported by David Powell, is playing the stellar role in "The Unforeseen," "Outcast," the first Empire picture, is to be released through the Mutual Exchanges, September 3.

CAMILLA DAHLBERG WITH METRO FOR "DRAFT 258."

Camilla Dahlberg, who originated the role of Bianca in "The Great Lover," with Leo Ditrichstein, has been engaged by Metro Pictures Corporation to play the important part of the woman spy in "Draft 258." Metro's new patriotic photodrama, which has already been put into production. Mabel Taliaferro is the star of "Draft 258," which was written by William Christy Cabanne and June Mathis.

Alexandra Carlisle

ALEXANDRA CARLISLE, who plays the star role in the new World-Picture Brady-Made, titled "Tides of Fate," is an English actress of very great celebrity for her rare physical beauty and her surpassing gifts in the art of acting.

Her greatest triumph in London was registered upon her appearance there in the leading role of "Everywoman" some years ago, when the most austere of the English critics hailed her as "the best actress and the most beautiful woman on the London stage."

Miss Carlisle came to America shortly after the production above mentioned and she has remained here ever since. She has been the "featured" player in several dramas and comedies, and last season was chosen by George C. Tyler for the central personage in "The Country Cousin," in which she made a genuine sensation during the long run in Philadelphia.

By an odd coincidence Miss Carlisle's first New York appearance in this drama

Alexandra Carlisle.

will occur at the Gaiety theater on the same date as the publication of her picture play, "Tides of Fate."

This drama contains a number of exceptionally thrilling episodes. In one of these a runaway saddle horse, upon which Miss Carlisle as the heroine is taking her morning spin, plunges from a high cliff into the river, from which she is rescued by "the wrong man," whom she marries from gratitude. Later there are two extremely striking battle scenes—one between bandits and the mounted police of Canada, and the other an engagement of United States troops with an overwhelming horde of Moros in the Phillipines.

"Tides of Fate" is a "big" picture in every sense of the term, and in the making involved an expenditure that would have amply justified its issuance as a ten-reel special but for the World's loyalty to the regular program policy.

ALICE BRADY LEAVES WORLD FILM CORPORATION.

Alice Brady has completed her contract with the World Film Corporation, and she declines to renew it. She severs her connections this week with that firm, of which her father, William A. Brady, is managing director, and she announces that she is now at liberty. She may accept any one of several offers that she has had from other motion picture producers, and she may possibly return to the legitimate stage. She has two plays under contract, and if she appears in them it may be under the direction of her father in his capacity as theatrical manager, but she is not to be any longer a star for the World Film Corporation which turns out "Brady-made Pictures." She has been with that company for two years, and in that time she has won wide popularity as a "movie" star. The World Film Corporation recognised this fact when her contract expired on Tuesday (Aug. 14) and it offered her a very large increase of salary, but the increase was not sufficient in her opinion, since she had already received large offers from other companies, and she declined to renew her contract. Negotiations have continued throughout the week, but Miss Brady has announced definitely that she has severed her connections with the World Film Corporation.

THE PARALTA PLAN BOOK.

The Paralta Plan book, which Paralta Plays, Inc., has been advertising very extensively in the trade papers of late as an aid to the development of picture theater patronage and the elimination of waste in the management of theaters, has been issued from the press and thousands of copies are now being sent to exhibitors throughout the country who filed their applications for them during the past three months.

This book comprises 64 pages. It reviews the economic history of the trade, it shows the 'leakage" which results from the present forms of picture distribution and shows how the four big points of the Paralta Plan will redound to the benefit of the exhibitor.

The book especially dwells on restricted, non-competitive territory, unlimited runs, repeat booking privileges without extra charge, and a twelve month contract, with cancellation privileges to the exhibitor which are exclusively his. Otherwise, under the Paralta Plan, the exhibitor is protected in every way from the conditions he now claims militate most against his interests. He can cancel a Paralta contract, whereas the company cannot cancel on him. The Paralta Plan book is very interesting reading to all concerned.

Grace Darmond.

WHEN Duty Calls," the seven-reel production with which Sanger and Jordan will make their initial bow in the producing field, is a stirring war photodrama in which Miss Grace Darmond takes the leading role. The picture is now in the making at the Norma Talmadge studios under the direction of Capt. Harry Lambart. Miss Darmond, probably the youngest leading woman in the film firmament, occupied the stellar role in Pathe's thrilling serial, "The Shielding Shadow," which is shortly to be seen in New York at one of the leading Broadway theaters. It was Miss Darmond's brilliant work in this picture, after it had been seen at a private view, which caused Sanger and Jordan to immediately offer her a contract as leading woman in "When Duty Calls" and several other pictures they contemplate producing.

Grace Darmond.

"When Duty Calls' is not a war picture in the sense that the audience is thrilled by the sight of marching soldiers and the usual scenes which accompany a film of this class, but it is a photodrama which will appeal to every mother in the country who has a son of draft age and is willing to send him to the front with a mother's blessing.

The young leading woman has a checkered career as bride and mother whose husband has answered the call of his country. At the same time she has ample opportunities of displaying the fine dramatic qualities which she showed she possessed in the Pathe serial, "The Shielding Shadow." Miss Darmond lays claim to being the most married star in filmdom, as in her brief twenty years she has been led to the altar no less than three hundred times. True, Miss Darmond's experiences have been in front of a motion picture camera, and at present there is a prospect that she will continue on her way as a blushing bride, at least in the movies, for some time to come.

H. NEWMAN OPENS IN OSSINING.

On Monday evening, Aug. 20, the Victoria theater threw open its doors to the public in Ossining, New York, under the management of H. Newman. Mr. Newman formerly ran the Majestic in Holyoke, Mass. The Victoria was formerly known as the Roe theater, but has been renamed by Mr. Newman, who has remodeled the lobby, added a fine new electric sign and made other improvements. He expects to run first run pictures, selecting his program from state rights and other features and in this way will secure an entirely different program from other theaters in his vicinity.

Among the Picture Theaters

Colonial Theater, Columbus, O.

Manager Marcus Has His House Decorations Harmonize With the Different Seasons of the Year—Admission Prices 10 and 20 Cents.

DO ATMOSPHERIC conditions in a photoplay house count? They do as is attested by the policy pursued by M. Marcus, who is the manager of the Colonial theater in Columbus, Ohio. The accompanying pictures of the stage, foyer and lobby give a very good idea of the floral decorations for summer used recently to beautify the Colonial. These embellishments have occasioned many favorable comments from the theater's large patronage, and it is the intention of Mr. Marcus to have the decorations conform with the different seasons of the year. The decorations, whether they are flowers, banners, festoons, or bunting, for any one season do not remain up during the entire period of that season, but are changed every two weeks or so.

Formerly used as a burlesque house and as the home of stock, the Colonial has been transformed into a veritable garden, and under the directing hand of its manager it has been developed as the ideal home of photoplays, playing to capacity audiences every day at ten and twenty cents. Mr. Marcus believes that appearances help make a theater, and it is not too much to say that for attractiveness, lobby effects, and stage settings, the Colonial compares favorably with any other theater between New York and Chicago.

Of special interest is the lighting system. Lights are changed each week, the colors so arranged as to harmonize with the settings and the particular picture shown. Everything in the house suggests quietude and harmony. The energetic young manager came to take charge of the Colonial after it had proven a failure as a photoplay house. He came with ideas of his own, and was given carte blanche to put them into execution. The result is that the Colonial is now on an excellent paying basis, and that its clientele is steadily growing.

Another element that made for the success of the Colonial is the musical entertainment. Music as an essential to the proper enjoyment of motion pictures was recognized by Manager Marcus as a direct necessity, and instead of the loud blare and the illogical orchestration so common in many photoplay houses, the music fits in and harmonizes with the picture.

Before the pictures constituting a show are screened for the public Mr. Marcus views each one privately. He also has the musical score selected for each picture tried out during the private running of the program to further satisfy him that there are no inconsistencies. Should any unsuitable cue be found in playing the selection which was not observed when it was picked, it is altered immediately, so that each score is in perfect harmony with the action in the picture, and in shape to be presented to the patrons of the Colonial.

St. James Theater, Asbury Park, N. J.

Rosenberg Opens 2,360-Seat Picture House on Jersey Coast —His Third Venture There—Typhoon Fan Ventilation System Used.

THE accompanying illustration is a photograph of a wash drawing of the new theater which was opened recently in Asbury Park, N. J., by Walter Rosenberg, manager of the Savoy theater, 112 West 34th street, New York City. This makes the third venture on the Jersey Coast for Rosenberg, for he controls and operates the Savoy theater, also in Asbury Park, and the Broadway at Long Branch.

The St. James has a seating capacity of 2,360, which entitles it to the distinction of being one of the largest motion picture houses in the State of New Jersey. Thomas W. Lamb, who was the architect of the Rialto theater, New York City, designed the St. James, and the exterior is built

Wash Drawing of St. James Theater, Asbury Park, N. J.

of red brick laid up in black cement with panels of yellow buff. A scheme of color decoration different from that common in decorating the interior of theaters has been inaugurated in the St. James. Instead of the usual gold, brown and red motif the color scheme is black and gold, which is calculated to eliminate whatever glare that may be produced from the ceiling and wall lights.

The dimensions of the structure are 100 by 156 feet, and it is proposed to operate the St. James all the year round. The Typhoon Fan system of ventilation is used, and a Moeller pipe organ furnishes the musical accompaniment to the pictures. Ample provision was made in building the St. James to house "legitimate" shows should it ever be decided to change the policy.

$80,000 PICTURE HOUSE FOR MADISON.

An $80,000 theater will be erected on East Mifflin street, Madison, Wis., taking the place of the Strand and running through to East Dayton street. Concrete, tile, marble and iron will be used in the construction of the playhouse, which is to be one of the largest and finest moving picture theaters in the northwest. It will be fireproof throughout.

The Lobby of the Colonial, Columbus, O., with Summer Decorations.   The Artistic Stage Setting at the Colonial, Columbus, O.   The Foyer of the Colonial Theater, Columbus, O., in Summer Dress.

Star Palace, Patchogue, L. I.

Oldest Theater on Long Island Still Going "Strong" After Twelve Years—Has Been Remodeled from Ttime to Time to Bring It Up to Date.

THE Star Palace, the oldest theater on Long Island, is at Patchogue, under the management of George T. Holmes. It has been under the same management since its inception twelve years ago. This is a long life for a motion picture theater. It began in 1905 in a small store which seated 116 persons. This was before the days of motion picture studios. Pictures were being made on the roofs of office buildings. Few pictures were as long as one thousand feet. The exhibition of a moving picture was mainly a stunt. And yet Mr. Holmes made good and has kept it up ever since.

The first building of the Star Palace was operated for two years. Then a larger house was built two doors below seating four hundred persons. This building was occupied until three years ago when the present building was erected.

The present building, the third Star Palace, is the largest theater in Suffolk County. It was erected at a cost of $30,000 and has a seating capacity of over fifteen hundred. It is a two-story concrete structure, the facade decorated with artistic plaster figures in relief. It carries a vertical electric

Star Palace, Patchogue, L. I.

sign bearing the word, "Palace," surmounted by a five-pointed electric star. The building is flanked by two ornamental columns for street lights standing at the curb. On each side of the arch, which gives entrance to the wide and spacious lobby, is an electric arc. The arch is set with electric lights. Altogether this arrangement gives a very attractive appearance by night, and serves to beautify the high road on which the theater is situated. The large lobby offers lots of space for the display of posters advertising the daily attractions. The admission prices are fifteen and twenty-five cents daily, both matinee and night.

This was the first theater on Long Island to have an orchestra. There are now six pieces in the orchestra. The stage is decorated with a special scene set made by the Lee Lash Studios. The size of the picture projected is seventeen by twenty-four feet. A Johns-Manville booth is used and Simplex projectors. This theater had the third Simplex that was built.

The publicity department of the theater is under the management of Earle Holmes, whose enterprise won for him second prize in the Bluebird advertising contest. As an example of what he can do, this is what happened when "The Eagle's Wings" was shown for two days for the benefit of the Red Cross. He used a Ford tractor as a street advertisement and thereby attracted one thousand children into the theater from the nearby village of Hagerman, L. I. Further, he induced a local weekly newspaper, "The Argus," to issue a special edition advertising the picture. This is an unusual feat. Mr. Holmes attributes the success of his theater directly to the Moving Picture World, from which he has gleaned many a money-making point.

MANY IMPROVEMENTS FOR GRAND OPERA HOUSE.

Always on the lookout for the comfort and convenience of their patrons, the O'Donnell-Eskridge Amusement Company, of Washington, Ind., at a cost of $3,000 has installed in their Grand Opera House there a new ventilating and air-cooling

system. Situated between the ceiling and roof of the building is a double set of eight-foot typhoon multiblade twin blowers, with ventilators located in another part of the building, which provide an outlet for the vitiated air. The fans are operated by a ten-horsepower electric motor. This equipment insures a constant supply of fresh, cool air at all times, which is particularly pleasing to the audience during the hot summer months.

The company also announces that late in the summer the upper part of the theater will be remodeled, the present balcony and offices removed and a new semi-circular balcony built, allowing an unobstructed view of the screen from every seat, and increasing the capacity of the house by about 350. Four new boxes will be added, new orchestra chairs installed, and the entire theater redecorated. As a result, Washington will have one of the most attractive and up-to-date houses in southern Indiana.

Opera House, Wolfville, N. S.

Town with Only 2,000 Population Maintains 500-Seat Photoplay Theater—Students of Seminary Attend Show in Body When Educational Film Is Run.

THE Opera House at Wolfville, N. S., formerly owned and managed by the late W. Marshall Black, has been taken over by several St. John men. A. E. Mason, formerly of the Imperial theater, has been appointed manager and is already in Wolfville. Mr. Mason has been for some years chief electrician and operator at the Imperial and will be qualified by his experience to manage the theater. He has a personal interest in the business.

The town of Wolfville has a population of 2,000, and is the center of a large farming district. There is a seminary there and when an educational film is run the authorities co-operate with the theater and announce the picture at the college, the students sometimes attending in a body.

The Opera House has perhaps the finest set of properties in the Provinces and can handle any of the better class of road shows. The house is used (as so many of our thea-

Interior of Opera House, Wolfville, N. S., Canada.

ters are) as a sort of social center, and on Sundays meetings of various kinds are held, recruiting, patriotic or lectures.

The house is decorated in old rose and cream. It possesses two picture machines and its own electric light plant. The city current is alternating, so a Mercury Arc Rectifier is used.

Music can be furnished by piano or organ, and the theater is equipped for orchestra. Admission is ten and fifteen cents, the management paying the war tax. The admission was raised recently to meet this tax. Only evening shows are held. The programme changes three times a week. There is a seating capacity of five hundred. The seats are opera chairs.

YOUNG BUYS GRAND THEATER AT LEXINGTON.

John C. Young, who for about two years has been associated with Clyde Wright as part owner of Wright's Grand theater, Lexington, Mo., has purchased Mr. Wright's interest in the house. Mr. Young, who will now assume full charge, is well fitted for his duties as he has had several years' experience in the motion picture business. This change is due to Mr. Wright's recent illness, together with the great increase in his duties as Justice of the Peace. He has proved himself to be an enterprising manager and a great believer in the efficiency of advertising, and his many friends regret to see him give up the business with which he has been associated for several years.

Old Mill Theater, Dallas, Texas

E. H. Hulsey Rehabilitates House Damaged by Fire—One of the Prettiest Theaters in the City—Uses No Gaudy Announcements in Lobby.

ON May 19 last the re-opening of the Old Mill Theater in Dallas took place. The original building was so badly damaged by fire on the night of February 24 that the structure had to be practically rebuilt. As can be seen from the accompanying view of the exterior the architectural design resembles that of a mill. There is the flanking column at each side, wide at the bottom and slightly narrower at the top, where an immense exhaust fan in each has been placed, calling to mind the fan shaped wind wheel which is so important a part in the old-time mills. Then further enhancing the illusion is the old fashioned shaped window in the columns and in the center part of the structure, and the gradually sloping roof which projects just a little beyond the front and back of the building.

One of the distinguishing features of the rehabilitated Old Mill is the attractive electrical display over the main

The Old Mill Theater, Dallas, Texas.

entrance. This shows a woman standing at the edge of the roof in a diving position. The next figure shows her in the air, while in the third position the figure is partly submerged in the "water." Each of the figures is outlined in colored electric lights, and the splash caused by the "body" touching the "water" is also brought out by the alternating lighting and dying out of incandescent lights. Then there is the water wheel of the mill and the "water" gushing under it and the spray from the blades as they leave the water. This is a two-side sign; that is to say, it can be seen from either direction on a line parallel with the building line.

The front of the Old Mill is faced with tapestry brick lined with white cement. There is an artistic canopy running the entire length of the building and extending to the edge of the sidewalk with art glass in the squares in the drop. In keeping with the handsome appearance of the front is the method in which the announcement concerning the current and future programs is made. All paper used is placed in glass covered brass frames. No gaudy posters are employed, but artistically painted signs, giving the names of the pictures, the featured players, and other data pertaining to the subjects. The flooring of the lobby is laid with large and small squares of tile in attractive design, and the box office has a wainscoting of marble which is topped with plate glass running along the sides and front. A pretty wood carved design bearing the name of the theater surmounts the glass sides and finishes off this part of the theater. The lobby as well as the front is abundantly illu-

minated, and four wide entrance doors lead into the auditorium. The doors are finished in mahogany. Each one is beautified with fifteen squares of beveled glass.

The fine impression of the house that is created upon the mind by the graceful lines of the exterior is not weakened one iota when the interior is approached. Here, too, the lines are graceful, and the various colors used in the decorations blend harmoniously. And so the conception that the Old Mill theater is a thing of beauty, a worthy addition to the list of excellent motion picture theaters in Dallas and a credit to the name of E. H. Hulsey, general manager of the company operating the house, and to the other members of the concern, is firmly entrenched in the mind of the observer.

A few words of detail on the embellishments of the interior will not be amiss. Silk tapestry of rosy hue adorn the walls, and the quiet elegance produced by this warm decoration is enhanced by the arrangement of ivory colored panels in relief. Ivory and gold is the color motif of the ceiling, and this has been relieved by hand painted floral effects. All electrical fixtures are finished in gold leaf while the draperies are in blue silk velour. This is in striking contrast to the ivory colored carpet, the plainness of which has been broken by figures in blue. Then there is the flower receptacles and bird cages in willow with stands to match, adding to the individuality of the Old Mill.

Each one of the 1,500 seats has a mahogany colored frame with Spanish leather upholstering. Indirect lighting is used, and a vacuum cooling system. Music is furnished by a large pipe organ. Until six o'clock a section is reserved

Interior of the Old Mill Theater, Dallas, Texas.

for children under twelve years and unaccompanied women. The uniform of the ushers smacks of the military, and each man is drilled in courtesy and politeness.

Capacity houses have been enjoyed since the Old Mill was re-opened, and the admission prices are 10, 15, 25 and 35 cents.

ALLENTOWN'S STRAND TO OPEN IN SEPTEMBER.

Situated in the heart of the City of Allentown, Pa., at the corner of Eighth and Hamilton streets, the Strand theater, representing an investment of over $100,000, is nearing completion, and will be opened early in September. The location of this house is admirable, as it faces the terminus of the trolley lines from Philadelphia and surrounding towns.

Gennert and Stuckert, who are the managers as well as the owners, have spared no expense in making this house, so far as beauty and comfort are concerned, one of the most attractive houses in that part of the state. The ventilating plant, which is being installed by the American Heating and Ventilating Company, will supply 25 cubic feet of air per minute for each patron.

Built of steel, brick and concrete, the building occupies a plot 46½ by 170 feet, and is equipped with a large number of exits so as to enable the theater to be emptied within a very short space of time. Another feature which not only adds to the safety but also to the comfort of the patrons is the wide spaces between the rows of seats. Other conveniences for the patrons include rest rooms, sanitary drinking fountains and a spacious foyer; in fact, the management is providing numerous new and novel features which should, together with the high class of pictures to be shown, insure a large clientele.

Motion Picture Educator

Conducted by REV. W. H. JACKSON and MARGARET I. MACDONALD

Interesting Educationals

One Floricultural Subject, One Marine, One Sport, and Four Travel.

Reviewed by Margaret I. MacDonald.

"Rose Breeding" (Universal).

IN THE Universal Screen Magazine No. 31 will be found some valuable information concerning the breeding of roses. For those who love flowers or are interested in the development and culture of roses this subject will be found unusually interesting. The illustration reveals the manner in which the seed from selected plants is fertilized, ripened and later germinated in sandy soil. The subject is well illustrated and sub-titled with care.

"An Under-Sea Garden" (Mutual-Gaumont).

In Reel Life No. 67 will be found some interesting views which have been photographed on the floor of the ocean at Miami, Fla., by E. B. Gray. In the picture are shown the coral reefs at the edge of the gulf stream, the plant life of the ocean, and the fish swimming about in their own domain. This is an intensely attractive subject which will find favor with all.

"Beach Sports in Southern California" (Paramount-Bray).

In the eightieth release of the Pictograph will be found some inspiring views of beach sports on the Californian coast. Among these is surf riding, which originated with the Hawaiians. Here we see men and women indulging hilariously in the sport of riding a plank over the waves. Splendid exhibitions of swimming are also included, and one of the features of the picture is the work of A. Dahlquist, a member of the San Diego Life Guards, who demonstrates some daring feats.

"Bruges, Belgium" (Mutual-Gaumont).

Views of the old city of Bruges, Belgium, comprise a part of Tours Around the World No. 40. Bruges is the capital of West Flanders and is of unusual interest on the screen at the present time because of Belgium's place in the great world war. The canals which intersect it have caused it to be known as "The Venice of the North" and add much to its picturesqueness. The city is noted for its wonderful chimes, and the places of interest which are shown are the famous belfry of Bruges, the Lion's Bridge, and the Gruthouse, a seignorial residence of the fifteenth century.

"The Land That Does Not Wiggle" (Educational-Bruce).

On his way through Texas and New Mexico Robert C. Bruce picked up a great deal of interesting material, photographing for us the idiosyncrasies of the "Land That Does Not Wiggle." Evidently the stillness of the sandy wastes and rocks over which he chose to travel impressed him in this manner. One of the first things in picture that impresses us is a sand storm. Then there is the little mission made of mud, and the chocolate colored houses with their chocolate colored inmates. There are typical New Mexico scenes in abundance, and views of the Rio Grande and cactus covered wastes. This is a remarkably attractive picture, at the close of which are some night scenes on the desert. Here we are reminded that because of its beautiful nights men answer the wail of the desert.

"The First American Apartment House" (Educational-Bruce).

"The First American Apartment House" appears on the same reel with "Nature's Theatricals," a study of the Grand Canyon. The apartment house referred to is that embodying the homes of the Cliff Dwellers, which were photographed by Mr. Bruce at the Canyon of El Rito de Los Frijoles, N. M. It has a courtyard 200 feet in diameter and possesses 180 rooms. On the walls in the back rooms there still exist the remains of adobe plaster used in lining them. The subject is unusually well illustrated in the usual interesting style of Robert C. Bruce.

"Nature's Theatricals" (Educational-Bruce).

"Nature's Theatricals" presents some of the most beautiful views of the Grand Canyon of Arizona that have ever been photographed. Here we see the tourists descending into the

canyon by way of the Bright Angel trail, and are given several views of the sides of the great abyss. Then we are told that only amateurs get their knowledge of the canyon by following the trail into its depths. Others of wider vision sit on the edge of the precipice and watch for "Nature's theatricals" in the play of the elements about its rim. Before and after the storm are beautifully described in film, and with our photographer we watch the mystery of the clouds as they pour like great white streamers from canyons into other canyons of greater mystery. A truly beautiful picture.

The School vs. The Theater

W. D. McGuire of the National Board of Review Points Out Wisdom of Utilizing Theaters for Film Entertainments.

IN SPEAKING of the work of the National Committee for Better Films to a representative of the Moving Picture World, W. D. McGuire, secretary of the National Board of Review, said: "It is not unusual in the development of many social movements, for dangers to crop up, that were not at first anticipated. The enthusiasm with which local committees are forming in different communities to further the Better Films Movement is also giving rise to a danger which may develop unless motion picture exhibitors show themselves willing to grasp the opportunity offered. I refer to the question frequently asked by these committees as to whether it is wise to give motion picture entertainments in the school buildings. We all recognize that the people are coming into their own as far as the schoolhouse is concerned. The time is rapidly passing when either the principal of a school or the local school board may consider the school as their personal property, and they no longer feel that they have the authority to deny the unlimited use of the school building, to the people of the community—the taxpayers—to whom the property really belongs. This was brought out forcibly at the Chicago convention of the National Council of Community Center workers whose slogan is the unlimited use of the schoolhouses by the people themselves.

"When it comes, however, to transferring the motion picture entertainment of the community to the school building, even as a community center, danger arises. The school stands for concrete education and this fact is very apt to be implied in the whole atmosphere of the place. It is particularly well-grounded in the minds of young people who spend so many hours a day under the schoolhouse roof. The motion picture theater, on the other hand, represents 'entertainment' in their minds and this type of entertainment while possessing educational value of a high order, nevertheless imparts its enlightenment, for the most part, sub-consciously rather than consciously. It is apt, therefore, to be more permanent.

"The local committee on Better Films, therefore, working for permanent results, will do well to utilize the motion picture theater as the field for their operations rather than attempt to transfer the entertainment to a school building where the surroundings do not especially lend themselves to entertainment as an end in itself. Whether or not the local committee is inclined to transfer its activities to the schoolhouse depends largely upon the measure of cooperation shown by the local theater manager. It is fortunate that in most localities up-to-date managers are quick to show the utmost cooperation, realizing that to work in the public interest is to their personal financial interest also.

"The National Committee for Better Films has urged from its origin the avoidance of the so-called educational pictures, at any rate as the backbone of the program. The finest dramas with a strong human interest element are those which appear month after month on the bulletin of the National Committee as having been used most successfully. There are conspicuous examples among producing companies making photoplays of this type consistently. It may be stated with reasonable assurance, that the entertainment which will not please the older people of the community will not be successful with young people. The heart, rather than the head, must govern in selecting the pictures. Strong, vital drama, presenting manhood and womanhood at its best, are needed. Lessons—'moral' or otherwise—should be avoided. Inspiration to act and think rightly is the best kind of education and the moving picture entertainment attracts thousands when pictures possessing these qualities are shown.

"The theater, not the schoolhouse, is the place for the motion picture show. Much is gained and nothing lost by using this natural channel for the entertaiments. It all depends on the cooperative spirit shown by the exhibitor."

White Plains Gets Busy
Local Committee for Better Films Makes Plans for Future Entertainment and Welfare of Community—Theater Manager Cooperates.

RECENTLY at White Plains, N. Y., a meeting was held to arrange for special moving picture shows for that city. A strong group of representatives of various women's clubs was organized to further the interest of the Better Films Movement in White Plains, and a local exhibitor was consulted. Unfortunately he allowed other matters to press upon his time to the extent that the women of the committee gained the impression that he did not wish to cooperate with them. They immediately turned their attention to the school building and started their plans to organize regular performances in the schoolhouse weekly. At this point the manager realized the opportunity that was slipping from him and assured the ladies that by a return to the original plan they could count on his utmost cooperation. Conference meetings have been held during the summer and the movement is well under way toward getting the first of the Better Film performances started at White Plains immediately after the opening of the schools in September. Mrs. R. P. Ray, wife of the city superintendent of schools, has been active in the movement since its origin. No one realises better than Mrs. Ray the advisability of using the regular theater for the special performances, and the danger of making the program "educational." The committee, headed by Mrs. A. K. Griffin, has the matter in charge. Publicity plans are being worked out and everything points to carrying out the plan most successfully. Mr. W. D. McGuire of the National Board of Review to whom we are indebted for this information says: "Frequently the motion picture exhibitor does not realize the Better Films Movement is his movement and that the organisation of a local committee is one of the best mediums of publicity his theater can obtain."

Moving Pictures in the Orient
Interesting Matter Gleaned from J. W. Allen, Paramount Representative Recently Returned From the Orient.

OUR San Francisco correspondent, T. A. Church, sends some interesting facts in connection with the moving picture's place in the Orient. These facts, learned in an interview with J. W. Allen of the Paramount Pictures Corporation, will be found good reading, and are as follows:

The Orient, the land of mysticism, but also the land of wonderful commercial possibilities, is succumbing slowly but surely to the charm of moving pictures. This is the news brought home by J. W. Allen, of the San Francisco branch of the Progressive Motion Picture Company, distributors of Paramount Pictures, who returned in July from a trip to China, Japan and the Philippine Islands, made for the purpose of studying conditions from first hand and of placing Paramount service. During his absence of six months and two days he secured a fund of valuable information that will be used to advantage and succeeded in booking a large amount of business, considering the present development of the field.

Mr. Allen was accompanied on the trip by his wife, and the first stop, after a brief visit to Honolulu, was made in Japan. From that city and other communities of the Insular possessions of the United States. There are several moving picture houses here and Paramount pictures are being shown in a splendid new one, the Lyric theater, on the main street of the city, opened on June 1. While prominent as a business thoroughfare, this street is one of the shortest of similar importance in the world; being but about four blocks in length.

From the Philippine Islands Mr. Allen and his wife went to Hong Kong, the British port in China, and then to Canton, Shanghai and the northern provinces, two months being spent in this country. Much has been written concerning the moving picture industry in China, but Mr. Allen found but

little to substantiate the reports that have come out of that country either concerning the number of theaters, their ownership or the methods of conducting them. "China, with a population estimated at four hundred million souls, has within its great confines only forty moving picture houses," said Mr. Allen, "or one for every ten million persons. On the face of it this country should present wonderful possibilities for moving pictures, and it does, but any development will be slow. Moving picture theaters are found in the treaty ports, but there are great cities in the interior where there are no theaters and none are wanted at the present time. A vast amount of poverty and ignorance must be overcome and changes made in local government before moving pictures will be popular." In many places attempts have been made to introduce this form of amusement, but without much success. Soldiers would insist on being admitted free to entertainments and would start disturbances which the civil authorities would be unable to quell, with the result that the latter in many cases are now refusing to grant permits to would-be exhibitors in order to preserve order. This is merely one of the many problems met with in attempting to introduce moving pictures in China and illustrates the fact that it is not solely a question of educating Chinese to appreciate screen productions.

During the stay of Mr. Allen in Japan he visited the leading cities, including Kobe, Osaka, Kyoto, Tokyo and Yokahama. He found that this country possesses splendid possibilities as a market for moving pictures. With this form of entertainment steadily growing in popularity. However, there are many problems to be overcome by the American manufacturer in marketing his products there and business cannot be transacted on American lines. Quite a few Japanese films are being made, but these do not approach the American product in quality. These native productions are divided sharply into two schools, those of the old, or Shogun days, which have to do with the legends and myths of old Japan, and those of the new Japan, whose actors play parts of modern dramas. Practically all of the work is done by men, it being very seldom that a woman portrays a character before the camera.

The wrestlers of Japan, long idols of the people, are commencing to appear on the screen. These are trained from boyhood for their future occupation and the course of training they receive and the system of feeding that is followed make giants of them and they appear almost like a different race, compared with the rest of the people, who are small.

One of the distinctive features of moving picture entertainments in Japanese theaters is the use of the film explainer, or kabutsan, as he is known. This personage occupies a prominent place on the stage and explains the action on the screen while the films are being slowly run through. He gives his interpretation of what the actors in the production are saying, runs the gamut of emotions, with deep bass tones for the villains, shrill shrieks for woe, and changes to suit the action of the picture. Frequently he gets an entirely different impression from that intended by the director of the picture, but if this is noticed by the audience it is never shown.

Moving pictures are projected in an entirely different manner in that country than in the United States, and machines of Japanese manufacture are used almost exclusively. These are sold at less than one hundred dollars gold, so there is no chance for any business there by American manufacturers under present conditions. Films are run through the machines at a very low rate of speed and the intermittent movement is supplanted by a device which serves the same purpose, but which does not admit of a fast motion.

Contrary to the general impression, but few of the Japanese sit on the floor in moving picture houses, but the parts of the theaters arranged for sitting in this manner are considered the best. Music is furnished by a native orchestra, which performs after the kabutsan has finished his work. All attempts to introduce American music has failed, being acceptable to no class of Japanese. The patronage is drawn almost exclusively from the middle class, the members of the old school not caring for modern invention and the poorer classes unable to go. Japanese exhibitors do not use film titles, leaving the interpretation to the kabutsan, but in China these are translated and are shown in both English and Chinese.

While in Tokyo Mr. Allen made a trade showing of Paramount pictures and the leading film men of the Empire were on hand to view them. A story of his trip appeared in the "movie magazine" published by the Katsudo-Shashin-Zasshi Publishing Co., with pictures taken at a welcome party tendered himself and Mrs. Allen at Mikawaya Hall on June 20, by Shiho Okamura, publisher of the Katsudo-Shashin-

Zasshi. The dinner served here included almost twenty courses and was an interesting experience, in which the manipulation of chopsticks formed no small part.

Mr. Allen is now attending to his former duties as manager of the San Francisco branch of the Progressive Motion Picture Company, but these have taken on a different aspect since his return from the Orient. Instead of being merely a distributing point for the Pacific Coast, in itself a territory of no mean importance, San Francisco has become the distributing center for the biggest territory in the world, serving five-eighths of the entire population of the globe. Paramount pictures have been placed in this new field and the seed that has been sown is expected to produce an abundant harvest in years to come, when the sleeping East awakens.

British Notes

THE most important news item of the week is an announcement by the Chancellor of the Exchequer (Bonar Law) respecting the increased entertainment taxes which should have come into operation the beginning of this month but which have been postponed until October. Mr. Law has made the following concessions: The admission tax of one penny to entertainments will apply up to and including seats of the value of four-pence instead of three-pence originally proposed. The duty on seats over the value of seven shillings and six-pence but under ten shillings will be one shilling and six-pence instead of two shillings. On admissions over half a guinea but under fifteen shillings, two shillings instead of three shillings, and on seats over fifteen shillings the duty payable will be at the rate of six-pence for each five shillings (or part of five shillings) over and above the two shillings on the initial fifteen. Upon introducing these amendments into the Finance Bill Mr. Law stated in Parliament that the Government has no desire to pose as a killjoy and it realises the necessity for legitimate entertainment at this time of nerve strain. The concession cannot be extended to six-pence seats because over eighty per cent. of the entire revenue from this source comes from tickets of six-pence or less. Mr. Law added that "the reduction of the higher priced tickets is to encourage higher forms of entertainment." The announcement has naturally given satisfaction in all sections of the trade but particularly to exhibitors. They are, however, determined to keep the entertainment duty at its present level if humanly possible, especially in regard to six-pence seats.

 * * *

What is claimed as the longest consecutive scene on a film appears in a new production by the Ideal Co. of Galsworthy's "Justice."

 * * *

Following upon the success of the Bainsfather humorous cartoons of trench life Film Booking Offices (Essanay-M. P. Sales) are preparing to similarly animate a number of Raemaeker's scathing records of German gentility.

 * * *

Mention of the enemy reminds me that the first German propaganda film to be publicly exhibited in Great Britain was put on last week at the Scala, the theater Chas. Urban is associated with. The film embraces life in the enemy's lines with several rather good close-up views of the Kaiser.

 * * *

The news of the sudden death of Sir H. Beerbohm Tree must have occasioned bitter disappointment to his many film producing friends in the States, particularly in Los Angeles, whither he had definitely planned to return in the autumn. The late Sir Herbert was the first great luminary of the "legit" theater to realise, seven years ago, that the cinema was more than an ingenious toy and to bestow his patronage upon it. Since this, his first appearance in Barker's "Henry VIII," down to the Triangle "Macbeth," the industry had a consistently firm friend in the famous actor-manager.

 * * *

The call upon the exhibitor to show on his screen slides and films in aid of war and other charities without including the large number of appeals from different Government departments has never been so great as now. So much so that a number of showmen are inclined to the opinion that they are being taken advantage of by charitable institutions out for free publicity. The Edinburgh branch of the Exhibitors' Association has decided to show no further films or slides

of this type until they have been approved by the secretary, and even then only upon condition that acknowledgment of the exhibitors' services is made in the press.

 * * *

D. W. Griffith, Robt. Harron, Lillian and Dorothy Gish left London the other evening for France to do the exteriors of a film "D. W. G." is producing for the French Government. As soon as these are completed they return to America to make the interiors and complete the subject, which is one of patriotic appeal.

 * * *

If there is one question more than another that a certain London newspaper keeps on flashing before its readers it is "when is Charles Chaplin going to enlist?" According to this paper and the inference of the articles the war will cease the day Chaplin appears in France, so perhaps this is one reason why its owner is visiting America to coerce Charlie into joining for immediate service. A telegram published on Saturday and attributed to the Los Angeles correspondent of the Boston "Christian Science Monitor," states that the famous comedian has already enrolled in the U. S. A. citizen army for training, cancelling all future arrangements for film production. All this makes interesting reading, but the balance of opinion, in the trade and out, concurs that Chaplin could render no better service than by keeping on, "keeping on."

 * * *

The moving picture biography, "The Life of Lord Kitchener," which has been occupying the Windsor Film Co. for nearly a year now, has been acquired, world's rights, by the London Independent Film Trading Co.

 * * *

The Vitagraph Co. announce this week the release of "Womanhood, the Glory of a Nation" and "The Suspect." The former was shown to the trade on Friday and the applause which greeted its exhibitors was torrential. "Womanhood" is certainly a worthy successor to "The Battle Cry of Peace."

 * * *

Entitled "The Re-birth of a Nation," the Gaumont Co. have prepared a one-reel, exclusive of a number of remarkable incidents photographed in Petrograd by their camera man during the recent revolution.

J. B. SUTCLIFFE.

MOBILIZE PARK SHOWS FOR WAR TIME.

This year the whole scheme of the Boston Park Shows has been changed and they are "mobilized for war service." Incidentally they are showing that motion pictures have definite usefulness to convey information to the people in times like these. Current record films are used, but not anything of a dramatic or story character. Four to six reels are run a night. The length of the program is an hour and a half to two hours. The singing of national or patriotic songs by the audience, with words thrown on the screen, is a prominent feature. Several sets of slides are used in each program, which makes it easy to emphasize whatever subject is current, as, for example, the Liberty Loan when that was being pushed; the Red Cross war fund campaign; recruiting for army, navy and Marine Corps and, later, food conservation.

The film material found to be especially desirable for the purpose includes the Universal, Pathe and Mutual News Weeklies, Selig "Following the Flag," Federal's "America Is Ready," Pathe's "Our Fighting Forces" and Metro's Army and Navy pictures.

FIRE UNDERWRITERS ISSUE BOOKLET.

The National Board of Fire Underwriters, with offices at 76 William street, New York, has prepared for the Council of National Defense a booklet giving directions for the prevention of fire. Its title is "Safeguarding Industry." The booklet contains twenty-four pages. Sixty-six thousand copies have been mailed to manufacturers, and the board states if any concern has been overlooked it will be glad to forward a copy on application.

The purpose of the publication is the highly important one of preventing fires in industrial plants working under the abnormal conditions of wartime emergency. The cover carries a signed statement especially written by President Wilson, as follows: "Preventable fire is more than a private misfortune. It is a public dereliction. At a time like this of emergency and of manifest necessity for the conservation of national resources, it is more than ever a matter of deep and pressing consequence that every means should be taken to prevent this evil."

Advertising for Exhibitors

Conducted by EPES WINTHROP SARGENT

Swagger.

THE Queen theater, Galveston, Texas, which does most things exceedingly well, did better than usual with an invitation card to "Womanhood." This was a private showing to launch the feature in Texas. The invitation idea is the reverse of new, but it is not often

The Queen Theatre

cordially invites you to attend the opening

performance of J. Stuart Blackton's

soul stirring preparedness drama

"Womanhood"

The Glory of the Nation

starring Alice Joyce and Harry Morey

Thursday, June 21, 1917

10.15 A. M.

Kindly Present This Card

that we get a card so well done, though done from type. We get few examples of Old English than we used to, but most jobs show the type instead of play impression. This card is printed from type, yet suggests engraving. It is done with Litho Shaded Script printed with a light inking. The effect is decidedly swagger and aids in creating a favorable impression in the minds of the recipients.

Cheating Itself.

The C. and A. Amusement Company, Pocatello, Idaho, gets out a twelve-page weekly for the three theaters under its management, but it takes a space only four by seven inches for the triple program. In so small a space there can be little display, at best, and here the printer complicates matters by setting it all in full face, and not

PROGRAMS AT OUR THREE HOUSES FOR WEEK OF JUNE 4TH TO JUNE 9TH

ORPHEUM	PRINCESS	OLYMPIC
Wm. S. Hart in "Wolf Lowry" First Art Triangle "The Gollie Market" Two Reel Vitagraph Comedy Life Story	MON., TUES., WED. Jess Sanford, Whirling Vaudeville Comedian in his Eleven-Minute Screen "THE CHOICE BOX" Overtime Heroes in Their Triumph in Finding Ace	MONDAY AND TUESDAY Kathlyn Williams & Bessie Peters in "THE HIGHWAY OF HOPE" Five Act Paramount "THE SOCIAL BUZZ" One Reel Triangle Comedy
WEDNESDAY AND THURSDAY Geo. M. Cohan in his own Production of "BROADWAY JONES" Seven Act Special Attraction As Advanced Prices	"Heart of the Army" Two Reels First Art Vitagraph Comedy	WEDNESDAY AND THURSDAY Peggy Hyland in "BABBETTE" First Art Vitagraph "Press Weekly"
FRIDAY AND SATURDAY Fine Pay in "THE MILLIONAIRE VAGRANT" Five Act Triangle Chas. Murray in "Her Fame and Shame," scream Keystone	YOUNG., FRI., & SAT. Hugo Hits, Hand Balance and Bronze Rings Brina & King, Comedy Singers and Talkers "Mystery of the Double Cross" Heroic Pathe News	FRIDAY AND SATURDAY Pauline Frederick in "HER BETTER SELF" Five Act Paramount "LOVE AND FIRE" One Reel Triangle Comedy

always with a good idea of what should be kept up. With twelve 8 by 12-inch pages there should be more space for the program announcement instead of merely a third of one page, and even a dub printer should know better than to use all full face where he is so crowded. That page three should be given to the editorial head and the three programs alone, which would permit a proper display, using one of the many forms of program shown in this department; for example, the Colonial, Camden, N. J., which would work well here. This chain of houses is almost too generous with its general reading. The house should come first always, no matter what the form. Recently all three houses bought Liberty Bonds with the day's taking. There was a patriotic parade where the Mayor ordered all business places closed in the afternoon, but between five and eleven the houses ran full blast and then bought Liberty Bonds. Naturally they got local mention, the daily paper giving them a three-line twenty-four-point head on the first page as part of the general whoop for the day. In the same paper there is the announcement of F. H. Richardson's tour and his comments on the town, for F. H. used to shove a locomotive through the town when it was only a narrow gauge road and a narrow gauge town. Now both are broad gauge.

Another Red Cross Scheme.

T. L. Little, of the Majestic, Camden, S. C., sends in a ticket used for Red Cross week with this explanation:

I am enclosing to you a coupon ticket that I am using for Red Cross Week, June 18 to 25, and which so far is meeting with unusual success.

The boy Scouts and the local branch of the Red Cross Society are both taking an active interest and selling these coupon tickets. I am taking my highest average week receipts and giving to the Red Cross all over and above that. I figure now that the Red Cross will receive as their part $100 for the seven days.

There is practically no inducement in cut rates, as the 80-cent coupon is sold for 70 cents, making the straight seven days at 10 cents, there being one 10-cent-au-cent day.

The ticket is a straight cardboard strip 2¾ by 6 inches, as shown, the stubs being perforated to permit them to be torn off, the first date being at the top. Presumably some box office stamp was used as a counter check; certainly some such safeguard should be used. Mr. Little is taking no chance. He gets his top receipts and turns over to the beneficiaries a stipulated percentage of their sales, or a percentage of all the takings above a certain sum. The straight commission basis is the best rule, since it requires them to work and yet gives them a direct check on results. But any scheme is good that declares the house in on the movement—for public good. Between the Liberty Bond sale and the Red Cross movement, the picture theaters have presented themselves in a wholly new light to the public.

		Monday, June 18th.
	"THE STAR SPANGLED BANNER"	
	10c ADMIT ONE 10c	
	American Red Cross Week	
		Tuesday June 19th.
	"THE BOTTLE IMP"	
	10c ADMIT ONE 10c	
	American Red Cross Week	
		Wednesday, June 20th.
	"IN AGAIN—OUT AGAIN"	
	10c ADMIT ONE 10c	
	American Red Cross Week	
		Thursday, June 21st.
	"THE MAGDALENE OF THE HILLS"	
	10c ADMIT ONE 10c	
	American Red Cross Week	
		Friday, June 22nd.
	"PATRIA" Last Episode.	
	10c ADMIT ONE 10c	
	American Red Cross Week	
		Saturday June 23rd.
	"THE GUN FIGHTER"	
	William S. Hart Special	
	10c ADMIT ONE 10c	
	American Red Cross Week	
		Monday June 25th.
	"The Adventures of Buffalo Bill"	
	10c ADMIT ONE 10c	
	American Red Cross Week	

This coupon ticket sold as a special benefit for the American Red Cross Society. Tickets are good on the day sold for only.

In purchasing this coupon ticket you are getting value received for your investment and at the same time helping one of the most deserving causes before the American public today.

Purchasers Name Must be Signed Here
PRICE 70c NOT TRANSFERABLE PRICE 70c
MAJESTIC THEATRE

Doubles on the Kids.

The City theater, Newark, N. J., has found it pays to cater to the children. It announces two special bills a week through vacation time. We print the announcement:

With the view of making the City theater attractive to its younger patrons during vacation days, Wednesdays have been selected to furnish special features for the children in addition to Saturday matinees. The success of the special children's matinee program on Saturday afternoons has not only warranted its continuance, but the setting aside of Wednesdays as well for a similar entertainment. The principal attraction now booked for this new departure on Wednesdays is little Mary McAlister in Charles Mortimer Peck's "Do Children Count?"—a series of twelve two-reel subjects, each unit a complete and distinct story in itself. Motor comedies, animated photographic comedy conceits enacted by toy dolls and manikins, in conjunction with Ditmar's celebrated animal pictures, are the selections for the entertainment of our younger clientele at the mid-week special children's show. These features will also be a part of the evening as well as the afternoon entertainment.

The present policy of presenting attractions for the children in addition to the feature for "grown-ups" on Saturday afternoon will be continued. The offerings for children Saturdays will be different than that presented on Wednesday. The programs will consist of the more pretentious children's productions and the better known juvenile subjects. These features will be presented at 1.00 and 3.00 P. M. at the matinee only, and will not form a part of the evening's entertainment.

It might be argued that there is too much propaganda on "Do Children Count?" but we think that it will be found that the pictures will interest the youngsters. Special catering to the kiddies through the summer is a lot better than kicking about poor business. The City is using a neat six page railroad with an informative front page and a space for the star feature there, and a well arranged inside form. The color combination—deep green on lemon—is rich and effective, but perhaps a bit too warm for summer.

Halfway.

Here is a trade advertisement we clipped from the program of the Queen. De Queen, Ark. It illustrates a nice point in advertising. The

SAVE THE

PRICE

of the admission to the show all this week. You can do it by buying one pair of shoes at Knights',

idea is good in that it offers a specific argument. You save money. How much? The cost of admissions to the theater for a week. But the display does not catch as well as would a

FREE

ADMISSIONS

All this week

That would get them started reading because it is something concrete. It is a definite promise and not a broad generality. Precisely the same thing holds good in writing your theater copy. Be definite in your statement. Get attention with a catchline, but make the line important. Think what you want to say, then say it in the most definite and attractive way you can plan.

Boxed Fronts.

The joint program of the Majestic and Colonial theaters, Jackson, Mich., offers some neat wrinkles. We rather like the front page arrangement, for example, in which the stories are boxed. The pages are eight by nine inches, almost too square, perhaps, and the side boxes are each an inch and a half wide. The middle box changes with the cut or may be omitted if the cut is too wide to make up well. The examples

show one with and one without the rule box. Both work well. The matter in these boxes runs all the way from advance notices to hints on theatergoing. It is all live material and not merely matter put in

there to fill up a space. It all means something to the house and the patron. The inside pages suggest the Kunsky houses in Detroit, which use much the same style program. We particularly like the page on the left, with the time table in the box. There might be room to date the days on both programs, but the weekly date is pretty close, though not close enough to link the day and date. A man may not stop to

figure out that in the week of June 24 Thursday is the 28th, and the idea is to get day and date in the memory at the same time. W. S. McLaren shows a nice judgment in his clip stuff, but it is by no means all clip. His original matter is smart and to the point. In announcing "The Slave Market" he starts in with the explanation that it is not another vice trust expose but a good old-fashioned pirate story. That is a far better line to take. The program runs eight pages with a generous support from the trade advertisers, who are not permitted, however, to intrude on the space needed by the house. It is the sort of program that makes business, and the fact that it is in its third volume speaks for itself.

Both if Possible.

W. H. Coon, of the Mission, Amarillo, Texas, writes:

I am sending you two of my programs for criticism. This is a town of about 18,000 and has three theaters. We put out 1,500 of these programs every week. Our house, which caters to the better class, has a seating capacity of 750, and employs a five piece orchestra. Knowing these things do you think hand bills or newspaper advertising would be the better? We have always used hand bills, but since every house in town is using them at present, we have not been getting the results from them lately that we secured in the past. You will notice the little cut in the center of our program which reads:

We began using this cut several months ago and have found it continuously. A few weeks ago another house began to use the same style of composition on all advertising matter, but the text reads, "Where all the people go to see the best show." What do you think ought to be done? We have done nothing—letting it "soak" into the public. Do you think that is best?

MISSION
WHERE AMARILLO GOES
TO SEE GOOD SHOWS

We have reproduced the cut in question, not that we think it would pay to take the matter to law, but because this appropriation of idea is so common and may sometimes be so important that it will be worth nothing that adaption does not always prove safe. If Mr. Coon has been using his trade mark only a few months it might be necessary to patent the design to enforce protection, but we think that as a general rule the copying of an established slogan with reproduction of the essential features of a design will be held at common law to be a colorable imitation and an attempt to trade upon the merit of the original. An injunction would probably lie against an infringer, but in the present instance it hardly seems worth while to force an issue. Had the design been in use for a year or so, and had it become identified with the house, it would pay to protect the rights. The better plan would be to let the matter lie dormant. The public will make its own deductions. At the same time it is well to remember that it is not necessary to be protected by patent to guard against an attempt to trade on reputation, though it is to be presumed that if a trade mark is worth while, it is worth entering with the patent office.

But the more interesting question is the relative value of newspaper and hand bill advertising. We take it that Mr. Coon by "hand bill" refers to the programs sent, and not to throwaways in the generally accepted sense of the word. We think that a program classes above the general run of distributed matter. It is entitled to a greater distinction, but it should be distributed in some more dignified manner to gain its greater credit. If it is merely dumped upon the front door step along with two or three others, it classes as a nuisance save in the minds of the fans. Given more importance, it might advantageously replace newspaper work, though if there is a daily paper of a considerable circulation, and there is a reading public, the fact that the house appeals to the better class would indicate the fairly generous use of the daily paper. For a long time Steve Farrar, who appealed largely to miners in Eldorado, Ill., found that circulars were best, but Steve has come over to colored programs lately. If he had a larger proportion of newspaper readers from which to draw, Steve would be all for the newspapers. The way to figure it is this: If there is a local paper, does it have a large local circulation? That, of course, means large as proportioned to the town. In a town of 5,000 persons a circulation, locally, of 900 would be large. Some towns have their local papers and yet most persons depend upon the dailies from the nearby cities. All through Maine, for example, the Boston papers have the advantage over the local sheets. It would not pay to advertise in the Boston papers a theater in a small town in Maine, but the Boston papers to some extent blanket the local issues. Here the distributed program would at least get into the house, where the local paper is not seen, and so would be a better publicity medium, but even where this is the case there should be some advertising in the local paper, and it should be well and carefully done, no matter what is used to supplement it. In a town of 18,000 it should be possible to use some pictorial paper advantageously posted. This would be better than hand bills, particularly if there are several sets of hand bills. Put up paper and make the boards distinctive so that it is easy to see that the paper refers to the attractions at the Mission. Supplement this with a program that has something to read on it other than the formal bill. The Mission program is a four pager with an ornamental front, a well and double middle and an atrocious back page of trade ads held together by apiece. There is no frame to hold it together and the announcements are so small in proportion to the page that they look positively lonesome. It would be better to take that back page for five dollar announcements and use half the space, running reading matter. Still better would be the use of reading matter on page two, with the program in the Theater Louisiana style on page three and with trade ads decently and respectably set on the back page, or the trade ads as they stand with a heading and a narrow column of text between. The ads run 3½ inches wide on a page 6½ inches wide. There is too much margin. That back page is enough to damn the entire issue. A program must be something people want to see, not something they merely tolerate. If it is the only one in town it may show some results, but if there is competition the best looking bill will be apt to get the more respectful attention, but it must be something that looks like a "really and truly" program and not an experiment on the part of an amateur typesetter. A 750 house in an 18,000 town should be able to use both newspaper advertising and a good program. There must be some printer in Amarillo who knows his trade and the elemental rules of getting out a good job. It will be harder work to supply copy for the right sort of a program, but it will pay.

Too Joyous.

Clearly Miss Pauline Carr has been reading of Douglas Fairbanks and the ample salary a smile brings to him, for she is beaming in the ballyhoo used for Keith's Hippodrome, Youngstown, Ohio. The feature was "Womanhood," and evidently the house tied up to the recruiting service, for the officer in the car is Captain Stanley Huntley Lewis. No

details are sent with the photograph, but these may be imagined. Note particularly the lettering on the car. Few exhibitors seem to realize that water color can be used on a car without damage if it is carefully washed off afterward. Direct lettering on the car is several times more effective than banners tied on. Directly under Capt. Lewis is "Recruiting Service," lettered upon a bursting bomb, while the hood is lettered with the title of the film story and fact that it has been adopted by the Naval Recruiting Service in its work. The sailor on the opposite running board seems to be in charge of some sort of machine gun. The collaboration with the Navy Department works well both for the house and the Department. More exhibitors should realize that they can help recruiting and themselves at the same time and this in many other ways.

Scott Starts Up.

Having gotten through with the special publicity work for Linder, L. J. Scott is back in the Chicago offices of Essanay, and those who know him from Kansas City days will be glad to see that he is starting up his aids to exhibitors. Mr. Scott knows from personal experience what will and will not make good for exhibitors. His press sheets are not filled with theories but experience facts, and while he says he does not want a comment on his first sheet—for "Do Children

Count?"—we do not see what he needs to be so blamed modest for. He will get better as he goes on, for that is his way, but his first contribution is nothing to be ashamed of. We do not grow jealous when the press men follow the lines of this department. We welcome every aid the exhibitor can get, and we are glad to see Mr. Scott where his material will go to Exhibitors generally and not merely to those in the limits of one exchange. Even if you do not use the Essanay features

his stuff is a good lesson in general advertising, but we think that many will be led to take up this Keys feature because the press work is made so easy. Here are some examples of preliminary advertising. The cuts in two cases seem to have been taken from a cut up larger plate, but the suggestions are good, and those two on the left we particularly like. But it is as a stunt man that Mr. Scott excels, and it is easier to write advertising than to evolve pulling stunts. Some of the stunts he suggests are new and the others are time tried, but particularly applicable to the present series. That's Scott—stunts that fit. We cannot copy his stuff with the same freedom we showed when his work had but a limited circulation, for you can get the Essanay sheet for a postal card, but we want to urge you to make sure you get on the Essanay mailing list. It will be worth while. One very practical stunt is a six page railroad folder for the series, printed in brown on cream laid paper with a blank page for the current house program. This is a new scheme, and a valuable one.

Special Ghost Stories.

The Universal special press sheet for "The Gray Ghost" is a good example of what it should be. It is printed only on one side, and not only gives a number of stories but gives stories of the sort that an editor will print without revision downward. One great trouble with these advance sheets, not alone the Universal but most others, has been the extravagance of tone of the stories. The real trick in press agenting lies in writing stuff that will be printed without undue revision. If you say a story is "superbly wonderful" the entire sentence is apt to be cut out because the copy reader will not bother to write in a new adjective. If you say that the story is of real interest the sentence is apt to stay in, and it is more profitable to the exhibitor to have printed the fact it is of real interest than to have no comment at all. It helps the exhibitor not at all to give him color printing and extravagant adjectives. It does help him to get stuff that his newspaper friends will be glad to print, and service to the exhibitor is the determining factor in sales. One thing that makes the Pathe serials so popular is the adroit press material. Of course there has to be that in the film which will make good, but it is real press work that sells the serial to the public, and so it is the press work that sells it to the exhibitor. This is a point we have been hammering on for several years, and yet it is only lately that there has been much evidence that it has reached home, and some producing exchanges still waste on fancy printing the money they might better put into press work. This does not mean that these press helps should not be well printed. It does mean that the first consideration should be the production of a grade of press matter that will enable the exhibitor to make a profit on his rental investment. The Universal sheet is a step in the right direction and something editors and exhibitors alike should welcome.

All in Red.

J. S. Woodhouse, of the Lagoon, Minneapolis, Minn., gets out a Fourth of July program in fiery red with firecracker border used as dashes. It is appropriate, but it is not easy to read red on white smaller than twelve point, and much of the program is in a small eight point. But it is appropriate for this once, and the program is very well laid. The front page is given to a Jazz orchestra which is featured. The second page also gives prominence to the band, giving the program by days. Page three has readers on the band and four has a story on six children to be seen at the Lagoon in a single week. It is an original story picked up from the program much as a Sunday editor picks his features from the daily news. The children are not all in the same play nor in the same company. It simply struck Mr. Woodhouse that he had some unusual kiddies in unusual numbers, so he made it a talking point. Page five starts off with talk of the plays for the week and then runs into a series of casts, dated, and with a few lines of comment on the play. It is not a formal program, but treats each play by itself. The titles are in eighteen point condensed Gothic (rather a trying face) with an eight point full face dated day and the cast, also in full face, with the comment in eight point Roman following. It is neat and orderly. This runs on the next page, with a page ad for "The Neglected Wife" on page seven and two weeks' advance programs on page eight. It all forms a meaty program that you can read without mentally tiring, and in black it would be easy on the eyes. He runs several slogans at the bottom of the pages. One is "If it's at the Lagoon it's good." It might be well to work the double phrase and run: "If it's good it's at the Lagoon. If it's at the Lagoon, it's good."

A NEW HELP FOR MANAGERS

The Photoplaywright

Conducted by EPES WINTHROP SARGENT

INQUIRIES.

Questions concerning photoplay writing addressed to this department will be replied to by mail if a fully addressed and stamped envelope accompanies the letter, which should be addressed to this department. Questions should be stated clearly and should be typewritten or written with pen and ink. Under no circumstances will manuscripts or synopses be criticised, whether or not a fee is sent therefor.

A list of companies will be sent if the request is made to the paper direct and not to this department, and a return stamped envelope is inclosed.

Triangle Scripts.

RECENTLY we published a letter from the Triangle Film Corporation asking that all scripts intended for Triangle be sent to the company at Culver City, California, and not to the executive offices in New York, where there are no facilities for handling scripts. The item was plain enough in view of other news stories of late, but to make it fully definite it should be noted that the Triangle is the Triangle and Ince is Ince. Mr. Ince is no longer making Triangles. If you intend your script for Ince production wait for announcement of his needs. Meantime, there is a better demand for scripts at Culver City than existed during the Ince regime, and the company promises action within ten days of receipt, but this does not mean within ten days from the time you drop your envelope into the letter box at home.

Credulous.

Lately some magazine stated that a woman was making a good thing selling plots given her by her little children. We did not see the statement in print, but take this from a boob letter, but if such a statement was ever made we believe that the originator of the fable could make Ananias look like a tongue-tied amateur. It is conceivable that now and then some kiddie with an uncanny imagination might evolve an idea capable of being built up into a plot, but that a woman should make a living by marketing these kid plots is unbelievable. It sounds like one of those lies used to sell the Producer's League junk. The point, however, is that it does not pay to believe all you read in the Motion Picture Magazines intended for the general public. It is written to be interesting, and not always does the author cling to the truth with the same fierce intensity that was practiced by G. Washington. Take it with a couple of pounds of salt.

Stories Count.

The other day we noticed that one of the really big New York theatres was taking all of a certain service save the comedies. Another brand, once favored, has been dropped. In one case the comedies are all written by a single hired hand; not a writer, but a hired man. In the other case the stories have become too deadly sameness because the star will accept only material running in the same narrow lines. In both instances the stories have practically become a detriment to their releasing affiliations because the stories are wrong. High priced players of real merit are failing to amuse because they lack material. And neither company realises that it is the stories or lack of them, that is to blame. Another brand is replacing these because here are offered stories that are stories and not mere excuse for pie throwing and stunt stuff.

Holding Back.

Evidently writing more for a confirmation of her own intention than with a desire for information, an author says:

I am by nature born to fight and do not believe in lying flat because sales are slow at present. If I do as you say many do, and stop sending in stories, won't the companies forget a writer? In every studio there must be someone who watches the writer's progress. I think it cowardice to stop.

We disagree with the writer of the above. Editors are not buying, not because, as this writer suggests, they are too poor to pay for scripts, but because they want to hold the job to themselves or because they are not able to judge scripts. Generally it is more a desire to hold the money in the family. Presently these grafters are going to be found out and then kicked out. Manufacturers will find that their much-admired staffs are the chief cause of hackneyed stories and unprofitable releases and will turn again to the great body of writers. There will again be a market. That is the time to be ready to rush in with a lot of really good stories. If you send them in now the chances are that some portion of the idea may linger in the memory of some unscrupulous staff writer and what merit your work has will be taken. Then when you send in to the new editor you meet the "done before," and are naturally suspected of having stolen your own idea. It may be cowardice to stay out of the market, but we are more inclined to believe that it is merely sound sense.

Originality.

We were talking to Marc Edmund Jones the other day and some of his ideas are just as crazy as ever, though he is not talking about them as much as in the days when "Marcemunding" was a synonym for visioning. We always walk soft when we pass Marc Edmund, for we do not know at which end he is loaded. It is just possible that what we now regard as freak writing may, some day, be evolved into the play of the future. At least he is one of the few with the courage of his convictions, and he is not ashamed to offer his freaks along with the bulk of his stuff which conforms to current usage. And if it is not Jones it will very probably be someone like him who will lead the way to the real photoplay. In spite of all that has been said and written, we are not yet arrived at the real photoplay form, and by form we mean the art and not the mechanics of writing. Photoplay form today follows too closely the drama and the action story. It must be made more individual, more distinctive, more original before it can properly claim its place as an art instead of a graft upon twin arts. Don't get too fantastic, but do not be afraid to give rein to your fancy. It may be you or Jones or Vachel Lindsay. It probably will not be one of the old time writers.

The Average.

Probably 95 per cent. of the writers of scripts stop with their tenth submitted story. That is an average. Some may write more and others not so many, but of every hundred starters it is safe to say that 95 of them between them produce about 550 plays and stop. The other five per cent. keep on. How many beginners, do you suppose, go into a box factory and master the work after spoiling only ten boxes? It is true that they are broken in on the different machines, and seldom make complete boxes, performing only certain of the operations, but even at that there are those who master the knack with a spoilage of material for but ten boxes. Manufacturers count a certain loss as a part of the cost of breaking in new hands. They expect it. They know it must come. And yet hundreds of would-be writers do ten stories and quit. Most of them, perhaps, should have quit before the first, but unquestionably some of them could master the business if they kept at it. It is because so few do that there is still some room for those left.

Deduction.

Take a long and sharp lead pencil. Now write down the name of Marguerite Clark. Now write down the name of some "vampire" who is more popular than Miss Clark. You cannot do it, can you? You cannot think of a single vampire who is more generally popular than Miss Clark. You cannot think of one who is as popular. You can think of players who are as clever as Miss Clark, perhaps, but you cannot think of one who is as popular. Now write down the Vampire plays in which Miss Clark has appeared. There isn't one, is there? Isn't it obvious that the clean play, well done, is the best seller? Then why not write more of these?

Bribery.

Lately a very new writer wanted to know if there was not "some gathering of those authorized to purchase stories." to which he could submit his story with a reading fee. It would take only an hour, he wrote, to read his five-reel cowboy play, and he was positive that once read, it would be bought, so he was willing to pay the reader for his time. This is the second cousin to the scheme of offering the editor a sales commission, but it is just as effective in spoiling whatever chance there may be. Such editors as still read with a view to acceptance are paid to do their work, and do it properly. If a story has merit, it will be read for that merit and not because an author slips a two-dollar bill into the envelope.

Drags.

All arts have their drawbacks. We have excesses of closeups and visions, but painting has its cubists and impressionists and literature its free verse. We might be worse off.

Technique of the Photoplay

By

EPES WINTHROP SARGENT

A book replete with practical pointers on the preparation of stories for the screen, answering the hundred and one questions which immediately present themselves when the first script is attempted. A tested handbook for the constant writer of picture plots.

"Straight-from-the-shoulder" information from an author with a wealth of real "dollars-and-cents" experience.

Published and For Sale by

THE MOVING PICTURE WORLD, 17 Madison Ave., N.Y

Schiller Bldg., Chicago   Haas Bldg., Los Angeles

Projection Department

Conducted by F. H. RICHARDSON.

Manufacturers' Notice.

IT IS an established rule of this department that no apparatus or other goods will be endorsed or recommended editorially until the excellence of such articles has been demonstrated to its editor.

Important Notice.

Owing to the mass of matter awaiting publication, it is impossible to reply through the department in less than two to three weeks. In order to give prompt service, those sending four cents, stamps (less than actual cost), will receive carbon copy of the department reply, by mail, without delay. Special replies by mail on matters which cannot be replied to in the department, one dollar.

Both the first and second set of questions are now ready and printed in neat booklet form, the second half being seventy-six in number. Either booklet may be had by remitting 25 cents, money or stamps, to the editor, or both for 40 cents. Cannot use Canadian stamps. Every live, progressive operator should get a copy of these questions. You may be surprised at the number you cannot answer without a lot of study.

Cannot Get Results.

Bert C. Evans, Saginaw, Mich., is in trouble, as follows:

> Would greatly appreciate your assistance in the following matter, as for some reason I am unable to get desired result. Data is: Two Powers' 6-B projectors, using 60 amperes D. C. Gundlach No. 1 projection lenses, having an effective opening of 1⅜ inches. Back focus of projection lenses, 3.5 inches; ¾ cored carbons above and 1₁/32 Silver Tip below. Project a 17-foot picture at 88 feet.
>
> Please advise what condenser combination should be used, both plano convex and Meniscus bi-convex; also distance from center of condenser combination to aperture. Enclosed find postage for carbon of department reply, and any additional information will be appreciated.

You say "result is unsatisfactory," but you do not advise as to in what way it is unsatisfactory. I can, therefore, only advise as to the proper lineup of the lenses and aperture distance. Using plano convex condensers you will need a 6½ next the arc, and a 7½ in front, with not to exceed 1/16 of an inch between the apexes of the lenses, and with about 15½ inches from center of condenser combination to aperture. With Meniscus bi-convex you will need either two 7½ lenses, or one 7½ and one 8½, with about 17½ inches between aperture and center of condenser combination. This advice is based upon the assumption that you use 60 amperes. A different amperage will require a different line-up. The reason I give two possible combinations for the Meniscus bi-convex is that the 60-ampere curve comes exactly half-way between the two. In your case I think I would advise the Meniscus bi-convex, because it increases distance Y, which is highly desirable. After installing the new condenser system, remove your objective lens and insert a sheet of white paper exactly the same distance the back surface of the projection lens was from the film. Open your machine gate and project the white light on this paper, and measure its dimensions. You can then see how it compares with your effective lens diameter, and govern yourself accordingly insofar as projection lens diameter be concerned. Will you kindly advise me as to how this works out in your case?

From Nova Scotia.

A. J. Mason, an old-time correspondent of the department, is here again with the following. He writes from Wolfville, Nova Scotia:

> You will doubtless be surprised to hear from me at the above address, but the way of the world is that we change. I have taken charge of the Wolfville Opera House, and am well pleased with the proposition. The theater is a mighty nice one for a town of 2,000; also it has a fine stage, and an operating room 12 x 14, equipped with Motiograph and Edison motor-driven projectors. There is a Mirroroid screen, and projection is first class, with a good operator, Everet Pineo, in charge. I feel that I can make more in this end of the game, though the business will have to be built up, having been run down by carelessness in management, and by poor pictures. (Poorly-selected programmes, Brother Mason means, I take it.—Ed.) The one thing which impressed me most when I arrived here four weeks ago (letter dated July 25.—Ed.) was a photograph of the Operator's Friend, F. H. Richardson, neatly framed and hung in the lobby along with the photos of other stars. The operator has your handbooks, second and third edition, which argues for good results on the screen.
>
> My former assistant has taken charge of projection at the Imperial (Friend Mason was chief operator at the Imperial theater, St. Johns, N. B., for a long while.—Ed.), and is, I believe, making good. He is deserving of success, and I most earnestly wish it for him. I left because I was told I was as high as I could climb, and that did not in the least meet with my views. I was receiving more than any of the other men, and friend employer well knew I could not secure any-other position as operator at the same or better money anywhere in the Provinces. The answer is that I am here, and well satisfied with the change.
>
> My operator works daytime at the automobile business, and is considered about the best man in these parts. But what they lack in this part of the province is knowledge of electrical equipment. They send batteries to St. John to be charged, for instance. Friend operator wants me to go in with him. Am not familiar with car wiring. Can you recommend some good work on that subject? Note with much pleasure account of your successful trip. It was amusing at times, and I was surprised, but well pleased at the interest taken in your most valuable lectures, which every right-thinking operator cannot deny are highly instructive.

Am well pleased to hear of Mason's graduation into the managerial class, and trust he will have all kinds of success. And, by the way, what's the matter with you Maritime Province men, anyhow? Have not heard from any of you in Heaven knows how long. If you want to crawl back into your hole you can do it, of course, but it really isn't necessary to yank the hole in after you. Have I got to come up there and poke you up again? I'm some considerable poker, you know!

Cannot say offhand just what book you need, but will look the matter up tomorrow and advise you as to what I discover. What happened to that organization the Nova Scotia men formed last fall? Did it go blooey, or what happened to it?

Reduce Your Lens Ports.

The lens port should only be as large as the actual, effective light ray which carries the picture. The picture-light ray is surrounded by a halo of reflected light which, if it escapes into the auditorium, will do nothing but injury to the projection.

To test this matter, project a film (the clear white light will not do) when the audience is not in the house, and place a cardboard in the light ray right up close to the operating room wall—in the lens port, for instance. You will probably be surprised to find your actual picture-bearing light is much smaller than you had supposed, and that a considerable halo of light surrounds it.

You should then reduce the lens port to a shape and dimension which will barely pass the light ray carrying the picture, and nothing more. Paint the operating room side of the mask dead black, so that the light it intercepts will not be reflected back into the operator's eyes. In making the test for size do NOT use a title, but a rather clear scene—one not too dense. The light which surrounds the picture ray often has the effect, though I am not certain as to just why, of lessening the sharpness of the picture. But even if it does not do this, it does no good and does do distinct harm.

Jimmy-the-Usher Patches.

Joe Welch, Indiana, sends in some "horrible examples," together with the following pointed remarks:

> Attached splices are from the subject, "Youth's Enduring Charm," received July 14 from Indianapolis branch of the Mutual Film Corporation. Would call your special attention to where Jimmie-the-Usher got a part spliced in wrong side to. The picture was shipped to us rewound, and presumably inspected, but this is what I encountered on the first run. I hope you will forward these to the main office of the Mutual.

All right, Indiana, I will do that little thing for you, and for the benefit of other operators and exhibitors receiving service from this apparently mismanaged exchange. It is even as Indiana says. A part of the subject was spliced in backwards. Such work is raw. It is outrageous. I have repeatedly said, and I again repeat: THE OPERATOR IS NOT EMPLOYED TO DO FILM INSPECTING, and to compel him to inspect and repair film is nothing less than an outrage and a swindle. The film exchange is presumed to sell service in shape to project. The theater pays for that kind of service. Is it getting what it paid for, when an operator finds such things as this, plus a mess of splices varying from ¼ to ½ of an inch wide? Well, scarcely. The exchange is not, then, fulfilling its part of the bargain, is it? It is selling one thing and delivering quite another, is it not? And this is distinctly dishonest, is it not, both as regards the operator, who must do the work of inspection and repair, without a cent of pay, and as regards the theater itself?

What It Looks Like and How to Use It

The accompanying drawing shows the "new" incandescent equipment being marketed by the Nicholas Power Company and also the instructions for adjustment which are sent with the equipment.

Two sets of condensers are provided in this equipment, the corrugated one being for motion picture work and the other for stereopticon. The required adjustments are given below:

1—With the special moving picture lens in position, move the lamphouse forward so that the distance between the aperture and face of the lens is about 7 inches.

2—Swing the left hand arm and receptacle into position with respect to the condenser lens and secure by tightening thumb-screw "G."

3—Seat the lamp in receptacle "N"; the first position of the lamp necessary is the placing of it so that the plane of the filament "O" is parallel with the front face of the lamphouse. This is obtained by a swivel motion of the receptacle "N" and base "M," after which it is secured in this position by tightening of thumbscrew "L."

4—Place the center of the lamp filament "O" on a level with the point "Q" by means of adjustment "H."

5—Center the filament "O" of the lamp, and the lens, with respect to side movement, by means of adjustment "K."

6—By means of adjustment "J" the lamp can be brought close to the condenser so that the proper spot can be obtained at the aperture.

7—The reflector is a very important factor in obtaining the maximum amount of light. After the lamp has been properly adjusted, it should be lit and the objective lens removed so that the image of the filament may be obtained on the screen. It is necessary, of course, to get as flat a field as possible, and the adjustment of the reflector provides for this. After placing the center of reflector in a horizontal plane with the filament "O," the reflector should be moved forward or backward by means of adjustment "B" until the reflected light is the same size as the filament image. It is then moved sidewise on stud "B" until the dark spaces between the filament images are filled with the reflected light. The reflector and mounting is then secured in position by turning up the thumbscrew "F."

The lamp is now adjusted and in position for operation, allowing, of course, for the usual slight movements of either or both the lamphouse or lamp, backward or forward, to obtain a good spot on the aperture and a flat field on the screen. The other arm is swung into similar position, and adjustments as above described repeated.

When the use of slides is desired, the lamphouse is moved over to the usual position on the sliding rods, and the other set of condensers swung into place.

It must be remembered that when this type lamp is used on the usual 110 or 220 volt D. C. or A. C. commercial service, the proper auxiliary appliances for reducing the voltage and maintaining a rated current flow must be employed. Satisfactory lamp performance cannot be expected unless the lamps are used with control apparatus equipped with means for accurately regulating the current. If these means are carefully used, the saving in lamp renewals will soon more than offset the slightly higher cost of accurate control devices.

A Law Needed.

We have many examples of freak legislation on the books, so why not add one which is needed. It might be a "freak" in one sense, but would act as a protection to the theater, the operator and to the public. I would arise to suggest a law, with severe penalty, absolutely prohibiting the sending out of any film to a theater in other than perfect mechanical condition as regards splices and sprocket holes. Of course friend film exchange manager instantly declares such a law to be impractical, in that he simply MUST send out uninspected film upon occasion; also there would be difference of opinion as to what constitutes "perfect mechanical condition." But it really is not so impractical as seems at first glance. Mr. Manager does not have to send out film in bad condition. He just thinks he does. I have managed an exchange, and am in position to say that, while conditions arise in which it is a big temptation to do so, it is really not at all necessary. And if it were it would be easy to insert an "uninspected" slip in, directing the operator to inspect and send in bill for the labor. As to disputes, why the court would settle them, would it not? That is what courts are for, I believe. Protection in this matter is needed, and is needed badly. The condition in which some exchanges send out film is shameful. True, there is little to complain of in this respect with regard to properly-managed exchanges, but unfortunately not all exchanges come under that category.

Sample Letter.

The following, which requires no comment other than to say it is one of the many received from local unions all over the country, speaks for itself. It comes from a live president of a live local—a good combination:

Colorado Springs, June 15, 1917.
The Moving Picture World,
   New York City:
Gentlemen.—Just a few lines to personally thank you for the visit and splendid lecture of our brother, F. H. Richardson, whom we had the pleasure of having with us June 9, which same we owe to the Moving Picture World, which cannot receive too much credit from managers and operators all over the country. The lecture was without a doubt the most interesting thing to which the writer ever listened; moreover, he never expects to again hear its equal, unless we are so fortunate as to hear Brother Richardson again. And this I sincerely trust may come about. Moreover, let me add that our entire membership, as well as our managers, enjoyed it every bit as much as did I, and all the talk since he left has been of the Moving Picture World and Richardson. Again thanking you for the great work you and Brother Richardson are doing for the good of the entire industry, I am, very truly yours,
                              O. C. HURT,
         President Local Union No. 62,
         I. A. T. S. E. and M. P. M. O.

With Regard to Shutters and A. C.

E. W. Humphreys, Woodstown, N. J., desires the following information with regard to the revolving shutter and alternating current. He writes:

Being the manager of a small-town house, with an operator who is rather indifferent as to results, I try to keep up with the Projection Department, and wish to compliment you on the able assistance you so often render to operators. We use alternating current, 60 cycle, through a Fort Wayne Compensarc. The projector is a Powers' 6A. Our current supply was recently changed from 133 to 60 cycle, and we are still using the three-wing shutter we used when the current was 133 cycle. Ought we change to a two-blader? I do not notice any unusual flicker on the screen, but if we can get a better picture with a two-blade shutter, why it's me for it. We had, of course, to change compensarcs when the current was changed.

Another thing: I notice you often speak of using glass in the port holes. I take it this refers to the observation ports only. Am I correct?

With regard to the port holes, you are not right. I mean there should be glass in all of them. The glass should be old photographic plates from which the emulsion has been thoroughly cleaned. The idea is to prevent pulling the foul, hot air from the auditorium into the operating room. The operating room should be supplied with FRESH air, pulled in from outside the building through a special air chute, or else forced in from the air chutes of the house ventilating system. For several reasons, however, it is best to have the operating room ventilation entirely separate from the main house ventilation system. The lens ports may be left open provided they be reduced to the size of the actual light ray.

As to the other matter, it is quite possible that you may use a three-wing shutter with 60-cycle current, or what is supposed to be 60-cycle, and if you are using it without any trouble, keep right on using it. The trouble with 60-cycle current and a three-wing shutter is that, especially if the cycle happens to be really be (as quite happens) a little less than 60, and you run your projector a trifle fast, its blades will, or may, get into synchronism with the alternations of the current. As you will see by consulting page 16 of the third edition of the handbook, or any standard textbook dealing with alternating current, two times each cycle the voltage of single-phase current sinks to absolute

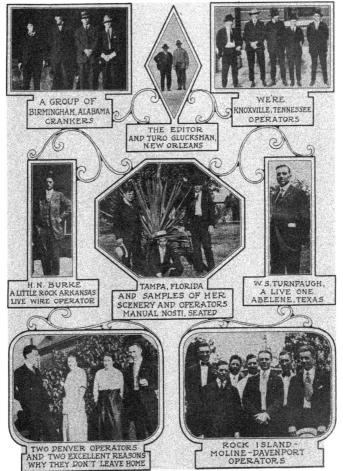

A GROUP OF BIRMINGHAM, ALABAMA CRANKERS

THE EDITOR AND TURO GLUCKSMAN, NEW ORLEANS

WE'RE KNOXVILLE, TENNESSEE OPERATORS

H. N. BURKE A LITTLE ROCK ARKANSAS LIVE WIRE OPERATOR

TAMPA, FLORIDA AND SAMPLES OF HER SCENERY AND OPERATORS MANUAL NOSTI, SEATED

W. S. TURNPAUGH, A LIVE ONE, ABELENE, TEXAS

TWO DENVER OPERATORS AND TWO EXCELLENT REASONS WHY THEY DON'T LEAVE HOME

ROCK ISLAND – MOLINE – DAVENPORT OPERATORS

zero, and at this instant or time the brilliancy of the crater is greatly diminished. If your shutter blades should happen for a space of time (it would be almost impossible that the blades would remain in synchronism with the alterations for more than a few seconds at a time) to cover the lens at the exact time when the crater is most brilliant, and uncover it when it is at its lowest point of brilliancy there would be a decided dimming of the light at the screen. Due to the improbability of the shutter remaining in synchronism for any extended period, the effect is usually that of a waving of the light—alternately brilliant and dim. If you have no such trouble, your shutter is not doing this and you should continue to use it.

Might Help.

Frank Shipley, Des Moines, Ia., has the following to say:

Enclosed find four dollars for autographed third edition of the handbook. I attended your lecture here, and desire to express my appreciation. Have not as yet heard of any resultant progressiveness, but don't belong to the local here, so don't know whether or not they are acting. To my mind the operator may get much good out of a study of "First Principles in Physics" books such as are used in public schools. I have one, and find it deals with many principles the operator comes into contact with. What do you think of the idea?

Why should the change-over sign be placed in the negative, as you advocate? I use a cross, scratched in a corner of the frame about five feet from the end. I receive films with unnecessary punch marks. Even find them at the beginning of the reel.

Well, brother Shipley, I am a little bit inclined to believe that it will require a pretty heavy jolt to wake up Des Moines as she ought to be waked. There was every indication of extreme sluggishness in that city. Do you mean you are not a member of the Des Moines local? Or that you do not belong to the I. A. If the latter, take my advice and "get in." If merely the former, why you might better put your card into the local union. It needs every live man it can get. As to the change-over sign in the negative, why if put there, then it would be in every positive, and no more trouble about it: moreover, it would be one universal sign, and everyone would soon come to recognize it. The negative is where it should be. Your cross mark is a mutilation, though a small one. But the next man will not know it is there, and will make his own—and so on. Do you see the point? I am very much afraid your copy of the Handbook was not autographed. And if so, it was my fault. Your letter was to the first mail received when I reached New York, and I thumbed through it hurriedly to give just such matters attention. Saw the four-dollar order and word Handbook. Gave address to office force and did not notice the autograph part. Sorry, old man. Yes, the books you mention have much of value, but I fear the average operator would be unable to apply it in his work. However, a study of the books certainly could do no harm.

Pictorial Photography.

The J. B. Lippincott Company has favored us with a copy of "Pictorial Photography," a 300-page cloth-bound book, by Paul L. Anderson, written in response to a definite and insistent demand for an authoritative work on American Photography.

The writer does not pose as an authority on photography, but it requires no exhaustive knowledge to see that the subject is, in this instance, handled ably and well. Mr. Anderson has put out a work which, while it shows his evident familiarity with the science of photography, and the principles which lie at the base of its structure, is couched in language so simple that the layman can readily understand and profit by what he reads. The work is replete with formulas, and will be of decided value to the amateur, as well as to the professional.

I can recommend this book to operators who are amateur kodakers. It will give them the precise information they want in that line; also the chapter on the lens will impart valuable understanding of lens action which will help them in their work—operating, I mean.

Port Shutters.

When in Tucson, Arizona, last April I visited the Tucson Opera House, W. W. Brumberg, Chief Operator, and noticed a very clever and effective method of fusing and of dropping the port fire shutters. Brother Brumberg, a live wire, by the way, promised to send in description thereof as soon as I returned to New York. He has kept his word.

The drawing consists of the main, upper sketch, and two detail sketches showing parts of the device. A-A are ordinary roller shade fixtures, such as one uses in the home. B is a suitable length of ordinary wooden curtain pole, 1¼ to 1½ inches in diameter, into which are driven iron pegs, such as a small nail from which the head has been amputated. These pegs are indicated by the letter F. O-C-C-O indicates the wall shutters, D-D the upper magazines of the projectors, E-E an iron lever, of suitable length, firmly attached to roller B, as shown in detail No. 1. G-G are film links inserted in master cord O by means of clamps such as are shown on page 225 of the Handbook, the same being indicated by the letter L. M is a film link inserted in the master cord, and located directly over the rewinder. N is a small ring attached to lever B.

The action is as follows: should either of the film links break or burn, master cord O would instantly be released at all points, which would cause weight N to pull lever E down, thus rotating roller B and dropping the rings to which port shutter cords are attached off pins F, causing the shutters to fall over the wall openings. The action

of the roller is shown in detail No. 2. H-H are metal pieces attached to bottom of upper machine magazines, as indicated in detail No. 1. I-I are similar pins attached to wall of room.

I believe a little study of the sketches will make the entire action clear, and that operators will have small difficulty applying the plan if it appeals to them. Incidentally I saw other more or less similar plans in different cities, and would like to have sketches and description of same. The film link in my judgment and opinion, the thing to use. It is far superior to metallic fuses, but must be placed intelligently if one is to receive the benefit. I saw one scheme which particularly appealed to me: An operator had inserted into the port shutter master cord, at the proper place, about eighteen inches or so of fine copper wire. He had then drilled a small hole in the center of the top of

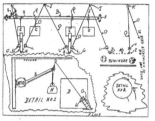

his upper magazine, doubled the wire in its center and passed it through the hole. He then rolled about an inch of film tightly and laid it over, or rather under the hole, pulling the wire tight. Of course should the fire get into the upper magazine, the bit of film under the wire would instantly burn, thus releasing the wire, and the master cord, which supported a roller somewhat similar to the one used by Brother Brumberg. Still another scheme I saw was to pass film link G into the lower front of the upper magazine through a very narrow slot. I would ask that these and other plans be sent in, to the end that they be set forth in the department for the benefit of all. Many thanks to friend Brumberg. By the way, Tucson, the wife thinks that Indian made wicker basket from San Xavier mission is just about the finest thing going. It occupies the place of honor on the mahogany (I strongly suspect the genuineness of the mahog part) pedestal, right square forninst the very frontest front window. Personally, aside from the kindness which prompted the gift, I didn't think such a much of it, but gee, you couldn't pry it and friend wife apart with a crowbar.

Motion Picture Photography[*]

Conducted by CARL LOUIS GREGORY, F. R. P. S.

Inquiries.

QUESTIONS in cinematography addressed to this department will receive carbon copy of the department's reply by mail when four cents in stamps are inclosed. Special replies by mail on matters which cannot be replied to in this department, $1.

Manufacturers' Notice.

It is an established rule of this department that no apparatus or other goods will be endorsed or recommended editorially until the excellence of such articles has been demonstrated to its editor.

Motion Picture Standards.

At the last meeting of the Society of Motion Picture Engineers held at the Sherman Hotel, Chicago, Monday and Tuesday, July 16 and 17, the following standards were formulated and approved with the recommendation that they be universally adopted by all manufacturers.

Film Speed: A film movement of sixty feet per minute through motion picture machines shall be considered a standard speed.

Frame Line: The dividing line between pictures on a motion picture film shall be exactly midway between the margins of perforations.

Projection Angle: The maximum permissible angle in motion picture projection shall not exceed twelve degrees (12°) from a perpendicular to the screen surface.

Projection Lenses: The outside diameter of projection lens tubes shall be of the following diameter: 38 mm., 46 mm. and 65 mm.

Projection Lens Foci: The focus of motion picture projection lenses shall increase in ¼ inch steps to 8 inches, and from 8 to 9 inches in ½ inch steps.

Projection Lens Mounting: Picture projection lenses shall be so mounted that the light from the picture aperture shall have an uninterrupted full path to the rear component of the lens.

Picture Aperture: The film picture aperture in a projection machine shall be 0.906 inch wide, and 0.6735 inch high.

Projection Lens Light: The standard height above the floor to the center of the projection lens of a motion picture machine shall be 48 inches.

Film Perforations: The dimensions and location of film perforation shall be in accord with the illustrating diagram herewith. (The diagram is not given here.)

Standard Picture Film shall be 1⅜ inches in width and carry a picture for each four perforations, the vertical position of the picture being longitudinal of the film.

Lantern Slide Mat Opening: A standard opening for lantern slide mat for use in conjunction with the motion pictures shall be 3 inches wide by 2¼ inches high.

Thumbmark: The thumbmark spot on a lantern slide shall be located in the lower left-hand corner next the reader when the slide is held so as to be read against a light.

Lantern Strip: A red binding strip shall be used on the lower edge of the lantern slide.

As these standards comply with the measurements now generally in use, and most of the variations from them were retained by dissenting manufacturers for trivial reasons, the principal one being that there was no recognized authority to recommend a universal standard. It is to be hoped that the few remaining cumbersome departures from standard practice will be speedily abandoned.

The frame time question has caused more annoyance than all the other points put together. The news weeklies will now have no excuse for putting out prints that require the framing lever to be shifted a half dozen times during the showing of a reel.

Camera men whose cameras frame differently than the adopted standard should have their frame line altered to correspond.

Film manufacturers who have not had their cameras lined up have often learned to their sorrow after using different cameras on a picture that expensive scenes could not be used or would have to be retaken in order to match frame lines. Happily most of them have already learned their lesson, and have adopted the frame line now recognized as standard. Unfortunately for a few of the old line companies their frame line is on the center of the perforations, but they will undoubtedly see the wisdom of conforming with the overwhelming majority and drop into line with the rest.

Of course the amount of expense involved in the mechanical work entailed may cause some of them to be tardy in agreeing with the

standard, but the cost is a mere bagatelle compared with the future saving in trouble and expense.

The future tendency will always be to conform to standard, and all those who fail to recognize that standardization is just as much for their benefit as it is for the industry at large will inevitably pay for their stubbornness in annoyance at being unable to use standard apparatus without expensive changes and in loss of business from their customers who will prefer to use standard apparatus which is designed to give sure fire results with standardized products.

Another feature of standardization that will save many deluded people a large amount of hard earned money is the fact that standardization will discourage many mad inventors with freak motion picture apparatus from foisting their abortions upon gullible people who can be made to believe that film should be run horizontally instead of vertically, or that a slight change in the dimensions of the picture frame or film will produce a miraculous improvement in motion pictures.

The woods are full of self deluded inventors, who have marvelous contraptions which are to revolutionize the picture business just as soon as some kind angel supplies the money for them to work out their ideas.

This little tirade, of course, does not apply to the hundreds of serious workers, who are, day by day, solving the problems that the industry presents with a sane inventive genius and a large admixture of hard work.

The work of the society fills a gap which has yawned unfilled in the industry since its inception, and will be of incalculable benefit and save time, material and money at a time when they are most sorely needed for the welfare of the nation.

Los Angeles writes:

Some time ago I noticed in your department an article concerning the new Akeley Moving Picture Camera. Is it being manufactured? By whom? And what will be the probable price?

Lately I have been trying to photograph against the light. There are two difficulties I have run up against. One is exposure; the other is the difficulty of keeping the sun out of the lens. In the majority of cases I have tried to use a lens shield, but find that unless the sun is fairly high in the heavens the sun shines fairly in the lens. In the matter of exposure, I find the faces especially are under-exposed. Then I have increased the exposure and ruined the picture again—over-exposure. I am only an amateur in this game, so if you can tell me how to arrive at a happy medium I will be very thankful. In my ordinary exposures I use the Harvey Meter as a guide, and find it the best thing out in that line, but am up a stump in this particular proposition so am writing to you.

The Akeley camera is not yet on the market. You can probably obtain further particulars from Mr. Carl Akeley, American Museum of Natural History, New York City.

In regard to exposure in back lighting: In calculating exposure for

Sketch No. 1.—Showing Back Lighting with Diffusion Reflector to Bring Out Shadow Detail.

back lighting it is usual to calculate the exposure for the lower tones in the picture, as the high lights where the sun strikes are always over-exposed. It is practically always necessary to use a lens hood or some sort of shield to protect the lens from the direct rays of the sun. When the sun gets low enough to be included in the picture it is then usually too dark for back lighting, and the effect then becomes either silhouette or moon light effect. It is customary in most back lighting effects to light up the shadows—by an inclined reflector placed between the foreground and the camera, as shown on rough sketch.

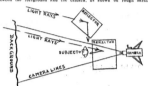

Sketch No. 2.—Ground Plan Showing Back Lighting with Two Diffusing Reflectors to Illuminate Shadow Detail.

Back lighting generally takes two to four times the exposure necessary in the same light when used in direct lighting.

Export Items

By E. T. McGovern.

J. M. ARAGON, of the Crest Pictures, announces that the premier of Joan the Woman in Buenos Aires has been a huge success and that the picture will continue indefinitely.

* * *

The Piedmont Pictures Corporation, formerly the Hawk Film Co., have secured the entire foreign rights on the Ivan Productions. These pictures are particularly adaptable to Latin American territory.

* * *

A deal recently closed with W. Fay Lynch of the Essanay Co. and F. H. Knocke and Jacob Glucksmann will bring the famous "On Trial" film to Argentine, Chile, Uruguay and Paraguay. A contract was also closed under which all Max Linder comedies will be distributed through Max Glucksmann of Buenos Aires.

* * *

Kurt W. Linn, export manager of the Universal, who has recently returned from a short vacation, reports a great demand for the new serial, "The Grey Ghost," throughout Latin America.

* * *

R. R. Nehls of the American Film Co. and B. J. Brandon of the Oceanic have just completed a contract which calls for over 1,500,000 feet of film a year for Norway and Sweden. This includes all the American Film Company's productions and the Frank Powell Pictures released by Mutual.

* * *

Francisco Elias has contracted to translate all Spanish titles for the Fox Pictures. Fox pictures are distributed through their own exchanges throughout the principal territories in South America.

* * *

The Bray Cartoons have been sold on contract to Argentine, Porto Rico and Mexico. Mr. Friend of the Bray Co. states that he expects to close for Brazil shortly.

* * *

At the Inter Ocean offices preparations are being made for the opening of "The Manxman" at the Criterion in New York and Louis Brock and Leon Schlesinger are preparing a comprehensive foreign sales campaign.

* * *

Senor Zeno Gandia of the Medal Film Co. of San Juan, Porto Rico, is paying a visit to the New York offices of his company in the Longacre Bldg.

* * *

Severo Norsa, the Argentine agent of our Spanish edition, Cine Mundial, writes that the interest in the publication becomes more intense with each issue.

* * *

J. H. Hallberg reports a keen interest in the 20th Century Generator in the Spanish-speaking countries.

Douglas Fairbanks is rapidly gaining in popularity throughout South America and his new Artcraft pictures should gain wide distribution in this territory. The Latin people have only seen a few of his Triangle pictures, but are already clamoring for more of this "personality plus" star.

* * *

E. M. Porter of the Precision Machine. Co. reports that July was a banner month for the "Simplex" in regard to export.

* * *

The fact that James M. Sheldon is the new president of the Empire All Star Film Co., as announced in last week's World, speaks well for the foreign business on these productions. Mr. Sheldon sold "Gloria's Romance" throughout the civilized world.

"DOUG" FAIRBANKS PULLS A BONE

Douglas Fairbanks has pulled a bone.

Yes, sir; the Artcraft star has pulled a bone—pulled it right out of the ground on an island "somewhere in the Pacific." And to prove that "Doug" pulled the bone Bennie Zeidman, than whom there is no more veracious fabricator, has mailed us the bone. It is the d-yes, bone we have ever seen. In fact, it is so dry that we are almost convinced that the "bone-dry" movement was named after the bone that Bennie sent us. But Bennie always did try to prove his assertions, and below is the assertion he wanted to prove, which was pasted on the bone:

"The remains of a prehistoric creature found by Douglas Fairbanks on an island 'somewhere in the Pacific Ocean' named in honor of the Artcraft star by a western Government official. The Douglas Fairbanks Island is now being registered in Washington."

We hate to doubt Bennie's word, and we further dislike to dash his hopes. We will grant him that Mr. Fairbanks found the bone. But we have had the said bone examined by one of New York's foremost specialists. He reports that the bone is the rib bone of a steer, otherwise known as Bull.

GAUMONT CHARACTER ACTOR DEAD.

The announcement last week of the sudden death of Charles W. Travis, well known as a character actor, came as a distinct shock to his friends in the Gaumont Company, where for so long a time Mr. Travis was a general favorite and a leading member of its stock company. Mr. Travis, who was born in Brooklyn in 1865, died in that city following a second apoplectic stroke. For nearly forty years he had been before the public as an actor, practically the last decade having been devoted to the silent drama. That he was an early recruit to pictures will be understood when one recalls that he played the part of the parson in "Davy Crockett," the first picture produced by the Bison Company. He also worked in the first independent picture that was ever produced by a firm releasing under the Carson brand. He later played character parts for the Universal Company, the Ramo Company, the Famous Players, the Fox Company, Humanology, and the Gaumont Company.

Among the Gaumont productions in which Mr. Travis scored were "The Devil's Darling," with Francine Larrimore, in which he took the part of the devil, "The Card Players," "The Idol of the Stage," "As a Woman Sows," "I Accuse," "According to Law," "The Quality of Faith," "Flames of Vengeance" and "Armadale."

FILM "TOM SAWYER" IN MARK TWAIN'S HOME.

The exterior scenes in "Tom Sawyer," Jack Pickford and Louise Huff's next Paramount production, will be taken in the very locality where Tom lived nearly 70 years ago. The Pickford-Huff company have betaken themselves to Hannibal, Missouri, where Mark Twain lived as a boy, and they will spend the next few weeks in taking the scenes for the story of "Tom Sawyer."

MUSIC CUE SHEETS FOR K-E-S-E PATRONS.

Music cue sheets will hereafter be provided on all features released through K-E-S-E. This service begins regularly with the release of Essanay's "Open Places," August 20, featuring Jack Gardner. K-E-S-E Service has engaged George W. Beynon, a widely known and accomplished musician, to select and arrange the music.

ROSE GOES TO BATTEN AGENCY.

Norman S. Rose has resigned from Artcraft's publicity department to become associated with the George Batten advertising agency.

Chicago News Letter
By JAS. S. McQUADE

"Perfection Pictures"

The Highest Standard in Moving Picture Art Yet Reached Most Likely To Be Announced Officially in the Near Future.

MANY surprises have marked the development of the moving picture industry since it became an industry and ceased to be a novelty or a mere plaything. And by "surprises" is meant important happenings, not mere rumors which have never been realized.

It may be questioned, however, if any of these former surprises will rank with one that is about to come in the near future, almost as certainly as anything human can be certain.

This will be nothing less than the merging some time ago of the interests of some of the foremost of America's producers with the aim of establishing a new high standard in the art of making moving pictures; and these pictures, it is expected, will so clearly demonstrate their superiority that they will be known as "Perfection Pictures."

It is understood that some of America's finest directors have been at work for several months past on these "Perfection Pictures" and that fifteen have already been completed, while as many more are now under way.

These productions are, and will be, comprised chiefly of light comedy-dramas, of five reels or more in length, which will be released at the rate of one a week, the first release to be made sometime in September.

It is said that appropriations have already been made which call for the expenditure of $1,700,000 on productions alone, for the first year.

It is also stated that many of America's foremost novelists, magazine story writers, and the cream of the authors of "best sellers" have been placed under contract, and that some of them have already supplied manuscripts for use in "Perfection Pictures."

Don't ask for names just now. They will be revealed in the very near future, in all probability.

New York Versus London as World's Film Center.

In the discussion which is now being carried on in the London trade press over the possibility of New York supplanting London as the world's film center, the latest issue of the Kinematograph to hand, at the time of writing, has the following expression from E. H. Montagu, European agent for the Selig Polyscope Co.:

It will do no good to grumble about the film export trade going to America. Changed conditions mean changed methods, and people here may as well make up their minds to the fact.
Personally, as the representative of the Selig Polyscope Co., I have first of all to consider the interests of my firm, and I may say I have voluntarily surrendered the right to work certain markets, because, under present-day conditions, it is cheaper and more satisfactory to work them from America.
The trouble with film dealers in this country is that for a long time they have made their money too easily. The experience spoiled them, and they seem unable to grasp the fact that in future they will have to work harder for smaller returns.
As for the agitation to keep London the film-distributing center of the world, it comes too late. The export trade in films is not merely going to New York. A great deal of it has already gone, and no amount of shouting will bring it back.

Chicago Reel Fellows' Club Dissolved and the Organization of Its Successor Discussed.

The first meeting of the reorganization committee of the Reel Fellows' Club of Chicago took place Wednesday noon, August 15, at the Hamilton Club. Messrs. Proctor, Nehls, Belford, Curtis, Ross, Russakov, Hopp and Stoddard were present.

President Proctor took the chair and the meeting at once engaged in the election of permanent officers of the reorganization committee. On a motion made and carried, the following officers were unanimously elected: President, R. R. Nehls; vice-president, R. O. Proctor; secretary, Mr. Stoddard, and treasurer, H. E. Belford. After the election Mr. Proctor resigned the chair in favor of Mr. Nehls.

The meeting then proceeded to a discussion of the present condition of the Reel Fellows Club and the most feasible plan to surmount the difficulties confronting it. Various plans were discussed by the committee, and the following resolutions were finally moved, seconded, and unanimously carried:

Resolved, that the Reorganization Committee of the Reel Fellows' Club of Chicago, pursuant to power vested in it, does hereby declare the Reel Fellows' Club of Chicago to be and the same is hereby dissolved.
Resolved, that this committee proceed at once to wind up the affairs of the Reel Fellows' Club of Chicago, and further
Resolved, that this committee proceed at once to the organization of a new club to be composed of the representative men of different branches of the motion picture industry.

The meeting then appointed a committee for the performance of the above duties, and after a motion duly made and carried, it was unanimously

Resolved, that this committee be equally divided into two sub-committees, known as the Organization Committee and the Finance Committee; that the president appoint all of the members of this committee to the respective sub-committees, and that the president be a member of both committees, and further
Resolved, that the duties of the Organization Committee be to draft and submit to this committee a constitution and code of by-laws for the proposed club and to formulate and submit a plan of organization for the same, and further
Resolved, that the duties of the Finance Committee be,
First: To wind up the affairs of the Reel Fellows' Club of Chicago, this committee being vested with full power to liquidate said club, provide ways and means for meeting the obligations of the same and to deal with the creditors and properties of that Club, and,
Second: To prepare and submit to this committee a financial budget for the proposed club, advising the necessary running expenses for a year of said club, and to make recommendations for the meeting of the same.

R. R. Nehls, presiding, then announced the members of the two sub-committees as follows:
Organization Committee, Messrs. Nehls, Curtis, Ross, Hopp, Russakov and Stoddard.
Finance Committee, Messrs. Nehls, Proctor, Bell, Rothacker, Heaney and Belford.

The first meeting of the Organization Committee was set for Thursday noon, August 16, at the Weiss restaurant, in the Consumers Building, and the first meeting of the Finance sub-committee was set for Monday noon, August 20, at Mr. Proctor's office, 207 South Wabash avenue. The next meeting of the Organization Committee was set for Tuesday noon, August 31, at the Hamilton Club.

Before adjourning the suggestion was made that each member of the Organization Committee prepare a roster of the candidates for charter membership in the new club, to be submitted to the committee at the next meeting.

Chicago Film Brevities.

Alfred Hamburger recently brought suit in the Circuit Court against Nathan Ascher, of the Ascher Brothers' circuit, for breach of contract, which involves over $75,000. The particulars of the suit have not been given out, but it is well known that there is a strong spirit of rivalry has existed for some time between these owners of large competing chains of picture theaters.

*   *   *

A special meeting of the Advertising Film Producers' Association will be held Monday, August 27, at the Rothacker Film Manufacturing Company's studios. The business taken up will include changes in the constitution and by-laws, standards of practice, the campaign for 1917-18, and other matters of importance connected with moving picture advertising. The Association is the recognized moving picture department of the Associated Advertising Clubs of the World.

*   *   *

How moving pictures are made was explained to members and friends of the Chicago Camera Club Wednesday evening, August 15, at the American Film Company's plant, this city, by Charles A. Ziebarth, superintendent of the company. Amateur photographers were also addressed by Mr. Ziebarth on the processes to which the raw film is subjected from its crude state until ready for projection on the screen.

"The Call to Arms," the original title of the patriotic picture on which Mary Miles Minter is now engaged, has been changed to "Her Country's Call."

Beginning Saturday, August 18, Alfred Hamburger will offer his first pre-release program of Paramount, "The Mysterious Miss Terry," in which Billie Burke is featured, according to his contract with that company, which gives him the right to first run of this make throughout the city. A similar contract also applies to Artcraft pictures.

Arthur S. Odin, who owned the Plaza theater at Lansing, Mich., about a year ago, has been at the training quarters for officers at Fort Sheridan for the past three months. Mr. Odin has had an important military career, having served as corporal in the 9th regiment, U. S. infantry, for many years. He was in the quartermasters' corps in Manila for a considerable part of that time, and has also seen service in Cuba. It has not been yet ascertained whether or not Mr. Odin succeeded in securing a commission. It is hoped so, as he is a splendid specimen of a man, both mentally and physically.

E. O. Gurney, auditor of the Universal and Bluebird exchanges, stopped over in this city last week while on an extended trip through the west, during which he expects to visit every Universal, Butterfly and Bluebird exchange before returning to New York.

The Longacre Film Co., through which the Alice Howell comedies will be released beginning September 1, has opened an office on the 15th floor of the Consumers Building.

The Studebaker will pass out of the control of Jones, Linick & Schaefer at the conclusion of a two weeks' run of "The Honor System," which will end Sunday, September 2. It is said that Oliver Morosco is aiming to secure this house for the production of his dramatic plays.

On Friday evening, August 17, a benefit presentation of "The Retreat of the Germans at the Battle of Arras" was given at Orchestra Hall, in aid of the First Regiment, Illinois Engineers. These British official pictures were secured by the Citizens Unit of the First Regiment, Illinois Engineers, through the courtesy of Pathe Exchange and Official Government Pictures, Inc., and the occasion marked their first projection on any screen in Chicago. Many of Chicago's leading families were represented in the boxes during the presentation, and numerous parties were present on the ground floor as the guests of other prominent people. The proceeds, which were large, will be devoted to buying extra equipment, clothing, mdicine, etc., for the First Regiment boys. Col. Jamieson, of the British Recruiting Mission in this city, pointed out the military features of the films to those in the large assemblage. Tom North, of Pathe Exchange, Inc., made the arrangements for the benefit.

"The Italian Battle Front," the only official war pictures of that country now in America, will be given a run of 12 days at the Auditorium theater, beginning Thursday, August 23. These pictures show fighting in the Alps, many thousands of feet above sea level; the campaign against and the fall of Goriзia, the great Austrian fortress, and Italy's battles among the clouds and on the sea. A forty-piece symphony orchestra will play the accompanying music.

A New York music publishing house has issued a song entitled "The Garden of Allah" in honor of the Selig super picture of that name. The front cover is illustrated with scenes from the Selig production.

Wm. N. Selig again desires to state that his company is not in the general market for scenarios, being overstocked with stories. The company is willing, however, to consider synopses for features of big, comprehensive themes.

The opening of "The Crisis" at the Garrick theater, Philadelphia, August 13, was a great success from accounts furnished by the Harris P. Wolfberg Attractions, which owns the rights in that territory. The Wolfberg Co. sent out letters to many exhibitors in adjacent country, inviting them to see the big film drama and promising to pay their expenses. By this means many attended and.bookings were largely increased in consequence.

Edward Trinz, nephew of Joseph Trinz, of the firm of Lubiner & Trinz, this city, and formerly manager of the West End theater here, called at the World office August 16. Mr. Trinz recently joined the Second Infantry regiment of the Illinois National Guard, which will leave in a few days for Fort Sam Houston, Tex., where it will remain encamped

for some time. He took advantage of this opportunity to say good-bye to all his brother exhibitors, through the courtesy of the Moving Picture World.

"The Retreat of the Germans at the Battle of Arras," under the management of Tom North, opened its run on Saturday, August 18, instead of Sunday, August 19, as previously announced. It was thought better to continue the big war picture after the benefit given the preceding Friday evening in aid of the First Regiment, Illinois Engineers.

A special meeting of the Chicago branch of the Motion Picture Exhibitors' League of America was held in its hall in the Masonic Temple building, Friday morning, when the new wage scale for operators, the music tax, and other matters were discussed.

James Vincent Directs "The Hidden Hand" for Pathe.

"THE HIDDEN HAND," the Pathe four-star serial which will be released in the early winter and which stars Doris Kenyon, and features Sheldon Lewis, Arline Pretty and Mahlon Hamilton, is being directed by James Vincent, who has to his credit, the production of many successful features. This is the first serial Mr. Vincent has directed, and he says he is surprised to find that the atmosphere, sets, story and acting required for a Pathe serial are of the kind that is required for the best features.

James Vincent

Mr. Vincent is a native of Springfield, Mass., and was educated in that city. He studied at the Emerson School of Expression in Boston, and took part in the juvenile lead in several dramatic productions, among them being "As a Man Thinks," with John Mason, and "The Man Who Stood Still," with Louis Mann. He took the part of Jack Hale in "The Trail of the Lonesome Pine," dramatized from the novel of the same name. He was leading man for Kalem for several years.

Director Vincent has to his credit the following features: "The Melting Pot," with Walker Whiteside; "Gold and the Woman," with Theda Bara; "Sins of Men," with Stuart Holmes; "Ambition" and "Love and Hate," with Madame Bertha Kalish; "Sister Against Sister" and "A Royal Romance," with Virginia Pearson, and "The Unwelcome Mother," adapted from Isben's "The Lady from the Sea," with Baroness Valkyrien.

Not only can Mr. Vincent show an actor or actress how a certain bit can be put over to the best advantage, but he also can tell when and the reason why. He has a thorough grounding of dramatic principles and believes that the universal language is pantomime, which is only sign language carried to its highest degree.

The story Mr. Vincent has to portray in "The Hidden Hand" is a dramatic one and Pathe expects big effects of his work. It is being produced under the supervision of G. A. Smith, formerly manager of Pathe's serial publicity department, who from his wide experience with serials knows what suits the public taste in chapter photoplays.

NEW THEATER AT TRAIL, B. C.

This week there was opened at Trail, B. C., the beautiful little Liberty theater. Trail is a prosperous little community with the mining business as its chief asset. M. P. Wetherall, formerly of Grand Forks, is in charge of the house. The house was opened with the subject, "Miss George Washington." They wrote the Famous Players Exchange as follows: "The house opened to S. R. O. with 'Miss George Washington.' Fine house, fine pictures, everybody happy."

News of Los Angeles and Vicinity
By G. P. HARLEMAN

Universal Studios Busy.

Many New Players Engaged—Eddie Lyons Marries—Other News from Big Film City.

UNIVERSAL CITY is always busy and many companies at work for Mr. Laemmle. We paid a visit this week to the big film factory and found the place a bee-hive of activity

During the past week a number of players have been added at the Universal plant and each has been assigned roles in current productions.

Among these may be mentioned Kenneth Harlan, who recently finished playing the juvenile lead in Lois Weber's latest production. He is now playing opposite Carmel Meyers in "The Dynast," which is being directed by Harry Solter.

Hal Cooley has returned to the Universal City fold. Cooley was with the Universal Company up to a year ago, when he went to the Keystone Company where he played juvenile leads. He also was with the American Company at Santa Barbara. Cooley has been assigned to the company directed by Elsie Jane Wilson in which Zoe Ray, the child actress, is featured.

Another player who has returned to Universal City is Rena Rogers, who will best be remembered for her work in Lois Weber's "Where Are My Children." Miss Rogers is also in Miss Wilson's company.

David Morris has become the leading comedian of Director Craig Hutchinson's aggregation of fun-makers. Morris has had a long experience both in the legitimate and before the camera.

Charles West, who is best known for his Biograph work under D. W. Griffith and who also was with that producer at the Fine Arts studios, is among the newcomers at the Big U City. West established an enviable reputation in the cinema world playing both juvenile and characters. He is now playing opposite Miss Grace Cunard, under the direction of Louis W. Chaudet.

Director Edward J. Le Saint, who is gathering a notable cast for a feature production, will have among his players Mildred Davis as his ingenue.

Eddie Lyons has joined the ranks of the benedicts. His marriage to Virginia Kirtley took place on August 1 and no one knew anything about it—not even the members of the Nestor Company, with whom he has been so closely associated—until the night of August 4, when it was announced at a beefsteak dinner given to the screen scribes of the motion pictures by Eddie Maier, of Los Angeles. About one hundred were present at the dinner and when the announcement was made the bridal couple was showered with congratulations.

Mrs. Lyons is no stranger to screen fans, for she has been in pictures for several years, appearing with the various companies.

Priscilla Dean, star of the Universal mystery serial, "The Gray Ghost," whose arm was fractured recently while performing a hazardous scene for the seventh episode of the story, again has taken up her work before the camera after an enforced illness of but ten days.

Although she was urged by Stuart Paton, her director, and Henry McRae, Production Manager of Universal City, to take a longer rest, Miss Dean thought her absence would handicap Paton in the filming of the serial and insisted upon picking up her part of the production at the earliest possible moment and her indomitable will and courage could not be denied.

Toreadors Corraled by Fred Palmer.

The Toreadors, that valiant bunch of hot air merchants, under the leadership of Fred Palmer, the comic scribbler, adjourned to the classic environment of Maier's Brewery, on Saturday last week. Charlie Murray and others made several speeches which were very good but not quite as fine as other things more tangible. The steaks were securely planked,

in fact we noticed that there was nothing that could be thrown around the room, however there were no casualties. Among those present were Ethel Davis, Lee Moran, Virginia Kirtley, Eddie Lyons, Mr. and Mrs. Roy Clements, Alice Lake, Franklyn Farnum, Mrs. and Mr. Fred Palmer, Miss M. E. M. Gibsone, Doris Schroeder, Mr. and Mrs. Ben Rothwell, Mr. and Mrs. M. Jonas, Mr. and Mrs. Carlyle Robinson, G. P. Harleman, Peter Milne, Mr. and Mrs. J. C. Jessen, Mr. and Mrs. Charlie Murray, Mr. and Mrs. Eddie Cline, Mr. and Mrs. A. L. Selig, Hal Cooley, Harry Wulze, Mr. and Mrs. Kenneth McGaffey, Miss Gene Crosby, Kenneth O'Hara, J. B. Woodside, Sam H. Comly, Allen Hulbert, "Pop" Hoadley, J. Grubb Alexander and the latest stenographic recruit to the navy, Clark Irvine, as well as others whom we missed in the haze.

Fox Company Films Elaborate Battle Scenes.

A BIG naval battle scene was staged by Director J. Gordon Edwards at Balboa Beach this week for the Fox production of "Cleopatra," in which Theda Bara is being starred. The scene is a reproduction of the famous battle of Actium. Participating in the conflict were the war vessels of Octavius Caesar and the galleys of Cleopatra and Antony. In reproducing the battle Mr. Edwards required the services of several thousand men.

About five thousand gallons of crude oil and inflammable materials were used to stimulate the burning of the fleet.

Anita King is with Balboa and will be starred in a series of five-reel features for release on the Mutual Program.

* * *

Mary Pickford, her director, Marshall Neilan, and the entire company will soon leave Los Angeles, according to an order received from New York. Miss Pickford's future productions will be produced at the Artcraft Studios in Fort Lee, N. J.

* * *

The wreath of hero reposes on the crown of Charlie Chaplin. The famous film comedian has rescued a little girl from drowning at Santa Monica. The child was swept into the ocean by a wave while she was watching Chaplin working before the camera.

* * *

Words come from New York that the Metro Pictures Corporation contemplates sending several of its companies to the Coast. We called up the Yorke-Metro Studios for particulars, but were informed by Pat Dowling, the local publicity representative, that the announcement was a little premature and that he himself was not as yet informed in regard to this matter.

* * *

Eric Campbell, the big heavy that plays opposite Charlie Chaplin, was married this week to Miss Pearl Gilman. The actor's bride is a sister of Mrs. W. E. Cory, wife of the well known steel magnate. The couple expect to go to Honolulu on a wedding journey sometime in December.

* * *

Reeves Eason and William Bradshaw were visitors at this office of the Moving Picture World prior to their departure for New York, where they will dispose of Mr. Bradshaw's Japanese travelog.

* * *

An auto driven by William Horsley, brother of David Horsley, plunged off the Canyon Pass, August 12. Mr. Horsley, his wife and son and Mr. and Mrs. Fred Dawes were injured, but fortunately none of them seriously. Mrs. Horsley and Mr. Dawes were taken to the Romona Hospital.

* * *

Balboa will send an expedition of camera men to the wilderness of Canada. Balboa wants some unusual scenery for use in a number of productions. The first expedition will be in charge of Cameraman E. L. Chindland, who has been instructed to go as far as he can before cold weather stops him.

The Mena Film Company is the name of a new film producing company in Los Angeles. The company is incorporated in New Jersey. Its officers are E. W. Kuehn, Toledo, president; J. G. Kuehn, Brooklyn, vice-president; Dr. L. W. Jones, Chicago, secretary-treasurer; R. R. Hollister, Pittsburgh, foreign director; C. C. Driscoll, Los Angeles, manager. The company is planning to produce motion picture feature films on popular subjects, and the first picture, which is in progress of production, will be an allegorical Biblical and modern story in a new and unique setting. The company's principal studios are located at Fountain avenue and Berendo street, Hollywood.

* * *

The Helen Holmes company is rapidly nearing the completion of the sixth episode of their serial, "The Lost Express." This chapter will be released under the installment title of "High Voltage." As the name implies, electricity plays an important part in the episode.

Upon the completion of "High Voltage," the company is to leave Los Angeles studios for the Yosemite Valley, where they are to make a number of scenes around the mines of that locality for use in the seventh and eighth episodes of the serial.

* * *

Fred Wilson, well known for his work with various of the Los Angeles film companies, has been secured by the Signal Film corporation for a several weeks' engagement during the production of "The Lost Express." Mr. Wilson is cast for an important character role in the serial.

* * *

A large Barbary Coast dance hall or "Honky-tonk" is being erected on the stage at the Lasky studio for the use of Wm. S. Hart in his first Artcraft production.

* * *

Jack Pickford and his company, under the direction of William D. Taylor, have departed for the wilds of Missouri to film some exterior scenes for his forthcoming production for the Morosco Company. The company will be gone for nearly a month.

* * *

Vivian Martin, having just completed a production at the Morosco studio under the direction of Robert Thornby, has been granted the long period of two days in which to rest and refresh herself for another attack on the silent drama, which will also be directed by Thornby at the Morosco studio.

* * *

Having made such a success in directing the battle scenes of "Joan the Woman" by means of a series of field telephones, Cecil B. DeMille has ordered a set to be used in Geraldine Farrar's forthcoming production equipped with the same instruments. Twelve telephone stations scattered throughout the village will be in constant communication with the director-general who stands on his platform with the receiver strapped to his head and the transmitter swinging from his breast. The cast of Miss Farrar's production includes Wallace Reid, Hobart Bosworth, Raymond Hatton, Theodore Kasloff, James Neill, Walter Long, Olga Gray and others.

* * *

Triangle-Keystone fans are soon to be treated to a new style of pantomime entertainment that should find instant appeal. Triangle-Keystone Director Henry Kernan and Jay Dwiggins, the veteran character comedian, have started work on a new series of comedies to be released on the Triangle program at regular intervals. Jay Dwiggins has been with Triangle-Keystone for a year, and will be remembered by many for his work with the late John Bunny in the old days. He will write all of his own stories and appear in the leading role. The series will be devoid of the slapstick tricks and will present human little stories that intersperse comedy with pathos and human touches.

* * *

Julian Eltinge and his company, under the direction of Donald Crisp, will shortly depart for the Columbia River, near Portland, Oregon, there to film exterior scenes for the feminine impersonator's second Lasky-Paramount production. The company will be gone about two weeks.

* * *

Aileen Allen, Triangle-Keystone champion diving beauty and professional swimmer, added another medal to her ever increasing collection last week when she won the Southern California high diving championship at Ocean Park, California.

* * *

Triangle-Keystone Director Robert Kerr has just finished a Triangle-Keystone comedy featuring Bob Millikin, Fritz Schade, Claire Anderson, Andy Anderson, Jack Henderson and Joey Jacobs, and has started another comedy with the same cast.

Olive Thomas, Triangle star, is being directed by Lynn Reynolds in her latest feature entitled "Broadway Arizona." Mr. Reynolds is the author of the story, and at the present time the company is shooting exterior scenes at Big Bear Lake, California.

* * *

Due to the illness of Louise Glaum, Director Walter Edwards of Triangle was called upon to find a substitute for his star. Belle Bennett, of the Triangle stock company, was selected and is now playing the lead in his feature supported by one of the strongest casts ever assembled in a Triangle production. Among the most prominent actors are Jack Livingston, Lee Hill and Jack Cunningham.

* * *

Under the direction of E. Mason Hopper, the Triangle company, headed by Walt Whitman, is engaged in producing a feature production entitled, "The Tar-Heel Warrior."

* * *

"Hill-billies" of the Kentucky Cumberlands offer most of the excitement in Margery Wilson's latest play, "Mountain Dew," which Director Tom Heffron finished shooting recently at the Triangle Culver City Studios. All the characters of mountain life are included in the cast, and Margery Wilson appears in the role of a girl who cannot read or write. Charles Gunn plays opposite Miss Wilson.

* * *

Fred J. Balshoffer, president of the Yorke-Metro, stood sponsor for a picnic given to a truckload of youngsters at one of the beaches near Los Angeles this week. In the absence of Mr. Balshoffer, who was laid up on account of injuries received in a recent automobile accident, the party was managed by Tom Walsh, assistant director.

* * *

The completion of the new stage recently secured by the Yorke-Metro company has enabled the art department, under the supervision of R. C. Godfrey, who is an expert in studio art and design, to commence the construction of an unusually elaborate ball room set for "Paradise Garden," the Harold Lockwood picture, which is under production by Fred J. Balshoffer.

* * *

The Apollo Theater in Hollywood, by arrangement of Manager Young, gave a pre-showing of "Under Handicap," the Yorke-Metro picture which features Harold Lockwood, produced for the Metro release this month. Members of the cast, including Harold Lockwood, Lester Cuneo, William Clifford and others, and also the studio force of the Yorke-Metro were present.

* * *

With a company of fifty people Director Rupert Julian went to Seven Oaks, California, this week to film scenes of "Julio Sandoval," a five-reel play. Monroe Salisbury and Ruth Clifford are the leading players. The story was written and prepared for the screen by Elliott J. Clawson.

* * *

Wallace Reid, the popular Lasky player, was temporarily discharged from military service this week by Draft Board No. 14 which met at the Hollywood Board of Trade. Reid claimed exemption on the grounds that he has a wife and six-weeks-old child to support. The board decided it would grant exemption from service to Reid until such a time that the baby has reached an age that will permit Mrs. Reid to resume her own professional work.

* * *

When the 17th Coast Artillery of Hollywood, California, was mustered into the Federal service and left Sunday morning, Aug. 5, for Fort Arthur, at San Pedro, it took with it fifteen men from Universal City, all of whom relinquished positions at the film capital to enter the service of Uncle Sam.

The list includes Leonard Clapham, W. B. Paquette and Stanley Fitz, who were playing in Universal's forthcoming serial "The Red Ace;" Dwight Robinson and Stanley McCullough of the general acting force; F. Quincy and Fred Burnworth of the film editorial department; H. Godwin and Herbert Kirkpatrick, cameramen; property clerks Henry Hathaway and Hugh Meisel; Mack Wright, technical man of Director Harry Solter's company; Bert Howell, a stage carpenter; Robert Klein of the laboratory, and Alfred Connors of the general stores department.

* * *

Geraldine Farrar, with the same portable dressing room which she used in her production of "Joan the Woman," has departed for the California mountains to film scenes in her forthcoming production which is being made under the direction of Cecil B. DeMille from the story by Jeanie MacPherson. This dressing room, no matter where it is set, contains all the comforts of Miss Farrar's room at the studio, even to a telephone.

Italian Letter

By Francesco Manelli.

NOTWITHSTANDING the war, which has caused a slump which amounts almost to a standstill in those industries not directly connected with the supply of munitions, the cinematographic industry has received a new impulse in spite of the increase in the cost of both raw material and labor.

This impulse is rather in the nature of an artistic revival in production than in strictly trade matters which are laboring under the disadvantage above cited, as well as the difficulty which confronts the exportation of Italian films, the rigorous Government censorship and American competition.

This new impulse has taken the form of the following of the example of Gabrielle D'Annunzio by many men of letters in devoting much of their time and effort to the production of scenarios for the adaptation of their literary or theatrical works to the screen. D'Annunzio himself has recently given to the screen "The Crusade of the Innocent," an original subject that, while it brought the author twenty-five thousand francs and is said to have cost the producers six times this figure, proved a failure both artistically and financially—an unfortunate contrast to the splendid success achieved by the same author's "Cabiria." Among the distinguished authors who are now writing for the screen will be found many who, but a short time ago, thought so lightly of the picture as to refuse to admit that it was vested with either artistic conception or idealism.

Their opinion on this point was probably influenced by the fact that the growing popularity of the motion picture had considerably reduced their earnings from play-writing—which had heretofore been one of the most lucrative fields of their endeavor.

Becoming convinced at last that the cinematographic industry did possess merits of its own, several of these literary lights organised a society of which the principal object was the forming of a Cinematographic Literary Trust, which was bound to publish only their own productions, each member bound himself to write three or four scenarios per annum and all agreed to pool the profits for equal division. This trust was formed under the name of the Silentium-Film and numbers among its members Marco Paraga, Renato Simoni, Giuseppi Adami, Giovanni Verga, Dario Niccodemi. Alfredo Testoni, all dramatists, a few theatrical-critics, and so far they have brought to light "Mimi and the Ragamuffins" by Adami, "Night of Tempest" by Praga, and have ready or in course of preparation "Illusion" by Simoni, "Happiness" by Testoni, "Enemy" and "Scampolo" by Niccodemi, "Angelus" by Giacomo, and "The Wolf Hunt" by Verga, which the Italian censor thought fit to suppress.

The other literary men are working on their own account or for such producing or publishing houses as may pay them best. Adami, of the Silentium trust, has also composed a work for the "Savoia-Film" which is entitled "How a Butterfly Died" and which was interpreted by the celebrated Italian lyric artiste Rosina Storchio. Ferdinando Russo, an exquisite Neapolitan dialectic poet and a celebrated novelist and journalist, has written two scenarios, "The Good Thief" and "The Memories of a Maniac," both of which have been presented with great success.

Another Neapolitan dialectic poet, Ernesto Murola, has given up the management of a dramatic company and passed also into the cinematographic literary world with an original work entitled "O Sole Mio ((My Sun)," portraying the Neapolitan surroundings, with musical accompaniment by the well known Maestro V. Valente.

Carlo Zangarini, known as a librettist, has given up part of his activity to cinematographic work. Among his most recent productions may be mentioned "From Dawn to Sunset," written for the Luna-Films."

Mario Corsi, the keen dramatic critic of the Tribuna, has already written for the Tespi-Film "The Woman Without a Heart," and is now preparing "Friar Sole," a cinematographic vision of the life and epoch of Saint Francis of Assisi.

Count Luciano Zuccoli has given up for the time being novel writing and journalism in order to write "The Old Flame," the interpretation of which he has intrusted to the celebrated French actress, Suzanne Armelle.

Even one of Italy's most eminent parliamentarians, who has also been more than once a minister, has specially composed for a cinematograph film "The Ruler" of Venice, a political and suggestive subject, "The Song of the Flowers." Other important original works are promised by Sem Benelli, Roberto Bracco, Mario Settimelli, Luigi Barsini and many others.

The writer, however, who has really distinguished himself in a very short time for quantity and quality of his productions is the well known journalist, Lucio D'Ambra, who in less than a year has written "Miss Cyclone," "The Chess King," "The Towers," "The Altieri," "They Called Her Cosetta," "Emir Circus Horse," and recently "The Wives and the Oranges," a subject which is out of the ordinary run for the strange nature of its conception and originality of its form, which were all well received by the public.

The public taste is on the verge of changing from bloodthirsty films, that have not as yet totally disappeared from the Italian cinematographic scene, such as the doings of the Apaches, the clever and shrewd deeds of the detectives.

Side by side therewith, and with the tendency to abolish them, there flourish subjects in which art is evident in the conception. Perhaps it may be that the reform of Italian cinematographic art is at hand, which at the same time will determine the reform of public taste. The Italian authors have at last condescended to enter the cinematographic field, which but yesterday they scorned and despised, tempted more by the aspect of lucre than by the desire to ennoble this form of art.

It is an unchallengeable fact that the entrance on the cinematographic scene of the above mentioned well known writers will at all events greatly influence the taste and habits of the public, however, always assuming that the literary and artistic productions of these gentlemen be not swayed by the dictates of a false and damaging commercial spirit, which means appealing to the public by pandering to its vilest instincts.

A proof of the tendency of the Italian public of today to break from the old style of the cinematograph is illustrated by the good reception given to the American films and especially those of the "Triangle Company." It is not the writer's object to draw comparisons between the films of other American companies which have been circulating in Italy and those of the Triangle that have been put on the Italian market but recently; but it must be admitted that the result of this enterprise is beginning to exceed the expectations of the Triangle manager in Italy, Ernest Bru, and his agent for the sale of the concession Kodato Rossi.

The enterprise has been well prepared with excellent advertising, and any new films which appear on the screen are accompanied and frequently preceded by articles in the Italian dailies, wherein are found unconditional praise instead of criticism.

Milan led and Rome followed, in according a magnificent christening to the Triangle, suffice it to record that within a fortnight no less than eight projections were given in presence of packed houses and an enthusiastic press. The debut took place with the film "The Coward." The local press at once recognised in this work, as well as in all the other productions of the Triangle, an unconditional superiority over the Italian productions and they also admired the novel method of advertising the trade mark of the Triangle, which is everywhere conspicuous, adorning hoardings at every street corner. It has been announced in print that the Triangle is the gospel of the cinematograph, and more particularly in Rome, the announcements bear a text similar to that of the National Loan: "Do Your Duty, See the Triangle Film!" and the people rushed and admired.

Perhaps the public does not admire completely and unconditionally, as the Italian public are still accustomed to the old familiar faces, real Italian types, such as Bertini, Borelli, Menichelli, divas of the Italian silent art; but the die has been cast, with the works of the Italian literature on one side and the films of the Triangle on the other, although elements in direct competition as it were, still they serve together to raise the Italian public taste, and to launch the national output in a field in which hitherto it had no competitors, and in which it now feels the necessity of fighting merely for existence and the necessity of improving.

"QUEEN OF THE SEA," NEW KELLERMANN PICTURE.

"Queen of the Sea" is the title decided upon for the new sub-sea picture in which the marvelous Annette Kellermann will be presented by William Fox as his premiere for the season of 1917-18.

Miss Kellermann and a company are now at Bar Harbor, Maine, and work has begun under the direction of John G, Adolfi. The new picture of which George Bronson Howard is the author will be entirely different in action and story to "A Daughter of the Gods."

Reviews of Current Productions
EXCLUSIVELY BY OUR OWN STAFF

"Efficiency Edgar's Courtship"

The First Venture of Taylor Holmes in the Silent Drama
Pronounced Success—Ably Supported by Virginia Valli,
Ernest Maupain and Rodney LaRock.

Reviewed by James S. McQuade.

THE stage creator of the roles of Bunker Bean and Frank
Craven, which won him high favor among dramatic theatergoers will capture a fine following among photoplay theater
fans by his first essay before the camera, if my opinion is
worth anything. In "Efficiency Edgar's Courtship," by Essanay,
Taylor Holmes has not only given us a delightful and mirthful
characterization of "Efficiency Edgar," but he has succeeded in
"putting over" comedy points and subtle humor in a singularly
effective way before the camera. In this Mr. Holmes is aided by

Scene from "Efficiency Edgar's Courtship" (Essanay).

clever subtitles, when the pictures alone are unequal to the
task of expressing the full meaning. The method of Mr. Holmes
is marked by a resourcefulness that is never lacking, whether it
be mobile facial expressiveness, intelligent gesture or in happy
"bits" of business. He is distinctly a comedian of the higher
class, who makes his appeal to the intelligence of the spectator
and not to his ordinary risibilities. Indeed, in this instance, he
is compelled to do so by the nature of the story itself; for a less
delicate handling of the part of Edgar would deprive the photocomedy of much of its cleverness and the spectator of much of
his pleasure.

"Efficiency" Edgar, or Edgar Bumpus as he was christened,
believes that efficiency in love-making is quite as desirable as
efficiency in business, and he employs it in his pursuit of Mary
Pierce whom he has selected as the adorable object of his love.
Mr. Pierce, her father, a grouchy old gentleman, is made to feel
sorely the effectiveness of Edgar's efficiency, as he is check-
mated at every move and is finally compelled to give his blessing to the young lovers. Young Mr. Wimple, a rival for Mary's
hand, self-centered and bumptious, also becomes an easy victim and drops out of the story unhonored and unsung.

The Mary Pierce of Virginia Valli is quite creditable and Rodney La Rock's Wimple is satisfying. In his characterization of
Mr. Pierce, the much-tried father of Mary, Ernest Maupain has
added another splendid type to his long list of character successes before the camera. His make-up in the role, as is his wont,
is an artistic study.

The production was in the care of Director Windorn, who is to
be congratulated for careful and highly intelligent work.

The release will be made September 3 through K-E-S-E, Inc.

"Nearly Married" for Madge Kennedy.

Madge Kennedy's second Goldwyn production will be the
famous stage success, "Nearly Married," by Edgar Selwyn,
Goldwyn having purchased this delightful farce comedy during the current week. "Nearly Married," when presented several seasons ago in New York, was an all-season success at
the Gaiety theater and played to tremendous audiences
throughout America. At the time of its stage presentation it
gave Bruce McRae one of the best roles of his career and also
brought the beautiful Ruth Shepley into greater prominence.

"Babbling Tongues"

Seven-Part Ivan Photoplay Is Thoroughly French in Subject
and Treatment and Contains Many Tense
Dramatic Moments.

Reviewed by Edward Weitzel.

ONE is at a loss at first to understand why William Humphrey and George E. Hall should have laid the scene
of their seven-part Ivan photoplay, "Babbling Tongues,"
in France and made all the characters French. The mystery
is cleared up, however, before the end of the picture, in fact,
most spectators will recognize, as soon as the story is well
under way, that only in the land of the tri-color could such a
combination of incidents flourish even in screen fiction. This
is not to say that "Babbling Tongues" is devoid of merit. It
is quite the reverse.

The story is peopled with high-strung individuals who seem
to care a great deal more for "dramatic values" than for common sense, and who never lose an opportunity to make the
most of the acting possibilities of their lives. Once started,
however, it moves smoothly along the track approved of by
the novelists and playwrights of France and contains many
tense dramatic moments. So well does it hold the attention
that it seems nothing short of impertinent to be told calmly,
at the finish, that the thing never happened at all, that our
sympathy has been obtained under false pretenses and the
almost tragic denouement is the trick of a writer for the
stage. The theater is the dwelling place of illusion—why
shatter the illusion with one stroke of the pen?

The finish is led up to in this wise: An elderly French gentleman, who has been saved from financial ruin by a friend,
marries a young wife, and then discovers that the son of his
benefactor is living in a garret and undergoing the usual
struggle of the unknown dramatist. He takes the young man
into his home, and his relatives, friends and servants try to
make him believe that the playwright and the young wife are
betraying his trust. He will not listen at first, and he is justified in this; but the tongue of scandal is too strong for even
innocence to counteract and keeps manufacturing apparent
evidence until the husband drives both wife and playwright
from his door and forces them into each other's arms. Before
they can reach the outer door, however, the scene shifts and
shows husband and wife and playwright sitting at a table
and smiling happily at one another. The dramatist has been
reading his last play to them, and made himself the hero of
the story. The thing never really happened at all!

The picture has been given a liberal production, and is ar-

Scene from "Babbling Tongues" (Ivan).

tistically directed by William Humphrey. The cast is an able
one, James Morrison, Grace Valentine and Arthur Donaldson
acting the playwright, the wife and the husband, respectively.
Other capable members of the cast are: Paul Capellani, Louise
Beaudet, Gladden James, Carolyn Birch, Richard Tucker and
Robert E. Hill.

"The Bridge of Fancy"

Little Mary McAlister, Supported by a Cast of Children in the Latest Episode of Essanay's "Do Children Count?" Series.

Reviewed by Arthur W. Courtney.

LITTLE MARY M'ALISTER'S latest episode in Essanay's "Do Children Count?" series is full of children and it is about children. Yet it is a picture that is too sophisticated for an audience of children. It will afford unlimited enjoyment to adults. It is the kind of picture that keeps lovers of children

Scene from "The Bridge of Fancy" (Essanay).

in a continual ripple of laughter from beginning to end. This episode was released August 15. The screen time is twenty-five minutes.

The picture is a fantastic dream of Little Mary's. But it is much better than most dream pictures. After her mother has kissed her good-night and left the room, Little Mary gets up, steals to her mother's room and comes back with her mother's new dress and hat. She always at her best when she is trying on grown-up clothes. Then she lies down on the bed in all her finery and dreams.

The dream is a delicious burlesque on the story of high society life where the multimillionaire betroths his daughter to a count. The daughter's true lover fights a duel with the count; afterward sets detectives on his trail, and at the betrothal banquet breaks in to announce that the count is an imposter. Jack Paul and Billie Paul are the children who take the leading parts in this burlesque. They are made up with false whiskers in burlesque style. Even Little Mary wears shoes too big for her. When the count takes her for a joy ride it is in a child's auto propelled by foot power. The children maintain the spirit of the burlesque with great realism. They make believe with out half trying and get good fun out of it.

Little Mary's awakening from her dream occurs when she is dreaming that she has fainted and is lying on a couch and that her true, soldier lover is bending over her and kissing her back to consciousness. She awakes to find that the true and only Bo-bo, her bull pup, has climbed on the bed and is licking her face. As this picture dissolves, the audience is as much surprised as Mary.

The sub-titles are very good. In the scene where the father is discussing the marriage settlement with the count, the count asks for a million dollars and then accepts ten dollars on account. The children act this picture better than adults could do because they maintain a serious demeanor through it all. This is the essence of true burlesque acting.

"The Law of the Land"

A Complete Piece of Paramount Artistry with Madame Petrova in the Leading Role.

By Louis Reeves Harrison.

"The Law of the Land," a Paramount subject released on August 13, has a basic idea which will be popular as long as there is rigid enforcement of laws originally enacted for elastic interpretation; its remarkable similarity to the De Saulles case acts as stimulant to close attention, and its artistry of directing and interpretation may be called complete, though there are some minor errors and a motif denied as modern by many critics, the old motif of many stage plays, that of woman's sacrifice in marriage for the honor of the family. In spite of its tendency to theatricalism, the mood of "The Law of the Land" is so admirably preserved by the fine cast and by exceptionally appropriate settings, many of the latter being works of art in themselves, that the whole effect, the illusion, is delightfully preserved. This is more difficult than producers realize, for we are in an era of serving dried fruit, whose live flavor has been evaporated in some other kind of performance.

at the dawn of an era when people will demand the fresh article.

Madame Petrova is entirely at home in her emotional role, but her eloquent eyelids lose effectiveness at times from a common studio fault, that of a make-up too obviously artificial, in this case ageing her and wholly unnecessary. She is otherwise in an almost constant state of mental revelation, an impressive exponent of screen psychology, at all times a marvel of dignified grace in movement. It would require an artist like Madame Petrova to portray a character rarely seen as yet, that of the modern woman of high intelligence, of as acute sensibilities as the traditional stage heroine, yet with a high-strung nervous temperament under the control of a sound, normal and well-trained mind. She exhibits many of the subtle half-disclosures of thought and feeling so essential in an interpretation of the up-to-date American woman, demonstrating a higher capability than is called for in any but the most recent stories of human life. In other words she rises to the opportunity afforded her, and goes beyond it with the unfailing intuition of a true artist. There is a romantic setting at the outset announced to be a scene in the Riviera—by this is generally meant the French Riviera—with a back drop portraying a promontory like that of Monaco, or of Cape Ferrat near Nice. It is entirely appropriate and very well done, but it plants the locality. There is only one gambling·casino of note in that neighborhood, that of Monte Carlo, familiar to an enormous number of good Americans, and the games there are roulette and trente et quarente. The latter only is a card game, and the pack is handled by the dealer. The old lady could not cheat at cards there, nor would she have been a private villa. But this is of small importance. It is remarked in the way of suggestive criticism—it does not mar the story, even to the initiated. The whole effect is one of superior and complete artistry, highly creditable to all engaged in the production.

"Durand of the Bad Lands"

Fox Makes Burlesque With Dustin Farnum as Wild Western Hero—It Amuses and Will Entertain.

Reviewed by Hanford C. Judson.

THERE is in the screen writings of Maibelle Hikes Justice, who has furnished the script for "Durand of the Bad Lands," Fox five-reel picture, released August 12, a marked feeling for character and liveliness of humor. Both of these traits are noticeable in this offering. Its hero, Durand, is played by Dustin Farnum, and it is he who performs the exploits. The character is modern with railroads and macadam highways. This bandit is wanted by the sheriff for many high crimes and misdemeanors. Both these men love the same girl and in the end the bad man proves the most desirable. It is he, for instance, who drives off a band of Indians who have jumped a caravan of settlers. That they should have taken the train is part of the humor. These bad reds have killed just exactly nineteen sturdy whites when Durand comes along in time to save three kids. The sheriff finds his holster on the field, and for the added crime of wholesale murder another thou' is added to the reward for his head. The Governor of the State is inspecting the border, probably as a military precaution, when the same band of Indians race the train and hold it up. The sheriff is on board, but he too has to hold up his hands. The chief runs away with the Gover-

Scene from "Durando of the Bad Lands" (Fox).

nor's daughter, but not until Durand appears—it is he who makes them scamper. He, too, is the man who races after the chief and saves the girl. The sheriff thereupon takes him up, pleas of the Governor notwithstanding. The trial is a comical bit, with the Governor waiting to reprieve the culprit after The Governor sits there melodramatically to turn the trick at the right time. There is a good deal of freshness in the "comic relief," and that parson must not be forgotten.

"Through Fire and Water"

Episode of Stingaree with a New, Breezy Story Makes Entertaining Picture—Has a Delightfully Humorous Incident.

Reviewed by Hanford C. Judson.

THERE is distinctly good quality in the story told by this episode of the Stingaree series, "Through Fire und Water." Its humor is the real article, freshly thought up, breezy and quite enjoyable. It's a picture that takes a spectator out of himself with a care-free tale. The ugly bad-man villain is seen crossing the desert. He

Scene from "Through Fire and Water". (Kalem).

lights a cigarette and drops off to sleep while his coat takes fire. Stingaree, the bad-man hero, sees his predicament and gives him the famous white coat to wear. A little group of incidents helps the bad man to recognize Stingaree, and he goes to the police to try for the reward. Howie's bucking horse takes him to a cabin where a pretty young woman gives him a meal. Stingaree, looking for Howie, learns that the man with the coat is helping the police. The girl in the cabin, who helped Howie, turns out to be the wife of the "ugly bad man, who has deserted her with all her money, 500 pounds, just the amount of the reward. Stingaree goes out and sees the chief of police and the bad man looking for him. He leads them a chase till at night they fall asleep, one on one side of a stream, one on the other. Then Stingaree changes horses with the chief and leaves his hat. The policeman, by the way, has the 500 on him. Then on the other side of the stream he makes the ugly bad man look, in the distance, like himself, Stingaree. When the sun rises and the two awake to go about their business, they look across and each thinks he sees Stingaree. There's a rifle fight and the ugly bad man, who needed killing, is shot. The reward is taken to the little woman. It's her money.

Official British Government War Pictures

"The Retreat of the Germans at the Battle of Arras" the Fourth Installment of These Remarkable Views From the French Battle Front.

Reviewed by Edward Weitzel.

THE latest installment of the Official British Government War Pictures consists of ten thousand feet of remarkable views from the French battle front, and are entitled "The Retreat of the Germans at the Battle of Arras." The large number of persons that have witnessed the previous pictures sent to this side of the ocean by our Allies in Great Britain need only to be assured that the latest films from the seat of the war are as interesting as the others to insure them equal success in all the picture theaters in this country. Actual warfare as it is now being carried on with the aid of big guns, "tanks," airplanes, bicycle corps and all the marvelous modern machinery that human skill has placed at the disposal of the millions of men now fighting for universal freedom is shown in these pictures, many of the views being taken during the heat of battle. Hundreds of thousands of feet of film were secured, some of it of so ghastly a nature as to prevent its being shown. Enough realism, in the shape of wounded soldiers being treated at a dressing station near the front, has been retained, however, and the joy with which the inhabitants of a village vacated by the retreating Germans welcome the advance guard of victorious English soldiers furnishes further proof of how rapidly the camera has followed the march of events.

The pictures taken from an aeroplane are especially interesting. Views showing the enemy's trenches and camps are included among them. As a finish the spectator is shown how the face of the earth looks to an airman when he is spiraling downward at the rate of seventy miles an hour.

It is the purpose of the British Government to make these views constitute a pictorial history of the British forces in the Great War, and every care is being taken to secure the best material possible. Another interesting fact in connection with these pictures is that over $200,000 has been contributed to the American Red Cross from the proceeds resulting from their exhibition in this country.

"Transgression"

Five-Part Vitagraph Blue Ribbon Feature With Earle Williams Is Fairly Interesting Melodrama.

Reviewed by Edward Weitzel.

MELODRAMA with a society atmosphere classifies "Transgression," a five-part Vitagraph Blue Ribbon feature written by J. Stuart Blackton and Cyrus Townsend Brady. The story turns on a situation that is hardly plausible, but, once it is accepted, it leads up to a well sustained climax, and competent acting by the entire cast, under the direction of Paul Scardon, insures the bringing out of the best points in the picture.

Hal Page, whose brother is mayor of the city, falls in love with a lady who is no better than she should be, and throws over an old admirer in order to accept an invitation to become Mrs. Hal Page. Hal's rival, whose name is Staley, meets him one night at the home of the lady and attempts to shoot him. The mayor's brother seizes a pistol belonging to the cause of the trouble, and when the smoke of battle clears away Staley is lying dead on the floor. Stephen Page arrives at this moment and takes charge of affairs. He hurries his brother off to Spain and tells the woman that the secret must be kept for all their sakes.

The next morning Staley's body is found in an alley. Later on the Shrefton woman marries a crooked politician, and when the District Attorney is about to convict him, his wife goes to the mayor and threatens to tell who killed Staley if Stephen Page does not have the case against her husband stopped. The mayor will not agree, and subsequent developments prove that Hal did not fire the fatal shot, but took the blame in order to shield the woman, Staley being killed in a struggle with her. A love affair which the mayor has with the daughter of the District Attorney is also brought to a happy end. The doubtful point is in having the woman about to give information that would lead to a searching examination into a case of manslaughter of which she herself is guilty.

The acting honors of the drama go to Billie Billings as Caroline Shrefton. Edwards Davis is excellent as the District Attorney, and Earle Williams, Webster Campbell, Mary Maurice, Corinne Griffith, Denton Vane and Jack Ellis keep the performance up to the mark.

"Hashimura Togo"

A Paramount Drama of Japanese Character Admirably Pictured by Wm. C. DeMille, with Sessue Hayakawa in the Leading Role.

Reviewed by Louis Reeves Harrison.

HASHIMURA TOGO is a very intelligent character portrayal with exquisite settings, both Japanese and American, in a story of attempted sacrifice on the part of Togo to save his family honor, while he becomes the unwitting instrument of saving an American heroine from a sacrifice at the altar to save her

Scene from "Hashimura Togo" (Paramount).

family honor. That both are saved is due to the acumen of an unheroic American newspaper reporter. The villainous trustee of an American girl's property attempts hypothecation by forging a note from her father to himself for the sum of $350,000.00. He uses this note to force a promise of marriage from the girl, although she is already engaged to a man she loves. On receiving her verbal promise to marry him, the villain tears the forged note up in her presence and throws the scraps in a waste basket.

Togo, who has sacrificed his own future to save a gu
brother in Japan is employed in the girl's household. He patc
the note together, writes in his own vernacular to the newspa
about it, and, in this way, the matter comes to the atten
of a plain ordinary reporter, who places it before the dig
attorney. Togo is taken before his own father, now an Ame
consular officer, and ordered to commit hari-kari. He is
when about to plunge a knife in his body by the real cu
confession, while the young American girl is saved at th
by discovery that the villain she is about to marry is th
and all turns out happily in the end. The release is r
for a clear glimpse of Japanese character and for the
manner in which it is handled by Mr. DeMille.

Triangle Productions

"Wooden Shoes," Five-Part Photoplay Star
Barriscale, and "A Pawnbroker's Heart," G
Keystone Comedy Featuring Chester Co

Reviewed by Edward Weitzel.

THE story which J. G. Hawks has utilized in "W
five-part Triangle photoplay starring Bessie
set against a picturesque background of Du
that has been reproduced with pleasing fidelity. T
bridges, quaint shops and quainter customs and costum
people are all there, just as they have been sketched and
by a long line of famous artists. Faithfulness to local color
of the chief virtues of this comedy-drama which serves
Barriscale as an interesting medium for the display of her abil
to enact a pretty little Dutch maiden in queer pointed cap,
stomping around in a pair of wooden shoes. At first sight the
unusual vivacity shown by Pampy seems a trifle inconsistent to
the character, but when it is known that she is one-half American the objection disappears.

The explanation of how this member of the Holland-
American line came to be reveals the fact that Pampy's father
was an American tourist, who married a native of the Dutch
village of Diepenveen and was disowned by his wealthy father.
The death of Pampy's mother and the loss of her father's health
forced the young girl to become the wage-earner of the family. Just previous to her father's death Pampy and a young
American artist fall in love with each other. The girl's grandfather relents shortly after his son's death and sends for Pampy.
The scheming mother of another Dutch maiden contrives to
pass off her own daughter as the wealthy heiress, but Pampy
arrives in time to secure her wealthy grandfather and the artist
for herself.

Not a novel story by any means, but clean in theme and entertaining throughout. The care with which it has been produced
has already been mentioned, and Bessie Barriscale as Pampy fits
the part most becomingly. Jack Livingston as the artist, J. J.

Scene from "Wooden Shoes" (Triangle).

Dowling as the bad man of the group, and Lon Likes as Hans
Dunkelberger constitute the star's leading support. Thomas S.
Guise, Howard Hickman, Will H. Bray, J. Frank Burke, Marga-
ret Thompson and Gertrude Claire are also competent.

"A Pawnbroker's Heart."

Keystone Comedies are known by their casts. With Chester
Conklin, Ben Turpin, Peggy Pearce, Caroline Rankin and Glen
Cavender to take care of the acting end of this rapidly moving
farce there is bound to be something, or someone, stirring all
the time. "A Pawnbroker's Heart" keeps pace with the Keystone reputation, the characters being reinforced by a number
of nicely behaved durmies. There is a plot that struggles man-
fully not to get lost in the general mix-up and just manages
to do it, and a crook finish that involves the robbery of the
office safe. The one object of rough house comedy is never
absent, however, and that is the one recommendation that has
any weight with the man out in front who has paid his money
to be amused.

Scene from "Miss Nobody" (Astra).

bedents. She only knows that the kindest folks in the world
are "Daddy" Crespi and "Uncle" Malone, pawnbroker partners.
The two old men send the girl to a fashionable school. Finally
pressed by her as to her identity, the kindly men lie and tell
her she is the daughter of a deceased English Earl. This leads
to many logical plot complications, and matters finally are
straightened out when an English Lord discovers through a
locket that the girl is his daughter. Thus the romance between
her and the Lord's ward is consummated.

Miss Hulette seldom has been seen in a more atractive role
than that of Roma. Cesare Gravina and H. G. Andrews have
the parts of the pawnbrokers. Their characterizations help
the production immeasurably. William Parke, Jr., is the hero;
Sidney Mather the heavy.

Director Parke has injected the same convincing and pleasing
atmosphere into this picture as he has injected into previous
productions. He is especially to be commended on his lightings.
The writer seldom has seen better or more effectively lighted
scenes than a few darkened room scenes in "Miss Nobody."

"Lonesome Luke's Wild Women."

Harold Lloyd and his co-workers have succeeded in presenting a very good comedy number in the two-reeler titled "Lonesome Luke's Wild Women." Especial note must be made of
th exteriors in this number. So beautiful are some of them
that they would need no human action at all to make them
good screen entertainment. But the action is there, too. Hal
Roach dircted the piece. Luke is aided in his comedy capers
by Harry Pollard and Bebe Daniels. Most of the scenes are
laid in an Oriental palace. These sets are sumptuous, and it
is on the thickly-upholstered divans that the "wild" women
are found. Luke and his pal, sailors, get into all sorts of
complications with the palace guards. It is not so much the
story as the incident and individual work of the players and
director that make this comedy worth-while.

"Pay Me"

Five-Part Western Melodrama on Jewel Productions Program Has Strong Story and Is Excellently Played by
Dorothy Phillips and Supporting Company.

Reviewed by Edward Weitzel.

THERE is good, red blood all through "Pay Me," a five-part
western melodrama written and directed by Joseph De
Grasse for Jewel Productions, with Dorothy Phillips as
the featured player. The story is full of primitive romance
and its movement is, for the most part, steadily forward. Joe
Lawson and Hal Curtis are partners in a mine, at the opening
of the drama. Both men are married, Lawson's child being

Triangle Program for August 26.

...essie Love in "Wee Lady Betty," a play of Irish life, and ...Devereaux and Anna Lehr in "Grafters," will be the ...n luminaries on the Triangle program for the week of ...t 26. Miss Love, whose characterization in "The Saw-...King" was credited as being one of the best recorded on ...e film, has in "Wee Lady Betty" another part designed ...abilities as an interpreter of juvenile characters.

...ornage has the chief role opposite Miss Love in this ...was written by J. G. Hawks and directed by ...er. The large cast of principals includes Charles ...Walter Perkins, L. Jefferies, Walter Whitman, ...g. Thornton Edwards, Alfred Hollingsworth and ...

...e a farcical treatment of swindlers who swindle ...ack Devereaux appears as the "silk-stockinged" ...ys more blue sky than can be located in the uni-...na Lehr is the alluring young person who con-...aud him, according to plans made by the young ...who aims to teach the boy a few lessons in busi-...Jack turns the tables and proceeds to teach the ...young lady and her confederates. Frank Currier, ...ard, George Siegmann and Robert Crimmins are ...supporting players. Arthur Rosson, assisted by ...son, directed the production under the supervision of ...wan. The play was picturized from a story by James ...ams.

Constance Talmadge at Work in "Scandal."

The first picture in which Constance Talmadge, who is the latest addition to the Selznick Constellation, will make her appearance as a film star is a powerful screen version of Cosmo Hamilton's sensational serial "Scandal," now appearing in the Green Book.

The role of Beatrix Vanderdyke, "the worst spoiled woman in America," gives Miss Talmadge a most unusual opportunity to show her talents. Indeed, it is a rare thing for a young screen star to be intrusted with the creation of a character so imbued with personality and abounding with opportunity for individual expression.

Cosmo Hamilton, whose "Blindness of Virtue" and "Sins of the Children" place him in the forefront of British novelists, has not only done his most powerful piece of work in "Scandal," but has also written a novel which abounds in the most remarkable way with elements which make for popularity.

Miss Constance Talmadge will therefore make her first appearance as a Selznick star in a play the sheer power and scope of which provide her with an ideal vehicle for her initial stellar venture.

The screen version of "Scandal" is being directed by Charles Giblyn, and in the notable company which has been collected in support of the young star are Harry C. Browne, J. Herbert Frank, Aimee Dalmores, W. P. Carleton, Ida Darling and Gladden James.

Work on the production has been going along steadily for the past two weeks in the Selznick Studio in the Bronx and on the beautiful estate of Commodore E. C. Benedict at Greenwich, Conn. Commodore Benedict has not only placed his mansion and grounds at the disposal of Director Giblyn and the "Scandal" company, but has also graciously played host on his famous steam yacht the Oneida, on which a number of the more important scenes of the play have been photographed.

Harry Keepers at camera; Wesley Ruggles, assistant director reading script; Frank Beresford, technical director; Dell Henderson, stage director; Harry Zeehand, chief electrician, preparing for opening up the lens on the first scene of the Charles Frohman stage success, "Outcast," in which Ann Murdock will be presented by Empire All Star Corporation.

...zation of Alice Heagan ...oyt and Neva Gerber ...by Lynn F. Reynolds. ...iewed by Ben H. Grimm.

...) proves "The Play's the Thing" in "Mr. Opp," a five-reel visualization of the novel of the same title by Alice Heagan Rice, also authoress of "Mrs. Wiggs of the Cabbage Patch." Without a big star, but with none the less capable players, Director Lynn F. Reynolds has succeeded in

Scene from "Mr. Opp" (Bluebird).

transferring to the screen a story whose humanness and substantiality is made evident in every foot of the five reels. As a whole the piece is a character study drawn with words by a master of her craft and limned on the screen by a master of his craft. No human note that could have been struck has been left unsounded; the uppermost chord is one of sympathy for vain, optimistic, lovable, self-sacrificing Mr. Opp. Arthur Hoyt takes the title role. He might have stepped from the pages of the book, so well does he fit and play the part.

The story deals with plain folks in a small town. Mr. Opp becomes the guardian of his half-witted sister. Through many vicissitudes he is optimistic, hoping for the best and fighting for the right. He starts a small newspaper, living more on the plaudits of the few inhabitants than on material pay. Finally he makes the supreme sacrifice—he gives up the girl he loves so that he may live a life of service to his sister. The picture follows the story of the novel closely with the exception of the ending, which, in the photoplay, is made more happy than that in the novel.

Director Reynolds' work cannot be too highly complimented. His atmosphere is always flawless and his artistry made evident at all times. His choice of types shows a keen and sympathetic knowledge of the needs of the story. The titles are exceptionally good. Neva Gerber takes second acting honors. She has the difficult role of the half-witted girl and does splendid work, as do also George Chesbro and George Hernandez.

Comments on the Films

EXCLUSIVELY BY OUR OWN STAFF

General Film Company.

THROUGH FIRE AND WATER (Kalem).—A continuation of the Stingaree series in two reels. It is a delightfully fresh and breezy story and is sure to make many friends among those who see it. For a longer notice see elsewhere in this issue.

DON'T LOSE YOUR COAT (Black Cat).—This is a two-reel, slapstick written and directed by the leading actor, Amedee Rastrelli. He is a farmer's son who comes to the city to marry an heiress. A funny situation comes at the end, where he gets his foot caught in a water pitcher.

THE MAINSPRING (Falcon).—This is an excellent four-reel mining story. It was directed by Henry King, the young man who plays the leading part. The beginning is strong, and action that holds the interest fills each reel. Seldom are so many good situations used in a single picture. It starts off as if it might be a detective story, but quickly changes to a story of adventure. The direction and acting is excellent. The fire in the mine, with which the picture ends, is handled with plenty of thrills. Careful workmanship abounds in this picture. Ethel Pepprell plays opposite Henry King.

THE FURNISHED ROOM (Broadway Star).—A two-reel O. Henry story. This is not as good as its immediate predecessors. It is a tragedy with a moving picture happy ending tacked on. The shock we get when we think that the boy has committed suicide by gas in the same room in which the girl did, is not corrected by seeing their meeting in the hospital with the prospect of both recovering. The story of the picture is merely a series of happenings. The girl goes from one theatrical agency to another searching for work and finds none. The only dramatic element is the final situation, the suicide. And this is not an entertaining situation on the screen. The boy by J. Frank Glendon; the girl is Agnes Eyres.

THE SOLE SURVIVOR (Selig).—A two-reel story of adventure in the jungles of Central America. This picture is a long time getting started. The early scenes are poorly directed. But from the time the hunter finds a girl, a prisoner in one of the mad scientist's cages, the interest is strong. When the hunter is put in a cage with a lioness who puts her paws on his chest as he lies on the ground, the interest is stronger. The story-within-a-story construction clogs up the action somewhat. The girl makes a startling change of clothes at the end while she is still in the jungle, where she was shipwrecked and has been a prisoner for two years. She changes from a wild animal's skin, in which she is very attractive, to up-to-date shirtwaist and skirt. In its best scenes, this is a bully wild animal subject.

HER HEART'S DESIRE (Selig).—A one-reel story of the old-fashioned type. It is full of incident but little else. At the reception after the girl's marriage to her first husband, the bride is fondled by one of the mess guests. This scene does not look quite right. A flock of sheep in the latter part of the picture makes an attractive background for the girl and her shepherd lover. At the beginning, a little child is knocked down by the girl's first husband in showing that he does not like children. This picture is only fair in its entertainment value.

Art Dramas, Inc.

THINK IT OVER (U. S. Amusement Corp.), August 13.—Catherine Calvert is featured in this five-part comedy-drama, supported by Richard Tucker. He is a middle-aged bachelor. She is a school girl with a wicked guardian. A review was printed in last week's issue.

Bluebird Pictures Corp.

THE SHOW DOWN, August 13.—A desert island and a shipwreck are important features in this five-part photoplay starring Myrtle Gonzales and George Hernandez. The story is pleasing and has been given a careful production. A longer review was printed on page 1231 of the issue of Aug. 25.

MR. OPP, August 20.—An excellent picturization of Alice Heagan Rice's novel of the same name. Lynn F. Reynolds' direction has made the photoplay as good a picture as is the book. Arthur Hoyt draws a fine character. There are smiles and tears in the picture, which is recommended to every exhibitor. A longer review is printed in the review columns.

Fox Film Corporation.

DURAND OF THE BAD LANDS, August 12.—A five-reel burlesque on the once popular wild west melo. It has some things in it that are quite new and most of all it is refreshing. It is not an ambitious picture, and one hardly worthy of any specially high commendation, except that it interests and amuses. It is not a scream; but surely it is entertaining. For a longer notice see elsewhere in this issue.

THE SOFT TENDERFOOT, August 12.—A lively comic burlesque with Tom Mix as the astonishing tenderfoot at the ranch. It is a

picture to kill worry and will furnish a good time. We can safely say that there isn't a dead yard in its two thousand feet. It is just stunts, but they are often very amusing.

Greater Vitagraph.

TRANSGRESSION, August 20.—A five-part Blue Ribbon feature with Earle Williams, this picture is a fairly interesting melodrama and is well acted by the entire cast. It is reviewed at length on another page of this issue.

BOBBY, THE PACIFIST, Aug. 27.—A very good addition to the one-part Bobby Connelly comedies, this release shows that there are times when the most ardent pacifist finds that the only thing to do is to fight. The small star acts with his usual effectiveness.

WORRIES AND WOBBLES.—A comedy number, by Lawrence Semon and Graham Baker. This centers about a married man who comes home with a jag and finds his wife waiting for him in anger and tears. A burglar appears and the police are called out. This has no particular plot and develops only a fair amount of humor, though well handled for this type of humor.

CHUMPS AND CHANCES.—This is an amusing one-part, roughhouse farce, written by Lawrence Semon and Graham Baker. Everyone works with a will all through the reel and risk life and limb with equal abandon.

Ivan Film Corporation.

BABBLING TONGUES, August.—William Humphry and George E. Hall are the authors of this seven-part photoplay, which is French in story and a good example of its class. The cast, headed by Grace Valentine and James Morrison, does it justice. A longer review is printed on another page of this issue.

Jewel Productions, Inc.

PAY ME, August.—Dorothy Phillips heads the cast of this five-part western melodrama, written and directed by Joseph De Grasse. The picture is red-blooded and is admirably acted and produced. A longer review is printed on another page of this issue.

Kleine-Edison-Selig-Essanay

EFFICIENCY EDGAR'S COURTSHIP (Essanay), September 3.—A high-class comedy of excellent merit. Taylor Holmes, in the title role, makes a pronounced hit and he is ably supported by Virginia Valli, Ernest Maupain and Rodney La Rock. On another page, in this issue, will be found a detailed review.

THE LITTLE CHEVALIER (Conquest No. 5).—This is the four-reel dramatic feature of this program. The story is by M. E. M. Davis. Shirley Mason plays the leading part. The action of the story takes place in Louisiana before the Revolutionary War. The boy and the girl are representatives of French families. The girl's father killed the boy's father in a duel in France. The girl, dressed as a boy, is The Little Chevalier, who defends the honor of her family. Later, when she is dressed as a girl, the boy meets her and falls in love with her. The part of the boy is played by Ray McKee. Richard Tucker is the villain, a secretary of the Governor of Louisiana, who attempts to prevent the marriage. This is a fairly interesting costume play.

A VANISHING RACE (Conquest No. 5).—This is a half-reel showing the domestic habits of the Blackfoot Indians. They are shown on their reservation in Montana. Interesting scenic shots are worked in. This picture shows how much squaws have to do around the tepee. Bona fide survivors of the Blackfoot Indians are the actors in this picture.

GOLD AND DIAMOND MINES OF SOUTH AFRICA (Conquest No. 5).—This is a half-reel showing how gold and diamonds are taken out of the earth in South Africa, with instructive street scenes in the cities of the district.

THE DINOSAUR AND THE BABOON (Conquest No. 5).—This is a half-reel manikin play by Willis H. O'Brien. The figures are very jerky in their movements. The comedy is low, but not vulgar. It is not especially interesting.

BIRDS OF A FAR-OFF SEA (Conquest No. 5).—This is a half-reel showing the bird life on an island three hundred yards square off the southern tip of Africa. There are Solan geese, cormorants and penguins. These are interesting scenes and beautiful, too.

SOLDIERS OF THE SEA (Conquest No. 5).—This is a full reel showing the activities of the U. S. Marines, interspersed with many strained patriotic sub-titles.

THE BRIDGE OF FANCY (Essanay), August 15.—A 25-minute episode in the "Do Children Count" series. Little Mary AcAlister heads a cast of children, among whom are Jack Paul and Ellis Paul, in a burlesque on the high society story of the millionaire's daughter, who is betrothed to a bogus count. This is an excellent picture for lovers of children. It is reviewed in this issue.

OPEN PLACES (Essanay), August 20.—This is a five-reeler written and directed by W. S. Van Dyke. Jack Gardner is a constable of the Royal North West Mounted Police. The story is about life on the northern border of the United States. Ruth King is a school teacher in Montana. She marries a bad man, but does not find out how bad he is until afterwards. Carl Stockdale is the husband. This photoplay lacks interest.

Metro Pictures Corporation.

MISS ROBINSON CRUSOE (B. A. Rolfe), July 30.—The star of this five-part comedy is Emmy Whelen, the English musical comedy star. The scenes are laid among the Thousand Islands and are often picturesque. The story is frothy and passably well acted. A longer review was printed on page 1228 of the issue of Aug. 25.

Odgen Pictures Corporation.

THE LUST OF THE AGES, August.—A pretentious subject in seven parts, featuring Lillian Walker. It is a preachment against the love of gold and the money power. The story branches in so many directions there is a failure to consolidate interest. The picture is reviewed on another page.

Paramount Pictures Corporation.

THE VARMINT (Lasky).—Jack Pickford and Louise Huff are co-stars in this five-part story of college life taken from Owen Johnson's well-known novel. The picture duplicates the success of the printed book. It was reviewed at length on page 1230 of the issue of Aug. 25.

HASHIMURA TOGO.—A story of Japanese character, with exquisite settings by Mr. DeMille and an admirable portrayal of the leading role by Sessue Hayakawa.

THE LAW OF THE LAND.—An unusually successful adaptation, artistically done throughout, of strong interest and with Madame Petrova very effective in the leading role.

Pathe Exchange Inc.

MISS NOBODY (Astra), August 19.—A five-reel subject that has all the elements that appeal. It is an especially good picture for neighborhood audiences, in that besides being entertaining it is thoroughly wholesome. The story tells of a girl who is educated by two old pawnbrokers. They tell her she is a lady, which leads to many amusing complications. It later develops that the girl really is a lady. A longer review is printed in the review columns.

THE DICE OF DEATH (Astra), Sept. 2.—Episode No. 9 of "The Fatal Ring" serial. The instalment moves rapidly and contains its full quota of excitement. The story develops to the point where the spectator is led to believe that Pearl has been stabbed by the plotters and closes at the most exciting moment.

LONESOME LUKE'S WILD WOMEN (Rolin), Sept. 2.—A two-reel comedy number, with Harold Lloyd, Harry Pollard and Bebe Daniels. It is a good number. The exterior scenes are very beautiful in themselves and the interiors, which show an Oriental palace, quite sumptuous. The release relies more on incident and the individual work of the players and director than the story. It tells of two sailors who reach a shah's palace and harem. Reviewed in the review columns.

CENTRAL COLORADO (Combitone), September 2.—A one-reel scenic-educational release of merit. Most of the footage of the reel is devoted to instructive and beautiful scenes showing gold mining in the Cripple Creek section of Colorado. Through the agency of the camera the spectator is brought through every interesting point of a gold refinery. The latter portion of the reel is devoted to footage containing well-photographed scenic views of the same general geographical section.

FINE FEATHERS (International), September 2.—A split-reel embracing an educational-industrial and a "Jerry on the Job" cartoon. The first sections shows from beginning to end the processes by which ostrich-plume fans and boas are made. The cartoon is especially funny. It shows Jerry in the uniform of a National Guardsman and his trials and tribulations in guarding the Mexican-American border.

OFFICIAL BRITISH GOVERNMENT WAR PICTURES.—The fourth instalment of the Official British Government War Pictures is called "The Retreat of the Germans at the Battle of Arras," and is equal in interest to the previous numbers. A long review will be found on another page of this issue.

Triangle Film Corporation.

GOLDEN RULE KATE, August 12.—This is a five-part Western melodrama in which the title role is excellently played by Louise Glaum. The story is full of interest and its possibilities have been fully realized by the producer and the cast. It was reviewed at length on page 1231 of the issue of August 25.

A PAWNBROKER'S HEART, August 19.—Chester Conklin and Ben Turpin are the principal peace-disturbers in this one-reel Keystone comedy, directed by Eddie Cline. It moves with the regulation Keystone speed and has its share of amusing situations. A longer review is printed on another page of this issue.

WOODEN SHOES, August 26.—The scenes of this five-part photoplay are laid in Holland, and the star, Bessie Barriscale, plays the owner of the pair of wooden shoes charmingly. The production is complete in every detail. A longer review is printed on another page of this issue.

Universal Film Manufacturing Company.

WHY THEY LEFT HOME (Joker), Week of August 72.—A comedy number, by C. B. Hoadley, featuring William Franey, Zazu Pitts, Lillian Peacock and Milburne Moranti. The country youth and his sweetheart join a show troupe and some entertaining comedy ensues. This contains a number of quiet chuckles and is quite amusing, though not unusual in plot.

THE HANDS IN THE DARK (Star Featurette), Week of August 27.—A two-reel subject, by E. M. McCall, featuring E. N. Wallack, Rex Roselli, J. Warren Kerrigan and Edith Johnson. This is a melodramatic offering, in which the hero quarrels with the girl's father. The butler, taking advantage of this circumstance, kills the old man and steals the jewels. The hero is sentenced to death and on the eve of execution a chase ensues to obtain a pardon from the governor on the grounds of new evidence. This has been done so often that it is hard to put new thrills into the situation. It is well handled and has the advantage of strong presentation. On last reel is also a short scenic, "Old French Towns."

THE HOUSE OF SHADOWS (Universal Special), August 27.—Episode No. 10 of "The Gray Ghost." This installment introduces a number of weird and mysterious happenings, in which The Gray Ghost appears simultaneously in two places. He first disappears from the place where he is lying, presumably dead, and then shows up in the house of mystery and at the police station. These new developments stir the interest considerably and keep the observer wondering what the solution will be.

BUSTING INTO SOCIETY (Joker), Rel. Week of August 27.—A comedy number, featuring Gale Henry and Milton Sims. The former is a poor girl with social aspirations and her lover is a hod carrier. The father wins a lottery prize and they break into social life. This has not a very strong plot, but contains some good burlesque touches and will bring numerous smiles.

JUNGLE TREACHERY (Bison), Rel. Week of August 27.—A two-reel subject, by W. B. Pearson, featuring Fred Church, Eileen Sedgwick, Fred Montague, Charles Brinley and others. The hero goes with a party to make a survey of some African jungle land. Adventures with wild beasts and war with the natives are interesting features. The night photography is good. This is stronger than the average two-reel subject.

THE WINNING PAIR (Gold Seal), Rel. Week of August 27.—A three-reeler featuring Ruth Stonehouse. It is unfortunate if she is to become associated with parts which require the telling of a number of falsehoods. Her hobby in this picture is collecting many pairs of boots for herself. At a country hotel she is mistaken for a "female drummer." She acts out the part with great success. The entertainment value of this picture is not high.

SCANDAL EVERYWHERE (Victor), Rel. Week of August 27.—A comedy number, by R. A. Dillon, featuring Max Asher as chief of the bell boys in a hotel. He flirts with the wife of one of the guests, who turns out to be a sleep walker. The humor is slightly rough and not particularly strong, though inoffensive. The closing scenes, where the characters bound up and down the skyscraper, are novel and interesting.

THE NIGHT CAP (Nestor), Rel. Week of August 27.—A one-reel comedy subject, by Virginia Kirtley, featuring Eddie Lyons, Lee Moran and Edith Roberts. The young man retires, on the eve of Eddie's wedding day, and Lee wears a girl's night cap. He is mistaken for a girl and trouble follows. A slightly risque situation, presented with just the right sort of juvenile humor to keep it from being offensive. A good comedy of the type.

PROPS, DROPS AND FLOPS (L-KO), Rel. Week of August 27.—A two-reel comic, featuring Gladys Varden, Bert Roach, Walter Stephens and Harry Griffith. The first reel introduces a number of stage hands and some chorus girls behind the scenes of a theater. Some of the incidental business is funny, but none of it very strong. The action in the second reel is better and holds the attention closely. There is a lot of good knockabout business and a number of interesting features, including the knife throwing and fire scenes. This will succeed with audiences who like plenty of comic action without much plot.

World Pictures.

THE LITTLE DUCHESS (Peerless), August 20.—The juvenile star, little Miss Madge Evans, contributes largely to the success of this five-part photoplay which deals with an orphan who becomes a member of the English aristocracy. The production is an all around good one. A longer review was printed on page 1229 of the issue of August 25.

PATHE PROGRAM FOR SEPTEMBER 2 FULL OF GOOD THINGS.

Baby Marie Osborne in a five-part Gold Rooster play, "Tears and Smiles"; Pearl White in the ninth episode of "The Fatal Ring"; Mollie King and Creighton Hale in the first episode of "The Seven Pearls"; "Central Colorado," which is the 21st installment of the "Know America" Pathe-Combitone series; Harold Lloyd in a two-reel "Lonesome Luke" comedy called "Luke's Wild Women"; a split reel international cartoon and scenic and the Hearst-Pathe News Numbers 72 and 73, make up the Pathe program for the week of September 2. In diversity of subject matter, quality of content and box-office value of the stars it would be hard to excel this program.

State Rights Department
Conducted by BEN H. GRIMM

Independent Producers Meet

Discuss Formation of Buyers' Organizations—Lee Organization Rapidly Forming—Final Meeting of Lesser Organization Called.

IMPELLED by the knowledge that two organizations of state rights buyers were forming, virtually every representative independent producer attended a meeting held in the Hotel Astor, New York, on Saturday, August 18. The meeting was held behind closed doors, and no definite announcements were made. It was learned, however, that the meeting was called by the producers of state rights pictures for the purpose of considering ways and means of "protection" against any possible attempts at arbitrary price-fixing or any other factor detrimental to their interests that might result in the event that an organization of buyers became powerful enough to dictate.

It was not given out just which of the producers attended or were represented at the meeting. It is known, however, that, since the formation of the First National Exhibitors' Circuit and the imminent formation of the organizations promoted by Sol L. Lesser and Joseph F. Lee, the producers have had their ears to the ground ready to "unionize" at short notice if need be.

Conjecture has it that the producers, if they organize formally and if the occasion arises, will fight as a unit to protect their interests against any possible dictatorial terms laid down by any organization of buyers. The life of the state rights market, they say, lies in its competition. If any group of buyers form a "trust," they say, then it will have to unite for strength.

As the situation looms up at present everybody on the producing side of the fence is marking time waiting for the buyers to start playing the music, and everybody on the buying side, besides watching each other, as a body is waiting for the producers to start playing the music. The situation may be likened to two boys ready to fight, each with a chip on his shoulder, but each too good a friend of the other to knock the chip off.

Lee Organization Rapidly Forming.

Joseph F. Lee announces rapid progress in his endeavor to bring together prominent state rights men in all parts of the country. The organization work has progressed to such a point, it is stated, that a representative has left New York on a tour that will, according to Mr. Lee, result in the acquisition as members of several of the biggest men in the field.

During the week there have been several conferences in which Louis B. Mayer, of Boston; Harry Crandall, of Washington, and Mr. Lee were the leading figures. Indications point to an early announcement of future plans.

Meeting of Lesser Organization Called.

The final meeting of the National Organization of State Rights Buyers—the organization promoted by Sol L. Lesser —has been called for Wednesday, August 22. It is announced that at this meeting all details that must be worked out before the organization begins active operations will be concluded.

Mr. Lesser still is confined to bed with typhoid fever, but is convalescing rapidly and is expected to be about in a few days. He is in constant touch with his lieutenants and despite his illness is directing the work of organization.

NETTER GETS "REDEMPTION" FOR OHIO.

Leon D. Netter, of the Masterpiece Film Attractions, Cleveland, has purchased "Redemption" for Ohio. Netter closed the "Redemption" deal almost at the same time that he purchased for the same territory "The Cold Deck," the new Hart picture. Masterpiece also controls in Ohio "The Garden of Allah," "Beware of Strangers." "The Ne'er-Do-Well and several others.

Hart Picture Selling Rapidly

Stephen A. Lynch Enterprises, Inc., Sell Big Block of Territory—Mayer, Lesser, Rosenberg and Netter Among Purchasers.

WITH about as little blaring of trumpets as a picture ever was given, the Stephen A. Lynch Enterprises, Inc., already have disposed of a great bulk of territorial rights to "The Cold Deck," a seven-reel Western subject in which William S. Hart is the star. The picture is the last one made by Hart while he was with the Triangle Film Corporation. Its production was supervised by Thos. H. Ince.

Louis B. Mayer, of Boston, has purchased the rights to the feature for Maine, New Hampshire, Massachusetts, Rhode Island, Vermont and Connecticut. Sol L. Lesser, acting for his All-Star Features Distributors, Inc., of San Francisco, directed from his sick bed the purchase of the film for California, Nevada and Arizona. Rights to "The Cold Deck" for Oregon, Washington, Idaho and Montana have been purchased by M. R. Rosenberg, of the De Luxe Feature Film Company, Seattle. Leon D. Netter, of the Masterpiece Film Attractions, Cleveland, purchased the subject for Ohio.

"DEEMSTER" SOLD FOR EIGHT MORE STATES.

The Arrow Film Corporation, through its president, W. E. Shallenberger, has disposed of "The Deemster" for two more territories, comprising eight States. D. P. Davis, acting for the All-Star Features, Inc., of Jacksonville, Fla., bought six Southern States, including North Carolina, South Carolina, Georgia, Alabama, Florida and Mississippi, and A. H. Blank, president of the Mid-West Photoplay Corporation, of Des Moines, purchased Iowa and Nebraska.

The Stillman Theatre, Cleveland, showed "The Deemster" last week and achieved wonderful results, it is reported. Cleveland critics waxed eloquent over the manifold beauties of story and production. Cleveland, it should be noted, has the largest Manx population in the world—not even excepting the Isle of Man. And by reason of this fact, rather than in spite of it, the financial returns in Cleveland mounted high.

WOLFBERG GETS "ON TRIAL."

It is announced at the offices of the Harris P. Wolfberg exchange, 603 Lyceum building, Pittsburgh, that the First National Exhibitors' releases would be distributed in Ohio through the Wolfberg exchanges. So far these releases consist of Essanay's "On Trial" and forthcoming Chaplin pictures.

Mr. Wolfberg, who also owns "The Crisis" and "The Deemster" for Ohio, Western Pennsylvania and West Virginia, will open offices in Cleveland and Cincinnati immediately.

Members of the Exhibitors' Circuit state that the distribution of their pictures was intrusted to Mr. Wolfberg because of his reputation for honest methods and square dealing with the exhibitor, and the high degree of efficiency of his exchanges.

SHORT FEATURES GETS OLD BIOGRAPHS.

Short Features Exchange, 729 Seventh avenue, New York, has purchased 50,000 feet of Biograph film. It is announced that the 50,000 feet are the pick of 300,000 feet examined. The pictures obtained include short subjects featuring Mary Pickford, Mae Marsh, Lillian Gish, Dorothy Gish, Blanche Sweet, Robert Harron, Henry Walthall and the whole list of other stars who had their start with the old Biograph company. Many of the pictures were directed by David W. Griffith and Mack Sennett. The exchange reports that the purchase included paper and other advertising matter.

HORSLEY STATE-RIGHTS MARY MacLAREN FEATURE.

Mary MacLaren Photoplays, made under her new contract with David Horsley, will be sold on the state rights basis. This is the announcement made by David Horsley in New York, where he has closed negotiations in four States for the first of her new seven-reel features, "The Counterfeit Soul." Mr. Horsley reports contracts signed for New York, New Jersey, New England and Pennsylvania.

BUYS "REDEMPTION" FOR NORTHWEST.

M. R. Rosenberg, of the De Luxe Feature Film Company, Seattle, has purchased "Redemption" with Evelyn Nesbit and her son, Russell Thaw, for Oregon, Washington, Idaho and Montana.

Unique One-Reel Star Series Announced

Photoplay Magazine Will Present Films Showing Big Stars Away From Studios—James R. Quirk Tells of Plan.

TWELVE single-reel subjects—one reel per month—of bizarre and unique views of the foremost players of cinemaland shortly are to be presented by the publishers of Photoplay Magazine under the title of Photoplay Magazine Screen Supplement. The twelve subjects will, in the very near future, be offered state rights buyers in the various territories.

Picture to yourself the contents of Photoplay Magazine come

James R. Quirk.

to life and you will have a fairly accurate idea of the nature of the newest novelty in motion pictures. Imagine scenes and closeups of such favorites as Mae Marsh, William S. Hart, Henry Walthall, Charlie Chaplin, Lucille Lee Stuart, Mr. and Mrs. Sidney Drew, Antonio Moreno, Bessie Love, Warren Kerrigan and a host of others in their homes, playing with their pets, swimming, motoring, fishing, mussing up in their dressing rooms and you will still further comprehend the sort of material that will be presented in Photoplay Magazine Screen Supplement. Exhibitors will not find it hard to appreciate the box-office possibilities that lie in this sort of an offering. These subjects will literally transport the fans to the homes of their favorites

and permit them for the first time to actually behold their idols doing the hundred and one things of which they are reputed to be fond, but which never heretofore have been seen on the screen.

"I am sure we have something wholly new, wholly different, to offer," said James R. Quirk, publisher of Photoplay Magazine, in discussing the forthcoming series presenting "The Stars As They Are." "It is not an idea conceived in a moment and executed the moment afterward, but the result of an idea which has been growing gradually and rounding into shape as time passed. We could have launched our first release months ago, but have refrained from doing so until we were sure of our ground—until we had collected material enough for months in advance and knew that the high standard we hit in our first release could be consistently maintained and even improved in subsequent issues. Right now we have on hand material enough for our first, nine releases and our cameramen are supplying it at a rate that will easily enable us to keep that far ahead of our release schedule.

"In offering these films we are going to give big exhibitors a chance to secure them for certain zones or territories, as well as state rights buyers. By that I mean if we receive a more attractive offer from John Doe, who conducts a string of fifteen or eighteen theaters in a certain territory, than we do from Richard Roe, who always snaps up a state rights bargain in that territory, John Roe, the exhibitor, will be given careful consideration when it comes to placing our franchise in that zone. Exhibitors controlling theater chains will thus be offered a chance to show the films in their houses as firstrun offerings and then to sub-lease them to other exhibitors in the territory at a price which will enable both the original lessees and the sub-lessees to make a profit.

"The trade is aware that Photoplay Magazine has always stood for quality—that it has begged, demanded and boosted for the better class, higher-grade type of photoplays—higher standards of direction, better photography and the employment of the foremost artists of the world. Now, therefore, its own debut in the film world as a manufacturer of films will have to bear out its past stand as a quality medium, and the trade may rest assured that nothing short of the best in every technical detail will be acceptable to it. The stars, of course, will be top-notchers—kings and queens of the cinema world. The camera work is in the hands of experienced, proven men of ability. The developing, tinting, toning and printing of Photoplay Magazine Screen Supplement will be handled by experts. The sub-titles will be as near perfection as money and brains can make them. In short, neither time, money nor effort will be spared to make our venture a real step in advance of anything that has gone before.

"The definite release date of our first Photoplay Magazine Screen Supplement has not yet been set, but within a week or two at most announcements will be made."

More "Parentage" Territory Allotted

Seng Will Inaugurate Bigger Campaign—"Parentage" to Go to Responsible Persons Only.

FRANK J. SENG, owner and distributor of "Parentage," announces that the Peerless Feature Film Exchange, of Philadelphia, will handle his unique feature in Eastern Pennsylvania, Southern New Jersey, Delaware, Maryland, District of Columbia and Virginia.

"Parentage" has been selected by the Stanley, the finest photoplay theater in Philadelphia, as its big attraction for the third week in September.

Commenting upon the large volume of direct inquiries for "Parentage" received from practically every buyer and exchangeman of prominence in the country and his reasons in particular for closing with the present holders of territorial contracts, Mr. Seng says: "When an exhibitor advertises he usually gets what he ought to receive—increased business. But his returns do not stop there. Every advertisement, rightly executed, creates good will and tends to establish his house as a factor in his community. In like manner do I regard the advertising that has already appeared and will continue to appear, featuring 'Parentage.'

"I am most sincere in my desire to create good will among state rights men and among exhibitors," says Seng, "hence my determination to spend exactly ten times more in each territory as it is disposed of than was set aside for the initial marketing campaign. And I would also like to impress the trade with the sincerity of my statement when I tell you that I have been more interested in the capabilities of the organizations who are handling 'Parentage' than in the size of the offers made."

To date, Mr. Seng says, he has found it advantageous to dispose of certain territories on a percentage basis, but a great many outright sales will be made and made as rapidly as the purchasers satisfy the owner of "Parentage" that they want to help the exhibitors make money and will co-operate with them to that end.

Exhibitors in the area of Greater New York who desire to book "Parentage" are referred to Lewis J. Selznick, of 729 Seventh avenue; those of New York state outside the metropolitan district should communicate with Veribest Pictures, Inc., 47 Swan street, Buffalo; those of Northern New Jersey should get in touch with Frank Gersten, Inc., 797 Times building, New York City; those in Eastern Pennsylvania, Southern New Jersey, Delaware, Maryland, District of Columbia and Virginia must look to the Peerless Feature Film Exchange of Thirteenth and Vine streets, Philadelphia, and Illinois and Wisconsin exhibitors should address their applications to the Lewis J. Selznick Productions, 110 South State street, Chicago.

"Garden of Allah" Sold for South

William N. Selig Also Announces Other Productions That May Be State-Righted.

THE All-Star Features Company, of Jacksonville, Fla., are the latest buyers of territorial rights for "The Garden of Allah," having purchased the rights to Georgia, Alabama, Florida, South Carolina, Mississippi, Tennessee, Louisiana and Arkansas.

Following the exploitation of state rights for "The Garden of Allah," the Selig Polyscope Company is turning its attention to several other big features which have been completed or are nearing completion. While William N. Selig has not definitely announced his plans concerning these latest features, it is presumed that several may be marketed along the lines of state rights successes such as "The Crisis," "Beware of Strangers," "The Garden of Allah," etc.

"The Garden of Allah" is another gripping drama bearing the diamonds trade-mark and presenting George Fawcett, the well-known star, as the lead. Mr. Fawcett takes advantage, it is said, of a large number of opportunities to perform clever character work. "The Railroader" was adapted by Gilson Willets from "Caleb Conover," the world-famous novel written by Albert Payson Terhune. Colin Campbell also directed this drama, which is said to carry some wonderful effects.

"The City of Purple Dreams" is another story filmed by the Selig Company and pronounced wonderful by those who have seen the play. It is adapted from the novel of the same name. Thomas Santschi stars and Colin Campbell was the director in charge. The scenic effects are said to be beautiful.

THIRD COMMONWEALTH COMEDY FINISHED.

"His Watery Waterloo," the third of the Commonwealth Comedies, was completed this week with Lou Marks playing the leading role supported by George Humbert, Leon Miller, Iva Edmondson, Leo Daly, Dorothy Gorden, Pauline Taylor and Irving Browning. The pictures were directed by Frank Donovan. Hughie Mack and Lou Marks are the Commonwealth stars. Both are famous for their comedy work and known throughout the world of motion pictures. A new one-reeler is being produced each week at the Commonwealth Studios in Cliffside, N. J., for early release.

Malitz Heads Piedmont Corporation

Is General Manager of Concern That Takes Over Hawk Film—Personnel of Piedmont Augurs Well for Future.

PIEDMONT PICTURES CORPORATION of New York, Paris, London, and Tokio, have taken over the business of the Hawk Film Company, and have opened new headquarters at 729 Seventh avenue, New York. Piedmont Pictures Corporation, as successor to the Hawk Film Company, operates now with a stronger and entirely paid-up capital, it is announced. Its object is to represent prominent producers as exclusive selling agents, and at the same time act as confidential purchase agents for prominent buyers throughout the world.

Felix Malitz, general manager, has a splendid reputation. As organizer and commercial manager of P a t h e Freres, for whom he has handled their entire American business as vice-president and general manager, he built up the entire Pathe Exchange organization in this country, and has for many years been generally connected with the film business in America and abroad. Assisting him are Joseph Lamy, export manager; Arthur Ziehm, Mr. Lamy's assistant; G. A. Enugler, manager of the distribution and s e r v i c e departments, and Harry Rubin, manager of the film and technical departments. These men are virile and young, yet long enough in the business to be thoroughly conversant with its various needs.

The Piedmont Corporation purposes to be an outlet for any manufacturer who will offer pictures which are sufficiently interesting to command the approval of the Piedmont expert export staff at the New York office. Their headquarters here acts as the dynamo whose power for real, live motion extends to every nook and corner of the world. Scores of salesmen and foreign correspondents in all the capital cities of Europe, North and South Africa, East and Far East assure a quick, courteous and satisfactory response to all.

The Piedmont Pictures Corporation also handles foreign productions in the United States. It is just about to put on the market a series of interesting British features dealing with the war viewed from the British side. These productions have met success all over England and the Allied countries, and should also appeal to the American public.

Noble Completes Feature

Director Finishes Special Length Picture Under Own Management Showing Son.

AFTER ten weeks spent in the making of a special picture which represents his idea of the acme of motion picture production from the standpoint of direction, acting, story and photography, John W. Noble has completed his first important contribution to the state rights market.

The drama, which is a bold treatment of a large and pertinent subject, is said to promise to cause a sensation by its clever presentation of a phase of the war little understood by persons as far removed from the trenches as Americans. It was thus the discovery of the story which prompted Mr. Noble to produce a special feature under his own management.

Mr. Noble's record as an army officer, who was promoted for brave and meritorious service in the face of the enemy while fighting for Uncle Sam in the Philippines, is as well known in army circles as his record for staging such productions as "Romeo and Juliet," "The High Road," and "The Awakening of Helene Ritchie," is known in the world of motion pictures. He has been on the lookout for an exceptional story ever since the beginning of the world war, because of his belief that a powerful drama inspired by the conditions in Belgium and France was sure to make its appearance sooner or later. The story selected suggested to him the drama he sought, and as soon as he had read it, he decided to make it the basis of a special state rights production staged under his own management; so that he could devote all of the time and money necessary to the creation of a picture worthy of a great subject, and also carry out his own ideas of what constitutes effective stage direction.

Jules Burnstein, who has sole charge of the business management of Mr. Noble's special feature, promises that it will interest producers and dramatists as much as it does exhibitors and the general public.

Lillian Walker Signs With Ogden

Eight Pictures Starring Her Will Be Made—Other Plans Announced.

LILLIAN WALKER has signed a two-year contract with the Ogden Pictures Corporation to appear in sixteen super-productions to be produced eight a year, at a salary said to be one of the largest ever paid to any star. The contract contains every detailed provision, providing for the proper exploitation of the productions. It requires that on each release a minimum sum of $12,500 shall be expended in advertising.

The company has placed at the disposal of Miss Walker a complete dressing room installed in a limousine. A provision unusual in contracts with stars appearing in motion pictures, but which is contained in Miss Walker's contract provides that she shall expend out of her own moneys a sum sufficient to provide a minimum of four new gowns and a complete change of wearing apparel suitable to each gown, for each production. All plays which are to be staged with Miss Walker are first to receive her approval and she is to have an equal voice in the casting of her leading supports.

Further plans of the Ogden corporation are made known in the announcement that four of the eight Walker productions to be made during the next twelve months will be made in the East and four in the West. The entire studio and technical staff will be employed by the Ogden studio in preparing the third production, while the second production is being made in the Eastern studio.

Work has already commenced on the second release, which promises to be as big a production as "The Lust of the Ages." No details as to the supporting cast or the character of the story are forthcoming and will not be given publicity until the company has completed the taking of the scenes. No expense will be spared in any of the operations connected with the Lillian Walker productions; a technical staff from the director and his assistants down to the merest property boy stand engaged for both studios. Lester Park, general manager of the company, will divide his time between the Western and Eastern studios.

HONEYMOONERS BEGIN WORLD TOUR.

Mr. and Mrs. E. Schayer.

For the purpose of obtaining a novel series of films, the Peter Pan Film Corporation is sending on a trip around the world E. Richard Schayer, founder, publicity manager for Lewis J. Selznick, and Mrs. Schayer. H. C. Allen, president of the Peter Pan Corporation, has adopted this method of producing pictures of especial interest. The party that is making the trip includes besides, the two principals, W. F. Aldrich, the cameraman, and Mrs. Aldrich and "Bill," Mrs. Schayer's Irish terrier.

The pictures will not be ordinary travelogues in any sense, it is announced. The idea is to get off the beaten track, and to make the films a record of personal, human experiences — not merely a series of views of foreign lands. They will be taken from the angle of the traveler trying to do and live as the natives of other countries, and will be full of humorous and human interest. The by-paths of the world are overflowing with picture material, and the best way to get it is not by making it but by really living it.

The new releases will be entitled "The Honeymooners," and while no definite time has been allotted to their production, it is expected that they will be completed in about two years. The party left New York on August 1 for San Francisco, from which place they sailed for Honolulu on the Matsonia, where they arrived on August 16. The first picture will be made in Hawaii and Mr. Schayer will recruit what company he needs from the natives.

BUD FISHER AN EXECUTIVE.

Bud Fisher, who has left his office to go to the Plattsburg Officers' Training Camp, came into the industry only a little over a month ago, knowing nothing about the distribution end of the business, and in that short space has accomplished an almost unprecedented sale of territory for the Mutt and Jeff Comedies. In fact, with the exception of a few straggling territories, he has sold out the entire world for the new series. He did this solely by the application of common sense and sound business principles of other commercial enterprises.

He has shown a keen perception of the intricate conditions of the industry, not only disposing of his cartoons to the advantage of the film corporation, but also to the advantage of the exchange. By selecting exchange men in harmony with his ideas, he has made it possible to work side by side and to obtain the most efficient results. Of course the exchanges have a tangible asset in addition to the films themselves in the tremendous advertising campaign that Mr. Fisher has inaugurated, whereby the Mutt and Jeff cartoons appear in 278 of the best dailies in the country and are seen daily by an audience of 17,-000,000 people. This is a large campaign.

FOREIGN BUYERS VISIT STUDIO.

One of the largest groups of foreign film buyers ever gotten together gathered at the King Bee Studios at Bayonne on Tuesday, August 14. Their activities practically cover the world of the industry. The party was organized by Mr. Garrett, president of J. Frank Brockliss, Inc., and consisted of Mr. Wainright, buyer for the English cinematograph trade; Mr. Mattsonn, the representative of the trade for Scandinavia and Northern Europe; Mr. Ono, representing Japan and the Far East; Mr. Cropper, who buys for the Middle West in the United States, and Madame Schuepbach, buyer for the Mundusfilm Company of Paris. Nat Spitzer, general manager of the King Bee Com-

Foreign Buyers at King Bee Studios.

pany, and Mr. Bernstein, the president of the same corporation, acted as hosts with. Mr. Garrett, who is known intimately to all. They met at the Brockliss offices and motored out to the studios at Bayonne, where they saw the comedian, Billy West, at work. Interesting entertainment was provided for them by Mr. Gildstrom, who directs the Billy West Comedies. He had concocted a scene in which the whole party appeared in conjunction with the company. Billy West himself entered into the spirit of the thing and was at his best. This scene Mr. Gildstrom promises to release in one of his forthcoming pictures.

SPITZER RETURNS FROM EXCHANGE TOUR.

Nat H. Spitzer, sales manager for the King Bee Company, has returned from a trip covering all the exchanges handling Billy West Comedies through the West and South. Mr. Spitzer is delighted with the outlook for the Billy West releases, and feels that conditions for them could hardly be better.

In an interview he gave a summary of his ideas on the situation in the Western and Southern markets.

"I found that the demand of the majority of the exhibitors who are guided by the likes and dislikes of their patrons was for booking short feature subjects, particularly comedy. Two-reel comedies of the better class are extremely popular throughout every section of the country, and since the various exchanges are demanding exorbitant rentals for their long features, which are beyond the reach of the average exhibitor, they are making up their programs from the shorter subjects, primarily a number of two-reelers and one-reelers. This is corroborated by the fact that the independent exchanges are demanding more and better shorter subjects. As an example of this our Chicago exchange has booked our pictures with the Lubliner-Trints circuit, the Ascher Brothers and the Hamburger chain of theaters of that city. That shows the present prevailing tendency.

"I am well satisfied with the progress that the Billy West Comedies are making at present, but in order to achieve them to the highest point of efficiency we have mapped out a national advertising campaign, the details of which are now being completed. This will include a series of novelty ideas for exhibitors, and for the exchanges, unique poster, and advertising matter as well as some new ideas in publicity."

BROCKLISS GETS FOREIGN RIGHTS TO LION COMEDIES.

The A. Kay Company announces that it has consummated a deal with the firm of J. Frank Brockliss, Ltd., whereby the latter secures the exclusive foreign rights to the Lion Comedies and the picturized versions of the famous Walt Mason stories.

The Lion Comedies, which are of a slapstick nature, are made by Masterpictures of Houston, Texas, under the supervision of Mr. Harold J. Binney, who for many years has been active in the production of comedies. The Filmcraft Corporation, which has arranged with the George Matthew Adams Service to picturize the famous Walt Mason stories and rhymes, recently entered into an agreement with the A. Kay Company to give the latter the world rights to their product to be known as the Walt Mason Stories.

Keenan and Edeson to Star

They Will Appear in "The Public Defender," to Be Produced by Harry Raver.

FRANK KEENAN and Robert Edeson have been engaged by Harry Raver to appear in a special production of "The Public Defender," by Mayer Goldman and Frank Harris of the New York bar. Alma Hanlon will be seen in the leading female role. An exceptionally strong cast has been secured for the new Goldman-Harris story, including John Sainpolis, Florence Short, William Green, J. K. Roberts, John O'Keefe, Irving Southard, Mrs. C. M. Heaten, Harry Mack, Jane Newcombe, J. J. Turner, Robert R. Lawrence, Louis Sterns, Blanche Thode, Edith Hartman, J. J. Tanner, James Gaylor, C. A. Ellwood, John Martin and James Sullivan. Burton King will direct.

The story is based on Mayer Goldman's book of the same name. It discusses a subject which seriously affects the rights and liberties of the masses. The basic idea is that it is as much the function of the state to shield the innocent as to convict the guilty, and that the "presumption of innocence" requires the state to defend as well as to prosecute accused persons.

Frank Keenan will be seen as the ambitious district attorney who has promised himself a seat in the Governor's chair. Robert Edeson will interpret the "Public Defender" who gives the accused an even break under the law. John Sainpolis is "The Murderer" of the story and Alma Hanlon is the girl who moves heaven and earth to save him from the electric chair.

Mr. Raver announces the production as the first of a series of exceptional pictures to be issued by him on an open-market basis under the brand name of "Important Productions."

STANDARD FILM BUYS COMEDIES.

The Standard Film Corporation, of which R. C. Cropper is president, has purchased distributing rights to the Christie Comedies for Iowa, Kansas, Missouri and Nebraska. These are a class of photoplays known as "society comedies," having as their principal ingredients attractive, youthful players, including in the case of the Standard's purchase, Betty Compson, Neal Burns and Billie Rhodes, and depending for their appeal on a certain freshness and breeziness of plot rather than upon the "eternal slapstick."

Mr. Cropper, in speaking of his purchase, said that he fully anticipated a remarkably strong demand for this class of film, and that his anticipations were being fully borne out by the eagerness of exhibitors to book the Christies. It will be remembered, in this connection, that the Standard recently bought the Middle West rights on the Billy West comedies also.

The Standard Film Corporation is one of the largest independent film exchanges in the Middle West, with offices at Chicago, St. Louis, Kansas City, Minneapolis, Omaha and St. Louis. Phil L. Ryan, the sales manager, is at present making a flying visit to the St. Louis office, as an exceptionally strong demand is expected in the territory of that office for the Billy West and the newly-purchased Christie Comedies. He is conferring with "Barney" Fegan, the genial and highly efficient manager who has succeeded J. Erwin Dodson in the St. Louis territory of the Standard.

LOCAL ADVERTISING FOR "THE LUST OF THE AGES."

In connection with the sales work of selling the territory of the Ogden film "The Lust of the Ages," in which Lillian Walker is starred, much attention is being devoted to sales ideas and plans for use among exhibitors. The theory behind this effort is that a picture provided with a sales plan is a picture many times more valuable to its state right owner and to its exhibitor.

So the enterprises which succeed in winning the rights on "The Lust of the Ages" for any given territory will find themselves in a position to let the picture practically sell itself. There will be prepared, in advance, everything that the exhibitor will want to know. There will be given to the exhibitor little stunts of all kinds, which he can use in his lobby, on his billboards, in his local newspapers for both editorial and advertising use. There will be ideas for his magazine, if he prints one, suggestions for envelope stuffing which can be sent out in his weekly mail announcements, and moreover, and perhaps of greater importance, there will be plans suggested for creating a local excitement.

In this connection it is interesting to note that the A. M. Swedy Company, who have been engaged to prepare the advertising for "The Lust of the Ages" is headed by Charles D. Isaacson, who was responsible for the campaign on "The Exploits of Elaine."

WARNER BROTHERS GET MUTT AND JEFF.

The Warner Brothers, who have been closely associated with all branches of the motion picture industry, last week acquired the rights for the Mutt and Jeff Comedies for New York and northern New Jersey from the Bud Fisher Films Corporation. They announce very successful booking for these comedies already, and predict great popularity for them in the new territory.

Manufacturers' Advance Notes

American Bids for Laboratory Work

Will Develop and Print for the Trade—Offers Ample Facilities.

MANY manufacturers of film will be interested in learning that this week the American Film Company, Inc., announces the opening of its huge laboratories to any in the trade desiring printing and developing work of the highest class. A weekly capacity of more than 1,500,000 feet of film

Manager Richard R. Nehls.

is claimed by the American plant in Chicago and apparatus of the latest type is available now for all who care to make use of it.

The American's productions, released through the the Mutual Film Corporation, have long been notable for their technical perfection. The same staff of experts which supervises the handling of the pictures in which are starred such screen favorites as Mary Miles Minter, Helen Holmes, Gail Kane, Juliette Day, William Russell, Charlie Chaplin and Margarita Fischer will have charge of all the commercial work undertaken for patrons of the American laboratories.

"Times without number we have been begged, implored and entreated by film manufacturers, state rights men, etc., to handle developing and printing for them, but have always had to refuse," said Manager Richard R. Nehls of the American Film Company, Inc., in discussing the matter with an interviewer in his Chicago office. "The increase in our facilities permits us, for the first time, to offer our laboratories to outsiders. Manufacturers who are spending huge sums for famous stars, high salaried directors, noted authors and stage settings that run into thousands of dollars, can now rest assured that the technical work on their productions can be handled by experts with all the care, skill and attention to detail that have made our own attractions notable in the motion picture field.

"Believing that a number of film makers are really seeking technical work of the highest class and will be satisfied with nothing short of that, we have arranged to offer our vast resources in the way of printing and developing to such of the trade as are seeking quality work. American film productions have always been praised for their tinting, toning, printing and developing. They are uniform in quality throughout. Every stage of the work is handled by experts. Ten years of experience is back of every print we turn out today. Our mechanical equipment is unexcelled. Every bit of apparatus in our huge laboratories is of the very best. The films that are offered us for development and printing will be handled by the same corps of experts that handle our own productions—the American features starring such favorites as Mary Miles Minter, Gail Kane, Juliette Day, William Russell, Margarita Fischer and Charlie Chaplin.

"In addition to all the above advantages, the central location of the American Company's plant (Chicago being the hub of the whole country) alone would justify any film manufacturer in placing his developing and printing work with us, purely on account of the saving in time and money in shipping his positive prnts to the exchanges. Hours of time and hundreds of dollars in transportation charges can be saved by printing and developing in Chicago and distributing positive prints from the most central point of the country."

Three Essanays for September

Larger Subjects Will Feature Taylor Holmes, Mary McAlister and Jack Gardner.

TAYLOR HOLMES, the stage star, heads Essanay's schedule of feature releases for September in "Efficiency Edgar's Courtship," released September 3. Little Mary McAlister will follow him in "Pants," and Jack Gardner will complete the monthly program of five-part pictures with the fourth of his series of Westerns, entitled "Men of the Desert."

"Efficiency Edgar's Courtship" will mark Taylor Holmes' first appearance as a screen star. His most recent stage production, "His Majesty Bunker Bean," ran an entire season in Chicago, duplicated that success on Broadway, and then toured the country. "The Million" and "The Commuters" were among his previous hits.

Trade showings of the picture are now in progress at all branch offices of the K-E-S-E Service.

"Pants" will be released September 10. The production is the first five-reel picture in which Mary McAlister has been starred. The idea of the story is that it takes something more than wealth to make a child happy.

"Men of the Desert" will be released September 24. Like its predecessors, 'Land of Long Shadows,''The Range Boss" and "Open Places,' this picture presents a story of the red-blooded West. Mr. Gardner is supported by Ruth King, Carl Stockdale and Essanay's original Western company formed for this series.

NEWARK UNIVERSAL IN NEW OFFICE.

The Newark office of the Universal Film Exchange of New York has moved to 25 Branford place. Here they are in more commodious and convenient headquarters and are in the position to give real service to exhibitors. M. H. Goldstein, formerly manager of the Mutual in Jersey, has been installed as manager.

DOROTHY BENHAM IN NEW WARREN SUBJECT.

Little Dorothy Benham, daughter of Harry Benham, who played one of the leads in Edward Warren's "The Warfare of the Flesh," is an industrious little lady in spite of the fact that she is only five years old on her next birthday. Ever since war was declared she wished to help wherever she could and she has recently turned her energies towards knitting for the "Sammies."

Little Dorothy is playing quite an important role in Mr. Warren's coming production, the title of which has not yet been announced, and when she appeared at the studio the other day

Little Dorothy Benham Doing Her Bit.

she not only brought her knitting with her but she insisted on working on it in her scene, although the scenario didn't exactly call for it. Mr. Warren did not want to discourage the little patriot and as it fitted in right well with her posing for the day he allowed her to continue her knitting. The incident not only adds a touch of novelty to the scene as shown on the screen, but is quite inspiring as well.

Goldwyn Names First Eleven Pictures

Mae Marsh Figures in Five, Maxine Elliott and Madge Kennedy in Two Each.

WHEN Goldwyn Pictures Corporation, almost a year ago, announced its intention of making a large number of costly productions, perhaps as many as a dozen, in advance of its first release the following September, few were willing to believe the new company.

With release of its first picture, "Polly of the Circus," but three weeks distant, Goldwyn announces the definite completion of seven productions, besides two other pictures in course of production and a tenth huge picture, with Mary Garden as the star, to be under way in a fortnight.

Considerably more than one million dollars has thus far been invested in the pictures made or in the making, this amount not being inclusive of any of the cost of distribution overhead or the operation of the Goldwyn branch offices.

Organization has been effected throughout the United States; Goldwyn Pictures Ltd. of Canada is actively operating in the Dominion, and arrangements are virtually completed for prompt operation of Goldwyn organizations in England, Australia, South America and other more distant lands.

To date, and as applied to future extensions, Goldwyn expects to own outright or control its offices in all parts of the world, so that Goldwyn Pictures will not at any time pass out from under the solicitous attention of the factors who produce them in America.

Thus far the completed Goldwyn Pictures are: Mae Marsh in "Polly of the Circus," by margaret Mayo; Madge Kennedy in "Baby Mine," by Margaret Mayo; Maxine Elliott in "The Eternal Magdalene," by Robert McLaughlin; Jane Cowl in "The Spreading Dawn," by Basil King; Mae Marsh in "Sunshine Alley," by Mary Rider; Maxine Elliott in "Fighting Odds," by Roi Cooper Megrue and Irvin S. Cobb; Mae Marsh in "Fields of Honor," by Irvin S. Cobb.

Pictures now in the making at Goldwyn's New Jersey studios are: Mabel Normand in "Joan of Platbush," by Porter Emerson Browne; Madge Kennedy in "Nearly Married," by Edgar Selwyn; Mae Marsh in "The Cinderella Man," by Edward Childs Carpenter. And, early in September, Mary Garden, just returning at that time from France, will begin work on "Thais," by Anatole France.

The order on which the productions have been named above is not necessarily the order in which they will be released. The thing of biggest import, perhaps, is the fact that not one penny of exhibitor money has been received or applied to production costs from the day the company was formed down to the present moment, and there will be no allotment of this policy. Goldwyn, from the outset, was, through its owners, prepared to finance itself. In pictures it has been more or less customary to expect the exhibitor through deposits, advances or money paid for franchises to provide producers with the money with which pictures were made. President Goldfish and his associates disapproved of this method from the start.

Next in importance is the Goldwyn policy of distribution and salesmanship which has resulted in the application of real merchandising principles to film renting and distribution.

"A TRIP TO CHINATOWN" (Selig).

"A Trip to Chinatown" is considered one of Charles Hoyt's merriest comedies, and the Selig Polyscope Company promises that not a laugh has been lost in the two-reel Hoyt comedy. "A Trip to Chinatown," released in K-E-S-E on Monday, August 20.

Scene from "A Trip to Chinatown" (Selig).

The comedy has to do with the adventures of a race track tout and policemen, the tout's enemy. Giving wrong tips on the races, the tout seeks the seclusion of a "Chink" laundry, hits the pipe and is immediately transported to the Orient, where he meets a beautiful Oriental princess. And oh, joy! the policeman is discovered to be a slave in the palace.

Then things begin to happen. Seeking revenge on the policeman, the tout persuades the princess to match the slave with a gigantic wrestler, a swordsman and a fierce lion. The slave overcomes them all and wins the admiration of the princess. The tout makes his escape, is pursued, discovered, and he awakens in the laundry and finds the policeman is again after him!

The all-star comedy cast that has proven so popular in previous Hoyt comedies contribute to the merry action of "A Trip to Chinatown." The players include Amy Leah Dennis, Wm. Fables, James Harris and Fanny Cohen. J. A. Richmond directed the production.

MAE MURRAY BUSY ON INITIAL BLUEBIRD.

Mae Murray and her director, Robert Leonard, are busy at Bluebird's studio in Universal City, Cal., preparing Mr. Leonard's screen version of "Princess Virtue," drawn from Louise Winter's magazine story of the same title. The principal members of Miss Murray's support have been conscripted by Production Manager Henry McRae because of their established reputation for excellent achievements. For Miss Murray's leading man Wheeler Oakman was selected as one of the most popular of the younger leading men of the screen.

Mr. Oakman has built up an enviable reputation for himself during an engagement of more than two years with Kathlyn Williams at the Selig studios. He played the leading juvenile role in Selig's "The Rosary" and "The Spoilers" and was the principal player in "The Ne'er-Do-Well." More recently he has been playing opposite Mabel Normand.

Another well known screen actor who has been engaged to support Miss Murray is Harry Von Meter, who had been with the American company for nearly four years before joining the Bluebird players. Paul Nicholson, Jean Hersholt, Gretchen Lederer, Clarissa Selwin will be others in Miss Murray's support.

EDITH STOREY COMMENCES WORK FOR METRO.

Metro Pictures Corporation has chosen as Edith Storey's first Metro vehicle "The House in the Mist," a novel by Octavus Roy Cohen and J. U. Giesy, authors of "The Matrimaniac" and other successes. A six-reel special production will be made of "The House in the Mist," work on which will begin immediately at the Metro studio, 3 West Sixty-first street, New York, under the direction of Ted Browning.

The role of Carma Carmichael affords Edith Storey boundless opportunities. In "The House in the Mist," in addition to her magnificent acting, Miss Storey will ride, shoot and swim. "The House in the Mist" is frank, out-and-out melodrama—a real mystery story—with a wonderful girl as its heroine.

A notable cast has been chosen to support Miss Storey in her initial Metro production. Bradley Barker will play Jack Carrington, the hero who shares the adventures of the heroine. Harry S. Northrup, Metro's popular "villain," well known on both stage and screen, will have an important role in "The House in the Mist." Another player of importance will be Frank Fisher Bennett, the Francois Leblanc of "The Jury of Fate." James J. Dunne, formerly of Thanhouser, where he was associated with George Foster Platt, will assist Tod Browning in directing "The House in the Mist."

SPLENDID OUTLOOK ON THE COAST.

Reports from Los Angeles, San Francisco and Seattle branches of General Film just to hand give a most promising outlook for motion picture business. Writing from the field, General Sales Manager S. R. Kent, who has been on a tour of inspection, says:

"I find conditions on the West Coast have much improved, and I think that our three offices out here are going to do a corking business in the next ten or twelve months. Also I find many exhibitors are trying to get away from the burden of high prices for over-rated features and are taking up our 'Variety Day' service."

The "Variety Day" service of General Film is the recently suggested idea of reserving one or two days a week for short subjects of feature quality to compose the whole show, instead of headlining a five-reel feature. The plan has been adopted with great enthusiasm by General Film exhibitors in many parts of the country. It seems to be particularly well liked on the Pacific Coast, where it has been longest in vogue. This is hailed as a sign of enduring popularity for the idea.

RUSHING WORK ON "MAGDA."

Clara Kimball Young is working fast on "Magda," her initial production with her own new organization under the management of Harry I. Garson. This haste and long hours is the result of the shift in plans to first produce "The Marionettes," over which a question as to the American rights was brought forth by the Charles Frohman Estate.

Supporting Miss Young is Thomas Holding, who was brought to this country by Hugh Ford, appeared in the Famous Players productions of "The Eternal City" and as leading man for Pauline Fredricks, covering a period of three years. Mr. Holding also played the lead with Jane Grey in "The Fighting Chance," "The Great White Trail," and others of the successful production. Others in the cast are Edmund Fielding, George Merlo, Edward Kimball, Alice Gale, Kitty Baldwin, Maude Ford and Valkyrian, all well known artists.

Emile Chautard, whose successful productions have rapidly brought him to the front as one of the foremost directors in America, is enthusiastic over the results already accomplished.

Mutual Offers Two Features a Week

President John Freuler Announces Schedule Involving $5,250,000 Worth of Pictures a Year to Commence September 3.

FIVE and a quarter of a million dollars worth of feature productions per year will be marketed by the Mutual Film Corporation, according to a policy effective September 3, it is announced from the Chicago offices of John R. Freuler, president of that concern. The Mutual has adopted a policy of "big stars only" for its feature productions, which, beginning in September, will be issued to exhibitors at the rate of two a week. Mr. Freuler also announces the complete schedule for two months of releases at this rate, including:

SEPTEMBER 3.—Mary Miles Minter in "Charity Castle," the first of a new series of Mutual-American productions starring the delightful actress and the first Minter picture under the direction of Lloyd Ingraham, late of Fine Arts.

Edna Goodrich in "Reputation," the first of the series of Mutual star productions, featuring the celebrated stage beauty. "Reputation" is the story of a small town girl who went to the city, met a he-vampire and came back with a Reputation. It was directed by John B. O'Brien.

SEPTEMBER 10.—Gail Kane in "The Specter of Suspicion," the fifth of the series of Mutual-American star productions in which the beautiful and talented Miss Kane plays the leading role. "The Specter of Suspicion" deals with a bride whose family closet is the abiding place of a skeleton and furnishes the basis for a thrilling drama. It was directed by Henry King, who scored such a big success with "Souls in Pawn," Miss Kane's latest photoplay.

Ann Murdock in "Outcast," the first of the Charles Frohman stage successes in motion pictures. Miss Murdock is one of the most famous of American actresses, the product of the school of the celebrated genius of the drama. "Outcast" is a picture adaptation of the Broadway hit. Miss Murdock is supported by an all star cast. The production is the first to be released from the Empire All Star studios.

SEPTEMBER 17.—Juliette Day in "The Rainbow Girl," which is the first star of Mutual-American productions starring the Broadway star, Juliette Day. Miss Day scored her most recent stage success in "Upstairs and Down" and has been at the American-Mutual studios since early in the summer working under the direction of Rollin S. Sturgeon.

Margarita Fischer in "The Girl Who Couldn't Grow Up," the fifth of the series of Pollard-Mutual star productions featuring Margarita Fischer. Miss Fischer has not appeared on the screen since the release of "The Devil's Assistant," early in the spring, closely following the completion of which she was taken ill.

SEPTEMBER 24.—William Russell in "Sands of Sacrifice," a corking five-reel drama starring the heroic Mutual-American star. "Sands of Sacrifice" is the first of a new series of William Russell productions directed as were the pictures of the previous series by Edward S. Sloman.

Julia Sanderson in "The Runaway," the second of the Frohman productions and the first of the series featuring Miss Sanderson. "The Runaway" is the picturization of the stage success of the same title in which Miss Sanderson scored on Broadway. It was produced under the direction of Dell Henderson.

OCTOBER 1.—Mary Miles Minter in "Her Country's Call," the second of her new series of Mutual-American star productions in which Miss Minter carries the role of a patriotic little girl. "Her Country's Call" was directed by Lloyd Ingraham.

Edna Goodrich in "Queen X," the second of the series of productions starring Miss Goodrich. "Queen X" is from the story by Edwin M. Stanton, assistant United States attorney of New York, who conducted a crusade against smugglers and put his experiences into a five-reel photodrama. The picture was directed by John B. O'Brien.

OCTOBER 8.—Gail Kane in "Southern Pride," sixth of the Mutual-American series starring the Broadway favorite, in which she plays the role of a beautiful Southern girl. The production was under the direction of Henry King.

Anita King in "The Girl Angel," first of a new series of Mutual Horkheimer productions starring the popular motion picture star. Miss King has played leading parts in "The Heir to the Hoorah," "Maria Rosa," "The Race" and "Golden Fetters." She has been engaged by the Horkheimer studios to produce a series of star productions for release on the Mutual schedule.

OCTOBER 15.—Juliette Day in "Betty and the Buccaneers," a story of pirates bold, produced at the Mutual-American studios under the direction of Rollin S. Sturgeon. "Betty and the Buccaneers" is Miss Day's second production under the contract for which she deserted Broadway for the camera.

Margarita Fischer in "The Miracle of Life," sixth of the series of productions starring the well-known and popular screen star.

OCTOBER 22.—William Russell in "The Sea Master," the second of the new series of William Russell productions, in which he appears as an entirely new sort of a hero. The picture was directed by Edward S. Sloman, who is responsible for staging the successful series of recent Russell productions.

Ann Murdock in "The Beautiful Adventure," the second of Miss Murdock's productions and the third release of the Charles Frohman stage successes in motion pictures. "The Beautiful Adventure" gives Miss Murdock a role admirably

suited to her abilities. It was staged under the direction of Del Henderson.

"This collection of pictures, now complete and ready for delivery to our half a hundred exchanges, represents a year of planning and effort and the most careful consideration of the picture market," observed Mr. Freuler.

"I am convinced that the motion picture theaters will find this fall and winter a particularly prosperous season. The circulation of money is lively and despite high living costs the people who constitute the big majority of motion picture patrons have more money to spend than ever."

THE WEEK'S WORK IN THE FOX STUDIOS.

Gladys Brockwell has just completed "The Soul of Satan," to be released August 20, for the William Fox productions. She will begin another feature shortly under the direction of Bertram Bracken. In the supporting company appear Bertram Grassby, Charles Clary, William Burress, Joseph Swickard, Gerard Alexander, Norbert Myles, Lucille Young, Frankie, Lee and Marie Kiernan.

The Foxfilm comedy issued on August 20 will be "A Domestic Hound." Hank Mann is the featured player.

Owing to changes which were imperative in George Walsh's cast, begun a short time since, has been titled "A Rich Man's Plaything." Randolph Lewis wrote the story and Carl Harbaugh is the director.

To make for the increasing comedy output of the organization two more "lots" and stages have been added to the grounds the company already occupies in Hollywood, Cal.

HARRY CAREY IN "STRAIGHT SHOOTING."

Harry Carey, widely known for his vigorous handling of western types, will make his first appearance in a Butterfly production on August 27, when he will be starred in "Straight Shooting," a drama of the cattle country. Molly Malone will be featured in Carey's support.

"Straight Shooting" has been written by George Hively and produced by Jack Ford. It tells the story of the warfare that used to be so common between the cattle barons of the 'open range" and the incoming settlers, or "nesters" as they were contemptously called.

"Thunder" Flint, overlord of a vast grazing territory which he holds in defiance of law and order, has sent forth the ukase that all settlers on land that he desires for his steers must vacate without delay or suffer the consequences. Flint is a power in the territory, one that no man has ever dared offend. But when his messenger delivers this ultimatum at the home of "Sweetwater" Sims, leader of the nesters, he meets with an unexpected rebuke from Joan Sims, the fearless daughter of the household.

As a result of this questioning of his authority, Flint has Ted Sims, the girl's brother, shot from ambush, and at about

Scene from "Straight Shooting" (Butterfly).

the same time he hunts up "Cheyenne" Harry, a notorious gunman of the plains, to lead an attack upon the nesters which will put them to rout. While the plans for this cowardly attack are maturing, however, Cheyenne meets Joan and her father by accident. Their desperate plight appeals to his latent manhood, and in a denouement which brings all of the range vagabond's better instincts into play, we find his talents for straight shooting and hard riding used to defeat the designs of his former chieftain. Carey has never had a role better suited to his straightforward style of acting.

Important Plans for "O· Henry"

"The Defeat of the City" Opens Four-Reel Series of the Famous Author's Stories.

ALL the curiosity that has been accumulating in regard to General Film's forthcoming O. Henry stories in more elaborate picture form is now to be satisfied. The title and release of the first four-reel O. Henry has been determined. It will be "The Defeat of the City," scheduled for September 1.

Other details of the plan for O. Henry pictures include the information that one four-reel picture is expected to be presented every two weeks, and that a series of at least ten may be expected.

Another bit of welcome news to the trade emanates from General Film in this connection. It is that the two-reel O. Henry pictures will continue, owing to tremendous demand for short-length features of high merit. Confirming hints that have been given already, Western O. Henry stories are being produced. These will be put into the two-reel division, and one of them will alternate every two weeks with a four-reel O. Henry. Many of the O. Henry stories with Western atmosphere were published in his "The Gentle Grafter" series, and for the initial release "The Atavism of John Tom Little Bear" has been chosen, it being one of the favorite Jess Peters adventures.

Three most competent Broadway Star Feature directors are now working to provide the O. Henry pictures for General Film. At the Eastern studio Thos. R. Mills, the first of several clever people to be made famous with O. Henry productions, and who directed over a dozen of the first twenty releases, has finished "The Defeat of the City." Also working at the Eastern studio is Martin Justice, who did "A Departmental Case," "The Coming Out of Maggie" and "The Discounters of Money," three already current two-reel subjects. At the Hollywood studio David Smith is doing the "Jeff Peters" stories and others with a Western setting.

HELEN HOLMES IN NEW MUTUAL SERIAL.

Helen Holmes, fearless daredevil of the screen, in the early chapters of the newest Mutual chapterplay, "The Lost Express," is going to set the nerves of even the most blase and thrill-hardened exhibitor atingle by her utter recklessness, performed with an apparent nonchalance that bids defiance to death.

In one of the earliest chapters of the new mystery serial dealing with the total disappearance of an express train while passing from one station to the next, down a perfectly straight stretch of single track line, Miss Holmes fights a hand-to-hand battle with three men on top of a rapidly moving passenger train. Just as she seems certain to be defeated in her struggle, she escapes by jumping and catching an overhead warning signal such as are placed on either side of low bridges, tunnels, etc., and thus is left dangling in midair while the passenger train bearing her enemies is whisked away from beneath her.

Announcement of the exact release date of the newest Mutual-Signal chapterplay starring Helen Holmes, and directed by J. P.

President John R. Freuler, Herbert Holmes, Florence Holmes, J. P. McGraw and Thomas Lingham.

McGowan, will be made within a few days. Exhibitors are already besieging Mutual Exchanges with applications for bookings on this forthcoming Helen Holmes thriller, for past Helen Holmes successes have thoroughly demonstrated the drawing power of this star and the theaters which have "stood 'em out" for night after night with previous serials built about the dare-devil personality of Miss Holmes are anxious to again line up the crowds in front of the box-office.

"THE DEAD LINE" FEATURES BEATRIZ MICHELENA.

In the role of Star Dowell in "The Dead Line," Beatriz Michelena is said to evidence a wider variety of Western accomplishments than shown in any of her previous photodramas of the untamed frontier: Horsemanship, for which she has always been renowned, is, according to studio reports, the very least of her troubles in this latest and most strenuous of her Western productions.

She whirls a revolver around her finger with all the nonchalance of a true cowboy and throws a lasso with undeviat-

Scene from "The Dead Line."

ing accuracy. When she ropes and "hog-ties" the boastful sheriff that rides into the mountains to arrest her she goes about it in a business-like manner that can leave no doubt as to the genuineness of her Western schooling. The producer is announcing her as the female "Bill" Hart, and predicts that her proficiency in "The Dead Line" will make the original "William" look jealously to his cowboy laurels.

The picture is being filmed in the Santa Cruz mountains and is scheduled for independent release early this coming fall. William Pike, Albert Morrison, Clarence Arper, Cliff Thompson, Jeff Williams, D. Mitzoras and Katherine Angus are among those who make up the supporting cast. George E. Middleton is the director.

"BETWEEN MAN AND BEAST" (Selig).

"Between Man and Beast," the two-reel jungle drama released by the Selig Company in General Film service on Monday, August 20, was directed by Colin Campbell from the story written by W. E. Wing. One thrilling incident in the drama is the care given a lost baby by a gigantic ape which carries the little one into a tree in search of food and then makes a home for the baby in a cave. Other animals of the jungle also participate in the action of the drama.

"Between Man and Beast" is the tale of the adventures in the heart of the jungle of a young man and his wife and baby. Pursued by a villain who plots their deaths, the little family becomes separated and then it is that the ape cares for the lost child.

Bessie Eyton is starred in the drama and is ably supported by Wheeler Oakman and others. The photography and wild animals' jungle scenes are said to be all that can be desired. Exhibitors are demanding realistic dramas of the jungle and the Selig Company is releasing a series of jungle pictures in General Film service that are not only produced by the best directors, but also exploit stars whose names bring in the money at the box office.

"HONOR SYSTEM" OPENS IN CHICAGO.

William Fox's stirring cinemelodrama, "The Honor System," which has been playing to capacity in the New York and New Jersey territory, will open its first engagement in the West on Monday, August 20, when it takes the screen at the big Studebaker Theatre in Chicago.

On August 26 this production will be available to exhibitors everywhere. Bookings for it can be made now at the nearest William Fox exchange. As "The Honor System" is a Standard picture, the policy that "You cannot book it until you see it" will apply.

LOEW SIGNS FOR CONQUEST PROGRAMS.

Marcus Loew has signed in behalf of eight New York theaters of his circuit, to show Conquest picture programs produced at the Edison Studios and released through George Kleine's K-E-S-E distributing organization. The theaters selected by Mr. Loew to show these pictures are: The New York Theater, Greeley Square, Lincoln, National, American, Orpheum, Boulevard and Avenue B.

Drama and Comedy in "U" List

President Carl Laemmle Writes Amusing Skit for William Franey—J. Warren Kerrigan Is Starred in Strong Tabloid Drama.

THE Winning Pair," a Gold Seal comedy drama, featuring Ruth Stonehouse and Roy Stewart, heads Universal's regular schedule of releases for August 28th. August 27th is Butterfly Day, as usual, signalized by the release of "Straight Shooting," in which Harry Carey is starred. Eugene B. Lewis as author and L. W. Chaudet as director are responsible for the "Winning Pair." The story details the adventures of Jack Croft and Beatrice Moore, son and daughter, respectively, of two gouty and grouchy shoe manufacturers, formerly business partners, but now bitter enemies, following some trivial difference in which neither would admit himself at fault. There are many amusing turns to the story which move at a rapid pace.

Eddie Lyons and Lee Moran will also be seen on the same date in a Nestor comedy entitled "The Night Cap." This ribtickler was written by Virginia Kirtley, who has recently become the bride of Eddie Lyons in real life. It details the unusual consequence following the night "at the lodge," when Eddie and his pal return home to find that the former's wife has gone out for an evening's entertainment with her mother. The boys are forced to break into the house, but are mistaken for burglars by an over-zealous policeman. Having finally cleared themselves to retire to bed only to find themselves in a still worse predicament. Roy Clements directed the production.

"Props, Drops and Flops," a two-reel L-Ko comedy, will be the offering for Wednesday, August 29th. This riotous sketch of life behind the scenes in a burlesque theater will add to the prestige of Neal Smith and J. G. Blystone as director and supervisor, respectively. In this unreal domain behind the footlights the head property man reigns an absolute monarch over the destinies of manager, artists, stage director and other workers of humbler sphere. When the assistant property man rebels chaos reigns until the fire department finally comes to the rescue with a watery but effective solution. The 87th issue of the Animated Weekly will be released on the same date.

J. Warren Kerrigan is the star of "Hand in the Dark," the feature scheduled for release Thursday, August 30. This tabloid thriller was written by E. M. McCall and William-Parker and was personally directed by Henry McRae, production manager at Universal City. Kerrigan is supported by Edith Johnson. The story has to do with a young man who is in love with the daughter of an immensely wealthy miser. When the father is mysteriously murdered circumstantial evidence makes it apparent that Kerrigan is the author of the crime.

The manner in which the girl in the case solves the mystery of her father's death, incidentally saving her lover's life, adds several unusual thrills to a well acted and adequately directed production. William Franey will be seen on the same day in a Joker comedy, entitled "Why They Left Home." This clever burlesque was written by Carl Laemmle during a recent visit to Universal City at Franey's special request, and bears witness to Mr. Laemmle's versatility. It is a caricature of life behind the scenes in a theater, and depicts the events that take place during the production of a melodrama with the rather significant title, "The Salary of Sin." Franey is capably suppressed by Lillian Peacock and Milburn Meranti. W. W. Beaudine is credited with the direction.

"Scandal Everywhere," featuring Max Asher and Gladys Tennyson, bears the date of Friday, August 31st. A Victor comedy, written by R. A. Dillon and produced by Craig Hutchinson in this production shows in a realistic manner the dire fate that overtakes a trifler with more susceptibility than discretion. The 34th issue of the Screen Magazine released simultaneously with the Asher Comedy will contain many timely subjects, including pictures of the new food conservation work for the Government.

On Saturday, September 1, Eileen Sedgwick and Fred Church will be featured in a two-reel Bison, entitled "Jungle Treachery," written and produced by W. B. Pearson and Rex Hodge. An unusually gripping story in an exploring expedition in Africa, this production has been widely heralded as a thriller with several wild animal scenes of great novelty. Gale Henry and Milton Sims will also be seen in a Joker Comedy known as "Busting Into Society," written by Tom Gibson and directed by Allen Curtis. The 16th issue of Current Events will make the third release for the day, bringing a week to a close with up-to-the-minute scenes of important happenings in the world of work and play.

NO RAGGED CLOTHES IN NEW FREDERICK PICTURE.

From the part of a scrubwoman, toiling with mop and brush in a seven-story office building to the young wife of a successful husband, playing about in Long Island summer society, Pauline Frederick makes a big jump from her last Paramount picture, "The Love that Lives," to her newest one, "Double Crossed," recently completed and scheduled for release in September. In "Doubled Crossed" Miss Frederick as Eleanor Stratton, beautiful young society matron, much in love with her young broker-husband, has a chance to display her beauty and charm, as well as some wonderful gowns and jewels. Miss Frederick will be supported by Crawford Kent, of recent musical comedy fame, as a new leading man. Others in the cast include William Riley Hatch, Clarence Handysides, Harris Gordon and Joseph Smiley.

"PANTS" (Essanay).

Jealousy has no place in the make-up of Little Mary McAlister, Essanay's juvenile star, who is soon to be seen in a five-reel feature of her own entitled "Pants." At a private showing of this feature recently she was an interested spectator, closely scrutinizing every scene regardless of whether she appeared in it or not.

At the finish when asked how she liked herself in it she said,

Scene from "Pants" (Essanay).

"Oh, I think I did pretty good in some parts, but wasn't my leading man just grand?"

She had reference to a boy about ten years of age who recently applied at the studio and stated so persistently that he felt he would make good if given a chance that he was finally cast for a part in "Pants." His work proved a surprise to everyone except Director Berthelet, who stated after the day that he considered the youngster a perfect foil for the little leading lady.

The combination of these two forms such an appealing team that in all probability they will work opposite each other in several of Mary's future photoplays.

MISS MINTER IN "CHARITY CASTLE."

Truly a sparkling production is "Charity Castle," the American Film publication of September 3. Of delicate texture, beautiful settings, tasteful appointments, rich in good humor, this first of Mary Miles Minter's productions under her new contract and directorship of Lloyd Ingraham, is offered by Samuel S. Hutchinson as something out of the ordinary even in high-standard American enfilments.

The story is by C. Doty Hobart; the screen adaptation by Doris Schroeder. In a word the plot may be stated as: How a happy little girl sets a certain little world aright after it had all but dried up through chronic grouchiness. As Charity, Miss Minter appears in a role different from any before given her—a combination role—that of an orphan, ward of a rich young spendthrift who knows the joys of living, and general peacemaker in aristocratic misunderstandings. That she is delightfully successful is the verdict of all the judges who have had previews.

In her spare time, Charity spins fairy yarns to the Prince, the four-year-old she has adopted. Clifford Callis, an endearing babe, plays the latter role.

Alan Forrest is cast as Miss Minter's chief support, the "goldcoast" youth who becomes her champion through the lure of fairyland. He is subsequently disinherited by his rich father and remains persona non grata until Charity redeems him.

Spottiswoode Aitken, the eminent character actor, is assigned an important part in the production, while Henry A. Barrows plays the grouchy millionaire.

Other members of the cast are Eugenie Forde, Aston Dearholt, Robert Klein, George Ahern and Gordon Russell.

WALLACE REID IN ROMANCE OF WAR.

War is the theme for "The Hostage," Wallace Reid's starring vehicle to be released by Paramount in September. Beulah Marie Dix, who wrote the internationally famous war sketch "Molloch," has again taken the war note as her subject and woven into a thrilling story a romance that is said to suit Reid especially well.

Reid is admirably suited for the part of the young lieutenant. His physical prowess and good looks are said to stand him in good stead in a most exacting role. Dorothea Abril in the part of Nathalia is Mr. Reid's new leading woman. She is one of the cleverest of the Paramount ingenues and her splendid work in "The Little American" with Mary Pickford is a matter of recent remembrance. In the cast supporting Mr. Reid are C. H. Geldert, Guy Oliver, Noah Beery, Gertrude Short and others.

H. H. Cudmore in New York

Is Introducing the Sheck Invention—An Improved Mazda Lamp for Theaters.

H. H. CUDMORE of Cleveland, Ohio, well known in electrical circles through his connection with the Mazda Lamp industries and recently made general manager of the Argus Lamp & Supply Company of Cleveland, will be in New York this week to personally superintend the installation of the New Sheck Adapters, by which motion pictures may be projected with Mazda incandescent lamps, in several of the larger motion picture theaters in the city. Motion picture people throughout the country are keenly interested in the practical demonstrations of the new Sheck Adapters, for they promise to revolutionize the motion picture business from the exhibitor's standpoint.

The new appliance which Mr. Cudmore will personally introduce in New York is the invention of Oscar M. Sheck of Cleveland, one of the best-known electrical engineers in the country. By his invention it is possible to use the Mazda incandescent lamps with the ordinary equipment in any motion picture theater.

H. H. Cudmore.

In discussing the merits of the Sheck invention with a number of electrical engineers who visited the Argus Company's plant in Cleveland recently, Mr. Cudmore said he was confident that the new device was the most important step that had been taken ahead in the motion picture business in a number of years.

"We are of the opinion," said Mr. Cudmore, "that the development of this new Mazda lamp and the co-incident invention of the Sheck Universal Adapter will revolutionize the entire field of motion picture projection. We have had lamps running in theaters for more than a year, and the proprietors of these theaters are enthusiastic over them.

"We claim that we give better screen illumination; that we do not tire the eyes; that We entirely eliminate flicker on the screen, and that we materially lower the cost of projection. One item of greatest importance is the fact that the new lamp method of projection does away with all the poisonous gases in the projection booth which have been proven so injurious to the health of operators."

The New York theaters where the new projection method will be demonstrated will be announced later, and the entire motion picture trade invited to see for themselves just what the lamps can and will do.

STRONG K-E-S-E PROGRAM FOR SEPTEMBER.

Kleine-Edison-Selig-Essanay program for September looks unusually attractive and was arranged, K-E-S-E's Publicity Department states, with a view of giving exhibitors every opportunity to "make good" with their patrons with the inauguration of their fall and early winter campaign.

"Efficiency Edgar's Courtship," released September 3, produced by Essanay, featuring their newest star, Taylor Holmes, who is credited with several big hits on the speaking stage, is the first September K-E-S-E release.

This will be following September 10 by another Essanay feature, "Pants," presenting fascinating little Mary McAlister, as star. "Pants" was written especially for this little girl who is scoring such decided success in the Essanay series, "Do Children Count?"

Mr. Kleine will announce the name of the K-E-S-E September 17 release in a few days and promises that it will be an exceptionally strong production.

"Men of the Desert," featuring Jack Gardner, an Essanay production, will be presented September 24.

LONGACRE DISTRIBUTING CHANGE OFFICES.

The Longacre Distributing Company, distributors for Alice Howell Comedies, has moved from the seventh to the fourth floor of the Mecca building. On August 20 the big subway and elevated station advertising campaign goes into effect. Mr. Kelly, the sales manager, feels that this campaign will go a long way toward gaining the popularity that Alice Howell Comedies are worthy of.

COMING FOX FEATURES.

Forthcoming Fox features include "Every Girl's Dream," a picturesque romance of old Holland with June Caprice in the stellar role. This will be released on August 27, and in it Harry Hilliard appears opposite Miss Caprice. This is the dainty Fox star's first production under the direction of Harry Millarde. In addition to Mr. Hilliard Miss Caprice's support includes Kittens Reichnert, Margaret Fielding, Marcia Harris, and Dan Mason.

On September 9 Mr. Fox will release the latest Virginia Pearson picture. This is "When False Tongues Speak," a gripping story by George Scarborough, known to every playgoer as the author of "The Lure," "At Bay," and other stage successes. In it Miss Pearson is said to have abundant opportunity for the exercise of those artistic abilities with which she is so highly endowed. In addition to an unusual and thrilling story, and a star of first magnitude for its interpretation, "When False Tongues Speak" was directed by Carl Harbaugh, which, in itself, is a guarantee of excellence. And Miss Pearson is supported by an admirable cast. This includes Mr. Harbaugh, Hardee Kirkland, Claire Whitney, Carl Eckstrom and William E. Meehan, famous as the comic crook in "Turn to the Right," and who portrays another crook in "When False Tongues Speak."

GRAND OPERA STAGED IN "THE LUST OF THE AGES."

The Ogden Pictures Corporation's initial release, "The Lust of the Ages," contains almost every element that enters into an extraordinary attraction; extraordinary, photographic effects and camera work, dramatic scenes, light comedy, heart interest and pathos, and even grand opera is portrayed. One and a half acts of the opera "Faust" is portrayed in the production, and Harry Havier, the director, was fortunate in securing the entire troupe of an Italian Repertoire company, then playing a short engagement at Ogden. The entire troupe was transported to the studios of the Ogden Pictures Corporation, together with that company's scenery and orchestra, and one act and a half of the opera "Faust" was photographed. This practical working out of another problem saved a tremendous amount of time and expense in rehearsals and completing the scenery necessary to be used in the scenes. It is this fidelity to details that is one of the marked characteristics of "The Lust of the Ages," and no subterfuge was resorted to to substitute the sham for the real.

"REPUTATION," EDNA GOODRICH'S FIRST MUTUAL PICTURE.

Edna Goodrich, famous beauty of the stage, will return to the screen September 3 in "Reputation," the first of her series of star productions for Mutual. Miss Goodrich has been at work for months on the series of photodramas which she is making under her contract with John R. Freuler, president of the Mutual Film Corporation. The first of the series was finished some months ago, but it was decided that the third must be well under way before the date of the first release was announced.

In the meantime great interest has been aroused in the forthcoming Goodrich pictures. In addition to "Reputation," "Queen X" has been completed and "A Daughter of Maryland" is so far under way that it will be finished before "Reputation's" release.

Scene from "Reputation" (Mutual).

The fourth of the series will be "American Maid," preparations for the production of which are already started. Miss Goodrich will be directed in "American Maid" by Albert Capellani, the noted stage manager who has but recently come into the Mutual organization.

Miss Goodrich is as well known as any woman who has appeared on the American stage in the last ten years. She is celebrated in America and Europe as a beauty. She is one of the wealthiest women of the stage and is commonly acknowledged to have been the highest salaried showgirl who ever appeared on Broadway.

Stage Plays in Pictures

Brady Says "Stage Hits" Make Most Enduring Screen Successes and Offers Some.

THE history of motion picture success," said William A. Brady, director general of World-Pictures Brady-made, that the biggest and most enduring hits are screen adaptations of stories which have been highly favored by the public in the speaking theater. This applies not alone to program features but to special price pictures, and the fact accounts for the oral theater. Between Sept. 17 and Oct. 15 we shall publish rights to stage plays.

"The World corporation has been exceptionally fortunate in acquiring these productions heretofore, and they have invariably turned out so very well as to more than justify our faith in them, going to show that there is little, if any, difference between the tastes of moving picture audiences and those that assemble in the 'regular' playhouse.

"All this is preliminary to the announcement that World Pictures will immediately present an altogether remarkable series of screen versions of dramas which have enjoyed big careers in the oral theater. Between Sept. 17 and Oct. 15 we shall publish no less than four such productions, and I desire to invite the closest of scrutiny as to their quality.

"The first of this series is 'Betsy Ross,' the title role of which is acted by Alice Brady. This story by H. A. Du Souchet, author of 'My Friend from India,' not alone had a notable stage career, but was widely circulated in book form. It carries a strong dramatic plot and faithfully reproduces certain events of importance in the history of our country.

"The second of the quartette is 'The Corner Grocery,' in which Madge Evans is featured with Lew Fields. The comedy which with serious touches was produced by Adolph Philipp in New York, where it had a record-breaking run, although under the disadvantage of being interpreted in a foreign tongue.

"Third in the set is 'Shall We Forgive Her,' the central personages of which are assumed by June Elvidge and Arthur Ashley, with John Bowers playing an important part. The stage version of 'Shall We Forgive Her' was written by Frank Harvey, a very well known contributor to the literature of the theater, and it has been played repeatedly throughout the country.

"Finally comes 'The Burglar' with Carlyle Blackwell, Evelyn Greeley and Madge Evans at the head of a particularly effective company. The story first appeared as a novel from the pen of Frances Hodgson Burnett, who was also the writer of 'Little Lord Fauntleroy.' It was made into a drama by Augustus Thomas, and quite possibly contributed more to the popularity of that justly famous author than any of his other plays.

"The qualities which made 'The Burglar' one of the very greatest successes in the history of the American stage have been fully preserved, and perhaps emphasized, in its transference to the screen. Certainly it never was played better than by Mr. Blackwell, Miss Greeley, little Madge Evans and the other members of the silent cast.

"I am willing to let my judgment of values stand or fall upon the assertion that 'The Burglar' is the best picture play in three reels that ever was published.

"Indeed, I will go further and donate ten thousand dollars from my personal funds to the Red Cross if within a space equal to that consumed in the production of these four World Pictures the same number of special price pictures of as good quality have been made—the decision to rest with a jury of exhibitors. This is a challenge for a comparison between regular World program fair price features of five reels each and an equal number of special price pictures no matter how long or pretentious."

SELIG PRODUCING "THE STILL ALARM."

"The Still Alarm," that sterling melodrama, known to thousands of theatergoers of the past decade, will be theatreproced on a lavish scale at the Selig studios, Los Angeles, under the direction of Colin Campbell. Always a play of spectacular appeal on the legitimate stage, it will prove much more so in the screen version, where effects not possible to produce on the stage will be shown in realistic vividness. This is one of the few successful stage plays that lends itself admirably to picturization, having a splendid plot and allowing much of the action to center about thrilling fire runs and other spectacular effects. The cast, which is a large one, will be headed by Thomas Santschi, Bessie Eyton and Fritz Brunette. Whole streets of substantial-looking buildings are being erected on the Selig lot for the forthcoming production for the sole purpose of being burned down.

RELEASE OF "RED ACE" AND "GRAY GHOST."

Owing to the great demand for serials in the fall the Universal Film Exchange of New York has decided to release the "Red Ace" and "Gray Ghost" in close proximity to each other. On August 27 the "Red Ace," starring Marie Walcamp, will be available to exhibitors, while the "Gray Ghost," starring Eddie Polo, will be open for bookings on September 17.

An advance showing on the "Red Ace" has been arranged for Monday, 11 a. m., at the Broadway theater. Universal announces that while Marie Walcamp did some very clever work in the famous serial "Liberty," in the "Red Ace" she surpasses all past efforts.

BRENON FINDS ACTOR TO PLAY KERENSKY.

Up in Yonkers there lives a young man named W. Francis Chapin who has been acting in pictures and plays in a small way for some time, but now is in a fair way to become famous. Herbert Brenon in finishing his feature "The Fall of the Romanoffs," which as the title indicates is an authentic version of the recent Russian Revolution interwoven with a charming romance and story of adventure and action. All of the central figures in the present Russian situation necessarily play parts in "The Fall of the Romanoffs," for the picture scenario is by

Scene from "The Fall of the Romanoffs" (Brenon).

such famous writers as the Czar, Czarina, Rasputin, Grand Duke Nicholas, Iliodor, Prince Felix and the other real characters who figure either in the Revolution or the events leading up to it.

The outstanding figure of the Russian Revolution, the one character whose prominence demanded an equal position in the picture was the new-found "Man of Iron," premier and military dictator, Alexander Kerensky, the absolute one man force holding the myriad of puzzled factions in Russia together. For weeks Brenon employes sought the actor for this role. Agencies have been combed and players by the score have been examined and rejected by the Brenon Studio, since the director insisted upon an exact double of "The Man of Iron." Finally the right actor was found—his name is W. Francis Chapin. He is not a Russian, but his resemblance to Kerensky is so startling that "The Man of Iron" seems to have stepped from the Brenon photogravure sections right to the Brenon screen. Mr. Chapin has been posing before the Brenon camera for the past week and with the taking of his scenes the big feature will be ready for assembling.

MACK SENNETT BEAUTIES WILL BE IN FRONT.

Mack Sennett's first Paramount comedies to be released the latter part of September will feature all the famous Sennett comedians and beauties—they call the bathing suit girls "Sennetts" out on the Pacific coast. The casts give slight idea of what to expect. In "Roping Her Romeo," Polly Moran plays a girl sheriff, Ben Turpin a wealthy waiter, Slim Summerville a gambler, and Ethel Tearle a girl from the city. Fred Fishback is directing.

In "A Bedroom Blunder" Charley Murray plays a "good natured husband who likes to flirt with the girls." The girls in the case are some more Sennette whose bathing suits add a touch of interest for the tired business man. Mary Thurman, a wife with some remarkable attractive costumes, plays a "young wife who loses her necklace." Wayland Trask plays her simple husband and Eva Thatcher plays Murray's equally simple wife. Eddie Cline is doing the directing.

"The Pullman Bride" features Gloria Swanson as "the girl in the case," a beach maiden of imposing and impressing beauty. Mack Swain as a "waiter posing as a man of wealth," and Chester Conklin as an adventurer. Clarence Badger is the director.

"THE CINDERELLA MAN" FOR MAE MARSH.

Goldwyn has purchased from Oliver Morosco and Edward Childs Carpenter, the author, the famous all-season New York success, "The Cinderella Man," and without any loss of time whatever Mae Marsh began work before the camera in this production this week.

The director of this production is George Loane Tucker, the successful English director, whose recent film productions under his own auspices have attracted widespread attention in the industry. Mr. Tucker's affiliation with the Goldwyn directorial forces has been impending for a long time, and his work with Mae Marsh may be expected to add still further to his reputation.

Triangle-Keystones of All Variety

Human Interest Comedies as Well as Slapstick Will Be Offered With Well-known Keystone Players for September Release.

THE Keystone plant is the busiest picture foundry in California at the present moment, more than twelve companies being engaged in turning out comedies for the Triangle company. An innovation in this famous brand of entertainment is promised in a series of comedies to be made by Director Henry Kernan and Jay Dwiggins, the veteran character comedian.

Dwiggins has been prominent in Keystones for a year and was for some time associated with the late John Bunny. He will write all his own stories and appear in the leading roles. The series will be devoid of the slapstick stunts which characterize most of the comedies. They will present human interest stories of a comic nature, described by Dwiggins as "lessons in how to enjoy living at the age of fifty." Caroline Rankin, the straw-figured Keystoner, will be the leading woman in these productions.

Other comedies now in the course of production will present the old-time riotous sort of entertainment which has become the steady diet of picture fans. Director Robert Kerr has just completed one of this type with Bob Milliken, Frits Schade, Claire Anderson, Jack Henderson and little Joey Jacobs, and is ready to start another with the same cast.

Aileen Allen, the diving nymph, who captured another medal for high diving at championship contest held at Ocean Park, California, will be featured in several aquatic stunts with the famous Keystone bathing girls in forthcoming releases.

The first September Keystone release is "A Shanghaied Jonah," presenting Billy Armstrong, Maude Wayne and Guy Woodward as the chief fun-makers.

Louise Fasenda, Charlie Murray and Slim Summerville head the company of "His Precious Life," scheduled for September 9.

The Keystone beauties will be out in force with the release of "Hula Hula Land" on September 16. Billy Armstrong, Maude Wayne and Guy Woodward are the featured players.

"The Late Lamented" is the lugubrious title of the September 23d issue, with Mary Thurman, George Binns and Claire Anderson acting as the chief mourners.

A production built along the lines of "Oriental Love" is listed for the week of September 30. It bears the title of "The Sultan's Wife" and presents Bobby Vernon, Gloria Swanson and Joseph Callahan in an Oriental laugh mixture.

INITIAL ELSIE FERGUSON SUBJECT FINISHED.

With the completion of the big Algerian street scenes for Elsie Ferguson's initial picture, "Barbary Sheep," early last week, the production of this super-photoplay drew to a close at the Famous Players-Lasky studio in Fort Lee. For practically two months work on this gigantic production has been in progress under the direction of Maurice Tourneur and it is announced that the film is the most elaborate ever staged at this studio in New Jersey.

Advance reports indicate that Elsie Ferguson will score an

Scene from "Barbary Sheep" (Artcraft).

immediate triumph as a photoplay star. One of the most beautiful women of the speaking stage, she has always been identified with the true dramatic art such as evidenced in her many famous stage characterizations. Her rare personal charm is faithfully reproduced by the camera, it is announced, and that her popularity of stageland will more than be duplicated on the screen is readily anticipated. Supporting her is an exceptional cast, including Lumsden Hare, Pedro de Cordoba, Macy Harlem, Alex Shannon, Maude Ford and many other talented artists of the cinema.

SELIG'S "A TRIP TO CHINATOWN."

Monday, August 20, is the release date in K-E-S-E for "A Trip to Chinatown," the merry comedy written by Charles Hoyt and presented by the Selig Polyscope company. The comedy cast includes Amy Leah Dennis, Wm. Fables, Charles Harris, with J. A. Richmond the director in charge.

The story of Hoyt's "A Trip to Chinatown" is one full of fun. A follower of the race track touts the wrong horse to the visitors. He is chased out of the betting ring by a policeman.

The tout is penniless and finally seeks comfort in a Chink's laundry, where he sniffs a narcotic and falls asleep and dreams. He dreams that he is transported to a palace where he meets a beautiful princess. Granted a personal slave, he recognizes in that attendant the policeman who chased him out of the betting ring. He thirsts for revenge.

First there comes a gigantic wrestler, who, after a fierce match, is overcome by the slave. A swordsman is produced. A brief but sharp engagement, and again the slave proves the victor. A potion causes the slave to fall in love with the old maid attendant, who really wishes the race course tout to attend her.

And then the slave is thrown to the lion, but makes the lion eat out of his hand. The bravery of the slave wins the love of the Princess, and the tout escapes just in time to awaken in the "Chink's" laundry and to be thrown out by the Chinaman. He falls right into the arms of the policeman and is jailed.

There are said to be a succession of clever situations and funny episodes, while the photography is all that can be desired.

"THE WAR AND THE WOMAN" (Pathe).

In "The War and the Woman" Thanhouser has contributed to the Pathe program a picture that is beyond all question the best that Florence La Badie has ever starred in—a picture that is justly entitled to the much abused word "big." It will be released as a five-part Gold Rooster play the week of September 16. Ernest Warde, son of Frederick Warde, the famous actor, not only directed the feature, but plays in it an important role so capably that his honors are even as actor and director.

"The War and the Woman" is a timely story, dealing, as it does, with a girl who, despite her alien parentage, is a true blue American. Her stepfather is suspected by the Secret Service of being a spy.

For intensity of dramatic action, for excellent acting, for artistically staged production, this picture is sure to be highly praised. Exhibitors showing Pathe Gold Rooster plays may be certain that their audiences will be highly pleased with it. It will undoubtedly play many "repeats."

"THE SPREADING DAWN" JUST COMPLETED.

After nearly three months of most exacting effort through the very hottest season of the year, Jane Cowl finally has emerged, tired but triumphant, from her first screen production for Goldwyn Pictures. Her vehicle, "The Spreading Dawn," from the story by Basil King, author of "The Inner Shrine," has just been completed at Goldwyn's Fort Lee studios.

For this picture Miss Cowl has been surrounded by an excellent cast, very largely of her own selection. It comprises players of note who have achieved success with her in some of her notable plays such as "Within the Law" and "Common Clay." Orme Caldara was engaged for Miss Cowl to play the leading male role opposite to her as in the two plays mentioned. In addition there are Henry Stephenson, Charles Hammond, Edith McAlpin, Lettie Ford, Marion Knapp and Antoinette Erwin in the cast.

CHANGES IN UNIVERSAL SCHEDULE.

Universal announces changes in its weekly schedule of releases which are designed to strengthen the list and meet the demands of a majority of exhibitors.

The Powers' cartoon that has been released on Saturdays will be withdrawn, and a two-reel Bison will be released regularly in its place. The plan of releasing a three-reel Bison on alternate Tuesdays will also be discontinued. All three-reelers shown on Tuesday hereafter will be of the Gold Seal brand. Victor comedies will be made in single reels instead of double-reel lengths, as heretofore. They will continue to be released on Friday, together with the Universal Screen Magazine.

These changes will be put into effect beginning the week of August 27.

GARSON ORGANIZES COMEDY COMPANY.

The Fun-Art Film Company has been organized by Harry I. Garson, who is also personal manager for Clara Kimball Young, to produce a series of two-reel pictures. Mr. Garson has signed a contract for five years with the well known and youthful vaudeville team of Ray and Gordon Dooley. These comedies will be known as the "Dooley series" and it is Mr. Garson's belief that he has a real find in this team of clever artists, who are nineteen and twenty years of age, respectively. The first release will be sometime in September.

Paramount Announces September Releases

Exceptional List of Stars and Authors Selected for Second Month of Star Series Distribution.

WITH the announcement of its September releases Paramount establishes more firmly than ever its determination to improve the quality of production and to place before the exhibitor under its new Star Series selective booking system an even higher grade of photoplay than that upon which it has established its reputation in the motion picture field.

For September there will be seven Paramount pictures starring Marguerite Clark, Pauline Frederick, Fannie Ward, Julian Eltinge, Mme. Petrova and George Beban. Among the authors of the August Paramount releases there appeared such international celebrities as Sir Arthur Wing Pinero, Owen Johnson, Wallace Irwin and George Broadhurst. The authors of the September productions are equally prominent, Gelett Burgess, Mary Roberts Rinehart, Charles Kenyon, Carolyn Wells, Beulah Marie Dix, Dolf Wyllard and Hector Turnbull being among those who contribute the basic stories for the month's selections.

September will mark the advent of Mary Roberts Rinehart upon the screen as an author, the adaptation of the first of her celebrated "Sub-Deb" stories, starring Marguerite Clark, being scheduled for release in the latter part of the month. This production will be called "Bab's Burglar," and the titles of the others in the series will be announced later.

The first production for the month will be George Beban in "Lost in Transit," which was written for Mr. Beban by Kathlyn Williams, the well known photoplay star. Wallace Reid follows Mr. Beban in "The Hostage," a timely story written by Beulah Marie Dix, well known playwright and author of "Moloch."

Charles Kenyon, whose "Kindling" made him world famous as a dramatic author and who has already written successful productions for Paramount, is the author of "On the Level," in which Fannie Ward will appear. Pauline Frederick, leaving her rags and tatters far afield, appears as a society belle in a powerful drama written especially for her by Hector Turnbull. It is called "Double Crossed," and has to do with political intrigue in high circles.

The next production in the list is "Exile," written by a poet and artist of literature, Dolf Wyllard. This is a story of the Far East starring Madame Petrova, which has been staged in an extremely comprehensive and absorbingly interesting manner by Maurice Tourneur. Gelett Burgess and Carolyn Wells furnished the literary inspiration for Julian Eltinge's first screen appearance. This, "The Countess Charming," written especially by these two celebrated authors in collaboration for Mr. Eltinge, is of course designed to give full scope to the remarkable dual personality of Mr. Eltinge which arises from his ability as a feminine impersonator.

As has already been stated, the seventh production to be listed for the month is Marguerite Clark in "Bab's Burglar," the first of the Mary Roberts Rinehart "Sub-Deb" stories.

Dwan Favors Timely Topics

Triangle Director Believes in Subjects Dealing With Current Life of American People.

ALLAN DWAN, who supervises all Triangle productions made in the east, is gradually putting into operation a distinct policy of picture making, which he correlates with the editorial policy of the Saturday Evening Post insofar as he aims to specialize in pictures treating of timely issues touching on the every day life of American people.

As indicative of his general policy of production, "The Food Gamblers," recently issued, is a striking example. It is entertainment that treats constructively of a national evil, and one which is receiving the attention not only of one class of people, but virtually every family in America. "A Successful Failure," "The Man Who Made Good" and "American, That's All," all treat of some particular phase of business life as faced by young America. "Grafters," which is scheduled for the August 26 program, is an amusing arraignment of the idle youth who believes he knows all the tricks of business.

Dwan does not take up masculine problems exclusively, as demonstrated by the announcement that "The Man Hater," the Saturday Evening Post story by Mary Brecht Pulver, is shortly to make its appearance in picture form with Winifred Allen in the leading role. It presents an entertaining study of feminine psychology.

Another Saturday Evening Post story now in the course of production in "Cassidy," by Larry Evans. Dick Rosson will appear as the boy of the streets to whom the author says. "There's many a man with God's own soul who never had a chance." Larry Evans in this story has depicted as vividly the squalid phase of New York life as did Dickens that of his London.

"The Haunted House," which will be released in September with Winifred Allen in the leading role, presents a picture of striking contrast to that of "Cassidy." The locale is a little New England village where bigotry and false prejudices still find root. Miss Allen appears as the housekeeper for a sullen, reticent uncle who works for the railroad.

A number of other plays are being put into production at this studio, situated on the old Clara Morris estate near the Hudson, and all of them are said to have subjects of actual news value.

Triangle Divides Exchange Work

One Branch to Have Charge of Sale and Release of Program Productions; Other to Handle Paralta Plays and Hart-Fairbanks Series.

DUE to the volume of increased business, the New York exchange of the Triangle Distributing Corporation has announced that hereafter the exchange will be divided into two separate departments, one having charge of the sale and release of productions appearing on the Triangle program and the other to handle special productions. The former will be known as the Program Department, and the latter as the Series Department.

The Series Department will have charge of all Paralta releases, and also the Fairbanks and Hart reissues, which are to be released September 2 and 16 respectively. Entirely distinct sales and service representatives will be located in each department, devoting their time exclusively to the special work of the respective branches. It had originally been planned to keep the exchange as one office, handling both the program and the specials from there, but the volume of business already undertaken made this arrangement impossible.

"THE CITY OF PURPLE DREAMS" (SELIG).

"The City of Purple Dreams" is the latest of Selig film features to arrive in Chicago from the Pacific coast. The drama is a faithful version of the book of the same name. Colin Campbell was the director in charge and Gilson Willets wrote the scenario. Some of the features of the film drama are described by those who have seen the play are said to include a succession of wonderful lighting effects, including a bird's eye view of Chicago after nightfall; a succession of elaborate interiors of a millionaire's home; the night at the opera and other effective details.

The plot of "The City of Purple Dreams" is laid in Chicago and many familiar scenes in the Windy City are presented. The players include Thomas Santschi, Fritzi Brunette, Frank Clark, Bessie Eyton, A. D. Sears, Eugenie Besserer, Cecil Holland, Harry Lonsdale, and others. The continuity of the story is said to be all that could be hoped for and the acting clever in every detail.

Colin Campbell staged "The City of Purple Dreams."

EFFICIENCY VIA EXPRESS.

In the 82d release of Paramount-Bray Pictograph, the "magazine on the screen," the subject, "Efficiency by Express," is a graphic story of the development and operation of one of the most important industries of this country. The Bray Studios, Inc., producers of this release, were privileged to have the co-operation of the greatest of all express companies, and many of the scenes were taken in the busiest express office in the world, where thousands of express shipments pour through daily, and where efficiency of the highest order is needed to keep the influx and outflow of parcels on the move.

VICTOR MOORE IN "EGGED ON."

Victor Moore releases August 20 his latest comedy by Lois Zellner, called "Egged On." Vic. is entrusted with a gunpowder formula, which has been put into egg shells to take to the American munition manufacturers. It is supposed to be the most deadly weapon of the kind invented, so in order that nothing should happen to the eggs, Vic. puts them in a hand-bag, which he keeps close to his side.

On arrival in the States he loses the bag and his wallet full

Scene from "Egged On" (Klever).

of money. He is unable to cable home, so he takes a job for five dollars as a sandwich man, advertising a clothing concern, to enable him to cable home for money. He is met by other sandwich men, who insist that he show his Union card, which he cannot, so they make him join the union. This costs him five dollars, and he is left flat again. Other misadventures overtake him. This farce is in line with the best pictures Moore has made.

Bluebird Features

Shifting of Stars and Directors Necessitates Change in Schedule.

WITH the prospect of a general shifting around of stars and directors in the Bluebird program, there comes from the city department of that organization reference to several productions either complete or under way that will be of interest to the exhibitor who includes "Bluebird Day" as a part of his weekly arrangements. The list of stars to be consistently presented in the series embraces Mae Murray, Dorothy Phillips, Violet Mersereau, Franklyn Farnum, Rupert Julian and Ruth Clifford, and Carmel Meyers. There will be occasional offerings by other prominent players, to provide variety and consistency to the program.

Franklyn Farnum will become a lone-star with the presentation in October of "The Maverick," a production by Joseph De Grasse. Mr. Farnum and Brownie Vernon will be seen together for the last time in "A Stormy Knight," to be released Sept. 17, and Miss Vernon will shortly appear as co-star with Herbert Rawlinson in "Sky High," directed by Elmer Clifton.

Dorothy Phillips, who has heretofore been directed alternately by Ida May Park and Joseph De Grasse, will have Miss Park as her sole director in future, starting with "Bondage," a prospect for the October schedule. Miss Park and Miss Phillips have begun work at Universal City upon "The Boss of Powderville," a story written by Thomas Addison.

Violet Mersereau is working on "The Girl by the Roadside," at the Bluebird Leonia (N. J.) studios, and Mae Murray is preparing her first Bluebird under direction of Robert Leonard on the West Coast. Rupert Julian will make a select number of features in which he will co-star with Ruth Clifford. These offerings will result in establishing the Julian productions among Bluebirds.

Carmel Meyers will become a new star in the Bluebird group when she is presented in "The Dynast," a production directed by Harry Solter, who has also prepared "Bitter Sweet," an Ella Hall feature for release among autumn Bluebirds. Kenneth Harlan and Charles Hill Mailes will be prominent in Miss Meyer's supporting organization. Among other features to become Bluebirds will be "The Man of God," directed by E. J. Le Saint and featuring William Stowell; "It's Up to You," a feature for Herbert Rawlinson and Brownie Vernon, and "The Cricket," produced by Elsie Jane Wilson, who gets credit, along with Ida May Park, as woman director of Bluebirds.

"THE BANKER" (Selig).

Charles K. Harris, the noted writer of songs and stories, claims that his best work is "The Barker," the Selig Red Seal play released on Monday, August 13, in K-E-S-E service. Mr. Fields claims "The Barker" is one of the best productions he ever appeared in. William N. Selig shared no expense in doing the picture, and with adequate support and good photography which are promised, "The Barker," should prove an unusually meritorious release.

"THE MARTINACHE MARRIAGE" (General Film).

The second of the new four-reel dramas from General Film comprising the Falcon Features is primarily a "heart" story. It is from a magazine romance by Beatrix Demarest Lloyd.

Scene from "The Martinache Marriage" (General Film).

Margaret Landis is featured as the heroine and Philo McCullough as the hero. The love interest is enacted against a strongly dramatic background.

In "The Martinache Marriage" the title refers to the name of the bridegroom, but there are two Martinache men to reckon with as eligibles for the hand of the girl. A very novel triangle is introduced, there being no problem, but a wholesome competition that is worked out in a human and pleasing way.

An excellent cast and production have given "The Martinache Marriage" under the supervision of H. M. and E. D. Horkheimer. Mollie McConnell, Leota Lorraine, Julien Beaubien, Vincent Beresford and Frank Brownlee are other members of the cast.

"THE AUCTION BLOCK," BY REX BEACH.

One of the country's most successful newspaper editors owes much of his success to the fact that he never overlooks the weather. When it is very hot and everybody knows it's hot, he has a first page "story" setting forth the hourly temperatures and other data of sweltering interest. When there is a

Scene from "The Auction Block" (American).

big storm or a cracking cold spell his readers are put in possession of all the details. The editor scores by telling his readers what they know all about.

Rex Beach has followed the same psychological process in making a motion picture from his splendidly successful novel of New York life, "The Auction Block." This picture, now undergoing the final polishing process, is to be released throughout the country by the Goldwyn Distributing Corporation under the terms of contract recently entered into between Mr. Beach, Benjamin B. Hampton, president of the Rex Beach Film Corporation, and Goldwyn.

MYSTERY PICTURE ON BLUEBIRD PROGRAM.

Rupert Julian and Ruth Clifford will be stars of the Bluebird release for week starting Sept. 17—a study in psychology, written by Elliott J. Clawson, and produced by Mr. Julian, and entitled "The Mysterious Mr. Tiller." There are so many unusual twists to the plot, plus a surprising outcome, that Bluebird believes the feature will create an unusual interest when shown to the public.

Mr. Julian and Miss Tiller" by Lloyd Whitlock, E. A. Warren, Fram Brownlee, Wm. Higby, Harry Rattenberry and Wedgewood Nowe. Another Rupert Julian picture, "The Desire of the Moth," arrived from the West Coast last week and was shown to Bluebird executives and will be prepared for release later on.

"Triumph," starring Dorothy Phillips, and "A Stormy Knight," having Franklyn Farnum and Brownie Vernon as stars, will be Bluebirds for Sept. 3 and 10, respectively. In "Triumph," William Stowell and Lon Chaney, who have always supported Miss Phillips in Bluebirds, will appear together in her company for the last time, other plans having been made for their future employment on the program.

"A Stormy Knight" will present Mr. Farnum and Miss Vernon as joint stars in Bluebirds. Mr. Farnum will hereafter go it alone, and Miss Vernon will have as her future screen-mate Herbert Rawlinson, who will be added to Bluebird's list of stars. There is a strong element of mystery in "A Stormy Knight" to precede the arrival of "The Mysterious Mr. Tiller."

L-KO FOR SEPTEMBER.

General Director J. G. Blystone of L-Ko Comedies has issued a series of merrymakers for September that promise, according to President Julius Stern, to maintain the best traditions of that popular program of comedies. Phil Dunham, who lately gave up acting as a featured L-Ko comedian, has supplied two subjects, and Noel Smith and Vin Moore have each directed one of the September shows.

"Backward Sons and Forward Daughters" is the title of Phil Dunham's release for September 5, with Lucille Hutton and Billy Bevan featured. The same director also produced the September 26 release, "Entangled Tanglements," with Miss Hutton and Mr. Bevan also featured.

Noel Smith directed "From Cactus to Kale," the September 12 release, in which Gladys Varden and Walter Stephens are supported by Katherine Young, Harry Griffith and Bert Roach. "From Ranch to Riches," the L-Ko for September 19, was produced by Vin Moore and will have Myrtle Sterling and Al Forbes featured.

Triangle Announces Features for September

Plays Starring Louise Glaum, Olive Thomas, Bessie Love, Dorothy Dalton, Margery Wilson and Others, Listed for Release Soon.

TRIANGLE opens the fall season with a flourish of stars in production of unusual stories, some of which have appeared in national magazines or in book form. Notable among these is "The Man Hater," by Mary Brecht Pulver, published in the Saturday Evening Post of June 9. It will reach the public in picture form on September 2 with Winifred Allen in the leading role, and will be shown first at the New York Rialto Theater. Jack Meredith had the role of the rugged blacksmith, the first man to attract consideration from the girl. A number of scenes in which the little star appears with the four children of which she is guardian gives a humorous, human appeal to the play. Albert Parker directed the production under the supervision of Allan Dwan. The cast includes, beside Miss Allen and Mr. Meredith, Harry Neville, Jessie Shirley, Marguerite Gale, Robert Vivian and little Anna Lehr.

Dorothy Dalton will appear the same week in "Ten of Diamonds," adapted for the screen by L. V. Jefferson from the story by Albert Cowles. Jack Livingston, J. Barney Sherry, Billy Shaw and Dorcas Matthews support the star. The story is designed to show how a woman's life may be directed by the man or men with whom she comes in contact. Miss Dalton vivifies the role of Neva Blaine, a cabaret girl in a cheap resort. Jack Livingston has the leading male role. Other important parts are presented by J. Barney Sherry, Billy Shaw and Dorcas Matthews. Raymond B. West was in charge of the direction.

A play that will be heralded by the Triangle company as an extraordinary program feature, warranting special attention from the exhibitor because of its unusual box-office value, is "Idolaters," starring Louise Glaum, which is scheduled for the week of September 9. It is similar in action to "The Wolf Woman," which is said to have been one of the most valuable box-office propositions ever put out by the company. George Webb was secured for the leading male role opposite Miss Glaum, and Hugo Koch was engaged for another important part. Other prominent players who appear are Thomas S. Cuise, Milton Ross, Dorcas Matthews and Lee Hill.

The production was placed in charge of one of Triangle's best directors, Walter Edwards, who carefully rehearsed the play with Miss Glaum.

"The Sawdust Ring" indicated what Bessie Love could do in a worthy play well directed. Following "Wee Lady Betty," to be released August 26, the little star, set to work on "Polly Ann," scheduled for place with "Idolaters" on the September 9 program. The story of "Polly Ann" is woven with bright threads of humor, the star shining in the role of a happiness-giver.

Margery Wilson in her first starring play, "Mountain Dew," will come to the screen on September 16. The locale of the story is Kentucky, the home of Miss Wilson, who appears as a mountain girl brought up where the law is made by feudist clans. Jullen Josephsen and Monte M. Katterjohn are the authors of the piece.

Belle Bennett, a new Triangle star, makes her bow in "The Judgment of the Guilty," by Edith Kennedy, on the same week that Miss Wilson appears in her first starring vehicle. It is a story of the West, presenting three forceful characters, that of two men and a woman.

Roy Stewart and William Desmond are presented on the program of September 23. Stewart in "Devil Dodger" is a Western gun man, whose daring gives him his satanic sobriquet. Desmond in the part of a young college man who turns detective, just as an experiment and because he is in need of a meal ticket, is the star of "Flying Colors," written by John Lynch.

"Broadway, Arizona," is the title of the next Olive Thomas play, now in the course of production. It will be released on September 30 on the same program with "The Hell Warrior," featuring Walt Whitman. Miss Thomas comes forth this time as a Western dance hall girl, as famous along Broadway, Arizona, as she is in real life along Broadway, New York.

BIG LINE OF ADVERTISING MATTER FOR NEW COHAN PICTURE.

An exceptional line of advertising and publicity matter for George M. Cohan's second photoplay, "Seven Keys to Baldpate," has been prepared by the exploitation department of the Artcraft Pictures corporation. A twenty-four sheet, which has been proclaimed by many to be the most attractive piece of paper prepared this season, shows the typical actor-author-producer in one of the big scenes of the photoplay. The line of lithographs includes one twenty-four sheet, two six sheets, two three sheets and three one sheets, all of unusual design and appearance. Attractive store cards, slides and a novelty key puzzle are other splendid business stimulators prepared by Artcraft for this film. A large assortment of newspaper cuts and mats of complete advertising layouts, together with special articles in mat form, have been prepared by the publicity department, and a complete press book containing ten pages of stories, ranging in size from squibs to lengthy interviews, gives the exhibitor plenty of material for his local publications.

Get Roach Comedies from Pathe

Big Distributing Company Announces a Number for Immediate Distribution.

ACCORDING to an announcement from Pathe, the big distributing company has scheduled for release during August, September and October a number of unusually strong comedies produced by Rolin under the direction of Hal Roach. They are: "Lonesome Luke, Mechanic," two reels, August 19; "Lonesome Luke's Wild Women," two reels, September 2; "Over the Fence," one reel, September 9; "Lonesome Luke Loses Patients," two reels, September 16; "Pinched," one reel, September 23; "By the Sad Sea Waves," one reel, September 30; "Birds of a Feather," two reels, October 7; "From London to Laramie," two reels, October 21.

The two-reel pictures are Lonesome Luke Comedies and the one-reelers will be known as Harold Lloyd Comedies. These will alternate with the Luke two-reelers till further notice, and a Lloyd one-reeler will be announced for the open dates in October.

In the Harold Lloyd one-reel comedies the star is seen in a characterization entirely different from anything he has yet done. It is absolutely distinct from "Lonesome Luke."

In all these pictures Harold Lloyd is supported by Bebe Daniels and Harry Pollard. Bud Jamieson also appears in most of them.

"Lonesome Luke, Mechanic," is a side splitting burlesque on the modern garage with Luke using the gasoline pump as a fire extinguisher.

"Lonesome Luke's Wild Women" shows Luke and Snub in incredible adventures at the Palace of the Shah on the "Isles of Gek."

"Over the Fence" is a splendid baseball burlesque in which Harold Lloyd as a studious young man comes to bat in the nick of time and saves the game. The first part shows him as the enterprising proprietor of a tailoring establishment of the "We-Press-'Em-While-You-Wait" variety.

"Lonesome Luke Loses Patients" shows the incorrigible funmaker as the Doctor Killem of an up-to-date sanatorium.

In "Pinched" he has many an embrace in the long arms of the law, is lodged in jail for a robbery he didn't commit and escapes only after a series of laughable adventures.

"By the Sad Sea Waves" introduces Lloyd as a pseudo-life saver who makes good against his will.

There will be one, three and six sheets, a stock one sheet, and a slide on the "Lonesome Luke" one-reel comedies and a one-sheet on the Harold Lloyd one-reelers.

"THE MYSTERIOUS MR. TILLER" (Bluebird).

Several months after "The Mysterious Mrs. M." arrived at theatres where Bluebirds are shown comes "The Mysterious Mr. Tiller" to cast the spell of uncertainty and suspense upon the screen. Elliott J. Clawson wrote this combination of psychology and detective business and Rupert Julian made the production. Bluebird is starring Mr. Julian and Ruth Clifford in the net result, set for release Sept. 17.

"The Mysterious Mr. Tiller" will be the third Bluebird in which Mr. Julian and Miss Clifford have jointly starred. "A Kentucky Cinderella" served to introduce them to the regular program and "Mother of Mine," set for release Sept. 3 as a Bluebird extraordinary, for the purpose of getting the right players to fill the exactions of specific roles. Sensations and surprises are promised in the unravelling plot and a "surprise finish" caps the climax. It is declared that "The Mysterious Mr. Tiller" will be among the best of fifty-two answers in the year to the question: "Why Bluebirds?"

Scene from "The Mysterious Mr. Tiller" (Bluebird).

Brownlee, E. A. Warren and Lloyd Whitlock will be supporting members of a cast selected from end to end to fit the Bluebird purpose of getting the right players to fill the exactions of specific roles. Sensations and surprises are promised in the unravelling plot and a "surprise finish" caps the climax. It is declared that "The Mysterious Mr. Tiller" will be among the best of fifty-two answers in the year to the question: "Why Bluebirds?"

Wedgewood Nowell, Harry Rattenberry, Wm. Higby, Fram

Exhibitors Promised Good Things

Grant Wilbur, Catherine Calvert, Jean Sothern and Marian Swayne in Coming Plans of Art Dramas.

DIFFICULTIES in revising the Art Dramas schedule, to allow the immediate release of the newly-acquired Crane Wilbur features, have at last been circumvented, and the new order of productions is here given forth for the first time. As far as is known, this order will be followed exactly.

According to the new schedule, exhibitors of Art Dramas may look forward to a rich variety of popular productions, headed by stars of ability and renown. Two Crane Wilbur Horsley pictures are promised in close succession, and there will be also Jean Sothern, Marian Swayne and Catherine Calvert, in plays of distinction.

"Think It Over," which was due for release August 13, is a U. S. Amusement Corporation production, in which Catherine Calvert is starred, supported by Richard Tucker and a cast specially selected for the various characters. This play is a breezy, swift-moving comedy, written by H. Blache and directed by him. This was followed by "The Little Samaritan," a much-heralded play which will, according to those in authority, live up to its advance notices, if not surpass them.

With Marian Swayne as star, Joseph Levering as director, and Reverend Clarence J. Harris as author, "The Little Samaritan" is made up of the same triple alliance which produced "Little Miss Fortune," the picture which was such a sensation all over the country.

"Behind the Mask," another U. S. Amusement Corporation Art Drama in which Catherine Calvert is starred, again supported by Richard Tucker, was directed by Mme. Alice Blache from the story by Charles Dazey, one of the most capable and clever scenario writers before the public. In this story he has constructed a plot which will astonish by its novelty. It was adapted to the screen by Frederick Rath.

The second Horsley-Art Drama starring Crane Wilbur will follow "Behind the Mask." This is "Blood of His Fathers," and is a scientifically correct study of heredity. Mr. Wilbur plays three characters in the course of the narrative. "Blood of His Fathers" is somewhat of a novelty in form in that it is told with a prologue, a device somewhat common in stage plays, but almost unknown to motion-pictures. The prologue takes place during the Civil War, and Mr. Wilbur is in that period of the story a disreputable captain of guerrillas, who wander the country pillaging and destroying. The remainder of the story is modern.

"Blood of His Fathers" was written by J. Francis Dunbar and directed by Harrish Ingraham, the two men who were responsible for the strength of story and excellence of production of "Eye of Envy," Mr. Wilbur's first Art Drama.

"Peg o' the Sea," a Van Dyke picture starring Jean Sothern, will follow this. Winifred Dunn wrote the story from which this is taken. The staging of the picture has been practically completed except for a few interiors. This week the company returned from Atlantic Highlands, where the sea scenes were taken. It is expected that the remainder of the photoplay will be completed by the end of the week.

An untitled picture in which Catherine Calvert is starred will follow this. The U. S. Amusement Corporation is at present working on the new play, and it is to be finished in a week or so. More details regarding its nature will be given in a later issue.

"Unto the End," third of the Horsley Art Dramas starring Crane Wilbur, is the next in order. This is a somewhat tragic drama, deeply moving in its wealth of pathos. It relates a story of love which endures, despite all obstacles and difficulties, until the death of the lovers. The last scene of "Unto the End" is said to be one of the most intensely emotional moments ever screened. The heroine, afflicted with leprosy, has been sent to an island in the Pacific—one of the Hawaiian group. Here her lover goes in secret, for no one is permitted to visit the dwelling of the living dead. He arrives to find her dying on the shore. Picking her up in his arms, he enters the sea, and wades out toward the setting sun until he and his mate have been swallowed up by the waves.

SELIG "WORLD LIBRARY NO. 15."

Historic Monterey, California, is presented in Selig World Library No. 15, released in General Film Service on Wednesday, August 22. In 1602, Don Sebastian Viscaino entered Monterey Bay and took possession of the soil in the name of King Philip III of Spain. Monterey was the capital of California when the latter was a Mexican province. California's first theater, first frame house, first brick building. The home of Robert Louis Stevenson. The old Custom House.

Latest African fashions include—a skirt made from bamboo leaves and without the slightest waste.

Tuna fishing in the Pacific is an important industry. Tons of the fish are caught along the Pacific Coast, where they swim in shoals. Some attain a length of fifteen feet, weighing about 1,500 pounds. The fish are cleaned at sea. Here is a 50-pound salmon. Securing salmon for spawning purposes.

The silk worm came originally from China. Mulberry leaves are its chief food. The silk secreting glands. The cocoon in which the chrysalis is killed is placed in warm water to soften the gum, allowing the silk fiber to be reeled. After being properly cleaned it is ready for spinning. The weaving machine. Ready for market.

Russian Art Film Attracts

Many Inquiries Received in Response to Advertising and Inspection.

PRELIMINARY announcement, made in the Moving Picture World last week by N. S. Kaplan, that his Russian repertory of the films would soon be released in the United States, has brought hundreds of communications to the offices of the Russian Art Film Corporation, in the Godfrey building, at 729 Seventh avenue, New York City. There appears to be a widespread interest in the project of presenting to American playgoers many new personalities in stories worthy of their abilities. Mr. Kaplan is enthusiastic at the response of the exhibitors who read the advertising pages of the Moving Picture World:

"The reception given to our general announcement amazes me," said Mr. Kaplan. "I had thought that the exhibitors of America would be interested to know what was being done in Russia to further the art to which they are devoted, but I had no idea that the response would be so conclusive. My desk is literally covered with telegrams and letters asking for particulars regarding the system of release that we shall follow in presenting Russian Art films to the trade in America. To all inquiries I have replied that I don't know; the reception given to the first picture which we present on Broadway in a few weeks will determine our plan of action. In Russia we have a motto or saying: 'Be sure you're right, then go ahead.'

"The Russian Art Film Corporation intends to be right before it goes ahead. We have completed the tremendous task of sorting and assembling for American production the greater part of the fifty negatives which I brought from Moscow. From half a dozen the final choice will be made as to the initial production. We don't say it will be the best picture drama of the lot—in fact, we believe that it will not be—but we promise that it will be representative of the generally high level of the art as it has been developed in the famous Moscow theater of Russia. We shall let the critical authorities and the exhibitors who know what their patrons want tell us what our policy shall be."

PRINT OF FIRST KERRIGAN PICTURES.

Carl Anderson, president of Paralta Plays, and other officers and directors of that corporation have seen a run of the first print of J. Warren Kerrigan's production of Peter B. Kyne's "A Man's Man." They express their approbation in very enthusiastic terms.

"A Man's Man" will be released through the Triangle Distributing corporation in September. Prior to the release a special invitation showing will be made.

"OUTCAST" (Empire-All Star).

At a final viewing of their first release, "Outcast," the Empire All-Star Corporation, who are releasing through the Mutual Exchanges, feel quite sure they have a picture that is going to be something of a surprise to those who believe that plays have to be materially altered for screen showing.

Much of the scenery was taken from the Frohman storehouse and costumes were faithfully reproduced. Miss Ann Murdock, who is starring in the film version, herself long a

Scene from "Outcast" (Mutual).

Frohman star, declares herself to be more than pleased. She and David Powell, who is playing "Geoffrey," the same role he played when on tour with the original "Outcast" company, often discussed various little incidents that cropped up, and their memory helped to straighten out many mooted questions.

Dell Henderson, who directed, declares that he asks for nothing better than that all plays should adapt themselves to the screen as well as "Outcast" has. And so those who declare that a good story is equally good whether it be used for magazine, stage or screen use, win their point.

"FROM CACTUS TO KALE" (L-KO).

Under the supervision of Director General J. G. Blystone of L-Ko comedies, the release set for September 12, under the title of "From Cactus to Kale," is said to have developed some of the most ingenious ideas Director Noel Smith has presented in the L-Ko series. "From Cactus to Kale" is another angle of the art of getting laughs out of Western comedy of the swift-moving, slap-stick sort. Gladys Varden and Walter

Scene from "From Cactus to Kale" (L-Ko).

Stephens will be leaders in the fun-making, with Katherine Young, Harry Griffith and Bert Roach strong in the support. This release is expected to maintain the L-Ko average as one of the best of September issues.

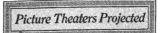

Picture Theaters Projected

CORONADO, CAL.—The Silver Strand theater, erected for John D. Spreckles and costing $80,000, has been opened to the public.

CORONA, L. I., N. Y.—Rex Theater Company, Inc., 138 Forty-first street, has plans by Gustave Erda, 826 Manhattan avenue, Brooklyn, for a one-story moving picture theater, 40 by 115 feet, to cost $12,000.

CLEVELAND, O.—Max Schoehtel has plans by George A. Grieble, 707 Park building, for a four-story moving picture theater and office building, 50 by 132 feet, to cost $150,000.

CLEVELAND, O.—Stork Amusement Company, 353 The Arcade, have plans by A. F. Jarowitz, Permanent building, for a one-story moving picture theater, 42 by 160 feet, to cost $50,000.

CLEVELAND, O.—C. A. Bressler, 1503 East 107th street, has plans by Nicola Petti, 307 Williamson building, for a one-story addition to his moving picture theater, to cost $8,000.

TOLEDO, O.—The Valentine theater will be converted into a moving picture house.

DELAWARE, OKLA.—Ralph Sullivan has purchased the interest of Lou Warwick in the Nusho theater. The new firm will be known as Green & Sullivan.

DUNCAN, OKLA.—Manager Burns of the Bungalow and Manager McDaniel of the Pastime have arranged to consolidate the two theaters.

FOSS, OKLA.—The Empress theater has been leased by Miss Alma Gilham and Miss Modelle Childress.

LONE WOLF, OKLA.—The interest of Goodson & Ziegler in the Elite theater has been purchased by Arthur Dirks.

TULSA, OKLA.—W. M. Smith has plans by George Kinkler for a modern theater building, to cost $150,000.

PHILADELPHIA, PA.—Temple Theater Company, incorporated with a capital of $10,000 by Frank J. Riera, Jr., H. Wolfender and Louis M. Stiles.

PITTSBURGH, PA.—The Ross Grove Amusement Company has been incorporated with a capital of $100,000 by J. Fred Allen, 9 Buffalo street, and C. E. Bronier and H. D. Montgomery, 1415 Union Bank building. The purpose of the company is to conduct amusement places of all kinds.

PHILADELPHIA, PA.—John E. Hardy has taken title to the two-story brick moving picture theater at 3716-18 Girard avenue, subject to a mortgage of $15,000. The property is situated on a lot 35.6 by 100 feet, and is assessed at $15,000.

COLUMBIA, S. C.—Broadway theater has awarded the contract to erect an addition to building, enlarge seating capacity, provide ladies' retiring room. Improvements to cost about $3,000.

CHATTANOOGA, TENN.—The Albert Amusement Company has been incorporated with a capital of $25,000 by W. S. Albert, W. V. Turley, O. F. Pennebaker, H. H. Miller and F. E. Stoops. The purpose of the company is to finance and operate theaters, amusement houses, parks, carnivals, etc.

CORSICANA, TEXAS.—J. B. Metcalf has the contract to erect an addition to a moving picture theater for M. L. Levine, to cost $35,000.

SANDERSON, TEXAS.—W. F. Bohlman will erect a moving picture theater and store building to replace structure lately damaged by fire. The new structure will be constructed of brick and concrete.

PETERSBURG, VA.—Century Amusement Company, Walter Sachs, president, will erect a fireproof theater, 50 by 136 feet.

RICHMOND, VA.—Sparklin & Childs, 215 Courtland street, Baltimore, are preparing plans for a one-story moving picture and vaudeville theater, 96 by 160 feet, to cost $250,000. The plans also include ten stores.

SEATTLE, WASH.—Pacific Theater Corporation has been organized with a capital of $100,000. The incorporators are: Newell & Miller, D. B. Worley and Thomas Wilkes.

KIMBALL, W. VA.—Charles K. Wagner, Catlettsburg, W. Va., has plans by W. H. St. Clair, Charleston, W. Va., for a three-story theater, 35 by 100 feet, to cost $30,000.

APPLETON, WIS.—The Appleton theater will be opened shortly.

BELOIT, WIS.—A commodious fireproof theater and business block to occupy the present Hamlin block is contemplated. The proposed new structure will cost about $100,000.

BERLIN, WIS.—J. B. McWilliams, who formerly conducted the Atlas and Gem theaters, has discontinued business.

LOOMIS, WIS.—A one-story town hall, 30 by 50 feet, to cost $3,000, to be erected here. Peter Kaufman, chairman town board.

MADISON, WIS.—T. H. Lunemann of Cedar Rapids, Ia., has purchased the interest of F. W. Fisher in the Majestic theater.

NEW RICHMOND, WIS.—The New Richmond theater is to be redecorated. T. J. McNally is the manager.

POYNETTE, WIS.—Lee Manly has assumed full control of the Cosmo theater, which he purchased recently.

RACINE, WIS.—Telligren & Brachman have leased the Baker block and will convert it into a theater. It will be used for moving pictures, vaudeville and the drama. The remodeled structure will be one of the finest theaters in the city. Work on the building will be commenced some time in October.

SUPERIOR, WIS.—Reopening of the Princess theater with the latest moving picture bookings will take place under the management of Frank C. Buckley, who recently took over the house.

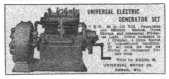

Trade News of the Week

GATHERED BY OUR OWN CORRESPONDENTS

Carry License Discussion to Supreme Court

In Dorchester, Mass., a Protest is Registered at the Erection of a Theater on Codman Square When Other Applications Were Turned Down.

By Richard D. Howe, 80 Summer Sereet. Boston, Mass.

BOSTON, MASS.—An appeal will be made to the Supreme Court of Massachusetts for a decision regarding the law giving the mayor of a city the right to issue licenses to erect moving picture theaters. This is the result of a bitter fight, which has been waged in the Codman Square district of Dorchester, a suburb of Boston, between the residents and city officials.

Applications have been made for three separate sites for motion picture theaters in this section of the city. Mayor James M. Curley of Boston refused two of the applicants, but the third application from a concern, of which Patrick Bowen, a former alderman, is at the head, seems practically assured a license. Mr. Bowen already has commenced construction of a beautiful theater in Codman Square without waiting for a permit from Mayor Curley. This action on his part has provoked determined resistance on the part of residents against the license being granted.

Rev. Alfred S. Isaacs, pastor of the Dorchester Temple Baptist Church, is leading the fight of the opposition against the erection of the theater. At a public hearing conducted in City Hall, Mr. Isaacs, among other things, charged "rotten politics" having a great deal to do with the partiality being shown Mr. Bowen.

The pastor declared he would produce witnesses that the petitioners for the license for the theater had secured the signatures through misrepresentation.

He stated the procedure had been first to present the petition in favor of the moving picture house and then, if the resident refused to sign it, he was visited a few days later by other men, with a petition for the construction of "a public building" in Codman Square. The "public building" petition, said Mr. Isaacs, was signed under the impression that it did not refer to the theater.

A petition bearing 1,600 signatures, many of them from school teachers, was presented by the remonstrants.

The mayor, after declaring that he was practically powerless to withhold the license—though he had done so on two previous occasions when moving picture theaters were projected in the same vicinity—he produced a ruling from Corporation Counsel Sullivan to support his claim. He withheld his decision on the matter.

Attorney Joseph F. Warren, one of the protestants, said he would take the matter to the Massachusetts Supreme Court for a ruling on the power of mayors of cities to grant or reject licenses for motion picture theaters.

W. S. Shapiro Now Heads Fox Exchange.

Boston, Mass.—An important change has taken place in the management of the Boston Fox office. William S. Shapiro has succeeded C. G. Kingsley, who has been transferred to the Indianapolis exchange

of the Fox organization to fill the vacancy left by Charles E. Phillips, who resigned and accepted a position with Harry Campbell, manager for Goldwyn in New England. Mr. Phillips was assistant under Mr. Campbell when the latter had charge of Fox's Hub office.

William S. Shapiro, the new Boston manager for Fox, has been connected with that organization for about a year and for several months was sales representative in Maine, New Hampshire and Vermont. Mr. Shapiro was very successful on the road, and when Charles Phillips was appointed manager of the Indianapolis office Mr. Shapiro was elected to be assistant to Manager Campbell. He temporarily took charge of the local office when Mr. Campbell joined the Goldwyn forces, but was soon relieved by C. G. Kingsley, who was sent from the Detroit exchange to take charge of the Boston office. Mr. Shapiro then appointed manager of the Fox Standard Productions at that time, but has now been given supreme control of the local exchange. He will also take charge of the standard pictures.

J. L. Reardon Will Open Boston Office for Selznick.

Boston, Mass.—J. Lester Reardon, formerly manager of the Vitagraph, V-L-S-E local exchange and owner of the Cross Street Orpheum, a moving picture theater in Somerville, Mass., has been appointed New England representative for Louis J. Selznick. Mr. Reardon will have entire charge of Selznick pictures in New England and plans shortly to open an office in this city. He is already on the lookout for a suitable location for an exchange. Mr. Reardon reports that he has been very successful since joining Mr. Selznick.

J. L. Levine Manager General Film Exchange.

Boston, Mass.—Jefferson D. Levine, one of the best known film men in New England, has been reappointed manager of the local office of the General Film Company. Mr. Levine was first given the managership of the Boston exchange last winter, when William H. Patten resigned the position, and was in charge up to a few months ago, when Frank Shirley, of the Wilkes-Barre, Pa., office was transferred to the local exchange. He continued with the General Film under Mr. Shirley and has now been given entire control of affairs in the Hub office.

Mr. Levine has been associated with the General Film for more than six years and during that time has been a valuable asset in the local exchange. He started as a poster clerk and was soon promoted to salesman. During his period on the road in New England, Mr. Levine established a lasting friendship with many of the most prominent exhibitors in his territory and

increased the sales of the company to a considerable extent. L. A. Hacking, at present a member of the Boston staff of the Vitagraph, who was formerly manager of the General in Boston, soon called him his assistant manager, in which capacity he continued until he was elected to take charge last winter, when William H. Patten left the organization.

Enlighten Thy Daughter Doing Splendidly.

Boston, Mass.—President Harry Segal, of the Supreme Photoplay Corporation, who is exploiting "Enlighten Thy Daughter" throughout New England, states that he has received heavy bookings and the big business seems sure to continue. He is also playing the picture on a percentage basis now, with two shows now on the road in different parts of New England, both of which are doing well.

Mr. Segal is being ably assisted by his publicity manager, Robert W. Cobe, who is getting out a great line of high-class literature and advance advertising matter on the picture. Mr. Cobe is a theatrical man of known ability, having been with several big companies on the road as press agent. He only recently returned from a flying trip through Maine, New Hampshire and Vermont. He states that his trip playing the picture on a percentage basis was entirely successful and he would have continued it but for the fact that he was called early in the draft and was forced to get back home and appear for examination for the new National Army.

Paramount Holds Picnic at Rocky Point.

Boston, Mass.—A number of the employees of the Paramount Boston office held a pleasant outing at Rocky Point, R. I., recently. The party traveled in an auto truck, covered with Paramount "onesheets," which attracted considerable attention enroute to the recreation grounds. The crowd enjoyed a perfect day.

Castle Square to Open With Pictures.

Boston, Mass.—Remodeling of the Castle Square theater, for many years the home of John Craig's stock company in this city, is going on rapidly, and it is planned to open the house in the near future, showing moving pictures only. Frank Ross, manager of the Lancaster theater on Lancaster street, has been selected to manage the new house. The Castle Square is situated in the South End and should prove a good location for a "movie" house, as there is no other house nearby. The shows will be run at popular prices.

Exhibitors See "Baby Mine."

Boston, Mass.—A large gathering of exhibitors and exchangemen flocked to the New England headquarters of the Goldwyn Pictures Monday, August 13, to view a private trade showing of "Baby Mine," the new Goldwyn production. It was the unanimous opinion of all present that "Baby Mine" is a wonderful picture. The new Goldwyn office is located at No. 40 Piedmont street, Boston.

Maritime News Letter

By Alice Fairweather, The Standard, St. John, N. B.

A Successful Woman Exhibitor.

MONCTON, N. B.—A successful woman theater manager is Mrs. R. H. Davidson, who for some years has been the proprietress of the Dreamland at Moncton, N. B. Mrs. Davidson has recently purchased the theater and quite a strip of land about it which makes her property come well up to the C. G. R. tracks. Later in the year she will renovate the house and improve it greatly in various ways.

As a woman Mrs. Davidson knows how to cater to an audience of women and children as well as to the many men who attend her theater. That she is fortunate in her choice of pictures is shown by the fact that her theater is so popular that special matinees are given for children or extra reels run for them on Saturdays. Mrs. Davidson uses Vitagraph, Metro, Famous Players, Mutual and other features.

Queens Rink to Be Picture Theater.

St. John, N. B.—There is to be another new theater in St. John, or rather an old building is made over into a theater. Robert Armstrong, who for many years managed the Queens rink, is turning that place of winter amusements into a motion picture theater. The theater will have a seating capacity of twelve hundred. The stage is to be very large so that special productions can be accommodated at dances given there. The admission price is to be five cents. No policy of pictures has as yet been decided upon.

F. G. Spencer Considers Building New Theater.

St. John, N. B.—F. G. Spencer of St John has leased the Hayden Gibson theater, Woodstock, N. B., one of the most up-to-date houses in the Maritime provinces. The new owner takes charge September 3. Mr. Spencer now controls the Lyric and Unique theaters, St. John; the Empress, Gem and Star in Amherst, N. S.; the Peoples and Prince Edward theaters in Charlottetown, Prince Edward Island; the Gem in Fredericton, the capital city of New Brunswick, and the Hayden-Gibson theater in Woodstock, N. B. The Princess (and, it is rumored, the Strand) in Truro, N. S. In fact, Mr. Spencer is a sort of theater king in the Maritime provinces. He also has in contemplation a new theater (The Strand) in St. John, to be built on King square. Accompanied by Mrs Spencer and several friends, Mr. Spencer is now on an automobile tour about Woodstock and that part of the Province. We do not know how many theaters he may gather in on his travels.

March-Golding Wedding Announced.

St. John, N. B.—There is a wedding which is of great interest to members of the theatrical fraternity in St. John, to take place in August. On the 19th of August Miss Kathleen Golding will be married to Reginald March, manager of the Specialty Import company (Pathe), St. John. Miss Golding is a niece of W. H. Golding of the Imperial theater and was for some time his secretary. Both have many friends in St. John who will wish them every happiness.

Notes Gleaned About St. John, N. B.

Visiting the Metro exchange in St. John, H. H. McArthur tells me that "The Great Secret" begins in the Academy at New Glasgow, shortly and at the Savoy, Glace Bay, the following week.

The Opera House, Pictou, N. S., used a Metro pictures and liked it so well that they sent for more. W. O. Wheaton is the manager there.

K. Keltie, of the Peoples theater, Yar-

Parcels Post Not a Perfect Film Carrier

Several Exchange Men in Washington Have Reason to Find Fault With Post Office Present Realities—Lost Film, Slack Service and Red Tape.

Clarence L. Linz, 622 Riggs Building, Washington, D. C.

WASHINGTON, D. C.—Washington's exchange managers are somewhat disappointed in the parcel post service, for as far as they are concerned it is not "panning out," according to a number of speakers at the meeting of the Washington Exchange Managers' Association, held recently. A number of cases were spoken of where the servic failed to come up to the expectations of the managers. One case in particular covered the loss of four reels of film. It was found where the reels had left the sending office and where they had failed to be received at the Washington office. Further than that, they are "just lost." This happened two months ago and nothing has been heard of the reels in all that time. They were not insured through the error of the sender of the films, so that the exchange cannot recover their value from the Government.

For the most part, the Washington exchanges have given up patronizing the parcel post service because of the lack of "service." Despite the difficulties incident to shipping through the express companies, the latter are far more satisfactory than the former. One of the chief complaints against the parcel post additional to the dissatisfaction over the loss and damage provisions is that if a shipment be refused by the consignee, instead of the postal authorities shipping it back immediately in conformity with the instructions contained on the top of the box, they hold it up and write the shipper of the circumstances and ask that stamps be sent to cover the cost of return transportation. This means a loss of time and consequent loss of rentals.

The exchange managers declare that there is too much idle talk and red tape involved in the parcel post business. Until it can be placed on the plane of the express companies, it is useless for them to avail themselves of the mails for the shipment of films. They declare that apologies do not make deliveries, and when films are lost or there is loss of time, it means money. If any serious difficulties arise between the exchanges and the express companies, it is a very easy matter to secure an adjustment through the New York offices of the companies and by appeal to the Interstate Commerce Commission. Nothing of this

mouth, N. B., is beginning to show Metro films, opening with Edmund Breeze in "The Weakness of Strength."

Harvey Watkins, superintendent for the Keith interests of Eastern Canada, paid one of his flying visits to St. John, N. B., lately.

Wm. Cranston, the Canadian manager for D. Griffith's spectacle, "Intolerance," and "The Birth of a Nation," was in St. John last week. "Intolerance" is booked at the Academy of Music, Halifax, for a three days' run.

C. A. Ganter, the general manager for Canada of the Mutual Film company, was in St. John recently on his way to Toronto. Mr. Ganter has been attending a meeting of the Mutual Managers' Association, which met recently in Chicago and was full of enthusiasm regarding the new policy of his company. With C. Kerr, the local manager of the Mutual, Mr. Ganter spent his few hours in St. John visiting some of the theater managers. It is hoped that some of the Mutual stars may be able to attend the convention.

W. H. Golding has just returned from a visit to Halifax where he found the Halifax exhibitors much interested in the coming convention in St. John and making preparations to attend.

nature can be accomplished where the mails are involved.

New Selznick Offices Chosen.

Washington, D. C.—The new Selznick offices, it is understood, will be located in the building at Eighth and G streets, northwest, which is being remodeled to make it desirable as a film exchange building. This property is controlled by Edmund K. Fox, who recently sent out announcements to the effect that he intended turning the building into one that would prove to be within the requirements of the new film regulations recently adopted by the Commissioners of the District of Columbia.

New Theater Planned for Richmond.

Richmond, Va.—Sparklin & Childs are now preparing plans for a large theater to be built in Richmond, Va., to cost about $200,000. The structure will measure 160 by 96 feet and be designed in the most up-to-date method.

Will Study Theater Advertising in South America.

Washington, D. C.—J. W. Sanger, an advertising investigator, counsel and writer of New York City, has just been chosen as the agent of the Bureau of Foreign and Domestic Commerce, of the Department of Commerce, to conduct an investigation of the advertising methods in vogue in Latin America. He will study all of the usual advertising methods in South America, paying particular attention, among other things, to electric sign and motion picture advertising. When the investigation is completed his conclusions and recommendations will appear in the form of a bulletin, and this bulletin, as well as his personal services in an advisory capacity when he returns to the United States, will be available to any American manufacturer or dealer who wishes to promote trade in Latin America by advertising. Any one interested in the forthcoming investigation desiring to consult with Mr. Sanger before he leaves for his trip may reach him at the Division of Commercial Agents, Room 405, Custom House, New York City.

Alaska Eager for Government Films.

Washington, D. C.—American motion picture films are meeting with fine favor in Alaska. As previously reported in this paper last fall the Bureau of Fisheries sent 100,000 feet of motion picture films to Saint Paul Island, Alaska. The films were selected chiefly with the view to affording recreation and instruction to the natives. They were rented and must be returned this summer. Agent Fassett, in charge of Saint Paul Island, in recommending recently that a new supply of pictures be sent to the island, stated that the value of the first lot has been almost immeasurable and that the natives would sacrifice anything to secure a continuance of the weekly entertainment afforded by the pictures. It appears that comedies, news and educational subjects are the most in demand. News pictorials on Saint Paul Island, it is said, need not be of current week's events to be of interest. Employees of the Naval radio station on Saint Paul Island have furnished the machines for showing the pictures and are willing to co-operate in this way another year. It is expected that arrangements will be made to send a second set of films for use during the coming winter season.

In answering advertisements, please mention The Moving Picture World

Philadelphia Season Opens With "Crisis"

Elaborate Arrangetemnts Made for the Opening of the Big Civil War Picture at the Garrick on August 13—Vacation Notes—Jottings.

By F. V. Armato, 144 N. Salford St., Philadelphia, Pa.

PHILADELPHIA, PA.—The opening of the new theatrical season will be marked by the first presentation beginning Monday afternoon, August 13, for an extended engagement, at the Garrick theater of the spectacular screen version of Winton Churchill's Civil War novel, "The Crisis." The picture will be shown in a manner to suggest Southern hospitality and Southern aristocracy. A double sextette of male and female voices will sing, and there will be music by a large orchestra. Miss Hazel Lee, as hostess, will receive visitors in the auditorium and will see to it that every one is made comfortable. An old Southern mammy will further lend variety to the suggestion of Southern solicitude, and she will be generous in her bestowal of temperance mint juleps. A cotton-picking scene will reveal a number of Southern darkies in plantation diversions. Thus it will appear that there will be much of a picturesque character in the exhibition.

Where They All Are Spending Hot Days.

Philadelphia.—Vacations and week-end trips are at present being indulged in by the prominent film men and exhibitors. During the hot spell Stanley W. Mastbaum enjoys the cool breezes at the St. Charles, Atlantic City. Abe Einstein we find cottaging at the shore with his family. Fred and Eugene Felt of the Locust and Belmont theaters, now have easy access to the Atlantic with the aid of their new Mercer car. Lewis J. Swaab and his son Mark are commuting daily to the shore. Mr. and Mrs. Herbert Effinger of the Strand spend the week-ends motoring from one seashore resort to another. Chas. Segal of the Apollo prefers to tour with his family in the vicinity of the mountains around Lancaster. J. M. Graver of the Liberty is taking his vacation and will visit the beautiful country parts up the state and then continue on his way through Maryland. Oscar Morgan of the Paramount was seen dancing on the Steel Pier in Atlantic City last week so naturally, it is easy to guess where he spends his idle hours. George Meeker of the World Film, although very busy, also likes the seashore. George Denhow, Fox; Robert Lynch, Metro; B. R. Thomas, Mutual; Max Milder, Peerless; Harry Schwalbe, Elec.; R. Garrick and Wm. Schenmaier, of the Interstate; A. Osborne, Pathe; Harold Rodner, Selznick, and Alen May of the Bluebird, are prominent exchange men, all of whom are owners of automobiles of various types which are busily engaged in running down to the nice cool spots near the shore or seeking the shade in the quiet of the mountains. Herbert Givens, Triangle; J. Hebrew, V-L-S-E; George Ames, Goldwyn; J. Buck, K-E-S-E, and Percy Bloch, of the General, are also prominent exchange managers who deserve their vacation whenever they may take them.

Royal Palace Theater Changes Hands.

Philadelphia.—Conveyance was made last week of the Royal Palace theater, 3716-18 Girard avenue, by Charles H. Colburn to John E. Hardy for a nominal sum, subject to a mortgage of $15,000. The property is a three-story brick structure on a lot 36.6 by 100 feet and assessed for $15,000.

Rialto Has New Organ.

Philadelphia, Pa.—The Rialto theater, under the direction of the Stanley Corporation, has installed a new organ. It is one of the finest of its style and it is the intention of the management not only to have special musical scores played

that accompany the big featured pictures, but talented artists will give special recitals at every performance. The new organ permits of a wide variety of imitations of various instruments and also has many other stops for voice and effects that make it complete and thoroughly enjoyable in tone and color.

A Fine Lecture on the Great War.

Philadelphia, Pa.—The Philadelphia public had an opportunity last week to hear M. Moncel Knecht deliver a lecture at Houston Hall, illustrated with moving pictures of the war direct from France. Mr. Knecht came to America with Viviani and Joffre, and is a member of the French Commission. He speaks English fluently and is an orator of rare ability. His subject was "The Effort of France and Her Colonial Empire and of Alsace-Lorraine." While the lecture was scheduled as one of the summer school entertainments of the University, the public was also welcome.

Chaplin Comedies on More Liberal Terms.

Philadelphia, Pa.—B. R. Tolmas, manager of the Mutual Exchange, announces that Chaplin Comedy releases in the future will be booked on a liberal arrangement in conjunction with their program.

Western Pennsylvania Theater Jottings.

Philadelphia.—M. Stiefel has made some improvements at the Lafayette theater on Kensington avenue, which included a new crystal fibre screen and two Powers' 6B machines.

Bryn Mawr.—The Bryn Mawr theater after extensive alterations and remodeling at the cost of $6,000, will reopen about Sept. 1 under the new management of W. H. Hassinger. A Kimball organ will also be installed as one of the many features of the house.

Allentown, Pa.—The new Strand theater, which will open here on September 1, will have a seating capacity of 1,000 and be of modern construction throughout. A pipe organ screen will be included in the up-to-date equipment.

York, Pa.—The Jackson theater here is reported to be prepared for their opening during the early part of September. The theater is of the 1,000-seat variety, handsomely furnished and of the best construction. R. C. Jackson & Co., of Lebanon, Pa., who are the owners of this house, also control a chain of theaters in this vicinity.

Charles A. Calehuff and F. R. Bloomfield will shortly start together for an extended business trip throughout the state.

Baltimore News Letter

By J. M. Shellman, 1902 Mount Royal Terrace, Baltimore, Md.

Special Showing of "The Slacker."

BALTIMORE, MD.—Through the courtesy of Charles E. Ford, manager of Ford's Opera House, arrangements were made by Harry Cohen, the live-wire Metro representative from the Washington office, for a private screening of "The Slacker" on Wednesday afternoon, August 15, at four P. M. Mr. Ford went to a great deal of trouble to decorate his playhouse with the national and state colors for the occasion and 1,500 invitation cards were sent out to the British and American recruiting officers and to the state, city and national officials, the greater majority of them being accepted. Special music was furnished by E. V. Cupero and an especially arranged orchestra. Mayor Preston and

his staff and many other notables attended and short speeches of a patriotic nature were made by the mayor and his former secretary, Robert E. Lee, during the intermission.

J. J. Hartlove's Big Balihoo.

Baltimore, Md.—To especially call attention to the dare devil of the screen, Tom Mix, in "Movie Stunts," on Thursday, August 9, J. J. Hartlove, manager of the Crescent theater, 1110-12 South Charles street, engaged Indian Joe and his two cowboys to appear in the lobby of the theater in their full Western regalia to balihoo the performance. The lobby was decorated with pelts, skins and banners. Five thousand handbills were issued and distributed and Mr. Hartlove states during the afternoon performance 1,000 people attended the show.

Actress Marries in Baltimore.

Baltimore, Md.—Baltimore was again the scene of a romantic marriage on Saturday, August 11, when Sarah V. Fox, of the "Follies of 1917" company, was married to Robert M. Wilson, a hero of the battle of the Marne, whose home is in Denver, Colo. The romance began shortly after Mr. Wilson returned to the United States last year, and met Miss Fox in Philadelphia.

Big Civic Auditorium Planned.

Baltimore, Md.—According to the Civic Center plans, which are now being drawn up for Baltimore, a vast municipal auditorium, which will have a seating capacity of about 14,000 people and be a one-story building, with architectural embellishments, is to be erected on the ground extending from Gay street back to the Fallsway. It is planned to have entrances both at the front and back and at the side, near the center, a smaller building will be built to seat about 3,000 people for smaller affairs.

Superba Is Improving.

Baltimore, Md.—David Braun, proprietor of the Superba theater, 908 Columbia avenue, which has a seating capacity of about 400, has had this playhouse closed for the past two weeks for alterations and improvements. A concrete floor is being placed in the theater, which is being generally renovated.

York Theater to Open.

York, Pa.—It is now announced by Professor Edward Gentzler, of this city, that he will open his East Lyric theater, which has a seating capacity of about 300, on September 1. This playhouse has been closed during the summer months and when reopened the Universal program will be used.

C. W. Sutton in Baltimore.

Baltimore, Md.—C. W. Sutton, proprietor of the Opera House in this city, visits Baltimore during the week of August 11 and called on his friends at the exchanges. While there Mr. Sutton booked "Pershing in France" for his theater.

New Theater at Buckhannon.

Buckhannon, W. Va.—About six weeks ago H. B. Young, of this city, opened up his new Main Street theater, which has seating capacity of about 500. It is stated to be a very pretty theater.

Business Notes.

Baltimore, Md.—I. Berman, proprietor of Berman's theater, Baltimore street and High, has had his house closed for several weeks and when opened will be improved.

P. Oletsky, manager of the Baltimore Film Exchange, is now in Atlantic City enjoying a vacation in his cottage.

M. Seigel, Bluebird representative in Baltimore, is now enjoying the sea breeze on his vacation at the Atlantic Hotel in Atlantic City.

Barnett Freeman, Universal representative, has just returned from a vacation which he enjoyed immensely.

William F. Stone, treasurer of the Maryland Censor Board, has been confined to his home since Saturday, August 11, with an attack of the measles.

Miss Rose Wood, of this city, is reported to have gone to New York to join the company of players supporting Marie Doro in photoplay presentations.

Harry Woods, manager of the Garden theater, on Lexington street at Park avenue, in the heart of the shopping district, has innovated the idea of starting his performances at noon in order to give the shoppers a chance to view the full show by 4 p. m., which consists of vaudeville and pictures.

North Carolina News Items

By D. M. Bain, Wilmington, N. C.

Savings Bank in a Picture Theater.

RALEIGH, N. C.—A freak picture show, the first of its kind probably in the country, will soon be seen in Raleigh. The Superba, operated by F. L. Allen, is closed for alterations and when re-opened will have built right in the center of its large lobby a savings bank—one of the both day and night variety.

Narrow alleyways on either side of the miniature bank building will furnish entrance and exit to the theater proper in the rear. In order to minimize the space occupied by the bank the vaults will be constructed underground, immediately beneath the bank, a narrow spiral stairway leading to the underground strong boxes of the banking institution.

The Superba has a very advantageous location on the busiest block in town, and this ingenius arrangement was the only method by which the day and night bank could obtain a coveted stand.

Wilmington's Royal Closes Summer Policy.

Wilmington, N. C.—The Royal theater, now presenting super-picture productions, will be closed for one week after August 25 and will reopen on Labor Day, playing vaudeville and tabloid musical comedy attractions, the super-productions after that date being transferred to the Grand theater, on North Front street. Both theaters are operated by the Howard and Wells interests.

President Warner at Wrightsville Beach.

Wilmington, N. C.—George C. Warner, of the Ideal theater, Columbia, S. C., is spending the week at Wrightsville Beach with Mrs. Warner and children. Mr. Warner is president of the South Carolina Exhibitors' Association and states that a large delegation of exhibitors from the Palmetto state will attend the joint convention at Ocean View, Va.

IN PITTSBURGH.

Harry Lande Now Controls Quality Film.

Pittsburgh, Pa.—Max W. Herring has disposed of his interest in the Quality Film exchange, 404-406 Ferry street, Pittsburgh, to Harry A. Lande, who is now sole owner of the concern. Mr. Herring announces that he is continuing in the film business and has already secured a number of subjects. He will announce his location in the near future.

Lyric at Uniontown to Be Handsomer.

Uniontown, Pa.—The Lyric theater, Uniontown, Pa., is being extensively remodeled by the owners, the Penn Amusement company. A handsome new front is being installed and the interior redecorated and newly equipped. Manager McCloskey states that the Imp theater, conducted by the same company, will be closed in the near future.

Pittsburgh Revises Picture Theater Tax

Legislative Committee of the League Gets Ordinance of 1913 on Licenses for Theaters Revised—More Favorable Requirements Secured.

From Pittsburgh News Service, 6104 Jenkins Arcade, Pittsburgh, Pa.

PITTSBURGH, PA.—A revision of the tax on moving picture theaters in Pittsburgh has been secured through the efforts of the Motion Picture Exhibitor's League legislative committee, which has been finally successful in having the 1913 ordinance fixing the license tax or fee for all public amusements amended favorably.

The new ruling permits all theaters having a seating capacity of less than 450 to charge a maximum price of 30 cents admission without any additional tax. Heretofore all theaters were compelled to pay a license of $35 per month, irrespective of their seating capacity, provided they at any time charged more than 10 cents admission. In other words, a house having a seating capacity of 500 or less and paying a license of $10 per month would have to pay $35 per month if at any time they charged more than 10 cents admission. A house of 300 seats, which paid $15 per month license, would likewise have to pay $35, provided there was an admission price of more than 10 cents.

As the ordinance reads now the seat grading is as follows: Two hundred or less, $10; 300 or less, $15; over 300, $35, provided that when the seating capacity of the house exceeds 450 seats the maximum charge of admission does not exceed 30 cents. If the maximum charge exceeds 30 cents admission they shall pay a license of $35.

In commenting upon the new tax schedule, Secretary G. A. Sahner, of the Pittsburgh Exhibitors' League, said that the picture theaters have been paying over two-thirds of the city licenses of amusements against the large theaters, baseball, skating, billiards, pool, carnivals, circuses, etc. He points out that all of these taxes come in direct competition with the picture business.

John McAleer Heads Pittsburgh F. I. L. M. Club.

Pittsburgh, Pa.—John McAleer, manager of the Independent Film exchange, local office of the Universal, has been elected president of the Pittsburgh F. I. L. M. Club, succeeding F. C. Burhans, who recently resigned. The choice of Mr. McAleer to head this thriving organization of the exchange men of the city meets with much approval, as he is exceptionally well fitted for the work. Mr. McAleer has been prominently identified in the past with various movements here, having been very active in the Pittsburgh Screen Club, and a year ago led the successful fight against a threatened censor ship law in West Virginia. Although the F. I. L. M. Club has been organized only about a year it has proven of great value to exhibitor and exchanges alike, and under President McAleer's able guidance the organization is expected to accomplish still greater things in bringing about harmony in the trade.

"Jack and the Beanstalk" Pleases Exhibitors.

Pittsburgh, Pa.—The notable fairy film, "Jack and the Beanstalk," the first juvenile on the Fox Standard program, was shown before a large and appreciative gathering of the trade on Sunday, August 11, at the Olympic theater. Fifth avenue. Pittsburgh. About four hundred exhibitors and their friends were present. A well-attended trade showing of the big William Fox production, "The Honor System," was also held recently at the Olympic.

Press Sponsor for Battle Film.

Penn avenue, Pittsburgh, one of the city's leading legitimate houses, will open an engagement of Pathe's big war film, "The Battle of the Ancre," the week of August 27. The showing will be under the auspices of the Pittsburgh Press, which paper will spend over $4,000 for publicity in various forms. The proceeds will be donated to the Regimental Fund.

"Fatal Ring" Serial's First Showing.

Pittsburgh, Pa.—The Pittsburgh Pathe exchange on Sunday, August 5, gave a very successful trade showing of the first three episodes of the new Pathe serial, "The Fatal Ring," featuring Pearl White, at the Liberty theater, East End. One of the latest Luke comedies was also shown with good effect. The Pathe exchange announces some of the first run bookings on the new serial as follows: Sheridan Square theater, East Liberty, Pittsburgh, three days; Strand theater, Erie, three days; Orpheum theater, Altoona, three days; Mercer Square, Grove City; Clarksburg; Thomas, Sharon; Colonial, Farrell; Shapiro, Mt. Union, and the Grand, Bradford.

Harris P. Wolfberg Opens More Offices.

Pittsburgh, Pa.—Right on the heels of the announcement that the First National has opened an office in Pittsburgh, and that additional offices will be opened in Cleveland and Cincinnati, it is learned that Mr. Wolfberg has purchased the rights to the Hall Caine masterpiece, "The Deemster," for Missouri and Kansas. This necessitates the establishment of offices in St. Louis and Kansas City. Mr. Rhea Johnson, who has covered the western Pennsylvania territory for the Wolfberg exchange for the past six months, has gone to Cleveland, O., to open a new office for Mr. Wolfberg. Mr. Johnson will be the Cleveland branch manager.

H. E. Stahler of the Wolfberg Attractions publicity department, is on a two weeks' trip over the eastern end of the territory. He will spend some time in Philadelphia, where "The Crisis" opens for a three weeks' run at the Garrick theater.

Morris Berger Ill.

Pittsburgh, Pa.—It is with much regret that the many friends of Morris Berger, of the Boulevard Film company, Pittsburgh, learn that he is ill with scarlet fever in a hospital at Detroit, Mich. Mr. Berger was stricken while on a vacation trip motoring around the Great Lakes.

John Isaac Completing a Theater at Lyndora.

Lyndora, Pa.—A new theater is being completed at Lyndora, Pa., by John Isaac, who announces that it will be ready for opening about September 1. The house is an attractive one, seating 350, and will offer high-class feature productions.

Pitt Theater Closes for Redecorating.

Pittsburgh, Pa.—The Pitt theater, Penn avenue and Seventh street, Pittsburgh, after a successful repeat run of "The Bar Sinister," on August 11 was closed for several weeks for extensive renovating and redecorating. It is expected to reopen this house of big features about Labor Day.

Joseph Spero Joins Specialty Road Staff.

Pittsburgh, Pa.—Joseph Spero, a pioneer film man of New York and formerly special representative for the Mutual, has joined the road staff of the Specialty Film company, Pittsburgh.

Loew Secures Two Big Ohio Theaters

The Stillman in Cleveland and the Valintine in Toledo, Each Seating About 1,500, Change Hands—Adolph Zukor Said to Be Interested.

From M. A. Malaney, 218 Columbia Bldg. Cleveland, O.

CLEVELAND, OHIO.—Marcus Loew, the Eastern theatrical man, has invaded Ohio. He has acquired control of two of the largest and finest theaters in the state, and it is reported that he is looking for more.

The theaters are the new Stillman in Cleveland and the Valintine in Toledo. Each seats about 1,500 and are among the most beautiful theaters in the United States.

It is understood that Loew is associated with Adolph Zukor in these enterprises. Mr. Zukor has been in Cleveland twice within the last month and has conferred with Manager Emanuel Mandelbaum of the Stillman, who retains his interest in the theater and will continue to manage it. The bookings, however, will be under the supervision of Mr. Loew.

The details of the Valintine deal have not as yet been given out, but it is reported that Indianapolis capital is represented in the new deal. The theater now is undergoing remodeling and alterations and will be opened soon.

High class pictures will be shown in both theaters, arrangements having been made to book many of the popular stars.

Goldwyn Offices Formally Opened.

Cleveland, O.—The Goldwyn offices have been formally opened on the fourth floor of the Standard theater building, Cleveland, where H. A. Bandy is in charge. The Goldwyn pictures have been booked in the Temple theater, Toledo, and also in a downtown Cleveland theater, the name of which cannot be announced publicly at present.

Sam Deutsch Adds to Sun Theater.

Cleveland, O.—Sam Deutsch, manager of the Sun theater, Cleveland, arrived back in town this week from a three weeks' trip by auto through the east, and immediately set to work to rebuilding his theater.

The Sun will be enlarged by three hundred seats and an elegant marquis will adorn the entrance. The house also will be redecorated.

General Film Offices Will Be Moved.

Cleveland, O.—The General Film company, after having been located at 1022 Superior avenue, East, Cleveland, for over five years, will move about August 20 to the fourth floor of the Standard Theater building on Prospect avenue, right in the heart of the film district.

Manager Flynn expects to take along a black cat which wandered into the exchange a few weeks ago and made itself at home among the posters advertising Essanay's "Black Cat" features. Flynn says all he has to do to draw business into the office is to allow the cat to sit in the doorway for a few minutes. It's a great mascot.

Cincinnati News Letter

From Kenneth C. Crain, 307 First-National Bank, Cincinnati, O.

Cincinnati News Weekly Company Expands.

CINCINNATI, O.—The Cincinnati Motion Picture Co., which has for five years been producing a regular news weekly covering the Cincinnati territory, besides engaging successfully in commercial moving picture work, is branching out into other cities. Clarence Runey is head of the company. Ira J. Hoffman, who has been with the company for some time, has gone to Louisville, Ky., and Indianapolis

to open up branches in those two cities and will be permanently located in one or the other, with extra cameramen working from the two offices to cover happenings of interest in the vicinity of those cities.

Goldwyn Gives Private Showing.

Cincinnati, O.—Manager C. C. Hite, in charge of the Goldwyn offices in Cincinnati, held the first of his private exhibitions recently at the Nordland Plaza theater of "Baby Mine." Special music added to the enjoyment of the performance, and the quality of the picture created a good impression among exhibitors who saw it. "Baby Mine" and other pictures are being booked by Mr. Hite for early showing in and around Cincinnati.

The Walnut's New Policy Making Good.

Cincinnati, O.—A successful week's engagement of a new Artcraft release, "Down to Earth," shows well for the new policy and the new pictures at the Walnut theater. As recently announced, the Walnut will run Artcraft-Paramount pictures for the coming year, admission 25 cents for the lower floor and 15 cents for the balcony. Manager Libson found it rather difficult when the Walnut was first turned over to pictures to get the crowds. Now they are not only coming, but are paying the highest regular scale of prices of any picture theater in Cincinnati.

The Faurot at Lima Makes Improvements.

Lima, O.—The Faurot theater, Lima's leading house, is being extensively remodeled, and when it is reopened for business, which will be the latter part of the month, it will be greatly improved. The chief change being made is the removal of the pillars which formerly obstructed the view on the lower floor. A new floor is also being constructed, and new decorations will freshen up the interior so that it will look like a new building. The work has been under way for some time and is being pushed rapidly in order to reach completion at an early date.

New Demand for Educational-Advertising Films.

Canton, O.— Educational-advertising films produced by various manufacturers for the purpose of showing how their goods are manufactured and used are coming into favor for a purpose which should be very beneficial to all concerned. Inquiries have been received by several local manufacturers who have produced such films asking that prints be loaned to the industrial department of the International Y. M. C. A. which desires to exhibit them at the various army cantonments soon to be opened. The films will be transferred from camp to camp by representatives of the Y. M. C. A. without cost to the producers, so that there will be no trouble or expense connected with the work, and the manufacturers have indicated their entire willingness to meet the situation, both from patriotic motives and for their own benefit.

Toledo Men Incorporate New Theater Company.

Toledo, O.—The Valintine Theater company has been incorporated by a number of local men, including Charles K. Friedman, Jacob Kruckman, George E. Dixon and Mark M. Gates, to construct and operate a large moving picture house. The company has a capital stock of $30,000.

Louisville, Ky.—J. G. Conner, representing the Indianapolis Mutual office, was in Louisville recently and closed a deal with L. J. Dittmar of the Majestic Amusement company to run the Mutual feature, "Souls in Pawn," featuring Gail Kane. This is the first time that a Mutual feature or anything other than a Paramount release has been shown in the Majestic, and is quite a feather in Mr. Conner's cap, and also speaks well for the picture.

Buffalo News Letter

By Joseph A. McGuire, 152 N. Elmwood Street, Buffalo, N. Y.

"Italian Battlefront" Pictures at Fort Niagara.

BUFFALO, N. Y.—As a compliment to Col. Samuel W. Miller, commander of the reserve officers' training camp at Fort Niagara, "The Italian Battlefront War Pictures" were shown in the open recently before the members and officers at the camp. William Moore Patch, in charge of the pictures, sent a special set of films the films have been the attraction at the Teck Theater, Buffalo. A guest at the opening night at the Teck was General Guglielmotti, a hero of the battles in the Trentino and on the Carso plateau. As he entered the box and removed his high military cap, the house, filled with local Italians, arose to greet him. An augmented orchestra played the Italian national hymn.

Among Western New York Film Men.

Buffalo.—A. W. Root, a former vaudeville agent, has taken over the Palace Theater, Olean, N. Y.

P. N. Zimmerman, of Buffalo, traveling representative of the Bluebird Photoplays, has returned from a motor trip to New York City and is spending two weeks at his cottage at Lake Chautauqua.

F. F. Peters, Hornell exhibitor, is summering at Cuba Lake. Mr. Peters and G. H. Christoffers, manager of the Victor Film, Buffalo, recently enjoyed the scenic beauties of Niagara Falls.

Mr. Hilkert, of Geneva, N. Y., is negotiating for the Johnson opera house property at Seneca Falls. He is interesting Buffalo capitalists to erect a $25,000 moving picture theater on the site.

William L. Sherry and H. F. Brink have several Western New York towns where they secured a fine lot of contracts for the new Star series of the Artcraft and Paramount services. The Buffalo headquarters of these services at 145 Franklin street have been enlarged, giving more office and shipping room.

The Colonial Theater, Rochester, is being remodeled.

Harry Marsey and Al Becker, Buffalo film men, have returned from a motor trip to New York.

A. J. Sardino, former manager of the Savoy Theater and later lessee of the Regent, both of Syracuse, has taken over the Hippodrome moving picture theater, that city. The house is being remodeled and redecorated.

It is said several of the Rochester exhibitors will use features daily after September 1, and advance their admission from five to ten cents.

F. S. Hopkins, manager of the Bluebird Photoplays, Buffalo, will also handle the Alice Howell Comedies for New York State.

"The bookings of these comedies are very satisfactory," said Mr. Hopkins.

Veribest Pictures, Inc., Moves Its Offices.

Buffalo, N. Y.—The Veribest Pictures, Inc., of which George R. Matthews is Buffalo manager, has moved to 47 West Swan street, this city. The location is central and on the first floor.

Ben Fitzer Will Travel for Goldwyn.

Buffalo, N. Y.—George A. Hickey, manager of the Goldwyn Distributing Corporation, Buffalo, has engaged Ben Fitzer as traveling representative of that concern. Mr. Fitzer has been with the Universal and the Artcraft.

Fire in Booth of Amherst Street House.

Buffalo, N. Y.—A film at a moving picture theater at 367 Amherst street, Buffalo, recently burned. The house was emptied quickly. Charles E. Reiner, the proprietor, put out the blaze in the operating booth before the arrival of the firemen. The damage totaled $200. J. C. Koons, the operator, had his hair singed.

STRAY NOTES FROM MIDWEST.

By Frank H. Madison.

Fred Solomon Heads Omaha General Film Office.

Omaha, Neb.—Fred Solomon has been made manager of the local office of the General Film company, succeeding C. W. Taylor, who has been made manager of the Omaha office of the Art-drama exchange. Solomon has been with the General Film company for six years, excepting the time that he was with the V-L-S-E and Mutual.

Theater Notes from Wisconsin.

Madison, Wis.—H. H. Linneman, of Cedar Rapids, Iowa, has purchased the Majestic theater from F. W. Fischer, who has conducted it for the past year.

Lone Rock, Wis.—L. J. Egan and Mr. Brophy have purchased the Harriet Opera House here from Lew Plus.

Milwaukee, Wis.—The Griffith spectacle, "Intolerance," is booked for a late summer date at the Davidson theater.

Superior, Wis.—The Savoy theater has changed to an exclusive policy, using Fox features three days and Triangle service for four days.

IN ONTARIO.

Camp Borden Theater Makes Assignment.

Toronto.—The Summer Theatres Company, Limited, operating the Strand theatre, Camp Borden, Ontario, has made an assignment to J. P. Langley, McKinnon building, Toronto, for the benefit of creditors. This theatre is a huge wooden structure seating 2,400 people, and it has been the principal place of amusement in Camp Borden, Canada's chief military camp. Last year, when there were as many as 34,000 troops in the camp, the Strand did a big business, but this season the number of soldiers in training here has dropped to a few thousand. The theater building was cut in half, but even then it proved too large for the patronage.

Toronto Visitors Will See Best Pictures

Local Theaters Have Prepared Excellent Programs for the Visitors to the Big National Fair at the End of August—Some of the Offerings.

By W. M. Gladish, 1263 Gerrard St., Toronto, Ont.

TORONTO, Ont.—As forecasted in Moving Picture World, many Toronto exhibitors, individually, have picked upon the weeks of August 27 and September 3 for the presentation of special attractions to form an opening of the season of 1917-1918.

Manager Clarence Robson of the Strand theater announces that he will have "Beware of Strangers," the seven-reel special, as his big attraction for the week of September 3. He has been changing programs three times each week during the summer months, but with the presentation of this subject he will return to his fall and winter policy of only one show for the week.

Manager Robson has just reorganized his orchestra, which is one of the best in Toronto. The new leader is Ernest Knaggs of the Toronto Symphony Orchestra and the various members are solo-musicians of that orchestra. Robson has signed up his music crew, for twelve months.

The Park theatre, Lansdowne avenue and Bloor street, one of the largest outlying houses here, is being painted and redecorated in anticipation of an "opening" about September 1.

Harry Pomeroy, manager of the Photodrome, is proceeding with the establishment of a dance hall, cabaret and model barber shop in connection with his theater for the coming fall and winter seasons.

These, and other "openings" already reported by the Toronto correspondent, will occur simultaneously with the holding of the annual Canadian National Exhibition in Toronto when the city will be crowded with thousands of out-of-town visitors.

"Nation" and "Intolerance" Pictures Still Doing Well.

Toronto.—B. S. Courtney of Toronto, formerly general manager of the Basil Film Corporation, has arrived in France as a lieutenant in a Canadian Forestry Battalion, according to a statement by William Cranston, the new general manager of the company. This corporation controls the Canadian rights for the "Birth of a Nation" and "Intolerance," both of which are still doing big business in the Dominion.

The very first time that the "Birth of a Nation" has been shown under canvas was at Trenton, Ontario, on August 2, 3 and 4, when it was presented in the airdrome there. This airdrome has a seating capacity for one thousand persons. Incidentally, there is only one theater building in Trenton and the Nation film had never been screened there before.

A second print of the "Birth of a Nation" has been doing one and two-night stands in the Canadian West, while the one Canadian print of "Intolerance" has been screened in various Western cities

during the mid-summer fairs. It was shown at Regina during the week of July 23 and at Saskatoon during the week of July 30. It was the attraction at the Walker theater, Winnipeg, during the week of August 13. The next stop will be made at Sault Ste. Marie, after which it will come back to Toronto for the two weeks starting August 25.

According to Manager Cranston, both the "Nation" and "Intolerance" pictures are good for at least another year in Canada. Mr. Cranston says that "Intolerance" has been making from $300 to $400 a day at the annual fairs in the Canadian West.

A Power's traveling outfit has been added to the mechanical equipment of the Western "Birth of a Nation" company. This was found necessary, says Mr. Cranston, because in many cases the projection machines in local theaters were in such a condition that the print was becoming damaged.

Roma Theater at Kitchener Damaged by Fire.

Toronto.—Fires in moving picture theaters in Ontario are not very frequent. The Roma theater, Kitchener, Ont., was rather seriously damaged by flames, however, on the night of August 7. The loss is estimated by L. Longo, owner of the theater, at $5,000. The fire started from unknown causes. The business at this theater had been very good all summer and the blaze will cause considerable inconvenience.

Banquet Held to Honor Ben Cronk.

Toronto, Ont.—The film people of Calgary were apparently glad to see Ben Cronk, for four years manager of the Allen theater there, leave for Toronto to assume the management of the new Allen theater here. They were not happy to lose Cronk, but they rejoiced because he was going to a big job. They liked him so well that they held a farewell banquet in his honor, the attendance at this celebration consisting of eighty-three exhibitors, exchange men, Shriners and others. They presented Ben with a valuable gold watch and a club bag, and before they were through they had said all kinds of nice things about him. Mr. Cronk has arrived in Toronto to take charge of the brand new house which is scheduled to open early in September.

Many Pictures Show Glories of Ontario.

Toronto, Ont.—One of the many features provided by the Ontario Government for the Canadian National Exhibition, Toronto, August 25 to September 8, will be a demonstration of the educational moving picture service. Director S. C. Johnston has had a number of cameramen out for some time taking pictures of Ontario's experimental farms, prison farms and other institutions. Among various other views will be those showing fruit-growing, mining, forestry, protection and road-making within the Province. Pictures showing the new farms in Northern Ontario of returned war veterans will be exhibited. One whole wing of the Educational Building has been turned into a moving picture theater for this demonstration.

More Business Notes.

Toronto, Ont.—Super Features, Limited, Toronto, reports record business in Canada for "The Whip." This picture has had two long runs at the Grand, Toronto, the second of which extended through the month of July.

Charles Stevens, general manager of Super Features, Limited, has purchased the entire Canadian rights for the seven-reel feature, "On Trial."

Atlanta's Rialto Reopens With Fairbanks

Will Be Suitable House for Goldwyn, Artcraft, Paramount Offerings, and Promises Many a Treat to Atlantans During Coming Season.

By Alfred M. Beatty, 43 Copenhill Ave., Atlanta, Ga.

ATLANTA, GA.—The Rialto theater, which has been undergoing extensive repairs, opened Monday morning, August 13, under the joint direction of Jake Wells and John Q Evins. The opening of this house inaugurates the plan of Mr. Welles and Mr. Evins to make Atlanta the home of the most superior motion picture theater from every standpoint.

All of the Goldwyn pictures are to be shown with all of the productions supervised or directed by D. W. Griffith, Cecil B. DeMille and Thomas H. Inc. The Rialto will be the home of the Paramount stars. Mr. Wells and Mrs. Evins have seen to it that the already beautiful theater has been completely renovated and a number of

important changes made.

The initial attraction this week is Douglas Fairbanks in "Down to Earth."

Joe Marientette, of the Goldwyn Film Co., spent several days this week in Nashville, Tenn., among theaters.

The Strand theater last week played Marguerite Clark in "The Amazons" the entire week. This theater is now under the management of Jake Wells and John Evins, who announce the Strand will in future be a theater playing a feature all week. Crowds are being turned away, the house playing to capacity. This is something unusual for Atlanta theaters for quite a while.

Nashville Elite Opens as Feature House

Crescent Amusement Company Overhauls Big Theater and Changes Program Service from Short Reels to Features—Higher Admission Asked.

By J. L. Ray, 1614 Stahlman Building, Nashville, Tenn.

NASHVILLE, TENN.—The Elite theater reopened its doors to the public on Monday, August 13, after extensive repairs and a complete renovation. Prior to its closing the Elite was one of the most popular of the few remaining five-cent houses on Fifth avenue, Nashville's leading amusement center, but with the reopening there comes into existence a new high-class feature house.

Owing to a wreck, the train bearing the initial program from Atlanta did not reach the city until many hours behind schedule time, and the formal opening was postponed until nine o'clock in the evening, by which time a large crowd had gathered at the doors.

The Crescent Amusement company, which operates the Elite, played a trump card in offering Marguerite Clark for the initial dates in the late Paramount production, "The Amazons." Douglas Fairbanks in his newest Artcraft subject is booked for the second week; both of these films run the entire six days, which in itself is an item worthy of mention in this city. Every indication points to the complete success of the Elite as a permanent feature house, it having followed the course of the Crescent and Fifth Avenue theaters in changing from short lengths to features.

In addition to an unusually attractive decorative scheme on the walls and ceiling of both auditorium and corridor, an immense typhoon fan has been placed over the entrance, augmented by a battery of wall buzzers placed at intervals of twelve feet along both sides, and the customary rotary fans suspended from the ceiling. This makes the Elite without doubt one of the coolest houses in the state.

The semi-direct lighting system is employed, which gives just the proper amount of light for easy access in and out of the aisles, without impairing the vision of the projected picture. An attractive feature of the house, which was not formerly in effect, is the use of white washable seat covers, which adds much to the comfort of the patrons, especially in summer weather. The floor has been covered with a heavy battleship linoleum, and the partitions at the back of the aisles upholstered with a durable leatherette fabric. All doors have been handsomely regrained, and heating apparatus gilded.

The large player orchestra has been removed from near the entrance and a modern Melville Clark Apollo player piano installed at the screen end, and is operated by hand during performances. This instrument was invented by a Nashville man and distributed by a local piano concern, the F. A. Leatherman company.

Wilder Theater Opens.

Chattanooga, Tenn.—The Wilder theater, located at the military camp at Chickamauga Park, was opened to the public on August 12. This theater has a seating capacity of 3,500, being largely for the purpose of furnishing the soldiers amusement. It is under the management of Will S. Albert of the Albert Amusement Company.

Majestic Rejoices at Open Booking.

Memphis, Tenn.—The Majestic Amusement Company, operating the Majestic theaters numbers one and two in this city, recently announced through the press that it was strongly in favor of the open booking plan, setting out its many advantages to the public, and stating that the most famous productions of the day would be brought to its houses at once. Among the larger features to come to the Majestic No. 2 in the near future are William Farnum in "A Tale of Two Cities," Alice Joyce in "Womanhood," etc., with an elaborate assortment of the most popular features, starring Theda Bara, Clara Kimball Young, Douglas Fairbanks, Wm. S. Hart, Valeska Suratt, Geo. M. Cohan, Mary Pickford, etc. The Majestic company is covering a wide field in Memphis, both from a standpoint of quality service and in the number of patrons it reaches through its four houses.

The Lincoln to Reopen.

Nashville, Tenn. — Nashville's negro population will be afforded another high-class amusement house in the Lincoln theater, which will be reopened on August 27 with moving pictures. This theater has been opened and closed a number of times during the past several years, its doors having been closed the last time since early spring. William Hartman, owner of the house, will run it as a moving picture house exclusively for negroes, and much of the equipment has been removed from the Excel theater, another negro house, and placed in the Lincoln. The Excel did business for a long time a few doors below the Lincoln on Cedar street, and one of the main reasons for closing the latter house was due to the fact that the other theaters in the same territory interfered with a profitable patronage. However, it is expected that with the Excel out of the way, the Lincoln will enjoy a successful run.

Wolfden Boosting "Hidden Hand."

Nashville, Tenn.—Mr. Wolfden, from the Atlanta office of William Fox, was recently in the city in the interests of the Fox productions, and paid a visit to several local managers. Wolfden is strong for "The Hidden Hand," which is being strongly pushed in this territory. Manager Milton Starr of the Bijou acted as escort to Mr. Wolfden over the city, and both he and the World man found him to be an agreeable sort of fellow.

Knoxville Strand Thrives.

Knoxville, Tenn.—According to local picture men the Strand, which was recently reopened here, is enjoying the best business of its existence. The Strand was formerly owned by Geo. N. Shorey, being known as the Gay, but since being taken over by the Signal Amusement company of Chattanooga has prospered under the new name. An admission scale of five cents for children and ten cents for adults has been established.

Kentucky News Letter

Ohio Valley News Service, 1404 Stark Bldg., Louisville, Ky.

Screens Helped J. L. Steurle Pile Up Votes.

LOUISVILLE, KY.—The power of screen advertising was shown in the recent race for honors in the local Democratic primary, in which Joseph L. Steurle, manager of the Walnut theater, and connected with the Broadway Amusement Enterprises, of which he is an officer, ran for city auditor on the Democratic ticket. This year the ticket was split into two factions, the machine candidate being one, while the Brumleve crowd opposed the old political machine. Mr. Steurle ran without support of either faction, being a sort of independent Democrat. However, the machine candidate triumphed with only 158 votes more than received by Mr. Steurle, while the third man was well up in the race. Mr.

Steurle at first thought he had been jobbed, and announced that he would contest the nomination, but later stated that he had found no indication of fraud, and was satisfied. He has shaken hands with the nominee and congratulated him on his election.

Mr. Steurle announced last week that he had resigned from the Walnut theater and the Broadway company, the resignation effective August 15, but has reconsidered this action and will continue with the companies as heretofore. This was Mr. Steurle's first political effort and was made possible largely through the co-operation of the local photoplay houses, who, with the exception of two theaters, ran slides for several weeks in boosting Mr. Steurle for the nomination. Running within one hundred and fifty-eight votes of the machine candidate testifies to the power of the screen, and also to the fact that Mr. Steurle had many friends, although he has never been before the public to any extent in the past.

Buckingham Theater Puts Off Opening.

Louisville, Ky.—For the first time within memory the Buckingham theater, the local burlesque house, will fail to open on the scheduled time, which had been advertised as Sunday, August 19. Manager Horace McCrocklin states that, due to a controversy between the Columbia Amusement and the Empire Circuit companies, no shows would start out on the Columbia wheel until the troubles had been adjusted, and in the meantime the Buckingham will remain dark. This theater is the only one in Louisville playing burlesque, and has the exclusive franchise at the present time. Its contract with the Columbia company has seventeen years yet to run, but as all of the burlesque road attractions of size are controlled by the Columbia people, there is small chance of any other house figuring on starting burlesque before the Eastern tangle is settled.

No Sunday Show at Nicholasville.

Nicholasville, Ky.—A pretty little row has been stirred up locally by W. C. Jackson, owner of the Savoy theater, which he recently purchased from Nave & Sparks. Whereas the theater had not been operating on Sunday, Mr. Jackson stated that, starting August 12, the theater would open at 1 o'clock Sunday afternoon and run until 6 o'clock, with a two-hour lay out until 8 o'clock so as not to interfere with churchgoers. However, the ministers formed a committee and protested. Mr. Jackson stated that he had the same privilege of running a picture amusement house on Sundays as the operators of the bathing beach did in charging for Sunday afternoon amusement there. The preachers protested to M. H. Nave, operator of the beach, who agreed to close on Sundays, and residents of the city will not be compelled to do any Sunday bathing at home or in an unfrequented portion of the river. A petition is now being circulated by the church people and will shortly be placed before the city council, this petition asking that the theater be closed on Sunday.

Liberty Theater at Mt. Sterling Open.

Mt. Sterling, Ky.—N. A. Wilkerson, owner of the Liberty theater, formerly the Paramount, recently reopened the house, which has been closed for a year or more. The theater has been remodeled inside and out and under Mr. Wilkerson's capable management should do well, as he has had much experience in the district.

Hopkinsville's Princess Brightens Up.

Hopkinsville, Ky.—Manager Stockley has reopened the Princess theater, which has been renovated and generally done over. The lighting fixtures have been replaced with more attractive ones, bronze rails installed around the balcony, and much paint has been used.

Film Snap Shots from the Middle West

By Frank H. Madison, 623 South Wabash Ave., Chicago, Ill.

Among Illinois Theaters.

FOREST CITY, ILL.—The Folly theater is putting out a monthly program in the form of a book mark. The Folly is running "Liberty" and conducting an essay writing contest for children.

LaSalle, Ill.—The Werner theater suffered a film fire.

North Chicago, Ill.—The library board has leased the Auditorium to Mr. Jeffries, who will use the building for a moving picture theater beginning September 1. If the venture is successful a year's lease will be taken.

Decatur's Avon Theater Changes Hands.

Decatur, Ill.—The Avon theater, opened last fall by Joseph Allman, has been leased to outside capital and Manager Carrier and the owner will take up activities in connection with the amusement business elsewhere. The house is closed at this writing and will be reopened after a general overhauling.

E. H. Gilley Heads Escanaba Mutual.

Escanaba, Mich.—Everett H. Gilley has been appointed manager of the Mutual Film exchange, with headquarters in this city. He will have charge of the business in the Upper Peninsula, succeeding Eugene Wilson, who has gone East.

Violet McMillan Home for a Rest.

Grand Rapids, Mich.—Violet McMillan, after completing several features at Universay City, came to her home here for a rest. She will spend her time at her cottage, "Folger Arms," at Whitefish Lake. Late in September she and John Folger, her husband and manager, will go into vaudeville with an act "In and Out of the Movies."

Theater Notes Across Michigan.

Holland, Mich.—The Royal theater closed for several weeks for remodeling has been reopened. The front and interior have been rebuilt and new lighting and ventilating systems have been installed.

Pontiac, Mich.—The redecorated Howland theater has been reopened. The color scheme is sage green, old rose, light tan and old ivory. Over the proscenium arch is an allegorical group suggested by the Swan Song from Lohengrin. Old rose silk hangings are used.

Escanaba, Mich.—The Strand theater has added six girls in white linen to the house staff to serve lemonade to the patrons.

Nashville, Mich.—A. J. Ferte has leased the Star theater from Charles Richardson.

Kalamazoo, Mich.—The Fuller theater has been reopened after undergoing redecorations. It started with feature pictures and will play pictures except when theatrical attractions are booked. Fred Stafford and George Spaeth will be managers.

Taylorville, Ill.—Construction of an addition which will increase the seating capacity of the Empress theater has begun. The changes also will provide room for the installation of a balcony should one be needed.

Lincoln, Ill.—Seven nights at the Lincoln Chautauqua will be devoted to moving pictures which have been selected by Manager Burnstine of the Star theater. Among the pictures selected by him are: "The Boy Who Cried Wolf," "The Message of the Mouse," "Lady of the Lake," "Hansel and Gretel."

Percentage Basis and the Average Exhibitor

World's Detroit Correspondent Asks Theater Managers for Their Opinions—Finds Half Are in Favor and Half Against Percentage Plan.

By Jacob Smith, 503 Free Press Bldg., Detroit, Mich.

DETROIT, MICH.—The Moving Picture World correspondent has been endeavoring to get interviews with leading exhibitors and exchange managers as to whether they would prefer to play a big feature on straight rental or percentage basis. The result has been an even break for both policies. Many exchange men would prefer to get straight rental on pictures which they are somewhat afraid of, and which, to their surprise, often turn out to be big drawing cards; other exchange men prefer to book on percentage only, as it invariably gives them the best end. Then again, the picture stands out on its own merits. Now then, from the standpoint of the exhibitor, he oft would rather book straight rental and take a chance on a picture drawing big business; while others would rather gamble with the exchange man. Where a picture is played on percentage, both the exhibitor and exchange usually go 50-50 on the extra expense of advertising and publicity.

Broadway-Strand Items.

Detroit, Mich.—Harry I. Garson, managing director of the Broadway-Strand Theater, Detroit, was home for a few days of last week, and during that time had frequent conferences with the Moving Picture World correspondent regarding future matters.

Mr. Garson announced that he was making comedies, and that if they turned out as good as the first—now being produced—they would be continued at the rate of two a month.

The Broadway-Strand theater will open with its Artcraft-Paramount policy on Sunday, August 26, with "The Amazons," featuring Marguerite Clark. The section attraction will be "The Varmint." The Broadway-Strand will take only the Fairbanks, Harts, Clarks, Fredericks and Jack Pickford pictures, as well as the Clara Kimball Youngs, for the first year.

Fox Manager Gives Private Views of New Film.

Detroit, Mich.—A trade showing of "The Honor System," "The Conqueror," "Jack and the Beanstalk" and "The Spy" is now being made through Michigan by Jos. Kaliski, Detroit manager for Standard pictures. A regular route has been laid out, and exhibitors in the vicinity of each town is invited to attend the screening. Mr. Kaliski says he has instructions from New York to adhere absolutely to the new policy "that the exhibitor must see Standard pictures before he can book them."

J. C. Fishman Gets Christie Comedies.

Detroit, Mich.—J. C. Fishman of the Standard Film Service, Detroit, announces another important acquisition for Michigan—the Christie comedies. Last issue we mentioned that the Standard had secured the Billy West comedies and the Art Dramas. This gives the Standard one of the best line-ups in Michigan, and for an independent exchange the Standard has made wonderful progress. Much credit is due Mr. Fishman and Harry Charnas, of Cleveland, who is general manager of the company. The Standard occupy offices in the Peter Smith building, but will soon move to the new film building.

Third Print of "The Slacker" Ordered.

Detroit, Mich.—Manager George Montgomery has been doing so well on "The Slacker," Metro's latest special production, that he has ordered a third print to ak¢,care of bookings in the upper peninsula.

Mr. Montgomery is getting ready for bookings on the new Charlie Chaplin pictures, as they are to be handled through the Metro exchange for Michigan, inasmuch as John H. Kunsky, member of the First National Exhibitors' Circuit, controls the Michigan Metro exchange, as well as the new Chaplin pictures.

William F. Klatt Makes Shining Success.

Detroit, Mich.—Among the men who have made good in Michigan is William F. Klatt, who has leased the Regent theater to Charles H. Miles for vaudeville and pictures. Mr. Klatt was one of the pioneers in the picture industry in Michigan, starting in on Monroe avenue, Detroit. He began just about the same time as did Caille & Kunsky, so that he is conceded to be one of the first exhibitors in the world. His first house was the Bijou. Prices were 5 cents; shows lasted about twenty minutes. The Bijou was a tremendous success. Then Mr. Klatt branched out and secured other theaters, forming the Detroit Theaters, Inc. Recently he disposed of the Vendome and Jewell theaters, and about two weeks ago leased the Regent—his biggest house—to Charles H. Miles. He still has the Rosedale and the Gratiot theaters. He owns all theater property outright, including land and buildings; he also has considerable other valuable property.

H. D. Goldberg Transfered to Cleveland.

Detroit, Mich.—Harry D. Goldberg, who for the past six weeks has been acting as agent for Lewis J. Selznick, has been transferred to Cleveland, Ohio.

Selznick Fails to Get Injunction.

Detroit, Mich.—The injunction suit of Lewis J. Selznick against the Harry I. Garson Productions, asking that the latter be restrained from doing business in Michigan, came up before the Detroit Circuit Court on Tuesday, August 14. The court refused to grant an injunction to Selznick as applied for.

Stockholders of New Miles-Regent Company.

The Miles-Regent Co. has been formed with a capital stock of $150,000 to conduct the Regent and Orpheum theaters, Detroit. The principal stockholders are Charles H. Miles, Tom Ealand and Fred T. Grennell. Of course, most of the stock is held by Miles.

If present plans materialize, Bryant Washburn may visit Detroit some time within the next ninety days. His pictures will be shown during the next 12 months at the Majestic theater, Detroit, and it may be that Manager M. W. McGee may be able to induce the Essanay people to let Washburn come over for a day or two and get better acquainted with the patrons of the Majestic. We will say this much for Bryant—he is becoming more popular every day right here in the Wolverine state. As exhibitors say, "he gets me the money."

"The Bar Sinister" has been booked by the Washington theater, Detroit, but no date has yet been set for the showing. "The Bar Sinister" is the first of the M. H. Hoffman Foursquare pictures to be shown in this state. George Weeks, division manager, says that first-runs through the territory have already been secured. He is gratified with business thus far, and looks for really big things during the coming fall and winter. D. Leo Dennison is in Cleveland for him, and Hal Smith in Cincinnati. Besides George has his old-time pep, and that means getting business when he goes after it.

Fire Prevention Bureau for Indianapolis

Commissioner of Public Buildings Plans for Inspection and Control of Film Industries—Got Ideas From Chicago and Cincinnati.

From Indiana Trade News Service, 861 State Life Bldg., Indianapolis, Ind.

INDIANAPOLIS, Ind.—Jacob H. Hilkene, commissioner of public buildings, announced this week that he will recommend the establishing of a fire prevention bureau as a part of the city government to assist his department in enforcing building ordinances for fire prevention, especially in relation to the motion picture industry.

The announcement was made by the building commissioner following his return from Chicago and Cincinnati, where he, with E. M. Sellers, manager of the Indiana Inspection Bureau, and H. H. Friedley, state fire marshal, went, at the expense of owners of motion picture exchanges and theaters in Indianapolis, to study methods for controlling the motion picture business in those cities.

Mr. Hilkene says Chicago has worked out a remarkable system for the control of the motion picture industry. The success of the law depends, however, on the efficiency of the fire prevention bureau and the system of inspection that has been established. Mr. Hilkene says the inspectors in this department are under civil service, and that the appointments are divided equally between the two leading political parties.

Mr. Hilkene says he will suggest that Indianapolis be divided into districts so that it would be possible to have a captain of the fire department in each district to serve on the fire prevention bureau. These captains, he says, could extend the inspection of property to all parts of the city and the inspection therefore could be made more thorough. He says he does not believe such a system would prove a big expense to the city.

The building commissioner announced that he also expects to make a few additional changes in the proposed ordinance governing the storage, handling and manufacture of motion picture films, which is now pending before the council. Although he said nothing definite on the subject, he intimated that he probably will support the insurance men in their demands that the motion picture exchanges be equipped with automatic sprinklers. The owners of the exchanges contend that if such a provision is inserted in the ordinance they will be forced to pay out money unnecessarily for fire protection. It is on this question that the exchange owners and the insurance experts have failed to reach an agreement.

Elkhart Exhibitors to Work with Censors.

Elkhart, Ind.—Managers of three of the four motion picture theaters now operating in Elkhart last week responded to an invitation to confer with the city administration's board of moving picture censors, and, at a meeting in the mayor's office, unhesitatingly agreed to co-operate with the board in preventing objectionable exhibitions in the future.

The theaters represented at the meeting were the Bucklen, the Family and the Hippodrome. The board of censors consists of Mayor Smith, Police Commissioners Brown, Earl and Machan, Chief of Police Riblet and Police Matron Fay.

An informal discussion was held regarding certain kinds of shows that had been offered in Elkhart recently and the censors announced the standard below which they think public exhibitions should not fall.

The managers of the three theaters agreed to hereafter refrain from showing so-called "white slave" films, or those revealing the nude human form, or, in short, most any production which seems to be in violation of the rule against "children under sixteen," etc. They also agreed to abstain from the use of objectionable advertising, after one of the

censors had pointed out that in his opinion some of the announcements thrown on the screen were immeasurably worse than the films themselves.

Manager Young Will Beautify Orpheum.

Gary, Ind.—V. V. Young, manager of the Orpheum theater and several others, has secured a permit for making extensive alterations in his theater at the corner of Eighth avenue and Washington street, the improvements alone to cost about $2,000. $10,000 in new equipment and scenery for the theater. He expects to reopen the house some time in the latter part of August or first of September.

More Indiana Holdings for Chicago Firm

Bankers and Merchants Theater Company Takes Over Isis at Kokomo—Spending $75,000 on the Variety at Terre Haute.

KOKOMO, IND.—Through a deal consummated last week the Isis theater, in South Main street, one of the most popular motion picture houses in Kokomo, was added to the chain of theaters owned and operated by the Bankers' and Merchants' Theater Company of Chicago. R. K. Mosiman, manager of the Alhambra Amusement Company, who engineered the deal, will remain in charge of the Isis for the new company. The terms of the deal have not been made public.

The chief reason for making the Isis a member of the Bankers' and Merchants' Theater Company chain, according to Mr. Mosiman, is to try to bring better shows for the local patrons. He says that with the power of the Chicago syndicate behind him he will be able to bring many exclusive film features to Kokomo that could not otherwise be obtained.

With the change in ownership, Mr. Mosiman also announced plans for extensive improvements in the building which it now occupies. A contract has already been let for the extension of the room, which it now occupies, clear back to the alley between Main and Buckeye streets. This will double the capacity of the theater, making it possible to seat more than 1,000 persons. Work on the improvements will be started in about two weeks, according to Mr. Mosiman.

The Bankers' and Merchants' company is at present the owner of the Orpheum theater in Fort Wayne, and the old Variety theater at present being torn down and a modern $75,000 theater to be erected on the site by the Chicago company. The company is also trying to arrange deals for several other theaters in towns near Kokomo, according to Mr. Mosiman.

Iowa News Letter

By Dorothy Day, Register-Tribune, Des Moines, Ia.

Paramount Film Office Opens in Des Moines.

DES MOINES, IA.—A. D. Flinton, district manager of the Kansas City Feature Film company, handling the Paramount and Artcraft pictures, was in town last week arranging with R. C. Ll Beau for the opening of the Des Moines office. It is understood that an office was secured on Eleventh and Locust streets, of which Ll Beau will be manager. Ll Beau has been the manager of the Des Moines Film & Supply company, a subsidiary branch of the Kansas City Feature company.

Trade Showing of Goldwyn Subjects.

Des Moines, Ia.—On August 22, A. H.

Gumbiner Brothers Buy Orpheum at Hammond.

Hammond, Ind.—Gumbiner Brothers, who own a chain of motion picture theaters in Chicago, have added another one to their list by purchasing the Orpheum theater here. The theater, which was constructed in 1911 at a cost of $100,000, has a seating capacity of 1,300 and is equipped for vaudeville as well as motion pictures. The new owners announce that they intend to make material improvements in the place.

C. A. Wagner Will Open Show at Elwood.

Upland, Ind.—C. A. Wagner, who has operated a motion picture theater here for the last fourteen months, has leased the show to George Day, of Muncie, and will move to Elwood, where he intends to open a moving picture house.

Mid-West Office in Des Moines Now Releasing.

Des Moines, Ia.—With the arrival of S. S. Schwarz, general auditor of the Mid-West corporation, the Des Moines office over the Garden theater began the shipping and complete booking of the Mid-West output in Iowa and Nebraska. This includes the Selznick, the First National Exhibitors' Circuit productions and all of A. H. Blank's state rights pictures.

Gladys Coburn has been engaged as film inspector, Helen Davidson as stenographer and William Jones as shipper. Schwarz will act as auditor and John J. Shipley will continue to sing the praises of the Mid-West productions.

Over the State with Exhibitors.

Indianola, Ia.—Walker & Thorpe have sold their Lyric theater in Indianola to Mr. Price, and have purchased the Star theater in Milo from the Newton Theater Supply company of Des Moines.

Minburn, Ia.—C. E. Bassett sold his Pleasant Hour theater in Minburn to Mrs. M. Bryant.

Fort Dodge, Ia.—D. B. Lederman, manager of the Des Moines-Laemmle Film service, has purchased the Strand theater in Fort Dodge from Messrs. Julius & Awe.

Onawa, Ia.—Kregston & Wonders purchased the Royal theater in Onawa from Messrs. Fairchild & Payne. This deal makes Kregston & Wonders owners of both photoplay houses in Onawa.

Marshalltown, Ia.—Wilbur Ingledue, owner of the Strand theater in Marshalltown, was drafted into service with the first army and will begin training at Camp Dodge in the first week of September. Being a perfectly normal young fellow and having no dependents, there was no chance for Wilbur.

Marshalltown, Ia.—Leo Muelhaupt of the Casino in Marshalltown has practically redecorated his house and is planning to run feature photoplays on the first half of the week and vaudeville the latter part of the week.

Some Metro Activities.

Des Moines, Ia.—The new Metro All Star productions will be open for book ings from the Des Moines Metro office beginning September 2. Metro has bee coming up on to its Iowa and Nebraska business this summer and greater business than ever is expected on these all-star attractions.

With big advance advertising "The Slacker' goes on at the Palace for a week's run the 19th of August. This is State Fair Week in Des Moines and the Palace management are looking forward to capacity houses.

Visitors and Des Moines Happenings.

Des Moines, Ia.—Joe Gerbracht of the Twin Star theater in Ames stopped off in Des Moines on his way home from an extended motor trip to the Lakes. He visited the Midwest and Mutual offices; in fact all the exchanges reported a call from Mr. Gerbracht.

L. A. Sheridan of the local Pathe exchange has purchased a new Dodge touring car and is spending some of his time visiting the nearby towns and rounding up Pathe business.

L. M. Mann, special representative of Triangle out of New York, stopped over in Des Moines on business. It is rumored that a Triangle office will be opened in Omaha in the near future.

TEXAS JOTTINGS.
By Kansas City News Service.

Heard Here and There in Texas.

Fort Worth, Tex.—The Carb-Bailey Amusement Company has been chartered with a capital stock of $10,000 by Merideth R. Carb, Cullen W. Bailey and D. Brown.

Fort Worth, Tex.—The Worth Amusement Company has been chartered with a capital stock of $4,000 by John T. Rogers, Joseph Casa and Frances Fay Dillon.

Cuero, Tex.—A. D. Evans has leased the Fox theater on Esplanade street here.

Dallas, Tex.—The contract for the steel construction of the new Majestic Theatre building has been let to Austin Brothers of this city and work will start immediately. The building will cost $100,000. The architects for the new building are Lang & Witchell. It will be located on Elms street near St. Paul street.

Fort Worth, Tex.—The Healy theater has been reopened by J. J. Dillon after being remodeled and improved upon in many ways. The name of the house will soon be changed.

Central City, Neb.—The Empress theater here has been sold to C. E. McDonald, who will manage the theater. It has been managed recently by Kerr Brothers.

Memphis, Tenn.—The Memphis Amusement Company has been chartered by W. L. Hall, E. O. Bailey, W. W. Fisher, C. S. Lancaster, W. Percy McDonald and C. N. Horton with a capital stock of $2,500.

MINNEAPOLIS NOTES.

Northwest Jottings About Theaters.

Bemidji, Minn.—Oliver Whaley has reopened the Elko theater here.

Aberdeen, S. D.—John Ritter has purchased the theater at Morristown, S. D., from C. C. Dunning.

Nashwauk, Minn.—Crockett Brown has opened the Unique theater.

Cando, N. D.—Robert Henkel has leased the Rex theater from Adolph Straub.

Butte, Mont.—The Broadway theater here has been closed to undergo repairs that will bring the house up to a standard few in the Northwest can excel.

Baker, Mont.—Nogren and Hamilton have opened the Lyric theater here.

Meetings of Two Exhibitors' Organizations

Associated Theaters Holds First Meeting for the Election of Officers at West Hotel—Northwest League's Regular Meeting Also on August 14.

By John L. Johnston, 704 Film Exchange Bldg., Minneapolis, Minn.

MINNEAPOLIS, MINN.—Two bands of exhibitors, each with really beneficial business to transact, were scheduled to meet here Tuesday, August 14.

The Associated Theaters body organized by Thomas J. Hamlin, former editor of "Amusements," was scheduled to hold its first meeting at the West hotel and incorporate for $100,000, elect officers and take the first step towards organizing. Representatives from six states were expected to attend the gathering.

The Northwest branch of the National league was scheduled to hold its regular weekly meeting, with some real action promised. The members of this body were expected to decide whether or not they would continue to use three and six sheets to advertise future productions. The action of those present on August 14 will mean united activity of the entire organization, and the elimination of three and six sheets will save exhibitors a mint of money in the future if the meeting decides to give the large paper "the air." One Minneapolis exhibitor operating two small theaters informed the writer he would save over a hundred dollars a month by adopting the use of one sheets exclusively, by tabooing threes and sixes.

Harry Cohen Still "Under Water."

Minneapolis, Minn.—Harry Cohen has arrived in Minneapolis again after two days spent in New York headquarters to select a new manager for the local Metro exchange. Harry has been in Minneapolis about once a week, every week since January 1, and many thought he would be able to pick a new "boss" right off the jump. However, applications for the position have been so numerous and there have been so many attempts at politics that Mr. Cohen is still "under water." Walter Strauss has been manager pro tem, succeeding William K. Howard, who left Saturday, August 11, for Jefferson Barracks, Mo., to enter Uncle Sam's regular army. Cohen is contemplating a race with Harry Sherman to see who eats up the most carfare between Minneapolis and New York.

Will Lee Horn Be Manager or Soldier?

Minneapolis, Minn.—"Am I, or am I not?" This interrogation is constantly issuing forth from the lips of Lee A. Horn. Mr. Horn is neither delirious or on the verge of insanity, but he has been appointed manager of the new Longacre exchange here, and due to the draft does not know whether he will be able to hold down the job or not. Lee has received a letter from Uncle Sam inviting him to a medical examination next week. Watch next week's edition for solution to this puzzle.

T. L. Hays Opens the New Garrick.

St. Paul, Minn.—Ruben & Finkelstein's tenth Twin City theater opened to the public here Sunday, August 12, when the New Garrick, formerly called the Strand, began a four-day run of "The Little American," featuring Mary Pickford. Messrs. Ruben & Finkelstein sprung a big surprise when they announced the manager for the new house. The executive in none other than Theodore L. Hays, perhaps the best known showman in the entire Northwest. Mr. Hays has been actively engaged in all branches of theatrical presentation for over twenty years, and was formerly owner of the Grand opera house and interested in the Bijou and Gayety theaters of Minneapolis.

Harry Hollander Becomes Fox Roadman.

Manager Eddie Westcott, of the Fox exchange, has secured the services of Harry Hollander as roadman for the exchange. Mr. Hollander was formerly with the local

exchange, but went to New York two months ago to do work on 'The Honor System's' eastern campaign. Stuart Achesom, of the publicity department of the Fox headquarters in New York, spent three days here last week planning a local publicity campaign on future Fox features.

M. MacIntyre Now With Rialto Supply.

Manager S. A. Louis, of the Rialto Theater Supply Co., has secured M. MacIntyre, former Fox road salesman, to cover the Northwest territory for his firm.

From the Twin City Exchanges.

Minneapolis, Minn.—The Friedman Film Corp. has purchased the rights to display "The Bar Sinister" in Minnesota, the Dakotas and Montana, according to an announcement by President Benjamin Friedman. The film will be shown to Northwest exhibitors in a few weeks at some downtown Minneapolis theater.

Manager Harry Graham, of the K-E-S-E exchange, has announced that bookings on "Do Children Count?" Essanay serial, featuring Little Mary McAllister, have not only exceeded expectations, but have eclipsed any record previously made by a serial from his office.

A. A. Hixon has resigned from the sales force of the Elliott & Sherman exchange, and is spending a short vacation before taking up new work, the manner of which his is not announcing.

Frank A. McInerny, former publicity manager for the Elliott & Sherman exchange here, and who went East three weeks ago to become publicity manager for Harry A. Sherman's enterprises, has returned. Mr. McInerney states that he enjoyed the trip, but failed to find Mr. Sherman. If records are correct, Mr. Sherman was half way between Minneapolis and New York when Mac started back home.

Manager H. J. Bayley, of the Greater Vitagraph exchange, has supplied each roadman with a chapter print of "The Fighting Trail" serial.

Edward J. Frye, manager of the XL Films exchange, of Great Falls, Mont., has returned West after securing the right to display several Lochren features in Montana. Mr. Frye also secured the Montana rights to "The Battle of Gettysburg," which he has been playing and dividing proceeds with the Red Cross.

Big Week for Picture Lovers.

Minneapolis, Minn.—Minneapolis moving picture followers had a "big" week beginning August 12.

"The Amazons," featuring Marguerite Clark, began a four-day run at the New Garrick at 20 cents admission.

Billie Burke in "The Mysterious Miss Terry" re-opened the Lyric.

Alice Brady in "Darkest Russia" was the attraction at the New Aster.

The Strand offered Florence Reed in "The Eternal Sin."

The New Unique presented Louise Glaum in "Golden Rule Kate."

Special musical numbers, including jazz music and pipe organ solos, was offered at each playhouse Sunday.

August 12 saw all downtown theaters enjoying an overflow business.

The New Lyric, which reopened August 12 after being closed a week, has been redecorated both inside and outside, and now presents an appearance more suitable to the high class of pictures presented at the theater.

Kansas City Exhibitors Face Car Strike

Downtown Theaters Lose Many Patrons When Street Car Men Go Out on Strike.—
Suburban Theaters Get the Benefit of Hindered Traffic.

Kansas City News Service, 205 Corn Belt Building, Kansas City.

KANSAS CITY, MO.—Trainmen on the Kansas City Railways, the company serving the city with street cars, struck Wednesday, August 8, and in the succeeding days when no city street cars were running the business of moving picture theaters was variously affected. Downtown theaters lost fully 25 per cent. of their business; there were far fewer transients than usual, and those downtown wanted to watch the excitement rather than attend a picture show. In the suburbs the reverse was the effect. People could not get downtown in street cars, and they visited their neighborhood shows.

Interurban street cars were running, but these did not pick up city passengers. The entire traffic was cared for by automobiles. Several thousand motor cars were put into jitney service—and this was another but minor factor in the effect on the theaters: the owners did not have time to drive over to their favorite theaters.

Universal Forms New Butterfly Company.

Kansas City, Mo.—The Butterfly pictures, that in the past have been handled by the Universal Film & Supply Co. will now be handled by a company to be known as the Butterfly Super-Photoplay Company. The new company will be managed by D. O. Reese. The offices of the company will be at 214 East Twelfth street, which is the home of the Universal company. It has been decided to buy two prints of each picture, beginning August 27.

J. E. Dodson Will Assist Manager Reese.

Kansas City, Mo.—J. Erwin Dodson, formerly manager of the Standard Film Corporation at St. Louis, Mo., has been made assistant to manager D. O. R. Reese, of the Universal Film & Supply Company here. He takes his new position August 15.

L. J. Doty Will Travel With Supplies.

Kansas City, Mo.—Leo J. Doty is again a member of the Universal company and will take a territory in Missouri and Kansas as a representative of the supply department.

John H. Morgan Goes to Southwestern Kansas.

Kansas City, Mo.—John H. Morgan, formerly of the supply department of the Universal Film & Supply Company, has been transferred from that department to a territory in southern Kansas.

George Leonard Heads Kansas City Triangle.

Kansas City, Mo.—George Leonard has been made branch manager of the Kansas City Triangle office. He will be directly responsible to the home office in New York City for the Kansas City territory, as he has charge of the road men and everything connected with the Kansas City branch. He succeeds C. D. Struble. Mr. Leonard comes here from Jacksonville, Fla. Assisting him is another new man, E. E. Reynolds, who is office manager. Mr. Reynolds was with the General Film Company at Chicago, Ill, for about six years and has had considerable other film experience.

Triangle Roadmen Attend Banquet.

Kansas City, Mo.—The road men of the Kansas City Triangle office were recently called to Kansas City to attend a banquet that was held at the Baltimore hotel.

Those attending were E. D. Lappey, E. W. Green, A. Kahn, H. M. Weinberg, Mr. Heinz, the sales manager from New York City, and the heads of the different departments, making a total attendance of fourteen men.

Kansas City Triangle Now in Moriarty Building.

Kansas City, Mo.—The Kansas City office of the Triangle Film Corporation has been moved from Nineteenth and Main streets to Twentieth and Grand avenue, in the Moriarty building. The company occupies the entire second floor, giving the office double the space of the former location.

Standard Film Announces Three New Men.

Kansas City, Mo.—The Standard Film Corporation announces the addition of the following new men who will work out of St. Louis, Mo.: Joseph Bloom, Thomas Leonhard and W. H. Hoppe.

W. C. Ansel Transferred to St. Louis Office.

Kansas City, Mo.—W. C. Ansel, southern Missouri representative for the Standard, has been transferred from that territory to the St. Louis, Mo., office.

J. H. Roth to Manage a Freuler Theater.

Oklahoma City, Okla.—J. H. Roth, formerly representative of Paramount and Art Craft in Oklahoma City, Okla., has resigned his position with the company to accept a position as manager of one of the Freuler theaters in Milwaukee, Wis.

A. W. Friemel Joins Kansas City Feature Film.

Kansas City, Mo.—A. W. Friemel, formerly with the General Film, has been added to the sales force of the Kansas City Feature Film Company. He is now working in the Kansas City office, as his territory has not yet been assigned.

W. S. Merrill Now With Triangle.

Kansas City, Mo.—W. S. Merrill, Southern Kansas representative of the General Film, has severed his connections with that company and is now with the Triangle Film.

A. W. Friemel Goes to Paramount.

Kansas City, Mo.—A. W. Friemel, Oklahoma traveler for the General Film, has resigned his position with that company. He is now with the Paramount company at Des Moines, Ia.

C. W. Hardin Goes to Atlanta.

Kansas City, Mo.—Charles W. Hardin, formerly manager of the Metro here, has gone to Atlanta, Ga., to assist in the taking of contracts for additional film for the E. and H. Film Distributing Company, of which he is part owner. The second Kansas City man to be associated in that office, the other being Paul Engler, who has been employed by the old International Film Company, the Greater Vitagraph and the Mutual.

Goldwyn Films at Private Showing.

Kansas City, Mo.—The projection manager of the local Goldwyn office having arrived this company held a series of private showings at the office, three being given on August 8, three on August 9, two on August 10, and one on August 11. The local exhibitors were invited to the showing, which was given on "Baby Mine," starring Madge Kennedy. A few out-of-town exhibitors were also present.

W. H. Rosenbloom in Kansas for Mid-West.

Kansas City, Mo.—W. H. Rosenbloom is now working the Kansas territory of the Mid-West Photoplay Corporation, having been transferred to that territory from the Nebraska territory.

With Theaters Across Kansas.

Wichita, Kan.—The Colonial theater here has been opened up under the management of Dan Hosmer, after a complete remodeling.

Eldorado, Kan.—The Opera House here will be remodeled into a first-class modern brick theater.

Ogden, Kan.—Steve Clark is erecting a fine new theater building here.

Burton, Kan.—Edgar G. Rollings will soon open a moving picture theater here in a new building having a seating capacity of 275.

Hutchinson, Kan.—The Pearl theater, at No. 7 North Main street, was badly damaged by fire August 3. The loss amounted to $3,500, of which $200 was on the building, the remaining being on the equipment and furniture.

Pleasanton, Kan.—W. E. Stepp is the new owner of the Regent theater here.

Garden City, Kan.—A new theater and office building will soon be erected here on Main street, for which the plans are now being drawn.

Theater Jottings from Missouri.

Slater, Mo.—Mr. and Mrs. William Jenkins of the Auditorium theater here gave a Red Cross benefit August 7, which netted the Relief Workers $185.70. The first part of the program consisted of an excellent Vitagraph feature, "Aladdin from Broadway." The second part was made up of Slater's best talent.

St. Louis, Mo.—The New Orpheum theater at Ninth and Pine streets, will be opened Labor Day, September 3, with E. J. Sullivan as manager.

St. Joseph, Mo.—The Crystal theater will open August 19, having been closed for redecorating.

St. Louis, Mo.—The Empress theater here has been completely redecorated and will reopen August 13.

New Theaters and Changes in Oklahoma.

Delaware, Okla.—Ralph Sullivan has bought the interest of Louis Warwick in the Nusho theater. The new firm will be known as Green & Sullivan.

Foss, Okla.—The Empress theater here has been leased by Miss Alma Gilham and Miss Modelle Childress, who will continue the shows at this theater.

Miami, Okla.—The Picher theater here has been leased by W. J. Cotter.

Bartlesville, Okla.—The Odeon theater has been purchased by Messrs. C. E. Oliver, Carl Drath and T. C. Steeper, who have already taken charge of their new holdings.

Ada, Okla.—J. F. Painter of Pranks, Okla., has bought the De Sota theater here from Charles Chauncey.

Clinton, Okla.—Charles Duffield is contemplating the opening of a large moving picture theater here.

Healdton, Okla.—The Healdton Amusement Company has been chartered here with a capital stock of $2,000 by G. W. Jennings, J. H. Smith and Fred C. Ryburn of this town.

Denver, Colo.—The Plaza theater was damaged by fire to the extent of $500 recently.

Santa Fe, N. M.—The Paris theater has been remodeled by the manager, who has made it thoroughly modern and up-to-date.

San Francisco Briefs.

Charles Rosenthal, of the M. & R. Feature Film exchange, recently made a visit to the new Los Angeles branch. Its latest release, the Ivan production, "Babbling Tongues," is being shown at the Rialto theater.

Chester Roeder, formerly with the Mutual exchange, is now filling a position with the Progressive Film exchange.

The Progress theater on Fillmore street recently broke all former records for attendance with "The Flame of the Yukon."

H. A. Oastler, of the American theater and Nixon opera house, Winnemucca, Nev., was a recent visitor there, having motored down for a two weeks' stay.

Lotz Out of Pathe Exchange.

San Francisco, Cal.—H. E. Lotz, for the past year manager of the local branch of the Pathe Exchange, Inc., has given up this position and left recently for New York to form new connections. Special Representative Charles A. Meade is in charge pending the selection of a new manager, and will probably remain here for several weeks. Before leaving Mr. Lotz was presented with a gold watch by employees of the local office.

Turner & Dahken Circuit Notes.

San Francisco, Cal.—"On Trial," the initial purchase of the First National Exhibitors' Circuit, was recently presented at the Tivoli opera house with great success, and will now be shown over the entire T. & D. circuit, after which it will be released to other houses that have booked it from Turner & Dahnken. It was not intended to show this production so early, but unforeseen conditions arose in connection with the screening of the "Curse of Iku" and "On Trial," and it was hastily substituted in its stead.

Fred Dahnken, Jr., president of the circuit, will go east shortly to attend a meeting of the First National Exhibitors' Circuit, and E. B. Johnson will also be off to attend to business connected with that organization about the 24th of August.

The new office building of the Turner & Dahken Circuit on Golden Gate avenue will be ready for occupancy within sixty days.

J. T. Turner, vice-president and general manager of the circuit, has returned from a three weeks vacation at Shasta Springs.

Universal Jottings.

San Francisco, Cal.—Dave Bershon, manager of the California Film exchange at Los Angeles, and formerly of this city, was a recent visitor here.

Leon Haas, of the local staff, is enjoying a vacation in the southern part of the state, and while away will explore the mysteries of Universal City.

Ed. Fowler, also of the local force, has returned from a vacation spent on the Russian River.

The patriotic spirit of the day has struck the fair employees of the California Film exchange, and during spare moments all are busy on needle work. Miss Stella Uri has joined a sewing club, while the others are merrily clicking their needles in knitting socks for soldiers.

Here and There Among the Theaters.

Oakland, Cal.—The Beach & Krahn Amusement Co. has awarded contracts for the construction of a moving picture theater on College avenue, near Shatter. This will be the third house in its circuit.

Redwood City, Cal.—A fire occurred recently in the Alhambra theater, which is being remodeled. Repairs will be made and the house reopened at the earliest possible date.

Reno, Nev.—The Majestic theater has been refurnished and opened as a vaudeville and moving picture house by the Nixon estate, K-E-S-E features being shown four times a week.

Hollister, Cal.—Stark & Hodges have purchased the Opal theater. They were formerly of Manteca and Lodi.

Association Gets Down to Constructive Work

United Motion Picture Industry of Northern California Holds Meeting—Industrial Insurance and Billboard Advertising are Discussed.

From T. A. Church, 1507 North Street, Berkeley, Cal.

SAN FRANCISCO, CAL.—The monthly meeting of the board of directors of the United Motion Picture Industry of Northern California, composed of film exchange men and exhibitors, was held at the Techau tavern on August 8, with a full attendance. Now that all matters connected with organization work are at an end and the campaign for membership has proved eminently successful, this new constructive work for which it was formed.

At the recent meeting it was pointed out that moving picture houses and film exchanges were being called upon to pay a much higher rate of industrial insurance for their employees than is the case for many other lines and it was decided to investigate this and make an attempt to secure a rate to conform more closely to the actual risk. The organization also hopes to correct some of the faults in the present system of billboard advertising so extensively used here. Much "dead" paper is being left on the local billboards, to the detriment of theater advertising, and it is desired to induce bill posters to remove the notices of special events as quickly as possible in order to make this form of advertising more effective. The strike of photo-engravers also came in for attention at this meeting, exhibitors doing newspaper advertising being seriously affected. At the present time many exhibitors are compelled to have cuts made outside the newspaper offices, a source of considerable expense, and the proposition of curtailing advertising of this kind during the strike was discussed.

Imperial to Advance Prices.

San Francisco, Cal.—Owing to the increased cost of film service, advertising and labor, the management of the Imperial theater has had to advance the price of admission to 10, 15 and 25 cents for matinees, and 15, 25 and 35 cents for evenings. This house was one of the pioneers in the 10-cent field and was also one of the first to inaugurate 10 and 20-cent prices. In discussing the advance, Manager J. L. Partington said: "Costs have been steadily mounting skyward and have reached such a point that a higher admission price is absolutely necessary. The public has become accustomed to paying more for everything else and will doubtless see the justice of the small increase asked for high-grade amusement." The Imperial has recently been redecorated, the exterior and lobby made resplendent by a new coat of paint, new lights installed and new furnishings added to the ladies' rest room.

Nat A. Magner Out of the Hospital.

San Francisco, Cal.—Nat A. Magner, of the film exchange bearing his name, has recovered sufficiently from the operation he recently underwent in a local hospital to be out and is again able to come down to his office. His rapid recovery is now expected.

Fine Organ for T. & D. Theater.

Berkeley, Cal.—A large Wurlitzer Hope-Jones unit orchestral organ has been installed in the T. & D. theater, conducted under the management of E. J. Merlin, at a cost of about $30,000, and this is now proving a great drawing card for this house. The task of removing the old instrument and installing the new one was accomplished with a minimum of inconvenience and a piano was used during the time there was no organ in operation. The new instrument was formally presented to the people of Berkeley at a free recital held on Saturday morning, with the well-known organist, Albert May Malotte, at the console. In addition to installing a new organ in this theater the owners are expending $10,000 in putting in a tea room and children's play room on the mezzanine floor and in renovating the house. On the first of September prices will be advanced to 15 cents for adults and 10 cents for children. This theater is one of the most important in the chain of houses conducted by the Turner & Dahnken circuit and is being kept up to the minute in its appointments and in the class of service rendered.

K-E-S-E District Manager Visits Coast.

San Francisco, Cal.—E. R. Pearson, district manager for the K-E-S-E, arrived in this city recently for a short stay and after inspecting the local exchange and putting in a profit sharing system, left to visit the Los Angeles branch. Before returning east he will return to this city to make another short stay. This is Mr. Pearson's first visit to this territory and he has enjoyed the trip immensely.

Infringement on "The Slacker" Claimed.

San Francisco, Cal.—When the Turner & Dahken circuit recently featured the Metro production, "The Slacker," and inaugurated a great advertising campaign, the management of the Strand secured the K-E-S-E feature, "The Man Who Was Afraid" and billed it as A Slacker, "The Man Who Was Afraid." The Metro Picture Corporation at once applied for an injunction against the New York & San Francisco Amusement Co., the Strand Theater company, D. J. Grauman and Sidney Grauman to prevent them from making use of the term "Slacker" in connection with a photoplay and was granted a temporary restraining order. It was claimed that the order was violated and the matter will be aired at an early date in the U. S. Federal District Court presided over by Judge Van Fleet.

Fine New House for Oakland.

Oakland, Cal.—The American theater, San Pablo avenue and Seventeenth street, was opened on August 4 by C. W. & Rex Midgley under very auspicious circumstances. This theater was formerly known as the Reliance, but had been closed for months and the new owners have remodeled and redecorated it, making virtually a new house of it. The exterior lighting has made this spot one of the brightest places in the downtown district. The large marquee is brilliantly illuminated, while a forty foot sign, with an animated border and bearing the name "American," surmounts the house. An animated clectric American flag, 5 by 15 feet in size also serves to attract attention, while a large illuminated sign two blocks away on another main thoroughfare directs attention to the location of the house. The theater, which has a seating capacity of 1,600, was packed at both performances on the opening night, the leading attraction being a Metro production, "The Haunted Pajamas." Many San Francisco exhibitors and film exchange men were present at the opening and the floral tributes were unusually plentiful. Music is furnished by an orchestra of twelve pieces, under the direction of John Warry Lewis, and the American quartette was an added feature on the opening night. The prices are 15 cents for the lower floor and 10 cents for the balcony, a pay-as-you-enter system being used, instead of a box office.

Says There is Money in Second Run Pictures

Seattle Exhibitor in Shopping District Raises Price and Changes from First Run Policy for Second Run Pictures—Makes a Success of It.

By J. S. Anderson, East Seattle, Washington.

SEATTLE, WASH.—Neither the war nor summer weather nor anything, except the car strike, have cut into the profits this summer of John Hamrick, manager of the Rex. Mr. Hamrick's theater is a house of about 600 capacity, situated on Second avenue in the very center of Seattle's shopping district. Until this year the Rex had always been operated as a first run house. In the early spring Mr. Hamrick decided to put on second run pictures. It was just a few months after the admission price had been raised from 10 to 15 cents, but the manager did not lower the price in spite of the fact that the nearest run houses in the city charge no more for general admission than 15 cents.

The programs at the Rex are composed only of those features which have played to extraordinary business during their first run in the city. The usual plan is to change twice a week, but when a picture warrants it, it is kept on a full week. For special reasons first run pictures are sometimes shown; as, for instance, after "Hell Morgan's Girl" had played a very successful second run at the Rex, a week or two later it was followed by "The Girl in the Checkered Coat," and the fact that the same cast appeared in this picture that had made such a hit in "Hell Morgan's Girl" was made the keynote of the advertising. Excellent business was the result. Mr. Hamrick has no trouble in getting the same admission price for his second run pictures that the first run houses charge, and the first week of the car strike is the only time this summer when his business has not been satisfactory. After that first week people found out that jitneys were just about as good as cars to ride in, and that the Rex was still showing good pictures, so the second week Mr. Hamrick's business came back to normal and has continued that way.

Seattle Paramount-Artcraft Notes.

Seattle, Wash. — Paramount - Artcraft's selective star series opened simultaneously in Seattle, Portland, and Spokane on August 12, with Margarite Clark in "The Amazons." It was shown at the Coliseum in Seattle.

Clarence Hill arrived from the San Francisco headquarters this week to discuss with H. G. Rosebaum, manager of the Seattle Paramount-Artcraft office, the question of opening a branch in Portland. The territory will be as nearly as possible equally divided. Portland is to have the southern Washington territory below Chehalis.

Guy Navarre, road representative, has just returned from a trip through the Oregon territory, having signed every town he visited.

Miss E. Erickson, formerly head stenographer at the Salt Lake City Triangle office, is now stenographer in the contract department of the Seattle Paramount-Artcraft office.

At the Seattle Triangle Exchange.

Seattle, Wash.—H. H. Hurn, manager of the Seattle Triangle office, reports that the "Flame of the Yukon" broke all Saturday and Sunday records at the Strand theater, Walla Walla, and that similar satisfactory reports regarding this feature are coming in from all over the territory.

Mr. Hurn called a meeting of his three salesmen, W. W. Armstrong, Ed. I. Hudson, L. T. Turner, last week to discuss the handling of the new Hart and Fairbanks reissues in which exhibitors have already shown much interest.

T. Thurston, cashier at the Triangle office, has gone on a short vacation to Mt. Rainier.

Other Notes From the Film Row.

Seattle, Wash.—Fred C. Quimby, Northwest supervisor for Pathe, left this week for Butte.

L. J. Schlaifer went to Eastern Montana this week. His partner, Melvin G. Winstock, was in Portland last week looking after the business of their features.

B. L. Daniels, of Coeur d'Alene, Idaho, wired to the Seattle G. A. Metcalfe store for two Power's 6B machines this week.

Spokane News Letter

By S. Clark Patchin.

Brief Notes of Local Film Circles.

SPOKANE, WASH.—Ruth Corwin, who recently appeared in "Soul Mates" at the Liberty, is a former Spokane girl. Students of the North Central High school, where she attended, made up a party and attended the theater in a body when the fact was learned.

Mary Pickford played to standing room at the Liberty in "The Little American." Among pictures which drew well in Spokane the week of August 6 were Norma Talmadge in "The Law of Compensation" at the Clemmer; Bryant Washburn in "The Golden Idiot" at the Casino; Mary Pickford in "The Pride Of The Clan," at the Lyric, and Louise Lovely in "The Gift Girl," at the Rex.

Coeur d'Alene Strand Burns.

Coeur d'Alene, Ida.—Fire of mysterious origin did damage to the extent of $30,000 in the building occupied by the Strand theater at 2 a. m., August 9. This building is now being remodeled by a syndicate of which M. B. Daniels is manager and the syndicate took over this and the Lyric of Coeur d'Alene recently.

The blaze started in the rear of the theater when no one was about and the stage and screen and orchestra equipment and many of the seats were burned. The building is owned by John B. Taylor and the furnishings by O. R. Shern. Mr. Daniels says the building will be rebuilt and pictures will be shown as soon as possible.

Ralph Ruffner's Interesting Career.

Spokane, Wash.—From messenger boy for the Western Union to a railroad telegraph operator, then entering the moving picture business on a piano stool, later to be manager of one of the most up-to-date moving picture houses in the northwest are a few of the experiences of Manager Ralph Ruffner, of the Liberty theater, Spokane, Wash., who now has a machine installed in his three-room office suite on the third floor of the building, and a screen covered by dark curtains to be used for showing him special run or open market pictures.

Additional to the above, Mr. Ruffner has been office boy in a railroad master mechanic's office, operator of a steam hammer in a railroad blacksmithy, office stenographer, city ticket agent, baseball player, a moving picture pianist and organist, and now, when he chooses, he handles the mammoth Wurlitzer, Hope-Jones organ of the Liberty with ease. He can handle any angle of the moving picture business from janitor to operator, decorator, general director, publicity and advertising man, and manager, and put in odd times amusing the patrons by furnishing music for them during the pictures. He is a live-wire at advertising, and is always working up something new to attract the attention of the thousands who pass and enter the theater daily and weekly. He is a good publicity man, and gets by with much free publicity .in newspapers here by various ingenious means.

Right now Mr. Ruffner is concentrating his efforts in and using his past experiences in his capacity as manager of the Liberty.

Should the regular operator be unable to work and no substitute be immediately available, Mr. Ruffner peels off his coat and goes to work. Aside from putting in about 16 hours a day at the theater or in connection with it, Mr. Ruffner keeps his muscles limbered up by playing with a 100-pound dumb bell which he keeps in his office, and can easily put it up several times with one hand then hold out at arms length with both hands.

In 1907 he was inveigled into the picture show business. A railroad friend induced him to play the piano at his Comet theater in Vancouver, Wash., across the river from Portland, and he later became manager of this theater. He hit on the idea of extending credit to the soldiers of the fort there, who were paid monthly, and each was allowed a credit up to $3 worth of seats a month. On pay day they squared their accounts—"sometimes"—according to Mr. Ruffner. He said the experiment cost him about $20,000, which he carries as souvenir paper and would sell cheap. He managed a small theater at Ranier, Ore., in 1914, then went to Butte, where he made a signal success of the American theater, and came to Spokane in the spring of 1915 to manage the Liberty, where fortune has continued to smile upon him.

Manager Ralph Ruffner at the Organ.

PRAIRIE STATE ITEMS.
By F. H. Madison.

Dakota Theater Notes.

Bismarck, N. D.—The Publicity Film company of this city has made for the State Fire Marshal a film which shows modern fire-fighting methods. This will be used by the marshal's office in educational work.

Morristown, S. D.—John Ritter has purchased the interest of C. O. Dunning in the moving picture show.

Among Nebraska Film Men.

Kearney, Neb.—Local exhibitors have ventured Sunday shows. There is a liberal patronage and it is likely that seventh day shows will become firmly established.

Omaha, Neb.—A daughter, Mona Virginia, has been born to Mr. and Mrs. George H. McCool. The father is booker at the local exchange of the Universal.

Havelock, Neb.—The Joy theater has been sold to R. W. Wolverton.

Omaha, Neb.—The Empress theater has added a ladies' rest room, fitted with Jacobean furniture, writing desk, lounge and chairs.

Longacre Gets Portland Connection.

Portland, Ore.—The Longacre Film corporation, releasing Alice Howell comedies under the brand of Century Comedies, has obtained a Portland connection and will open offices with Bluebird at the exchange of the Film Supply company of Oregon. Gus Metzger, manager, reports that his company will also take care of the distributing company's affairs in Seattle and Spokane.

Eastern Triangle Manager Visits.

Portland, Ore.—Gerald Payne, reputed to be the youngest exchange manager in the District of Columbia, honored Portland with a visit August 8, when he stopped off a few hours between trains en route from Los Angeles to the East. He called on several of Portland theaters using Triangle service, and expressed his opinion that business seemed much better than he had anticipated it would be. He was agreeably surprised with the city.

Organist Writes a Song.

Portland, Ore.—E. H. Hunt, organist at the People's, has written and published a patriotic popular song called "Swat the Kaiser," which had its premier presentation at the People's when it was sung by the Portland Ad Club Quartette. Needless to say it went over big.'

New Portland Censor Board Meets.

Portland, Ore.—The new censor board appointed by Mayor George L. Baker in an effort to minimize the heretofore alleged censorship unfairness held its organization meeting August 7. Gus A. Metzger, manager of the Universal exchange, has been made a member of the board since the list of appointees was made public last week. A committee consisting of C. W. Meighan, manager of the People's theater; Gus Metzger, and W. P. Ready was appointed to formulate a new set of rules for the guidance of the viewers of the board. It is anticipated that these rules will give everybody a fair deal.

Pathe to the Front.

Portland, Ore.—That local exchanges are receiving patronage in preference to out-of-town exchanges is evidenced by the way the Pathe exchange is coming into favor with Portland exhibitors. Manager W. W. Kofeldt has finally landed Gold Rooster features in the People's theater, Portland's big first run house, to start September 16. He has also placed "The Fatal Ring" at the Pantages, and 'The Battle of the Somme" at the Majestic.

C. E. Waite, traveler for Pathe, recently returned from a trip South, and reports business much better than expected.

Portland Exhibitors Do Exhanges' Work

Object to Requirement of Exchanges to Make Collections—Have to Keep Wires Hot With Changing Shipping Orders—Long Distance Shipments Blamed.

By Abraham Nelson, Majestic Theater Bldg., Portland, Ore.

PORTLAND, ORE.—Oregon exhibitors are getting tired of doing office work for Seattle exchange. To obviate long distance shipments, the cause of much complaint by Oregon theater men, and loss of business to Seattle exchanges, the distributors recently hit upon the plan of putting in a lot of small circuits throughout the territory. The circuit scheme is not new, of course, but of late it has become quite popular as a means of quieting exhibitors' complaints about high express rates on shipments to and from Seattle.

The circuit plan worked all right as long as the circuits remained intact as the road was originally arranged them, but when one exhibitor happened to drop out the wires began to hum between Seattle and the remaining members of the circuit, and the exhibitors had shipping instructions to worry about. Of late exchanges have become more presumptious and are ordering exhibitors to ship films C. O. D. to circuit members. The C. O. D. amounts vary each week, according to the way the slow pay circuit member sends his check to the Seattle office, and the member making the shipment to him must receive a notice of the amount each week.

It is causing a lot of dissatisfaction among Oregon exhibitors to be compelled to worry about this routine work for the exchanges just to save express charges on long distance shipments, and they are looking forward to the establishment of more exchanges in Portland.

Goldwyn Holds Trade Showing.

Portland, Ore.—C. F. Hill, new manager for Goldwyn, temporarily moved his sales force down from Seattle for the accommodation of Portland and Oregon exhibitors, and held a trade showing of the first productions released under the new brand. The cosy Sunset theater was the scene of the exhibitions on August 9, 10 and 11 before and after the regular shows. The regular Sunset organist was in attendance at all performances.

Nearly every exhibitor in Portland viewed "Baby Mine," and a number of out-of-town men were also present. Among these were George Bligh, Bligh theater, Salem; A. H. McDonald, Rex theater, Eugene; W. S. Humphrey, Savoy theater, Eugene; Henry E. Morris, Star theater, McMinnville; E. M. Thurber, Orpheum theater, Marshfield; W. A. Long, Star theater, Oregon City; C. C. Ferguson, Baker theater, Newberg, and several others.

Harry C. Arthur, traveling representative for Goldwyn, was in Portland assisting Mr. Hill. Mr. Arthur resigned his position as traveler with Fox to accept the Goldwyn appointment. He recently completed a trip south from Portland, and reports excellent business. He says that the Percy-Moran Company, owning the new Rialto in Medford, were the first exhibitors in the Pacific Northwest to sign a Goldwyn contract.

Local Pictures Go Well.

Portland, Ore.—The People's Amusement Company patronized home industry during the week of August 5, and showed a program consisting entirely of Portland made photoplays. Manager Meighan, of the People's theater, intended to show the pictures during the first split of the week only, but the venture proved so successful that they were retained the full seven days.

The photoplays consisted of a six-reel drama, "A Nugget in the Rough," and a two-reel polite comedy, "The Tale of a Dress." They were produced by the American Lifeograph Company under the direction of Louis Macloon, formerly with Brenton-Holmes in Chicago. Both pictures make use of the excellent Oregon scenery

to very good advantage. Ruth Weyland, Hazel Hansen, and Harold Grady are featured.

G. E. Jackson Is Appointed Manager.

Portland, Ore.—With the coming of A. S. Kirkpatrick, formerly Portland Mutual manager and now personal representative of John R. Freuler, with headquarters in Chicago, formal announcement of the appointment of George E. Jackson, former Mutual road man, to the office of manager of the Portland branch was made. H. H. Brownell, well known in Portland film circles, is the new traveler out of the Portland office.

Oscar Hanson, booker, will leave Aug. 16 for a tour of the Mutual offices to install a uniform booking system in all of them. This system has been worked out in the Portland office during the past few years.

Mr. Kirkpatrick is making the present tour for the purpose of systematizing operation in all the Mutual offices, and is delivering a personal message from President Freuler to the branch managers of Mutual west of Denver. The managers east of the Rockies were called in conference in Chicago.

The Portland film fraternity was on hand a hundred per cent. strong to greet Mr. Kirkpatrick on his visit here. His rise in the film circles in Portland were rapid. His resigned a position as efficiency expert with the City of Portland to take up the same line of work with the Mutual when C. J. Kerr was manager of the Portland office. He afterwards became branch manager for Metro, then traveling representative for Mutual, and within a few months manager.

Mr. Kirkpatrick is returning to Chicago by way of San Francisco and Los Angeles.

New Mutual Manager for Butte.

Butte, Mont.—With the transfer of management of the Mutual office here, to the position of traveling representative out of Seattle it is announced that G. W. Whitney has been made manager. The Mutual office is enjoying excellent business.

With the Exhibitors.

Grants Pass, Ore.—The Bijou theater, Caldwell Bros., will discontinue pictures in their house for a short time and run a season of stock. While the summer slump has not been as bad this year as usual the theater managers feel that a little variety in shows will be welcome. The Bijou will resume pictures about Sept. 1.

Roseburg, Ore.—The Majestic theater, Frank Boles, is doing exceptionally well this summer.

Marshfield, Ore.—The Noble theater, Bob Marsden, is installing a new Johns organ.

Coquille, Ore.—The Scenic theater has been reopened by C. A. Pendleton.

Albany, Ore.—E. R. Cummings, the new manager of the Globe, recently made a trip to Seattle to arrange service. Mr. Cummings came to the Globe from Marshfield, where he was manager for E. M. Thurber at the Orpheum.

Emmett, Idaho.—J. M. Houston opened the new Emmett theater here September 3.

Portland, Ore.—Pete Sabo reports new installations of equipment at the Crystal theater, Astoria, and the Arcade, Springfield. W. J. White, owner of the Arcade, has sold his Springfield house.

Portland, Ore.—Sam Bernstein, who recently sold the Gem, has purchased the Elite theater in Rose City Park.

Calendar of Daily Program Releases

Releases for Weeks Ending September 1 and September 8

(For Extended Table of Current Releases See Pages 1438, 1440, 1442, 1444.)

Universal Film Mfg. Company

RELEASE FOR THE WEEK OF AUGUST 27.

GOLD SEAL—The Winning Pair (Three Parts—Dr.)	02641
NESTOR—The Night Cap (Comedy)	02642
L-KO—Props, Drops and Flops (Two Parts—Comedy)	02643
UNIVERSAL ANIMATED WEEKLY—Weekly No. 87 (Topical)	02644
STAR FEATURETTE—Hands in the Dark (Two Parts—Drama), and Old French Towns (Short Scenic)	02645
JOKER—Why They Left Home (Comedy)	02646
VICTOR—Scandal Everywhere (Comedy)	02647
UNIVERSAL SCREEN MAGAZINE—Issue No. 34 (Educational)	02648
UNIVERSAL CURRENT NEWS—Issue No. 15 (Topical)	02649
JOKER—Busting Into Society (Comedy)	02650
BISON—Jungle Treachery (Two Parts—Drama)..	02651
UNIVERSAL SPECIAL—The Gray Ghost, Episode No. 10—Title not decided (Two Parts—Dr)....	02652

RELEASES FOR THE WEEK OF SEPTEMBER 3.

GOLD SEAL—The Empty Gun (Three Parts—Drama)	02654
NESTOR—Looking 'Em Over (Comedy)	02655
L-KO—Backward Sons and Forward Daughters (Two Parts—Comedy)	02656
UNIVERSAL ANIMATED WEEKLY—Weekly No. 88	02657
STAR FEATURETTE—A Dream of Egypt (Two Parts—Drama)	02658
JOKER—Officer, Call a Cop (Comedy)	02659
VICTOR—The Curse of a Flirting Heart (Comedy)	02660
UNIVERSAL SCREEN MAGAZINE—Issue No. 35 (Educational)	02661
UNIVERSAL CURRENT EVENTS—Issue No. 16 (Topical)	02662
JOKER—A Gale of Verse (Comedy)	02663
BISON—The Lure of the Circus (Two Parts—Comedy-Drama)	02664
UNIVERSAL SPECIAL—The Gray Ghost (Episode No. 11—Two Parts—Drama)	02665

Mutual Film Corporation

WEDNESDAY, AUGUST 29, 1917.

MUTUAL—Mutual Weekly No. 139 (Topical)	05737

THURSDAY, AUGUST 30, 1917.

CUB—Jerry's Eugenic Marriage (Comedy)	05738
GAUMONT—Reel Life No. 70 (Subjects on Reel: Using The Abalone, A Little-Known Industry of the Pacific Coast; A Boy and a Rope; Handling the Mail; Beach Sports of California; "The March of Science" and "What a Bachelor Sees at a Wedding" are animated drawings from "Life"..	05739

MONDAY, SEPTEMBER 3, 1917.

MUTUAL STAR PRODUCTION—Charity Castle (American—Five parts—Drama).

MUTUAL STAR PRODUCTION—Reputation (Five parts—Drama).

WEDNESDAY, SEPTEMBER 5, 1917.

MUTUAL—Mutual Weekly No. 140 (Topical).

THURSDAY, SEPTEMBER 6, 1917.

CUB—Jerry Tries Again (Comedy).

GAUMONT—Reel Life No. 71 (Subjects on reel: A Watering System for a Small Farm; Pets Which Will Never Be Popular; Handling the Mail, Parcel Post, Money Orders, etc.; The Five Senses in Business and Pleasure; A Leaf from Life; "Fresh Advances in the Champagne District").

MAE MURRAY.

PRODUCTIONS

FIRST RELEASE
TO BE ANNOUNCED
SOON ▲ ▲ ▲ ▲ ▲

JAMES MONTGOMERY FLAGG

DIRECTION OF ▲▲
ROBERT LEONARD
FOR ....

BLUE BIRD FILMS

Stories of the Films

General Film Company, Inc.

BROADWAY STAR FEATURE.

THE ATAVISM OF JOHN TOM LITTLE BEAR (One of the O. Henry Series—Two Parts).—The cast: John Tom Little Bear (Al Jennings); Jeff Peters (Dan Duffy); Blinkly (J. Abraham); Roy Conyers (Roberto Turnbull); Mrs. Conyers (Marye Brittain); Mr. Conyers (H. E. Smith). Directed by David Smith.

John Tom Little Bear, an educated Indian, Jeff Peters, a medicine fakir, and Mr. Blinkly, a would-be actor, are resting in camp. The Indian is cooking a steak, when from the bushes opposite a tiny cloud of smoke appears. The Indian staggers and extracts from his chest a tiny bullet. He runs to the bushes and drags therefrom a boy of nine years of age holding a tiny rifle in his hands. Using stragetic means the fakir obtains from the obstinate child his name and address. It transpires that the boy, Roy Conyers, ran away from home in order to shoot redskins and that the conductor set him off the train at Kansas. After a few days the Indian becomes sincerely attached to the boy, who confidingly tells John Tom that "Papa is a bad man." The fakir advises that the boy's mother should be telegraphed, and accordingly next day Mrs. Conyers arrives.

That night at the hotel the Indian becomes greatly attracted to Mrs. Conyers, but later he confides to Jeff that he realizes only too well the racial distinction. So he determines to seek the white man's surcease—whiskey. Events move rapidly. Mr. Conyers suddenly turns up at the hotel and kidnaps the boy. When the Indian learns of this he gives a frenzied shriek and chases the kidnapper. Mrs. Conyers is frantic with grief and Jeff is striving to comfort her, when suddenly the Indian appears with the boy in his arms. He explains that he has run fifteen miles. Mrs. Conyers hurries her precious treasure indoors, and Jeff leads the exhausted Indian back to camp. Jeff then picks from the Indian's belt a man's scalp, and he visualizes the grim adventure which the Indian must have experienceed in order to rescue the boy. He knows also that John Tom Little Bear may be "Red without—but White within."

FALCON FEATURES.

THE PHANTOM SHOTGUN (Four Parts).—The cast: Van Buren Courtland (R. Henry Grey); Elizabeth Kennedy (Kathleen Kirkham; Frank Marshall (Barney Furey); Hamilton Forbes (Frank Brownlee); Betty Marshall (Gloria Payton); Patton (F. H. Gibson Gowland); Larkins (Wm. Marshall); Harding (Bruce Smith); Capt. Lloyd (Capt. J. E. Nicholson). From story by Stanley Clisby Arthur. Directed by Harry Harvey.

Van Buren Courtland, partner of Hamilton Forbes, loves Elizabeth Kennedy, Forbes' secretary, who is also loved by Forbes. Forbes has Courtland arrested for forgery and, professing friendship, finances his defense. An important state witness becoming confused, Courtland is freed, and after accusing Forbes, goes west to find the bribed witness.

Elizabeth promises to marry Forbes, having been told by him that Courtland is dead. Courtland, seeing the announcecment of the engagement, comes east to stop the marriage, but is told by Larkins, a reporter, that the marriage has taken place, and he is persuaded to leave the city. Larkins, who has all along suspected Forbes of the frame-up, follows Courtland to the pier and sees Elizabeth and Forbes boarding the ship. Fearing trouble, Larkins goes along too. Elizabeth is overcome when she sees Courtland. When he explains matters to her she quarrels with Forbes and moves to another stateroom. That night Forbes is killed and Courtland suspected. Patton, a deck steward, is recognized by Larkins as an escaped convict who had been sent to prison on the false testimony of Forbes. Suspected of the murder, Patton denies his guilt to Larkins, but admits he saw the murderer.

That night Patton is also killed and an attempt is made upon Courtland's life. It is known that a shotgun is used in each case, but none can be found on board. The crew mutiny and the phantom gun saves the captain's life. Larkins is the next to be shot and wounded. Finally, the stateroom of Frank Marshall, a passenger, is fired into. Larkins promises to solve the mystery and flips a penny which rolls under the berth. In reaching for it with Marshall's cane the cane breaks, disclosing a hidden shotgun. Marshall confesses, saying that when his sister died, having been ruined and deserted by Forbes, he had sworn to kill her betrayer "in his happiest hour." Patton had witnessed the murder and Larkins' investigations were becoming alarming, so both had to be shot. Elizabeth and Courtland are now free to marry.

THE MARTINACHE MARRIAGE (Four Parts).—The cast: Sara St. Ypriex (Margaret Landis); Mrs. Martinache (Mollie McConnell); Hermia Martinache (Leota Lorraine); Irene Lawson (Julien Beaubien); Col. Horace Martinache (Philo McCullough); Eric Martinache (Vincent Berresford); Lord Sayle (Harl McInroy); Roscoe Vandercourt (Frank Brownlee). From story by Beatrix Demarest Lloyd. Directed by Bert Bracken.

In Paris Horace Martinache, wealthy young American, aids a ragged young flower girl who was knocked down by his machine. Placing her in a hospital he leaves money to pay for her education when she recovers, and sails for home without further thought of the affair.

Some years later Martinache, still a bachelor, learns that his nephew, Eric, during a trip abroad has fallen in love with an actress and is bringing her home to gain his mother's consent to their marriage. The mother and sisters of the young heir to the Martinache millions are horrified and ask Col. Martinache's aid to break up the match. The latter consents, but orders a a genteel and diplomatic method. Madame Martinache is to invite the actress, Sara St. Ypriex, to be her guest in the household, the theory being that seeing a great deal of each other will cause the lover's devotion to cool. Sara becomes a guest at the mansion and is introduced to the social set which passes its week-ends under the hospitable Martinache roof.

Her beauty earns her new suitors, an Englishman, a nobleman of mediocre character, and Roscoe Vandercourt, a rather strong personality. To make the cure absolute Col. Martinache consents to join the house party and pay attention to the charmer. Sara is agreeably startled to discover in him her benefactor, she having been the flower girl of Paris. Col. Martinache is unaware of the coincidence, however, and his love, encouraged by the deeply grateful girl, becomes reality instead of pretense. Matters are aided when she is annoyed by the nobleman and by Vandercourt. Eric shows his fickleness when Col. Martinache is discovered in Sara's room after his response to cries of alarm, Vandercourt, her attacker, having just escaped. Col. Martinache is now committed more than ever to protect her happiness. He proposes and is accepted, while Vandercourt, now discovered to be an international crook, is removed by an avenging hand, Sara's father having traced him to America after a prison term served as the result of treachery.

KALEM.

THROUGH FIRE AND WATER (An Episode of "The Further Adventures of Stingaree"—Two Parts).—The cast: Stingaree (True Boardman); Howie (Paul C. Hurst); Kate Proctor (Edythe Sterling); Billy Shuster (Ray Hanford); Sergeant D'Aeth (Hal Clements). Directed by Paul C. Hurst.

Stingaree and his partner, Howie, while riding across Old Man Plain in the bush country of Australia, save the life of Billy Shuster, a worthless vagabond, when that individual drops a lighted cigarette, falls asleep, and catches fire. Shuster's coat is destroyed by fire, and Stingaree gives him his white one.

At their camp, Howie attempts to break a wild colt, but the horse runs away with him and finally throws him. The accident is seen by Kate Proctor, the "hired help" of Mr. and Mrs. Brockton. She helps Howie to the house and bandages his wounded arm. Stingaree, searching for Howie, arrives at the house. He finds a revolver on a side table, and Kate explains that it belonged to her husband, who has stolen her money and left her. From her description of the man, Stingaree recognizes him as no other than the man he has befriended. Shuster, having recognized Stingaree and read of the 500 pounds reward offered for his capture, is now at the troopers' barracks setting Sergeant D'Aeth on the track of the bushranger.

Stingaree rides back to the spot where he met Shuster, and there, to experience the keen delight of throwing Sergeant D'Aeth off the track, he makes new tracks in place of the old ones which have been obliterated. He rides to a stream, which he enters and rides through. Sergeant D'Aeth and Shuster, following his tracks, reach the stream. They decide that each one shall take a side of the stream and search for the tracks until nightfall. Then they shall camp for the night and meet in the morning. By evening neither has found trace of the bushranger, so they make separate camps for the night.

Before dawn, while both his pursuers are sleeping, Stingaree pays them a visit. Coming to D'Aeth camp, he trades hats with the sergeant, and also appropriates his coat. Now, with Stingaree's fancy striped hat, and a white shirt, the sergeant could easily be mistaken for the bushranger. Then Stingaree visits Billy's camp with the sergeant's horse (which he had exchanged for his own) and changes the sergeant's horse for Billy's. Taking Shuster's hat with him, Stingaree hides in the bushes to await results.

When the two pursuers awake they are astounded at the traisformations. And when Shuster sees the sergeant on Stingaree's horse, with a white shirt and Stingaree's hat, he mistakes D'Aeth for the bushranger. D'Aeth, seeing Shuster on his horse and wearing Stingaree's white coat, mistakes him for Stingaree. Both open fire, and Shuster is the victim.

Stingaree returns to Kate with the 500 pounds reward which he appropriated from the sergeant. He tells her that her husband, whom he found fatally wounded after a flight from the troopers, sent it to her.

SPARKLE COMEDY.

HER PEIGNOIR (One Reel).—The cast: Ami Simple (Tom Mulgrew); Janice Simple (Estelle Wynne); Mrs. Gay (Mrs Herbert); Mr. Gay (Hamilton Crane). Directed by Charles Pitt.

Ami Simple and his wife never tire of telling their neighbors, Mr. and Mrs. Gay, of their wonderfully happy and eugenic marriage. One morning Mrs. Simple, struck by a stunning new peignoir in Vogue, decides to have one and goes at once to her dressmaker. Ami returns home to lunch and cannot get in. With the aid of Gay he breaks in through the window and finds a note on the table which reads: "Have gone to have my peignoir cut out. Janice."

Horrified at the terrible news, Ami calls up the hospital and is told that Mrs. Simple is undergoing ether. Rushing to the hospital he bends over the bed and finds the patient is another Mrs. Simple. He shows the note to the superintendent, who calls in several doctors for discussion. After trying in vain to discover from their medical books what a peignoir is, they conclude it is some terrible new disease and assure Simple that his wife has probably gone to a specialist. Overcome, Simple enters a saloon and manages to take the edge off his sorrow.

Meanwhile Janice returns and Mrs. Gay asks her if the operation was successful. Explanations follow and Janice unwraps a bundle and shows what a peignoir is. Simple wends a crooked path home and when he, too, is told what a peignoir is he flops to the floor.

JAXON COMEDY.

TOUGH LUCK (One Reel).—Pokes and Jabs are behind with their board and are held up by the boarding housekeeper at the point of a pistol. Jabs tells her that they have money hidden in their room and she agrees to wait till they go up and get it. Mrs. Ham goes to market and returns just in time to catch the delinquents about to skip. Jabs escapes, but Pokes is caught by the hair of his head and made to work out the double board bill as cook, waiter and scrub woman. Pokes tries to escape one night, but Mrs. Ham hears the commotion and, mistaking it for burglars, notifies the police.

The cop arrives just as Pokes drops out of the window. They grapple and in the scuffle the cop loses his helmet, revealing Jabs. Mrs. Ham from the window recognizes the pair and is furious. Looking about for a weapon of vengeance, she seizes the packed trunk and hurls it at them. It hits Pokes in the head. Jabs does his duty and arrests Pokes, who appears in court the following morning a wiser and smaller man.

"As good as gold." "As white as snow." "As fine as silk." Why do other papers in this field invariably try to compare with the standard of the MOVING PICTURE WORLD? There's a reason.

SELIG.

SELIG WORLD LIBRARY NO. 14.

Vast Vineyards of California—The grape is the oldest of cultivated fruits. Its culture in California was begun by the Spanish missionaries about 1770. The grapes are picked by hand, placed in boxes and hauled to the wine presses. When grapes come to the winery they are run through a machine which crushes the grapes but not the seeds. Juice is strained from the pulp and placed in reservoirs. Here's some choice fruit.

The American Rattlesnake—The rattlesnake of Southwestern America is one of the most deadly of poisonous serpents, ready to defend itself, it seldom leads an attack. It feeds on rats, squirrels and rabbits.

The Clay Industry—The clay used is a hydrous aluminum silicate, and is formed from the decomposition of aluminous rocks. Women are employed to cast small statues. Toy animals cast from clay. Casting vases. A statuette sculptor.

The Buddhists Pagodas of Burma—About nine-tenths of the total population of Burma are Buddhists. Although banished from Hindustan, Buddhism prevails in China, Siam, Mongolia and Japan, and its adherents are said to number 147,000,000. The Shoay-Dagon at Rangoon, Burma, is the most venerable Buddhist Pagoda in the world, 970 feet high and supposed to have been built 585 B. C. The Pagoda and surrounding shrines are covered with gold leaf. A Pagoda contains some relic of Buddha, or one of his disciples, such as a bone, a tooth, or a hair. Pagodas at Mandalay, India.

THE SOLE SURVIVOR (Two Parts).—The cast: Joan Darcy (Bessie Eyton); John Gaunt (Charles Clarey); The Mad Scientist (Lafayette McKee); His Slave (Roy Watson); Thomas Wynn (Charles Wheelock). Written by James Oliver Curwood. Directed by F. J. Grandon.

Five young men meet at the home of Thomas Wynn and propose that they shall meet again there five years from that date at nine o'clock in the evening if they are alive.

The years pass and the appointed day is at hand. Only three of the five arrive on time. A letter is received from the fourth, who is dying from a bullet wound in a Bombay hospital. The three friends drink a toast to John Gaunt, the fifth and last man, "wherever he may be."

Then Gaunt appears in tattered clothing and tells a strange story. For three years he had buried himself in the wilds of Central America, in search of gold. He became lost in the jungle. He was captured by a mad scientist, who showed Gaunt a beautiful maiden imprisoned in a cage. The girl was classified by the scientist as one of his "specimens."

Gaunt tells a startling story of his hardships, of thrilling adventures and of his escape. He says that on the Coast settlement he was believed to be insane, and asks his friends to go with him to the rescue of the white girl imprisoned in jungle wilds. They go to the rescue and find the girl just in time to save her from death.

Gaunt has learned to love the girl and on the homeward journey asks her for her hand in marriage.

HER HEART'S DESIRE (One Reel).—The cast: Andres (Wheeler Oakman); John Fordyce (J. F. McDonald); Carolyn Carter (Bessie Eyton); Mrs. Carter (Lillian Hayward). Written by Lanier Bartlett. Directed by Colin Campbell.

Carolyn Carter obeys the commands of her mother, who is socially ambitious, and marries John Fordyce, a wealthy, disreputable rounder. Carolyn soon discovers, as so many women have before her, that a loveless marriage for gold only causes sorrow.

Matters go from bad to worse and finally Carolyn divorces Fordyce and goes away to live among the simple folk, between the mountains and the sea. There she meets Andres, a young shepherd, who is tending his flocks. Andres longs for an education and the beautiful stranger instructs him in book lore. Then it is that love enters the game and joins the hearts and hands of Andres, the shepherd, and Carolyn Carter, and finally she realizes her heart's desire of marriage for love and children.

Universal Film Mfg. Co.

GOLD SEAL.

THE WINNING PAIR (Three Parts—Release Week of August 27).—The cast: Beatrice (Ruth Stonehouse); Jack (Roy Stewart); John Croft (Alfred Allen); Ezra Moore (Harry Dunkinson); Gerald McLaughlin (Kingsley Benedict); Mrs. Ezra Moore (Evelyn Selbie); Hotel Clerk (Jack Dill); Mose Cohn (Walter Belasco). Written by Eugene B. Lewis. Produced by L. W. Chaudet.

Beatrice was the twenty-year-old daughter of Ezra Moore, grouchy old millionaire shoe manufacturer. Years before he had been in partnership with John Croft, but the partnership had been dissolved over a trivial matter and the two men had not spoken since. John Croft, Jr., or "Jack," a good-natured youth of twenty-four, is in love with Beatrice.

Jack is cut off by his dad, on his refusal to forget Beatrice. Holding herself in some degree responsible for Jack's embarrassing financial condition, Beatrice pays a call on the superintendent of her father's factory, with the result that Jack goes to work for Ezra Moore.

Ezra Moore specialized in men's shoes and John Croft in women's footwear. Beatrice, a "bug" on shoe leather, always kept on hand a supply of from fifteen to twenty pairs of the "fanciest make." As her father did not manufacture her style of shoes, she bought them wholesale from the Croft factory. The bill for Beatrice's shoes amounted to $380, and when her father received it he became greatly aggravated. The old man pointed out to his daughter how she had been flim-flammed on the prices, and what the prices should have been. To show that she was a good business woman, Beatrice had the Croft concern cut down the price of her shoes to meet her father's figures.

Moore had the gout in a bad way and his physician ordered him to the seaside to recuperate, and Beatrice was obliged to go along. The separation from Jack got on her nerves, so she issued orders to the head of her father's factory to give Jack the territory that embraces the seaside resort. One night, while at a week-end country party, Beatrice gets word that Jack will arrive the following day. She can't wait for the morning train. On the pretext that the message is from her father, that he has taken a sudden turn for the worse, she packs her trunk, which contains her full complement of footwear, and leaves for the seaside. On the way her car is wrecked and she is obliged to take refuge in a prominent hotel. The attaches of the hotel assume that she is a saleswoman and this suspicion is confirmed when her shoe trunk falls and bursts open, scattering her footwear over the floor. The trunk is put in the sample room. That night, Gerald McLaughlin, head of a large string of shoe stores, comes in with Jack and the latter is told about the line of shoes a new "drummer" has brought to town. Jack consults the register and wonders what Beatrice can be doing there.

The following morning Beatrice learns from Jack that she is supposed to be a shoe drummer. This appeals to her, and she decides to go through with it. The result is that she lands a half-million-dollar order from McLaughlin for his twenty-six stores. She sends the order to Jack's father. It is followed by a personal letter from McLaughlin to Croft, congratulating him on having such a saleswoman.

Later Jack learns that an army purchasing agent is about to place an order for 350,000 pairs of shoe. With the aid of Beatrice he secures the order and sends it to Moore's factory. The constant effort of Jack and Beatrice has been to effect a reconciliation between their fathers.

VICTOR.

SCANDAL EVERYWHERE (Rel. Week of Aug. 27).—The cast: The Western Man (Max Asher); The Soubrette (Gladys Tennison). Scenario written by R. A. Dillon. Produced by Craig Hutchinson.

The soubrette in the country hotel is flirting with a guest. The manager tells the detective to watch her, and she is bawled out for her acts. She leaves the hotel and outside meets Max and his wife. She flirts with Max, and his wife catches them and, bawling Max out, pulls him into the hotel. Max goes to the hotel desk to register, and catches the detective watching him. He slams the detective's head on the hotel desk and, going upstairs, shoots at him when he sees the detective examining the register for his name.

The detective grabs a water pitcher to throw it at Max, who shoots the pitcher out of the detective's hand. Max goes to his room, while the detective, to spy upon him, bores a hole from the room above and sends the plaster down on Max. Max shoots up at the ceiling, and then goes upstairs, to find the soubrette in the room, she returning after the detective vacated it.

She invites Max in, and he orders refreshments when the bell hop comes in answer to Max's shooting at the push button in the room. The detective takes the bell hop's uniform and, disguising himself, serves the drinks. Instead of a horse's neck drink he brings up the head of a horse (papier mache), and Max starts shooting at him.

The detective runs out and tells Max's wife where her husband is. She goes to the room. Max looks for his money and finds it gone. The soubrette, who has taken it, shoves the money in the detective's pocket, and Max, finding it there, starts shooting at him. They go down in a chase to the lobby where, back to the room again, Max jumps at the chandelier where the detective is hanging, and, missing the detective, hangs there and falls with the chandelier to the floor.

He goes right through the floor, down into the dining room. He goes right through the dining room table and into the lobby, where some cops mistake him for the detective, and he flees, followed by everyone. Max doubles on them, then meets his wife. That lady proceeds to take good care of him in a way he did not expect.

JOKER.

WHY THEY LEFT HOME (Rel. Week of Aug. 27).—The cast: Ira Dewberry (William Franey); Mary Mandrake (Zasu Pitts); Flossie Flatter (Lillian Peacocke); Jack Dawson (Milburn Moranti); Character Man (Burt Law); Ira's Father (Bobby Mack). Scenario written by C. B. Hoadley. Produced by W. W. Beaudine.

Ira, who is employed at the oil station, falls in love with Flossie, wife of Jack, as they drive by. Ira later announces to his father that he is going to the city, and does. Mary, his ex-fiance, learns he has gone to the city and consoles the father of Ira by announcing that she, too, is going to bring Ira home.

In the city Ira meets Hank, a property man in a theater, who invites him to come with him behind the scenes. Mary has wandered into the same theater. A drama, entitled "The Salary of Sin," is on, and during the action Jack threatens Flossie if she does not marry him. Flossie scorns Jack, and Jack thereupon steals a sum of money from a desk, places it under a rug and accuses Flossie of stealing it. Ira recognizes the principals. He takes the action literally, as does Mary, in the orchestra section. Ira has seen Jack place the money under the rug. It looks black for the accused Flossie, but Ira rushes on the stage, interrupts the performance and accuses Jack of stealing the money. There follows a struggle, much to the amusement of the audience and the consternation of Mary, who flees the theater. Ira is thrown out and, explaining to Hank, is told that Flossie has children older than Ira and has been married three times. Ira is disillusioned and Mary, happening on the scene at this critical period, the twain are reunited—happier and wiser.

BUSTING INTO SOCIETY (Rel. Week of Aug. 27).—The cast: Lizzie (Gale Henry); Rupert (Milton Sims); "Lonesome" Larry (Charles Dorien); Father (Charles Haefili); Mother (Mrs. George Hernandez). Scenario by Tom Gibson. Produced by Allen Curtis.

Rupert helped Lizzie hang the clothes on the line until it broke, and then they repaired to the kitchen, where the feminine head of the family, very much the worse for wear, hung over the ironing board. Lizzie would not hear the pleas of her Rupert to be married, for Rupert was only a hod-carrier. There must have existed in the mind of Lizzie some faint premonition of the riches to be hers, for a few minutes later the male head of the family, also very much used, burst in upon the group with the startling information that his lottery ticket had copped the grand prize and that thereafter no more ironing boards for them.

Rupert and his hod were quickly relegated to the back yard by Papa, and he and Lizzie, with, of course, Mama, went to live in a brownstone front. They wanted to get into society bad. So when the Grand Duke Larry comes along they plan a big feed for him. Larry, however, has his eyes only on their jewels, and after giving the silver the once over and dining in state, he holds them up and is about to make a get-away when the trusty hod-carrier looms on the scene.

He has, in all truth, been sticking around Lizzie pretty much despite being thrown out of the back, front and side doors a couple of dozen times, and when he sees the Grand Dooke's change of front he hops through the window and makes him come through. He covers him with the bread knife until the arrival of the officers of the law, and then the reunited family sit down and do justice to the rest of the ducal dinner, with Rupert the prospective son-in-law and hero of the hour.

NESTOR.

THE NIGHTCAP (Rel. Week of Aug. 27).—The cast: Eddie Latelywed (Eddie Lyons); Edith Latelywed (Edith Roberts); Lee Malatrops (Lee Moran). Scenario written by F. A. Palmer. Produced by Roy Clements.

When Eddie Latelywed went to the club, Edith, his wife, hurries over to her mother's home. The two women settle down to a quiet evening, except for the continual stream of advice and warning against the "wiles" of husbands that the worldly-wise mama gives.

Midnight finds the boys at the club somewhat unsteady—with divers highballs to their credit. They leave and, finding the last car gone, they commandeer a cab which stands alone, the driver having left it temporarily. The drive home is productive of laughable incidents and, arriving at Eddie's house (he having invited Lee to spend the night), Eddie discovers that he has forgotten his key, and the couple attempt to get in via the window. Inside, Eddie finds that he has but one clean pair of pajamas, so Lee dons Edith's lacy nightgown.

Edith and her mother, weary of waiting, start home. By the time they arrive the boys are asleep. They go in and Edith sees the arm and head of Lee, who has put her nightcap on, and thinks the worst. Eddie wakes up, grabs a pistol, thinking burglars are in the house, and, seeing his wife, he drops the pistol and starts to embrace her. But mother-in-law is on the job. She picks up the gun and takes a shot at the form in bed. Lee jumps up, explanations follow, and mama's plans and suspicions are foiled with the couple embracing.

STAR FEATURETTE.

HANDS IN THE DARK (Two Parts—Rel. Week of Aug. 27).—The cast: Jonathan Brewer (E. N. Wallack); Helen (Edith Johnston); Howard (J. Warren Kerrigan); Butler (Rex Roselli). Scenario written by William Parker. Produced by Henry McRae.

Helen, daughter of Jonathan Brewer, came to speak to her father regarding her love affair, but before she could make herself heard the old man, a miserly sort of a person, believed she came to request more jewels, and so paid no attention to her. A half hour before Howard, a clerk, and Helen's lover, had been sent from her father's house, accused of wanting to marry her for the possession of the jewels and coins, for which the old miser, in the neighborhood, was more hated than revered.

But Brewer is not long left to rub together his thin fingers over his earthly possessions, for he is killed. Mutely accused by his cigarette case found in the room, Howard is arrested, then convicted, and the day for his execution is set.

To the mountains with her aunt and butler Helen goes, and on the morning of the execution a forest fire routs them from their beds. The butler, acting suspiciously, arouses the girl, who follows him with a gun and, as the flames creep near, she sees him hastily dig up a bag filled with the precious stones. She covers the man with a gun and the rest comes easy. After a record run to the city and to the death chamber, the fire having broken all connections with the telephone to the city, Helen makes the trip, and she saves the life of her sweetheart.

L-KO.

PROPS, DROPS AND FLOPS (Two Parts—Aug. 29).— Shortly after the day began in the property room of the U-Funny theater there entered Griffith, the company's manager, with his associates from town. There was Mrs. Morris, the heavy, and Gladys, the soubrette. Bert, the head prop man, and Walter, his assistant, made a grab for Gladys, who was none other than the affianced of Griffith. Her suitcases and trunks received first attention, despite Mrs. Morris' fondness for both the property man and his assistant, and when her foot caught in a board in the stage and dangled into the prop room there was almost a stampede as to who should come to her assistance first. The climax arrived when Walter and Gladys were discovered in a small canoe in the middle of the lake by Griffith. The boat is overturned and, with the aid of a passerby, the two vacationists are lassoed, and almost dragged over the bridge's railing to safety. Griffith, unable to stand it longer, enters the water, when the rope is snapped, and there ensues a lively fight, with all emerging and seeking refuge in the park until their clothing dries.

A weary Willie passing along, with a penchant for stealing clothes, further complicates matters so, when the trio does finally arrive, much the worse for wear and tear, at the U-Funny theater, where the curtain is already up, some more things begin to happen. Mrs. Morris is justified in feeling slighted, and she plans a few stunts herself, which deprive Gladys of some of the spotlight, especially as she has arrived after Walter, taken from his duties as head prop man, is mustered into soubrette service. Bert finally helps out and becomes a target for the heavy, who hurls knives, daggers, hatchets and other delicate things at his head, shoulders and limbs, to show that she is an A No. 1 marksman, each time just missing a part of Bert's quivering flesh. Finally, when it comes to throwing the burning torches, a fire is started, and while the firemen are arriving other things start to happen, with Gladys, Walter and Mrs. Morris mixed up in the melee. Bert is finally rescued, after a very horrible experience, and Gladys and the chorus find that they have left little of their original abbreviated wardrobes.

ANIMATED WEEKLY.

ISSUE NO. 85 (Aug. 16).

Cliff Dwellers Are Not Extinct! Uncle Sam Has Thousands.—Soldiers living like famous Indian tribe are fit and ready to go to France—Balboa Park, San Diego, Cal.

War Detained Dutch Sailors Hold Life Boat Races on Hudson.—Crews of ships held by President's order have a holiday and regatta—New York City.

Minus Speech and Hearing, These Boys Are Real Soldiers.—Instructor—a deaf and dumb West Pointer—puts mutes through complete drills.—State School for Deaf and Dumb, Alpine, Texas. Subtitles: They can't hear nor speak, but will fight when needed! Reviewed by state officials.

Southern Hospitality Extended Jackies of Britain and America.—Mr. and Mrs. Wm. Sloane entertain 400 sea fighters at their country home.—Norfolk, Va. Subtitle: Never pick a scrap with a man who can play!

War's Latest Wonder.—Wireless controlled submarine dives, rises, launches torpedoes and is uncanny in its possibilities.—Los Angeles, Cal. Subtitles: Robert A. Norton, Harvard graduate engineer, and his wonderful invention. From an aero, battleship or fort this new sea terror can be made to enter the Kiel canal. Without a man on board it launches its own torpedoes. Speed submerging.

Creator of New Child Method of Learning Demonstrates Her Work.—Madam Montessori, in America to aid child victims of the war, shows the proper application of her methods.—San Diego, Cal.

Cartoons by Hy Mayer.

BISON.

JUNGLE TREACHERY (Two Parts—Rel. Week of Aug. 27).—The cast: Betty (Babe Sedgwick); Nathan Briggs (Charles Brinley); Bob (Fred Church); Big Bill McPherson (Fred Montague); Stenographer (Willard Wayne). Produced by Rex Hodge and W. B. Pearson.

Betty had always been a child of nature. Born in the heart of East Africa, she lived with her father, Nathan Briggs, a squatter on English territory, until now always happy.

Big Bill McPherson, the territorial surveyor to the English Government, is trying to persuade his son, Bob, just out of college and anxious to prove his worth, not to go to Africa, as two parties have already been lost there. But knowing that, if he can survey one hundred miles inland, the Government will pay him five thousand pounds, Bob heads an expedition into Africa, leaving with three men.

Nathan is prospering and has to account to no one. He hates the English, as did Betty until recently, and he is surprised to hear from a native that there is an English camp over the ridge. Betty is sent to find out what the men are in the neighborhood for, and on the way falls down a slide and sprains her ankle. The country is full of wild animals. At twilight the beasts of the jungle come forth for their prey and Betty finds herself in danger. She begins to scream for help. Bob hears the cries. He finds Betty and carries her to his tent, where he makes her comfortable and then proceeds to question her as to how she happens to be in East Africa.

Nathan has become anxious about Betty and starts out to search for her, after ordering the natives to get their forces together to attack the Englishmen. Nathan finds Betty at the tent. He swears vengeance. Betty warns Bob to prepare for fight, and by the time the natives arrive the Englishmen have made breastworks from where they fire. They are victorious in the ensuing fight.

Meanwhile, Nathan returns to his cottage. A lion, being attracted by the odor of meat, has entered the house, and as Nathan enters the door backwards, watching the fight in the distance, the animal pounces on him. He is found badly wounded and, knowing that he is about to die, sends for Betty, begging her forgiveness and confessing to Bob that it was he who had kept the English out of the territory, but pleading with him to take care of Betty.

Bob later drives the first survey line into British East Africa, and returns to introduce Mrs. McPherson to Big Bill, who is as happy over the outcome as they.

UNIVERSAL CURRENT EVENTS.

ISSUE NO. 14 (Aug. 17).

Ships! and More Ships!—Embargo on steel exports speeds up shipbuilding in America, —Pittsburgh, Pa. Subtitles: Placing ribs. Putting on the "skin."

Society's Daughters Now Expert Farmers—Girls of famous Bryn Mawr College raise produce for Uncle Sam on twenty-acre farm—West Chester, Pa. Subtitles: The sweated brow of labor. The old axe in new hands. An expert says "Some Farmers!" Canning.

Ready for Commissions in Uncle Sam's Big Army—1,200 Coast Artillery student officers receive finishing touches—An American Fort. Subtitles: Fitting in a manly way for a man's size job. The 12-inch mortars handled skilfully. "Long Liz" obeys them like a pet pup. A meal for "Long Liz." 1,070-lb. projectile and 325 lbs. of powder.

World's Largest Log Raft Makes Thousand Mile Pacific Trip—800 ft. long, 52 ft. wide, it is towed from Columbia River, Oregon, to San Diego, Cal.—United States West Coast. Subtitles: Like a huge turtle it is on its way to help Uncle Sam. 300 tons of chains used to bind it. Some logs.

Modern Mercuries on Motorcycles Furnish Thrills—Up hill or down the motorcycle corps meets and surmounts obstacles.—Somewhere near Pittsburgh, Pa. Subtitles: Off for the tests. Here he comes. But you never can tell. Zip! There goes another one.

Reviews of New York Troops Find Them Fit and Ready for France—Officers at Plattsburg and famous 12th New York makes gallant showings on inspections. Subtitles: Plattsburgh officers' training camp. These are some of the men who will command our boys in France.—Central Park, New York City. Major General O'Ryan inspects and reviews the 12th New York—the Fighting Dozen. Well, "Little Old New York" here comes your boys and they are coming back to you victorious. Their outfit je complete. Like the men, their arms also are in fighting trim.

Where War Has Been the Scars Remain— But, France is making her German prisoners repair part of their fearful destruction.—Cracenne, France. Subtitles: This was beautiful Cracune. Ribecourt, France.—Work of reconstruction being done by men who destroyed Temporary village—the old town will be permanently rebuilt. Sanitation is compulsory.

France's Fighters in Paris Celebrate the Fall of the Bastille—Soldiers, sailors, aviators—all tried and proven—show form that stopped them at the Marne.—Paris, France. Subtitles: President Poincare and general staff on way to reviewing stand. These fellows would rather fight than eat. French marines, when built, these boys lacked just one thing—a sense of fear. Aviators—While these used their legs their comrades soared above on wings. The famous French 75's that gave the enemy the jolt of its life.

"So You Thought That I'd Stand Your Bullying. Always?" Subtitle: And there's more coming to you.

UNIVERSAL SCREEN MAGAZINE.

ISSUE NO. 35 (Sept. 7).

Engineering—Panama the Second, the Great New Salmon Bay Lock of the Lake Union Canal at Seattle, Washington, Rivals Those at Panama and is One of the Greatest Structures in the World. Built by Army Engineers at a Cost of Over $5,000,000. Subtitles: When filled the lock basin contains 150,000,000 gallons of water and will accommodate vessels drawing 36 feet of water. All of the machinery is operated by electricity. Electrical pump lowers the level of the water, from that of Lake Union to sea level, in about four minutes. These immense gates weigh 210 tons each; when sea level is reached they are immediately closed in order to retain the water. Raising the water to the Lake Union level of 14 feet. The water is forced into the chamber from the bottom. Water has now reached Lake Union level and the gates open for the passage of tug or log barge.

Nature Study—Evolution of the Butterfly. No Other Insect Furnishes a More Conspicuous Example of Nature's Mystic Wonders Than the Butterfly. Subtitles: Search for the caterpillars on any green vegetation. Put them in a glass jar covered with cheese-cloth for ventilation, and feed them on leaves of same plant on which they were found. When the caterpillars are full fed and sluggish they should be transferred to an old box containing leaves and pieces of twig. They set to work and spin their cocoons. Inside the cocoon the caterpillar gradually evolves into a chrysalis. Three specimens of cocoon. To harden the birth of the butterfly, the cocoon is cut open and the chrysalis taken out. The butterfly breaks out of the chrysalis unaided and emerges to freedom. As soon as its wings are dry it flies.

Industry—Hydraulic Mining. One of the Oldest and Most Economical Methods of Mining. It is Frequently Employed in Extracting Gold, the World's Most Precious Metal, from the Rough Ore. Subtitles: Tremendously powerful stream tears out 100 tons of earth per day. Its direction is controlled with comparative ease by means of levers. The ore is washed down over many miles of mountain-side through sluice box to stream. The stream is then dredged and the ore hoisted up by a series of endless chain carriers. The cars carry the ore to the crushing machine. A novel and expeditious method of dumping. The crushing machine. This thoroughly pulverizes the ore for the smelting process. The molten gold as it comes from the smelting pot. It is molded into sizable ingots. Nothing "phoney" about this!

Screen Oddities—Penyugal Springs, Age-Old Fires in the Bowels of the Earth Heat the Waters of Penyugal Springs to a Boiling Temperature and Send Them Effervescing to the Surface. Curious Natural Phenomenon in Northern California. Subtitles: It is a time-honored custom among travelers to test the cooking efficiency of the springs. Fresh "hen fruit" serves the purpose. A few dips and they are hard boiled. Eggs are also quickly poached. "Couldn't be better, thank you!"

Art—Miracles in Mud. Produced by Willard Hopkins, Noted Sculptor. "Some Trade Mark."

Mutual Film Corp.

CUB.

JERRY'S EUGENIC MARRIAGE (August 30).—The cast: Jerry (George Ovey); Marie (Claire Alexander); Expressman (George); Pete (C. E. Feehan); Postman (Tom Riley).

Disconsolate, with only Pete, his old-time chum, for companionship, Jerry reads of the recent wedding of a man to a millionairess, effected through a newspaper want ad. To him comes the thought that he might be able to put through a similar deal. Jerry writes an ad calling for a beautiful wife, accomplished and affectionate, and clearly states he has no objection to one of wealth.

Jerry selects the picture of Marie as his prospective bride and travel far to come. Marie joins Jerry and together they go to a minister. Jerry offers his stamps for his fee. The ceremony is about to be performed when the clergyman demands Marie's eugenic certificate. They agree to visit the Eugenic Bureau. Marie is put through a severe test that results in her rejection by the physician. She departs for the railroad station to return to her home, while Jerry decides that matrimony is a pretty tough proposition.

GAUMONT.

REEL LIFE NO. 70 (Aug. 30).—The majority of people post a letter and give no thought to the intricate system required to speed it to its destination. To show what happens to the missive after it is placed in the box is the mission of "Handling the Mail," a leading section of Gaumont's "Reel Life" No. 70. After seven descriptions of various methods of collection, the work of handling the letter at the post office is described. How money orders are handled is also shown in this section.

"Using the Abalone," a little-known industry of the Pacific coast, is an entertaining series of pictures of the abalone shells, which are so popular in making jewelry, furnishing ornamentation for various articles, and as salad forks, jewel caskets, etc. The shells are removed from the rocks by deftly administered electric shocks, a method which brings the shell away intact.

"Beach Sports of California," will fascinate every one who loves the great out-of-doors. The pictures show fair bathers riding the "sport-fish," the newest sport of California beach resorts. There are also pictures of girls dancing on the beach.

A fourth section shows Bobby Feinberg, aged nine years, doing the difficult lassoo stunts which one associates with Will Rogers on the stage and with the cowboy stars of the Wild West shows. There are also two animated drawings of a humorous nature, founded upon pictures which have appeared in "Life." These are "The March of Science" and "What a Bachelor Sees at a Wedding."

PATHE EXCHANGE, INC.

HEARST-PATHE NEWS NO. 65 (Aug. 11). Great Lakes, Ill.—The Russian Mission visits the Naval Training Station to see how America turns out her splendid sea fighters. Subtitles: Five thousand Jackies are assembled to greet the distinguished savoys. They review the sturdy, courageous boys who will soon man Uncle Sam's mighty warships.

New York City.—A portable field hospital, like those used in the war zone, is established by the Rockefeller Institute as a training station for American medical units. Subtitles: The wards are light and airy and in case of aerial attack the walls are let down to facilitate quick exit. Dr. Alexis Carrel, the famous surgeon, will teach Army doctors his miraculous treatment for gangrene.

San Diego, Cal.—The ship scarcity cannot halt the building of Army camps, as the needed lumber is floating down the Pacific on rafts. Subtitles: Some rafts are 800 feet long and defy the biggest U-boats. From a distance they look like huge turtles.

Boston, Mass.—New England welcomes the Belgian Mission, and soldiers, sailors and marines join in a great tribute to the visitors. Subtitles: Russian sailors, here to purchase mine sweepers for their country, march in the parade. The envoys of bleeding Belgium, whose wrongs have stirred the world in heartfelt sympathy.

After the U-Boat.—A Western inventor plans an ingenious wireless submarine to wrest the supremacy of the deep from the ruthless foe. Subtitles: The undersea boat can submerge on short notice. And the all-important torpedo, sent on its deadly mission by the invisible electric waves.

Spartanburg, S. C.—New York's National Guard will soon be able to start training, for its cantonment is rapidly nearing completion. Subtitles: The 22nd Engineers are getting things in shape. The most welcome news—news from home.

Yellowstone Park, Wyo.—Nature's wonders in the great West come into their own as the war keeps tourists from visiting the European resorts. Subtitles: Hymans Terrace and the Grand Canyon. The park abounds in picturesque falls.

The Fall of the Bastille.—Inspiring scenes mark the celebration in Paris of the 128th anniversary of the birth of French liberty, which the nation is now struggling to save. (Official French War Pictures). Subtitles: In 1870 her liberty was successfully assailed, and at the Strassburg monument she mourns the loss of Alsace and Lorraine. But in 1917 France is resolved that her freedom shall not be crushed, and her warriors are nobly battling for its security. The heroes of the war are honored by President Poincare. Liberty shall triumph.

Denver, Colo. (Local).—Colorado celebrates its 41st anniversary as a part of the Union with a great patriotic demonstration. Subtitles: Cowboys and cowgirls take part in the parade. In the city square, where flags are presented to the State National Guard.

Cleveland, Ohio (Local).—Recruits of the Fifth Ohio Infantry parade at the ball grounds to show that they are ready for their equipment. Subtitle: The morning dip keeps them in trim.

HEARST-PATHE NEWS NO. 66 (Aug. 15). Washington, D. C.—Herbert Hoover assumes the office of Food Administrator, resolved to wage war on food speculators and extortionists. Subtitle: He asks the co-operation of all people to help conserve the food supply by preserving perishable fruits and vegetables.

New York City.—The police force is mastering the art of jiu jitsu; woe to the criminally inclined caught violating the law. Subtitles: Sergeant Shaw shows the bluecoats the new "telephone" hold, which enables a policeman to phone and keep the prisoner. Good work.

A Western Fort—The American Mission to Free Russia returns after a thorough investigation of affairs in the new democracy. Subtitles: The members of the party, who bring encouraging reports of the unification of all factions to save the newly won liberty. Ex-Senator Elihu Root, who headed the Mission.

Havre, France.—Slowly but surely the Teuton line retreats and M. Viviani, who recently visited America, visits the reconquered cities. Subtitles: Back to the bosom of France the fiery orator welcomes the liberated people. The little ones are not forgotten and there is a gift for each. They are free once more—free children of France.

London, England.—King George and Queen Mary attend services at Westminster Abbey in celebration of the great British offensive. Subtitles: British women are forming a "Legion of Honor" and many leave for service at the front. The youth of the nation also rallies round the Union Jack.

San Francisco, Cal.—The dream of a floating palace at last comes true as the Exposition building "Virginia" is removed to Santa Venetia. Subtitle: The removal of the structure intact is an engineering feat.

Toronto, Ont.—The Allies prepare for the grand struggle in the air, and thousands of aviators are in training at the Royal Camp. Subtitles: The expert birdmen study the various parts of the machine. A company of scouts set to reconnoiter the enemy's positions. Whizz the world looks like to the aviator. Remarkable scenes taken by a Hearst-Pathe News cameraman from an aeroplane.

Rockford, Ill.—Like a magic city the new cantonment springs up rapidly under the vigorous drive of an army of patriotic carpenters. Subtitles: Trench diggers dig the ditches for the water mains. Through fields of thriving corn and ripening wheat, macadam roads will soon wind their way. Student officers complete their training course and are ready to lead the National Army.
Cartoon (Magazine Section).—Growing Fast.

MISS NOBODY (Astra—Five Parts—Aug. 19).—The cast: Roma (Gladys Hulette); Crespi (Cesare Gravina); Malone (A. G. Andrews); Jack Thurston (William Parks, Jr.); Roland Fabor (Sidney Mather). Directed by William Parke.
In the life of Roma there was only one thought, who was she? She was nobody. Ridiculed by her schoolmates, she begs her guardians to tell her the truth. With her happiness at stake, they convince her that she is a distinguished English lady. Vacation time at hand, Roma is greeted into society as Lady Partington. She wins the heart of Jack Thurston, a young Englishman. Roland Fabor, a gentleman burglar, admires her. Lord Pembroke, Thurston's uncle, pays him an unexpected visit and learns of his attentions to Roma. Pembroke is an old friend of the Partington family and he knows that Partington never had a daughter. Becoming suspicious, he places a detective on the trail of Jack. Praising her guardians, Roma has Jack visit them. Unfortunately they are pawnbrokers, and this to Jack seems peculiar. Becoming furious at Jack's actions, Roma denounces him and accepts Fabor against her guardians' wishes, as they know his true character.
At a reception given in Roma's honor, Fabor shows his true colors by stealing a necklace from one of the guests, and immediately leaves and goes to Roma's guardians to have it redeemed. To prove to Roma what he is, they hold Fabor and phone her. Suspecting something, Fabor escapes, leaving the necklace behind. As the detective walks in, Roma has the necklace in her hand and is accused of theft. Pembroke is notified by the detective that he has the goods on Roma. In the presence of Jack, Roma pleads with Pembroke to assist her. She shows him her locket. Opening the locket he steps back astonished.

THE FATAL RING Episode No. 9, "The Dice of Death"—Two Parts—Astra—Sept. 2).—The cast: Pearl Standish (Pearl White); The Priestess (Ruby Hoffman); Richard Carslake (Warner Oland); Tom Carlton (Henry Gsell).
Unaware of danger and ignorant of the fact that the Violet Diamond is not within the safe, Pearl Standish endeavors to open it. The result is an explosion which wrecks the room and hurls Carslake and Pearl to the floor. Tom and Spider learn Pearl's whereabouts. Dopey Ed, Carslake's henchman, regains his senses and shakes Carslake. His first thought of Carslake. Regaining consciousness, Pearl sees Ed. She throws herself upon him. Pearl opens his hand and the Diamond falls to the floor. Picking the Diamond up, Pearl rushes to the other room, only to be encountered by Ed again, and is knocked to the floor. Tom and the Spider arrive. Dopey Ed sees them and eludes them by jumping through the window. As they pass Carslake, he appears to be unconscious. Going to Pearl, they revive her. Carslake rises and, seeing the Diamond on the floor, picks it up and escapes.
The next afternoon Carslake, unaware of Dopey Ed's attempt to double cross him, plots with him to regain the setting for the Diamond. He sends his men to Pearl's home and by a trick they draw Pearl out into the garage. Binding her hand and foot, they bring her to Carslake's den.
Tom, worried, returns to the Standish home in an attempt to persuade Aunt Ella to prohibit Pearl's further quest for the ring. The phone rings and Tom answers it. Carslake is speaking. "The setting for the Diamond is in the top drawer of her dresser. Bring it to the Grand Central at three o'clock." Tom consents. Tom is at the station at the appointed time and, placing the setting in the ring, passes it into Carslake's pocket. Wiggsey Benson, a successful pickpocket and one-time confederate of Carslake, sees the incident between Carslake and Tom. Walking up to Carslake, he shakes him by the hand and at the same time fetches the envelope from his pocket. Realizing his loss, Carslake immediately follows Benson, and is in turn followed by Tom.

Tracking him to an apartment, Carslake enters, while Tom remains outside.
Pearl finds herself locked alone and, in looking for a means of escape, she accidentally touches a wainscoting. Its secret compartment opens and to her surprise she finds the Violet Diamond. Overjoyed, she attempts to escape, but as she is about to go down the stairs she trips and falls to the bottom. Carslake's men bring her back and, wrapping her in a quilt, they place her on the sofa. She appears to be unconscious. Carslake left instructions that if he did not return by three o'clock, Pearl should be killed, and the hour was not very far off. Carslake had followed Benson into the apartment. Closing the door behind him, he is astounded to see the Priestess and her adherents. Carslake tries to struggle with the Arabs, but is finally subdued. Death staring him in the face, Carslake promises to get the Diamond for the Priestess. Looking at his watch he sees it is near three, so he warns the Priestess to hurry. Grabbing a knife from her hand, Tom follows them. Nearing his den, Carslake sees Tom's taxi behind him. Sending one of the Arabs off the machine, Carslake has him fire and puncture the tires of Tom's machine. Arriving at his den, Carslake jumps off the machine and rushes in. Throwing the door back, he sees his man plunging the dagger in the wrapped up form on the sofa.

Miscellaneous Subjects

K-E-S-E.

EFFICIENCY EDGAR'S COURTSHIP (Essanay—Five Parts—Sept. 3).—The cast: Edgar Bumpus (Taylor Holmes); Mary Pierce (Virginia Valli); Mr. Pierce (Ernest Maupain); Wimple (Rodney LaRock).
Efficiency wins success in business; why not in love? Edgar Bumpus, a rising young man, applies this reasoning to his courtship of Mary Pierce. He first eliminates Wimple, his closest competitor, who plays a guitar, by learning to play a saxophone, which makes louder noise, and by sending Mary flowers and candy each time Wimple calls on her. The plan works O. K., until the saxophone disturbs Mr. Pierce's slumbers. He and Edgar clash and the latter is forbidden to visit Mary any more.
Edgar employs a clipping bureau to send news items to Mr. Pierce which tells of the troubles young girls get into when their fathers refuse to let them have bank. One eloped with a milkman; another disappeared. This has no effect upon Mr. Pierce, however, except to make him hate Edgar more. However, the youth's persistence finally wins Mary's love. Then Edgar plays his trump card. He sets Mary to sign a legal agreement to forfeit $10,000 to him, unless she marries him. The two then confront Mr. Pierce with this document. Rather than lose the money, he consents to lose his daughter, the only stipulation being that Edgar will throw away his saxophone. Thus efficiency triumphs.

CONQUEST PICTURES.

T. HAVILAND HICKS—FRESHMAN (Three Parts—On Program No. 7—Aug. 25).—The cast: T. Haviland Hicks (Lay McKee); Jack Merritt (Albert Macklin); Theophilus Opperdyke (James Turbell); Brewsters (William Sherwood). Scenario by Raymond B. Dakin.
T. Haviland Hicks contracts an intimate friendship with Theophilus. They are freshmen. Hicks is saturated with good humor. Theophilus' main characteristic is timidity and the least excitement makes him faint. The sophomores, indignant at Hick's abuse of the banjo, prepare to haze him. Theophilus overhears their scheme and warns Hicks. Hicks hurls a defy at the sophomores to the effect that they are welcome to haze him, but if they fail to do so, Theophilus and himself are to be secure from hazing for all time.
They accept the defy and on the appointed night repair to his room wrapped up in pillow cases. Hicks smashes the drop light against the wall and the room is steeped in darkness. When a light is secured, Hicks is not to be found and the sophomores conclude that he has dived through the window. In fact, he is right among them, wrapped up in a pillow case. The duped sophomores plan to avenge themselves. Hicks gets wind of their scheme and awaits developments with absolute calm.
On the fated night the sophomores drag Hicks out of bed and carry him off to their

lair. They proclaim him to be the original "missing link" and urge him to do an imitation of a monkey; but he dives through a window into a tennis net held ready for the purpose by a number of freshmen. The pursuing sophomores encounter a superior number of freshmen and are roughly handled.

Thereupon the sophomores post a defy, daring Hicks and his class to substitute the freshman colors for the sophomore colors, which will be found floating from the flag pole at a stated hour. Hicks dons a coat of mail, disguises Theophilus as a gorilla and succeeds in routing the sophomores and hoisting the freshman colors. Hicks becomes the most famous man at college.

"GALLEGHER" (Two Reels—On Program No. 7.—Two Parts—Aug. 25).—The cast: Gallegher (Andy Clark); Stephen Hade (Jack Willard); Dwyer (William Wadsworth); Detective Heffinger (Lou Stearn).

Gallegher is a fighter by birth, a student of crime by choice, and an office boy at the "Press" by necessity. His ambition, however, is to become another Sherlock Holmes. A sensational murder case is just going the rounds of all the newspaper offices. A millionaire has been murdered and the disappearance of Stephen Hade, his secretary, together with a large sum of money, leaves no doubt as to the perpetrator of the crime. A photograph and a full description of the murderer appear in every paper, and a reward of $5,000 is offered for the apprehension of the criminal. Particular attention is drawn to the fact that the index finger on Hade's right hand is missing. The reporters of the "Press" are advancing their theories of how Hade is most apt to be caught. Gallegher listens. His theory is that Hade will always be found wearing gloves of which one finger will be stuffed with cotton. The only man on the staff Gallegher respects is Dwyer, the sporting editor, who has just received information of a championship fight that is to be staged at the Eagle Inn at Torresdale on Wednesday.

The office of the "Press" receives a visitor in the person of Mr. Heffinger of the Secret Service. Gallegher is so engrossed on the detective's conversation that he neglects his office duties and even accompanies him to his hotel, where he astounds him by his knowledge of criminals, and his offer of assistance towards the apprehension of a notorious forger on whose trail Heffinger is just bent.

On his way back to the office he passes the railway station, where he sees a man wearing gloves with the right index finger standing out in a peculiar way. Gallegher decides to stick to his trail and follows him to Torresdale and thence to Eagle Inn. There he learns that Hade is going to attend the championship fight, which is to be staged in a big barn at the inn without the knowledge of the police.

Gallegher dispatches a telegram to Heffinger, asking him to meet him at the station, and then hurries back to Philadelphia and to the home of Dwyer to convey the news to the sporting editor. Dwyer sends a note to the city editor urging him to hold back the forms for the next morning's issue as long as possible. Accompanied by Gallegher, he hurries to the station, where they meet Heffinger. They get to Eagle Inn. Dwyer is admitted to the barn, while Gallegher and Heffinger climb to the hay loft, whence they can look down into the arena. While the fight is going on the police break into the barn and arrest everybody, including Dwyer. Heffinger secures Hade and being of the Secret Service is permitted to leave with his prisoner.

Gallegher stealthily secures the "copy" from Dwyer's pocket and, by pretending to be the son of the innkeeper, is permitted to get out of the barn to take leave of his father before he is taken to prison. When Gallegher reaches the outside he leaps into a cab and drives away at top speed. What with cold and excitement at the hands of policemen he encounters on the way, it is only by dint of grit and cunning that he succeeds in reaching the office of the "Press" just as the city editor is about to give the order to close the forms.

YOUNG SALTS (600 Feet on Program No. 7 —Aug. 25).—This subject reviews the life of the marine. At the Culver Naval School the day begins at six o'clock. The morning is spent in such exercises as boxing, racing, scaling fences and playing tennis. This is followed by a Cutter Drill. In the afternoon a race is usually held between cutters, water sports play an important part in the life of a marine. The film shows the men giving remarkable exhibitions of fancy diving—sliding down the shute, and of the unique "chain dive." It ends with a series of scenes which show that marines are not only sailors, but crack soldiers as well.

HOLY LAND (400 Feet on Same Reel as Foregoing).—This scenic of the Holy Land opens with a view of the Garden of Gethsemane, now a Russian monastery. Other views include a panorama of Jerusalem from the

---

Fill Up Our Soldiers' Pipes

America's fighting men need tobacco to make trench life a little more comfortable. Here's a chance to treat the boys at the front.

"Our Boys in France Tobacco Fund" has been organized to furnish "smokes" for the American soldiers and sailors in active service.

All labor and administrative expenses are contributed, so that every cent you give goes to pay for tobacco which is purchased in large quantities at a low price.

One dollar buys four packages of tobacco and sends them to France. Each package, costing twenty-five cents, has a retail value of forty-five cents, and keeps a man in "smokes" for a week. Every dollar sent to "Our Boys in France Tobacco Fund" buys a bundle of tobacco that would cost $1.80 at your cigar store.

In every package is a post card addressed to a contributor to the tobacco fund. In accepting the package the soldier or sailor agrees to send on the card a message to his benefactor in the United States. According to the plan, every person who gives a quarter gets his receipt from a fighting man in France.

The work of this fund is approved by the Secretary of War and the Secretary of the Navy.

Send as many dollars as you can spare. Write your name and address clearly.

"Our Boys in France Tobacco Fund"

19 West 44th Street

New York City

Mount of Olives; of the busy mart in what was once the Pool of Siloam; of lepers and beggars waiting for alms; of the ancient Wailing Place of the Jews at whose walls men and women are forever wailing, as they did thousands of years ago. Among other scenes are Christian Pilgrims carrying the cross along the way to Calvary; the Gate of Damascus; a caravan going through the desert, and the little town of Bethlehem. Views of the latter include women making cakes and using goatskins as churns, people picking olives on the hills around Bethlehem, and tending their flocks today, just as they did centuries ago.

TURNING OUT SILVER BULLETS (1,000 Feet on Program No. 7—Aug. 25).—These pictures were taken at the Philadelphia Mint by permission of the United States Treasury Department. We see raw material transformed into a fiery liquid, cast into ingots and pressed into rolling mills, where it undergoes twenty-eight different operations. Another machine pounds out the blanks, which are smoothed, cleaned and rounded off at the edges, at which stage they are cast into the coining machine that stamps out the finished coin. This is examined for defects, counted and weighed by machine.

ART DRAMAS, INC.

THINK IT OVER (U. S. Amuse. Corp.—Five Parts—Aug. 13).—The cast: Alice Rowland (Catherine Calvert); Henry Whitworth (Richard Tucker); George Baring (A. Lloyd Lacic); James Baring (Eugene Borden); Mrs. Martin (Auguste Burmester). Written and directed by Herbert Blache.

The action of this comedy-drama centers around Alice Rowland, an orphan under the guardianship of George Baring, an unscrupulous man, desirous of her fortune. To gain his ends Baring tries to force Alice to marry his son, James. Alice, however, is under the care of Henry Whitworth, an old friend of her mother's, who, although he has no legal jurisdiction over her, nevertheless thwarts the plans of her guardians in several instances. Baring spirits Alice away from Whitworth and confines her in his own home. She escapes and flees to Whitworth in the middle of the night. Both realize that her guardians can claim her legally, and for a time both are confronted with the problem of escaping them. Alice comes to an amazing decision, which startles Whitworth out of his wits. It is that she shall marry him and thus dissolve the guardianship.

FOX FILM CORP.

THE SOUL OF SATAN (Five Parts—Aug. 19).—The cast: Miriam Lee (Gladys Brockwell); Joe Valdez (Bertram Grassby); Calvert Carson (Charles Clary); Alden Lee (William Burress); "Chicago" Stone (Josef Swickard); Fanny Stone (Gerard Alexander); Jim Calvert (Norbet Myles); Hazel Valdez (Lucille Young); Miriam's brother (Frankie Lee); Miriam's sister (Marie Kiernan). Directed by Otis Turner.

The story centers about Miriam Lee, whose life of drudgery is unrelieved until Joe Valdez enters it. She does not know that Joe in years past had eloped with Jim Calvert's wife and had been driven from the mining settlement where the event took place. Calvert had sworn he would find Valdez and have his revenge. Miriam's intimacy with Joe has its inevitable result. Her father forces her from the house, and Joe, simulating sympathy, offers marriage. Joe stages a fake ceremony, but the girl suspects nothing. She rejoices in being joined legally (as she thinks) to the man she has always loved, despite his faults. Joe prospers as the manager of a high-class gambling club, and Miriam herself becomes known as Myrtle Beaumont, Queen of the Night. Through her Joe has been able to win huge amounts from the rich men she has lured to his establishment.

When "Lucky" Carson arrives in New York, Joe plans to ensnare him. He sends Miriam on her usual errand, but "Lucky" understands the game she is to play, and goes through with it. In the incidents which ensue Carson recognizes...

nizes Joe Valdes and telegraphs to Calvert in the West. Then Valdes comes face to face with his bitterest enemy. Miriam, who has prided herself on having been a faithful wife, now learns that she has never been a wife at all. And in the silence of the night, as Joe Valdes lies dead from a pistol shot of Calvert's, Carson tells his tale of love to Miriam.

A DOMESTIC HOUND (Foxfilm—Two Parts —Aug. 13).—The cast: Hank (Hank Mann); Shorty (J. C. Weldon); Mrs. Hank (Eva Nelson); Mrs. Shorty (Katherine Griffth); The Ingenue (Rena Rogers); The Heavy (Harry Moody); The Cop (Harry O'Connor); The Man-with-Money (Robert Kortman). Hank is the hound. He has an able assistant domestic hound in Shorty. Both Hank and Shorty are at the beach on a vacation, but they are handicapped in their sightseeing trip by the presence of their wives. The hounds make several attempts to visit the pretty ingenue who has just come from the bath-house attired in her bathing suit. They do succeed in escaping from the hotel at which the spouses are staying and meet the ingenue on the beach. Unfortunately for the hounds, however, the "Heavy" thinks 'enough of the ingenue to resent the intrusion. He' shows his resentment plainly. Hank's face shows it also, when the "heavy" finishes. In the chase that follows, Hank and Shorty run faster along that beach than a man whose clothes have been stolen. Being only mortal, they grow weary of flight and seek refuge under two beach umbrellas. When they find their wives are the holders of the umbrellas, the outlook does not seem particularly rosy to the hounds. They flee with more determination, if less speed, than before. That evening the two wander to a roof garden. Hank did not know that a man who had a grudge against him had dropped a big roll of bills in his pocket. Consequently, the hound begins dispensing greenbacks right and left until wiyen, "heavy," cop and the owner of the money appear. Hank and Shorty leave the scene via balloon.

JACK AND THE BEANSTALK (Standard Pictures—Ten Parts).—The cast: Francis and Jack (Francis Carpenter); Virginia and Princess Regina (Virginia Lee Corbin); Prince Rudolpho (Violet Radcliffe); the King of Cornwall (Carmen Fay DeRue); Blunderbore, the giant (J. G. Tarver); the Giantess (Vera Lewis); Francis' Father (Ralph Lewis); Francis' Mother (Eleanor Washington); Virginia's Mother (Ione Gleason). Adapted for the screen by Mary Murillo. Directed by C. M. and S. A. Franklin.

William Fox's version of 'Jack and the Beanstalk" requires a modern setting, or prologue, before Jack's adventures begin, bringing the film story right down to every-day reality. Jack, at first, is just a healthy, normal kiddie, who, in modern life is known as Francis, and his little neighbor is called Virginia. When we first meet them in the picture the mothers have gone to an afternoon tea, leaving Francis and Virginia with a nursemaid. She does the most natural thing in the world—reads them a story of "Jack and the Beanstalk." Then the wonderful idea comes to Francis. He is quite sure that all that is necessary to find the enchanted forest is to go and look for it. He has his toy automobile, too. And so he conspires with his little playmate, Virginia, and they start forth, with their dog "Sport," to find the place in the woods where the terrible giant lives.

Fortunately the children take plenty of wraps with them, for the inevitable dark creeps upon them and even the courage of the giant-seeker is taxed a bit as he listens to the screeching of the owls and he feels that sleep is creeping upon him. He cares tenderly for his little friend as she gathers her tiny robes about her, and finds the softest place on the ground. Then Francis himself succumbs, and the Dream God waves his magic wand, and lo, and behold, Francis becomes the Jack of Beanstalk fame, and Virginia is the Princess Regina.

Everybody knows the age-old story of "Jack and the Beanstalk." Jack sells his mother's cow for a sack of beans. Instead of being delighted with his bargain she scolds him roundly and throws the seeds out of the window. They are magic seeds, however, and sprout immediately. The next morning the seeds have become a wonderful vine, which grows until it has reached the clouds.

Jack is filled with the spirit of adventure and, besides, his fairy godmother has told him that fortune awaits him if he but climb the stalk. Jack starts out and finally reaches the top, arriving in a country where a terrible giant dwells. Here again Jack's fairy godmother meets him and tells him he must slay the giant and secure all his riches, thus avenging Jack's father. While in the lands above the clouds Jack meets Princess Regina, whom he rescues from the giant. Jack finally causes the terrible giant's death and marries the Princess —and they live happily ever afterward.

in the epilogue Francis and Virginia, who are asleep in the wood, are found by their distracted parents and taken home.

METRO PICTURES CORP.

THE GIRL WITHOUT A SOUL (Rolfe—Five Parts—Aug. 13).—The cast: Unity Beaumont and Priscilla Beaumont (Viola Dana); Hiram Miller (Robert Walker); Ivor (Fred Jones); Dominic Beaumont (Henry Hallam); Henrietta Haleman (Margaret Seddon); Louise (Margaret Vaughan). Written and directed by John H. Collins.

Dominic Beaumont, mender of violins, lives in a country village with his twin daughters, Unity and Priscilla. Priscilla has inherited a talent for music from her mother. Unity is skilled in household duties. On account of her lack of artistic temperament her father considers her "a girl without a soul." Ivor, a traveling musician, is attracted by Priscilla and gives her music lessons. He tells her that she has a great future before her. She is unsuspicious of the man's true character, and knows nothing of the girl Louise, whom Ivor also promised "to make," but who now lives in the city in abject misery.

Unity's sweetheart is the village blacksmith, Hiram Miller. To Hiram has been entrusted the church fund for a new organ. Hiram obtains Beaumont's permission to pay for a term at boarding school for Unity. Ivor tells Priscilla the only thing that stands in the way of her success is the lack of funds. Priscilla thinks of the money in Hiram's desk and steals it.

In Hiram's absence the church committees go to his rooms to get the money to pay for the organ, which has arrived. They find the money gone. On Hiram's return to town with Unity from her graduation, he is accused of stealing the money entrusted to him. In vain he protests. Miss Haleman, on the committee, is also the village storekeeper, and she says that Hiram has plenty of money to buy dresses for young women.

Unity secretly a note sent by Ivor to Priscilla, telling her where to meet him, so that they may elope. Donning Priscilla's cape, Unity keeps the appointment, and thinking she is her sister, Ivor takes her to a country hotel. He tells her that through a misunderstanding the minister will not be able to marry them until the morning, but asks at once for the money. The disappearance of the money is then clear to Unity. She denounces Ivor, locks him in the room and escapes. When she confronts her sister, Priscilla confesses to having stolen the money. She gives it to Unity, who promises to shield her.

Hiram is placed on trial. Everything looks black for him, when Unity rushes in with the money. She is accused of the theft. She protests her innocence, but refuses to say who is the guilty person.

Ivor has escaped from the inn and comes for Priscilla. He asks at once for the money. Realizing that it is more for the money than herself that he has returned, she leaves him and rushes to the courthouse, where she tells the truth. Hiram slips from the courthouse, and goes in pursuit of Ivor. He overtakes the musician and takes him back to the village. He hands Ivor over to the authorities.

Priscilla tells her father: "You have always misjudged Unity—it is she who has the soul, not I. I've been narrow and selfish, but I'm going to do better now."

GREATER VITAGRAPH.

BOBBY, BOY SCOUT (Aug. 8).—The cast: The Boy Scout (Bobby Connelly); his Mother (Mabel Ballin); Capt. Barnacle (William Shea).

The picture opens with Bobby engaged in scrubbing his little ragamuffin dog. Then it switches to his mother, who has just been ordered out of her seaside cottage because of inability to pay the rent. She tells Bobby that they must move and the folks below, saddened, goes for consolation to his friend, old Captain Barnacle. The old sailor hears Bobby's story and, to get his mind of it, takes him for an outing on an island across the bay.

On the island, they prepare to cook dinner and Bobby is sent to gather twigs for the fire. While thus engaged, he sees a pair of gun runners loading rifles on a boat and while he is watching the operations of one the other comes up and makes him a prisoner.

Bobby is tied hand and foot and left in a cave. From the men's conversation, he learns that they are violating the federal law and the Boy Scouts' oath comes to his mind. He gets free from his bonds and, finding a large-calibre revolver, loads it with cartridges he had taken from the Captain's rifle. He surprises the smugglers at the mouth of the cave and commands them to throw up their hands. They, believing the gun unloaded, rush for him and he fires, narrowly missing one of the men.

Captain Barnacle, hearing the report of the shot, rushes to the cave and there helps Bobby make the men prisoners. They are taken back to the mainland and turned over to the federal officers. Later, Bobby is given a reward by the government for his action and the money saves his mother from losing her cottage.

BOBBIE, MOVIE DIRECTOR (Aug. 16).—The cast: Bobby, screen star (Bobby Connelly); Bobby's leading lady (Aida Horton); Bobby's mother (Mabel Ballin).

The picture opens with Bobby trying to work in a new picture when he does not feel like working and the director is despairingly trying to show the little star how to make a proper entrance. Bobby slips away to an adjoining studio, where Anita Stewart and a lot of grown-up Vitagraph stars are putting on a grand ball room scene. He keeps right on moving away from that director until he runs across a friendly driver of a fish wagon who carries him to where a lot of boys are playing marbles. Bobby is happy. He gets into the game and is having a great time until Aida, the leading lady, perched on a gate, recognizes him.

"I know you," she pipes. "You're Bobby Connolly, who plays in the movies."

The boys all crowd about Bobby. The truant star admits the assertion and adds, when asked what he can do, that "I am a director." Furthermore, he orders them to follow him to the beach where he will show them what sort of a director he is and overrules their decision that little Aida shall not come along.

They all pile into a boat and on reaching the "location" Bobby proceeds to direct the picture "Pokyhauntus," with Aida in the leading role and himself as "John Smith—Injun." Bobby makes real Indians of them and with an old cigar box for a camera leaves little to the imagination.

Meanwhile, Bobby has been missed at home and so has his leading lady and all other members of the "Pokyhauntus" cast. Bobby's mother appeals to Capt. Barnacle, who stops the director and his company through his field glasses and goes to the rescue.

BOBBY, PHILANTHROPIST (Aug. 20).—The cast: The Philanthropist (Bobby Connelly); The Ragged Dan (Aida Horton); Bobby's Mother (Mabel Ballin); Captain Barnacle (William Shea).

Bobby one day sees a big, rough man cruelly treating a kitten. Without hesitating, the youngster steps up to the man and upbraids him for his cruelty and takes the kitten away. The second occasion of Bobby's chivalry comes a few days afterwards when Booby sees a crowd of boys bullying a newsgirl. Rolling up his sleeves and not stopping to count the odds against him, he pitches into the gang. The little girl, Miss Aida Horton, Vitagraph's 3-year-old, gamely backs up her champion, but Bobby is getting worsted when a policeman happens along and the boys scatter.

Bobby then listens to the girl's story; she is afraid to go home. He promptly takes her to his home, where his mother welcomes her and decides to keep her as Bobby's sister, when she learns she is a waif whose parents are unknown. The little girl is named Mary and Bobby proudly takes her to Captain Barnacle to whom he introduces her as a "good scrapper."

BOBBY, THE PACIFIST (Aug. 20).—The cast: Bobby (Bobby Connelly); Her (Aida Horton); Captain Barnacle (William Shea); Bobby's Mother (Mabel Ballin).

Bobby comes on two boys fighting and when he tries to interfere, the older one turns on him and strikes him. Bobby rolls up the sleeves of his Boy Scout coat and prepares to do battle. Then he recalls the injunction of his pastor, of turning the other cheek when your tormentor hits you on one. He drops his arms and the boy in disgust hits him again and walks away. To make matters worse, his sweetheart has witnessed it all.

A few days later, a ball, thrown in play, strikes a rough man in the face and Bobby, running away, takes refuge in a deserted house. He discovers it is the headquarters of a band of kidnappers and that six little sweetheart is a prisoner in the next room.

Bobby realizes his opportunity is at hand to show her and his playmates he is not a "'fraid cat." He ties a rope across the top of a flight of stairs, and luring the kidnappers from the room knocks them over the rope and down the stairs. Then he barricades the door from the inside and heliographs to Captain Barnacle for help. The captain arrives just as the kidnappers break into the room.

BOBBY'S BRAVERY (Sept. 3).—The cast: Bobby (Bobby Connelly); His Teacher (Mabel Ballin); Steve (George Forth).

Bobby is in love with his school teacher, Miss Cynthia, and dreams he is a big, brave knight and rescues her from a robber band. To demonstrate his bravery, he persuades the school yard and frightens the children out of their wits. Then Bobby decides he will be a knight and his school chums his loyal warriors. So he "knights" them all by a most

---

---

impressive oath and arms them with staves. All that is needed now is a bold robber to try to steal Miss Cynthia.

Sir Bobbie and his band are in the woods when the teacher and Steve, who is in love with her, pass, and Bobby hears Steve say something about stealing her and carrying her off. Steve, of course, is a bad robber, and Sir Bobby's work is cut out for him.

One night Steve takes Cynthia for a walk in the woods, and Bobby and his band are on hand to capture the robber. The boys all wear masks and have a sack to tie over Steve's head. The "robber" and Miss Cynthia are seated on a rock and she has just said "yes" when Bobby gives the word. The boys descend on Steve and get the bag over his head, but the man, after a brief struggle, throws them off. All flee but Bobby, and he is a much abashed Sir Galahad who stands before Miss Cynthia and tells her the whole story. But she and Steve are too happy not to forgive Bobby and his henchmen, for the youngsters, meeting later, vote to disband after taking a new and more solemn oath to remain "bachelors fourever."

TRANSGRESSION (Five Parts—Aug. 20).—The cast: Stephen Page (Earle Williams); Hal Page (Webster Campbell); Mrs. Page (Mary Maurice); Kent Hayward (Edward Davis); Marion Hayward (Corinne Griffith); Carline Shrefton (Billie Billings); James Reede (Jack Ellis); Burt Staley (Denton Vane). Directed by Paul Scardon.

Hal Page becomes infatuated with Carline Shrefton, a woman who lives by her wits. Because of his inheritance she makes a play for him, and throws down her first suitor, Burt Staley.

Both men meet at her house one night; a quarrel starts between them and Staley is killed. Hal's brother, Stephen Page, is Mayor of the city. He arrives at the house, and when Hal confesses his guilt he spirits him out of the city, and arranges things so that Staley's body is picked up in an alley the next day.

One year later Steve is engaged to marry Marion Hayward, daughter of the district attorney. Hayward is about to convict a crooked political band headed by Jim Reede; who, strange to say, is married to Carline. The latter goes to the Mayor and threatens to expose him unless he gets district attorney to let up on her husband.

He refuses. She goes to the district attorney, who also refuses to let duty interfere with friendship. She sends for reporters and just when it looks as though exposure must come, Hal mysteriously turns up. He tells all that he did not kill Staley—took blame to shield the woman Carline. Staley was killed in a struggle with Carline.

Hayward verifies what he says, then sends for Carline and she breaks down under grilling. She signs a confession exonerating Hal. Reede is sent away.

proctocior, who is none other than "Bill" Lawson, son of the "Killer," whom he deserted. Bill
bests Jepson, and brings on a general fight
between the lumberjacks and the employees of
the Nugget. Just as Curtis, with murder in his
heart, aims his gun at the "Killer," a shot rings
out and cheats him of his vengeance. Hilda,
who has been persecuted and abused by White
from the day she ran away with him, is the
murderess.

On his deathbed White tries to make what
amends he can for his many misdeeds. He dies
without his son's becoming aware of his identity.
tell him that Marta is not his daughter, but
that of Curtis, and the two young people go
forth into life together.

BUTTERFLY PICTURES.

THE LAIR OF THE WOLF (Five Parts—
Aug. 20).—The cast: Margaret Dennis (Gret-
chen Lederer); Oliver Cathcart (Joseph Gir-
ard); Jim Dennis (Chester Bennett); Raymond
Taylor (Val Paul); Robert Shepherd (Chas.
Mailes); Bess Shepherd (Peggy Custer); Steve
Taylor (Donna Drew); Old Man Taylor (George
Berrell). Scenario by E. Magnus Ingleton.
Produced by Chas. Swickard.

Oliver Cathcart's manners are perfect, thinks
Margaret Dennis, a widow, as she enters his
office with her son, Jim, to secure a position
from the latter. Cathcart has a charming personality, but behind it lies a sensual and
brutal nature. He is feared by his employees,
among whom is Raymond Taylor, a young man
whose family has been ruined in a financial
deal with Cathcart. His mother died as a result and his father, Old Man Taylor, is now a
drunkard, depending entirely upon the eighteen-year-old sister, Steve. Raymond and the
old man vow to get revenge on Cathcart. Jim
learns of Cathcart's bad reputation. Later
when she announces that she is going to marry
Cathcart, Jim makes his mother choose between
him and Cathcart, and tells her he never wants
to see her again. They go to a country estate
called "The Pines," but by the villagers, "The
House of Gloom." Here Margaret learns of
her husband's true character.

The garden of "The Pines" is cared for by
Robert Shepherd, a good man who worships
his daughter, Bess. Near them live the Tay-
lors. Steve and Bess are good friends. Old
Man Taylor pals with The Man With the
Crutch, a short, thin, sinister, lame man, who
also craves vengeance on Cathcart because of
the latter's treatment of a sister. He and
Taylor can revenge together, and finally the
cripple offers to pay Taylor for committing the
murder.

Meanwhile, Steve, full of romance and a
longing for adventure, and with the ten dollars she has earned by washing, sets out,
dressed in boy's clothes, leaving a note to
say that she has gone out to see the world.
Raymond visits his people and also Milly, Margaret's maid, and his sweetheart. Margaret
gives him a message to take to Jim. Cathcart catches Raymond and Jim talking. He
fires Raymond because he will not say what
they were talking about. Jim wires his mother
that he will come to see her.

Margaret, having borne Cathcart's brutality
long enough, will not let him in when he
arrives at "The Pines." He sends Shepherd to
the village for a locksmith, but Shepherd goes
only a short distance, for he meets a man
who proffers to give the message to the locksmith.

Jim arrives and promises to take his mother
away the next day. When he leaves by way
of a French window he is seen by Milly and
Taylor. He gets caught in a rainstorm and
seeks shelter in a deserted hut, where Steve is
now trying to sleep. He thinks Steve a boy
and they become friends. Raymond finds the
note by Steve and, thinking Cathcart responsible, goes to the village tavern to find his
father and there tells the landlord that Steve
has gone away and that Cathcart has discharged him. Raymond starts out to "get"
him.

That night Cathcart is killed. Milly testifies to seeing Jim lurking about "The Pines,"
to the message sent him by Margaret and to
the wire received from Jim. Margaret hires
one of the best lawyers available and he soon
learn's that Jim's only chance is in finding
Steve, who can furnish the only conclusive
evidence in his favor, for she knows he was a
mile away from the house at the time of the
murder.

Margaret can bear the suffering of her son
no longer and says she killed Cathcart, but
Jim urges the court not to believe her. Then
the landlord who heard Raymond's threat to
"get" Cathcart testifies, and suspicions is cast
at Raymond. Robert Shepherd confesses that
he killed Cathcart, because, returning to the
lodge the night he was sent for the locksmith,
he found Cathcart there struggling with Bess.
Cathcart's brutality to her aroused for the
first time in his life an overpowering passion
of hate, which could be wiped out only by
killing. Steve, having read an advertisement
that a man's life depended upon her and that
she was wanted in court, arrives and relates
her story. It frees Jim. Shepherd is acquitted
on the plea of temporary derangement.

Some time has passed. An odd wedding
takes place in the deserted hut where Jim and
Steve first met. The only witnesses of the
ceremony are Raymond and Milly. Old Man
Taylor, because of the shock to his weak mentality, caused by the murder of Cathcart, dies.

STRAIGHT SHOOTING (Five Parts—Aug.
27).—The cast: "Cheyenne" Harry (Harry
Carey); "Thunder" Flint (Duke Lee); "Sweet-
water" Sims (George Berrell); His Daughter
Joan (Molly Malone); His Son (Ted Brooks);
Danny Morgan (Hoot Gibson); Black-Eyed
Pete (Milt Brown). Produced by Jack Ford.

"I am only a girl—not a fighter. But I
would not wage war on women or—old men,"
said Joan. Danny Morgan uncovered, stared
at her with open admiration, then stuttered:
"Neither will I. I'm with you." "Thunder"
Flint, cattle king, had reached a cruel resolve
—to drive the Nestors out of the country. To
find "Cheyenne" Harry for "the work," Harry
is found asleep in a saloon, where every one
is afraid of him as a "gunman." Harry agrees
to meet Flint in Diablo.

At their rendezvous near Diablo, Black-Eyed
Pete and his gang are splitting the spoils of a
marauding expedition. Harry meets two of the
outlaws, who tell him they are cached up near
the Big Rock. They seem to be friends.

Danny and Ted, "Sweetwater" Sims' son,
enter the saloon at Diablo together. There
they come upon Harry, who, hearing that Ted
is a Nestor, begins insulting him and shoots
at both of them, but they escape. Flint does
not laugh at all his trust in "Cheyenne" Harry,
and seeks for "Placer" Fremont, a gunman
of unsavory reputation. Fremont and Harry
meet at the saloon; each is suspicious of the
other; each handles his gun while he drinks.
Flint enters and sizes up the situation. Harry
asks Flint if Fremont is another "killer" he
has imported. Flint introduces Harry and Fremont, who merely extend a casual greeting.
Flint is surprised and assures them that there
is no cause for trouble, as they are both on
the same job and there is plenty of work to
be done.

Ted and Danny ride to the cabin to tell Sims
that Flint's "killers" have arrived and to prepare for trouble. Joan is greatly agitated.
The next day Ted goes for a bucket of water
and finds a sign warning the public that the
spring is private property and that trespassers
will be shot on sight. Fremont, hidden in a
tree, raises his rifle and fires at Ted, who rolls
down the bank—dead. Joan tells her father
where Ted has gone; they rush to the spring
and are grieving over the body of the boy
when Harry rides by. The father tells Harry
that he supposes he is one of the "killers,"
come to gloat over their "dirty work," but
Harry insists that he did not know of their
trouble, that he is a man and doesn't make
war on children and old men. Harry tells Joan
that if this is a sample of the work he was
brought here for he's through, and from now
on she can count on him whenever she needs
him. Harry later informs the foreman that
he's through with Flint and his outfit.

When Flint hears that Harry cannot be depended upon, he sends Fremont to Diablo for
"get" Harry. But Danny, hearing these instructions, warns Harry, who lays for Fremont, and, in the act of being shot, kills Fremont. Flint and his gang start out that night.
Danny has told Sims and Joan of the coming raid, and the girl rides out to warn all
the Nestors, who ride from all directions to
the cabin. Harry meets Joan and tells her
that there are so many of the raiders that
unless they get help they are lost. He rides
to the camp of Black-Eyed Pete, where he asks

for help. The outlaws rush to the battle, arriving in time to save the Nestors.
The next day while Joan is caring for Danny's wounds, Sims asks Harry to remain at the cabin, but Harry declines, saying that there is something "just over yonder" which keeps calling to him. He tells Sims that he will let them know at sundown. Danny comes to him as he is thinking out his problem. Harry tells him to go back to the little girl. Joan is disappointed at urst to see Danny instead of Cheyenne, who is left facing the setting sun alone.

CHRISTIE FILM CO.

HER MERRY MIX-UP (Aug. 7).—The cast: The Girl (Margaret Gibson); Her Husband (James Harrison); Her Friend (?) (Ethel Lynne); Her Brother (Eugene Corey); Basement Ben (Eddie Gribbon).
Margaret, in clandestine consultation with a book agent regarding a birthday gift for her husband. Jimmy, is discovered when he returns home unexpectedly. She sends the agent hurrying off and refuses to reveal his identity to her husband, who leaves the house in anger. Ethel, to whom he tells his troubles, later sees Margaret get into a taxicab with her brother, who is spending an hour or two with her between trains. Notified of this, Jimmy, who does not know the brother, follows the pair to a cafe, and later sees Gene kiss Margaret good-bye.
In the meantime, Basement Ben, the bold burglar, burgles the bungalow of James and Margaret, and when Gene decides to pay a final visit to his sister's home, hides in a closet with the swag. As Gene sits awaiting his sister's return a bill collector calls, and also decides to wait. When the furious Jimmy is seen coming up the walk flourishing a gun, the two take refuge in the same closet that holds the burglar, and all crouch in fear and trembling while Jimmy rages outside. His jealous suspicions are confirmed when he finds on the library table a bouquet of flowers bearing a loving message from the giver, but really left at Jimmy's house by mistake.
While he is out of the room, Margaret and the book agent arrive to make a final decision on the gift for Jimmy, and when Margaret hears her husband approaching she hastily shoves the agent into the closet, which is already full to overflowing. Jealous Jimmy shoots through the closet door when he finds the book agent's hat on the library table, and the four trembling ones file into the room. After explanations are made, Basement Ben quietly sneaks out with his loaded suit case, only to run into the arms of a cop.

A SMOKEY LOVE AFFAIR (Aug. 14).—The cast: The Girl (Betty Compson); The Boy (James Harrison); The Detective (Eddie Gribbon).
Jimmy starts from the office for a two weeks' vacation at the beach. On the train he sees Betty, also bound for the seashore, and attempts to become acquainted with her. Meeting with continued rebuffs, he resolves to win her in spite of everything, and when they arrive at the beach he follows her to the hotel, and incidentally arouses the animosity of the house detective. Jimmy secures a room across the hall from Betty's, and when she orders her breakfast served in her room the persistent Jimmy bribes the waiter to exchange coats with him, so that he may take the tray in to her. Betty calls the house detective, and has Jimmy ejected. When she goes for a ride on the board walk in a motor chair, it is Jimmy who turns up as the driver, and narrowly escapes arrest.
At length the love-sick swain hits upon a means of gaining her favor, and decides to rescue her from a fake fire. Lighting a towel, he places it against her door, and when the smoke pours into her room she is glad to be carried out by her heroic suitor. When she discovers his deception she is furious, and returns to

her room. By chance a real fire breaks out, and when Jimmy again cries out a warning at her door she refuses to respond. In desperation he at length breaks in her door, and Betty picks up a shoe and knocks him senseless. At this juncture she is hurried out by firemen, and when she discovers that the hotel is really on fire she returns with the men to rescue the unconscious Jimmy. A kiss restores him to consciousness, and Betty nurses her hero back to health.

SELZNICK PICTURES.

THE LESSON (August).—The cast: Helen. Drayton (Constance Talmadge); "Chet" Vernon (Tom Moore); John Galvin (Herbert .eeyes); "Tub" Martin (Walter Hiers); Henry Hammond (Joseph Smiley); Mrs. Hammond (Lillian Rambeau); Ada Thompson (Dorothy Green); Harriet Reeves (Christy Walker). Direction Charles Giblyn.
In a small American town, Helen Drayton, the belle of the neighborhood, has for a long time been "going with" Chet Vernon, but while she likes Chet she is inclined to rebel at not being allowed a wider range of choice. So she welcomes the visit of John Galvin, a young architect. A swift courtship is followed by an elopement, and Helen finds herself keeping house for a young husband who has still to make his place in the world. But while Galvin can always find plenty of money to spend downtown, he is stingy with Helen, expecting her to finance a whole wardrobe with a ten dollar bill. Through Mrs. Hammond, wife of one of Galvin's business acquaintances, Helen finds a means of getting money by exercising her talents for interior decorating.
Meanwhile Chet Vernon, tired of the lack of opportunities in the little town, also comes to the city. With a mutual friend he calls on Helen, and they arrange a theater party. Galvin excusing himself on the ground of important business. After the theater Chet, Helen and their friend go to a cafe, and Chet sees Galvin buying wine for Ada Thompson, the niece and secretary of Hammond. He does not tell Helen, however.
The Hammonds invite Helen and Galvin to their seashore house for a house party, and Galvin's attentions to Ada Thompson are very noticeable. Helen suspects nothing, however, until one afternoon, passing a secluded summerhouse, she sees something which causes her to rush to her room, pack her grip and hurry to the city. Galvin follows her, and in a stormy scene she tells him that he has not even been supporting her.
Helen then embarks in her decorating business on a large scale, obtains a divorce and eventually finds happiness with her girlhood sweetheart.

EDUCATIONAL FILMS CORP.

THE LIVING BOOK OF NATURE (By Raymond L. Ditmars—Babies of the Farm).—A pleasing picture of pigs, kittens, calves, infant birds and the like, and prepared along sympathetic and entertaining lines. The theme couples the lives of the commoner creatures with animals of the wilds and displays their play, tribulations—and dangers. Everybody is interested in baby animals, and the wonderful clarity of photography in this picture imparts the nearest possible impression to life itself upon the screen.
Attractive titles, brimful of information, but radiating freshness and vigor, flow through the scenes.

WORLD PICTURES.

THE GUARDIAN (Five Parts—Aug. 27).—The cast: James Rokeby (Montague Love); Marie Dacre (June Elvidge); Fenwick Harvey (Arthur Ashley); William Donavan (William Black); Chief Conlin (Robert Broderick).
James Rokeby is the president of a national bank at the time the story opens, but in his earlier days he was a burglar. Donavan, the keeper of a notorious dive, knows this and

Stronger Light

The light from an Alternating Current arc comes alternating from both carbons, while from a Direct Current arc it always comes from the same carbon. The Direct Current arc can therefore be arranged so that the maximum amount of its light always passes through the lens, while it is impossible to do this with an Alternating Current arc. A Direct Current arc also gives off more light for the same current than an Alternating Current.

If your electric service is only Alternating Current, a

Westinghouse-Cooper Hewitt Rectifier Outfit

will convert it into the Direct Current you need. It saves you money and satisfies your patrons. Write for Folder 4285-C for more particulars.

'Westinghouse Electric & Mfg. Co.
East Pittsburgh, Pa.

milks Rokeby regularly for large 'sums of money. When Rokeby's ward, Marie Dacre, becomes infatuated with a young fortune hunter, the latter falls into the clutches of Donavan and when Marie finally turns the fortune hunter down the two men form a diabolical plot to get the girl's money. This plot almost succeeds, but is finally frustrated in a remarkable manner by Rokeby. Then Rokeby's long love for his young ward meets the reward it merits.

PARAMOUNT PICTURES CORP.

PARAMOUNT-BRAY PICTOGRAPHS. — The 80th release of the Paramount-Bray Pictographs shows the working of the Fansworth Institute of New York City, where the deaf and dumb are taught to hear and talk by means of the sense of feeling.

Otto Luck is also seen in this number, in "A Flivvered Romance," perhaps the most amusing cartoon in which this unique character has yet appeared.

The beach sports in southern California showing scores of girls in bathing suits that are not considered conventional at all bathing beaches, also makes an excellent hot-weather attraction.

PARAMOUNT-BRAY PICTOGRAPHS. — The 81st release of the Paramount-Bray Pictographs contain, for the first time after a long absence, another of the inimitable Colonel Heeza Liar animated cartoons. The Colonel is seen as a temperance advocate, but an unfortunate experience in the movies causes him to relinquish his ideas on the subject.

"A Day at Coney Island" is also shown in this release; a subject that is of great interest to millions all over the country who have never been fortunate enough to visit the great amusement centre.

A land and water submarine, the invention of Simon Lake, makes an exceptionally interesting feature of this issue, inasmuch as it is an amplification of the under-water boat.

A series of interesting and instructive views of the tea industry in China and Ceylon are also contained in this number.

IVAN FILM PRODUCTIONS, INC.

BABBLING TONGUES (Six Parts—August.— State Rights Production).—The cast: Paul, a young author (James Morrison); Theresa Moreau (Grace Valentine); Jose Moreau, Theresa's husband (Arthur Donaldson); Louis Moreau, Jose's brother (Paul Capellani); Marie Moreau, Louis' wife (Louise Beaudet); Felix, their son (Gladden James); Henrietti, his sister (Carolyn Birch); Viscount de Bellepine (Richard Tucker); M. Etienne Le Moyne (Robert E. Hill). Written by William Humphrey and George E. Hall. Directed by William Humphrey.

Jose Moreau, a rich merchant about forty years of age, is ideally married to Theresa, a beautiful woman in her early twenties, who adores him. He is a generous and kindly man and upon the death of an old and honored friend, to whose assistance in the past he owes his present fortune, he adopts into his house, hold the son of the friend, Paul. Paul is twenty-six years old; he reads poems and writes plays, and is a thoroughly fine fellow. Paul feels an almost filial affection for Mons. Jose and a wholesome brotherly friendship for Theresa. He accompanies Jose and Theresa everywhere in the social world; he sits in their box at the opera, acting as Theresa's escort when her husband is detained by business.

Society, with sinister imagination, begins to look askance at the triangulated household; tongues begin to wag; and gossip grows. Tidings of the evil talk about town are brought to Mons. Jose by his brother, Louis, who advises that Paul had better be requested to live in quarters of his own. Jose repels the suggestion as insulting; but Louis persists that only by such a course may the family name be rendered unimpeachable upon the public tongue.

Paul, to still the evil rumors, goes to live in a studio alone. This simple move on his part suggests to everybody that he have had a real motive for making it. Gossip increases, instead of diminishing; and the emotions of Theresa and Jose and himself are stirred to the point of nervous tensity. Mons. Jose, in spite of his own sweet reasonableness, begins subtly to wonder if there could be, by any possibility, any basis for his brother's vehemence. Louis' wife, Marie, repeats the talk of the town to Theresa, and turns her imagination inward, till it falters in self-questioning. The world at large whispers unthinkable and tragic possibilities to the frantic and self-searching mind of Paul. He resolves to seek release in leaving for foreign shores. But before he can sail away he overhears, in a fashionable cafe, a remark which casts a slur on Theresa, and strikes the speaker of the insult in the face.

A duel is forthwith arranged to take place in a vacant studio adjacent to Paul's. When

Censorship
is the
Bogey Man
of the
Moving Picture Industry

KEEP THE PICTURES CLEAN
AND KEEP THEM OUT OF
POLITICS

WE DO NOT BELIEVE
THE AMERICAN PEOPLE
WANT CENSORSHIP

WE WILL NOT SHOW
OBJECTIONABLE FILMS
IN THIS THEATRE

. This is one of the set. .

We have prepared and are distributing at cost

A Set of Nine Anti-Censorship Slides

(All Different)

As a means of self preservation Exhibitors everywhere should constantly fight the proposed discriminatory control of their business.

Picture theatre patrons can aid materially in the fight and will if the subject is kept constantly before them.

The set of nine slides, carefully packed, will be sent postpaid on receipt of $1.80.

Address

MOVING PICTURE WORLD

17 Madison Avenue
New York City

Mons. Jose learns about it, he is troubled by the idea that another man should be fighting for his wife, and rushes forthwith to wreak vengeance himself on the traducer. Theresa hears the news, and in order to prevent both her husband and Paul from endangering their lives, she rushes to Paul's rooms to urge him to forestall hostilities. Meanwhile her husband encounters the slanderer, and is severely wounded. He is carried to Paul's studio. Hearing people coming, Theresa hides herself in Paul's bedroom, where she is discovered by her husband's attendants. Jose, wounded and enfevered, now at last believes the worst. Paul seeks and slays Jose's assailant. But now the whole world credits what the whole world has been whispering. In vain Paul and Theresa protest their innocence to Louis and his wife. In vain they plead with the kindly and noble man they both revere and love. Jose curses them, and dies believing in their guilt. Then at last, when they find themselves cast forth isolate by this entire world, their common tragic loneliness draws them to each other. They are given to each other by the world. The insidious purpose of babbling tongues has been accomplished; Paul takes Theresa for his own.

TRIANGLE FILM CORPORATION.

THEY'RE OFF (Five Parts—Aug. 19).—The cast: Rita Hackett (Enid Bennett); Randolph Manners (Rowland Lee); Daniel Hackett (Melbourne MacDowell); Judge Peterson (Walter Whitman); Uncle Mose (Samuel Lincoln). Directed by Roy Neill.

While Daniel Hackett, millionaire broker and turfman, with his daughter Rita was on a tour of the South their machine broke down near an old Southern mansion. Rita expressed a desire of owning a home-like it. Hackett became angered when told by the owner, Randolph Manners, that it was not for sale, and informed him that he usually got what he went after. Hackett, learning that the young Southerner was heavily interested in the tobacco market forced him, through his Wall street manipulations, to sell the estate and everything else he owned.

The new owners took possession. Rita found an old crinoline dress which she put on. Thus garbed she accidentally ran into young Manners and the colored servant, Mose. Recognizing the dress as his dead mother's wedding gown, he ignored her. Realizing what she had done, Rita determined to see Randolph and explain. Learning that he had taken a temporary residence in the old training quarters, Rita feigned a fall from her horse near the place. Randolph ran to her assistance and took her to his cabin. Rita burst out laughing and Randolph, realizing the trick she had played on him, became angered. Mose left them alone. When Rita learned how her father had forced the estate from him she determined to regain it for him.

Upon returning to the mansion, her father presented her with the deed to the estate, which she refused, explaining that she had learned how he had obtained it. He was dumbfounded, but instead gave her a black horse, Satan, which he had entered in the coming race, explaining that another one of his horses, Wasp, would win but that Satan would take second place.

Rita found Randolph worried over the fact that his horse, Vixen, had gone lame and could not be entered in the race, but consoled him by telling of her scheme to point Satan up with white feet and enter him in the race against Wasp, she to be the jockey. Despite Ran dolph's protests, Rita made him accept a bill of sale for Satan. Rita won the race and also Randolph. Hackett, upon trying to purchase Satan, was told that the mansion would be the only consideration, and agreed. Upon learning that the horse was Satan and the jockey Rita, he became indignant, but after noting the very apparent interest between Rita and Randolph, decided that he hadn't lost anything, anyway.

WOODEN SHOES (Five Parts—Aug. 20).— "Pampy," a Dutch girl, has an invalid father dependent upon her for support. With her companion, Hans, the tot boy, she proves a quaint sight as she clutters up and down the cobbled street in her wooden shoes selling flowers to the tourists who visit the village and serving as their guide. "Pampy's" father dies, leaving her alone and penniless with her only hope for the future being to get to America where her grandfather will provide for her.

"Pampy's" father, before his death, had written to the grandfather about "Pampy," but the answer had been intercepted by the unscrupulous proprietress of the inn where "Pampy" stays. Later on we find her and her companion in America, having come over in the steerage. How "Pampy" found her grandfather as well as the artist for whom she had posed in Holland and whose interest in her from their separation had developed into a strong love, makes one of the most charming stories ever transferred to the screen.

Classified Advertisements — NOTE TERMS CAREFULLY

Remittances must accompany all orders for classified advertisements as follows: One dollar per insertion for copy containing twenty words or less. Five cents per word on copy containing over twenty words. Each word to be counted including names and addresses.

NOTICE TO ADVERTISERS:—The Publishers expect that all statements made in every advertisement will bear the strictest investigation.

SITUATIONS WANTED.

POSITION WANTED by up-to-date motion picture lady organist. Best city references. Address Organist, care M. P. World, N. Y. City.

OPERATOR, strictly experienced, desires position, first-class theater. Handle any equipment, perfect projection, go anywhere. Eugene Barker, Watertown, South Dak.

MAN AND WIFE, violin and piano, at liberty for pictures or stock. Experienced, absolutely deliver the goods. Large library, references. Box 454, Cedar Rapids, Iowa.

MOVING PICTURE MACHINE operator, manager; six years experience New York, three years former employer, references. Address Reliable, care M. P. Woyld, N. Y. City.

MANAGER—Years of New York City experience, all phases of business. Exempt from draft, desires connection. Will go anywhere. E. G., care M. P. World, N. Y. City.

CAMERAMAN, with Bell and Howell camera, will be at liberty soon; wants feature work.' Address, Cinema, care M. P. World, N. Y. City.

CAMERAMAN, experienced in composition, art, lighting in motion picture photography; moderate salary, consistent with best results; permanent engagement. Willing to travel anywhere; studio or location. References; am exempt.' H., care M. P. World, N. Y. City.

A-1 PIANIST—Director, composer, arranger. Member A. F. of M. Vaudeville and pictures a specialty. Charles Jerreld, 41 Eastern Ave., Springfield, Mass.

OPERATOR, strictly experienced, desires position, first-class theater only. Handle only best equipment, perfect projection guaranteed. Henry Alsman, Dyersburg, Tenn.

HIGHLY EFFICIENT and experienced theater organist at liberty September 1st. Expert motion picture accompanist. Address, Efficient, care M. P. World, N. Y. City.

HELP WANTED.

OPERATOR—Perfect projection or don't answer. Simplex machines, direct current; three matinees, no Sundays, eighteen dollars. Utopia Theater, Painesville, Ohio.

EQUIPMENT WANTED.

WANTED—Power's 6A head, in any condition, for experimental purposes. Matzinger, Optical Goods, 1123 Broadway, N. Y City.

EQUIPMENT FOR SALE.

GUARANTEED MACHINES—Slightly used type 6-1917 model, Simplex motor drive, factory guarantee, at reasonable prices. Room 206, 1482 Broadway, N. Y. City.

FOR SALE—A full moving picture house equipment. 300 opera chairs, machines, operating booth, fans, and miscellaneous equipment. Reasonable price to quick buyer. Must vacate at once. Address Box 23, Norwalk, Conn.

FOR SALE—Two Simplex motor-driven, up-to-date machines in perfect running order, complete for immediate use, $250 each, including all extras. Walter S. Hodgman, 356 West Van Buren Street, Chicago, Ill. Tel. Harrison 3403.

FOR SALE—Two 6A Power's machines, rotary converter, piano, five hundred and sixty-five chairs. All excellent condition. Address Box 372, Elmira, New York.

CAMERAS, ETC., FOR SALE.

PROFESSIONAL CAMERAS, tripods, perforators, printers' developing outfits, rewinders, Tessars, effects, devices, novelties, experimental workshop, repair, expert film work titles. Eberhard Schneider, 14th St. & Second Ave., N. Y. City.

TO ALL INTERESTED IN M. P. CAMERAS SEND AT ONCE FOR SPECIAL CATALOG ON THE UNIVERSAL AND ALL OTHER MAKES OF MOTION PICTURE CAMERAS. Just Out! You cannot afford to be without it. Free for the asking. Send postal at once. We have recently equipped the following with complete outfits: James Herrick, San Diego, Cal.; Dr. Brockinridge, Racine, Wis.; Wallace Carlson, Camimated Nooz Cartoonist for Brays Paramount Studios, Chicago; Fred Parrish, Madison, Wis.; Francis Schwaegerle, Cincinnati, O.; Charles Pierce, Ottumwa, Iowa; Frank Schmidt, Commercial Studio, Chicago, and several others. You, too, will purchase your outfit of us if you knew the value and service rendered by our Motion Picture Camera Department. Quality, value and service in all our transactions makes our store the motion picture camera headquarters of America. Send for latest book on motion pictures, "How to Make and Operate," by Bernard E. Jones, worth its weight in gold to all interested in motion picture photography. Postpaid for $1.10. The famous Northern Light, complete in case, $52.50, list, $68. Telegraphic orders receive our prompt attention. BASS CAMERA COMPANY, Charles Bass, president. 109 Dearborn St., North, Motion Picture Camera Department, Chicago, Ill.

PITTMAN PRESWICH model, Zeiss F:3.5, 50 mm. Six magazines, cases, tripod, everything complete, $150. Bryniarski, 117 Oxford Place, Plainfield, N. J.

DAVID STERN COMPANY, INCORPORATED. "EVERYTHING IN CAMERAS." PIONEERS IN THE MOTION PICTURE FIELD—SPECIAL————400 ft. Williamson M. P. Camera, Heitar lens, F:4.5, Williamson Claw Movement. OUR PRICE, $135.00. EXCLUSIVE DISTRIBUTORS FOR THE DAVSCO, AGENTS FOR THE UNIVERSAL. WRITE OR WIRE FOR OUR SPECIAL PROPOSITION. DAVID STERN COMPANY————"Everything in Cameras." In business since 1885. 1027-1029 R Madison St., Chicago, Ill.

FILMS, ETC., FOR SALE.

FILMS—Better class commercial films available on the leasing basis consisting of comedies and dramas, two-reel Westerns and dramas, three-reel dramas and five-reel features. Posters for each film. Formerly most prominent brands on the market. Exceptional opportunities for commercial exchanges. Address Consumers Film Trading Company, Room 518, 220 South State St., Chicago, Illinois.

WEEKLY SHIPMENTS OF FILMS FOR SALE—We will sell outright twenty reels of single-reel comedies and two and three-reel features or one five-reel feature and ten reels of one, two, and three-reelers with a nice assortment of clean paper on each subject at $100.00 a week or shipment. All films are in splendid condition shipped subject to examination. Send $10.00 to guarantee express charges, will ship C. O. D. each week. Wire or write at once. Chicago Film Trading & Exporting Co., 4th floor Shops Bldg., Chicago, Illinois.

SIX-TWEEDLEDUM COMEDIES, including five single reels and one two-reeler only slightly used. Like brand new. Large quantity of new paper on each subject. To dispose of same quickly will sell for $30.00 per reel. Cost $110.00. Send 10 per cent. of purchase price to cover express charges. Will ship balance C. O. D. subject to examination. United Film Service, 17 No. Wabash Ave., Chicago, Illinois.

MUSICAL INSTRUMENTS FOR SALE.

SEEBURG picture instrument, style "S," good as new, at great sacrifice; used few months. Cash or easy payments. Address Queen Theater, Knoxville, Tenn.

MISCELLANEOUS.

SUPER SCENARIOS wanted, five reels up. Liberal compensation for big stuff. No costume war or period stories. Please be original, no hash. J. W. Townley, 500 Fifth Ave., N. Y. City. Room 402.

Producers and Exchangemen

Kindly read article on page 1349 and ACT AT ONCE. Films will go forward by first steamers through the Quartermaster's Department. THIS IS AN APPEAL FOR FILMS FOR OUR SOLDIER BOYS. What have you on your shelves to donate? MOVING PICTURE WORLD.

?????????????????????

INDEX

TO CONTENTS

TO ADVERTISERS

In Answering Advertisements, Please Mention THE MOVING PICTURE WORLD

Do we need
to say anymore?
Let us send you
catalog of the
best Projector
made

List of Current Film Release Dates

ON GENERAL FILM, PATHE AND PARAMOUNT PROGRAMS

(For Daily Calendar of Program Releases See Page 1422.)

General Film Company, Inc.

(Note—Pictures given below are listed in the order of their release. Additions are made from week to week in the order of release.)

BROADWAY STAR FEATURE.

A Departmental Case (One of the O. Henry Series—Two parts—Comedy-Drama).
A Little Speck in Garnered Fruit (One of the O. Henry Series—Two parts—Comedy-Dr.).
The Gift of the Magi (One of the O. Henry Stories—Two parts—Comedy-Drama).
The Coming Out of Maggie (One of the O. Henry Stories—Two parts—Comedy-Dr.).
The Venturers (one of the O. Henry Series—Two parts—Comedy-Drama).
Discounters of Money (One of the O. Henry Series—Two parts—Comedy-Drama).
The Furnished Room (One of the O. Henry Series—Two parts—Drama).
The Defeat of the City (One of the O. Henry Series—Four parts—Drama).
The Atavism of John Tom Little Bear (One of the O. Henry Series—Two parts—Drama).

ESSANAY.

Two Laughs (Black Cat Feature—Two parts—Comedy-Drama).
Our Boys (Black Cat Feature—Two parts—Comedy).
Seventy and Seven (Black Cat Feature—Two parts—Comedy-Drama).
Pete's Pants (Black Cat Feature—Two parts—Comedy).
Vernon, the Bountiful (Black Cat Feature—Two Parts—Comedy-Drama).
The Long-Green Trail (Black Cat Feature—Two parts—Comedy-Drama).
Don't Lose Your Coat (Black Cat Feature—Two parts—Comedy).
Star Dust—Black Cat Feature—Two parts—Comedy-Drama).
Twelve Cylinder Speed of the Leisure Class (George Ade Fables—Two parts—Comedy).

FALCON FEATURES.

The Mainspring (Four parts—Drama).
The Martinache Marriage (Four parts—Dr.).
The Stolen Play (Four parts—Drama).
The Phantom Shotgun (Four parts—Drama).
His Unpolished Self (Four parts—Drama).

KALEM.

The Ghost of the Desert (An episode of "The American Girl"—Two parts—Drama).
The Man of Stingaree (Episode of "The Further Adventures of Stingaree"—Two parts—Dr.).
An Order of the Court (Episode of "The Further Adventures of Stingaree"—Two parts—Dr.).
At the Sign of the Kangaroo (an episode of the "The Further Adventures of Stingaree"—Two parts—Drama).
Through Fire and Water (Episode of the Further Adventures of Stingaree—Two parts—Drama).
A Bushranger's Strategy (Episode of the Further Adventures of Stingaree—Two parts—Drama).
The Stranger at Dumcrief (Episode of "The Further Adventures of Stingaree"—Two parts—Drama).
A Champion of the Law (Episode of "The Further Adventures of Stingaree"—Two parts—Drama).

GEORGE KLEINE.

Nearly a Husband (One-Reel George Bickel Comedy).
Some Statue (One-Reel George Bickel Comdy).

JAXON COMEDIES.

(Pokes and Jabs).
Pearls of Paulina.
Ploughing the Clouds.
(Second Series.)
Counting 'Em Up.
The Baggage Man.
Spilling the Coin.
Tough Luck.
Play Ball.
Love Letters.

SELIG.

Selig World Library No 10 (Educational).
A Daughter of the Southland (Two parts—Dr.).
The L.-X. Clew (Drama).
Selig-World Library No. 11 (Edu.).
The Toll of Sin (Two Parts—Drama).
The Bush Leaguer (One part—Drama).
Selig-World Library No. 12 (Educational).
The Smoldering Spark (Two parts—Drama).
The Love of Madge O'Mara (Drama).
Selig-World Library No. 13 (Educational).
A Man, a Girl and a Lion (Two parts—Drama).
Her Perilous Ride (One part—Drama).
Selig World Library No. 14 (Educational).
The Sole Survivor (Two parts—Drama).
Her Heart's Desire (One part—Drama).
Selig World Library No. 15 (Educational).
Between Man and Beast (Two parts—Drama).
Her Salvation (One part—Drama).
The Love of Madge O'Mara (Drama).
Pioneer Days (Two parts—Drama).
In After Years (One part—Drama).

RAY COMEDIES.

A Laundry Mix-Up.
A Peaceful Flat.
Cheating His Wife.
A Bathtub Marriage.

SPARKLE COMEDIES.

Bertie's Bath.
A Night of Enchantment.
(Second Series.)
An Attorney's Affair.
Her Peignoir.
Those Terrible Telegrams.
The Stag Party.
Bragg's Little Poker Party.
Mixed Flats.

Pathe Exchange, Inc.

RELEASES FOR WEEK OF AUGUST 5.

Captain Kiddo (Lassilda—Five parts—Drama).
The Neglected Wife (Episode No. 13, "Revolting Pride"—Two parts—Drama).
The Fatal Ring (Episode No. 5, "Danger Underground"—Two parts—Astra).
Know America No. 18—Stray Shots in the Lone Star State (Scenic-Combitone).
Lonesome Luke—Messenger (Two Parts—Comedy-Rolin).
Hearst-Pathe News No. 64 (Topical).
Hearst-Pathe News No. 65 (Topical).
Iska Werreh (Abe Kabbible Cartoon), and How a Phonograph Record is Made (Educational) (International) (Split Reel).

RELEASES FOR WEEK OF AUGUST 12.

The Streets of Illusion (Five parts—Drama—Astra).
The Neglected Wife (No. 14—"Desperation"—Two parts—Drama—Balboa).
The Fatal Ring (No. 6—"Rays of Death"—Two Parts—Drama—Astra).
Know America No. 19—"Southern Colorado" (Scenic—Combitone).
Hearst-Pathe News No. 66 (Topical).
Hearst-Pathe News No. 67 (Topical).
Bringing Up Father—"He Tries His Hand at Hypnotism (Cartoon Comedy), and Sardine Fisheries at Monterry (Edu.) (International) (Split Reel).

RELEASES FOR WEEK OF AUG. 19.

Miss 'Nobody (Five parts—Drama—Astra).
The Neglected Wife (No. 15—"A Sacrifice Supreme"—Two parts—Drama—Balboa).
The Fatal Ring (No. 7—"The Signal Lantern"—Two parts—Drama—Astra).
Along the Baltic Sweden (Scenic—Sweafilms), and Japan, the Religious (Colored Scenic) (Split Reel).
Jerry on the Job—"On the Border" (Cartoon Comedy), and "Fine Feathers" (Edu.) Split Reel).

Lonesome Luke, Mechanic (Two parts—Comedy—Rolin).
Hearst-Pathe News No. 68 (Topical).
Hearst-Pathe News No. 69 (Topical).

RELEASES FOR WEEK OF AUGUST. 26.

Iris (Five parts—Drama—Astra).
The Fatal Ring (No. 8, "The Switch in the Safe"—Two parts—Drama—Astra).
Know America No. 20—Near Pike's Peak, Colo. (One reel—Scenic—Combitone).
Hearst-Pathe News No. 70 (Topical).
Hearst-Pathe News No. 71 (Topical).

Paramount Pictures Corp.

BLACK DIAMOND COMEDY.

June 11—Her Fractured Voice.
June 25—Auto Intoxication.
Aug. 6—Susie the Sleepwalker.

FAMOUS PLAYERS.

June 28—The Little Boy Scout (Five parts—Drama).
July 2—At First Sight (Five parts—Drama).
July 9—The Love That Lives (Five parts—Drama).
July 23—The Long Trail (Five parts—Drama).

KLEVER KOMEDY.

July 2—Oh Pop!
July 16—The Wrong Mr. Fox.
July 30—Motor Boating.
Aug. 13—Summer Boarding (Comedy).

LASKY.

July 16—What Money Can't Buy (Five parts—Drama).
July 26—The Squaw Man's Son' (Five parts—Drama).
July 30—The Crystal Gazer (Five parts—Dr.).

MOROSCO AND PALLAS.

June 21—Heir of the Ages (Pallas—Five parts Drama).
July 5—Big Timber (Five parts—Drama—Morosco).
July 19—Cook of Canyon Camp (Five parts—Drama).
Aug. 2—A Kiss for Susie (Five parts—Drama).

PARAMOUNT-ARBUCKLE COMEDY.

May 21—A Reckless Romeo (Two parts).
June 25—The Rough House (Two parts).
Aug. 20—His Wedding Night (Two parts).

PARAMOUNT-ARTCRAFT.

Aug. 5—The Amazons (Five parts—Drama).
Aug. 5—The Varmint (Five parts—Drama).
Aub. 12—Seven Keys to Baldpate (Five parts—Drama).
Aug. 12—The Law of the Land (Five parts—Drama).
Aug. 19—The Mysterious Miss Terry (Five parts—Drama).
Aug. 19—Haskimura Togo (Five parts—Dr.).
Aug. 26—Close to Nature (Five parts—Drama).
Aug. 26—Little Miss Optimist (Five parts—Drama).

PARAMOUNT-BURTON HOLMES.

Aug. 6—Geysers of Yellowstone (Scenic).
Aug. 13—Wonders of Yellowstone (Scenic).
Aug. 20—Tropical Nassau (Scenic).
Aug. 27—Madrid to Madeira (Scenic).
Sept. 3—Norway (Scenic).

PARAMOUNT BRAY PICTOGRAPHS.

June 11—Subjects on Reel—Soldiers of the Soil; Travelling Forts; Repairing a Submarine Cable; Cartoon—Evolution of the Dachshund.
June 18—Subjects on Reel—Unmasking the Medium; On Duty with the Coast Guards; Scientific Stock Breeding; Bobby Bumps' Submarine Chaser.

Producers.—Kindly Furnish Titles and Dates of All New Releases Before Saturday.

The Day is Passed

when patrons will tolerate projection with an alternating current arc. You cannot expect them to tolerate poor projection when your competitors are offering something better. Do not look upon the purchase of

Wagner

WHITE LIGHT

Converters

as an expense. It is an investment that will increase your profits. You can get more light with less current from a Wagner Converter, if you are now using alternating current.

Send at once for Bulletin 10923 and prices. Don't let another day of poor projection drive your patrons to competitors. Send today for information.

Wagner, Quality

Wagner Electric Manufacturing Company,
Saint Louis, Missouri

List of Current Film Release Dates

ON UNIVERSAL, METRO AND TRIANGLE PROGRAMS

(For Daily Calendar of Program Releases See Page 1422.)

Universal Film Mfg. Co.

ANIMATED WEEKLY.
July 11.—Number 80 (Topical).
July 18.—Number 81 (Topical).
July 25.—Number 82 (Topical).
Aug. 2.—Number 83 (Topical).
Aug. 9.—Number 84 (Topical).
Aug. 16.—Number 85 (Topical).
Aug. 23.—Number 86 (Topical).
Aug. 30.—Number 87 (Topical).
Sept. 6.—Number 88 (Topical).

BIG U.
July 2.—The Mad Stampede (Drama).
July 9.—The Punishment (Drama).

BISON.
July 4.—The Wrong Man (Two parts—Dr.).
July 9.—Double Suspicion (Two parts—Drama).
Aug. 6.—The Soul Herder (Three parts—Dr.).
Aug. 20.—Squaring It (Three parts—Dr.).
Aug. 27.—Jungle Treachery (Two parts—Dr.).
Sept. 3.—The Lure of the Circus (Two parts—Comedy—Drama), and Sierra Winter Sports (Scenic).

GOLD SEAL.
July 9.—A Limb of Satan (Three parts—Drama).
July 16.—Six Shooter Justice (Three parts—Drama).
July 23.—A Soldier of the Legion (Three parts—Drama).
July 30.—Right of Way Casey (Three parts—Drama).
Aug. 13.—A Wife's Suspicion (Three parts—Dr.).
Aug. 27.—The Winning Pair (Three parts—Dr.).
Sept. 3.—The Empty Gun (Three parts—Dr.).

IMP.
July 4.—The Girl in the Limousine (Drama).
July 9.—Hattoo of Headquarters (Drama).

JOKER.
July 9.—Kitchenella (Comedy).
July 16.—He Had 'Em Buffaloed (Comedy).
July 23.—Canning the Cannibal King (Comedy).
July 25.—The Southette.
July 30.—The Battling Bellboy (Comedy).
July 30.—The Stinger Stung (Comedy).
Aug. 6.—O-My the Tent Mover (Comedy).
Aug. 6.—The Vamp of the Camp (Comedy).
Aug. 13.—Out Again, In Again (Comedy).
Aug. 13.—Back to the Kitchen (Comedy).
Aug. 20.—Behind the Map (Comedy).
Aug. 20.—Mrs. Madam Manager (Comedy).
Aug. 27.—Why They Left Home (Comedy).
Sept. 3.—Boating Into Society (Comedy).
Sept. 3.—Officer, Call a Cop (Comedy).
Sept. 3.—A Gale of Verse (Comedy).

L-KO.
July 9.—Hearts and Flour (Two parts—Comedy).
July 16.—Burt Scandal (Two parts—Comedy).
July 23.—The Sign of the Cucumber (Two parts—Comedy).
July 30.—Blackboard and Blackmail (Two parts—Comedy).
Aug. 6.—The Little Fat Rascal (Two parts—Comedy).
Aug. 13.—Rough Stuff (Two parts—Comedy).
Aug. 20.—Street Cars and Carbunkles (Two parts—Comedy).
Sept. 3.—Backward Sons and Forward Daughters (Two parts—Comedy).

NESTOR.
July 9.—Minding the Baby (Comedy).
July 16.—A Dark Deed (Comedy).
July 23.—Seeing Things.
July 30.—Married by Accident (Comedy).
Aug. 6.—The Love Slacker (Comedy).
Aug. 13.—The Rushin' Dancers (Comedy).
Aug. 20.—Move Over (Comedy).
Aug. 27.—The Night Cap (Comedy).
Sept. 3.—Looking 'Em Over (Comedy).

POWERS.
July 9.—Monkey Love (Cartoon Comedy) and In the Rocks of India (Dorsey Educational).
July 16.—Box Car Bill Falls in Luck (Cartoon Comedy) and in the Heart of India (Educational).
July 23.—Hammon Egg's Reminiscences (Cartoon Comedy) and in The Land of Light and Gloom (Dorsey Edu.).
July 30.—The Good Liar (Cartoon) and "In Monkey Land" (Ditmar's Edu.).
Aug. 6.—Seeing Ceylon with Hy Mayer (Travlaugh).
Aug. 13.—Doing His Bit (Cartoon Comedy), and Algeria, Old and New) (Scenic) (Split reel).
Aug. 20.—Colonel Pepper's Mobilized Farm (Cartoon Comedy), and "The Home Life of the Spider (Ditmar's Edu.) (Split Reel).

STAR FEATURETTE.
July 23.—The Beautiful Impostor (Two parts—Drama).
July 30.—The Woman Who Would Not Pay (Two parts—Society—Drama).
Aug. 6.—The Untamed (Two parts—Drama).
Aug. 13.—Cheyenne's Pal (Two parts—Drama).
Aug. 20.—The Golden Heart (Two parts—Dr.).
Aug. 27.—Hands to the Dark (Two parts—Dr.), and Old French Towns (Short Scenic on Same Reel).
Sept. 3.—A Dream of Egypt (Two parts—Dr.).

VICTOR.
July 9.—Meet My Wife (Comedy).
July 9.—The Paper Hanger's Revenge (Comedy).
July 9.—Kicked Out (Two parts—Comedy Drama).
July 16.—One Bride Too Many (Two parts—Comedy-Drama).
July 30.—Where Are My Trousers? (Two parts—Comedy).
Aug. 6.—Like Babes in the Wood (Two parts—Juvenile Comedy).
Aug. 13.—The Brass Girl (Two parts—Comedy-Drama).
Aug. 20.—A Five Foot Ruler (Two parts—Comedy-Drama).
Aug. 27.—Scandal Everywhere (Comedy).
Sept. 3.—The Curse of a Flirting Heart (Com.).

UNIVERSAL SCREEN MAGAZINE.
July 9.—Issue No. 27 (Educational).
July 16.—Issue No. 28 (Educational).
July 23.—Issue No. 29 (Educational).
July 30.—Issue No. 30 (Educational).
Aug. 6.—Issue No. 31 (Topical).
Aug. 13.—Issue No. 32 (Topical).
Aug. 20.—Issue No. 33 (Educational).
Aug. 27.—Issue No. 34 (Educational).
Sept. 3.—Issue No. 35 (Educational).

UNIVERSAL SPECIAL FEATURE.
July 15.—The Gray Ghost (Episode No. 3.—"The Warning"—Two parts—Drama).
July 22.—The Gray Ghost (Episode No. 4—"The Fight"—Two parts—Drama).
July 29.—The Gray Ghost (Episode No. 5.—"Plunder"—Two parts—Drama).
Aug. 6.—The Gray Ghost (Episode No. 6, "The House of Mystery"—Two parts—Drama).
Aug. 13.—The Gray Ghost (Episode No. 7) (The Double Floor) (Two parts—Drama).
Aug. 20.—The Gray Ghost (Episode No. 8, "The Pearl Necklace"—Two parts—Dr.).
Aug. 27.—The Gray Ghost (Episode No. 9—Title Not Reported—Two parts—Drama).
Sept. 3.—The Gray Ghost (Episode No. 10—Title not decided—Two parts—Drama).

UNIVERSAL CURRENT EVENTS.
July 14.—Issue No. 9 (Topical).
July 21.—Issue No. 10 (Topical).
July 28.—Issue No. 11 (Topical).
Aug. 4.—Issue No. 12 (Topical).
Aug. 11.—Issue No. 13 (Topical).
Aug. 17.—Issue No. 14 (Topical).
Aug. 24.—Issue No. 15 (Topical).
Sept. 1.—Issue No. 16 (Topical).

Metro Pictures Corporation.

METRO PICTURES CORP.
June 25.—Aladdin's Other Lamp (Five parts—Drama).
July 2.—The Trail of the Shadow (Five parts—Drama).
July 9.—Peggy, the Will o' the Wisp (Five parts—Drama).
July 30.—Miss Robinson Crusoe (Five parts—Drama).
Special.—The Slacker (Seven parts—Drama).
Aug. 6.—The Jury of Fate (Rolfe—Five parts—Drama).
Aug. 13.—The Girl Without a Soul (Five parts—Drama).

YORKE FILM CORP.
July 16.—The Hidden Spring (Five parts—Dr.).

METRO COMEDIES.
July 9.—Lest We Forget (Drew).
July 16.—Blood Will Tell (Rolins).
July 23.—Mr. Parker—Hero (Drew).
July 30.—Henry's Ancestors (Drew).
Aug. 6.—His Ear for Music (Drew).
Aug. 13.—Her Economic Independence (Drew).
Aug. 20.—Her First Game (Drew).
Aug. 27.—The Patriot (Drew).

Triangle Film Corporation.

TRIANGLE PRODUCTION.
July 8.—A Strange Transgression (Five parts—Drama).
July 8.—Time Locks and Diamonds (Five parts—Drama).
July 15.—The Sawdust Ring (Five parts—Dr.).
July 15.—The Mother Instinct (Five parts—Dr.).
July 22.—A Successful Failure (Five parts—Drama).
July 22.—Sudden Jim (Five parts—Drama).
July 29.—In Slumberland (Five parts—Drama).
July 29.—Borrowed Plumage (Five parts—Dr.).
Aug. 5.—The Food Gamblers (Five parts—Drama).
Aug. 12.—An Even Break (Five parts—Drama).
Aug. 12.—Master of His Home (Five parts—Drama).
Aug. 12.—Golden Rule Kate (Five parts—Dr.).
Aug. 19.—Wee Lady Betty (Five parts—Drama).
Aug. 19.—They're Off (Five parts—Drama).
Aug. 26.—Wooden Shoes (Five parts—Drama).
Aug. 26.—The Jinx Jumper (Five parts—Drama).

TRIANGLE KOMEDY.
July 8.—His Thankless Job.
July 8.—A Joy of Fate.
July 15.—His Sudden Rival.
July 15.—The House of Scandal.
July 22.—His Fatal Move.
July 22.—An Innocent Villain.
July 29.—Sole Mates.
July 29.—His Perfect Day.
Aug. 5.—A Matrimonial Accident.
Aug. 12.—His Cool Nerve.
Aug. 12.—A Hotel Disgrace.
Aug. 19.—A Love Chase.
Aug. 19.—His Hidden Talent.
Aug. 26.—Their Domestic Deception.
Aug. 26.—Her Honey Love.

KEYSTONE.
July 8.—Dangers of a Bride (Two parts).
July 15.—A Clever Dummy (Two parts).
July 22.—She Needed a Doctor (Two parts).
July 29.—Thirst (Two parts).
July 29.—His Uncle Dudley (Two parts).
Aug. 12.—Lost—a Cook (Two parts).
Aug. 19.—The Pawnbroker's Heart (Two parts).
Aug. 26.—Two Crooks (Two parts).

Producers.—Kindly Furnish Titles and Dates of All New Releases Before Saturday.

List of Current Film Release Dates

MUTUAL PROGRAM AND MISCELLANEOUS FEATURES

(For Daily Calendar of Program Releases See Page 1422.)

Mutual Film Corp.

CUB.

July 12—Jerry at the Waldorf (Comedy).
July 19—Jerry's Star Bout (Comedy).
July 26—The Red, White and Blew (Comedy).
Aug. 2—Jerry's Big Stunt.
Aug. 9—Jerry on the Railroad (Comedy).
Aug. 16—Beach Nuts (Comedy).
Aug. 23—Jerry on the Farm (Comedy).
Aug. 30—Jerry's Eugenic Marriage (Comedy).

GAUMONT.

Aug. 2—Reel Life No. 66 (Subjects on Reel: Making Machine Guns; Beads of Rose Petals; Saving a Wrecked Steamship; Keeping the Boys Home; Leaves from "Life"). (Mutual Film Magazine).
Aug. 7—Tours Around the World No. 40 (Subjects on reel: Down the Senegal River in French West Africa; Bruges, Belgium; Fishing Villages of France) (Travel).
Aug. 9—Reel Life No. 67 (Subjects on reel: An Undersea Garden; A Colored Baptising; Electricity from the Heart; The Tallest Boy on Earth; Making Schools Safe; Animated Drawing from "Life"; "Not a Shadow of a Doubt"; "A Bomb and a Boomerang" (a war cartoon) (Mutual Film Magazine).
Aug. 16—Reel Life No. 68 (Subjects on Reel: Young Men's Christian Association; Learning to Be a Soldier; The Absent-Minded Dentist; An Animated Drawing from "Life" (Mutual Film Magazine).
Aug. 23—Reel Life No. 69 (Subjects on Reel: Hunting Alligators for Their Skins; Harvesting Potatoes on the Eastern Coast; Coney Island Thrills; Oil from Japan; Something Going to Happen; An Animated Cartoon from "Life."
Aug. 30—Reel Life No. 70 (Subjects on Reel: Using the Abalone, a Little Known Industry of the Pacific Coast; A Boy and a Rope; Handling the Mail; Beach Sports of California; "The March of Science" and "What a Bachelor Sees at a Wedding" are animated drawings from "Life."

LA SALLE.

July 10—When Lula Danced the Hula (Com.).
July 17—The Kissing Butterfly.
July 24—A Match in Quarantine.
July 31—Man Proposes (Comedy).
Aug. 7—Pigs and Pearls (Comedy).
Aug. 14—The Widow's Might (Comedy).

MUTUAL WEEKLY.

July 11—Number 132 (Topical).
July 18—Number 133 (Topical).
July 25—Number 134 (Topical).
Aug. 1—Number 135 (Topical).
Aug. 8—Number 136 (Topical).
Aug. 15—Number 137 (Topical).
Aug. 22—Number 138 (Topical).

MUTUAL CHAPLIN.

April—The Cure (Two parts—Comedy).
June 22—The Immigrant (Two parts—Com.).

MONMOUTH.

July 6—Jimmy Dale alias The Grey Seal (Chapter No. 16—"The Victory"— Two parts—Drama).

MUTUAL STAR PRODUCTIONS.

July 9—Mary Moreland (Powell—Five parts—Drama).
July 16—Betty Be Good (Horkheimer—Five parts—Drama).
July 23—Melissa of the Hills (Five parts—Dr.).
July 30—Pride and the Man (Five parts—Dr.).

Aug. 6—Souls in Pawn (American—Five parts —Drama).
Aug. 13—Bab the Fixer (Horkheimer—Five parts—Drama).

MUTUAL SPECIAL.

July 23—The Great Stanley Secret (Chapter No. I, The Gipsy's Trust—Four parts—Drama—North American).
uly 30—The Great Stanley Secret (Chapter No. II, "Fate and the Child"—Four parts —Drama—North American).

SIGNAL PRODUCING CO.

July 9—The Railroad Raiders (Chapter No. 14—"The Trap"—Two parts—Dr.).
July 16—The Railroad Raiders (Chapter No. 15, "The Mystery of the Counterfeit Tickets"—Two parts—Drama).

Feature Releases

ART DRAMAS, INC.

July 16—When you and I Were Young (Apollo —Five parts—Drama).
July 23—The Millstone (Erbograph—Five parts —Drama).
July 30—Eye of Envy (Five parts—Drama).
Aug. 13—Think It Over (U. S. Amusement Corp. —Five parts—Comedy-Drama).

ARTCRAFT PICTURES CORP.

July 2—The Little American (Five parts— Drama).

BLUEBIRD PHOTOPLAY, INC.

July 30—The Little Terror (Five parts—Dr.).
Aug. 6—The Clean-Up (Five parts—Drama).
Aug. 13—The Show Down (Five parts—Dr.).
Aug. 20—Mr. Opp Five Parts—Drama).
Aug. 27—The Charmer (Five parts—Drama).
Sept. 3—Triumph (Five parts—Comedy-Dr.).

BUTTERFLY PICTURES.

July 30—A Wife on Trial (Five parts—Dr.).
Aug. 6—Follow the Girl (Five parts—Dr.).
Aug. 13—The Midnight Man (Five parts—Dr.).
Aug. 20—The Lair of the Wolf (Five parts— Drama).
Aug. 27—Straight Shooting (Five parts—Dr.).
Sept. 3—Who Was the Other Man? (Five parts —Drama).

CINEMA WAR NEWS SYNDICATE.

July 22—American War News Weekly No. 12 (Topical).
July 29—American War News Weekly No. 13 (Topical).

EDUCATIONAL FILM CORP.

July 25—Among the Sennosi (Educational).
July 30—Living Book of Nature (Water Fowl).
Aug. 1—Chink and the Chinese No. 4 (Scenic and Educational).
Aug. 6—Living Book of Nature (Mounting Butterflies).
Aug. 8—Alaska Wonders in Motion No. 4 (Scenic and Educational).

FOX FILM CORP.

Special Release—Jack and the Beanstalk (Ten parts—Drama).
July 22—The Innocent Sinner (Five parts—Dr.).
July 29—Wife Number Two (Five Parts—Dr.).
Aug. 4—Wrath of Love (Five parts—Drama).
Aug. 11—Durand of the Bad Lands (Five parts —Drama).
Aug. 18—The Soul of Satan (Five parts—Dr.).
Aug. 25—Every Girl's Dream (Five parts—Dr.).

FOXFILM COMEDIES.

July 9—Bing! Bang! (Two parts).
July 23—A Soft Tenderfoot (Two parts).
Aug. 6—A Domestic Hound (Two parts).

GREATER VITAGRAPH (V-L-S-E).

Aug. 13—Mary Jane's Pa (Five parts—Drama).
Aug. 20—Transgression (Five parts—Drama).
Aug. 27—The Divorcee (Five parts—Drama).
Aug. 6—Bobby, Boy Scout (Comedy-Drama).
Aug. 13—Bobby, the Movie Director (Comedy).
Aug. 20—Bobby, Philanthropist (Comedy-Dr.).
Aug. 27—Bobby, Pacifist (Comedy-Drama).
Sept. 3—Bobby's Bravery (Comedy-Drama).

KLEINE-EDISON-SELIG-ESSANAY.

Aug. 8—The Little White Girl (An Episode of the "Do Children Count?" Series— Two parts—Drama).
Aug. 11—Conquest Program No. 5 (Subjects: The Little Chevalier (Four parts— Drama); Birds of a Far-Off Sea (500 feet); A Vanishing Race (500 feet); Soldiers of the Sea (One Reel); Gold and Diamond Mines of South Africa (500 feet), and The Dinosaur and the Baboon (500 feet).
Aug. 15—The Barker (Selig—Five parts—Dr.).
Aug. 15—The Bridge of Fancy (One of the "Do Children Count?" Series—Two parts -Drama).
Aug. 18—Conquest Program No. 6 (Subjects: The Customary Two Weeks (Four parts—Drama); The Story of Plymouth Rock (1,000 feet); The Grand Canyon of Arizona (500 feet); The Four P's (500 feet); Nature's Perfect Thread Spinner (500 feet); The Magic of Spring (500 feet).
Aug. 20—Open Places (Essanay—Five parts— Drama).
Aug. 22—The Kingdom of Hope (One of the "Do Children Count?" Series—Two parts—Drama).
Aug. 24—A Trip to Chinatown (Selig-Hoyt Comedy—Two parts).
Aug. 27—The Lady of the Photograph (Edison —Five parts—Drama).
Aug. 25—Conquest Program No. 7 (Subjects: Haviland Hicks, Freshman (Three parts—Drama); Gallagher (two parts—Drama); Turning Out Silver Bullets (One reel); Young Salts and the Holy Land (Combined in one reel).
Sept. 3—Efficiency Edgar's Courtship (Five parts—Drama—Essanay).
Sept. 3—A Midnight Bell (Hoyt Comedy—Two parts).

SELZNICK PICTURES.

The Lash of Jealousy (Drama).
The Lesson (Drama).
The Moth (Drama).
The Wild Girl.

STANDARD PICTURES.

Aug. 19—The Spy (Ten parts).
Aug. 26—The Honor System (Ten parts).
Sept. 2—Jack and the Beanstalk (Ten parts).
Sept. 16—The Conqueror (Ten parts).

WHOLESOME FILMS CORPORATION.

Sept. 3—The Penny Philanthropist (Five parts —Drama).
Sept. 3—Cinderella and the Magic Slipper (Four parts—Drama).

WORLD PICTURES.

July 16—The Beloved Adventuress (Five parts —Drama).
July 16—When True Love Dawns (Brady-International—Five parts—Drama).
July 23—A Self-Made Widow (Five parts—Dr.).
Aug. 6—The Iron Ring (Five parts—Drama).
Aug. 13—Souls Adrift (Five parts—Drama).
Aug. 20—The Little Duchess (Five parts—Dr.).
Aug. 27—Her Guardian (Five parts—Drama).
Sept. 3—The Marriage Market (Five parts— Drama).

Producers:—Kindly Furnish Titles and Dates of All New Releases Before Saturday.

List of State Rights Pictures

(For Daily Calendar of Program Releases See Page 1422.)

Note—For further information regarding pictures listed on this page, address State Rights Department, Moving Picture World, and same will be gladly furnished.

ARIZONA FILM CO.
May—Should She Obey (Drama).

BERNSTEIN FILM PRODUCTION.
Humility (First of "Seven Cardinal Virtues"—Drama).
June—Who Knows? (Six parts—Drama).

J. FRANK BROCKLISS, INC.
U. S. Navy (Five parts).
Terry Human Interest Reels (900 Feet Every Other Week).
Russian Revolution (Three parts).
Land of the Rising Sun (10,000 feet—Issued complete or in series of 2,000 feet or 5,000 feet).

BUD FISHER FILMS CORP.
Mutt and Jeff Animated Cartoons.

CAMERAGRAPH FILM MFG. CO.
June—What of Your Boy? (Three parts—Patriotic).
June—The Automobile Owner Gets Acquainted With His Automobile (Educational).

CARONA CINEMA CO.
May—The Curse of Eve (Seven parts—Dr.).

CENTURY COMEDIES.
May—Balloonatics.
May—Neptune's Naughty Daughter.
May—Automaniacs.
June—Alice of the Sawdust (Two parts).

BENJAMIN CHAPIN PRODUCTIONS.
(The Lincoln Cycle Pictures.)
My Mother (Two parts).
My Father (Two parts).
Myself (Two parts).
The Call to Arms (Two parts).

CHRISTIE FILM CO.
July 2—Almost a Scandal (Comedy).
July 9—The Fourteenth Man (Comedy).
July 16—Down By the Sea (Comedy).
July 23—Skirts (Comedy).
July 30—Won in a Cabaret (Comedy).
Aug. 7—His Merry Mix-Up (Comedy).
Aug. 14—A Smokey Love Affair (Comedy).

CINEMA DISTRIBUTING CORP.
June—The 13th Labor of Hercules (Twelve single parts).

CORONET FILM CORP.
Living Studies in Natural History.
Animal World—Issue No. 1.
Animal World—Issue No. 2.
Birdland Studies.
Horticultural Phenomena.

COSMOFOTOFILM, INC.
March—The Manx-Man (Eight parts—Drama).
June—I Believe (Seven parts—Drama).

E. I. S. MOTION PICTURES CORP.
Trooper 44 (Five parts—Drama).

EMERALD MOTION PICTURE CO.
May—The Slacker (Military Drama).

EUGENIC FILM CO.
April—Birth (A Picture for Women Only).

EXPORT AND IMPORT FILM CO.
June—Robespierre.
June—Ivan the Terrible.

FACTS FILM CO.
April—The Big Question (Drama).
April—How About You (Drama).

FAIRMOUNT FILM CORP.
June—Hate (Seven parts—Drama).

FLORA FINCH FILM CO.
"War Brides" (Two parts—Comedy).

FRATERNITY FILMS, INC.
May—Devil's Playground (Nine parts—Drama).

FRIEDMAN ENTERPRISES.
A Mormon Maid (Six parts—Drama).

FRIEDER FILM CORP.
June—A Bit o' Heaven (Five parts—Drama).

FROHMAN AMUSEMENT CORP.
April—God's Man (Nine parts—Drama).

JOSEPH M. GAITES.
August—The Italian Battlefront.

GOLDIN FEATURES.
A Bit of Life (One Reel Comedy-Drama).

GRAPHIC FEATURES.
April—The Woman and the Beast (Five parts—Drama).

F. G. HALL PRODUCTIONS, INC.
May—Her Fighting Chance (Seven parts—Dr.). (Mr. Hall has world rights to this picture.)
May—The Bar Sinister (Drama). (Mr. Hall has world rights to this picture.)

HANOVER FILM CO.
April—How Uncle Sam Prepares (Topical).

HILLER & WILK.
April—The Battle of Gettysburg.
April—The Wrath of the Gods (Drama).

HISTORIC FEATURES.
June—Christus (Eight parts—Drama).

ILIDOR PICTURES CORP.
June.—The Fall of the Romanoffs (Drama).

IVAN FILM PRODUCTIONS.
Apr. —One Law for Both (8 parts—Drama).
August—Babbling Tongues (Six parts—Dr.).

JEWEL PRODUCTIONS, INC.
Pay Me (Drama).

KING BEE FILMS CORP.
June 15—Dough Nuts (Two parts—Comedy).
July 1—Cupid's Rival (Two parts—Comedy).
July 15—The Villain (Two parts—Comedy).
Aug. 1—The Millionaire (Two parts—Com.).
Aug. 8—The Genius (Two parts—Comedy).
Aug. 15—The Modiste (Two parts—Comedy).

A KAY CO.
Some Barrier (Terry Cartoon Burlesque).
His Trial (Terry Cartoon Burlesque).
Terry Human Interest Reel No. 1 (Character As Revealed in the Face).
Terry Human Interest Reel No. 2 (Character As Revealed in the Eyes).

KLOTZ & STREIMER.
June.—Whither Thou Goest (Five parts—Drama).
June—The Secret Trap (Five parts—Drama).

MAYFAIR FILM CORP.
Persuasive Peggy (Drama).

M-C FILM CO.
April—America Is Ready (Five parts—Drama).

MIL-KS.
April—The Test of Womanhood (Five parts—Drama).

MOE STREIMER.
June—A Daughter of the Don (Ten parts—Drama).

B. S. MOSS MOTION PICTURE CORP.
January—In the Hands of the Law (Drama).
April—Birth Control (Five parts—Drama).

NEVADA MOTION PICTURE CORP.
June—The Planter (Drama).

NEWFIELDS PRODUCING CORP.
Alma, Where Do You Live? (Six parts—Dr.).

OGDEN PICTURES CORP.
August—The Lust of the Ages (Drama).

PARAGON FILMS, INC.
The Whip (Eight parts—Drama).

PETER PAN FILM CORP.
Mo-Toy Troupe (Release No. 2—"Jimmy Wins the Pennant").
Mo-Toy Troupe (Release No. 3—"Out in the Rain").
Mo-Toy Troupe (Release No. 4—"In the Jungle Land").
Mo-Toy Troupe (Release No. 5—"A Kitchen Romance").
Mo-Toy Troupe (Release No. 6—"Mary and Gretel").
Mo-Toy Troupe (Release No. 7—"Dinkling of the Circus").
Mo-Toy Troupe (Release No. 8—"A Trip to the Moon").
Mo-Toy Troupe (Release No. 9, "Golden Locks and the Three Bears").
Mo-Toy Troupe (Release No 10, "Dolly Doings").
Mo-Toy Troupe (Release No. 11 "School Days").

PUBLIC RIGHTS FILM CORP.
June—The Public Be Damned.

PURKALL FILM CO.
July—The Liar (Six parts—Drama).

RENOWNED PICTURES CORP.
June—In Treason's Grasp (Five parts—Drama).

REX BEACH PICTURES CO.
March—The Barrier (Nine parts—Drama).

SELECT PHOTOPLAY CO.
May—Humanity (Six parts—Drama).

WILLIAM N. SELIG.
April—The Garden of Allah.
May—Beware of Strangers (Eight parts—Dr.).

FRANK J. SENG.
May—Parentage (Drama).

SHERMAN PICTURE. CORP.
July—Corruption (Six parts—Drama).
August—I Believe.

JULIUS STEGER.
May—Redemption (Six parts—Drama).

SUPREME FEATURE FILMS, INC.
May—Trip Through China (Ten parts).

ULTRA FILMS, INC.
A Day at West Point (Educational).
West is West.
Rustlers' Frame-Up at Big Horn.

UNIVERSAL (STATE RIGHTS).
May—The Hand that Rocks the Cradle (Six parts—Drama).
June—The Cross-Eyed Submarine (Three parts—Comedy).
June—Come Through (Seven parts—Drama).

E. WARREN PRODUCTION.
April—The Warfare of the Flesh (Drama).

WHARTON, INC.
June—The Great White Trail (Seven parts) (Drama).

WILLIAMSON BROS.
April—The Submarine Eye (Drama).

Producers.—Kindly Furnish Titles and Dates of All New Releases Before Saturday.

Convention at Ocean Beach, Va.

August 30th, 31st, Sept. 1st

THIS will be the most important gathering of Exhibitors ever held in the South. President Percy W. Wells expects a big attendance from North Carolina. President Geo. C. Warner, of the South Carolina League, will be present with other exhibitors from his state. Harry Crandall will head a delegation from Washington, and Guy Wonders, vice-president of the American Exhibitors' Association, will be over with a large delegation from Maryland.

All exhibitors should attend whether members or not, as matters of great importance will be considered.

MOTION PICTURE EXHIBITORS' LEAGUE OF VA.

JAKE WELLS, President   CHESLEY TONEY, Secretary

Richmond, Va.

We Can Make Your Theatre More Popular

The popularity and success of any place of entertainment depends largely upon its pleasing appearance.

Let us brighten up your theatre. We are expert specialists in this line and carry an immense variety of papier mache and floral decorations especially adapted to theatres.

Send for our illustrated catalog

The Botanical Decorating Co.

Manufacturers of
Artificial Plants and
Theatrical Decorations
208 W. Adams St., Chicago

"NEWMAN" BRASS FRAMES AND RAILS

Read what C. A. Morrison of The Princess Theatre, Hartford, Conn., says about Newman Quality:

Gentlemen:
We have purchased quite a number of Brass Frames and Easels, together with Brass Ticket Rail and Three-Sheet Brass Poster Frames of your Company.
All of these goods reached us in perfect condition and the quality was the best. I have told several other managers in the city of your goods and in several instances orders have been sent you—all of which goes to show that your best advertiser is a satisfied customer.
PRINCESS THEATRE CO., Inc.,
C. A. Morrison, Mgr. Hartford, Conn.

INSIST ON THE NAME "NEWMAN" WHEN BUYING FRAMES
Write for New 1917 Catalog.

The Newman Mfg. Company

Established 1882
Frames, Easels, Rails, Grilles, Signs, Choppers, Kick Plates, Door Bars
717-19 Sycamore Street, Cincinnati, O.
68 W. Washington Street, Chicago, Ill.
Canadian Representative—7. Malone, Rialto Theatre Bldg., Montreal, Canada.
Pacific Coast—G. A. Metcalfe, San Francisco, Cal.

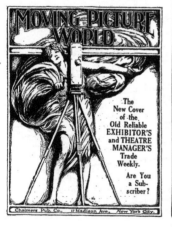

The New Cover of the Old Reliable EXHIBITOR'S and THEATRE MANAGER'S Trade Weekly.

Are You a Subscriber?

Chalmers Pub. Co., 17 Madison Ave., New York City.

You can afford

to use, and we can afford to manufacture, *only* the *best* film. With the product *right*, chemically and physically, "clearest pictures" follow as a matter of course.

It is easily identifiable by the stencil

"EASTMAN"

in the margin.

EASTMAN KODAK COMPANY,
ROCHESTER, N. Y.

F. H. RICHARDSON'S
MOVING PICTURE HANDBOOK

Published by
The Moving Picture World

THE latest edition of a volume on the technical side of the moving picture industry which has achieved the distinction of being one of the most widely read technical books ever published.

Technical because its subject matter is technical but written in a fluent, easy, everyday style which makes it easily understood by all classes of readers.

Of Inestimable Value to Moving Picture Operators and Managers.

On Sale at Offices of the
MOVING PICTURE WORLD
17 Madison Avenue, New York
Schiller Building, Chicago
Haas Building, Los Angeles

$4.00 the Copy
Postage Paid

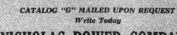

MOVING PICTURE WORLD

Founded   By J. P. Chalmers in 1907

Chalmers Pub. Co.,   17 Madison Ave.,   New York City.

PETROVA PICTURES

FIRST RELEASE:
on or about Oct. 22, 1917.

Petrova Picture Company
Frederick L. Collins.. President
25 West 44ᵗʰ Street.. New York

Essanay pictures
are winning the
highest praise
from critics and
public alike.
Your patrons are
entitled to the
best! Get them
at any K. E. S. E.
office.

Geo. K. Spoor.

BUTTERFLY PICTURES Present

RUTH STONEHOUSE

"The EDGE of the LAW"

A POWERFUL STORY OF A GIRL
WHOSE BETTER NATURE OVERCAME
A FAGIN'S EFFORTS TO MAKE
HER A CROOK 🦋🦋🦋🦋🦋
DIRECTED BY L.W. CHAUDET
BOOK THROUGH ANY BUTTERFLY EXCHANGES
OR DIRECT TO UNIVERSAL FILM MAN'F'G CO.
CARL LAEMMLE PRES...1600 BROADWAY
NEW YORK CITY

Story by
MAUDE
PETTUS

GEORGE LOANE TUCKER
presents

THE MANX-MAN
BY
HALL CAINE
NOW PLAYING
CRITERION THEATRE
BROADWAY & 44th ST, NEW YORK CITY
PRICES-25¢-50¢-$1.00
JUSTIFIED CAPACITY

THE MANX-MAN CO. INC.
HENRY J. BROCK, Pres.
220 WEST 42nd STREET
NEW YORK CITY

Producer and Story
getting acquainted.

This Thrilling Romance
of Metropolitan Life,
By one of the most
Distinguished American
Authors, will be
Herbert Brenon's next
Selznick-picture

Herbert Brenon

visualizes

the passing of
autocracy

the advent of
democracy

Czar Nicholas II.

now an exile
in Siberia

Alexander Kerensky

Foremost citizen of
the Russian Republic

in the

the FALL of the ROMANOFFS

with ILIODOR

Produced by Special Arrangement
with Mr. Lewis J. Selznick and the
Herbert Brenon Film Corporation

Address All Communications
ILIODOR PICTURE CORPORATION
729 Seventh Avenue

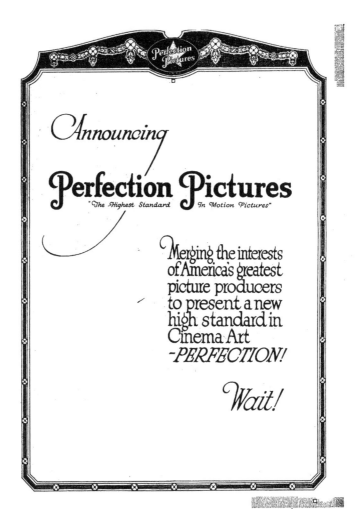

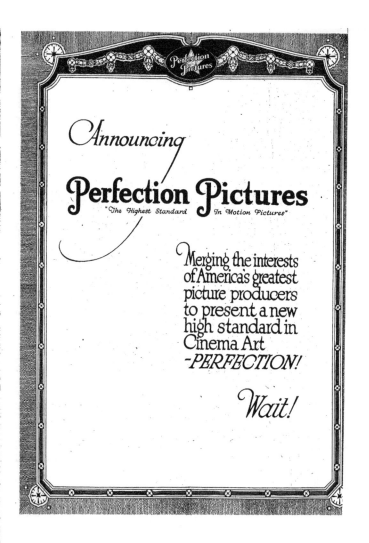

CLARA
KIMBALL
YOUNG
and
Her Own Company

THIS supreme screen favorite is the first to be announced in the list of great screen stars and directors, whose productions are to be released and marketed through SELECT PICTURES CORPORATION, details of which organization are presented on the following page.

Clara Kimball Young will be seen as the star of eight pictures to be released during the coming year. The great following which this splendid emotional actress gained with "The Common Law," "The Price She Paid," and "The Easiest Way" will eagerly welcome her appearance in the first of these eight productions — "Magda," a photoplay adapted from the famous play of the same name.

Distributed by
Select Pictures Corporation
729 Seventh Avenue, New York City

Select Pictures

WITH this announcement SELECT PICTURES CORPO-RATION introduces itself. SELECT PICTURES will offer to exhibitors the productions of the screen's most brilliant stars and directors. The first of its presentations is described on the preceding page.

SELECT stands for what its name implies; a medium for the distribution of the most select, the most choice, the most individual productions of film manufacturers anywhere and everywhere.

SELECT has advantages not shared by any other distributing organization in the film industry. Its producers are stars and directors whose places as great box-office attractions have been won through years of diligent service to the motion picture public of the world. SELECT'S personnel is composed of men who have fashioned successful careers because their progressive ideas have coincided constantly with the ideas of the progressive exhibitors.

SELECT PICTURES enters the field of photoplay distribution fully grown, its stars and directors bearing names that are household words throughout the land. Its organization is composed of branches situated in all the large cities of the United States. The following SELECT exchanges are now open for bookings:

New York Sol. J. Berman, Mgr. 729 Seventh Avenue	Cleveland Sam E. Morris, Mgr., Columbia Bldg.	Dallas C. C. Ezell, Mgr., 1919 Main Street
Philadelphia M. Milder, 1335 Vine Street	Detroit To be announced	Denver Hugh Rennie, Mgr., 1541 Welton Street
Boston S. H. Steinfeld, Mgr., Address to be announced	Chicago 110 South State Street	Los Angeles H. H. Hicks, Mgr., 736 South Olive Street
	Des Moines A. H. Blank, Garden Theatre Bldg.	
Buffalo C. R. Rogers, Mgr., 86 Exchange Street	Kansas City W. H. Bell, 920 Main Street	San Francisco X. K. Stout, Mgr., 985 Market Street
Washington V. P. Whitaker, Mgr., Address to be announced	Minneapolis H. A. Rathner, Mgr., Film Exchange Bldg.	Seattle B. R. Keller, Mgr., 1541 Welton Street
Pittsburgh C. F. Schwerin, Mgr., 1201 Liberty Avenue	Atlanta Walter Price, Mgr., 61 Walton Street	Cincinnati Sam E. Morris, Mgr., 502 Strand Theatre Building

Select Pictures Corporation

729 Seventh Avenue   New York City

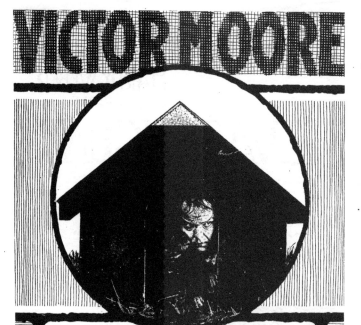

"THE CINDERELLA HUSBAND"

By Thomas J. Gray

Released August 27

OUR exhibitors everywhere are calling Kleyer Komedies "the single reel comedies with a story." Instead of being an insult to the intelligence of even an average man Victor Moore Comedies are really very funny, and "The Cinderella Husband" is a fair example.

Give single reel comedies a chance. You will find these safe, sane and funny. The best theatres show them—why not you?

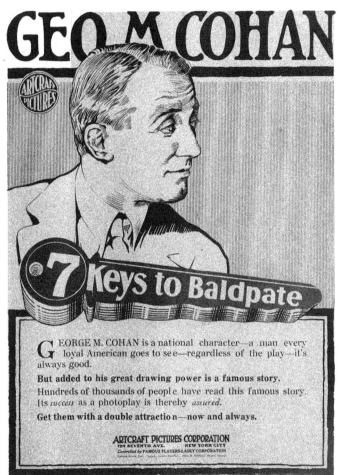

G EORGE M. COHAN is a national character—a man every
  loyal American goes to see—regardless of the play—it's
always good.

But added to his great drawing power is a famous story.

Hundreds of thousands of people have read this famous story.
Its *success* as a photoplay is thereby *assured*.

Get them with a double attraction—now and always.

ARTCRAFT PICTURES CORPORATION
729 SEVENTH AVE.   NEW YORK CITY
Controlled by FAMOUS PLAYERS-LASKY CORPORATION

MARY PICKFORD
in
"Rebecca of Sunnybrook Farm"

A Play That Ran Six Years

PUBLIC DEMAND has prompted "Little Mary" to appear in the famous story by Kate Douglas Wiggin and Charlotte Thompson.

ARTCRAFT PICTURES CORPORATION
729 SEVENTH AVE.   NEW YORK CITY
Controlled by FAMOUS PLAYERS-LASKY CORPORATION

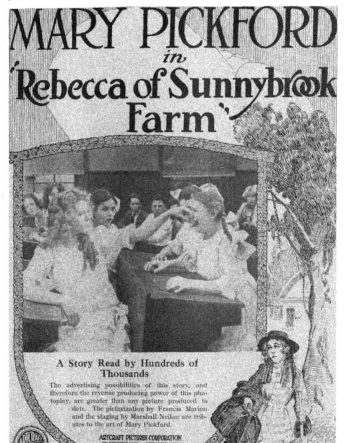

MARY PICKFORD
in
'Rebecca of Sunnybrook Farm '

A Story Read by Hundreds of Thousands

The advertising possibilities of this story, and therefore the revenue producing power of this photoplay, are greater than any picture produced to date. The picturization by Francis Marion and the staging by Marshall Neilan are tributes to the art of Mary Pickford.

ARTCRAFT PICTURES CORPORATION
729 SEVENTH AVE.   NEW YORK CITY
Controlled by FAMOUS PLAYERS-LASKY CORPORATION

GEORGE BEBAN
in "Lost in Transit"

A WONDERFUL love story—a gem of a photoplay. Teeming with heart-throbs — touched with pathos. The quaint humor and heart interest is introduced by one of the greatest actors on the American screen. His pictures have become unusually popular. His ability to sway the public from weeping to shrieks of laughter in a moment has no small part in the great success of his pictures.

A Paramount Picture

Anna Katharine Green

We can offer no
strong'er proof
of the standard
to be set in *Paramount*
serials than this:
that Anna Kath-
arine Green is
the author of
<u>the first</u>

*Paramount
Serial*

Exhibitors know the value of that name ····· Ready in October

Paramount Pictures Corporation
FOUR EIGHTY FIVE FIFTH AVENUE AT FORTY FIRST ST,
NEW YORK, N.Y.
Controlled by FAMOUS PLAYERS-LASKY CORP.
ADOLPH ZUKOR, Pres.   JESSE L. LASKY, Vice-Pres.   CECIL B. DeMILLE, Dir. Gen.

Anna Katharine Green
and the first
Paramount Serial

The world's most
famous author of
mystery stories and
the world's most fam-
ous producers are
working together to
make *Paramount's
first Serial* the
most satisfying pro-
duction ever thrown
on a screen

Exhibitors know that means a Picture and the Power behind it
Ready in October

Paramount Pictures Corporation
FOUR EIGHTY FIVE   FIFTH AVENUE   AT FORTY FIRST ST.
NEW YORK, N.Y.
Controlled by FAMOUS PLAYERS-LASKY CORP.
ADOLPH ZUKOR, Pres.   JESSE L. LASKY, Vice-Pres.   CECIL B. DEMILLE, Dir. Gen.

Paramount-
Mack Sennett
Comedies

Are You a Real Showman?

Mack Sennett is the man who
put the come in Comedy. He
taught *most* of the good screen
comedians *most* of what they
know.

You see the *new* tricks for the
first time in Paramount-Mack
Sennett Comedies — every *real*
showman knows their value —
he wouldn't be without them.

Paramount Pictures Corporation
FOUR EIGHTY-FIVE   FIFTH AVENUE   & FORTY-FIRST ST
NEW YORK
Controlled by FAMOUS PLAYERS-LASKY CORPORATION
Adolph Zukor, Pres.   Jesse L. Lasky, Vice-Pres.
Cecil B. DeMille, Director General.

Paramount
Pictures

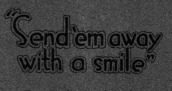

"Polly Of The Circus"
Cost $250,000

A ND GOLDWYN presents this to the
exhibitors of America at the regularly
scheduled price with the hope and the
certain knowledge that every exhibitor playing
it will reap immense profits.

A production so big that it would make a fortune if handled separately—a picture so fine
that many who have seen it say: "Why do you
let it go out to exhibitors at regular contract
prices?"

And it is *true* that it is worth double or triple
the price you pay for it under a Goldwyn contract. . . . But a group of skilled and earnest people have worked a year to make this
and other pictures like it, firm in the belief
that exhibitors everywhere will support a company capable of such achievements as *Goldwyn
Pictures.*

These productions *are worth more than we ask
for them* and they will make more money for
exhibitors than any pictures now being made
by any other producing organization in the
world.

Advisory Board:
SAMUEL GOLDFISH
    Chairman
EDGAR SELWYN
IRVIN S. COBB
ARTHUR HOPKINS
MARGARET MAYO
ROI COOPER MEGRUE
ARCHIBALD SELWYN
CROSBY GAIGE
PORTER EMERSON BROWNE

Goldwyn Pictures
Corporation

16 East 42nd Street,   New York City
Telephone: Vanderbilt 11

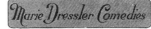

"The Stars As They Are"

TWELVE single-reel peeps into the lives of the shadow players—a new high class subject every month, beginning soon! The title: PHOTOPLAY MAGAZINE SCREEN SUPPLEMENT. Picture the contents of Photoplay Magazine—the world's leading motion picture magazine—come to life, and you will appreciate the box-office value in Photoplay Magazine Screen Supplement. Imagine how the fans will enjoy "off-the-screen" pictures of such favorites as Mae Marsh, William S. Hart, Charlie Chaplin, Henry Walthall, Mary Charleson, Bessie Love, Edith Storey and a host of others—many stars in each release.

Superb photography, the world's greatest stars, regular "Oh Boy!" sub-titles, and absolute perfection in printing and developing are matters of course in Photoplay Magazine Screen Supplement. Applications are invited from the foremost State Rights buyers, foreign buyers and exhibitors controlling theatre chains, for exclusive territory on these twelve de luxe motion pictures. Wire or write

Edith Storey —at Home.

JAMES R. QUIRK, Publisher
PHOTOPLAY MAGAZINE
CHICAGO, ILLINOIS

"Out!"—Says
the Umpire

PHOTOPLAY MAGAZINE·
SCREEN SUPPLEMENT

Applications for territory are invited

APPLICATIONS are now invited from State Rights Buyers and prominent Exhibitors, for territorial rights to
PHOTOPLAY MAGAZINE SCREEN SUPPLE-
MENT—twelve de luxe single reel subjects. Each release
presents unique and unusual views of numerous stars. A proposition that stands alone—without competition. Nothing like it
on the screen. Wire applications for territory stating full details
of your ability to distribute these subjects to high class theatres.

JAMES R. QUIRK, Publisher
PHOTOPLAY MAGAZINE
CHICAGO, ILLINOIS

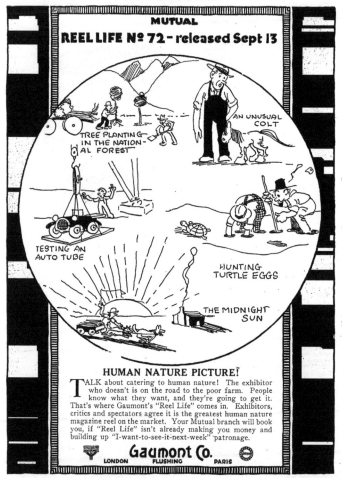

HUMAN NATURE PICTURE!

TALK about catering to human nature! The exhibitor who doesn't is on the road to the poor farm. People know what they want, and they're going to get it. That's where Gaumont's "Reel Life" comes in. Exhibitors, critics and spectators agree it is the greatest human nature magazine reel on the market. Your Mutual branch will book you, if "Reel Life" isn't already making you money and building up "I-want-to-see-it-next-week" patronage.

Gaumont Co.
LONDON   FLUSHING   PARIS

Mutual Pictures
for the Coming Year

By JOHN R. FREULER, *President Mutual Film Corporation*

In this statement I am privileged to announce to Exhibitors throughout America the plans of the Mutual Film Corporation for the coming year—plans which I believe will mean much to those interested in box-office receipts.

For the Season of 1917-1918, the Mutual Film Corporation will release eight Mutual Pictures—"BIG STARS ONLY"—every month—*Two Big Star Features Each Week.* These attractions will include the Charles Frohman Successes in Motion Pictures and a complete new variety of high class feature productions by prominent authors and playwrights.

Among the stars to be presented in these coming Mutual Pictures are Mary Miles Minter, Ann Murdock, Gail Kane, William Gillette, Julia Sanderson, William Russell, Olive Tell, Juliette Day, Edna Goodrich, Margarita Fischer, Anita King and others.

These attractions will be of the highest class in every respect. They will be directed by such noted directors as Albert Capellani, Rollin Sturgeon, Lloyd Ingraham, Edward Sloman, John B. O'Brien, Henry King, Dell Henderson and Harry Pollard.

They will be leased to Exhibitors under the Mutual's New Service Contract, providing from five to ten reels daily—one to seven days each week—or they may be booked in series of stars, on open booking or on a basis of two or more Mutual Pictures—"BIG STARS ONLY"—each week regularly.

This new Mutual Policy for 1917-18 has just been put into effect i. all our exchanges. Exhibitors who have not yet received detailed information regarding booking dates, prices, etc., should communicate immediately with the nearest Mutual Exchange, before the territory is closed.

Raise your admission to 15c and play Mutual Pictures—"BIG STARS ONLY"—under the new Mutual Policy of TWO-A-WEEK.

President
Mutual Film Corporation

trade journal re-
viewers say after wit-
nessing the opening
installments of Signal's
greatest serial:

WILLIAM J. McGRATH In

Directed by ﹁
J. P. McGowan

Motion Picture News Says:

"Here is Helen Holmes once again in a railroad story—not a repetition of previous Helen Holmes productions, but *something new!* It has a mystery angle that is as fresh and as new as a dime out of the mint. *It is the ideal
serial with every chapter a whetter of appetite for what is to come.* As one looks at it he is forced to commend inwardly and
outwardly too, the creative ability of Frederick Bennett, well known war correspondent, who wrote the scenario, and the genius
of J. P. McGowan who directed it. It is a Helen Holmes picture in the first place and that gives it a great get-away. Then, to
cinch the prediction of its success, is that all-absorbing, new and tantalizing mystery tang that is bound to pervade it to the end."

Exhibitor's Herald Says:

". . full of action and suspense. There is no reason why this serial should not excel any of the previous
Helen Holmes railroad photo-novels. There is thrill after thrill and every foot of celluloid contains action."

Motography Says:

"It is 'su e-fire.' The mystery element should make it interesting to even those who do not care
primarily for railroad thrills."

Exhibitor's Trade Review Says:

"There are no dull moments, no dragging, there is plenty of quick action and an unbroken chain of thrills."

Booking Now at All Mutual Exchanges! WIRE!

—Until WE Saw Them . . "

The Classic of Adventure and Mystery Plays

BESSIE BARRISCALE
in "Madam Who?"

By HAROLD MacGRATH   Direction of REGINALD BARKER

The Master Drama of American History

Madam Who?
She grasps the rim of despair.
She scorches her soul with the fires of hate.
Even her love she denies,—
For the sake of HER COUNTRY'S HONOR.

A Woman's wits stacked against the brains of 2,000,000 Men. SHE WINS? Romance—Intrepitude—Tremendous Suspense— and the most powerful Snap Finish ever conceived by Play-building Genius.

The Superlative Box Office Drawing Card

The Play That Will Outlive the Screen

BESSIE BARRISCALE
in "Rose o' Paradise"

By GRACE MILLER WHITE, Author of "Tess of the Storm Country"   Direction of JAMES YOUNG

The Most Unusual Story Told in the Most Unusual Way

BESSIE BARRISCALE *is* Jinnie, the Angel of Paradise Road. She smiles through tears of happiness. She makes your heart glad with an exquisite warmth that radiates from her unending faith in God's handiwork.

What "Home, Sweet Home" is to the Ear and Mind,
"ROSE O' PARADISE" is to the Eye and Heart.

Box Office Note:

The most extraordinary Nation-Wide publicity campaign for "ROSE O' PARADISE" *has been launched. It will cause the public to DEMAND that you show this picture.*

Sold Under Either
Star Series Booking Method
or
The Paralta Plan

TRIANGLE

▼ The Triangle Code

Story. Triangle will secure the best stories that are written — stories that have been widely read — stories by the best known authors in the country — stories with a "punch."

Production. Triangle has always stood for high quality in production — pictures with a real box office value. This same high standard will be absolutely maintained.

Price. Triangle productions will be sold at prices that will enable an exhibitor to pay for his film service and other expenses and retain a profit for himself. The small town as well as the city exhibitor will be considered. No exhibitor need advance admission prices for Triangle plays.

Star. Triangle has made stars and will continue to make them. Read over the list of the stars of to-day and see how many were made by Triangle. Triangle stars, moreover, will be offered at a price that guarantees a profit to the exhibitor.

Equipment. Triangle studios at Culver City and Hollywood, Cal., are the finest in the country. No producing company has at its command studio facilities that are the equal of Triangle's.

Trade Mark. The Triangle trade mark is a real asset to exhibitors, for in the minds of the public it stands for motion picture quality.

Triangle is a business proposition for business men. *Watch Triangle grow.*

THE TRIANGLE DISTRIBUTING CORPORATION
1457 Broadway, New York

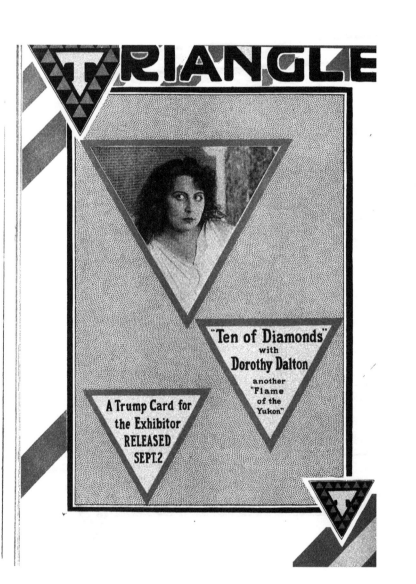

TRIANGLE

"Ten of Diamonds"
with
Dorothy Dalton

another
"Flame
of the
Yukon"

A Trump Card for
the Exhibitor
RELEASED
SEPT. 2

"The Man Hater"
with
Winifred Allen

A Saturday Evening-
Post Story by
Mary Brecht
Pulver

A Picture it will
pay to advertise
RELEASED
SEPT. 2

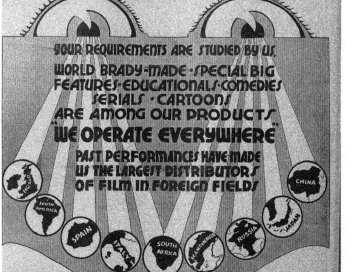

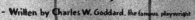

Pathé

MOLLIE
KING
star of
The SEVEN PEARLS

She proved her worth
in "Mystery of the Double
Cross", "The On-the-Square
Girl", "Kick In" and
"Blind Man's Luck",
all successful.

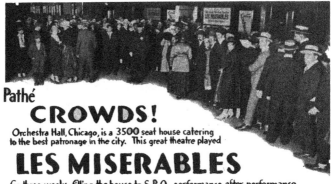

Pathé

CROWDS!

Orchestra Hall, Chicago, is a 3500 seat house catering to the best patronage in the city. This great theatre played

LES MISERABLES

for three weeks, filling the house to S. R.O., performance after performance.

When Victor Hugo's great classic was first brought out in this country four years ago it played 26 weeks in New York, proving the extraordinary hold that the immortal story has upon the public. Today revised, improved and brought up to date, millions wish to see it where thousands saw it before.

"What was the marvel of dramatic skill four years ago remains a marvel. You cannot doubt the worth of the motion picture after you have seen 'Les Miserables'. Exquisite detail."—*Oma Moody Lawrence in Chicago Post.*
"Infinately better than most of the present day pictures."—*Louella Parsons in the Chicago Herald.*
"This picture is a marvel, and marvellously well played. Hugo's story is presented faultlessly."—*Mae Tinee in Chicago Tribune.*
"The crowded house at Orchestra Hall, on Sunday night, the line reaching out on the avenue from the box office is recommendation enough for 'Les Miserables'. It was a warm night and a myriad of counterattractions, but the Hall had as many as it could hold."—*Chicago Examiner.*

This wonderful attraction will be released Sep. 9 in 8 parts!

Ask the nearest Pathé Exchange about it.

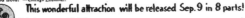

Pathé

Like all Pathé serials it has hit the bull's eye of popular approval

The Neglected Wife

with

Ruth Roland

Produced by Balboa   Written by Mabel Herbert Urner

RUSSIAN ART FILM CORPORATION

Personalities Your Patrons Will Learn to Love

IVAN MOZUKIN, NATALIA LESIENKO, VERA COLODNA, MLLE. CARALLI, ANNA NELSKA, ZOYA KARABANOVA and OLGA ZOVSKA are players with personalities selected by the deposed Czar of Russia because of their ability and trained at the Government expense. As personalities they are sure to become favorites with American audiences as they have become established in the hearts of their countrymen.

A distinguished dramatic critic says:

"The stage is a field in which the Russians have attained superlative excellence, and the Moscow Art Theatre is known all over the world as the pioneer in intelligent realism and one of the foremost theatres of the world."

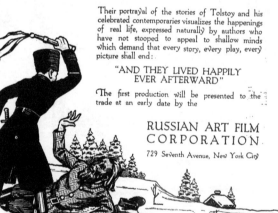

LOEW
of Moving Picture Theatre Circuits

OKS
COMEDIES
HOWELL
LOEW Theatres

The following branches are now open and ready to do business on Century Comedies.

Communicate with the Office nearest to you

Albany—Longacre Dist. Co., 559 Broadway
Boston—Longacre Distributing Co., 13 Stanhope St.
Buffalo—Longacre Distributing Co., 35 Church St.
Butte—Longacre Distributing Company, 52 E. Broadway
Chicago—Longacre Distributing Co., 220 So. State St.
Cincinnati—Longacre Distributing Co., 401 Strand Thea. Bldg.
Cleveland—Longacre Distributing Co., 856 Prospect Ave.
Charlotte—Longacre Distributing Co., 307 W. Trade St.
Calgary, Alt.—Canadian State Right Features, 407 W. Eighth Ave.
Dallas—Consolidated F. & S. Co.—Super Features Dept., 1900 Commerce St.
Denver—Longacre Distributing Co.
Des Moines—Longacre Distributing Co., 75 Broadway
Detroit—Longacre Distributing Co., 702 Mulberry St.
Smith—Longacre Distributing Co., 24 S. 6th St.

Indianapolis—Longacre Distributing Co., 58 W. New York St.
Kansas City—Longacre Distributing Co., 806-7 Shubert Bldg.
Los Angeles—Longacre Distributing Co., 822 So. Olive St.
Minneapolis—Longacre Distributing Co., 266 Film Exchange Bldg.
Milwaukee—Longacre Distributing Co., 133 Second St.
Montreal—Canadian State Right Features, 295 St. Catherine St.
New Orleans—Consolidated F. & S. Co.—Super Features Dept., 914 Gravier St.
New York City—Longacre Distributing Co., 1600 Broadway.
New Haven—Longacre Distributing Co., 228 Meadow St.
Newark—Longacre Distributing Co., 25 Branford Bldg.
Omaha—Longacre Distributing Co., 1122 Farnum St.
Oklahoma City—Longacre Distributing Co., 116 W. 2nd St.
Philadelphia—Fairmount Feature Film Exchange, 1302 Vine St.
Pittsburgh—Longacre Distributing Co., 938 Penn Ave.

Portland—Longacre Distributing Co., 405 Davis St.
Phoenix, Ariz.—Longacre Distributing Co., 117 No. 2nd Ave.
San Francisco—Longacre Distributing Co., 125 Golden Gate Ave.
St. Louis—Longacre Distributing Co., Olive Street
Springfield, Mass.—Longacre Distributing Co., 326 Dwight St.
St. John, N. B.—Canadian State Right Features, 87 Union St.
Toledo—Longacre Distributing Co., 436 Huron St.
Toronto—Canadian State Right Features, Co., 56 Exchange Place
Salt Lake City—Longacre Distributing Co.
Vancouver, B. C.—Canadian State Right Features, 711 Dunsmuir Ave.
Winnipeg, Man.—Canadian State Right Features, 40 Aikens Bldg.
Washington—Fairmount Feature Film Exchange, 419 No. Ninth St.
Wichita—Longacre Distributing Co., 157 No. Market St.
Atlanta—Consolidated Film Supply Co., Rhodes Bldg.

NOTE: Century Comedies distributed exclusively throughout the United States and Canada by the Longacre Distributing Company (Home Offices), Mecca Building, New York City.

Alice Brady Pictures, Inc.

Watch for further developments

Courtesy of VANITY FAIR   Copyright 1917 by Alfred Cheney Johnston

FOLLOWING THE LEAD

of the MOVING PICTURE WORLD ·any amount
of so-called exhibitor helps have been advertised.

Every publication having any bearing whatever on the
moving picture industry claims a department through
which they want to help the exhibitor if he will send
his address and the name of his house. *It sounds good,*
but—Just think for yourself a moment.

The exhibitors of today are *just as intelligent* and in many cases
know more and are *better posted* in the show business than those
who have appointed themselves advisors.   So *why waste your time.*
If you had a physical ailment you wouldn't run up any brown stone
stoop and ring the bell because some doctor put an attractive sign out,
would you?   Of course you wouldn't.   You would look for a doctor
who really knew more than you did about every thing physically.

Your business should be treated similarly—it is just as important to life
as your body.

When troubles are encountered in the exhibiting end of the motion
picture business, look for expert advice—take out your copy of the
MOVING PICTURE WORLD and study its special departments,
They are compiled and edited primarily for the exhibitor.

The MOVING PICTURE WORLD is the oldest trade paper in the
business. It started with the industry.   It has a well-known and expert
staff of moving picture specialists who have studied the picture business
and know what is needed.

If you haven't sent in your renewal, DO IT NOW—or if you are
not yet a subscriber, begin today. No successful exhibitor would be
without the "WORLD."

Subscription Rates
Domestic, $3.00; Canada, $3.50; Foreign, $4.00

Mme. ETROVA *in*
TO THE DEATH

AROLD OCKWOOD *in*
UNDER HANDICAP

THEL ARRYMORE *in*
THE LIFTED VEIL

RANCIS X. BUSHMAN *.*
and BEVERLY BAYNE *in*
THEIR COMPACT

Mme. ETROVA *in*
SILENT SELLERS

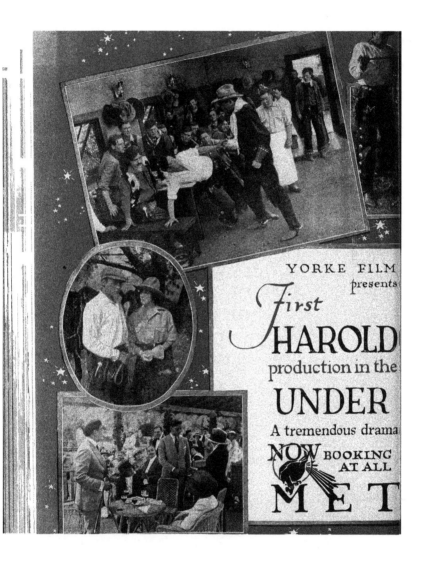

YORKE FILM
presents

First

HAROLD

production in the

UNDER

A tremendous drama

NOW BOOKING
AT ALL

MET

CORPORATION
the

LOCKWOOD
BIG STAR SERIES

HANDICAP
in Seven amazing Acts
Directed by
Fred J Balshofer
R O EXCHANGES

GEORGE K. SPOOR

presents

Little

Mary McAlister

the most winsome child actress

in

"PANTS"

Screen Time 65 Minutes

A picture that will delight children and grown-ups alike! They will laugh and cry over the joys and sorrows of this little girl and live over again the happy days of the rag doll and the old swimmin' hole.

THE TREMENDOUS SUCCESS

of

Little Mary McAlister

in

"Do Children Count"

a series of twelve
independent plays

assures you of a screen triumph in her *new* picture, "PANTS."

released through the K. E. S. E.

Essanay

1333 Argyle St., Chicago

• K·E·S·E •

Entered at the General Post Office, New York City, as Second Class Matter

Founded by J. P. CHALMERS in 1907.

Published Weekly by the

CHALMERS PUBLISHING COMPANY

17 MADISON AVENUE, NEW YORK CITY.

(Telephone, 3510-3511 Madison Square)

J. P. Chalmers, Sr............................President
J. F. Chalmers.............................Vice-President
E. J. Chalmers.....................Secretary and Treasurer
John Wylie........,......................General Manager

The office of the company is the address of the officers.

CHICAGO OFFICE—Suite 917-919 Schiller Building, 64 West Randolph St., Chicago, Ill. Telephone, Central 5099.

PACIFIC COAST OFFICE—610-611 Wright and Callender Building, Los Angeles, Cal. Telephone, Broadway 4640.

SUBSCRIPTION RATES.

United States, Cuba, Mexico, Hawaii, Porto
  Rico and Philippine Islands.................$3.00 per year
Canada .... 3.50 per year
Foreign Countries (Postpaid)................ 4.00 per year

Changes of address should give both old and new addresses in full and be clearly written. Two weeks' time should be allowed for change.

ADVERTISING RATES.

CLASSIFIED ADVERTISING—One dollar for twenty words or less; over twenty words, five cents per word.

DISPLAY ADVERTISING RATES made known on application.

NOTE—Address all correspondence, remittances and subscriptions to MOVING PICTURE WORLD, P. O. Box 226, Madison Square Station, New York, and not to individuals.

"CINE-MUNDIAL," the monthly Spanish edition of the Moving Picture World, is published at 17 Madison Ave. by the Chalmers Publishing Company. It reaches the South American and Spanish-speaking market. Yearly subscription, $1.50. Advertising rates on application.

(The INDEX to this issue is on page 1588.)

Saturday, September 8, 1917

Facts and Comments

WILLIAM JOHN WATKINS, a long time and regular editorial contributor to the MOVING PICTURE WORLD, passed from this life on August 22, after a brief illness, at a hospital in Brooklyn, N. Y. The deceased was one of the oldest employees of the Vitagraph company in point of service, having joined that organization in 1900 and continued with it almost to the day of his death. His intimate knowledge of the motion picture business and his early newspaper training made him a valuable commentator on trade subjects. The files of this paper indicate that his first contribution appeared in the issue of February 13, 1909, under the pen name of "The Man About Town," for his identity was never disclosed. From that time until the current issue, with but few omissions, his articles appeared regularly and were read with considerable interest. His last contribution was written the week before his death and appears in this issue. The deceased was a man of education and ability and made many friends. The MOVING PICTURE WORLD regrets his untimely demise and the consequent severance of long and pleasant relations.

* * *

A VERITABLE fever of organization seems to have struck the motion picture business. This week's news contributes no less than four efforts among various branches of the trade to get together. Two organizations are of state right buyers; one is of state right producers, and the fourth is of exhibitors on lines similar to both the Exhibitors' League and the First National Circuit. Two seem to have accomplished the work of organization and the others give promise of accomplishing as much. After that time only can furnish proof of their utility. Altogether these efforts indicate a desire to standardize the methods of production and distribution of motion pictures, an end greatly to be hoped for in the present state of affairs.

* * *

OPINION in some localities near big camps is, it is reported, reluctant to permit motion picture shows to open Sundays. The soldiers off duty need these places of innocent amusement and the military authorities will perhaps insist that they have them. What the official arrangements in the matter are to be has not been reported as we go to press, but that any arrangements are needed throws a shaft of light into the mental workshops of people who are so hide-bound as to oppose these shows. What some people see is what they have always seen and their make up is such that they'll never see anything else. 'Tis also a safe bet that a majority of them never saw the inside of a picture theater.

* * *

SYSTEMATIZING and classifying the information necessary today in any line of business is no easy task, but is, as a matter of fact, a science. The matters covered in each weekly issue of the MOVING PICTURE WORLD are so varied, cover so many different subjects that are of especial importance to every theatre manager that they become invaluable if located at the moment they are desired. It is more than anyone can expect to do, however, to read weekly so much that is pertinent and know just where to lay a finger on it when required. We index as fully as space permits, but some system of filing paragraphs under main heads and sub-divisions for music, projection, advertising, etc., becomes imperative for those who would secure the fullest benefit from this trade paper.

* * *

AN exhibitor living in a small village where he can get 250 patrons out to two shows a week will probably do better not to try for a show every night. In places where there is not a great deal of amusement, expectation of picture show night helps advertise it. It may become the village center of interest on two nights of each week. Of course such an exhibitor has to have some other means of livelihood, as he can hardly expect to net more than $10 a week unless he runs it in connection with a candy and ice cream store. In that case he will probably get two dimes from each patron on show nights and the work involved in the show business is like a hobby to him. It may grow, for he is learning a very profitable trade—that of the showman.

The Exhibitor's Mirror ▣ ▣ ▣ ▣ ▣ ▣ By Louis Reeves Harrison

HOLDING up the mirror to nature " is an expression which has become so fixed in minds critical that it seems to have warped some of them. Not to select an illustration from reviews of our moving pictures, because criticism has not greatly advanced beyond the art of production in this field, we may go to the columns of those who shape the destinies of literature for an example of how critical judgment may be twisted out of shape by limited comprehension of what is meant by "holding up the mirror." A man whose taste is correct in many instances thus reviews a novel which he has evidently read with appreciative pleasure.

"The people of this story are made to talk just as people do talk, and to act just as people do act," and so on, with several paragraphs devoted to the "true to life idea," which besets the amateur when he first begins to wonder where he is at. As a rule, considering how people do talk and do act, is the "true-to-life" stuff fit to print? John wakes up in the morning and manages to remember that this is the day for him to change his shirt. He washes the front of his face, all that *he* can see, swipes at his hair with a brush, goes to breakfast and reads his paper while consuming eggs and coffee. Intense *action!*

He now makes a memo of some things he will forget before the day is over and starts for his place of business, following exactly the same route he does every week day of his life. He pursues the same route, does the same general character of work for about half he thinks he ought to get for it, tells a friend at lunch how the business *ought* to be run, with cynical comment on the boobs he has to work with and for, then there is an afternoon grind. He may meet a friend on the way home and they *talk*. "Hello Tom!" "Hello Dick! How's things?" "Oh, so-so. How's things with you—ain't seen ye in a long time." "I'm at the same old place. Wher've-ye been keepin' *yourself?*" and the invariable formula ad infinitum. Hold up the mirror to the way people *do talk and do act* and you only glimpse the periscope. It takes imagination to picture the submarine, just as it did when Jules Verne did *not* hold up the mirror to his times, when he wrote "Twenty Thousand Leagues Under the Sea." An author who knows his business may exhibit the periscope for the sake of plausibility, but he goes beneath the surface and into the very heart of a complicated mechanism for its true nature and submerged purposes.

Hamlet neither acted nor talked as did the people of his time. Like every true artist, Shakespeare was not engaged in holding up the mirror to such habitual, and more or less artificial manifestations of our inner selves. The true artist does not use a pocket mirror from a lady's vanity bag, nor a shaving glass of distortion. The Immortal Bard went beneath the surface and reflected for all time the secret workings of the human heart and mind. He pictured the battlefield of past habit and present aspiration, the eternal struggle of·man with his ancestors.

The time is coming, if it is not already here, when the exhibitor may decide upon the character of what is presented at his theater. He should rise above the narrow limitations of personal preference to high ground of broad scope and vision. This will not be easy, but it is bound to become a big factor in our growth of production and presentation. This is a form of esthetic drama, an impressionist form, its natural tendency away from the unbeautiful and toward the tremendous effect of deep character analysis as opposed to strained and theatrical imitation.

Keep One Eye on the Padding. If there is material

enough in a release to fill five reels there will be no injection of extraneous matter, the picturing of scenes foreign to the subject and of characters not essential to the dramatic telling of the story. There must be a firmness of connection between the parts of a feature play, and it usually implies a single line of action from beginning to end, following the movements of one leading character. This makes the telling clearer to the audience. A confused audience is apt to be a bored one in time.

Keep One Eye on Consistency. Not only should the different parts of a play be firmly connected, but there must be an agreement of a harmonious nature between parts so united. A consistent story is what might be called a successful combination of complex motives and situations which fit nicely into each other. The keen critic gives close attention to the coherency of all parts because those releases which stand a second showing and achieve a certain permanence are made of beautifully welded materials, which stand together in a well-united whole effect.

Give Attention to Setting. The drama of character development and soul crisis is opening up to our audiences undreamed-of vistas of beauty and absorbing human interest, but it can be made puerile, if not entirely spoiled, by careless grouping of studio properties, whose ugliness and inappropriateness distract attention, jarring every nerve in the spectators, tearing the illusion to shreds. There is almost as great need of artists in the studio as in the construction of plays for exclusive screen presentation. One can *feel* whether or not the background is in accord with the scene being portrayed, and its influence on the imagination becomes powerful when it accords with the play's mood.

Look Out for Stale Stuff. The mortgage to be foreclosed on the home; all at stake on a race horse; the villain's dying confession of a crime fastened on the innocent hero; the poor little neglected ingenue in curls who wears a pretty frock in the last act; the sacrifice of a young heroine to a scheming villain for the "honor" of the family; the interrupted wedding between villain and heroine; the two people who look exactly alike; the mistaken identity; the unexpected return of the hero supposed to be dead in battle or drowned at sea. There is an ocean of it on tap.

Shun the Blind Alley. A large number of modern screen stories start out as though they were leading through interesting scenes to some definite end—they seem to have a decided aim, but they end next to nowhere. This is largely due to the fact that they are adaptations of movement without comprehension of motive in the original work. The types in such releases do not represent the characters clearly; the audience becomes confused, and presently the original purpose is diverted by some change made in the studio. If it is a mystery story—it must be a mystery up to the final solution. No play can fix audience attention when it wavers—it must stick to its keynote.

The Weakest Spot can be easily determined by a little quiet thought after watching a private exhibition. Aside from the embrace of two people at the end, does the story have any definite meaning—does the whole composition produce an effect on you? If it is a director's hodgepodge of scenes taken more or less at random and patched up in the finishing room, you may have a· feeling of having been at a table bright with flowers and after-dinner speeches, without having eaten anything. The surest test of a play is its firmness of definite purpose.

Look at Ourselves, Our Friends and Others *By Sam Spedon*

HONESTLY! In the past didn't the people in the picture business remind you of a lot of inexperienced men suffering from nervous prosperity? Men who suddenly found themselves in a business that gave them more or less prominence, without the necessary balance to sustain their position and command the respect of those with whom they associated.

Exhibitors.

They reminded us of the Irishman who attended a wedding and when introduced to the bridegroom as the best man, called him a liar and tried to prove it by licking him. They never conducted their business along business lines, they didn't know how. They agitated everything and everybody. They called the producers, exchange men and themselves liars and other things; organized, spoke in many tongues and never got anywhere.

It Is Different Now.

The old time circus with the sideshows, the shell and three-card monte games is a thing of the past. The days of the ballyhoo and the "ringers" are no longer with us. God be with the fast approaching days of a real "simon pure" business and everything else that goes with it.

Think It Over.

Two church members had a quarrel; one used profane and insulting language to the other. The profane brother was brought up before the consistory of the church on charges preferred by the offended member. The charge was dismissed with the following decision: "Some men swear a little and some men pray a little, but neither of them means anything by it."

Don't Rush Into Print.

When will men who pretend to be business men learn to use their brains and not take things to heart, the petty politics, jealousies and grievances that are nine time out of ten tempests in a tea-pot or a case of spleen. Every once in a while the papers are requested to champion somebody's grievance. Some one has cast an aspersion on his personality or something else. Immediately he wants to rush into print and say worse things about the other fellow. Then the other fellow want the papers to do the same thing for him, to keep up an incessant barking of accusations and denials, which never look well in print. These requests are not confined to individuals, they sometimes come from organizations whose statements are not tempered with judgment and do not use discretion in defining their position clearly or logically, regardless of drawing the papers into their personal or political differences.

Independent Producers.

This term reminds us of the old days of the "Patents Companies." We thought it had become obsolete. It sounds like a contradiction between a combine and an unrestricted opposition. Why not use another term like—unaffiliated. The exhibitors who are looking for a less expensive program no doubt will be glad to know the difference between the high priced and a program that comes within their means. We presume that is the reason for the organization of the socalled "independent producers" without desire to create opposition

or confusion. All producers today are independent, or should be, with free rein to compete with each other in quality and price. The exhibitors' preference depends upon their pocketbooks and what will prove most profitable in their theaters.

Have a Look.

At a theater in New York there is comedy being presented at one of the theaters in vicinity of Times Square, entitled "Business Before Pleasure." If you are interested in moving pictures and want to see ourselves as others see us don't fail to take it in when in the Metropolis. It is a full of thought matter. It will make a hit with you because it expresses in actions and the living presence what has often been said in mere words. We are not saying this on the strength of a pass, we paid for our ticket and want another when we feel in need of another good laugh.

Always Two Sides
By SAM SPEDON.

WE ARE in receipt of a letter from an exhibitor in Sheridan, Wyoming, owner of a theater seating six hundred and fifty, with a six-piece orchestra. We quote from his letter:

"Hark ye! All faithful subjects will this day (5th day of August, 1917), present themselves body and soul (and don't forget your bank-roll) at the nearest exchange, at which time you will surrender your birth-right and anything else that you may have in your possession. If you don't do this we will strangle you and throw you to the wolves of competition. This is our 'New Policy' and you will find it more equitable than the old one, inasmuch as we make the deposit system easier. Under our old system you deposited the amount of the cost of the last four pictures that you used, now all you have to do is to deposit one-fourth of the cost of the last picture of about twenty-five or thirty stars.

"We got several of these notices. Did you get yours? P. T. Barnum was right. One every minute, we answer the roll-call now. Who's next? But—We have jumped the traces and it is now up to the exhibitors to get busy and trample this blood-sucking parasite who sits in his office in New York demanding his pound of flesh. Shylock was a philanthropist in comparison."

The quotations from the foregoing letter are plainly a travesty on the "new policy" as set forth therein. For the benefit of those who may not know the actual conditions of the "new policy" of which Sheridan complains we give the following illustration: The "new policy" salesman goes into a town of three theaters and offers his star features at a set figure to one exhibitor, who says he can use twenty-four of the features a year; the second exhibitor agrees to use forty-eight and the third exhibitor agrees to book the whole output of the "new policy" company. Naturally the salesman signs up with the third exhibitor to the exclusion of the other two. This is business. On the other hand, if three exhibitors are approached and one wants twelve, the second wants twenty-four and the third wants forty-eight, the third fellow gets the first choice of stars. This again is business.

Why Not Try This?

It is not necessary to book any number of star features under the "new policy" week after week. They can be booked a month or two apart if need be. It has occurred to us that high priced star features could be introduced in a regular program once a month, or every second month, during the year as a special or exceptional attraction, which they advertised to be. This would give the exhibitors a chance to show them occasionally and test them without the necessity of going to any great or continued expense. Of course we grasp the competition argument from Sheridan, that the "New Policy" company wants to create with opposition houses. Again it is up to the exhibitors to destroy this competitive opposition by agreeing to make a proposition to the distributing companies that the exhibitors will use the "new policy" star features alternatively. If this proposition is not accepted no harm is done; they can go right on without them. It strikes us as we indite this article that many difficulties of this kind could be adjusted by the combined or concerted action of the exhibitors. You can lead a horse to water but you can't force him to drink.

All Rests With Exhibitors.

Upon the face of such a "new policy" as this letter implies it looks the imposition of a hardship upon the exhibitors who are now struggling under expenses that leave them the bare margin of a living profit. But according to our Sheridan correspondent the exhibitors have met the situation by refusing to accept the "new policy," which is the wise and only logical thing to do. If the exhibitors stand in an organized unit and will not compete with each other in Sheridan, or any other place, then they have mastered the situation and there is no reason to complain. If exhibitors do not hold together in any locality and are willing to compete with each other, the fault lies with the exhibitors and not the distributors.

The Other Side.

We must not forget that the producers of high priced star features, and particularly the one to whom the Sheridan letter refers, are trying to meet a demand for better pictures, which are presumably produced by the best players, writers and director. Necessarily these are expensive mediums and luxuries in the making and exhibiting; just as stage stars and plays of high order are. The producers cannot force anyone to exhibit their pictures. It appears to us that these star feature producers are willing to take a chance in "high art" for art's sake and employ high priced stars, plays and directors for the betterment of motion pictures, hoping to reap a pecuniary reward as well as artistic and public appreciation. For this they should be commended. If Sheridan or any other place cannot indulge in "High Art" and contribute to the producers' reward he (the producer) will have to look elsewhere for it. There is plenty of art in the market and, as we have said before, there is no occasion to be disturbed.

The American Exhibitors' Association Will "Show Us"

THE general manager, C. C. Pettijohn, of the American Exhibitors' Association, is very much elated over the association's progress within the six weeks of its inception. In a clear cut statement Mr. Pettijohn announces that already it has as many, if not more, members pledged than the National League. "By the first or tenth of September we will be in comfortably appointed offices in the Times Building, New York, thoroughly equipped to carry out the Association's business and proceed under full operation without interruption".

We must give Mr. Pettijohn credit for his enthusiasm

and devotion to the work he has undertaken. His voluntary reduction of his own salary from ten thousand dollars to five thousand that the difference might be devoted to the general running expenses of the Association's establishment, inspires confidence in the man's sincerity and dispels the many adverse criticisms and rumors we have heard.

The Association is to be commended for its avowed purpose not to accept moneys or contributions from outside sources, to ask no favors from anyone or of any trade paper outside the publication of news of the Association and such publicity as conform to its policies. And not to affiliate with any other organization that might compromise its fundamental purpose as a representative exhibitors' association, working primarily for the exhibitors, in accord with the whole industry, for constructive and not destructive ends.

"Let me tell you something," to quote Mr. Pettijohn, "we mean to show you. And when we do there will be no need to say anything. Keep your ear to the ground. After the convention at Ocean City, Virginia, I hope to publish a full list of our members and then you will see and believe."

William J. Watkins Dead

Old Time Moving Picture Man and Contributor to Moving Picture World Succumbs to Pneumonia.

WILLIAM J. WATKINS, for seventeen years connected with the Vitagraph Company of America, died of pneumonia at the Brooklyn Heights Hospital on Wednesday, August 22. William John Watkins was born in New York City on August 21, 1861, received his education at the public schools and later took a law course at Columbia College. In early manhood, he was associated with a prominent law firm; then moved to Shenandoah, Pennsylvania where he was for eighteen years connected with the local paper, "The Herald". At Shenandoah he became active in politics, being defeated for mayor by one vote.

In 1900 he entered the employ of the Vitagraph as bookkeeper and general office man at 116 Nassau street, New York City. Three years ago he was transferred to the studio in Brooklyn in charge of the extras, which position he filled until some four months ago, when in the wholesale dismissal of employees, he was with others of the "old guard" let out. Since then he has worked on and off as "extra". And it was while doing some work of this kind that he contracted a cold which developed into pneumonia and led to his death. The fact that most of the old hands were reinstated, while he, one of the oldest employees was not, preyed on his mind and helped to hasten his demise.

The body reposed at Harry T. Pyle's undertaking establishment on Thursday, where his old friends and associates paid their last tribute. The different departments of the Vitagraph Company and friends formerly with the company sent floral offerings. The body was removed to Point Pleasant, New Jersey, on Friday, where funeral services and burial took place on Sunday, August 26.

Though not generally known to the readers of the Moving Picture World, the deceased had been a contributor to this paper for many years, writing under the signature of "The Man About Town" various observations concerning the trade and the men engaged in it. His last contribution appears in this issue.

ABRAMSON FILMING NEW PLAY.

Ivan Abramson, director general of Ivan Film Productions, is now deeply engaged in filming his new play, "Sins of Ambition." Ivan Abramson's reputation as portrayer of problem plays is well established, and the announcement that with the production now in the making, he has begun on a new line of problems, is quite an interesting statement to the trade. He feels that because of the fact that most directors have not carte blanche in producing their stories, they are greatly hampered when an occasionally problem play is placed in their hands to produce. Not so with Mr. Abramson.

In "Sins of Ambition" Mr. Abramson presents to the public his treatment of the new line of problems which the trade can expect from time to time. At this time he is not quite ready to divulge more than the title of the picture as regards to the cast and expense—is the most elaborate thing yet undertaken by him for Ivan Film Productions.

Activities of War Committees
OF THE MOTION PICTURE INDUSTRY

THE prominent motion picture men who were recently appointed as state chairmen of the National Committee by President William A. Brady of the National Association of the Motion Picture Industry, at the request of the President of the United States, have promptly taken up the work of organising the exhibitors in their respective states for the purpose of utilising the film and screen to spread broadcast throughout the nation information in regard to the plans and purposes of the various departments of Government during the period of the war.

Of the forty-eight chairmen appointed by President Brady on July 3 only four have not been heard from, this celay being due to the fact that the exhibitors appointed in these localities are away from home and therefore not aware of their selection as representatives of the National Committee.

In a majority of the forty-four other states and the District of Columbia the organisation of exhibitors is now well under way, and in several states conventions of the exhibitors have been held which have established new records for attendance, indicating their desire to aid in this patriotic work.

One of the first state chairmen to take up the work was Charles H. Bean, of Franklin, who brought the subject to the attention of his fellow-exhibitors in New Hampshire in the form of a circular letter which was sent to every exhibitor in the state. It was as follows:

Dear Brother Exhibitors of New Hampshire:

At the request of William A. Brady, through the President of the United States, I have accepted appointment as state chairman of the National Committee representing our state and it will be my duty to carry out such suggestions or requests as may be sent to me by the War Co-operation Committee of the National Association, comprising the most representative men in the industry, which is now considering plans of which you will be advised in due course of time.

The President of the United States has honored and recognised the motion picture industry as a great force in assisting the United States Government in the present world crisis.

The exhibitors of the United States have been asked to work especially with the committee on public information, and there will be two methods in distributing information.

Our screens (showing slides and short films).

Four-minute talks in our theaters.

The motion picture industry has been under severe criticism in the past—perhaps ofttimes rightly. The industry is asking for special consideration by the people in the way of liberal legislation. I believe everything asked for, in reason, will be granted if the motion picture industry shows itself worthy.

Do your bit big and help carry on this splendid work.

Inclosed find a card. Will you kindly fill out the same and mail to John B. Jameson, Concord, N. H.?

I am sure there will be a generous response from every exhibitor in the state.

                    CHARLES H. BEAN,
Representative for the Motion Picture Exhibitors of New Hampshire.

P. S. Inclosed you will find copy of letter from President Wilson to William A. Brady.

The postal card referred to contained the following pledge:

I pledge myself that I will do all I can to help with my screen and theater in this great world crisis.

Name ....
Theater ....
Town or City ....

In a report to President Brady on August 20, State Chairman Bean says he per cent. of the exhibitors in his state and feels confident the rest will respond, as several are known to be away from home on business trips or on vacations. A convention of the exhibi-

tors of New Hampshire was held at Manchester on August 16, presided over by Mr. Bean, and despite a pouring rain there was the largest attendance ever recorded by the Motion Picture Exhibitors' League of that state. A resolution was adopted offering the fullest possible support and co-operation to the President and the various Federal Departments by the motion picture theaters of New Hampshire. Ernest H. Horstmann of Boston, treasurer of the National League, addressed the meeting, setting forth the many ways in which the members of the state league could assist the Government at this time.

Similar activities have been undertaken by Herman J. Brown, state chairman of the National Committee in Idaho, who has advised President Brady in a letter dated August 13 that he has already undertaken the organisation of exhibitors in accordance with the suggestions contained in the announcement which accompanied his appointment.

The circular which State Chairman Brown, who is president of the Idaho Theater Men's Association, sent to the theater owners and managers contained the following pertinent statement:

Your president has accepted the position of state chairman of the National Association of the Motion Picture Industry, at the request of William A. Brady. This means a whole lot of work and no pay for me. It means that I will have to do ten times as much as any other exhibitor in the state in Government war co-operation matters. I accepted this for the good of the industry in this state and to help increase its growing dignity. We now have a chance to make the motion picture business a respected business, to take it forever out of the clutches of the petty politicians, to attain to a power that will mean the death of the bum politicians that attack us. We have this chance, but it means that we must get in and realise that an organisation can't live on wind and shirkers. You will soon be called on, as I will be called on, to get busy for the United States Government.

The organisation will have to report the theaters who are doing the work of the Government, which says "We depend on the motion picture theaters as on no other institution." It will also have to report the theaters who refuse to do the right thing. I have already assured the president of the National Association of the Motion Picture Industry that Idaho will be on deck 100 per cent. strong.

Letters have also been received from the following state chairmen advising as to their plans for organising the exhibitors in response to the appeal of President Brady: John E. Rickards, Phoenix, Ariz.; H. M. Thomas, Omaha; A. B. Momand, Shawnee, Okla.; H. T. Nolan, Denver; C. W. Meighan, Portland, Ore.; A. W. B. Johnson, Birmingham; Saul S. Harris, Little Rock; Frank A. Garbutt, Los Angeles; Theodore Jelenk, Wilmington; H. M. Crandall, Washington; Howell Graham, Chattanooga; C. D. Cooley, Tampa; William Oldknow, Atlanta; George K. Spoor, Chicago; F. J. Rembusch, Shelbyville, Ind.; C. E. Glamann, Wellington, Kan.; Lee L. Goldberg, Louisville; Alfred S. Black, Rockland; Louis B. Mayer, Boston; E. M. Clarke, Natchez; Thomas Furniss, Duluth; H. Charles Hespe, Jersey City; H. B. Varner, Lexington, N. C.; B. J. Sawyer, Cleveland; Charles H. Williams, Providence; H. B. Hurst, Deadwood, S. D.; E. H. Hulsey, Dallas; Edward J. Fisher, Seattle; A. D. Flintom, Kansas City; F. A. Hornig, Baltimore, Md.

WAR CONVENTION OF BUSINESS MEN.

The National Association of the Motion Picture Industry has received an invitation to send delegates to a special meeting of the Chamber of Commerce of the United States to be held at Atlantic City, N. J., September 18 to 21. The call for this meeting is issued by President R. G. Rhett, who sets forth in a statement accompanying the invitation the reasons for holding the meeting at this time and the subjects which are to be considered.

In view of the prominent part which the motion picture industry has already taken in connection with the war activities the film men will be in a position to relate their activities during the past three months at this meeting, which is to be made the occasion for the business men of the nation to meet in a convention to consider their part and share in the war, with a view to the formulation of generally approved lines of procedure. Consequently this is more than a special meeting, and has been designated as "The War Convention of American Business."

The National Association will be entitled to several delegates at the meeting to be held at Atlantic City, and the invitation will be presented for consideration at the forthcoming meeting of the Board of Directors.

The Roll of Honor

WILLIAM KALISKA, former manager of the Allendale theater and at one time assistant manager of the Strand, Buffalo, when Harold Edel guided the destinies of the last-named house, has received a commission as captain at Madison Barracks. "Bill"—we mean Captain W. Kaliska—has been receiving the handshakes, "good-lucks" and other farewell greetings from the film men in Buffalo. He says he expects to meet all of them "somewhere in France" in 1918.

* * *

H. S. Mandelbaum, who was formerly connected with the Cleveland branch of the U. T. E. Corporation, is about to leave for a Southern training camp. He was one of the first to respond when President Wilson asked for volunteers. He is with Battery A, Ohio Light Artillery.

* * *

Paul Diemer, who represented the Gaumont Company at the first training camp this season at Plattsburg Barracks, N. Y., has been ordered by the government to hold himself in readiness for extended field service. Mr. Diemer was commissioned a second lieutenant of artillery this month.

* * *

Richard C. Travers, the prominent Essanay player, reported at the officers' training camp at Fort Sheridan, Ill., August 27. Mr. Travers traveled through the south until that time, making personal appearances. He served in the Boer war. He is no newcomer to the war game. He served in the service in France, while another recently was killed on the firing line.

* * *

F. S. Fountain, formerly manager of the Seattle Paramount office, is now on active service with the United States Engineering Corps.

* * *

R. L. Tracy, of the Cortlandt theater, San Francisco, after three months in the First Reserve Officers Corps has been commissioned a captain.

S. A. LYNCH GOES TO THE COAST.

Stephen A. Lynch, President of the Triangle Distributing Corporation, left New York on Friday of last week for California. Mr. Lynch's visit to the Coast may have something to do with the many rumors that have been circulating for the past three or four weeks relative to the big things that are about to be done in Triangle. Inquiries at the office of the Triangle Distributing Corporation fail to reveal the purpose of his visit to the West, but the opinion prevails that Mr. Lynch has some very definite objects in mind. It can be said that Stephen A. Lynch, who has many business interests, would not take the time to make a trip across country unless the outcome of the trip had to do with some very important matters. Those connected with the motion picture industry are awaiting with interest announcements from Triangle, which will no doubt be made within a very short time.

FLORENCE PRINTY WILL SUPPORT WILBUR.

Crane Wilbur's leading woman in "Unto The End," one of the series of Art Dramas which David Horsley is producing, is Florence Printy, a recruit from the legitimate stage. Miss Printy displays marked ability as a screen actress. Miss Printy portrays a chorus girl, named Goldie Gay, with whom Jim O'Neil, the character played by Mr. Wilbur, falls madly in love.

Francis Ford, director and star of "The Purple Mask," "The Broken Coin," and other popular serials, will have the featured part in the new Butterfly picture, "Who Was the Other Man?" released September 3. Mae Gaston will be seen in the role opposite Ford.

Colleen Moore, Bluebirder

COLLEEN MOORE has been added to the galaxy of youthful beauties of the Bluebird West Coast studios, among whom may be mentioned Ruth Clifford and Carmel Myers. All three of these young girls have not yet passed "sweet sixteen" and each is a brunette with unusual fair complexion. Miss Moore was assigned by Production Manager MacRae to the Rupert Julian Company, and she has gone to Seven Oaks in the San Bernardino Mountains, where Director Julian has started production upon a new Bluebird photoplay entitled "Julio Saudoval," in which the new addition to the Bluebird forces will play the ingenue role.

Little Miss Moore was born in Michigan, going to Florida when a little child. There she was educated in a convent at Tampa. From early childhood the little lady was interested in theatricals and before she was twelve years old she organized a dramatic club, in which she was a veritable Pooh Bah, serving as director, manager, villain, leading woman, etc.

About a year ago, while visiting in Chicago with her mother, she met D. W. Griffith, who immediately recognized excellent screen material in her and sent her to California to make her appearance in Fine Arts pictures. The day after her arrival she was cast in "The Bad Boy" with Robert Harron. Then followed "The Old Fashioned Young Man," also with Harron, after which she appeared with Wilfred Lucas in "Hands Up," one of the last photoplays made by the Fine Arts before it ceased operations as a producing organization.

Miss Moore is only five feet three inches in height and weighs exactly one hundred pounds. She says she will never grow any taller and doesn't want to tip the scales at any more than her present century weight. "Mother has bought me a copy of 'Eat and Grow Thin,' and that little book is going to be a constant reminder to me to remain at one hundred pounds," said Miss Moore with determination indicated in every word.

Colleen Moore.

U. S. AMUSEMENT STUDIOS ENLARGED.

The United States Amusement Studios, at Fort Lee, N. J., are being extensively remodeled and enlarged. Although this studio is known to be one of the most complete and modern in the country, United States is anxious to have it second to none, and plans were just completed by a competent contractor. Work was started as soon as "Behind the Mask" was completed.

The new plans will give almost double the floor space of the present arrangement. New lightings are being installed, extra scene docks are being built, and some large open air stages are to be shortly constructed. The effect will be practically to make the place into an entirely new studio, with every modern improvement.

MOUNTAIN ROMANCE FOR VIVIAN MARTIN.

Mountain romances are something of a specialty with Vivian Martin, who seems to be particularly happy in her interpretation of heroines who work out their destinies in the hollows of the hills amid sylvan surroundings. In "The Sunset Trail" added to the September releases of Paramount, Miss Martin appears as a lonely little girl who longs for youthful associates in her California mountain home.

From the reports of those who have witnessed the filming of "The Sunset Trail" it affords Miss Martin with a part that is not only suited to her particular style of acting, but gives her much new material. It offers, likewise, a splendid opportunity for the others in the cast.

Chicago News Letter

By JAS. S. McQUADE

Operators' New Scale.

AT a special meeting of Chicago Local, M. P. E. L. of America, held in its hall in the Masonic Temple, Friday, August 17, the following subjects were brought up for discussion:

The new wage scale of operators' union, Local 110, I. A. T. S. E.; the proposed music tax on moving picture theaters; the new scale of wages of the Chicago Federation of Musicians, and the proposed reduction of electric light bills in certain picture theaters.

After discussing the new wage scale for operators fully, it was finally decided to appoint a special committee of the Chicago Local to act with the executive committee of that body in a joint meeting with like committees of Local 110, to take up and adjust the proposed scale at a meeting in League headquarters, in the Masonic Temple, Tuesday afternoon, August 21.

President Joseph Hopp appointed the following members on the special committee to represent the League: Nathan Ascher, Geo. D. Laing, Harry C. Miller, L. Sigel and Ludwig Schindler.

For the operators, at the Tuesday meeting, there were present: Joseph Armstrong, president; Fred Havill, vice-president; Al. Johnstone, secretary, and Tom Molloy, business agent. There were also present the members of the new wage scale committee, with Mr. Hitchcock as chairman.

These committees went over the proposed new scale of wages very carefully and exhaustively. After a session of three hours they agreed on a number of revisions and on everything pertaining to the wage scale except the clause relating to small houses, which seat less than 300 people. In such cases the League committees were of the opinion that the compensation for operators should be less than the figure which the new scale provides. It is expected by members of the League committees that this matter will be adjusted fairly, and this is all the more likely, judging from the good spirit that prevailed throughout the discussion.

Regarding the music tax on picture theaters, President Joseph Hopp was informed by President Joseph Winkler, of the Chicago Federation of Musicians, that the members of that organisation were in harmony with the members of the Chicago Local M. P. E. L. of America, to combat the tax, and President Winkler assured Mr. Hopp that his organization would take immediate action to co-operate with the Chicago Local.

This action by the Chicago Federation of Musicians follows closely that taken by similar federations in New York and Boston, where the members have refused to play any music listed as copyrighted by the Society of Authors and Composers.

The question of the new wage scale of the Chicago Federation of Musicians, which affects only the larger theaters, and that referring to electric light bills in certain theaters, after considerable discussion at Friday's special meeting, were referred to the executive committee of the Chicago Local, which will make a report at the next regular meeting of the League, which will be held on Thursday, Sept. 7, in its hall, in the Masonic Temple.

Prospects Promising for New Chicago Reel Fellows' Club.

At the first meeting of the Organisation Committee of the Chicago Reel Fellows' Club, held Thursday, August 16, there were present: Messrs. Stoddard, Bell, Haag, Belford, Nehls and Ross.

It was decided to disband the old club and to reorganise on a more solvent and a firmer basis. It was also agreed that the membership of the new club would be restricted to a higher class of film men and others interested in the film business.

The members of the Committee decided to give up the old club rooms and to store the furniture; also that the new organization would assume the indebtedness of the old, and that all bills payable would be protected.

The first meeting of the Finance Sub-Committee of the Club was held Monday noon, Aug. 20. Messrs. Proctor, Nehls, Bell and Belford were present. Plans were discussed for liquidating the debts of the old club, but nothing definite was decided upon. The meeting was then adjourned.

A full meeting of the Re-organisation Committee is announced for Monday, Aug. 27.

The Italian War Pictures at the Auditorium.

These remarkable registrations of the camera opened at the Auditorium, Thursday evening, August 23, and were viewed by a great gathering that taxed the seating capacity of the largest theater in America. The dense throng of spectators served to show the intense interest taken in the tremendous campaign waged on the Italian front by citizens of awe, because of the almost insuperable obstacles and conditions encountered and overcome by the Italian soldiers.

Following are excerpts from Kitty Kelly's review, which appeared in the Examiner:

> These first Italian war pictures, stamped with officiality by their government, turn a new light on the incredible difficulties of this warfare. The first section is devoted to the Alpine battlefront, and reveals, in scaling the snowclad heights, in transporting guns, ammunition and other supplies, unutterable effort, indomitable will. The persistence shown by these men in struggling through heavy snows, reaching dizzy heights in baskets swung on wire ropes, snowshoeing into action, laboriously by hand dragging heavy guns up the slippery slopes—till artillery is planted at a 12,000-foot altitude—is breathtaking. Hannibal is out-Hannibaled, and, incidentally, Cabiria out-Cabiriaed.
>
> The pictures are excellently photographed and effectively assembled, illuminated with forceful subtitles, mainly quotations from different writers commenting on the situations disclosed. There is a scenic introductory effect and an orchestra that keeps colorful accompaniment.

Chicago Film Brevities.

An advance showing of Essanay's fine photo comedy, "Efficiency Edgar's Courtship", in which Taylor Holmes makes his initial bow in moving pictures, was given at Orchestra Hall, Friday morning, August 24, to a large invited audience. The use of Orchestra Hall was granted George Kleine for the occasion, through the courtesy of Messrs. Wessels and Voegeli, managers of Orchestra Hall, and Pathe Exchange, Inc. The large auditorium was fully occupied, and everybody present was effusive in praise of Taylor Holmes and the supporting cast in Essanay's sparkling production. The presentation was accompanied by Lynne Hazzard's orchestra, an unusual distinction for the private and trade showing of a picture.

* * *

Watterson R. Rothacker, president of the Rothacker Film Mfg. Co., was recently appointed a member of the advisory committee of the American Red Cross Bureau of Motion Pictures, by Evan Evans, director of that organisation.

* * *

"The Sin Woman", an Owl feature, in which Irene Fenwick appears in the lead, has been announced as the leading attraction at the Ziegfeld theater for the week beginning Saturday, August 25.

* * *

"The Retreat of the Germans at the Battle of Arras", the latest war picture exploited by Pathe Exchange, Inc., and Official Government Pictures, has been shown to large crowds all through the week, beginning Saturday, August 18. The critics of the Chicago daily press have devoted large space to these films, which are described as possessing tremendous interest. Strange to say, the run will terminate Saturday evening, August 25, the time, in my opinion, being altogether incommensurate with the value of the films and their great popularity.

The benefit presentation of these pictures, given Friday evening, August 17, in aid of the First Regiment, Illinois Engineers, under the patronage of the Citizens' Unit of that regiment, was a most successful affair. After paying for newspaper advertising (which was very liberal), billboards, mailing circulars, etc., etc., fully $1,500 was netted by the Citizens' Unit. The entire proceeds were devoted to the regiment in question by Pathe Exchange, Inc., and Official Government Pictures, Inc.

Thursday evening, August 23, Manager North, for the interests mentioned, extended an invitation to the Chicago British Committee on allied recruiting and the members of foreign consulates in the city to attend the presentation of the pictures. Addresses were delivered by prominent members of the committee during the evening. For the information of inquirers, it may be stated that these pictures have a length of 4,850 feet.

* * *

Merl La Voy, the Chicago cameraman, who took many of the pictures now being shown under the title of "Heroic France", left for the Balkan states last week as a member of a Red Cross mission in aid of Serbia.

* * *

Adolph Zukor, president of Paramount, was in the city last week. He came on to attend the wedding of a relative.

* * *

Oliver Morosco stopped over in the city last week on his way from Los Angeles to New York, and during that time saw his stage production of "Upstairs and Down", at the Cort theater.

* * *

Aaron J. Jones has secured the rights to "The Mormon Maid" in the states of Illinois and Indiana, for the Central Film Company.

* * *

"Within the Law", a Vitagraph feature on which Major Funkhouser has placed his ban, was given a private showing at the Studebaker theater, Thursday morning, August 23. About two thousand invitations were sent out to experts and prominent citizens. Several addresses were delivered on the occasion by speakers interested in prison reform among women. It is the desire of the Vitagraph Company to secure the opinions of people competent to judge the picture before bringing mandamus proceedings against the city. The stage production of this title was successfully shown in the city some time ago without any interference. Judge McKenzie Cleland was present and said, "It's a very good picture, I think."

* * *

It is going the rounds here that Henry B. Walthall has formed the Henry B. Wathall Pictures Corporation and that he will begin work soon in Hollywood, Cal.; also that Mary Charleson will be his leading woman and Reginald Barker the director.

* * *

Bryant Washburn, Essanay's popular comedy star in the Skinner series, has been pressed into the service of Uncle Sam's national army from division 55 in this city. Some unkind things appeared in the city papers regarding Mr. Washburn for his claiming exemption from service; but he states that he has at all times been willing to do his duty to his country as a soldier. "If I have been accepted for military service, I am more than willing to go and do my bit, as becomes a true, loyal American", says Mr. Washburn.

* * *

It has just been announced that one of the largest theater buildings yet constructed in Chicago will be erected in the near future at the northeast corner of Marshfield Ave. and W. 47th St. The structure in which the theater will be included will occupy a lot 121 by 208 feet and will be two stories high. The building, in addition to the theater, will include four stores and a number of offices. James Svehla, a furniture dealer, will build the structure, the estimated cost of which is $250,000. It is said that the moving picture theater when completed will seat over 3,000 people, and that Jones, Linick & Schaefer may take over the theater on a long term lease.

* * *

"The Honor System", by Fox, now showing at the Studebaker, is making a big record. The production has been highly praised by Chicago photoplay critics and the crowded houses daily testify to the popularity of the photoplay.

* * *

Joseph Hopp, Peter J. Schaefer, Alfred Hamburger and Robert R. Levy left Friday to attend the meeting of the officers and executive committee of the M. P. E. L. of America, which was held in New York Saturday, August 25. On Monday, August 27, they attended the meeting of the M. P. E. L. held in New York City.

* * *

Thos. J. Furniss, member of the National Executive Committee of the M. P. E. L. of America, was in the city Thursday, August 23, accompanied by Mrs. Furniss. They visited the officers' training quarters at Fort Sheridan, where their son is now in training, and left the same evening for New York.

* * *

David Rogers of Minneapolis, national organizer of the M. P. E. L. of America, spent a short time in the city Thursday, August 23, and left the same evening for New York City, where he attended the meeting of the national executive committee and the officers of the League on Saturday.

* * *

Edgar Hopp, son of Josph Hopp, on the office staff of Hopp & Co., dealers in moving picture supplies, has enlisted in the United States navy and starts with the rank of first class yeoman. He is at present stationed in the paymaster's department at the Great Lakes Naval Station.

* * *

The Chicago Federation of Musicians, following the lead of their organisation in other large cities, has taken a stand against the music tax on picture theaters and will co-operate with the Chicago branch of the M. P. E. L. of America to combat the tax.

* * *

Juliette Day, the popular star of the American Film Co., Inc., returned recently to Broadway to fill a stage engagement with Klaw & Erlanger. Just before leaving Santa Barbara, Miss Day donated her high-priced touring car to the American Red Cross, to be disposed of at auction. The machine was purchased by a wealthy mining man, who paid for it several times more than it was really worth.

Marion Davies in "Runaway Romany"

MARION DAVIES is in the motion pictures to stay. At least, the young star who left the cast of "Oh Boy" at the Princess Theater, New York, several weeks ago, to make her film debut in her own story, "Runaway Romany," has decided not to return to the musical comedy stage for the present and this week begins work on her second photoplay.

Following the completion of "Runaway Romany," which is now nearly ready for Broadway showing, Miss Davies went to the mountains for a brief vacation, intending to resume her part in "Oh Boy." But last week she came back to see how she looked in motion pictures and was convinced that the opinion of competent critics was right and that she had a promising career in photoplay if she wanted to pursue it. She surprised the officers of the Ardsley Film Corporation by announcing her change of heart and they immediately submitted to her several scenarios by authors of reputation who are familiar with her stage career and see in her an excellent type for the screen.

Marion Davies.

After going over the scenarios Miss Davies eliminated all but two, then finally she selected the medium for her second picture and is now up Long Island Sound filming the first scenes. It is announced that the company to be seen with Miss Davies in the new play, when completed, will be equal in ability and fame to the players who appeared with her in "Runaway Romany." This company, an unusual one for an untried star in motion pictures, included Joseph Kilgour, Pedro De Cordoba, Matt Moore, Ormi Hawley, Gladden James and Boyce Combe. Many of these players are now engaged in other productions but Miss Davies intends that as long as she remains in photoplay her productions companies must maintain the standard set by this famous group of actors of stage and screen in her motion picture debut.

News of Los Angeles and Vicinity
By G. P. HARLEMAN

Theaters and Copyrighted Music
Must Have Permission by American Society of Composers, Authors and Publishers to Play Copyrighted Music in Public.

LOS ANGELES motion picture theaters and other places of amusement received an unpleasant shock on Thursday, August 16, in the form of a letter from Philip Cohen, local representative of the American Society of Composers, Authors and Publishers. The gist of the letter is an ultimatum demanding that the prevalent practice of playing copyrighted music without permission must cease and requesting theaters to get a special license from the organisation or face prosecution. The letter reads as follows:

Dear Sir—The public performance of copyrighted musical numbers in a motion picture theater, without permission of the copyright owner, subjects the proprietor of such establishment to very serious penalties. Under the decision of the Supreme Court of the United States, rendered on January 22, 1917, in the case of Victor Herbert et al vs. The Shanley Company, the unlicensed performance of a copyrighted musical composition, in a motion picture theater, infringes the exclusive right of the owner of the copyright to perform the work publicly. We inclose herewith a copy of the opinion of Justice Holmes.

This society was organized to protect composers, authors and publishers against such rendition of their compositions and for the purpose of licensing the public performance of the works of the members who comprise most of the well known authors, composers and publishers of America, England, Italy and Austria.

Licenses are issued from this office and we recommend your application as early as possible, stating whether for an individual, co-partnership or organization. Inclosed herewith you will find application blank for license, upon the basis of which declaration a contract license will be issued for your establishment.

If no license is secured, then you are hereby notified to prohibit the rendition upon your premises of any works of the members of this society.

The penalty under the copyright act for the public rendition of copyrighted musical works without the owner's consent as is indicated by the enclosed contract of the copyrighted law.

The license for motion picture theaters, we are informed, is to be made 10 cents per year for each seat so that a house seating 500 will be required to pay the sum of $50 per annum, 900 seats $90 per year, etc. In cabarets a flat charge of $15 a month is to be made. Hotels will pay from $5 to $15 per month according to class and business.

Some of the best known song writers and composers of the world belong to the society, including Victor Herbert, Ernest R. Ball, Jerome D. Kern, Irvin Berlin, Carrie Jacobs-Bond, George M. Cohan, Earl Carroll, Harry Carroll, Silvio Hein, Chauncey Olcott, Jean Schwarts, Albert von Tilzer, John Philip Sousa, Rudolph Friml, Franz Lehar, etc.

Douglas Fairbanks in Wyoming
Popular Artcraft Star and Large Company on Big Cattle Ranch Filming Scenes for "Man from Painted Post."

DOUGLAS FAIRBANKS and a large company arrived in Wyoming last week and have pitched their tents on the Riverside Ranch, thirty miles from the Laramie Railroad station in Wyoming, where the exterior scenes of "The Man from Painted Post" are being staged by Joseph Henaberry, assisted by Millard Webb, under arrangements with James House to use the Riverside Ranch, which includes 160,000 acres of land and 25,000 head of cattle, taking advantage of the real West for scenic purposes.

Fairbanks has secured Sam Brownell, champion bucking broncho rider of the world, Tommy Grimes, the fearless steer roper, Johnny Judd, fancy rope artist, Jay Miller, Tom Yarberry, Bill Baker, Charley Self and Bill Brown.

In addition to this group of champions who were featured in the recent Frontier Day Celebration, Fairbanks was accompanied from Los Angeles by H. A. Strickland, champion bare-back bucking broncho rider, Jack Padgan, Bill Crawford, Ed. Burns, Charles Stevens, Fred Burns, who held the trick roping championship for five years until 1912, Edgar Metchen and Charles McPherson.

Among the players who support Mr. Fairbanks in "The Man from Painted Post" are Frank Campeau, the Western character actor, and at one time the best known player of his type on the speaking stage, as the result of creating Trampus in "The Virginian" and Tony in "Ari-

zona"; Eileen Percy, known for her work in Wild and Woolly"; William Lowery, who played with Mr. Fairbanks in "Reggie Mixes In," one of his first screen productions, and Rhea Haines, identified with Morosco-Jack London pictures.

New Policy for Triangle Pictures
The Advertising of Stars and Individuals Will Be Subordinated to Productions.

STRICT adherence to facts and constructive exploitation that will keep public and exhibitor alike informed of production activities in studios and distributing organization plans will be the keynote of future Triangle Film Corporation publicity.

Advertising of stars and individuals will not be eliminated, but subordinated to the finished production and the exploitation of the brand under which they are exhibited. Casts will be selected for their ability to play the roles assigned rather than for individual fame or personal reputations, and no whim of star or director will be permitted to interfere with the quality on the screen.

Los Angeles Film Brevities.

Juliette Day, the American Film star, has left Santa Barbara for New York, where she will appear in a Klaw & Erlanger production. Miss Day may return to the American Film Company after her New York contract expires.

* * *

Robert Leonard has commenced production on "The Princess Virtue," in which Mae Murray is to be starred, from a story written by Louise Winter.

* * *

Samuel A. McKee, proprietor of McKee's Cafe, has filed suit for $100,000 in the Superior Court, against the Universal Film Company and the Superba Theater Company. The plaintiff alleges that the cafe in question is shown at four different intervals during the running of the moving picture "The Double Standard", and the inference is that vice and evil of social character exists in cafes of that description.

Presiding Judge Finlayson issued a temporary injunction restraining the theater from showing any scenes involving the cafe.

The plaintiff also alleges that since the initial showing of the film his cafe has been held up to ridicule, contempt and hatred and that the ill-will of the public will continue unless the picture is constrained by court.

Sub-titles stating that cafes in cities are traps and pitfalls, dangerous to the morality and welfare of the young and inexperienced girls, are shown in the picture and the complainant alleges that showing of the exterior cafe follows immediately after such captions, thereby inferring that his is one of the places referred to.

Al Nathan, manager of the Superba theater, exhibited the picture without the scenes in question being displayed and stated that the deleted picture would continue to be shown throughout the week. The case comes up for a hearing next Monday.

* * *

The Triangle-Keystone studios have long been famed for their generous collection of blonde beauties, but now another hue has entered the field and promises to run the first named a close race for popularity. The blondes have been in the majority for a year or more, but if the present pace keeps up the Titian-haired members of the comedy studio are going to outnumber them. The red-haired section now includes Myrtle Lind, Marie Manley, Clara Roberts, Nina Trask, Ruth Churchill, Myrtle Reeves and Dorothy Hagar. The rivalry is becoming so keen that the girls are planning on organizing a basket-ball team or tug-of-war or something, and in the event that they do it has been suggested that they bill their contents, "Peroxide vs. Henna".

* * *

M. J. Doner, former technical director at the Triangle Culver City studios, is engaged at the National studio in Hollywood in modeling some elaborate decorative casts, illustrative of scenes in the company's nine-reel production, "Tarzan of the Apes".

* * *

A new Christie comedy has been started this week under the working title, "A Blessed Blunder", with Betty Compson, who has just returned from a month's vacation, in the leading role. Jay Belasco plays opposite Miss Compson, and Harry Rattenberry, who has been absent from the studio for several weeks, also returns as a member of the cast. Other parts are taken by Jean Hathaway and Robert Mc-Gowan.

* * *

Al. E. Christie, director of Christie comedies, has just completed "When Clubs Were Trumps", with Margaret Gibson as the star and the production is now in the cutting room.

* * *

Mary Pickford is to have a new job, that of referee in a fist fight between Charlie Chaplin and Douglas Fairbanks, who is about 100 pounds heavier than the comedian, which will be staged at the Mason Opera House next Sunday evening.

The burlesque fight is part of a program offered for the benefit of the French-American emergency hospital, and arranged by Mrs. Frank Wright of London.

Other stars of the film world who will take part in the entertainment are Julian Eltinge, Wallace Reid, Louise Huff, Raymond Hatton, Mae Murray, Jack Pickford, Olive Thomas and Hughie Mack.

Edna Purviance, Lottie Pickford, Teddy Sampson, Gertrude Selby, Anna Luther and Dorothy Dalton will sell programs.

* * *

Another new comedy man to join the Universal Company is Al Santell, who has been added to the directing staff to alternate with Director Craig Hutchinson in staging comedies in which Dave Morris and Gladys Tennyson are the principal players. Last year Mr. Santell wrote and directed Kolb and Dill feature pictures, produced by the American Company and lately has been putting on the Ham and Bud pictures for the Kalem Company.

* * *

Claiming that the Fox Film Company had staged a mine disaster so realistically that when the mine exploded they were injured and their property damaged, four residents of Klondike Park this week sued for nearly $50,000 damages in Federal Judge Trippet's court.

The plaintiffs are Walter L. Dunham, Andrew J. Dunham, William Foster and Lillian E. Comfort.

In December, 1916, when the Fox people were filming "One Touch of Sin", and in January, 1917, when William Farnum was making "The Conqueror", "it is alleged the complainants were injured by the blowing up of mines, high explosives and bombs on the Los Feliz road". The film corporation has entered a general denial, setting out the non-dangerous character of the explosions complained of, asserting that instead of the dynamite being used nothing more dreaded than black powder was employed. The attorneys for the film company declare that they will bring into court as witnesses 150 "extras" who were working in the scene and were not injured, to testify that the explosion was harmless.

* * *

A patriotic play centering about the heroism of a little girl of the slums, to be called "Doing Her Bit", soon will be in course of production at the Triangle Flm Corporation's Culver City studio under the direction of Jack Conway. The cast has not yet been selected.

* * *

Enid Bennett, the former Ince star, has filed suit in the Superior Court for cancellation of a contract alleged to have been made with Thomas H. Ince personally, and for an injunction restraining the New York Motion Picture Corporation from hampering her in her work.

Miss Bennett entered into a two years contract with Mr. Ince in July, 1916. Since that time, Mr. Ince has severed his conection with the New York Company, and Miss Bennett, saying that she was not aware of the fact that Mr. Ince was the agent of another company, refused to carry out the old contract handled by other persons.

Her salary was $200 per week, according to the complaint, and her work for Mr. Ince was satisfactory. However, she does not want to continue the work under the supervision of others, she said.

* * *

Among the many new players recently engaged to work at Universal City are Mattie Cummont and Henry Murdock, who will be under the direction of William W. Beaudine.

Mattie is the short, roly-poly woman who has been working recently with the Fox Company and with Max Linder. She is known as one of the foremost comediennes of the French legitimate stage and photoplay fans with good memories may recall her in French Pathe comedies.

Henry Murdock has been working with the Kalem Company for a year or more, first with its Florida company and more recently with Ham and Bud in California.

* * *

John Schoenberg, who formerly led the orchestra at Al Levy's Watts Tavern, has been engaged by F. J. Balshoffer, to play exclusively for Yorke-Metro pictures while under production. Schoenberg is said to be one of the best "atmosphere violinists" now engaged in the new occupation of playing for pictures, and will be a valuable addition to the Lockwood company.

* * *

Production is finished at the Culver City plant of the Triangle Film Corporation on "Broadway Arizona", the sensational drama of New York life and Western adventure in which Olive Thomas is starred under the direction of Lynn Reynolds.

* * *

We are informed that Thomas H. Ince has leased the old Continental studios at 5813 Santa Monica Boulevard, and will put three new companies to work there at once.

* * *

Out on the three-acre lot of the Mena Film Company in Hollywood, the big moments in the lives of the early Egyptians is being lived these two weeks under the direction of Howard Gaye. Work has just begun on the multiple reel feature, preparations for the making of which have been in progress for more than a year. E. W. and J. G. Kuehn, men of eastern capital, are at the head of the Mena Company's affairs. The four principals to appear throughout the four episodes of the production are Virgina Chester, Amy Jerome, Frank Whitson and Alfred Garcia. Only a small number of the suporting cast will appear in all four episodes, new support being chosen for each one. It is estimated that the production will take two months in the making.

* * *

Wheeler Oakman has been chosen as leading man opposite Mae Murray in the first production of the Mae Murray Company under Robert Leonard's direction. The company has gone to San Diego for the making of its initial scenes.

* * *

Crane Wilbur has turned story speculator. He became so fascinated with a serial story that he requested an option on the story's picture rights. This was granted him and he's now purchasing the serial, though he admits that "now he's got it he does not know what to do with it." The chances are, however, that Mr. Wilbur will identify himself with the hero of the fascinating story.

* * *

One of the results of President S. S. Hutchinson's current visit to his American Film Company plant at Santa Barbara was the signing of a year's contract with Director Lloyd Ingraham, who has just completed his second Mary Miles Minter story.

* * *

Vola Vale is the latest member of filmdom to don the wide sombrero and do "Westerns". Miss Vale's first appearance in such a role will be opposite Charlie Ray in his first Artcraft release now in the process of production at the Thomas H. Ince studios.

* * *

James Harrison, leading man in Christie comedies, who recently enlisted in the Hollywood company of the Field Artillery, has been assigned to duty at the harbor defenses at San Pedro, Cal., and is already actively at work in his new role. Harrison's successor at the Christie studio is Jay Belasco, who has been engaged by Director Al Christie for leading parts opposite Betty Compson and Margaret Gibson. As Belasco's name appears in the draft list, Mr. Christie may find it necessary soon to seek still another leading man.

* * *

William V. Mong who has just completed a state rights feature for the Crest Motion Picture Company, entitled "The Chosen Prince", has been added to the ranks of the Triangle Company. Mr. Mong's first production will be a story of the Canadian Northwest and features Margery Wilson.

* * *

Director General J. Gordon Edwards completed the William Fox, Theda Bara Superpicture, "Cleopatra", on Monday, August 13. The picture is now being cut and is expected to be shipped to New York the end of the month.

* * *

Gladys Brockwell has started a new picture under the direction of Bert Bracken, who has been recently engaged by William Fox to supersede Otis Turner in the directing of Miss Brockwell.

* * *

The Sunshine Comedy Company, of which Henry Lehrman is the supervising director, is at work on turning out several laugh makers. Tom Mix has started a new comedy under Mr. Lehrman's direction.

* * *

E. R. Pearson, district manager of the K-E-S-E, has left his Chicago headquarters for an extended tour along the coast and is now in Los Angeles visiting for a week with E. H. Silcocks, the local manager of the K-E-S-E Exchange. Mr. Pearson, Mr. Silcocks and Mr. V. R. Day, the local manager of the Essanay Company, took an auto trip to San Diego recently, and while there were the guests of Manager Bush of the Superba Theater, aboard his yacht.

* * *

Crane Wilbur is adding to his picture fame according to reports from exhibitors who are enthusiastic over his new David Horsley productions now being released through Art Dramas. Particular praise is resulting from his work in "The Eye of Envy" while previews of "Devil McCare", a Western comedy-drama, just completed, promise even greater approval of Mr. Wilbur's art.

* * *

Clair DeWitt, assistant director of George Ovey in Cub Comedies, has passed his physical examination under the draft regulations for a part in Uncle Sam's army.

* * *

The producing staff of the National Film Corporation, who recently left Los Angeles for New Iberia, La., have transferred their base of operation to Morgan City, where the Company is now at work on the production "Tarzan of the Apes", under the direction of Scott Sidney. The city officials have donated for the use of the company a large warehouse with trackage at one side and a boat landing at the other, so that transportation for location work is reduced to a minimum. A large storeroom has also been secured opposite the hotel, where a force of property men are working in conjunction with the technical staff. Director Sidney, in view of the desires of local merchants, has agreed that his biggest scenes, requiring the participation of several hundred negroes, will be made on Sundays, so that the usual commercial activities of the city will not be interfered with. A large number of negroes have migrated to the North within the past year, and the wage scale for cannibals has jumped from a dollar a day to $1.75.

* * *

"Mother" Lule Warrenton returned to the Universal fold this week. Mrs. Warrenton is one of the best known character actresses of screendom and was associated with the Universal Company for more than three years before she left that organization to produce children's photoplays for the Frieder Film Corporation in Lankershim. Mrs. Warrenton enjoyed a long experience in the spoken drama before going into motion pictures and at one time had her own stock company. In the cinema world she has played with many of the leading stars and for a time directed feature children's pictures at Universal City.

BIOGRAPH STUDIO FOR PETROVA.

Petrova Picture Company, the organisation that will produce and market Madame Petrova's personally-supervised pictures, announces that the distinguished Polish actress has leased the Biograph Studio, New York City, until arrangements have been completed for a permanent Petrova studio. The production of the first picture will begin September 3. Madame Petrova has selected George Irving to direct her first picture. Mr. Irving was chosen because of his splendid work in the direction of "The Witching Hour" and "Jaffray." Another example of his art will be seen in "Raffles," John Barrymore's recently-finished picture.

Two unusually strong stories are now being prepared for production. One is a story written by Madame Petrova, which furnishes a splendid vehicle for her talent; the other is a popular novel full of dramatic situations. These two stories will be the first and second Petrova pictures; both will be in seven reels.

AL GRIFFIN WITH ROLIN.

Al Griffin, for five years technical director with the Essanay Co. and later for some time with Rex Beach, has been secured by the Rolin Co. as technical director on the "Lonesome Luke" comedies, the Harold Lloyd comedies and the "Toto" comedies, all on the Pathe program.

Alice Brady Forms Own Company

Player to Make Eight Pictures a Year—Has Already Begun Work in New York Studio.

THE sequel to the announcement that Alice Brady has left the World Film Company comes in the news of the incorporation in Albany of the Alice Brady Pictures, Inc., August 25, with a capitalisation of $250,000.

Arrangements have been concluded for a studio in the vicinity of New York, and work on her first picture has been begun. It is announced the first production of the company will be the screening of one of the most successful plays in the history of the legitimate theater, a play that almost every film maker in America has tried to produce. Early announcement will be made of the method of distribution adopted by the company. Miss Brady expects to produce eight pictures a year, and her first production will be ready for release October 15.

T. Wigney Percyval

T. WIGNEY PERCYVAL, co-author of "Grumpy" and "The Little Lady in Blue," and incidentally one of the best known actors on the English stage, was lured into the movies this season. Mr. Percyval holds that there is no field so full of "copy" for the novelist and playwright as the movie territory. The only globe-trotters these days are motion picture actors, he declares. They are the only professional travelers left.

The first picture Mr. Percyval played in was "She", laid in Africa. But the long sea voyage to this far away country was obviated by the fact that Florida is so close at hand —and full of native sons of Ham.

"We arrived in our Africa, which is near Tampa, Florida", he said, "and in due course on, and the director gave instructions for us to make up.

T. Wigney Percyval.

"I asked, naturally enough, where we were to dress. The director waved his hand expressively. He took in the whole landscape. 'Anywhere,' he said.

"I proceeded to hunt a convenient cave in which to change myself from an Englishman to an African prime minister. After wandering around an hour I came across a bungalow. I rapped. No response. I tried the blinds. All were securely fastened.

"At last, finding one unlatched, I opened it and went in. The house was deserted. So I adjusted my dressing case and mirrors, made up comfortably and donned my robes of state in privacy.

"I continued to use the bungalow day after day. I called at my house. One day I was dressing when I heard steps on the veranda.

"A man strolled to the window. I had been using as my door and greeted me with 'Hello, are you living here now?'

"I replied in the same tone, 'I am.' I wasn't sure what his position was, but I waited for him to explain his intrusion on my premises.

"'Just dropped by,' he said casually, 'to see who is living here now. Used to live here myself in happier days,' and he was gone.

"What was his story? I find myself often wondering. Who figured in those happier days?

"I lost him, for he disappeared as suddenly as he arrived, and I am in private life no detective, though I did recently play the part of an English detective in 'Sylvia of the Secret Service' with Mrs. Castle. But I played a stupid English detective.

"I shall continue in the 'movies', in addition to my literary work", Mr. Percyval concluded; "it is the one field of romance, adventure, that has not yet been scratched by the novelist. I mean the experiences of motion picture actors in the strange, new countries they are exploring right here in the United States of America".

Raver Resigns as Art Dramas Head

Will Give His Whole Time to His Own Productions—To Exploit European Spectacles.

THE resignation of Harry Raver, president of Art Dramas, Inc., has been tendered his organization. A successor has not as yet been announced. No changes in the releasing make-up of the program are indicated in the action of Mr. Raver, his reasons for vacating the executive chair being said by him to be personal.

"My resignation need occasion no surprise," said Mr. Raver, "as I have for some time contemplated turning over the reins to one whose sole time and energy could be devoted to the details, leaving me free to supervise my American productions and, as well, the exploitation of a new series of twenty or more European spectacular and novelty productions which I have recently imported, one of which, 'The Warrior,' has just closed a successful run at the Criterion Theater."

Mr. Raver has just completed an important production of "The Public Defender," by Mayer C. Goldman and Frank W. Harris, two prominent members of the New York bar, starring Frank Keenan, Robert Edeson, Alma Hanlon, John Sainpolis and Florence Short. This is to be followed by others of the same type and personnel.

Richard Bret Harte

BRET HARTE wrote of California's first great industry, gold mining, and made the gold camps forever famous, and now a Bret Harte is writing for California's last and greatest industry, the production of motion pictures. His name is Richard Bret Harte, grandson of the famous author, and he has just been added to the scenario staff of the Triangle Culver City studios.

The young Mr. Bret Harte believes that if his grandfather were alive today, he would be one of the foremost scenario writers, and he points to the classical stories, "Solomy Jane" and "The Luck of the Roaring Camp", as examples of what the elder artist might have done for the newest method of dramatic expression.

His training for dramatic writing is unusual. While born in Philadelphia, his residence in America was short, for his father took him to England as a little child. He was educated in prominent schools in England and Belgium, later engaging himself with art studies in the Beaux Arts in Brussels. While clever with his pencil, he prefers his typewriter.

Richard Bret Harte.

And the typewriter he prefers is by no means a usual one. It speaks nine languages. He is a rapid writer, having done special work for the New York and Philadelphia papers, and considerable magazine work. He is a member of the staff of the Overland Monthly, the magazine founded by his grandfather.

His father was an intimate friend of Dion Boucicault, the Irish dramatist, and was considered an authority on French and English drama. His father's connection with the stage offered unusual advantages to Richard Bret Harte to absorb the fundamentals of dramatic contruction.

CHADWICK ON TOUR.

I. E. Chadwick, general manager of Ivan Films, left Saturday, August 18th, for a tour throughout the country in the interest of the Ivan Film Productions, visiting the different distributors, energising their efforts for the fall campaign.

Mr. Chadwick will not return until the early part of September, and as he is, while attending to business, also trying to get a few deep vacation breaths, his staff at the home office wish him all the enjoyment that he can get while away and hope to see him back in his usual vigor, which those who know him say is sufficient to make things hum.

Olive Tell

THERE are very few stage or screen stars today who can lay claim to have started at the top of the ladder, rather than to have experienced all the bitter before reaching the sweet things in life. Still, Olive Tell, now starring in film features for the Empire All-Star Corporation, and who is actively engaged in filming "The Unforeseen," under the direction of Albert Capellani, spent a year in the Sargent Dramatic School after finishing her education abroad, and from there to the stage, where she played in leading parts from the first, having been engaged by Frohman. Miss Tell has appeared in "Husband and Wife," "Cousin Lucy," "The King of Nowhere," "The Intruder," "Romance" and "Under Pressure," for the stage, while her film work has been limited to three pictures, "The Smugglers," with Donald Brian; "The Silent Master," with Robert Warwick, and her present feature. Miss Tell was also the featured leading woman with the Manhattan Players in Rochester, N. Y., where she played a summer engagement for three

Olive Tell.

consecutive seasons, terminating her present season early to start work for the Empire All-Star productions.

Exceedingly beautiful and talented, Miss Tell brings to the screen one of the most charming personalities of the theatrical world. Accomplished, an expert pianist and golfer, she can be seen at prominent week-end parties of the smart set, and very few golf matches among the women folk at Forest Hills Gardens, L. I., draw much attention unless Miss Tell is a competitor, and she has already won several trophies on the links. Much interest is being manifested in Miss Tell's first starring vehicle, which will be released by the Mutual Film Corporation.

HUMISTON INJUNCTION INEFFECTIVE.

The injunction granted Mrs. Grace Humiston by Supreme Court Justice Ordway two weeks ago to restrain the Universal Film Mfg. Co. from releasing the issue of the Animated Weekly containing pictures of Mrs. Humiston taken at the scene of the Cocchi murder, has been withdrawn upon refusal of the plaintiff to provide a bond of $2,500. Evidently in much doubt regarding the outcome of the case. Mrs. Humiston thought it best not to put up the sum required, thereby rendering the injunction ineffective. The Universal has withdrawn the issue of the Animated Weekly containing the pictures from circulation, however.

The decision of Justice Ordway that news films such as these features, as any private citisen who happens to appear before the lens of a camera while a parade or other news event is being taken will have the right to sue for damages if the picture is released commercially.

The decision of Justice Ordway that news films such as class as newspapers seems likely to stand, and may cause considerable loss to the various film concerns manufacturing the Animated Weekly are not to be considered in the same

ANDERSON GOES TO COAST.

Monday afternoon, August 20, Carl Anderson, president of Paralta Plays, Inc., left for Los Angeles to look over the important Western interests now controlled by his corporation and allied companies. He will be gone four weeks. This is Mr. Anderson's first visit to the West Coast since the formation of the Paralta Corporations in February and March last.

With the Henry B. Walthall Company added to the Kerrigan and Barriscale Companies as producing units at the Paralta studios, this plant will become a busy place. These companies do not, however, represent its capacity, and at least four more organizations can work there with substantially separate accommodations for each.

Reviews of Current Productions

EXCLUSIVELY BY OUR OWN STAFF

"Straight Shooting"

Stirring Five-Reel Butterfly Number Features Harry Carey
—A Powerful Story of Western Plains.
Reviewed by Robert C. McElravy.

THE old days of the West live again in such exceptionally realistic offerings as "Straight Shooting." It tells a picturesque narrative of the days when cattlemen made war upon homesteaders. Harry Carey is featured in the familiar role of "Cheyenne Harry," a bad man with a good heart. He has previously done some splendid work in this part, but this number is a step ahead both for himself and his supporting company of rough riders and Western character performers. The story itself, written by George Hively and produced by

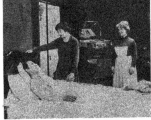

Scene from "Straight Shooting" (Butterfly).

Jack Ford, is a clean-cut, straightforward tale, whose thrilling moments would seem fictitious except for the fact that they are bolstered up by actual tradition. It would be hard to get into the pictures any more striking or tragic incidents than have actually occurred in the warfare of the range. Both the author and the director are to be congratulated upon having selected compelling scenes and situations for the production. The Western panorama is set forth in clear, attractive photography and the riding and fighting episodes are enacted with dash and enthusiasm. So successful is the offering that it deserves to rank with "The Virginian" and "Whispering Smith." It has not the humor of the former, but it has a strong human quality and rivals the latter in intensity and conviction.

George Berrell and Molly Malone play the old settler and his daughter, whose home is made the scene of numerous stirring events. Others in the cast are Duke Lee, Vester Pegg, Ted Brooks, Hoot Gibson, Milt Brown and a large cast of rough riders.

"The Jury of Fate"

Mabel Taliaferro Gives Fine Characterization of Dual Role in a Story of the Canadian Forests.
Reviewed by C. S. Sewell.

EXCELLENT characterization of two contrasting roles mark the work of Mabel Taliaferro, who is cast both as Jeanne Labordie, a charming, unselfish girl, and as her twin brother, Jacques, who is pampered and selfish, in "The Jury of Fate," a Metro-Rolfe picture released August 6.

The story by Finis Fox, adapted by June Mathis, is laid for the most part in the heart of the Canadian forests, somewhere in the northern part of Quebec. Henri Labordie's wife dies after giving birth to twins, and he makes an agreement with his friend, Duval Hebert, that Jeanne, when old enough, shall marry Hebert's son Louis. Jacques is the favorite of his father, who, when the girl grows blind, is fast becoming blind; and in order to lessen the blow, Jeanne masquerades as Jacques, after he is accidentally drowned. The father dies soon after and, carrying out his request, she goes to his friend Hebert, learns of the agreement, and agrees to marry Louis Hebert, a weak-natured, dissipated youth, although she is in love with Duncan, a surveyor, whom she has met in the north woods. On the night

before the wedding Louis returns from a trip to the north bringing Duncan, who believes that Jeanne has deceived him. Louis hears their conversation, denounces Jeanne, and is killed by being thrown over a banister in a fight with Francois Le-Blanc, a halfbreed friend of Jeanne's. LeBlanc and Jeanne return to the forests, and, through the unselfishness of LeBlanc, who himself loves Jeanne, a reconciliation is brought about between Jeanne and Duncan.

There are many beautiful woodland views, and Director Tod Browning has made excellent use of double exposures, Miss Taliaferro playing opposite herself in a number of scenes. Much of the heart interest is supplied by F. F. Bennett as Le-Blanc, the halfbreed, in love with Jeanne, a part reminiscent of Poleon Doret in "The Barrier." Albert Tavernier as Henri Labordie, Bradley Barker as Louis Hebert, and H. F. Webber as Duval Hebert are satisfactory in their respective parts, and the photography is excellent.

"Tides of Fate"

World Film Corporation Releases Subject Featuring Alexandra Carlisle in Story of Real Life.
Reviewed by Robert C. McElravy.

REAL life, with melodramatic trimmings at odd moments, is the chief impression made upon the observer by this five-reel feature. It follows the fortunes of a girl named Fanny Lawson, capably portrayed by Alexandra Carlisle. It is Fanny's fate to be rescued from a watery grave by an adventurer named Stephen King. A captain of the mounted police, named John Cross, is recuperating from an illness in the neighborhood. He falls in love with Fanny, but she has given her heart to King and eventually marries him and goes to the city. Scenes are then shown in rapid succession, picturing the lives of the three principals. At first the observer is conscious of a certain abruptness in the direction, owing to the number of plot threads woven into the story, but this course was apparently necessary and is readily excused when the threads once more unite and the plot comes to a satisfactory climax.

King turns out to be an experienced counterfeiter, who has served a term in prison. After the marriage he becomes indifferent to Fanny and leaves her. Government agents search her apartments and find King's counterfeiting plates. The wife, although entirely innocent, is sent to prison as an accomplice and serves two years. John Cross in the meantime is having adventures with the mounted police in Canada, where he is court-martialed for alleged cowardice. Later he goes to the Philippines, where he redeems his honor. He and Fanny eventually meet again in a New York boarding house, and are in love with one another when King appears. The latter becomes

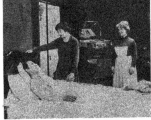

Scene from "Tides of Fate" (World).

wildly jealous and starts trouble. He is fatally shot by a policeman during the melee, but before his death confesses to his various crimes and clears Fanny's name.

The story is adapted from "Creeping Tides," by Kate Jordan. There is perhaps no special strength about the presentation, although certain scenes grip the attention closely. These include the court-martial, the prison theatrical entertainment and

Fanny's escape, the battles in the Philippines, and the fight at the close.

Others in the cast are Frank Holland, William A. Sheer, Charles Graham, Jane Kent and Walter Ryder.

"The Seven Pearls"

Mollie King and Creighton Hale Featured in Pathe's New Serial—First Two Episodes Promise Fascinating Story.

Reviewed by Ben H. Grimm.

WITH the adventurous materiality of the East working at cross purposes with the mysterious craftiness of the Orient, Pathe's new serial, "The Seven Pearls," gets off to a fast and fascinating start in the first two episodes. The two chapters shown for review promise a good serial. Mollie King and Creighton Hale, who already have established themselves in serials, are the featured players in this one. Leon Bary, Henry Gsell and John J. Dunn are also prominent players. Charles W. Goddard wrote the story and scenario. The serial

Scene from "The Seven Pearls" (Astra).

was produced by Astra and the first episode will be released September 2.

"The Sultan's Necklace."

The first chapter, in three reels, is titled "The Sultan's Necklace." It plants the leading characters and gets into the story proper in short order. Mollie King is seen as an American girl who has been brought up in Turkey as the daughter of Honest Bey, a former Ambassador. Through an adventure she meets a young American. Later the young American innocently steals a pearl necklace left in the Bey's care by the Sultan. The Sultan demands that the girl become an inmate of his harem. Her alternative is to recover the necklace within six months. The young American learns that he has been inveigled into a gang of international crooks. The action shifts to New York. The girl continues her search for the necklace, the seven pearls of which have been given to seven different persons. A mysterious character enters the action here. He is apparently the member of a secret Oriental order. The pearls are well-distributed in the first chapter and at the close the spectator is anxious to know more.

"The Bow String."

In the second chapter, titled "The Bow String" (two reels), the story moves along more rapidly, the characters having been planted. The chapter turns chiefly around the efforts of the girl to acquire the pearls. The chapter gets its title from the fact that the girl is threatened with the bow string, the contrivance used in strangling women of the harem who flirt. The girl is constantly watched by a lieutenant of the Sultan. In the episode one of the gang of crooks makes the girl's acquaintance. He is caught by her in a house as he is stealing a painting. He overpowers her and is about to make way when the hero enters. The girl gets two of the pearls, but they are taken from her by her guard.

"The Divorcee"

Alfred Vosburgh Gives Excellent Performance as Militant Parson in Blue Ribbon Feature.

Reviewed by George Blaisdell.

THE notable factor in "The Divorcee," a Blue Ribbon release of August 27, is the performance of Alfred Vosburgh as a militant parson. What not too often happens on the screen we have here a player who looks a minister of the gospel. He neither overplays nor underplays the part. His Rev. Jerry Ferguson, the Reno minister in a campaign against the divorce evil or the evil divorce laws, has the face and the bearing of a man of breeding and education. Yet, too, we see he is a man of action, who can ride and shoot, who can impress other men of action with the fact that he is one of them.

Rufus Steele has written a comedy-drama around the divorce colony of the Nevada town which in other days was known the country over as a temporary abiding place of those anxious to be quickly freed from the bonds of matrimony. Mr. Steele has given us some good situations and some excellent titles—the sort that reveal the hand trained in phrasing, in putting something worth while into a few words. As one reviewer remarked, the story picks up sharply when the red blood comes into evidence. And he had the clergyman in mind.

Mary Anderson is Wanda Carson, who goes to Reno to visit a brother who permanently lives in the town. Wanda decides that in order to see anything of the restricted life in the place it will be necessary to enroll as one of the divorcees. To further her scheme she claims as her own the little daughter of her cousin. Then she meets the parson, riding afield arrayed in all the stage cowboy panoply presented him by his in-the-rough friends. The story twists humorously and seriously following the revelations to the minister of one of the genuine divorcees and to Wanda of the depredations of an honest-to-goodness highwayman, the two principals meanwhile concealing their identity from each other.

The action rapid and interesting in the second half of the subject atones for the absence of this quality in the opening. The ending is one that will "send 'em away smiling."

"Pants"

Charles Mortimer Peck's Story Produced by Essanay, with Little Mary McAlister in the Lead, Assisted by a Cast of Clever Players.

Reviewed by James S. McQuade.

LITTLE MARY McALISTER will please her many admirers in "Pants," a five-reel production by Essanay, the story being specially written for Little Mary by Charles Mortimer Peck. While everybody who sees "Pants" will be deeply interested in the amusing escapades in which Little Mary figures, those of us who are zealous for a well constructed plot cannot help wishing that the strong climax, which occurs early in the third reel, could have been avoided, as the spectator's interest for some time afterward is somewhat dulled.

However, as Little Mary is the sun around which every other person in the cast revolves, and seeing that she is delightful, even with faulty construction of plot, we refuse to permit our pleasure to be marred by any technicality.

There is a beautiful lesson for children and grownups also in the screen story of "Pants," as well as a rich fund of humor. Let it be known that "Pants" is the nickname of a wealthy little girl called Betty, whom our Little Mary McAlister impersonates. Betty has an ogre of an aunt, who forbids her playing with the lowlier children of the tenements, and as these are the only playmates at hand, it can readily be guessed that

Scene from "Pants" (Essanay).

Betty will be obliged to mope and cry her eyes out from sheer loneliness, unless she can find a way. Her good uncle champions her one day and tells her to go to the beach and play, promising to stick by her.

On this occasion she wishes to play with the boys; but they are intent on bathing and rebuff her by singing, "Ah-h, we don't want no girls! We're goin' to do something girls can't do," and they rush off and out of sight. In her wanderings Betty chances on a boy's clothing, and finding the role of a girl irksome, she appropriates the pants and a hat, leaving instead her frock and hat. The sequel reveals mirthful complications that are best told by the pictures.

The scene showing Betty entertaining a crowd of her young tenement friends—begrimed and foot-dirty, in her beautiful home, brings laughter and the joy akin to tears; for Betty's kindness makes the whole world kin.

These are only two of the numerous pleasing and mirthful incidents in "Pants," which will be released through K-E-S-E, Inc., Sept. 16.

"The Lust of the Ages"

Ogden Pictures Corporation's Initial Subject Is a Pretentious Subject, Stronger as a Spectacle Than as a Drama.

Reviewed by George Blaisdell.

THE Ogden Pictures Corporation gave a trade showing of its first production on Friday, August 17. In "The Lust of the Ages," a seven-part picture, Lillian Walker is featured. The subject is a spectacular preachment—on the titular side it is a homiletic discourse on the evils of money grab-

Scene from "The Lust of the Ages" (Ogden).

bing; on the dramatic or picture side it is a story within a story, with the same principals employed in each.

The picture will appeal to those who "dearly love a lord," who are interested in portrayals or persons of wealth and of social position, who enjoy looking upon the habitations of those above the average in means, and who are attracted to mob scenes, of throngs. It will not appeal to those who care for, first of all, a straight and simple story. It lacks heart interest—if there is in the seven reels a situation that makes the pulse beat faster or one that gets under the skin, this writer failed to register it. In presentation there are many photographic novelties, touches that add to the picturesqueness of the subject.

Miss Walker has the role of Lois Craig, a young woman reared in wealth, her father a money grabber, her mother a lover of the home and the family circle. The father dies, and the invalid mother, with recollection of her own experience, warns the daughter against her fiance. Lois discovers her intended husband is of the same stamp as was her father and breaks the engagement, recommending to the young man the perusal of a novel she has written. The reading of the book is undertaken, and we see on the screen the working out of the story.

In the subsidiary tale Miss Walker is shown as a shepherdess in love with a man of the vicinity. The army of Mammon invades the Valley of Content and forces the inhabitants to remove beyond the snow mountains. There had been a series of introductory symbolic scenes, visualizing the story told in Lois' book, in which are revealed the manner in which wealth is wasted, the immoral entertainments that contribute to this end, the destitution of the poor. There is a scene of the prostitute on the street corner, followed by a representation of Christ chastising the money changers. Then, too, there is a present day reminder of the war, in which Miss Walker, as a daughter of the King whose country for forty years has been preparing for hostilities, prevails upon her fiance, a prince, to utilize a liquid fire invention for the destruction of the accumulated gold, with the result that both are executed when detected. The "location" of the Valley is a scenic treat.

It is after finishing this book that Byron Masters, the young financier, played by Jack Mowers, decides to renounce his former beliefs and to take Lois' view of life. The somewhat extended outline of the story will show that there are many angles to the theme of the picture, angles that divide the interest.

MARY MILES MINTER IN "CHARITY CASTLE."

Mary Miles Minter, the "Crown Princess" of the motion picture, whose success in heart interest drama has been of a phenomenal sort, is starred in a new five act dramatic fantasy, "Charity Castle," produced under Mutual-American auspices for release Septembe, 3. It was written by O. Doty Hobart. Director Lloyd Ingraham, one of the leading men of his profession, studied the play for several weeks with Miss Minter and the author before it was decided to place "Charity Castle" in rehearsal.

BILL GILLESPIE JOINS ROLIN.

Bill Gillespie, for three years with the Selig Company and late of the Chaplin studio, is the latest recruit to the Rolin players. Shortly after he signed up he presented the name of a candidate for starring honors in 1935. Her name is Margaret Ann Gillespie and she has just arrived.

"The Mysterious Miss Terry"

A Famous Players-Paramount Production, with Billie Burke.

Reviewed by Louis Reeves Harrison.

THE Mysterious Miss Terry" is self-announced to be founded on the mystery of a certain lady's identity. It strikes a true keynote at the beginning, and its artistic purpose should be unfalteringly firm to the end, the mystery of her identity being the element of suspense on which audience attention depends. This it fails to do. A well-dressed young lady alights from a cab in a city street and tells the driver to wait for her—she is "going around the corner." She there enters what has the appearance of being a magnificent country mansion and fills a valise with loot. even robbing a wall safe, during the temporary absence of the sole caretaker. She makes a successful getaway when he returns and drives to her boarding house, where she pays her overdue bill from the stolen money. Among the table boarders are three men who make various efforts to help and to entertain her. The four are at a private repast when she asks each to make a wish. One wants a few hundred dollars to become a cowboy, one enough to go into "society," the third, nominated as an "author", wants money to publish his book, some typed pages bound at the edge like a play-broker's script, and rolled up like one.

Lack of knowledge of authorship seems to be this story's weak spot. The mystery is not preserved as promised. The mysterious lady is of the highest society and worth millions. Unable to command congenial surroundings, she has sought them in the boarding house under an assumed name. The story now drifts away into a comedy burglary, complicated with a real one, during which the "author" is shot. The mysterious lady takes care of him and provides him with a remunerative position. She gratifies the wishes of the other two men and is arrested for robbing her own house before she reveals herself to the "author" who wanted money to publish his book. She finally marries the distinguished gentleman who had never written anything for which a publisher would pay him, and this vehicle for talented Billie Burke is at an end.

The actress deserves something better than a vehicle, she is delightful in screen comedy with intelligent characterization, and she is good in every dramatic opportunity in this story of mystery which gives up mystifying at the very moment it should be intensifying its plainly announced object. There is good material in the comedy burglary. In fact there is enough material in the play for a well-constructed five-story house, but it has been put together without the plans of a skilled architect. The settings and the effective picture contrasts, light and shade effects, are all good, and there has been an honest effort to keep up to the Paramount standard. That sincerity counts for much, but it has to be supplanted with skill in all three departments of artistry to reach a front place.

"Grafters"

Triangle Cast, Including Jack Devereaux and Anna Lehr, Appear in Crook Story Containing Devious Twists and Turns of a Humorous Character.

Reviewed by Robert C. McElravy.

THIS five-reel subject, written by James W. Adams and produced by Arthur Rosson and Allan Dwan, is another of the familiar "thief comedies" which have been so much in vogue recently, both on screen and stage. It rings in some new changes of the farcical sort and certain developments

Scene from "Grafters" (Triangle).

will furnish an enjoyable surprise for those who have not seen too many of this particular type of offering. Even observers who have become familiar with plots of the sort will follow the story with interest.

Jack Devereaux appears as Jack Towne, a young millionaire whose uncle is constantly advising him to be on guard lest he become the victim of grafters. The youth is over-confident and sure of himself, so in order to teach him a lesson the uncle employs certain persons to work a swindle upon him. Anna Lehr appears as the girl in the case, who lures the young man on. Jack at first falls a victim to the game, but later turns the tables on his uncle and the crooks as well. He saves his uncle from a real holdup and later forgives the girl for her deception and the usual love affair follows.

The number is given adequate presentation throughout. Most of the scenes occur in the city, but others take place at a country inn, to which the girl has enticed the young man.

The others in the cast are Frank Currier, Irene Leonard, George Seigmann and Robert Crimmins.

"Outcast"

Hubert Henry Davies Play Given Excellent Six-Part Picturization for Mutual Program with Ann Murdoch in the Leading Feminine Role.
Reviewed by Margaret I. MacDonald.

THE famous Charles Frohman stage success "Outcast" has been filmed for the Mutual program by the Empire All-Star Corporation with Ann Murdoch in the leading feminine role. The production is one of good calibre, and has been artistically directed by Dell Henderson. By reason of the nature of its plot and characters the picture, which is in six parts, could not be recommended among the class chosen for Better Film programs. While by reason of its artistic and entertaining qualities it will be found an excellent box-office attraction.

The two principal figures in "Outcast" are a man and a woman whose experiences in love have been similar. When the paths of these two people cross the woman has become a woman of the streets and the man a drunkard. The soul of the woman being the first to awaken, she lifts the man, and together they renounce the evils to which each has fallen. The jarring note in the morale of the play is the difference which the picture gives of love without marriage. When the man decides to discard the woman and return to an old love, his discovery of the shallowness of the love of the last-named not yet divorced from her husband, causes him to turn again to the "outcast" whose forgiveness he easily wins.

The action of this picture is unusually realistic, which together with its play on human emotions will tend to make it popular.

"The Charmer"

Ella Hall Featured in Five-Reel Bluebird—Directed by Jack Conway—Released August 29.
Reviewed by Ben H. Grimm.

BLUEBIRD'S release for August 29, "The Charmer", a five-reeler in which Ella Hall is featured, is just an ordinary picture. The picture runs along at an easy-going and sometimes slow gait, and the viewer is at no time moved to any great extent by what is going on on the screen. There is no really big situation. The story is only mildly entertain-

Scene from "The Charmer" (Bluebird).

ing and ofttimes rather obvious. There is scarcely enough story to bear the burden of five reels. However, the film should make more or less of a hit with juveniles, inasmuch as it centers chiefly around a child who is orphaned when the ship upon which she is traveling is torpedoed. The torpedoing is done by titles.

The story was written by J. Grubb Alexander and scenarioized by Fred Myton. Miss Hall has been seen in much more compelling roles than she has in this picture. Jack Conway, who directed the piece, has rather overdone in footage those double-exposure scenes in which a child's beliefs in fairies are visualized on the screen. Miss Hall is seen as an orphan who is adopted by a small-town old maid after the latter has "won" the orphan at a church fair. There are many extraneous bits of fairly humorous child stuff introduced into the action. The girl meets her Prince Charming in the boy who has been sent to his parents' house in the small town. His wealthy mother

plans to divorce her husband. The "co-respondent" fails to appear at the trial and Ambrosia, the girl, says that she is the correspondent. The Court soon becomes aware of the fact that the child has confused "co-respondent" with "correspondent", and her appearance in the witness chair leads to the husband's explanation that he told the girl that he, too, was in love with a Lady Fair (his wife), but a wicked witch (Society) iced her heart. A reconciliation instead of a divorce takes place and the girl, ousted by the old maid, gains a home with the reunited parents of her Prince Charming.

The photography is excellent and many scenes in the piece are very pleasing to the eye.

In the cast with Miss Hall are Belle Bennett, Martha Mattox, James McCandlas, George Webb and Frank McQuarrie.

"A Bushranger's Strategy"

Latest Two-Reel Episode of Kalem's "The Further Adventures of Stingaree" Is Fair Number.
Reviewed by Ben H. Grimm.

THE latest two-reel episode of Kalem's "The Further Adventures of Stingaree" series is a fair number. The story, while interesting, is somewhat slow in its unfolding on the screen, but in the latter part of the picture the

Scene from "A Bushranger's Strategy" (Kalem).

action speeds up to a satisfactory pitch. The release follows the same general lines as those that have gone before. True, Boardman is seen as Stingaree, the gentleman bushranger, and Paul C. Hurst as Howie. The latter also directed.

E. W. Hornung's story tells of how Stingaree and Howie come across a lone violin player in the wilderness. They take him to their camp. A former show girl searching for a man, is forced to go afoot when her horse goes lame. True, the violin player slips away from camp and binds her. It develops that the violin player is a police spy, but Stingaree has outguessed him and the troopers find only the violinist's horse, where they expected to find the two bushrangers. It develops that the violinist is the man who stole the show girl's money. Stingaree and Howie outwit the police, get the violinist alone, and recover the girl's funds. They send the violinist, barefoot, out on the desert.

Other players than those mentioned are Edythe Sterling, Barney Furey and Jack Waltemeyer.

"Little Miss Optimist"

Pallas-Paramount Five-Part Subject a Well Played All Around Story of Hard Luck and Good Cheer.
Reviewed by George Blaisdell.

THERE is good philosophy in "Little Miss Optimist", the five-part Pallas subject released by Paramount August 26. The picture is wholesome in tone, with a distinct church atmosphere. The latter is not offensively so, if the expression may be used, having in mind the main interests and recreations lie in other directions. If it were not for the murder committed, the piece is one that might well be shown within the walls of a church. It is a good human, all-around story, one that should go well in any house.

Vivian Martin is well cast in the role of Maizie-Rosie Garden, the freak name bestowed on the heroine by Gardner Bunting, author of the story. Maizie is a cheerful little person, one who believes happiness to a large degree consists not in what you have, but in what you hope to have. Her philosophy has to take some pretty rough bumps, but it withstands it.

Tom Moore is Deal Hendrie, a down-and-outer, befriended by Maizie, but who comes back under the inspiration of her friendship. Charles West is Ben Cardin, the brother of the heroine, who seems to have more than his share of hard luck. Ernest Joy is John West, a coal merchant, who befriends Hendrie. Charles Gerard is Winter, the embezzling bookkeeper of West, who in a struggle with his employer kills him.

Robert Thornby directs the picture. The story is well hooked up. A battered dime figures much in the tale, and every time it enters it makes more sure the conviction of the murderer. The moment of Winter's uncovering is dramatic. Maizie, hiding from the police, has taken shelter in the church, subsisting on the food left in haste by the members of the guild when they learned of the death of West. She parts

Scene from "Little Miss Optimist" (Paramount).

the curtains in front of the pulpit, sees Winter shifting the battered dime he has taken from the body, lifting from the plate a good one for it. She denounces the murderer, upsetting the services. A policeman takes Winter away, the organist lover declares himself, and all is well.

"His Wedding Night"

A Two-Part Paramount-Arbuckle Comedy with Fatty as a Soda Clerk in a Country Drug Store.

Reviewed by Arthur W. Courtney.

IN FATTY ARBUCKLE'S latest two-reel comedy, "His Wedding Night," ice cream is held on thick. This picture is full of laughable bits. Some are just glorified jokes, as when one stops eating watermelon to pick seeds out of his ears. But these scenes are funny nevertheless, even when the material is old.

Fatty is a soda clerk in a country drug store. After juggling an egg and milk he strains it through a comb and brushes off the foam with a hair brush. The India rubber egg is a good bit. He provides beer for a customer with a wink; also an individual bar-rail, a cuspidor and a sprinkling of sawdust. Two sissies appear in this picture. One sprays himself with sample perfume and is provided with a bathtub and towels and a stream from a siphon. Fatty substitutes chloroform for the perfume. This gets him one girl. But another he invulnerable—she even drinks it. A negress comes in for powder and is asked whether she wants face, gun or bug. She says she is not a bug, so she gets charcoal. In the gasoline episode a Ford is charged twenty-six cents a gallon, and when a Rolls-Royce comes up Fatty turns over the ticket and charges a dollar. The chauffeur does not object. He peels a bill off a big wad. Fatty gives him change from a still bigger wad, then sprinkles the road with gasolene.

Fatty overcomes a rival suitor, who then plans to kidnap the bride. Instead of the bride he gets the sissy who delivered the bridal gown and who has put it on to show how it hangs. This comedy will get a laugh out of everyone.

"The Lady of the Photograph"

Shirley Mason Attractive in Five-Part Comedy Drama for K-E-S-E Produced by Edison Company.

Reviewed by Margaret I. MacDonald.

THE Lady of the Photograph" is founded on a story of which a great deal might have been made. The production in five parts, which was made at the Edison studios, and there is a feeling that the comedy situations, which in themselves are good, do not "get over". Shirley Mason is charming in the role of a young American heiress who while visiting in England meets her fate when she falls into a pond in quest of a water lily. Raymond McKee as Ferdy Latimer, a disinherited Englishman, is quite the type, and Royal Byron as John Brown, who made millions in soap, plays exceptionally well. Others of the cast, William Calhoun, Jane Harvey, Dudley Hill and Gerald Pring, do good work in the supporting cast.

As the story runs Marjorie Van Dam, visiting in England, falls accidentally into a lily pond on the Latimer estate and is rescued by Ferdy, the disinherited member of the family.

The mutual attraction between the two is discouraged by the girl's parents, who are looking for wealth and social position in a match for their daughter. Ferdy starts out for America to make good, but failing to make the progress expected he attempts suicide in the river and is rescued by John Brown soap millionaire, who in return for his services requests Ferdy to help him to win the girl he loves, who turns out to be Ferdy's sweetheart. In disguise he undertakes the mission and finally attempts suicide again. The end of the matter is that Ferdy comes into his own through the death of another relative and is accepted by Marjorie's parents and the socially ambitious John Brown marries his stenographer.

"The Little Samaritan"

Five-Part Erbograph Comedy-Drama on Art Dramas Program Featuring Marian Swayne—An Excellent Story of Church Life in a Small Town—Written by a Clergyman.

Reviewed by Arthur W. Courtney.

THE five-part Erbograph comedy-drama "The Little Samaritan", released on the Art Dramas program, is an interesting story of church life in a small town. The story was written by the Reverend Clarence J. Harris. The director, Joseph Levering, sometimes forgets he is dealing with church people. The church board has women on it. One of the men is proprietor of a cigar store. The heroine, who is all that a church member should be, scrubs the dog on Sunday afternoon. The young minister comes to town in a cutaway coat that he wears to church on Sunday. He enters the main door, leaves his walking stick and gloves in the pulpit and puts on his hat before he leaves the body of the church. He puts on a high clerical vest on Monday.

Marian Swayne is Lindy, a Polly Anna orphan living with her grandmother, a fine old character type. She is warned to avoid Jim. His mother runs the choir and keeps Lindy from joining. Lindy's best friend is the old skinflint deacon's wife. The new minister comes to town and puts up at Lindy's house. Lindy's dream is produced in a highly artistic manner, and, thank goodness, it does not run through the remaining four reels.

Lindy gets Noah, an old negro, another fine character type, the job of sexton. The deacon comes to Lindy's grandmother for the interest. She is five dollars shy. The next day Lindy pays. The minister and the deacon discover that the collection money has been stolen. Noah and Lindy each think the other is guilty, so both confess. But neither is guilty. The solution concludes an entertaining story.

"The Defeat of the City"

The First Four-Part O. Henry Story on the General Film Program, a Simple Tale Glorifying Country Life—J. Frank Glendon and Agnes Eyre in the Leading Parts.

Reviewed by Arthur W. Courtney.

THE first four-reel O. Henry story, "The Defeat of the City", is not different from the two-reel stories we have had. It is simply an O. Henry story done in four reels instead of two. The adaptation was done by Will Courtney. Thomas R. Mills was the director.

J. Frank Glendon has the leading part. He is a country boy who comes to the city, makes good as a lawyer, becomes a "prominent clubman", and marries one of the four hundred. Agnes Eyre is the bride. She plays well in the first reel.

The story is not dramatic. It is a simple narrative with two mild O. Henry surprises. The first comes in the third reel. The wife finds a letter addressed to her husband in a book in the library. She goes at once to his office. It looks as if there would be a scene. But the letter is from his mother. He has never told his wife that his mother lives on a farm. The satire is not especially well done. What the husband says and what the wife says when they decide to visit the farm are still subtitles.

The second surprise is at the end. After the husband has spent the day cutting capers on the old farm he is sure his wife is displeased. He nerves himself for her opinion. She says: "I thought I married a gentleman, but—I find I married a man." Those who like a simple tale glorifying country life to the discomfiture of all dwellers in cities will be pleased with this subject. This is a Broadway Star Feature on the General Film program.

"The Silent Witness"

Authors Film Seven-Part Production Is Strong in the Final Two Thousand Feet.

Reviewed by George Blaisdell.

THERE is a dramatic closing in "The Silent Witness", adapted from the play by Otto Hauerbach, the seven-part picture produced by Harry Lambart for the Authors' Film Company, and being released by M. H. Hoffman, Inc. The part of the picture that stands out is in the final two thousand feet. Two reels at least might be eliminated with profit from the remainder. The whole subject does not impress on the side of direction.

Gertrude McCoy plays Helen Hastings, one of the leading roles—in her case an emotional one—that of a mother who, through a supposed death in a fire, is debarred from being a wife. Miss McCoy is one of the older favorites of picturegoers and her reappearance on the screen will be welcomed by them.

Frank L. A. O'Connor is Richard Morgan, in early life the fiance of Helen, and who loses track of her when she leaves home immediately on reading the misreport of his death, later to appear as the district attorney of the county where, on trial for murder, is the son of the two. Morgan has no knowledge there is a son until the mother appears before him. It is in the clearing up of the tangles as we see them unspun in the latter part of the story that we come to the real drama, and here it surely is worth while. Mr. O'Connor and Miss McCoy constitute a strong team. Good support comes to them too from Edwin Fosberg, who has the role of the ambitious assistant district attorney.

Others in the cast are Junius Mathews, who was none too happily cast as the eighteen-year-old son of Morgan and Helen—Mathews' stature was not a part of that of his parents—Aphie James, Helen May, Roulet E. Cotton and Jack Sherrill.

There is one tragedy in the course of the story, but it will hurt the feelings of no one. It is one of those cases where it was "coming to him". The ending is of the happiest.

Falcon Features

The First Three of a Series of Four-Part Photoplays—Released on General Film Program.

Reviewed by Arthur W. Courtney.

THE first three Falcon features are: "The Mainspring," "The Stolen Story," and "The Martinache Marriage." These are four-reel photoplays made by H. M. and E. D. Horkheimer and released on the General Film program. The first one was released on August 17.

"The Mainspring" is a mining story of adventure written by Louis Joseph Vance. "The Stolen Story" is a dream story based on hypnotism with the addition of a Trilby episode. "The Martinache Marriage" is a love story told against a background of robbery, murder and suicide.

These are strong melodramatic stories that open with incident and follow it up with a wealth of incident expertly arranged to maintain a mild suspense to the very end. They keep one guessing all the time. Large casts are skilfully handled. The stories are magazine stories, machine-made but mechanically perfect. They plunge into a welter of incident and relationship based on sound narrative structure. They are photoplays of action in the true sense.

Especially noteworthy is the treatment of crime. Invariably all the preliminaries of the act are omitted. This not only eliminates the repulsive features but increases the suspense. Every crime is a mystery. This is more pleasant than knowing perfectly well just how it was done.

These are absorbing photoplays with a clearly marked individuality.

Busy Days at Metro

Fall Season Commences With New Productions for Thirteen Celebrated Stars.

METRO'S studios start the fall season of picture-producing with work going at full blast. Every one of Metro's thirteen stars is busy creating a new character to add to the portrait gallery for the delight of his particular following, and each is surrounded by a small army consisting of supporting cast and studio workers, with a master-director for every group.

The talents of both novelists and trained scenario-producers have been enlisted to provide all these stars with adequate material and the public with good stories. Prominent among them are Louis Joseph Vance, Mabel Wagnalls, Octavus Roy Cohen and J. U. Giesey, well known collaborators; Jackson Gregory and George Gibbs, novelists of world-wide reputation, and among the scenario writers represented are William Christy Cabanne, author and director; June Mathis, who has written innumerable successes; Lionel Barrymore, John H. Collins and George D. Baker, all author-directors of note.

Nazimova, the celebrated Russian dramatic star, has begun preparations for her initial Metro offering, "The Rose Bush of a Thousand Years", which George D. Baker will direct.

Ethel Barrymore is engaged in the production of "Life's Whirlpool", an intensely dramatic story written and directed by the star's brother, Lionel Barrymore, formerly himself a Metro star. This five-part feature production will be presented by B. A. Rolfe. In the supporting company are such well known players as Paul Everton, Alan Hale, Walter Hiers and Ricca Allen.

Francis X. Bushman and Beverly Bayne have gone "on location" to make the exteriors of their new production written by Max Brand. Charles Brabin is directing this super-feature, which Albert Shelby Le Vino has adapted for the screen.

"Draft 258," by William Christy Cabanne and June Mathis, is the name of the new patriotic production. Mabel Taliaferro will have the leading role. Walter Miller, Millicent Fisher, Camilla Dahlberg and Eugene Borden are prominent in Miss Taliaferro's support.

Emily Stevens is engaged in a production adapted by Mary Murillo from the story by Charles A. Logue, George D. Baker is directing. Earle Fox, Frank Currier, Paul Everton and Ricca Allen are among the prominent members of the cast.

Edith Storey is hard at work on a picture version of "The House in the Mist", a gripping adventure story by Octavus Roy Cohen and J. U. Giesey, adapted by June Mathis. Tod Browning is directing. The cast includes Harry S. Northrup, Bradley Barker, Kempton Greene and Frank Fisher Bennett.

Emmy Wehlen has just begun work in a picturization of Louis Joseph Vance's story, "Nobody", with William C. Dowlan as director, and Benjamin S. Kutler as his assistant. Miss Wehlen's cast includes Florence Short, Ilean Hume, Herbert Hayes, Boyce Combe and Virginia Palmer. Charles A. Taylor has made the screen adaptation of the Vance novel.

Viola Dana has chosen Joseph Arthur's old-time stage success, "Blue Jeans". John H. Collins is directing this production, the screen version of which has been made by June Mathis. Robert Walker, Sally Crute, Augustus Phillips and Clifford Bruce are included in the unusually strong cast.

Harold Lockwood has begun work in "Paradise Garden", another "book" story from the pen of George Gibbs. Fred J. Balshofer is directing it. "Paradise Garden" has a "different" sort of hero, and a "different" sort of story, which the popular star will be able to invest with his own engaging personality. Pretty Vera Sisson has been engaged as leading woman.

Mr. and Mrs. Sidney Drew, creators and co-stars of Metro-Drew comedies, are just completing a playlet devoted to the subject of food conservation. It is called "The Patriot", and is fully up to the Drew standard. Mr. and Mrs. Sidney Drew will continue to complete one comedy a week.

Mme. Petrova is the star in "The Silent Sellers", a powerful five-part feature production directed by Burton L. King. In this production Mme. Petrova has an opportunity to display emotional ability, and also wears some of the most beautiful gowns in which screen patrons have ever seen her appear. Favorites in the cast are Mahlon Hamilton, Violet Reed and Henry Leone.

Italian War Films Draw Crowds

"The Italian Battlefront" Fills Forty-fourth Street Theater—Fort Pitt Corporation Sponsoring American Tour.

WITH film men generally sceptical as to the drawing power of war films, the official war pictures of the Italian government, "The Italian Battlefront," in less than a month's time, have completely shattered all previous experiences and opinions in the trade, according to the announcements of the Fort Pitt Theater Corporation. Not only have the pictures played to capacity business wherever they have been presented, but at the Forty-fourth Street Theater, New York, the gross has exceeded that of practically every legitimate attraction on Broadway. This business has been maintained so consistently at every performance that William Moore Patch, president and managing director of the Fort Pitt Theater Corporation, under the direction of whom the American tour of the films has been placed, was last week negotiating for another theater in New York in which to extend the run.

The pictures have been received with equally substantial support in Pittsburgh and Buffalo. They are now playing at the Tremont theater, Boston, to sitting and standing capacity, and at the Auditorium, Chicago, seating 4,000. Not the least remarkable phase of the success of the films is the fact that the astute members of the trade concede the pulling power of these particular war pictures, notwithstanding their previous misgivings as to pictures of this character. These runs have been in no way forced. The advertising has not been extensive, nor have there been any unusual methods employed in the way of exploitation. The results have been due strictly to the intrinsic entertainment of the pictures, and the demand which word-of-mouth advertising has been created. As a matter of fact, the runs in each of the cities have been absolutely free of paper, save the usual courtesies to the press, with prices ranging to $2.00 up, standing room has been at a premium at every performance for the past three weeks at the Forty-fourth Street theater, New York—this notwithstanding the warm weather.

The explanation for this reversal of all precedent regarding war pictures, seems to be due to the fact that "The Italian Battlefront" differs essentially from any other pictures of like nature which have thus far been presented in this country. They depend upon heroism, rather than horrorism for their appeal. The magnificent natural scenery of the Alps, in which most of the footage was filmed, provides them with an additional interest, not common to their contemporaries. With these two attributes, Mr. Patch, in assembling the picture, has so blended suspense with thrills, and drama, with the romance and lighter side of the war, that there is gained an affect which, in swiftness of action and absorption of incident, is as dramatic and intense as that of any scenario ever filmed.

To Film Chinese Comedies.

Six one-reel comedies, translated from the Chinese by Robert B. Carson, will be the initial offering of the Screen Craft Photoplay Company, launched last week by George W. Shepard, head of a big turnpiking concern. Mr. Carson will also direct the making of the pictures.

The star will be Charlie Fang, who appeared in the serial. After the six films are completed, a series of twelve five-reelers will be made. The offices of the new company are located at 205 Fifth Ave., New York.

Comments on the Films
EXCLUSIVELY BY OUR OWN STAFF

General Film Company.

A BUSHRANGER'S STRATEGY (Kalem).—A two-reel episode of "The Further Adventures of Stingaree" series. The release is a fair one. The story tells of a lone violin player who gets to Stingaree's camp. Stingaree rightly figures him for a police spy. Howie and Stingaree outwit the troopers and obtain for a lost show girl the funds that the violinist-spy stole. They send the spy, barefoot, across the desert. True Boardman and Paul C. Hurst have the leading roles. Reviewed at length elsewhere in this issue.

STAR DUST (Black Cat Essanay).—A 29-minute story of a poor girl at a girl's college. She has no soldier sweetheart. All the other girls have. Each girl is shown in a separate scene kissing a letter from a soldier. Then follows a garden scene where each girl is with her soldier. More separate scenes of kissing. The second reel is a story written by the heroine expressing her lonesomeness. The picture ends with the realization of what she had hoped for, but thought was only star dust, romance, that she should have a soldier. Virginia Valli simply walks through the picture. She is not the lonesome girl. A newspaper clipping shown on the screen is not in the midst of a press sheet. This is a lugubrious story.

PIONEER DAYS (Selig).—This is an historical two-reel picture of the Indian massacre at Fort Dearborn (the site of Chicago) on August 15, 1815. This is an instructive picture. It is entertaining. And it is done on a big scale. In the course of the massacre several persons are tapped on the crown with tomahawks. Kathlyn Williams has a prominent place in the latter part of the picture. This subject is very well done.

HER SALVATION (Selig).—This is a one-reel drama of the old days. Most of the scenes take place in a tough dance hall. A good girl, Nance O'Shaughnessy, goes to her first dance and meets the human spider. One night he goes home with her. Her father finds her struggling with him in her room. A wicked woman, Mame Ryan, neglects her husband and little boy to go to the dance hall. It is customary for her little boy to call for her, take her home drunk, and put her to bed. Sandy comes from the country and warns Nance of "dance hall evils." But she will not listen. Nance and Sandy come upon Mame one day on a pier that as she is about to commit suicide. They take her to her home. Her husband wants to put her out. But Sandy remonstrates with him and he relents. The picture ends with the marriage of Sandy and Nance. The incidents of the story are weakly strung together. This is not a picture that will entertain an intelligent audience.

SELIG WORLD LIBRARY NO. 15.—This reel treats three subjects. A scenic of Monterey, California, shows among other points of interest the home of Robert Louis Stevenson. Tuna fishing in the Pacific, also brief scenes of mussel hunting, and salmon and rock cod fishing, ending with taking the eggs from the female salmon for spawning purposes is in the middle of the reel. The end is an account of the different processes in the silk industry from the laying of the eggs by the moth to the finished cloth. A fuller account of these subjects will be found in the Motion Picture Educator.

THE STOLEN STORY (Falcon).—If you like dream stories, this four-reeler will please beyond anything you have ever seen. The amanuensis of a blind playwright dreams that a play broker has such hypnotic power over her that he compels her to dictate a play that the playwright has discussed with her. This story is told with such power that it-rivets the attention and holds it from beginning to end. Observe that when the dream ends, a dissolve is not used. The director has succeeded in increasing the suspense in ways unfamiliar to photoplay patrons.

THE MARTINACHE MARRIAGE (Falcon).—This four-reeler is a love story told against a very exciting background of melodrama. It begins with a robbery in a low restaurant in Paris. Mystery envelops the thief's daughter all through the picture. Toward the end she is unjustly accused of murder. Her father, who is the guilty one, when he finds that she is accused, writes a confession and commits suicide. There is nothing vulgar about the crime in this picture. It is done in high French style. Margaret Landis, who plays the leading part, wears a "trying" straight black velvet gown that will interest the women.

THE DEFEAT OF THE CITY (Broadway Star).—The first four-part O. Henry story with J. Frank Glendon and Agnes Eyre in the leading parts. It is a simple tale of how much better it is to live on a farm than in the city. It does not hold the interest well. It is reviewed in this issue.

Bluebird Photoplays, Inc.

THE CHARMER, August 20.—Ella Hall is the featured player in this five-reel offering. The picture is ordinary, but probably will hold more than ordinary interest for juveniles. It told how an ordinary girl meets her Prince Charming and later reunites his parents, who are at the point of divorce. A longer review is printed in the review columns of this issue.

Butterfly Pictures.

THE LAIR OF THE WOLF (Butterfly), August 20.—A five-reel offering, written by E. Magnus Ingleton and produced by Charles Swickard, and featuring Gretchen Lederer, Joseph Girard, Donna Drew, Val Paul and others. This tells a complicated and at times melodramatic story. The events center about a man named Cathcart, admirably portrayed by Mr. Girard. Cathcart possesses a brutal nature and marries a widow, only to neglect her. In the course of the story he is murdered, but has so many enemies that numerous people are suspected of the crime. The manner in which the truth is brought to light carries the interest very well.

STRAIGHT SHOOTING (Butterfly), August 27.—A splendid five-reel Western subject, featuring Harry Carey, Molly Malone, George Berrel and others. This tells a stirring story of the old West when cattlemen and settlers were at war with one another. Reviewed at length elsewhere.

Greater Vitagraph.

THE DIVORCEE (Blue Ribbon), August 27.—As is pointed out in a review on another page this five-part subject is a story of the divorce colony at Reno, Nevada. The subject has been handled in a semi-humorous vein by Rufus Steele, the author, yet in the latter half he has injected much real drama.

JUST WHAT BOBBY WANTED.—A one-reel comedy with Bobby Connelly. This was written by Charles M. Seay. Bobby wants a little sister. He finds Aida Horton, the daughter of a drunkard. He takes her to his father's barn and improvises a bedroom for her there. This is only a fair number. Bobby has adopted Aida before in this series, and that was a more interesting picture.

Kleine-Edison-Selig-Essanay.

A DOG IN THE MANGER (Selig), August 6.—William Fables and James Harris have the leading parts in this Hoyt comedy. They portray respectively A. Jackson Bright and Colin Early. J. A. Richmond directs these two worthies in their efforts to accumulate money in ways not recognized as legitimate. Their machine for making sausages from the live dog works perfectly when one of the partners is on the inside to feed out the finished butcher's product, as the other is on the outside to push in the live material and turn the crank. There is a lively chase and getaway as the police interrupt a sale nearly completed. There follow much slapstick when the two volunteer as hotel employes to take the place of striking help. The picture is fast and contains amusing moments.

A TRIP TO CHINATOWN (Selig), August 20.—This is a two-reel version of a Hoyt farce. William Fables plays the leading part. He makes a trip from a Chinese laundry by way of an opium pipe to an Oriental realm where Amy Dennis is queen. The talent of the realm performs for his entertainment. There is an Oriental dance, a snake charming act and a tank episode. This starts with a dive by two girls in white one-piece suits. The queen's swordsman turns out to be a sissy. James Harris is a slave. He is put in a den where he makes friends with a human lion from whose paw he extracts a thorn. This is a fair slapstick comedy.

PANTS (Essanay), September 30.—The story of this mirthful, five-reel production was specially written for Little Mary McAllister, and in it she endears herself still more strongly to her numerous friends— both grownups and little ones. Little Mary is supported by a strong cast. A detailed review appears on another page in this issue.

Metro Pictures Corporation.

THE JURY OF FATE, August 6.—A five-reel Rolfe picture. The story is laid in the Canadian forests, and affords Mabel Taliaferro opportunities for excellent characterization of a dual role, that of a selfish French Canadian boy and his unselfish, whole-hearted sister. An interesting story, with beautiful outdoor scenes. Reviewed elsewhere in this issue.

Mutual Film Corporation.

BEACH NUTS (Cub), August 16.—In this rather entertaining farce-comedy Jerry follows his sweetheart, her father and her father's choice of a husband for her to the beach. There he gets mixed up with a policeman who has an eye on the girls, and eventually manages to elope with the lady of his choice in an automobile.

ON THE FARM (Cub), August 23.—This number of the Jerry comedies shows Jerry in the employ of a moving picture company which is on the lookout for a "thank-you" location. This is found on a farm which there is also a pretty daughter. Jerry, as usual, fascinates the girl and is given rough handling by the girl's sweetheart. A very ordinary comedy.

REEL LIFE NO. 70 (Gaumont), August 30.—In this issue of Reel Life will be found some interesting subjects, namely, "Using the Abalone," "A Boy and a Rope," showing the dexterous manner in which a boy of nine years uses a lassoo, "Beach Sports of California," and "Handling the Mail." A couple of short animated cartoon studies finish the reel.

OUTCAST (Empire), September 10.—A six-part adaptation of the Frohman success of the same name which was written by Hubert Davies. Ann Murdock is the star and does splendid work in the role of the woman of the streets who recognises the predicament of another outcast, a man, and lifts him along with herself to a better level. The morals of the play is not to be recommended for Better Film programs, but the production, which is reviewed in full elsewhere, is unusually entertaining and well made.

Paramount Pictures Corporation.

EGGED ON (Klever), August 20.—This is a one-reel comedy with Victor Moore in the leading part. He is entrusted with a new explosive packed in egg shells to deliver to the government. On the journey an heiress he meets gets his valise and puts the eggs in an incubator when she gets home. Vic arrives too late to prevent the explosion. The story is bolstered up with other incidents. Vic tries to earn five dollars to send a cable for money when he loses his valise. He wears a dress suit with a tailor's advertisement on the back. The heiress pretends to return his eggs to him, but really substitutes real eggs, which are hatched when he opens his valise in the government office. This is a fair comedy. No eggs are thrown.

LITTLE MISS OPTIMIST (Pallas), August 26.—Vivian Martin has the lead in a good wholesome story. It is interesting all the way, with a dramatic denouement. It is reviewed in another column.

HIS WEDDING NIGHT (Arbuckle), August 20.—A two-reel comedy of the knockabout variety located in a country drug store where Fatty is the soda clerk. Watermelons and ice cream are thrown, and chloroform and iodine are used in large quantities. Two sissies appear. One dresses in a bridal gown and is kidnapped instead of the bride. Try as one might, he could not help laughing at this picture.

Pathe Exchanges, Inc.

THE SULTAN'S NECKLACE (Astra), September 2.—First chapter of the new "The Seven Pearls" serial. The number promises a good serial. It tells of an American girl brought up in Turkey who must recover a seven-pearled necklace or become a member of the Sultan's harem. Mollie King, Creighton Hale and Leon Bary are the featured players. Reviewed at length in this issue.

THE BOW STRING (Astra), September 9.—Second episode of "The Seven Pearls" serial. The story moves along faster in this episode and promises much adventure and a fascinating story. In the issue the girl is confronted with the bow string, the contrivance used in strangling women of the harem who flirt. In the number the girl gets two of the pearls but to have them snatched from her at the close.

OVER THE FENCE (Rolin), September 9.—A one-reel comedy featuring Harold Lloyd. The number is a good one and shows the comedian as a baseball player. The comedy hits Mr. Lloyd injects into this reel are immense. We see him as the star player of a fast baseball team. Bebe Danles is also seen on the screen, as are also the other important members of the Lonesome Luke company.

MAKING A WAR POSTER (International), September 9.—A split-reel embracing an industrial-educational and Katzenjammer cartoon. The first half shows the making of a war poster from the time it is conceived by the artist until it comes off the lithographer's press and is posted. The cartoon shows the Katzenjammer kids up to some new and, if possible, funnier pranks.

Triangle Film Corporation.

GRAFTERS (Triangle), August 26.—A five-reel crook story, treated in a farcical way, featuring Jack Devereaux, Anna Lehr and others. This keeps the humorous side up and follows the prevalent order of "thief comedies." Reviewed at length elsewhere.

A NOBLE CROOK, (Triangle-Keystone).—A typical two-reel comedy, featuring Harry Gribbon as a kind-hearted crook who keeps the avaricious banker from foreclosing the mortgage and marrying the widow's daughter. A number of amusing comedy situations are strung along through this, and there is a lively chase at the close, participated in by an auto, a train and an aeroplane.

World Pictures.

THE GUARDIAN (World Film-Peerless), August 27.—A five-reel subject, written by W. B. M. Ferguson and produced by Arthur Ashley. This tells a story of well-rounded interest, simple in plot but brought up to rather strong interest by the excellent work of the three leading performers, Montagu Love, June Elvidge and Arthur Ashley. It concerns a girl whose guardian has a black past, but to save a truly good man. She becomes acquainted with a crook who learns of the guardian's past and tries to supplant him in the girl's affections. In the end the girl falls in love with her guardian and marries him.

TIDES OF FATE (World Film), September 17.—A five-reel story of real life, with numerous interesting melodramatic situations strung through it. It tells the story of a girl beloved by two men and contains plenty of plot interest. Reviewed at length elsewhere.

Universal Film Manufacturing Company.

THE LURE OF THE CIRCUS (Bison), Week of September 3.—A two-reel subject, by W. B. Pearson, featuring Fred Church and Eileen Sedgwick as a young blacksmith and his sweetheart who have aspirations to join a circus. She attempts bareback riding and he tries lion taming. Some good comedy situations result. The action is a little strung out, but holds the interest well.

OFFICER, CALL A COP (Joker), Week of September 3.—A one-reel comedy, by A. F. Stables, featuring William Franey, Jaret Eastman and Percy Pembroke. The scenes occur in a Chinatown section, where the girl is made captive. Yawning trap doors also catch a cop and the hero in search of the girl. Diverting and quite amusing in a knock-about burlesque sort of way.

A DREAM OF EGYPT (Star Featurette), Week of September 3.—A two-reel number of certain unusual qualities, by Myrtle Stedman. Lena Baskette plays the part of a little girl who dreams she is in Egypt, where she saves her mother from the wicked Shiek. This is strong on Oriental atmosphere and the settings and costuming are attractive. The dancing scene toward the close is well staged. Claire MacDowell is also in the cast. A pleasing number.

A GALE OF VERSE (Joker), Week of September 3.—A comedy number, by Tom Gibson, featuring Gale Henry and Milt Sims. Gale plays the part of a country poetess who insists upon reading her poetry aloud to everyone. She goes to the city and gets on a newspaper, where she assists in rounding up some counterfeiters. A typical offering, with a funny idea back of it.

THE CURSE OF A FLIRTING HEART (Victor), Week of September 3.—A "flirtation" comedy, by C. B. Hoadley, featuring Max Asher, Lillian Peacock and others. Max and his wife are each caught flirting on the beach by an amateur camera man and see themselves on the screen next day. Some of the beach costumes are a little breezy, but the action is inoffensive and contains funny moments.

BACKWARD SONS AND FORWARD DAUGHTERS (L-KO), Week of September 3.—A knockabout comic, in two reels, featuring Billy Bevan and Lucille Hutton. The former plays a country youth in the city, who falls in love with a restaurant cashier. Some of the action in this is funny, but there is not enough plot to hold the attention well. Some of the restaurant scenes are also disgustingly dirty and unattractive. The number is below this company's average.

ANIMATED WEEKLY, NO. 85 (Universal), August 22.—Contains an entertaining assortment of news topics in pictorial form, including Madam Montessori's child methods, Canadian flood scenes, and many war views.

CURRENT EVENTS, NO. 16 (Universal), August 24.—War sidelights in France, Italy, England and this country are included in this. Also return of the Root mission from Russia and other live features.

Three Artcraft Stars for October

Douglas Fairbanks, Geraldine Farrar and William S. Hart in One Month's Productions.

UNDOUBTEDLY the greatest array of motion picture attractions ever offered in one month by a distributing organization is announced as the October releases of Artcraft. Douglas Fairbanks, Geraldine Farrar and William S. Hart, three box-office names in productions extraordinary, are scheduled for release during this month.

The first offering will be Douglas Fairbanks in a photoplay entirely different from anything in which he has appeared on the screen to date. The original title of this picture, "Fancy Jim Sherwood", has been changed to "The Man From Painted Post". A comedy-drama of exceptional action and true Western atmosphere, this photoplay offers the energetic player new opportunities to disclose not only situations of typical Fairbanks construction, but incidents of stirring dramatic qualities.

Artcraft's second offering marks the return to the screen of Geraldine Farrar, favorite of screen and operatic stage. As her initial Artcraft vehicle a spectacle in which it is expected she will score even a greater triumph than in "Joan the Woman" has been given her. "The Woman God Forgot" is the new production, from the pen of Jeanie Macpherson, and staged under the direction of Cecil B. De Mille.

As its third release is the Hart-Ince offering, "The Narrow Trail", a typical William S. Hart subject, written by himself for the great popularity of this Western "Bad Man" is the result of unusual ability and individuality. In "The Narrow Trail" Hart not only gives himself a vehicle particularly adapted to his capabilities, but also affords his admirers, the Fritz, a big opportunity to display its merits. In the part of an outlaw Hart gives a thrilling characterization carrying throughout a certain human appeal which makes him the most beloved "villain" on the screen.

FILMING O. HENRY'S "GENTLE GRAFTER".

After careful preparations to engender an atmosphere of O. Henry not previously done for the screen, word has now progressed well along into the filming of the famous American author's "Gentle Grafter" stories, which concern the adventures of Jeff Peters, itinerant fakir. The first picture is "The Atavism of John Tom Little Bear", which General Film announces for release on September 8. It is a two-reeler. Another very strong story soon to follow this one in two-reel form is "The Last of the Troubadours", one of the most startling of O. Henry's Western stories.

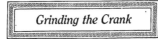

Grinding the Crank

With Thornton Fisher

HOW'D it go today?" I asked a fellow who doubles for the big ones. "Pretty soft today," says he. "All I did was to jump from a seventy-foot chimney, fall off a horse, drop off a train, fall under a buzz car and swim two miles. Pretty soft today, but I may have to work tomorrow."

* * *

Scene—Movie theater.
Time—7:45 p. m.
Characters—Mother and young hopeful of six seasons.
Young hopeful as subtitle is flashed—"What's 'at say?"
Mother—"John and Mary leave for ——."
Y. H.—"What they doin' now?"
M.—"Sh-h, Just watch."
Y. H.—"Where they goin', huh?"
M.—"Keep still and watch."
Y. H.—"Now what they doin', huh?"
M.—"Sh-h."
Y. H.—"What'sa letter say?"
M.—"You wouldn't understand."
Y. H.—"Looka! Indians! Whathey doin', huh?"
M.—"Keep quiet and see."
Y. H.—"What's he hittin' her for?" :
M.—"For goodness sake, keep still."
Y. H.—"Now what they gonna do, huh,"
M.—"WILL you keep still?"
Y. H.—"What we gotta go home for, huh?"
And still they wonder why Ma is using hair dye to restore it to its original hue.

* * *

Song for Quartet. Heart Interest Stuff.

A mother sits in sadness thinking of her only child
Who's working in the movies far away (far away)
While on the window sill stands a moving picture "still"
And through her tears this dear old soul did say.

CHORUS.

They've went and took my darling child
From this, our dear old house and
Are starving her to death each month
On a measly forty thousand.

S'funny, but the film fan doesn't care what color socks the camera man wears, or what the property man's favorite breakfast food is.

* * *

An unfortunate thing almost occurred last week at an eastern studio. An extra man was struck by a falling beam from a burning building and rendered unconscious while the cameraman was grinding. It looked for a second as though the beam would miss his head and spoil the picture.

TO THE READER WHO CAN GUESS THE NAME OF THIS WELL KNOWN PLAYER WE WILL GIVE A BOX OF SAFETY MATCHES.

It might discourage some publicity gentleman to know that there exists in this country a few individuals in an obscure little mountain village who never saw a moving picture and don't know whether Charlie Chaplin is the name of a book or Mary Pickford the title of a song. Nevertheless we've been through some territory lately where the sinking of the Maine was the latest news they've had recently.

* * *

Advertisements received too late for our forms:
Wanted: By a young man, position as scenario writer. Have had five years experience as plumber's assistant, but am tired of work.   G. E.
For Sale Cheap: Projecting machine by exhibitor with several parts missing.   Q. S.

* * *

G. Iva Payne, the famous producer, had a sudden attack of the heart one day last week. It seems that Mr. Payne was engaged at the time signing up O. Hava Sole, the international star. Mr. Sole had just remarked that he would walk to and from the studio, and did not wish the company to furnish him a car or a valet. At this point Mr. Payne collapsed.

* * *

"The Man Who Couldn't Behave" was released last week. The State gave him a new suit and a five case note, and wished him luck.

* * *

Guess we'll "cut"?

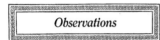

Observations

BY OUR MAN ABOUT TOWN

IT IS very unfortunate that at this period, when plans should be discussed and in the making for the fall and winter season, the motion picture exhibitors of the country are again divided and the time that should be spent in the formation of a campaign for the mutual benefit of all concerned in the business is being wasted by criminations and recriminations in one of the most important branches of the great industry. The situation confirms the conclusions of some of the most conservative and profound thinkers in the business, which may be summed up in the brief statement that it is more difficult to keep the exhibitors within the boundary of bona fide cooperation and mutual effort than it is to control or influence any other branch of the business. One fortunate phase of the situation is that the rupture in the ranks of the exhibitors comes at a time when the common enemy of the motion picture industry finds himself too busy lobbying for and against legislation that does not bear upon the motion pictures. When the common enemy is stripped for battle on the censorship and other questions, the exhibitor is an important factor in the army of defense, his cooperation in the attacks upon forts ignorance, incompetence and graft in the past being second in value to no other branch of the industry. But this service could never have been rendered by the exhibitors individually. They demonstrated their power only when invited, when they went into battle after joint conference on the issues at stake and the best methods to adopt in the campaign against unreasonable legislation and oppression.

* * *

It would seem that in view of the important events that arise in the motion picture business from time to time, and the necessity that exists for complete amalgamation of the various branches of the industry to meet such events, it should not be a difficult matter for the exhibitors to get together and adjust their differences. It would seem so, but it isn't. In spite of declarations made by some very intelligent and able men in the field, the motion picture business is entirely distinct from any other lines of business, both as to methods and results; and the most peculiar branch of it is that embracing the exhibitors. It has always been the most difficult to handle and efforts to maintain a genuine spirit of good fellowship and trade cooperation has been almost disastrous to the nerves of many a good man.

* * *

With all due respect for the men in the exhibitors' field who are actuated by sincere and bona fide motives, records show that exhibitors are a composite of jealousy, partiality and avarice. Good fellows as a whole? Yes, but too many of them lacking that spirit which will permit them to temporarily make a personal sacrifice in order that benefit may accrue to their organization, or the industry as a whole. Some are too frequently intoxicated by acquirement of popularity or power. Others sour because lack of personality or misconception of policy places distinction beyond their grasp. There seems to be a woeful lack of that sublime gift or acquirement known as liberality of the mind, which results in misfortune for the organization which could be made a power for the benefit of the members, individually and collectively.

* * *

Too many of the exhibitors fail to get out of their minds that the motion picture business does not belong to the sphere of the manufacturers' union, the trades union, the retail merchants' association, or any other similar organization. Those who have been very active and conscientious in bringing the exhibitors into one organization, have always maintained that if the principle were properly absorbed the members would find that they partook more of the fraternal spirit than any other organization arising from the amalgamation of those engaged in business circles. But, say some of the organizers, it seems almost impossible to inject the spirit of fraternity into many of the members. At least they fail to manifest its absorption, unless they be in attendance at some social affair. When it comes to a convention or some important meeting many of them take pride in displaying scalping knives and promising to hang to their belts the scalp of anyone who "gets too gay and tries to constitute himself the whole cheese."

The spirit that occurred at the convention in Chicago between the Exhibitors' League of America and the bolting faction, now known as the American Exhibitors' Association, was a serious one. Efforts to bring the factions together by conservative advisors failed and the seceding faction is found applying for admission to the National Association. The situation is a delicate one for the latter to be in, but as its members represent the brainiest men in the moving picture industry the result will no doubt be in full accord with the principles of reason and justice. It is sincerely hoped that no error of judgment will be made in the decision, so that should either of the factions lose in the controversy there will be no excuse for evading submission to it. There is an element in the ranks of the exhibitors that is hoping for a speedy settlement of the questions before the National Association, and there is reason to believe that it will have been settled before this goes to press. But speedy action is not to be so much wished for as established unanimity. Many more difficult questions involving far more vital issues have been adjusted in the past and as a united organization is essential to the exhibiting business, it is not improbable that the Chicago break may be effectually knitted and healed.

* * *

In putting a provisional restriction on the exportation of moving picture films from this country, the Government has taken a very sensible step. It is not difficult to determine what makers of films are making genuine exportations—that exporting films only for exhibition purposes, and none of the companies are so devoid of patriotism as to sell junk films to be used in the manufacture of munitions for the German armies, especially since their attention has been called to the matter by the Government. It is regretted, however, that the junk films must be held by the companies. There is a suffering public wishing that the Government could make an appropriation for the cleaning off the shelves of all such junk. Reference was made in these columns last week to the rank imposition that is forced upon an unsuspecting public by cheap and unprincipled people who are not deserving of the title "exhibitor," and since that time makers and exhibitors of bona fide war films have been obliged to protest through the press against false billing, advertising and exhibition of faked war films. If the Bureau of Licenses cannot see its way clear to deal with these fake show people the police and government officials may be able to devise means by which the offenders may be effectually dealt with, either by compelling them to exhibit only genuine films, or closing the places. The newspapers are not permitted to knowingly publish fake war pictures and cheap show men should not be allowed to display fake war pictures either inside or outside the house. It is a fraud and creates false impressions that are likely to cause trouble.

* * *

During the recent very hot spell of weather many local theater managers complained of a big falling off in business, which complaint was not as justified as one the patrons have against the houses. It is not improbable that the local authorities will be after some of the houses. Some managers make a marked display of signs announcing that the interior of the houses are far cooler than the atmosphere outside. Some signs give the difference as twenty degrees, some thirty and not a few have put the difference as high as forty. A very indignant genteman seated in a picture and vaudeville house on one of the very hot afternoons was so warm over and under the collar that he gave the management notice he would file complaint with the authorities. "I know I was not obliged to come into your place," said the patron, "but I was induced to enter by your misleading sign outside regarding the temperature. Perhaps I will not be able to hold you on that," continued the irate patron, "but I'll tell you where I have got you. You have plenty fans, but to save current you operate them against the houses. I'll tell you what I'll do," added the man as he shook an index finger at the manager, "but you keep those fans working when its hot or I'll spring a thermometer on you some time and get the Board of Health to look into your ventilating apparatus."

ENID BENNETT FINDS A STORY.

It is announced a final selection for the first Paramount picture starring Enid Bennett, the charming Australian actress, has been made at the Ince studios. It is furthermore reported the story is one embodying all of those qualities which are most eminently suited to the capabilities of the star.

Popular Picture Personalities

WHO'S WHO IN THE MOVING PICTURE WORLD
Compiled by the Statistical Department.

LITTLE, Anna. Born in Sisson, California. American parentage. Is five feet, six inches tall and weighs 125 pounds. Dark complexion, brown eyes, dark hair. Miss Little is silent about her stage career other than to tell that she made her stage debut in 1909 and was for four years on the speaking stage. In 1913 she turned to pictures and in the past four years she has played with the Ince, American, Selznick and York-Metro companies, the latter being her present connection. It is as an Ince player that she is perhaps best known, for she was one of the original Ince group. Some of her best parts were in The Battle of Gettysburg, The Black Box serial, Immediate Lee, Land o'Lizards and The Silent Master. And what do you suppose she specially likes to do? All out door sports? Wrong! Her fad is reading K. C. B. in the Hearst papers (advertisement) but she likes press notices, too, we think; most players do.

LYON, Benjamin B., Jr. Born in Atlanta, Ga. American parentage. Is 5 feet 10½ inches tall and weighs 143 pounds. Dark complexion, dark brown hair and blue eyes. Though born in Atlanta, Mr. Lyon's parents removed to Baltimore, Md., when he was four years old and it was here that he first attracted public attention by his work as an amateur. In the summer of 1914 he played with the Poli stock in that city; his professional debut. His picture debut was made October 9, 1916, in a Famous Players production, the title of which he does not recall. Later he went to the Edison company, playing in the Conquest pictures and is now; with less than a year's experience in pictures, a juvenile lead for the Metro. Off duty he divides his time between his high-powered car and the swimming pool, for he is an expert driver and you can leave off the second letter and still be correct. He both dives and drives.

MINTER, Mary Miles. Born in Shreveport, La. American parentage. Is but two and a half inches over five feet and weighs 110 pounds. Blonde complexion, golden hair and blue eyes. Miss Minter made her stage debut in November, 1907, at the age of five, and has played about every child role in the stock repertoire. She also originated child parts in Cameo Kirby, Hanele, A Fool There Was, with Robert Hilliard; A Woman of Today, with Mme. Kalich, and in The Littlest Rebel, with the Farnums. Has also played Shakespearian roles with her sister in private entertainments. She made her picture debut December 15, 1915, in The Fairy and the Waif, a World production. She has also played with Metro and is now one of the bright particular stars at the American studios at Santa Barbara. Miss Minter has won an unusual success for a child of her age, due largely to her naturalness.

KING, James Wallace. Born in Florence, South Carolina. His father was English-Scotch and his mother English-German. Is five feet eleven inches tall and weighs 150 pounds. Dark complexion, black hair and gray eyes. Mr. King made his stage debut in September, 1913. He was for two years in musical comedy and for a year with a minstrel troupe. He made his debut in pictures in May, 1917, in The Village Villain, produced by the Master Pictures, of Houston, Texas, and with startling frankness he writes that he has played no notable parts and does not even add "as yet." Of course three months in pictures does not make for a very elaborate record of past performances, but even at that—! Mr. King sets down as his fads riding, swimming, singing and athletics and adds that he dances. That is an improvement upon all out-door sports, though some singing should be classed as an outdoor sport. We do not know as to Mr. King.

BILLINGTON, Francelia. Born in Dallas, Texas. Her father was an Englishman and her mother an American. She is five feet six and one-half inches tall and weighs 135 pounds. Light complexion, light brown hair and gray eyes. Miss Billington is an old-time picture player, for she has been in pictures all of four years, starting in 1913 in Strathmore, a Majestic, if we remember. At any rate she has played with Majestic and Universal and is now with the American. Some of her best liked parts have been in Naked Hearts, My Fighting Gentleman, The Masked Heart and Pride and the Man. In spite of this predominance of "heart" plays, Miss Billington has no heart, for she ignores a whole lot of nice blank lines in her questionnaire and does not even tell whether she has any fad. Perhaps her fad is not filling out the blanks in questionnaires. Who can tell? It certainly looks that way.

Music for the Picture

Conducted by CLARENCE E. SINN

The Music Copyright Question.

THE drastic tax on music being imposed by the American Society of Composers, Authors and Publishers has stirred up a feeling of bitter resentment among the exhibitors of moving pictures. And this feeling is not without reason. The music publishers declare emphatically that the movement was fostered and engineered by the authors and composers primarily and that they—the publishers—were compelled to come in as a matter of self-preservation. That part of the question doesn't matter now. The fact remains that the publishers are affiliated with the prime movers (the authors and composers) and that all three must sink or swim together—with the odds in favor of swimming for a time at least. The publishers also assert that the bulk of the revenue from the music tax goes to the authors and composers and a relatively small part to the publishers. That does not interest us so much at present. We don't care so much who gets it, as who gives it.

For the past twenty-five years the music publishers have been frantically creating an artificial condition in the trade which was bound to result sooner or later in chaos. They entered a business which was comparatively small, safe and conservative. By over-stimulation they created a business which became inflated, top-heavy, and bound to fall of its own weight. Each firm employed an expensive staff (under salary) to promote their songs and create a public demand for the same. Not only that, a staff of piano players were maintained in each house to teach these songs, a staff of arrangers to make free orchestrations (if the free published arrangements did not happen to lay in the singer's range) and in many cases a bonus or premium was paid to singers for singing these songs. The tons of free music which has been distributed to band and orchestra leaders (usually in specially made arrangements) must amount to an enormous figure. The music publishers taught everybody connected with the show business to regard free music as a right and not a privilege. They have taught us that we were doing them a favor in playing and singing their music—and quite often we were. For a while the profits were big. The writers of successful songs were engaged and placed on the staff of one firm or another—to keep a competitor from getting his future output. Royalties were fair; in some cases generous. But the ever-growing competition and fierce rivalry brought an ever-growing expense. Of the stream of money flowing in, another large stream flowed out. And this last stream has been steadily increasing, while the first—if it has not been diminishing—has certainly not been growing. Authors and composers are now getting as low as one-half of one per cent. in royalties—when they get anything. And now the present decade is expected to repay the sinners for their own mistakes made in the past.

So far as the authors and composers are concerned, they are not the wolves we are apt to picture in our first burst of indignation. They are trying to get what they consider a proper remuneration for their work and talent. So far as the publishers are concerned, they are perhaps the victims of circumstances; said circumstances being created by themselves collectively, and later, suffered for individually.

And now we are to hold the bag.

Nobody will dispute that the writer or producer should have a fair recompense for his efforts; the more worthy his efforts the greater his recompense. Nobody will begrudge the publisher a fair profit for his investment, nor a fair remuneration for his services. All of these people are at the very foundation of the show business. They furnish the biggest part of our working tools and they have a right to pay for the same. But we resent being coddled along all these years, receiving goods for nothing which in the very nature of things should have been paid for, and then suddenly held up and told to "stand and deliver." To deliver not only the price of the goods, but a big premium besides in the shape

of royalties (or as they prefer to call it, a "music tax"). Now I don't believe anybody would object if the so-called "free list" were stopped entirely. It should never have existed in the first place. Musicians and others should be willing enough to pay the price for their music. It constitutes a part of their working tools. But we do object to paying not only for the music, but for the privilege of using it. The argument that in playing the music in public we are "selling it" to the audience may be sound in law, but under present conditions is most unfair in principle.

Why in the name of common sense did they not, if the business did not pay, why, I say, did they not cut out the free music and charge a price for their goods which would make it pay; make it pay everything including royalties which are a legitimate part of the expense?

Exhibitors all over the country are trying to get together (I won't say "organising") for the purpose of fighting this condition. It is respectfully suggested that exhibitors will do well to move carefully. Don't let your indignation run away with your judgment. It is not wise to send your money to any fund for fighting this condition unless that fund is for the sole purpose of getting this law repealed. It has been suggested that exhibitors seek injunctions on the A. S. of C., A. & P. charging restraint of trade. It has been suggested that they be fought as a "trust." The publishers assert that inasmuch as there is no price fixing among them, there is no trust and no restraint of trade. I am informed by a Chicago attorney that the Society's position is sound in law.

This law is a Federal law and as such we are bound to obey it. We have only two courses open to us in opposition to it. We can refuse to use their music or we can work to have the law repealed. Don't spend your money on anybody who tells you you can do anything else, for you will only waste it if you do.

Moving picture theaters are not so dependent on popular music as they think they are. It is true, we like to keep up to date and give our patrons the newest and the best, but in music for the picture the newest is not always the best. Generally the "popular" number has nothing whatever to recommend but its newness. Lots of the old music is available and does not come under this copyright protection. Mr. G. Schirmer has stated in an open letter that his copyrighted musical publications (with cited exceptions) may be publicly performed without restriction. Please do not take this too literally. Mr. G. Schirmer has a splendid catalog, the late music so reduce the sales and profits as to compel the society to try some other tactics. Probably they will take off the tax and increase slightly the cost price of the music. If one exhibitor in a neighborhood pays the tax and uses the popular stuff, and the other exhibitors become frightened at a possible chance of losing some trade thereby—well, they will all run for a license. It is this very thing upon which the society is building its hopes. Will the exhibitors stick together for a common cause? The society thinks not. Will each exhibitors try to get the better of his rival in business, if only for a week or a day? The society thinks he will. We can only wait and see.

Motion Picture Educator

Conducted by REV. W. H. JACKSON and MARGARET I. MACDONALD

The Educator Review

No Results—A Future.

By Rev. W. H. Jackson.

IT has always been the custom of the Moving Picture Educator to look for and expect some special results from the annual convention of the moving picture interests—results which could be turned to good account in behalf of the advance of educational moving picture work. In past years there has always been some general, if not detail, developments upon which the Educator could mould specific advantage; at times there have been emphatic and important events or efforts, which were capable of being used to bring about things more or less progressive in the educational world of moving pictures. Last, but not least, yet of vital importance, was the fact that conventions are usually mapped out with the object of bringing marked progressive and educational progress in the whole realm of moving picture endeavor. Judging by these former standards the convention at Chicago was a conspicuous and lamentable FAILURE.

As empty as Mother Hubbard's cupboard there is absolutely nothing to be found that can in any way be turned to advantage in any branch of the moving picture advance, indeed, retrogressive work of those responsible for the management of the precious days spent in selfish destructiveness rather than dignified unselfish constructiveness.

An Opportunity Lost.

It would seem that never before in the history of moving pictures was a convention held under such favorable auspices and weighted with golden opportunities. The days of evil and dire criticism which marked the early growth of the picture industry have been supplanted by a universal appreciation of their value and a world-wide desire for their development. The President of the United States has publicly asked for the benefit of their far-reaching, constructive and enlightening influence. It seemed, however, that the personal desires of a little President within the narrow conception of his own personal ambitions and immediate financial gains were to take precedence of the wishes of the great President of the world's greatest nation.

The policy of rule or ruin has always resulted in ruin, it rules for a brief moment and is then buried under the ruins with which it seals its own eternal destiny. It may be well, however, too feel that the loss of the opportunity for this convention to seize the immediate opportunity presented to it, may yet prove of greater good. Who can tell what little and unprofitable results would have resulted from national use of the moving pictures under the leadership of that spirit which dominated the Chicago Convention, truly the time would surely have followed when shame would have covered the fact of the moving picture world.

A New Opportunity.

Judged from every standpoint upon which a convention assembles, debates, decides and sends forth its beneficial results to the members dependent upon its activities, we have found the Chicago convention a great waste of time, of labor, of talent, of money and of opportunity!—notwithstanding this the whole realm of moving-picturedom is far richer as a result of this notorious meeting—it is richer in experience, who can say but that it is not an experience much needed. The resultant crisis brings with it a new opportunity. New men—and stronger—have come to the front, new issues are found pregnant with new possibilities; new disclosures of smaller and selfish issues which in time might have become cancerous, leading to new ideas of a larger and surer vision.

It is a most remarkable thing that just at the precise moment when the moving picture is being called to the assistance of the whole world and it is found coincidentally that:

The World Needs the Moving Picture.

A shaking of those forces in control may prove as necessary as shown in many national capitals; we have seen how men in present command have had to make way for "men of the hour."

In more ways than one *this is the hour of the moving picture*, and no one man, or even a limited set of men, can claim to meet the situation; the great democracy of thought inherent with the world's greatest educator is summoned to action, and, freed from the thralldom of every semblance of autocracy, individual or collective; the forces that control the moving pictures can now be mobilised in fairness and safety to meet the great requirements made upon them. It is a wonderful truth that had those forces which sought to control the Chicago convention been successful, the power of the moving picture today would have been so crippled that they could not have answered the three calls from the President, the Nation and the World.

Interesting Educationals

Three Industrial Subjects, Two Travel, One Topical and One Zoological.

Reviewed by Margaret I. MacDonald.

"Using the Abalone" (Mutual-Gaumont).

THE abalone industry is now one of considerable importance on the Pacific coast, making an interesting screen subject. In Reel Life No. 70 a fine illustration of how the abalone is gathered and the various uses the shell is put to will be found. We learn that the abalone clings tenaciously to the rocks, and that the modern effective method of detaching it is by the application of an electric battery, the shock causing it to relax its grip. An exhibition is also given of the buffing and polishing of the shells and of various beautiful articles made from them, among these is a jewel box inlaid with abalone shell, a salad fork, and jewelry set with pearl blisters sometimes found in the abalone.

"Harvesting Scallops." (Universal).

In Screen Magazine No. 32 will be found some interesting views photographed along the shore of Long Island, showing a scallop fleet off for a day's work. The fishermen are shown hauling in the nets, selecting the best and throwing the small ones back to the beds to grow, and unloading the day's harvest. Then there are scenes in the sorting shacks, with an expert opener at work. An interesting feature of the picture is the collecting of starfish which prey upon the scallop. For this purpose a kind of mop is dragged from the side of the boat, to which they attach themselves.

"Fine Feathers" (Pathe-International).

A nicely illustrated description of how the plumes of the ostrich are utilized for fans and boas has been presented by Pathe. Here we learn how the beautiful tail and wing feathers of the ostrich are clipped at certain periods of the year, and of how they are treated, and finally converted into said articles combined with other essentials in the shape of ivory, or silk by way of foundation. An interesting half reel.

"In Tropical Nassau" (Paramount-Holmes).

Burton Holmes in his travels in the Bahama Islands managed to snap some intensely interesting material in the vicinity of Nassau, the principal city of the Bahamas. In the city, as we arrive on Sunday, we find the colored police force marching to church. We discover that no color line is drawn here and that the whites and blacks attend divine service out of doors side by side. A garden party at the Colonial hotel gives us a chance to look over the socially elect. One of the most interesting things in the picture is the opening of a Royal palm bud, aided by the gardener. The natives climb cocoanut trees for our benefit, and we are later introduced to the wonderful silk cotton tree from which a fibre called Kapok is obtained. The baths are also interesting, as well as other sights which Mr. Holmes has filmed for us.

"Madrid to Madeira" (Paramount-Holmes).

The scenes gathered by Burton Holmes during his visit to Madrid and Madeira take us first to the heart of Madrid to wl 2 the city's easternmost gate once stood, known as "Ti.. Gate of the Sun," as the present Spanish name of the street implies. Here we watch the various types of Spanish population as they pass in the crowded streets, including different kinds of conveyances. The arena comes in for a share of attention, and also the Royal Palace with its beautiful grounds. Barcelona is next visited, giving a glimpse of the daily life of the citizens, and also Lisbon and other seaport towns, until at last we arrive at the Madeira Islands, where we learn of the lovely vineyards, and of the famous Madeira wines. A trip on a funicular railway to a position 2,000 feet elevation is delightful.

"Handling the Mail" (Mutual-Gaumont).

Reel Life No. 70 contains a comprehensive illustration of how the mail is handled in a large city. We see the postmen starting out on their respective routes from the 8th avenue branch of the New York postoffice, we learn that in some places mail can be posted on street cars, and we are shown all the details in connection with the collecting, sorting, stacking, postmarking and transportation between branch postoffices and the main postoffice. A pneumatic tube used for the purpose of shooting mail to the main postoffice from an uptown branch is also shown.

"Biography of a Stag" (Educational-Ditmars).

An unusually interesting number of the Ditmars series throws light on the life and habits of a stag. We learn from the picture that the male of the species is ordinarily ferocious, and by hanging a dummy to a tree an illustration is given of what he would do to a human being in one of his fierce charges if given an opportunity. What is left of the dummy when the stag's ire is abated is not worth mentioning. The shedding of the stag's antlers is attractively illustrated, and also the growth of the new ones, which are soft and velvety for some months. During this period the stag is docile, being temporarily deprived of his weapons, for the growing antlers are tender and easily injured. This picture is especially pleasing.

Selig World Library

First Five Numbers Contain Subjects of Interest Illustrated Briefly but Comprehensively.

THE majority of our readers are now familiar with the fact that the interesting Selig release known as the World Library has taken the place of the Selig-Tribune, a former weekly news reel. And it may be of further interest to know the class of subjects included in this new release which made its initial appearance some time back. For this purpose we here give a brief resume of the contents of the first five numbers.

In Number 1 of the Selig World Library we have a glimpse into the Granite Dells of Arizona, after which we are greeted familiarly from the screen by Champ Clark, William Hale Thompson, Jeanette Rankin, and General Pershing, and are introduced to the home of Franklin MacVeagh of Washington which was thrown open to one of the recent European missions, and also to the homes of other prominent individuals. In the number are also included scenes on an Indian tea plantation, and the birth of a butterfly. This latter subject is especially well illustrated.

Number 2 acquaints us with the Ainos of Japan, a people little known, who are particularly hairy and who have been driven into the northern part of Japan by the superior strength and numbers of the yellow race. They live by fishing and hunting. Locations of famous paintings introduce scenes which feed the eye and the imagination. These locations are at Amalfi, Italy, and in the vicinity of the Matterhorn. American ruins present several interesting views of the Alamo, and of various old missions, including the mission of San Juan, and that of the Espado.

Number 3 opens with a peep into jungleland where a huge and aged snake is forced to consume by way of a meal 55 pounds of meat. This is followed by views of the homes of the cliff dwellers. A brief sketch of the whaling industry, shows the capture of a whale by th modern harpoon gun method. We see also the cutting up of carcass, and are informed in subtitle of the chief products of the whaling industry, which are sperm oil and baleen or whalebone.

Number 4 opens with glimpses of famous architecture, in-

cluding the Piazzo del Duomo at Pisa, Italy, and also the Campanile or leaning tower, the topmost story overhangs its base by 13 feet. Sheep herding in New Mexico shows the rounding up, counting, shearing and final dipping of the sheep for the extermination of ticks. The sacking of the wool and the transporting of it to the depot form the closing scenes. A short sketch on elephants, including a few scenes illustrating their usefulness as beasts of burden, and some views of Independence Hall, Philadelphia, and the Betsy Ross house are also included in this number.

Some novel scenes showing human figures in a game of chess on a huge chess board placed for the purpose in a Chicago square open No. 5, which also includes a look into Uncle Sam's money shop, a short study of seals and glimpses of public buildings and places closely associated with the life of George Washington.

New Brand of Educationals

W. L. Brind Enters the Market With the First of a Series of Educational Pictures, Entitled "All About Bees."

W. L. BRIND, F. Z. S., has entered the market on his own account and intends producing one educational picture a month to be released through J. Frank Brockliss, Inc. Mr. Brind, who is a serious student of zo-ology, has chosen as his first subject the honey bee, and has entitled the 914 feet of film pertaining to the busiest insect, "All About Bees". The picture, which makes its appearance under the brand name of the Brind Educational Films, is the first of a series and lives up to its title; for when we have finished viewing the picture most of us know more about bees than we ever did before. The subtitles have been worded pleasingly and carefully carrying the information necessary to make clear the animated illustrations.

The opening scene of the picture shows the worker bees beginning the day's work, ready to gather honey and pollen from the flowers. This is followed by a street in "Bee City" showing long rows of box hives, and a glimpse into a foraging round of the bees, a bed of golden glow in an old orchard. An interesting closeup showing several bees extracting honey from the red clover is followed by a microscopic view of the tongue of a bee, with which it gathers honey. The picture also shows a large bee farm which produces thousands of pounds of honey yearly, on which men are kept busy all the time tending the bees. It explains the difference between the drone, the worker bee, and the queen bee which is not generally understood; and in fact there is little, if any, information concerning the bee that has been overlooked in this picture. Magnified closeups of the antenna or "feeler" of the bee and of its sting are interesting. Scenes showing the remarkably bold manner in which a West Indian "Bee Man" handles bees, washing his face with them, and even sprinkling them over his naked body reminds us that even a bee knows who its friends are. The smoking of the bees previous to the removal of the honey, and close views of the removal of the frames are among the last ones in the picture.

Mr. Brind is to be congratulated on the comprehensiveness and entertaining quality of his screen exploitation of the honey bee; and we do not hesitate to say that it is the best picture on the subject that has been offered.

Red Cross Benefits in Church

Rev. W. H. Jackson of the Moving Picture World Editorial Staff Converts Church Into Moving Picture-Show for Benefit of Red Cross Fund.

THE example which the Rev. W. H. Jackson of the editorial staff of the Moving Picture World has set, and which was given due publicity in a recent issue of the New York Tribune, is a good one for others of the clergy to follow. According to the Tribune, Mr. Jackson, who is the pastor of the Oyster Bay Reformed Church at Brookville, L. I., has kept his parish "at the concert pitch of patriotism ever since the outbreak of the European war." Every Monday evening he turns his church into a motion picture playhouse, taking charge of the performance himself. This performance, according to the Tribune, is a "crack-up, lively, instructive performance, given at the rate of fifty cents per adult, and twenty-five cents per child." These performances are given for the benefit of the Red Cross fund, and have added materially to its bulk. "We do it to stimulate the neighborhood," Mr. Jackson is quoted as saying, "to entertain and instruct, and to secure funds to make up any deficits. I use only such pictures as are shown as will stimulate patriotism, and those of the highest class. The whole neighborhood responds. In this manner we have solved the problem of using pictures as a continuance of the Red Cross work, so that the patriotic and active spirit may be maintained throughout the entire period of the war, with financial profit to the Red Cross."

ITEMS OF INTEREST.

The S. S. Film Company, of 220 West 42nd street, New York City, have produced a feature picture for the New York State Woman's Suffrage Party. While the picture is essentially a propaganda production, it is said to have a strong story running through it, and it is hoped that as well as working out its individual purpose, it will prove a satisfactory attraction for the exhibitor. It will receive its first public showing at the convention in Saratoga on Aug. 29, when it will be exhibited before Governor Whitman, Mayor Mitchel and numerous officials of the State, after which it is the intention of the Suffrage Party to give it the widest possible distribution throughout New York State, and probably throughout the country. This picture, we understand, is being made free of charge for the Suffrage Party by the S. S. Film Company.

In noting the advance of the Industrial Film we find that the E. I. S. Motion Picture Corporation has closed a contract with the Hendee Manufacturing Company for the filming of their plant. The picture will exploit the manufacture of the Indian Motorcycle, which is a product of the Hendee Manufacturing Company's factories. It is interesting also to note that "The Story of a Loaf of Bread," made by the E. I. S. for the Ward Baking Company, has been run in the regular program of 700 theaters in New York City.

CHARLES MILLER DIRECTS NORMA TALMADGE.

Charles Miller, who for two years directed many of Triangle's greatest productions, has been engaged by Joseph M. Schenck to direct the Norma Talmadge photoplays. The first effort of Mr. Miller's new affiliation will be Grace Miller White's "The Secret of the Storm Country," on which Miss Talmadge will begin work next week in Ithaca, N. Y., where the original scenes of the story were laid.

Mr. Schenck's attention was called to Mr. Miller through the splendid work he did under the Triangle banner, for Bessie Love in "The Sawdust Ring," for Dorothy Dalton in "The Flame of the Yukon," and for Bessie Barriscale.

Before he became identified with the world of films Mr. Miller was a well-known leading man and appeared in Henry B. Harris, Klaw and Erlanger and Frohman productions. For several years he was manager of the Castle Square Opera House in Boston. He has been a familiar figure on both sides of the curtain through his activities as actor, manager and author.

NEW MANAGER FOR ATLANTA K-E-S-E BRANCH.

Harry R. Bannister has been appointed manager of George Kleine's K-E-S-E Branch at Atlanta, succeeding J. T. Ezell. Mr. Bannister possesses every qualification, making a successful manager, and it is expected that K-E-S-E service at Atlanta will thrive under his direction.

Bar Harborites Watch Miss Kellermann

Summer Idlers at Maine Resort Take Much Interest in Making of "Queen of the Sea."

WITH all the society of Bar Harbor watching the making of "Queen of the Sea," the new William Fox subsea fantasy with Annette Kellermann, little thought is given to the enormous amount of preparation necessary to begin the picture. Society sees only the spectacular parts of the making of the film—the actual taking of scenes. It does not realize that for months Director John G. Adolfi and his assistant, John W. Kellette, worked out the dramatic features, but spent an almost equal amount of time in preparing.

How thoroughly the preparedness went was shown during the taking of some water scenes in which hundreds of young women and men took the part of mermaids and mermen. They are compelled to remain for long periods of time in the icy cold waters of the ocean and even with the greatest of care accidents will happen. One of the mermaids became exhausted and before the lifeguards could reach her had gone down twice. The lifeguards dived in and brought her to the surface unconscious. Instantly one of the pulmotors which had been provided was working on the girl and in a few minutes she had been restored to consciousness.

In addition to two local physicians who are always within call, a diminutive Red Cross unit is constantly on location. In addition there is a late model stretcher for the transportation of those too badly injured to walk. Those picturesque rocks which abound in Bar Harbor are extremely treacherous and in addition to being slippery as glass at the water's edge are covered with barnacles which are sharper than the proverbial serpent's tooth.

During the work here six seven passenger automobiles and four immense motor trucks have been in use to transport the company to and from their hotels and the location.

To secure settings for "Queen of the Sea" days were spent in the Congressional Library at Washington and in many private libraries in an effort to make historically correct every detail of the picture. Even Grecian mythology was invaded and every article used is not only historically but fabrically correct. Even the rocks had to have barnacles put where no barnacle had ever appeared before.

Stalactite and stalagmite formations were studied in order that even the cave scenes might be absolutely right. After this was found it devolved upon the technical department might reproduce it. In Bar Harbor the company had a crew of stage carpenters, scenic artists and everything essential to the making of the production.

In making a picture like "Queen of the Sea," the weather conditions are not alone to be considered. Another element enters into it and this is the tides. There is a rise and fall of fifteen feet.

With work done for the day, the activities of the director, his assistant and his camera men do not cease. They spend half the night planning out the work for the following day.

That society is interested in the making of "Queen of the Sea" is shown by the immense crowds which have daily witnessed the work from the vantage points afforded by the rocks. Everybody who is anybody in Bar Harbor society has driven out to the location and spent not one day but many.

TEXAS GUINAN IN TRIANGLE PLAYS.

Texas Guinan, whose name and personality are known wherever musical comedy thrives, has deserted the stage for the studio and will shortly be featured in Triangle pictures. As "The Merry Widow," "The Bell of Avenue C," "The Hoyden" and "The Kissing Girl," Texas Guinan has drawn a following of theater patrons from coast to coast who will be eager to see the favorite on the screen. It is believed that the star possesses a personality that will be effectively projected from pictures. She is noted for a spontaneous charm, the ability to establish an intimacy with her audiences, and a smile that has flashed from the pictorial section of virtually every magazine.

Miss Guinan first came into prominence in the role of Alan-a-Dale in De Koven's opera, "Robin Hood." Her immediate success caused the Shuberts to give her a contract providing a four-years' starring engagement. This was renewed six years later, and upon its expiration, two months ago. Miss Guinan affixed her name to a contract with the Triangle Film Corporation.

Advertising for Exhibitors

Conducted by EPES WINTHROP SARGENT

For the Dog Days.

MANAGER Charles Decker, of the Majestic, Grand Junction, Colorado, has evolved a neat hot weather advertisement. It is set in eighteen point display, single column, with a thirty-six point head in three lines. It runs:

DON'T STAY HOME ON ACCOUNT OF THE HEAT!

DO JUST THE OPPOSITE—GO TO THE MAJESTIC TO KEEP COOL.

SAFEGUARD YOUR HEALTH!

BREATHE PURE AIR!

DO YOU KNOW THAT THE MAJESTIC HAS A LARGE VENTILATING PLANT IN THE BASEMENT WHICH FORCES 13,000 CUBIC FEET OF COOL WATER WASHED AIR INTO THE THEATER EVERY MINUTE?

ASK US TO SHOW YOU THIS PLANT. YOU DON'T REALIZE THE SIZE OF IT AND DO YOU REALIZE THAT PURE AIR IS JUST AS ESSENTIAL AS PURE FOOD, TO KEEP YOU IN GOOD HEALTH?

YOU DON'T SWEAT AND SWELTER IN THE MAJESTIC. YOU DO ENJOY THE PROGRAM IN COMFORT.

IF YOU WOULD KEEP COOL AND HEALTHY—PLAY THE MAJESTIC.

VISIT THE VENTILATING PLANT—WE WILL GLADLY SHOW YOU ANY TIME.

This is good stuff to run, but only if you can take the doubter down cellar and show him the plant you advertise. That is what counts, and an advertisement unbacked by the ventilator is apt to be boomerang. There is always a chance to talk about your ventilation, summer and winter, but in the hot months it is better to tell why your house is cool than merely to state that it is. A couple of years ago there used to be a lot printed about ventilation, probably because the well ventilated house was then almost a novelty, but the very fact that it is no longer new is the precise reason why you should remind your patrons now and then of the care you take.

All but the Dates.

The Princess, DeLand, Florida, gets out a four page program that is not pretentious, but rather well done save that the days are not dated and you have to turn back to the front page to figure the showing of any feature that attracts your attention. It would help, too, to get the middle pages framed. It looks rather unfinished, but the type outfit makes the titles fairly yell at you the moment the page is turned; big, black italic letters that have nothing on the page to fight them. There is no ornate display, but it is a program that talks to you for all of that. The back page carries a few house points tersely and strikingly told. Probably DeLand offers no elaborate press service, but the management has done the best it could with what it could get, and the printer has helped all he was able. It makes a good start. One change that might be made is pulling in the waste space at the head of the inside pages, each of which is now decorated by a large Old English "Program." It is scarcely necessary to waste this space telling the intelligent reader that it is a program, and instead there might run a line or two of comment on the stories.

Hanging Up a Record.

Lee L. Goldberg, of the Big Feature Rights Corporation, Louisville, Ky., writes:

In Beaver Dam, Ky., which is listed on the Rand McNally map as having 800 population, we played, on June 1), to 520 people. Also bear in mind the fact that it was a warm and cloudy day. The chances are that had the weather been favorable, every one of the 800 people in Beaver Dam would have been on hand at the Opera House to see "THE CRISIS."

I think our business there speaks volumes in praise of both "THE CRISIS" and the progressive management of the theater under Mr. John H. Barnes, who, by the way, is a prominent banker.

It's not the size of the town that counts but hustling management. Nothing is too big for a big small town man, and we would rather run a good feature in a small town than a large one, for the small town will more readily respond to intensive advertising.

From an Old Chum.

Melvin G. Winstock writes from Seattle that he finds that he can sell film to exhibitors as well as he could to the general public, and so he is selling film. The best film salesman is always the man who can show the exhibitor how to clean up with a feature, and Winstock surely possesses that information. He has had a pretty long siege of illness, but now he is able to make faces at doctors and is in the state rights business for himself. Here's all good wishes.

Slides and Things.

No optician is going to pay the Dixwell, New Haven, Conn., a commission on sales due to poor slides. L. H. Rossiter, the advertising manager, sends in some sample slides that are pretty things to see. We have suggested before that we think Mr. Rossiter does his own printing. Certainly he never said us nay, though he does not write letters. These slides seem to have been printed up at the house. They are not unlike those sent out by the companies some years ago, printed on oiled paper and intended to be sealed between to cover glasses, but these are house matters, and they give a clean and elegant appearance on the screen.

Whenever you think of motion pictures think of this design.

Whenever you see the design think of the best motion pictures.

The design stands for the DIXWELL THEATRE.

The DIXWELL THEATRE stands for the best in Motion Pictures.

This slide is evidently adapted from Picture Theatre Advertising. The others mainly refer to house matters, though a couple are better slides for coming attractions than can be had from any of the slide companies. A five dollar press, a few fonts of six, eight, ten and twelve point type, some carefully chosen ornaments to be used in moderation and intelligence, and you have a slide outfit that will give dignity to your house, and at the same time you can do a surprising lot of house printing even on a five dollar press. We show three samples of Mr. Rossiter's work. The one on the right has the too-common fault of keeping the

play title down. The Burton Holmes cut is a good attractor, since it belongs, but "The House of Lies" is more important than the travelogue and should have been given at least a ten point display, similar, perhaps, to those titles in the middle example. That on the right is done in red and black, the Paramount frame and the house title being in black and the rest in red. Here, too, the titles are overshadowed by the illustrated song, and the illustrated song is too old to be featured these days. Mr. Rossiter has adopted Mr. Blanchard's "Orpheum Bill," which reminds us that Mr. Blanchard has been quiet for some time. Boy, page J. M. Blanchard.

Purely Personal.

Will Jay Emanuel please write and tell us how he likes being a Benedict? Replies will be considered as strictly confidential if he desires.

Printed in Bulk.

We are indebted to Tarleton Winchester, of the Pathe Exchange, for a new wrinkle, originated by Fr. H. Blair, of the Lyric, Mena, Ark., and the Dallas Pathe Exchange. It is a season ticket for a serial; not any particular serial but any one the house happens to be running.

Chapter	1	2	3	4	5	6	7	8	9

NO.

This Season Ticket is good for all chapters of

Mystery Double Cross SERIAL

This ticket is not transferable and will be taken up if used by other than original purchaser.

ADULT TICKET.   Original Purchaser.

Chapter	10	11	12	13	14	15	16	17	18

The value of the idea lies in the fact that instead of having to print up tickets in excess of the probable demand to meet the possible demand for each serial, the tickets can be printed in five thousand lots at a small cost and used for the current serial as needed. We think it would be better to name the house, and to use some box office validating stamp. Where a serial runs fewer, chapters than the number printed in the margin, the excess should be punched out *before* a sale to avoid dispute as to whether or not each number is good for an admission. The name might more neatly be filled in with a rubber stamp, and where more than one serial is running at a time, or even where there is but one, it would be handy to rubber stamp a huge number in colored ink on the face of the ticket, using one for the first serial so handled, two for the next and so on. The name of the subject should be stated, as shown here, the number merely facilitating the handling of the tickets at the door. It would probably help sales for exchanges to offer exhibitors these tickets free. The cost of a couple of hundred would not be much and it would be a good talking point for film salesmen.

Again the Pharisees.

The Princess theater, Argenta, Arkansas, favors us with a copy of the Arkansas Democrat of recent issue. It seems that the public spirited citizens arranged a free Sunday showing of pictures for the soldiers, and the Ministers' Alliance, of Little Rock, and Argenta frothed at the mouth and remarked "for money and worse they would rob and blight our soldier boys and send them penniless and diseased into the trenches." This might have sounded natural a few years ago, but most ministers have more sense these days. Today things are different. The Y. M. C. A., the finest example of practical Christianity that could be imagined, not only uses the pictures, but several branches actually conduct picture shows regularly as a source of income, and ministers the world over use the picture in the pulpit to drive home their texts. But it is too late to start to defend the pictures; they have acquitted themselves, but the latter portions of Elmer E. Clarke's brilliant editorial are worth reproducing as a resume of what part the pictures are playing in the life of the soldier. After explaining that the performance was a free one, so that the soldiers would not be robbed, even of their ten cent pieces, he goes on:

The Ministerial Alliance is making a serious charge against men as public spirited as they are, and men whose integrity is just as high. Now that they have assumed to attack the motives of men of high standing, it is fair to call upon them for their proof.

The Arkansas Democrat asks the Ministerial Alliance to give the names of persons who are contending that Little Rock and Argenta must have beer and red light districts for the soldiers. The statement of the Ministerial Alliance would make it appear that those who have favored Sunday moving pictures for the soldiers were also the ones who were contending that there should be beer and red light districts for the soldiers.

The Arkansas Democrat has been a leader for Sunday recreation for the soldiers and has advocated the Sunday moving pictures. Does the Ministerial Alliance mean to charge that the Arkansas Democrat is contending that beer and the red light districts should be brought here for the soldiers? With all due respect to the ministers for the good they do in their pulpits, such a charge is false.

Myron A. Kesner, field secretary of the War Department Commission on Training Camp Activities, has advocated Sunday moving pictures for the soldiers. Does the Ministerial Alliance mean to charge that Mr. Kesner has favored and is favoring the introduction of beer and the red light districts for the soldiers?

Major General Leonard Wood, in command of the Southeastern Military Department, in which Little Rock and Argenta is located, while in this city asked the co-operation of the people of Little Rock and Argenta in furnishing wholesome recreation for the soldiers, especially on Sunday. He said he favored church for them, but declared that if $35,000 or 40,000 soldiers are turning loose in a town on Sunday without something provided for them to do trouble will follow.

The war department officials at Washington have seen the programs for recreation and amusement provided by the Little Rock and Argenta Federation on Training Camp Activities and have praised them. These programs have been sent to other cantonment cities with suggestions that they be followed there. No objection has been heard from the War department to Sunday moving pictures.

The War Department HAS objected to providing beer and red light districts for the soldiers just as have others in favor of Sunday movies for the men in training.

But let it be understood once for all that the men who are advocating Sunday movies for the soldiers have motives just as high as have the members of the Ministerial Alliance.

There is no reason for grumbling with the ministers because they disagree with others in their opinion on certain subjects. But the ministers in their statements should be just as careful as others not to impute wrong motives to persons who are just as clean in their motives and just as public spirited as are the ministers.

Evidently the pictures have become linked with beer and the red lights in the minds of the reverend gentlemen, but the general public no longer accepts the pictures as the third member of this trio.

A Puzzling Puzzle.

Lee L. Goldberg, of the Strand and Mary Anderson, Louisville, Ky., sends in two papers showing the advertising for those houses, which are now being managed by Lee and Joseph Goldberg for the B. F. Keith interests. One sample is an advertisement for "The Fatal Ring" that is more of a puzzle than most of these contests. You are required to read several hundred words on the new Pathe offering and then form a seventeen word sentence from the bunch. There is no particular clue as to which words to use, and we think that the puzzle will therefore defeat its own aims. You have your choice of several hundred words, of which seventeen can be formed into a specific sentence, and you get two free tickets for a correct solution. Personally we should prefer to pay our way in. The puzzle is entirely too blind, and the solver is required to work completely in the dark. Few people will work long ever so involved a matter. Most of them will read the stuff over once, but if they lay the paper down sore at the task required of them it will not do much good. The contest should be more simple and give more of a chance of winning. In such a case the scheme would be a good one, for most persons like a puzzle though few care to spend more than a couple of months winning two theater tickets. The Mary Anderson News mentioned long ago in these pages, still continues, with the Strand running a similar news on the opposite side of the page, each house getting two columns, and the paper runs the regular photoplay department in between. The Mary Anderson has stuck to this form of newspaper advertising longer than any other house we recall. Most exhibitors find the cost too great, but it is better advertising than a similar space in display, particularly if the stuff runs on the page with the paper's own department—always providing that the house stuff is equally readable. Here the advertising ends seem to have a shade the best of it, for both sections are played up well for notes and comment.

The Mary Anderson overlaps its serials, the first chapter of "The Double Cross," Evidently the Pathe serials pay here. The Herald runs the story version of each serial and gives the house considerable free advertising in return for equally free advertising for the newspaper.

No Poetry.

Gordon H. Place is now settled down in the Editorial chair of Reel Reels in place of George E. Carpenter, and he even tries to versify like Carpenter—and he does—like Carpenter. Perhaps he is even more so. This is a sample:

WHO IS HE?

Frolicksome Fatty, funny film favorite,
Always a-laughing, agile, athletic;
Tempestuous tumbler, talented troglodite,
Temperamentally tender, traumatic, timely;
Yearningly youthful, yielding young yokel;

Absolutely alluring, ambitious, adventuresome;
Rough-housing realist, red-hot reel regent;
Butcher boy, bravo, benevolent barbarian;
Undaunted, uproarious, uxorious, unequalled;
Classic comedian, cheerfully comical;
Kaleidoscope, keen, knightly kisser;
Lively laugh-launcher, languishing lover;
Eccentric, expensive, entertainer elite.

Outside of that he is doing well. We are still waiting to hear from George Manager Carpenter, however. We should like to see some samples.

Only Half the Idea.

The Third Street theater, Easton, Pa., uses this paragraph on its Kraus program covers:

The photographs on the front page of this program are good enough for framing? You can't get a better one for less than twenty-five cents. These programs are free—are you on the mailing list? If not, leave your name and address at the box-office.

That's half the idea. The other half of the idea is not to smear the house name on the front in too large a type. A neat imprint in copperplate gothic in about the second smallest of the six point sizes would be a lot better and would be more likely to be kept on the print if it is framed. The house type used is entirely too large for the space it fills, and the big idea of those Kraus programs is that they are so well done that they serve as well as photographs for collections. They are of real photographic value and much to be preferred to colored covers, but they should be left free of imprint or else printed in keeping with the quality of the picture.

Starting Well.

W. M. Johnson, of the Franklin theater, Oakland, California, in sending in his first program writes:

I am enclosing the first number of what is to be a weekly program for our theater. I should like your criticism on the layout—the makeup. My idea is to have something that the patrons will take home and treasure rather than glance over it and throw it into the gutter. For this reason I have reserved the last page of my program for chit-chat and anything pertaining to pictures and players appearing at our house that might be interesting to the play-going public.

We wish we could show you the inside pages of this program, but the color scheme will not reproduce. It is the always good combination of brown ink on deep cream paper, but the layout is unusual. A double bill is advertised. On page two there is a two-line head and a short column of talk of one feature. This is set thirteen ems with a half inch space at the sides, and almost two inches top and bottom. Set in a ten point type the matter would fill the panel and crowd it, but in an eight it looks so small and compact that you do no realize that it says a lot. On the other side there are two boxes made of triple rule. These lie above and below a scene cut. The top merely gives the title and the Bluebird cut. The bottom starts with "An Odd Inheritance," which is a better catchline for the Clock than the familiar "The Story." You are over on the back page before you know it, and you carry with you a memory of the two subjects because you have not been made to read more than you are willing to read. The house changes twice weekly, and evidently the program is to be devoted to a single bill and not the bill for the week. This is costly, but it is not costly if it pays, and we think it will pay if succeeding issues are equally well done. We hope that Mr. Johnson will send in a proof on white paper some time. The brown ink will serve if the paper is white, and the printer will not mind running a couple of white sheets through the press if asked.

Warning Note.

So many newspaper editors are writing and telling William Lord Wright that his Selig Pastepot and Shears is good that there is danger that presently he'll have to use hair oil on his head to enable him to slide into his office. But Bill has worn the city editor's collar and knows that editors like press agents who do not always write of their own attractions and are willing to pay for favors with fillers. That's one thing too few press agents understand. It goes for the exhibitor press agents, too. Give the editor something besides the press story you want him to run and he'll be more apt to run the press story. "Pay" him for the free stuff with items he can use and cannot otherwise get, and you'll find that he will be less free with his blue pencil.

Heaven Forbid.

In a recent program the Royal theater, Enid, Okla., asks, without punction:

Special 5 part Metro "Would you Sacrifice a Mother" with good Vaudeville.

Most assuredly not. Even a fairly poor mother is too good to sacrifice to "Good vaudeville" of the sort a picture theater can afford to show for five and ten cents. We would not sacrifice any mother even though it were, as announced in the same program:

This is the highest class entertainment ever pulled off at the Royal.

The h. c. e. consists of Mary Pickford "with the Roe sisters in vaudeville, music and singing." You have to turn back to the first page to find that Miss Pickford is to be seen in "The Little American." The program box gives it all to the vaudeville act. The Roe sisters seem to be local favorites, but in a program the title of Pickford should be announced, and the printer should be asked to help with the breaking up of the lines.

Side Heads.

A program editor writes that he wants to run paragraphs in his paper, "and I don't want to use headlines, and I don't want them without," he concludes. Evidently he does not want to use paragraphs large enough to need special heads and yet does not want to run them without. In this case the answer is simple. Set the first few words of each paragraph in full face or all capitals, and separate the paragraphs with four points of lead. The full face looks better, but generally it costs to cut the full face in and adds to the expense, when caps may be used instead. This is a very common device, and gives a slightly bigger show, which run under a general head or with no heading at all. It is particularly good for program fillers of short length.

No Wonder.

No wonder some exhibitors say that business is bad. A Newark exhibitor recently ran Mary Pickford in "The Little American" first run, the films of General Pershing in France and "Paid in Full" all for ten cents. That is plain criminal. You cannot keep on liking pictures in such wholesale quantities.

We Like This.

For once the Third Street theater, Easton, Pa., seems to have coaxed the printer to act human and do a good job; possibly because they did not ask fancy work, but we like the arrangement better than most of the stuff the Third Street has offered, and in the past couple of years we think that the Third Street has led the line for innovations. The new program runs for two weeks on a four pager, a page to a week, with an illustrated front and "Do Children Count?" on the back. The layout is not a new idea, but we like the way they have worked it. Reading the left hand column you get the features at a glance while

the right hand boxes give the brief details. It will be some time before the Third Street can beat this program form, which works well with any average size.

Request Cards.

The Elmwood, Buffalo, N. Y., encloses a request card with a recent program. It is a 2¼ by 3½ card printed:

ELMWOOD
THEATER
ORCHESTRA AND ORGAN REQUEST CARD.
Please play the following selections:

....

....

....

Name ....

Address ....

Sending the card out with the program may possibly attract new business and appeal to the old as well. The only trouble is that too many requests may come in, and it is not a good plan to load down the musical program with request numbers.

Reacts.

Look out for fake press work for the films you use. We have just put down a house organ containing a story. It's a good story if you never see the film, but if you ever do it is such an outrageous lie that it will react against the house and not against the film. No manager can afford to permit his patrons to believe that he is a stupid come-on, eager to swallow anything, nor yet to shake their faith in the value of his word on films. Lay off the too lurid stuff. It will pay. We are coming to more careful press work, but there is still a lot of stupid stuff written apparently in the belief that exhibitors are all stupid. And when you do get stung on an item, write your exchange and the head of the releasing company, as well and make a kick. If all exhibitors did that it would soon be possible to get really good dope.

A NEW HELP FOR MANAGERS

The Photoplaywright

Conducted by EPES WINTHROP SARGENT

INQUIRIES.

Questions concerning photoplay writing adressed to this department will be replied to by mail if a fully addressed and stamped envelope accompanies the letter, which should be addressed to this department. Questions should be stated clearly and should be typewritten or written with pen and ink. Under no circumstances will manuscripts or synopses be critized, whether or not a fee is sent therefor.

A list of companies will be sent if the request is made to the paper direct and not to this department, and a return stamped envelope is inclosed.

The Scope of Photoplay.

BRANDER MATHEWS is one of the few commentators on the drama who writes of photoplay with an open mind. He does not always write from full information but from what he knows he neither seeks to decry the new art form nor to find in it something with which to replace all other forms. He is judicial and generally keen. His comment on the various forms of play is worthy of note. In the North American Review for March he writes:

Perhaps it is going a little too far to assert that the disappearance of the ultra-sensational melodrama is due solely to the competition of the moving picture which can present the same kind of story with a far greater wealth of detail. Yet it is beyond question that the movie can satisfy the ruder likings of the mob for coarse-grained happenings far more successfully than the most inventive and ingenious stage manager can ever hope to do. But while melodrama has had a long and interesting history, it is not one of the higher and more important forms of the drama. Indeed, it is frankly an inferior form because it contents itself with story-telling for its own sake, never hesitating to sacrifice character to situation. Its appeal is to the emotions but mainly to the senses, and more especially to the nerves, whereas true drama, the drama comic or serious, which is really worth while, appeals both to the emotions and to the intellect; it uses situation mainly to reveal character.

In a melodrama or in a farce we are interested very much in what happens and very little in the persons to whom these misadventures happen. In a comedy or in a tragedy we are interested mainly in the persons themselves, in what they are rather than in what they do. However powerful the situations may be in which they are immeshed, we are always watching them to see how their characters are going to react and to reveal themselves under the stress of unforeseen circumstance. In melodrama and in farce we are quite satisfied to find characters painted in the primary colors, but a few bold strokes, presented in profile as it were, whereas in comedy and tragedy we expect the rotundity of real life, the complexity, the delicate colors and the finer shadings of a subtler art. We demand from the dramatist who essays the higher forms that he shall be able to "convince the taste and console the spirit." And Mr. Howells was right when he declared that this was precisely what the moving picture could not do. So long therefore as it labors under this total disability the moving picture can never be a real rival of the drama.

Certain kinds of melodrama the movies can do better than the regular theater; certain kinds of farce also. But comedy and tragedy are wholly beyond its reach; and equally unattainable by it are the social drama and the problem-play. It is true, of course, that the moving picture director can take comedy and tragedy; social drama and problem-play and that he can translate them on the screen; but what has he succeeded in presenting? The mere story, the empty sequence of events, void of nearly all the humanity that gives it meaning. He can take "Hamlet" and put it into pictures but he has to leave out all that lifted "Hamlet" above the violent melodrama out of which Shakespeare made it. He can take "Macbeth," which has a good story picturesquely set forth, and he can show the succession of incidents with the utmost splendor. But he cannot show what gives all its value to this external shell of episode. He can make visible the marching of Macduff's army, and the coming of Birnham Wood, but he cannot disclose the conflict in the soul of Macbeth himself; he cannot make us shudder at the slow and steady disintegration of a noble character under the stress of recurring temptation. All that the moving picture can do to a masterpiece of Shakespeare is to rob it of its vitality and its significance and to reduce it to the purely spectacular level of "The Birth of a Nation" and of the "gross and palpable" triumphs of the "black art," as Mr Howells has termed it.

Mr. Mathews is a student of the photoplay theater rather than of the real art of photoplay writing. He writes of what he sees and does not go beyond. As he earlier pointed out, the photoplay has largely replaced melodrama because it can picture, and show as actual happening that of which the stage play can only tell. Here he makes his point well. The photoplay of Othello gains vividness because it can visualize the tales of daring by means of which Othello won Desdemona. Here photoplay gains for the dramatist's creation. It does lose, unless an excess of leader is employed, the literary quality of the dramatist, and photoplay can never replace the spoken drama for this reason, but it can, and does, offer a greater flexibility of thought expression than Mr. Mathews dreams of. We do not say that this has been done because no one has as yet risen to a full appreciation of photoplay. David W. Griffith has not done this because he is a trickster of the stage, employing the tricks of the stage merely adapted to the new environment. Some of his one-reel productions show him in a far more favorable light than "The Birth of a Nation" or "Intolerance" where he seeks to cover lack of thought with splendor of the Loke Belasco, his is the triumph of trickery; of stage effect. He does not realize photoplay possibilities to the full. Rather it is Hugo Munsterberg who points the way in his book, "The Photoplay." He finds in the cut back and the vision and the close-up the true factors whereby we may arrive at individuality of thought in photoplay, and through these means, intelligently done, it is possible to show the steady disintegration of Macbeth's character as surely and as clearly as we can depict the coming of Birnham Wood, but to do this we must have a man who is free from the traditions of stage and studio alike, who comes to his work with reverence and love, who is not a third rate stage director nor yet a photoplay actor lately risen from the ranks. He must be, at heart, a photoplay producer, working a new art by its own methods and not the discarded mechanism of the stage. He must be able to use and yet not abuse the vision and close-up. He must have a vital reason for each cut-back and not merely cut two scenes, one into the other, to get a large number of scenes. And everything he does must be intended for showing on the screen. We are sick—ghastly sick—of these stories of six miles of film made for a six thousand foot production. That does not argue intelligent direction. It is the work of a man who does not know what he wants trying to find out, and the result can only be imperfect and incomplete. There will be no perfect plays until there comes into existence a class of men who can write perfect continuities and others who can realize these scripts in action from the continuity, with nothing added nor subtracted. Then, and not until then, shall we have good photoplays, and in those days there can be no complaint that photoplay is merely an imperfect visualization of stage plays or current fiction, nor will it be written that the producer but imperfectly translated the borrowed theme. Fewer themes will be borrowed, for the artist-producer will know that not all plays are suited to the screen any more than all these are suited to the stage or will make interesting fiction. He will select only such themes as lend themselves to the medium in which he works, but he will give those themes so adequate a production that there will be felt no lack of the finer qualities that give to the spoken play and the printed story their charm and appeal. Photoplay will never supplant the spoken drama. It can and will rise to an equal level, but not until there comes into being a class of artist-producers to replace the present day men with their little bags of cheap tricks. Mr. Matthews writes dispassionately of what he sees, but apparently he does not see beneath the surface.

The Time to Work.

Just now ice is selling at higher prices per ton than it did last winter, but last winter the ice man was stocking his house against the time he could sell ice at a profit. In the same way now is the time to be writing good plays against the day they come in demand again. Get your storehouse full against the time of need, but don't try to peddle ice when coal is more in demand.

Your Troubles.

Don't spoil what little chance you have of selling by telling your troubles to the editors. We know one man who was ruined by a lawsuit and another who is hurting his standing by sending in scripts with long letters telling all his troubles to the editors. It will not influence the editor to buy scripts and it may, and often does, cause him to return the stuff unread because he has spotted the author.

Projection Department

Conducted by F. H. RICHARDSON.

Manufacturers' Notice.

IT IS an established rule of this department that no apparatus or other goods will be endorsed or recommended editorially until the excellence of such articles has been demonstrated to its editor.

Important Notice.

Owing to the mass of matter awaiting publication, it is impossible to reply through the department in less than two to three weeks. In order to give prompt service, those sending four cents, stamps (less than actual cost), will receive carbon copy of the department reply, by mail, without delay. Special replies by mail on matters which cannot be replied to in the department, one dollar.

Both the first and second sets of questions are now ready and printed in neat booklet form, the second half being seventy-six in number. Either booklet may be had by remitting 25 cents, money or stamps, to the editor, or both for 40 cents. Cannot use Canadian stamps. Every live, progressive operator should get a copy of these questions. You may be surprised at the number you cannot answer without a lot of study.

Get Into the Papers.

Brother W. W. Brumberg, Local Union 298, Tucson, Arizona, sends in clipping from the Arizona Daily Star, Sunday, July 22 issue, with the following note:

What do you think of it, Brother Richardson? At last we are recognized in a literary way!

What do I think of it? Why I think it is a corking good stunt. The article in question is headed: "If You Like the Show It's the Fault of the Operator." The writer then proceeds in the first really intelligently written article I have ever seen in a daily paper, dealing with the operator and the operating room, to call attention to the importance of the operator and his work in the scheme of affairs as applied to the public. The writer says, in part:

The moving picture operator is one of the most important factors in the great moving picture business. Next time you go to a show and are pleased with the program, and feel that you should stop and tell the manager as you go out that you are pleased, don't forget to say a word about the projection, for ten to one there was a good operator in the booth. If there hadn't been you would not have liked the show no matter how laughable the comedy or stirring the drama. Consider the movie operator; he is worthy of your consideration.

As in the case of a piano-player, if the record is merely pumped through not much in the way of real music is obtained. But the one who operates a mechanical piano with feeling can get results that approximate the effects of a musician. The same applies to the hand-turning of a motion picture projecting machine when judgment is used in regulating the manner of screening a film.

Photoplays are recorded on a narrow strip of celluloid. The individual pictures are one inch wide by three-quarters of an inch deep. That makes sixteen pictures or exposure to the foot of film. A reel means a thousand feet of exposed film or 16,000 pictures less that amount of footage given to subtitles, which may be anywhere from a hundred to two hundred feet in the average photoplay. Usually twenty minutes is allowed for projecting a reel, though sometimes it is done in less time. Unless it be comedy, the result is not satisfactory to the spectator.

Improvements are being made right along on the many different types of projecting machines in use. The aim is to get a flickerless succession of pictures on the screen to reproduce perfectly the animation of real life. Owing to the intense heat of the electric light used the film is not permitted to stop a fraction of a second or it would burn.

To guard against fire all cities have strict regulations covering the construction of projection booths. They are built of sheet-iron and asbestos. Lanterns are equipped with safety slides to cut off the light should anything stop the unwinding.

At the other end of the theater stands the screen. This may be of any material that will give a white surface. Screens vary in size, the average being fourteen by eighteen feet. The little film scene thrown on it would be enlarged 48,384 times. Sometimes the enlargement exceeds even this, depending on the size of the screen.

As a result of the popularity of the motion picture projection is a new line of work and gives employment to many men at good wages. The projector must be an electrician and a skilled mechanic. In most places the craft is organized and many municipalities license motion picture machine operators. Besides "grinding," the projector has plenty to keep him busy.

He must watch his lights continually, keep his picture "framed"—centered on the screen—and use discernment every minute of the time if the people are to be pleased. They are not slow to manifest impatience when the projection is not up to standard.

It is the positive film which is projected. In the unreeling it often tears, when repairs must be made. The projector has to watch his lens for the proper focus. All in all the work is hard on the eyes because of the brilliancy of the lights and sometimes the booths are hot to work in.

Notwithstanding, the work has its rewards and is interesting. Yet not many people stop to think how much of their pleasure in a picture and impression of a film favorite depends on the projection.

I have printed considerable of the article to the end that those who wish may use it as a basis for a similar article for their home paper. The limelight, my brother, may be sneered at by those who do not enjoy its glare, but it has a tremendous value just the same. The man of today who plays the modest roll and hides his light under a bushel may be admired by a small circle of friends with whom he comes into direct personal contact, but he is not apt to burn up much gasoline. Once educate the public as to the importance of projection and there will be a demand for high class work, because friend patron will be able to locate the trouble when twelve-year-old Willie shoots a bunch of jumping shadows at the screen; also he will demand the elimination of the aforesaid shadows, which mean the elimination of dear little Willie and the substitution, in his stead, of an operator. And the change will, to the amazement of the manager, prove a splendid investment, because while Willie and his shadows are low in first cost, they bring in little at the box office. I don't know who posted the Arizona reporter, or who got him started on the job, but he certainly did it up brown. Other articles should try and get similar work from other cities and towns should try and get similar articles into their home papers. If desired I will publish a series of such short articles in this department, which may be lifted bodily and given to the local scribe.

Most Excellent Device.

While in Lincoln, Nebraska, Brother R. A. Lindsay presented to me two devices which have, it seems to me, very distinct merit. The one consists of an ordinary near-ivory toothbrush handle, which has been cut off just behind the brush and filed sharp at both ends. It is then used to scrape emulsion from the tension springs. Strikes me it is a most excellent and efficient tool for the purpose. Certainly the steel of the springs, or shoes, could not be in the least degree roughened, and the blade is an extremely important point, since any roughing of the polished steel will only serve to aggravate the trouble.

The other implement consists of a safety razor blade set in a spool as per sketch. Cut off about one and one-half inches from the harlue end of a broom handle and saw a slot in it at an angle as shown. Bore a hole, in proper position, and insert a handle. Then wedge a safety razor blade in the slot. The advantage of this tool is that you may remove the emulsion, when making a splice, at one swipe, and at the same time have a perfectly straight edge, since you lay the blade edge on the film crosswise of the length of the film. The secret of success with this implement is, keep the blade edge perfectly sharp; and for this pur-

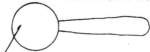

pose it is necessary to have a small but good oil stone on the rewinder bench, so you may touch up the edge occasionally. It is a dandy little tool and just the thing for the purpose. Brother Lindsay says: "Use Enders or Keen Kutter blades."

Rise Above the Average.

In moving picture operating, as in everything else, there is plenty of room at the top. The ladder of fame, however, is always crowded at its lower rungs, because while sliding down hill, or even walking along the level is easy, it takes labor to mount a hill. There are many kinds of men. There is the constitutional shirker. The lazybones whose ambition rises not one inch above three meals a day and a place to sleep. He envies the man who is far up on the ladder, but makes no effort to raise himself because that would require work. There are many men who will work and slave under orders from another man.

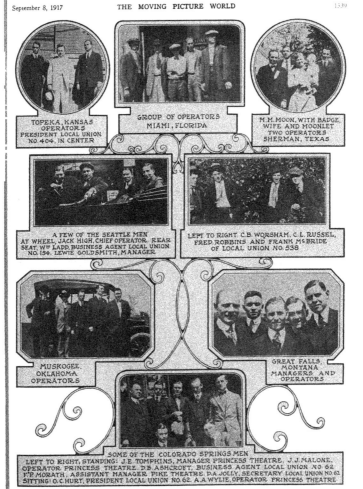

TOPEKA, KANSAS
OPERATORS
PRESIDENT LOCAL UNION
NO. 404, IN CENTER

GROUP OF OPERATORS
MIAMI, FLORIDA

M. M. MOON, WITH BADGE,
WIFE AND MOONLET
TWO OPERATORS
SHERMAN, TEXAS

A FEW OF THE SEATTLE MEN
AT WHEEL, JACK HIGH, CHIEF OPERATOR. REAR
SEAT, WM LADD, BUSINESS AGENT LOCAL UNION
NO. 154. LEWIE GOLDSMITH, MANAGER

LEFT TO RIGHT, C. B. WORSHAM, C. L. RUSSEL,
FRED ROBBINS AND FRANK McBRIDE
OF LOCAL UNION NO. 538

MUSKOGEE,
OKLAHOMA
OPERATORS

GREAT FALLS,
MONTANA
MANAGERS AND
OPERATORS

SOME OF THE COLORADO SPRINGS MEN
LEFT TO RIGHT, STANDING: J. E. TOMPKINS, MANAGER PRINCESS THEATRE, J. J. MALONE,
OPERATOR PRINCESS THEATRE. D. B. ASHCROFT, BUSINESS AGENT LOCAL UNION NO. 62
F. P. MORATH, ASSISTANT MANAGER PIKE THEATRE, D. A. JOLLY, SECRETARY LOCAL UNION NO. 62
SITTING: O. C. HURT, PRESIDENT LOCAL UNION NO. 62, A. A. WYLIE, OPERATOR PRINCESS THEATRE

Place them under a foreman and they will almost work their fingers off to please. But that is their sole ambition. Without a boss they would scarce raise a finger. To them the idea of earning advancement through hard work and initiative is as a strange language. They know it not. Others will work hard just so long as the boss is looking, but once his back is turned their ambition ceases instantly, replaced by the how-little-can-I-do-and-get-by idea. They, of course, never get anywhere. They "hold their job" until the boss gets wise, and then move on, cursing their "hard luck."

But here I am, meandering around like a lost sheep. What I really want to say is that the man who takes up operating for his profession should understand very thoroughly that his success or failure lies in his own hands. He should also understand that success does NOT consist in delivering a screen result which will just barely hold his job and get him the union scale. The union scale is a very excellent and very necessary thing, but it is only a minimum which must be paid the poorest men. The real man will strive to create for himself a market at advanced figures. He will not be satisfied with the dead level. He will have self confidence and initiative. He will seek to prove to friend manager that he is WORTH more than the man down the street. To do this he must work and study. He must experiment. He must apply brains to his work. The process will be long, and will at times be discouraging, but persistence will win. But it may not be quite so slow in future as in the past, because theaters are increasing in size and in excellence. That means better jobs. It means a higher type of theater manager. It means more machinery and better machinery. And in the end it will mean a demand for higher intelligence and skill in the operating room, and then is when the student, the hard working grubber, will win out and raise himself above the average. But the drone will never win anything but the chance to exist. He will never forge ahead in operating or in anything else.

And (whisper) maybe one reason for low wages is to be found in the fact, for fact it is, that, taken as a class, operators cannot claim any very extended scientific knowledge of their business. Is this not so?

Mind you I do not mean that friend manager is going to rush up, fall on the skilled man's neck and weep. He is not that variety of hairpin. By and large he is a business man, and is in the market to purchase service as cheaply as may be. But no man will dispute the fact that high grade service sells better than low grade, and Mister Manager is slowly awakening to the fact that, when it comes to operating, there is service and service; also that the high grade man may be cheaper than the low grade one even at an advanced figure. Witness the fact that we have operators in well organized cities all over the country receiving more than, and some almost double, the union scale, because while the manager can get plenty of men at the scale, he cannot get the class of service he wants at that figure. And where that condition exists why are not YOU the one to get the job? Ask yourself that pointed question, and hold close communion with yourself until you get the answer. Get out of the rut. Be a winner. Rise above the dead level of the average.

From Little Rock.

L. B. Herring, Little Rock, Arkansas, shies his hat into the ring as follows:

In June 9 issue C. E. Linstruth, Carthage, N. Y., tells us a test lamp will not burn to c. p. across the arc lamp terminals, when taking current through a rheostat, and the are not burning. With regard to this, a rheostat designed to deliver 25 amperes when working in conjunction with a D. C. projection arc, has approximately 2.5 ohms resistance. Using an ordinary 16 c. p. incandescent carbon filament globe, which pulls about .5 of an ampere, you would get (Ohms law) a drop of (C X R = E): ½ x 2½ = 1¼ volts drop through the rheostat, and this would not be sufficient to seriously affect the c. p. of the lamp.

In the same issue, under the caption "Can You Dope It Out," you present a problem, as follows: on a 110 volt line, with three 25 ampere rheostats connected thus:

CUTTING ADDITIONAL RESISTANCE
IN MULTIPLE (PARALLEL)WITH RESISTANCE
ALREADY IN USE, HAS SAME EFFECT AS
INCREASING DIAMETER OF RESISTANCE
WIRE WOULD HAVE.

And right there friend Herring gets his dates twisted, or at least seems to, for he first says we would get nothing at the arc, and then says we would get fifty amperes. His figures are, however, correct. The single rheostat would have about 2.5 ohms resistance and the two in multiple exactly half as much as the single resistance alone, hence there would be a total rheostatic resistance of 2.5 plus 1.25 ohms, equals 3.75 ohms opposed to the line voltage of 110. In addition to this there would be the arc resistance, which would be somewhere in the neighborhood of fifty volts drop, or that number of volts divided by amperes flowing as expressed in ohms. And right there is the sticker, for how can we determine the arc resistance without first knowing amperage, and how can we determine amperage without first having accurate knowledge of arc resistance. The mere fact that they are twenty-five amperes rheostats proves nothing, because they are

now hitched in series with each other, and we must therefore take the entire combination as a base. Perhaps the following will be as nearly accurate as we could figure it. The rheostat combination presents a total resistance of 3.75 ohms in itself. If two and one-half ohms in series with an arc supplies 25 amperes then 3.75:2.g:25::X, which simple problem gives up 16 amperes plus. Am I right or wrong in figuring the matter in that way? Brother Wallis, Hamilton, Ontario, figures it out at 16.5333 plus amperes. His knowledge of the connection is beyond criticism, but, after remarking that the arc amperage and resistance are unknown quantities, divides 62 (110 — 48) by 3.75, the total resistance of the combination. This may be correct, but I must confess I don't quite follow his line of reasoning at this point.

John Solar, Watertown, N. Y., also sent in an approximately correct reply in another form, but he assumes an arc voltage, which has, I think, led him into error. His answer is 17.6 amperes. Chas. B. Stears, Vancouver, B. C., had the right idea, btu got twisted in his figures.

New York City Operators Attention.

In an endeavor to complete the organization of Greater New York City operators, Local Union 306 I. A. T. S. E. & M. P. M. O. has lowered the initiation fee, for a limited period only, to twenty-five dollars. Also to show its good faith in making it entirely possible for every competent New York operator to join, the fee will be accepted as follows: $6.25 with the application, $6.25 when he is examined, and the balance, $12.50 when he is initiated.

On January first the initiation fee will be raised to $75.00, the intention being merely to give the operators who have objected to joining on the score that the initiation fee is too high to get in on the "ground floor." Twenty-five dollars is, by comparison, very reasonable indeed. Many unions in far smaller cities than New York are charging $100.00.

The editor is not in favor of a too-small initiation fee. Experience has shown that the man who "gets in for a song," drops out at the slightest pretext. He figures he can drop out for a year, save his dues, join again and actually save money. But with a seventy-five or one hundred dollar fee it is very different. When a man has that sum invested he is mighty careful what he does. A hundred dollars is a lot of money to the operator. It represents a whole month of hard work. It is harder to get him in at that figure than for a small fee, but once in he is there to stay. It is quite true that many managers who are not over anxious to have their operator join the union (though they themselves may be enthusiastic members of the Exhibitors Union), claim that a fifty or one hundred dollar initiation fee is "robbery." They point with righteous indignation, to the fact that their own initiation fee in their union (League) was a mere, piffling five dollars, or maybe only one. And they are exhibitors too! Yep, Mr. Exhibitor, that may all be true, but by the time your union (League) has done for exhibitors what the I. A. T. S. E. & M. P. M. O. has done for operators, it will be justified in charging a respectable initiation fee. Meanwhile the last objection each can possibly be raised by the New York City outsider to joining is temporarily removed, and it is up to him to get inside the fold. Don't stand outside and whine like a kid with a sore toe, saying "The union isn't run right!" Get in, where you belong, and help run it right. It may not be perfect; in fact most human institutions are not, but it is the best thing you have, and the sooner you are inside the better it will be for both you and the union. Get busy!

They Don't Work Out.

It is amazing what a number of inventions reach the office of the editor, and how very few have any real merit, notwithstanding the fact that the average inventor is thoroughly imbued with the idea that he has a world beater. Recently a correspondent in Italy wrote concerning an incandescent lamp, which he firmly believed would revolutionize projection. It, so he said, gave a marvelous amount of illumination from an extremely small filament. I advised him to forward one or more of the lamps to a well known Cleveland corporation, and now have their report on same. Briefly it is to the effect that the lamps closely resemble those used in the Pathescope Home Moving Picture Machine, which same cannot be recommended for anything greater than a six foot picture.

I mention this incident becase it is fresh in memory, the report on the lamps only having come in today. I could mention dozens of others, quite similar, which have occurred recently, and the record of eight years would run into the hundreds; I almost said thousands. I am right now investigating the merits of an invention which, if it works out, ought to revolutionize the projection of pictures. But there is the rub—if it works out! I am hoping that it will, but am industriously engaged in believing it will not. In the vernacular, I am from Missouri.

And there are some rather sad incidents in this connection. Some time ago an operator insisted that I examine a projection machine he had evolved, which was, according to his enthusiastic imaginings, going to be a world beater of the nth power. Having grave suspicions as to what was coming I did my best to sidestep. I tried to shoo him off on some one else, but it was no go. I was the elected one, and no other would do.

So, I finally consented, and set a time. The stupendous wonder was in his home, but when I arrived it seems some unforeseen thing had occurred which prevented its performance. His wife, almost with tears in her eyes, hoped I would find it good, for, said she, "he has spent every cent he could rake and scrape for three years in perfecting it, and in the process had reduced his family almost to actual hunger."

A cursory examination told the story and told it unmistakably. The machine was a conglomeration of ideas, some already patented, some entirely in use, and none new. Bluntly, the machine was not worth a single copper, except what it would bring far old iron. Now here was a sad duty. If I told the truth it would probably make of the man a mortal enemy, but would prevent his spending more money—throwing good money after bad; also the wife would hate me as the man who had pricked their bubble of wealth. On the other hand I could be non-committal, and thus escape a disagreeable duty—and one which fails to the lot of this editor oftener than you might imagine. And what would YOU have done in such circumstances? The fault of course lay with the man himself in not having ascertained what had already been done along the lines he proposed to follow. What I did was to intimate to the woman that under no circumstances ought any more money be expended on the machine, and then I told the man the plain, unvarnished, baldheaded truth. It hurt like using caustic, but there was nothing else to do, so I did it. I gave him such data as would enable him to prove many of the things I told him, and let it go at that.

But to get back to my subject, it is a fact that a comparatively insignificant number of the many ideas sent in are of value. Still there is an occasional one, and that one is the wheat among the chaff. It is to be devoutly hoped that the one I spoke of as under investigation will prove to be of the latter, but——? So far as projection machines which utilize present principles, it is extremely doubtful if a projector of such extraordinary value as to force it into an already well-covered field could be evolved by an individual. He would be working alone, probably hampered for capital and proper machinery, and in competition with several large, splendidly equipped corporations. That the individual, working alone, might easily evolve a valuable, or an even extremely valuable improvement as applied to present projectors, is quite possible, but I would strongly advise against attempting to "invent" a whole projector, unless it be one in which entirely new principles are involved—such as, for instance, a non-intermittent machine, the practicability of which, by the way, I shall believe when I see it in actual commercial form.

One possible avenue for inventors might be a rewinder which will be reasonable in price, geared to rewind in not less than ten minutes (but with a special arrangement whereby film may be rewound rapidly upon occasion), with an automatic cutoff to stop friend motor when the rewinding is finished. Such a machine, if reasonable in price and well made, would have the undivided and enthusiastic support of this department, since rapid rewinding works many thousands of dollars of damage to films every month.

Aisle Lighting.

The Brookins Company, Cleveland, Ohio, noticed an article in the Department, and was moved to write thusly:

We notice the lighting diagram on page 931, August 11 issue. Permit us to say that, after giving eleven years to the study of interior illumination we conceived the idea of lighting theatre aisles from a little above the floor level, thereby making it possible to eliminate all exposed lights during the performance. Enclosed circular will give you an idea of what our proposition is, and any further information will be gladly supplied.

The fact that eleven years was consumed in a study of interior lighting does not necessarily prove that the student is qualified to pose as an authority on *moving picture theatre lighting*. To give competent advice as regards moving picture theatre lighting one must not only understand the correct principles of interior lighting, but must also understand, and very thoroughly understand that subject AS APPLIED TO THE PROJECTION OF MOTION PICTURES. Lighting which would be ideal for a dramatic theatre, fails utterly to meet the requirements of projection.

After having studied this subject pretty closely for some considerable time, and having viewed many hundreds of moving picture theatres, lighted in almost every imaginable way, ranging from very nearly perfect to simply awful, I am convinced the two things to receive first consideration are (A) conceal all lights from the screen, (B) conceal all lights from the eyes of the patron.

In addition to this there must be no bright spots, either on ceiling, wall or floor, which same will be within view of any patron as he or she look at the picture on the screen. The light must be *evenly distributed*, and should be projected either straight downward or ahead. Given these conditions, with the direct rays prevented from reaching the screen, it is amazing what an amount of light there may be without any apparent injury to the picture.

The Brookins plan fails in two important particulars. First, while it lights the aisles, it does not supply any light to the auditorium itself, leaving the patron at the end of the row of seats without a ray of light by which to find his or her seat. Second, it spots the aisle with bright patches of light, and this is trying to the eyes of the patron seated in a dark auditorium and looking over these bright spots at a picture in the distance. The Brookins plan has value, I should imagine, in some ways, but I cannot agree with its employment as a sole means for moving picture theatre lighting, or with its use at all in that connection, unless the light be so diffused that it will cover the whole aisle floor with a subdued glow of light, without bright spots.

Non Intermittent Projector.

And now comes Christian Andersen, Portland, Oregon, who, being duly unsworn, declares and says that he is the inventor of a projection machine which uses a continuously-running film, and delivers a first-class result on the screen. He asks us to have some friend in Portland examine it and report his findings. The thing is done, according to Andersen, by means of a moving prism, which synchronizes with the film movement. I cannot, of course, pass any intelligent judgment until I have actually seen the method by which the synchronism of movement is accomplished, but it must, perforce, be a movement which will not be affected by wear to any appreciable extent. However, I will have the machine examined, and if it seems to warrant investigation, will try and have same sent to New York City for further, personal investigation. Until then I have nothing to say concerning the feasibility to Friend Andersen's projector, except to hope that which seems too good to be true, really is true.

Good Stunt.

Brother J. O. Thomas, Vancouver, B. C., has evolved what looks to yours truly like a corking good stunt, and one which might well be adopted by all machine manufacturers. It consists of an arm attached to the lamphouse door, as per illustration. To the end of this arm,

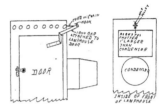

by means of a hook, is attached a flexible wire cord, or a very small metal chain. This cord, or chain, passes into the lamphouse through a small hole located near its top. It then passes over a small metal pulley, and down, attaching to the upper end of an asbestos shutter, which is thus made to raise or lower as the lamphouse door is opened or closed. The shutter may or may not slide in loose grooves, but grooves are to be preferred. The hook where the cord, or chain, attaches to the bar, is in order that the same may be detached after the last show at night, and lowered over the condenser. It is a good stunt, and one which may easily be installed by any operator.

Booklets Free.

This department has been informed that some party, to us unknown, is selling the little booklet put out by the Nicholas Power Company under the title "Hints to Operators." According to our information the fee asked is small, but there should be none at all as these books are issued by the Power Company gratis. Moreover the books contain copyrighted matter the use of which is given with the understanding the books would not be sold. The party selling is therefore not only coming pretty close to operating a fraud, but is laying himself liable under the copyright law. The booklet "Hints to Operators" may be had without money and without price by addressing the Nicholas Power Company, whose address may be had by referring to their advertisement on the back cover page of each week's issue of the Moving Picture World.

Motion Picture Photography*

Conducted by CARL LOUIS GREGORY, F. R. P. S.

Inquiries.

QUESTIONS in cinematography addressed to this department will receive carbon copy of the department's reply by mail when four cents in stamps are inclosed. Special replies by mail on matters which cannot be replied to in this department, $1.

Manufacturers' Notice.

It is an established rule of this department that no apparatus or other goods will be endorsed or recommended editorially until the excellence of such articles has been demonstrated to its editor.

Fixing Baths.

Hypo is one of the cheapest chemicals used in photography, and yet one of the most important. It is also the most common, and yet the most misused salt in the photographic laboratory.

Photography with gelatine emulsions would be almost impossible were it not for this cheap solvent of the silver haloid salts. Before its introduction the highly poisonous cyanide of potassium was the agent used. Potassium cyanide attacks not only the haloid salts, but, at a slower rate, the reduced metallic silver which forms the image and gelatine as well.

Hypo, or sodium thiosulphate, to give it the correct chemical name by which it is seldom called, has practically no effect upon either the reduced silver image or upon the gelatine unless allowed to act for an undue length of time or at a too high temperature.

Chemically the difference between sodium sulphite and sodium thiosulphate is that hypo contains one more atom of sulphur in a molecule than sodium sulphite.

One of the methods of manufacturing hypo is the solution of pure sulphur in sodium sulphite liquor, from which liquor the hypo is then crystallized out.

The chemical bond which holds this sulphur is easily broken, and under certain conditions the hypo solution breaks down and deposits this sulphur in a finely divided state in the hypo bath. This condition is manifest by the milky appearance of the bath and may be the result of a number of things. Acids and acid salts are the commonest causes of sulphur precipitation. Formaldehyde as hardener will also bring about this condition.

A bath which is precipitating sulphur liberates it in nascent form, at which time it is capable of attacking the finely divided particles of metallic silver which form the photographic image and converting it into silver sulphide. This is a process intentionally used in the sepia toning of photographic prints, but a highly undesirable thing for negatives, as the opacity of the image to actinic light is thereby greatly increased.

It is common practice in most laboratories to use a plain hypo bath with an acid short stop between the developer and the hypo. Even though hypo is cheap, still there is no sense in wasting it, especially as the more economically it is used the more valuable it becomes. Used hypo is worth money on account of the silver which it contains and the more silver it takes up the more valuable it becomes and the easier it is to recover the dissolved silver.

It is a common practice in most places to empty a portion of the hypo tanks each day and then "freshen" the bath with more hypo and water. This is decidedly wrong. Each developing tank should have two hypo tanks, one containing an old and the other an entirely fresh bath. The developed film should go into the old bath for five minutes then be finished in the fresh bath. When the old bath becomes so saturated that it does not remove most of the milkiness in five minutes it should be run into the precipitating tank and an entirely fresh bath mixed; whereupon the former fresh tank becomes the old bath and the new solution the fresh bath.

Hypo forms with silver haloids two distinct compounds. Both of these compounds are transparent, but one is soluble with difficulty and the other is very soluble. In the first compound, one molecule of hypo unites with one molecule of silver haloid, while the next, and easily soluble compound, is the same as the former with an additional molecule of hypo. An old or used bath tends to form this insoluble compound in the emulsion and consequently makes it exceedingly difficult to wash, but as soon as it strikes the fresh bath it takes up an additional molecule of hypo and becomes, as the term is, thoroughly fixed.

These are proven chemical facts ascertained years ago by two distinguished French photo chemists, A. Lumiere and M. Seyewits, and it seems very strange that so little attention has been paid to their investigations, the results of which have been widely published in photographic literature.

*Copyright, 1917, by the Chalmers Publishing Co.

They demonstrated that a film, fixed in fresh hypo and soaked in water for five minutes, contained only a small fraction as much hypo as a film fixed in an old bath and washed for an hour in running water. By this method of two baths every ounce of use is extracted from the hypo and the smaller volume of concentrated silver-hypo solution renders the silver recovery much easier.

For the precipitation of the silver from the hypo two capacious tanks of concrete should be constructed a good distance away from the building; for the chemical used as a precipitant, when acted upon by an acid, produces a gas, the smallest quantity of which being present in the atmosphere of the dark room, fogs sensitive emulsion just as surely as sunlight would.

The two tanks should each be of sufficient capacity to hold at least a week's run of spent hypo; the top level of the lower one being below the bottom of the upper one. Each tank should be provided with a series of cocks or outlets or an adjustable syphon, whereby the liquid can be drawn off at any desired level and a weatherproof, but easily removable, cover and, if the size of the tanks warrants, a small flight of steps for the laborer who shovels the silver sludge into barrels.

On account of the disintegrating action of the hypo solution the concrete should be protected by a heavy coat of asphalt.

The upper tank has an inlet pipe from the dark room through which it receives its charge of solution and all its outlets drain into the lower tank. The lower tank in turn drains into the sewer.

The precipitating solution is liver of sulphur or the cheapest commercial grade. It comes in large chunks of the fused chemical, varying in color from light brown to dark brown, according to the purity. Chemically it is a mixture of indefinite polysulphides of sodium and potassium, and the precipitate which it forms with the silver is silver sulphide, a dirty brownish black appearing substance. Liver of sulphur is very soluble in water but, on account of the large impervious pieces in which it comes, it takes a long time to dissolve unless broken up, and breaking it up is no pleasant job, as it has the quintuple fragrance of ancient eggs. It is a good plan, therefore, to have a stout barrel or hogshead with a snug-fitting cover in which are placed water and chemical enough to have a saturated solution constantly on hand.

Where it is not possible to have tanks on different levels, a small bronze centrifugal or rotary pump and electric motor will take care of the solution nicely. When the upper tank is two-thirds full of hypo solution and sulphuret solution, stir with a wooden paddle and pausing once in a while to let the precipitate settle a little, and take a glass full of the supernatant liquid and add a little of the sulphuret solution to see if there is any further precipitation. If it produces a dark brown cloudy precipitate it is necessary to add more precipitate, but if the precipitate is only slightly cloudy or absent the precipitation is complete and the tank should be allowed to settle until the next day, when the clear supernatant liquid may be carefully decanted into the lower tank. However careful you may be, you will find that it is impossible to remove all of the supernatant liquid with a portion of the precipitate escaping into the next tank. It is to remedy and save this escaping precipitate that the lower tank was constructed. The lower tank is now allowed to settle and the clear liquid allowed to run into the sewer. This precipitation may be repeated until the accumulation of sludge in the bottom of the tank is sufficient to warrant putting it into tight barrels for transport to the reducer.

If any acid is used in the hypo do not fail to run enough spent developer solution into the tank to make sure that all the acid is neutralized and that the solution is decidedly alkaline. If this is not done the acid will react on the liver of sulphur and foul the whole neighbor-hood with the abominable odor of sulphuretted hydrogen or hydrogen dir sulphide, which has rotten eggs backed off the boards for fragrance.

Reducing solutions and silver intensifying baths may also be run into those tanks for recovery of their silver content.

Plain hypo should be used only after a weak acid short stop made as follows:

Water .... 10 gallons
Acetic acid (No. 8) .... 32 ounces

The acid neutralizes the alkaline salts which the gelatine of the emulsion has absorbed from the developer and stops action of the developing agent almost instantly. If the film is transferred directly to a plain hypo bath the developer with which the emulsion is saturated will continue to act after the film has been immersed in the hypo, as it takes considerable time for the hypo to penetrate the deeper layers of the gelatine coating and prevent further developing action by combining with the unreduced haloids.

The use of an acid fixing bath has a number of advantages. The acid neutralizes the alkaline salts of the developer, the alum hardens the gelatine of the film and renders it more resistant to reticulation and frilling from high drying room temperatures and the sulphite present retards the precipitation of sulphur from the acid hypo bath.

(To be continued.)

Hobart to Write for Paramount

Noted Humorist, Playwright and Author Engaged to Prepare Original Screen Plays.

ADDED to the growing list of noted authors who are writing original photoplays for Paramount and Artcraft stars is George V. Hobart, one of the most successful of American playwrights, who has just been engaged by Jesse L. Lasky, vice-president of the Famous Players-Lasky Corporation, to prepare exclusive screen material for that organization.

Mr. Hobart will devote the greater portion of his time to this work, and he has already completed one original script. He is now engaged in writing a highly dramatic photoplay for Sessue Hayakawa, which, it is said, possesses an intensity and interest that marks it as a genuine novelty. Hobart has been giving much study to the peculiar quality of Hayakawa's work.

That Mr. Hobart will bring to the screen the same degree of originality and cleverness that has won for him a high place in the ranks of American authors and dramatists goes without saying. He takes a keen interest in motion pictures and looks forward with no little pleasure to seeing his first photoplay on the screen. It is probable he will contribute a number of vehicles within the next few months, as he is an unusually prolific writer.

The career of Mr. Hobart makes entertaining reading. His beginnings were humble and came by the newspaper route. Twenty-two years ago he was a telegraph operator in the offices of the New York Evening Sun. Prior to that he had worked as a railroad telegrapher. Attention was first attracted to his literary ability by a number of clever verses which he contributed to the columns of the Sun.

The now famous "Dinkelspiel" stories appeared first in the Baltimore News and were afterward translated to the vaudeville stage. He wrote numerous other sketches and in many of his earlier efforts May Irwin appeared on the "big time."

Among the plays to his credit may be named "Sally in our Alley," "The Candy Shop," "Moonlight Mary" and "Our Mrs. McChesney," in collaboration with Edna Ferber. This year's "Follies" owes its clever libretto to Hobart.

SUPPORTING CAST FOR LOCKWOOD PICTURE.

The supporting players who are to appear with Harold Lockwood in the picturisation of the George Gibbs novel, "Paradise Garden," have been chosen by Fred J. Balshofer as follows: Virginia Rappae, as Marcia VanWyck; Catherine Henry, Miss Gore; Olive Bruce, Miss Wetherby; Harry de Roy, as Christopher; B. A. Sprotte as Henry Ballard; George Hupp, as Jerry Benham (Harold Lockwood) at the age of ten; Violet Eddy as Miss Redwood, Jerry's governess. Vera Sisson, who played the feminine lead in The Hidden Spring, also has a leading part in the new story, that of Una Habberton, a settlement worker. Lester Cuneo plays the heavy man of the story, Jack Ballard; and William Clifford is to be seen as Roger Canby, tutor to Jerry Benham, the hero of the play. The part of Marcia Van Wyck, which is to be played by Virginia Rappae, was the most difficult to fill, the producer having spent three weeks in a search for the exact type of "juvenile vampire" which is called for in the novel.

FINIS FOX JOINS BROTHER IN PICTURE FIELD.

Finis Fox, a promoter of large business interests, secretary and assistant general manager of the White Crown Fruit Jar Co., of Louisville, Ky., has given up active participation in these interests to master the details of the motion picture industry. He will first be associated with his brother, Edwin Carewe, one of Metro's directing staff, in the producing of multiple reel pictures at Metro's Super-Feature studio.

For some time Mr. Fox has evinced an interest in motion pictures. He is the author of "The Jury of Fate," recently produced by Metro with Mabel Taliaferro as star, and of several other photo-dramas not yet ready to be released.

GRIFFIN RETURNS TO THE NICHOLAS POWER COMPANY.

Herbert Griffin, who left the Nicholas Power Company last June to accept a position in Detroit, has again joined the staff of the Power Company selling batteries. Prior to leaving the Power Company, Mr. Griffin traveled throughout the country boosting the Cameragraph for five years, and his return as traveling representative will be welcome news to exhibitors and supply men throughout the industry.

At the Leading Picture Theaters

Double Bill at the Strand, Cohan at the Rialto—Other Feature Productions Week of August 26.

Strand Theater.

THE Strand Theater presents again a double feature bill. The second and final installment of the official British war pictures of "The Retreat of the Germans at the Battle of Arras," the first part of which attracted crowds that taxed the capacity of the spacious playhouse last week, will be shown. In the second installment the performances of the tanks, the sustained activities of the British artillery and soldiers advancing through the barrage of German fire, during which shells burst close to the camera, are seen. The film concludes with a thrilling photograph of a spinning descent in an aeroplane from a height of 13,000 feet.

The photodramatic feature is a Triangle picture entitled "The Ten of Diamonds" in which Dorothy Dalton enacts the stellar role. The cast includes Jack Livingston, J. B. Sherry and Dorcas Matthews. The story is by Albert Cowles. The Strand Topical Review contains some interesting news pictures taken in this country and abroad.

There is an excellent musical program. Among the soloists are Henri De Caux, the celebrated tenor, who will sing the Barcarolle from "The Masked Ball"; Helen Scholder, the 'cello virtuoso, will play Popper's "Tarentella"; Arthur Depew and Ralph H. Brigham will be heard in solos on the grand pipe organ. The concert orchestra, under the direction of Carl Edouarde, will render excerpts from "La Boheme" and also play appropriate incidental music to the subjects projected on the screen.

Rialto Theater.

George M. Cohan is seen for the first time on the Rialto screen this week in his successful mystery farce, "Seven Keys to Baldpate". This was one of Mr. Cohan's most notable stage successes and those who saw it will recall with delight its fun and thrills, and its rapid sequence of surprises. Anna Q. Nilsson plays opposite the star, and in the supporting cast are Purnell Pratt, Frank Losee, Eric Hudson and Carlton Macy.

Goldmark's brilliant "Sakuntala" overture will be played by the Rialto orchestra, with Hugo Reisenfeld conducting. In honor of the star of the feature picture, selections from his popular musical comedy "George Washington, Jr.", will be played as an added number. Paul Doret, French tenor, will sing "At Dawning", by Cadman, and Alberto Bachman, violinist, will render "Fantasia Apassionata" by Vieuxtemps. Profesor Firmen Swinnen will contribute a solo on the grand organ.

Mr. and Mrs. Sidney Drew will be seen in "The Patriot", a comedy concerned with the conservation of food bearing the indorsement of Mr. Hoover, the food administrator. A beautiful combitone picture showing scenes in Central Colorado will supply the scenic portion of the programme, and the Rialto Animated Magazine will furnish the news of the day from all sources.

Eighty-first Street Theater.

At the Eighty-first Street Theater there will be shown on Monday, Tuesday and Wednesday Jack Devereaux and Anna Lehr in a stirring play of love and action, "The Grafters", Hugh Fay, in a merry mix-up. "Her Donkey Love", is an added attraction. Thursday, Friday, Saturday and Sunday Bessie Love will be seen in "Wee Lady Betty", a sparkling, modern play of the Emerald Isle. Polly Moran, with Keystone funmakers, will be seen in a sidesplitting comedy, "His Uncle Dudley", produced by Mack Sennett. The vaudeville on the same bill will be of prominence and quality.

Other Special Productions Showing.

At the Globe Theater "The Spy", the sensational Fox story of German intrigue, succeeds "Jack and the Beanstalk".

At the Forty-fourth Street Theater "The Italian Battlefront", official war subject, is still drawing large houses.

At the Criterion "The Manxman" is still holding forth.

At the Broadway "Sirens of the Sea", a Jewel production, succeeds Pay Me".

DOROTHY DALTON IS READY FOR WORK.

Dorothy Dalton is ready to begin her first Paramount production under the direction of Thomas H. Ince. She has been spending a vacation of three weeks at Arrowhead Springs, Cal.

Miss Dalton is an enthusiastic and skilled golfer, and at Arrowhead Springs found an eighteen-hole course of which she made full use.

Walthall to Have His Own Company

Pictures Will Be Made at Paralta Studios in Hollywood and Released by Triangle Distributing Corporation.

HENRY B. WALTHALL has become a star-manager at the head of his own independent producing company. He will personally select the subjects for production. This situation was brought about on August· 20, through negotiations conducted between N. William Aron-

Henry B. Walthall and Carl Anderson Signing Contract. N. W. Aronson Standing.

son, Mr. Walthall's personal ·manager, and Carl Anderson, president of Paralta Plays, Inc.

Mr. Walthall will head a corporation to be called the Henry B. Walthall Pictures Corporation, now being formed. The production of Mr. Walthall's pictures will be made at the Paralta studios in Hollywood, and will be. released by the Triangle Distributing Company on. the star series plan.

Mr. Walthall has left for Los Angeles. His first vehicle has been selected and will be put in production the moment he reaches Hollywood. Mary Charleson, who has been his leading woman in several productions in which he had recently appeared, will play leads in the new company.

Mr. Walthall is regarded by competent critics as one of the most finished actors on the screen. He is 36 years of age, and became a moving picture actor in 1910. He had played on the legitimate stage before that, making his debut in the Murray Hill Theater stock company under the management of the late Henry V. Donnelly.

Mr. Walthall worked for Biograph in the summer of 1910 and went to England with Henry Miller in September to play in "The Great Divide." It was not a hit and the company returned in November. He then went to Mr. Griffith, who engaged him permanently. From that day to this he has never played a part in spoken drama. He remained with Mr. Griffith during the time that director was producer for Biograph and went with him in 1913 to the Majestic. During the past two years Mr. Walthall was leading player for Essanay, appearing in this company's feature plays.

GAUMONT MEN WED.

Despite the fact that just at present the Gaumont Company is not producing·photoplays, romance is not dead at the Flushing studio. It is very much alive, as witnesseth the announcements simultaneously of the engagements of two of the Gaumont cameramen, Walter Pritchard and Otto Pilts. What increases interest in these announcements is that the young men are to marry cousins.

Mr. Pritchard is to marry Miss Ethel May Blair, of Corona, L. I., and Mr. Pilts is to marry her cousin, Miss Celia Mae Spalding of Prattsville, N. Y.· No date has been set for the weddings.· Mr. Pritchard has just returned from a ·vacation with Miss Blair at the present home of her parents at Cleveland, O., and Mr. Pilts soon leaves for an outing in the Catskills, Miss Spaulding's home being in the heart of these mountains.

Both Pritchard and Pilts live in Bayonne, N. J., and make the trip daily to and from the Gaumont plant. They are now looking for twin houses so that the inseparable 'cousins will have only a back fence to separate them. The men are wedded, one might say, to Bayonne, but the brides-to-be are urging them to find homes in Flushing so that they·will not have to leave so early in the morning and so that they will return earlier at night.

E. K. Lincoln Entertains Press

Former Vitagraph Player Gives Outing to Eighteen Representatives of Motion Picture Press at His Estate in Berkshires.

E. K. LINCOLN, former Vitagraph player, and whose latest screen-experience was as the star of the "Jimmie Dale, Alias the Grey Seal" series, gave eighteen representatives of the motion picture press. an outing on his 4,500-acre estate in the Berkshires over the week-end, beginning Saturday, August 18. The party left New York for Springfield, Mass., in a special car on Saturday morning.

E. K. Lincoln.

Nine reluctantly returned Monday afternoon, some on Tuesday, and a few are.yet to be heard from.

To say that Mr. Lincoln is a superlative host is putting it mildly. When the bunch arrived at Springfield they were met by Mr. Lincoln and three automobiles. An hour's trip over the mountain roads through gorgeous scenery brought the party to Mr. Lincoln's country house. From then on until it was time to go home the group of writers owned the place. Tennis was the most popular pastime with some, while others spent much of the time in the lake that nestles on the Lincoln estate— that is, the bunch did those things when they were not eating, which was most of the time.

Mr. Lincoln showed the boys his place by means of motor trips and hikes. Chief interest centered in his kennels. At the mountain house Mr. Lincoln has only about fifty valuable dogs. He also has another place on which he houses more than 500 ribbon-winning canines.

Those who were the guests of Mr. Lincoln were: Gerald Duffy, Picture Play Magazine; William Barry, Motion Picture News; Walter McRaig, Motion Picture Classic; Charles Condon. Motography; Ben. H. Grimm, Moving Picture World; Peter Milne, Motion Picture News; C. A. Kracht, Morning Telegraph; Rudolph Cormier, Exhibitors' Trade Review; William Beecroft, Exhibitors' Herald; Mr. Thompson, Dramatic Mirror; Edwin M. LaRoche, Motion Picture Magazine; N. Boneil, New York Clipper; Colgate Baker, New York Review; Jack Edwards, Billboard; Lumiere, the photographer, and T. E. Letendre, business manager for the trip.

JACK MEADOR WITH LONGACRE.

In line with their policy to inaugurate a nation-wide advertising and news-publicity campaign for their new. Alice Howell Century comedies, the Longacre Distributing Company has made Jack Meador their general press representative. Mr. Meador, a publicity promoter, newspaper and magazine writer of wide experience, has an extensive acquaintance among newspaper men throughout the country. which will be a valuable aid to him in his new work.

He was formerly a reporter on the Record-Herald and Tribune of Chicago. Ten years ago he came to New York to join the staff of the New York Herald. . He went to Europe in 1912 in the interests of The Authors' Inter-Ocean Magazine and Newspaper Syndicate. Later he was made the president of the syndicate. with headquarters in Paris. When the war broke out and the company suspended business on account of the conditions in the manuscript market, Mr. Meador returned to newspaper work, representing the London Times and New York Times as a special correspondent in France. Two years ago he returned to America to direct a publicity campaign for the Colt machine gun. His success in this work in getting articles in English, French, South American magazines of ·national reputation, ·as well as American periodicals, attracted considerable attention. Since our entrance in the war, he has been doing special Sunday newspaper stories and scenario writing.

The Motion Picture Exhibitor

WRITE US EARLY AND OFTEN

THE MOVING PICTURE WORLD carries the most complete record of Exhibitors' News. This department aims at being the fullest and fairest chronicle of all the important doings in the ranks of organized exhibitors. To keep the department as complete and as useful as it is now we request the secretaries of all organizations to favor us with reports of all the news. Coming events in the ranks of the organized exhibitors are best advertised in this department of the Moving Picture World.

American's State Directors to Meet

Will Convene at Ocean View, Following the Virginia Session
Closing on September 1.

GENERAL MANAGER Charles C. Pettijohn, of the American Exhibitors' Association, has notified President Percy W. Wells, of the North Carolina organization, that a meeting of the state directors of the A. E. A. will be held at Ocean View, Va., on Saturday, September 1, in conjunction with the convention of exhibitors from Southern states, which comes to a close on that date at Ocean View.

Among the state presidents and leaders in the A. E. A. who are expected to attend the directors' meeting are: Harry M. Crandall, District of Columbia; Frank J. Rembusch, Indiana; Guy Wonders, Maryland; Sam Trigger, New York City; I. M. Mosher, New York State; Fred J. Herrington, Pennsylvania; George C. Warner, South Carolina; Percy W. Wells and H. B. Varner, North Carolina, and Harry Bernstein, Virginia.

Jake Wells, president of the Virginia League, who has planned the Ocean View convention, states that the convention is to be in no way confused with the meeting of the A. E. A. directors, which is an entirely separate affair. The purpose of the convention proper, as outlined by Mr. Wells, is to promulgate and perfect an organisation of the adjacent states to be represented, for the purpose of handling matters of purely local significance. The meeting of the A. E. A. directors was an event planned afterward by Manager Pettijohn, who saw in this large gathering of exhibitors an opportunity for furthering the interests of the new association.

It was reported to Mr. Pettijohn that Lee A. Ochs would attend the Ocean View convention, and the general manager of the American Exhibitors' Association expressed great satisfaction, stating that "my organisation desires nothing better than a face to face comparison of its personnel with that of the old League". It is quite likely the convention will assume lively proportions from the presence of leaders of both organisations, each endeavoring to enroll new members and strength for their respective bodies.

MICHIGAN A. E. A. CONVENTION.

The Michigan branch of the American Exhibitors' Association will hold a convention at Detroit, Mich., on September 5 and 6. There will be many entertainment features provided for visiting delegates and all exhibitors are urged to attend and to bring their wives.

Henry B. Varner in New York

Southern Exhibitor Talks with Messrs. Williams and Pettijohn Over Washington Situation.

HENRY B. VARNER, motion picture exhibitor and editor of several Southern newspapers, was in New York August 21, 22 and 23. Mr. Varner is the man who labored for his brother exhibitors in Washington on the tax question.

On August 21 he sat in a conference with John D. Williams, general manager of the First National Exhibitors' Circuit, and Charles C. Pettijohn, general manager of the American Exhibitors' Association. It is known that the tax situation is not as yet "out of the fire", Mr. Varner refused to confer with anybody upon this subject excepting those who represented exhibitors only. No details of the conference were given out.

Mr. Varner has been appointed chairman of the legislative committee of the American Exhibitors' Association. The association is to be congratulated upon securing Mr. Varner in this capacity. Mr. Varner is personally acquainted with many of the officials at Washington, and is peculiarly fitted for these duties.

Mr. Varner left New York on the 23d for Washington, where he will represent exhibitors until the tax question is finally settled.

New Exhibitors' Body Planned

Herbert Lubin Chief Mover in Plan to Form Co-operative Exhibitors' Circuit.

HERBERT LUBIN, former holder of the Metro franchise in Canada, is the prime mover in a proposed organization of exhibitors and state rights men. Meetings are scheduled in the Hotel Astor for several days the current week. It has been learned that the proposed organization will have as have some of the characteristics of the First National Exhibitors' Circuit and some of the characteristics of the Motion Picture Exhibitors' League and the newly-formed American Exhibitors' Association. The tentative title of the organization is Exhibitors' Co-operative Circuit.

No announcements are forthcoming from any of the men already lined up with the scheme. It is known that telegrams were sent to some of the most powerful exhibitors and state rights men in the country, and that many are coming to New York to be present at the meetings. It is understood that the promoters of the organisation already have planned the purchase of the world rights to a big picture. Mr. Lubin, who was an important mover in the negotiations that resulted in Mme. Petrova's signing with Superpictures, Inc., declares that the organisation will be well on its way toward completion in all details within a week.

Franchise holders in the proposed organization, it is understood, will share the profits of any picture purchased and exploited by the organisation. Pictures will be rented to members at low rates, it is said, and the exhibitor may, in the event that a picture is very successful, get back almost his whole rental price. Every one concerned with the proposed organisation says that when definite announcements do come they will carry news of vast importance to the industry.

Coming League and Other Exhibitors' Conventions

(Secretaries Are Requested to Send Dates and Particulars Promptly)

Virginia Exhibitors at Ocean City..August 30, 31 and Sept. 1
   Chesley Toney, secretary, Richmond.

Michigan, American Exhibitors' Association at Detroit .... September 5 and 6
   King Perry, secretary, 204 Brietmeyer Bldg., Detroit, Mich.

Maritime Provinces League at St. John, N. B................................September 9 and 10

Brooklyn Exhibitors Hold Meeting

National Executive Committee Attends in a Body—Twenty Local Managers Are Sued by Music Publishers.

A T a largely attended meeting of the Brooklyn local of the Exhibitors' League held at the Duffield theater on Saturday evening, August 25, it was decided to fight the tax imposed by the music publishers' society. What stirred the forty exhibitors present was the announcement that action has been taken by the society against twenty exhibitors in Brooklyn alone. The members of the National Executive Committee came over from Manhattan on the invitation of the local officers and on the assurance they would be afforded an opportunity to follow the proceedings of a "regular" branch. They thus were enabled to receive in person a vote of thanks unanimously extended to their committee for its action in voting to defend the suits instituted against the Brooklyn exhibitors. Some of the exhibitors offered to place on sale in their lobbies the sheet music of the independent music publishers.

For the first time there was publicly revealed word of the negotiations that have been in progress between the city administration and the organizations of the Bronx, Manhattan and Brooklyn looking to a centralization in the license department of authority over motion picture theaters. Under the new arrangement an exhibitor formally accused of a violation of the city ordinances will be haled before the license commissioner and his case will be heard and determined before that one tribunal. The League officials given credit for accomplishing this result were John J. Wittman of the Bronx, Lee. A. Ochs and Louis Blumenthal, of Manhattan, and Louis Levine and William Brandt, of Brooklyn. Under the new plan all children's cases will now go before the license commissioner. By exhibitors this is considered to be one of the important angles of the agreement.

League Executive Committee Meets

Large Attendance at Gathering in New York, but Proceedings Are Not Revealed.

T HE executive committee of the Motion Picture Exhibitors' League of America held meetings in New York on August 25 and 26. Up to Monday afternoon no word of the two days' proceedings had been permitted to escape to the trade press. It was said there would be another session Tuesday, August 28.

In attendance at the sessions were Frank D. Eager, Nebraska; Alfred S. Black, Maine; Eugene M. Clarke, Mississippi; Daniel Chamberlain, North Dakota; Alfred Hamburger, Illinois; Peter J. Schaefer, Illinois; Robert Levy, Illinois; Hector M. E. Pasmezoglu, St. Louis; N. C. Rice, Iowa; C. E. Glamann, Kansas; Louis L. Levine, Brooklyn; Thomas Furniss, Minnesota; Louis L. Blumenthal, New Jersey; Thomas Howard, New York; J. H. O'Donnell, Pennsylvania; Sam Grant, Massachusetts, 1918 convention manager; Milton N. Goldsmith, general counsel, New York, and these officers: President Lee Ochs, First Vice-President Joseph Hopp, Illinois; Second Vive-President William Isenberg, Mississippi; Financial Secretary William Sweeney, Illinois; Executive Secretary William Brandt, New York; Treasurer Ernest Horstmann, Boston Organizer D. G. Rodgers, Minnesota.

SHEA DECLARES HIMSELF WITH A. E. A.

A telegram received at the headquarters of the American Exhibitors' Association from I. M. Mosher says:

"Mike Shea is with us and has promised to assist us in every possible way. You have authority to use his name for the good of the association."

Mr. Shea is the owner of the big Hippodrome in Buffalo.

N. A. M. P. I. Re-elects Brady

Meeting of the Board of Directors Picks Officials for Ensuing Year—Recognition Refused American Exhibitors' Association.

A MEETING of the board of directors of the National Association of the Motion Picture Industry was held at the offices of the Association, Times Building, New York City, on Monday, August 27, nearly all the directors being present. The annual election of officers was held, with the following result:

President, William A. Brady; vice-presidents, Adolph Zukor, R. A. Rowland, J. A. Berst, William L. Sherrill, J. H. Hallberg, Thomas Furniss, Arthur James; secretary, F. A. Elliott; treasurer, J. E. Brŏulatour.

The matter of the application of the American Exhibitors'

Association for recognition as an organisation was rejected by a vote of 24 against and 5 in favor.

These firms were elected to membership: Bray Studios, Pathe Exchange, Inc., Norma Talmadge Films, Selig Polyscope, Inter-Ocean Film Corporation, Standard Engraving Company, Ivan Pictures Corporation, Harry Rapf, Mayfair Film Corporation, Ogden Pictures Corporation.

KENT BACK FROM TOUR.

Sidney R, Kent, General Sales Manager of General Film Company, has returned to New York City after spending six weeks among branch offices of the company. Los Angeles, San Francisco, Seattle, Denver and many other cities were visited by him.

One of the objects of Mr. Kent's trip was to install advanced merchandising methods in the exchanges. A large part of his time was devoted to effecting special coordination of branch activities in distributing product in line with important new projects which are being directed from headquarters.

PAUL BRYAN TO HANDLE GAUMONT PUBLICITY.

Extended leave of absence having been granted Harry King Tootle, publicity manager of the Gaumont Company, Flushing, N. Y., his work will be taken over by Paul M. Bryan. Mr. Bryan is editor of "Reel Life," Gaumont's Mutual magazine in film which is issued weekly. Mr. Tootle's leave is for the duration of the war. He has left for Plattsburg Barracks, N. Y., where he is a member of the Sixth Company of the Eighteenth Provisional Regiment of the training camps for officers.

VIOLA DANA TO STAR IN "BLUE JEANS."

Metro Pictures Corporation has acquired the motion picture rights to "Blue Jeans," Joseph Arthur's famous old stage success, for the use of Viola Dana. Miss Dana will play the exacting part of June, originally played by Jennie Yeamans at the old Fourteenth Street theater. John H. Collins will direct the production which B. A. Rolfe will present, and the screen adaption has been made by June Mathis. John Arnold is cameraman.

FILM SALVAGE PLANT BURNS.

The plant of the Levine Company at Passaic, N. J., where old motion picture film was treated for the extraction of the silver in the emulsion, was burned on August 24. The loss was estimated at $50,000.

EASTERN FILM COMPANY PLANT BURNED.

The plant of the Eastern Film Company at Providence, R. I., was destroyed by fire on August 24. The loss was total and is estimated at $100,000.

Officers and Directors of the Newly Organized Associated Theaters Inc., With Headquarters at Minneapolis, Minn.

From left to right, bottom row: William S. Smith, Secretary, Menomonie, Wisconsin; H. L. Hartman, President, Mandan, North Dakota; Forest Scoor, Vice-President, Forest City, Iowa. From left to right, top row: Thomas J. Hamlin, General Manager, Minneapolis, Minnesota; Charles W. Gates, Chairman Board of Directors, Aberdeen, South Dakota; Henry F. Green, Treasurer, Minneapolis, Minnesota. These exhibitors incorporated a $100,000 booking organization Tuesday, August 14, in Minneapolis, to book film and handle supplies and equipment for one thousand theater-members in the Northwest.

State Rights Department
Conducted by BEN H. GRIMM

Producers Plan Central Exchange

Propose to Have One Exchange Where All State Rights Films Will Be Bought and Sold—Organization Not Yet Completed.

MORE than twenty producers of state rights pictures or their representatives met in the Hotel Astor on Wednesday night, August 22, for the purpose of perfecting an organization whose chief aim will be the centralization under one roof of the sales power of all members. The plan is one of the most advanced and sensible that has yet been suggested in state rights marketing, and resembles in broad, general lines the plan of operation of the Real Estate Exchange of New York. Under the proposed plan every picture available for any territory can be viewed at the one place and, if desired, any deal or deals may be consummated on the floor of the exchange. In the one exchange there will be a print of every picture that is for sale for any territory, and a sample of every piece of advertising matter connected with the film. Thus a buyer coming to New York can go into the exchange and there see the entire stock of available pictures, doing away with the present necessity of his having to spend several days in getting around to the various offices.

The meeting Wednesday was held behind closed doors. Those who attended were sworn to secrecy, as they were at the producers' meeting of a week before. The organization has not been completed, but matters have advanced to the point where papers are in the hands of attorneys, and indications are that definite and certain details soon will be forthcoming. According to all of the men questioned it is but a matter of a few weeks, at the most, before the exchange becomes a material factor.

Under the proposition submitted before the producers a manager of the exchange shall be appointed at a minimum salary of $7,500 a year. It shall be the duty of the manager, the proposal states, to compile and keep alive lists of state rights buyers, independent exchanges, exhibitors, etc. The manager also shall render any possible service to members and others and facilitate the sale of pictures to the end that the producer shall consummate any transaction. The manager, may, on occasion, act for the producer and complete any deal. The manufacturer may have as many sales representatives on the floor of the exchange as he desires.

The expenses of the exchange shall be met by a treasury fund raised through commissions to the exchange on pictures sold. Five per cent. of the net amount paid for a picture shall be turned into the treasury. The term "net amount," according to the proposal, shall mean the gross sum received from a buyer, less the cost of prints delivered.

Another proposal is that the organization regulate the medium of advertising, the members to agree not to patronize any publication devoted to motion pictures other than those specified by the organization. It is also a proposed object to patronize only those lithographers, printers, engravers, slide houses, etc., that are listed with the organization—concerns who make special prices to members because of the volume of business given the concern by the organization. Members of the organization, it is understood, will decide on a certain laboratory or laboratories to do the work of all members.

Members may report any grievances against any director, actor, actress, exchange man, exhibitor, and the like. An executive committee of five members, it is proposed, will pass on all grievances. Members will refuse to do business with anyone found guilty of unfair practices toward the organization or any member of the organization. It is proposed in the plan considered Wednesday that every member contribute, in advance, his share of a fund large enough to pay the expenses of the exchange for three months, by which time, it is believed, the exchange will not only be paying its own expenses, but paying dividends to its members.

The proposals submitted have not yet been voted on. Wednesday's session was given up almost wholly to discussions of the various clauses in the prospectus, but no clause was adopted. It was generally agreed, however, that the organization must be formed with as little delay over details as possible.

Among the concerns represented at the meeting were: William L. Sherrill, Frohman Amusement Corporation; Duplex Films, Harry Rapf, A. H. Jacobs Photoplays, Inc., Arrow Film Corporation, Harry Rapf, Wharton, Inc., Mayfair Film Corporation, Crystal Film Corporation, Ogden Pictures Corporation. Edward Warren Productions, Paul Cromelin. Cosmophotofilm: Jesse Goldburg, Williamson Brothers, Advance Film Corporation (Ralph and John Ince), John W. Noble, Authors Film Corporation, and others.

Lesser Organization Formed

State Rights Distributors, Inc., Has Fifteen Members—Two Territories Being Contested For—Will Buy Negatives.

UNDER the title State Rights Distributors, Inc., the organization of state rights buyers promoted and sponsored by Sol L. Lesser, matured on Wednesday, August 22. Fifteen men, representing all of the territories in the United States with the exception of two, and the whole of Canada, are represented in the organization, whose aim it is to purchase negative rights on pictures. The Lesser organization follows closely in its working scheme that of the First National Exhibitors' Circuit. Each franchise holder will be taxed his pro-rata share on any films bought by the organization.

Mr. Lesser was elected president. Louis R. Mayer, of Boston, was made treasurer. Louis Haas, of New York, is vice-president, and Leon D. Netter, temporary manager and secretary.

The members of the organization as given out by Mr. Netter are: Nathan Hirsh, Civilization-Pioneer Film Co., Greater New York and New York State; Louis B. Mayer, American Feature Film Co., Boston, New England States; Daniel M. Vandawalker and Henry L. Dollman, Indianapolis and Chicago, Illinois and Indiana; Sydney B. Lust, Washington, D. C., Delaware, Maryland, Virginia and District of Columbia; Master Photoplays Co., Newark, New Jersey; W. S. Butterfield, Battle Creek, Michigan; S. A. Lynch Enterprises, Inc., entire South (11 states); A. D. Flintom, Yale Photoplay Co., Kansas City, Mo., Missouri, Kansas, Iowa and Nebraska; M. Rosenberg, De Luxe Feature Film Co., Seattle, Washington, Oregon, Idaho and Montana; All Star Feature Distributors, Inc., San Francisco, California, Nevada and Arizona; Monarch Feature Film Co., Toronto, Canada and Alaska; Harry Schwalbe, Peerless Feature Film Co., Philadelphia, Eastern Pennsylvania, and Harry Grelle, Supreme Photoplay Productions, Pittsburgh, Western Pennsylvania and West Virginia.

The directors of the organization are Mr. Lesser, Louis Haas, Henry L. Dollman, S. A. Lynch, J. J. Allen, C. D. Struble and Louis B. Mayer.

The purchasing committee consists of seven members. Five out of the following seven members will pass on pictures: Nathan Hirsh, Mr. Mayer, Daniel M. Vandawalker, Mr. Lynch, Mr. Netter, Mr. Lust and Mr. Allen.

"All features purchased will be distributed throughout the United States and Canada through forty offices now in active operation", reads the statement issued by Mr. Netter. "The entire United States and Canada are covered except the Minnesota and Colorado territories, both of which are being actively contested for.

"The need of an organization of this kind has already been made evident by the fact that already we have under consideration negatives of five big productions. Business transacted through this organization will be done on a strictly cash basis.

Mr. Lesser still is confined to his bed in Dr. Stern's sanitarium. He is suffering from typhoid fever and is expected to be fully recovered in about ten days.

LEE ORGANIZATION PROGRESSING.

Rapid progress in his plan to form an organization of state rights buyers is reported by Joseph F. Lee. During the week Mr. Lee received wires from all over the country indorsing his plan. In many cases the senders of the telegrams indicated that they would be in New York within a week. Mr. Lee says that the proposition now looks as if the first definite steps would be taken within a few days, at which time there will be several big out-of-town buyers in New York, several of whom are coming solely for the purpose of meeting with other believers in Mr. Lee's plan.

"Shame" Noble's First Special

Zena Keefe and Niles Welsh Featured in Timely Subject—Showing Soon.

JOHN W. NOBLE'S first production for the state rights market, titled "Shame," has been cut and edited and will be introduced by a regular trade showing at an early date. Zene Keefe, who is featured, with Niles Welch as her leading man, plays the part of a girl who is the innocent victim of circumstances brought about by war conditions. The story opens with a prologue which takes place during the drafting of the countries' young manhood, and has a most striking and unusual climax which plunges the audience into the middle of an exceptionally original drama.

The title is a particularly fitting one, as it applies to the drama in a double sense and suggests the bigness and the importance of the subject which deals with the attitude of the world in general and society in particular, toward the innocent victims of war conditions and the children who share the fate of their unfortunate mothers. "Shame" is said to be a powerful plea for tolerance on the part of the world for the victims of war who, although far removed from the battle

John W. Noble.

front, deserve the same consideration as the wounded heroes of the trenches. By means of an intensely dramatic story Mr. Noble, whose services as an officer in the United States Army has given him a deep understanding of his subject, brings home to his audience the criminal folly of those uncharitable members of society who fail to appreciate the effects of the strain of war upon those in close touch with it, and who do not realize the extent of the hero worship inspired by the soldiers in the hearts of those for whom they fight.

Jules Burnstein is acting as business representative for Mr. Noble in the marketing of the picture.

BERNSTEIN IN NEW YORK TO SELL TWO FILMS.

Isadore Bernstein, of the Bernstein Film Productions, has arrived in New York for the purpose of disposing of the two big features, "Humility" and "Loyalty", which he recently completed. His agents, Shepard & Van Loan, are negotiating with several people for the sale of these features. While both are up to the Bernstein standard of photography and direction, "Loyalty" seems to be the favorite at the present moment, for it deals with the drug evil and has one of the finest characterizations of a "dope" fiend ever seen on the screen. It should be a big box-office attraction for this reason, aside from the fact that it is supported by an excellent cast, has beautiful photography and good direction.

The cast includes Betty Brice, Murdock McQuarrie, Jean Hathaway, and Jay Morley, who gives the excellent impersonation of "Hugh Gordon", a man who is addicted to the drug habit.

ECKERT MANAGING CLEVELAND EXCHANGE.

T. M. Eckert, for the past six months a member of Pathe's Pittsburgh branch, has been made manager of the new Cleveland office of the Harris P. Wolfberg Attractions. Mr. Wolfberg is exercising great care in choosing the men for his organization. This is essential because, as Mr. Wolfberg explains, "each of my men must be a specialist, not only in selling big productions to the exhibitor, but in helping the exhibitor sell to the public. We are classed as state rights buyers, but I am proud to say that we call ourselves state rights distributors and are striving to live up to that name".

"A MORMON MAID" SOLD FOR TWO STATES.

Jones, Linick & Schaefer, and Ascher Bros., of Chicago, have purchased through Hiller & Wilk the Illinois and Indiana rights to the Friedman film, "A Mormon Maid". The feature will be given a long run at a leading downtown theater, and an endeavor will be made to have Mae Murray, the star, present at the picture's Chicago premiere. It is announced that an extensive advertising campaign will herald the feature in Illinois and Indiana.

Earlier Co-operation Wolfberg's Idea

Pittsburgh Operator Believes Producer and Prospective Buyers Should Plan Advertising Together.

HARRIS P. WOLFBERG, the state rights operator of Pittsburgh, has a few ideas that probably account for his rapid rise in the film industry. One, in particular, is his belief that the proper time for co-operation between the producer and the independent buyer to begin is before the producer plans his advertising campaign or disposes of a single state. Some film men may regard this as a revolutionary statement, but Mr. Wolfberg cites many instances where a much greater success could have been made possible if this policy had been pursued.

"It is the state rights buyer", says Mr. Wolfberg, "who is in constant touch with the exhibitor. He sees at first hand how every picture goes over, in the town of one thousand as well as in the largest cities. If there is a failure he knows when the picture is at fault and when it is the advertising that is to blame.

"Take the matter of advertising: Every producer tells the state rights man that 'a complete advertising campaign already has been prepared'. Whether this includes anything else or not, it always includes the posters. And when the paper arrives the distributor is greeted by several styles of posters depicting gruesome sick-room or death-bed scenes—paper that the wise exhibitor often refuses to buy. Doubtless these scenes are taken from highly dramatic parts of the film and are full of interest when one views the entire picture. But they are placed on the posters because the manufacturer is in love with his work—not by reason of any inherent advertising value they may possess.

"The whole point is this", continued Mr. Wolfberg; "too often a man will estimate the public taste by his own likes and dislikes. Each of us, in a way, is a sort of a Funkhouser, of Chicago, in this respect. There is no reason why we should allow this human weakness to injure us longer. The state rights field has grown rapidly. There are now prominent and responsible men in nearly every territory. The manufacturer or producer who looks ahead knows which of these buyers he wants to handle his pictures. If he is a producer of massive, high priced productions, he wants a distributor who is specializing in handling high priced attractions—one who has an established clientele for big stuff. While your picture and advertising are still in the making, why not call in the men who are the logical ones to handle it, and get their ideas on how best to take off the rough edges, what to use as the slogan and what scenes to use on the posters?

"Since the strength of the independent field lies in each distributor's prerogative of buying or rejecting any picture presented for his approval, wouldn't there be fewer pictures rejected if the distributor were given a voice in these matters before it was too late to make any changes? The distributor then will have none but himself to blame in case of failure and, on the contrary, will take a personal pride in making a huge success of any picture which is being exploited according to his own ideas and methods.

"We are on the right track now. We are gradually getting together, but let's do it earlier in the game. It's too late when the stage is set and the curtain is up".

HARRY BERG ON TRANS-CONTINENTAL TOUR.

Harry Berg, of the Overland Film Company, left New York Saturday on a transcontinental trip to visit the leading state rights buyers of the country. Mr. Berg, who is a comparatively newcomer in the state rights field, has already established himself as one of the live wires of the industry. Before entering the motion picture business he had a long and comprehensive training in the theatrical game, having been connected with many of the leading producers and for more than a decade held a responsible position with a leading vaudeville manager.

Mr. Berg brings to the picture business a thorough knowledge and understanding of the requirements of the exhibitor, and in his presentation of the feature photoplays on a territorial basis considers only their value from the box office point of view.

On the trip he will carry two prints of "Man's Law", a multiple-reel feature starring Irving Cummings, soon to be released on the state rights plan, which will be shown to the big buyers in the principal cities he visits. He plans to stop at Chicago, Minneapolis, St. Louis, Denver, San Francisco, and will spend considerable time in Los Angeles. While in Los Angeles he will complete negotiations already under way for the signing of long term contracts with several stars who will appear in productions to be made by the Overland for the state rights market.

"13TH LABOR OF HERCULES" SOLD FOR CANADA.

The Cinema Distributing Corporation, 220 West Forty-second street, New York, of which Henry J. Brock is president, announces that the series of the Panama-Pacific Exposition known as "The 13th Labor of Hercules," has been sold for the Dominion of Canada to Charles Stevens, general manager for Superfeatures, Ltd., 59 Victoria street, Toronto, Ont.

Washington Exchange Widens Field

Exhibitors' Film Exchange Expands Field to Include Entire South—Territory Has Been Neglected, Is Belief.

FOR the purpose of better handling a territory that it believes has been more or less neglected, the Exhibitors' Film Exchange, of Washington, D. C., has expanded its field of operation to include the entire South. Formerly the exchange operated only in the territory comprised by Delaware, Maryland, District of Columbia and Virginia. Under the new arrangement the field covered will include, besides the states mentioned, North Carolina, South Carolina, Georgia, Alabama, Mississippi, Florida and Tennessee.

The decision to expand was reached after a conference taken part in by Harry M. Crandall, F. Ferrandini, H. Bernstein and A. Dresner, directors of the Exhibitors' Film Exchange. They believe that the South has been overlooked in the past, and further believe that with proper working it can be made one of the most lucrative territories in the country. They state that under the new arrangement they will be able to quote to a producer a blanket price for the entire block of Southern states, including also the Washington territory, or can quote prices for what is now known as the Southern territory and what is now known as the Washington territory.

Offices will be opened in the principal cities and exchange centers of the South. An effort already is on foot to line up the exhibitors under a co-operative plan, and missionary work in the South already is well under way.

SPITZER ANSWERS "WHAT'S WRONG WITH MARKET?"

"What is wrong with the States rights market?" Nat M. Spitzer, sales manager for the King-Bee Corporation, was asked. "In the first place", Mr. Spitzer said, "it lacks a proper foundation. Up to the present time business has been done by the average state rights distributor on a very loose basis. The general procedure seems to be to make a picture, and spend a little or a great deal of money upon it. This depends on whether it is the desire of the company to 'gyp' their stockholders, or, if it is their own money that they are spending, to cut expenses to the last detail.

"The next step is to splurge out in a lot of inconsistent advertising, and to spend more or less money unnecessarily, as the case may be. And the final move is to place an exorbitant price upon the rights for the various territories, and if the picture isn't 'there,' it gets cold, waiting for buyers. It's a bloomer. The company goes 'bust.' However, another springs up in its place, for they're just like mushrooms; they come up over night.

"These are the methods that are doing the harm to the industry. We must seek a firmer business basis. We must reach a higher standard. There are too many wildcat schemes, and too few built upon really sound business principles. It is just a phase of the tremendous criminal waste of our industry.

"That's what is the matter with the present state rights market—unsound principles, and a waste of materials.

"My policy is to try to overcome this tendency, and we certainly have done so as far as the King-Bee is concerned. In the first place, we don't produce pictures that are not up to a certain standard, for Mr. Bernstein and Mr. Gildstrom personally pass on every script before it is finally accepted. We run our whole organization on a principle of efficiency, and every dollar paid out in expense brings in a certain amount of profit on the other side of the ledger. Therein lies the secret of our success."

BIG EXPLOITATION FOR "GREAT WHITE TRAIL."

Extensive plans are in the making for the exploitation of "The Great White Trail", the new Wharton super-feature, in Canada. John C. Green, controlling the rights for the Dominion and for Alaska, has left Ithaca for his offices in Galt, taking with him three prints of the picture and more than a ton of advertising material, which he intends to distribute through Canada on the Golden Rule principle.

"And that ton of advertising stuff is only to be the beginning", says Mr. Green. "I'll just be getting a good start by the time that is used up, and calling for three or four times as much".

Mr. Green intends to open the picture in one of the big houses of Canada for a run. It then will be distributed through Regal Films, Limited, of Toronto.

"MAN'S LAW" SOLD FOR SEVERAL STATES.

The Overland Film Co., 729 Seventh avenue, New York, sponsors for the latest Irving Cummings picture, entitled "Man's Law", announce that the rights to New York and Northern New Jersey have been sold to the Mammoth Film Corporation. Harry G. Segal, general manager of the Globe Feature Film Co., of Boston, has purchased the picture for the New England States. Mr. Mattson, representing John Olsen & Co., has purchased the rights for Norway, Sweden and Denmark. U. One contracted for the rights for Japan for his organization in Tokio.

MOTOY STUDIO FOR NEW YORK.

H. C. Allen, the President of the Peter Pan Film Corporation, has returned to New York from Chicago, where he completed the arrangements for the moving of the Motoy studio from that city to New York. While there he met R. M. Vandivert, the vice president of the organization, who had been on the ground for several days. Mr. Vandivert has been making an extensive trip for the study of exchange conditions throughout the country, and has reported so great an increase in business as to justify the change. Mr. Allen had already made partial arrangements and has only awaited the assurance of Mr. Vandivert on the question.

"I have felt the necessity for some time", Mr. Allen said, "of having our main studio here in the city, where I can keep in closest touch with the production. While we were getting started and doing business on a comparatively small scale, this was not so necessary, but with the tremendous growth of our bookings and our increase of production, it seems best to centralize as far as is possible.

"At present we are releasing through the Educational Film Corporation of America, which controls the territory of Greater New York, New York and Northern New Jersey; the Standard Film Service Company for Southern Ohio and Kentucky; the Standard Film Service Company for Cleveland and Northern Ohio; the Lea Bel Company for Illinois, Indiana and Southern Wisconsin; M. R. Dick for Minnesota, North and South Dakota, and Northern Wisconsin; Standard Film Service for Michigan; Metropolitan Film Company for New England; Metro Film Service Company for Virginia, Maryland, District of Columbia, North Carolina and Delaware; Mayer & Rosenthal for California, Arizona and Nevada; William T. Binford for Wyoming, Utah, Colorado, and New Mexico. We have the country pretty well covered and are now completing arrangements for taking up South America, beginning probably at Buenos Aires. Mr. Woolwidge left this week for London to attend to the details of our new English office, and will remain over there some time studying the conditions of the foreign market.

"Our present plans are to release 1,000 feet each week, composed of two 500-foot novelties, the novelties to be released on alternate weeks. After September 1 a one-reel subject will be released in addition to this program, and after December 1 this plan will be augmented by a further release of one reel a week.

"The Peter Pan Company is sending a wedding party on a trip around the world to make a series of travel pictures, and will begin to release these at an early date. The party is already at work in Honolulu. These will be released in addition to our other program."

TERRY COMPLETES FOURTH HUMAN INTEREST REEL.

Terry has just completed his fourth of the Terry Human Interest Reel series. The name of the fourth episode of this series of animated human interest sketches is called "Character as Revealed By The Ear", and continues as part of the studies of that eminent delineator of character, Jessie Allen Fowler. The first of the Terry Human Interest Reel series is called "Character As Revealed By The Nose", and was released a short time ago. The second of the series is entitled "Character As Revealed By The Eyes". The third of the series deals with the mouth and lips and is known as "Character As Revealed By The Mouth".

WELCH MADE BUD FISHER MANAGER.

Bud Fisher has selected J. Edward Welch as general office manager of the Bud Fisher Films Corporation. Bud goes to war this month, and as H. A. Brock, the former manager, has been called to the Quartermasters' Department of the Army, it was necessary to find a man of ability to look after the affairs of the organization.

When Mr. Welch came to New York from Baltimore, where he had been an exhibitor, he met Mr. Fisher, who immediately saw his possibilities, and offered him a place in his company. Since that time, under Bud's careful training, he has become an excellent exchange man, and has a remarkable knowledge of the conditions of the American market.

HILLER & WILK HANDLING "ALMA".

Conspicuous among several big feature pictures that Hiller & Wilk, film brokers, have arranged to handle for the early autumn is "Alma, Where Do You Live", the six-reel version of the famous play of the same title.

Supporting Ruth MacTammany in the screen interpretation are George Larkin, Jack Newton, John Webb Dillon, Frank McNish, Mattie Keene, Marian Kenmaire, Walter Mack, George Gaston, Joseph Phillips and other well-known screen favorites.

PIEDMONT BUYS "WHIP" FOR FOREIGN CLIENT.

The Piedmont Film Corporation has purchased for a foreign client through Hiller & Wilk "The Whip". The sale covered the rights for India, Ceylon and Burma.

"The Whip" Offered World-Wide

Paragon Films, Inc., Announce Big Melodrama Ready for Sale in Open Territories.

PARAGON FILMS, INC., announce that "The Whip" is now being sold not only for states but for world rights, and thereby hangs a story. "The Whip," made from the famous melodrama into a spectacular picture of eight reels, was first released early last spring. It ran for a considerable time at the Park theater in New York, attracting a great deal of attention and afterward it ran in San Francisco and one or two other big centers with equal success. It was all ready for state rights release, but just about that time the United States entered the great war, and conditions were so uncertain that Paragon Films, Inc., practically withdrew "The Whip" from the market. It has been held until the present time and now it is being released for the world market with a new big hoorah and with every indication of tremendous success.

"The Whip" is now released by Paragon Films, Inc., of 912 Longacre Building, New York, for the states that were not sold at the beginning and for various parts of the world. It has great possibilities for both markets because of the fame it attained during its sensation runs in the two world capitals, London and New York.

These territories still are open: Pennsylvania, Illinois, Ohio, Missouri, Kansas, Nebraska, Iowa, Colorado, Utah, North Dakota, South Dakota, Nevada, Wyoming, Wisconsin, Minnesota, New Mexico, West Virginia, Maryland, District of Columbia, Delaware, Virginia, North Carolina, South Carolina, Florida, Georgia, Tennessee, Alabama, Louisiana, Mississippi, Texas, Arkansas and Oklahoma. Also the rights to these continents: Europe, except Great Britain and Scandinavia; all of South America, with Mexico and Cuba; all of Asia, except Japan, and all of Africa, except British South Africa.

The following sales have been made, and in each case the buyer has reported great success within his territory: New York State, bought by Marcus Loew; New Jersey, bought by the Civilization Film Corporation of New Jersey; Oregon, Washington, Idaho and Montana have been bought by the De Luxe Feature Film Co., of Seattle; California and Arizona have been bought by All-Star Feature Distributors, Inc., of San Francisco; Kentucky and Indiana by Robert Lieber; New England by American Feature Film Co.; Canada by SuperFeatures, Ltd., of Toronto; Great Britain and Ireland by Theater Royal, Drury Lane, Ltd., of London; Australia, New Zealand, the balance of Australasia, Hawaiian Islands and South Africa by Samuel Krellberg, and Scandinavia by the Interocean Film Co. In some cases the men and corporations who bought these rights have elected to book "The Whip" as a regular theatrical attraction at the very best theaters in their territory. Robert Lieber has done this in Kentucky and Indiana with the best kind of results. The American Feature Film Co. booked "The Whip" over the Poli circuit of theaters through New England, and it drew such large crowds everywhere that now they are booking it back over the same circuit. In cities where there are no Poli theaters they release it regularly. Under both arrangements "The Whip" has proved to be a great moneymaker.

SMALLWOOD STATE-RIGHTING COMEDIES.

Arthur N. Smallwood, of the Smallwood Film Company, announces that the Aubrey Series of two-reel super-comedies featuring James Aubrey, will be released on the state rights plan.

Beginning in October a two-reel subject will be released monthly, for ten months. They will be sold as a series to state rights buyers, with the provision that they be sold to the exhibitor in the same way.

"Arrangements are in the course of completion whereby the Aubrey Series will be advertised in a big way through one hundred newspapers in the largest cities", said Mr. Smallwood. "The publicity attached to the series will measure up favorably with that given the best exploited serials. We have secured Aubrey's services on a three-year contract. We will give the state rights buyer and the exhibitor every chance in the world to cash in big on James Aubrey. Of course, we expect to cash in ourselves, but we are willing to wait until the second year for our profits. We will invest our money in newspaper space, believing that in this way we can best serve our customers and, at the same time, insure our own profits".

MILTON J. SCHWARTZ JOINS SHORT FEATURES.

Milton J. Schwartz has joined the selling staff of the Short Features Exchange. Mr. Schwartz comes to Short Features after several years of experience as an exhibitor, in which branch of the motion picture business he made good. His experience as an exhibitor naturally gives him a big advantage over the average film salesman, inasmuch as he knows the exhibitor's wants. Although a young man, he has matured him. He honestly believes in the short picture, and emphatically declares that it is just as important to the exhibitor's program as the feature itself. He allied himself with the Short Features Exchange because, as an exhibitor, he had discovered their drawing power. Now his business is to convince other exhibitors of their drawing power, and no doubt he will make good in this field of the game as he did as an exhibitor.

Beynon Engaged for "Lust of Ages" Score

Ogden Corporation Also Announces Advertising Matter Ready on Lillian Walker Subject.

THE Ogden Pictures Corporation has engaged George W. Beynon to prepare a complete and original musical score for the production 'The Lust of the Ages", in which Lillian Walker is starred. Mr. Beynon, after viewing the picture, stated that of the hundreds of musical scores prepared by him he does not recall a single photoplay production which lends or adapts itself to so much originality as "The Lust of the Ages". The score is for an orchestra ranging from four to forty pieces.

The distribution of the musical score is one of the many novel advertising appurtenances issued in connection with "The Lust of the Ages". A film card containing a reproduction of a chest of gold, around which are cubes or frames of positive film, being scenes from the production, which are beautifully tinted and toned, is an added novelty. These film cards, when hung in the lobby where daylight is profuse, or in front ot an electric bulb, will give an unusual effect to those viewing it and is also employed by film salesmen handling the production in order to present to theatergoers in concrete form an idea of the beauty of the photography, tinting and toning and the massiveness of interior settings and the scenery employed in the production.

A heavy circular cardboard, ten inches in diameter, containing on one side a reproduction of a twenty dollar gold piece and on the other side a picture of Lillian Walker, is an unusual window card issued in connection with the production. These replicas of the twenty dollar gold piece can be devoted to various uses as, for instance, tacking them on to the four corners of the lithographs and billboards, hanging them in lobbies, putting them in windows of stores and nailing them to telegraph poles and other places. A further novelty consists of an advance trailer which, contrary to usual trailers, does not contain altogether scenes from the release, but various poses of Miss Walker in various characters showing the wide range of her versatility in make-up.

KLOTZ & STREIMER PLANNING FALL CAMPAIGN.

Klotz & Streimer, who are selling "Whither Thou Goest" on a state rights basis. Mr. Klotz, president, is negotiating with two well known directors to produce for his concern. Klotz states that he was encouraged to market state rights from the demand he has for "Whither Thou Goest", which is proof that there is a market for clean, wholesome productions, if produced by a capable director and a cast to fit the story. Mr. Streimer is about to close for stories of well-known plays which were produced successfully on the speaking stage and which are adapted for the screen. Streimer has engaged one of the best script writers to work in conjunction with the director on the scenario. The second picture will be ready to be shown about September 15.

"SIRENS OF THE SEA" AT BROADWAY.

"Sirens of the Sea," a super-feature of Jewel Productions, Inc., began an engagement at the Broadway theater, New York, on August 26, with Louise Lovely and Jack Mulhall in the leading roles. The scenario follows the story of Grace Helen Bailey, and Allen Holubar is the director.

The feature, in five reels, is said to be most elaborate, many

Scene from "Sirens of the Sea" (Jewel).

of the scenes being laid off a strange island in the Pacific. The story has to do with the discovery of a small child in a fishing net, by Wellington Stanhope and his wife, who dwell in a villa built by the ancient Greek sculptor, Ceres. The dramatic incidents develop when, grown to womanhood, the wife is wooed by a millionaire cruising in search of adventure and by his friend.

Manufacturers' Advance Notes

Mutual Initiates Two a Week

Begins a Run of Sixteen Subjects with Edna Goodrich's "Reputation" and Mary Minter's "Charity Castle."

MUTUAL opens its schedule of two star productions a week September 3, when it will release "Reputation," the first of a series of feature productions starring Edna Goodrich, stage beauty, and "Charity Castle," the first of a new series of Mutual-American pictures, starring Mary Miles Minter.

The studios producing features for Mutual release have spent a strenuous summer in preparation for the elaborate plans of John R. Freuler, president of the Mutual Film Corporation, to put into the market two five reel features a week. Mr. Freuler and the executives of the various producing companies have been in close touch all through the hot season, selecting stories, supervising direction and overseeing the most minute detail of production that there would be no hitch in the "two a week" plan and that the standard of the releases would conform to the high standard which the chief of Mutual had laid down.

That the preparations have been made carefully is evidenced by the fact that before the middle of August Mutual was in a position to announce a release schedule of two five-reel features a week for eight weeks. Every one of the sixteen productions is either completed or in the last stages of completion.

"Reputation" is from the story by John Clymer, Miss Goodrich carries the role of a small town girl who goes to the city to "make good" and returns, unblemished, but with a reputation. The play is admirably suited to Miss Goodrich's talents. It provides her plenty of opportunity for display of the vivacity, the deep emotion and her beauty.

"Charity Castle" is a five-act dramatic fantasy in which Mary Miles Minter plays the role of fairy princess. It is another modern fairy story, different to a marked degree from the others in which Miss Minter has starred and which have been such tremendous successes. In "Charity Castle" she is a child of the slums, who takes her little brother and her smile to the home of a confirmed crab. The old grouch turns his gloomy domicile into "Charity Castle" with Miss Minter as the princess royal.

Mutual's schedule for the week of September 3 carries one comedy, a one-reel Cub starring George Ovey. "Jerry Tries Again" shows Jerry's further efforts to secure a bride via the want ad route. Reel Life No. 71, Mutual's film magazine, released September 6, shows a watering system for a small farm, shows how the United States Government handles its mail, takes visitors on a visit to a skunk farm conducted by a fifteen-year-old girl, and shows how the five senses are more acutely developed by various businesses and by various pleasures. The reel carries an animated drawing from Life, entitled, "Fresh Advances in the Champagne District."

"Mutual Weekly," the weekly news reel, will carry, in addition to pictures of the history events which are taking place in America, glimpses of the American soldiers in their camp in France.

HEARST-PATHE NEWS TO DEPICT LIFE IN CANTONMENTS.

Relatives and friends of soldiers boys who have enlisted, or been drafted, into the great national army, will have an opportunity to see them at work in the training camps in vivid motion pictures.

Kendall Banning, director of the Division of Pictures of the Committee of Public Information, has granted permission to the Hearst-Pathe News cameramen to visit all of the cantonments throughout the United States, where the soldiers are training. Several cameramen will be assigned at various times to each of the training camps where they will spend several days picturing the defenders of the nation in the preliminary work that they must undergo prior to their departure for the battlefields of Europe. The work of these cameramen will form one of the most important connecting links of American history. Men who are rookies today, and who may later occupy high positions in the events, will be shown undergoing the grinding detail of camp life. Such pictures of the Civil War, had they been taken, would be of inestimable value today.

As rapidly as the pictures are taken they will be forwarded to Washington to be passed by the official censors, after which they will be shown each week in the releases of the Hearst-Pathe News.

"THE RAILROADER" (Selig).

"The Railroader" is a Selig version of Albert Payson Terhune's world-famous novel, "Caleb Conover," which has been read and enjoyed by hundreds of thousands of readers in all parts of the country. George Fawcett, the famous star, enacts the title role and is supported by a clever cast of players, among whom can be named Bessie Eyton, Frank Clark, William Robert Daly, Thomas Santschi and others.

The story of "The Railroader" is a tense drama of human interest. Caleb Conover is a railroad section boss who, with indomitable will, follows the iron rule of "what I want I take." He rises by his own efforts. He takes his mate by main force, he seizes an opportunity to make a million dollars on a real estate investment and later becomes political boss of an entire

Scene from "The Railroader" (Selig).

state and his wealth is reputed to amount to sixty millions of dollars.

But too late Caleb Conover realises that wealth and power are not everything; that the trampling down of the rights of the people; the violations of friendship; and the usurpation of the rights of others cannot in the end but react upon the perpetrator. The end comes dramatically but logically. Deserted by his quondam friends, his son a saphead and his daughter disgraced, a prison term staring him in the face, Caleb Conover realizes that there is a divinity that shapes our ends.

Attention is called by the Selig Company to the wonderful sets presented in this drama and an all-star cast, including Thomas Santschi, Bessie Eyton, Fritzi Brunette and others, cleverly support Mr. Fawcett in a gripping drama of human interest.

William N. Selig expects to announce plans for the exploitation of "The Railroader" in the near future.

REAL AMERICAN SPIRIT IN RAY'S PICTURE.

The sort of stuff that makes Americans respected in every clime and which is asserting itself today in the preparations for the great conflict is featured in Charles Ray's first Paramount picture, which is being produced under the supervision of Thomas H. Ince. The title of the picture is "The Son of His Father," and it depicts the efforts and final success of a rich man's son, Gordon Carlboy, when he is given five thousand dollars and told to "go to it," by his dad, who has become disgusted with the lad's spendthrift traits.

The story of "The Son of His Father" is by Ridgewell Cullum and it is directed by Victor Schertzinger. Vola Vale, who has played with Sessue Hayakawa in "Each to His Kind" and with George Behan in "The Bond Between," supports Ray in his first production.

SIMPLEX FOR AUSTRALIA.

From far away Australia L. H. Cornell, operator Grand Theater, Perth, West Australia, writes that his Simplex Projectors are giving satisfaction in every respect and of course, the Precision Machine Co. will be pleased to learn they have added another member to the Simplex Boosters' Club.

Rodeo Champions in New Fairbanks Picture

Many Leaders of Western Sport to Be Seen in "The Man From Painted Post," a Cattle Rustling Story.

IN "The Man From Painted Post", Douglas Fairbanks' newest Artcraft picture, there will be seen a great collection of Western champions. Following the recent Rodeo in Cheyenne, Mr. Fairbanks immediately engaged the winners of the first prizes for his next release, including Sam Brownell, champion bucking broncho rider of the world; Tommy Grimes, the fearless steer roper; Johnny Judd, fancy rope artist; Jay Miller, Tom Yarberry, Bill Baker, Charley Self and Bill Brown. In addition to this group of experts he engaged H. A. Strickland, champion bareback bucking broncho rider; Jack Padgan, Bill Crawford, Ed Burns, Charles Stevens, Fred Burns, who held the trick roping championship for five years until 1913; Edgar Metchan and Charles McPherson. Every cowboy in the new Fairbanks production has distinguished himself in one of the various accomplishments of the plainsman, and is well known among the followers of Western sports.

This entire party, together with the cast and the technical staff recently journeyed from Los Angeles to Laramie, Wyoming, and then to James House's Riverside Ranch, which has been leased by the Fairbanks organization for the film. The ranch is conceded to present the most beautiful scenic displays of Wyoming and includes 150,000 acres of land and 35,000 head of cattle.

The story is a comedy drama of the cattle rustling days handled in a novel manner. The vehicle discloses the energetic Douglas in a role unlike anything in which he has ever appeared on the screen and gives him an opportunity to present various dramatic situations in addition to many original incidents of typical Fairbanks creation.

Among the supporting players is Frank Campeau, the well known Western character actor. Joseph Henaberry is directing the picture, assisted by Millard Webb.

THREE ADE COMEDIES RELEASED.

The first three George Ade "Fables in Slang" have been listed for release by General Film as follows: September 1, "The Twelve Cylinder Speed of the Leisure Class"; September 8, "The Wandering Boy and the Wayward Parents"; September 15, "What Transpires After the Wind-Up." There are to be fully twelve George Ade "Fables in Slang" picturized for this series at the rate of one each week.

"THE ADVENTURER" SHOWS CHAPLIN A CONVICT.

Charlie Chaplin will next be seen as a bestriped convict in "The Adventurer." The last few scenes of his forthcoming picture are being "shot" at Los Angeles. Many scenes from "The Adventurer" were taken along the Sierra Madre coast range, where Chaplin, in the role of an escaped convict, flees over the rocky coast pursued by armed guards, of whom big Eric Campbell is the chief.

The forthcoming Mutual-Chaplin special is declared to be quite the funniest thing the international comedian has yet done. The idea around which it is built provides so many humorous situations and so many opportunities for Chaplin

Scene from "The Adventurer" (Mutual).

to work in those subtle bits of humor which makes his pictures so uproariously comical that it cannot help being a masterpiece of comedy.

The idea on which "The Adventurer" was built was the one in which he made his first start on the picture which eventually turned out to be "The Immigrant." Chaplinlike, he got started on the one, the other popped into his head and he began work, full steam ahead, on the new idea. In the meantime he evolved the idea of "The Adventurer," put a lot of new touches into it, so that really it could not be identified by the parent germ from which it is descended.

Essanay Using Animated Titles

Innovation in "The Golden Idiot" May Become Fixture in Coming Releases.

AN innovation which has caused favorable comment has been introduced by Essanay into recent photoplays. It is called the animated sub-title. One of the chief causes for criticism of sub-titles, particularly where any quantity are used in a feature, is the fact that many persons read them at a glance, and are then forced to continue to watch several yards of the same title being run off for the benefit of those who read more slowly.

This has resulted in every possible sub-title being eliminated in the past, in spite of the opinion of many that this portion of a subject can be made one of its greatest assets. For this reason Essanay considered it important to provide a form of leader that would add to the pleasing qualities of the film without in any way detracting from the entertainment of those who had found cause for complaint.

The animated sub-title is the result, and it has been hailed as a novelty. It was first introduced to the public in "The Golden Idiot," a recent success featuring Bryant Washburn. Those who have seen it will appreciate the interest aroused by the conversation which took place between the characters that were shown in a blocked off corner of the screen without interfering with the action. The success of this innovation means that it will undoubtedly play an important part in future releases of the Essanay Company.

LE SAINT MAKING "THE MAN OF GOD."

Director E. J. Le Saint, who produced a number of exceptional feature pictures a year ago for the Universal, has rejoined that company and has started work on the filming of "The Man of God," a western story by J. Grubb Alexander and Fred Myton of the Universal writing staff.

Stella Razetto, well known screen actress, who in private life is Mrs. Le Saint, will be behind the camera as co-director. The cast for Le Saint's current production easily might be called all-star. William Stowell, who played the leading male role in "Pay Me!" will have a prominent part in the picture, as will Helen Gibson, the daredevil leading lady of the recent railroad dramas filmed at Universal City. Hector Dion, whose screen popularity dates from the time he played leads with Florence Turner in Vitagraph pictures and extends through engagements with Reliance, Biograph and Thanhouser, has been engaged for Le Saint's company.

Another new personage in Universal films is Miss Mildred Davis, formerly leading lady of one of the Mutual companies, who will play the principal ingenue role in "The Man of God." Betty Schade, Millard Wilson and Alfred Allen, each of whom has played leads in Universal pictures, will also have prominent parts in Le Saint's new production.

ART DRAMAS FOR SOUTHERN DISTRIBUTION.

One of the biggest deals ever consummated by Art Dramas, Incorporated, since its inception was closed this week by Arthur F. Beck, general manager of the concern. The deal involved the disposing of franchise rights on Art Dramas for practically the entire South. The States covered by the contract are North Carolina, South Carolina, Florida, Georgia, Alabama, Mississippi and Tennessee.

The company which purchased the franchise was organized by Atlanta capital solely to exploit Art Dramas. It is known as the E. & H. Film Distributing Company, and has central offices in Atlanta. Other offices in all parts of the large territory are being formed as fast as possible.

E. H. Harden is the president of the E. & H., and P. A. Engler will be general manager. Both men are known throughout the Southern territory as veteran film men who are experienced in catering to the exhibitor's wants, and who have been extremely successful in the exploitation of big features.

APOLLO STARTS WORK ON MYSTERY TALE.

According to announcement from Harry Raver, president of Apollo Pictures, Inc., releasing on Art Dramas Program, his company will shortly begin work on a mystery story of unusual nature and novel plot, which will deal with the adventures of a crook known as "T." The title of the production has not yet been decided.

Mr. Raver is of the opinion that this story is one of the most amazing and surprising dramas ever conceived, and he is confident it will cause a sensation. It is completely out of the beaten track of mystery stories, according to announcement.

"THE FALL OF THE ROMANOFFS" COMPLETED.

Herbert Brenon took the last scene of his forthcoming production of the events which led up to and immediately preceded the Russian revolution, which he has entitled "The Fall of the Romanoffs" at his studio on Hudson Heights, Wednesday, August 20. Already the assembling, cutting and titling has so far progressed that the exhibition will be completed in its entirety by September 6, when a private showing at the Ritz Carlton will be held. Five of the eight reels have been corrected and titled, and are ready for release.

Current Triangle Bill

First Fall Releases, Scheduled for September 2, Include Saturday Evening Post Story.

"TEN OF DIAMONDS," by Albert Cowles, and "The Man Hater," a Saturday Evening Post story by Mary Brecht Pulver, are listed as the first fall releases from the Triangle Film Corporation, appearing on the program for the week of September 2. "Ten of Diamonds," which is being featured at the Strand Theatre, New York City, this week, concerns a girl of a cheap tenderloin cafe who is metamorphosed into "a lady" at the caprice of an idle young rich bachelor, who aims to play a trick on society by presenting her as a wealthy tourist spending the winter in New York. He also intends to use her as a weapon of vengeance against a society man who has humiliated him. The woman from the streets upsets these plans, however, by becoming mistress of her own destiny.

"The Man Hater" was published as a story by Mary Brecht Pulver in the Saturday Evening Post of June 9. It is issued as a picture by Triangle on September 2. Winifred Allen has the role of the fascinating man-hater. She is supported by Jack Meredith, Harry Neville, Jessie Shirley, Marguerite Gale, Robert Vivian and little Anna Lehr. The production was directed by Albert Parker, assisted by Thomas F. Tracey, under the supervision of Allan Dwan.

The Triangle comedies for this program are "His Fallen Star," with Harry McCoy, Frederick Bertrand, Gladys Tennyson and Eddie Sutherland, and "His Foothill Folly" with Ray Griffith, Eleanor Field and Frank Bond.

"His Fallen Star" is the story of astronomers looking for a new star, and of a young genius, Harry McCoy, who invents, with the aid of a box of fireworks, one for them. The inventive youth thereby wins the near-sighted astronomer's daughter as a bride. The other comedy, "His Foothill Folly" is a burlesque of the Western bad-man pictures. This Keystone gunfighter has his own private graveyard, his own particular brand of stimulant and his evangelical girl. It is described as a melodrama of laughter.

"A Shanghaied Jonah," featuring Maude Wayne, Billy Armstrong, Guy Woodward, and the mermaid contingent of the Keystone camp is the Keystone two-reeler that will enlighten picturegoers during the first week of the fall. It is the fable of the ill-fated Jonah brought up to date.

PATHE POSTPONES RELEASE OF "THE SEVEN PEARLS."

"The Seven Pearls," Pathe's new serial, featuring Mollie King, Creighton Hale and Leon Barry, announced for release September 3, has been postponed until September 16. The delay in release was made at the request of many exhibitors throughout the United States who wished to find place on their program for this serial, but were unable to do so if it was released as originally scheduled.

VICTOR MOORE IN "THE CINDERELLA HUSBAND."

Victor Moore will release August 27 his newest comedy, entitled "The Cinderella Husband." It is based on the idea of the fairy tale, but written in an up-to-date manner by Thomas J. Gray.

Vic is discovered in the opening scene at the wash tub in the kitchen working his head off. Like Cinderella in the

Scene from "The Cinderella Husband" (Klever).

fairy tale, the best he gets is the worst of it. He is a slave in the house with a capital "S" and his wicked brother-in-law, who is more "law" than "brother" helps add to his misery.

It happens that there is a carnival in the town, and the Queen of the carnival is to pick her own King in a very unique way. Every man present is to put one of his shoes in the basket, and the Queen, blindfolded, will pick out a shoe. Whoever the shoe fits will be the King of the Carnival.

This is a unique picture which Moore has made, and is full of real genuine laughter. The picture is presented with a very large supporting cast.

"THE LOST EXPRESS" (Signal).

The Mutual Film Corporation will release "The Lost Express," a fifteen chapter, thirty-reel photodrama starring Helen Holmes on September 17. "The Lost Express" was produced by the Signal Film Corporation under direction of J. P. McGowan. The production will be released a chapter a week for fifteen weeks. Helen Holmes has won international repute by the thrilling escapades in which she has figured before the camera in a series of highly successful chapter dramas.

Scene from "The Lost Express" (Mutual.

Her successes have all been staged by McGowan, past master of the art of creating thrills. In staging "The Lost Express," he had the active assistance and co-operation of the author, Frederick R. Bennett.

"The Lost Express" is built around a baffling scientific mystery. An express train, carrying a carload of highly valuable documents, leaves its terminal under armed guard. It never reaches the next station. Members of the crew are found, bound and gagged, in the bottom of a lumber wagon.

For the first time in her career of exciting escapades, Miss Holmes goes to the bottom of the sea in a diver's suit.

"MARRIED IN NAME ONLY" (Ivan).

"Married in Name Only," dramatized by Ivan Abramson and Edmund Lawrence is, as far as an official of the Ivan Film Company states, the last of the sex problem picture that Mr. Abramson has prepared for the camera.

The picture has been now concluded, and Mr. Lawrence, who directed the production, has finished cutting and titling same, and is so pleased with the picture that he enthusiastically announces that it is the best thing he ever done.

Scene from "Married in Name Only" (Ivan).

When one considers Mr. Lawrence's position, having been for many years with Kalem, bringing out the best they have ever made, and just lately severed his connection as director of Mme. Petrova, "Married in Name Only" judging from above ought to be a remarkable picture.

Gretchen Hartman, who is now playing the lead in the big nine reel production, "Les Miserables," is the female star, featured in conjunction with Milton Sills, who has the leading male part.

Five Fox Releases for September

R. A. Walsh's "Betrayed" Heads the List, to Be Issued the Day Before Labor Day.

MIRIAM COOPER, Virginia Pearson, George Walsh, and Dustin Farnum, are announced as the players starred in William Fox's first four feature releases during September. The productions are: September 2, R. A. Walsh's drama, "Betrayed," with Miriam Cooper; September 9, Virginia Pearson in "When False Tongues Speak"; September 16, George Walsh in "The Yankee Way"; September 23, Dustin Farnum in "North of Fifty-three." It is probable "A Rich Man's Plaything," in which Valeska Suratt has the chief role, will be issued on the last day of the month.

"Betrayed" centers about Carmelita Carrito, whose worldly condition is that of a peon, whose soul is that of an aristocrat, whose heart is that of a coquette.

In "When False Tongues Speak," by George Scarborough, Hardee Kirkland is seen opposite Miss Pearson, and the company includes Claire Whitney, Carl Eckstrom and William E. Meehan.

"The Yankee Way" is described as a "star-spangled comedy." It presents the genial George Walsh, supported by Enid Markey, Joe Dowling, Charles Edler, James O'Shea, Ed Sedgwick, Edward Cecil and Tom Wilson. Richard Stanton is the director.

"North of Fifty-three" was taken from the story of that name by Bertrand W. Sinclair. The picture, with the inimitable "Dusty" Farnum, as "Roaring Bill" Wagstaff, will undoubtedly have the same wide vogue as that enjoyed by the novel. Winifred Kingston gives her always brilliant interpretation in the role opposite Mr. Farnum.

"BROADWAY, ARIZONA" (Triangle).

Production work has been finished at the Culver City plant of the Triangle Film Corporation on the drama of New York life and Western adventure, in which Olive Thomas will be starred under the direction of Lynn Reynolds.

The name of Miss Thomas' new piece is "Broadway, Arizona," and the action of the story is all that the name implies. Elaborate settings, which vary from luxurious scenes of metropolitan life to the rugged beauty and grandeur of the Southern California mountains, make the screen offering one of picturesque quality. Miss Thomas plays the part of an actress who achieves sensational popularity on the gay White Way, and is later compelled to create a Broadway for herself when failing health banishes her to a Western desert town.

The exterior scenes of the production were filmed in the Big Bear lake country in Southern California, which is famed for its beautiful scenery. Director Reynolds is said to have secured some unusual photographic effects that will make the whole piece one of rare beauty.

"FLIRTING WITH DEATH" (Bluebird).

Herbert Rawlinson and Brownie Vernon appear as joint stars on the Bluebird program for the first time, week starting September 24, in a sensational comedy drama entitled "Flirting With Death." Waldemar Young and Frank Dazey furnished the story under the original title of "Sky High," and Mr. Young made the scenario from which Elmer Clifton directed the feature.

Mr. Rawlinson has appeared in earlier Bluebirds, having

Scene from "Flirting With Death" (Bluebird).

co-starred with Ella Hall in "Little Eve Edgarton," and he was the hero of "The Eagle's Wings," the industrial preparedness feature Bluebird released on State rights. Miss Vernon has become extremely popular as co-star with Franklyn Farnum in a series of releases that terminated when Mr. Farnum cut loose as a lone star on the program.

"Flirting With Death" is the first of several features in which Mr. Rawlinson and Miss Vernon will star under Elmer Clifton's direction. The hero is a soldier of fortune who has ventured into the circus business to establish a bankroll and

in his pursuit of the nimble dollar he finally is forced to negotiate a sensational airship flight and parachute drop to "put across" a deal that assures his fortune and the hand of his beloved.

Director Clifton has represented the sensational "punch" of the picture with skill and effectiveness, and Rawlinson accepts the hazard with thrilling realism. Two reels of circus scenes, taken while a touring show was halted in transit, reflect the life and daily adventure of showmen in actual scenes. "Flirting With Death," it is declared, reflects real circus life and depicts the real character of showmen besides offering a fetching love theme and sprinkling excitement through many fleeting thrills and sensational episodes.

"The Woman God Forgot" a Spectacle

Geraldine Farrar's Initial Artcraft Subject Expected to Create Greater Sensation Than "Joan"—Gigantic Sets Used.

IN addition to its spectacular scenes Geraldine Farrar's initial Artcraft production, "The Woman God Forgot," now being staged by Cecil B. De Mille, promises to prove a super-photoplay of unusual beauty. One of the elaborate scenes discloses the largest aviary in the world especially built for this film. A number of views present the huge private swimming pool and garden of Montezuma's daughter. The garden and pool were inclosed in a wire netting fifty feet high and 400 feet long to prevent the escape of thousands of rare birds which filled the foliage.

Last week Director De Mille took a company of 200 people by special train into Yosemite.

In building the gigantic pyramid, the highest set ever used in a motion picture, a force of carpenters and stonemasons were busy nearly two weeks working night and day. This one set covers an area of over two square miles and is the site of an immense battle in which a thousand persons take part. The interior views of an Aztec temple also offer novel scenes, the huge sacrificial room with its flaming altar being reproduced in the exact size of the chamber in which the high priest sacrificed his human victims to the Aztec gods.

A stirring romance between the Aztec princess and the Spanish captain for the Cortez army, disclosing many exceptional dramatic situations, fastens the spectator's interest upon the leading characters of the play in the development of the story. The production demands much of the histrionic talents of the famous Farrar and that it will prove her greatest cinema characterization, not excepting "Joan," is readily anticipated. The photoplay will be ready for release within a month.

"MADAM WHO" (Paralta).

Bessie Barriscale's company is busy at the Paralta studios at Hollywood producing her second Paralta production, "Madam Who," which will be released through the Triangle Distributing Corporation in October.

It is founded on Harold McGrath's mystery romance of the same title. This story was first published about a year ago in a popular magazine and created something of a sensation among readers of light fiction.

In subject it is very timely. The heroine, Jeanne Dupree, loses her father and two brothers in war. She becomes a military spy and discovers a band of spies of the enemy within the lines of her army. In attempting to capture them she, herself, is captured by the enemy, who are masked and apparently unknown to each other except by number.

They are loathe to kill her and one suggests that she be forced to marry one of them. In the face of death Jeanne consents and is married by one of the masked men, who is really a clergyman.

Jeanne is left bound and gagged, but escapes and swears to run down and capture the masked spies. This is the motive of the dramatic action of the story, and in the accomplishment of her purpose the young girl has many thrilling adventures which will be as thrillingly depicted on the screen.

Miss Barriscale is supported by Ed Coxen as John Armitage; Howard Hickman as Henry Morgan; Joseph J. Dowling as Parson John Kennedy, and David M. Hartford as Allen Crandall of the secret service. Other parts are played by Fannie Midgeley, Nick Cogley and Bert Hadley.

HOLMES PICTURE SLATED FOR FIRST RUNS.

Owing to the favorable time selected for the release of "Efficiency Edgar's Courtship," the first Taylor Holmes picture by Essanay, this subject is slated for a number of first runs. So phenomenal was his success in his recent stage production, "His Majesty Bunker Bean," that a deal is now pending whereby his first feature will be shown throughout an entire circuit heretofore devoted exclusively to stage attractions.

This photoplay was originally prepared for release earlier in the fall, but these houses were closed for the summer, and it was not considered advisable to open them for the run of the one picture. Now that they are about to open for the regular season, it was thought possible to make a place for this attraction before the stage productions start.

It is expected this will popularize this comedian more quickly than would be possible if his first subject were to be shown for its first run in the usual manner.

William Fox Making "Les Miserables"

William Farnum Being Starred in a Standard Picture, Directed by Frank Lloyd.

ONE of the most important announcements William Fox has made this year is that a complete and superb cinema version of "Les Miserables" is under way.

Work on this great photodrama has gone forward for some time at the big Fox studios at Fort Lee. William Farnum is appearing as Jean Valjean in Victor Hugo's immortal classic. Mr. Farnum is infusing into his portrayal of the famous Valjean a fineness of characterization, a depth of artistry seldom achieved, and worthy of this master figure of literature.

The photoplay is being screened under the direction of Frank Lloyd, who directed "A Tale of Two Cities." Mr. Lloyd is well equipped for the successful and satisfying transference of "Les Miserables." The players supporting Mr. Farnum have been selected with great care, and special attention also is being given the photography. In the filming of Hugo's classic are required scores of night scenes. Mr. Fox is desirous of producing in "Les Miserables" a drama which shall be the perfection of workmanship.

The threescore years which have passed since the publication of "Les Miserables" have brought it more and more praise from critics and laymen. "Les Miserables" is, without question the most splendid epic and dramatic piece of fiction ever created. That is the manner in which Swinburne, the famous poet, described it. It is the epic of a soul transfigured and redeemed, purified through heroism and glorified through suffering; the tragedy and the comedy of life at its darkest and its brightest, of humanity at its best and its worst.

"Les Miserables" will be a William Fox Standard Picture, and the second of the number in which William Farnum will appear.

FIVE DIRECTORS MAKING L-KO'S.

The studios of L-Ko Comedies, at Hollywood, Cal., are scenes of great activity. Under the general supervision of J. G. Blystone, five directors are working overtime to stack up releases against the rainy season. Phil Dunham and Archie Mayo have lately been added to Mr. Blystone's staff to increase production.

Mr. Dunham formerly was a featured comedian in L-Ko but lately turned to directing, with Frank Clark as his assistant. At present Mr. Dunham is working on a comedy in which he will be featured but there will, meanwhile, be shown "High Class Nonsense," Sept. 26, in which Mr. Dunham directed Lucille Hutton and Billy Bevan, as well as "Backward Sons and Forward Daughters," Sept. 5, with the same players featured.

Vin Moore, directing Myrtle Sterling and Al Forbes; Noel Smith, with Gladys Varden as his star; and Dick Smith, directing Eva Novak, are all busy with forthcoming L-Ko's. Gladys Varden will appear Sept. 12, supported by Walter Stevens, Katheryn Young, Bert Roach and Harry Griffith in "From Cactus to Kale." Myrtle Sterling will be star of the Sept. 19 release, "A Prairie Chicken," with Al Forbes heading the support.

Hughey Mack, who lately joined General Director Blystone's forces to be a featured comedian, is working under the direction of Noel Smith in his first picture. Archie Mayo, the latest addition to the directing staff, has not, as yet, been assigned to his company, but he will be at work next week upon his first release.

President Julius Stern, of the L-Ko Corporation, is making plans for an original advertising campaign to boost the L-Ko product through Universal exchanges. His idea involves an altogether novel scheme that has not, previously, been associated with comedy releases. L-Ko is preparing for a lively season.

"BAB'S DIARY" IS FIRST OF "SUB-DEB" SERIES.

In order that the Paramount screen adaptations of the "Sub-Deb" stories starring Marguerite Clark may follow in chronological sequence the order in which they were originally published, the first of the series will be "Bab's Diary" instead of "Bab's Burglar," as previously announced.

Miss Marguerite Clark in the role of the capricious and wholly delightful Bab is fitted with a part that is seemingly made expressly for her. She romps through a series of adventures that provide the most delectable comedy situations. "Bab's Diary" is a September Paramount release under the new Star selective booking plan. The series is the work of Mary Roberts Rhinehart, and the adaptations have been made with particular care so that none of the originality and flavor of the stories have been lost. J. Searle Dawley is directing the productions.

SELIGS ON K-E-S-E.

William N. Selig announces advance releases of two reel comedies in K-E-S-E service as follows: "A Midnight Bell," written by Charles Hoyt, released Monday, September 1; "A Contented Woman," written by Charles Hoyt, released Monday, September 17; "A Bear Fact," released Monday, October 1. Each of these comedies is said to carry not only a plot of merit but a succession of funny incidents. The Charles Hoyt farce comedies, released every two weeks in K-E-S-E service, have proven exceedingly popular with the people. Each comedy is enacted by a capable cast.

MOZUKIN IN "THE PAINTED DOLL."

As the first personality of the cinema to be presented to American playgoers the Russian Art Film Corporation has selected Ivan Mozukin, regarded as the foremost player in the famous Moscow Art Theater, which means in Russia. Mozukin will be seen in "The Painted Doll," a representative film drama selected from the more than fifty negatives which N. S. Kaplan brought from Moscow several weeks ago. In his

Scene from "The Painted Doll" (Russian Art).

support will be seen two other prominent personalities, Natalia Lesienko and Tanya Fetner.

For his premiere here Mozukin will have a role which requires a makeup that conceals the features so much admired by the matinee girls of Russia. This he does not hesitate to do whenever the role requires it. In fact, one of Mozukin's most popular roles finds him creating a character of eighteen years and then developing it through the various stages of manhood to eighty. He is a product of the most rigid artistic system in the world, but a system that makes for the greatest flexibility once the aspirant has qualified. Mozukin, under this system, was selected at an early age by his government and trained for years at government expense. Now approaching the zenith of his development, he is said to be a composite of the abilities of half a dozen prominent American players. He portrays a hero with as much ease as does Francis X. Bushman and he can be as much of a villain as Stuart Holmes. It is predicted that American audiences will like him.

"MAGDA" (C. K. Y.)

In her determination to do bigger things in a bigger way Clara Kimball Young seems to have struck in "Magda" a particularly happy vehicle for her talents. The picture has

Scene from "Magda" (C. K. Y.).

been completed. "Magda," by Herman Sudermann, is the story of a girl whose father believes that the father's will is the will of the whole household.

In the accompanying illustration Valkyrien is seen in the role of the sister standing by Miss Kimball and at the other side is Edward Kimball, the father of the player.

"Magda" is Miss Young's initial production with her own organization under the management of Harry I. Garson.

Paramount to Release Serial in October

Unnamed as Yet, It Is from Pen of Anna Katherine Green and Will Star Kathleen Clifford.

PARAMOUNT is going in for serials. This great motion picture organization announces it will release in October a fifteen-episode mystery drama that will reach in every detail the Paramount quality. Starred will be Kathleen Clifford, vaudeville and musical comedy star, who is making her motion picture debut. The story is the work of America's greatest builder of mysteries, Anna Katharine Green, who possesses the faculty for jamming her stories full to the brim with gasps and throbs.

This serial is the first story Mrs. Green ever has written for motion picture production. It is not a dramatization of any of her previous works, but a brand new tale with the famous Green tangles and apparently unsolvable secrets. It will not be published in book form until after the release of the final episode. Exhibitors are thus protected so that the public may learn the details of the final twist in the plot only by seeing every episode through to the end.

Paramount is using every effort to make its first serial the finest production of its kind. The fifteen episodes are nearly completed, and none will be released until it has passed every test and has met every requirement demanded by every Paramount picture.

The title has not been selected. It will be announced shortly. Mrs. Green has not yet written the final chapter of the story, and only she knows the final twist that will solve the many complications into which she has thrown her interesting characters.

Special service, more thorough than that offered by producers of any other serial, will be given by Paramount exchanges to all exhibitors booking this serial. The publication of a new Anna Katharine Green tale is in itself a literary event, and the fiction story will be widely exploited by the hundreds of newspapers throughout the country that will print it as a news feature of unusual value, not merely as "just another serial story."

Kathleen Clifford is one of the tiniest actresses in motion pictures—and one of the bravest. She was chosen for the first Paramount serial because she was one of the few actresses with genuine dramatic talent who actually possessed athletic ability and a daredevil spirit.

"THE DEFEAT OF THE CITY" HEARTFUL.

In choosing "The Defeat of the City" as the first of the famous O. Henry stories to be picturized in four-reel form, thought was taken of the intensity of the heart interest and the wealth of human appeal assembled by the gifted author in the plot. None has ever rivaled O. Henry for the dramatic depth that he can put into an apparently superficial situation. Always he succeeds in gripping the reader and the beholder of his stories done for the screen. And in "The Defeat of the City," seizing upon one human attribute, Pride, and so dissecting it that he reveals the true and the false to be millions of miles apart, he subtly reveals it to his audience in one offhand, yet tremendous climax.

"The Defeat of the City" by O. Henry is a plain story of American life gaily told. It is such a story as one beholds unseeing every day until a master touch discloses its vibrant beauty.

For his masterful presentation of several preceding heroes

Scene from "The Defeat of the City" (General Film).

in the O. Henry productions for General Film, J. Frank Glendon is cast as Robert Walmsley. Another of the favorite Broadway Star Features players, Agnes Eyre, plays Alicia. Frank Chapman as the old father of Robert and Mrs. Fisher as his mother, and Frank Heath, Alice Rodier and Virginia Spraggins as brother and sisters, are also cast. Thomas R. Mills directed the picture.

Every four-reel O. Henry release will be followed by a two-reel release.

FOREST CONSERVATION IN GAUMONT REEL.

Outstanding features of the week of September 10 among the single-reel pictures which Gaumont will release through Mutual are the war pictures which will form a part of Mutual Weekly No. 141 and "Tree Planting in the National Forests," a section of "Reel Life" No. 72. The Mutual Weekly is released September 12. In view of the fact that it is not made up until the date of release, in order to incorporate the latest news pictures, no forecast of the contents can be made at this

Scene from Reel Life No. 72 (Gaumont).

time. It is a certainty, however, that it will contain battle pictures from the western front taken by the cameramen of the Societe des Etablissements Gaumont and rushed to this country by the first available steamer.

"Reel Life" No. 72 is released September 13. Its leading section is "Tree Planting in the National Forests." Most of the pictures were taken at the Wind River Nursery in the state of Washington. Millions of pine trees are here grown from seeds and when three years old are set out upon the mountain slopes which have been denuded of vegetation by forest fires. This is a remarkable picture as it shows just what is being done to protect the country from floods and soil loss.

Other pictures upon the same reel are "An Unusual Colt," a small Shetland pony, "Hunting Turtle Eggs," an exposition of the habits of turtles when they come to the beach to deposit their eggs, "Testing an Auto Tube," a remarkable exhibition of the tensile strength of an inner tube, and a picture from Alaska of "The Midnight Sun."

HAROLD LLOYD IN TWO FUNNY COMEDIES.

Admirers of the Rolin comedies on the Pathe program, and they are many, have some good things to look forward to the weeks of September 9 and 16. On September 9 comes the first of the new one-reel Harold Lloyd comedies. "Over the Fence" is the title, and it is a laughable burlesque on the national game. Lloyd proves a scream as a baseball pitcher, and by many impossible plays is winning his own game when he sees his best Sunday girl sitting in the bleachers with his dearly hated rival. Then all bets are off. Snub Pollard and Bebe Daniels also figure prominently in the cast with all the other Rolin favorites.

The week of September 16, "Lonesome Luke Loses Patients" will be released. In this comedy we find "Luke" running a sanitarium which is a regular bonanza because of the big staff of hand-picked beauties whom he has secured as nurses. The sanitarium is very popular with men whose wives do not stack up in the pulchritude class. In this fact lies the undoing of the sanitarium. Wives visiting husbands who have suddenly complained of being ill after seeing Luke's nurses find that their hubbies need chaperones. Harold Lloyd as the doctor is in one of his funniest parts. Ably assisting him are Snub Pollard and Bebe Daniels.

FIRST WHOLESOME SUBJECT READY.

"The Penny Philanthropist" by Miss Clara E. McLaughlin, the first release of the Wholesome Films Corporation, now is practically completed.

Director Guy McConnell, with an able cast headed by Ralph Morgan of the "Turn to the Right" company, has been putting in long hours at the Wholesome Studios on the north side, Chicago.

M. J. Weisfeldt, General Manager of the Wholesome Films Corporation, announces that the film will be ready for release within the month.

Eddie Foy, Jr., son of the inimitable Eddie, the world's greatest father, has been an interested spectator at the Wholesome Studios during the production of "The Penny Philanthropist." Young Foy is a close friend of Director Guy McConnell. He has been in Chicago with his father's vaudeville troupe and seized the opportunity to visit his old friend McConnell.

Drama and Comedy on Universal's Program

Lon Chaney, Lyons & Moran, Lena Baskette, Max Asher, Gale Henry and Eileen Sedgwick Some of the Favorites to Be Seen First Week of September.

THE Empty Gun", a Gold Seal drama, produced by Joseph De Grasse, who directed "Pay Me!", one of the biggest Western dramas of the year, heads the Universal schedule, beginning Tuesday, September 4th. The Butterfly picture released the day previous under separate booking arrangments will be the Francis Ford mystery play, "Who Was the Other Man?" The De Grasse production was written by J. Grubb Alexander and Fred Myton, and features Lon Chaney, Claire McDowell and Sam De Grasse. It tells a poignant story of the life in a mining town. A woman has been tricked into marrying the wrong man.

"Locking 'Em Over", a Nestor comedy, featuring Eddie Lyons, Lee Moran and Edith Roberts, will be released the same day with "The Empty Gun". This hilarious trio have a story excellently suited to their various styles of funmaking in the script written by Fred Palmer and produced by Roy Clements.

Wednesday, September 5th, is L-KO Comedy Day, with "Backward Sons and Forward Daughters" as the two-reel feature, headlining Billie Bevan and Lucille Hutton. The latest celluloid chuckle-starter, done under the personal supervision of J. G. Blystone, maintains the full speed limit in action and implication throughout its hundred odd scenes.

The 88th issue of the Universal Animated Weekly, released at the same time, is also notable for the amount of movement crowded into one reel, although unlike the L-KO brand, it all relates to actual news events of the day.

Lena Baskette, widely known as "Pavlowa, Jr.", is the star of the feature for Tuesday, September 6th. "A Dream of Egypt", written by Myrtle Stedman and Nan Blair and produced by Marshall Stedman, is the name of Lena's starring vehicle. The play tells a picturesque dream story of ancient Egypt, in which the little girl saves her mother's life by dancing before the king who has captured them. Lena is adequately supported by Betty Schade, Fred Montague and Walter Belasco.

William Franey will be seen on the same day in a Joker comedy entitled, "Officer, Call a Cop!", written by Arthur F. Statter and directed by W. W. Beaudine. Throughout the tangled course of events pictured, many amusing scenes are laid in Chinatown. Janet Eastman and Milburn Moranti also have prominent parts in the story.

"The Curse of a Flirting Heart" is the title of the Victor comedy in which Max Asher again appears under Universal auspices on Friday, September 7th. C. B. Hoadley wrote the script, which has been produced by Craig Hutchinson. Lillian Peacock has the featured part in support of Asher. Several striking bathing scenes are shown, as much of the action transpires at the beach.

The 35th issue of the Universal Screen Magazine, bearing the same date, will contain many novel illustrated articles on subjects of wide appeal.

Eileen Sedgwick and Fred Church will be featured in a two-reel Bison comedy-drama on Saturday, September 8th, entitled "The Lure of the Circus." W. B. Pearson wrote and produced this novelty, which pictures the adventures of a country lad and his sweetheart who obtain employment in a circus as animal trainer and bareback rider, respectively, to escape the drudgery and monotony of small town life.

Gale Henry and Milton Sims are also scheduled for appearance on the same bill in a Joker comedy entitled "A Gale of Verse", written by Tom Gibson and directed by Allen Curtis.

Breezy and timely in theme and presentation, the 17th issue of the Universal Current Events will bring the week to a close.

CONSERVATION AND PREPAREDNESS.

Universal shows several subjects in the Screen Magazine, released September 21, sure to arouse interest in the great work of conservation now being carried on by the government. A graphically illustrated lecture on the best method of canning and preserving corn is shown through co-operation with the Department of Agriculture. The New York City Food Aid Committee has become so interested in this department that it has requested the editor of the Screen Magazine to make a complete reel of similar subjects to use in the propaganda work now being carried on.

The campaign to prevent the high death rate among babies is also given much valuable material in the series of pictures contained in this release, showing many of the most interesting methods now being employed to keep the coming generation in good health and spirits.

There are also a number of spirited scenes illustrating the way in which women are being trained to take the places of men in such unique fields as wireless telegraphy and the various mechanical trades.

GENERAL CHANGES LOBBY CARDS.

For its new four-reel subjects, including the Falcon Features and the O. Henry de luxe subjects, General Film has adopted the 11x14 size of pictures for the lobby display frames as favoring the artistic treatment. There will be a title card and six photographic reproductions of scenes in each set of this display material.

Century Comedies

Plans for Distribution Completed by Longacre Distributing Company—Many Advertising Helps.

WITH the plans for the distribution of the new Alice Howell Century comedies completed, three names in the film world have been brought together. They are Alice Howell, Century comedies, and the Longacre Distributing Company. Miss Howell is going to make the Century comedies and Longacre is going to see that her big public has an opportunity to enjoy them. Among their plans are many novel aids to exhibitors seeking these super-comedies.

Longacre proposes to issue twelve of these comedies a year. At least ten are guaranteed. J. G. Blystone, whose range in the comedy field is unlimited, will be in charge of the direction of Miss Howell's pictures. Being the only young woman to have attained world-wide distinction in the "slapstick" end of the business, Miss Howell occupies an unusual position among stars of the film world.

"Her Bareback Career", one of the first and most thrilling of her new comedies, has entered upon its second week at the Broadway theater in New York. Others that will follow soon are "Automaniacs", "Neptune's Daughter", and "Balloonatics".

The Longacre plan calls for the division of the territory into districts. The "district rights" will be sold in each of these divisions. The Century comedies will be furnished to exhibitors regardless of any other service which they may be receiving, for Longacre has no affiliation with any other film service. For the benefit of those purchasing district rights, Longacre designates a district as a town, or in the case of a large city, a section of the city, in which there is either one theater which draws from the entire populace, or two or more theaters, which run in competition to each other, and to which only one of the so-called "first-run" of a picture can be sold. This constitutes the selling plan of Longacre, and the prices are already scheduled in every district.

Longacre exchanges have already been established in all of the principal cities, Boston, St. Louis, Philadelphia, Salt Lake City, Kansas City, Minneapolis, Indianapolis, Atlanta, New Orleans, San Francisco, Los Angeles, Spokane, Butte, Omaha, Oklahoma City, Chicago, Des Moines, Dallas, Wichita, Portland, Cleveland, Washington, D. C., Toledo, Denver, Pittsburgh, Buffalo and Milwaukee among others. Screenings are held in all of the districts in these cities, and tremendous enthusiasm for the Alice Howell productions has already been shown.

As part of its service, Longacre issues a clever campaign book called "The Boost-er Book", which is filled from cover to cover with publicity stunts, press stories, talks on comedies as program features, descriptions of the novel and original advertising matter, and every help known to the trade. There is also a folder, gotten up in a striking style, announcing the new series of Century comedies, which has been mailed to every exhibitor in the country. A remarkable line of advertising material of all kinds has been prepared, including life-sized cut-outs of the famous comedienne, novel heralds—the first a balloon to advertise one of her first releases, "Balloonatics".

"BACKWARD SONS AND FORWARD DAUGHTERS" (L-Ko).

Comedian Phil Dunham having turned from acting in L-Ko's to producing those merrymakers will show his first release on the program September 5. Lucille Hutton and Billy Bevan will be the featured ones with a large company of L-Ko beauties to enliven the various incidents. "Backward Sons and Forward Daughters" is the title, and the laughs will be pro-

Scene from "Backward Sons and Forward Daughters" (L-Ko).

voked under many unusual circumstances. Antics on land and under water will involve the players in hilarious scenes, and L-Ko is sponsor for the promise that Phil Dunham is just as good as a director as he was in the role of featured comedian on J. G. Blystone's staff of players.

Bluebird Fills Out Year's Program

Five Scattering Weeks Only Remain in Which Dates Have Not Been Set.

WITH the exception of five scattering weeks Bluebird has made tentative adjustment of its program until the first of the year. These open weeks will be filled by productions designed especially to supply the right sort of feature to give the series diversity and strength in its entirety. September, October and the early week of November are booked solid, although in several instances the release titles have not been definitely selected—but all the subjects are either completed or in process of production.

"Triumph", on Labor Day, starts the regular theatrical season (when exhibitors will have organized opposition) with a heavy dramatic subject introducing Dorothy Phillips as the star of a Joseph De Grasse production. In this Mr. De Grasse will appear for the first time as an actor, joining William Stowell and Lon Chaney as Miss Phillips' chief support.

"A Stormy Knight" will be the September 10 release, presenting Franklyn Farnum and Brownie Vernon as joint stars for the last time among Bluebirds. Hereafter Mr. Farnum will be an individual star and Miss Vernon will appear with Herbert Rawlinson. Exhibitors will have this special advertising point to emphasize in announcing "A Stormy Knight."

"The Mysterious Mr. Tiller", September 17, will have Rupert Julian and Ruth Clifford as co-stars in a sensational combination of mystery and psychology. Mr. Julian directed the work from Elliott J. Clawson's scenario and has introduced some new twists in photoplaying and camera trickery that promise surprising results, reduced to the screen.

"Flirting with Death", September 24, will have the new Bluebird combination—Herbert Rawlinson and Brownie Vernon—in the star parts. Here is another sensational issue, largely comedy drama, but thrilling in execution. Elmer Clifton, who formerly directed Franklyn Farnum and Miss Vernon, presents "Flirting With Death" as the first of a number of Rawlinson-Vernon Bluebirds.

"Bitter Sweet", October 1, will have Ella Hall as star in a story of Belgium's distress, translated to America for the happy ending. On October 8, with Joseph De Grasse as his director, Franklyn Farnum will be introduced as a lone star in "The Maverick", a Western drama, in which Lon Chaney will be featured in Mr. Farnum's support. Dorothy Phillips will appear in "Bondage" October 15 and "The Desire of the Moth" will have Rupert Julian and Ruth Clifford as stars October 22.

Violet Mersereau is just finishing at Fort Lee her presentation of "The Girl By the Roadside", directed by Theodore Marston, to be ready for release October 25. Then will come an event of importance to Bluebird exhibitors in the introduction of Mae Murray to the program, directed by Robert Leonard, with "The Princess Virtue" her initial offering. Another star, new to Bluebirds, will be introduced a week later in the person of Carmel Myers, who will be seen in "The Dynast", a feature especially written for the occasion.

RUTH ROLAND IN MYSTIC ROLE.

"The Stolen Play", third of the series of four-reel dramas, the Falcon Features has Ruth Roland as the star, with Wm. Conklin and Edw. J. Brady also among the principals. A most unusual offering is discovered in this General Film release. It carries a thoroughly sustained atmosphere of mystery and intrigue. An intense conflict of motives follows the theft of a play early in the action and leads to climax after climax.

Miss Roland is cast as the secretary of Charles Edmay, a blind playwright of distinguished success. With the aid of an agent, Alice Mason, he undertakes desperately to secure it. At the same time the playwright and his secretary have become under great nervous stress while bringing the play to completion. With the circumstances the audience is quickly put into the mood for startling developments.

"The Stolen Play", was written by D. F. Whitcomb and directed by Harry Harvey, supervised by H. M. and E. D. Horkheimer. Lucy Blacke, Harry Southard, Ruth Lackaye and Makato Inokuchi are members of the cast.

The next Falcon Feature will be "His Unpolished Self", from a story by Horace Annesley Vachell, featuring Henry Ainley.

NELL SHIPMAN INDEPENDENT.

Nell Shipman wishes it generally known that she is not under exclusive contract to any one for either her services or her scenarios. Miss Shipman has long realized the great difficulty of procuring suitable material for original and picturesque feature plays, and her six months' trip to the West Indies was undertaken upon her own initiative with a view to procuring "somewhat different" material for leading producers.

In this she was eminently successful, and although some of her stories of "The Spanish Main" and "Bucaneering Days" have been disposed of, her "piece de resistance" is being retained until arrangements can be made with one of the foremost directors for its sensational production.

Nell Shipman is at present in California concluding a contract for delivery of a number of photo dramas, but will soon return East to supervise the production of one of her more recent stories, which is to be released on the open market.

PATHE PROGRAM FOR WEEK OF SEPTEMBER 9.

Florence LaBadie in "War and the Woman", easily the best picture she has ever done, Pearl White in a strong serial episode, and a Harold Lloyd one-reel comedy are features of Pathe's program for the week of September 9.

Pearl White stars in the tenth episode of "The Fatal Ring" serial, entitled "The Perilous Plunge". This is probably the best episode yet of a serial that is breaking all records. It is said that a large number of Pathe offices have already beaten their average on "The Iron Claw".

Harold Lloyd is the star in "Over the Fence," the one-reel comedy produced by Rolin under the direction of Hal Roach. This is not a Lonesome Luke comedy. It shows Harold Lloyd, creator of the Lonesome Luke character, in an entirely new characterization, one absolutely distinct from Luke and yet, if possible, even funnier.

"Over the Fence" is a baseball burlesque in which Harold Lloyd is a studious young man. He comes to bat in the nick of time and saves the game. The first part shows him as the enterprising proprietor of a tailoring establishment of the "We-press-'em-while-you-wait" variety. He tires of pushing the needle, goes to the ball game and then things happen thick and fast.

The "Know America" Combitone Scenic release is entitled "Colorado's Scenic Wonders", and an International cartoon and scenic split reel, Heart-Pathe News No. 74 and No. 75 complete the program.

SELIG SUBJECTS FOR GENERAL FILM.

The Selig Polyscope Company announces an unusually excellent program for release in General Film Company for the week of September 9. On Monday, September 3, "The House of Mystery," a two reel melodrama of mystery and adventure will be released. The plot is from the versatile pen of Mary Roberts Rinehart and features an exceptional cast of players among whom can be named Thomas Carrigan and Adrienne Kroell. There is said to be plot, counter plot and tense action.

On Saturday, September 8, "The Convert of the North." a gripping one reel drama, will be released. It is an exciting romance of the Canadian Northwoods and was written by Gilbert Parker. Bessie Eyton, Wheeler Oakman and other well known players participate in a drama said to be filled with atmosphere and clever action.

The Selig World Library, a Reel Magazine, continues to appear every Wednesday in General Film service. It presents the strange and startling from all parts of the world.

MISS PICKFORD GETS POLICE GUARD.

If there is anyone who does not believe that Mary Pickford is a person of importance and worthy of attention and consideration, all they have to do is to ask Mayor James Rolph and the police department of San Francisco. Miss Pickford and her company visited the Bay City to film some scenes last week. When Miss Pickford approached her automobile the first morning to go on location she found it surrounded by a cavalcade of fifteen mounted policemen. The police gave a salute, and the lieutenant informed her that Mayor Rolph had heard of her arrival in the city to do some work and had provided the police for her protection during her stay in the city.

Wherever Miss Pickford goes to film scenes she is immediately recognized and surrounded by crowds which frequently interfere with the work of the players. Mayor Rolph, remembering the sensation Miss Pickford had caused when she appeared in San Francisco to assist in the sale of liberty bonds, placed the police department at her disposal.

FAREWELL TO "FIGHTING 69TH."

A remarkable number of human interest scenes of the famous 69th regiment on its way to Berlin, via Mineola, L. I., pictured in Universal Animated Weekly No. 86, just released, shows what New York City thinks of the "Fighting Irish." The Universal cinematographer was the only cameraman to accompany Col. Hine and his boys throughout the long line of march and the results obtained are well calculated to arouse any American audience to the highest pitch of patriotic enthusiasm.

Another topic of timely interest is the arrival of the imperial Japanese War Mission at San Francisco. Viscount Ishii and his distinguished Oriental colleagues are officially welcomed with full military honors and are quite evidently delighted with the reception. The student officers at Fort McPherson, Ga., are shown on their final hike and there are several other timely items depicting America at war.

ANOTHER O. HENRY STOCK SLIDE.

While continuing the special advertising plan for each O. Henry release, General Film is also providing another stock slide. The novelty about this slide is in utilizing a greatly admired crayon bust of O. Henry (William Sidney Porter), drawn by E. A. Bushnell from the best portrait in existence of O Henry. It is used by courtesy of Doubleday, Page & Co.

Essanay Announces Fall Program

Holmes and Washburn to Make Regular Appearance—Ade to Provide More Fables.

TAYLOR HOLMES heads Essanay's fall program in "Efficiency Edgar's Courtship," to be released September 30. Mr. Holmes is one of the best known interpreters of subtle humor on the speaking stage, having been responsible for such tremendous successes as "His Majesty, Bunker Bean," "The Third Party," and other audible comedies. In presenting him to patrons of the screen, Essanay has given him the same type of characterization, as well as the broader field for its portrayal which motion picture productions afford.

Mr. Holmes will appear again in October in "A Fool For Luck." This comedy-drama is an adaptation from the story by Kennett Harris called "Talisman." The following month, November, he will be presented in "Two Bit Seats," an adaptation from a magazine story.

Bryant Washburn's three Skinner pictures already are on the screen, and, according to reports from K-E-S-E headquarters, are demonstrating by their success the public's desire for pictures of a lighter vein. Mr. Washburn will be released in another comedy-drama in October, the title of which will be "The Fibbers." His November release will be announced shortly.

In addition to pictures featuring these two stars Essanay is releasing September 10 "Pants," a comedy-drama in five parts, with Little Mary McAlister as the lead. This child recently has been seen all over the field in "Do Children Count?" a series of child dramas. She also was a member of the all-star cast in Essanay's Super-feature, "On Trial," She is scheduled for another picture of the comedy-drama type in October.

George Ade, the famous Hoosier humorist, is providing his inimitable "Fables in Slang" for filming by Essanay. These pictures will be two reels in length and released one each week through the General Film Service. The first is entitled "The Fable of the Twelve-Cylinder Speed of the Leisure Class."

Picture Theaters Projected

HAWTHORNE, CAL.—The Inglewood theater has been opened to the public. The house has seating capacity for 600 persons. G. S. Bell is the proprietor.

SAN PEDRO, CAL.—William Dorner has disposed of his interest in the Globe theater to C. B. Cannon.

TULARE, CAL.—L. W. Willis has disposed of his interest in the Lyric airdome and theater to L. E. Galvan.

VALLEJO, CAL.—The Rex theater has been purchased by A. M. Bowles.

HARTFORD, CONN.—P. Arthur King has the contract to make interior alterations to the Hartford theater for J. Wise. The improvements will cost about $8,000.

WATERBURY, CONN.—Mill Engineering & Construction Company, 111 W. Main street, have the contract to make alterations to a theater building for John Moriarty, 137 E. Main street. The improvements will cost $8,000. Work has already been started.

COEUR D'ALENE, IDAHO.—A syndicate which controls moving picture houses in Wallace, Kellogg, Mullan and Wardner has leased the Lyric and Strand theaters. The owners are B. L. Daniels, W. A. Simmons, George M. Wilson and F. F. Moe. The Strand will be remodeled at a cost of about $1,500.

CHICAGO, ILL.—The Woodlawn Theater Company, Alexander Simpson, president, will erect a modern moving picture theater at 535-55 Sixty-third avenue.

DECATUR, ILL.—Aschauer & Waggoner, Citizens' Title & Trust building, are preparing plans for alterations to a moving picture theater, to cost $8,000.

GOSHEN, IND.—H. F. Klobr contemplates converting lower floor of his new building on E. Lincoln avenue into a moving picture theater.

HAMMOND, IND.—Gumbiner Brothers, owners of a chain of theaters in Chicago and other cities, have purchased the Orpheum theater and will make a number of improvements. The house will be conducted as a moving picture and vaudeville theater.

NEW ALBANY, IND.—The Royal theater has been purchased by Tom Barnett.

ALLERTON, IA.—Majestic theater has been opened to the public. It will be devoted to high-class pictures.

ALGONA, IA.—W. H. Hodges has disposed of his moving picture business.

BEVERLY, IA.—The property at the corner of Federal and Chapman streets has been purchased by the Enterprise Amusement Company as a site for a modern iron, steel and concrete theater building. It will be known as the Beverly.

DES MOINES, IA.—Kratech & Kraetch are preparing plans for a moving picture theater to be erected at the corner of Eighth and Locust streets.

FAYETTE, IA.—Charles Halverson has purchased the interest of T. J. Leahy in the Princess theater.

LANSING, IA.—Manager Ruprecht has closed the Princess theater, leaving the town without a moving picture house.

IOWA CITY, IA.—Garden theater will reopen shortly under the management of J. H. Lake of Des Moines.

KAMRAR, IA.—L. A. Miller has disposed of his moving picture business to H. E. Ryland.

KINGSLEY, IA.—Reliance theater on Main street will be opened by Jesse Schofield.

MARSHALLTOWN, IA.—The Casino theater has been redecorated and reopened under the management of Mr. Muelhaupt.

SIOUX CITY, IA.—The Orpheum theater located on Nebraska street has reopened under the management of Roy. C. Emery.

SHELBY, IA.—Charles Albertus has purchased the moving picture business of W. C. Howland.

WEST UNION, IA.—Charles Halverson has disposed of his interest in the Princess theater to T. J. Leahy.

BURTON, KANS.—Edgar G. Rollings will establish a moving picture theater here, having a seating capacity for 275 persons.

GARDEN CITY, KANS.—A new theater and office building will be erected on Main street.

HOISINGTON, KANS.—A new moving picture theater will be erected at the corner of Main and First streets, having seating capacity for 800 persons. L. E. Baker is interested.

JUNCTION CITY, KANS.—Fogel Construction Company have the contract to erect the new Columbian theater at the corner of Tenth and Washington streets.

PORTLAND, ME.—Nickel Amusement Company, 565 Congress street, have plans by Thomas W. Lamb, 644 Eighth avenue, New York, for an addition 132 by 129 feet, and alterations to their moving picture theater, store and office building, to cost about $100,000.

BALTIMORE, MD.—Thomas Moore has plans by Blanke & Zink, 648 Equitable building, for a two-story theater building, 98 by 105 feet, to cost $100,000. The theater will be known as the Victoria.

ROXBURY, MASS.—David J. Segel has plans by J. Marsden Parks for a new brick, stone and terra cotta theater at 738 Huntington avenue, 175 by 250 feet, to cost $250,000.

DETROIT, MICH.—C. H. Miles has leased the Regent theater from William R. Klatt.

HOUGHTON, MICH.—The Star theater has been remodeled.

LOWELL, MICH.—Earl Wright has purchased the interest of H. V. Warner in the Empress theater.

MANISTEE, MICH.—The Ramsdell theater will be reopened under the management of John Strenach, Jr.

NASHVILLE, MICH.—The Star theater has been leased by A. J. Fette from Charles Richardson.

PONTIAC, MICH.—The Howland theater has been redecorated and reopened.

ALBERT LEA, MINN.—The Royal theater is being remodeled.

BEMIDJI, MINN.—Oliver Whaley of the Harding-Whaley Company announces that the Elko theater will be reopened to the public and the Grand theater closed until September.

BEMIDJI, MINN.—The Grand theater has been remodeled and reopened. Pictures are now being shown every Saturday and Sunday evenings.

CROOKSTON, MINN.—W. M. Ferguson and Prof. Charles Pflock have taken over the Bijou theater on South Main street and will conduct it as a moving picture house.

CUYUNA, MINN.—The management of the Grand theater at Crosby plans to establish a moving picture house here at an early date.

MAHOMEN, MINN.—Lawrence L. Kreider has purchased the Grand theater from Lee Gallagher.

MINNEAPOLIS, MINN.—Charles Branham, formerly of Duluth, has been appointed manager of the Strand theater in this city.

MINNEAPOLIS, MINN.—The new Emerson theater at the corner of Twenty-sixth avenue N. and Emerson avenue has been completely redecorated. E. H. Bohlig is the new owner and manager.

PAYNESVILLE, MINN.—The moving picture theater erected here for Hartigan and Hood has been opened to the public.

PERHAM, MINN.—Lux theater has been opened under the management of A. J. Lucking and A. E. Eggers.

RUSHFORD, MINN.—M. Radke has disposed of his moving picture business to O. K. Quarve, manager of the opera house.

ST. PAUL, MINN.—A new $15,000 pipe organ is being installed in the New Garrick theater, formerly the Strand.

VIRGINIA, MINN.—The Grand theater has been opened under the management of the United Picture Show Corporation of Minneapolis.

Trade News of the Week

GATHERED BY OUR OWN CORRESPONDENTS

Boston Filmdom Doings Last Week

R. W. Cobe Made Manager of the Globe Feature Film Exchange—Famous Boston Theater to Be Entirely Rebuilt—Notes of Interest.

By Richard Davis Howe, 80 Summer St., Boston, Mass.

BOSTON, MASS.—Robert W. Cobe, who has been associated with the Globe Feature Film Corporation since last September, the time the film organization commenced doing business, has been appointed exchange manager. The appointment was made by General Manager Harry G. Segal as a result of the good work and the great increase of sales accomplished by Mr. Cobe recently. Mr. Cobe was formerly assistant to President Segal.

Globe Feature Film Adds to Sales Forces

Boston, Mass.—The Globe Feature Film Corporation of this city has increased their sales force, having taken on three new salesmen. The men are Frank J. Larkin, who is covering western Massachusetts, New Hampshire, and Vermont; W. H. Leahy, representing in the state of Maine, and T. E. Leahy, who is traveling with Al Lewis, manager of the "Enlighten Thy Daughter" road show, which is playing this picture on a percentage basis in Maine, New Hampshire, and Vermont.

General Manager Segal has just returned from New York, where he purchased the New England rights for several big productions.

New Goldwyn Exchange's Good Points.

Boston, Mass.—The new Goldwyn exchange on Piedmont street, this city, is practically completed. It is located in an ideal section, and receives a great quantity of sunlight. It runs back half way to the next street, giving space in which to store various film supplies.

The private office of Manager Campbell has been established on the first floor, and next to this is the office of his booker and private stenographer. In the center of the main floor a number of typewriter desks have been placed. Publicity Manager Joseph Di Pesa will also have a desk on the first floor. The shipping room is on the first floor on the left hand side of the building, with easy access to the street.

On the second floor is the projection room, large and roomy, with a new screen and a new Power's machine. The re-wind room on this floor is large and light, enabling the girls to work in a pleasant room. Manager Campbell has had eight large racks built on this floor, where photographs, cuts, paper, etc., are stored. There are four vaults capable of storing hundreds of films, and an elevator to send films from the second floor to the shipping room. Everything has been built for convenience, and is up-to-date in every respect. There are four lavatories on the second floor.

Will Rebuild Famous Boston Theater.

Boston, Mass.—The famous old Boston theater, one of the oldest and largest theatrical houses in New England, is about to be torn down and rebuilt. The Boston theater is one of the old landmarks of this city, and for many years has been the home of legitimate plays.

Plans for the remodeling have been drawn up by A. Paul Keith and Edward F. Albee, to cost about $1,000,000.

According to present plans the new theater in the busy downtown section of the city will be the largest theatrical house in Boston. The main entrance and box office will be located on Washington street as at present. It is planned to tear down the Arcade at No. 162 Tremont street and rebuild it as a Tremont street entrance.

It will have 4,000 seats. It will be fitted with boxes. No definite date has been set to commence work. It is believed though that it will start shortly.

Charles Phillips Comes Back to Travel for Goldwyn.

Boston, Mass.—Charles Phillips, well known in New England film circles and more especially in this city, where for more than a year he was assistant manager of the Fox Film Corporation under Harry Campbell, has joined his former employer, who is now at the head of the Goldwyn interests in New England, with offices at No. 49 Piedmont street, Boston. Mr. Phillips will leave shortly on a road trip.

Mr. Phillips was associated with Harry Campbell for over a year in the Boston office of the Fox organization. Several months ago he was promoted and transferred to the Indianapolis exchange where he took charge of affairs. But just so soon as Mr. Campbell joined the Goldwyn forces he set about to get Mr. Phillips to go with him.

With the acquisition of Mr. Phillips, the Boston office of the Goldwyn organization, the local office is rapidly getting into shape and before long things will be in full swing. Mr. Campbell only recently appointed Frank Vine, former Boston manager of the International Film Service, a salesman in this territory; Mr. Vine on his several road trips has turned in good results, and Manager Campbell is highly pleased at the success attained by his men.

Two New Fox Pictures Shown.

Boston, Mass.—A large gathering of exhibitors and exchange men attended the private trade showing of two of the new Standard productions, "The Honor System" and "Jack and the Beanstalk," both of which were held at the Fenway theater, through the courtesy of Manager Stanley Sumner of the Fenway. Exhibitors expressed their approval of the pictures to Manager William S. Shapiro of the local Fox office. Mr. Shapiro is planning to conduct a sweeping advertising campaign for the Standard pictures and intends to run advertisements in every leading publication in New England.

Strand at Fall River Nearly Ready.

Fall River, Mass.—Construction of the new Strand theater in this city by Jannings Brothers is nearing completion and will probably be ready so that the management may put on a show Columbus

Day at the latest. The Jannings Brothers, Nathan and A. I., are owners of the Plaza and Palace theaters in this city also. They plan to make the new Strand one of the finest theaters in New England.

Joseph M. Darling drew the plans for the new house and Charles F. Grinnell & Company are building the theater. It will have a seating capacity of 1,800, with 1,000 seats on the ground floor and the remainder in the balcony. The cost is estimated at $60,000. An up-to-date cooling system will be installed for use during the summer months, and many other modern accommodations will be made in the new house. It is planned to have the picture booth located between the floor and the balcony.

Jannings Brothers will have a large orchestra and brand new organ for their new enterprise. The program will consist of moving pictures and vaudeville.

Charles Mailley Takes Brighton Theater.

Boston, Mass.—Charles Mailley, former manager of Gordon's Scollay Square theater, Boston, has taken over the Brighton theater in Brighton and reports that he is doing a good business.

Soldiers and Sailors See "Italian Battle Front" Free.

Boston, Mass.—The management of "The Italian Battlefront," the interesting war pictures showing at the Tremont theater in this city, has extended a very welcome courtesy to soldiers and sailors of New England. Any man in uniform may attend the performance free by applying to the box office for tickets between 2 p. m. and 8 p. m. On behalf of the Italian Government, William Moore Patch, directing the American tour of the Italian pictures, will be the host, and any soldier, sailor or marine in uniform will be the guest.

There are two exhibitions daily, matinees at 2:15 and evenings at 8:15. There is an orchestra of forty pieces.

Italy's purpose in throwing open exhibitions to the uniformed men is to let those men who are soon to fight for liberty profit by the experiences of the fighters on the Italian front.

Goldwyns for Six-Day Runs in Worcester.

Boston, Mass.—Manager Harry F. Campbell, of the local Goldwyn exchange, is pleased. Together with his two sales representatives, Charles Phillips and Frank Vine, he has closed large contracts recently, and reports of sales come to the Boston office every day.

The three theaters are B. F. Keith's in Portland, Maine; B. F. Keith's in Lowell, Mass., and Nathan Gordon's Park theater, Worcester, Mass. This year is the first time that a theater in Worcester has been a six-day run house. Besides the Park theater is one other with a six-day run program, the Strand, which subscribes for the Artcraft service. The new policy seems to meet with the approval of moving picture fans in that city. Mr. Campbell, himself, closed the contract for the two Keith theaters, with R. D. Larsen in charge of the Keith interests in this city, and Harvey Watkins associated with B. F. Keith. Several other contracts for shorter runs have been signed up by Manager Campbell and his two salesmen.

Pine Tree State Letter

By J. P. Flanagan, 151 Park View Ave.,
Bangor, Me.

Adolphi Enjoying Tides and Fogs.

BAR HARBOR, ME.—The William Fox
Company, which is filming an elaborate photoplay at Bar Harbor, is to spend
many dollars on this production. Director
Adolphi is highly pleased with the scenery
about Bar Harbor, but the recent fogs and
rains have dampened his enthusiasm.
Tidal conditions have hampered the players and the water is very cold indeed, but
in spite of difficulties the work is progressing. High tides three times swept
away a set costing $4,500, known as the
"Cavern of Despair." Billy Noel and Ed
Carroll, garbed in seal suits, made admirable seals. Miss Kellermann, who in
private life is Mrs. James R. Sullivan,
works every sunny day at the Sun Rocks.
The sunburned and barnacle injured players have been taken care of by local physicians and are now convalescent. Curious
spectators should not bring cameras, as
the Fox Company wishes to reap the pictorial benefits of its million-dollar outlay.

Film Shows Maine Boys in Camp.

Bangor, Me.—More than 9,000 Augusta
people saw the film of the Maine National
guardsmen at the Colonial theater last
week. The film, which was taken by Daniel M. Maher, of Bangor, shows the daily
life of the Second Maine Infantry and
First Maine Heavy Artillery in camp at
Augusta and Brunswick. The title of the
picture is Maine Sammies Preparing for
the Front. It will be shown in Bangor
and other Maine cities.

Trenton Theater Incorporated.

Trenton, N. J.—The Trenton Grand
Theater Company of New Jersey was incorporated August 6 with an authorized
capital of $5,000. J. Irving Davidson, of
139 East State street, is named as registered agent. The concern will operate
theaters. The incorporators are John R.
D. Bower, J. Irving Davidson and S. A.
Peoples.

Newark Universal Has Important Changes

Office Is Moved to New Quarters—M. H. Goldstein Succeeds S. E. Fried as Manager—Additions to the Staff of the Exchange.

By Jacob J. Kalter, Newark, N. J.

NEWARK, N. J.—The Newark office of
the Universal Film has undergone
some radical changes. In the first place
the local exchange has moved from its
former quarters at 286 Market street to
more convenient offices at 25 Branford
place. In these new quarters the Universal will be in a better position to
inaugurate and maintain a more efficient
system of booking and of handling films
and posters. They are directly opposite
the Keeney theater, and is in the heart of
the downtown business section.

Another important change is the leaving
of Manager S. E. Fried, who is succeeded
by M. H. Goldstein. Mr. Goldstein comes
here from New England, where he acted
as supervisor and manager of both the
New Haven and Springfield exchanges of
the Mutual film. He is a man possessed
with some excellent ideas concerning the
film industry. Talking to the correspondent of the Moving Picture World, Mr.
Goldstein said: "You may tell the Jersey exhibitors for me that they are assured of a square deal when they do business here. Candidly, I admit but three
years' experience in the film industry, but
I've had a world of business experience,
which stands me in good stead now."

As assistant to Mr. Goldstein, Henry
Cole, of the Mecca branch of the Universal, has now joined the Newark office. He
will act as general representative. Mr.
Cole also has some decided innovations
for the Jersey exhibitors. He has had
printed a novel folder, and has been the
recipient of many congratulations on it.

Louis Kutinsky will remain as representative with the local exchange. Mr.
Kutinsky will cover West Hudson territory.

Miss Gertrude Barnett has joined the
staff as office assistant and stenographer.
Miss Barnett is well known to all Jersey
exhibitors, having been connected with
the Fox Company. Miss Barnett also was

with the New Jersey Exhibitors' League,
and with the Pathe exchange.

Jerry Kraker will assume charge of the
film and poster department, and will have
as his assistants Moe Grubel and Moe
Coleman.

Unpatriotic Protests Against Four-Minute Men.

Newark, N. J.—That a movement to boycott moving picture theaters where the
Four-minute Men are delivering their
talks on the war is in evidence in this
city, was the statement made at a meeting last Friday of the organization of
speakers. If this discrimination is shown,
the Four-Minute Men will take steps to
combat it. At the meeting, however, no
sufficient proof was given, and the campaign managers were skeptical as to the
veracity of the statement.

The Motion Picture Exhibitors' League
of New Jersey at a meeting last week approved the Four-Minute idea, and appointed a committee to co-operate with the
speakers.

The Strand theater, 118 Market street,
has agreed to allow a patriotic song, written by a local man, to be sung this week
as part of its program.

The theater managers are doing all in
their power to aid the movement, but
nevertheless people sympathizing with
Germany perhaps will get up and go out
when the speaker is announced. The
Newark Evening News, in a recent article,
declared that this was due probably "to
the fact that moving picture patrons visit
the theaters to see and not to hear."

Frank Keeney on Vacation.

Spring Lake, N. J.—Frank A. Keeney,
proprietor of the Keeney theater, Newark,
one of a chain of Keeney theaters, was enjoying a brief vacation at this place last
week.

Showing of "I Believe."

Newark, N. J.—A private showing of the
religious film, "I Believe," was given Friday morning at the Fox Terminal theater,
Park place, exclusively for members of
the clergy. The firm of Frank Gersten,
Times building, New York, control the
northern New Jersey rights to the film.
Herbert H. Yudkin represents the concern
in this territory.

Fire at Warren Square.

Newark, N. J.—Small boys and matches
was the cause of a small fire at the Warren Square theater, 465 Warren street, last
Friday. W. F. Conway is the tenant. The
entire moving picture stage and part of
the building was damaged by the flames
and water.

"The Slacker" at Goodwin.

Newark, N. J.—For the entire week of
August 13, the Metro patriotic production, "The Slacker," featuring Emily Stevens, was the attraction at the Goodwin,
863 Broad street. Mrs. L. H. Webbe, who
runs the Goodwin, advertised the film extensively, and the box office results were
exceedingly good.

Union Hill Amusement Corporation Starts.

Union Hill, N. J.—The P. & K. Amusement Company, with registered offices at
8 Bergenline avenue, filed articles of incorporation August 2. Edward Hollander
is named as agent of the concern, which is
capitalized at $25,000. The corporation is
empowered to operate moving picture
theaters. Besides Mr. Hollander, the incorporators are Hyman Kaplan and Herman Kerkelmer.

Baltimore Sees Good Business This Fall

Many Theaters Are Reopening—Serials and Short Subjects Are Popular—Stars and Features Also Getting Hearty Reception.

J. M. Shellman, 1902 Mt. Royal Terrace, Baltimore, Md.

BALTIMORE, MD.—While the summer
has evidently worked great hardships
on many of the exhibitors in Baltimore,
still it can be seen by the way these theaters are again opening their doors that
the coming season will probably be a good
one. F. Oletzky, manager of the Baltimore
Film exchange, states that he expects a
big coming season, for many places are
now reopening, and from his observations
the business is gradually picking up every
day. The serials and short subjects are
going very good, and the demand for this
class of pictures seems to be greater now
than it has been for a long time. Arthur
B. Price, Triangle representative in Baltimore and manager of the Rialto theater,
says the Hart and Fairbanks releases are
meeting hearty receptions in this city.

Harry Woods Aids British Recruiting.

Baltimore, Md.—Through the courtesy of
Harry Woods, manager of the Garden theater, Lexington street at Park avenue, the
British Recruiting Mission in Baltimore
was given great assistance on Friday afternoon and night, August 24. Around noon
on this day the 16 members of "The Boys
in Blue" act, then running at this theater,
headed by a band and eight members of
the mission, paraded through the business
section, and ended up at Hopkins Place,
where a drill was given and appeals for
recruits made. During the evening performance at the theater, after this act was
completed other speeches and appeals were
made, it was called "British Night" at the
theater. Recruiting cards are being posted

in the lobbies of the downtown theaters by
the mission.

Enthusiasm at Trade Screening of "The Spy."

Baltimore, Md.—Due credit should be
given L. A. DeHoff, manager of the New
theater, 210 West Lexington street, for the
interest he is taking in donating his beautiful playhouse so frequently for trade
screenings of big features. These
premiere views are usually held on Sunday nights, and a noticable fact is that they
have been extremely well attended. The
latest showing of this kind occurred Aug.
19, and on this occasion the William Fox
production, "The Spy," was shown to an
audience numbering about 450, composed
of the members of the Charcoal Club, an
artist's organization of Baltimore, and
many exhibitors and their friends. Special music for the occasion was rendered
in a beautiful manner by Prof. E. V. Cupero and his symphony orchestra. This
wonderful exploit of the horrible German
spy system was received with great enthusiasm by the assembled people.

Bridge Theater Criticism Contest.

Baltimore, Md.—During the week of
August 20, on the days that Louis Schlichter ran Mary Pickford in "The Little
American" four prizes were offered for the
best opinions turned in on this picture.
The motion picture editors of the Baltimore papers acted as the judges.

S. Lust Joins National State Rights Buyers

Gives Up Washington Selznick Office and Will Cover Territory in Connection with National Organisation of State Rights Buyers.

By Clarence L. Lenz, 622 Riggs Building. Washington, D. C.

WASHINGTON, D. C.—Sidney B. Lust has just announced that he has disposed of his interest in the business in this territory covering the Selznick Attractions to Mr. Selznick following the entrance into the home company of Adolph Zukor. As previously noted in the Moving Picture World, Selznick and Brenon pictures are hereafter to be handled by a separate exchange in this city under the management of Vivian Whitaker. The latter is temporarily located with Mr. Lust pending the putting into shape of the quarters which he has just selected.

Mr. Lust is joining with a number of other state rights buyers in what is to be known as the National Organization of State Rights Buyers. It is understood that the United States is to be divided up into twenty-six territories, and allotments made to that number of men. The plan originated, so it is said, with Sol Lesser. It is intended to buy negatives and make distribution of films in accordance with the requirements of the respective territories. A meeting to go over details was held in New York during the week.

The territory consisting of Maryland, Delaware, Virginia, North Carolina and the District of Columbia, now handled by Mr. Lust, would be covered by him as a member of this organization. In addition, he is arranging for a large number of feature films to market in addition to those he is already handling, including "20,000 Leagues Under the Sea," booked for an indefinite run at the Leader theater here; "Civilization," "Witching Hour," Ella Wheeler Wilcox series, Billy West two-reelers, the Mutt & Jeff comedies and others.

Mr. Lust also announces that E. W Balderson, heretofore in charge of the office, has been appointed traveling representative of the exchange, and will cover the District of Columbia, Virginia and North Carolina. He is succeeded as office manager by R. W. Fuller, of Dallas, Texas, a recent arrival in Washington.

Permit Granted to Build New Theater.

Washington, D. C.—The securing of a permit to build last week met at rest all rumors that have from time to time arisen to the effect that Harry Crandall for some reason or another would be unable to go ahead with the building of his new Metropolitan theater, which is to be located at Tenth and F streets, Northwest. The building inspector's office has issued a permit to Crandall's Theater Company to erect such a theater at a cost of $200,000. R. W. Geare is the architect, and the contract has been awarded to F. L. Wagner, who is going ahead with the construction work.

With a view to incorporating in this theater building all of the very latest in equipment and construction, Mr. Crandall and the architect have been making trips to other cities, studying all of the recently erected theaters. Both of these gentlemen and Mr. Crandall's associates in the company are well pleased with the outlook, for they fully expect to have a building that is as modern as it is possible to secure.

Propose Theater Ship for Men of Navy.

Washington, D. C.—There is a deal of discussion around Washington concerning matters of entertainment for the soldiers and sailors who are going to participate in the war. The latest proposal is a theater ship for the entertainment of the naval personnel afloat. Such a feature has been adopted profitably, it is said, for the British grand fleet. In additon to the regular forms of recreation that prevail on board individual ships there have been provided a theater ship, a large floating place of amusement. This is brought alongside any war vessel that makes application therefor, and a performance given. It is said that this might be done in our own navy, utilizing the talent on board the ships for vaudeville and securing pictures for motion picture exhibitions, attaching the theater ship to the fleet.

James H. Butner Leaves for Atlanta.

Washington, D. C.—It was with regret that the film men of Washington last week parted company with James H. Butner, former manager of the local Triangle exchange, who has gone to Atlanta, Ga., to join the forces of Jake Wells, presumably to handle the state rights pictures that the Wells organization will secure in the future.

When seen for a brief moment by the Moving Picture World correspondent, Mr. Butner stated that he could not outline the work connected with his new position other than to say that he would probably assume charge of the exchange feature of the Wells interests.

Mr. Butner came here about a year ago, after an absence of some years, to open the Washington Triangle office. He had a host of friends in the city, for he had previously been engaged here in newspaper work with the Associated Press. He foresaw the great opportunities of the film business, and accordingly entered it, obtaining a position as salesman, then as manager of an exchange in Philadelphia. He joined Triangle and made periodic trips to Washington from the Philadelphia office until he opened the new branch.

He had hardly become established in Washington before his fellow exchange managers sought him out as president of their little, though thriving organization, and he served in that position until a couple of weeks ago, when, on severing his connection with the Triangle Distributing Corporation, he presented his resignation. In consideration of the excellent service he had rendered the Washington Exchange Managers' Association, he was elected an honorary member with all of the privileges of a regular member despite the fact that he will be located out of the city.

A. Van Roley Reopens Casino Theater.

Washington, D. C.—The Casino theater, at Seventh and F streets, Northwest, has been reopened by A. Van Roley, of New York. "Feature pictures of an unusual type," are advertised for this house, and the first offering was "Twilight Sleep." The afternoon exhibitions were restricted to women, and. the evening performances to the men.

Mr. Van Roley states that later on he may employ vaudeville specialties of equal novelty with the pictures of unusual type.

Theaters Near Camps Expect Sunday Shows

Military Authorities, It Is Understood, Will See That Exhibitors Are Permitted to Keep Open for the Soldiers on Sundays.

By D. M. Bain, Wilmington, N. C.

CHARLOTTE, N. C.—From Chillicothe, Ohio, where fifty thousand troops are now assembling in training camps, comes the word that the military authorities have notified city officials that theater proprietors are to be allowed to open their theaters on Sundays just the same as on the other six days of the week, this is in order to provide adequate amusement facilities for the soldiers.

This announcement has created much interest here, as well as elsewhere throughout the South where eight large training camps will soon be in full operation with a total of something like $60,000 troops, all told, assembling for training. Speculation is being indulged in as to whether like action will be taken here, or whether this will only be done in districts close to places where Sunday shows are already allowed, and where, therefore, there would not be so much opposition to the Sunday showing of pictures.

Certain it is that should the War Department give the shows here and throughout the South where training camps are located the privilege of remaining open on Sundays such an avalanche of protests would descend upon the heads at Washington and from the Ministerial Associations as would cause to pale into insignificance the many other "obstructionist" movements since the war began. In Charlotte, particularly, where it is unlawful to sell a soft drink or a cigar on Sunday, opposition would be strong and insistent, and it is doubted if even the exigencies of war used as an argument would dissuade certain elements of the city's leading citizens from opposing the open Sunday. Theater managers locally, upon the first hint of such a possibility, have started hurried investigations, and a statement will probably be forthcoming within the near future. While the local magnates would, of. course, welcome the seventh day of revenue, the sentiment generally is that they would not welcome any such movement did it not coincide with the views of their regular patronage.

A Freak Bill Against Serving Special Drinks in Pictures.

Wilmington, N. C.—A freak bill introduced at the last session of the North Carolina Legislature, but which, through some prank of fate never came up for final passage, has just been unearthed. The bill introduced by Representative Withrow, reads as follows:

"A bill to prohibit showing drinking scenes in moving picture shows."

"The General Assembly of North Carolina do Enact:

"Section 1. That any person, firm or corporation engaged in the business of exhibiting moving pictures who shall within the State of Carolina exhibit a picture in which there is a scene showing any person or persons indulging in the drinking of spirituous, vinous or malt liquors, or intoxicating bitters, shall be guilty of a misdemeanor, and for each offense shall be punished by a fine of not more than $5 or imprisonment not more than thirty days.

"Section 2. That this act shall be in effect and be in force from and after the first day of August, 1917."

The effect such a bill would have had in the state, had it passed and become a law, can easily be seen, and it would have caused the censoring and re-editing of everything in the picture line from Chaplin's latest comedy to Pathe's "The Life of Our Saviour."

Fred Young Visits Wilmington.

Wilmington, N. C.—Fred W. Young, representing the Serial Department of Atlanta Mutual exchange, was a visitor in the city last week. W. M. Sipe, now covering this territory for Atlanta Triangle office, is in the city this week.

PHILADELPHIA NEWS LETER.

By F. V. Armato, 144 North Salford street, Philadelphia, Pa.

F. W. Seymour Comes to Manage.

Philadelphia Triangle.

PHILADELPHIA, PA.—W. F. Seymour arrived from New York last week to assume management of the Triangle Distributing corporation, and arrange the distribution of the Paralta films. Herbert Givens, who retires from the post with his best wishes of all concerned, promises to make known his new appointment at an early date and will spend the next few weeks on his vacation at the seashore.

World Correspondent Drops in at Mutual Office.

Philadelphia, Pa.—Every exhibitor who visits the Mutual exchange will be glad to see Ruth Stanton back at her desk again. She has just returned from her vacation with a healthy complexion of tan and red together with an abundant supply of smiles which she will distribute to Mutual exhibitors.

Falcon Four-Reel Picture Ready.

Philadelphia, Pa.—Percy Bloch, of the General Film, will shortly announce the release date of the new Falcon four-reel feature each week. The first feature will be "The Main Spring," featuring Henry King.

K-E-S-E Manager Sees Bright Outlook.

Philadelphia, Pa.—A. G. Buck of the K-E-S-E has made a considerable increase in bookings this summer over last spring and is perfectly confident of the future.

Ridge Avenue Theater Closes for Paramount and Fox.

Philadelphia, Pa.—Ben Shindler of the Ridge Avenue theater has closed for the first showing of Paramount and Artcraft Pictures in his neighborhood and for the first presentation of Fox features in North Philadelphia.

Harris Hana Starts New Policy.

Philadelphia, Pa.—Harris Hana of the Pastime, considered one of the most successful and most conservative exhibitors in this city, has completed arrangements for the presentation of Paramount and Artcraft pictures for the first showing in his neighborhood. In conjunction with the showing of his new program he will also inaugurate a big newspaper advertising campaign.

Jerome Abrams Opens Foursquare Office

Philadelphia, Pa.—The Foursquare Pictures, Inc., exchange opened here recently under the management of Jerome Abrams, who hails from New York. Up to the present time he has met with considerable success in booking "The Bar Sinister," "Fighting Chance," "Whither Thou Goest" and the "Silent Witness," his latest release.

Plans for "Betsy Ross" Release.

Philadelphia, Pa.—George Meeker, of the World, is looking forward to the release of the super production "Betsy Ross," starring Alice Brady, with great expectancy. He is planning for its presentation on an elaborate scale and is making extensive preparations for the big event.

Some Big Films for Reading This Season

Reading, Pa.—Frank Hill of Reading reports that a generally fair condition of affairs is existing there during the summer. He negotiated for large productions which he expects to show during the coming season at the Lyric.

Dixie Theater Much Improved.

Philadelphia, Pa.—James E. Seerey and Cornelius Keeney have completed extensive alterations in their Dixie theater at Manayunk where they also have rebuilt a new and up-to-date projection room under the able direction of Lewis M. Swaab, who also furnished two motor driven Simplex machines and other equipment.

Big First Runs at the Benn.

Philadelphia, Pa.—Marcus A. Benn, one of the pioneer exhibitors in this territory, has booked the first run in his neighborhood of Triangle, Fox, Metro, and Selznick productions. He announces that he will shortly spend at least $1,500 beautifying his Benn theater and will also add to it the very latest equipment. Mr. Benn is a great believer in the early showing of big productions when obtained through the Stanley corporation .

K-E-S-E Pittsburgh Film Exchange Grows

Quarters at 123 Fourth Avenue Are to Be Enlarged and Made Very Attractive—S. Wheeler Joins the Selling Staff of the Exchange.

From Pittsburgh News Service, 6104 Jenkins Arcade, Pittsburgh, Pa.

PITTSBURGH, PA.—The quarters of the K-E-S-E Service, 123 Fourth avenue, Pittsburgh are to be considerably enlarged, and Manager C. K. Campbell is planning to make the exchange one of the most attractive and up-to-date in the city. The adjoining space, formerly occupied by the Unicorn exchange, will be added, about doubling the size of the office and giving more room for expansion.

Samuel Wheeler, formerly booker at the Fox and Triangle exchanges in this city, has joined the selling staff of the K-E-S-E, working out of the Pittsburgh office.

Cameraphone Breaks Record with "Somme" Picture.

Pittsburgh, Pa.—The East Liberty Cameraphone theater, Pittsburgh, last week broke all previous house records with Pathe's "Battle of the Comme." The same subject has been placed in the Cambria theater, Altoona, Pa., for showing September 6, 7 and 8. "The British Tanks" will play at the Cambria September 13 and 14. The Altmeyer theater, McKeesport, will run the Pathe war pictures for five days, beginning August 27. This house has also contracted for the Gold Rooster Features.

L. A. Snitzer to Manage Goldwyn Road Staff.

Pittsburgh, Pa.—The local Goldwyn branch, sixth floor of the Seltzer Film building, Pittsburgh, has installed a handsome and commodious projection room, and same has been nicely equipped under the direction of Manager C. C. McKibbin. James B. Clark, head of the Rowland & Clark theaters, Pittsburgh, has contracted for the Goldwyn pictures, to be shown at the Regent theater, East Liberty, the finest of the R. & C. chain. Each release will be run three days.

L. A. Snitzer, for the past year and a half with the Pittsburgh Triangle exchange, has resigned to become manager of the road staff of the local Goldwyn office.

Horace Conway Comes to Wolfberg Exchange.

Pittsburgh, Pa.—Horace Conway, formerly manager of the Milwaukee branch of the General Film Company, is now a member of the Harris P. Wolfberg forces. Mr. Conway will probably be stationed at the Pittsburgh office, Lyceum Theater building, operating in Western Pennsylvania and West Virginia.

M. Teplitz Buys Out Amalgamated Film

Pittsburgh, Pa.—M. Teplitz, of the Specialty Film Company, Film Exchange building, Pittsburgh, has purchased the entire stock of films, paper and equipment of the Amalgamated Film Service, formerly the Unicorn, at 126 Fourth avenue. Same was sold at a constable's sale. The stock included over two hundred and fifty reels of film.

Notes from Pittsburgh Fox Exchange.

Pittsburgh, Pa.—J. C. Ragland, manager of the Standard Picture department of the Pittsburgh Fox exchange, reports excellent bookings on "The Honor System," the first release on this new program. Among the contracts already approved are the following: Majestic theater, Erie, one week; Grand theater, Homestead, one week; Robinson Grand. Clarksburg, W. Va., three days; Majestic, Rochester, two days; Bentley, Monongahela, two days; Majestic, Charlerot, two days.

Another trade showing of Fox Standard

pictures drew a large attendance of exhibitors on Sunday, August 19, when "The Conqueror" and "The Spy" were presented at the Olympic theater, Fifth avenue, Pittsburgh. They met with much appreciation and were declared exceptionally strong subjects. The next trade showing will be "Camille," featuring Theda Bara.

Park to Run "Her Condoned Sin."

Erie, Pa.—The Park opera house, Erie, has joined the film ranks and will shortly begin an engagement of "Her Condoned Sin," with a large augmented orchestra and advanced admission prices for September. Extensive advertising plans have been made by the Park theater management.

A. M. Weir's New Theater to Open.

Charleston, W. Va.—The handsome new theater being completed by A. M. Weir, at Charleston, W. Va., will be thrown open about September 1, it has been announced. A name has not yet been selected. This theater will be one of the finest exclusively picture houses in the state.

Trade Notes in Pittsburgh.

The Famous Players exchange gave a largely attended trade showing of the great film spectacle, "Joan the Woman," featuring Geraldine Farrar, at the Regent theater, East Liberty, on Sunday afternoon, August 26.

The Anton theater, Monongahela, Pa., has been improved by the installation of a handsome Seeburg orchestral organ at a cost of $4,000.

A report is current in local moving picture circles that the Empire theater property, East Liberty, Pittsburgh, has been purchased by the Harris & Davis amusement interests.

More Baltimore Notes

Camp Meade to Have Theater.

Baltimore, Md.—Word is now going along the line that negotiations are being made with the Government to permit a large theater at Camp Meade, where 40,000 men will shortly be assembled for military training. A number of prominent Baltimoreans are associated with the matter behind which, it is stated, is a large New York theatrical corporation. Vaudeville and motion pictures will probably be the attractions, while standard productions may also be given. As the camp will be a permanent establishment, a large sum of money may be used for erecting the playhouse.

Business Notes from Baltimore.

Baltimore, Md.—The Patterson theater, 1202 Laurens street, which has been closed for some time, was reopened to the public on August 26. Robert L. Mead is now managing this house.

Baltimore, Md.—L. Hasslinger, the proprietor of the Daisey theater, Collington avenue and Gay street, states that he will reopen his theater to the public on September 1.

Baltimore, Md.—During the week of August 20, Douglas Fairbanks in "Down to Earth," packed them in at the Parkway theater, 3-9 West North avenue. The extensive improvements which are being made in this beautiful playhouse are in no way interfering with the schedule of performances.

Baltimore, Md.—Manager F. C. Schanberger opened the Maryland theater with Keith vaudeville and motion pictures on Monday, August 20, for the season.

Film News in Buffalo Last Week

"Four-Minute Men" Are Using Picture Theaters to Instruct Buffalo—Soldiers and Sailors Get Free Shows—Local Notes of the Film Trade.

By Joseph A. McGuire, 152 North Elmwood St., Buffalo, N. Y.

BUFFALO, N. Y.—The "Four-Minute Men and Women" are delivering peppery, punchful speeches in several of Buffalo's moving picture theaters this week They are telling the audiences that while our troops are going to the front housewives have a grave responsibility, and that Buffalo must help Uncle Sam feed the boys in France. The following are some of the points covered by the lecturers:

The fear of famine has caused many wars and also has won many victories; it is therefore, the duty of the housewife to sign the Hoover pledge at once and premise to carry out the advice of the food administrator in the conduct of the household wherever possible.

This city (Buffalo) has a food conservation comittee, a home economic expert, and a community kitchen where "canning" —quite different from the kind so familiar to film men—may be followed on a pretentious scale.

Lectures have been given in the following theaters: Variety and Colonial; Allendale, Eastern Star, Abbott, Pastime and Grant; Tri-It, Colonial, Savoy, Victoria, Rialto and Orpheum; Columbia, Rialto, Victoria and Grant; New Arcadia, Como, Orpheum and Variety; Eastern Star, Abbott and Pastime. The audiences received the speakers enthusiastically.

Soldiers Enter Free at the Academy and Regent.

Managing Director Michaels of the Academy and Regent theatres, Buffalo, under the auspices of the Evening News, is entertaining hundreds of local soldier boys, who, when in uniform, are being admitted free to performances in both houses. The Buffalo Evening News arranged for the "wide-open-door" policy for these stouthearted devotees of the screen. So well did the soldiers take advantage of the favor that at nearly every performance of the Academy and Regent, these houses looked as if they were located a stone's throw from some military barracks.

Vocational School's Methods Shown in Film.

Buffalo, N. Y.—Moving pictures showing the work at Buffalo's vocational schools are being shown at Shea's Hippodrome. The schools are busy training youths to be able to work at the local plants, which are working night and day on war orders.

Buffalo Film Men Who May Soon Be Soldiers.

Buffalo, N. Y.—Among the Buffalo film men who were included in the draft were H. E. Hughes, who handles features at his own office; Manager Keating, of the Jubilee theater, and Leo Davidson, of the Mutual.

J. M. Gerchof Will Run Park Pavilion in Corning.

Buffalo, N. Y.—J. M. Gerchof, formerly road representative of the Mutual, Buffalo, was a caller. Mr. Gerchof has the honor of having made the first suggestion that the Buffalo Screen Club be formed early last year. He didn't stop with the suggestion, but got busy at that time and helped with the organization, Mr. Gerchof has just secured a contract to manage as an evening amusement place the Denison Park pavilion in Corning, N. Y. The park is owned by that city.

According to the contract he is to provide free moving pictures and other entertainment from 7:30 to 9 o'clock each evening for the benefit of the citizens of Corning. From 9 o'clock to midnight the pavilion will be conducted by him as a high class dance hall. Mr. Gerchof visited the

local exchanges for his first quota of pictures and equipment.

"Believe me, I need the Moving Picture World every week," said the Corning man.

Clarence Williams Managing Modern Features.

Buffalo, N. Y.—Clarence Williams, formerly road representative of the Modern Features, Buffalo, has been appointed manager of that exchange.

C. J. Rose Is Metro Road Man Now.

Buffalo, N. Y.—C. J. Rose, formerly with the Mutual, is now road representative of the Metro, Buffalo.

Stray Jottings About Bison City.

Bruce Fowler, manager of the Olympic theater, Buffalo, has returned from his vacation at Angola-on-the-Lake.

During the summer the Mutual exchange, Buffalo, opens at 8:30 o'clock in the morning and closes at 5 o'clock in the afternoon. Several of the employees have cottages at Crystal Beach.

Ira B. Mosher, manager of the Palace theater, Buffalo, has returned from a two weeks' motor trip.

T. W. Dooley, representing the Super Film Attractions Co., Syracuse, was a Buffalo caller.

Atlanta News Letter.

By Alfred M. Beatty, 43 Copenhill Ave., Atlanta, Ga.

The Forsyth Will Reopen Labor Day.

Atlanta, Ga.—The Forsyth theater, Atlanta's big playhouse, which has been closed for the summer, is undergoing a sys-

tematic overhauling, and will re-open Labor Day with Keith vaudeville and motion pictures, as formerly.

The house has been repainted and redecorated, the seats all put in good condition, and it will be as cozy and comfortable as ever. George H. Hickman will again be in charge.

It is understood the Lyric will continue all winter as the home of popular-priced family vaudeville and motion pictures, although no definite announcement has been made.

E. A. Schiller Travels Much These Days.

Atlanta, Ga.—E. A. Schiller, southern representative of the Loew interests, left Atlanta Monday night for New Orleans, where he will remain ten days in the interest of widening the Loew circuit in the South.

Mr. Schiller has just returned from New York, where he advised with the home office of the Loew circuit in regard to extending the time in this territory and also discusses plans for building of a new Loew house in Atlanta. It is expected that on his return from New Orleans definite announcement will be made of all the plans decided on.

Geo. L. Schmidt Back at Alamo No. 2.

Atlanta, Ga.—George L. Schmidt, who has been in Rome, Ga., for recent weeks managing a motion picture theater, is again back in Atlanta and managing the Alamo No. 2, where he was so successful for many years. Mr. Schmidt has hundreds of friends in Atlanta and all over the South. He has seen service as a motion picture theater manager in many Southern cities, in all of which he has been uniformly successful.

Hank Cassidy Back on the Job.

Atlanta, Ga.—Hank Cassidy, who has been in a hospital in Chattanooga several weeks, has recovered, and returned to Atlanta Sunday.

Mr. Cassidy will return to his duties as advertising manager of the Wells' motion picture houses in Atlanta.

McMahan & Jackson Sue Adams Express

Ask Damages of $633 for Delay of Picture on Which Expensive Advertising Had Been Put Out—Hope to Teach a Lesson in Promptness.

By Kenneth C. Crain, 207 First National Bank, Cincinnati.

CINCINNATI, O.—Exchange men and exhibitors alike have for many moons had their grievances against the express companies, the exchange men being the recipients of many kicks from exhibitors on account of the failure of films to arrive on the date booked, due solely to carelessness on the part of employes of the express companies. Of late there has been a decided tendency to do something more than merely complain of these delays, several suits being recorded in various Ohio courts where advertised features were delayed in shipment and were therefore not shown.

One of the latest of these cases was filed a short time ago in Cincinnati by McMahan & Jackson against the Adams Express Co., Charles Rettig, lessee of the moving picture exhibiting rights of the Sorg opera house, at Middletown, O., being joined also as a plaintiff.

According to the petition filed, in which damages of $633.77 are asked, "How Molly Made Good" was advertised for exhibition at Middletown on January 20 last, and the express company failed to deliver the film, although it was shipped in ample time. The expense of the advertising and a reasonable estimate of the profits of the exhibition are sought to be recovered. A few more suits of this sort, moving picture men declare, will make the express companies a little more careful to see that films are delivered promptly.

Fox Office a Busy Place These Days.

Cincinnati, O.—Activities at the Fox offices here are progressing without any

let-up, the work of getting the new system thoroughly established, and the routine made necessary by the several big releases recently sent out, giving Messrs. Conant and Knoepfle plenty to do. Mr. Knoepfle returned shortly from a three-day trip over the territory around Cincinnati, visiting exhibitors, while Mr. Conant, besides staging a great special showing of "Jack and the Beanstalk" for exhibitors, at the Hotel Gibson, in Cincinnati, has also arranged for private screenings of two other Fox Standard releases, "The Honor System" and "The Spy." P. C. Mooney, district manager, was in Cincinnati not long ago to look things over in this territory on one of his swings around the circle of five offices now under his supervision.

"Barrier" Has Splendid Week's Run.

Cincinnati, O.—The Selznick production of "The Barrier," a film version of one of Rex Beach's most successful books, had a splendid week's run at the Grand opera house at the advanced prices which have prevailed there during the entire summer season, the size and comfort of the big theater, with its splendid location, being factors which have kept up attendance even when other considerations were not favorable. "The Barrier" had much of the same sort of thrill as "The Spoilers," the first great Rex Beach moving picture success, and drew almost as well.

Manager Hite Feels Optimistic.

Cincinnati, O.—Manager C. C. Hite, who is rapidly getting things in splendid shape in this territory for Goldwyn pictures, returned from a recent trip to Indianapolis enthusiastic over a trade showing there of "Baby Mine" and other Goldwyn releases. Similar private exhibitions in Cincinnati have resulted in excellent bookings of the new pictures, and Mr. Hite feels highly optimistic over the success of the productions in this vicinity.

Movie Baseball Team Plays at Outing.

Cincinnati, O.—A "movie baseball team" organized by I. W. McMahan from some of the leading members of the exhibiting and exchange ranks in Cincinnati, helped to furnish a leading feature at the annual outing of the Chamber of Commerce at Coney Island recently, playing a highly exciting if not entirely errorless game with another team of business men. The line-up as announced in advance by Capt. McMahan, who himself assumed the onerous duty of pitching, was as follows: John Huebner, Jr., shortstop; Ned Hastings, catcher; Haines, first base; H. Serkovich, right field; Gus Mueller, center field; H. Levine, left field; C. C. Hite, second base; Charles Weigel, third base.

Demand for Sunday Shows in Chillicothe

Chillicothe, O.—Local moving picture exhibitors, who for some time have not been opening on Sunday on account of the success with which the authorities invoked the old Ohio "blue laws," are contemplating securing acquiescence in Sunday performances in the future, on account of the demand for wholesale recreation for the thousands of soldiers who will be in training at the cantonment, as well as for visitors and officers' families. The ice was broken recently, by way of experiment, by a band concert at one of the theaters on Sunday, at which admission was charged, and in view of the desire of the local authorities to make all conditions satisfactory for the soldiers, it is felt that there will be no trouble later on about Sunday opening.

Soldiers Guests of May's Opera House.

Piqua, O.—A military audience, consisting of all of the soldiers in Piqua at the time, saw "The Man Who Was Afraid" at May's opera house, on the special invitation of Manager Kress. The picture was felt by Mr. Kress to be one which would be especially pleasing to the soldiers, as it deals with the National Guard, and the enthusiasm of the boys proved that he was right.

Editing Motion Picture Films.

After a motion picture film has been developed and printed it is sent to the general manager or to the director to be "edited". Like an author's manuscript in the hands of an editor, it is shortened here and there, the captions altered, some parts entirely "cut" or deleted and the whole film dressed up to suit the ideas of the men closest in touch with the theater-going public.

The editing takes place in the projection room, says the Popular Science Monthly, but the altering—cutting the film and changing it—is done in the cutting and assembling room by men who do nothing else. Sometimes the men in the cutting room ("cutters", in the trade lingo) are so overwhelmed and confused with orders issued by the studio officials that they are compelled to ask for additional explanations. Needless to say this wastes much time.

By means of the phonograph, however, one motion picture company is eliminating this waste and saving money. As the director watches a picture in the projection room he utters his editing orders into the transmitter of a dictating machine. The film is then sent back to the cutting room with the phonograph record.

Youngstown, O.—The management of the Park theater recently entertained members of a local G. A. R. Post at a special performance of "The Birth of a Nation."

New Ontario Inspector Pleases Film Men

New Inspector of Moving Picture Theaters Is Popular with Exhibitors—Was Assistant Inspector Under Mr. Newman—John Leonard Will Assist Him.

By W. M. Gladish, 1263 Gerrard Street, East, Toronto.

TORONTO, ONTARIO.—Moving picture men in Ontario are in high glee as a result of the appointment of Otter Elliott as inspector of moving picture theaters in Ontario. Mr. Elliott's regime starts under most auspicious circumstances because there is scarcely a film man in the province who does not admire him. Mr. Elliott served as the assistant inspector under the late Mr. Newman, and he was naturally in line for the post.

John Leonard, of 105 Concord avenue, Toronto, has been selected to succeed Mr. Elliott as assistant inspector. This, too, is a happy selection. Mr. Leonard is a returned soldier, having served with the First Signaling Station until he was wounded at Ypres on June 28, 1916. Mr. Leonard is also a practical theater man, having served considerable time as a projection machine operator and otherwise.

Changes in Canadian General Film.

Toronto, Ont.—Some important changes have been made in the Canadian organization of the General Film, which directly affect the Toronto branch of the company. J. F. Clancy, the Toronto district manager for the past three months, has been promoted to the position of business manager for the whole company and will make his headquarters in Montreal. F. H. Wells, who has been general sales manager, has become the manager of distribution.

Mr. Leslie MacIntosh, formerly a Toronto salesman for the General, has been appointed manager of the Toronto office.

The General Film is now releasing twenty-five reels each week through its various branch exchanges.

Phil Kaufman Becomes Vice-President of Globe Film.

Toronto, Ont.—The important news has been released that Phil Kaufman has become vice-president of the Globe Film Company, 221 Yonge street, Toronto. Mr. Kaufman was Toronto district manager of the Famous Players for a number of years and is one of the best known exchange men in Canada.

Announcement was also made a short time ago that Maurice Kaufman, formerly Montreal manager for the Famous Players, had become associated with the Globe Company. The two are brothers. Phil Kaufman has just made an important business trip to New York for the Globe Company, which has been distributing Ivan productions and many special releases throughout Canada. The Globe is one of the youngest film exchange companies in Canada. Closely associated with it are the Globe and Rialto theaters in Toronto, two of the most important downtown houses.

The Globe Film Company recently acquired the Canadian rights to Evelyn Nesbit's "Redemption," the first release of which was booked by Loew's theater, Toronto. Second run went to the Photodrome, Toronto, for the two weeks of the Canadian National Exhibition, August 27 to September 8.

The company recently moved into handsome new headquarters over the Rialto theater, Yonge street.

Two Toronto Newspaper Men Enter Local Picture Field.

Toronto, Ont.—Two Toronto newspapermen have taken up duties in the local moving picture field. Harold Hutchinson, formerly of the Toronto World, has become assistant treasurer of the Strand Theater Company, while George Mitford, also of the World, has also become publicity manager for the Regent theater, Toronto.

M. M. Davis Gets Executive Job at Fox Montreal Office.

Montreal, Que.—Maurice M. Davis has been appointed assistant manager of the Montreal branch of the Fox Film. He was formerly associated with the Famous Players in Montreal.

A. H. Fischer Now General Sales Manager of Independent.

Toronto, Ont.—Abe H. Fischer, formerly president and general manager of the United Photoplays, Limited, has become general sales manager of the Independent Film & Theater Supply Company with branches in Toronto, Montreal, Winnipeg and elsewhere. This company has just acquired a number of state right features, the first of which is "God's Man."

Theaters in Canada Expect Prosperous Season.

Toronto, Ont.—More and still more theaters are being renovated in anticipation of great business next fall and winter.

Montreal, Que.—Extensive improvements are being made in the National Biograph, Notre Dame street, West Montreal.

Toronto, Ont.—The lobby of the Colonial theater, City Hall square, Toronto, has been remodeled and the house has been otherwise refitted.

Windsor, Ont.—The Favorite theater, Windsor, under the management of Clyde Curry, is undergoing extensive renovations. Mr. Curry promises that his house will be one of the nicest in western Ontario when alterations are completed.

Kitchner, Ont.—The Roma theater, Kitchner, which was almost totally destroyed by fire, is being rebuilt under the direction of Leo Landry.

Ottawa, Ont.—The Flower theater, Ottawa, which was closed in June, will be reopened before September 1. A number of changes have been made in the structure during its darkness.

Toronto, Ont.—Plans have been drawn by B. Woolson, 186 Queen street, East, Toronto, for the alteration of the premises at 1184 Queen street, West, into a moving picture theater, the expenditure to be $1,100.

Studio Being Altered.

Newark, N. J.—The Chelsea Securities Investment Company, owner of the building situated at 261 Washington street, has secured a permit for alterations to the moving picture studio there occupied by the Washington Studios of the Newark Film Corporation. The estimated cost of the work is $2,000.

Goodwin to Show Goldwyn.

Newark, N. J.—The Goodwin theater, under the management of Mrs. L. H. Webbe, will be the first in Newark to show the new Goldwyn pictures. Announcement of this fact has already been made. The first feature will probably be shown the week of September 9.

Plenty of Business in Louisville Already

Soldiers Won't Be Coming Till September, but Even the Workmen on the Camp Site Have Helped Local Business Markedly.

By Ohio Valley News Service, 1404 Starks Bldg., Louisville, Ky.

LOUISVILLE, KY.—Louisville moving picture exhibitors, together with practically everybody else in Louisville, are busy getting ready for the soldiers, the first group of which are due to arrive at Camp Zachary Taylor, just outside of the city, early in September. There are to be about 40,000 troops stationed at this camp and they will enjoy a five-cent car fare to the downtown theater district.

Of course, there will be moving pictures for the men at the Y. M. C. A. halls in the camp, at the big Army Auditorium, and probably at the entrance to the camp, but the downtown exhibitors do not appear to be the least disconsolate over the prospects of getting their full share of the business that undoubtedly will be developed. The men can stay in the camp and go to picture shows among the soldiers all they want to. The only way they can get a girl and go to a show will be to come to town. Even if the soldiers themselves were not to be counted on for patronage, they are going to bring unusual prosperity to the city. An evidence of this has been shown during the construction of the camp. Here were about 10,000 laborers and the payroll has been around $250,000 a week. There was a lot of this money that went out of the city to the dependents of the workmen in other places, but enough of it was distributed in Louisville to give the retail merchants some of the best business they have had in months.

The soldiers, although they will not draw as much money, will not have to send it home because few will have dependents, and there will be many times more soldiers than there have been workmen. In looking ahead, planning for the kind of pictures that the boys will want, the exhibitors are reported to be proposing to provide pictures away to a considerable extent from the military. Pictures of the war in Europe and scenes as close to actual action as possible will be considered very desirable, but ordinary military stuff, it is figured, will hardly pull because most of the boys will have been fed up on military things by their hard training at the camp.

Light Cretonnes Make Theater Seem Cool.

Louisville, Ky.—Several of the Louisville theaters have been more comfortable, speaking psychologically, this summer than has been the case before. This statement applies especially to The Strand and the Mary Anderson, as well as to Keith's. At all of these houses the heavy velvet, plush or other rich hangings have been supplanted by cretonnes of light color and texture. Of course, curtains do not increase the actual warmth when they are used merely for ornaments inside a theater, but they "look hot," as the womenfolk say, and the result is much the same. They also have become encrusted with dust during the long winter and, even if they are good enough to go back up next winter, they will be all the better for a rest and a trip to the cleaners. The light cretonnes look cool and fresh and add a great deal to the mental comfort of the patrons of the houses. Besides that they are comparatively inexpensive.

Majestic Theater Advertises Coming Features.

Louisville, Ky.—Louis J. Dittmar returned from New York to announce that he had closed a contract for presentation at the Majestic theater of the All-Star Paramount program. Mr. Dittmar made the announcement with pardonable pride and by use of extended advertising space

and readers gave the announcement in detail to the Louisville public. Stress is laid in this publicity on the stars who will be seen during the coming months on the Majestic screen.

Power Company's Bad Coal Dims Theaters.

Louisville, Ky.—Some of the Louisville houses, principally those on the outskirts, were inconvenienced by partial failure of the Central Station electric service some nights ago. This followed complete suspension of the street lights, which were shut off when the attendants at the central station power house found their steam going down. The service to residences and business houses grew indifferent, especially away from the central part of the city, until the steam was raised in another power unit at the power house. The difficulty, it was explained, was due to the fact that, having had to buy everywhere to get sufficient coal to continue operations with, the lighting company got some that would not do the work required of it. Before the situation was discovered and corrected service was very considerably reduced.

Savoy at Nicholasville Continues Sunday Shows.

Nicholasville, Ky.—W. C. Jackson, manager of the Savoy theater, continues to give Sunday programs, under the authority of the Board of Council. Petitions are being circulated addressed to the council, urging withdrawal of its consent and noting the fact that the manager of the local bathing beach has agreed to close the beach on Sunday. Mr. Jackson's position is simply this—he has been given the privilege by constituted authorities to run his theater on Sundays and proposed to do so.

Good Pictures Pay in Falmouth.

Falmouth, Ky.—The Duncan theater, Elmer Woodhead, proprietor, is another example of a theater in a small city which proves that good pictures can be made to pay. Since taking charge of the theater Mr. Woodhead has made numerous improvements in the house and in the film service. The house shows much the same pictures as are seen on the screens of the larger cities. Mr. Woodhead has recently completed showing of the serial "Patria," and Paramount stars are frequently seen, as well as Mary Pickford and Charlie Chaplin. On Saturday night, August 18, Mr. Woodward added a vaudeville bill to the program.

Cleveland News Letter.

M. A. Malaney, 218 Columbia Bldg., Cleveland.

Screeners to Roast Corn Cobs.

CLEVELAND, OHIO.—The Cleveland Screen Club is making arrangements for a big corn roast and picnic to be held the middle of September.

This event will probably be at Willoughby-beach, which has a fine dance hall and beach, and will be the second outing of the club this summer.

The club in the future will have its weekly luncheons and meetings in a private dining room at the Colonial theater. Arrangements for the picnic will be completed at the meeting August 22.

At the regular monthly business meeting of the screeners the following new members were elected: Miles F. Gibbons and J. H. Norwood of the K-E-S-E, exchange; G. G. Rich of the Famous Play-

ers; S. A. Gerson, Buckeye Poster Company; Ike Merris, Home theater; W. J. Brant, Stillman theater; J. E. Beck, Vitagraph exchange.

Babyland Film Making New Picture.

Cleveland, O.—The Babyland Film Company of Cleveland, maker of children's pictures with amateur actors, is now making a new picture called "The Adventures of Jack and Jill." Last spring this concern made a three-reel picture of the famous fairy tale, "Puss in Boots."

Making Use of Local Events.

Cleveland, O.—Charley Hutsenpiller, manager of the Virginia theater, is surely of the live Cleveland exhibitors. Re-

Charles Hutsenpiller.

cently the merchants of his vicinity had a big picnic and he took moving pictures of it. A few days later he exhibited these pictures and enormous crowds attended the theater. These occasional local interest pictures give a big lift to a theater in the eyes of many patrons. The habit of going to any theater is easily acquired when the show is worthy. There is hardly anything better than to get local faces on the screen now and then. It may bring some in who have never visited it before, and even if the possible patron misses the picture he hears about it and it helps him remember the house. He may drop in just to see if something else is doing.

Two New Exchanges to Locate Here.

Cleveland, O.—Cleveland shortly will have at least two more film exchanges. The Four Square Pictures people are now in the city looking for suitable space and expect to open up shortly. The offices will be in charge of D. Leo Dennison, who was formerly with the Paramount. George W. Weeks, of Detroit, will have supervision over the Ohio territory and an office also will be opened soon in Cincinnati.

The Jewel Productions, Inc., will open up offices in Cleveland within a month. This is a big state rights marketing company, recently formed in New York.

Sam Schultz's Exchange Prospers.

Toledo, O.—The Consolidated Film service of Toledo is doing a nice business under Sam Schultz, one of the owners. Besides a large number of one and two-reel subjects, he has many five-reel features. Sam is a hustler and says he will have a large number of new pictures for the coming fall and winter.

Barnett Film Moves Office.

Cleveland, O.—The Barnett Film Attractions, handling "Jean the Woman" and "Twenty Thousand Leagues Under the Sea," has moved from the Sincere building to larger quarters at 722 Columbia building, from which offices they have started their fall and winter booking.

IN DETROIT.

Foursquare Picture at the Washington.

Detroit, Mich.—"The Bar Sinister," the first of the Hoffman Foursquare Pictures to be released in Michigan, has been booked for a solid week at the Washington theater, Detroit. It will then play a week at the Liberty theater. Division Manager George W. Weeks says the outlook is very bright both in Michigan and Ohio, and that he is sure of numerous fall bookings.

Notes of the Trade in Detroit.

The new Charlie Chaplin comedies, to be released through the First National Exhibitors' Circuit, will play one week each at the Madison theater, Detroit.

Dave Mundstock, of the Strand Features, Detroit, is back from a ten days' trip in New York, where he bought some new Chaplin comedies, and a series of two-reel W. S. Hart reissues. Mr. Mundstock will have a big assortment of film attractions for the coming fall season.

The Regent theater, Detroit, closes August 26 and will reopen Sept. 3 with vaudeville and pictures, policy to be continuous from noon to 11 p. m. Tom Ealand, at present manager of the Orpheum, will be in charge of the house.

F. J. Stafford, formerly operating the Central theater in Pontiac, has leased the Fuller theater, in Kalamazoo. George Spaeth continues as manager.

A. I. Shapiro, Detroit manager of the Goldwyn Co., has been taken in the draft, but has asked for exemption. Mr. Shapiro has landed many fine contracts so far and they are from the very best theaters in the state. The Madison, Detroit, has the first run in town.

H. I. Garson Gets Court Order.

Detroit, Mich.—Although Harry I. Garson won the injunction suit started by Lewis J. Selznick to restrain him from doing business in Michigan, the court has decreed that the Garson exchange must send to Selznick 42½ per cent. of the receipts as per the original contract.

Robert Cotton Sticks Fast to Program.

Detroit, Mich.—There is only one policy that dominates Robert Cotton, World Film manager at Detroit, and that is—World Pictures-Brady Made—one a week. Regardless of all the independent releases and the talk of open booking, Mr. Cotton is convinced absolutely that the program is the only system, and he proves it by saying that he has not had a single cancellation in many weeks, regardless of all the open-booking agitation. "World-Brady-Made customers don't want to give up our program—they want to keep it," he said. "They know that we are giving consistent pictures week in and week out—their patrons like them—and we don't ask a fabulous price for them. We want our clients to offer their patrons good pictures, consistent, dependable—and not poor stories, fair productions and high-salaried stars."

Mr. Cotton has been in charge of the World exchange at Detroit for several years, coming here originally as special representative. He was formerly in other lines of commercial business, and when it comes to genuine salesmanship—the kind Charles Schwab talks about—hats off to Brother Cotton, who certainly is "there."

Big Detroit Contract by Artcraft-Paramount

Close to $135,000 Worth of Bookings Secured from Three Leading Theaters in Automobile City—How the Program Is Divided.

By Jacob Smith, 718 Free Press Building, Detroit, Mich.

DETROIT, MICH. — Artcraft-Paramount can certainly feel elated over the deal which they put over in Detroit, Friday, August 17, and which involves close to $135,000 worth of bookings in three leading theaters—the Majestic, Washington and Broadway-Strand. In short, the deal is this: the three houses mentioned are splitting up the Artcraft-Paramount list of pictures, each taking about one-third of the entire program. For instance, the John H. Kunsky theaters get Douglas Fairbanks, the D. W. Griffith productions and others. The Broadway-Strand gets Mary Pickford, W. S. Hart, Pauline Frederick and the De Mille productions. The Majestic theater gets Marguerite Clark and the Stuart Blackton series, as well as others. Each house will play all features not less than one week. The Arbuckle and Sennett comedies will go to the Broadway-Strand.

Represented in the deal were Al Lichtman, general manager for Artcraft-Paramount, and John H. Kunsky, representing the Kunsky interests; Harry I. Garson, representing the Broadway-Strand, and Frank Westbrook, representing the Majestic theater.

It is positively the biggest booking deal ever made in the city of Detroit—it represents about $135,000 worth of bookings b.tween the three first-run houses, and means that the three leading theaters will book out of the same office.

As they would say in the land of slang, "it was some deal."

Bookings with the three houses mentioned will be in operation by the early part of September, although the Broadway-Strand started its new booking arrangement Sunday, August 26, with "The Amazons" owing to it having previously been contracted. Future Marguerite Clark pictures go to the Majestic.

Several New Theaters Building in Detroit.

Detroit, Mich.—Theaters under construction at the present time in Detroit are the De Luxe, at Kercheval and Parkview; the Farnum theater in Hamtramck section; a theater in Springwells section, and one on West Fort street, between Military and Cavalry, which will seat 2,000 people. Louis Smilansky, with offices in the Chamber of Commerce, is building the West Fort street theater. All will be in operation by January 1 or thereabouts.

Percentage Basis Good for Small Houses

Flint, Mich.—Opinions vary as to whether percentage or straight rental is the best proposition for the exhibitor booking big feature attractions. The larger exhibitors would prefer to play pictures on straight rental, while the smaller ones prefer percentage basis. For instance, Charles Garfield, of the Orpheum theater in Flint, would much prefer to play straight rental, and take the gamble himself of cleaning up rather than playing on percentage and giving the big end to the man with the picture. But the smaller exhibitor, expressing the views of R. Sargent of West Branch, is that he cannot afford to take the chance of paying big rental, hence must rely on percentage.

World Man Finds Colonial Theater Top-Notcher.

Detroit, Mich.—The World correspondent made a trip through the new Colonial theater, Woodward at Sibley streets, Detroit, one day last week, and he must say that the Colonial is one of the finest houses in the middle west from the standpoint of being fireproof and modern. It is being built both for vaudeville and pictures. The house will seat 1,700, of which 800 seats are on the main floor. The picture booth is built on the roof of the building—that is, the roof at that place drops down sufficiently to make the booth in proper line with the stage, and yet it is outside. The policy of the Colonial will be vaudeville and pictures, showing continuously from 1 to 11 p. m. daily. The Colonial will open around Sept. 20. William Newkirk is to be the house manager, and he is already on the job. C. A. Hoffmann and Graham Hoffmann are building the Colonial. They now operate the Palace theater on Monroe avenue. Prices at the new house will be from 10 to 25 cents for the regular seats and 50 cents for the boxes.

Two New Men With Detroit Vitagraph.

Detroit, Mich.—J. M. Duncan, manager of the Vitagraph exchange in Detroit, announces two important appointments: L. G. Parkhurst as his assistant and L. E. Davis as city salesman. Mr. Parkhurst was formerly manager at Detroit for Pathe and for the past six months has been in Kansas City for Pathe. Mr. Davis has been with Pathe for several years in Detroit, and enjoys the unique distinction of being the highest paid film salesman in Detroit. Both men will prove of great value to the booking department of Vitagraph in Michigan, and Manager Duncan says he is very much pleased over their acquisition.

Let Exchanges Get Film Back Quickly.

Detroit, Mich.—Michigan film exchange managers have asked the World to call attention to the laxity of exhibitors in sending back their film on time. Of late quite a number of theaters have had to remain dark because film booked to them was delayed in transit or because some exhibitor had delayed in shipping the film as per instructions. If exhibitors all over the country would bear in mind that their inattention to the prompt shipment of film means loss to the exchange and some other theater they would probably be more careful in this matter. SHIP YOUR FILM PROMPTLY AND GET THE ADDRESSES CORRECT ON THE SHIPPING BOX. The carelessness of one exhibitor may mean the rerouting and changing of bookings for twelve or fifteen houses.

Robert Cotton, World Film, Detroit.

Indianapolis Alhambra Much Beautified

Barton and Olson Have Spared no Expense in Making the New Picture Theater Acceptable—Notes About the Firm.

From Indiana Trade News Service. 361 State Life Bldg., Indianapolis, Ind.

INDIANAPOLIS, IND.—Another important milestone in the amusement affairs of the Hoosier capitol was passed Saturday evening, August 18, in the opening of the new Alhambra theater, which is devoted entirely to photoplays and motion pictures of high quality.

The Alhambra is one of the Barton & Olson chain of theaters and this firm, one of the pioneers of the motion picture field, has spared no expense in rebuilding the house. Located in the very heart of the business and shopping district of the city, it is the second largest motion picture theater in Indianapolis and one of the best in the entire state.

Seats for 1,200.

The Alhambra now has a seating capacity of more than 1,200. There are 700 seats on the lower floor, 500 in the balcony and sixty comfortable loge seats. The new chairs, solid leather upholstered, are of the latest design for the theater patron's comfort. The loge chairs are of the very best of wicker.

The cost of rebuilding the Alhambra, which now has an additional width of fif-

Reading from Left to Right:
Charles Olson   Benjamin Barton
And in Center, Edwin Booth

teen feet, exceeds $40,000. There are many innovations, among them being a mezzanine floor, elegantly furnished with every convenience, including free telephones and writing desks. A ladies' rest room and a gentleman's smoking room are in the basement, which also houses a music room for orchestra rehearsals, a private projection department for the inspection of picture subjects, a recreation room for employes and the manager's office.

Operator's Booth and Projection.

Messrs. Barton and Olson have given careful attention to the subject of picture projection. The operating booth is equipped with two new Simplex machines, spot and flood lights. The booth is fireproof in

every detail and, as an extra precaution, is protected with fire ventilating shafts and automatic shutters.

The picture, size 13 by 16 feet, is thrown upon a specially prepared screen, built in Philadelphia, and the only one of its kind to be installed in the middle west. In abolishing eyestrain, it is said to be far superior to even a mirror screen. The screen forms the background of a stage upon which singers and concert artists who may be employed will appear.

The Ventilating System.

One of the most complete ventilating systems ever installed in a theater is one of the important new features. The air is washed and cooled before being forced into the house. Individual ventilators are located under each seat. Large exhaust fans, perfectly noiseless in operation, draw the air out of the house, thus keeping fresh, cool air in constant circulation. Sixteen silent fans also are stationed in the house and no matter how warm it may be outside, a temperature near 70 can easily be maintained in the theater.

Music, Programs and Policy.

The policy of presenting clean, high-grade pictures of artistic quality, always adhered to by Messrs. Barton and Olson, will be in effect at the Alhambra at all times. The program is to be sufficiently diversified, according to the management, to please even the most exacting of patrons. In addition to the featured photoplay, educational films, travelogues, high-class comedies and other picture novelties will be interpreted.

Music is furnished by a ten-piece concert orchestra under the direction of Charles Worthy, whose long experience in arranging instrumental programs for photoplay purposes, admirably fits him for the post. Jesse G. Crane presides at the pipe organ.

The Alhambra now offers a continuous performance, starting at 10 o'clock each morning and terminating at 11 o'clock at night. The program is changed twice weekly, on Sundays and Thursdays. One price—10 cents—prevails for all seats in the afternoons. In the evenings the lower floor and loge seats are 15 cents and the balcony 10 cents.

The Firm of Barton & Olson.

Messrs. Barton and Olson, the owners, have during the last seven years become the biggest theatrical firm in Indianapolis. Doing business under the name of the Central Amusement Company, they own and operate the Lyric theater, devoted to popular vaudeville and pictures; the Alhambra and the Isis, both picture houses, and are summer lessees of the English opera house, where they present vaudeville during the summer months. They are also interested in various other enterprises directly or indirectly affiliated with amusements.

Mr. Barton started in the motion picture business at a time when there was only one picture show in operation in Indianapolis, and that a small place called the Vaudette on South Illinois street. He is president of the Central Amusement Company, also president of the Indianapolis Motion Picture Exhibitors' League, and a director of the Motion Picture Exhibitors' League of Indiana.

Mr. Olson, vice-president and treasurer of the company, was internationally famous as an athlete, and champion light heavyweight wrestler of the world before he engaged in the theatrical business. He founded the Central Film Service Company in Indianapolis, bought control of and reorganized the Buckeye Film exchange of Cincinnati. He is also heavily interested in the Peoples Amusement Company, which owns a string of theaters throughout the state. Edwin Booth, who has managed the theater for the last year, will continue in that position.

May Proh'bit Smoking in Theaters

Indianapolis, Ind.—An ordinance that will prohibit the smoking of tobacco or the lighting of a match in all theaters, including motion picture houses, was to be introduced before the Indianapolis city council Monday night, August 20. The ordinance was prepared by Jacob H. Hilkene, commissioner of public buildings who says the passage of such a measure is necessary for the public safety.

A fine of not to exceed $25 was to be provided for each violation of the ordinance, and theater managers will be made liable to arrest if they permit smoking in their theaters.

"It has been called to my attention recently," said Mr. Hilkene, "that men have been smoking in some of the downtown theaters. This practice has got to stop, because it is not safe and because it is not sanitary."

Exhibitors and Union Temporarily at Odds

Indianapolis Operators Ask for a Double Shift and Better Working Conditions—Rabbi Has Been Chosen to Act as Arbiter in the Dispute.

INDIANAPOLIS, IND.—Trouble has broken out in this city between the Indianapolis Motion Picture Exhibitors' Association and the Motion Picture Operators' Union, as a result of a disagreement over working conditions, and so far has not been adjusted.

A threatened walkout of about seventy union operators, which was scheduled to take place Thursday night, August 16, at midnight, was averted by a temporary restraining order granted by Judge T. J. Moll, of Superior Court. The hearing on the motion, which was scheduled to take place the next day, was postponed for one week after the representatives of the exhibitors' association had informed the court that if a postponement was granted a compromise probably could be reached.

The strike order, according to the members of the union, followed when the exhibitors' organization refused to grant the union demands for a double shift of operators and what they term better working conditions. The representatives of the exhibitors' association say they have been

willing at all times to arbitrate any differences, but they insist that the present demands of the operators are unreasonable.

Rabbi Feuerlicht Chosen Arbiter.

Rabbi Morris M. Feuerlicht was chosen as arbiter, following the expiration of a three years' contract on August 1, and the exhibitors maintain, the operators agreed to continue working until the difficulty should be adjusted. Instead, they say, they learned that the strike order had been issued and they immediately petitioned the court for a temporary injunction.

Officers of the operators' union refuse to discuss their plans since they had the restraining order has been served on them. It is thought, however, that some sort of a compromise will be affected in a few days and everything will turn out satisfactory. A meeting of representatives of the two organizations will be held this week to try to thrash the matter out.

MORE KENTUCKY NOTES.

Insurance Board Lets Up on Small Theaters.

Frankfort, Ky.—The Kentucky Insurance Board, which has charge of enforcement of the new fire insurance code adopted last year, is looking after the interests of the exhibitors in the small towns where there is no organized fire protection. It was provided in the new law that in such communities the insurance agents might increase the rates by ten per cent. In practice, however, it has been found that this plan has resulted in unduly high rates and the board has called a halt on the practice.

Woman Patrons in Paducah Get Hoover Cards.

Paducah, Ky.—Managers of the local moving picture theaters are co-operating with the movement of the big organization looking toward conservation of the food supply of the country. Here the managers have all been supplied with the Hoover pledge cards and are distributing them to the women folk who come to see the pictures. This action was taken with a view of getting the widest possible distribution of the cards by which it is hoped that it will be possible to hold down the consumption of foodstuffs and eliminate waste altogether.

N. A. Wilkerson's New Liberty Makes a Hit.

Mt. Sterling, Ky.—The new Liberty theater, under the management of N. A. Wilkerson, has made good. This was formerly the Paramount theater and, since Mr. Wilkerson has taken charge, has been remodeled and redecorated and is reputed to be one of the coolest and most comfortable houses in the eastern part of the state.

Gurnee Theater Company Formed.

Lexington, Ky.—The Gurnee Theater Company, with capital stock of $25,000, has been incorporated by Nelson van Houten Gurnee, president of the company in charge of the Ada Meade theater and other amusement places, T. C. Fuller and V. H. Fuller. The headquarters of the company will be in Lexington and it will operate a circuit of theaters.

Clyde Gaines Again a Picture Man.

Winchester, Ky.—Clyde Gaines, former prominent exhibitor, who for a time dropped out of moving picture circles to take care of his large eastern Kentucky oil interests, out of which he has made considerable money, is again in the ring, having reopened a theater at Irvine, Ky., which replaces the building burned a few months ago in the big fire. The new Gaines theater is a larger and better house in every way than the one burned and one of the best in the section. However, he has not stopped with the one house, but has purchased the Lyric of Pineville, Ky., paying $16,000 to Col. C. W. Metcalfe, who purchased the property two years ago at a commissioner's sale. He takes possession of the new theater on September 1.

The new house at Irvine, Ky., cost $21,000 to erect and equip. Mr. Gaines now has the money to back his theatrical ventures in the way they should be backed, and is figuring on securing a chain of good small houses in the eastern section of Kentucky in the large oil, lumber and coal districts, where the population is growing rapidly and where high wages are paid, and there are few amusement enterprises of the exclusive jitney. Irvin within a two-year period has jumped from a town of 300 people to one with 6,000 inhabitants, due to the big oil boom, and Pineville has advanced as rapidly due to lumber and coal.

New Theater Association in the Northwest

Associated Theaters, Inc., of North Dakota, with Offices in Minneapolis, Will Do General Theatrical Business for Its Stockholders.

By John L. Johnston, 704 Film Exchange Bldg., Minneapolis, Minn.

MINNEAPOLIS, MINN.—Tom Hamlin's dream has at last been realized, for Tuesday, August 14, the Associated Theaters, Inc., was organized under the laws of the State of South Dakota for $100,000. H. L. Hartman, Mandan, N. D., president of the North Dakota Exhibitors' League, is president of the Associated Theaters, Inc.; Forest Secor, Forest City, Iowa, is vice-president; Charles W. Gates, Aberdeen, S. D., is chairman of the board of directors; Henry P. Greene, Minneapolis, is treasurer; William S. Smith, Menomonie, Wis., is secretary, and Thomas J. Hamlin, Minneapolis, is general manager of the corporation.

Offices have been opened at 810 Lumber Exchange, Minneapolis, and the new body will, if present plans carry, do all that any exhibitor could wish—buy, sell and equip complete theaters, rent film, make slides and film, book vaudeville and road attractions, and handle paper. The corporation will operate without the use of C. O. D.'s and advance deposits, and according to plans, hopes to eliminate much express expense.

The organization hopes to have 1,000 theaters listed before December. Exhibitors are required to buy only enough stock to cover the price of ten days' film rental, and bills will be rendered them for service only at the end of each week. It is said that almost 200 theaters, with but one exception all out of town houses, have signed up with the new body. The new organization is not formed, according to its officers, to "beat out" any other body, but is formed only to serve the exhibitor in the best possible way.

The Year's Big Joy Feast Coming.

Minneapolis, Minn.—There is one time every year that all Minneapolis' filmdom gets together and business jealousy is forgotten. And—only one. That time will arrive Thursday afternoon, August 23, when exhibitors and exchange men will meet at the sixth annual picnic. The merry festival will be held at Spring Park, Lake Minnetonka, this year instead of at Parker's Lake, and several committees have worked diligently to assure the picnickers a good time.

Film Flashes Around the Twin Cities.

Minneapolis, Minn.—Frank Woskie, former roadman for the Supreme and Favorite exchange here, has returned from Baltimore, where, with Ted Karatz, he was interested in the exploitation of "The Spoilers." He expects to be out on the Northwest trail for some local exchange again shortly.

Manager Eddie Westcott, of the Fox exchange, showed "Jack and the Beanstalk" to local exhibitors at the Lyric Monday morning, Aug. 20. Mr. Westcott has had Fox offices in the Jewelers' exchange enlarged and rearranged.

Moran and Wilson, theatrical lobbyists de luxe, have moved their studios from the Jeweler's exchange to the Loeb arcade.

Charles Branham, new manager of the Strand, is developing Dick Long's orchestra by leaps and bounds, and now on every hand one sees placards reading: "That Strand orchestra just won't let your foot keep still. Hop to it." Incidentally the Strand box office is checking up a few more fifteen centses.

Hugh C. Andreas, Lyric theater manager, has increased the size of his orchestra to ten pieces.

Fred Meyer, General exchange manager, has announced the coming release from his exchange of George Ade's "Fables in Slang" short films that made a tremendous hit here some time ago.

Newt. Davis, Bluebird manager, has booked "Mother o'Mine" in the Lyric, Minneapolis, and New Majestic, St. Paul.

St. Paul gets the first showing of Brenon's "The Lone Wolf," Manager Harry Rathner, of the Selznick exchange, having booked the film in the New Garrick for three days beginning Aug. 23.

C. P. Sheehan and C. W. Eckhardt, representing the Fox headquarters in New York, spent two days with Manager Westcott, of the local Fox offices, last week on their transcontinental tour.

Manager J. Earle Kemp, of the Westcott Film Corp., has returned from Milwaukee, where "Intolerance" began a two weeks' run at the Davidson theater to a good business. Tom Burke, of the Westcott forces, will display the new Rex Beach travel pictures to Twin City exhibitors at some downtown theater next week.

Mr. and Mrs. Dale McFarland, of the Independent exchange, have returned from a ten-day vacation trip to Yellowstone National Park.

Mr. and Mrs. S. A. Louis, of the Rialto Theater Supply Co., are spending their vacation in the Northern Minnesota country.

S. N. Robinson, of the Film Library and Exchange, distributing Christie comedies, has opened a branch office at Room 2, Babcock building, Billings, Mont. B. F. Shearer is in charge of the branch.

Earl C. Sly, of the Lochren Film Service, has returned from North Dakota, where he took several thousand feet of commercial film for a local farm machinery factory.

Bert Barnett, Sr., Comes Back with State Right Film.

Minneapolis, Minn.—Bert Barnett, Sr., one of the oldest and most popular exchange managers the Northwest has ever had, returned to Minneapolis true to our predicting. Mr. Barnett controls the rights to display "Joan the Woman," featuring Geraldine Farar, in the Dakotas, Minnesota, Wisconsin, Ohio, and Michigan. He has opened up offices at 404 Film Exchange building here to cover the four Northwest states, and Bert Barnett, Jr., is in charge of offices at Detroit and Cleveland. Leo Eckstein, former Paramount roadman out of Wilwaukee, will direct the feature in Wisconsin, while Mr. Barnett, Sr., will look after Minnesota and the Dakotas personally. Miss Mayme Lucia, former Paramount exchange booker, has been secured by Mr. Barnett for his "right hand man." The Barnetts owned the Famous Players All Star Feature exchange here until January 1 last, when the business was sold to the Paramount.

Honor William Howard, Soldier of the Republic.

Minneapolis, Minn.—William K. Howard, who resigned as manager of the Metro exchange here recently to join the Signal Corps of the United States Army, was the guest of Mill City exhibitors and exchangemen at a banquet in his honor at Schick's, Aug. 12. The banquet was of the North Dakota variety, H Two O being the exclusive beverage. About fifty men were present, and Mr. Howard was presented with a handsome marine wrist watch. Following the feast, Mr. Howard, with C. L. Booth, motored to St. Mary's, Ohio, where Mr. Howard bid good bye to his parents. He then went to Jefferson Barracks, Mo.

Many Texas Theaters Find Business Slack

Continued Drought Takes Life Out of the Small Town Trade—War Draft Also a Factor—Better Business Prospects Seen.

By Douglas Hawley, Times-Herald, Dallas, Texas.

DALLAS, TEXAS.—As a result of continued drouth in some fifty West Texas counties, 35 per cent. of the motion picture houses in that section of the state have been compelled to close their doors.

Childress, Quanah and several other towns in Western Texas of more than ordinary importance in the matter of population and business have been seriously affected by the continued dry spell. It may be remarked, however, that at this writing showers have been reported from various points close to that section and the fervent hope is that the worst is over.

It may have been the effect of the drouth; it may have been the effect of the draft or war conditions in general, but the dull business has even been felt in the larger towns. Theaters in Dallas, Fort Worth, Waco, Houston and San Antonio all have suffered. Places with established reputations for showing the best that there is have done pretty well—everybody else has been traveling a rocky road for the last several weeks. However, there is promise for the future. If the picture business in Texas is to be affected for better or for worse by crop conditions, then this is the lean season of but short duration, for rarely has Texas as a whole ever made a total failure cropwise. Its "come-back" is proverbially the strongest that there is.

Manager Reed Shows Exhibitors Fox Films.

Dallas, Texas.—With Charles Wurz and E. H. Wachter, from the home office, on hand, exhibitors' showings of the Fox features, "The Conqueror," "Jack, and the Beanstalk" and "The Honor System" were made at the Jefferson theater (now not operating) at Dallas last week. More than a hundred Texas picture men were in attendance and expressions of full satisfaction were heard. The local showing was made under arrangement of Dallas Manager G. C. Reed of the Fox Corporation.

Perhaps They May Be Soldiers.

Dallas, Texas.—The war draft is making rifts—or threatening too—in the ranks of the motion picture men in Texas. Lawrence Stuart, manager of the "Old Mill" Hulsey theater, at Dallas, has had his number drawn, and is not offering exemption claims. Herschel Stuart, assistant to Mr. Hulsey, has also been drawn, but Hulsey, it is understood, is urging an industrial exemption claim before the district board on the part of his able lieutenant. W. C. Dugger, manager Triangle Company's Dallas branch, it is declared, is carrying brain pictures of khaki coats, soldiers' shoes and shoulder straps, and may be a member of the second officers' training camp at Leon Springs, which opens the latter part of the month.

Some Hits in Dallas Theaters.

Dallas, Texas.—"Sudden Jim," with Charles Ray, was a popular picture shown at Dallas during the last week—one of the few, along with Margurite Clarke, in "The Amazons," which brought out excellent attendance. The former was shown at the Old Mill and the latter at the Queen, both Hulsey theaters.

A Texas woman—Corinne Griffith, with Earle Williams—in "The Stolen Treaty," has been a good drawing card at the Washington theater the last week. Miss Griffith is good looking and shows her ability as an actress. Controversy as to her residence has sprung up between four Texas towns. The truth is she is a native of New Orleans, but was, just prior

to entering the pictures, a resident of Mineral Wells—Texas health resort—for several years. Her mother still resides there.

Dallas Censors Forbid Two Films.

Dallas, Texas.—"The Mother Instinct," with Petrova, and "The Little Lost Sister," have been two films frowned upon by the Dallas censor during the last week. The former had been billed, but was not shown. The latter was forbidden after a private showing. The two were first pictures condemned by action of the new board of censors, appointed by the city administration, which came into office on May 1.

Eight Censors Use Passes Liberally.

Dallas, Texas.—Eight members of a board of censorship, all expecting—and receiving—free passes to the picture shows, is going pretty strong in the opinion of not a few people—not only those in the business but others as well. Nevertheless that's the condition in Dallas. All eight members of the board have their passes and they do not hesitate to use them. There has been no complaint on the part of picture theater managers, but it is understood that the manager of a local vaudeville house has made a strenuous sotto voce objection. At this writing it is not known whether this latter has issued the eight passes asked for.

H. G. Morrow Leaves the Dallas Paramount.

Dallas, Texas.—Hoyt G. Morrow has resigned from the sales managership of the Artcraft-Paramount, Dallas, Texas, branch. After a vacation trip with Mrs. Morrow through Colorado he will return to Dallas to take a position with another distributing organization. He has devoted the past twelve years to the motion picture business and has an extensive acquaintance in the South and Southwest.

Iowa Film News Letter.

By Dorthy Day, Register-Tribune, Des Moines, Ia.

Butterflies Going Over Big in Iowa.

DES MOINES, IA.—D. B. Lederman, veteran manager of the Laemmle Film Service in Des Moines, is enthusiastic. He says that when the Butterflies were released in May the bookings came in so strong by June 1 he had to order his roadman to quit selling them, as all dates were filled until the 20th of August. About the 10th of August he started selling again and now every available date is filled until November.

Charles B. Wells, formerly manager of the K-E-S-E office in Minneapolis, and who is now managing the Isis theater in Cedar Rapids, is also enthusiastic over the Butterflies, while the Strand, in Fort Dodge, is equally satisfied.

Garden Books Bessie Barriscale Paralta Output.

Des Moines, Ia.—The Garden theater, of this city, seemingly intent on securing all of the better pictures on the market, have booked the Bessie Barriscale pictures from the Paralta.

Douglas Fairbanks Takes Des Moines by Storm.

Des Moines, Ia.—Des Moines people have certainly taken the Douglas Fairbanks smile and the Fairbanks stunts to heart by the way in which they await

the coming of his pictures. John Shipley, publicity man for the Garden, realizes the great popularity of the star and in his ads always refers to him as "Doug." The Garden showed "Down to Earth" the week of the 19th.

Fred Theile Chief Booker at Triangle Office.

Des Moines, Ia.—Fred Theile, formerly of the General Film Exchange in Des Moines and Omaha, is now chief booker at the Triangle office in Kansas City. Mr. Theile is well known in this territory.

Harry Weinberg Covering Missouri for Mid West.

Des Moines, Ia.—Manager Blank, of the Mid West Photoplay Corporation of this city, announces that Harry Weinberg, formerly roadman for Triangle in Nebraska, is now covering Missouri for the Mid West office in Kansas City.

R. L. White Makes Hurried Trip to Georgia.

Des Moines, Ia.—R. L. White, Iowa roadman for the K-E-S-E, has been called to Georgia by the serious illness of his mother at her home there.

Heard at the Exchanges.

Des Moines, Ia.—Paul Le Bar, pianist at the Garden theater in Des Moines, is leaving the Garden orchestra to play at the Orpheum, Des Moines' finest vaudeville house, on its opening date, the 26th of August.

J. A. Pickler, new owner of the University theater in Des Moines, has a versity theater in the Selznick and other Mid West pictures at his suburban house. Mr. Pickler purchased the University from W. H. McDowell some five weeks or so ago.

The Pathe exchange are receiving many inquiries over the booking dates on "To-Day" and "The Mad Love," the Robert Warwick features to be released through Pathe. Exhibitors seem to be anxious to run the Warwick pictures.

The Mid West Photoplay office have received just exactly 380 requests from the Iowa exhibitors for advance news and release dates on the Chaplin pictures for the Exhibitors' Circuit.

Odds and Ends from Over Iowa.

Ellsworth, Ia.—The opera house in Ellsworth, Ia., formerly operated by the Ellsworth Amusement Company, has been closed down for extensive repairs.

Stratford, Ia.—V. Landers, owner of the Simplex theater, in Stratford, has gone on a three weeks' vacation, leaving the theater in the care of his nephew.

Grand Junction, Ia.—Fred Hughart, of the Eagle theater, in Grand Junction, has installed an up-to-the-minute model of the Motiograph. This is the second that Mr. Hughart owns, and he is now able to run his pictures straight through with no interruption.

Creston, Ia.—Hood & Snyder have purchased the Lyric theater, in Jewel, from George Patterson. Mr. Patterson is giving his entire time now to the operation of the Grand theater in Story City, having heretofore been managing both houses.

Creston, Ia.—William Weldon has purchased the Willard theater, in Creston, from C. H. Hoffman, who had owned it five or six months.

Iowa City, Ia.—The Garden theater, in Iowa City, has been closed for some time, but it is to be reopened soon by J. H. Lape, who is redecorating the theater from

top to bottom. He has been to the Mid
West office in Des Moines and arranged
for the big Selznick pictures and is also
planning to show Goldwyn pictures.

Marshalltown, Ia.—Leo Meulhaupt, of
the Casino theater, in Marshalltown,
opened Sunday the 19th with "On Trial."
The Casino has been redecorated and M.
Meulhaupt will show feature pictures the
first half of the week and vaudeville the
rest of the time.

Hubbard, Ia.—Knowes & Boeke have
closed the Electric theater, in Holland,
during the hot weather, and are planning to reopen the 1st of October.

Radcliffe, Ia.—Dan Ertel, of the opera
house, in Radcliffe, took a trip to Green
Mountain last week to visit his son, who
is a successful farmer near there.

Boone, Ia.—M. J. Lockard is planning
to open the Palace theater, formerly
called the Gem, and closed by the former
manager, Mr. Allinson, this spring, about
the 15th of September, with the Pathe
picture "The Vicar of Wakefield." Mr.
Lockard has remodeled the new Palace,
put in an entirely new front and is erecting a splendid looking balcony. The former Gem will be one of Boone's finest
photoplay houses.

Rippey, Ia.—The Electric theater, in
Rippey, has been closed by its owners,
Parr & McCain, and the building is being
torn down.

Wheatland, Ia.—J. C. Robertson has
sold the opera house, in Wheatland, to Mr.
Otto Lahann.

Des Moines Visitors and News of Film People.

Des Moines, Ia.—T. J. Acklin, of the
opera house, in Swan, Ia.; C. L. Allen, of
the Elite theater, in Pella, Ia.; J. A. Shales,
of the Past Time theater, in Brandon,
were visitors at the Pathe exchange last
week.

A. C. Schunemann, of the Isis theater, in
Webster City, was a caller at the Mid
West office and the Mutual exchange.

With Middle West Picture Theaters.

Topeka, Kan.—The Majestic theater will
be remodeled and redecorated before its
opening on Labor Day.

Arkansas City, Kan.—Roy Burford,
manager of the Rex theater, will build a
new balcony in his theater.

Clarence, Mo.—The Star theater has
changed hands.

St. Louis, Mo.—Charles W. Daniels will
be the new manager of the Gayety theater.

Omaha, Neb.—Paul LeMarquand and W.
LeDoux, lessees and managers of the Empress theater, have leased the Brandeis theater.

Claremore, Okla.—The Claremore, a new
theater east of the Sequoah Institute, has
been opened. L. H. Brophy is the manager.

Pauls Valley, Okla.—J. W. Groves, formerly of Edmond, has taken charge of the
Regal theater, and will reopen it shortly.

Lawton, Okla.—The Koehler Amusement
Company has been chartered, with a capital
stock of $3,000, by C. T. Wetherell, J. W.
Powell, and C. R. Johnson.

Mitchell, S. D.—The Gale, a new motion
picture house, has been opened by Mr. Dix,
the manager.

Garretson, S. D.—J. W. Tillman has sold
the Princess theater to Mr. Peterson, of
Edgerton.

El Paso, Tex.—The new Alameda theater
will be completed and ready for occupancy
the last of August. J. C. Ontiveros is the
manager.

Waco, Tex.—A theater for soldiers to
be known as the Old Glory will be opened
at Nineteenth and Summer streets near
the main entrance to the Government training camp. P. G. Cameron, of Dallas, will
be at the head of the company.

Austin, Tex.—Marvin Halden has taken
the place of F. Gale Wallace as manager
of the Majestic theater.

Kansas City Picture Notes Last Week

Longacre Distributing Company Opens an Office for Century Comedies—News Notes from Local Exchanges and Theaters in Middle West.

By Kansas City News Service, 205 Corn Belt Bldg., Kansas City, Mo.

KANSAS CITY, MO.—The Longacre Distributing Company, handling the
Century Comedies featuring Alice Howell,
has opened offices on the third floor of the
Shukert building here. There is considerable demand for these comedies in
Missouri and Kansas, the territory that
will be covered by the new exchange.
Several of the theaters in Kansas City in
the downtown districts have made inquiries
in regard to getting the franchise for the
comedies. The manager of the exchange
has not yet been selected.

H. C. Phillips One of Goldwyn Staff Now.

Kansas City, Mo.—H. C. Phillips, formerly of the Vitagraph company here, is
now with Richard P. Robertson, manager
of the Kansas City Goldwyn office, as bookkeeper and cashier.

C. W. Hinson Gets Triangle Sales Staff Job.

Kansas City, Mo.—G. W. Hinson has
been added to the sales force of the
Southern Triangle Pictures Corporation.
He will work on a Kansas territory. He
was formerly with the Metro company.

F. Donigan Goes on Road.

Kansas City, Mo.—F. Donigan has been
taken out of the poster department of
the Southern Triangle Pictures Corporation and has been given a territory in
Kansas.

Fred Thiele Will Be Assistant at Omaha Triangle.

Kansas City, Mo.—Fred Thiele, head
booker at the local Triangle office, will soon
go to Omaha, Nebraska, to work as assistant manager of the Triangle office that is
now being opened there.

"Flame of the Yukon" Passes in Kansas.

Kansas City, Mo.—The local Triangle
office was successful in the second effort
to have the picture, "The Flame of the
Yukon," passed by the Kansas State Board
of Review.

Omaha Triangle Office Will Handle Nebraska and Iowa.

Kansas City, Mo.—The Triangle offices
announces that all the accounts of the company in Iowa and Nebraska will be handled
through the office of the company at Omaha,
Nebraska, which is now being installed.
All shipments to said accounts will be
made from this office.

Emmett Crozier Out of Feature Film Company.

Kansas City, Mo.—Emmett Crozier,
publicity manager of the Kansas City Feature Film Company, has severed his connections with that company. His plans for
the future are unknown.

C. L. Matson Will Handle Feature Film Publicity.

Kansas City, Mo.—C. L. Matson has been
made publicity manager for the Kansas
City Feature Film Company to succeed
Emmett Crozier, who resigned. Mr. Mat-
son is well acquainted in the territory,
having conducted theaters in Iowa and
Wisconsin. He was formerly assistant to
Mr. Crozier.

W. C. Rider Goes to Salt Lake City.

Kansas City, Mo.—W. C. Rider, who has
been handling the Arbuckle comedies for
the Kansas City Feature Film Company,

has resigned his position with the company. He will go to Salt Lake City, Utah,
for a short vacation before beginning his
work there, which will be with a moving
picture concern.

C. Knickerbocker Transferred to Fox St. Louis Office.

Kansas City, Mo.—Charles Knickerbocker, salesman working out of the
Kansas City Fox office, has been transferred to the St. Louis, Missouri, office of
the company.

Lewis Waldman Now Shipping Clerk for General.

Kansas City, Mo.—Lewis Waldman, formerly with the General Film at Charlotte,
North Carolina, has been made shipping
clerk at the Kansas City office.

Falcon Feature, "The Main Spring," Shown.

Kansas City, Mo.—The General Film recently gave a private review of the first of
the Falcon features, "The Main Spring," at
the Wonderland theater here. The showing
was attended by local and out-of-town exhibitors.

Bluebird Offices Moved Down Stairs.

Kansas City, Mo.—The Bluebird Photoplay Corporation has moved into more
spacious offices on the third floor of the
Shukert building from the sixth floor of
that building. The new location will give
the company double the space that it had
formerly. The office will be shared with
the Longacre Distributing Company.

Crystal Theater Finds Bluebirds Good.

Ottawa, Kan.—W. A. Millington, manager of the Crystal theater at Ottawa,
Kansas, recently made a 52-week contract
with the Bluebird company after showing four pictures produced by that company. The four pictures were "The Little
Orphan," "The Kentucky Cinderella," "A
Little Terror," and "The Girl in the
Checkered Coat." He has never shown a
Bluebird before, which makes the signing
of the contract all the more unusual.

Universal Exchange Issues Weekly Magazine.

Kansas City, Mo.—The Universal Film
and Supply Company is now issuing a
weekly magazine devoted to the work of
the exchange at Kansas City. This magazine containsin formation in regard to
future releases of Butterfly features,
serials, and the Universal regular weekly
program. The paper is edited by L. B.
Douglas, publicity manager of the company here. The paper has a circulation of
about 1,000, as each exhibitor in the territory is forwarded a copy each week.

Texas Theater Jottings.

Denison, Tex.—E. H. Hulsey, who recently took charge of the Kyle theater, is
remodeling it, and will open the last of
August.

Deming, Tex.—C. T. Jones has purchased
a lot 75x145 feet, and will erect a motion
picture theater to cost $8,000, which will
have a seating capacity of 2,000 persons.

Austin, Tex.—The Shannan Amusement
Company has been chartered with $3,500
capital stock.

Sherman, Tex.—The Gem theater has
been remodeled. Among the improvements
made is a new front to the building.

San Francisco Theaters Revise Prices

Will Keep Step with Times in Asking More for Admissions—New Policies Announced by Theatres and Better Service.

From T. A. Church, 1507 North St., Berkeley, Cal.

SAN FRANCISCO, CAL.—The movement toward higher admission prices at local moving picture theaters has taken a definite shape and within a short time a revised schedule of rates will be placed in effect at a number of the leading downtown houses. The five-cent theater has long been practically out of existence here ang the indications are that the ten-cent house will follow in its wake. The increased cost of film service, theater supplies and labor is cutting seriously into the profits of all houses and theater managers declare that they must take in more money, and at once.

In a public statement on this question Howard J. Sheehan, manager of the Rialto theater, recently said: "The conditions surrounding the exhibiting of motion pictures have changed to such an extent during the last few months that the Rialto, in order to meet the new state of affairs, which is due largely to changes in the producing end of the business, has been practically forced, if it would continue to exist, to reconstruct its entire plan of doing business. We have now arrived at a point where, if we are to continue to give our patrons the same high class entertainment that they have learned to expect from us, it is necessary that we make radical changes in our policy. And the very first change is an increase in the price of admission, which will be 15 and 25 cents, with 35 cents for the loge chairs, instead of 10, 20 and 30 cents, as heretofore." Mr. Sheehan notes, however, that with the increase in prices to be shown and the method of showing them will also be raised. The Rialto will show the new Standard pictures of the Fox Film Corporation, and instead of making a weekly change of program, as has been the case in the past, will keep these on the screen as long as there is a demand for them.

The Imperial theater has also announced an increase in admission prices to 15, 25 and 35 cents, and is likewise planning to improve its program and its service. With the film offerings at its command Manager J. L. Partington expressed the belief that the public will willingly pay the small increase.

The Turner & Dahnken circuit, which conducts a chain of ten theaters, is also planning to advance admission prices at most of these, and other theater owners in this part of California are preparing to put new prices in effect.

Sheehan and Lurie Get Strand Theater.

San Francisco, Cal.—The Strand theater, conducted as a moving picture house for the past six months by Sid Grauman, and operated by him for several years previous to this time as a vaudeville house, is to be taken over at an early date by Sheehan & Lurie, owners of the Rialto theater, all arrangements for the transfer having been completed. Sid Grauman has been a leading figure in the local amusement field for many years, and his father, D. J. Grauman, who is associated with him, was one of the first to show moving pictures here. A fine theater is being erected at Los Angeles for Sid Grauman and associates and he will go there to assume its management as soon as his business affairs are settled here.

E. O. Child Becomes Pathe Manager.

San Francisco, Cal.—E. O. Child, who handled the series of McClure pictures in this territory, and who has been enjoying a ranch life for the past eight weeks, has returned to this city to accept the management of the local branch of the Pathe Exchange, Inc., succeeding H. E. Lotz, who

recently resigned and left for the East. Mr. Child is one of the most popular exchange men in this territory and his return to the business is hailed with delight by his many friends. Special Representative Charles Meade, who has been here for the past five weeks with his wife, will shortly resume his tour of Pathe offices, but leaves with a tinge of regret, as he has become enamoured with the cool summer climate of this city.

Goldwyn Making Flying Start.

San Francisco, Cal.—The local officers of the Goldwyn Distributing Corporation are now in about a completed form, the latest addition being a glass enclosed private office for Manager C. Mel Simmonds. District Manager Harry Leonhardt is here and an active campaign for business has been launched, following a trade showing of the first two releases. J. L. Frazier recently made a tour of the San Joaquin valley and lined up a number of fine houses, including the Kinema, Fresno; the Monache, Porterville; the Elite, Merced; the Ashby, Hanford, and the Star, Modesto. He will start out again shortly and will visit the towns along the south coast. William Benard is covering the territory north of San Francisco and he also sending in good reports. A first run has been secured in San Francisco at the T. & D. Tivoli opera house.

Big Simplex Installations.

San Francisco, Cal.—The Breck Photoplay Supply Company recently received a shipment of fifteen Simplex machines installed to special order, twelve of these to be installed in local houses and three to be sent out of town to a theater now in course of construction. The machines are finished in white enamel, giving them a very striking appearance, the idea being that of Louis R. Greenfield, of the Kahn & Greenfield circuit. The operating rooms of this concern are models of their kind and it is the delight of members of the houses to show them to patrons of the houses conducted by it. The initial installation of three machines will be made in the Progress theater on Fillmore street, and three each will be installed in the New Mission and the New Fillmore theaters. The latter house is now closed, owing to rebuilding operations, but will be opened again in September. The balance of the big order for machines is divided between the Imperial theater, of this city, and the new Liberty theater being erected at Fresno, Cal., by James Beatty and associates.

Nat A. Magner to Go to the Orient.

San Francisco, Cal.—Nat A. Magner is closing out his local film interests and plans to leave for the Orient about the middle of September, where he will be the sole Selig representative, handling all of the Selig productions. His stock of films has been purchased by Davis Bros., who are enlarging their quarters at 187 Golden Gate avenue, to handle the added business, and he is making a short business trip to Los Angeles. Upon his return he will make a flying visit to Chicago and will then sail from this port for the Far East.

California Film Exchange Notes.

San Francisco, Cal.—E. H. Goldberg, for five years with the California Film exchange, at Los Angeles, has been placed in charge of the Bluebird office at San Francisco, succeeding A. Markowitz. L. F. Zellinsky is a new salesman out of the local office and he has been bringing in some fine contracts.

Dave Bershon, who was here recently with his family on a visit from Los Angeles, where he is branch manager, has returned home by auto.

John Pervia, of the shipping staff, has been enjoying a vacation and is now back at work again, filled with his usual ginger.

Carl Laemmle, president of the Universal Film Manufacturing Co., is expected here late in August.

Two huge billboards at the entrance to Film Row have been leased by Manager Markowitz and exhibitors cannot enter or leave the district without seeing the attractive paintings on these. A late one represents a great crowd making for the nearest Bluebird theater.

A large contract has been signed between Manager M. L. Markowitz and the Honolulu Film Company for Universal and Bluebird service on the Hawaiian Islands. The Honolulu Film Company is a new concern incorporated with a capital stock of $3,000 by Toru Masuhara, William F. Wallace, Mataji Nagamori and Isami Ta Kano. The concern controls a circuit of theaters and will sub-rent films after it has made use of them.

Notes From Progressive Exchange.

San Francisco, Cal.—The new offices recently taken over by the Progressive Motion Picture Company in the Pacific building have been remodeled and are now being occupied. Separate rooms have been made for the bookkeeping and booking departments and local Manager J. W. Allen has been given another private office. A private telephone exchange has been installed and considerable new office equipment added.

Harold N. Harshman, of the single reel department was married on August 13 to Miss Agnes S. Campbell of this city.

Miss Marie Cooper, of the bookkeeping department, has been sent to the new Portland office to assist Manager C. M. Hill.

D. K. Reed, formerly of the Los Angeles branch, is now the feature booker at the home office, and Mr. Lohman has been promoted to the office of chief booker.

"Come Through" Scores a Success.

San Francisco, Cal.—The Strand theater has met with great success in its run on "Come Through," which is controlled personally in this territory by Morris L. Markowi z.

Supply Business Picking Up.

San Francisco, Cal.—Local dealers in machines and theater supplies state that business has been showing quite an increase of late. G. A. Metcalfe recently sold two Power's 6B Cameragraphs, a Westinghouse motor generator set and full operating room equipment to the Rosebrook Amusement Company, which will open a new theater at Piedmont in September. Power's machines, to the Fetters Hot Springs and the Mount Shasta Amusement Company of Etna Mills. A large lot of lobby display equipment was purchased by W. M. Englehart, of Truckee, who was recently here on a visit.

Mutual Representative Visits Golden Gate.

San Francisco, Cal.—A. S. Kirkpatrick, of the home office of the Mutual Film, spent a short time at the local branch recently. The sales force of this office has been augmented by H. Von Emmel.

San Francisco Jottings.

Thomas O'Day, of this city, is erecting a theater near Camp Freemont to have a seating capacity of 1,500. It is on the edge of the great army camp in the suburbs of this city.

Otto Laurelle, a veteran exhibitor of San Francisco, and Charles Rasmussen, a well known dealer in moving picture houses, have opened the Oriental theater, in the heart of Chinatown. With a Chinese girl in the box office and a Chinese attendant at the door, this house has a real Oriental air and the patronage is largely from Chinatown.

John Bromberger, a musician of note, has been made manager of the Panama theater on Market street. He was a witness of a hold-up recently, but was not molested, other than being compelled to elevate his hands.

The Alhambra theater, on Market street. Sam Gordon, proprietor, will change shortly from straight pictures to moving pictures and vaudeville.

A pay-as-you-enter system has again been installed at the T. & D. Tivoli opera house.

Jules E. Smith, of the Butler theater, Tonapah, Nev., was a recent visitor, having been spending a vacation in California.

H. D. Maugle, western division manager of the Greater Vitagraph Company, paid the local branch a visit about the middle of August.

Northern California Notes.

Oakland, Cal.—Phil Doll, of the Circle theater, with Frank A. M. Bowles, who recently took over the Rex theater, has sold his interests to J. Marsh.

Alterations are being made and a full operating room equipment installed by Walter G. Freddey, of San Francisco.

Petaluma, Cal.—The Gem theater has been destroyed by fire.

Vallejo, Cal.—A. M. Bowles, who recently took over the Rex theater, has sold his interests to J. Marsh.

Great Organ for California Theater.

San Francisco, Cal.—The organ for the new California theater at Fourth and Market streets, San Francisco, Cal., which will be opened to the public on November 1, arrived recently and the event was regarded of such interest and importance by the management of the house that a parade was organized, and headed by a band of music the twenty-one large auto trucks required to move the parts making up the great instrument covered the downtown district.

This instrument, which required five large cars to bring it from the factory, is a Wurlitzer Hope-Jones Unit Orchestra, and is the largest ever turned out by the company. It cost more than $50,000 at the factory, and the installation will bring the cost up to about $10,000 more. Many unique features have been incorporated in its manufacture and it has five complete sets of marimbaphones, which will be heard for the first time in this theater. Manager Eugene Roth, under whose direction this house is being built, promises a genuine musical treat to the patrons of this new theater.

The services of Bruce Gordon Kingsley, an organist of international fame, who gave a series of thirty-three eminently successful concerts at the Panama-Pacific International Exposition in 1915, have been secured for a period of three years at a large salary and the musical programs are already commencing to receive attention.

The console of the organ is located in the center of the orchestra pit and is placed on an automatic elevator which permits the organist to rise to the level of the stage when rendering concert numbers and allowing the audience to see the intricate console, with its four manuals. Five large organ chambers house the tone parts of the instrument, which duplicate the music of any instrument ever made. The contact room in the basement occupies a space of ten by twenty feet and is surrounded on three sides by plate glass, it being the intention of Manager Roth to permit the public to inspect the working of the marvelous electric keys which manipulate the instrument.

Producing Company Organized in Spokane

C. J. Ward Is Taking Steps to Incorporate Washington Motion Picture Company —Finds Northwest Better than California for Studio Sites.

By S. Clark Patchin, E1811 Eleventh Ave., Spokane, Wash.

SPOKANE, WASH.—"An investigation of several weeks convinces me we have found, here, conditions more favorable for the production of moving pictures than in California," said C. J. Ward, manager for Tyrone Power, and who is taking steps for the incorporation of the Washington Motion Picture Corporation. Continuing he said:

"With a contract for the services of Mr. Power for the next few years, I have been in a position to complete the essentials for a profitable enterprise.

"We are completing the organization of our company and will at once file articles of incorporation. A board of directors will be elected within the next few days and we will be able to announce within two weeks where we will construct the studios.

"I feel confident that within 60 days the production of pictures will be under way. After spending next week in Spokane Mr. Power will proceed to New York City, where I have contracted for him to accept a limited engagement at the Manhattan opera house. While he is in New York we will arrange to take part of the pictures for a production entitled "A Man and His Brother," in which Mr. Power will appear."

A Neat Small Town Theater.

Douglas, Wyo.—Exhibitor Irwin A. Erdman, of the Princess theater, at Douglas, Wyo., sends to the Moving Picture World the accompanying picture of his pleasing

Princess Theater, Douglas, Wyo.

Princess theater. It seats 600 persons and serves a town of 1,600. "It would do Mr. Richardson's heart good," writes the manager, "to see our operator eat up his projection department in your publication. The handbook he calls his bible."

Artillerymen Are Guests of Theaters.

Spokane, Wash.—C. E. Stilwell, manager of the Stilwell Theaters Company, is keeping open house at all of his theaters for members of the field artillery being organized in Spokane. They are at liberty to visit the Class A, Rex, Unique and Casino with the exception of Saturday afternoons and Sundays.

Notes From Spokane Filmdom.

Spokane, Wash.—Ellis Cohen, of New York City, representing the "Gray Ghost," being put out by the Universal, is spending a few days in this territory. He is visiting W. Potter, manager of the Universal. Mr. Potter has just completed a trip through Western Montana and reports business good.

J. H. Baum, of Portland, Ore., who has spent 30 days in Spokane territory with "20,000 Leagues Under the Sea," returned to Portland.

P. L. Carroll, manager of the Pathe exchange, is covering his territory along the Great Northern Railway, and reports business good.

Seattle News Letter.

lly S. J. Anderson, East Seattle, Wash.

Special Concerts a Drawing Card at Clemmer.

SEATTLE, WASH.—With the opening of "The Whip" at the Clemmer theater on Sunday, August 19, the eight-piece Russian Orchestra was enlarged by the addition of a harpist and another violinist. The orchestra is also giving two special concerts a week in the evening in addition to the regular Tuesday and Friday afternoon concerts. M. Guterson and his Russian Orchestra since their coming to Seattle a year and a half ago have won a large following among the music lovers of the city, and these special concerts have become one of the Clemmer's greatest drawing cards.

Regular patrons of this theater have also welcomed with enthusiasm the return of the Drew comedies to the program. Slapstick comedies do not as a general rule appeal to the high class patronage which the house draws, but the funny situations in the Drew comedies and the funnier mannerisms of Sidney always appeal to them. The Hearst-Pathe News is also a very welcome attraction which has returned to the Clemmer program.

Motion Picture Business Booming in Java.

Seattle, Wash.—According to A. W. Walker, of the firm of Robinson and Walker of this city, exporters and importers to Java, the motion picture business in this and other islands of the Dutch East Indies is flourishing. Messrs. Robinson and Walker make a specialty of exporting film to this section of the Orient, and so keep in close touch with conditions in the industry there. Many fine new bioscopes, as the motion picture theaters are called in the Orient, are being erected; and the inhabitants are demanding better pictures to be shown in them. Motion picture shows are just coming into their own as the most popular amusement of the people, and the natives are crazy about them.

Seattle Exchange Notes.

Seattle, Wash.—J. F. Paine, special representative from the New York office, is spending several days this week at the Seattle Triangle office. With S. P. Peck. head of the booking department, ill and two stenographers away on their vacation, H. H. Hurn, manager of the office, is busy.

Melvin G. Winstock, of the L. J. Schlaifer Attractions Company, will leave next week for Portland, where he will open headquarters for a month.

L. Ernest Ouimet, president and general manager of the Specialty Film Import, Limited, of Canada, with headquarters in Montreal, spent a day or two in Seattle this week. Mr. Ouimet handles the Pathe films for Canada, and while here he obtained Alexander Pantages' signature to a contract for Pathe pictures for all his houses in Canada.

Visitors on Film Row.

Seattle, Wash.—Among the exhibitor visitors to Seattle this week were: Hector Quagliotti, Colonial theater, Vancouver; I. L. Williams, Orpheum and Monroe theaters, Snohomish; A. H. McDonald, Rex, Eugene, Oregon; George Hunt, Page, Medford, Oregon; H. T. Moore, Colonial, Tacoma; A. C. Anderson, Apollo, Tacoma; C. E. McKee, Orpheum, Everett.

Portland Suburban Houses Plan Price Raise

Exhibitors Propose to Charge Fifteen Cents for Evening Shows—Raise Will Be Simultaneous—High Cost of Features the Reason.

By Abraham Nelson, Majestic Theater Bldg., Portland, Ore.

PORTLAND, ORE.—A movement is on foot among suburban exhibitors to raise the evening admission price to 15 cents The raise has been talked of since the downtown theaters went to 15 cents for matinees as well as for evening performances several months ago, but it has not until now been whipped into concrete shape.

At meetings of suburban exhibitors held at the club rooms of the Motion Picture Exhibitors' League of Oregon propositions to charge 15 cents on Sundays have been made at various times, also further propositions to raise to 15 cents for certain brands of features. Owing to the fact that competing exhibitors would be unable to obtain sufficiently strong pictures on the 15-cent days, it has been concluded that a general raise of fifteen cents for every night in the week will be the only practical thing.

Suburban exhibitors agree that unless additional revenue is got at the box office several nights in the week, at least, they are not going to make any money at film quotations recently received from several big producers. The need for a raise in price has become so urgent that even the most active competitors are getting together on the proposal plan.

Another incentive toward the price raise is the demand by certain producers that their product be not run at less than 15 cents.

General Film To Return to Portland.

Portland, Ore.—After an absence from Portland of about six months the General Film Company will again open an office here. The exact location had not been selected at the time of this writing, but negotiations have been going on for quarters in the film exchange building on Ninth and Burnside. It is reported that the new manager will be a San Francisco man who has met with a great deal of success in the southern territory. Manager L. A. Todd, of the Seattle office, was in Portland August 17 to arrange details.

Cameraman Returns from Strenuous Trip.

Portland, Ore.—Jesse J. Sill, popular Portland cameraman, is back in the Rose City resting after a strenuous jaunt through Glacier National Park, Montana. He has been absent over a month, accompanying Robert C. Bruce, scenic director for the Educational Films Corporation, in search of new material. The next trip will be made through Rainier National Park, Washington.

Former Owner Returns.

Seaside, Ore.—O. Cacheralis, who conducted the Orpheum for several seasons, has again taken charge of the showhouse. Ed Berg, who managed it for Tom Gekas, having left. The seaside season is about 45 days late, but has turned off very good.

Julian Eltinge Makes Films in Portland.

Portland, Ore.—Julian Eltinge, the famous female impersonator and now Lasky star, made his first stage appearance at the People's theater here since his entry into film stardom some months ago. This popular star was just as much, if not more, enthused over the success of his appearance before a photoplay audience as he was during his appearance on the "legit" stage a few months ago, when it cost his audience two dollars a seat. In fact he was so pleased with his reception at the People's that it was at his own suggestion that he went back for a second personal appearance.

Mr. Eltinge and company of 20, under the direction of Donald Crisp, arrived from Los Angeles, Aug. 13, on the steamer Beaver. Production manager Fred Kley was

highly impressed with the grandeur of the Columbia River Highway and the Oregon scenery generally, and he promised to have his players in Oregon again this fall. The production upon which Mr. Eltinge was working when in Portland was "The Clever Miss Carfax," in which he is being supported by Miss Daisy Robinson.

Eugene Theater Gets New Owner.

Eugene, Ore.—The lease of the Eugene theater has been transferred from H. F. Hollenbeck to J. A. Morrison, a moving picture man from Canada. Big moving picture features and road shows will be featured in the house. New projection equipment, supplied by the Service Film Company, of Portland, was recently installed.

I. W. W's. Cause Theater Closing.

Portland, Ore.—Col. Warden, Orpheus theater, Klamath Falls, Oregon, was a recent visitor on Film Row, and stated that I. W. W. troubles in the Southern Oregon town had compelled him to close his house temporarily. The industrial troubles have caused a closing of the mills for the time being.

Majestic Books Goldwyn.

Portland, Ore.—The first run theater in Portland to run Goldwyn pictures will be the Majestic. Manager J. J. Parker recently signed up for this brand with C. F. Hill, of the Seattle Goldwyn office. The first picture will be "Polly of the Circus," which is scheduled to show at the Majestic Sept. 15.

Sumpter Theater Burns.

Sumpter, Ore.—The Electric theater was destroyed August 13 when a fire wiped out the business section of the town doing over $200,000 damage. The Electric theater was the only showhouse in this picturesque mining town, and was owned by Herbert L. (Cap.) Davies, a veteran showman.

Brief Oregon Theater Items.

Corvallis, Ore.—A Sunday closing fight that has been going on here for some time will be put direct to the people at the polls Sept. 4.

Portland, Ore.—Herman Wobber, Progressive Motion Picture Company, San Francisco, was in Portland for a few days supervising the installation of the new Paramount office.

J. A. Berkowitz was in Portland with "The Argonaut," and A. W. Watson with "War On Three Fronts."

Bert Latz, manager for Universal at Seattle, and Joe Baum, traveler, were visitors at the local Universal office.

Exhibitors visiting Portland exchanges recently were: Sam Whitesides, Corvallis, Ore.; O. C. Smith, Dallas; F. A. Watrous, Forest Grove; F. H. Park, Molalla; O. Phelps, Hillsboro; C. J. Pugh, Falls City; John Wesley, Scio.

MORE SEATTLE NOTES.

French Official War Pictures at the Strand.

Seattle, Wash.—The French Official War Pictures, which opened at the Strand theater Sunday, August 19, have been showing to big business. The success of these pictures is undoubtedly due, partly, to the big advertising given the British Official War Pictures during their showing at the same house a few weeks ago. Mr. Smythe has added to his collection of war

relics which he displayed in front of his theater during that showing and has an army man to explain about them. This was one of the most effective of the many forms of advertisement which he employed for the British pictures.

E. R. Redlich Will Take Charge at Metro

Seattle, Wash.—C. J. Kerr has resigned as manager of the Seattle Metro office, and E. R. Redlich, now manager of the Toronto Metro office, will arrive in Seattle within a week to take charge of this territory. Before leaving this city last spring to go to Toronto Mr. Redlich was coast division manager for Fox and had been in the film business here for years. Exhibitors and exchange men will be glad to welcome him back, for everyone who had dealings with him liked him.

Until Mr. Redlich arrives Harry Lustig, Metro special representative, is managing the Seattle Metro office, assisted by E. F. Rosenberg, special advertising man for Metro.

J. S. Clemmer Member of Committee on Four Minute Men.

Seattle, Wash.—James Q. Clemmer, of the Clemmer theater, has been appointed to serve on the committee of the Four Minute Men for Seattle. Mr. Clemmer will have charge of the arrangements for the four minute speeches in the theaters.

More Theater Notes for Middle West.

Russellville, Ark.—The Crescent airdome is being razed and the site will be covered by a new $25,000 theater, of which Oscar H. Wilson is to be the owner. Mr. Wilson has already negotiated a lease with E. H. Butler to take charge of the new theater upon its completion.

Des Moines, Ia.—C. C. Taft, A. Frankel, and Ira R. Thomas have leased the lot at the corner of Eighth and Locust streets for a motion picture theater.

Shelby, Ia.—W. C. Howland has purchased the motion picture theater of Charles Albertus.

Kingsley, Ia.—Jesse Schofield will open the Reliance theater soon.

Council Bluffs, Ia.—Peter Steenhusan has become the proprietor of the opera house.

Kamrar, Ia.—L. A. Miller has sold his motion picture house to H. E. Ryland and his wife.

Onawa, Ia.—Krigstin & Wonder have purchased the motion picture theater formerly operated by Fairchild & Paine.

Milo, Ia.—J. G. Tharp is now manager of the Star theater.

Spencer, Ia.—H. B. Gray has purchased the Fraser theater.

Allerton, Ia.—The new Majestic theater has been opened. Mr. Lane is the proprietor.

Fayette, Ia.—Charles Halverson has sold the Princess theater to T. J. Leshy.

Stories of the Films

General Film Company, Inc.

FALCON FEATURES.

THE STOLEN PLAY (Four Parts Drama). The cast Sylvia Smalley (Ruth Roland); Leroux (Edw. J. Brady); Charles Edmay (Wm. Conklin); Alice Mason (Lucy Blake); Foster (Harry Southard); Mrs. Edmay (Ruth Lackaye); Togo (Makato Inokuchi). Story by D. F. Whitcomb. Directed by Harry Harvey under the supervision of H. M. and E. D. Horkheimer.

Edmay, a blind playwright, is engaged to marry Sylvia, his amanuensis. Leroux is anxious to produce a play that Edmay has about finished, but the playwright is reluctant to sell. Leroux plans to secure the play. Working over the play Sylvia has become nervous and Edmay morbid. Leroux sends Alice Mason, his agent, to steal the script and he abducts Edmay and Sylvia. Alice has an encounter with Togo, the playwright's valet, and accidentally killed him. Leroux has hypnotic ability, and placing Sylvia in a trance gets a dictation of the completed play, while Edmay is detained in a wine cellar. Leroux learns to love Sylvia which leads to a stormy scene with Alice who is infatuated with him.

Alice starts to leave Leroux's house but is pursuaded to remain as a caretaker of Sylvia. Leroux discovers that in a hypnotic state Sylvia is capable of great dramatic powers, and at the play's premiere she takes the leading role with success. The effort is too great, however, and she succumbs to exhaustion. Leroux revives her, she realizes her position and so reproaches him that he releases Edmay from his prison and permits her to escort him home.

Overheard by Alice, Leroux plans a dramatical end of his career; placing a tool of his, Foster, under hypnotic control Leroux commands him to wall up the entrance to the underground prison and leave the country forver. Leroux enters the vault and is walled up alive. At the approach of his death Alice reveals herself to him in the vault where she had secreted herself to die with him. At this apparent climax the story takes a different turn and concludes in an explanatory manner.

ESSANAY.

DON'T LOSE YOUR COAT (Black Cat Feature—Two Parts)—At Hick's Corner, Farmer Jones strikes oil and gets rich. He goes to the city to celebrate. At the hotel a matrimonial agent is seeking to escape from a dozen women whose affections he has tampered with. While Jones is taking a bath, the crook exchanges clothes with him and, disguised as a farmer, gets away. Jone is forced to put on the agent's clothes. He starts to see the sights but the women, mistaking him for their Nemesis, make a dash for him. Then a chase begins which does not end until the farmer gets back to Hick's Corner.

SPARKLE COMEDY.

BRAGG'S LITTLE POKER GAME.—Late one night Bragg gets a message that a poker game is in progress at a friend's, and manages to leave the house without waking his wife. Soon after a burglar enters the house, followed by a cop. The burglar gets into the twin bed vacated by Bragg and when the cop appears says, "Hist! don't wake my wife." The policeman leaves the room determined to wait for the burglar. In the meantime the poker game is raided and all are arrested except Bragg, who escapes and arrives home only to be captured by the cop. He protests that he is Bragg, but his wife, half asleep, says that her husband is in the next bed, and Bragg is led away. Later Mrs. Bragg finds out her mistake and the real burglar is taken by the police.

At the station the members of the raided poker party, who are all in one cell, discover that in the scrimmage a pack of cards has been saved and, with additional partners, the game is continued.

JAXON COMEDY.

PLAY BALL.—Pokes and Jabs, clerks in the brokerage office of Adam Fossil, are both smitten with the charms of Edna, the stenographer. Fossil also indulges in an occasional flirtation with her.

The baseball season is about to begin and the enthusiasm of Pokes and Jabs is aroused to concert pitch by announcements of the opening game. Old Fossil catches them playing an imaginary game and fires Jabs and [illegible] to work posting the ledger. Pokes resorts to a little liquid refreshment to brighten his spirits. Edna has a headache and is excused for the afternoon. Pokes writes himself a letter stating his grandma is seriously ill, and is also excused. He meets Edna and they go to the ball game. In the midst of an exciting play Edna discovers the boss is directly behind them, and Pokes sneaks off to another section.

Meantime Jabs has entered into a plot with Bill Blutch to rob Fossil's safe. The game is at its height. The last inning score tie and two men out, three men on bases, when the heaviest hitter has an argument with the umpire and is ordered out of the game. Pokes offers to take his place and hits the first ball so hard that it flies into Fossil's window, hitting Jabs on the head just as he has lit the fuse to blow up the safe. Pokes scores a home run and the stands go wild with delight.

The safe explodes and the noise arouses Pokes from his slumber. Rushing through the offices, he finds everything going on as usual. Returnning to the counting room he throws the bottle of rye out the window, repeating to himself, "never again."

SELIG.

BETWEEN MAN AND BEAST (Two Parts). The cast: Milbank (Wheeler Oakman); Blackmoor (Roy Watson); Mrs. Milbank (Bessie Eyton); Baby Alma (Lucile Carter); Chimp (Sally Edwards); Nig (A. S. Stecker). Written by W. E. Wing. Directed by Colin Campbell.

Blackmoor, an adventurer, who trails Milbank, accompanied by his wife and his faithful black, into the jungle, is inspired by two motives, first to locate the mining claims that Milbank's father had discovered, and second to cause the death of the party, so that he will secure the gold. The Milbanks locate the cabin of the old man, but they have arrived too late, for he has passed away. Young Milbank starts alone to locate his father's mining claims. Blackmoor follows after first setting fire to the shack which houses Milbank's wife and child. Nig, the faithful native, saves the woman and baby from death.

Milbank, attracted by the fire, returns finding it in ashes and his loved ones gone. Blackmoor picks up Milbank's hat and finds in its lining a description of the locations.

Mrs. Milbank falls asleep in the forest. An ape carries away her child. The mother starts in pursuit, dropping her shawl. The ape proves a kindly guardian for the little one. Eventually comes Milbank and his anguished wife whom he has found. They are astonished to discover the child alive and well in the care of the ape. In addition they find a rich mining claim.

Blackmoor finds his stolen data useless for the mines the paper represent are worthless.

HER SALVATION.—The cast: Sandy McCarthy (Joe King); Pat McGuire (Wheeler Oakman); Ryan (Frank Clark); Dicky (Roy Clark); Nance O'Shaughnessy (Bessie Eyton); Gertie, her friend (Gerti Ryan); Mame Ryan (Eugenie Besserer). Story by Honore Willsie.

Nance, a little Irish American girl from the great East Side, works in a laundry where she meets Pat McGuire, a spieler for a cheap dance academy. Sandy McCarthy, a nice lad from the country, comes to the city to make his way and, meets Nance.

Mame Ryan, who frequents dance halls, loves Pat McGuire, who has no use for her. One night he strikes a woman and his action opens Nance's eyes, for she is inclined to favor the man. Ultimately Sandy McCarthy meets Pat McGuire and whips him.

The Celtic instincts of Sandy and Nance draw the pair together more strongly and they conclude to marry.

BROADWAY STAR FEATURE.

THE FURNISHED ROOM (One of the O. Henry Series—Two Parts).—The cast: The Girl (Agnes Eyres); The Boy (J. Frank Glendon).

The boy and girl live in the country. The girl has a voice and is anxious to go to the city and become a great singer. She is encouraged to go by an unscrupulous promoter. She tells the boy and they quarrel. She goes to the city to learn that her voice is only mediocre. Too proud to confess defeat, she struggles to exist in the big city without success. The boy learns of her plight and comes to bring her back. Like the characters in Evangeline the boy and girl just seem to miss each other by an eyelash each time. The girl gives up the fight and writes home to the boy to come and take her. The letter returns with no answer. She feels he has forgotten her. She attempts suicide which is unsuccessful, and taken to a hospital in a dying condition. Boy is just about to attempt suicide in same way when the odor of mignonette stops him. It is the girl's favorite perfume and he knows she has been in the room. Learns, all, and goes to the hospital and finds her. They are happily reunited.

THE DEFEAT OF THE CITY (One of the O. Henry Series—Four Parts).—The cast: Robert Walmsley (Frank Glendon); Alicia Van Der Pool, his bride (Agnes Eyre); "Old Man" Walmsley (Frank Chapman); Ma Walmsley (Mrs. Fisher); Tom, Robert's younger brother (Frank Heath); Millie and Pam (Alice Rodier and Virginia Spraggins). Directed by Thos. R. Mills.

Robert Walmsley, at the end of six years in the city, has won fortune, fame—and Alice Van Der Pool, a "daughter of the old burghers—high and cool and white and inaccessible." So Robert feels that he has achieved the ultimate end of success and happiness.

Alice finds a letter written to Robert by his mother—a letter straight from home, full of farm lore and gossip. She prevails upon Robert to take her for a visit to the farm. Robert is dismayed at the prospect, fearing Alicia will be shocked at the crudeness of his rural atavism. Theer his wife sits silent and immovable while Robert cuts ridiculous capers. Alicia presently ascends to her room. Robert, suddenly feeling that he is disgraced in her eyes, and that he has been unmasked by his own actions and that "all the polish, the poise, the form that the city has given him has fallen from him like an ill-fitting mantle at the first breath of a country breeze," grows quiet.

Presently he follows Alicia upstairs—prepared to meet his fate. He knew the rigid lines that a Van Der Pool would draw. She is standing at the window, in the twilight. Robert silently takes his place beside her. "Robert," said the cool, calm voice of his judge, "I thought I married a gentleman—" Alicia steps closer to Robert. "But," she continues, "I find that I have married—something better—a man. Bob, dear, kiss me, won't you?"

Mutual Film Corp.

CUB.

JERRY TRIES AGAIN (One Reel—September 6).—The cast: Jerry (George Ovey); Marie (Claire Alexander); Expressman (George George); Pete (C. E. Feehan); Postman (Tom Riley); Policeman (Harry Jackson); Physician (Harry De Roy); Minister (Louis Fitzroy).

Disappointed over his failure to marry Marie by reason of the ruling of the Eugenic Bureau, Jerry's only consolation is a large and growing accumulation of postage stamps he received in answers to an advertisement he inserted in a daily paper for a wealthy wife.

Jerry meets several candidates for his lot in life and leads them to the Eugenic Bureau, where one after the other they are disqualified.

Jerry finally makes the mistake of his life and sends for six girls to meet him at one time. He leads his collection of would-be brides to the examining physician who promptly rejects all but one, a large, healthy but heavy maiden. The disappointed girls are furious. They wreak vengeance upon Jerry with their fists and umbrellas, but he escapes with his abundant prize to the minister. All seems clear for a happy ending when the minister demands Jerry's certificate. He rushes to the bureau for examination. He is immediately rejected.

JERRY'S WHIRLWIND FINISH (September 13).—The cast: Jerry (George Ovey); Hank (George George); First Cop (Gordon McGregor); Second Cop (C. E. Feehan); Third Cop (Harry Riley). Written and produced by M. H. Fahrney.

Jerry becomes affected by the wiles of a park flirt who has been lavishing attention upon a large and enthusiastic collection of bench-warmers, to say nothing of several park policemen. Jerry presses his suit, but when discovered by one of her policemen friends, is temporarily routed. Jerry finds a telephone wagon nearby where he procures a coil of rope and succeeds in lassoing the cop and the girl and pulling them into a deep pool. A whirlwind chase ensues, participated in by the entire police force.

Jerry drops from the second-story window of a house into the vacant saddle ordinarily occupied by a mounted policeman and dashes away to freedom. The cops in their flivver run out of gasoline, but make the grade by hoisting a sail, and continue the chase. Jerry rides headlong into the arms of Shoot-em-up-Bill, a bad man, who exhibits a $5,000 sack of gold. "Shoot-em-up" commandeers Jerry and his horse and together they ride into town. Shoot-em-up puts the gold in a safe, and Jerry runs to a room overhead. Safe-crackers blow up the safe, the force of which shoots the gold up through the floor into Jerry's arms. The mast on the flivver waiting below provides the means of Jerry's escape from yet another difficulty.

GAUMONT.

REEL LIFE NO. 71 (Sept. 6).—"The Five Senses—in Business and Pleasure." While in no sense to be regarded as a dramatization of the five senses, the pictures show how the world's work and the world's play are rendered easier and pleasanter by the development of the senses. The dictaphone, the phonograph and the Braile system are some of the means of demonstrating the senses. Then the delicate work of the diamond buyer, the coffee taster, the perfume blender is pictured.

A continuation of the postoffice pictures which began in a recent number shows how parcels post and money orders are handled. The spectator of this reel is taken "behind the scenes" and shown the immense amount of work required in handling these two branches of Uncle Sam's postal system.

"Pets Which Will Never Be Popular" is the title of a section which records a visit to a skunk farm. The one of the five senses most in evidence here cannot be transported to the screen, and the millions of people who visit the farm via these Gaumont pictures will be highly instructed without suffering any ill effects. An interesting feature of this picture is that the farm is conducted by a fifteen-year-old girl. She appears in a number of the scenes.

"A Watering System for a Small Farm" pictures a method of irrigation possible where intensive farming is followed. Pipes supported on posts about six feet from the ground are perforated, and the water flows through these holes to the soil below.

"Fresh Advances in the Champagne District" is a humorous animated drawing founded upon a picture in "Life," the leading magazine of wit and satire.

REEL LIFE NO. 72 (Sept. 13).—How the Government is Planting Trees to Conserve the Nation's Water Supply.—To prevent Americans having such barren, arid areas as China is cursed with, the United States Government has undertaken the work of reforestation of mountain areas devastated by forest fires. It is, thanks to the forests, that our rivers do not carry down the soil of the mountain sides, that they retain the water that otherwise would come down in great floods. Pictures of the work of the national foresters are shown. Most of the views are of the Wind River tree nursery in the State of Washington. How the pine cones give up their seeds, the planting, the transplanting of the small trees, and the camps of the foresters are shown in an interesting manner.

"An Unusual Colt" is a picture of a Shetland pony which weighed only twenty pounds when five weeks old. Its hoof was the size of a silver twenty-five-cent piece. This picture will be particularly pleasing to children. It is only a short section of the reel.

"Hunting Turtle Eggs" shows the habits of the loggerhead turtle which comes out of the ocean at night and lays her eggs in the sand. When it is on the nest, the pictures illustrate how it is captured by turning it over on its back. One hundred or more eggs are found in a nest.

"Testing an Auto Tube" is an interesting illustration of how the inner tube of an automobile can lift a weight of 2,290 pounds. The unusual method is adopted of having the tube lift the automobile which the tire is to support when inflated.

A picture of "The Midnight Sun" completes the reel.

MUTUAL STAR PRODUCTION.

CHARITY CASTLE (American—Five Parts—Sept. 3).—The cast: Charity (Mary Miles Minter); the Prince (Clifford Callis); Merlin Durand (Alan Forrest); Zelma Verona (Eugenie Forde); Simon Durand (Henry A. Barrows); Elmer Trent (Ashton Dearholt); Graves (Robert Klein); Lucius Garrett (Spottiswoode Aitken); Bill Turner (George Ahearn); Sam Smith (Gordon Russell). Directed by Lloyd Ingraham.

"Charity" is a little girl who has been orphaned with her little brother, popularly called "The Prince," these two falling into contact with Merlin Durand, the young son of Simon Durand, a millionaire, who being a miser as well as a millionaire, objected to "Sonny" Durand's scheme of expenditure. At the time the story opens "Sonny" has been told to get out and hustle for a living.

Charity is so sorry that she takes "The Prince" into her confidence. These two youngsters invade "Old Man" Durand's library, with the intention of pleading with him to "please be good to Sonny," but "The Ogre," as Durand was known, had gone away and the servants had departed for a holiday.

Finding the castle uninhabited but filled with good things, Charity and "The Prince" decided to make the best of conditions, so they invited Lucius, a vaudeville actor; Bill, the Badlands burglar; and Sam "the bum" to spend an evening with them.

It is this gathering that "Old Man" Durand interrupts when he returns from taking the "water cure" and discovers "The Prince" master of ceremonies. There is trouble in the wind, but Charity intercedes with "The Ogre," who is so impressed that he forgets the offenses of his son when Charity champions the latter, and all ends happily.

REPUTATION (Five Parts—September 3).—The cast: Constance Bennett (Edna Goodrich); John Clavering (William Hinckley); Edmund Berste (Frank Goldsmith); Mrs. Berste (Carey Lee); Nellie Burns (Esther Evans); Mrs. Williams (Nellie Parker Spaulding); Mrs. Clavering (Mrs. Brunage). Directed by John B. O'Brien.

Constance Bennett is reared in a small town by a maiden aunt, and is the sweetheart of John Clavering, son of the local grande dame. Constance goes to New York, where she becomes a model in a suit and cloak house. Edward Berste, her employer, forces his attentions upon her, and Mrs. Berste becomes suspicious and later wildly jealous.

Constance returns to the home town to escape the attentions of Berste and men of his type. Berste, however, follows her there. She has established a store of her own, and before a crowd of customers Mrs. Berste walks in and accuses Constance. The girl faces ostracism at home. She is turned out of the church. In despair she returns to New York. She meets Berste and visits the cabarets with him. They return to her apartment, where she traps him into an avowal of love. She has summoned his wife and exposes him. Berste seeks to retaliate and hires a woman to trap Constance. She goes to dine with them in a hotel and finds herself alone with Berste. Clavering has returned from Mexico and has followed her. She fights with Berste, and Clavering bursts into the room. A pistol is fired. Berste is mortally wounded. Constance faces trial for murder and is acquitted. She returns to the home town as Clavering's bride.

MUTUAL WEEKLY.

WEEKLY NO. 138 (Aug. 22).

The Recapture of Kut.—Turkish trenches again in the hands of the British.

Atlanta, Ga.—Baseball fan keeps invalid wife confined at home posted on baseball scores. Carrier pigeon, with scores attached to leg, is sent home after each inning.

Denver, Col.—State honors her soldiers. Colorado celebrates Admission Day by presenting each soldier with $10 gold piece.

Copenhagen, Denmark.—The king of Denmark dedicates the Royal Palace of Christiansborg.

Glendale, L. I.—Edna Goodrich, Mutual Film Corporation's beautiful star, who will shortly appear in the photoplay "Reputation," finds time, between the taking of scenes, to make bandages for the Red Cross.

Somewhere-in-America. — Our soldier boys learn the art of trench digging, and how to make themselves comfortable in their dug-outs.

New York City.—New styles in milady's shoes. Courtesy of J. Miller, New York. Subtitles: Tan Oxford—wing tips. Satin beaded evening slipper. Sport shoe, tan, with buckskin top.

Conejo, Cal.—Uncle Sam goes into the hog-raising business. Food for National Army assured.

An-Atlantic-Port.—Sea lane guards put in here for supplies. Cruisers in war paint anchor here to give "Jack" a day of play.

South City, Cal.—Motorcycles climb rocky grade. Many try but few succeed in negotiating 78-degree hill.

Alameda, Cal.—Big pottery goes up in flame. Loss, $750,000.

Washington, D. C.—Mrs. Lansing entertains other cabinet ladies at luncheon composed entirely of dried foods. Subtitle: Mrs. Clark and Mrs. Lansing seem to enjoy the menu.

San Diego, Cal.—Army lumber travels 1,500-mile ocean voyage in huge log raft. Eight million feet for U. S. N. A. camp.

Venice, Cal.—Government investigates new aero propellor. It can be adjusted for pulling power to meet all atmospheric conditions and also lift an airplane at the rate of 2,000 feet a minute.

Fort Meyer, Va.—Eighteen hundred student officers receive their commissions. Subtitles: The President and Mrs. Wilson arrive, escorted by Major-General Scott. The student body passes in review. Receiving their diplomas from Secretary of War Baker.

MUTUAL WEEKLY NO. 139 (Aug. 29).—Seattle, Washington.—Big steel freighter is launched. New vessels will replace those sunken by submarines.

Los Angeles, Calif.—"Movie" cameramen mobilize for war service. The great war will be visualized to millions at home by moving pictures.

San Francisco, Calif.—Mikado's envoys reach U. S. for war conference. Viscount Ishii heads the Commission.

Quincy, Mass.—This Little City is Determined to Have Cheaper Food. Grasping middlemen eliminated by establishment of public market bringing producer and consumer together.

San Francisco, Calif.—Norman Ross Wins Golden Gate Swim. Choppy Sea makes the going hard.

New York City.—Speedway Triumph Won by De Palma. 40,000 see him win from Oldfield and Chevrolet. Subtitles: Chevrolet changes a tire in 11 seconds. De Palma, the winner. Oldfield, the veteran.

Boston, Mass.—G. A. R. Veterans Meet Here. Old troopers parade for last time.

New York City.—Belgian Commission Welcomed by the Metropolis. Delegation, headed by Baron Moncheur, greeted by Mayor Mitchel and City Officials.

New York City.—"Fighting 69th" off to Camp. Troopers start on first lap of journey to France. Subtitles: Some of the boys missed the boat, and had visions of the guard house when Miss Ann Murdock, Mutual's star playing in "Outcast," came along and gave them a lift to the nearest R. R. station, where they took a train for camp, arriving on time.

Paris, France.—General Pershing Visits an Ammunition Factory.

Paris, France.—The American Battalion Leaves Here for Headquarters Camp Near the Front.

Brandford, Conn.—Passengers Trapped in Cars and Mangled. 19 dead, 40 injured in head-on trolley crash.

Down in Virginia.—The Watermelon Season Is at Its Height.

Universal Film Mfg. Co.

ANIMATED WEEKLY.

ISSUE NO. 86 (August 22).

Tank bombards eligibles for recruits. Carries an appeal and assurance to men who are *needed NOW* by Uncle Sam.—Chicago, Ill. Subtitle: "Don't *wait* to read of America's victory—get into uniform and *help hasten it.*"

Finish training course with nine-day hike.—Fort McPherson student officers, "Marching through Georgia," pleases natives.—Near Atlanta, Ga. Subtitle: Quiet in a "scrape" with friends—but with the enemy?—that's different!

Secretary McAdoo entertains "Four-Minute Men."—Group of orators who, in four-minute speeches, will inform the public on vital issues, are honored.—Washington, D. C. Subtitle: In moving picture theaters and elsewhere these men will speak for the Government TO the people. Congressman Kahn, of Conscription and Food Bills fame—a loyal aid of President Wilson—a SIMON-PURE AMERICAN! "The Best of Friends Must Part!" Here we see "Joe" Cannon—but where, oh *where* is the famous cigar.

De Palma, now world's speed king.—At 110 miles per hour in his aviation-type motor Packard he beats Chevrolet and Oldfield.—Sheepshead Bay Speedway, N. Y. Subtitles: Off to a flying start! "Neck and neck!" Breaking records at 110 miles an hour. The winner-up, Louis Chevrolet. Barney Oldfield and his famous golden submarine, which was out-distanced early in the race.

Imperial Japanese Mission here for war conference.—Headed by Viscount K. Ishii, distinguished Orientals are welcomed to America.—San Francisco, Cal.—Subtitles: Left to right: Asst. Secy. of State Long, Viscount Ishii, and Cavin McNab. Military honors for our Eastern ally. Viscount Ishii pleased at reception.

Heated cities "overflow" into the sea.—Millions, during record season, make the ocean—in spots—a VERY crowded pond.—Atlantic City, N. J. Subtitle: When he's on the beach there's room in the ocean for others.

Gas mask demonstration in heart of metropolis.—Various types in use on French front shown in Union Square.—N. Y. City. Subtitles: May look freakish, but what of style when life is at stake? "Woof! Woof!"

By chat and chart our fighters learn French.—Prof. of Gordon-Detwiller Institute aids soldiers in simple and practical way to use French military and other terms.—Cicero, Ill. Subtitles: As he pronounces, his class repeats.

When Venus steps forth, crowds flock around.—Fashion parade at Columbia Beach proves no *ONE* section of America has a corner in beauty.—Portland, Ore.

"Fighting 69th," N. Y., start for France.—Cheered by millions, the "Fighting Irish" start for way station on road *TO BERLIN!*—New York City. Subtitles: No city ever gazed on braver! 2,000 strong, determined on victory, this regiment carries the CIVILIZED world's best wishes with it! Irish men o' war! Col. Charles De Laue Hine, who will take them "Over the Top" to victory.

Cartoons by Hy Mayer.

GOLD SEAL.

THE EMPTY GUN (Three Parts—Week of Sept. 3).—The cast: Frank (Lon Chaney); Mary (Claire McDowell); Jim (Sam De Grasse). Story by J. G. Alexander and F. Myton. Produced by J. De Grasse.

Frank, riding through the storm, approaches the station, to give ten thousand dollars worth of gold, which he has just brought from the mine, into safe keeping. Dave the agent hears him, and when he finally appeared, disappointment awaited Frank.

"I can't take charge of the money," says Dave. "I'm sorry, Frank, but the train is late, and the gold can't go on tonight. I saw two suspicious-looking characters hanging around here, and I won't take the responsibility."

Mary, formerly beautiful, but now haggard from work and loneliness, stands at the window of her dilapidated shack clenching a letter which says: "Dear Frank—You and I know it was you, and not Jim, that started me on the downward path, but I did not know you persuaded me to accuse him so that you could marry that innocent thing you were both in love with." Mary can hardly keep back the tears and when Frank enters, she keeps her back turned, even when he remarks he supposes she is crying again because she is sorry she married him. After putting the gold in a drawer, Frank leaves the shack.

Shortly afterward Mary goes and stares at the gold, then fingers the revolver which lies near by, and sits by the fire, lost in revery.

Jim knocks at the door. Mary asks who it is, but Jim will only answer: "A stranger lost in the storm." She opens the door. Both are startled and delighted. Jim picks up the gun and asks what she is doing with an empty gun. Laughing, he loads it.

Mary shows Jim the note and he is angry. She sees he still loves her and pleads with him to take her away. Jim takes her in his arms. Then, thinking of Frank, determines to make him account for the past. He leaves to find Frank.

Frank is attacked by one of the tramps, but overpowering him, exchanges clothes with him and hurries to the shack.

The wind from an open window blows out the lamp. Mary hears a noise and sees only a man's eyes, and when he enters the room she orders him to stop, but he only smiles. As he still approaches, Mary fires and he springs at her; they struggle.

Jim, undecided as to the direction of the station, returns to ask Mary. He jumps into the struggle, but the stranger is getting the best of the fight; he breaks away, picks up a heavy object and swings it above his head to strike Jim, who has already been knocked to the floor. Mary picks up the gun again and fires at the stranger, who sinks to the floor. Jim puts his arms around Mary; he removes the mask from the man's face, and both are horrified to see Frank.

"It is the judgment of the Highest Court," says Jim, solemnly.

BISON.

THE LURE OF THE CIRCUS (Two Parts—Week of Sept. 3).—The cast: Bud (Fred Church); His Father (Doctor Crane); Lily Wright (Eileen Sedgwick); Bringley (Kewpie Morgan). Story and production by W. B. Pearson.

"Shoeing mules is all you're fit for, so get busy." So spoke Bud's father, the village blacksmith, as his son was treating him to the story of his talents as an animal trainer.

"Well, I'll show you some day," muttered Bud, and just that minute Lilly, his sweetheart, rushed up with a circus ad, looking for a girl to ride bareback and a man to learn lion taming. It looked like Providence, and Bud dropped his work at once.

Bud and Lilly are employed, Bud with the understanding that he is to start taming the young lions first and thus get used to them. But the men around the arena make fun of Lilly in her riding outfit, and the horse leaves her in the ring hanging on the end of a pole. She soon loses much of her ardor for her new profession. Bud also has his troubles, for when he starts training some cubs, the mother lion gets away and comes after him and he climbs wildly up the cage wall. Then Al, the trainer, comes to his rescue and chases the lions away, but just for fun, lets them out again and they run after Bud, pursuing him until he has climbed over a fence.

Meanwhile, Bringley has dropped a plug of tobacco near Charlie, the elephant, who eats the plug. Then, infuriated with such treatment, Charlie pulls his chain loose and makes his way to the office where Lilly is just telling Bringley that she doesn't want to ride horses any more. Charlie knocks the office building over; Lilly and Bringley are lost in the wreckage. Lilly finally meets Bud outside the arena, and together they return to the blacksmith shop.

"I'll train mules, pop," says Bud, pulling on his leather apron.

VICTOR.

THE CURSE OF A FLIRTING HEART (Two Parts—Week of Sept. 3).—The cast: Max (Max Asher); Mrs. Max (Lillian Peacock). Story by C. B. Hoadley. Produced by Craig Hutchinson.

"If he flirts all the time with strange women, I don't see why I shouldn't flirt with strange men," says Mrs. Max, as she puts on her best hat and goes out.

In a park where the mayor of Bugville is flirting with a swell-looking woman, Mrs. Max seats herself behind her parasol. Max comes along, sits beside his wife and starts a flirtation, neither knowing the other, but Max discovers his error and flees. A cameraman is going about the town shooting local scenes. Max picks up an acquaintance with a young woman who is hanging out clothes; they decide to go to a picture show. Mrs. Max becomes friendly with this same neighbor's husband and they also go to the picture show, sitting directly in front of Max and his friend.

Max and the neighbor have been chased out of a barn by a mule while trying to hide from Mrs. Max. Max crouches in the crowd as he enters the show. The neighbor hides behind Mrs. Max's skirts as he goes in. The manager of the show receives word that the films for his program missed the train.

The operator writes on a slide and flashes on the screen: "There's a man in the house with another man's wife and the husband is looking for him." Max and the man with Mrs. Max both sneak out of the show and later return, Max being seated by his own wife and the neighbor by his.

The mayor and his wife are also in the show. Because of the lack of regular films, the local views, taken by Professor Shutter, are shown on the screen. All the scenes of the different flirtations are shown; the mayor chased by a bull; the episode with the mule; a prominent old maid and a man flirting; Max and his wife flirting behand the parasol.

"Never again for ours!" vow Max and his wife.

STAR FEATURETTE.

A DREAM OF EGYPT (Two Parts—Week of Sept. 3).—The cast: Dorothy (Lena Baskette); Her Mother (Betty Schade); Her Father (Albert MacQuarrie); the Prince (Fred Montague); Prince's Confidant (Walter Belasco). Story by Myrtle Stedman. Directed by Marshall Stedman.

Dorothy was a little girl whose great passion was dancing. She was never tired of looking at a book in the library called "Mysterious Egypt," which told the story of a famous dancing girl and a Prince. "I know what I'll do," she exclaimed. "I'll get a shawl out of the attic, and play I'm the beautiful dancer."

Draping the shawl around her, she starts to dance. She imagines she is the girl in the picture. Her mother watches her, but tells her she must change her dress, as her father will soon be home for dinner.

The father brings home a beautiful statuette of a little Egyptian dancing girl, as a surprise for his wife and child. It is placed on a pedestal at the foot of the stairway. Dorothy is delighted and gazes at it enraptured. Later, Dorothy creeps down-stairs and dances before the statuette.

Dorothy has a wonderful dream. She is the statuette dancing girl; her mother is her sister and her father the sweetheart of her sister. All of them are poor Egyptians. The child dances on the street while her sister sells flowers, and her sweetheart works in the markets of Cairo. A prince falls in love with the sister and desires her for his harem and, because the flower girl refuses, the prince has her seized and taken to his palace.

Dorothy tells the sweetheart what has happened. She makes up her mind to gain entrance to the palace to plead for her sister. Slipping by the guards, she comes to the palace and begs the prince to let her sister go. When he refuses, she begins to dance. The prince is fascinated and at last says he will let her sister go, but she will be held to dance for him. Meantime, the sweetheart has gotten help and fights with the guards.

The prince orders the sister released, but she refuses to leave the child. Then the sweetheart gains admittance to the palace and rescues the two girls, just in time to have the slaves tear the child away from him.

The prince demands that the child dance. She obeys, but finally falls exhausted to the floor at the foot of the raised dias on which the prince is seated.

"Wake up, Dorothy! You've fallen out of bed and pulled the covers with you!"

With these words in her ears, Dorothy wakes from her dream of old Egypt.

JOKER.

OFFICER, CALL A COP! (Week of Sept. 3).—The cast: Bow Nee (Milburn Moranti); Sweeney (William Franey); Evelyn Dale (Janet Eastman). Story by A. F. Statter. Directed by W. W. Beaudine.

"Good day, officer. Nice weather, isn't it?" said Evelyn Dale to Sweeney, as she dismissed her machine at the entrance to Chinatown, and passed down the street to deliver some tracts on "The Social Uplift."

Sweeney looked after her with a sigh, which changed to a gasp of fright, as the girl was suddenly surrounded by a band of Chinks, who dragged her into their lair.

"Stop thief!" began Sweeney, starting to rush to the spot. His spirit was willing, but his feet were weak, and they headed him in the opposite direction, landing him in a familiar saloon.

In the meantime, Evelyn was beating furiously on the panels of an underground chamber. Sweeney had a shot of his favorite beverage, and began to remember the credit of the force of which he was so conspicuous an ornament. Soon he was on his way to the place from which Evelyn had disappeared.

Thud—kerplunk! Sweeney knew no more. When he came to, Bow Nee was offering him a pipe and a pill, and the unsuspecting cop accepted both with resignation. Blissful dreams were his, but a rude awakening followed when the police raided the joint.

"I rescued Miss Dale! I discovered the den! I put out Bow Nee! I done it all!" And Sweeney got away with it, too, until, just as Mr. Dale was handing over the reward for his daughter's rescue, the pesky opium pipe had to fall out of his uniform.

"The cooler for you with the Chinks!" said the heartless captain, and Sweeney's pipe dream was over.

A GALE OF VERSE (Week of Sept. 3).—The cast: Lizzie Loose (Gale Henry); Jerry (Milton Sims); Phoney Felix (Charles Haefli). Story by Tom Gibson. Produced by Allen Curtis.

"And while the bats go batting through,
My love for you will still be true."

Lizzie Loose had just finished reading this masterpiece to the editor of the Caterwaul, and he came to long enough to murmur: "Too good for us, I fear—too highbrow, you know."

"But you can't send me away like that. The stars told me to come to you," said Lizzie, fixing her cross-eyed glance upon him.

Just then a letter was handed to Ye Ed. It was from Lizzie's paternal parent, and said that he would give a hundred plunks to the man who could make Liz go back to the farm. Jerry, the star reporter, pricked up his ears. He wanted a hundred dollars, and he was used to hard work. He frames it with the Ed to send Liz on a phoney assignment to an empty house, while he will appear in a series of different make-ups and scare her from the job. But Liz didn't have her long ears for nothing, and she overhears the plot.

In the cellar of the house lives Phoney Felix and his band of desperate counterfeiters. Jerry is seized and condemned to death. The composer's stone is suspended over his head with the rope in the flame of a candle.

Lizzie arrives. She thinks the whole thing is a frame, so she sails in and does up the gang. The police are attracted by the row

(*Continued on page* 1580.)

Calendar of Daily Program Releases

Releases for Weeks Ending September 8 and September 15

(For Extended Table of Current Releases See Pages 1590, 1592, 1594, 1596.)

Universal Film Mfg. Company

RELEASES FOR THE WEEK OF SEPTEMBER 3.

GOLD SEAL—The Empty Gun (Three Parts—Drama)	
NESTOR—Looking 'Em Over (Comedy)	02654
L-KO—Backward Sons and Forward Daughters (Two Parts—Comedy)	02655
UNIVERSAL ANIMATED WEEKLY—Weekly No. 88	02656
STAR FEATURETTE—A Dream of Egypt (Two Parts—Drama)	02657
	02658
JOKER—Officer, Call a Cop (Comedy)	02659
VICTOR—The Curse of a Flirting Heart (Comedy)	02660
UNIVERSAL SCREEN MAGAZINE—Issue No. 35 (Educational)	02661
UNIVERSAL CURRENT EVENTS—Issue No. 16 (Topical)	02662
JOKER—A Gale of Verse (Comedy)	02663
BISON—The Lure of the Circus (Two Parts—Comedy-Drama)	02664
UNIVERSAL SPECIAL—The Gray Ghost (Episode No. 11—Two Parts—Drama)	02665

RELEASES FOR THE WEEK OF SEPTEMBER 10.

GOLD SEAL—The Perilous Leap (Three Parts—Railroad Drama)	02667
NESTOR—The Boulevard Speed Hounds (Comedy)	02668
L-KO—From Cactus to Kale (Two Parts—Comedy)	02669
UNIVERSAL ANIMATED WEEKLY—Weekly No. 89 (Topical)	02670
STAR FEATURETTE—To the Highest Bidder (Two Parts—Society Drama)	02671
JOKER—Short Skirts and Deep Water (Comedy)	02672
VICTOR—In the Clutches of Milk (Comedy)	02673
UNIVERSAL SCREEN MAGAZINE—Issue No. 36 (Topical)	02674
UNIVERSAL CURRENT EVENTS—Issue No. 18 (Topical)	02675
JOKER—Nearly A Queen (Comedy)	02676
BISON—The Texas Sphinx (Two Parts—Western Drama)	02677
UNIVERSAL SPECIAL—The Gray Ghost (Episode No. 12—Title not decided—Two Parts)	02678

Mutual Film Corporation

MONDAY, SEPTEMBER 3, 1917.

MUTUAL STAR PRODUCTION—Reputation (Five parts—Drama)	05730-31-32-33-34
MUTUAL STAR PRODUCTION—Charity Castle (American—Five parts—Drama)	05735-36-37-38-39

WEDNESDAY, SEPTEMBER 5, 1917.

MUTUAL—Mutual Weekly No. 140 (Topical)	05740

THURSDAY, SEPTEMBER 6, 1917.

CUB—Jerry Tries Again (Comedy)	05741
GAUMONT—Reel Life No. 71 (Subjects on reel: A Watering System for a Small Farm; Pets Which Will Never Be Popular; Handling the Mail, Parcel Post, Money Orders, etc.; The Five Senses in Business and Pleasure: A Leaf from Life; Fresh Advances in the Champagne District)	05742

MONDAY, SEPTEMBER 10, 1917.

MUTUAL STAR PRODUCTION—Outcast (Frohman—Six parts—Drama)	05743-44-45-46-47-48
MUTUAL STAR PRODUCTION—The Bride's Silence (American—Five parts—Drama)	05749-50-51-52-53

WEDNESDAY, SEPTEMBER 12, 1917.

MUTUAL—Mutual Weekly No. 141 (Topical)	05754

THURSDAY, SEPTEMBER 13, 1917.

CUB—Jerry's Whirlwind Finish (Comedy)	05755
GAUMONT—Reel Life No. 72 (Subjects on reel: An Unusual Colt; Hunting Turtle Eggs; Testing an Auto Tube; Tree Planting in the National Forests; The Midnight Sun)	05756

IGGER
ETTER
USINESS

You are doing your part in the furthering of your interests in the United States and Canada; but what of that vast and fertile territory in South and Central America?

The Republic of Argentine, with a population of 15,000,000 people and over 1,000 first-class theatres, is just an example of the great opportunity offered in this growing market.

the Spanish edition of the Moving Picture World,

is selling film, projection machines, generators, cameras and other accessories in this territory and is willing and capable of producing a new volume of business for you.

The opportunity is at hand—grasp it ! ! !

Address

Spanish Department
Chalmers Publishing Company
17 Madison Avenue,   NEW YORK CITY

(Continued from page 1577.)
and arrest the bunch. Lizzie wins the big reward for the capture of Phoney Felix. She remembers Jerry just in time and, rushing to him, blows out the candle and saves him.
"But if I untie you, you'll have to marry me," she whispers coyly.
"Marry you? To get out of here I'd marry the —— himself," and Lizzie takes that for a compliment.

NESTOR.

LOOKING THEM OVER (Week of Sept. 3).— The cast: Eddie (Eddie Lyons); Lee (Lee Moran); Eddie's Wife (Edith Roberts). Story by Lyons and Moran. Directed by Roy Clements.
Eddie is married, but plays the cafes regardless. Lee is married and realizes it every minute. Eddie persuades Lee to go out for a night, and by means of a ruse Lee gets away from the house.
While they are enjoying themselves at a cafe with two pretty entertainers, Lee wife's brother and a friend arrive from the West. They are hungry and get the two wives to go to go to a cafe for something to eat. They go to the same cafe that Lee and Eddie have chosen. Two husbands see their wives with the strange men, and flee to the kitchen for a consultation.
They decide to stay and watch their wives. Donning waiter's clothes, they proceed to wait on the party. Their jealousy is aroused more and more as they watch their wives dance with the two men. Finally their anger leads them to crown the two men with dishes of soft food, and a chase and general scramble ensues.
"Forgive me, darling. I didn't have a bit of a good time without you," says Lee.
"Forgive me, sweetheart. He's only my brother," says wife, and so peace is restored once more.

UNIVERSAL CURRENT EVENTS.

Issue No. 15.—Aug. 23.
Famous Speeder Known as "The Blue Streak" Ready to Fly in France.—Polly Rice Pierce, society girl, now a daring aviatrix, New York City. Subtitle: A masterful mistress of the air. From her new French military tractor she "spills" bombs with accuracy.
Troops Reviewed by Gen. Edwards, Commander of Northeastern Department, Fort Ethan Allen, Vt. Subtitle: Gen. Edwards and staff keenly interested.
"Coal Goes Up, Must Come Down."—True of hoisting tower used in construction of 8,-000,000 gallon reservoir. Subtitle: But just suppose it refused to stay down!
Like Fathers Like Sons.—Some Italian fighters hold mountain climbing race, Cuglieri, Cagliari Province, Italy. Subtive: watch those mountain squirrels!
Canada's Troops at Famous Westminster Viewed by Royalty. Subtitle: Britain's ruler inspects the fighting Canadians.
These Masons Will Aid War's Wounded.— Masonic Ambulance Corps leaves for American Lake, Wash. to prepare for France, San Francisco, Cal. Subtitle: Mayor Rolph presents a guidon to this unique unit.
One of These Two Baby Parades Should Make America Wake Up.—One was a gay one with fine kiddies and proud mothers, London, England. Subtitles: The other "parade" followed the "humane" visit of zeppelins. The hearses are filled with child victims.
Elihu Root and Others of Mission to Russia Welcomed on Return.—Received at City Hall by Mayor Mitchel, where warning speech stirs throng. New York City. Subtitle: Left to right: Geo. Hugh L. Scott, Nathan Straus, Elihu Root, Mayor Mitchel, Admiral Glennon, and Comptroller Prendergast.
Solves Problem That Expensive Gasoline Offers.—Colored genius of the South decides to ignore the Oil Trust and reverts to the Old Rainbarrel, Richmond, Va. Subtitles: "O! Cos she has to haa a little watah! An' den ah slips 'er a little kole. Twen de two de steam is riz. An' now ah'm ready. Cum on Mister Millionaire wid hoah rawls rooster!"
Uncle Sam Now a Real Fishmonger.—To teach practical economy he catches grayfish and sells them at cost, Norfolk, Va. Subtitle: The Grayfish was considered inedible until the "Old H. C. of L" taught us different.
After Five Months in the Field the Famous 71st Returns.—Greeted by thousands at Van Cortlandt Park after a campaign guarding bridges and water systems of State, New York City. Subtitle: The ladies of the Red Cross canteen know their needs.

General Petain Visits and Reviews France's Fighters at the Front.—Subtitles. Gen. Petain decorates the 410th Infantry. Gen. Feraud decorates the 1st Cavalry Cyclists. Gen. Petain congratulates the Commanders.

Miscellaneous Subjects

BLUEBIRD PHOTOPLAYS, INC.

THE CHARMER (Five Parts—Aug. 20).—The cast; Mr. B. Webster Opp (Arthur Hoyt); Willard Hinton (George Chesbro); Jimmy Fallows (George Hernandez); John Mathews (Jack Curtis); Guinevere Gusty (Neva Gerber); Miss Kippy (Elsie Maison); Mrs. Gusty (Anna Lockhart). Screen version of Alice Heagan Rice's novel. Scenario and direction by Lynn F. Reynolds.
Daniel Webster Opp, egotistical, vain and with only a smattering of education, is the epitome of cheerfulness and optimism. He has ventured into many careers and has made a failure of all of them, until he becomes a traveling salesman for a St. Louis show firm. Just when promises are golden, Opp receives word that his stepfather has died and he must go at once to his old home to settle the estate.
He is met at the hotel in Cove Junction by his brother, Ben, who demands that a settlement be made on the basis of D. Webster taking the homestead while Ben shall have the few dollars in cash that complete the estate. In this arrangement Ben plans to send Kippy Opp to an institution for the feeble minded. As a result of the ravages of fever Kippy at the age of twenty-four has only the mind of a child.
D. Webster Opp decides to sacrifice himself to the care of his sister. He gives Ben the money and settles down in the old homestead to start life anew. An Cove Junction boasts no newspaper, Mr. Opp establishes The Opp Eagle. His optimistic editorials are read by a wealthy promotor who goes to Cove Junction to investigate the possibilities of getting coal from the ground in that vicinity.
Mr. Opp's plan for a "Greater Cove Junction" enthuses the populace, and he is chosen as the community head in forwarding schemes to make the town famous and prosperous. John Mathews, the promoter, addresses an assembly of the townsfolk, promising to co-operate with them in developing the coal lands if the citizens will invest with him in the Turtle Creek Development Co., which he undertakes to form. Mr. Opp's enthusiasm leads the citizens to invest, and Cove Junction begins to boom.
With Guinevere Gusty, the village belle, Mr. Opp has fallen in love, proposes marriage and is accepted. This happens before Willard Hinton, because of threatened blindness, is compelled to abandon his position as private secretary to John Mathews. Hinton decides to remain in Cove Junction and goes to board at the home of the Widow Gusty. This move ends Mr. Opp's matrimonial aspirations, for Guinevere falls in love with Hinton and Mr. Opp releases the girl from her engagement.
John Mathews returns to Cove Junction and at a meeting of the stockholders declares that the coal lands have been found to be unproductive of profit, but offers a plan to sell out to a rival corporation. All the stockholders, except Mr. Opp, agree to sell. Mr. Opp declares the whole transaction to be dishonorable, preconceived by Mathews to trick the rival company into buying a worthless proposition. He, however, is voted down and the sale is consummated.
Then and there Cove Junction's boom begins to wane. Hinton, having married Guinevere, makes a proposal to buy the Opp Eagle and retain Mr. Opp as an employee. Seeing his last hope vanishing, Mr. Opp sells out on the day the townsfolk have set for a banquet to do honor to the man who has done so much to advance the prosperity of Cove Junction. Mr. Opp finds himself the hero of an occasion that brings to his heart the measure of satisfaction and praise for which he is so hungry. He is then and there nominated for the office of Mayor and the story ends with Mr. Opp finding in the homage of his fellow citizens with a life of devotion to the brain-sick Kippy.

THE CHARMER (Five Parts—Aug. 27). The cast: Ambrosia Lee (Ella Hall); Charlotte Whitney (Belle Bennett); Cynthia M. Perkins (Martha Mattex); Don Whitney (James Mc-Candlas); Franklin Whitney (George Webb); Judge D. W. Appleby (Frank McQuarrie). Story by J. Grubb Alexander and Fred Myrton. Directed by Jack Conway.

When an enemy torpedo sank a great trans-Atlantic liner, Ambrosia Lee was left an orphan. The only lifeboat heard from after the catastrophe came ashore, with Ambrosia and her two charges—Caesar, a black little imp, and a pet monkey.

The refugees were taken to the general store in Peentucket where the male population were wont to gather for the purpose of assembling 'round the stove and adjusting the fate of the nation. Judge Appleby, supreme in finally settling disputes, ruled that Ambrosia should be contributed to the war bazaar that was then being held in the basement of the parish church.

The wheel of fortune was designated as the means of deciding who should win the prize, and the lucky number was held by Cynthia Perkins, a spinster of rigid New England disposition. Ambrosia, once established in her new home, resumed her communication with fairies that had been interrupted by the disaster on shipboard. A copy of Grimm's Fairy Tales supplied the medium for passing many hours in dreaming of the day when Prince Charming should come to claim her.

The immediate necessity of washing dishes and doing housework was reluctantly observed, but she was always waiting for an event that, suddenly and unexpectedly brought her Prince—and a great deal of trouble to boot. Don Whitney was her Prince Charming and he had been sent to Peentucket because his father and mother were not getting along first class in their matrimonial arrangements.

Mr. Whitney sent Don to his boyhood home and when Mrs. Whitney started her divorce she took the lad elsewhere, leaving Ambrosia forlorn. Ambrosia, having heard of the domestic storm in the Whitney family, had written a letter to Mr. Whitney, telling him the fairies would adjust matters and all would be well.

Mrs. Whitney's lawyer had arranged for a hired co-respondent to give the testimony that should free her from her husband, but when it came to trial the said co-respondent failed to appear. When Ambrosia heard that the trial could not proceed for want of a co-respondent, she remembered the letter she had written Mr. Whitney. Adjudging herself eligible as a "correspondent" Ambrosia took the witness stand—and had explained to her the meaning of the two words she had confused in communion with the fairies.

The interpretation Mr. Whitney gave to the Court as to the contents of Ambrosia's letter touched Mrs. Whitney's heart and impelled her to withdraw her suit. When Cynthia Perkins heard of Ambrosia's "outrageous conduct" she turned her out upon the cold, cold world. When the Whitneys heard of Ambrosia's distress they adopted the child and we leave the little orphan and Don Whitney happy in the extreme.

BUTTERFLY PICTURES.

WHO WAS THE OTHER MAN? (Five Parts—Sept. 3).—The cast: Herbert Cornell (Duke Worne); Senator Washburn (Wm. T. Horne); Marion Washburn (Mae Gaston); Wanda Bartell (Beatrice Van); James Walbert, and Ludwig Schumann (Francis Ford).—Story by J. Lowe. Produced by Francis Ford.

"Prettiest Girl I ever saw," says Ludwig Schumann of the Secret Service, as he catches sight of the young American at the desk of the Grand Hotel in Paris.

He learns she is Marion, the daughter of Senator Washburn of Texas, and is engaged to marry Herbert Cornell, a favorite of Washington society, to whom her father has only one objection. He thinks Herbert has played the role of society butterfly too long, and it is time to prove he is made of sterner stuff. Therefore, he consented on the condition that Herbert take charge of the delivery of the plans for an international canal, and see that they reach the proper hands.

Schumann is about to address Marion, when a young American enters. The spy is struck with the resemblance of the newcomer to himself. His stare attracts the stranger, who is also astonished at the likeness.

The American is James Walbert. He sees Marion, and is attracted by her beauty. A small, dark man enters the hotel and gives Walbert a paper as he passes. Walbert realizes the occurrence is unusual, and goes to his room. He opens it and finds a woman's photograph, with instructions to take the steamer on which she is sailing that evening for America. Walbert, knowing that he has

been mistaken for the other, decides to go through with the undertaking.

Schumann meets the dark man, who says: "You will have to hurry if you want to make that steamer tonight."

"What on earth are you talking about?" says Schumann, and is disconcerted to discover the agent has given the message to the wrong man. He accosts to the other's room, and Walbert looks up to see the muzzle of a revolver covering him.

"Hand over the instructions you received," says a curt voice, and Walbert, bowing to the inevitable, raises his hands above his head. An interruption occurs, and Walbert overpowers his double, ties him securely, rushes for the nearest exit and springs into a taxi.

On the steamer he sees Marion Washburn, the then Wanda Bartell, whom he recognizes from the photograph as his intended confederate. He makes himself known to her. Walbert realizes Marion is far more charming than he thought at first sight. He learns of her engagement to Herbert Cornell with a distinct pang.

Arrived in New York, Walbert and Wanda report at the headquarters of the Black Legion. They have learned that the plans have been intrusted to Cornell, and instruct Wanda to play the old, old game.

It is the ancient passion of jealousy which Wanda calls to her aid. It is not hard for her to contrive an accidental meeting with young Cornell, and the upshot is an invitation to her rooms, and a toast to their better acquaintance. He remembered nothing after drinking the toast, and Wanda relieved him of the plans he carried. Then, as she contemplated his death-like face, a sob burst from her, and she covered her face with her hands.

"Heaven help me! I love him!" she confessed.

"That's one reason why you'll hand me those plans. And the other is this:"

The voice was that of her "confederate," and "this" was the badge of the United States Secret Service. Snatching up Cornell's half empty glass, the woman drained it and fell at Walbert's feet.

Walbert left the room, however, determined on rounding up the Black Legion single-handed. For days Marion had been disturbed by the sense of impending trouble. Many small things combined in her mind into a certainty that Herbert, and possibly Walbert, were in danger. Meeting him on his way to the docks, she had a sudden inspiration.

Walbert, entering unsuspiciously after giving the password, was not prepared for the attack launched against him. Schumann had escaped, and wirelessed the news of the impersonation to headquarters. No match for the dozen men, Walbert was putting up a splendid fight when the police summoned by Marion burst into the place. The Black Legion had held its last meeting.

FOX FILM CORP.

EVERY GIRL'S DREAM (Five Parts—Aug. 25). The cast: Gretchen (Jude Caprice); Jane Cummings (Kittens Reichert); Carl (Harry Hilliard); Hulda (Margaret Fielding); Mrs. Van Lorn, Gretchen's mother (Marcia Harris); Mynher De Haas (Dan Mason). Scenario by Adrian Johnson. Directed by Harry Millarde.

Olenberg, a town in Holland, is famed for its pretty girls. One of these is Gretchen, who lives with her foster mother, Mrs. Van Lorn. Gretchen is beloved by everyone. Carl, a woodchopper, particularly loves Gretchen, too, is a foster child. Mynher De Haas, the town lawyer and capitalist, loves Gretchen and despite his fifty years cannot understand why the girl will not consider him as a suitor.

Mrs. Van Lorn prefers the lawyer. Incidentally the lawyer holds a mortgage on the Van Lorn homestead. But Hulda, a dark beauty, is determined Gretchen will not have Carl. Every time she finds them together she notifies Mrs. Van Lorn who drags Gretchen away and leaves Carl and Hulda.

One day De Haas comes to pop the question. As he is making a fervent plea a friend fastens a fishhook to his wig. When he gets up off goes his wig. Gretchen laughs heartily. Mynher leaves in a rage. Determined to make the Van Lorn family pay for the insult he looks for the mortgage in his pocket. It's not there. He has Gretchen arrested as the thief. At the same time Carl is in the woods. A carriage approaches. On nearing Carl it stops and a liveried attendant gets out. Noticing a birth mark like a fleur-de-lys on Carl's back he calls another attendant, seizes the youth and throws him into the carriage. They drive off.

The next day finds Gretchen on her way to the stocks, to pay for her theft. Mynheer is following her. Just as the girl is to be locked in the lawyer finds the mortgage. He asks that Gretchen be freed. When the populace learns of his mistake they put him in the stocks, and free Gretchen.

That evening a courier enters the town seeking a lost princess. The lucky girl has among her trinkets a beautiful locket. Hulda finds the locket in Gretchen's trunk. Hulda is proclaimed the princess. In a carriage in the square, she is told, is the prince she is to marry. The carriage door opens and out steps an old, wrinkled man.

Hulda runs off, crying she isn't the princess, that Gretchen is the girl and that she stole the locket. Gretchen is placed on the throne.

But the old man wasn't the prince. The prince, no other than Carl, comes from the coach and sits beside Gretchen. After the town's celebration a messenger announces that Carl's father has died and Carl is king.

While the people hail him, Carl gathers Gretchen into his arms and asks her to be his queen. Then Gretchen awakes and finds it was only "Every Girl's Dream".

GREATER VITAGRAPH.

THE DIVORCEE (Five Parts—Aug. 27). The cast: Wanda Carson (Mary Anderson); Rev. Jerry Ferguson (Alfred Vosburgh); Sam Carson (Filny Geoffriend); Mrs. Pelham-Wilson (Jean Hathaway).

Wanda comes to Reno to visit her brother but he is away on business and in her search for excitement she decides to play tag up-to-date divorcee. She makes up a story of marital infelicity which wins her the sympathy of the colony in which she becomes the leader, although in her heart she disapproves of the fast, careless lives they live.

Fond of horseback riding, she meets a young minister whom she mistakes for a cowboy. Riding is just a diversion with him, however, his main purpose being the repeal of laws which makes for easy divorces. She champions the cause of the divorcees and replies to the minister's attacks in press and open meeting, although he is unaware of her identity.

She is frequently put to embarrassment in maintaining her pose and is nearly exposed when her women friends demand that she show her marriage certificate. Her wit saves her, however, when she produces the child of a woman companion who accompanied her to Reno and of whom they knew nothing and challenges the divorcees to show such good proof.

Meantime, the friendship of the minister has grown into love, when Wanda in disgust breaks all relations with the divorcees, who inform the minister that the woman he admires is one of them and has a little girl in the bargain.

Wanda riding out to meet the cowboy minister is witness to a stage hold-up and is convinced that the minister is the robber. She hurries to warn him of a posse' approach and he, under a misapprehension, believes she is fleeing from an angry husband who has found her retreat. And so the two race ahead of the sheriff with bullets falling about them, until finally cornered.

Explanations follow and the sheriff, an old friend of the minister, quickly vouches for him. It might have gone harder with the "divorcee," only her brother Sam, also a friend of the sheriff, happens to be in the posse and she is speedily relegated to her rightful position of a very attractive and unmarried young woman who loves only the minister.

SOLDIERS OF CHANCE (Five Parts—Sept. 3). The cast: Billy Mountain alias Captain Josslyn (Evart Overton); Josephine Winton (Miriam Fouche); Dolores (Julia Swayne Gordon); Philip Winton (Charles Kent); Peter Lawler (Charles Henderson); Yawkey (Denton Vane).

Lawler, the promoter, has Winton, the girl's father absolutely in his power financially, when Billy Mountain, unrecognized as Lawler's enemy, arrives in New York. He needs money to start a revolution in South America to exploit mahogany concessions, and gets

Lawier on his yacht intending to force him to sign away valuable securities. Miss Winton and her father also go on the yacht.

Lawier, defiant, refuses to sign any papers and the party finally arrives at the South American estate of Mountain, who starts the revolution. Lawier joins the federal forces and betrays Mountain, who is captured, along with he girl, and sentenced to death the following day.

Miss Winton gets word to the revolutionists of Mountain's plight and agree to marry Lawier if he will, postpone the execution one day. By forced marches, Mountain's men arrive before the palace just as he is about to be shot. There is a battle in which the federals are put to rout and Mountain and Lawier meet face to face. The latter is killed by one of Mountain's followers and the father is cleared of the stigma of a murder with which he has been charged, by the arrival of the man he was supposed to have killed. Mountain and the girl have learned to love each other.

JEWEL PRODUCTIONS, INC.

SIRENS OF THE SEA (Five Part). The cast: Sybil (Louise Lovely); Gerald Waldron (Jack Mulhall); Julie (Carmen Myers); Hartley Royce (Wm. Quinn); Wellington Stanhope (Sidney Dean); Mrs. Stanhope (Helen Wright); Haji (Evelyn Selbie). Story by Grace Helen Bailey. Produced by Allen Holubar.

In the night a terrific storm arises off a strange island and a ship is cast furiously about, sending forth rockets in an appeal for help. As the sun begins to appear, fishermen start drawing in their nets. The rocky shore is strewn with wreckage among which the old beachcomber, Haji, is picking up driftwood. As Wellington Stanhope and his wife, who lives in the Grecian villa, come down to the beach, the fishermen have opened their nets and discovered a tiny blonde child. Haji mutters and looks across the sea. The Stanhopes take the child and try to resuscitate it, and when the tiny girl opens her eyes, they conclude God has sent this little one to fill the void in their hearts.

Fourteen years later Sybil has blossomed into womanhood. Her school chums are spending their vacation at the villa. Julie, a cold, calculating girl, is jealous of Sybil. They go to a nearby island where they start undressing behind rocks, preparatory to going in swimming. Sybil takes their bathing suits. The girls don sea-weed and chase Sybil, then start playing ukuleles and dancing. They are seen by Gerald Waldron, who, bored with society, has found a means of escape on his yacht, but has been unable to escape Hartley Royce, who finds Gerald's money much to his liking. The boys find that there is so much island noted on the map and figure that they have made a discovery. Gerald says it is an enchanted island and over yonder sits Lorelei and her sirens. Destruction or not, he is going to Lorelei. Hartley determines to go back also.

Gerald and Hartley fall in love with Sybil; Julie rages and finds herself relegated to second place. By a sudden change of Sybil. A fortnight goes by. Julie and Hartley plot to separate the lovers. Julie insinuates that Sybil is not the daughter of the Stanhopes. Hartley tells Sybil not to worry about Gerald, who has a sweetheart in every port.

It is Sybil's eighteenth birthday and a celebration is in progress. After failing Julie her plan, Sybil gives away to go for Haji, to induce her to tell the fortunes of the young people. Julie informs Hartley, who follows Sybil. She tries to elude him, but he gains and passionately catches her in his arms. She rushes to the top of a cliff and, though she warns him, he rushes toward her and she jumps into the sea. After several moments of horror, he picks up her cloak which has been washed to shore, and returns to the villa. Gerald is frantic. After hours of fruitless searching the dawn finds him hopeless and exhausted. He has heard Haji saying Sybil came from the sea and has gone back to the sea; that she is the spirit of the Greek sculptor, who, lured by the sirens, left his wife and child, and the wife drowning herself and the child, cursed the land and water "until true love shall reign again."

Gerald and Hartley start out to find the girl, each in a different direction, and to each is accorded a series of startling adventures, which end with the sailing of Sybil and Gerald for America.

K-E-S-E.

PANTS (Essanay—Five Parts—Drama—Sept. 10).—Little Betty has a luxurious home, an army of servants and the costliest of toys. But she hasn't what a child wants most of all —other children to play with. The result is that she runs away and joins a group of children from the ghetto district on the beach. In play she exchanges clothing with a little boy. That evening Betty doesn't return home. Her maiden aunt—an over-zealous guardian—is frantic. She notifies the police. The same evening the father of the boy, who has lost his position and is facing starvation, decides to turn burglar. He steals into the home of Betty's father. The household is awakened and the intruder captured. At that moment the police arrive with the boy whom they have mistaken for Betty on account of the little girl's clothing which he wears. All are utterly bewildered. The denouement comes with Betty's entrance at this juncture, garbed in the boy's clothes. She likes the boy and on her plea he and his father are liberated. The experience teaches Betty's father that his little girl should have more than his wealth can afford her; that is, other children to play with.

CONQUEST PICTURES.

(On K-E-S-E Program.)

THE PRINCESS NECKLACE (Edison—Four Parts—September 1—On Program No. 8).—The cast: The King (William Calhoun); the Princess (Kathleen Townsend); the Stranger (Wallace MacDonald); the Little Girl (Susan Mitchell); the Girl (Dorothy Graham); the Shepherd (Roy Adams).

Once in a country called Happyland there lived a good and wise King. To his beautiful daughter, Princess Loree, the King presents a priceless pearl necklace. A mysterious stranger arrives. He meets the Princess and they fall in love at first sight. He reveals to her that he comes from a country where the people are forever in gloom and he is here to learn the secret of happiness. He meets with a number of adventures which teach him some of the principles of happiness, but not its Master Secret.

One day a goblin takes the necklace and brings it to his chief, who hides it in the wall of the Goblin's Cave. The Princess and the people are grief-stricken and the stranger decides to find it. He enters the Enchanted Woods and after a series of adventures reaches a secret passage which leads him into the Cave of the Goblins. The chief of the goblins r~un-lenses to return the necklace if the stranger will brave any perils that may confront him. The latter consents and passes undaunted through them all.

He obtains the necklace and returns it to the Princess, whose happiness is restored. The King is willing to give him half his kingdom as a reward, but all the stranger asks is to be allowed to speak to the Princess one hour every day for seven days. At the end of the seventh day he leaves, promising to return shortly.

Weeks pass. The King informs the Princess the newly-crowned King of Roseland is coming to pay homage to Happyland and that she had better don her finest apparel and help him entertain the illustrious guest. The King of Roseland arrives and the Princess is happy, for in him she recognizes the Stranger. She inquires if he has discovered the Master Secret. He answers in the affirmative, saying true happiness consists in deeds that bring happiness to others, and in the realization of one's ideals —love crowning all.

THE PUZZLING BILLBOARD (Edison—850 feet—September 1—On Program No. 8). This is a puzzle story arranged by Sam Lloyd of a billboard or rather of the evolution of a word thereon from pants to nails. On the surface there seems to be no connection between pants and nails; yet it is as easy as eating pie to make nails out of pants if you know how. The first word advertises the product of a clothing man. But he has made his reckoning without the host—or rather a number of hosts. For a florist, a furrier, a jeweler, a plumber, a dry-goods man, a carpenter, a physician, a lawyer, a mason, a ship's chandler and a hardware man happen along one after the other, and by merely pasting over one letter of the word on the billboard with a different letter, each alters the word into an advertisement of his own product. The film is ingeniously arranged so as to give the onlooker a chance to use his wit in guessing the next word on the billboard. In the end a goat comes along and eats up the poster. This goat is a puzzle in itself. Is it a rear goat? Who knows?

IN OLD ENGLAND (Edison—250 feet—September 1—On Program No. 8). This scenic is interesting by virtue of the marked contrast between the rural scenery of Albion and that of our own country. We still boast pristine forests and regions untrod by man. But England is a tight little isle, teeming with population. Nature there bears no aspect of rugged grandeur. Everything, be it sward or tree or brook, is trimmed down to a nicety—according to model. Everything is orderly and prearranged as things in Toyland. We gain this impression as we follow the tourists along English roads, past quaint little houses, where everything is peaceful and serene and unruffled, down the banks of the Thames, under bridges and through massive locks.

THE BLIND FIDDLER (Edison—One Reel—Sept. 1—On Program No. 8—With Viola Dana as the Fairy).—The blind fiddler is playing his weird and haunting music outside his hut, but he is very unhappy. He sighs: "Ah if I could only see my lovely wife, how happy I would be." A fairy is moved by his prayer and restores to him his sight. But the world he has imagined so beautiful bursts repulsively on his sight. He sees a man beating his dog unmercifully. His wife turns out to be old and ugly. The disillusionment affects his genius and his violin is deprived of its haunting, almost human witchery. He cries out in despair for the return of his blessed darkness. The fairy restores to him and therewith his happiness.

WOODCRAFT FOR BOYS (Edison—400 feet —September 1—On Program No. 8). This film shows that many schools have complete courses in woodcraft for boys. Two-day canoe trips are part of the course. While out camping, the boys enjoy the simple life, living in tents, taking their daily swim and cooking their own meals. Matches are not needed, and it is a treat to watch the boys starting a fire without them. The flapjacks they turn out would arouse the envy of a Broadway chef. Their bodies are hardened by such sports as racing, swimming and spear throwing. In the evening they dance around the camp fire and indulge in such simple games as knocking each other off the stool. The ending of this split reel shows a boy blowing the bugle and the camp breaking up.

SHIPPING LIVE FISH (Edison—200 feet— September 1—On Program No. 8). (Photographed at a New York aquarium under the auspices of the New York Zoological Society.) Fish breathe oxygen from the water. If a fish is placed in a small amount of water he soon exhausts the oxygen and dies of suffocation. The New York Aquarium has solved the question of supplying the oxygen on long-journeys even when fish are placed in small jars. The jar is first filled with pure sea water. The fish to be shipped are placed in it and the jar is inverted in a tank full of water. Sufficient oxygen is then admitted to force out one-third of the water. The jar is tightly corked under water and hermetically sealed with waxed linen. The jar is then packed in a barrelful of sawdust or excelsior, addressed and shipped to its destination. The fish will live for more than fourteen days in a jar of small size. It is therefore possible to ship them from New York to any part of the United States and to most parts of Europe.

THE BROOK (Edison—400 feet—Sept. 1—On Program No. 8). This famous poem by Tennyson is made the subject of a scenic comprising a tableau of pictures that interpret the mood of the poem. We follow the falls bickering down the valley and the brook as it chatters over stony ways in little sharps and trebles, as it steals by lawns and grassy plots and murmurs under moon and stars in brambling wilderness, as it hurries down the hills past town and under bridges, winding in and out with here and there a foamy flake until it joins the brimming river.

OGDEN PICTURES CORPORATION

THE LUST OF THE AGES (Seven Parts—August).—Edmund Craig, obsessed with the ambition to acquire wealth, pays scant attention to his wife and daughter, Lois. Mr. and Mrs. Craig reap their harvest, but in different ways. Craig, in the excitement of the hour and in the moment of consummating a large financial transaction, is stricken with heart disease and dies.

Lois completes her education at a female "Freshwater" college and is awarded the literary prize as a result of her book, which she has entitled "The Lust of the Ages." Professor Mason, a kindly, elderly gentleman, marvels at the strength of the work, and prevails upon Lois to permit him to have it published. Lois shortly after her graduation becomes the fiancee of Byron Masters, a whole-souled American. Masters is the chairman of the Board of Trustees, whose financial contributions permit Professor Mason to keep his college open. Professor Mason for his commencement lecture, chooses the subject, "The Iniquities of Wealth Wrongfully Applied," and inveighs against monopolies and aggregations of wealth generally.

Masters is the head of a combination seeking to control important railway lines and, hearing Mason's address, determines to remove him as president of the college and forwards him a notification to that effect.

Professor Mason delivers the first copy of Lois Craig's novel to her in the garden of her home and there also tells her of his removal by Byron Masters. Lois protests and tells Professor Mason she will have him restored. She calls on Masters and when she realizes that he, too, is obsessed with the lust for gold, and with the lesson of her mother's experience in her mind, tells Masters they could never be happy and terminates the engagement. She leaves with him her book and asks him to read it.

Masters commences to read the book and the photoplay then visualizes what Lois Craig has written. She proves the dissipation and squandering of wealth, immoral entertainments held by those of the rich, the want and privation of the poor, the reason that girls are driven to immoral deeds and then traces the history of the lust of all ages from the time of the ancient days, when there was no money and wealth was acquired through the medium of barter and exchange. There was then known a habitation called the Valley of Content, but the army of Mammon invaded this peaceful valley and, re-

---

knows where Tom is. Pearl offers him $5,000 to save Tom's life, and starts for her camp in the Adirondacks with "The Spider." The next morning Tom is captured by the Priestess and her followers, and the camp is set on fire just before Pearl and "The Spider" reach it. Pearl and "The Spider" are locked in the burning cabin, while Tom is led away captive by the Priestess and her followers.

TRIANGLE FILM CORPORATION.

WEE LADY BETTY (Five Parts—Aug. 19). The cast: Wee Lady Betty (Bessie Love); Roger O'Reilly (Frank Borzage); Fergus Mc-Clusky (Charles K. French); Shamus Mc-Teague (Walter Perkins); Lanty O'Dea (L. Jefferies); The O'Reilly (Walter Whitman); Mrs. O'Reilly (Aggie Herring); Connor O'-Donovan (Thornton Edwards); Father Dan (Alfred Hollingsworth); Michael O'Brien (J. P. Lockney). Story by J. G. Hakwa. Directed by Charles Miller.

On the Isle of Kilcroney Wee Lady Betty ruled O'Reilly Castle with a stern hand and a big heart. Their fear of the Wee Lady was next to the fear of the ghost of "Slasher" O'Reilly. Sir Daniel O'Reilly, the rightful owner died, leaving the castle to Roger O'Reilly, who announced that he was coming to take possession. The tenants would not have this as the Wee Lady had been good to them, but she told them to receive the new master kindly.

Not having the wherewithal to provide for her aged father, the Wee Lady contrived a scheme. Feigning to leave the castle, she had her father returned after dark the same night and she installed in the haunted chamber, keeping the key. The next day when Roger arrived with his mother his reception was a chilly one, the villagers believing that he was responsible for the Wee Lady's supposed departure. The Wee Lady Betty in the guise of a maid showed them through the place, paying particular stress on the haunted chamber and the ghost of "Slasher" O'Reilly.

When Roger had gone, his mother demanded to see the haunted room, so the Wee Lady got into an old suit of armour and said "Begone!" Mrs. O'Reilly fainted. The Wee Lady found that she had developed a strong liking for Roger but was thrown into despair when he declared he would call on the door of the chamber. While getting food to her father that night she heard a door open and behind Roger entering the room. Once more she got behind the armour and said "Begone!" and her answer was a shot from Roger's pistol, grazing her arm. There was a loud noise outside and Roger rushed from the room, not knowing the work his pistol had done. The villagers had stormed the castle and were rushing up the steps when Roger appeared at the top. A fight ensued when the Wee Lad- appeared and commanded them to leave. They left the castle, leaving the Wee Lady Betty and Roger clasped in each other's arms.

A PAWNBROKER'S HEART (Triangle Key-stone—Two Parts).—The cast: Glen Cavender (Boss of Pawnshop); Caroline Rankin (His Wife); Chester Conklin (Clerk in Pawnshop); Peggy Pearce (His Wife and Cavender's Maid); Ben Turpin (Janitor in Pawnshop).

Peggy didn't figure that [ee]dine her husband with the choicest cuts from the Cavender steak was anything but proper, but it led to complications. Glen essayed to go into the kitchen and bawl out Peggy for sending little more than a bone to the family table. Mrs. Glen misconstrued the situation, and Peggy was canned.

In the pawnshop, Conklin and Turpin doing their best to get their salaries with as little effort as possible. Peggy comes in and secrets herself with Cavender, in an effort to get her job back, it starts something, for Mrs. C. and Peggy's hubby don't get the angle. A band of crooks plan to rob the pawnshop. Clothing store dummies play an important part, and two bags, one with and one without cash, figure prominently in the plot.

GRAFTERS (Five Parts—Aug. 26). The cast: Jack Towne (Jack Devereaux); Mark Towne (Frank Currier); Doris Ames (Anna Leher); Mrs. Ames (Irene Leonard); The Menace (George Siegmann); "Laughing Louie" (Robert Crimmins). The story of "Grafters" details the efforts of Mark Towne to teach his nephew, who has just inherited a million dollars, to beware of

swindlers. The nephew, Jack, falls so easily for scarce strangers who specialize in selling blue sky, that he eventually engages a band of crooks to swindle Jack in a small way, and so teach him through the wisdom of experience to take care of the rest of his money.

At the head of the band of conspirators is Doris Ames, a young woman who is working to save her mother from the poor house, and she and Jack fall in love. In due course Doris finds the rest of the conspirators are planning to make a good haul from Jack while they are at it, and determines to defeat their aims. At about the same time Jack engages a band of detectives to trap the crowd. From this situation, fun follows fun, to a thrilling end.

TEN OF DIAMONDS (Five Parts—Sept. 2). Neva Blaine, a cabaret girl in a cheap cafe in a great city, at the price of every youthful and womanly hope has retained her virtue. Her coldness, cynicism, hate and disillusionment form a background for her frantic efforts to help young girls who enter the cafe with men who prey. Between her songs at the cabaret she habitually tells her fortune with playing cards.

Into her life came Warren Kennedy, wealthy society man. He was to have been married to Blanche Calloway, a social butterfly, when his enemy, Ellis Hopper, intrigued against him. Hopper succeeded in getting Miss Calloway to wed his son, leaving Kennedy shamed amid the wedding guests at a great church. Hopper further humiliates him by personally delivering the note in which the girl tells of her treachery.

To forget the tragedy of his love, Kennedy began a night of debauchery, ending in the dive where Neva worked. She was selected to get his money. Instead, she fell in love with him.

A plot of revenge occurred to Kennedy. He determined to educate Neva in social affairs, launch her as a wealthy tourist, have her trap his enemy in to marriage, and then he, Kennedy, would feel his revenge on exposing her origin and Hopper's plight.

She does her part successfully, winning Hopper but loving Kennedy, who rejects her efforts to become more than a friend to him. She despises Hopper. On the day of the wedding, she delays preparations to write a note to Kennedy, imploring him to save her from the unwelcome bridegroom. Kennedy informs her it is either Hopper or the slums for her future.

In desperation she prepares to suffer the wedding, when she determined on a tragic relief. She secured a bottle of wine, spilled much of the contents over her wedding dress, so the odor was offensive, then pretended drunkenness and reeled through the fashionable crowd toward the altar.

The guests fled from her. Hopper horrified denounces her. She returned to her room, abject in her woe. Then Kennedy could not resist she forces that drew him to her. He went to her room, they exchanged vows of love, and both their lives were made happy.

THE MAN HATER (Five Parts—Sept. 2). The cast: Phemie Sanders (Winifred Allen); Joe Stull (Jack Meredith); Phemie's Father (Harry Neville); Phemie's Mother (Jessie Shirley); Lucy Convey, the Widow (Marguerite Gale); The Doctor (Robert Vivian); Phemie's Little Sister (Anna Lehr). Story by Mary Brecht Pulver. Directed by Albert Parker.

Despite her hatred for the other sex, Phemie assumes charge of her little brothers blacksmith, in order to escape the tyranny of her drunken father. When her parents die, Phemie Sanders marries Joe Stull, a stalwart and sisters, taking them into her own home. She still declines to give her husband any affection, for she told him frankly before their marriage that she could not love him.

In desperation, he attempts to awaken her jealousy by writing notes to himself on lady's stationery and signing the scheme. A pretty widow named Lucy Conver moves into the home across the street from the Stull's and commences a flirtation with Joe. Phemie's attitude toward this affair gives a humorous twist to the story, proving that all women are more or less inconsistent, particularly where men are concerned.

Classified Advertisements   NOTE TERMS CAREFULLY

Remittances must accompany all orders for classified advertisements as follows: One dollar per insertion for copy containing twenty words or less. Five cents per word on copy containing over twenty words. Each word to be counted including names and addresses.

NOTICE TO ADVERTISERS:—The Publishers expect that all statements made in every advertisement will bear the strictest investigation.

SITUATIONS WANTED.

POSITION WANTED by up-to-date motion picture lady organist. Best city references. Address Organist, care M. P. World, N. Y. City

AT LIBERTY—Union operator and electrician, I. A. T. S. E. September 10th, account Park closing. Ten years' experience, handle any outfit, go anywhere. Sober, reliable, married, reference. State all in first. Operator, care M. P. World, N. Y. City.

EXPERIENCED orchestra leader, violinist, with organist on Wurlitzer and American Master organs. Two years present theater, seek change. Large repertoire for pictures. Address Musicians, 32 Victoria St., Montreal, Can.

CAMERAMAN—Originality, thorough experience. Now with government. Own Pathe professional camera outfit complete. Go anywhere. 613 Eleventh St. P. O., Washington, D. C.

ORGANIST, highly efficient and thoroughly experienced, open for theater engagement. Expert motion picture accompanist. Address Efficient, care M. P. World, N. Y. City.

EXPERT projection operator, open September 5th; ten years' experience; Ultra results. Go anywhere. Rene Robert Laurier, Cape May, N. J.

OPERATOR, strictly experienced, desires position first-class theater only. Handle only best equipment. Perfect projection guaranteed. Henry Alsman, Dyersburg, Tenn.

VIOLINIST and orchestra leader, experienced in picture and vaudeville. Fine library, married, no bad habits. J. Harry Hurley, 710 Fox St., Denver, Colo.

COLORED LADY desires permanent studio connection. Have played "maid" parts before. References. J. R., care M. P. World, N. Y. City.

HELP WANTED.

UNION ORGANIST wanted for Indiana city, 90,000 population, experience in picture playing on Wurlitzer-Hope-Jones. State salary and experience first letter. Address L. G. Barnes, care Lyric Theater, Kalamazoo, Mich.

ORGANIST, thoroughly experienced with picture playing two-manual Hillgreen Lane organ; three matinees, no Sunday shows. State price and references. Utopia Theater, Painesville, Ohio.

THEATERS WANTED.

WANTED—To lease theater of 500 seats in Central States, with privilege of purchase. J. Lake, Marseilles, Ill.

THEATERS FOR SALE OR RENT.

FOR SALE—On account of being drafted, will sell swell picture house, southern city of 15,000. Big paying proposition. Price, $4,000, $2,000 cash, easy terms balance. Address R. K. L., care M. P. World, N. Y. City.

FOR SALE—Only motion picture theater in Menominee, Michigan. Population ten thousand. Seating four hundred and fifty. Popular, doing good, nicely equipped. Needs management. Write or wire owner, Campbell, care Strand, Escanaba, Mich.

THEATER—Moving picture, money maker, absolutely modern. 100 per cent. guaranteed. Fine 50,000 city, central Western State. 300 seats. If looking for cheap, run-down place—don't reply. Address C. O. L., care M. P. World, N. Y. City.

EQUIPMENT FOR SALE.

GUARANTEED MACHINES—Slightly used type S-1917 model, Simplex motor drive, factory guarantee, at reasonable prices. Room 206, 1482 Broadway, N. Y. City.

FOR SALE—A full moving picture house equipment. 300 opera chairs, machines, operating booth, fans, and miscellaneous equipment. Reasonable price to quick buyer. Must vacate at once. Address Box 23, Norwalk, Conn.

BARGAINS—Two Power's friction speed controllers, motors, 110 volts, direct current. Fort Wayne compensarc. Address 208 So. Market St., Canton, Ohio.

CAMERAS, ETC., FOR SALE.

PROFESSIONAL CAMERAS, tripods, perforators, printers' developing outfits, rewinders. Tessars, effects, devices, novelties, experimental workshop, repair, expert film work titles. Eberhard Schneider, 14th St. & Second Ave., N. Y. City.

WILLIAMSON Professional camera, perfect condition. Goertz F:3.5 cellor, 200-foot capacity, tripod, four extra magazines; a bargain for $150.00 complete. Will ship for inspection on receipt of $10.00 to cover express charges. Balance C. O. D. Hofmann, 1194 First Ave., N. Y. City.

DEVELOPING tanks, racks, printers, polishers, drying drums, cameras, tripods. Electric lights, home projectors. Low prices. Ray, 326 Fifth Ave., N. Y. City.

200-FOOT Ernemann, Tessar lens and direct focusing. Tripod and extras, $130. Full particulars. Address Hew, care M. P. World, N. Y. City.

DAVID STERN COMPANY, INCORPORATED. "EVERYTHING IN CAMERAS". PIONEERS IN THE MOTION PICTURE FIELD———

SPECIAL———

SPECIAL———400 ft. Ernemann Model B, forward and reverse take-up, without change of brits. Finest movement, gear drive, regular and trick crank, 2-in. F:3.3 and Telephoto lenses, in revolving lens mount. Focusing tube through camera. OUR PRICE—$225.00. EXCLUSIVE DISTRIBUTORS FOR THE DAVSCO. AGENTS FOR THE UNIVERSAL. WRITE OR WIRE FOR OUR SPECIAL PROPOSITION. DAVID STERN COMPANY———"Everything in Cameras". In business since 1885. 1027-29 R Madison St., Chicago, Ill.

WRITE AT ONCE to the Motion Picture headquarters of America. The greatest assortment of used bargains ever offered. Note prices and act at once———200 ft. Professional Ernemann with prismatic focusing device, regular and trick crank, Ernon F:3.5 lens, including heavy panoram and tilting top tripod, $135.00———300 ft. Urban Professional with F:3.5 lens, three magazines, heavy panoram and tilting top tripod; an exceptional bargain; price complete, $110.00———200 ft. Universal, second hand, but perfect condition, equipped with 50 M. M. Tessar, F:3.5 lens. A Snap. Price, $195.00———200 ft. capacity U. S. Professional, regular and trick crank, perfect condition, equipped with 50 M. M. Tessar F:3.5 lens, complete. $120.00———Every machine guaranteed. Act promptly and follow the crowd to the greatest camera center to the United States. Telegraphic orders receive prompt attention———BASS CAMERA COMPANY M. P. Camera Dept., 109 N. Dearborn St., Chicago, Ill.

FILMS, ETC., FOR SALE.

FILMS—Better class commercial films available on the leasing basis consisting of one-reel comedies and dramas, two-reel Westerns and dramas, three-reel dramas, and five-reel features. Posters for each film. Formerly most prominent brands on the market. Exceptional opportunities for commercial exchanges. Address Consumers Film Trading Company, Room 518, 220 South State St., Chicago, Illinois.

WEEKLY SHIPMENTS OF FILMS FOR SALE —We will sell outright twenty reels of single-reel comedies and two and three-reel features or one five-reel feature and ten reels of one, two, and three-reelers with a nice assortment of clean paper on each subject at $100.00 a week or shipment. All films are in splendid condition shipped subject to examination. Send $10.00 to guarantee express charges, will ship C. O. D. each week. Wire or write at once. Chicago Film Training & Exporting Co., 4th floor Shops Bldg., Chicago, Illinois.

FILMS, ETC., WANTED.

HAVE you good feature you can't sell? Have new plan percentage booking gets money. Ray, 326 Fifth Ave., N. Y. City.

INDEX

TO CONTENTS

TO ADVERTISERS

In Answering Advertisements, Please Mention THE MOVING PICTURE WORLD

MICHIGAN STATE CONVENTION

OF THE

American Exhibitors' Association

DETROIT, MICHIGAN
SEPTEMBER 5-6

With a free Auto Ride, Theatre Party, Smoker and Cabaret. Want every Exhibitor to come, bring his wife and have a good time.

KING PERRY, Secretary
204 Brietmeyer Building, DETROIT, MICH.

ARE YOU

Saving Your Money

TO INVEST IN THE

NEXT ISSUE

OF THE

LIBERTY LOAN

?

List of Current Film Release Dates

ON GENERAL FILM, PATHE AND PARAMOUNT PROGRAMS

(For Daily Calendar of Program Releases See Page 1578.)

General Film Company, Inc.

(Note—Pictures given below are listed in the order of their release. Additions are made from week to week in the order of release.)

BROADWAY STAR FEATURE.

A Little Speck in Garnered Fruit (One of the O. Henry Series—Two parts—Comedy-Dr.).
The Gift of the Magi (One of the O. Henry Stories—Two parts—Comedy-Drama).
The Coming Out of Maggie (One of the O. Henry Stories—Two parts—Comedy-Dr.).
The Venturers (one of the O. Henry Series—Two parts—Comedy-Drama).
Discounters of Money (One of the O. Henry Series—Two parts—Comedy-Drama).
The Furnished Room (One of the O. Henry Series—Two parts—Drama).
The Defeat of the City (One of the O. Henry Series—Four parts—Drama).
The Atavism of John Tom Little Bear (One of the O. Henry Series—Two parts—Drama).

ESSANAY.

Two Laughs (Black Cat Feature—Two parts—Comedy-Drama).
Our Boys (Black Cat Feature—Two parts—Comedy).
Seventy and Seven (Black Cat Feature—Two parts—Comedy-Drama).
Pete's Pants (Black Cat Feature—Two parts—Comedy).
Vernon, the Bountiful (Black Cat Feature—Two Parts—Comedy-Drama).
The Long-Green Trail (Black Cat Feature—Two parts—Comedy-Drama).
Don't Lose Your Cost (Black Cat Feature—Two parts—Comedy).
Star Dust—Black Cat Feature—Two parts—Comedy-Drama).
Twelve Cylinder Speed of the Leisure Class (George Ade Fables—Two parts—Comedy).

FALCON FEATURES.

The Mainspring (Four parts—Drama).
The Martinache Marriage (Four parts—Dr.).
The Stolen Play (Four parts—Drama).
The Phantom Shotgun (Four parts—Drama).
His Unpolished Self (Four parts—Drama).

KALEM.

The Mark of Stingaree (Episode of "The Further Adventures of Stingaree"—Two parts—Dr.).
An Order of the Court (Episode of "The Further Adventures of Stingaree"—Two parts—Dr.).
At the Sign of the Kangaroo (an episode of the "The Further Adventures of Stingaree"—Two parts—Drama).
Through Fire and Water (Episode of the Further Adventures of Stingaree—Two parts—Drama).
A Bushranger's Strategy (Episode of the Further Adventures of Stingaree—Two parts—Drama).
The Stranger at Dumcrief (Episode of "The Further Adventures of Stingaree"—Two parts—Drama).
A Champion of the Law (Episode of "The Further Adventures of Stingaree"—Two parts—Drama).

GEORGE KLEINE.

Nearly a Husband (One-Reel George Bickel Comedy).
Sea Statue (One-Reel George Bickel Comedy).

JAXON COMEDIES.

(Pokes and Jabs).
Pearls of Paulina.
Ploughing the Clouds.
(Second Series.)
Counting 'Em Up.
The Baggage Man.
Getting the Coin.
Tipbath Jute.
Play Ball.
Love Letters.

SELIG.

Selig World Library No. 10 (Educational).
A Daughter of the Southland (Two parts—Dr.).
The L.-X. Clew (Drama).
Selig-World Library No. 11 (Edu.).
The Toll of Sin (Two Parts—Drama).
The Bush Leaguer (One part—Drama).
Selig-World Library No. 12 (Educational).
The Smoldering Spark (Two parts—Drama).
The Love of Madge O'Mara (Drama).
Selig-World Library No. 13 (Educational).
A Man, a Girl and a Lion (Two parts—Drama).
Her Perilous Ride (One part—Drama).
Selig World Library No. 14 (Educational).
The Sole Survivor (Two parts—Drama).
Her Heart's Desire (One part—Drama).
Selig World Library No. 15 (Educational).
Between Man and Beast (Two parts—Drama).
Her Salvation (One part—Drama).
Selig World Library No. 16 (Educational).
Pioneer Days (Two parts—Drama).
In After Years (One part—Drama).

RAY COMEDIES.

A Laundry Mix-Up.
A Peaceful Riot.
Cheating His Wife.
A Bathtub Marriage.

SPARKLE COMEDIES.

Bertie's Bath.
A Night of Enchantment.
(Second Series.)
An Attorney's Affair.
Her Fatquest.
Those Terrible Telegrams.
The Stag Party.
Bragg's Little Poker Party.
Mixed Nuts.

Pathe Exchange, Inc.

RELEASES FOR WEEK OF AUGUST 12.

The Streets of Illusion (Five parts—Drama—Astra).
The Neglected Wife (No. 14—"Desperation"—Two parts—Drama—Balboa).
The Fatal Ring (No. 6—"Rays of Death"—Two parts—Drama—Astra).
Know America No. 10—"Southern Colorado" (Scenic—Combitone).
Hearst-Pathe News No. 96 (Topical).
Hearst-Pathe News No. 61 (Topical).
Bringing Up Father—"He Tries His Hand at Hypnotism (Cartoon Comedy), and Sardine Fisheries at Monterey (Edu.) (International Split Reel).

RELEASES FOR WEEK OF AUG. 19.

Miss Nobody (Five parts—Drama—Astra).
The Neglected Wife (No. 15—"A Sacrifice Supreme"—Two parts—Drama—Balboa).
The Fatal Ring (No. 7—"The Signal Lantern"—Two parts—Drama—Astra).
Along the Baltic Sweden (Scenic—Sveslims), and Japan, the Religious (Colored Scenic) (Split Reel).
Jerry on the Job—"On the Border" (Cartoon Comedy), and "Fine Feathers" (Edu.) Split Reel).
Lonesome Luke, Mechanic (Two parts—Comedy—Rolin).
Hearst-Pathe News No. 68 (Topical).
Hearst-Pathe News No. 69 (Topical).

RELEASES FOR WEEK OF AUGUST. 26.

Iris (Five parts—Drama—Hepworth).
The Fatal Ring (No. 8, "The Switch in the Safe"—Two parts—Drama—Astra).
Know America No. 20—Near Pike's Peak, Colo. (One reel—Scenic—Combitone).
Hearst-Pathe News No. 70 (Topical).
Hearst-Pathe News No. 71 (Topical).

Releases for Week of September 2.

Tears and Smiles (Lastilda—Five parts—Drama).
The Fatal Ring (Episode No. 9, "The Dice of Death") (Two parts—Drama—Astra).
Lonesome Luke's Wild Women (Two parts—Comedy—Rolin).
Know America No. 21, "Central Colorado" (Scenic-Combitone).
Scenic and Cartoon (International Split Reel—Title not reported).
Hearst-Pathe News No. 72 (Topical).
Hearst-Pathe News No. 73 (Topical).

Paramount Pictures Corp.

BLACK DIAMOND COMEDY.

June 25—Auto Intoxication.
Aug. 6—Susie the Sleepwalker.
July 9—Wits and Fits.
July 23.—The Rejuvenator.

FAMOUS PLAYERS.

July 9—The Love That Lives (Five parts—Drama).
July 28—The Long Trail (Five parts—Drama).

KLEVER KOMEDY.

July 16—The Wrong Mr. Fox.
July 30—Motor Boating.
Aug. 13—Summer Boarding (Comedy).
Aug. 20.—Egged On.

LASKY.

July 26—The Squaw Man's Son (Five parts—Drama).
July 30—The Crystal Gazer (Five parts—Dr.).

MOROSCO AND PALLAS.

July 19—Cook of Canyon Camp (Five parts—Drama).
Aug. 2—A Kiss for Susie (Five parts—Drama).

PARAMOUNT-ARBUCKLE COMEDY.

June 24—The Rough House (Two parts).
Aug. 20—His Wedding Night (Two parts).

PARAMOUNT-ARTCRAFT.

Aug. 5—The Amazons (Five parts—Drama).
Aug. 5—The Varmint (Five parts—Drama).
Aub. 12—Seven Keys to Baldpate (Five parts—Drama).
Aug. 12—The Law of the Land (Five parts—Drama).
Aug. 19—The Mysterious Miss Terry (Five parts—Drama).
Aug. 19—Hashimura Togo (Five parts—Dr.).
Aug. 26—Close to Nature (Five parts—Drama).
Aug. 26—Little Miss Optimist (Five parts—Drama).
Sept. 3—Rebecca of Sunnybrook Farm (Five parts—Drama).
Sept. 10—Barbary Sheep (Five parts—Drama).
Sept. 10.—The Hostage (Five parts—Drama).

PARAMOUNT-BURTON HOLMES.

Aug. 20—Tropical Nassau (Scenic).
Sept. 2—Madrid to Madeira (Scenic).
Sept. 2—Norway (Scenic).
Sept. 10—Hong Kong and the Pearl River (Scenic).

PARAMOUNT BRAY PICTOGRAPHS.

June 25.—No. 73. Subjects on reel. Fencing in Japan; American Match Making; States; Otto Luck to the Rescue (Cartoon).
July 2.—No. 74. Subjects on reel. Mechanical Operation of the British Tanks; Sports and Pastimes of the American Cowboys; Picto-Puzzles; War-time Economy.
July 9.—No. 75. Subjects on reel: Water Sports in Beautiful Hawaii; Unmasking The Oldest Railroad in the United States; Going to Sea in the Heart of New York; Bobby Bumps' "Fourth" (Cartoon).

Producers—Kindly Furnish Titles and D ates of All New Releases Before Saturday.

List of Current Film Release Dates

ON UNIVERSAL, METRO AND TRIANGLE PROGRAMS

(For Daily Calendar of Program Releases See Page 1578.)

Universal Film Mfg. Co.

ANIMATED WEEKLY.

July 11.—Number 80 (Topical).
July 18.—Number 81 (Topical).
July 26.—Number 82 (Topical).
Aug. 2.—Number 83 (Topical).
Aug. 9.—Number 84 (Topical).
Aug. 16.—Number 85 (Topical).
Aug. 23.—Number 86 (Topical).
Aug. 30.—Number 87 (Topical).
Sept. 6.—Number 88 (Topical).
Sept. 13.—Number 89 (Topical).

BISON.

Aug. 6.—The Soul Herder (Three parts—Dr.).
Aug. 20.—Squaring It (Three parts—Drama).
Aug. 27.—Jungle Treachery (Two parts—Dr.).
Sept. 3.—The Lure of the Circus (Two parts—Comedy—Drama), and Sierra Winter Sports (Scenic).
Sept. 10.—The Texas Sphinx (Two parts—Western Drama).

GOLD SEAL.

July 16.—Six Shooter Justice (Three parts—Drama).
July 23.—A Soldier of the Legion (Three parts—Drama).
July 30.—Right of Way Casey (Three parts—Drama).
Aug. 13.—A Wife's Suspicion (Three parts—Drama).
Aug. 27.—The Winning Pair (Three parts—Dr.).
Sept. 3.—The Empty Gun (Three parts—Dr.).
Sept. 10.—The Perilous Leap (Three parts—Railroad Drama).

JOKER.

July 16.—He Had 'Em Buffaloed (Comedy).
July 23.—Canning the Cannibal King (Comedy).
July 23.—The Soubrette.
July 30.—The Battling Bellboy (Comedy).
July 30.—The Stinger Stung (Comedy).
Aug. 6.—O My the Tent Mover (Comedy).
Aug. 6.—The Vamp of the Camp (Comedy).
Aug. 13.—Out Again, In Again (Comedy).
Aug. 13.—Back to the Kitchen (Comedy).
Aug. 20.—Behind the Map (Comedy).
Aug. 20.—Mrs. Madam Manager (Comedy).
Aug. 27.—Why They Left Home (Comedy).
Aug. 27.—Busting Into Society (Comedy).
Sept. 3.—Officer, Call a Cop (Comedy).
Sept. 3.—A Gale of Verse (Comedy).
Sept. 10.—Short, Skirts and Deep Water (Comedy).
Sept. 10.—Nearly a Queen (Comedy).

L-KO.

July 16.—Surf Scandal (Two parts—Comedy).
July 22.—The Sirn of the Cucumber (Two parts —Comedy).
July 30.—Blackboard and Blackmail (Two parts —Comedy).
Aug. 6.—The Little Fat Rascal (Two parts—Comedy).
Aug. 13.—Rough Stuff (Two parts—Comedy).
Aug. 20.—Street Cars and Carbuckles (Two parts —Comedy).
Aug. 27.—Props, Drone and Flops (Two parts—Comedy).
Sept. 3.—Backward Sons and Forward Daughters (Two parts—Comedy).
Sept. 10.—From Cactus to Kale (Two parts—Comedy).

NESTOR.

July 16.—A Dark Deed (Comedy).
July 23.—Seeing Things.
July 30.—Married by Accident (Comedy).
Aug. 6.—The Love Slacker (Comedy).
Aug. 13.—The Rushin' Dancers (Comedy).
Aug. 20.—Move Over (Comedy).
Aug. 27.—The Night Cap (Comedy).
Sept. 3.—Looking 'Em Over (Comedy).
Sept. 10.—The Boulevard Speed Hounds (Comedy).

POWERS.

July 16.—Box Car Bill Falls in Luck (Cartoon Comedy) and in the Heart of India (Educational).
July 23.—Hammon Egg's Reminiscences (Cartoon Comedy) and in The Land of Light and Gloom (Dorsey Edu.).
July 30.—The Good Liar (Cartoon) and "In Monkey Land" (Ditmar's Edu.).
Aug. 6.—Seeing Ceylon with Hy Mayer (Travelaugh).
Aug. 13.—Doing His Bit (Cartoon Comedy), and Aigleria, Old and New) (Scenic) (Split reel).
Aug. 20.—Colonel Pepper's Mobilized Farm (Cartoon Comedy), and "The Home Life of the Spider (Ditmar's Edu.) (Split Reel).

STAR FEATURETTE.

July 23.—The Beautiful Impostor (Two parts—Drama).
July 30.—The Woman Who Would Not Pay (Two parts—Society—Drama).
Aug. 6.—The Untamed (Two parts—Drama).
Aug. 13.—Cheyenne's Pal (Two parts—Drama).
Aug. 20.—The Golden Heart (Two parts—Dr.).
Aug. 27.—Hands in the Dark (Two parts—Dr., and Old French Towns (Short Scenic on Same Reel).
Sept. 3.—A Dream of Egypt (Two parts—Dr.).
Sept. 10.—To the Highest Bidder (Two parts—Society Drama).

VICTOR.

July 9.—The Paper Hanger's Revenge (Comedy).
July 9.—Kicked Out (Two parts—Comedy Drama).
July 16.—One Bride Too Many (Two parts—Comedy-Drama).
July 30.—Where Are My Trousers? (Two parts—Comedy.)
Aug. 6.—Like Babes in the Wood (Two parts—Juvenile Comedy).
Aug. 13.—The Brass Girl (Two parts—Comedy-Drama).
Aug. 20.—A Five Foot Ruler (Two parts—Comedy-Drama).
Aug. 27.—Scandal Everywhere (Comedy).
Sept. 3.—The Curse of a Flirting Heart (Com.).
Sept. 10.—In the Clutches of Milk (Comedy).

UNIVERSAL SCREEN MAGAZINE.

July 16.—Issue No. 28 (Educational).
July 23.—Issue No. 29 (Educational).
July 30.—Issue No. 30 (Educational).
Aug. 6.—Issue No. 31 (Educational).
Aug. 13.—Issue No. 32 (Topical).
Aug. 20.—Issue No. 33 (Educational).
Aug. 27.—Issue No. 34 (Educational).
Sept. 3.—Issue No. 35 (Educational).
Sept. 10.—Issue No. 36 (Educational).

UNIVERSAL SPECIAL FEATURE.

July 15.—The Gray Ghost (Episode No. 3—The Warning"—Two parts—Drama)
July 22.—The Gray Ghost (Episode No. 4—"The Fight"—Two parts—Drama).
July 29.—The Gray Ghost (Episode No. 5—"Plunder"—Two parts—Drama).
Aug. 6.—The Gray Ghost (Episode No. 6, "The House of Mystery"—Two parts—Drama).
Aug. 13.—The Gray Ghost (Episode No. 7) (The Double Floor) (Two parts—Drama).
Aug. 20.—The Gray Ghost (Episode No. 8, "The Pearl Necklace"—Two parts—Dr.).
Aug. 27.—The Gray Ghost (Episode No. 9—Title Not Reported—Two parts—Drama).
Sept. 3.—The Gray Ghost (Episode No. 10—Shadows—Two parts—Drama).
Sept. 10.—The Gray Ghost (Episode No. 11—Title not reported—Two parts—Drama).

UNIVERSAL CURRENT EVENTS.

July 14.—Issue No. 9 (Topical).
July 21.—Issue No. 10 (Topical).
July 28.—Issue No. 11 (Topical).
Aug. 4.—Issue No. 12 (Topical).
Aug. 10.—Issue No. 13 (Topical).
Aug. 17.—Issue No. 14 (Topical).
Aug. 24.—Issue No. 15 (Topical).
Aug. 31.—Issue No. 16 (Topical).
Sept. 7.—Issue No. 17 (Topical)..

Metro Pictures Corporation.

METRO PICTURES CORP.

July 2.—The Trail of the Shadow (Five parts —Drama).
July 9.—Peggy, the Will o' the Wisp (Five parts—Drama).
July 30.—Miss Robinson Crusoe (Five parts—Drama).
Special—The Slacker (Seven parts—Drama).
Aug. 6.—The Jury of Fate (Rolfe—Five parts—Drama).
Aug. 13.—The Girl Without a Soul (Five parts—Drama).
Aug. 27.—To the Death (Five parts—Drama).

YORKE FILM CORP.

July 16.—The Hidden Spring (Five parts—Dr.).
Sept. 3.—Under Handicap (Seven parts—Drama).

METRO COMEDIES.

July 16.—Blood Will Tell (Rolins).
July 23.—Mr. Parker—Hero (Drew).
July 30.—Henry's Ancestors (Drew).
Aug. 6.—His Ear for Music (Drew).
Aug. 13.—Her Economic Independence (Drew).
Aug. 20.—Her First Game (Drew).
Aug. 27.—The Patriot (Drew).

Triangle Film Corporation.

TRIANGLE PRODUCTION.

July 15.—The Sawdust Ring (Five parts—Dr.).
July 15.—The Mother Instinct (Five parts—Dr.).
July 22.—A Successful Failure (Five parts—Drama).
July 22.—Sudden Jim (Five parts—Drama).
July 29.—In Slumberland (Five parts—Drama).
July 29.—Borrowed Plumage (Five parts—Dr.).
Aug. 5.—The Food Gamblers (Five parts—Dr.).
Aug. 5.—An Even Break (Five parts—Drama).
Aug. 12.—Master of His Home (Five parts—Drama).
Aug. 12.—Golden Rule Kate (Five parts—Dr.).
Aug. 19.—Wee Lady Betty (Five parts—Drama).
Aug. 19.—They're Off (Five parts—Drama).
Aug. 26.—Wooden Shoes (Five parts—Drama).
Aug. 26.—Grafters (Five parts—Drama).
Sept. 2.—Ten of Diamonds (Five parts—Drama).
Sept. 2.—The Man Hater (Five parts—Drama).

TRIANGLE KOMEDY.

July 22.—His Fatal Move.
July 22.—An Innocent Villain.
July 29.—Sole Mates.
July 29.—His Widow's Might.
Aug. 5.—His Perfect Day.
Aug. 5.—A Matrimonial Accident.
Aug. 12.—His Cool Nerve.
Aug. 12.—A Hotel Disgrace.
Aug. 19.—A Love Chase.
Aug. 19.—His Hidden Talent.
Aug. 26.—Their Domestic Deception.
Aug. 26.—Her Donkey Love.
Sept. 2.—A Fallen Star.
Sept. 2.—His Foot-Hill Folly.

KEYSTONE.

July 22.—She Needed a Doctor (Two parts).
July 29.—Thirst (Two parts).
Aug. 5.—His Uncle Dudley (Two parts).
Aug. 12.—Lost—A Cook (Two parts).
Aug. 19.—The Pawnbroker's Heart (Two parts).
Aug. 26.—Two Crooks (Two parts).
Sept. 2.—A Shanghaied Jonah (Two parts Comedy).

PARALTA.

Rose O' Paradise.
A Man's Man.

Producers.—Kindly Furnish Titles and Dates of All New Releases Before Saturday.

List of Current Film Release Dates

MUTUAL PROGRAM AND MISCELLANEOUS FEATURES

(For Daily Calendar of Program Releases See Page 1578.)

Mutual Film Corp.

CUB.

July 19—Jerry's Star Bout (Comedy).
July 26—The Red, White and Blew (Comedy).
Aug. 2—Jerry's Big Stunt.
Aug. 9—Jerry on the Railroad (Comedy).
Aug. 16—Beach Nuts (Comedy).
Aug. 23—Jerry on the Farm (Comedy).
Aug. 30—Jerry's Eugenic Marriage (Comedy).
Sept. 6.—Jerry Tries Again (Comedy).

GAUMONT.

Aug. 7—Tours Around the World No. 40 (Subjects on reel: Down the Senegal River in French West Africa; Bruges, Belgium; Fishing Villages of France) (Travel).
Aug. 9—Reel Life No. 67 (Subjects on reel: An Undersea Garden; A Colored Baptizing; Electricity from the Heart; The Tallest Boy on Earth; Making Schools Safe; Animated Drawing from "Life"; "Not a Shadow of a Doubt"; "A Bomb and a Boomerang" (a war cartoon) (Mutual Film Magazine).
Aug. 16—Reel Life No. 68 (Subjects on Reel: Young Men's Christian Association; Learning to Be a Soldier; The Absent-Minded Dentist; An Animated Drawing from "Life" (Mutual Film Magazine).
Aug. 23—Reel Life No. 69 (Subjects on Reel: Hunting Alligators for Their Skins; Harvesting Potatoes on the Eastern Coast; Coney Island Thrills; Oil from Japan; Something Going to Happen; An Animated Cartoon from "Life."
Aug. 30—Reel Life No. 70 (Subjects on Reel: Using the Abalone, a Little Known Industry of the Pacific Coast; A Boy and a Rope; Handling the Mail; Beach Sports of California; "The March of Science" and "What a Bachelor Sees at a Wedding" are animated drawings from "Life."
Sept. 6—Reel Life No. 71. Subjects (on reel: A Watering System for a Small Farm; Pets Which Will Never Be Popular; Handling the Mail; The Five Senses; Drawing from "Life."

LA SALLE.

July 24—A Match in Quarantine.
July 31—Man Proposes (Comedy).
Aug. 7—Pigs and Pearls (Comedy).
Aug. 14—The Widow's Might (Comedy).

MUTUAL WEEKLY.

July 18—Number 132 (Topical).
July 25—Number 134 (Topical).
Aug. 1—Number 135 (Topical).
Aug. 8—Number 136 (Topical).
Aug. 15—Number 137 (Topical).
Aug. 22—Number 138 (Topical).
Aug. 29—Number 139 (Topical).
Sept. 5—Number 140 (Topical).

MUTUAL CHAPLIN

April—The Cure (Two parts—Comedy).
June 23—The Immigrant (Two parts—Com.).

MUTUAL STAR PRODUCTIONS.

July 16—Betty Be Good (Horkheimer—Five parts—Drama).
July 23—Mellen of the Hills (Five parts—Dr.).
July 30—Pride and the Man (Five parts—Dr.).
Aug. 6—Souls in Pawn (American—Five parts —Drama).
Aug. 13—The Fuel of Life (Horkheimer—Five parts—Drama).
Sept. 3.—Reputation (Goodrich—Five parts— Drama).
Sept. 3.—Charity Castle (American—Five parts Drama).

MUTUAL SPECIAL.

July 23—The Great Stanley Secret (Chapter No. 1, The Gipsy's Trust—Four parts—Drama—North American).
July 30—The Great Stanley Secret (Chapter No. 2, "Fate and the Child"—Four parts —Drama—North American).

SIGNAL PRODUCING CO.

July 9—The Railroad Raiders (Chapter No. 14—"The Trap"—Two parts—Dr.).
July 16—The Railroad Raiders (Chapter No. 15, "The Mystery of the Counterfeit Tickets"—Two parts—Drama).

Feature Releases

ART DRAMAS, INC.

Aug. 7—Eye of Envy (Five parts—Drama).
Aug. 13—Think It Over (U. S. Amusement Corp. —Five parts—Comedy-Drama).
Aug. 27—The Little Samaritan (Erbograph —Five parts—Drama).
Sept. 3.—Behind the Mask (U. S. Amusement Co.—Five parts—Drama).

BLUEBIRD PHOTOPLAY, INC.

Aug. 6—The Clean-Up (Five parts—Drama).
Aug. 13—The Show Down (Five parts—Drama).
Aug. 20—Mr. Opp (Five Parts—Drama).
Aug. 27—The Charmer (Five parts—Drama).
Sept. 3—Triumph (Five parts—Comedy-Dr.).
Sept. 3.—Mother O' Mine (Five Parts—Drama —Special).
Sept. 10—A Stormy Knight (Five parts—Comedy-Drama).

BUTTERFLY PICTURES.

Aug. 6—Follow the Girl (Five parts—Dr.).
Aug. 13—The Midnight Man (Five parts—Dr.).
Aug. 20—The Lair of the Wolf (Five parts— Drama).
Aug. 27—Straight Shooting (Five parts—Dr.).
Sept. 3—Who Was the Other Man? (Five parts —Drama).
Sept. 10.—The Little Pirate (Five parts— Drama).

CINEMA WAR NEWS SYNDICATE.

Aug. 4—American War News Weekly No. 14 (Topical).
Aug. 11—American War News Weekly No. 15 (Topical).
Aug. 18—American War News Weekly No. 16 (Topical).

EDUCATIONAL FILM CORP.

Aug. 6—Living Book of Nature (Mounting Butterflies).
Aug. 5—Alaska Wonders in Motion No. 4 (Scenic and Educational).
Aug. 13—Living Book of Nature, "Animals in Winter" (Ditmars).
Aug. 15—The Hard, Hard Road to Adventure (Bruce).
Aug. 20—Living Book of Nature, "Ancestors of the Horse" (Ditmars).
Aug. 22—China and the Chinese, No. 5.

FOX FILM CORP.

Special Release—Jack and the Beanstalk (Ten parts—Drama).
July 29—Wife Number Two (Five parts—Dr.).
Aug. 4—Wrath of Love (Five parts—Drama).
Aug. 11—Durand of the Bad Lands (Five parts —Drama).
Aug. 18—The Soul of Satan (Five parts—Dr.).
Aug. 25—Every Girl's Dream (Five parts—Dr.).
Sept. 1—Betrayed (Five parts—Drama).
Sept. 9.—When False Tongues Speak (Five parts—Drama).

FOXFILM COMEDIES.

July 29—A Soft Tenderfoot (Two parts).
Aug. 6—A Domestic Hound (Two parts).

GREATER VITAGRAPH (V-L-S-E).

Aug. 13—Mary Jane's Pa (Five parts—Drama).
Aug. 20—Transgression (Five parts—Drama).
Aug. 27—The Divorcee (Five parts—Drama).
Aug. 6—Bobby, Boy Scout (Comedy-Drama).
Aug. 13—Bobby, the Movie Director (Comedy).
Aug. 20—Bobby, Philanthropist (Comedy-Dr.).
Aug. 27—Bobby, Pacifist (Comedy-Drama).
Sept. 3—Bobby's Bravery (Comedy-Drama).
Sept. 3.—Soldiers of Chance (Five parts.— Drama).
Sept. 10.—An Alabaster Box (Five parts— Drama).

KLEINE-EDISON-SELIG-ESSANAY.

Aug. 13—The Barker (Selig—Five parts—Dr.).
Aug. 15—The Bridge of Fancy (One of the "Do Children Count?" Series—Two parts —Drama).
Aug. 18—Conquest Program No. 6 (Subjects: The Customary Two Weeks (Four parts—Drama); The Story of Plymouth Rock (1,000 feet); The Grand Canyon of Arizona (500 feet); The Four P's (500 feet); Nature's Perfect Thread Spinner (500 feet); The Magic of Spring (500 feet).
Aug. 20—Open Places (Essanay—Five parts.— Drama).
Aug. 22—The Kingdom of Hope (One of the "Do Children Count?" Series—Two parts—Drama).
Aug. 20—A Trip to Chinatown (Selig-Hoyt Comedy—Two parts).
Aug. 27—The Lady of the Photograph (Edison —Five parts—Drama).
Aug. 25—Conquest Program No. 7 (Subjects: T. Haviland Hicks, Freshman (Three parts—Drama); Gallagher (Two parts—Drama); Turning Out Silver Bullets (One reel); Young Salts and the Holy Land (Combined in one reel).
Sept. 3—Efficiency Edgar's Courtship (Five parts—Drama—Essanay).
Sept. 3—A Midnight Bell (Hoyt Comedy—Two parts).
Sept. 1—Conquest Program Nos. 8 (Edison). Subjects: The Princess' Necklace (Four Parts—Drama); The Puzzling Bill-Board and Its Old England (Split Reel); The Brook, and Woodcraft for Boys; Shipping Live Fish (Split reel); The Blind Fiddler (One reel).

SELZNICK PICTURES.

The Lash of Jealousy (Drama).
The Lesson (Drama).
The Moth (Drama).
The Wild Girl.

STANDARD PICTURES.

Aug. 19—The Spy (Ten parts).
Aug. 26—The Honor System (Ten parts).
Sept. 2—Jack and the Beanstalk (Ten parts).
Sept. 16—The Conqueror (Ten parts).

WHOLESOME FILMS DRAMA.

Sept. 3—The Penny Philanthropist (Five parts —Drama).
Sept. 3—Cinderella and the Magic Slipper (Four parts—Drama).

WORLD PICTURES.

July 16—When True Love Dawns (Brady-International—Five parts—Drama).
July 23—A Self-Made Widow (Five parts—Dr.).
July 30—Youth (Five parts—Drama).
Aug. 6—The Iron Ring (Five parts—Drama).
Aug. 13—Souls Adrift (Five parts—Drama).
Aug. 20—The Little Duchess (Five parts—Dr.).
Aug. 27—Her Guardian (Five parts—Drama).
Sept. 3—The Marriage Market (Five parts— Drama).
Sept. 10—Betsy Ross (Five parts—Drama).

Producers.—Kindly Furnish Titles and Dates of All New Releases Before Saturday.

List of State Rights Pictures

(For Daily Calendar of Program Releases See Page 1578.)

Note—For further information regarding pictures listed on this page, address State Rights Department, Moving Picture World, and same will be gladly furnished.

ARIZONA FILM CO.
May—Should She Obey (Drama).

BERNSTEIN FILM PRODUCTION.
Humility (First of "Seven Cardinal Virtues"—Drama).
June—Who Knows? (Six parts—Drama).

J. FRANK BROCKLISS, INC.
U. S. Navy (Five parts).
Terry Human Interest Reels (900 Feet Every Other Week).
Russian Revolution (Three parts).
Land of the Rising Sun (10,000 feet—issued complete or in series of 2,000 feet or 5,000 feet).

BUD FISHER FILMS CORP.
Mutt and Jeff Animated Cartoons.

CAMERAGRAPH FILM MFG. CO.
June—What of Your Boy? (Three parts—Patriotic).
June—The Automobile Owner Gets Acquainted With His Automobile (Educational).

CARONA CINEMA CO.
May—The Curse of Eve (Seven parts—Dr.).

CENTURY COMEDIES.
May—Balloonatics.
May—Neptune's Naughty Daughter.
May—Automaniacs.
June—Alice of the Sawdust (Two parts).

BENJAMIN CHAPIN PRODUCTIONS.
(The Lincoln Cycle Pictures.)
My Mother (Two parts).
My Father (Two parts).
Myself (Two parts).
The Call to Arms (Two parts).

CHRISTIE FILM CO.
July 2—Almost a Scandal (Comedy).
July 9—The Fourteenth Man (Comedy).
July 16—Down By the Sea (Comedy).
July 23—Skirts (Comedy).
July 30—Won in a Cabaret (Comedy).
Aug. 7—His Merry Mix-Up (Comedy).
Aug. 14—A Smokey Love Affair (Comedy).

CINEMA DISTRIBUTING CORP.
June—The 13th Labor of Hercules (Twelve single parts).

CORONET FILM CORP.
Living Studies in Natural History.
Animal World—Issue No. 1.
Animal World—Issue No. 2.
Birdland Studies.
Horticultural Phenomena.

COSMOFOTOFILM, INC.
March—The Manx-Man (Eight parts—Drama).
June—I Believe (Seven parts—Drama).

E. I. S. MOTION PICTURES CORP.
Trooper 44 (Five parts—Drama).

EMERALD MOTION PICTURE CO.
May—The Slacker (Military Drama).

EXPORT AND IMPORT FILM CO.
June—Robespierre.
June—Ivan, the Terrible.

FAIRMOUNT FILM CORP.
June—Hate (Seven parts—Drama).

FLORA FINCH FILM CO.
"War Prides" (Two parts—Comedy).

FORT PITT CORPORATION.
The Italian Battlefront.

FRATERNITY FILMS, INC.
May—Devil's Playground (Nine parts—Drama).

FRIEDMAN ENTERPRISES.
A Mormon Maid (Six parts—Drama).

FRIEDER FILM CORP.
June—A Bit o'. Heaven (Five parts—Drama).

FROHMAN AMUSEMENT CORP.
April—God's Man (Nine parts—Drama).

JOSEPH M. GAITES.
August—The Italian Battlefront.

GOLDIN FEATURES.
A Bit of Life (One Reel Comedy-Drama).

GRAPHIC FEATURES.
April—The Woman and the Beast (Five parts—Drama).

F. G. HALL PRODUCTIONS, INC.
May—Her Fighting Chance (Seven parts—Dr.). (Mr. Hall has world rights to this picture.)
May—The Bar Sinister (Drama). (Mr. Hall has world rights to this picture.)

HANOVER FILM CO.
April—How Uncle Sam Prepares (Topical).

HILLER & WILK.
April—The Battle of Gettysburg.
April—The Wrath of the Gods (Drama).

HISTORIC FEATURES.
June—Christus (Eight parts—Drama).

ILIDOR PICTURES CORP.
June.—The Fall of the Romanoffs (Drama).

IVAN FILM PRODUCTIONS.
Apr. ——One Law 1er Both (8 parts—Drama).
August—Babbling Tongues (Six parts—Dr.).

JEWEL PRODUCTIONS, INC.
Pay Me (Drama).

KING BEE FILMS CORP.
June 15—Dough Nuts (Two parts—Comedy).
July 1—Cupid's Rival (Two parts—Comedy).
July 15—The Villain (Two parts—Comedy).
Aug. 1—The Millionaire (Two parts—Com.).
Aug. 8—The Genius (Two parts—Comedy).
Aug. 15—The Modiste (Two parts—Comedy).

A KAY CO.
Some Barrier (Terry Cartoon Burlesque).
His Trial (Terry Cartoon Burlesque).
Terry Human Interest Reel No. 1 (Character As Revealed in the Face).
Terry Human Interest Reel No. 2 (Character As Revealed in the Eyes).

KLOTZ & STREIMER.
June—Whither Thou Goest (Five parts—Drama).
June—The Secret Trap (Five parts—Drama).

MAYFAIR FILM CORP.
Persuasive Peggy (Drama).

MILES.
April—The Test of Womanhood (Five parts—Drama).

MOE STREIMER.
June—A Daughter of the Don (Ten parts—Drama).

B. S. MOSS MOTION PICTURE CORP.
January—In the Hands of the Law (Drama).
April—Birth Control (Five parts—Drama).

NEVADA MOTION PICTURE CORP.
June—The Planter (Drama).

NEWFIELDS PRODUCING CORP.
Alma, Where Do You Live? (Six parts—Dr.).

OGDEN PICTURES CORP.
August—The Lust of the Ages (Drama).

PARAGON FILMS, INC.
The Whip (Eight parts—Drama).

PETER PAN FILM CORP.
Mo-Toy Troupe (Release No. 2—"Jimmy Wins the Pennant").
Mo-Toy Troupe (Release No. 3—"Out in the Rain").
Mo-Toy Troupe (Release No. 4—"In the Jungle Land").
Mo-Toy Troupe (Release No. 5—"A Kitchen Romance").
Mo-Toy Troupe (Release No. 6—"Mary and Gretel").
Mo-Toy Troupe (Release No. 7—"Dinkling of the Circus").
Mo-Toy Troupe (Release No. 8—"A Trip to the Moon").
Mo-Toy Troupe (Release No. 9, "Golden Locks and the Three Bears").
Mo-Toy Troupe (Release No 10, "Dolly Doings").
Mo-Toy Troupe (Release No. 11 "School Days").

PUBLIC RIGHTS FILM CORP.
June—The Public Be Damned.

PURKALL FILM CO.
July—The Liar (Six parts—Drama).

RENOWNED PICTURES. CORP.
June—In Treason's Grasp (Five parts—Drama).

REX BEACH PICTURES CO.
March—The Barrier (Nine parts—Drama).

SELECT PHOTOPLAY CO.
May—Humanity (Six parts—Drama).

WILLIAM N. SELIG.
April—The Garden of Allah
May—Beware of Strangers (Eight parts—Dr.).

FRANK J. SENG.
May—Parentage (Drama).

SHERMAN PICTURE CORP.
July—Corruption (Six parts—Drama).
August—I Believe.

SKOBELOFF COMMITTEE.
The Great Russian Revolution.
Behind the Battle Line in Russia.

JULIUS STEGER.
May—Redemption (Six parts—Drama).

SUPREME FEATURE FILMS, INC.
May—Trip Through China (Ten parts).

ULTRA FILMS, INC.
A Day at West Point (Educational).
West in West.
Rustlers' Frame-Up at Big Horn.

UNIVERSAL (STATE RIGHTS).
May—The Hand that Rocks the Cradle (Six parts—Drama).
June—The Cross-Eyed Submarine (Three parts—Comedy).
June—Come Through (Seven parts—Drama).

E. WARREN PRODUCTION.
April—The Warfare of the Flesh (Drama).

WHARTON, INC.
June—The Great White Trail (Seven parts) (Drama).

WILLIAMSON BROS.
April—The Submarine Eye (Drama).

Producers.—Kindly Furnish Titles and Dates of All New Releases Before Saturday.

Fire=safety
for your audience

Safeguard your patrons against the dangers of sudden fire and panic. Provide against emergencies by hanging J-M Fire Extinguishers along the walls of your theatre, so your employees can make short work of a blaze. You'll find it a paying policy to protect your audiences.

Fire-safety for your investment, too—for unless you snuff out the fire before it has a chance· to g r o w dangerous, your losses may run to big figures.   And the Johns-Manville Fire Extinguisher will smother any incipient fire, whether from grease, oil, gasoline, or ·electric arcs. It's a real investment in safety, at minimum cost.

Discharged by simple hand pumping—or in close quarters where there's no room to pump, by air pressure previously pumped up and released by opening the nozzle. This valuable two-way operation is an exclusive Johns-Manville feature.
The Johns-Manville ·Fire Extinguisher is examined, approved and labeled by the Underwriters' Laboratories, Inc., under the direction of the National Board of Fire Underwriters.

Price in United States:
East of Colorado, $10.00
Brass or Nickel Finish,
Bracket included
$10.50 Colorado and West

Dominion of Canada:
$12.00 East of Calgary
$12.50 Calgary and West

H. W. Johns-Manville Co.
NEW YORK CITY
10 Factories—Branches in 54 Large Cities

Johns-Manville
Fire Extinguisher

In answering advertisements, please mention The Moving Picture World

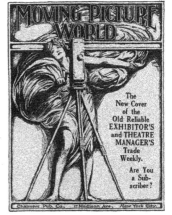

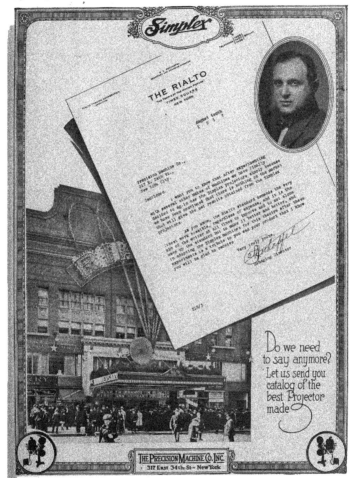

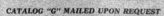

Goldwyn pictures

The most talked-of
motion picture product
in the entire world

And deservedly so,
because they are
the best.

Essanay's new comedy
drama vein in
pictures has hit
the psychological
need of the hour.
Give your patrons
what. They want
by booking these
pictures at any
Kleine distributing
exchange today.

Geo. K. Spoor.

For all Exhibitors
73 Universal Exchanges now specializing on the

Twice-A-Week News Service
UNIVERSAL ANIMATED WEEKLY
UNIVERSAL CURRENT EVENTS

EXTRA
EXTRA

New York's thrilling "GOOD-BYE" parade to her soldiers, with wonderful Fifth avenue scenes, released on our Twice - A - Week-News-Service WITHOUT ONE CENT EXTRA COST TO EXHIBITORS.

—enabling all Exhibitors to secure the combined big winners—The Universal Animated Weekly—and—The Universal Current Events—for months first with the biggest news events of the entire world.

Compare our release dates with competition and you'll see how far in advance the "U" Animated is. This plus the popularity of the "U" Screen Magazine has given to Exhibitors the week's biggest crowd-getter —the Universal's TWICE-A-WEEK-NEWS-SERVICE, especially now during war time.

The demand for the "U" TWICE-A-WEEK-NEWS-SERVICE has prompted us to offer OPEN BOOKINGS. Things have changed in News Weeklies. Time was when the loudest shouter and biggest Trade Paper advertiser got the business. Exhibitors can't be bunkoed any more, by mere loud talk or lavishness in advertising spaces. Exhibitors have demanded the best news first. The Universal's TWICE-A-WEEK-NEWS-SERVICE is the answer. It is sweeping the country, delighting millions and bringing the crowds to thousands of theatres. It has no competition. There's nothing like it. You can book the TWICE-A-WEEK-NEWS-SERVICE thru any Universal Exchange or communicate with the

UNIVERSAL
ANIMATED WEEKLY
1600 Broadway **New York City**

In Answering Advertisements, Please Mention the MOVING PICTURE WORLD.

GEORGE BEBAN

in

"Lost in Transit"

TEEMING with romance—touched with pathos. An exhilarating love theme that will carry an audience spellbound to the end.

Everybody likes a good love story—everybody is going to see George Beban in this one.

Let them know you have it and the rest is easy.

Picturized by Gardner Hunting.
From the story by Kathlyn Williams.
Directed by Donald Crisp.

A Paramount Picture

J. STUART BLACKTON

SERIES

"The World for Sale"

"TEKEWANA"

the proud old Indian chief, who fairly breathes the spirit
of the Great Northwest, is fittingly typified by one of his
own blood, CRAZY THUNDER in this story of the Great
Northwest and racial conflict

By Sir Gilbert Parker

Thousands of the readers of this author's books will want
to see this picture.

Paramount Pictures Corporation
FOUR-EIGHTY-FIVE   FIFTH AVENUE   FORTY-FIRST ST
NEW YORK
Controlled by FAMOUS PLAYERS-LASKY CORPORATION
ADOLPH ZUKOR, Pres.   JESSE L. LASKY, Vice-Pres.
CECIL B. DeMILLE, Director General

Paramount Pictures

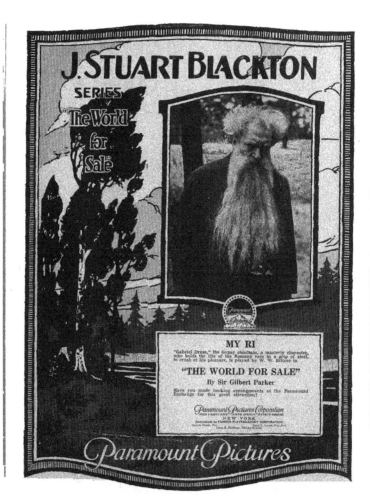

WALLACE REID
in "THE HOSTAGE"

A Timely Story
of military life with the trenches left out. Crammed with romance, adventures and a rare touch of humor that makes the grim profession of the god Mars take on a sunnier aspect.

You'll be doing yourself and your patrons a good turn when you show a picture like this in these times.

Picturized by Beulah Marie Dix
Staged by Robert Thornby
Presented by Jesse L. Lasky

Paramount Pictures Corporation
FOUR EIGHTY-FIVE FIFTH AVENUE &-FORTY-NINTH
NEW YORK
Controlled by FAMOUS PLAYERS-LASKY CORPORATION
ADOLPH ZUKOR, Pres.　JESSE L. LASKY, Vice-Pres.
Cecil B. DeMille, Director General

A Paramount Picture

Who is "Number One"?
BY ANNA KATHARINE GREEN

the Story
A brand-new story
brim-full of hair-crisping
situations and baffling
intrigue by that arch-
priestess of mystery—
Anna Katharine Green

the Picture
A fifteen episode serial
into whose making and
marketing will be put the
genius that has made
Paramount Pictures
stand alone

the Combi-
nation
Two great powers—Anna
Katharine Green and
Paramount — are at the
Exhibitor's service in

Who is "Number One"?
BY ANNA KATHARINE GREEN

the first
Paramount Serial

READY IN OCTOBER

Paramount Pictures Corporation
FOUR EIGHTY FIVE   FIFTH AVENUE   & FORTY FIRST ST.
NEW YORK, N.Y.

Controlled by FAMOUS PLAYERS-LASKY CORP.
ADOLPH ZUKOR, Pres.   JESSE L. LASKY, Vice-Pres.   CECIL B. DeMILLE, Dir. Gen.

Kathleen ......

the Star

The rest of her name is Clifford ✧ She is the lovely, brilliantly daring star of the first *Paramount Serial* ·········

Who is *"Number One"?*
BY ANNA KATHARINE GREEN

the Girl

A spring-time girl is Kathleen ✧ She flits through Anna Katharine Green's startling creation like a tinted butterfly

Number One

The biggest story ✧ the daintiest star and *Paramount* promotion ✧ Make Who is *"Number One"?*
BY ANNA KATHARINE GREEN

number one on your serial list ··············

Ready in October·

Paramount Pictures Corporation
FOUR EIGHTY FIVE   FIFTH AVENUE   AT FORTY FIRST ST.
NEW YORK, N.Y.
Controlled by FAMOUS PLAYERS-LASKY, CORP.
ADOLPH ZUKOR, Pres.   JESSE L. LASKY, Vice-Pres.   CECIL B. DEMILLE, Dir. Gen.

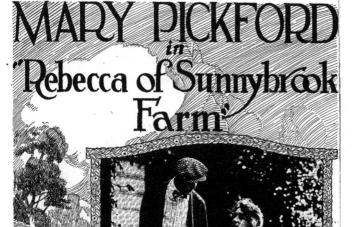

MARY PICKFORD
in
'Rebecca of Sunnybrook Farm'

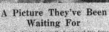

A Picture They've Been Waiting For

Thousands of people know the heroine of this famous story and want to see her come to life on the screen. Hundreds of thousands will want to see "Little Mary's" interpretation of "Rebecca." Millions will want to see this famous story just because it's a Mary Pickford picture.

You don't care why they want to see it—it's enough to know that everybody will want to.

From the play by Kate Douglas Wiggin and Charlotte Thompson. Picturized by Frances Marion. Staged by Marshall Neilan.

ARTCRAFT PICTURES CORPORATION
729 SEVENTH AVE.   NEW YORK CITY
Controlled by FAMOUS PLAYERS-LASKY CORPORATION

Elsie Ferguson

ARTCRAFT PICTURES CORPORATION
729 SEVENTH AVE. NEW YORK CITY
Controlled by FAMOUS PLAYERS-LASKY CORPORATION

in "Barbary Sheep"

From the Novel by Robert Hichens
Scenario by Charles Maigne
Directed by Maurice Tourneur

A DISCOVERY

That is the judgment of all who have seen this wonderful star in this superb picture

Adapted from the popular novel

"BARBARY SHEEP"

By ROBERT HICHENS
Picturized by Charles Maigne
Staged by **MAURICE TOURNEUR**

Elsie Ferguson's great histrionic ability has had wide scope—to the end that this piece of work will go down in film history as one of the greatest attractions of the time.

You will want to secure all the Elsie Ferguson Artcraft Pictures now.

Geo.

"7 Keys to Baldpate"

(From New York World)

The World Says—

'BALDPATE' ON SCREEN CROWDS THE RIALTO

"Seven Keys to Baldpate," in moving picture form, was shown at the Rialto theater yesterday before crowds that packed the house several times In the evening several hundred persons were so anxious to see the film that they waited over an hour outside the theatre until the first crowd left and the second showing began.

"Seven Keys to Baldpate" is one of the best examples of George M. Cohan's playwriting skill. Those who have never seen it on the stage should certainly seize the chance afforded by its reflection on the moving picture screen; while more fortunate persons — and many were among the spectators last night—may greet the story as an old friend.

Why Shouldn't the Yankee Doodle Boy—

GEORGE M. COHAN
in
"Seven Keys to Baldpate"

By GEORGE M. COHAN
founded on the novel by Earl Derr Biggers
(Published by Bobbs Merrill & Co.)
Directed by Hugh Ford

Crowd YOUR theater?

Cohan

TERROR extraordinary screen story ROMANOFFS

THE CZARINA (Nance O'Neil)

ARENA (Pauline Curley)

ILIODOR (himself)

RASPUTIN (Edward Connelly)

KERENSKY (Charles Chaplin)

PRINCE FELIX (Conway Tearle)

GRAND DUKE NICHOLAS (Charles Craig)

FEOFAN (William O'Shay)

SONIA (Mlle. Marcelle)

ANNA (Betty Glantz)

THE CZAR (Alfred Hickman)

THE KAISER (George Duneburg)

Produced by Special Arrangement with Mr Lewis J. Selznick and the Herbert Brenon Film Corporation

Address All Communications
ILIODOR PICTURE CORPORATION
729 Seventh Avenue

PHOTOGRAPHED BY
J. ROY HUNT

Coming:

Perfection Pictures
"The Highest Standard   In Motion Pictures"

Screen Literature!
Especially chosen
stories-the best works
of contemporary fic-
tion. Produced with
great care. ~ Plays
aptly branded –
-*PERFECTION!*

Details Next Week!

Coming:

Perfection Pictures

"The Highest Standard ƍ In Motion Pictures"

Five and six reel productions from the pens of prominent authors -staged by competent directors-produced by America's pioneer picture producers. ∽ Attractions described in one word- -*PERFECTION!*

Details Next Week!

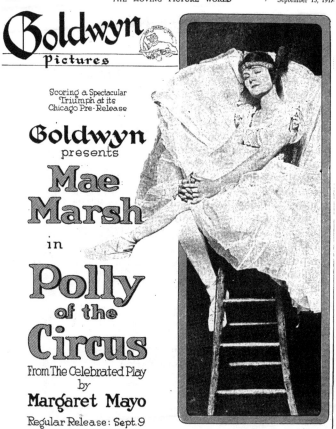

Goldwyn
Pictures

Scoring a Spectacular
Triumph at its
Chicago Pre-Release

Goldwyn
presents

Mae
Marsh

in

Polly
of the
Circus

From The Celebrated Play
by
Margaret Mayo
Regular Release: Sept. 9

Here Is A Screen Combination That Guarantees Assured Profits for Exhibitors

Goldwyn pictures

The Next Great Box Office
Favorite Who Will Make
Exhibitors Tremendous Profits

Goldwyn
presents

Madge & Kennedy
in

Baby Mine

From The Celebrated Play
by
Margaret Mayo

"Goldwyn" Has More Than Fulfilled Its Promises of Magnificent Productions" Boston Record

Goldwyn Pictures

Goldwyn
presents:

The International Beauty

Maxine Elliott
in

The Eternal Magdalene

by Robert McLaughlin

The First Great Morality Play of The Screen – Greater Than The Huge Stage Successes "Everywoman" and "Experience"

The New York City Press Said:

The Evening World.

"Circulation Books Open to All."   "Circulation Books Open to All."

NEW YORK,   TUESDAY,   AUGUST 14, 1917.   14 PAGES

"THE MANXMAN"
A STRIKING PICTURE OF HALL CAINE'S NOVEL

"The Manxman," Hall Caine's famous novel, had its first screen presentation at the Criterion Theatre last night, and ran such successful opposition to hot weather that it kept a capacity audience literally bound to the chairs for two hours.

"The Manxman" is an unqualified success. It is a big, gripping picture, filled with the stern, grim characters with which Mr. Caine peopled his novel. From the point of photography and setting, it is as near perfect as the most enthusiastic picture fan could wish. When frequent applause greets scenes in which the only action is provided by drifting clouds, or angry waves breaking on the rugged Manx coast—scenes in which humans play no part—sufficient has been said of the picture's photographic merits.

As for the cast, which is large, much might be written. The characters are as real as if Mr. Caine himself had suddenly discovered somewhere on the Isle of Man the men, women and children he put in his story and turned them over en masse to George Loane Tucker expressly for the purpose of making a motion picture. It would be difficult to single out any individual in awarding the laurels, but if this were to be done, Fred Groves, the Pete of the picture, would win without question. He has brought to the part an interpretation and a skill at delineating what this author wrote into the character that has seldom been seen on Broadway. Elizabeth Risdon as Kate Cregeen and Henry Ainley as Philip Christian complete the list of principals with well nigh perfect acting. Practically the same might be said of the remainder of the huge cast, even including three children, ranging apparently from six months to five years in age.

With story, cast, photography and setting on such a high plane of merit, it only remained for Mr. Tucker to add to the whole the element of the spectacular. This was not lacking, for the big scenes showed 11,000 people in the camera's range, including a regiment of real British soldiers, survivors of the Battle of the Marne. In these scenes the same skilful direction was evident.

The story of "The Manxman" is too well known to be dwelt upon. The picture is new to New York, but it is safe to say that few real picture fans will fail to see it.

MR. FOREIGN BUYER

Our Organization is welded
together like an endless chain.
Our Productions are worthy
of our reputation—
Our Reputation is our big asset.
Our Productions are Standard
and are selected by experts who
know your requirements as
well as you know them yourself.

INTER-OCEAN FILM CORPORATION

Henry J. Brock, Pres.   Paul H. Cromelin, Vice-Pres.

220 W. 42nd St.   NEW YORK CITY

"THE WORLD OUR FIELD"

LARGEST DISTRIBUTORS OF FILMS IN FOREIGN FIELDS

In this month's Mutual releases you see an example of the "Big Stars Only" Policy adopted by the Mutual Film Corporation. We open the season of 1917-18 this month with a further fulfillment of our pledge of "Big Stars Only."

The week of September 3rd we present Mary Miles Minter in "Charity Castle" and Edna Goodrich in "Reputation."

The week of September 10th we present Gail Kane in "The Bride's Silence" and Ann Murdock in "Outcast"—first of the great Charles Frohman Successes in Motion Pictures.

The week of September 17th we present Juliette Day, the charming ingenué of "Upstairs and Down" in "The Rainbow Girl" and Margarita Fischer in "The Girl Who Couldn't Grow Up."

The week of September 24th we present William Russell in "Sands of Sacrifice" and Julia Sanderson in "The Runaway"—second of the Charles Frohman Successes in Motion Pictures.

Eight big feature attractions for September—*Two Mutual Pictures—"Big Stars Only"—Every Week!*

Is this not a splendid demonstration to the Exhibitors of America of the fulfillment of our pledge —"Big Stars Only"? There is value—*sound, substantial box-office value*—in these high class Mutual Pictures. The intelligent Exhibitor will see in these attractions his opportunity for *higher admission prices and bigger profits.*

President
Mutual Film Corporation

"Big Stars Only"
Value in Mutual Pictures

AMERICAN FILM COMPANY, INC., *Presents*

GAIL KANE *in*
"THE BRIDE'S SILENCE"

A powerful five-act mystery drama. By
Daniel F. Whitcomb. Directed by Henry
King. Released the week of Sept. 10th.

One of the most baffling mystery stories ever
unfolded on the screen. An attraction that
should be held for a run of from three days
to a solid week at any theatre. Now booking
at all Mutual Exchanges.

Produced by
AMERICAN FILM COMPANY, INC.
SAMUEL S. HUTCHINSON, President

Distributed by
MUTUAL FILM CORPORATION
JOHN R. FREULER, President

HELEN
HOLMES

Filmdom's foremost serial star—known the world
over as the most daring actress in Screenland—
admired and worshiped by hundreds of thousands
of picture-goers—performs still more wonderful and
dangerous exploits in "The Lost Express"—the
big 15 chapter mystery serial, directed by J. P.
McGowan. Released September 17th. Now booking at all Mutual Film Exchanges.

Produced by
SIGNAL FILM CORPORATION
Samuel S. Hutchinson, *President*

THEY SAY

H. H. LUSTIG, *Manager Angela Theatre, Cleveland, Ohio, Says:*—"I attribute the remarkable increase in my Sunday receipts to Helen Holmes and I prefer a serial starring Helen Holmes to any other serial on the market."

WILLIAM D. SCOVILLE, *Manager Idle Hour Theatre, Kansas City, Mo., Says:*—"Why shouldn't I be Helen fishing? Featuring her in serials, in Sundays has made that my best-paying day. Despite being on a 5c street, Helen Holmes day is always a 10c day with me."

IN THE LOST EXPRESS

Directed by
J·P·M^cGOWAN

JEWEL

PRODUCTIONS INC.

JEWEL Productions are a direct answer to the national demand of the show-man to "get away from the old and give us something new."

Jewel Productions, Inc., is not a producing concern. Its sole business is to market fine pictures. It will buy negatives outright or it will book them for the producer on percentage, solely on the basis of merit.

We may release a picture a month —or not more than five or six a year— entirely according to the supply of pictures that are up to the high standard we hope to maintain.

We have thus far acquired the rights to only five pictures after examining a large number.

🙟

One was made by Edwin Thanhouser, with the intention of selling it on the state rights plan; but we secured the world's rights.

🙟

Three are from the Universal Film Manufacturing Co.

🙟

One is from Lois Weber.

🙟

All are of the calibre referred to in the trade as "state rights" quality—a quality that will stand the acid test of a Broadway run.

🙟

We have given our offices four of these great plays as a beginning. The fifth we will hold back until later in the season. The four that are now ready for bookings are:

🙟

"Come Through"—George Bronson Howard's greatest melodrama.

🙟

"The Man Without a Country"—the patriotic classic.

🙟

"Sirens of the Sea"—the picture beautiful.

🙟

"Pay Me"—a big drama of the West.

🙟

You may see these plays and arrange for bookings at any of the following offices, already established:

🙟

In New York—Jewel Productions.
　　1600 Broadway.
In Chicago—Jewel Productions.
　　220 S. State St.
In Pittsburgh—Jewel Productions.
　　1201 Liberty Ave.
In Detroit—Jewel Productions.
　　205 Griswold St.
In Cleveland—Jewel Productions.
　　112 Prospect St.
In Portland, Ore.—Jewel Productions.
　　401 Davis St.
In San Francisco—Jewel Productions.
　　121 Golden Gate Ave.
In Omaha—Jewel Productions.
　　1504 Harney St.
In Los Angeles—Jewel Productions.
　　822 S. Olive St.
In Canada—State Right Features.
　　106 Richmond St., W—, Toronto.

🙟

If there is no Jewel Office as yet in your territory, address requests for bookings to the nearest office in the foregoing list, or else write direct to the Home office of Jewel Productions, Inc., at 1600 Broadway, New York City. We are opening other offices as rapidly as possible and will advertise them from time to time.

🙟

We will not bore you with extravagant statements about our pictures. We THINK we have bought the best the market affords. We will stand or fall on their merits and on whether you think our judgment is good.

HENRY KRAUS
Premier Actor of France

"Production tremendously satisfactory", "A marvel presented faultlessly". "One of those rare things that delight eye and mind alike", "Striking in its atmosphere".

The splendid commendation of a great picture given above was not written by the Pathé Exchange but by the trained and critical observers of the largest newspapers in Chicago.

It played to S.R.O. performance after performance at Orchestra Hall, Chicago, one of the two finest houses of the country.

Pathé

in the eight reel masterful production

LES MISERABLES

"Fills a long felt want", "Proves
the worth of the motion picture", "Exquisite detail", "Classic
in quality", "The picture shows
results that it is doubtful could
be achieved in this country."

Such unanimous and highly complimentary opinion from unbiassed journalists
proves that Pathé is right in saying that
"Les Miserables is one of the greatest pictures of all time."

This super-attraction will
be released September 9th.
Book it and get the business.

Pathé

Pathé

The last lingering doubt of the skeptic and the pacifist as to why the United States is at war will vanish when they see

IN THE WAKE OF THE HUNS

Churches wantonly destroyed, tens of thousands of fruit trees leveled to earth, houses sacked and dynamited, inhabitants outraged, pavements lost in mine craters scores of feet deep, mile after mile of desolation and unnecessary and wilful destruction, and through all the victorious sons of immortal France pursuing the beaten and retreating enemy! Better than miles of word description, graphic in the extreme, timely and of vast interest to all are these Official French War Pictures. As a box office attraction they are all-powerful. Everyone in your community will wish to see them. Your local newspaper should be willing to play them up big!

Ask the nearest Pathé Exchange about them - quick!

Two smashing, sensational reels!

B.A. ROLFE *presents*

The third of the
GREAT STAR SERIES
ETHEL
BARRYMORE
Directed by George D. Baker
in a 5 *Act* Drama de Luxe

Produced by
METRO
PICTURES CORPORATION

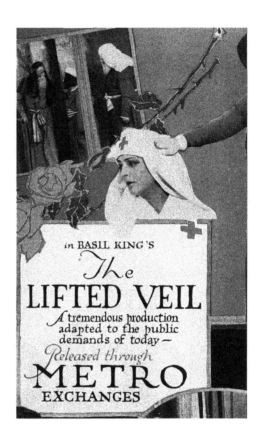

Announcing

PHOTOPLAY MAGAZINE SCREEN SUPPLEMENT

*T*WELVE single-reel journeys to the homes of the players—screen views of such stars as Douglas Fairbanks, Charlie Chaplin, Bessie Love, Viola Dana, Mabel Talliaferro, Henry Walthall, Mr. and Mrs. Sidney Drew, Lucille Lee Stuart, William S. Hart, Warren Kerrigan, and countless others, as they live, frolic and indulge their pet hobbies when away from the studios.

Positively the greatest box-office attraction ever offered the state rights buyer, or the exhibitor who operates a chain of theatres and is seeking subjects to play his circuit and, later, sub-lease to other exhibitors.

All the Profits to the Red Cross!

All the profits from the sale of territorial rights to Photoplay Magazine Screen Supplement will be turned over to the American Red Cross. Photoplay Magazine is not in the film business for profit, and much of the credit for these pictures must be given the manufacturers who have so generously permitted the filming of their stars. Bids for these twelve single-reel subjects are arriving in every mail. You may still be able to secure exclusive territory for what is sure to be the most talked-about feature on the screen, and at the same time "do your bit" for the Red Cross. Wire or mail your application TODAY!

JAMES R. QUIRK, PUBLISHER

PHOTOPLAY MAGAZINE

CHICAGO, ILLINOIS

PHOTOPLAY
MAGAZINE
SCREEN
SUPPLEMENT

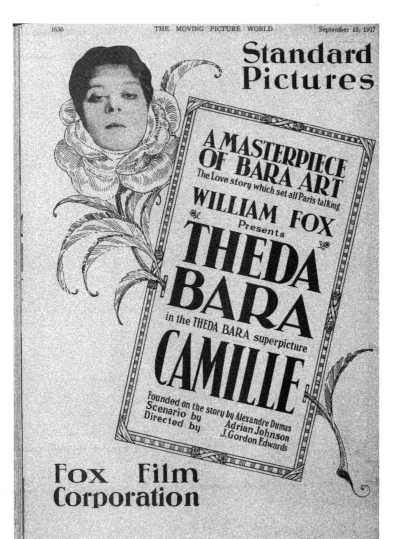

STANDARD PICTURES

JACK AND THE BEANSTALK

Beginning of the Fox Kiddies

Cost
$500,000
to make
1300 CHILDREN.
1 GIANT — 8 ft. 6 in.
Castles and Cities Built.
8 Months to Film _
EVERLASTING AS TIME
IS THIS PICTURE FOR
ALL CHILDREN BETWEEN
THE AGES of 5 and 90

Direct from Its Big New York Run at the Globe Theatre
NOW BOOKING AT ALL FOX EXCHANGES

STANDARD PICTURES
FOX FILM CORPORATION

U.S. NAVY
FOX EXCLUSIVE FEATURES
WILLIAM FOX
PRESENTS
JUNE CAPRICE
THE SUNSHINE GIRL
BUSHELS OF JOY AND LAUGHTER
WHEREVER SHE APPEARS
THE CAPRICE SMILE BRINGS:
HAPPINESS TO YOUR PATRONS
SUCCESS TO EXHIBITORS
MONEY TO THE BOX OFFICE
BOOK JUNE CAPRICE
AND BE JOYOUS, TOO
FOX FILM CORPORATION

FOX EXCLUSIVE FEATURES

JUNE CAPRICE
THE SUNBEAM OF THE FILMS

IN BUOYANT AND JOY-OUS PORTRAYALS

A MESSENGER OF GLADNESS IN CHARMING PICTURIZATIONS OF YOUTHFUL LOVE AND ADVENTURE

THE PUBLIC LOVE CAPRICE PICTURES

BOOK THEM NOW AND WATCH THE BOX OFFICE RESULTS

FOX FILM CORPORATION

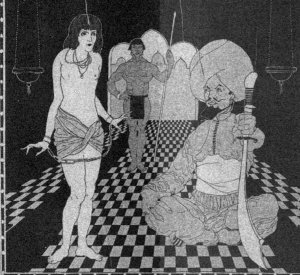

WILLIAM FOX *PRESENTS*

A DAUGHTER *OF THE* GODS

WITH ANNETTE

KELLERMANN

THE PICTURE BEAUTIFUL

BREAKING ALL RECORDS IN PRESTIGE
AND PATRONAGE IN ALL LARGE CITIES

ADMISSION PRICE 50¢ TO $2.00

FOX FILM CORPORATION

"Its Real

WILLIAM A. BRADY,
Director - General
WORLD PICTURES
present

"RASPUTIN, THE BLACK MONK"

Seven Stars

Montagu Love, June Elvidge, Arthur Ashley, Henry
Hull, Julia Dean, Irving Cummings, Hubert Wilke

Directed by Arthur Ashley

The Russian Revolution

Origin—
RASPUTIN"

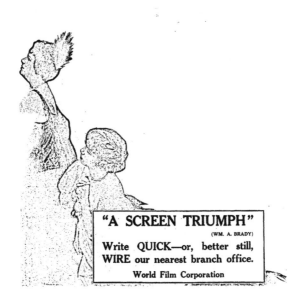

"A SCREEN TRIUMPH"
(WM. A. BRADY)

Write QUICK—or, better still,
WIRE our nearest branch office.

World Film Corporation

Madame

PETROVA

In Her First Petrova Picture

"The Greater Way"

TO BE RELEASED ON OR ABOUT OCT·22·1917·

Petrova Picture Company
Frederick L. Collins..President
25 West 44ᵗʰ Street New York

PCo.
INC.

PETROVA PICTURES

FIRST RELEASE:
on or about Oct. 22, 1917.

Petrova Picture Company
Frederick L. Collins.. President
25 West 44ᵗʰ Street.. New York

Louise Glaum
in
"IDOLATERS"

Big advertising possibilities in this play—Display the
"stills" and you've sold the show.

Released Sept. 2

TRIANGLE DISTRIBUTING CORPORATION
1457 BROADWAY, NEW YORK

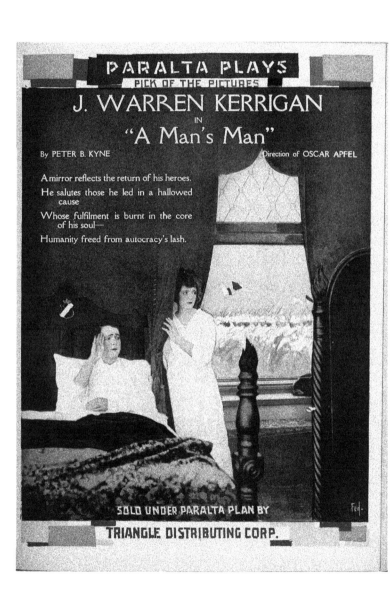

PARALTA PLAYS

PICK OF THE PICTURES

J. WARREN KERRIGAN

IN

"A Man's Man"

By PETER B. KYNE   Direction of OSCAR APFEL

A mirror reflects the return of his heroes.

He salutes those he led in a hallowed
cause

Whose fulfilment is burnt in the core
of his soul—

Humanity freed from autocracy's lash.

SOLD UNDER PARALTA PLAN BY

TRIANGLE DISTRIBUTING CORP.

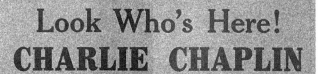

GENERAL FILM COMPANY,

GEORGE
ADE
NEW FABLES
IN SLANG

By America's
greatest humorist.

ONE EVERY WEEK
FOR ANY PROGRAM

Sept. 1: "The Fable
of the 12 Cylinder
Speed of the Leisure
Class."

Sept. 8: "The Fable
of the Wandering
Boy and the Way-
ward Parents."

Sept. 15: "The Fable
of What Transpires
after the Wind-Up."

Distributed Exclusively by General Film Co.

GENERAL FILM COMPANY,

The Fastest Stepping
Detective Story
Ever Screened

THE
PHANTOM
SHOT GUN

by Stanley Clisby Arthur
with
KATHLEEN KIRKHAM
and R. HENRY GREY

FALCON

Distributed Exclusively by General Film Co.

GENERAL FILM COMPANY,

The Beloved Characters of "O. Henry"

Al Jennings as "John Tom Little Bear," and Roberto Turnbull

"John Tom Little Bear"

"O-ho!" says John Tom, "I see. You're the Boy Avenger. And you've sworn to rid the country of the savage redman!"

The educated Indian whose aspiring soul was dismayed by race inequality—who loved a white woman hopelessly—who reverted to savagery in his hour of crisis.

"John Tom Little Bear," the newest 2-reel O. Henry masterpiece.

Book "THE DEFEAT OF THE CITY," the magnificent heart-interest O. Henry story, first one of four reels.

BROADWAY STAR FEATURES
Distributed Exclusively by General Film Company

Entered at the General Post Office, New York City, as Second Class Matter

Founded by J. P. CHALMERS in 1907.

Published Weekly by the

CHALMERS PUBLISHING COMPANY

17 MADISON AVENUE, NEW YORK CITY.

(Telephone, 3510-3511 Madison Square)

J. P. Chalmers, Sr.............................President
J. F. Chalmers........................Vice-President
E. J. Chalmers.....................Secretary and Treasurer
John Wylie................................General Manager

The office of the company is the address of the officers.

CHICAGO OFFICE—Suite 917-919 Schiller Building, 64 West Randolph St., Chicago, Ill. Telephone, Central 5099.

PACIFIC COAST OFFICE—610-611 Wright and Callender Building, Los Angeles, Cal. Telephone, Broadway 4640.

SUBSCRIPTION RATES.

United States, Cuba, Mexico, Hawaii, Porto Rico and Philippine Islands................$3.00 per year
Canada .... 3.50 per year
Foreign Countries (Postpaid)................ 4.00 per year

Changes of address should give both old and new addresses in full and be clearly written. Two weeks' time should be allowed for change.

ADVERTISING RATES.

CLASSIFIED ADVERTISING—One dollar for twenty words or less; over twenty words, five cents per word.

DISPLAY ADVERTISING RATES made known on application.

NOTE—Address all correspondence, remittances and subscriptions to MOVING PICTURE WORLD, P. O. Box 226, Madison Square Station. New York, and not to individuals.

"CINE-MUNDIAL," the monthly Spanish edition of the Moving Picture World, is published at 17 Madison Ave. by the Chalmers Publishing Company. It reaches the South American and Spanish-speaking market. Yearly subscription, $1.50. Advertising rates on application.

(The INDEX to this issue is on page 1752.)

Saturday, September 15, 1917

Facts and Comments

WE have called attention many times already in these columns to the ways in which the present executive of the League and the coterie of his friends now in control are merely using that organization as a booster for the publishing venture of President Ochs and his friends. The latest attempts along this line include consideration by the so-called executive committee of the League on how best to promote the circulation of Ochs' paper and a ruling by the same committee prohibiting the giving out of any information on League matters by the League Secretaries or any individual member, all such news only to be given out in the future through the office of Ochs' paper. If this is not making the League merely a tail to the President's kite, what would be your answer to the riddle? The great majority of thinking and successful exhibitors throughout the country are not likely to be fooled by the tactics of these few politicians under the guise of exhibitor organization.

* * *

ON Page 1348 of our issue dated September 1, we published a short article on the N. A. M. P. I. by-laws, which is worth a second reading in view of the recent vote of that organization refusing to admit to membership a large, representative and influential body of exhibitors. We counted on fourteen League votes as sure to be cast against admitting other exhibitors into the organization, but we certainly are at a loss to understand by what line of reasoning the other directors voting against the motion felt justified in taking such action. Playing into the hands of a few at the expense of the many and at the cost of fair play and justice is surely poor policy, that cannot be justified even by the prospect of securing 50 per cent. of exposition profits. As members of this association we are compelled to enter this protest against the majority vote in this case. Majorities are not always right nor minorities always wrong. These by-laws should be amended to prevent a very small and unrepresentative body of exhibitors from refusing representation to the great majority of exhibitors of the country.

* * *

THERE threatens to be another flood of publicity on the so-called "open booking" plan. Wonder if anyone knows what anybody thinks the "open booking" plan means? What the theater manager wants is a plan whereby he can get good pictures—good average pictures—with regularity to show his patrons and get them with the least trouble and expense to himself. Dependability is the big idea, and the plan that doesn't comprehend that idea is not worth fussing about. The producer who will make interesting pictures and rent them at a fair price will get the business, no matter what he calls his "plan."

* *

There is really only one "plan" that deserves attention; it is the plan that will reduce the cost of distribution to a minimum. The high cost of stars is with us to stay for many days to come, so that if there are to be any reductions made they must come out of the cost of administration and distribution. Conservation, efficiency, forethought and a few other cardinal virtues common to almost any other business one might mention, would reduce manufacturing and distributing costs to a fraction of the present figures in many instances. Competition should, in the natural course of business, give this advantage to the exhibitor. Such a "plan" would receive immediate attention from the exhibitors. As for the rest of them—camouflage.

* * *

A SUBSCRIBER closed a recent letter with the following: "Have learned that an established policy backed up by common sense business principles and plenty of advertising makes for success." We might add that above plan will make for success in moving picture exhibiting perhaps more surely than in any other line of business one might know of. The idea that brains are not necessary in the moving picture business certainly does not apply to the exhibiting end of the business.

Don't ☒ ☒ ☒ ☒ ☒ ☒ ☒ ☒ ☒ ☒ ☒ ☒ ☒ *By Louis Reeves Harrison*

THERE are all sorts of trade combinations in prospect or in embryo, some of them made necessary by extortionate demands of actors and directors who think they ought to get it all, or ·by new and changing conditions in distribution, while some are the natural outgrowth of strife for superiority. The grouping of interests may stimulate growth and improvement when it results in a higher test of skill, but, as in the past, it will only prove self-destructive when designed to throttle competition. It is through natural love of superiority, emulation, and through the stimulus of intelligent criticism that we expect to completely win public confidence.

No producer who sincerely desires to improve his product objects to capable criticism—it may hurt for the time, but it pays in the long run to have the good qualities and demerits of a product clearly defined and separated. Just so it helps for one concern to rival competitively another, especially when the desire to equal or surpass another is actuated by honorable motives. Competition in business, however, is very different from that in artistry. Any concern, or group of concerns, which attempts to boycott artistry will soon find itself clear out of the game.

Money is an overpowering factor in ordinary commercial rivalry, and it is a big factor in stimulating the sculptor, the author, the dramatist, the painter—it may be used to advantage to quicken creative genius in any field, but not obstructively. Real creative genius is as sensitive as it is rare. Opposition withers and blights it, only encouragement and nourishment can bring it to full flower. Constructive talent may do what it is told, but the creative kind works by impulse, to less advantage when compelled. The marked distinction between these two is seldom understood.

The motion picture public is sometimes easily amused, some portions of it, but it also easily forgets the superficial representations of life and movement. A man may go to the movies for occasional amusement merely to watch the unfolding of plot in a story, and idly conjecture how it is all to turn out, but he is not strongly enough impressed to care much whether he goes back again. The characters in ordinary screen plays merely drift through some oft-repeated incidents to an inevitable conclusion, one more or less foreseen from the beginning. Such is the commonplace photodrama turned out regularly for routine distribution.

It is in the very breath of creative genius to abandon this machine-made humdrum, to follow some troubled heart through all the vague and mysterious workings of destiny to an end which cannot be foreseen at any stage of development, though it be the most natural end in the long run. Such stories are fascinating pages from the book of the human soul. They have the snap and vigor of a strong pulse in high action. It is when they drag along by the old accepted routes that they become weak or tiresome. The man who goes to the movies may be living a drama, or he may be trudging along in weary commonplace. In both cases he is most deeply impressed by revelation of what has been going on in his spirit without being conscious of it, which is artistry's true appeal.

There is little of this dramatic essence in the stuff turned out by scenario editors, though they may be capable of fine work.' They buy an "idea," meaning a plot or a situation, even from an amateur, and work out a machine-made scenario. Any editor who buys on a synopsis basis is on a par with a publisher who would buy the script of a novel on reading a brief summary, or a reader of stage plays who would do such an insane thing. There are none such.

The successful actor, especially one boosted into prominence by producers and exhibitors alike, will form his own company and begin to write his own plays. He may be a playwright, but this tendency will naturally be to keep himself in the limelight as much as possible, transforming an otherwise good story into a dull vehicle for his specialties. A really good actor can portray character without using the drama for a vanity box, a mere publicity scheme to get all there is while the getting is good. He might prevent other dramatists from working, but he would naturally be among the last to encourage them.

At a time when there is crying need of original stuff, when professional authors have turned cold on the whole moving picture proposition, nothing is to be achieved by clogging the source of creative work. The very men we want, those who have an unfailing font of invention and have mastered the thousand technical difficulties of intelligent authorship, who might double public interest in this new medium, will adhere to the older ones, where there is no boycott of any kind, where genius is SOUGHT, not merely tolerated, where it is recognized and adequately compensated.

The aloof attitude of producers and professional writers, with both at fault, has been responsible for much of the quackery now being forced on the exhibitor and on the public. Authors should know more about screen requirements than they do about details comparatively mechanical of studio craftsmanship, without which their stories often become ineffective, while producers should place a higher value on the profound insight into human nature required of successful authorship. The great composer of music must master his medium before he can use it to advantage, but mastering the medium does not mean successful composition unless the true creative gift is behind it all.

Exactly the same condition we are in has existed in our theatrical world, when adaptations were the rule and native talent at a discount. A talented critic of the time says, "Surely we have been very stupid not to suspect the actual fact in the case, not to realize that there are among us plenty of men peers or superiors of England's Pinero, Shaw, Jones and Hope; of France's Rostand, Donnay, Coppe and Porte-Rich; of Germany's and Austria's Suderman, Fulda and Hauptman; of Norway's Ibsen, Italy's Giacosa, Belgium's Maeterlinck, and Russia's Ostrovsky. Why in the school of nations should we wear the fool's cap"?

Why in the school of arts should this new and beautiful medium of expression dubbed "the movies" wear the fool's cap, when there are men in this line of work capable of writing magnificent dramas for screen representation if they were given time to do so and suitable reward for the time and labor expended?

Timely Thoughts ☒ ☒ ☒   ☒ ☒ ☒ ☒ ☒   ☒ ☒ *By Sam Spedon*

Twenty-Four to Five.

TO AN individual exhibitor the National Association of the Moving Picture Industry may not mean much, but to exhibitors as a body it should mean a great deal. We believe it does, both individually and collectively. Wm. A. Brady, the president of the N. A. M. P. I., expressed himself in favor of the association admitting the American Exhibitors' Association to its membership, but by a vote of the majority of the board of directors the A. E. A. was rejected. The vote was 24 to 5, and the twenty-four dissenting votes comprised fourteen directors from the National Exhibitors' League and ten votes from other branches of the industry. We held the same opinion as Mr. Brady, that the A. E. A. should be admitted under a certain section of the association's by-laws.

The A. E. A. claims that it can act more freely unaffiliated with the National Association. We hope it can, but we believe there would be a greater chance of harmony between the A. E. A. and the National League if they were all members of the National Association of the industry. Besides, we believe if the two exhibitor bodies were members it would strengthen the National Association in the accomplishment of good for the whole industry. According to parliamentary precedent, we must abide by the decision of the majority, but, like Paddy with King William's nose, we still have our own opinion.

A Flight of Fancy.

Thought expression produces other thoughts that develop into ideas, take form and establish facts. Here is a thought expressed a few days ago: Will any of the many organizations recently formed ever assume the proportions of an exclusive club on the Stock Exchange when it may cost a good round sum to become a member?

It sounds like a pipe dream. Greater things have come to pass. We never can tell to what heights and flights anything in the moving picture world might ascend. Better get in while the getting's good.

Somewhat Different View.

A well known theatrical man said: "Moving pictures haven't hurt the legitimate theater at all; the stage is as popular as ever. In my opinion they have hit periodicals more than anything else. Persons who were in the habit of staying at home every night reading magazines now go to the 'movies' and spend an occasional fifteen cents and evening in that way." Looks feasible.

Another County Heard From.

An exhibitor from the South said: "I have had no difficulty in securing star features at a price commensurate with the earning capacity of my house; even the biggest companies are willing to make fair concessions. I have a theater of five hundred and fifty seats, in a city of 15,000, with several theaters of different grades. We have no competitive opposition, which proves that exchanges will meet conditions where organized consolidation of responsible exhibitors exists."

From 5 to 10 and 10 to 15.

The increase in admission prices from five to ten cents and ten to fifteen cents does not mean that the public is being charged more for what they formerly paid the smaller price. It means that the public is paying more for better service, better pictures, and more comfortable theaters. The public today demands, no matter how small the house, attractiveness, cleanliness, and all the comforts of home. These things, with the increased price of help and materials, make an increase in price of admission necessary. You don't have to get it from the public, it is willing to pay what the service is worth, providing you give it what it wants. Formerly it had to be satisfied with five cent quality, now it wants higher quality and better service; it is educated up to it.

Some exhibitors make it possible for those of limited means, particularly women who wish to take the children, to see the shows by retaining the five and ten cent admission for matinees up to 6 p. m., which strikes us as a very fair arrangement under the present advance in the cost of everything else.

Always With Us.

"You don't happen to know of a position in the film business for a young man with 90 per cent. ability? If you do, we know of several who can fill that kind of a job. We have a few on our waiting list, and there are more to follow. We have a lot more with 95 per cent. gall and 5 per cent. ability." This is from the contents of a letter we received about two years ago from a friend of ours in an employment agency.

The woods are full of them, and the film business sequestered something like fifty per cent. of them. It is a little different now. Most of those employed have to produce and make good, the army and navy are willing to take the rest of them. Easy jobs and easy money are getting scarcer every day.

Should "Honor" Funkhouser

WE rise to protest against the opprobrium that is being heaped upon our esteemed collaborator, Major M. L. C. Funkhouser, censor of Chicago. Motion picture men have greatly misunderstood the efforts of the Major. While his seeming opposition to pictures of a certain class has occasioned recourse to law to enable them to be shown in Chicago, it should be borne in mind that the columns of publicity his actions breed in the Chicago papers could scarcely be obtained in any other way. Not even the Chicago sob sisters in chorus could produce such results. You might kittykelly a picture to a fareyouwell and it would not mean a thing in the young lives of Chicago's highbrows. But let Major Funkhouser so much as raise his eyebrows and, bluey, the picture is lifted to the power of popularity. Let it be known that we believe Major Funkhouser's usefulness has been greatly underrated and his efforts meanly recompensed; therefore, in justice to him and as a slight recognition of his services to the trade, we hereby recommend that he be decorated with the red badge of courage and nominated for life membership in the Almighty Press Agents.

"POP" HOADLEY WRITES WAR STUFF.

C. B. Hoadley has written a very amusing one-reel comedy, entitled "Dodging the Draft," just filmed at Universal City under the direction of Craig Hutchinson. Dave Morris and Gladys Tennyson have the leading roles.

National Association Holds Meeting ▧ ▧ ▧ ▧ ▧ ▧

Elects Officers and New Members — To Give Films to the Soldiers in France

THE first meeting of the recently elected board of directors of the National Association of the Motion Picture Industry, which is to serve until the annual meeting in June, 1918, was held at the organization's headquarters, Times Building, Monday, August 27, with President William A. Brady in the chair.

Thirty-two of the forty-two members of the board were in attendance. This was the largest and most representative meeting of the board since the organization of the National Association in August a year ago. The following were present: William A. Brady, William L. Sherrill, Adolph Zukor, Samuel Goldfish, Walter J. Moore, Lee A. Ochs, Alfred Hamburger, N. C. Rice, C. E. Glamann, Alfred S. Black, Thomas Furniss, Eugene M. Clarke, Frank Eager, Louis L. Levine, Louis F. Blumenthal, J. H. O'Donnell, Dan Chamberlain, Hector Pasmezoglu, Robert Levy, J. A. Berst, Arthur S. Friend, P. A. Powers, Richard A. Rowland, J. E. Brulatour, J. H. Hallberg, Joseph F. Coufal, Arthur James, William A. Johnston, Joseph F. Lee, Thomas G. Wylie, Fred J. Beecroft and George Irving.

Following the reports of the officers and committee, the members proceeded to elect new officers for the ensuing year and the following were unanimously elected: William A. Brady, president; vice-presidents, Adolph Zukor, J. A. Berst, William L. Sherrill, Thomas Furniss, R. A. Rowland, J. H. Hallberg and Arthur James. J. E. Brulatour was re-elected treasurer and Frederick H. Elliott was re-elected secretary for the ensuing year.

The following companies and individuals were unanimously elected to membership: The Bray Studios, Inc., Producer Class C; Pathe Exchange, Inc., Producer Class A; Norma Talmadge Film Corporation, Producer Class A; Selig Polyscope Company, Producer Class A; Inter-Ocean Film Corporation, Standard Engraving Company, Pictures Corporation, Producer Class B; Harry Rapf, Producer Class B; Mayfair Film Corporation, Producer Class B; Robert Welch, George Gould, Frances Klein, J. S. Judd, William McCormack, E. Kendall Gillett, and H. A. Wyckoff.

The application of the American Exhibitors Association for affiliation under Article 2 of the by-laws was denied by a vote of 24 to 5.

The secretary's report reviewed the activities of the association since the last meeting of the board. Practically all of the secretary's time, as well as that of the office staff, had been devoted to the work of the War Co-operation Committee in carrying out instructions from Mr. Brady, who was requested by President Wilson to mobilize the industry, and in the perfection of the organization of the national committee. It was reported that all of the twenty-eight state chairmen appointed on July 3 had accepted and were actually engaged in the organisation of the exhibitors for the purpose of carrying out the instructions received from the motion picture committees, the chairmen of which are in constant communication with the members of the Cabinet, federal offices, Red Cross war council, Council of National Defense and the four-minute men.

A report was presented by R. H. Cochrane, chairman of the advertising trailer committee, that at the Chicago convention of the national exhibitors the proposition contained in the set of resolutions in regard to showing advertising trailers was rejected. Members of this committee were present and suggested that the committee should be continued in power, with a view to carrying out the plan at some future time.

Resignation of the Mutual Film Corporation as a member of Distributor Class No. 4 was presented and tabled by unanimous request and referred to President Brady for action. The resignation of the Billboard Publishing Company as a member of the general division was accepted. An invitation from the United States Chamber of Commerce to the association requesting it to send delegates to the War Convention to be held at Atlantic City, September 17-21, was presented and President Brady was authorized to appoint delegates to attend this important meeting.

The Inter-Ocean Film Corporation in an application for membership requested a new classification for exporters of motion pictures, which was granted, as was also the application of the Standard Engraving Company in a new classification for engravers.

It was decided to invite all individual state right buyers to join the association as members of the general division, Class 5, entrance fee $10, annual dues $5.

A resolution was adopted requesting President Brady to appoint a committee to confer with the committee of the National Exhibitors League in regard to the holding of future expositions. The following committee was appointed: William A. Brady, ex-officio; Arthur S. Friend, J. E. Brulatour, William A. Sherrill, J. A. Berst, Gabriel L. Hess and J. H. Hallberg. The joint committee went into session immediately following the directors' meeting.

Mr. Brady stated that in view of the increase of the board of directors from thirty to forty-two, it is his opinion that the executive committee should be increased from nine to twelve. This action necessitates an amendment to the by-laws, and the directors decided to call a meeting of the members of the association to be held at headquarters on Thursday, Sept. 20.

Uncle Sam's soldiers will be provided with film entertainment while they are encamped on French soil, through the good offices of the National Association. At the suggestion of President Brady many of the leading manufacturers and distributors guaranteed to contribute films to a distributing agency to be conducted under governmental control, for the entertainment of the soldiers.

President Brady was empowered to name a man to assume charge of this agency and to offer his services to the government, and it is considered possible that in view of the great value of such an agency the man in charge will receive a commission from the president.

Adolph Zukor, president of Famous Players-Lasky Corporation, asserted he was heartily in favor of this move, but suggested that instead of giving old films, the manufacturers should contribute new pictures. Messrs. Rowland, Berst, Brady, Powers and Hess signified their willingness to participate in this arrangement.

Brady Personal Representative of President.

President Brady made a spirited speech and was heartily applauded. He reviewed the work of the association for the past year, declaring his belief it had accomplished wonders. Again he appealed for the getting together of exhibitors. The president made the flat declaration that his appointment by Mr. Wilson to mobilize the industry for service was in his individual capacity and not as president of the N. A. M. P. I. and that he was responsible only to the President of the United States. He said further in that position he would recognise any individual he felt impelled to recognise. Mr. Brady spoke as follows:

Gentlemen: In accepting this office for another year I would like to have it understood at the outset that I am doing it at great inconvenience to myself. I feel that since it seems to be your desire that I should continue for another twelve months that it is my duty to do so, and therefore I accept the office.

I feel, however, in accepting it, and with no intention of boring you in the slightest as to what I've got to say—I will put it in as short a manner as I can—I feel as I felt in Chicago, and I want it distinctly understood by the exhibitor directors who are in the room, that never in any way, shape, manner or fashion have I participated in any politics connected with the Exhibitors' League of America or connected with the American Exhibitors' Association, and I also make this statement in advance, that during the next twelve months, if I live, I shall follow the same rule—that I know nothing but good of the National Association as a whole. I know nothing of the quarrels that may come up between any of the factions in the National Association.

I shall rule honestly and in a fair-minded fashion to the best of my ability on any question that may come up before this association, no matter who it hurts, whether it be the biggest man in this business or the smallest man in the business.

Having that distinctly understood as a so-called platform as to what I want to do, I want to proceed further and say that I feel at the end of the first year of this association that we have accomplished wonders. We are not in debt to any extent that can't be wiped off in an hour. We have succeeded in almost everything that we have attempted, except one thing, that is, the complete organization of the motion picture industry as a national unit, and the principal reason why that has not been accomplished has been the troubles and dissensions among the exhibitors.

I believe at this stage of the game that it is the duty of every exhibitor in the United States to get together in some fashion that you know better than I how to do, and form yourselves in one great, big national group. I feel that it is a great mistake for the exhibitors, either as an association or two associations, either collectively or individually, to stand apart from the National Association.

I received a circular this morning from the American Exhibitors' Association. In one of their clauses, in fact, the first clause in summarizing what they intend to do, is this statement: "Are the exhibitors of this country going to run their own business or are they going to see it run to ruination by senseless censors, idealists, reformers and self-seeking gentlemen in other branches of the industry?"

After having passed through twelve months, I would like to ask the gentleman who wrote that sentence what he means by "self-seeking gentlemen in other branches of the industry?" I have mixed up with fights in associations of this kind since I was 20. Never in those years of experience have I ever seen men stand together at times when they were needed to stand together as these or other "self-seeking gentlemen in other branches of this industry."

I am not for any branch of this industry. I don't depend for a living upon any branch of this industry, therefore, I can speak fearlessly to any man in this room, and I say to you that the exhibitors who have been connected with this association during the last twelve months would not be men, would not be honest men, if they did not testify to the fact that every time that a proposition has come before this association that the exhibitors have received every bit of value they were entitled to. (Lee A. Ochs—"Right.").

There never has been a time in the twelve months where a great crisis has come up, as for instance the rows we had in Albany, and after all, Albany is the principal capital city in the United States, because if the reformers and the tax legislators there had succeeded in doing what they proposed to do, in which they almost succeeded in doing, every state in the Union would have followed in their footsteps and the tax that would have been put upon the industry would have been something almost impossible to prejmage. I say that we went there as a group. I say that the producer, the exhibitor, the distributor and the miscellaneous class fought just as finely, came forward with their money just as quickly, as any class in the business.

Who would have suffered in that glaring instance of adverse legislation? The National Association of America.

We went forward, nearly two hundred men, on a special train, every man paying his own expenses, and put before the legislators at Albany as dignified and intelligent a group of men as they have met representing any industry during the last session.

I testify here to every man in this room and to every exhibitor in America that the manufacturer, that the producer, that the distributor, that every branch here is willing to stand with the other branches, and I claim that those men are not against the exhibitor. I claim that they are for the exhibitor, that upon the success of the exhibitor depends their business, and never have I found one iota of an attempt to injure the exhibitor, but rather a unanimous and solid attempt to benefit the exhibitor. Therefore, I say at the beginning of the second twelve months of this association, that we should all get together.

Before we pass beyond this question of affiliation you will have to take notice of the fact that it places your president in a very embarrassing position. As the American Exhibitors' Association quote in their letter, they tendered to me, as the representative of the President of the United States, their co-operation, and I accepted it, as I will accept the co-operation of any exhibitor, actor, director, producer or distributor in the United States. I will accept their co-operation without regard to any association that exists in the motion picture business.

I might state that at one time last month Mr. Bush of the Exhibitors' Trade Review attended here in company with Mr. Ochs, and he put the question direct to me as to whether I had received the appointment from the President of the United States because I was president of the National Association of the Motion Picture Industry, or whether I had received the appointment as an individual, and I told him straight that I had received the appointment as an individual, and I desire that every man in this room will appreciate that fact—that I am not responsible to the National Association of the Motion Picture Industry, nor to the Exhibitors' League, nor to the American Exhibitors' Association, nor to any collective members or individual members of this association. You may reconsider my re-election as your president if you will, but I am responsible only to the President of the United States to mobilize this industry for effective co-operation with the different heads of the government in the prosecution of the war, and if, in the carrying out of my national duty, I am compelled to recognize any association or any individual I shall do so.

N. A. M. P. I. and League Get Together

In Future the Two Organisations Will Go Fifty-Fifty on all Expositions, Balls, Etc.

AT a joint meeting of the committee representing the National Association of the Motion Picture Industry, and the National Motion Picture Exhibitors League of America, held August 27, consideration was given to matters pertaining to the promotion of future motion picture expositions.

After a careful survey of the situation it was finally decided to schedule two expositions for 1918, the first one to be held in New York City, during the month of February, and the second to be held in Boston at the time of the annual convention of the National Exhibitors' League, which begins on July 14. The promoting and management of both expositions will be under the direction of a joint committee, members of which will be designated by each organization, and it is the purpose to plan these two trade showings so that they will compare favorably with the annual shows and expositions held by other leading industries of the country. The same co-operation is to be effective in the case of balls and other public functions.

The National Association of the Motion Picture Industry was represented at the meeting by President William A. Brady, ex-officio, Arthur S. Friend, J. E. Brulatour, William L. Sherrill, J. A. Berst, Gabriel L. Hess and J. H. Hallberg. The National Motion Picture Exhibitors League was represented by Lee A. Ochs, president, ex-officio, Ernest H. Horstmann, Alfred S. Black, J. H. O'Donnell, Eugene M. Clark and Frank D. Eager. Present also by invitation was Sam Grant of Boston, manager of the 1918 Exposition.

It is expected that permanent committees will be appointed within a fortnight so that preliminary arrangements can be made for the New York exposition in February, which will include the selection of a building, date and manager.

No expositions of the motion picture industry have been held in New York during the past two years, and it is contended that a well organised and conducted exposition, at which every big producing and distributing corporation as well as supply and equipment companies, will be represented, showing the growth of the industry, will attract big crowds and prove a money maker for the promoting organizations.

The Expected Happens in Chicago

"The Spy" Held Up—Fox Sues to Restrain Mayor and Funkhouser From Interfering With Production.

THE Mayor of Chicago, William Hale Thompson, and M. L. C. Funkhouser, second deputy superintendent of police, who has charge of film censorship in that city, are named in a bill of complaint just filed by the Fox Film Corporation in the United States District Court for Northern Illinois.

The bill asks the court for an injunction to restrain Mayor Thompson, Mr. Funkhouser and Herman J. Schuettler, general superintendent of police, from preventing the production if Chicago of William Fox's film drama, "The Spy."

Funkhouser, having viewed the picture, refused to give it a permit, declaring (the bill states) "that the acting in the play was in places too powerful and too dramatic, and that it made the sweat stand out on his brow."

It had been planned to present this photoplay at the big Studebaker theater on August 26, but Major Funkhouser has declined to issue a permit unless certain scenes are deleted.

Mr. Fox, however, would not consent to the elimination of the scenes desired, because they were vitally necessary to the patriotic mission of the piece, and because, he asserted, the scenes could be condemned only as the result of a short-sighted policy.

"Mayor William Hale Thompson," the bill reads, "has repeatedly expressed himself publicly and privately as opposed to the war and opposed to the prosecution thereof by the United States."

The bill for the injunction establishes the point that since the outbreak of hostilities between the United States and Germany, President Wilson has specifically requested that film producers and distributors organize and mobilize to co-operate with the Government in waging war and in bringing it to a successful conclusion. "The primary purpose of 'The Spy,'" the bill continues, "is to arouse American patriotism and to encourage enlistments."

"Major Funkhouser," the bill proceeds, "heretofore has refused permits for motion pictures depicting the events of the war and the conduct of the war by Germany on the ground that it would offend Germans living in Chicago, and since the declaration of war he has established a rule in his department against issuing permits for such pictures."

Judge Straightens Out Mr. Funkhouser.

In the United States District Court, in Chicago, on August 31, Judge Samuel Alschuler issued an order restraining city officials from interfering with the presentation of "The Spy," the Fox subject which had been banned by the police censor of Chicago. Judge Alschuler ruled that Second Deputy Funkhouser's objection to the picture was not within the meaning of the ordinance creating the bureau of censorship; in other words, the issue involved in the case of "The Spy" was not one of morals and consequently Mr. Funkhouser had no jurisdiction.

SING SING PRISONERS SEE "POLLY OF THE CIRCUS".

Mae Marsh and the great photospectacle, "Polly of the Circus", the first of the Goldwyn productions to be released, will have for their initial showing east of the Mississippi the most remarkable audience in the United States, the members of the Welfare League of Sing Sing prison. Chairman E. J. Meagher of the Welfare League has written to President Goldfish of the Goldwyn Pictures Corporation asking that Goldwyn's first production be screened in the prison auditorium for the benefit of the shut-in men of Sing Sing. President Goldfish immediately consented, and "Polly of the Circus" will be shown to the prisoners on Sunday, Sept. 2.

The Motion Picture Exhibitor

League Executive Committee Meets

Decides to Co-operate with N. A. M. P. I. on Trade Functions—To Fight the Payment of Music Royalty.

A REGULAR meeting of the executive committee ot the Motion Picture Exhibitors' League of America was held at the Astor on August 26 and 28. There was a full attendance of members. Several important matters were taken up. On Monday, August 27, the League members of the board of directors of the National Association of the Motion Picture Industry attended a stated meeting of that organization. One of the important results of the latter gathering was a decision to hold all expositions, balls and trade functions under the joint auspices of the League and the Association, the two bodies sharing equally in the profits.

The question of deposits was considered, and after passing a long resolution, in which it was declared bills should be presented in all state legislatures the coming year, whereby all deposits would be insured against loss, the meeting decided to hold the matter in abeyance pending a conference with the manufacturers.

By formal resolution the committee declared the League should pay a reasonable amount of money to the National Association in the way of dues.

It was decided to ask Ludwig Schindler, general manager of the recent Chicago exposition, as to the status of the receipts of the big show and to take steps to have the money transferred to the League as soon as it may be available. The committee appointed to have charge of the matter were Peter Schaefer, chairman; Alfred Hamburger, Lee A. Ochs and Joseph Hopp.

Frank D. Eager moved that a committee be appointed with full power to consider the question of a division of profits with the National Association on all trade functions. The

Officers and Members of Executive Committee of Motion Picture Exhibitors' League of America.

Standing, left to right—Robert Levy, Chicago; Peter Schaefer, Chicago; Sam Grant, exposition manager, Boston; Milton Goldsmith, counsel, New York; N. C. Rice, Iowa; C. E. Glamann, Kansas; Alfred Hamburger, Chicago; Louis Blumenthal, New Jersey; Dan Chamberlain, North Dakota; Thomas Furniss, Minnesota; A. B. Black, Maine; Eugene M. Clarke, Mississippi. Seated—J. H. O'Donnell, Pennsylvania; David Rodgers, Minnesota; Frank D. Eager, Nebraska; William J. Sweeney, Chicago; Hector Pasmezoglu, Missouri; Lee A. Ochs, New York; Joseph Hopp, Chicago; William Iseeberg, Mississippi; William Brandt, New York; Ernest Horstmann, Massachusetts.

Coming League and Other Exhibitors' Conventions

(Secretaries Are Requested to Send Dates and Particulars Promptly)

motion prevailed, and the president appointed Lee A. Ochs, Ernest Horstman, Alfred S. Black, J. H. O'Donnell and Louis Blumenthal.

The committee decided to issue a general appeal in favor of the assessment of $3 on each theater in order to fight the demands of the American Society of Composers, Authors and Publishers that exhibitors pay royalties on copyrighted music. Nathan Burkan, general counsel, and President Maxwell, of the society, appeared before the committee and declared any exhibitor who played music copyrighted by any member of their society would be haled to court and prosecuted. Notice was served the society would search the country for evidence of violations. The call to exhibitors by the committee followed the remarks of the two officials of the society.

Peter Schaefer announced that Marcus Loew had joined the Manhattan branch of the Exhibitors' League.

Hector Pasmezoglu, of St. Louis, called the attention of the committee to the labor situation in his city as regards the union musicians. He declared the American Federation of Musicians is compelling theaters to place additional men in the orchestras, according to the price of admission. He charged the musicians with assuming a dictatorial manner and threatening that if the demands are not complied with the musicians will be withdrawn. On a motion by Mr. Eager the president of the League was instructed to communicate with Samuel Gompers, president of the American Federation of Labor, submit the whole question to him and endeavor to learn if the St. Louis musicians were acting within their rights in attempting to dictate how many musicians should be employed by an exhibitor.

Also, on a motion by Mr. Eager, the president and executive secretary were instructed when communicating with locals to secure all available information as to taxes and licenses paid in the various localities, wages paid to operators and musicians, number of hours and conditions of labor, data as to costs of electric lighting and fire insurance, the populations of the towns and number of exhibitors, and all possible information, and that this be collated and placed on file for the benefit of the committee at its next meeting.

The question of a trade show in New York the coming winter was taken up and the whole matter was referred to the joint committee of ten of the League and the National Association.

Virginia Exhibitors' Convention

Enthusiastic Meeting at Ocean View in Which Representatives From Other Southern States Join—Votes to Affiliate With A. E. A.

VIRGINIA Motion Picture Exhibitors held a notable convention at Ocean View, Va., on August 30, 31 and September 1. The organization convened as a branch of the Motion Picture Exhibitors' League, and adjourned as an integral part of the recently organized American Exhibitors' Association. Seventy-five exhibitors were present, and fifty representatives of the exchange and manufacturing branches of the business were in attendance.

President Wells, of the State League, called the meeting to order at 1.30 o'clock Thursday afternoon. Addressing the convention Mr. Wells explained the objects for which it had been convened, and introduced Charles C. Pettijohn, general manager of the American Exhibitors' Association, who addressed the assemblage upon the principles of the new organization, and expressed a sincere desire that the exhibitors of Virginia and the other States represented would decide to become part of it. He was followed by Percy Wells of North Carolina, Harry Crandall of Washington, D. C., and Sam Trigger of New York.

President Wells stated that the Virginia State organization would enter upon its immediate duties, and the other members from other States withdrew. The committee on by-laws and constitution presented and read their constructions, and each section was considered separately. This occupied the remainder of the afternoon.

The reading of the by-laws and constitution was finished and referred back to the committee on Friday morning for revision as corrected, which was done very quickly, and the by-laws and constitution was adopted as read.

The motion was made and carried that the name of the Motion Picture Exhibitors' League of Virginia be changed to the American Exhibitors' Association of Virginia. This was followed by a motion that the A. E. A. of Virginia request charter from the National A. E. A., which was unanimously carried.

Election of State officers being in order the nominating committee presented the following names: President, Jake

Wells, Richmond; vice president, E. D. Heines, Roanoke; treasurer, C. E. Geogheghan, Chase City; secretary, Chesley Toney, Richmond. All of whom were unanimously elected.

The convention reassembled as a whole at 3 o'clock. Mr. Pettijohn was again introduced by President Wells, and read the following telegrams, addressed to various officers of the A. E. A.:

Columbia, S. C.
South Carolina solid. Nearly one hundred now for A. E. A. Can't withdraw from League because never joined it. Your principles correct. We depend on you.—Geo. C. Warner, Pres. S. C. League.

Owensboro, Ky.
Chairmanship for state accepted. Sure all exhibitors in Kentucky will be in new league in ten days. Look to you for protection and accomplish needed reforms. Forty-one in now.—Geo. A. Bleich.

Indianapolis, Ind.
Passed three hundred mark for A. E. A. last night. Will keep Indiana in first place if we have to build more theaters. Boys recommend you withdraw the 217 from old league and put in 3012 in A. E. A.—Fay Andrews, Secy.

Cleveland, O.
Six members joined since you left. Pay for same so as to have all in good standing. Money on hand to refund. Success to A. E. A. from Ohio.—J. H. Simpson.

Buffalo, N. Y.
Assured of sixty Buffalo and surrounding theater owners. Enthusiastic over A. E. A. Success to convention.—I. Mosher.

Lexington, N. C.
Impossible to attend meeting. North Carolina is solid for A. E. A. More than one hundred in so far. All my personal energy and best wishes with you.—H. B. Varner.

American Exhibitors' Association stands first in Arkansas. As president of Independent Arkansas League I assure you of our hearty co-operation. Anything I can do to assist the cause have no hesitancy in calling on me.—Saul Harris.

Detroit, Aug. 29.
Your invitation to attend the Motion Picture Exhibitors' Convention received and thank you very much.
I am very sorry that I cannot attend as it is impossible for me to get away at this time. I have been out on a membership tour for the A. E. A. and have been very successful. We have now a better organization than we ever had in the League, and I expect to have 90 per cent. of the exhibitors in Detroit in by Oct. 1. We have not had a single complaint on our action in withdrawing from the League and joining the A. E. A.
With best wishes for the success of the convention and hoping to meet you all at the First Convention of the A. E. A. in Detroit in 1918, I am—Peter A. Jeup.

Providence, R. I., Aug. 31.
Telegram received. Accept your request to act as temporary chairman. About seventy-five feel sure of half.—Chas. F. Williams.

President Wells, in a stirring address, set forth the need of securing funds for immediate use in working out the objects of the A. E. A., and when he concluded seven members of the A. E. A. there and then subscribed one thousand dollars to the Association for emergency. Suggestions were offered to further augment the treasury by Fred Herrington, Sam Trigger, Percy Wells and Harry Crandall, all of which were referred to the Committee of Ways and Means.

On Friday, August 31, at 1.30 P. M. over two hundred guests sat down to a sumptuous shore dinner given by Messrs. Otto and Jake Wells. The ball on Friday night was attended by two thousand guests, and the following screen stars: Alice Brady, June Elvidge, Kitty Gordon, Marguerite Snow, Madge Evans, Rose Tapley and King Baggot.

The closing session on Saturday was marked by the appearance at the last moment of Lewis J. Selznick, who is on a tour of the States in behalf of his film interests. The convention then adjourned without delay.

A. E. A. to Fight Deposit System

Pettijohn Declares Action of N. A. M. P. I. in Refusing Affiliation Leaves New Association a Free Hand.

NOW we are ready for our first great fight in the exhibitor's behalf, against the advance deposit system." This was the reply of Charles C. Pettijohn, general manager of the American Exhibitors' Association, when informed that the directors of the National Association of the Motion Picture Industry had voted against the offer of affiliation made by the association.

Mr. Pettijohn was emphatic in declaring that the action of that body in no way affected the aims and purposes of the A. E. A. in working for the betterment of all branches of the industry, particularly where the exhibitors were concerned, and asserted that the vote of the delegates from the Motion Picture League clearly indicated that it was too closely allied with the manufacturing interests of the trade to be called a representative exhibitors' organization.

As evidence of the stand to be taken in all questions pertaining to the best interests of the trade, Mr. Pettijohn has written William A. Brady, President of the N. A. M. P. I., pledging the support of the American Exhibitors' Association in all matters that will aid the Government in the successful prosecution of the war and assuring him that in every movement that tends to improve any part of the industry will have the backing of the association.

Mr. Pettijohn issued the following statement regarding the action of the National Association of the Motion Picture industry in refusing the offer of affiliation with the American Exhibitors' Association.

"At a meeting of the directors of the N. A. M. P. I., held Monday, August 27, the offer of affiliation on the part of the American Exhibitors' Association as set out in our communication of August 15, was rejected. The offer made the following stipulations:

"First—The American Exhibitors' Association on July 20, 1917, tendered through William A. Brady, not as President of the National Association of the Motion Picture Industry, but as the designated official, by reason of his selection by President Wilson, our hearty co-operation and services to help carry on the work set aside by the Government for the motion picture industry during the present crisis. We are building a business organisation of exhibitors to the end that this may effectively be done and good results obtained.

"Second—We care not whether we have one or fifty votes either as directors or members of the National Association of the Motion Picture Industry, because voting inside the industry cannot interest us.

"Third—We are asking nothing of you, and are offering only our affiliation and assistance in a stand with the other branches of the industry for what is healthful and against that which unjustly attacks.

"Fourth—On the other hand, we will not at any time, by any unit vote or combination of votes, permit ourselves to be bound to support any act, measure or effort that is not for the best interests of real exhibitors of America, who comprise our membership, nor for or against any faction in any other branch of the industry that may hereafter develop.

"Fifth—We desire to have it clearly understood that our services are tendered, and that no application is made at this time for votes, or for any change in the by-laws of your organization.

"Sixth—We ask that the directors at the meeting August 27, 1917, either promptly reject our proffer of affiliation, assistance and co-operation in such manner as our position may be clearly and definitely interpreted by our officers and entire membership.

"We are informed that the fourteen delegates representing the Motion Picture Exhibitors' League voted solidly against it, and that seventeen of the other gentlemen present voted twelve for and five against. We are also informed that others present did not vote. It may have been that our offer to work harmoniously with the other branches of the industry was not sufficient, and it may have been that our plain statement that we would not co-operate with any movement which we did not feel was for the best interest of the exhibitors was retaining too much latitude on our part. We shall maintain that attitude, however, irrespective of the action of any other organisation or branch of the industry. We feel that it was the proper premise to stand upon, and we still maintain that position.

"We regret the offer was not accepted in the spirit in which it was tendered, but the refusal will not conflict in any way with our plans to build up a real exhibitors' organization which stands for exhibitors only, and which will in no way be allied with the manufacturers either directly or through the medium of a trade paper which depends upon the manufacturer's advertising for its support.

"One thing is certain. This alliance upon the part of the gentlemen representing the other exhibitors' association, and men interested in other branches of the trade has relieved this association of certain embarrassments. Our acts are now free. Our pathway is clear to make a fight for exhibitors only without fear or favor of the manufacturer. To the five directors who voted in favor of the co-operation of this organisation that stands for exhibitors we extend our thanks and sincere appreciation.

"There are some manufacturers who really want a business men's organisation of exhibitors. There are others who do not care for one, and some who positively 'will not stand for one.'"

REMBUSCH TO HEAR COMPLAINTS.

The complaint department of the American Exhibitors' Association will be handled by Frank J. Rembusch of Indiana. He is recognised as one of the best informed exhibitors on trade questions and will gladly answer the inquiries of the exhibitors on all questions pertaining to the industry. He should be addressed, 412 Indiana Trust Bldg., Indianapolis, Ind.

Each suggestion and complaint will receive his personal attention and exhibitors are invited to write him regarding any angle of their business. Any movement for the betterment of exhibitors will receive his hearty support, and every communication will receive careful attention on his part. Such matters as can not easily be taken up in the Western offices will be forwarded to New York for investigation and a report made after the investigation has been concluded.

Horstmann Corrects Percy Wells

Record Bears Out Statement of Former That Massachusetts Cast but Nine Votes at Chicago.

Editor Moving Picture World:

In a statement issued by Percy Wells on Page 354 of the issue of The Moving Picture World of September 1 he makes a statement that Boston voted 30 delegates at the last convention held in Chicago. This is certainly an absolute misstatement of the facts as the records will show that in every case Massachusetts voted but nine votes. The other Leagues comprising the New England States were voted by their respective presidents who accompanied us to Chicago. Massachusetts, as Mr. Wells admitted, is entitled to nine votes, and that is all it voted.

Massachusetts has always been a lover of "fair play," and has always gone into the battle and come out with its shield untarnished. E. H. HORSTMANN.

Treasurer M. P. E. L. of A.

Boston, August 29, 1917.

[At the evening session on the opening day of the recent convention of the Motion Picture Exhibitors League of America in Chicago Mr. Wells was named as one of a committee of three to act as tellers on a vote to be taken. His note book shows that Massachusetts at that time cast nine votes.—Ed.]

GOLDWYN SHOWS "POLLY OF THE CIRCUS."

Several members of the Moving Picture World staff have been permitted an advance viewing of "Polly of the Circus," the first Goldwyn release. The subject was shown last week at the New York exchange, 509 Fifth avenue. Among those present were Vice President Fred B. Warren, of Goldwyn, who received for his company the congratulations of those in attendance. There seemed to be no doubt in the minds of the men and women who followed the fortunes of Polly through the eight reels, that the initial release of Goldwyn will make a strong impression on the photoplay public. "Polly" will not be formally reviewed in this journal until after the regular presentation at the Strand, but there is no hesitation in saying here that the production is above the average, that it is an all-around picture, that it represents a keen blending of the spectacular and of heart interest, as well as containing novel effects in night photography.

CLARA KIMBALL YOUNG BOMBARDS SOLDIERS WITH CHOCOLATE.

All work stopped at the Thanhouser studio Thursday, where Clara Kimball Young has been busily engaged on "Magda," while this enthusiastic little lady occupied a point of vantage to help speed the boys in khaki on their way. At each period of rest Miss Young showered the tired and perspiring soldiers with chocolate, which was welcomed in an enthusiastic and grateful manner.

Miss Young is very much interested in soldiers' kits, and will devote most of her spare time in providing comforts for the boys abroad. She insists that each kit must be well supplied with chocolate, which is so dear to the soldiers' hearts.

ANITA STEWART IN NEW COMPANY.

Anita Stewart, former Vitagraph star, has signed a contract with Louis B. Mayer, of Boston, to appear in a number of big features. Few details regarding the signing of the contract are forthcoming from Mr. Mayer or his associates. Mr. Mayer states that distribution plans and production plans will be made known within a week.

MARY PICKFORD TO REFEREE BOXING MATCH.

Mary Pickford, at the Mason Opera House, Los Angeles, at the benefit given for the French Emergency Hospital fund, will act as a prize fight referee. Miss Pickford has offered to referee the terrific fistic encounter which is to be conducted by Charlie Chaplin and Eric Campbell, his "heavy."

Activities of War Committees
OF THE MOTION PICTURE INDUSTRY

THE Department of Agriculture, in co-operation with the war committee of the motion picture industry, has arranged for the display during the next three or four weeks at motion picture theaters in Illinois, Massachusetts, New York and Pennsylvania of lantern slides dealing with the canning, preserving, drying and pickling of perishable food products. This action was taken as a result of reports received by the department that a large surplus of perishable fruits and vegetables was accumulating in the big population centers and that there was great danger that large quantities would go to waste.

The following letter has been sent by the Secretary of Agriculture to motion picture exhibitors:

The help of motion picture exhibitors in your State is urgently needed at this time in bringing before their patrons the importance of conserving perishable fruits and vegetables. I am informed by agencies of this department which are in close touch with conditions that in your State a large surplus of perishables is accumulating, much of which will be wasted unless extraordinary effort is made to conserve for later use that which cannot be promptly consumed. In the emergency which our country is facing the waste of any of this food would be deplorable.

I am taking the liberty of inclosing four gelatine sheets dealing with the canning, drying, preserving and pickling of perishable products. You will be rendering a definite public service, and the Department will greatly appreciate it, if you will place these between cover glasses and project them on your screen between motion picture reels for a period of from one to three weeks, depending upon the number of runs you make. you, patronage and other local conditions. It is important that they be shown immediately. While it would be preferable to display all of them at each show, they may be divided, if necessary, using Nos. 1 and 2 during one program and Nos. 3 and 4 when the program is changed. Since it was necessary in order to save time and expense to provide gelatine slides, will you please ask your operator not to leave them in the machine long enough to melt them?

The loyal support which the entire motion picture industry is giving to the Government in this emergency convinces me that you will be willing to assist it in this important matter.

Very sincerely yours,
D. F. HOUSTON, Secretary.
Approved and recommended by the committee of the Motion Picture Industry co-operating with the United States Department of Agriculture.
S. A. LYNCH.
LOUIS L. LEVINE.
W. R. ROTHACKER.

The National Association of the Motion Picture Industry has also in a general letter requested that all theaters insert the contents of the slides in house programs for a period of four weeks.

These Are the Slides.

The slides sent out by Secretary Houston are as follows, with the exception that the second paragraph of No. 1 is repeated in each of the others:

WAR MESSAGE NO. 1.

Let nothing be wasted. Preserve, can, pickle, or dry all surplus perishable fruits and vegetables possible to lessen the world's food shortage.

For instructions, write to the State Agricultural College, your County Agent, or the U. S. Department of Agriculture, Washington, D. C.

WAR MESSAGE NO. 2.

Canning and drying are very simple processes requiring small, cheap equipment. Easy to do in a city house or apartment.

WAR MESSAGE NO. 3.

Tin cans are scarce. Put up perishable foods in glass jars or bottles. Dry such vegetables as beans, carrots, beets, peas and okra.

WAR MESSAGE NO. 4.

Dry fruits and vegetables in the sun, in or over a stove, or by an electric fan. Pack in plain or paraffin paper bags or cartons, in empty cergal boxes or coffee cans.

Offer Films to Soldiers in Europe

National Association Formally Agrees to Supply New Subjects for Entertainment of Men of Foreign Service.

IN line with the spirit of co-operation with the Government in the prosecution of the war as suggested recently by President Wilson, the board of directors of the National Association of the Motion Picture Industry at its recent meeting in New York offered to supply regularly to the American troops in Europe all the latest motion pictures. These films will be sent to the soldiers without cost to the Government except such minor expense as may be involved in the transportation of the prints, and possibly the outlay necessary for projecting machines, in case these are not given.

P. A. Powers, a director in the National Association, was delegated to proceed immediately to Washington and present the matter to the authorities of the War Department. Mr. Powers interviewed Secretary of War Baker, who was much impressed by the possibilities for the entertainment of the troops contained in the offer of the association. Steps are now being taken to clear the tracks for the acceptance of the offer.

Mr. Powers tried to get in touch with Raymond B. Fosdick, chairman of the commission on camp activities, but Mr. Fosdick was out of the city. He will take up the whole question with Mr. Hammer, the representative in New York of Mr. Fosdick, and attempt a solution of the difficulties at present in the way of an acceptance by the Government of the Association's offer.

The chief significance of the proposition of the manufacturers lies in the fact that if the Government accepts the offer to establish an agency in Paris in charge of an officer of the War Department the troops will have the benefit of the newest films, enabling them to keep right up to date as to what is going on at home in motion pictures. It will be recalled that already the Government has accepted the offer of the Goldwyn company to supply one print of each subject to be released by that concern.

LOWRY TO SHOW "FOR THE FREEDOM OF THE WORLD."

Ira M. Lowry will present for a trade showing at 10:30 o'clock on the morning of September 10 his eight-part production of Captain Edwin Bower Hesser's story, "For the Freedom of the World." No pretense of a new theme is made. It is the old game of love with three players, one of whom must lose. For screen purposes, however, variation and importance are attained in the production by the employment of patriotic and military atmosphere.

E. K. Lincoln is featured in the character of a young American enlisting in the Canadian army, with Barbara Castleton furnishing a charming Canadian society girl to be wooed and won and Romaine Fielding in the unenviable role of a typical slacker. To Mr. Fielding was also entrusted the direction of "For the Freedom of the World," under the personal supervision of Mr. Lowry.

Why Be a Wolf? Asks Nat Brown ▨ ▨ ▨ ▨ ▨

Paralta Man Advises Exhibitors to Choose the Best in Programs, in Open Booking and in Selective Stars

ONE man says program booking is the only rational system on which to conduct a moving picture theater. Another man says the open booking plan is the only one to follow. Another man says that the selective star series method will assure success. Another man says none of these are right; he can't state any other plan, but he is sure they are all wrong.

Why not seek the truth? Why be a wolf? The truth is that each of these plans possesses essentials of right, valuable if appreciated and properly applied. Why not combine the real benefits of all plans and profit by them?

The program system is unquestionably the most logical, for it furnishes substantial assurance of the basis of a strong bill and eliminates a very important element of doubt. No sane man would build or lease a dramatic or vaudeville house without knowing where his attractions are coming from, and the general merit of what he has to depend on to draw people to his theater.

The manager of a dramatic house depends on the productions provided by his booking exchange; the vaudeville manager is in the same boat, with this difference—he can strengthen the bill by books of his regular exchange by putting on a star act, or "big headliner."

The moving picture manager who books a program is in just the same position as the vaudeville man. He puts on a good program bill, but, being enterprising and desiring to give his patrons an entertainment they will appreciate and talk about, he puts in a star feature film, secured either on the open-booking system or under the selective star series method.

What is the result? He has a well balanced bill, and puts on a show that sends his patrons away with the opinion that he is a generous provider and is deserving of support.

The program will ever be the real foundation of moving picture exhibition, for it is certain in contract and of fixed charge. It enables an exhibitor constantly to secure the foundation of his bill under such conditions, and at such price, as will enable him to figure with some degree of certainty just what his operating charges are going to be on the week, and to what expense he can reasonably go to provide special star attractions.

The merit of program pictures, like the real merit of star feature pictures, varies somewhat. A big legitimate star may have an exceptionally strong vehicle one season and a mediocre play the next. The same condition prevails in all picture production. An absolute standard of excellence in a program cannot be maintained, but average merit can.

The open booking system appeals strongly to the man who has not experienced its uncertainties. He thinks, at first blush, that he can be a real "picture picker"; display not a little discrimination and make a big record for selecting the best productions made.

From the moment he enters into this proposition he goes back to the days, practically, when theatrical business was transacted on the curbstones in front of the old Morton House at Broadway and Union square. He abandons system, safety and certainty, and enters into a "catch-as-catch-can" contest with conditions of a most uncertain nature.

Nothing stays fixed, and in his effort to get things where something can be considered as nailed to the floor he soon finds everything in chaos; and, to cap the climax, like the old-time manager of the palmy days before the theatrical syndicate injected real business into the theatrical world he may find himself with two or three pictures booked for the same day in his anxiety to see to it that he gets all the good things.

Open bookings (indiscriminate of various makes and subjects) will never prove successful or satisfactory to the manager of a moving picture theater, for he has nothing to gain by it as a system except an advance in rentals.

Because of lack of responsibility behind most open booking features—a program name carries responsibility which must be met in quality—a manager depending on the open booking system for success will be forced to see run a large part of what he books.

Imagine what that means! He will spend much of his time in a projection room selecting what he may desire to play, whereas, under a program booking contract he knows he will get good pictures, for the program cannot afford to kill itself by putting out bad pictures.

Many fine pictures get on the market through open booking channels. They cannot be disregarded, and here is where the wise booking manager will avail himself of conditions favorable to him in the open-booking system and use them to his advantage. Combination of the valuable parts of the open booking system with the program system, wisely made through the selection of big features offered in open market, bring together two elements which are important to a well balanced moving picture theater management.

The argument for the star series selective method is also a strong one. This system makes for certainty to both producer and exhibitor. On the one hand the producer is proceeding on that certainty which comes from knowing just what his market is, and what he can get for his pictures. On the other hand, the exhibitor can secure a series of pictures of a star most popular with his patrons, under such conditions, and at such cost, that he is enabled to so figure his other bookings that he can "cut his coat according to his cloth."

The producer cannot afford to take the great speculative chances entailed in the tremendous salaries of stars, the great amounts now demanded for adequate subjects and the growing cost of production created by the constant public demand for greater things, without full and complete advance knowledge, so far as lies in human power, of the disposal of his product and the price he will get for it.

Entering into a contract with a star of established drawing power in these days is something of a responsibility, combined with other contingent obligations which run into hundreds of thousands.

A producer cannot fairly be expected to take these chances without knowing the most important of all things to any rational business enterprise—how he is to get his money back with a profit reasonable in the light of the hazard he takes.

The selective star series method is really a step forward, meeting public demand for constant advancement in quality of entertainment. The history of the theater, in this respect, is being repeated in the moving picture. Competitive production and public demand means constantly bigger and better things; and these can only be provided on such a basis as the selective star series method of booking makes possible.

So, instead of the adherents of any one of these systems getting out in the open and shrieking his views with the vehemence of an intolerant fanatic, he would far better study in what way the other fellow's idea may hook up with his.

"Why be a wolf?"

That's one of the great troubles with this business—this habit of seeing where the other fellow may walk a little lame, and then the whole pack jumping on him and eating him up in critical moment.

There is virtue in most all plans for the distribution of moving pictures. Why not combine these virtues and reject the errors. Such a course would not only help the producer and distributor greatly, but it would help the exhibitor—much of the uncertainty under which he now operates would be eliminated.

Most exhibitors are not trained showmen. They read the views expressed by producers and distributors, and try to come to a conclusion which will be right and helpful in the conduct of their business.

How can exhibitors come to any definite and stable conclusion about anything, when one producer or exhibitor may argue one thing and another man may say another thing in reference to the same proposition, and a third man may argue, in the face of obvious truth, that the other two are wrong, and with the Rev. Jasper of Mississippi he agrees that "de sun do move"?

"Less critical conversation and more practical sense," would seem to be an important impression yet to be made on some moving picture producing distributing minds.

Join the best of the program plan, the open-booking plan, the selective star series plan, and a very nearly perfect system will be evolved. This will mean the full protection of the interests of everybody—producer, distributor and exhibitor.

Help it along. "Why be a wolf?"   NAT I. BROWN.

Embargo on Films

Motion Pictures Among Articles Listed by President
Wilson—Exporters Must Obtain Licenses.

FILMS are to be prohibited of export from the United
States under the proclamation just issued by President Wilson, extending the list of commodities subject to the provisions of the limited embargo law, unless
the exporters shall first obtain a license.

In his proclamation the President stated the public safety
requires that, except at such time or times and under such
regulations and orders, and subject to such limitations and
exceptions as the President shall prescribe, until otherwise
ordered by the President or by Congress, the articles named,
including films, shall not, on and after August 30, be ex-
ported or shipped from or taken out of the United States
or its territorial possessions to Abyssinia, Afghanistan, that
portion of Belgium not occupied by the military forces of
Germany or the colonies, possessions or protectorates of
Belgium, Bolivia, Brasil, China, Chile, Columbia, Costa
Rica, Cuba, Dominican Republic, Ecuador, Egypt, France
and her colonies, possessions or protectorates; Guatemala,
Haiti, Honduras, Italy and her colonies, possessions or
protectorates; Great Britain and her colonies, possessions
or protectorates; Japan, Liberia, Mexico, Monaco, Monte-
negro, Morocco, Nepal, Nicaragua, the colonies, possessions or protectorates of The Netherlands; Oman, Panama,
Paraguay, Persia, Peru, Portugal and her colonies, possessions or protectorates; Roumania, Russia, Salvador, San
Marino, Serbia, Siam, Uruguay, Venezuela (excluding any
portion of the foregoing occupied by the military forces of
Germany or her allies), or any territory occupied by the
military forces of the United States or by the nations associated with the United States in the war.

"The purpose and effect of this proclamation," a statement from President Wilson said, "is not export prohibition
but merely export control. It is not the intention to interfere unnecessarily with our foreign trade; but our own
domestic needs must be adequately safeguarded and there is
the added duty of meeting the necessities of all the nations at war with the Imperial German Government. After
these needs are met, it is our wish and intention to minister to the needs of the neutral nations as far as our
resources permit. It is obvious that a closer supervision
and control of exports is necessary with respect to these
European neutrals within the sphere of hostilities than is
required for those countries further removed."

The administrative processes will be simplified by this action, it is said, and the policy of minimizing the interruption
of trade will be continued.

Applications for export license should be made to the
Exports Administrative Board, 1435 K street, Northwest,
Washington, D. C., or to the branch office at 11 Broadway,
New York; or they may be filed at any of the branch offices of the Bureau of Foreign and Domestic Commerce,
of the Department of Commerce, at Boston, Chicago, St.
Louis, New Orleans, San Francisco and Seattle, where
blank application forms may be obtained. Licenses will be
issued at the branches of the Bureau of Foreign and
Domestic Commerce in all cases possible, but in certain
cases it will be necessary for applications to be forwarded
to the office of the Exports Administrative Board in Washington.

Licenses will ordinarily be good for sixty days, unless
revoked prior thereto, and at the expiration of that time
must be renewed to be valid.

It was reported some time ago that large quantities of
old films were being bought up by German agents and were
being shipped into Germany to be converted into high explosives. American exporters and others were urged to
be very careful to see that the good offered by them to
foreign buyers should not go to the people who would
either send them to Germany or her allies, or to others for
that purpose. Under the proclamation of President Wilson,
it will be impossible practically for such a thing as this to
again occur, for suspicious looking cases will be scrutinised
and examined carefully.

SALLY CRUTE IN "BLUE JEANS."

Pretty Sally Crute, a favorite motion picture player, has
been engaged to play Sue Eudaly in the special screen production which Metro Pictures Corporation will make of the
old-time stage success, "Blue Jeans," with Viola Dana as
star. Sue Eudaly was a vampire in the days before there
were any vampires, formally so-called, and to Miss Crute
has been entrusted the task of presenting to theatre-goers
of to-day the splendid charms of the wicked Sue Eudaly of
twenty-odd years ago.

At the Leading Picture Theaters

"Efficiency Edgar" Showing at the Rialto, "Rebecca of
Sunnybrook Farm" at the Strand.

The Rialto.

AT the Rialto, the week of September 2, Clarence Bud-
dington Kelland's "Efficiency Edgar" will be presented, with Taylor Holmes in the title role. It is a
story with an idea back of the usual romance—that of a
business man who decides to apply to his personal affairs
the same efficiency methods that he has applied with great
success to his business. Aiding Mr. Holmes in the fun-
making are the well known players, Virginia Vallie, Ernest
Maupin and Rodney La Rock.

In the Rialto Magazine, a feature of timely events that
makes a history of great value, there will be shown among
other pictures of the moment those taken a few days ago
at West Point which are rather more intimate and interesting that the usual views shown of this famous military
academy. A new "Mutt and Jeff," and a new Mr. and
Mrs. Sidney Drew comedy promise an exceptionally fine
program.

Many requests have come to Dr. Riesenfeld for Puccini's
"La Boheme," and this with a revival of Leo Fall's operetta
"The Dollar Princess," will be the two most important con-
tributions by the big orchestra.

Greek Evans will sing, in English, "The Two Grenadiers,"
for which some special lighting and scenic effects have been
devised by Mr. Rothapfel. Madame Felicia French will
sing the aria from "Ernani" by Verdi.

The Strand.

One of the most pretentious film offerings ever presented will make its initial appearance at the Strand
theater, where Mary Pickford will be seen in her newest
Artcraft picture, "Rebecca of Sunnybrook Farm," by Kate
Douglas Wiggin and Charlotte Thompson.

Some interesting views from the French battle front also
will be shown. Manager Edel has made special arrangements whereby new French battle pictures will be shown
every week at the Strand. Victor Moore will be seen in
his latest farce entitled "Camping." The Topical Review
contains the latest news pictures of interest from this country and abroad.

The musical program is headed by Henri De Caux, the
tenor, who will sing "Celeste Aida." Helen Scholder, the
'cello virtuoso who created a sensation at the Strand last
week, will be heard again in Popper's Mazurka No. 1 and
Drage's Serenade. The Strand concert orchestra, under the
direction of Carl Edouarde, will play Liset's "Prelude." This
will be the last week of the Strand concert orchestra.
Commencing Monday, September 10, the new symphony
orchestra will inaugurate the afternoon symphony concerts which will be given every week day at 2:15 preceding
the regular program of motion pictures and vocal and instrumental selections.

Eighty-first Street Theater.

At the Eighty-first Street theater for the entire week
Douglas Fairbanks will be seen in his own story, his newest,
funniest offering, "Down to Earth," presenting his own
optimistic view of life.

At Other Broadway Houses.

At the Globe "The Spy," the Fox spectacular story of
German intrigue in the United States, continues for the
week.

At the Criterion "The Manxman" is running indefinitely.

ANOTHER GROUP OF SPARKLE COMEDIES.

Another series of Sparkle Comedies is now ready for
General Film distribution. As in the preceding groups
there are six subjects, the producer, Jaxon Film Corporation, finding significant response in issuing its product in
compact series.

The new Sparkles are "Hearts and Harpoons", "Toodles",
"Bangs Renigs", "Triple Entente", "Whose Hosiery" and
"Wrong Wrights". The first of these is ready September
20, the others following in order and insured for delivery
without a break each week.

Like the first and second series of Sparkle Comedies the
new releases are refined farce comedies with each a clever
story and snappy production. Care has been taken to get
good people, far above the average of players in one-reel
pictures, and a reputation for consistent excellence is being
clinched with each succeeding group.

Chester Beecroft Returns

Says He is the Only American "Film" Man Who Has Visted Russia and Other Belligerent Countries in Two Years.

CHESTER BEECROFT of 501 Fifth avenue, New York, who has been touring Europe in the interests of his film exporting and importing business for the last four months, returned to America on a Scandinavian-American liner, landing on August 30. Mr. Beecroft left New York on the steamer which carried General Pershing and the first American expeditionary forces to the battle-front in France and enjoyed the exceeding good fortune to witness the entrance of the American commander and his staff into London and later on into Paris.

It is said that Mr. Beecroft is the only American commercial traveler and possibly the only traveler of any class whatsoever whose passport shows the successful entrance and departure to and from England and France, a return departure from England, then Norway, Sweden, Denmark, Finland and Russia, during the last two years of the war. In making this extraordinary voyage over more than twelve thousand miles of water Mr. Beecroft passed through the majority of the most dangerous submarine and mine areas in the world, including two trips across the Atlantic by different routes, two through St. George's Channel, two across the Straits of Dover, one through the Irish Sea and the North Atlantic, twice across the North Sea and once through the Skager-Rak and Kattegat.

In course of these thrilling voyages, some of which were made in small freight boats under the most trying circumstances, Mr. Beecroft's vessel was twice attacked and once sunk by submarines. Mr. Beecroft does not hesitate to state his reasons for risking his life in so perilous a voyage. He says that conditions in the foreign film markets have changed so rapidly and so completely during the last year that no one on this side possessed any definite knowledge of the subject and that so many mistaken impressions had gained credence here that the American manufacturers were bewildered and had no way of basing a definite policy for the foreign distribution of their pictures. So many conflicting statements had been made by those who knew a litle and those who pretended to know much, that in many cases extraordinary prices out of all proportion to the possibilities of the market were being asked. Sometimes these prices were absurdly high and sometimes absurdly low, few people indeed having any idea as to what kind of picture was suited to the various countries in which they were endeavoring to make a sale. It frequently happened that a product which had absolutely no chance of being placed in a certain specific market at any price at all was being held at a price which was peculiarly suited and which consequently would net the buyer or distributor a handsome profit were being slyly coaxed away by the "wise ones" at a figure far below their worth.

It was this state of affairs, so unfair to the American manufacturers of today, and so inimical to the American product of the future, that determined Mr. Beecroft to go abroad, despite all hazards, to study first hand and to learn from actual observation the exact conditions which obtained in the principal European markets. Mr. Beecroft found, among other things which will be of particular interest to picture producers here, that the film business is far from enjoying the full confidence in certain official circles and that the American manufacturer should use the utmost caution and make most thorough investigation, as an unfortunate association, however innocent the action of the seller may be at that time, is almost certain to have a

Chester Beecroft.

most serious effect upon the standing and future activities of the manufacturer or seller himself.

While abroad Mr. Beecroft closed several important contracts and considers his journey to have been even more successful than anticipated. He, no doubt, has many friends in the business who will be glad to hear of his safe return.

Tanya Fetner, Russian Actress

TO a public ever on the alert to discover some new favorite in the films there is a promise in the announcement of the Russian Art Film Corporation that in its first release a young woman who bears the unfamiliar name of Tanya Fetner will appear. Miss Fetner plays the title role in "The Painted Doll," which has in its cast two of the most popular players in Russia, Ivan Mozukin and Natalia Lesienko. In Russia Miss Fetner is merely one of the company at the famous Moscow Art theater. She is undergoing the usual course of training which has evolved all the great Slav stars of the stage, which means that until she becomes a star herself in her native land she must play the parts assigned to her, whether on the speaking stage or in the motion picture.

When Mozukin assembled his cast for the Pushkin drama he selected Miss Fetner for the part of Tanya, wife or a plodding engineer in the employ of the most brilliant man of the profession in Russia. While her husband works and works under the direction of this man, played by Mozukin,

Tanya Fetner.

the pretty wife fascinates his employer. Kresslof, the name of the character created by Mozukin, despises the social aspirations of his wife, they are separated for long periods and he yearns for feminine associations. He finds them in Tanya, who is ambitious and looks beyond her own narrow sphere.

In the development of this familiar story the famous Russian poet and dramatist departs from obvious methods and keeps up the suspenses by numerous original devices of the author of great artistry. The role of the young wife at once excites the sympathy of the audience and is condemned as it deserves. Miss Fetner in her delineation of the character always emphasizes the better side of her nature and suppresses the weakness born of ambition for a larger life. Trained in the most comprehensive school in the world, she never overacts and her appearance on the Russian Art Film programme in "The Painted Doll" is expected to achieve the succcess in America that is always waiting for the artist of talent. "The Painted Doll" will be presented to the trade in a few weeks.

GRAHAM BAKER MANY SIDED.

As an antidote for the serious work of writing one Big V slapstick comedy each week, Graham Baker, of the Vitagraph scenario staff, has relieved his sombre moments by picturing "The Grell Mystery," in which Earle Williams is appearing under the direction of Paul Scardon; adapting "The Flaming Omen" for Mary Anderson and Alfred Whitman; and writing titles for "An Alabaster Box," featuring Marc MacDermott, and assisting in the direction of "For France," a thrilling spectacle featuring Edward Earle and Betty Howe.

Mr. Baker's versatility will be appreciated in the fact that "The Flaming Omen" is a play with a deeply religious motive; "The Grell Mystery" is a detective play; "An Alabaster Box" is a story of country life; and "For France" is a patriotic picture. To fill in his spare moments, Mr. Baker reads and passes on all comedies submitted to the Vitagraph for sale.

War Cameraman's Kit

Leon H. Caverly With Marine Corps in France Describes the Methods and Needs of the Cinematographer at the Front.

AN old-time "weekly" motion picture cameraman, Leon H. Caverly, who is now "somewhere in France" with the Fifth U. S. Marines, writes an interesting letter to the Moving Picture World regarding the methods he employs in taking photographs, both still and motion, and what a cameraman at the front needs in the way of a "kit." Here are his directions:

"Motion Picture World, New York, N. Y.

"Gentlemen: I am taking the liberty to send you a description of the outfit which I am now using in the capacity of war cinematographer for the U. S. Marine Corps, thinking that it may be of interest to some of your readers. For the benefit of some of my brother photographers who are interested to know what constitutes a complete equipment for the war photographer, I herewith list the following equipment which I have thus far found adequate for all conditions at the front.

"As one is often obliged to carry his outfit on 10-mile hikes, weight and bulk are very important factors. Developing and printing movie film while in the field is entirely out of question, but with the aid of an Eastman developing-tank and a pail of water, which, by the way, often has to be carried a mile, good results can be secured on all stills. As ice is very hard to obtain I have found the water cool enough for all photographic purposes early in the morning when it has had ample time to cool over night. By using one ounce of alum to a barrel of water and allow it to stand over night we get, by draining off the top, very good washing water. This method has to be resorted to many times owing to one's inability to secure fresh running water.

"To return to the proper outfit for recording every phase of modern warfare we must divide such pictures into two classes, moving and still pictures. I am now using a Pathe (Outside Model), with the magazines enclosed. A Debree Moy or Bell & Howell are all equally good for this class of work. My outfit is fitted with the Goerz Michrometer mount adjusted to take the 2-inch, 3-inch and 6-inch lenses. A set of color screens to fit these lenses will oftentimes allow one to secure artistic results, but are not a real necessity.

"The ball-bearing tripod manufactured by the New York Motion Picture Apparatus Company is considered the best on the market, although any good substantial tripod with panoramic and tilting top will do. Extra retorts sufficient to carry 3,000 feet of film will more than prove sufficient for any day's work.

"Leather cases for one's equipment should be especially made of extra heavy hand-sewed leather with brass bound corners as they secure unusually severe treatment in transit.

"Eastman's negative film should be ordered in separate cans of 400 feet each, and only opened as needed for immediate use. Development should follow at the earliest possible moment for best results.

"Light values I find about the same as in America at this season of the year. "X" backed film may be used during cold weather, and should static appear, cotton soaked with ammonia or a weak solution of glycerine placed in the corner of the retort will prevent this bugbear of the cameraman. A metal crank has also been recommended as a preventative of static, and I believe, has been used to good result. Loading retorts under blankets for a dark room is but one of the many tricks the camera man has to resort to in his long line of inconveniences.

"Still pictures offer far less difficulties, and armed with the 3-A Eastman Kodak Special fitted with a 6.3 Zeiss Tessar in Optimo, also a 3-A Graflex and F4.5 Tessar, complete my outfit of still cameras. Good aerial pictures can be secured only with the proper equipment, and this I have found possible by using the Eastman Aeroplane Camera. Owing to the extreme high speed of the aeroplane it becomes necessary to use a much faster exposure, both on account of this fact, and also that one is traveling at a tremendous rate of speed. Regardless of what class of photography is being covered in the events of actual warfare, one is constantly up against all kinds of difficulties which have to be overcome in one hundred different ways as they come up from time to time.

"The strict censorship on all mail returning to the States prevents my going further into detail in regard to what I am actually photographing, still you can judge my location to some extent when I tell you that the roar of battle is distinct here both day and night. I am sorry that I cannot accompany this article with a series of photographs, but upon my return to the States will be pleased to go further into detail and offer such pictures as you may care to accept for publication, with the permission of the Publicity Bureau.

"With your kind permission I will take this opportunity to send my regards to all my brother crank turners, from somewhere in France. Very sincerely yours,
"LEON H. CAVERLY."

Louis Rosenbluh Comes Back

Famous Manager of Greater New York Exchange Will Handle Fox Standard Pictures in the East.

WITH the announcement by the Fox Film Corporation of the inauguration of Standard Pictures, comes the further news that the chief executive of their distribution in the East will be Louis Rosenbluh, well-known in film circles throughout the country, and particularly in the New York territory, where he has for years conducted his successful operations.

Mr. Rosenbluh's re-entry in the field of film distribution brings back into the fold one of the strongest personalities in the industry, as well as it recalls to the trade a career

notable for its spectacular features. Ten years ago Mr. Rosenbluh, in co-operation with William Fox, entered the exchange business with their Greater New York Film Rental Company on Fourteenth street.

At the height of its success came complications with the Motion Picture Patents Company, and there ensued a long controversy in the United States Courts. To the credit of the Greater New York Film Rental Company came a striking victory over the Patents Company, which, as every exhibitor knows, has made the film rental situation easier for the exhibitor.

Recently the Greater New York Film Rental Company was sold. Mr. Rosenbluh has

Louis Rosenbluh.

looked carefully over the film manufacturing market for the organization which he believed was producing the class and type of pictures that the exhibitor demanded. He aimed high and found his haven in Standard Pictures under the banner of Fox Film Corporation.

Mr. Rosenbluh describes the situation as follows:

"Not until I viewed the first Standard Pictures on the screen did I decide that I had found films that were worth my conscientious recommendation, and which would retain for me the confidence which my customers have always had in any product I recommended to them. Apart from that, as a pure proposition of dollars and cents, Standard Pictures are the first proposition I saw that merited unquestionably the effort that I intend to put into them."

This brings back into the field a man whose every move has always had a reason, and having satisfied himself, as he outlines above, Mr. Rosenbluh is now busy with his staff, getting into shape a home befitting this high opinion of Standard Pictures. These quarters will occupy the seventh floor of 130 West Forty-sixth street, where the old friends and the new will be welcome to come in and renew acquaintance.

SYLVIA BREMER LEADING LADY FOR HART.

As William S. Hart's leading lady in his initial Artcraft picture, "The Narrow Trail," Thomas Ince has selected Sylvia Bremer, the popular Australian actress. Miss Bremer has won fame, not only on the stage of her native country, but in a series of plays that enjoyed long periods of financial and artistic success in America.

Universal Gets Government Contract

Official Films, Showing Work of Department of Agriculture, to Be Distributed By Big U Organization at Reasonable Price.

UNIVERSAL this week signed a contract with the officials of the United States Department of Agriculture to distribute all motion pictures showing the work and activities of the department during the coming year.

This is considered one of the most important deals of the kind and significant in showing that the national government is fully alive to the power of the motion picture as an agency of enlightenment. It is also a striking indorsement of Universal's distributing facilities, as many other companies were competing for the contract.

A number of pictures have already been completed by the Department of Agriculture, and others will be made with the co-operation of Universal, as the contract provides that the services of scenario writers, producers, directors, actors and actresses and others shall be furnished by the distributing organization whenever needed. Operators are also to be provided for the exhibition of pictures in foreign lands.

Some of the pictures already made show the work of the forestry bureau in fighting fires and caring for the immense tracts of wild land under government supervision. There are also many beautiful and picturesque studies of the agents of the department at work among the sheep and cattle ranches of the west, and a reel devoted to the work of road building under various circumstances is highly instructive, besides possessing many splendid bits of photography.

One of these features will be released every two weeks, bearing the notice, "Official Film of the United States Department of Agriculture, Distributed by the Universal Film Manufacturing Company."

Special advertising matter and lithographic paper will also be issued for the series in co-operation with the department.

Any scenes that are of particular timeliness will be utilized in issues of the Animated Weekly, Current Events and the Screen Magazine. It is planned, however, to edit the original films so as to bring out all of the dramatic and human interest qualities in the subjects handled.

Each feature released will thus be the official expression of one of the most interesting phases of work carried on by the government of the United States, presented in a way to interest and educate all classes of citizens.

Charges for this service will be made reasonable enough to meet the purse of any exhibitor in the business.

WELL KNOWN WRITERS DOING PATHE SCENARIOS.

Gladys Hulette's latest picture, "Miss Nobody", which has been very well received, was written by Jos. F. Poland, the author of the story "The Fraud", which being put into scenario form by Howard Irving Young, was produced as a Pathe Gold Rooster play by the Astra Company, under the title of "Miss Nobody". Mr. Poland is an author of ability and particularly successful at injecting "human interest" into his stories.

Mr. Young, who did the scenario, has just completed his course of training at Ft. Myer and is now an officer in the Reserve Army.

The previous Gladys Hulette Gold Rooster play, "The Streets of Illusion", was written by John B. Clymer and Harry O. Hoyt. The scenario was prepared by Philip H. Bartholomae, the well known dramatist.

INFORMATION WANTED.

On behalf of some of its readers, the Moving Picture World desires information as to the present address of the Hall of Fame Publishing Company, Inc., or of Harry Ash, who was connected with that company. For a time they occupied an office in the Brokaw Building, near 42d street, New York, and were soliciting copy for a publication which was to be devoted to leading moving picture artists, publication of which was promised before the end of last year. Mr. Ash is said to be a relative of a well-known film director, and his father was believed to be interested in the company also. All information will be considered confidential, if desired.

GOLD KING DOUBLES FACTORY.

President Jones of the Gold King Screen Company, announces that their factory has doubled its capacity. The Gold King Screen will be handled by picture theatre supply houses exclusively in future.

Selznick on Tour

Will Spend Six Months Meeting Exhibitors of Every Section of the United States—Starts With Five States Convention at Ocean View, Virginia.

LEWIS J. SELNICK left New York Friday afternoon, August 31, by Old Dominion Steamship for Norfolk, from which place he will proceed to Ocean View, Va., where the five states exhibitors convention is being held. Mr. Selznick will address the convention by special request of the exhibitors, invitation having been extended by H. M. Crandall, owner of the important Crandall chain of theaters in Washington, and Jake Wells, owner of the Colonial Theater in Richmond and a great chain of theaters in the South, who came to New York to urge Mr. Selznick to attend the convention.

Five states convention is a get-together organization formed by the exhibitors of South Carolina, North Carolina, Virginia and Maryland, with the District of Columbia included. This organization includes in its membership some of the livest operators of motion picture theaters in the South Atlantic territory, and they are especially interested in the Open Door policy of which Lewis J. Selnick has been the pioneer.

Mr. Selznick, before leaving New York, expressed himself as unusually pleased that the Southern exhibitors wanted to meet him and to have him address them, as many of these men were adherents to the closed program system when Mr. Selznick began preaching the open door policy.

But this is only the beginning of an extensive tour which Mr. Selznick intends making. In the interest of the Select Pictures—the new distributing corporation which has just been formed—Mr. Selznick will spend six months touring every part of the United States and meeting the exhibitors in every city and town of importance. This will occupy about half of Mr. Selznick's time during the coming twelve months, and it is the first instance of a producer of the highest quality pictures taking steps to put himself into personal touch with exhibitors throughout the land.

Mr. Selznick draws an apt comparison between conditions in the film industry and the banking business.

"There was a time," he says, "when the president of a bank always hid himself away behind a closed door at the rear of the banking offices. Neither depositors nor borrowers, nor anyone except his intimate friends could reach Mr. Bank President. Now, however, all that has passed. The bank president today sits in an open office near the entrance to the bank, and it is part of his business—one of the most important part of his business—to meet the patrons of his bank."

Just such an evolution has taken place in the motion picture industry, contends Mr. Selznick. "The producer used to be an unknown quantity to the exhibitor as far as personal acquaintance is concerned, but the time for that has passed. Today the producer and the exhibitor must get together for their own good and the good of the industry; and I am going out to meet the exhibitor in his home town."

Mr. Selznick looks for great results from this pilgrimage of friendship, during which he will bring home to every exhibitor in- America the tremendous importance of Selznick Pictures and of Select distribution.

SALISBURY RETURNING FROM CHINA.

Edward A. Salisbury, according to advices just received by the Moving Picture World, stating that he is returning to America on the Steamer Siberia Maru after his extended trip through Japan and China for Prizma. From present indications, backed by the assurances from this noted photographer-explorer, Dr. Salisbury has not only obtained the most valuable records ever photographed in these countries, but he has preserved for the first time in color the customs, habits and costumes of these interesting peoples of the Orient.

Dr. Salisbury had the good fortune to be in Pekin at the time of the recent uprising. Concerning this he cabled Carl H. Pierce recently: "I have the only camera here. Have fine close-ups of the fighting, bursting shells, etc. Large footage;" following this up with another message: "My camera is the only one in Pekin during all the trouble and I have taken several thousand feet and am still taking. It is all in color. Taken for The Prizma, Inc."

Doubtless this is the first time in the history of the world that a revolution in China or in any other country on the globe has been taken in color and the Prizma people are enthusiastically awaiting Dr. Salisbury's arrival, because it is expected that these views of bursting shells and other battle scenes will give Americans and the public at large a better idea of actual fighting conditions as they exist than anything yet offered for the screen.

Billy the Exhibitor

While Appreciating the Benefits of Properly Prepared Press Matter, He Hands Out a Joke to the Publicity Man Who Sells Himself to the Boss.

By E. T. Keyser.

BILLY had a pipe in the southwest corner of his mouth, a pair of shears in his right hand and a paste brush in his left, the waste basket was overflowing and his office looked like the editorial room of a country paper just about to go to press.

"Gee, I am glad to see you," he observed with that portion of his mouth not holding the pipe. "I have a few observations regarding press agents that would sour in my system if I didn't get them out pretty quickly."

"What is the brand of calamity that is making you so exceedingly glad to see me on a busy day?" I asked.

"See that waste basket?" said Billy. "It's full of press dope that was fired at me by misguided individuals who imagined that I had any particular interest in the fact as to whether the plans of various picture companies were formulated after hard and laborious study, who did the studying, and also why he thinks his concern is the greatest that ever came down the pike or ever will come and incidentally how, when or why the- boss of the aforementioned concern is one of the greatest minds in the picture field today."

"Then you don't care about personal reminiscences of that sort?" I inquired.

"I certainly do not," said Billy with much emphasis. "I don't care the forty-second part of a rap whether the boss stayed up all night to figure out a program or a policy or whether it came to him in the guise of an acute attack of indigestion produced by a Welsh rabbit having the wrong reaction on a lot of ill-assorted wet goods.

"Neither do I care how big or how grand is the celebrated Mr. B. Unkum. The only thing I care about is information I can spread to my fellow-townsmen that will make them want to come in to see the- picture and make them want to come so badly that they will leave tangible evidence of their desire in the box office.

"Neither do I care how many near accidents stars, staresses and would-be stars experience in the course of a week or a rehearsal. Perhaps if one of them jumped off a cliff and was spattered over the surrounding landscape, thereby creating a universal interest in the afore-demised's last picture I might gain a fuller house if the news was tactfully spread abroad, but otherwise you cannot expect anyone to buy an extra admission because Molly Molasses narrowly escaped drowning by not embarking on a boat that ran ashore two days later."

"Then you don't like the line of press work that is being handed out?" I asked.

"A great deal of it, no," said Billy, 'and still there is enough of good stuff written by fellows who know their business to help me get out my house organ and liven up my program, but I notice that this line of matter comes from men who have held their jobs down long enough to be able to distinguish between what will help an exhibitor increase admissions, and what the boss will like because he finds his name mentioned in nineteen assorted places.

"The trouble seems to me that just about the time a press agent gets wise to the kind of dope that helps exhibitors, the boss's first cousin by his fourth wife comes along and wins the experienced man's job away and has to be taught all over again and by the time he really begins to make good the boss's fourth wife becomes an angel and some relative of number five succeeds to the job."

CHAPIN PHOTOGRAPH IN LINCOLN HOUSE.

O. H. Oldroyd, noted as the owner of the house in which Lincoln died in Washington, D. C., which contains the famous Oldroyd Lincoln Memorial collection, requested a photograph of Benjamin Chapin for framing in the Lincoln House just after the Lincoln Cycle was given a private showing in the National Capitol.

Mr. Chapin felt so pleased with the request that he immediately arranged for a special sitting at his studio, and the portrait has been sent to Mr. Oldroyd by special messenger with a note explaining "The Lincoln Man's" gratification at being able to find place in the Oldroyd Lincoln collection.

RATH GOES TO YAPHANK.

Frederick Rath, scenario editor for Apollo Pictures, Inc., has been called in the draft. He was passed by the medical board and enters the military service on September 19. The chairman of the district board has selected him to have charge of the drafted men from his district when they entrain for Camp Upton at Yaphank, L. I.

Prompt Rebuilding of Eastern Studio

Jaxon Film Corporation's Progress Unchecked by $65,000 Fire at Providence, R. I.

BY a fire that started from undetermined causes at 3 a. m. on August 23, the extensive plant of the Jaxon Film Corporation at Providence, R. I., was damaged to the extent of $65,000. By 3 p. m. work had been resumed making pictures. On the second day following, Saturday, ground had been broken for rebuilding.

The fire destroyed the main studio building at the plant,

Main Studio of Jaxon Film Co., Which Was Gutted by Fire.

but left the laboratory unscathed. The company is enabled to go along with its regular work from having an outdoor studio and a small indoor studio left. The work of making Sparkle Comedies and Jaxon Comedies for release through General Film Company will therefore not be interrupted. A serial which the company is producing will not be delayed much. However, considerable film which was being handled on government contract was destroyed in the building which was burned, entailing a setback which will be costly. Arrangements have already been made to replace this film.

The new building is to cost $75,000. The company has also a studio at Jacksonville which can be used if necessary.

Defective insulation of electric wiring is supposed to have caused the fire.

TRIANGLE WANTS EXHIBITORS' CRITICISMS.

"The Triangle Film Corporation will organise an exhibitors' service department at the Culver City studio, which will be maintained solely for the purpose of studying exhibiting conditions and co-operation with exhibitors from the studio end," says Manager Davis. "The individual and community needs of the exhibitors will be investigated from every viewpoint, and sincere effort will be made to determine the most satisfying kind of pictures and the methods of production that will best please exhibitor and public alike.

"Right now I want to take occasion to appeal to every exhibitor in the country to communicate their needs, suggestions and complaints to me at the Triangle Culver City, California, Studio, and I will see that they are given immediate attention by this department. We do not expect to satisfy or please every exhibitor, but our efforts will be directed toward securing the best results obtainable for the majority."

JUDGE WILLIS BROWN WRITES FOR UNIVERSAL.

Judge Willis Brown, widely known throughout the United States as a juvenile authority and educator, has been lured into the motion pictures. That is, the founder and first judge of the Utah juvenile courts and the originator of the Boy City movement, has written a number of stories for the screen which are to be produced by Universal. The first of these stories to be filmed is entitled "Nancy's Baby," in which Violet MacMillan will be starred on the Butterfly program. A series of boy stories will follow. It is in connection with his Boy City idea that Judge Brown has made the greatest contribution to the advancement of children, particularly boys.

The Roll of Honor

EARL METCALFE, announcement of whose appointment as a lieutenant in the officers reserve corps of the United States Army was recently made, was born and raised near Fort Thomas, Kentucky. Lieutenant Metcalfe was a graduate of the Plattsburg camp. At one time he was a captain in the Kentucky National Guard, and has organized many drill organizations. He has appeared in many military and naval characters on the screen. When with the Kalem company he was one of the first players to don a uniform in a war time subject. Also with Lubin he appeared in many military dramas. His last appearances on the screen before departing for Plattsburg were in a Mutual serial, in which he played the leading male role, and with Art Dramas. Lieutenant Metcalfe, who is twenty-eight years old and married, has been assigned to the National Army at Camp Upton, Long Island.

Lieutenant Earl Metcalfe.

* * *

Edward J. McCloskey, formerly Moving Picture World correspondent for Boston and vicinity, and well known in moving picture and newspaper circles, has enlisted in Uncle Sam's Navy, and has been assigned to transport duty. Mr. McCloskey was given a fine send-off the other night in Boston when he departed for New York, where he goes on to one of the world's greatest liners, now a transport, as a yeoman. Mr. McCloskey for two years has been on the reportorial staff of the Boston American. Before that he was a member of the force of the Atlanta staff of General Film. When Edward J. Farrell took over the Southern office of General Film he took. Mr. McCloskey South with him as his secretary and assistant manager. On Mr. Farrell's return to Boston, Mr. McClockey left the film business and returned to active newspaper work.

* * *

William Cunningham, owner of the Orpheum and White Way theaters at Fredonia, Kan., has left his houses in charge of Mrs. Cunningham to take up work with the Red Cross.

* * *

Mr. Kindley, of Kindley & Perry, who conduct the Drexel theater at Coffeyville, Kan., has joined the aviation corps.

* * *

Mannie Gottlieb, former manager of Favorite Features exchange, Minneapolis, Minn., is now drilling with Aero Squadron No. 72 at Kelly Field, South San Antonio, Texas.

* * *

R. H. Zerbel, manager of the Marquette opera house, Marquette, Mich., was recently in Detroit bidding his friends goodbye. He has enlisted in New York University Hopsital Unit, and is now somewhere in France.

* * *

Arthur W. Metcalfe, who played a prominent role in the recent Essanay production, "The Golden Idiot," as well as numerous other pictures, has resigned from Essanay and is now training in the Canadian army. Mr. Metcalfe joined the First Battalion, Forty-eighth Highlanders, and is at Camp Borden, Ontario, preparatory to sailing for the front. Mr. Metcalfe is a native of England. He played in several London stage hits before crossing to this country. He has been with the Essanay company two years.

MRS. ALLEN WALKER WITH NOBLE.

Mrs. Allen Walker, who will be remembered for her characterization of Mother Camillo in "The Call of Her People," supporting Ethel Barrymore, has signed with Director John Noble and will appear in a new picture supporting Arnold Daly. For the first time in many years Mrs. Walker will be seen in other than a character part, her "gypsy" and "hag" soles having made her famous in that particular line of work.

Larry Peyton Hero of "The Red Ace"

LARRY PEYTON, one of the best known and most popular leading men in the films, who plays the leading role opposite Marie Walcamp in the new Universal serial, "The Red Ace," announced for release early in October, is an actor of wide experience. Originally "intended for the farm" by his father, who was a tobacco planter in Kentucky, his early training and education were anything but conducive to a career behind the footlights or before the cameraman. With a thorough foundation in the way of elementary education, he was sent to the Colorado Agricultural College, where he started in to learn all the fine points of stable sanitation, mechanical milking, and the rotation of crops.

But, notwithstanding all the lavishing of money and attention upon his agricultural education, Larry always had a hankering for the stage. So it was not strange that the embryo farmer, once beyond the influence of immediate parental association, soon found his way behind the footlights. His debut, in an "ornamental" part, was made at the Curtis theater in Denver, but it was not long before the manager of the stock company gave him something to say.

Larry Peyton.

He worked hard those first three months, at the end of which period he went to Chicago and obtained, through a friend, a part in "Human Hearts," that rugged old melodrama known to almost every town in America boasting an opera house. He toured throughout the West in this production, and was later associated with many traveling companies. One of his last roles in the spoken drama was that of Stephen Brice in "The Crisis."

But in spite of his success, Peyton longed for work in the out-of-doors. "I never could accustom myself to the speaking stage," he said the other day, "notwithstanding its fascination for me—it always seemed such a cramped place for a man to work in. I suppose that was due to the fact that I had lived so long in the open, and when a chance came for me to get into the movies I lost no time in availing myself of it. I would never think of going back to the stage."

Before joining the Universal, Peyton appeared in productions of Kalem, Balboa, Lasky and others, and has played important roles with Marguerite Clark, Blanche Sweet and Geraldine Farrar, appearing with the last named as Gaspard in "Joan the Woman." He is fully six feet tall and of fine physique, proving the ideal hero of "The Red Ace."

FOX FILM CORPORATION TAKES MORE SPACE.

To keep abreast of the need for more space, due to the expansion of its business, especially within the last year, extensive alterations are being made in the Leavitt Building, at 130 West Forty-sixth street, New York, after the completion of which Fox Film Corporation will occupy the entire seventh floor.

The primary reasons for taking greater area, in addition to that it already has, is the rise of Mr. Fox's Standard Pictures and the growth of the Fox Special Features, which are released weekly. It is only a few years since the company occupied a single floor.

This space has increased steadily until the offices now require five floors. The corporation also maintains an enormous loft, or storehouse, in the downtown section of New York.

CONNOR HEADS MUTUAL IN INDIANAPOLIS.

The Mutual Film Corporation has appointed J. G. Connor, formerly a salesman, as temporary manager of the Indianapolis branch office.

MOVING PICTURE WORLD
NEWS REEL for AUGUST

Chicago News Letter

By JAS. S. McQUADE

Pictures for War Purposes

An Interesting Chat With John R. Freuler on Patriotic and Other Films.

DURING an interview with John R. Freuler, president of the Mutual Film Corporation, last week the conversation touched on the desire of producers to render willing and intelligent service to the Government in the present crisis. Mr. Freuler is chairman of the war co-operative committee of the N. A. M. P. I., in connection with the Navy Department, and he is in favor of the production of features the stories of which would meet the requirements of the Navy and War Departments. The secretaries of these departments are exceedingly busy men just now, but if each could outline the needs of the hour in his department so that they could be embodied in a feature story for production, the producers of the country are ready to do their share in making films that will give these needs the widest publicity.

Regarding the "four-minute men," who deliver speeches in picture theaters throughout the country, Mr. Freuler is of the opinion that much better results could be obtained if the subject matter of these speeches was turned into story form and visualized. By this means more can be told on the screen in four minutes than could be done in a speech that would take half an hour to deliver, besides, the screen story would be more vivid and lasting. This method would also avoid causing complaints from exhibitors, as is now the case in several instances, where the speakers sometimes take up fifteen minutes instead of four. Mr. Freuler intends taking up this subject in the near future with George Creel, civilian chairman of the committee on public information.

There is no doubt that producers will be glad to make special patriotic feature pictures, if the Government departments will outline the special needs that are to be met and which should be given the widest publicity. Devotion to country by those who offer themselves at the front should be equaled at least in willing service by those who remain at home. It is understood, of course, that these special patriotic features are to be released and rented just like other features, and that in themselves they have the attractiveness to win liberal patronage.

Mr. Freuler incidentally mentioned "Our Country's Call," in which Mary Miles Minter plays the leading role, and which will be released October 1. This photoplay story has deep human interest and strong patriotic appeal. Indeed, the dominant note is patriotism. It was produced by the American Film Company, Inc., under the direction of Lloyd Ingraham.

Speaking of the Charles Frohman players now being visualized, Mr. Freuler was much pleased with the outlook. The first of these, "Outcast," with Ann Murdock in the leading role, will be released September 10, and this

John R. Freuler

will be followed by "The Runaway," in which Julia Sanderson stars, the release date being September 17.

"Please Help Emily," which as a play had fine vogue in this country and is still showing in England, is now being produced at the Empire studios, Long Island, with Ann Murdock in the lead. Olive Tell, one of Charles Frohman's stars, is now working in "The Unforseen," another successful Charles Frohman play. The announcement that William Gillette will soon begin work in "Secret Service" at the Empire studios will be received with great acclaim by exhibitors throughout the country.

Mr. Freuler makes no bones in saying outright that he is never satisfied with business; but on this occasion he was compelled to state that he had no cause to complain. And well he may refrain from complaining; for no less than 100 new customers—in the Chicago territory alone—have been secured within the last two weeks in view of the two features a week released, which include Charles Frohman plays and the product of the American Film Company. This, Mr. Freuler concedes, is most encouraging at the present time.

D. W. Griffith Champions England's Natural Light.

At various times we have either read, or have heard it said, that the natural light in England was poor for producing purposes. Now no less an authority than D. W. Griffith explodes the statement, as is shown by the following paragraphs from a recent interview which appeared in the Weekly Dispatch, of London, England:

"There is nothing to compare with the variety of color in an English landscape. You have old walls of between 300 and 400 years old which only time could have painted. The winding lanes have unexpected lines and changing beauty. In the new country the houses are all exactly like each other; in the old country, in the villages, there are so many different shapes and styles of houses that you wonder how it is possible for them to have been invented. Let the people in the States see moving pictures of your English country life—the pastoral simplicity of the villages.

"It is absolute nonsense to say that your lighting here is a handicap. Some of the pictures we have already taken here are the most beautiful we have made anywhere. The light is as good as in the States, and, what is more important, it lasts longer. In the States we have to stop at six o'clock; it gets darker much sooner. Over here we have taken pictures as late as nine o'clock in the evening. Here, too, we can get much more artistic effects because of your long, varying twilight. It is the most beautiful twilight imaginable."

Peel Off the Cotton Wool.

The untiring activities, of late, of Major Funkhouser in the censorial field, as shown in his attitude toward "The Little American," "Within the Law" and "The Spy," all films to which no loyal American can take exception, have aroused great hostility to his methods in Chicago.

The Second Deputy, by some fancied God-bestowed wisdom, assumes the right to prevent adults, no matter how enlightened, from viewing pictures on which he has placed his ban. He predicted for the release of "The Little American" great injury to the feelings of Americans of German origin, and other ills; but I have talked with a number of these citizens and they have testified that they had not suffered any ill effects. The truth is these men are good Americans and don't give a snap for the Kaiser. America is their country and their sons are going to the front for her.

The Major is getting what he richly deserves from all sides, a sample of which is furnished by the following editorial from the Chicago Post, which appeared under the title, "Peel off the Cotton Wool":

The delicate sensibilities of Chicago's public are being tenderly protected. We are not allowed to see anything that might shock or horrify. We are not permitted to feel a little of the reflected anguish of Europe. Broken bodies and shed blood are the commonplaces of France and

Flanders, but pictures that would help us to visualize something of what our allies have suffered are kept from our gaze.

We understand that the pictures showing the tanks in action at the battle of the Ancre were subjected to the "cut out" process and all unpleasant scenes eliminated before permission was given for their local production. And now the guardian of our innocence refuses to allow "The Spy" to be shown until the "close-ups" are expunged that show a loyal American suffering torture because he refuses to disclose secrets greatly desired by the Berlin police and the German war office.

It is about time we peeled off the cotton wool. This nursery care which we are now enduring makes mollycoddles of us. We cannot hope to live in isolation from the pain of the world—and we should not hope to.

The banned picture contains no horror that the Kaiser's vassals have not inflicted numberless times on their victims. Many things more cruel have been done. It is part of the needed education of the American people to know about these things, and to know about them in a way that will make us feel them.

Major Funkhouser's services as a shock absorber for Chicago are tiresome, harmful, and ought to be ended.

Chicago Film Brevities.

Director J. A. Richmond recently completed "A Midnight Bell," of the Selig-Hoyt comedy series, and is now engaged in the production of "A Contented Woman," another of the Selig-Hoyt comedies, which will be released Monday, Sept. 17. The first mentioned was released Monday, Sept. 3.

* * *

Mary Miles Minter took second place, with 1,000 votes, for the first week of the popularity contest now being conducted by Photoplay Art Magazine. Gail Kane, Juliette Day, Charlotte Burton and Kathleen Kirkham, other American Film Company stars, also secured high places on the list of contestants.

* * *

Colin Campbell, dean of the Selig directors, recently returned to the Selig Los Angeles studios from his summer vacation and is now engaged in the production of "The Still Alarm," in which Thomas Santschi plays the lead. Other prominent Selig players in the cast are Bessie Eyton and Fritzi Brunette.

* * *

Sidney E. Abel, manager of Chicago Vitagraph branch office, is circulating a petition for signatures which asks that Major Funkhouser be removed as film censor, or that the censorship be likewise applied to newspapers, sermons and stage dramas. "Within the Law" (Vitagraph) is still held up by the Chicago censor.

* * *

It has been announced that Henry B. Walthall's productions will bear the Paralta brand and that they will be released through the Triangle Distributing Corporation.

* * *

Peggy O'Neil, the well known star in the stage success, "Peg O' My Heart," has been selected to play the lead in "The Penny Philanthropist." She arrived in the city last week and began work at the Wholesome Films studio under the direction of Guy McConnell. Ralph Morgan, who is a popular figure in the cast of "Turn to the Right," which has been turning many away at Cohan's Grand and which is now in the thirty-third week of its run, is playing opposite Miss O'Neill.

* * *

In a recent interview, in England, D. W. Griffith announced that he has already produced a picture in that country which will be worth 100,000 men to the cause of the Allies when shown in the United States.

* * *

"The Spy," a patriotic production by Fox, in which Dustin Farnum plays the lead, has been forbidden public showing in Chicago by Major Funkhouser. A special invitation presentation of the picture, which was attended by many prominent Chicago people, was given at the Studebaker Monday morning, Aug. 27, and the consensus of opinion was decidedly in favor of the Funkhouser ban being lifted. An appeal to the courts will be made for permission to have it shown here. The photoplay critics of the Chicago dailies, who saw the picture at the Studebaker, are all in favor of its being presented in Chicago. Kitty Kelly writes: "The picture is strongly American—strongly anti-enemy, which is in this case anti-German. It's perfectly respectable, so far as that section of the ordinance goes, and certainly should not arouse any race riot or prejudice among American citizens—the only kind of people there is room for in the country at present."

* * *

Wm. N. Selig, president of the Selig Polyscope Co., recently forwarded a composite film to the National Association of the Motion Picture Industry, New York, which is intended for use in a nation-wide campaign for legislative

uses. The first part of this film shows the famous fight in "The Spoilers," in its entirety, which is considered the most realistic fistic event ever shown in a photoplay; the second part shows Tom Mix in some of his most sensational cowboy feats on horseback, and the third shows Kathlyn Williams in several of her hair-raising adventures with wild animals. Everyone who has seen this Selig composite film has pronounced it a strong attraction.

* * *

Friday, Sept. 7, is the date of the next regular meeting of Chicago Local, M. P. E. L. of America, in their hall, on the fifth floor of the Masonic Temple. As Messrs. Joseph Hopp, Peter J. Schaefer, Robert R. Levy, Alfred Hamburger and William J. Sweeney—who attended the recent meeting of the officers and national executive committee of the M. P. E. L. of America in New York—will have some interesting statements to make, a large attendance should mark the occasion.

* * *

W. R. Rothacker, president of the Rothacker Film Manufacturing Company, left for New York City Thursday, August 30, where he will remain for about a fortnight on business.

* * *

The Italian war pictures, entitled "The Italian Battle Front," are continuing to do a crowded business at the Auditorium. Through their influence hundreds of alien Italians have applied at the recruiting stations either to enlist under Uncle Sam or to be sent back to Italy to enlist under King Victor.

* * *

"Efficiency Edgar's Courtship," by Essanay, has been receiving favorable criticism from the local press generally during the week. Taylor Holmes comes in for numerous compliments and high praise for his work in the title role.

Mae Marsh

THOUGH she got her start in motion pictures more or less by accident there is no question but what Mae Marsh, the famous little celebrity and star in "Polly of the Circus," the first Goldwyn release, found the vocation she was best fitted for. Her rise in motion pictures has been meteoric.

Miss Marsh is one of the youngest of the stars of the screen. She is only twenty years old. She was born in Santa Fe, N. M., where her father was an officer of the Santa Fe railroad.

The "accident" by which Mae Marsh became associated with motion pictures occurred in Los Angeles. She was in a studio watching her sister, Marguerite, rehearse for a production being directed by D. W. Griffith. The director was attracted by the little girl sitting on a box in the corner and asked her if she would like to go into motion pictures. With a nod of her head Mae Marsh entered upon a great future.

Within three years she was featured in "The Birth of a Nation," and a year later in "Intolerance." Last September Samuel Goldfish, president of Goldwyn Pictures, induced Miss Marsh to join the company he was forming. He admits she

Mae Marsh.

was the inspiration for the formation of the Goldwyn corporation. The following is a partial list of the big picture productions in which Miss Marsh has appeared either as the star or in important roles, and covers a period of five years: "The Birth of a Nation," "Intolerance," "The Wharf Rat," "The Little Liar," "The Marriage of Molly O.," "Hoodoo Ann," "The Wild Girl of the Sierras," "The Escape," "A Child of the Paris Streets," "Judith of Bethulia," "The Sands of Dee," "A Temporary Truse," and "Man's Genesis," the latter her first "hit" and the one responsible for her permanent engagement by the Biograph Company.

News of Los Angeles and Vicinity
By G. P. HARLEMAN

Yorke-Metro Coming East
Balshofer's Company Will Make Pictures in Eastern Studios For Three Months.

IN ORDER to complete the production, "Paradise Garden," which was begun in the Hollywood studios of the Yorke Film Corporation, the Harold Lockwood company, under the direction of F. J. Balshofer, will this week go to New York, where scenes of the picture requiring locations in New York City will be filmed.

Following the completion of "Paradise Garden" in New York, Mr. Balshofer's company will probably undertake the production of several Lockwood comedy-dramas before returning to the Los Angeles studios. Stories are now under consideration, and it is probable that either two or three of these will be produced in the East.

Since bringing the Harold Lockwood company to California about a year ago, the Yorke-Metro company has produced six pictures at the Hollywood studios. According to Balshofer, this is an ideal location for the making of most of the Harold Lockwood features. The Yorke-Metro studios in Hollywood will therefore be closed only temporary, or until perhaps the first of 1918, when it is expected that the Lockwood company will have returned from the East.

Those who are leaving Los Angeles for New York this week are Harold Lockwood; Fred J. Balshofer; Lester Cuneo, heavy man; Richard V. Spencer, scenario editor; Tony Gaudio, cameraman; Ben Pierpaolo, assistant; and Wiley J. Gibson, business manager.

Crane Wilbur to Go on Tour of United States.
Crane Wilbur, whose present contract calling for appearance in a series of pictures for the Art Dramas expires August 22, will leave Los Angeles early in September, to begin the first lap of a nation-wide tour, in which he will make personal appearances at a large number of motion picture theaters throughout the country. Mr. Wilbur will fill the first engagements of his personal tour in the southern and middle-western states and will continue through the leading cities for an extended trip of several months duration. The route of his tour is being arranged by Carlyle R. Robinson, who accompanied J. Warren Kerrigan on the first extensive tour of this kind to be undertaken by a motion picture star.

Los Angeles Film Brevities.
Work on the seventh episode of "The Lost Express" the Signal-Mutual serial feature, Helen Holmes is progressing rapidly, Director General J. P. McGowan having "shot" 180 scenes in two days.

For scenes in this episode Mr. McGowan took the Helen Holmes company to Delmar, California, where a number of locations about the Saratoga Inn were used.

* * *

Sherwood Macdonald, former director of Jackie Saunders, Horkheimer Mutual star, is having his first experience at "shooting the baby" as, in studio vernacular they call photographing the baby star, Gloria Joy.

* * *

Anita King, Balboa's new star, has begun work in a five reel feature under direction of Edgar Jones, who has just completed "The Twisted Thread" for Horkheimer Brothers. Miss King's first story is "The Girl Angle" by L. V. Jefferson. Miss King will be the featured star in a series of six photoplays all to be produced under the management of E. D. Horkheimer and for release by Mutual.

* * *

Jack Dillon, formerly of the Vogue and Keystone Companies, has joined the Triangle Film Corporation directorial staff and soon will begin the production of a picture in which Olive Thomas will play the leading role.

* * *

Mildred Delfino, the Triangle actress who was dangerously injured while working in support of Miss Margery

Wilson at the Hartville ranch studio several days ago, is recovering rapidly and soon will return to her studio duties at Culver City.

* * *

Mr. and Mrs. Harry Todd, and daughter Margaret, Harold Lloyd, Marie Mosquini and Gil Pratt were guests at a reception and dinner given by Bebe Daniels, leading lady of the Rolin, at her seashore home at Ocean Park, Sunday, August 19.

* * *

Al Griffin, for five years technical director with the Essanay Company and also with Rex Beach for a long period, has been engaged by the Rolin Company as technical director.

* * *

Deep inroads are being made into the ranks of the Rolin Company by the National call to the colors. Three of the boys have already appeared before the examining board and have been found physically fit for the selective army. They are Hal Roach, Director-General of the company; Herb Kerrigan, assistant director to Mr. Roach and Harry "Snub" Pollard of the Harold Lloyd Company. Dwight Whiting, treasurer, secretary and manager of the Rolin, has just been notified to appear for examination.

* * *

The Harold Lloyd Company, under the direction of Alf Goulding, has started the filming of a new one reel comedy featuring Harold Lloyd. He is being supported by Bebe Daniels and Harry "Snub" Pollard.

* * *

Josephine Sedgwick, who recently joined the Triangle Culver City studio playing forces as a stock woman, has done such creditable work in the first production in which she appeared that she has been elevated to the rank of a leading woman and will play opposite Roy Stewart in the Western star's next picture.

In her new position Miss Sedgwick will be one of the youngest leading women enrolled under the Triangle banner, but she has been engaged in dramatic work since childhood. She was in vaudeville several seasons with members of her family as one of the "Five Sedgwicks" and has been before the camera two years. Her previous appearance in a Triangle picture was in support of Belle Bennett in "Ashes of Hope," which will be released in the near future.

* * *

George Stone, Beulah Burns, Thelma Burns and the celebrated Triangle Kiddies soon will be seen again in a production which has been begun at the Triangle Culver City studio under the direction of William V. Mong.

Margery Wilson is the featured player in the cast and is supported by George Chesboro, but the youngsters have prominent parts in a counter plot that will enable the many admirers to enjoy their work.

* * *

"The Firefly of Tough Luck" is the new drama E. Mason Hopper is directing at the Triangle Culver City studios. Walt Whitman and Alma Reuben are playing the leading roles.

* * *

Four hours a day was the limit of work for the Triangle Company directed by Lynn Reynolds, while in the vicinity of Victorville, shooting scenes for the Olive Thomas Company, "Broadway Arizona," due to the fact that the mercury around Victorville is on speaking terms with one hundred degrees in the shade, and no shade to be found.

* * *

With activities at the Triangle-Keystone studios in Hollywood, California, slipping along in two-four time, comes the announcement that the famous song writer and director, Harry Williams, will again be with the comedy forces, starting Monday.

Harry Williams has three stories under consideration, his initial production with the Triangle-Keystone studios to be determined as soon as his company has been organized and decided upon. It is likely that he will make his first comedy with Max Asher, who has just signed a Triangle-Keystone contract. Asher is a well known figure in film comedy, his most recent work being with Universal.

* * *

With five companies in operation turning out one and two reel comedies, and another to start next week, the scenario staff at the Triangle-Keystone studios have found little else .o do but work and work hard. Headed by Albert Glassmire, the Triangle-Keystone writing staff now includes Walter McNamara, Walter Fredericks, Harry Wulze, and Anthony Coldowey.

* * *

Enid Markey is finishing her work with the Fox company, a special engagement opposite George Walsh. Her future plans are not fully developed, but she is already considering several things.

* * *

Margarita Fischer has completed her work in "The Girl Who Would Not Grow Up" and promises to pay Los Angeles a short visit soon. The film is a bright comedy written for Miss Fischer, has been made in and around San Diego. It is likely that Miss Fischer will stick to this line.

* * *

Henry King brought his wife, Gypsy Abbott, to Los Angeles to submit to an operation and the plucky little lady, now in a Los Angeles hospital, is reported as getting along nicely. Miss Abbott was unable to see herself in the preview of "Lorelei of the Sea" in which she did capital work.

* * *

Ten Los Angeles film exchanges will soon be extablished, with convenient offices and supply facilities in a six-story reinforced concrete building at 720-24 South Hill street, alterations to be made by Lawrence B. Burch and Dr. W. Jarvis Barlow, lessees of the building. Plans have been made by architect Frauenfleder for remodeling of several floors of the building for motion picture firms.

* * *

The Los Angeles photoplay colony was a large contributor of talent for a benefit performance given at the Mason Opera House for the French Wounded Emergency Fund. Among those who gave their bit to entertain the audience were Raymond Hatton, Louise Huff, Wallace Reid, Mary Pickford, Charlie Murray, Eric Campbell, Charlie Chaplin, Harry Carol, Julian Eltinge and Hughie Mack.

* * *

W. Todd Martin, of Australia, is registered at the Hotel Alexandria. He is here to buy feature films for release on the Australian market.

* * *

Dan Cupid continues to be a happy busybody at Universal City and a few nights ago the little god of love was chief guest at the wedding of Miss Eileen Sedgwick and Justin H. McCloskey.

* * *

Miss Sedgwick has been featured during the past year in Bison thrillers in which lions, leopards and other beasts of the jungle contribute to the exciting scenes.

* * *

McCloskey came to Universal City from New York a year and a half ago and at present is assistant to Director George Marshall, producer of western pictures.

* * *

The filming of the sixth episode of the latest Universal serial, "The Phantom Ship," has begun under the direction of Francis Ford. Ben Wilson is the featured player with a large supporting cast headed by Neva Gerber, Kingsley Benedict, Duke Worne and Elsie Van Name.

* * *

Director Eugene Moore is rapidly nearing the completion at Universal City of a five-reel drama entitled "O'Connor's Mag." The production, the story of which was written by Charles J. Wilson, Jr., features Edith Roberts. Others in the cast are P. S. Pembroke, Francis McDonald, Harry Mann and Marie Van Tassel.

* * *

With Eddie Lyons and Lee Moran as his principal players, Director Harry Edwards is filming a two-reel Nestor comedy, "The King Was Crowned," at Universal City.

* * *

Frank H. Spearman's story, "The Run of the Yellow Mail," is under production at Universal City by Director George Marshall in three reels. The leading role is played by Helen Gibson, supported by Val Paul, Buck Connors, G. Raymond Nye and Wadsworth Harris. R. A. Dillon prepared the scenario.

* * *

"The Ghost Girl" is the title of a five-reel comedy-drama being produced at Universal City under the direction of

Jack Wells. Donna Drew plays the leading role. Miss Drew has in her support Casson Ferguson, Claire Du Brey, Fred Montague and Victor Rottman. The story was written by Patricia Foulds and prepared for the screen by Charles J. Wilson, Jr., and George Hively.

* * *

The Universal western company under the direction of Jack Ford is filming a five-reel drama entitled "Bucking Broadway." It features Harry Carey with Molly Malone. playing opposite. George Hively wrote the story and prepared the screen version also.

* * *

With an all-star cast of players headed by Dorothy Phillips, William Stowell and Jack Mulhall, Miss Ida May Park of the Bluebird studios is filming a five-reel drama entitled "The Boss of Powderville." Miss Park prepared the scenario from a story written by Thomas Addison, and which appeared in "Adventure."

* * *

Frank Borsage, who has just joined the Universal company, will make his first appearance opposite Brownie. Vernon under the direction of Allen J. Holubar in "The Twisted Soul," a five-reel feature production. Borsage before entering the motion pictures was on the legitimate stage for several years playing in various stock companies.

* * *

With Ruth Clifford and Monroe Salisbury as his principal players, Director Rupert Julian is filming a five-reel drama at the Bluebird studios. This photoplay, which is being produced under the working title of "Julie Sandovel," was written by Elliott J. Clawson.

* * *

A five-reel drama, dealing with the backwoods, is under production at Universal City by Director E. J. Le Saint. It is entitled "The Wolf and His Mate" and features Louise Lovely. The story was written by Julia Maier and was prepared for the screen by Doris Schroeder. Hart Hoxie, Hector Dion, George O'Dell, Betty Schade and Georgia French appear with Miss Lovely in this production.

* * *

Al Santell, who is directing Victor comedies at Universal City, is engaged in the filming of a one reel farce comedy entitled "The Pink Pajamas." Gladys Tennyson and Dave Morris are the principal players.

* * *

The production of the sixteen-episode serial, "The Gray Ghost," is nearing completion at Universal City, Director Stuart Paton now being engaged on the fourteenth installment of the story. The action is largely carried by Priscilla Dean, Eddie Polo, Harry Carter and Emory Johnson.

* * *

Director Allen J. Holubar has under production at Universal City a five-reel drama entitled "The Twisted Soul." featuring Brownie Vernon. Supporting Miss Vernon are Frank Borsage, Murdock MacQuarrie, Joseph Girard and Miles McCarthy. The story was written by J. Grubb Alexander and Fred Myton.

* * *

To the cast supporting Miss Mae Murray in "The Princess Virtue," which includes Wheeler Oakman, Harry Von Meter, Gretchen Lederer, Jean Hersholt and Clarissa Selwynn, has been added Paul Nicholson, popular star of the musical comedy stage. This engagement marks Nicholson's first screen appearance since the perfection of motion pictures. He is, however, one of the pioneers of screen acting.

* * *

David Horsley is expected to return to his Los Angeles studios early next week after nearly a month's business trip in Eastern states.

* * *

The Cub Comedy featuring George Ovey has just completed the filming of "Officer Jerry," written and directed by Milton H. Fahrney. The action is somewhat unique in that Jerry is called upon to enact a "cop" role, the sight of a policeman to Jerry ordinarily being the high sign 'to. "beat it."

* * *

Director Thomas Ricketts will this week complete the filming of Mary MacLaren's second feature photoplay made under her contract with David Horsley.

* * *

Harrish Ingraham has nearly completed "The Child of M'sieu," a five-reel drama featuring Baby Marie Osborne for the Pathe program. The camera work executed by William Nobles promises many new efforts as the result of a number of experiments made recently under a new lighting process.

Export Items

By E. T. McGovern.

LEROY GARFINKLE, New York representative of the Sociedad General Cinematografica, has just closed a deal by which his company controls the rights in Chile, Uruguay, Paraguay and Argentina for the Triangle Pictures.

* * *

Myron Selznick has moved his office to the 8th floor of the Godfrey Bldg., and is handling the film advertising service. There is a rumor afloat that Myron may go into the foreign rights selling field.

* * *

Felix Malitz, General Manager of the Piedmont Pictures Corp., is receiving regularly extremely interesting films from France and England showing current topics. His latest arrivals were films showing General Pershing and the American troops in Paris on July 4th and the celebration of July 14th by the French troops.

* * *

Alexander Beyfuss, President of the Iliodor Picture Corporation, informs us that the demand for foreign rights on "The Fall of the Romanoffs" has exceeded his utmost expectations. No contracts will be closed until the showing is made to the trade at the Ritz-Carlton Hotel.

* * *

Fred Warren of the Goldwyn Pictures, reports a continued demand for the rights on his pictures from the Spanish speaking countries.

* * *

The Fleitzer Film Co. of 220 W. 42nd Street, have received five Danish five-reel features for exploitation in the United States and South American territories.

* * *

Jacob Gluckmann has moved from the third floor of the World's Tower Building to suite 407, the same building, into more spacious quarters and invites offers from producers for distribution through Max Glucksmann of Argentina.

* * *

The Russian Art Films, now being exploited in the United States, are open for negotiations for distribution in the South American markets.

* * *

The Universal is inaugurating a campaign through its export department for the sales in South America of "Twenty Thousand Leagues Under the Sea." This picture should have a strong appeal to the Spanish and Portugese speaking people.

* * *

J. Frank Brockliss is preparing to return to England. He will leave his office in capable hands for the erection of a larger export trade than ever before. The Billy West Comedies are a great attraction to foreign buyers and a number of sales have been consummated.

* * *

The Bray Cartoons have been sold for Mexico. There seems to be a strong demand for these laugh-provoking pictures in the Latin-American fields. They now are contracted for in Argentina, Uruguay, Paraguay, Chile, Porto Rico and Mexico.

* * *

The Precision Machine Co. reports a rapidly increasing demand for the Simplex in the South American countries. A big contract is now in contemplation with one of the largest importers in this territory for the exclusive agency of these projectors.

COMPETITION FOR JUVENILE REVIEWERS.

William Fox is offering prizes of $500, to be distributed in five awards of $100 each, for the best written reviews on "Jack and the Beanstalk." Any boy or girl under 14 years of age is eligible and is invited to compete in the contest, which begins with the announcement.

The reviews should be written on only one side of the paper and should be sent to the Fox Kiddies Editor, 130 West Forty-sixth street, New York City. All communications regarding the contest should be addressed to the same office.

Australian Notes

THE censorship trouble has been largely remedied, and all concerned are much more satisfied than they were three months ago. The board has reaffirmed its decision regarding productions of a salacious and harmful nature, and such pictures are not to be allowed to be imported.

* * *

Owing to the great success of his first production, Beaumont Smith, formerly well-known in the theatrical line, has completed a second film subject. A comedy entitled "Hayseeds in Sydney," which is a burlesque on the Australian bush farmer who brings his family to this city. The chief sights of our premier village are shown.

* * *

The Southern Cross Film Company has been registered in Sydney, and will produce short stories. The present program of production consists of two single-reel comedies and several one and two-part dramas. The head of the new concern, J. Goudet, is at present organizing an efficient staff of helpers for all branches of his venture.

* * *

John F. Gavin is likely to give up producing features and devote his energy to two-reel dramas. The great number of features imported monthly from America hardly gives the Australian producer a chance, as his production must be much better than the imported stuff to be marketable. Gavin has therefore decided to produce program fillers, and hopes to finish one subject each week. He has secured a large studio in the I. O. O. F. buildings, Pitt street, Sydney, and is fitting it up with all the latest apparatus.

* * *

Australasian Films, Ltd., this week presented on behalf of the Commonwealth Government a series of war films under the general title, "Australian in Action." This included the "Australians at Posieres," "The Battle of the Marne," and "The Tanks at the Ancre." Some very original advertising stunts were tried, one of which was a motorcar disguised as a tank, which went round the streets. The "Disguise" was done on a very elaborate scale, and the effect was most realistic.

* * *

"The Barrier" is the current attraction at the Sydney Lyceum. E. J. Carroll's very efficient publicity manager has put over a great advertising campaign in connection with this subject, and the result has been very satisfactory. The picture is undoubtedly a good drawing card.

* * *

Hoyt's Limited has opened a new exchange for a brand of English features, the ideal productions. These are shown first at the same firm's city theater. Two subjects have already been released: H. B. Irving in "The Lyons Mail" and Albert Chevalier in "The Fallen Star."

* * *

"The Honor System" closed a month's very successful run at the Sydney Theater Royal last week. The big Fox feature has been very favorably commented upon in all quarters. The Farnum de luxe attraction, "A Tale of Two Cities," is the current special attraction at the same theater.

* * *

Australian Feature Films, Ltd., distributors here of Paramount features, have announced that, starting shortly, all features will be released on the open market basis. The news that Ince and Sennett productions would be released through this exchange, conveyed in a full page newspaper advertisement last week caused much amazement to all in the film business. THOS. S. IMRIE.

Sydney, N. S. W., Australia, July 24, 1917.

EAGLE TO DIRECT SKATER.

The Commonwealth Pictures Corporation has secured the services of Oscar Eagle to direct their first production featuring Charlotte, the international ice skater. Mr. Eagle arrived in Chicago August 27 and commenced work immediately.

Grinding the Crank

With Thornton Fisher

VACATION is over! Gosh, where did those two weeks go so rapidly?

* * *

News report from the Coast says that little Mary Pickford's maid started a free-for-all at the Pickford home. Somebody called the police. Nobody thought of calling the cameraman.

* * *

THE FILM FOOLOSOFER SAYS" OUR IDEA OF NOTHING SURROUNDED BY OZONE IS THE EXTRA MAN WHO THINKS THAT HE WAS SUPPORTED IN THE CAST BY THE STAR."

Met the first guy yesterday who said he never had attempted to write a scenario. Otherwise he was all right.

I WONDER WHERE THE REST OF OUR CROWD IS?

I SPENT A DIME TO SEE THE PICTURE—SIT DOWN!

THEY OUGHTN'T TO ARREST A MAN FOR DOING THAT.

Chicago has recovered from its convention, but it will never look the same.

Let's sing a tune.
It's the funniest thing I ever did see;
In fact I may say that by far
It's the cleverest comedy that ever was filmed.
Who me! Why of course I'm the star!

* * *

J. Fillam Foote, the director, when interviewed concerning the work of a certain extra in his recent release said !!!???

GOOD LUCK MY BOY!!

I SHALL SUCCEED!

FATHER, I COULDN'T MAKE IT GOOD!

AUTHOR

BEING THE BRIEF TALE OF THE PRODIGAL SON—ARIC

M—UTUAL-METRO.
O—GDEN PICTURES CORPORATION.
V—ITAGRAPH.
I—NTERNATIONAL.
N—EWS REEL.
G—AUMONT-GOLDWYN.

P—ARAMOUNT-PATHE.
I—VAN.
C—OSMOFOTO FILMS.
T—RIANGLE-THANHOUSER.
U—NIVERSAL.
R—EX.
E—SSANAY-EDISON.
S—ELIG.

* * *

What Every Man Connected With Pictures Hears.
"Oh! Do you know Bill Hart personally?"
"Tell me, is it true that Gertie Gimpus is married?"
"I'd just love to be in a picture to see how I'd look!"
"I have a friend who'd take fine in moving pictures!"
"Does Charlie Chaplin really get what the papers say?"
"See that actor on the screen there? Well after seeing him on the street, I must say the camera certainly is lenient with him!"
"It must be nice to know the actors people read about!" etc., etc., etc.

* * *

There goes the elevator, so I guess we'll go.

OH YES—I SEE—I SEE—I DIDNT GET IT AT FIRST!

GET THIS THIS TIME—WATCH ME. JOE—MORE PEP—THE WAY YOU DID IT WAS AS FUNNY AS A CRUTCH, REMEMBER YOU'RE AS SOUSED AS A MACKEREL—NOW TRY IT AGAIN!

ANYBODY WHO'D LAUGH AT THAT COMEDY AINT RIGHT! TELL YA!

IF THAT'S GOT A LAUGH IN IT—IT'S A LIZARD

THE FUNNIEST THING THAT COULD HAPPEN TO THAT GUY WOULD BE TO HAVE A TREE FALL ON HIM!

THE DIRECTOR TRYING TO SHOW THE COMEDIAN HOW TO BE FUNNY.

Spokes from the Hub

By Marion Howard

COMMEND me to "The Sawdust Ring" for pure fun and kid stuff which pleases young and old alike. Why have we not seen the youngster Harold Goodwin before? Strikes me he shared the honors with Bessie Love. Here we get real circus life in action, the young pair traveling with a genuine company, and it was some show when Bessie got in the ring with her burlesque stunt. Nothing deep or new in the plot, but it is good entertainment, and that is what we go to the theater for. One of the funniest things in this was the dream indulged in by the kids, the horse and the dog, worked out for our edification. On the same program at the Exeter theater was George Beban in "The Cook of Canyon Camp" and who had a penchant for flapjacks, otherwise known as griddle cakes. Beban's methods are about the same and he had splendid support in Helen Eddy. It was a joy to see the fine work of Monroe Salisbury. I had not seen him since "Ramona," in which he scored as Alessandro. He had a sympathetic part and deserved all that came to him later, thanks to the cook. The outdoor scenery was excellent.

* * *

Is it not questionable taste for acrobats and other persons doing stunts to drape their bodies with "Old Glory"? It "sure is," at this time, when our flag is held in such high respect the world over—even our enemies have a secret regard for what it spells. I saw a short subject Sunday night, picturing a man on a skyscraper wearing our flag in a questionable manner, and I was glad to hear a few hisses round me. What are directors thinking of to so offend good taste! I have seen my first "Scarlet Runner" with Earl Williams and enjoyed it as all did. We are to get the series each week at the Exeter, which runs good Universal short stories Sundays.

* * *

"The Second Mrs. Tanqueray" went well at the Fenway, though it is somewhat of a tragedy, as all know who have seen the speaking play. Sir George Alexander, Hilda Moore (who is so like Mrs. Pat Campbell in this character) and a finished array of English players gave us an artistic treat. The interiors were pretentious and beyond criticism; still it is not a picture one cares to see twice because it lacks lightness and good finale.

* * *

The Hub is just now enjoying 'The Italian Battlefront' picture, one of the best attractions of its kind, put on at the Tremont theater, the first home of "The Birth of a Nation" here and which is one of our coolest theaters. So much has been written in this publication and by the critics all I can say is 'them's my sentiments, tew." We have a very large Italian colony—40,000 at least, and I hope all will be able to see this.

* * *

The Community Picture Bureau is doing a tremendous business in its new quarters, and has placed pictures in army camps in New England and other pictures as far away as San Diego, Vancouver and Montana. It does not make any pictures, but supplies the calls from far and near for clean, virile pictures and selects them and it knows what's what. Mrs. William Foster and a large staff are busy well into the night filling orders. This bureau is a Hub institution and unique.

* * *

Glad to see that Rex Beach is making his own titles; that Lillian Walker is getting busy on new pictures, but why such a title as "The Lust of the Ages"—why the misleading word. "lust"? What if it has naught to do with sex, is it a good box office word?

* * *

We had fun over the Motoy doll pictures and liked the novelty.

* * *

"Her Strange Wedding" was some picture and oh, my, doesn't Fannie Ward wear some stunning gowns? Edythe Chapman is one of my favorites, a graceful, well-groomed woman who makes a capital society mother.

* * *

Do we need such plays as "A Strange Transgressor"? It pointed no moral, had no comedy in it to relieve the tension felt in front, and was not especially wholesome. We

are surprised at this Triangle offering, though it was superbly acted and put on. Louise Glaum made a fascinating member of the demimonde class, so much so that a man said to his companion, "Gee, I don't blame John Hampton, for she has class." The redeeming part was centered around the kid and here we had some good touches, showing the great mother love willing to sacrifice her all for the sake of the lad. Still, the play apart from this is unreal.

* * *

I saw two splendid pictures of late, one "Time Locks and Diamonds," from the Triangle studios and in contrast to the one just mentioned, for here we get William Desmond and looking for all the world like William Gillette, in a part which suits him evidently. We get a lot of suspense in this, some trickery and good twists. Mildred Harris is better in this than in recent pictures and we liked the ending.

* * *

"Forbidden Paths" with the Japanese actor was another Lasky picture to go well here, with Vivian Martin, Tom Forman and others, and here we get the stoicism of the Japanese wonderfully displayed by Hayakawa. It was a fine bit of acting, as we learn to expect at his hands.

* * *

We liked "The Stolen Treaty" as we do all plays with the secret service sauce as spice. Earle Williams has some support in Corinne Griffith, and doesn't she film well!

* * *

Again I went to see "The Little American," and got a bit more of the picture at the Fenway as Manager Sumner did not cut the offending reel picturing the Red Cross nurse after the vile attack which might better be eliminated, as it is a blot. Mrs. Ayer did not use it at her theater—hence my remark in my last letter. What a wonderful picture Artcraft has given us here, and not a bit of it overdrawn. Good idea to have these scenes presented as they exist somewhere in France and Belgium—yes and in more harrowing detail. We get enough here in this to open the eyes of the indifferent to the type of system we are up against in dealing with the enemy. Raymond Hatton is some actor and wonderfully versatile—here as the young French officer wearing the medal of bravery, sacrificing his arm and with a sorrow in his heart because he could not win the "Little American." He was an artist all through. Only last week I saw him in another rôle vastly different as a king in that delightful picture, "What Money Can't Buy." I wonder no critic has mentioned his make-up, as he looked like Charles Dickens when he came to this country fifty years ago. It was startling. The titles were great and got a hand.

* * *

Another pair of gems is "The Uneven Road" and "The Lighted Lamp" given to delighted fans by the Essanay company. In the first named where little McAlister figures as a blind child there were two features to hold attention and which have passed unmentioned. One was the unconscious influence of that child (wandering along the street led by her wonderful dog) upon the lascivious mind of the man bent on moral destruction in her home. Of course, "hubby" returned suddenly, but there was the earlier transformation in the man who suddenly realised the mother's would-be sacrifice for the child. Will you who have seen this ever forget the closing picture of Mary and the dog eating ice cream and the knowing look of the dog toward the house? Edwin Arnold seems a dependable man for "The Lighted Lamp." The opening scene was of the cave man order, but I liked best the camp with the lonesome men thinking of the absent ones when the juice of "Home Sweet Home" was turned on in the machine. These plays are novel in idea and well worked out. This is the day of the short story well sandwiched on the program.

"TOM SAWYER" NEARLY READY FOR RELEASE.

Boys of all ages, from ten to ninety, will welcome the advent of Tom Sawyer, the immortal boy, in motion pictures, and the much-loved juvenile hero, who seems to symbolize the real boy character as no other has ever done, will strut bravely across the screen when Jack Pickford portrays the character in his forthcoming Paramount production. The fact that Louise Huff, the other member of the famous "kid" duo, will interpret Becky, is assurance these two figures will be adequately rendered to the last degree of perfection. The filming of the exteriors at Hannibal, Missouri, the place where Mark Twain spent his own boyhood—seventy years ago—has been accomplished. Hannibal Cave figures in the picture and many other spots made familiar through the author's work.

British Notes

A S INDICATION of the hold the moving picture has upon the industrial classes in northern England the suggestion has been made by the Kinematograph Exhibitors' Association that the time is opportune for the industry to possess direct parliamentary representation. There are several areas in industrial districts, it is pointed out, where a candidate, apart from political currents, would be well supported in championing the cause of the national amusement, the kinema. In view of the momentous issues before the nation at the present day this may be too optimistic an estimate of his chances, nevertheless, by association with the labor interests now in office with the moving picture as the main plank in the election platform, the return of a candidate does not seem improbable. The Exhibitors' Association, being now a registered trade union, has much to gain by affiliation with the central organisation of trade unions, controlled in politics only by the Labor party, and negotiations to this end have already been opened. Speculation is rife in the trade as to who will be the first "Movie M. P." Many names have been mentioned, but popular selection favors either A. E. Newbould (chairman of the Exhibitors' Association) or W. Gavazzi King (secretary of the association).

* * *

Samuel Goldfish's undertaking, Goldwin Pictures, proposes a strong campaign for its features on the British market. R. S. Edmondson (American Film Releases) has found temporary office accommodation at his new and commodious premises just off Wardour St. for the preliminary work and advertising. Goldwyn's London address until further notice is 16 Great Chapel street, London, W. I.

* * *

Film production is as a strange black art to the Irish peasant people. The colleens of Mullinahone, near Clonmel, were horrified a few days ago at the extravagance of a director of the Film Company of Ireland in rebuilding a thatched cottage, only to burn it down again. The scene was one of many recorded in the Clonmel district for inclusion in a new feature play entitled "Knocknagow."

* * *

A supplementary order of the Privy Council has placed carbons and dry cells upon the list of articles which must be imported into the country by special license only.

* * *

Admiral Jellicoe recently stated that the number of ships in the navy now was in excess of 4,000. From this can be gathered a conception of the immensity of the task of supplying the fleet with moving picture films apart from the gigantic task of distribution. The Lord Mayor of Liverpool has raised a substantial fund for the provision of further Kinematograph outfits for the senior service, while today (July 23rd) sees the opening in London of "navy week." For the next few days many theater and kinema theater proprietors are devoting a day's proceeds for this and other comforts for our sailors.

* * *

The final sitting of the Kinema Commission took place at Westminster last Monday. The Bishop of Birmingham presided and announced that the report (a 500-page volume) would be issued within the course of a few days. He specially thanked the trade for the assistance given the Commission, particularly by Messrs. Newbould and King.

* * *

Printed histories of the great war are as numerous as flies, but it has been left to the instigation of Pathe Freres to make a moving picture anthology illustrative of the progress of the European conflagration since the assassination of the Austrian arch-duke three years ago. War pictures are apt to pall unless of some great battle, but this cannot be attributed to the Pathe "History of the War." It is comprised of the brightest and most interesting selections from miles of negative taken by Pathe cameramen on six war fronts. Mr. Balfour and Lord Derby attended the trade shows last week and warmly commended Messrs. Pathe on the coherence of the animated history.

* * *

The motto of the successful film producer has long been 'The Play's the Thing," but it looks as though this slogan is to be steadily usurped by the intervention of the song theme into the gentle art of filmongery. A popular song does not usually embody a plot, but it does have a theme for the nucleus of a story. One of the most successful British subjects, "My Old Dutch," was a simple story written around Albert Chevalier's famous ballad of Cockney life. Now the Ideal Co. is almost ready with another champion tear-enticing melody of last decade, namely, "Asthore," while International Exclusives have visualised that super-sobber, "Daddy." Cannot someone produce a song-story from a humorous favo i e by way of a change?

* * * r t

D. W. Griffith still keeps in or about London, and has been engaged in Kent taking scenes for a forthcoming drama featuring the sisters Dorothy and Lillian Gish. One scene is of a society garden party, and among the people whom Griffith persuaded to appear in the scene were Lady Paget, Lady Drogheda, Miss Elizabeth Asquith and the Princess of Monaco.   J. B. SUTCLIFFE.

Indian Notes

By S. B. Banerjea.

R ECENTLY certain leading film manufacturers of America requested the American consul in Calcutta to furnish them with a list of all the bioscope theaters in India. This news has caused some uneasiness in the English bioscope world in India, one of the organs of which has suggested that both British and native proprietors should combine for mutual protection, as the Americans mean the sort of enterprise in the near future which will harm their interest. It adds: "If American promoters intend after the war to open up in various towns in India, they or any others, not British subjects, should be impeded by a special theater tax, or be similarly handicapped by a tax on receipts. So far India has managed very well without American theatrical enterprise, and we have yet to discover that this country is pining for it."

* * *

Now, there are not many picture houses in India. Only Calcutta, Bombay, and Madras boast of half a dozen picture theaters, while Delhi—the Imperial city—Lahore, Mussooric, Darjeeling, and certain other cities have only one theater each. These theaters, I must state, are owned by natives mainly. It must not be concluded that the Indians are not patrons of the bioscope. In fact, they will gladly patronize any decent show. But where is the enterprising showman to cater to their wants? If now Americans come here and open picture houses they will simply mean a war. If you, Mr. Grumbler, have the means, why don't you open picture theaters in the leading cities and towns of India? If you have not the necessary means or cannot command the necessary capital, your rival is sure to occupy the field.

* * *

When the Picture House of Calcutta, which is owned by natives, opened the other day we were told that we would get the best Universal and other American films. We have too much of Pathe in the Elphinstone, and thought that we might now expect a variety of American films. It is understood that, owing to certain reasons, the policy of the Picture House has undergone a change. This policy, we are assured, has been crowned with success, and that large audiences are now greeting the all-British films. I prefer not to discuss the new policy of Messrs. K. D. Bros., the proprietors of the Picture House, but will only remark that they have acted a bit hastily, as they will find out sooner or later.

* * *

Referring to the trial scene, which is a feature of "God's Witness," the leading paper of Asia remarks: "It was a splendid story, but we wish the Americans would be a little less free with their maker's name in movie titles." Obey this order, ye American film manufacturers, otherwise ye run the risk of banishment from India!

* * *

I would advise some enterprising American dealer to secure the great Red Cross film, "The Sick and Wounded in Bombay," for exhibition in his country. It shows that India is trying to move with the times. The rights for premises just off Wardow St. for the preliminary work and is 16 Great Chapel St., London, W. I.

India and Burma have been acquired by the Royal Opera House of Bombay. I think the American rights have not been disposed of yet.

* * *

Calcutta has at last got its board of film censors. It consists of three members—one a representative of the police, and one each from the Trades Association and the European Association. Every Thursday morning they visit one or other of our bioscope theaters and pass the weekly program. It is to be regretted, however, that no native is on the board. The bioscope theaters are mostly patronised by natives, and it stands to reason, therefore, that a representative Indian should have been among those selected. The censorship has been established on the score of morality. Now, many European manners and customs are repugnant to the Indians. Take the film, "Midnight at Maxim's," for instance. It is objectionable in Indian eyes, but Europeans do not object to it. No wonder it has not been withdrawn. But if an Indian were on the board he would have insisted upon its withdrawal. The Indians found little or nothing objectionable in "Who Pays," but only three or four episodes of this series were shown. I need not multiply instances. Suffice it to say, however, that on the board of censor the Indian and not the European element should have predominated. I should add that the board is a tentative measure. It has a life of one year only, but it will be made permanent. The Calcutta vigilance committee, to which the board is mainly due, has just issued a report of its activities, which contains much interesting reading. Already I hear the wails of the proprietor of a leading bioscope theater of Calcutta. He has been compelled to take off certain films. He has had a fling at the "crank brigade" in his paper recently, and hopes that its interference will not influence the Government toward any decision which will unduly tie the hands of proprietors and managers. He specializes in all British films.

* * *

We have had a succession of Gold Rooster plays at the Elphinstone. By way of variety, Mr. Madan is now showing us the big Balboa film, "The Red Circle." It is bound to draw big houses. At the Picture House we have had the opportunity of seeing the Bluebird photo drama, "The Girl of Lost Lake," "The Secret of the Swamp," and "Barnaby Rudge." At the Bijou we witnessed "The Black Orchid," "Ultus and the Secret of the Night," and the Selig film, "The Hare and the Tortoise." This theater had to withdraw "The Chalice of Sorrow" after showing it for one day only. Mr. Bandmann is showing "The Battle of the Seine" to crowded houses. At the New Alexandra cinema (Kristma Theater) of Hyderabad, which was opened last January, "The Woman Who Did," "Pearl of the Ganges," "She," and other all British and several Chaplin, Keystone, and L-Ko films have been shown with success.

* * *

The Essanay company's decision to announce the running time of film instead of its length has been approved by Mr. Incasse and other Bioscope theater proprietors. Mr. Incasse suggests that the Essanay action should be copied by all other film manufacturers, and that Bioscope managers should also notify the time table of the feature film in their program. At any rate he has begun doing so. I hope Mr. Madan will follow suit.

BLACKTON RESIGNS FROM VITAGRAPH.

Having completed the taking of scenes for his first production for Paramount, "The World for Sale," a screen version of Sir Gilbert Parker's widely-read novel, J. Stuart Blackton has formally resigned as vice-president and secretary of the Vitagraph Company of America, with which he was so long associated.

Commodore Blackton feels that inasmuch as he will henceforth devote all his time to his own productions, he would be unable to properly fill the offices he has held with Vitagraph.

CHARLES MILLER NEW DIRECTOR FOR NORMA TALMADGE.

Charles Miller, who for two years directed many of Triangle's greatest productions, has been engaged by Joseph M. Schenck to direct the Norma Talmadge photoplays. The first effort of Mr. Miller's new affiliation will be Grace Miller White's "The Secret of the Storm Country," where the original scenes of the story were laid. Mr. Schenck's attention was called to Mr. Miller through the splendid work he did under the Triangle banner, for Bessie Love, in "The Sawdust Ring," for Dorothy Dalton, in "The Flame of the Yukon" and for Bessie Barriscale.

Arthur Leslie's Book

"Who's Who and Why: The 100 Leading Lights of the Screen" Is Well Received By Newspaper Editors.

WHO'S Who and Why: The 100 Leading Lights of the Screen" is both the title and the description of a compact biographical cyclopaedia of photoplayers just prepared and published by Arthur Leslie.

As its name implies, it is selective in its scope and aims only to include the actors and actresses of the screen who have won assured position as recognized favorites, or those who have given proof that they will soon take their place with them. As the "Why", in its titular "Who's Who and Why" indicates, this book does not limit itself to the dry details of the player's professional career, but gives his or her life history in such manner as to throw informing light on the causes that have led, or are leading, to the winning of success. In these intimate personal details of early work and early struggle that are here given may be found a deeper interest than in the later records of achievement. It is a book that will be of the greatest aid to every editor controlling a department devoted to photoplays and photoplayers, and the one purpose that led to its compilation was to fill a need that has been felt in every newspaper office. Wide recognition of this fact is already coming from editors throughout the country.

The book is inscribed "This work is respectfully dedicated to Carl Laemmle, President of the Universal Film Manufacturing Company, whose fine courage and broad vision made the motion picture world safe for democracy." Leslie refers to the fight made by Mr. Laemmle as the first big independent producer.

Vivian Rich with Universal

VIVIAN RICH, one of Universal's latest acquisitions, is at present playing opposite Neal Hart in a five-reel feature entitled "The Bumble Bee." Miss Rich says that when she graduated from high school her parents wanted her to go to college, but she had a longing for the stage and prevailed upon her father and mother to permit her to gratify her ambition in that direction. There was no serious objection upon their part, as both had been theatrical people themselves.

One of the first productions in which Miss Rich appeared was "The Country Girl" at the Herald Square Theater, New York. The same season she joined Gus Edwards in vaudeville and after a time with his company came with her mother to the Pacific Coast. That was in 1913, and she joined the American Company, subsequently playing under the banner of William Fox.

Among the notable features in which she has appeared are "Holly House," "Pastures Green" and "The Little Troubadour," in all of which she played leads. Miss Rich also appeared opposite William Farnum in 'The Price of Silence.'

Vivian Rich.

Vivian Rich is a great reader. She is seldom to be seen without a book, and her dressing room looks like a small library. Occasionally she tries her hand at a short story, and has had some success in inventing scenarios. Nearly all outdoor sports appeal to her, motoring being her special hobby; but, unlike most girls, she is a thorough mechanician and can overhaul her own car like a paid expert.

CARMEL MYERS WITH JEWEL.

Carmel Myers, one of the most beautiful women of the screen, has joined the forces of Jewel Productions, Inc., and made her first bow as a Jewel star in "Sirens of the Sea" at the Broadway theater. It is understood that Miss Myers will shortly be featured in an important Jewel production.

Motion Picture Educator
Conducted by REV. W. H. JACKSON and MARGARET I. MACDONALD

Interesting Educationals

One Topical Subject, Four Travel, Two Zoological, Two Industrial and One Historical.

"Efficiency Via Express" (Paramount-Bray).

THE manner in which our express packages are handled on their way from one part of the country to another is shown in the 82d release of the Paramount-Bray Pictograph. Here we learn that in one of the largest express offices in the country some 50,000 packages arrive per day. These packages must also leave this office and start on their several journeys on that same day; and in order to do so and to avoid congestion remarkable efficiency is necessary in the handling this immense mass of material, including live stock, plants and all the other kinds of things that travel by express. When waggons come to the terminal a crew is ready to unload it. The packages are then tossed onto a wide endless belt which precipitates them onto a tremendous revolving cone. Around the base of this cone stand forty-eight men, each man representing one of the forty-eight states of the Union, and so expert are they that as the packages slide down the slippery sides of the cone they are picked out and properly sorted into the bins of the proper states. Back of the bins again stand boys who reassort the packages according to counties, cities, towns and villages. The subject is well illustrated and interesting.

"Alaska Wonders in Motion No. 3" (Educational).

This interesting reel opens with views of the village of Kenai which was founded 160 years ago by a tribe of the same name. A number of types of this tribe are shown, and we are told that many of them go blind because of the number of months to which they are subjected to darkness, having only three months in all the year when they have daylight. Some good views illustrative of the fishing industry are given, and remarkably well-photographed scenes in which the interest is focused on the ice-floes in the neighborhood of Miles Glacier, showing the constant dropping of immense pieces of ice into the water below. This Alaska series is an unusually good one, and can be relied upon to interest an audience. Other scenes of interest are the interior of a Russian church, and the Million Dollar span on Copper River between Miles and Childs glaciers.

"China and the Chinese No. 5" (Educational).

One of the principal features of this number illustrates the cotton industry as it exists in China. Here the laborers work at picking and hauling the cotton for a few cents a day. We are shown their primitive methods of spinning and weaving the cotton, and later a more modern method to photograph which the side had to be taken from the small factory in order to get enough light by which to make the picture of a girl at work at a loom The making of bamboo and grass rope introduces us to other primitive methods. Then there is pictured a feast day, and the elaborate funeral of a rich Chinaman. A leaning pagoda 1,300 years old is among the other interesting sights of the picture and also a view of the Loo Chow pagoda, the largest and most beautiful in China.

"Norway" (Paramount-Holmes).

In his trip to Norway Mr. Holmes lands us at Bergen, where he gives us a closeup view of the genuine Norwegian at the fish market of this typical Norse city. A journey by rail takes us from Bergen along the shores of the famous Norse fiords through the most beautiful of scenery. In carioles we make the trip through the Romsdal, alighting now and then at the very steepest places, or to gaze at the splendors of such waterfalls as the Voringfos or to photograph Alpine lakes snuggled in the heights of the mountains. One of the delights of the trip is a cruise on the Telemarken Canal, which your steamboat passes through in about 30 minutes of actual time. The famous Trondhjem cathedral and the hotels at Balholm are also interesting sights. Finally we arrive at Hammerfest, the most northerly of all the cities of the earth, where we meet the Laplander with his reindeer. A delightful scenic.

"Historic Monterey, California" (General Film-Selig).

In World-Selig Library, No. 15, is a good series of pictures of points of interest in Monterey, the capital of the province under Mexican rule. The first theater (built as a hotel), the first frame house, and the first brick are shown. The most interesting view is the home of Robert Louis Stevenson. The custom house, which has had the flags of Spain, Mexico and the United States over it, is shown. Also the rose bush planted by General Sherman. He fell in love with a senorita when he visited the city and when he left, he planted a rose bush, saying that he would return when the roses bloomed.

"Animals in Winter" (Educational-Ditmars).

This picture opens with a delightful winter scene showing a herd of buffalo feeding at the Zoo in winter. The scene is especially effective, photographed as it is with the winter landscape as a background. This is followed by several scenes at the Zoo during a blizzard, with sheep huddled together on a rocky slope. Then we are introduced to the walrus in his winter quarters and learn that his icy surroundings are the height of his ambitions. The same is true of the Polar bear, who sniffs the approach of the winter season with evident delight. The tropical gorilla taking a carriage ride well muffled up to protect him from the elements is amusing. The picture closes with some amusing scenes showing the feeding of the beckoning bear.

"Ancestors of the Horse" (Educational-Ditmars).

The various species of the horse family as shown in this picture, which has been carefully arranged by Raymond L. Ditmars, are the Celtic horse which roamed a part of Europe during the ice age, the Norse or Scandinavian horse of the same period, the wild horse of Mongolia with colt, and the kiang or wild horse, of Tibet. Then there is the Chapman zebra with its colt, the Abyssinian zebra with narrow stripes and the mountain zebra with wide stripes. An interesting number.

"The Silk Industry of Japan" (General Film-Selig).

In World-Selig Library, No. 15, silk is traced from the egg of the moth to the finished cloth. The moths are shown laying eggs. Then after a gorge of mulberry leaves, they are shown making cocoons. The process of reeling this silk from the cocoons as they float in a pan of warm water, is shown, followed by the spinning and weaving processes. Four thousand yards of silk may be taken from a single cocoon. We have often read of these processes, and we can say that they mean much more as pictured here.

"Tuna Fishing in the Pacific" (General Film-Selig).

In World-Selig Library, No. 15, is a picture of how tuna fish are caught in the Pacific. They are pulled into the boat, knocked on the head with a club and cleaned at sea. Some of these fish reach a length of fifteen feet and weigh fifteen hundred pounds. Fish of this size are not shown. Other fishing subjects shown in brief scenes on this reel are: Mussel hunting, and salmon and rock cod fishing. A fifty-pound salmon is shown. An interesting feature is the securing of salmon for spawning purposes. Taking the eggs from the female is shown clearly. The subtitle calls this "despoiling the female." This has a criminal connotation. It is as if one should speak of stealing hens' eggs instead of gathering them. The correct expression for taking the eggs from the female salmon is "stripping them."

"Pioneer Days" (Selig).

This is a two-reel historical picture of the massacre of the whites at Fort Dearborn settlement (the site of Chicago) by the Indians on August 15, 1815. The picture begins with scenes about the fort. Then follows the evacuation and the attack by the Indians. In the course of the massacre several persons are tapped on the crown with tomahawks, but the picture is not bloody. This is an instructive picture. It is entertaining. And it is done on a big scale.

Russia to the Front

Rialto Theater Gives Up Whole Program to Depicting Scenes Relative to Russia's Freedom Preluded by Scenes on the Russian War Front.

THE unusual program exhibited in the Rialto theater, New York City, the week of Aug. 20th, is deserving of more than a passing comment. The management, alive to the importance of a picturization of Russia's awesome position of having at last entered the gateway of freedom after centuries of serfdom, gave up the entire program of an entire week to the exhibition of the Skobeleff Committee's motion pictures of the Russian campaign on the Caucasian front, the Southwestern front, the Russian Revolution and the famous first celebration of Russian independence held May first, 1917.

These pictures are not only well photographed, but have the quality of conveying more clearly, more impressively than anything else possibly could, the immense significance of the Russian Revolution in world civilisation. One could scarcely view these scenes in which surging masses of individuals of all classes joined hearts as one in celebrating what was not only the greatest event in the history of their country, but one of the greatest events in the history of the whole world, without being aroused to a high degree of enthusiasm and admiration for the heroes of the hour.

The program opened with Tschaikowsky's "March Slav" splendidly rendered by the Rialto orchestra, introducing scenes on the Caucasus front showing the transporting of supplies and wounded soldiers over the mountains. The "Plastun" Cossacks in a flanking movement in the rear of the Turks presents some effective scenes which are followed by a view of Anatolia as seen from an aeroplane. With the Russian fleet on the Black Sea we see the destruction of a causeway bridge, breaking communication between the Turkish army and Trebisond and the destruction of a floating mine by machine guns, as well as much else of interest. The fall of Trebizond is also well depicted, showing Mr. Kaiser, United States Consul, at the head of the people of Trebizond, who carrying a white flag of truce went out to meet the commander of the Russian detachment, to hand over to him the keys of the city. The desecration of the monastery of Pochayev, showing how the German soldiers, respecting not even the dead, opened the tombs and threw the corpses from their coffins in search of treasure, and the replacing of the bodies and re-bricking of the tombs by the Russian soldiers, testifies to the grossness of German soldiers.

The remainder of the program had to do with scenes relative to the Russian Revolution and encompassed the funeral procession of the four hundred victims in Mars Field, Petrograd, when the entire population of the city turned out to pay a final tribute to the heroes of the Revolution. Views of the fortress of St. Peter and St. Paul, the gala jubilee session of the State Duma, April 27th, 1917, and scenes showing the celebration on Mars Field on May 1st, 1917, encompass a wealth of material to make the thoughtful individual stop and think. Pictures of the Czar, the Czarina and the entire Royal family of Russia, who, according to a subtitle, "are now in an armored railway coach on their way to Siberia", are also included in the collection.

The weight of this program was relieved by interpolations of Russian music well rendered by the Rialto orchestra and a Russian male chorus.

New Suffrage Film

"Woman's Work in War Time" Title of Propaganda for New York State Woman Suffrage Party Made by S. S. Film Company.

J. CHARLES DAVIS, JR., of the S. S. Film Company, 220 West 42d Street, New York City, recently produced for the New York State Woman Party, a propaganda film which is not alone destined to fulfil the purpose for which it was made, but is a credit to its maker.

This statement is not intended to convey the idea that the two-part picture, "Woman's Work in War Time", is an elaborate production with a big story, for it is not. On the contrary the story interest is very slight. We are introduced first to a much domesticated mother whose daughters are enthusiastic workers for the suffrage cause. The daughters in a successful attempt to convince the mother that their cause is a just one, and that women are at the present time actively engaged in important work for the nation, taking the places of men who must answer their country's call to battle, afford an opportunity of exploiting the subject on the screen. For this purpose Mr. Davis has photographed the various recently acquired activities of women, such as farming, making ammunition, working in locomotive shops, and working as conductors on trolley cars. Some scenes showing the food conservation classes at work at the War Service Department of the New York State Woman Suffrage Party are also included in the picture. Scenes at the headquarters of the Suffrage Party picture Mrs. Norman Whitehouse and her associates discussing important matters; and, in closing the picture, the son of the house having gone to war a splendid view of the soldiers marching down Fifth avenue is given.

During a conference of the New York State Woman Suffrage Party which was held at Saratoga on Aug. 29th and 30th, this film was exhibited before Governor Whitman. It is expected that it will be given immediate distribution throughout New York State by the A. Kay Company, of 729 Seventh avenue, New York City.

Retreat of the Germans

Official Government Pictures Taken on the British Front at the Battle of Arras Shown at Strand Under Direction of Pathe.

THE Pathe Exchange, Inc., is responsible for the presentation of the Official Government Pictures of "The Retreat of the Germans at the Battle of Arras", which have been seen at the Strand theater in two instalments during the past two weeks. These pictures are remarkable for the fact that they bring us extremely close to the actual battle. They repeat without any startling gruesomeness the story of how a great battle is conducted. They suggest again the dreadful efficiency embodied in the British tank; and in fact we are face to face with the realism of battle as we view these pictures. We see men obedient to the battle call emerging from their dugouts to man the big guns for an attack on the enemy's positions and the various maneuvers and rushing forward of troops and artillery in pursuit of the retreating Germans. There is nothing singularly spectacular about these pictures. They are merely as true a statement as a merciless camera can give of things as they happened at the Battle of Arras.

The Call of the World

The Moving Picture Must Put Forth Its Full Power in the Service of Humanity.
By Rev. W. H. Jackson.

Under the caption of "A Call" many pictures have been put upon the market and readily accepted by the public as filling certain very necessary conditions, revealing certain requirements and meeting with acceptable and often profitable responses. "The Call of Nature" has been made and met; "The Call of the West" and "The Call of the Wilds" have each in turn had their messages instructive, helpful and entertaining by means of the moving picture. A new call has now come in a more concrete form and from a far wider field than any yet imagined by any scenario writer. This call is not for a certain kind of picture from a certain locality and for a certain purpose however laudable; it is a world call for the whole powers of the moving picture to put forth its greatest efforts in the service of humanity.

The Call from the Nations.

All the great nations of the earth have called upon the moving picture to assist them in seeing that which the human eye cannot see and to record indelibly all the varied scenes of domestic, commercial, industrial activities both for peace and war. In war the activities of a nation are exercised to the utmost degree and to the last detail. Every nation has become one vast unit through the amalgamation of all its powers and forces for concentration upon one purpose and objective.

The moving picture has been seized upon as being at once a time saver, illustrator, teacher and recorder; it would seem difficult to find an occasion of necessity which the pictures do not fill their new, yet all important task, and that they do so with thoroughness and efficiency is only a natural result of their applied powers.

In addition to the numerous unofficial uses of the camera, every government has taken official cognizance of the need of the times and official pictures of the natural activities and especially the war scenes are being exactly recorded.

The great nations have organised and equipped moving picture departments, so that faithful reproductions of all stages of the war's progress may be permanently recorded. How different to former years when the description of an intrepid war correspondent alone was sufficient of the artist to produce a few pictures of important events for the walls of the nation's art galleries. Now any selected scenes may be faithfully reproduced while the whole relationship of scenes and events become an eternal chronicle.

The Call of Governmental Departments.

As if in subdivision of the work of the nation, the departments of the Government find the need of the moving picture and call for its particular and specific aid. Answering this call in the United States the moving picture industry is now positively mobilised into War, Navy, Treasury, Agriculture and other permanent departments, including the new commissions, such as Food Control and Training Camp. In a word, there is no department, either permanent or special, which is without its associate branch in moving picture work. The work of these departments must of necessity be most helpful and far-reaching and the help given by the pictures beyond computation. When the government saw the wisdom of mobilising the moving pictures it secured at the same time the interests of the whole people, for are they not inseparable, and from the fact that the pictures are the great leaders of the people, we can safely paraphrase an old saying and declare that "as go the pictures so go the people," and when the government secures the picture help they secure the people also.

The Call of the Red Cross.

Patriotism and Humanity are nowhere linked together as in the Red Cross; the two highest attributes of human character are found in the theory and practice of the Red Cross movement; nowhere else are God, Country and Man blended in happy unison for the good of all. The Red Cross has asked for money by the millions of dollars and has been fully answered. The Red Cross has asked for trained volunteers by the thousands and has received a noble response; now this same organisation calls for the moving picture to bring its influence to in further spreading its gospel of help to all mankind and the moving picture is going to reply to the fullest extent of its great abilities. To secure twenty millions of members is the first object of this new call to show America's teeming millions how, while patriotism is compelled to fight battles, humanity can minister to all those needs the curse of war imposes upon all. Never was a nobler work placed before or upon any power than that which is here made the objective of the moving picture and never will any response be more thorough and acceptable.

The Call of the People.

Race, creed, color and language are one in the interpretation of the moving picture. This is another link in the chain of mutual purposes now dominating the civilised world, and the peoples of the earth are calling upon the moving pictures to do three things: Aid them in that war which is to destroy war and make democracy safe for all; keep them enlightened as to the progress of all the many sided events of that war and become the eternal historian, chronicler and illustrator, so that in ages yet to come because of the moving picture, "generations yet unborn" shall receive an education which shall lift them into a realm of knowledge so superior to our times that, beginning where we leave off the benefits of our struggles, aims and victories shall be the seed from which shall spring up a newer, brighter and safer world.

EXPERT REVIEWING.

"A Pleasing Role." While the ability required to review a picture is of no mean order, the power of descriptive language should run parallel with the ability to discern. The art of the reviewer was recently the subject of some sarcasm in a certain moving picture trade paper which tried to ridicule—without cause and without effect—the reviews of one of its contemporaries; to this same paper we are indebted for what their own reviewer considers "A Pleasing Role."

The latest release of a picture in which Madam P. takes a leading part, we find she fills the role of a young lady who is compelled to marry a man she despises to save her mother from a scandal consequent upon her cheating at cards.

Her married life being one of prolonged and intense misery, which she endures for the sake of her boy, who is a

victim of the father's cowardly hate, until unable longer to endure his treatment the wife, seeking to defend the boy from further abuse, shoots the father and so tragically puts an end to a life of such brutal associations. This is the "Pleasing Role" which our neighborly reviewer describes as being so well filled by Madam P. Just in what way it is "pleasing" we are not enlightened; possibly our ignorance prevents us from seeing the point, but we learn the lesson that when a woman becomes the wife of a coward and a brute and enacts a tragedy to defend her home from his continued abuse, she is filling "A Pleasing Role." W. H. J.

TRUE AND "FAKE" FRENCH OFFICIAL WAR PICTURES.

Edmond Ratisbonne, head of the French Official Pictorial Service in the United States, has had his attention called to certain war pictures advertised as "French Official" and showing gruesome or faked scenes of prejudicial character.

The French Official pictures, handled in this country by Mr. Ratisbonne, who is the delegate of the Photographic and Cinematographic Division of the French Army, are very carefully edited and titled, and are patriotic, educational and intensely interesting from the American as well as the French point of view.

It is unfortunate that certain unscrupulous parties are using 'patched up" Official pictures with other pictures which are not official, and which give a distorted and undesirable impression, and are offering these pictures to the exhibitors as "French Official."

Mr. Ratisbonne wishes to call the attention of all patriotic exhibitors to the fact that these are times when the performances of the Allied Armies must not be misrepresented, and that they should co-operate with him by preventing the exhibition of "pirated" pictures.

All owners of bona fide Official French war pictures may obtain the written endorsement of Mr. Ratisbonne; and all exhibitors showing such pictures are urged to demand such evidence before booking pictures which are represented to them as French Official. W. J.

WEEK'S RUNS AT NEW YORK'S ACADEMY.

Arrangements have been made to show William Fox's three big Standard pictures, "Jack and the Beanstalk", "The Spy", and "The Conqueror", at the Academy of Music, New York, after the runs of these productions at the theatre for the entire week. The doors will be opened at ten o'clock each morning, and inasmuch as the historic playhouse seats more than 3,100 persons, new attendance records will probably be established.

"The Spy", now at the Globe for a limited engagement of two weeks, will then take the screen for the entire week of September 9, at the Academy. During the week of September 23, "The Conqueror", R. A. Walsh's American drama with William Farnum in the stellar role, will be the attraction.

The policy at the Academy of Music, of which John Zanft is managing director, has been hitherto to make a wid-week change in programme.

Popular Picture Personalities
WHO'S WHO IN THE MOVING PICTURE WORLD
Compiled by the Statistical Department.

MALONE, Molly. Born in Denver, Colorado. Her father was Irish and her mother English. Is five feet two inches tall and weighs 108 pounds. Fair complexion, chestnut hair and dark brown eyes. Miss Malone has had no stage experience, making her debut directly before the camera in 1915 in The Little Angel of Canyon Creek. He is at present a Universalist, but has been with the Vitagraph, Lubin and Lasky Western companies. Some of the best remembered plays in which she has been seen are The Girl in the Garret, The Red Stain, The Telltale Clue, The Lawyer's Secret and Mountain Blood. Miss Malone writes that swimming, tennis and riding are her pet fads, but the thing she loves the most is her work, and she adds "truly," with a line under the truly to make it emphatic, because she did not have time to run down to the notary and hold up her right hand and solemnly swear.

KING, Henry. Born in Christiansburg, Va. American parentage. Is half an inch over six foot mark and weighs 184 pounds. Fair complexion, brown hair and blue eyes. Mr. King made his stage debut in February, 1903, and for ten years played in stock and productions. In stock he has played in New York, Cleveland, Buffalo and Chicago. He has also appeared in The Lion and the Mouse, The Devil, Graustark and for a season played a round of Shakespearian parts. In January, 1913, he made his debut in pictures in the lead in Love and War in Mexico, a Lubin West-Coast production. He remained with Lubin for a year, then went to Balboa, where he remained for three years and ten months, and is now with American. He has been director and co-star of Should a Wife Forgive and with Little Mary Sunshine in Joy and the Dragon and Twin Kiddies. Likes swimming, motoring and all out door sports.

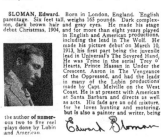

the author of numerous two to five reel plays done by Lubin and American.

SLOMAN, Edward. Born in London, England. English parentage. Six feet tall, weighs 165 pounds. Dark complexion, dark brown hair and gray eyes. He made his stage debut Christmas, 1904, and for more than eight years played in English and American productions, including the lead in The Wolf. He made his picture debut on March 10, 1913, his first part being the juvenile lead in Universal's The Severed Hand, He was Trine in the serial Trey o' Hearts, Prince Hassan in Under the Crescent. Aaron in The Vengeance of the Oppressed, and had the leads in many of the Lubin productions made by Capt. Melville on the West Coast. He is at present with American at Santa Barbara and directs as well as acts. His fads are an odd mixture, for he loves hunting and motoring, but is also a painter and writer, being

PERIOLAT, George E. Born in Chicago. His father was born in France and his mother in Ireland. He is five feet ten inches in height and ten pounds shy of the 200 mark when he gets on the scales. Brown hair and blue-gray eyes. Mr. Periolat was for eighteen years on the speaking stage, and will be best remembered in his stage work through appearances in Otis Skinner's Prince Otto and Julia Arthur's More Than Queen. He is a veteran of the pictures as well, for he made his camera debut away back in 1909, appearing initially in Forgiven. He is at present with the American, at Santa Barbara, but he has signed the payrolls of Essanay, Selig and Universal. Some of his best known plays have been Oil on Troubled Waters, The Man from Nowhere, A Diamond from the Sky and Annie for Spite, but he has literally hundreds of well-played parts to his credit. Likes swimming, music, etc. What does etc. mean?

KANE, Gail. Born in Philadelphia, American parentage. Is five feet five inches tall and weighs 140 pounds. Dark complexion, brown hair and eyes. Miss Kane is now with the American, but has also played for the World Film. She is best known as a dramatic actress, for her connection with the pictures has been comparatively recent. She was one of the stock of the Little Theater in New York and has figured largely in George M. Cohan productions. Some of her best dramatic roles have been in Arizona, Seven Keys to Baldpate, Anatol and The Miracle Man. Of her picture career Miss Kane says nothing, evidently feeling that it is too recent to need repetition, and she does not say a word about her fads, ignoring the fact that a hardworked cuss has to make these paragraphs run twenty-four lines whether the player says anything or not, but it is safe to say that she likes all outdoor sports and is devoted to her work. Selah!

Advertising for Exhibitors
Conducted by EPES WINTHROP SARGENT

Maine Advertising.

E VIDENTLY Maine advertisers should be represented by a minus rather than a plus sign. Recently we discussed the advertising in Waterville and spoke of the work down the river, but the other day we got a file of the Daily Kennebec Journal and went over it systematically. This paper is published in Augusta and serves a considerable territory; most of the towns being represented by weekly papers or being too small even to support a once-a-week. The entire advertising in the average issue would not make a single regular advertisement for many western houses.

Because of the large proportion of space given the nearby towns there are special headings for the leading points, and three house ads appear below these headings, but without definite indication. Gardiner, for example, has two houses. One of these recently reopened after a shut down and actually splurged to the extent of six inches of space in the form of a two threes that shows:

The Strand Will Reopen
On Saturday

7 reels of high class motion pictures. George Walsh in, "THE ISLE OF DESIRE," and a Fox 2 reel comedy. Matinee at 2.45, Evening 7 and 8.30.

This ran for two insertions and then the house dropped to the level of its opposition and runs on with three inches daily, each house getting 1½ inches across two columns. The paper seems to require that all ads be cut off by double rule and the measuring is done between these

---

THE STRAND :|: WEDNESDAY AND THURSDAY

Metro Pictures Presents the Supreme Screen Favorites Harold Lockwood and May Allison in "MISTER 44," a Metro Wonderplay of Exquisite Charm in Five Parts.

Two Reel Comedy, Pathe Weekly Showing European War News in Motion Pictures

Coming Friday and Saturday Clara Kimball Young in Her Latest Production, "THE EASIEST WAY" in Seven Parts.

Johnson Opera House - TODAY

Sessue Hayakawa in "THE JAGUAR'S CLAWS," a smashing, fighting story of the border. Sessue Hayakawa as a Mexican bandit heads an all-star cast.

JUVENILE CHARLIE CHAPLIN

Pictograph & Bray Cartoon   Twelve Reels Friday & Saturday

---

rules, so the actual advertisement is only 1 3/16 inches deep, including two point rule. As the stuff is on the Gardiner page there is no town name in the advertising. Only the stringer in Augusta would go around looking for the Johnson Opera House in that town.

The City Opera House, Waterville, takes from an inch and a quarter to an inch and three-quarters deep. The Silver does not advertise, apparently, save in the local paper. Having the page to himself, Mr. Kelliher does not trouble with rule work save to box in with a light line the house title.

The Colonial, Augusta, has the same type of advertisement as the Gardiner houses and generally takes the same three inches a day divided between two columns, but the Fourth of July brought out nine inches in which to announce the Pershing picture in two four and a halfs. Sometimes this regular advertising runs as high as two threes, and the house seems to gauge its space by the attraction. Mabel Taliaferro got 36 inches for "A Magdalene of the Hills," four nines being used. Moreover, it is a very well set advertisement; the first really good advertisement for a motion picture we have seen in a Central Maine newspaper.

But even the Colonial, livelier than the rest, does not appear to have declared in on Dollar Day in Augusta, where Charles Decker, of Grand

WILL HER VERDICT BE YOURS?

At any rate, you will enjoy a wonderfully good, intensely interesting and gripping story when you see

MABEL TALIAFERRO
In Her Latest Superb Metro Wonderplay

"A Magdalene of the Hills"
FRIDAY ONLY
AT THE COLONIAL

Because she states it is her best, we will show it to you for your verdict.

Junction, Colorado, for example, actually inaugurated a dollar day. There were two dollar days in succession and the house did not seem to know it, to judge from the newspaper advertising.

Other houses in the smaller towns do not advertise. Even the summer park within the ten cent fare limit, does not announce its attractions. They all seem to trust to word of mouth advertising or the desire for amusement. None of them go after business. No wonder they do not do better business, yet they complain because they cannot draw better. It is entirely their own fault. There must be some real live wires in the state—there used to be—but if there are, we would be glad to get some examples of their work. It would be a novelty.

Makes Its Border.

The Grand theater, Faribault, Minn., sends in a window card for Miss George Washington, nicely done in red and blue. The card is 14 by 22 inches and has a home-made patriotic border. Evidently they had on hand a lot of white stars with dark grounds. These are about eighteen points square. By putting three bits of three-point rule be-

---

Special Offer

From 9 a. m. until 10 a. m. (one hour) Monday, June 18th, we will give with every Cash Purchase of $1.50 or over a ticket to Marguerite Clark in "Miss George Washington" at the Grand Theatre Monday night

Our Sale Still Continues On

Coats   Suits   Children's Coats   Wash Dresses   Wash Goods
Bath Towels   Bed Spreads   Long Cloth

REMEMBER—We will give tickets for only one hour, 9 to 10 Monday morning next, and only on Cash Purchases of a $1.50 or more. One ticket to a customer. No telephone orders. No C. O. D. No charge.

---

tween the stars, they get an effective running border, printing the star backgrounds in blue with the stripes in red. It is not a flag border, the use of which is prohibited, but it is striking and timely. This red, white and blue will not reproduce, as the blue takes too white, but in the original the display is excellent, both as to copy and type composition. In connection with the showing of the subject a local dry goods house gave a free ticket to every woman purchasing goods to the value of $1.50 or more to the evening performance, and took four sevens in the local paper to advertise that fact, giving the house considerable publicity both in the advertisement and the accompanying reader, while paying straight box office prices for the tickets. This, of course, is the ideal condition, but if your matinee business is poor and you want to build up you can arrange with some local store to work in with you, perhaps paying half price for the tickets and guaranteeing a certain amount of publicity. Show this reproduction to your prospect if he is in doubt as to how it works, and point out that the shopping public will be more apt to read an announcement of free tickets than straight bargain dope. It works good to both house and store.

Good Ideas.

The ideas slip now being sent out with all Bluebird press sheets is good advertising. Generally there is offered one or more street stunts and the copy for a post card or form letter, but the point is that the ideas are calculated to work instead of getting the user into trouble with the police, which is the chief trouble with many of the schemes. That is one point to be watched. If you expect to use a traffic impeding stunt see the chief of police in advance and tell him what you want to do, and ask if you may. Generally you can, save in the larger cities, and it is better to have a permit than a summons given you.

A Rush Drawing.

Gordon F. (100%) Fullerton, of the Liberty, Seattle, Wash., sends in a new cut example and writes:

Thank you for the story on the Liberty, which you ran in the MOVING PICTURE WORLD of July 7. The suggestions for the use of the Benday are very good. Had it not been for the simple reason that the feature was picked at the last minute, and I had to get an idea for the cut and have the drawing made in a little more than an hour, I would have had more details and finishing touches. We appreciate your criticisms because we want to improve our work.

We are enclosing "FLAME OF THE YUKON" Sunday ad. It is a wonderful picture. We have tried to get the atmosphere of the picture in the drawing. This is another one of those rush order drawings, turned out while you wait, and it might have been better. In spite of the fact that the temperature hovered around ninety degrees (equivalent to 130 degrees in the east), the crowds jammed the theater all day Sunday and were standing out in the streets by night to see this feature.

If you will turn to the issue for July 7 you will see an hour-glass cut for The Witching Hour. The black masses were unrelieved by white save the figure eight of the glass itself. In the cut reproduced here there is less black on any one mass, though probably the artist used no more ink on the other cut. Here the black is better distributed, and so a better display is gained. But Benday, when it is needed should take no more time than plain black, and Benday is effective where too solid a mass is to be avoided. We think that had this been cropped slightly above the title with another box of type above that, the advertisement would have shown as well, since the top part contributes but little to the atmosphere. The main point, however, is that a display drew a turnaway. More than that no manager can ask. An hour is a pretty limited time for drawing. Under the circumstances, the artist has done well, but he should get more time and be encouraged to study the subject ahead. Here he got the main idea well—that of an Alaskan dance hall girl, but we think that sun must have been the one that brought the 90 degree weather. But what does Mr. Fullerton mean about 130 degrees back east?

Catch Up Matinees.

Lately we had the Luncheon Matinee. Now it's the catch-up. This is part of the front page of the Lagoon theater, Minneapolis:

To Every Woman and Her Husband.

Dear Madame:

So wonderfully interesting has proven "The Neglected Wife"

featuring Ruth Roland, and so thoroughly am I convinced every woman and man should see this great serial photoplay in its entirety, we have arranged to give a "CATCH-UP" matinee on WEDNESDAY, JULY 11, at the LAGOON theater, at which every adult woman will be given FREE ADMISSION.

On this occasion the first three episodes, consisting of six reels, will be shown. You are cordially invited. REMEMBER, there will be no charge for this Wednesday Matinee.

The fourth episode of the serial will be shown Wednesday evening and Thursday matinee and evening. The CATCH-UP matinee will enable those who did not see the opening chapters to see the picture in its entirety from the beginning and follow it consistently to the end. It is going to be a very fascinating and pleasant entertainment for thousands of women, for aside from the entertainment the Lagoon theater is delightfully cool on hot summer afternoons.

This is in typewriter type, and is signed by the manager, J. S. Woodhouse. Since the letter is addressed to "every woman and her husband" the salutation should be changed to match. Repetition of the first of a serial is not at all a new idea, but calling it a catch-up matinee gives it a new kink.

Growing.

The Colonial, Camden, N. J., is closed for a brief period to permit the enlargement of the auditorium. Mrs. A. R. Woodruff is a steady and consistent advertiser. She has worked her house program into a model of its kind, and she goes after business intelligently. Instead of making a "poor mouth" and joining the general cry that she is slaving to keep the exchanges prosperous, she is increasing her auditorium to take care of the crowds that seek admittance. Good advertising backed by good bills and courteous management will bring money and more money to a house. No kick of poor business comes from the real hustlers. If your own business is poor advertise more and advertise more intelligently. You cannot pull business with no advertising and films so old they are ready to drop apart. We saw a year old Chaplin the other day, and it was in wretched shape, yet it was a feature of a house that tries to bolster up poor business with a musical comedy stock company that is even worse than the business. It cannot be done that way. Mrs. Woodruff knows the way, and so she has to add more seats.

Program Stuff.

Here is an unusually good program reader. It is by E. F. Coe, of the Theater Louisiana, Baton Rouge, La., the home of the model program. Mr. Coe seldom runs general copy in his small folder, but when it does it is all there. You can adapt this to your own facts:

SOMEBODY HAS SAID:

"The greatest preacher of them all is the ant—and he says nothing!" But then the ant has nothing to advertise. Theater Louisiana offers a good show every day. The best in pictures perfectly presented and projected. A comfortable house at all times. Typhoon ventilation; air changed twice every minute; fresh air too, from fifty feet above the street. And last but not least, courtesy at all times and a marvelous ability to listen to criticism—sometimes called "kicks." These we do not get often, but they are appreciated when they come, and finally, be sure of this, that we are striving to please, and we thank you most heartily for your generous patronage in the past.　　　　F. E. COE, Manager.

There is nothing extravagant about this. It is all plain, common sense stuff that sounds as if Mr. Coe meant it, as undoubtedly he does. If Mr. Coe can write as well as this it would pay him to take half the back page each issue just for a chat and change weekly.

Just So—What?

This is by L. J. Scott in the Essanay house sheet:

WHAT COULD HE EXPECT?

A PATRON RECENTLY ATTENDED A THEATER ON THE NORTH SIDE OF CHICAGO TWO NIGHTS IN SUCCESSION. THIS HOUSE IS LOCATED IN ONE OF THE MOST THICKLY POPULATED DISTRICTS WHERE COMPETITION IS KEEN. ONE PROJECTOR WAS OUT OF FOCUS, A DIRTY FRINGE SURROUNDED THE APERTURE PLATE OF EACH MACHINE, AND THE LENS ON THE SLIDE PROJECTOR WAS COVERED WITH A SMEAR OF GREASE THAT ALMOST OBLITERATED THE SLIDES. THE SECOND NIGHT NO ATTEMPT HAD BEEN MADE TO REMEDY THE FAULTY PROJECTION.

AND YET THE MANAGER OF THIS SHOW IS WONDERING WHY BUSINESS IS BAD.

Just so. Why shouldn't business be bad. The exhibitor would not expect to sell decayed bananas for the price of fresh fruit, but to too many anything on a film seems to be a picture no matter how rainy it may be or how poorly projected.

Real Time Tables.

The Third Street theater, Easton, Pa., has another good wrinkle. It is a pocket size folder captioned

Time
Table
July 1917
Pennsylvania
Lehigh Valley
Central Railroads
and
Third Street Theater

Below is the explanation that it shows the trains running to and from Philadelphia and New York and the features at the theater for the second half of July. The second page gives the schedule to and from Philadelphia, trains of all the roads being listed in chronological order, saving the consultation of three time-tables in order to discover the next train. Page three gives the trains to New York and the back page lists the features. This is something that is really valuable to the recipient, for even the man who does not expect to travel likes to have a time table. Linking the house with the railroad and even semi-public institutions is an excellent scheme. The Third Street management keeps thinking winter and summer.

An Improvement.

C. H. Bayer, of the Opera House, Leighton, Pa., has turned to a nice folder program that is about as neat as anything he has done. The card is 3 by 4½ inches, a nice buff, printed in a warm brown. The front page is really artistic. There is a small cut of a player to the left with a strip of border and the type choice is excellent. The days are dates and stars are set in roman caps with titles in full face. Evidently Mr. Bayer was fortunate in getting hold of a printer who takes a pride in his work, and between them they have turned out a model issue. We hope to reproduce one as soon as we can get one on white stock. Mr. Bayer does not make the error of trying to tell too much in small space. He has just one line of brief comment for each play, but the line tells something. "A tear or two and more than a few smiles," means more than "Thrilling society drama" or any other of the bromides. Mr. Bayer has a program that is worth holding to for a time.

Too Extravagant.

The Lafayette theater, Baltimore, Md., is inclined to be too effusive. Where everything is "splendid," nothing is good, and it is better to use a sliding scale of adjectives. One announcement, for example, starts off: "This program combines some of the grandest selections in picturedom for this week." The next week they have "intense interest in every subject, elements of suspense constantly before your eyes and startling plunges of mystery and love." That sounds almost too good to be true. Next week the bill is "So vividly interesting, breathless action, thrills, suspense, heart interest, romances, so intensely dramatic, enacted by the cream of popular players." That is so glittering that it means nothing at all. It is not even a grammatical sentence. A more temperate announcement would be more convincing to the average patron. "Grand" should never be used. Its erroneous use always cheapens a statement. The same lack of continuity of thought is apparent in the detail program, and the proofreading is poor. Take this for Tillie Wakes Up:

Some comedy drama, you begin to chuckle, it spreads to joy, the merriment it creates when Marie makes for the witching waves and her dizzie feeling from the effects of old "Scotch," says nothing saying nothing about her seated on a cake of ice, when Tillie wakes up. What wild experiences and hilarious moments caused by these spashlardn effects can only be known, when you see this photoplay. Don't miss this fun.

Lindley Murray himself could not parse that. Another announcement tells that the heroine was the hero's "all in," instead of "all-in-all," which is something else again. Greater care would give the program infinitely greater value as advertising material. The present phrasing is apt to convey the suggestion that a management so unfamiliar with good English is not apt to know how to run a good show. This probably is not true, but that is the impression the stranger prospect is apt to receive.

Booming West.

Phil L. Ryan, of the Standard Film Corp., Kansas City, asks for a personal letter of criticism on a mailing sheet for Billy West Comedies. We trust that the carbon of this copy will suffice. The sheet is 17 by 22 inches, printed as a whole on one side and in half and sixths on the other. The full sheet is rather awkward to handle for mail use, but it folds well and one of the sixths is printed for the address. It is done in a gray brown and yellow and the use of tint suggests three colors. As an example of good press work it qualifies and the general argument is good, though we think that too much stress is laid upon sending for the campaign book. This sheet should be the salesman and not the campaign book. Some of the argument is too extravagant to be convincing. For example, the statement is made that Director Gilstrom's salary is "the largest paid to any individual man in the business with the exception of Charles Chaplin and Douglas Fairbanks." Not only does this put West in the position of the tail to the dog, but the statement is so utterly at variance with the facts that your credence is weakened and you can believe nothing that is said. No exhibitor is going to swallow such a statement as that, and it weakens the entire sheet.

Bottled Up.

John C. Green, Galt, Canada, Canadian handler of the Wharton features, uses a bottle cut-out to advertise "The Great White Trail." The bottle has no bearing on the release, but the label reads:

PEP
and
PUNCH

The Sure cure

Open me up
and look me over.

Cut-outs are costly, but they generally attract, and if they can be picked up at a bargain almost any cut-out can be made to apply to a release. Personally we prefer glass bottles with extractable corks, but this idea is neatly done. Inside there is a neat typographic idea that can be used when there are three stars, one of whom is the feature. Here the principal name is set in 36 point with the supporting stars in two eighteen point lines, one at either side.

English Programs.

Arthur Peel, of the Queen's, Nelson, England, sends in a new ad, vertising booklet and writes that he proposes to issue this monthly. It is 3 by 4½ inches, a heavy tint cover and eight pages in blue on white inside, making twelve in all. This carries portrait cuts and announcements of coming attractions and supplements the house program. This last is a six page folder, a rather awkward size unless one is used to it, but a standard British form. The full sheet is 11 by 17 inches folded to get a six page railroad. The two changes for the

week stand on either side of the musical program in the center, and there is plenty of space for the trade advertising. The front page carries a sketch design and there is some film chat on the other pages in the program space; giving reading on every page of advertising. The small booklet, because of the portraits, is apt to be retained, and it is small enough to class as a vest pocket. It admirably supplements the weekly program by attracting prior interest.

Parkway Programs.

The Parkway, Baltimore, is one recent program used cuts two inches wide by an inch and a quarter high in spaces 3½ by 4½. Making these special cuts from stills showing close-ups gives a much better effect than could be had from portrait vignettes or the regulation scene cuts supplied by the manufacturer. The pages of the Parkway are always well laid out, and a neat looking page is the first gun in the campaign. You must have an attractive page if you would have it read in the proper frame of mind. The McHenry, a sister house, uses a six page railroad style, taking the inside for the three changes of bill and the back for house talk and full information from times of feature showing to the free ice water.

A Voting Idea.

H. G. F. Nerge suggests a new adaptation of the voting scheme. In place of the checked ballot he contemplated using the half of a ticket given the patron in many houses as a seat identification, though the common duplex ticket will work as well, or a card may be specially printed and handed the patron on entering. The essence of the scheme is a series of boxes near the exit, the slots being lettered "for" and "against" the feature or features. Where but a single feature is used, the idea works well, but with two or more features and but a single vote, the patron is left undecided and is apt to vote erratically. It should be remembered, in all voting schemes of this sort, that some people will vote adversely through a misdirected sense of humor, and a certain allowance should be made for this fact.

One Good Maine Man.

We were pleasantly surprised the other day to pick up a good advertisement at the Belgrade Lakes, Maine. It was only a four by eight throwaway, printed on one side, but well printed from clean and well selected type. It advertised the Acme theater to the campers and hotel guests, and must have been distributed broadcast, for we picked a couple out of the road.

The Photoplaywright

Conducted by EPES WINTHROP SARGENT

INQUIRIES.

Questions concerning photoplay writing addressed to this department will be replied to by mail if a fully addressed and stamped envelope accompanies the letter, which should be addressed to this department. Questions should be stated clearly and should be typewritten or written with pen and ink. Under no circumstances will manuscripts or synopses be criticised, whether or not a fee is sent therefor.

A list of companies will be sent if the request is made to the paper direct and not to this department, and a return stamped envelope is inclosed.

Bill Wright Writes.

THE story from William Lord Wright, now of the Selig Staff, throws some light on certain closed markets. Selig is not buying much now because he bought so liberally in the past. He has a stock on hand that supplies his present needs. Now he wants only the most striking and the most timely stuff. Only lately a former employee said that the Selig company had thousands of dollars worth of stuff in its vaults. Selig still wants the biggest and most important stuff, but is not in the market for what might be termed "good average stuff," for this was bought in the market when the average was considerably higher than it is now. Mr. Wright says :

According to William N. Selig, president of the Selig Polyscope Company, that company is not in the regular market for scenarios, although ready to consider any unusual idea or story that can be developed into a feature production. Stories or ideas dealing with comprehensive subjects or timely questions are always worthy of consideration. Two of the recent releases of the Selig Company are criterions. "Beware of Strangers," filmed with all the care and expense for which the Selig Company is noted in big stuff, dealt with the operations of Mann Act blackmailers, and polished swindlers. The work of these crooks filled the public prints some months ago and it remained for the Selig Company to present a drama that has proven both artistically and commercially popular. Another drama soon to be released by the Selig Company is entitled "Who Shall Take My Life?" Miss Maibelle Heikes Justice became interested in the pros and cons of the Capital Punishment question—a question that is being universally discussed. She secured consent of the authorities to visit Sing Sing, and did so as the guest of Thomas Mott Osborn, then Warden. She is said to be the only woman who ever received permission to visit the Death House of Sing Sing and converse with the prisoners there. She then wrote a seven-reel feature protesting against Capital Punishment, and in the drama she used the atmosphere she gained during her visit to the prison. The production is said to be a strong plea against Capital Punishment, also carrying a dual love story.

One occasionally reads of the dearth of material for motion picture plays. The Selig Company claims enough plot material to supply all needs for years to come, and that is one reason why the company is not in the open market. Mr. Selig finally passes on all stories accepted by his company, and he early realized the wisdom of buying good material. For years he has paid authors the prices they have asked for their work, and those writers who may complain today have been the ones who yesterday importuned the Selig Company to buy their stuff and sold it.

In the Selig Company vaults are both stories and poems from practically all of the famous writers of the present day. Not only novels but short story rights to pictures are owned by Mr. Selig. At a moment's notice he can supply a director with a tale by a well-known author, for a feature film, a five-reeler, or interesting stuff for one, two and three-reelers.

Get It All.

Now and then the boob letters are lightened by something real. Here's a line from a man whose work is selling and whose vocation indicates the possession of real brains. He says:

Of course every photoplaywright in America should read your page every week. I do, and it has been untold assistance to me in my work. But he should also read the Moving Picture World from "kiver to kiver." In the issue of June 9th I ran across a little ten-line article which proved to me in just five seconds that one of the best ideas I ever had had been anticipated by an earlier and perhaps better author. When the first pangs of disappointment had passed away I realized with a deep feeling of thankfulness that by reading that one item I had saved myself many days and nights of hard but absolutely unproductive labor; for, with the other fellow "beating

me to it," my script would not have been worth the paper it was written on.

There are two big facts in this letter. In the first place he does not say his idea was stolen. He is able to understand that another might have the same idea, particularly since he has not submitted his, but the main point is that he reads the entire paper, and reads it carefully. Do you? You should. It saves trouble in many ways.

Psychology.

"I have too much psychology in my stories," complains a writer. "My plots are all dependent upon the thoughts and emotions of my characters rather than their actions." The inference is that the ideas find visual expression in drab action. Perhaps this is true, but the fault may be with the thinker and not with the thought. Perhaps the writer takes too seriously the psychology of his stories without giving heed to the action rising from those stories. The desire of a man for wealth, for instance, the subordination of all else to this desire, taken by itself is purely mental and not physical, but this desire surely can find symbolism in pictured action if the author is careful not to make the thought superior to action. Suppose that we conceive the idea of a man who sacrifices everything to a desire to be wealthy. As a psychological study of character, this would scarcely be interesting, even in words, but this desire, the striving and the result are all capable of being pictured in action as clearly as his mental processes may be described in words. We have a wealthy person as the symbol of his desire. We have the woman he loves as the symbol of his renunciation. By a skillful handling of these symbols and the lesser factors, we can indicate as clearly in action as in words the struggle and the sacrifice he makes. All photoplay really is, is the substitution of action symbols for word symbols. You express avarice in the five letters, g r e e d. You can express it more forcefully by showing the result of greed, the deliberate putting away of happiness and contentment for power and wealth; the marriage for money instead of for love, the severance of home ties that bind ambition. Idea is the spring which gives movement to action, but any person should be able to replace words with action if only they strive to arrive at a proper appreciation of the value of idea, and can come to realize that the exact and definite expression of an idea in words is seldom as effective and graphic as the showing of the results of that idea in happenings. To say that a man discarded love to marry money conveys an idea. Building up we can tell just how he came to put wealth above affection, but if we use words to do this we merely leave the reader to put into picture the thoughts we express in language where, by realizing the picture ourselves we can put on paper words conveying actions that, done into pictured action, will make the play. The trouble with the writer seems to be that he values idea too highly and action not sufficiently. He fails to see that the apparently indirect expression of the idea in action is really the most complete and understandable expression of the thought. Photoplay should be the most complete expression of thought. It will be when its possibilities are fully understood. The author seeks to convey through his work pictures. The sculptor seeks to reproduce life. The artist paints pictures of life and often seeks, more or less unsuccessfully, to convey the idea of motion. The photoplay writer writes in life-motion. He realizes the goal for which the others all have striven. It is a pity that so few realize fully their wealth of opportunity and use their wonderful resources only to convey the simplest and most banal ideas.

You Can't Fool Pop.

C. B. Hoadley, better known as Pop Hoadley, one of the original Insquefers and one of the best old scouts in the photoplay end, is how reading comedies for the Universal. He writes that there is a small market for comedies at the Big U, but adds: "One must be acquainted with the needs of the various companies to get by with it. I have a good staff, and we supply nearly all of the stuff, with a script from the outside now and then. Good comedies are becoming scarce. Most of the stuff submitted is of the musty, mouldy brand, and the dubs are trying to peddle me my own stuff, written several years ago." You cannot fool Pop with old stuff. He was in the game when it was young and he has a memory that is the despair of his assistant. He remembers all his own stories and all the stories of others, and if he buys it must be brand new, and a thing is not brand 'new merely because you never heard of it before. It is brand new only if Pop never heard of it, and there are few comedy ideas he has never heard of before, so send him only the stuff so new that you're a bit surprised at its newness yourself.

Projection Department

Conducted by F. H. RICHARDSON

Manufacturers' Notice.

I T IS an established rule of this department that no apparatus or other goods will be endorsed or recommended editorially until the excellence of such articles has been demonstrated to its editor.

Important Notice.

Owing to the mass of matter awaiting publication, it is impossible to reply through the department in less than two to three weeks. In order to give prompt service, those sending four cents, stamps (less than actual cost), will receive carbon copy of the department reply, by mail, without delay. Special replies by mail on matters which cannot be replied to in the department, one dollar.

Both the first and second sets of questions are now ready and printed in neat booklet form, the second half being seventy-six in number. Either booklet may be had by remitting 25 cents, money or stamps, to the editor, or both for 40 cents. Cannot use Canadian stamps. Every live, progressive operator should get a copy of these questions. You may be surprised at the number you cannot answer without a lot of study.

Reopens Charter.

Carl Gilbert, secretary-treasurer Sioux City, Iowa, Operators' Local Union No. 355, I. A. T. S. E. & M. P. M. O., writes as follows:

Will you kindly have the following published in next issue of the department:
The Sioux City Motion Picture Operators' Union, Local No. 335, I. A. T. S. E., will reopen its charter September 1st, and it will remain open until January 1, 1918. During this period the initiation fee will be $25, but on January 1st the fee will be raised to $50. This action is taken for the benefit of those operators working within the jurisdiction of this local who may wish to join. Application should be made to Carl Gilbert, Secretary, P. O. Box 834, Sioux City, Iowa.

It is impossible to get anything into the "next issue" after its receipt. In matters of this kind we expedite publication as much as it is possible. I would strongly recommend to all operators within the jurisdiction of the Sioux City local that they take this opportunity to climb aboard the band wagon and become members of the international organization. It is to be regretted that Brother Gilbert did not send a list of towns within the jurisdiction of the local.

An Invention.

From L. S. Baluta, Roaring Creek, Pennsylvania, comes letter and patent papers (Patent Number 1,232,753), descriptive of an invention by friend Baluta, who also sends crudely made working models. He asks that the invention be criticised in the department; also for our personal opinion as to its merits, or possible improvements.

The invention consists of a metal clasp designed to engage the outer diameter of an ordinary wooden reel hub, an elastic band attached thereto, of length sufficient to reach beyond the outer diameter of the metal reel-side, and a metal clasp attached to the outer end of the said elastic band, the latter being so made that the film may be readily shoved under and thus engaged with the end of the band, though not so firmly but that it will readily pull loose at the end of the rewinding process. The whole is intended to facilitate threading the machine by making it easy to attach the film to the lower reel while the reel is in the magazine.

In the illustration, 3 is the aforesaid elastic band, 1 the metal clasp designed to slip over and engage the reel hub, and 12 is the film clasp. In figures 2 and 3 full detail is given, so that I think you can readily grasp the idea, as well as its practical operation. So far a slot G in the upper illustration, and dowel (don't know what else to call it) in figure 3 be concerned, I think they are unnecessary and impractical. They do not exist in the models sent. Ends of clasp 4 can be bent at right angles and have a saw-tooth edge which will provide ample anchorage, always supposing the clasp to be made of spring steel. Band 3 can be riveted to clasp 1 on its flat surface, extending clear around the clasp to prevent out-of-centering effect. Clasp 12 should be made of best grade spring steel, and there ought to be a slight shoulder between screws 8 and clasp 2, figure 3, in order that the film be engaged a little more firmly than it is likely to be with the plain, flat surface.

The thing seems to be practical, but there would, I am afraid, be more or less trouble through weakening of clasp 2, due to the necessarily very short bend, and the liability of operators when in a hurry

to raise the clasp up to slip friend film under—not supposed to be necessary, but will be done just the same—and raise it too high, thus ruining the clasp. I would suggest that neighbor Baluta send two of these devices to each of the following operators, requesting them to make report to the department: W. O. Woods, Market Street theater,

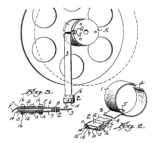

Fig. 3.

Fig. 2.

San Francisco, who can also report as to its probable marketability, he being connected with a firm making and dealing in theater specialties; Chief Operator Strand theater, New York City; E. A. Shields, Chief Operator Isis theater, Denver, Colorado.

Measuring the Intermittent.

A. G. Rollins, St. Louis, Missouri, propounds the following:

I have received much benefit from the, or rather from "our" department. Just what the profession would have done without its help in years gone by I do not know, and I believe operators, as a class, do not properly appreciate what a tremendous help it has been, or in how many ways it has aided them. To my mind, immense as has been its aid in improving the technical knowledge of the operator, it has done an even greater work in making of the business of operating respectable in compelling the operator, often against his own will, to respect his own profession, and pounding into the mind of the manager the fact that projection is, when all is said and done, one of his very greatest assets.

And now, having eased my mind of that load, may I ask a question? You often speak of the relation of intermittent speed to shutter blade width, and the importance of the operator measuring and comparing the various intermittents and their speed ratio. I think, however, it would help many of us if you would go further and explain the whole matter, including illustrated directions for measuring intermittent speed. It may seem childishly simple to you, friend Richardson, but to me, and I am sure to many more, it is almost anything else. May I hope to see a complete answer to this, my first question, in the columns of our department soon?

You certainly may, Brother Rollins. A request so courteously made is doubly deserving of attention; moreover I agree that the matter needs elucidation in the department. It is one of more than passing importance; also it is one very little understood by operators in general. In Memphis, Tennessee, the secretary of the local union did not even know what I mean by ratio of intermittent speed, and, in consequence of lack of knowledge on that and other points, he was cutting an unnecessarily large percentage of his light. And this same is true in very many cases.

The measuring of the ratio of intermittent speed is a very simple matter. But first let me explain that ratio of intermittent speed means the ratio the time the intermittent is moving and pulling down the film bears to the time it is at rest, and the picture being projected to the screen. Therefore it means the ratio of the time the main shutter blade must cover the lens to the time the lens is open, hence, while it does not necessarily mean the ratio of light to darkness (percentage of light cut), it has a direct and important bearing thereon, and does mean the ratio of light to darkness it is possible to obtain under a given local condition.

Examining the drawing we note mark A, B. C. A is a slight, but plainly visible scratch mark made on the machine frame, at any convenient point beside and as close as possible to the outer rim of the flywheel. We now turn the flywheel until the intermittent sprocket just barely begins to move. We must be very particular about this, and very carefully locate the precise point at which the sprocket begins to move. If we are to use our test as indicating the speed of the intermittent movement of a particular type of machine, then it will be well to use a new mechanism, and to be sure the intermittent is in proper adjustment.

Having located the precise point at which the intermittent sprocket

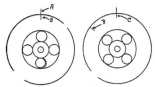

begins to move, make a slight, but plainly visible mark on the rim of the flywheel, exactly opposite mark A on the frame. Mark B ought to be made on the outer diameter of the wheel, so it will come just as close as possible to mark A, because any variation, however slight, will affect the result. To locate the point of first movement of the sprocket an extremely accurate method is to set a straight strip of flat spring steel, such as the steel the main spring of a watch is made from, about three of four inches long, so that one end rests against one of the sprocket teeth and the other against any temporary stop, as shown in the second illustration.

But the steel must be not less than three inches long, and must be very light, since the parts must not be put under strain. Of course when the sprockets move the spring steel will instantly bow, either up or down. I suggest this as a very accurate method, but the beginning of movement may be detected quite accurately either by using a condensing lens as a magnifier, or by sense of touch.

Having located the point of first movement, and made mark B, we now turn the flywheel until the intermittent sprocket just barely ceases to move, using due care to locate this point with the same accuracy, and make scratch mark C.

We now have our ratio of movement laid out on the rim of the flywheel, and are in position to measure it at will. This may be done in several ways. One is to take a compass having very sharp points, and set it to just register the distance from marks B to C. Having done this, just "step" the compass on around the diameter of the wheel, and if you find there are just six "steps," including the distance between marks B and C, then the movement is a one to five, which means that the film will be at rest exactly five times as long as it is moving. You may also measure the circumference of the wheel with a steel tape line (an ordinary tape will not serve), and then measure the distance between marks B and C. Divide the first by the last and the answer will be the number of divisions. Suppose, for instance, the circumference of the wheel to measure exactly nine inches, and the distance between marks B and C to be exactly one and one half inches. Dividing nine by one and one half we get six, hence we conclude the movement to be a one to five.

Applying this to the shutter, it means that the lens must be covered by the main blade during one sixth of the period of time elapsing from the time the intermittent sprocket begins to move until it begins to move next time, qualified by the fact that the lens need not be entirely closed until the film has moved considerably, and may be opened before the film has actually come to rest. On the other hand, with a one to six movement the lens must only be covered one during one seventh of each picture cycle, which is a very distinct gain in picture brilliancy and in other ways. Of course I fully understand, Mr. Pick-It-To-Pieces, that in practice other things besides speed of intermittent have to do with necessary shutter blade width, but that fact does not in any way affect or alter the matter with which we are now dealing. If a certain local condition, due, for instance, to wide picture at short throw, necessitates a certain added width of shutter blade it will add just that much

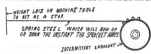

to the comparatively narrow blade of the fast intermittent machine, or to the already comparatively wide blade of the slow intermittent. Summed up, the faster the intermittent the narrower may the cut-off blade of the revolving shutter be, hence the less percentage of light will be cut off.

As against this, however, the faster the intermittent the greater the strain on the star and cam, on the intermittent sprocket teeth and on the film sprocket holes. Experience has proven, however, that film sprocket holes will stand up well with a one in six movement, and the

same is true of the mechanism, always provided it be well made and properly hardened. But with these latter matters we have nothing to do, other than to set forth the facts as we have found them. It is very necessary that operators understand these matters, and understand them thoroughly. And the more thoroughly you understand them the more valuable will you be to your employer and to the moving picture industry. You will find machine manufacturers who will argue for fast intermittent movement, while other manufacturers will argue for slow. It is for you, Mr. Operator, to understand, and be in position to intelligently weigh such arguments. There are other important reasons why speed of intermittent is of great importance, under certain local conditions. Let us hear from some of you as to your views in this matter; also tell us what would be most desirable in this respect in a house having short throw and wide picture, and why.

Better Be Careful.

J. R. Gralledale, Chicago, Illinois, wants information concerning a new projector. He asks:

> Will you please advise me as to whether or not the Stern Moving Picture Machine is a good machine. It is made in Philadelphia, and its makers claim big things for it.

Claims, friend Gralledale, are easy to make—much easier than a projector. If the makers of the machine in question had a really excellent article, it is reasonably certain this department would have heard from them. The fact that we have not heard from them is not conclusive evidence that their projector has no merit, but it certainly does incline one to the idea that it is not up to the standard. That a manufacturer of a really superior projection machine would place his machine on the market without first having presented its points of excellence to the Projection Department is extremely unlikely. It has been the experience of eight years that those who have projection apparatus of merit let no grass grow under their feet in getting it to the Department, in order to secure its approval, which costs not one red cent. On the other hand the manufacturer of inferior apparatus invariably keeps it away from us as long as possible.

There are plenty of excellent, standard projection machines on the market, neighbor Gralledale, and I would advise you to stick to goods of known value and merit, until such time as the manufacturer in question takes the trouble to present his goods for examination. We will then tell you precisely what he has, and you won't have to buy a pig in a poke.

From Texas.

D. Prather, San Angeleo, Texas, sends forty cents for the first and second sets of questions, and says:

> Am operator in the Lyric Theatre. We have two machines, one a Power's 6-A and one a Baird. The latter is a wonder in producing a flickerless picture. We have a large concrete operating room and a 110 foot distance of projection. The current is A. C., which we change to D. C. by means of a Mercury Arc Rectifier. Have just finished remodeling the house all over, and it certainly has helped a lot. We have just ordered 250 new opera chairs, and when they are in our seating capacity will be 600. It is 500 now. Have the very best programme we can buy and it gets the crowd, both at matinee and night.
>
> You will receive bill for renewal in good time, Brother Prather. And now as to the questions (which have been sent): Some few who ordered the second seem to have the mistaken idea that the answers accompany them. If that were true it would make a book worth at least $2.00, if not more. The reason I still continue to sell the booklets is that the operator who gets them will have a guide to study. It he starts at the beginning and studies those questions, he will have acquired a wide range of technical knowledge by the time he has finished with them.

Glad to know your theatre is doing well, which means that Messrs. Robb and Rowley and their operator are also doing well. Come again when the spirit moves.

Working for Nothing.

From a town in the state of Washington comes the following:

> I wonder if other theaters in this state get film like I do. I am enclosing just a few of many faults amputated from the last 100 feet of "The Pride of the Clan," received from the Progressive Film Corporation recently. I mailed a lot of them to the Progressive, explaining what a world of trouble it put a fellow to. This thing of doing a lot of work for nothing gets very monotonous in course of time. Never hear of other operators making complaint—Washington men, I mean—and am wondering if I am the only goat. What is your idea of an exchange giving this kind of service?

My opinion of such mis-managed exchanges has been set forth so often that it hardly requires repetition. I wonder what sort of howl one of the exchange mis-managers who do this sort of thing would put up if he rented a house, at a good, stiff rental, on the presumption it was in good order, only to find the roof leaked like a sieve, and when he demanded that the roof be fixed the landlord told him to "fix it himself." Or if the wall paper all fell to pieces and the landlord told him to "fix it himself, or go to the devil!" Oh, yes, Mr. Exchange manager, the cases are precisely analogous. The landlord rents you a building under the presumption that it is in usable condition—in good order. You rent a theater films on precisely the same assumption. The landlord has just as much right to tell you to "fix it yourself," as you have to tell the operator the same thing. But I believe this form of outrage on the part of irresponsible, incompetent exchange managers will never cease until one of two things happen, viz.: Sending out films in anything but first class mechanical condition is prohibited (as it ought to be prohibited) by law, or the operator gets strongly enough organized to put a stop to it himself.

Figuring Resistance.

A. W. Reynders, Sioux City, Iowa, makes the following inquiry:

As a subscriber to the Moving Picture World and owner of a handbook, which is very good indeed, I would like to have an answer to the following: What would be the resistance of the following. Please give formula for figuring it.

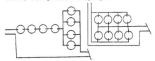

In the first connection you would have a series of four 8-ohm coils, making a total of 32 ohms, and a multiple of four 8-ohm coils in series with the 32 ohms. The placing of four coils in multiple would actually offer the resistance of one coil divided by four, so that the multiple would actually offer 8÷4=2 ohms, which, added to the 32, makes a total of 34 ohms opposed to the voltage. In the second sketch we have eight 8-ohm coils in multiple, and eight divided by eight equals one ohm. In dealing with a multiple, if the coils or resistances all have equal resistance, just divide the resistance of one by the number of resistances, or coils, and the result will be the resistance opposed to the current. If the rheostats have unequal resistance, then add the total of them all together and divide by the number of rheostats. The result will be the total resistance opposed to the arc. In these calculations no account has been taken of the arc resistance.

Probably a Loose Lens.

J. B. Stine, Covington, Indiana, is in trouble. I shall make my own suggestion, and ask operators who may have experienced similar trouble, and who may be able to suggest a different solution, to advise. Friend Stine writes:

Have been a constant reader of the World for several years; also possess one of your handbooks, but have recently bumped into a projection proposition for which I have been unable to find either remedy or cause, though I have diligently searched my files of projection dope from A to 4c. My present operator has had no previous experience with such a trouble, and I have had two high class operators trying to dope it out, but their success is represented by 0. So here I am, hat in hand, making my best bow and asking the Main Guy himself to get on the job.

Some time ago I remodeled my house, increasing the distance of projection to 124 feet. Machine is a Power's 6-B, taking A C through Bell & Howell Compensarc, from a 110 volt, 60 cycle supply. Had to get a Gundlach-Manhattan half size or No. 2 projection lens, with the special Power shutter for large diameter lens. Picture is 14 feet. And now for the disease, which is really not so easy to describe on paper: The shutter seems to be in time, as there are no streaks either up or down from title letters, nor do we have what is commonly termed a "travel ghost" (Streaks up or down is precisely what travel ghost is, neighbor Stine. —A.). but there is a blur of all objects—a shaded-out effect very similar to a ghost, which sometimes appears on the left one third of the screen, and sometimes on the lower one third, while the upper part and center is usually, though not always, clear. This condition does not always obtain, there being times when the picture will run absolutely perfect for several consecutive minutes.

Have tried all combinations of condenser lenses, using for a time, a 8½-8½ bi-convex set, but recently changed to 7½-9½ meniscus bi-convex, which gives us a beautiful, white light, almost equal to direct current. In using this set we have the lamphouse back as far as it will go, and get a clearly defined spot which looks good. Am using ¾ National cored carbons above and below. Smaller size seemed to pencil down to a point, and would not hold steady arc. If you can help us it surely will be appreciated. Enclosed find 4 cents, stamps, for carbon of department reply.

It seems to me, neighbor Stine, your trouble can only be due to one of two or three things. Take that lens out and shake it sharply, listening for a rattle which would denote a loose lens. But failure to hear the rattle should not stop you from taking the lens combinations out and examining the mounts. But before you even do this, take off the revolving shutter and project a light scene in some film, holding a piece of thin white writing paper over the front of the projection lens. It may be, and probably will be, found that the actual picture ray is very much smaller than the lens diameter. If so, then, with a pencil, while the film is running (the white light will not do), trace the outline of the picture ray on the paper. Then, using that as a pattern, cut a mask from black cardboard and place it in front of the projection lens, so as to just allow the actual picture ray to pass out, and nothing else. You may find that this will stop your trouble (though I hardly think so) and at the same time allow you to trim down on your main shutter blade considerably. Next, stop up the lens port in the operating

room wall with black cardboard, or sheet metal—preferably the latter, and project a film (not the white light, but a film scene), marking the exact outline of the actual picture-carrying ray on the cardboard or metal, after which cut out the mask thus indicated. If these things stop the trouble, well and good. The next thing is a search for a loose projection lens.

I could not advise as to your condenser combination unless I knew your amperage. Ordinarily I would say you are wrong, but you have a rather long focal length projection lens, and maybe it is all right. The chart says that with 60 amperes A C a 7½-7½ meniscus bi-convex set, with 2½ inches from center of condenser combination to film, is correct. The trouble with the 7½-9½ is that you have too great a distance from crater to lens. Suppose you try two 7½ lenses and let us know the result. They must be set close together, of course. Sorry your reply was somewhat delayed, but I'm just beginning to get half way straightened out after the Long Hike.

Information Wanted.

Under date July 7, Nebraska, asks:

Will you kindly tell me how to take the jump and side motion out of a picture, and what carbons to use on a A C; also what amperage and what make of lens. Please let me know at once, as my picture has a bad jump. Sprocket is new, as is also aperture plate. Enclosed find two cent stamp; also fifteen cents for your book.

New brother, don't get insulted when I tell you you ought to secure a position under a competent operator and serve at least a year apprenticeship. While it is true you are in a comparatively small city, still photoplays which cost many thousands of dollars to produce are placed in your hands for reproduction, and the art of artists, than whom there are none better, is dependent entirely upon your skill for proper reproduction upon the screen. Nor is this all, for the patrons of four theater pay admission to see photoplays properly reproduced upon the screen, and still, beyond all this, you may be wasting, and probably are wasting money of your employer, since you cannot possibly work efficiently or intelligently unless you understand the apparatus, and your letter seems to indicate an almost total lack of knowledge thereof. As to fifteen cents for "my book," why you had me puzzled, but I guess you mean a copy of the Moving Picture World, which is $3.00 per year, or $1.50 for six months. I am returning your stamps. Carbon copies of department reply are four cents, not two. Even at that the carbon copies cost me a great many dollars a year more than they bring in. However, I am glad to supply them. And now to your queries: You have not even told me what kind of machine you have, so how I can direct you how to eliminate side motion, other than to say that to remove any side motion there may be in the intermittent sprocket, see that the guide rollers at top of the gate (if there are any) fit the film snugly, but without buckling it, and be sure there is no side motion to the machine itself. As to the jump, if it occurs regularly four times to every revolution of the crank the trouble lies in either your intermittent sprocket or its shaft. Be sure of the faces of your sprockets, particularly the intermittent sprocket, are perfectly clean. Dirt on face of intermittent sprocket is apt to make the picture jump. You should have described the "jump" very carefully, which you did not do. Am sorry your reply was so long delayed, but the letter came while I was away and was buried under a mass of correspondence. It should have been kept separate. As to carbons, why I could hardly take space to re-publish tables covering this. Would suggest that you procure a handbook from the Moving Picture World, price $4.00. It is precisely what you need. 700 pages dealing with practical projection in terms which you, or any other man, can understand. With this book and a year of apprenticeship you will be a thoroughly competent operator, provided you study, as well as work. The carbon-size tables for A C and D C will be found on page 287 of the handbook.

Wonder What's Up?

From San Francisco, California, comes a postcard, on one side of which are pictures of the exterior and interior arrangements of what seems to be a real swell hotel, and on the opposite the following : Hello Rich! Just on a trip to Frisco with a few chinks, en route to Hong Kong. Toro Glucksman. Huh, I am real curious to know what my old friend Toro, of New Orleans, is doing chaperoning a mess of ex-pig-tails around over the scenery; also whether it is only the crevices (joke! A Chink is a crevice, isn't he?) who are en route to the Flowery Kingdom, or is Glucksman also bound thenceward?

Motion Picture Photography*

Conducted by CARL LOUIS GREGORY, F. R. P. S.

Inquiries.

QUESTIONS in cinematography addressed to this department will receive carbon copy of the department's reply by mail when four cents in stamps are inclosed. Special replies by mail on matters which cannot be replied to in this department, $1.

Manufacturers' Notice.

It is an established rule of this department that no apparatus or other goods will be endorsed or recommended editorially until the excellence of such articles has been demonstrated to its editor.

Fixing Baths (Continued).

WHERE acid short stop alone is used the acid carried over from the short stop may cause sulphur precipitation and the sudden neutralization of the alkaline carbonates of the developer, by a strong acid short stop, liberates bubbles of carbonic acid gas in the gelatine film, causing small round blisters. Where the short stop is made weak to avoid these blisters it becomes rapidly exhausted from the neutralization of the acid by the alkaline developer and must be often renewed to accomplish its purpose.

Plain hypo also becomes rapidly discolored by the old developer carried into it by the film. Acid hypo prevents staining of the film and remains clear much longer than plain hypo.

Sulphurous acid is a strong decolorising agent and the acid fixing bath contains a certain amount of free sulphurous acid produced by the action of the acetic acid upon the sodium sulphite present.

Acid Hypo Fixing Solution.

Dissolve completely:

Water	10 gallons
Hypo	21 pounds

Then mix the following acid hardener separately and after it is thoroughly dissolved add it to the hypo solution above:

Water	40 ounces
Sodium sulphite (dessicated)	4 ounces
Alum (white, not chrome)	8 ounces
Acetic acid (No. 8)	24 ounces

When this acid hypo solution is run into precipitation tanks for silver recovery it is highly important that enough spent developer be also run into the recovery tanks to neutralize all of the acid present or the acid will react with the sulphide used for precipitating and produce an awful stench of liberated hydrogen disulphide.

When the fixing of the film is complete, wash it thoroughly and immerse for two minutes in a glycerine bath—water, 10 gallons (40 litres); glycerine, 32 fluid ounces (1 litre)—to maintain the flexibility of the film.

These formulas are given in the small quantities of 10 gallons each so as to render the calculation of larger quantities relatively simple. Most developing tanks hold very nearly some multiple of ten gallons, thus rendering the calculation for a 20, 40, 60 or 80 gallon tank the simplest kind of mathematical calculation.

By mixing the same amount of chemicals in a smaller quantity of water, a good stock solution may be mixed for the development of still picture negatives.

The following acid hardening bath has an even greater hardening action than the first, but may be objected to on account of its green color, and some claim that it is slightly more liable to sulphur precipitation than the plain alum bath. That is probably untrue, as either will remain clear as long as they will mix thoroughly if they are properly compounded.

The following formula for chrome acid hardener is for addition to ten gallons of 1 to 4 plain hypo solution:

Water	2	gallons
Sulphite of soda (des.)	2	lbs.
Sulphuric acid, C. P.	5	ounces
Chrome alum	1½	lbs.

Be sure to mix in the order given, and when adding to the hypo stir well and add slowly, otherwise precipitation may take place.

To insure permanency and perfect hardening, film should remain in this bath for twenty minutes, or at least twice as long as it takes for the milky appearance of the silver haloid to disappear from the back of the film.

Films from a properly mixed chrome alum bath will withstand the warmest of wash water.

(The End.)

*Copyright, 1917, by the Chalmers Publishing Co.

Motion Picture Nomenclature.

The motion picture has brought into use a number of words and phrases peculiar in their significance when used in connection with the industry.

Many of them have a self-evident application while others are either ambiguous or have entirely different meanings as used in various studios.

The Society of Motion Picture Engineers has undertaken to define a few of the more common terms met with in the industry. It is to be hoped that they will lengthen the list in the near future, as there are yet many words which are still in need of concrete definitions and which are, therefore, used loosely and indiscriminately.

The following list gives the definitions which have been approved by the society:

Cine—A prefix used in description of the motion picture art or apparatus.

Condensers—In an optical projection mechanism, the lens combination which gathers the diverging rays of the luminant and converges them into the objective.

Douser—The manually operated door in the projecting machine which intercepts the light before it reaches the film.

Frame (noun)—A single picture of the series of a motion picture film.

Frame (verb)—The adjustment of the relative position between the aperture and the pictures on the film to bring them into register with each other.

Intermittent Sprocket—The sprocket (in motion picture apparatus) which engages the film to give it intermittent movement at the light aperture.

Lantern Picture—A still picture projected on a screen by means of an optical lantern.

Lantern Slide—The transparent picture from which a lantern picture is projected.

Magazine Valve—The film opening in the magazine of a motion picture projector.

Motion Picture—The synthesis of a series of related picture elements, usually of an object in motion.

Motion Picture Film—The ribbon upon which the series of pictures are recorded.

Motion Picture Projector—An optical lantern equipped with mechanisms for suitably moving motion picture film across the projected light.

Negative Stock—Light sensitive film intended for motion picture camera use.

Negative—The exposed film, after being exposed in a camera.

Objective—The image-forming member of the optical system in picture apparatus.

Positive Stock—The light, sensitive film intended to be printed upon through a negative.

Positive—The developed film, after being printed through a negative.

Print—Same as "positive."

Projecting Lens—The lens (in an optical machine) which images the picture on the screen.

Reel—The flanged spool upon which film is wound for use in projecting machines.

Reel—An arbitrary unit of measure for film—approximately a thousand feet of length.

Rewind—The process of reversing the winding of a film, usually so that the end to be first projected shall lie on the outside of the roll.

Rewinder—The mechanism by which rewinding is accomplished.

Safety Shutter (also known as the fire-shutter)—The automatically operated door (in a projecting machine) which intercepts the light when the machine runs below normal speed.

Screen—The surface upon which a picture is optically projected.

Shutter—The obscuring device, usually a segmental revolving disc, employed to intercept the light during the movement of the film in motion picture apparatus.

Shutter—Working Blade (also known as the cutting blade or obscuring blade)—That segment which intercepts the light during the movement of the film at the picture aperture.

Shutter—Intercepting Blade (also known as the flicker blade)—That segment which intercepts the light one or more times during the rest or projection period of the film.

Sprocket—The revolvable toothed member (in motion picture mechanism) which engages the perforations in the film.

Take-up (verb)—The process of winding the film (in a motion picture machine) after it passes the picture aperture.

Take-up (noun)—The mechanism which receives and winds the film (in a motion picture machine) after it passes the picture aperture.

Throw—The distance to the screen from the objective of a lantern or a motion picture projecting machine.

Still—A picture printed from a single negative.

Florence Short in Metro's "Nobody"

FLORENCE SHORT, dramatic actress and artist's model, has been engaged for the part of Mrs. Standish in Metro's screen version of "Nobody," Louis Joseph Vance's novel, which has been adapted by Charles A. Taylor for the use of the exquisite Metro star, Emmy Wehlen, William C. Dowlan will direct the production.

Miss Short is intensely patriotic, and divides her time between patriotic duties and her work at the studios. She gives several hours each day to the Stage Women's War Relief, where she is in charge of the surgical dressings department.

Florence Short.

Mrs. Standish, the part played by Miss Short in the Wehlen production, is a new kind of "vampire," a society woman who steals her own jewels in order to claim the insurance she has placed on them.

Because of her brunette beauty, directors insist on casting Miss Short in villainess roles. Her introduction to the stage was in the part of "Passion" in "Experience." Holbrook Blinn happened to see her in this part, secured for her a "bit" in the McClure picture, "Pride," and her success in this justified her engagement for leading adventuress roles with Apollo. Among her pictures have been "Pride and the Devil," "The Law That Failed," and "The Mystic Hour."

Miss Short has played prominent parts in successes on the speaking stage, notably in "Sinners," "Damaged Goods," with Richard Bennett, and "The Real Thing," with Henrietta Crossman. She has posed for paintings by Robert Henri Glackens, Sloane, Maynard and other artists, being often chosen for Italian and Spanish types.

Miss Short was born in Springfield, Mass., but removed with her family to New York when she was only six years old. Later she attended the Finch School for Girls. Miss Short is a member of the Gamut Club for professional women.

SMALLWOOD COMES BACK.

Arthur N. Smallwood, who will release the Aubrey Series of two-reel Super-Comedies featuring James Aubrey, formerly featured as Heine, in the "Heine and Louie Series," issued by Pathe, and in "Big V" Comedies by Vitagraph, announces that his producing organisation has been fully recruited. The pictures will be made under Mr. Smallwood's personal supervision and will be released on the state rights plan. The direction of the Aubrey series will be in the capable hands of C. Jay Williams and Wm. A. Seiter, who will act as co-directors on every production. Archer McMackin will be editor-in-chief of the Scenario Department.

PHYSICAL CULTURE FEATURES FAIRBANKS.

Douglas Fairbanks is featured in the August issue of Physical Culture. The author classifies the player as 100 per cent alive, and suggests to any reader if he desires fully to comprehend the meaning of that expression he should see Fairbanks on the screen. The story covers eight pages, and is an interesting illustrated review of the comedian's work as well as containing much on the personal side. One of the statements that may attract attention sets forth that Fairbanks smokes little, mostly for the camera, and that his strongest drink is orange juice.

FRANCIS FORD IN BUTTERFLY FEATURE.

"Who Was the Other Man?" is a rapidly moving story of international intrigue in which Ford plays a dual part. Jessie Lowe and William Parker are the authors of the script, which has been directed by Ford with his customary vigor of treatment.

WANTS LARGER TYPE IN TITLES.

"Mostly all, if not all, of the best photoplays produced today have one glaring error in common, i. e., the type of print in the facsimiles of both written and typewritten letters is so small that it becomes an utter impossibility for the patrons sitting in the further removed seats from the picture sheet to read them. Now, when the letter contains, as it does in most pictures, a vital part of the story, the person or persons who cannot read the writing lose the continuity of the story and the tale becomes disconnected and in some parts impossible of explanation. Cannot something be done to remedy this error? It seems a pity to me to spoil a good story for the sake of omitting the use of larger type. Very truly,   "WILLIAM KATZ,

       "Manager 'The Stanley,' Philadelphia, Pa."

UNIVERSAL TO AID IN SAFETY FIRST CAMPAIGN.

The services of the Universal Screen Magazine have been enlisted by Francis W. Hugo, New York's energetic Secretary of State, to assist in the "Safety First" campaign inaugurated some time ago through the State Automobile Bureau for the purpose of lessening the number of automobile accidents. The pictures, which will be released shortly, were taken in New York City under the personal supervision of C. L. Grant, manager of the publicity bureau of the Secretary of State's office.

The film starts with flashes of the Safety First folder issued by the bureau and Secretary Hugo and Chief Redmond of the automobile department, followed by a number of graphic pictures of automobile accidents.

"ITALIAN BATTLEFRONT" FORCED OFF BROADWAY.

Notwithstanding that the business of the official Italian war films, "The Italian Battlefront," which have been playing at the Forty-fourth Street Theater, for the past four weeks, is said to have broken all records, not only for war pictures, but for any other film production, with the exception of "The Birth of a Nation," the management was forced to bring the run to an end on Saturday, September 1. This was due to the unparalleled demand for theaters which exists on Broadway now, every house having at least three or four attractions waiting to get in.

SPECIAL GENERAL FILM HERALD.

To cover important new announcements a special edition of the General Film Herald has just been distributed. It contains data and forecasts on the new four-reel O. Henry stories, the new George Ade "Fables in Slang" and the Falcon Features, four-reel dramas. The newest Selig releases and the complete "Further Adventures of Stingaree" from the Kalem Company are also represented in this edition.

SIX NEW JAXON COMEDIES.

General Film announces a high-voltage group of six new Jaxon Comedies for release beginning November 14. All these subjects feature Jaxon's best comedians. The titles are "Speed Demons," "The Collectors," "Jolly Tars," "Wild Injuns," "Deviled Crabs" and "The Triple Cross." These are one-reel subjects.

"LIKE WILDFIRE" STOLEN FROM CONSOLIDATED.

Manager Depinet of the Consolidated Film and Supply Company, Dallas, Texas, writes that the Butterfly picture "Like Wildfire" has been lost or stolen from his Houston, Texas, office. It disappeared on August 10, and has not been located since. Exhibitors and exchanges are requested to watch for it. The number is 868.

GENERAL MOVES CLEVELAND OFFICE.

A change in location that will be beneficial has been made by the Cleveland branch of General Film. This office, formerly at 1022 Superior avenue, has removed to 809-811 Prospect avenue in the Standard Theater Building, where Branch Manager J. E. Flynn will be in closer touch with his trade.

HARRY I. GARSON HURRIES WEST.

Harry I. Garson, manager of Clara Kimball Young, and the Broadway Strand in Detroit, hastened West last week on an important theater deal, which, it is said, will change the moving picture theater map in Detroit.

BEBE DANIELS RECOVERS.

Bebe Daniels, whose piquant little personality has been pleasing admirers of the "Luke" comedies ever since their inception, has returned to the Rolin Studio after an illness of two weeks.

Reviews of Current Productions
EXCLUSIVELY BY OUR OWN STAFF

"Betrayed"
Dash and Suspense Keep Fox Picture Alive From the Start
—Hobart Bosworth and Miriam Cooper With
Competent Cast Stir Things Up.
Reviewed by Hanford C. Judson.

IF PUNCH is wanted, the new Fox release "Betrayed" is a good place to find it. The story deals with a Border raid, but the viewpoint is wholly from the Mexican side. There is nothing in it to excite a feeling of animosity between Americans and Mexicans, but it is full of matter to keep the nerves tingling. The villain, whom Hobart Bosworth's sensible acting makes amply satisfactory to the spectators, is a villain to the Mexicans as well as to the Americans. The senorita, Miriam Cooper, seems to love him and does a good deal of

Scene from "Betrayed" (Fox).

satisfactory posing in her Mexican way, for while her nature must play at capriciousness, she really is true to her shiftless singing lover at the expense of both the blustering bandit and the young Americano lieutenant. The weakness of the plot is that part of it is a dream and we are not shown clearly where the dream begins. There is consequently a couple of hundred feet where we are left dangling in the air, so to speak, before we can get our bearings again after we find that things we thought were real were solely in the dream of the fair senorita.

The quality of it comes largely from the able directing of William Walsh who keeps not only his small scenes where two or three players have the stage, but the large scenes in which there is riding and fighting, filled with dramatic suspense. His scenes also are largely free from those trite bits that show a director's lazy mind and which, not long ago, disfigured many pictures of all makes or nearly all. This is an excellent popular offering and will win favor with all kinds of spectators. Its realism comes near spoiling romance in the early scenes; but there is always in it a subtle touch of humor which rises to fun now and then as when the Papa of the senorita disgusts the bandit by his table manners—the bandit is no Chesterfield either.

"The Girl Without a Soul"
Viola Dana's Clever Acting in Dual Role, the Outstanding
Feature—Ably Assisted by Robert Walke.
Reviewed by C. S. Sewell.

AS a result of her splendid work in "The Girl Without a Soul", the Metro-Rolfe five-reel picture released August 13, Viola Dana will gain many admirers. Cast in the dual role of twin sisters whose temperaments are entirely different, she does excellent work in delineating the two characters, particularly in the scenes where, by means of double exposure, both appear simultaneously on the screen.

Dominic Beaumont, a mender of violins, lives in a country village with his twin daughters, Priscilla, who has inherited her mother's musical talent, and Unity, who, because of her lack of artistic temperament, is called by her father, "a girl without a soul". Ivor, a traveling musician, persuades Priscilla

to elope, by painting a glowing picture of the wonderful career that awaits her. The necessary money is obtained by theft from Hiram Miller, Unity's sweetheart, who has been entrusted with funds for purchasing an organ for the village church. Unity, masquerading as Priscilla, meets Ivor, and unmasks his plot. Hiram is arrested, and at the trial Unity, who has secured the money, returns it, but refuses to name the thief; Priscilla, however, confesses, exonerating Hiram, and is freed by the Judge, who lays the blame on Ivor's sinister influence.

Adequate settings and good direction characterize the work of Director John H. Collins, who also wrote the story, and there is an unexpected punch near the end of the picture, where Hiram breaks away from the authorities, leaps on horseback, and by taking a short cut, intercepts Ivor who has fled in an auto, gives him a thrashing and brings him back to the court.

Robert Walker gives a fine performance as Hiram Miller, and Fred Jones is good as Ivor. The rest of the cast, including Henry Hallam as Dominic Beaumont, Marguerite Seddon as Henrietta Hateman, the village storekeeper, and Margaret Vaughan as Louise, the girl whom Ivor has cast aside, are entirely satisfactory.

"Men of the Desert"
A Western Picture of the Higher Type, by Essanay, Featuring Jack Gardner, With a Strong Supporting
Cast—Written and Directed by
W. S. Van Dyke.
Reviewed by James S. McQuade.

THE old type of Western picture has faded out; but that did not mean that a ban was placed by the screen on all stories of Western plot and action. William S. Hart has proved that conclusively, and Jack Gardner, under W. S. Van Dyke's direction, is furnishing additional proof that the atmosphere and real types of the West still retain their old glamor to make the spectator's blood tingle, his heart beat faster and to hold his interest with the steady rein of a fearless rider.

"Men of the Desert" is the best thus far of the Gardner series. Everyone familiar with the long strife between the cattlemen and the sheepmen of the great ranges of the old West, in which the cowboys and the sheep herders were the militant forces, can recall the bitterness of the struggle. It was really a battle for existence on the part of the cattlemen; as wherever sheep graze, it is impossible for cattle to subsist. It can, therefore, be expected that "Men of the Desert" abounds in thrills and in types of men who laughed at fear and scorned danger.

Jack, impersonated by Jack Gardner, is a cowboy who holds that his allegiance to law is higher than that which he owes to his calling; and so we find him relieving a cowardly sheriff.

Scene from "Men of the Desert" (Essanay).

of his office in order that he may arrest and bring to justice the murderer of a sheepherder who was shot while protecting his flock, by one of the Flying O cowboys. Mason (Carl Stockdale), the leader of the Flying O outfit, acknowledges to Jack that he knows the murderer, and is at once arrested and jailed. Much to the astonishment he is subjected to such harsh treatment that he gives the name of the guilty man.

May (Ruth King), daughter of the owner of the Flying O,

holds Jack in high accord at first, but learns to love him for his bravery and fearlessness and for his gentleness to women. Jack's boldness in arresting the murderer makes her fear for his safety, as she knows that "the Flying O cowboys, led by Mason, will never rest until they release the prisoner and kill his captor. They succeed in the first, but May frustrates them in the second undertaking by a ruse that is as novel as it is exciting and clever.

The praiseworthy acting of the principals will appeal to everyone, as will the various well-staged scenes which show the climaxes of the story. So also will the scene which shows Jack's method of popping the question to May. This is not only Western in method, but (it strikes me) it is decidedly original and most enjoyably amusing.

The release will be made September 24, through K-E-S-E, Inc.

"Who Was the Other Man?"

Francis Ford and Mae Gaston Appear in Five-Reel Butterfly Subject Which Deals With Activities of Foreign Spies.

Reviewed by Robert G. McElravy.

FRANCIS FORD plays a double role in this five-reel offering, appearing as James Walbert, an American secret service man, and Ludwig Schumann, a foreign spy. Both characters are introduced early in the story, when Schumann is about to leave Paris to come to this country. The instances of double exposure photography are carefully handled, though something of confusion exists in the observer's mind regarding the identity of the two individuals. Fortunately for the story this doubt is a helpful thing, and is partly intentional.

The events which follow the sailing of the supposed Schumann for America are quite entertaining, though no particular thrills develop until the final reel is reached. He finds a woman confederate on board, named Wanda, and they begin paying marked attention to a young man named Herbert Cornell and his sweetheart, Marion Washburn. This latter couple have the entree to Washington society and the plotters make good use of their opportunity.

In the course of the story the principals are seen at a social function in Washington, where Wanda gives Herbert some drugged wine and relieves him of important government documents, which she turns over to the supposed Schumann. She is then seized with remorse, for she had really fallen in love with Herbert, and kills herself. In the final reel, which contains more action than the others, the spy is discovered to be, not Schumann, but the American secret service man. This final reel does much to strengthen the general effect of the

Scene from "Who Was the Other Man" (Butterfly).

number, which is brightly pictured but only moderately entertaining in story interest in the early reels.

The cast is an agreeable one throughout, Mae Gaston being attractive in the part of the heroine. Others appearing are Duke Worne, Wm. T. Horne and Beatrice Van.

"Lorelei of the Sea"

M. Philip Hansen Presents Six-Reel Picture Produced by Henry Otto—Tyrone Power and Frances Burnham Featured—Released on State Rights.

Reviewed by Ben H. Grimm.

PHOTOGRAPHICALLY beautiful, sometimes artistically pleasing, but with far too little story value to hold up its footage, "Lorelei of the Sea", a six-reel picture produced by Henry Otto, is presented for release on the state rights basis by M. Philip Hansen. The production lacks the substantiality necessary to hold interest at such time as the consciousness is not enthralled by mere physical beauty. In those scenes in which nymphs disport about waterfalls and subterranean caves Mr. Otto has proven himself no less an artist

than did he in his production of similar scenes in "Udine." But in "Lorelei of the Sea" there is an overabundance of beautiful scenes and not enough action. No matter how great an appetite we have for beauty, too much will give us indigestion. The scenes that tell the story proper have been allowed too much footage; the picture would be vastly improved if judiciously cut at least a thousand feet. The excess footage allowed to remain in the print shown for review retards the tempo to a very slow pace.

From the standpoint of mere beauty there are scenes in the picture which, if transferred to canvas, would be worthy of lining the walls of a palace.

Tyrone Power and Frances Burnham are the featured players. Mr. Power is seen as a villager on Seal Island, the Pacific haven of a group of refugees. Miss Burnham is ostensibly his daughter. It is in the visualization of the latter's dreams and imaginings that we see the Lorelei at play. Although there are nude figures in the picture, they are at all times far enough away from the camera to make us see them only in their beauty. It is also due to Mr. Otto's handling that the scenes showing the nymphs are art in every sense of the word, and incapable of giving offense to even the most prudish. There is absolutely nothing unwholesome in the picture.

Two of the refugee youths are in love with the girl, who is known as Lorelei. Paul (Mr. Power) is made the leader of the islanders. Young Dorian, son of a wealthy pearl agent, comes to the island on his yacht. He hears the Lorelei song

Scene from "Lorelei of the Sea" (Marine).

and his boat is wrecked. He is rescued by Lorelei. Mutual love develops. Dorian is believed by his companions to have been drowned, but his father comes to Seal Island and finds him. It develops that young Dorian and Lorelei are stepbrother and step-sister. Jay Belasco has the role of young Dorian. Mr. Otto is seen as his father. Others in the cast are John Oaker, Gypsy Abbott and Winnifred Greenwood.

The story was written by Richard Willis. Camera work was done by James Crosby.

"Soldiers of Chance"

Evart Overton and Miriam Fouche Featured in Five-Reel Vitagraph Blue Ribbon Feature—Released September 3.

Reviewed by Ben H. Grimm.

THERE is plot action in every foot of the five reels of "Soldiers of Fortune", a five-reel Vitagraph Blue Ribbon Feature released September 3. Evart Overton and Miriam Fouche are the featured players. The picture was directed by Paul Scardon from a story by James Oliver Curwood. The photoplay is out-and-out melodrama. It makes no pretense of being anything else, and as such holds the interest from start to finish. The story is full of adventure and has all the elements of stories such as are seen in magazines as the Popular, Adventure, and the like. Love, revenge, South American revolutions, and other elements popular in this type of story all have their place in the picture.

In the film the story progresses rapidly, and shows a clever hand at plot building on the part of Mr. Curwood. The actors who were selected for the screen interpretation of the story carry it over with a dash. The one thing that mars the film is the fact that many of the battle scenes are quite badly out of focus.

Mr. Overton is seen first as Captain Josslyn and later as Billy Mountain (his real identity). Tis one enemy is Peter Lawler (Charles Henderson). Lawler holds a confession made by Philip Winton (Charles Kent) that he killed a man. Winton's daughter is coveted by Lawler. Billy gets Lawler on his yacht and forces him to become a stoker. War springs up between Billy and the girl, but she has promised to marry Lawler if he does not make her father's confession known. The plot complications come thick and fast and here and there is a fine degree of suspense. Lawler gets into the good graces of the republic's president. Billy's forces attack the

Federal soldiers and win- the battle. Lawler is killed. It develops that the man Winton thought he killed is alive.

Mr. Scardon has used some very effective lighting in darkened room scenes. His direction meets every need of the story. Others than those mentioned who are seen on the screen are Julia Swayne Gordon and Denton Vane.

"Mother O' Mine"

Five-Reel Blue Bird Tells Strong Story of Young Man Whose Personal Ambition Made Him Forget Love for His Mother.

Reviewed by Robert C. McElravy.

A STRONG story is unfolded in this five-reel number, written and produced by Rupert Julian and put into scenario form by Elliot J. Clawson. Mr. Julian appears to advantage in the leading role and is supported by a good cast, which includes Mrs. Ruby La Fayette, Elsie Jane Wilson, Ruth Clifford and W. E. Warner.

The story is one that brings both smiles and tears. It is

Scene from "Mother O' Mine" (Bluebird).

developed in a quiet, effective manner and rounds up with a pleasing climax. The chief idea is perhaps new to the screen, though familiar in fiction. It concerns an elderly woman who comes to the city to see her son, unexpectedly, and arrives in the midst of a social affair. The son really loves his mother and is delighted to see her, but her plain, old-fashioned appearance makes him just a little ashamed of her, as he moves in high society and is engaged to a girl "bred in the purple."

Mrs. La Fayette gives a splendid portrayal of the sweet old lady, being exactly that herself to all appearances, and gets a firm hold on the sympathies. Her appearance at the reception has been carefully led up to, many scenes having been shown at the old country home where she has waited a long period of years for the return of her son.

The son welcomes her joyously and then later succumbs to the false pride which induces him to tell his sweetheart that the old lady was once his nurse. The mother hears this and that night slips away from the house and returns to her country home. The son follows in a repentant frame of mind and with a firm resolution to devote future years to the care of his mother. He even breaks off the engagement with his sweetheart, but the latter, who knows the truth, follows with her own mother and there is a reconciliation at the country home.

The production is splendidly made and is one that should prove successful wherever shown.

Conquest Program

Excellent Material Contained in Number Six, Consisting of Nicely Chosen Variety of Subjects.

Reviewed by Margaret I. MacDonald.

THE thing that strikes one after viewing No. 6 of the Edison Conquest programs, which are now being released by K-E-S-E, is the careful arrangement and excellent quality of the material of which it consists.

"The Customary Two Weeks"

which is the opening number is a four-part drama of more than the ordinary amount of interest. It is well made and is a proof of the virtue of fitting the film to the story and not the story to the film. The story moves at a lively pace and no attempt is made to drag in unnecessary scenes for the mere purpose of filling in footage, as is so often the case in productions of five reels and over. The plot hinges about the career of a young man who, feeling himself an indispensible adjunct of the firm by which he is employed, becomes the butt of an unscrupulous manager when he makes an effective interference in the case of an aged employee who is discharged by this man with the "customary two weeks". A fine lesson

in the art of advertising and salesmanship is contained in the story when fate makes these two men competitors for a big order of goods.

"The Story of Plymouth Rock"

covers the story of "The Courtship of Myles Standish" as told in Longfellow's poem, as well as giving a clear but brief delineation of the history of the Pilgrim Fathers from the time of their persecution in England to the establishment of their little colony in America. This picture is in one reel.

"The Grand Canyon of Arizona"

contains some fine views of this wonderful spot, showing the descent of a party of tourists four thousand feet below its rim to the Colorado river. Scenes on the Bright Angel trail, and at the Hermit House, as well as of the clouds gathering about the rim of the canyon, are interesting. At the time when this picture was photographed a snow storm had invaded the canyon, adding considerably to its beauty from a photographic viewpoint.

"The Four R's"

brings us in touch with the art of the fourth R, which is riding, and introduces some tremendously interesting scenes at the Culver Riding Academy.

"Nature's Perfect Thread Spinner"

gives one of the best illustrations of how the silk worm spins itself into a silk cocoon, from which it emerges a short time afterward in the form of a beautiful moth, as we have seen. This moth, the picture tells us, lays 200 eggs and then dies. The moth in the act of laying these eggs is an interesting and unusual sight.

"The Magic of Spring"

is a delightful short bit in which a young man falls asleep in a park on a beautiful spring day and dreams that he is a son of Pan, pursuing a beautiful maiden, who eventually comes to him of her own accord. He awakens to find the idol of his dreams beside him. The scenes of this picture are inspiringly beautiful.

Pathe Pictures

"Tears and Smiles," Five-Reel Gold Rooster, Featuring Baby Marie Osborne, and "Lonesome Luke Loses Patience," Two-Reel Rolin Comedy.

Reviewed by Ben H. Grimm.

O BVIOUSLY a photoplay builded around the particular talents and charm of Baby Marie Osborne is "Tears and Smiles", a five-reel Pathe Gold Rooster picture released September 2. The picture follows the same general lines of

Scene from "Tears and Smiles" (Pathe).

former Lasalida productions in which the diminutive star was featured. In this production most of the burden of entertaining falls on the shoulders of Miss Osborne, and she carries off honors easily and in a manner that will please her followers to no inconsiderable degree. The little colored boy who has acted as a foil for little Miss Osborne in several preceding releases also is seen in this picture, and the two get over considerable touchingly humorous situations. The incidents knotted into the thread of the story aids the picture's entertaining power to no little extent.

Baby Marie is seen as the child of a drunken father who beats his wife. The baby runs away when her mother is taken to the hospital and is adopted by a wealthy, childless couple. Through the tot's diplomacy the mother is given a position as the baby's governess. The father gets out of jail and kidnaps his child. This gives the adopters a knowledge of the baby's mother's relationship to the child. Baby is rescued and the drunken father is shot in a struggle with a policeman. Meanwhile the wealthy man's wife has died from an overdose of headache powders. Later this leaves the way clear for a marriage between the broker and the baby's mother.

Baby Marie is surrounded by a company of capable players. Philo McCullough is seen in the leading male role. Marian Warner and Katherine MacLaren also have important parts.

The picture was directed by William Bertram. He has introduced some very pretty backgrounds for his action and has given the story fitting screen interpretation. Photography and other technical details are satisfactory.

"Lonesome Luke Loses Patience."

"Lonsome Luke Loses Patience", a two-reel comedy made by the Rolin Film Company for release by Pathe on September 9, contains a full quota of laughs. Harold Lloyd this time is seen as the conductor of a sanatarium. He is surrounded by a score or more of pretty girl nurses, which fact helps the number. Most of the action is confined to scenes in the sanitarium, which is the haven for several "ill" old men. There is enough speed to keep things going, with a whirlwind finish along toward the 800-foot mark. Harry Pollard and Bebe Daniels also are seen on the screen.

"The Marriage Market"

Five-Reel World Film-Peerless Production Tells Strongly Entertaining Story, With Melodramatic Finish.

Reviewed by Robert C. McElravy.

RARELY does a five-reel offering contain so much action as this number, written by Clay Mantley and directed by Arthur Ashley. There is a wealth of plot material and it has been so smoothly and carefully put together that one situation follows another without awkward breaks of any sort. It is highly entertaining and there is no lack of conviction until perhaps in the melodramatic scenes at the close, but even here the interest is held so strongly that the absence of entire plausibility is readily excused.

June Elvidge does excellent work in the leading feminine role. She plays the part of Helen Grant, daughter of a Wall street speculator who commits suicide after financial failure. The girl, in a vain effort to save her father just before his death, sells herself to Bradley Spayden, a young speculator on the street, though at the time she is in love with another man named Richard Marlowe. After her father has killed himself the girl remains true to her bargain, though her husband treats her cruelly. From this point the story moves forward in breathless fashion, showing the girl's attempt to grin financial independence on the street, her appeal to Eric Foxhall, and the latter's murder under complex circumstances. The court scenes are the ones which are rather lacking in conviction, but they are merely incidental to the main story. The girl, through a happy turn of events, is at last restored to her own lover.

The opening scenes of this story are particularly strong, showing an auction sale of thoroughbred horses. The stock market scenes are also pleasing. As a whole the production is one of rather exceptional interest in many ways.

Others in the cast are Arthur Ashley, Carlyle Blackwell,

Scene from "The Marriage Market" (World).

Frederick Truesdell, Jack Drumler, Charles Duncan, Eugenie Woodward and Lewis Edgard.

No Date Set for New Chaplin.

The date of the release of "The Adventurer", Mutual-Chaplin Special No. 12, has not yet been set and will not be decided until the film reaches the executive offices of the Mutual Film Corporation from Los Angeles and is viewed by President John R. Freuler.

"The Stranger at Dumcrieff"

Latest Two-Reel Episode of Kalem's "The Further Adventures of Stingaree" is Interesting

Reviewed by Ben H. Grimm.

E. W. HORNUNG has written another interesting story in "The Stranger at Dumcrieff," latest two-reel episode of Kalem's "The Further Adventures of Stingaree" series. Paul C. Hurst has given the story fitting screen interpretation with himself and True Boardman in the leading roles. This

Scene from "The Stranger at Dumcrieff" (Kalem).

time Stingaree is instrumental in vindicating a young preacher who has been maligned by a former cell-mate; also the gentleman bushranger brings together two hearts that were separated by the criminal's story.

The story progresses toward its climax at a pace that keeps the spectator just one jump behind and always interested. There is just enough heart interest, enough suspense and enough of the other necessary photoplay elements to make the release attractive.

Besides Mr. Boardman and Mr. Hurst there are in the cast G. A. Williams, Edythe Sterling, Edward Hearn, Frank Jonason and Barney Furey. Photography, locations, etc., are up to the high standard of this series.

"Sirens of the Sea"

Louise Lovely, Carmel Myers, and Jack Mulhall in a Five-Part Jewel Photoplay Suggested by the Legend of the Lorelei.

Reviewed by Arthur W. Courtney.

THOSE who go to see the five-part Jewel photoplay, "Sirens of the Sea," to see the beauty of the female form revealed will not be disappointed. Louis Lovely in a bathing suit entertains about twenty of her school girl chums. She takes them to the seashore; then tells them that they must undress behind the rocks. When there is nothing but bare arms and shoulders and legs in sight, she runs off with their clothes and gives them seaweed to drape themselves in. Nothing could be fairer.

Jack Mulhall comes along on his yacht with a good-for-nothing companion (played by William Quinn). They come ashore and Mulhall pairs off with Louise and Quinn with Carmel Myers, who has the part of an artificial girl of the fashionable set jealous of Louise. One night Quinn chases Louise down by the shore and she jumps off a cliff. Mulhall goes in search of her in a rowboat, gets exhausted and has a beautiful dream. He dreams that Louise, who came out of the sea no one knows whence, has gone back to the sea to the haunts of the sirens. The scenes of the sirens swimming about in their grottos are indeed very beautiful. After this the picture drags. A handful of scenes like Mulhall kissing Louise, and the sirens, in Greek bathing suits, dissolving out of and into the sea are repeated to the point of tedium and beyond. The story of the dream does not hold the attention. It was written by Grace Helen Bailey, and adapted and directed by Allen Holubar. This picture is clean, and beautiful.

Change in Standard Releases.

Through a change just decided upon by William Fox in the order of release of several of his most pretentious Standard Pictures, it becomes necessary to make revision in the schedule. Instead of "Cleopatra" being the first of the Theda Bara Superpictures issued to exhibitors, the initial production of the series will be Miss Bara's "Camille", directed by J. Gordon Edwards, released September 30.

The release dates of the first of the Standard Pictures are: August 19, "The Spy"; August 26, "The Honor System"; September 2, "Jack and the Beanstalk"; September 16, "The Conqueror"; September 30, "Camille".

"Seven Keys to Baldpate"

Entertaining Comedy-Melodrama of Artcraft Production, With George M. Cohan.

Reviewed by Louis Reeves Harrison.

IN many respects "Seven Keys to Baldpate" is of high merit. Mr. Cohan's interpretation of an author who is called upon to write a novel in twenty-four hours in order to win a large wager, is highly intelligent and effective. He does not

Scene from "Seven Keys to Baldpate" (Artcraft).

fall into studio and stage errors about the writer of fiction, but acts like one in minute details quite as well as in psychology. When to this is added the fascination of his genial personality, his performance dominates the entire work. He is interesting every moment he appears on the screen, and he lucidly conveys an infinite variety of thought and feeling by subtle methods rather than by the broad ones of the stage. Concessions have been made in the settings to theatricalism, but not offensively so. Only in the grouping of characters is this fault shown.

Those same settings are admirably selected, but they might be less impressive if it was not for some exceptional photographic work, nicely adjusted composition and powerful contrasts of light and shade. Artistic photography ranks second to Mr. Cohan's performance. The story held tight before a large Rialto audience until the concluding scenes, where the story-within-a-story idea seemed to act as an anti climax. There was a slump when it was seen that the supposedly real characters were fictitious ones. In a play of such general high merit it might be worth while trying the effect of ending as though the experiences depicted were those the author passed through. It might easily give more "zip" to the conclusion. The general impression, however, was favorable, and, as it stands, the story will please.

Robert Leonard Begins Mae Murray Bluebird.

Out in Universal City Robert Leonard, who will direct Bluebird's new star, has begun work on the interiors for "Princess Virtue," the feature designed to introduce Miss Murray to the program Nov. 5. The scenes are laid in France, among ultra fashionable folk, and at exclusive watering places, thus making the scenic requirements unusually exacting. Massive sets are under construction, and the exteriors will be made at Coronado Beach, Cal., the famous Pacific Coast resort. Bluebird intends to introduce Miss Murray to the program with every possible adjunct that may be expected to make for an immediate success for her productions. To that end a careful selection of her support has resulted in the engagement of Wheeler Oakman, Paul Nicholson, Jack Vosburg, Harry Von Meter, Gretchen Lederer and Clarissa Selwyn.

"Every Girl's Dream"

Fairy Tale—Like Quality in Its Story—Pretty Interior Scenes—June Caprice, a Good Cast, and a Remarkable Dog Player.

Reviewed by Hanford J. Judson.

THE new William Fox picture, "Every Girl's Dream," will please a good many in almost any general audience; but there is nothing sure-fire about it. The spectators at the Academy of Music, New York, seemed to take interest in it, but it is too long for a costume picture with so slight a plot as is this.

In the little Dutch village of Olenberg a baby girl, Gretchen (June Caprice), is found by the watch. The burgomaster makes Frau Van Lorn (Marcia Harris) adopt her, and as she grows up she has a hard time with the crabbed old woman. A silver box was found with her, and this she still keeps.

She is loved by Carl (Harry Hilliard), who is also a foundling, but whose foster parents are kind to him. We are let into the secret that he is a stolen prince. A comical old mynher (Dan Mason) takes a fancy to Gretchen and offers to buy her, as his wife by paying off Frau Van Lorn's mortgage. Through this and through the jealousy of Hulda (Margaret Fielding) much trouble comes to poor Gretchen. She is falsely accused of theft and Carl can't save her and she is put in jail. While Carl is mourning, he is taken away to the palace and finds that he is the king of the country. There is still a bit more of well

Scene from "Every Girl's Dream" (Fox).

built suspense before Carl and Gretchen are seated on a throne together.

The picture is helped by excellent character work. Margaret Fielding also deserves credit for good work in the not elaborate part she fills. The center of the picture is, of course, Caprice, with her remarkably trained dog. It is surely a pretty picture and it has many praiseworthy qualities.

A Couple of Mutuals

"The Bride's Silence" Melodrama Featuring Gail Kane, and "Charity Castle," With Mary Miles Minter in the Feminine Lead, Excellent Offerings.

Reviewed by Margaret I. MacDonald.

"The Bride's Silence."

GAIL KANE plays realistically in a well made melodrama for the Mutual Program, entitled "The Bride's Silence". The production, which is in five parts, was made at the American studios and is unusually creditable. It is a well

Scene from "The Bride's Silence" (Mutual).

staged, well-dressed play which guards its secret to the end, and affords a large amount of live entertainment.

The story opens on a scene in which a woman enters from between velvet portieres with a dagger in her hand. This sets the ball of mystery rolling, and not until the very close of the story are we sure that the son of the house, whose murder is disclosed also at the opening of the story, has not been murdered by his own sister. Sharing with us in dread silence, the belief that the woman, who has become the bride of the prosecuting attorney, and has inspired this suspicion by becoming hysterical in her sleep, are her husband and her father. Carefully guarding what they believe to be her secret they take her away to a secluded spot where the world will not be the wiser of the fact that her mentality is shaken; and there they remain until the arrival of a telegram revealing the secret which the bride has striven to keep, that another woman bearing the family name has committed the murder in revenge of a wrong. The story is a good one well told.

"Charity Castle."

Mary Miles Minter has been afforded an excellent vehicle for her talent in "Charity Castle", a five-part comedy-drama from the American studios. The story is one that will appeal to children as well as adults. The story is one that will appeal to children as well as adults, and is wholesome and amusing. While the plot of the story may be reminiscent the general entertaining quality of the production makes it acceptable.

According to the story the extravagant son of a grouchy, gouty old man, at a moment when his father has turned him out of his house with orders not to return until he can show that he is able to earn a week's salary, finds himself face to face with a peculiar situation. His charwoman dying and her two attractive children left alone, he decides in the goodness of his heart to adopt them, not counting the cost. One day the little girl, who is a believer in fairy stories and all beautiful things, discovering his identity and also the fact that he is in financial trouble because of bills which he is called upon to pay on their behalf, starts out, accompanied by her little brother, for his father's house, which she afterward names Charity Castle, to try to mend the situation. Some amusing incidents occur when the children, alone in the great house, from which the master and servants had gone vacationing, make friends with a burglar, a "bum" and a down-and-out actor. Of course the story ends with the grouch arriving on the scene and being converted to a happier and kindlier frame of mind by the children. The son, returning after having actually earned a week's salary, is reinstalled in his father's affections.

"Idolaters"

Louise Glaum and Strong Supporting Company Appear in Five-Reel Triangle Story of the Vampire Type.

Reviewed by Robert C. McElravy.

THIS five-reel offering, written by John Lynch and Monte M. Katterjohn, and directed by Walter Edwards, represents the voluptuous, exotic type of narrative, usually designated as the "vampire" story, in a high state of development. Nothing is wanting in the way of appropriate settings, sensual atmosphere and intense, fervid acting to carry out the traditions in this sort of production. It is, in fact, so true to type that for many observers the end of the story is in sight long before the last reel has finished its revolutions.

The plot is stronger than that many of the kind and deals with an interesting set of characters. It begins with the chance meeting of two girls in a Chicago station, each of them bound for New York City with the express intention of becoming an actress. In the course of the story both succeed. Anita Carew wins by dint of hard work and then gives up the stage to marry a young playwright. Viola Strathmore wins by a different method. Her success is brought to her by the aid of an "angel," a wealthy old man who has fallen into her clutches. Later she appears in a play written by Anita's husband, whom she lures to his destruction. The inevitable tragedy is

Scene from "Idolaters" (Triangle).

led up to in masterly fashion, though such situations never get far away from a certain artificiality. The young playwright is murdered and Viola also meets death afterward at the hands of her jealous Egyptian servant.

Louise Glaum is strong in the part of Viola, utilizing all the seductive methods permissible for carrying out her ambitions. She times the arrival and departure of her various admirers by a wrist watch. Dorcas Matthews does some appealing and effective work as Anita Carew, and Lee Hill has

a few good bits as Borul, the Egyptian. George Webb has the leading masculine role as the playwright. Others in the cast are T. S. Hill, Hugo Koch and Milton Ross.

"Triumph"

Dorothy Phillips as a Stage-Struck Country Girl in a Five-Part Bluebird.

Reviewed by Arthur W. Courtney.

IN THE five-part Bluebird, "Triumph," Dorothy Phillips is a stage-struck country girl. She gets only as far as the country railroad station, where she meets a traveling troupe waiting for a train. One of the actors tells her a story

story runs four reels. It is a tragedy. Dorothy Phillips plays the part of the young actress that the story is about. She is loved by the manager of the show and the author. After the dress rehearsal the author goes to her dressing room to run over the love scene. It should go more smoothly. The manager finds them and calls off the show. The actress goes to the manager's rooms to plead with him to let the show on. He finally consents (we quote the press book) after setting his own price upon the girl's ambition. When he immediately attempts to bind the bargain, the girl stabs and kills him. This murder is followed by two suicides.

The succession of scenes after this when the girl is taking curtain calls at the theater and the author is lying dead at home, after writing a confession to the murder of the manager, brings out dramatic irony strongly. It is the best part of the photoplay. In the girl's death scene in the play she uses a real dagger and kills herself. When we are brought back to the railroad station where the actor is telling this story to the stage-struck country girl. When he finishes she changes her mind about going to the city. Thus the photoplay is injured at the end by the anti-climax.

The audience is cheated at the beginning of the story within the story. This made to seem a continuation of the outside story. Some like this manner of construction. It is not clear why Dorothy Phillips should be the only person in costume at the first rehearsal of the play unless it is to show her understanding as an ingenue. However, the tragic story within the story would make a very good photoplay without the outside story. This photoplay is a screen version of a magazine story written by Samuel Hopkins Adams. In the cast are Lon Chaney, William Stowell, William J. Dyer and Claire Dubrey. It was directed by Joseph De Grasse. It was released September 3.

"The Cinderella Husband"

Victor Moore in a Modernized Version of the Fairy Story—A Good Klever Comedy That is Not Too Rough.

Reviewed by Arthur W. Courtney.

A GOOD Klever Comedy that is not too rough is "The Cinderella Husband," written by Thomas J. Gray. Vic lives with a "brutess" of a wife and her brother. The first part of the picture shows Vic doing the housework. There are some good bits here. Then the trio attend a meeting where the king of a carnival is to be selected. Each man puts a shoe in a basket. The queen, blindfolded, takes out a shoe and the one that the shoe fits is acclaimed king. Vic makes a very funny king. We are sorry that he had to sit on his sharp-pointed crown. When the brother-in-law villain blows up the throne it raises Vic very high in everyone's estimation. This picture is bound to bring laughs. The interest of the picture is in Victor Moore's characterization. It is very well done.

"The Ten of Diamonds"

A Triangle Five-Part Production Featuring Dorothy Dalton Proves to Be Unusually Entertaining.

Reviewed by Margaret I. MacDonald.

THE reason why "The Ten of Diamonds," from a story by Albert Cowles, proves intensely entertaining, is principally because its presentation is psychologically correct. The chief feminine character in the story is not of the type that we might wish our daughters or sisters to emulate, yet as a stray bit of human driftwood we find Dorothy Dalton's portrayal of her very fascinating.

According to the story, a cabaret dancer of the rougher type takes the offer of a handsome stranger who comes to her as she is reading her fortune in cards with the

will appeal directly . . . their entertainment from Bluebird. These increased efforts will be applied about October first, when fixed stars on the program will begin regular appearances on dates to be definitely fixed far ahead.

Ella Hall, announced to appear Oct. 1 in "The Spotted Lily", will very likely then make her final appearance among Bluebirds. Harry Solter, who directed Miss Hall in this feature, has been assigned to the development of Carmel Myers as a Bluebird star, "The Dynast" being now in process of production as Miss Myers' initial release, Nov. 12. This will introduce two new stars to the program on successive weeks—Mae Murray, in "The Princess Virtue", coming out Nov. 5, under the screen management of Robert Leonard.

Further releases in October will start a regular routine of appearance for each principal eight weeks intervening, while Bluebird's eight fixed stars take their regular turn on the schedule. Franklyn Farnum will be introduced as a lone star in "The Maverick" (directed by Joseph De Grasse) Oct. 8. Chief in his support will be Lon Chaney and his leading lady will be Claire Du Brey. Both of these players moved over with Director De Grasse from the Dorothy Phillips company. Isola Forrester and Mann Page furnished the story of "The Maverick".

Miss Phillips, directed by Ida May Park, who will make all future Dorothy Phillips Bluebirds, will offer "Bondage", Oct. 15, as her tenth production since joining Bluebird as many months ago. In this feature Miss Phillips will have William Stowell as leading man, to be featured along with Gretchen Lederer and Gertrude Aster in the supporting company. "Bondage" was created for the screen exclusively by Miss Park from a story Edna Kenton suggested .

Rupert Julian and Ruth Clifford will be presented Oct. 22 in "The Desire of the Moth", a third offering in the series of "Rupert Julian Bluebirds" to be especially featured on the program hereafter. Monroe Salisbury makes his first appearance in this feature, working opposite Miss Clifford. The story came from Eugene M. Rhodes, Elliott J. Clawson furnished the scenario and Mr. Julian has directed a feature that created great enthusiasm among Bluebird executives when it was first screened for their consideration.

Violet Mersereau, directed by Theodore Marston, is finishing the Oct. 29 Bluebird at Leonia, N. J., where Robert L. Hill is assisting in producing "The Girl by the Roadside" from John C. Brownell's version of Varick Vanardy's "best seller" of the same title. During the past week Miss Mersereau and her company have been finishing up some exteriors, to complete the work of production.

Anna Little to Support Wallace Reid.

"Nan of Music Mountain" is to be seen on the screen. This will be welcome news to the thousands who have delighted in the breezy novel which has long held a record among the best sellers. It will be a Paramount picture, and will have as its star none other than Wallace Reid, whose latest picture, "The Hostage," is a September 10 Paramount release. An announce-

ment of particular interest in this connection is that Anna Little, former Ince star, and who will be seen with Conway Tearle in J. Stuart Blackton's forthcoming production of Sir Gilbert Parker's novel, "The World for Sale," has been engaged by Jesse L. Lasky to support Wallace Reid in the picture.

New Faces in Forthcoming Triangles

All Departments Have Been Augmented by Addition of New Players, Directors and Scenario Writers.

MORE than twenty new players, scenario writers and directors have been added to the Triangle Culver City forces since the reorganization of the company, and it is reported that negotiations are now under way to obtain the services of several more stars and production experts. Among the most important of those recently engaged is Richard Bret Harte, grandson of the famous writer. Mr. Harte will devote his time to preparing original stories for the screen, drawing on a rich fund of experiences during his life in this country and abroad.

Texas Guinan, whose engagement has been officially announced, is already a favorite of the public by reason of her musical comedy success. "The Devil Dodger," a forthcoming western drama, will present Roy Stewart as gunfighter for the first time in the Triangle program. Stewart is master of all the tricks of horsemanship, it is said, having owned and operated a ranch in Mexico prior to the disturbances there some time ago.

Belle Bennett is another "find" for whom a wide popularity is predicted. Her first appearance before the Triangle cameras was in "Valley of Fear," to be released the middle of September. She is now working on "Ashes of Hope," a play similar in locale and action to "The Flame of the Yukon," one of Triangle's greatest successes. Arthur Hoyt, whose most recent appearance was in the title role of "Mr. Opp," has become a member of the Triangle Players' Company and will appear in roles of the type which he has interpreted with remarkable success during the past.

Claire MacDowell, featured in numerous recent plays produced by other companies, has been added to the Triangle lists for leading roles. Ruth Stonehouse, already one of the film favorites of the day, has started work on a Triangle production, the title of which has not been decided upon. Margery Wilson, who has long attracted attention for her work in Triangle plays, comes forth as a new star in "Mountain Dew," on the program for the week of September 16.

Among the other new names that appear on the roster of the stock company is that of George Cheseboro, who has played leading roles in numerous productions, his most recent being in support of Arthur Hoyt in "Mr. Opp." He will act as leading man for Olive Thomas in "Broadway, Arizona," just completed. George Hernandes, George C. Pearce, Gloria Madien, Carolyn Wagner, and others whose names are known to the film fans, will shortly appear in Triangle offerings.

The directorial staff has been augmented by the addition of Lynn F. Reynolds, Jack Conway, E. Mason Hopper, Ferris Hartman, Thomas H. Heffron and William V. Mong. Cliff Smith, who has directed William S. Hart in many of the star's western dramas, now being reissued, has been assigned to the direction of plays featuring Roy Stewart, Walter Edwards, one of the best known of Triangle directors, having completed "Idolaters," with Louise Glaum, is now directing Belle Bennett in "Ashes of Hope."

George Ade Fables Begin

"The Twelve Cylinder Speed of the Leisure Class" First of Essanay's New General Film Series.

WITH the naming of the first releases in the new George Ade "Fables in Slang" series General Film reports extraordinary attention for these comedies being manifested by exhibitors. There will be twelve of these American humorous subjects in approximately two-reel lengths. The releases come one a week.

The opening number of the current series is "The Twelve-Cylinder Speed of the Leisure Class". The story concerns the sudden rise to wealth of Mr. and Mrs. Basker, plain, homespun people of the Middle West. A terrific pace is set them by their more modern son and daughter. Particularly happy types for the Baskers have been found by Essanay in George Bean and Frankie Raymond.

The succeeding subjects in the Ade series of comedies are "The Wandering Boy and the Wayward Parents" and "What Transpires After the Wind-Up".

"The Neglected Wife" Contest.

The work of sorting out and reading the great mass of answers submitted by serial fans throughout the country in the contest on "The Neglected Wife", Pathe's serial, is practically completed, and the judges are now considering the merits of less than 100 of the 50,000 answers received, to decide as to who will obtain the prizes. The prizes to be awarded consist of the first prize of $1,000, a second prize of $500, and five additional prizes of $100 each.

Mabel Herbert Urner, the author of "The Neglected Wife", J. A. Berst, vice-president and general manager of Pathe Exchange Inc., and Lewis Joseph Vance, a well known American writer, are the judges who will make decision in this contest.

Comments on the Films
EXCLUSIVELY BY OUR OWN STAFF

General Film Company.

THE STRANGER AT DUMCRIEFF (Kalem).—A two-reel episode of "The Further Adventures of Stingaree" series. E. W. Hornung has written an interesting story and Paul C. Hurst has screened it fittingly, with True Boardman in the leading role. Stingaree is this time instrumental in vindicating a young minister who has been maligned by a former cell-mate, and also brings together two hearts that were separated by the story. Reviewed in this issue.

TWELVE-CYLINDER SPEED OF THE LEISURE CLASS (Essanay).—A two-reel George Ade fable about a middle class family that is visited by the scourge of war. Juicy contracts make them rich. The father dresses up like a safeblower disguised as John Drew; and the mother takes orders from a maid whose cost of arms is French but whose map is Killarney. They go to Palm Beach. The humor of the picture is in their attempts to ape the rich. Some of the sub-titles are very funny. The moral of the fable is not clear.

IN AFTER YEARS (Selig).—A one-reel drama. In the first part a reminiscent passage is very well done. The heroine sees the events of her past life enacted in the fireplace. Her lover goes to hunt in the jungle. He is attacked and wounded by a tiger. This part is very exciting. He recovers. Camels and elephants figure in the jungle scenes, with a very interesting tiger.

WORLD SELIG LIBRARY. No. 16.—Four subjects are treated in this reel. The best part is the harvesting of wheat on a 25,000-acre farm in North Dakota. Threshing 2,000 bushels a day is shown; the use of tractors, plowing eight furrows at once, and the use of grain elevators. The reel begins with the instruments in the Government weather bureau, and ends with an arsenic squad going out after grasshoppers. The short subject on this reel is the breeding of silver foxes at $6,000 each. The foxes are camera shy. They scarcely give an idea of what a silver fox looks like.

THE HOUSE OF MYSTERY (Selig).—A two-reeler with John Cossar in the cast. It bears a resemblance to a photoplay seen two years ago in which there was a circular staircase with a secret chamber at the top. The story of this picture is quite incoherent.

A MAN OF HIS WORD (Falcon).—A four-reeler set in England. The story is about a run on a bank. The hero is an Englishman of a family which has headed the bank for six generations. He is brought back from France, where he has spent twenty years, to take charge of the bank. He helps a good-for-nothing rival banker and nearly causes the collapse of his own bank. This is a fair photoplay.

THE PHANTOM SHOTGUN (Falcon).—A four-reeler directed by Harry Harvey and featuring Kathleen Kirkman and R. Henry Grey. The story was written by Stanley Clisby Arthur. It is a mystery story set on shipboard where a number of passengers are strangely shot. It takes two reels to work up to this situation. It is fairly entertaining.

JOHN TOM LITTLE BEAR (Broadway Star).—A two-reel O. Henry story adapted by Harry Southwell and directed by David Smith. Al Jennings has the leading part. He is an Indian college graduate associated with two fakirs in the exploitation of a patent medicine called Sum-wat-ah. A child joins them. They find his mother. John Tom falls in love with her, gets intoxicated and puts on his war paint. He visits the hotel where mother and child are. He meets the father, who has separated from the mother and has returned to kidnap the child. John Tom kills the father and scalps him. The story centers about the Indian's reversion to type under alcoholic intoxication. The beginning is dull and full of sub-titles. The end is somewhat repulsive. The Indian staggers in with the dank scalp hanging at his belt.

Art Dramas, Inc.

THE LITTLE SAMARITAN (Erbograph), August 27.—A five-part comedy-drama of church life in a small town. The story, written by a clergyman, is excellent. Marian Swayne has the leading part. Reviewed in last week's issue.

Bluebird Photoplays, Inc.

MOTHER O' MINE, September 3.—A strong five-reel subject, written and produced by Rupert Julian, who plays the leading role, supported by Mrs. Ruby LaFayette, Elsie Jane Wilson, Ruth Clifford and W. E. Warner. The number contains a great deal of humor and pathos and is one that should have wide appeal. Reviewed at length elsewhere.

Butterfly Pictures.

WHO WAS THE OTHER MAN? September 3.—A five-reel subject featuring Francis Ford in the double role of foreign spy and American secret service man, supported by Mae Gaston and others. This deals with the activities of foreign spies in Washington. The story is only moderately entertaining at the start, but reaches a pleasing climax. The cast and photography are pleasing. Reviewed at length elsewhere.

Fox Film Corporation.

THE DOMESTIC HOUND, August 6.—A Hank Mann picture full of rough comedy that made a number of good laughs at the Academy of Music, New York. It is the usual Hank Mann stuff. It isn't polite comedy, but it gets by with most, or seems to.

BETRAYED, August 26.—Plenty of action and well directed story, with humor, realism, romance and dash. It will be a sure winner with most audiences and will please every audience probably. For a longer notice, see elsewhere in this issue.

EVERY GIRL'S DREAM, August 25.—A costume picture in five reels, telling a slight but pretty romance half like a fairy tale. It is well put on and has many attractive qualities, but is rather long for the substance of the plot and this makes it seem slow in action. A longer notice will be found on another page of this issue.

Jewel Productions, Inc.

SIRENS OF THE SEA, August ...—A five-part photoplay suggested by the legend of the Lorelei. Louise Lovely, Carmel Myers and Jack Mulhall have leading parts. The first two reels are very fine. After that Mulhall has a dream that does not hold the interest well. It is composed of a monotonous succession of similar scenes. This picture is clean. The best parts are the swimming scenes, with about twenty girls, in the first two reels. Reviewed in this issue.

Greater Vitagraph.

WHEN BOBBY BROKE HIS ARM.—A one-reel Bobby Connelly picture written and directed by Charles M. Seay. Bobby with a fractured arm visits his grandma in the country. He and Aida Horton fall in love with a calf, Gladys Pansy. The calf is sold to a butcher; but when the children learn of this they take it away from the butcher's shop where it is tied up. They plan to join a circus. Bobby will be a lion-tamer, Aida a bare-back rider, and the calf, a horse. Bobby's mother arrives and affairs are straightened out. This picture is fairly entertaining.

SOLDIERS OF CHANCE (Vitagraph), September 3.—A five-reel melodrama by James Oliver Curwood. Evart Overton and Miriam Fouche are featured. The film has story action in every foot of film. It tells of adventure in South America and of the revenge on an unworthy captain. The love interest is there, too. A longer review is printed in the review columns of this issue.

GALL AND GOLF (Vitagraph).—A one-reel comedy produced by Lawrence Semon, who also takes the leading role. The comedy is mostly devoted to footage, showing Mr. Semon in attempts at clowning. The number does not go over very well, its only laughs being in the scenes showing the golf balls flying around. A few pretty girls help a little. A mediocre release.

SLIPS AND SLACKERS (Vitagraph).—A one-reel Lawrence Semon comedy written by Graham Baker. He is a slacker who is scared by the methods of testing recruits. These scenes are very funny. He compels the scrubwoman to marry him. Then he finds that she is worse than war. The best part is where he sits on a target that has been freshly painted. When he gets up the recruits mistake him for the target and begin practice.

M. H. Hoffman, Inc,

THE SILENT WITNESS, August.—A seven-part picture, produced by the Authors Film Company and featuring Gertrude McCoy and Frank L. A. O'Connor. As pointed out in a review on another page the story has merit in its last third, the first five thousand feet lacking the interest to sustain that amount of footage.

Kleine-Edison-Selig-Essanay

CONQUEST PROGRAM NO. 6 (Edison), August 18.—This program contains an excellent four-part comedy-drama entitled "The Customary Two Weeks," wholesome and entertaining, a one-reel historical picture, "The Story of Plymouth Rock," scenes in "The Grand Canyon of Arizona," "Nature's Perfect Thread Spinner," which is a 500-foot illustration on the silk worm, and "The Magic of Spring," a delightful fantastical bit. This is a good program all through and has been reviewed at length elsewhere.

THE LADY OF THE PHOTOGRAPH (Edison), August 27.—A five-reel comedy-drama featuring Shirley Mason. The star is attractive and the story is a good one; but the latter has not been handled well and the comedy does not always get over. A full review of the picture will be found elsewhere. The cast is a good one.

A MIDNIGHT BELL (Selig), September 3.—A two-reel version of a Hoyt farce directed by J. A. Richmond. William Fables, James Harris and Amy Dennis are in the cast. The story is about a fire in a country town where the fire chief and chief of police are both in love with the girl to be rescued. Much of the humor depends on the fire hose. A very funny incident is where a rope is thrown up to a window and the chief of police pulled down. This is a knockabout with laughs. It is free from the objectionable features of its predecessors.

THE KINGDOM OF HOPE (Essanay), August 22.—A two-reel episode of the "Do Children Count?" series, with Little Mary McAlister as the child of pacifist parents. She and Ellis Paul shame their parents by enlisting. This is not an interesting picture.

Marine Film Corporation.

LORELEI OF THE SEA (Marine), August.—A photographically beautiful, sometimes artistically, pleasing six-reel picture that has far too little story value to hold up its footage. Tyrone Power and Frances Burnham are featured. There are many scenes showing nymphs disporting about waterfalls, etc. The picture is wholesome and clean. It was produced by Henry Otto. A longer review is printed in the review columns of this issue.

Metro Pictures Corporation.

THE GIRL WITHOUT A SOUL, August 13.—Viola Dana does some very fine work in this five-reel Rolfe production, in which she plays the part of two sisters having opposite temperaments. The direction and photography are good, and she is ably assisted by a competent cast. A review appears on another page of this issue.

THE PATRIOT (Drew), August 27.—An excellent patriotic comedy offering featuring the Drews. In this number Mr. and Mrs. Henry become very patriotic, and food as they are of good living, decide to support the administration in conserving food. Mandy, the colored cook, is taken into their confidence and turns out to be more patriotic than her employers. Very funny.

Mutual Film Corporation.

CHARITY CASTLE (American), September 3.—A Mary Miles Minter picture; in which the star has been given a better opportunity than usual. The story is somewhat reminiscent, but is well done and interesting. It is a picture that children will like as well as adults, and has been reviewed at length elsewhere. The story tells how a little girl regenerates an old grouch and cements sundered family relations.

REEL LIFE NO. 71 (Gaumont), September 6.—The subjects in this number of Reel Life are "A Watering System for the Farm," a short but interesting bit; "Pets Which Will Never Become Popular," introducing a skunk farm and its young mistress. This is also a short length. "Handling the Mail" shows us how the parcel post department is managed, and also the money order and postal savings departments. A short length on "The Five Senses," with a couple of cartoons from "Life" close the reel.

THE BRIDE'S SILENCE (American), September 10.—A well-made five-part melodrama featuring Gail Kane. A full review of the production appears elsewhere. Suffice it to say that the story is a good one, and has been produced in a manner to create suspense. The picture is well dressed, artistic, and holds its secret to the end.

REPUTATION (Goodrich).—A five-part production featuring Edna Goodrich. It is not the fault of the story or of the supporting cast that this production is not up to the mark. The picture is badly made. It tells the story of a young girl who goes to the city to try to make good, and is harassed into leaving her position by a loosed-moraled employer. The wife of this man, believing the girl to be at fault, ruins her name in her own town. Later when again she tries to make her way in the world a trap is set for her by some associates of the man's. In the end she triumphs by luring the man on and exposing his perfidy to his wife. As the story is told on the screen it has an unwholesome tinge.

REEL LIFE NO. 72 (Gaumont), September 13.—This number contains some interesting matter, the most interesting of which is "Tree Planting in Our National Forests"; "An Unusual Colt," presents a tiny Shetland pony in the arms of a little boy; "Hunting Turtle Eggs" tells some interesting things about the loggerhead turtle, and shows a nest of eggs being unearthed in a sand bank. "The Midnight Sun," photographed at a far northern point of Alaska, presents an unusual sight.

Paramount Pictures Corporation.

THE CINDERELLA HUSBAND (Klever).—Victor Moore in a good one-reel comedy written by Thomas J. Gray. First we see Vic doing the housework. Then he is elected king of a carnival. Victor Moore does some good comedy character acting.

Pathe Exchange, Inc.

HEARST-PATHE NEWS NO. 68, August 19.—Arrival of Japanese Mission on Pacific coast; championship auto races at Sheepshead Bay, N. Y.; Fourth of July celebration of U. S. Soldiers in China; British women doing their "bit," and other interesting items comprise this reel.

HEARST-PATHE NEWS NO. 69, August 26.—An interesting feature shows Greeks at Athens cheering arrival of French officers; there are also views of 165th U. S. Infantry at Mineola; German Liner Kronprinzessin Cecile being overhauled for U. S. service; National Army men drilling on Governor's Island, N. Y., and harvesting of gigantic wheat crop in California.

TEARS AND SMILES (Lasalida), September 2.—A five-reel picture featuring Baby Marie Osborne. Miss Osborne holds up her end in a

masterly fashion, although she hasn't got a particularly strong story to work with. The story tells of her being adopted by wealthy folks and later scheming to get her mother with her. The supporting cast is good. A full review is printed in the review columns of this issue.

LONESOME LUKE BOSSES PATIENTS (Rolin), September 9.—A two-reel comedy in which Harold Lloyd is featured. The film contains a full quota of laughs. The action is confined to scenes in a sanatarium which old men attend, and in which are a score or more of pretty girl nurses. There is enough speed to the comedy to carry it through. Reviewed in this issue.

THE SHORT CIRCUIT (Astra), September 16.—Episode No. 11 of "The Fatal Ring." Pearl White gets over several thrills in this chapter—one when she leaps from a galloping horse to a tree, another when she jumps from the horse into an automobile, and a third when she catapults from a bridge to the top of a speeding train. The story progresses rapidly. Pearl escapes from the burning building, but thinks Tom has perished. She gets possession of the violet diamond and learns that Tom is a prisoner. Carslake holds her up and gets the diamond. Pearl, aided by the foresters, rescues Tom.

OUR NATIONAL PARKS—GLACIER PARK (Pathe).—A split-reel sharing American scenery with Japanese. The first half of the reel is devoted to beautiful scenes in the vicinity of Triple Divide Mountain. Ice and snow on the mountain tops in summer are shown in all their grandeur. Close-up views give us an insight into what Nature does when she dresses her mountains in white. The latter half of the reel contains beautiful "shots" in Pathecolor at gorgeously pretty Japanese gardens. We get a thorough idea of the horticultural skill of the Japanese through the views obtained by the cameraman.

MAKING MARINE OFFICER (International), September 2.—A split-reel combining a visualized article outlined by the title and a 500-foot animated cartoon titled "Happy Hooligan Gets the Razoo." The first half of the reel shows us just how this country is training youths to become officers. The pictures were taken aboard the training ship Newport and show the boys learning seamanship. A few excellent scenes show the men climbing up ratlines. The "mass overboard" drill is also interesting. The cartoon brings Hooligan and his brother Gloomy to a cannibal island. It is quite funny.

Triangle Film Corporation.

THE TEN OF DIAMONDS (Triangle), September 2.—A five-part production of entertaining quality featuring Dorothy Dalton. The picture is presented in a manner psychologically correct, and therefore carries weight as a box office attraction. It is not, however, a picture of entirely wholesome moral atmosphere. A full review will be found elsewhere.

IDOLATERS (Triangle-Kay-Bee), September 9.—A five-reel offering of the vampire type, by John Lynch and Monte M. Katterjohn. Louise Glaum is featured in the leading role, which is effectively rendered for this type of part. The story is one of the sensuous sort, leading up to a series of tragical events. It is lavish in settings and well produced. Reviewed at length elsewhere.

HIS COOL NERVE, August 12.—A comedy number of average strength, involving the adventures of Harry McCoy as an iceman and a fickle lover, handled in such a manner as to get a number of laughs. Much of the comedy is supplied by an exceedingly thin spinster, whose bank account finally secures for her a stout husband.

Universal Film Mfg. Company

THE PERILOUS LEAP (Gold Seal), September 10.—A three-reel subject, by T. Shellay Sutton, featuring Val Paul, Helen Gibson, O. C. Jackson, George Williams and George Routh. This tells of opium smuggling. The girl performs some daring feats on a swiftly-moving freight train in going to the rescue of the hero, a secret service agent. The story could well have been told in two reels, as some of the opening scenes are not essential. At the same time the subject has considerable strength and works up to an exciting close.

SHORT SKIRTS AND DEEP WATERS (Joker), September 10.—A burlesque number, by Tom Gibson, featuring Gale Henry and William Franey as leaders in an "Anti-Sin" society. They visit the beach and attempt to regulate the length of bathing costumes. This is characteristic and contains some fairly good humor of the type.

BOULEVARD SPEED HOUNDS (Nestor), September 10.—An original and unusually funny comedy, by Fred A. Palmer, featuring Eddie Lyons and Lee Moran. They are pinched for speeding and fool the cop by making believe Eddie's wife is ill from childbirth; Lee poses as the wife and uses a small dog for the baby. A delicate situation handled with just right comedy touch to get it over in good style.

TO THE HIGHEST BIDDER (Star Featurette), September 10.—Whether or not the author of this two-part picture took his idea from the play called "The Marriage Market" is of slight importance, for whatever its origin this production will make satisfactory entertainment. Mary Fuller plays a country girl who offers herself to the highest bidder. A first rate story well presented by Miss Fuller, Averill Harris, Clara Beyers and others.

IN THE CLUTCHES OF MILK (Victor), September 10.—A comedy number, by Craig Hutchinson, featuring Max Asher, Gladys Tennison and Harry Mann. There is a great deal of "boozing" in this number, but not much point to the action, which keeps it from being very funny. It has but few really strong moments; the chase scenes at the close are best.

NEARLY A QUEEN (Joker), September 10.—A typical Gale Henry number, which brings the usual number of laughs. She plays the part of a waif left in a far land by some sailors. Twenty years later she poses as queen. The hero and the villain clash over her. This gets up some amusing burlesque action and is quite entertaining.

A TEXAS SPHINX (Bison), September 10.—This is a two-reel Western drama with a surprise plot. Harry Carey holds up a stage. One of his victims, sworn in as deputy sheriff, tracks down his partner and puts him in jail as a noted outlaw in disguise. Harry Carey turns out to be a ranger, and the deputy sheriff is the real outlaw. This picture leads up to a very strong climax.

FROM CACTUS TO KALE (L-KO), September 10.—A two-reel comedy number that has a quite fast and furious finish. There is not much to the earlier parts of the picture, the scenes of which are devoted mostly to a restaurant where the Weasel starts things. When the Weasel inherits money and comes to the city he starts some more things. The chase that finishes the picture is a good one. During the course of it an auto plunges into the sea. A fair comedy of its type.

ANIMATED WEEKLY, NO. 86, August 29.—Recruiting with a tank in Chicago, training in Georgia, visit of the Imperial Japanese Mission, and various other entertaining features are included in this number.

CURRENT EVENTS, NO. 16, August 31.—A number filled with timely pictorial subjects, including views of Uncle Sam's coast defense, the dog show at Atlantic City, the Dolly sisters posing as "iron workers," swimming instructions at Silver Bay, and others.

THE FLAMING METEOR (Universal Special), September 3.—Episode No. 11 of "The Gray Ghost." Very interesting developments mark this episode. The Gray Ghost has a mental control of some sort over the girl, but it develops that the maid, who is in love with him, is overcome with jealousy and she threatens to kill The Gray Ghost. This installment, which is full of pleasing incidents, closes with the maid about to shoot the master criminal.

World Film Corporation

THE MARRIAGE MARKET (Peerless), September 3.—A brisk, well-constructed five-reel number, with a melodramatic close, featuring June Elvidge, Arthur Ashley, Carlyle Blackwell and others. The story deals with the paddock, the financial district and also has a pleasing social side. It has a swift-moving plot, not entirely convincing in certain of the latter scenes, but very enjoyable. Reviewed at length elsewhere.

To Show "Fall of Romanoffs"

Brenon's Picture Dealing With Incidents of the Russian Revolution to Have First Screening at Ritz Carleton.

INVITATIONS are out for the premier showing of Herbert Brenon's screen creation "The Fall of the Romanoffs," scheduled for Thursday evening, September 6, in the ballroom of the Ritz-Carleton Hotel, New York City. It is expected that many notables will be present. The showing begins at 8.30 o'clock.

The relation of the subject of this picture to events that have transpired in Russia within the past few months has aroused considerable interest in it, undoubtedly, and many will be curious to learn just how faithfully and with what insight Mr. Brenon has handled his theme. Much will be expected of the producer, who presumes to portray as historical facts events of so recent occurrence and to base conclusions upon them. As a record of those events—if it is a record—"The Fall of the Romanoffs" should be of inestimable value.

As an inference of the importance of the Brenon picture we append the impressions of Julian Johnson, a writer and critic of known ability, connected with the Department of Exploitation of the Herbert Brenon Film Corporation, which may be fairly said to indicate the character of the subject. Mr. Johnson says:

"Herbert Brenon's screen production 'The Fall of the Romanoffs' is the first big and significant record, literary or pictorial, which the Great War has inspired. It should be as enduring as the events which it reproduces are far-reaching.

"One can think, immediately, of many pictures which the war has caused to be painted; of the multitude of books which the conflict has caused to be written; of the inspired poems, of the messages of authors from Maeterlinck to Kipling, of the earnest efforts of every great artistic mind. But what have these men —and women—succeeded in? Impressions. Nothing more.

"To rely on the ever-ready motion picture phraseology, there has been but one 'complete sequence' in the war; and but one enduring effect has been registered so far on the changeless film of eternity. That sequence effect, result, or what you will, is the Russian revolution.

"Be the Western finish what it may, regarding crowns and boundaries; be the final result the overthrow of a dynasty and indemnity, or be it pacifism and disarmament, Russia is free. She has changed from a barbarous despotism to militant democracy, and so far there is no promise of any single result in the war which will be so great.

"And the nucleus, the kernel, the causation of all this, has been registered in Brenon's film. These absolute realities form the plot, the personality, the thrill, the suspense, the romance, the terror, the big living drama of 'The Fall of the Romanoffs.' The title of the picture itself is history.

"Forgetting what the fall of the Romanoff dynasty means to the world, let us see what the picture means to motion picture progress. It is the second of two great historic scrolls worthy preservation for the instruction of future generations. The first was 'The Birth of a Nation,' in which Mr. Griffith made a long-dead day live again, and showed the horrors of fratricide in so convincing a manner that it is quite probable that this photoplay alone might prevent a civil war. Here was a record of the past, made to live again by the touch of a man of genius. It is quite true that practically none of the present generation knew by direct personal contact anything about Civil War men and Civil War times, but the transcript was enough—it was art enough, humanity enough to plunge any twentieth century boy or girl unreservedly into the events of fifty years ago.

"Mr. Brenon, however, has taken the most significant episode of the moment, and has told its meaning in a universal language. This is the first and only historical document which is equally understandable in Singapore, Naples, Belfast, New York and Clay Center. This picture is destined to go around the world, proclaiming what the Russian revolution means to all peoples. To all peoples! you say; what concern is the Russian revolution to all peoples?

"Russia is, next to China, the world's most populous country. While the vast body of its agriculturists have not been progressive, the nation is not at all to be compared to China in its inertia and lack of imaginative force. Contrariwise, Russia is the most potential country on the face of the earth. Its millions are children of imagination, invention and ambition. Even in their darkest hours of slavery great poets, great composers, great painters and great generals have arisen among them, and the fame of their art and their valor has gone around the world. Liberty to Russia will prove a flame in a tinder forest; and an exposition of the source of Russian liberty, as well as the cause of Russian slavery, is of interest to every living man and woman who is above the level of tearing raw meat and wearing a geestring.

"Why? Because Russia, in peace, is going to be the world's most stupendous competitor. Her countless thousands are going to make life a matter of hustle for everybody else on the globe, and the pre-eminent question is going to be: 'How did this happen?' Brenon is telling you how it happened—now.

"It chanced that the greatest romance and the most unbelievable melodrama are wound up inextricably in the final throes of Russian autocracy, and the first struggles of the new-hatched freedom. Rasputin, the strangest, the most diabolic, the most gigantic figure since the Middle Ages, was the wielder of empire in empire's final wild flare, and Brenon's story picks up Rasputin at his very dawn, and follows him to his doom. He is the central figure—the demon—if you please—of a great tableau of love and hate which embraces the Czar, the Czarina, the reactionaries, such revolutionists as Korniloff and Kerensky, and the beauties of the Imperial court."

PREPARATIONS FOR ONCOMING L-KO'S.

General Director J. G. Blystone, of L-Ko Comedies, back from a fortnight of refreshing rest amid the Sierra Nevadas, has set to work upon a series of comedies with his staff of assistants speeding up the preparations for a series of lively fun-makers. Noel Smith, Phil Dunham, Dick Smith, Archie Mayo and Vin Moore have all been instructed to work fast before it starts raining for a Los Angeles winter.

Just now Noel Smith is working out a comedy that centers around a dancing school, with Gladys Varden, Walter Stevens and Bert Roach leading in the festivities. Dick Smith has rebounded from a siege of pleurisy and is making up for lost time with Eva Novak, Bob McKenzie, Chester Ryckman and Eddie Barry doing comedy stunts to enliven the L-Ko series.

Phil Dunham, having tried his hand at both acting and directing, is now combining his talents in a two-reeler that will have Lucille Hutton and Billy Bevan featured with Mr. Dunham playing a part as well as showing them how to do it. As he was a favorite comedian in L-Ko's before he took to directing, Mr. Dunham will find his audience waiting for his return to the screen.

Vin Moore is working on a mining comedy, starring Myrtle Sterling with Al Forbes featured. Miss Sterling has her work cut out for her as a Western belle who cleans up a mining camp, reforms a dance hall and does a comedy "white wings" in the village street. Hughie Mack is nearing the finish of his first L-Ko, with Noel Smith directing him and the new featured comedian in L-Ko's is trying to make his first comedy serve as an effective introduction.

Exhibitors who get their comedies through Universal sources are promised a series of L-Ko's that will cleverly maintain the average set by past releases in that series.

SOUTHWESTERN ART DRAMAS TAKES LARGER QUARTERS.

Southwestern Art Dramas, Inc., distributors of the Art Dramas program throughout the State of Texas and the Southwestern territory, has taken larger and more convenient quarters at 1911½ Commerce street, Film Row, Dallas, Texas.

Announcement is also made by this company of the acquisition of James J. Harvey, well known salesman throughout the New Orleans territory, to do special work and help exhibitors with Art Dramas in that section. Mr. Harvey has an enviable record and is one of the best liked film men in New Orleans. He was formerly connected with the Central Feature Film Company of New Orleans.

State Rights Department
Conducted by BEN H. GRIMM

Lee Organization Completed
Roster Includes Big Operators—Foreign Buyers Also Join —Body Comprises Three Classes.

JOSEPH F. LEE announces that the organization of state rights buyers promoted by him is completed. Numbered on the organization's membership roll are some of the biggest operators in the United States. Also, under Mr. Lee's promotion and through his efforts and the efforts of Jacques Kopfstein, several independent foreign buyers have joined the organization. There will be three distinct classes of franchise holders under the plan of operation: those who handle nothing but the big special state rights features, those who handle the "commercial" five and single-reel films, and those who handle foreign territories on all pictures.

Mr. Lee gives it as his belief that the success of the special feature attraction depends largely on the representatives in the territories having suitable theaters to exploit them properly. Those who have already signed in the special attraction class are: Louis B. Mayer, controlling the New England States, also the Park theater, Boston; Harry Samwick, New York and State; Sid Gruman, of San Francisco, who controls the Empress theater circuit, and who at present has in course of construction in Los Angeles a theater that will have cost a million dollars, controlling California, Arizona and Nevada; A. Dresner and Harry Crandall, of the Exhibitors' Film Exchange, Washington, controlling District of Columbia, Delaware, Maryland and Virginia; Jack Lannon, general manager of the Greater Features Co., controlling Washington, Oregon, Montana and Idaho.

The remainder of the territory, according to Mr. Lee, merely awaits confirmation. The foreign department, in charge of Mr. Kopfstein, includes the following: Sociadad General Cinematografica, Argentina, Chile, Uruguay, Spain, Portugal and New Guinea, Leroy Garfinkle, representative; The Pan American Film Service Company, Mexico and Cuba, Thomas & Kapfstein, representatives; Charles Thompson, Philippine Islands, Peru, Bolivia and Brazil, U. Ono, Japan; Progressive Film Company of Australia, Australia, William Schmidt and C. Lippman, representatives; Scandinavian Film Company, Scandinavia and Russia; David P. Russell, Great Britain, and Royal Cinema Corporation, Switzerland.

There will be no directors of the organization, it is announced. Simplicity and efficiency will be the keynote. Each man in his respective territory will act as a selling agent. He alone will judge what he will use and purchase. He will not be forced to take anything that he does not believe will prove a box-office winner in his territory.

With the addition of the foreign representatives it will be the purpose of the organization to purchase as much of the United States and Europe at one time as is possible, paying cash for same. Mr. Lee, general manager of the organization, is seeking permanent quarters where it is hoped American and foreign buyers can be gathered under one roof. Temporary quarters are at suite 1103, Longacre building, New York.

BACKER ON TRIP TO WEST.

Franklyn E. Backer, president of the Mammoth Film Corporation, left for the West on Wednesday, August 29, to oversee his numerous activities on the Coast. His first point will be Denver. From there Mr. Backer will visit all the important cities in his territory, finally meeting in San Francisco a number of capitalists who are discussing with him the early formation of a novel producing company, based upon lines which will be especially attractive to the exhibitor. A new and beautiful star is looming on the horizon in connection with this company.

One year ago Mr. Backer started in the state rights field with one picture, "The Fall of a Nation." Today he controls the output of ten big features in New Jersey and New York, and the Western rights in a big film. Mr. Backer attributes his success to the motto of his exchange, which is: "A square deal and a carefully selected picture."

BUYS "LUST OF AGES" FOR NORTHERN JERSEY.

Franklyn E. Backer, president of the Mammoth Film Corporation, has purchased the Northern New Jersey rights to the Ogden Pictures Corporation's "The Lust of the Ages." The deal was consummated by Mr. Backer and Jesse Goldberg, of the Ogden Corporation, between the time it took a Pennsylvania train to reach Harrison from New York. Mr. Backer was en route to Denver when overtaken by Mr. Goldberg.

"The Warrior" for State Rights
General Enterprises, Inc., Purchase Italian Film Featuring Maciste from Harry Raver.

NEGOTIATIONS have been closed by Herbert Lubin and Arthur H. Sawyer between General Enterprises, Inc., 1600 Broadway, New York, and Harry Raver, whereby the General Enterprises, Inc., becomes the owner of the American and Canadian rights for "The Warrior."

This Italian picture features Maciste, the giant who reached prominence through his wonderful feats of strength and daring in "Cabiria," and whom the New York Times calls "The Fairbanks of Italy." "The Warrior" shows Maciste at his best in a great story, a combination of farce-comedy and drama of which the New York American says, "a succession of laughs, weeps and cheers."

General Enterprises, Inc., plans to distribute the picture throughout the United States and Canada on the territorial or state rights plan. Mr. Raver had received numerous offers for different territories, but his plan has always been to sell the entire rights for the United States and Canada to one purchaser.

"The Warrior" ran four weeks at the Criterion theater, New York, and proved a tremendous box office attraction.

Attractive advertising matter is being made up by the General Enterprises Inc. and plans are under foot to run the picture at another Broadway theater for an indefinite run.

"THE LUST OF THE AGES" FOREIGN RIGHTS SOLD.

Although the Ogden Pictures Corporation's initial release, "The Lust of the Ages," in which Lillian Walker is starred, has been exploited, or offered for sale, through advertising in the trade journals for but three weeks, and although but two weeks have elapsed since the trade showing of that production, sixty-two per cent. of the entire would have been sold on this as well as the succeeding seven Lillian Walker super-attractions. All of the foreign markets with the exception of three of the belligerent Central Powers have been disposed of.

Jesse J. Goldburg, exploitation and production manager, stated: "We do not intend either advertising or giving publicity to the individual territory sold until the entire world has been disposed of; then we shall pound away through the medium of every worthy trade journal to the end that the exhibitors may know with whom to deal. In any event, although sixty-two per cent. of the world has been sold, our contracts provide the release by the exchange cannot take place before September 25.

WOLFBERG ENGAGES ADVERTISING MAN.

In line with the recent avowal from the Harris P. Wolfberg offices that co-operation with the exhibitor is being developed to the highest degree, comes news of the engagement of J. L. Ellman to take complete charge of this department. Mr. Ellman is an advertising man with many original ideas, and for the past year has been with the Reuble-Brown Advertising Agency of St. Louis. During this period he played a prominent part in "putting over" some of the biggest advertising successes of the year. Mr. Ellman will be located at the Pittsburgh office, but his work will take him over the entire territory—Ohio, Western Pennsylvania, West Virginia, Missouri and Kansas.

CLAIRE WHITNEY TO STAR IN SPECIALS.

Several big producers of state right specials have approached Claire Whitney to star in big specials, it is reported. Miss Whitney has starred under the Fox banner for the last three years, where she established herself as a big favorite.

Among her big successes were "Life's Shop Window" and "The Ruling Passion," also supporting William Farnum in "The Plunderer" and "The Nigger." Her versatility has enabled her to play the winsome and sweet ingenue in "Heart and Soul" with Theda Bara to the fair-haired "vamp" in Virginia Pearson's next picture, "When Lying Tongues Speak."

Miss Whitney is enjoying a well earned vacation after her strenuous labors at the Fox studios.

HOFFMAN BUYS "ONE HOUR."

M. H. Hoffman has purchased from Harry Rapf the American rights to "One Hour," a six-reel love romance distinctly out of the ordinary. Some persons will be inclined to term it "sensational," for the reason that the events crowded into a single hour in the lives of the hero and heroine of the story are unique and extraordinary.

Star Series Profits to Red Cross

Net Earnings of "Photoplay Magazine Screen Supplement" to Be Given for War Relief, Says Quirk.

JAMES R. QUIRK, publisher of Photoplay Magazine, who is about to issue twelve single-reel motion pictures on a state rights basis, under the title "Photoplay Magazine Screen Supplement," announces that all the profits from the sale of these de luxe motion picture subjects are to be turned over to the American Red Cross. All of the net profit received from the sale of territorial franchises on Photoplay Magazine Screen Supplement will be donated to the fund for aiding war-stricken Europe—helping Uncle Sam's soldiers and sailors to be more comfortable.

"In these strenuous times, when the whole civilized world is struggling in defense of humanity, when every man, woman and child is being called upon to aid the cause in which we have taken up arms, I feel that the least Photoplay Magazine can do is to contribute its bit toward alleviating the sufferings of those who are stricken," said Mr. Quirk. "The idea of making and distributing pictures of the stars as they are—unique and unusual views of the players 'off-the-screen,' under the title 'Photoplay Magazine Screen Supplement,' was not conceived with a thought of profit. We aimed solely to increase and augment our service to the picture fans of the country—to give them in motion pictures glimpses of the things they have read about the players doing in the pages of Photoplay Magazine.

"I want to thank the manufacturers who have co-operated to make this idea a success. Without their whole-hearted belief in the proposition it would have been impossible. I am sure every one of them will be with us strong on this idea of increasing the public interest in the stars, and at the same time helping the most worthy cause in the world. I am going to make sure these pictures reach the highest degree of excellence. They are going to reflect Photoplay Magazine throughout the country in a wonderful way, and I want that reflection worthy of the high ideals of the magazine itself. If I were not assured that the pictures reached this high ideal they would never be released.

"We have the pictures ready, and though many of them have been difficult to secure, we are not going to exploit them for profit. It is my plan to turn over every cent received from the sale of territorial rights on these twelve de luxe single-reel subjects to the American Red Cross—after deducting, of course, the sum necessary to cover the cost of the undertaking. This does not apply to any one release of Photoplay Magazine Screen Supplement, but to the entire series of twelve subjects, which are to be released within a period of a year.

"I am more than glad to assure every buyer of territorial rights on 'Photoplay Magazine Screen Supplement' that his money will not only secure for him what I believe to be the greatest box-office attraction ever offered him, but also will enable him to participate pro rata on what I hope may be a generous donation for the relief of the sufferers of all nations."

HOFFMAN TOURING FOURSQUARE CIRCLE.

Swinging around the Foursquare circle is the occupation which M. H. Hoffman, vice-president and general manager of M. H. Hoffman, Inc., is now following. Mr. Hoffman left New York on Monday, August 27, and the following day arrived in Chicago. From that city he sent the following wire to P. V. R. Key, his manager of sales and advertising:

"Chicago Hoffman-Foursquare Exchange will be established next week. Exhibitors here united in endorsing our policy of reasonable profits on strong features, and want our combined product. After visiting our exchanges in St. Louis, Cincinnati, Cleveland, Detroit, Pittsburgh and Philadelphia will return to New York. Toronto and Montreal Foursquare Exchanges will be next in order of establishment."

According to Mr. Key, Mr. Hoffman will personally proceed at once to finish starting the Hoffman-Foursquare service stations, and before the end of September not less than three other cities will be added to New York, Boston and those mentioned in the paragraph preceding.

"Mr. Hoffman's plans for exhibitors," said Mr. Key, "are certainly more than liberal. He feels that the quickest and surest way to build up a permanent patronage is to give big values for a sum considerably under what would ordinarily be regarded as reasonable.

"The Hoffman-Foursquare idea is to approach seriously the price question—among others to be corrected. And when we say we purpose putting our prices for each feature to the exhibitor on a basis allowing us only a small margin of profit, Mr. Hoffman intends to abide by that decision."

ATLANTA EXCHANGE MOVES.

The E. & H. Film Distributing Company of Atlanta, Georgia, has moved from 65 to 73 Walton. The firm has purchased all the fixtures of the Artcraft office, which was formerly at this address, and at the same time took over all the films controlled by the Strand Film Company, consisting of about twenty state rights features, including "The Ne'er-do-Well."

The E. & H. Film Company consists of two men—Chas. W. Harden and F. A. Engler. Mr. Harden has for several years been associated with several of the big film companies. Mr. Engler, the other member of the firm, is also an old film man.

"Today" and "Mad Lover" for State Rights

Pathe Offers Buyers Pictures Starring Florence Reed and Robert Warwick, Respectively.

PATHE announces that "Today," starring Florence Reed and "The Mad Lover," starring Robert Warwick, are for state rights sale.

It is with full appreciation that the important state rights buyer demands productions that are "special" in every way—stories, stars, cast and direction—that Pathe offers these two photoplays, which are looked upon as state rights propositions extraordinary.

"It is no exaggeration to say," stated a Pathe official, "that judged from every angle and by every standard that makes a picture great, 'Today' is not merely one of the great pictures of the year, but one of the greatest that has ever been made, from a standpoint of box-office value."

Harold Edel, managing director of the Strand theater, New York, called it one of the three or four best pictures he has ever seen. The picture was greeted by newspaper and magazine critics as a bigger hit than the play by George Broadhurst and A. S. Schomer, which played to tremendous business on Broadway for over a year.

Florence Reed, who has proven herself to be a splendid moving picture actress, says it is the best film she has ever appeared in. Her interpretation of the role of Lilly is a wonderful piece of screen acting. The picture was produced by Harry Rapf under the direction of Ralph Ince.

Robert Warwick is one of the most popular dramatic stars on the screen. The title, "The Mad Lover," is also a box office asset. Elaine Hammerstein, who made a hit with Mr. Warwick in "The Argyle Case," is the leading woman. Leonce Perret, the famous French producer, not only directed the picture but also wrote the story.

A. KAY DISTRIBUTING MASON COMEDIES.

The A. Kay Company has acquired from the Filmcraft Corporation the distributing rights to the Walt Mason Comedies, and has already started plans for the disposition of these pictures in state rights territory. Since the announcement that the A. Kay Company were to act as agents for the Filmcraft Corporation, numerous inquiries have come into the offices of the A. Kay Company from state rights buyers.

S. L. Rothapfel, of the Rialto theater, after seeing several of the Walt Mason stories, unhesitatingly placed his stamp of approval on them and gave it as his opinion that exchange owners, exhibitors and the public would be quick to appreciate the amusement and actual money value of such a line of clean, natural, humorous stories from a genuine poet-author who, during the past twelve years, has endeared himself to the hearts of millions of newspaper and magazine readers.

At present "The Dipper," "True Love and Fake Money," "Hash" and "Bunked and Paid For" are ready for release, and Filmcraft announces that these releases will be followed up regularly with others taken from the best of Walt Mason's stories.

HEARST-PATHE NEWS SHOWS DEPARTING GUARDSMEN.

By a fine bit of enterprise on the part of the Hearst-Pathe News many persons in New York, Newark, N. J., Albany, Newburg and Poughkeepsie who were unable to see the magnificent send-off which New York City gave the departing National Guard, saw the parade just the same, but on the screen. Pictures taken by a large squad of Hearst-Pathe News cameramen were speedily developed, edited, titled and printed and then put out as a "special" in the cities mentioned the night of the same day the parade was held—Thursday, August 30. This special was 400 feet long and was greeted with cheers by every audience to which it was shown.

Sixty-six of the most prominent theaters in New York City showed this special, among them the Strand. Much favorable comment was heard among exhibitors as to the interesting character of the film and the great speed with which it was issued.

"REDEMPTION" BOOKING BIG IN NEW YORK.

Announcement has been made by Nathan Hirsh, president of the Civilization-Pioneer Film Corporation, controlling the rights for Greater New York and New York State to Julius Steger's production, "Redemption," that a heretofore unattained record has been broken in booking the feature, inasmuch as twenty copies have been booked for September 10, the date of release. The picture has been booked by the entire Loew and Keith circuits, the Eighty-first Street theater, Mt. Morris theater, and other leading theaters in the territory.

The Civilization-Pioneer Film Corporation also controls the exclusive rights to "Hate" and the Williamson Brothers' production, "The Submarine Eye."

"A MAN OF HIS WORD" (Falcon Feature).

George Loane Tucker is the producer of the fifth of General Film's series of Falcon Features, "A Man of His Word." It is a picturization of the famous play "Jelf's," by Horace Annesley Vachell. In this picture Henry Ainley, who does such conspicuous work as a principal in "The Manxman," is the featured lead. Opposite him plays Mary Dibley, one of the most versatile of the English actresses of the film.

Italian War Pictures Breaking Records

Chicago and Boston Follow New York in Acclaim of Films Controlled by Fort Pitt Theater Corporation.

CHICAGO has rallied to the first and only authentic Italian war pictures, "The Italian Battlefront," with audiences that have packed the big Auditorium from pit to dome at every performance. Beginning with the initial performance, when the entire house of four thousand seats was sold out two hours before the opening, with prices ranging from 50 cents to $2.00, the picture has played to a business exceeding that of any other production ever presented in Chicago, save one, according to announcement from the offices of the Fort Pitt Theater Corporation.

Notwithstanding the pace set by the opening performance, which was attended by Lieutenant-General Guglielmotti, one of the highest ranking officers of the Italian army, who, with his entire staff, went from Washington to Chicago for the premier, and Major-General Thomas H. Barry, Commander-in-Chief of the Central Department, who has since left for active service abroad, together with the Italian, French, British, Belgian, Russian and Japanese consuls, the picture has consistently maintained the high level of business with which it started.

This has no doubt been due to the fact that in common with the New York, Boston and Pittsburgh reviewers, the Chicago critics have heralded the production in a manner almost unprecedented. In Boston the films broke a long-standing precedent. For the first time in the history of the city, a Sunday night performance of a moving picture was held in a legitimate theater. A special dispensation, suspending Boston's ordinance having to do with exhibitions in a legitimate theater on Sundays, was obtained through the influence of Mayor Curley.

The chief executive of the city, together with Governor McCall, General Clarence Edwards, commanding the New England Department, and his entire staff, as well as many other notables, attended the opening performance of this production. They were so impressed with the inspiring and patriotic character of the picture that when a request was made by the management to exhibit the production on Sunday evening, it was readily complied with.

"REDEMPTION" BREAKS RECORDS IN CANADA.

"Redemption," with Evelyn Nesbit and her son, Russell Thaw, is reported to have broken all records for attendance at Loew's Yonge Street theater, Toronto. This is one of the largest and finest theaters in Canada, with both a theater and roof garden. It was packed continuously for a solid week with "Redemption," and the picture will probably be brought back for a return engagement later.

"Redemption" has also been engaged for an entire summer season's run at the Brighton Beach Music Hall, the vast amusement palace at New York's summer resort. It is playing to capacity at Gordon's theater, Rochester, where it was held over for an additional week because of big business.

Territory for "Redemption" has been selling very fast lately. The De Luxe Feature Film Company has bought the rights for Washington, Oregon, Idaho and Montana. The Exhibitors' Film Exchange has bought Maryland, Delaware and Virginia. The best proof that the picture is a remarkable business proposition is furnished by Jones, Linick & Schaffer, of Chicago, who bought the rights for the State of Illinois, and found that the bookings were so heavy that they have purchased the film for Indiana.

PRE-RELEASES PROPEL "MOTHER O' MINE."

"Mother O' Mine," the third "Bluebird Extraordinary," was released throughout the country Labor Day on starlights lines, although during the previous week it was shown on pre-release in several localities. The feature was shown two days at Marcus Loew's New York theater, during the benefit week for The Sun's tobacco fund for U. S. Soldiers in France.

Rupert Julian, who directed the production, is co-star with Ruth Clifford, while Ruby La Fayette, a veteran actress, made her bow before the moving picture camera, at the age of seventy-three, in the mother role. "Mother O' Mine" is the third "Bluebird Extraordinary" distributed independent of the program. "The Eagle's Wings," an industrial preparedness feature that is being widely used as a patriotic incentive to enlistment, and "Hell Morgan's Girl," a story of the San Francisco fire, being the others. Herbert Rawlinson is star of "The Eagle's Wings" and Dorothy Phillips stars in "Hell Morgan's Girl."

WILLIAM HARTMANN OPENS NEW YORK OFFICES

William C. Hartmann has opened offices on the fifth floor of 218 West Forty-second street, New York, where he will conduct a general motion picture film business, specializing in state rights features and comedy productions. Mr. Hartmann's first offerings will be a series of high class farce comedies produced along new and original lines.

There will be four separate and distinct subjects, each under an individual trade mark, and one of each of the series will be produced monthly. The stories are by writers of national reputation.

Each subject or series will be worked out with a star performer having a world-wide reputation. The first of one of the subjects will be ready for screening within a week.

Peter Pan Increases Output

R. M. Vandivert Tells of Novelties Additional to Motoy Comedies—Will Release 2,000 Feet a Week.

R. M. VANDIVERT, vice president and general manager of the Peter Pan Film Corporation, has recently returned from an extensive trip covering all the distribution centres of the United States. The purpose of this trip was to establish the exact status of the short subject upon the present day program. Mr. Vandivert has made a keen analytical study of the market conditions, and has submitted in his report to H. C. Allen, president of the organization, that there is a brilliant future in store for the short subject throughout the country.

"As regards our future plans," said Mr. Vandivert, "we have decided to launch into the short subject on a very elaborate scale. The first step toward this end was the moving of the studio from Chicago to New York. We have contracted for

Scene from One of the Motoy Comedies.

the services of one of the most virile and capable men in the novelty field—C. P. Jaeger, who is our director-in-chief. George W. Hanlon, a son of one of the famous Hanlon Brothers, has been engaged to assist him in the production.

"We have given very considerable thought to the type and character of short subjects that we could add to our program of Motoy Comedies in order to make the Peter Pan short features the leading factor in the independent field. To this end we have selected the Black Magic Comedies, which are a series of novelties in which everything is black and white, the actors either in white against a black background, or in black against white.

"The Mirror Comedies, the Shadographs, and the Honeymooners' are our other releases, the last being a series of foreign pictures, which Mr. and Mrs. Richard Schayer are taking on their wedding trip around the world.

"Our sales plan already is complete. Commencing September 15, the Motoy Comedies and the Black Magic will be released as a single reel, alternating each week with Shadograph and Mirror Comedies as a single reel. In addition to this the 'Honeymooners' will be released in a 1,000-foot reel each week, thus enabling us to give the exchange a weekly output of 2,000 feet of high-class novelty pictures.

DESERET BUYS "DEEMSTER" FOR ELEVEN STATES.

J. L. Adams, acting for the Deseret Film Corporation, of Salt Lake City, Utah, and W. E. Shallenberger, president of the Arrow Film Corporation, have signed contracts whereby "The Deemster" becomes the property of the Deseret Film Corporation in eleven Western states—Colorado, Utah, Wyoming, New Mexico, Washington, Oregon, Idaho, Montana, California, Arizona and Nevada.

This leaves only one group of states on 'The Deemster' available. It has not been decided what policy will be pursued by the Arrow offices for the immedia e future, as nothing has been produced or obtained to follow the Hall Caine feature.

Commenting on the sale, Dr. Shallenberger expressed himself as highly pleased with the result, and stated that he was delighted with the knowledge that his picture would be in such efficient hands for exploitation throughout the Western half of the United States.

LION COMEDIES BOUGHT FOR WEST.

The Peerless Film Service, of Los Angeles, has closed a deal with the A. Kay Company, in which it becomes the exclusive distributors of Lion Comedies for California, Nevada and Arizona.

Manufacturers' Advance Notes

LITTLE ZOE RAE IN "THE LITTLE PIRATE."

Little Zoe Rae will be the star of the Butterfly feature to be released September 10. "The Little Pirate" is the title of the picture in which Zoe will have the lead, supported by Gretchen Lederer, Frank Brownlee, Charles West, Lillian Peacock and Burwell Hemerick.

Directed by Elsie Jane Wilson from the story by Norris Shannon and Elliott J. Clawson, "The Little Pirate" brims with human interest, and offers the small leading lady the best part she has depicted up to date on the Butterfly program.

It tells the story of a married couple who become estranged when the wife refuses to allow her husband to raise some necessary cash on the bonds that are held in trust for their

Scene from "The Little Pirate" (Butterfly).

small daughter, Margery. Virginia Baird not only fails to comprehend the vital urgency of the request, but when she overhears a conversation in which her husband's lawyer advises him to utilize the bonds without consulting her, she decides to place them in the hands of Charles West, a friend of long standing. This leads to an open rupture, and Virginia leaves the house. Margery tries to console her father, and failing in this, she sets out that evening on her pony to bring her mother home again. But she is held up on the road by Captain Kidd, Jr., who adopts her forthwith as his trusty first mate, and the two children take up their residence in a grass hut on a nearby island, where they live a life of gay piracy until they finally take part in a denouement that brings happiness to all the principals in the story—except the unfortunate villain responsible for the act of grand larceny, which furnishes most of the suspense to the plot.

"MEN OF THE DESERT" (Essanay).

The public mind generally associates the feuds of old with the mountaineers of Kentucky and Tennessee, yet history will show that perhaps the most terrific of these internecine quarrels were fought out on the great deserts of the West. For a quarter of a century, up until as late as 1895, cattlemen and sheepmen fed their factions against each other in bloody battles for the possession of the best grazing lands. Deeds of heroism beyond the ken of the Easterner were but a part of the ordinary day's work in the thrilling lives of these people.

"Men of the Desert," the fourth of Essanay's series of Western photodramas, is a picturization of such a feud. It will be released through the K-E-S-E service September 24. It is being given trade showing now at all branch offices of the K-E-S-E.

Jack Gardner, the former musical comedy star, takes the lead as the nomadic cowboy who attempts to restore law and order to the feud-stricken desert. Ruth King, as the daughter of one of the feud leaders, is his leading woman. Carl Stockdale heads the remainder of the supporting cast, which is made up largely of cowboys and ranchmen noted for their daring horsemanship.

"Men of the Desert" will have a screen time of sixty-five minutes, approximately.

VIRGINIA PEARSON'S TENTH PICTURE.

Virginia Pearson appears in her tenth production for Fox Films in "When False Tongues Speak", a big surprise drama, which William Fox will release on September 9. The unusual scenes scattered through the picture make it one of the year's most distinctive features.

The supporting company includes among the principals Carl Harbaugh, who also directed Miss Pearson in the film; Hardee Kirkland, Carl Eckstrom and William Meehan. Meehan had a prominent role in "Turn to the Right", the big comedy success, which has been running at a Broadway theater for a solid year.

"THE PHANTOM SHOT GUN" (Falcon).

What some enthusiasts have described as "the fastest-stepping detective story ever screened," is presented in General Film's current Falcon Feature release, "The Phantom Shot Gun".

This is the fourth of the four-reel dramas scheduled under the Falcon brand and is one of the most admirable subjects for holding an audience spellbound that has so far been found in a detective story. It is a detective story unlike so many others which have a great wealth of mystery without the varied action of a typical drama. In "The Phantom Shot Gun" developments are continuous. Situations and new mysteries come one right after the other until suddenly the guilty person is discovered in a most cleverly built up denouement.

The story is by Stanley Clisby Arthur, noted magazine writer. The hero is Courtland, broker, a partner of Hamilton Forbes, who appears as the villainous element as far as the love interest is concerned. Both men are in love with Elizabeth Kennedy, their secretary. Forbes gets Courtland out of the way by nearly framing up a conviction for forgery. At the last moment a bribed witness becomes stampeded and flees, and Courtland sets out to find him to clear his name. Forbes makes Elizabeth believe Courtland is dead and she consents to marry him. They are on their honeymoon trip abroad an ocean vessel when Courtland, with Larkins, a newspaper reporter, comes aboard by chance, and the whole situation becomes dynamic. On the voyage Forbes and a half dozen others are shot down by an invisible gun. Forbes, Elizabeth

Scene from "The Phantom Shotgun" (General Film).

and others are in turn suspected. On the fourth day out Larkins, who has been a silent investigator all along, turns up the murderer with a brilliant stroke of detective work.

Kathleen Kirkham is featured as Elizabeth and R. Henry Grey as Courtland. Frank Brownlee, Wm. Marshall, Gloria Payton, J. E. Nicholson, Barney Furey and Bruce Smith are other members of a most excellent cast. The play was directed by Harry Harvey, supervised by H. M. and E. D. Horkheimer.

The next Falcon Feature will be "His Unpolished Self" from the great play "Jelfs" by Horace Annesley Vachell. This is a George Loane Tucker production, and features Henry Ainley and Mary Dibley.

Art Dramas Fall Program

Crane Wilbur, Catherine Calvert, Jean Sothern and Marian Swayne to be Seen in Strong Features.

ART DRAMAS offers exhibitors a fall program of exceptional strength, with a wide range of stars and subjects. The schedule is typical of Art Dramas in that it possesses marked variety. Crane Wilbur, Jean Sothern, Catherine Calvert and Marian Swayne, Art Dramas stars of proven ability and certain drawing power, are represented in a list of features, whose stories are original and technically perfect.

Crane Wilbur will be seen in a Horsley feature, "Blood of His Fathers"; Jean Sothern in a Van Dyke production, "Peg O'-the Sea"; Catherine Calvert in "Behind the Mask", produced by the U. S. Amusement Corporation, and Marian Swayne in "The Little Samaritan", an Erbograph picture.

"Blood of His Fathers" tells an unusual story, treating of the subject of heredity. In construction, too, it is out of the beaten track of motion pictures, necessitating the portrayal of three distinct characters by Mr. Wilbur. In the prologue, laid in Civil War days, the Horsley star portrays the role of a questionable captain of predatory guerillas. In its later development the story is entirely modern and of compelling interest. J. Francis Dunbar is credited with the authorship of "Blood of His Fathers", while the direction was in the capable hands of Harrish Ingraham.

"The Little Samaritan" is an elaborate production in which Marian Swayne is fitted with a role, similar to that which she so successfully interpreted in her former Art Dramas vehicle, "Little Miss Fortune", and "The Road Between". Miss Swayne's character is that of a little orphan in a New England village. Babbling tongues fire the minds of the small-minded villagers against her and heap down upon her unhappiness and misery. But she battles against the odds and finally is blessed with a bountiful reward. The story is replete with interesting details and strong situations and affords the appealing little star a wide scope in which to display the charm and ability which placed her at the top almost overnight.

Joseph Levering directed, while the story was especially written for Miss Swayne by the Rev. J. Clarence Harris, a practicing minister, also wrote "Little Miss Fortune."

"Behind the Mask", starring Catherine Calvert, is said to be the best production yet made by the U. S. Amusement Corporation. This picture, written by Charles T. Dazey, author of many film classics, is, like most of Mr. Dazey's screen stories, a marvel of workmanship. It is, indeed, such a perfect example of the best in the photodramatic art that Mme. Alice Blache, who directed, cited it to the Columbia University journalistic students in connection with her lecture on scenarios recently as a desirable form of study. "Behind the Mask" was adapted to the screen by Frederick Rath.

Next in order is "Peg O' the Sea" by Winifred Dunn. Jean Sothern, star of this picture, is seen as the daughter of an old fisherman, living in a New England fishing village. In her slackers and rain hat she makes an appealing picture. Comedy is mingled with pathos and the splendid coast scenes give the picture a background of rare beauty. Miss Sothern, her director, Eugene Nowland, George Wiley, president of Van Dyke, and the others of the company spent several weeks in the Atlantic Highlands "shooting" these scenes.

SELIG RELEASES BY GENERAL FILM.

William N. Selig announces the following releases in General Film service:

"The Victor of the Plot", a two-reel drama, of British Army in India, featuring Miss Bessie Eyton, supported by an all star cast.

"The Voice That Led Him", a one-reel drama, will be released Saturday, September 15. This is a gripping drama of the African jungle, with Kathlyn Williams in one of her most sensational roles. A number of wild beasts are engaged in the scenic action.

On Monday, September 17, "The Law, North of 65", is the two-reel Selig release. In this, a strong drama of the Canadian Northwest, winsome Bessie Eyton is seen in an entirely new characterisation. Colin Campbell is the director.

"Vengeance Versus Mercy" is the title of a single reel drama announced for release Saturday, September 22. It is a gripping drama of vengeance thwarted by mercy, showing the infinite power of even a mere memory of a woman once loved, in the heart of a man.

The Selig Company promises excellent photography and strong plots. The principals announced speak for themselves.

TRIANGLE RESTORES MUSIC CUES.

The music cue sheet accompany each picture, which was lately eliminated from the Triangle service in order to ascertain whether or not it was of value to the exhibitor, has been restored in response to the demand for it. The number of requests indicate positively the value of this feature. It has become an essential part of the service provided exhibitors in connection with the showing of the picture. The Triangle policy of providing service men and every conceivable aid to theaters booking Triangle pictures demands a thorough investigation of the value of all material, insuring that effort is not being misdirected. The demand for the music cue is gratifying to those responsible for this service policy, for it proves that service is scarcely second in importance to the quality of productions.

West Pointers Graduate Early

1918 Class Which Will Help Train Half-Million Soldiers Shown in Gaumont-Mutual Weekly, Sept. 5.

WEST POINT cadets who, under normal conditions, would have continued as students until June, 1918, were graduated on August 30, ten months ahead of time. Interesting views of these 154 highly trained young officers, who will aid in the instruction of the first 500,000 selective draft army, are shown in Gaumont-Mutual Weekly No. 140, released Sept. 5.

The remainder of this reel is filled with current news events of general interest. Monster celebrations in New York City and elsewhere in honor of the members of the National Guard who are leaving for Southern encampments prior to embarking for France; military activities throughout the United States; and scenes on the actual battle ground, in France, are shown. The Mutual Weekly is fortunate in being able to obtain weekly shipments of news negative direct from the Societe des Etablissements Gaumont, whose large force of military cameramen co-operate with the French Government in the taking of these authentic war pictures.

Among other subjects of current interest, Governor Stephens, of California, is shown amid the giant redwoods of that state inaugurating the opening of the California State Highway. In Denver, women are acting as conductors and motormen on the city tramway. In New York City Bill Snyder, famous animal trainer of the Central Park Zoo, is teaching women to take the place of the park attendants.

JEWEL PRESENTS "MAN WITHOUT A COUNTRY."

"The Man Without a Country", Edward Everett Hale's appeal to patriotism, is the basis of a multiple reel photoplay produced by the Thanhouser Film Corporation which Jewel Productions, Inc., will present at the Broadway theater, beginning September 9, featuring Florence LaBadie and H. E. Herbert, supported by an excellent cast.

The version is the work of Lloyd Lonergan, after the story written by Mr. Hale in the summer of 1863.

Ernest C. Warde, the producer of many well-known photoplays, including "The Vicar of Wakefield", is responsible for the staging of the Hale story.

Mr. Herbert made his first appearance on Broadway five years ago, as Billie Burke's leading man in Pinero's "Mind-the-Paint-Girls"; he had a leading role with Blanche Bates in "The Witness for the Defense", with Grace George in "Half an Hour" and with Mrs. Patrick Campbell in Shaw's "Pygmalion" and "The Second Mrs. Tanqueray".

VICTOR MOORE IN "SEEING THINGS."

Victor Moore releases on Sept. 3 a distinctly different comedy called "Seeing Things", written by Edward McWade. Vic has been in a sanitarium for some time for the "cure", he having had "too many mornings after the night before." He is almost well and his doctor is about to discharge him, hoping that the change will also cure him of an optical delusion that he has. It seems Vic has a delusion that a certain "Gloomy Gus" looking creature is always following him wherever he goes and this serves to get him into no end of trouble. The doctor wires this fact to Vic's wife and prepares to start Vic on his way. Vic after bidding good-bye to the other inmates goes, only to be so he thinks followed by his friend "Gloomy Gus." He feels

Scene from "Seeing Things" (Klever).

that he is with him all the way home, and he certainly has his troubles with him.

Vic arrives home much to the delight of his wife but much to the disgust of his mother-in-law. It is not very long after his arrival home that the "optical delusion" again starts working, and poor Vic gets himself into lots of difficulties, and at the finish gives it up as a bad job.

This comedy is unlike anything that Moore has made, and is distinctly novel. It should more than please the "Moore Fans", and give them lots of laughs.

Border Drama Heads U List

Helen Gibson, Mary Fuller, Lyons & Moran, Max Asher, Harry Carey and Alice Lake Give Class to Releases for Week of September 10.

FOLLOWING the release, on Monday, September 10, of the Butterfly feature, "The Little Pirate", starring Little Zoe Rae, the week's schedule of Universal pictures opens on Tuesday, the 11th, with a Gold Seal drama, entitled "The Perilous Leap". The scenario was prepared by George Hively from a story by T. Shelley Sutton, and J. D. Davis directed the production. Helen Gibson and Val Paul have a lot of thrilling work to do in this story of opium and Chinese smugglers, and they are ably supported by a fine cast. The scene is laid near the Mexican border.

On the same date Eddie Lyons, Lee Moran and Edith Roberts appear in a rollicking Nestor comedy, "The Boulevard Speed Hounds". As Clinton Syx and Steele A. Ryde, they are arrested for speeding, but stall the officer with the pretext that Syx is a doctor, hastening to Ryde's wife. The cop is suspicious and demands to see the wife. So the bluff has to be carried out, the utmost being made of the comedy opportunities. The real wife appears on the scene at a most embarrassing moment and adds to the amusing complications.

On Wednesday, September 12, Gladys Warden, Walter Stephens and Harry Griffith are presented in a two-reel L-Ko comedy, "From Cactus to Kale", in which the action rapidly shifts from a small town restaurant to a palatial residence in the metropolis and finally out into the very middle of the ocean. The plot involves the kidnapping of the weak-kneed heir to a fortune, and employing him as a stalking horse in the operation of obtaining a large amount of money. The climax is reached when the victim of the conspirators gathers his cohorts and starts in pursuit, several buildings being demolished in the chase. Universal Animated Weekly No. 89 is scheduled for release on the same date.

Mary Fuller is the star of the feature for Thursday, September 13. "To the Highest Bidder" will be the title of her vehicle, a swiftly moving drama of a country girl who is determined to get away from the deadly monotony of her surroundings to the city, where she will be able to make a career for herself. She carries out this determination, but becomes entangled in a Bohemian set, and after spending all of her funds one day announces at a party that at the end of the month she will sell herself to the highest bidder. The outcome of this unusual situation is both surprising and satisfying to the most jaded picture fan. Emmett Campbell Hall and Catherine Carr wrote the play, which has been ably directed by Lucius Henderson.

"Short Skirts and Deep Water" is the rather startling title of the Joker comedy released on the same day, featuring Gale Henry, William Franey and Milburn Moranti. It deals with the efforts of the Anti-Sun Society to enforce the rules regarding the wearing of décollette bathing apparel on the beaches. Allan Curtis and Tom Gilson prepared the script, which has been produced with many hilarious effects by Curtis.

Max Asher and Gladys Tennison are the featured players in "The Clutches of Milk", a Victor comedy released Friday, September 14. Written by Craig Hutchinson and C. B. Hoadley and put on by the former, the piece details the amusing mix-up that occurs when a husband of one of Max's numerous flames writes him a letter declaring that he intends to put him out of the way, via the poison route. The thirty-sixth issue of the Universal Screen Magazine will be released at the same time as the Asher comedy.

Saturday, September 15, will be signalized by the release of "The Texas Sphinx", a Bison drama of the Southwest, featuring Harry Carey and Alice Lake. The story was written by T. S. Sutton and George Hively and produced by F. A. Kelsey. It provides Carey with the sort of vigorous character, reflecting the color and primitive strength of the open range, that has already built up an enviable following for him. Alice Lake is both a beautiful and appealing foil for Carey's sunburnt type of hero.

"Nearly a Queen" is the Joker comedy in which Gale Henry and Milton Sims appear on the same day. Allen Curtis and Tom Gibson are also responsible for the authorship and direction of this tale of the strange adventures of a waif who is beguiled into believing herself the daughter of ancient kings. The eighteenth issue of Universal Current Events completes the list of releases for the week, with its usual quota of timely scenes, strikingly photographed.

SELIG'S WORLD LIBRARY NO. 17.

The Selig-World Library No. 17, released in General Film service on Wednesday, September 5, is of unusual excellence, according to the Selig Polyscope Company. The famous beach resorts on our Atlantic Coast are pictured, including the homes of millionaires at Newport.

The mussel pearl industry is another interesting picture. Fishermen drag mussels from the bed of White river, Arkansas, and the value of the pearls discovered amounts to thousands of dollars yearly. Out of the shells pearl buttons are made, and this is the most profitable part of the industry. In Africa, the wife must be her husband's barber. The primitive method of pulling out the hairs is still in practice.

Java possesses a soil of astonishing fertility and a vegetation unsurpassed in its luxuriance. One of the chief articles of export is sugar. Preparing the soil, the plant, the harvest of sugar cane, the manufacture of sugar.

"A MIDNIGHT BELL" (Selig).

"A Midnight Bell" is the title of the latest Charles Hoyt comedy to be released by the Selig Polyscope Company, Monday, September 3, in K-E-S-E. Those who have been permitted to view this two reel comedy pronounce it as being one of the best of the Selig-Hoyt series that have proven so popular.

A comical story of rural life is "A Midnight Bell", involving the rival affections of the Punktown Chief of Police and Ezekiel Slover, chief of the fire department, for the heart and

Scene from "A Midnight Bell" (Selig).

hand of Amy Grey, the village belle. The rivalry is not confined to love making, however, for professional jealousy crops out between the two village functionaries and this leads to many and varied developments.

J. A. Richmond, responsible for the popular Selig-Hoyt comedies, is the director in charge and the cast includes William Fables, James Harris and Amy Leah Dennis.

The fire at Punktown's city hall is said to be among the funniest of motion picture episodes and carried out with all the enthusiasm and the blunders so common in "tank towns".

The K-E-S-E reports that the Selig-Hoyt comedies are increasing in popularity and that their rebookings are common with many of the K-E-S-E exchanges.

Following "A Midnight Bell" the Selig Company announces the following Hoyt comedy in two reels for release Monday, September 17, "A Contented Woman". For release in K-E-S-E service Monday, October 1, "A Bear Fact". This comedy was not written by Charles Hoyt but is said to be a clever comedy in every detail.

FOUR COMING FOX FEATURES.

Miriam Cooper, Virginia Pearson, George Walsh and Dustin Farnum, four William Fox stars, are announced as the principal players in the first four feature releases during September. This group of films consists in a photoplay comedy drama of a thrilling romance in Mexico, a mystery photoplay of suspense and action built around present day life in New York City, a refreshing and fast moving story of a love affair which began in a Chicago cabaret and ended with a wedding ring in a Balkan principality, and a powerful visualization of a big man's struggles in the great snows of the Northwest.

These are the productions, with the dates of their release: September 2, R. A. Walsh's drama "Betrayed", with Miriam Cooper; September 9, Virginia Pearson in "When False Tongues Speak"; September 16, George Walsh in "The Yankee Way"; September 23, Dustin Farnum in "North of Fifty-three".

"Betrayed" has a score of deft, unusual touches.

While it is necessary to dwell lightly on the story of "When False Tongues Speak", that the novel twists shall remain undisclosed until the screening the fact that the script was written by George Scarborough is conclusive evidence of its merit.

"The Yankee Way" is described as a "star-spangled comedy". It presents the genial George Walsh as Dick Mason, a young millionaire who happens into cabaret just in time to end one flirtation and start one of his own.

"North of Fifty Three" was taken from the story of that name by Bertrand W. Sinclair. The picture, with the inimitable "Dusty" Farnum as "Roaring Bill" Wagstaff, will undoubtedly have the same wide vogue as that enjoyed by the novel.

AMERICAN MADE WARES IN DEMAND.

The scarcity of foreign made motion picture machines and equipment has created a demand upon the American manufacturers for such wares. The Precision Machine Company recently received orders for twenty-eight Simplex Projectors to be delivered to the Scandinavian countries. A special letter of assurance from the British Embassy was granted for these shipments, so that there would be no delay in the projectors reaching their destination. Other equipment such as screens, generator sets, carbon, etc., were also purchased to be used in the above countries.

General Forecasts "O. Henry"

Releases for September and October Include Five Four-Reel Features and Four Two-Reelers.

WITH three directors working at one time on the new "O. Henry" Broadway Star Features, the production of these dramatic releases is definitely established for two months ahead, announces General Film. Five of the very greatest of O. Henry's intensely human stories will be filmed and distributed during this period in the four-reel feature form. A number of the shorter stories that carry all the inimitable sentiment of the great author's characteristic treatment will also be ready within the same span.

The big O. Henry features will be these, named in the order of distribution: "The Defeat of the City", with J. Frank Glendon and Agnes Eyre, directed by Thomas R. Mills; "Blind Man's Holiday", with Carlton King and Jean Paige, directed by Martin' Justice; "The Duplicity of Hargraves", with Charles Kent, J. Frank Glendon and Myrtis Morgan, directed by Thomas R. Mills; "The Ruler of Men" and "A Night in New Arabia".

The new series of two-reel O. Henry stories starts with the "John Tom Little Bear" story, with Al Jennings, Dan Duffy and little Roberto Turnbull, followed by "The Last of the Troubadours", with S. E. Jennings, Dan Duffy and Nolan Leary. These are directed by Dave Smith. Succeeding them will be "The Lonesome Road" and "Law and Order".

"JACK AND BEANSTALK" IN ST. LOUIS.

"Jack and the Beanstalk", William Fox's cinema spectacle, which concluded its run on Broadway on August 26, opened at the Belasco Theater in Washington, D. C., on that date. A week later the picture will go into the Garrick Theater in St. Louis, while still showing in Washington.

"RASPUTIN, THE BLACK MONK" (World).

"Rasputin, the Black Monk", is the title of a newly completed World-Picture Brady-Made about to be published on the World program. This photoplay has been in preparation for several months under the direction of Arthur Ashley, with a most unusual assemblage of star players. These include Montagu Love, June Elvidge, Arthur Ashley, Henry Hull, Julia Dean, Irving Cummings and Hubert Wilke.

Mr. Love appears in the name part; Miss Elvidge personates the wife of Rodin (Mr. Ashley), the early leader of the revolutionists, betrayed by Rasputin; Mr. Hull is seen as Kerensky, the hero of the hour in Russia, to whom the young American actor bears a quite striking likeness; Miss Dean is the Czarina's favorite lady in waiting under such hypnotic fascination for the black monk that she eagerly performs his bidding in all things; Irving Cummins plays a gallant young prince whose influence, thrown to the revolutionists at the crucial moment, enables him to overthrow the Government and accomplish the freedom of their country; and Mr. Wilke portrays the Czar whose rule is ended in the final episodes of the new drama.

It is declared that the present exposition of the conditions and influences which led to the great upheaval is entirely authentic, and that many details are brought to light for the

Scene from "Rasputin, the Black Monk" (World).

first time, even to certain state secrets which have been guarded heretofore with the greatest care.

"Rasputin, the Black Monk", is described as an exceptionally "big" picture in theme and production. Several immense scenes have been built outside the studio from photographs brought to America by returning representatives of World-Pictures Brady-Made who had been in Petrograd for a long time prior to the culmination of the movement for freedom. In addition to the star cast large numbers of "extras", horses, etc., are employed in the several imposing spectacular episodes.

"CAMILLE" (Fox).

Theda Bara in a sumptuous picturization of "Camille" is the latest announcement of William Fox to the motion picture public. Once more the makers of Fox pictures have delved into the masterpieces of literature. "Camille", the story of Alexandre Dumas fils, has behind it a long history of success. Its engagements in every civilized country of the world. It has been acted on every great stage of Europe and both

Scene from "Camille" (Fox).

Americas, and, in book form, it has brought tears to the eyes of men and women all 'round the globe.

Theda Bara, as the unhappy Parisian girl who sacrifices herself on the altar of convention, has surpassed all her previous work in this production.

"Camille" has just been completed, under the direction of J. Gordon Edwards. Parisian life has been followed in every detail, so that the atmosphere of the story fits admirably with the acting in it.

"Camille" is the most famous French novel of the nineteenth century. The original story, known as "The Lady of the Camellias", was published in 1848. A year later its author recognised the dramatic possibilities of the piece and made a new version, which was acted on the Parisian stage in February, 1852. Its success was enormous.

The Fox version of this tremendously successful story play will be released to exhibitors on September 30.

"SANDS OF SACRIFICE" (American).

Human sympathy and devotion blend pleasantly in William Russell's next publication for the American, the issue of September 24, entitled "Sands of Sacrifice". Centered in "Big Bill". Darcey (Russell), they are played interchangeably between the two leading supporting characters, Nora Farnes, later Mrs. Darcey (Francelia Billington), and Billy's pal, the invalid "Sammy" Goode (John Gough).

When Nora is placed in compromising straits, "Big Bill" gets her out in marriage, and when "Sammy" is told he is going to die unless he burns out the poison in the hot sands of the desert, Darcey packs him off with him to the wilderness.

Mr. Russell had a hot time making the film. He and Gough, Director Tod Sloman, cameraman, assistants, etc., did the desert scenes in the midst of the July torrid wave which seared and parched California to the limit of endurance. But photographic conditions were excellent and some splendid exposures were made.

The same holds true of the mountain scenes, several in particular being magnificent panoramas of the famous "hairpin" curve of the San Bernardinos, down which Darcey's roadster races. Much of the scenery was obtained in the "big tree" country and has been reproduced in accordance with the American's high standard of workmanship.

Coming in the fall hunting season, the interiors of Darcey's mountain lodge will be specially interesting. These sets were built with great care and expense, and when shown will excite the envy of the sportsmen of the Adirondacks.

"THE AWAKENING OF RUTH" (Edison).

"The Awakening of Ruth", by Julien Hubbard, the five-reel Edison feature, one of the first Perfection Pictures to be released through the Kleine System on September 17, is a story of unusual charm and variety. Shirley Mason, Viola Dana's younger sister, is given an excellent opportunity to snow her subtle and versatile art and she is ably supported by George Forth and Donald Hall.

The suspense of the story is sustained through a plot in which life on an island off the Florida coast and the complex existence of the Great White Way are cunningly interwoven.

The love interest predominates and technically the pictures exhibit the perfection of detail which characterizes all of the Edison productions. This release cannot fail to be popular with all ages and classes.

"The Angel Factory" Heads Pathe Program

First Appearance of Antonio Moreno—"Seven Pearls" Serial Begins—Other Features for Week of September 16.

PATHE'S program for the week of September 16 marks the first appearance of Antonio Moreno as a Pathe star. It also brings Mollie King in the first episode of "The Seven PPearls" serial, Pearl White and a Lonesome Luke two-reel comedy as other features.

Antonio Moreno, one of the most popular male stars on the screen, is seen in "The Angel Factory." Opposite him is Helene Chadwick, who has been rapidly coming to the fore. Other important members of the cast are Suzanne Willa, Margaret Green and Armand Lopez. The story deals with a little East Side girl whose father is a drunkard and whose mother is a sloven. It tells how she comes into contact with the superintendent of a settlement house and finally develops into the kind of woman it was intended that she should be. The picture works up to a big punch at the end with a shooting and circumstantial evidence pointing to the guilt first of the heroine and then of the hero.

Mollie King stars in the first episode of the "Seven Pearls", entitled "The Sultan's Necklace". The story tells how the Sultan's necklace is stolen, how Ilma, a beautiful young American girl, must recover the seven pearls contained in it, or see her guardian die and herself enter the Sultan's harem. Creighton Hale appears opposite Mollie King.

Pearl White stars in the 11th episode of "The Fatal Ring", entitled "The Short Circuit", another thrilling chapter of a serial that is a guarantee of twenty weeks' big business. It is a knockout wherever shown according to all reports. The story tells how Pearl succeeds in recovering the Diamond from Carsake in an unusually interesting fashion, and how he in turn takes it from her. Warner Oland does especially good work.

Lonesome Luke is seen in "Lonesome Luke Loses Patients", a two-reel comedy produced by Rolin. Lonesome Luke is the Doctor Killem of a twentieth century sanitarium. An idea of the laughs in it can be seen from the following titles: "I hope you'll get well—or something". "This part requires practice and 'sang froid'—whatever that is". "My middle name is Cuddle". "He swallowed a buffalo nickel and it's kicking him". "I feel like a camel on the eighth day".

There is a Pathe scenic on the program entitled "Triple Divide Mountains, Glacier Park" and "Japan, the Floral" (colored). There is also an International cartoon and scenic split reel and Hearst-Pathe News No. 76 and No. 77.

INSTALLING SHECK ADAPTERS.

H. H. Cudmore, general manager of The Argus Lamp & Appliance Company, manufacturers of the Sheck Universal Adapters for Mazda projector lamps, in company with R. P. Burrows, manager commercial section, engineering department, National Lamp Works of General Electric Company, Nela Park, Cleveland, who has been directly responsible for the commercial development of the newly designed Mazda projector lamps, recently visited the cities of St. Paul and Minneapolis and made several successful installations of the Sheck Universal Adapter with Mazda projector lamps in motion picture theaters. Successful installations were made in the "Cozy" theater, Seventh and Smith streets, St. Paul, Minn., of the Model "A" Sheck Universal Adapter with the 30-ampere 28-30 volt 600 Watt Mazda projector lamp, using the newly designed type "T" Ft. Wayne compensarc for directly controlling alternating current for the successful operation of Mazda projector lamps.

This theater was especially selected as being typical of all motion picture theaters of six hundred seats and under using alternating current where the Sheck Universal Adapter and Mazda projector lamps will successfully replace carbon arc projection apparatus and effect a current saving of at least two-thirds the cost of operating carbon arc projection apparatus.

A successful installation was made in the "Gem" theater, St. Paul, Minn., utilizing model "A" Sheck Universal Adapter with the 30-ampere Mazda projector lamp in connection with the newly designed Ward-Leonard 110 volt direct current rheostat.

All exhibitors who have seen these practical demonstrations of the Sheck Universal Adapter for Mazda projector lamps were very well satisfied and pleased and a large number of orders were placed with distributing agents for the Sheck Universal Adapters in the northwest territory.

Mr. Cudmore and Mr. Burrows contemplate visiting all of the prominent cities of the United States within the next few months for the purpose of making practical trial demonstrations of the Sheck Universal Adapter for Mazda projector lamps.

BILL DESMOND IN "FLYING COLORS."

William Desmond, the most popular of the Triangle stars, is to be seen in "Flying Colors," as a Yale athlete who puts into practical use some of the gymnastic stunts which made him a star at university field meets. In the cast supporting the star are: Golda Madien, Jack Livingston, Laura Sears, J. Barney Sherry, George W. Chase, John Lockney, Bert Offerd, Mary McIvor and Ray Jackson. The story was written by John Lynch and R. Cecil Smith, and produced under the direction of Frank Borzage.

Initial Hart Picture Nearing Completion

"The Narrow Trail," a Thrilling Drama of Western Bandit Life—Fritz, Hart's Famous Horse, Plays Opposite Actor.

WILLIAM S. HART'S initial Ince production to be released by Artcraft Pictures in October is now rapidly nearing completion at the Lasky studio in California. The photoplay, "The Narrow Trail," offers a dramatic Western story involving the life of a bandit and his great love for his beautiful pinto, the fastest horse in the community. Appearing opposite the star, with almost human intelligence, is Fritz, Hart's famous horse. The story allows for a great heart appeal, which is most effectively brought out by the splendid actor and his pony.

The exteriors for "The Narrow Trail" were staged in the range of mountains south of Los Angeles, and work is now being finished on several interiors at the Lasky studio, which will complete the production. One of the thrilling bits of play is a fight between Hart and two other members of the cast. The scene was staged last week at the Lasky studio, and is expected to become established as the greatest rough and tumble scuffle ever staged before the camera. Hart, as well as his opponents, were severely bruised as a result of this encounter in which blood flowed. Many other tense scenes of equal effectiveness have been staged which are contrasted with views of the bandit and his horse disclosing various pictures of particular human charm.

The story for this production is the creation of William S. Hart himself, and is adapted to the screen by Harvey F. Thew, of the Famous Players-Lasky staff. During Hart's recent trip across the country, when he appeared personally before many audiences, he received so many requests for information regarding his popular horse that the star decided to feature the animal in his next picture. Fritz was purchased by Hart from an old Indian several years ago for a trifle. At this time the animal was nothing but a raw-boned pony. As a result of great care from the hands of the actor himself the pony developed, not only in one of the swiftest horses on the West Coast, but became one of the most beautiful animals ever screened, but exceptional supporting cast has been given the star, including Sylvia Bremer, the talented beauty who appeared with him with such distinction in "The Cold Deck."

"ARMS AND THE GIRL" COMPLETED.

"Arms and the Girl," the latest Billie Burke picture for Paramount, has been photographed in its entirety. The film is now being cut and assembled—in itself no mean task, as many scenes had to be taken over and over to insure getting perfect results. This picture will be one of the most spectacular, according to the belief of those responsible for its production, ever turned out by Paramount. Director Joseph Kaufman has permitted no opportunity of enhancing the war scenes and rendering them realistic to escape his attention. One member of the cast who saw the battle of Arras in films declared that some of the scenes were almost paralleled in "Arms and the Girl," despite the fact that the director had not seen the actual war picture.

"COMPLICATED COMPLICATIONS" (L-Ko.).

Director Phil Dunham, of L-Ko, having graduated from General Director Blystone's acting forces, shows how well he can produce pictures as well as create laughs on his own account in "Complicated Complications," set for distribution through

Scene from "Complicated Complications" (L-Ko.).

Universal sources Sept. 26. Lucille Hutton and Billy Bevan will be the featured players in an oddly-conceived and amusingly-executed two-reel laugh-maker. While it is fair to presume that the methods for surprising laughs out of audiences have been pretty well covered by the producers of rough-house comedy, it is declared that Phil Dunham has discovered a few remaining wrinkles in the game that will be first exploited in his initial L-Ko.

Change in Triangle Program

Substitutes "Idolaters" for September 2—September 9 Releases Include Bessie Love in "Polly Ann" and Winifred Allen in "The Haunted House."

OWING to the fact that the cutting and sub-titling of "The Man Hater", the Saturday Evening Post story starring Winifred Allen, has not yet been perfect, that play has been taken off the Triangle schedule for September 2, and "Idolaters", starring Louise Glaum, substituted. "Idolaters" is the story of a woman who worships the false god of vain success, setting aside all else to satisfy her ambition. The action parallels the lives of two women who are determined to win places for themselves on the stage. One proceeds to four-flush her way, the other to make good by hard work.

This is the production for which Triangle built an elaborate Egyptian setting, representing the apartment of "the peacock woman", played by Miss Glaum, who, as "vanity", wears innumerable gowns of bizarre fashion.

The tale of a ghost that turned human is the theme of "The Haunted House", an Allan Dwan production, featuring Winifred Allen, which will be presented on the program for September 2. The locale is a New England village, where superstition continues to stalk in the minds of the austere residents. Denied the ordinary pleasures of youth, the girl of the story devotes herself to imaginative fancies. Being of a sensitive, spiritual temperament, she believed the spirits of the wood commune with her, as they did with Joan of Arc. The mystery of the haunted house, which holds in awe the superstitious villagers, is not penetrated until one night a young desperado, seeking refuge, dares to invade its premises and finds the ghost to be exceedingly human.

As a small-town slavey who becomes a barnstorming Bernhardt, Bessie Love makes her appearance in "Polly Ann", the other release for September 9. She is an orphan inmate of a poor farm until the village tavern keeper engages her as slavey of all work. When a fly by night company of players comes to town, Bessie is smitten by the romantic demeanor of one of the actors. She determines to become a player and proceeds to give her version of Ophelia, Portia and other great characters of dramatic literature. Later she becomes an heiress and experiences a real adventure, as romantic as any ever presented by the strolling players.

"His Precious Life", featuring such famous Keystoners as Louise Fazenda, Charlie Murray, Slim Summerville, Dora Rogers and Wayland Trask, will be released by Triangle on the week of September 9.

"A Warm Reception", with Alatia Morton, Marianne de la Torre, Pietro Bianchi, Pat Kelly, Jack Dillon and Larry Bowes, is the Triangle comedy accompanying "Polly Ann".

"A Dark Room Secret" will be the supplementary feature with "The Haunted House". The comedians of this one-reeler are: Elizabeth De Witt, Lillian Biron, Harry Depp, Lloyd Bacon, Marie Manley and Ben Horning.

BOYS' PRANK HELPED CHAPIN.

Boys will be boys, but their pranks can be an inspiration, Benjamin Chapin has discovered. The result is "The Call to Arms" chapter of the Lincoln Cycle and here is how: Mr. Chapin found himself ready to do a scene showing Willie and Tad Lincoln, but the boys who were to play the parts had disappeared. There is a swimming hole near the Chapin studio at Ridgefield Park, New Jersey, and Mr. Chapin's own knowledge of youthful ways led his steps to it. But "Willie and Tad" were not there. At length he discovered them stealing into the studio with soaking wet bath towels under their arms. They had beaten him to it, but a Chapin lecture on "Lateness" followed just the same. At the conclusion of it Mr. Chapin sat down.

Were the late actors impressed? Did they give way to tears? As we have said, Mr. Chapin sat down. But he also stood up. He didn't relish sitting on wet towels. He thought it a corking "situation", however, and that is why you find the incident repeated in "The Call to Arms" and get a big laugh from a little happening.

"If nothing else, this incident should show how laugh currents are worked up in production," says Mr. Chapin. "They are likely to come to one at any time and nothing should be overlooked if usable."

CAST FOR GOLDWYN'S "CINDERELLA MAN."

Casting Director Adolph Klauber of the Goldwyn Pictures Corporation has completed the list of principals for Mae Marsh's new screen vehicle, "The Cinderella Man," and work upon Edward Childs Carpenter's whimsical story is already well under way at the Fort Lee studio.

Barring "Margie," which Mae Marsh will play, the most important part in the new Goldwyn film is "Tony", he is the socalled "Cinderella man," who lives all alone in his garret under the eye of his former butler, until "Margie" slips across the roof one Christmas Eve from her aristocratic house to bring him friendly cheer—and food. For "Tony," Mr. Klauber has selected Tom Moore.

In George Fawcett Goldwyn has secured an admirable "Caner". Another distinguished character actor, who has left the legitimate stage for the screen, is George Farren, who will play "Sewell".

Alec B. Francis has been chosen for the part of "Romney". Others in the cast are Louis R. Grisel, Elizabeth Aarionsm, Mrs. J. Cogan, Dean Raymond and Harry Scarborough.

Fine Production of "On the Level"

Strong Cast and Admirable Story Make This Paramount Picture Unusually Attractive.

When "On the Level" is released September 10 as a Paramount feature it will be found that, in addition to the star, Fannie Ward, there is a cast which throughout is of unusual strength, a story that is both thrilling and convincing, and a production leaving nothing to be desired. In the cast are such well known and popular players as Jack Dea, Harrison Ford, Lottie Pickford, James Cruze, James P. Mason, James Neill, Edythe Chapman, Jane Wolff and Henry Woodward.

The direction of George H. Melford is a guarantee of the excellence of the picture in this respect, while the fact that the story was written by Charles Kenyon, the well-known playwright, and the screen arrangement by Marion Fairfax, assures its perfection.

SHECK SALES MANAGERS.

H. A. Brereton has been appointed sales manager of the Argus Lamp & Appliance Company, 222 Euclid avenue, Cleveland, manufacturers of the Sheck Universal Adapter for Mazda projector lamps.

H. L. Nebeker, formerly manager of the Chicago office of the Victor Animatograph Company, manufacturers of semi-portable motion picture projection machines, has been appointed Chicago district manager. Mr. Nebeker will handle all of the business in the Chicago district territory and Indiana and territory adjacent to Chicago.

A large stock of Sheck Universal Adapters for Mazda projector lamps and the necessary current controlling apparatus will be carried in Chicago to take care of the extensive demand for their products, at 708-10 First National Bank building.

SAME CAST IN ALL "BAB" PICTURES.

For the five big five-reel productions, starring Marguerite Clark, and adapted from the "Sub-Deb" stories by Mary Roberts Rinehart, the same cast will be used throughout, according to Hugh Ford, Eastern production manager, who has just completed his arrangements for these exceptional Paramount productions.

The principal players in the "Sub-Deb" or "Bab" pictures, and who will appear in each of the five big productions, are Marguerite Clark as Bab Archibald, Leonora Morgan as Jane, Nigel Barry as Carter Brooks, Richard Barthelmess as Tommy, Frank Losee and Isabel O'Madigan as Mr. and Mrs. Archibald, Helen Greene as Leila, Guy Coombes as Harry and Jack O'Brien as Harold.

"THE SPOTTED LILY" (Bluebird).

Ella Hall makes another appearance as a star among Bluebirds with the release of "The Spotted Lily," on Oct. 1. This feature previously referred to as "Bitter Sweet" is a story of pathetic sacrifice, having the outrage of Belgium as its basis, with its final scenes translated to the United States for the happy ending. J. Grubb Alexander wrote the story, Fred Myton prepared the scenario and Harry Solter, veteran among moving picture directors, made the production. In Miss Hall's

Scene from "The Spotted Lily" (Bluebird).

support, Charles Hill Mailes will play the role of a Roman Catholic priest who suffers indignities through his protection of a defenseless girl, and finds recompense in the surety of his charge's future happiness in America. There is just enough battle and carnage to develop the motive of the plot, but while they last the war episodes are sharp and sensational. Ella Hall, who has made an enviable name as an interpreter of juvenile roles, finds opportunity to display her more widely developed talents in playing the part of a little girl and, later, her mother grown up.

Paramount Chooses Serial Title

"Who Is Number One?" Will Be the Name of the Fifteen-Episode Mystery Drama.

PARAMOUNT has selected the title for its first serial. The fifteen-episode mystery drama, starring Kathlen Clifford, is to be called "Who Is 'Number One'" and the story by Anna Katharine Green, great writer of mystery fiction, will bear the same title when it is published in book form after the serial has completed its run.

Paramount has demanded that its first serial satisfy in every particular the standard that exhibitors have learned to expect from Paramount pictures. A corps of motion picture expert writers, art directors, photographers, producers, editors and artists are concentrating their efforts toward making "Who Is 'Number One'?" a serial of undisputed quality.

Thousands of feet of retakes are being made, entire episodes are being reconstructed in order that no part of any episode shall drop into the category of ordinary serials. Paramount realizes the importance of gaining for its serials the same confidence that exhibitors place in its other productions, and "Who Is 'Number One'?" will not be shown anywhere until the entire fifteen episodes have passed every test.

When "Who Is 'Number One'?" is ready—some time in October—exchanges will be furnished prints of the entire production, so that if exhibitors choose they can see every reel of the serial before they sign a contract.

GAUMONT FOR WEEK OF SEPTEMBER 17.

The Gaumont-Mutual Weekly which will be released September 19 will contain the usual unusual scenes of timely news interest which the public confidently looks for in this news reel. As the Weekly is an up-to-the-latest-minute release, it is not possible to say in advance just what happenings will appear in a number until it "goes to press". But a staff of enthusiastic news-photographers stationed all over the world, including the military cameramen of the Societe des Etablissements Gaumont who are with the American expeditionary forces in France and on the battle front, insure that spectators of the Mutual Weekly will receive the earliest possible photographic advice of the march of our boys toward Berlin.

"Reel Life," the Mutual film magazine, does not show news events, but longer, fuller subjects which are current at all times. Issue No. 73, which will be released September 20, contains three subjects which are real features: "Running an Airplane Without Danger" shows how aviators can learn to fly before they leave the earth. "Student Officers" illustrates how the young commanders of our new army are learning the up-to-date methods of modern warfare. "The Principle of the Gyroscope" is a rare, scientific article so clearly pictured that no one can see it without being entertained. A picture of the weaving of President Wilson's portrait in fabric, and an animated drawing from America's leading humorous weekly, "Life," showing how you feel when a big car passes your "flivver", complete the reel.

CABANNE FINISHING "DRAFT NO. 258."

Although Director Wm. Christy Cabanne's contract with Metro expired on September 2, he will continue with that organization until the completion of his newest war picture, "Draft No. 258." The possibilities and magnitude of this production were not realized until Director Cabanne had gotten well into it. He estimates now that it will be a picture seven or eight reels in length, with stupendous scenes and groupings.

There will be no definite announcement of Director Cabanne's plans until after "Draft No. 258" is finished. The dynamic director has a number of offers under consideration, but has decided to take his time in making a decision. Several propositions for the production of his own pictures on a basis of state rights have made the most direct appeal to him so far.

The conspicuous position which Director Cabanne occupies in the motion picture world among producers and exhibitors, to whom he has never offered a failure, and the further fact that he has been the author and director of some of the most popular of screen dramas, makes his future plans of general interest. His most recent picture, "The Slacker," of which he was author and director, is playing to crowded houses from Coast to Coast.

"THE BRIDE'S SILENCE" (Mutual).

Gail Kane, the Broadway star who is making a series of pictures for the Mutual release at the studios of the American Film Company, Inc., Santa Barbara, is starred in "The Bride's Silence", a five-reel mystery drama, scheduled for release September 10.

"The Bride's Silence" is the fifth of Miss Kane's Mutual productions. It was staged under the direction of Henry King. The story is by Daniel Frederick Whitcomb, author of "Little Mary Sunshine" and more than two hundred other successful motion picture productions. The story involves a prominent New York family. Miss Kane is supported by Ashton Dearholt, a stage and screen actor of note; Henry A. Burrows, James Lee Farley, Robert Klein and Lewis J. Cody.

"THE YANKS ARE COMING!" IN UNIVERSAL CURRENT EVENTS.

Universal covered the big military parade in New York, August 30, with six of the best cameramen on the staffs of the Animated Weekly and Current Events. Every interesting feature in connection with the greatest mustering of armed troops that the city has witnessed since Civil War days was pictured, from the start at 110th street to the disbanding of the husky 30,000 at Washington Square. Although the parade

Scene from "Current Events No. 17" (Universal).

was not over until three o'clock, the Universal version was shown on the screens of the Broadway and other leading New York theaters the same evening. Some 450 feet of selected views have also been incorporated in the 17th issue of Current Events, released September 1.

Besides picturing Manhattan's farewell to her boys, the Universal scored a beat on competing news weeklies by securing permission to send a cameraman with the 22d Engineers to Spartanburg, S. C. In this way, the entire journey of Colonel Vanderbilt's famous regiment will be pictured from the time it left Fifth avenue until it turns into cantonments prior to its embarkation for France.

This issue of Current Events will also contain a series of exclusive views of the graduating exercises at West Point.

"WHO SHALL TAKE MY LIFE" (Selig).

Thomas Santschi and Fritzi Brunette enact important roles in "Who Shall Take My Life?" the Selig feature film written by Maibelle Heikes Justice, and presenting a convincing plea against the evils of capital punishment. The drama not yet presented to the general public is said to be one of the most gripping productions of the film world. Santschi enacts the role of "Big Bill" O'Shaughnessy, a bridge tender, while Fritzi Brunette plays the part of a girl of the underworld who loves the bridge tender and, when cast aside, becomes embittered and revengeful. How the web of circumstantial evidence enmeshes "Big Bill" O'Shaughnessy, how the girl finally confesses her part in the plot against him, how the bridge tender is led to the electric chair and then—Well, "Who Shall Take My Life?" is a stirring and convincing plea for the abolishment of capital punishment.

"Who Shall Take My Life?" and the propaganda it advances has been endorsed by the Maurice Kovnac, National Secretary of the Anti-Capital Punishment League of America; former Warden Osborne, of Sing Sing Prison; members of the Anti-Capital Punishment League of Chicago, all of whom have viewed the film.

EDITH STOREY IN DUAL ROLE.

In "The House in the Mist", the forthcoming Metro wonderplay in which Edith Storey will make her bow to Metro screen patrons, the favorite star will be seen as both mother and daughter, first in fascinating crinolines and powdered hair, and later in the mode of the present moment.

In this story, adapted by June Mathis from the novel of Octavus Roy Cohen and J. U. Giesy, the mother of Carma Carmichael marries the wrong man. She marries Roger, a carefree ne'er-do-well, whereas it is his brother, Quincy Carmichael, who has a heart's devotion to offer her. She makes her choice between the two at a costume ball where the guests are garbed in the manner of 1832. Miss Storey has never looked more attractive than she does in the full panniers and silk brocades of that period. The ballroom scene is a brilliant one, resplendent in laces, frills and powdered wigs, with men and maidens dancing the minuet and quaint old-fashioned "square" dances.

Later, as Carma Carmichael herself, Miss Storey appears in modern evening gowns and "sport" clothes. Plenty of incident is arranged for the Cohen-Giesy story, and Tod Browning, who is directing the production, has developed it in terms of good red-blooded action.

Two Mutual Features for Sept. 10
Ann Murdock and Gail Kane Are Starred in Five and Six-Reel Subjects.

THE first of the Frohman Empire All-Star subjects will be released on the Mutual Film Corporation's schedule September 10 when Ann Murdock returns to the screen in "Outcast", a six-reel picturization of the Broadway success. On the schedule with "Outcast", under President John R. Freuler's policy of "two star productions a week", will be released "The Bride's Silence", a five-reel American Mutual drama starring Gail Kane.

"Outcast" is a screen adaptation of Hubert Henry Davies' startling and sensational play, which scored a hit on Broadway with Miss Murdock in the stellar role. The picture was directed by Dell Henderson. Miss Murdock is supported by a notable cast, which includes most of the original company of players who appeared in the play.

"The Bride's Silence" is the fifth of the series of American Mutuals starring Miss Kane, who deserted the footlights of Broadway to go to Santa Barbara to make pictures for Mutual. The picture was originally announced under the working title of "The Unafraid". It was directed by Henry King. It is an unusual and thrilling mystery story by Daniel Frederick Whitcomb. Miss Kane's return to the screen has been justified by the success of the series of productions in which she has recently been starred.

"Jerry's Whirlwind Finish", a one-reel Cub comedy, is on the Mutual release schedule for Thursday, September 13. The picture features George Ovey, the funny man of the Cub's. On Wednesday will be released Mutual Weekly No. 141, carrying current news, on September 13 Reel Life No. 72, the Mutual-Gaumont screen magazine, will be released. It shows "Tree Planting in the National Forests," most of the pictures being taken in the Wind River nursery of Washington. "Hunting Turtle Eggs" is another subject covered, while "Testing an Auto Tube" shows a remarkable exhibition of the strength of the inner tube of motor tires, the experience of motorists notwithstanding. The reel carries an interesting picture of the midnight sun from Alaska.

"LOST IN TRANSIT" ABOUNDS IN HUMAN INTEREST.

While patrons of the photodrama have grown accustomed to expecting genuine touches of human interest in all of George Beban's productions, it is safe to say that they will be agreeably surprised when "Lost in Transit" is shown, for it contains a greater amount of those features which appeal to human sympathy than anything in which he has heretofore appeared. September 3 is the release date of "Lost in Transit," and the fact that it is from a story by Kathlyn Williams, also a Paramount star, is an added feature of interest. The scenario was prepared by Gardner Hunting, and the direction was most capably handled by Donald Crisp.

In the supporting cast, besides Bob White, the child actor, are Helen Eddy, who has been seen so often in Mr. Beban's pictures for Paramount; Henry Barrows, Pietro Sosso, Vera Lewis, Frank Bennett and others.

The settings are extremely realistic, and not a point has been overlooked that would tend to make the picture more pleasing or natural.

HARTFORD THEATER SAFE ROBBED.

A. C. Morrison, managing director of the Majestic theater, Hartford, Conn., writes that the safe of his house was broken into on August 2 and $100 in charge taken. It is believed that the house was entered by someone who had the keys. The last person seen about the place was Guy Bottume, eighteen years old, who had been employed as doorman. He came to the theater on the night of the robbery to polish some brass and disappeared from Hartford the same night, leaving about 4 a. m. on a bicycle. Bottume is of light complexion, wore a blue suit and a straw hat at the time of his disappearance. It is thought he might be working in New York City. A warrant has been issued for Bottume's arrest and ten dollars will be paid for information leading thereto. Information may be sent to A. C. Morrison, owner of the Majestic theater, or to the Chief of Police of Hartford, Conn.

Guy Bottume.

EVELYN NESBIT'S SECOND PHOTOPLAY.

A company of forty people has left New York for the Adirondacks, where Miss Evelyn Nesbit, assisted by her son, Russell Thaw, and a cast of excellent players, will begin her second photoplay, under the personal direction of Julius Steger. The title of this picture is "The Greater Love," by James M. Starr, the scenario version of which has been made under Mr. Steger's supervision.

PATHE FRENCH WAR PICTURES SHOWS DESTRUCTION BY GERMANS.

Under the title of "In the Wake of the Huns," Pathe will release on September 23 the first authoritative pictures taken under French Government supervision of the occupation by French troops of the territory recently evacuated by the Germans after the battle of Arras. As a contribution to history, as well as for its great interest and timeliness, this two-reel picture ranks very high. Unlike many of the war pictures which have found their way to this country, "In the Wake of the Huns" is beautifully photographed. The cameraman or cameramen who took these views were artists. By intelligent selection of foregrounds there is a wonderful effect of depth obtained in the longest "shots," as well as those with more limited backgrounds.

The havoc in the evacuated territory is almost beyond belief. Stately chateaux, churches, city halls—all manner of buildings, both public and private—are shattered apparently beyond repair. Particularly interesting are the scenes of the Germans, when they abandoned the section, blew it up, for what reason it is hard to say. Such senseless destruction is all too apparent in almost every scene in these pictures.

NEWMAN BRASS INSTALLATIONS.

The Newman Manufacturing Company, of Cincinnati, Ohio, with branch factory located at 68 W. Washington street, Chicago, Illinois, have recently furnished the New Rialto Theater of Brockton, Mass., with the entire equipment of brass work, including a brass ticket booth, special brass Unit, frames to fit around the corners of lobby, and brass railing work and brass ticket chopper.

Mr. Papoulegs, the owner of this new theater, wanted only the very best brass work which he could obtain and selected the Newman Manufacturing Company to do this work for him. He had them build special hinged one sheet frames to fit the entire length of his lobby, which is 71 feet long. These one-sheet frames are made with lion heads and leaf ornaments on the face of frame, making same very attractive.

The Newman Manufacturing Company are also furnishing the Dusenbury Theaters, at Columbus, Ohio, namely the Grand and Vernon, with special Unit frames to fit around the corners, made of corrugated moulding. This is the very latest style of display frames. This concern is running a night shift in order to take care of orders and thus give prompt service.

EMMY WEHLEN IN "NOBODY".

Exquisite Emmy Wehlen, one of the most delightful of Metro stars, has commenced work on her new Metro wonderplay, "Nobody", a screen version of the novel of the same name by that prince of story tellers, Louis Joseph Vance. Charles A. Taylor has adapted the story for the screen. Directing "Nobody" is William C. Dowlan, and assisting him is Benjamin S. Kutler. "Nobody", published by the Charles H. Doran Co., was originally issued in serial form under the title "An Outsider". This "Outsider" is Sally, who up to the time the story opens has been a shop-girl in a department store. So well does the role of Sally fit Miss Wehlen that Mr. Vance might easily have written the story with her in mind.

A capable cast has been chosen for the star for this production. Herbert Hayes will play Trego, the western millionaire. Florence Short will play Mrs. Standish, the clever society woman who steals her own jewels. Ilean Hume, the clever and pretty Metro player, will have the part of Lucy Spode, a young worker in New York's art colony. Virginia Palmer and Boyce Combe are other members of the cast.

BROWNIE VERNON IS A BUSY LADY.

Since her elevation to stardom, in conjunction with Franklyn Farnum, on the Bluebird program, Brownie Vernon has found nothing dull, from a professional standpoint, in her moving picture life. She appeared in seven exciting comedy-dramas, as co-star with Mr. Farnum and when it was decided to continue Farnum as a lone-star on the program Miss Vernon was transferred to Elmer Clifton's company as co-star with Herbert Rawlinson.

"Flirting With Death", the first Rawlinson-Vernon Bluebird, will be released Sept. 24, and a second Bluebird, "It's Up to You", has just been finished for the same stars. Now Miss Vernon has begun work under Allen Holubar on "The Twisted Soul", in which she will be individually starred.

"UNDER FALSE COLORS."

On September 23 Pathe will release another Gold Rooster play, in which Frederick Warde and Jeanne Eagels have the leading parts. It is called "Under False Colors," written by Lloyd Lonergan, directed by Emile Chautard and produced by Thanhouser. The last time these two stars appeared in the same production was in "The Fires of Youth," which was more than ordinarily successful and was very well received by the critics. The story is most timely, dealing as it does with Russia just prior to the dethronement of the czar.

Petrova Organization Completed

Many Well-Known Experts Join the Staff of Petrova Pictures—Baron Dew.tz Engaged.

MADAME PETROVA has announced the personnel of the staff that will assist her in the production of Petrova Pictures. An innovation, so firmly grounded on hard common sense that it will probably be adopted by all studios seeking to produce perfect dramas, is revealed in Petrova's engagement of an art connoisseur-regisseur, in the person of Baron Dewitz, to see that the actors appearing in Petrova Pictures dress, bow, eat, fence, write telegrams, telephone and dance in strict accordance with the social customs and practices of the country in which the scene of the play is laid.

The Baron's first duties will be to co-operate with Director George Irving in making the big spectacular scenes and the locale of her first picture absolutely authentic and correct. A regisseur can best be described as "a consulting technical director." His work consists of removing all of the little inconsistencies which are apt to creep into the film, and which, to an exacting audience, are inexcusable. A few years ago such defects would have passed without a murmur, but today the engagement of the Baron is Petrova's answer to the public's just requirements. It is therefore safe to say that when an audience views a scene in Petrova Pictures it can be sure that it is an accurate representation.

Other experts who will assist Director George Irving in the production of Petrova Pictures are: Robert North, studio manager, who brings to his new work a fund of experience gained while serving in this capacity with other companies. Harry B. Harris, camera man, was associated with Petrova in former pictures, and assisted her director, Mr. Irving, in the production of "Raffles." Mrs. Emma B. Clifton will be the continuity writer for Petrova's first picture, the story having been written by Petrova herself. Mrs. Clifton has collaborated with Petrova on former occasions. Messenier, from the Biograph Studios, will be Petrova's technical director.

It has been decided by Frederick L. Collins, president of Petrova Pictures Company, to present Petrova Pictures to the public through one of the most powerful, yet dignified publicity campaigns in the history of motion pictures. The plans embrace magazine, newspaper, billboard, and direct-by-mail advertising on a countrywide scale. Daniel M. Henderson, who has had charge of advertising campaigns for McClure Pictures and Superpictures, will manage the advertising and general publicity campaign for Petrova Pictures.

Madame Petrova has engaged Miss Beulah Livingstone as her personal representative, in charge of her special publicity work. Miss Livingstone was formerly associated with Thomas H. Ince as his general publicity representative in the launching of "Civilization" in New York. She was general publicity representative last season for Henry W. Savage, and previous to that conducted special publicity campaigns for David Belasco, F. Ray Comstock, Elizabeth Marbury and others. She also handled the New York publicity for Arthur Hopkins when he had Mr. and Mrs. Vernon Castle on their whirlwind dancing tour of twenty-four cities.

New Fairbanks-Artcraft Picture Finished

"The Man From Painted Post" to Be First Artcraft Release in October—Star and Company to Arrive in New York Early Next Week for New Production.

A TELEGRAM received at the New York headquarters of Artcraft Pictures from John Fairbanks, general manager of the Douglas Fairbanks company, announces the completion of "The Man From Painted Post," which has been in the course of production during the past month in Wyoming. The entire Fairbanks organization is highly enthusiastic over its newest offering.

Replete with the swift action and thrills of a story dealing with the cattle rustling days of the West, together with the most beautiful scenic displays of Wyoming, the latest Fairbanks-Artcraft picture discloses the popular exponent of the smile in a role said to be quite different from any of his previous screen efforts. In addition to being a typical Fairbanks vehicle of the rapid-fire variety, the story allows the player a great opportunity of proving his dramatic ability. Various scenes of tense interest afford the star a chance to display his versatility as an actor. In contrast to these situations are many humorous bits showing the experiences of Douglas as a supposed "tenderfoot" among the cowboys.

Douglas Fairbanks and his company is expected in New York early next week for the production of several scenes of his next Artcraft picture. The company will remain in New York only long enough to film the desired scenes, after which it will return to California to finish the picture.

"THE LOST EXPRESS" (Mutual).

Helen Holmes' latest Mutual-Signal fifteen chapter photonovel "The Lost Express," the first chapter of which will be released on September 17, is without doubt the most thrilling adventure drama in which the intrepid young star has appeared on the screen.

The story, which was written by Frederick B. Bennett, is based on the amazing disappearance of an express train between way stations on an absolutely straight piece of railway track with no switches or sidings. How this train is disposed of by a band of robbers constitutes the mystery of a drama that is as full of mystery as it is of adventure, and which is engrossingly interesting in every one of its fifteen episodes.

The new photonovel has been directed by John P. McGowan, who has directed most of Miss Holmes' plays and one of the most widely traveled men in the motion picture world. McGowan knows how to get the right atmosphere in "outdoor stuff," and his genius in the selection of locations for "thrillers" is not to be outdone.

Included in the cast of "The Lost Express" are Leo D. Maloney, Thomas Lingham, William Brunton, Edward Hearn, Al J. Smith, Andrew Waldron, V. O. Whitehead, S. A. Sues, R. V. Phelan, Clyde Roe, William Behrens, Charles U. Wells and Lenren Maxem, all regular actors in the star's support.

ALL KEITH THEATERS BOOK PATHE WAR PICTURES.

One of the largest bookings made for motion pictures was that consummated the last days in August by the B. F. Keith circuit and the Official Government Pictures, distributed by Pathe, for a showing of these war pictures that will be over 5,000 days and will amount to almost a quarter of a million dollars.

All the theaters on the Keith circuit will show these latest pictures of the war. Beginning Monday, September 17, and continuing for three weeks, these pictures will be the headline feature of the Keith vaudeville houses.

Picture Theaters Projected

FRESNO, CAL.—Hippodrome Circuit has leased the Fresno theater for a period of ten years. L. L. Cory, owner of, the building, will expend about $25,000 for improvements.

LOS ANGELES, CAL.—R. H. Arnold Company have the contract for the theater under construction at the corner of Third street and Broadway. The project represents an investment of $100,000.

LONG BEACH, CAL.—Palace theater, managed by William J. Fahey, is being remodeled.

MANTECA, CAL.—Steve Pelton, of San Jose, has leased space in the Palm building. He will fit it up as a moving picture theater.

OAKLAND, CAL.—A moving picture theater at the corner of Piedmont street and Linda avenue, to be known as the New Piedmont, will be opened to the public shortly by D. C. Rosebrook.

PORTERVILLE, CAL.—Extensive improvements will be made to the Monarche theater.

SAN FRANCISCO, CAL.—Weeks & Day are preparing plans for a theater to be erected on Broadway, near Stockton street. It will be known as the New Broadway and have seating capacity for 2,000 persons. It will be conducted under the management of Max Blumenfield.

SAN FRANCISCO, CAL.—An addition will be built to the St. Francis theater.

SAN JOSE, CAL.—Theater will be erected on the site of the Auditorium, with seating capacity for 1,800 persons. M. Blumenthal, of San Francisco, is the lessee.

BRIDGEPORT, CONN.—Feuer-Sagerstein Theatrical Enterprise Corporation has been incorporated with a capital of $30,-000. The purpose of the company is to construct, buy and own various moving picture theaters. At present the company owns the Hippodrome theater in this city and a theater in Bristol, Conn.

WILMINGTON, DEL.—Theater which Rush & Andrews are erecting will be completed about November 1. It will be known as the Vanderbilt.

CHICAGO, ILL.—James Svehla will erect theater at corner of Marshfield avenue and Forty-seventh street, with seating capacity for 3,000 persons and costing $250,000. Theater will be operated by Jones, Linick & Schaefer.

CHICAGO, ILL.—E. P. Wach, 5311 S. Kedzie avenue, is having plans prepared for a one-story moving picture theater and store building, 50 by 60 feet and 42 by 60 feet, to cost $13,500.

CHICAGO, ILL.—J. A. Loranger, 111 W. Washington street, has plans by Paul F. Olsen, 127 N. Dearborn street, for a one-story moving picture theater, 75 by 125 feet, to cost $60,000.

COOKSVILLE, ILL.—Profit and Stagner, of Anchor, have taken over the moving picture theater formerly conducted by O. J. Breidenbach.

EAST ST. LOUIS, ILL.—Theater erected on Main street by Maurice V. Joyce and Ernest Schmalzried has been completed.

MORRIS, ILL.—M. J. Hogan, Jr., and R. L. Davison, of Seneca, owners of the Dreamland theater, have purchased the Royal theater.

PETERSBURG, ILL.—Elite theater has been remodeled, redecorated and reopened to the public.

TAYLORVILLE, ILL.—Joseph McCarthy, owner of the Empress Picture theater, contemplates expending about $10,000 in remodeling the structure.

MARION, IND.—Grand theater has been opened to the public under the management of W. D. Clark.

ROCHESTER, IND.—J. F. Dysere plans to erect a moving picture theater, with seating capacity for 500 persons.

BURLINGTON, IA.—Grand opera house has been reopened to the public.

KINGSLEY, IA.—Jesse Schofield has purchased the Hoops theater.

MILO, IA.—J. G. Tharp is the new proprietor of the Star theater.

ONAWA, IA.—Fairchild and Payne have disposed of their moving picture theater to Krigstin and Wonder.

POMEROY, IA.—George Hockeschwender has disposed of his moving picture business to Richard Moore.

SPENCER, IA.—Fraser theater, formerly conducted by William Fraser, has been taken over by D. J. Strow and H. B. Gray, of Fort Dodge. Mr. Strow is the principal owner.

BROCKTON, MASS.—Rialto theater, at 56 Main street, has been opened under the management of William J. Papouleas. The house has seating capacity for 1,200 persons. Up-to-the-minute system of ventilating is a feature.

DETROIT, MICH.—Colonial theater, at the corner of Sibley street and Woodward avenue, will be opened to the public on September 17.

JACKSON, MICH.—Mrs. Mary E. Jackson has purchased the Crown theater on West Main street and plans to remodel the structure.

MINNEOTA, MINN.—Crescent theater has been opened under the joint management of George Benson and E. B. Kiley.

MONTEVIDEO, MINN.—Star theater has been leased by E. E. Marsh.

NEW RICHLAND, MINN.—Faust theater has been closed for two weeks during which time it will be redecorated.

PRESTON, MINN.—Edward Johnson has disposed of his moving picture business to Mr. Smelzer.

STAPLES, MINN.—Palace theater has been leased by A. A. Green.

TRACY, MINN.—Walter Heine has disposed of his interest in the Colonial theater to T. H. Webb.

WALTHAM, MINN.—O. W. Root of Brownsdale has purchased the moving picture business of E. E. Dennis.

HATTIESBURG, MISS.—A new moving picture theater will be opened here in the near future by the Tri-State Amusement Company of Meridian. The house will be under the management of C. R. Hatcher.

AURORA, MO.—A. L. Johnson has disposed of his moving picture house to Ernest Williamson of Pittsburg, Kan.

KANSAS CITY, MO.—Work has been started remodeling a theater building for the Columbian Amusement Company, southwest corner Twelfth and Wyandotte streets. The improvements will cost about $4,000.

OAK GROVE, MO.—An airdome having seating capacity for about 400 persons has been erected here by D. F. Trigg and N. W. Lemasters.

SEDALIA, MO.—The Sedalia theater has been remodeled at a cost of $6,000. The house will be devoted to high-class pictures and vaudeville. Jack Truitt is the manager.

ST. LOUIS, MO.—Frank G. Root has purchased ground on the west side of Broadway, between Lafayette avenue and Soulard street, and will improve it with an addition to his present moving picture theater.

ANACONDA, MONT.—The Broadway theater is to be remodeled at a cost of about $100,000.

BAKER, MONT.—The Lyric theater has been opened by Mogren & Hazelton.

BUTTE, MONT.—Broadway theater is to be completely remodeled, new seats installed and the entire inerior changed. It is estimated that the improvements will cost about $100,000. The house will be devoted to high-class pictures and vaudeville.

LIVINGSTON, MONT.—Arcade theater, formerly conducted by Dorman-Kellogg, has been taken over by G. H. Howard.

OUTLOOK, MONT.—Star theater, formerly conducted by Joe Cairns, has been leased by J. L. Burns and H. Tschen.

WINNETTO, MONT.—W. E. Dickson has the contract to build an addition to the Aridto theater.

AMHERST, NEB.—A new moving picture house, with seating capacity of 250, has been opened here by William Buettner.

CENTRAL CITY, NEB.—C. E. McDonald has purchased the Empress theater from Kerr Brothers.

HAVELOCK, NEB.—The Joyo theater has been purchased by R. W. Wolverton.

GENEVA, NEB.—Grand theater has been taken over by J. E. Zimmer.

IMPERIAL, NEB.—George Brewer has disposed of his interest in the Imperial theater to A. C. Norman.

LINCOLN, NEB.—George Tobin, 1948 J street, has the contract to erect a one-story moving picture theater, 50 by 140 feet, for Nellie C. Buck, to cost $15,000.

NEBRASKA CITY, NEB.—The Empress theater, formerly conducted by E. W. Blakeslee, has been taken over by George Stevenson.

OMAHA, NEB.—Paul Le Marquand and W. Le Doux, lessees and managers of the Empress theater, have leased the Brandies theater.

SEWARD, NEB.—A building is being remodeled here for Fred and Will Hayland for a moving picture theater.

SEWARD, NEB.—Will and Fred Mayland, of Omaha, have opened a moving picture theater here. The house has seating capacity for 500 persons.

ASBURY PARK, N. J.—The St. James is the name of a new moving picture house opened here by Walter Rosenberg. It has seating capacity for 2,300 persons.

HACKENSACK, N. J.—James Tracey, northeast corner Main street and Salem place, contemplates making alterations to his moving picture theater.

PASSAIC, N. J.—Harris Brothers, 184 Fourth street, have plans by Abram Preiskel, Hobart Trust building, for a one-story and balcony moving picture theater, 75 by 100 feet, to cost $60,000.

TYRONE, N. MEX.—Robert Belb has leased the moving picture house formerly conducted by Simon B. Casey.

CORINTH, N. Y.—Tiffany & Conrad, Phelps building, Binghamton, N. Y., are preparing plans for a one-story and gallery moving picture theater, 50 by 90 feet, to cost $12,000.

Trade News of the Week

GATHERED BY OUR OWN CORRESPONDENTS

Week's News from Boston Film Territory

Globe Feature Film Works Out Complete Scheme for Percentage Basis for Its Pictures in New England—Paramount-Artcraft Changes—Notes.

By Richard D. Howe, 80 Summer Street, Boston, Mass.

BOSTON, MASS.—An important change in the policy of the Globe Feature Film Corporation, which went into effect September 3, is announced by General Manager Harry G. Segal. Under the new plan all feature productions released through this organization will be sold to the exhibitor on a straight percentage basis.

A careful survey of the entire New England territory has been made by General Manager Segal and Exchange Manager Robert W. Cobe, each city and town has been figured down to a certain specified percentage basis. The figures for the new proposition have been derived not from the estimated population of the city or town, but from the actual industrial conditions of the community.

Mr. Segal states that while prices may fluctuate, the price to the exhibitor will remain the same. It is announced that productions will cost the exhibitor the same amount on release date as one year later. One price will be set and there will be no bargaining on sales.

One, two or three-day runs will cost the exhibitor the same identical price and no reductions or excess charges will be made to exhibitors playing a three-day run or the man using a one-day run. All charges will be the same.

Frank McKay Will Be Fox Sales Representative.

Boston, Mass.—Frank McKay, formerly manager of the Kriterion Film Company, of this city, has resigned his position and joined the Boston office of the Fox Film Corporation as a sales representative in Massachusetts and along the Cape. Mr. McKay succeeds Samuel Steinfeldt, who has been appointed New England manager for the Louis J. Selznick Enterprises.

Changes in General Officers and Staff of Paramount-Artcraft.

Boston, Mass.—Several important changes have been made in the Boston, New Haven, Conn., and Portland, Me., offices of the Paramount and Artcraft Pictures Corporation as a result of the new selective series booking plan of these concerns.

The general management of the joint business in New England is in the hands of Harry Asher, formerly manager of the Boston office, and he will now have supervision over all of the New England offices of the two concerns.

Manager Asher brings to Boston as publicity manager of the two interests John P. McConville, a Portland, Me., newspaper man and formerly secretary to former Governor Curtis of Maine. An account of Mr. McConville's experience and a picture were recently printed in this paper.

Joseph A. McConville, a brother of John P. McConville, who was formerly assistant manager of the Boston office of Paramount, has been advanced to branch manager of the New England office of both Paramount and Artcraft.

George K. Robinson, formerly Paramount publicity manager, becomes sales manager in the Boston office of both concerns, and Samuel Bernfield, continues as branch manager for Artcraft.

Other changes include: A Barry, formerly Paramount booker, becomes booker for both interests; Moxley Blumenberg, the Portland, Me., manager, becomes manager for the Maine, New Hampshire and Vermont interests of Artcraft and Paramount, and Henry T. Scully takes over the whole of Connecticut, a part of Rhode Island and Massachusets, as his district in the management of the joint interests, with headquarters in New Haven.

Dudley Street Theater Has New Manager.

Roxbury, Mass.—Hanford Wallins, former manager of the Mystic theater, Malden, Mass., has been installed as the new manager of the Dudley Street theater in Roxbury. Mr. Wallins is a well known moving picture exhibitor and is one of the oldest moving picture men in New England. He succeeds Hugo O'Neil, who has become a salesman for the Universal Film Company in Boston.

S. J. Steinfeldt Heads New England Selznick.

Boston, Mass.—General Manager Arthur S. Kane, of the Louis J. Selznick Enterprises, Inc., has appointed Samuel J. Steinfeldt to represent the Selznick productions in New England. For some months Mr. Steinfeldt has been a sales representative in Massachusets for the Fox Film Corporation under Manager William D. Shapiro, of the local exchange. He was greatly missed by that organization.

J. Lester Reardon, owner of the Cross Street Orpheum theater in Somerville, Mass., and former manager of Greater Vitagraph's Boston office, who a few weeks ago was appointed head of the New England Selznick office, remains with the Selznick Enterprises as an assistant to Manager Steinfeldt.

General Manager Kane located the new Boston offices of the Selznick company temporarily at No. 69 Church street, in the exchange of the R. W. Lynch Enterprises.

Manager Steinfeldt has taken on Max Carmusion, formerly Maine, New Hampshire and Vermont representative of the Universal, as a New England salesman. Mr. Carmusian is a widely known roadman and should be a big asset to the Selznick people.

M. J. Coyle Joins Eastern Feature Staff.

Boston, Mass.—Herman Rifkin, president and general manager of the Eastern Feature Film company of this city announces the acquisition of M. J. Coyle, an experienced roadman, to his staff of New England sales representatives. Mr. Coyle has been assigned to the Massachusetts territory and feels sure of success in his new appointment. He turned in good results his first week at work.

General Manager Rifkin states that his long list of features, for which he controls the New England distributing and states rights for, are doing a fine business. His newest Ivan picture, "Babbling Tongues," is going over exceptionally. Mr. Rifkin has closed a deal with the Ivan people to handle all of their productions in this territory.

Waterbury's New Rialto Opens Sept. 3.

Waterbury, Conn.—The new Rialto theater in Waterbury, Conn., formerly the Bijou, opened September 3. The new moving picture house, with a seating capacity of about 1,400, is one of the most beautiful theaters in Connecticut and is magnificently furnished throughout. Every thing has been arranged for the convenience of the theater's patrons.

Manager Nichols has planned a grand opening for his new theater and has booked "The Honor System" for the initial night.

Fire Destroys Eastern Film Studio.

Providence, R. I.—A large amount of valuable film went up in flames when fire destroyed the studio of the Eastern Film Company, here, on Thursday, August 23. The loss is estimated at $100,000.

The Eastern Feature Film Company for some time has been producing film for the general market. The company officials would not state when they could resume business.

Exhibitor Hawes Was on His Job.

Boston, Mass.—The alertness of Manager Charles Hawes of the Puritan theater, a moving picture house on Washington street, this city, averted a possible panic in the theater when the blowing out of a fuse caused a flash of flame to burst forth frightening the audience.

Some excited person in the audience shouted "fire" and women and children rushed for the exits. Many were caught and trampled upon before they could be rescued. Manager Hawes immediately leaped upon the stage of the theater and, shouting to the excited audience, told them to keep their seats. His quickness prevented more serious consequences. Manager Hawes and Special Officer John E. Smith quieted the crowd and the performance was resumed.

M. H. Hoffman Chooses Boston Offices.

Boston, Mass.—The New England head-quarters of the M. H. Hoffman Productions, Inc. will be at No. 16 Piedmont street, which is the general office of the Federal Feature Film Corporation, of which Samuel V. Grand is president and general manager.

A private trade showing of two important Hoffman features, "The Fighting Chance" and "The Sin Woman" attracted a large number of exhibitors to the Fenway theater, this city, where the run-offs were made, through the courtesy of Manager Stanley Sumner of the Fenway.

Halifax Family Theater to Play Up Pictures

Has Been a Vaudeville House With an Occasional Picture—Contracts for Universal Output and Begins With "Red Ace."

By Alice Fairweather, The Standard, St. John, N. B.

HALIFAX, N. S.—Some decided changes have taken place in the Family theater, known as "Acker's", in Halifax, N. S. This has been a vaudeville house, with just an incidental picture. Beginning August 25 L. R. Acker will show entirely Universal pictures, with four acts only of vaudeville. He has booked the Universal service for twenty-six weeks and asked for an option later.

He starts the serial, "The Red Ace", on the same date and through the week will use as a feature Bluebird, Butterfly and L-Ko comedies. G. A. Margetts, of St. John, has just returned from Halifax and will go back this week to start the advertising campaign. I believe the Herald and Mail, leading morning and evening papers, are to carry a large space, starting off the pictures thoroughly.

The theater is to be redecorated throughout, the seats upholstered in cretonne, new seats put in the balcony, new electric light fixtures installed and a regular little palace made of the house. An American decorator is doing the work.

The owners of the building are making several necessary alterations to comply with the building and fire regulations of the City of Halifax.

G. A. Margetts Will Manage U. State Rights.

St. John, N. B.—G. A. Margetts has been appointed manager of the Universal for the Maritime Provinces. He will handle at least twelve big productions during the year besides the Alice Howell Comedies. Mr. Margetts continues as manager at the St. John office of the company as well.

It is expected to have one of the comedies here for screening during the coming convention.

Local 497 Gets Charter.

Halifax, N. S.—The moving picture machine operators and theatrical stage employees of Halifax have secured a charter in the International alliance of Theatrical Stage Employees of United States and Canada. The number of this local is 497, and the charter gives it jurisdiction over all operators and stage employees in the Maritime provinces. The officers elected for the ensuing year are:

F. P. Metzler, president; Tom S. Daley, vice-president; H. J. Ward, financial secretary; A. A. MacDonald, corresponding secretary, Strand theater, Halifax; W. B. Fox, recording secretary; A. Flynn, J. O'Brien, E. Harrington, trustees; M. Lannigan, sergeant-at-arms.

Mr. Daley, the vice-president, is a former St. John boy, having been operator at the Gem theater, St. John, for some time.

Perkins Interests Get Government Films.

St. John, N. B.—Allan Christie, manager of the Perkins Electric and the Independent Film and Theater Supply companies, has received news from Montreal that this company has been appointed by the British Government to handle all official films, such as British cinema war weeklies and all big war pictures. The company expects to have four prints. The first is to be the arrival of the United States Fleet in British waters. This picture is exclusive and an official Government picture. It has been booked by the Imperial theater, Montreal. "The Battle of Arras" will probably be shown in Halifax very shortly, and the fleet picture will be in St. John in September. Allan Christie has just returned from Halifax, where he was in the interests of the electrical side of his business. He states that business in that line is fair.

Jottings from Maritime Provinces.

St. John, N. B.—C. J. Godet, of Happyland theater, Prince Edward Island, was in St. John last week. Mr. Godet is an ardent horseman and was one of the judges at the races run at Moosepath, St. John, N. B., recently.

Charlottetown, P. E. I.—J. G. Armstrong, who is associated with F. G. Spencer in the capacity of treasurer, is visiting C. J. Gallegher, of the Prince Edward theater, Charlottetown, P. E. I., for some weeks.

St. John, N. B.—F. G. Spencer, of St. John, is traveling from one of his new theaters to another and is personally superintending the remodeling and decorating of all three (Amherst, Woodstock and Fredericton).

Truro, N. S.—The Princess theater, managed by A. A. Fielding, for F. G. Spencer, St. John, has had a new projection booth added to it. This is said to be the finest booth in the Maritime Provinces.

St. John.—R. G. March, of the Specialty Film Import, has come back from a trip through Nova Scotia, where he did some good business. N. W. Mason, of the Academy of Music Co., New Glasgow, has booked Pathe features and the serial, "The Fatal Ring", for New Glasgow. At Pictou, W. O. Wheton, of the Opera House, will show "The Fatal Ring", as will D. A. McKay, of the Bijou, New Waterford, N. S.

St. John.—At the office of the Specialty Film Import many inquiries are being received regarding the new Pathe serial, "The Seven Pearls", featuring Mollie King and Creighton Hale. This serial will be released in this territory the week of September 17.

West St. John, St. John.—William Smith, of the Empress' theater, West St. John, last week closed with the Pathe Exchange for no less than three of their serials and will run an all-Pathe program, features, comedies, weeklies and serials. The serials are "The Double Cross Mystery", "The Fatal Ring" and the "Neglected Wife".

Yarmouth, N. S.—K. Keltie, of Yarmouth, is in St. John arranging for his programs.

Moncton, N. B.—Mrs. R. H. Davidson will close her house, the Dreamland, August 25, for one week, when the theater will be redecorated and a number of new seats installed. Mrs. Davidson has booked from G. A. Margetts "The Voice on the Wire" and Butterfly features.

Pine Tree State News

By J. P. Flanagan, 151 Park View Avenue, Bangor, Me.

Kellermann Players Net $4,000 for Hospital.

BAR HARBOR, ME.—Society paid more than a dollar a minute to admire itself and see Annette Kellermann do a three or four-minute swimming exhibition, at the fashionable Bar Harbor Swimming Club.

The exhibition was for the benefit of the Bar Harbor Hospital and Miss Kellermann, who is here making a new sub-sea picture "Queen of the Sea"—consented to give the performance. Nearly $4,000 was raised and this will enable the hospital to keep open throughout the year.

Miss Susette Sturgis arranged the affair and every cottager in Bar Harbor was there. The congestion of automobiles at the entrance to the club house was so great that many of the box holders were unable to get in to the beginning of the exhibition, which was delayed in order that as many as possible might be present.

After the swimming exhibition, which was repeatedly applauded, Miss Kellermann was given a reception on the lawn and a tea by Mr. and Mrs. Herbert L. Satterlee, Mrs. William Lawrence Green, wife of the president of the club, and other prominent social leaders.

The boxes, holding five persons, sold for $50, while the reserved seats were disposed of for $6 each.

Neal W. Cox President of Gold Moon Pictures.

Portland, Maine.—An error in our report of the officers of the Gold Moon Pictures Corporation has been noticed. We give a correct list of the officers of that company as follows: President, Neal W. Cox; vice president, E. T. Rundlett; treasurer, Sumner E. Coleman; clerk, Percy B. Maxon. The office of the Gold Moon Corporation is at 502 Congress street, Portland, Maine.

Handsome New Theater Promised Baltimore

Parkway Theater Company Plans a 2,000-Seat House in the North Avenue and Charles Street Section—Will Be the Homewood.

By J. M. Shellman, 1902 Mt. Royal Terrace, Baltimore, Md.

BALTIMORE, MD.—The announcements were made last week that Baltimore is to have one more large and handsome theater in the North avenue and Charles street section. The Parkway Theater Company, Harry W. Webb, president, plans a playhouse to have a seating capacity of 2,000. This company is now operating the Parkway, Strand and McHenry theaters and the new building will probably be called the Homewood. It will be on the northeast corner of Charles street and Lafayette avenue. According to the present arrangements of the company work will begin immediately and it is thought that the new theater will be ready for the public about January 1.

On August 24 the Homewood Amusement Company filed incorporation papers with the State Tax Commission, its capital being $100,000 preferred and $190,000 common stock. Among the directors of the new company are George A. Finch, Howard M. Emmons and Edward C. Sandell. The last named is of the Lord Calvert Theaters Company and it is understood that he will manage the new house. Blanke & Zink are the architects and the

general design will be on the Colonial lines. Work will be rushed so that the new house may be opened by December 1.

A. M. Seligman Goes to Pittsburgh Theater.

Baltimore, Md.—Affable and courteous, A. M. Seligman, who has acted as treasurer at Nixon's Victoria, 415 East Baltimore street, since that theater was taken over from Pierce & Scheck, last October, and has many friends in this city, will shortly leave for Pittsburgh, where he will become associated with the management of the Nixon theater.

Beautiful New Theater for Hanover.

Hanover, Pa.—On Friday, September 14, the Strand, a new and beautiful motion picture theater, will be thrown open to the public. It is the new $800,000 building now nearing completion. M. Schaeffer will be the proprietor.

This theater is fireproof throughout. The seating capacity is 498, with standing room for 200. The chairs will be the orchestra type, upholstered with green leather, which carries out the general color scheme of the decorations. The auditorium of the theater will be decorated very artistically by a series of dark green panels with trimmings of gold leaf. The woodwork will probably be done in white with the walls of old ivory, the cornice being done in old ivory and gold. A mellow glow of light is obtained by the indirect system.

The operating room is equipped with metal doors. Two Power's 6B projection machines have been installed. The throw to the screen is 90 feet and it is a Mirror screen measuring 13 by 16 feet.

Perfect ventilation has been obtained by building a system of eight ventilators, each measuring about three feet across, on each side of the theater, each of which is equipped with a powerful exhaust fan. The lobby is trimmed with marble.

Theater at Red Lion Reopens.

Red Lion, Pa.—Robert Quigley, proprietor of the Photoplay theater of this city, announces that he will reopen this playhouse on Saturday, September 1. This house has been closed during the summer months, and while dark Mr. Quigley has greatly improved its appearance by having it thoroughly repainted and overhauled.

Huntingdon Theater Changes Hands.

Baltimore, Md.—J. Coghlan has given up the management of the Huntingdon theater, 225 West 25th street, and Mr. Simpson has leased the playhouse for a period of five years. The Huntingdon has been greatly improved, having been entirely repainted, new frames having been built on the front for paper, and the lighting system entirely rearranged. This house has a private dynamo which furnishes all the current needed to run the machines and the lights.

Vitagraph $1,000 Essay Prize Awarded.

Baltimore, Md.—On Tuesday night, August 28, the $1,000 prize for the best essay written on "How America Should Prepare," which was offered by the Vitagraph Company in connection with its production "Womanhood, the Glory of a Nation," was awarded to Henry H. Bliss, of Baltimore, at the New theater, 210 West Lexington street. The presentation of the money, which was in one-dollar notes, was seen by many of the patrons of this house. President Albert E. Smith of the Vitagraph, was represented on this occasion by Nat S. Stronge, the publicity director for this company. Mr. Bliss is a widower who is employed in the engineering department of the Pennsylvania Railroad. He is a true patriot and his two stalwart sons resemble him in this respect, for they are connected with the Aviation Corps at Fort Myer, Va. Just before the affair was staged L. A. DeHoff, manager of the New theater, entertained several of his newspaper friends and Mr. Stronge at a very enjoyable little dinner at the Rennert Hotel.

Garden Ballroom to Open.

Baltimore, Md.—It is announced by Harry Woods, manager of the Garden theater, Lexington street at Park avenue, that the beautiful ballroom of this house will be reopened to the public on Saturday, September 15.

Bridge Theater Contest Coming.

Baltimore, Md.—Through a misunderstanding it was stated in last week's issue that Louis Schlichter, manager of the Bridge theater, ran a criticism contest for his patrons during the week of August 20 on Mary Pickford in "The Little American." This was wrong, for the contest will be held on September 12, and four prizes will be awarded, $5, $3, $2 and $1 each. The essays are limited to 200 words.

Stanley Theater Organization Has Outing

Over 200 Persons Connected With the Stanley Theaters and Exchanges Enjoy a Picnic at Doylestown—Merry-Making and Athletics.

By F. V. Armato, 144 North Salford Street, Philadelphia, Pa.

PHILADELPHIA, PA.—The first Stanley outing, including the employees of the Stanley theaters and those of the exchanges belonging to this organization, was held on Sunday, August 26, at the National Farm Schools, near Doylestown. The happy crowd, 200 strong, were fully prepared to start the day with merry making of all sorts. Headed by a committee, consisting of B. F. Tickner, Jules W. Catsiff, David S. Fuhrman and Miss C. W. Wachwits, they assisted in amusing the crowd with their various contests.

A strong line-up for a ball game was headed by Robert Lynch, captain of the exchange men's team, which was pitted against Captain Jules W. Catsiff's team of theater employees. The game has hotly contested until the eighth inning when the theater employees' team gracefully retired in favor of the exchange mens' team, who were leading by the score of 10 to 6. H. Tyson and Bill Bethel on more than one occasion brought home the bacon by driving out home runs at opportune moments and making several spectacular plays.

A general rumpus was started by a pie-eating and watermelon contest. Bert Tickner succeeded in consuming more watermelon than the rest of the party and David Fuhrman and Jules Catsiff ran a dead heat in the pie-eating contest. Miss Anna Laverty and Miss C. W. Wachwits were two of the popular girls present who attended to witness this massacre. The theaters represented were The Stanley, Great Northern, Imperial and Rialto, and the exchanges represented were Metro, Goldwyn, Selznick and Peerless.

Allentown's Hippodrome Reopens September 10.

Allentown, Pa.—The Hippodrome, now being remodeled by George Bennethum at a cost of $40,000, when completed will be one of the finest houses in the state. The opening is expected to take place on or about September 10, the equipment will be entirely of the latest type and everything will have an up-to-date finish. This is the theater which Mr. Bennethum recently bought for $97,000. A $10,000 billiard room will be on the second floor and a fine tonsorial parlor with six chairs will be in the basement to make this place a huge success.

State Moving Picture Censorship Changes.

Harrisburg, Pa.—Eleven changes in the staff of the State Board of Censors for moving pictures have been made, without official announcement. Charles E. Bell becomes chief clerk in place of Joseph Berrier, transferred to inspector; J. A. McLaughlin, first assistant chief clerk, vice R. W. Read, removed; Maude M. Ely, second assistant chief clerk; Thomas Watson, chief inspector, vice Henry W. Lewis, removed; R. F. Costello, advanced to inspector; William E. Conner made inspector; E. Fred Dummel and Daniel McDonald, operators; James J. Brennen, janitor; Mary Leatherberry, clerk, as substitute for Francis Sears, enlisted, and R. W. R. Work, chief operator, as substitute for Samuel Johnson, enlisted.

Exhibitor Rappaport Aids Cigarette Fund.

Philadelphia, Pa.—Charles Rappaport, one of our prominent exhibitors, aided Sergeant C. R. Tracey, of Truck Company No. 3, who is camping at Mt. Gretna, in collecting the sum of $68 for their cigarette and tobacco fund. Many of the prominent exchange men and exhibitors contributed freely to the fund.

Philadelphia Theaters Use Street Car Ads.

Philadelphia, Pa.—Street car advertising is being indulged in by a large number of theaters, among whom are such houses as the Iris, Lafayette, Logan, Auditorium and the 56th Street theaters.

E. Millegan Traveling With Submarine Film.

Philadelphia, Pa.—E. Millegan, the traveling road representative, is on a tour throughout the state with the new Peerless production, "20,000 League Under the Sea", which has met with such wonderful success here.

Special Films Shown in Philadelphia.

Philadelphia, Pa.—During the week of August 27, the following new photoplay attractions made their debut here." An intensely human story, gripping in every situation, and splendidly portrayed, makes "The Honor System," a Wm. Fox production, at the Stanley, one of the season's film masterpieces. It has been booked for a two-week engagement at the above theater, starting from August 27. The Regent opened with "The Girl Without a Soul," in which Viola Dana is the attractive heroine, this picture already having won local approval. During the last part of the week Mary Anderson will be the star in "Divorcee." For the opening week of its new season the Strand is offering the ever-popular Douglass Fairbanks in "Down to Earth", this will be replaced in the latter part of the week by "The Law of the Land", another new production in which Olga Petrova appears. At the Arcadia this week is H. B. Warner in "God's Man", a gripping film by George Bronson Howard. The Palace has one of its best attractions of the season in the presentation of the new Herbert Brenon picture, "The Lone Wolf," from the well known novel by Louis Joseph Vance. This cast is headed by Hazel Dawn and Bert Lytell. The Victoria will divide the week with "The Silent Witness", in which Gertrude McCoy is the heroine. This will be followed on Thursday by Mme. Petrova in "To the Death", in which she appears as Blanca, a Corsican girl. The Great Northern opens the week with "The Golden Fool", which features Bryant Washbrun. The Leader starts the week with a double bill, including "The World Apart' and "His Wedding Night," with Fatty Arbuckle the feature. The Alhambra opens its regular season with Enid Bennett in "The Mother Instinct".

"The Crisis" Begins Its Third Week.

Philadelphia, Pa.—"The Crisis" entered on its third week beginning Monday, August 27. It has now played to almost 50,000 persons in Philadelphia. Persons have crowded the Garrick to see this film version of Winston Churchill's popular novel and to enjoy the additional treat provided by the theater management.

"Redemption", a Success.

Philadelphia, Pa.—At the Forrest theater the screen production, "Redemption", with Evelyn Nesbit and her son, Russell Thaw, has reached its last week. The presentation of Evelyn Nesbit in pictures has excited an interest only equaled by the appreciation of her work. The picture has proven very popular. The story of the film is built largely around the star's own tragic experience and critics say that accounts for the realistic way in which she plays. Miss Nesbit has proved herself a very earnest artist and the public is recognizing her as such.

The Week's Trade News in Pittsburgh

Jewel Productions, Inc., Opens Office—Longacre Distributing Takes Room in Blue-Bird Exchange—Business Changes Noted Last Week.

From Pittsburgh News Service, 6104 Jenkins Arcade, Pittsburgh, Pa.

PITTSBURGH, PA.—The Jewel Productions, Inc., have established a Pittsburgh branch office in the Seltzer Film building, 1201 Liberty avenue, with Fred Flarity, one of this city's most able film men, in charge as manager.

Mr. Flarity was at the head of the local branch of the General Film for the past year and a half.

The Jewel exchange was thrown open for business August 27, but the installation of the equipment and furnishings has not yet been completed. Manager Flarity plans to make the quarters among the finest in the city. It has been announced that the release date of the first offering of the new exchange, "Come Through," a seven-part feature, will be September 15. The production has been screened for the local trade and met with much approval.

Walter F. Kinson Heads Pittsburgh's General Film.

Pittsburgh, Pa.—Walter F. Kinson, recently with the Mutual in this city, has been appointed manager of the General Film office here. Mr. Kinson is a film man of broad experience and one of the best known of the younger managers in Pittsburgh. He was at one time manager of the local office of the General for several years and his return is welcomed by many of his old associates and friends.

Longacre Distributing Office Opens.

Pittsburgh, Pa.—The Longacre Distributing Company has opened an office in the quarters of the Bluebird exchange, Film Exchange building, Pittsburgh, for the handling of the new Century Comedies. Sidney Lenchner, of the Pittsburgh Bluebird sales staff, has been placed in charge. The new productions, in which Alice Howell is featured, will be released monthly, the first, entitled "Balloonatics," being scheduled for release Sept. 1.

F. J. Herrington Running for City Office

Pittsburgh, Pa.—Local exhibitors and exchange men have received with much approval the announcement by Fred J. Herrington of his candidacy for City Council. Mr. Herrington is one of the foremost figures in the moving picture industry and a pioneer exhibitor. The entire trade is assuring him of its support in the coming election, as he is a tireless champion of the picture interests. Mr. Herrington has a large following throughout the city, and his election to the important office of Councilman is regarded as practically certain.

Samuel Sivitz on Road to Recovery.

Pittsburgh, Pa.—Samuel Sivitz, publicity manager of the Rowland & Clark theaters, with offices in the Westinghouse building, Pittsburgh, has been seriously ill for several weeks, but is now on the road to recovery. M. J. C. Kornblum, formerly manager of this department, is in charge during Mr. Sivitz's absence.

Local Notes of Passing Interest.

Manager Burhans, of the Fox exchange, reports that contracts have been renewed by the Olympic theater, Fifth avenue, and the Cameraphone theater, East Liberty, for the Fox regular weekly feature service.

The Theatorium, Brookville, Pa., was closed September 1 for extensive remodeling and renovation, and indications are that when the improvements are completed the theater will be one of the most attractive in its locality. Manager J. M. Scribner states that the house will be formally reopened in about three weeks.

George Schweitzer, manager of the Century Family theater, East Ohio street, Northside, Pittsburgh, and president of the Motion Picture Exhibitors' League, has just returned from his vacation, which he spent on an extended tour in his new automobile.

The Leader Film Service, 804 Penn avenue, Pittsburgh, has purchased the Western Pennsylvania and West Virginia rights on the notable film production "Ignorance," featuring Earl Metcalf and Mary Moore.

Newark News Letter.

By Jacob J. Kalter, 25 Branford Place, Newark, N. J.

Remodeled Newark Theater Reopens.

NEWARK, N. J.—After several months of extensive remodeling and renovating the Newark theater, at 196 Market street, will reopen its doors September 2 to an invited audience composed of city officials, press representatives and others to the number of 2,500. The theater in its new dress is hardly recognizable.

The property on which the show house is situated was sold two years ago by the H. C. Miner estate to the Beaver & Market Realty Corporation, of which Max Spiegel is president and Edward Spiegel acting director. The concern has spent over $400,000 in improving the theater, which has been practically reconstructed, steel and reinforced concrete being the principal materials used.

The proscenium arch has been set back to provide larger capacity, the old boxes have been removed and boxes of a recent design have been substituted and the old gallery and balcony have been replaced by one large balcony. The inaugural attraction is Mary Pickford in "Rebecca of Sunnybrook Farm."

John B. McNally, well known local theatrical man, will assume active management of the house. Mr. McNally has been resident manager of the Keeney theater here and more recently has managed the Strand theater. He is exceedingly active in the various theatrical organizations. Mr. McNally will be assisted in his new duties by George Turner, also well known locally.

F. D. Allison Managing Strand.

Newark, N. J.—Frank D. Allison is now the manager of the Strand theater, 113 Market street, owned by the Frank Hall interests. Mr. Allison hails originally from Pittsburgh, where he owned and managed several moving picture theaters, including the Pastime, the Dreamland and the Homewood.

Montclair Has Open Air Theater.

Montclair, N. J.—An open air theater that has been constructed on the grounds of the Montclair High School will be opened September 6. A concert will be the initial attraction. The funds from the affair will be expended in the beautifying of the grounds adjacent to the outdoor theater.

"Jack and the Beanstalk" at the Terminal.

Newark, N. J.—The William Fox "Jack and the Beanstalk" was the attraction at the Terminal theater, Park place, during the week of September 2. A children's special matinee will take place daily at 10 a. m. Manager Moe Kridell has had beautiful twenty-four sheets posted up over the city and has employed other methods of advertising the feature.

Operators Represented at Paterson.

Paterson, N. J.—The Moving Picture Operators' Unions of Newark and Hudson County were represented at the annual convention of the New Jersey State Federation of Labor August 20, 21 and 22. John R. Walsh, Reginald Cooper and Jack B. Higginson represented Newark Local 244, while Hudson County Local 384 elected Edward Dougherty, Anthony Boscarelli and E. W. Bordman as its delegates.

Lyric Theater Reopens.

Newark, N. J.—The Lyric theater, 211 Market street, was reopened August 25 by the owner and manager, Dr. R. G. Tunison. The house has undergone extensive improvements during the summer months.

S. Pfirschbaum With Adler.

Newark, N. J.—Semi Pfirschbaum has become the right hand man for Lester Adler, manager of the World Film, Strand theater building. Semi was formerly connected with the Royal Features Film Company, and more recently with the various film delivery companies.

Children's Matinee at City.

Newark, N. J.—One of the most popular innovations at the City theater, Seventh and Orange streets, is the children's matinee, which is held twice a week, Wednesday and Saturday. Managing Director Leon O. Mumford arranges only pictures which have a direct appeal to the children for these shows. At present the Edison Conquest Pictures are being featured. This house is the only one in the Roseville section showing these educational reels.

Obtains Patent on Machine.

Montclair, N. J.—Frank L. Dyer, of this city, has secured a patent on a motion picture projection machine.

Wilmington, N.C., 5 Cent Shows Charge 10

Jitney Theater Raises Its Price Under Stress of War Times—Old Days Recalled When a Show Was Somewhat Different from Now.

By D. M. Bain, Wilmington, N. C.

WILMINGTON, N. C.—Effective next Monday, Sept. 3, the Bijou, which has the honor of having been the first motion picture house in the South, and which has the unique record of never having changed admission charges of strictly five cents during the twelve years of its existence, will change its policy and increase admission price to ten cents.

The Bijou was started in a tent on the same site of the present building, by Messrs. Howard & Wells, pioneers in the motion field in the South. Sawdust carpeted the floor, a few incandescents strung from pole to pole, were the illumination, and in winter during a big coal heater gave the heat, and it had a phonograph ballyhoo out front. In its early days, before the public had learned to grasp the meaning of the flashing pictures, the operator acted as spieler, spelling from the porthole of the booth a description of the action as it was unfolded on the screen. Three reels of pictures was then considered a whale of a show, and only one reel was changed daily, giving one new reel and one repeater every day. An illustrated song, of course, was necessary to complete the program, together with that other relic of a prehistoric past, a slide bearing the readings. "Just One Minute Please, to Change Reels." The Bijou building was erected on the same lot five years ago, and has been one of the most successful theaters in the South, from which the owners have enlarged their activities to the point where they control all five of the Wilmington theaters at present.

Prosperity Comes to Charlotte, N. C.

Charlotte, N. C.—Charlotte last week enjoyed their first season of "war prosperity" attributable to the immense army of workmen employed at the cantonment grounds erecting the mammoth city for the forty thousand soldiers who will soon invade the place for training. The first pay day for the three thousand workmen was Saturday, September 25, and $130,000 was loaded on to a large van from the Realty National Bank, and escorted by soldiers with drawn bayonets was taken to the cantonment camp office where it was distributed to the men. Saturday night a general invasion of the city took place and the shows did the biggest business in their careers, records being smashed all down the line. Proprietors of Charlotte's theaters are very optimistic over the outlook for the biggest season in the history of the city, with the coming next month of the soldiers and theatrical stocks are on a big boom.

"Womanhood" Breaks Record of Strand.

Fayetteville, N. C.—Manager H. T. Drake of the Strand, Fayetteville's most modern and newest theater, reports all house records broken with "Womanhood" this week, due to co-operation of the War Department in putting it over big. Mr. Drake notified the Adjutant General at Washington of his date, and Corporal Williams was sent down from Washington to assist in staging the mammoth patriotic spectacle in a proper manner. A tent was rigged up in the lobby of the theater, with stacked guns, bayonets and small cannon much in evidence. Mr. Drake is attending the convention at Ocean View, Va., this week.

Local Notables at Ocean View Convention.

Wilmington, N. C.—Messrs. Percy W. Wells, B. H. Stephens and Marx S. Nathan, of this city, are attending the Film Convention and Exposition at Ocean View, Va., this week. Word from Harry Bernstein, of Richmond, who has charge of the picture stars promised will be there except Pearl White, who was unable to leave location in the Adirondack mountains to attend.

DETROIT JOTTINGS.

The formal opening of the New Adams theater, Detroit, devoted to stock and the property of John H. Kunsky, took place Saturday, Sept. 1, to big crowds. R. O. McGaw is the house manager for Mr. Kunsky.

Milton Bryor, formerly Pathe salesman in Detroit, has been transferred to Chicago.

George W. Weeks, division manager at Detroit for Foursquare pictures, is back from Chicago, where he had a conference with M. H. Hoffman.

Unless granted exemption it looks very much as if A. I. Shapiro, Goldwyn manager at Detroit, will see training within the next 30 days, inasmuch as he is in the first selective draft and passed an excellent physical examination.

Jules Levy, now covering the state for General, has booked service into 90 per cent. of the houses he calls on, which is a mighty good record.

Earl H. Rathbun, of the State Film Co., Detroit, has been examined for the first draft, but will probably be exempted owing to dependents.

Detroit Operators Dissatisfied With Scale

Demand Increase in Wages of From $3 to $5 a Week—Got Increase Last Year— Put Joker About Rejecting Slides in Demand.

By Jacob Smith, 713 Free Press Building, Detroit, Mich.

DETROIT, MICH.—A serious problem confronting the motion picture business of Detroit right now is the demand of the union operators for increased wages, a new schedule of hours and several other demands that are meeting with opposition from the exhibitors. The latter have been holding daily conferences, some with members of the union in an endeavor to come to some amicable understanding, but up to the time of writing no final agreement had been reached from both sides.

In the first place, the increase in wages amounts to from $3 to $5 per week. Last year the unions were granted an increase, and the new agreement is for one year only. Then there is a schedule of hours which is not considered fair to the industry for the reason that some theaters operate on a different schedule of hours than called for in the agreement. Then again the union demands 80 cents per hour for all overtime, with not less than $3 for extra matinees and not over three hours' work. Another clause in the contract gives the union the final right to reject any slides to be thrown on the screen other than the regulation theater slide. This is resented by exhibitors, who feel that they have a right to be the final judge of what goes on their screen, being their property and not that of the operators' union. However, this is a clause which will be readily stricken out, inasmuch as it was put in the agreement only as a "joker," as one operator expressed it.

Exhibitors grant that the operators are entitled to some wages, but they also feel that inasmuch as they are now paying increased taxes, increased film rental, and that last year the operators refused to carry film, putting them to an expense of $3.50 per week extra, they are going pretty near the limit. We trust that by the time our next letter is ready the whole matter will be satisfactorily adjusted on both sides.

Two More Theaters May Be Started.

Detroit, Mich.—A number of new theaters are contemplated for the city of Detroit, which is very encouraging to the industry in the face of building conditions, such as the high prices for materials, labor and the uncertainty of getting orders properly filled.

The DeVoe Construction Co., with offices at $21 Book building (a Chicago company, which financed large Detroit offices), are considering the erection of a theater seating 1,800 on Grand River avenue, about a mile past the Grand Boulevard, in a district that is growing very rapidly. They plan to own and operate the enterprise.

Another theater is under consideration for the east side by the Schram Amusement Co., who now operate the Bijou, Monroe and Bernhardt theaters, and who are building the Farnum theater in Hamtramck district.

Theaters under construction right now at Detroit are the Farnum, the DeLuxe, one at Fort and Military, and another in Springwells for J. L. Selling.

Palace Theater at Flint Has Premier.

Flint, Mich.—The Palace theater, in Flint, Mich., was officially opened on Thursday evening, August 30, with vaudeville and pictures. Several dozen Detroit exhibitors and exchange managers were on hand for the opening to extend felicitations to Col. W. S. Butterfield, the owner. Frank Butterfield is the house manager. The new Palace seats about 1,500 on two floors, although most of the seats occupy the main floor. The booth is 34 by 50 feet and is equipped with Power's

machines and a Hertner transaverter. Most of the equipment was installed by Ray Branch of the United Theater Equipment Co. The Hertner transverter was installed by M. S. Bailey, the New Michigan representative. The policy will be six acts of vaudeville and short reels of film. Quite a crowd of noted theatrical men from Chicago and New York were also on hand for the opening.

Exchanges Moving Into Film Building.

Detroit, Mich.—The first exchange to move into the new film building, Detroit, at John R and Elizabeth streets, will be the Mutual. Next will follow the K-E-S-E and possibly Pathe. By the 1st of October most of the exchanges in town will be over there, exclusive of Paramount, Metro and the John H. Kunsky enterprises. The building is the finest of its kind in the country, with fireproof steel and concrete vaults, safes and everything right up to date to conform to the building code.

M. S. Bailey Exploiting Hertner Transverter.

Detroit, Mich.—M. S. Bailey, formerly manager of the Universal branch in Detroit, is back in the picture business, but this time in the supply end of it. He is also president of The Metropolitan Co., specializing in cartoon film advertising. Mr. Bailey has offices at 903 Peter Smith building, and has already secured the exclusive state agency for the Hertner Transverter, made in Cleveland. He is going to make a strong drive for business and has already made several important sales. J. H. Chambers, sales manager for Hertner products, was in Detroit last week and closed up the deal with Mr. Bailey. The latter has other lines for which he is now endeavoring to secure the Michigan sole agency.

O. Henry and Other Short Films in Big Demand.

Detroit, Mich.—Dave Prince, manager of the General Film, Detroit, is confident that short subjects are coming back. He said to the World: "We are doing an enormous business on O. Henry, Stingaree and Black Cat subjects, all two reels each, and we expect to do equally as well with the new four-reel Falcon Features and the new four-reel O. Henry subjects. I don't say that exhibitors want a program of short subjects seven nights a week, but surely out of the seven they can easily devote two nights to such a program, and give their patrons something away from the long feature. The best indication that short subjects are coming back is the big business our exchange is doing."

Interesting News Notes from Detroit.

J. M. Duncan, manager Vitagraph exchange, Detroit, reports heavy bookings on "The Fighting Trail."

M. W. McGee, manager Majestic theater, Detroit, returned August 28 from a two weeks' motoring trip to Chicago.

J. O. Brooks, manager of the Madison Film exchange, Detroit, reports that bookings are heavy for fall and winter on "The Crisis," "Enlighten Thy Daughter," "Idle Wives" and "On Trial." Mr. Brooks, by the way, will also be special field representative for the Columbia Booking exchange, another Kunsky enterprise, which will book vaudeville to theaters.

Buffalo Feels Need of Exchange Building

Fifteen or More Exchanges Now in the City Are Scattered—Film Center Would Add Efficiency and Solve Rent Problems.

By James A. McGuire, 152 N. Elmwood St., Buffalo, N. Y.

BUFFALO, N. Y.—The opinion has frequently been expressed that Buffalo is sorely in need of a film exchange building. This city has developed into a live film center in the past few years. The fifteen or more exchanges are scattered here and there about the downtown business section, and it is generally conceded that for efficiency reasons they would have many special advantages if concentrated under one roof.

Some other cities the size of Buffalo boast of such buildings, whose tenants are delighted with the benefits derived from having the film industry so centralized. The exhibitors, express companies and the exchange men are quick to realize that this concentration offers advantages over Buffalo's plan of having the exchanges spread over a wide area. Buffalo's capitalists are often alert when it comes to dropping their surplus coin into some wildcat venture, but they seem to sink into a state of coma when urged to consider the erection of a fireproof film exchange building in this city.

Some of the local exchange men say their present facilities are adequate, while others claim their location are far from satisfactory. New exchanges coming to Buffalo often have a great difficulty in finding suitable quarters. Many of the landlords object to the presence of film in their buildings on the ground that it means a sharp advance in the insurance rates. They say that film vaults, no matter how fireproof, are objected to by the other tenants.

It is said a new "film building" in Buffalo would be a paying investment from the beginning and would soon have its full quota of tenants. Such a structure, it is said, would attract more exchanges to this city, and as competition is the life of trade, such an enterprise would thus give a powerful impetus to the local film industry.

Manager C. H. Williams Announces Staff Changes.

Buffalo, N. Y.—C. A. Williams, recently chosen manager of the Modern Features, Buffalo, has made these appointments in his staff: Miss Rebecca Rappeport, assistant manager; Miss Annette Frey, inspector; Hiram Hatch, shipper; Victor Zebil, transferred from the office to the road.

Operator Shafer Wins World Film Prize.

Ogdensburg, N. Y.—E. J. Shafer, operator of the Strand theater, Ogdensburg, won the World's monthly operators' contest for keeping his films in the best condition.

H. E. Lotz Heads Buffalo Triangle.

Buffalo, N. Y.—H. E. Lotz has been appointed manager of the Triangle Film, Buffalo. Mr. Lotz, who was born in Buffalo, left this city twelve years ago to enter the moving picture business in the West. He was with the General Film Co. for two years in the capacity of general manager in Canada, and had supervision of all the Canadian branches. Later he came to the United States as special representative of the same company in the east and south. Last year Mr. Lotz resigned from the General to become branch manager of the Pathe in San Francisco.

Tag Day Nuisance Condemned.

Buffalo, N. Y.—The Buffalo Chamber of Commerce, of which some of the moving picture men are members, has adopted a resolution against "tag day," conducted in the streets for charitable purposes. Local showmen for a long time have been opposed to "tag days." These were quite the vogue not very long ago and were so overworked that they became a nuisance. Solicitors were accustomed to run rampant in the streets, hold up citizens for funds, follow them into the lobbies of the theaters and elsewhere, and hold up business men and their staffs. Local theatrical men realize that unscrupulous persons have been using "tag days" as a means of collecting and pocketing funds and condemn the system as no longer countenanced by progressive cities.

Veribest Pictures Opens Offices.

Buffalo, N. Y.—The Veribest Pictures, Inc., which has opened offices at 43 West Swan street, has begun a campaign on the feature, "Parentage." This company has other attractions, such as "God's Man," "Morman Maid," and "Whither Thou Goest?" The offices are being fitted out elaborately. The Veribest policy will be two features a month, beginning in October.

Buffalo Expects Good Fall Business.

Buffalo, N. Y.—Buffalo film men are alive with enthusiasm for the coming season. There is every indication that business through Western New York will be brisk and attractive. One of the new films commanding attention is "The Slacker," released by the Metro. This new war picture has proved a wonderful aid in securing recruits in Buffalo. The Metro plans to release one big feature a month. The K-E-S-E reports that the Little Mary McAllister pictures, "Do Children Count" are proving a success.

Changes in K-E-S-E Buffalo Staff.

Buffalo, N. Y.—J. V. Allen has been transferred from the New York office of the K-E-S-E as assistant to Louis Green, Buffalo manager. L. A. Schaeffer, formerly booker, has been appointed salesman to work out of the Buffalo office of the K-E-S-E.

Have Responded to Bugle's Call.

Buffalo, N. Y.—Among the patriotic young film men who have answered the "bugle call" are H. Lawrence, Isadore Wartikowski and John Child of Buffalo. Mr. Lawrence is a salesman for the Mutual, Buffalo, and Mr. Wartikowski was night shipper on the same force. Mr. Child has been with the World Film for two years. He left Saturday for New York City. George Landis, formerly of Chicago and Indianapolis, is taking Mr. Child's place, covering Western New York.

Relven Theater Company Incorporated.

Buffalo, N. Y.—The Relven Theater Company has been incorporated in Buffalo to do a theatrical and realty business, with a capital stock of $10,000. The incorporators are Walter W. Newcomb, Fannie M. Mumerson and Irving L. Fish, of this city.

Notes of Trade from Buffalo.

Buffalo, N. Y.—Charles L. Taylor, of Metro, Buffalo, is touring New York State in his automobile.

Mr. and Mrs. J. Savage, of the Como theater, Buffalo, have returned from an extended auto trip through the east. They visited Boston, New York, Philadelphia.

All the employees of the Victor Film Co., Buffalo, have returned from their vacations.

Cleveland News Letter

From M. A. Malaney, 218 Columbia Bldg., Cleveland, O.

A Romance in Cleveland's Filmdom.

CLEVELAND, O.—The fade out in the last reel of a real moving picture romance occurred in Cleveland last Wednesday afternoon, when Miss Helen Muckley, photoplay editor of The Leader, became Mrs. John DeKoven Hilt, formerly photoplay editor of that paper, who recently received a commission as a lieutenant in the officers' reserve.

Miss Muckley met Mr. Hill when he was "doing" movies about a year ago and she was working in the Sunday department of the paper. She wished to write about films, so Mr. Hill took her to screenings and soon she was assisting him in his daily work.

Whether this was a "labor of love" or duties imposed by the managing editor, we won't say, but along about last Valentine Day Mr. Hill presented Miss Muckley with a handsome engagement ring as her valentine. Miss Muckley immediately started to wear it—in the little plush box, so no one working on the paper or film men saw it. The engagement was kept a secret until last Wednesday, when Lieutenant Hill returned from the officers' camp at Fort Ben Harrison, Indiana, and obtained the wedding license. The same day in St. John's Episcopal Church the wedding occurred, and Mrs. Hill, who had just returned from a vacation the previous week, plunged into her work, forgetting any such thing as a honeymoon.

New Gaiety Theater Has Its Premier.

Cleveland.—Max Lefkowich, one of the pioneer exhibitors of Cleveland, was in his glory Thursday night, August 23, when his new Gaiety theater was formally opened to the public.

Max has operated the little Wonderland theater on East Ninth street for many years. The new house, which seats close to 500, is only a few doors south of the Wonderland.

The Gaiety has all the modern improvements. There is a long lobby leading to the auditorium, which is in the rear of the building.

At the opening Max showed the Standard Film Company's production of "The Girl Who Doesn't Know," with Marie Empress in the title role. The equipment was furnished by the Oliver Motion Picture Company.

Jewel Productions Opens Offices.

Cleveland.—The new Jewel Productions, Inc., have opened up quarters here at 812 Columbia building, in charge of A. J. Mentz, a well-known film man of the Middle West.

The first production, "Come Through", will be ready for release shortly.

Leon J. Bamberger, who is establishing the offices, also has announced that an exchange will be located in Cincinnati.

The Stillman Will Remain Picture House.

Cleveland.—Marcus Loew came to Cleveland recently and left the same night, after looking over his latest theater project—the Stillman.

Mr. Loew announced that the Stillman would not show vaudeville, but will continue pictures and the prices will be lowered. He also stated that Jack Kuhn, of New York City, has been made manager of the theater.

Elyria Theater Wants New Name.

Elyria, O.—Melton Phelps, manager of the Strand theater, Elyria, together with Chris Neufer, Sam Sadaris, H. A. Dykeman and John Grumbos, have taken over the Elyria theater, formerly the Opera House and will show pictures in it. They will install new equipment and a prize has been offered for the best name for the house to be suggested to the Daily Telegram, an Elyria newspaper.

Trade Notes in Cleveland.

Cleveland.—Agnes Eyre, a young moving picture actress, who was seen in Cleveland last week in "To the Death", featuring Mme. Petrova, is spending her vacation in Cleveland, staying at the Ford residence, on Euclid Heights.

Cleveland.—The Consolidated Film Company, Cleveland, now has a complete laboratory and an expert cameraman, who is taking many local pictures for exhibitors in northern Ohio.

Dayton Weekly News Letter
By Paul J. Gray, Alhambra Theater Building.

Clay E. Brehm to Manage Keith's Strand.

DAYTON, OHIO.—According to an announcement made Saturday, the 25th, Clay E. Brehm has been appointed manager of the Strand theater here. Mr. Brehm is very popular in Dayton through having served in managerial capacities with the World Film and also the Universal Film. He was at one time manager of the World Film Exchange in New York and made quite a success with it. The Strand is one of Dayton's largest theaters and it takes a twenty-four man staff to keep things going fast in a theater that seats eighteen hundred, with balcony and gallery. The house is operated by the Keith interests and runs Paramount and Artcraft pictures, first run exclusively. If advance notices are lived up to the Strand will be one of Dayton's best managed theaters.

Little Things Are Often Best Publicity.

Dayton, O.—A novel way to restore lost articles to his patrons is practiced by Bert Frala, manager of the Alhambra theater in Dayton. On a big night when the house was filled a small boy turned in a diamond ring that he found in the theater. Not knowing who the ring belonged to and knowing that the party that lost the ring was probably not aware of it, Mr. Fiala quickly made a slide which read as follows:

Did you lose a diamond ring?

We found one.

About two minutes after the slide came off the screen a lady came to the box office and described the ring perfectly. The boy received a liberal reward and the theater too, for next day everybody within a radius of ten squares of the theater knew of the incident and advertised the theater in a way which no paid advertising can do.

Mr. Fiala is to be complimented on his quick action and also for creating something better than a press story for publicity.

New Dayton Theater Nearly Ready.

Dayton, O.—The new Dayton is rapidly nearing completion and will soon be opened. The Dayton will seat 2,500 and will be the most modern theater in Ohio.

Jottings in Dayton.

Dayton, O.—Assistant Manager George Wilson, of the Standard Film Co.'s office in Cincinnati, was in Dayton last week and reports that the Billy West comedies are going strong in this section. While in Dayton Mr. Wilson secured eight contracts for the Billy West comedies.

Dayton, O.—Through having held a private exhibition of their latest serial, "The Fighting Trail", at the Globe theater last week, the Vitagraph Co. has contracted with quite a few Dayton exhibitors to run this picture in its entirety. This is a new departure in Dayton and as appreciated by exhibitors here, as a few of them are too busy to go to Cincinnati, where the nearest Vitagraph exchange is.

Globe Films Limited Establishes Offices

Arthur Cohen Heads Film Corporation—Office in Rialto Building on Yonge Street, Toronto—Personnel of the Globe Staff.

By W. M. Gladish, 1263 Gerrard Street, East, Toronto.

TORONTO, ONTARIO.—A Canadian development of prime importance has been the establishment of the Globe Films, Limited, with officers in Toronto and Montreal. The chief of staff is Arthur Cohen, who is also head of the Globe Securities, Limited, operating the Globe and Rialto theaters, Toronto. In addition, Mr. Cohen is the "resigned president" of the Moving Picture Exhibitors' Association of Ontario. He is not the whole works, however, as he has gathered about him some of the most able exchange men in the country. His associates include Phil. Kauffman as vice-president, who was formerly general sales manager for the Famous Players Film Service, and Harry Kauffman, of Montreal, who has become general manager of the Globe company. Harry Kauffman remains in Montreal.

The Globe interests recently acquired possession of the second and third floors of the Rialto building, 219 and 221 Yonge street, Toronto. During the past few months the company has absorbed two Canadian exchanges, All-Features and the Peerless, and has also secured the Canadian rights for Ivan and King Bee releases, in addition to a number of state rights attractions, chief of which is "Redemption". The company already has four prints of "Redemption" in constant use in Eastern Canada alone. A new De Luxe edition of "The Spoilers" has also been secured for early release. One of the principal bookings for "Redemption" is that of the St. Denis theater, Montreal, the largest theater in Canada, for the week of September 17. The Photodrome, Toronto, also took this feature for two weeks, starting August 27.

When Phil Kauffman left the Famous Players Film Service he was presented with a large diamond stick pin by fellow officials and employees. He was succeeded as general sales manager by I. Soskin, who has been with the Famous Players for a considerable period. The Globe company has also closed with Mr. Humble, a Toronto writer and advertising specialist, as manager of the publicity department. There are two road men attached to the Toronto office also.

Globe Films, Limited, is in a position to negotiate for large or small state rights propositions for the whole of Canada. President Cohen is particularly anxious to secure the largest independent releases available.

A recent change has been made in the management of the Rialto theater, Toronto, which is closely associated with Globe interests. W. J. Stewart, formerly manager of the Casino, Ottawa, has become manager of the Rialto in succession to R. E. Willis, who has returned to Winnipeg to manage the Rex. The manager of the Globe theater, Toronto, is T. Coulson.

The plans of the Globe company include the opening of branches in Western Canada before the end of the present year.

Herman Fischer Will Look After U. State Rights.

Toronto.— Herman Fischer formerly manager of the United Photo-Plays, Limited, has joined the force of the Canadian Universal. Mr. Fischer has taken charge of the State Rights Features Department at the Universal headquarters here and will look after the distribution of a number of attractions, the Canadian Rights Features Department of the "U". These include the special releases, "God's Law" and "Come Through", Century Comedies, featuring Alice Howell, will also be handled in Canada by the State Rights Features Department of the "U". Special managers for the distribution of these pictures from Universal branches

from Coast to Coast in Canada are to be appointed, it is announced.

Attractive Fronts and Favorable Business.

Toronto.—A very noticeable increase in attention to lobby displays by exhibitors of Toronto has taken place during the past three or four weeks. Most everybody is doing it now and the theater managers are enthusiastic in their belief that the attractive fronts have caused a substantial increase in business. Judging by statements of various managers, there is scarcely a theater in town which has not enjoyed far greater patronage this summer than during the 1916 hot season. Not one Toronto theater had a special lobby display during the summer of 1916, and therefore attention to this detail is more than probably responsible for increased attendance this year.

Toronto theaters which have had special lobby decorations this summer include the Strand, Rialto, Globe, Photodrome, His Majesty's, Red Mill and Colonial. Outside of the big Regent, these are practically all of the downtown theaters of the city.

T. J. Peart Starts Theater at New Toronto.

Toronto.—T. J. Peart, 591 Indian road, Toronto, has started the construction of a two-story moving picture theater and office building at Fifth street and Lake Shore road, New Toronto. The structure, which will cost $20,000, will include the theater, three stores and accommodation for a number of offices. The theater will seat 400 people. New Toronto has become a hustling industrial center, several large factories having been erected in the vicinity during the past year. The theater building will be of brick construction, with hardwood floors, etc., and will be ready before Christmas, it is announced.

Sam J. Massoud Buys Empress Theater.

Toronto.—Sam J. Massoud has purchased the Empress theater, 317 Yonge street, Toronto, and has made a number of improvements in the house. The ventilation arrangements have been improved and new equipment includes an organ costing $2,500. Massoud has decided on two changes of program each week and performances are given from 1 p. m. to 11 p. m. During his opening week Manager Massoud gave a nine-reel show.

Notes of the Trade in Ontario.

Orangeville, Ont.—Dr. T. G. Phillips, 185 St. Clair avenue, West, Toronto, has offered his moving picture theater at Orangeville, Ontario, for sale or rent. Orangeville is a wide-awake Ontario town and the house would make a fine opening for a hustler.

Toronto.—Announcement is made by General Manager Mulhall, of the Atlas Films of Canada, Limited, that A. Dunbar is no longer associated with that company as a director.

Toronto.—Harold Hitchinson, formerly of the Toronto World, has become assistant treasurer of the Strand theater, Toronto.

Toronto.—Many Toronto exhibitors witnessed the special presentation of the first four episodes of the new Greater Vitagraph serial, "The Fighting Trail," at the Strand theater, Toronto, on Wednesday evening, August 22.

Memphis Foresees Good Picture Season

Road Shows Have Been Hit by War Conditions—Special Shows Will Have their Place; But the Mainstay Will Probably Be Pictures.

By J. L. Ray, 1014 Stahlman Building, Nashville, Tenn.

MEMPHIS, TENN.—Operators of theaters playing big stage productions are of practically the same opinion as the vaudeville and moving picture managers in West Tennessee, to the extent that the road shows in 1917-1918 will suffer materially from the war and its consequences. This city being in a direct line of the high-class productions from Chicago to New Orleans, will receive its share of the best shows, but the general opinion prevails that another unusually successful season for the moving picture and combination vaudeville and picture houses will arrive with the cold weather.

All three of the larger Memphis theaters will be open in September. The Lyceum, under the local management of Mr. Stainback, is on the Loew Circuit, and will step from its summer to the winter season shortly. The Orpheum, on the circuit of the same name, opened its winter season August 27, and will continue to run under the active supervision of Manager Arthur Lane. The moving pictures at this house have been one of the bright spots on its program all season, and under no circumstances could the management consider removing this service from the daily performances. News and travel pictures have in the past proven a stimulus to patronage. The policy of the Orpheum will be as it has been for the past several winters, namely two performances every day, consisting of three sets of moving pictures and several vaudeville acts.

Manager Frank Gray will be in charge of the Lyric. This house will operate as a legitimate, but it is understood that a few of the largest screen productions may be worked into the bookings as the opportunities arise.

The straight moving picture houses, too numerous to mention, will continue to run as usual, with a number of improvements contemplated for the larger uptown houses. These, in addition to the new theaters put up during the summer, will furnish a battery of substantial moving picture shows for Memphis.

Open Booking Also Has Its Disadvantages.

Nashville, Tenn.—In conferring with local theater managers as to the respective merits of open booking and contract program service, it has been pointed out by one Nashville manager that while there are a number of advantages to be derived from the open booking plan, at the same time it carries its disadvantages.

"For instance," said the theater man, "I have just returned from the Southern film market centers, where I went into booking arrangements with a number of exchanges for the coming season. I found at one exchange that service which I formerly paid a moderate price for had materially increased. It looks as if they had set out to make up on the two good pictures they made each month what they would naturally lose on the bad ones. Of course, everybody will pick out the two good ones each month, which will rush the number of prints in circulation, and create a one-sided arrangement, so to speak." This is a phase of the open booking question which might not have appealed to many of the theater managers, but is worthy of note. The majority of the Tennessee managers, however, are strongly in favor of open booking.

Strand Will Reopen With 35-Cent Seats.

Nashville, Tenn.—Manager Carson Bradford announces that the Strand theater will close on September 3 for a period of one week, during which time a complete remodeling and renovation will be undertaken. A number of high-class attractions have been lined up for the reopening, the first of which will be "Within the Law." Manager Bradford intends to book a big Vitagraph picture after the house is reopened, and will institute a 35-cent admission price—the first of the kind to be charged in Nashville, but the picture will be nine or ten reels in length and based upon an unusually strong theme.

Fire Inspectors at Memphis Busy.

Memphis, Tenn.—Seeking to reduce the possibility of fire loss to a minimum, a score of trained underwriting engineers, representing the Conservation Association of Tennessee, will conduct an immediate survey of local warehouses, grain elevators, groceries, store rooms, and adjacent moving picture houses, being authorized by the United States Government to take these steps as a means of protection to the food supply of the country. It was pointed out that the loss by fire resulting from burning film in projection machines has caused fires over the United States from year to year, and while modern apparatus has brought this loss down to a much lower figure than in the past, at the same time the danger incident to certain moving picture theaters was apparent.

Cotton States Convention Filmed.

Memphis, Tenn.—The entertainment and business features incident to the convention of the Cotton States Convention Association will be recorded in moving pictures by a cameraman connected with the Majestic Amusement Company. A novelty in connection with the pictures will be the fact that all photography will be taken at night by the aid of flares, being in charge of D. B. Griswold, of the Majestic company. The films will be displayed first at the Majestic theater, and later over the South.

Nashville Orpheum to Reopen.

Nashville, Tenn.—The Orpheum theater, under the management of William H. Moxon, will be opened to the public on September 10, instead of Labor Day, September 3, as previously planned. Mr. Moxon has been in New York, but will return shortly and set to work on his plans for the winter. Some minor repairs will be made to the theater, but the larger items, such as painting and redecorating, were attended to prior to its closing several months ago, and the interior is still in good shape.

Columbia Another Long Show Town.

Columbia, Tenn.—The Vogue theater of this town is another moving picture house showing from seven to nine reels for a ten-cent admission. A goodly sprinkling of comedy relieves the performance of any tediousness which might be prevalent if the entire show was composed of drama. A recent program consisted of two reels of the serial, "Patria," a two-reel Lonesome Luke, a single reel Big V Comedy, Pathe News Reel, and Mutt & Jeff Cartoon. Columbia is a good picture town all the year around.

War Time Prices for Seats in Louisville

Fifteen Cents or More for a Seat Is the Rule Now—Changes in Policy in Several of the Big Theaters—Ready for the Soldiers.

By Ohio Valley News Service, 1404 Starks Bldg., Louisville, Ky.

LOUISVILLE, KY.—All of the large theaters of Louisville are now charging war time prices with the exception of the Mary Anderson, and the management of that theater expects to increase the ante to fifteen cents within a few days, the matter being under consideration. The Alamo theater has gone from a dime to fifteen cents, while the Majestic has been getting fifteen cents and the Strand twenty cents for some time past.

Some Big Pictures Ready for Release in Louisville.

Louisville, Ky.—The Big Features Rights Corporation has secured several new pictures which will be released in this district shortly. The principal pictures are "On Trial," seven reels, state rights in Kentucky and Tennessee; "One Law for Both," in eight reels, Kentucky, Indiana and Tennessee; "Babbling Tongues," seven reels, Kentucky, Indiana and Tennessee; and "Two Men and A Woman," five reels, Kentucky and Tennessee. This list constitutes a formidable array of big new features, and coupled with the new Chaplin releases handled by the local company in this territory, gives a good list of material to boost for the present time.

C. N. Koch Plans to Film Army Scenes.

Louisville, Ky.—C. N. Koch, manager of the Rex theater, recently returned from Clarksville, Tenn., where he made a two-reel picture of the Odd Fellows' home. Mr. Koch is now planning to make a series of army pictures at the local cantonment, these pictures to be released through the string of theaters controlled by the Broadway Amusement enterprises.

Louisville Ready for Soldiers.

Louisville, Ky.—The cantonment at Louisville has been completed, and drafted soldiers from Kentucky, Indiana and Illinois will be located here within a few days according to the press. It is estimated that between 40,000 and 50,000 men will be located here, and prospects are for the local moving picture theaters handling the largest business on record. It is thought that every theater in the downtown district, and all of those near the camp will do capacity business, while the few vacant theaters will be placed in operation as soon as the camp is occupied. Just now the outlook is far more favorable than ever before in the moving picture or other theatrical field.

Several Important Leases Expire.

Louisville, Ky.—As stated several weeks ago some big changes are likely to be made shortly in local moving picture circles. Starting September 1, the Walnut and Casino theaters were darkened. The lease of the Princess Amusement Co. on the Casino, the oldest Fourth avenue house in operation, expired on August 31. However, it is rumored that arrangements will be made to continue operations at the house. At the Walnut theater a ten-year lease expired, and the owners refused to rent the house at the old figure except on a sixty-day clause in the lease and this was refused as it would make it impossible to book pictures ahead for any length of time.

Theater Jottings in Oklahoma.

By Kansas City News Service.

Bartlesville, Okla.—Carl Gregg has recently bought the Lyric theater here. He will open with "Within the Law" on September 3.

Geary, Okla.—Rex Dunn, of Shattuck, has recently purchased a moving picture theater at Geary.

Lawton, Okla.—The Temple, a new moving picture theater here, has been formally opened to the public.

Miami, Okla.—The Miami Business Men's League will lease the city park from the city for five years, upon which there will be erected an open-air theater.

Cincinnati News Letter.

From Kenneth C. Crain, 307 First Nat. Bk. Bldg., Cincinnati.

Myrtle Theater Will Become Store.

CINCINNATI, O.—The Myrtle theater, on Woodburn avenue, Walnut Hills, one of the smallest of the Hynicka holdings, has finally been disposed of, after being on the market for several years, and will no longer be used as a photoplay house. It has been leased by a florist. The house was one of the first picture theaters in the Walnut Hills district, and did fairly well until the popularity of the Orpheum, a few blocks away, took most of the business in that section.

"Four-Minute Men" at Cincinnati Theaters.

Cincinnati.—The "Four-Minute Men" are again at work in the moving picture houses, emphasizing the need for the whole community assisting the Government in the great work of carrying on the war. The following theaters are being visited by the speakers: The Strand, Forest, Orpheum, Keith's, Walnut, Norwood Plaza, Family, Lyric and Grand.

Cincinnati Film Men Pleased With Fox Method.

Cincinnati.—The announcement by the Fox Film Corporation that exhibitors' deposits hereafter are to draw four per cent. interest has been well received here, and bids fair to dispose of the irritation which the deposit system has caused, at least as far as this company is concerned. The chief objection of reliable exhibitors to the system has been that they were deprived of the use of their money, and the allowance of interest will meet this objection. Walter Lamford, head of the publicity department of the company, was in Cincinnati lately, visiting this among other western offices.

Notes of the Trade Around Cincinnati.

Cincinnati.—George M. Cohan in "Seven Keys to Baldpate", of the stage version of which he was the producer, was the Artcraft offering at the Walnut for a week, meeting with marked success, as Cohan appears in only a few film productions, and the public seem anxious to see the famous actor-author-composer-manager-producer.

Cincinnati.—The usual engagement of the Lyman H. Howe pictures, which serves to mark the end of the summer season of pictures at the Lyric and the beginning of the regular season, started on Sunday, August 26, the travel offerings of the Howe organization for this season being the remarkable pictures taken in the Antarctic regions by the Shackelford expedition. Higher prices prevail for this engagement than for the summer moving pictures, but the houses are always large.

Hamilton.—The Grand theater, which has had a splendid summer season of moving pictures, is being prepared for its regular winter season of vaudeville and pictures combined by complete redecorating, white and gold, with green draperies, furnishing an attractive color scheme. Manager Goodwin also announces that a larger orchestra than ever before will be employed.

Youngstown.—The management of the Grand Opera House reports a pronounced hit by the Metro patriotic production featuring Emily Stevens, "The Slacker".

Akron.—The marked success of the first week's engagement of "The Birth of a Nation" at the Colonial was instrumental in bringing about a second week's run of the great feature. In spite of the high prices charged, ranging up to $1 at night, afternoon performances and $1.50 at night, full houses were the rule during the entire run.

Camp Gordon Makes Boom City in Georgia

Atlanta Feels a Bit Left-Out Through Lack of Transportation to the Camp Site —Chamblee Becomes a City.

By A. M. Beatty, 43 Copenhill Ave., Atlanta, Ga.

ATLANTA, GA.—While the people of Atlanta and especially many moving picture exhibitors, are awaiting to find whether or not they are to be isolated from Camp Gordon by lack of transportation facilities, the people of Chamblee, Ga., are preparing to do what Atlanta expected to do—take care of the 40,000 soldiers who will begin arriving at Camp Gordon on September 5.

This became evident Wednesday when it was learned that over forty stores have already been built at Chamblee and between fifteen and twenty more are planned, that more motion picture houses and other amusements will be established, that two hotels have been projected and that what was little more than a hamlet is soon to be a thriving city in its own right.

Even more interesting was the statement by a citizen of Chamblee that these enterprises are in large measure being financed by business men in Macon, Jacksonville, Columbia, Chattanooga and cities other than Atlanta, and that these men are preparing to reap the "golden harvest" which Atlanta merchants and theatrical men expected to reap, but which they are not going to reap unless a way is provided for the soldiers to come eleven miles to the city of Atlanta.

It isn't that Chamblee wants to take anything away from Atlanta. On the contrary, the people of Chamblee would be delighted to see the Georgia Railway and Power Company build a double track extension. As proof of this fact, the Chamblee committee on public safety has invited the power company not to stop its extension on the edge of Chamblee, as it plans to do, but to continue the line right on up to the Chamblee depot. The town of Chamblee will be glad to give the power company a right-of-way through Chamblee.

Sixty days ago Chamblee, Ga., was only a mile in circumference and consisted of one main street, one postoffice, one depot and two stores. Now it has forty shops already established and is surveying and grading for fifteen more.

Camp Gordon has been the making of Chamblee, but even that which has been done could not have been done if the citizens of Chamblee had not been enterprising and farsighted enough to see what was coming and patriotic enough to co-operate to the fullest with the Government authorities.

When the Government wanted to move some houses from the camp site of the Southern Railroad the people of Chamblee said "Go Ahead!" Now the Government has returned good for good by announcing that property owners can begin erecting permanent structures on the town side of the railroad, assured that the Government will not want this land.

H. R. Bannister Now Heads Atlanta K-E-S-E.

Atlanta, Ga.—Harry R. Bannister has been appointed manager of George Kleine's Kleine - Edison - Selig - Essanay branch at Atlanta, succeeding J. T. Ezell. Mr. Bannister possesses every qualification for making a successful manager, and it is expected that K-E-S-E service at Atlanta will do well under his direction.

C. A. Nathan Now With New York Concern.

Atlanta, Ga.—C. A. Nathan, after traveling the South, from Atlanta headquarters, for six months, on "The Crisis," has moved to New York City. Mr. Nathan will have charge of New York City and State for the Jewel Productions, 1600 Broadway. While in the South Mr. Na-

than made many good friends among the exhibitors, as also exchangemen.

Bob Northey Now Running Grand Theater.

Greenville, Ga.—Bob Northey, who has been leader of the Bonita theater orchestra about a year, has resigned and will assume the management of the Grand theater, Greenville, S. C.

Strand Film Company Changes Hands.

Atlanta, Ga.—The E. & H. Film Distributing Company, who for the past year has been distributing "The Crimson Stain Mystery" serial in the South, announced this week that it had purchased the Strand Film Company, at 73 Walton street, and will in the future be located in the office formerly occupied by the Strand Company.

Charles W. Harden, president of this company, was formerly district manager for the Fox Film Company in the South, and more recently of the Metro offices in Kansas City, Mo. Paul A. Engler was formerly manager of the Fox Film office in this city, and later connected with the International Film forces. They state they have decided to locate in Atlanta due to the wonderful prospects of business conditions for the coming season, especially in the amusement business.

Walter Hiers at the Rialto in Person.

Atlanta, Ga.—Walter Hiers had the chance to see himself as others saw him, and incidentally perhaps heard what others thought about him when he appeared at the Rialto theater, in person, to make a little talk Friday and Saturday about his work in the silent drama.

Hiers is one of the few comedians of prominence in the screen world who hail from Georgia. He was born in Cordele, Ga., and at the age of 14 he moved to Savannah. At present he calls New York his home.

He has been engaged in making a picture in Charleston, S. C., and getting time for a short vacation came to Atlanta to see his aunt and her husband, Mr. and Mrs. J. A. Bishop, 88 Columbia avenue. He is appearing at the Rialto at the request of the management. In "The Mysterious Miss Terry", which stars Billie Burke, he plays the comedy lead.

Death of Howard Winburn.

Atlanta, Ga.—Funeral services for Howard Winburn, pianist at the Vaudette theater, and widely known musician, who died Saturday following an attack of acute indigestion, were held Monday.

Mr. Winburn's death came as a distinct shock to his many friends in this city. Born in Atlanta, Mr. Winburn had spent practically all his life here. For a number of years he has been at the Vaudette theater, as leader of music. Mr. Winburn was an Elk and a Mason.

Atlanta Trade Jottings.

Atlanta, Ga.—The first authentic motion pictures of the landing of American troops in France was shown at the Savoy theater Monday. It was the arrival of the first army divisions on French soil and filled the Savoy to capacity.

Billie Burke played at the Rialto all this week in the first of her Paramount pictures, "The Mysterious Miss Terry." This is thought by many Atlantians to be the best picture the famous star has ever done.

LaGrange, Ga.—A. Ginsberg, proprietor of the Strand, LaGrange, Ga., was in Atlanta this week looking over some feature pictures.

Film Jottings in Kansas City Territory

Prominent Visitors—Changes in Personnel at City Exchange Offices and Among the Road Men—With Local Exhibitors—Other Notes.

By Kansas City News Service, 205 Corn Belt Bldg., Kansas City, Mo.

KANSAS CITY, MO.—The local Vitagraph office was the host on August 27 to Walter W. Irwin, vice-president and general manager of the Greater Vitagraph Company, New York City, and to H. Naugle, western division manager, with headquarters at Los Angeles. Mr. Irwin is on his way to Denver. The salesman working out of the Kansas City office called in to meet Mr. Irwin were George Ware, J. B. Lowe, William Darnell, C. F. Doles and Joseph Fox. Roy R. Wert, formerly president of the Oklahoma Exhibitors League of Oklahoma, from Enid, Okla., and several out-of-town exhibitors were also visitors at the office. A meeting was held in the afternoon at the Hotel Muehlbach, after which Mr. Irwin visited several of the local theaters.

C. D. Struble Takes Over Yale Photo Play.

Kansas City, Mo.—C. D. Struble, formerly branch manager for the Southern Triangle, is now handling the picture, "Joan, the Woman," for A. D. Flintom. He has also taken over the Yale Photo Play Corporation, which is handling only big, high class state right productions. Mr. Struble recently returned from New York City, where he made arrangements for some big state rights pictures, which will be announced at a later date.

Columbia Theater Opens for Super Features.

Kansas City, Mo.—The Columbia theater here has been reopened after being closed the entire summer. The theater will show super-features at an admission price of 25 cents. The theater will open with "Civilization," which will be followed by other big productions never shown in this territory before. It will be operated by the Columbia Theater Amusement Company, the former owners, and will have the same manager in charge. The music for the present will be furnished by a Wurlitzer pipe organ, although an orchestra will be furnished later. The theater has been remodeled and renovated. There has also been a new cooling plant installed.

General Auditor J. J. Rotchford in Kansas City.

Kansas City, Mo.—J. J. Rotchford, general auditor of the General Film Company, from the home office at New York City, is now working at the Kansas City office. He will be in Kansas City for several weeks.

S. L. Huldeman Gets Territory for General.

Kansas City, Mo.—S. L. Huldeman has been added to the sales force of the General Film Company. He will work in Kansas, Missouri and Oklahoma.

Ed. J. Eskay Gets Missouri for Mid-West Film.

Kansas City, Mo.—Ed. J. Eskay is taking over the Missouri field for the Mid-west Film Corporation. He was formerly at the Artcraft office in Chicago, Ill.

M. P. Moore Appointed Cashier at Vitagraph Exchange.

M. R. Moore, formerly of the Mutual Oil Company of Kansas City, has been made cashier at the Kansas City Greater Vitagraph office.

Joseph Fox Becomes Vitagraph Salesman.

Joseph Fox, formerly with the Mid-

west Film Corporation, has been put on the sales force of the Greater Vitagraph Company. He is at present specialty man for the Kansas City office.

J. B. Howard Joins General's Sales Forces.

Kansas City, Mo.—J. B. Howard is now a member of the sales force of the General Film Company. He formerly represented "Civilization" in this territory. He is an experienced man and will work in parts of Kansas, Missouri and Oklahoma.

Recent Visitors in Kansas City Were:

J. G. Tyndale, Elite theater, Iola, Kan.; Lewis Marcus, Majestic theater, Council Bluffs, Ia.; M. W. Reinke, Orpheum theater, St. Joseph, Mo.; Lee Gunnison, Crystal and Royal theaters, Atchison, Kan.; Robert Holmes, Royal theater, Emporia, Kan.

New Exclusive Theater Will Be Exceptional.

Kansas City, Mo.—A new exclusive motion picture theater is being built at Eleventh and Main streets, Kansas City, Mo., by Harding Bros., of Omaha. It is in the heart of the shopping district and will be about fifteen hundred. The ground, building and equipment will be an investment of $700,000. The theater will be open some time this year.

Mr. Sam Harding, owner of the Princess theater, Omaha, is one of the oldest exhibitors in the state, and says his new theater in Kansas City will be one of the most modern and equipped theaters in this country. One of the important features will be a $25,000 Austin organ, and the seats will be of the highest quality, installed by the American Seating Company, and they take special feature of the house will be the ventilation on which Mr. Harding says they have spared no expense.

Supreme Film Closes Kansas City Office.

Kansas City, Mo.—The Supreme Film Corporation has discontinued its office here at 215 Gayety building. Frank Sailsberry, who was the manager of the office, is now handling "Civilization" throughout Kansas, Nebraska and Oklahoma. All business formerly handled by the Kansas City office will be taken to the Pittsburgh, Pa., office of the Supreme Film Corporation.

Son Born to George Bowles.

Kansas City, Mo.—George Bowles, manager of the local Bluebird office, reports the birth of a son, George III, who weighed eight pounds at birth. The youngster was recently given a present of $10 by R. G. Cropper, president of the Standard Film Corporation, and who was at one time manager of the Universal office here. Mr. Bowles has recently received his exemption papers from the Government.

Missouri Theater Changes and Notes.

Excelsior Springs, Mo.—The Auditorium theater here has been sold to C. V. Tanner by S. H. Snively.

St. Louis, Mo.—Work on the new Melba theater here is progressing nicely. This theater will have a seating capacity of 1,400.

St. Louis, Mo.—William Goldman is building an addition to his motion picture house at 2812 North Van Deventer street.

Independence, Mo.—The Lewis theater here was slightly damaged by fire a short time ago.

Among Kansas and Arkansas Theaters.

Howard, Kan.—J. F. Tonken, of the Princess theater, has taken his wife to Tulsa, Okla., to place her under expert treatment for a long sickness.

Arkansas City, Kan.—Roy Burford has closed the Rex theater in order to put in a balcony in his house and to do other remodeling.

Eureka, Kan.—The Isis theater here has been sold by William Shively to C. H. Barrow, who is also the owner of the Isis theater at Augusta, Kan.

Madison, Kan.—Otto Focht, manager of the Royal theater here, will soon reopen his picture house, which has been closed for some time, owing to the electricity plant of the town being out of commission. He will begin with the "Fall of a Nation".

Coffeyville, Kan.—Mr. Kindley, of Kindley & Terry, who are operating the Drexel theater here, has left for service in the aviation corps.

Solomon, Kan.—H. C. Collins has sold the Cozy theater here to W. W. Brown.

Humboldt, Kan.—A new brick theater building has been erected here recently.

Hutchinson, Kan.—The Pearl theater, recently damaged by fire, is being remodeled and will be opened about September 1.

Satanta, Kan.—A moving picture theater was opened here recently.

Penalosa, Kan.—A. T. Ware has opened the Electric theater.

Notes from the Texas Field.

Plainview, Texas.—The Ruby theater is being remodeled.

Dallas, Texas.—The Liberty Film Company has been chartered with a capital stock of $10,000 by H. Clogenson, B. F. Yancey and J. C. Deane, all of Dallas.

Leesville, Texas.—Ground has been broken for a new moving picture theater building that is soon to be built here. The building will be of brick.

Waco, Texas.—The Queen theater here, which was recently destroyed by fire, will be immediately rebuilt by J. E. Horne, the owner of the building.

San Antonio, Texas.—A new film exchange handling 250,000 feet of film will soon be opened here with S. J. Smith, of New York City, as manager.

Indiana Trade News Letter.

From Indiana Trade News Service, 861 State Life Bldg., Indianapolis, Ind.

One Four-Minute Man Sees His First Show.

COLUMBUS, IND.—In addition to doing many other things since the war broke out, patriotism has taken the Rev. W. H. Book, pastor of the Tabernacle Christian Church, of this city, to his first moving picture show.

The Rev. Book has always been opposed to the class of pictures shown frequently at local photoplay houses, and had the distinction of being about the only person in the city who had never attended a single show. But the call of his country came and he put patriotism first, and answered the call. He was selected as one of the "four-minute men" and spoke between reels last Saturday night at the Crystal theater.

The Rev. Book said he had seen moving pictures of religious work in churches, but last Saturday was his first experience inside a real moving picture theater. As it was his first opportunity he decided to make the best of it, arriving at the theater when the show started and remaining nearly the entire evening. Following the show, the Rev. Book said he spent a most enjoyable evening and was somewhat surprised to see the large number of his church members in attendance.

E. E. Norman, manager of the Crystal, and Ernest Rogers, manager of Crump's Theater, have agreed to the proposals of the local council of defense and have made arrangements to permit the four-minute men to make speeches at the theater any time the committee may ask.

Joe Gavin to Run the Isis Theater.

Indianapolis, Ind.—The recent announcement of the appointment of Joe Gavin as house manager of Barton & Olson's Isis Theater, on North Illinois street, is welcome news to legions of Indianapolis amusement patrons, whom Mr. Gavin has served for many years. Mr. Gavin began his theatrical career as treasurer for Dickson & Talbott, working in the old Grand and Park Theaters. When the Valentine Company secured the lease on English's opera house, some twenty years ago, Mr. Gavin was made resident manager. He was treasurer of the Indianapolis baseball club from 1896 to 1900, and again from 1908 to 1910. His last theatrical work was the management of the Illinois theater, of which he was the owner.

Progress Film a New Producing Company.

Indianapolis, Ind.—The Progress Film Company, established recently with home offices in the Indiana Pythian building, in this city, has filed incorporation papers with the secretary of state to engage in the manufacture and production of motion picture plays. The capital stock is announced at $20,000. The directors are Louis M. Emmons, Carey L. Smith and Elizabeth D. Kimball.

The first photoplay to be filed by this concern, it is announced, will be entitled "Society". It is the plan in this film to depict society events of all kinds—events in which the acme of American fashions and styles may be shown as a further proof of the superiority of American fashions. "Society" will be filmed in this city and will be given its premier showing in the principal theaters of Indianapolis before being released throughout the country.

One of W. F. Warneford's Lobbies.

Lawrenceville, Ind.—Theforegoing photograph shows a view of the lobby dis-

Lobby of Gem Theater at Lawrenceburg, Ind.

play used for the showing of "Womanhood", by W. F. Warneford, manager and owner of the Gem theater at Lawrenceburg, Ind. Mr. Warneford is one of the foremost exhibitors in the state and spends a great part of his prime sitting up late at night figuring out attractive lobby displays for his theater. Judging from the success he is enjoying the most skeptical could be convinced that "advertising pays".

Goshen, Ind.—James Bources and S. Reynolds, motion picture exhibitors of South Bend, were in Indianapolis last week negotiating with H. F. Kidder for his double room on East Lincoln avenue, which was formerly a portion of the Irwin theater, destroyed by fire early last winter. If successful in closing the deal with Mr. Kidder the two men expect to open a modern motion picture theater in the place. An Elkhart exhibitor has also been trying to lease the room, it is reported.

Twin City Film Men Enjoy Big Picnic

Cold Drizzle Didn't Dampen Baseball or Other Outdoor Sports—Many Amusing Events on Program—Who Were and What They Did.

By John L. Johnston, 704 Film Exchange Building, Minneapolis, Minn.

MINNEAPOLIS, MINN.—The front line had nothing on Spring Park, Lake Minnetonka, for activity Thursday, August 23, when Minneapolis and St. Paul exhibitors and exchangemen got together for their seventh annual picnic and field day. A damp polar breeze and a little damper drizzle failed to check the festivities and all of the events went off as per schedule. Hardly had the boat carrying the merrymakers from the street car to the island docked when ball players began to gather on the diamond and at the end of five innings of play Newton Davis' Bluebirds had warbled a three to nothing victory over Ira Mantike's pet exchangemen's aggregation. Frank Thayer, manager of the Calhoun theater, Minneapolis, and A. A. Hixon, Metro, made up the Bluebird battery, and this pair, aided by Mortensen's heavy clubbing, did much to put the Bluebirds on the long end of the score.

The other athletic events on the program brought out some sterling material. Lee Horn, Long Acre exchange boss, ran away from a good field in the 100-yard dash; Ira Mantzke, Mutual, nosed out Horn in the 50-yard sprint, and Horn and Thayer came back and won the men's three-legged race hands down. Joe Cohen, Lagon, Minneapolis, won the fat men's wobble, otherwise known as a race. Mrs. Margaret Chambard, Art Dramas, was a double winner among the ladies. She was a victor in both the ladies' free for all and married women's races and finished second in the hop, skip and jump. Ethel Mortensen, Mutual, won the ball throwing contest, and Ethel Swanson, of the Selznick exchange, proved the best jumper among the feminine contingent. In a special professional 100-yard dash Fred Meyer, general manager, beat out Otto C. Stelzner, Minneapolis Star theater sprinter, in a neck-and-neck race. The two demons of the cinder path raced on a winner-take-all basis. Mr. and Mrs. W. Al Steffes, of the Minneapolis Northern theater, were winners in a prize old-fashioned waltz contest. The Steffes plan to build a school with the prize money received and name it "Castles-on-the-Mississippi."

Mike Conhaim and a select bevy of bathing Venuses, Hugh C. Andress, Minneapolis Lyric manager; Eddie Westcott, Fox; Frank Burke, Westcott exchange; Harry Rathner, Selznick; Henry Breilein, Breilein theaters, St. Paul; Lew Francis, Dolly McCallum, Jack Elliott, Tom Hamlin, Clyde Hitchcock, Ira Mantzke, George Law, Harry Cohen, Art Lund, Olga Mortensen, Bill Cutter, Henrietta Oftedahl and Mr. and Mrs. Ben Blotcke were among the many prominent film people much in evidence at the picnic.

H. J. Breilein Leases Arcade Theater.

St. Paul, Minn.—Henry J. Breilein, owner of the Verdi, Faust and Victoria theaters on University avenue here, has leased the Arcade theater on Dayton's Bluff. The Arcade, a two-year-old, handsome, neighborhood house, has been managed by William Cutter, former K-E-S-E roadman. William Maitland, Mr. Breilein's chief of staff, is expected to look after the Arcade's destinies.

What Is Booked for Fair Week.

Minneapolis, Minn.—Manager Hugh C. Andress, of the New Lyric theater here, will offer "The Barrier", by Rex Beach, as a special Minnesota State Fair week feature, September 1 to 9. Twenty-five cents admission will be charged.

Manager Lowell V. Calvert, of the New Garrick, will offer Mae Marsh in "Polly of the Circus" for Fair Week.

Manager Charles G. Branham, of the Strand, has booked "The Slacker" for Fair

Week at regular prices. He has added to the bill personal appearances every evening of Egbert Van Alstyne, popular song writer, and Walter King, soloist. Mr. Branham has secured John Howard, formerly organist at the Covent Garden, Chicago, to play the organ at his theater in the future.

Geo. F. Bromley Stops Over.

Minneapolis, Minn.—George F. Bromley, former star University of Minnesota athlete, stopped off here two days recently on his way to Omaha, where he will open a Triangle branch exchange. Mr. Bromley has recently seen service with the Chicago Triangle and Fox exchanges. A few years back he was considered one of the greatest footbal linemen in the country.

F. O. Fredrickson With Pathe.

F. O. Frederickson, former Vitagraph and Elliott-Sherman exchange broker, is now located with the Pathe Exchange, Inc., at Kansas City, Mo.

A. A. Hixon Again on Metro Sales Force.

Minneapolis, Minn.—No permanent manager for the local Metro exchange has been appointed—yet. A. A. Hixon, former assistant manager of the exchange, has joined the sales force again. It is rumored he may be put in charge of the Milwaukee office, recently vacated by Daddy E. H. Hoyt, resigned.

Notes at the Film Exchanges.

Minneapolis, Minn.—Manager Bayley, of the Greater Vitagraph, has booked "The Fighting Trail" in the Minneapolis Pantages and St. Paul Hippodrome theaters for first run.

Harry Rathner has announced that he will distribute Clara Kimball Young's "Select" features in the Northwest. This was predicted two months ago.

Manager Ralph Bradford, of the Goldwyn exchange, is calling attention to the large number of Goldwyn twenty-four sheets displayed in and around the Twin Cities.

Manager Charles Stombaugh, of the Standard Art Dramas exchange, has been called to the bedside of his father, who is seriously ill at Lincoln, Neb.

Acting Manager Strauss, of the Metro exchange, has booked first-run Metro features in The Strand, Minneapolis.

Manager C. L. Peavey, of the Paramount exchange, has booked fifteen first-run Paramount features not included in other Twin City first-run contracts in The Strand, Minneapolis. Keystone-Sennett comedies and Arbuckles are much in demand at the Paramount exchange, Mr. Peavey reports.

Manager Benjamin Friedman, of the Friedman Film Corp., has booked "The Bar Sinister" in Thomas Furniss' Rex theater, Duluth, Minn.

Manager Harry Graham, of the K-E-S-E, has booked Taylor Holmes' "Efficiency Edgar's Courtship" to Charles G. Branham, of the Minneapolis Strand.

Dan Michalove, Minneapolis Triangle manager, has received word from his home in North Carolina to report to a Minneapolis medical board for draft examination. Mr. Michalove has also received word that President Freeman, of the Triangle exchange, is to visit him shortly.

Levi Chandler, former Universal and Bluebird exchange man, has been appointed assistant manager of the New Garrick theater, St. Paul, Minn.

New Policies in Crescent City Theater

New Orleans Has Several Picture Houses of the Highest Grade—What Is Being Offered—Smaller Houses Dropping Out.

By N. E. Thatcher, 3301 Canal St., New Orleans, La.

NEW ORLEANS, LA.—With the return of the summer vacationists the outlook for the motion picture business for the coming season takes on a most hopeful appearance. Marked changes are to be noted in the lineup of theaters and in the policies of their owners and managers. There is a growing death list of store shows. Alert managers are bending every endeavor to present attractive theaters and the best programs possible during the winter months.

It behooves them to do so. With the opening of the magnificent Strand theater a few weeks ago, a new mark was set for the exhibitors. The Strand is managed by men who make the showing of pictures a profession and not a mere occupation. Success is their natural reward. The Diamond theater has made a record for itself and its bank account by adhering to the fixed policy of showing only such pictures as meet with the personal approval of the management, regardless of the picture's relation to any or no program. The Triangle theater's manager started on the road to much greater achievements when he opened the house. In fact Ernst Boehringer may be regarded as the pioneer in modernizing the motion picture business in New Orleans.

Policy of Leading Houses.

On September 1 Marcus Loew launched the Crescent theater as a motion picture enterprise, using vaudeville acts at certain hours of the day as an added attraction. A feature production and single and special reels will make up the program. The opening offerings were of Paramount service, and other brands will also probably be shown later on. The Crescent will be one of the units in the Loew circuit of theaters.

Upon the same day the Palace theater which is the old Triangle, made notable as a motion picture house under the Boehringer regime, opened as a motion picture theater under the direction of the Orpheum circuit. The program of each of these theaters is to begin showing pictures at 11 o'clock in the morning and to continue until 11 at night. At stated intervals vaudeville acts will be introduced and prices are to range from 5 to 30 cents.

The Strand theater is presenting a program of feature and special pictures interspersed with high class music under the direction of Don Phillipini at the head of thirty-five expert musicians. The Strand entertainment is very similar to that of the Rialto theater in New York. Every appliance of the pleasure and comfort of the patrons of the Strand has been provided and the house has leaped into immediate and widespread popularity. Managing Director Cornelius was the first motion picture theater manager to inaugurate the noonday musical concert, rendered by the full Phillipini orchestra and the great pipe organ, and these concerts have attained statewide reputation and incidentally have proven to be a very noticeable aid to the cash box. The Pearce interests are tightening up their exhibition forces and are planning an aggressive campaign with special features for the winter months.

New Liberty Theater Coming Along.

Still another element to be reckoned with before the season is ended will be the Liberty theater, which is being built for the Boehringer Amusement Company under the supervision of Ernst Boehringer. Work was advancing rapidly upon this theater when the government commandeered the steel frames for the structure and an unavoidable delay was thus caused. Manager Boehringer took the delay with greater good humor than he usually displays when his enterprises fail to run smoothly, and he is pleased to do one of his "bits" to help his country in this manner. A reserve force of workmen are held in readiness to proceed with the building upon the moment of the arrival of new steel, which is now on the way.

In addition to the activities in motion picture circles in the downtown sections the suburban houses are manifesting marked activity. Much improving and remodeling is under way and the new and pretentious houses recently opened are building up remarkably liberal patronage.

Pearce Interests Take the Dreamworld.

New Orleans, La.—On October 1 the Josiah Pearce & Son's interests will take over the Dreamworld theater at the corner of Canal and St. Charles streets, but no announcement has been made as to the future policy in the operation of the house. The Dreamworld is one of the pioneer houses of the city and in its early days was a good money maker for its owner, Herman Fichtenberg. Later it passed under the control of the Saenger Amusement Company, along with the Picto, a small theater adjoining. The Saenger interests still control the Picto and rumors of new enterprises are numerous.

Notes of Interest in the Crescent City.

New Orleans, La.—The Dreamland, one of the Pearce smaller houses, on St. Charles street, was closed on August 23 and the furnishings were removed. The lease on the building had expired.

The Symphony orchestra of the Strand theater, under the direction of Don Phillipini, at the request of Mayor Behrman, of New Orleans, gave a concert at Camp Nicholas on Sunday, August 26, at which over 2,000 soldiers and their friends were delighted. Manager Cornelius of the Strand is endeavoring to arrange another concert at the earnest solicitation of the soldiers.

The Avenues theater, which was the old Mercedes, on St. Cloud street, has been remodeled and reopened. This house is in a good suburban neighborhood and it has been enjoying a liberal patronage since its rehabilitation.

C. E. Tandy, at the head of the Southern Paramount Pictures Corporation, which controls the output of the Paramount production for eleven Southern states, was a recent visitor to New Orleans.

The Diamond Film Company has opened a suite of magnificent offices in the Audubon building and the work of renovating the studios on Bayou St. John is well under way. A contract for the making of the first five-reel feature has been signed with Richard C. Travers and negotiations are under way for securing the services of a leading lady. The best actress that money can secure is sought.

Prairie State News Letter

By Frank H. Madison.

New Booking Association Contemplated in Omaha.

OMAHA, Neb.—Suburban exhibitors contemplate the organization of The Exhibitors Booking association for the protection of mutual interests.

Private Showing of "Jack and the Beanstalk."

Omaha, Neb.—Club women interested in moving pictures for children were given a private showing of the Fox film "Jack and the Beanstalk", at the Rhollf theater. Mrs. W. S. Knight, chairman of the moving picture committee of the Omaha Woman's club said: "This is the most elaborate program thus far produced for boys and girls, unless it is 'Alice in Wonderland.' Those interested in the work appreciated the thought and planning which is leading producers to be willing to expend vast sums of money for our young people, a most important part of the film business."

Nebraska Theater Notes.

Imperial, Neb.—A. C. Norman has purchased the Imperial theater from George Brewer.

Omaha, Neb.—Moving pictures are proving a popular attraction at Manawa Park.

Falls City, Neb.—Company E's mess fund is $150 richer as the result of special shows by the World theater and the Airdome. Films of the company's Farewell Day were the feature.

Theater Jottings from the Dakotas.

Sioux Falls, S. D.—S. J. Smith has sold a half interest in the Princess theater to H. J. Updegraft, until recently owner and manager of the Gem theater at Pipestone, Minn.

Forman, N. D.—Walloch & Hobbins are now operating the moving picture theater here, Millard Dada having sold his interest to Hobbins.

Florence, S. D.—The new Florence opera house has been opened.

Lake Preston, S. D.—W. H. Owen has sold his moving picture theater here.

Grand Forks, N. D.—John Bertram, manager of the Grand theater since its erection and manager of the Grand theater since 1905, has resigned to accept a position as booker for the Western Vaudeville Managers' Association.

Sioux Falls, S. D.—"The Birth of a Nation" played a four-day return date at the Orpheum theater.

Mitchell, S. D.—Manager Dix has opened the Gale theater on Main street.

Garretson, S. D.—The Princess theater has been sold by J. W. Tillman to Mr. Peterson of Edgerton.

Wisconsin Theater Notes.

By Frank H. Madison, 623 S. Wabash Ave.

MADISON, WIS.—Fred Flom, owner of a building at 20 E. Main street, is remodeling it into a moving picture theater, seating 450.

Durand, Wis.—George Harrington has sold the Grand theater to A. N. Storey.

New Richmond, Wis.—F. J. McNally is now manager of the New Richmond opera house.

Chippewa Falls, Wis.—Opening of the new Rex theater was planned for September 10, featuring the schedule which originally called for a Fair week opening.

Illinois News Letter

By Frank H. Madison, 623 S. Wabash Ave., Chicago, Ill.

Nu-Movie-Lite Company Formed.

PEORIA, ILL.—Articles of incorporation have been filed by the Nu-Movie-Lite Company with a capital stock of $100,000. The incorporators are M. M. Livingston, Charles W. LaPorte and Hiram Todd. The company will manufacture the Nu-Movie-Lite, an electrical appliance for all standard projectors which is said to eliminate the use of carbons. Livingston is the inventor. The concern also will make a combination stereopticon flood light and spotlight, designed by Livingston. All the stock has been sold to Peoria men, it is announced.

New Houses and Changes in Illinois.

Rock Island, Ill.—Rock Island's ninth moving picture theater, the Fifth Avenue, has been opened by C. J. Larkin at 2520 Fifth avenue. It seats 500, is modernly decorated, lighted and ventilated and has rest rooms, a confectionary booth near the entrance is an innovation. One afternoon and two evening shows will be given.

Morris, Ill.—M. J. Hogan, Jr., and R. L. Davison, owners of Dreamland theater at Seneca, have purchased the building in which the Royal theater of this city is located. The Royal has been under the management of Lee Osmanson, but the new owners of the building announce they will operate it in conjunction with the Seneca house.

Cooksville, Ill.—Profit & Stagner of Anchor, Ill., have purchased the moving picture theater here from O. J. Breidenbach.

East St. Louis, Ill.—The moving picture theater on Main street erected for Maurice V. Joyce is nearing completion.

Streator, Ill.—Manager C. A. Day gave an entire day's receipts to the Red Cross fund. He ran the "Pershing in France" pictures as a special attraction.

Galena, Ill.—Dreamland theater has been re-opened with a new dress. The Paramount, "Each to His Kind," was the initial attraction.

Streator, Ill.—The old Lyric theater has been remodeled into a store building.

Springfield, Ill.—The Majestic vaudeville theater will use the Universal weekly this season.

Havana, Ill.—"Les Miserables" in films was a feature attraction at the Chautauqua assembly held at Quiver Lake park near here. Moving pictures were used extensively on the fifteen-day program.

Cairo, Ill.—The Bijou theater is co-operating with local merchants who are giving with purchases tickets which will be honored by the Bijou.

IN MICHIGAN.

Manager and Usher Burned Trying to Save Film.

Belding, Mich.—Manager Frank Joslin of the Empress theater and Earl Wright an usher were badly burned when they rushed into the operating room in an attempt to save films from fire. The blaze did $750 damage to the theater. The films were valued at $600.

Michigan Theater Changes and Notes.

Battle Creek, Mich.—Lipp & Cross have sold an interest in the Rex theater to E. J. Wheelock, who has been connected with the house for two years. Wheelock has assumed the management. The theater has been redecorated.

Jackson, Mich.The Crown theater on West Main street has been sold to Mrs. Mary E. Jackson of this city.

Grand Rapids, Mich.—The entire Grand Rapids battalion headed by its band attended the first presentation of "The Slacker" at the Majestic Gardens. All house attaches were in uniform during the week. Civil War veterans were admitted free.

Calumet, Mich.—The Calumet theater has booked "The Barrier" for early in October.

South Range, Mich.—The Star theater has been redecorated with a view to booking vaudeville and other shows this winter.

Houston's Hour of Terror---Texas Notes

Exhibitor Polmanakes of the Crown Theater Tells of Turmoil When Negro Troops Run Amuck—Drought Partly Broken.

By Douglas Hawley, Times-Herald, Dallas, Texas.

DALLAS, TEXAS.—Theodore Polmanakos, of the Crown at Houston, told of the reign of terror which existed there as a result of the outbreak of negro troops. Much was carried in the papers, says the Houston theater man, but only those who were in the city know the actual feeling which existed and the actual terrorization of the people which resulted.

"'Twould have made a picture full of action, wouldn't it?" it was suggested to Mr. Polmanakos.

"It might have," he said, "but it would have required a man nervier even than Charley Van Loan's Gabby to have ground a crank while the actual shooting was going on."

The city was soon quiet after the outbreak, says Mr. Polmanakos, and within a few hours was back at its normal temperature, despite the seriousness of the situation. It will be remembered that negro troopers of the twenty-fourth infantry, stationed here, ran amuck, and that seventeen people were killed.

"Down to Earth" Makes Record at Old Mill.

Dallas.—Douglas Fairbanks in "Down to Earth", played to the biggest business Hulsey's Old Mill theater has done in some time, on its five-day run here. Observant local critics declared it to be the best thing the versatile player has done. As this is written, Arbuckle's "Wedding Night" is beginning a run at the same theater, which bids fair to set a new mark for that cherubic scion of avoirdupois.

J. D. Wheelan Comes Back with Newport Theater.

Dallas.—Away back in the pioneer days, when folks scoffed and predicted that the motion picture "craze" was an ephemeral thing of faddish conceit, doomed to exist for but a span, J. D. Wheelan entered the business as a local exhibitor. The ephemeral didn't ephem, and Wheelan got rich. He got out of the business later, and has been taking life easy. But now he's back again. His name is back of the reopening of the Newport theater, Dallas, closed for the last several months. The theater is a small one and not elaborate, but it enjoys an ideal location and is doing well, apparently.

Drouth Broken in Parts of Texas.

Dallas.—A number of sections of the heretofore drouth stricken region in West Texas have been blessed with life-restoring precipitation, and as a result the feeling is much better. The effect is noticeable in a number of managers from what is inelegantly termed "the sticks" calling on booking agencies and branch houses in Dallas during the last week.

Fox "Siren" Too Daring.

Dallas.—Valeska Suratt, daring and dashing, has been ruled a bit too daring and somewhat too dashing as "The Siren" in the Fox film of that title, for Dallas motion picture patrons, by Mrs. Ethel Boyce, the Dallas censor. The picture was condemned for local showing. Under requirements of the local ordinance, a private showing was made, after which the censor acted. It is the third film which has come under the ban here during the last month.

West Wants Western Stuff.

Dallas.—They like Western stuff in the West, just the same is in the East, according to J. B. Dugger, V. L. S. E. branch manager here. Mr. Dugger is now on a Western trip, called out by the prospect

for big business with "The Fighting Trail", a recent V. L. S. E. release. Incidentally, Dugger named the picture. His suggestion for a title was selected from the many sent in.

H. E. Fulgham Back With Vitagraph.

Dallas.—H. E. Fulgham is back on the road in the interest of Vitagraph. Mr. Fulgham has been on duty in the local office for the last several months.

Texas Trade Notes of Interest.

Dallas.—Joseph Clemons, of the Tivoli, Beaumont, and J. A. Holton, of the People's at Port Arthur, booked new stuff through local branches during the week and declared themselves satisfied.

Houston, Tex.—Oh, yes, there are lady owner-managers in Texas. Witness: Miss Edith Johnson, of the Liberty and Keith at Houston, booked several new things through Dallas branches during the last week and reported conditions and the prospect for the fall entirely promising.

Brenham, Tex.—W. A. Stuckert, of The Rex at Brenham, Tex., was another South Texas manager who said that section of the state was in good condition.

Iowa Film Trade News

By Dorothy Day, Register-Tribune, Des Moines, Ia.

"The Slacker" Does Big Business in Des Moines.

DES MOINES, IA.—The Palace theater in this city surely cleaned up on "The Slacker" the week of the 19th. J. Milios-kowsky, who is usually reticent in his praise of pictures, went so far as to openly state that his business was something wonderful on the big Metro success. He would have held the picture over into the week of the 26th if it had been possible for the local Metro office to have obtained prints.

The picture is not only going big in Des Moines, but all over Iowa and Nebraska exhibitors are writing in and seeking dates on the feature. It is being booked in all of the smaller towns for more than two days, where no picture has ever been shown more than but one day.

News of Film People and Des Moines Visitors.

Des Moines.—J. S. Skirboll, general manager of the Metro out of Pittsburgh, Kan., spent one day in Des Moines, last week, visiting his brother, William N. Skirboll, manager of the local Metro exchange.

Charles B. Orr, of the photoplay house in Bagley, Ia.; William Gleason, of the Little Gem in Duncomb, Ia., and the Misses Gerbracht, of Ames, Ia., were callers at the Universal exchange in Des Moines last week. Miss Ada and Miss Della Gerbracht are the sisters and partners of Joe Gerbracht in the ownership of the Twin Star theater in Ames.

C. W. Stombaugh, formerly manager of the General exchange in Des Moines, and now manager of the Standard office in Minneapolis, stopped over the latter part of the week, on his way home to Minneapolis after attending the burial of his father in Lincoln, Neb.

George Fowler, of the Unique in Menlo, Ia., and Charles Owens, of the Past Time in Bagley, Ia., were callers at the Pathe this week.

Charter Oak, Ia.—C. C. Cooper has purchased the Royal theater in Charter Oak from William Probasco.

Ackerman & Harris Circuit Is Extending

Takes Ten Year Lease on Cory at Fresno—To Build New Hippodrome in San Jose
—Takes Over the Strand at Stockton.

From T. A. Church, 1507 North Street, Berkeley, Cal.

SAN FRANCISCO, CAL.—Ackerman & Harris, who conduct the circuit of Hippodrome theaters on the Pacific Coast, and who already have fourteen houses under their control, are making preparations to add several new ones in California at an early date. This increased activity on their part has made necessary the securing of larger office quarters, and within thirty days they will remove from the Humboldt Bank building, where they have made their headquarters for years, to what will be known as the Circuit building on O'Farrell street, opposite the Alcazar theater, where a building is being fitted up to meet their particular needs. The Hippodrome shows are made up of vaudeville and moving pictures, with the latter receiving special attention.

A ten year lease has been taken on the Cory theater at Fresno, Cal., and it is planned to open this in October, after extensive alterations have been made by the owner of the property, L. L. Cory. The front of the house will be changed the interior redecorated, a marquise installed and other improvements made at an estimated cost of $25,000, under the direction of Eugene Mathewson, an architect of Fresno.

Contracts have also been signed for a new Hippodrome theater at San Jose, Cal. A two-story, reinforced concrete theater with a seating capacity of 2,000 will be erected by T. S. Montgomery, adjoining the Montgomery hotel, and opposite the T. & D. theater. This house, in a complete form, will cost about $150,000. The architects are Binder & Curtis.

The old Strand theater at Stockton, Cal., has also been taken over, remodeled and enlarged, and will be opened on August 29 as the Hippodrome theater, the initial moving picture to be shown to be the "On the Square Girl," with Mollie King. The circuit has also arranged to place its acts in the Wigwam theater in the Mission district, San Francisco, which is to be changed on September 2 from a stock to a vaudeville and moving picture house, the first picture offering to be "Lonesome Luke's Wild Women."

Theater Deal Falls Through.

San Francisco, Cal.—The deal whereby the Strand theater was to pass from the possession of Sid Grauman and D. J. Grauman to the proprietors of the Rialto theater, of this city, struck a snag at the last moment and will probably not be consummated. In speaking of the matter Sid Grauman states that a decision has virtually been arrived at not to dispose of the house, but to operate it in conjunction with the one to be opened shortly at Los Angeles. He said, "We have a fine theater in an ideal location and have about decided not to dispose of our interests here, where our name is an asset. Business is increasing in fine shape and it looks as though we would experience a wonderful fall and winter season".

Lasky Company Makes Coast Trip.

San Francisco, Cal.—A company of players from the Lasky studio at Los Angeles were recent visitors here to take scenes for the "Clever Miss Carfax", featuring Julian Eltinge. The company came up the coast by boat and went as far as Portland, Ore., but adverse weather conditions prevented the taking of as many scenes as was desired. Mr. Eltinge was to have appeared in person at the Porter theater, in this city, but the boat was late and he was compelled to postpone the engagement. The company was in charge of director Donald Crisp and in addition to Julian Eltinge included H. B. Carpenter, Ernest Joy, Noah Beery, Fred Church, Miss Daisy Robinson, Miss Marie Stark.

Goldwyn Author in Town.

San Francisco, Cal.—Roy Cooper Megrue, author of "Fighting Odds", in which Goldwyn will feature Maxine Elliott in its third release, is here for a short stay and will shortly go on to Los Angeles, having come by way of the Northwest. Harry Leonhart, the Western division manager for Goldwyn, is making a visit to the Seattle branch.

"British Tanks" Draw Crowds.

San Francisco, Cal.—Howard J. Sheehan, of the Rialto theater, advises that all former records at this house were broken during the recent engagement of the Pathe "Tanks at the Battle of Ancre." This showing is considered a remarkable one in view of the fact that this week also marked an advance in admission price from 10, 20 and 30 cents to 15, 25 and 35 cents.

Turner & Dahnken Activities.

San Francisco, Cal.—E. B. Johnson, secretary of the Turner & Dahnken circuit, will leave shortly for New York to attend a meeting of members of the First National Exhibitors' Circuit. While away he will also attend to details in connection with the opening of an exchange in that city. This is to be ready for business on November 1 and is to be in charge of Ralph Clark, manager of the T. & D. theater at Oakland.

This circuit has purchased the California, Arizona, Nevada, New York and Hawaiian Island rights to "The Curse of Iku", which is now being shown with great success in the local territory.

The new organ in the T. & D. theater at Berkeley is proving to be a strong drawing card and music is being featured as never before. Clarence A. Tufts is the organist and the services of well known solo artists are being secured from time to time to lend variety to the program.

A free recital marked the opening of the new orchestral organ at the T. & D. opera house on August 18. This organ has been entirely reconstructed and enlarged and is now one of the finest in the West. The opening concert was rendered by Gordon Bretland.

E. H. Kemp Installing Many Machines.

San Francisco, Cal.—Edward H. Kemp is busily engaged in installing Motiographs in Y. M. C. A. buildings at army camps in this territory and expects to put in about thirty in all. He has sold three Motiographs to be installed in the new California theater, these to be built especially for this house. A traveling equipment, with a portable electric lighting plant, has also been fitted up for use in Mexico.

New House for North Beach.

San Francisco, Cal.—Sam Gordon has sold his interests in the old Penny Arcade on Broadway and a new fireproof theater with a seating capacity of 2,000 is to be erected on the site for the Broadway Theater Company. The architects are Weeks & Day, Phelan building, and the theater will be conducted under the management of Max Blumenfeld.

Babies Are Tickets.

San Francisco, Cal.—During the recent engagement of "Skinner's Baby" at the Strand theater, manager Sid Grauman extended an invitation to mothers to attend the Thursday and Friday matinees, the only ticket required being a baby in arms. Hundreds accepted the invitation and baby buggies filled the lobby and all the available storage space in the house. Mothers were asked to check their tickets should they become obstreperous, but only a few found this necessary, the behavior of the little tots being most exemplary. The ticket takers had instructions to punch no tickets, but to smile at every baby, regardless of race or disposition.

Australian Film Man Visits San Francisco.

San Francisco, Cal.—N. Crown, formerly of Dallas, Tex., but for the last three years located in Australia, arrived here recently to secure films to be taken to that country. He is negotiating for the Pathe release, "Les Miserables", the Hart feature, "The Cold Deck", and productions of a like character. He reports that so many men have left Australia that the theaters in many of the small towns have been closed, but that business is good in the larger places.

Pathe Exchange Notes.

San Francisco, Cal.—C. A. Meade, the special Pathe representative, who has been here for several weeks, has left for a brief stay at Los Angeles.

Nick Turner, formerly a well known exhibitor of northern California, and later connected with local film exchanges, has returned from an Eastern trip and has joined the Pathe sales staff.

H. Stuart has become assistant bookkeeper at the local office and Gilbert Moyle has been appointed cashier, replacing L. Adler, who has been transferred to the Dallas branch.

Sol Lesser Gets New Film.

San Francisco, Cal.—Sol L. Lesser has purchased the California, Arizona and Nevada rights to "The Cold Deck", featuring William Hart, and the All Star Distributors, Inc., is now booking this production locally. "The Garden of Allah" recently had a successful run at the Lyric theater at San Rafael and will shortly be shown here for the first time.

Demanding Safer Operating Rooms.

San Francisco, Cal.—Officials of the local Department of Electricity have been visiting the operating rooms of local houses of late and have insisted on improvements that have necessitated the purchase of considerable new equipment. The use of fireproof rewinds has been especially insisted upon.

Frisk Makes Theater Sales.

San Francisco, Cal.—Fred Frisk, of the United Theater Exchange, has effected the sale of the Rex theater at Santa Clara, Cal., from Hoots & McDaniel to John G. French, formerly of Angels Camp, and has sold a one-half interest in the Larkin theater of this city for Charles M. Goodwin to Louis C. Werner.

Selznick Offices Being Improved.

San Francisco, Cal.—Now that the uncertainty in regard to the plans of the Lewis J. Selznick Enterprises has been dismissed arrangements are being made to place the local offices on a permanent basis. A large film vault is to be installed at once and the quarters in the Easton building.

California Newslets.

Hollister, Cal.—The Opal theater has been taken over by Stark & Hodges.

Angels Camp, Cal.—E. A. Watkins has purchased the Angels theater.

Sacramento, Cal.—The Nippon theater has been opened by C. Rohrer.

Willows, Cal.—The Opera House will be opened by R. W. Claman.

Spokane News Letter

By S. Clark Patchin, E1811 Eleventh Ave.,
Spokane, Wash.

Tyrone Power Addresses Spokane Audience.

SPOKANE, WASH.—Tyrone Power, Shakespearean actor and moving picture actor, swooped down on Spokane for the week of August 19 and was royally entertained by the people of the city, who hope to have him and C. J. Ward, his manager, establish a producing moving picture studio here.

In an address before the Spokane Transportation Club, Wednesday, August 22, he said:

"The man who would continue to play Shakespeare is on a direct road to the motion picture came along and said 'Eat'; and actors must eat. Ministers would fill their houses better if they had the Bible stories prepared for the screen, and when they announce their texts have the pictures, depicting the text, thrown on the screen. Some say they are oposed to pictures, yet on their windows and walls are highly colored Bible pictures and statuary.

"Whether I come here or not to make pictures someone is going to, for your scenery is ideal and conditions are most wonderful. You have a vast amount of virgin scenery here that has not been used up like the California scenery has. Things are ideal and it seems a great shame that it has not been taken advantage of sooner."

Pantages Theater Being Rebuilt.

Spokane, Wash.—Work on reconstructing the Pantages theater in Spokane has been started by Earl B. Newcomb, of Seattle, the contractor. The Pantages circuit shows are being produced in the American theater, which was dark, and are drawing large crowds. The house has just booked the Vitalgraph serial, "The Fighting Trail," which will start to run September 10. Additional to its moving picture portion of the program Ottavia Handworth, a moving picture actress, appeared on the stage the week of August 19.

Majestic Theater Changes Hands.

Spokane, Wash.—The Majestic moving picture theater, of Spokane, which was incorporated, has changed managements. On August 18 J. C. Knipe, C. Bowman and H. W. Koons purchased the controlling interest in the place and Mr. Knipe is the acting manager, taking the place of A. H. McMillan, manager, who will take up other duties after September 1. The purchase price was not made public.

Film Men From Seattle Visit Spokane.

Spokane, Wash.—F. A. Hill, representative of Goldwyn, with offices in Seattle, visited Spokane managers during the week of August 20.

G. A. Ferris, manager of the Vitagraph exchange in Seattle, and Ashley McRea, traveling representative of the company from the same office, gave private showings of "The Fighting Trail" and "The Common Law" in the Clemmer and Lyric theaters, August 23, to exhibitors from outside of the city. Mr. McRea announced that several good bookings resulted from showing the pictures to the men of the Inland Empire towns.

PORTLAND, ORE., NOTES.

C. W. Meighan Leaves the People's.

Portland, Ore.—C. W. Meighan has resigned his position as manager of the People's Amusement Company to accept the position of manager of the Columbia theater and publicity expert for both the Columbia and Liberty theaters.

Exchanges Make New Demands

Oregon Exhibitors See Serious Problems Ahead in Dealing With Exchanges— Raise in Prices—New Schedules Require Two Days' Run of Films.

By Abraham Nelson, Majestic Theater Building, Portland, Ore.

PORTLAND, OREGON.—The reorganization that has been going on among certain film distributing companies has struck home in the usual and customary place, to wit, the ultimate consumer, the exhibitor. The past few weeks have found certain exhibitors in a frenzy to grab one or two certain picture programs and those programs have been demanding prices among the small showmen that by far top anything ever before asked, even in the palmy days of General Film monopoly.

To an exhibitor who for the past year or more has maintained an every day change policy, a film concern makes this demand: I—— for our films in your locality for two days?

"But," says the exhibitor, "I change every day and never show a film two days."

"That makes no difference," answers the exchange, "the price of our service is I—— for your locality whether you run the picture one or two days."

All of which, the exhibitor believes, is a polite way of saying that the film rental charged by the distributing concern is about twice what it was before.

Nevertheless, competing exhibitors in a locality have, for the past few weeks, been engaged in a throat-cutting bidding fray for certain film service, which, it is argued by the onlooker, must eventually result disastrously even for the winner. Men who have held one brand of service for years are trembling for fear their competitors will take it away from them and the competitors are not backward about admitting that they are out to get it if possible.

One of the exchanges in question states that the increased salaries paid to stars and the increased cost of production are responsible for the increased charges in rental of service. However, the situation as it confronts film exchanges themselves appears to the exhibitors in the territory to be a most delicate one, and it is their opinion that only the exercise of excellent judgment and the most painstaking efforts to give the exhibitor a square deal will solve the perplexing problem in a manner that will guarantee the future prosperity of the distributors as well as the present. The activities of the old General Film regime still rankle in the breasts of Oregon's exhibitors.

No Sunday Express Deliveries in Portland.

Portland, Ore.—Starting August 26, Portland express companies will not make any Sunday deliveries and exhibitors who get their shows from Seattle will be compelled to personally call at the express offices to get their Sunday programs. The action by the express companies is a war measure, in line with the "one delivery a day" plan adopted by the Portland merchants. Neither will the express companies pick up film for out-of-town shipment after five o'clock. The rule applies to Portland, Seattle, Tacoma and Spokane.

The situation is just another argument in favor of Seattle exchanges putting branches in Portland so that its exhibitors can be effectively served.

W. E. Tebbetts Learns a Lesson.

Portland, Ore.—Ask W. E. Tebbetts, the popular owner of the Alhambra theater, whether two projecting machines are an absolute necessity or the old way of doing business, and his answer will be "necessity" in positive tones.

After putting on faultless pictures for four years with a single machine, using

2,000-foot reels, Mr. Tebbetts enjoyed the disheartening experience of the old stand-by breaking down on a Sunday afternoon. Pete Sabo, projection expert, could have fixed it in 15 minutes, but he was out of town. Finally Charles Pumphrey was routed up from his Sunday dinner a few miles away and a temporary machine was secured after a few hours' delay.

Needless to say, Mr. Tebbetts bought a second machine the next day.

Ed. Hudson Leaves Triangle.

Portland, Ore.—Ed. Hudson, popular traveller in the Portland territory, has resigned his position with Triangle to accept one as travelling representative with Goldwyn.

During his connection with Triangle, Mr. Hudson has built up a reputation for square dealing, making personal service a selling point of his product. In that way he has established a regular clientele among the exhibitors in the territory.

Jack Hovick a Wise Money Spender.

Portland, Ore.—Jack Hovick, Jensen & Von Herberg publicity expert, holds an enviable position. He has the opportunities to spend just as much, if not more,

John Hovick in His Den at the Liberty Theater.

money on advertising than any theatrical ad writer in the Pacific Northwest or on the Pacific Coast. Whole newspaper pages of Jensen & Von Herberg advertisements every few days is nothing in his young life. Recently he startled the staid Portlanders with a cut of Olive Thomas a page long. However, Mr. Hovick spends his bosses' money judiciously, as the business at the Portland Liberty and Columbia and the Seattle theaters for which he writes publicity will testify.

Goldwyn Goes Over Big.

Portland, Ore.—H. C. Arthur, Jr., road man for Goldwyn, was a recent caller at the League rooms and reports excellent business down the Willamette Valley and a big clean-up for Goldwyn.

Mr. Arthur reports that Maude Munson, the new owner of the Rainbow theater at McMinnville, has inaugurated a new policy in her theater and hereafter will show only the highest class of pictures. Increased admission prices are charged.

Calendar of Daily Program Releases
Releases for Weeks Ending September 15 and September 22

(For Extended Table of Current Releases See Pages 1754, 1756, 1758, 1760.)

Universal Film Mfg. Company

RELEASES FOR THE WEEK OF SEPTEMBER 10.

GOLD SEAL—The Perilous Leap (Three Parts—
Railroad Drama) 02667
NESTOR—The Boulevard Speed Hounds (Comedy). 02668
L-KO—From Cactus to Kale (Two Parts—Comedy). 02669
UNIVERSAL ANIMATED WEEKLY—Weekly No. 89
(Topical) 02670
STAR FEATURETTE—To the Highest Bidder (Two
Parts—Society Drama) 02671
JOKER—Short Skirts and Deep Water (Comedy).. 02672
VICTOR—In the Clutches of Milk (Comedy)....... 02673
UNIVERSAL SCREEN MAGAZINE—Issue No. 36
(Topical) 02674
UNIVERSAL CURRENT EVENTS—Issue No. 18
(Topical) 02675
JOKER—Nearly a Queen (Comedy).............. 02676
BISON—The Texas Sphinx (Two Parts—Western
Drama) 02677
UNIVERSAL SPECIAL—The Gray Ghost (Episode
No. 13—Title not decided—Two Parts)........ 02678

RELEASES FOR THE WEEK OF SEPTEMBER 17.

GOLD SEAL—The Pullman Mystery (Three Parts—
Drama) 02680
NESTOR—Welcome Home (Comedy).............. 02681
L-KO—A Prairie Chicken (Two Parts—Comedy).... 02682
UNIVERSAL ANIMATED WEEKLY—Weekly No. 90
(Topical) 02683
STAR FEATURETTE—The Right Man (Two Parts—
Drama) 02684
JOKER—Hawaiian Nuts (Comedy)............... 02685
VICTOR—Marathon Maniacs (Comedy)........... 02686
UNIVERSAL SCREEN MAGAZINE—Issue No. 37
(Topical) 02687
UNIVERSAL CURRENT EVENTS—Issue No. 19
(Topical) 02688
JOKER—Circus Sarah (Comedy)................ 02689
BISON—The Last of the Night Riders (Two Parts—
Drama) 02690
UNIVERSAL SPECIAL—The Gray Ghost (Episode
No. 13—Title not decided—Two Parts—Drama) 02691

Mutual Film Corporation

MONDAY, SEPTEMBER 10, 1917.

MUTUAL STAR PRODUCTION—Outcast (Frohman—
Six Parts—Drama) 05743-44-45-46-47-48
MUTUAL STAR PRODUCTION—The Bride's Silence
(American—Five Parts—Drama) 05749-50-51-52-53

WEDNESDAY, SEPTEMBER 12, 1917.

MUTUAL—Mutual Weekly No. 141 (Topical)....... 05754

THURSDAY, SEPTEMBER 13, 1917.

CUB—Jerry's Whirlwind Finish (Comedy)......... 05755
GAUMONT—Reel Life No. 72 (Subjects on reel: An
Unusual Colt; Hunting Turtle Eggs; Testing an
Auto Tube; Tree Planting in the National For-
ests; The Midnight Sun)..................... 05756

MONDAY, SEPTEMBER 17, 1917.

MUTUAL STAR PRODUCTION—The Girl Who
Couldn't Grow Up (Pollard—Five parts—Drama)
05757-58-59-60-61
MUTUAL STAR PRODUCTION—The Rainbow Girl
(American—Five Parts—Drama) 05762-63-64-65-66
SIGNAL FILM CORP.—The Lost Express (Episode
No. 1—"The Lost Express"—Two Parts—Drama)

WEDNESDAY, SEPTEMBER 19, 1917.

MUTUAL—Mutual Weekly No. 142 (Topical)....... 05767

THURSDAY, SEPTEMBER 20, 1917.

CUB—Officer Jerry (Comedy)................... 05768
GAUMONT—Reel Life No. 73 (Subjects on Reel:
Weaving the President's Portrait; Running an
Aeroplane Without Danger; The Principle of the
Gyroscope; When a Big Car Goes By (Animated
Drawing from Life) (Mutual Film Magazine)... 05769

Stories of the Films

General Film Company, Inc.

SELIG.

PIONEER DAYS (Two Parts).—General Herald of Fort Dearborn (LaFayette McKee); Black Partridge, an Indian Chief (Charles Clarey); Toinette, a French girl (Adrienne Kroell). Written by C. E. Nixon. Directed by Oscar Eagle.

In June, 1812, England declared war against the United States and secured the co-operation of the northern Indians as mercenaries and proceeded to devastate what was then the northwestern frontier.

At the mouth of the Chicago River stood Fort Dearborn, named in honor of General Nathaniel Dearborn, and established by the order of General Wayne. After the war with England started, General Wayne instructed General Heald to evacuate Fort Dearborn and go to Detroit.

Before he carried out this order Heald infuriated the hostile Indians in the vicinity by dampening all the surplus powder, emptying casks of liquor in the Chicago River and throwing all surplus muskets into a deep well at the fort.

On August 15, 1812, the men, women and children of Fort Dearborn started overland for Detroit. The hostile Indians attacked the troops and the famous Fort Dearborn massacre resulted, in which women, children and soldiers were slaughtered by the savages.

This massacre, together with other historical data of pioneer days, are thrillingly presented.

WORLD LIBRARY 'NO. 13 (August 22). Historic Monterey, California.—In 1602, Don Sebastin Viscaine entered Monterey Bay and took possession of the soil in the name of King Philip III. of Spain. Monterey was the capital of California when the latter was a Mexican province. California's first theater, first frame house, first brick building. The home of Robert Louis Stevenson. The old Custom House over which have flown the flags of three nations, Spain, Mexico and Old Glory. The famous Sherman rose.

Latest African Fashions.—

A skirt in perfect taste;
It's made like Eve's,
From bamboo leaves—
Without the slightest waste!

Tuna Fishing in the Pacific.—Many tons of tunnies are caught along the Pacific Coast, where they swim in shoals. Some attain a length of 15 feet, weighing about 1,500 pounds. rock cod are caught in great numbers. A fifty pound salmon. Securing salmon for spawning purposes.

The Silk Industry of Japan.—The Silk worm came originally from China. Mulberry leaves are the chief food of the silk worm. The silk secreting glands. The cocoon in which the chrysalis is killed, is placed in warm water to soften the gum, allowing the silk fiber to be reeled. After being properly cleaned it is ready for spinning.

ESSANAY.

OUR BOYS (Black Cat—Two Parts).—The downfall of Bobbie Browbeat, the bully in the little country school, presents a crisis in the life of Miss Patience, the teacher. Bobbie's cruelty to the smaller children leads Average Fellows and Howard Herows to trounce him severely. The affair winds up in a fight in the school and the teacher, learning the real cause, suspends the bully.

Bobbie induces his father, a school trustee, to "get" Miss Patience's job. The other children enlist on her side, and with their parents, threaten to "get" the jobs of the trustees if the teacher is discharged. The trustees changed their minds quickly.

STAR DUST (Black Cat—Two Parts).—The cast: Polly Parker (Marguerite Clayton); Capt. John Hastings (Mark Ellison).

Every girl has a soldier sweetheart these days; that is, every girl except Polly Parker. At her big university she alone is loveless and unloved. To a crowd of girls one day she reads a story she has written of Mary, a girl just like herself, who pines for a soldier's love.

Mary read of Captain John Hastings' return from the front and writes him, explaining her plight. An exchange of letters followed, then photographs. Finally the Captain was ordered back to the front. He took Mary with him as his happy wife. As Polly finishes the story she remarks that it is only "star dust"—a happy dream, but her audience is gazing across the campus in wonderment. There comes Captain Hastings for Mary, who, in reality, is Polly, herself. The "star dust" comes true.

FALCON FEATURES.

HIS UNFINISHED SELF (Four Parts).—The cast: Richard Jelf (Henry Ainley); Thomas Jelf (Charles Rock); James Palliser (Gerald Ainley); Sir Jonathan Dunne (Philip Howland); Adam Winslow (Hubert Willis); Perkins (George Bellamy); Tom Harkaway (Douglas Munro); Hon. Archibald Moll (Hayford Hobbs); Countess of Skene and Skve (Gwynne Herbert); Lady Fenella Hull (Mary Dibley); Dorothy (Christine Rayner). From "Jelf's," a play. By H. A. Vachell.

Dick Jelf, who has been ranching in Arizona, is recalled to London by his uncle to take over the direction of the banking house of Jelf's. There is much misgiving among the representatives of finance.

Through Jim Palliser, also a banker, Dick meets Lady Fenella Hull and her aristocratic, though impoverished, family. Fenella is engaged to Palliser, but his bank is shaky and her mother insists on the engagement being broken. Dick is captivated by the beautiful girl, but she complains to her mother of his crudeness. However, she recognizes his strength and agrees to marry him.

Dick's unconventionality scandalizes Sir Jonathan Dunne, president of the Bankers' Association, but the ex-rancher shows brains and adaptability. The crisis comes when Palliser, faced by ruin, begs Dick to help him and Dick does so out of his own resources, for Jelf's bank must not be connected with Palliser's. Soon after Dick finds Jim Palliser making love to Fenella, but he keeps his word, even when Palliser telephones to a financial paper that Jelf's bank is supporting Palliser's. The news that Jelf's Bank is backing a rotten concern like Palliser's causes a run on the bank which Dick faces alone. A panic-stricken mob surges at the doors. Tom Harkaway, who is known by every sporting man to have £200,000 in Jelf's, can't trust his money with one who has been "fool enough to back Jim Palliser."

When the outlook is darkest, Fenella who has tried to induce Palliser to make amends, comes and stands at Dick's side. When the last moment comes and the cash is exhausted, Harkaway, impressed by Dick's honesty and courage, checks the crowd with a hasty bellow, telling them to leave their money where he is going to leave his—with an honest man. Then Sir Jonathan, who has been watching Dick closely, induces the Bankers' Association to stand by Jelf's, and the old bank weathers the storm and Dick wins the girl.

SPARKLE COMEDY.

THE STAG PARTY. The cast: Sally (Effie Shelley); Billy Barlow (Tom McEvoy); Bob Temple (Tom Mulgrew); Grace Gilmore (Mildren Bright). Story by Mae A. Hitchcock.

Billy Barlow sends Sally a note inviting her to go motoring 'but drops it, and his sister Betty puts it in his overcoat. Billy finds Sally out, and thinks she does not love him. Meantime Bob Temple and Grace Gilmore have planned to elope and ask Billy to help them. On the night of the elopement Sally gives a stag party for her girl friends and Betty provides herself and several others with clothes from her brother's wardrobe. Billy is astonished to find his clothes gone. Finding Betty's invitation to the stag party he sees a chance of getting even with Sally and chooses the police a description of the clothes, saying the thieves are at Sally's house. He starts out in his pajamas and overcoat, but is arrested for speeding. He phones Bob to bring him some clothes.

Meantime the police arrive at Sally's and they are all brought to the station house. Billy has been released, and hearing of the raid he and Bob race to the station house. Explanations follow and Bob, Grace and Billy hasten to the minister's. Grace still wearing male clothing. At the depot Grace and Bob pick up the wrong suit case and discover on their arrival at the hotel that Grace has a bag full of men's clothes while Bob has the bag containing Billy's pajamas. After mutual explanations, Billy and Sally race to the minister's and are married.

KALEM.

A BUSHRANGER'S STRATEGY. An Episode of "The Further Adventures of Stingaree" (Two Parts).—The cast: Stingaree (True Boardman); Howie (Paul C. Hurst); Signor Corelli (Barney Furey); Jane Ryder (Edythe Sterling); Sergeant Whipple (Jack Waltemeyer). Story by E. W. Hornung. Directed by Paul C. Hurst.

Stingaree and Howie are surprised to meet, near this camp, an Italian violinist, who introduces himself as Signor Acamporo. Stingaree recognizes the name as that of a master musician and is delighted at the meeting. Himself a violinist, the gentleman bushranger rejoices at the opportunity of hearing such a celebrated performer. But Howie suggests "If this feller's worth a barrel o' money, why not hold him for ransom?" The signor makes no objection to this, as he realizes that to be held for ransom by the famous Stingaree will be a great advertisement when he returns home. The bushrangers take the musician to their camp, and Stingaree appears disappointed when he hears the Italian play.

Jane Ryder, a former show girl, arriving in the bush country, finds that her horse has gone lame, and is forced to abandon him and proceed on foot. Approaching the camp of the bushrangers, she finds a handkerchief that the Italian musician has dropped, and appears to recognize it. The signor, while playing for Stingaree, sees Jane dodging through the bushes. Awaiting his opportunity, he slips away and waylays the girl. He binds her hand and foot, and hearing the bushrangers calling, hurries back to the camp.

While the Italian is enjoying a repast Jane manages to free herself and is soon lost in the bush country. Stingaree, again listening to the signor play, instructs Howie to fetch the Italian's horse.

Troopers of the New South Wales Mounted Police hear the strains of the signor's violin and approach. Coming in sight of the violinist, he signals them to approach further, and they surround the bushranger's tent. They see it move, and believe the bushranger to be inside. Rushing inside, they find the Italian's horse. Stingaree has escaped.

Riding away from camp, Stingaree and Howie meet Jane. She tells them her story. Penniless and desperate, she is following a man who had stolen the money she had saved to return to her home in England. He was the orchestra leader in the show in which she played. From her description, Stingaree knows that the fake Signor Acampora is the man. Riding off, he finds the Italian who, with the troopers, has resumed the search for the bushrangers. He takes him back to Jane and hands over to the girl the money which he finds hidden in the Italian's violin. Then, compelling the signor to take off his boots and socks, he gives him a canteen of water and sends him forth barefooted.

The feet of the troopers' accomplice are soon cut and scratched as he trods over the rough ground, while Jane thanks the bushrangers and accepts the loan of Stingaree's horse to ride back to town.

THE STRANGER AT DUMCRIEFF (Episode of "The Further Adventures of Stingaree)—Two Parts. The cast: Stingaree (True Boardman); Howie (Paul C. Hurst); John Stewart (G. A. Williams); Edith Stewart (Edythe Sterling); Stephen Hope (Edward Hearn); Jerome Moffitt (Frank Jonasson); Sergeant Deane (Barney Furey). Directed by Paul C. Hurst.

Just as Stephen Hope, the youthful minister of Dumcrieff, becomes engaged to Edith Stuart, a stranger calls. The minister recognizes him as Jerome Moffitt, who recalls to the days when they were cell-mates in prison. Moffitt demands money, and when refused spreads the news that the minister is an ex-convict. The villagers plan a public denunciation of Hope.

Stingaree enters the village in a disguise to purchase ammunition. He recognizes Hope as a man who once befriended him when Stingaree lived in England and plans to vindicate him. With Howie, Stingaree meets Moffitt, invites him up to his cabin and gives him several drinks until his tongue is sufficiently loosened to tell the story of Hope's arrest and conviction for a crime Moffitt himself committed.

The public denunciation of the minister at the Sunday service has begun when the bushrangers arrive with Moffitt. While Howie keeps guard outside, Stingaree holds up the church and forces Moffitt to tell the story of Hope's conviction. They are interrupted by the arrival of the mounted police. Hope persuades Sergeant Deane to allow the bushranger to complete his mission. Deane waits in the sacristy, facing the altar where Stingaree is standing. But Howie sneaks in and overpowers the trooper. After vindicating the minister, Stingaree is able to make a getaway.

Stingaree and Howie ride to their retreat, satisfied with their day's work, while Hope is reunited to his sweetheart.

Universal Film Mfg. Co.

ANIMATED WEEKLY.

ISSUE No. 87 (Aug. 30).

Marine "Masked Ball" Prepared for Sea Wolves.—Spbmarine Chasers Built by United States for France Invisible at a Distance.—An American Navy Yard. Subtitle: A Keen Eye and a Steady Hand and the Subsea Boat Will Be Found!

Opera Star Sings to Troops.—Governor Edge Introduces Miss Anna Case to Jersey Guardsmen.—Sea Girt, N. J. Subtitle: Left to right: Col. Landin, Anna Case and Governor Edge.

Armour Co. Ice Plant Burns.—War Plot Suspected in $400,000 Fire at Largest Ice Plant in World.—Round Lake, Ill. Subtitle: 100,000 Tons of Ice Destroyed.

British Volunteers From America.—Major General Sir Fancis Lloyd Commends Patriots in Review on Horse Guards Parade.—London, England.

Review of Princeton University Warriors.—Brigadier Gen. Chas. W. Barber Inspects Student Soldiers. Subtitles: Realistic Bayonet Drill. Charging Dummies.

3,000 Car Strikers Parade with Wives and Babies.—Plea for "Living Wage" Makes One of the Most Spectacular Labor Demonstrations Ever Held.—San Francisco, Cal.

Wreck of Grain Steamer Spokane.—Loaded with Wheat, Big Freighter Collides with Pier and Sinks.—Sault Ste. Marie, Mich. Subtitle: Salvagers at Work.

Making Comfort Kits for "Sammies."—Red Cross nurses preparing to ship boxes to U. S. soldiers in France.—Pittsburgh, Pa. Subtitles: "Needles and Pins, Needles and Pins."

When a man enlists his troubles begin—

UNTIL he gets a comfort kit.

Teaching the Soldiers to Cook.—Public school instructor volunteers four days a week to educate 22nd Engineers in culinary art.—New York City. Subtitles: Flipping Flapjacks. Tough as Leather? Not on Your Life!

Welcoming Japanese Envoys at Capital.—Secretary Lansing and Other Officials Cordially Greet Baron Ishii and the Imperial War Mission.—Washington, D. C. Subtitles: Escorted by Cavalry Along Pennsylvania Avenue. The Visiting Diplomats of the Mikado.

Cracks of the Racket Play Patriotic Tennis.—War turned the National Championship Tournament into a Brilliant Exhibition Benefit for the Tennis Ambulance Sections in France.—Forest Hills, L. I. Subtitles: Miss Molla Bjurstedt (left), National Woman Champion, and Miss Mary K. Browne, the Tennis Wonder-Girl of California, Three Times Former Champion. East Versus West—Robert Lindley Murray, of California, winning the tournament from Nathaniel W. Niles, of Boston.

Fighting Sixty-ninth Has 25,000 Callers.—Famous Irish-American Regiment from New York, now the 165th, plays and prays on its first Sunday at Camp Mills, L. I. Subtitles: Rev. Father Duffy, Chaplain of the Regiment, Celebrating the Mass. At Field Mass on Hempstead Plains.

Cartoons by Hy Mayer, world famous caricaturist.

UNIVERSAL CURRENT EVENTS.

ISSUE NUMBER 16 (Aug. 31).

Giant Bulldog Guardians of Uncle Sam's Shoreline Thunder Defiance at Democracy's Enemies.—These have been used to train new coast artillery officers in the difficult art of big gun handling. Subtitle: Some shells are large and some are small, but they only have one mission—to put a kink in Kaiserism.

Dances of the Old Days Versus Broadway Winners.—Ned Wayburn puts his beauties in the "Ziegfeld Follies" chorus through stunts for benefit of National Convention of Dancing Masters.—McAlpin Hotel, N. Y. City. Subtitle: This is what grandfather paid good money to see. "Swanee River." "Watch Your Step!" "Oh, You baby!"

Dogs Do "Their Bit"—for patriotic cause. Elite of canine society display themselves at show for benefit of the Red Cross.—Atlantic City, N. J. Subtitles: Rip Van Winkle, Junior. Highbrows from Boston. Fluffy-fluff-fluff of the Powder-Puff Class.

Eagles Make the Eagle Scream! Patriotism Reaches High Pitch at Annual Convention of Order. Mammoth parade is the feature event of festive week at Buffalo, N. Y. Subtitle: They didn't want anybody to miss "Old Glory."

"As Iron Workers We Are Good Dancers!" That's What the Dolly Sisters Say. When they aren't dancing and acting on Broadway these talented twins do movie stunts on hotel roof.—New York City. Subtitle: "When it's 99 in the shade heating rivets is perfectly adorable!" "Iron working is such a nice, lady-like job—we love it!"

Learn to Swim on Dry Land.—Y. M. C. A. gives complete course of instruction to boys before allowing them to enter water.—Silver Bay, N. Y. Subtitle: The stroke is first taught. Theory is immediately followed by practice! You can take a post-graduate course in fancy diving. Look at this!

Benny Leonard Fights for Uncle Sam—But Not in France. Champion lightweight boxer gives a war benefit exhibition at Monument Grounds. Washington, D. C. James J. Corbett, master of ceremonies (left), gives the "Glad Hand" to Benny. Subtitle: The little champion displays a full line of the "mule-kick" wallops that won him fame.

Russian Diplomats Welcomed by Aged "Boys in Blue." G. A. R. Veterans march miles through torrid city streets to honor distinguished visitors.—Boston, Mass. Subtitle: They proudly display the flag of the republic THEY fought to save.

"Safety First" Is a National Slogan—But Wrecks Sometimes Happen.—Steel coaches prevent great loss of life as train leaves rails at high speed.—Seabrooke, La.

Bevy of Daring Beach Venuses Sport Fearlessly with Sharks.—Only these don't bite and make great surf-sleds.—Ocean Park, Cal. Subtitle: Three charming dare-devil experts. Whoops, my dear! Tao higher the better!

Bravest Nation-Martyr in All History Sends Mission for Munitions to Wage Fight for Freedom.—Marked tribute paid to members of Belgium War Mission upon arrival in nation's metropolis, New York City. Subtitles: Mission arrives at City Hall. Marines and sailors forming honor guard pass in review. Baron Moncheur, head of Mission, and Mayor Mitchel.

VICTOR.

IN THE CLUTCHES OF MILK (Victor—Sept. 10. The cast: Max (Max Asher); his niece (Gladys Tennyson); Dick (Chester Bennet). Story and production by Craig Hutchinson.

Max refuses to let his niece marry Dick, because he says Dick is not a moral fellow. Max proceeds to make love to the maid. He receives a letter and, not having his spectacles, has his niece read its contents. Some one threatens to beat him up for being a "woman chaser." Max is frightened. A bum comes to see him, but his niece says her uncle left for Europe—to be gone five years.

Dick arrives and is told that the niece can't marry him, so he decides to kill himself and rushes to the drug store for poison. Max is getting drunk and very flirtatious. Terrified at Dick's threat, his girl takes the bottle to tell Max about it. She hides the poison, after tearing off the label and goes back to Dick. Max discovers the bottle and takes a drink, which causes him to cough. The niece rushes out. Seeing the bottle, she yells that Max has drunk poison. Dick is dumfounded. Max rushes out, partially dressed. He snatches a bottle of milk from a wagon, but the milkman gives chase. A crowd carries Max to a doctor's house, where the doctor prepares to use the stomach pump. But the drug clerk rushes in to tell them that he gave Dick the wrong stuff—ipecac instead of poison.

STAR FEATURETTE.

TO THE HIGHEST BIDDER (Two Parts—Sept. 10).—Story by Emmett Campbell Hall. Directed by Lucius Henderson.

Rose Weston looked up from her uncongenial task of churning butter, as Robert Wayne, her sweetheart, came up the path.

That night the family is gathered in the sitting-room. Robert and Rose's father talk "crops." Rose's fat brother is engaged in brushing flies from his forehead; her mother is sewing. Rose bangs at the piano unmercifully.

"Rose, child, what is the matter? Hush!"

"I am tired of stopping, hushing, being quiet, living in the country, listening to talk of crops!" She rushes blindly from the room.

Later Robert hands Rose a letter. She is still angry, so he kisses her and leaves.

Next day Rose receives a letter from a former schoolmate, Esther, who deplores the fact that the girl is going to marry a farmer, settle down in the country and be an old "drudge." Shortly, thereafter, Rose's father hands her a cheque for $300, which has been left her by an uncle. In the night, Rose slips from the house, having left a note saying that she is going to the city and Robert ought to be glad to get rid of her.

Rose goes to the apartment of Esther, where there is in progress a Bohemian party. The girl drinks her first glass of wine.

There follows many auto trips and suppers. Rose's funds are becoming very low. She announces, to friends, at the close of a day spent in the woods, that, at the end of a certain time, she will sell herself to the highest bidder.

Meanwhile a prospector has met Robert and discovered a copper mine, which the two develop. Robert comes to town, and with his partner is seated in a restaurant where there is a gay party. He is attracted to one of the women, and when she turns he sees that she is Rose. His partner tells him of her declaration to sell herself to the highest bidder.

Rose sees Robert and starts to speak to him. He repulses her. When she arrives home she finds him waiting for her. He remonstrates with her and she orders him out of the place.

The day of the auction draws near. Robert gives his partner a blank cheque telling him to bid anonymously for the woman.

The auction is at hand. Rose, mounted on a chair, goes under the hammer. Suitors bid for her. One offers riches in India; another spreads jewels at her feet; another lures her with the promise of making her a prima donna; Robert's friend offers wealth, in the form of a cheque, in behalf of an absent friend.

A message arrives. Rose announces that every one is outbidden.

Robert is dejected when his partner tells him the outcome of the sale. He packs up and goes back to the farm.

In the garden he meets Rose. She shows him her father's note, telling her he forgives her for having left home and explains this is a higher bid than any for her.

They are happily reunited, each the richer for their experiences.

NESTOR.

THE BOULEVARD SPEED HOUNDS (Sept. 10).—The cast: Clinton Syx (Eddie Lyons); Steele A. Ryde (Lee Moran); G. Rabum Quick (Harry Nolan); Cherrie Sundae (Ray Godfrey); Mrs. Clinton Syx (Edith Roberts). Story by F. A. Palmer. Produced by B. George.

"You're under arrest! Stop!"

"But this is a physician," Ryde explains. "Wife's ill."

The cop becomes suspicious. He demands to see friend wife. Syx has to carry the bluff through and Ryde gets into the wife's bed. The cop sees the form in bed (and something else), which he believes is a baby.

The cop demands that he be allowed to get the wife's signature. Ryde has resumed his own clothes and hurries to borrow "a wife." He secures his fiancee, who happens to be passing, gets her upstairs and into the bed. The cop is satisfied. BUT—when he has gone, the real wife returns, and the girl is still in the house. After considerable excitement and sundry narrow escapes she meets the girl and finds her to be an old friend, the fiancee of her hubby's friend. All, thenceforth, is well with the Syx's and affairs are amicably settled.

GOLD SEAL.

THE PERILOUS LEAP (Gold Seal—Three Parts—Sept. 10).—The cast: Joe Mead (O. C. Jackson); "Dad" Shannon (George Williams); Pete Larkins (George Routh); Effie (Helen Gibson); Ned Donnely (Val Paul). Story by S. Sutton, produced by J. D. Davis.

Joe Mead stood on the porch of "Honest" Dad Shannon's shack, to all intents an agent of a munition factory in search of quicksilver, but, in reality, the head of a clique of smugglers.

Dad Shannon believed in everybody, despite the fact that he knows Le Crus, not far from the Mexican border, is infested with opium smugglers and Chinese.

He allows the "mercury" to be located in his shed, for Joe says the government is in need of it. Joe warns "Dad" to keep the affair a secret.

Pete Larkins, a renegade brakeman and member of the band, is in love with Effie, Shannon's daughter, but she cares nothing for him. But when she meets Ned Donnelly of the Secret Service, the attraction is mutual.

Ned warns the inspector to watch Mead. That night the inspector sees Mead and "Dad" lifting boxes from an auto and carrying them into the shed. The inspector approaches the shed and breaks the locks. He finds the boxes contain opium.

Mead meets Pete, who warns the former that Ned is in town and the two men hasten to look after their stuff. They see some one is in the shed and, when the inspector comes out Mead fires and misses, then the inspector shoots and both men fall wounded, while Pete takes the guns and runs away. "Dad" rushes out and Ned and Effie join him. Ned concludes some one has tried to murder the men, for there is no weapon about.

Later Pete tells "Dad" it will go hard if they find the opium in his shed, but he is willing to keep quiet if "Dad" will let him marry Effie. Effie offers to marry Pete to save her father. Ned receives word that Pete is identified as a member of Mead's gang. He stops to watch him. Ned then urges Shannon to make a clean breast of the whole affair. Shannon tells Ned Pete agreed to take the opium away and promises to help Ned catch the culprits.

Pete moves the stuff to the railroad yard and prepares to send it out on No. 7, along with some Chinamen. Effie informs Ned and he rushes to the depot where Pete is just reaching the car. Ned holds Pete up with his gun, but a Chinaman suddenly jumps from the car onto

Ned, who is overpowered and thrown into the car. Effie has seen this act. She swings onto a car as the train passes, but is seen by Pete who runs to her, trying to prevent her from reaching the top of the car. They struggle. She gets away and climbs to the top of the car, but is caught and Pete tries to throw her in the refrigerator car as they go under a bridge. Effie trips Pete, then grabs one of the girders and swings from the train, dropping onto the train several cars away from Pete, who seeing her trick, runs after her.

Meanwhile, Ned has had a desperate fight with the Chinaman, who is trying to knife him. Escaping, he climbs to the top of the car and sees the struggle between Pete and Effie. Ned knocks Pete from the train and catches Effie as she swoons. Finally the train is stopped. Pete is forced to confess to everything, exonerating "Dad," and Ned and Effie plan to be married.

JOKER.

SHORT SKIRTS AND DEEP WATER (Sept. 10).—The cast: President of Anti-Sin League (Gale Henry); Deacon (William Franey); Judge of Police Court (M. Moranti). Story and direction by Allen Curtis.

The president of the Anti-Sin League has called a meeting to discuss the shortness of bathing suits. Her right-hand man is the Deacon. He is bent on getting evidence, but falters upon seeing divers types of loveliness which the bathing suits adorn.

The president is a fire-brand and takes her fight to the Police Judge. She convinces him the short-skirted suit must go.

The Deacon is observed by the president and determines to teach him a lesson. Donning a bathing suit with a long skirt, she veils her face and starts to lure the Deacon. He is taken off the yarn with which the bathing suit was made becomes entangled on a nail and the skirt is unraveled to an alarming shortness by the time she is seen by the Deacon. He follows and she proposes a boat ride. They land on an island, where she discloses her identity and maroons the Deacon.

While waiting she is run down by the police boat, searching for violators of the new law, and is arrested and locked up for ninety days. Remembering the Deacon, she manages to escape disguised as a policeman and arrives in time to take the penitent Deacon aboard her boat.

NEARLY A QUEEN (Sept. 10)—The cast: Belinda (Gale Henry); Felix (Milton Sims); Stranger (Charles Haefili), Story and production by Allen Curtis.

It is the morning of a terrible storm off a lonely island. A baby girl has been washed ashore and is adopted by an island couple..

Grown to womanhood, there comes a stranger who tells her she is the daughter of kings, that she has a palace and wealth awaiting her. Felix, her lover, is forgotten as she makes plans to go to her throne. But—she has reckoned without the cupidity of the stranger. He plans to get rid of the princess and have the throne to himself. His accomplices lure her aboard their boat, tie her in a sack and dump her overboard. Felix, however, is a stowaway, and manages to get her to shore. The stranger again come upon them. He is bested in the fight and Belinda is taken away. She is tied in an abandoned cabin and the place set afire. Felix tries to put the fire out, but before he can succeed, is made a captive by the plotters.

Felix's dog comes to the rescue and frees Felix who is amazed to find the cabin. Nothing daunted, he digs in the embers and finds her unharmed. She is still the "Queen" and instead of winning commendation, he gets nothing but abuse. Trying to explain, he follows her back to the village where they come upon the stranger explaining that a mistake has been made, that he is the King. The "King" spies Belinda and she is once more set upon, but this time Felix defends her valiantly. The fight is interrupted by the arrival of a couple of guards from a nearby asylum. They take Napoleon away with them, explaining to Belinda that his mania seems to be threes.

Belinda is the laughing stock on account of the airs she put on. But Felix gets on the job and once more they are happily reunited.

L-KO.

FROM CACTUS TO KALE (Two Parts—Sept. 10).—Directed by Noel Smith.

Gladys, the waitress in the restaurant, offers Walter a pail of water. He has had a bad time of it when he is mistaken for a cow and almost branded. He is inclined to be comforted, however, by Gladys, until the cook with floury gestures announces the house's slogan: "Shot at sunrise if you flirt with the waitress."

Walter is kicked out and lands on a cactus bush. He returns with a handful and throws it at the cook. The fight is on and the place is almost demolished.

In a sitting-room the no longer young Miss Young reclines on a sofa, and Harry gives the paper the once over. They both jump to their feet when he reads a certain paragraph and make a rush for the depot. But the train has already steamed out, carrying a mustached gentleman who carries some very precious papers.

Harry and Miss Young pursue the train in an auto and board it at the tank station. Miss Young engage the mustached gentleman in conversation. She winks to Harry. He follows to the rear end platform where he administers to Miss Young's companion a dose of chloroform and hurls him from the train.

The couple arrives in the town and Gladys and Walter make for the restaurant. They take Walter and tell him piles of gold await him in the city.

Walter, once arrived in the Metropolis, indulges in diversions, which almost put the precious trio in very bad. However, Walter and Miss Young land the young gentleman in a house, where there are a number of strange-looking inmates. One gives Walter the combination of a safe, after which he fails dead. When the couple see Walter has the safe's combination they attempt to wrest it from him, after having installed him as master in a large house, where he is giving a large dinner party. He is eating principally with his knife and shooting from the table live crabs and lobsters.

Meanwhile the mustached gentleman has picked himself up from the embankment, brushed off the dust from his coat and made his way into town and into the good graces of Gladys. He tells her Harry and Miss Young have kidnapped him and in order to pursue the trio and arrive just as the conspirators are wresting the fortune from the safe. They rush through the house, hands, arms, pockets filled

with bank notes, Gladys, Walter and the mustached gentleman hot in pursuit. The race gathers momentum and grows as it continues through the streets, demolishes whole buildings and ends in the middle of the ocean, where the lovers are reunited.

BACKWARD BONS AND FORWARD DAUGH. TERS (Two Parts—Sept. 3).—Directed by Phil Dunham.

Billy, supposed to saw wood, was possessed of other plans. He went fishing.

Lucille was rich. She held a mortgage to the soil where Billy was fishing. The Bevans, proud parents of Billy, were about to be ejected.

"I have a plan," said Lucille as she broke in upon them. "Your son", exclaimed the unhandsome spinster. They found Billy. But he had other plans.

Billy took Lucille for a boat ride, during which he managed to drop her in the middle of the lake, a stone about her throat. Then he packed his belongings and beat it for town.

In the hash house of the sweltering city he found employment and love, in the person of the proprietor's daughter. But Lucille, recovering, got on the job.

Bill had no intention of giving up his sweetheart, but he could not confide to her that a former would-be flame devoured corn flakes at one of her father's tables.

"Quick, a mustache from the wigmaker", Bill appealed to a fellow slave. As they are cooing at the desk, Lucille has penetrated Bill's disguise and rushes toward him, throwing herself into his unwilling arms. "Out of my way", exclaims Bill, grabbing up about a dozen and a half plates, which he manipulates with telling effect.

A marconi battle follows, with more dishes thrown and a complete demolishing of the place.

Lucille goes back to the farm, much the worse for wear, and Bill takes into his arms the fair form of his beloved. The mortgage is lifted from the homestead, and Bill's parents welcome his bride. Lucille takes courage again in the smiles of a lean ledger, sure that he has at last found in love a much-needed and long-coveted meal ticket.

UNIVERSAL SPECIAL.

THE GRAY GHOST (Episode No. 11—"The Flaming Meteor"—Two Parts—Sept. 3).—The cast: Morn Light (Priscilla Dean); Wade Hildreth (Emory Johnson); His Secretary Marco (Eddie Polo); The Gray Ghost (Harry Carter); Cecelia (Gypsy Hart); Arabian (Howard Crampton); Jerry Tryon (Lou Short); Williams (Francis Macdonald). Story by A. S. Roche. Directed by Stuart Paton.

Moonlight, Hildreth and Marco, stealing through the underbrush, suddenly paused in terror. Three weird shapes were approaching them. They moved as if encased in metal, as indeed they were. With indrawn breath came a sensation in the throat of each of the fugitives. They saw a stream of vapor coming from the mouths of the figures, which moved upon them.

"It is poison gas!" cried Marco. "Fly for your lives!" The sky grew darker and darker, and the whole atmosphere seemed charged with deadly fumes. Suddenly there came a crash. The sky seemed to split and a meteor plunged head on crashing the figures to the ground.

Cecelia, Morn Light's maid, had watched with jealous attention the progress of the Gray Ghost's infatuation. Now she searched him out, and informed him she knew the secret which enabled him to confront with such indifference the menace of his enemies.

"I'll inflict upon you the fate you reserved for me!" she cried, advancing with upraised knife; for she had learned that only a knife stab to the heart could kill him. As she approached he gave the signal, and she was surrounded by his henchmen and quickly discovered. She fell into passionate sobbing, while he left her to seek Morn Light, who had been discovered wandering on the island. His object was to obtain the ring Hildreth had given her, and he exerted the mysterious influence he possessed to attain his end. Morn Light never knew why she acceded to his demands, but she was powerless in his hands. She was about to hand him the ring when Cecelia spoke.

"You're 'covered", she said coldly, and the master thief, turning, saw a revolver in her hands.

UNIVERSAL SCREEN MAGAZINE.

ISSUE NO. 36 (Sept. 14).

"The first subject shows how inland sea-birds and myriads of sea-fowl live on Bird Island in the center of the great Salt Lake and keep the identity of the species intact. There is first a launch laden with nature students, leaving for Bird Island, and a flock of California gulls. An afternoon siesta of thousands of pelicans on the surface of the lake, groups of sandhill cranes, blue heron and handsome specimens of the gull family, together with fine views from the summit of Bird Island, make this interesting.

What We Eat, the second subject, shows the various ways of making butter on the farm, from the separation of milk and cream to the moulding of one-pound prints of butter.

Better Babies—For a perfect peach of a specimen, little Miss Romaine Williams is seen being put through a third degree, just loving all manner of exercises to make sturdy and vigorous arms, shoulders, legs, spine and knees.

A splendid preparedness subject reveals the making of shrapnel and other shells, from the rough castings down to the Government inspection of them and mobilization for shipment to the front. Willie Hopkins contributes a number on "Swat the Fly".

BISON.

THE TEXAS SPHINX (Two Parts—Sept. 10).—The cast: Jim Cranman (Harry Carey); Bob Giles ("Hoot" Gibson); Dave Baxter (Ed. Jones); Steve (Vester Pegg); Elsie (Alice Lake); Dick Lonagan (Bill Gettinger). Story by T. S. Sutton. Produced by F. A. Kelsey.

Everybody knew Sheriff Baxter of Maverick was considerable of a coward and a "softie". The stage coach approaches Maverick, with one lone passenger. Two men see it. One wants to rob it, the other demurs. The first man, Giles, decides to rob it alone. He does so, taking the money he finds in the possession of the lone passenger, who is Dick Lonagan. Giles returns to his companion, Cranman, and goes to Ballinger, where Pete Howell recently robbed the postoffice. Cranman proceeds after the stage coach to Maverick. The stage coach driver makes known the holdup.

Lonagan is introduced as a cattle buyer from El Paso. He says he is broke and is taken home by McGibben's daughter, and immediately takes a liking to her. Cranman arrives and is seen by the Sheriff, who becomes suspicious of him, but McGibben tells him he is not the holdup man. The Sheriff gets the idea that Cranman is the man who is wanted in Ballinger, and confers with McGibben. Cranman meets Elsie. Elsie likes Lonagan and Cranman is unable to warn her against him, although he believes Lonagan to be a bad character.

Lonagan calls on the Sheriff and the Sheriff tells him that he suspects Cranman of being the bandit. He encourages the Sheriff's belief. The Sheriff decides to "get" Cranman. Elsie learns of this, and is cautioned by her father to stay away from Cranman. Lonagan presses his suit, favored by the father. Elsie agrees to marry Lonagan. Lonagan insists that the Sheriff arrest Cranman, and, believing the Sheriff afraid, he agrees to arrest him, giving the Sheriff the reward and the glory.

Lonagan lays for Cranman and covers him. No one but the Sheriff and Elsie (unseen) sees this. Elsie is not quite satisfied that Cranman is guilty. Lonagan places Cranman in jail; then urges Elsie to leave with him on their honeymoon in Oklahoma.

Meanwhile Giles arrives in Maverick. He overhears a conversation and learns Cranman is in jail. The Sheriff, Lonagan and McGibben meet Giles. He is recognized as the hold-up man. Giles admits Cranman is his partner, but does not reveal his character or business. Giles is denounced as the robber. Lonagan attempts to cover Giles, but the latter is too quick for him.

Giles disarms the men, keeping them covered, leads them up to the jail and explains that they held up the stage to get the evidence on Lonagan; that he is Pete Howell, and that they have the money he took from Ballinger. Giles turns over photo of Howell to Sheriff and convinces him.

family and jealous of the family name, believes a member of that family responsible for the murder of Nathan Standish, her brother, who is mysteriously stabbed from behind a portiere.

Sylvia discovers the knife with which the deed was perpetrated and hides it. Bobbins, the footman, known to have hated Standish, comes under suspicion of the crime. To preserve the Standish name, Sylvia allows Bobbins to be dragged away to jail.

"Bull" Ziegler, a detective, suspecting that the surface indications concerning the murder are false, pursues his investigations privately, to the horror of Sylvia, who is haunted by remorse. On the insistence of her father, Sylvia marries Paul Wagner, the district attorney. Her fear of an exposure is thus emphasized.

Meantime Ziegler has become convinced that Bobbins is innocent, and that an effort is being made to convict him of another's crime. He suspects Sylvia. Having pursued the young wife to a retreat in the mountains, to which she has been sent by her husband, Ziegler is in time to witness the clearing up of the mystery and the clearing of the Standish name of the crime, through confession of a girl suicide that Chester Standish had been her betrayer and that she had killed him in revenge after secreting herself in his home.

OUTCAST (Empire—Six Parts—Sept. 10).— The cast: Geoffry (David Powell); Valentine (Kathryn Calvert); Hugh (Richard Hatteras); Tony (Jules Raucourt); Mr. Guest (Herbert Ayling); Lord Moreland (Reginald Carrington); Mrs. Guest (Kate Sergeantson); Taylor (H. Ashton Tonge); Gerald (V. L. Granville); Beulah (Maud Andrew); Miriam's father (James Malaidy); Miriam (Ann Murdock). Directed by Dell Henderson.

Miriam, a beautiful girl without near relatives, meets, loves and is betrayed by a handsome adventurer who later abandons her to marry an old woman with money. When the child is born, Miriam finds herself without friends or funds.

Compelled to take to the street for funds to save her child from starvation, she sells herself for naught, because the child dies. She buries her hopes with the baby and, despairing of any future for herself, adopts the life of a courtesan.

Taken up by Geoffrey Sherwood, a London barrister who has been jilted by his fiance, Miriam becomes Sherwood's mistress. She hopes he will marry her, but as time goes on and the influence of his former fiance is re-established, this hope lessens. Valentine is married to a man of great wealth, but remains unhappy. Sherwood convinces her that all must be over between them. He then offers marriage to Miriam, and after being wed in a little Scottish kirk they start for Buenos Aires.

THE RAINBOW GIRL (Five Parts—Sept. 17). —The cast: Mary Beth (Juliette Day); Richard Warner (George Fisher); Amos (Charles Bennett); Christiana (Lilian Hayward); Plugger (Louis Morrison; Mme. Lavatenne Du Bois (Emma Kluge); Eva Bangaway (Marie Robertson).

Mary Beth never was grum or grouchy, not even when her daddy came home to say his job was gone and he was too old to get another. She said: "Don't be sad. Here's my money to tide things over."

Mary had been saving a small legacy to get a musical education, but she gladly sacrificed herself to make her daddy comfy. To help out a little letter, Mary put an ad in the paper for a roomer for the attic.

Richard Warner, a poor musician, was looked upon as a joke where he tried to sell his songs. He needed a room and took the one in Mary Beth's attic. They fell in love at once. Both lied and said they had sweethearts and some day that they both had sweethearts and some day they hoped to patch things up.

Poor Richard got shabbier and shabbier and finally hungry. He just couldn't put his ballads over. He was desperate, so came home and chancing to find a book which quoted Pliny as saying it was fine to commit suicide, turned on the gas and closed the windows. But a plate of biscuits and a pot of tea saved him from the great beyond. Mary Beth brought them up and when he had eaten them he felt so good that he wanted to live.

It was well he did, for the next day Mary took his song about the rainbow girl to Old Plugger,

the music publisher, and sold it. Now Richard had lots of money, yet he wasn't happy.

He was thinking about that sweetheart of Mary Beth's. He wanted to see the thing squared up, so he said, "I'll give her up and get out." But Mary Beth caught him in his exit.

"Aw, I fibbed," admitted she.

"Well! well, so did I," he breathed, close in her embrace. Can't you hear the sweet wedding bells.

SIGNAL.

THE LOST EXPRESS (Signal—Chapter 1—Two Parts—Sept. 17). The cast: Helen Thurston (Helen Holmes); Pitts (Leo Maloney); The Baron (Thomas G. Lingham); Vaiques (V. O. Whitehead); Charles Bonner (William Brunton); Francis Murphy (Edward Hearn); General Thurston (John McKinnon).

Helen Thurston is the daughter of General Thurston, inventor-financier—man of wealth. Thurston owns a new invention for granulating gasoline, a mechanical invention affecting combustion, without which granulated gas is useless.

Thurston's mansion is outside Capital City near Landpert. With him live his daughter, Helen, and Gaston Pitts, private secretary. Thurston regards Pitts as a future husband for Helen, who distrusts the man.

The representative of a foreign government, Vaiques negotiates for rights to Thurston's process. Thurston is obdurate. Vaiques hires crooks to obtain the device. In this gang are "The Lench," "The Baron" and "The Hare." "The Hare" has a harelip. He resembles Pitts but for that deformity.

This gang burglarizes the Thurston place. Helen gives the alarm. General Thurston is paralyzed by a bullet wound.

Helen hires an express train to transfer the invention and models to a city bank vault. The express train completely disappears between stations from a single line of rail with no switches. Helen rescues the crew of the missing train in a desperate leap from a speeding engine to a wagon pulled by runaway horses.

CUB.

OFFICER JERRY (Cub—One Reel—Sept. 20). —The cast: Jerry (George Ovey); Bill (George George); Pete (Gordon MacGregor); Jack (John J. Hayes); Tilly (Beulah Booker); Bess (Eva Southern). Written and produced by M. H. Fahrney.

Jerry becomes enamoured of a maid servant in the home of a wealthy newly married couple. His flirtation is interrupted by the arrival of Jack and his bride. Jerry sticks around while Jack opens a letter from Bill, a wild-eyed gun man who is enraged at Jack's marriage to Bess. Bill threatens Jack's life and Jack writes a note to the police demanding protection. Jerry gives the letter to Tilly who has been granted an afternoon off. Jerry meets Tilly and promises to mail the note. Tilly leads Jerry to a dressmaker's where several dummies appeal to his sense of humor. Jerry and Tilly select a seat in the park where they expect seclusion but the inevitable cop drives Jerry from his new found love. Jerry opens the letter he promised to mail. A sergeant appears. Jerry peaches on the amorous cop who is fired. Jerry runs to the dressmaker's where he steals a dummy. Returning, he throws the dummy in the lake, rushes up to the humiliated cop and points to the dummy and tells him it is Tilly. The boy discards his uniform, leaps in the lake and drags the dummy ashore while Jerry does his uniform and applies to Jack as preserver of the peace.

Tilly recognizes Jerry, serves him a repast in the kitchen while Bill and his chum Pete arrive and make matters uncomfortable for Jack. His bride covers Pete while Jerry, roused to action, covers Bill. The real cops arrive, ending the family's and Jerry's troubles.

BUTTERFLY PICTURES.

THE LITTLE PIRATE (Five Parts—Sept. 10).—The cast: George Drake (Charley West); John Baird (Frank Brownlean); Virginia Baird (Gretchen Lederer); Margery (Zoe Rae); Butler (Mr. Titus); Maid (Lillian Peacock); The Boy (Burwell Hemerick). Story by N. Shannon. Produced by Elsie Jane Wilson.

Over the home of John Baird a pall has

fallen. Baird faces financial ruin. Weary and haggard he arrives at his attorney's offices. "Get those securities of Margery's and raise a few thousand on them to tide you over," suggested the attorney.

Baird explained his plight to Virginia, his wife, asking for the securities of Margery, their child, but she refused to give them up.

Virginia asks Drake to get the securities, and, though reluctant, he consents. Drake has just bought a new auto and asks Virginia to go for a spin with him. A hearing is burned out and the mechanic informs Drake it will take about an hour and a half to fix it. Virginia is hungry, so they go to a roadhouse, not knowing it is a notorious place. Virginia suggests Drake phone Baird of their predicament, but he says it is unnecessary.

That evening Baird tells Virginia he knows Drake is almost a member of the family, but others may put a meaning upon the easy companionship between them. Virginia says she is sorry she refused to let him have the securities, which she now offers him. Baird says he will get them from the bank, but she says she sent Drake for them. Baird is furious, saying she confides in Drake and mistrusts her husband, and insists she must think a great deal of Drake. Virginia, dumb with outraged pride, leaves the room. Baird has already received word that, thanks to an unknown friend, they have weathered the storm.

Drake has placed the securities on the table of his room when Baird arrives and asks for them. Drake goes to his room, only to find them gone, and the butler declares he has no idea who could have taken them.

Virginia has, meanwhile, left a note, saying she has gone to her Aunt Sarah's until he regains his reason and begs her forgiveness. Margery comes to him that night. Baird tries to comfort her. The child writes a note to her mother, saying everybody forgives her and loves her very much, so to come right back home again, and signs it, "Your Loving Husband." Margery dresses, leaves the house quietly and rides away on her pony.

A voice commands her to halt, and a blunderbuss is pointed at her through the bushes. It is a boy playing that he is Captain Kidd and searching for buried treasure. Margery joins his band and they row across the lake into his cave. Margery and "Captain Kidd" see a man bury something and then hurry away. They dig up what he buried and are disgusted to find only a package of papers, which "Captain Kidd" puts in his pocket. They eat most of their supplies, and terrified by stories the boy reads, Margery finally begins to cry and wants to go home. Meanwhile, the pony has returned home, and Baird is frantic. Searchers find hair ribbon in the lake. Baird goes to tell Virginia. Both forget their own troubles in the new one.

Captain Kidd and Margery finally start home in the boat, which begins to leak rapidly. At last there is a happy reunion. Margery shows the papers and declares the butler buried them. Though the butler jumps into the lake to escape, the detectives catch him.

Baird receives word that Drake is the friend who has kept him from ruin. Baird shakes hands with Drake, whom Margery hugs and kisses, declaring that when she grows up she is going to be a pirate's wife.

FOX FILM CORPORATION.

BETRAYED (Five Parts—Sept. 2).—The cast: Carmelita Carruti (Miriam Cooper); Carpi, her father (James Marcus); Leopoldo Juarez, outlaw (Hobart Bosworth); Pepo Esparenza, lover (Monte, Blue); William Jerome, U. S. A. (Wheeler Oakman). Directed by R. A. Walsh.

The story of "Betrayed" centers about Carmelita Carrito, whose condition is that of a peon, but who remains an aristocrat and a coquette at heart, despite Carpi, her fat, filthy father. Carmelita has a lover, Pepo, but her affection goes aglimmering when the bandit, Leopoldo Juarez, raids her home. Leopoldo's personality impresses her in a never-to-be-forgotten way.

After Leopoldo departs, Carmelita sits by the window looking silently at the soft Mexican moonlight. Gradually she falls asleep and dreams.

An American army officer, William Jerome, is searching for Juarez. Carmelita is fascinated by the Gringo, and tells him Leopoldo is to meet her at the brook.

Leopoldo intercepts the note and arranges a counter plan. He is enraged by the girl's duplicity. He expresses fear lest she catch cold in the evening breeze and forces her to don his coat and put on his hat.

An instant later Jerome, seeing the pair through the bushes, thinks Carmelita is Leopoldo and shoots the woman he loves. The American goes to his death before the firing squad. Then the heartless Carmelita whispers to Pepo, her first lover, that he must get the Americans.

Carmelita awakes. United States troopers, aided by Pepo, are closing in on her house. There the bandit, Leopoldo, has taken refuge.

So Pepo captures Juarez and receives the reward.

M. H. HOFFMAN, INC.

THE SILENT WITNESS.—The cast: Sarah Blakeley (Aphie James); Helen Hastings (Gertrude McCoy); Bud Morgan (Junius Mathews); Janet Rigsby (Helen May); John Pelham (Edwin Fosberg); Wilbur Weldon (Roulet E. Cutton); Travers (Jack Sherrill); Richard Morgan (Frank L. A. O'Connor). Adapted from the play by Otto Hauerbach.

The opening scenes are laid in Denver, presenting Janet Rigsby in love with a college student, who later meets his death through a fire. Shortly after, Janet leaves her home and within a short time a son is born to her. Her circumstances through these years are not of the best, but she manages to send her son (Bud Morgan) through college.

While in college he becomes acquainted with the other students, the most of whom are sons of wealthy families. Among these is one who casts a slur on the poor boy's mother. This causes a fight and Bud Morgan kills—as he believes—his adversary. He is held for murder and his father (unaware at the time of his relationship to the prisoner) is the District Attorney. During the trial the facts are brought about so as to clear the boy from the charge of murder and finally bringing his father and mother together.

K-E-S-E.

A MIDNIGHT BELL (Selig—Two Parts—Sept. 3).—The cast: Lemuel Tidd, chief of police (Wm. Fables); Ezekiel Slover, chief of the fire department (James Harris); Amy Grey, the village belle (Amy Dennis); Jonathan Grey, her father (Fred Eckhart); Steve Larabee, Lemuel's right-hand man (Frank Hamilton); Nap Keene, Ezekiel's leading fire fighter (Jim West). Story by Charles Hoyt. Directed by J. A. Richmond.

Lemuel Tidd, chief of police, and Ezekiel Slover, chief of the fire department, are bitter rivals for the hand of Amy Grey. The two resort to all manner of tricks and deceptions in order to gain an advantage.

When fire breaks out in Punktown, the fire department saves the chief of police in a marvelous manner and saves Amy Grey by a still more wonderful feat, by sliding down a stream of water from the fire hose. After both the chiefs have extended themselves to the limit, they drag themselves away from the noise and confusion to resume their listless lives and to give their future strictly to the duties of their respective offices namely, caring for the safety and happiness of Punktown.

PARAMOUNT PICTURES CORP.

EGGED ON (Klever—Aug. 20).—The story tells of Vic's misadventures with a gunpowder formulae which he is intrusted to bring to America from Europe. To guard his secret Vic puts the plans in some eggshells which he keeps in a handbag. He loses the handbag and the wallet, however, and is forced to take a job as a sandwich man in order to earn $5 to cable home.

Just as he has earned enough money to send a cable he is forced to give it up to become a member of the sandwich men's union. While parading on the avenue with the restaurant advertisement he is met by an heiress who insists he have lunch with her. Through a series of manipulations, Vic manages to get another man's coat, but he never does regain his lost formulae. They had been mistaken for real eggs and placed in an incubator to be hatched.

PATHE EXCHANGE, INC.

TEARS AND SMILES (Lasalida—Five Parts—Sept. 2).—The cast: Little Marie (Baby Marie Osborne); Bertrand Greer (Philo McCullough); Marie's Mother (Marian Warner); Louise, a society favorite (Katherine MacLaren). Directed by Wm. Bertram.

"Now see what you've done! Poor Mama," said Marie to her father, who in a drunken stupor

---

had flung Marie's mother across the room, where she collapsed and fell to the floor. Angry at the child's accusation, he attempted to seize her, but she ran out of the house. A policeman after a terrific fight arrested Marie's father. Later her mother was taken to a hospital.

Nowhere to go, Marie wandered into a park. She suddenly saw a dog. Picking him up she whispered that they were going to be friends. Her happiness was disturbed by the arrival of a maid, who claimed the dog. Marie refuses to part with her find. Unable to separate them, the maid brings them to the home of Bertrand Greer, a well-to-do broker. Bored with his continual plea for her to adopt a child, his wife finally consents. At this moment Marie was ushered in. Fascinated, Greer adopts Marie.

Marie's mother recovers and pays her a secret visit. Marie begs her mother to take her back, but she refuses, as she is unable to care for her. Finally Marie has her maid dismissed and has Greer hire her mother without letting it be known just who she is.

Sunshine reigns until Marie's father is released from prison. He writes a note telling her if she does not return he would steal the child, and carried out his threat. Greer learned of this and also the truth of Marie and her mother. Rushing to her old home, Greer and the mother find Marie's father had been shot by an officer.

Greer's wife takes an overdose of headache medicine and when Greer arrives he finds her dead. Marie and her mother enter. Greer is deep in thought when suddenly Marie steals over to him. Taking her mother's hand, she places it in Greer's. Her mother tells him she is going to leave. Grasping her hand tighter, and looking at Marie, he begs her to remain.

HEARST-PATHE NEWS No. 69 (Aug. 25).
San Francisco, Cal.—The ties of friendship between America and Japan are more firmly cemented with the arrival of the Japanese Envoys. Subtitles: They are entertained by Mayor Rolph and other Western leaders. They visit General Liggett at the Presidio and get their first glimpse of Liberty's new forces.

Enos Mills, Colo.—Conventionalities of life bore Miss Agnes Lowe, so she wanders forth into the wilds of nature, a true daughter of Eve. Shy even of the camera.

Seabrooke, La.—Two lose their lives when the fast Cincinnati Express is derailed and narrowly escapes a plunge into the lake. Subtitles: The track is soon cleared to enable resumption of traffic.

A Coast Fortification.—Hidden in many secret places along the seabeards lie these huge mortars, ready at a minute's notice to repel invasion. Subtitles: Approved by Committee on Public Information. Frequent tests keep the guns in trim. The shell weighs 1,075 lbs. and requires 325 lbs. of powder. These powerful disappearing guns are a source of relief to many anxious shore dwellers.

New York City.—Farms in the country, farms in back yards, farms atop skyscrapers, farms everywhere is in answer to the Nation's call. Subtitles: The old fashioned well, the indispensable feature of every farm, is not forgotten. 'Way up yonder in the cornfields.

San Francisco, Cal.—Big waves and a strong tide make the fifty-five entries in the swim across the Golden Gate battle hard for victory. Subtitles: Numerous boats watch out for the safety of the swimmers. Norman Ross covers the difficult course in 21:13 minutes.

Battle Creek, Mich.—The barracks at Camp Custer, National Army cantonment for this district, will soon be ready for the embryo soldiers. Subtitles: Major Ganseer, German by birth, but a true-blooded, loyal American citizen and soldier. The 33rd Michigan Regiment does not wait for quarters to be finished and is already engaged in vigorous sham battles. On the march.

Oyster Bay, L. I.—Colonel Theodore Roosevelt greets the Envoys of bleeding Belgium, whose rights he has so ardently championed. Subtitles: Oh, for a chance at the ruthless invaders who rode roughshod over the little kingdom.

Boston, Mass.—Veterans of the Grand Army of the Republic, six thousand strong, mobilize once again for the annual encampment. Subtitles: Age has bent their bodies, but the hearts of the Boys in Blue still beat warmly for America. Old Glory was their standard.

Cincinnati, Ohio (Local).—The boys of the Third Ohio Infantry in the Federal Service since the call to the border, leave under secret orders. Subtitle: Off to duty.

St. Louis, Mo. (Local).—The famous Clendenen Dancing Girls give an exhibition of the famous

Grecian art at the Municipal Theatre. Subtitle: On with the dance; let joy reign unconfined!

San Antonio, Tex. (Local).—Uncle Sam's boys vie with each other in athletic prowess at a meet held here for the benefit of the Red Cross. Subtitle: The hurdle race is closely contested.

Washington, D. C. (Local).—Mrs. Robert Lansing, wife of the Secretary of State, entertains other Cabinet ladies at a novel luncheon of dried foods. Subtitles: The food before it was prepared. These present are, left to right: Mrs. Redfield, Mrs. Scott, Mrs. Clark, Mrs. Lansing, Mrs. Pomerene, Mrs. Daniels.

HEARST-PATHE NEWS, NUMBER 70 (Aug. 20).

Mineola, L. I.—The 165th U. S. Infantry, made up of the N. Y. "Fighting 69th," holds its first field mass in training camp. Subtitles: Hundreds of friends and relatives take advantage of the privileges of visiting day. Proud of her soldier daddy.

Overbrooke, Pa.—The rapid advance in railroading is emphasized by the installation of huge electric locomotives on Eastern lines. Subtitle: The engine can develop 7,000 horsepower. Note the ease with which it gets under way. The steam locomotive looks rather small against the new type.

Chicago, Ill.—Wartime interest in marksmanship brings out a very large field for the Grand American trap-shooting meet. Subtitles: Every shot a hit, the standard of the U. S. A. Women vie with the men in sharpshooting skill.

An Atlantic Port.—The German liner Kronprinzessin Cecilie, taken over by the U. S., is placed in drydock for thorough overhauling. Subtitles: Scraping the bottom to remove deposits accumulated during the three years of internment. Captain Robertson, who will command the big vessel under the Stars and Stripes.

Athens, Greece.—The sympathies of the Greek people in the war are clearly indicated as crowds cheer the arrival of French officers. Subtitles: Allied troops join in the great celebration. Leaders of the new government pledge fidelity to the Greek constitution.

Bayside, L. I.—A closely contested tub race is one of the features of the war sports carnival given by the Bayside Yacht Club. Subtitles: Some people discover that a canoe can be easily overturned.

New York City.—Men drafted for the National Army, eager to start on their new duties, get preliminary course on Governor's Island. Subtitles: They drill with wooden guns. Miss Liberty gazes down upon her stalwart sons who soon will battle for her safety.

Gloucester, N. J.—Shipyards are fast attaining the pace set by U-boats, and for each ship sunk there will be another to take its place. Subtitle: This new tanker, Desdemona, is ready for service in the Allied cause.

Sacramento, Cal.—The largest wheat crop ever raised in this district is ready for war needs and the work of harvesting is rushed. Subtitles: These monster machines make quick work of the threshing. Scores of wagons are required to haul the wheat to the elevator pits. Uncle Sam's land army, upon whom may depend the final decision in Democracy's struggle.

San Francisco, Cal. (Local).—The British Recruiting Mission, headed by General W. A. White, arrives to open up the campaign in the West. Subtitle: They review American troops at the Presidio.

Fort Oglethorpe, Ga. (Local).—Four thousand men of the U. S. Army Medical Units participate in a grand review on McDonald Field. Subtitles: Some of the different kinds of wagons used.

THE FATAL RING (Episode No. 11—"The Short Circuit"—Two Parts—Sept. 17).—The house caves in, Pearl extricates herself and the body of the Spider from the smoking debris. She tries to rouse him, but he is all in. Half dragging the Spider, Pearl finally manages to escape without being injured.

The Spider recovers, Pearl starts back into the flames, half-sticed by the smoke. Looking around, she sees Tom's watch and chain! Meanwhile, Tom, a prisoner of the Order of the Violet God, saves the priestess' life when she is bitten by a spider, and she grants him any favor in her power. Tom requests that Pearl be told of his whereabouts. The Priestess consents.

In the city Carniake gloats over his possession of the Violet Diamond, but is interrupted by the arrival of the telephone man, who wishes to fix the wires. The 'phone rings and the man tells Carniake the call is for him. Unsuspecting, he drops the Diamond on the table. Picking up the 'phone, he receives a shock and endeavors to drop it, but is unable to do so. The man takes the Diamond and escapes. The housekeeper cuts the wires and saves Carslake. Searching the man's coat, which he left behind, Carslake finds this note: "Sapper—Get the Diamond. Bring it to me at Pearl Standish's lodge in the Adirondacks." Carslake leaves immediately. Gravins, one of the priestess' spies, starts on his mission to Pearl, meets Carslake; informs him where he is going and learns of the diamond. He advises he will send Pearl on the trail, but she need never reach Tom.

Sapper gives the Spider the diamond. He unwraps it and gives it to Pearl. Pearl learns of Tom's whereabouts and starts off. Galloping along, Pearl sees Carslake and his henchman rushing towards her. She is about to pass a low hanging bow. Reaching up, she grabs hold of it, letting her horse run from beneath her. Carslake catches her and demands the diamond. She hands it to him. Worried over Tom, Pearl gains the assistance of some constabulary officers. At sundown Tom is to die, according to the decree of the Secret Order. The Priestess takes the scimitar and is ordered to carry out the death sentence. She looks at it in horror and starts towards Tom. Raising the knife, she is about to strike as the film fades out; the cavalry gallops towards the den.

Pearl fires and hits the Priestess in the hand. She drops the knife and flees. Pearl rushes to Tom and unbinds him. 'Now that I have you, I simply must get the diamond," says Pearl. Carslake and his adherent catch a train as Pearl comes galloping towards the station. Seeing that she has missed the train, Pearl jumps into a machine and passes the train. She jumps out and on to the railing of the bridge. As the train is passing beneath, she drops on to the train and goes into the coach where Carslake is. Pearl speaks to the astounded Carslake. "The Diamond, please." Carslake smiles as his adherent comes behind Pearl and holds a stiletto at her ribs as the film fades.

SEVEN PEARLS (Episode No. 2, "The Bow String"). Two Parts.
Harry Drake discovers that the masked figure who held him up is Ilma. When they realize the intruder has departed, they discover the pearl has disappeared. Harry tries to comfort Ilma. He tells her that he loves her, but she tears herself away from him saying, "Love me? Do you realize how I must pay for those pearls?" She then tells Harry she must go into the Sultan's harem or see her father killed, if she cannot recover the pearls.
Harry offers to co-operate with her and Ilma suggests he pretend to join Grady's gang. He agrees to do so.
Ilma is traced by the Sultan's executioner, to Harry's apartment. Standing outside the door, he overhears their conversation. Nemesis, who secured the pearl from Harry and Ilma, has been overcome by the executioner who takes the pearl from him.
Harry again tells Ilma he loves her and is about to kiss her when he hears a knock at the door. He looks through the keyhole and assures Ilma no one is there. She points to the floor, starting back in terror as she sees a bow string, used to strangle women of the harem who flirt, slipped under the door. Later the pearl is mysteriously returned to Ilma, and Harry, gambling for Jack's pearl, loses his own.
That night, a member of the gang, sneaks into a rich man's residence. He is followed by Ilma. Entering a room used as a picture gallery, decorated by suits of armor, Jack dons one of the suits. Drawing his sword, he starts to cut out one of the pictures. He is interrupted by Ilma, who demands his pearls. He tells her he cannot get at them through his armor. He overcomes Ilma and, tying her to a chair resumes his work.
The door opens, and a second figure in armor enters. Jack fumbles for his gun but is unable to get it from under his armor. The strange figure draws his sword and he and Jack fight like knights of old. Jack is overpowered. The stranger proves to be Harry. Recovering the pearls, Harry gives them to Ilma, and starts towards the window after Jack, who tries to escape. Ilma backs towards the curtain. In an instant some unknown throws a curtain over her head, takes the pearls and escapes.

TRIANGLE FILM CORP.

IDOLATERS (Five Parts—Sept. 9).—The cast: Viola Strathmore (Louise Glaum); Curtis de Forest Ralston (George Webb); Anita Carew

(Dorcas Matthews); Berul, Egyptian servant (Lee Hill); Burr Britton (T. S. Guise); Druce Winthrope (Hugo Koch); Oscar Brent, stage manager (Milton Ross). Story by John Lynch and M. Katterjohn.
Two girls become acquainted while waiting in a railroad station on the way to New York, where both expect to make careers. Violet Strijk-er, flashly dressed, expresses her opinion that girl must four-flush to get ahead in the world, while the other, Anita Carew, believes that success is attained only by work.
The two are brought together later in a strange situation. Violet, under the name of Viola Strathmore, has gained success as an actress through the friendships of masculine admirers. One of these men is a young playwright, Ralston, whom Anita has married. In a vain attempt to keep his affection, Mrs. Ralston visits Viola to plead with her. She is spurned by the audacious beauty, and her pride is crushed when her husband makes his appearance in the apartment, shamelessly boasting of his love for Viola.
In Ralston's play, "Vanity," Viola makes her great hit, but it is not lasting, for the man who has financed the production turns against her when he discovers her faithlessness. In a moment of mad fury Viola kills Ralston, whom she believes to have caused her downfall. Her only friend is the Egyptian servant, who has cherished a certain love for her.
The climax comes when this barbaric lover defies the law that seeks to punish her, and the woman reaps the penalty of her lustful career.

WORLD FILM.

TIDES OF FATE (Five Parts—Sept. 3).—Fanny Clawson is rescued from a runaway horse and a watery grave by Stephen King, a newcomer to the village. He is a flashy, agreeable adventurer, and Fanny's gratitude turns to love. When Claudia's husband, Ezra Nelson, the mayor of the town, expresses a doubt regarding King's character Fanny upholds King.
Captain John Cross, of the Northwest Mounted Police, is spending his vacation in the village. He is attracted by Fanny, but she has eyes for King only. On the day of his return to duty, Cross experiences a keen disappointment when he reads of the engagement of Fanny to Stephen King.
Ezra shows King a report from a private detective that King has served a prison term for counterfeiting. King denies this. He urges Fanny to marry him and go to the city at once.
In the Northwest, a year later, the Mounted Police round up a band of train robbers, and Cross, still suffering from the effects of his nervous breakdown, loses his nerve and deserts. Charged with cowardice, Cross is discharged without honor. Fergus, his friend, not believing Cross cowardly, resigns his commission to go with the dishonored man.
King's indifference to his wife, and the mystery with which he surrounds his occupation cause her unhappiness.
The appearance of a new counterfeit note results in the Government agents following a clue to the corner grocer, from where it is traced to Fanny.
In accordance with instructions received from King, urging her to express him the iron ore which he has hidden under the couch, Fanny pulls out a heavy box, speculating as to its contents. The Government agents come upon her with the box, which contains counterfeiter's plates. She is arrested and convicted on circumstantial evidence. Hoping to retrieve the past, Cross, accompanied by Fergus, enlists in the service of Uncle Sam. In the Philippines, they are among the soldiers sent to quell an uprising among the Moros. Cross, single-handed, volunteers to go for aid. Fergus follows. The natives are put to rout.
King escapes to the coal district, where he bides among the miners. At the prison entertainers give a performance. One, noting Fanny's distress, secures her services in helping to dress. After hearing her story she persuades Fanny to escape in a suit of boys' clothes.
At the mines, King gambles and loses his wealth. The boss discharges King. The following day, after an accident, one of the miners is brought up dead. Because of the watch he wears, engraved "Stephen King," he is identified as King.
Broken in spirit, Fanny arrives at the home of Claudia, who makes her welcome. Fanny reads of the death of Stephen King, the notorious counterfeiter. Relieved, she looks forward to a

---

He is going over the top! and he needs a smoke to cheer him up!

Americans, our fighting men in France need tobacco. They are giving their lives to defend you. Do your part to make them comfortable during the dreary hours in the trenches.

Twenty-five cents provides enough tobacco to make one of our gallant defenders happy for a week. $1.00 sends a month's supply.

Prominent magazines and newspapers stand back of this movement. The War and Navy Departments endorse it.

A War Souvenir for You

In each package is enclosed a post card addressed to the donor. If these come back they will be war souvenirs much treasured.

Mail Coupon Today

"OUR BOYS IN FRANCE TOBACCO FUND"

19 W. 44th St.   New York

Gentlemen:
I want to do my part to cheer up the American soldiers who are fighting my battle in France. If tobacco will do it—I'm for tobacco.

(Check below how you desire to contribute)

I send you herewith ...., my contribution toward the purchase of tobacco for American soldiers. This does not obligate me to contribute more.

I enclose $1.00. I will adopt a soldier and send you $1.00 a month to supply him with "smokes" for the duration of the war.

Name.................................
Address...............................

For the fullest and latest news of the moving picture industry in Great Britain and Europe.
For authoritative articles by leading British technical men.
For brilliant and strictly impartial criticisms of all films, read

THE BIOSCOPE

The Leading British Trade Journal with an International Circulation
85 Shaftesbury Avenue, London, W.
Specimen on Application

---

new life, but her brother-in-law drives her from the house.

Their terms of enlistment having expired, Cross and Fergus return to America. Ill with fever, Cross remains in New York while Fergus continues to the Northwest. Under an assumed name, Fanny is living in New York. Cross rents a room in the same boarding house. Weakened by the journey, Cross drops a bottle of medicine and groans. The landlady and Fanny rush to his aid. Weeks pass, and with the return of his health, comes love for Fanny.

A Sergeant from the Mounted brings the news that Cross' commission has been restored at Fergus' intercession. His name cleared, Cross proposes to Fanny, who recalling her prison record, fears to share her disgrace with the man she loves, and does not give him an answer.

Later Fanny is seen by King, the fugitive from justice. He follows her to the boarding house, where he demands money. When she refuses, there is a struggle and Cross comes to her aid. Fanny calls for police, and in an attempt to escape King is shot by the policeman. In his dying confession, he clears Fanny of the counterfeiting charge, saying she had no knowledge of his work.

Cross tells Fanny King has cleared her name. They start life anew.

THE MARRIAGE MARKET (Five Parts—Sept. 10).—At an auction sale of thoroughbred horses, Helen Grant bids against Eric Foxhall for Dandy Dick. The horse goes to Helen for five thousand dollars. Foxhall, learning of activity in steel, requests the stock Grant had pledged to him. Grant stalls him off. Foxhall goes to Beale and Marlowe to purchase Southland stock. Here he is shown the stock certificate which Grant had left as security. Beale promises to secure the stock for Foxhall if he can. Foxhall is enraged to find it is the same stock for which Grant had given him a receipt as security for the loan. He confronts Grant, threatening to arrest him. When Helen learns of her father's predicament, she determines to do all in her power to save him.

She goes to Bradley Spayden for a loan of a hundred thousand, offering a pearl necklace and their home, but Spayden says she is the thing he desires most. Putting aside her love for Marlowe, she agrees to marry Spayden. He writes a check for a hundred thousand, payable to Mrs. Helen Grant Spayden. They are married and Helen rushes to her father's office. With the check she buys from Foxhall her father's receipt for the stock certificates. Foxhall remarks she sold herself cheaply—he would have paid a million! Marlowe denounces Helen. A shot rings out—her father ignorant of the fact that Helen has saved him, has killed himself. Richard pleads with Helen to annul the marriage before it is too late, but she decides to stand by her bargain. At his club, Spayden regards his marriage as an occasion for getting drunk. As time passes, Helen learns the full meaning of disillusion. Spayden exhibits her to his maudlin friends as the best little thoroughbred he ever owned. Mortified beyond endurance, Helen sells her jewels, and has Beale invest the money for her.

Beale advises Helen she must have five thousand dollars to safeguard her investment. She decides to sell Dandy Dick. She phones Foxhall. He asks her to come to his house. She writes Beale to have Marlowe meet her at Foxhall's at eight-thirty, that she may give him the money to cover her investment. She realizes his insinuation, and when he attempts to embrace her, she spurns him.

Not finding Helen at home, Spayden learns she has gone to Foxhall's.

The struggle between Helen and Foxhall ends in her shooting him with his revolver. There is a furious ringing of the doorbell. Foxhall rushes Helen into the bedroom. He pulls out his cigarette case, showing a bullet imbedded in it. Spayden rushes in, demanding to know where Helen is. They hear a noise in the next room. Spayden strikes Foxhall down, and drags Helen out. Believing she has killed Foxhall, she swoons. Spayden picks up the revolver and shoots Foxhall. He falls back dead. Horrified, Spayden leaves through a window.

Richard Marlowe finds Helen and Foxhall, both apparently dead. Helen comes to, and Richard believes she has killed Foxhall. He takes her to his mother's home. Marlowe is arrested for the murder of Foxhall, and pleads guilty. In the days of her convalescence, all knowledge of Marlowe's trial is kept from Helen. Marlowe is pronounced guilty. Helen hears a newsboy calling an extra, and discerns Marlowe's name. With the aid of her nurse, she rushes to court, declares Marlowe innocent, saying she killed Foxhall. Among the spectators are Spayden and Grimes, Foxhall's butler. As Helen confesses, Spayden starts to sneak out, but Grimes yells to have him stopped. Spayden is brought back, and Grimes swears he saw Spayden kill Foxhall. Grimes tells his story.

For fifteen years he has been in the service of Foxhall, whom he hated and despised. After Spayden left, Grimes stole the money Foxhall had prepared for Helen. Spayden denies the story, but is dragged off by attendants. In

another room, he shoots himself. Helen and Richard are reunited.

BETSY ROSS (Five Parts—Sept. 17).—Betsy Griscom, living in Philadelphia at the beginning of the Revolution, is the daughter of a Quaker. Clarissa, her sister, wearing Betsy's cloak, keeps tryst with Clarence Vernon, an officer in General Howe's Army. On her way to meet Joseph Ashburn, owner of a trading vessel, Betsy meets Clarissa. Taking the wrap from her, Betsy goes on to her trysting place. When Joseph expresses a fear that her father will not consent to her marriage, Betsy is for declaring war on her father. Vernon sees Betsy in Joseph's arms, and he believes Clarissa is playing him false. When Betsy has left, Vernon says Mistress Griscom is his. In the duel, Vernon is struck down by Joseph. The town crier, Ketch, urges Joseph to escape. Throwing his hat and cloak into the river, Joseph departs.

Joel Radley, a renegade, finding Vernon wounded, realizes he will be well paid for befriending the rich officer. When Ketch calls for help, Radley kills him. Vernon comes to and Radley shows him Ketch's body, saying Vernon had killed the crier. Radley assures him he will save him if paid well. Radley helps Vernon to his home. Radley compels Vernon to introduce him as a trusted friend, saying he will make a valuable spy for General Howe.

Betsy learns Joseph has been drowned. A year later she marries John Ross, who is afterward killed. Then Betsy becomes proprietress of an upholstery shop. Later Joseph, under the name of Nathaniel Wheatley, has become aide to General Washington. Clarissa is driven from her home and Betsy cares for her.

Disguised as a Dutch vender, Vernon comes to Philadelphia. His resignation from Howe's Army has been accepted and he is waiting to join the American Army.

Betsy suspects Vernon is a spy, when Clarissa tells her she saw him in disguise. As Lieut. Wheatley, Joseph comes to Betsy's shop. Both are startled. Washington commissions Betsy to fashion the country's first flag. Joseph confesses he is a murderer. She promises not to betray him. Unable to go to Clarissa, Vernon urges his mother to reassure her. When the minister accuses Betsy of harboring a scarlet woman, she swears the child is her own. Mrs. Vernon insinuates Betsy's shop is a harbor for spies. Vernon peers through the shop window, and when Joseph is about to shoot, Betsy says a shot may alarm someone who is ill upstairs. Joseph believes she is harboring either a lover or a spy.

Betsy spurns the money offered by Mrs. Vernon, who says her son denies the marriage to Clarissa. Vernon rushes in. He is being pursued by American guards. He pleads with Betsy to hide him. Betsy sits in a chair and covers Vernon with the flag. Betsy smuggles Vernon into a closet. Washington calls to get the finished flag. Joseph asks to be permitted to retain the guard. When he refuses to explain why, he is placed under arrest. Washington gives him a letter to Benedict Arnold, ordering Joseph to report his arrest in person to Arnold. Arnold sends Joseph back to Washington with papers which had been captured on an enemy messenger.

Realizing that through his love for her, Joseph is being dishonored, Betsy confesses there is a spy in the house—her sister's husband. Joseph returns. Washington tells him his position has been explained by Betsy, and asks Betsy to turn her prisoner over to Joseph. When Joseph sees Vernon, he realizes he is not a murderer. Vernon is tempted to go to Clarissa, but he steels himself and leaves with Joseph. Betsy assures Clarissa that she has seen Vernon and heard from his lips that she is his wife. The next morning Betsy comes upon the packet which Joseph had brought from Gen. Arnold. She reads Vernon's name and realizes it must be his discharge from Gen. Howe's Army. Knowing his life is in jeopardy, Betsy rushes to Washington, only to find Joseph has taken Vernon to Gen. Arnold. Believing Vernon already convicted by the Court Martial, General Washington writes a release, with which Betsy goes on an adventurous ride to General Arnold's headquarters.

Radley is suspected by the Americans and arrested. Thrown into Vernon's cell, he confesses he killed Ketch. Vernon is found guilty. Radley is also sentenced to be shot. Betsy arrives, but is told the spy has been executed. As the body is carried out, Betsy finds it is not Vernon but Radley. As the squad aims to fire at Vernon, Gen. Arnold stops the execution, and Vernon is permitted to return to his wife and child, an honorable American. Joseph looks on, unable to understand the relation between Betsy and Vernon. Betsy explains, and his faith restored, Joseph folds Betsy in his arms.

Classified Advertisements   NOTE TERMS CAREFULLY

Remittances must accompany all orders for classified advertisements as follows: One dollar per insertion for copy containing twenty words or less. Five cents per word on copy containing over twenty words. Each word to be counted including names and addresses.

NOTICE TO ADVERTISERS:—The Publishers expect that all statements made in every advertisement will bear the strictest investigation.

SITUATIONS WANTED.

OPERATOR, strictly experienced, desires position first-class theater only. Handle only best equipment. Perfect projection guaranteed. Henry Alsman, Dyersburg, Tenn.

HELP WANTED.

WANTED—Violinist with up-to-date library for small orchestra; also pianist for high-class theater in Iowa. Playing best picture attractions, road shows and vaudeville. Seven-day town, matinee and night. Only capable artists answer, stating your experience and salary for permanent position year round. Iowa, care M. P. World, N. Y. City.

BUSINESS OPPORTUNITIES.

FOR SALE—Theater and store building, store rents for one hundred twenty-five per month. Address J. Rantschler, Harlem, Mont.

THEATERS FOR SALE OR RENT.

FOR SALE—Only motion picture theater in Menominee, Michigan. Population ten thousand. Seating four hundred and fifty. Popular, doing good, nicely equipped. Needs management. Write or wire owner, Campbell, care Strand, Escanaba, Mich.

THEATER TO RENT IN WORCESTER, MASSACHUSETTS (THE CITY OF PROSPERITY). CITY OF 175,000 PEOPLE. CENTRALLY LOCATED, SEATING 1,100. APPLY F. W. TAYLOR, 438 MAIN ST.

EQUIPMENT FOR SALE.

GUARANTEED MACHINES—Slightly used type S-1917 model, Simplex motor drive, factory guarantee, at reasonable prices. Room 206, 1482 Broadway, N. Y. City.

FOR SALE—A full moving picture house equipment. 300 opera chairs, machines, operat-

ing booth, fans, and miscellaneous equipment. Reasonable price to quick buyer. Must vacate at once. Address Box 23, Norwalk, Conn.

USED opera and folding chairs, large quantities in stock; also upholstered; all in excellent condition. Bargains. Atlas Seating Co., 10 East 43d St., N. Y. City.

$125,000 BUYS my complete, good-as-new, 110-volt, direct-current, motor-drive Power's 6A moving picture machine, with rheostat and lenses. H. David, 711 So. Kedzie Ave., Chicago, Ill.

3,000 OPERA CHAIRS, steel and cast frames, 60c up. All serviceable goods, cut prices on new chairs. Six standard asbestos booths. Send for weekly list of close outs and save half. J. P. Redington, Scranton, Pa.

144 VENEERED CHAIRS, twenty inch, suitable for moving picture theater or lecture hall. Price, 75c each. D., care M. P. World, N. Y. City.

FOR SALE—6A Power's machine, used 30 days. New 50-ampere tube. H. L. Salmon, 2725 No. Clark St., Chicago, Ill.

FOR SALE—Complete outfit, 400 chairs, Simplex and Motiograph, 1917; Mazzville booth, coils, fans, screen, etc. whole or part. Bargain. Write Crawford, 822 Wood St., Wilkinsburg, Pa.

CAMERAS, ETC., FOR SALE.

PRESTWICH M. P. Camera, not much used, good condition. Zeiss Tessar lens, tripod, about 4,000 feet Florida views. Also printing machine. All in good shape, bargain to early buyer. W. F. Hitchins, 366 Centre St., Bloomsburg, Pa.

DAVID STERN COMPANY, INCORPORATED. "EVERYTHING IN CAMERAS." PIONEERS IN THE MOTION PICTURE FIELD. SPECIAL——600 ft. U. S. Professional Automatic Dissolve, Forward and reverse, regular and trick crank with Pan. and Tilt Tripod. $250.00. EXCLUSIVE DISTRIBUTORS FOR THE DAVSCO. AGENTS FOR THE UNIVERSAL. WRITE OR WIRE FOR OUR SPECIAL PROPOSITION. DAVID STERN COMPANY

"Everything in Cameras." In business since 1885. 1027-29 R Madison St., Chicago, Ill.

TO ALL INTERESTED IN MOTION PICTURE CAMERAS. WRITE AT ONCE FOR BEST BARGAIN LIST OF USED UNIVERSAL CAMERAS. LARGEST SELECTION IN THE COUNTRY, NEW AND USED. PRICES: 1915 MODELS, $185.00; 1916 MODELS FROM $200.00 to $225.00. 1917 MODELS FROM $225.00 to $260.00. Write for special proportions on new Universals. Prompt shipment, telegraphic orders shipped five minutes after receipt. Our list of satisfied customers grows every week. Latest buyers of Bass Bargains: A. N. Harlow, Chattanooga, Tenn. J. L. Schrode, LaSalle, Ill. R. P. Hildebrand, Des Moines, Iowa. Several others. You, too, will be pleased at our prompt, satisfactory service. Quality cameras only. Our complete sixty-six page camera catalog ready for distribution, free on request. The latest and best book on Motion Pictures, "How to Make and Operate," postpaid, $1.10. WRITE TO CAMERA HEADQUARTERS OF AMERICA AT ONCE. BASS CAMERA COMPANY, CHARLES BASS, PRES., 109 NORTH DEARBORN ST., CHICAGO, ILL. MOTION PICTURE CAMERA DEPT.

PHOTO CINES camera complete with 2" lens, magazines, tripod and tilt regularly $300; our price, $175. Like new. Ernemann Model B, four magazines, 2" lens, like new, $275. Universal camera, four magazines, 2" lens, $250, exactly like new. Also the largest stock in the United States of other motion picture cameras, printers, tripods, etc, both new and second hand, at the right prices. Motion Picture App. Co., 110-114 West 32d St., New York City.

FILMS, ETC., WANTED.

WANTED—The following subjects in good condition: The Great Train Robbery, 1 reel; Convict King, 3; Highbinders, 2; Fight for Right, 2; Convict Hero, 3; Chinatown Mystery, 2; Convict 4287, 2; The Light of New York, 5, and Charles Chaplin comedies. Select Film Co., 145 West 45th St., N. Y. City.

In answering advertisements please mention The Moving Picture World

---

A Welcome Visitor Each Week in Every Business Home Where Moving
Pictures Are of Interest

The Moving Picture World

Is Admirably Adapted to Carry Any Little
Message Which You May Wish to Send

Our Classified Advertisements at Five Cents Per Word

Will Produce Remarkable Results — One Dollar for Twenty Words or Less

Send Copy, with remittance, to CHALMERS PUBLISHING CO., 17 Madison Avenue, New York City

INDEX

TO CONTENTS

TO ADVERTISERS

List of Current Film Release Dates

ON GENERAL FILM, PATHE AND PARAMOUNT PROGRAMS

(For Daily Calendar of Program Releases See Page 1738.)

General Film Company, Inc.

(Note—Pictures given below are listed in the order of their release. Additions are made from week to week in the order of release.)

BROADWAY STAR FEATURES.

The Gift of the Magi (One of the O. Henry Stories—Two parts—Comedy-Drama).
The Coming Out of Maggie (One of the O. Henry Stories—Two parts—Comedy-Dr.).
The Venturers (one of the O. Henry Series—Two parts—Comedy-Drama).
Discounters of Money (One of the O. Henry Series—Two parts—Comedy-Drama).
The Furnished Room (One of the O. Henry Series—Two parts—Drama).
The Defeat of the City (One of the O. Henry Series—Two parts—Drama).
John Tom Little Bear (One of the O. Henry Series—Two parts—Drama).
Blind Man's Holiday (One of the O. Henry Series—Four parts—Drama).

ESSANAY.

Our Boys (Black Cat Feature—Two parts—Comedy).
Seventy and Seven (Black Cat Feature—Two parts—Comedy-Drama).
Pete's Pants (Black Cat Feature—Two parts—Comedy).
Vernon, the Bountiful (Black Cat Feature—Two parts—Comedy-Drama).
The Long-Green Trail (Black Cat Feature—Two parts—Comedy-Drama).
Don't Lose Your Coat (Black Cat Feature—Two parts—Comedy-Drama).
Star Dust—Black Cat Feature—Two parts—Comedy-Drama).
Twelve Cylinder Speed of the Leisure Class (George Ade Fable—Two parts—Comedy).
The Wandering Boy and the Wayward Parents (George Ade Fable—Two parts—Comedy).

FALCON FEATURES.

The Mainspring (Four parts—Drama).
The Martinache Marriage (Four parts—Dr.).
The Stolen Play (Four parts—Drama).
The Phantom Shotgun (Four parts—Drama).
His Unpolished Self (Four parts—Drama).

KALEM.

An Order of the Court (Episode of "The Further Adventures of Stingaree"—Two parts—Dr.).
At the Sign of the Kangaroo (an episode of the "The Further Adventures of Stingaree"—Two parts—Drama).
Through Fire and Water (Episode of the Further Adventures of Stingaree—Two parts—Drama).
A Bushranger's Strategy (Episode of the Further Adventures of Stingaree—Two parts—Drama).
The Stranger at Dumcrieff (Episode of "The Further Adventures of Stingaree"—Two parts—Drama).
A Champion of the Law (Episode of "The Further Adventures of Stingaree"—Two parts—Drama).

JAXON COMEDIES.

(Pokes and Jabs).

(Second Series.)

Counting 'Em Up.
The Baggage Man.
Getting the Coin.
Tough Luck.
Play Ball.
Love Letters.

(Third Series.)

Speed Demons.
The Collectors.
Jolly Tars.

SELIG.

A Daughter of the Southland (Two parts—Dr.).
The L.-X. Clew (Drama).
Selig-World Library No. 11 (Edu.)
The Toll of Sin (Two parts—Drama).
The Bush Leaguer (One part—Drama).
Selig-World Library No. 12 (Educational).
The Smoldering Spark (Two parts—Drama).
The Love of Madge O'Mara (Drama).
Selig-World Library No. 13 (Educational).
A Man, a Girl and a Lion (Two parts—Drama).
Her Perilous Ride (One part—Drama).
Selig World Library No. 14 (Educational).
The Sole Survivor (Two parts—Drama).
Her Heart's Desire (One part—Drama).
Selig World Library No. 15 (Educational).
Between Man and Beast (Two parts—Drama).
Her Salvation (One part—Drama).
Selig World Library No. 16 (Educational).
Pioneer Days (Two parts—Drama).
In After Years (One part—Drama).
The House of Mystery (Two parts—Drama).
Selig World Library No. 17 (Educational).

RAY COMEDIES.

A Peaceful Flat.
Cheating His Wife.
A Bathtub Marriage.

SPARKLE COMEDIES.

(Second Series.)

An Attorney's Affair.
Her Peignoir.
Those Terrible Telegrams.
The Stag Party.
Bragg's Little Poker Party.
Mixed 'Ites.
Hearts and Harpoons.
Toodles.
Bangs Reniga.

Pathe Exchange, Inc.

RELEASES FOR WEEK OF AUG. 19.

Miss Nobody (Five parts—Drama—Astra).
The Neglected Wife (No. 15—"A Sacrifice Supreme"—Two parts—Drama—Balboa).
The Fatal Ring (No. 7—"The Signal Lantern" —Two parts—Drama—Astra).
Along the Baltic Swede (Scenic—Seasfilms), and Japan, the Religious (Colored Scenic— Split Reel).
Jerry on the Job—"On the Border" (Cartoon Comedy), and "Fine Feathers" (Edu.— Split Reel).
Lonesome Luke, Mechanic (Two parts—Comedy —Rolin).
Hearst-Pathe News No. 68 (Topical).
Hearst-Pathe News No. 69 (Topical).

RELEASES FOR WEEK OF AUGUST. 26.

Iris (Five parts—Drama—Hepworth).
The Fatal Ring (No. 8, "The Switch in the Safe"—Two parts—Drama—Astra).
Know America No. 20—Near Pike's Peak, Colo. (One reel—Scenic—Combitone).
Hearst-Pathe News No. 70 (Topical).
Hearst-Pathe News No. 71 (Topical).

RELEASES FOR WEEK OF SEPT. 2.

Tears and Smiles (Lasilida—Five parts— Drama).
The Fatal Ring (Episode No. 9, "The Dice of Death") (Two parts—Drama—Astra).
Lonesome Luke's Wild Women (Two parts— Comedy—Rolin).
Know America No. 21, "Central Colorado" (Scenic—Combitone).
Scenic and Cartoon (Top/-national Split Reel— Title not reported).
Hearst-Pathe News No. 72 (Topical).
Hearst-Pathe News No. 73 (Topical).
Happy Gets the Razoo (Happy Hooligan Cartoon Comedy), and "Making a Marine Officer" (Educational) (International Split Reel).

RELEASED FOR WEEK OF SEPT. 9.

War and the Woman (Thanhouser—Five parts— Drama).
The Fatal Ring Episode No. 10, "The Perilous Plunge"—Two parts—Drama—Astra).
Know America No. 22, "Colorado's Scenic Wonders" (Scenic—Combitone).
Over the Fence (Comedy—Rolin).
Happy Hooligan in the Zoo (Cartoon Comedy); and "From Rookie to Regular" (Educational) (International Split Reel).
Hearst-Pathe News No. 74 (Topical).
Hearst-Pathe News No. 75 (Topical).
Les Miserables (Special—Eight parts—Drama).

Paramount Pictures Corp.

BLACK DIAMOND COMEDY.

Aug. 6—Susie the Sleepwalker.
July 9—Wits and Fits.
July 23—The Rejuvenator.

FAMOUS PLAYERS.

July 9—The Love That Lives (Five parts— Drama).
July 23—The Long Trail (Five parts—Drama).

KLEVER KOMEDY.

July 16—The Wrong Mr. Fox.
July 30—Motor Boating.
Aug. 13—Summer Boarding (Comedy).
Aug. 20—Egged On.
Aug. 27—The Cinderella Husband.

LASKY.

July 26—The Squaw Man's Son (Five parts— Drama).
July 30—The Crystal Gazer (Five parts—Dr.).

MOROSCO AND PALLAS.

July 19—Cook of Canyon Camp (Five parts— Drama).
Aug. 2—A Kiss for Susie (Five parts—Drama).

PARAMOUNT-ARBUCKLE COMEDY.

June 25—The Rough House (Two parts).
Aug. 20—His Wedding Night (Two parts).

PARAMOUNT FEATURES.

Aug. 5—The Amazons (Five parts—Drama).
Aug. 5—The Varmint (Five parts—Drama).
Aug. 12—The Law of the Land (Five parts— Drama).
Aug. 19—The Mysterious Miss Terry (Five parts —Drama).
Aug. 19—Hashimura Togo (Five parts—Dr.).
Aug. 26—Close to Nature (Five parts—Drama).
Aug. 26—Little Miss Optimist (Five parts— Drama).
Sept. 3—Lost in Transit (Five parts—Drama).
Sept. 10—The Hostage (Five parts—Drama).
Sept. 10—On the Level (Five parts—Drama).
Sept. 17—Her Double Cross (Five parts—Dr.).
Sept. 17—Exile (Five parts—Drama).

PARAMOUNT-BURTON HOLMES.

Aug. 20—Tropical Nassau (Scenic).
Aug. 27—Madrid to Madeira (Scenic).
Sept. 3—Norway (Scenic).
Sept. 10—Hong Kong and the Pearl River (Scenic).
Sept. 17—Canton and Shanghai (Scenic).

PARAMOUNT-BRAY PICTOGRAPHS.

July 9—No. 75. Subjects on reel: Water Sports in Beautiful Hawaii; Unmasking the Mediums; Going to Sea in the Heart of New York; Bobby Bump's "Fourth" (Cartoon).
July 16—No. 76; Subjects on Reel: The Key to Beauty; Otto Luck and the Ruby Rasmatas (Cartoon); The Latest Kinks in Canning.
July 23—No. 77; Subjects on Reel: Testing Men for Air Fighting; A Study in Fox Hounds; Land of Make Believe; "Sic 'em Cat" (Cartoon).

Producers—Kindly Furnish Titles and Dates of All New Releases Before Saturday.

List of Current Film Release Dates
ON UNIVERSAL, METRO AND TRIANGLE PROGRAMS

(For Daily Calendar of Program Releases See Page 1738.)

Universal Film Mfg. Co.

ANIMATED WEEKLY.

July 18—Number 81 (Topical).
July 25—Number 82 (Topical).
Aug. 2—Number 83 (Topical).
Aug. 9—Number 84 (Topical).
Aug. 16—Number 85 (Topical).
Aug. 23—Number 86 (Topical).
Aug. 30—Number 87 (Topical).
Sept. 6—Number 88 (Topical).
Sept. 13—Number 89 (Topical).
Sept. 20—Number 90 (Topical).

BISON.

Aug. 6—The Soul Herder (Three parts—Dr.).
Aug. 20—Squaring It (Three parts—Drama).
Aug. 27—Jungle Treachery (Two parts—Dr.).
Sept. 3—The Lure of the Circus (Two parts—Comedy—Drama), and Sierra Winter Sports (Scenic).
Sept. 10—The Texas Sphinx (Two parts—Western Drama).
Sept. 17—The Last of the Night Riders (Two parts—Drama).

GOLD SEAL.

July 23—A Soldier of the Legion (Three parts—Drama).
July 30—Right of Way Casey (Three parts—Drama).
Aug. 13—A Wife's Suspicion (Three parts—Drama).
Aug. 27—The Winning Pair (Three parts—Dr.).
Sept. 3—The Empty Gun (Three parts—Dr.).
Sept. 10—The Perilous Leap (Three parts—Railroad Drama).
Sept. 17—The Pullman Mystery (Three parts—Drama)..

JOKER.

July 23—The Soubretta.
July 30—The Battling Bellboy (Comedy).
July 30—The Stinger Stung (Comedy).
Aug. 6—My the Tent Mover (Comedy).
Aug. 6—The Vamp of the Camp (Comedy).
Aug. 13—Out Again, In Again (Comedy).
Aug. 13—Back to the Kitchen (Comedy).)
Aug. 20—Behind the Map (Comedy).
Aug. 20—Mrs. Madam Manager (Comedy).
Aug. 27—Why They Left Home (Comedy).
Aug. 27—Busting Into Society (Comedy).
Sept. 3—Officer, Call a Cop (Comedy).
Sept. 3—A Gale of Verse (Comedy).
Sept. 10—Short Skirts and Deep Water (Comedy).
Sept. 10—Nearly a Queen (Comedy).
Sept. 17—Hawaiian Nuts (Comedy).
Sept. 17—Circus Sarah (Comedy).

L-KO.

July 23—The Sign of the Cucumber (Two parts —Comedy).
July 30—Blackboard and Blackmail (Two parts —Comedy).
Aug. 6—The Little Fat Rascal (Two parts—Comedy).
Aug. 13—Rough Stuff (Two parts—Comedy).
Aug. 20—Street Cars and Carbunkles (Two parts —Comedy).
Aug. 27—Props, Drops and Flops (Two parts —Comedy).
Sept. 3—Backward Sons and Forward Daughters (Two parts—Comedy).
Sept. 10—From Cactus to Kale (Two parts—Comedy).
Sept. 17—A Prairie Chicken (Two parts—Com.).

NESTOR.

July 23—Seeing Things.
July 30—Married by Accident (Comedy).
Aug. 6—The Love Slacker (Comedy).
Aug. 13—The Rushin' Dancers (Comedy).
Aug. 20—Move Over (Comedy).
Aug. 27—The Night Cap (Comedy).
Sept. 3—Looking 'Em Over (Comedy).
Sept. 10—The Boulevard Speed Hounds (Comedy).
Sept. 17—Welcome Home (Comedy).

POWERS.

July 23—Hammon Egg's Reminiscences (Cartoon Comedy) and in The Land of Light and Gloom (Dorsey Edu.).
July 30—The Good Liar" (Cartoon) and "In Monkey Land" (Ditmar's Edu.).
Aug. 6—Seeing Ceylon with Hy Mayer (Travelaugh).
Aug. 13—Doing His Bit (Cartoon Comedy), and Algiers, Old and New) (Scenic) (Split reel).
Aug. 20—Colonel Pepper's Mobilized Farm (Cartoon Comedy), and "The Home Life of the Spider (Ditmar's Edu.) (Split Reel).

STAR FEATURETTE.

July 30—The Woman Who Would Not Pay (Two parts—Society—Drama).
Aug. 6—The Untamed (Two parts—Drama).
Aug. 13—Cheyenne's Pal (Two parts—Drama).
Aug. 20—The Golden Heart (Two parts—Dr.).
Aug. 27—Hands in the Dark (Two parts—Dr.), and Old French Towns (Short Scenic on Same Reel).
Sept. 3—A Dream of Egypt (Two parts—Dr.).
Sept. 10—To the Highest Bidder (Two parts—Society Drama).
Sept. 17—The Right Man (Two parts—Drama).

VICTOR.

July 9—Kicked Out (Two parts—Comedy Drama).
July 16—One Bride Too Many (Two parts—Comedy-Drama).
July 30—Where Are My Trousers? (Two parts —Comedy).
Aug. 6—Like Babes in the Wood (Two parts—Juvenile Comedy).
Aug. 13—The Brass Girl (Two parts—Comedy-Drama).
Aug. 20—A Five Foot Ruler (Two parts—Comedy-Drama).
Aug. 27—Scandal Everywhere (Comedy).
Sept. 3—The Curse of a Flirting Heart (Com.).
Sept. 10—In the Clutches of Milk (Comedy).
Sept. 17—Marathon Maniacs (Comedy).

UNIVERSAL SCREEN MAGAZINE.

July 23—Issue No. 29 (Educational).
July 30—Issue No. 30 (Educational).
Aug. 6—Issue No. 31 (Topical).
Aug. 13—Issue No. 32 (Topical).
Aug. 20—Issue No. 33 (Educational).
Aug. 27—Issue No. 34 (Educational).
Sept. 3—Issue No. 35 (Educational).
Sept. 10—Issue No. 36 (Educational).
Sept. 17—Issue No. 37 (Educational).

UNIVERSAL SPECIAL FEATURE.

July 22—The Gray Ghost (Episode No. 4—"The Fight"—Two parts—Drama).
July 29—The Gray Ghost (Episode No. 5—"Plunder"—Two parts—Drama).
Aug. 6—The Gray Ghost (Episode No. 6, "The House of Mystery"—Two parts—Drama).
Aug. 13—The Gray Ghost (Episode No. 7) (The Double Floor) (Two parts—Comedy).
Aug. 20—The Gray Ghost (Episode No. 8, "The Pearl Necklace"—Two parts—Dr.).
Aug. 27—The Gray Ghost (Episode No. 9—Title Not Reported—Two parts—Drama).
Sept. 3—The Gray Ghost (Episode No. 10—Shadows—Two parts—Drama).
Sept. 10—The Gray Ghost (Episode No. 11—"The Flaming Meteor"—Two parts—Drama).
Sept. 17—The Gray Ghost (Episode No. 12—Title not reported—Two parts—Drama).

UNIVERSAL CURRENT EVENTS.

July 21—Issue No. 10 (Topical).
July 28—Issue No. 11 (Topical).
Aug. 4—Issue No. 12 (Topical).
Aug. 10—Issue No. 13 (Topical).
Aug. 14—Issue No. 14 (Topical).
Aug. 24—Issue No. 15 (Topical).
Aug. 31—Issue No. 16 (Topical).
Sept. 7—Issue No. 17 (Topical).
Sept. 14—Issue No. 18 (Topical).

Metro Pictures Corporation.

METRO PICTURES CORP.

July 9—Peggy, the Will o' the Wisp (Five parts—Drama).
July 30—Miss Robinson Crusoe (Five parts—Drama).
Special—The Slacker (Seven parts—Drama).
Aug. 6—The Jury of Fate (Rolfe—Five parts—Drama).
Aug. 13—The Girl Without a Soul (Five parts—Drama).
Aug. 27—To the Death (Five parts—Drama)..
Sept. 10—The Lifted Veil (Five parts—Drama).
Sept. 17—Their Compact (Seven parts—Drama).

YORKE FILM CORP.

July 16—The Hidden Spring (Five parts—Dr.)
Sept. 3—Under Handicap (Seven parts—Drama).

METRO COMEDIES.

July 23—Mr. Parker—Hero (Drew).
July 30—Henry's Ancestors (Drew).
Aug. 6—His Ear for Music (Drew).
Aug. 13—Her Economic Independence (Drew).
Aug. 20—Her First Game (Drew).
Aug. 27—The Patriot (Drew).
Sept. 3—Music Hath Charms (Drew).
Sept. 10—Rubbing It In (Drew).
Sept. 17—Henry's Ancestors (Drew).

Triangle Film Corporation.

TRIANGLE PRODUCTION.

July 22—A Successful Failure (Five parts—Drama).
July 22—Sudden Jim (Five parts—Drama).
July 29—In Slumberland (Five parts—Drama).
July 29—Borrowed Plumage (Five parts—Dr.).
Aug. 5—The Food Gamblers (Five parts—Drama).
Aug. 12—An Even Break (Five parts—Drama).
Aug. 12—Master of His Home (Five parts—Drama).
Aug. 12—Golden Rule Kate (Five parts—Drama).
Aug. 19—Wee Lady Betty (Five parts—Drama).
Aug. 19—They're Off (Five parts—Drama).
Aug. 26—Wooden Shoes (Five parts—Drama).
Aug. 26—Grafters (Five parts—Drama).
Sept. 2—Ten of Diamonds (Five parts—Drama).
Sept. 2—The Maus Hater (Five parts—Drama).
Sept. 9—Idolators (Five parts—Drama).
Sept. 9—Folly Ann (Five parts—Drama).

TRIANGLE KOMEDY.

July 22—An Innocent Villain.
July 29—Sole Mates.
July 29—His Widow's Might.
Aug. 5—His Perfect Day.
Aug. 5—A Matrimonial Accident.
Aug. 12—His Cool Nerve.
Aug. 12—A Hotel Disgrace.
Aug. 19—A Love Chase.
Aug. 19—His Hidden Talent.
Aug. 26—Their Domestic Deception.
Aug. 26—Her Donkey Love.
Sept. 2—A Fallen Star.
Sept. 2—His Foot-Hill Folly.
Sept. 9—A Dark Room Secret.
Sept. 9—A Warm Reception.

KEYSTONE.

July 29—Thirst (Two parts).
Aug. 5—His Uncle Dudley (Two parts).
Aug. 12—Lost—A Cook (Two parts).
Aug. 19—The Pawnbroker's Heart (Two parts).
Aug. 26—Two Crooks (Two parts).
Sept. 2—A Shanghaied Jonah (Two parts Comedy)."

PARALTA.

Rose O' Paradise.
A Man's Man.

Producers.—Kindly Furnish Titles and Dates of All New Releases Before Saturday.

List of Current Film Release Dates

MUTUAL PROGRAM AND MISCELLANEOUS FEATURES

(For Daily Calendar of Program Releases See Page 1738.)

Mutual Film Corp.

CUB.

Aug. 9—Jerry on the Railroad (Comedy).
Aug. 16—Beach Nuts (Comedy).
Aug. 23—Jerry on the Farm (Comedy).
Aug. 30—Jerry's Eugenic Marriage (Comedy).
Sept. 6—Jerry, Tries Again (Comedy).
Sept. 13—Jerry's Whirlwind Finish (Comedy).

GAUMONT.

Aug. 16—Reel Life No. 68 (Subjects on Reel: Young Men's Christian Association; Learning to Be a Soldier; The Absent-Minded Dentist; An Animated Drawing from "Life" (Mutual Film Magazine).

Aug. 28—Reel Life No. 69 (Subjects on Reel: Hunting Alligators for Their Skins; Harvesting Potatoes on the Eastern Coast; Coney Island Thrills; Oil from Japan; Something Going to Happen; An Animated Cartoon from "Life."

Aug. 30—Reel Life No. 70 (Subjects on Reel: Using the Abalone, a Little Known Industry of the Pacific Coast; A Boy and a Rope; Handling the Mail; Beach Sports of California; "The March of Science" and "What a Bachelor Sees at a Wedding" are animated drawings from "Life."

Sept. 6—Reel Life No. 71. Subjects on reel: A Watering System for a Small Farm; Pets Which Will Never Be Popular; Handling the Mail; The Five Senses; Drawing from "Life."

Sept. 13—Reel Life No. 72; Subjects on Reel: An Unusual Colt; Hunting Turtle Eggs; Testing an Auto Tube; Tree Planting in the National Forests; The Midnight Sun.

LA SALLE.

Aug. 7—Pigs and Pearls (Comedy).
Aug. 14—The Widow's Might (Comedy).

MUTUAL WEEKLY.

Aug. 8—Number 136 (Topical).
Aug. 15—Number 137 (Topical).
Aug. 22—Number 138 (Topical).
Aug. 29—Number 139 (Topical).
Sept. 5—Number 140 (Topical).
Sept. 12—Number 141 (Topical).

MUTUAL CHAPLIN

June 23—The Immigrant (Two parts—Com.).

MUTUAL STAR PRODUCTIONS.

Aug. 13—Bab the Fixer (Horkheimer—Five parts—Drama).
Sept. 3—Reputation (Goodrich—Five parts—Drama).
Sept. 3—Charity Castle (American—Five parts Drama).
Sept. 10—Outcast (Empire—Six parts—Drama).
Sept. 10—The Bride's Silence (American—Five parts—Drama).
Sept. 17—The Rainbow Girl (Five parts—Dr.).
Sept. 17—The Girl Who Couldn't Grow Up (Five parts—Drama).

Feature Releases

ARTCRAFT PICTURES CORPORATION.

Aug. 12—Down to Earth (Five parts—Comedy-Drama).
Aug. 26—Seven Keys to Baldpate (Five parts—Drama).
Sept. 3—Rebecca of Sunnybrook Farm (Five parts—Drama).
Sept. 10—Barbary Sheep (Five parts—Drama).

ART DRAMAS, INC.

Aug. 13—Think It Over (U. S. Amusement Corp. —Five parts—Comedy-Drama).

Aug. 27—The Little Samaritan (Erbograph —Five parts—Drama).
Sept. 3.—Behind the Mask (U. S. Amusement Co.—Five parts—Drama).
Sept. 10—Blood of His Fathers (Horsley—Five parts—Drama).
Sept. 17—Peg o' the Sea (Van Dyke—Five parts —Drama).

BLUEBIRD PHOTOPLYS, INC.

Aug. 13—The Show Down (Five parts—Drama).
Aug. 20—Mr. Opp (Five Parts—Drama).
Aug. 27—The Charmer (Five parts—Drama).
Sept. 3—Triumph (Five parts—Comedy-Dr.).
Sept. 3—Mother O' Mine (Five Parts—Drama —Special).
Sept. 10—A Stormy Knight (Five parts—Comedy-Drama).
Sept. 17—The Mysterious Mr. Tiller (Five parts —Drama).

BUTTERFLY PICTURES.

Aug. 13—The Midnight Man (Five parts—Dr.).
Aug. 20—The Lair of the Wolf (Five parts— Drama).
Aug. 27—Straight Shooting (Five parts-Dr.).
Sept. 3—Who Was the Other Man? (Five parts —Drama).
Sept. 10—The Little Pirate (Five parts— Drama).
Sept. 17—The Spindle of Life (Five parts—Dr.).

CINEMA WAR NEWS SYNDICATE.

Aug. 18—American War News Weekly No. 16 (Topical).
Aug. 25—American War News Weekly No. 17 (Topical).
Sept. 1—American War News Weekly No. 18 (Topical).

EDUCATIONAL FILMS CORP.

Aug. 13—Living Book of Nature, "Animals in Winter" (Ditmars).
Aug. 15—The Hard, Hard Road to Adventure (Bruce).
Aug. 20—Living Book of Nature, "Ancestors of the Horse" (Ditmars).
Aug. 22—China and the Chinese, No. 5.
Aug. 27—Living Book of Nature, "Orong Volunteers" (Ditmars).
Aug. 29—First American Apartment House and Nature's Theatricals (Scenic and Educational).
Sept. 3—Living Book of Nature, "Kangaroos and Their Allies" (Ditmars).

FOX FILM CORPORATION.

Special Release—Jack and the Beanstalk (Ten parts—Drama).
Aug. 4—Wrath of Love (Five parts—Drama).
Aug. 11—Durand of the Bad Lands (Five parts —Drama).
Aug. 18—The Soul of Satan (Five parts—Dr.).
Aug. 25—Every Girl's Dream (Five parts—Dr.).
Sept. 2—Betrayed (Five parts—Drama).
Sept. 9—When False Tongues Speak (Five parts—Drama).
Sept. 16—The Yankee Way (Five parts—Dr.).

FOXFILM COMEDIES.

July 23—A Soft Tenderfoot (Two parts).
Aug. 6—A Domestic Hound (Two parts).

GOLDWYN PICTURES CORP.

Sept. 9—Polly of the Circus (Eight parts— Drama).
Sept. 23—Baby Mine (Six parts—Drama).
Oct. 7—Fighting Odds (Six parts—Drama).

GREATER VITAGRAPH (V-L-S-E).

Aug. 13—Mary Jane's Pa (Five parts—Drama).
Aug. 20—Transgression (Five parts—Drama).
Aug. 27—The Divorcee (Five parts—Drama).
Aug. 6—Bobby, Boy Scout (Comedy-Drama).
Aug. 13—Bobby, the Movie Director (Comedy).
Aug. 20—Bobby, Philanthropist (Comedy-Dr.).

Aug. 27—Bobby, Pacifist (Comedy-Drama). Drama).
Sept. 3—Bobby's Bravery (Comedy-Drama).
Sept. 3—Soldiers of Chance (Five parts —Drama).
Sept. 10—An Alabaster Box (Five parts— Drama).
Sept. 17—For France (Five parts—Drama).
Sept. 17—Favorite Film Features: "Winning the Stepchildren" (One Reel Drama) "Goodness Gracious" (Two Reel Comedy).

KLEINE-EDISON-SELIG-ESSANAY.

Aug. 18—Conquest Program No. 6 (Subjects; The Customary Two Weeks (Four parts—Drama); The Story of Plymouth Rock (1,000 feet); The Grand Canyon of Arizona (500 feet); The Four P's (500 feet); Nature's Perfect Thread Spinner (500 feet); The Magic of Spring (800 feet).
Aug. 20—Open Places (Essanay—Five parts— Drama).
Aug. 22—The Kingdom of Hope (One of the "De Children Count?" Series—Two parts—Drama).
Aug. 20—A Trip to Chinatown (Selig-Hoyt Comedy—Two parts).
Aug. 27—The Lady of the Photograph (Edison —Five parts—Drama).
Aug. 25—Conquest Program No. 7 (Subjects; T. Haviland Hicks, Freshman (Three parts—Drama); Gallagher (Two parts—Drama); Turning Out Silver Bullets (One reel); Young Salts and the Holy Land (Combined in one reel).
Sept. 3—Efficiency Edgar's Courtship (Five parts—Drama—Essanay).
Sept. 3—A Midnight Bell (Hoyt Comedy—Two parts).
Sept. 1—Conquest Program No. 8 (Edison). Subjects: The Princess' Necklace (Four Parts—Drama); The Puzzling Bill-Board, and In Old England (Split Reel); The Brook, and Woodcraft for Boys; Shipping Live Fish (Split reel); The Blind Fiddler (One reel).
Sept. 10—Pants (Five parts—Drama—Essanay).
Sept. 17—The Awakening of Ruth (Five parts— Drama—Edison).
Sept. 17—A Contented Woman (Hoyt Comedy— Two parts).

SELECT PICTURES CORP.

Magda (C. K. Y. Corp.).

SELZNICK PICTURES.

The Lash of Jealousy (Drama).
The Lesson (Drama).
The Moth (Drama).
The Wild Girl.

STANDARD PICTURES.

Aug. 19—The Spy (Ten parts).
Aug. 26—The Honor System (Ten parts).
Sept. 2—Jack and the Beanstalk (Ten parts).
Sept. 16—The Conquerer (Ten parts).

WHOLESOME FILMS CORPORATION.

Sept. 3—The Penny Philanthropist (Five parts —Drama).
Sept. 3—Cinderella and the Magic Slipper (Four parts—Drama).

WORLD PICTURES.

Aug. 13—Souls Adrift (Five parts—Drama).
Aug. 20—The Little Duchess (Five parts—Dr.).
Aug. 27—Her Guardian (Five parts—Drama).
Sept. 3—Tides of Fate (Five parts—Drama).
Sept. 10—The Marriage Market (Five parts— Drama).
Sept. 17—Betsy Ross (Five parts—Drama).

Producers—Kindly Furnish Titles and Dates of All New Releases Before Saturday.

List of State Rights Pictures

(For Daily Calendar of Program Releases See Page 1738.)

Note—For further information regarding pictures listed on this page, address State Rights Department, Moving Picture World, and same will be gladly furnished.

ARIZONA FILM CO.
May—Should She Obey (Drama).

BERNSTEIN FILM PRODUCTION.
Humility (First of "Seven Cardinal Virtues"—Drama).
June—Who Knows? (Six parts—Drama).

J. FRANK BROCKLISS, INC.
U. S. Navy (Five parts).
Terry Human Interest Reels (900 Feet Every Other Week).
Russian Revolution (Three parts).
Land of the Rising Sun (10,000 feet—Issued complete or in series of 2,000 feet or 5,000 feet).

BUD FISHER FILMS CORP.
Mutt and Jeff Animated Cartoons.

CAMERAGRAPH FILM MFG. CO.
June.—What of Your Boy? (Three parts—Patriotic).
June.—The Automobile Owner Gets Acquainted With His Automobile (Educational).

CARONA CINEMA CO.
May—The Curse of Eve (Seven parts—Dr.).

CENTURY COMEDIES.
Sept. 1—Balloonatics (Two parts—Comedy).

BENJAMIN CHAPIN PRODUCTIONS.
(The Lincoln Cycle Pictures.)
My Mother (Two parts).
My Father (Two parts).
Myself (Two parts).
The Call to Arms (Two parts).

CHRISTIE FILM CO.
July 9—The Fourteenth Man (Comedy).
July 16—Down By the Sea (Comedy).
July 23—Skirts (Comedy).
July 30—Won in a Cabaret (Comedy).
Aug. 7—His Merry Mix-Up (Comedy).
Aug. 14—A Smokey Love Affair (Comedy).

CINEMA DISTRIBUTING CORP.
June—The 13th Labor of Hercules (Twelve single parts).

CORONET FILM CORP.
Living Studies in Natural History.
Animal World—Issue No. 1.
Animal World—Issue No. 2.
Birdland Studies.
Horticultural Phenomena.

COSMOFOTOFILM, INC.
June—I Believe (Seven parts—Drama).

E. I. S. MOTION PICTURES CORP.
Trooper 44 (Five parts—Drama).

EMERALD MOTION PICTURE CO.
May—The Slacker (Military Drama).

EXPORT AND IMPORT FILM CO.
June—Robespierre.
June—Ivan, the Terrible.

FAIRMOUNT FILM CORP.
June—Hate (Seven parts—Drama).

FLORA FINCH FILM CO.
"War Prides" (Two parts—Comedy).

FORT PITT CORPORATION.
The Italian Battlefront.

FRATERNITY FILMS, INC.
May—Devil's Playground (Nine parts—Drama).

FRIEDMAN ENTERPRISES.
A Mormon Maid (Six parts—Drama).

FRIEDER FILM CORP.
June—A Bit o' Heaven (Five parts—Drama).

FROHMAN AMUSEMENT CORP.
April—God's Man (Nine parts—Drama).

JOSEPH M. GAITES.
August—The Italian Battlefront.

GOLDIN FEATURES.
A Bit of Life (One Reel Comedy-Drama).

F. G. HALL PRODUCTIONS, INC.
May—Her Fighting Chance (Seven parts—Dr.). (Mr. Hall has world rights to this picture.)
May—The Bar Sinister (Drama). (Mr. Hall has world rights to this picture.)

HILLER & WILK.
April—How Uncle Sam Prepares (Topical).
April—The Battle of Gettysburg.
April—The Wrath of the Gods (Drama).

HISTORIC FEATURES.
June—Christus (Eight parts—Drama).

ILIDOR PICTURES CORP.
June.—The Fall of the Romanoffs (Drama).

IVAN FILM PRODUCTIONS.
Apr.—One Law for Both (8 parts—Drama.)
August—Babbling Tongues (Six parts—Dr.).

JEWEL PRODUCTIONS, INC.
Pay Me (Drama).
Sirens of the Sea.

KING BEE FILMS CORP.
July 1—Cupid's Rival (Two parts—Comedy).
July 15—The Villain (Two parts—Comedy).
Aug. 1—The Millionaire (Two parts—Com.).
Aug. 15—The Goat (Two parts—Comedy).
Sept. 1—The Fly Cop (Two parts—Comedy).
Sept. 15—The Star Boarder (Two parts—Com.).

A KAY CO.
Some Barrier (Terry Cartoon Burlesque).
His Trial (Terry Cartoon Burlesque).
Terry Human Interest Reel No. 1 (Character As Revealed in the Face).
Terry Human Interest Reel No. 2 (Character As Revealed in the Eyes).

KLOTZ & STREIMER.
June.—Whither Thou Goest (Five parts—Drama).
June—The Secret Trap (Five parts—Drama).

MANX-MAN COMPANY.
The Manx-Man (Eight parts—Drama).

MAYFAIR FILM CORP.
Persuasive Peggy (Drama).

MOE STREIMER.
June—A Daughter of the Don (Ten parts—Drama).

B. S. MOSS MOTION PICTURE CORP.
April—Birth Control (Five parts—Drama).

NEVADA MOTION PICTURE CORP.
June—The Planter (Drama).

NEWFIELDS PRODUCING CORP.
Alma, Where Do You Live? (Six parts—Dr.).

OGDEN PICTURES CORP.
August—The Lust of the Ages (Drama).

PARAGON FILMS, INC.
The Whip (Eight parts—Drama).

PETER PAN FILM CORP.
Mo-Toy Troupe (Release No. 4—"In the Jungle Land").
Mo-Toy Troupe (Release No. 5—"A Kitchen Romance").
Mo-Toy Troupe (Release No. 6—"Mary and Gretel").
Mo-Toy Troupe (Release No. 7—"Dinkling of the Circus").
Mo-Toy Troupe (Release No. 8—"A Trip to the Moon").
Mo-Toy Troupe (Release No. 9, "Golden Locks and the Three Bears").
Mo-Toy Troupe (Release No 10, "Dolly Doings").
Mo-Toy Troupe (Release No. 11 "School Days").
Moy-toy Troupe (Release No. 12, "Little Red Riding Hood").
Moy-toy Troupe (Release No. 13, "Puss in Boots").

PUBLIC RIGHTS FILM CORP.
June—The Public Be Damned.

PURKALL FILM CO.
July—The Liar (Six parts—Drama).

RENOWNED PICTURES CORP.
June—In Treason's Grasp (Five parts—Drama)

REX BEACH PICTURES CO.
March—The Barrier (Nine parts—Drama).

SELECT PHOTOPLAY CO.
May—Humanity (Six parts—Drama).

WILLIAM N. SELIG.
April—The Garden of Allah.
May—Beware of Strangers (Eight parts—Dr.).

FRANK J. SENG.
May—Parentage (Drama).

SHERMAN PICTURE CORP.
July—Corruption (Six parts—Drama).
August—I Believe.

SKOBELOFF COMMITTEE.
The Great Russian Revolution.
Behind the Battle Line in Russia.

JULIUS STEGER.
May—Redemption (Six parts—Drama).

SUPREME FEATURE FILMS, INC.
May—Trip Through China (Ten parts).

ULTRA FILMS, INC.
A Day at West Point (Educational).
West is West.
Rustlers' Frame-Up at Big Horn.

UNIVERSAL (STATE RIGHTS).
May—The Hand that Rocks the Cradle (Six parts—Drama).
June—The Cross-Eyed Submarine (Three parts—Comedy).
June—Come Through (Seven parts—Drama).

E. WARREN PRODUCTION.
April—The Warfare of the Flesh (Drama).

WHARTON, INC.
June—The Great White Trail (Seven parts) (Drama).

WILLIAMSON BROS.
April—The Submarine Eye (Drama).

Producers.—Kindly Furnish Titles and Dates of All New Releases Before Saturday.

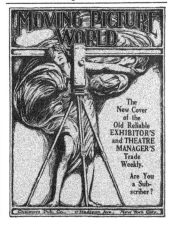

A Look Behind the Scenes

On Curtis Street, Denver

where there are more Moving Picture Theatres crowded into two blocks than anywhere else in the world.

When Mr. F. H. Richardson, the noted Projection Expert, visited Denver recently, he wrote in the Moving Picture World:

"I didn't get a chance to visit a single Denver Theatre, and she has some beauties, too, to say nothing of the Curtis Street White Way, which for two blocks would actually make Broadway at 42nd Street at 11 p. m. look shady by comparison.

"It hasn't the tremendous size of New York's White Way . . . but what there is of it is a stem-winding, double-back action humdinger, and, what's more, the entire show is composed of the illumination on the fronts of the Curtis Street colony of Moving Picture Theatres."

Now let us

do what Mr. Richardson didn't have time for, and find out what "makes Denver's White Way go."

Here it is:

Simplex Projection in every Theatre on Curtis Street
Simplex Projection for a seating capacity of nearly 20,000
Simplex Projection delighting 75,000 pairs of eyes daily

Now that you know what is back of Denver's White Way you need no longer wonder why it is such a success, why it compares so favorably with New York's White Way.

And of course you can't overlook that what the Simplex is doing for these Denver Exhibitors it will do for you—if you let it.

Let us send you Catalog "A." Then we'll tell you at the same time what Simplex Distributor can help you to the equal of Denver's projection.

Get in touch with the Simplex Distributor. He's the friend of the Exhibitor.

THE PRECISION MACHINE CO., INC.
317 East 34th St— New York

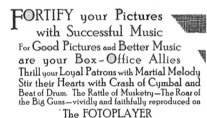

Goldwyn
pictures

The Last Words
Have Been Said
When you Say:
Goldwyn
Pictures

The pictures now
giving the greatest
satisfaction are
Essanays. Seeing
is believing.
Look and you
will book —
at any Kleine
Exchange.

Geo. K. Spoor.

Tense Timely Thrilling

"The RED ACE"

The UNIVERSAL Master Serial
featuring
Dashing, Daring, Fascinating
Marie Walcamp

CONSIDER THESE FACTS, Mr. Exhibitor, in booking "THE RED ACE." The Universal's great serial "LIBERTY" played from Coast to Coast, in many towns repeat, in some towns four and five times, and in every town Exhibitors positively cleaned up.

We could give you the names of hundreds who cashed in BIG MONEY on "LIBERTY." Now — in "THE RED ACE", you get the same STAR, Marie Walcamp — you get the same director, Jacques Jacquard, and you get even greater thrills, more tense situations, wonderful struggles, adventures, romance and a beautiful love story. "THE RED ACE" is a whale of a serial There is *no serial on t e market* that surpasses the RED ACE. We will guarantee it to pack your house. BOOK IT *NOW* thru any of our 73 Universal Exchanges.

Jack Mulhall

Zoe Rae

Molly Malone

Edith Roberts

Harry Carey

Louise Lovely

Butterfly Stars

BLUEBIRD Photoplays

Present

FRANKLYN FARNUM

in

"A FOOL FOR LUCK"

Production by Joseph De Grasse
Story by Isola Forrester and Mann Page

The story of a man who was willing to "try anything once" and his
ultimate success in getting a square deal for himself and others.

Book through your local BLUEBIRD Exchange

BLUEBIRD Photoplays, Inc.   1600 Broadway, New York

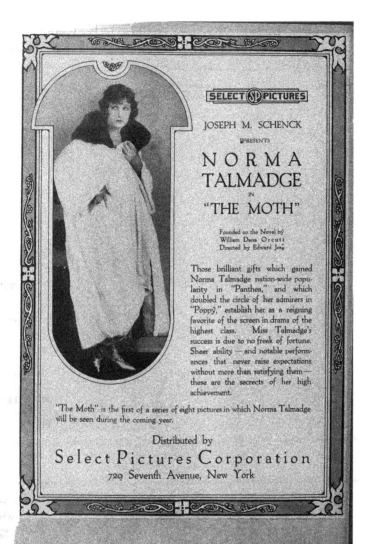

SELZNICK🌐PICTURES

LEWIS J. SELZNICK
PRESENTS

RITA JOLIVET

The International Star, in

"LEST WE FORGET!"

Directed by LEONCE PERRET

THE distinguished stage artiste, RITA JOLIVET, is shown in this picture as the center of a powerful drama, the scenes of which reflect international events at the beginning of the European war. Based on actual occurrences in the memorable summer of 1914, the play presents as its central picture the torpedoing of the Lusitania. RITA JOLIVET was one of the survivors when the Lusitania was destroyed by a German submarine, and in this picture she lives over again the memorable scenes that accompanied the sinking of the ill-fated steamer. Running through the photoplay is a tender love story. Miss JOLIVET, supported by a notable cast, in this picture displays to advantage those talents which have made her a star of international repute.

Produced by

Rita Jolivet Film Corporation
729 Seventh Avenue, New York

WHAT OTHER PEOPLE SAY

———— OF ————

LILLIAN WALKER

"The Darling of the Screen" in

"THE LUST OF THE AGES"

From the book by Aaron Hoffman
Directed by Harry Revier

"THE LUST OF THE AGES" is all of a big "special" and will rank high as a State Rights money-getter for the three best of reasons: A worthy story, superlative production and a widely-known and talented star appearing a her best.

The surprise and wonder start with the first clicks of the projector and endure through the seven reels, while the spectator sits transfixed at the strength, beauty and true artistry with which the thing is treated.—GRAVES in MOTOGRAPHY.

From first to last of that sort that will make sure appeal to feminine audiences. Particularly charming and strikingly well done. Should be billed as a special attraction.—EXHIBITORS' TRADE REVIEW.

Ingeniously directed and photographed along original lines. A timely story. It ranks as one of the most important photoplay productions of the present day.—JOLO in VARIETY.

Pretentiously produced and excellently staged, "THE LUST OF THE AGES" is a picture decidedly above the average run and is imaginatively and picturesquely presented. Miss Walker's many admirers will be delighted by her return and be glad to see her in a picture that has many claims to the unusual.—SUNDAY TELEGRAPH.

An interesting bit of artistry and decidedly different from the ordinary routing productions. It has an element of romance, but beneath it all there is a thought which will reach home. The interest is held throughout, and any fan will consider this a production worth while. Miss Walker's work in this production will not soon be forgotten.—WID.

Exceptionally good State Rights feature. Entirely different from the average run. Miss Walker's work is above criticism.—NEW YORK REVIEW.

The film will sell itself because it is a criterion of photographic art, beautiful to the eye, and holds the attention throughout. It is one of the pictures which can be warmly endorsed.—L. H. in BILLBOARD.

A production that will stand the scrutiny of the classes and registers with force. There is a certain grandeur about this production that holds. Some of the best work ever shown on the screen comes to light in this production. Miss Walker's work will elicit praise from her many admirers. If there is any reason why the exhibitor in any locality cannot book this feature and "cash in," the reviewer has failed to recognize it.—KELLY in MOTION PICTURE NEWS.

A pretentious subject with many novelties, touches that add to the picturesqueness of the subject.—MOVING PICTURE WORLD.

An excellent interpretation, both for beauty and direction of an absorbingly interesting story, and the interest is not permitted to lag for a moment. Miss Walker displays her customary ability and charm. Exhibitors managing any class of theatre may rest assured that "THE LUST OF THE AGES" will meet with instantaneous success.—F. T. in DRAMATIC MIRROR.

Lillian Walker has done nothing so good as her portrayal of Lois Craig in "THE LUST OF THE AGES," nor has any screen actress been allotted a more delightful character to portray. Her work stamps her as one of the screen's foremost players. The episodes of "THE LUST OF THE AGES" are tremendously gripping with much heart interest.—EXHIBITORS' HERALD.

Above is the verdict of the keen-sighted, discriminating critics upon whom the trade relies. We can say no more.

Franchises for the remaining seven Lillian Walker productions to be produced during the year are being awarded to the State Right purchasers of the initial production.

Address all communications to

OGDEN PICTURES CORPORATION

Eastern Executive Office

Phone—Bryant 1820.

729 Seventh Avenue, New York City, Room 1202

METRO PICTURES
CORPORATION presents
An extraordinary
BIG STAR SERIES
production
FRANCIS X
BUSHMAN
and
BEVERLY
BAYNE

COMPACT

by CHARLES. A. LOGUE

*Produced under the
personal supervision of*
MAXWELL KARGER and
directed by Edwin Carewe

Madame
PETROVA
in her first
Petrova Picture

PETROVA PICTURES

FIRST RELEASE:
on or about Oct. 22, 1917.

Petrova Picture Company
Frederick L. Collins.. President
25 West 44" Street.. New York

MARY PICKFORD
in
"Rebecca of Sunnybrook Farm"

The New York Herald says:—

"Mary Pickford is big hit at Strand."

From the famous play by
KATE DOUGLAS WIGGIN
and CHARLOTTE THOMPSON.

Picturized by Frances Marion
Staged by Marshall Neilan

ARTCRAFT PICTURES CORPORATION
729 SEVENTH AVE. ... NEW YORK CITY
Controlled by FAMOUS PLAYERS-LASKY CORPORATION
ADOLPH ZUKOR, Pres.   JESSE L. LASKY, Vice-Pres.
CECIL B. DeMILLE, Director General

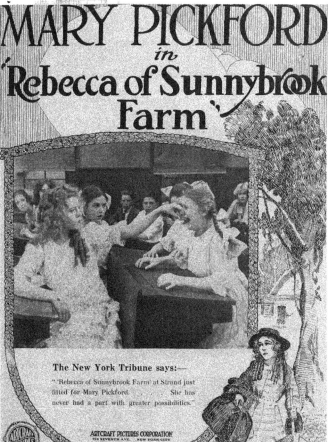

MARY PICKFORD
in
'Rebecca of Sunnybrook Farm'

The New York Tribune says:—

"'Rebecca of Sunnybrook Farm' at Strand just fitted for Mary Pickford.   She has never had a part with greater possibilities."

FAIRBANKS
"The Man from Painted Post"

—is just a big hearted citizen who will tickle your sense of humor and make you glad you're alive.

Gladder, in fact. Think of your returns on his last picture, and how your patrons liked it, and the way your newspapers wrote it up, or the "class" your house gets by showing all the new Artcraft-Douglas Fairbanks Pictures. The next one will be advertised—everywhere as

DOUGLAS FAIRBANKS
in
"The Man from Painted Post"

Story by Jackson Gregory,
Picturized by Douglas Fairbanks,
Staged by Joseph Henaberry

AN ARTCRAFT PICTURE

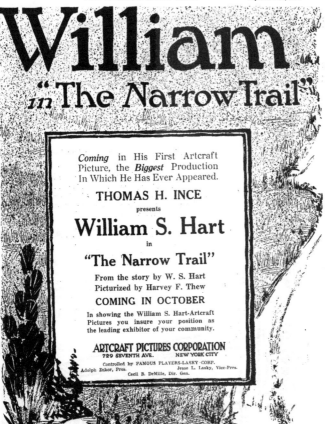

William

in The Narrow Trail

Coming in His First Artcraft Picture, the *Biggest* Production In Which He Has Ever Appeared.

THOMAS H. INCE

presents

William S. Hart

in

"The Narrow Trail"

From the story by W. S. Hart
Picturized by Harvey F. Thew

COMING IN OCTOBER

In showing the William S. Hart-Artcraft Pictures you insure your position as the leading exhibitor of your community.

ARTCRAFT PICTURES CORPORATION
729 SEVENTH AVE.   NEW YORK CITY

Controlled by FAMOUS PLAYERS-LASKY CORP.
Adolph Zukor, Pres.   Jesse L. Lasky, Vice-Pres.
Cecil B. DeMille, Dir. Gen.

S. Hart

ARTCRAFT PICTURES

"Anything Goes"

in a Paramount-Mack Sennett Comedy—
only one rule—good taste—for comedies—they are for ladies and gentlemen,
you know—by ladies and gentlemen, for
ladies and gentlemen, with ladies and
gentlemen—with the accent on the
ladies—1, 2, 3—we're off—

"Roping Her Romeo"
"A Bedroom Blunder"
"A Pullman Bride"

Remember, we all like to laugh.

Kipling put it "Biddy O'Grady and
the Colonel's lady are sisters under
the skin."

Most of them girlies, and none of them
twenty, and you can't fool a camera—
come and see.

Paramount Pictures Corporation
FOUR EIGHTY-FIVE FIFTH AVENUE at FORTY-FIRST ST
NEW YORK
Controlled by FAMOUS PLAYERS-LASKY CORPORATION
Adolph Zukor, Pres., Jesse L. Lasky, Vice-Pres., Cecil B. DeMille, Director General

Like a May Morning

is

Kathleen — the
starry-eyed her-
oine of *Para-*
mount's first serial --- She
dances ~ a daring saucy sunbeam
through the dark plots and in-
trigues of

Kathleen Clifford

Who is "*Number One*"?
BY ANNA KATHARINE GREEN

a mystery serial of unqualified
strength woven around the hate
and fury of a woman scorned

A campaign of far-reach-
ing and irresistible ad-
vertising and promotion
is behind this rare com-
bination of author, star
and producer

READY IN OCTOBER

Anna Katharine Green

Polishing a Diamond

The usual five-act feature is completed in six weeks The first *Paramount Serial* - - -

Who is "Number One"?
BY·ANNA·KATHARINE·GREEN

was begun early in last January and is not yet finished!

It takes a long time to cut and polish a diamond

♦ That is the parallel by which to judge Anna Katharine Green's great serial of mystery and a woman's jealous hate

READY IN OCTOBER

VIVIAN MARTIN
"Little Miss Optimist"

A Magnet for Millions

VIVIAN MARTIN has an attractive force called CHARM. In "Little Miss Optimist" that charm is given the widest opportunity to enthrall your patrons. It is reinforced by a story that would be billed by most producers as an attraction extraordinary.

We call it "A Paramount Picture"—it has all of the quality that that name implies.

Picturized by GARDNER HUNTING
Directed by ROBERT THORNBY

A Paramount Picture

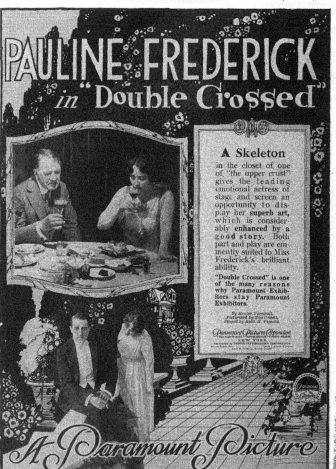

PAULINE FREDERICK
in "Double Crossed"

A Skeleton

in the closet of one of "the upper crust" gives the leading emotional actress of stage and screen an opportunity to display her **superb art,** which is considerably **enhanced by a good story.** Both part and play are eminently suited to Miss Frederick's brilliant ability.

"Double Crossed" is one of the many reasons why Paramount Exhibitors stay Paramount Exhibitors.

By Hector Turnbull
Pictureized by Eve Unsell
Staged by Robt. G. Vignola.

Paramount Pictures Corporation
FIVE FIFTY-SEVEN FIFTH AVENUE NEW YORK
Controlled by FAMOUS PLAYERS–LASKY CORPORATION

A Paramount Picture

CARNEGIE HALL

Sunday Evening, January 21st, 1917, at 8.30
Monday Afternoon, Jan. 22d, 1917, at 3.00
1916-1917

BURTON HOLMES TRAVELOGUES
Under the direction of
LOUIS FRANCIS BROWN

QIAN ROCKIES
OGUE IN THREE PARTS BY
ON HOLMES

Nobody questions the quality of Burton Holmes Travel Pictures—*they are proven.*

But do you realize their attraction value for a certain class of people. These same pictures that are shown in Carnegie Hall at $2.00—*you can show to your patrons at your prices—for example—*

Regina to the Rockies
Beautiful Banff
With the Stony Indians
Exquisite Lake Louise
The Yoho Valley
On the Great Glacier

Is this series a good buy?

Paramount Burton Holmes Travel Pictures

Paramount Pictures Corporation
FOUR EIGHTY-FIVE FIFTH AVENUE AT FORTY-FIRST ST.
NEW YORK
Controlled by FAMOUS PLAYERS-LASKY CORPORATION

THE WARRIOR

THE *SMASHING SEVEN* REEL
COMEDY-DRAMA
featuring MACISTE
The giant hero of "CABIRIA"

STATE RIGHTS

The biggest "Sure-Fire"
Money-Making State Rights
Proposition Ever Offered.
Four Weeks Capacity
Business at
**CRITERION THEATRE
NEW YORK**

LAUGHTER - THRILLS - CHEERS - TEARS

Not a Battle Picture, But a Human Story full of
Heart Interest, Suspense and Side-Splitting Comedy

"Some Warrior, Maciste. He Out Fairbanks Fairbanks." *N.Y. Times*	"Such a demonstration seldom has been seen before at the Criterion Theatre." *N.Y. Tribune*
"Laughs, Tears, Cheers." *N.Y. American*	"I think it immense; Ought to make a lot of Money." *A.H.Woods, Theatrical Producer*

NOW READY FOR BIDS from STATE RIGHTS BUYERS

HERBERT LUBIN **GENERAL ENTERPRISES, INC.** ARTHUR H. SAWYER
1600 BROADWAY, New York ··· Telephone **BRYANT 5692**

The Sidney Drews at Home

America's Greatest Stars

—Stars famous wherever motion pictures are
screened—stars like Douglas Fairbanks, Charles
Ray, Emily Stevens, Louise Glaum, Dorothy Dalton,
Viola Dana, Margaret Thompson, William Russell,
Mr. and Mrs. Sidney Drew, Mary Miles Minter,
Bessie Love, Annette Kellerman and hosts of others
—"The Stars As They Are"—are presented from
a new and fascinating angle in

PHOTOPLAY MAGAZINE
SCREEN SUPPLEMENT

Positively the greatest series of single-reel de luxe motion
pictures ever assembled—the kind of attractions exhibitors not only
book for themselves, but recommend to their brother exhibitors—
now offered state rights buyers and chain theatre owners. Superb
photography—unique sub-titling—an absolute novelty—nothing
like it ever before screened.

Applications for territory are arriving daily. Zone franchises
will be issued at an early date. To receive consideration make
your application without delay. Wire or write

JAMES R. QUIRK, PUBLISHER
PHOTOPLAY MAGAZINE
CHICAGO, ILLINOIS

RIANGLE

Margery Wilson

in

"Mountain Dew"

Released
Sept. 16

A sparkling new
star in a play
of mountain
charm and
fresh-
ness

William Desmond
in
"Flying Colors"

Released
Sept. 16

Yale athlete turns so-
ciety detective and
with daredevil
stunts captures
a thief, a bride
and an in-
come

nifred Allen
in
"The
nted House"

Released
Sept. 9

The tale of a ghost
that turns human
and falls in
love with a
thief

Keystone Comedy

"Hula-Hula Land"

Released
Sept. 16

by Peter B. Kyne   Direction of Oscar Apfel

A Man's Man.
He is no respecter of persons or pomp.
Braid of gold.—fine feathers.
To him they are meaningless.
Is a man TRUE?—No one may tell by his skin.
Deep in his heart lies the worth of a MAN.

Sold Under Either Star Series Booking Method, or The Paralta Plan.

"Ask Any Triangle Exchange"

No, you are mistaken! We're not shaking our fists at you; we're only trying to be emphatic—talking with both hands.

We believe what we have to say to you in the Paralta Plan book is of great importance to your interests as an exhibitor, and so we adopt one of the strenuous methods of the most forceful personality in American public life to impress this fact on your mind and talk with both hands.

Some exhibitors have not yet sent for the Paralta Plan book. It only costs one's name and address on a one-cent postal card. Are you one of them? If so, why?

Real wise men get all the information they can about their own business from every possible source. Why not be a real wise man?

You have heard much about working on system. This book not only tells you of a system that will work in your interests, but it also tells you how another SYSTEM is working against you day and night.

Write for the Paralta Plan book. It is only sent on request. Read it and know every angle of your own business. Knowing "all his game" made Rockefeller a billionaire.

"Ask any Triangle Exchange."

ARALTA PLAYS INC.

CARL ANDERSON, President   **ROBERT T. KANE,** Vice-Prest.
HERMAN FICHTENBERG, Chairman Directors   **HERMAN KATZ,** Treas.
          NAT. I. BROWN; Secretary and Gen'l Manager.

729 SEVENTH AVENUE
NEW YORK CITY -

Goldwyn's New Message to the Small Exhibitor

MORE than a thousand of the smaller exhibitors of the nation have signed for Goldwyn Pictures — quality productions at prices they can afford to pay. At prices that will leave them a profit.

There are *eighteen thousand* motion picture theatres in the United States—the great majority of them *small* theatres. It is our ambition to have all of the smaller exhibitors of the nation solidly behind Goldwyn Pictures—liking them, playing them and making a profit on them.

And here is news for you: By playing Goldwyn Pictures you can make your small theatre *a large theatre.* For Goldwyn productions will bring the best people in every community in America to your box offices. *And they will go away pleased.*

At this moment, when our productions are the most talked-of motion pictures in America, there are still thousands of exhibitors who can increase their profits and their prestige by signing Goldwyn contracts.

Goldwyn Pictures Corporation

16 East 42nd Street,   New York City
Telephone: Vanderbilt 11

Goldwyn Pictures

Goldwyn
presents:

Mae Marsh

In

Polly of the Circus

By Margaret Mayo

'At the very top as an artistic achievement. Containing all the refinements and dramatic values and all of the elements of popular appeal that should be embodied in "the perfect picture."

Goldwyn Pictures

Speaking for Chicago

Oma Moody Lawrence, motion picture critic of the *Chicago Evening Post*, telegraphs to Goldwyn the following enthusiastic approval of Madge Kennedy in "Baby Mine":

Congratulations on Madge Kennedy's first Goldwyn Picture, "Baby Mine" which opened at the Colonial today. The critics at the advance showing here agreed it was a credit to Goldwyn and the industry. Make more like it. We don't care how hard we work looking at Madge Kennedy if she continues in the present form.

Goldwyn

presents

as its second remarkable release on September 23rd, throughout North America.

Madge Kennedy
in
Baby Mine

By Margaret Mayo

Kitty Kelly in *The Chicago Examiner* says: "Madge Kennedy is what Samuel Goldfish predicted—a comedy mine... A comedy gold mine for the exhibitors of America... 'Baby Mine' is a path-pointer for the new comedy era."

Goldwyn Pictures Corporation

16 East 42nd. St.   New York City

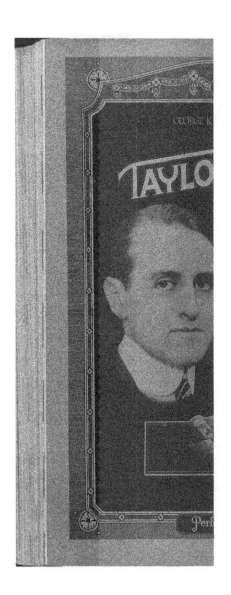

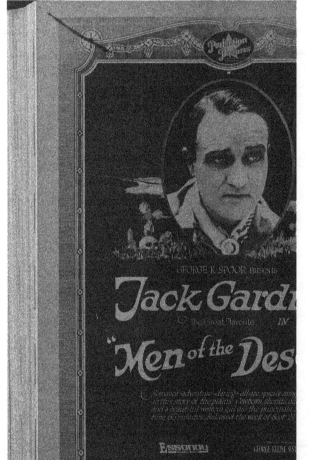

GEORGE K SPOOR PRESENTS

Jack Gardn
The Great Favorite   IN

"Men of the Des

Romance-adventure-daring-all are spicely mingl
in this story of the plains Cowboys, sheriffs, out
and a beautiful western girl are the principals
time 66 minutes Released the week of Sept 30

Essenay   GEORGE KLEINE SYSTE

Perfection Pictures

GEORGE K. SPOOR PRESENTS

Taylor Holmes

Filmland's newest twinkler. IN

"*Fools For Luck*"

Four-leaf clovers, horseshoes, rabbits feet, and swastikas are all jinxes when compared to the luck that followed the hero of this comedy-drama. Based on Kennett Harris' Saturday Evening Post story "Talismans." Screen time 66 minutes. Released the week of Oct. 8th.

Essanay   GEORGE KLEINE SYSTEM

Perfection Pictures

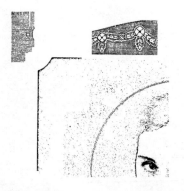

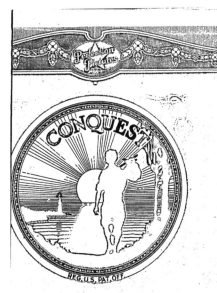

Let Your Theatre Benefit By This
Saturday Evening Post Campaign

Put this big national advertising campaign to work for your theatre. The first of these national advertising bombs is fired in the issue of the Saturday Evening Post dated Sept. 22nd. Millions of people will see it: They will be looking for the theatres showing Perfection Pictures—"The Highest Standard in Motion Pictures." Let your box-office benefit by this publicity. Bring the people to your theatre to see the films in which they are interested. The value of a Perfection Picture contract will be tremendous in your territory. Don't let your competitor get ahead of you. Arrange today to show Perfection Pictures in your theatre. Wire or write your nearest Kleine Exchange for details.

GEORGE KLEINE SYSTEM

Sole distributors of Perfection Pictures throughout America

Perfection Pictures

Pathé

Not only are Pathé serials the best written, the best produced, the best acted, <u>but they are the best advertised</u>. In the chief cities of the land as well as many others the principal news—papers publish the novelizations of the serials and carry the extensive help-the-exhibitor advertising.

The following is only a <u>partial</u> list of <u>Sunday</u> news-papers which will publish the novelization of

ℑhe SEVEN PEARLS
WITH
MOLLIE KING
AND CREIGHTON HALE

New York American	Baltimore American	St. Paul News
Boston American	Albany Knickerbocker Press	Syracuse Herald
Atlanta Georgian	Washington Times	Milwaukee Leader
Chicago Examiner	Louisville Herald	Richmond Times Dispatch
San Francisco Examiner	New Orleans Item	Houston Chronicle
Los Angeles Examiner	Omaha News	Rochester Picture Play News
Philadelphia North American	Minneapolis News	Indianapolis Star

Such co-operation, united with the unequalled feature quality of the serial, insure to the exhibitor wide public interest and a consistently large attendance.

Additional lists of newspapers advertising "The Seven Pearls" will be given later. There is a newspaper in <u>your</u> section which will have this advertising.

Produced by Astra – Written by Charles W. Goddard, the famous playwright

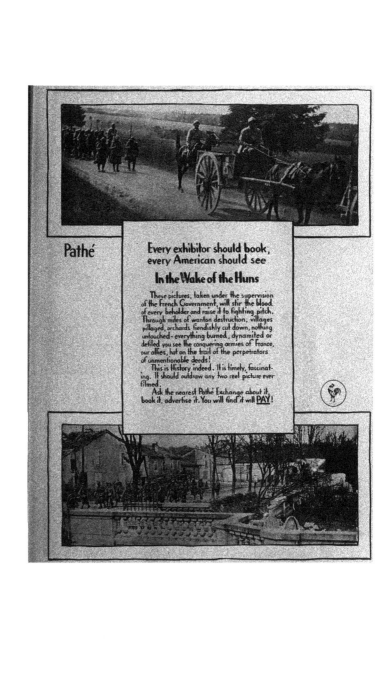

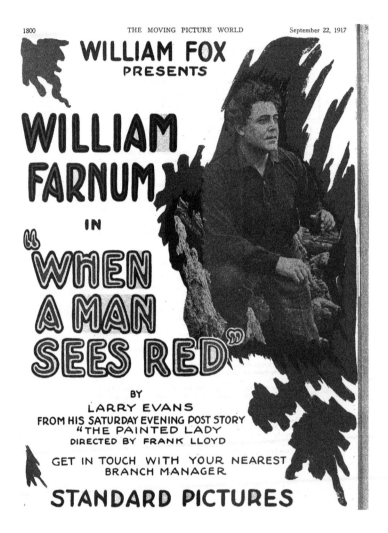

WILLIAM FOX
PRESENTS

WILLIAM
FARNUM

IN

"WHEN
A MAN
SEES RED"

BY
LARRY EVANS
FROM HIS SATURDAY EVENING POST STORY
"THE PAINTED LADY
DIRECTED BY FRANK LLOYD

GET IN TOUCH WITH YOUR NEAREST
BRANCH MANAGER

STANDARD PICTURES

THIS IS HOW A MAN LOOKS —

—WHEN HE SEES RED

MR. EXHIBITOR:—
THIS IS HOW MAD YOU'LL LOOK IF YOUR COMPETITOR GETS THIS PICTURE AND EVERYBODY GOES BY YOUR DOOR

ACT QUICK

Standard Pictures

A MASTERPIECE OF BARA ART

The Love story which set all Paris talking

WILLIAM FOX

Presents

THEDA BARA

in the THEDA BARA superpicture

CAMILLE

Founded on the story by Alexandre Dumas
Scenario by   Adrian Johnson
Directed by   J. Gordon Edwards

Fox Film Corporation

WILLIAM FOX
PRESENTS

GLADYS BROCKWELL

THE FIRST
LADY OF
CINEMALAND

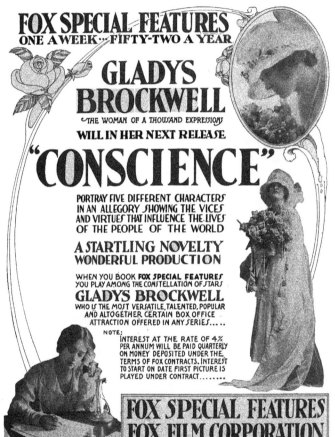

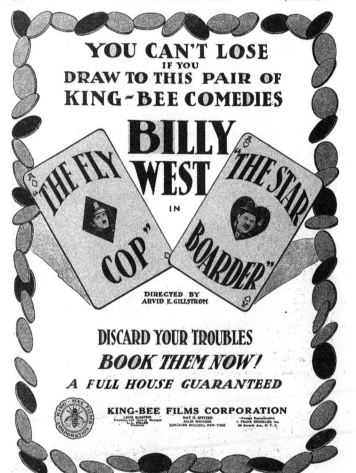

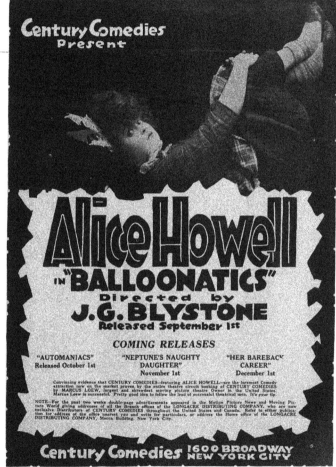

AMERICAN FILM COMPANY, INC., *Presents*

Juliette Day

The Star of "Up and Down" IN

"The RAINBOW GIRL"

A five-act drama of intense heart appeal. By *Jere F. Looney*. Directed by *Rollin S. Sturgeon*. Released the week of Sept. 17th.

First of the Juliette Day Series of American Pictures—"*Big Stars Only*." Presenting this popular stage favorite in the role of a cheer-up lady, who brings joy and romance into the life of an humble worker in "Tin Pan Alley". The kind of a picture that sends patrons home radiating happiness and good will. Book the entire series of Juliette Day American Pictures at your nearest Mutual Exchange.

Produced by
AMERICAN FILM COMPANY, INC.
Samuel S. Hutchinson, Pres.

Distributed by
MUTUAL FILM CORPORATION
John R. Freuler, Pres.

D PICTURE PLAYS COMPANY *Presents*

arita Fischer

IN

'The Girl Who Couldn't Grow Up

A five-act comedy-drama. Written and produced by Harry Pollard ~ Released the week of September 17th

Pretty Peggy Brockman, despite her dad's millions, was a regular tom-boy. Her sisters set their caps for Lord George Raleigh, but Peggy preferred Wiggins, his valet. ~ And then—Wiggins proved to be the real Lord George after all. A sure-fire attraction of the type for which Margarita Fischer is famous. Booking NOW at all Mutual Exchanges.

Produced by
POLLARD PICTURE PLAYS COMPANY

Distributed by
MUTUAL FILM CORPORATION
John R. Freuler, Pres.

BIG
STARS
ONLY

WAY

EL MORTON

tures. The play
season. In six
cted by an all-
Mutual Exchanges.

tures:

ANN. MURDOCK

BIG
STARS
ONLY

Book These Laugh Producers!

"A CONTENTED WOMAN"
Released in K-E-S-E September 17

"A MIDNIGHT BELL"
"A TRIP TO CHINATOWN"
"A DOG IN THE MANGER"
"A RUNAWAY COLT"
"A RAG BABY"
"A DAY AND A NIGHT"
"A BRASS MONKEY"
"A HOLE IN THE GROUND"

LEW FIELDS

in

"THE BARKER"

Charles K. Harris' Drama of Circus Life Is
Getting the Money for the Wise Exhibitor.

BOOK THEM ALL IN
K-E-S-E

Selig Polyscope Company
Chicago, Ill.

Entered at the General Post Office, New York City, as Second Class Matter

Founded by J. P. CHALMERS in 1907.

Published Weekly by the

CHALMERS PUBLISHING COMPANY

17 MADISON AVENUE, NEW YORK CITY.

(Telephone, 3510-3511 Madison Square)

J. P. Chalmers, Sr..............................President
J. F. Chalmers...........................Vice-President
E. J. Chalmers....................Secretary and Treasurer
John Wylie..........................General Manager

The office of the company is the address of the officers.

CHICAGO OFFICE—Suite 917-919 Schiller Building, 64 West Randolph
St., Chicago, Ill. Telephone, Central 5099.

PACIFIC COAST OFFICE—610-611 Wright and Callender Building, Los
Angeles, Cal. Telephone, Broadway 4640.

SUBSCRIPTION RATES.

United States, Cuba, Mexico, Hawaii, Porto
Rico and Philippine Islands.................$3.00 per year
Canada .... 3.50 per year
Foreign Countries (Postpaid)............... 4.00 per year

Changes of address should give both old and new addresses in full
and be clearly written. Two weeks' time should be allowed for change.

ADVERTISING RATES.

CLASSIFIED ADVERTISING—One dollar for twenty words or less;
over twenty words, five cents per word.

DISPLAY ADVERTISING RATES made known on application.

NOTE—Address all correspondence, remittances and subscriptions to
MOVING PICTURE WORLD, P. O. Box 226, Madison Square Station,
New York, and not to individuals.

"CINE-MUNDIAL," the monthly Spanish edition of the Moving Picture World, is published at 17 Madison Ave. by the Chalmers Publishing Company. It reaches the South American and Spanish-speaking
market. Yearly subscription, $1.50. Advertising rates on application.

Saturday, September 22, 1917

Facts and Comments

SPURRED on, no doubt, by the attempts of the music
composers to bleed the picture theater managers by
way of a graded yearly tax for permission to play
music already bought and paid for, we now have the
musicians' unions trying to dictate to the picture theater
managers how many men they may employ in their
houses. If we are not mistaken, a similar attempt was
made by this same dictatorial body some time since on
the legitimate theater owners and managers. Instituting
a policy of killing the goose that lays the golden egg
seems to be the long suit of some of the leaders of our
unions, with consequent loss and very often serious readjustment of living conditions to the rank and file of their
own members. Unless the theater owners and managers

present an unflinching front against such unwarranted
and illegal encroachment of their rights, nothing but choas
and ruin all round can be the result.

* * *

AGAIN referring to this new "stand and deliver"
policy of the music composers, we would refer
theater managers once more to the article on this
subject on page 1530 of our issue of September 8.
Managers can secure all the music they really need and
for which no royalty or "music tax" can be demanded.
The composer and publisher of music are entitled to their
share, but said share can only be equitably secured by
placing it on the first cost and not by any additional tax
for so-called performing rights. As a matter of fact,
the publishers and composers have only themselves to
blame for present unsatisfactory conditions and they
seem to be going at the readjustment on an altogether
unjust basis.

* * *

THE unanimity of condemnation of the recent vote
of the N. A. M. P. I. in refusing membership to
a large body of exhibitors indicates quite conclusively that this action was not based on justice and right
principles. That the action was dictated by a mistaken
policy of self-interest on the part of those who desired to
curry favor with the small body of exhibitors who mainly
represent their own narrow interest in this city becomes
more and more evident as the question receives further
consideration. Fortunately the vote does not adversely
affect the great body of exhibitors throughout the country, who are, after all, the real backbone of the exhibiting
side of the industry. Refusing exhibitors representation
in the N. A. M. P. I. just means that much of a loss to
the latter body, to our way of thinking.

* * *

LAYING out a business policy that is worthy of the
name and not primarily intended as a get-rich-
quick scheme is surely not as easy as one would
think, judging from the mistakes that are continually
made along this line. No matter whether it is the business policy of an exhibitor for his theater or that of an
exchange with his patrons or the bigger and further
reaching policy of a producing combination that affects
all branches of the industry. We have had examples
galore of the foolishness of over-reaching; we have
seen theaters driven to the wall through trying to gouge
the public, we have seen large business in the renting
and exchange end of things go down the hill for the
same reason. Treat your public fair and square, "give
them all you can for a dime and they will give you all
the dimes they can" was the good old motto of a successful exhibitor. We hear a lot today about "open booking"
and various other kinds of exchange "policies," but no
policy will be permanent that does not look ahead to the
extent of building up the business of its clients while building up its own. All attempts at securing exclusive control of this big industry or anything like it are bound to
fail and their promoters should be able to see that success
itself would mean eventual failure.

* * *

IN PHILADELPHIA the I. A. T. S. E., Local 307,
has passed a resolution to provide $100 to the de-
pendents of every member of the Local who dies in
honorable discharge of his duties in the United States
service during the war. This will be raised by levying
one dollar on every active home member of the Local.
One of the greatest benefits that the struggle in which
we have taken up our part is already bringing to us is
the awakening of brotherhood and solidarity and responsibility for our individual share. Those who go pluck
the flower of service, but its sweetness extends to the
senses of everyone whose heart is in the right place.

Miss Mollycoddle 🎞 🎞 🎞 🎞 🎞 🎞 🎞 🎞 By Louis Reeves Harrison

IF SCREEN subjects are to be vital, if we are not to deliberately avoid noticing great changes taking place in our midst, necessary as air to our existence, contributing heavily to our development as a race, we should not fail to recognize a remarkable evolution in womanhood at home and abroad. We need not give much serious attention to violent and erratic efforts at enfranchisement, but we cannot shut our eyes to certain steady and irresistible changes taking place in the mother half of humanity, which may be for our benefit or detriment, according to circumstances we help to create by the production and exhibition of moving pictures.

Standing as we do in a vestibule of progress, it is permitted to glance back at the fine mothers many of us have known with pride and affection, but only that we may more deeply realize a responsibility we share in common for mothers of the future. We may thus face the other way with intelligent comprehension of what present conditions are leading to, what sort of false mental images we are setting up before the people in our repetition of two stale types, that spectral relic of Slavic superstition, the "vampire," and that listless lollypop of exaggerated ineptitude, the curly-haired, treacle-smeared simp, Miss Mollycoddle, the ingenue.

Some of us who have been a long time very much alive, who have travelled other lands than this, have never seen a woman bearing the slightest resemblance to the vampire of stage and screen—she has long been discarded in fiction. To the common run of men she is the morbid imaging of some disappointed boob, the vengeful conception of some weakling Adam, who tried to blame it all on Eve. What a small-town ideal of womankind! The only place to exploit her is in farce-comedy.

What do our women represent? For one thing the average member of the mother sex lives a far cleaner life than the average male. She helps him to live right from the time he lisps at her knee to the last days of his grouchy old age, whereas he has been known to devote the energy of ingenuity at his command to bringing her down morally to his level, not even after he is married, but usually so. Once in a while a girl hits back at him as hard as he gives it to her. That is when he bawls it out all over the lot, so that everybody may hear, "she is a vampire." He renders some such service to his kind as the "Pass-a-fist" does.

Forget the vampire, and let us turn to the other type, one set up persistently as the ideal to which we all aspire, the intelligent and healthy wife, the mother of a race hardy, resolute and energetic, Miss Mollycoddle, who embraces the innocuous hero in the last act. She is representative of something to some people. There is Mrs. Bulge, for instance, rotund, weepy, overfed product of table, rocking-chair and bed. Mrs. Bulge leaves the dirty dishes in the sink and goes to the movies of an afternoon. She thinks Miss Mollycoddle is a "little dear," and she really does not mean to pun on the high cost of squab stars to the average producer.

There is also thirteen-year-old Chewing-gum Mabel, of lanky legs and ardent hopes. She sees herself reflected in the "little dear" of colorless character and thinsoup emotions. How grand to be rescued from the humiliation of having to ride in trolley cars by a young Wall Street millionaire in dress suit and shiny pumps and carried away in his twin-six to a paradise of bridge whist and late suppers! She fairly dotes on her favorite Miss Mollycoddle and says of her on the way to the soda fountain, "I think she is just simply too sweet for anything."

One brilliant little artist has shown unusual talent. She interprets all sorts of roles with skill, and she has a vast amount of personality, which enables her to put zip into the characters she impersonates. In imitation of this successful actress we have been flooded with ingenues of doll faces and curls irrespective of native ability or consistency of performance. Worse, the average ingenue is not representatively American except in rare cases, and she is not at all representative of the new womanhood.

There are a lot of changes taking place in our ideas of family life, deeply concerning the modern woman, and progress in standards of education and intelligence have so greatly elevated our ideas of what woman should be and can be that she has become an object of tremendous interest to all classes of people except those mummies who believe that the world is standing just where it was when they were really alive. It is among the masses that these new ideas are taking hold, the very people who are counted upon as steady patrons of the moving picture show. The modern young woman does not wait for some man to come along and rescue her from pitiful dependence. She does the rescuing herself.

All this is changing our conditions of marriage, sometimes to the disadvantage of the man who earns only a moderate salary, quite as often to his benefit, but this new individualism of the woman, bearing upon important questions of marriage and divorce, upon the future of her offspring, upon our world status as a great race, cannot be expressed through negative and colorless types any more than through unnatural ones. The fact should be faced that we are up against new social conditions, and our bright young girls should be portrayed as they are, not as they were in the days of the good little girl and the bad little girl. She of today is as composite as we are.

We are just beginning to realize that woman can fight. This is a dangerous subject, but a recent writer on it declares that she has been sticking a bayonet in her husband for many years; not only that, but turning it around inside of him, very much to his discomfort. Ask any married man if this is not true. She likes a fight better than he does, and she doesn't care much where it takes place or who knows it. We ought to occasionally portray her as she is, not always as we think she ought to be. She is here, just one of us, with her full share of the primitive instincts, impelling her for good or bad, moved by the same influences which affect us, quite as capable as we are of improvement.

It would at least add variety to our screen stories if we had a few examples of the modern intelligent woman offered now and then, at least so that she is recognizable as a product of existence as we know it, and not as it has been plotted out according to set types. She is all types in one. If she must be idealized, let it be in physical perfection, not an amazon, but the kind of a woman who responds to the masculine conception, which is certainly not that of the mollycoddled kind.

In that every twelfth marriage ends in divorce, with more pending, lies optimism for stories dealing with men and women after that eternal embrace in the last act of the photoplay. The real end is not there—it is the beginning of comedies, dramas and tragedies without number.

Do Something ▨ ▨ ▨ ▨ ▨ ▨ ▨ ▨ ▨ ▨ ▨ By Sam Spedon

To Everybody.

PROBABLY others have thought these same thoughts. Probably some have already put them in operation. Probably there are others to whom they will be a discovery. To some they may be a revival. We will let it go at that. Audiences change every four years. If they didn't, you wouldn't have been making and showing pictures for the past ten years and we wouldn't have been writing. If they didn't change, there would be no hope for motion pictures and publications in the future. There is nothing new under the sun.

To the Exhibitors.

Until the exhibitors, exchangemen and the pro-ducers—the three great factors of motion pictures—get down to an established business basis of organization they cannot do business safely and sanely. The exhibitor cannot look for relief until he can decidedly calculate the number of patrons within his reach, in his immediate territory; the capacity of his theater; what profit he can make after he has paid cost of film service; the running and upkeep of his theater. When he can do this and make it clear to the exchangemen that he can afford to pay but so much for his pictures, then, not till then, will he be relieved from the excessive prices asked by the salesmen sent out to make a record for themselves and the interests they represent. To accomplish this for the benefit of all, particularly its members, the national organization should have each and every exhibitor send in or secure in some other way the above-mentioned information and keep it on file with a record of the management's responsibility. In this way the organization could arrive at what would be an equitable price for productions or service, based on its knowledge of what the exhibitors could afford to pay in each territory and class of theater. It would also enable the organization to become acquainted with the character of the theaters represented by its membership.

To Exchangemen and Distributors.

With this same information the exchange would not be sending out salesmen on "gypping" excursions to establish records for themselves. Furthermore, it would make the salesmen more secure in their positions, by showing their business superiors that it is impossible to do business where it doesn't exist and get prohibitive prices where possibilities are limited. It would also enable the exchange manager to figure on the amount of business he might reasonably expect from the exhibitors and the different territories. In other words, he could work intelligently and would not be susceptible to the "fairy tales" told by the smart salesmen who promise much and produce little. He would do business on a safe and sane basis.

To the Producers.

With this knowledge in hand, the producer could estimate what he should expend in the making of a picture. He would know he could or could not employ high-priced stars with or without proportionate returns. If he could not afford the expense, he would naturally tell them he could not engage them and would have to employ less expensive ones. He would not indulge in "pipe dreams" and "brain storms" of golden harvests and Eldorados. Such knowledge would bring the stars to a realization of facts and do away to a great extent, if not entirely, with extravagant salaries demanded and paid by producers. If these facts were known, all producers would be led to estimate in this way and stars would determine that one producer could not safely afford to pay more than another. They would wisely decide, all things being equal, to stick and not change, as they have in the past, from one company to another. The stars might conclude that their value as actors, their drawing power and past records should be considered. So they would; but with the facts before them they would face an insurmountable barrier to excessive demands.

Our great benefit to be derived from an exact knowledge of business conditions would be the making of better pictures that would stand on their own merits, story and direction, and not entirely upon the greatness of the stars employed.

Another benefit would be that the exhibitors, be they few or many, who demanded or expected high-priced stars would have to pay the high price to enable the producer to pay the stars. Thus it would devolve upon the exhibitors to decide. This brings us to our first premise. Exhibitors are the base of operations and must furnish or present the facts to the other two branches of the industry if they hope to get what they want.

Don't Forget the Public.

It sometimes makes excessive and extravagant demands as well as the stars and other individuals. Certain classes of it want the best and first choice. The question to decide is: How many in the localities of your theaters will pay for it, or can afford to pay for the choice? If they can do it, then, Mr. Exhibitor, it is again up to you to get the price and pay the producers for it. If your public can't or won't pay you, then it will have to wait and take second or third choice, according to the returns of your box office. When you acquaint the distributor, the producer and the public with the facts and take them into your confidence, the motion picture business will be conducted on a safe and sane business basis.

May Be Right at That.

At a recent convention a well-known producer and exhibitor said: "I will be glad when the exhibitors organize and lay down some well-defined and formulated terms upon which the distributor can do business and eliminate existing differences between him and the exhibitor. If the exhibitors can say and mean what they say, they will insure us and themselves against failure."

They Don't Know.

The foregoing assertion prompts us to believe that the distributors and producers don't know just where they are at and want the exhibitors to tell them. We feel sure that the man who made the assertion would not listen or take heed to an individual exhibitor if he were to tell him what could be done. We presume he meant exactly what he said: he would be glad if an organized body of exhibitors, big and strong enough, would tell the distributors and producers where they are at.

Activities of War Committees
OF THE MOTION PICTURE INDUSTRY

REPORTS which are being received from the State chairmen of the National Committee, appointed by President William A. Brady of the National Association of the Motion Picture Industry, indicate widespread enthusiasm in the plan to mobilise the exhibitors throughout the country in aid of the government's war policies.

Striking evidence of this fact is contained in an announcement from President Brady to the effect that every one of his appointees in the forty-eight States have now accepted and are busily engaged in making up lists of the motion picture theaters so as to inform their managers of the plans of the War Co-operation Committee, and that they may be prepared to show on their screens slides or trailers received from the motion picture committees of the National Association acting in conjunction with the members of the Cabinet and the various Federal departments, the Council of National Defense, the Red Cross War Council and the Committee on Public [I]nformation.

Rapid progress is being made in the organisation of the exhibitors in many States following the successful campaign which was inaugurated last June under the auspices of the National Association and the Exhibitors' League in connection with the Liberty Loan, and the splendid service rendered by the industry in this instance will be greatly augmented in the future, as new theaters are being listed which have only been opened during the past few months.

In this connection a novel plan as set forth in the following letter has been successfully worked out by Herman J. Brown, state chairman of Idaho, which will interest the chairmen in other states:

I have made arrangements to reach villages so small that our association has no record of the theaters and managers. I did this through letters to the postmasters and was surprised that fly specks on the map all seem to be on deck with some place to show pictures and someone to show them. The postmasters to call personally on the reluctant exhibitors.

My experience has convinced me more than ever that the screen has the press skinned a mile, as "burgs" of 150 population have a show at least once a week but no paper within a hundred miles.

C. W. Meighan, state chairman of Oregon, has made notable progress in the organisation of the exhibitors, according to report contained in the following letter to President Brady:

In pursuance with the instructions contained in your favor of the 4th, I am now having prepared with all possible care a list of representative motion picture exhibitors from every city, village, town and hamlet in our state; men whom I know will be pleased to serve with unselfish devotion the cause which you have so generously undertaken to promote.

It may interest you to know that even before you formed the National Committee our exhibitors in Oregon were exerting every possible effort to co-operate with the government. That their work was effective is attested by the fact that the screen in Oregon is given great credit for the splendid over-subscription this state showed in Liberty bonds, Red Cross subscriptions, and for the fact that it stands first among all the states in the matter of voluntary enlistments. Our Portland district is the only one in the United States, I am told, which contributed so many voluntary enlistments that no men at all were taken by the government on the first draft. Concerted wo[r]k on the part of motion picture theaters is credited with contributing largely to this splendid showing.

I tell you this so you may know that to every extent within the power of our exhibitors in this state you may count upon our fullest, heartiest and most cheerful co-operation.

As state chairman I shall look forward to your various communications and suggestions from time to time and shall be more than pleased to have an opportunity to put them promptly into execution.

C. W. MEIGHAN,
Chairman of the Oregon State Committee for War Co-operation, President Motion Picture League of Oregon, Manager People's Amusement Company.

The western states are not the only ones in which active work is under way. Many of the middle west and eastern states are being organised by the state chairmen, and in some localities this campaign apparently affords the first real opportunity for perfecting an exhibitors' organisation.

H. M. Morrison, of the Majestic and Princess theaters, Hartford, Conn., and state chairman of the National Committee, is now engaged with plans for effecting the first organization of exhibitors in that state. Mr. Morrison is vice president of the Hartford local, which comprises all the theaters in the state capital, and similar organisations are proposed for New Haven, Bridgeport, Waterbury, Stamford, New London, Meriden and Danbury. Chairman Morrison will issue a call for a general meeting of all the exhibitors of the state at an early date, when the purposes of the War Co-operation Committee of the National Association will be placed before them by President Brady, who is to be invited to attend the conference as guest of honor.

Cabanne to Stage Red Cross Pageant
Prominent Ar[ti]sts of Opera, Stage and Screen to Participate in Great Open-Air Patriotic Spectacle.

WHAT is expected to be one of the most ambitious open-air spectacles produced in this country is the national pageant of the American Red Cross, which will be staged in the beautiful open-air theater on Rosemary Farm, at Lloyd's Neck, Huntington, L. I., on the afternoon of October 5.

The Rosemary Pageant, as the production is now termed for working purposes, was written for the Red Cross by Joseph Lindon Smith, author, traveler and lecturer of Boston, and Thomas Wood Stevens, head of the department of dramatic arts of the Carnegie Institute of Technology at Pittsburgh and president of the American Pageant Association. It will be directed and produced by Mr. Stevens, who was the author and director of the pageant of St. Louis, the pageant of Newark, and the pageant of the Old Northwest. He will be assisted by a number of the foremost pageant directors in the country, including Mrs. John Alden Carpenter, Paul Chalfin, Ben Ali Haggin, Prince Pierre Troubetzkoy and Mrs. Harry Payne Whitney. Interested in the theatrical side of the production also are E. H. Sothern and William Faversham, while Daniel Frohman is the casting director.

The Rosemary Red Cross Pageant is to be divided into two parts—the first devoted to a series of symbolic scenes representing achievements of the several Allied Nations—the second a dramatic statement of the Allied cause in the present war. The first half is magnificently spectacular, the second half is essentially dramatic in character.

Episodes of ancient, medieval and modern times of the various lands will be depicted and the characters appearing in the numerous scenes will be portrayed by hundreds of the best-known stars of the opera, stage and screen. Among the prominent professionals who have already been enrolled in the cast of the pageant are Mme. Frances Alda, George Arliss, Miss Blanche Bates, Miss Ethel Barrymore, Barney Bernard, Holbrook Blinn, John Barrymore, Miss Constance Collier, Miss Hazel Dawn, Robert Edeson, William Faversham, Miss Irene Fenwick, Miss Mary Garden, Ernest Glendenning, Miss Kitty Gordon, Hale Hamilton, Miss Gladys Hanson, Miss Marie Horn, Shelly Hull, Miss Rita Jolivet, Walter Jones, Howard Kyle, Ernest Lawford, Mrs. Ernest Lawford, Miss Eva Le Gallienne, Miss Edith

Wynne Mathison, Major -Wallace McCutcheon, Mr. Mortimer, Miss Margaret Mower, Miss Julie Opp, Gabriel Perrier, William Rock, Miss Zelda Sears, Vincent Serrano, Hassard Short, E. H. Sothern, John Philip Sousa, Miss Frances Starr, Paul Swan, Miss Mabel Taliaferro, Miss Alma Tell, Miss Olive Tell, Ernest Truex, Miss Helen Ware, Jack Wilson, Miss Frances White and Miss Marjorie Wood.

For the reason that the Red Cross has planned to make the Rosemary Pageant a national affair and that it is practically impossible to produce and present such a spectacle to the people of every city, it has been arranged to perpetuate the entire pageant on the screen with the original all-star cast as staged and produced in the magnificent Rosemary Farm open-air theater.

The filming of this spectacle will be under the direction of Wm. Christy Cabanne, who has produced some of the masterpieces of the screen, and a seven-reel feature film will be the result of his work. This picture will be shown in every city and town, and in this way the Rosemary Pageant will be brought direct to all the people and will also be a source of revenue to the Red Cross, as the distribution and exhibition of the film will be made for the sole benefit of the American Red Cross.

Working headquarters for the scores of prominent men and women who are giving their time and energy to the Rosemary Pageant have been established at 71 West Twenty-third Street, in offices that have been donated to the Red Cross.

Industry Aids Food Conservation

Chairman Friend of Auxiliary Motion Picture Committee Outlines Importance of Work.

THE motion picture industry in its every phase is being enlisted by the United States food administration to get the whole American people lined up on the food pledge, "which gigantic job must be done," according to the Government's plan.

The motion picture division of the food administration, which is in charge of Arthur S. Friend, treasurer of the Famous Players-Lasky Corporation, is having produced a series of short subjects which will forcibly visualize the fact that "Food will win the war."

Every motion picture exhibitor in the country is being personally urged to lend his hearty co-operation in this movement and to show the pictures in his theater and also to become a member of the food administration. Exhibitors are being impressed with the fact that by lending their co-operation to the Government in placing these pictures on the screen they will not only be doing their country a great service but they will win for their theaters a higher respect in their immediate communities, and for themselves a sense of gratification because they are materially contributing to the greatest cause or their lives.

"Getting the whole American people lined up on the food pledge is a job that must be done," said Mr. Friend. "The wheatless meal, the meatless meal, and the clean plate must be with us until peace returns.

"This is a sales job. It calls for leadership. Every reader of a newspaper, trade journal and every motion picture lover may consider himself a leader and begin his sales work by selling the food pledge to himself.

"There is a tremendous necessity for food conservation. Not that people shall eat less, but that they waste nothing. Nothing in the world will send this message 'across' to the hearts of the millions of motion picture lovers in this country so forcibly as the visualizing on the screen in a series of pictures the singular fact that the world war can be won by saving food.

"We know how we would save food in Germany—under a dictator. But here the food pledge is entirely voluntary. We are put upon honor. Nobody prescribes what we shall eat, or how much, but ourselves. Nobody keeps a record of our performance but ourselves. In just the measure that we are honorable in this matter are we Americans. That is the sales sense of the food-saving proposition. Now sell it to yourself, and then sell it to those who look to you for leadership.

"Every exhibitor who will co-operate with this movement at this time will be doing the Government a tremendous service, and it is the plan of the food administration to serve him in every respect, so that he, too, will benefit through the assistance he renders in this movement."

The Gold King Screen Company, of Altus, Okla., has announced that the price of their screen will advance to 75 cents on and after November 1, 1917. They state the advance prices in materials have forced them to raise the price.

ELLIOTT SUBJECT FOR FIGHTING IRISHMEN.

At the suggestion of Maxine Elliott, her first Goldwyn production, "The Eternal Magdalene," was given its first outside showing for the entertainment of the soldiers of the 165th Regiment the evening of September 2 at Camp Mills, near Mineola, L. I. It was received with the cheers of the 3,700 men and officers who saw it from the natural amphitheatre where it was shown.

This was the first opportunity offered to Goldwyn Pictures to carry out its offer to provide motion picture entertainment for the soldiers in their encampments both here and in Europe.

Shortly after registration had closed for the draft army, Samuel Goldfish, president of Goldwyn Pictures, in a letter to the secretary of war, Newton D. Baker, offered to provide prints of Goldwyn productions for the soldiers. This offer was accepted with thanks by Mr. Baker and the matter was placed in the hands of Raymond B. Fosdick, who is at the head of the commission which has jurisdiction over the recreational activities of the troops.

CHANGES IN MUTUAL BRANCH MANAGERS.

The Mutual Film Corporation has announced several changes in the managerships of branch offices.

J. L. Merrick, manager at Seattle, has been appointed manager at Los Angeles, to succeed T. C. Malcolm, whose resignation was effective August 29.

C. P. Merwin, former booker at the Seattle branch, has been appointed manager of the office.

A. C. Field, manager of the Escanaba branch, has been transferred to the sales force of the Milwaukee office and C. K. Olson, formerly a salesman at the Minneapolis branch, has been appointed branch manager at Escanaba.

B. Whitman, formerly salesman at Winnipeg, has been named branch manager at Winnipeg, succeeding J. H. Boothe, whose resignation became effective September 2.

PEIL RETURNS TO SELIG.

Edward J. Peil, a former Selig player and one of the screen's very best exponents of genteel though none the less deep-dyed villainy, has rejoined the Selig Company's acting forces after a long absence, and will be seen in the important heavy role in "The Still Alarm," now in course of production at the Los Angeles studio, under Colin Campbell's direction. Mr. Peil, among other things, will pay for his screen misdeeds in this feature by being defeated in a thrilling fistic encounter with the hero, played by Thomas Santschi.

EMILE CHAUTARD TO DIRECT MME. CAVALIERI.

An announcement of more than ordinary interest is that Mme. Lina Cavalieri, the beautiful operatic star, will be directed in her first Paramount picture, "The Eternal Temptress," by the eminent French expert, Emile Chautard. This has just been decided upon and work will begin the first part of September upon the production, which is an original play, written expressly for Mme. Cavalieri by Mme. Fred de Grisac, whose work is almost too well known to need mention.

TWO MORE WELL-KNOWN PLAYERS FOR FOX.

Eugenie Forde and Marjorie Daw, famous on the shadow stage, have begun work under the William Fox standard in Hollywood, Cal., in a new picture starring Gladys Brockwell.

Miss Forde was well known for her performances in the legitimate before she came to the films. She appeared for more than fifteen years with such footlight favorites as George Munroe, William Faversham and Chauncey Olcott.

E. O. BROOKS RETURNS TO NEW YORK.

Edgar O. Brooks, for the past two years connected with the Mutual Film Corporation in Chicago, has resigned that position and returned to New York. Brooks paid the Moving Picture World a call upon his arrival and let it be known that he was going to take a few weeks to look around before making another connection. He is looking as though the climate of the Windy City agreed with him.

CIRCLE THEATER CELEBRATES FIRST YEAR.

The Circle Theater of Indianapolis, Ind., celebrated its first anniversary during the week of September 3, augmenting the occasion by showing the first Goldwyn subject, "Polly of the Circus." Special stage settings were devised by Manager McCormick and an unusual music program was arranged by Max Weil, orchestra leader.

The Motion Picture Exhibitor

Michigan Exhibitors Meeting

Greatest Convention Picture Men of That State Have Ever Held—Affiliated With A. E. A.

THE meeting called for Tuesday, Sept. 4th, at the Hotel Statler, Detroit, Mich., was a huge success—not only because it brought out a large attendance but due to the fact that it resulted in the abandonment of the State branch of the Motion Picture Exhibitors' League and the formation of a new and greater state association which is to be affiliated with the new American Exhibitors' Association. Michigan is 100 per cent. against the Motion Picture Exhibitors' League because it no longer has confidence in that organization due to its "gag" methods and tyrannical policy as displayed at the recent national convention in Chicago.

The Detroit meeting just referred to was attended by about 75 exhibitors, city and state, and they were owners of large and small theaters. They came to discuss the proposition of a new and greater state association. They listened attentively to the stories by delegates to the national convention of the disgraceful, embarrassing and shameful way they were treated on the convention floor, and when they were all through with their stories, there wasn't a man in the hall that was not more earnest than ever in breaking away absolutely from the national organization.

A vote was taken as to what should be done and everyone present unanimously voted "yes" to a motion made, calling for the formation at once of a temporary state association to be affiliated with the American Exhibitors' Association and the appointment of a committee to work out the proper by-laws and constitution so that steps could be taken in the near future for making it a permanent association. Until such time, S. A. Moran, of Ann Arbor, will act as president, and Claud Cady, of Lansing, as secretary.

A discussion came up regarding the coming convention at Detroit of the American Exhibitors' Association, which is scheduled to meet in Detroit some time during the summer of 1918. While the association will hold its meetings in Detroit, it will be up to Detroit and Michigan exhibitors to decide as to whether they want to hold an exposition, as well as to work out the matters relative to entertainment. A committee and state exhibitors will be appointed to take up these questions during the next ninety days, and to then report to Manager Pettijohn of the national organization. As far as he is concerned, we understand it is perfectly agreeable, although the final yes or no is right up to Michigan and no one else. If the Michigan exhibitors feel that they can successfully conduct such a stupendous affair without losing money, no doubt they will entertain such a proposition, but it will be thoroughly looked into and investigated before any final action is taken.

The principal speakers of the Detroit meeting were Frank Rembusch, of Shelbyville, Ind., and an officer of the American Exhibitors' Association, and Fighting Sam Bullock, of Cleveland, Ohio. They sure did talk straight from the shoulder and what they said carried considerable weight and made a favorable impression—so much so that when they concluded their talks, there wasn't an exhibitor present that did not agree with them that the American Exhibitors' Association was organized along the right lines. The point made by both gentlemen was that the new national organization had but one thing in mind—and that was "business." Some of the things touched upon by Mr. Rembusch were membership, clean pictures, censorship, Sunday opening, our president, need of economy, cost of programs, over buying, length of program, complaint department, advance deposit system, all exhibitors are welcome, our general manager, this is not a one-man organization and maintenance. Sam Bullock of Cleveland in his talk practically reiterated the statements made by Mr. Rembusch. He was given a rousing ovation upon the conclusion of his remarks, as was Mr. Rembusch. Both remained in the city until the next day and were shown around the town via motor car.

In the evening there was a big theater party for the ladies at the Washington theater to see "On Trial" given complimentary by J. O. Brooks and John H. Kunsky. At 11 p. m. there was a big stag smoker for the men at an east side restaurant, which was attended by nearly 250 exhibitors and exchangemen. It was positively the largest joint gathering of tradesmen held in the State of Michigan. The smoker was a huge success, thanks to the untiring efforts of King Perry, secretary of the Detroit association, who had full charge of all entertainment features.

F. I. L. M. Club Visits League

Delegation Attends Session of Manhattan Local and Urges Co-operation Between Exhibitors and Exchangemen.

THE meeting of the Manhattan Local No. 1, Motion Picture Exhibitors' League of America, was held on September 5 at headquarters, 218 West Forty-second Street, New York, President Martineau presiding. The meeting was opened with an address by one of the four-minute men—Mr. Williams, secretary—who took for his subject the co-operation of the exhibitors in and around Greater New York. Mr. Williams said he hoped the picture men would continue their help in the future as they had in the past.

The next matter taken up was the matter of expressage of film. A committee, composed of exchange men representing the F. I. L. M. Club, was present. Mr. Chadwick acted as spokesman. The committee hoped for a better feeling between exhibitors and exchangemen, a solution of the problems of the film delivery system, and for the elimination of film thievery. A committee was appointed, with power to act, for further discussion with a view to a final settlement of the delivery system. This committee, consisting of Messrs. Haring, Brecher and Wolf, met Monday at 2 o'clock at local headquarters.

National President Ochs told of the work accomplished by the National Executive Committee. This was followed by a discussion of the music tax situation.

In a discussion as to the advisability of taking up new headquarters, it was suggested that the local take an entire building with four floors, located between Forty-sixth and Forty-ninth Streets, near Broadway. It was further suggested that the building be shared with the F. I. L. M. Club, thereby creating a better feeling among all parties interested. The division of the building was suggested as follows: One floor for a restaurant, one for a lounging or billiard room, and the other two floors for separate meeting rooms, such as one for exhibitors and one for exchangemen, thereby reducing expenses. A committee was appointed, with power to co-operate with a committee from the F. I. L. M. Club.

The meeting was well attended and harmonious. The resignation of Samuel H. Trigger as a member of Local No. 1 was tendered by William Hilkemeier and Morris Needles and was accepted.

Pettijohn Enthused

Rapid Growth of Sentiment Among Exhibitors in Favor of A. E. A. Interests Him.

"THE action of the exhibitors' convention at Ocean View, Va., illustrates that the exhibitors of the country have awakened to the fact that the American Exhibitors' Association is made up of men who have the interests of the owners of motion picture theaters at heart," said Charles C. Pettijohn, general manager of the A. E. A.

"Before the State organizations represented at the Virginia convention became affiliated with our organization the delegates carefully studied our plans and principles and then unanimously applied for membership in the American Exhibitors' Association.

"The fact that as State bodies in Virginia, Indiana, North Carolina, Oklahoma, Michigan, South Carolina, District of Columbia, Arkansas, Idaho, Nevada, Oregon, Washington, Georgia, Kentucky and other States, they have joined the A. E. A. speaks for itself.

"Already our organisations in Illinois, New York, New Jersey, the New England States and Pennsylvania are very strong and growing rapidly.

"What impresses me most is that we have succeeded in interesting men who have heretofore no interest in exhibitors' organisations. We realise that meeting with the approval of the exhibitors as we have, it is up to the officers of the association to merit this confidence which is piling upon us in leaps and bounds. We all recognise our responsibilities and will work unceasingly to the end that we may be able to maintain the standard of efficiency as set out in our platform, pledging the making of this organisation a powerful weapon in the hands of exhibitors for exhibitors only.

"I can't help but be pleased and elated over our success. It is really wonderful the way the exhibitors are responding. Their responses fully convince me that they have wanted this kind of an organisation badly, else we would not have received this practically unanimous vote of approval."

During the past week, Mr. Pettijohn has been deluged with personal letters from exhibitors, applications for membership, checks for dues and inquiries calling for further information.

Maritime Provinces League Election

Officers for the Coming Year Chosen at the St. John Convention—Affiliation With Any American Organization Rejected.

AT A LARGE gathering of exhibitors of the Maritime Provinces of Canada at St. John, N. B., held September 8, 9 and 10, the following officers were elected to serve during the coming year:

President, Narcisse V. Gastonguay of Halifax; vice-president, Fred G. Spencer of St. John; secretary, J. M. Franklin of Halifax; treasurer, J. G. B. Metzler of Halifax; vice-president for Nova Scotia, N. W. Mason of New Glasgow, N. S.; vice-president for New Brunswick, W. H. Golding of St. John, N. B.; vice-president for Prince Edward Island, C. C. Gaudet, Charlottetown, P. E. I.

A motion to consider the question of affiliation with an American national organisation was laid upon the table until the next convention.

RAYNOR TO MANAGE NEW YORK MUTUAL.

W. E. Raynor, manager for George Kleine and the K-E-S-E. New York Exchange, has resigned his position to take up the management of the New York Branch of the Mutual Film Corporation.

Mr. Raynor first came to New York four and a half years ago to introduce "Quo Vadis" for Mr. Kleine, which was the first big moving picture road show. Since then Mr. Raynor has handled Mr. Kleine's various enterprises in the East and was finally made branch manager for the K-E-S-E. N. Y. Exchange.

The severing of business connections have been pleasant on both the part of Mr. Kleine and Mr. Raynor. Mr. Raynor has the good wishes of all the leading exhibitors in this territory with whom he is personally acquainted.

PETTIJOHN ATTENDS MARITIME CONVENTION.

Charles C. Pettijohn, general manager of the American Exhibitors' Association, left New York Friday to attend the convention of the Motion Picture Exhibitors' League of Canada, to be held at St. John, N. B., Sept. 8th, 9th and 10th. Mr. Pettijohn received an invitation from W. C. Golding, president of the Canadian exhibitors' organisation.

OKLAHOMA GOES OVER TO A. E. A.

L. W. Brophy, secretary of the Oklahoma Motion Picture Exhibitors' League, wired the Moving Picture World, under date of September 5, as follows:

"At the Motion Picture Exhibitors' League meeting at the Lee Huckins Hotel, Oklahoma City, on August 28, our members assembled unanimously voted to quit the league and to make application for a charter in the American Exhibitor's Association—a business organisation. There were fifty members present."

At this meeting A. B. Momand, of Shawnee, was chosen president, and H. W. McCall, of Oklahoma City, vice president. L. W. Brophy continues as secretary. He operates the Yale theater at Muskogee.

ONTARIO EXHIBITORS TO JOIN A. E. A.

The motion picture exhibitors of Ontario are organising under the leadership of M. Mannist, of the Royal theater, Fort Williams. Ont., and when their organisation is completed they will apply in a body for a charter in the American Exhibitors' Association. Mr. Mannist is a wide-awake exhibitor who recognizes that the only way the exhibitor can accomplish any reforms is through concerted action with a body that is composed entirely of exhibitors who have no connections with the manufacturer.

He is also avowedly opposed to the advance deposit system, which method of doing business by the producer is being fought by the American Exhibitors' Association.

JAKE WELLS ATTENDS CIRCUIT MEETING.

Jake Wells, president of the American Exhibitors' Association, has been attending the meeting of the First National Exhibitors' Circuit at the Hotel Astor. Charles G. Pettijohn, general manager of the A. E. A., was his guest at the dinner of the Exhibitors' Circuit at the Hotel Astor, Wednesday, September 5.

VARNER WATCHING LEGISLATION.

H. B. Varner, chairman of the legislative committee of the American Exhibitors' Association, has been in New York for several days attending to matters connected with the A. E. A. He left for Washington, where he will look after legation which affects the exhibitor. Mr. Varner was most enthusiastic over the hearty response of exhibitors in all parts of the country in becoming members of the American Exhibitors' Association.

"At last," he said, "we have a sound business organisation of exhibitors only—men who are in no way affiliated with the manufacturers and who can work together for the betterment of the exhibitor without fear of any interference from the producer. I freely predict that the American Exhibitors' Association will prove to be the organisation that all real exhibitors have been looking for since they entered the motion picture business."

IRVING THEATRE, CHICAGO, OPENS.

The Irving theater, a new 1,800 seat house, opened at Crawford avenue and Irving Park boulevard, Chicago, Saturday evening, September 1, with Mary Miles Minter in "Charity Castle," the first of Miss Minter's new series of Mutual-American productions.

The Irving theater is located in the heart of Irving Park, one of the most populous of Chicago's neighborhoods. It is one of the largest and most modern theaters outside of the Chicago loop and one of the most completely equipped picture theaters in the United States. Careful attention has been paid to every detail of construction and equipment. The decorations are dainty tints of blue and pink on a cream background.

The theater cost $200,000 and will be devoted exclusively to motion pictures. The management has announced a policy of showing only the highest type of productions and selected "Charity Castle" for the inauguration of its policy.

ANOTHER FRANKLYN FARNUM BLUEBIRD.

Director Joseph De Grasse, having completed his first production, with Franklyn Farnum as the star, is now turning to a second feature, entitled "The Winged Mystery," in which Mr. Farnum will play a dual role. Claire Du Brey will continue as leading lady, and the support will also include Sam De Grasse and Charles Hill Mailes. Incidentally Sam De Grasse is a brother of the producer, and although they have each been long employed in pictures, this is the first engagement Joe and Sam have ever played together.

Brady Misinformed

Arthur F. Beck Takes Exception to William A. Brady's Views on Successful Pictures.

WILLIAM A. BRADY'S recent statement to the effect that the biggest and most enduring hits are adaptations of stage play successes is held to be invalid by Arthur F. Beck, general manager of Art Dramas.

"Mr. Brady seems to be misinformed," said Mr. Beck. "While it is true that some of the most successful pictures are adaptations of successful stage plays, still there have been just as many, if not more, really big and enduring successes which were especially written for the screen.

"As proof of this, I need mention only one picture which was not adapted from a stage success. I mean 'Cabiria.' Surely, 'Cabiria' is entitled to be classed as one of the biggest and most enduring hits.'

"Then there are 'Civilization,' 'Intolerance,' 'The Battle Cry of Peace,' 'Womanhood,' 'Joan, the Woman,' 'Traffic in Souls,' 'Neptune's Daughter,' 'A Daughter of the Gods,' 'The Soul of a Woman,' and 'The Spoilers.'

"Then there is that notable instance of a success that had its origin purely as a scenario—'The Cheat,' by Hector Turnbull. Here is a photoplay that reverses the usual order of things. It was such a phenomenal success that it was dramatized, which seems to be conclusive proof that the screen is capable of doing big things without looking for aid from the legitimate stage.

"And again: What about Mary Pickford's successes, such as 'Rags,' 'Hearts Adrift,' 'Poor Little Peppina,' and many others? And, finally, take the Fairbanks pictures—tremendous successes and written for the screen.

"I might go on to enumerate hundreds of substantial screen successes which were not adapted from the stage. But what's the use? It seems to have been pretty well established by now that what the public is looking for is good entertainment. If it can be found in play adaptations, well and good. On the other hand, the public has found excellent entertainment in original photoplays and book adaptations. And, Mr. Brady's statement to the contrary notwithstanding, the demands of the screen are leaning more and more to original works of photoplaywrights. In fact, the scripts of our big special pictures today are originals. A majority of the big special pictures today are originals.

"It seems to me that Mr. Brady's statement could do a lot of harm. Never in the history of motion pictures have we been more in need of the stimulus that goes with original works. As has been said many times before, no art can ever be truly great unless it evidences creative ability."

MARGUERITE SNOW MAKES SOUTHERN TOUR.

MARGUERITE SNOW, motion picture star extraordinary, and known the length and breadth of the world for her wonderful film portrayals, not only attended the convention of the Virginia State Exhibitors' Association at Ocean View, Va., but she made such a decided impression on the delegates that she was immediately signed for a personal appearance tour of the principal cities of the South, being the only motion picture star present offered such a contract.

Although there were no less than twelve of the most prominent stars of filmdom present, when the members of the association held a session to determine which of the stars would be asked to make a personal tour of their various theaters, Miss Snow received 22 of the 24 votes cast, and being such an unanimous choice, was engaged within the hour.

As a result Miss Snow left New York for Martinsburg, W. Va., Sept. 7, opening at the Central Opera House the following day with an afternoon and evening appearance. The tour is to extend for four weeks, and is being booked by J. Henkel Henry, manager of the Empire theater of Winchester, Va., who also holds an option for four additional weeks of Miss Snow's time, providing it does not interfere with her picture engagements.

ED ROSENBAUM, JR., KING BEE PRESS AGENT.

Nat H. Spitzer, general manager of the King-Bee Film Corp., presenting Billy West in two reel comedies, announces the engagement of Ed. Rosenbaum, Jr., as head of their publicity department. Mr. Rosenbaum has resigned from the executive staff of Elliott, Comstock and Gest to take charge of this department.

For four seasons he handed the publicity of the Ziegfeld Follies, then "The Winsome Widow," "Good Brian, "Madame Sherry," Anna Held, "Very Good Eddie" and many others.

Not Under the Law

Judge Altschuler Says Funkhouser Had no Authority to Hold Up "The Spy."

THE Fox Film Corporation obtained a preliminary injunction restraining Major Funkhouser, the Chicago censor, from refusing to issue a permit for the showing Chicago of "The Spy." In the decision handed down by Judge Samuel A. Altschuler, in the United States District Court, Chicago, the court says in part:

"From a perusal of his (Funkhouser's) affidavit, I find and conclude there is nothing that he there which, under the ordinance, would be considered as immoral or obscene or unlawful or otherwise objectionable, but that the objection consists wholly in the horrifying nature of the tortures which are portrayed as inflicted upon the hero of the play, and his ultimate execution, and shooting by a firing squad. Now, I do not believe that from his own portrayal of the play, on his own depicting in his affidavit of the facts upon which he bases his conclusion, his action is within the authority of the ordinance."

The ordinance referred to in the decision is that city ordinance which prohibits the exhibition of immoral, obscene or unlawful pictures. According to Judge Altschuler, "The Spy" does not come under that category. In this connection the decision reads:

". . . Now, this finding, therefore, that it is not immoral or obscene or otherwise objectionable under ordinance as to adults it seems to me of itself would place the picture in the category of those which do not come within the prohibition of 1627.'"

The decision concludes: ". . . I am satisfied that from the showing here that the statement made in the affidavit is apparently a truthful and sincere statement of Mr. Funkhouser on which he has assumed to act and to refuse the permit, and that accordingly the chief of police has refused the permit upon grounds wholly outside of those enumerated in the ordinance, which alone gives them the power and the right to refuse the permit, and under these circumstances I believe that the preliminary injunction prayed for should be granted."

HOAGLAND BACK WITH PATHE.

An announcement of more than passing interest to the trade is that from Pathe to the effect that J. A. Berst, Vice-President and General Manager of Pathe Exchange, has engaged H. C. Hoagland, recently general manager of the Selig Co. to act as film editor with supervision over the titling, cutting and film editing departments. Mr. Hoagland was for five or six years with the old Pathe Freres in Jersey City, holding in succession the positions of publicity and advertising manager, editor of the Pathe Weekly, manager of the film department and later after the resignation of Mr. Berst to accept the presidency of the General Film Co., acting general manager of Pathe Freres. Mr. Hoagland thus brings to his new position an unusually broad experience gained in every branch of the film business and one that makes him an unusually valuable man. His engagement illustrated Mr. Berst's policy to make the Pathe film department second to none in the business.

Mr. Hoagland comes of a family distinguished in private and public endeavor since the Colonial period. His father is the Rev. Warren L. Hoagland, one of the most prominent ministers of the Methodist Episcopal Church. His grandfather on his mother's side was a cousin of ex-President Grover Cleveland; his great-uncle on his mother's side was Orestes Cleveland, several times mayor of Jersey City, and several times U. S. Congressman from New Jersey. Before Mr. Hoagland went with Pathe Freres he was advertising manager of a large Newark, N. J., department store and later was advertising manager for a well known and largely advertising specialty house.

BLUEBIRD HAS ANOTHER MARY MAC DONALD.

Mary Mac Donald, who has made considerable progress upon the speaking stage before she entered pictures, has been engaged by Bluebird for a position of prominence in one of their stock companies. "Mary Mac Donald" is a name that has figured in Bluebird's announcements, since Lois Weber took a novice of that name, changed it to Mary Mac Laren and established her as an "over night" star in "Shoes." The name of "Mary Mac Laren" was created and copyrighted for the purpose of moving pictures, and it is barely possible that when Mary Mac Donald reaches the screen, she will be heralded, after the fashion of her predecessor, as "Mary Mac Laren."

Universal Increases Forces

More Actors, Actresses and Directors Engaged During Past Month Than at Any Similar Period During the Year.

MORE additions have been made to the acting and directing forces at Universal City during the past month than at any similar period throughout the present year. Among the leading men who will be seen in important productions shortly are: Charles West, Frank Borzage, Casson Ferguson, Hart Hoxie, Kenneth Harlan, David Morris and Hal Cooley. The first five of these actors have already won wide recognition for effective dramatic work, while Morris and Cooley are equally well known as comedians.

Charles West, who will shortly be seen in support of Zoe Rae in "The Little Pirate," gained his first experience as a member of D. W. Griffith's famous Biograph stock company, appearing later in Fine Arts' productions when Griffith was in control of that organization.

Frank Borzage, who is also a newcomer to the Big U. plant, is now appearing opposite Brownie Vernon in Allen Holubar's production of "The Twisted Soul." Every picture fan of three years' standing will vividly recall Borsage as the young American sailor hero of Thomas H. Ince's "Wrath of the Gods," the remarkable Japanese play with Tsuru Aoki and Sessue Hayakawa. Borsage also appeared in many western features as a member of the American company, and gained some prestige as a director before coming under the Universal banner.

Casson Ferguson, now nearing the completion of his first Universal lead opposite Donna Drew in "The Ghost Girl," directed by Jack Wells, has played with the American and other well-known film companies, besides having won his spurs on the legitimate stage.

Hart Hoxie appeared in several of the Lois Weber productions made a year or more ago at Universal City. Hoxie will make his present debut to Universal patrons in Edward J. Le Saint's current production.

David Morris, who has been advanced to the position of leading comedian of Craig Hutchinson's Victor Comedy company, has had a long career on both stage and screen. He was recently seen in support of Max Asher.

Hal Cooley returns to the Universal fold to take an important part in "The Cricket," the Zoe Rae play now being produced by Elsie Jane Wilson. Cooley was a member of the Universal forces a year ago, when he left to do juvenile leads with the Keystone Company. He has also appeared in American productions at Santa Barbara.

Among the actresses and comediennes of achievement and especial promise who have been engaged for Universal productions during the past month might be mentioned Rena Rogers, Gladys Tennyson, Rosemary Theby, Beatrice Burnham and Mildred Davis.

Rena Rogers will be remembered for her striking characterization in Lois Weber's especial production, "Where Are My Children?" She will also be seen shortly in the Zoe Rae vehicle, directed by Elsie Jane Wilson.

Gladys Tennyson, who will be seen in the leading feminine roles of Victor comedies during the coming months, is a Texas girl, and did good work in Keystone and Christie comedies before joining the funmakers at Universal City.

Rosemary Theby becomes a Universalite for the second time. She is equally adept in comic and dramatic roles, and after completing her present work with Eddie Lyons and Lee Moran will be featured in more pretentious productions.

Beatrice Burnham, although but seventeen years of age, has had several years' experience acting for the films. She will be attached to the Nestor comedy company, appearing in support of Lyons and Moran when Miss Theby finishes her engagement with that team of favorites.

Mildred Davis, who has the ingenue role in "Man of God," the production being put on by E. J. Le Saint, owns to eighteen summers. She is an attractive blonde, and is said to possess authentic emotional ability.

Besides E. J. Le Saint, who is filling a return engagement on Universal's producing staff, Harry Harvey has recently been added to the directing forces.

For some time past associated with Pathe, Harvey has many notable productions to his credit in the widely advertised serials, "Neal of the Navy," "The Red Circle," and "Who Pays?" He also directed some of the best western pictures released by that company.

Zittel to Manage International

Hearst Appoints Well Known Vaudeville Publicity Man to Take Charge of His Film Company.

C. F. ZITTEL, famous throughout the country as "Zit" of the New York Evening Journal, has been appointed by William Randolph Hearst as general manager of the International Film Service, Inc. Mr. Zittel's appointment as head of the International will not in any way interfere with his duties as head of the theatrical department of the New York Evening Journal from 224 West 47th street to the general offices of the International, which occupy the entire sixteenth floor of the Godfrey Building at 729 Seventh avenue.

Mr. Zittel assumed his new position last week immediately upon returning from a vacation in the Adirondacks.

"It is too early," he said, "for me to outline a policy of what the International probably will do. But we are going to do big things. Mr. Hearst is never satisfied unless he is doing big things.

"The International expects to begin producing within a short time. The Hearst organization controls the output of the foremost writers of today. Their works, which originally appear in the eight magazines owned by Mr. Hearst, will be utilised in motion pictures, prepared for the screen by foremost scenario writers. Other plans are being worked out, the details of which will be announced later on."

Mr. Zittel has been with the Hearst organization for twelve years, having taken charge of the Dramatic Department of the New York Journal in 1906. He made that department a power, and the New York Evening Journal was soon recognised as one of the foremost theatrical authorities in the country. In February of 1913, Mr. Zittel, foreseeing the remarkable future of the motion picture industry, established a motion picture department in the New York Evening Journal which has been as successful as the theatrical department.

In assuming the general management of the International, Mr. Zittel will divide his time between that organization and the theatrical department of the New York Evening Journal, surrounding himself with a corps of able assistants in both of these organizations.

Brings New Names to Screen

Empire All Star Corporation Introduces Many Players Who Have Never Been in Pictures Before.

THE Empire All Star Corporation is introducing many well-known names to the screen who have heretofore remained adamant to all offers to forsake the footlights even for a short time. Ferdinand Gottschalk, whose list of stage successes is too long to enumerate, is one of them. He is now with the organization that is busily engaged in transforming the late Charles Frohman's stage successes into noteworthy screen productions. In "My Wife" Mr. Gottschalk is playing for the screen the same role that he created on the stage, and many people will welcome his screen "Gibby."

Warburton Gamble is another who makes his initial bow to the screen. All those who saw the late Sir Herbert Tree in "Colonel Newcome" last season will remember the acting of Mr. Gamble, whose "Sir Barnes Newcome" was a performance to be hugely enjoyed and forever remembered. Miss Eileen Dennes, who with Mr. Gamble is appearing in "The Unforeseen," starring Miss Olive Tell and featuring Mr. David Powell, is another screen debutante. Miss Dennes originally started out to be a dancer, and with the end in view spent a whole year with the great Pavlowa studying and appearing in her company both in London and New York.

Hubert Druce, the deservedly well-known English actor, is yet another member of the Empire All Star Corporation to make his first appearance in the motion picture world. He as is Amy Veness, John Harwood, Rex McDougal, Edward Fielding, Norman Trevor, and, last but first to be remembered, Miss Julia Sanderson.

Miss Sanderson has refused to even consider any offer from motion picture managers so often that it was generally considered hopeless to suggest "getting" Miss Sanderson for any production however noteworthy. But the name of Charles Frohman still stands for all that is best and most successful now, as it did when he was alive, and it was through this that Miss Sanderson was persuaded. Her first picture, "The Runaway," is scheduled for release through the Mutual exchanges Sept. 24.

Thomas Meighan Continues With Famous Players-Lasky

Hero of Many Paramount Pictures Renews His Contract; Will Be Seen Shortly With Billie Burke in "Arms and the Girl."

IT will be welcome news to the thousands of admirers of Thomas Meighan that he is to continue to appear in Paramount productions, having just signed a new contract with the Famous Players-Lasky Corporation. Mr. Meighan will next be seen in "Arms and the Girl," in support of Billie Burke, with whom he has appeared since her association with Paramount. His last picture with her was "The Mysterious Miss Terry."

Prior to his appearances in Billie Burke's screen vehicles, Thomas Meighan was leading man for Pauline Frederick in a number of her most successful pictures, including "Sapho," "S l e e p i n g Fires" and "Her Better Self."

Mr. Meighan's first L a s k y picture was "The Fighting Hope" in support of Laura Hope Crews. He was leading man for Charlotte Walker in "The Trail of the Lonesome Pine" and "Kindling." He was seen in "Armstrong's Wife" with Edna Goodrich, "The Sowers" with Blanche Sweet, "The Clown" in support of Victor Moore, "The Dupe" in support of Blanche Sweet, and "Common Ground," in which Marie Doro had the leading feminine role.

Thomas Meighan.

Still other Paramount pictures in which Mr. Meighan has appeared are "The Secret Sin" with Blanche Sweet, "Blackbirds" with Laura Hope Crews, "Out of Darkness" with Charlotte Walker, "The Immigrant" with Valeska Suratt, and "The Heir of the Hoorah" with Anita King.

Personality is the thing that, coupled with his undoubted ability and versatility, has made for Mr. Meighan a host of admirers who welcome his every appearance on the screen. He is the exact type for a leading man, of fine presence, athletic and with an ever-ready smile.

MADAME PETROVA ANNOUNCES CAST.

Madame Petrova is making the Biograph studio a hive of activity as she produces the first of the pictures to be made under her personal supervision. In spite of Petrova's exacting work and the countless details involved in making a play filled with spectacular scenes, it is practically assured that the first Petrova picture will be ready for release by the latter part of October.

Petrova has personally selected the following cast: Thomas Holding, leading man; Anders Randolf will play the part of Frans Jorn, an artist; Henri Leone plays the part of a police agent; Richard Garrick plays the part of Graham West, secretary of the American Minister; Carl Dietz plays the part of a secret service operative; Warren Cook has the part of the American Minister to Belmark; Anita Allen is the maid.

STRONG SUPPORTING CAST FOR DOROTHY DALTON.

Dorothy Dalton is more than pleased with the cast chosen to support her in her first Paramount-Ince picture which is now being filmed at the Thomas H. Ince studios. The players who will appear in the picture in support of the beautiful and talented star include Thurston Hall, a leading man with long experience on the legitimate stage; William Conklin, who has an enviable reputation through his past work for the screen; Dorcas Matthews, a talented young actress who has for some time been under Mr. Ince's management; Adele Farrington, an accomplished player, with both film and stage experience, together with several others.

Sing Singers Loudly Applaud "Polly"

Goldwyn's First Production Is Seen By Prisoners, Who Greet Mae Marsh and Margaret Mayo.

SING SING prison, through its Mutual Welfare League, gave Mae Marsh, Margaret Mayo and Goldwyn's big photo-spectacle, "Polly of the Circus," a tumultuous reception the night of Sunday, September 2, when the big motion picture had its eastern premiere in the presence of its star and author and a group of guests.

The chapel of the prison, on the second floor of the big dining hall, has seating accommodations for 800 prisoners, but there were 1,200 in the room when Miss Marsh, Miss Mayo, Edgar Selwyn and other Goldwyn officers arrived.

Presentation of the picture began at 7.45 o'clock following the introduction of Miss Marsh and Miss Mayo to the large and temporarily silent audience. Both star and author were greeted by a storm of applause.

Sing Sing's projection room is equipped with one machine, which necessitates a moment of intermission between each reel. At the conclusion of each reel the big prison audience gave unmistakable evidences of its approval of "Polly of the Circus" by prolonged applause, and during the running of the exciting horse race the white-shirted audience could be seen half rising from the seats and each time the white horse ridden by Mae Marsh forged ahead applause and cheers were given so loudly that they could have been heard half a mile away beyond the prison walls.

During an intermission one of the League officers made announcement that Goldwyn Pictures Corporation hereafter would place Sing Sing prison on its regular circuit—all Goldwyn Pictures, as released, being at the disposal of the League.

Brady Finds a "Kerensky" Too

HENRY HULL, the young actor who plays the role of Kerensky in "Rasputin, the Black Monk," is said to bear an almost startling resemblance to the Russian idol of the hour. Young Hull, however, is not a product of the Czar's former domain—in fact, has never been nearer than the Atlantic seaboard to Russia.

He was born in Kentucky, where his father, Will Hull, was a very well known newspaper man. His brothers, Howard and Shelby Hull, have met with unusually fine success as actors.

When William A. Brady, director-general of World-Pictures Brady-Made, was casting about for an actor to impersonate the leading male role in "The Man Who Came Back," then about to be produced at the Playhouse, he found he had assigned himself to no easy task. To fill the bill properly the actor must be not only the possessor of real dramatic power, but manifestly youthful—two qualities which rarely go together.

In young Henry Hull he finally discovered the material he sought, and on the opening night a brilliant young leading man was added to the list of Broadway favorites. Since then Mr. Hull has supplemented his stage work by appearing in several World Pictures with quite marked success. It was Mr. Brady who detected the likeness between Mr. Hull and the photographs of Kerensky when looking for a recognised player to fill this important place in the "Rasputin" cast. Several photographs of the actor as he is shown in the Kerensky characterization making the impassioned address which swayed the Russian Duma in unrestrained unison toward the revolution, have the effect of stamping the director-general's choice as altogether felicitous.

Henry Hull.

Griffith Returning

Completes Successful Trip to Europe After Many Triumphs —Has New Picture Under Way.

AUTHORITATIVE announcement was made September 5 that D. W. Griffith, who has been in Europe since March 17, has completed his labors on the other side and is to return to America the last week in September. Mr. Griffith went to London to personally oversee the presentation there of his "Intolerance" at the Theater Royal, Drury Lane, London.

"Intolerance" in London proved the greatest motion picture success the British stage has ever known and crowned its triumph by being given at a gala performance in Drury Lane before King George and Queen Mary. Other occupants of the royal box on this occasion were Queen Mother Alexandria and Princess Mary and the younger sons and daughters of the Duke of Fife, members of the British royal family.

Mr. Griffith was presented to their Majesties. At that meeting he also grouped the royal family in an impromptu scene on the stage of the famous old theatre and took moving pictures of them. He has also been busy doing some work for both the British and French governments and has taken actual views of the war at numerous points along the western front. With these activities and the great success of "Intolerance" in Europe his time has been so occupied that his original visit which was only intended to last six weeks stretched over as many months. 'Intolerance' has been seen by nearly everybody of prominence in London, Paris and Rome, and Mr. Griffith has completed arrangements for its presentation in the principal cities of England, France and Italy.

With "Intolerance" launched upon its phenomenal run in Europe Mr. Griffith called Robt. Harron, Dorothy and Lillian Gish to England along with William Bitzer, his camera man, and together these prominent lights of the American motion picture world have been working upon a story which will be Mr. Griffith's next presentation. The European scenes have been completed and Mr. Griffith and his forces are hurrying home to complete the production for presentation the coming winter. A studio has been secured in California and the big production will be rounded out there. As Mr. Griffith was on the battle front in France for several months, it is a safe conjecture to say that his forthcoming production will deal in a powerfully dramatic way with the present world war.

General Adopts a "Little Man"

Quaint Emblem Suggested by "K. C. B.," the Clever Humorist of "Ye Town Gossip" Fame.

BECAUSE a noted newspaper humorist had a hunch which he could not make use of in his own work, General Film Company is the gainer by a new totem or emblem. It has a visualized "General Film," in the form of the accompanying cut.

This emblematic "General Film" is the suggestion of "K. C. B.," known all over the country as "the little man with the funny hat," and whose "Ye Towne Gossip" column in the Hearst newspapers in Boston, New York, Chicago, Atlanta, Los Angeles, San Francisco and elsewhere is as well known as the newspapers themselves. Although he hides himself under the famous initials, Kenneth C. Beaton as his name really is, has from the outset made himself a tangible personality to his readers by the daily illustration at the bottom of his column showing himself as "the little man." And a very accurate portrait it is, as regards his features, those who know him personally can testify.

To a General Film official with whom he has been long acquainted "K. C. B." said recently, "I dreamed the other night that I saw General Film marching down Fifth avenue all by himself with a sword. I suppose he was on his way to war, or whatever it is he was on his way to, and I liked him. He was a nice little man."

Then "K. C. B." described him. An artist was put to work and the result is General Film's own "little man," or "Gen. Film."

Gilson Willets With Pathe

GILSON WILLETS, well known novelist and traveler, who for a number of years has been associated with the Selig Company as scenario writer, has been engaged by Pathe, and has already started work in his new position in the Pathe scenario department. This is not the first time that Pathe has made use of Mr. Willets' talents. The rights to his novel "The Double Cross" were purchased by Pathe for adaptation into a serial which was later put out under the title "The Mystery of the Double Cross." In his review of his novel for the New York American, Edwin Markham, author of "The Man With a Hoe," characterised it as by far the greatest American mystery novel that had ever been written.

Mr. Willets is the author of twenty other books, among them "The First Law," "His Neighbor's Wife," "Anita the Cuban Spy," "The Workers of a Nation," "The Rulers of the World,"~"The Inside History of the White House," etc. In addition to his books Mr. Willets is a prolific magazine writer and has had published over a thousand different articles in such media.

Gilson Willets.

As a scenario writer Mr. Willets has many successes to his credit, among them the first motion picture serial, "The Adventures of Kathlyn" and the special features, "The Thundering Herd," "The Lily of the Valley," "I'm Glad My Boy Grew Up to Be a Soldier," "I Hear Her Calling Me," etc.

Mr. Willets has had a very busy and interesting life. He began his literary career at the age of nineteen and at twenty-one published his first book. When hardly more than a boy he became editor of Current Literature. In search of literary material he traveled in all parts of the world. Among his exploits at this stage of his career were traveling for three months through the length and breadth of India in famine and plague time, making a sledge journey of 500 miles through Northern Russia, Finland, Lapland and Sweden and crossing Northern Mexico on horseback. More than any other man can he claim credit for preserving Niagara Falls from despoilation at the hands of greedy commercial interests. His articles in Leslie's Weekly on "The Raps of Niagara" started a country wide agitation to save the Falls.

Mr. Willets comes of an old colonial family of distinction. His ancestor, Thomas Willets, was first mayor of New York in 1665. Two and a half centuries ago the family owned a large tract of land on Lond Island which extended from Willets Point to Hempstead. At the latter place Mr. Willets was born, the fourth of the same name in direct line. He is a member of many of the leading New York Clubs, among them the Aldine, Fencers, Republican and St. Andrew's Golf Club.

Mr. Willets' engagement is indicative of the policy of J. A. Berst, vice-president and general manager of Pathe Exchange, to build up the scenario department of Pathe to the point where it is admittedly the strongest and best balanced in the business.

MONTAGU LOVE CONTINUES WITH WORLD.

Montagu Love has been re-engaged for World-Pictures Brady-Made under a contract covering the next twenty-four months. During this period Mr. Love will be either "starred" or "featured" in all productions in which he takes part, and the agreement also provides for a substantial increase in the monetary compensation for his services.

Mr. Love has been a member of the World Film Corporation's acting forces for something more than a year. During the early stages of his term he played a wide variety of roles chiefly of the kind technically known as "character parts," and in these he displayed such unusual and dexterous versatility that the patrons of World Pictures began to ask for plays in which he was cast.

Sir Gilbert Parker Guest of Commodore Blackton

Noted Author, Whose Works Are Being Filmed for Paramount, Combines Business With Pleasure at Harbourwood.

KEENLY enjoying every moment of the time, Sir Gilbert Parker, the gifted English novelist, and M. P., whose books have sold into the millions and a number of whose most popular works are now being filmed by J.

Sir Gilbert Parker and Commodore Blackton.

Stuart Blackton for Paramount, recently was the guest of Mr. Blackton, at the latter's beautiful country estate, Harbourwood, at Oyster Bay, Long Island.

It was a combination of business and pleasure, however, for at intervals seated on the spacious veranda of the Casino, overlooking the blue waters of the Sound, the author and producer discussed in detail the forthcoming production of "The World for Sale" as well as future pictures to be made from the Parker novels.

Sir Gilbert witnessed a private projection of "The World for Sale" the other night at Oyster Bay and expressed himself as delighted by the outcome of the careful and artistic work that had been devoted to the production.

"Of course," said Sir Gilbert, "when I had read Commodore Blackton's scenario, I felt easy in my mind as to the story, at least. It was a masterful piece of work. I frankly confess I could not have done it. Were someone to offer me five thousand dollars now to write a three-reel scenario—much less a seven-reel one—I would have to decline. I simply haven't got that peculiar talent. It is an art in itself.

"As I say, I was confident the story would be right, because I had read the script. I was, to say the least, astonished. Every bit of the story that was essential to the plot was there, yet most wonderfully condensed. The few necessary changes that had been made, resulting from the absence of dialogue, have not marred the work; it is a direct, concise and wholly entertaining rendition of my book.

"Then I saw the picture screened, as you call it. And I marveled again. I confess I had been a bit anxious as to one or two of the characterizations, but I was agreeably surprised in every respect. I can only repeat that I marveled. The types selected to play the leading roles—such as Ingolby and Fleda Druse, Marchand, the French villain, Jethro Fawe, the Gypsy and of course the Ri, Gabriel Druse, had evidently been picked with the utmost care and attention the requirements of the unusual parts called for in the story. I can hardly say enough in praise of Mr. Blackton's efforts in this direction."

As a matter of fact, when Sir Gilbert saw the picture screened, it was without the subtitles, which have been taken entirely from the author's own lines.

"Since I have seen an example of Commodore Blackton's work," went on Sir Gilbert, "I feel safe in leaving my books in his hands for translation into motion pictures. Any author may feel as I do with him. It is a relief to know that intelligence and artistic perception will mark every production made under his supervision."

Sir Gilbert Parker will watch the filming of one or two more scenes in one of the later pictures, now under way, and will return shortly to England.

At Leading Picture Theaters

Programs for the Week of Sept. 9 at New York's Best Motion Picture Houses.

"POLLY of the Circus," the first of the new Goldwyn pictures to be released, was the principal photodramatic feature at the Strand the week of Sept. 9, with Mae Marsh in the title role. It tells a story of a little circus orphan who is raised by Toby, the clown. Polly is hurt in an accident and has to remain behind while the show goes on. She is taken to the home of the minister, where her presence in the house is turned into a scandal by the narrow-minded village gossips. Everitt Shinn, the artist, designed the settings, and Margaret Mayo, the author, personally aided Charles Horan, the director of the picture, in his work. The Strand Topical Review, Educational and Travel features and a new comedy were also shown.

The soloists were Mlle. Verba, Herbert L. Waterous, Arthur Depew and Ralph H. Brigham.

"Barbary Sheep" at the Rialto.

At the Rialto Theater Elsie Ferguson made her motion picture debut in "Barbary Sheep" for Artcraft Pictures under the auspices of Adolph Zukor. Adapted from Robert Hichins' most popular book since "The Garden of Allah," the romantic story of Algeria, tells of the infatuation of an English noblewoman for a dark-skinned army officer, and is charged with the passion, and swift action that befit a novel of this kind. Supporting the star is an exceptional cast of players, including Pedro de Cordoba, Lumsden Hare, Macy Harlam, Alex Shannon and Maude Ford. The scenario was adapted from the book by Charles Maigne.

The soloists were Gaston Hubois, Marion Rudolfo, and Greek Evans.

Eighty-first Street Theater Bill.

At the Eighty-first Street Theater for the entire week Evelyn Nesbit and her son, Russell Thaw, were seen in "Redemption."

"The Man Without a Country" at the Broadway.

Edward Everett Hale's patriotic classic, "The Man Without a Country," has been put into screen form by Thanhouser and opened an engagement at the Brodway Theater last Sunday night.

GENERAL OPENS IN PORTLAND.

Owing to continued pressure in the northwest Pacific field from exhibitors attracted by the quality of General Film's product, the company has just opened a branch office in Portland. This office will relieve the Seattle office of the growing bulk of business in the Oregon district.

In accordance with its policy of making promotions from its own organisation wherever recognition is earned, General Film has placed in charge of the Portland office Mr. W. E. Matthews. Mr. Matthews is a successful, energetic and popular salesman, who had been for some years with the San Francisco office of the company. He has taken charge, and Portland is now permanently on the General Film map.

FIRE SHUTTER CASE WILL BE APPEALED.

The Moving Picture World is advised by J. A. LeRoy, one of the plaintiffs in the case of C. R. Baird and J. A. LeRoy against the Nicholas Power Company, that the decision reported in the Moving Picture World of September 1 is not final but that it was in the nature of an interlocutory decree and that he wishes to inform the readers of the World, upon advice of counsel, that the case will be carried to the Court of Appeals in due and proper course.

HERMAN MANDELBAUM GETS INTO UNIFORM.

Herman Mandelbaum, son of Henry J. Mandelbaum, manager of the Cleveland branch of the United Theater Equipment Company, has left for a camp in Alabama, as a member of the artillery company recently organised in the Forest City. Mr. Mandelbaum was for years with the equipment and supply house and is well known among the exhibitors of Ohio, who wish him the best of success.

NEW OPERATORS' SCALE FOR NEW YORK.

Henry I. Sherman, recording secretary of New York Operators' Union 306, I. A. T. S. E., announces that a new wage scale for motion picture operators will go into effect Monday, September 24. The new scale will appear in full in the Projection Department for the issue of September 29.

Abel to Represent Select Pictures

Resigns From V-L-S-E Chicago Branch and Will Travel for New Distributing Company.

SYDNEY E. ABEL has been appointed Special Representative of Select Pictures Corporation and begins work in the interest of Select exchanges Sept. 10. Mr. Abel has resigned his position as manager of the Chicago branch exchange of Vitagraph V-L-S-E.

Mr. Abel has made an enviable record in conducting branch exchanges in the Middle West. He started with the Cleveland Exchange two years ago after the Vitagraph V-L-S-E organization was effected.. The splendid showing which he made in selling V-L-S-E product in the Cleveland district in six months' time brought him promotion to the managership of the Chicago exchange, which position he has held ever since. In Chicago Abel established a record for big sales. He is credited with having put over the V-L-S-E in that territory.

Prior to his connection with the Vitagraph interest, Sydney Abel spent four and a half years with the Mutual Film Corporation as branch manager in various eastern cities. He was in charge of the Pittsburgh exchange when the Vitagraph brought him into their fold. Abel is a Minnesota man, having been born in St. Paul, but for several years past has resided in Chicago.

Sydney E. Abel.

He is of a most genial disposition and has a host of friends among exhibitors and salesmen throughout the country. Aside from putting over big sales of pictures, Abel has one love that is dear to his heart—his Paige car. He is an enthusiastic motorist and spends most of his spare time burning gasoline in the interest of real sport.

With Select pictures Abel will act as a first aid to sales, much of his time being spent on the road visiting exchanges in the various cities.

WANTS RECORD KEPT OF INSURED PARCELS.

Exhibitors and exchange managers are soon to be requested by their local postmasters to install a system whereby an accurate record may be kept of all insured parcel-post shipments received at the theaters and exchanges.

This request will be made at the instance of the office of the Third Assistant Postmaster General at Washington, which has just issued a letter in which it is asked that, in view of the fact that insured parcels are now delivered without record being made at post offices of address, the postmasters take up with those who receive large numbers of insured packages the matter of putting in a system of checking the receipt thereof, so as to make sure that their answers as to whether a particular article has been received are correct.

In the case of parcels being received that do not bear the name and address of the sender, the department asks that a record be made by the recipient of the number of the parcel, the date of receipt and the office of mailing, in order that when inquiry is made regarding such parcels the fact of their receipt may be reported. The attention of patrons of this service is also to be directed to the necessity for extreme accuracy in such cases.

Director Dillon Has Had Much Experience

Man Who Will "Put On" Next Ann Pennington Picture for Paramount Has Turned Out Many Comedies in Past.

AN all around experience, dating from the earliest days of the motion picture, is possessed by Edward Dillon, whose first Paramount picture will be a comedy drama in which diminutive Ann Pennington, the "Follies" beauty, will be starred. Nor is his experience limited to the films, for he was at one time an actor himself. He served two seasons with Otis Skinner, a season with Dustin Farnum and Ada Rehan. Oddly enough, he began his stage career as a horseback rider in racing melodramas, once exceedingly popular.

For eight years Dillon served with D. W. Griffith, varying from drama to comedy, in which latter field he displayed remarkable talent for devising unique situations and getting the most out of every opportunity. The old Biograph comedies were directed by him for some time, in the days when Mack Sennett, Mabel Normand, the late Fred Mace, and Del Henderson were familiar figures in those productions. When Griffith left the Biograph, Dillon went to the Reliance - Majestic and

Edward Dillon

started a new brand of comedies till the Triangle was formed. He created the Triangle comedies and later put on longer pictures.

"The new Ann Pennington film," said Mr. Dillon, "will be notable for the opportunities it gives the star to wear some stunning gowns, fetching bathing costumes in the swimming scenes, etc. She will also have a chance to display her powers at dancing and high diving. I am putting a lot of original material into the picture, and though it is too early to divulge the character of the plot I may say that it will be something out of the ordinary in comedy-drama, with novel sets and plenty of real action.

KEENE THOMPSON WITH FAIRBANKS.

Douglas Fairbanks last week engaged Keene Thompson, the well-known magazine contributor, as a member of his scenario department in the production of Artcraft pictures. Mr. Thompson started his professional career as a comic artist on the staff of the New York World, when still in his knickerbockers, at the age of 15. His first fiction work followed shortly, when he sold a story to the New York Sun, followed by having the Scrap Book accept one of his manuscripts.

Thompson has written advertising copy for such accounts as the Singer Sewing Machines, Ingersoll Watches, Regal Shoes, American Tobacco Company, etc., and then entered the free-lance fiction field. He has sold over six hundred short stories, novelettes and verses, and was approached by Douglas Fairbanks, after accepting one of Keene's film stories, "Far From the Maddening Girls," written in conjunction with Gerald C. Duffy, editor of Picture Play Magazine.

JEWEL CARMEN COMES EAST.

Jewel Carmen is now an outstanding feature of the landscape around the William Fox studios at Fort Lee, N. J. She is playing Fantine in the film version of "Les Miserables," now in the making.

Miss Carmen has been in motion pictures almost four years, but she has earned a good part of the love which photoplay fans hear her since her advent into William Fox films about twelve months since. She has played in the role opposite William Farnum in "The Conqueror," as Lucy Manette in "A Tale of Two Cities," and in the leading feminine roles of "American Methods" and "When a Man Sees Red."

Traveling Cameramen Get Thrills

Willard Vander Vere and Assistant Return from Trip Through West Indies—Arrested as Spies at St. Pierre.

WILLARD VANDER VERE, a Gaumount cameraman, and his assistant, Norton Willis, have returned to the United States after spending several months in the West Indies taking scenic and educational subjects. The trip was highly successful and, according to Mr. Vander Vere, somewhat exciting. It was while at Martinique, a French possession and under martial law, that the most thrilling incident occurred. Mr. Vander Vere and his assistant had left their ship to take advantage of an unexpected opportunity to visit this interesting island. Securing an automobile they had journeyed from Fort de France to the ruined city of St. Pierre and Mt. Pelee, some twenty miles away.

Arriving at St. Pierre they prepared to take some pictures of that famous old city, once known as "Little Babylon," when a gendarme suddenly appeared from an old ruin and demanded an explanation. "He talked for several minutes with his mouth and hands," said Mr. Vander Vere, "but we could not understand a word he said. In a general way I guessed what he wanted, so we got into our machine and he

Vander Vere and a Curious Native

guided us back to Fort de France, where we went to the police headquarters and were brought before a number of officials in gold braid, tassels and plumed hats. Other officers came in and they talked to, at, of, and about us, for two solid hours. I was asked for my passport, but I had left it on the ship. This looked bad for us. Fortunately Willis had his, which helped some, but there was I in a French possession under martial law, known to have taken photographs of the island, claiming a questionable name and with no passport to show.

"After a while I got them to send for the American Consul, who arrived half an hour later. To him I explained the situation, and he pow-wowed with the officials, with the result that we were freed with a warning. Speaking to the consul afterward I was informed that I had been taken for a spy and that the officials were deciding to shoot me.

Vander Vere said that they were again arrested in Barbados, B. W. I., for taking pictures in a certain vicinity that was barred to photographers, but that they cleared themselves and left for Trinidad the next day. "Everything went fine in Trinidad," said Mr. Vander Vere, "till I started to take views along the waterfront. I had to develop my negative and show the officials that I was not photographing anything that would be of value to the enemy. While in the country districts I was held up several times, but upon showing my permit I was allowed to continue. One reason for my being allowed a great deal of liberty with the camera in Trinidad was because it was my second visit and I was known to a great many of the people.

"I found so much of interest in Trinidad that I stayed several months. Among the subjects taken were 'West Indian Life,' 'The Cocoanut,' 'Monkey Tricks,' 'Indian Industries,' such as basket making and jewelry making, making cocoanut bread, scenes of the Mohammedan mosque and types of worshipers. An interesting comparison is of the Mohammedan and Hindu priests; another is that between Port of Spain, the present capital, with its 60,000 inhabitants, electric cars, asphalt streets, electric lights and handsome residences, and the town of St. Joseph, the ancient Spanish capital, with a few hundred people, its unpaved streets and small huts. In fact, it is like being in a different world, although Port of Spain is but ten miles distant."

Mr. Vander Vere visited the islands of St. Thomas and St. Croix just prior to their purchase from Denmark by the United States and took the pictures that Gaumont released on the day that the Danish commissioner received Uncle Sam's check for the purchase price—$25,000,000.

GIVEN A BEAUTIFUL WATCH.

VISITING film men who meet E. V. Richards, Jr., general manager of the Saenger Amusement Co., Inc., in his native lair in New Orleans, and ask him the time of day will get at least passing glimpse of a "watch what is a watch," recently given him by his subordinates in the Saenger Company as a token of the appreciation and esteem in which he is held

by the men who work with him and meet him from day to day.

Mr. Richards—or "Rich" to his many friends throughout the South—is the foundation upon which the big Saenger organization was constructed, the building having been begun in Shreveport, La., some years ago. He has been much in the limelight recently because of the amalgamation of the Saenger and the Fitchenburg interests in the South and because of the opening of the beautiful new Strand theater in New Orleans, the construction, equipment, and advance plan of operation of which he personally plotted and supervised.

The beautiful watch given Mr. Richards is of platinum, studded with diamonds, the designs being a monogram of the recipient's name and the insignia of the Shrine, F. A. O. M., Mr. Richards being a member of El Karujah Temple of Shreveport, La. The presentation, very much in the nature of a surprise, took place at a recent weekly conference of the Saenger employees and was made by Will Gueringer, formerly general manager of the Fitchenburg motion picture interests, but since the amalgamation of the two companies, Mr. Richards' assistant.

REAL "SPEED DEMONS" IN COMEDY.

In the new series of six one-reel Jaxon Comedies just announced the initial release carries about a dozen cut-ins of an honest-to-goodness auto world's championship race. This comedy, dated for September 14, is "Speed Demons." Besides Pokes and Jabs in their burlesque of automobile strenuousness, Barney Oldfield and Ralph De Palma figure as racers in deadly earnest. The automobile color for this film was obtained July 21 at Providence, when De Palma and Oldfield held their historic meeting before a tremendous crowd.

The Jaxon Film Company, whose Eastern studios are at Providence, had special facilities for covering the Narragansett Park event, and had several cameras on the scene.

Burton Holmes and H. T. Cowling Making the Paramount-Burton Holmes Travelogues in the Blue Mountains of Australia.

Henry J. Brock Killed in Auto Accident

Pioneer Film Man and Foreign Market Specialist Dies When Pinned Under Car.

HENRY J. BROCK, who was one of the best known and most loved men in the motion picture industry, was killed in an automobile accident that occurred near Kingston, N. Y., on Friday afternoon, September 7. Mr. Brock was on his way to Kingston to his home in Buffalo. In the automobile with him were Herry Brouse, a well known exhibitor of Ottawa, and Emery Hylandt, a friend of the Brock family, Mr. Brock was at the wheel when the car suddenly turned turtle and pinned Mr. Brock underneath. He was killed instantly. Mr. Brouse and Mr. Hylandt were injured seriously. They were taken to the Kingston Hospital. Mr. Brock was forty-six years old. He had been identified with the motion picture industry for upwards of eleven years. He began his career on the amusement field when he gave up a profitable wholesale clothing business in Buffalo to become associated in the exhibiting of motion pictures with Mitchell H. Mark, his brother-in-law, who now controls the Strand theater in New York. The two men founded the Mark-Brock enterprises. The venture proved an immediate success, and was one of the insti-

The Late Henry J. Brock.

tutions that founded the penny arcade system in the early days of motion pictures. The firm soon widened its activities until it controlled theaters throughout Northern New York and Canada. Mr. Mark later withdrew from the firm, leaving Mr. in control of Mr. Brock.

Still holding his interests in the theaters, Mr. Brock became president of the Kinemacolor company. In this position he made many friends and broadened the field of his activities to a wide extent. After his association with Kinemacolor Mr. Brock began to specialise more in the foreign market. He made several trips to Europe, and at the time of his death had the entire foreign market at his finger tips. For the past few years Mr. Brock had been wonderfully successful in the handling of big features, and he controlled the rights to South America, Central America, Great Britain and Canada on the best products of American producers. He operated on a large scale and was successful in all his undertakings. He owned or controlled a great many motion pictures.

At the time of his death Mr. Brock was president of the Inter-Ocean Film Company, the Manxman Company and the Cinema Distributing Company. He, also owned the Academy and· Regent theaters, in Buffalo, and the Strand and York theaters, in Toronto.

He is survived by his widow and four children—two girls and two boys, ranging in age from five to eighteen years—his mother and four sisters.

Representatives of every branch of the motion picture field and other amusement enterprises attended the funeral, which was held from Mr. Brock's late residence in Richmond avenue, Buffalo, on Sunday afternoon. Details of the funeral were in charge of Mr. Mark, who hurried to Kingston as soon as he had heard of the accident.

Among the bearers at the services were Hiram Abrams, of Paramount; Felix Feist, Joseph M. Schenck, of the Loew interests; George W. Newgrass and Fred Newman, business associates of Mr. Brock, and Paul H. Crumelin, vice-president of the Inter-Ocean Film Corporation.

Among the others who attended the funeral were Gus and Leo Schlessinger. M. S. Epstien, Eugene Kaufman, Madge Maloney and Edith Schulhoff. Miss Maloney had been in the employ of Mr. Brock for fifteen years and was his chief auditor. Miss Schulhoff was his private secretary.

Circuit Forms Release Plans

First National Members Form National Distributing Organ. ization—By-Laws Revised—Schwalbe to Supervise Exchanges.

THE First National Exhibitors' Circuit, during meetings held several days last week at the Hotel Astor, New York, formed new release plans and formed a national distributing organization. The by-laws of the organization were amended and revised to cover the new plan. Harry M. Schwalbe, of Philadelphia, was appointed general supervisor of the exchanges that in future are to be controlled by the Circuit. The representative member of the Circuit in each respective district will open an exchange. All exchanges in all probability will be supervised from a headquarters in New York.

Many matters of importance were considered and acted upon during the meetings. One revision of the by-laws allows a greater leeway in the purchase of pictures. The purchase of two or three productions by national stars also is being considered. One or two contracts are said to have been signed, but members of the organisation decline to either affirm or deny that such is the case.

Among those who attended the meetings at the Astor were: T. L. Tally, of Los Angeles, who was instrumental in the Circuit's signing Charlie Chaplin; Harry M. Schwalbe, Philadelphia; Aaron J. Jones, Chicago; Nat Ascher, Chicago; Robert Lieber, Indianapolis; E. H. Hulsey, Dallas; E. B. Johnson, San Francisco; E. V. Richards, Jr., New Orleans; William Sievers, St. Louis; E. Mandelbaum, Cleveland; A. J. Gilligham, Detroit; Lynn S. Card, New Jersey; Nathan H. Gordon, New England; J. B. Clark, Pittsburgh; Jake Wells, Norfolk; J. H. Blank, Des Moines; Henry Brouse, Ottawa; W. H. Bewetts, Vancouver; Tom Moore, Washington; J. H. Kunsky, Detroit, and W. H. Swanson, Denver.

Lloyd Lonergan Retires

Thanhouser Scenario Writer Decides to Take a Rest from His Labors.

LLOYD LONERGAN, who wrote the first scenario for the Thanhouser Company, and has been connected with that institution since it was started in 1909, retired, on September 1. He is going to Cape May, New Jersey, for a rest, and intends to put business to one-side until his return.

Of the hundreds of stories Mr. Lonergan has written, "The Million Dollar Mystery" was easily the most famous. Not only did he evolve the name and prepare the script of this serial, but the selection of the director and the cast was done by him, and every detail of the production was in his hands. Mr. Lonergan was more lucky than many authors, for he had a large financial interest in his "brain child," and shared in the tremendous returns that came to the stockholders.

The latest picture from the pen of Mr. Lonergan is "The Man Without a Country," suggested by Edward Everett Hale's patriotic story. This photoplay, a six-reeler, was made by Thanhouser, and will be released by Jewel Productions, Inc. Some of his other recent productions are "The Woman in White," "Mary Lawson's Secret," with Charlotte Walker; "Under False Colors" and "The Heart of Ezra Greer," in both of which Frederick Warde starred; "A Modern Monte Cristo," featuring Vincent Serrano, and "Her Belover Enemy."

J. H. GENTER DEAD.

A letter from the J. H. Genter Company, Inc., of Newburgh, N. Y., makers of Mirroroid screens, brings the news that J. H. Genter, president and treasurer of the company, died very suddenly at his home in Newburgh on Wednesday evening, September 5. Heart failure is given as the cause of death which was as unexpected as it was sudden, for Mr. Genter was apparently in the best of health.

The deceased was thirty-eight years of age. He was born in Albany, N. Y., but had made his home for the past twelve years where he founded the business which bears his name. A widow and son of twelve survive. The funeral services were held on Sunday, September 9.

BASS CAMERA COMPANY ISSUES CATALOG.

The Bass Camera Company, of No. 109 North Dearborn street, Chicago, has issued a new and complete catalog covering their line. The catalog has been compiled along lines that make its contents accessible in minimum time. All accessories are listed in alphabetical order, making the catalog self-indexing.

Chicago News Letter

By JAS. S. McQUADE

Traveling Picture Tent Shows Hurting Country—Town Exhibitors in Mississippi and the South.

CLYDE MARTIN, widely known among exhibitors as the first traveling musician who played musical accompaniment for moving pictures, is at present touring the south in that capacity. I have just received a letter from him that is well worthy of appearing in print, as it shows the prosperous condition of exhibitors in Mississippi and some of their drawbacks, the traveling picture tent show being one of the chief.

Mississippi exhibitors should certainly organise and have laws passed that will protect them against these itinerant competitors. Moving picture theater owners are tax payers and contribute to the growth and attractiveness of their communities. The small license paid by the tent show picture does not compensate the community for that which is tained by the responsible, resident theater-owner. The town officials should be guided by ordinances that will protect the regular licensed exhibitor and resident from these traveling mountebanks. Following are paragraphs from Mr. Martin's letter:

"I am playing through the south, my first trip down here since 1912, and the change in the picture business in this territory is certainly astonishing. In fact, I think the business in the small towns of the Delta of Mississippi would open the eyes of some of the Northern exhibitors in the smaller towns. Everywhere I have found regular theaters, regular managers and the fifteen-cent admission. They are getting fifteen cents for regular attractions and twenty and twenty-five cents for features. Cotton prospects are wonderful and all exhibitors are doing good business.

"The only drawback which the Mississippi managers have is the road show competition. This territory is infested with a swarm of cheap tent shows. Several of the towns have passed laws regarding tent shows that have protected the exhibitor to a certain extent. I should think that this form of opposition would be enough to impress the exhibitor that organization is needed to protect their interests.

"This week, I am playing Cleveland, Miss., a town of two thousand population, and it would do your heart good to see the projection and the theater, and to meet the manager, R. T. Megibben. This house, The Regent, has a seating capacity of four hundred and he needs every seat. On Tuesday he ran 'The Masque of Life' at twenty-five cents admission, and packed them in. Wednesday and Thursday he has 'Womanhood,' at fifty cents admission, and I would bet a box of those favorite Havanas of yours that he will pack two shows each day. But 'Every silver lining has its cloud,' and in this case the cloud is formed by three tent shows which are billed in the town within the next ten days.

"But, notwithstanding all this, business is good in the South."

"Denver Dixon," Cowboy Actor, Tours Australasia for Two Years with Selig Western Pictures.

"Denver Dixon," the cowboy actor who figured prominently in Selig pictures a number of years ago, has just returned to Chicago after a two-years' trip through Australasia. During that time he has visited every city and town of importance in New Zealand and Australia, and has "showed" in 600 picture theaters.

Mr. Dixon carried with him two Selig films, "The Days of the Thundering Herd" and "The Diamond S Roundup," and at each presentation of these he delivered a lecture, entitled "What an American Cowboy Really Is."

While delivering this lecture and showing the films in a theatre at Adelaide, the Governor of South Australia and his wife, Lady Galloway, were present and gave high praise to the Selig pictures. Lady Galloway also told Mr. Dixon that previous to hearing his lecture she had never known why American cowboys wear fringes on their chaps, a something about which many millions of Americans are also ignorant.

Moving pictures are extremely popular in Australia and New Zealand, Mr. Dixon states, and the theaters are, as a rule, superior to those in America. The presentations are made with great care, both as to projection and the accompanying music.

American pictures are much preferred and Western subjects are in high favor. Pictures produced in Australia are inferior, owing to the lack of high-class directors, Mr. Dixon says.

Douglas Fairbanks Goes East to 'Film Several Scenes in "Reaching for the Moon."

Douglas Fairbanks stopped over in Chicago about an hour Tuesday, September 4, on his way from Los Angeles to New York. It was at first intended to entertain him at lunch in the Blackstone Hotel, but the brief time made it necessary to substitute instead the Hotel Dearborn, which is beside the La Salle depot, the point of departure eastward.

Max Goldstine, division superintendent of Paramount-Artcraft, stationed in this city, was the host. He had assembled over a score of representatives of the daily press and trade journals to meet the guest of honor, who was accompanied on the trip by his brother, John Fairbanks, who fills the position of business manager, and Bennie Ziedman, press representative. During lunch the author and star of "Down to Earth" gave an informal address, interspersed with some of his funny stories, which put everyone present in good humor.

Mr. Fairbanks stopped over at several towns on the way from Los Angeles before reaching the Windy City. These included San Bernardino, Gallup, New Mexico, where he was greeted at the station by several hundred children, who presented him with an American flag; Albuquerque, where a crowd of 2,000 people had assembled to do him honor, and at Dodge City, Ia., where Dick Crawford presented him with a gun which had been active in numerous holdups.

In New York, Mr. Fairbanks will take several scenes at Sherry's and Rector's for one of his near, coming productions, "Reaching for the Moon." The story of this picture has to do with modern life from the psychologic viewpoint.

Moving Pictures and Japanese Cops.

Mae Tinee, photoplay critic of the Chicago Tribune, treated her readers the other day to an amusing story showing how the police in Japan regulate moving picture theaters. Taking all in all we are thankful to be in Chicago.

Here is the story:

"Many lively comedies are being enacted in the picture houses of Tokio, a Japanese correspondent informs me—more comedies than are thrown on the screens. It seems that the police have been appointed guardians and that they take their duties seriously, congregating outside in numbers that would indicate that a political meeting was going on within. They watch carefully all who go in and make no bones about preventing them.

"A boy who declared he was 16, it is said, was told by the police that he appeared to be only 15. Whereupon he was compelled to go home and get the family register before he would be permitted to enter. The police also took serious exception to a married couple sitting in different parts of the house and spoke to the management about it.

"'If they are married,' said they, 'why don't you keep them together?'"

Chicago Film Brevities.

Thomas J. Furniss, member of the national executive committee of the M.P.E.L. of America, stopped over in the city, Saturday, Sept. 1, on his return from New York, where he attended the meetings connected with the officials of the League and the meeting of the N.A.M.P.I. Mr. Furniss left for Duluth the same evening, accompanied by Mrs. Furniss.

* * *

Sidney E. Abel, manager of Vitagraph's Chicago office for

a year and a half, resigned his position Saturday, Sept. 1, and has been succeeded by H. J. Bayley, formerly manager of Vitagraph's Minneapolis office.

* * *

Margarita Fischer has just signed a contract with President S. S. Hutchinson, of the American Film Co., Inc., and will begin work in a new American feature on Sept. 10. The name of the picture has not yet been announced.

* * *

Miss Lottie Pickford made a brief stop-over in the city Thursday forenoon, Sept. 6, on her way from Los Angeles to New York. It is understood that during her stay in New York Miss Pickford will consider a flattering offer from Pathe Exchange, Inc., to appear again under the Pathe banner.

* * *

Luman C. Mann, who is well known in Chicago film circles, and who was formerly a member of Company H in the First Regiment Illinois National Guard, has been appointed observer in the aviation corps now stationed at Fort Sill, Okla. While with Company H, of which he was a noncommissioned officers, Mr. Mann produced a one-reel picture describing general camp life, entitled "With the Illinois Troops" or "A Day with the Second Battalion First Illinois Infantry." Mr. Mann, who left for Fort Sill Wednesday evening, Sept. 5, made arrangements with the Lea-Bel Company, 612 Schiller Building, to handle the picture just mentioned.

* * *

At the New York meeting of the officers and members of the executive committee of the M.P.E.L. of America, the music tax was brought up, and after a brief discussion, was referred to a special committee appointed at the time to meet the situation and to confer with the national president of the Federation of Musicians.

* * *

Leon J. Bamberger, general publicity manager of Jewel Productions, Inc., was in town during the week and established a Chicago office for the company. The Jewel Productions, Inc., is not a producing company, being engaged in the buying of features and in their sale to exhibitors. The Chicago office is on the 15th floor of the Consumers Building, and Eli Van Ronkel has been appointed manager. Mr. Van Ronkel is a brother of I. Van Ronkel, manager of the Bluebird Exchange, this city, of which he has been assistant manager for some time.

* * *

"A Stormy Knight," a Bluebird feature, had a week's run at the Playhouse theater, Michigan avenue, from Sept. 1 until Friday, Sept. 7, inclusive. Manager I. Van Ronkel, of Bluebird Photoplays, Inc., donated 15 per cent. of the gross receipts of the week to the tobacco fund for American soldiers now in France.

* * *

"Rebecca of Sunnybrook Farm" (Artcraft), with Mary Pickford, began a run for one week at the Ziegfeld theater, Saturday, Sept. 8. This fine feature was directed by Marshall Neilan, who will be remember long as the author and director of "The Country that God Forgot" (Selig).

* * *

The war council of the Y. M. C. A. has made an appeal to moving picture producers for industrial moving pictures, which are intended to be shown in the military camps in this country and in France, and in the prison camps of Switzerland. It is estimated that the attendance in military training camps in this country will be over 250,000 a week, while the number of prisoners in Switzerland who will be entertained will be over 30,000. The appeal for such pictures has also appeared in the commerce reports of the U. S. Government, and the heads of film companies as well as business men who have had industrial moving pictures made especially for their lines, are directed by the government to write to Arthur M. East, secretary of the moving picture bureau of the Association, New York City.

* * *

"Within the Law" (Vitagraph), with Major Funkhouser has refused a "white" permit, and for which Vitagraph firmly refuses to accept a "pink" permit, will reach a hearing in the Circuit Court (Judge Robert E. Crowe presiding), Saturday, Sept. 15.

* * *

The case of "The Spy," the Fox picture which had been refused a "white" permit by Major Funkhouser, was given a hearing in the United States District Court, before Judge Samuel Alschuler, Friday, Aug. 31, and an order was issued restraining the city officials from interfering with its exhibition. Judge Alschuler ruled that the objection of Major Funkhouser to the picture was not within the meaning of the ordinance providing for the censorship of moving pictures. "There is nothing in the ordinance providing for

the censorship of pictures which states a permit may be refused a picture simply because of the horrifying nature of one scene," ruled Judge Alschuler. "Objections to pictures are allowed when they are of an immoral or suggestive caliber." An order permitting the showing of "The Spy" was issued Saturday morning, Sept. 1, by Judge Alschuler.

* * *

Hazel Daly, popular throughout the country for her impersonation of "Honey" in Essanay's Skinner comedy series, has been engaged by Wm. N. Selig, president of the Selig Polyscope Co., to take the leading woman's role in "Brown of Harvard," the production of which will soon begin at the Selig Chicago studios.

* * *

Dick Travers, the popular moving picture player, is now at the officers' training camp, Fort Sheridan. He is the third in the family to join the ranks of the allied troops. His younger brother is now in service in France, and another brother has been killed at the front, in action.

* * *

"The Italian Battle Front" closed at the Auditorium Sunday, Sept. 9, after a remarkably successful run. The opening date was Thursday, Aug. 23.

* * *

Winfield Sheehan, general manager of the Fox Film Corporation, spent several busy days in the city last week in connection with the big Fox programs that will prevail during the year opening September 2. All social and sex problem stories have been strictly eliminated from the Fox programs, Mr. Sheehan assured me, which will be supplanted by stories with a particular appeal to women and striving and vigorous plays for men. "Kiddie" series for children, which have become so popular will, of course, be continued and carried into still higher favor. Mr. Sheehan motored all of the way from New York City, stopping off at various points on the way to attend to the Fox interests.

* * *

Cecil Holland, the Selig player who appeared in the cast of "The Crisis," has joined the colors, and will go to the front in France with the contingent from the Pacific Coast.

* * *

James Bradbury, who took leading roles in "A Milk White Flag" and other Hoyt plays filmed by the Selig Polyscope Co., is at present appearing at the La Salle theater, this city, in the role of Judge Carter, in "Oh, Boy!" Mr. Bradbury scored a great success as the Sand Diviner in "The Garden of Allah," and has been at the Selig Los Angeles studio for some time. Since his return to Chicago he has been kept busy greeting his many friends in the city.

* * *

The marriage of Miss Margaret M. Tighe to Mr. Thomas J. Hackett, both of Chicago, has been announced to take place Tuesday morning, September 18, at Holy Cross Church, Sixty-fifth street and Maryland avenue. The marriage will be solemnized by the Rev. D. D. Hishen. Miss Tighe has been on the city office staff of George Kleine for the last eight years, and was one of the most popular and valued members. Indeed, so intimate was Miss Tighe's knowledge of the office routine, she has been known for a long time as Miss "Efficiency" Margaret. Personally, I am indebted to Miss Tighe for her intelligent assistance on many, many occasions, and I take this opportunity to thank her sincerely and to wish her all happiness in the years to come.

Vitagraph Seeks Injunction

Gets Temporary Restraining Order from Justice Mullen Against Anita Stewart and Louis B. Mayer— Returnable September 11.

RECENT announcements in the trade press to the effect that Louis B. Mayer has secured the services of Anita Stewart, and had formed a company to exploit her in pictures has raised a protest from the Vitagraph Company, which claims that Miss Stewart is still under contract to play in Vitagraph pictures, and that said contract does not expire until January 31, 1918.

In support of these contentions the Vitagraph Company has brought an action against Miss Stewart and Mr. Mayer to restrain them proceeding with their plans to produce pictures featuring Miss Stewart, or to give publicity in any manner to such plans before the expiration of the existing contract between the Vitagraph Company and Miss Stewart.

Upon hearing the complaint and affidavits of the plaintiff, Justice Mullen of the Supreme Court, New York County, granted a temporary injunction on September 6, which order is returnable at 10.30 o'clock on Tuesday, September 11, when a motion to make it permanent will be argued.

News of Los Angeles and Vicinity
By G. P. HARLEMAN

Carl Laemmle Arrives at the Coast
Will Replace Drafted Stars With Men Under Draft Age— To Send Several Companies to Orient.

WE are now engaged in developing young men under the draft age to take the place of our young leading men who have been called to the colors."

Carl Laemmle, president of the Universal Film Manufacturing Company, imparted this information to a representative of the Moving Picture World upon his arrival at Universal City from New York, for a stay of a month or more, when asked if the mobilization of the liberty army would not have a serious effect upon the ranks of the young men who play leads in Universal pictures.

"For a time," continued the head of the Big U organization, "there was every indication that the necessity of filling Uncle Sam's wants would cripple us as far as the young leading men were concerned, but we hit upon the idea of replacing them with the younger men and we are meeting with gratifying success.

"We have in our organization excellent material in the ambitious youngsters, quite a number of whom have been with us for several years and, being familiar with the exacting requirements of cinema production, they are fitting into the leading roles in a most satisfactory manner.

"Youth is a wonderful thing and we all admire it both in real

Carl Laemmle.

life and when it is presented to our view on the screen, and that is why in all of the Universal productions we make every effort to obtain a cast containing young people who we believe form the most alluring combination for our patrons—youth, naturalness and acting ability."

Mr. Laemmle said that the motion picture industry is in a most prosperous condition, new theaters being constructed in every part of this country and in the Canadian dominions, thus causing a corresponding increase in the demand of the product of the various manufacturing concerns.

"We are going full tilt, day and night," said Mr. Laemmle, "and one of the objects of my visit at this time is to arrange for doubling the capacity of the laboratories at Universal City, so that we will have no difficulty in meeting the ever-increasing demand. We are doing an unusually large business with China, Japan, India and Australia just now and Universal films are being transported to twenty-one different foreign lands, our agents having met with wonderful success in the countries across the seas where American films have become so popular. It is our intention to send several companies to the Orient in the near future to film on an elaborate scale a number of pictures in the atmosphere of the Far East."

The Universal president brought with him from New York a number of new stories by well-known authors and these are to be made into feature productions.

"Comedy will prevail to a large extent in the forthcoming photoplays," said Mr. Laemmle; "these are serious times, you know, and in their diversion the people must find much of the lighter side of life. That's the reason we are going to inject all the comedy we can into our future productions."

Johnson Chief at Culver City
Will Have Dictatorial Powers Over Triangle Productions From Scenario Department to Market.

JULIAN JOHNSON, until recently editor of the Photoplay Magazine and a former Los Angeles drama critic, has been appointed editor-in-chief of the Triangle Film Corporation, and is en route to Los Angeles to assume his post.

The position was created for Mr. Johnson by H. O. Davis, general manager and vice-president of the Triangle Film Corporation, and is one of exceptional responsibility. He will be held responsible for all pictures produced at the Triangle Culver City studio from the time they leave the scenario until they are ready for marketing.

"It is a new department for us," stated Mr. Davis. "No such position has been open in our company until now. I saw the need of a final supervisor or editor-in-chief, and I simply created the post. Of course, I first made certain that we could obtain Mr. Johnson's service.

"He will act as sort of a middleman between our script editor, Mr. Cunningham, and myself. His word on the stories will be final, and a picture will not be released until he has placed his O. K. on the film following the cutting operation. The new system will, I think, eliminate a lot of waste and will work for the betterment of Triangle pictures.

"Mr. Johnson is rated among the best newspaper and magazine writers of the country, and my opinion of him is expressed by the dictatorial powers which have been granted him."

At the Paralta Studios
Henry Walthall Arrives—President Anderson Visiting the Studios—Vice-President Robert T. Kane Drafted.

HENRY WALTHALL, who has recently signed up with Paralta Pictures, Inc., arrived at the local studios Sunday, August 26. Oscar Apfel, who has directed the Warren Kerrigan Company, will be Mr. Walthall's director. Kerrigan is now up and around again and doing very nicely considering that he sustained a bad fracture of the leg only four week's ago. Mary Charleson has been selected to play opposite Walthall in his first production. The story and supporting cast has not been selected as yet. Carl Anderson, the president of the Paralta, arrived in the city last week and reported himself as delighted at the progress his organization has made. Robert T. Kane, vice-president of the Paralta Pictures, Inc., who came out here to open up the Pacific Coast studios, has been drafted and expects to join the colors in a very short time. He has been working for several weeks to put his affairs in such order as to be able to leave for the front on a moment's notice. The vice-president of the Paralta Pictures, Inc., did not claim exemption.

G. R. Warren Now Horsley Manager.

G. R. Warren has been appointed manager of productions of the Horsley studios in Los Angeles, and will assume immediate charge.

Mr. Warren, who is recognized as one of the most capable all-around men in the picture business, began his career in the legitimate drama, through which he graduated to executive positions in the administration side of the profession. Early in the development of moving pictures Mr. Warren was first associated with Mr. Horsley in what has since become the Universal Film Company.

W. A. S. Douglas and Norman Manning have severed their affiliations with the Horsley organization. Mr. Douglas was associated in the conduct of the Lasalida Company and Mr. Manning was manager of the studio.

Mary MacLaren Injured.

The car of Mary MacDonald MacLaren, the David Horsley star, was wrecked by another machine last week and Miss MacLaren suffered painful lacerations and bruises. Although her beauty will not be impaired, she will be confined to a hospital bed for several weeks to come.

Los Angeles Film Brevities.

C. M. and S. A. Franklin, who are directing the Fox Kiddie Features, are engaged in the production of "The Mikado," for which a version has been arranged by Bernard McConville. The original story has been carefully preserved, with an addition of a great deal that lends atmosphere to it and that conveys a strong impression of the real Nippon life. The two famous little players, Francis Carpenter and Virginia Corbin, take the leading roles.

* * *

. . William Russell has commenced work on a western comedy-drama written by his director, Edward Sloman. The initial scenes are being made in the American Film Studio at Santa Barbara, though the majority of this new Russell feature will be made in mountain locations.

* * *

E. W. and J. G. Kuehn, president and vice-president, respectively, of the Mena Film Company, have decided to remain in Los Angeles until the completion of their first multiple-reel feature, "By Super-Strategy." Brooklyn is the Kuehn home.

* * *

J. P. McGowan, of the Signal Corporation, started shooting Saturday morning scenes for the seventh episode of "The Lost Express," which has been given the instalment title of "The Race With the Limited." Director McGowan will take the entire Helen Holmes company to San Diego, where a number of scenes in and around the big hotels will be made.

To secure several scenes for the sixth episode of the "Lost Express," just completed, Director-General McGowan took the entire Helen Holmes company on a hurried trip to Santa Barbara.

* * *

In her production of Mary Roberts Rinehart's "K," now nearing completion, Lois Weber has selected an unusually strong and well selected cast of popular players to appear in her second independent release. The stellar role of Sidney will be played by Mildred Harris. True Boardman, of Stingaree fame, will play the title role of "K," while he and Miss Harris are being supported by Albert Roscoe (Dr. Max), Hal Clements (Dr. Ed), Zella Caull (Charlotta), Carl Miller (Joe Drummond), George French (Schwitter), and Jean Bernoudy (Tillie), and a host of others. It has not yet been decided whether it will be marketed as one of her new independent releases or on the states rights plan.

* * *

That poverty comes high is proved by the setting for "Doing Her Bit," which Ruth Stonehouse is starring in, under the direction of Jack Conway. In this a block from a New York tenement district has been reproduced at the Triangle's Culver City studio at a cost of nearly $50,000. In "Doing Her Bit," Miss Stonehouse, the new Triangle star, is shown as the sister of a slacker, and as a result of her tireless effort not only the wayward brother, but many other war dodgers in the tenement district are imbued with a spirit of patriotism which carries them into the recruiting station and Uncle Sam's liberty army.

* * *

Film fans with a taste for the melodramatic will be able to get their fill of thrills and incidentally witness the screen debut of Roy Stewart as a star when the new Triangle actor's first picture, "The Devil Dodger," which just has been completed, is released.

Stewart appears in the role of a bad man of the worst type, who shoots from his hip and fears neither man, beast nor devil.

* * *

A good idea of the amount of money consumed in film alone in a modern motion picture plant may be gained from the following data furnished by Peter Shamray, laboratory manager of the former Triangle-Fine Arts plant, now the producing center of Triangle-Keystone comedies.

The Eastman company recently sent out a notice to the trade to the effect that they would be unable to ship film on account of the shortage of tin cans, brought about by the war, and urging all producing plants to return the empty containers they had on hand, for which a liberal price would be paid.

An inventory of the film cans in the Triangle-Keystone plant revealed the fact that, in a period of a little over two years, the Triangle-Fine Arts studios had used 8,142 cans of raw stock. Each can contains 2,000 feet of film, making a total of sixteen million, two hundred and eight-four feet. The cans, when crated, made twelve truck loads.

Until recently, the freight on empty cans to New York was more than the containers themselves were worth, but the price of tin has mounted so rapidly that at the present time the revenue on the empties effects a saving not to be scoffed at. What is more important than the monetary saving, however, is the insurance that the Triangle-Keystone studios will not be held up on account of inability to procure raw stock.

* * *

The Universal Nestor company, under the direction of Roy Clements, is filming a two-reel comedy at Universal City entitled "Trial Engagement." The principal roles are played by Eddie Lyons and Lee Moran, supported by Donna Drew.

* * *

Ida May Park is rapidly nearing the completion of a five-reel special feature production, "The Boss of Powderville," written by Thomas Addison and prepared for the screen by Miss Park. William Stowell plays the "Boss" and Dorothy Phillips has the star feminine role. Jack Mulhall plays the "juvenile." Lon Chaney and Alfred Allen also have important parts in the photoplay.

* * *

When Mae Murray, with her director, Robert Leonard, came to the Bluebird studios recently, Production Manager Henry McRae set about to secure for the celebrated star with the American Company for nearly four years before th best supporting cast available. For her leading man he was forunate in obtaining the services of Wheeler Oakman, who is one of the most popular of the younger lead men of the screen.

Oakman has built up an enviable reputation for himself during an engagement of more than two years with Kathlyn Williams at the Selig studios. He played the leading juvenile role in Selig's "The Rosary" and "The Spoilers," and was the principal player in "The Ne'er-Do-Well." More recently he has been playing opposite Mabel Normand.

Another well-known screen actor who has been engaged to support Miss Murray is Harry Von Meter, who had been with the American Company for nearly four years before joining the Bluebird players. He played the heavy lead in several of Mary Miles Minter's productions and was one of the featured players with Gail Kane in "Whose Wife?"

* * *

A one-reel comedy entitled "Out of the Bag," is being produced at Universal City under the direction of Al Santell. Harry Mann is the featured player.

* * *

Allen Curtis, director of Universal Joker comedies, is staging a new one-reel comedy, "Rain and Rascality." Gale Henry and William Franey, supported by Milburn Moranti, play the leading roles.

* * *

Rosemary Theby is to become a member of the Bluebird company, directed by Joseph De Grasse and playing opposite Franklyn Farnum. The first Bluebird in which Miss Theby will appear will be "The Winged Mystery." The stbry is by O. D. Stuart and it has been scenariozied by William Parker.

* * *

"The Twisted Soul" is the title of a five-reel photoplay production at Universal City by Director Allen J. Holubar. The featured role is played by Brownie Vernon. Others who have important roles are Frank Borsage, Murdock MacQuarrie and Joseph Girard. The story was written by Fred Myton and J. Grubb Alexander.

* * *

Director Stuart Paton is filming the fifteenth and final episode of the Universal serial, "The Gray Ghost," with Priscilla Dean, Eddie Polo, Harry Carter and Emory Johnson as his principal players. The serial was adapted for filming by Paton and Karl R. Coolidge, from the book, "Loot," written by Arthur Somers Roche.

* * *

With Louise Lovely as his featured player, Director Edward J. Le Saint is producing a five-reel drama entitled "The Wolf and His Mate." Supporting Miss Lovely are Hart Hoxie, Betty Schade, Hector Dion and George O'Dell. The story was written by Julia Maier and prepared for the screen by Doris Schroeder.

* * *

Ben Wilson and Neva Gerber are the principal players in the Universal serial, "The Phantom Ship," being produced at Universal City by Director Francis Ford. The company is filming the sixth episode at the present time.

* * *

Neva Gerber was operated upon for appendicitis at the Clara Barton Hospital, Los Angeles, on August 23. The operation was a success, but it will be at least a month before Miss Gerber will be in satisfactory condition for the resumption of her work and then only to play in scenes requiring but little effort on her part.

How Pictures Look to a Legionaire

Interesting Letter from Bennett Molter, Who Describes Exhibitions in Sound of the Guns.

BENNETT MOLTER, formerly of Metro's directing staff, the only moving picture man "at the front," who is an aviation pilot, will return soon to America to take his examinations for a commission. The American aviator was slightly injured recently in a fall which, however, had no power to lessen his enthusiasm for the service. Robert J. Huntington, at the Metro Studio, 3 West Sixty-first street, has just received a letter from Mr. Molter which proves conclusively that his enthusiasm for motion pictures has not lessened, either. Here are some interesting facts about the pictures shown to the men in the service abroad, quoted from Molter's letter to Huntington:

At the Front—Flanders.

My Dear Bob: I am back at it again, but not so strong as before my smash. Looking back, I sure was in luck. The British have a battery of heavy caliber guns near us, and have taken over an old barn in the village in which a regular motion picture show is given daily. It is run under the auspices of the British Expeditionary Forces Canteen Cinema Supply.

A charge of thirty centimes, 6 cents, is made for soldiers, and a franc for officers. They have a portable dynamo and projection machine, etc. And all the subjects are American. Can you beat it? Last night I had the pleasure of seeing the "M" in Metro tumble around, and the stars take their places, and then the Drews, in "At the Count of Ten." Sidney Drew got many laughs, especially when he repeatedly touched the money he succeeded in borrowing to his forehead, nose and lips. Believe me, Bob, it was a real treat for me to see the old faces again, to imagine big Bob Kurrie at the crank, Eddie Shulter running around back of the set, and maybe you looking on. It took me back to Sixty-first street for an hour or so. And all the time the picture was on we could hear the "boom, boom" of the cannonading. Metro is sure "At the Front."

The program is an all-comedy one, generally three single-reelers and then two two-reelers. They love the westerns, especially the trick stuff in chases, etc. A real picture would fall flat, because they don't want to have to think, but comedies give them something to laugh at and make them forget the hardships of the trenches. One day a week the civilians are allowed to attend the show, but on the others days, only troops. They begin the run at 6 o'clock and finish at 8—two hours; change the program twice a week, Sundays and Thursdays. On conversation with the lieutenant in charge, I find he pays $24 a week for this service, and his overhead for petrol, etc., is about the same, but he takes in from 750 to 1,000 francs a week. The balance above the expenses is used to finance new shows of a similar nature in other portions of the British front.

Gee, but I would like to be back in the good old U. S. A. That —— Drew picture has made me homesick. Regards to Cabanne and Pop and Billy. BEN.

HAL ROACH IN NEW YORK.

Hal Roach, director general of the Rolin Film Co., and the man who is personally in charge of the direction of Pathe's new Toto comedies and the well known "Lonesome Luke" and Harold Lloyd comedies, is now in New York on a business visit to the Pathe offices. Mr. Roach brought with him the second Toto comedy which was shown to the Pathe film committee. The report on it was to the effect that it easily ranks as one of the best laugh producers that has ever been made and that Toto is destined to be a great favorite.

Mr. Roach reports the engagement by Rolin of a number of new players, directors and technical men. The company has shown an uninterrupted and rapid growth from the time when its product was first placed upon the Pathe Program two years ago.

NEW GLADYS BROCKWELL CAST ANNOUNCED.

One of the finest companies of motion picture players that has been seen this year in a feature production is that which has been gathered together under the direction of Bertram Bracken for Gladys Brockwell's new William Fox drama.

In the cast are Eugenie Forde, Marjorie Daw, Harry Lonsdale, Douglass Gerrard, Edward Cecil, Colin Chase and Bert Grassby. Gerrard has acted in and directed many films; Lonsdale was with Mansfield in "Beau Brummel," with Nat Goodwin for five years, and with E. S. Willard for twelve; Edward Cecil and Grassby have been in several Fox plays.

Douglas Fairbanks Arrives on Broadway

Met by Reception Committee at Grand Central Station— Expresses His Delight at Being Back in Typical Fairbanks Style.

IN order to spend two days in New York for the production of a few scenes of his newest Artcraft picture, Douglas Fairbanks, accompanied by his players and technical staff crossed the continent from Los Angeles, arriving in Manhattan last Wednesday. With his famous smile in full play the energetic Douglas expressed his delight in being back among the tall buildings by performing a somersault over the tonneau of S. L. Rothapfel's car which awaited him, while the Universal Weekly cameraman, the Underwood & Underwood Syndicate Newspaper photographer and reporters recorded proceedings. Spying a New York copper the athletic once again leaped out of the car, hurdling over the rear end and with a shout, landing on the shoulders of the surprised copper. Grasping the wielder of the nightstick around the neck Douglas expressed his delight in seeing one of New York's finest in a no uncertain manner.

At the depot a reception committee of well known filmites awaited the arrival of Fairbanks and his company, including Al. Lichtman, general manager of Artcraft, S. L. Rothapfel, managing director of the Rialto theater, John Emerson, director-general of the Fairbanks forces, Emil Shauer of the Famous Players-Lasky offices, and Pete Schmid, of Artcraft.

The trip cross country proved a never-to-be-forgotten event for the popular Douglas. At San Bernardino one of the greatest crowds ever seen at the station greeted the Artcraft star and during the fifteen minute stop-over Douglas autographed articles ranging from the inside hat-band of a straw hat to the tongue of a tennis shoe. At Gallup, N. M., 200 school children presented the popular actor with an American flag which had been waving over their school house for fifteen years. At Alberqueque a troop of soldiers and a tribe of Indians gave him a rousing reception. Dodge City presented him with a gun that boasts of ten notches, formerly owned by Dick Crawford, the one time notorious bandit. Kansas City, Toledo, Cleveland and Chicago offered him similar receptions. Douglas was accompanied by John Fairbanks, Eileen Percy, Mrs. Douglas Fairbanks and Douglas, Jr., Victor Fleming, Bennie Zeidman, Joseph Henaberry, Millard Webb, Bill Shay, Keene Thompson, Edwin Tanake and Deliah Dowd. The party made the trip in a special car, which took them back to the Coast after a two day stay in New York.

R. A. WALSH TO DIRECT GEORGE WALSH.

Probably for the first time in screen history a motion picture director, R. A. Walsh, will direct his own brother, George Walsh, in a feature production. The film play is now in process of construction at the big William Fox studios in Hollywood, Cal. Unusual interest will attach to the production, of course, because of the alliance of the two Walshes on a single work.

George Walsh has appeared in an even dozen photoplays and R. A. Walsh has directed nine subjects for the Fox organization.

Both George and R. A. Walsh were born in New York City. The former attended Fordham and Georgetown Universities, while the latter holds a degree from Seton Hall College.

NORMA TALMADGE RETURNS TO NEW YORK.

Miss Norma Talmadge has returned to her own studio at 318 East 48th street to make the interiors of her new picture, "The Secret of the Storm Country." Ithaca, New York, witnessed in detail the filming of the rugged exteriors of this screen story, a sequel to Grace Miller White's "Tess of the Storm Country," which also appeared in film form. Miss Talmadge spent several weeks in Ithaca with her supporting cast. The entire company returned to New York early this week. Niles Welch and Helen Dahl will appear in her new picture.

W. T. KINSON WITH GENERAL AT PITTSBURGH.

A new manager for the General Film Company exchange at Pittsburgh is announced. He is W. T. Kinson, who was for two years the Mutual representative in Pittsburgh. Mr. Kinson has always had an excellent record in the motion picture distributing world and comes to his new position with excellent prospects for usefulness.

Among the Picture Theaters

Morelock Leases the Liberty

Will Open House on September 30 as High Class Photoplay Theater—Productions Booked to Determine Admission Prices—Reserved Seat Accommodation for Patrons.

A. E. MORELOCK, former owner and manager of the Pageant theater, Delmar avenue, St. Louis, Mo., has concluded a long-term lease on the Lorelei Building at Olive street and Taylor avenue, and will open it September 30 as a high-class motion picture theater. The Liberty has 1,600 seats, all on one floor, 250 being loge, or box, seats arranged in a unique manner on each side of the main cir-

Liberty Theater, St. Louis, Mo.

cle and raised to a position that puts them in a direct line of vision with the screen.

The interior decorations of the theater are in white and colored tile, the sides and ceilings being finished in lattice lacings of hardwood painted in old gold and white enamel. The lobby is especially striking, with solid marble wainscoting and ceramic tile floor. Mr. Morelock will operate the Liberty on a new policy of program, only one show being given in an evening. The doors will be opened at 7 p. m., but the regular performance will not begin until 8. The hour preceding the feature will be taken up by musical concerts, soloists, lectures, and slides of an educational nature. The regular program will last until 11.

Spacious Interior of Liberty Theater, St. Louis, Mo.

Only high-class features of the larger and better kind will be shown. Admission will be based on the strength and merits of the productions screened, and tickets will be sold on the reserved seat coupon plan, enabling patrons to reserve seats in advance by telephone or in the usual manner.

Mr. Morelock has had wide experience in all lines of amusement business. He entered the field in St. Louis in September, 1915, when he erected The Pageant, one of the biggest and best equipped theaters in the city. His new

house is in a fine location, being in a high-class residence and business district known as the West Side Rialto, at Delmar and Kings Highway. Mr. Morelock says he is in the market for productions that will stand a week's run or more, and will either rent outright or book on a percentage basis.

Princess Theater, Argenta, Ark.

On Front of House and Extending Across the Street Is Big Electric Sign Emblazoning Theater's Name—Letters Are Four Feet in Height—Managed by Louis Rosenbaum.

ARGENTA, located just across the river from its sister city, Little Rock, the capital of Arkansas, has one institution of which every one of its 15,000 inhabitants is proud. It is an amusement resort—the Princess theater—a strictly modern and fireproof structure, equal to any in the state. Louis Rosenbaum is the manager. Constructed at a cost of $15,000 and furnished in the most up to date theater furniture at no less expense than $7,500, the Princess is "nifty," cosy and and a really hand-

Princess Theater, Argenta, Ark.

some place of amusement. It is located on Main street on the busiest block in the city, between Second and Third streets.

The interior of the theater is striking. The walls are beautified with oil paintings and in the ceiling are six large domes with an indirect lighting system that in no way affects perfect pictures and at the same time make the theater light as day. A ventilating system that changes the air in the theater every three minutes has been installed, thereby making the auditorium a real airdome on the hottest summer day.

One Motiograph and one Power's 6B machine are used. A Wagner Transformer permits the use of direct current, and the Gold King screen leaves no room for improvement along these lines. Music is rendered by a $3,000 player piano.

A large electric sign with the word, "Princess," has been hung across the street. The letters are four feet high and 196 lights illuminate it so that it can be plainly seen for a distance of several blocks. Not only does the management believe in giving the patrons the best in theater furnishings, but also strives to furnish them with the best motion pictures on the market. Program is changed daily.

The Princess seats 650 persons. A balcony, seating 150, is provided for the negroes. That no part of the theater may present the appearance of anything but a comely playhouse, the same care in equipping the balcony was used as in the lower floor. The balcony and lower floor are supplied with twenty-two electric fans. The auditorium is steam heated. In fact, nothing has been overlooked to install everything that appertains to a first-class playhouse.

New Liberty Theater, Portland, Ore.

Jensen and von Herberg Transform Playhouse Into a Shrine of Photoplays and Music—Magnitude of Sumptuous Settings Elicits Unbounded Praise—Spacious and Luxurious Rest-rooms for All Patrons—Seats 2,100.

"THE grandest in the West"—thus Jensen and von Herberg characterise the latest acquisition to their already pretentious circuit of photoplay theaters. "The grandest in the West" is the Portland, Oregon, Liberty Theater, and the people of this City of Roses call it a shrine of photoplays, music, and allied arts.

And the Portland Liberty may be called a shrine, for, since its opening on July 17, patrons of photoplay have thronged its portals, and once within have reveled in its grandeur, effused over the magnitude of its sumptuous settings, and gloried in the fact that this photoplay palace has graced their city.

The motif—one usually speaks of decorations alone as having a motif, but with the Liberty it may be said that the

plays against the center lights and drops into the fountain's base where the goldfish swim. The floor of the inner lobby is carpeted in a rich gray, which color is also used on the stairway and ramp. The patron can enter the auditorium from this inner lobby either by going through the curtain hung entrances to the lower floor or by selecting the ramp or stairway to the balcony.

On the mezzanine floor is the reception room. The architecture of this room is of the Georgian period and it is handsomely and harmoniously furnished. Here the patron is impressed by the vista effect of heavy French mirrors showing through arbors of hanging flowers, reflecting latticed balconies and radiant color beyond the fancy of the most vivid imagination.

The walls of the auditorium are decorated with frescos from famous paintings, to which are added canvas reproductions of the work of the artist Fraganard. The general decorative color scheme harmonizes with the other fittings of the theater, of course, and is burnt orange, gray and black. The decorations, the settings, the effects, are the work of Percival Collins, of Seattle, under whose direction several

Exterior View of the New Liberty Theater, Portland, Ore.

Luxurious Reception Room at New Liberty Theatre, Portland, Ore.

whole theater casts a spell over the patron that seems to be impelled by a sensuous something to which that term may be properly applied. The motif of the Liberty, then, is from the Italian, tempered a bit with the atmosphere of rose-fragrant Portland, and ever spreading until, even beyond the ripple of the water falls symbolic of Oregon's great outdoors, the spectator is caught and held and thrilled by its witchery. Such is the motif.

On both sides of the velvet curtains of burnt orange which hide the screen are replicas of Oregon's famous water falls, Multnomah and
Bridal Veil.
Here water ripples in true outdoor fashion over miniature rocks and under fairy bridges.

To the left and to the right of the stage are the organ lofts where the notes from the big Wurlitzer Hope-Jones Unit Orchestra come forth from behind Italian Garden sets, vine hung pergolas and trellised balconies, replete with palms and floral decorations in most profuse varieties.

In the spacious inner lobby, the patron passes a fountain in sculpture, a reproduction of the Boy and Goose masterpiece by Verraccio. Here a stream of water constantly

other of the Jensen and von Herberg theaters have been decorated. A gentlemen's smoking room, provided with comfortable lounging chairs, has its entrance from the mezzanine floor.

The Portland Liberty is as perfect mechanically as it is artistically. The three stage curtains of burnt orange colored velvet, over 200 yards in area, are controlled by motors from the operating room. When the center curtain is down
hiding the
screen, the side
curtains are
drawn back, disclosing the cascading water
falls on each
side of the stage
set. Then when
the picture is to
be projected,
the center curtain parts and
the side curtains
close the wings.

The throw is
122 feet from
the operating
room on the
lower floor; and
a perfect picture is projected. The operator is in charge
of both stage
sets and projection. He has at
hand dimmers
for various purposes and myriads of colored
lights throughout the theater
are under his
control. The
front of the
Liberty is
graced with an
electrically
lighted replica

Interior of New Liberty Theater, Portland, Ore., Looking Toward Stage. Note the Beautiful Falls at Each Side of Curtain, and the Trellised Balconies Behind Which Are the Pipes of the Big Wurlitzer Hope-Jones Unit Orchestra.

of the goddess after which the theater is named. This stands above the elaborate marquee and shows for blocks up and down Portland's Broadway.

To those who have known the Liberty in the days when it was the Orpheum, Empress, T & D, and James' Broadway, mention of a few of the big changes might be of interest. The outside lobby has been shortened by perhaps 20 feet and the result is the magnificent inner lobby with the Boy and Goose fountain. The left hand stairway has been converted into a ramp leading to the balcony, the former loftlike mezzanine has been divided into rest rooms, the ceilings have been arched, and French mirrors have been fitted into the walls.

The old, big, gloomy auditorium has been made comfortable, cosy and cheerful by the removal of the theater boxes and the installation of Italian garden sets, balcony effects and rows of loges across the middle of the house. The new decorative scheme, frescos and hidden lights have added an inviting atmosphere that was formerly lacking.

found to be most desirable in a strictly high class moving picture house. Added to these are many innovations, so that the Madison stands out today as one of the most up to date theaters in the country.

The Madison seats 3,600 on the main floor and in the spacious balcony. Between the two elevations is a mezzanine —the architect calls it a well—for the convenience of those who come between shows and desire to sit around in comfort until the beginning of the next picture. The seating arrangement is such that the entire screen is in a direct line of vision from all parts of the house.

The decorative scheme of the Madison is from the Italian renaissance. Tapestry panels cover the walls, and a color scheme of green, gold and old ivory is carried out in every bit of work. The stage setting differs from all others. It is a complete dome, and the pillars and dome are colored with a combination of the three primal hues. Lighting effects are arranged at the top, bottom and sides, so that

Capacious Foyer of New Liberty Theater, Portland, Ore. Note the Boy and Goose Fountain in Center, Which is a Reproduction of the Original Sculpture by Verraccio.

The opening of the theater on the afternoon of July 17 was most auspicious. Shortly after the lunch hour, the crowd began to gather under the marquee and by two o'clock, the opening time, the people were lined up Broadway to Washington street. The performance began with a showing of the Statue of Liberty as the sun rises on New York harbor. The electrical effects were given full play while the short piece of film was being projected, and Oliver C. Wallace, at the organ, had his audience on its feet cheering. Then came the feature, "The Flame of the Yukon."

The Liberty is operated by the Liberty Theater Corporation, of which Jensen and von Herberg are the managing directors. J. G. von Herberg was personally present at the opening. The direct management of the theater is in the hands of E. J. Myrick, whose successful direction of the Portland Columbia has placed it in an enviable position among the Rose City's photoplay theaters.

The new Liberty is the sixth Jensen and von Herberg house on the Pacific Coast. It seats 2,100 and about $48,000 was expended making the alterations preliminary to its opening, a sum approximately $10,000 in excess of the first estimate. A newer and bigger Hope-Jones Wurlitzer is now being built for the theater, to be delivered in October.

Madison Theater, Detroit, Mich.

Kunsky's Magnificent Picture House the Embodiment of Everything Modern in Theater Construction, Architecture and Furnishings—Seats 3,600—Property Represents Investment of $500,000.

THE Madison, which is situated at Broadway and Grand Circus Park, Detroit, is a John H. Kunsky creation. The structure faces the park on Witherell street. The original plan called for an expenditure of $250,000, but when the doors were opened upward of $500,000 had gone into the property. Mr. Kunsky cast about a long time before he was able to secure the piece of land he wanted, and considering it the best of any possible location in the city, he built a theater which adds to Detroit's fame.

In the Madison is combined everything that has been

Interior of Madison Theater, Detroit, Showing Arrangement of Mezzanine Floor.

any desired effect can be produced—beautiful sunsets, winter scene, cold moonlights or the glare of the tropical sun.

The orchestra pit also is new, being in three elevations, similar to the concert arrangement, and in full view of the spectators. The pipe organ cost $50,000, and is probably the largest in any theater this side of New York.

The lighting arrangement is such that the house is never dark; that is to say, during the time it is open

A Section of the Mezzanine Floor, Madison Theater, Detroit.

to the public. The orchestra is under the direction of Eduard Werner, and the organist is Arthur H. J. Searle, of London. M. Harlan Starr, formerly of the Washington, is manager of the Madison.

Associated with Mr. Kunsky in this and other enterprises is George W. Trendle, corporation lawyer. The financial welfare of Mr. Kunsky's enterprises and many of the important business details have been consummated under his direction and with his advice.

The location of the Madison being most central, Mr. Kunsky has arranged for a continuous performance from 12 o'clock noon until 11 o'clock at night. The start of each of the set performances during those hours is at 12 o'clock, 2, 4, 5:45, 7:30 and 9:15 o'clock.

Music for the Picture

Conducted by CLARENCE E. SINN

Improvising (Part II)

IN ISSUE of July 28 (page 637) Moving Picture World, was shown an example of progression from one chord to another through means of one note held in common by both chords. Example 33 illustrates the tonic chord of C. and shows four other chords (or keys) each having a note which is contained in the chord of C. In the illustration (Ex. 33) the note in question is "C" which—as shown—is also contained in the chords of A minor, F major and the dominant 7th of the key of G major. (This note "C" is also found in the chords of F minor and the dominant 7th of the key of G minor.) A sort of relationship is thus established between the chord of C and other chords containing the note "C."

Observe the two other notes in the chord of C ("E" and "G"). Each one of these notes may be found in other chords beside the chord of C. Example 34 shows three

Key of G. Key of E♭ Key of D.

Key of A. Key of E. Key of B.

Ex. 34.

chords (besides the C chord) containing the note "G," and three containing the note "E."

These notes in the chord of C (viz.: "C", "E" and "G") being also found in chords of other keys, establish a more or less close relationship with those other keys. Examples 33 and 34 illustrate simple and natural progressions from the chord of C to the following keys.

Through the note "G;" Key of G, key of E-flat and key of D (through dominant 7th of key of D).

Through the note "E;" Key of A, key of E.

Trough the note "C;" Key of A minor, key of F major, key of A-flat major and key of G (through dominant 7th).

In the last measure of example 34 we find a progression from key of C to the key of B natural. In all previous examples in modulating from one key to another I have endeavored to give preference to modulation through dominant 7th's. That is, when using an intervening chord between. From the key of C to that of B natural is a half tone progression downward. Descending chords by halftones is difficult. In an earlier article a table was shown giving one means of this progression. To go directly to the dominant 7th of B natural from the chord of C makes too great a contrast to give pleasant results. I have used instead another chord as a pivot in modulating from C to B

Harsh; unpleasant.   A little better.

Ex. 35.

natural. For this particular progression (downward in halftones) one will find it preferable to use two or more intervening chords.

In Ex. 35 I have shown the progression (pivoting on the

note "E") from the chord of "C" to the dominant 7th of B natural. Next, from the chord of "C" to another chord (augmented 6th) to key of B natural. The two examples in the lower part of Ex. 35 show progressions through two intervening chords—all pivoting upon the note 'E.'

The Garden of Allah.

E. James, Chicago, writes: "Can you kindly give me any information regarding the exquisite incidental music to the 'Garden of Allah' (Selig Special)?"

The music incidental to this artistic Selig production was compiled by Mr. Harry Alford of Chicago, Illinois. A great part of the music is original with Mr. Alford, and was composed by him especially for this picture. Mr. Alford conducts a bureau for arranging, copying and composing music, and is the best equipped for work of this sort of any man in the west. He has made musical settings and orchestral scores for a number of special pictures, among them the "Garden of Allah." Numerous inquiries similar to the one above have been received concerning this picture, and the writers will please consider this an answer to all.

New Picture Music.

Mr. Joseph Carl Breil, the man who composed and compiled the music for "The Birth of a Nation," has, through Chappell & Co., Ltd., issued a brand new collection of incidental music for use in playing for the picture. This collection contains twelve original numbers presented in a novel form. Nine of these numbers are divided into parts marked "A," "B," and "C." Each of these lettered themes is complete in itself, yet related to the others. The idea being that a chosen theme can be amplified or carried to its logical conclusion through one or both of the succeeding themes. For example, No. 7, is arranged in this manner:

1 (A)—To depict a conspiracy or burglary with (B) consequent tumult or escape.

2 (A)—A dismal forest or desert scene with (B) pursuit by wild beasts or bandits.

3 (A)—An approaching storm and (B), its unleashing.

A dainty little conceit is No. 10, opening with a recitative in which the music seems to ask a question. It is divided thus:

"The question" (A) a doubtful or embarrassing moment followed by (B) threat, decision or resolution.

Mr. Breil has a number of other good things to his credit, having compiled and composed the incidental music to "Intolerance," and other pictures; has composed the music to the opera "The Legend" (anew work), and will be best remembered as composer of the music to the playlet, "The Climax," a success of some years ago. His song, "The Climax," is still a popular number among the better class of soprani.

NEW THEATER AT RADFORD, VA.

The new Colonial Theater at Radford, Va., is nearing completion and will open Oct. 10 with the "Birth of a Nation." The new house will have a seating capacity of about seven hundred. It will be a decided credit to a city of five thousand population. The management will offer both pictures and legitimate, keeping open all the time with pictures when other shows are not booked. The city has been without a large house for years and is looking forward to the opening. It will be run under the management of Painter and Lane.

ALMA RUEBEN IN "THE FIREFLY OF TOUGH LUCK."

Alma Rueben, whose beauty and finished delineations have attracted remark from critics and fans, will from henceforth be featured in Triangle plays, the first one selected for her being "The Firefly of Tough Luck," in which Walt Whitman, the veteran character actor, will also have a leading part.

British Notes

D. W. GRIFFITH shortly intends to revive "The Birth of a Nation" for another season at Drury Lane Theater. Since its introduction to British audiences two years ago its progress from London, around the leading provincial theaters, then back to London, has been rather slow but of undoubted certainty. Particularly in Lancashire, Yorkshire, the Tyneside and Scotland has the Clansman story developed into a prime favorite, and repeated runs have been the rule rather than the exception. Now, while "The Birth of a Nation" is to reappear at the national theater, its successor, "Intolerance," commences its first provincial tour.

* * *

The Fox superfilm, "A Daughter of the Gods," was also launched upon an extensive provincial and suburban tour last week, after a short season at the London Opera House (now known as the Stoll Picture Theater). At its first engagement at the Royal Artillery Theater, Woolwich, it proved a refreshing attraction to the munition makers.

A growing complaint against imported picture plays from America is of hustle. In one or two recent productions I could name to such a noticeable degree is the action of the story speeded up that only the discretion of the operator could save the situation. It is an axiom of the successful film maker that the photoplay must be the embodiment of life and movement, but at the same time a picture play that reflects things in an unnatural manner fails in its purpose. A Wardour street exchange manager advises me that he received a subject a few weeks ago keyed up in action to such a pitch that when projected below the normal speed it was converted from first-class drama into third-rate slapstick. He overcame the speed difficulty by judicious padding.

A celebrity in any sphere of art or industry who has never seen a film exhibition must be relegated to the plane of the dodo, both in rarity and ideas. Such, however, is the proud boast of a well-known concert vocalist who attended a kinema for the first time the other day. The film shown was Essanay's "Burning the Candle," starring Henry B. Walthall. After the show the famous singer admitted to a group of copy-thirsty pressmen being agreeably surprised to find an entire absence of flicker and ventured the opinion that the average line of posters outside kinema shows did the films rather less than justice. Rather singularly the celebrated singer complained of hustle in the picture. "It struck me very much that there was too much hurry about it. Over and over again I wanted longer to study the facial expression of the characters. Walthall has a particularly mobile face, and it was annoying when one was watching its changes of expression to find the film switching off suddenly to another incident. There was not enough use of the dramatic pause to enable one to study the thoughts of the characters. The heroine was treated with the same brusqueness, just a fleeting glance of her changes of expression. I wanted more time to take it in."

* * *

Joseph R. Darling, of the Fox Film Corporation, left London last week-end for South America. He anticipates returning to London via New York at the end of the year.

* * *

Censor Films is the name of a new renting exchange that has opened at 101 Wardour street and will work southern territory upon several first-class exclusives, notably "The Fall of a Nation," "The Witching Hour," and "God's Man," in addition to productions of the Frohman Corporation. The new undertaking is identified with Bolton-Stewart's International Pictures and will act as agents for that firm in London and district.

* * *

The short career of the only registered trade union of the industry, the Kinematograph Exhibitors' Association, is already becoming schismatic. A number of exhibitors in the northern provinces have, one can not say other than indiscreetly, abandoned the exhibitors' association in favor of a rival association, the Provincial Entertainment Proprietors and Managers' Association. I asked one well-known exhibitor his reason for breaking away from the old association. He replied that there was considerable dissatisfaction among provincial members with the policy of the general council of the exhibitors' association. The provinces are dominated too much from London, he alleged, and the interests of northern exhibitors are subservient to those in the metropolis and the south. Two other exhibitors opined that recent attitudes of the exhibitors' association on questions affecting their welfare were passive or even dormant, and this view generally summarises the complaint of the wayward ones. Nevertheless, the breach is an unfortunate one, occurring at the commencement of a new phase in the career of an association better organised, better fitted, and better able to serve the exhibitors' interests than ever before. To abandon a ship before there is any probability of it sinking and after acting as guarantors for its passage is decidedly not playing the game.

* * *

John D. Walker (Walker's World Films) has secured another feather for his cap in the capture for the British market of the Arbuckle (Fatty) comedies. The first of the new series, entitled "The Butcher Boy," will be shown to the trade within the course of a few days.

* * *

D. W. Griffith has been scouring the countryside on the outskirts of Greater London in search of prospective locations for dramatic subjects. The belief held by American producers that production in Great Britain is handicapped by the climate and inferior lighting is entirely a myth, says "D. W. G."

* * *

It is not unlikely that a new edict about to be issued by the Railway Executive Committee, the joint board of control of British railroad companies, will give the kinema theater business a decided impetus at the expense of the legitimate theater. Touring theatrical companies after September will not be allowed to travel with scenery and effects and artists will be allowed to travel on Fridays only. No discrimination is made between the barnstorming fraternity and royal opera. While this may not cause any appreciable difference in London, its effect in the provinces can be imagined, for by far the majority of the companies on the road, whether revues, music-hall sketches, musical shows, or melodrama, deprived of their own special scenic effects, would be shorn of half their attractiveness. Sunday is the present general day for theatrical companies on tour to make the change over from one theater to another. In the height of the pantomime season close upon a thousand such changes are made, involving as many journeys from one town to another, very often long distances. The substitution of Friday for Sunday will do away with the Saturday matinee at most theaters, in addition to the loss of one business day. The proposed regulations are naturally meeting with strenuous opposition from the theatrical associations.

* * *

It is expected that the funds of the British American Overseas Ambulance will benefit considerably from a charity matinee at the West End Kinema Tuesday, Aug. 7. The kinema will be open all day free. Whether visitors will get out free is, of course, another matter.

* * *

The London Film Company has not been particularly active at its Twickenham studio since G. L. Tucker finished "The Manxman." Now, however, another W. W. Jacobs comedy is well under way, as that master of nautical satire and dialogue would say. The title is "The Persecution of Bob Pretty" and the length only one reel.

* * *

Additional regulations will shortly be drafted into operation governing the importation of films into France. Although a film dealer may procure a license from the War Department allowing him to export films to France, it will be necessary for the purchaser of the films to have an import license before they can be admitted into that country. Any American firm likely to be affected can obtain full information from the department of the Minister of Commerce, Paris.

J. B. SUTCLIFFE.

UNFAIR COMPETITION SQUELCHED.

The William Abrahamson Theater Company of Duluth, Minn., haled the members of the Brunswick Theater Company of the same city into court the other day on the charge of unfair competitive methods in that the latter company placed misleading advertising in the local newspapers. An injunction was asked and secured from a local justice which remedied the evil complained of. The Abrahamson company had advertised the picture entitled "The Slacker" for two weeks when the Brunswick company came out with large advertisements for the "The Man Who Was Afraid" in which the words "The Slacker" were most prominent. The court ruled that the Brunswick had no right to the use of the words "The Slacker."

Motion Picture Educator

Conducted by REV. W. H. JACKSON and MARGARET I. MACDONALD

Interesting Educationals

Four Travel Subjects, One Zoological, Four Topical, One Economic, One Forestry, One Agricultural, One Industrial, and One Art Subject.

Reviewed by Margaret I. Macdonald.

Glacier National Park (Pathe).

BELONGING to the Pathe series, entitled "Our National Parks," this number does its delightful best to exploit for our benefit the beauties of Glacier National Park. While but half a reel is given over to scenes in this beautiful stretch of mountains and ice and snow, this half reel is tremendously convincing. Many of the scenes contained in the picture are in the vicinity of Triple Divide Mountain. Close-up views of the mountains give us an insight into what Nature does when she dresses them in snow. The last half of the reel is devoted to Japanese Gardens, which are presented in all the glory of color photography. Through this latter subject we get a thorough idea of the horticultural skill of the Japanese.

"The Snows of Many Years" (Educational).

Scenes photographed on and in the vicinity of Eliot Glacier give us an excellent idea of "The Snows of Many Years." There, as the fearless mountain climbers traverse the dangerous wastes of ice and snow which comprise the glacier, we are treated to close-up views which show us the layers of ice and snow representing passage of the years. Very fantastical, too, is this beautiful field of ice in the mountain tops, with its crevasses worn by mountain streams, and its grottos and queer-shaped spears of eternal ice. The picture is one of the Bruce series, but not one of recent release.

"In the Hanging Glacier Country" (Educational).

Isella Glacier and vicinity is the spot to which we owe the beauty of this picture, which shows us Railroad Creek, the Mary Green Cabin, and other interesting sights of mountain travel before we finally ascend with the cameraman and his party to where this great mass of ice which moves at the rate of about 400 feet per year still holds its equilibrium. One thousand feet below the glacier is Horton Lake, into which great pieces of the glacier are seen to drop in the months of August and September. This is an enjoyable scenic number which will appeal to the adventurously inclined.

"In Hong Kong" (Paramount-Holmes).

In one of his journeys in the Orient Burton Holmes visits the wonderful Chinese city of Hong Kong. Hong Kong, he explains to us, is one of the most important commercial ports of the world, and one of the most beautifully located, rising as it does from the water's edge and dominated by "The Peak," that lovely suburb in the clouds, its park and residential sections forming an abiding place for the vast European colony of Hong Kong. Hong Kong is an island, and the name of the actual city is Victoria, we are told; and we are given a glimpse of "The Peak" and of other interesting points about the city. A view of the port, and of the busy streets with its throngs of busy people are all interesting sights.

"Nature's Perfect Thread Spinner" (Edison).

One of the clearest illustrations of how the silk worm spins its 1,000 yards of beautiful silk thread per cocoon will be found in the Edison Conquest Program No. 6. In this illustration we are privileged to watch the spinner at close range enclosing itself in a dextrously-fashioned silken enclosure. The substance from which this cocoon is made comes from two glands in the mouth of the silk worm. We are also shown what appears to be an X-ray of the cocoon after the worm has spun itself in, and later we see a beautiful white moth emerge from the cocoon. This moth lays 200 eggs and then dies. The young silk worms hatching from the eggs and feeding on the leaves of the mulberry tree are also shown.

U. S. Government Weather Bureau (World-Selig).

The instruments that the Government uses in forecasting the weather are shown at the beginning of World-Selig Library No. 16. The barometer, the anemometer which measures the velocity of the wind, and weather vanes that record electrically are shown. The instruments are not photographed so as to be instructive. The views are as so many "stills," even though some of the instruments are in motion.

"Saving the Babies" (Universal).

In No. 37 of the Screen Magazine will be found some interesting views taken in one of the several hundred health stations maintained by the New York Department of Health. Here we learn that the pedigree of each baby is taken when it is first brought in. They are weighed and examined each time they are brought to the station, and their progress is carefully noted. Milk in proper ratio to the age and condition of the baby is given out each day. The picture contains some interesting and healthy looking specimens of babyhood as a result of careful feeding and proper care.

"Handling the Mail, No. 2" (Mutual-Gaumont).

In Reel Life No. 71 will be found the second instalment of "Handling the Mail." This time we are shown in detail just what happens to parcels which we have weighed, stamped, and handed in at the post office for safe transportation to their destinations. This also includes the customs department, where all foreign parcels are opened, the contents valued, and the packages resealed. Following this cards are sent to the owners of the parcels apprising them of their whereabouts and amount of duty due. The postal order and postal savings departments are also explained in detail.

"Making a Merchant Marine Officer" (Pathe-International).

The pictures contained in "The Making of a Marine Officer" were photographed aboard the training ship "Newport" and show the boys learning the art of seamanship. A few excellent scenes show them climbing up ratlines. The "man overboard" drill is also interesting.

"Canning Corn" (Universal).

At a time when the necessity for food conservation is so great, a public demonstration of even one method of accomplishing this is of great value. The Screen Magazine No. 37 contains such a demonstration, teaching the thousands of women who view this number how to can corn for use in the winter months. In the first place, according to the picture, the ears of corn are subjected to a blanching method, after which they are dipped in water at a temperature of 50 degrees. The corn is then cut from the cobs with a sharp knife and put at once in hot jars, after which a level teaspoonful of sugar or salt is added, and the jars filled with boiling water. The jars are then placed in a covered tin receptacle and cooked for three hours after the water begins to boil. The scenes of this picture are presented by courtesy of the United States Department of Agriculture.

"Tree Planting in Our National Forests" (Mutual-Gaumont).

Comparatively few in an audience know anything about the manner in which the regeneration of our national forests is conducted. This they can learn from a series of scenes on the subject included in Reel Life No. 72. Here we are shown the barren wastes of charred timber which result from the great forest fires that from time to time ravage the forest growth of many years. We learn that the pine cones are dislodged by careful hands from their hiding places under leaves and hollow logs and are broken up, then sifted through a sieve. In this way the seeds of the pine tree are obtained and are furthermore put through a machine for the removal of the chaff before planting them in shallow beds, which are then carefully covered by wire screens. When the plants are two inches high the screens are lifted, and some time later they are removed from these beds, their roots trimmed, and transplanted. When they are two years old they are ready for shipping. Views of planted territory with the young trees well under are also shown. This picture is unusually instructive and interesting.

Harvesting Wheat (World-Selig).

The magnitude of a 25,000-acre wheat field in North Dakota can be appreciated by seeing World Selig Library No. 16. A threshing machine that handles 2,000 bushels a day and tractors at different jobs are shown. The plowing of eight furrows at once is one of the views. The grain is followed to market as far as the grain elevators, the operation of which is shown. This is an instructive picture.

"Goat Ranching in America" (Paramount-Bray).

In the eighty-third release of the Pictograph we learn more than most of us ordinarily know about goats. We learn that great ranches of these animals are kept in America for the purpose of supplying the large amount of goat's milk which the demand requires. Goat milk, which is supposed to contain no tuberculosis germs, is fed to babies with good results. It is also used in the manufacture of certain kinds of cheese. We are shown a herd of goats grazing contentedly on sage brush, and are told that cattle would starve on pasturage on which goats thrive. It costs 5 cents a day to feed a goat which yields five quarts of milk per day.

"Art in Bookbinding" (Paramount-Bray).

In the eighty-third release of the Pictograph will be found some wonderfully interesting and well-illustrated details regarding the art of bookbinding in its finer forms. The renovation of old manuscripts calls for skilled workmanship, and we are allowed to gaze familiarly at the busy hands of selected workers as they remove the dust of ages, resew, recover and regild priceless volumes. The only person in the world who can bind a book entirely by herself is presented to us. This turns out to be a young lady of artistic bent, who has charge of one of the costliest private libraries in the world. One marvels at her skill, especially in the finer work of fixing, with tools for the purpose, designs of ancient pattern on volumes of fabulous value.

Another "Romeo and Juliet"

This Time the Souls of the Shakespearian Lovers Will Saunter Forth Enveloped in Animated Clay.

SOME of our readers no doubt will be familiar with the artistic animated clay work, or statuette cartoons, made by Helena Smith Dayton. These have followed different lines from scenes and individual figures in metropolitan life to the fads of the wealthy. Wonderfully clever have been the efforts of this artist to instil the soul of an idea into the lifeless substance of clay.

It is interesting to note that by way of novelty and also abeyance to the artistic spirit of the thing, the S. S. Film Company are producing a series of animated clay figure pictures, the first of which will be the Shakespearean play, "Romeo and Juliet," with Mrs. Dayton as the artist. We understand that the greatest possible pains have been taken to make a faithful version of the play. All the sets are specially built and are said to be as correct as the sets used in any stage production of the same play. The costuming of the clay figures will also be historically correct.

It is expected that the picture will be handled by the Educational Films Corporation of America, 729 7th Avenue.

A Patriotic Comedy

The Sydney Drews Concoct a Patriotic One-Reeler Which, Comic Though It Is, Hits the Nail of Common Sense Square on the Head.

Reviewed by Margaret I. Macdonald.

THE "Patriot" is the title of a comedy which features the inimitable Mr. and Mrs. Sydney Drew, and which was written by them. The picture is, of course, in one reel, as are all of the Metro-Drew comedies, and has been made with an eye to fitting the present situation. The plot centers about the food conservation problem, making Mandy, the colored cook of Mr. and Mrs. Henry of the play, one of the chief exponents of this thing which has by force of circumstance become one of the cardinal virtues.

As the story of the picture runs, Mr. and Mrs. Henry, who are fond of good living, have become ardent patriots. In the first year of their married life they have had some fifty-seven cooks, all of whom were temperamental; but at last an angel has been sent them in the shape of Mandy, who caters religiously to their appetites. Mandy's first jolt from the patriotic side comes one day when she finds in the ice box the chicken, which she has carefully prepared and sat up four hours the night before to serve as a part of a late supper to her master and mistress on their return from a patriotic ball. At this point Mandy's education has begun, and

at last, to the delight of Mr. and Mrs. Henry, Mandy not only has become a full-fledged food conservationist herself, but has educated all the cooks in the block, and has seen to it that Mrs. Henry wears the badge of honor also.

The picture will make an excellent comic number for a patriotic program, for, in spite of its comedy, it carries a real lesson.

Lesson in Advertising

Edison Conquest No. 6 Contains a Four-Reel Feature in Which Will Be Found a Wholesome Lesson in the Business of Honest Advertising.

THE Customary Two Weeks" is a four-reeler of merit appearing on No. 6 of the Edison Conquest Programs, which are being leased through the K-E-S-E. The excellent lesson in honest advertising methods which it contains prompts a special notice for the production as one based on fine wholesome principles, and one which is of special value for exhibition before boys and young men. The manly spirit of the hero as pitted against the baser principles of his opponent is an inspiration for good.

The production pictures a conflict between two young men which has arisen through the championing by our hero of the cause of an old employee of the firm. The affair leads indirectly to the hero of the story losing his position, after which he has a desperate time to gain another. Finally, when he has been given an opportunity with another big firm in the capacity of traveling salesman, he is sent, after having made good in a small way, to land a million-dollar order. His old enemy, representing the firm for which he had worked previously, becomes his competitor for the order, proceeds to knock the goods of every other firm in the market, and loses out thereby. The hero of the story wins by opposite legitimate methods of presenting his goods. A love thread running through the story adds to its interest.

E. W. Hammons Drives More Nails

For the Success of the Educational Films Corporation of America—Corrals Ditmar's Negatives and Lassoes the Latest in Cartoonists.

IT was necessary to chat a while with E. W. Hammons, vice president of the Educational Films Corporation of America, to get a look in at the real facts of the case; in other words, to find out just the latest triumph of this progressive organization. There were only a couple of choice bits at the time with other important matters in a state of crystallization, not yet to be spoken about.

We all know, of course, that the Raymond L. Ditmars series of animal pictures known as "The Living Book of Nature" have for more than a year been distributed exclusively by the Educational Films Corporation of America. Readers will be glad to learn that the contract of this corporation with Mr. Ditmars has been renewed for a period of five years. And in addition to this the control of the Ditmars negatives has been ceded to them for the same period with an increase in the number of prints to be supplied.

The Educational Films Corporation of America has also been quick to make negotiations with a couple of young cartoonists, B. E. and V. I. Whitman, an exhibition of whose work at the Rialto theater, New York City, a short time ago caused considerable furore. Cartoon subjects by these young artists will hereafter be affixed to certain educationals released by the Educational Films Corporation of America.

Merger of Viewpoints

Purpose of Conference to Be Held at Scudder School, at Which National Board of Review Will Listen to What Producers Have to Say.

THE Review Committee of the National Board is formulating plans for a series of round-table conferences in co-operation with the Scudder School, 72d street and Riverside Drive, New York. The purpose of the conferences will be to secure for the members of the National Board a clearer comprehension of the point of view of the makers of motion pictures. Some of the leading motion picture directors are expected to address the conferences, and it is hoped that a more complete understanding of their work by the National Board will result. Such conferences will also furnish an opportunity to demonstrate to the directors what, in the estimation of the National Board, a "better film" consists of or does not consist of, as the case may be. It is hoped that the producing directors will come to see that the Better Films Movement is not a movement for educational pictures, but, on the contrary, one looking to the production of the highest types of film entertainments.

Advertising for Exhibitors

Conducted by EPES WINTHROP SARGENT

An Exhibitor's Catechism.

SOMEONE on the staff of the Moving Picture Weekly, the Universal's house organ, has prepared a series of questions to be asked of himself by the exhibitor. They are worth reprinting in case you passed them over the first time. Here they are:

What causes the crowd to pass my theater up in favor of my opposition?

Am I showing the right kind of pictures?

Am I doing the right kind of advertising?

Am I fighting hard enough to get business?

What do I do to hold on to business when I do get it?

Are my business methods such as to win friends for me?

Have I been successful in making friends of my patrons?

Is my personality a liability or an asset?

Have I been sufficiently attentive to my customers?

What kind of employees are on my payroll?

Are they helping me, or are they hindering me in my effort to make my theater a paying investment?

Is my theater the kind of a place I would allow my own children to attend?

Does it present an inviting appearance, both inside and out?

Is the ventilation everything it should be?

Is it comfortable both winter and summer?

Is it kept in spotless condition?

Have I paid sufficient attention to the musical end of my shows? Or are my musicians the "don't-give-a-darn" variety who play ragtime stuff during intensely dramatic scenes, and "Hearts and Flowers" during comedy pictures?

What is the condition of the films I show?

Am I saving at the spigot and wasting at the bunghole by getting old stuff that costs me little—and that pleases my patrons about as much as it costs?

What have I done to make my theater one of the community's social centers?

Am I a member of the local merchants' organization?

Have I ever attempted to get the local merchants to co-operate with me for mutual benefit?

What have I done to get such special business as various social, fraternal and religious organizations could be made to yield?

Am I paying more for my pictures than the seating capacity of my house warrants?

Am I charging the proper admission price?

Is it too high? Too low?

Have such big special features that have cost me higher prices brought me as much business as regular program features bring?

Did they please my patrons as much?

What percentage of my trade comes from the immediate vicinity?

What percentage comes from outside the community?

What am I doing to attract the latter class?

To what extent is my opposition cutting into my trade?

Why should people who would find it mere convenient to patronize me attend my opposition?

Are my patrons satisfied with the shows I am presenting?

Have I ever taken such steps as would enable me to know accurately my patrons' likes and dislikes?

Would it be worth my while to offer little prizes for suggestions that would help me make my theater more popular?

Do I keep a set of books, so that I may know at all times exactly where I stand?

Where do I stand?

Am I in the business best suited to my peculiar talents?

Would I do better in some other line?

What are the prevailing conditions in this community?

What is the outlook for the next year?

Is the community going back? Is it progressing?

Is the location of the house against me?

Is there any way in which the handicap of location can be overcome?

Are my cashier and ticket taker courteous and reliable?

Which pictures, according to my box office receipts, have brought me the most money?

Which brand yields the poorest receipts?

Which players, according to the same authority, are most popular with my patrons?

What am I doing to build up my matinees?

Am I exerting any effort to make Saturday mornings productive by presenting special children's performances?

Is my projection all that it should be?

Are my projection machines up to date?

Is my operator the right man for the job?

Is my screen suited to the peculiar requirements of my theater?

Which are my best days?

Which are my poorest days?

Why?

What can I do to build up my attendance on these days?

Have I given the business as much of my personal attention as it deserves?

Have my personal habits injured my theater to any extent?

How many of these questions can you honestly answer in a way that will be satisfactory to yourself? Of course if you can answer the first question by saying that you are really getting the opposition's business, then you do not have to worry, but if you feel that you are not getting all the available business, run down the list. Answer the questions intelligently. For example one asks if the big special features bring as much as a regular service. Don't merely look at your books and find that you took in an extra hundred or so on the day. Look back and forward. See if people held back for the feature. See if receipts increased or diminished following the big show. You cannot say that you made an extra hundred if you find that the big show killed your regular business two hundred dollars. In such a case you lost one hundred dollars instead of gaining that sum.

Look at the question of what business you are getting outside your territory. It is no great credit to you to bring in the patron from next door or three blocks down. Any dub should be able to do that. But can you make your house so pleasant that patrons seek your house in preference to that of your opposition? This does not necessarily mean a bigger house or even a better house. It does mean a better run house. It does mean that you can answer to your satisfaction questions about your help, your projection, your program and your advertising. It doesn't mean buying a few pots of artificial flowers or an electric fountain for the foyer. It does mean making the house cordial and restful. Have it smell clean and sweet, with the cleanliness of soap and water and not the sweetness of some powerful disinfectant masked by an artificial scent. Don't cover up your dirt. Sweep it out. Don't mask your vitiated air. Sweep it out. And along with it sweep out the discourteous usher or the grouchy doorkeeper.

And ponder long and seriously that question as to your personal habits. Do you smoke cigars—possibly bad ones—all over the house, either before or during the performance? Have you the common trick of grabbing people by the arm to shove them around instead of directing them with a gesture? We know of one house where the women patrons complain that the manager gets their light dresses dirty by grabbing their arms in the dark to lead them to the aisles. We have seen the handprints on white dress sleeves. The manager is merely eager to give the fullest service, but he grabs his patrons with his unwashed hands instead of putting in a couple of indirect lights to enable patrons to make their own progress to the aisles. Women cannot make a scene, but they can, and many of them do, avoid a repetition of the annoyance.

If you can answer all these questions to your own satisfaction and still are not making money, answer them to someone else and see if they are convinced. That may be the trouble. You are not trying to please yourself in the conduct of your house. They count—you don't count. You are there to please your patrons. They count—even the smallest tot with the plugged nickel counts for more than your whims and fancies. Whoever wrote that article for the Universal seems to know the game. The result has been worth while.

Precisely.

We lift this from Paramount Progress because it is so close to the secret of success:

When you get right down to the beef and beans of life, it's the fellow that does a little hard work, a little hard thinking, a little planning, and carries it out that makes the big success in life.

Picture theaters are no longer automatic money-making machines. You must work for your money, and the harder you work, the more you can make, if you direct your efforts in the proper direction, but there must be direction. A dog chasing a cat is doing more than a puppy chasing its own tail, and advertising is precisely like the picture theater. It is not an automatic money-maker. It must be good advertising.

For Your Program.

We like this line from the Stillman program. It will serve to run on any news weekly.

If you've failed to read the newspapers—no matter. The latest news is here and you're right by while it happens.

It would be difficult to express it more neatly than that. Too many exhibitors fail to realize what a business-builder the news weekly can be made if they use a recent date. Thirty day stuff is no longer news; it's history.

An Avant Courier.

The scheme of using an advance card is not new to traveling men, but not many film men seem to use the scheme. Maurice M. Davis, of the General Film, of Canada, sends in the post card he sends in advance

of his coming. It is well drawn, but his name appears only on the aeroplane and in letters only about 1/32 of an inch in height, which will confuse new prospects. It would be better to print the name larger and clearly and to use in place of the "I will be dropping in your town very soon," "about" instead of "very soon." Then the approximate date can be filled in.

Letting Others Help.

A couple of years ago several exhibitors brought in dealers to work with them on a double page display for Shoes. The idea was widely exploded at that time, but so far but a single exhibitor, The Hip, Phoenix, Arizona, has seen that Skinner's Dress Suit gives as good a chance at the clothing dealers. The house got four tailors and a shoe store to come in with it on a double middle page in the daily paper. All of the clothing ads hinged on the luck the dress suit brought Skinner and the shoe man added that shoes are necessary to make a smart costume complete. Here was a chance thrown away, and yet there are scores of chances to do the merchants a good turn while helping them to help you advertise your attraction. Trade advertising that is coupled with amusement advertising always pulls better, and here was a fine chance for anyone—and only one man in Arizona seems to have seen that opportunity. This cut can do little more than

give a general idea, but paste it above your desk and watch for the next chance if you have already booked with Skinner.

Brief but Efficient.

The Circle, Washington, D. C., uses a small four pager, the pages three by six inches, but they make good use of this rather limited space and do just as much as they could on a five by seven. They use the same copy but hold down the type sizes, getting the same relative display. This is possible because they print in a shop provided with display faces in the smaller sizes. In the latest example a couple of the compartments are a bit crowded, but the general effect is good and the program is efficient. The back page is held for house talk. The entire page is not filled, but runs about one-half of the space. This

gives the patron the suggestion that he is not asked to read too much, and on a small program the device is good. On a larger size it is better to set double column and fill the page, breaking up the paragraphs, but for a small space, the single column and the partly filled page form a better combination. They handle the matter of varying prices very nicely. Perhaps this clip will help others:

It has ever been our slogan to show a Program that was "Consistently good," and with this object in view we have spared neither trouble nor expense to secure the best obtainable pictures. Our regular price of admission is 10c., but occasionally, on stated evenings, the price of admission to the CIRCLE will be 15c. This increase in the price of admission when BIG PICTURES or POPULAR STARS are shown is not actuated by any desire on our part to take advantage of your eagerness to see the best pictures. It is dictated by necessity. The explanation of this necessity lies in the fact that film actors and actresses who become popular favorites realize their drawing power and demand fabulous salaries. In turn film producers demand high rental for the films and the exhibitor is thus constrained to increase the price of admission.

The best way to explain the increased price is to tell the truth. It's all right to say that this or that feature is so much bigger than the average that it is worth more, but when you say that you must charge more because there is an increase all along the line, starting with the star's salary, then you have a concrete argument that you can prove. People cannot see why they should pay more merely because a picture is better. They can understand the higher admission if they are told the real reason.

For Pickers.

We forget just where this clip from the program of the Garfield theater, Chicago, originally appeared, but it seems to have been lifted from a recent periodical. The management picked up or adapted the one paragraph that gives the essence of the idea. Constructive criticism—not merely complaint—is something that every manager should welcome and appreciate. Run this in your program or on your screen. You'll find out things about your own house that will surprise you:

DON'T GROWL—KICK!

Talk with anybody in the management of an institution that serves the public and you will find the average American will growl, but he seldom complains. When something is wrong he will argue the matter with a ticket-seller, usher or doorman. They have no authority to set things right. The public will not go to the trouble of sending an orderly complaint to the management. An intelligent complaint will often clear up difficulties for you. You must know how to gather yourself for a kick and how to land it in the right place.

You can find a lot of good program material in magazines and newspapers if you'll only look for the stuff. This paragraph had nothing to do with picture theaters, but deals merely with the value of the kick properly landed instead of shot at random, but it suits no business more accurately than the business of selling entertainment, for here the merchant of pleasure must give satisfaction from every angle to draw return business, and it is only the steady patronage that counts. Encourage suggestion, but do not seek to create kickers. Ask them to help you run your house; not to run it for you.

Poor Counting.

The Cozy, Schenectady, N. Y., remarks "5,000 feet of film, with 12 pictures to the foot, means 60,000 pictures that will please the eye," etc. They must be getting film that has gone through one of those operating "booths" in the care of one of those careless operators that Brother Richardson has been scolding. But we are inclined to think that so many persons now know that there are sixteen frames to the foot that they will think the management a bit slow. It is just a slip of the pen, but it is apt to have a bad effect. The general program is well done, but some little points might be improved. There is a cut of Baby Osborne on the front page, but no line to connect with a picture in which she appears, advertised on the third page. Most persons can figure it out, but there should have been a caption line to connect the portrait with the "appearance of the star. An oddity is a credit line at the bottom of the last page announcing "This program is written by J. P. Arthur, 24 Cedar St." The union label and office imprint and address follow. Mr. Arthur writes well, but he does not always show good judgment in placing his material in the form. An announcement of a change of service is run casualty on the third page instead of being featured on the front as a matter of real importance. Generally speaking, the program is well done.

Darn that Comp!

The festive compositor and the foolish proofreader have been at it again. Charles Decker, of the Majestic, Grand Junction, Colorado, booked House Peters and Kathlyn Williams in "The Highway of Hope" and ran a strip across the top of the front page, above the heading, announcing "Two real stars in a real play." And the printer got it "two rear stars." They treated more respectfully Mr. Decker's

DON'T STAY HOME
ON ACCOUNT OF
THE HEAT

Do just the opposite—go to the Majestic to keep cool.
Safeguard your health.
Breathe pure air.

There follows an explanation of the ventilation system winding up with "Pure air is just as essential as pure food to keep you in good health." We like that last. It is forceful and it's true.

Hardwick Hustle.

Hardwick Brothers, of Clovis, N. M., have another new one. It is a very simple idea—once you think of it. This is it:

"WITHIN THE LAW"
PERSONALLY GUARANTEED

BRING THIS CARD WHEN YOU BUY YOUR TICKET

We have every confidence that "Within the Law" will meet with your approval. When you purchase your ticket, this card will be stamped. After seeing "Within the Law" and you do not think that it is worth the money, tell us why on the back of this card, mail it to Hardwick Bros., and we will refund the difference between the price of the ticket you purchased and a fifteen cent ticket. No refund will be made unless card is in by the 23d. This is our "personal guarantee" of absolute satisfaction.

Name.......................... Address....................

You must write your reasons on back of this card.

The way it works is very simple. The cards are sent to out-of-town patrons with a form letter that runs in part:

Mr...............................,
Texico, New Mexico.
"PERSONALLY GUARANTEED" entertainment.

Dear Sir:

They tell us about page advertisements in the magazines that cost five thousand dollars for a single insertion, so that we may understand that this is the day of worth-while advertising. It is—this letter represents something over thirty thousand dollars of our money.

In other words, we are putting everything back of the guarantee which we give you on "PERSONALLY GUARANTEED" entertainment. If this entertainment does not make good, we will have to close up, lose our property, our business, our everything.

So you may be sure that we are not offering "PERSONALLY GUARANTEED" entertainment without first making sure that it is of the highest quality. You may be sure also that when you spend your money for "PERSONALLY GUARANTEED" entertainment you will get full value for every cent, regardless of the price.

The first of these "PERSONALLY GUARANTEED" entertainments is "WITHIN THE LAW." It is a Vitagraph production in nine parts and features the greatest combination of stars before the public today. They are ALICE JOYCE and HARRY MOREY, whom you recently saw in "WOMANHOOD." But "WITHIN THE LAW" is better than "WOMANHOOD," being the successful photodramatization of the greatest success that Broadway has ever known. It ran for sixteen months in one theater in New York, and nine road companies played to over two and a half million dollars' receipts in the U. S. and Canada alone. These are only proofs of the high quality of the production.

This personal guarantee we look upon as a service to you. When an attraction is so advertised you know that you are going to get full value for your amusement money, for we, HARDWICK BROS., theater managers, within your easy reach, stand back of "PERSONALLY GUARANTEED" entertainments. If they are not right you have only to call us to account. It's our thirty thousand that protects you, because it's right here on Main Street, day and night.

Come and see "WITHIN THE LAW." Look over the first of these personally guaranteed 'entertainments, the entertainment that protects you with our dollars and our word. You will find that our guarantee has not been misplaced.

There was about half a page additional about the attraction and the house. About 250 of these letters were sent out on house letter heads. For the local campaign eight young women, who were intelligent and good talkers, were schooled in a selling talk. The reviews from all the trade papers were read to them and they were provided with a selling talk, running about 500 words, which they were to translate into their own language. The city was divided into districts, and one girl was assigned each district. She called upon every family and left a card at each home. The scheme worked so well that it will be repeated with other big attractions. The value of the personal appeal cannot be underestimated, and while it costs money it is worth more than the cost, and it should be remembered that the cost will cover much more than the original production. It lasts and brings in money long after the particular film boomed has passed down the line.

The Hardwicks literally smeared the newspapers. In one issue there were 65 column inches of display advertising in four different spaces, more than a column reader with a double column cut, and twelve readers. There was one or more mentions of the play on seven out of the eight pages of one issue of the local paper in addition to other matter about the house. As preparation about twenty-four different slides were used for the screen, and the slides were the sort with a punch, not the "greatest ever" type, not like these.

If you want to stop the girls from stealing, give them a chance. No honest girl can live decently on six dollars a week, and buy food and clothes and pay room rent and car fare. ALICE JOYCE says

"WITHIN THE LAW."

SEE IT! ! !

The Hardwick Brothers demonstrate what others know: that you can pay a rental price for a feature and get your money back, or you can add advertising to rental and make much more money. But advertising is something more than space in a newspaper. It is hammering all along the line and in every way possible.

Lobby Specials.

The Triangle Magazine has some good stuff on lobby work, dealing mostly with the painted signs used in lobbies. Their story is too long to be used in full, but these paragraphs are worth while pasting up for general reference:

As to actual colors used on the signs, much of that may be left to the painter, although one has to be careful that his combinations are not too shrieking or too "futuristic" for the good of the institution in which they are to be used. The same caution may be expressed with regard to the type of letter used and the "decorations" employed to fill in odd corners. The same style of letter should generally be used throughout any one sign, and the ornaments should be in keeping with the subject and the general display. It is also wise to avoid the same kind of letter that nearly everyone else is employing. However, that does not mean trying to create a peculiar form of type for use in the theater alone. It is virtually impossible to create a new kind of letter to be used in brush work that will not be so fantastic that it will be hideous. There is nothing smart or clever in ugliness.

Triangle on several occasions has detailed a scientific series of experiments once carried on to determine the degree of legibility in colored advertisements of various combinations. It was there declared that the most legible (if not the most effective) combination is black on yellow. Then follow green on white; blue on white; white on blue; black on white; yellow on black; white on red; white on green; white on black; red on yellow; green on red and red on green, the degrees of legibility following in the order named. One unusual combination that was lately put into effective use at a New York theater, for its lobby signs, is blue on orange. By trying out combinations the theater manager will find one that will be distinctive for his purposes and also pleasing to the eye. Pleasing the eye is important. One may attract attention with the shriek of a steam whistle, but it will not necessarily please the public. Red and black letters on a white ground is a pleasing combination, but it is not the only one.

Notice how low down white on black is. Also the famous red on yellow, once supposed to be the last word in poster work.

Like Suggestions.

J. E. Cooney, publicity man of the Winchester Avenue theater, New Haven, Conn., sends in some house programs and asks for comment. The programs are the familiar five by seven size. Each carries a front page portrait cut linked to the showing of that star during the week by some proper comment as "Here Thursday," "In a beautiful drama of the Orient on Wednesday," and similar lines. Inside day and date is indented to the left of the text in a large type and the back is reserved for chatter. Enough outside comment is mixed with the remarks on the current films to make it all read and readable. The front carries the house information as to times of showing and admission prices. There is little comment to be offered, for Mr. Cooney seems to have followed good examples, but it might help to discard the house advertisement on the back and make a page of two column chat running down to the underline at the bottom and referring in some measure to that underline. This would give the opportunity for sufficient type to create a more intimate feeling between the editor and the readers, which, in turn, would give force to what the editor has to say. Win the reader's confidence with friendly chat, hold it by never betraying confidence, and that back page could be made to work harder than the other three pages put together, but the other three pages are needed for a backing.

Bettered.

Film Forecast, the Pittsburgh organ of Rowland and Clark, has come out in a new dress and looks much better, for the imprint is cleaner and the make-up improved slightly. One departure worth while is a page editorial on one of the coming plays. This is signed by the editor and its authoritative form of statement impresses the reader with the merits of the film. The trade advertising is still a bit too obtrusive, giving a choppy make-up, but trade advertising is what pays the freight.

The Photoplaywright

Conducted by EPES WINTHROP SARGENT

INQUIRIES.

Questions concerning photoplay writing addressed to this department will be replied to by mail if a fully addressed and stamped envelope accompanies the letter, which should be addressed to this department. Questions should be stated clearly and should be typewritten or written with pen and ink. Under no circumstances will manuscripts or synopses be criticised, whether or not a fee is sent therefor.

A list of companies will be sent if the request is made to the paper direct and not to this department, and a return stamped envelope is inclosed.

Merwin on Scripts.

BANNISTER MERWIN writes from his home on the Thames: I urging some spare hours the other day I went through your last edition of Technique of the Photoplay more carefully than I have yet had opportunity. My point of view of your point of view holds certain considerations which I should like to talk over with you at some length if there were opportunity. My points are not opposed to yours, but tangential. For example, your chapter on continuity.

Strong insistence upon complete continuity means dullness. Now the question how far we are to go with our approximate continuity can only be solved by more or less arbitrary conventions. In so far as we become slaves to those conventions we again tend to dullness. Don't you suspect, as I do, that we make a shibboleth of continuity? Personally I believe that we should aim to make every scene that is to fill a time gap a really significant scene. If it is necessary to show a man leaving a house, construct the story in such a way that something rather important happens as he leaves the house. But if such a scene is not practicable surely we should get our continuity matter, as such, down to the narrowest margin compatible with the prevention of a jarring and confusing break. Suppose that Jones is talking with Brown in one scene and in the next scene Jones is talking with Smith in a room at the other end of town. Surely it is enough if we give the conclusion of the first scene—show Jones winding up his business with Brown, then leaving, and give Brown five seconds alone with some significant bit of action; then go to Smith's office, show Smith alone for a few seconds and then Jones entering. It all depends upon the interest of what you make Brown and Smith do in the brief periods when they are alone in their respective offices. The point to remember is, *continuity is not an attempt to approximate in one's play the actual time in which all the movements of the characters would take in real life, but it is an endeavor to prevent the spectator from suffering mental confusion.* If we satisfy this point we do all that we should do.

My present notion of the best construction for long feature stories follows somewhat the lines of the stage play. Teh line of climactic development should be a series of ascending waves. After each crisis or climax there should be a slight lull. And the first few hundred feet, like the first ten minutes of a play, should be devoted to getting your audience acquainted with your characters and their relationships. To place a very important action in the first few hundred feet before the audience knows who the characters are or what they are to one another tends to create confusion. People will later say, "Oh, was he the one who did that?" Of course the characters must do things in those first few hundred feet, but they should be things that express their characters interestingly rather than things that have important significance in the plot development. Perhaps I put the point a little too strongly, for there are always exceptions, but you will know what I mean.

The thing is to look at one's own work from the viewpoint of the audience, and continually ask one's self such questions as, "Is it clear? Can I follow it without confusion of mind? Does it constantly keep my interest stimulated?"

Now the question of breaking one's scenes with close-ups and varied shots from different angles. Of course, we all do this in preparing our scripts. But lately I have wondered whether it would not be better to leave the breaking up of the scene to the producer, except in very obvious cases. You see, I am now speaking as a producer as well as a writer. The value of the close-up almost always is governed in practice by floor conditions. I mean by this several things. For one thing, if the cast is not the ideal cast you have had in mind when writing the play the character you have set down for a close-up may not be able to express what it is essential to express in that particular close-up. The producer must then find some other means of punctuating the situation. For another thing, no producer is likely to build a set and handle his people in it in exactly the way you have conceived. For that matter no two producers are likely to handle the set and the characters in the same way. It follows that very often the producer can secure a natural close-up in the course of the action where you have called for a special close-up scene. And on the other hand the producer may find that he needs a special close-up scene at a point where your conception of the movements of the characters has not made it appear necessary. Anyhow, the close-up is an interpretation.

If, as I hold, the producer is an interpreter, would it not be better to leave this matter of close-ups to him, and write your scene straight, with emphasis on the points that should be brought out most strongly? I don't say that this surmise is right; I merely am wondering. In any event we do not want to see the close-up overdone. We don't want too much of the Griffith staccato. It leads to what a certain friend of mine once called Tom Lawson's method of muck-raking— "The method of universal emphasis."

There is another belief that has become strong in me during the last year or two. It is that just as a knowledge of actual stage conditions is almost essential to the writer of plays for the stage so a knowledge of actual studio conditions is almost essential to the writer of photoplays. The writer should learn not in the picture house, where he is bound to be more or less under the illusion, but on the studio floor. I don't mean that he cannot get a start without this knowledge. But he cannot reach his full development until he knows the studio. This is a hard saying, but I believe that this is true. I append a sheet of manuscript to show you a form I have been using lately in my work. It seems to work well, and I find it easy to write. These are action scenes and not acting scenes.

Scene 30.—A road close to the cliffs, Night.

Action.—Walters, Aymond, and Hand drive on in the wagon. They stop, and Hand gets down, taking a lantern (a powerful electric hand-lantern) from the wagon. He walks toward the cliff.

Scene 30A.—On the cliff. Night.

Action.—Hand moves toward the edge of the cliff from behind the camera. He stands holding the darkened lantern and looking out to sea.

Scene 30B.—A view out to sea (night). Shoot downward at first, then pan slowly upward until the horizon is included. Then hold.

Scene 31.—At sea. Night.

Action.—A German submarine lies almost awash, with a small boat ready to put off from it. Commander, officer, and men are on the upper works. The commander is looking toward shore through binoculars.

Back to Scene 30A.—Hand signals with his lantern.

Scene 30D.—A view out to sea (night). Shoot downward at first, then pan up to the horizon, as in Scene 30B. Three times a light appears and disappears on or near the horizon.

(Note: You can get this effect of the appearing light in one of two ways. [1] Double exposure—studio—black cloth with hole in it through which light appears. [2] When you get to your bold of the horizon you have virtually a still. By putting a black dot on your still near the horizon line and duping your still you can get the effect.)'

Back to Scene 30A.—Hand turns back toward the wagon.

Back to Scene 30.—Hand rejoins Walters and Aymond at the wagon. They begin to take the tins of oil from the wagon and carry them down the path to the beach.

We think that Mr. Merwin takes more seriously than we intended certain general rules, one of which was that to see the same man in two rooms without leaving the house suggested that he was in the same house. This did not mean that he was actually to be bundled out of doors to get him to the next house. We do believe, however, that the ten feet for closing and opening might better be a six or eight foot break scene. We have italicized Mr. Merwin's definition of continuity, since it is better than our own. If you have a copy of technique paste it in.

Another point is that we suggested that some important action should open the picture, but not something setting the key too high. Most assuredly there should follow the introductory phases, but we have too many pictures like that recently described by William Lord Wright in Belig's Paste Pot and Shears, in which the seven-part story would have been better "had not the first five reels been used to introduce the story."

Revision.

The only revision bureau that can help you to success is the studio continuity writer. If your idea is worth changing he will change it for you, and he'll probably change it even though it may not need it.

Projection Department

Conducted by F. H. RICHARDSON

Manufacturers' Notice.

IT IS an established rule of this department that no apparatus or other goods will be endorsed or recommended editorially until the excellence of such articles has been demonstrated to its editor.

Important Notice.

Owing to the mass of matter awaiting publication, it is impossible to reply through the department in less than two to three weeks. In order to give prompt service, those sending four cents, stamps (less than actual cost), will receive carbon copy of the department reply, by mail, without delay. Special replies by mail on matters which cannot be replied to in the department, one dollar.

Both the first and second sets of questions are now ready and printed in neat booklet form, the second half being seventy-six in number. Either booklet may be had by remitting 25 cents, money or stamps, to the editor, or both for 40 cents. Cannot use Canadian stamps. Every live, progressive operator should get a copy of these questions. You may be surprised at the number you cannot answer without a lot of study.

Oil.

The receipt of a new lot of oil from a Pennsylvania company, with request that I test it, and recommend if found good, recalls to me the fact that it is time I gave you all another talking to about lubrication. The projection machines in use in this country alone are worth, something more than $6,000,000, and I think there is no doubt but that these machines and their vital parts would last one-third longer if they received proper lubrication, or rather if they were lubricated with oil in every way best suited to the work. If this is true, then it will be seen, merely by glancing at the machine value, the waste through inefficient oil is something pretty huge. At least, it is well deserving the careful consideration of operators. It is, of course, not to be expected that the average operator can or will conduct a series of elaborate tests in order to determine the relative efficiency of different oils. The great majority of the men could not do this, and do it intelligently, if they would. How, then, are they to secure oil which they can feel satisfied will give satisfactory service?

The matter is quite simple. In the first place we may promptly discard all drug store oils. They are made to sell, and you can have no possible way of knowing what they are, except that they vary from poor to very poor. They are expensive in first cost, and very, very expensive in damage to machinery. Three in One oil, for instance, is advertised to oil fine rifles, typewriters and to polish furniture with. Is it likely to be efficient to oil a machine which sees heavy service? Ask yourself that question! Is not the reply pretty obvious? Do we polish furniture with an oil having high lubricating qualities?

Having rejected the drug store as a possible source of supply, we may then consider other possible oils, one of which is that sold by the manufacturer of projection machines. Such oil may be relied upon as having at least fairly well to the work, with the notation that the same oil is sold for use in Edmonton, Alberta, as is sold for use in Miami, Florida. The other, and really best, supply source is to purchase oil from the local light and power company, securing the same oil they use for their generators. As I have time and again pointed out to you, the light and power company simply must have good-oil for its generators. It must be an oil light enough to not clog the oil rings when the generator is shut down in cold weather, and must have high lubricating qualities, else the generator bearings will very soon begin to buck. You will probably be able to get this oil at a very reasonable price, probably very much less than one-half of what you pay for the drug store variety, and it will, if used intelligently, last very much longer—also your machines will last very much longer. In closing, let me again reiterate one of my many-times repeated statements, viz: never use but one drop of oil on a moving picture machine bearing. An added drop does no good, and does do much harm, for an oil soaked machine means oil smeared films, and films are worth approximately $125 per foot, which valuable property is intrusted to your care under the presumption that you are an operator, not a sloppy slob—that you know your business and, knowing it, attend to it intelligently and well.

Interesting Installation.

The editor has been informed that Operator F. H. Avery, Home theater, Portage, Wisconsin, is a reg'lar feller, and an operator of the high-voltage type. As I understand the matter, he has an installation containing many inventions of his own, and that it is most complete. Have written Brother Avery and asked him to contribute description for the department. Will await his reply with interest.

Floor Paint Wanted.

Frank Gwinn (or at least Gwinn is what it seems to be), Shreveport, Louisiana, desires information with regard to a floor paint, as follows:

This is the first time I have attempted to break into the Projection Department, though I have read it for the past three years, and get from it much benefit and enjoyment. And now I have an axe to grind myself. My operating room is floored with asbestos, which same is soft and spongy. What can I paint it with to get a good, hard surface? Please advise through the department. I carry a card in the Shreveport local No. 222, I. A.

Um, well, I'm not at all certain you haven't got me sticked. I really don't know whether a thin Portland cement paste, mixed half fine, sharp sand and half cement, would do the trick or not, but I think not. I believe the best thing to do would be to run in an inch and one-half of cement finish. It does seem to me there was something published about just such a paint as this a long time ago, but I cannot remember what it was, nor can I seem to find any record of it. If any brother can offer anything on this subject, let him get out his pencil and paper and be heard.

Later: I have been thinking this matter over. Here is a mess I saw used for a somewhat similar purpose once upon a time. It worked all right, and maybe it would do the trick for Shreveport. I dunno. Might try it anyhow—just a little at first, to see how it comes out. Asphaltum varnish and shellac, mixed equal quantities, the shellac to be tolerably thin before mixing with the asphaltum. Having thoroughly mixed the two, thin down with benzine until it is quite thin. Apply plenty of it, and be sure no matches are lighted in the room, and that the arc is not struck for at least half an hour after the job is complete. By that time all fumes will have evaporated. I do not say this will work, but I am inclined to think it will. Undoubtedly shellac alone would do the trick, but it would be too expensive.

Wants to Be Correct.

Edwin L. Benton, LaCrosse, Wisconsin, sends in newspaper clipping concerning our address to the men of LaCrosse last July, and asks:

In what issue of the World did that table you referred to in your address appear, and can I obtain a copy? Am interested in cutting down my shutter, and want to know my lens system is right before I start.

It was not a "table," Brother Benton, but a chart. It appeared in March 17 issue, this year. You may obtain copy by remitting fifteen cents, stamps, to the Moving Picture World, Box 226, Madison Square Station, New York City. You are quite right in wanting to be sure you are right before proceeding. Study your lens system closely. Get you a Handbook, unless you already have one, and study it closely. Take time to do a little experimenting on your own hook. It will prove to be interesting, and the more knowledge you acquire the better operator you will be.

Non-Flam Film.

The Stout Machine Company, Rockford, Illinois, manufacturers of the Portoscope projector, desire information concerning non-inflammable film. They write:

We have under way negotiations which will call for the use of a great deal of non-flam film, and are trying to gather information concerning same. The following is what we would like to know: Names of manufacturers of non-flam film stock, both in this country and abroad. Which are the ones that are most transparent, flexible and most likely to give best satisfaction, all things considered? Do you know of any producers of pictures intended primarily for use in churches and schools which are printed on non-flam stock? We are dealing with an institution which will have their own pictures taken and printed on non-flam stock, but will want to use other suitable pictures, also printed on non-flam film.

If you are dealing with a company which will produce pictures on non-flam film we would like to have particulars ourselves. So far as myself, or others in position to know are aware, there is no available non-flam film stock, in any quantity at least, except some the Pathe company holds for its own use, which same is not for sale. So far as known no non-flam film stock is being made. It is, to all intents and purposes, a non-existent material. You may have this statement verified by addressing the Eastman Company, Rochester, N. Y., or the Pathe Exchange, J. A. Berst, General Manager, 25 West 45th street, New York City.

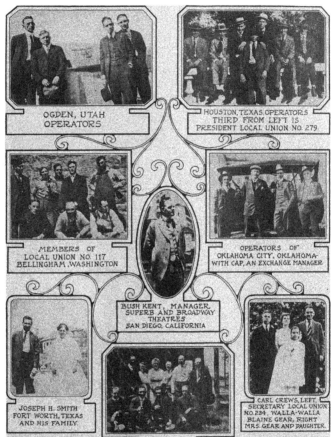

OGDEN, UTAH
OPERATORS

HOUSTON, TEXAS, OPERATORS
THIRD FROM LEFT IS
PRESIDENT LOCAL UNION NO. 279

MEMBERS OF
LOCAL UNION NO. 117
BELLINGHAM, WASHINGTON

OPERATORS OF
OKLAHOMA CITY, OKLAHOMA
WITH CAP, AN EXCHANGE MANAGER

BUSH KENT, MANAGER
SUPERB AND BROADWAY
THEATRES
SAN DIEGO, CALIFORNIA

JOSEPH H. SMITH
FORT WORTH, TEXAS
AND HIS FAMILY

CARL CREWS, LEFT,
SECRETARY LOCAL UNION
NO. 234, WALLA-WALLA
BLAINE GEAR, RIGHT
MRS. GEAR AND DAUGHTER

A DENVER, COLORADO GROUP, LEFT, STANDING, OTTO THUM, COMMISSIONER CITY OF
DENVER. FIRST ON RIGHT OF SCENERY, HARVEY GARMAN, CLERK DENVER CITY COUNCIL
NEXT COMES RALPH MOSER, CITY BOILER INSPECTOR, AND LAST THE CITY ELECTRICIAN

What Twelve Degrees Drop in Projection Means.

Simon Arkin, New York City, contributes the following:

Having had my attention drawn, by an article in the projection department, to the fact that the maximum allowable pitch in projection adopted by the Society of Projection Engineers and expressed in degrees (twelve degrees being the maximum

adopted), will not be understood by the moving picture industry, I have drawn a sketch for your benefit.

Looking at the drawing you will see that the standard, as adopted, will mean an allowable drop of 21.256 feet, or approximately 21 feet and 3 inches, or 255 inches, in 100 feet of distance. For each ten feet of throw the 12 degree drop means 2.1256 feet, or 25.5 inches. Expressed another way, the maximum drop in projection must not exceed 21.256 per cent. of the throw.

Friend Arkin, who is a consulting engineer, did not quite understand me. I did not mean that we could not figure out what twelve degrees drop stood for in inches, but that if it had been expressed in inches per foot in the first place, a lot of unnecessary trouble would have been avoided; moreover, it is not every operator or manager who could figure the thing out. The idea I sought to convey to my esteemed colleagues in the Society was that it would be well to avoid unnecessary little-understood expressions and make things perfectly plain. But we are nevertheless indebted to Arkin for the sketch and explanation. It has at least saved this editor the labor of figuring the thing out for himself, as he had intended to do for the benefit of all.

Wants More Light.

C. Elmer Dietrich, Tunkhannock, Pennsylvania, seeks the following information:

We are not getting enough light. We are about to install two new Simplex projectors with the same rheostats we are now using, and are afraid the light will be the same. We are now using two No. 6 Power's, projecting a 15 foot picture at 90 feet current 133 cycle, 110 volt. The rheostat delivers 45 amperes. The current will be changed to 60 cycle in about fourteen months, and I don't wish to invest in any apparatus which will be useless after the change is made. Kindly advise me what we can do to get a better light. Using ⅝ cored National carbons.

Assuming that it is possible to, and that you do line up the optical systems of your Simplex, including revolving shutter, the same as the Power's, the mere changing from Power's to Simplex will have no effect on your screen brilliancy. The advice I would give you would depend on things you have not set forth. If you are getting current on what is known at a "flat rate," then all that is necessary is to hitch a twenty-five ampere, 110 volt rheostat in multiple with the 45 ampere one you are now using. This will only involve the purchase of two 25 ampere, 170 volt rheostats, which won't be a very serious matter, and will give you almost anything you want, up to sixty, or maybe sixty-five amperes —you must understand that the average rheostat does not really deliver its rates capacity after it has been in use a short while.

On the other hand, if you are on meter rate, and the rate is high, it is quite another matter. In that event it would be expensive to use current through rheostats, and the higher the amperage the greater the waste—for you must understand that, when using 110 volt alternating current through resistance, much more than half the power is wasted, and all the waste registers on your meter. Using 60 amperes it would stack up something like this: wasted in the resistance, about 4,000 watts; utilized in the form of light at the arc, about 2,600 watts. And this would be pretty expensive. Suppose, you pay six cents per K. W. hour, and run an average of seven hours per day. You would be wasting about (4x6)x7=$1.68 per day in the resistances and that multiplied by 425 days (one year and two months) means something like—umph, well, figure it out for yourself, substituting the actual-hours per day you run, the number of days per year you run and the actual rate you pay per K. W. hour.

There are several things you may do. First you may install a semi-reflective (metallic surface) screen, if you have not one already. Second, you may decrease the size of your picture, which will increase its brilliancy, since it will have the effect of concentrating the light upon a smaller surface. You now have about 170 square feet of screen to cover with picture. With a twelve foot picture this would be reduced to 108 square feet, which would mean that your available light would be covering 62 square feet less surface, with corresponding gain in brilliancy, except that there will be some added loss between aperture and lens over what there is now, though not nearly enough to counter-balance the gain at the screen. In fact, by getting the new objective (you would require one to change your picture size) with proper opening and carefully matching the optical system, including revolving shutter, to the local conditions, you might have no added loss at all between aperture and lens.

Third, you could get a sixty or seventy ampere A. C. economizer (low voltage transformer) and run both machines off it, using one of your rheostats to warm up the carbons, making the connection as illustrated in figure 100, page 251 of the handbook. It is quite possible you might arrange with the United Theatre Equipment Corporation or Mr. Lewis M. Swaab (address will be found in their advertisement on

another page) to purchase an economizer, allowing you a very substantial sum for it in exchange for sixty cycle economizers or a motor generator set (which latter is what you should have) later on, when the change in the current cycle is finally made. The use of A C for projection is out of date. In order to get anything like equal brilliancy you must use almost double the amperage necessary with D C. Get a motor generator set after the change is made, in my advice. It is even possible Swaab or the United might sell you a motor generator set with a 133 cycle motor, under agreement to exchange the motor for a 60 cycle one later at a reasonable, agred-upon-at-the-time-the-bargain-is-made figure for the exchange, but this agreement should be in writing.

In Bad Condition.

Ohie sends us some samples of film faults he finds in his service and says:

Am running two Power 6-A projectors and thus far have obtained pretty good results on the screen. Have your hand-book, second edition, and it helps a whole lot. Attached you will find a few samples of what I cut out of an "inspected" Universal film. This was a particularly bad example, in that whereas the first hundred feet was right side to, the rest of the reel was wrong side to. Our service comes from the Victor Film Service, Cleveland, Ohio.

No exchange manager who has any right conception of what is due his customers, of what is due the film producer, or what is due the industry itself, or who cares for the safety of theatre patrons, would send out films in such wretched condition as is evidenced by the samples sent in by Ohio. My compliments to the mismanager of the Cleveland Victor Film Service. To say there was not time to inspect the film is no excuse. There was no 'Film not inspected—operator inspect and send bill for labor to exchange' slip in the shipment.

To Renew Our Friendship.

Daniel Constantino, Easton, Pennsylvania, writes as follows:

Just a few lines to renew our friendship. We last met on the night you addressed the managers and operators of Easton last fall. I was then assistant to Earl Roberts, but since then have become chief operator at the Strand. Have two Power 6As, motor driven. The operating room is just about ample size for the two machines. Am projecting a picture a trifle wider than sixteen feet, at 82 foot throw, with a five and one half foot drop in the projection. Use meniscus bi-convex condensers. Am a member of local union 203, I. A.

All of which requires no comment, except to say I am glad to hear you are getting ahead. I remember the Easton men well, and enjoyed my visit with them. Maybe I'll drop in again some of these days when you're not looking for me, so keep your eye on the screen, and don't get caught with a fault thereon.

For the Hot Days.

Here is a scheme for hot days. I think it requires no special comment other than to say that the fan wings should not be made any larger than the proportion shown. Strikes me, too, they would be more

effective if placed on the other side of the shutter. They will not add enough extra strain to the gears to amount to anything.

Unnecessary Fighting.

From Edward J. Cooper, manager, Phoenix, Arizona, comes a letter, which I only quote in part, because its full publication would, I think, serve no good purpose, and might stir up additional bitterness and ill feeling. I quote the letter, in part, because I wish to use it to point a moral for the benefit of others. Friend Cooper says:

Noticed your remarks, July Fourth issue, concerning the trip you did not make through our city, and wish to throw a little light on conditions as they existed in Phoenix at that time, and do now exist. Had I personally known it was possible to have you include Phoenix, I would have gotten busy with the exhibitors, and have insisted that you include the capital city of Arizona, for all exhibitors here are live wires. So far as the union was concerned, however, under the conditions existing, it would have been impractical for it to invite you, without the assistance of the exhibitors. Along about the first of the year everything in Phoenix was union, and we were getting along very well. About that time the Columbia was contracted to play "Intolerance," and right there the union pulled a foolish play which resulted in every house in the city, except one, a "girl show," employing non-union operators (Cooper says "go open shop," but I think he means just what I have said, and that I included the stage hands, too. Open shop really, at least in a case of this kind, means non-union.—Ed.). The stage hands made an unnecessary demand, which cost the Columbia a lot of money which literally meant the entire profit on the big picture. This deal was pulled after the theater was packed to the doors, although it was understood there would be two weeks' notice of any change in the then existing conditions. Of course, there was nothing to do but concede the point under the conditions, or else dismiss the audience. So Mr. Mauk gave in, but next day there was a hurried meeting of exhibitors and every house except the one spoken of went non-union. * * * I am not writing this from a prejudiced viewpoint, because this thing took place before I took the management of the Columbia. * * * The union now feels that it made a mistake and has been back many times, trying to fix things up. At present there are but two of its members left in the city.

The Phoenix Amusement Company is getting along very well. It has, as you will see by the letterhead, added two more houses to the circuit, and is now negotiating for two more, which will make it one of the largest circuits in the entire West. I followed your trip throughout, and you must have enjoyed it. If you ever start this way again without letting us know your route, and including Phoenix therein, we will boycott the World, which, by the way, has by far the largest circulation in this territory.

All right, Neighbor Cooper, next time Phoenix will be graced with my presence for one day. I've been there twice already, before the days of moving pictures. I've seen the Phoenix mix-up. I have had to change Cooper's lines considerable, but think I have his meaning clear. If he has been made to say anything he did not really say, that is my fault, for I have misunderstood.

Now, I know nothing whatever about the real merits of this case, because I do not know what demands the men made. Perhaps the demands were, as Cooper says, unreasonable. Perhaps, also, they were not, when all things are considered. But one thing seems certain, viz.: the Phoenix union committed an unpardonable blunder in the method of approach, always supposing Friend Cooper to have set the facts forth as they are, and we have no reason to suppose he has not. The only possible excuse for such a method (making a demand without notice, where it was understood two weeks' notice would be given) would be a case where something in the proposed presentation of the play violated international I. A. laws, and even that would not, under any ordinary conditions, justify a union in pulling, or threatening to pull its men after the audience is assembled. Mind you, it is no pleasant thing for me to take up a matter of this kind in this way. Nor am I necessarily condemning the Arizona local. I would have to know ALL the circumstances before I could do that. But this I feel should be said: It is very easy to, by the use of wrong tactics, kick up more unnecessary trouble in one day than can be remedied in two years. Where there is prospect of a demand being made which will entail an argument, the union should never attempt to catch the managers unawares and butt it through, except in possible cases where the union is dealing with managers who are themselves known to seize unfair advantage. A union is a business organization, pure and simple, formed to protect and advance the interests of its members. It should deal with theater managers as business men, in a business way. Strong arm methods are still, it shames me to say it, necessary in isolated cases, but even in such instances, nine times out of ten, if the matter be carefully taken up, by very carefully selected committees, more would be accomplished in the long run by argument and diplomacy than by force.

There is, however, one phase of this matter which needs a little one-overing. It often occurs that an I. A. rule, or law, which seems at first glance to be oppressive and unjust, and which really may be just, that, insofar as the individual case be concerned, is, nevertheless, a very important and very necessary, as well as a very just law. It is possible that this particular demand on the part of the Phoenix union was due to some such law as this, which the union had no power within itself to waive, and the violation of which would bring upon the local and its individual members severe penalties. But, even so, there still could be no real, legitimate excuse for threatening to tie up a show after the audience had assembled. That is not only taking an unfair advantage (assuming that no demand had previously been made on the Columbia) of the theater, but violates the right of an innocent party, the audience.

The editor of this department and this department stands for organization. The editor is himself an active member of the I. A. T. S. E. and M. P. M. O., and an honorary member of several locals. Neither himself, or this department, however, will defend any union in an action which is wrong, because that would not be true friendship to the union itself.

In this case, however, regardless of everything else, if the union sinned it has paid the penalty. It has suffered amply for any fault it may have committed, and I would suggest that Phoenix managers and exhibitors ought to now prove their broad mindedness by forgetting the whole thing, holding no rancor against those they have, according to Friend Cooper's statement, defeated. The men should, on the other hand, accept their defeat gracefully, taking profit by the mistakes of the past. There is no use fighting forever over a lost cause, and keeping ill feeling alive. If you must fight, fight like the devil (but fairly) until victorious or defeated, and then promptly proceed to forget it. If I have not made all this very clear, just try and understand my meaning, and that I am trying to give you a little lecture for the good of all concerned.

Operators Deserve a Cussing.

Verne P. Clement, Brevard, North Carolina, expresses his opinion of certain matters as follows:

I look for the World every week, and am an enthusiastic reader of its pages. In a recent issue appeared a letter from a Florida operator who complained of film reaching him in bad condition. And you make take it from me as a statement of fact that I know something about that particular thing. I am compelled to work for hours on some programmes in order to get them in shape to run. However, I don't think the fault lies altogether with the exchange. I believe some operators are due to get a little cussing. If every operator would send film back in the same condition it is received, the next man would not have such a hard time. I have been operating about one year in a town of fifteen hundred. Have one Power 6A, with a 6 x 14 foot operating room. Have been having a little trouble with up and down movement in my picture. Can you help me to locate the trouble?

Operators should by all means take proper care of film while in their charge, and should, so far as possible, repair damage done by them, but that fact does not relieve the exchange from making a thorough inspection and thoroughly repairing films before sending them out to a customer. It is their duty so to do. It is a part of the service they sell, and to sell a thing and not deliver it smacks of dishonest methods.

As to the movement in your picture, you should have described it very much more in detail. If the movement is regular, occurring four times to each turn of the crank shaft, then the trouble lies in your intermittent, and it is probably due to (A) Dirt on face of intermittent sprocket. (B) Intermittent sprocket not true. (C) Intermittent sprocket loose on shaft. (D) Intermittent sprocket shaft sprung. If the movement is irregular, it may be due to any one of several causes, and I would have to have it very closely described before attempting to tell you which one it is. Be sure, also, that it is not in the films themselves.

A Change in Projection Machine Manufacture.

This department is officially notified by the Stout Machine Company that the Portoscope, formerly manufactured and sold by the Picture-Scope Company, 565 West Washington street, Chicago, will in future be made and sold by them. The Stout Machine Company is located at 814 South Main street, Rockford, Illinois.

The Portoscope is a good machine of its kind, and we wish the Stout Machine Company success in its new field.

Incidentally the company asks for authoritative information with regard to transparent screens. In reply to this, the Mirror screen, made by Frank J. Rembusch, Shelbyville, Illinois, is the most efficient of any, but rather costly and very fragile. The Optigraph Company, Chicago, 1010 First National Bank Building, makes, or did make, a transparent screen. There was a screen known as the Trans Lux, made by the Trans Lux Company, 251 Washington street, Brooklyn, but whether or no they are still doing business, I cannot say. That is the sum of my knowledge as to transparent screens just at this time. There are so little used that I have not kept up to date on them, I am sorry to say.

Motion Picture Photography*

Conducted by CARL LOUIS GREGORY, F. R. P. S.

Inquiries.

QUESTIONS in cinematography addressed to this department will receive carbon copy of the department's reply by mail when four cents in stamps are inclosed. Special replies by mail on matters which cannot be replied to in this department, $1.

Manufacturers' Notice.

It is an established rule of this department that no apparatus or other goods will be endorsed or recommended editorially until the excellence of such articles has been demonstrated to its editor.

Sepia Toning.

THE usual method of sepia toning is that of immersing the film in a solution which changes the metallic silver image to a haloid or ferricyanide salt, which is in turn converted to the brown sulphide. Since the conversion of the image to a haloid salt causes the emulsion to whiten so that it resembles unexposed film and the sulphide solution "develops" the image again, this process is often termed re-development.

Films for re-developing should possess a blue-black tone and should be thoroughly washed (to eliminate Hypo) and be perfectly dried. Films which have been over-exposed and under-developed do not give successful results in Sepia toning. A print to produce a pleasing brown should have just the correct exposure, or perhaps a little less than normal, and be developed completely; that is, one in which the image seems to come to its full density in the normal time and which will not gain further with continued development; except, of course, that if the development is too prolonged there will be a chemical fog slowly produced by the continued action of the developer. Two solutions are required for the production of Sepia-toned films.

Sepia tone is one in which the silver image has been converted to a pleasing tone of brown, and in which the high lights are clear, transparent films. The solutions are made up as follows:

No. 1. Bleaching Solution.

Potassium Ferri Cyanide	1½	lbs.
Potassium Bromide	1½	lbs.
Water	10	gallons

No. 2. Re-developing Solution.

Sulphide (not Sulphite) Soda	12	ozs.
Water	10	gallons

Manipulation.—(1) Immerse the rack of film in the bleaching bath, letting it remain until the entire silver image has turned to a creamy yellow, allowing it to remain until the yellow image has practically the same appearance from the back as well as the front of the film. This operation will take place in from one to two minutes.

(2) Rinse thoroughly in clear, cold water in a rinsing tank.

(3) Place in the developing solution until original detail of the picture returns, except that the image is now brown instead of black. This takes about thirty seconds. The films should not be allowed to remain in this solution any longer than is necessary to complete the developing action, as the sulphide is a strong caustic and has a tendency to soften the emulsion, and in hot weather to produce reticulation.

(4) Wash for half an hour before drying.

In warm weather, if troubled with softening of the emulsion or with reticulation, rinse the film quickly as it comes from the re-developer, and then immerse for five minutes in a hardening bath composed of

Acid Hardener	3	qts.
Water	10	gallons

Then remove from this bath and wash as usual.

If properly carried out, the density and graduation of the sepia-toned film will not be affected by re-development, although many studios make a slightly lighter print for sepia than for a straight print.

The acid hardener is the same formula as that used in the preparation of acid hypo fixing bath, given recently in this department.

While intensification and reduction of motion picture films is not, as a rule, advisable on account of the tendency of granularity in the image, caused by the use of the solution, it is often desirable to give an added snappiness and contrast to a negative film by a slight intensification. One of the best methods of intensifying a negative and one which has practically no tendency to granular image, is the sepia re-development.

While the method of intensification by re-development is comparatively new, yet it is a most effective and simple means of intensifying film negatives. It may be used in exactly the same manner as for producing sepia tones on positive film. Negatives intensified by re-development are

*Copyright, 1917, by the Chalmers Publishing Co.

built up evenly without undue contrast and without the chance of staining. They are, moreover, more permanent than a straight developed negative, as they will never be subjected to brown staining such as is often seen in old negatives which have been kept in damp vaults for some time. The advantage of being able to use toning bath for two different purposes is obvious, the results in either case being all that could be desired.

On account of war prices the cost of the bleaching bath has reached an alarming height. The following bleaching bath is cheaper but cannot be kept in a wooden developing tank unless it is well protected with parafin, asphalt, or Probus paint, as it attacks the wood and precipitates. A slate or soapstone tank is best for this solution.

Permanganate Bleach.

A

Potassium permanganate	1½	ounces
Sulphuric acid (C. P.)	9	fluid ounces
Water	6	gallons

B

Sodium chloride (common salt)	3	ounces
Water	2	gallons

Solutions A and B should be prepared separately and mixed together for use after dissolving. Do not use table salt but the coarser brine salt, as table salt generally contains flour or starch to prevent caking in damp weather when exposed to the air in salt cellars.

When the film has been bleached white the gelatine will have a permanganate stain. Rinse it thoroughly and place in a 1% solution of sodium bi-sulphite which will clear it of the stain. Rinse again and re-develop in the re-developing solution first given.

The explanation of the process is very simple. The permanganate and acid acts as a reducer in dissolving the metallic silver, but in the presence of sodium chloride the dissolved metallic silver is immediately transformed into a silver chloride and remains in the film.

Quick Work and Double Exposure.

The modern cameraman finds it necessary, in order to keep up with the times, to have at his disposal a number of devices which, a few years ago, were seldom, if ever, used.

Many beautiful effects, which, when properly used, add a greatly enhanced value to the beauty of the photography and lend to the capable director a variety of effects hitherto not at his command, may be obtained by a few comparatively simple devices.

In the old days it was seldom that even the common fade out was used. Today there is scarcely a picture in which the simple fade out does not occur at least once, and generally several times. On account of the number of different devices used in securing similar or nearly similar effects, there has been a confusion in the nomenclature used in designating the different effects; therefore, it will not be amiss to explain briefly in this regard the terms used and the means of distinguishing between the various effects and the apparatus by which they are produced.

Fade-out and fade-in: These terms are open to the criticism of being too general in their application, but, being the oldest form of an effect in motion pictures and having the sanction of long usage, designate, respectively, the even fading of the entire picture within the frame to blackness and the general transformation of a picture filling the entire frame from total obscurity to brightness.

This effect may be obtained in several ways: First, by closing the iris diaphragm in the lens while turning; second, by a dissolving shutter; third, by a graduated screen; fourth, by chemical means.

The first method is probably the commonest, but is open to the objection that most iris diaphragms do not close entirely and that it is therefore impossible to make a complete fade, especially in a brightly lighted location. There is also the objection that, as the diaphragm closes, the depth of focus increases, and there is a very perceptible sharpening of the focus as the image darkens, giving the unpleasant suggestion that the scene was not as sharply focussed as it could have been.

No matter what stage of development has been reached in the attainment of artistic effects by the "fuzzytype" school of still-photography, cinematography has not yet reached the stage where "fuzzytype" results can be tolerated in the picture. The psychology of vision permits one to view a motionless landscape or a still life through half-closed eyelids for the attainment of an artistic effect, but a moving object demands open-eyed attention and sharply focussed eyes to delineate its contour, and the inability of the eye to sharpen the definition of an out-of-focus picture results in an irritation to the eye which is not only a mental abomination but an actual and harmful physical eye-strain. On the other hand, razor-blade sharpness in every plane of a motion picture is not always essential nor is it natural. The human eye only discerns clearly those objects which are in the plane on which it is focused, and it is an insurmountable law of physics that no lens should be in focus at all distances, whether it is a photographic objective or the cornea of the human eye.

(*To be continued.*)

Reviews of Current Productions
EXCLUSIVELY BY OUR OWN STAFF

"Rebecca of Sunnybrook Farm"

Artcraft Presents Mary Pickford in a Delightful and Humanizing Comedy of Decided Artistry.

Reviewed by Louis Reeves Harrison.

REBECCA of Sunnybrook Farm" can easily run the gauntlet of close inspection and sharp criticism without fear.

It is complete and satisfying in every department, the kind of artistry destined to bring millions to the picture shows who do not now attend. The author, the director and the brilliant little artist who plays the title role are in a harmony of creative and interpretative effort which delights the eye, the mind and the heart, now a beautifully composed picture effect, now a flash of wit or humor in subtitle, and again a revelation of tender sympathy which stirs one's kindest sensibilities. Miss Pickford is given far higher opportunity than could be

Scene from "Rebecca of Sunnybrook Farm" (Artcraft).

attained in any "vehicle," and she easily rises to the dramatic heights afforded her. She becomes a dominating figure through ability, instead of having everything thrown her way.

The play, to begin with, addresses refinement. The influence of any such story upon the public reacts for good or evil upon the exhibitor and producer alike. It is not a question of satisfying the vulgar and morbid tastes of this or that group of spectators, but of addressing the higher standards of millions upon millions of Americans who read the magazines of high quality, who have been disgusted with low standards in moving pictures. "Rebecca of Sunnybrook Farm" is not superior in subject matter, nor in plot, nor in many other respects to other pictures, but in logic of construction—it is developed along lines which appeal to rational minds. It is an attempt to entertain the great majority of intelligent people, and it reaches out to the minority primitive minds without vulgarity. It is thus a success both ways. The circus scene is a scream—it will convulse the average audience—yet there are moments of tender pathos, and even a touch of melodrama in the storm, but there are no flashy characterizations of the theatrical kind.

As a consequence, Miss Pickford does not have to be theatrical. She does not have to sterilize her personality. She uses it brightly to stimulate the imagination, expressing temperamentally a variety of thought and feeling, ranging from the depths of sorrow to the heights of youthful spirits and good humor, with a lot of kindly sympathy interspersed. This is made possible by the high quality of the medium. The greater consistency of ideas throughout impels the actress to greater naturalness, to more effective characterization and emotional denotement. Play and player unite in an effort indispensable for the advancement of this new art of ours. They make it an instrumentality for humane advancement and, at the same time, raise the standard of motion picture entertainment.

The recently completed Alice Brady photoplay for World Pictures is now called "A Maid of Belgium" instead of "The Refugee," as at first.

Pathe Pictures

"War and the Woman," Five-Reel Melodrama Featuring Florence La Badie, and "The Angel Factory," Five Reel Astra Production Featuring Antonio Moreno.

Reviewed by Ben H. Grimm.

BECAUSE war is uppermost in the minds of all at the present time, "War and the Woman," a five-reel Thanhouser melodrama featuring Florence La Badie, is an acceptable offering and should get over. Considered solely on its merits as a photoplay and aside from its association of ideas with that which is most vital to us just now, the picture is not so much. There are no battle scenes. Philip Lonergan wrote the story and scenario. He has given us a highly imaginative story of, as he terms it, "what might have been"—what might have happened had a foreign enemy invaded this country. Miss La Badie is seen in the role of a girl whose stepfather is suspected of being a spy. She leaves him and, through a series of circumstances marries John Barker (Wayne Arey), after she has rescued him from an aeroplane accident. John is called to duty. The foreign enemy invades the country and takes over the Barker country home. The girl is made a servant because of her refusal to meet the advances of the commander of the invading army. John, now an aviator, gets leave to search for his wife. He gets through the lines and plans to rescue the girl. She manages to elude the invaders as they are at a Bacchanalian dinner. She lights a fuse connected with a dynamite charge in the cellar. The house blows up and the girl is carried away in her husband's airplane.

One touch that could have been left out is that in which President Wilson is shown purchasing books. The actor who plays the part bears a striking resemblance to the President, but it is doubtful if the incident will take well. Another incident that might have been left out is that showing one of the girls who had been "invited" to the invaders' dinner, and who too obviously had been ravaged.

Miss La Badie is thoroughly capable in her part, as is also Mr. Arey. Other important parts are in the hands of Tom Brooks, Grace Henderson, Arthur Bower and Ernest C. Warde, who also directed. Mr. Warde directed with his usual skill.

"The Angel Factory."

At all times interesting and with an idea that scratches below the surface, "The Angel Factory," a five-reel Astra production, is a good photoplay. Into the picture have been kneaded all the elements that make for interest, and the whole is served in a fitting manner. Antonio Moreno is the featured player.

Scene from "The Angel Factory" (Astra).

Opposite him is Helene Chadick, a young woman who shows rare promise. Much interest in the picture centers in the types obtained for even the smaller character parts, and the production given Lucien Hubbard's story by Director Lawrence McGill. The picture shows that the author knows the slums and knows how slum inhabitants act; also that the director was in sympathy with the story.

Mr. Moreno has the part of a wealthy young man who conducts a settlement house which has been dubbed "The Angel Factory." Miss Chadwick is seen as a virtuous slum girl who is more or less carried away by the adventurous charm of a gang leader. The settlement worker's efforts to uplift, despite his society's fiance's objections, lead the latter to invite the girl, now the youth's protege, to a dance. The girl carries off honors at the dance. The gang leader becomes jealous of the settlement worker and, as he attempts to shoot his rival, is himself killed. The girl is first accused of the murder. Later the settlement worker is accused. During this part of the picture there is a fine degree of suspense worked up, which is finally dispelled when Sailor Bill, a man whom the youth had helped, and who finally had given in to his whiskey craving, confesses. The youth's society fiance jilts him, and he and the girl of the slums confess their mutual love.

The character portrayals are excellent. Important players besides the leads are Armand Cortes, Laura West, Margaret Greene, Suzanne Willa and Franics X. Conlan.

"Fools For Luck"

Taylor Holmes Makes Second Hit in Photocomedy Adapted from Kenneth Harris' "Talismans."

Reviewed by James S. McQuade.

WHEN Kenneth Harris wrote "Talisman's," he aimed at making each of the characters fit into his or her niche in real life as closely as possible. In other words, the story impresses one as a matter-of-fact story, which will remind the spectator of incidents in his own life or in the lives of people whom he has known, without any attempted exaggeration. Naturally the hero of the story is placed at a disadvantage under these somewhat prosaic conditions, especially in the judgment of people who revel in melodramatic, or unreal life; but to those who have learned to look for a faithful reflection of life on the screen "Fools For Luck" will be gladly welcomed and Essanay will be credited with another success in which Taylor Holmes is the leading figure.

At this point it is timely to remind Mr. Holmes that in the early reels of this picture, in certain scenes, he can be justly accused of over-acting the role of Philander Jepson, an oversight that is emphasized by contrasting the simple, natural treatment of the part of Brunhilda by Helen Ferguson.

Essanay's foreword to this photo comedy prepares the spectator for what is to come in the following words: "This is a darn fool story about good luck, bad luck, love and other silly things. If you are not a little bit superstitious, please pass out quietly, and maybe the box office will give your money back —maybe." I have very little fear, however, that any one of the many hundreds of thousands who will view this picture will take the chance, for it is exceedingly pleasing to stay. There is such a gratifying, pleased feeling in one's heart to watch the self-redemption of Philander, who has been a firm believer in rabbit foot, and other good luck charms and superstitions. We see him get down to bedrock and begin building the foundations of character on his own best efforts, and we joyfully watch him as he throws gambling and his gambling friends aside and devotes himself, heart and soul, to the nursing of his job. And this leads him back again to Brunhilda,

Scene from "Fools for Luck" (Essanay).

whose father had forbidden him his home, because he was "going straight to the devil, with a clear track."

Mr. Holmes will add to his following by his screen creating of fine comedy points before the camera is again pleasingly evidenced. In the love scenes between Philander and Brunhilda, Mr. Holmes shows great tenderness and devotion. While Helen Ferguson's Brunhilda cannot fail to win a host of admirers.

Robert Bolder and Frankie Raymond, as the father and mother of Brunhilda; John Cossar, as the boss who fired Philander; James C. Carroll, as the succeeding boss, who gave Philander another chance, and Ed Cooke, as the barroom waiter, who advised Philander to jump in the lake, are the other members of a capable cast.

The release will be made through K-E-S-E, Inc., October 8.

"The Little Pirate"

Five-Reel Butterfly Subject Features Zoe Rae in Story of Reviewed by Robert C. McElravy.

A STRONG juvenile interest is uppermost in this five-reel number, written by Norris Shannon and produced by Elsie Jane Wilson. It has a simple, direct plot, which could easily have been encompassed in a less number of reels, but which, nevertheless, holds the interest firmly as presented.

"Scene from "The Little Pirate" (Butterfly).

Zoe Rae, a child actress well known to the films, has the part of Margery Baird, daughter of a business man in temporary financial straits. The father is trying to raise some money to tide him over a crisis and his suspicions are aroused by the disappearance of some securities in the hands of a man named Drake. The latter individual is also the cause of trouble between Baird and his wife. This latter phase of the story constitutes the chief adult interest in the number.

It is after the quarrel and separation of Baird and his wife that little Margery ventures out upon the exploit which brings up the chief incidents of the story. She is riding through the woods on her pony, which she leaves temporarily in order to pursue a rabbit. The pony runs away and Margery then meets the boy pirate, played by Burwell Hemerick. The latter attempts to terrorize her, but only makes her fall in love with him. Then they decide to leave civilization and take a boat for the pirate island.

The remainder of the story is concerned with the efforts of two sets of grieving parents to get trace of the missing children. The latter for a time enjoy life on the island, turning up the missing "securities" in their search for treasure. They attempt to return in a leaky boat and considerable excitement ensues before they are rescued.

Others in the cast are Charley West, Frank Brownlee, Gretchen Lederer, Mr. Titus and Lillian Peacock.

George Ade Fable

The Fable of "The Wandering Boy and the Wayward Parents" an Amusing Two-Reel Essanay.

Reviewed by Arthur W. Courtney.

THE second of George Ade fables made by Essanay in two reels, "The Wandering Boy and the Wayward Parents," is a splendid photoplay in every respect. It was directed by Richard Foster Baker.

This fable points the moral that if you want to see city life you must go to the country. Rodney La Rock plays the part of the country boy just returned home from college. This is the best piece of acting we have seen him do. He is the life of the picture and he makes it very funny indeed. Magna Anderson plays opposite him as the millionaire's daughter, who considers it her duty to bring Maeterlinck to the masses. Her part is more or less of a burlesque, but it, too, is a scream.

The photoplay shows the college boy coming home. He finds nothing to do. He gets an invitation to the city. He goes and gets into social uplift work. He helps clean up the morals of the city. He has not time for even such conventional temptations as musical comedy. He visits his parents and finds that they have gone to the bad. Father is head of the house committee of a fashionable club that runs a blind pig. He returns to the city to live a clean life with the girl who likes to read aloud from the Belgian playwright.

"Polly of the Circus"

Goldwyn Initial Production a Great Picture—Mae Marsh in Margaret Mayo Story Shines Her Brightest.

Reviewed by George Blaisdell.

IN "Polly of the Circus," Goldwyn's initial production, we have a great picture. It makes a twin appeal—to the eye and better still to the heart. If Adrian Gil-Spear's development of Margaret Mayo's story has been somewhat slow it has been sure. The eight reels may be divided into two equal

Scene from "Polly of the Circus" (Goldwyn).

parts. The first half is pure entertainment, or nearly so. The last half is sterling drama. It grips and it deeply stirs. The spectacular, of which there is much, is subsidiary. It rounds out, it complements the whole; but what dominates, holds tight, is the growing affection of Polly for the "sky pilot" toward whom at first sight she displayed nothing but scorn—a perfectly natural attitude on the part of the girl reared among the big tents.

Mae Marsh shines as Polly. It is over five years since we saw her first in a big role—and her portrayal of Lilywhite in "Man's Genesis" was one of the first pieces of work she did for the screen. As Polly she displays the same talent evidenced in the earlier characterization, and in addition the art that she has acquired in a busy half decade under exceptionally keen instruction. Polly enters the story as a girl untamed, inured to the hurlyburly of the show and accustomed only to the ways of men and women who act and speak frankly. She emerges a woman—softened by contact with men and women of quieter ways, of education, of simpler life, and touched by love.

The opening of the picture is addressed to those boys and girls whose childhood is far behind them; it is an effective appeal, made stronger by reason of the charming bits of village scenery. There is brought out the fascination for mankind that inheres in the annual circus, with its strange humans and animals. We are intoduced to the two boys and the girl who figure in the main story. The first touch of real drama comes when Polly, injured in the ring, is brought to the home of the boy "Skinnay," now the village preacher. Indignant parishioners declare the girl of the circus must not enter the parsonage. "This is the Lord's house, and while I dwell in it none shall be turned away," says the pastor, and the matter is settled.

Right here the story really begins. Polly's first day, a Sunday, in her new home is full of interest. In her bed, pulled to the window, she can look in on the services in the church and hear the minister, as well as see him. There is rare comedy when Polly, catching the eye of the speaker, furiously waves her arms to him. It is a tragic situation for the preacher and for one of the protesting ancient members of the choir who has witnessed the action. The home life of the parsonage, with its two negro servants, is finely shown. Polly, convalescent, romps with the children—and with the pastor—studies and leans more and more on her protector.

Vernon Steele is Big Jim, the minister, a fine character, and he gives an equally fine characterization. Wellington Playter is Big Jim, the Boss Canvasman, the protector of Polly and in love with her, a strong performance. Charles Eldridge's identity is concealed under the make-up of Toby the clown. Mr. Eldridge is at his best. George Trimble is Barker, the portly owner of the show, a convincing ringmaster. There is a long supplementary cast, among them the villagers and church members, the latter of whom are made to show us the most uncharitable sort of persons—an interpretation that very likely will be resented in communities that best know that non-cosmopolitan type.

On the dramatic side there is much to commend. The ever new story of Ruth and Naomi is effectively told by the pastor to his injured visitor; that its influence on Polly is marked we have abundant proof later. If any screen horse race has in its suspense ever matched Bingo's battle to be first under the wire we did not see it.

On the pictorial side the subject is notable. Charles T. Horan directed. To Everitt Shinn is given the credit for the art direction. George W. Hill was the photographer. There are many examples of night stuff, all of them unusual and remarkably effective—of the show, of street scenes.

"Polly of the Circus" will go strong in any house.

A Pair of Triangles

Bessie Love in "Polly Ann," a Five-Part Comedy-Drama by J. G. Hawks and R. Cecil Smith, and William Desmond in "Flying Colors," by John Lynch and R. Cecil Smith.

Reviewed by Edward Weitzel.

"Polly Ann."

THE humors of New England village life are entertainingly set forth in "Polly Ann," a five-part photoplay written by J. G. Hawks and R. Cecil Smith and produced by the Triangle, with Bessie Love in the title role. The bewitching Bessie appears as a neglected orphan whose only home has been the poor farm until she is hired out to the proprietor of the village tavern and made to do most of the work about the place. The story follows along the accepted lines laid down for this class of screen and stage romance, and Polly Ann's fairy prince arrives in due time and carries her off to the city and a life of ease and luxury. Before this happens, however, she goes through a series of amusing experiences; she even becomes a member of a one-night-stand show troupe and plays one of the little Princes in Richard the Third.

The engagement of the company is not a success, but Polly departs with them when the star and his support jump their board bill and flee in the faint light of early dawn. The attentions of the handsome leading man becoming too insistent, the ex-slavey is glad to be rescued by the real hero. The plot is mainly valuable by reason of the opportunities it gives Miss Bessie to play a simple hearted but clear headed little waif whose good fortune at the finish will be welcomed by everyone in front of the screen. The amount of charm, sly humor and human nature that the actress puts into her creation will be easily anticipated. The supporting company, consisting of Rowland Lee, Walt Whitman, John Lockney, William Ellingford, David Foss, Alfred Hollingsworth and Josephine Headly, portray the various New England types with the proper amount of realism. Charles F. Miller's direction of the picture adds materially to its worth.

"Flying Colors."

The moral to be learned from "Flying Colors," a five-part photoplay written by John Lynch and R. Cecil Smith and directed by Frank Borzage, is not to pull a long face when down on one's luck but to encourage a genial smile. William Desmond, who has the leading role in this picture, is a living example of the force of the above precept and, as Brent Brewster, a famous college athlete who turns detective when forced to by circumstances, illustrates that a pleasant look, backed up by a firm will and strong muscles, is quite sure to make any young chap come out with flying colors. Brewster is sent to keep his eye on a house party, the mistress of the place having been robbed of her jewels. The first thing he does is to fall in love with the sister of his hostess. He then gets down to busi-

Scene from "Flying Colors" (Triangle).

ness, and fastens the robbery upon a certain Captain Drake, a high class crook of English birth, who is also endeavoring to carry off the object of Brent's newly awakened affections.

"Flying Colors" was evidently written with William Desmond in view and proves an excellent fit. It is good entertainment of its class, and is assisted in this end by the acting of Golda Madlen, Jack Livingston, Laura Sears, J. Barney Sherry, Geo. W. Chase, John Lockney, Bert Offerd, Mary McIvor and Ray Jackson.

"Lost in Transit"

Pallas Five-Part Subject Is a Typical Beban Picture, One With Smiles and Tears.

Reviewed by George Blaisdell.

IT'S a real Beban picture we have in "Lost in Transit," a Pallas five-part subject released on September 3—just the sort we look for when we see George Beban on the bills. There are smiles in good measure for the first 3,500 feet, but in the remainder these are not in evidence. For 1,500 feet it is tense

Scene from "Lost in Transit" (Paramount).

drama—of life on the pathetic side artistically portrayed. There's a baby in this story, too—very much in it, by the way. Bob White is an interesting youngster, but it is likely his natural attractiveness is very much increased by his contact with the leading player; Beban surely has a way with him when he is engaged in securing the confidence of a little one. The actor is a natural-born playmate, and the entertainment he radiates extends beyond his immediate subject. In this instance, by the way, there is a suspicion the relationship between the two is more than casual. The resemblance is marked.

Mr. Beban is Niccolo Darini, an Italian junkman, with a wagon —and a white horse; a thoroughbred by no means, but just good-natured, plodding, plugging old plug. The animal looks wise, too, when his master whispers in his ear. The baby enters the story when its mother lifts it in among the rags in Niccolo's cart and disappears. From this point on the baby is right up in front. He is not turned over to the "peleece"—he becomes a part of the life of Niccolo.

Helen Eddy plays opposite Mr. Beban, and plays in her always finished manner the smaller part that falls to her. Vera Lewis is Mrs. Flint, the matron of the children's home who takes the baby from Niccolo and passes it off on Mr. Kendall for the reward of five thousand dollars. Henry Barrows is Kendall, who for two and a half years refused to look on the face of his child because its mother had died at its birth, only to suffer the loss of the little one by kidnapping when his heart softened.

Kathlyn Williams has given us a story of real human interest and Donald Crisp has so directed it as to bring out the best drama in it. "Lost in Transit" possesses the rare faculty of sending 'em away in a happy and also in a melting mood.

"Under Handicap"

Harold Lockwood in Eight-Part Yorke Photoplay Has Congenial Role—Released on Metro Program.

Reviewed by Edward Weitzel.

ALTHOUGH handicapped by an unmusical title, the eight-part photoplay produced by Yorke and named "Under Handicap," is a well made picture and has a pleasing story. It is the familiar one of the rich man's son who goes the pace, until his father comes to his senses and refuses to keep up the supply of necessary coin. Thrown on his own resources, the young man, having the right material hidden away in his backbone, turns to and works out his own salvation. In the present photoplay he again follows the beaten trail and heads for the West. Once there, he meets just the sort of young woman to inspire him with a desire to show her that he is a real man, and before the end of the last part succeeds in downing his enemies, completing an important piece of engineering work and winning the heart of the Western heiress.

The importance of intrusting the part of the hero to the right type of actor has not been overlooked in the casting of the photoplay. As Greek Conniston, the young man with too much money to spend, Harold Lockwood fills all the requirements of the character. Anna Little is uncommonly attractive as Argyle Crawford. The picture was directed by Fred S. Balshofer.

Two Kalems

"A Champion of the Law," Last of the "Stingaree" Series, and "Politics in Pumpkin Center," a "Ham" Comedy.

Reviewed by Ben H. Grimm.

KALEM'S "The Further Adventures of Stingaree" series finished up with "A Champion of the Law," a two-reeler that is more full of thrills than have been any of the preceding episodes. Also it brings to the screen almost the entire roster of Kalem players. The story is not so connected as it might have been, but the "punch" is there nevertheless. In the last chapter Stingaree, through a series of melodramatic circumstances, becomes one of those who defend a house against a band of outlaws. Incidentally he is brought face to face with his sweetheart from England. The end shows the gentleman bushranger sailing for home with his sweetheart. His defense of the house, set upon by the bandits has earned for him a pardon.

True Boardman finishes his Stingaree role with his usual ease. Paul C. Hurst is the Howie that is left in Australia. The cast includes Marin Sais, Chris Lynton, Edythe Sterling, Edward Hearn, Ronald Bradbury, Hart Hoxie, Frank Jonasson and Edward Clisbee.

Mr. Hurst, who directed, has succeeded in obtaining some good night scenes, showing various groups around campfires. The number is one that finishes the series in a fitting manner.

"Politics in Pumpkin Center."

Ham and Bud are responsible for a number of laughs in this one-reel comedy. Ham is the mayor, first chief and everything else in a rural town. Bud is the assistant everything. Henry Murdoch is the cause of Ham's deposition. Bud takes his place. Considerable fun is had with a flivver, which changes from a fire engine to a police patrol quite often.

"A Stormy Knight"

Franklyn Farnum Is Featured in a Bluebird That Holds Well for Three Reels and Then Lets Down.

Reviewed by George Blaisdell.

THERE is real interest in the first three reels of "A Stormy Knight," the five-part Bluebird released on September 10 and featuring Franklyn Farnum. Brownie Vernon is in the cast, but her appearances are so widely spaced it can hardly be said she is featured. What counts much in the picture is the fine night storm stuff. It seems to be a foregone conclusion that the more some directors get away from the attempted illusion of tinting down for night scenes the more some others will have to meet their work and give us the genuine article. In the opening of the picture there are also shown some remarkable views of banks of clouds, seen from the mountain tops above. It will be sure to make a hit.

The subject gets well started as a melodrama, but the action toward the ending diverges to the farcical. Throughout the story one is curious to know what it's all about; at the denouement he is informed that all of the seeming plots and counterplots have been designed solely for the sake of interesting the hero in a young woman—all ordinary means having failed. Mr. Farnum's smile lacks the illusive quality that may

Scene from "A Stormy Knight" (Bluebird).

be noted in the case of its obvious inventor. Perhaps the fault lies in overworking it, in smiling when the observer cannot in the immediate situation discover any occasion for evidence of pleasure.

Others in the cast besides the two principals are Jean Hersholt as Dr. Fraser, Hayward Mack as Richard Weller and Frank McQuarrie as Mr. Weller. The story is based on Jack Cunningham's tale of "The Fourth Glove." Waldemar Young made the adaptation and Elmer Clifton directed.

"Betsy Ross"

Alice Brady in Five-Part Peerless Photoplay Founded on Stage Drama by Henry A. Du Souchet—Released by World Film Corporation.

Reviewed by Edward Weitzel.

THE character of Betsy Ross, the young woman who made the first American flag, is an appealing one, as shown in the five-part photoplay produced by Peerless and released on the World Program. Henry A. Du Souchet, the author of the story, first fashioned his work for the spoken stage, and the

Scene from "Betsey Ross" (World).

screen version shows many traces of its origin. Although history gives the making of the flag as the most important event in the life of Miss Betsy, the playwright uses it merely as an incident, her personal affairs of the heart taking up the larger part of the action. Through a misunderstanding, due to Betsy's sister wearing her cloak, the heroine's lover thinks she is untrue to him and fights a duel with his supposed rival, leaving him for dead. This is the means of tying the usual dramatic tangle, which is only straightened out after Betsy has had several opportunities to exhibit her courage and loyalty. George Washington and Benedict Arnold also figure in the cast of characters.

The direction of the picture was intrusted to Travers Vale and George Cowl, and reflects credit upon them both. Alice Brady finds the character of the historic flag-maker quite in her way. Her personal charms offer sufficient excuse for her lover's devotion, and she acts the part excellently. The supporting company is a large one and consists of such well schooled actors as John Powers, Lillian Cook, Eugenie Woodward, Kate Lester, Frank Mayo, George MacQuarrie, Robert Cummings and Nellie Fillmore.

"To the Death"

Olga Petrova Appears in a Melodramatic Story of a Woman's Revenge—Tragic in Theme, but With a Happy Ending.

Reviewed by C. S. Sewell.

CORSICAN revenge is the basis on which "To the Death," the five-part Metro production released August 27, starring Olga Petrova, is founded. The story, tragic in theme, has been given a happy ending, which, while tending to weaken it, makes it more acceptable to a majority of audiences.

Bianca Sylva (Olga Petrova), a lace maker in Calvi, Corsica, is sent to Paris by a sculptor who is impressed by her talent while watching her modeling in clay. She meets Robert Dumont of the Secret Service and they are attracted to each other. Dumont is warned to go to Corsica and watch Laporte, who is engaged in government work. Some time later Bianca, who has achieved success, is suddenly called home. She finds her sister dying and discovers the note which lured her to her destruction, signed "Pierre Renard," and vows vengeance "to the death." On returning to Paris, she meets Laporte, and agrees to sacrifice herself upon his promising to find "Pierre Renard." On learning that Dumont is Renard, she stabs him, and goes with Laporte, who then boasts that it was he who signed Renard's name to the note. Detectives break in and arrest Laporte for treason, while Bianca rushes back to her studio and finds that Dumont will recover.

While the work of the star in this picture is good, she is not afforded as great opportunities as in some of her other productions. Evelyn Brent is attractive as Rosa, the younger sister, and the rest of the cast, including Wyndham Standing as Laporte and Mahlon Hamilton as Dumont, are satisfactory. The story was written by Madame Petrova and L. Case Russell, and the production directed by Burton L. King.

"The Fall of the Romanoffs"

Herbert Brenon's Eight-Part Picture Novel of the Russian Revolution Has the Absorbing Interest and Dramatic Sweep of the Actual Events.

Reviewed by Edward Weitzel.

AMONG the many excellences to be found in "The Fall of the Romanoffs," Herbert Brenon's eight-part picture novel, based on the Russian Revolution, one attribute stands out in bold relief—the swift onrush of events. Realizing that the multiplicity of amazing happenings which have taken place since Rasputin, the Sacred Devil of Russia, came in contact with the unhappy ruler and his family, offered an embarrassment of historical facts, Austin Strong and George Edwardes-Hall, the writers of the scenario, and producer Brenon, have hurried the action from one salient episode to another and dispensed with the minor detail generally found in works of fiction. In this way the historical events of several years have been compressed into an eight-part picture, and its effect on the beholder is as if he himself were an actor in the scenes that have but recently been added to the pages of history.

It is hardly necessary to outline the plot of "The Fall of the Romanoffs." Rasputin, the illiterate sled driver who rose to power on the ladder of religious superstition, is the dominant figure of the novel. Other characters from life are Nicholas II, the Czarina, the German Emperor, Grand Duke Nicholas, Alexander Kerensky, and Iliodor, the Siberian monk who attempted to overthrow Rasputin, and was himself obliged to flee from Russia. The fictitious characters and events that have been introduced to assist in telling the story fit in admirably with the selection of material from the actual course of affairs. In tracing the rise and fall of Rasputin, the self-styled prophet, the overthrow of the Romanoffs is also shown; and the amazing power commanded by this drunken, licentious mountebank fascinates the spectator, despite his better judgment. Rasputin's effect upon the fate of a great nation when ruled by a man whose only qualification is one of birth, offers a potent argument in favor of democracy. The spectacle of the Czar and Czarina listening to this charlatan as to one inspired and allowing him to direct matters of state as well as their private lives, strengthening the conviction that absolute monarchs are no longer needed on this war-rent world.

To Herbert Brenon belongs a large share of the credit for putting "The Fall of the Romanoffs" before the public in an able and impressive manner. The reproduction of the scenes, episodes, characters, and all that goes to make up the life of the country, has been accomplished with convincing skill. Palace and hut, noble and peasant, the lone figure of the Czar or the rabble in the streets clamoring for freedom—the director has placed them on the screen in exact counterpart and made them do his bidding in an absorbing story which he wisely classifies as a picture novel. One touch of theatricalism mars his work. In the banquet scene, which ends with the killing of Rasputin, a soldier enters the room on horseback and rides his mount down the length of the long table. A very good circus trick, but out of place in this scene.

The cast could hardly be bettered. Edward Connelly as Rasputin gave a character study, based upon actual knowledge of the man, that was finely conceived and adroitly executed. Charles Craig's performance of the Grand Duke Nicholas was equally meritorious, and Conway Tearle as Prince Felix, Nance O'Neil as the Czarina, Alfred Hickman as the Czar, R. Payton Gibbs as Baron Frederick, Mlle. Ketty Galanta as Anna, Pauline Curley as Princess Irena, Mlle. Marcelle as Sonia, William E. Shay as Theofan, George Denueberg as Wilhelm II., Master Lawrence Johnson as the Czarevitch, and W. Francis Chapin as Alexander Kerensky, sustained their roles with commendable ability. Iliodor, the Russian monk, appeared in person and was surprisingly excellent before the camera.

Vitagraphs

"An Alabaster Box," Five-Part Blue Ribbon Feature Featuring Alice Joyce and Marc MacDermott, and "The Fighting Trail," Serial by J. Stuart Blackton and Cyrus Townsend Brady.

Reviewed by Edward Weitzel.

"An Alabaster Box."

IT was a foregone conclusion that a story by Mary F. Wilkins Freeman would contain sound character drawing and be wholesome of theme. Both of these qualities are found in "An Alabaster Box," a five-part Vitagraph Blue Ribbon feature, written by Mrs. Freeman and Florence Morse Kingsley, and directed by Chester Withey. The leading character of the drama is Andrew Bolton, the "big man" of a New England village, whose energy and push keep the place alive and furnish employment for nearly all the inhabitants, but whose financial failure is brought about by the refusal of his fellow townsmen to support him when he tries to enlarge his business interests, and he is sent to prison for embezzlement. Years after his daughter, who was a young child when her father was convicted, returns to the village under an assumed name, and becomes the Lady Bountiful of the place, a fortune having been left her by an uncle. Her father also returns and when his old neighbors learn the truth they turn on his daughter and try to wreck the old Bolton home where she is now living. Bolton tries to defend the house, and falls dead from excitement. An interesting love interest runs through the story.

Alice Joyce fits the character of Lydia Bolton to a nicety, and

Marc MacDermott plays Andrew Bolton with the necessary force and finish. Harry Ham, Patsy De Forest and Frank Crane have other important roles and act them properly. The production is adequate, and Chester Withey has directed it with skill.

"The Fighting Trail."

The opening installment of "The Fighting Trail," the new Vitagraph serial in fifteen episodes, written by J. Stuart Blackton and Cyrus Townsend Brady, is called "The Priceless Ingredient," and deals with a struggle to control a powerful explosive the use of which would go far in settling the Great War. One ingredient is very difficult to obtain, a young mining engineer named John Gwyn, having a secret source of supply. The Central Powers attempt to gain possession of it, and stop at nothing in their efforts. With a motif such as this, it should be easy to build up a powerful story, and vindicate the claims of the Vitagraph that the serial is one of the best adventure tales ever filmed.

The cast has been well selected. William Duncan has the brawn and brains to portray the mining engineer, and Carol Halloway, as Nan Lawton, his sweetheart, appears as a Western heroine of the particularly fearless type. George Holt, Joe Ryan, Walter Rodgers, H. Ducrow and Charles Wheelock are prominent members of the cast.

World Film Prepared for Emergencies

Its Reserve of Brady-Mades Carry It to February, 1918— List of Available Subjects.

WORLD Pictures, Brady-made, are now completed for publication far beyond the beginning of 1918. This is the result of steady accumulation in following out the policy long ago established by Director General William A. Brady, under which the rate of manufacture has been considerably in excess of the volume of issue.

The outcome has been brought about not by speeding up the making of each picture—which might have affected the quality of the product to some extent—but by increasing the number of plays simultaneously in process of production. For months the World studio and outdoor stage at Fort Lee have been occupied constantly by at least six working photoplay companies all the time.

The situation thus developed places World Pictures in a very advantageous position. It enables the director general to correct any minor defects that may come to notice on repeated private showings of a given picture, permits of a complete shift of publications whenever a particularly timely play comes along (as for instance "Rasputin, the Black Monk"), and supplies a constantly swelling list of tangible assets.

Further, in case of any sudden upheaval of general business affairs, the World interests would find it possible to cease making a serious of releases. Of course, no such situation is at all likely to arise, but the World executives obviously perceive the advantage of being ready for emergencies, unforeseen and otherwise.

Following are the World Pictures Brady-Made, in the order of their publication up to and including the week of February 11 of next year:

September 24, Ethel Clayton in "The Woman Beneath;" October 1, Lew Fields and Madge Evans in "The Corner Grocer;" October 8, all star cast, headed by Montagu Love, June Elvidge, Arthur Ashley, Julia Dean, Henry Hull, Irving Cummings and Hubert Wilke in "Rasputin, the Black Monk;" October 15, Carlyle Blackwell, Madge Evans and Evelyn Greeley in "The Burglar;" October 22, Alice Brady in "The Maid of Belgium;" October 29, June Elvidge and Arthur Ashley in "Shall We Forgive Her;" November 5, Ethel Clayton in "The Dormant Power;" November 12, Madge Evans in "The Little Patriot;" November 19, Carlyle Blackwell and Evelyn Greeley in "The Good for Nothing;" November 26, Kitty Gordon in "Her Hour;" December 3, June Elvidge and Arthur Ashley in "A Creole's Revenge;" December 10, Montagu Love in "The Beast;" December 17, Ethel Clayton in "Easy Money;" December 24, Carlyle Blackwell and Evelyn Greeley in "The Ladder of Fame;" December 31, Kitty Gordon in "The Divine Sacrifice;" January 7, June Elvidge in "The Way of the Strong;" January 14, Alice Brady in "The Spurs of Sybil;" January 21, Madge Evans in "True Blue;" January 28, Ethel Clayton in "Stolen Hours;" February 4, Carlyle Blackwell and Evelyn Greeley in "Almost a King;" February 11, Kitty Gordon in "Making a Man Pay."

This list insures a definite program for twenty-one weeks, which is said in the offices of World Pictures to embrace a much greater number of releases than were ever made in advance by any other picture producing company.

NEW FARRAR SPECTACLE FINISHED.

The new Geraldine Farrar motion picture spectacle, staged under the personal direction of Cecil B. De Mille, "The Woman God Forgot," has been finished in California and marks the initial Farrar release through Artcraft Pictures. The last scenes for this production were staged in the Yosemite when Director De Mille took 300 people by special train to this beautiful section for several immense exteriors.

Supporting the famous diva in "Woman God Forgot" are many of the artists who appeared with her in "Joan," including Wallace Reid, Raymond Hatton, Hobart Bosworth, Walter Long, Charles B. Rogers, Olga Grey, as well as Theodore Kosloff, the Russian dancer. The story is by Jeanie Macpherson, who also wrote "Joan."

A Three-Star Mutual Week

Mutual's Schedule for the Week of September 17 Contains Three Productions of Unusual Interest—Fischer, Day and Holmes Featured.

MARGARITA FISCHER, whose productions has been interrupted by illness, is starred in "The Girl Who Couldn't Grow Up," a five-reel comedy drama listed for September 17. Juliette Day, who deserted the footlights of Broadway for the Santa Barbara studios, is released in "The Rainbow Girl," a five-reel drama on the same date.

"The Lost Express," the first chapter of "The Lost Express," fifteen chapter Signal-Mutual photonovel, is scheduled for first run on Monday, September 17. The schedule for the week includes "Officer Jerry," a one-reel Cub Comedy, Mutual Weekly, the current events reel and Reel Life, the one-reel magazine of the film.

Miss Fischer comes back in pants. "The Girl Who Couldn't Grow Up" is a rollicking comedy and provides Miss Fischer with a role well suited to her abilities. She wears middy and trousers, an over-sized dress suit and adorable pajamas. She is a mischievous college girl, loved by a British nobleman who masquerades in his valet's place while his valet is being lavishly entertained by the girl's stepmother and her daughters at papa's home in the mountains.

The plot brings in a dozen intricate and comical situations which provide Miss Fischer with splendid chances for fast comedy action. The picture isn't all funny, for there are a lot of serious situations and Miss Fischer wears her most becoming gowns in most becoming style.

Miss Fischer's illness interrupted the production of "The Devil's Assistant," and she has spent most of the summer recuperating. "The Girl Who Couldn't Grow Up" shows that she has regained her health and her energy and that she is the same beautiful Margarita who scored so heavily in "The Pearl of Paradise" and "Miss Jackie of the Navy."

Miss Day, star in "Upstairs and Down," during its successful run on Broadway, went to the Pacific Coast early in the spring to produce a series of pictures for the American Film Company for Mutual release, and "The Rainbow Girl" is the first completed for presentation. "The Rainbow Girl" deals with a couple of young folks who loved each other but thought that the other loved somebody else.

Miss Day's value at the box office lies in her fame on the legitimate stage, but that is quite sufficient to attract the crowd. When Broadway will part with its money, night after night, to see an actress and she reaches the point where she is styled a hit, photoplay fans want to see her on the screen. Miss Day is declared to screen well and she is known to be a clever little actress. "The Rainbow Girl" is a crack story. The picture was directed by Rollin S. Sturgeon.

"The Lost Express," the serial release for the week of September 17, has been pronounced a corking photo-novel by the reviewers who have seen the opening chapters. It opens-ing—with the mysterious disappearance of a trainload of valuable documents. A band of pirates has raided the laboratories of old General Thurston to steal his formula for granulated gasoline and the old general himself has been shot in the fight. His daughter Helen, played by Miss Helen Holmes, orders that the documents in his safe be removed to a safety vault in a nearby city and charters a train to take them. Between stations the whole train disappears.

"The Lost Express" will be released, a chapter at a time, for fifteen weeks. The chapters are in two reels each. The production was directed by J. P. McGowan, celebrated for his stage management of photo-melodrama starring Helen Holmes, acknowledged to be the most fearless of motion picture actresses. It was produced by the Signal Film Corporation.

The Cub comedy "Officer Jerry," released on September 20, gives George Ovey the role of a masquerading policeman in which he goes through a series of humorous situations. Reel Life No. 73, the release of September 20, carries scenes showing the making of army rifles, running an aeroplane without danger, portrays the principle of the gyroscope and animated drawings from Life. Mutual Weekly, scheduled for September 19, includes current events up to the time the reel is assembled.

ESSANAY-CHAPLINS TO BE REISSUED.

Essanay has bowed to the call of the public for its famous Charlie Chaplin comedies and will put out new prints of all the Essanay-Chaplin productions. The first one will be offered on September 15, and one a month will be issued thereafter. "The Champion," with a screen time of approximately thirty minutes, will head the program.

This will be followed by other equally humorous comedies, including "In the Park," "By the Sea," "A Woman," "Shanghaied," "Work," "A Jitney Elopement," "The Bank," "A Night in the Show," and others. They will be distributed through the General Film Company, Inc.

These comedies were all made in the heyday of Chaplin's popularity and have been held by both critics and the public to be very best of his pictures.

The Essanay Company has issued a warning that it will prosecute any person making, distributing or renting spurious company in its fight for picture honesty if exhibitors will kindly report such abuses.

Comments on the Films
EXCLUSIVELY BY OUR OWN STAFF

General Film Corporation.

SELIG WORLD LIBRARY NO. 17 (Selig), September.—In this number of the Selig World Library will be found the following subjects well illustrated: "The Mussel Pearl Industry"; "American Beach Resorts," and "The Sugar Industry of Java."

THE WANDERING BOY AND THE WAYWARD PARENTS (Essanay).—A George Ade fable in two reels. This is a very amusing subject that will entertain the intelligent. Rodney La Rocq does the best work we have seen him do. The moral of this fable is that if you want to see city life you must go to the country. A review of this picture is printed elsewhere.

Artcraft Pictures Corporation.

REBECCA OF SUNNYBROOK FARM (Sept. 3).—A gem of motion picture production, resourceful in all departments, with Mary Pickford in what may be justly called her finest impersonation. A screen story well calculated to please old patrons and bring a host of new ones to the theater.

Bluebird Photoplays, Inc.

TRIUMPH, September 3.—A five-part photoplay from a story by Samuel Hopkins Adams; directed by Joseph De Grasse. In the cast are Dorothy Phillips, Lon Chaney, William Stowell, William J. Dyer and Claire Dubrey. The tragedy is told as a tragic story within a story with a happy ending. The inside story has some strong moments. The story hinges upon a theatrical manager's improper advances to the leading lady of his show. This is followed by a murder and two suicides. A review of this photoplay was printed in last week's issue.

A STORMY KNIGHT, September 10.—Franklyn Farnum is featured in this mystery story. Opposite him is Brownie Vernon. The story gets away to an excellent and a picturesque start, but the interest lets down in the last two reels. The subject is reviewed in another column.

Butterfly Pictures.

THE LITTLE PIRATE, September 10.—A five-reel story, by Norris Shannon, featuring Zoe Rae, Burwell Hemerick, Gretchen Lederer and others. This will perhaps make its strongest appeal to children, as it concerns a boy and girl who run away to become pirates. The story interest is moderately strong and the presentation is consistent. Reviewed at length elsewhere.

Greater Vitagraph.

BOBBY'S SECRET (Vitagraph).—This is a one-reel Bobby Connelly picture with Aida Horton poor again and lame. The story was written and directed by Charles M. Seay. It is a clumsy story within a story. The inside story is fairly entertaining. Bobby's parents leave him in care of the maid who begins to receive presents of jewelry from an admirer. When the parents return, Bobby's bank that had ten ten-dollar gold pieces in it is found empty. The maid is accused, and then Bobby tells the long inside story, the main story. He finds the poor lame girl, and takes her to a hospital and pays for the operation. The best scene is where a dog, thrown into the river in a weighted bag, is rescued by Bobby's pal and taken home for Aida.

Kleine-Edison-Selig-Essanay

MEN OF THE DESERT (Essanay), September 24.—This is a Western picture that is certain to win high favor. It is of the new Western type, affording much that is satisfying to the spectator. Jack Gardner, Ruth King and Carl Stockdale play the principal roles with fine spirit. Director Van Dyke is to be complimented for the art and care bestowed on the production. A detailed review appears in last week's issue.

FOOLS FOR LUCK (Essanay), October 8.—A clean, wholesome photocomedy, abounding in mirthful incidents, in which Taylor Holmes and Helen Ferguson appear as the lovers—ably directed by Lawrence Windom. An extended review appears on another page in this issue.

Metro Pictures Corporation.

TO THE DEATH, August 27.—A five-part Metro production, presenting Olga Petrova in a story of Corsican revenge, tragic in theme, but having a conventional happy ending. A review is printed on another page of this issue.

MUSIC HATH CHARMS (Drew), September 3.—This is not the best of the Drew comedies by any means. At the same time it is capable of getting a laugh. The subject is presented amusingly, and deals with the effect which the music played at the wedding ceremony has on the bride. In one instance Mr. Henry learns by accident of the quadru-

pletics were the result of the playing of the quartette from "Rigoletto"; and when on the anniversary of his own marriage his wife in reminiscent tones reminds him of the various things which happened on their wedding day, among them the playing by the orchestra of the sextette from "Lucia" a closeup of Mr. Henry's face suggests nervous prostration. We venture to say that none but the Drews could present such a subject in comedy without offense.

Mutual Film Corporation.

MUTUAL WEEKLY NO. 138 (Gaumont), August 22.—Items of interest in this issue show us our boys learning the art of trench digging, motorcycles climbing a rocky grade, Colorado honoring her soldiers, and presenting each with a $10 gold piece, army lumber taking a 1,500 mile journey on a log raft, and 1,800 student officers receiving their commissions at Fort Meyer, Va.

MUTUAL WEEKLY NO. 139 (Gaumont), August 29.—The launching of a big steel freighter at Seattle opens this number. Other interesting sights are the mobilization of camera men at Los Angeles for war service, the speedway triumph at New York City won by De Palma, General Pershing visiting French munition factory, and Norman Ross winning the swimming championship at Golden Gate, San Francisco.

REEL LIFE NO. 73 (Gaumont), September 20.—The subjects in this number of Reel Life are "Weaving the President's Portrait"; "Running an Aeroplane Without Danger;" "The Principle of the Gyroscope," and "Student Officers." An interesting and well-illustrated number.

Paramount Pictures Corporation.

LOST IN TRANSIT (Pallas), September 3.—A typical George Beban subject, with lighter touches and pathos. A fine picture, as is set forth in a review in another column.

Pathe Exchange, Inc.

WAR AND THE WOMAN (Thanhouser), September 9.—A five-reel war melodrama featuring Florence La Badie. The picture tells an imaginative story of what might have been had a foreign enemy invaded this country. There are no battle scenes. Spies and other war followers are seen in the picture. It is melodrama pure and simple, and as such should interest. A longer review can be found in the review columns.

THE ANGEL FACTORY (Astra), September 23.—A five-reel picture featuring Antonio Moreno and Helene Chadwick. It is at all times interesting and has an idea that scratches below the surface. While the story centers around a girl of the slums and a wealthy settlement worker, it carries the idea of uplift. The story is full of suspense and interest. Reviewed in the review columns of this issue.

THE AIR PERIL (Astra), September 30.—Chapter No. 3 of "The Seven Pearls" serial. The story speeds up considerably in this number, and Mollie King in the role of Ilma creates more mystery and goes through more adventure. The chapter ends showing her bound to a balloon that is released by a man who murdered his brother for one of the pearls.

Universal Film Mfg. Company.

ANIMATED WEEKLY, NO. 87 (Universal), August 29.—An entertaining and diversified number, picturing various war activities on land and sea, burning of an Armour ice plant in Illinois, car strike in San Francisco and other features.

CURRENT EVENTS, NO. 17 (Universal), September 8.—Graduation exercises at West Point, annual baby parade at Asbury Park, bathing suit styles in Chicago and many war scenes are included in this instructive number.

A PRAIRIE CHICKEN (L-KO), Rel. Week of September 17.—Myrta Sterling is featured in this two-reel comic, playing the part of a fat, roly-poly Western girl who goes East to visit relatives. She shocks the effete Easterners with her uncouth ways, and some amusing situations result. This is free from offense and is well up to the average of this company's productions.

HAWAIIAN NUTS (Joker), Rel. Week of September 17.—A comedy number, by William Beaudine, featuring Gale Henry, William Franey, Ed Baker and Milton Sims. Franey is designated by a secret order to procure a certain valuable snake. The plot rather fizzles out, but there are some very amusing situations of a nonsensical sort.

CIRCUS SARAH (Joker), Rel. Week of September 17.—A comedy number, by Tom Gibson, featuring Gale Henry and Milton Sims. The circus manager, in financial straits, meets Gale and invites her to do bareback riding. Her awkward attempts at this are funny, though there is not much to the plot as a whole. It makes a fair subject.

THE PULLMAN MYSTERY (Gold Seal), Rel. Week of September 17.—A three-reel subject by Robert von Saxmer, featuring Hayward Mack, Molly Malone, Ray Hanford, Larry Peyton, T. D. Crittenden, Fred Montague and Josephine Sedgwick. The story is of the melodramatic type and has no particular plot novelty. The action and continuity are good, however, and it makes a fairly strong offering. It begins with a murder committed during some labor troubles. The hero, accused of the crime, impersonates a man supposed to be dead, but in the end reveals his true identity. The real murderer then makes a confession of his crime. There is the usual love story.

WELCOME HOME (Nestor), Rel. Week of Sept. 17.—A comedy subject, by Fred A. Palmer, featuring Eddie Lyons, Lee Moran and Edith Roberts. Lee Moran is amusing in the part of the hobo who observes the "game laws" and refuses to shoot snipes under two inches in length. The plot is not particularly strong, but the subject proves quite entertaining. The close is rather conventional.

THE RIGHT MAN (Star Featurette), Rel. Week of September 17.— A two-reel subject, by M. McCall, featuring J. Warren Kerrigan, E. M. Wallack, Edith Johnson and Charles Cummings. This tells of a young bank clerk, in love with the president's daughter, who is found guilty of embezzlement, though the job was put up on him by another. He goes West and later a friend tells him the true facts. He hastens back home, just in time to interrupt the wedding of the girl to the real villain. This makes a good offering of the slightly melodramatic sort, and is enacted by a pleasing cast.

MARATHON MANIACS (Victor), Rel. Week of September 17.—A comedy number, by Craig Hutchinson, featuring Dave Morris, Max Asher and Gladys Tennison. This has a "sporting" flavor, most of the scenes transpiring in a training quarters. It is an amusing and successful offering of the type. The reel closes with a footrace.

THE LAST OF THE NIGHT RIDERS (Bison), Rel. Week of September 17.—A two-reel subject, by Jack Cunningham, featuring Fred Church, Eileen Sedgwick, Frank Lanning, Leonard Clapham and others. This begins with the incendiary firing of a tobacco warehouse by some Southern night riders, and the story deals with the efforts of the hero and his father, the sheriff, to bring the miscreants to justice. The plot is melodramatic at times and none too convincing. At the same time the scenes are picturesque and the action good.

THE POISONED RING (Universal Special), Rel. Week of September 17.—Episode No. 12 of "The Gray Ghost." This is an eventful number, in which the arch villain fulfils his threat to call upon the commissioner of police. He does so and by a trick escapes with the valuable pearls. The ring is also returned to Morn Light, but has been poisoned, and the last reel closes just as she is about to place it on her finger.

Hart's Initial Artcraft Finished

"The Narrow Trail," to Be Released Next Month, Marks Double Debut of Star as Author and Artcrafter.

WILLIAM S. HART'S initial Ince-Artcraft production, "The Narrow Trail," has been finished at the Lasky studios in California. This photoplay marks a double debut for "Big Bill," so to speak, in that it presents him for the first time as an Artcraft star and also presents his initial endeavor as an author. The story was scenarioized by Harvey Thew. In writing the tale Mr. Hart has not forgotten the popularity of his Pinto pony, Fritz and has given his horse particular opportunity to display his talents for the benefit of his many admirers.

The story has to do with Ice Harding, a notorious Western bandit, whose beautifully marked pinto makes him an easy mark for the members of the law who are hunting him and his gang. The wonderful speed and endurance of the animal keeps the outlaw safe from the sheriff and his posse, but finally the animal causes considerable trouble for its master, who refuses to part with his best pal. A romantic theme is also involved in the story when the outlaw falls in love with his ideal of a girl and turns over a new leaf only to be suddenly confronted with the belief that his new faith has been shattered. Among the thrills offered in the picture are daring feats in horsemanship, a stirring fight between Hart and two opponents, and an exciting horse race with crowded grandstands, offering a surprise climax to the story.

"MADAM WHO" MISS BARRISCALE'S FIRST RELEASE.

Bessie Barriscale's first Paralta release will not be Grace Miller White's "Rose o' Paradise," as at first announced. Instead, Harold MacGrath's "Madam Who," Miss Barriscale's second Paralta production, will be presented in October and will be followed by "Rose o' Paradise."

Mrs. White's story may be termed an emotional optimistic romance in which the principal characters, "Jinnie Singleton," played by Bessie Barriscale, "Lafe Grandeken," acted by Howard Hickman, and "Peg," impersonated by Edythe Chapman, are beset by poverty, intrigue and danger and yet they form a "Happy in Spite" club, in which they find inspiration to see in every disappointment and disaster—"it happened for the best."

Mrs. White's story has attracted much attention because of her very beautiful handling of its optimistic theme. The result has been that over one hundred "Happy in Spite" clubs have been formed throughout the country.

A nation-wide publicity campaign in connection with "Rose o' Paradise" and its optimistic club has been inaugurated and will reach and interest over one million people before the picture is released. A special picture edition of the story will also be issued to further the promotion of these "Happy in Spite" clubs.

"The Pullman Mystery" Leads Universal

Mystery Drama, Several Rollicking Comedies and Three Big News Features Complete Strong List for Week of September 18.

THE PULLMAN MYSTERY," a Gold Seal drama, released Tuesday, September 18, heads Universal's schedule for the week of the 17th. On the previous day, released under other arrangements, "The Spindle of Life," is the regular Butterfly feature for the week. "The Pullman Mystery" was written by Robert Von Saxmar and Jack Cunningham, Charles Swickard being the director in charge. An excellent cast, including Molly Malone, Larry Peyton, Hayward Mack and Ray Hanford, is provided. The story is built around the masquerading adventures of Paul Dustin who, an innocent suspect of a murder, the immediate circumstances of which seemed to incriminate him, dons the clothing of a suicide whose body he discovered in a compartment by his losing fight for the affections of the heroine, confesses with his dying breath; and Dustin is able to clear himself of suspicion in the mystery of the Pullman car.

A clothes-changing episode, under decidedly different circumstances is one of the high spots in the Nestor one-reel comedy, "Welcome Home," released on the same date. Eddie Lyons and Lee Moran are the chief fun makers, with Edith Roberts playing the part of Eddie's innocent wife, who didn't get Eddie's letter announcing his return—because Eddie never mailed it.

The release for Wednesday, September 19, is a rattling good two-reel L-Ko comedy entitled "A Prairie Chicken," directed by Vin Moore. Merta Sterling plays the part of the "Chicken," who pays a visit to her blase city relatives and gives them a shock upon shock by indulging in all her ranch accomplishments, even to shooting at the feet of the butler. She squares herself with the family when she gives chase to a thief who has stolen her aunt's jewels, pursues him to the edge of a drawbridge, ropes him and recovers the jewels.

Thursday, September 20, is the date of release of another of the popular J. Warren Kerrigan features in two reels, this one being entitled "The Right Man," by E. M. McCall and William Parker, directed by Henry McRae. It is a highly exciting story of the rivalry of two suitors for the same fair lady's hand. They are employees of the same bank, and the president's daughter is the girl in the story. One of the rivals tampers with some bank notes, casting suspicion upon the other, who loses his job, girl and all. But truth finally prevails and the marriage of the girl to the wrong man is prevented, after a series of thrilling adventures, in the nick of time. It was filmed under the direction of W. W. Beaudine.

"Marathon Maniacs," a Victor comedy, is scheduled for Friday, September 21. Max Asher, Dave Morris and Gladys Tennyson are featured and a riotously funny "Marathon race" is staged. Universal Screen Magazine No. 37 is scheduled for the same day.

For Saturday, September 22, a thrilling Bison drama, "The Last of the Night Riders," is the offering. As the name implies, it is a story of the night-riding days in Kentucky, in which the course of true love is decidedly ruffled by the enmity between the riders and the officers of the law. "Circus Sarah," a Joker comedy, written and produced by Allen Curtis, the scene of which is laid under the "big top," completes the bill.

October Keystone Comedies Completed

Girls and Favorite Comedians Are Prominent in Two-Reel Triangle Mirthmakers.

DUE to the system recently inaugurated at the Triangle west coast studios, productions are being made a month or two in advance of their release dates in order that they may be at the exchanges in time for exhibitors' pre-release showings. With new directors and players already added to its large staff, the Keystone company has been in a position to complete all October productions during August and early September.

"His Crooked Career" with the blond Keystone siren, Claire Anderson, and the character comedian, Fritz Schade, is scheduled as the first October release, the week of the 7th. Robert Milliken, who is best in pictures a comparatively short time, flashes forth as a new type of the comedy species in this Keystone.

The Keystone beauties in a fashion show will be one of the features of "Pearls and Perils," released October 14. A classic dancer, Alice Maison, is among the featured players, who include Dora Rogers, Alatia Morton, Harry McCoy, George Hall and Lloyd Bacon.

Dale Fuller, George Binns and Maude Wayne are the comedy trio appearing in a picture called "A Hindu Hoodoo," the October 21 feature. Binns is a get-rich quick gentleman of the Wallingford school. By day he is a city editor; at night he is Swami Swobodi, crystal-gazer. Guy Woodward, Eddie Gribbon and Mal St. Clair also have important roles in the picture, which was directed by H. Raymaker.

Myrtle Lind and Jay Dwiggins are the victims of "A Seminary Scandal," the comedy scheduled for the last week in October. They are supported by two of the Keystone featherweights, Caroline Rankin and Martin Kinney. The Keystone beauty squad will be represented by Rose Carter. Aileen Allen, the champion driver, is another siren of the bathing scenes.

State Rights Department
Conducted by BEN H. GRIMM

Foreign Buyers Explain Aims
Organization Hopes to Eliminate Middlemen—New Credit System Planned—Affiliated With Lee Organization.

THE formation into an association of the foreign film buyers resident in this country, and the affiliation of that body with the organization of state rights buyers promoted by Joseph F. Lee, marks a departure in the manner of handling films for foreign exploitation. The prime purpose of the new foreign buyers' organization, which became such mainly through the efforts of Jacques Kopfstein, will be the centralization of the buying of films for the foreign market. Under the plan the individual broker and dealer in foreign rights is eliminated. The buyers now will deal direct with the manufacturers through their organization.

The association will rent offices, where each of its members will be housed. Vaults, packing and shipping rooms will be engaged, to be used for the joint benefit of all the members. A screening room will be built, to be used only for association purposes and exclusively for the use of members. Notices of films offered for the foreign market will be posted on the board and in this wise it will be possible for all members to view a film at one time and make a combination offer for all territory outside the United States and Canada.

The greatest problem which today confronts the foreign buyer is the transfer of credits from abroad to this country, and the long delays necessitated by the prevailing system of money transfers. "Cash against documents" often causes film to be held up for a long period. As a consequence, the foreign buyer must have large sums of money tied up in the banks here in order that he can get delivery of film, and where transfers are slow or the buyer operates on a limited amount, he is almost certain continually to change his schedule of releases and shipments because of this unfortunate condition. Mr. Kopfstein is negotiating with one of the largest American banking houses engaged in the foreign business to act as factors to the members of the association, and if satisfactory arrangements are concluded, members of the foreign buyers' association will be enabled to operate on about one-quarter of the ready cash capital they have required heretofore.

The following countries, comprising ninety-five per cent. of the film buying foreign territory, are represented in the new organization: France, Francisco Elias; England, David P. Russell; Italy and Switzerland, The Royal Cinema Corporation; Australia and New Zealand, the Progressive Film Company of Australia; Scandinavia, the Scandinavian Films Company; Phillipine Island, C. W. Thompson; Cuba, Santos and Artigos; Central America, the Las Americas Company; Mexico, Kopfstein and Thomas; Spain and Portugal, Alfonso and Guinea; Brasil, Frederick H. Knocke; Argentine, Chile and Uruguay, The Sociadad General Cinematografica (Leroy Garfinkle, representative); Japan, U. Ono; Russia, David P. Rissell; Peru and Bolivia, Charles Thompson; India, Symington, Cox and Company; The Far East, David P. Howells; the West Indies, Frederick H. Knocke, and Greece, Alexander Stathopoulo.

Offices for the new association will be engaged jointly with the Lee state rights organization at a very early date.

NEW YORK RIGHTS ON "TODAY" AND "MAD LOVER" SOLD.

Pathe announces that the rights for the state of New York on "Today," with Florence Reed, and "The Mad Lover," with Robert Warwick, have been sold to the Civilization-Pioneer Film Corporation.

"Today" is the refutation of the theory which once held that a successful play suffered by transportation to the screen. In the opinion of competent critics "Today" as a picture is as great as the play was as a play. The punch, the vitality which Messrs. Broadhurst and Schomer put into the situations and dialogue of the spoken drama is retained and accentuated in the feature. Miss Reed adds materially to the laurels which she has gained as an emotional star of the first magnitude. It is called Ralph Ince's best work.

"The Mad Lover" enjoys with "Today" the distinction of being called by Harry Rapf, the producer, the two best pictures he ever made. Leonce Perret, who wrote and directed it, put into a rare beauty and finish. Elaine Hammerstein plays opposite Mr. Warwick.

MICHIGAN RIGHTS TO "WRATH OF GODS" SOLD.

The Dawn Masterplays Company, of Detroit, has purchased through Hiller & Wilk the Michigan rights to "The Wrath of the Gods," the reissue in which Sessue Hayakawa is the star.

Blumenthal Buys "Loyalty" and "Humility"
Entire Foreign Rights to Bernstein Production Purchased by Export and Import Executive.

THE Export and Import Film Corporation, Inc., have bought the world rights to the Isadore Bernstein productions "Loyalty" and "Humility," excepting the United States and Canada, and are at present negotiating for the sale of the entire territory. Ben Blumenthal, president of the organization, has had years of experience in Europe with the foreign market, and is one of the keenest judges of picture sales possibilities in the business. He has taken the rights to these pictures feeling that they are assured immediate success in the foreign field.

"We have bought these pictures," he said, "because they have a moral value and purpose, and although like all American made pictures, they have the happy ending, their structure and lesson cannot but appeal to the European audiences. I am glad to see that the American producer is finding courage enough to teach a definite moral lesson, undisguised, while possessing the ability to do it interestingly and convincingly. The pictures are well produced and well acted and filled with thrills from beginning to end. The foreign markets are demanding the American product at present, and we look confidently toward a brilliant future for these new releases.

"I feel that 'Loyalty' will present a great appeal to the foreign audience. It is the powerful story of a man conquering a great weakness with the help of a true woman. It is an arrangement of snobbery and the sham of false social position, which will not let itself see the real things that count in life. Under the pressure of the present crisis, people are daily realizing the futility and danger of this false attitude, and the picture will help to bring home the lesson. Added to this fact, the story, although crammed with thrills, does not see-saw up and down over climaxes, but maintains a tremendous dramatic tension, so dear to the European heart.

"The people abroad go to the theater not only to be entertained, but to be made to think, but they do not wish a problem merely presented and left to them to solve. They want it entirely worked out to a logical conclusion, and it is here that these pictures will successfully pass the test."

"A MORMON MAID" SOLD FOR NEW ENGLAND.

The Boston Photoplay Company has purchased the New England rights to the Friedman Enterprise feature, "A Mormon Maid," in which Mae Murray is the star. This is the feature which created so much discussion when it was shown at the Park theater, New York. It deals with pioneer days in Utah and it served to bring Mae Murray into the lime light as one of the few charming photoplay stars.

In addition to owning the New England rights to "A Mormon Maid" the Boston Photoplay Company controls the New England rights to "Joan the Woman," "The Common Law," "The Foolish Virgin," "The Price She Paid," "The Easiest Way," "War Brides," "Panthea," "The Argyle Case," "The Libertine," "Where Are My Children," "Wars' Women," "The Dumb Girl of Portici," "The Conquest of Canaan" and "Twenty Thousand Leagues Under the Sea."

LUST MAKES SEVERAL PURCHASES.

Sidney B. Lust, of the Super Film Attractions, Washington, D. C., has purchased "The Whip" for the District of Columbia, Delaware, Virginia, Maryland and North Carolina. The deal was negotiated for Paragon Films by Hiller & Wilk, as also was the deal whereby Mr. Lust obtained from the Lynch Enterprises, Inc., the rights for the same territory to "The Cold Deck." On his shopping trip Mr. Lust also purchased the rights to "The Wrath of the Gods."

SPITZER OPENS NEW YORK EXCHANGE.

Nat. H. Spitzer, sales manager of the King-Bee Films Corporation, announces that the Billy West Comedies are in such great demand that they have decided to open their own exchange for the State of New York. All the other state rights have been disposed of. King Bee releases two comedies a month.

FRIEDMAN ON WESTERN TRIP.

Benjamin Friedman, head of the Freidman Enterprises, Inc., left Minneapolis on Sunday, September 8, on a tour of exchanges of the Middle West and West. He will work in the interests of the Friedman Enterprises' "The Mormon Maid" during the trip.

ALBERT SCOWCROFT RETURNS TO OGDEN.

Albert Scowcroft, president of the Ogden Pictures Corporation, left New York for Ogden, Utah, Friday, August 31, after having seen the establishment of the Eastern executive office of that company well on its way. Mr. Scowcroft, before leaving, stated that his visit to the East was for the purpose of securing a competent Eastern manager of productions and general representative.

"Our Eastern organization now is completed," said Mr. Scowcroft, " and the second Lillian Walker extraordinary attraction will be made in the East; the third will be made at Ogden, Utah; the fourth at Los Angeles, and the remaining four of the first year's series also will be made in the East. I shall report to my co-directors the wonderful progress we have made and will present to them a plan of enlarged operations that will call for a scheme of advertising, publicity and exploitation the like of which never has been attempted in the exploitation of any individual star. We know we have made no mistake up to this point. What those plans are, however, cannot be given to the trade at this time, excepting to say that we hope to teach the photoplay public a few additional startling innovations that will convince them of the wonders that motion pictures can really perform. Several such innovations, we are advised by our attorneys, are patentable and we have already applied for patent rights on them. When I state that I hope to present to the world, through the medium of Ogden Pictures, a stereoscopic form of photography that will present the characters of the screen almost as if they were in the flesh and on the stage, you can well appreciate what I have in mind."

Mr. Scowcroft will return to New York at the completion of the production now being made in the East.

"THE FATED HOUR" READY.

Victoria Feature Films, 220 West Forty-second street, New York, have contracted to release Clines' six-reel sensational drama, "The Fated Hour," in the United States and Canada. It will likely be offered to state right buyers and the sales campaign will commence Sept. 15.

The picture had a big foreign run and is considered one of the few of the larger features that have attracted attention in Europe in the last year.

The punch of the picture is a thrilling fire scene, depicting the destruction of a theater. This particular effect is reported to never have been secured with such realism before. The star, Minichelli, has attained much publicity abroad.

"We had this ready for the market in June," stated a Victoria representative, "but it was not thought to be the best time to launch such a big picure. The result was that we locked it up in our vault, and it will stay locked there until Sept. 15."

A. KAY GETS LION HUNT FILMS.

The A. Kay Company announces that it has closed a deal with Bob Bakker, the celebrated lion hunter, in which it has secured for universal distribution the hunter's famous motion pictures of "Hunting Mountain Lions in Montana." The pictures are a distinct novelty and depict in master fashion the hunting of mountain lions in the rough, mountainous sections of the Rockies.

Bob Bakker comes from Libby, Montana, and holds the unique distinction of having captured more mountain lions than any man in America, and since most hunters are not over anxious to attempt to wrest these laurels from him, his championship and record are most likely to remain his for many years to come.

LESSER BUYS "TODAY" AND "THE MAD LOVER."

Sol L. Lesser has added to his ever-growing list of features the new seven-reel production, "Today," featuring Florence Reed, and the six-reel feature, "The Mad Lover," with Robert Warwick, for exploitation in California, Nevada and Arizona. The deal was consummated through his associate, Mr. Leon D. Netter, during Mr. Lesser's illness.

Mr. Lesser has now so far recovered from the attack of typhoid fever that Mr. Netter, who has been with him constantly, has found it possible to make a trip to Cleveland for a few days. From present indications, Mr. Lesser will be out of the hospital within a week.

LUST PLACES MOTOYS IN SEVEN THEATERS.

Sidney B. Lust, of the Super Film Attractions, Washington, D. C., distributor of the Peter Pan Film Corporation's Mo-Toy Comedies for Maryland, Delaware, Virginia, North Carolina and District of Columbia, announces that these comedies have been placed in the following theaters: Garden, Strand, Lyric and Navy, Washington; American, Hopewell, Va.; Strand. Petersburg, Va., and American, Norfolk, Va.

INTERNATIONAL VAMPIRE IN METRO-DREW COMEDY.

Evelyn Dumo, "the international vampire," will be seen in the forthcoming Metro-Drew comedy, "The Unmarried Look," in the role of the newest and smartest type of vampire. She is the "lady buyer" from "the provinces," in the big city to get a new stock of goods for her firm, and all the amusement possible for herself.

STANDARD MAN GETS ST. LOUIS CONTRACTS.

Phil L. Ryan, sales manager of the Standard Film Corporation, paid a visit to the organization's St. Louis office, which resulted in the securing of several large contracts from the local theater men on the Billy West comedies, which the Standard is handling throughout the Middle West. Mr. Ryan's visit extended over a period of sixteen days, a part of which time was given over to the consideration of the many new angles of the sales problem in the St. Louis territory, which is now under the management of "Barney" Fegan.

Mr. Ryan, who is also advertising manager of the Standard, gives considerable credit to a persistent advertising policy for his success in selling the Billy West comedies not only in St. Louis, but in other cities served by the Standard as well. "We have," said Mr. Ryan, "virtually created this question in the mind of the theatergoer: why has not my theater manager booked the Billy West comedies? And the theater manager is not the last person in the world to sense the existence of this question, either as is illustrated in the case of Messrs. Cella & Tate, the leading exhibitors of St. Louis, who operate the Columbia and several other theaters there.

"Cella & Tate have arranged with us for the Billy West comedies for a run of fourteen days in their theaters, and Mr. Cella was frank in admitting that, aside from the value of West as a drawing card and a comedian, he was booking him because of the accumulative interest-force of advertising that we have placed in the St. Louis and surrounding papers."

STRAND BOOKS FIRST WALT MASON STORY.

The Short Features Exchange of New York announces that it has arranged with Manager Harold Edel of the Strand theater, New York, whereby "Bunked and Paid For," the first of the series of Walt Mason Stories, which are now being made by the Filmcraft Corporation, was shown at that theater during the week commencing September 9. Mr. Edel expressed himself as highly delighted with the picture, and his placing it on the Strand program confirms the fact that he was well pleased with it.

RENOWNED OPENS PROJECTION ROOM.

Further evidence of the activity of the Renowned Pictures Corporation, located on the fourth floor of the Mecca Building, 1600 Broadway, is demonstrated by the opening of the new and up-to-the-minute projection room in their suite of offices. No effort has been spared to make an improvement over the projection rooms now being used in the trade. The result is a comfortable and handsomely furnished projection room where pictures can be screened under the most ideal conditions.

The projection room is at the disposal of the trade; perfect projection by a competent operator is assured.

"THE STAR BOARDER" (King-Bee).

Billy West, King-Bee's comedy star, has just completed his ninth two-reeler, entitled "The Star Boarder." In this number Billy is seen as the star boarder in a boarding house, in which most of the other boarders are pretty girls. But there are

Scene from "The Star Boarder" (King-Bee).

janitors, cooks, cows and lots of other things around the house in which Billy is the star boarder, and each furnishes the comedian with laugh-making possibilities that are taken advantage of to the full. Many of the scenes of "The Star Boarder" were made at a well-known seashore resort. Gil Gilstrom, Billy's director, has injected into the latest King-Bee release comedy action enough to satisfy even the most laugh-hungry appetite.

Zena Keefe Star in "Shame"

Considers Her Best Work Done in John W. Noble's Big Feature—Most Dramatic Role of Career, She Believes.

ZENA KEEFE, who in spite of her long stage career and many notable appearances in important picture productions, still enjoys the distinction of being one of the youngest stars in the theatrical firmament, will soon be seen in the leading role of the special state rights feature "Shame," recently completed by John W. Noble.

The new Zena Keefe vehicle, which is in seven reels, and which is said to represent ten weeks of Mr. Noble's greatest

Zena Keefe.

effort as a director, is considered by the beautiful little star as the most ambitious production in which she has ever appeared. "I deserve very little credit for my work in 'Shame,' although I must confess that I think it the best I have ever done," said Miss Keefe. "Every actress looks forward to a time when she will be given an opportunity to play a really great part in a powerful drama. I was just lucky enough to get my wish, that all. Can you imagine a girl being placed in more dramatic situations than the little daughter of the hero of the trenches in 'Shame'? Why, I simply had to act."

Miss Keefe is one of the interesting personalities of the stage that, starting as mere tots, practically grow up behind the footlights and act as naturally as they walk. She starred as a child, being closely identified with the remarkable success of "The Fatal Wedding" and later becoming an established vaudeville headliner. Her long engagement with the Vitagraph comedy made her a prominent screen star. Her experience there was followed by notable appearances in feature pictures, of which "Enlighten Thy Daughter" and "One Hour" are now enjoying exceptional popularity. Notwithstanding the fact that her stage and screen record equals that of many of the older stars, Miss Keefe is only twenty-one years of age, having been born in San Francisco on June 26, 1896.

More Cities Acclaim Italian War Films

William Moore Patch Announces Extraordinary Business—Chicago Run Extended—Plans Another New York Engagement.

PILING UP the success which has marked its presentation everywhere, the official Italian war pictures, "The Italian Battlefront," opened at the Garrick theater, Philadelphia, last week, to crowds which, on the first day, blocked Chestnut street, in a vain effort to gain admission. The production accomplished that which has never been achieved by any other picture shown in that city—the complete sell out of the house for a solid week in advance. The opening performance was attended by the Mayor of the city and other important public dignitaries, including the various foreign Consuls of the Allies stationed in Philadelphia.

As in the instance of Chicago, the run in Philadelphia is proving doubly remarkable, because of the presence of so many Americans in the audience. Although Philadelphia has a large Italian population, the interest and support accorded these war films by its native public easily equalled that given to them by the Italians. As has been pointed out before, this seems to be due to the fact that "The Italian Battlefront" is totally unlike any other war series heretofore presented in this country, introducing suspense, dramatic action, beauty, heroism and thrills, rather than horror.

William Moore Patch, under whose direction the American tour is being conducted, stated upon his return from Philadelphia to New York that the Chicago run, in the Auditorium theater had been extended to September 9, and that arrangements were being made whereby these pictures would be returned to the Forty-fourth Street theater, New York, where they played to unparalleled business for four weeks. Mr. Patch said that the only reason the New York run had been interrupted was because of the total inability to obtain a theater along Broadway for Labor Day week.

Arrangements are already being made in quite a number of Western states, including Cleveland, St. Louis, Kansas, and in the East, Baltimore, Providence, Washington, Norfolk and similar centers.

Lubin and Sawyer Active

Heads of General Enterprises Inc., Plan "Warrior" Campaign—Negotiate Contract for Washington Film Building.

THE activities of General Enterprises, Inc., have attracted considerable attention in film circles during the past few weeks and interest culminated last week in the announcement by the firm that the United States and Canadian rights to "The Warrior" had been secured. The prime movers of General Enterprises, Inc., A. H. Sawyer and Herbert Lubin, propose to allot territorial rights to the master feature starring Maciste, the Herculean lead of "Cabiria," and already offers from prominent buyers are pouring into headquarters at 1600 Broadway, New York. A technically-planned exploitation campaign has been laid out by experts to properly assist the showmen who will exhibit "The Warrior," and many advertising novelties of a "different" nature have been devised. This trilling and timely feature controlled by General Enterprises, Inc., has been unanimously declared by New York theatrical and film critics a worthy successor to the famous "Cabiria," and Maciste actually outdoes himself in feature of strength and hair-raising, death-defying stunts.

Of equal importance is the statement issued by A. H. Sawyer to the effect that General Enterprises, Inc., has successfully negotiated a contract for the erection of a modern film building in Washington, D. C. This deal, highly significant to the Southern film trade, was closed Saturday, September 1, with Alonzo C. Mather of Chicago. The structure, to be known as the Mather building, will be a ten-story affair, completely equipped with vaults, a series of projection rooms, telegraph offices, express facilities, etc., and will be the last word in construction of this nature. Construction will commence on the new building Tuesday, September 4, located at 916 G street, N. W., Washington, D. C.

The new organization rapidly is increasing its scope in the buying of film rights and in line with this progress the foreign rights to the McClure Series of "The Seven Deadly Sins" have acquired. This series, starring eminent players of the silent and spoken drama, has met with sweeping success in this country and the securing of the foreign rights is considered a coup by wise film men.

HOFFMAN ABOLISHES RELEASE DATES.

"Ancient methods of booking subjects on release dates have been done away with by Hoffman-Foursquare exchanges," declared M. H. Hoffman, president and general manager of his organization, on his return a few days ago from his Western trip. "From now on there will be no such thing as a release date in any of our service stations.

"Every Hoffman-Foursquare exchange will be ready at any time to supply the demands of the exhibitor, and will release any desired feature the moment prints and advertising material are ready for runs. Because of this, exhibitors need not look for release dates on any picture we control. They merely have to examine our list of subjects available and act accordingly.

"There is one thing, however, I wish to emphasize: the elimination of release dates does not mean that there will be no protection of first, second or third runs in territories or towns. Each run will be amply guarded by our division and branch managers, whose instructions to salesmen will be clear in this most important matter.

"It is my belief that this policy—which I regard as a long step in the direction of advancement—will work to the advantage of both exhibitors and public. When an exhibitor requires a certain production we have we will see to it that he gets it. The fact that some of our pictures may not suit his need of that particular moment will not prevent him from getting those, of later production, which he can use.

"Priority runs, as one may readily see, can and will be protected under our system as well as any other. It is simply that our method has all the advantages of the old system and none of its disadvantages. An exhibitor interested in the tail-end feature may have it; 'the last will be first' whenever he says the word."

SCHWARTZ OBTAINS SHORT SUBJECTS.

Eddie Schwartz, of the Federal Feature Film Company, announces that he has just secured a large assortment of one, two and three-reel pictures from several film companies, for exploitation in New York State. The pictures consist of one-reel comedies, scenics and educations, two-reel comedies and dramas and a number of three-reel dramas. Several of the two and three-reelers are features in themselves, and each one of them is strong in plot and in cast. With this new addition of short subjects to his list of features, Mr. Schwartz plans to inaugurate a new service, which he will call the Federal's Short Picture Service. The new service department which Mr. Schwartz plans to put into effect will cater only to the wants of exhibitors who are desirous of obtaining short pictures of merit. Mr. Schwartz will manage this department in conjunction with his other duties, and will see to it that every exhibitor gets what he wants at a price within the reach of his pocketbook.

Manufacturers' Advance Notes

Beach Pictures on Separate Contract

Goldwyn Announces Its First Story by Author Will Be Ready for Trade Showing in Two Weeks.

THE productions of Rex Beach Pictures Corporation, which are to be distributed exclusively by Goldwyn, will be issued to exhibitors on contracts separate from those of the regular Goldwyn subjects and will be maintained as a distinct selling unit.

The officials of the Beach company—Mr. Beach, Benjamin B. Hampton, president, and Larry Trimble, director—announce that "The Auction Block" will be ready for the trade in a few days. Goldwyn plans to have enough prints for trade showings delivered to each of its branches in the United States and Canada within two weeks. The task of cutting and titling the film has proved to be a large one. More than 18,000 feet of film were exposed in the making of the picture, virtually all of which was good. Mr. Beach, who is doing his own subtitles, finds that brief conversational excerpts from the book serve to thread the picture story together. The continuity was so carefully done that even with a great deal of cutting he has not found it necessary to insert more than occasional explanatory leaders.

VICTOR MOORE IN "CAMPING."

Victor Moore gets back again to the "family series" in his Sept. 10 release called "Camping," written by Thos. J. Gray. Vic is a lover of fresh air, and decides that the best way to get it is to go "camping." He manages to induce his wife to go along with him and take the kids. He also takes his nephew, and two nieces. After equipping them with camping outfits, and also loading his Ford up with the necessary camping things they make a start. The car looks like a moving circus and the kids have the time of their young lives. Vic encounters many troubles en route to the camping place, the last one being the climbing of a mountain, which is very exciting and funny. He eventually arrives at a spot he thinks will do. The tent is put up, and camping life is en in full blast. Everything would have been ideal if it was not for a "would be" Indian who tries to scalp Vic. He nearly scares the daylight out of Vic, and only the arrival of an old hermit and the kids save him. They knock the spots out of the Indian, and the hermit takes him off in his custody. By this time the nightfall is coming on, and Vic and the family get in the sleeping bag, to get into the arms of Morpheus. It had to pick out that night to rain, and rain it does, as it never did before. Vic unfortunately built

Scene from "Camping" (Klever).

the trench around the tent the wrong way, and consequently the water runs in the tent instead of out. Added to this comes a gale, which blows the tent away, and they are all left standing in their "nighties." Vic makes them all get under the Ford, which he says is like a rich uncle, it always comes in handy. "Camping" is the funniest "family" comedy Moore has made, and it is "chucked" full of laughs and ridiculously funny situations.

"THE CONQUEROR" (Fox).

In "The Conqueror," a Standard picture with William Farnum in the stellar role, which he presented at the Globe theater Monday night. September 10, William Fox believes a new standard has been set in motion picture prodiction—a standard which, going further than the thrill and the spectacular in which "The Conqueror" abounds, affords a new and higher plane for dramatic exposition through the medium of the screen.

"The Conqueror" picturizes the heroic life and romantic times of General Sam Houston, known to every American as the Liberator of Texas. It is a cross-section cut out of American

Scene from "The Conqueror" (Fox).

history in the making, and it holds intense interest for every citizen and resident of these United States.

There is probably no more romantic figure in American history than Sam Houston, and there is unquestionably no actor better equipped artistically as well as physically for the portrayal of Houston than William Farnum. Mr. Farnum's is said to be a masterly interpretation of a role in which his admirers will like him best.

Given Henry Christeen Warnack's engrossing, virile story, and the enormous facilities afforded by the unlimited resources of the Fox producing organization, it needed but the master hand of R. A. Walsh, the famous Fox director and the man who staged "The Honor System," to make of "The Conqueror" a photodramatic masterpiece. This Mr. Walsh has done.

"The Conqueror" was photographed in California, Texas and Mexico. It was six months in the making. In the making of the picture were 450 Sioux Indians secured through the Department of the Interior from the Pine Ridge Agency, and for whose safe return at the end of their artistic labors a bond of $50,000 was deposited. There were also Mexican soldiers, negroes from Southern plantations, Texas Rangers and regular Cavalrymen.

Prominent in Mr. Farnum's support are Jewel Carmen, who appears as Eliza Allen; Charles Clary, J. A. Marcus, and William Eagle Shirt, Chief Birdhead and Little Star, Indians all.

HOLUBAR STARTS NEW PLAY.

Director Allen J. Holubar's next production will be entitled "The Twisted Soul," the story of which is by J. Grubb Alexander and Fred Myton. It is a psychological drama in which heredity figures to a considerable extent and it will be produced in five reels.

Director Holubar's star in "The Twisted Soul" will be Miss Brownie Vernon, who although the only woman in the production, will be supported by an unusual cast, among whom will be Murdock MacQuarrie and William Garwood, two former well-known actors and directors at the Universal Company, who have returned to the fold.

Garwood will play the lead opposite Miss Vernon and the principal character lead will be in the hands of MacQuarrie, who ranks high in the cinema world for his remarkable character portrayals.

Others in the cast will be Myles McCarthy, whose legitimate stage work is well known; Joseph Girard and Charles Hill Mailes.

A Five-Star Pathe Week

Appearing in Features and Serials—French War Pictures, Cartoons and Scenics Complete Program.

THE Pathe program for the week of September 23 is characterized by two unusually big features, a very funny comedy and two strong serial episodes. The Box office stars who appear on this program are Frederick Warde, Jeanne Eagles, Mollie King, Pearl White and Harold Lloyd.

The five-reel production of the week is Frederick Warde and Jeanne Eagles in "Under False Colors." It is an original story by Lloyd Lonergan, produced by Thanhouser under the direction of Emile Chautard, with one of the best starring combinations ever seen on the screen—the best known Shakespearian actor in America in the role of a modern financier, and the most charming young leading woman on the American stage in the role of a beautiful Russian countess, forced to take refuge in the United States under a false passport.

"The Bow String" is the title of the second episode of "The Seven Pearls" serial in which Mollie King is featured with Creighton Hale and Leon Bary.

The suspense of the first episode is heightened in the second, one of the features of which is a fight between two men dressed in armor and thus disguised as knights of old. As Ilma (Mollie King) starts toward the curtain, a hand steals out from behind it, takes the pearls and before she is able to untangle herself the indistinguishable figure steals out and escapes.

Pearl White stars in the 13th episode of "The Fatal Ring," entitled "The Desperate Chance." This chapter is characterized by breathless suspense and many thrills. At the point of a revolver in a fight on top of a fast moving train, Carslake and Pearl both fall off. Carslake rises and starts after the train, leaving Pearl lying prone across the track. With a northbound train only fifty yards from Pearl, Tom Carleton, after an exciting race in his automobile, manages to pull the switch in time to save her. Learning where Carslake is hiding, Pearl, accompanied by the Spider, Tom, and detectives, invades the house. After a terrific fight, Carslake opens a trap door in the roof and climbs out. Pearl comes out of the trap door as Carslake gets to the edge of the roof by the iron girder. As he starts over the girder Pearl pursues him. Thinking that this is a good chance to get rid of her, Carslake seizes her and as the film fades out, starts to bend her back, back, back.

The second big feature of the week is the three-reel Official French War Film entitled "In the Wake of the Huns." Pathe calls attention to the drawing power of this title "plastered all over town on the most striking paper you ever saw and advertised big in the newspapers."

"In the Wake of the Huns" is official. It is the first French picture of its kind to be seen in this country, and it is safe to say that the interest of the people of America is greater in what the French are doing than in the activities of any other belligerent, except Uncle Sam itself. These pictures show the actual French territory which has been recovered in the great Allied advance and in which the American troops will see their first action.

It is an impressive historical document, which is so absorbingly interesting that though it is only three reels in length it deserves the featured position in any theater's bill.

Harold Lloyd is seen in "Pinched," a one-reel comedy, produced by Rolin. It is one of the funniest of the Lloyd comedies. In it the star and Snub Pollard manage to get their clothes and identities mixed and both land in the police station with "a-laugh-a-foot" complications.

International cartoon and Scenic, and Hearst-Pathe News No. 78 and No. 79 complete an unusually strong program.

HERBERT BRENON AT WORK ON "EMPTY POCKETS."

The filming of Rupert Hughes' popular novel, "Empty Pockets," is now progressing rapidly at Herbert Brenon's Hudson Heights studios. "Empty Pockets" will be the Brenon production to immediately follow "The Fall of the Romanoffs."

In "Empty Pockets" Mr. Brenon has another swift moving romance. The story is built around the murder of a debonaire millionaire, "Merry" Perry Merithew, who is found dead on the dirty tin roof of an East Side tenement. Strands of a woman's red hair are clutched in his hands. This is the only clue. The mystery involves four Titian haired girls: one a millionaire's beautiful daughter; another a model installed by the dead man in a Central Park West apartment, the third the unscrupulous daughter of a bankrupt society matron, and the fourth a cabaret dancer married to a thug.

One of the thrilling incidents is a midnight motor chase back and forward across the island of Manhattan and ending at the edge of Spuyten Duyvil Creek. This is said to be one of the most thrilling things to yet reach the screen.

For the role of the heroic Doctor Worthing, Mr. Brenon has selected Bert Lytell, who scored so decidedly as the Lone Wolf. Reviewers pronounced him the genuine find of the past screen season.

Barbara Castleton has been selected to play Muriel Schuyler, the daughter of a money king, who is involved in the murder mystery. Miss Castleton is looked upon by Mr. Brenon as a distinct discovery.

Mr. Lytell and Miss Castleton have the principal roles. The other parts will be enacted by equally well known players since Mr. Brenon is a believer in the well balanced cast, rather than the top-heavy star cast.

"THE SPINDLE OF LIFE" (Butterfly).

Ben Wilson is the featured player of "The Spindle of Life," the Butterfly picture scheduled for release September 17th. He will be capably supported by Neva Gerber, Richard La Reno and Hayward Mack, who have prominent parts in a well-selected cast.

"The Spindle of Life" is a picturization of Sidney Robinson's novel, "Gladsome," arranged for the screen by Karl Coolidge and produced by George Cochrane.

It tells the story of the unconventional meeting of Gladsome

Scene from "The Spindle of Life" (Butterfly).

Harrison, an interesting young tomboy heiress, and "Alphabet" Carter, crown prince of America's financial realm, in a quaint seacoast town. Gladsome's mother, a wealthy widow, tries to bring her daughter up according to the latest approved mode of the smart set, but Gladsome would rather knock around in overalls with her old pals, the fishermen, than drink pink tea out of a Soissons tea-cup. This is a sore trial to mother, who would like to see Gladsome safely married to Vincent Bradshaw, the tiresomely correct son of her financial adviser.

One day on the sands Gladsome meets an interesting stranger, and they strike up a friendship which develops along unexpected lines, when the girl asks the "sandman" to help her devise a way to foil her mother and the ubiquitous Bradshaw. The way out of the resulting tangle is the occasion for considerable fun, interspersed with some good dramatic work, in which both Wilson and Miss Gerber score.

THE WEEK IN THE FOX STUDIOS.

William Fox's present schedule of releases calls for the issuing of "When a Man Sees Red," the powerful extra-reel drama with William Farnum in the stellar role during October. Frank Lloyd was the director. He filmed the picture from the story "The Painted Lady," by Larry Evans.

Jewel Carmen, who played opposite Mr. Farnum in this production, as well as several others, has been transferred from the Fox studios in California to the plant at Fort Lee, N. J., where Mr. Farnum is making "Les Miserables." Miss Carmen will have the role of Fantine in the production.

Work is progressing rapidly on Virginia Pearson's new starring vehicle, and on the first of a series of eight light comedy dramas starring the magnetic Jane and Katherine Lee. Miss Pearson's picture is to be called "Thou Shalt Not Steal," and is being directed by William Nigh. In the supporting cast are Claire Whitney, Eric Mayne, Robert Elliott, John Goldsworthy, Victor Delinsky, Dan Mason, Dan Sullivan, Lemuel Kennedy, Martin Faust and Mathilde Brundage.

The Lee children's subject is almost completed. Kenean Buel, who screened the highly successful "Two Little Imps," is again in charge of the direction.

George Walsh, the man who made the smile famous, has started another production on the West Coast. It will be his thirteenth photoplay.

The release for September 9 will be "When False Tongues Speak," in which Virginia Pearson has the chief part. The story is by George Scarborough and the direction is by Carl Harbaugh. Hardee Kirkland is the leading man.

"MEN OF THE DESERT" SHOWN BY K-E-S-E.

Trade showings of "Men of the Desert," the fourth of Essanay's series of Western photodramas, featuring Jack Gardner, the musical comedy star, are in progress at all branches of the George Kleine distributing system. This picture, presenting a screen version of the Taylor-Norris feud, one of the most notorious of the West, is said to be the strongest unit of this series. It will be released September 24.

Mr. Gardner is supported by Ruth King, Carl Stockdale and the remainder of the company, which has been seen with him in "Land of Long Shadows," "The Range Boss," and "Open Places." The picture was staged on the plains of Arizona and presents many picturesque settings. It has a screen time of approximately sixty-five minutes.

What Triangle Offers for September 16

"Mountain Dew" Has Kentucky Locale and Kentucky Star; William Desmond in "Flying Colors" Is Other Feature of the Week.

MARGERY WILSON'S first starring play, "Mountain Dew," will be released on the Triangle program for the week of September 16, together with "Flying Colors," in which William Desmond is starred.

Being a Kentucky girl, Miss Wilson is naturally adapted to her role in "Mountain Dew," which has as its locale the Blue Grass state. Miss Wilson is seen as a wild sprite of the mountains who knows nothing of "larnin'" and is not worried over the deficiency.

The Triangle comedy accompanying "Mountain Dew" is entitled "His Baby Doll." The players featured are Claire Anderson, Mal St. Clair, George Binns, Florence Clark and James Donnelly.

In "Flying Colors" Bill Desmond has the role of a Yale athlete who puts to practical account some of the dare-devil stunts he learned at college. A one-reel Triangle comedy will be presented as a demitasse for the program of which "Flying Colors" is the feature. It bears the title of "His Unconscious Conscience" and features Hugh Fay, Tom Perese, Phyllis Hoover, Wm. Irving, Geo. Jeskis, James Spencer and Jack Perrin.

"Hula-Hula Land" is the Keystone comedy for the week and brings forth the Keystone bathing girls, this time in grass skirts and strings of beads. Billy Armstrong, Maude Wayne and Guy Woodward disport at the head of this band of ukelele maids.

GAUMONT'S "REEL LIFE" NO. 74.

Californians regulate their watches when they reach their offices at 9 a. m., Chicago men perform this duty at 11. New Yorkers and other Easterners wait until they are ready for luncheon, at 12 o'clock. Strange though it may seem, all these timepieces are checked up at the same moment. The determining of exact noon by the Naval Observatory at Washington, for flashing throughout the United States, forms a most interesting subject which is shown in Reel Life No. 74, released the week of September 24.

President Washington's spectacles differed greatly from the curved lenses of to-day, which science has enabled even the poorest to wear. The manufacture of glasses which duplicate the best natural sight is another section of this film magazine.

That many are willing to fight if they can be assured of good bread is shown in 'The Soldier's Staff of Life," which depicts the use of a portable bread-maker which the government used in seeking recruits. Last year the bean-eating aphides contributed to the shortage of another army aphid, but this year we need too many beans to humor these plant' lice, and so scientists have sicked lady-bugs onto them. Scientists are also working to get rid of the lamprey, a fish which has killed thousands of others because of its blood-sucking proclivities. These three subjects add to the variety of this issue of Reel Life.

"So Easy," an animated drawing from the leading humorous weekly, Life, closes a highly entertaining reel.

CANADIANS LOOK ON "POLLY OF THE CIRCUS."

A large audience crowded the Regent theater, Toronto, on Thursday, August 30, at an invitation showing of the first Goldwyn production, "Polly of the Circus." Prominent exhibitors from all over Ontario made a flying visit to the city for the purpose of seeing the results of a year's efforts on the part of the Goldwyn producing forces.

At the screening were prominent city officials, representatives from all of the city newspapers, besides practically. every exhibitor in the city. The Regent Symphony orchestra, under the leadership of John Arthur, gave the musical setting. The audience showed its appreciation of the picture by hearty applause.

Among the out-of-town exhibitors who made the trip to the city especially to see the picture were: Clyde Curry, Favorite theater, Windsor; J. A. Walsh, Walkerville; John C. Green, Temple theater, Galt; William Stewart, Patricia theater, London; T. W. Logan, Majestic theater, London; Dr. Robinson, Empire theater, Peterboro; Ernest Moule, Brant theater, Brantford; F. Pursel, Lyric theater, Simcoe; James Sullivan and Jack Sullivan, King George theater, St. Catherines; J. Brady, Princess theater, Sarnia; Meighan and Roneigk, Academy theater, Lindsay; Mr. Simpson, Apollo theater, Guelph; Leo Longo, Roma theater, Kitchener.

"ANTICS OF ANN" NEW PENNINGTON PICTURE.

Ann Pennington has begun work on her new Paramount. picture, a charmingly written little comedy entitled "The Antics of Ann." Edward Dillon is directing the production and a number of the interior scenes already have been made. It offers the young star an opportunity of proving that she is a comedienne of no small skill and in addition permits of her wearing many fetching costumes, including something new in the way of satin pajamas and bathing suits that were never made for the water, but which are nothing short of bewitching.

SELIG RELEASES ON GENERAL FILM.

"Over the Top to Victory" is the title of one of the latest of motion pictures announced by William N. Selig for release in General Film service. on Monday, Sept. 24. The production is in two reels and should prove particularly interesting to the mothers and fathers, the wives, sisters and sweethearts of the young men who have become soldiers.

"Over the Top to Victory" is said to present as details of the development of America's young men into soldiers who will defend their country's honor in the battlefields of Europe. From daybreak until "Taps" are sounded, we follow the citizen-soldiers through their drills and pastimes.

For release Saturday, Sept. 29, the Selig Company announces the one-reel drama, "The Angel of Poverty Row," with winsome Bessie Eyton as the star. Colin Campbell directed this production, which is said to possess many of the characteristic touches which have made Colin Campbell famous as a director.

On Monday, Oct. 1, the Selig Company announces the release of a two-part Western drama entitled "The Rustler's Vindication," with daring Tom Mix performing many of his death-defying feats. Myrtle Steadman is also seen in an important part.

"The Witness for the State" is the title of the Selig one-reel release in General Film service for Saturday, Oct. 6. Bessie Eyton and Eugenie Besserer both have important parts in this one-reeler, which was also produced by Colin Campbell.

ACTIVITIES AT L-O STUDIOS.

With five directors working, General Director J. G. Blystone is turning out a supply of L-Ko's to last through the bad weather that is bound to come on the Pacific Coast. Noel Smith, Archie Mayo, Dick Smith, Phil Dunham and Vin Moore are rushing matters as expeditiously as possible.

Lucille Hutton has written a story which will be entitled "A Giddy Girl's Love," when it eventually becomes an L-Ko from Mr. Blystone's scenario. This is the first time Miss Hutton has done more than to act in other people's stories. If the expected success attends her first efforts as a screen novelist, she will probably write her own material hereafter.

Vin Moore has just completed a Western comedy and has started another feature with beginnings in Mexico and a finish in San Francisco. The work required a special steamer, on charter, to carry Myrtle Sterling and her company, as well as figuring in the scenes.

Because of the increased production of L-Ko's a new studio is under course of construction, with an addition to the main stage, occupying 80 x 120 feet. A new wardrobe department is also being outfitted, to meet the extra demands of five active producing organizations.

Hughie Mack, latest addition to the L-Ko comedy leaders, has just finished his first release. It will be sent along to exhibitors early in October through Universal exchanges.

LOIS WEBER HAS "THE TIME OF HER LIFE."

"The Time of Her Life" is the alluring title of the first of the new Lois Weber productions, which is now completed and ready for release. Any production by Lois Weber is an event of interest and curiosity to all exhibitors and film fans who look with confidence for something unusual and worth while in all plays bearing her name. "The Time of Her Life" will prove no exception to the rule, save that in this—her first independent production—this "dean" of directors has forsaken propaganda only to demonstrate the more dramatically the influence of home upon character and one's subsequent life and career. In her new play Miss Weber takes for her principal characters two girls working side by side in a big department store, to show how the influence of their respective homes so widely distinguishes their destinies. It is a big theme, handled with that fearless fidelity to facts and yet that unswerving idealism in purpose which distinguish all Lois Weber's productions. Mildred Harris, the former Fine Arts ingenue, is seen in the stellar role, supported by Helene Rosson, Kenneth Harlan, Adele Farrington, Gertrude Astor and Alfred Allen, of "Hell Morgan" frame—some cast. As for the play—well, see for yourselves, and remember it's Lois Weber's choice for the first independent release.

ALADDIN THE NEXT FOX KIDDIES RELEASE.

An early release of William Fox's kiddies pictures will be the picturization of "Aladdin and the Wonderful Lamp." This fairy story film has just been completed, and those who have seen the uncut film believe the picture will even surpass "Jack and the Beanstalk," the first Fox kiddies picture which has been so favorably received throughout the country since its most successful run at the Globe theater in New York in August.

It was felt by those who had seen "Jack and the Beanstalk" that the acting of Francis Carpenter and Virginia Lee Corbin and the other children could not be bettered, but in "Aladdin" they have even gone beyond their work in "Jack." According to those who have seen the film the portrayal of those eastern characters is a revelation.

In one of. the scenes the lamp is rubbed and a palace appears on the burning desert. And the desert itself gives to one an atmosphere ̦that is romantic, mysterious and oftentimes consuming.

Paramount October Releases

Marguerite Clark, Billie Burke, Vivian Martin, Charles Ray, Dorothy Dalton, Jack Pickford, Louise Huff, Sessue Hayakawa and Ann Pennington Among Stars Listed.

SOME inkling of the tremendous drawing power and wide variety of entertainment to be furnished by Paramount under its new "Star Series' selective booking system of distribution can be gained by that company's announcement of its releases for the month of October. The October list of Paramount releases furnishes a striking example of the combined strength represented by the various producing forces in addition to the tremendous producing organization already built up and perfected by Famous Players-Lasky. The October schedule marks the first appearance of a Blackton production on the Paramount schedule and also contains the first of the Paramount-Ince photoplays in addition to embracing such stars in its roster as Marguerite Clark, Billie Burke, Vivian Martin, Jack Pickford, Louise Huff, Sessue Hayakawa and Ann Pennington. The stellar forces of the Thomas H. Ince organization are represented by Dorothy Dalton and Charles Ray. In the Blackton production, which is an adaptation of Sir Gilbert Parker's celebrated novel, "The World for Sale," the principal roles are played by Anna Little and Conway Tearle. The tentative arrangement of the schedule is as follows:

"The Ghost House," starring Jack Pickford and Louise Huff, directed by Wm. C. DeMille, leads off. This is a story which has to do with an old haunted house and a band of criminals—which is enough to tell at present. Suffice that it is a picture calculated to thrill as well as entertain.

"Arms and the Girl," from the successful stage play, has as its bright particular star the lovely Billie Burke. This picture deals with the invasion of a Belgian town by the Germans and the scenes depicting this particular event are said to be so near the actuality as to be positively startling. Needless to say, in the stellar role, Miss Burke gives a charming performance. Joseph Kaufman directed the film and Thomas Meighan, who played opposite Miss Burke in her first Paramount picture, also supports her in this one.

"The Trouble Buster"—with Vivian Martin in the star role—is, as the title implies, another of the optimistic films for which Miss Martin is already famous. It is a "cheer-up" story with plenty of action.

"The Call of the East," starring Sessue Hayakawa, the eminent Oriental actor whose popularity in Paramount pictures is unquestioned, gives him a splendid chance for his dramatic ability, because it is a tale of modern Japan with a plot based on the racial conflict. Margaret Loomis supports Hayakawa, while Tsuru Aoki, Jack Holt and other well known Paramount players appear in the cast. The story is by Beulah Marie Dix and George Melford is director.

"The World for Sale," by Sir Gilbert Parker, directed and produced by J. Stuart Blackton, is a picture with a carefully chosen cast of type actors, and headed by Conway Tearle and Anna Little.

"Bab's Burglar," second of the "Sub-Deb" stories by Mary Roberts Rhinehart, directed by J. Searle Dawley, and starring Marguerite Clark, will further establish the popularity of the star in the role of ingenuous Barbara Archibald.

"The Son of His Father," offers Charles Ray, among the most popular of all the younger stars. The Ince picture is directed by Victor Schertzinger and stages a thrilling hand-to-hand fight that is said to be a "hummer."

Dorothy Dalton will make her first appearance in Paramount-Ince pictures in "The Price Mark," an exceptionally powerful drama such as those with which the name of Mr. Ince and Miss Dalton have already been indelibly associated.

Ann Pennington, the Ziegfeld Follies star, who has already made an enviable reputation in Paramount pictures, returns to the screen after a successful season upon the stage in "The Antics of Ann," a delightful comedy written especially for her.

From the foregoing list of attractions it need scarcely be repeated that October is certain to be a memorable month in the history of Paramount, where every month is notable. It is the logical beginning of the Fall season in motion pictures and a more auspicious opening could hardly be desired, and while it is to be expected that Paramount should take front rank position, it is at least worthy of note that in the October list there appear the names of not only several new stars—new that is on the Paramount schedule, but already established favorites with the film-going public; several authors of world wide prominence, and, withal, a series of offerings that should supply every exhibitor's need.

GREAT FIGHT IN "WHEN A MAN SEES RED."

A motion picture director's word is law to the players in his company. Actors carry out his commands by instinct. While making the Fox production of "When A Man Sees Red," one of the Standard pictures soon to be released, William Farnum stood facing G. Raymond Nye, preparatory to the great fight scene. Nye, like Farnum, was known affectionately as "Bill." Suddenly Frank Lloyd, who directed the picture, called out: "Hit him Bill!" The two players both struck, and went at it hammer and tongs. When Lloyd was asked afterward which "Bill" he meant he smiled.

"THE NURSE OF AN ACHING HEART" (L-Ko).

Eva Novak, Chester Ryckman, Eddie Barry and Bob McKenzie are featured in the forthcoming L-Ko that General Director J. G. Blystone has captioned "The Nurse of an Aching Heart." In this work Archie Mayo shows himself for the first time as a director of L-Ko's. As this is his first L-Ko, it may be his last one, for the reason that the Board of Examiners in Hollywood, Cal., have given him his "number" and he awaits the final call to arms. As the title would indicate, "The Nurse

Scene from "The Nurse of an Aching Heart" (L-Ko).

of an Aching Heart" is located in a hospital where Eva Novak, as a nurse, does some heroic work. Comedy situations have been created in abundance amid unusual surroundings, and it is promised that L-Ko standards are well maintained.

PEGGY O'NEILL IN "THE PENNY PHILANTHROPIST."

Peggy O'Neill, famed as the creator of the title role in the big Broadway success, "Peg O' My Heart," has been signed by Wholesome Films Corporation to play the lead in that organization's first feature production, "The Penny Philanthropist."

Miss O'Neill will have ample opportunity in this feature to display on the screen all that charm which has made her success on the speaking stage.

Miss Clara Laughlin, one of America's best known women writers, is author of "The Penny Philanthropist," and Guy W. McConnell will personally supervise the production.

Miss O'Neill will have playing opposite her Ralph Morgan, a young convert from the speaking stage, whose work in "Turn To The Right" was one of the best dramatic characterizations of the year. The story of "The Penny Philanthropist" is replete with a humaneness, virile and yet gentle, carrying a message of good deeds in a manner compellingly interesting and entirely unique.

O. HENRY'S "BLIND MAN'S HOLIDAY."

Scarcely a better story could have been chosen for picturization than O. Henry's "Blind Man's Holiday." This is the second of the 4-reel de luxe features released through General Film Company, as a departure from the already famous two-reel subjects from the great short story author's repertoire. "Blind Mans' Holiday" has its scene laid in New Orleans. Incidentally there is another New Orleans four-reel story to follow this one in another month, "The Enchanted Kiss." Before that, however, there will be one with a Washington atmosphere, "The Duplicity of Hargraves," also in four-reel form.

In "Blind Man's Holiday" the story is that of Lorison, a young man who is the victim of extreme moods. His romance is one of psychological peculiarities handled in a most telling and lucid fashion, an art which O. Henry more than any other popular short story writer has mastered. Added to that O. Henry puts sentiment into the story that irresistibly sways the emotions. This story also has one of O. Henry's most triumphant "happy endings."

ESSANAY-HOLMES COMEDIES.

Essanay has completed the production of three pictures in which Taylor Holmes, the stage comedian, is featured. A fourth is now in the filming process.

"Efficiency Edgar's Courtship," the first of this series, and, incidentally, the star's initial screen vehicle, was released September 3. The second picture, entitled "Fools For Luck," will be released October 8.

This picture will be followed in November with the release of "Two-Bit Eats," and "The Small Town Guy" will be the title of the December releases.

In line with the policy recently announced by George K. Spoor, president of Essanay, that his organization henceforth will produce only pictures of a lighter vein in an attempt to offset the gloom of war, all Holmes pictures will be comedy-dramas. The George Kleine System will distribute these films.

Triangle Aims for Variety

Kiddie Features, Patriotic Plays, Western Dramas, and Comedies of All Varieties Now in the Course of Production.

DIVERSITY of subjects, having an appeal for all classes, ages and professions, is to be a feature of the Triangle policy, according to a schedule recently evolved, which provides for kiddie features, western dramas, stories of business, patriotic plays, mythical fables, and comedies ranging from those of human interest drama in five parts—to the fast and furious burlesques in one and two-reel comedies. These will be presented in rotation, with the intention of providing exhibitors with a program which, like the leading national magazines, will have something of interest for everybody.

During the past few months the Triangle Distributing Corporation has issued plays in keeping with this policy. The Triangle September schedule has been carefully arranged with plays of contrasting type succeeding one another. "Idolaters," a drama of city life with a designing adventuress as the chief character, is followed by "The Haunted House," which presents a spiritualistic girl living with her fairy fancies in a quiet New England village. "Polly Ann," the next release, is described as a play of gladness, recounting, as it does, the humorous experiences of a little orphan. "Mountain Dew" is a story of a girl of the Kentucky Cumberlands who learns the secrets of love and "larnin'" at the same time. A Yale athlete who becomes a society detective is the central figure of "Flying Colors." The following week, September 23, presents "The Devil Dodger," a western drama with the new bad man star, Roy Stewart. This is followed by "Broadway, Arizona" with Olive Thomas as the gay young chorus girl who is abducted and carried to the western mountains where she creates a Broadway of her own.

The October productions are being completed and the order of their release is now being planned. The schedule will lead off with "Ashes of Hope," a drama that is said to be similar in action and spirit to "The Flame of the Yukon." "Doing Her Bit," a patriotic play, is another feature of the month which was devised with an eye to timeliness of appeal. About October 21 Alma Rubens will come forth as a star in "The Firefly of Tough Luck," scenes of which are now being filmed on the deserts of Arizona. The Triangle kiddies, headed by Georgie Stone, Beulah Burns, and Thelma Burns will appear in support of Margery Wilson, who stars in a gypsy role of "Wild Sumac."

RITA JOLIVET PICTURES TO BE "LEST WE FORGET."

"Lest We Forget" is the title which has been selected for the great screen drama of international events in which Rita Jolivet is starred. This picture depicts occurrences at the beginning of the war and especially the early German invasion of Belgium and France, the sinking of the Lusitania, and deals with secret service in France, England and America, and shows the co-operation between the British and American foreign offices in handling German spies on both sides of the Atlantic.

Miss Jolivet is surrounded by a notable cast, among whom are included Hamilton Revelle, an actor whose prominent work has scored in many Broadway productions. Roger Lytton, who so capably portrayed a German spy in "The Battle Cry of Peace," again is seen as an agent of the Wilhelmstrasse in "Lest We Forget!" Mr. Lytton holds an officer's commission in the American army. He was excused from duty at Plattsburg for a period of weeks in order to allow him to take part in Miss Jolivet's great photoplay. At the conclusion of the scenes in which he is required he leaves at once for a military camp, from which he is scheduled to depart at a very early date for France.

The actual taking of the scenes in the picture has been proceeding since July 7 and will not be completed for another month. At present Director Leonce Perret is working in the large village—a duplication of a French coast town—which has been erected on the Watson farm in Westchester County. Many of the scenes in the picture are laid in this village. When these scenes have been filmed the destruction of the village by German bombardment will be photographed. This is one of the spectacular moments in the picture.

CANADIAN RIGHTS FOR ART DRAMAS SOLD.

Another big deal was consummated last week by Art Dramas, Incorporated, when contracts were closed for the distribution rights of the Art Dramas pictures for all Canada.

Despite its importance, the final arrangements were made in record time between Arthur F. Beck, general manager of Art Dramas, and George F. Perkins, a prominent Canadian exchange man, who immediately formulated plans for the exploitation of the Art Dramas Program in his territory.

Mr. Perkins is a veteran film man and is known as one of the most capable men in the business. He owns the Independent Film and Theater Supply Company, which handles a vast amount of business throughout Canada, and has exchanges in Toronto, Montreal and Winnipeg, Canada.

Mr. Perkins has engaged A. Fischer, who accompanied him on the trip to New York, as general manager. Both were in conference at the Art Dramas executive offices, and matters of distribution were discussed at length.

Also accompanying Mr. Perkins and Mr. Fischer was George Rotsky, general manager of Montreal's two leading theaters, the Holman and the New Grand. Mr. Rotsky arranged to run Art Dramas in his houses.

GAUMONT PROGRAM FOR WEEK OF SEPTEMBER TWENTY-FOUR.

On the road to Berlin, via France! Our soldier boys are everywhere—in camp, on the high seas, even at the very edge of battle! And wherever they may be there you will find Gaumont cameramen to keep the home folks posted as to their movements. The people have come to look forward with eager expectancy to the release of the Gaumont-Mutual Weekly on Wednesday of each week, and they can safely expect that when Weekly No. 143 is released on September 26 they will not be disappointed in its contents. As the Weekly is "made up" at the last moment, like a daily newspaper, it is not possible to predict its contents.

One day later the Gaumont film magazine, "Reel Life," will be released. It is the policy of the Gaumont Company to make the subjects in this release as diversified as possible, no two similar subjects appearing in a single issue. "Reel Life" No. 74, which will reach the public on September 27, contains a half dozen subjects of such dissimilar nature that no spectator can fail to be entertained. "The Correct Time" shows how the U. S. Naval Observatory determines exact noon each day and flashes it throughout the country. "Beans and Lady-Bug" illustrates how the common lady-bug is working to prevent a shortage in the food which makes Boston famous. Contrarily, "The Lamprey," a blood-sucking fish, is doing its best to deplete the food supply. In "Making Eyeglasses" we are familiarized with a novel industry, and shown how even the poorest of us may duplicate the best natural sight. "The Soldier's Staff of Life" enabled Uncle Sam to gain many recruits. "So Easy," an animated drawing from Life, America's leading humorous magazine, completes the reel.

"SINS OF AMBITION" (IVAN).

"Sins of Ambition," Ivan Film Productions' play now in making, written and directed by Ivan Abramson, promises to be a super-feature of exceptional quality.

As usual, Ivan Abramson has gathered around him a stellar cast, the names of which are sufficient to guarantee the artistry to be developed upon the screen. Wilfred Lucas, for a long time with the Triangle Fine Art Films, and known as leading man in "Hell-to-Pay Austin," "Orpheus in Our Square," and lately appearing in the leading male part of "The Food-Gambler," has been entrusted with a big part in "Sins of Ambition." Co-starring with him we find such screen favorites as beautiful Leah Baird, charming Barbara Castleton and James Morrison, all of honors. Other well-known stars appearing in the picture are Madaline Travers, Anders Randolf and Edward Lawrence.

The picture will, Mr. Abramson says, be an epoch-making one, both on account of its exceeding timeliness and exceptional dramatic action. While it has to deal with a great international question, yet it is in no sense whatsoever a military picture, as its basic proposition is to show the philosophical side of the sins of ambition and the consequences when ambition oversteps its boundaries.

HOW TO RAISE STRONG CHILDREN.

Bernarr Macfadden, widely known as the editor of Physical Culture, has made an agreement with Universal whereby he will demonstrate feats of strength and methods of physical development for the average man or woman in future issues of the Screen Magazine.

In the 39th issue, to be released shortly, Macfadden gives some highly entertaining scenes in which he and his children take part. He is an advocate of the training of children from their earliest babyhood, and in the case of his own family shows that normal children can soon be developed into prodigies of health and strength. His three-year-old son is shown punching the bag, turning hand springs and performing other feats ordinarily far beyond the ability of a child so small. The boy's ten-year-old sister demonstrates that she possesses the stamina and agility of a boy of fifteen by chinning herself fourteen times on a horizontal bar. Macfadden maintains that his system of strenuous but judicious training from the earliest days of the child's life not only builds muscle but gives fine poise and completely banishes fear. Directions are given for the building of inexpensive apparatus that can be erected and utilized in any backyard.

"SUNSET TRAIL" IS A PLAY OF THE GREAT OUT-DOORS.

Vivian Martin appears in a new Paramount picture, "The Sunset Trail," September 17th, and in addition to the fact that it is a story with a genuinely interesting plot, many unique situations and a splendid cast in support of the charming young star, it is notable because of the exceptional photography and the spirit of the great outdoors which it possesses.

Beulah Marie Dix made the scenario of the photoplay from a story by Alice McIver and George H. Melford directed it. Cameraman Percy Hilburn will come in for a good share of praise when the picture is exhibited owing to the remarkable work he has done in perpetuating in celluloid scenes of its exquisite scenery in the mountains and the views of sunsets and drifting clouds which were found in the locations chosen for many of the scenes. Harrison Ford appears as the sweetheart of Bess and the others in the cast give entirely adequate performances.

MME. OLGA PETROVA IN "EXILE."

Oddly enough the title of "Exile" is derived from the name of a town—or colony—a Portuguese settlement. This is the picture in which Mme. Petrova will appear September 17, under the Paramount banner. It is a Lasky production, directed by Maurice Tourneur, and is said to be a really "red-blooded" picture, with a world of opportunity for the star as well as the exceptional supporting cast, together with settings that are far beyond the ordinary.

The story is by Dolf Wyllarde, with a scenario prepared by

Scene from "Exile" (Paramount).

Charles E. Whittaker. It deals with the efforts of a young American engineer, played by Mahlon Hamilton, to bring better conditions in the lonely colony. He encounters the Chief Justice of the place, Peres, an unscrupulous wretch who becomes realistic in the hands of Wyndham Standing. Claudia, portrayed by Mme. Petrova, is the wife of Peres and when the engineer secures a hold over the official he undertakes to gain his way with Claudia. He learns, however, that she is genuinely in love with him and refuses to take advantage of the situation with the result that Peres is permitted to go unscathed. But he is afterward lynched by the furious natives against whom he has long plotted and the American saves Claudia. They watch the Arabs departing over the desert and turn back to finish out their own span in mutual happiness.

The scenes in the Portuguese-Arabian colony, the startling situations and the splendid acting of all concerned should render "Exile" an unusually strong attraction. Others in the cast beside those mentioned are Warren Cook, Charles Martin and Violet Reed.

"IN THE WAKE OF THE HUNS" (Pathe).

Pictorial evidences of the progress the French are making in regaining the northern part of their land from the Germans is shown in the Official French War Pictures titled "In the Wake of the Huns," which will be released by Pathe September 23.

These pictures are different from any other war pictures shown, because, while they show war as it really is they also show France recovering herself from the blows struck by the Germans. They depict the French army rebuilding the railroads, the bridges and the roads. They show the ruin left by the Germans, in the orchards, in the villages, in the cities and the devastation of churches and other public buildings.

One of the features of the film is the picture of the Château de Coucy. This chateau was built over six hundred years ago and many famous events in French history happened under its roof and around its walls. The pictures show the chateau as it was before its occupation by the Germans. These pictures, of course, were taken before the war broke out. Then is shown the devastation wrought by the Germans when they were forced to evacuate the chateau and it typifies in a measure the wantons spite that is being taken out on French monuments and on France itself by her invaders.

Troops in action, troops on the march, troops moving forward to engage the enemy are shown and will arouse the enthusiasm of American audiences.

"TILLIE" THE SCRUB-LADY" IS FINISHED.

Compressing 459 comedy scenes into 1,800 feet of motion picture film is likely to be a fast-moving whole, Marie Dressler has demonstrated this with "Tillie, the Scrub-Lady," the first of her two-reel comedies for Goldwyn distribution. The subject, titled and finally cut, is being printed for trade showing at all the company's branch offices.

Marie Dressler has substituted "plot" for "pie," so that her audiences may not feel compelled to laugh when they feel perfectly sure they oughtn't to.

CURRENT EVENTS IN ANIMATED WEEKLY.

Practical lessons in the art of cooking and handling food, demonstrated by a corps of experienced cooks for the benefit of the new American army, furnish one of the most interesting features of the 87th issue of the Universal Animated Weekly, just released. These pictures were posed exclusively for the Animated Weekly, and present many human interest bits, besides imparting much valuable information.

In the same issue, Anna Case, whom many consider the most beautiful of the younger American singers, is shown singing for the New Jersey troops encamped at Sea Girt. Some effective close-ups of Miss Case are pleasingly introduced.

The recent championship tennis match between Molla Bjurstedt and Mary K. Browne, at Forest Hills, L. I., has been graphically recorded in a series of views bound to stir the blood of any spectator who has ever wielded a racquet.

Other subjects that help make this number notable are scenes taken during the recent parade of street car workers with their wives and babies in San Francisco; pictures of the wreck of the grain steamer Spokane at Sault Ste. Marie, Michigan; the review of British volunteers from America, recently held in London; and the ceremonies in connection with the welcoming of the Japanese envoys in Washington. Brief, snappy subtitles add considerable interest to the reel, which is concluded, as usual, with one of Hy Mayer's timely cartoons.

MARY GARDEN SAILS FOR HOME.

Mary Garden, famous opera prima donna, has taken ship from France for home. Upon her arrival here she will be met by officials of Goldwyn Pictures and will go at once to the Goldwyn studios at Fort Lee to begin work in the splendid motion picture production of "Thais."

Miss Garden will not get into the swing of her work, however, until she has made a little concert tour she herself suggested. She wants to sing at least once for the soldiers in every northern cantonment before her camera engagements keep her close to the studios.

The script of "Thais" has been completed in the Goldwyn scenario department and awaits Miss Garden's approval. In the picturization the story of the opera has been deviated from but slightly—only enough, in fact, to lift the principal character a shade above the estate of a courtesan.

"THE MAVERICK" (Bluebird).

Franklyn Farnum makes his first appearance as a lone star in Bluebirds on Oct. 8, presenting a sensational comedy-drama, tentatively titled "The Maverick." William Parker prepared the scenario from a story furnished by Isola Forrester and Mann Page and Joseph De Grasse directed the production. Mr. De Grasse previously supervised the screen appearance of Dorothy Phillips in the Bluebird series but has now undertaken the direction of Mr. Farnum during his progress as an individual star.

Claire Du Brey, who has worked herself up from playing humble "maids" in Dorothy Phillips' company, has also been transferred to the support of Mr. Farnum as his leading lady.

Scene from "The Maverick" (Bluebird).

Lon Chaney, previously featured in Miss Phillips' support, has an important character role in "The Maverick" and will continue in the De Grasse company for more Farnum pictures. Mr. St. John, Margery Lawrence, Sam De Grasse, Eugene Moore, Wm. Dyer and D. A. Appling are other members of Mr. Farnum's support.

"The Maverick" has a plot that starts in the East and winds up in the West where Farnum cuts a sensational dash as a "tender foot" ranchman.

THE SCREEN SHOWS A NEW EVA TANGUAY.

Those persons who have long been familiar with that dynamic personality of the vaudeville circuits, Eva Tanguay, will be surprised to find an entirely new Eva when they see her in "The Wild Girl," the first screen production in which Eva Tanguay has come before the public. For the Eva of "I don't care" fame is lost among the hundred other Evas who play the central character in "The Wild Girl."

Miss Tanguay, experienced artist that she is, has not made the mistake of cutting her screen heroine after the pattern of her vaudeville self. The problem of characterization in the photoplay has been made clearly and fully by the eccentric little artiste. Eva Tanguay of the music halls has disappeared and a new—and dare we say greater?—Eva has come in her place.

The story of "The Wild Girl" is based on a suggestion by George M. Rosener, and was directed by Howard Estabrook. The play has been given a costly production and is unusually handsomely mounted. Miss Tanguay's screen debut will be made in a picture well worthy of the fame of its star.

EDNA GOODRICH IN "AMERICAN MAID."

With the completion of "Reputation," "Queen X" and "A Daughter of Maryland," her first release of the series of star productions which she is to make for the Mutual Film Corporation, Miss Goodrich is at work at her studio on Long Island under Albert Capellani's direction in "American Maid," a five-reel patriotic picture. "Reputation" was released on Sept. 3 and met with an enthusiastic reception from exhibitors and their patrons.

The other forthcoming Goodrich productions are "Queen X," written by Assistant United States District Attorney Edwin M. Stanton of New York; "American Maid," scenarioized by Hamilton Smith from a story by Julius Rothschild, and "A Daughter of Maryland," scenarioized by Anthony Kelly from a play by Samuel Morse.

LOYALTY IS THEME OF "DOUBLE-CROSSED."

Loyalty to her husband, even when she discovers that in his past there is a black spot which is cropping up to menace their happiness, forms the theme of "Double-Crossed," in which Pauline Frederick will appear September 17th. This is a Paramount picture produced under the direction of Robert G. Vignola, with the same attention to detail, the same richness of settings and excellence of support that characterizes all Paramount productions.

Hector Turnbull, author of "The Cheat," is responsible for the scenario of "Double-Crossed," and in the cast are such well-known players as Crawford Kent, Clarence Handyside, William Riley Hatch, Harris Gordon and Joseph Smiley. This picture will appeal to women particularly because of the exquisite gowns that Miss Frederick wears and the fact that it is a story which touches the home so deeply.

MARGUERITE CLARK AT WORK ON THIRD "BAB" PICTURE.

After a brief rest, Marguerite Clark begins work this week on the third in the Paramount series of "Sub-Deb" stories by Mary Roberts Rhinehart, which are being filmed under direction of J. Searle Dawley from the stories originally published in The Saturday Evening Post. The first story, "Bab's Diary," will be released on the 24th of this month and in October "Bab's Burglar," also completed, will be placed on the market. The idea is to follow in regular sequence the order of the stories as published in the Post and for the entire series the same cast will be used in support of Miss Clark.

CANTON, ILL.—John Silvernail has leased space in the Blackaby building on South Main street. He will equip it as a moving picture theater.

CHICAGO, ILL.—Dahl, Stedman & Co., 11 S. La Salle street, have the contract to make alterations to the Suedebaker theater for the Studebaker Theater Company.

CHICAGO, ILL.—Haymarket theater, at 722 W. Madison street, has been acquired by Francis and Augustus Biedler and Emma B. Camp from Mrs. Clara A. Avery.

CHICAGO, ILL.—Marshall & Fix, 706 Lincoln parkway, are preparing plans for interior alterations to the Powers theater.

SALEM, ILL.—Princess theater will be closed while improvements are being made.

FOWLER, IND.—Edward Martin has disposed of his interest in the Fowler theater to Andrew La Fountain.

MUNCIE, IND.—Vaudeville theater, on South Walnut street, has been remodeled and reopened to the public.

CRESTON, IA.—W. Weldon has purchased the Willard theater.

DES MOINES, IA.—The Auditorium has been leased by A. P. Rainsburg.

ROCK RAPIDS, IA.—Strand is the name of a new moving picture theater opened here by R. W. Steen.

TOLEDO, IA.—W. B. Persons, of Wall Lake, has purchased the Grand theater from C. E. Olson.

WHEATLAND, IA.—Otto Lahann has purchased the interest of J. C. Robertson in the A-Muse-U picture theater.

LEXINGTON, KY.—Gurnea Theater Company has been incorporated with capital of $25,000 by T. C. Fuller, V. H. Fuller. and others.

BOSTON, MASS.—A. Paul Keith and Edward F. Albee will have the Boston theater on Washington street torn down. A new structure to cost $1,000,000 will be erected on the site, with seating capacity of 4,000.

ADRIAN, MICH.—Garden Theater Company has taken over the Croswell theater. The building will be remodeled.

MANISTIQUE, MICH.—Extensive improvements will be made to the Geno theater.

NEGAUNEE, MICH.—Members of Iron Mountain Lodge of Odd Fellows are considering using their building on West Iron street for theater purposes.

BELLE PLAINE, MINN.—Paul Grossman has purchased the moving picture business of Frank Weiss.

BLUE EARTH, MINN.—J. F. Brinkman and C. E. Steele are proprietors of the Royal theater.

OSLO, MINN.—Bert Lee has purchased the interest of Mr. Olson in the Lyric theater.

OSSEO, MINN.—Masonic lodge recently taken over by Heesen Brothers, will be converted into a theater.

ASHLAND, MONT.—Moving picture theater will be opened here under the management of Carl Risvald.

Picture Theaters Projected

PAYSON, ARIZ.—Moving picture house has been opened here by Floyd Gardner. Pictures will be shown two or three times a week.

MIAMI, ARIZ.—Theater to cost $45,000 will be erected here.

RUSSELLVILLE, ARK.—A new $25,000 moving picture theater will be erected on the site of the Crescent Airdome on Main street by Oscar H. Wilson. Lessee, E. H. Butler.

FRESNO, CALIF.—Theodore Keech has leased the Liberty theater.

SANTA ANA, CALIF.—Clune's theater has been leased by Mr. and Mrs. L. A. Schlesinger.

STOCKTON, CALIF.—D. S. Rosenbaum will expend $2,000 in remodeling interior of Strand theater.

THOMPSONVILLE, CONN.—Nathan Shitsky, owner of the Majestic theater, has formed a business partnership with Clarence D. Burbank, owner of the New Franklin theater.

BLUE ISLAND, ILL.—Lyric is the name of a new moving picture theater opened here under the management of Fitzpatrick & McEvoy. House has seating capacity for 1,000 persons.

With Greatest Sorrow
it becomes our painful duty
to announce the death of
Our Esteemed President

Mr. Henry J. Brock

Which occurred on
September 7th, 1917

Inter Ocean Film Corporation

Addresses of Home Offices and Film Exchanges

ARTCRAFT PICTURES CORPORATION.

Releasing All Artcraft Productions.

Executive Offices:
729 Seventh Avenue, New York.
With branch offices as follows:

Atlanta, Ga............51 Luckie Street
Boston, Mass........8-14 Shawmut Street
Buffalo, N. Y.........146 Franklin Street
Chicago. Ill........220 South State Street
Cincinnati, O....107-109 West Third Street
Cleveland, O.....Standard Theater Bldg.
Dallas, Tex.............1912 Main Street
Denver, Colo..........1747 Welton Street
Detroit, Mich.....278 E. Jefferson Avenue
Kansas City, Mo....22nd & Grand Avenue
Los Angeles, Cal...Marshall-Strong Bldg.
Minneapolis, Minn........16 N. 4th Street
New Orleans, La.......814 Perdido street
New York. N. Y..........729 7th Avenue
New York, N. Y........71 W. 23d Street
Philadelphia, Pa.......1219 Vine Street
Pittsburgh, Pa....13th St. & Penn. Ave.
Portland, Me...........85 Market Street
Portland, Ore.....9th & Burnside Streets
San Francisco, Cal......445 Pacific Bldg.
Salt Lake City, Utah..133 E. 2nd South St.
St. Louis, Mo......14th & Locust Streets
Seattle, Wash..........1200 4th Avenue
Washington, D. C......525 13th St., N. W.

CANADA.

Famous Players Film Service, Ltd.,
Calgary ....Elma Block
Famous Players Film Service, Ltd.
Montreal, Que..158 St. Catherine St. West
Famous Players Film Service, Ltd.,
Toronto, Ont.........12 Queen St. East

AUSTRALIA.

Australian Feature Films, Ltd.,
Sydney, N. S......192 Castlereagh Street.

ART DRAMAS, INC.

Art Dramas, Inc., releases the following brands: Apollo, Erbograph, Horsley,
U. S. Amusement Corporation, Van Dyke.

Executive Offices:
1400 Broadway, New York.
With branch offices as follows:

E. & H. Film Distributing Co.,
Atlanta, Ga...............85 Walton Street
Boston Photoplay Company,
Boston, Mass..........193 Pleasant Street
Standard Film Corporation,
Chicago, Ill.....207 South Wabash Street
Standard Film Service Company,
Cincinnati, O.....14 West Seventh Avenue
Standard Film Service Company,
Cleveland, O.............Columbia Bldg.
Southwestern Art Dramas, Inc.,
Dallas, Tex............1812 Main Street
Standard Film Corporation,
Des Moines, Iowa....702 Mulberry Street
Standard Film Service Company,
Detroit, Mich...............Smith Bldg.
Standard Film Corporation,
Kansas City, Mo.......1306 Walnut Street
Sol Lesser,
Los Angeles, Cal...514 West Eighth Street
Standard Film Corporation,
Minneapolis, Minn....406 Film Exch. Bldg.
Standard Art Dramas Film Exchange,
New Orleans, La.........608 Canal Street
Modern Feature Photoplays, Inc,
New York City.........729 Seventh Avenue
Standard Film Corporation.
Omaha, Neb..........1417 Farnham Street
Electric Theater Supply Company,
Philadelphia, Pa.......1321 Vine Street
Liberty Film Renting Company,
Pittsburgh, Pa..........938 Penn Avenue
Sol Lesser,
San Francisco, Cal....191 Golden Gate Ave.
Standard Film Corporation,
St. Louis, Mo...304 Empress Theater Bldg.

CANADA.

Independent Film and Theater Supply Co.,
Montreal, Quebec.......7 Phillips Square

FOX FILM CORPORATION.

The Fox Film Corporation releases the following brands: Foxfilm Comedies, Fox Special Features, Standard Pictures.

Up-to-Date Lists of the Larger Groups of Distributors Arranged in Alphabetical Order.

F OR the convenience of our readers and subscribers we are publishing herewith up-to-date lists of the head offices and branch exchanges of all the larger groups of film renters. The lists are arranged alphabetically by companies and also by cities. The film brands handled by each group are also listed alphabetically at the beginning of each list. Exhibitors are requested to file this copy for future use, as we will only be able to publish the lists at intervals on account of the space required. Time will usually be saved by corresponding with the nearest branch office, but matters may be taken up with the head office direct when desired. In all your correspondence with any of these offices, kindly refer to the Moving Picture World.

Executive Offices,
130 West 46th Street, New York City.
With branch offices as follows:

Atlanta, Ga..............111 Walton Street
Boston, Mass........10-12 Piedmont Street
Chicago, Ill..............Mallers Building
Cleveland, Ohio....760 Prospect Avenue
Cincinnati, Ohio........412 Vine Street
Dallas, Texas......1907 Commerce Street
Detroit, Mich..........407 Smith Building
Denver, Colo...........1442 Welton Street
Indianapolis, Ind'...222 N. Illinois Street
Kansas City, Mo.........928 Main Street
Los Angeles, Cal...734 South Olive Street
Minneapolis, Minn.....527 First Avenue N.
New York, N. Y......130 West 46th Street
Newark, N. J.....Strand Theater Building
New Haven, Conn....Poli's Theater Bldg.
New Orleans, La.......632 Common Street
Omaha, Neb........315 South 16th Street
Philadelphia, Pa........1333 Vine Street
Pittsburgh, Pa.......121 Fourth Avenue
Salt Lake City, Utah...McIntyre Building
San Francisco, Cal...243 Golden Gate Ave.
Seattle, Wash........1214 Third Avenue
St. Louis, Mo.........3432 Olive Street
Syracuse, N. Y.......445 S. Warren Street
Washington, D. C....305 Ninth St., N. W.

CANADIAN OFFICES.

Montreal, Que...322 S. Catherine St. W.
Toronto, Ont........12 Queen Street, East
St. John, N. B.,
Bank of B. N. A. Bldg., 1-5 Market Sq.
Vancouver, B. C.,
506-9-10 Orpheum Theater Building
Winnipeg, Man.......Phoenix Block

UNITED KINGDOM.

London, Eng....74-76 Old Compton Street
Liverpool, Eng..........16 Manchester Street
Manchester, Eng.,
28 Deansgate Arcade, Deansgate. E.
Newcastle-on-Tyne, Eng.20 Westgate Rd.
Leeds, Eng................29 Albion Place
Birmingham, Eng.1-3 Temple St. New St.
Cardiff, Wales.......9 and 3-a Wharton St.
Glasgow, Scotland.....78 Dunlop Street
Dublin, Ireland,
Dame House, 24-25 Dame Street

AUSTRALIA.

Sydney, N. S. W.Symond Bldg., 194 Pitt St.
Melbourne, Victoria,
Elizabeth and Little Collins Streets
Adelaide ....Peel Street

SOUTH AMERICA.

Rio de Janeiro, Brazil...Caixa Postal 989
Sao Paulo, Brazil.Rua Santa Ephigenia 77
Buenos Aires, Argentine,
951 Calle Corrientes
Rosario, Argentine......San Lorenzo 912
Montevideo, Uruguay,
Care Colonial and River Plate Bank
Lima, Peru .(fox- Chili, Peru, Bolivia).

SPAIN AND PORTUGAL.

Barcelona...........Ronda Universidad 14

SCANDINAVIA AND RUSSIA.

Stockholm, Sweden,
Metropolitan, 3 Hollandaregat
Christiania, Norway.......4 Startingsgade

NEW ZEALAND.

Wellington, N. Z.........65 Willis Street

GENERAL FIRM CO., INC.

The General Film Company, Inc., releases the following brands: Broadway Star Features (the O. Henry Series), Essanay (black Cat Feature, George Ade "Fables in Slang" and Chaplins), Falcon Features, Kalem (series and comedies), George Kleine (George Bickel comedies), Jaxon Comedies (Pokes and Jabs), Selig (short subjects), Ray Comedies, Sparkle Comedies.

Executive Offices,
440 Fourth Avenue, New York City.
With branch offices as follows:

Albany, N. Y............48 Howard Street
Atlanta, Ga............111 Walton Street
Bangor, Me............133 Franklin Street
Boston, Mass........28 Ferdinand Street
Buffalo, N. Y..........123 Pearl Street
Chicago, Ill........235 North Clark Street
Cincinnati, Ohio..........514 Elm Street
Cleveland, Ohio..1022 Superior Ave., N. E.
Dallas, Texas........2017 Commerce Street
Denver, Colo.........1448 Champa Street
Detroit, Mich..........100 Griswold Street
Indianapolis, Ind...24 W. Washington St.
Kansas City, Mo......921 Walnut Street
Los Angeles, Cal...738 South Olive Street
Minneapolis, Minn....509 Hennepin Ave.
New Orleans, La.......242 Baronne Street
New York, N. Y.......71 West 23d Street
Omaha, Neb........1508 Howard Street
Philadelphia, Pa........1208 Vine Street
Pittsburgh, Pa.........1201 Liberty Avenue
St. Louis, Mo..........3601 Olive Street
San Francisco, Cal..256 Golden Gate Ave.
Seattle, Wash..........819 Third Avenue
Washington, D. C...7th and E Sts., N. W.
Wilkes-Barre, Pa....50 E. Market Street

CANADIAN OFFICES.

GENERAL FILM COMPANY, LTD.
Executive Office:
242 Bleury Street, Montreal, Quebec.
With branch offices as follows:
St. John, N. B..........122 German Street
Toronto, Ont...........171 King Street W.
Vancouver, B. C........440 Pender Street, W.
Winnipeg, Man...........220 Phoenix Block

GOLDWYN DISTRIBUTING CORPORATION.

Releasing all Goldwyn Productions.

16 East Forty-second Street.
With branch offices as follows:

Atlanta, Ga..............75 Walton Street
Boston, Mass......40-44 Piedmont Street
Buffalo, N. Y............200 Pearl Street
Chicago, Ill........110 South State Street
Cincinnati, O........217 East Fifth Street
Cleveland, O..403 Standard Film Building
Dallas, Tex............1922 Main Street
Denver, Colo.........1440 Welton Street
Detroit, Mich.Room 404, Peter Smith Bldg.
Kansas City, Mo.......1120 Walnut Street
Los Angeles, Cal...912 South Olive Street
Minneapolis, Minn..16-18 N. Fourth Street
New York, N. Y.......509 Fifth Avenue
Philadelphia, Pa....Cor. 13th and Vine Sts.
Pittsburgh, Pa.......1201 Liberty Avenue
San Francisco, Cal......985 Market Street
St. Louis, Mo...........3312 Lindell Blvd.
Seattle, Wash..........1200 Fourth Avenue
Washington, D. C..10th and G Sts., N. W.

CANADIAN OFFICES.

GOLDWYN PICTURES, LTD., OF CANADA
Executive Office:
21 Adelaide St., W., Toronto, Ont.
With branch offices as follows:
Calgary..............315 MacLean Street
Montreal, Quebec.......337 Bleury Street
St. John, N. B...........19 Market Square
Toronto, Ont.........21 Adelaide St., W.

Vancouver, B. C......304 Orpheum Block
Winnipeg, Manitoba.......48 Aiken Block

GREATER VITAGRAPH, INC.

Greater Vitagraph, Inc., releases the following: Big V Comedies, a Bobby Connelly series release, two Favorite Film Features, a two-reel episode of "The Fighting Trail" and a Multiple Reel Feature.

Executive Offices:
1600 Broadway, New York City.

With branch offices as follows:
Atlanta, Ga............111 Walton Street
Boston, Mass...........67 Church Street
Chicago, Ill...Adams St. and Wabash Ave.
Cincinnati, O....N. W. Cor. 7th & Main St.
Cleveland. O......2077 East Fourth Street
Dallas, Tex........1900 Commerce Street
Denver, Colo.......1433 Champa Street
Detroit, Mich.........44 E. Larned Street
Kansas City, Mo....13th and Walnut Sts.
Los Angeles, Cal...643 South Olive Street
Milwaukee......Third and Grand Avenues
Minneapolis, Minn...608 North First Ave.
New Orleans, La....347 Carondelet Street
New York City..........1600 Broadway
Omaha, Neb.......1111 Farnum Street
Philadelphia, Pa....229 North 12th Street
Pittsburgh, Pa......117 Fourth Avenue
San Francisco, Cal....986 Market Street
Salt Lake City, Utah...62 Exchange Pl.
St. Louis, Mo.......3630 Olive Street
Seattle, Wash...........415 Olive Street
Syracuse, N. Y.......117 Walton Street
Washington, D. C....710 Eleventh Street

CANADIAN OFFICES

Montreal, Canada........401 Bleury Street
St. Johns, N. B...167 Prince William Street
Toronto, Ontario.......15 Wilton Avenue
Winnipeg.............114 Phoenix Block

KLEINE-EDISON-SELIG-ESSANAY.

Kleine - Edison - Selig - Essanay releases the following brands: Edison (Conquest) Program and Multiple Reel Features), Essanay (Multiple Reel Features, Kleine Multiple Reel, two-reel Comedies and "Do Children Count!" series), Selig (Multiple Reel Features and Hoyt Comedies).

Executive Offices:
63 East Adams Street, Chicago, Ill.

With branch offices as follows:
Atlanta, Ga.........71 Walton Street
Boston, Mass........14 Piedmont Street
Buffalo, N. Y........Palace Theater Bldg.
Chicago, Ill.....207 So. Wabash Avenue
Cincinnati, O........128 W. 7th Street
Cleveland, O........2077 E. 4th Street
Dallas, Tex.....1812½ Commerce Street
Denver Colo........729 18th Street
Detroit, Mich........Peter Smith Bldg.
Indianapolis, Ind.....Lyric Theater Bldg.
Kansas City, Mo........208 Ozark Bldg.
Los Angeles, Cal.....642 So. Olive Street
Minneapolis, Minn.....16 No. 4th Street
New Orleans, La......714 Poydras Street
New York, N. Y.......729 7th Avenue
Philadelphia, Pa......1309 Vine Street
Pittsburgh, Pa........123 4th Avenue
St. Louis, Mo........3315 Olive Street
Salt Lake City, Utah..127 E. 2nd South St.
San Francisco, Cal...182 Golden Gate Ave.
Seattle. Wash....204 Orpheum Thea. Bldg.
Washington, D. C.......6th & F Sts. N. W.

CANADIAN OFFICES.

Toronto, Ont. Canada..39 Adelaide St. W.
Montreal, Que., Canada,
    6 McGill College Avenue

METRO PICTURES CORPORATION.

The Metro Pictures Corporation releases the following brands: Columbia, Drew Comedies, Metro, Popular Plays and Players, Quality, Rolfe, Yorke.

Executive offices:
1476 Broadway, New York City.

With branch offices as follows:
Metro Pictures Corporation of N. E.,
Boston, Mass...........60 Church Street
N. Y. Metro Film Service,
Albany, N. Y..........Enterprise Bldg.
N. Y. Metro Film Service,

Buffalo, N. Y............Palace Theater
Southern Metro Pictures Corp.,
Chattanooga, Tenn...7 Chamberlain Bldg.
Metro Picture Service,
Chicago, Ill.............410 Mallers Bldg.
Metro Film Service, Inc.,
Cincinnati, O.........7th and Main Streets
Metro Pictures Corp.,
Dallas, Tex. .....1905½ Commerce Street
Metro Pictures Corp.,
Denver, Colo........1721 California Street
Metro Pictures Corp.,
Des Moines, Ia........920 Walnut Street
Metro Pictures Service,
Detroit, Mich............75 Broadway
Metro Pictures Service,
Kansas City, Mo........928 Main Street
Metro Pictures Corp.,
Los Angeles, Cal........820 Olive Street
Metro Pictures Service,
Minneapolis, Minn. ....807 Produce Exch.
Southern Metro Pictures Corp.,
New Orleans, La.....713 Paydros Street
N. Y. Metro Film Service, Inc.,
New York, N. Y......729 Seventh Avenue
N. J. Metro Film Service,
New York............7 West 23d Street
Metro Film Exchange,
Philadelphia, Pa. ......1331 Vine Street
Metro Pictures Service,
Pittsburgh, Pa........938 Penn Avenue
Metro Pictures Corp.,
San Francisco, Cal.......55 Jones Street
Metro Pictures Corporation,
Salt Lake City.......18 Post Office Bldg.
Metro Pictures Service,
Washington, D. C....7th and D Sts., N. W.

CANADIAN OFFICES.

Metro Film Service, Ltd.,
Montreal, Canada..8 McGill College Avenue
Metro Pictures Service, Ltd.,
Toronto...............263 Yonge Street
Western Metro Service,
Vancouver, B. C.........Orpheum Theater

GREAT BRITAIN.

Ruffells Exclusive, Ltd.,"
London, England ....9 Long Acre

MUTUAL FILM CORPORATION.

The Mutual Film Corporation releases the following brands: Chas. Frohman's Successes in Moving Pictures, Cub, Gaumont, La Salle, Monmouth ("Jimmie Dale alias the Grey Seal" serial), Monogram ("The Shorty Hamilton" series), Mutual Chaplin, Mutual Special ("The Great Stanley Secret" serial), Mutual Star Production, Mutual Weekly, Niagara ("The Perils of Our Girl Reporter" series), Signal Producing Company ("The Lost Express" serial), Strand Comedy and Vogue Comedy.

Executive offices:
220 South State street, Chicago, Ill.

With branch offices as follows:
Albany, N. Y.............733 Broadway
Atlanta, Ga........146 Marietta Street
Baltimore, Md..........412 E. Baltimore
Boston, Mass..........39 Church Street
Buffalo, N. Y..........106 Pearl Street
Butte, Mont..........126 Granite Street
Chicago, Ill........Consumers Building
Cincinnati, O..........224 E. 7th Street
Cleveland, O....750 Prospect Avenue, S. E.
Dallas, Tex..........1807 Main Street
Denver, Colo........1724 Welton Street
Des Moines, Ia........Cohen Building
Detroit, Mich.....97 Woodward Avenue
El Paso, Tex.,
Cor. W. San Antonio Ave. & S. Santa Fe St.
Escanaba, Mich....1019 Ludington Street
Fargo, N. D............119 Fifth Street
Houston, Tex.......805 Franklin Avenue
Indianapolis, Ind....North Illinois Street
Kansas City, Mo........328 Main Street
Los Angeles, Cal...825 South Olive Street
Memphis, Tenn.........230 Main Avenue
Milwaukee, Wis...301 Enterprise Building
Minneapolis, Minn...22 North Sixth Street
New Orleans, La......816 Perdido St.
New York City, Mutual Film Exchange,
    71 W. 23rd Street
New York, Western.....126 W. 46th Street
Oklahoma City....Box 978, 715 Walker St.
Omaha, Neb..........1413 Harney Street
Philadelphia, Pa........1219 Vine Street
Pittsburgh, Pa..........420 Penn Avenue

Portland, Ore........9th and Davis Street
Salt Lake City, Utah..123 E. South Street
San Francisco, Cal.......177 Golden Gate
St. Louis, Mo...........1311 Pine Street
Seattle, Wash........1933 Third Avenue
Washington, D. C....419 Ninth St., N. W.

CANADIAN OFFICES:

Toronto, Canada........15 Wilton Avenue
Calgary, Canada.......702 4th St. W.
Montreal, Canada......345 Bleury Street
St. John, Canada........39 Waterloo Street
Vancouver, Canada...963 Granville Street
Winnipeg, Canada,
    48 Aiken Block, McDermott Avenue

PARAMOUNT PICTURES CORPORATION.

The Paramount Pictures Corporation releases the following brands: Arbuckle Comedies, Black Diamond Comedy, Furton Holmes Travelogue, Bray Pictographs, Famous Players, Klever Comedy, Lasky, Morosco, Pallas.

Executive Offices:
485 Fifth Avenue, New York City.

With branch offices as follows:
Southern Paramount Pictures Co.,
Atlanta, Ga............61 Luckie Street
Famous Players Film Co. of N. E.,
Boston, Mass..........10 Shawmut Street
Wm. L. Sherry Feature Film Co.,
Buffalo, N. Y..........145 Franklin Street
Famous Players Film Service,
Chicago, Ill..........220 So. State Street
Famous Players Film Service,
Cincinnati, Ohio......107 West 3rd Street
Famous Players Film Service,
Cleveland, Ohio.....Standard Theater Bldg.
Texas Paramount Pictures Co.,
Dallas, Texas ......1902 Commerce Street
Notable Feature Film Co.,
Denver Colo..........1749 Walton Street
Famous Players Film Service, Inc.,
Detroit, Mich...278 East Jefferson Avenue
Kansas City Feature Film Co.,
Kansas City, Mo........2024 Broadway
Progressive Motion Picture Co.,
Los Angeles, Cal......Marsh-Strong Bldg.
Famous Players Star Feature Film Co.,
Minneapolis. Minn....Produce Exch. Bldg.
Famous Players Film Co. of N. E.,
New Haven. Conn....121 Meadow Street
Southern Paramount Pictures Co.,
New Orleans, La........814 Perdido St.
Wm. L. Sherry Feature Film Co.,
New York City, N. Y..729 Seventh Avenue
Famous Players Exchange.
New York City, N. Y..71 West 23d Street
Famous Players Exchange.
Philadelphia, Pa.........1219 Vine Street
Famous Players Film Service,
Pittsburgh, Pa......Penn Ave. & 12th St.
Famous Players Film Co. of N. E.,
Portland, Me..........85 Market Street
Notable Feature Film Co.,
Salt Lake City. Utah..133 E 2nd So. Street
Progressive M. P. Co.,
San Francisco, Cal.......645 Pacific Bldg.
Progressive M. P. Co.,
Seattle. Wash...........Central Bldg.
Famous Players Exchange,
Washington, D. C......525 13th St. N. W.

CANADIAN OFFICES:

Famous Players Service, Ltd.,
Calgary, Alberta, Canada...12 Elma Block
Famous Players Exchange, Ltd.,
Montreal. Canada..198 St. Catherine Street
Famous Players, Ltd.,
Toronto, Canada....12 Queen Street East

PATHE EXCHANGE, INC.

Pathe Exchange, Inc., releases the following brands: Astra, Hearst-Pathe News, International, Lasallda. Rolin, Thanhouser.

Executive Offices
25 W. 45th St., New York City.

With branch offices as follows:
Albany, N. Y..........298 Broadway
Atlanta, Ga..........111 Walton Street
Boston, Mass. ....7 Isabella Street
Buffalo, N. Y..........269 Main Street
Butte. Mont........114 W. Granite Street
Charlotte, N. C.......3 S. Graham Street
Chicago, Ill..........220 South State Street
Cincinnati, O....124 East Seventh Street
Cleveland, O. ..750 Prospect Avenue, S. E.
Dallas, Texas ....2012½ Commerce Street

Denver, Colo. ....1229 16th Street
Des Moines, Iowa..316 West Locust Street
Detroit, Mich. ....40 Larned Street E.
Indianapolis, Ind. .....224 N. Medidian St.
Kansas City, Mo. ....928 Main Street
Los Angeles, Cal........732 South Olive St.
Milwaukee, Wis.........174 Second Street
Minneapolis, Minn. ....608 First Ave. N,
Newark, N. J..........6 Mechanic Street
New Orleans, La......836 Common Street
New York, N. Y......115 East 23d Street
Omaha, Neb. ....1417 Harney Street
Philadelphia, Pa. ....1235 Vine Street
Pittsburgh, Pa. ....938 Penn Avenue
Portland, Ore. ....392 Burnside Street
Salt Lake City, Utah....68 S. Main Street
San Francisco, Cal.....985 Market Street
Seattle, Wash. ....810 Third Avenue
St. Louis, Mo.........3210 Locust Street
Washington, D. C......501 F Street, N. W.
Spokane, Wash..12 S. Washington Street

CANADIAN OFFICES, PATHE BRANDS.

SPECIALTY FILM IMPORT, Ltd.
Executive Offices
313 Bleury Street, Montreal, Quebec.
Calgary, Alberta..Leeson & Lineham Blk.
St. John, N. B.........167 Prince William
Toronto, Ontario .....56 King Street W.
Winnipeg, Man........342 Donald Street
Montreal-.............313 Bleury Street
Vancouver, B. C.....563 Granville Street

TRIANGLE DISTRIBUTING CORP.
The Triangle Distributing Corporation
releases the following brands: Triangle-
Plays, Trinagle Komedies, Keystone Com-
edies, Paralta Plays.
Executive Offices
1457 Broadway, New York City.
With branch offices as follows:
Atlanta, Ga.........51 Luckie Street
Boston, Mass.......49-50 Melrose Street
Chicago, Ill......5 South Wabash Avenue
Cincinnati, Ohio......215 East 5th Street
Cleveland, Ohio......704 Sincere Bldg.
Dallas, Texas......1814 Commerce Street
Denver, Colo.......1425 Champa Street
Detroit, Mich..........71-75 Broadway
Kansas City, Mo....19th and Main Streets
Los Angeles, Cal....643 South Olive Street
Milwaukee, Wis...172 Toy Bldg., 24 Street
Minneapolis, Minn....16-18 N. 4th Street
New Orleans, La....340 Carondelet Street
New York, N. Y........1457 Broadway
New Haven, Conn....130 Meadow Street
Omaha, Neb......16th and Harney Streets
Philadelphia, Pa.......1227 Vine Street
Pittsburgh, Pa........414 Penn Avenue
St. Louis, Mo........3320 Lindell Boulevard
Salt Lake City, Utah..58 Exchange Place
San Francisco, Cal...111 Golden Gate Ave.
Seattle, Wash........1206 Fourth Avenue
Washington, D. C.....708 13th St., N. W.

UNIVERSAL FILM EXCHANGES.
The Universal Film Manufacturing Com-
pany releases the following brands: Ani-
Ohama, Neb......12th an Harney Streets
mated Weekly, Big U. Bison, Butterfly
Pictures, Gold Seal, Imp. Joker. L-Ko.
Nestor, Powers, Rex, Star Featurette,
Universal Current Events, Universal
Screen Magazine, Victor.
Executive Offices,
1600 Broadway, New York City.
With branch offices as follows:
Consolidated Film & Supply Co.
Atlanta, Ga. ....Rhodes Bldg.
Albany, N. Y........Rex Film Exchange
New England Universal.
Boston, Mass.......12-19 Stanhope Street
Victor Film Service,
Buffalo, N. Y.........35 Church Street
Universal Film Exchange,
Butte, Mont. ....52 East Broadway

Universal Film Exchange,
Charlotte, N. C....307 West Trade Street
Laemmie Film Exchange,
Chicago, Ill...........17 So. Wabash Ave.
Universal Booking Office,
Chicago, Ill..........220 South State Street
Cincinnati-Buckeye Co.,
Cincinnati, Ohio ......531 Walnut Street
Universal Supply Company,
Cairo, Ill. ......6th & Washington Aves.
Cleveland, Ohio......Victor Film Service.
Consolidated Film Supply Co.,
Dallas, Texas......1900 Commerce Street
Universal Film Exchange,
Denver, Col..........1422 Welton Street
Laemmle Film Exchange,
Des Moines, Ia......918 Locust Street
Universal Film Exchange,
Detroit, Mich. ......101 West Fort Street
Universal Film Exchange,
Escanaba, Mich.
Universal Film & Supply Co.,
Fort Smith, Ark.
Consolidated Film Supply Co.,
Jacksonville, Fla. ......330 Forsythe Street
Central Film Service,
Indianapolis, Ind....113 West Georgia St.
Universal Film & Supply,
Kansas City, Mo. .....214 East 12th Street
Universal Film Exchange.
Harrisburg, Pa. ....5 So. 4th Street
Consolidated Film & Supply Co.,
Houston, Tex. ....801 Franklin Street
Universal Film Exchange,
Milwaukee, Wis.........133 Second Street
Consolidated Film Supply Co.,
Memphis, Tenn. ......226 Union Avenue
Laemmle Film Service,
Minneapolis, Minn. ...717 Hennepin Avenue
Universal Film Exchange,
New Haven, Conn. ....229 Meadow Street
Consolidated Film & Supply Co.,
New Orleans, La. .....914 Gravier Street
Universal Film Exchange,
Newark, N. J.........25 Branford Place
Universal Film Exchange,
New York City.........1600 Broadway
Universal Film Exchange,
New York City. ....115 East 23d Street
Universal Film & Supply Co.,
Oklahoma City, Okla.116 West 2nd Street
Universal Film Service,
Omaha, Neb. ....1123 Farnum Street
Universal Film Exchange,
Grand Rapids, Mich...68 So. Division Ave.
California Film Exchange,
Los Angeles, Cal.....736 So. Olive Street
Interstate Film & Supply Co.,
Philadelphia, Pa. ....1304 Vine Street
Eagle Projection Co.,
Philadelphia, Pa. ....1304 Vine Street
Universal Film Exchange,
Philadelphia, Pa.....223 West 13th Street
Universal Film Exchange,
Phoenix, Ariz........117 No. 2nd Street
Independent Film Exchange,
Pittsburgh, Pa. ....938 Penn Avenue
Film Supply Co.,
Portland, Ore. ....401 Davis Street
Universal Film Exchange,
Saginaw, Mich. ....4 Mercer Bldg.
Universal Film Exchange,
Salt Lake City, Utah...56 Exchange Place
California Film Exchange,
San Francisco, Cal..121 Golden Gate Ave.
Film Supply Co.,
Seattle, Wash. ....217 Virginia Avenue.
Universal Film Supply Co.,
Spokane, Wash...16 So. Washington Street
Universal Film Exchange,
Springfield, Mass........326 Dwight Street
Universal Film & Supply Co.,
St. Louis, Mo.........2116 Locust Street

Toledo Film Exchange,
Toledo, Ohio.........439 Huron Street
Washington Film Supply Co.,
Washington, D. C....419 9th Street N. W.
Universal Film Exchange,
Wichita, Kan.........209 East 1st Street
Exhibitors Film Service,
Wilkes-Barre, Pa. ....61 So. Penn Street

CANADIAN OFFICES.
Canadian Film Exchange,
Winnipeg, Manitoba, Canada,
....................40 Aikens Bldg.
Canadian Film Exchange,
St. Johns, N. B., Canada...87 Union Street
Canadian Film Exchange,
Calgary, Alta., Canada.497 Eighth Avenue
Canadian Film Exchange,
Vancouver, B. C., Canada...711 Dunsmuir
Canadian Universal Film Co.,
Montreal, Canada..205 St. Catherine Street
Canadian Universal Film Co.,
Toronto, Canada......106 Richmond Street

FOREIGN OFFICES.
Universal Film Mfg. Co.,
Tokio, Japan,
14 Sanchore, Minamidenmacho, Kiobashi
Universal Film Mfg. Co.,
Bombay, India,
Hesra House, Sandhurst Rd., Girguam
Excelsior.
Buenos Aires, Argentina..........Lima 691
E. Martinez y Gunche,
Buenos Aires, Argentina......Bogata 2879
Universal Film Mfg. Co.,
Manila, P. I...........206 Roxas Bldg
Universal Film Mfg. Co.,
Singapore, S. S...........62 Orchard Road
Agencia Cinematographica Universal,
Rio de Janeiro........25 Rua Treze de Maio
Universal Film Mfg. Co.,
San Juan, P. I............Tetuan Street
Universal Film Mfg. Co.,
Bandoeng, Java ....Z. W. 37 Pasirkliki
Universal Film Mfg. Co.,
Havana, Cuba ....Edificio Campoainor

WORLD FILM CORPORATION.
The World Film Corporation releases
the following brands: Brady-International.
World Pictures-Brady Made.
Executive Offices:
130 West 46th Street, New York City.
With branch offices as follows:
Atlanta, Ga..........145 Marietta Street
Boston, Mass.........41 Winchester Street
Buffalo, N. Y.........269 Main Street
Chicago, Ill......207 South Wabash Avenue
Cincinnati, O..N. W. Cor 7th and Main Sts.
Cleveland, Ohio.........Belmont Building
Dallas, Texas.......1905 Commerce Street
Denver, Colo..........1753 Welton Street
Detroit, Mich........97 Woodward Avenue
Indianapolis, Ind....294 N. Illinois Street
Kansas City, Mo......411 Ozark Building
Los Angeles, Cal..823 South Grand Avenue
Minneapolis, Minn-Produce Exchange Bldg.
New Orleans, La........815 Union Street
New York, N. Y.........130 W. 46th Street
Omaha, Neb. ....1508 Harney Street
Philadelphia, Pa.........1314 Vine Street
Pittsburgh, Pa.........938 Penn Avenue
St. Louis, Mo.........3626 Olive Street
Salt Lake City, Utah...135 E. 2nd Street
San Francisco, Cal...164 Golden Gate Ave.
Seattle, Wash.........1801 Fifth Avenue
Washington, D. C.......1004 E St., N. W.

CANADIAN OFFICES.
Regal Films, Ltd.,
37 Yonge Street, Toronto, Ont.

The attention of EXHIBITORS and THEATER MANAGERS is called to the preceding lists
of Film Exchanges, covering the larger groups of film renting offices and the majority of best
known brands of films. Keep this list for reference, as we will only publish same occasionally on
account of space required. Time will be saved by corresponding with the nearest branch office
for whichever brands you desire, but correspondence may be sent to the executive office whenever necessary. It will facilitate matters if you will refer to the MOVING PICTURE WORLD in
all your correspondence.

Trade News of the Week

GATHERED BY OUR OWN CORRESPONDENTS

"Jack and the Beanstalk" Pleases Boston

Newspapers and Public Accord Fox Big Fairy Tale Feature the Warmest Welcome at the Majestic Theater—What Dailies Said About It.

By Richard Davis Howe, 80 Summer Street, Boston, Mass.

BOSTON, MASS.—The great Fox feature film, "Jack and the Beanstalk," got a big welcome in Boston. Here are what the leading daily papers had to say of the first day's run at the Majestic theater:

Harlow Hare, in the Boston American: "There was a large audience on hand which wasn't youthful by any means, but the big folks seemed to enjoy the picture as much as the children."

Cortlandt Marsden, in the Traveller, said: "The work of that youngster, Francis Carpenter, as Jack, was a revelation. 'Jack and the Beanstalk' is well worth seeing."

Salita Solano, in the Journal: "Film to delight the imagination of every child who ever lost himself between the covers of a book of fairy tales."

The Globe: "The most fertile imagination never travelled faster or reached greater heights than this William Fox production of the oldest of fairy tales. Thrills and enchantment combined to the complete joy and satisfaction of the juveniles and to the admiration of their elders."

A large amount of space was purchased in the Boston papers for the exploitation of the picture at the Majestic, one of Boston's largest legitimate theaters in the downtown district. The picture drew large crowds. Some specially good press work was done by Joseph DiPesa, who was retained by the Fox interests to look after the publicity end of the run.

Premier of Waterbury's Rialto.

Waterbury, Conn.—The new Rialto theater in Waterbury, Conn., was opened on Labor Day, with William Fox's feature production, "The Honor System." There was a capacity crowd all day. The Rialto is one of the finest show houses used for motion pictures in New England. It was formerly the Bijou, which was torn down and rebuilt into the Rialto. The theater seats 1,400. Manager Nichols is booking only the very best productions for this house.

Joseph Mack on Manager Campbell's Staff.

Boston, Mass.—Harry F. Campbell, manager of the Boston Goldwyn exchange, has completed the personnel of his office by adding to his sales and office staff, and now has everything in readiness for a great drive.

Joseph Mack, one of New England's foremost film salesmen, has become a member of the Boston exchange and will represent the Goldwyn productions in western Massachusetts, Worcester inclusive, and the territory east of the Connecticut river handled by the local office. This territory is very familiar to Mr. Mack, who has a wide acquaintance among the moving picture men in this vicinity.

Mr. Mack is one of the most popular film men in New England and controls the Onset theater in Onset, Mass., which he personally manages during the summer months. He was formerly sales representative for the World Film in the Bay state, under Stanley Hand, manager until a few months ago when he was succeeded by George M. A. Fecke. He was the winner of a sales contest conducted by Manager Hand, turning in the largest amount of business for a two months' period.

Goldwyn Gives List of New Contracts.

The following is a partial list of theaters in New England that have signed up contracts for Goldwyn productions through Harry F. Campbell, manager of the local office:

Three day runs—Harvard, North Cambridge; Olympia, Lynn; Olympia, New Bedford; Rialto, Brockton; Broadway, Lawrence; Music Hall, Pawtucket, R. I.; Union Square, Pittsfield; Davis, Norwich, Conn.

Two day runs—Olympia, Chelsea; North Shore, Gloucester; Park, Woonsocket, R. I.; Opera House, Willimantic, Conn.; Empire, New London, Conn.; Central, Westerly, R. I.; Empire, North Adams; Gorman, Framingham; Orpheum, Gardner, Mass.

The Bowdoin Square's Sunday Evening Shows.

Boston, Mass.—Manager Al Somerby, of the Bowdoin Square theater, in the west end of the city, has inaugurated a new program for his patrons on Sunday evenings. The entire bill of moving pictures will consist of Paramount productions. There will be vaudeville in addition to the picture program. Last Sunday Manager Somerby played "Out of Darkness," with Charlotte Walker, and "Hearts and Flowers," with Mrs. Thomas Whiffen and Beulah Poynter. A record-sized audience was in attendance at this performance and many favorable comments were heard from patrons as they passed out of the theater regarding the new policy.

Manager Farrell Pleased With New Pathe Serial.

Boston, Mass.—"The Seven Pearls," the new Pathe serial, bids fair to do unprecedented business in New England. The interest with which the chapter picture is being received by local exhibitors indicates that the new serial will go over bigger than any other chapter photoplay ever exploited in New England. Manager Edward J. Farrell, of the Boston Pathe exchange, states that he is very well pleased with the bookings that are coming in every day, some from his sales representatives and others direct from the exhibitors.

The release date of the serial has been changed from Sept. 3 to Sept. 16.

Manager Farrell's staff of salesmen, Frank J. Grady in greater Boston; J. J. Donnelly in Connecticut and Rhode Island; H. I. Goldman in Western Massachusetts

and A. E. Penn in Maine and New Hampshire, are all working hard to put this new serial over in grand style and make it a record-breaker for business.

Frank J. Grady Leading Pathe Salesman.

Boston, Mass.—Frank J. Grady, Pathe sales representative in Eastern Massachusetts, is receiving the congratulations of many of his friends today, having achieved the honor of being the champion salesman of the entire Pathe forces of the country for the month past. He turned in more business than any other roadman for Pathe in the United States. Mr. Grady has achieved this feat several times since joining Pathe a little over a year ago.

Straight Pictures at Colonial Theater.

Haverhill, Mass.—Keon Brother's Colonial theater, one of Haverhill's finest theatrical houses, has reopened under an entirely new policy. The management has arranged a six-day program of pictures and on Sundays will run moving pictures and vaudeville. The picture program will consist of Metro productions, Conquest films and open market pictures.

During the summer months, while the house was closed down for repairs, Keon Brothers employed the services of two well-known club women to make a complete canvass of the city, visiting every house in an effort to find out at first hand just what the people of the city wanted at the Colonial. They unanimously acclaimed the straight moving picture policy, which is expected to be successful.

Al Couture Takes Scenic Theater.

Rochester, N. H.—The Scenic theater, a moving picture house in this town, was sold last week to Al Couture, owner of the Crown theater, Manchester. The Scenic was formerly owned and managed by L. H. McDuffee and has always been a very successful enterprise.

Moses Demers Buys Globe Theater.

Holyoke, Mass.—The Globe theater in this city has been taken over by Moses Demers, former manager of the Grand theater, also located in this city. The Globe is a house of about 600 seats, while the Grand has a seating capacity of 500.

SHORT NEW ENGLAND NOTES.

Meriden, Conn.—Manager J. Belasco of the Life theater, in Meriden, Conn., has booked the Ivan production, "Babbling Tongues," from General Manager Herman Rifkin of the Eastern Feature Film company of this city.

Boston, Mass.—Manager L. A. Watrous, of the Boston office of the Vitagraph, announces that the new V-L-S-E serial production, "The Fighting Trail," is making a tremendous hit with New England moving picture exhibitors in general.

Boston, Mass.—The Hyde Park theater, in Hyde Park, a suburb of Boston, which has been closed during the summer months, reopened Labor Day. The theater has been completely renovated both in the interior and on the exterior and has been greatly improved upon.

Seattle Film Trade News and Theater Notes

Clemmer Theater Has Big Success on Reopening for New Season—Changes Among Exchange Offices and Jottings About Local Exhibitors.

By S. J. Anderson, East Seattle, Wash.

SEATTLE, Wash. — The show at the Clemmer theater the last week in August, advertised as the Fall Opening, was a big success from the points of view of both business and satisfaction of patrons. Few programs shown in Seattle have been so widely and so favorably commented on. To begin with, Guterson's Russian orchestra had been augmented by four pieces. A special concert was given every afternoon and twice each evening. In all the newspaper advertisements the Clemmer is now labeled as "The House of Music," but this description was not adopted until the people had already begun to think of it as such.

The feature on the opening program was "The Whip," and the audiences became so enthusiastic that they cheered again and again during the showing.

The "filler" was a travel picture showing the Columbia Highway in Oregon. The clear photography was commented upon by all who appreciate beautiful pictures. Beverly B. Dobbs, a Seattle cameraman, was the photographer.

With this week's bill the admission price after 6:30 has been raised to 20 cents. Fifteen cents will remain the price of admission to the matinees.

H. Sussman Buys Out Waring & Finck.

Seattle, Wash.—H. Sussman, president of the Peerless Film service, has bought Waring and Finck's supply store at 1014 Third avenue. The deal includes the transfer of the agency of the Motiograph machines to the purchaser. Mr. Sussman will carry out the plans of Waring and Finck in moving to the new location built for them on film row at 2020 Third avenue, which will be completed by September 15. The new store will be known as Sussman's Theater Supply Company and will be operated as an altogether separate business from the Peerless Film Service, which will continue at 216 Seneca street.

Mr. Sussman has engaged as manager of the supply store E. L. Shwetzer, for the past two months manager of the G. A. Metcalfe store in this city. Mr. Shwetzer knows every phase of the exhibitor's business, having been both an operator and an exhibitor. He came to Seattle directly from the San Francisco headquarters of G. A. Metcalfe. Mr. Sussman has been receiving congratulations on his good fortune in securing the services of so able a manager.

For several years Mr. Sussman has conducted the Peerless Film Service, buying and renting short-length films and dealing in certain lines of theater supplies. It was an unpretentious business, but he continually made good at it, until he has been enabled to buy one of the best supply businesses in Seattle. Progressive business men like to see a man make something big out of a little thing. Therefore some of Seattle's film men have named Mr. Sussman "The Little Giant."

H. W. Finck, one of the former owners of the supply store, has been wanting to get away to the officers' training camp at the Presidio in San Francisco for some time. He left the day after he sold out to Mr. Sussman. After the war he expects to return to some phase of the motion picture business in Seattle. Mr. Waring will probably enter some branch of studio work in Los Angeles immediately.

New Manager for Seattle "U" Office.

Seattle, Wash.—B. R. Latz has resigned as manager of the Seattle Universal office and will leave next week for Portland to take charge of the office of the Jewel Productions in that city. John R. Meldrum, formerly Bluebird representative in Butte, has arrived in Seattle to take Mr. Latz's place. Mr. Meldrum opened the first office in Seattle of the Film Supply Company,

the organization that handles the sale of Universal pictures in this territory. This was in 1912, and he remained until 1915, so he is not a stranger in this new location.

Select Pictures Takes Over Selznick Productions.

Seattle, Wash.—The Lewis J. Selznick exchange in Seattle, which has been taken over by the Select Pictures Corporation, will handle all Selznick productions, including those formerly handled in this territory by the De Luxe Feature Film Company. The De Luxe company will, however, continue to serve exhibitors who still have deposits on their Selznick pictures. The Select Pictures' Seattle branch will also handle Clara Kimball Young, Norma Talmadge and Constance Talmadge releases. B. R. Keller will remain as manager.

E. R. Redlich Takes Management of Seattle Metro.

Seattle, Wash.—E. R. Redlich has returned to Seattle from Toronto to become manager of the local Metro office. H. L. Lustig, division manager, will remain in the city to help Mr. Redlich get settled in the new building at 2002 Third avenue. B. F. Rosenberg, Metro representative, spent last week in Spokane. He reports that first, second, and third runs of Metro pictures have been signed for in that city. Mr. Lustig reports tremendous business in this territory on "The Slacker" and that Metro's prospects for all fall and winter business is very encouraging.

Two New Houses Open in September.

Mansfield, Wash.—Theodore Radtke will open a new house of 350 capacity on September 25. He has purchased his entire equipment from the Sussman Supply Company of Seattle, including two of the 1918 De Luxe models of the Motiograph.

Zillah, Wash.—A. S. Hillyer will open a new motion picture theater this month. Mr. Hillyer purchased his outfit from the Sussman Supply Company of Seattle. He will also use the De Luxe model of the motiograph projection machine.

Idaho Exhibitor in Seattle Hospital.

Seattle, Wash.—R. S. Tucker, manager of the Strand theater, Moscow, Idaho, is confined in the Providence hospital in Seattle.

H. C. Arthur, Jr., and J. E. Hudson With Goldwyn.

Seattle, Wash.—E. I. Hudson, formerly road man for Triangle, is now with Goldwyn. He has the western Oregon territory and will have his headquarters in Portland. H. C. Arthur, Jr., is the new Goldwyn representative for eastern Washington, northern Idaho, and northwest Montana.

Exchange Notes From Seattle.

Harry Leonhardt, western division manager for Goldwyn, with headquarters in Los Angeles, stopped for a few days in Seattle this week while on a tour of the western offices.

C. F. Hill, manager of the Seattle Goldwyn office, is carrying on an extensive publicity campaign through billboards. He already has 46 boards on the leading car lines of Seattle covered with 24-sheets.

Eugene L. Perry, Fox special representative from New York, was in Seattle in conference with A. W. Eden, Seattle manager. J. L. Merrick, manager of the Seattle Mutual office, had a conference recently with J. F. Dippy, manager of the Vancouver office, and F. S. Marshall, manager

of the Calgary office. The two Canadian managers spent several days in Seattle.

The productions of the Frohman Amusement Company will be handled in this territory from the Seattle Mutual office.

Mike Rosenberg, president of Greater Features, has just returned from his trip to New York. While there he bought the latest Hart picture, "The Cold Deck," and "Redemption," starring Evelyn Nesbit.

H. A. Johnson, of the H. A. Johnson Company, returned to Seattle this week after several weeks in New York and Chicago.

S. J. Ekre, salesman for Selznick, who has just returned from a trip through his territory, wishes it announced that he is eating regularly since joining the Selznick forces.

Supply Store Manager Receives Bad Cut.

Seattle, Wash.—Dr. P. Metcalf, of the O. A. Metcalf supply store of this city, had to spend two days in a hospital last week as the result of splitting too much kindling early in the morning. It would seem that Dr. Metcalf tried to add his hand to the kindling pile. The tendons of the thumb and index finger were cut, and the operation of sewing them back together was a long and painful one.

Tacoma Exhibitor Drafted.

Tacoma, Wash.—Clarence Summerville, manager of the Melbourne and Hippodrome theaters, two houses operated by Eugene Levy of Seattle, has been selected in the draft and will go to American Lake to begin training on September 5.

Snapshot taken by Seattle World Correspondent of H. D. Nangle, Vitagraph Coast Division Manager, and G. A. Faris, Vitagraph Seattle Manager. Mr. Faris is the one casting his eyes at the "chicken" off stage. Mr. Nangle is the perfectly proper looking gentleman on the right.

Exhibitor Visitors to Seattle.

Seattle, Wash.—Among the exhibitors visiting Seattle's film row this week were: Henry Newman, Arcade theater, Hoquiam; W. D. Gross, Coliseum, Juneau, Alaska; E. A. Rupert, Dream, Aberdeen; J. D. Ferrel, Colonial, Ellensburg; E. A. Halberg, Lincoln, Port Angeles; E. I. Zabel, Bay, Olympia; Chas. Stillwell, Stillwell Theaters Company, Spokane; J. G. Gregg, Dreamland, Dayton.

Maritime News Letter
By Alice Fairweather, The Standard, St. John, N. B.

March-Golding Wedding a Brilliant Affair.

ST. JOHN, N. B.—The wedding of Miss Kathleen Golding and Reginald George March, manager of the Specialty Film company, took place Wednesday, August 25. Mr. March is a son of the late Rev. H. G. March, of Montreal. Miss Golding is the daughter of J. N. Golding, Jr., and a niece of Walter H. Golding, of the Imperial theater, St. John. The ceremony took place in the Germain Street Baptist church in the presence of many friends. After a bridal tour through the Annapolis valley, N. S., Mr. and Mrs. March will reside on Sydney street, St. John.

K. Keltie Leases Strand Theater.

Truro, N. S.—It seems that there was some hitch in the sale of the Strand theater, Truro, N. S., and K. Keltie, of Yarmouth, has become the lessee and will run it on his own behalf. Mr. Keltie is well known as a very successful manager.

Notes From Famous Players Exchange.

St. John, N. B.—Visiting the Famous Players exchange I gleaned the following items:

M. Bernstein has returned from a trip to Montreal and tells me that the Monarch Film company will have here "The Garden of Allah," "Beware of Strangers," "The Submarine Eye," and "The Public Be Damned," all for release in this territory.

Alfred Gaudet, late of the Empress theater, Moncton, and formerly of the Birth of a Nation company, has joined the Monarch Film company as one of its sales force for the maritime provinces.

"Joan, the Woman," is to play at the Casino, Halifax, for four days.

Edwin Lynn, of the Casino theater at Sydney, has signed a new contract with the Famous Players for Artcraft and Paramount pictures.

Mat Nowland, of the Russel theater, Glace Bay, has also a new contract for the Mary Pickford franchise, the Russel Arbuckle franchise and the George Cohan pictures. N. W. Mason, of the Roseland theater, New Glasgo, has renewed his Paramount contract.

Halifax, N. S.—Ackers Family theater opened with the new Universal service on Monday, August 25. The picture was "The Man Who Took a Chance," featuring Franklyn Farnum, and it went very well.

BALTIMORE JOTTINGS.

Ford's Gives Annual Treat to Cripples.

Baltimore, Md.—Last year, about this time, the annual treat which has been given by Charles E. Ford, manager of Ford's Opera House, to the children at the Kernan Hospital for Crippled Children, could not take place owing to the outbreak of infantile paralysis. But on Wednesday afternoon, August 29, about twenty-five of them that were able to travel in automobiles were brought in to the theater and greatly enjoyed the treat of viewing Howe's Travel Pictures.

Business and Personal Jottings.

Greenwood, Del.—Mr. Hausman, proprietor of the Auditorium theater, in this city, visited Baltimore last week and called on his friends at the exchanges.

St Michaels, Md.—The proprietor of the Electric Rainbow theater, of this city, F. Wrightson, took a run up to Baltimore last week to look over the situation.

Dallastown, Pa.—W. Bigler, proprietor of the Auditorium theater, in this city, announces that after Saturday, September 1, he will open his playhouse to the public every night in the week.

New Newark Theater Has Brilliant Premier
Theater Recently Rebuilt at a Cost Reaching Up in the Hundred Thousands Is Opened September 1—Mayor of City Makes Speech.
By Jacob J. Kalter, 25 Branford Place, Newark, N. J.

NEWARK, N. J.—One of the most notable premiers of a showhouse took place Sept. 1, when the new Newark theater at 195 Market street was opened to an invited audience. The lobby was completely converted into a fragrant bower by the floral tributes.

Representing the management, Joseph J. Fiske, a local newspaper man, introduced Max Spiegel, president of the Market and Beaver Realty Company, owners of the theater.

The old Newark theater has been completely demolished, and now in its place is the modernly-constructed moving picture house, seating about 2,500. The chairs are upholstered red panne plush.

Music an Important Adjunct—Prices.

The musical program plays an important role at the new house. The orchestra, in charge of Warde Johnson, who was musical director of the Strand in New York, consists of twenty-five able musicians. A large Austin pipe organ has also been installed and two accomplished organists have been employed to play it. At the premier Miss Grace Hoffman, operatic soprano, sang, and Mery Zentay, violinist, played. Music forms no little part in the program of the Newark.

As the opening program, Mary Pickford, in "Rebecca of Sunnybrook Farm," was the feature. In addition, the British War Pictures were also exhibited. The week of Sept. 9 will bring Elsie Ferguson in "Barbary Sheep."

The program will be changed twice a week, Thursdays and Sundays. There will be a continuous performance from 11 o'clock in the morning until 11 o'clock in the evening. The matinee prices are 10, 15, 25, 35 cents, while in the evening, 15, 25, 35 and 50 cents are the prices.

Personnel of the Firm.

The men behind the enterprise control the Strand theater, New York. The officers are Max Spiegel, president; Henry Waterson, vice-president; A. B. Stupel, secretary; Dr. Richard G. Tunison, treasurer, and Edward Spiegel, acting director. John B. McNally will be the resident manager of the new playhouse, and he will have as his assistant George F. Turner. Mr. McNally is well known locally.

L. S. Card Booking Corporation Formed.

Newark, N. J.—For the purpose of acquiring the new Jersey rights to the new Chaplin comedies and the other releases of the First National Exhibitors' Association, Inc., there has been incorporated under the laws of New Jersey the L. S. Card Booking Corporation. The concern has opened offices in Suite 605, G o d f r e y building, 729 7th a v e n u e, New York City. The first Chaplin release is expected early in October. The officers of the concern are Lynn S. Card, president; Jacob F a b i a n, vice-president; Samuel Sobelson, secretary; Edward I. Church, treasurer. Louis D. Lyon will be the manager of the exchange. Mr. Lyon was associated with Mr. Card in the running of the Newark branch of the Mutual, and later with the Civilization Film Corporation. Lynn S. Card, the president of the new

Lynn S. Card.

booking company is one of the most popular of the Jersey film exchange managers. An excellent likeness of Mr. Card is herewith reproduced. Mr. Card was manager of the Newark branch of the Mutual, and left that position to become manager of the Civilization Film Corporation. After making a tour of the United States in the interests of the Frank Hall Productions, Inc., Mr. Card returned to New York, where he formed the new booking concern.

New Burlington Amusement Company.

Jersey City, N. J.—The Burlington Amusement and Development Company has been incorporated here under the laws of New Jersey. It is capitalized at $125,000, and is authorized to operate theatrical enterprises. Peter Bentley, of 75 Montgomery street, is the registered agent. The incorporators are James J. Higgins, Peter Bentley and Arvilla Ullmeyer.

New Organ for Carlton.

Newark, N. J.—The $15,000 Hope-Jones Unit Orchestra recently installed in the Carlton theater, Market and Halsey streets, is meeting with the approval of the patrons. Louis P. DeWolfe, the manager, reports exceptionally good business for this time of the year. Mr. DeWolfe has just returned from a vacation spent in New England.

"Polly of the Circus" Here.

Newark, N. J.—The first Goldwyn release, "Polly of the Circus," was at the Goodwin theater, under the management of Mrs. L. H. Webbe, during the week of Sept. 9. During the week of Sept. 2, Evelyn Nesbit in "Redemption" was the feature.

Strand Adds Vaudeville.

Newark, N. J.—The Strand theater, 118 Market street, has added eight acts of vaudeville to its regular program. Feature photoplays will be shown in conjunction with the vaudeville. Frank D. Ellison is the manager of the theater.

Belmont Square Closed.

Newark, N. J.—The Belmont Square theater, 1 Belmont avenue, is closed. The foreclosure of a mortgage was the cause. On Thursday afternoon, August 16, a public sale was held at the theater, and a good portion of the equipment was sold to meet the indebtedness.

Loew's Opened Labor Day.

Newark, N. J.—Loew's Market theater, 99 Springfield avenue, reopened for the season Labor Day, September 9. Eugene Meyers was the resident manager last year. The house is a combination vaudeville and moving picture theater.

Park View to Reopen.

Newark, N. J.—The Park View theater, Watson and Badger avenues, is closed temporarily for repairs and a complete renovation. Floyd Longyear, the new manager, announces that the house will reopen August 20.

Forrest Theater Books "Redemption."

. Philadelphia, Pa.—"Redemption," starring Evelyn Nesbit and her son, Russell Thaw, will have its premier at the Forrest theater and be put on as a first class theatrical attraction.

"Redemption" has been booked for a limited engagement of two weeks, beginning Monday, August 20. An extensive publicity campaign is in charge of Abe Einstein, who previously met with great success at the same house when "20,000 Leagues Under the Sea" was offered.

Philadelphia Theaters May Raise Prices

Film Circles Have a Feeling that the Price of Admission Is Too Low—Changes in Personnel at Exchanges—Trade Notes.

By F. V. Armato, 144 North Salford St., Philadelphia, Pa.

PHILADELPHIA, PA.—There is talk among the local exhibitors of an increased admission charge. Promise of concerted action cannot be pinned down aywhere ,but the movement seems to be "in the air," and the general feeling is that in th late autumn all the photoplay theaters will raise their prices.

The cost of exhibiting is going up all around and it looks as if the customer, as usual, will have to pay the bill.

Moving pictures have steadily been coming into more popular favor, though, and it may be that no serious objection will be registered.

General Manager F. W. Buhler, of the Central Market Street Amusement Co., announces that admission prices at the Victoria theater will advance from .10 and 20 cents to 15 and 25 cents, while the Fairmount will also increase its price from 10 to 15 cents. However, the percentage of increase of prices among local exhibitors is expected to be large and should take effect in the very near future.

Charles Wanamaker Now With Nixon-Nirdlinger.

Philadelphia, .Pa.—Announcement is made that Charlie Wanamaker, for several seasons resident manager of the Garrick theater, has become associated with Fred G. Nixon-Nirdlinger in his theatrical and motion picture interests as personal representative. Mr. Nirdlinger, who has just returned from a tour of the Far West, has many interests in a theatrical way in this city.

Will Run "Jack and the Beanstalk" for Month.

Philadelphia, Pa.—Al Boyd, to whom I was talking the other day, told me he is so confident of the future that he has enlarged his pretty little Arcadia theater so that it will seat six hundred persons, and that he contemplates an innovation in October that should be looked upon with interest. It is nothing less than the running for an entire month of "Jack and the Beanstalk."

M. D. Starkman Goes to Metro as Salesman.

Philadelphia, Pa.—M. D. Starkman, formerly of the Mutual forces, has joined the Metro staff of salesmen and will shortly begin a tour of the neighboring towns.

I. A. T. S. E. Local 307 Will Provide War Insurance.

Philadelphia, Pa.—A noteworthy resolution presented by Walter Murray, of the Local 307, I. A. T. S. E., was unanimously adopted at the first meeting. It provides that in the event of any of its paid-up members who have enlisted or have been drafted into Uncle Sam's service should be killed or die in the defense of his country, the organization will pay $100 to the deceased member's family or dependents. This patriotic and humane donation is made up by a voluntary assessment fund of $1, being contributed by each of its members.

Thomas Love Feels Exclusive.

Philadelphia, Pa.—A general complaint was made to representatives of the daily newspapers by Thomas M. Love, manager of a large theatrical syndicate, regarding the advertising of photoplays under the head of amusements. He suggested the placing of sub-headings, like vaudeville, photoplays, burlesque and others, in the columns of the newspapers so readers could easily distinguish the various forms of amusements. However, as zoological gardens, musical and vocal concerts and a number of other classifications would be necessary, the newspaper men voted that the idea of any change would be impracticable and not. in accord with the original heading of amusements, which has stood for all forms of amusements for over half a century.

Attractions Passed and Coming.

Philadelphia, Pa.—During the week of Sept. 3 interesting photoplay announcements disclose the following photoplay schedule:

"The Honor System" will enter upon its second and final week at the Stanley. This big Fox spectacle was acclaimed by the press and public as one of the greatest human-interest dramas ever shown.

At the Arcadia the attraction for the first three days of the week will be "The Marriage Market" with Carlyle Blackwell and June Elvidge as the stars. The feature of the last half of the week will be Taylor Holmes in his first screen comedy, "Efficiency Edgar's Courtship."

The Palace will present "Betsy Ross," a World feature, starring Alice Brady, during the first three days of the week and Earle Williams in "Transgression" during the last part.

Norma Talmadge, in the "Moth," has been booked a solid week at the Victoria. "Souls Adrift," will be shown for two days.

First-run Paramount and Artcraft pictures to be presented by the Strand will be Billie Burke in "The Mysterious Miss Terry" and Sessue Hayakawa in "Hashimura Toga."

At the Locust, Geraldine Farrar in "Joan, the Woman," will be shown during the entire week.

"The Italian Battlefront," war pictures, will begin its engagement at the Garrick theater beginning Monday, Sept. 3, for a limited engagement.

The Stanley Co. announce that for the week of Sept. 10 Mary Pickford, in "Rebecca of Sunny Brook Farm," will have its first presentation at the Palace, 1218 Market street, and at the Arcadia, 16th and Chestnut streets.

Sabolsky and McGirk Open Fall Season.

Manyunk, Pa.—The Empress, one of the most popular and commodious amusement places in Manayunk, begins its fall season with high-class vaudeville and films, under the direction of Sabolsky and McGirk, who have won success in other sections. The vaudeville bills will be changed on Mondays and Thursdays and the pictures daily.

Margaret Mayo Expected at the Stanley.

Philadelphia, Pa.—Margaret Mayo, who enjoys the reputation of being one of the most artistic playwrights in this country, and who is now one of the advisory board of the Goldwyn Pictures, will visit this city Monday, Sept. 10, when her great picture, "Polly of the Circus," will have its first presentation at the Stanley theater. As this is the first time .for many years that Miss Mayo has been seen in this city and as this marks the inauguration of the Goldwyn Pictures in Philadelphia, this gifted woman will be tendered a dinner, served with the famous golden Bellevue service set, and reception by Stanley V. Mastbaum, in the Bellevue-Stratford Hotel at six o'clock. Miss Mayo will be greeted and introduced to the dramatic critics of the newspapers and she will be made welcome. in that true hospitable style which Mr. Mastbaum is famous. After the dinner Miss Mayo will be escorted to the Stanley theater.

Business Notes from Philadelphia.

Philadelphia, Pa.—Some very interesting and noteworthy films which were presented at a recent entertainment for the benefit of the sailors and marines were the K-E-S-E Conquest Pictures. An entire program consisting of seven reels made up the splendid show. A noteworthy picture included was a four-reel feature entitled "The Little Chevalier."

Philadelphia, Pa.—H. M. Kendrick, of the Fairmount, has returned from his vacation, which he spent in New York, making frequent visits to Asbury Park. Beginning September 2 the Fairmount will increase its price of admission to 10 cents and 15 cents.

Philadelphia, Pa.—General Manager Herbert Effinger, of The Strand and The Leader, reports very favorable business upon the opening of the new season with Paramount and Artcraft pictures.

Philadelphia, Pa.—Abbott Oliver, after a successful tour with "Intolerance," will begin his season's projection work at the Nixon's Colonial, beginning Sept. 3.

Philadelphia, Pa.—Charles Segal of the Apollo theater is making preparations for the fall season to show a large number of exclusive masterpiece productions.

Philadelphia, Pa.—E. Elliott, of Atlantic City, paid the Paramount office a visit last week and reported good business at the seashore. He is now using first-run Paramount productions with good results.

Philadelphia, Pa.—Lewis M. Swaab made a big sale of nine Simplex moving picture machines to Mr. George Bennethum last week.

Buffalonians Want the Six Cent Pieces

Cheaper Theaters Would Find the Proposed Coin Much More Advantageous Than the Jitney—Many Other Good Uses for It.

By Joseph A. McGuire, 152 N. Elmwood St., Buffalo, N. Y.

BUFFALO, N. Y.—Is the time-worn expression "the nickel show" to be relegated to the past in Buffalo and other cities and to be replaced by a new term, "the six-cent show"? This is a question which local film fans are considering as a result of a bill introduced at Washington by Representative Linkham of Massachusetts, authorizing the coinage of a six-cent piece. Many Buffalonians, especially in the mercantile lines, are. writing to their representatives advocating passage of the measure. It has been pointed out that the general use of the six-cent coin would popularize the sale of many articles, which for a long time have been selling at a meagre profit at five cents. Of course in line with this change would be the six-cent picture show.

Buffalonians for a long time have been educated to a knowledge of the increased cost of giving " a nickle show."

Under the present system, however, if the price were raised to six cents, patrons of such houses would object to paying the extra penny because of its inconvenience. The searching for the extra penny or the receiving of four pennies in change from a ten-cent piece would get on the nerves of patrons and would be out of step with their rapid way of doing. business. If the proposed coin is introduced, it would be an easy to pay a six-cent admission as it is to pay five cents. The possibilities of the proposed six-cent coin are therefore being fully realized by the men who run five-cent theaters in the Buffalo territory.

Shea's Hippodrome Enters Third Year.

Buffalo, N. Y.—Shea's Hippodrome, Buffalo. recently celebrated its third anniversary. This theater is regarded as one of the most luxurious picture houses in

America. The management has just closed a contract giving the Hippodrome first run of Douglas Fairbanks, William S. Hart, Pauline Frederick, Marguerite Clark, and a long list of other stars, as well as the Arbuckle and Keystone comedies. This house has a concert orchestra of twenty-six soloists, who offer carefully selected incidental music for each production. The overture is changed twice a week. Matinee prices on the orchestra floor have been advanced from ten to fifteen cents.

The International a Host to Company.

Niagara, N. Y.—Howard C. Carroll, manager of the International theater, Niagara Falls, recently gave a theater party in honor of Company E, Third New York Infantry of that city. The company paraded the streets before the show in uniform for the first time.

Matinee Prices Go Up at Shea's.

Buffalo, N. Y.—At the opening of the fall season at Shea's theater, Buffalo, there was a change in matinee prices. The same prices which formerly prevailed on Saturday at 25, 50 and 75 cents, will now be charged throughout the week. The evening prices will remain unchanged.

Rialto Reopens September 2.

Buffalo, N. Y.—The Rialto, formerly the Family theater, Buffalo, opened for the season Sunday, September 2. Many improvements have been made in the house. Manager Harry Marcy announces that he will present only high class productions. The initial offering was "Parentage," which was well received.

Buffalo Jottings.

Various war scenes showing how soldiers greatly enjoy their "smokes" were shown in Buffalo recently. The purpose was to arouse interest in a campaign in which thousands of packages of cigarettes, tobacco, pipes, etc. were collected for Buffalo boys who are going to the front.

Manager Weinberg of the Elmwood moving picture theater, Buffalo, recently distributed miniature pictures of Emily Stevens, who appeared in "The Slacker" at that house. Back of each picture was this information about the production: "A patriotic drama of the times. No war scenes, BUT it makes the old yearn to be young. It makes the young spring to the nation's call."

J. M. Sitterly, of the Popular Cinema, Buffalo, has a new motor car, in which he will cover his territory.

Sherman S. Webster has bought a new auto, in which he is touring Western New York, introducing a new policy for the Select Film Co.

E. R. Price, formerly of the Triangle, Buffalo, is visiting friends in New York City

Western New York Notes.

Seneca Falls, N. Y.—Mr. Hilkert, of Geneva, has closed a deal for the Johnson opera house, Seneca Falls. On the site he will erect a new picture theater with a seating capacity of 1,000. The house will be ready for business by December 1, 1917.

Bradford, N. Y.—Thomas Breaky, of the Star theater, Bradford, called at the Victor office, Buffalo.

Salamanca, N. Y.—Dr. Robbins, of the Strand, formerly the Palm theater, Salamanca, reports a god business during opening week. The policy of the Strand is to play high class attractions only.

Gouverneur, N. Y.—William Gauthier, of the Gouverneur opera house, was a Buffalo visitor.

In answering advertisements,

please mention

The Moving Picture World

New Canadian Triangle Service Company

Headquarters of New Distributing Organisation Are in Montreal—Branches Being Opened in Winnipeg, Vancouver and Other Cities.

By W. M. Gladish, 1263 Gerrard Street East, Toronto.

MONTREAL, QUE.—An announcement made at Montreal, Quebec, by the Triangle contains the information that entirely new distribution arrangements for the whole Dominion have been made by the company. The interests of E. A. Fenton, of Montreal, holder of the Triangle distribution rights in Canada, have been purchased outright, it is announced, and a Canadian company, known as the Triangle Film Service, Limited, has been incorporated, with headquarters in Montreal. Robert E. Wells is named as the district manager of the company in charge of the Montreal headquarters.

Branches of the Triangle service, are being opened in Winnipeg and Vancouver to take care of the Western Canadian territory.

Announcement is also made that first run of Triangle pictures in Canada will be seen at the Holman theater, Montreal, and seventeen other houses of Montreal are already booking Triangle releases.

A branch office of the Triangle has been in operation in Toronto for almost a year. This office also becomes a part of the new Triangle Film Service, Limited.

Bert Mason Goes to K-E-S-E at Montreal.

Montreal—A third salesman has been added to the staff of the Montreal K-E-S-E office in the person of Bert Mason, who was formerly associated with the Mutual branch in Montreal. The other outside men under Manager Arthur Reddy are Arthur Larente and Phil Magher. Announcement is made that the K-E-S-E in Montreal is now releasing seventeen reels per week.

Notes From Famous Players' Office, Calgary.

Calgary, Alberta—N. M. Trafton, who controls the Orowpay circuit of houses in Fernie, Nelson and Trail, has arranged for the Artcraft productions in these towns, as well as several special features booked by the Famous Players in Canada.

Mr. Dawson of Vancouver is in the city looking after his interest in the 'Ne'er Do Well" during its engagement at the Grand theater, Calgary, for one week.

C. G. Bowker, Empress theater, Mcleod, was in Calgary and arranged for some of the Famous Players specials.

A. W. Warner, who controls the theaters in Prussia and Prelate, Sask., was in Calgary and arranged for several of the special features, as well as regular service from the Famous Players Film Service, Ltd.

Big Films During Fair Week at Toronto.

Toronto.—Picture fans of Toronto had a wealth of good productions from which to choose during the week of September 3. In fact, the quality of the various attractions constitutes a record for any place in Canada. The larger features included: "Intolerance"—Massey hall.
"The Daughter of the Gods"—Grand opera house.
"The Barrier"—Regent theater.
"Beware of Strangers"—Strand theater.
"Redemption"—Photodrome.
"The Page Mystery"—Loew's.
"The Candy Girl"—Hippodrome.

New Policy at Toronto's Regent.

Toronto, Ont.—Upon the completion of the first year's operation of the Regent theater, Toronto, on September 1st, Manager Roland Roberts announced a new policy for the big downtown house. One of the principal features of this is a new scale of prices. At evening performances the new price for ground floor seats is 35c instead of 25c and 15c. Matinee prices, except on Saturdays and holidays, are 15c and 10c, and on the special days the matinee prices are 25c and 15c. Reserved loge chairs at evening performances are 50c.

New program features include a symphony orchestra every afternoon for half an hour, starting at 4:15, and the presentation of a solo number at every performance by a special artist. Manager Roberts also announces that he will insist on absolutely first run pictures simultaneously with New York release dates whenever possible. Shows will be held five times daily, starting at 12:15, 2:15 and 4:15 in the afternoon and during the evenings at 7:00 and 9:00 o'clock.

As a start for the new Regent year, Manager Roberts presented "The Barrier" during the week of September 3, and the first Goldwyn, "Polly of the Circus," was shown during the week of September 10. Programs will be changed weekly.

Small Toronto Theater Burns.

Toronto.—It is very infrequent that a fire occurs in a moving picture theater in Ontario during the course of a performance. One of these unusual experiences occurred, however, when the small theater at 1035 Gerrard street East, Toronto, was partially destroyed on Saturday afternoon, September 1. The operator was rewinding a reel when the fire started. G. T. McNally, the proprietor, was painfully burned about the hands and face when he attempted to extinguish the blaze at close quarters. The audience made its escape quickly and without mishap through the various exits.

The feature picture which was destroyed was Clara Kimball Young's "The Price She Paid." The loss to the building amounted to $400.

W. Yates Making Good at Royal Theater

Toronto.—The Royal theater, King street West, Hamilton, Ontario, has prospered since the recent change in ownership and management. The house has been taken over by W. Yates, who announced that he had served his apprenticeship in showmanship with some of the best houses in New York. Manager Yates made a number of alterations and improvements in the building, did a little advertising, increased the quality of the pictures and has already begun to count growing receipts.

New Corona Theater Begins.

Toronto.—The New Corona theater, Fort William, Ontario, was opened on Monday, September 3, under the management of William H. Chadderton. Programs will be changed twice each week, according to the adopted policy.

Exhibitors' Association Has Club Rooms.

Toronto.—Club rooms for the Exhibitors' Association of Ontario have been opened over His Majesty's theater, Yonge street, Ontario.

STRAY NOTES FROM NEW ENGLAND.

Marblehead, Mass.—The Warwick, a moving picture theater in this town, has shut down for the summer. The Warwick is a comparatively new house, built a few months ago. The management will open it again in September.

Boston, Mass.—The Hyde Park theater in Hyde Park, a suburb of Boston, has closed and will open again early in September.

Meat Cutters May Trouble Sunday Theaters

Want Closed Meat Shops and Butchers Threaten to Invoke Blue Laws to Aid Their Cause by Closing Up Everything in Sight.

By Kenneth C. Crain, 307 First National Bank Building, Cincinnati, O.

CINCINNATI, O.—For the first time a threat of the enforcement of the old Ohio blue laws, involving Sunday closing, has been heard in Cincinnati as a result of the conflict between members of the Meat Cutters' Union and the Cincinnati Retail Grocers' and Butchers' League. The union men want all shops selling meat to remain closed on Sunday, so as to give them a full day of rest, while there are some retailers who desire to remain open, and these threaten that if they are forced by the union to close they will invoke the old laws to close the picture shows and other places of amusement and refreshment on Sunday.

Several Ohio cities have enforced the blue laws against picture shows, and are now without moving pictures on Sunday, but Cincinnati has heretofore been totally without trouble of this sort. The union representatives declare that they will get warrants under the Sunday laws against all grocers and meat retailers who remain open on Sunday hereafter, and if this is done the retaliatory measures referred to may be taken against the photoplay houses as well as the other theaters, thus bringing up the question in the local courts.

S. W. Hatch Takes Charge of K-E-S-E Offices.

Cincinnati, O.—Manager S. W. Hatch, for a long time associated with the Mutual and the Vitgraph offices in Cincinnati, being manager of the latter ever since C. E. Holah left, has taken charge of the K-E-S-E organization in this territory, being succeeded at the Vitagraph office by A. H. McLaughlin, of Chicago.

One of Mr. Hatch's first acts at the K-E-S-E was to arrange to move the exchange several blocks east, to 111 East Seventh street, which is just around the corner from the new Film Exchange building, is near other exchanges as well, and is only two blocks from the theatrical center. The move has not yet been completed, but is to take place shortly, giving the K-E-S-E branch much better quarters in every respect than those it has been using on West Seventh street.

Manager Wessling Pleased With New Features.

Cincinnati, O.—Manager W. S. Wessling, of the Pathe exchange, was highly elated recently at news from New York that his company has purchased the distribution rights to a pair of big features, "To-Day," made from the successful play of that name, and "The Mad Lover," featuring Florence Reed and Robert Warwick. Manager Wessling has already made arrangements for the first showing of these pictures, a pair of downtown houses having taken the first run as soon as they were offered.

Manager Harry Hawn Killed By Auto Accident.

Akron, O.—Harry Hawn, manager of the Casino Park theater for some years, and booking agent for the Meyer's Lake theater, was almost instantly killed when an automobile in which he and three companions were riding skidded against a tree. Mr. Hawn's skull was fractured. He had been for years prominent in theatrical circles, and was also a prominent member of the Elks.

"Nation Film" Coming Back to the Grand.

Cincinnati, O.—The Grand opera house is about to close the most successful summer season it ever had, starting the usual run of stage attractions for the fall season with "Dew Drop Inn." This, however,

is a little early, so it is to be followed by a week's return engagement of "The Birth of a Nation," which had a remarkable success at its long run early in the season, going far toward making the Grand's summer period of pictures the record-breaker it was. The opportunity to secure the big Griffith picture for another week was promptly seized, as the crowds were still coming when the early run closed, and indications are that the week will be a successful one. The same prices as originally prevailed are scheduled.

Orphans Visit the Lyric as Guests.

Cincinnati, O.—Manager Herbert Heuck, of the Lyric theater, brought the moving-picture season of the house to a fitting close by entertaining the city's orphans with a free view of the Lyman Howe travel pictures, which featured the final two weeks of the season. All told nearly 2,000 children participated in the treat, each institution sending its children on the day appointed for them, and they formed an enthusiastic part of the audiences.

Short Notes of the Trade.

Piqua, O.—The management of May's opera house co-operated recently with a number of local merchants, who issued admission tickets with a certain amount of purchases made at advertised sales, and the net result was highly gratifying all around. The house entertained unusually large crowds, while the merchants participating in the sales reported considerable increases in business.

Lima, O.—The "four-minute men" have been addressing audiences at local theaters with talks on the necessity of unanimous co-operation in war-time work, all of the houses giving time to the speakers. Among those used were the Orpheum, the Star, the Lyric, the Dreamland, the Royal, the Star, the Majestic and the Empire.

CLEVELAND NOTES OF INTEREST

By M. A. Malaney, 218 Columbia Building, Cleveland, O.

AKRON, OHIO.—The exhibitors of Akron have formed an organization known as the Akron Screen club. There are 28 active theaters here and nearly all of the managers have joined. The following officers have been elected: Robert Miller, Waldorf theater, president; J. H. Moore, Ideal theater, secretary; C. H. Belden, Thornton theater, treasurer. Their first social affair will be a supper September 16 at Young's restaurant, a summer place near Akron.

Henry Morris Dies.

Cleveland.—Henry Morris, well known among the film men of Cleveland, died recently, aged 67. He was financially interested in Cleveland theaters and at one time managed the Crown, on East 105th street. Mr. Morris was the father of Sam Morris, of the Selznick Pictures, and Isaac Morris, manager of the Home theater; also Mrs. L. H. Kilk, wife of the present manager of the Crown.

Atlanta News Letter

By A. M. Beatty, 43 Copenhill Ave., Atlanta, Ga.

Atlanta's Beginning of Prosperity.

ATLANTA, Ga.—Exhibitors here are beginning to feel good, since transportation facilities seem to be well provided for soon, to and from Camp Gordon, and this will give the forty thousand soldiers

stationed there an opportunity to come to Atlanta. Already the moving picture theaters are beginning to feel the increased attendance, and much doubt is expressed, with the transportation facilities now being provided pouring soldiers into Atlanta during the evening hours whether the theaters can take care of them. It looks like boom days for Atlanta exhibitors.

Chamblee Church's Free Pictures for Soldiers.

Chamblee, Ga.—One of Chamblee, Georgia's, municipal activities in connection with the entertainment of the soldiers at Camp Gordon will be presentation of a free moving picture show every Monday evening at 7:30 o'clock at the Chamblee Methodist Church. Chamblee, Ga., has grown from a few houses to a city, since the establishment of Camp Gordon, and is sporting four moving picture theaters. They are, however, crude affairs.

"Modern Mother Goose" at Loew's Grand.

Atlanta, Ga.—The big feature film, "Modern Mother Goose," which Loew's Grand theater has brought to Atlanta especially for the entertainment of the children, had its first public showing at a children's matinee at Loew's Grand theater Friday morning. The theater played to capacity Friday and Saturday.

Alice Brady Appears in Person at Loew's

Atlanta, Ga.—Alice Brady, charming star of the Alice Brady Pictures, Inc., and recently of World Film, known and admired by thousands of Atlantians through her appearance upon the picture screen at Loew's Grand theater, in World Film pictures, appeared in person upon the stage of Loew's Grand Tuesday, Aug. 28.

Loew's Grand theater secured for first showing in the South, Miss Brady's newest picture, the historical drama, "Betsy Ross," to be shown coincidental with Miss Brady's appearance in person. Though Miss Brady was seen in person only on Tuesday, her new picture was shown at all performances on Monday, Tuesday and Wednesday.

Children Flock to See "Jack and Beanstalk" Lobby.

Atlanta, Ga.—Every child in Atlanta, so it seemed, came out Sunday, Aug. 5, to see "The Village of Cornwall," which had grown overnight in the lobby of the Criterion theater and which was on exhibition Sunday only, as it was cleared away before the opening of the doors Monday morning for the first performance of the big film spectacle, "Jack and the Beanstalk." Manager Willard Patterson spent much time and trouble getting the village ready and the kids saw with delight the most elaborate and lavish lobby exhibit ever attempted in Atlanta.

This miniature village was complete in every respect. Houses, barns, fences, roads, trees, shrubbery, churches, cattle, sheep and the cow that was sold by Jack for the beans. Even the enormous beanstalk was there, and hovering over all inhabitants of this tiny village was the giant, his bulky form towering over everything. One more play like this and Atlanta children will place Willard Patterson in the same class as Santa Claus.

J. H. Butner Arrives in Atlanta.

Atlanta, Ga.—J. H. Butner, who was for the last year, manager of the Washington branch of the Triangle, has arrived in Atlanta and taken charge of the First National Exhibitors' Circuit, Inc., headquarters being temporarily established at the Lyric theater. The Atlanta branch will serve exhibitors in North and South Carolina, Georgia, Florida, Alabama and Tennessee.

Mr. Butner is delighted in being transferred to Atlanta, and the good fellowship that exists on exchange row among the exchangemen.

IN LOUISVILLE.
Worth a Passing Glance.

Louisville. Ky.—When the Walnut theater went dark at the end of a fortnight's showing Audrey Munson in "Purity," it closed on the two best weeks in the history of that theater. Not only, according to the management of the theater, were the attendance records broken, but the total box office receipts exceeded those of any other two weeks.

After having run tabloid musical comedy attractions through the summer at the Casino. Judge W. Allen Kinney, head of the Princess Amusement Co., has dispensed with the side issue. The Casino has gone back to straight pictures again.

During the showing of "The Slacker" at the Strand, Louisville, the management of the house had a "Camp Zachary Taylor Day," in honor of the soldiers stationed at the army camp just outside the city. On the day in question admission was free to every man in uniform. The house was well filled and very few of the soldiers came alone.

Lee Goldberg has just returned to Louisville from New York where he spent some time looking into forthcoming attractions. He was joined there by Col. Fred Levy, president of the Big Features Rights Corporation, and Mrs. Levy, and spent some time doing the studios. In New York, among others, Mr. Goldberg met Miss Marguerite Clark, and had the pleasure of recalling to her that she opened the Mary Anderson theater.

Kentucky Exhibitors Answer War Appeal
State Committeeman Lee Goldberg Finds No Lack of Patriotism—Gets Hearty Response All Over State—May Divide Territory.
By Ohio Valley News Service, 1404 Starks Building, Louisville, Ky.

LOUISVILLE, KY.—Lee Goldberg, general manager of the Big Features Rights Corporation, and the Kentucky war committeeman named by William J. Brady, has been in communication with all of the exhibitors in Kentucky and has obtained from them their promise to co-operate in every way possible to acquaint the people with the real inwardness of the war and to help war movements.

All of the exhibitors have agreed to use slides to help along the Red Cross work, food conservation and other allied movements. One of the big pieces of work which the exhibitors will help along will be the floating of the Second Liberty Bond issue, the selling campaign of which is to be undertaken in the near future. For this campaign not only the Louisville theaters, but the houses all over the state will use slides and such views as may be provided.

In the way of food conservation, most of the theaters of the state either have or will make provisions for the appearance of talkers who will spend four minutes at intervals telling those who have come to see the pictures what the food conservation movement means. In Louisville the theaters have or will set aside days on which parts of the receipts will be given to patriotic causes.

Mr. Goldberg is finding that there is a good deal of routine work attached to his office and it is likely that he will shortly divide the state into districts over each of which a sub-committeeman will be appointed.

Theatrical Season Began Labor Day.

Louisville, Ky.—Labor Day saw Louisville's theatrical season opened with Macauley's, the Gaiety and B. F. Keith's theaters bright, while the Buckingham, the burlesque house, hoped soon to be able to announce its premier. The summer vaudeville at Fontaine Ferry Park still continues, in addition to the moving picture theaters, all of which are operating except for the Walnut. This latter house is still dark, on account of the differences over the rent between the owner and the Broadway Amusement Enterprises interests.

In spite of the many amusement places in Louisville, all of them continue to be freely patronized and capacity houses are the rule. There is every indication that this will be a busy winter in Louisville. It is very noticeable that admission in all of the theaters and the moving picture theater crowds are peppered with the khaki of the men and officers stationed at the camps.

The retail merchants are already feeling present prosperity and one of the largest houses in the city reported that its August business this year was three times that of August of last year.

Big Features Go to the Mary Anderson.

Louisville, Ky.—A change that amounts to a complete switch has been announced by the management of the Keith photoplay theaters in Louisville for the winter. The Mary Anderson theater, which has been a 10-cent house, showing the popular pictures, with two and three changes of program weekly, becomes the feature house of the company, while the Strand, which has been the big features house, will take the popular-priced pictures, with two and three changes of program weekly. Prices at the Mary Anderson will be 20 cents and 15 cents, and those at The Strand will be 15 cents and 10 cents. This arrangement began on the first week of September with the Essanay production of Cohan & Harris' "On Trial." The Mary Anderson will also have the first of the new Chaplin series.

Ben Ali Shows "Joan" at 20 Cents.

Lexington, Ky.—For the first time in the history of motion picture in Lexington, prices have been put to a high figure. In connection with its showing of "Joan The Woman," the Ben Ali theater showed at a schedule ranging upwards from 25 cents, and had full houses all along.

Capitol Theater Advertises Stars.

Frankfort, Ky.—The Capitol theater of this city used a full-page newspaper advertisement announcing that it had contracted for the Paramount and Artcraft programs, the first of the offerings being Douglas Fairbanks in "Down to Earth" and the next Marguerite Clark in "The Amazons." The text of the advertisement discussed the Strand in New York, described as the "best known picture theater in the world," and closed with "The Capitol is Your Strand."

Exchange's Bad Policy Hits Everyboay
Dayton Branch of Fox Lets Bigger Theater Snatch Program from Smaller House and the Consequence Is That No One in City Sees Fox Pictures.
By Paul J. Gray, Alhambra Theater, Dayton, Ohio.

DAYTON, OHIO.—Quite a surprise will be evidenced when the announcement is made that there is at present no house in Dayton presenting Fox features first-run exclusively. The Lyceum, which formerly ran the Fox features really made the program in Dayton, and after developing the stars into drawing cards, the Strand suddenly took the program away from the smaller house. As the Lyceum seats about five hundred and the Strand about eighteen hundred, it can be readily seen that no competition could be offered by them. The Strand did not run the program very long, until they dropped it in place of Artcraft, and, in consequence, the Fox people have no first-run house in Dayton.

It is rumored that the New Auditorium, which will open in the next few weeks, is to run the program; another rumor has it that the Columbia, another large house a square away, is to present first-run Fox features in Dayton. As it has been over three weeks that these conditions have been in effect, the people of Dayton are surely missing some good pictures, as the writer had the privilege of witnessing a private exhibition of "The Honor System," and thinks it a very good ten-reeler. If the rest of the new Fox pictures are to continue in the standard set by the "Honor System," it is hoped that some theater manager will book the program soon.

New Superintendent a Speedy Man.

Dayton, O.—Before being appointed superintendent of the Strand here, one of the largest picture houses in Dayton, Rudolph Yost, formerly assistant treasurer of B. F. Keith's theater, had the reputation of being the fastest ticket racker in the state. This is quite a record in a busy box office, and is something to be proud of. It is hoped that Mr. Yost will make another good record at the Strand and excel in some line there.

Projectors in Dayton's Schools.

Dayton, O.—In the future all school buildings erected in Dayton will be equipped with the latest model projectors,

two new schools now being built have this plan in operation, which is only another proof that the moving picture is the leader of them all in up-to-date education.

Negro Situation Troubling Ohio.

Dayton, O.—Almost directly following the recent agitation concerning the showing of the "Birth of a Nation" in Ohio comes the news that the negro problem in this state is growing more acute every day. When one hears all the popular "Dixie" songs that are going the rounds and also thousands of victrolas over the country expounding the fact that Dixie is the dearest place in the world, it would naturally lead one to believe that there is quite a bit of affection in the hearts of Northern whites that is directed toward the black man and that is going to waste. Such is not the case, however, and when remembrances of the Illinois riots are refreshed it also pictures the sentiment of most Ohio people.

At least two-thirds of Governor Cox's Labor Day speech is taken up with the negro question, which indicates the deep feeling throughout the state. It seems that thousands of colored people have been induced to move to Ohio from the South, with promises of good jobs, low rent, etc., by employment agencies who do this only for the money that is in it. Estimates show that on one day this month over a thousand colored people arrived in Cincinnati from the Southern states. There are already demands from several labor unions that this influx be stopped, as it is proving to be a nuisance, for in the winter most of these people will be dependent on the general public for a living.

An excerpt from Governor Cox's speech on Labor Day gives the majority of people reason to be calm, as evidences are given that the question will soon be solved.

Exhibitors in residence districts will hardly find that this situation complicates their problems; but in other neighborhoods they may find matter in it worthy their careful consideration.

Nashville Local Union Gets Concessions

Wins Fight to Place Union Operators in All Local Houses Through Agreement of Crescent Amusement Company with I. A. T. S. E.

By J. L. Ray, 1014 Stahlman Building, Nashville, Tenn.

NASHVILLE, Tenn.—After two years and a half of vigorous agitation on the part of organized labor unions in this city, the Crescent Amusement Company, through its president, Tony Sudekum, has come to an amicable agreement with Local No. 626, I. A. T. S. E. of which Wm. J. Crane is secretary, whereby the Crescent company has agreed to work union labor in its several houses located in Nashville. Heretofore these houses have maintained a strictly non-union policy, but largely through the influence and instrumentality of Lee Murkin, a member of Local No. 46, Stage Employees, a satisfactory agreement has been reached between the union men and President Sudekum. The agreement is already in force, having taken immediate effect, but contracts were drawn up following the verbal understanding, for a period of four years, August 31, 1917, to August 31, 1921, inclusive.

A voluntary feature of the agreement, on the part of Mr. Sudekum, was an increase in salary accorded the men in the employ of the Crescent Amusement Company, averaging two to three dollars per week. This was not called for, by the operators, but holds forth in the written contracts. The houses affected by this action are the Fifth Avenue, Crescent, Elite, Rex, and Alhambra theaters, all located on Fifth avenue.

The victory of the union, however, is not limited to the Crescent company, but extends also to the suburban districts. L. E. Marshall, operating the Colonial, at Second avenue South and Carroll street, and the Dixie, for colored people, located at First avenue and LaFayette street, has signed similar contracts for one year. These theaters, up to two months ago, had been operating in sympathy with the union, but withdrew, and have just been brought back into the old working scale. Robert Haury, manager of the Peafowl theater, Fourth and Meridan streets, has closed one year contracts with the local union. This leaves only three Nashville houses outside the local, which are under the control of Henry Mouseon, operating the Central theater for white people, and the Liberty and Royal Palace for negroes. The union, however, will not let up on these three houses until some kind of a satisfactory understanding is reached, according to the secretary of Local No. 626, and it is expected that they will fall in line within a short time.

The Nashville local consists of forty-three members, and Secretary Crane has been in charge since February. Prior to that time Fred Carter held the secretaryship, but is now out of the city and no longer connected with this organization. His brother, Frank Carter, has had much to do with the success of the union policy in connection with the suburban houses, however, and is responsible for a large part of the union's achievements. The majority of the credit is being given to Lee Murkin by the operators, who, while not an operator himself, is an enthusiastic union man, being connected with the Princess theater as stage carpenter.

Elite Runs Billie Burke Whole Week.

Nashville, Tenn.—The Elite theater, recently opened as a moving picture feature house, ran "The Mysterious Miss Terry," featuring Billie Burke, for the entire week of August 27th, with prices set at 10 cents daytime, and 15 cents night. This is the third week of running a single picture at the Elite, something which is a rare occasion in Nashville, and will be followed next week by a Mary Pickford Artcraft subject.

Sunday Nuisance Case Decided.

Nashville, Tenn.—A decided victory has been achieved by amusement owners in Nashville through the decision of Special Judge Robert E. Blake, of the Second Circuit Court, who has ruled that Sunday baseball in this city can not be considered a public nuisance. It was pointed out at the time that if the courts decided in favor of the baseball club, that no nuisance was committed by an athletic contest of this kind on Sunday, certainly the operation of theaters on Sunday would not be a nuisance. Should the local theater managers decide at any future time to wage an active fight for Sunday opening, they will have a splendid basic ground to work upon.

Lincoln Theater Opens for Negroes.

Nashville, Tenn. — Entirely renovated, both inside and out, and under new management, the Lincoln theater for colored people opened for business on August 27th as a feature and comedy house. The Lincoln is located on Cedar street, and has experienced a varied career as a vaudeville and moving picture theater, but under the new plan will show moving pictures exclusively. The management promises to furnish the negro population with a high-class line of film attractions for the fall and winter season.

Gaumont Obtains Wrestling Rights.

Birmingham, Ala.—J. P. Harding, staff photographer for the Birmingham News, and representative of the Gaumont Company, secured rights to take a moving picture of the Lewis-Zbyszko wrestling match on Labor Day.

Prairie State News Letter

By Frank H. Madison, 623 E. Wabash Avenue, Chicago, Ill.

Film Men and Theaters in Nebraska.

OMAHA, NEB.—Carl Laemmle, president of the Universal Film Mfg. Co., while in Omaha declared that at all points visited on his trip to the West he had found business great.

Lincoln, Neb.—As a special fair week venture, N. H. Cinberg, of the Magnet theater, and F. D. Eager, of the Orpheum, Lyric and Wonderland theaters, leased the Lincoln Auditorium for the showing of "The Little American." Prices of 10 and 25 cents were secured.

Omaha, Neb.—C. E. Schmidt, who has been assistant manager of the local Pathe offices, has gone to New York City to become connected with the office of the business manager of the Pathe Company in that city.

Geneva, Neb.—Mrs. Edith Harting has sold the Grand theater, moving picture theater, to J. E. Zimmerman.

Norfolk, Neb.—The Lyric has been reopened by Fred Laun and Carl Dregor.

Happenings in the Dakotas.

Dickinson, N. D.—Manager Davis, of the Ray theater, has announced that he will remodel that house so as to increase the seating capacity. Davis is also said to be interested in a plan to erect a new 25 x 140 fireproof theater on Sims street.

Lakota, N. D.—Manager Enny has sold his interest in the Star theater to Geo. Steig.

Dickinson, N. D.—The Dickinson opera house, which was damaged by fire, causing a loss of $7,000, will be modernized when repairs are made, according to H. L. Reichert, the owner.

Langdon, N. D.—Alvin Orton has taken over the interest of his brother, Morris Orton, in the Electric theater.

Mandan, N. D.—Manager H. L. Hartman, of the Palace theater, made a Sunday opening with "The Life of Our Savior."

Sioux Falls, S. D.—Old Soldiers' Day at the Princess theater, when "The Slacker" was shown, was featured by attendance of members of the G. A. R., W. R. C. and Catholic Cadets.

Midwest News Letter

By Frank H. Madison, 623 S. Wabash Ave., Chicago, Ill.

Illinois Exhibitors and Theaters.

CANTON, ILL.—John Silvernail, formerly interested in the Dreamland theater, has leased the Blackaby building on South Main street and will open a moving picture theater.

Salem, Ill.—The Princess theater, under the management of Mrs. Sadie Sweet, was closed until Sept. 17 for redecoration, installation of new projection apparatus, new front and a larger operating room.

Galesburg, Ill.—The sale at auction of the Auditorium, one of Galesburg's oldest theaters, has been announced. The moving pictures is blamed for making theatrical attractions unprofitable.

Jottings from Michigan.

Negaunee, Mich.—Local Odd Fellows have been contemplating remodeling a building on West Iron street into a moving picture theater. The building has been vacant several months and statewide prohibition in May will throw other store buildings into the renting field.

Lansing, Mich.—Manager Claude E. Cady has had the Colonial theater on East Michigan avenue overhauled and redecorated.

Grand Rapids, Mich.—The Grand Rapids Herald is putting out a Pictorial News reel. It has been booked by the Tokio theater at Muskegon and the Robin Hood theater at Grand Haven.

Grand Rapids, Mich.—Another return date of "The Spoilers" marked the reopening of The Majestic Gardens on Sept. 2.

Hancock, Mich.—The Kerredge theater has installed two new projectors.

Bay City, Mich.—The Bijou theater, which formerly played pictures the last half of the week has a new policy of vaudeville seven days a week.

Heard in Wisconsin.

Sheboygan, Wis.—The Palace theater, at South Eighth and Clara avenues, closed since June, has been leased by Relschl & Mallman. It has been remodeled. Five cents admission will be charged.

Randolph, Wis.—The Opera House has been leased by Thomas Lawrence and Richard Jenkins, who will conduct a moving picture show.

La Crosse, Wis.—The La Crosse theater has been reopened and will play this season feature pictures, vaudeville and theatrical attractions.

Notes of the Trade in Detroit.

Detroit, Mich.—Manager J. M. Duncan, of the Vitagraph exchange in Detroit, has already booked more than $8,000 worth of business on the new Vitagraph serial, "The Fighting Trail."

We note that Col. W. S. Butterfield, president of the State Film Co., Detroit, is a member of the State Rights Distributors' Association, recently organized in New York.

The Majestic theater, Detroit, has signed for the Triangle reissues of Hart and Fairbanks, running each a full week. The Drury Lane theater, Detroit, has taken second run.

Both the Regent and Orpheum theaters, Detroit, used first-run Triangle features the week of Sept. 2.

Frank Gruber has taken over the lease of the Temple theater, East Jordan, Mich.

J. S. Greenberg City Salesman for General.

Detroit, Mich.—J. Stenton Greenberg has been appointed city salesman in Detroit for the General. Jules Levy continues as state representative, and Dave Prince is manager of the exchange.

A Successful Middle West Showman.

Battle Creek, Mich.—The sound business sense of a policy of "satisfaction guaranteed", as applied to what is known as "show business", is no better exemplified than in the career of W. S. Butterfield, more familiarly known as "Colonel" Butterfield of Battle Creek. On this policy has depended the upbuilding of a large circuit of theaters, comprising both motion picture and vaudeville houses, as well as an important participation in the amusement affairs of Michigan. Colonel Butterfield started in as an usher and soon advanced himself to the position of treasurer in an upstate New York theater. Along came old man "Wanderlust" and before long Colonel Butterfield

Col. W. S. Butterfield.

was a manager for one of Charles E. Blaney's then numerous traveling attractions.

His success with Blaney led him to branch out for himself and the result was the introduction of Ross Stahl and William Bonelli to the one-night stands. After several seasons with various road shows, the Colonel found himself one summer's day in Battle Creek. He decided that a vaudeville theater would be a valuable adjunct to the town's attractions.

The Hamblin opera house, which had welcomed Booth and Barrett to Battle Creek was vacant, owing to the recent opening of a fine new theater for the traveling shows. So the Colonel leased the theater, borrowed some opera chairs, sent to Chicago for some vaudeville acts, and laid the cornerstone of the present Butterfield circuit. At the present time this circuit includes two theaters in Battle Creek, one in Kalamazoo, one in Jackson, one in Ann Arbor, one in Lansing, three in Flint, three in Saginaw, and one in Bay City. In addition Colonel Butterfield is an active partner in theaters located in Waterloo, Iowa; Davenport, Iowa; Rockford, Illinois; Chicago, Illinois; Green Bay, Wisconsin, and Hammond, Indiana, as well as other theatrical holdings scattered through the Middle West.

The rapid evolution of the motion picture field attracted the Colonel's attention in the past few years, with the result that he is gradually coming into prominence in that division.

J. M. Erickson Now With Artcraft.

Detroit, Mich.—John M. Erickson, manager of the program department of the Fox Film exchange in Detroit, has resigned to become connected with the city sales staff of the Artcraft-Paramount exchange in Detroit.

E. J. Taylor With Artcraft.

Detroit, Mich.—E. J. Taylor, former salesman in Michigan for Artcraft, has joined the K-E-S-E in the same state.

Joe Fertie Joins Foursquare.

Detroit, Mich.—Joe Fertie, former salesman for Metro, is now salesman for Hoffman Foursquare Pictures in Michigan.

Michigan Filmdom Starts Its New Season

Flint Sees Premier of Butterfield's New Palace—Kunsky Opens Legitimate Theater—State's Biggest Theater Will Add Vaudeville.

By Jacob Smith, 718 Free Press Building, Detroit, Mich.

DETROIT, MICH.—The past week was an important one from the theatrical standpoint in the state of Michigan. Two brand new houses opened up, while the largest theater in the state reopened under a new policy.

First, there was the opening of the New Palace theater in Flint, owned by Col. W. S. Butterfield. The opening took place Thursday evening, August 30, and the affair was very successful. The policy of the Palace theater is vaudeville, Col. Butterfield shifting motion pictures to the Garden, and a combination of big features and road attractions to the Majestic in that city. The Palace seats about 1,500 and has a very complete motion picture booth, fully equipped with Power's machines and a Hertner transverter. After the night shows, Col. Butterfield entertained about 100 of his friends at a banquet in the Hotel Dresden, followed by informal vaudeville and dancing. Those from Detroit who went to the opening were J. O. Brooks, Art Hoganson, Eddie Murphy, Harry S. Lorch, Earl H. Rathbun, Jos. Kailaha, John M. Erickson, A. I. Shapiro, Harry Zapp and Jacob Smith (Moving Picture World), all from Detroit. There was also present two trainloads of Chicago vaudeville agents and managers, as well as a number of the managers of Butterfield theaters in other Michigan cities.

Second, the New Adams theater, Detroit, opened Saturday evening, Sept. 1, with dramatic stock. This house is owned by John H. Kunsky, making his tenth theater in Detroit. It is his first house devoted to this type of amusement, most of his other theaters being devoted to motion pictures. The Adams is a beautiful playhouse, seating about 1,800, and the sales of season tickets already assures Mr. Kunsky of another big theatrical success.

Third, the reopening of the Regent theater, Detroit. In the past this house has been devoted to motion pictures, but under the new lease to C. H. Miles it is devoted to vaudeville and pictures. The opening took place Labor Day, and the theater was packed to capacity at every show. If the opening is any criterion, the Regent is certain to continue with its present policy. The opening picture attraction was a Triangle feature, "They're Off." For the second week Mr. Miles is using the "Battle of the Tanks," Pathe release. Tom Ealand, manager of the Orpheum theater for Mr. Miles, is also managing and directing the Regent under the new lessee.

Operators Win an Increase in Wages.

Detroit, Mich.—The wage discussion between the union operators and the exhibitors in Detroit has been satisfactorily adjusted. The new contract at first demanded by the unions, effective Sept. 1, had a number of clauses which exhibitors considered unreasonable. Arbitration committees were appointed by both sides for a joint conference, and after several meetings, all matters were mutually fixed up. The operators get a wage increase, but eliminate the undesirable features of the new contract, which settles the wage scale for union operators until Sept. 1, 1918.

Mutual Exchange in New Film Building.

Detroit, Mich.—The Mutual exchange moved on Sept. 1 from 97 Woodward avenue, Detroit, to the new film building, at John R and Elizabeth streets, being the first film company to move to the new building. The Mutual occupies the greater portion of the second floor. Partitions are now being installed and it will probably be the 15th of the month before everything will be in its proper place. Other exchanges will be moving this month, so that by Octobr 1 most of the film companies will be doing business at the film building.

Joseph Horwitz Passed Cigars Recently.

Detroit, Mich.—"Hustling" Joe Horwitz, Universal salesman in Detroit, recently celebrated his 57th birthday, which was an occasion for "passing the cigars" among his many exhibitor friends. Mr. Horwitz came to Detroit several months ago direct from the New York office, where he had been in the life insurance business for 20 years. The Universal wanted a real salesman to locate in Detroit and build the city business to the point where it should be. Joe had made a success of the life insurance business by absolutely adhering to square principles so why wouldn't the same principles apply to his

Joseph Horwitz.

selling film. So he consented to go to Detroit.

When he started to call on the Detroit exhibitors Universal had 31 accounts. On August 18, Universal was supplying service of one kind or another to 121 Detroit theaters—and Joe says he is not through yet, although the town has only about 140 houses.

In consideration of his splendid work, Universal bought Joe a five-passenger automobile, which enables him to call on from 12 to 15 exhibitors every night. Joe has "57 varieties" of pep—and for a man of 57 summers he is a wonder at selling film.

W. O. Kenan Has Enlarged His Theater.

Adrian, Mich.—The Crescent theater, Adrian, Mich., operated by W. O. Kenan, is being extensively remodeled and enlarged to 400 seats. Mr. Kenan has been conducting the house for eight years and has a big success of that institution. He will take into partnership his son-in-law, Vincent J. Williams, who will be active in the management of the Crescent. No less than ten thousand dollars will actually be spent in fixing up the Crescent, during which time, the house will be closed. A new 20-year lease has been taken of the property by Messrs. Kenan and Williams.

Detroit's Duplex Will Be a Garage.

Detroit, Mich.—The theater equipment of the Duplex theater, Detroit, was sold at public auction on Sept. 4 to satisfy a judgment against that playhouse. This means "good-bye" to the Duplex as a theatrical enterprise. We will likely see the building converted into a garage.

Two Houses Charge 7 Cents.

Detroit, Mich.—This city now has several seven cent theaters—the Comique and the Rosebud, operated by the Woodward Amusement Co. Heretofore these houses have had a six cent admission price. "Increased expenses and increased film rental are the reasons for the advance," said Bert Williams, general manager.

Jewel Opens Temporary Offices.

Detroit, Mich.—The Jewel Productions, Inc, have opened temporary offices at 120 Broadway, in charge of Harry A. Bugle. Later he will have offices in the new film building.

Airdome Season in St. Louis Draws to Close

Mosquitoes Seek in Vain for the Thin Haired Patron—Legitimate Theaters Brush Up Stock Promises—Picture Houses Brighten.

By A. H. Giebler, 4123 Westminster Pl., St. Louis, Mo.

ST. LOUIS. MO. — It's getting along toward the shag end of summer here in St. Louis, and the baldheaded fans are happy because the shows will be moving back indoors pretty soon.

Downtown, in the treeless sections, the airdomes are not so bad from an insect standpoint, but out in the neighborhoods, where there are lots of leaves and grass, the bugs are fierce on a chap whose cranial foliage is getting thin, and even those who have hair find their whole evening spoiled when they have to go home and spend half an hour digging the katydids out of their ears.

Not Applause for Wild Cat Feature.

There was a "wild-cat" feature salesman here this summer who rented his unprecedented attraction to an airdome exhibitor out in the bug belt. Along about the last reel the "wild-catter" came in from the outside, stopped, and listened a minute.

"Gee, it's going great, ain't it?" he said to the exhibitor.

"It is not," grumbled the exhibitor, "it's a rotten show."

"But listen to that!" said the W. C. "Hear 'em applaudin' !"

"Applaudin' hell!" said the exhibitor. "They ain't applaudin', they're slappin' skeeters"!

Otherwise things are pretty brisk and the outlook for fall and winter business is promising.

Promises by the Legits as Usual.

The regular stage people are getting into print with their annual predictions of a revival of the drama. The newspapers are coming out with the usual this-time-of-the-year stories on the brilliant winter season that is about to burst upon us.

It is curious how hope springs eternal in the dramatic editors' breasts. They have been sitting back and watching the regular drama die of slow starvation for the last six years and they can't see the signs of dissolution yet.

Last year there was only one theater outside of the vaudeville and burlesque houses that kept its doors open all season, and the signs do not look any better for the future; yet, in the face of this, they whet up their fountain pens and rave about the momentous dramatic events that are about to happen to us, and predict a return of the old days when some of the regular houses were so arrogant that they did not have telephone connections with the common herd for fear some one might want to reserve a seat in advance.

Let 'em rave! We read their dope with our tongue in our cheek and the salt cellar handy.

The advance drama stuff is the same as it was last year. We are to get all of the great New York successes. And we will! We'll get 'em—we've got 'em before, and there's no earthly reason why we shouldn't get 'em again. Nobody in New York wants 'em any longer. They are all a year and a half and two years old, and they have worn themselves out utterly and completely.

They'll send us the New York shows with the original casts, the original scenery and the original costumes, just as they were bought two years ago without ever having been to the dry cleaners. They do that to give us the real New York atmosphere!

Same old jokes, same old songs we have been listening to in the four-a-day vaudeville houses all summer. And then some of these regular drama birds can't understand why St. Louis is a poor show town.

Houses Open for Fall Season.

The Jefferson will open next week, and the Garrick—which has been renamed the Shubert-Garrick, why, the Lord only knows; nobody will ever call it that—is to begin a brilliant season of speaking stage plays right away. But to make sure, they are opening with pictures, "Jack and the Beanstalk."

The Columbia has started a twelve-hour continuous grind with a half picture and half vaudeville bill.

The picture houses are booming and getting ready for what looks like good business for fall and winter.

The New Grand Central has just finished a two weeks' run of "Within the Law," and have "On Trial," the first of the First National Exhibitors Circuit releases on the screen this week.

The Lyric are stepping along with their usual first run Paramounts.

Hector M. E. Pasmezoglu, of the Congress, is pleasing big audiences with a mixture of Triangle, Paramount, Fox and Vitagraphs.

Skouras Brothers, out at the Pageant, are doing a nice business.

The Kings theater is reigning again with first run Triangles, and A. E. Morelock is getting ready to break into the game with the beautiful new Liberty theater, which will open very shortly with big stuff.

Down on the South Side, the Shenandoah, the Juniata, and the Arsenal are holding their own, and Freund Brothers, with the big Cinderella, are handling crowds of more than the usual size.

Joe Mogler, up on Ninth and Bremen, reports prosperity at the Mogler and the Bremen.

The Lindell is pleasing the North Side patrons.

Jack Sweeney, of the Central, is still winning with his "pictures with a punch."

St. Louis Exchanges Steady.

With the exchanges things are somewhat quiet. There hasn't been a new manager appointed for a whole week. It got so for awhile that a person going into any of the St. Louis offices didn't ask where is the manager, but who is the manager. There have been twenty-seven changes in exchange heads in this town in the last few months.

Walter Irwin, head mogul of the Vitagraph, was in town for a day two weeks ago and said things look mighty good hereabouts to him.

Walter Sanford, head publicity dopester for Fox, was here for a few days, arranging for the first appearance of "Jack' and the Beanstalk."

Mr. Sanford is an old-timer in these parts, having been manager of the Olympic for a number of years before he joined out with the movies. Everybody was glad to see Walt except the World correspondent, who didn't get to see him and is sore about it.

More About What's Going On.

St. Louis, Mo.—Roy Bettis has come all the way up here from Texas to help Syd Baker sell Foursquare features. Roy is a nice looking boy, doesn't look at all like we thought people from Texas looked. He isn't bowlegged from riding a horse, as all the Texas folks we see in the movies are, and he doesn't wear a wide hat, nor pants with hair down the sides, nor "pack" a gun.

Roy has been in the picture game quite a spell, he says, and from a kind of bright look about him we draw an idea that he'll make good. Syd Baker says he is going out on the road with "The Sin Woman," which isn't as bad as it sounds, the same being only a picture. Roy's address will be at the Fouraquare Pictures Corp., Empress Theater Bldg., if any of the folks down in Texas want to write to him.

Little Levy is a Live One.

Leo (Little) Levy, who is pretty well known hereabouts as a chap whose size and weight doesn't seem to have anything to do with the number of contracts he brings in, has gone down to 3547 Olive street and got a job from G. F. Hennessy selling Bluebird features and Alice Howell comedies. Levy used to work for the Bluebird people, so it's like coming back home for him, and he says he's glad to get back, and Hennessy says he's glad to have him, and so exerybody's happy.

Hoffman Not at all Stuck Up.

St. Louis, Mo.—M. H. Hoffman, high mogul of the Foursquare Pictures Corp., dropped off the Cannon Ball when it stopped at the depot here for water last Thursday, and went to see Syd Baker, who runs the office for him here. He and Syd got so interested talking that he stayed over till the evening train. We were introduced to Mr. Hoffman and were pleased to meet him. He is a nice man to talk to and knows a lot about pictures and is not a bit stuck up like some of those New Yorkers.

Star Boarder at the King's'll Stay.

A. F. King, auditor at the Universal exchange, has just taken a new boarder at his house. The newcomer didn't bring any personal property along when he came, but Mr. King and his wife liked his looks so well that they got him a brand new outfit of everything to wear and a rattle and some more things to play with, which pleased the little chap so well that he decided to stay, and Mr. King says he is already the star boarder.

New Paramount Office in Fine Location.

St. Louis, Mo.—The K. C. Feature Film Co., formerly the Monarch Feature Film Co., distributers of Paramount pictures, will move from the Gayety Theater building at 14th and Locust streets, where it has been located for several years, to the building formerly occupied by the Vandeventer Trust Co., at 3929 Olive street. The new Paramount offices are in a fine location, being just a little over a block from Film Row. Both floors of the building have been leased, each of which has a floor space of 35 by 80 feet. The offices are now being put in shape.

G. E. McKean, the manager, says that the new quarters will be fitted up in the most modern style and every facility for the prompt and efficient handling of films will be installed.

Lafayette Theater Enlarged for New Session.

St. Louis, Mo.—The Lafayette theater, at Lafayette and Jefferson avenues, is being remodeled for the fall and winter season. The Lafayette is one of the first high class neighborhood houses to be built in St. Louis, and at the time of its erection its six hundred seats were considered ample for the patrons. The new alterations will increase the capacity to 800, and include a new lighting system for the front and lobby. The Lafayette is operated by the Athenian Amusement Company, with E. Pasmezoglu as manager.

"Jack" On the Job at Garrick.

St. Louis, Mo.—"Jack and the Beanstalk" opened at the Shubert-Garrick theater on Sunday, Sept. 2, with admission prices of 25 and 50 cents at matinees, and 25 cents to one dollar in the evening.

Kansas City News Letter

By Kansas City News Service, 205 Corn Belt Bldg., Kansas City, Mo.

Southern Triangle Gets New Territory.

KANSAS CITY, Mo.—The Southern Triangle Pictures Corporation will now have charge of the Triangle accounts in the northern-half of Oklahoma, this business being taken from the Dallas, Texas, branch of the Triangle company. This change affects 129 accounts.

Additions to Southern Triangle Forces.

Kansas City, Mo.—The Southern Triangle has made several additions to the Kansas City office, including two salesmen and a booker. The new travelers are D. R. Patterson, formerly with the World Film, and F. G. Sherrick, formerly with the General Film, at Des Moines, Iowa. Mr. Patterson will work a southern Missouri territory and Mr. Sherrick will have northern Missouri.

The new booker is W. G. Miller, who was formerly the head booker at the Dallas Paramount office. He succeeds F. Thiele, who has gone to Omaha, Neb., to manage the Triangle office there.

R. H. Fairchild Goes on Road for General Film.

Kansas City, Mo.—R. H. Fairchild, for the last few months head booker at the Kansas City General Film Co. office, has taken a territory in Oklahoma for the company. He takes charge of his territory the week of September 9, succeeding A. W. Friemel, who is now with the Kansas City Feature Film Company.

W. R. Pittenger New Booker at General Film.

Kansas City, Mo.—W. R. Pittenger has been made head booker for the General Film Co. here, succeeding R. H. Fairchild. Mr. Pittenger was formerly with the General at Oklahoma City, Oklahoma, and with the Mutual at Kansas City.

Morris Spiecer Reopens New Center Theater.

Kansas City, Mo.—The new Center theater, Fifteenth street and Troost avenue, has reopened under the management of Morris Spiecer. The opening attraction will be the Triangle, "Wolf Lowry."

There will be a daily change of program, a different picture being run each day. The theater will show Paramount, Artcraft, Fox, Triangle, Bluebird, Metro and K-E-S-E pictures at family prices of five and ten cents.

Clayton W. Potter Weds.

Kansas City, Mo.—Clayton W. Potter, northern Kansas representative of the Universal Film and Supply Company, was married August 31 to Miss Ionia Cushwa. They will live at 4714 Morrill avenue, Kansas City, Mo.

Reissues of Hart and Fairbanks Pictures

Kansas City, Mo.—The first of the reissues of the William S. Hart and Douglas Fairbanks pictures are out the week of September 3. There are 25 of these pictures.

Jottings From Kansas City Exchanges.

Kansas City, Mo.—J. H. Blowitz, Kansas representative of the Kansas City Feature Film Co., was a visitor at the Kansas City office of the company this week. He reported that the conditions in his territory were very good.

F. Warren, treasurer of the Standard Film Corporation, and Phil Ryan, sales manager of the company, have gone to Chicago, Ill., to confer with C. W. Stonebaugh, the manager of the office there. They will be followed by R. C. Cropper, the president of the company.

C. W. Potter, northern Kansas representative of the Universal Film and Supply Company, has returned from a flying trip covering ten towns in his territory. He had remarkable success with serials in the places he visited as he landed five contracts for "The Voice on the Wire," and the same number of contracts for "The Gray Ghost."

A. D. Flinton, district manager for Paramount and Artcraft and president of the Kansas City Feature Film Company, has gone to New York City, where he will spend a vacation of two weeks. He is accompanied by his family.

Leon J. Bamburger, formerly head of the sales promoting department of the General Film Co., and now special representative of the Jewell Producing Co., was a visitor in Kansas City this week.

Minneapolis Letter on Week's Film News

M. R. Dick Sells Out to H. E. Pierce—New Exchange Opens to Distribute "Robinson Crusoe"—Pictures Shown Fair Week—Notes of Trade.

By John L. Johnston, 704 Film Exchange Building, Minneapolis, Minn.

MINNEAPOLIS, Minn.—Despite the fact that the Minnesota State Fair brought a bumper business to all Twin City photoplay houses during the week of September 3, there is not a great deal to write about; for, peculiar as it may seem, there was only one change of exchange managers during the entire week.

M. R. Dick Sells Out.

M. R. Dick, who for two years has operated a state rights exchange at Room 814 Produce Exchange building, sold his business to Harry E. Pierce of Duluth, Minn. Mr. Dick controlled territorial rights on "The End of the World," "Siberian Travel Pictures," Motoy comedies and other films. He has joined the Barnett Attractions exchange and will again act as first lieutenant to Bert Barnett, Sr., whom he once worked for at the old Famous Players All Star Feature exchange controlled by the Barnetts.

"Robinson Crusoe" Exchange Opened.

Mr. Pierce has secured the right to distribute H. W. Savage's "Robinson Crusoe" in four Northwest states and will operate the exchange under the name of H. E. Pierce Amusement Co., Inc. "Robinson Crusoe" will be shown to film patrons of the Northwest for the first time September 7 at the Zelda theater, Duluth. Mr. Pierce has been engaged in the theatrical and film booking and theater managing field for a score of years and he was chief executive at Duluth's largest downtown theater for 14 years.

Some of the Big Shows of Fair Week.

Minneapolis, Minn.—Film fans were offered some good bills here during fair week.

The New Lyric played "The Barrier" a week at 25 and 50 cents to a good business. Special music by an enlarged orchestra was also offered.

Manager Charles G. Branham of The Strand offered "The Slacker," Egbert Van Alstyne, the popular song writer and his soloist, Walter King, in person. The admission price at the Strand remained at 15 cents. Special jazz music and other numbers were offered by an enlarged orchestra.

Manager L. V. Calvert of the New Garrick showed Mary Pickford in "Rebecca of Sunnybrook Farm." Pathe news and a comedy. The admission price remained at 20 cents.

Manager William Cook of the New Aster offered Theda Bara in "Heart and Soul" and Bessie Love in "Wee Lady Betty," fair week.

Manager Arthur Gostie, of the New Unique, had Charlie Chaplin in a multiple reel revue and "The Grafters."

Manager Engler, of the Crystal, showed "Ignorance."

The St. Paul Theater Bills.

Manager Hays, of The New Garrick, offered George M. Cohan in "Seven Keys to Baldpate" the first half of the week and followed this with Pauline Frederick in "Double Crossed." Special music was offered for both bills with admission prices unchanged.

Manager Goldman's show was Fannie Ward in "The Crystal Gazer" at the New Princess and William Russell in "Pride and the Man" at the New Majestic.

Manager Campbell, of the Blue Mouse, offered Naomi Childers in an Art Drama release, "The Auction of Virtue."

Manager Gilosky, of the Alhambra, had Dorothy Dalton in "Ten of Diamonds" and Charlie Chaplin in "The Count."

Manager Morton Nathan, of The Starland, offered Clara Kimball Young in "The Savage Instinct" the first half and "War's Women" the last half.

Manager Julius Reisman, of The Dale, provided Wilfred Lucas in "Jim Bludso" and Douglas Fairbanks in "In Again—Out Again."

Manager Westcott's Boy Gets a Playmate.

Manager Eddie Westcott, of the Fox exchange, became the proud papa of a handsome baby girl last week. Mr. Westcott is delighted over the arrival of a playmate for his sixteen-months-old baby boy.

Grace Polk Editor of Semi-Weekly.

Minneapolis, Minn.—Manager Calvert, of the New Garrick theater here, has issued a handsome semi-weekly house organ edited by Miss Grace Polk, Ruben & Finkelstein's press representative etoile. The magazine, twelve pages thick, contains information about the stars appearing at the theater at date of issuing, musical programs and advance notices. It is printed on a high grade stock and two colors are used.

Liberty Theater Reopens.

Minneapolis, Minn.—Manager Lebedoff opened the Liberty theater, 1613 Sixth avenue North, Saturday, Sept. 1, to a good business.

"Slacker" Suit in Duluth.

Duluth, Minn.—Manager Abrahamson, of the Zelda theater here, was successful in a suit to restrain the Lyric theater management from advertising "The Man Who Was Afraid" as "The Slacker." "The Slacker," a Metro production, was booked at the Zelda, and Mr. Abrahamson's claim that to advertise another film of a different name as "The Slacker" for opposition's sake was unlawful was upheld by Judge Cant.

Exchange Jottings From Minneapolis.

Minneapolis, Minn.—Manager Wilson, of the American Maid exchange, has booked "The Deemster" in Ruben & Finkelstein's New Princess, St. Paul.

Manager Conhaim, of the Supreme exchange has received several new prints of "Where Are My Children?" for fall demand.

Ed. Redlich, recently appointed manager of the Metro exchange, Seattle, spent two days visiting Manager S. N. Robinson, of the Christyfield Film Library and Exchange here last week.

Fred Benna, manager of the Laemmle-Universal exchange at Fargo, N. D., conferred with Manager Julius Bernheim at the local Universal offices last week.

Hal J. Hawkins, formerly of the Lochren exchange, has joined Joseph Santley's "Oh, Boy" company, now playing in Chicago.

A. H. Nixon, of the Metro exchange, paid a flying visit to several Wisconsin cities last week and returned home with a handful of contracts. Incidentally it must be said the permanent manager for the Metro exchange has not as yet been selected. Harry Cohen is still present, smiling as usual.

Dallas Woman Applies for Operator's Card

Local Union Puts Matter of Admitting Fair Operator Up to National Officers—She Asks Why She Wouldn't Be a Good Picture Operator.

By Douglas Hawley, Times-Herald, Dallas, Texas.

DALLAS, TEX.—Would a picture look any better if the reel was operated by a lady? The question presents itself in the possibility of a woman operator for some Dallas show.

Miss Louise Millet has applied for membership in the Dallas union of motion picture machine operators. There was no precedent under which officials of the union might act in the matter, and consequently the fair one's application has been referred to national officers of the union.

"Why shouldn't a woman operate a motion picture machine?" she asked, answering a question as to how she came to select the profession, in the ranks of which thus far the Southwest knows only men.

"There are women bank presidents—there are women street-car conductors in some cities. Right here in Dallas, they tell me, women bill collectors are more efficient than the men. Why shouldn't a woman prove just as efficient in the operation of a picture machine as a man? I've qualified before the city electrician, and I mean to have a position if the union will accept my application for membership."

At Fort Worth Walk Out.

Fort Worth, Tex.—Fort Worth faces a strike of machine operators. Men in two theaters there—the Byers and Majestic—walked out on the night of August 30, demanding time and a half for overtime, double time for holidays and eight hours a day, with opening time at 8:30 and closing 11 p. m. The present rate of pay is said to be $25 per week for six days.

Incorporators of Liberty Film Company.

Dallas, Tex.—Charter of the Liberty Film Company, of Dallas, has been filed with the Secretary of State at Austin. Capital stock is $10,000 and the incorporators are H. Clogensen, B. F. Yancey and J. C. Deane, all of Dallas. Clogensen and Deane are both photographers, the former with wide previous experience in the motion picture field. It is planned to make marketable film in Dallas and Texas territory.

Exhibitors' Circuit Files Texas Charter.

Dallas, Tex.—Charter of the First National Exhibitors' Circuit of Texas, with headquarters at Dallas, has been filed with the Secretary of State at Austin. Capital stock is given at $15,000. Incorporators are E. H. Hulsey and Hershel Stuart, of Dallas, and S. T. McDonald, of Galveston. Hulsey operates a chain of theaters in Texas, and Stuart is his general manager. No announcement has yet been made as to the intentions of the new concern, or what its line of endeavor will be.

"Garden of Allah" Shown Privately.

Dallas, Tex.—Six general agents for shows saw a special reeling of the Selig "Garden of Allah" at the Old Mill theater here during the last week. J. M. Hathaway made the showing for E. H. Hulsey and others. Among the film folk who were present there were Wm. H. Horton, of Ringling Bros.; L. H. Heckman, of Hagenbeck-Wallace; C. W. Finney, of Jess Willard's "101" show; George Meghan and David Jarrell, of Yankee Robinson shows, and Emma C. Miller, W. K. Peck, Murray Pennock and Jack Henitz, of Al. G. Barnes' circus. All were loud in praise of the picture.

F. R. Newman Gets Honor.

Greenville, Tex.—F. R. Newman, of Greenville, Tex., has been appointed by E. H. Hulsey, of Dallas, as a member of the state board of war co-operative effort in the motion picture field. Work of organ-izing the state under the Wm. A. Brady plan is rapidly progressing.

Iowa News Letter.

By Dorothy Day, Register-Tribune, Des Moines, Ia.

Rumor of New Chain of Theaters.

DES MOINES, IA.—The film men of Des Moines are talking of the persistent rumor that a large syndicate of successful exhibitors in the eastern part of the state are strongly contemplating erecting a very large and up to the minute picture house in Fort Dodge, Waterloo and Mason City. At the present time this syndicate controls five first class houses and it is the aim to have a string of twelve or fifteen houses of the better sort all through Iowa.

"Twenty Thousand Leagues" Fourth Big Week.

Des Moines, Ia.—During Fair Week, Zach Harris, owner of the Iowa rights for "Twenty Thousand Leagues Under the Sea," leased the Coliseum and showed his picture evenings. This made the fourth big week for this picture in Des Moines, an unprecedented run of any picture except the "Birth of a Nation."

Des Moines Exhibitor Works Trick on Fair Visitors.

Des Moines, Ia.—To the discredit of Des Moines exhibitors, one of the biggest of them worked a low down trick on visitors to the fair, during the whole week of the State Fair. Realizing how well people from the country enjoy vaudeville as well as motion pictures and how quickly they would grasp at an opportunity to see both for a dime, this man placed a one-sheet prominently in his lobby. The sheet was on white cardboard and at the top there were several photographs of vaudeville performers, a couple dancing, a comedian, a monologist and the like for eight pictures. Then in the center of the sheet in large brightly colored letters about eight inches in heighth was the word vaudeville with above it in letters less than an inch in size "Some people like—" and then just below the prominent word of "Vaudeville" were the same small lettered words, "but, we show pictures, only."

The trick worked all too well, the visitors flocking in and waiting for the vaudeville to start until their patience exhausted they would leave in a great rage. The film men of the town ridiculed this exhibitor and openly denounced him, but he seems to have little honor when it comes to making money. The vaudeville sign was kept in the lobby throughout the entire week, hoodwinking the public who read only the big word and glanced at the pictures. There ought to be some way of 'getting' such exhibitors.

False "Slacker" Picture Causes Trouble.

Des Moines, Ia.—The local Metro exchange is having considerable trouble with exhibitors over the state, booking contemporary "slacker" pictures and advertising them as "The Slacker." In some cases rival exhibitors in the same town where the original "The Slacker" is running will advertise other pictures on the same order as "The Slacker."

In two cases it has been found necessary to prosecute exhibitors on the grounds that the exhibitor was not only defrauding the public but infringing on a copyrighted title. In one case an injunction was obtained that prevented the exhibitor from not only calling the picture "The Slacker" but from even showing the other film. Another time the erring exhibitor came half way and showed "The Slacker" picture after it had already been shown in another house. A circular letter has been mailed all over the state warning exhibitors from advertising any rival picture by the Metro title.

Notes From Midwest Office.

Des Moines, Ia.—A. Kahn has resigned from the selling force of the Triangle and will handle the Mid West productions in the western part of Iowa.

John J. Shipley, publicity manager of the Mid West office, took "The Lone Wolf" print into the eastern part of Iowa last week for a private trade showing of the successful picture.

Theaters Aid in "Smokes for Our Soldiers."

Des Moines, Ia.—The Des Moines Evening Tribune, the largest evening paper in the city, has opened a campaign for "Smokes for Our Soldiers," placing red, white and blue barrels in the cigar stores in the city and all over the state. Much publicity has been given the campaign and when the Majestic and Casino theaters placed a barrel in their lobbies they naturally received much press notice. In addition to the pledge of the barrels the two theaters offered five per cent. of their proceeds to the purchasing of "smokes" for the barrels. Zach Harris also placed a barrel in the lobby of the Coliseum and gave ten per cent. of his proceeds to the purchasing of smokes. The stunt popularized all three places of amusement during Fair Week, and the Majestic and Casino barrels will be maintained until the close of the Tribune campaign.

Laemmle Exchange Happenings.

Des Moines, Ia.—F. P. Peckenpaugh, salesman for the Bluebird office in this city, has given up the film business entirely.

Edgar Peel, for five years head booker at the Laemmle office, is the proud daddy of a fourteen pound boy, Gordon Leslie Peel.

George N. Wood has taken charge of the shipping department of the Laemmle Film Service and will be assisted in his work by W. R. Peacocke. D. W. Haskell is a new poster man at the same office.

Theater Notes Across Iowa.

Waterloo, Ia.—Nick Webber has sold the Princess in Waterloo to C. W. Martin of Cedar Rapids.

Fort Dodge, Ia.—Edward Awe, formerly owner of the Strand with Mr. Julius, has been appointed house manager of the Strand by Dan W. Lederman, manager of the Laemmle Film Service in Des Moines, who recently purchased the theater.

Pomeroy, Iowa.—Richard Moore of the moving picture theater of George Hochschwender, the Isis.

Newhall, Iowa.—A motion picture machine has been installed in the opera house here.

Wheatland, Iowa.—Otto Lahann has bought the interest of J. C. Robertson in the A-Muse-U moving picture theater here.

Bloomington, Neb.—The Bloomington moving picture theater has changed management.

State Fair Brings Many Visitors.

Des Moines, Ia.—The Iowa State Fair, held in Des Moines the week of August 24, brought many exhibitors over the state into the city. E. F. Johnson of the Opera House in Guernsey, Mr. Johnstone of Johnstone and Morrow of the Opera House in Barnes City, Mr. Kenworthy of Kellog Kenworthy of the Lyric in Fort Dodge, Joe Gerbracht of the Twin Star and Ames, F. W. Stegge of the Princess in Pocahontas, John Snyder of the Vernon in Renwick, Frank Davison of the Opera House in Boneparte, J. C. Breem of the Opera House in Pella, W. C. Treloar of the Treloar Opera House in Ogden, and Fowd McLuen of the McLuen theater in Guthrie Center, were reported from the Pathe exchange.

PACIFIC COAST NOTES.

E. M. Asher Now With T. & D.

San Francisco, Cal.—E. M. Asher, for quite a time with the All Star Feature Distributors, Inc., is now with the Turner & Dahnken circuit in the film exchange department. He is meeting with good success in placing the "Curse of Iku" and "On Trial," and will shortly begin on the Charlie Chaplin campaign.

Nat Magner's Trip Postponed.

San Francisco, Cal.—Nat A. Magner, who planned to leave for the Orient at an early date to handle all of the Selig productions, will not be able to get away as quickly as he anticipated. He recently underwent a serious operation at a local hospital and has been advised by his doctor not to attempt so strenuous a journey at the present time. It is expected, however, that he will be able to get away after a rest of a month or two.

Davis Bros. Buy State Rights.

San Francisco, Cal.—Davis Bros. have purchased the California, Arizona and Nevada rights to six two-reel productions based on the poems of Ella Wheeler Wilcox and formerly owned by Warner Bros. These have never been shown in this territory. They have also purchased the rights for these states to a five-reel production, "At the Front With the Allies," and a new two-reel picture, "Beasts of the Jungle."

Exhibitors Are Arranging Service.

San Francisco, Cal.—The fall season is opening up in splendid shape in the country districts and many exhibitors have been here of late arranging for service, purchasing new equipment and getting ideas. Among these have been: C. H. Douglas, of the Elite, Merced; William McKee, Theater Visalia, Visalia; Robert Davis, Lyric, Stockton; K. A. Adelberg, Marysville; George Bailey, Turlock; W. R. Claman, Orland; John Daly, of the Broadway and Majestic, Chico; Frank Vesely, Salinas; J. McCabe, Liberty, Coalinga; B. L. Waite, Minor, Arcata; John Ratto, Jackson; T. C. Reavis, Cline, Santa Rosa; W. Englehardt, of the Masonic, Truckee; F. G. Meisner, M. & M. theater, Healdsburg, and H. A. Meder, Valhalla, Gardnerville, Nev.

Big Demand for Reissues.

San Francisco, Cal.—Manager B. F. Simpson, of the local Triangle branch, states that the demand for the Douglas Fairbanks and William Hart re-issues has been very heavy and that the last week in August marked the biggest business ever done at this exchange. The re-issues of the productions featuring these stars have been booked, among others, to the following houses: Strand theater, San Francisco; Kinema theaters, Oakland and Fresno; Goddard's J Street theater, Sacramento; Lyric theater, Stockton, and U. C. theater, Berkeley. William Desmond was a recent visitor here.

Brief San Francisco News.

Morris L. Markowitz recently made a trip to Los Angeles, accompanied by Carl Laemmle.

Fred S. Peachy, formerly manager of the Film Exchange Board of Trade of San Francisco, and a well known exchange man, was married recently to Miss Blanche Goll.

Miss Muriel Harris has joined the office staff of the Pathe exchange.

The Theater St. Fracis, on Geary street, will be opened shortly by B. C. Mix. Extensive alterations have been made and a pipe organ installed.

Arthur Wobber has succeeded Joe Huff in the management of the Odeon and Unique theaters on Market street.

Newton Levy, manager of the Mutual exchange, made a trip to Reno, Nev., late in August.

Four Minute Men in California Theaters

United Motion Picture Men in Northern California Appoint Committee of Film Men to Supervise the Patriotic Campaign.

From T. A. Church, 1507 North Street, Berkeley, Cal.

SAN FRANCISCO, CAL.—Arrangements have been completed for the inauguration of a campaign of Four Minute Men in local houses under the authority of the Committee on Public Information, Washington, D. C. This subject was made the principal item of business at a meeting of the United Motion Picture Industry of Northern California held late in August, and a committee was appointed to take this matter up with exhibitors, arrange for speakers and supervise the campaign generally. This committee consists of Louis Reichert, manager of the local Metro exchange, who will represent the film exchange interests, and Eugene H. Roth, of the Portola theater, who will represent exhibitors. They have appointed Jesse H. Steinhart, a local attorney, chairman of the local committee, with authority to arrange for the services of speakers.

Bar to "Clansman" Removed.

San Francisco, Cal.—By a ruling of the State Appellate Court the attempt of negroes at Oakland, Cal., to stop the exhibition, of "The Clansman" has been quashed and this production may now be shown in California without further hindrance. The ruling was handed down in the case of D. R. Wallace against the Macdonough Theater Company, F. A. Geisea, owner, and D. W. Griffith and Thomas Dixon, Jr., lessors. The Alameda County Superior Court refused to grant an injunction and the matter was then appealed to the higher court, with the result that the action of the lower court was upheld.

Injunction in Infringement Case.

San Francisco, Cal.—The Metro corporation has secured a permanent injunction against the New York & San Francisco Amusement Co., the Strand Theater Company, D. J. Grauman and Sidney Grauman to prevent them from making any use of the name "Slacker" in connection with a photoplay. This injunction was secured on the showing that during the run of "The Slacker," a Metro production, the term "Slacker" was prominently used by the owners of the Strand theater in advertising another picture.

New Manager for K-E-S-E.

San Francisco, Cal.—W. O. Edmonds, who has had charge of the K-E-S-E exchange in this city since the opening of this branch, has tendered his resignation and will leave at once for Reno, Nev., where he will take charge of the Majestic theater, conducted by the Nixon estate. He will be succeeded here by Meyer Cohen, who has filled the position of head salesman at the Los Angeles office for some time, and who also has a wide acquaintance in the local field. When Mr. Edmonds goes to Reno he will take with him Architect M. V. Politeo, and plans will be considered for remodeling and enlarging the Majestic. It is also planned to erect a large amusement place with tea rooms, dancing floors, hanging gardens, soft drink parlors and the like on property adjoining this house owned by the Nixon estate.

Higher Prices With Increased Attendance.

San Francisco, Cal.—The new schedule of prices at the Imperial theater has been a success beyond all expectations, and instead of there being a falling off in patronage, as was expected by Manager J. A. Partington, there has been an increase in attendance since these were announced, with a marked gain in receipts. More seats at 35 cents are now being sold than was ever the case at 20 cents and on two occasions during August all former records for attendance and for receipts were broken. This is considered remarkable especially since a street car strike is in progress here that interferes with night business to a considerable extent. Business has shown a gain of almost thirty per cent. since the higher scale of admission prices was placed in effect.

R. A. Duhem Finds Business Brisk.

San Francisco, Cal.—Ray A. Duhem, of the Duhem Motion Picture Manufacturing Co., reports that business has been quite active of late, both in the line of camera work and in finishing and developing. He was commissioned to make a three-reel picture covering the recent visit of the Imperial Japanese mission to this city and accompanied the party headed by Viscount Ishii to Mount Tamalpais, the Yosemite Valley and other scenic spots in Northern California. One print of the film made has been sent to the President of the United States and another to the Emperor of Japan.

"The Lone Wolf" Makes a Hit.

San Francisco, Cal.—The Selznick release, "The Lone Wolf," has met with such favor here that the management of the Strand theater has retained it for a second week's run. Bert Lytell, who portrays the leading role, has for years a stock company idol in this city, and many of his former admirers came to see him in his first film appearance.

Changes in K-E-S-E Sales Force.

San Francisco, Cal.—H. W. Korper, who has been with the local K-E-S-E branch since the first of the year as outside salesman, has resigned and will leave for Chicago shortly to accept an important position.

Miss Irene Miller has been added to the traveling staff and is now on the road for K-E-S-E visiting exhibitors and appearing before women's clubs, educators and public bodies in the interests of the Conquest series.

Photoplayer Company Issues House Organ.

San Francisco, Cal.—The American Photoplayer Company has commenced the publication of a monthly house organ entitled "Fotoplayer Notes." This is edited by Jack Levy, of the recently inaugurated publicity department, and is designed to bring the various departments and branches of the company into closer touch with each other. Considerable space is given in the initial number to the new organ recently installed in the T. & D. Tivoli opera house.

New Exchange Making Improvements.

San Francisco, Cal.—The Select Pictures Corporation, which has succeeded the Lewis J. Selznick Enterprises, has taken over the former quarters of this concern at 985 Market street and is installing a large film vault and making other improvements of a permanent nature. District Manager Ben S. Cohen is making a short visit to Seattle to be present when the branch at that point moves into its new building.

R. B. Quive Off On Vacation.

San Francisco, Cal.—R. B. Quive, manager of the local branch of the Greater Vitagraph, has left for Chicago on a short vacation trip, the first in several years, and will attend a family reunion. Before leaving he gave a trade showing of the new serial, "The Fighting Trail," and started an active campaign on this. Western Division Manager H. D. Naugle is in charge of the local office during the absence of Mr. Quive.

Brief Northwest Items.

Weiser, Idaho.—M. E. Heath, who formerly conducted the Baker theater, Baker, Oregon, is now engaged in the theater business here.

Oakland, Ore.—Dr. H. H. Owens is preparing to reopen the Bungalow theater Sept. 8. Dr. Owens recently made a trip to Portland to arrange service.

Portland, Ore.—Among the visitors on Film Row during the week of August 25 were H. H. Hurn, Triangle, Seattle; E. E. McDonald, Arcade theater, Dayton, Oregon; W. H. Durham, Grand, Camas, Wash.; E. E. Hettum, Majestic, Kalama, Wash., and Henry Gravenkamp, Peoples, Mt. Angel, Ore.

Notes Gathered at the Exchanges.

Portland, Ore.—Joe Merrick, popular in Portland territory as traveler for General a year or so ago, and until recently Seattle manager for Mutual, was a recent visitor in Portland en route to Los Angeles to take charge of the Mutual office there. The Portland boys are congratulating Mr. Merrick on his well earned promotions.

R. C. Montgomery, traveler for World Film, who has been quite a stranger in these parts, returned to Portland recently. His absence has caused a big and successful offensive movement for business throughout the remote sections of the territory.

The Paramount office is proud of showing three first run pictures in the big downtown theaters at the same time. The Liberty ran "Hashimura Togo," The Columbia Billie Burke in "Mysterious Miss Tarry" and the Peoples' Petrova in "The Law of the Land."

Miss Joe Donnelley, who is managing Lamson's Film Exchange in Seattle, was in Portland recently with "The Barrier," which had a successful second run at the Star. The first run was at the People's in July. Miss Donnelley is reputed to be one of the cleverest "film women" in the business and has a host of friends in this territory.

S. L. Warner, of Warner Bros., who is promoting a co-operative film distribution plan among the exhibitors in the United States, was a recent visitor in Portland in the interests of his proposition.

With the Oregon Exhibitors.

Castle Rock, Wash.—Geo. Kramberger has sold the Dreamland theater to Fred Ragins.

North Bend, Ore.—Denny Hull has completed remodeling the Joy theater and has installed two new projectors supplied by Pete Sabo, of Portland.

Bandon, Ore.—Mrs. E. A. Hartman has opened her theater and is reported to be doing a dandy business.

Mill City, Ore.—F. E. Merrill has sold the Opera House to Bragg and Moran and will retire from the amusement business.

Albany, Ore.—The Rolfe theater, which was recently destroyed by fire, will reopen in about 60 days. Until a few weeks ago the owners were undecided upon the policy of remodeling.

Strand Drops Back to a Dime.

Portland, Ore.—The Strand, Portland's photoville theater, has again put its admission price down to a dime. A few months ago, after making extensive alterations in the theater, the admission was raised to fifteen cents, the price charged in regular photoplay theaters. The Strand shows a program of four acts of vaudeville and a first run photoplay.

Edwin F. James Back in Town.

Portland, Ore.—Edwin F. James, former owner of the Majestic and James' Broadway theaters, has returned to Portland after spending several months in Great Falls, Montana, in promotion work.

Exchanges Now in Portland Are Prosperous

Distributors Now in Oregon Territory Are Enjoying Fall Rush—New Exchanges See the Advantages of Portland's Location.

By Abraham Nelson, Majestic Theater Bldg., Portland, Ore.

PORTLAND, OREGON.—"Our only regret," said C. M. Hill, manager of the new Portland Paramount office, "is that we did not establish a distributing agency in Portland sooner. We now have customers on our books who have never before been users of Paramount service. They objected to the long haul that was heretofore necessary when Oregon territory was served out of other cities than Portland. We are highly gratified with the business our new office is doing and with the enthusiasm with which exhibitors have welcomed our coming to Portland."

As proof of his assertions, Mr. Hill showed the World correspondent a stack of contracts a hand or more high, all signed since the opening of the new office.

Paramount is not the only exchange that is enjoying prosperity, however. W. W. Kofeldt, manager for Pathe, reports the month of August the best in the history of the exchange, topping every record for business.

Manager George E. Jackson, Portland Mutual manager, reports the fall business opening excellently with a record number of contracts for Mutual service being signed during the last two weeks in August.

The indications are that the exhibitors in the territory are waking up to the advantages of doing business with local exchanges and doing away with long hauls on films.

Jewel Productions Opens Office.

Portland, Ore.—Jewel Productions, Inc., has opened headquarters in Portland in the office of the Film Supply Company of Oregon. The office is in charge of Bert Latz, who has the title of Northwest manager. The Portland office will handle Jewel productions in Oregon, Washington, Idaho and Montana and as far east as the Dakotas. Mr. Latz has been with the Film Supply Company and the Universal people in this territory, having at one time been traveling representative out of Portland. He left the Universal office in Seattle to become manager for Jewel. John Meldrum succeeded Mr. Latz in Seattle as Universal manager.

Guy Matlock Makes a Pilgrimage.

Portland, Ore.—It isn't very often that Guy Matlock, manager of the Pendleton Amusement Company at Pendleton, Oregon, travels very far. He stays pretty close to his business in the Round-up city. But he came to Portland the other day to pay his respects to his fellow exhibitors and was seen on Film Row with George Bligh, he of Salem. Mr. Bligh is second vice-president of the Oregon Exhibitors' League and Mr. Matlock is fourth vice-president, so they undoubtedly had a perfect right to be in each other's company.

Mr. Matlock's company controls four theaters in Pendleton and he reports all of them prosperous. His purpose in being in Portland was to line up the big services.

Columbia Theater Fixes Up.

Portland, Oregon.—E. J. Myrick, supervisor of the Jensen -& Von Herberg interests here, is making improvements in the Columbia theater that will make this house a strong bidder for popularity against the big Liberty, the other Jensen & Von Herberg theater in Portland. A split velvet curtain, the same style as is in use at the Liberty, new lighting system, decorations, carpets and draperies are being fitted into the theater. Mr. Myrick is personally supervising the improvements, the details of which are being at-

tended to by Percy Collins of Seattle, the man who designed the interior of the Liberty.

The Liberty will take up the fashion show idea successfully used at the Columbia last winter and each Monday living fashion models will be exhibited.

New Mutual Manager at Portland.

Portland, Ore.—George E. Jackson, who was recently selected manager of the Portland office of the Mutual Film Corporation, entered

George E. Jackson.

the film industry in 1915 as salesman for Mutual at Minneapolis office. Mr. Jackson worked out of the Minneapolis and Fargo offices of Mutual for about a year and a half, when he was transferred to the Pacific Northwest territory. Prior to becoming a film salesman, he was traveller for the American Tobacco Company for five years.

As travelling representative for Mutual out of Portland, Mr. Jackson has made a host of friends in the film fraternity who are glad to hear of his promotion to managership.

Alex Tagg Will Run Only the Big Ones.

Astoria, Ore.—Alex Tagg, who owns the Jewel theater, Astoria, Ore., was a recent visitor in Portland, booking service, and has announced the new policy of his theater. Mr. Tagg believes there are now enough "big" pictures in the market to run this class exclusively and has made his bookings accordingly. He reports business good in Astoria.

C. Morton Cohen Back in Portland.

Portland, Ore.—S. Morton Cohen, always a real factor in the theatrical situation of the country, is back in Portland after a protracted stay in the East and in California. Whether he has any plans for New Portland enterprises is not divulged. Mr. Cohen controls the Photoville theater in Los Angeles and was the man who originated photoville at the Portland Strand several years ago.

Charles Schram Takes a New Hold.

Oregon City, Ore.—Charley Schram, the veteran theater man here, is planning a big season next year and is preparing for it by making many changes in the theater. New projection equipment has been installed and he is now throwing a much better picture than formerly. Other improvements along the lines of decorations and general building repairs have been started which, when completed, will put new "pep" into the old Grand.

Soldiers Admitted Free.

Portland, Ore.—For a week prior to the departure of Oregon troops to the American Lake cantonment, the Portland downtown theaters admitted soldiers in uniform free. The invitation was extended through the Motion Picture Exhibitors' League of Oregon at the suggestion of the ladies' auxiliary of the Oregon military bodies. Although the exhibitors urged the soldiers to make full use of the free admission courtesy the boys were most considerate and did not abuse the privilege.

Stories of the Films

General Film Company, Inc.

KALEM.

POLITICS IN PUMPKIN CENTER (Ham and Bud Comedy).—The cast: Ham (Lloyd V. Hamilton); Bud (A. E. Duncan); The Girl (Juanita Sponsier); The Father (John Stepping); Weary Willie (Henry Murdock).

Election day in Pumpkin Center is over, and the same old gang is in again. Ham has been elected to every office, from mayor to fire insurance agent, and Bud is his assistant in every office. Ham's first official act is to make the town "bone dry." That does not prevent him from storing up a few cold bottles in his own house.

When Weary Willie meanders into town and finds these bottles in the mayor's wine cellar, he proceeds to empty them, and very soon shows the effects. He is arrested for breaking the prohibition law and brought up for trial before Judge Ham. The villagers clamor that the tramp show them where he got the "stuff." When Willie leads them to the mayor's home, it's all up with the mayor. Ham is bounced, and Bud is given the job.

Planning revenge, Ham makes out a fire insurance policy and tries to set fire to his house. But Bud, as the official fire department, proves too much for him, and Ham tears up the policy in despair. Just then his house catches fire by accident. Although Bud effects a thrilling rescue of the occupants, the house burns to the ground, and Ham looks for his policy that will enable him to collect the insurance. He is about to pick up the torn policy to put it together again, when a breeze carries it right into the fire, and Ham decides that politics in Pumpkin Center is a bad business.

ESSANAY.

THE FABLE OF THE TWELVE-CYLINDER SPEED OF THE LEISURE CLASS (A George Ade Fable) (Two Parts).—The cast: Mr. Basker (George Besa); Mrs. Basker (Frankie Raymond); Their Son (Rodney LaRock); Their Daughter (Hazel Coats); Her Husband (William Brotherhood).

In a Town where "Flivs" are still called Automobiles, enjoying the Comforts of Hard Labor, were Pa and Ma Basker. Ma's pride is her Geraniums was only equaled by his Interest in the factory on the River bank. They split Fifty-Fifty on their Affection for their Progeny, which totaled One of Each.

Though they were bursting with Rube Health, when Son succeeded in Hooking a contract which converted the Shop into a War-Baby it was hardly a Task to persuade the Old Folks to Knock Off and Live Up to the dignity of their Sudden Accumulations.

Seeing America first to them meant taking a Limited and stopping off where the Lights Dazzled the most. Cabarets, Dansants, à la Cartes and Golluf took the place of Church Socials, Spelling Bees, Chicken Suppers and Raising Vegetables in their Round of Pleasure.

For an excuse to Settle back in the old Grind, Pa Basker would have Split a large hunk of that Contract, but as it was he had to live up to his Income Tax.

SELIG.

SELIG WORLD LIBRARY NO. 16.
U. S. Government Weather Bureau.—The bomb meter, a mercurial instrument for indicating atmospherical pressure per unit of surface. Rules for forecasting the weather and for messuring elevation. The anemometer is an instrument that registers the velocity of the wind. The weather vane, which electrically records the direction of the wind. Delicate instruments are housed in a shelter, tower, and a triple register

records their readings. Testing official thermometer for low temperature and accuracy.

The Great Wheat Harvest of the U. S.—The U. S. leads the world in wheat production, which is the most important of the cereal industries. Harvest hands leaving for the fields. Wheat farms of western States are largest in the world, some possessing 20,000 acres. These farms are divided into sections and worked by separate crews. One section of a North Dakota farm operating fourteen reapers. Modern machines will thrash from 1,500 to 2,000 bushels of wheat in a day. A novel device which threshes the standing grain and leaves the straw as fertilizer. Tractors are used to pull a combination reaper and thresher. Steamships transport the grain to huge elevators. Preparing for the winter crop. A tractor with eight plows. A young Dakota with her heritage.

Breeding Silver Foxes—Animals sought by trappers for their valuable fur are now scientifically raised on a big ranch. Some of the foxes are valued at $6,000 each.

Arsenic Squads to Save Crops.—Agricultural interests send men to destroy grasshoppers and army worms attacking crops. Mixing the poison. Mr. Grasshopper greedily eats the mixture.

IN AFTER YEARS.—Lucile Danvers (Eugenie Besserer); Her Sister (Lyllian Brown Leighton); Stephen Landers (Wm. Stowell). Written by E. K. King. Directed by E. A. Martin.

"In After Years" is the story of a woman whose youthful loveliness and charm begin to succumb to the ravages of time and whose soul surrounds the jealousies and ambitions of prestige to become interested in the shadowed lives of the unfortunate, so that they can enjoy what the generosity of unselfish wealth can bring to them.

Universal Film Mfg. Co.

UNIVERSAL CURRENT EVENTS.

ISSUE NO. 17 (Sept. 8).

For Immediate Service in France West Point Graduates 152 Fighters.—Secretary of War Baker reviews them and presents diplomas and stirring advice—West Point, N. Y. Subtitles: Here is developed the brains of the American Army. The arrival of the Nation's war chiefs. Review of the entire cadet body. No finer display of men that can be found. Secretary Baker presents the diplomas. It was West Point's most glorious day—except for the rain. The graduating commanders of our new forces, who finished their rigid training nine months ahead of time. Secretary of War Baker and Chief of Staff Hugh L. Scott.

Kiddies and Khaki Combine in Patriotic Pageant at Jersey Resort.—War turns the famous annual baby parade into a brilliant military fete—Asbury Park, N. J. Subtitles: Liberty (Miss Grusilla Taylor) makes a spectacular entrance. Presentation of colors to New Jersey soldiers. Master William Thompson, prize winner, as "Our Billy Sundae."

It's Never Too Late for Bathing Suits—in Chicago.—Here are the new fall styles in—ah—dimples and near-the-water costumes. Chicago, Ill. Subtitles: President Wilson's Chicago double, whose name is Westphall, assisted Miss Columbia in reviewing the revelations.

"Good Luck, Boys!" Good Night. Kaiser Bill!"—Two million New Yorkers yell wild farewells to 30,000 guardsmen marching off to the front—New York City. Subtitles: The city's $50,000 farewell dinner to the 30,000 at Van Cortlandt Park. There was turkey and fixin's for all. Mrs. Charles E. Hughes, Mrs. Cornelius Vanderbilt, Jr. and Mrs. John Purroy Mitchel saw to it that things ran smoothly. Tramp, tramp, tramp: The boys are marching, keen to fight for Liberty. Major General O'Ryan, Divi-

sion Commander, and his staff, leading the parade. Col. Cornelius Vanderbilt, commanding the 22d Engineers. Fifth Avenue was a cheering turmoil. At the reviewing stand—Governor Whitman, Theodore Roosevelt and Mayor Mitchel. Full of pep, the lads seemed eager to get into the game at once. The emblem of their hearts. And they'll play a star part in making this world safe for democracy. A field supply train, seen from the Flatiron Building. Did they want a drink? They did. They got it. Beware! the Sammies are coming! "Good-bye, New York—till we meet again!" The object of this war is to deliver the free peoples of the world from the menace and the actual power of a vast military establishment controlled by an irresponsible government, which, having secretly planned to dominate the world, proceeded to carry out the plan without regard either to the sacred obligations of treaty or the long-established practices and long-cherished principles of international action and honor; which chose its own time for the war; delivered its blow fiercely and suddenly; stopped at no barrier of law or mercy; swept a whole continent within the tide of blood—not the blood of soldiers only, but the blood of innocent women and children also, and of the helpless, of the poor—and now stands balked but not defeated, the enemy of four-fifths of the world.—From President Wilson's reply to the Pope.

ANIMATED WEEKLY.

ISSUE NO. 88 (Sept. 5).

British Recruiting Chief Visits Great Southwest—Sir William White, distinguished Briton, honored in pretty West Coast City—Los Angeles, Cal. Subtitles: Gen. White and his staff of recruiting officers, who have done fine work in America. Mayor Woodman welcomes Gen. White.

Sea Wolf Gets the "Verdi."—Italy's daring merchant ship—430 feet long—succumbs to assassin's undersea stab. Somewhere in the Atlantic. Subtitle: The "Verdi" in New York Harbor.

When They Go After 'Em, They Get 'Em.—Two Prussian man hawks brought to earth by American Eagles—in the Vosges. Subtitles: When our complete flying force is at work, this will be an every-day occurrence! These birds of prey must be bagged—Civilization demands it!

Society Sees Diving Venus Dive.—When annette Kellermann performed for charity, the fashionables paid in $4,000 and crowded to board her—Bar Harbor, Me. Subtitle: The cheapest seat in the famous swimming club is $5.

Women Win New Honors in Trap Shooting Meet.—There were 800 pigeon hunters at the big American event, and the slaughter was terrific—South Shore, Chicago. Subtitles: Marc Aris, of Thomasbare, Ill., national champion. Look out! Mrs. Topperwein, a Texas professional, hit 91 targets out of 100.

Uncle Sam's Tars Enjoy Work and Nature.—Beautiful Balboa Park scene of activity while boys await orders to fight—San Diego, Cal. Subtitle: No hotel boasts a more wonderful dining room.

Twenty-second Engineers Arrive at Southern Camp.—Crack command goes into final training for the trip "Over There"—Spartanburg, S. C. Subtitle: Arrival of advance guard and supply train.

Selected for Honors in France. 30,000 Thrill Millions.—New York's boys, not yet in uniform, ready for service in the New National Army.—New York City. Subtitles: The flag's honor will be upheld! You'll hear from them when they get a crack at the enemy. And the enemy thought we could not raise an army!

Over the Cameraman's Shoulder in the War Zone.—Unusual views of action that were made under extraordinary conditions. Subtitles: The only voice of democracy that makes autocracy listen. It will talk the enemy into submission. These boys peep out from under their canvas, flags blankets and hand the enemy a few reminders that the world is not ready for fake "peace" bids. After the reminders are delivered bridges are constructed so that the invincible French infantry can add emphasis to the message. You have heard of straws? Watch this! The man whose earthly kingdom was ravaged, only to establish for him his people a vaster kingdom in the heart of civilization. With the French Minister of Munitions, Mr. Albert Thomas, in Rumania. At Harlem Station, With Gen. Berthelot and the presidents of council, Mr. Thomas awaits the arrival of the king. The ancient ceremony of bread and salt. Gen. Berthelot is decorated for bravery. The king of Rumania and Mr. Thomas review the troops leaving for the front.

STAR FEATURETTE.

THE RIGHT MAN (Two Parts—Rel. Week of Sept. 17).—The cast: Morgan Green (J. Warren Kerrigan); Frank Case (E. N. Wallack); Lillian Manley (Edith Johnson); Edward Manley (Harry Griffith); Fred Rose (Charles Cummings). Scenario by William Parker. Produced by Henry McRae.

Morgan Green, teller, and Frank Case, cashier, are both in love with Lillian, the daughter of the bank president, Edward Manley. She loves Morgan and promises to marry him, and while Manley is in favor of him, still he counsels them to wait until Morgan has a better position. Frank thinks there is a chance for him.

One day Frank, in revenge, tampers with a bundle of bank notes which are sent in for a factory payroll and leaves Morgan's knife beside the bundle. Later Morgan is accused of theft, and, while he denies it, the evidence is so strong that he is thought guilty. Through the pleadings of Lillian, who believes him innocent, Morgan is only dismissed from the bank, and he leaves for a ranch town nearby.

Left with a clear field, Frank ingratiates himself with Manley. When the bank commissioners deliver the ultimatum that unless the capital of the bank is increased it will have to close its doors, Manley accepts the proffered aid of Frank. He then persuades Lillian that, through a sense of obligation, she should accept him as a husband. She finally consents, though she still loves Morgan.

Fred Rose, a bank messenger in the firm, knew of Frank's act in connection with the stolen bank notes. Theratening him with exposure, Fred compels Case to give him a vacation. He goes with his invalid sister to the same town in which Morgan is staying. Soon after the latter rescues the little sister from a runaway at risk of his own life.

Fred feels that he must tell Morgan of Frank's act and does so. It is now about noon, and the marriage of Frank and Lillian is to take place in three hours. With much evading of constables and farmer deputies, they at last reach the Manley home just in time to stop the wedding. A few hours later a wedding takes place in which Lillian and Morgan are the principals.

L-KO.

A PRAIRIE CHICKEN (Two Parts—Rel. Week of Sept. 17).—The cast: Mrs. De Coin (Fay Holderness); Her Son (Al Forbes); Her Daughter (Kathleen Emerson); The Prairie Chicken (Merta Sterling); Count Notta Cent (Al Edminston). Directed by Vim Moore.

"Sending my daughter to you for visit. Arrives 3 p. m. today. Hank." Mrs. De Coin read the telegram and passed it to her daughter and her son.

About 3 o'clock there was a frightful disturbance in the driveway, and an auto appeared, upon the radiator of which was perched a striking figure, in wide-brimmed hat, chaps and flannel shirt, with a big gun in each hand. It was Brother Hank's daughter, who had shot up all the traffic cops in her progress from the station to her aunt's home. Mrs. De Coin and Kathleen were horrified, but Algernon, the son, found a strange attraction in the apparition.

They made her put on "civilized" clothes, but she insisted upon wearing her guns over them. She slept on the floor and insisted upon Al's giving her a ride on the tea wagon.

Count Notta Cent was arranging for the kidnapping of Kathleen, Mrs. De Coin's daughter, while she was joy riding. Mert, the young girl from the West, saw the affair from her room. She dropped from the balcony onto her horse and chased the machine. Catching the branch of a tree, she swung off it into the car, beat up the count and rescued the girl. The delighted mother could no longer withhold her blessing from the couple, Al and Mert, and it was planned to celebrate the engagement with a ball.

A barefoot dancer was engaged as entertainer. Mert, at first shocked, then decided to draw attention to herself by dancing with the butler, who was detailed to hold up her train. She landed the poor man in the fountain, and, tiring of her hoopskirts, rushed upstairs to put on her chaps. Mrs. De Coin, in the meantime, catches her servants robbing the safe. A chase follows the cry of "Stop thief!" all the way to the roof. The thief drops the jewels down a gutter pipe, and they fall into Mert's lap. She gives chase, too, and finally catches the man on the edge of a drawbridge just going up in the air. She roped him, pulls him down, restores the jewels to her aunt, and plunges the thief into the river, where he finds a watery grave.

UNIVERSAL SCREEN MAGAZINE.

ISSUE NO. 37 (Rel. Week of Sept. 17).

Fashions in aviation suits is the first subject of the Universal Screen Magazine, Issue No. 37. We see a suit of black bearskin and an overcoat of sheepskin, such as is the regulation wear of Uncle Sam's airmen. W. H. Bleakly, United States Instructor, shows a one-piece linen suit, which he fancies, and "Doc" Allen, formerly of the British Royal Flying Corps, shows us one of leather-lined muskrat skins.

The making of armadillo baskets from the shell of the quaint little animals found in Southern Texas comes next. A demonstration of the proper way to can corn, as it is done in the United States Department of Agriculture by the cold-pack method follows. We are instructed to apply for further information to the Director of Extension, College of Agriculture.

"Better Babies" is taken up again by the Screen Magazine, with views of the milk stations maintained by the New York Department of Health. Women wireless operators, working in the classes conducted at Hunter College, New York, takes care of preparedness in this issue.

A "Miracle in Mud," by Willie Hopkins, the Screen Magazine's wizard sculptor, finishes the reel. It is called "The Kaiser's Thermometer," and is a timely satire.

JOKER.

HAWAIIAN NUTS (One Reel—Rel. Week of Sept. 17).—The cast: The Ukelele Nightingale (Gale Henry); Professor Jasbo (Milton Sims); Happy Unlucky (William Franey); The Blackhand Chief (Milburn Moranti). Written and adapted for the screen by R. A. Dillon. Produced by W. W. Beaudine.

Bill is chucked out of the recruiting office and feels that there is no place for him in a disjointed universe. Wandering down the street, he sees a man approach another and slip him a wad of bills after making some strange passes in the air.

"Good enough to try, anyway!" says Bill, and, going up to the man, he waves his hands in imitation of the motions. The next thing Bill knows he is on his back in a den, with a lot of sinister ruffians bending over him. The chief asks him if he wants to join his blackhand band.

"I join any kind of a band but a Joiman band," says Bill, and he is initiated at once. Then comes the drawing of lots. Bill has no idea what it is for, but he doesn't want to be left out of anything. So, in a moment, he finds himself commissioned to take a ukelele filled with dynamite to the chief's inamorita. She is a lovely lady, with a passion for Professor Jasbo, who teaches the ukelele, and who, the chief fears, has stolen her heart away from him.

They are in the midst of a party when Bill arrives. A message from the chief lets him into the charmed circle at once, and he joins the group on the floor, having placed the dangerous instrument out of harm's way. There is a pause for refreshments, and in the scramble for the eats Bill mixes the instruments and brings back the loaded one to the chief instead of Jasbo's. The chief strikes a chord, and the whole gang goes up in smoke.

CIRCUS SARAH (One Reel—Rel. Week of Sept. 17).—The cast: Sarah (Gale Henry); Rudolph Ringtail (Milton Sims); Animal Trainer (Charles Haefli). Scenario by Tom Gibson. Produced by Allen Curtis.

Sarah, who lives in Cucumber Center, has a desire to become a circus queen. When the big show comes to town, Sarah takes all her savings and goes to the circus grounds. When she sees Rudolph Ringtail, the owner of the show, she faints right into his arms and murmurs "Yes" to his unspoken question. Rudolph had previously seen Sarah stuff a stout pocketbook into her stocking, so he does not mind. He calls a convenient minister, and the two are made one.

"And now, dearie, a little something to tip the minister," he prompts her. She hands out her bag. In it is a choice collection of powder puff, buttons, samples, a piece of gum, but no money. Rudolph all but faints when Sarah tells him that she spent all her money.

However, the show must go on, so he determines to make use of his bride. Elvira, the Bareback Queen, is sick, and Sarah has to take her place. Sarah, in powder-puff skirts and tights, is a riot, but the only trouble is that the crowd mistakes her for a new clown. Things look pretty bad, when a disgruntled employee hitches the elephant to the big top, and the animal pulls the whole show away by main force.

"At least, we have each other, darling," says Sarah but Rudolph goes into melancholy madness on the spot.

VICTOR.

MARATHON MANIACS (One Reel—Rel. Week of Sept. 17).—The cast: Max (Max Asher); Whiskers (Dave Morris); Pearl (Gladys Tennyson). Produced by Craig Hutchinson.

Max and Whiskers both love Pearl, an athletically inclined young woman, who takes a keen interest in sports. There is to be a marathon race in which Max and Whiskers are the favored ones in the betting, and they are training faithfully for the race, but each one has decided to put something over on the other. They revert to tricks in the training quarters.

On the day of the race Max plants an automobile out on the course and hides it. Whiskers secures a fleet horse and hides the animal in a safe place. Max and Whiskers watch each other. They drop out of the race, and Max finds the hidden horse of Whiskers and puts a sharp burr under the saddle. Whiskers has found some nitroglycerine, which he puts in the radiator of the car of Max. They both ride for it and have harrowing experiences with the horse and the machine.

The Marathon runners are plodding along, and the judges are perched in a stand over the road. Pearl is follswing in her automobile. The race finishes with Max and Whiskers arriving at the tape at the same time, Max in the motor car and Whiskers on the horse. The stand of the judges is knocked down in the confusion, but Max loses as Whiskers feebly staggers under the wire—winner by a whisker.

NESTOR.

WELCOME HOME (One Reel—Rel. Week of Sept. 17).—The cast: Eddie (Eddie Lyons); Lee (Lee Moran); Edith (Edith Roberts). Scenario by Fred Palmer. Produced by Roy Clements.

Eddie writes a letter to his wife, Edith, telling her that he will be home tomorrow at 10.30, and that he will see her at the station. He forgets to mail the letter. When he arrives at the station in his home town, he is surprised not to find his wife and consoles himself with the reflection that she wants to surprise him at home. So home he starts.

Eddie has two unpleasant encounters with the bum who tried to take his satchel at the station. The latter makes a getaway on a car, goes to a back door for a handout, finds that there is no one at home and that the back door is unlocked and goes in. It happens to be Eddie's home. Eddie arrives and goes in the front way. Lee hears him coming and hides. Eddie comes through the house, finds the back door unlocked, locks it and goes upstairs for a bath. Lee, finding door locked, starts out the front way, but has a desire to see what is upstairs. He sneaks up, finds Eddie is in the bath, changes his clothes for the ones Eddie left in the adjoining room to the bath room, and starts away, when Edith returns from shopping.

Lee hides, but finally gets away, only to be caught by an officer outside and taken to the jail hospital. Edith hears Eddie in the bath room, thinks it is a burglar, calls a cop, has Eddie arrested. Later both are in a hospital ward at the jail recovering from the clubbings they received, when Edith calls to find Eddie, whose grips she has found in the house. She is directed to Lee, who had Eddie's clothes and papers on him when arrested. The mistake is discovered and Eddie is finally welcomed home by Edith.

BISON.

THE LAST OF THE NIGHT RIDERS (Two Parts—Rel. Week of Sept. 17).—The cast: Bob Pritchard (Frank Lanning); Ted Pritchard (Fred Church); Jim Hoyle (Leonard Clapham); Sue Hoyle (Eileen Sedgwick); Orrin Black

(Noble Johnson). Scenario by Karl Coolidge. Produced by Henry McRae.

Jim Hoyle, an independent tobacco grower, is reading to his wife an account of the fire of the company's warehouses, where a year's supply of tobacco was stored, when Bob Pritchard, his friend the sheriff, with his son Ted, rides into view. The two men continue the discussion of the raids of the Night Riders upon the company's property, while the two young people, Jim's daughter Sue and Bob's son Ted, wander away into the garden, where Ted asks the all-important question. They return to find their fathers quarreling bitterly, and to hear Jim say that the riders are right and that he is going to join them.

Bob is furious, calls his son, tells him to have nothing more to do with the Hoyles, and rides away. As summer approaches, the raiders increase their activities. Bob overhears two of them whispering; one says, "Felton Woods this afternoon at four." Bob determines to investigate.

Meantime, Ted rides near the Hoyle home and whistles for Sue, who quickly goes to him, her father being away. While the two young people are talking, Orrin Black, a neighboring grower, sees them and informs Jim. Jim is furious and raves at Sue, while Black stands trying to get her attention, but she ignores him.

Bob creeps near enough to the group of men, among whom are Jim and Black, to hear them say: "Tomorrow night at the entrance to Box Canyon." Bob gathers together his deputies, instructing them not to fire until the raiders have passed into the canyon, where the deputies can hold them there until morning.

That night, when the raiders are cornered in "The Box," Ted and Sue are with Mrs. Hoyle, who is taken ill. Ted rushes for a doctor, who sends a young fellow to find Jim at once. Ted comes upon Bob, who is covered by Jim. Jim hears Ted asking for him and the reason for so doing. Bob exchanges hats and coats with Jim and has him wear his badge, while Bob puts on the black mask. Ted is taken prisoner by some of the raiders. Black is told to lock him in a shack, and later, when the raiders decide to blow up the warehouse and make a dash for freedom, Black again offers to place the bomb, but instead of putting it near the warehouse, he puts it by the shack, and the explosion immediately occurs. Bob joins the deputies, and they rush to the shack, where they find a body and think it is Ted's.

Bob dashes to Jim's home with the news. Jim is amazed. He enters the bedroom and sees Sue and Ted seated by Mrs. Hoyle's bedside.

Bob is bewildered. Ted tells him that the dead man must be Black, who tried to get rid of him because of Sue, but in the fight Ted overpowered him and escaped.

UNIVERSAL SPECIAL FEATURE.

THE GRAY GHOST (Episode 12—Two Parts—Rel. Week of Sept. 17).—The cast: Morn Light (Priscilla Dean); Hildreth (Emory Johnson); Gray Ghost (Harry Carter); Marco (Eddie Polo); Arabin (Howard Crampton); Cecelia (Gypsy Hart); Jerry Tryon (Lou Short).

"Give me the ring," said the Ghost, and Morn Light obeyed him, when a bullet from Cecelia's revolver crashed past her head and buried itself in the wall of the house. Morn Light fled to her room, while the Ghost seized the half-crazed maid by the arm. She fought him angrily, and, snatching the ring from his hand, tried to break away. Then she pointed the revolver straight at him, but he smilingly said:

"Have you forgotten the only way to kill me?"

Hildreth had followed Morn Light to her room, and the sound of the shooting seemed to restore her senses. She told him that she remembered nothing of what had taken place, and he was more puzzled than ever.

Marco followed Cecelia, and, concealing himself, managed to overhear her telling the crooks her plan to kill Morn Light.

"I have a ring," she said, "the exact duplicate of Hildreth's, which is infected with a deadly poison so that the smallest scratch will cause death."

As Marco was hastening to his friends with this news, he was held up and almost overpowered by several desperate men. He fought them off, and, climbing up a water pipe, escaped by crossing a telephone wire hand over hand.

At the police commissioner's all was in readiness for the visit of the Ghost. His appearance was greeted by the commissioner, but he was immediately covered by the revolvers of Arabin and Tryon, who had concealed themselves, awaiting his promised call for the necklace.

"The safe is open for you," said the commissioner suavely, bowing low.

As the master criminal turned to it, the two men emerged from their hiding place and called to him to hold up his hands.

"Only the Gray Ghost himself can catch me!" he cried, pushing them aside as if they had been children. He then dived into the safe and shut the door. When they opened it, all trace of him had disappeared. Another mystery!

GOLD SEAL.

THE PULLMAN MYSTERY (Three Parts—Sept. 18).—The cast: Robert Cheney (Frederick Montague); Mrs. Cheney (Mrs. Witting); Kathleen (Molly Malone); Kenneth Post (T. D. Crittenden); Jean Hardy (Ray Hanford); Paul Dustin (Lawrence Peyton); Lucille Crallen (Josie Sedgwick); Drake Dunn (Hayward Mack). Scenario by Jack Cunningham. Produced by Charles Swickard.

Drake Dunn, who is employed in the factory of Robert Cheney, has been offered the position of superintendent of the factory of Crallen in Los Angeles. He calls his sweetheart, Kathleen, and asks her to go with him as his wife. She consents. Jean Hardy, a chemist, is also in love with Kathleen. He meets Paul Dustin, the secretary to Robert Cheney, and takes him to a club operated by the workmen of the factory. Jean tells Paul that the men are dissatisfied and will strike if their demands are not met. Paul promises to speak to his employer about the matter, and leaves for Mr. Cheney's residence. He is not at home when Paul arrives, so he sits down and begins to put some of his ideas of the justice of the workmen's demands into the form of a speech, writing it down on the typewriter. Cheney came in and read words accusing employers in general and himself in particular. Angry, he told Dustin that he was a traitor and threatened to call the police. He then lost his temper and attacked the young man, who tried his best to keep him off without doing him harm. Cheney was backed toward the door of the conservatory, when suddenly he relaxed in Paul's grasp, his body became limp, and with a groan he fell to the ground.

Mrs. Cheney, attracted by the noise, rushed in and accused Paul of murdering her husband. The police entered, but Paul managed to escape. In the drawing room of a Pullman on the train approaching the station was Kenneth Post, reading over a letter from his cousin, recommending him to the care of Thomas Crallen, head of the big factory in Los Angeles, to which Drake Dunn had just been appointed superintendent. Post was discouraged because of failing health. Taking out a revolver, Post placed it to his temple. A moment later Paul, reaching the train, fell against the door, which opened with him. He picked up the letter lying beside the body and read: "His doctors are trying to frighten him to death. Give him something to do to keep his mind off himself." The letter was addressed to Thomas Crallen. The temptation was too great for Paul. He removed the clothes from the body and threw the body out of the window as the train crossed a bridge.

Some weeks later Paul, as Kenneth Post, was established as a member of the Crallen company. Having met Crallen's daughter Lucille, Drake Dunn, already tiring of Kathleen, was more than half in love with her. Kathleen was neglected by Drake and had no friends. Jean Hardy had not been able to resist the temptation to follow her to Los Angeles, and she feared the consequences of his meeting her husband. Drake was becoming suspicious of Paul. For one thing, Miss Crallen was too fond of him to suit the superintendent. He happened to see a picture of the supposed slayer of Robert Cheney, whose unrecognized body had been found in the river. The picture was the image of the so-called "Kenneth Post." He, therefore, planned to introduce Hardy and to watch the two men. Their meeting confirmed his suspicions, and he went straight to Crallen with the story.

By this time Lucille was engaged to "Kenneth," and her father refused to believe the story without proof. Hardy, crazed by Kathleen's unhappiness, plans to kill Drake. Paul finds out his plans and follows Drake in the hope of warning him. He misses him and Hardy succeeds in breaking into Drake's house, where he fires, wounding Drake in the arm. Paul has followed with the police. Hardy exclaims: "You'll never get me!" and shoots himself. As he is dying, he confesses to the murder of Robert Cheney. He was in the conservatory and fired through the window into Cheney's back. This clears Dustin, who then confesses to having taken the name of Kenneth Post. He returns all the property found on the train, and Crallen accepts him as a son-in-law. Drake's love for Kathleen revives under her tender care of his wound.

Mutual Film Corp.

SIGNAL.

THE LOST EXPRESS (Chapter II.—The Destroyed Documents—Two Parts—Sept. 24).—The mysterious disappearance of the express train in broad daylight throws the railway organization into a turmoil. Light engine searching crews start from both ends of the short line to locate "The Lost Express." They report no trace of it. The mystery grows. Meantime Valquez and his gang—the only persons who know what has become of the missing train—are in possession of General Thurston's documents and models. They discover that the principal blue print is missing.

Detective Murphy, chief of the railway secret service, holds a consultation with Helen. Murphy is elated when Helen tells him that one of the robbers has a harelip.

Valquez refuses to pay for the Thurston formula until it is complete. The thieves undertake to return to where they have hidden the train and find it. Detective Murphy pursues and is shot. Helen follows Murphy, rescues him in an unconscious state and takes him to a hospital.

Leaving the hospital, Helen sees "The Hare." She pursues him. He boards a moving train. Helen races her car to a bridge over the track. When the train passes, she drops on the roof. Crawling along the car top, Helen sees "The Baron" and "The Hare" sitting near a window in the smoker. Between them lies the all-important paper—the missing blueprint.

MUTUAL STAR PRODUCTION.

THE GIRL WHO COULDN'T GROW UP (Pollard Picture Plays Co.—5 Parts—Sept. 17).—The cast: Peggy Brockman (Margarita Fischer); Herbert Brockman (John Stepling); Mrs. Brockman, her stepmother (Jean Hatheway); Lord George Raleigh (Jack Mower); Wiggens, his butler (Joseph Harris); Tia Ana, the Brockman cook (Lule Warrenton); Iris Stanley (Leota Lorraine); Bertha Stanley (Marjorie Blinn). Written and directed by Harry A. Pollard.

Peggy Brockman and her father live happily on their ranch until the father marries, and the stepmother and her two daughters begin to make life miserable for Peggy. Lord Raleigh, traveling in his yacht incognito, has stopped near the Brockman home for a few days' fishing and is discovered by the socially ambitious Mrs. Brockman and deluged with invitations. He commissions his valet to serve in his stead.

Peggy is forbidden to attend Mrs. Brockman's masked ball in the nobleman's house. She steals away to put a crimp in the party by disabling his shore boat. Through a mishap she finds herself on board the yacht with the real Lord Raleigh. Police, hunting a runaway girl, pursue them to the garden party, where they have sought refuge. Peggy is put in college for the prank and the nobleman enrolls also. One night she climbs into the boys' dormitory by mistake and finds herself in Lord Raleigh's room. He has, on an avowal of love from her, previously secured a marriage license. They escape the dean, but have been discovered and decide to get married to prevent scandal. On the way from the justice's house they are pursued and land in jail. Peggy's horrified family, dragging the bogus Lord Raleigh, arrive at the cell and to the consternation of Mrs. Brockman and her daughters, Lord Raleigh admits his identity and announces that Peggy is his bride.

MUTUAL WEEKLY.

Issue No. 141 (Sept. 12).

Moscow, Russia.—M. Kerensky, new Prime Minister, visits the revolutionary troops. Loyal soldiers promise their leader to continue fighting. Subtitle: All newspapers were suppressed; the news was printed on sheets. The method of distributing the news sheets is shown in this section of the film.

In Champagne.—A German aeroplane, in flames, falls behind the French lines.

Columbus, Ohio.—"Some Flyer!" That's the verdict of the student aviators at Ohio State

(*Continued on page* 1896)

Calendar of Daily Program Releases

Releases for Weeks Ending September 22 and September 29

For Extended Table of Current Releases See Pages 1905, 1906, 1907, 1908.)

Universal Film Mfg. Company

RELEASES FOR THE WEEK OF SEPTEMBER 17.

GOLD SEAL—The Pullman Mystery (Three Parts—Drama)	02680
NESTOR—Welcome Home (Comedy)	02681
L-KO—A Prairie Chicken (Two Parts—Comedy)	02682
UNIVERSAL ANIMATED WEEKLY—Weekly No. 90 (Topical)	02683
STAR FEATURETTE—The Right Man (Two Parts—Drama)	02684
JOKER—Hawaiian Nuts (Comedy)	02685
VICTOR—Marathon Maniacs (Comedy)	02686
UNIVERSAL SCREEN MAGAZINE—Issue No. 37 (Topical)	02687
UNIVERSAL CURRENT EVENTS—Issue No. 19 (Topical)	02688
JOKER—Circus Sarah (Comedy)	02689
BISON—The Last of the Night Riders (Two Parts—Drama)	02690
UNIVERSAL SPECIAL—The Gray Ghost (Episode No. 13—Title not decided—Two Parts—Drama)	02691

RELEASES FOR WEEK OF SEPTEMBER 24.

GOLD SEAL—The Master Spy (An Episode of The Perils of The Secret Service) (Three Parts—Drama)	02693
NESTOR—Taking Their Medicine (Comedy)	02694
L-KO—Title not decided (Two-Reel Comedy)	02695
UNIVERSAL ANIMATED WEEKLY—Weekly No. 91 (Topical)	02696
STAR FEATURETTE—A Romany Rose (Two-Reel Drama)	02697
JOKER—Marble Heads (Comedy)	02698
VICTOR—Your Boy and Mine (Comedy)	02699
UNIVERSAL SCREEN MAGAZINE—Issue No. 38 (Topical)	02701
UNIVERSAL CURRENT EVENTS—Issue No. 20 (Education)	02702
JOKER—The Fountain of Trouble (Comedy)	02703
BISON—The Dynamite Special (Two Parts—Dr.)	02703
UNIVERSAL SPECIAL—"The Gray Ghost" (Episode No. 14—Title not decided (Two Parts—Drama)	02704

Mutual Film Corporation

MONDAY, SEPTEMBER 17, 1917.

MUTUAL STAR PRODUCTION—The Girl Who Couldn't Grow Up (Pollard—Five parts—Drama) 05757-58-59-60-61	
MUTUAL STAR PRODUCTION—The Rainbow Girl (American—Five Parts—Drama) 05762-63-64-65-66	

WEDNESDAY, SEPTEMBER 19, 1917.

MUTUAL—Mutual Weekly No. 142 (Topical)	05767

THURSDAY, SEPTEMBER 20, 1917.

CUB—Officer Jerry (Comedy)	05768
GAUMONT—Reel Life No. 73 (Subjects on Reel; Weaving the President's Portrait; Running an Aeroplane Without Danger; The Principle of the Gyroscope; When a Big Car Goes By (Animated Drawing from Life) (Mutual Film Magazine)	05769

MONDAY, SEPTEMBER 24, 1917.

MUTUAL STAR PRODUCTION—The Runaway (Frohman—Six Parts—Drama) 05770-71-72-73-74-75	
MUTUAL STAR PRODUCTION—Sands of Sacrifice (American—Five Parts—Drama) 05776-77-78-79-80	

WEDNESDAY, SEPTEMBER 26, 1917.

MUTUAL—Mutual Weekly No. 143 (Topical)	05781

THURSDAY, SEPTEMBER 27, 1917.

CUB—Jerry's Big Deal (Comedy)	05782
GAUMONT—Reel Life No. 74 (Subjects on Reel: The Soldiers' Staff of Life; The Correct Time—as Determined by the U. S. Naval Observatory; Beans and Lady Bugs; The Lamprey—A Blood-Sucking Fish; Making Eyeglasses—So Easy (An Animated Drawing from "Life").	

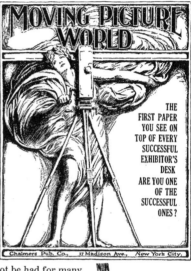

(Continued from page 1893)

University after seeing Ruth Law do some stunts.

The French Offensive in Flanders.—Belgian, English and French are united in a mutual effort. Subtitles: Big trucks loaded with shells keep the roads alive with traffic. Ammunition is plentiful. The big artillery is hammering away at the German trenches. King Albert of Belgium, with General Anthoine, visits the French position.

Camp Gordon, Ga.—Building a barracks in 8 hours. Two hundred men break all construction records. Buildings begun in the morning—finished by afternoon.

Charleston, W. Va.—U. S. Government will build projectile and armor plant. Secretary of the Navy Daniels, breaks ground for $8,000,000 plant.

Washington, D. C.—America's sons who will battle for democracy get rousing send-off. President Wilson leads parade of National Army on way to training camp. Subtitle: In New York, Mayor Mitchel leads the way amid great demonstration.

Ayer, Mass.—First drafted men arrive at Camp Devon and undergo final examination.

San Diego, Cal.—Old exposition grounds now a naval training station. "Jackies" enjoy meals in the most beautiful a la fresco dining-room—in the finest climate on earth.

Temecula, Cal.—Oldest Red Man raises Stars and Stripes over mission he helped to build. Pala Indians celebrate 100th anniversary of the founding of historic church.

GAUMONT.

REEL LIFE NO. 74 (Sept. 27).

The Soldier's Staff of Life.—The government has perfected a portable bread-maker for the army with one of which a baker's corps can supply 40,000 soldiers. These bread-makers were recently exhibited in some of the large cities, resulting in many enlistments.

The Correct Time.—As determined by the U. S. Naval Observatory: One of the branches of scientific research of the U. S. Naval Observatory, at Washington, D. C., is the determining of correct time. This is based over the wires of the Western Union every day at exact noon, when millions of timepieces are regulated.

Beans and Lady-Bugs.—Last year those infinitesimal insects, the aphides, destroyed thousands of dollars' worth of beans. This year, with so many soldiers to be fed, there must be no bean shortage, and so scientists have found an aphicide. They have discovered that these 'little insects are "pie" for the common lady-bug; and now, the lady-bugs are placed on the bean vines and left to do their best.

The Lamprey.—A blood-sucking fish. Unlike the lady-bug, the lamprey does its best to destroy the food supply. Many of the inland waters of the Northwest have been almost depleted of fish because of this eel-like suctorian, which lives on the blood of other fish.

Making Eyeglasses.—Many interesting scenes are shown of the testing of eyesight, and the grinding and mounting of scientific, toric lenses. So Easy.—An animated drawing from "Life." The facility with which one can say "Charge it," until the end of the month arrives in the form of a demon with bills, is cleverly illustrated.

Miscellaneous Subjects

ARTCRAFT PICTURES CORP.

REBECCA OF SUNNYBROOK FARM (Five Parts—Sept. 3).—The cast: Rebecca Randall (Mary Pickford); Adam Ladd (Eugene O'Brien); Hannah Randall (Helen Jerome Eddy); Mr. Cobb (Charles Ogle); Emma Jane Perkins (Marjorie Daw); Jane Sawyer (Mayme Kelso); Mrs. Randall (Jane Wolff); Miranda Sawyer (Josephine Crowell); Rev. Jonathan Smellie (Jack MacDonald); Minnie Smellie (Violet Wilkey); Mr. Simpson (Frank Turner); Mrs. Simpson (Kate Toncray); Clara Belle Simpson (Emma Gerdes).

Rebecca Randall and her large family of brothers and sisters live at Sunnybrook Farm.

---

which is principally remarkable for the size of the mortgage it carries. The task of taking care of all the children is too much for Mrs. Randall, so finally Rebecca is sent away to her two aunts, Miranda and Jane Sawyer, who are strict New England folk. She agrees to sell soap in aid of a fund to buy a banquet lamp for Rev. Smellie.

Rebecca meets young Adam Ladd, and, much to her astonishment, he purchases enough soap to pay for the banquet lamp. When Rebecca tells him about Mrs. Simpson and her lack of a wedding ring, Adam reaches into his pocket, brings forth his mother's wedding ring and gives it to Rebecca to present to Mrs. Simpson. Owing to his bounty, Rebecca thinks that Mr. Ladd is Mr. Aladdin, the hero of the wonderful lamp.

With the children of the village, Rebecca gets up a circus in which she is the bare-back rider, but is routed by Aunt Miranda just as she is doing her most daring stunt.

Rebecca is sent to school, but by her clever verse disgraces the aunt's family, so they decide to send her to boarding school. She returns a beautiful young girl. Adam's admiration for her has grown into love for the young woman. One of the aunts passes away, and later Rebecca learns that the railroad has purchased Sunnybrook Farm.

Rebecca has the Simpson family taken care of and all the Randall children well provided for. When everyone else is happy, Adam Ladd reminds her that when a little girl she had told him she intended to marry him when she grew up.

BUTTERFLY PICTURES.

THE SPINDLE OF LIFE (Five Parts—Sept. 17).—The cast: Gladsome (Neva Gerber); Mrs. Harrison (Jessie Pratt); Jason (Ed. Brady); "Hooky" (Richard La Reno); James Bradshaw (Winter Hall); Vincent Bradshaw (Hayward Mack); "Alphabet" Carter (Ben Wilson). Story from the novel "Gladsome," by Sidney Robinson. Scenario by Karl Coolidge. Produced by George Cochrane.

Mrs. Harrison and her daughter, Gladsome, arrive at their palatial summer residence in Harborport. Mrs. Harrison is a confirmed social climber, and her financial adviser, James Bradshaw, encourages her mania, as he hopes to trade his aristocratic but impoverished son for his client's wealthy daughter.

Mrs. Harrison's cherished idea of social distinction conflicts with her daughter's idea of living, so Gladsome, soon after arriving, makes for "Hooky" and the fishermen, with whom she has been on terms of intimacy since she was a girl in short dresses. Bradshaw and Vincent, his son, are on hand to greet the arrivals, but Gladsome is missing. They find her mingling with her fishermen friends, who have just given her a set of oilskins. The elder Bradshaw takes her away and insults the fisherman. A quarrel results, and Bradshaw forbids them to cross his property, which has saved them a long walk to their work night and morning.

In the city "Alphabet" Carter, a powerful person in the financial world, is advised by his doctor to cease work and take a vacation. He decides upon Harborsport, and arrives on the night that the fishermen have determined to take the right of way by force. Gladsome championing them against the Bradshaws. Gladsome is mixed up in the scrap, and when the police arrive she is carried off with the fishermen. In her oilskins the police have taken her for a boy. When her mother is informed of her daughter's arrest, she, Bradshaw and his son, race to the police station and rescue Gladsome. Some time later Gladsome meets Carter, and a mutual attraction springs up between them. This later ripens into love, and when Gladsome tells Carter that Bradshaw is planning to have her married to his son, Vincent, the money man suggests that she marry him. Gladsome is delighted. Carter is called to the city, where he discovers Bradshaw's operations with Mrs. Harrison's money and lays his plans to ruin the man in order to teach him a lesson and to save the Harrison fortune. Bradshaw, finding the formidable "Alphabet" Carter against him, tries to rush the marriage of his son to Gladsome to cover his loss of the Harrison money.

The little job of ruining the Bradshaws all completed, Carter returns to the beach. Gladsome meets him and they plan to get married that evening, for Bradshaw has announced the engagement dinner for that very night. The ceremony is held in "Hooky's" cottage. When

---

Mrs. Harrison learns of the wedding, she is perturbed beyond measure, but undergoes a revulsion of feeling when told of how Carter had saved her fortune.

BLUEBIRD PHOTOPLAYS, INC.

TRIUMPH (Five Parts—Sept. 3).—The cast: Nell Baxter (Dorothy Phillips); Paul Neihof (Lon Chaney); Dudley Weyman (William Stowell); David Montieth (Wm. J. Dyer); Lillian Du Pont (Clair Dubrey); Rupert Vincent (Clyde Benson); Ida Mayne (Helen Elder). Scenario written by Fred Myton. Directed by Joseph De Grasse.

Nell Baxter's friends and neighbors declared that fame and fortune awaited her behind the footlights. Stealing away from home, Nell made her way to the railroad station and there came upon a traveling theatrical company. To one of the men she confided her ambition.

It is late summer on Broadway when managers are selecting the players for their productions. An amateur from a small country town approaches the stage door of one of the big theaters and asks if there is any chance of her securing employment. It so happens that the ingenue of the company then rehearsing has sent word to the management that she has married and determined to leave the stage. The manager of the company sees Nell and decides that she shall have the part. There is a playwright who has tried without success to have this manager produce one of his plays. The leading lady, in love with the author, has tried her own wiles upon the manager but has failed to accomplish the coveted purpose.

Nell succeeds so well with the small role that has been assigned her that the manager, in pressing his attentions upon her, promises that he will advance her upon the stage as a return for her affections. She has met the impoverished playwright and has fallen in love with him, and, in the circumstances, it is she who is again chosen to urge the manager to produce the playwright's work. Aiming to advance himself further in the good graces of Nell, the manager agrees to produce the play and give the leading role to her.

Meanwhile, the leading lady, who has formerly basked in the good graces of the manager, becomes jealous of Nell and plans vengeance. When the author is in Nell's dressing room, rehearsing a love scene in his play that he wishes to be acted with preciseness, the jealous woman brings the manager to the dressing room door and discloses Nell and the playwright in affectionate embrace. Angered, the manager declares that the production shall then and there be abandoned.

The playwright, his constitution undermined by dissipation, feels the shock of disappointment. He goes to his apartment and sends for a doctor. The doctor gives him a stimulant, with the warning that an overdose would be fatal. When Nell realizes that her ambition to "triumph" upon the stage has been frustrated, she goes to the manager's apartments to plead that he shall reconsider.

The opening performance has been set for that night, and Nell pleads with the manager to let the show go on. He consents after setting his own price upon the girl's ambition. When he attempts to find the bargain, the girl stabs and kills him. Then she descends to the apartments of the playwright and makes a confession of her crime. Before being killed the manager has telephoned to his stage director that the performance shall proceed, and now the young playwright begs the girl to go on with the play and settle for her crime afterwards. She leaves for the theater, the playwright calls up the police, confesses the crime of murder over the telephone, takes the overdose of stimulant that kills him and the two dead men are found exactly as the circumstances have been telephoned to the police. At the theater the climax of the play is approaching. Nell senses that something has gone wrong with the playwright and overhears the truth when two members of the company are discussing the tragedy.

The curtain is up; it is time for the big scene of the play and to make the premier a success for the dead author's sake, the girl heroically goes on and attains her longed-for triumph. But the thunders of applause fall upon deaf ears—the girl has stabbed herself as a climax of the "big scene" and dies while the bravos of the audience resound through the theater.

FOX FILMS CORP.

BETRAYED (Five Parts—Sept. 2).—The cast: Carmelita Carrito (Miriam Cooper); Carpi, her Father (James Marcus); Leopoldo Juarez, outlaw (Hobart Bosworth); Pepo Esperanza, Lepo

---

(Monte Blue); William Jerome, U. S. A. (Wheeler Oakman). Directed by R. A. Walsh.

Carmelita Carrito was in love. The lucky man was Pepo Esperanza, Mexican like herself, an inhabitant of the same little border village of San Lepo. In spite of her fat, crude father, Carmelita had the soul of an aristocrat. Somewhere in her make-up there reposed the spirit of a Carmen. For Carmelita was nothing if not a coquette. The fame of the great bandit, Leopold Juarez, had traveled all over Mexico. When he made a raid on the larder of Carmelita's 'dobe home, therefore, it was natural that the girl should be somewhat impressed by his commanding personality.

The strange events of that day on which Leopold made his raid quite excited the girl. At night she sat by her window and looked lazily out at the Mexican moonlight. Gradually she fell asleep, and she dreamed. Leopoldo returned. She realized for the first time that she was in love with him. An American army officer, William Jerome, was at that very moment nearing her house in search of the man who had raided the territory of the United States.

Jerome came to Carmelita's home. Once more the fickle girl changed her mind and her heart. Now she was in love with the American. As the days passed, she grew to know the Gringo better and to love him more deeply. Finally she wrote him a note. Leopoldo, she said, would be beside her at a neighboring brook. Jerome could creep upon them and pick off his man with a single revolver shot. Then she would be his, body and soul.

Leopoldo intercepted the note, but allowed it to go to Jerome and arranged a counter scheme. When he met her at the brook, he craftily urged her to don his own coat. Then he placed his hat on her head. Jerome, seeing the party through the bushes, thought Carmelita was Leopoldo, and shot the girl he loved. Jerome was taken prisoner and shot. With fainting breath, the heartless Mexican girl whispered to her first lover, who had returned. He must get the Americans at once. Leaping swiftly upon his horse, Pepo rode off in the distance.

Then Carmelita awoke. She was just in time. American troopers, aided by Pepo himself, were closing in on her house. There the bandit, Leopoldo, had taken refuge. And Pepo himself captured Leopoldo and received the reward; and he and Carmelita lived happily ever after.

WHEN FALSE TONGUES SPEAK (Five Parts—Sept. 8).—The cast: Mary Page Walton (Virginia Pearson); Fred Walton, her husband (Carl Harbaugh); Piatt Sinclair (Hardee Kirkland); Helen Lee (Claire Whitney); Eric Mann (Carl Eckstrom); Jimmy Hope (William E. Meehan). Directed by Carl Harbaugh.

Married life proves an empty dream for Mary Page Walton. She knew Fred Walton was no angel, but thought he would mend his ways. Mary closed her eyes to most of her husband's doings. At last, Piatt Sinclair, her husband's lawyer, tells her she should start divorce proceedings.

Sinclair acts on Fred's suggestion. Fred is having an affair with Helen Lee. She thinks he—posing as a single man—loves her. Mary refuses to sue and, to escape the unhappiness of her home, organizes a settlement house in the slums. Eric Mann, a reporter, is assigned to cover Mrs. Walton's social work. His great interest in the work brings them much in each other's company. Sinclair returns to Mrs. Walton one evening to see if she has changed her mind. He finds Eric there interviewing the social worker. Sinclair rushes to Walton, whom he finds with Helen. Taking him aside, he tells him a tale of what he saw in his home. Sinclair's fine imagination adds much color to Eric's business call.

Walton, feeling hurt, tells Sinclair to start suit. When Eric learns of the case he angrily tells Sinclair he will have him disbarred. Sinclair decides to drop the suit. Meantime Mary is living at the settlement house. One night she returns to her home for some of her effects. Walton was giving a little "at home" for Helen. Jimmy Hope, a crook, was also in the house—on a professional call—but had been surprised on his way out and forced to hide behind a fire screen. Walton hides Helen in a closet. The wife hears a rustle and approaches to open the door. She grasps the knob and pulls. Helen, on the inside, pulls, too. Walton finally pushes Mary into the hall. Just then Sinclair is admitted.

Eric now comes up the walk, hears the rumpus inside and stops, uncertain whether to enter. The door opens. Eric leaps into the shadows. Mary hastily comes down the steps and hurries off. Helen now flees from the home. She is followed by Sinclair. As Eric is about to enter the

---

open door, he sees the crook leap out of a window and disappear. The reporter rushes in and
finds Walton dead on the floor. He summons
the police and—is arrested.

The next morning finds Mary on a train going
back to mother. Helen is sitting beside her,
also going home. The morning papers arrive.
Mary learns her husband has been murdered.
She collapses, and Helen tries to calm her. In
curiosity Helen opens the paper and finds a picture of the slain man. She recognizes Walton,
whom she knew under another name. Then she
collapses. Mary suspects Helen is the murderer
and has her brought back for trial.

Meantime, Jimmy Hope has been arrested for
a robbery. While Mary and Helen are at the
police station, the district attorney and Sinclair
enter. Sinclair at his own request, has been
appointed special prosecutor for the case. He
asks that Eric be brought out for a hearing. By
mistake the turnkey brings in Hope.

On seeing Mrs. Walton, Helen and Sinclair,
Hope gasps. Thinking he is to be accused of
murder, he squawks. Jimmy, from behind the
fire screen, had seen all the happenings of the
mysterious night. He traces the movements of
each person in the tragedy and names the person who killed Walton.

GREATER VITAGRAPH.

AN ALABASTER BOX (Five Parts—Sept. 10).
—The cast: Lydia Orr (Alice Joyce); Harry
Bolton (Marc MacDermott); Jim Dodge (Harry
Ham); The Child Lydia (Aida Horton); Fanny
Dodge (Patsy De Forest); Wesley Elliott (Frank
Crane). Authors, Mary E. Wilkins Freeman
and Florence Morse Kingsley. Director, Ches-
ter Withey.

Lydia Bolton is only a child when financial
difficulties overtake her father. His fellow-
townsmen do not give him support and he goes
to the wall. Andrew Bolton goes to prison an
embezzler, crushed by everyone. Lydia is taken
in charge by an uncle and the old Bolton mansion, once a proud landmark, is left to neglect.

Time has not tempered the disposition of the
community when Lydia Bolton comes back, her
identity hidden in the name of Lydia Orr. She
opens her purse first at a church festival, but
her generosity is rewarded only by disparaging
remarks and open hints of ulterior motives. She
lives at the same boarding house as the young
minister and tongues of scandal are at once
loosed.

Then she purchases the old Bolton mansion,
her childhood home, and offers to buy at un-
reasonably high prices all antique furniture in
the town. There is a rush to get all the girl's
money, but a few decent folks seek to protect
her and at once the town is split in two hostile
camps.

The minister has a sweetheart and she is
jealous of Lydia, which adds to the complexity
of her troubles. And in the midst of it all,
Bolton, his prison term ended, steals back to
town. Lydia and a few loyal friends seek to
hide his identity, for a time, at least, but the
senile old man eludes them and goes to the
country store and proclaims himself.

All the pent-up hatred against him now is
turned against the daughter and the towns-
people utterly blind to all she has done for them
and the town, rush to the old Bolton home to
wreck it and lynch Bolton. The old man, aided
by the minister and Lydia's sweetheart, are
striving to protect the girl when Bolton falls
dead. This tragedy disperses the mob and
finally Lydia's enemies come to see her and her
efforts in their true light.

PARAMOUNT PICTURES CORP.

HOLMES IN THE BAHAMAS (Aug. 20).—In
this Paramount-Burton Holmes Travelogue are
seen the beautiful and the unusual things that
are to be found in the Bahama Islands. The
points of interest in this release include the old
sugar mill, the colored police force of the island,
and open-air church services, where blacks and
whites worship together.

Another interesting section of the travelogue
shows a fashionable garden party of the socially
elect at the Colonial Hotel. The opening of a
Royal Palm bud, one of the beautiful specimens
of the flora with which the islands abound;
natives shaking down cocoanuts from the trees,
"Bath House Mary," a local celebrity, and native
dances, to which Mr. Holmes applies the line,
"On with the dance; let joy be unrefined," are
other features in this issue.

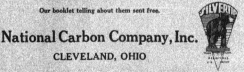

Asilomar, Cal.—Simultaneously with the call of the Nation's warriors to arms, American women mobilize in the country's service. Subtitles: The flag—for one and all.

The Flanders Advance.—For days before the attack huge guns of the allies keep up an incessant fusilade to weaken the enemy's positions. Subtitles: An endless stream of shells to the front assures an adequate supply. Under cover of their barrage the troops calmly launch their bridges across the streams. Soon the first lot of prisoners begins to trail in. Onward—ever onward to the Rhine.

Philadelphia, Pa.—The National Army is ready. Throughout the land cities fittingly honor their soldier sons, regulars of the U. S. A. Subtitles: G. A. R. veterans, heroes of wars gone by, cheer the gallant fighters of 1917. Minneapolis pays warm tribute to her drafted men and National Guardsmen. New York's quota to America's Honor Legion.

Hoch the Kaiser.—Cartoon.

THE ANGEL FACTORY (Astra Film Corp.— Five Parts—Rel. Week of Sept. 16).—The cast: David Darrow (Antonio Moreno); Florence Lamont (Helene Chadwick); Her Mother (Laura West); Betty Montague (Margaret Greene); Tony Podesta (Armand Cortez); Marie Lacey (Suzanne Willa); Sailor Bill Benson (Francis J. Conlan). Directed by Laurence McGill.

In the tenement section of New York there stood a building which was called "The Angel Factory." It had been erected by David Darrow, who devoted all of his time trying to enlighten the people and make them see the bright side of life.

In his slum work David came in contact with Florence Lamont, a girl of the poor. His friendship with her brings with it the uncompromising hostility of a gang leader, Tony Podesta, who is in love with Florence. She shuns him. It also causes David's fiancee, a girl of society, to become jealous of Florence. Thinking, perhaps, that, if she invites Florence to her home to meet her friends, she will cause Darrow, and then he will forget her. On the contrary, Florence acts demurely, and to Betty's astonishment, she is greatly admired by the young men at the reception. Podesta learns of Florence going out with Darrow and decides that he has been fooled long enough. Unfortunately, that night Darrow stops at the factory. Florence bids him good night and goes upstairs. Podesta has followed them home and, seeing Darrow at the window, draws his revolver and is about to fire, when suddenly someone fires and kills him. Hearing the shot, Darrow runs to the body of Podesta. As he is bending over the body, a detective grabs him by the arm and accuses him of the murder. Florence rushes to the scene and explains that she was the one that fired the shot. Showing them her revolver with one shot missing, they are convinced, but on summoning the broker where she purchased the revolver, they find that he filled the gun with blanks. About to leave, the detective picks up the revolver dropped by Podesta. Turning the revolver over in his hand, he sees Darrow's name. Immediately he releases Florence and on circumstantial evidence arrests Darrow.

Sailor Bill, whom Darrow had befriended and brought into the factory, disappeared after the murder. Florence remembered that he and Podesta had not been friendly lately and perhaps he was the one. Searching all over for Bill, Florence finally found him dying in a old seaman's lodge. She implores him to tell her if he killed Podesta. He refused to speak, but when Florence tells him that Darrow is held in prison accused of the crime, he begs to be taken to him at once. At the prison Bill acknowledges that he killed Podesta, a few seconds after the confession he dies. Darrow's fiancee calls off the engagement after she reads of Darrow being accused of murder. This only brought great joy to him, because it released him from a promise made to his father. Florence learns of the broken engagement and consents to teach Darrow how to make a home.

WAR AND THE WOMAN (Thanhouser—Five Parts—Rel. Week of Sept. 9).—The cast: John Braun (Tom Brooke); His Stepdaughter (Florence La Badie); John Barker (Wayne Arey); His Mother (Grace Henderson); Commander of the Invading Army (Arthur Bower); Lieut. Fredericks (Ernest C. Warde). Written by Philip Lonergan. Directed by Ernest C. Warde.

John Braun, an alien under suspicion, and his stepdaughter, Ruth, are accused by the secret service of giving information to one of America's enemies. Braun professes that he is innocent, and is dismissed. Up to the interview, Ruth knew nothing of Braun's actions, but on their way home he acknowledged that he was a spy, and that he wished to have her assist him, but she declined.

The revelation caused Ruth to change her opinion of Braun, and she decided to leave him. She walked to the rear platform of the train and jumped off. Ruth got on unhurt and started off across the country. She had not gone far when an aeroplane crashed to earth. Ruth saw the form of an American aviator entangled in the wreckage. While at the hospital, Ruth called to see the injured John Barker,

a wealthy young American, and it was in this
way that she met his mother, who considered that
Ruth had rendered her a service she could never
repay.

Ruth had the misfortune of losing her position
through a detective who had traced her and informed her employer she was a spy. Her funds
gone, she endeavored to find work, but was unsuccessful. She wanders out into the country
and collapses on a railroad track. She was
saved from death by a brakeman. John's mother
learned that Ruth was ill, and had her brought
to her home. After her recovery Ruth and John
were married.

The war became serious, and John was called
to duty. After his departure Ruth was notified
that the enemy was approaching. Everyone fled
and through a mishap Ruth was left behind. The
troops arrived and took possession of the home.
Among them was Ruth's father, who insisted
that she give him information. She promised
to aid them, with the one thought in mind, that
she might obtain their plans, but she was discovered and made a maid in her own home.

John was granted a leave and came to see
Ruth. By putting on an officer's uniform, he
gained admittance. He saw Ruth and slipped
her a note, telling her to meet him that night.
That night at dinner one of the men was about
to tear the American flag to pieces when Ruth
snatched it from him and fled from the room.
She ran down into the cellar. Thinking she
went on the roof, they climbed out. Ruth had
concealed some dynamite in the cellar. Lighting
the fuse, she rushed to John. As she was about
to climb into the machine, she gazed back, only
to see the house blown into a million pieces.

THE FATAL RING (Episode No. 12.—"The
Desperate Chance,"—Two Parts—Sept. 23).—
Pearl attempts to force the Violet Diamond from
Carslake. Carslake's adherent attacks Pearl,
and allows his master to escape from the car in
which Pearl had cornered him. The master villain leaves over the roofs of the train and is pursued by Pearl. She overtakes him, and after a
desperate fight on the car roof, she is overcome
and thrown to the ground from the fast-moving
train. She falls helpless across the tracks.
Carslake gloats in triumph as the train on which
he is riding takes the siding to allow the express
the right of way.

Tom, following after Pearl in an automobile,
sees her danger, but is unable to flag the fast-
approaching train. In a race with death, he
manages to throw the switch so that the express
is shot on another track, and Pearl is saved.

Tom takes her to her home in the city, and
later one of the Spider's men learns that Carslake is hiding in the home of a friend of his.
Pearl, accompanied by the Spider, Tom and detectives, invades the house. After a terrific fight,
Carslake reaches the roof of the house through
a trapdoor. Pearl comes out on the roof after
him just as Carslake has knocked out Tom, who
preceded her. She sees Carslake run to the edge
of the roof and start over to the next building
on a narrow iron girder. Pearl pursues him,
and Carslake turns at bay, when she is halfway
across the iron girder. Deciding that this is a
good chance to get rid of her, Carslake seizes
her and is about to throw her to the earth several
stories beneath, when the episode ends.

THE SEVEN PEARLS (Episode No. 2—The
Bow String—Two Parts—Sept. 23).—The cast:
Ilma (Mollie King); Harry Drake (Creighton
Hale); Handsome Jack (Henry Gsell).

About to phone the police, Harry discovers the
masked woman to be Ilma. Learning her story
and realizing that it was she he had robbed, he
pledges himself to win back the pearls. Outside
the door a mysterious man is spying on Ilma
and Drake. Suddenly he is attacked by Nemesis,
a man of unscrupulous character. In the struggle Nemesis is overpowered. About to kill him,
the spy sees a peculiar ring on a bracelet, which
is on his arm and decides not to. Hearing a
knock, Drake opens the door, much against
Ilma's wishes. Ilma sees the spy. His arms
are folded; she recoils. Drake attempts to protect her, but she bids him not to interfere. The
spy takes Ilma by the arm, and they walk off,
leaving Harry astounded.

Handsome Jack, one of the gang, whose specialty is the stealing of valuables, carries his
pearl with him, as Harry learns. Jack wishes
to gamble his pearl against the one Harry is
supposed to have. Ilma likes the idea, and as
she mysteriously found a pearl in her room, she
gives it to Harry. Drake shakes dice with Jack
and loses the pearl. To console him, Jack offers
to let him in on a burglary job, but Harry
scorns it. Ilma, who has been following Jack,
manages to meet him through a flirtation, and
decides on desperate means. That night Ilma
follows Jack to a Riverside residence. Stealing
into the house, she finds Jack dressed in armor.
She holds him up. He agrees to give her the
pearls. Turning a bit, Jack matches the gun
from Ilma's hand and is about to escape, when
Harry enters. Drawing two swords, they fight
like two knights of old. Harry recovers the
pearls and gives them to Ilma. Jack escapes
and Harry follows him. As Ilma is admiring
the pearls, a curtain is thrown over her head,
and the pearls are taken from her.

Classified Advertisements   NOTE TERMS CAREFULLY

Remittances must accompany all orders for classified advertisements as follows: One dollar per insertion for copy containing twenty words or less. Five cents per word on copy containing over twenty words. Each word to be counted including names and addresses.

NOTICE TO ADVERTISERS—The Publishers expect that all statements made in every advertisement will bear the strictest investigation.

SITUATIONS WANTED.

OPERATOR, strictly experienced, desires position first-class theater only. Handle only best equipment. Perfect projection guaranteed. Henry Alsman, Dyersburg, Tenn.

AT LIBERTY—A-1 pianist, drummer, with bells, xylophones, effects. Cue pictures. References. Union. Box 142, Winchester, Ohio.

OPERATOR desires position, at present employed—past two years in high class vaudeville house. Good habits, interview, communicate. C., care M. P. World, N. Y. City.

OPERATOR and electrician, with experience, wants position in first-class theater. Perfect projection guaranteed, reference furnished. Exempt from military service. Will go anywhere. State everything in first letter. Address W. C. Morrow, Livingston, Ala.

ORGANIST—Wurlitzer. Now employed, desires change. Sober, reliable, A-1 picture player. F. X. Keenan, 156 S. Tenn. Ave., Atlantic City, N. J.

EXPERIENCED motion picture organist, desires position in New York. Must be pipe organ. L., care M. P. World, N. Y. City.

BUSINESS OPPORTUNITIES.

FOR SALE—Theater and store building, store rents for one hundred twenty-five per month. Address J. Rantschler, Harlem, Mont.

THEATERS FOR SALE OR RENT.

THEATER TO RENT IN WORCESTER, MASSACHUSETTS (THE CITY OF PROSPERITY), CITY OF 175,000 PEOPLE. CENTRALLY LOCATED, SEATING 1,100. APPLY F. W. TAYLOR, 438 MAIN ST.

TWO theaters in town close together. Central States, good proposition. Address Theaters, care M. P. World, N. Y. City.

MOVIE FOR SALE—One of the brightest and most attractive propositions in State of Iowa; admission 10 and 15 cents; seating capacity 350; only theater in town; real estate 5 years old; price six thousand; good business. Lewis, 580 Ellicott Square, Buffalo, N. Y.

MOVING PICTURE HOUSE, Newport, R. I.; admission, 5 and 10c; seating capacity 587. This proposition is run mostly by hired help, as the owner spends the winter in Boston, and under these conditions, clears $85 per week over and above all expenses. This is the only straight picture house in town, showing eight reels; price, eight thousand. Lewis, Moving Picture Broker, 580 Ellicott Square, Buffalo, N. Y.

THEATERS WANTED.

I WANT to rent a moving picture theater, equipped ready for business. Give full particulars. A. E. Read, 28 Cornell Ave., Massena, N. Y.

EQUIPMENT FOR SALE.

GUARANTEED MACHINES—Slightly used type S-1917 model, Simplex motor drive, factory guarantee, at reasonable prices. Room 206, 1482 Broadway, N. Y. City.

FOR SALE—A full moving picture house equipment, 300 opera chairs, machines, operating booths, fans, and miscellaneous equipment. Reasonable price to quick buyer. Must vacate at once. Address Box 28, Norwalk, Conn.

USED opera and folding chairs, large quantities in stock; also upholstered; all in excellent condition. Bargains. Atlas Seating Co., 10 East 43d St., N. Y. City.

3,000 OPERA CHAIRS, steel and cast frames, 60c up. All serviceable goods, cut prices on new chairs. Six standard asbestos booths. Send for weekly list of close outs and save half. J. F. Redington, Scranton, Pa.

FOR SALE at your own figure, one Wotton transverter, 110 volts, 60 cycles, in good running order; also switchboard for same and electric baseball game board for stage. If taken at once, fifty dollars takes the whole outfit. F. O. B. Salamanca. Address Strand Theater, Salamanca, N. Y.

CAMERAS, ETC., FOR SALE.

DAVID STERN COMPANY, INCORPORATED. 'EVERYTHING IN CAMERAS.' PIONEERS IN THE MOTION PICTURE FIELD. SPECIAL—400 ft. U. S. Professional Automatic Dissolve. Forward and reverse, regular and trick crank with Pan. and Tilt Tripod, $230.00. EXCLUSIVE DISTRIBUTORS FOR THE DAVSCO. AGENTS FOR THE UNIVERSAL. WRITE OR WIRE FOR OUR SPECIAL PROPOSITION. DAVID STERN COMPANY 'Everything in Cameras.' In business since 1885. 1027-29 R Madison St, Chicago, Ill.

TO ALL INTERESTED IN MOTION PICTURE CAMERAS. WRITE AT ONCE FOR BEST BARGAIN LIST OF USED UNIVERSAL CAMERAS. LARGEST SELECTION IN THE COUNTRY, NEW AND USED. PRICES: 1915 MODELS, $185.00, 1916 MODELS FROM $200.00 to $225.00. 1917 MODELS FROM $225.00 to $260.00. Write for special propositions on new Universals. Prompt shipment, telegraphic orders shipped five minutes after receipt. Our list of satisfied customers grows every week. Latest buyers of Bass Bargains; A. N. Harlow, Chattanooga, Tenn. J. L. Schrode, LaSalle, Ill. R. F. Hildebrand, Des Moines, Iowa. Several others. You, too, will be pleased at our prompt, satisfactory service. Quality cameras only. Our complete sixty-six page camera catalog ready for distribution, free on request. The latest and best book on Motion Pictures, "How to Make and Operate," postpaid, $1.10. WRITE TO CAMERA HEADQUARTERS OF AMERICA AT ONCE. BASS CAMERA COMPANY, CHARLES BASS, PRES., 109 NORTH DEARBORN ST., CHICAGO, ILL. MOTION PICTURE CAMERA DEPT.

PATHE Professional outfit complete for most exacting studio work. Better than new. Could not be duplicated under $850. Make offer this week. Hall, 68 West 97th St., N. Y. City.

FILMS, ETC., WANTED.

WANTED—The following subjects in good condition: The Great Train Robbery, 1 reel; Convict Hero, 3; Chinatown Mystery, 2; Convict 4287, 2; The Light of New York, 5, and Charles Chaplin comedies. Select Film Co., 145 West 45th St., N. Y. City.

WANTED—Motion picture negative pertaining to outdoor and athletic sports of all descriptions. No current events. Magazine subjects. Pathe frame line. Physical Culture Photo Plays, Flat-Iron Bldg., New York City.

FILMS, ETC., FOR SALE OR RENT.

STATE RIGHTS "Prince of Darkness," just released, five reels of thrills, wonderful big pape. Phax Pictures, 1476 Broadway, N. Y. City.

SIX-TWEEDLEDUM COMEDIES, including five single reels and one two-reeler, only slightly used. Like brand new. Large quantity of new paper on each subject. To dispose of same quickly will sell for $30.00 per reel. Cost $110.00. Send 10 per cent. of purchase price to cover express charges. Will ship balance C. O. D. subject to examination. United Film Service, 17 No. Wabash Ave., Chicago, Illinois.

FOR SALE—Forty thousand feet of synchronized grand opera films; records optional. Big bargain. Kaufman, Rm. 1006 Candler Bldg., 220 West 42d St., New York City.

MUSICAL INSTRUMENTS FOR SALE.

NEW SEEBURG photo player with $150.00 worth of music rolls, $450.00 cash. Pitts Pipe Organ Co., Omaha, Neb.

MISCELLANEOUS.

PATENTS—Free search through Patent Office records and report as to patentability. Send sketch and description of your invention. Prompt and personal service. Attorney fee returned if application not allowed. Frank M. Stephen, Riggs Bldg., Washington, D. C.

SCENARIOS WANTED—Strong two-reel Western stories for male lead. Mail to Great Western Film Corporation, 520 Van Nuys Bldg., Los Angeles, Cal.

INDEX

TO CONTENTS

TO ADVERTISERS

List of Current Film Release Dates
ON GENERAL FILM, PATHE AND PARAMOUNT PROGRAMS

(For Daily Calendar of Program Releases See Page 1894.)

General Film Company, Inc.

(Note—Pictures given below are listed in the order of their release. Additions are made from week to week in the order of release.)

BROADWAY STAR FEATURES.

Discounters of Money (One of the O. Henry Series—Two parts—Comedy-Drama).
The Furnished Room (One of the O. Henry Series—Two parts—Drama).
The Defeat of the City (One of the O. Henry Series—Four parts—Drama).
John Tom Little Bear (One of the O. Henry Series—Two parts—Drama).
Blind Man's Holiday (One of the O. Henry Series—Four parts—Drama).
The Last of the Troubadours (One of the O. Henry Series—two parts—Drama).
The Duplicity of the Hargraves (One of the O. Henry Series—Two parts—Drama).
The Lonesome Road (One of the O. Henry Series —Two parts—Drama).

ESSANAY.

Vernon, the Bountiful (Black Cat Feature—Two Parts—Comedy-Drama).
The Long-Green Trail (Black Cat Feature— Two parts—Comedy-Drama).
Don't Lose Your Coat (Black Cat Feature— Two parts—Comedy).
Star Dust—Black Cat Feature—Two parts— Comedy-Drama).
Twelve Cylinder Speed of the Leisure Class (George Ade Fable—Two parts—Comedy).
The Wandering Boy and the Wayward Parents (George Ade Fable—Two parts—Comedy).
What Transpires After the Wind-Up (George Ade Fable—Two parts—Comedy).
What the Best People Are Not Doing (George Ade Fable—Two parts—Comedy).

FALCON FEATURES.

The Mainspring (Four parts—Drama).
The Martinache Marriage (Four parts—Dr.).
The Stolen Play (Four parts—Drama).
The Phantom Shotgun (Four parts—Drama).
His Unpolished Self (Four parts—Drama).
A Man of His Word (Four parts—Drama).
The Secret of Black Mountain (Four parts— Drama).

KALEM.

At the Sign of the Kangaroo (an episode of the "The Further Adventures of Stingaree"— Two parts—Drama).
Through Fire and Water (Episode of the Further Adventures of Stingaree—Two parts— Drama).
A Bushranger's Strategy (Episode of the Further Adventures of Stingaree—Two parts— Drama).
The Stranger at Dumcrieff (Episode of "The Further Adventures of Stingaree"—Two parts—Drama).
A Champion of the Law (Episode of "The Further Adventures of Stingaree"—Two parts —Drama).
Politics in Pumpkin Center (Ham and Bud Comedy).

JAXON COMEDIES.

(Pokes and Jabs).

(Second Series.)

The Baggage Man.
Getting the Coin.
Tough Luck.
Play Ball.
Love Letters.

(Third Series.)

Speed Demons.
The Collectors.
Jolly Tars.
Wild Injuns.
Deviled Crabs.
The Triple Cross.

SELIG.

The Bush Leaguer (One part—Drama).
Selig-World Library No. 12 (Educational).
The Smoldering Spark (Two parts—Drama).
The Love of Madge O'Mara (Drama).
Selig-World Library No. 13 (Educational).
A Man, a Girl and a Lion (Two parts—Drama).
Her Perilous Ride (One part—Drama).
Selig World Library No. 14 (Educational).
The Sole Survivor (Two parts—Drama).
Her Heart's Desire (One part—Drama).
Selig World Library No. 15 (Educational).
Between Man and Beast (Two parts—Drama).
Her Salvation (One part—Drama).
Selig World Library No. 16 (Educational).
Pioneer Days (Two parts—Drama).
In After Years (One part—Drama).
The House of Mystery (Two parts—Drama).
Selig World Library No. 17 (Educational).
The Convert of the North (One part—Drama).
The Victor of the Plot (Two parts—Drama).
The Voice That Led Him (One part—Drama).
Selig World Library No. 18 (Educational).

RAY COMEDIES.

A Peaceful Flat.
Cheating His Wife.
A Bathtub Marriage.

SPARKLE COMEDIES.

(Second Series.)

Those Terrible Telegrams.
The Stag Party.
Bragg's Little Poker Party.
Mixed 'Nuts.
Hearts and Harpoons.
Toodles.
Bangs Resigs.
Triple Entente.
Whose Hosiery.
Wrong Wrights.

Pathe Exchange, Inc.

RELEASES FOR WEEK OF AUGUST. 26.

Iris (Five parts—Drama—Hepworth).
The Fatal Ring (No. 8, "The Switch in the Safe"—Two parts—Drama—Astra).
Know America No. 20—Near Pike's Peak, Colo. (One reel—Scenic-Combitone).
Hearst-Pathe News No. 70 (Topical).
Hearst-Pathe News No. 71 (Topical).

RELEASES FOR WEEK OF SEPT. 2.

Tears and Smiles (Latilda—Five parts— Drama).
The Fatal Ring (Episode No. 9, "The Dice of Death") (Two parts—Drama—Astra).
Lonesome Luke's Wild Women (Two parts— Comedy—Rolin).
Know America No. 21, "Central Colorado" (Scenic-Combitone).
Scenic and Cartoon (International Split Reel— Title not reported).
Hearst-Pathe News No. 72 (Topical).
Hearst-Pathe News No. 73 (Topical).
Happy Gets the Razoo (Happy Hooligan Cartoon Comedy) and "Making a Marine Officer" (Educational) (International Split Reel).

RELEASED FOR WEEK OF SEPT. 9.

War and the Woman (Thanhouser—Five parts— Drama).
The Fatal Ring Episode No. 10, "The Perilous Plunge"—Two parts—Drama—Astra).
Know America No. 22, "Colorado's Scenic Wonders" (Scenic—Combitone).
Over the Fence (Comedy—Rolin).
Happy Hooligan in the Zoo (Cartoon Comedy) and "From Rookie to Regular" (Educational) (International Split Reel).
Hearst-Pathe News No. 74 (Topical).
Hearst-Pathe News No. 75 (Topical).
Les Miserables (Special—Eight parts—Drama).

RELEASES FOR WEEK OF SEPT. 16.

The Angel Factory (Astra—Five parts—Drama).
The Fatal Ring (Episode No. 11, "The Short Circuit"—Astra—Two parts—Drama).
The Seven Pearls (Episode No. 1, "The Sultan's Necklace"—Astra—Three parts—Drama).
Triple Divide Mountains (Glacier Park) (Scenic Half Reel) and Japan, the Floral (colored) (Pathe-Educational) (Pathe split reel).
Lonesome Luke Loses Patients (Rolin—Two parts—Comedy).
Hearst-Pathe News No. 76 (Topical).
Hearst-Pathe News No. 77 (Topical).

Paramount Pictures Corp.

BLACK DIAMOND COMEDY.

Aug. 6—Susie the Sleepwalker.
July 9—Wits and Fits.
July 23—The Rejuvenator.

FAMOUS PLAYERS.

July 9—The Love That Lives (Five parts— Drama).
July 23—The Long Trail (Five parts—Drama).

KLEVER KOMEDY.

July 30—Motor Boating.
Aug. 13—Summer Boarding (Comedy).
Aug. 20—Egged On.
Aug. 27—The Cinderella Husband.

LASKY.

July 26—The Squaw Man's Son (Five parts— Drama).
July 30—The Crystal Gazer (Five parts—Dr.).

MOROSCO AND PALLAS.

July 19—Cook of Canyon Camp (Five parts— Drama).
Aug. 2—A Kiss for Susie (Five parts—Drama).

PARAMOUNT-ARBUCKLE COMEDY.

June 25—The Rough House (Two parts).
Aug. 20—His Wedding Night (Two parts).

PARAMOUNT FEATURES.

Aug. 19—The Mysterious Miss Terry (Five parts —Drama).
Aug. 19—Hashimura Togo (Five parts—Dr.).
Aug. 26—Close to Nature (Five parts—Drama).
Aug. 26—Little Miss Optimist (Five parts— Drama).
Sept. 2—Lost in Transit (Five parts—Drama).
Sept. 10—The Hostage (Five parts—Drama).
Sept. 17—On the Level (Five parts—Drama).
Sept. 17—Her Double Cross (Five parts—Dr.).
Sept. 17—Exile (Five parts—Drama).
Sept. 17—The Sunset Trail (Five parts—Dr.).
Sept. 24—The Countess Charming (Five parts— Drama).
Sept. 24—Baby's Diary (Five parts)—Drama).

PARAMOUNT-BURTON HOLMES.

Aug. 20—Tropical Nassau (Scenic).
Aug. 27—Madrid to Madeira (Scenic).
Sept. 3—Norway (Scenic).
Sept. 10—Hong Kong and the Pearl River (Scenic).
Sept. 17—Canton and Shanghai (Scenic).
Sept. 24—Picturesque Peking (Scenic).

PARAMOUNT-BRAY PICTOGRAPHS.

July 23—No. 77; Subjects on Reel: Testing Men for Air Fighting; A Study in Fox Hounds; Land of Make Believe; "Bic 'em Cat" (Cartoon).
July 30—No. 78, Subjects on Reel: Training Members of New York's Police Force; Scientific Stock Breeding Farm at Purdee University; Sam Lloyd Animated Picture Puzzle.
Aug. 6—No. 79, Subjects on Reel: Stars of Yesterday; Unmasking a Medium; Cartoon—Bobby Bumps at an Amusement Park.

Producers.—Kindly Furnish Titles and Dates of All New Releases Before Saturday.

List of Current Film Release Dates
ON UNIVERSAL, METRO AND TRIANGLE PROGRAMS

(For Daily Calendar of Program Releases See Page 1894.)

Universal Film Mfg. Co.

ANIMATED WEEKLY.

July 25—Number 82 (Topical).
Aug. 2—Number 83 (Topical).
Aug. 9—Number 84 (Topical).
Aug. 16—Number 85 (Topical).
Aug. 23—Number 86 (Topical).
Aug. 30—Number 87 (Topical).
Sept. 6—Number 88 (Topical).
Sept. 13—Number 89 (Topical).
Sept. 20—Number 90 (Topical).
Sept. 27—Number 91 (Topical).

BISON.

Aug. 20—Squaring It (Three parts—Drama).
Aug. 27—Jungle Treachery (Two parts—Dr.).
Sept. 3—The Lure of the Circus (Two parts—Comedy—Drama), and Sierra Winter Sports (Scenic).
Sept. 10.—The Texas Sphinx (Two parts—Western Drama).
Sept. 17—The Last of the Night Riders (Two parts—Drama).
Sept. 24—The Dynamite Special (Two parts—Drama).

GOLD SEAL.

July 23—A Soldier of the Legion (Three parts —Drama).
July 30—Right of Way Casey (Three parts—Drama).
Aug. 13—A Wife's Suspicion (Three parts—Drama).
Aug. 27—The Winning Pair (Three parts—Dr.).
Sept. 3—The Empty Gun (Three parts—Dr.).
Sept. 10.—The Perilous Leap (Three parts—Railroad Drama).
Sept. 24—The Master Spy (An episode of "The Perils of the Secret Service"—Three parts—Drama).

JOKER.

Aug. 6—O-My the Tent Mover (Comedy).
Aug. 6—The Vamp of the Camp (Comedy).
Aug. 13—Out Again, In Again (Comedy).
Aug. 13—Back to the Kitchen (Comedy).
Aug. 20—Behind the Map (Comedy).
Aug. 20—Mrs. Madam Manager (Comedy).
Aug. 27—Why They Left Home (Comedy).
Aug. 27—Busting Into Society (Comedy).
Sept. 3—Officer, Call a Cop (Comedy).
Sept. 3—A Gale of Verse (Comedy).
Sept. 10.—Short Skirts and Deep Water (Comedy).
Sept. 10.—Nearly a Queen (Comedy).
Sept. 17—Hawaiian Nuts (Comedy).
Sept. 17—Circus Sarah (Comedy).
Sept. 24—Marble Heads (Comedy).
Sept. 24—The Fountain of Trouble (Comedy).

L-KO.

Aug. 6—The Little Fat Rascal (Two parts—Comedy).
Aug. 13—Rough Stuff (Two parts—Comedy).
Aug. 20—Street Cars and Carbunkles (Two parts —Comedy).
Aug. 27—Props, Drops and Flops (Two parts—Comedy).
Sept. 3—Backward Sons and Forward Daughters (Two parts—Comedy).
Sept. 10.—From Cactus to Kale (Two parts—Comedy).
Sept. 17—A Prairie Chicken (Two parts—Com.).
Sept. 24—(Title not reported).

NESTOR.

July 23—Seeing Things.
July 30—Married by Accident (Comedy).
Aug. 6—The Love Slacker (Comedy).
Aug. 13—The Rushin' Dancers (Comedy).
Aug. 20—Move Over (Comedy).
Aug. 27—The Night Cap (Comedy).
Sept. 3—Looking 'Em Over (Comedy).
Sept. 10.—The Boulevard Speed Hounds (Comedy).
Sept. 17—Welcome Home (Comedy).
Sept. 24—Taking Their Medicine (Comedy).

POWERS.

July 23—Hammon Egg's Reminiscences (Cartoon Comedy) and in The Land of Light and Gloom (Dorsey Edu.).
July 30—The Good Liar (Cartoon) and "In Monkey Land" (Ditmar's Edu.).
Aug. 6—Seeing Ceylon with Hy Mayer (Travelaugh).
Aug. 7—Seeing Ceylon with Hy Mayer (Travelaugh).
Aug. 13—Doing His Bit (Cartoon Comedy), and Algeria, Old and New) (Scenic) (Split reel).
Aug. 20—Colonel Pepper's Mobilized Farm (Cartoon Comedy), and "The Home Life of the Spider (Ditmar's Edu.) (Split Reel).

STAR FEATURETTE.

July 30—The Woman Who Would Not Pay (Two parts—Society—Drama).
Aug. 6—The Untamed (Two parts—Drama).
Aug. 13—Cheyenne's Pal (Two parts—Drama).
Aug. 20—The Golden Heart (Two parts—Dr.).
Aug. 27—Hands in the Dark (Two parts—Drama), and Old French Towns (Short Scenic on Same Reel).
Sept. 3—A Dream of Egypt (Two parts—Dr.).
Sept. 10.—To the Highest Bidder (Two parts—Society Drama).
Sept. 17—The Right Man (Two parts—Drama).
Sept. 24—A Romany Rose (Two parts—Drama).

VICTOR.

July 16—One Bride Too Many (Two parts—Comedy-Drama).
July 30—Where Are My Trousers? (Two parts Comedy).
Aug. 6—Like Babes in the Wood (Two parts—Juvenile Comedy).
Aug. 13—The Brass Girl (Two parts—Comedy-Drama).
Aug. 20—A Five Foot Ruler (Two parts—Comedy-Drama).
Aug. 27—Scandal Everywhere (Comedy).
Sept. 3.—The Curse of a Flirting Heart (Com.).
Sept. 10.—In the Clutches of Milk (Comedy).
Sept. 17—Marathon Maniacs (Comedy).
Sept. 24—Your Boy and Mine (Comedy).

UNIVERSAL SCREEN MAGAZINE.

July 30—Issue No. 30 (Educational).
Aug. 6—Issue No. 31 (Topical).
Aug. 13—Issue No. 32 (Topical).
Aug. 20—Issue No. 33 (Educational).
Aug. 27—Issue No. 34 (Educational).
Sept. 3—Issue No. 35 (Educational).
Sept. 10.—Issue No. 36 (Educational).
Sept. 17—Issue No. 37 (Educational).
Sept. 24—Issue No. 38 (Educational).

UNIVERSAL SPECIAL FEATURE.

July 22—The Gray Ghost (Episode No. 4—"The Fight"—Two parts—Drama).
July 29—The Gray Ghost (Episode No. 5—"Plunder"—Two parts—Drama).
Aug. 6—The Gray Ghost (Episode No. 6, "The House of Mystery"—Two parts—Drama).
Aug. 13—The Gray Ghost (Episode No. 7) (The Double Floor) (Two parts—Drama).
Aug. 20—The Gray Ghost (Episode No. 8, "The Pearl Necklace"—Two parts—Dr.).
Aug. 27—The Gray Ghost (Episode No. 9—Title Not Reported—Two parts—Drama).
Sept. 3—The Gray Ghost (Episode No. 10—Shadows—Two parts—Drama).
Sept. 10.—The Gray Ghost (Episode No. 11—"The Flaming Meteor"—Two parts—Drama).
Sept. 17—The Gray Ghost (Episode No. 12—The Poisoned Ring—Two parts—Drama).
Sept. 24—The Gray Ghost (Episode No. 13—Title not reported—Two parts—Dr.).

UNIVERSAL CURRENT EVENTS.

July 28—Issue No. 11 (Topical).
Aug. 4—Issue No. 12 (Topical).
Aug. 10—Issue No. 13 (Topical).
Aug. 17—Issue No. 14 (Topical).
Aug. 24—Issue No. 15 (Topical).
Aug. 31—Issue No. 16 (Topical).
Sept. 7—Issue No. 17 (Topical).
Sept. 14—Issue No. 18 (Topical).
Sept. 21—Issue No. 19 (Topical).

Metro Pictures Corporation.

METRO PICTURES CORP.

July 9—Peggy, the Will o' the Wisp (Five parts—Drama).
July 30—Miss Robinson Crusoe (Five parts—Drama).
Special—The Slacker (Seven parts—Drama).
Aug. 6—The Jury of Fate (Rolfe—Five parts—Drama).
Aug. 13—The Girl Without a Soul (Five parts—Drama).
Aug. 27.—To the Death (Five parts—Drama).
Sept. 10—The Lifted Veil (Five parts—Drama).
Sept. 17—Their Compact (Seven parts—Drama).
Sept. 24—His Curiosity (Drew).

YORKE FILM CORP.

July 16—The Hidden Spring (Five parts—Dr.).
Sept. 3.—Under Handicap (Seven parts—Drama).

METRO COMEDIES.

July 23—Mr. Parker—Hero (Drew).
July 30—Henry's Ancestors (Drew).
Aug. 6—His Ear for Music (Drew).
Aug. 13—Her Economic Independence (Drew).
Aug. 20—Her First Game (Drew).
Aug. 27—The Patriot (Drew).
Sept. 3—Music Hath Charms (Drew).
Sept. 10—Rubbing It In (Drew).
Sept. 17—Henry's Ancestors (Drew).
Sept. 24—The Silent Sellers (Five parts—Dr.).

Triangle Film Corporation.

TRIANGLE PRODUCTIONS.

July 29—In Slumberland (Five parts—Drama).
July 29—Borrowed Plumage (Five parts—Dr.).
Aug. 5—The Food Gamblers (Five parts—Dr.).
Aug. 5—An Even Break (Five parts—Drama).
Aug. 12—Master of His Home (Five parts—Drama).
Aug. 12—Golden Rule Kate (Five parts—Dr.).
Aug. 19—Wee Lady Betty (Five parts—Drama).
Aug. 19—They're Off (Five parts—Drama).
Aug. 26—Wooden Shoes (Five parts—Drama).
Aug. 26—Grafters (Five parts—Drama).
Sept. 2—Ten of Diamonds (Five parts—Drama).
Sept. 2—The Man Hater (Five parts—Drama).
Sept. 9—Idolators (Five parts—Drama).
Sept. 9—Polly Ann (Five parts—Drama).
Sept. 16—Mountain Dew (Five parts—Drama).
Sept. 16—The Haunted House (Five parts—Dr.).

TRIANGLE KOMEDY.

Aug. 5—His Perfect Day.
Aug. 5—A Matrimonial Accident.
Aug. 12—His Cool Nerve.
Aug. 12—A Hotel Disgrace.
Aug. 19—A Love Chase.
Aug. 19—His Hidden Talent.
Aug. 26—Their Domestic Deception.
Aug. 26—Her Donkey Love.
Sept. 2—A Film Star.
Sept. 2—His Foot-Hill Folly.
Sept. 9—A Dark Room Secret.
Sept. 9—A Warm Reception.
Sept. 16—His Baby Doll.
Sept. 16—His Unconscious Conscience.

KEYSTONE.

July 29—Thirst (Two parts).
Aug. 5—His Uncle Dudley (Two parts).
Aug. 12—Lost—A Cook (Two parts).
Aug. 19—The Pawnbroker's Heart (Two parts).
Aug. 26—The Crooks (Two parts).
Sept. 2—A Shanghaied Jonah (Two parts—Com.).
Sept. 9—His Precious Life (Two parts—Com.).
Sept. 16—Hula Hula Land (Two parts—Com.).

PARALTA.

Rose O' Paradise.
A Man's Man.

Producers.—Kindly Furnish Titles and Dates of All New Releases Before Saturday.

List of Current Film Release Dates
MUTUAL PROGRAM AND MISCELLANEOUS FEATURES

(For Daily Calendar of Program Releases See Page 1894.)

Mutual Film Corp.

CUB.

Aug. 9—Jerry on the Railroad (Comedy).
Aug. 16—Beach Nuts (Comedy).
Aug. 23—Jerry on the Farm (Comedy).
Aug. 30—Jerry's Eugenic Marriage (Comedy).
Sept. 6—Jerry Tries Again (Comedy).
Sept. 13—Jerry's Whirlwind Finish (Comedy).
Sept. 20—Officer Jerry (Comedy).

GAUMONT.

Aug. 23—Reel Life No. 69 (Subjects on Reel: Hunting Alligators for Their Skins; Harvesting Potatoes on the Eastern Coast; Coney Island Thrills; Oil from Japan; Something Going to Happen; An Animated Cartoon from "Life."

Aug. 30—Reel Life No. 70 (Subjects on Reel: Using the Abalone, a Little Known Industry of the Pacific Coast; A Boy and a Rope; Handling the Mail; Beach Sports of California; "The March of Science" and "What a Bachelor Sees at a Wedding", are animated drawings from "Life."

Sept. 6—Reel Life No. 71. Subjects on reel: A Watering System for a Small Farm; Pets Which Will Never Be Popular; Handling the Mail; The Five Senses; Drawing from "Life."

Sept. 13—Reel Life No. 72; Subjects on Reel: An Unusual Colt; Hunting Turtle Eggs; Testing an Auto Tube; Tree Planting in the National Forests; The Midnight Sun.

Sept. 20—Reel Life No. 73 (Subjects on Reel: Wearing the President's Portrait; Running an Aeroplane Without Danger; The Principle of the Gyroscope; When a Big Car Goes By (Animated Drawing from "Life.")

MUTUAL WEEKLY.

Aug. 8—Number 136 (Topical).
Aug. 15—Number 137 (Topical).
Aug. 22—Number 138 (Topical).
Aug. 29—Number 139 (Topical).
Sept. 5—Number 140 (Topical).
Sept. 12—Number 141 (Topical).
Sept. 19—Number 142 (Topical).

MUTUAL STAR PRODUCTIONS.

Aug. 13—Bab the Fixer (Horkheimer—Five parts—Drama).
Sept. 3—Reputation (Goodrich—Five parts—Drama).
Sept. 3—Charity Castle (American—Five parts—Drama).
Sept. 10—Outcast (Empire—Six parts—Drama).
Sept. 10—The Bride's Silence (American—Five parts—Drama).
Sept. 17—The Rainbow Girl (Five parts—Dr.).
Sept. 17—The Girl Who Couldn't Grow Up (Five parts—Drama).
Sept. 24—Sands of Sacrifice (Five parts—Dr.).
Sept. 24—The Runaway (Five parts—Drama).

SIGNAL.

Sept. 17—The Lost Express (Episode No. 1, "The Lost Express"—Two parts—Dr.).

Feature Releases

ARTCRAFT PICTURES CORPORATION.

Aug. 12—Down to Earth (Five parts—Comedy-Drama).
Aug. 26—Seven Keys to Baldpate (Five parts—Drama).
Sept. 3—Rebecca of Sunnybrook Farm (Five parts—Drama).
Sept. 10—Barbary Sheep (Five parts—Drama).

· ART DRAMAS. INC.

Aug. 13—Think It Over (U. S. Amusement Corp. —Five parts—Comedy-Drama).
Aug. 27.—The Little Samaritan (Erbograph —Five parts—Drama).
Sept. 3.—Behind the Mask (U. S. Amusement Co.—Five parts—Drama).
Sept. 10—Blood of His Fathers (Horsley—Five parts—Drama).
Sept. 17—Peg o' the Sea (Van Dyke—Five parts —Drama).

BLUEBIRD PHOTOPLAYS. INC.

Aug. 13—The Show Down (Five parts—Drama).
Aug. 20—Mr. Opp Five Parts—Drama).
Aug. 27—The Charmer (Five parts—Drama).
Sept. 3.—Triumph (Five parts—Comedy-Dr.).
Sept. 3.—Mother O' Mine (Five Parts—Drama —Special).
Sept. 10—A Stormy Knight (Five parts—Comedy-Drama).
Sept. 17—The Mysterious Mr. Tiller (Five parts —Drama).
Sept. 24—Flirting With Death (Five parts—Dr.)

BUTTERFLY PICTURES.

Aug. 13—The Midnight Man (Five parts—Dr.).
Aug. 20—The Lair of the Wolf (Five parts—Drama).
Aug. 27—Straight Shooting (Five parts—Dr.).
Sept. 3—Who Was the Other Man? (Five parts —Drama).
Sept. 10.—The Little Pirate (Five parts—Drama).
Sept. 17—The Spindle of Life (Five parts—Drama).
Sept. 24—The Edge of the Law (Five parts—Drama).

CINEMA WAR NEWS SYNDICATE.

Sept. 1—American War News Weekly No. 18 (Topical).
Sept. 8—American War News Weekly No. 19 (Topical).
Sept. 15—American War News Weekly No. 20 (Topical).
Sept. 22—American War News Weekly No. 21 (Topical).

EDUCATIONAL FILMS CORP.

Aug. 20—Living Book of Nature, "Ancestors of the Horse" (Ditmars).
Aug. 22—China and the Chinese, No. 5.
Aug. 27—Living Book of Nature, "Orong Volunteers" (Ditmars).
Aug. 29—First American Apartment House and Nature's Theatricals (Scenic and Educational).
Sept. 3—Living Book of Nature, "Kangaroos and Their Allies" (Ditmars).
Sept. 5—Land What Does Not Wiggle Much (Scenic and Educational).
Sept. 10—The Animals of Australia (Living Book of Nature).

FOX FILM CORPORATION.

Special Release—Jack and the Beanstalk (Ten parts—Drama).
Aug. 4—Wrath of Love (Five parts—Drama).
Aug. 11—Durand of the Bad Lands (Five parts —Drama).
Aug. 18—The Soul of Satan (Five parts—Dr.).
Aug. 25—Every Girl's Dream (Five parts—Dr.).
Sept. 2.—Betrayed (Five parts—Drama).
Sept. 9.—When False Tongues Speak (Five parts—Drama).
Sept. 16—The Yankee Way (Five parts—Dr.).
Sept. 23—North of Fifty-Three (Five parts—Drama).

FOXFILM COMEDIES.

July 23—A Soft Tenderfoot (Two parts).
Aug. 6—A Domestic Hound (Two parts).

· GOLDWYN PICTURES CORP.

Sept. 9—Polly of the Circus (Eight parts—Drama).
Sept. 23—Baby Mine (Six parts—Drama).
Oct. 7—Fighting Odds (Six parts—Drama).

GREATER VITAGRAPH (V-L-S-E).

Sept. 3—Bobby's Bravery (Comedy-Drama).
Sept. 3.—Soldiers of Chance (Five parts— —Drama).
Sept. 10.—A' Alabaster Box (Five parts—
Sept. 17—For France (Five parts—Drama).
Sept. 17—Favorite Film Features: "Winning the Stepchildren" (One Reel Drama); "Goodness Gracious" (Two Reel Comedy).
Sept. 24—The Bandit's Double (Five parts—Drama).
Sept. 24—Favorite Film Features, "The Reincarnation of Karma" (Two parts—Drama) and "A Lesson in Jealousy" (One Reel Comedy).

KLEINE-EDISON-SELIG-ESSANAY.

Aug. 20—Open Places (Essanay—Five parts—Drama).
Aug. 22—The Kingdom of Hope (One of the "Do Children Count?" Series—Two parts—Drama).
Aug. 24—A Trip to Chinatown (Selig-Hoyt Comedy—Two parts).
Aug. 27—The Lady of the Photograph (Edison —Five parts—Drama).
Aug. 25—Conquest Program No. 7 (Subjects: T. Haviland Hicks, Freshman (Three parts—Drama); Gallagher (Two parts—Drama); Turning Out Silver Bullets (One reel); Young Salts and the Holy Land (Combined in one reel).
Sept. 3—Efficiency Edgar's Courtship (Five parts—Drama—Essanay).
Sept. 3—A Midnight Bell (Hoyt Comedy—Two parts).
Sept. 1—Conquest Program No. 8 (Edison), Subjects: The Princess' Necklace (Four Parts—Drama); The Rustling Bill-Board, and In Old England (Split Reel); The Brook, and Woodcraft for Boys; Shipping Live Fish (Split reel); The Blind Fiddler (One reel).
Sept. 10—Pants (Five parts—Drama—Essanay).
Sept. 17—The Awakening of Ruth (Five parts—Drama—Edison).
Sept. 17—A Contented Woman (Hoyt Comedy— Two parts).
Sept. 24—Men of the Desert (Essanay—Five parts—Drama).

SELECT PICTURES CORP.

Magda (C. K. Y. Corp.).

SELZNICK PICTURES.

The Lash of Jealousy (Drama).
The Lesson (Drama).
The Moth (Drama).
The Wild Girl.

STANDARD PICTURES.

Aug. 19—The Spy (Ten parts).
Aug. 26—The Honor System (Ten parts).
Sept. 2—Jack and the Beanstalk (Ten parts).
Sept. 16—The Conqueror (Ten parts).
Sept. 30—Camille.

WHOLESOME FILMS CORPORATION.

Sept. 3—The Penny Philanthropist (Five parts —Drama).
Sept. 3—Cinderella and the Magic Slipper (Four parts—Drama).

WORLD PICTURES.

Aug. 13—Souls Adrift (Five parts—Drama).
Aug. 20—The Little Duchess (Five parts—Dr.).
Aug. 27—Her Guardian (Five parts—Drama).
Sept. 3—Tides of Fate (Five parts—Drama).
Sept. 10—The Marriage Market (Five parts—Drama).
Sept. 17—Betsy Ross (Five parts—Drama).
Sept. 24—The Woman Beneath (Five parts—Drama).

Producers.—Kindly Furnish Titles and Dates of All New Releases Before Saturday.

List of State Rights Pictures

(For Daily Calendar of Program Releases See Page 1894.)

Note—For further information regarding pictures listed on this page, address State Rights Department, Moving Picture World, and same will be gladly furnished.

ARIZONA FILM CO.
May—Should She Obey (Drama).

BERNSTEIN FILM PRODUCTION.
Humility (First of "Seven Cardinal Virtues"—Drama).
June—Who Knows? (Six parts—Drama).

J. FRANK BROCKLISS, INC.
U. S. Navy (Five parts).
Terry Human Interest Reels (900 Feet Every Other Week).
Russian Revolution (Three parts).
Land of the Rising Sun (10,000 feet—Issued complete or in series of 2,000 feet or 5,000 feet).

BUD FISHER FILMS CORP.
Mutt and Jeff Animated Cartoons.

CAMERAGRAPH FILM MFG. CO.
June—What of Your Boy? (Three parts—Patriotic).
June—The Automobile Owner Gets Acquainted With His Automobile (Educational).

CARONA CINEMA CO.
May—The Curse of Eve (Seven parts—Dr.).

CENTURY COMEDIES.
Sept. 1—Balloonatics (Two parts—Comedy).

BENJAMIN CHAPIN PRODUCTIONS.
(The Lincoln Cycle Pictures.)
My Mother (Two parts).
My Father (Two parts).
Myself (Two parts).
The Call to Arms (Two parts).

CHRISTIE FILM CO.
July 9—The Fourteenth Man (Comedy).
July 16—Down By the Sea, (Comedy).
July 23—Skirts (Comedy).
July 30—Won In a Cabaret (Comedy).
Aug. 7—His Merry Mix-Up (Comedy).
Aug. 14—A Smokey Love Affair (Comedy).

CINEMA DISTRIBUTING CORP.
June—The 13th Labor of Hercules (Twelve single parts).

CORONET FILM CORP.
Living Studies in Natural History.
Animal World—Issue No. 1.
Animal World—Issue No. 2.
Birdland Studies.
Horticultural Phenomena.

COSMOFOTOFILM, INC.
June—I Believe (Seven parts—Drama).

E. I. S. MOTION PICTURES CORP.
Trooper 44 (Five parts—Drama).

EXPORT AND IMPORT FILM CO.
June—Robespierre.
June—Ivan the Terrible.

FAIRMOUNT FILM CORP.
June—Hate (Seven parts—Drama).

FLORA FINCH FILM CO.
"War Pride" (Two parts—Comedy).

FORT PITT CORPORATION.
The Italian Battlefront.

FRATERNITY FILMS, INC.
May—Devil's Playground (Nine parts—Drama).

FRIEDMAN ENTERPRISES.
A Mormon Maid (Six parts—Drama).

FRIEDER FILM CORP.
June—A Bit o' Heaven (Five parts—Drama).

FROHMAN AMUSEMENT CORP.
April—God's Man (Nine parts—Drama).

JOSEPH M. GAITES.
August—The Italian Battlefront.

GOLDIN FEATURES.
A Bit of Life (One Reel Comedy-Drama).

F. G. HALL PRODUCTIONS, INC.
May—Her Fighting Chance (Seven parts—Dr.). (Mr. Hall has world rights to this picture).
May—The Bar Sinister (Drama). (Mr. Hall has world rights to this picture).

HISTORIC FEATURES.
June—Christus (Eight parts—Drama).

M. H. HOFFMAN.
September—Silent Witness (Seven parts—Drama).

ILIDOR PICTURES CORP.
June—The Fall of the Romanoffs (Drama).

IVAN FILM PRODUCTIONS.
Apr. —One Law or Both (6 parts—Drama).
August—Babbling Tongues (Six parts—Drama).

JEWEL PRODUCTIONS, INC.
Pay Me (Drama).
Sirens of the Sea.
The Man Without a Country (Drama).

KING BEE FILMS CORP.
July 1—Cupid's Rival (Two parts—Comedy).
July 15—The Villain (Two parts—Comedy).
Aug. 1—The Millionaire (Two parts—Com.).
Aug. 15—The Goat (Two parts—Comedy).
Sept. 1—The Fly Cop (Two parts—Comedy).
Sept. 15—The Star Boarder (Two parts—Com.).

A KAY CO.
Some Barrier (Terry Cartoon Burlesque).
His Trial (Terry Cartoon Burlesque).
Terry Human Interest Reel No. 1 (Character As Revealed in the Face).
Terry Human Interest Reel No. 2 (Character As Revealed in the Eyes).

KLOTZ & STREIMER.
June—Whither Thou Goest (Five parts—Drama).
June—The Secret Trap (Five parts—Drama).

MANX-MAN COMPANY.
The Manx-Man (Eight parts—Drama).

MARINE FILM CORP.
August—Lorelei of the Sea (Drama).

MAYFAIR FILM CORP.
Persuasive Peggy (Drama).

MOE STREIMER.
June—A Daughter of the Don (Ten parts—Drama).

B. S. MOSS MOTION PICTURE CORP.
April—Birth Control (Five parts—Drama).

NEVADA MOTION PICTURE CORP.
June—The Planter (Drama).

NEWFIELDS PRODUCING CORP.
Alma, Where Do You Live? (Six parts—Dr.).

OGDEN PICTURES CORP.
August—The Lust of the Ages (Drama).

PARAGON FILMS, INC.
The Whip (Eight parts—Drama).

PETER PAN FILM CORP.
Mo-Toy Troupe (Release No. 7—"Dinkling of the Circus").
Mo-Toy Troupe (Release No. 8—"A Trip to the Moon").
Mo-Toy Troupe (Release No. 9, "Golden Locks and the Three Bears").
Mo-Toy Troupe (Release No. 10, "Dolly Doings").
Mo-Toy Troupe (Release No. 11 "School Days").
Moy-toy Troupe (Release No. 12, "Little Red Riding Hood").
Moy-toy Troupe (Release No. 13, "Puss in Boots").
Mo-Toy Troupe (Release No. 14—"Jimmie the Soldier Boy").
Mo-Toy Troupe (Release No. 15—"Jimmie and Jam").
Mo-Toy Troupe (Release No. 16—"In Japoland").

PUBLIC RIGHTS FILM CORP.
June—The Public Be Damned.

PURKALL FILM CO.
July—The Liar (Six parts—Drama).

RENOWNED PICTURES CORP.
June—In Treason's Grasp (Five parts—Drama).

REX BEACH PICTURES CO.
March—The Barrier (Nine parts—Drama).

SELECT PHOTOPLAY CO.
May—Humanity (Six parts—Drama).

WILLIAM N. SELIG.
April—The Garden of Allah.
May—Beware of Strangers (Eight parts—Dr.).

FRANK J. SENG.
May—Parentage (Drama).

SHERMAN PICTURE CORP.
July—Corruption (Six parts—Drama).
August—I Believe.

SKOBELOFF COMMITTEE.
The Great Russian Revolution.
Behind the Battle Line in Russia.

JULIUS STEGER.
May—Redemption (Six parts—Drama).

SUPREME FEATURE FILMS, INC.
May—Trip Through China (Ten parts).

ULTRA FILMS, INC.
A Day at West Point (Educational).
West is West.
Rustlers' Frame-Up at Big Horn.

UNIVERSAL (STATE RIGHTS).
May—The Hand that Rocks the Cradle (Six parts—Drama).
June—The Cross-Eyed Submarine (Three parts—Comedy).
June—Come Through (Seven parts—Drama).

E. WARREN PRODUCTION.
April—The Warfare of the Flesh (Drama).

WHARTON, INC.
June—The Great White Trail (Seven parts) (Drama).

WILLIAMSON BROS.
April—The Submarine Eye (Drama).

Producers.—Kindly Furnish Titles and Dates of All New Releases Before Saturday.

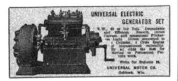

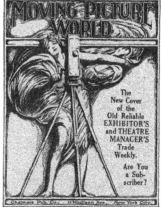

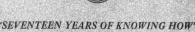

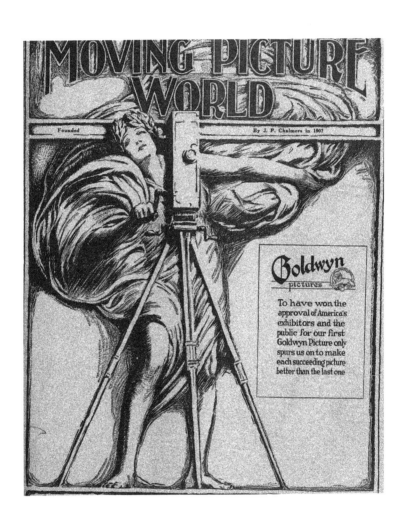

MOVING PICTURE WORLD

Founded   By J. P. Chalmers in 1907

Goldwyn
pictures

To have won the
approval of America's
exhibitors and the
public for our first
Goldwyn Picture only
spurs us on to make
each succeeding picture
better than the last one

PRODUCTIONS INC.

Of an importance almost equal to the superior merit of JEWEL PRODUCTIONS is the rapidly growing facilities for booking in every section of the country.

The number of Exchanges is increasing daily, and—for the first time in the history of films—this growth is in response to a pressing demand.

The announcement of JEWEL Productions, unaccompanied by extravagant statements or mouth-filling adjectives, struck a responsive chord in the mind of every progressive theatre manager. The demand and the establishment of convenient JEWEL Exchanges followed.

JEWEL Productions already released include:

"Come Through"—George Bronson Howard's greatest Melodrama.
"Sirens of the Sea"—The Picture Magnificent.
"Pay Me"—The Big Drama of the West.
These three produced by the Universal.
"The Man Without a Country"—The Patriotic Classic.
Produced by Thanhouser.

These pictures may be booked thru any of the following JEWEL Exchanges, or the home office. Address as below:

Soon to be released
"The Price of a
Good Time"
Produced by
LOIS WEBER

JEWEL Productions (INC.)

Detroit, Mich., 59 Elizabeth Street
New York, N. Y., 1600 Broadway
Pittsburgh, Pa., 1201 Liberty Avenue
Cleveland, Ohio, 112 Prospect Street
Chicago, Ill., 220 So. State Street
Portland, Ore., 405 Davis Street
San Francisco, Cal., 121 Golden Gate Avenue
Los Angeles, Cal., 822 So. Olive Street
Omaha, Neb., 1504 Harney Street

Denver, Colo., 1422 Welton Street
Kansas City, Mo., 1025 Main Street
Oklahoma City, Okla., 116 West 2nd St.
Indianapolis, Ind., 56 W. New York St.
Philadelphia, Pa., 1304 Vine Street
Boston, Mass., 60 Church Street
Washington, D. C., 419 No. 9th Street
Toronto, Canada—State Right Feature, 106 Richmond Street.

Taylor Holmes
has taken the
film world by
storm — in Essanay's
"Efficiency Edgar's
Courtship," declares
every critic. Not
a dissenting voice!
The most unprecedented
praise ever offered.
Read! Read! Read!

Geo. K Spoor.

The One Best Bet of the Week—

Neal Hart in "The Ninth Day"

THE night you show Neal Hart in "The Ninth Day" mix with your audiences in the lobby as they pass out, and you will learn a lot about this virile actor's drawing power. You'll learn that when it comes to crowding five reels into three the Universal Western pictures show how it should be done, and you'll find that your public's appreciation proves that they can distinguish the real thing from the fakerino—when it comes to Western pictures.

Because Neal Hart is genuine, and George Marshall, who, with Harvey Gates, wrote this big three-reel Gold Seal, and who also directed it is a producer of punches —plus. Neal is a private in the U. S. A., and in love with Janet Eastman, the storekeeper's daughter. Mexican Joe, who also desires her, has no apparent business, but always has coin. To get Neal as a rival out of his way he proposes a smuggling game across the border, and is to meet that shrewd youngster on patrol at night. Neal, suspicious, hides a friend near by. As the negotiations proceed, the friend sneezes and a smuggler shoots in the direction of the sound. Neal's enmity is thus revealed and Joe and his gang make him a prisoner in a deserted cabin. Neal, in the hut, overhears plans to blow up the post in nine days. How he escapes to warn the people, the wild riding and the fight that follows makes a tremendous climax that will arouse your audiences to a frenzy of excitement. This is a big three-reel picture that you cannot boost too strongly. Released week of October 8th. Book thru any Universal Exchange.

Or Book these Funny Comedies and Powerful Dramas!

OF COURSE you've got to have comedies if you want to get the money. No matter what kind of an entertainment you give you need comedy like the Nestor one-reel "Hot Applications," featuring Eddie Lyons and Lee Moran. Or perhaps you'd prefer a two-reeler. There's the L-KO "The Nurse of an Aching Heart," a screaming stunt laugh-getter. Be that as it may, you can't make a mistake with either of the Jokers—Wm. Franey and Gale Henry in "The Wart on the Wire," a burlesque detective drama, or Max Asher in "Rainstorms and Brainstorms," back of the scenes stuff—or, for the matter o' that, you'll like Ruth Stonehouse, who, in "A Walloping Time" (Victor one-reel), will give your patrons one. If you are showing the straight dramatic subjects better book that railroad thriller, Helen Gibson, in "Saving the Fast Mail" (Bison), with stunts to make your hair curl. For a marvelous juvenile-grown-up feature—great for a matinee special, book Lena Baskette in "A Prince for a Day" (two reels). All released week of October 8. Get in touch with your nearest Universal Exchange or Universal Film Manufacturing Co., Carl Laemmle, President—"The Largest Film Manufacturing Concern in the Universe"—1600 Broadway, New York.

2·a·Week News Service

The two greatest news weeklies in the world today—the news service that is always first—that is today packing theatres in every land—bears the brand of the

UNIVERSAL

President Wilson in the Draft Parade, Washington, D. C.

In addition to covering all the world's greatest and most interesting events—the Universal Two-a-Week News Service is the only one that thoroughly covers the big subject—the one nearest the heart of the people—AMERICA'S ARMY AND NAVY.

Universal Animated Weekly

"Get It First" is the famous slogan of the Universal Animated Weekly. That is why millions of people throughout the land—friends and relatives of our nearly two million men under arms—will pack any theatre showing this famous one-reel feature. Book the Animated and show your patrons their friends on duty at home and abroad.

Universal Current Events

The world's events that are making history are shown every week in Universal Current Events. Visiting foreign commissions; the army camps; activities on the battle fronts abroad; fascinating happenings from all over the world just as they took place. You can't get all the great news in pictures unless you book the UNIVERSAL Two-Week News Service.

It is what the people demand. It is up to you to supply them. It is a splendid way to do your bit—showing the boys away from home to the folks at home. Now is the golden time to book. Don't let your competitor beat you to it. Book thru any Universal Exchange, or write direct to the UNIVERSAL ANIMATED WEEKLY, 1600 Broadway, New York.

ANNOUNCEMENT.

MAE MURRAY

IN   SUPER-
BLUEBIRD
PHOTO~PLAYS

BLUEBIRD PHOTOPLAYS INC.
1600 BROADWAY   NEW YORK CITY

Pauline Frederick

in "Double Crossed"

Pauline Frederick's *drawing power* and *popularity* are not equaled by any other emotional actress of the stage or screen.

The author of "The Cheat," Hector Turnbull, also wrote "Double Crossed." This is an indication of the *intense* dramatic conflict in this production—the story of a young society matron who sacrifices her honor and position to save her husband from disgrace.

Scenario by Eve Unsell.
Staged by Robert G. Vignola.

Paramount Pictures Corporation
FOUR EIGHTY-FIVE FIFTH AVENUE FORTY-FIRST ST
NEW YORK
Controlled by FAMOUS PLAYERS-LASKY CORPORATION

A Paramount Picture

Paramount Pictures

The Truth conservatively stated is Paramount's advertising policy, but the Critics are lavish in their praise.

Kathleen Clifford

"We're Breaking Our Rule," say

many newspapers, "in contracting for the novelization of Who is *Number One*"?

but we are forced to it by the great fame of
Anna Katharine Green and the fact that it
is to be produced as a serial by *Paramount*"

The largest and most influential list of newspapers that ever backed a serial will be pushing and pulling for the first *Paramount Serial*

READY IN OCTOBER

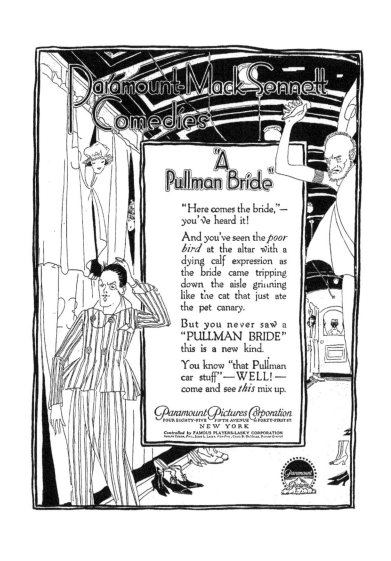

SELECT ⓈⓅ PICTURES

offers to Exhibitors who book

"THE PUBLIC BE DAMNED!"

exceptional opportunity to benefit from the nation-wide publicity which is now being given this picture and the entire subject of food conservation and price regulation by governmental and private campaigns now being energetically pushed. Give your audiences a chance to see the picture on which HERBERT HOOVER, now official Food Administrator of the United States, has placed his emphatic approval—*and help yourself while doing a patriotic duty!*

Distributed by

SELECT PICTURES CORPORATION
729 Seventh Avenue, New York City

SELZNICK ⬛PICTURES

HARRY WEBER
PRESENTS

EVA
TANGUAY

VAUDEVILLE'S
MOST FAMOUS
CYCLONIC
COMEDIENNE

First Time on the
Screen

IN

"THE WILD GIRL"

See it and go wild with her!

Director, HOWARD ESTABROOK

Watch for Date of Release

DISTRIBUTED BY
SELECT PICTURES CORPORATION
729 Seventh Avenue, New York City

GEO. M. COHAN

7 Keys to Baldpate

When Artcraft *advertised* that this picture was a good one and would draw well—it was the *truth* conservatively stated.

But the critics are so *lavish* in their *praise* that we take this space to insure your getting *their ideas* also.

The World (New York)
"Baldpate" on screen crowds Rialto—packed house several times. In the evening several hundred persons waited over an hour outside.

The American (New York)
As a motion picture the story is no less entertaining, and Hugh Ford, the director, has retained all the tricks of construction which made the play the theatrical novelty of its season.

The Herald (New York)
George Cohan has done his best work in "Seven Keys to Baldpate," presented yesterday in the Rialto Theatre.

The Tribune (New York)
"Seven Keys to Baldpate" loses nothing in screen version at the Rialto.

The Sun (New York)
This mixture of comedy and melodrama loses none of its punch through its transfer from the legitimate stage.

Story by George M. Cohan.
From the novel by Earl Derr Biggers. (Published by Bobbs-Merrill Co.)
Directed by Hugh Ford.

Book and take care of this picture properly and it will advertise and take care of you.

ARTCRAFT PICTURES CORPORATION
729 SEVENTH AVE.   NEW YORK CITY
Controlled by FAMOUS PLAYERS-LASKY CORPORATION
ADOLPH ZUKOR, Pres., JESSE L. LASKY, Vice-Pres., CECIL B. DeMILLE, Director General

"It's a Corking Idea!"—

"It's a corking idea—I think so much of it that I want to pin down my usual territory right now." That's what one of the biggest, best-known, most efficient state rights buyers in the country writes after reading the first announcement of

PHOTOPLAY MAGAZINE-SCREEN SUPPLEMENT

It didn't take him a minute to appreciate the box-office possibilities of twelve single-reel subjects presenting such stars as Douglas Fairbanks, William S. Hart, Bessie Love, Warren Kerrigan, Henry Walthall, Charlie Chaplin, Louise Glaum, Dorothy Dalton, Mary Miles Minter, Lucille Lee Stuart, the Sidney Drews, Charles Ray, Viola Dana, Mabel Taliaferro and a host of others; "the stars as they are"—many stars in each release. He *knew* such attractions would book like wildfire. He demanded a territorial franchise right then. Many, many other applications have been received. More are arriving daily. If your want exclusive territory on the greatest state rights attraction ever offered, wire or write

JAMES R. QUIRK, PUBLISHER

PHOTOPLAY MAGAZINE
CHICAGO, ILLINOIS

William Russell and His Chinese Cook "Bin"

What Exhibitors Say of Mutual's New Fall Features
—"Big Stars Only"

By JOHN R. FREULER

THE WEEK OF SEPTEMBER 3rd marked the start of a new chapter in film history. That week the Mutual Film Corporation began the new season of 1917-1918 by releasing two amazing box-office attractions—Edna Goodrich in "Reputation" and Mary Miles Minter in "Charity Castle."

Letters have come to me from prominent exhibitors everywhere praising the high quality of these new productions. Manager F. L. Newman, of the Royal Theatre—one of Kansas City's finest houses—says of "Reputation": "I think it is as fine a production as I have ever seen. The lighting effects and photography are excellent. The story could not be better. The introduction of the dancers in the cabaret scene is wonderful, also the way Miss Goodrich had the opportunity to display beautiful gowns.

Manager Leo A. Landau, of the Butterfly Theatre, Milwaukee, Wis., writes regarding "Reputation": "In point of story, scenery, cast, settings, star, titles, in fact, in every particular, I would call it a 100 per cent production. No exhibitor can desire more than 'Reputation' gives."

These letters are conclusive proof of the box-office value of the new Mutual Pictures. Eight of these big star attractions in five or six reels are released by Mutual this month—*two each week!* The week of Sept. 10th: Ann Murdock in "Outcast"—first of Charles Frohman Successes in Motion Pictures, and Gail Kane in "The Bride's Silence." The week of Sept. 17th: Juliette Day in "The Rainbow Girl," and Margarita Fischer in "The Girl Who Couldn't Grow Up." The week of Sept. 24th: William Russell in "Sands of Sacrifice," and Julia Sanderson in "The Runaway"—second of the Charles Frohman Successes in Motion Pictures.

Those fortunate exhibitors who have secured exclusive territory for the showing of these new Mutual Pictures—"Big Stars Only"—for the coming 52 weeks are assured big box-office returns. If you haven't talked to your Mutual manager recently or reviewed some of these new attractions, you're resisting opportunity.

President
Mutual Film Corporation

A tensely dramat
in five acts. Dire
ward Sloman. R
week of Septen

"Sands of S

A story of the big ou
laid amid the giants c
on the scorching sand
Depicting a good wom
the life of a reckless
feared neither God nor
of a picture you'll be
Booking NOW at all M

Produced
AMERICAN FILM CO
SAMUEL S. HUTCHINSO

Distributed
MUTUAL FILM CO
JOHN R. FREULER, F

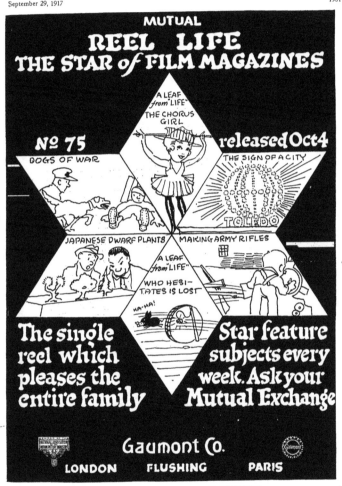

Goldwyn Pictures

The National Verdict Is:

NO LONGER an organization of promises, and at last *a company of definite achievement*, Goldwyn Pictures Corporation takes pleasure in quoting for the benefit of the trade and all lovers of good pictures, the important motion picture and amusement journals, the critics of the great daily newspapers and powerful exhibitors in several sections of the country about the first Goldwyn production, "Polly of the Circus."

FROM AMERICA'S GREAT DAILY PAPERS:

NEW YORK TRIBUNE: There is only one criticism of "Polly of the Circus." It is going to make us all dreadfully dissatisfied with the usual photoplay. Goldwyn's first production is a picture of wonderful charm and power.

NEW YORK SUN: 'Polly of the Circus" is a good augury that the name of Goldwyn shall not perish from the earth.

NEW YORK WORLD: This first Goldwyn production is a rare combination of pictorial and story-telling effectiveness.

NEW YORK EVE. TELEGRAM: The artistic merit of "Polly of the Circus" is beyond question.

NEW YORK EVE. POST: This first Goldwyn picture should appeal to all who appreciate wholesome entertainment.

PHILADELPHIA PRESS: Goldwyn's first production is a triumph of the screen. . . . A continuous series of thrills.

PHILADELPHIA NORTH AMERICAN: Goldwyn has arrived in more senses than one. "Polly of the Circus" has a strong claim on the "ideal picture" distinction.

CLEVELAND PLAIN DEALER: Goldwyn's great first release, "Polly of the Circus," is a picture you will see twice. It is an unusual play and presents Mae Marsh in a role that fits her like a glove.

CHICAGO EVE. POST: The whole production is a work of art, not merely a vehicle for the exploitation of a star.

NEW YORK AMERICAN: "Polly of the Circus" is a triumph for Goldwyn, for Margaret Mayo and lovely Mae Marsh.

NEW YORK EVE. SUN: This first Goldwyn picture gives promise of many good things to come.

NEW YORK HERALD: Here is a production of the highest order, and the work of Mae Marsh reveals all of her appealing powers.

NEW YORK TIMES: "Polly of the Circus" is a sincere effort to improve the motion picture art.

NEW YORK EVE. MAIL: You will thrill with every tenth or twelfth turn of the camera crank.

NEW YORK GLOBE: "Polly of the Circus" is leagues ahead of the average picture. Mae Marsh possesses all of her old-time appeal.

NEW YORK EVE. WORLD: As a Goldwyn picture, "Polly of the Circus" is even greater than it was as a great stage success.

PHILADELPHIA PUBLIC LEDGER: "Polly" is something of real and unusual beauty. It is a memorable production.

PHILADELPHIA INQUIRER: "Polly of the Circus" reaches the highest points strived for by previous producers.

PHILADELPHIA EVE. LEDGER: "Polly of the Circus" is a gem of cinema art. Progress is written over the whole film. It has a refinement of handling almost new to motion pictures.

CLEVELAND LEADER: The lighting and effects and thrills in "Polly of the Circus" must have given the people who achieved them supreme satisfaction as artistic work most creditably done. . . . Goldwyn sets a high standard for itself.

MINNEAPOLIS JOURNAL: Here is a magnificent production that will pack to capacity the motion picture theatres of the world.

BOSTON EVE. RECORD: Here at last is art in the movies. The outstanding features of "Polly of the Circus" are its unparalleled lighting effects, its wonderful night photography and its exquisite settings and backgrounds.

NEW ORLEANS TIMES-PICAYUNE: Brains win. "Polly of the Circus" is by far the greatest motion picture presentation that has ever been shown in the city of New Orleans. Mae Marsh is new and more appealing than ever before. Brains directed her. Brains adapted the story to the screen, and brains made it so clear and effective that there has never been a screen subject that approached closer to perfection than this one.

ALICE COON BROWN, OHIO STATE JOURNAL: "Polly of the Circus" is an exceptional film. If the other Goldwyn pictures are as well done as this one, all of us have a lot that is worth while to look forward to.

Maxine Elliott Releases Are Shifted

GOLDWYN will present Maxine Elliott for her screen debut in "Fighting Odds," by Roi Cooper Megrue and Irvin S. Cobb instead of in "The Eternal Magdalene," as previously announced. "Fighting Odds" will be released everywhere October 7.

Despite enthusiastic indorsement of "The Eternal Magdalene" by the National Board of Review, censor boards in Pennsylvania and the city of Chicago raise certain objections to the production —objections with which, quite naturally, Goldwyn disagrees in entirety.

But, rather than cause our exhibitor customers inconvenience through late delivery of the scheduled picture, Goldwyn brings forward "Fighting Odds" and will thresh out the points at issue in the two localities.

"Fighting Odds" is a powerful emotional drama of Big Business and a wife's loyalty and devotion to her husband who is made the catspaw of unscrupulous financiers. This big play gives Miss Elliott the finest dramatic opportunity she has ever had, and millions of people will welcome her to the screen in this big role.

The same big campaign of exploitation being conducted throughout America for "The Eternal Magdalene" is now being duplicated for "Fighting Odds."

Goldwyn Pictures

Goldwyn

presents

The Internationally Famous
Beauty and Theatrical Favorite

Maxine Elliott

in

Fighting Odds

By Roi Cooper Megrue
and Irvin S. Cobb

The Most Widely Advertised Feminine Personality in
All The World in a Drama of a Beautiful Wife's Loyalty and Devotion.

The Swiftest Farce-
comedy ever made for
the screen is Goldwyn's
second production
introducing

Madge Kennedy
in
Baby Mine

By Margaret Mayo

Released September 23rd

This young and beautiful Star is the freshest and most charming
personality that has come from the stage to the Screen

Madge Kennedy Is The Next Box-office Sensation to Reap Profits for Exhibitors

Goldwyn
presents

Under a Policy of
Wide Open Booking

George Loane Tucker's
remarkable production
of

Hall Caine's
greatest story

The Manx-Man

with
Elisabeth Risdon
and Henry Ainley

This remarkable production is exclusively distributed throughout North America by Goldwyn by arrangement with the late Henry J. Brock.

Bookings and reservations are now being accepted at all Goldwyn branch offices and trade showings will be held in each branch as quickly as possible. It is available to all exhibitors on the open booking plan. This splendid picture played to capacity for one month at the Criterion Theatre, New York City.

Goldwyn Distributing Corporation
16 East 42nd Street   New York City

RUSSIAN ART FILM CORPORATION

PRESENTS

OLGA ZOVSKA

and the renowned company of stars from

THE MOSCOW ART THEATRE

in a repertory of plays by famous authors.

"PICTURES THAT ARE DIFFERENT"

OLGA ZOVSKA

TRIANGLE

STAR SERIES
AT POPULAR
PRICES

NORMA TALMADGE
and
FRANK KEENAN
in
*THE TRIANGLE PLAYS THAT
MADE THEM FAMOUS*

Nine Keenan productions will be re-issued at intervals of four weeks, commencing with "The Sin Ye Do," October 7.

Seven Norma Talmadge features, one every four weeks, commencing October 21 with "The Devil's Needle."

EACH SERIES BOOKED SEPARATELY ON SAME
PLAN AS HART AND FAIRBANKS PLAYS

TRIANGLE

Roy Stewart

in

"THE DEVIL DODGER"

Released September 23d

Out of the West comes a new
gunman ready to round up the
crowds for your theatre.

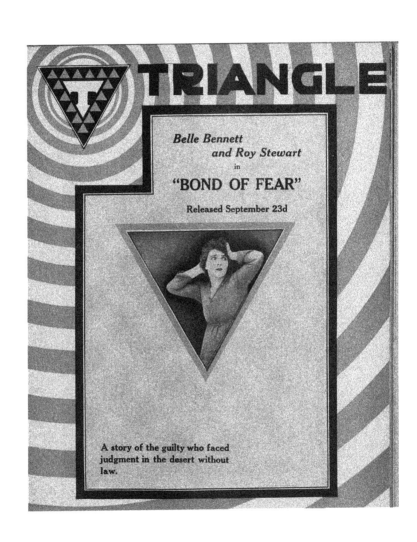

TRIANGLE

*Belle Bennett
and Roy Stewart*

in

"BOND OF FEAR"

Released September 23d

A story of the guilty who faced
judgment in the desert without
law.

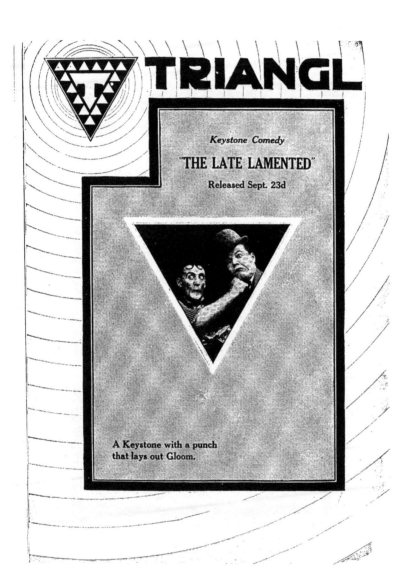

TRIANGL

Keystone Comedy

"THE LATE LAMENTED"

Released Sept. 23d

A Keystone with a punch
that lays out Gloom.

J. WARREN KERRIGAN
in "A Man's Man"

Directed by Oscar Apfel   Written by Peter B. Kyne

Sold Under Either Star Series Booking Method, or The Paralta Plan.

He fights
The merciless louts
Of a hellish breed.
He stakes his life
On the aim
Of his gun.
He fights
For right—
For friendship—
For love.
But he always
Fights fair.

More Action than the Falls of Niagara
More Stuff than the Encyclopaedia Britannica

And a Song of Love
As Tender as a Sprig of Thistledown Blown by the
Gentle Gust of an Autumn Breeze

The Goliath of Box Office Record Breakers

Herbert Brenon
will present

B E R T LYTELL

as Dr. Worthing in his picture story of

"EMPTY POCKETS"
by **Rupert Hughes**

Julian Johnson in October Photoplay says "If ever a star was born full-fired, such a visual birth was Bert Lytell's, the Lone Wolf in Brenon's picture of that name."

ANNOUNCEMENT

immediate sale of territorial rights for

Herbert Brenon's

the remarkable visualization of living beings, the weaknesses of a **Czar**, the schemes of a **Kaiser**, the cunning of a **Rasputin**

with one of the most exceptional casts ever assembled

RASPUTIN, THE SACRED DEVIL OF RUSSIA
AND SONIA, ONE OF HIS ACCOMPLICES

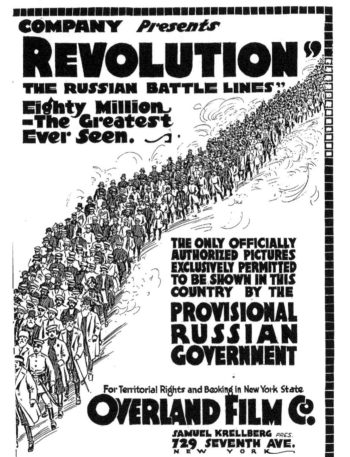

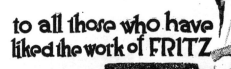

to all those who have
liked the work of FRITZ

ON AUGUST 29, 1917, Fritz made his last appearance before the camera in the closing scene of "The Narrow Trail," my first Thomas H. Ince production for Artcraft. Hereafter, he will live in retirement with all the comforts of horse life.

I have ridden Fritz constantly for more than two years, and he has served me so faithfully, and has been so steadfast and courageous whenever called upon to perform a hazardous feat, that I feel all who have been so kind to us in our work upon the screen will know and understand my motives. I love the old fellow dearly, and cannot, after all his loyalty, subject him further to a chance of injury.

I wish to tell all who like the little Pinto that he will be right with me wherever I may go—until the Boss Ranger comes along and summons one or both of us across the Big Divide.

With deepest gratitude from Fritz and myself.

William S. Hart

Please don't worry about me. I'm going to be with the boss just the same.

FRITZ.

BRYANT WASHBURN

The Popular Star of "Skinner's Dress Suit"

Presented by GEORGE K. SPOOR

in

"THE FIBBERS"

From the story by James W. Adams. Presenting a ragged hobo in the role of a Fairy Prince to a young couple who were battling the wolf at their door — and deceiving each other the while.

Proving that "fibbing"—even of the harmless, well-meant sort—is a dangerous pastime. Featuring the famous star of the "Skinner" Pictures.. Screen time 65 minutes. *Released October 15th.*

PRODUCED BY

Essanay

DISTRIBUTED THROUGH

GEORGE KLEINE SYSTEM

LITTLE MARY McALISTER

Presented by GEORGE K. SPOOR

in A Quaint Little Comedy-Drama Entitled

"PANTS"

The kind of picture that always satisfies. Scenes laid in the home of a millionaire and in the squalid tenement district of a big city. Featuring Filmdom's foremost child star — the heroine of the "Do Children Count?" Series.

Brimming over with human interest and a direct-to-the-heart appeal. Not a juvenile story —but one that will please both old and young. Screen time, 68 minutes. Now playing to capacity business at the best theatres.

PRODUCED BY
Essanay

DISTRIBUTED THROUGH
GEORGE KLEINE SYSTEM

SHIRLEY MASON

Presented by Thomas A. Edison, INC., IN

"THE APPLE TREE GIRL"

A film version of George Weston Mason's story as published in "The Ladies Home Journal." Has been read by millions. Now you can bring it to them on the screen of your theatre.

An entrancing heroine whose desire it is to make everybody admire her. An ideal role for Shirley Mason— Screenland's most winsome ingenue. Five reels. *Released October 1st.*

PRODUCED BY

Thomas A. Edison, INC.

DISTRIBUTED THROUGH
GEORGE KLEINE SYSTEM

The Meaning
Of This Mark

The design pictured above is a symbol of all that is finest and best in the way of short motion picture subjects. Like the Sterling mark on silver or the name Pierce-Arrow on a motor car, the pictured trade mark stands for quality—it is the insignia of

In Conquest Programs exhibitors can secure a diversified program that is sure to contain something of interest to every patron. Feature stories in three or four reels—the works of such celebrities as Robert Louis Stevenson, Richard Harding Davis, Ralph Henry Barbour—snappy comedies, laughable cartoons, scenics of amazing beauty, novelties in microscopic photography that baffle description, are regularly found in Conquest Programs. They are truly "Films for all the family." A new Conquest Program, comprising a total of seven reels, is released each week. Nine Conquest Programs are now available at the exchanges of the GEORGE KLEINE SYSTEM.

PRODUCED BY

Thomas A. Edison,
INC.

DISTRIBUTED THROUGH

GEORGE KLEINE SYSTEM

Robert Louis Stevenson's Famous Story

Presented by *Thomas A. Edison*, INC. *as*

THE FEATURE OF CONQUEST PROGRAM NO·9

Lives there a man or boy who has not thrilled to the famous story by Robert Louis Stevenson titled "Kidnapped"? It is numbered among the classics of literature of all ages. Millions have reveled in its adventure — its romance — its breeziness. Now in motion pictures it is doubly attractive.

Conquest Program No. 9, released the week of Sept. 8th, also includes an uproarious comedy "Friends, Romans and Leo"; a novelty in the way of an animated silhouette titled "Little Red Riding Hood"; a beautiful scenic depicting quaint Provincetown, Cape Cod; and a microscopic study of the minute forms life found in pools and ponds.

PRODUCED BY

Thomas A. Edison,
INC.

DISTRIBUTED THROUGH

GEORGE KLEINE SYSTEM

An amazing drama, the greatest
work of a tremendous star —
Wonderful

EMILY
STEVENS

in the E. Phillips Oppenheim master piece

A SLEEPING
MEMOR

Directed by
George D. Baker
under the personal
supervision of
Maxwell Karger

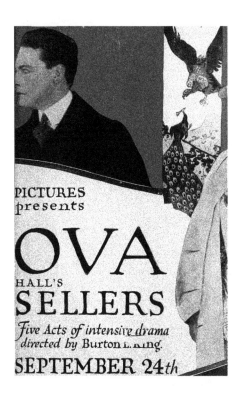

PICTURES
presents

OVA

HALL'S
SELLERS

*Five Acts of intensive drama
directed by Burton L. King.*

SEPTEMBER 24*th*

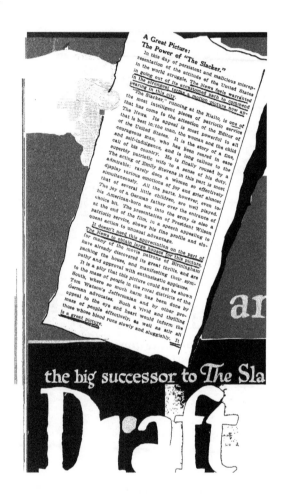

A Great Picture:
The Power of "The Slacker."

In this day of persistent and malicious misrepresentation of the attitude of the United States in the world struggle, The News feels warranted in going out of its accustomed path to commend in the strongest terms a motion picture now appearing in this city.

"The Slacker," running at the Rialto, is one of the most intelligent pieces of patriotic service that has come to the attention of the Editor of The News. Its appeal is most powerful to all of the United States. It is the story of a fine, courageous man, who has been reared in ease and self-indulgence, and is long callous to the call of his country. He is finally roused by a superbly patriotic wife 'to a sense of his duty.

The acting of Emily Stevens in this part is most admirable. rarely does a women so effectively display various emotions of joy and grief almost simultaneously. All the parts, however, even to that of several little children, are well played. The Joy of a German father over the entrance of his American-born son into the army is also a choice bit. The presentation of President Wilson at the end of the film, in a speech appealing to patriotic service, shows his fine profile and eloquent action to unusual advantage.

It doesn't need this appreciation on the part of The News to obtain large houses for this picture, for many of the movie patrons of Birmingham have already discovered its great thrills, and are packing the house, and manifesting their sympathy and approval with enthusiastic applause.

It is a pity that this picture could not be shown to the mass of people in the rural districts of the South, where so much harm has been done by Tom Watson's Jeffersonian and by other pro-German advocates. Such a vivid and thrilling appeal to the eye and heart would inform the mass of people effectively, as well as stir all those whose blood runs slowly and sluggishly. It is a great picture.

the big successor to The Sla

Draft

Everybody in the World has been Startled by the Revelations

—of his amazing experiences at the German Court up to the time the United States entered the great war by

JAMES W. GERARD

Former Ambassador to Berlin

The spies and treachery he tells of sends a shiver down your back and you begin to wonder who your neighbor is.

EVERY PERSON IN EVERY CITY—MAN, WOMAN *and* CHILD —IS INTERESTED *in this* VITAL SUBJECT

WILLIAM FOX'S
Vital and Timely
Motion Picture
with
DUSTIN FARNUM

is spreading throughout the land startling revelations in motion picture form of the Kaiser's system of spies, who number thousands in America alone.

YOUR PATRONS

are reading every day of attempts to blow up bridges and public utilities by spies in their own neighborhood —how a Swedish diplomat was tricked into sending code messages to the Kaiser for one of his spies.

THIS IS A
BIG SITUATION,
MR. EXHIBITOR!

The People Demand Information.
Spies Are Everywhere.

BOOK "THE SPY" NOW AT YOUR
NEAREST FOX EXCHANGE and GIVE
YOUR PATRONS WHAT THEY WANT

STANDARD PICTURES
FOX FILM CORPORATION

STANDARD PICTURES

ALADDIN AND THE
WONDERFUL
LAMP

THE MOST THRILLING
FAIRY TALE EVER TOLD

PLAYED BY THE MOST TALENTED
CHILDREN EVER ON STAGE OR SCREEN

MAGNIFICENT PRODUCTION·
WONDERFUL ACTORS

DIRECTED BY C.M. AND S.A. FRANKLIN

FOR YOUNG AND OLD

MR. EXHIBITOR—RUB THIS MAGIC
LAMP IN YOUR THEATRE AND
WISH FOR ALL THE GOLD
YOU WANT AND YOU'LL
GET IT

Globe Theatre, N. Y.
Broadway Showing
at $1.00 Scale
September 24

FOX FILM
CORPORATION

Madame
PETROVA
In Her First
Petrova Picture
To be released on or about
October, 22, 1917

Petrova Picture Company
Frederick L. Collins, President
25 West 44-Street, New York.

CUB   **CUB**

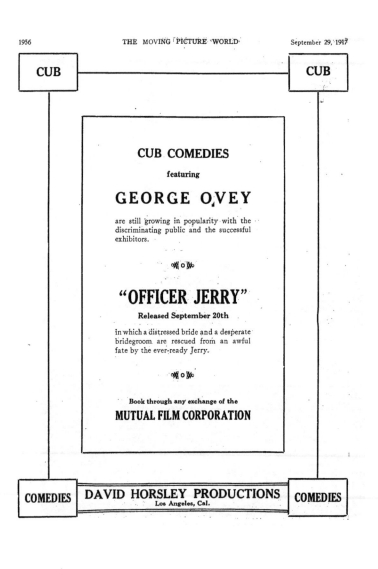

CUB COMEDIES

featuring

GEORGE O.VEY

are still growing in popularity with the
discriminating public and the successful
exhibitors.

"OFFICER JERRY"

Released September 20th

in which a distressed bride and a desperate
bridegroom are rescued from an awful
fate by the ever-ready Jerry.

Book through any exchange of the

MUTUAL FILM CORPORATION

COMEDIES | **DAVID HORSLEY PRODUCTIONS** | **COMEDIES**
Los Angeles, Cal.

LOUISE LOVELY

FEATURES

The Unique Little French-
Australian Star
with the
Sweet and Winsome
Personality

Now Under the Direction
of
Edward J. LeSaint

IN PREPARATION
"The Wolf and Its Mate"

Book the Smashing New York Sensation, the Picture Beautiful

LOUISE LOVELY
IN THE
"SIRENS OF THE SEA"

Jewel Productions, Inc.
405 Mecca Bldg., N. Y. C.

GENERAL FILM COMPANY,

Another FALCON Feature

THE SECRET OF BLACK MOUNTAIN

by JACKSON GREGORY

with VOLA VALE

and Philo Mc Cullough

A Virile Drama
of the West

Supervised by
H.M.&E.D.Horkheimer

FALCON
FEATURES

Distributed Exclusively by General Film Co.

GENERAL FILM COMPANY,

"The Three C Comedies"

Fresh, Original,
One-Reel Productions
with the
Conquering Comedian

LOU MARKS
The Galvanic Eccentric

Pretty PEARL SHEPARD
the Most Piquant Girl in Pictures

And the Convulsing Nondescript

OOM PAUL
Possessor of the Most Bizarre
Physiognomy Ever Unearthed

Together with a Great, Sweet,
Irresistible Group of Lively Lassies.

EVERY EXHIBITOR KNOWS HE CAN
COIN MONEY WITH COMEDIES LIKE THESE

The "Three C Comedies" Will Do It!

The Commonwealth Comedy Co., Inc.
1545 Broadway, New York City
Jos. S. Klein, Pres.; Arnold A. Klein, Vice-Pres.; Chas. W. Kesler, Secy.

DISTRIBUTED EXCLUSIVELY BY GENERAL FILM CO.

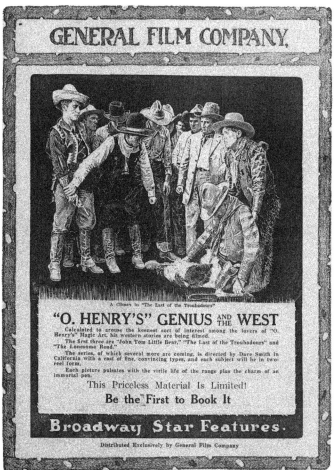

GENERAL FILM COMPANY,

A Climax in "The Last of the Troubadours"

"O. HENRY'S" GENIUS AND THE WEST

Calculated to arouse the keenest sort of interest among the lovers of "O. Henry's" Magic Art, his western stories are being filmed.

The first three are "John Tom Little Bear," "The Last of the Troubadours" and "The Lonesome Road."

The series, of which several more are coming, is directed by Dave Smith in California with a cast of fine, convincing types, and each subject will be in two-reel form.

Each picture pulsates with the virile life of the range plus the charm of an immortal pen.

This Priceless Material Is Limited!

Be the First to Book It

Broadway Star Features.

Distributed Exclusively by General Film Company

Entered at the General Post Office, New York City, as Second Class Matter

Founded by J. P. CHALMERS in 1907.

Published Weekly .by the

CHALMERS PUBLISHING COMPANY

17 MADISON AVENUE, NEW YORK CITY.

(Telephone, 3510-3511 Madison Square)

J. P. Chalmers, Sr.............................President
J. F. Chalmers...........................Vice-President
E. J. Chalmers...............Secretary and Treasurer
John Wylie.............................General Manager

The office of the company is the address of the officers.

CHICAGO OFFICE—Suite 917-919 Schiller Building, 64 West Randolph St., Chicago, Ill. Telephone, Central 5099.

PACIFIC COAST OFFICE—610-611 Wright and Callender Building, Los Angeles, Cal. Telephone, Broadway 4640.

SUBSCRIPTION RATES.

United States, Cuba, Mexico, Hawaii, Porto
Rico and Philippine Islands................$3.00 per year.
Canada ....3.50 per year.
Foreign Countries (Postpaid)................4.00 per year

Changes of address should give both old and new addresses in full and be clearly written. Two weeks' time should be allowed for change.

ADVERTISING RATES.

CLASSIFIED ADVERTISING—One dollar for twenty words or less; over twenty words, five cents per word.
DISPLAY ADVERTISING RATES made known on application.

NOTE—Address all correspondence, remittances and subscriptions to MOVING PICTURE WORLD, P. O. Box 226, Madison Square Station, New York, and not to individuals.

"CINE-MUNDIAL," the monthly Spanish edition of the Moving Picture World, is published at 17 Madison Ave. by the Chalmers Publishing Company. It reaches the South American and Spanish-speaking market. Yearly subscription, $1.50. Advertising rates on application.

(The INDEX to this issue is on page 2054.).

Saturday, September 29, 1917

Facts and Comments

ENTER the screen novelist! The classification of the moving picture is moving forward slowly, but in the right direction. The custom of placing all screen fiction under the heading of photoplays has continued too long, and the correct designation of the contributions of the camera must result in a broader knowledge of screen playwriting among both picture dramatists and laymen. As pointed out in a recent article in the MOVING PICTURE WORLD, many screen stories follow the novel in form and should be called picture novels. The producer of "The Fall of the Romanoffs," recognizing that his story contains all the elements of the historical novel, gives it its proper classification, thus blazing a much desired trail. The picture novel has now come into its own.

THE attention of our readers is once more directed to the lists of film exchanges throughout the country that we printed on pages 1674 to 1676 in last week's issue of the MOVING PICTURE WORLD. As these lists also give the brands handled by each group of exchanges, they form handy references for theater managers in selecting programs or in securing any production they may desire. On account of the space required we will only be able to print the lists occasionally, consequently last week's paper should be filed for reference.

* * *

FROM Boston to Seattle and in between the note of optimism that pervades the correspondence of representatives of the MOVING PICTURE WORLD is most encouraging. Every indication seems to point to a season of good business ahead for the exhibitor in all sections of the country. The increasing popularity and distribution of American films in many parts of the foreign market mean that the American producer is also getting a good share of the export business of the world. As we have said above, this is all most encouraging from a trade point of view providing it is not made the excuse for boosting prices all along the line.

ATTEMPTS to arbitrarily determine what is the best and most profitable length of feature to make are like similar attempts to fix a certain sort of program as being the most successful. Many subjects may be much better in eight or nine reels than in five, while many five-reel productions would really be too long in less than half their present footage. To the average theatergoer variety is ten times more acceptable than a continuous theme, just as the short story and the newspaper number hundreds of readers to one for the book of five or six hundred pages. Right here, we believe, is the kernel of the reason for the drawing power of many of our longer multiple reel subjects. There is sufficient variety in the development of the plot or action to make the audience forget that they are sitting through eight or more reels. Fixing a hard and fast rule as to length of feature or certain style of program would be a sure method of defeating the object in view, namely, the securing of the greatest possible amount of public interest and approval. This can only be done by variety, variety in length of subjects and in style of programs.

* * *

THERE are at least two brands of foolishness that we run into most every week. One is represented by those who would treat the exhibitors as infants to be led every step of the way and as men who can be made to believe any cock and bull story if properly presented. If this paper were to run short some week of the worth while news of the trade necessary to fill our columns and was to use up about five times as much paper to print all the matter we receive from the various publicity concerns in the industry, our readers would realize that there are many more in this foolish class than they ever dreamed of. The other foolish class are those who try to fry their own fish by telling the exhibitor that he is altogether independent of all other branches of the industry, that they all must come to him, etc., etc. The whole industry working together has a great virgin field that it has not yet reached and which affords scope for the best of united efforts, viz.: transforming into picture patrons the great big majority of our population which does not now frequent picture houses. We have what is now freely admitted to be a more direct and a much more interesting medium than books and newspapers, yet only used by possibly a fifth or at most a fourth of the American public and used much less frequently even by those than it might be.

Sane Business Acumen   By Louis Reeves Harrison

THERE are some very stupid assumptions about exhibitors and the public, and one of them is that writers must play down to a low order of intelligence. The founder of this paper was not of that opinion. He took it for granted that his readers knew just as much as he did; nothing too good for them would ever find its way into these columns, and whenever a writer had that opinion it was because he was behind the times. There are producers who have a nervous fit about getting over the heads of "the people," while those people are laughing tolerantly, when not in derision, at his efforts to put forth screen products in words of one syllable.

Another stupid assumption is that nothing good can come from dramas originated especially and only for the screen. The prevailing idea at this time is that we must "import" our stories from literature and from the stage. It is a drawback to have old art traditions hitched to this young art, and, keep this in mind, *the future success of motion picture production lies in its opportunities, not in its drawbacks.*

A very large number of our directors and actors have come to us from the stage, and they can greatly benefit from the training they have received *when they do not impose on moving pictures the artistic codes and methods they have borrowed from the theater.* It is almost time for us to provide our own materials, our own systems, our own principles and *our own standards.* We shall have a true moving picture art when we make it so in all the technics as well as in business organization. Every once in a while, when watching a new release from the viewpoint of a motion picture critic, I feel intuitively that an otherwise charming screen story is spoiled by theatrical grouping of characters, by stagey settings, and by the mannerisms of limelight and footlight actors.

Others feel the same way, to judge from the effect on large audiences. The impression made is that of artificiality, whereas, on the stage itself, supreme effort is made to dispense with everything which contributes to the unnatural because it tends to destroy the illusion. Stage affectations are far from useful in presenting to the mental eye alone our screen illusions of reality. It is to be seriously questioned if a producer, or an exhibitor either, for that matter, has really any shrewd insight into the demands of his patronage when he attempts to limit the splendid opportunities of this new art to the exactions of an older one.

Outside of producers and exhibitors of biased judgment, we are up against business organization and a distributive system which tends very strongly to be conservative. It is in the very nature of cautious business men to stand by the established order of things. A part of the name of holding on to money is to go slow about innovation and change. Good business organization is wisely preservative within its own field of action, and it is of value in production when it protects from unnecessary waste and loss, but it is not very well posted on the response of artistry to audience needs.

When a business organization fails to grasp the true relation between source of supply and consumer, as it usually does when there is an art intervening, it operates directly against its own survival. Inaugurated as a helping agency, it becomes a hindering one. The result has been to establish standards of stage drama and literature for those of the screen, to the injury of moving pictures and to the alienation of people who might easily love fine moving pictures for themselves. The new art is one of

expression in its own language, by its own methods. To dress it up in the old clothes of some parent art is more or less fatal to its individual charm.

Many of the plans unfolded for business reorganization in the production and distribution of moving pictures are sound as far as they go, but they lack breadth of comprehension. They are based on addressing an audience which has not been carefully studied, which is different and far larger than that of the theater, and which has been erratically and imperfectly served up to the present time. For instance, our show is given in the theater of the many. That "many" is falsely judged to be one of limited intelligence, or generously uncritical. False premises to begin with.

There is today no prejudice of importance among our people against moving pictures except that which the pictures themselves furnish. That is to say that existing prejudice is not against the art itself, but against its unsatisfactory examples. Our theaters can only succeed in a large way through immediate contact and close sympathy with our people. They must present what is in harmony with the whole thought of the nation, of what we are planning and thinking about, more of an advance agent of human minds and hearts than a reflection of what has already been presented.

What is to happen is of far deeper interest to all of us than what has happened. Most of us are glad to throw off the old chrysalis and spread our wings in some more perfect shapes for a new flight. Hence our intense fondness for what is new and original. Here is an audience demand rarely grasped by men who most sincerely believe that they possess sane business acumen. We lose sight of the charms and beauty of the life we are motoring through when our attention is entirely confined to driving at full speed. Swift movement may be a pleasure to the man at the wheel but his guests are not permitted to enjoy the change of scene and variety of experience which the ride is supposed to provide.

Is it sane business acumen to play down to the weaklings instead of to people as normal and intelligent as ourselves. *Is it sane business acumen* to "import" from other arts anything which puts a limitation on the opportunities of our own? *Is it sane business acumen* to restrict our scope and freedom of movement with the hampering methods of a boxed-in performance? *Is it sane business acumen* in the visualization of dramas not to consider the relation of the source of supply to the consumer? *Is it sane business acumen* to drive, drive, drive, at top speed in all departments, blind to the main object, that of *entertainment?*

Business organization fails entirely to grasp its opportunities when it disregards the main purpose for which it was created. The first and foremost object of any motion picture organization is to study the needs of our people as a whole and determine how they can be most delightfully satisfied. To grow and flourish we must strike our roots deep into the soil of American intelligence. This is not an easy matter. We cannot do it by borrowing right and left at random, and we must raise ourselves to higher levels of good taste, rather than try to drag it down.

We will all realize some day that this new art belongs to the people. They made it possible; they discovered it; they supported it, and they may yet take it into their own hands and make it deal objectively with the lives we are all living. We are not giving our best friends, the common people, the consideration they truly deserve.

Great Doings in Canada 🎞 🎞 🎞 🎞 🎞 🎞 🎞 *By Sam Spedon*

WE are mighty glad we went to the convention of the exhibitors of the maritime provinces of Canada, held at St. John, N. B. We heard a lot of things about the film business thereabout that make us believe it is indeed the Arcadia of the industry.

No Advance Deposits.

We were told there is only one distributing concern in that territory that asks for an advance deposit. One salesman told us he wouldn't ask for payment on delivery if it wasn't for an occasional cancellation on an agreement before the film was delivered.

For Instance.

"Once in a great while," the salesman said, "I travel one hundred and twenty-five miles at considerable expense, make a contract and when I returned to my office in Montreal I find a cancellation awaiting me. If it weren't for this rare instance I would trust any exhibitor with whom I do business. We have on the whole the finest and most upright class of exhibitors anywhere in the world."

Confidence.

There appears to be a bond of confidence between the distributors and exhibitors throughout the provinces. This was evidenced by the harmony and freedom of speech on questions relating to both, discussed in open convention.

For That Reason.

Everything at the convention and in connection therewith was carried out according to schedule, not a hitch in the whole program. The only discussion of any length was the question of affiliating with an American exhibitors' organization. This was discussed pro and con and it was decided, as conditions were different from those in the States, that the matter be laid on the table until the annual convention of 1918.

Board of Censors.

Even the censors in Canada work in perfect accord with the exhibitors. The final decision is left to the chairman of the board, and as he is a very fair-minded man, well-read and just, his decisions are always accepted as final. Pictures that are historically correct and scenes that are true to life, no matter how tragic in their picturization, are considered in accordance with facts and necessary to depict the truth and historic accuracy. Nothing but the vulgar, lewd and that which caters to the morbid and immoral is taboo.

Deserve the Best.

While at the showing of a feature picture exhibited at the Imperial theater in St. John, we overheard an exhibitor remark: "That's the best feature I have ever seen in Canada. Most of them with the exception of Pathe are so old and shop worn they give us a bad impression. If they showed them all in as good condition as this one it would make a big difference in our choice of features." This would indicate that the home offices of the exchanges do not give the Canadian exhibitors the consideration they deserve and do not know that they are dealing with some of the finest men in the exhibition field—men who deserve the best for audiences through-

out the provinces, that very nearly reach the one hundred per cent. class.

Montreal Conditions.

We were informed by an exchangeman and exhibitor from Montreal that conditions there are somewhat different in that "locality than anywhere else in Canada." In the first place, they said, it is a cosmopolitan city and territory. The exhibitors comprise Greeks, "Canucks," French Canadians and those from the States. We have found it impossible to organize to any extent and the demand for pictures are necessarily varied. We have a fertile field and good business but a difficult one to cater to and a very hard one to deal with, because we have to present our productions to our customers in the way they can best understand and appreciate them. We are striving to bring all the exhibitors into our league and hope eventually to succeed."

Prince Edward Island and Nova Scotia.

The delegates from these provinces were most enthusiastic over the condition of their business. They were full of "pep" and told us business was good, with bright prospects of bigger patronage this fall and winter. Some of them were enlarging and others were redecorating and improving their theaters. They were unanimous in testifying to the response they had received and were receiving from the public in its appreciation of giving it the best, also in its acknowledgement of the benefits of motion pictures, in educating, entertaining and promoting the welfare and happiness of the people.

Cheerfulness Prevails.

We went to Canada with some apprehension of war-cast gloom hanging over it. If it were there, no doubt it was, the people did not wear it on their sleeves. We were received with such good cheer and accorded such hospitality we were completely disarmed, made to feel so much at home, we felt as if we had known our hosts all our lives and were visiting our closest friends and neighbors. We want to go there some more and make a longer stay.

Allied Patriotism.

At the Saturday matinee and evening showing of an American war picture in Keith's Imperial theater, the audiences were vociferous in their applause whenever the Stars and Stripes were in evidence. At the close of the picture when the orchestra played the American and British anthems everyone in the audience stood up in acclamation of their allied interest in the establishment of peace on earth and good will among men.

An Equitable Contract
By SAM SPEDON.

AT a convention in the South a motion was made by a delegate to have the executive committee of the organization draw up an equitable contract between the distributors and exhibitors, the same to be presented to the board of directors for its approval. Now we hear that the National Association of the Motion Picture Industry is to frame an equitable contract between the producers and players. Quite a coincidence. The first will be comparatively easy, because it is a purely business proposition based on cost of production.

and profits governed by local conditions. The second is an entirely different matter, based upon temperament and personal valuation against the estimate of that valuation by the producers. We recall the remark of the old fellow to a consequential young men who was applying for a position and extolled in self praise his many qualifications for the job. The old fellow said, "Young man, I would like to buy you at my estimate and sell you at your own."

An equitable contract between producers and players would only affect the individual players who are obliged to work by the job. Most of the stars have formed their own companies and are in reality individual producers. An equitable contract would not reach the source about which there is most complaint, the high cost of star features and advanced rental prices.

We mentioned the contract between distributors and exhibitors first, to remind the framers of the equitable contract between producers and players that they must not fail to consider the exhibitors in the drafting of it. The article we published in last week's issue of this publication entitled "Do Something" might assist.

The Music Tax Question

ALL exhibitors are interested in the music tax question, which has become a considerable issue because of the energy with which the American Society of Composers, Authors and Publishers are prosecuting violations of the copyright act which gives to composers of music the exclusive right to perform their works for profit in public places. Because of that interest we direct the attention of our readers to articles by Clarence E. Sinn and C. C. Pettijohn published this week in the Department of Music for the Picture.

Mr. Sinn calls attention to the advertised statements of certain publishers that exhibitors are at liberty to use music published by them because they are not members of the Composers and Authors Society, and warns the exhibitor that it is the author and composer who control the copyright and not the publisher, so that the statements in question are misleading and likely to get the exhibitor who heeds them into trouble.

Mr. Pettijohn in answering a puerile editorial in a trade publication alleged to be "of, for and by the motion picture exhibitor," makes all too plain the futility of any attempt to combat by process of law the position of the American Society of Composers, Authors and Publishers. Mr. Pettijohn cites the decision of the Supreme Court of the United States, upon which authority the American Society is acting. He also quotes the opinions of several well known lawyers who corroborate his own opinion, and Mr. Pettijohn is himself a lawyer of known ability.

All this leads to but one conclusion: That the tax imposed by the American Society of Composers, Authors and Publishers has the sanction of law, sustained by the highest tribunal of the land; that any attempt to combat the provisions of the Copyright Law as affecting the rights of the composers of music is defeated before it is commenced.

As a further conclusion it must be said for the information of exhibitors generally that any appeal for funds to fight the Music Tax law is without justification; that it is born of ignorance and will avail those who contribute the sum total of nothing. Without a great stretch of imagination the taking of three dollars, or any other amount for the purpose stated might well be characterized as "obtaining money under false pretenses."

The Moving Picture World does not hesitate to warn exhibitors to disregard all such appeals and advises all who have contributed to request that their moneys be returned to them.

We append a list of the members of the American Society of Composers, Authors and Publishers whose copyrighted productions are subject to the Music Tax:

Abrahams, Maurice Music Co.
Bond, Carrie Jacobs & Son
Broadway Music Corporation
Daly, Jos. M. Music Pub. Co.
Enoch & Sons
Feist, Leo, Inc.
Forster, F. J. A.
Harms, T. B. & Francis, Day & Hunter
Harris, Charles K.
Jerome, William Publishing Corp.
Kalmar & Puck Music Co.
Karczag Publishing Co., Inc.
Remick, Jerome H. & Co.
Richmond, Maurice Music Co.
Ricordi, G. & Co., Inc.
Shapiro, Bernstein & Co., Inc.
Stern, Jos. W. & Co.
Von Tilzer, Harry Music Pub. Co.
Waterson, Berlin & Snyder Co.
Witmark, M. & Sons.

There are many reputable publishers who deal in non-copyright music, so that exhibitors should have no trouble in getting all the music they require that is not subject to tax.

"Eternal Magdalene" Held Up

Controversy With Censors Leads Goldwyn to Substitute "Fighting Odds" as First Maxine Elliott Subject.

After all, Maxine Elliott's debut on the screen as a Goldwyn star will be in the big emotional drama "Fighting Odds," by Roi Cooper Megrue and Irvin S. Cobb—and there's a reason. To get to the point quickly, "The Eternal Magdalene," previously announced as the first of Goldwyn's Maxine Elliott productions, has been challenged by the Pennsylvania board of censors and the Chicago censor board. Both bodies find points in the picture which they protest and which Goldwyn pointedly denies constitute any violation of good taste. Nevertheless, as "The Eternal Magdalene" has been announced for release on October 7 and that date is close at hand, Goldwyn has determined to fully protect all of its contract customers among the exhibitors of the United States by substituting Miss Elliott's other picture in its stead.

This means that "The Eternal Magdalene" and the points at issue with the two censor organizations can be threshed out and adjusted without holding up any Goldwyn customers or disarranging their playing dates. Goldwyn insists that "The Eternal Magdalene" made, as it has been, into a great morality play by Arthur Hopkins, in no way tends to endanger public morality and in this contention finds itself sustained by a most enthusiastic indorsement of the picture in its entirety by the National Board of Review, which exercises the censorial function for America as a whole. The National Board of Review, it will be recalled, declared that "the world as an audience owed Goldwyn a vote of thanks for making this remarkable picture."

In "Fighting Odds" Miss Elliott obtains an introduction to picture audiences of the world under most favorable conditions. In this picture she is equally charming and beautiful in the role of the Magdalene, and she figures as the heroine of a powerful emotional drama by two of America's foremost dramatic authors, Mr. Megrue and Mr. Cobb. "Fighting Odds" is the story of big business and a wife's loyalty to a husband who is made a catspaw to a big financial leader. The scenes of this play are laid in Detroit and New York, and Henry Clive, enacting the role of the husband, is a big manufacturer of automobiles with a business code and a friendliness for labor that suggest the modern wage policies of Henry Ford. Insuring the widest exploitation for this lovely star's debut, Goldwyn is maintaining its special publicity men throughout the country to exploit this picture in advance. In its advertising announcement this week Goldwyn frankly explains the reason for this change in releases and the attitude of the two censor boards.

EDNA PURVIANCE'S ILLNESS DELAYS "THE ADVENTURER."

Charlie Chaplin has resumed work at the Lone Star studio, Hollywood, Cal., on the last scenes of his twelfth Mutual special, "The Adventurer," which was delayed, first by the illness of the famous comedian himself and more recently by an indisposition of Edna Purviance, Mr. Chaplin's leading woman.

Miss Purviance, who had been in the Good Samaritan hospital near Hollywood, since August 19, appeared at the studio looking little worse for her illness, which is declared to have been due to the strain of continuous rehearsal.

Mr. Chaplin's new play is considered by the world's highest priced comedian to be his best production under the epoch-making $670,000 a year contract with the Mutual Film Corporation.

The Motion Picture Exhibitor

WRITE US EARLY AND OFTEN

THE MOVING PICTURE WORLD carries the most complete record of Exhibitors' News. This department aims at being the fullest and fairest chronicle of all the important doings in the ranks of organized exhibitors. To keep the department as complete and as useful as it is now we request the secretaries of all organizations to favor us with reports of all the news. Coming events in the ranks of the organized exhibitors are best advertised in this department of the Moving Picture World.

Maritime Provinces Convention

Large and Enthusiastic Gathering of Canadian Exhibitors at St. John, N. B.

By Alice Fairweather.

THE convention of the Maritime Provinces Exhibitors' League at St. John was, as was stated by several of the distinguished guests, characterized by a spirit of fair-mindedness and good fellowship to a remarkable degree. The attendance comprises about seventy-five exhibitors and a large number of exchange men, with two general managers and several representatives from the Montreal and Toronto head offices.

N. V. Gastonguay,
New President Maritime Province Exhibitors.

The business sessions of the league began at 2 p. m. at the Knights of Pythias Hall, with President W. H. Golding in the chair. After the welcoming remarks the matter of the unfinished business from last year was taken up and a motion relating to the league's joining with the Motion Pictures Exhibitors' League of America was moved. It was decided that in the existing state of affairs in the American leagues it would be unwise to affiliate with any league in the United States, and the matter was left over until the next annual convention.

The Nominating Committee, W. C. McKay, St. John; F. G. Spencer, St. John; D. W. Dimock, Campbellton; R. G. McAdam, Halifax, and N. W. Mason, New Glasgow, was appointed. The retiring president, W. H. Golding, in his address after welcoming the visitors, stated that one of the most serious difficulties confronting motion picture men today in the Maritime Provinces is the prohibitive prices asked for films and the inequitable contracts under which they are sold. "There are evils in the cash deposit arrangements and the dictating of a box office policy, together with a seeming disregard for the safety of the individual showman and his theater by producing magnates in their wild gambling for stars and features," he said. "The decrease in the patronage of moving-picture houses, due to enlistments and bereavements, make the demand for fancy prices come at a most inopportune time, when business is at its lowest ebb in Canada. Smaller places cannot make a big profit by handling big features at Broadway prices." Mr. Golding ended on a high note of patriotism, reminding the exhibitors that the Empire is at war and that their aims must not be only to make money, but to assist their country in every way possible as well. He thanked all his co-workers, and said that he retired with good-will to all.

G. A. Margetts, Maritime Province representative of the Canadian Universal Film Company, spoke on the matter of damaged films, diverting of shipments and other difficulties between the exhibitor and exchanges.

The following were elected officers for the coming year: President, N. V. Gastonguay, Halifax; vice-president, F. G. Spencer, St. John; secretary, J. M. Franklin, Halifax; treasurer, George Metzler, Halifax; vice-president for Nova Scotia, N. W. Mason, New Glasgow, N. S.; W. H. Golding, St. John, for New Brunswick, and J. J. Gaudet, Summerside, for Prince Edward Island.

D. A. McKay of New Waterford, N. S., spoke against the percentage system of playing film attractions. He introduced a resolution favoring a flat rental, but it was not passed.

C. F. Givan, of Sussex, advocated the publishing of a monthly paper giving league news and candid reviews of the films. He offered to publish this free of charge for the first three months. It was felt by those present that the existing trade papers covered the ground pretty thoroughly and that we had the Canadian Motion Picture Digest for the local news.

The question of a standardized contract was brought forward by R. H. McAdam, of Halifax, and was thoroughly discussed. It

W. H. Golding,
Retiring President.

is felt that the contracts at present are far too one-sided and that there are many clauses which might make them fairer to the exhibitor. A contract drafted by Mr. McAdam was left with the executive, who will discuss it with an exchange committee.

A resolution was passed that the board of censorship in the Maritime Provinces establish a physical censorship of films and refuse to allow any to be shown which they considered not to be in a fit condition. It was also recommended that the license of any operator habitually careless and destructive be canceled.

Merrick Nutting, in a bright speech full of common sense, spoke on the evils of under and over advertising and the necessity of taking trade papers to learn about the right pictures to buy; also the need to study one's clientele.

A resolution recommending the appointment of a legislation committee was moved by W. C. McKay, St. John. This committee will have from five to seven members, who will have power to study all legislation regarding matters of importance to the league that may come up in municipal, federal or provincial bodies.

The New Brunswick Telephone Company placed its wires at the disposal of the Maritime Province delegates, and the St. John Street Railway placed all cars at the disposal of the visitors.

N. V. Gastonguay, on taking the chair, made a happy address, paying warm tribute to the retiring officers, the energetic W. H. Golding and S. C. Hurley, the indefatig.

Motion Picture Exhibitors' League of the Maritime Provinces.

able secretary, and hoping that Halifax would show as good, if not a better, record next year.

S. C. Hurley,
Retiring Secretary.

Secretary S. C. Hurley, in his report, said that forty of the eighty theaters in the Maritime Provinces are members of the league (many of these theaters are owned by one man). More than fifty visitors had registered at the league's office in the city, 360 letters had been sent out by the secretary. He expressed the thanks of the league to the trade papers, the "Moving Picture World, the Canadian Motion Picture Digest and the daily press, mentioning especially the work of Miss Alice Fairweather of the St. John Standard. Thanks were due also Miss Kathleen Magee, who had assisted greatly with the secretarial work.

Treasurer G. J. B. Metzler, in his report, showed that the league had a credit balance of $221.49, and was in a healthy state financially. Mr. Metzler received a vote of thanks for his excellent report.

The evening's session program contained splendid addresses from Miss Rose Tapley, F. H. Richardson, Sam Spedon, C. C. Pettijohn and W. Stephen Bush, who spoke on "Organisation," with the text that "it is the exhibitor who is the most important factor in the industry," and he must be first considered.

Miss Tapley spoke from the standpoint of the producer, and urged the necessity of supporting those companies who make the clean, high type of pictures. She spoke of truthful advertising, and, in closing, paid a graceful tribute to the Maritime Provisional Exhibitors' League, saying that in all her travels she had never known a stronger organisation or met fairer, more reasonable men than those engaged in the industry here. She urged the exhibitor to state his grievances to the producer, and if it were a just grievance the matter would be righted; for the producer and the exhibitor, too, must stand shoulder to shoulder. Miss Tapley received an ovation, and her address was greatly appreciated.

F. H. Richardson, the projection expert of the Moving Picture World, spoke upon that subject in a very interesting way. He made a most humorous speech, which was greatly enjoyed.

Another excellent and clever address was given by Sam Spedon of the Moving Picture World, who spoke on some old times in the studios and the value of that strength which comes from unity.

Miss Belle Bruce, whose attractive personality made quite an impression, made a pretty little speech, thanking the league for the warmth of her reception.

Sunday W. H. Donaldson, of the Billboard, made a short speech upon the advisability of joining an American league.

C. C. Pettijohn made a fine address on the future of the motion picture and the need of the elimination of the filth stuff. He gave good advice in a very capable speech, and was listened to with deep attention.

Sunday's excursion up the St. John River was a delightful success. Many pictures were taken by professionals and amateurs, and all voted it a very fine affair. Lunch was served on board and a stop of an hour, made at Brown's Flats, one of the beauty spots of the famous St. John River. A meeting was held on board at which speeches were made by F. H. Richardson, Alfred McGinley, Editor of the St. John Standard (and an ex-censor); J. M. Franklin, R. D. McAdam, C. F. Givan of Sussex, A. E. Wall of the Nova Scotia Board of Censors, and Miss Alice Fairweather, motion picture editor of the St. John Standard, and others.

Sunday evening's meeting, to which admittance was by invitation, was well attended by an interested audience to listen to speeches by Miss Tapley, Miss Belle Bruce, W. Stephen Bush, C. C. Pettijohn, Sam Spedon and F. H. Richardson. Walter H. Golding, manager of the Imperial Theater, presided, and the Imperial Orchestra furnished music. Entertainment was provided for the New York guests after the evening's program.

Monday Miss Tapley and Miss Bruce were the guests of honor at a luncheon given by Miss Alice Fairweather of the St. John Standard, to which were invited the president and officers of the Women's Canadian Club, officers of the Local Council of Women and of the St. John Art Club. This was a very delightful affair, given at the Sign of the Lantern Tea Room.

The afternoon was given up to automobile trips about the suburbs of St. John. A very animated picture was taken by Mr. Warcanteen of the Universal.

Miss Tapley and Miss Bruce spoke at the Imperial Theater on Monday evening to very large audiences. They spoke at the Lyric and Unique Theaters Tuesday evening. Miss Tapley made an address before the members of the Women's Canadian Club on Tuesday afternoon after the show. She gave her talk illustrated, and after the address an informal reception was held on the stage.

CANADIAN EXHIBITORS JOIN AMERICAN ASSOCIATION.

Although the members of the Maritime Provinces Exhibitors' League decided to put over till next year action on the question of affiliating with an American organisation the latest reports indicate that there has been a change of sentiment on the part of the Canadians. Remaining after the close of the convention, General Manager Charles C. Pettijohn, of the American Exhibitors' Association, made a personal canvass of the exhibitors of St. John, N. B., with the result on Tuesday evening he was able to announce that the leading exhibitors of that city, W. H. Golding, F. G. Spence, and Fred Winter of Moncton, had joined the American Exhibitors' Association. It was further announced that S. C. Hurley had been appointed president for the Maritime Provinces and that twenty-five other exhibitors had signed.

Second Annual Convention at St. John, N. B., September 8 and 9.

It is explained by Mr. Pettijohn that the appointment of Mr. Hurley is in the nature of a provisional president, subject to the action of the general convention of the Association at Detroit, Mich., next year.

CLEVELAND EXHIBITORS MAY REORGANIZE.

Unless the proposed new wage scale of the operators, just offered, results in the exhibitors of Cleveland, Ohio, getting together for a fight, there will probably be a reorganization of the local league and an affiliation with the American Exhibitors' Association.

Ever since the split at the Chicago convention, not more than a handful of exhibitors have gathered for the weekly meetings and, in fact, most of the times the meetings were not held.

President Slimm and other influential Cleveland league exhibitors have joined the American Exhibitors' Association and it would not be surprising to hear of a reorganization meeting called shortly.

War Tax Bill Passes Senate

Picture Theaters Charging Less Than Twenty-five Cents Exempted—Joker in the Sliding Scale.

By C. L. Linz.

THOSE of the moving picture theaters having a sliding scale of prices, raising admissions above their regular prices when showing the large features, will, after November 1, be subjected to a tax equivalent to fifty per cent. of the amount in excess of their regular admissions, under the provisions of the general revenue bill passed by the Senate on September 10, while all other moving picture theaters making a charge for admission of twenty-five cents or less will be exempted from the so-called "War Tax on Admissions" as contained in the bill.

This measure was passed by the House of Representatives on May 23. That body provided for a tax equivalent to one cent for each ten cents or fraction thereof of the amount paid for admission to any place, including admission by season ticket or subscription, to be paid by the person making such payment, and a tax of five cents for each admission of each person, except in the case of a bona fide employee and children under twelve years of age and municipal officers on official business.

The five-cent tax contained in the second section of the above paragraph was rejected by the Senate Finance Committee, and later by the Senate itself, and an amendment was adopted which, in the case of moving picture shows, limited the application of the tax to those shows making a charge of more than twenty-five cents for a single admission.

The proposed tax on houses having a sliding scale of prices was aimed primarily at the legitimate theaters, but the motion picture houses must have a care to see to it that they do not run afoul of the new law. It behooves the exhibitors to carefully read the following provisions of the bill as they stand adopted by the Senate:

Sec. 700. That from and after the first day of November, nineteen hundred and seventeen, there shall be levied, assessed, collected, and paid (a) a tax of 1 cent for each 10 cents or fraction thereof of the amount paid for admission to any place, including admission by season ticket or subscription, to be paid by the person making such payment: PROVIDED, That the tax on admission of children where an admission charge for such children is made shall in every case be 1 cent; and (b) a tax of 1 cent for each 10 cents or fraction thereof paid for admission to any public performance for profit at any cabaret or other similar entertainment to which the charge for admission is wholly or in part included in the price paid for refreshment, service, or merchandise; the amount paid for such admission to be computed under rules prescribed by the Commissioner of Internal Revenue, with the approval of the Secretary of the Treasury, such tax to be paid by the person paying for such refreshment, service, or merchandise; and, in addition to the above, (c) upon tickets of admission to theatres, operas, and other places of amusement, sold at news stands, hotels, and places other than the ticket offices of such theatres, operas, or other places of amusement, at not to exceed 50 cents in excess of the sum of the established price therefor at such ticket offices plus the amount of any tax imposed under clause (a) of this section, a tax equivalent to five per cent of the amount of such excess, and if sold for more than 50 cents in excess of the sum of such established price plus the amount of any tax imposed under clause (a) of this section, a tax equivalent to thirty per cent of the whole amount of such excess, such taxes to be paid by the person, corporation, partnership, or association selling such tickets; and, in addition to the above, (d) a tax equivalent to fifty per centum of the amount for which the proprietors, managers, or employees of any opera house, theatre, or other place of amusement sell or dispose of tickets or cards of admission in excess of the regular or established price or charge therefor, such tax to be paid by the person, corporation, partnership, or association selling such tickets. In the case of persons having the permanent use of boxes or seats in an opera house or any place of amusement or a lease for the use of such box or seat in such opera house or place of amusement there shall be levied, assessed, collected, and paid a tax equivalent to ten per centum of the amount for which a similar box or seat is sold, for performance or exhibition at which the box or seat is used or reserved by or for the lessee or holder. These taxes shall not be imposed in the case of a place the maximum charge for admission to which is five cents, or in the case of moving picture shows and outdoor general amusement parks, main gates, shows and rides therein, the maximum charge for admission to which is twenty-five cents.

No tax shall be levied under this title in respect to any admission all the proceeds of which inure exclusively to the benefit of religious, educational, or charitable institutions, societies, or organizations, or admission to agricultural fairs, nor in respect to admissions to bona fide Chautauquas and Lyceum courses which are contracted for and guaranteed by local companies, associations, or individuals.

Sec. 701. That every person, corporation, partnership, or association receiving any payments for such admission shall collect the amount of the tax imposed by Section 700 from the person making such payments, and shall make returns and payments of the amounts so collected, at the same time and in the same manner as provided in Section 503 of this Act.

Every person, corporation, partnership, or association, liable to the tax imposed by subdivision (c) or (d) of Section 700, shall make monthly returns under oath in duplicate and pay the tax imposed by such subdivisions to the Collector of Internal Revenue for the district in which is located the principal place of business. Such returns shall contain such information as the Commissioner of Internal Revenue, with the approval of the Secretary of the Treasury, may by regulation prescribe.

TWO NEW UNIVERSALITES.

Verna Mersereau and Jack Mower, two young players holding forth unusual promise, were added to the acting forces at Universal City last week. Miss Mersereau, despite the similarity of names, is not a sister of Violet Mersereau, nor is she in any way related to the golden-haired star of Bluebird productions. She was associated with the Lubin Company for a while and later with the David Horsley Company. The new Miss Mersereau is an attractive brunette and her initial work with Director George Marshall, to whose company Miss Mersereau has been assigned by Production Manager Henry McRae to enact a heavy role, has created an excellent impression.

Jack Mower, who will appear opposite Donna Drew in the company directed by Jack Wells, will be favorably remembered as the hero of "Jackie of the Navy," playing opposite Marguerite Fischer. He also had the lead with Lillian Walker in "The Lust of the Ages." Mower is a product of the natural school of acting, and has a distinct and pleasing personality.

Music for the Picture

Conducted by CLARENCE E. SINN

The Copyright Proprietor.

EXTRACT from the copyright law relating to public rendition of musical works: **Section 25.**

That if any person shall infringe the copyright in any work protected under the copyright laws of the United States such person shall be liable:

(a.) To an injunction restraining such infringement.
(b.) To pay the *copyright proprietors* such damages as the copyright proprietor may have suffered, due to the infringement, as well as all the profits which the infringer shall have made from such infringement, etc., etc.

This law is intended to protect the producers of original musical compositions. The primal producer is, of course, the composer. He is the sole proprietor until he disposes of his property, and then the buyer becomes sole proprietor. The copyright law is designed to protect him (the proprietor) in "the monopoly that the law intends him to have." As to the publisher's rights, there is still some controversy, though I am informed that the recent court decision is plain on this point. Here are two different points of view:

G. Schirmer (Inc.) is sending the following notice to music dealers:

Gentlemen:—We write to advise that the copyright numbers of Friml and Herbert published by our firm are allowed to be played in public without the payment of a fee. We are not a member of the Society demanding fees for the performance of copyright works by small orchestras in restaurants and places of amusement.
G. SCHIRMER (Inc.) Wholesale Department.

Here is an extract from an open letter to G. Schirmer (Inc.) signed by Victor Herbert, Harry B. Smith and others:

G. Schirmer (Inc.)—Gentlemen:—The announcement in your circular letter and advertisements that your copyright musical publications may be publicly performed in hotels, cabarets, restaurants and other resorts is absolutely misleading insofar as it relates to any of our respective compositions published by you, as you do not own or control the performing rights of any of our works nor the right to authorize the playing or singing thereof by anyone. As a music publisher, your rights in our works are strictly limited to their publication in sheet music form and to their reproduction in music records and rolls. You have no right to grant to theatrical managers, hotel, cabaret or other amusement proprietors public performance rights in our works. We propose to prosecute proprietors of restaurants and other places of entertainment using any of our works published by you, unless such persons secure from the America Society of C. A. & P. a license to publicly perform the same.

In response to letters sent to various publishers, Mr. Glen MacDonough, Secretary for the American Society of Composers, Authors and Publishers, wrote me a courteous letter, saying, among other things:

The house of Schirmer publishes works by Victor Herbert, but Schirmer *does not own the performing rights.* Victor Herbert, being a member of the Society, benefits from his performing rights, while his publisher has no interest. The same applies to other publishers in America who issue foreign works. The foreign composer, being a member of the Society by treaty, the American publisher (non-member of the Society) having no interest, nor a right to give permission to perform.

All this leads up to a question which may or may not come to an issue. For example, many American publishers issue standard music from the pens of the old masters. These are usually called re-prints, and a large part of them were printed in this country before a treaty was made with European countries regarding copyright protection. Publishers on this side of the water could publish any musical composition which had made a success in Europe without paying royalties unless the composition was also copyrighted in this country—which was seldom the case at that time. The American publishers simply "appropriated" the foreign composers' music, and copyrighted it under their own names. Look over the old catalogs of almost any American publisher. You will find compositions by Grieg, Offenbach, Mendelssohn, Schubert, Gounod, Wagner, Balfe, Verdi—a host of names representing the world's best music—all of them copyrighted by American publishers. You can buy

the Suppe overtures copyrighted by Carl Fischer, copyrighted by Oliver Ditson, copyrighted by half a dozen American publishers; all holding (or claiming) copyright proprietorship over the same identical pieces. In what does their copyright proprietorship consist? On what do they base their claim for protection? Possibly on the "arrangement" of numbers—the orchestration. The composers of most of the old music pased away long before the American Society of Composers, Authors and Publishers was thought of. But their works are included in the catalogs of some of the publishers who are members of the Society. I don't believe it is their intention to try to collect a fee for the public performance of such works, but if they should do so, it will be interesting.

Carl Fischer publishes about everything of merit from the old composers (as well as the modern) and Carl Fischer is not a member of the Society. If you want to play safe you can select hundreds of numbers from the Fischer catalog, but be careful that the composer is an old one. Be sure he has been "de-composing" long enough.

The Federation of Musicians.

Local No. 10 (Chicago) of the American Federation of Musicians some time ago discussed the advisability of taking some action on the music tax question. Several plans were considered—some of which found their way into print—but no permanent action was taken. A letter from Joseph N. Weber (President of the national body) was sent to the various locals, a copy of which is here appended:

Ordered that all members be and they are hereby prohibited from playing all copyrighted musical compositions, whether from printed or written copies, or from memory, in any case where charges may be made by the composer or the American Association of Composers, Authors and Publishers, unless the members are directed by their employer to play such compositions.

This leaves it up to the musicians to supply themselves with music which does not come under the restrictions imposed by the society until such time as the employer decides to pay the tax, or otherwise. The Federation of Musicians is not contemplating any further action in the matter at present.

The Carl Fischer Music Publishing Company.

A letter from the above house contains this;

We wish to advise you that we are not members of either the American Society of Composers and Authors or of the French Society, and that there are no limitations on the performing rights of any of the compositions published and copyrighted by us. We have in our catalog, however, four works the copyright of which is not in our name, to wit:—
Dubussy, "Arbesquest" (I and II).
Puccini, "La Boheme" (Fantasie).
Leoncavallo.
Pagliacci (Selections).
and as we are somewhat in doubt as to our performing rights in these numbers, we would not advise you publicly perform them unless you have been licensed by the copyright proprietors or the Society of C. A. and P. to do so.

Mr. Fischer also calls attention to the Witmark catalog taken over by his house some time ago. He says:

Not only are M. Witmark & Sons the owners of the copyrights of the orchestra and band compositions which we issue in their behalf, but they are also members of the American Society of C. A. and P. It is therefore necessary for a leader who contemplates using any of the Witmark prints to write direct to Witmark as to their stand with regard to that particular composition.

Suggested Music.

Here are a few old standards issued by Carl Fischer: Grand Opera Album (selections from Standard Operas; arranged by Charles J. Roberts.
Album of Overtures (standard).
Album of Strauss Waltzes.
Album of Waldteufel Waltzes.

The Sam Fox Publishing Company, Cleveland, Ohio, also

issues some very clever little concert numbers which are worth your while. Mr. Fox is not a member of the society, and I am told he asserts that he has no intention of joining. I am informed that none of his composers are members. (Sam Fox Library Orchestra Folios.)

Send Stamps.

Correspondents wishing answers to their letters will kindly send postage stamps. Two cents may not mean much to you, but in the aggregate they amount to a great deal to me.

Music Copyright Question

General Manager of American Exhibitors' Association Shows Futility of Opposing Existing Law on Subject.
By C. C. Pettijohn.

THE "running and not fighting" editorial in the Exhibitors' Trade Review last week is thoroughly in keeping with its policy to misrepresent and mislead exhibitors. The American Exhibitors' Association has no official organ, but we do appreciate the support of the numerous papers who believe we are right. This Association did not intend to say or do anything that might in the least discourage any man or set of men engaged in any fight for the exhibitor. We are compelled, however, after the publication of this intentionally misleading article to make this statement:

The organisation of music composers and publishers, as the American Society of Composers, Authors and Publishers, comprising most of the well-known composers and publishers of America, England, Italy and Austria, was established for the purpose of issuing licenses to playing resorts to play the copyrighted music of its membership. This society is operating under Section 1, Sub. Div. e of the Copyright Act, which secures to a musical author the exclusive right to perform the copyrighted musical composition publicly for profit.

The Supreme Court of the United States, in the case of Victor Herbert, the composer, against the Shanley Company, the cabaret restaurant on Broadway and 43d street, decided that the playing of copyrighted music in the dining room of a restaurant for the entertainment of guests during meal time by an orchestra was an infringement of the composer's copyright, the court holding that whether or not an admission fee is charged for entering the place of entertainment makes no difference.

The court said in January, 1917:

"If the rights under the copyright are infringed only by a performance where money is taken at the door they are imperfectly protected. Performances not different in kind from those of the defendants could be given that might compete with and even destroy the success of the monopoly that the law intends the plaintiffs to have. It is enough to say that there is no need to construe the statute so narrowly. The defendant's performances are not eleemosynary. They are part of a total for which the public pays, and the fact that the price of the whole is attributed to a particular item which those present are expected to order is not important. It is true that the music is not the sole object, but neither is the food, which probably could be got cheaper elsewhere. The object is a repast in surroundings that to people having limited powers of conversation or disliking the rival noise give a luxurious pleasure not to be had from eating a silent meal. If the music did not play it would be given up. If it pays, it pays out of the public's pocket. Whether it pays or not, the purpose of employing it is profit, and that is enough."

The question as to whether this decision applies to motion-picture theaters was submitted by the First National Exhibitors' Circuit, Inc., to A. L. Jacobs, a well-known theatrical lawyer, for his opinion. After a very careful consideration, Mr. Jacobs reached the conclusion that the decision in the Shanley case applies with equal force to motion-picture theaters.

The Brooklyn League of Motion Picture Exhibitors, we are reliably informed, submitted the same question to Edmund Wise, another well-known copyright specialist, practicing in New York City, and he expressed it as his opinion that it is a violation of the copyright laws to play in any motion-picture theater copyrighted music without the consent of the copyright owners.

The question was then tested in the case of Raymond Hubbell against Royal Pastime Amusement Company before Judge Julius M. Mayer of the United States District Court, Southern District of New York, involving the playing of "Poor Butterfly" in the Regent Theater, a motion-picture house in the Borough of Manhattan, New York City. Judge Mayer in that case sustained the complaint of the composer against the picture house.

The decision of the Supreme Court of the United States in Herbert vs. Shanley proceeds upon the theory that the owner of a musical copyright enjoys two distinct rights: First, the right to publish and sell the composition and various arrangements thereof for different instruments; second, to publicly perform it for profit. I believe Congress intended to accord to the creator of the composition a monopoly for twenty-eight years.

The musical entertainment is an integral part of some motion-picture attractions, and in a great many cases the musical program is a distinctive feature of the house.

In the American Society we find such names as Victor Herbert, John Philip Sousa, Raymond Hubbell, Irving Berlin, Jerome D. Kern, Ray Goetz, Ernest Ball, Gus Edwards, Rudolf Frimi, Sylvio Hein, Edgar Leslie, Theodore Morse, Jack Norworth, A. Baldwin Sloane, Puccini, Mascagni, Leoncavallo, and hundreds of others. These men being artists are not difficult to approach or to negotiate with. If we do not blink at the facts and fairly recognise that these composers are daily conceiving and creating melodies which appeal to our public and which we need in our theaters for its entertainment, then why should we not meet these men in a spirit of fairness and concede to them that they have created something we want in our business. Considering the matter in that light, and relying upon the expression of their representatives as to their willingness to meet us half way, would it not be best to meet in conference and adjust our differences?

The American Society has been very active in enforcing the rights of its members, and has proceeded under both the civil and criminal provisions of the law.

Under Section 28 of the Copyright Act it is a misdemeanor, punishable by imprisonment for not exceeding one year, or for a fine of not less than $100 nor more than $1,000, to wilfully and for profit infringe any copyright or to aid or abet such infringement.

More than one hundred civil actions have been brought for the recovery of penalties, provided for by Section 25 of the Copyright Act, against exhibitors. The law provides that the damages recoverable for the infringement of a copyright shall not be less than $250 nor more than $5,000, upon the basis of $10 for every infringing performance in a case of a popular number, and in the case of an operatic composition, $100 for the first and $50 for every subsequent infringing performance. Costs will be allowed in all cases against the infringer, and a counsel fee may be awarded in the discretion of the court.

It has been the policy of this Government to give monopolies to authors and inventors upon the theory that by giving to them a monopoly of their works the progress of science and the useful arts will be promoted. Since phonograph records and rolls were introduced into the market commercially Congress has amended the copyright laws by compelling the manufacturers to pay a royalty to the composers. The tendency has been toward a more complete protection of authors and composers.

No honest lawyer should advise a client to engage in litigation he knows cannot be successful.

Mr. Brandt of Broklyn, the executive secretary of the M. P. E. L., is now under arrest for copyright violation, and Mr. Ochs, the president of the M. P. E. L., is collecting the $3 per exhibitor. Draw your own conclusions.

The American Exhibitors' Association is willing to meet the American Society of Composers, Authors and Publishers on behalf of motion-picture exhibitors. We have many differences. We will meet you in an open session. You hear us and we will hear you respectfully and conceding that we both have rights.

BRILANT SELLS "THE ALIBI" TO BRADY.

Arthur M. Brilant, author of "The Alibi," a powerful society drama, has sold the screen rights to his play to the World Film Corporation through William A. Brady, director-general. Alice Brady will play the leading role. At the same time Mr. Brilant is carrying on negotiations with a big firm of legitimate producers for the presentation of "The Alibi" as a three act play on Broadway shortly. Mr. Brilant is at present busy finishing a serial contracted for by a well known firm, and will shortly begin work on a ten reel feature for a state righting organisation.

Producers' Employment Bureau

Separate Corporations to Be Organized for the Purpose of Engaging Players—To Support Agencies.

AT A MEETING of the Producers' Branch Committee of the National Association of the Motion Picture Industry, held on Saturday, September 8, the report of a special committee, which was appointed at a previous meeting to investigate the possibility of establishing a service bureau, was received and adopted.

Gabriel L. Hess, secretary of the Goldwyn Pictures Corporation, as chairman submitted the report on behalf of the committee, the other members of which are R. H. Cochrane of the Universal Film Mfg. Company and Joseph W. Engel of Metro Pictures Corporation.

After a very thorough survey of the situation, covering a period of three months, the committee recommended the incorporation of a small company to be known as the Service Bureau of the National Association of the Motion Picture Industry, Inc., which will serve as an employment agency for the engaging of artists and players whenever the service of an agency is required, and all members of the Producers' Branch Committee have agreed to use this bureau in engaging their artists and studio employes. Application has been made for a license as an employment agency, and this department will be under the supervision of the license bureau of the City of New York as well as of the State Department of Labor.

Negotiations have been practically concluded for the services of an expert in this line to manage the bureau, and leases have been prepared for spacious quarters in a centrally located building which will be convenient for everyone desirous of enlisting the bureau's aid.

It is proposed that a uniform contract shall be adopted by the service bureau in employing artists and other help required in any branch of the industry, definite forms to be prepared for long term contracts as well as daily and weekly service.

The service bureau will be amply financed by the producer members and the net profits over and above the expense of operation are to be paid into the treasury of the National Association of the Motion Picture Industry.

There are many benefits to be derived through the establishing of an efficiently conducted service bureau, and it is contended that this new department of the National Association will greatly strengthen the industry and make cooperation much more easy. As evidence of the desire of many actors and actresses to negotiate for employment directly through the Producers' Committee of the National Association, it was stated that many applications have been received at the general offices during the past month, which will be turned over to the manager of the Service Bureau.

N. A. M. P. I. MEETING CALLED.

Will Vote on Proposition to Increase Membership in Executive Committee.

A special meeting of the members of the National Association of the Motion Picture Industry will be held at the headquarters, in the Times Building, Thursday morning (September 20), at eleven o'clock, when an amendment to the by-laws is to be voted upon, providing for an increase in the membership of the Executive Committee from nine to twelve members. The Board of Directors has recommended this action, but ratification by the entire membership is necessary before the present committee can be enlarged.

Immediately following the members' meeting the Board of Directors will convene for the September quarterly meeting, which is the first to be held under the amended by-laws. The important subjects which are on the calendar for consideration at this meeting include reports of the committees on Expositions, the All-Star Picture and the Service Bureau. The establishing of a Film Theft Bureau is to be considered, also plans for proceeding with the organisation of Advisory Committees in important film centers. President Brady will review the activities of the various sub-committees of the War Corporation Department, which are acting in conjunction with the federal departments. Matters pertaining to the legislative work this fall will receive attention by the directors, and a report regarding the possibility of an affiliation with the Pacific Coast Producers' Assocation will be presented.

President Brady will also file his nominations for membership on the Executive Committee for approval by the Directors.

Levine Representing Western Circuit

H. Z. LEVINE, widely known director of publicity and advertising, has established an agency that will negotiate purchases for several Southern and Middle Western independent distributors as well as handle the sales and exploitation campaigns for big special productions to be released in October. The headquarters will be at Suite 514,

Candler Building, 220 West 42d street. Mr. Levine, who will personally direct the activities of the new agency, has had practical experience in every branch of the industry and has been associated in one capacity or another with some of the leading companies. He has occupied the position of director of publicity both here and abroad, and personally directed on the ground intensive campaigns for serial attractions in England, Scotland, France and Germany. He has conducted elaborate sales campaigns in this country and has crossed the continent several times in the interest of superfeatures. He has been purchasing agent, film editor, and in the early days of the business did

Harold Z. Levine.

everything around a film plant except turn a crank. Mr. Levine was associated with the Blaches, Universal in Europe, Fox and Triangle. Prior to his film affiliations he was on the Brooklyn Eagle.

"We are in the market for a few pictures of quality," said Mr. Levine in discussing his new venture. "My clients want the best, and those who have nothing but junk to offer are persona non grata. We also want it made clear that we are not going to work boths ends against the middle. We are paid by our clients for our experience and good judgment and will not exact commissions for sales effected."

Abrams on Four Months' Tour

President of Paramount to Visit Exhibitors in All Towns Over Twenty Thousand—Prime Purpose to Establish Personal Contact.

WHAT is by far the most extended tour of the country and the widest survey of distributing and exhibiting conditions ever undertaken by a motion picture executive was inaugurated Monday, September 10, when Hiram Abrams, president of the Paramount Pictures Corporation, began a four-month trip to exhibitors all over the country in behalf of Paramount and Artcraft Pictures. Mr. Abrams' tour has been so arranged as to permit him to visit exhibitors in all towns of over twenty thousand population.

The prime purpose of the trip is to establish a point of personal contact between Mr. Abrams and exhibitors in all parts of the country, looking toward a better mutual understanding, a more sympathetic and logical appreciation, on the parts of the distributing and exhibiting elements of the trade for the problems of each other and a greater degree of service and a higher standard of cooperation by Paramount and Artcraft toward their clients. It is understood officially that Mr. Abrams will devote the greater part of his conferences with exhibitors to the solution of their local problems and the seeking of business fundamentals upon which can be based an advanced and more advantageous code of relationship that will in the future be applied to the industry in a national way, with the betterment of the exhibitors' collective interests and the strengthening of their investments always as the desired consummation.

B. P. Schulberg, general manager of Paramount, will accompany Mr. Abrams on his trip, and will compile a statistical chart graphically illustrating the results and information which the conferences will disclose, to be utilised as a basis for the constructive work that will follow immediately upon the termination of the trip.

"Polly" Gets Great Reception

First Goldwyn Production Released in Eighty Cities on Same Date Makes Great Impression on Record-Breaking Audiences.

GOLDWYN'S picturization of Margaret Mayo's great play, "Polly of the Circus," with Mae Marsh as the star, has gone over big. The first release of this new producing concern, now nearly a year old, got a rousing welcome in New York, Philadelphia and more than eighty other cities throughout the United States, where the picture was shown simultaneously.

While the owners of the Strand Theater, New York, looked for big business at the opening night's showing of the first Goldwyn release, they were not quite prepared for the rush. "Polly of the Circus" broke all recent Strand attendance records and kept the theater packed inside and with a lobby filled to overflowing throughout its first day at the greatest of metropolitan picture theaters.

Harold Edel, manager of the Strand, made elaborate preparations for the first showing of "Polly." For weeks the lobby of his theater had been dressed with attractive paintings, done by great artists to announce the production to the audiences. On the stage for the presentation he had ordered a distinctive drop, which show a circus lot and the big tent with the main entrance.

Out of this entrance stepped the ringmaster of "Polly of the Circus," George S. Trimble. He wore his ringmaster costume and high hat, and, removing his hat, he announced the beginning of the production in the florid language of the circus ring, ending by expressing the Strand management's appreciation of Goldwyn Pictures, which henceforth will be shown first in this theater.

Signor Arians and Carl Edouarde, the musical conductors of the Strand, had labored for weeks in preparing a musical accompaniment for the production and the orchestra was enlarged to forty-five pieces, or full symphonic strength, to make the presentation of "Polly of the Circus" memorable. As at previous invitation showings, the big scenes of the picture evoked audible enthusiasm from the audience. The exciting horse race scene brought the spectators out of their chairs.

Throwing every resource at his command behind Goldwyn Pictures Stanley V. Mastbaum, the Philadelphia exhibitor and theater magnate, made the opening presentation of "Polly of the Circus" at his Stanley Theater a memorable piece of showmanship from every angle. Mr. Mastbaum's organisation had conducted a brilliant newspaper advertising campaign in all of the Quaker City dailies within the prior week in sole behalf of "Polly of the Circus," and Goldwyn Pictures have been launched with greater force and received greater acclaim than almost any pictures ever before exhibited in the Philadelphia territory.

The triumph of Mae Marsh and the great film was marked in every section of the country. All existing house records, in money and attendance, were broken at the Standard Theater, Cleveland, and Manager Joseph Grossman was so enthusiastic over his opening that he telephoned Goldwyn at midnight on his opening night to congratulate Samuel Goldfish and his associates on the successful launching of the big producing company.

At the St. Denis Theater, Montreal, just taken over by N. L. Nathanson and his associates, all previous money records for a day were eclipsed, and the newspapers of the Dominion's big city are lavish in their praise of the Goldwyn standard of production.

In Columbus, Ohio, the Messrs. Dusenbury, owners of the Grand Theater, who are to play "Polly of the Circus" at a later date because of previously booked pictures, could not wait for a public verdict, but held a special showing of the production for newspaper publishers, the Ohio Board of Censors and members of the Governor's staff. The newspapers, without waiting for the public showing of the production, gave it laudatory notices.

Both in newspaper reviews and exhibitor telegrams a note is emphasized that Goldwyn productions are even better than its press agent promises in that everything that has been promised in quality of production has been exceeded in the production itself.

LEGISLATION ON ADVANCE DEPOSITS.

We heard in New York, from one who knows, that already a bill has been framed to be introduced in the next legislature obliging distributors who ask an advance deposit to place the deposit in a trust company and pay the exhibitors six per cent. on their deposits.

Lasky Returns to Coast

After Six Weeks in New York Vice-President of Famous Players-Lasky Corporation, Goes to Western Studios.

FOR the purpose of holding many vital conferences on producing matters Mr. De Mille and the heads of the Famous Players-Lasky studios, as well as with Thomas H. Ince and Mack Sennett, who are now producing for Paramount, Jesse L. Lasky, vice-president of the Famous Players-Lasky Corporation, left this week for California. It is his plan to spend six weeks at each side of the continent attending to the activities of the many producing organisations. Prior to his departure for the Coast, Mr. Lasky stated that he was more than satisfied with the progress of work at the Eastern studios, where stars of Paramount and Artcraft are all busily engaged on forthcoming productions. Marguerite Clark is doing a "Bab" story—third of the Mary Roberts Rinehart "Sub-deb" tales, published in the Saturday Evening Post; Pauline Frederick is at work on "Mrs. Dane's Defense." Ann Pennington is finishing "The Antics of Ann"; Lina Cavalieri has started work on "The Eternal Temptress," and Billie Burke has finished "Arms and the Girl." These are all to be Paramount releases. For Artcraft, Elsie Ferguson is to do Agnes and Egerton Castle's "Rose of the World."

In the west Coast studios Geraldine Farrar is working on "The Devil's Stone" for Artcraft. William S. Hart and Douglas Fairbanks are busy on new productions; George Beban is at work on a new one, and "Tom Sawyer" is being filmed, with Jack Pickford in the title part. These two latter are Paramount attractions of the near future. Vivian Martin will do "Mary Gusta" for Paramount, and Sessue Hayakawa is filming "The Secret Game."

Mary Pickford is working on "The Little Princess" for Artcraft. This is from the story by Francis Hodgson Burnett. Julian Eltinge is at work on "The Clever Mrs. Carfax" for Paramount, and Wallace Reid will do "Nan of Music Mountain" for the same company.

Mr. Lasky declares that things are running with the greatest smoothness in all departments of production.

ANDERSON BACK FROM THE COAST.

Carl Anderson returned from the Hollywood studios of the Paralta organisation last Sunday (the 9th inst.), accompanying S. A. Lynch, president of the Triangle Distributing Corporation, on his journey from the West Coast.

Mr. Anderson expressed himself as very much pleased over the organisation of the Paralta studios, as it has been developed since May last. In that brief time one of the ablest technical staffs in the country has been brought together, accommodations for five producing units have been provided and four big star feature productions have been completed.

In addition to this, two big stages have been built, 50 by 200 feet, one open-air and the other enclosed; a great property building has been constructed, and other departments for the making of special properties have been added to the original Clune studio plant, which Paralta leased.

AUBREY M. KENNEDY, MANAGER OF PRODUCTION

Aubrey M. Kennedy, since the middle of last winter manager of Goldwyn's studios in West Fort Lee, N. J., has been appointed to the newly created position of manager of productions, which gives him opportunity to accelerate Goldwyn's progress in the efficient production of the company's annual output of twenty-six big pictures.

As a result of Mr. Kennedy's elevation the position of business manager has been created at the studios and into this office steps H. J. Flint, a newcomer in the Goldwyn ranks, who takes over the executive and plant detail duties formerly performed by Mr. Kennedy.

Hard work and faithful attention to the task of helping Goldwyn make good its advance promises of ten or more finished productions before the date of its initial release of "Polly of the Circus" caused the Goldwyn executives to reward Mr. Kennedy with a larger field for his efforts.

SCREEN CLUB OFFICIAL TICKET UP.

In anticipating the annual election of the Screen Club, which will occur in December, the following nominations for officers for the coming year have been posted: President, Joseph W. Farnham; vice presidents, Frank Powell, Edgar Lewis, B. A. Rolfe; recording secretary, George Blaisdell; corresponding secretary, Anthony F. Kelly; treasurer, W. C. Smith; members of Board of Governors, George D. Baker, Max Mayer, C. J. Williams, John Harvey.

Brady Comes Back at Beck

Faith Is Still Unshaken in His First Proposition—Says It Is a Cinch.

WITHOUT the faintest intention of precipitating a controversy," said William A. Brady, director general of World-Pictures Brady-Made, "I remain unshaken in my belief that the most successful and enduring motion pictures are those which reach the screen by way of the speaking theater. I observe that a previous declaration along these lines has brought out an expression of opinion very much to the contrary, supported by the names of a number of motion pictures which owe nothing to the oral stage.

"To begin with, some of the plays quoted in the list to which I refer were never conspicuously successful, and not one of them ever had the vogue of, let us say, 'The Birth of a Nation,' which came to the screen from the theater, and to the theater from a printed novel.

"Then let us glance for a moment at the record of World Pictures derived from the stage and very successful without exception. These include 'After Dark,' 'Alias Jimmy Valentine,' 'As in a Looking Glass,' 'As Ye Sow,' 'The Ballet Girl,' 'The Boss,' 'The Builder of Bridges,' 'A Butterfly on the Wheel,' 'The City,' 'Col. Carter of Cartersville,' 'The Cotton King,' 'The Cub,' 'The Dollar Mark,' 'The Face in the Moonlight,' 'The Family Cupboard,' 'A Gentleman from Mississippi,' 'The Man of the Hour,' 'The Man Who Found Himself,' 'Mother,' 'Mrs. Wiggs of the Cabbage Patch,' 'Old Dutch,' 'Over Night,' 'The Pit,' 'The Rack,' 'The Social Highwayman,' 'Blue Grass,' 'The Master of the House,' 'La Vie De Boheme,' 'Husband and Wife,' 'Forget-Me-Not,' 'Bought and Paid For' and a few others.

"Without singling out any one or more of these plays, but bunching the whole lot, I can securely defy anyone to name a similar number of dramas writen exclusively for the screen and produced by any one management, registering anything like the drawing power of this collection.

"It seems to me to be a perfectly plain, obvious proposition that if you go before the public with a picture version of a play that has already been seen and liked by a great number of people, you have got your patronage assured before the doors are opened. If this is not the fact, then there is absolutely nothing in publicity or advertising, no use in building up the confidence of the people in the article you are about to offer.

"I will go further and say that when your photoplay is made from a successful stage drama, which in due course was dramatized from an immensely circulated novel, the value is increased immeasurably. This is the situation with our forthcoming picture, 'The Burglar,' starring Carlyle Blackwell and featuring Madge Evans and Evelyn Greeley.

"As previously stated, our photodrama was produced from the stage play of the same name by Augustus Thomas, which in its time was seen and applauded by pretty much all the theater patrons of the entire country. Mr. Thomas wrote his drama closely following Mrs. Frances Hodgson Burnett's story, 'Editha's Burglar,' which was read all over the world, having been translated into no less than six languages.

"Will anyone seriously contend that any number of original scenarios, prepared for the screen direct, have a chance to make as great and enduring a success as is practically sure to be registered by 'The Burglar'? It is absolutely open-and-shut that on the one side of this proposition we find an outside chance, and on the other a cinch."

GREENE RETURNS FROM ARGENTINA.

Edward Greene, who left New York in November, 1916, to supervise the film department of the North American Film Service in Buenos Aires, arrived on September 4th to act as assistant buyer to L. R. Thomas.

Mr. Greene says that prevailing conditions in Argentina today are similar to those of New York—overcrowded and overdone. Projection is good in most of the theaters.

North American Films Service are the representatives in Argentina, Chile and Uruguay for Metro, World, Universal and many other well-known brands.

INCE USES OLD BIOGRAPH STUDIO.

The old Biograph studio in Los Angeles, a cinema pioneer of Southern California, after a long period of disuse, has been taken over temporarily by Thomas H. Ince, and is now being used for the filming of photo-dramas which he will release through Artcraft and Paramount.

At Leading Picture Theaters

Programs for the Week of September 16 at New York's Best Motion Picture Houses.

"The Countess Charming" at The Rialto.

JULIAN ELTINGE in "The Countess Charming," written by Gelett Burgess and Carolyn Wells, headed the program at The Rialto the week of Sept. 16. For his first appearance as a Paramount star Mr. Eltinge was provided with a dual role, alternating a young business man and a Russian countess. The effect of these successive impersonations is completely mystifying to the other people in the story. Florence Vidor, Edythe Chapman, Tully Marshall, Mabel Van Buren and other clever players assist the star. Donald Crisp directed the picture.

The Animated Magazine, a scenic of the Canadian Rockies and a comedy were also on the bill. The soloists were Count Lorrie Grimaldi and Gloria Gale.

"Double-Crossed" at The Strand.

The principal photo-dramatic feature at The Strand was "Double-Crossed," a Paramount picture, starring Pauline Frederick. A devoted young wife learns of a youthful slip on the part of her husband. What happened when she found out his crime and how a new and deeper understanding was brought about between them is told in the picture. In the supporting cast are Crawford Kent, Riley Hatch, Clarence Handyside, Harris Gordon and Joseph Smiley. The picture was produced under the direction of Robert G. Vignola. Victor Moore was seen in his latest comedy, "In Bed—In Bad." A chapter of Raymond L. Ditmars' "Living Book of Nature," "Mounting Butterflies," and the Strand Topical Review were also on the program. Henry De Cayx and Norma de Mendoza were the soloists.

"The Man Without a Country" at the Broadway.

The second week of the engagement of the Jewel feature, "The Man Without a Country," at the Broadway, shows that the public interest in the picturization of the Edward Everett Hale patriotic classic is on the increase.

"RUNAWAY ROMANY" NOVELIZED FOR NEWSPAPERS.

The novelization of "Runaway Romany," Marion Davies' motion picture play, has been finished by her and forty metropolitan newspapers have agreed to print it simultaneously on September 16.

Among these are the Minneapolis Tribune, Rochester Democrat and Chronicle, Syracuse Post-Standard, Memphis Commercial Appeal, Louisville Courier Journal, St. Louis Republic, Columbus Dispatch, Buffalo Times, Toledo Blade, Worcester Telegram, Philadelphia Record, Boston Herald, Newark Star-Eagle, Milwaukee Sentinel, Des Moines Register and Leader, Dayton News, Detroit Journal and Providence Tribune.

Miss Davies has begun work on her second moving picture and has signed a contract with the Ardsley Art Film Corporation for two additional pictures.

KERRIGAN OUT OF HOSPITAL.

J. Warren Kerrigan has left the Cottage hospital at Santa Barbara, Cal., where he was taken when his right leg was broken below the knee by the fall of his horse four weeks ago. He remained at the hospital three weeks. The physicians then decided that he had progressed so favorably that it would be safe for him to return to Los Angeles.

Walking by the aid of crutches, and resting his leg on supports on the train, he made the journey without mishap. He was met at Los Angeles station by Robert T. Kane, vice-president of the Paralta Plays, Inc., and Robert Brunton, manager of the Paralta studios at Hollywood, and a number of his company. Mr. Kerrigan will remain at the home of his mother in Hollywood until he is sufficiently recovered to resume his work before the camera. His physicians state he will be able to walk without a crutch in two or three weeks.

"THE FALL OF THE ROMANOFFS" AT THE BROADWAY.

Herbert Brenon's latest production, "The Fall of the Romanoff's is to be shown at the Broadway Theater, New York City, where it will have a two weeks' running, beginning Sunday afternoon, September 23. The engagement will be a limited one owing to the fact that it is impossible at this time of the season to get a theater and that the bookings for the Broadway Theater have been made in advance.

Perfection Pictures—Announces Plans ▨ ▨ ▨ ▨ ▨

High-Class Stories by Known Authors Will Be Produced—New Process of Manufacture Utilized—Ample Advertising Aids Proposed

AN ANNOUNCEMENT of extraordinary interest in the film world comes in a statement which heralds the release of a new brand of feature pictures, to be presented one each week, beginning in September, under the brand name of Perfection Pictures, and which are to be backed up by one of the largest national advertising campaigns ever attempted in behalf of any motion picture project.

Perfection Pictures will represent the master efforts of three of America's pioneer producers, George K. Spoor, president of the Essanay Film Manufacturing Company; Thomas A. Edison, Inc., and George Kleine. They will be examples of a new high standard in cinema art—light dramas and comedy dramas of the cheerful vein, so much in demand at the present time. They will be released through the George Kleine System of exchanges, one each week for the first year,

Thomas A. Edison.

either on the open booking plan or on a contract for the full fifty-two pictures.

Perfection Pictures will be particularly notable for their stories and the quality of their photography. The stories will be furnished by many of America's greatest authors, while all Perfection Pictures will be made by the Perfection process—a new and wonderful invention for the development of films, which promises an evolution in the film industry. By reason of this process, which has taken four years to perfect, Perfection Pictures will excel any other pictures in the matter of clearness, brilliancy and ease of viewing.

The exact details of the Perfection process are, of course, a trade secret. An indication of the care which has been taken in developing it, however, is the fact that a huge machine weighing fifteen tons and costing $100,000 has been perfected by the world's foremost laboratory experts and is being used exclusively in the manufacture of Perfection Pictures. This wonderful film processing device ranks among the mechanical marvels of the world, paralleling the great printing presses of the present day in its importance. The results obtained by its use will be instantly perceptible on the screen. An invention of still greater magnitude, that will revolutionize motion photography, is also to be announced soon in connection with Perfection Pictures.

Among the attractions already made or in course of production are stories by such noted authors as Clarence Budington Kelland, Peter B. Kyne and Kennett Harris, all of Saturday Evening Post fame; George Ade, and many others. It is said that many months have been spent in searching the literary market for stories of the type desired for Perfection Pictures, and that eight productions—each in

George K. Spoor.

five or six reels—are finished and approximately ten more are now in work.

Perfection Pictures are being made in the studios of the Essanay Film Manufacturing Company, Thomas A. Edison, Inc., and George Kleine. Enough super de luxe attractions are completed or in process of production to insure a regular release of Perfection Pictures at the rate of one a week for a period of a year, beginning in September. That the utmost in the way of stories, stage settings, costumes and properties may be expected in Perfection Pictures is assured by the fact that appropriations of several million dollars have been made for productions alone during the first year.

This is exclusive of a fund of $300,000, which has been set aside as an advertising appropriation for the first year. Full pages are to be used each month in the Saturday Evening Post, the first full-page announcement appearing in the issue of Saturday, September 22. In addition, large space will be used in other national magazines and in newspapers throughout the country.

Under the brand of Perfection Pictures exhibitors will find a new type of photoplay entertainment — light, pleasing comedy - dramas and dramas from the pens of the world's greatest authors and playwrights — film stories created in the minds of such literary celebrities as Clarence Budington Kelland,

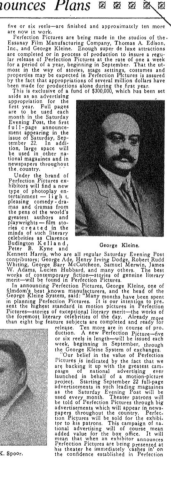

George Kleine.

Peter B. Kyne and Kennett Harris, who are all regular Saturday Evening Post contributors; George Ade, Henry Irving Dodge, Robert Rudd Whiting, George Barr McCutcheon, Samuel Merwin, James W. Adams, Lucien Hubbard, and many others. The best works of contemporary fiction—stories of genuine literary merit—will be found in Perfection Pictures.

In announcing Perfection Pictures, George Kleine, one of filmdom's best known manufacturers, and the head of the George Kleine System, said: "Many months have been spent in planning Perfection Pictures. It is our intention to present the highest standard in motion pictures in Perfection Pictures—stories of exceptional literary merit—the works of more than eight big feature subjects are completed and ready for release. Ten more are in course of production. A new Perfection Picture—five or six reels in length—will be issued each week, beginning in September, through the George Kleine System of exchanges.

"Our belief in the value of Perfection Pictures is indicated by the fact that we are backing it up with the greatest campaign of national advertising ever launched in behalf of a motion-picture project. Starting September 22 full-page advertisements in such leading magazines as the Saturday Evening Post will be used every month. Theater patrons will be told of Perfection Pictures through big advertisements which will appear in newspapers throughout the country. Perfection Pictures will be sold for the exhibitor to his patrons. This campaign of national advertising will of course mean added value for the box office. It will mean that when an exhibitor announces Perfection Pictures are being presented at his theater he immediately 'cashes in' on the confidence established in Perfection

Pictures through this tremendous national advertising campaign.

"Each theater playing Perfection Pictures will be further assisted through a line of advertising helps of superior value. Posters in all sizes will be done in five and six colors by master poster artists. Lobby photos of a new and attractive style will be available. Press sheets, cuts, slides, advertising helps of every imaginable sort, will still further augment the exhibitor's appeal to his patrons.

"I want to emphasize the fact that contracts for Perfection Pictures will be issued with the greatest care. Only exhibitors of the highest standing—those who can qualify for the ability to present Perfection Pictures properly—will be granted Perfection Picture contracts. To such exhibitors ample protection will be given for exclusive territory free from competition. Perfection Pictures will be booked on open booking—any picture, any time—or on a contract for fifty-two Perfection Pictures a year. Perfection Pictures are the kind of attractions any theater can play for runs of from three days to a solid week. The high type of stories presented assure capacity business not for one night only, but for many nights. Perfection Pictures are their own best advertisements. They are the kind that theater patrons enjoy themselves to the utmost and then recommend to their friends.

"Territory will be allotted quickly. Exhibitors seeking protection on the showing of Perfection Pictures in their vicinity will find it advisable to visit the nearest exchange of the George Kleine System without delay and make their reservations. The demand is certain to be tremendous, and exclusive franchises for the showing of Perfection Pictures will be issued as rapidly as exhibitors can qualify and at prices which are certain to allow each franchise holder to make big profits for himself."

President George K. Spoor, of the Essanay Film Manufacturing Company, refers to the new type of story that will be found in Perfection Pictures. "In these war times," he said, "the public is seeking to counteract the tragedy and sorrow of the great world by viewing the light and cheerful type of story on the screen and in its reading matter. Essanay has been striving along this line for Perfection Pictures. Light comedy-drama, pictures which cheer rather than depress; stories that present normal life, with all the little touches of humor that creep into our daily lives, will be found in the Perfection Pictures made at the Essanay studios.

"We have carefully combed the literary market of the entire world for stories of the kind referred to. That we have been successful in our quest is indicated by the fact that we have contracted for, and in many cases have already begun production on, the works of such acknowledged humorists and cheerful fiction writers as George Ade, Henry Irving Dodge, Clarence Budington Kelland, Robert Rudd Whiting, George Barr McCutcheon, Samuel Merwin, and many others."

Speaking as the representative of Thomas A. Edison, Inc., L. C. MacChesney said of the Perfection Pictures to be contributed by the Edison laboratories: "Every exhibitor knows the vast resources of the Thomas A. Edison, Inc., studios. Edison has always been a big factor in the motion-picture industry. The product of the Edison studios has always ranked high from the standpoint of entertainment, technical perfection and story value.

"Authors whose names are found on the contents pages of America's foremost magazines are providing the manuscripts for the Perfection Pictures being made by Thomas A. Edison, Inc. 'The Awakening of Ruth,' our first Perfection Picture, was written by Lucien Hubbard. Peter B. Kyne, a regular contributor to the Saturday Evening Post and periodicals of that grade, provided the manuscript for another Edison-made Perfection Picture. 'The Apple-Tree Girl,' another Perfection Picture from the Editor studios appears in the pages of the Ladies' Home Journal. All of these stories have been read by hundreds of thousands. Now in Perfection Pictures, the exhibitor is afforded an opportunity of attracting all these readers to his theater to see the stories enacted on the screen."

As stated above, many productions are already completed, and a dozen or more are in course of production. All the exchanges of the George Kleine System are prepared to screen prints of the earlier releases of Perfection Pictures, and reservations can be made now by exhibitors seeking exclusive franchises for the showing of the new brand of films in their respective territories.

Jewel Carmen Comes to Broadway

TO COME East, leaving California's sunny shores as flat as you found them, and to arrive in New York to find yourself appearing at a big Broadway theater, is by way of being a unique experience. The only thing necessary to complete the experience being to discover that you have made a hit in that same big Broadway playhouse. That's what Jewel Carmen found when she arrived in New York from the William Fox California studios. Miss Carmen, as you may know, is the personable young woman now appearing on the screen at the Globe, opposite William Farnum in the Fox picture, "The Conqueror." And Miss Carmen has scored a sizable personal hit, for her Eliza Allen, beloved of Sam Houston, "The Conqueror"—otherwise Mr. Farnum—is one of the most interesting and deftly done screen heroines of the season.

Jewel Carmen.

Miss Carmen has been in motion pictures about four years, but she has earned the greater part of the generous following which is hers since her initial appearance in Fox films some twelve months ago. Immediately upon joining the Fox forces Miss Carmen's blonde beauty arrested the eagle eyes of those who do the casting, and she was forthwith assigned the role of Lady Manette, also opposite Mr. Farnum, in that excellent picturization of "A Tale of Two Cities." She also played opposite Mr. Farnum in "American Methods," and again in "When a Man Sees Red," a screen adaptation of Larry Evan's Saturday Evening Post story, "The Painted Lady," which will be an early Fox release.

She was born in Danville, Kentucky, educated in Portland, Oregon, has done most of her picture work in Los Angeles, and says she likes New York immensely. There is every indication that New York is prepared to like Jewel.

HARRY HILLIARD LEAVES FOX.

Harry Hilliard, leading man of the Fox Film Corporation, has severed his connection with that company. His contract still has a year to run. Two years ago Mr. Hilliard left the legitimate stage after a successful season with Florence Reed in "The Yellow Ticket" to join the Fox Company.

His first picture was with Vivian Martin, "Merely Mary Ann," and established him as a favorite with motion-picture audiences.

Following his work with Miss Martin he played with Miss Suratt in "The New York Peacock," and later co-starred with June Caprice in "Caprice of the Mountains," "Patsy" and several other pictures.

In supporting Miss Theda Bara he attained his greatest success, playing with her in "Gold and the Woman," "Her Greatest Love," and "Heart and Soul." His Romeo to Miss Bara's Juliet in the Fox production of the Shakespearian tragedy served to gain for him many new admirers.

Mr. Hilliard is at present considering several offers, both from theatrical and motion-picture producers.

EARLE FOX ENGAGED BY TRIANGLE.

Earle Fox, one of the most popular of male players in pictures, has been engaged for the leading role opposite Winifred Allen in a Triangle production, "From Two to Six," now being made under the supervision of Allan Dwan at the Yonkers studio. A novel feature of the play, which is the work of the well known magazine writer, Arthur Stringer, is that the entire production takes place in a single afternoon, as the title indicates.

Metro-Yorke Company in New Quarters

Busy Week for President Fred J. Balshofer Getting His People Settled in New York.

FUTURE Metro-Yorke wonderplays starring Harold Lockwood will be made at the Metro Super-Feature studio at 645 West 43rd stret, New York. This was decided by Fred J. Balshofer, president of the Yorke Film Corporation, soon after his arrival from California a week ago. Mr. Balshofer has abandoned his California headquarters and hereafter will direct all his activities from New York.

The past week has been a very busy one indeed for Mr. Balshofer. In addition to making the foregoing noted arrangements for a studio, Mr. Balshofer has established business headquarters in the Metro offices. These are, in charge of Wiley Gibson, as business manager, who came from California with Mr. Balshofer and Mr. Lockwood along with Richard V. Spencer, scenario writer; Lester Cuneo, the Yorke "heavy"; William Clifford, character actor; John Schronberg, violinist; and Antonio Guadio, cameraman. He also made an addition to his staff in the person of Harry H. Poppe whose duties will be to look after the publicity for the Yorke company's activities.

Between getting settled the matter of future homes for his acting and business organizations, Mr. Balshofer has found time to superintend some changes he desires made at the studio; to make some additional scenes requiring a New York background for "Paradise Garden," the last picture he made on the Coast; to cut the negative of that subject; and to confer with his associates in the preparation of his next production.

Alterations are being made at the studio to suit the demands of Mr. Balshofer's next picture, the name of which he is not yet ready to announce. It is to be made from a story by a well-known author and Mr. Balshofer expects with it to equal, if not excel, his current effort, "Paradise Garden," which he regards as one of his biggest productions.

"Paradise Garden" is a seven reel picture adapted by Mr. Balshofer and Richard V. Spencer from the romantic novel of the same name by George Gibbs, author of a number of popular books. It will be released October first as a Metro wonderplay de luxe. Harold Lockwood is the star.

BARKER JOINS PARALTA PERMANENTLY.

Reginald Barker has become permanently connected with the Paralta Plays organisation, and will be sole director of Bessie Barriscale's photo dramas. During the past two months he has been directing her production of Harold MacGrath's secret service war romance, "Madam Who," on which he is now putting the finishing touches.

Since last November up to within a few days Mr. Barker's permanent plans for the future were very much in doubt. The early expiration of his contract with another company became known and from that moment this young producing genius was made a target for record-breaking offers from almost every organization in the moving-picture industry. Recognizing value, each concern strove desperately to capture him, many sending agents from New York to the Pacific Coast to personally negotiate a deal. Mr. Barker gracefully declined all offers pending a careful consideration of each proposition.

Seven weeks ago, on the expiration of his contract, Mr. Barker became director of Miss Barriscale in the production of Harold MacGrath's "Madam Who," not because it was the most lucrative of the many opportunities offered him, but because it gave him a chance to carry out some of the more pretentious ideas he had long entertained.

During the recent visit of Carl Anderson, president of Paralta Plays, to the Pacific Coast, a consultation was held between him and Mr. Barker and Robert T. Kane, vice-president of Paralta Plays, which resulted in agreements under which Mr. Barker will continue permanently as Miss Barriscale's director.

J. FRANK BROCKLISS SAILS FOR LONDON.

J. Frank Brockliss was the guest of honor at a theater party given at the Eltinge Theater, New York, on Thursday night, September 6. In the party were the executives of the King-Bee Films Corporation. Preceding the theater entertainment a very enjoyable informal dinner was arranged by Louis Burstein, president of the King-Bee Company. Among the guests were Nat. H. Spitzer, L. L. Hiller, Jacob Wilke, Arvid Gilstrom, Ed. Rosenbaum, Jr., and S. Garrett. Mr. Brockliss, who represents the King-Bee Billy West Comedies abroad, sailed for London on Saturday, September 8.

JOE AND SAM DE GRASSE AT LAST GET TOGETHER.

Director Joseph De Grasse, of the Bluebird studios, has been staging photoplays for more than six years, and his brother, Sam, has been acting in front of the camera for a like period, but in all that time they had never been able to get together on a picture until Brother Joseph filmed his latest Bluebird production, "Anything Once," in which Franklyn Farnum will be starred, as the October 8 release.

Samuel and Joseph De Grasse.

They have made a continuous effort for years to work together and came very near to putting it over on several occasions. Something, however, always happened to upset their plans.

Joe was overjoyed and so was Sam when it was decided that the latter was to play a role in "Anything Once," but both kept their fingers crossed and knocked wood every once in a while until the production was actually under way. Although the occasion has been referred to as "the De Grasse" reunion, there is still George Felix to be accounted for before the assembly of the De Grasses would be complete. Felix is one De Grasse who has stuck to the stage more than he has to pictures. He has long been identified with vaudeville with the team of Felix and Barry and with Barry Girls, taking occasional flyers into screen comedies.

To Bluebird, however, the importance of "Anything Once," in association with the directorial activities of Joe De Grasse comes in the announcement of Franklyn Farnum as a lone star, with Mr. De Grasse his director.

It was Joe De Grasse who introduced Louise Lovely to Bluebirds, early in the series, and it was this same skillful and experienced director who brought out Dorothy Phillips last fall and directed her until lately Ida May Park (who in association with Mr. De Grasse) became screen manager for Miss Phillips and Joe De Grasse became Franklyn Farnum's director.

FINGER PRINTS TO CORRECT CARELESS WORK.

George A. Rush, manager of Herbert Brenon's studio at Hudson Heights, N. J., has just applied the finger-print system to the development of negative film. Everybody "in the know" of the screen world realises the difficulty encountered by studio managers through injury to negative films during development. Despite rules and official precautions, upon development a negative will be found to have gathered a number of finger marks. This is largely due to the lack of care of the developers. Employees have realised that there was no way to trace their carelessness.

Usually these finger prints caused slight harm, but occasionally they marred a big scene, making the cutting of the damaged part necessary. This, of course, hurt the finished product, since a re-take of the scene is then impossible. Mr. Rush has been studying the finger-print evil for some time. Recently he hit upon the idea of applying the police finger-print system to the trouble. Under the direction of Lieutenant John Simons, of the North Bergen, N. J., police department, Mr. Rush has taken finger prints of the various employees of the Brenon developing department. Judging from results attained with the negative of "The Fall of the Romanoffs" Mr. Rush has solved the problem. The developed negative failed to have a single finger print mark.

Triangle to Produce Plays Abroad

Will Shortly Dispatch Companies to the Orient for Filming Productions Suitable for Market There.

BECAUSE of the imperativve demand for pictures from the Orient and South America, Triangle will send companies of players and directors to India and China for the purpose of filming plays that will appeal to these foreign patrons and bring a new type of production to Americans. Later, a company will go to Buenos Ayres to produce plays of distinctly South American atmosphere.

"We are supplying not merely America and the European continent, but literally all the world," said H. O. Davis, vice-president and general manager of the Triangle Film Corporation, in connection with the statement of the extensive producing activities now being planned by Triangle.

"Virtually all the cinema producers in this country are today sending a tremendous number of films to the Orient," continued Mr. Davis. "The celluloid is proving a potent tie of friendship and understanding between the Mongolian and the Caucasian. Film shadows, bringing modern ideas and democratic principles, are doing more than could armed forces to bring reform to China and to make it an integral part of the world instead of a sort of pariah among nations.

"There are more than six hundred motion picture theaters in China alone. The number in Japan is just as great. Virtually no film is made in either country. European manufacturers are at a standstill because of the war. Thus the United States is supplying the market.

"In the city of Shanghai there are five motion picture theaters with an average of 700 seats. Their admission prices range from twenty-five to sixty cents, according to location. Canton is another big buyer of films. Six theaters are now running there with combined seating capacity for 4,200 people. Another theater, now near completion, will accommodate 1,100 patrons. The Chinaman pays well for his entertainment, but he likes a long show. One five-reel drama is not enough for him. An evening must offer him at least three hours of diversion; so the program usually consists of two long films and a couple of short comedies.

"The foreign trade has taught us that the whole world is pretty much akin. Climate and the color of a man's skin doesn't alter his primal feelings. What pleases American usually pleases India and South America. Romance, adventure, tragedy and comedy are everywhere. Our foreign exhibitors invariably demand the dramas which were successes here.

"We have learned, however, to leave the Oriental features out of our home-made plays. India, for instance, has about 500 castes. These are distinguished sometimes by the folding of a turban, again by the color of a cloak. The problem is too involved for our American directors. We will therefore send companies with American stars and directors to India and China for regular stock work. Later we will invade South America. Our directors, working in the actual locale of the picture, can acquire accurate details. In this way we will satisfy our foreign market and at the same time give America an introduction to Oriental life and manners.

"This move of Triangle is merely in stride with the progress of the motion picture industry. It is only a decade since the days when thrills, accidents, collisions and marathon chases were the vogue. We no longer strive for miraculous 'stunts' except for comedy purposes. We have also been eliminating from our pictures all reference to creeds of religion. It is our purpose to entertain, not to preach. Yet we cannot escape the role of pedagogue entirely.

"I was amused recently at the complaint of a furniture dealer in one of the small towns of Northern California. He had an excellent stock. I commented upon it as I stopped for a purchase. His reply was rather surly.

"'Yes,' said he, 'but there's no money in the business any more. The movies have put us out. Used to be when my stock got low I just wrote for a carload of tables and chairs and bedroom sets. But that don't do for our farmers any more. No, sir; when they get married and go to housekeeping 'round here they come to me and want a set of furniture like they saw in some picture show down at the theater. The farmer's daughter, instead of just asking for a parlor set, wants Looey the Fourteenth!'

"This statement of the furniture dealer is just another proof that provincialism is being eliminated and a universal standard of life adopted. Motion pictures are completing the work started by the railroad, the telegraph, the cable, and the telephone."

Rhea Mitchell Joins Paralta

THE recent visit of Carl Anderson, president of Paralta Plays, Inc., to the Paralta studios at Hollywood, Cal., resulted in the conclusion of negotiations which had been going on for some time between Rhea Mitchell and this company in reference to her starring under the Paralta banner.

Contracts were duly signed, and Miss Mitchell will very shortly make her debut as an independent star at the head of her own company in a modern morality play by Hayden Talbot. Miss Mitchell's productions will be released by Paralta through the Triangle Distributing Corporation.

Miss Mitchell and her company will be acorded the same accomodations at the Paralta studios in Hollywood that are enjoyed by Bessie Barriscale, J. Warren Kerrigan and the Henry B. Walthall organizations. Miss Mitchell and company will have the benefit of the same general staff, headed by Robert Brunton, production manager; R. Holmes Paul, art director, and Robert T. Kane, vice-president of Paralta, as general supervising manager.

Miss Mitchell is 21 years of age, and has been connected with the stage and screen since her fifteenth year. She was born in Portland, Oregon. At

Rhea Mitchell

the age of fifteen her family moved to Spokane, where she made her first appearance on the stage, playing the ingenue role in "The Blue Mouse," produced by the Baker Stock Company.

In the fall of 1913 Miss Mitchell made her first appearance on the screen. She joined the New York Motion Picture Corporation as a leading woman. Her first part was in a two-reel production called "A New England Idyll," which was directed by Reginald Barker. She continued with the New York Motion Picture Corporation until 1915, when she joined the American Film Company at Santa Barbara. Miss Mitchell's last appearance was in a special production called "Whither Thou Goest," in which she made a striking personal hit as co-star with Orrin Johnson.

Miss Mitchell will be seen in eight Paralta star feature films each year.

NEW PATHE BRANCH MANAGERS.

Though still a young man, E. O. Child, just appointed manager of Pathe's San Francisco office, has been in the theatrical business for considerably more than fifteen years, since during that length of time he managed companies and was then assistant to the general manager of the Western Vaudeville Managers' Association in Chicago, the Western connection of the U. B. O.

He was manager of the Orpheum Theater, San Francisco, and the Orpheum Theater, Salt Lake City, Utah. He was then with the General Film Company and Essanay and was branch manager for V. L. S. E. in Pittsburgh, then San Francisco representative of McClure Superpictures, which concluded its career to join Pathe. Big things are expected of Mr. Child in his new position, and it looks as if he is going to live up to all expectations.

N. I. Filkins, who has been a salesman in Pathe's Buffalo office for the last two or three years, has been appointed manager of that office, succeeding J. W. Fuller, who has been appointed assistant manager of Pathe's office in St. Louis.

L. E. Kennedy becomes manager of Pathe's Los Angeles branch. Mr. Kennedy was for some time connected with that office in the capacity of salesman and he has a reputation of being one of the best, if not the best, film salesman in the Los Angeles territory.

An African Film City

A Big Studio at Killarney Commences Picture Production in Johannesburg.

Well inside the municipal boundary of Johannesburg, says the Johannesburg Sunday Times, a new hive of activity is coming to life. When completed, it will be a city in miniature. Everybody and everything connected with it will be dedicated to making films—for the pleasure and profit of South Africa and other countries.

Pictures of all kinds will be produced in the city, and it will contain handsome stone buildings and native kraals, an artificial river, a lake, and even a zoo. And not only will pictures be produced, but the films themselves will be manufactured here from raw materials.

The founders of the city are the African Films Production, Ltd., and they could hardly have chosen a healthier or more delightful site, and the future residents could not wish for more charming surroundings of kopjes and veld. Altogether the city will cover an area of 26 acres.

The building which now adorns the veld, and which occupies a space of 172 feet by 114 feet, is entirely of stone. There is an air of stability and permanence about it which indicates that an important industry has come to stay.

Contained in it are offices for the chairman, the general manager, the secretary, for the scenario editor and writers, for poster artists and the editor of the African Mirror, and six offices for the producers. There are dressing and bath rooms and a dining room and green room for the actors, a reading room and library, a mess room where workmen will get their luncheons free, and a kitchen.

Then there are store rooms, a carpenters' shop, places where girls will be employed in the making of props and a studio for the scenic painters, who just now, with the aid of carpenters, are building Windsor Castle for a great Zulu war picture. Downstairs in the basement the technical work is being done, and there are spacious rooms for cutting negatives, developing, washing, drying, perforating and assembling the films, mixing chemicals, printing and so forth. Here also are the electric motors, a heating chamber and a miniature theater.

Not far from the building is an open-air stage, 90 feet by 60 feet, and adjoining this the foundations have been laid for another large edifice which will contain a warehouse for the scenery and props of the special picture under production, and quarters (including a kitchen) for the use of the natives. Another stage for indoor work of the above dimensions is also being constructed, this being enclosed with glass.

There will be an educational film house with a camera playing all day, where the movements of a fly, a fish, a lizard, or the unfolding of a flower may be recorded.

Splendid stables are to be built—the finest in South Africa —also a garage for motor vehicles, and a wagon house for vehicles ranging from a Kruger coach to a 'ricksha. Native villages are to find their place here, from the Zulu mushroom huts to the mud contraptions of the Hottentots, even Bushmen's caves not being forgotten.

What is perhaps the most interesting feature of all is the manufacture of the film base, the film itself as apart from the picture. Only in California are the films made today, because they have to be dried in the open air and a dry climate is essential for the operation. Firms have tried to start the industry in England and France, but their efforts have resulted in failure. With its dry atmosphere, the Transvaal is regarded by experts as a particularly good place for the purpose.

Not only will the films for bioscope pictures be manufactured here, but also it is intended to meet the South African demands of professional and amateur photographers, and after that to build up an export trade.

Thus the Film City of Johannesburg, when in full running order, will cover enterprises which should offer occupations to hundreds of people, and will play no insignificant part in industrial life. The scheme includes residences for those engaged in the work of all branches of film production.

TO ENLARGE COMPANY.

W. A. King, representing Barker Bros., Los Angeles, Cal., manufacturers of the K B Motion Picture Camera and Projector, is in New York arranging for the formation of a new organization for the manufacture of the camera and projector in the east. A new office will be opened shortly in the Times Square section, where it is also desired to locate the factory.

Louise Glaum Visits New York

LOUISE GLAUM, Triangle's siren star, arrived in New York this week from Los Angeles for a vacation of ten days before commencing work on a series of spectacular productions at the Triangle Culver City studio. This is Miss Glaum's first trip to New York since she commenced her picture work four years ago in Los Angeles. She has been with Triangle since its inception, appearing in no less than twenty features. Her latest role was that of the vanity woman in "Idolaters," released t h e first of this month. With the exception of short rest periods between productions the star has had no time for anything but her work during the past two years.

Louise Glaum.

"I am a stranger to the gay white way," remarked Miss Glaum, "although I am supposed to know all about it after frequenting innumerable of its cafes—in my pictures.

"I came to rest, which shows just how little I know of New York. I am making a tour of the shops to secure gowns for my coming plays, which will be quite different from any of the recent ones. I had not seen my last play, 'Idolaters,' until it was shown for me in the Triangle projection room the other morning. I was terribly shocked by myself."

Miss Glaum's intention to visit the city was kept secret at her request, as she did not wish to make personal appearances, but rather to enjoy a genuine outing.

PATHE CLUB HAS AN END-OF-THE-SUMMER OUTING.

One hundred and five strong, the Pathe Club went by a specially chartered steamer on Sunday, September 9, to Glenwood Landing, Long Island, for an all day outing. Athletic contests for handsome prizes afforded much amusement to every one, and the many persons who were seen limping the next day afforded proof not only of the many entrants in these contests, but also of the whole hearted way in which they participated.

Dinner was had at Karatsonyi's Hotel. After dinner those persons who were still able after the violent exercises of the morning took part in a ball game, the distinguishing feature of which was a "Skinny Shaner" score.

Members of the club from the Twenty-third Street Exchange, the studio in Jersey City, and the factory at Bound Brook were present in force. A pleasant feature of the outing lay in the fact that the many young women employed in the clerical and stenographic departments of the Pathe Exchange were invited along as guests of the club and accepted the invitation to a girl. Among the associate members of the club who were present were Tom Wiley of the Novelty Slide Co., Fred Ruttenberg of the Wyanoke, and Harold Davis of the Chronicle Press.

President of the club, J. A. Berst, and Mrs. Berst were present and took a hearty interest in all the various amusements of the day.

P. A. Parsons was chairman of the committee on arrangements; J. W. Kyle, the secretary of the club; L. E. Franconi and M. W. Davidson, all appointed by President Berst for special duties, worked hard to make the outing a success.

BILLY REED DROPS IN.

Billy Reed, veteran operator for many years with the old Vitagraph organization, but now the star operator at Stanley Mastbaum's Colonial Theater, Atlantic City, N. J., paid a call at the Moving Picture World office on Friday, September 14, while on his way back to the job. Billy has been spending his well earned vacation in Boston, his home town, where he says he met up with many of the old-timers.

Some Good Stunts in Equipment

Devices Exhibited at the Safety and Sanitation Exposition Which Are of Interest to the Up-to-Date Exhibitor.

By E. T. Keyser.

THE American Museum of Safety and the National Safety Council held a joint Safety and Sanitation Exposition at the Grand Central Palace, New York City, from September 10 to 15, inclusive, and the picture theater proprietor who did not attend passed up a mighty good opportunity to become acquainted with several devices which would save him money, trouble and cuss words, if installed in his house.

Just to help out the non-resident of the metropolis who could not attend and simultaneously to rub the lost bet into the Gothamite who wouldn't the following description of what particularly appealed to the World man is written.

Of course, our old friend, Nick Powers, was there with both feet, or, rather, in two places, the projection room and the exposition floor, but, as he is getting his elsewhere, we will pass him by here with the mere mention that he constituted one of the bright lights of the affair.

As an illustration of the heavy blow which they are prepared to hand out to bad atmospheric conditions in picture theaters and elsewhere, the Typhoon Fan Company, of 1544 Broadway, New York, had three six-foot ventilating fans installed at the head of the entrance staircase and another of equal size in their booth. The beauty of a Typhoon fan lies in the fact that it will pull a crowd of admission paying people into a house on a hot night with the same celerity that it expels the hot foul air.

Speaking of atmospheric conditions, the Powers Regulator Company, of New York, Boston, Chicago and Toronto, showed a device which would permit the theater manager to settle the temperature at which he desires to keep his auditorium and rest assured that the auditorium, whether full, half full or empty will stay at that temperature without further worry on his part or effort on the part of the attendants.

Anyone who has ever skidded down a slippery flight of steps or anyone who has been confronted with the possibility of paying damages to the skidder would have appreciated the safety offered both parties by the stair treads exhibited by the American Mason Safety Tread Company, of Lowell, Mass. These treads, which may be applied to new or old stairs, are so constructed that they are non-slippable down to the last bit of their life and are built to be self-draining and do not permit foreign substances, which may be thrown upon them, to diminish their safety.

As a fire preventive, the automatic alarm shown by the Aero Fire Alarm Co., of 6 Church street, New York, holds much of interest to both exhibitors and producers. The device consists of one or more detectors which ring a gong when a fire starts and indicate on an annunciator just where the blaze is located. The detectors may be distributed in the auditorium, the operating room and anywhere else desired and will allow the watchman or attendants to get on the job of extinguishment without loss of time in locating an incipient blaze.

As a means of utilising the first few minutes of the conflagration's career to put an effective quietus upon it, the Pyrene Manufacturing Company, of 52 Vanderbilt avenue, and the Fire Gun Manufacturing Company, 17 Battery place, both of New York, and the Fyr-Fyter Company, of Dayton, Ohio, displayed assortments of hand fire extinguishers calculated to kill a fire while it was borning.

The danger of shock or burn by an open switch was what caused the Detroit Fuse & Manufacturing Company, of Detroit, to produce the Square "D" steel enclosed switch which protects both operator and equipment and which is provided with a safety lock-off which prevents closing the circuit while repairs are being made.

The Metropolitan Electric Manufacturing Company, of Long Island City, New York, also exhibited a line of the Naro-Safety Panel boards which are safe from shock or sparking and in which each circuit is removable and replaceable without interfering with other circuits, thereby endearing themselves to the heart of the house manager who desires comething safe, simple and compact with a capital C.

NEW LOIS WEBER PICTURE.

"The Price of a Good Time" is the title of the new Lois Weber feature to be released in the near future. It is said to be superproduction, marked by unusual color effects and night scenes said never to have been surpassed on the screen.

Earl Brunswick

TO HAVE appeared with Richard Mansfield is the enviable distinction that Earl Brunswick lays claim to, having supported Mansfield in "Old Heidelberg" and in "Ivan, the Terrible." He has had a thorough training in legitimate dramatic productions and has traveled over prac-

Earl Brunswick.

tically all of the states, as well as through Canada, Mexico and Cuba. For a time he was also associated with a brother in vaudeville and is especially well known throughout the Southern States. He is a native of Mount Vernon and early deserted a promising mercantile career for the stage. Among his first appearances in films was as lead in the film production, "Dear Old Girl." He recently played in the Goldwyn feature, "Baby Mine," and has just appeared under Director W. Christy Cabanne in the new Metro war picture, "Draft No. 258." In this latter production he plays the juvenile heavy in which he takes the part of a Socialist. Like many other graduates from the speaking stage, Mr. Brunswick has become an enthusiast in regard to the artistic possibilities of the moving picture.

"THE MAN WITHOUT A COUNTRY" AT THE BROADWAY.

The premiere of the Thanhouser version of Edward Everett Hale's patriotic masterpiece, "The Man Without a Country," was made the occasion of a gala evening at the Broadway theater, Sunday, when Jewel Productions, Inc., presented the feature with Florence LaBadie and H. E. Herbert in the stellar roles.

The flag-draped boxes were filled with government and city officials, together with men of the Army and Navy, including, Brig. Gen. Eli D. Hoyle and his staff, Capt. Charles A. Adams, U. S. N., and men of the U. S. S. "Recruit" and a large detachment of boy scouts. The patriotic fervor of the occasion was heightened by the patriotic verse of James L. Heron, secretary of the Canadian Club, one of a series of speakers furnished by the Mayor's Committee of National Defense to contribute speakers each evening at the Broadway during the two weeks' New York run of the timely feature. Etta Weiman gave vocal numbers.

Lloyd Lonergan wrote the present day version after the Hale classic and Ernest C. Warde, who did "The Vicar of Wakefield" and other highly successful cinema adaptations, is the director.

Jewel Productions, Inc., two weeks ago acquired the picture from the Thanhouser Film Corporation and will offer it for distribution as the fourth of a standard series which they will offer to the trade, the first being "Come Through"; the second, "Pay Me," with Dorothy Phillips, and the third, "Sirens of the Sea."

G. R. WARREN APPOINTED NEW HORSLEY MANAGER.

G. R. Warren has been appointed to the position of Manager of Productions by David Horsley, and will assume immediate charge of the Horsley studios in Los Angeles. Mr. Warren is recognized as one of the most capable all-around men in the picture business. His career opened in the legitimate drama, through which he graduated to executive positions in the administration side of the profession. Early in the development of moving pictures Mr. Warren was first associated with Mr. Horsley in what has since become the Universal Film Company. Mr. Warren's appointment is the result of years of observation by Mr. Horsley of his accomplishments and exceptional qualifications.

Chicago News Letter

By JAS. S. McQUADE

Bryant Washburn Exonerated

Essanay Player's Claims for Exemption from Draft Proved to Be Justified.

BRYANT WASHBURN has at last been exonerated from any suspicion of an ignoble motive in his claim for exemption from the national army, judging from the affidavits disclosed by Thomas J. Dawson, chairman of the exemption board of District 55. Washburn's case has been given considerable notoriety since the day he was called before the board to answer his call in the draft. After being pronounced physically fit by the examiners, he registered a claim for exemption on the grounds of having dependents, and was subsequently granted a certificate of release by the local board. This action of the local authorities was met with severe criticism by certain government officials and an investigation was begun by agents of the Department of Justice.

Reports all unfavorable to Washburn were circulated regarding his financial standing and the ability of his wife to support herself without his aid. By the recent disclosure, however, of the affidavits submitted in the case it was made clear that Mrs. Washburn, due to physical disability, is absolutely dependent upon her husband and that the family's present circumstances will not permit him to enter the army service.

The affidavits were furnished by Mrs. Mabel Washburn, his wife; her mother and father, Mr. and Mrs. W. S. Chidester; Dr. Joseph Zeisler, George K. Spoor, president of Essanay, and R. O. Proctor, Chicago manager of Art Dramas and now acting as a government agent. The affidavit made by Dr. Spoor denied the rumor that Mrs. Washburn, formerly an actress, had a contract with his company. The other affidavits corroborated the statement made by Mr. Washburn in his exemption claim.

Thomas J. Dawson, chairman of the exemption board, who has supported Washburn in the matter, made the following statement in tribute to him:

"Washburn had the right the same as any other American to claim exemption and on the evidence he was entitled to it.

"It was unfair to the board and unfair to him and humiliated us all before the public. Washburn is in every way a man. When he appeared before the board he helped us in every way possible to go into his life, financial and otherwise. He should not be martyred because he is an actor."

Mr. Washburn will continue with Essanay. "The Fibbers," a five-reel comedy in which he plays the lead, was completed last week and is to be released through the George Kleine System, October 15.

Dempsey Tells of War Experiences.

Frank Dempsey, formerly traveling representative for K-E-S-E, who returned to this country from France a few weeks ago, tells an interesting story of his experiences during six months of service in the American Ambulance Corps.

Mr. Dempsey sailed for France on February 4, reached Paris February 14, and left for the front February 24. His first real taste of war was in the battle of Mt. Cornillet, where Section 13, of which he was a member, received the army citation, the first to be given to an American section for bravery. Section 13 also received six Croix de Guerres (medals for bravery).

In the battle of Mt. Cornillet, Mr. Dempsey witnessed the destruction of a tunnel in which 1,300 Bosch soldiers were caught digging their way underneath the French lines. He also witnessed the bombardment of hospitals by German planes, and did service in the battle at Rheims.

Mr. Dempsey reports that the French government is circulating one and two-reel comedy pictures in some places for the amusement of the poorer classes. It is not an uncommon sight at night to see a picture projected from the side of a house with the aid of a white sheet and a calcium light outfit. In Paris the larger houses are doing good business at one franc admission. Very few houses are open after 9.30 p. m.

Mr. Dempsey sailed from Bordeaux August 11, and reached New York August 22. He intends to again enter the picture business in Chicago, where he will remain until called for service in this country.

Clune Has New Production.

The W. H. Clune production, "The Eyes of the World," based on the novel of that name, written by Harold Bell Wright, will have its premiere in Chicago, Friday, September 21, at the Auditorium theater. The Chicago showing follows the exploitation of the picture for several months in the states west of Denver, where Mr. Clune's representatives say it played to excellent business wherever shown. Chicago is the first city east of Denver to witness the presentation of the latest Clune production. An extensive advertising campaign is now being conducted under the supervision of Spencer E. Rogers, Mr. Clune's personal representative, who will have charge of all the details of the presentation of the subject during its engagement at the Auditorium. Numerous departures from present exhibiting methods are promised by him. An elaborate setting specially built for the occasion will occupy the Auditorium stage, and a large symphony orchestra will furnish the musical accompaniment.

Chicago Brevities.

James S. McQuade, our good friend and side-kick, is off on his holiday. He left Saturday, September 8, taking a train eastward, and will be in and around New York until Saturday, September 22.

* * *

Success of an effort now being made by local film men to have Major Funkhouser ousted from the censor board would permit undue privation in some instances. The Fox film, "The Spy," which was denied a permit by the major, and which is now being shown in a "Loop" theater under an injunction issued by the United States courts, is doing such good business that it has been secured for an indefinite run, despite the fact that eleven other prints have been booked by Chicago houses for the week of September 16.

The local office of the Fox Film Corporation has closed a contract with Ascher Bros. for the rental of "The Honor System," "Jack and the Beanstalk," "The Conquerer," "When a Man Sees Red," "Camille" and "Aladdin and the Wonderful Lamp" for a minimum run for two days of each subject in all houses of the Ascher circuit. The contract is said to represent one of the largest rental figures ever paid in this territory.

* * *

David G. Rodgers, national organizer for the M. P. E. L. of America, arrived in the city from the east on Thursday, September 6. Mr. Rodgers is on a tour in the interests of the League. He left New York, Monday, August 27, and spent several days in Harrisburg and Pittsburgh before reaching Chicago. In the cities visited Mr. Rodgers found excellent business conditions, especially in Harrisburg, where admission prices have been recently advanced from 10 to 15 cents. During his visit Mr. Rodgers attended the regular meeting of the Chicago local, held Friday, September 7. He was given the privilege of the floor, and his remarks were confined to business of the League. He left Chicago for Minneapolis on September 14, where he intends to remain several days before continuing on to Des Moines, Ia., Omaha and Lincoln, Neb., Kansas City, Mo., and St. Louis. His present plans are to leave St. Louis in time for the Kansas state convention to be held in Manhattan, October 16.

* * *

At the meeting of the Chicago local, held September 7, further discussions of the music tax and a new wage scale of the Operators' Union, Local 110, were entered into and later referred to various committees, who are to confer with the other side and report at the next meeting.

* * *

After spending a few days in New York, Aaron A. Jones and Nathan Ascher returned to this city on Thursday, Sept. 13. During their visit they closed a contract with Mr.

Griffith's representative to show "Intolerance" at Jones, Linick & Schaefer's Orpheum theatre and at the Ascher Brothers' circuit of theaters. The picture will be shown at the Orpheum about the middle of October, and will run for three days or a week, at 25 cents admission. After the run at the Orpheum the picture will be shown at each of the Ascher theaters for three days at 25 cents admission.

* * *

"Babbling Tongues," the Ivan production owned in this territory by the Unity Photoplays Co., and the Rex Beach travel pictures have been booked by a number of prominent exhibitors in this territory. The latter are being booked in series of 16 reels for delivery one reel each week, at a fixed figure for the entire set. Favorable newspaper criticisms of "Babbling Tongues" by the Chicago newspaper critics gave the bookings on the Ivan feature a big boost.

* * *

Jack Meredith, late of the Triangle, has been engaged by the Commonwealth Pictures Corporation to support "Charlotte," the famous ice skater, in a new feature subject now being produced at the studio of the Rothacker Film Manufacturing Co. Mr. Meredith will be remembered for his fine work in "The Man Hater" and such productions as "Poppy" and "Panthea," in which he played opposite Norman Talmadge. Courtland J. Van Duesen, formerly of the Vitagraph Co., has also been secured to co-operate with Oscar Eagle in the direction of the production, which will be about five reels in length. The name of the subject has not yet been given out.

* * *

Bernarr MacFadden, the well known Chicago physical culturist, who has conducted the Healthotorium resort at Forty-second and Grand Boulevard for a number of years, will next demonstrate his methods of physical development through the medium of the Universal Screen Magazine. Mr. M cFadden will be seen in the thirty-ninth issue to be released Monday, Sept. 17. Some very interesting scenes in which his children take part have been incorporated in the first release. Mr. MacFadden has endeavored to put in picture form his theory that children trained from babyhood can be developed into health and strength prodigies.

* * *

Harry Beaumont, former director of the "Skinner" series for Bryant Washburn, has been drafted for the national army. Mr. Beaumont will not claim exemption. He has signed a contract with the Selig Polyscope Co. to produce "Brown of Harvard," and will try to finish the production before he is called. "There is no reason," said Mr. Beaumont, "why a moving picture actor should be spared any more than anyone else. I want to do my duty and I think every man should accept the draft, whether he be a laborer on the streets or a high-priced actor in a moving picture studio."

* * *

"Barbary Sheep," the latest Artcraft release, starring Elsie Ferguson, will have its first showing in Chicago on Monday, Sept. 17, at the Ziegfeld theater.

* * *

The Playhouse on Michigan avenue opened the week of Sept. 8 with the Jewel production "Sirens of the Sea," with Carmel Meyers and Louise Lovely in the leading roles. The production is booked for an indefinite run and has been shown to good business since the opening.

* * *

During the week of Saturday, Sept. 1, 15 per cent. of the gross receipts at the Playhouse, amounting to $112.50, was donated to the Chicago Daily News tobacco fund for the American soldiers in France, by the Bluebird Photoplays, Inc. I. Von Ronkel, Chicago manager for Bluebird, is responsible for the consideration.

* * *

Carl Laemmle made a brief stop-over in this city Friday, Sept. 14, on his way from New York to Universal City.

* * *

Thomas J. Meighan, the well known Famous Players-Lasky star, who recently renewed his contract with that organization, spent a short vacation in Chicago last week prior to beginning work on his next picture. On Tuesday evening Mr. Meighan and his wife, known professionally as Blanche Ring, were guests at a dinner and theater party given by Max Goldstine, local Artcraft manager. Mr. Meighan left this city for New York on Wednesday, Sept. 12.

* * *

According to information received by the Selig Polyscope Co., "The Crisis" has played to almost 50,000 persons at the Garrick theater, Philadelphia, where the production is entering its third week of an indefinite run.

Richard R. Nehls, general manager of the American Film Co., Inc., this city, has been receiving congratulations from his many friends and brothers in the trade on his recent acceptance in Masonry. He took his first degree on Wednesday, Sept. 5, at the Birchwood Lodge.

* * *

The Bass Camera Co., this city, has just received the distribution privileges in the middle west for the K B camera and projector manufactured by Barker Bros., Inc., of Los Angeles. W. A. King, representing the Barker Co., arrived in Chicago Sept. 12, to complete negotiations. The Bass-Camera Co. is now issuing its first catalogue for the year 1917-18. It is nicely illustrated and comprised of 64 pages in two sections. Mr. Bass writes that the catalogue has been compiled for the purpose of aiding the amateur in obtaining the highest grade photographic accessories and cameras. The company carries a complete line of Eastman, Ansco and Rexo products, together with several makes of moving picture cameras, among them the Universal and U. S. Cinematograph.

* * *

The new Seeburg-Smith Unit orchestra manufactured by the Seeburg Piano Co., is now on display at the company's showrooms in the Republic Building, this city. To accommodate the instrument it was necessary to add several hundred square feet of floor space to the already spacious display rooms occupied by the company. Mr. Seeburg is very enthusiastic over the possibilities of the instrument for accompaniment to moving pictures. Four of the larger types have been sold to exhibitors since negotiations were closed with the inventor for the manufacturing rights.

* * *

Chicago's west side is to have another large moving picture theater now in course of construction at Twenty-sixth street and Harding avenue. It is being erected for Henry W. Browarski. The t ilding will front 200 feet on Twenty-sixth street and 180 feet on Harding avenue. It is to cost in the neighborhood of $215,000. It will be two stories high, with stores and offices on the first floor, in addition to the theater. A restaurant will occupy the second floor. The structure is designed according to the Spanish renaissance style with polychrome terra cotta and faced brick. Special attention has been given to the exterior lighting, over 4,000 lights to be placed so as to outline the building and its various entrances. The contract for the interior process relief decoration has been awarded to the Decorators Supply Co., of this city. The project is being financed by the G. H. Gottschalk Co. Henry L. Newhouse is the architect. Thanksgiving day ' set for the formal opening.

FIRE RAZES NEW ORLEANS EXCHANGE.

Fire destroyed virtually all of the merchandise and office fixings of the Consolidated Film & Supply Company, 914 Graver street, New Orleans, on Wednesday afternoon, September 5. The fire started through defective wiring. Flames first broke out in the ceiling and ate their way through the exchange. None of the many films stored in the vault were injured by fire. About twenty reels were destroyed by water. Half of the firm's paper department also was burned. No one was hurt.

By rapid, cool and efficient work on the part of the Consolidated's employes every exhibitor got his show on time from the exchange. As soon as the rooms had cooled sufficiently a cable was strung from the power plant to the exchange. A temporary office a few doors away had been opened within an hour after the fire started.

Plans already have been made for remodeling the old quarters, which will be ready in about three weeks.

NEW PLAYERS TO SUPPORT OLIVE THOMAS.

Lillian Langdon, one of the best known "mother" actresses of the screen, and Monte Blue, who appeared in juvenile roles in Triangle-Fine Arts productions, have been engaged to support Olive Thomas in a forthcoming Triangle production. Mrs. Langdon has played important roles with several companies, and was at one time a member of the famous stock company at the Triangle-Fine Arts plant. Monte Blue's last appearance on the Triangle program was in "Hands Up."

Jack Dillon is directing Miss Thomas and her company in the new play, which bears the working title of "Frankly Chaste." It will be released the latter part of October or early November.

LOS ANGELES

News of Los Angeles and Vicinity
By G. P. HARLEMAN

Billy Sunday Visits Motion Picture Studios
Appreciates the Wonderful Growth of the Industry and the Great Educational Value of the Pictures.

BILLY SUNDAY has been visiting the motion picture studios this week.

On Wednesday Mr. Sunday, his son and business manager, George Sunday, and his secretary, Bob Matthews, visited the Lasky studios in Hollywood, where he returned the call of Mary Pickford, who attended the services in his tabernacle on Tuesday night.

The great evangelist is anxious to correct a false impression which has been gained by the public concerning his attitude with respect to the motion picture industry. Like everything else, there is good and bad in this business, he said.

"I want to be as quick to praise as I am to condemn," he said, "and in discussing an institution like the motion picture industry, which means so much to Southern California, I desire above all other things to be perfectly fair.

"The moving pictures can be made a powerful influence for clean living. By the same token they can work incalculable harm unless high standards are adhered to. Motion pictures are rightly included among the greatest educational factors we have today. Until now I never really appreciated the wonderful growth of the industry."

Mr. Sunday will visit Universal City on Tuesday next week and great preparations have been made there for his reception. It is rumored that the famous evangelist recently turned down an offer of $500,000 to appear in a series of pictures.

Triangle Studios Busy
Start Fall Producing Campaign—Ten Companies Working at Culver City.

WITH ten directors and companies hard at work in almost every section of California, the Triangle Film Corporation studios at Culver City, California, have started fall producing.

Westerns, comedy dramas, melodramas and various other dramatic combinations of love and human interest are marshaled in the onslaught for the fickle public's favor, involving the efforts of fifteen scenario writers and scores of lesser film luminaries who are all doing their bit.

The first offering in a series of "vampires in real life" is being filmed under the direction of Walter Edwards. Miss Belle Bennett plays the feature role, supported by Lee Hill and Texas Guinan. The temporary title of the new story is "Fuel of Life." Maude Reeves White is the authoress and Grant Wallace picturised the story.

Exclusive Studio Quarters Built for Fox Kiddies.

What will soon be an institution that will doubtless be copied far and wide wherever the welfare of the young is kept clearly in mind is the new children's rest room at the William Fox studio in Los Angeles. This rest room Mr. Fox regards as one of the important features of the new buildings that are being erected exclusively for the little people who create the Fox Kiddie Features.

The care that is given to the children while they are working at the William Fox studio is of the very highest and most scientific order. They have their individual dressing and retiring room, play rooms and school and gymnasium and baths and swimming pool, and not the least important, their rest room. Beside it is a play room, where the children have numberless toys and games. But the rest room is one to which they may retire and remain in comparative quiet when they feel so disposed. They are allowed to bring some of their simpler toys into it, as it has been shown that children are inclined to be more calm when some of them are in sight, but here they must not romp or disturb each other.

Each child has a place to sleep that is apart from the rest room. The latter is a place for them to loll about and talk while waiting for the announcement of the day's work and where they can go to between times without actually falling into slumber. Periods for the latter in their private rooms are carefully prescribed and adhered to.

Douglas Fairbanks and Billy Sunday to Stage Benefit Ball Game.

A monster benefit for the soldiers at Linda Vista and other military camps in the south will be staged at Washington Park on Monday afternoon, September 24, when Billy Sunday and Douglas Fairbanks meet at the head of their rival ball clubs.

Douglas Fairbanks, who is in New York, wired Billy Sunday a challenge Thursday, this week, and the great evangelist lost no time in wiring back his acceptance. The game will be staged on the twenty-fourth, so as to give the rival managers time to get in great shape for the battle.

A monster program will be arranged for that day and there will be several special stunts arranged by the committee to be put on before the ball game.

The money taken at the gate will go toward purchasing sporting goods for the soldier and sailor boys who are ready to do their bit for the Stars and Stripes. It is the ambition of both Billy Sunday and Douglas Fairbanks to pack the park on that day and turn over to the boys enough footballs, baseballs, bats, gloves and other sporting goods to keep them busy during their idle moments.

Billy Sunday was formerly a member of the Chicago Cubs and one of the greatest outfielders in the game. On that day he will play his old position, center field, and endeavor to show some of the present day crop of gardeners how the old American game should be played.

Triangle-Keystone Comedians Entertain Departing Draft Contingent.

Triangle-Keystone comedians furnished the merriment for Los Angeles' farewell to the first contingent of the Liberty Army on September 1. Five automobiles decorated with flags and Triangle-Keystone pennants, and filled with Keystone beauties and comedians in make-up formed a conspicuous part of the long street parade.

At Exposition Park in Los Angeles, where the Home Defenders' League tendered a barbecue to the departing soldiers, Robert Milliken and his troupe entertained with comedy hokum and the famous Keystone beauty squad was the object of thousands of admiring eyes.

The comedians who took part were: Bob Millikin, Andy Anderson, George Hall, Ward Caulfield, Clarence Kenecke, George Gray, M. Bianci, George Allen, Earl Rodney, Johnny Hayes and little Joey Jacobs. The girls included Rose Carter, Rae Godfrey, Claire Anderson, Caroline Rankin, Miss Hart, Beatrice Lovejoy, Blanche Payson, Marie Manley, Myrtle Reeves, Myrtle Lind, Alatia Marton, Dale Fuller, Maude Wayne, Peggy Pearce, Ruth Langston and several others.

Los Angeles Brevities.

B. F. Rolfe, general manager of the Metro Pictures Corporation, arrived in Los Angeles on Wednesday, September 5. We have not had an opportunity to see Mr. Rolfe, but we are informed that Metro intends to operate seven companies here and bring out several of their most prominent stars and directors. Among those mentioned as scheduled for the coast are Viola Dana, the Barrymores, Emmy Whelen and Mabel Taliafero. The Yorke-Metro studios are temporarily closed, Fred Balshofer and Harold Lockwood having gone to New York, where they will remain for several months. Studio location for the new Metro companies has not as yet been announced.

It is also reported that Pathe intends to produce on a large scale in California and send nine companies to Los Angeles. It is reported that the Pathe interests have leased the Kalem studios in Glendale and will soon bring out a number of their most prominent stars, including Pearl White, Gladys

Hulette, Ruth Roland and many others. C. R. Seeley, Pathe's business manager, arrived in the city this week, but we have not been able to get hold of him in time for this News Letter.

* * *

Director General J. P. McGowan of the Signal Corporation this week finished the eighth chapter of the "Lost Express," which will be released under the installment title of "The Looters."

* * *

Ella Hall, petite cinema star, became the bride of Emory Johnson, also a popular film artist, at Hollywood, California, on the afternoon of September 6.

The wedding took place at the residence of Rev. E. P. Ryland and only the members of the two families, in addition to the bridesmaid and best man, were present; Miss Elsie Choen being the former and Harry Carter acting as best man.

The young couple started on a honeymoon trip by auto to San Francisco. They will remain there for ten days, returning to the south by way of the Yosemite Valley.

The bride is well known on account of her splendid Bluebird characterisations, and Johnson also has made an excellent reputation as an actor, his latest work of importance being in the thirty-two-reel Universal serial, "The Gray Ghost," in which he plays one of the leading roles. Johnson finished his final scene in the serial at Universal City at 2 p. m. and at 3 p. m. he was married.

* * *

For the first time in its history, the California State Fair Association has set aside a day in honor of a motion picture star. Friday, September 14, having been named "Helen Holmes Day." The dainty and daring Signal actress will start the two engines that are scheduled to make a head on collision for the benefit of fair patrons.

* * *

Carl Laemmle, president of the Universal Film Manufacturing Company, who arrived recently from New York for a month's stay, left Universal City a few days ago on an automobile trip which will last a week. During his seven days' absence from the film capital the Big U chief will motor to Santa Barbara, San Bernardino, Riverside, Pomona, Pasadena, San Diego and other cities of the southland, visiting the exhibitors in the various places and obtaining first-hand information as to photoplay conditions and the wants of the theater people. Mr. Laemmle will remain several days at Coronado before returning to Universal City.

* * *

Director Joseph De Grasse of the Bluebird studios is filming a five-reel drama entitled "The Winged Mystery," written by O. D. Stuart and prepared for the screen by William Parker. Franklyn Farnum is the featured player and has a dual role. Rosemary Theby plays opposite Farnum and the other important parts are in the hands of Claire Du Bréy and Sam De Grasse.

* * *

A one-reel comedy, "The Smuggler's Last Smuggle," is being filmed at Universal City by the Joker Company under the direction of Allen Curtis. William Franey and Gale Henry play the leading roles.

* * *

Having just completed "One Shot Ross," a Western "thriller" that centers about a two-gun bad man, Roy Stewart, cowboy star, again has started work at the Hartville ranch studio on another production of pioneer days which has been temporarily titled, "Guardian of El Dorado." Cliff Smith, who assisted William S. Hart in all of his Triangle productions, is directing Stewart. Jack Cunningham, scenario editor of the Culver City studio, is the author of the piece and the story was prepared for the screen by Alvin H. Neitz.

* * *

Eighteen actors and actresses play more or less important roles in "The Stainless Barrier," recently begun under the direction of Thomas Heffron, most prominent among them being Jack Livingston, J. Barney Sherry, Mary McIvor, Irene Hunt and Jessie Hallett. Jack Cunningham picturised the story, which was written by Louis Schneider.

* * *

Charles Gunn, formerly Olive Thomas' leading man in "An Even Break," and one of the most popular Triangle players for more than a year, is to be featured in a piece just begun by Ferris Hartmann. Laura Sears assumes the leading feminine role and Mildred Delfino, who but recently recovered from serious injuries received while she was supporting Margery Wilson in "Wild Sumac," will also play an important part. George du Bois Proctor, one of Triangle's most successful script artists, prepared the screen version of the story, which was written by Mildred Considine.

* * *

Director Lynn Reynolds departed this week for Santa Barbara, where he will produce a society drama featuring Fritzi Ridgeway and George Hernandez. The name of this piece has not yet been announced. Reynolds is the author as well as the director.

* * *

George Arling is back on the Triangle-Keystone staff and is doing a picture with Ray Griffith, Myrtle Lind and Martin Kinney under the direction of Reggie Morris.

Mr. Arling will be welcomed back by Keystone fans and will be remembered for his former work with the late Fred Mace. Mr. Arling's most recent work was with Fox.

* * *

Joseph (Baldy) Belmont is also back on the Triangle-Keystone "lot," and is waiting for a story. He will probably be directed by William Beaudine, who will start with Triangle-Keystone next week. This will bring the total of companies now engaged in making Triangle-Keystone comedies up to seven, and it is likely that one or two additional companies will be added later.

* * *

Triangle-Keystone's song writer-director, Harry Williams, is at work on his first comedy since resuming work with Triangle-Keystone. His cast included Eddie Gribbon, Rose Carter, Marie Manley, Mal St. Clair and Blanche Payson.

* * *

The first Lois Weber production, "Did You Ever Have a Good Time?" which will be released in the near future on a State's rights basis, will be marked by some noteworthy beautiful color effects. This part of the work has been done by Mr. Jack Bloom, the inventor and sole owner of the color process, first used and made famous in "Intolerance." Mr. Bloom is now affiliated with Miss Weber and will have entire charge of the tinting and coloring of her pictures.

Lois Weber's screen version of "K," Mary Roberts Rinehart's novel, is rapidly nearing completion, and Miss Weber is highly pleased with the excellent work done by the cast. True Boardman, in the title role of "K," Albert Roscoe as Dr. Max, and Mildred Harris as Sidney, all have had exceptional opportunities to display their artistry to the best advantage. In preparing the scenario, Miss Weber made every effort to follow the action of the novel as nearly as possible.

* * *

A new Lehrman comedy has been completed for William Fox that is believed to be the best that the famous director has ever put upon the screen. It brings out a new chapter in the development of motion picture humor.

"The distinctive feature of this new comedy," said Mr. Lehrman when the final touches were given, "is that it presents a comedy that is interesting and clever from the standpoint of the story. It has hundreds of funny incidents that are new and will inevitably cause the wildest sort of laughter, but without them a decidedly good and absorbing story has been told."

* * *

Jack Jevne has been added to the scenario staff at the Triangle-Keystone studios. Mr. Jevne is one of the best comedy writers in the business and has had considerable experience on the stage as a juvenile lead. He is also a short story writer of considerable note.

* * *

Triangle-Keystone Director Reggie Morris has been shooting scenes this week in a big cafe set for a forthcoming Triangle-Keystone comedy featuring Ray Griffith, Alatia Barton, Martin Kinney and Myrtle Lind. Between scenes Bob Millikin and Frits Schade, who were both vaudeville artists before joining Keystone, put on an "act" for the benefit of the fifty or more people working in the scene.

* * *

The final scenes in the sixteenth and last episode of the Universal serial, "The Gray Ghost," were made this week by Director Stuart Paton. The principal roles throughout the serial were played by Priscilla Dean, Eddie Polo, Harry Carter and Emory Johnson. Paton and Karl Coolidge collaborated in writing the scenario from the book entitled "Loot" by Arthur Somers Roche.

Spokes from the Hub

By Marion Howard

WHEN I saw "To the Death" I could not but feel that if Mrs. L. Case Russell, the author, had been present when it was directed she would not have allowed one "fool" thing to go forth. This was the scene when the villain (in cave man fashion) seized the heroine and took her outdoors, thence to a hotel, with his armful, but where did he drop her long enough to make a change in dress and to don an up-to-date hat? There was one big murmur all around me over this inconsistency. The plot seemed a good one with one or two new ideas in it, and was well cast and photographed, but Petrova is as icy as ever.

* * *

"Tides of Fate" had good sea stuff and served to show us Alexandria Carlisle in her first picture seen here. She made a hit and was a picture even in a hobble skirt and other long gowns. When I criticised this, someone said: "Well, the play is set back five years in the first reels." William A. Sheer in a thankless part was splendid all through.

* * *

"The Varmint" is a sure winner anywhere, and how Jack Pickford has developed! The college scenes are intensely interesting, so full of red blood and realism. Don't know when I've enjoyed Theodore Roberts so well.

* * *

"Mme. Bo-Peep," a Triangle winner, was liked, and pictured Western scenes galore, notably a sheep ranch. Seena Owen is some rider.

* * *

Burton Holmes has taken us through the Yellowstone and we have thus saved a lot of cash.

* * *

A recent winner here is "Sudden Jim," with Charles Ray, whom we all dote on. Reviewers have dealt well with this offering—a clever adaptation of a good story read by millions. We get a strong lesson here in self-reliance and the will power to make good.

* * *

"The Squaw Man's Son" was a good vehicle for "Wally" Reid, but too melodramatic and lacked plausibility for a Paramount picture. However, the acting was excellent and I was glad to see Dorothy Davenport playing in company with her "hubby," though she was some vampire. Here, too, we had Donald Bowles, so long in stock on the Pacific Coast. His mother is one of New England's best beloved women, the Rev. Ada Bowles, long past eighty, residing in old Gloucester, where for generations her family reared their own. She takes pride in the success of her boy.

* * *

Why do not all first class theaters put on the "Do Children Count" series? What excuse is there for denying your public a right to see something more than worth while? I heard a fool reason the other day when at the General Film Exchange. An exhibitor said he did not like the title, as it might seem to his public that it was suggestive. Isn't that the limit, and from the lips of an apparently decent clean-minded man? How easy to tell his public on a slide something to the contrary. The very title is of itself an advertisement, for intelligent persons know well that children do count everywhere, and these pictures point it out dramatically. Adults and kiddies alike are enjoying the series, which are a credit to Essanay and to the theaters showing them.

* * *

Perhaps I had a day off, but I did not care for "Mary Jane's Pa," although I sat it through twice to get the merits. It was clean and a good small-town play, and Eulalie Jensen was capital, but somehow I could not make Marc MacDermott fit into the part. The house liked it, and that's enough for the box office. Give me such plays at this season as "Slumberland," featuring the Triangle kiddies and Thelma Salter, a dainty girl, ably supported by young Stone.

* * *

Jean Sothern is a favorite for all who like youth and talent, combined with the added asset—beauty. "A Mute Appeal" was novel in theme and well worked out, with the inevitable happy ending the fans so like. Donald Cameron fitted into the part. In this play there were stunning out-

door scenes in the South and its wildwoods, while the mutes were perfect in their delineations. Good Art Dramas picture.

* * *

We have had a treat in the music offered of late in some of the theaters. At the Fenway young Del Castillo of Cambridge has given rare organ music in the absence of the house orchestra. He is of Spanish descent and inherits his musical ability from his mother, a musician of note. At the Exeter we have had Mary White-Mullen as soloist, much to our delight, as she has a powerful voice, and as a man said last night, "She is a beauty, no mistake." Martell, at the Park, too, is an organist worth hearing. At this house we get some big voices like Mary Desmond of the Metropolitan Opera Company, Mme. Calvert and such. It is refreshing, too, to again hear the old songs, marches, etc., now that the copyright ban is on, and if the players but knew it we like them far better than some of the modern music, so why not save the tax and dig up old-timers?

* * *

Like all Triangles, "Borrowed Plumage" had original features, and Bessie Barriscale made good as the versatile heroine. There was good soldier stuff and where is there another actress to so fit the role of queen of the kitchen as the dame in this picture? She is not listed in the cast, but should be, for it was a big hit in facial expression. I like especially the delicate manner in depicting John Paul Jones and his defense when branded a pirate, which he never was at any time.

* * *

Well, I liked "The Amazons," which ought to be good for a "repeat" any time for its novelty and splendid settings. For a Paramount it had Keystone features rather surprising, such as climbing to the roof and sliding down a rope to reach the gymnasium for a rendezvous, but it was plausible and had no slapstick features. The spectacle of seeing dainty Marguerite Clark do a trapeze stunt, and dropping on tree boughs from a window, a la Fairbanks, was some fun and a big hit with the house. Norton and Menjou had "silly ass" parts and made the most of it, but William Hinckley was unusually good, first as the English aviator and later as the lover. A perfectly safe picture to put on in any theater, for the personality of Miss Clark is so compelling.

* * *

Don't know when we have enjoyed a better picture in lighter vein than "Little Miss of Fortune," with Marian Swayne, who has ever made good. True, there were some inconsistencies, but who cares, since the idea works out so well. Especially noticeable was the character work of the old lady—"Granny" of the poorhouse. It was pathetic and artistic. The small town indoor scenes were funny, picturing the antics of an audience at an amateur show. I anticipate another rural play in "The Little Samaritan" for Miss Swayne, who is recalled with pleasure on the speaking stage.

* * *

No better comedy has ever been put on the screen than "Baby Mine," which you have all seen. So much has been said of this that further comments are like twice-told tales. Goldwyn has set a great pace, which speaks well for our future enjoyment, since other producers must look to their laurels.

* * *

"Redemption" went strong here, but was not rightly exploited in the press, which dwelt too much on the Thaw end and failed to say that this is a play featuring mother love and sacrifice, also the redemption of the "man in the case."

* * *

"The Last of the Carnabys" is strong, and little Hulette repeats her work in "The Shine Girl," one of the gems of last year. I do wish directors would not give us prolonged deathbed scenes as in this case, as it detracts from our pleasure and remains an impression hard to efface. Glad to see William Parke's boy making good as an actor and under the direction of his capable father, a local favorite.

* * *

Howell Hansel has given us a treat in "The Long Trail," with Lou-Tellegen and Mary Fuller, whom I had not seen for some time. It is nearly all outdoor with, snow, dog sleds, and other cool accessories. "Nice on a hot night to see, old man," said one next to me.

* * *

We are glad to learn that Charlie Miller is to direct Norma Talmadge the coming two years. Mrs. Miller writes me from California that they have a son at Harvard; that she is to motor to New York this week and will visit the Hub soon.

War and Exports 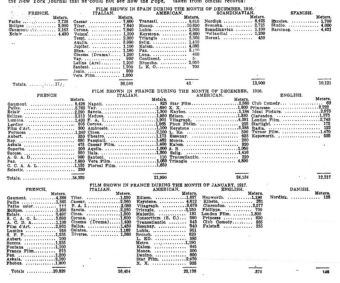 By F. G. Ortega

Businesslike Methods Will Be Necessary in the Immediate Future, if American Producers Are to Hold the Foreign Trade After European Competition Is Resumed

THE war will not last forever. The statement may sound foolish, but most of our producers and distributors seem to be doing business under the impression that these are normal times.

As the single mention of peace is originating more fights among civilians than any one word in the dictionary, nothing would have been more gratifying than to make our few remarks on export without trespassing on this dangerous ground.

But the subject cannot be avoided. Even at the risk that the whole assumption should be labelled by our London friends as a pro-Hun scheme, we will have to admit that the war cannot last forever.

Will it last ten years? Will it last five, two, one year more? How long will it last?

* * *

Some people think, that the Pope, horrified by some new atrocity, had an impromptu talk with his secretary and decided then and there to write to his friends in belligerent countries. This is the way in which many respectable citisens are explaining the peace note. In fact, a worthy bishop of one of the Protestant churches puts his veto on the whole proceeding, announcing in an article written for the New York Journal that he could not see how the Pope,

a private individual without diplomatic representation, might influence the powers. It is wonderful that such a thing could be said by a man of distinction in a country like this where everybody reads two or three newspapers a day.

The truth of the matter is, and it has been officially admitted, that His Holiness had been consulting with every belligerent and neutral country for months before sending the note, that the rulers knew it by heart before it was delivered and published, and that, if it does not mark the actual beginning of the end, it at least reveals a general desire to discuss peace terms.

* * *

A buyer from one of the South American Republics stated in the office of the Cine-Mundial, our international organ, that it would not take the European producers six months to recover the Latin-American markets after the war is over. "If a radical change is not established at once," he said, "the American manufacturers will lose our markets quicker than they captured them. Why, these gentlemen seem to be copying the methods of the German politicians. I asked the president of a well-known film company how much he would take for the exclusive rights for Brazil on one of his pictures, and what do you think he did? He brought out a map. We did not do any business, but I had the pleasure of telling him what I thought of the map as a basis for calculating the value of a picture."

* * *

"L'Arte Muta," the well-informed Italian trade paper, in an article published recently, reviews with alarm the strides made by American producers during the past six months. It prints the following statistical tables, taken from official records:

FILM SHOWN IN SPAIN DURING THE MONTH OF DECEMBER, 1916.

FRENCH.	Meters.	ITALIAN.	Meters.	AMERICAN.	Meters.	SCANDINAVIAN.	Meters.	SPANISH.	Meters.
Pathe	7,725	Caesar	7,800	Transatl.	8,616	Nordisk	8,425	Excelsa.	1,700
Eclipse	3,600	Tiber.	7,640	Monop.	10,650	Svenska.	2,725	Studio.	4,000
Gaumont	2,163	Corona.	7,640	Lubin.	2,000	Scandinavian	1,100	Barcinog.	4,421
Eclair	4,430	Volsca.	1,200	Keystone.	6,600	Hollandial	1,200		
		Tespi.	2,000	Triangle.	3,360	Boreal.	450		
		Aquila.	3,980	Selig.	1,450				
		Jupiter.	1,100	Kalem.	4,085				
		Etna.	1,160	Psa.	3,150				
		Cinema (Drama)	1,200	Luna.	400				
		Vay.	900	Continent.	5				
		Latina (Ars)	1,200	Broncho.	2,050				
		Santoni	1,200	L. K. O.	700				
		Jesio.	900						
		Vera Film	1,600						
Totals	17,2		36,080		43		13,900		10,121

FILM SHOWN IN FRANCE DURING THE MONTH OF DECEMBER, 1916.

FRENCH	Meters.	ITALIAN.	Meters.	AMERICAN.	Meters.	ENGLISH.	Meters.
Gaumont.	8,426	Napoli.	825	Star Film.	2,360	Club Comedy	60
Pathe.	5,765	Vay.	1,690	X. X.	1,800	Princesse.	2,222
Eclair	2,230	Savoia.	1,300	Kaybee.	1,184	Ideal Picture	2,975
Eclipse.	1,213	Medusa.	1,950	Edison.	1,280	Clarendon.	1,375
Lumina.	1,400	F. A. 1.	1,905	Vitagraph.	4,391	London Film.	2,743
Lordier	805	Corona.	1,965	Pinn Film.	20	Starlight.	175
Film d'Art.	300	Ambrosio.	1,100	Keystone	3,385	Radia.	122
Formosa	1,240	Cines.	2,100	L. Ko.	500	Turner Film.	1,470
Aubert.	350	Theatro.	1,175	Essanay.	635	Kepsworth.	535
Roy.	680	Pasquali.	1,462	Monca.	200		
Askala.	475	Caesar Film.	1,460	Kalem.	830		
Superba.	200	Aquila.	1,000	A. B.	1,050		
Succes.	950	Itala.	1,300	Selig.	1,416		
A. G. A. D.	980	Santoni.	110	Transatlantic.	220		
Pas.	1,890	Vera Film.	1,060	Triangle.	4,890		
C. C. A. A. L.	1,135	Floreal Film.	1,650				
Selectic.	280						
Totals.	34,389		21,990		24,134		12,217

FILM SHOWN IN FRANCE DURING THE MONTH OF JANUARY, 1917.

FRENCH.	Meters.	ITALIAN.	Meters.	AMERICAN.	Meters.	ENGLISH.	Meters.	DANISH.	Meters.
Gaumont.	4,366	Tiber.	1,550	Edison.	1,827	Hepworth.	1,196	Nordisk.	125
Pathe	1,565	Caesar.	2,060	Keystone.	4,612	Kineto.	261		
Pathe color	???	F. A. I.	2,085	Vitagraph.	3,670	Clarendon.	3,577		
Eclipse.	1,950	Savoia.	2,250	Triangle.	3,150	Philipps.	700		
Eclair.	3,497	Cines.	1,500	Majestic.	181	London Film.	1,800		
S. C. A. G. L.	3,690	Corona.	1,600	Consortium (S. C.)	590	Princess	630		
A. C. D. A.	1,100	Cinema (Drama)	1,400	Transatlantic.	948	Club Comedy.	885		
Film d'Art.	2,965	Salica.	1,450	Essanay.	940	Falstaff.	335		
Lumina	910	Galatea.	1,169	Lubin.	951				
S. P. F.	1,235	Diverse.	1,360	Bronch.	620				
Aubert.	100			L. KO.	585				
Succes.	1,235			Metro.	1,390				
Fontana	1,100			Kalem.	645				
Franco Film.	575			Monca.	200				
Pas.	1,200			Domino.	600				
Askala.	3,160			Star Film.	2,470				
Phobus.	1,900			X. X.	925				
Totals	29,829		16,454		25,138		874		125

Value of the film shown in Great Britain during the year 1916:

American .... 19,425,000 francs (About $3,885,000)
English .... 2,417,500 francs (About   483,500)
French .... 1,787,500 francs (About   337,500)
Other countries .... 1,108,750 francs (About   221,550)

* * *

Severo Norsa, Cine-Mundial correspondent in Argentine, makes in his last letter the following statement, based on official data: "In the first three months of the current year (1917), 4,958,940 feet of film were imported during the same period of last year. Although the increase is not very large, the situation, as a whole, is extremely favorable for the American producers. At the beginning of 1916, the film imported was mostly of European brands, all of which have virtually disappeared from the market. It can be said, therefore, that, excepting an insignificant percentage of French and Italian pictures, the five million feet imported are made up of American brands."

* * *

We are not in possession of exact data on other Spanish and Portuguese-speaking countries, but Argentine may be taken as a representative example insofar as the popularity of American pictures is concerned. Now then, Argentine, with about the same number of inhabitants as the cities of New York and Boston, is, according to the figures quoted above, a better market than France with a population of nearly forty millions. In fact, Argentine absorbs considerable more foreign film than most European countries. Chile, Bolivia, Uruguay and Peru are more or less dependent on Argentine.

Spain and Portugal, which may be considered a single unit for all commercial purposes, are a better market than Argentine.

Cuba and Porto Rico, with about three hundred theatres running daily, is another good market. As far as the American producer is concerned, as profitable as France.

Mexico, in peace times, is a better market than Argentine. Mexico is rapidly becoming normal again.

Venezuela, Colombia and the Republics of Central America, if properly handled, should absorb as much film as Argentine.

Brasil and Argentine run neck to neck in film consumption.

At this very moment the Spanish and Portuguese-speaking markets of the world are absorbing nearly as much American film as Great Britain, although, excepting two or possibly three New York concerns, the American Moving Picture Industry has made no intelligent effort to develop its trade there. If the business were gone after with a tenth of the energy displayed in this country, they would soon be at the head among our foreign customers, above Great Britain proper and second in importance only to the British Empire.

* * *

It should be stated plainly that the introduction of American film in Latin-America, and almost absolute control of the business in some of the Republics, have been caused by the war and nothing else.

The claims so often heard about the attraction exercised by our perfect plots, unexcelled beauty of the stars, well-balanced casts, superior technique and so forth have had nothing to do with the case. These merits are acknowledged today and will help to retain what we have already won, but they did not bring a single buyer to this country.

The foreign buyers came here simply because the war drove them out of business in Europe. The restrictions were so many and the shipments so uncertain that conditions became unbearable.

They came to this country to buy in large quantities, to open up new markets for American product, to pay, as a rule, higher prices than in France or Italy for brands and "stars" that meant less in their territories than Galatea or La Tortajada in New York, and on top of all this with the prospect of a long and costly struggle at home to eliminate the prejudice, prevailing at that time, against our artistic production.

At the present time, after two years of constant effort, we find the American film introduced in every Spanish and Portuguese-speaking market and in actual control of some of them. But this has been accomplished IN SPITE of the American producers, who have stuck to the take-it-or-leave-it system, and it would be fatuous to disguise the fact that a feeling of resentment has arisen among many of the foreign exchanges and their representatives in this country.

* * *

Are these foreign film men right in their contention that it

is impossible to do business with American producers in a business-like way?

Now we said at the beginning of these notes that the war could not last forever, and it seems pretty certain that it will not last a year longer.

Is it not about time, therefore, that the American producers and distributors gave some serious thought to the question of holding on after the war to what they have acquired during the past two years?

Or will they be satisfied to relinquish these markets as soon as Europe is ready for business again?

Today our stars are familiar to the public and generally admired, our brands are known, some have become famous and considered superior to anything produced in Europe, but owing to our haphazard methods in dealing with Latin-America, amounting to absolute non-cooperation in most cases, it can be stated, without fear of exaggeration, that as surely as the war cannot last forever, we will have to give up our preponderance in those markets if this policy of aloofness—or lack of policy—is not changed.

And the change, to be effective, will have to take place before the war is over—NOW.

Mexico Picture-Wild

Cameraman Robert A. Turnbull Finds Business Improving in the Land of Revolutions—Large Returns to Exhibitors.

ROBERT A. TURNBULL, an American cameraman who has been traveling in Mexico, writes an interesting letter regarding conditions in that country. The general impression is that Mexico is torn from one end to the other with internal strife, but Mr. Turnbull reports that things have quieted down in many states and that business is good. Motion pictures are especially liked by the Mexicans and the profits are good as his report shows. The letter follows:

"I came here from the United States about three months ago to do some motion picture work for the Mexican Government and send a little news about the American films in this country. 'Joan of Arc' is here and playing to packed houses, and the prices are, of course, much higher than in the States. 'Civilization' was also here last month and the owner cleaned up $10,000 in gold in a few towns. This man tells me that the film was shown in Mexico City and there it covered its cost in one month and also made $12,000 profit.

"Mexico is just picture wild, and most of the pictures shown here are French and Italian. Max Linder is the favorite. The shows start at 9 p. m. and continue until 12 p. m. They have a very funny way of charging admission: First you pay for the first two reels, then if you care to stay for the rest of the show a collector comes and you pay so much more. They call this 'Tandas.' First tanda means first part of the show, of course you can buy all of the show at one time and you save that trouble.

"Mexico City has now three studios producing pictures and no doubt it is the coming country for the game. I have offers to go with one of these studios.

"Things are shaping up very fine. I have been to three states and find that they are working and very peaceful, took some scenics through the states of Campeche, Tabasco, and Yucatan, and the wonderful Maya Indian ruins which date back to the year 1,000 A. D. One man, a millionaire, makes pictures as his hobby. He produced a picture called '1810,' which is the Mexican Independence year. He built the forts, houses, streets, canons, etc.—everything a la Griffiths; even imported some scenic artists from Cuba to do the sets. It cost him about $6,000 in gold. He took the picture, developed it, cut it, and showed it, all by himself and he had never seen a motion picture studio in his life. It was a one man business and he paid for all the expense, even hired a cook and took him to his hacienda so that the actors could have their eats. In one of the scenes he used 1,000 regular soldiers.

"I saw the picture on the screen and it was not bad at all, the photography was perfect. Out of this ten-reel feature he has made $7,000, that goes to show how these people will go to see any kind of a picture. They are easy to please and will pay the price.

"Anything I can do for you while here will be gladly done. Will be in Los Angeles by the fifteenth of September, but will return to Mexico City. I was cameraman for Lubin and on the Mutual program for the last two years, and made 'The Planter,' in Guatemala, with Tyrone Power."

Brazil As a Film Producer 🌑 🌑 🌑 🌑 🌑 🌑 🌑 🌑 🌑

*First Attempts Have Not Given Great Promise
—Possibilities of Large Profits Inducing
Further Efforts*

Rio de Janeiro, Brasil, August 8.

SEVERAL efforts have been made by local capital to form producing companies in the Brazilian field, but the most serious organization has not been able to get results expected. The great American companies' success has led some men of money to believe that all they have to do is to throw a few acts on the screen and become rich overnight. A film put on here recently did not follow closely the rules of the game, and nothing more was heard of it.

A French name for the film, an American actress for the leading part, a Brazilian supporting company, Brazilian scenes the plot of German villainies, the place Belgium—all this international mixture failed to put the film across. "Le Film du Diable" was the title. The Brazilian male lead made no attempt to make up the German part he essayed; his Francis Ford whiskers plainly put him out of the part. The film began by showing several flashes telling what the poor film industry was trying to do for Brazilians. After this the audience expected to go on with the play, but the screen was further occupied by a long series of scenes in and around Rio de Janeiro. These had nothing to do with the play.

Briefly the story was that of a young woman taken over by the officer of a German regiment invading Belgium. She is made the plaything of the officer after his troops had killed all the members of her family. She escapes after a time and is seen by friendly soldiers and taken to the shed where they are lodged. While asleep her spirit is made to leave the body and go out to seek revenge for the infamies perpetrated against her and her parents. Just outside she meets his Satanic majesty, who gives counsel as to what she should do. Here the spirit of evil and the spirit of good come to blows. The spirit of good is represented by a naked woman, who constantly confronts the devil.

The naked woman appears always in the distance, but toward the end of the film there is a close-up showing her talking to the devil. The woman who played this part was plainly agitated by her emotions, and did poor justice to the part through nervousness. The girl returns to her place in the shed, and the line on the screen puts an end to the misery of the audience by saying: "The rest of this play will appear soon." Nothing more has followed.

There were some beautiful backgrounds made up from the many landscapes around Rio de Janeiro. The leading woman did a good bit of work in an unattractive part. Not one of the male characters could be called interesting. The aid of the press—which is ever ready to give advice and offer suggestions—was not invoked before the play was put on. A few changes here and there would have done wonders.

Another and more serious attempt is being made by the Sociedade Anonyma Brasil-Film to portray interesting plays. This company has gone into the field better equipped than any other. It appreciates the necessity for organization and equipment. Its staff is made up of Dr. Octavio de Sousa Leão, G. Maxwell de Souza Bastos and Humberto Taborda. The artistic director is Eduardo Victorino. The latter was quoted as saying that his company would be equipped to produce any and all classes of film with the best photographic and artistic accompaniments. The company is said to count on the best work of native authors, which, in conjunction with the excellence of the marvelous landscapes and other beauties of Brazil, should guarantee success. No secret is made of the fact that the organizers and directors of the new company will adapt foreign processes to local needs, depending on the natural methods of expression of its actors to make its plays appreciated.

The company plainly seems to fear lack of capital, but the success of American enterprises is mentioned to show that success comes to those who invite it. The European war did not keep American companies from going ahead. The Moving Picture World is quoted to show that the United States counts some thirty big moving picture companies, and the new Goldwyn organization is cited to prove that money is to be made in the film game. The capital of the Goldwyn company is said to be $3,000,000, and the director is quoted as saying that these fabulous figures should

stimulate Brazilians to their best efforts to produce films for local consumption. The director thinks that local capital will be difficult to obtain. Artistically, he thinks the "art of gesture and of facial expression is a little more difficult" in the making of films than in theatrical productions. If it be true that a good film actor must have a good mimicry, then it is equally true that he must possess a good oral expression. Due to the briefness of many film scenes, and lack of time for good preparation of dialogues, expression is sometimes necessarily more intense, more rapidly executed. This, claims the director, makes impossible the development of an actor. (It should be noted that up to this point the necessity of making good film actors was not appreciated.) When asked if the making of actors was a question of time, Mr. Victorino said:

"We are bringing from Italy and France three women and two men. These will serve as models, and our own artists will be formed after them."

Some of the higher schools of Brasil are using the moving picture as part of the study course. Mr. Victorino thinks the use of films should be extended to the lower schools by order of the educational authorities, giving studies in geography, history, agricultural and general information. The company has already received and read more than forty subjects for its production, but only two have actually been filmed, "In the Abyss" and "Between Two Loves." The latter was not received with any particular fervor, and the former was hardly noticed. The director claims for "Between Two Loves" (Entre Dois Amores) that it is a simple study of characters. Mingled with scenes of beauty in Rio de Janeiro, of picturesque landscapes, of scenes of simple rural life, there is shown a struggle of hearts because of the defects or blemishes of education. Love, naturally, permeates the picture, from which comes forth a delicate emotion.

The program of the Brasil-Film includes works of science and propaganda. The director says the company has in preparation a large work for the benefit of commerce and industry in Brazil.

Worth special mention here is the success of the Nacional Film. Incidents of importance are shown the day after the event—the arrival of the American fleet, the various receptions and the big parade on the Fourth of July were projected in several theaters in a remarkably short time. Any happening of local interest is sure to be taken and distributed. J. H. C.

Scene from "Madame Who?" (Paralta).

TERRISS JOINS VITAGRAPH.

Tom Terriss has been specially engaged to play opposite Miss Alice Joyce and direct her productions. The first picture, which he is now working upon, is a Robert W. Chambers story, entitled, "Anne's Bridge," to be followed by one of Mr. Chambers' most successful stories. Mr. Terriss left the head of his own corporation as the Vitagraph made such an attractive proposition.

Russia a Profitable Field

N. S. Kaplan Says Revolution Has Removed One Obstacle to American Productions—Rest Up to Producers.

THE opening of a new market for American made film productions, one that will eventually prove to be very profitable, is seen in late news despatches from Russia by the representative of the Moscow Art theater in this country, N. S. Kaplan. From his studios last week he received details of one very tangible result for good already made possible by the revolution. The democratisation of the Russian stage and screen is assured under the new regime. This means, says Mr. Kaplan, that not only will the wealth of Russian artistic production be available for the entire world, but that the obstacles hitherto placed in the way of the revelation of foreign achievement will be to a certain extent eliminated.

"When I say that Russia will prove a profitable field for American motion picture producers," said Mr. Kaplan, "I do not overlook the difficulties in the way of final success. American films have been shown in Russia, usually with little success. This lack of appreciation of your productions may be traced to two causes. One the revolution has just eliminated. The other is up to the American producer.

"Russian audiences must be studied by the producer who is not familiar with their demands. As I have said so many times the Russian playgoer insists on two things; he must have a story that is based on a foundation of realism and truth, and he demands that the players be artists. If I may say so, these essentials are often lacking in the best of American productions. Here the theatergoing public is a composite of so many different elements that a picture play generally has an appeal to one element or another. Russia is Russia, where the people have been forced to stifle aspirations, to repress their human feelings and to cringe before the oppressor. This heritage of centuries has left its mark. The Russian must be educated out of his bondage. When the American producer perceives this and selects carefully from such productions as he may make those which portray real life then he will find an enthusiastic reception in Russia.'

Mr. Kaplan compares the system by which the stars of the screen are developed in America and in Russia to emphasize his point that the failure of films made here is due to some extent to the American policy of accepting stars who have not justified their position either by experience or ability.

"But the main point of my prediction that America will find a profitable field for its film output in Russia is the announcement that has just come to me regarding the abolition of strict government direction of the stage. My studio manager tells me that the artistic management of the imperial theaters is to be autonomous. This means that a large number of theaters will have a wider range of selection than formerly. American promoters have found that even if they had an attraction that found favor in Russia they soon exhausted the available theaters for presentation. This, I believe, will be changed under the new regime. The greater the opportunity given the greater will be the possibilities of successful export of the screen productions of the United States in Russia.

"Another point, perhaps a frivolous one, is suggested by the overthrow of the monarchial form of government. Hitherto it has been well nigh impossible for many lovers of drama to obtain seats at the theaters. The government subsidized the playhouses and in return exacted more than half the capacity in reservations for the various dignitaries of the court. The best way to obtain a pair of seats in the old days was to be some kind of a relative of some attache of the court. The system discouraged enthusiasm for the drama among those who would have made it profitable. Now the bars are down and there is a splendid nucleus for a great theatergoing public in the new republic.

"Anything that applies to the dramatic stage in Russia applies to the screen as well. There is no fine distinction there. I hope to arrange while I am here for the exchange of Russian Art films and the best American productions. I believe the two peoples can form an alliance of art that will be everlasting."

KATE PRICE IN COMEDY SERIES.

Kate Price, the jolly comedienne and screen favorite of long standing, is to appear again before her motion-picture public in a series of six of the "Sparkle" comedies released through General Film Company. With her as co-actor will be seen Billy Rugh, one of the best character comedians of the film.

New Sales Manager for Select

C. E. Shurtleff, Formerly with Pathe and V-L-S-E, Comes Into the New Organization.

Arthur S. Kane, general manager of Select Pictures Corporation, is rapidly strengthening the sales staff of that organization. He has just brought into the Select camp C. E. Shurtleff, who assumes position as sales manager for Select Pictures.

Mr. Shurtleff is well known in the trade because of the special work which he has done for the Pathe organisation. As special representative for Pathe during the past year Mr. Shurtleff organised a sales system which proved remarkably effective. He spent much time organising and reorganising the Pathe sales force and bringing it up to a high standard of efficiency. He first entered the Pathe organisation as manager of the Cleveland branch.

Three years ago Mr. Shurtleff joined the World Film Corporation, afterwards leaving it to go with the V-L-S-E as branch manager, being in turn in charge of exchanges at Detroit, Cincinnati and Cleveland, at which points he made a high record for sales and business transactions. It was to join Pathe that he relinquished his V-L-S-E connection.

With Select, Mr. Shurtleff will devote his energies especially to producing a highly efficient sales corps, and to this end intends to make a comprehensive study of fields covered by Select exchanges.

"Intensive cultivation of territory is an important phase of the program which I expect to follow in handling Select Pictures. I am strongly impressed with the value of the personal equation in selling pictures, and I believe that both exchange managers and salesmen should thoroughly acquaint themselves with the personnel of the exhibitors throughout the territory which they are expected to cover, and should make a thorough study of the conditions existing in each locality in order to more intelligently supply that locality's needs. With this object in view I shall doubtless spend about half of my time in the field getting acquainted with exhibitors and keeping in close touch with our branch executives and with their sales forces," said Mr. Shurtleff.

"Nothing can quite equal the personal sizing up of conditions on the spot, and by following this method it is my hope to make the distribution of pictures through Select exchanges as near perfect as it is possible to bring picture distribution when the rapidly changing conditions in all the various territories are considered.

"In the short time that I have been with Select I have already become impressed with the tremendous opportunities which this organization holds forth to live exhibitors, and also to its own many employees."

BEBAN SIGNS NEW CONTRACT WITH PARAMOUNT.

Hiram Abrams, president of Paramount Pictures Corporation, has just announced the completion of arrangements whereby the famous impersonator of Latin types, George Beban, will remain as one of the galaxy of stars who are engaged in making pictures for Paramount, and that at least two more Beban productions will be released following "Lost in Transit," which went to exhibitors September 3d.

During his period of activity in Paramount pictures Mr. Beban has done some of the most appealing, wholesome and thoroughly satisfying photoplays that have ever been produced. In each and every one there has been pre-eminently featured a type of Latin character which in itself was worthy of commemoration in the annals of dramatic representation. It is conceded that Beban is an artist without a peer in his line, and he has had the advantage of excellent vehicles, splendid support and productions, to which the most careful attention and sumptuous investiture has been given.

MARIE DRESSLER GOES TO CALIFORNIA.

Marie Dressler and her staff quit the Goldwyn studios at Fort Lee last week for California and sunlight. Accompanied by her director, her secretary and her cameramen, the famous comedienne is Hollywood-bound in a private car. When she will return is a matter for conjecture.

Prints of "Tillie, the Scrub Lady" are being prepared and will soon be ready for distribution for trade showings throughout the country. Miss Dressler has approved the scenario for her second comedy, and work on it will begin with her arrival at Los Angeles. She will make eight pictures a year for exclusive distribution by Goldwyn.

Motion Picture Educator

Conducted by REV. W. H. JACKSON and MARGARET I. MACDONALD

Interesting Educationals

Two Travel Subjects, One Zoological, Four Industrials, One Sociological, One Scientific, and One Military Subject.
Reviewed by Margaret I. MacDonald.

"In Old Canton and New Shanghai" (Paramount-Holmes).

TWO of the most interesting cities of China are Canton and Shanghai, to which Burton Holmes takes us in this release of his travel pictures. In Canton we see much that belonged to the old regime, as well as much that pertains to the progress associated with the new. As we jog through the narrow streets of Canton in a coolie-carried chair we realise that in these streets no wheeled vehicle could navigate, and we gaze on sights and types totally unfamiliar to many of us. Once in a while we see school boys drilling, which suggests to us the spirit of a new China. And we will even see a corps of Boy Scouts. There is also to be noticed the new woman of China, whose feet are larger than those of her sister of the old regime. Then we meander on to Shanghai, which is an international city. Here we see British tramways crowded with Chinese, while British East India policemen direct the traffic. We will notice, too, the absence of pigtails, for the Chinaman of the Republic has cut off his pigtail. There are trolley cars in Shanghai, another mark of progress in contrast to the man-trundled vehicles so common in Chinese cities.

"Historic Monterey" (Educational).

This picture presents in an interesting way the scenes of beauty along the Bay of Monterey and also about the town. The well-known seventeen-mile drive is, of course, included, and at various points of interest along the way progress is halted while we stop to gaze at Point Joe, Point Lobos, or the Lone Cypress tree. It will be remembered that one of the charms of this drive is the fringe of cypress trees, with delightful glimpses of the shore. This is a beautiful scenic number.

"The Orang Volunteers" (Educational-Ditmars).

Among his charges at the Zoo, Raymond L. Ditmars discovered an unusually precocious orang; and in a picture, to which he has skilfully added a patriotic touch, he has shown us many of the animal's clever tricks. He starts him out husking corn on a patriotic farm and shows him to us at the close of a strenuous day mopping his brow with a handkerchief. He throws stones with curious dexterity, and is then given lessons in rifle shooting. To this form of bombardment he does not take very readily, for after experiencing for the first time the recoil of a gun he shows the white feather and returns to his former method of stone throwing. One of the most amusing things in the picture is the clever manner in which the orang dressed in soldier's uniform stretches himself out on the ground to take aim in true military fashion. This picture is one of Ditmars best.

"The Mussel Pearl Industry" (General Film-Selig).

The scenes of this picture, which will be found in No. 17 of the Selig World Library, were taken at the White River, Arkansas. The mussel pearl industry has grown to be an important one, netting those who engage in it large sums of money. The mussel pearls, which are obtained by steaming open the shells, are used in the making of jewelry; while the shells which form the most profitable part of the mussel are used in the manufacture of pearl buttons.

"The Sugar Industry of Java" (General Film-Selig).

In this picture, which is a part of the Selig World Library No. 17, we learn how the sugar cane is planted, as well as how it is converted into the sugar we use. The cane is cut into short pieces, which are planted in mud beds prepared in trenches. Then the harvesting of the sugar cane is shown,

and its transportation to the mills, where it is put through a crushing machine and its juice later put through an evaporating process and treated with sulphuric acid and lime to remove impurities. This subject is well illustrated.

"The Production of Fine Table Salt" (Universal).

In Screen Magazine No. 33 will be found a good illustration of the method in which fine table salt is manufactured. We learn from the picture that the brine is forced up by compressed air into large centrifugal tanks, where it is allowed to remain for forty-eight hours in order that the impurities may settle. The brine is then run through hot vats for evaporation purposes. The evaporation process completed a scraper is placed in the vat, which pushes the salt onto a belt which carries it to the centrifugal drivers, where it revolves at the rate of from 850 to 1,000 revolutions per minute. This machine also automatically weighs the salt and places it in bags for the purpose, which are then passed on to operators, who sew the bags.

"Helping Men Go Straight" (Universal).

The work of the industrial schools and prison reformatories in connection with the Department of Corrections of the City of New York is a wonderful and important one, as is shown in the scenes photographed at one of these institutions for the Screen Magazine No. 33. The picture shows how the boys arriving at the farm are made to feel at home. Before they are put to work on the farm each boy is thoroughly examined by a doctor and reported on. We are shown the various branches of farming which these boys are taught to do, including the care of chickens, pigs and cows. They are taught how to raise the finest vegetables and fruits, and are then shown how to can these for winter use. We also see the boys at recreation, and learn that drilling is one of the principal daily exercises. There is much to interest in this subject, as illustrated in the Screen Magazine.

"Preparation of Pasteurized Milk" (E. I. S.).

A picture of possibly two reels, showing the method used by one of our large dairy concerns in pasteurizing milk, was made by the E. I. S. Film Company and exhibited at the Strand Theater, New York City. The picture opens with views of cattle grazing, and draws attention to some fine specimens of breeding stock. Then we are taken to the stables, which are receiving one of their two daily cleanings. Here we see the cows washed and milked, after which the milk is weighed and placed in clean receptacles. The exact details of the pasteurization of the milk are then shown, when we feel perfectly satisfied that the manner in which the milk at this dairy is handled is perfectly sanitary.

"The Principle of the Gyroscope" (Mutual-Gaumont).

An interesting and clearly defined explanation of the gyroscopic principle as applied to the monorail car and the motion of the earth will be found in Reel Life No. 73. The demonstration is given by Professor Newkirk of the University of Minnesota, with a miniature monorail car suspended on a wire, and the gyroscopic bar-bell and dumb-bell, as well as with a miniature body representing the earth turning on its axis.

"Student Officers" (Mutual-Gaumont).

In Reel Life No. 73 we have a good illustration of how student officers are trained to undertake the details of coast defense. Here we see them being instructed on how to manipulate a fleet of battleships on a dummy map 50x50. The use of big guns in coast defense work and the laying out of fort cities is interesting by way of instruction. The sending up of aerial observation kites and the movement of an artillery corps across a temporary bridge, which can be erected or displaced at will, are also features of interest.

Co-Operative Work for Better Films

National War Council of Y. M. C. A. and National Committee for Better Films to Co-operate on Movement.

WITH THE co-operation of P. F. Jerome, Director of the Equipment and Supplies Division of the National War Work Council of the Y. M. C. A. of the United States, comprehensive plans are being worked out by the National Committee for Better Films to take steps in the way of creating organizations of affiliated committees in cities where up to this time there has been but little interest in the Better Film Movement. The secretaries of various social welfare organizations, it is expected, will take an active part in calling conferences of groups of individuals in each locality looking to the formation of a definite committee which will adopt a program for co-operation with some local exhibitor. The plan presupposes that exhibitors will welcome the co-operative support thus assured them. The present plan of the Committee is to cover the following states systematically: West Virginia, Virginia, North Carolina, Tennessee, Florida, Alabama, Mississippi, Texas, Oklahoma, Iowa, Michigan, Wisconsin, Minnesota. Already correspondence is under way, and the outlook is hopeful for active results.

FOUR MINUTES.

Operating under the authority of the Committee on Public Information of Washington, there has been organized in New York City a patriotic committee under the title of "Four Minute Men," whose particular work in the cause of national defense will be that of making four-minute talks in the moving-picture theaters. The brief talks must be of great importance, the brevity demanding both a force and thoroughness which shall attract and become effective. Each speaker will be duly authorized and a standard policy of subjects and subject-matter required. The necessities of the war, truths desired to be promulgated by the Government will be given first importance, and the moving-picture houses afford abundant occasions for reaching large numbers of people effectively. Again we gladly help!

W. H. J.

ITEMS OF INTEREST.

A correspondent writes that moving pictures are to be exhibited in the school houses in Jones County, Mississippi, under the auspices of the Farm Demonstration agents, T. J. Cook and G. E. Hailes.

* * *

The Russian Parents' League, said to have a membership of some 50,000 in more than 200 cities and towns of Russia, has become interested in the subject of motion-picture films for schools, and has asked the American consulate-general at Moscow for catalogues and instructions in the use of such films. While the inquiry does not promise a large business, as the league will undoubtedly take most of the pictures it displays in order to present a familiar background and setting, there is an opportunity for friendly co-operation between American and Russian educators, with possibly incidental business. The address of the league is Vserossisky Roditelsky Soyus, Balchug No. 15, apart. 7, Moscow, Russia. The English language may be used in correspondence.

* * *

The following are longer dramatic pictures for young people which have been used successfully for special programs in theaters:

Artcraft—"Wild and Wooly," "The Little American"; Bluebird—"A Kentucky Cinderella"; Metro—"Lady Barnacle," "The Slacker"; Mutual—"The Immigrant"; Triangle—"The Clodhopper," "Paws of the Bear," "American—That's All," "The Sawdust Ring"; Pathe—"Fires of Youth"; Paramount—"A Roadside Impresario," "The Cook of Canyon Camp"; K-E-S-E—"The Man Who Was Afraid."

SELECTING CAST TO SUPPORT MABEL NORMAND.

Among the players already selected by Casting Director Adolph Klauber to surround Miss Normand and to carry out this idea of straight comedy are Robert Elliott, a favorite screen player since his appearances on the stage as leading man to Margaret Illington; William Fredericks, the character player; Joseph Smiley, well known for his work as actor and director during the last months of the Lubin Company, and John Webb Dillion, seen recently with Fox in "The Darling of Paris."

Intolerance for Picture Houses

Griffith Decides to Offer Mammoth Production for Popular Exhibition.

BY CABLE arrangements, completed within the past few days, D. W. Griffith will present his great spectacle, "Intolerance," this season in the representative picture theaters of America. This means that the same care and elaborateness which were shown in the handling of the Griffith spectacles on their special tours of the country will be carried out when "Intolerance" is transferred to the regular picture field.

It is nearly four years since Mr. Griffith has been a direct contributor to the screens of the representative motion picture theaters. In the interim he has built up a greater following for his newer form of art than had been dreamed possible in photoplays up to the time "The Birth of a Nation" was launched upon its phenomenal career. Perhaps no one man associated with the art of the camera had done so much to elevate the tone of pictures and to increase their popularity as Mr. Griffith. It is fitting that his return to his favorite field will be with his crowning achievement, "Intolerance."

Great plans are being made by Mr. Griffith's forces to present his production in a way that will further add to the popularity of the picture theaters. It will be handled by experts in every branch and given on the same magnificent scale that has marked the Griffith productions from the time the director-producer made his first venture outside the confines of the popular-priced houses.

Limited engagements will be booked in the representative motion picture theaters of the principal cities of the country. This opens up a new and larger field for Mr. Griffith, and is made possible by the many splendid picture theaters that have been built since he began to make his elaborate productions. At the time Griffith's first big schemes of spectacular offerings were being formulated the opportunity to show his productions was so limited that he was forced to go to the old-line theaters and make a new place for the art of photoplays. Picture theaters have breasted up with modern requirements in the new art since then, and Griffith's return to that fold is an event which thoroughly demonstrates the advancements which have been made in the past four years.

Experts who have grown up in the Griffith organization will lay out a complete campaign and every detail looking to the success of the presentation will be attended to. This will cover the advance promotion, the advertising, the atmospheric projection and the musical accompaniment of the most remarkable motion picture spectacles the world has ever seen.

Distributing offices for the bookings of "Intolerance" have been opened at 508 Longacre Building, and the scheme of presenting this spectacle under the new conditions will be entirely separated from any other venture with which Mr. Griffith is identified.

VIOLET HEMING IN BLACKTON PICTURE.

That Commodore J. Stuart Blackton intends to engage only stars of recognised merit for his forthcoming productions for Paramount is evidenced by the fact that Violet Heming, well known on the stage and on the screen, has been engaged by Commodore Blackton to star in his adaptation of Sir Gilbert Parker's novel, "The Judgment House." Violet Heming, who will play Jasmine in "The Judgment House," is one of the best known of the many celebrated English actresses who have come to this country. She has already appeared in one Paramount picture and recently played opposite H. B. Warner in "The Danger Trail." She made a great success in the leading role of the great war drama, "Under Fire," in which she appeared with William Courtney, and has to her credit a large number of success-ful stage appearances. Wilfred Lucas and Florence Deshon, both film players of recognised ability, are to appear in support of Miss Heming, while Conway Tearle, famous on the stage and screen, and one of the most popular leading men of the day, will play opposite Miss Heming.

NOTABLE CAST FOR "NEARLY MARRIED."

Comedians of note are in the cast supporting the Goldwyn comedienne, Madge Kennedy, in the filming of "Nearly Married," Edgar Selwyn's successful comedy, which is near-ing completion at the Goldwyn Fort Lee studios. Among them are Frank Thomas, Mark Smith, Alma Tell, Richard Barthelmess and Hedda Hopper.

Popular Picture Personalities

WHO'S WHO IN THE MOVING PICTURE WORLD

GIBSON, Helen Rose. Born in Cleveland, Ohio. Her father was Swiss and her mother a German. Weighs 140 pounds and is five and a half feet tall. Dark brown hair and hazel eyes. Miss Gibson made her debut away back in 1914 —which is far back in Pictureland,

and then she worked for the Bison-101 company. Later on she went to Kalem and is now with the Universal. Some of her appearances have been in The Test of Courage, The College Boys' Special and the Longpoint Feud. She writes that her fads are driving, riding, skating and camping. Camping is all right around Universal City; no one can ask for a better camping location than most any part of southern California, but it is unlikely that she gets much chance to indulge in skating in a place where snow is as scarce as ice is said to be in another and even warmer locality than California.

Helen Rose Gibson

HOWELL, Alice. Born in New York City. Irish parentage. Is five feet, two inches tall and weighs 130 pounds. Fair complexion, red hair and brown eyes. Miss Howell has not been upon the speaking stage, but started in pic-

tures with the Keystone, later going to L-Ko and now heads her own company known as Century Comedies. Considering the fact that her first appearance with Keystone was in January, 1914, in Beans to Billions, her rise to stellar honors has been rapid, but she has a sense of humor that gets over and she is not afraid to take chances or to make herself look ugly, indeed she prefers to look in character and sends a character picture even for reproduction. Many women think they are born comediennes, but few stand the test of time. Miss Howell has stood the test. Her fads are motors, horses, dogs and not filling in questionaires. The latter seems to vie with all out door sports.

Alice Howell

ARMAND, Aida. Born in Buenos Aires. American parentage. Three feet, six inches tall and weighs 43 pounds. Light complexion, golden brown hair and brown eyes. Little Miss Armand is only four years old, and has most of her

career before her, but she has already made a name for herself as a dancer and reciter at social affairs, and she was the little ragged girl in the Clara Kimball Young production of The Foolish Virgin and the smallest model in The Runaway with Julia Sanderson. She is studying classical dancing under competent teachers and wants to be an interpretive dancer some day. She is also fond of drawing, and has quite a repertoire of recitations for so small a tot. She likes motoring and swimming and can go through the water like a Kellermann, though perhaps not so fast yet. Perhaps some day she will be specializing in Mermaid pictures and beating Miss Kellermann.

Aida Armand

MULHALL, John Joseph, ("Jack"). Born in New York City. Irish parentage. Is five feet, eleven inches tall and weighs 154 pounds. Ruddy complexion, dark brown hair and blue eyes. Mr. Mulhall made his stage debut in 1909,

and has played stock, including the West End Stock in New York City, with James K. Hackett in "The Grains of Dust," and with Ned Wayburn productions. In April, 1913, he went over to pictures and his first screen appearance was with the Biograph stock in the days of its greatest popularity, the first picture being "The House of Discord." He is now a member of the Universal, playing leads. Some of his best liked plays have been The Gang's New Member, The Terror, Mr. Dolan, of N. Y., Fighting for Love and Playing Safe. True to form, he likes all out door sports, but he has another liking for "plays without a heavy vamp," and a large community rises to endorse his choice.

Jack Mulhall

FORTH, George J. Born in Philadelphia, American parentage, for the Forths settled in the Cumberland valley of Pennsylvania in 1742. Five feet 11 inches tall and weighs 170 pounds. Dark complexion, brown hair and eyes. Mr.

Forth has no stage record, but he has been busy since he made his debut in pictures in March, 1917. Since then he has played in Vitagraph, Thanhouser and Edison productions, including The Sixteenth Wife with Peggy Hyland, Bobby's Bravery with Bobby Conelly, The Heart of Ezra Greer with Frederick Warde, The Girl from the Sea, with Shirley Mason and Roger Kendall in O. Henry's A Municipal Report. That is going some for a few months. Mr. Forth for the past five years has been personally stage managing his stock farm in Maryland, and still is owner and manager of a 350-acre estate there. He specializes in blooded stock. Is an all round athlete and is musically inclined.

George J. Forth

NOTICE.

Players are invited to send in material for this department. There is no charge of any sort made for insertion, cuts, etc. This is a department run for the information of the exhibitors, and is absolutely free to all players with standing in any recognized company. No photograph can be used unless it is accompanied by full biographical data and an autograph in black ink on white paper. If you have not received any, ask for a questionaire and autograph card. Send all three.

STATISTICAL BUREAU,
Moving Picture World.

17 Madison Avenue,
New York City.

Haas Building,
Los Angeles.

Advertising for Exhibitors
Conducted by EPES WINTHROP SARGENT

Editing Film.

CONTRIBUTING to the Saturday Evening Post a series of stories on the Motion Picture industry, Rob Wagner has in turn told the stories of the director, the actor, the script writer and the rest. One late story deals with the experiences of an exhibitor. In the story he is made to say that he had houses in the Middle West, but the Wagner stories have been picked up on the Pacific Coast, and this story reads more nearly like the story of a live Pacific exhibitor. Probably most of the readers of this department have read the story and others interested can procure the issue. It is not our purpose to brief the article here, but to speak of what Mr. Wagner's exhibitor calls "film-assassins." The term is apt, for there is a growing and all too frequent tendency on the part of exhibitors to usurp the functions of the cutter and editor. We are not saying that many exhibitors cannot edit film more intelligently than many editors, but this is not the point. It is not a question of fitness but of results. To cut even a one-reel story is no light matter, and it should take more than a day to properly trim the last run of a five-reel picture, and many of these cuts would require new leader, yet an exhibitor will trim a five-reel story in an hour and never dreams of bridging the cuts. Many exhibitors speak with pride of their work, but even the best jobs are butchery and worse. It is unfair to the patron and to the producer alike. Let the producer stand on what he has done and let the patron see the film as he would have the patron see it, and not as the temporary renter thinks it should be seen. If a story is too palpably padded, do as Mr. Wagner's exhibitor does, and pass it over for another subject. In these days of rebookings and return dates the first-run fetich is impotent. Book only films of which you know, and having booked them—leave them alone. It would be bad to change the film if your patrons alone suffered, but all who come after you must suffer, too. If the scenes are properly trimmed the opening and closing are properly timed. Cutting out and replacing means the sacrifice of several frames; at least two frames for each splice, and presently the entrances are all wrong and the entire film looks botchy and inexpert. It is almost as bad as cutting out and saving bits of scenes that you take a fancy to, perhaps a pretty landscape, a closeup of some star or the risque scene. More than one exhibitor has from 500 to 2,000 feet of such material, stolen from exchanges, that he runs off for the delectation of his friends. It is a condition of affairs that should be stopped, and film cutting for any purpose other than repairing a break should be penalized, but it will not be possible to exact penalties until the exchanges so change their plans that proper inspection is made possible. There is something radically wrong on the entire system of release that is based upon dates. At least the exhibitors can help to the extent of keeping their hands off the film and giving others a chance to see the story as the director planned it and not as some not always competent authority thinks it should be arranged. Let's lay off it.

Here's a New One.

Now and then someone strikes something really new. F. S. Workman, of the Brainerd (Minn.) Amusement Co., sends in a cast sheet with this note:

Inclosed find a cast which we are giving away each day. We have these changed according to program, which is sometimes daily, and our patrons are so pleased with them that I am

passing the idea along. The ads pay the cost of the program, and the work of getting them up is nothing compared to the return to your feelings from the compliments paid by the patrons.

The casts are about four by five inches, printed on good grade white paper on one side only. The examples shown give those for two changes of showing how the space works for large and small cuts. These casts can be used with a weekly program and will, in a large measure, reduce waste on these larger issues. Moreover, they are a real convenience to the patron, since they are small and handy. Mr. Workman has evolved a winner and the wonder is that no one thought of this scheme before.

Starts a Program.

J. H. Ziegler, of the Bluebird theater, Orangeburg, S. C., sends in number five of a new program and writes:

This is one of your ideas that was taken from your book, "ADVERTISING FOR EXHIBITORS." We in the near future intend to make it larger and more interesting for the readers. In other words, to make a thing like this go you have to give them a large quantity of good, interesting items about the stars and plays; in this way you will make your program so popular that they will be waiting with eagerness to receive a copy of it. We will let you hear from us, from time to time, so that you may see our progress—with it.

We think your book, "ADVERTISING FOR EXHIBITORS," covers every branch of advertising that could be wished for by any exhibitor, and that every exhibitor should have one of these valuable books in his possession; there is unlimited amount of good advertising stunts in it. If we couldn't get another one like it, we wouldn't part with it for ten dollars.

The program is 5½ by 8½, in brown on white. The cut shows the front page and the two inside pages. The back carries the formal pro-

gram with dated days. Where the back page program is used, we think it is a better form to omit the dated days over the stories and instead treat them as headed news items running into "to be shown Thursday, September 6," or whatever the date may be. The form shown in the cut is good where the formal program is not used, but it is better to use the formal program and omit the heavy dates over the readers, using instead of the "William Fox presents" something more on the order of a news head, such as

Old and New.

The Hardwick Brothers, Clovis, N. M., are offering some old and some new ideas in a new program. The old idea is to give out a monthly program and offer to accept the same as five cents on the last day of the month. This is to insure the program being held through the period of its life. The announcement reads: "This program is worth 5 cents to you." A better catch line would be a twelve or even eighteen point. "We will pay you—" running down to an eight-point announcement to get

We Will Pay You

To keep and read this program. It is good for the month of September. Note the attractions day by day, and on September 30th we will accept this program as five cents on the purchase of any ticket.

New ideas are plentiful. One points out that for five cents a head a worried parent may bring children to the matinee and shop in peace and comfort, and another paragraph words the old "If you like the show tell your neighbor, if not tell us." The new form is better and runs:

If there are pictures that you would like to see tell us. We will try and get them for you. It is our business to please and amuse you. If you don't like the show tell us. Don't tell your neighbor; he can't improve it, but we can by getting what you want.

This carries a real argument instead of being merely a catch phrase. The program itself is decidedly neat, a vest pocket (though a bit large), on thin but stiff card. It is a bit costly, but it has to last a month, and it pays to make it last. If you spend four dollars a thousand for a one-week program it is worth six for better stock to run a month, and you save ten—if the program is held for a month.

Credit, Please.

The Stillman theater program is running a half column a week on how to write photoplays. When they lift stuff bodily from our photoplay department they might give a credit line now and then.

Makes His Own.

Evidently Ralph Ruffner means what he says when he declares that the stuff the manufacturers give him to work with is not good. He doesn't merely say it and keep on using the stuff. He says it and then proves it by getting something better. He writes—in all capitals:

WHEN I CALL IN A GOOD PHOTOGRAPHER TO SHOOT OUR LOBBY AND PAY THE BILL OUT OF MY OWN POCKET JUST TO FURNISH YOU WITH MAGNUM OPUS, I'M JUST FAR ENOUGH WEST TO BE INSTILLED WITH THE DEVOTION THAT WHAT IS WORTH DOING IS WORTH DOING WELL, AND AS LONG AS THE TRACK IS FAST AND MY WIND GOOD I'M GOING TO CHASE IT DOWN TO SEE IF IT REACHES YOU. THERE ISN'T A DAY GOES BY BUT WHAT I SEE HANDIWORK OF SOME ONE SOUL WHO IS COMPLETELY OUT OF TUNE WITH THE UNIVERSE FROM THE STANDPOINT OF USABLE STUFF FOR THE PICTURE THEATER MAN. I HAVE ARRIVED AT THE POINT WHERE I'M GOING OFF ON A TANGENT OF MY OWN. THE PHOTO HEREWITH IS EVIDENCE THEREOF, WITH THE KNOWLEDGE THAT MOST EVERY THEATER FROM THE ATLANTIC TO THE ORIENT USES THE SAME TOOLS TO WORK WITH, BE IT ONES, THREES, SIXES IN LITHOS OR HOME MADE CARDS, BANNERS OR SIGNS; A BUNCH OF PHOTOS, CUT-OUTS AND THE LIKE, I, FOR ONE, PRAYED FOR AN INSPIRATION THAT WOULD LEAD ME TO

A SOLUTION OF THE PROBLEM, AND THE ANSWER IS FOUND IN THE LARGE TERRA COTTA PEDESTALS AND FLOWER BOXES. IF YOU WILL COMPARE THIS PHOTO WITH THE ONE SENT YOU SOME TIME AGO OF A DOUGLAS FAIRBANKS' LOBBY YOU WILL SEE HOW VERY FAR AWAY WE REALLY HAVE DEPARTED FROM THE OLD ORDER OF THINGS. THE COLOR SCHEME IS BLUE AND IVORY WHITE, AND ALL WERE MADE TO OUR ORDER. THEY WEIGH ABOUT A THOUSAND POUNDS EACH. LETTERING OF THE ATTRACTION CAN BE DONE ON THE FACE OF THE FLOWER BOX ITSELF OR PLACED ON A PATTERNED CARD TO FIT THE RECESS, AND CHANGED AS OFTEN AS NECESSARY. THEIR COST IS CONSIDERABLE, BUT IT IS ALL IN THE GAME. WE HAVE ACCOMPLISHED THAT WHICH WE SET OUT TO DO—TO PRESENT SOMETHING DIFFERENT, ARTISTIC AND ATTRACTIVE, TO DO IT WITHOUT THE AID OF FRAMES, PHOTOS OR BALLYS.

Somewhere around here is a cross-page cut of the Liberty lobby. There is a large glass dome that does not show in the reproduction because we cannot spare the space for glass, but we have reproduced the lobby in single column more than once. The reproduction to which Ruff specifically refers is a cross-page cut in the issue for March 31 of this year. If you have your file handy turn to that date and compare the present lobby with the last. One is the lobby of a picture theater, the other is the lobby of a theater. Not many Broadway houses offer as good a display. Just take this issue in your hand and go out and compare the picture with your own lobby. Not all houses can afford thousand pound flower boxes, but no house is too small to make some effort at decoration to avoid the old nickelodeon look.

Ruff is right. The majority of the stuff put out by the makers of film is rotten. Just plain rotten. No other word seems to fit. People of discernment and good taste are supposed to be appealed to by the sort of paper that would disgrace an old style Gus Hill or Al Woods melodrama. It is stuff that a self respecting manager hesitates to put on the boards and will not permit in the lobby. Many companies now pay particular attention to their helps for exhibitors. Bill Hines, of Paramount, for example, was a regular theatrical press man fifteen years back. He knows what the house needs and can give it. Other Paramount men have had similar experience. Other companies have similar men. Essanay, for example, has L. J. Scott, who came up from the small town theater through the larger house and the exchange to his present position. He knows. On the other hand there are too many still who merely suit themselves instead of seeking to suit the exhibitor. *If the manufacturer of film played the houses on sharing terms it would not be three months before conditions were completely changed.* Then he would get money only if he helped the house make money. But now he seems to figure that when one exhibitor goes broke another man with money will take the house, and the rentals will go on.

Ruffner solves the problem in his own way. He gets out his own lobby displays, has his own drawn designs for the advertising, his own ballyhoos, and more and more he works to the quiet, refined side, because he finds that this brings him the better income. He can afford to because he has a large house and a large clientle. But what about the little man who is almost wholly dependent upon the manufacturer for his publicity material? The condition is all wrong.

We do not mean to say that a manufacturer should supply ornate lobby displays with each film, offer free photographs and all sorts of special matter, but each manufacturer should see to it that the paper is of the right sort and not the dead, odorous stuff that is all too common. It is hard to get directors to supply the proper stills, but they cannot make the manufacturer realizes that the man is working for him and not be for his employees. The press man can get out good paper if only he gives more time to his work, and with proper paper probably houses would use more. Certainly the live wires would because they would find it good business to do so, but the day is passed when the spectacle of a man in dress clothes choking a woman in no clothes at all is regarded as "strong." It is too common to be strong any longer, and we have even seen it get a laughing comment.

If we had a house and belonged to the league we would make a fight for paper worth while, and we think that we would get it in time. Meanwhile the exhibitor individually must do the best he can, and he can do pretty well if he will do a little slinking. Ruff is "raising a holler" about bad paper, but he is not waiting for his kicks to bring results—he cannot afford to. In the meantime he is getting out his own displays, and is making business through these displays. If you cannot afford concrete flower boxes, you can adapt the idea. Don't blame *all* the bad business on the manufacturer's lethargy. Do your own share meanwhile. Get your own lobby looking so attractive that you can send a photograph of it to the manufacturer and write "Do you expect me to put your punk paper in this beautiful lobby?"

Show the manufacturer that you are not merely kicking, but kicking with a reason, and he will be more apt to wake up himself. This department, it closely followed, will help you to get better, but you must learn to apply the ideas to your own use. And remember that variety is the chief appeal. Do not stick to a single idea. Vary your appeal. The Kashimn house in Montreal gets out some remarkably good displays, but they are all the same sort and have come to be a sort of open and Eden Musee. If you had a trick butcher shop for Arbuckle, and it paid, as probably it did, do not have a mechanical effect for the next attraction. Get something else—something different. It is novelty that counts. If you have had photograph frames in your lobby for three or four months take them out for a week. Nail photograph albums of the cheaper sort to light tables. Put the stills for the next attraction in these and post a card inviting the passer by to look them over. He will for the novelty of the thing. And before the novelty is exhausted get something else. Keep kicking for better helps, but meantime help yourself, and you will be more apt to find your prayers answered by the manufacturers. Ruff sets a good example. Follow his lead.

Found It Out.

J. H. Kennedy, of the Pavilion, Lemoore, California, in sending in his communication adds:

We have been trying to do without the Moving Picture World the last three months, but find that we cannot do so. It is certainly a great help to us as well as the operator.

I am enclosed herewith one of latest advertising stunts. We send out about 300 of these postals every week, besides advertising in the newspapers and using a float about town.

That's the sort or letter we like to get. The man who changes over and finds that he cannot do without the Moving Picture World *knows* the real value of the paper, and knows that it offers more material of real value, intelligently presented, than any other publications or the lot of them. He has found that others papers may look the same, or even better, but after he has tried out the stunts and suggestions he begins to realise that something besides bushwa and printers' ink is necessary to get out a trade paper that is really worth while. The poet card inclosed suggests Jay Emmsuel's old layout (before he used dated days), with the date running down the side of the card in the shape of a line reading "A glimpse of what we have in store for you the week of July 8th." This is not as good as dated days. We would suggest that each day be dated and that a Roman be used in place of the full face body type, using the full face for titles and stars, or the stars may be put in italics. This full face works better than usual, because it is opened with lead, but a clean cut Roman would be better still for so small a card. The post card is the most economical form of mail advertising, since it requires no envelope and the stock is furnished free. It works so well that where the card is regularly used it would pay to provide some clip or frame into which the regular patrons may slip their received. Perhaps some company will think out something of this sort. Meantime it is possible to get spring clips with a celluloid advertising button about the size of a half dollar, and these might be used, one being given each person on the mailing list, perhaps when the address is turned in, as a premium for the name.

Booming McCormick's Booming.

The Pathe Exchange has issued a special six page, newspaper size folder showing how S. Barrett McCormick boomed "The Tanks in Action at the Battle of Ancre." It makes a fine advertisement for this striking release, but it does a great deal more than this. It shows that with any attraction of merit good newspaper work will fill the house, in spite of the weather. The film played the Circle, Indianapolis, the last week in June. It broke the house records for attendance and receipts. The same can be done with any other strong feature, provided

it is done well. A vital news subject is as good as a Pickford or a Fairbanks, providing you can get the feature. We are carefully saving our copy of the sheet. It is a study in advertising and advertising methods worthy of preservation. If you have not received a copy write the Pathe Exchange for one. Mr. McCormick is an old newspaper man—old in service rather than in years—who was pleading for ten cent shows in Denver when Denver was the deadest show town in the country. Later he went back and ran a quarter house in that same town and made so good that he was brought East to a more responsible charge. His entire success has been based upon advertising, but he knows that advertising is something more than putting any old copy into a given space in the newspapers. He knows that it must be the best and strongest argument he can conceive for that space and that it must be backed up by production, house, presentation and in every other way possible. He adroitly uses every department of the paper from the editorials to the society slush and he works hardest for the stuff that costs him nothing because he knows it is worth something. Get this campaign stuff, study it, and do as much as you can afford to do with your own next big subject. It will pay you so well that you will keep on doing it.

Artcraft's Organ.

Artcraft celebrates its first anniversary by inaugurating a house organ, Artcraft Advance, that carries a well designed cover in colors and some good reading inside. The best thing in the entire sheet is one of the ears on the editorial page that reads:

He profits most who serves the best.

If there were nothing else in the paper it would be worth while just for this compact guide to exhibiting, but the twelve pages is well edited (by Norman S. Rose) and swings into line with the rest of the house organs. Did it ever occur to you that the distributors find it plays to get out a house organ and that a house organ might pay you as well? It is the most personal form of general appeal. Note, too, that these house organs talk about themselves and not about general topics. Make your house organ talk about your house as well as your films. Help your patrons to realize how good your house is. It can be done.

Booming Himself.

The shoemaker's children are always out of their shoes and the tailor's boy has a hole in his trousers, but George Wotherspoon is a publicity artist who believes in taking his own medicine in liberal doses. He has concluded a two years' contract with a Western theatrical firm and is ready to book in elsewhere. To make himself known he has sent out a booklet of twenty-four pages and cover giving a brief account of himself and offering samples of every class of press work from phrases to page ads. The idea is unique. He does not say that he is good, but he proves it by his past performances. Here's success to a man who has ideas.

What About the Organs?

It has been more than a year, we think, since any exhibitor has written in about his free organ recitals? What has become of them? Time was when many houses featured their organs, some of them even giving special free recitals on Sundays when local laws did not permit Sunday shows. More houses than ever now using organs and yet few, if any, seem to be using the organ recital as a business booster. Get up a series of invitation affairs. Invite the literary and musical societies, the clubs and lodges, school children and their teacher. Have programs suitable for each type of guest and you'll be surprised at the talk you'll get—and talk means business.

Neatly Put.

In its monthly calendar the Elite theater, Merced, California, announces an increase in prices by saying:

We believe in preparedness and are compelled to offset our increased expenses by a few changes August 1st. On and after this date children between five and fifteen years will be charged 10 cents. Children under this age will be admitted free, but must refrain from exercising their vocal chords. Our patrons object.

This is so well put that no one can object, where "Crying children must be removed" would assuredly garner the maternal goats.

A NEW HELP FOR MANAGERS

Picture Theatre Advertising

By EPES WINTHROP SARGENT (Conductor of Advertising for Exhibitors in the Moving Picture World)

 TEXT BOOK AND A HAND BOOK, a compendium and a guide. It tells all about advertising, about type and type-setting, printing and paper, how to run a house program, how to frame your newspaper advertisements, how to write form letters, posters or throwaways, how to make your house an advertisement, how to get matinee business, special schemes for hot weather and rainy days. All practical because it has helped others. It will help you. By mail, postpaid, $2.00. Order from nearest office.

Moving Picture World, 17 Madison Ave., New York

Schiller Building   Haas Building
Chicago, Ill.   Los Angeles, Cal.

The Photoplaywright

Conducted by EPES WINTHROP SARGENT

INQUIRIES.

Questions concerning photoplay writing addressed to this department will be replied to by mail if a fully addressed and stamped envelope accompanies the letter, which should be addressed to this department. Questions should be stated clearly and should be typewritten or written with pen and ink. Under no circumstances will manuscripts or synopses by critized, whether or not a fee is sent therefor.

A list of companies will be sent if the request is made to the paper direct and not to this department, and a return stamped envelope is inclosed.

Analysis.

ABOUT the best study in plotting we know of is the editorial advertisement of the Popular magazine appearing in the back of each issue. The editor is talking of stories to come, but most of these announcements are studies in plotting. In a recent issue the editor explains that publications are of two sorts—"class" and "punch". Class he describes as "fiction that might have been written by a professor of English who had devoted his spare time to psychological study," which has the drawback of being "either an exhibition of hairsplitting as regards human emotion and character or a good enough study of still life". Passing on he comes to "punch" in these words:

And now we come to the school of fiction with the "punch". The idea on which this is based is sounder, if less elegant. Fiction should have "punch", and lots of it. The great difficulty with the fiction of plot and incident is that too often it has little else. It is badly written. It gives no clear impressions or visualizations. It tells us nothing that we don't know, and, what is more, it tells us many things that we know to be untrue if we stop to think about them. The whole fault is not with the idea itself, but with the people who are trying to put the punch into the fiction. In almost every case the man writing or buying and publishing this sort of work imagines himself above his task. He is not consulting his own taste; he is consulting the taste of an imaginary public—a collection of beings without reflection, discrimination, or powers of reasoning. He feeds them clothing-store advertisements for heroes, and calendar pictures for heroines. His villains have been cast aside as worn out by writers of melodrama ten years ago. Incident he gives you, but it is purely physical incident, such as automobile chases, explosions, fist fights, and murders. All these things have their place, but our idea of action and incident is something with more pith and meaning to it. Ask the purveyor of these wares why he does it, and he tells you that he would like to do something better—he means the "classy" stuff—but that this is what the public want. All the readers want or understand is clatter for action, clamor for conversations, and murder for emotion.

The writer is talking of fiction in print and not fiction in film, but he accurately describes the attitude of too many motion picture purveyors, manufacturers, editors and directors, who affect to look down upon the cheap tastes of their patrons, who offer the mechanical punch instead of the mental appeal and then curse the flatheads because they cannot appreciate even this.

A more intelligent appreciation and less of the spirit of contempt would doubtless bring better results, but it is difficult to make the average producer and manufacturer realize that his cheap little tricks should be put back into the bag and sent to storage while he labors for a more intelligent appeal. Even the children are no longer thrilled by the purely mechanical punch. It is no longer possible to excite even the ten and twelve year olds with train wrecks and aeroplane flights. The appeal should lie in the reason for the flight or the wreck, but most producers believe that the wreck alone is sufficient. It is a pity that there exists no system for gathering the opinions of the patrons. Did such a system exist, makers of film stories would be shocked at the results. People these days mostly go to the pictures in spite of their poorness, rather because of their merits. It is only a question of time when this failure to appreciate the real taste of the public will result in the creation of newer and more successful brands.

Not Quite Right.

H. Tipton Steck, in his article in the big issue, seems to suffer from aberration of memory when he remarks that he was instrumental in pushing along to us our first photoplay check. He also claims first payment to Emmett Campbell Hall, and to have used the first idea of Roy McCardell. Mr. Steck never took one of our stories for Essanay, and we did not even send a story to Essanay until more than a year after we had purchased a half reel comedy from Mr. Steck for the use of the Lubin company. More than that Lubin took the first story Emmett Campbell Hall sold, and Roy McCardell's first idea was turned out for the Biograph company back in the last century,

for Roy was the first paid script writer in the business, and "wrote the ideas for the Mutoscope that were also put out as Biograph film because it did not cost anything.

Building Up.

As we sit here writing we can look out on the surface of a small lake. This morning the water was like glass, but the wind came up and has grown in intensity, working on the water until there is now a decided ripple. By afternoon it is probable that there will be whitecaps on the waves, and the water will be dashing up on the beach. You cannot say just when the change came. First there was the occasional ripple on the surface, then the ripple became permanent, and now and then some gust made an extra large wave. It is the same way with a story. Start with placidity and work up to a storm, not immediately; not violently, but so gradually that you sense only the fact that the story grows more tense because the facts have become more vital. You cannot do that with machine-made sensation. The turmoil must rise from the story or you are like a small boy trying to create a storm with an oar blade. You can make an awful fuss for a moment in one locality, but it will not be convincing. It cannot be more than a small boy splashing about.

Adapting.

Here's an adaptation of the loose leaf idea to adaptation. One man who has gained some reputation in this line takes a pack of blank cards. As he reads the book he makes a separate note of each essential fact on one of the cards. When he has compiled his reading he reads a second time for story alone. Then he takes the cards and distributes the facts into their proper place in the film story and proceeds to write his script. It often happens that a chance paragraph in the middle of the book gives a fact that in the film should appear earlier in the story than the first stated fact. By using the cards he is able to place the fact in its proper position, and he is also able to discard the non-essential facts. In adaptation the chief trouble lies in the proper orientation of facts. Phil Lang used to tell of his adaptation of a place in which the last line in the last act was the first scene in his screen version.

Suitability.

Lately an actor who came into pictures about a year ago told us that he was trying to get the rights to a certain story by a well-known author. "Just that one," he qualified. "The set is no good for pictures, but that one would make a peach of a story." He was right. There was just one story in a series of a dozen or more that would work into pictures. The rest were interesting fiction stories, but they did not have the making of motion pictures in them. The actor failed to get his single story because the entire series had been purchased by one of the large companies. Possibly this company knows that there is but one picture story in the lot, but they are looking to the author's name and the fact that the stories were printed in a widely circulated magazine to bring them back their money. There is no question as to the advertising value of the pictures, but the camera stories are not yet ready, and yet they brought about the same price as another series from the same magazine that will lend themselves excellently to pictures. Even at this late day manufacturers are not yet ready to make picture stories, but are still fooling around with experiments. Both of the authors have written directly for the camera and have failed. Both could write for the camera if given coaching and encouragement, but manufacturers seem to prefer the second hand but advertised stuff.

Substitutions.

If you go into a grocery and ask for a pound of best butter, you will resent the efforts of the grocer to sell you oleomargarine. You want the best butter and not an imitation. You cannot exactly blame the grocer for trying to sell the substitute if he has no real butter, but you will not buy the oleo and you'll go somewhere else next time you want more butter. That's about the way a reel editor feels when he asks for only the best scripts and gets all sorts of junk. He wants what he wants and unless that is what you have to sell he wants none of your goods. Make certain that your scripts make more than good for their pure food label before you ship them out.

Projection Department

Conducted by F. H. RICHARDSON

Manufacturers' Notice.

IT IS an established rule of this department that no apparatus or other goods will be endorsed or recommended editorially until the excellence of such articles has been demonstrated to its editor.

Important Notice.

Owing to the mass of matter awaiting publication, it is impossible to reply through the department in less than two to three weeks. In order to give prompt service, these sending four cents, stamps (less than actual cost), will receive carbon copy of the department reply, by mail, without delay. Special replies by mail on matters which cannot be replied to in the department, one dollar.

Both the first and second set of questions are now ready and printed in neat booklet form, the second half being seventy-six in number. Either booklet may be had by remitting 25 cents, money or stamps, to the editor, or both for 40 cents. Cannot use Canadian stamps. Every live, progressive operator should get a copy of these questions. You may be surprised at the number you cannot answer without a lot of study.

Defends the Exchange.

L. D. Lumpkin, Local Union 626, I. A., Barnesville, Georgia, grabs his trusty cudgel, shies his hat into the ring and hands us the following:

Have just read August 18 issue of The World, taking special note of A. D. Hoatling's article with regard to condition of service received from Atlanta branch of the Vitagraph. I request that you have him send you some of the faults he has cut out, for the reason that I have been running service out of the Vitagraph Atlanta branch for the past six years, and am running it at present: also I have run the two subjects he named, less than sixty days ago, and I can say that if all exchanges kept up the physical condition of their films as the Atlanta Branch of the Vitagraph does, we would have no trouble to speak of. I have been running their service which is more than a year old here in this house (Palace Theater) since January first, last, and have not had a picture which required inspection as yet. Of course you will find a sprocket hole broken once in a while, but never two together, and when even one is broken it is invariably trimmed—or at least that is the way I have found it. In view of these facts I would have to see some of the faults Friend Hoatling cut out before I could believe his statement. I readily agree that films should be in such condition that the operator will have no need to inspect and repair them, and if he must do so, then certainly he ought to be paid for the work. If I trust you will investigate this matter fully.

That would be an extremely difficult matter, Brother Lumpkin. Moreover, it would be of little use to ask Brother Hoatling to send in faults. If he would be dishonest enough (a thing I am by no means prepared to concede) to send in a dishonest report of film condition, then it would be but a step further to get film faults to send in, even

Group of Exhibitors, Managers and Operators of Springfield, Mo., Taken at Time of Editor's Visit, but Mislaid and Overlooked.

if he had to make them. You seem to forget, however, that Hoatling sent copies of his letters to the exchange, together with the originals of the exchange managers' replies along with his letter to the department. Surely you would not imagine that an operator would go to the length of writing the exchange twice if his only object were to send in a dishonest report to this department. That theory does not hang together very well. Now do not get me wrong. I am not questioning your honesty. While it would be improbable, still it is within the range of possibility that your service has been all that you claim it to be, and at the same time Hoatling's service was exactly as he described it. This department has no axe to grind in matters of this kind. It has no grudge against the Vitagraph Atlanta branch, or against any other exchange. It simply seeks to protect the operator, the theater and the industry at large against the manifest outrage of films sent out in wretched physical condition, or, for that matter, in any other condition than that of ready-to-run. It also seeks, and intends to continue to seek, to protect the operator against the rapacity of exchange managers who try to force him to do their film inspecting and repairing free of charge. As to the present case, why, I would suggest the following: Operators receiving service from this exchange make careful note of name of each subject for one week, make a record of the exact condition of the films, the time the reels were received, and whether received direct from the exchange or not. These reports should be O. K.'d, if possible, by the theater manager, and forwarded to this department, accompanied by all faults cut out, each bunch of faults tagged with name of subject, and, if possible, the number of the reel, if more than one in the subject. I know this will involve some trouble, but if you want this non-inspection outrage cleared up, you must take a little trouble. Personally I would particularly like to see this case threshed out to a finish, because I don't want to do injustice to any one.

And while we are at it, here is another letter bearing on the same matter. It is from New Hampshire.

Was pleased to read the letter from A. D. Hoatling, Deland, Florida, August 18 issue, and what you had to say concerning same. You both hit the nail squarely on the head, and the high note you struck when you asked the exchange manager why he doesn't do it (get a lot of inspecting done for three dollars) was fine; nor do I believe Saint Peter will close the Big Gate in your face for it, either. I have myself done a lot of kicking, and have written many letters to exchange managers, who do not even bother to reply. Also I have paid good money for service, with guarantee that it would be in first class condition. The guarantee was always by word of mouth; also it was always composed entirely of hot air. The films come with no leaders, no tail pieces, with sprocket holes by the hundred broken, with loose patches, and many times with one or more total breaks, left by the operator who ran them last for its sp up. I have even found the last part of one reel of a multiple-reel subject spliced to the front end of another reel, with nothing to tell where or how to get it together again, except by careful examination and matching up scenes. There is not a week that I do not work from two to four hours every Tuesday and Friday, doing inspector's work free of charge. I am both operator and manager, and must put down the coin for supposed-to-be service, even to a two-cent postage stamp on posters sent, which I find to be repeats and which I must return, at my own expense, and then fight to get credit for them. If you use this, please omit name of town, as I have to deal with exchanges, and they can make it even more unpleasant for me than it now is.

And this case is but one of many. The man is paying his good money for one thing, and getting quite another. It is unfair; it is indecent; it in not good business from the exchange man's viewpoint, and is a dagger in the back of the moving picture industry. How much longer is the fifth industry of the country to endure such unbusinesslike methods? And the pity of it is that exhibitors have it entirely within their power to call a swift halt on the sending out of film in imperfect condition.

Must See It.

H. W. Floyd, Capron, Oklahoma, sends in patent papers covering his invention, designed to attach to the projector and obviate the necessity for rewinding. He asks for our "honest opinion" with regards to its merits.

For the benefit of Friend Floyd, and others, let me say that it would be foolish to venture an opinion on something I have not seen in operation, or to form an opinion from a description, no matter how complete, or from patent papers and drawings. Such an opinion would have no value whatsoever. If you want my opinion, Friend Floyd, you will have to send on a well made, practical working model, and even then I might not be able to venture a decided opinion on a thing of this kind without first having watched it in actual theater projection work over a considerable period of time.

Interesting Theories.

Our old friend, John Griffiths, Ansonia, Connecticut, proceeds to stir the optical pool as follows:

> The following comments on light ray action are written with the general idea of getting them out of my system, rather than to immediately inflict them upon the department readers. Perhaps I have unconsciously fostered the idea that the projection of motion pictures cannot be successfully accomplished except with the crater in focus, or near-focus at the aperture, in contradistinction to stereopticon projection, in which the crater is in focus either within or near the projection lens.
>
> As a matter of fact, the projection of motion pictures may be accomplished in a number of different ways, dependent upon the arrangement of the apparatus and the amperage used. The chart published March 17th issue was designed for use under conditions as found in ordinary practice, and with the apparatus arranged in the usual way. In many matters I am in perfect accord with friend Martin's conclusions, whereas, judged by published data only, we seem to be at variance.
>
> Where low amperage is used, with consequent crater of small area, such as, for instance, an experimental outfit, or for demonstrating purposes, it is entirely practical as well as very efficient to project motion pictures in the same manner as stero slides are projected, provided always that the focal length of the projection lens be short enough, because with the crater image within the projection lens the plane of the condenser beam through which the film is passing is even in density, whereas, if the projection lens were of longer focal length, then, in order to advance the crater image to a point within the lens, it would be necessary to bring that portion of the condenser beam which is not of even density ahead far enough to reach the film, and, as this portion of the condenser beam carries the blue ghost, it follows that the blue ghost would be in focus at the screen, and would inevitably show thereon.
>
> One very effective method of projection motion pictures with very light amperage would be to use a two-inch-diameter condenser, and duplicate the projection of slides exactly, by having the lamphouse snug up against the machine head, so that the condenser would not be more than ½ inch from the film. This would be ideal motion picture projection, but unfortunately it does not lend itself to heavy amperage, owing to excessive heat. Under this plan there would be practically no loss of light, except the absorption which takes place in the glass itself, and the necessary loss by reasen of the revolving shutter. Spherical aberration would cut no figure at all, and long focal length projection lenses would represent no difficulties. The method would be to either mount the condensers where the cooling plate now is, and have the mount water cooled, or else mount the condenser in the usual place on the lamphouse (And bring the lamphouse forward, I suppose he means, though he does not say so.—Ed.). In the former case a thin, circular piece of mica could be placed in front of the arc, with the dowser between the crater and mica. The crater position would, under these conditions, be from 1½ to two inches from the arc condenser, which would give the condenser the same collective power as the regular 4½-inch lens now used. The E. F. of the condenser combination would be about two inches, varying slightly, according to the focal length of the projection lens, so as to place the crater image within the projection lens, and small enough to pass through without obstruction. The plane of the condenser beam which would be in focus at the screen would be ½ inch in front of the front plane of the front condensing lens, therefore, it would be perfectly even in density. Also the beam is converged entirely within the lens, so that if A. C. be used, both craters will give effective illumination, and if the projection lens diameter be ample it would require a much-neglected arc to show discoloration on the screen.
>
> It will thus be seen that motion pictures may be projected on precisely the same principle as we employ in stereopticon projection. There are other possible methods also, but for modern operating conditions they are useless, unless unusual amperages be used. I believe the chart in March 17 issue about fills the bill. I believe you will find that where the chart seemed to fail with the lower amperages it was due to an insufficient Y distance to correspond with the small crater area, and in all probability the spot was not an approximate image of the crater, which same is essential if the chart is to prove a success.

I print this as an interesting topic for study. That there would be more heat at the film with the film ½ inch from the condenser is not true, but to bring an electric arc of any considerable amperage 1½ inches from even a two-inch condenser would be something else again. Personally, I have never given this phase of motion picture projection any thought. I know and knew that it could be done. In fact, it is being done in at least two small "home" projectors. The writer believes, however, that insofar as theater projection be concerned, the thing is merely interesting. I do not think it is practical. I do, however, think there are decided possibilities in the matter of a corrected condenser. I believe condenser breakage can be stoppd, though it is, to date, confined strictly to "believing." That is one of a number of things I hope some day to find time to experiment with. Seems to me a properly directed air blast of proper volume ought to do the trick, and the possibilities that a corrected condenser would open up are very great.

Motor Cutoff.

J. M. Lenny, Harrisburg, Pennsylvania, says:

> Note in recent issue, cut of rewinder made by Frank Bell, Palestine, Texas, and that you suggested to him the addition of an automatic cutoff, so that the motor will be automatically stopped when the film is rewound. Would you be kind enough to tell me, through the department, how this can be done, as the cut accompanying original article is not sufficiently clear to enable me to dope it out.

Sure, Mike! I'll do that little thing for you. The automatic cutoff had not been installed when the photograph accompanying the other article was made. There are several ways in which the motor may be automatically stopped upon completion of the rewinding, and the best methods are through a magnetically controlled switch. But I don't remember just how that is done, and have not the time, nor have I the energy, during this hot weather, to dope it out. So I will give you a very good mechanical method, and ask those who use the magnetic to send in a description, if they will be so kind.

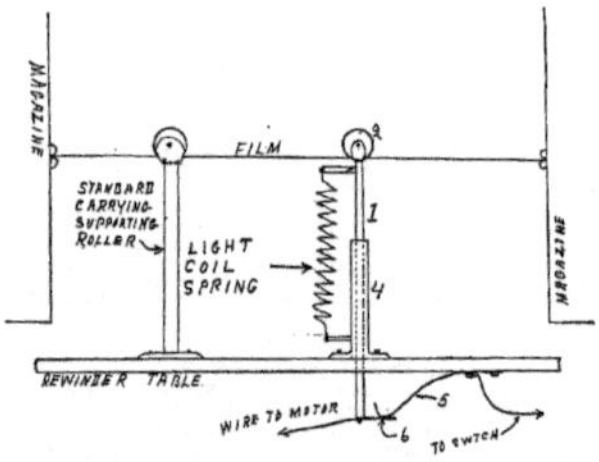

The sketch isn't a very good one, viewed from the artistic standpoint, but it is nevertheless very easily understood. 1 is a standard, carrying roller 2 at its upper, and copper plate 6 at its lower end. 4 is a hollow standard carrying standard 1 as shown. 5 is a copper contact, attached to rewinder table on under side, with insulation between, of course, since otherwise friend Inspector would put up an awful howl. The supporting roller shown is not absolutely necessary, but advisable. The action is simple. Contact 6 is attached to standard 1 by screws, under one of which is attached one end of one of the motor circuit wires, the same having been cut for the purpose, The other end is attached to contact 5 by one of its holding screws. When there is no film, the rewinder standard 1, being unsupported, drops, the action being aided by the coil spring. I personally don't think the spring necessary, and if it is used it must be a *very* light one. Standard 1 ought to be square in shape. When the film is in, tension applied to the tail reel (reel from which the film is being wound) and the motor is started by raising standard 1, the film, being drawn taut, standard 1 is held up, by the film, and thus contacts 5 and 6 are held together. As soon as the rewinding is completed roller 2, no longer being supported by the film, drops, thus opening the motor circuit at contacts 5 and 6. Roller 2 should be so made that it bears only on the film track, and if it is of ample diameter all the better. Standard 4 may be made of heavy steel metal, bent over a convenient form. The whole thing is practical; also it may all be constructed by the operator, without any expense to speak of. I would, however, prefer the magnetic action, and will publish description of same as soon as received.

A New Book and a Good One.

I have just been looking over "Modern Theater Construction," by Edward Bernard Kinsila, published by the Moving Picture World. The book contains 269 pages, is substantially bound in cloth, printed in plain type, on good paper, and is illustrated. So much for the mechanical end of it. The book itself seems to be a general treatise on theater planning and construction, and as such is well worth its price to exhibitors and managers. In one particular it is unique, viz.: it is the only work of the kind I have seen which did not burst forth into pure, unadulterated drivel and arrant nonsense when its author reached the chapter dealing with the operating room. Brother Kinsila does not go into details concerning the operating room very much, but what he does say is essentially correct. I am not an architect, but, taken as a whole, "Modern Theater Construction" is, it seems to me, well worth its price, which same is $3.00.

Can It Be Possible?

Last week a New York City exhibitor called me up and anxiously inquired as to what he could use to mix black paint with to paint the interior of his operating room, to which I replied: "Turpentine and boiled linseed oil." But, to my astonishment, he told me he would not be allowed to use paint mixed with either turpentine, oil or both.

I really have not the time or energy to chase down every rumor of fool "rules" promulgated by fire departments and other city authorities, concerning operating rooms, but I really wonder if there exists a public official with a dome roofed with solid ivory so thick that he would actually issue as thoroughly and completely idiotic an order as that? If such a one exists I would be more than glad to have his name, and to know the position he is attempting to occupy. Probably, if he really exists, we shall soon hear of an order from him prohibiting the use of oil to lubricate the projectors, because lubricating oil will, given proper inducement, b-u-r-n! Another item of danger lies in the language used by operators in speaking of this type of official. It is often lurid enough to set almost anything on fire, except, possibly, asbestos.

New Union Scale.

September 8, 1917.

Moving Picture World:

I am herewith enclosing the wage scale that was adopted by Local 306 on Wednesday, September 5, 1917, and is to go into effect on Monday, September 24, 1917.

Trusting that you may find space enough to squeeze same into your next edition and thanking you for past favors and wishing the World the best of luck and success for the future, I am,

Very respectfully yours,

HENRY I. SHERMAN,

Recording Secretary, 306 I. A.

MINIMUM WAGE SCALE OF THE MOVING PICTURE OPERATOR'S UNION, LOCAL 306 I. A. T. S. E.

Class 1.—All houses charging from 5 to 10 cents admission:

From 9 a. m. or later to 11 p. m. daily, 2 shifts, each shift not
  to exceed 7 hours per day per man, each man to receive not
  less than.. $24.50

From 10 a. m. or later to 11 p. m. daily, 2 shifts, each shift not
  to exceed 6½ hours per day per man, each man to receive not
  less than.. 22.75

From 11 a. m. or later to 11 p. m. daily, 2 shifts, each shift not
  to exceed 6 hours per day per man, each man to receive not
  less than.. 21.00

From 11 a. m. or later to 12 midnight daily, 2 shifts, each shift
  not to exceed 6½ hours per day per man, each man to receive
  not less than.. 23.75

From 12 noon or later to 12 midnight daily, 2 shifts, each shift
  not to exceed 6 hours per day per man (not later than 12
  midnight), not less than.. 21.00

From 2 p. m. or later to 11 p. m. daily, 1 hour for supper, not
  less than.. 28.00

From 5 p. m. or later to 11 p. m. daily, not less than........... 21.00

From 5 p. m. or later to 11 p. m. daily, 2 matinees per week,
  1 hour for supper.. 24.00

Extra matinees... 1.50

1 day's work (Class 1), not less than 3 nor more than 8 hours,
  at pro rata at the rate of 6 days per week.

Supper hour, first hour.. 1.00

Supper hour, second hour... .50

Overtime per hour.. .75

Overtime per half hour... .38

Operators working in film exchanges, studios or laboratories shall not work more than 8 hours per day and shall receive the same scale as Class 1.

Class 2.—All houses charging not more than 50 cents admission:

From 9 a. m. or later to 11 p. m. daily, 2 shifts, each shift not to
  exceed 7 hours per day per man, each man to receive not
  less than.. 29.40

From 11 a. m. or later to 11 p. m. daily, 2 shifts, each shift not
  to exceed 6 hours per day per man, each man to receive not
  less than.. 25.20

From 2 p. m. or later to 11 p. m. daily, 1 hour for supper, not
  less than.. 33.60

1 day work (Class 2), not less than 3 hours nor more than 8
  hours, at pro rata at the rate of 6 days per week.

Supper hour, first hour.. 1.20

Supper hour, second hour... .60

Overtime per hour.. .90

Overtime per half hour... .45

Vaudeville and burlesque houses, not more than eight hours,
  with 1 hour for supper, not less than............................ 33.60

All houses and hours not specified in Class 2 shall be rated at
  60 cents per hour.

Class 3.—All houses charging over 50 cents and giving two or more
  performances (per day):

Lectures, clubs and all other special performances................ 5.00

Setting up and taking down a machine............................... 2.50

Setting up and taking apart a booth................................ 2.50

Class 4:

All school performances.. 4.00

Any house not employing a steady operator and running a week
  or more, 1 man at each machine, not more than 8 hours per
  day per man, each man to receive not less than................... 30.20

No man is permitted to work more than 8 hours per day.

Prices and hours not provided for in this schedule shall be referred to the executive board of this union.

To recognize 7 days as constituting a week, except when calculating the salary for a fraction of a week, when 6 days shall constitute a week.

All operators will entirely confine themselves to operating moving picture machines only during working hours.

All members of this union holding a position as manager or being an exhibitor can relieve union operators for supper hour only.

Extremely Doubtful.

J. B. Simon, Pine Bluff, Arkansas, makes the following inquiry:

Please advise me as to your opinion of the value of the Super-Light shutter, made by the Super-Light Shutter Co. New York City, N. Y. They claim it will increase the screen illumination by as much as 30 per cent. Inasmuch as its purchase

represents quite an investment, will you kindly investigate and advise?

I have done violence to one of my rules, and have invited the Super-Light people to present their goods for examination and test. Will advise as soon as they have done so, but the chances are ten to one that if they could have made good on their claim, they would have needed no invitation. They would have presented their shutter to this department about the first thing they did after getting it ready to market. If they still fail to present it, I would advise you to only purchase after testing the shutter out in your own theater. The chances are all against the validity of their claims.

Patent Intermittent Sprocket.

There have been several attempts to so construct an intermittent sprocket in which the teeth may be renewed without renewing the whole

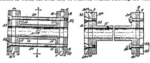

sprocket, but to date none of them have seemed to have value. And now comes one, John Domerhuisen, New York City, and presents the following:

Am inclosing patent papers of an invention which bears directly upon an idea you have long been hammering upon, viz.: frequent renewal of intermittent sprocket. My invention introduces a sprocket which may, in so far as the teeth be concerned, and that is, of course, the vital point, be renewed at a minimum of expense; also the renewal element may be made of better material, and the hardening process may be brought to a greater state of perfection. Does this merit your attention?

Anything which presents any possible points of superior merit, and which is not obviously impractical, either from the manufacturing or some other standpoint, "merits my attention", and gets it too.

As to the article in question, it is not for me to pass judgment. I see no reason why better material could be used than in a whole sprocket, but can see that it might, and probably would, very much simplify the hardening problem. But there are other and exceedingly weighty matters to consider, the first of which is the element of weight. It seems to me the sprocket you propose will, of necessity, be very much heavier than those now in use, and that a very considerable portion of this added weight will come near its rim. Now, an intermittent sprocket must start from absolute rest, overcome inertia and attain high speed, and then overcome velocity and come to absolute rest sixteen or more times per second, therefore, any added weight, no matter how slight, must be reckoned with, particularly if it comes at or near the outer diameter. Then, too, an intermittent sprocket must be mechanically true, and the question arises, can a sprocket thus constructed be made perfectly true? It would seem to me doubtful. Take the one item, the holes for screws, 24. These would, of necessity, have to be made and finished before tempering. Suppose the tempering shrank the metal ever so slightly, and shrank it unevenly. What then? Modern sprockets (intermittent) are finished *after* tempering, by grinding, and the grinders run at the speed of about 20,000 revolutions per minute. You could not grind these holes, could you?

These are a few of the questions which present themselves when this matter is examined. On the other hand, such a sprocket would be very much easier for the operator to renew, since there would be no delicate hub pins to drive out; also, if the plan worked out satisfactorily, the parts would be interchangeable, and the turning of the sprocket teeth or installation of a new set would be a comparatively simple operation. please understand that I am not passing judgment on this matter. I am not competent to do so. Only a manufacturer of projectors could give an authoritative opinion on a thing of this kind. I am merely presenting the matter to you, amiable reader, making such remarks as occur to me while so doing. Anyhow, the thing is interesting—maybe it is also practical, I don't know. The two illustrations show two possible methods of construction.

Motion Picture Photography*

Conducted by CARL LOUIS GREGORY, F. R. P. S.

Inquiries.

QUESTIONS in cinematography addressed to this department will receive carbon copy of the department's reply by mail when four cents in stamps are inclosed. Special replies by mail on matters which cannot be replied to in this department, $1.

Manufacturers' Notice.

It is an established rule of this department that no apparatus or other goods will be endorsed or recommended editorially until the excellence of such articles has been demonstrated to its editor.

Trick Work and Double Exposure (Continued).

LET us not forget, however, that the human eye has a lens of extremely short focus and accommodates itself almost unconsciously so that in taking near objects with a large-apertured objective the fuzziness of a distant background is very much greater to the longer-focused wide-apertured lens objective than it is to the human eye and that the selection of a background very close or very dark gives a much better effect than the exaggerated mushiness of a brilliantly lighted distant background.

The shutter fade-out gives the best effect, as the image fades uniformly and completely away. The shutter fade-out is a mechanical device by which, while the shutter is revolving, one blade advances over the shutter opening until it is entirely closed, thereby gradually decreasing the successive exposure from normal to nothing. Its range being always the same, renders it much superior to the diaphragm fade-out, as the diaphragm fade-out may be from the largest aperture at one time and from F 16 at another, and it is practically impossible to give a properly graded fade-out from a small stop, as the arc of movement from a small stop to closure is too short.

The Bell-Howell camera is practically the only well-known make of camera in which the shutter dissolve, or fade-out, as it is variously known, is incorporated in the original instrument. Such a shutter can be installed in any make of camera by a competent mechanic, and, while the cost will probably range around a hundred dollars or more, no photographer who has used one would part with it for twice its cost. A shutter fade-out may be either hand operated or automatic. In the hand operated shutter dissolve the shutter opening is controlled by a lever with a graduated arc which indicates the shutter opening. The automatic dissolve is operated by a push button, which throws in a clutch on a screw, which operates the shutter, while a dial indicator shows the closing or opening of the shutter blades. It is open to the objection that it works at one speed only and consequently produces a fade-out of only one certain length, while a hand-operated dissolve may be varied to any desired extent.

The graduated screen fade-out is not much used and consists of strip of glass sliding in a race or grooveway as close in front of the lens as possible. This strip of glass varies in intensity from clear glass at one end to complete opacity at the other. To make one of these strips, place an unexposed contrast plate in a holder in the dark room and insert the slide into the holder just far enough to cover about one inch of the plate. Place it facing a distant incandescent lamp and have some one turn it on at a word of command, at which time slip the slide home slowly and evenly. On development you will have a plate clear at one end where protected by the slide, with a deposit increasing in density to the other end. With a good glass cutter, this can be cut into several strips, each wide enough for your purpose. Cut another similar strip of clear glass for a cover and bind or cement them together to protect the graduated screen. Slip the clear end in the groove in front of the lens and take the scene which you wish to fade out through this. When the fade out is to occur, slide the glass strip slowly across the lens until the opaque portion covers the aperture.

A graduated screen fade-out mechanically operated by clockwork is manufactured by the Universal Camera Co. and sold by Burke & James, Chicago.

In using the graduated screen it is essential that a hood be used which prevents any stray light from falling on the screen, or there will be a decided degradation in your negative, due to light scattered by the screen.

The chemical method of producing fade-out is a last resort, as it is a very difficult method to obtain an evenly graduated fade-out, owing to the uneven action of the chemicals. It is a very valuable aid to have in reserve, however, as a fade-out may be placed anywhere it is thought desirable after a picture is taken.

To produce a chemical fade-out make up one of the following formulas:

Cyanide of potash... 1 oz.
Water .... 20 oz.
or
Ferricyanide (red prussiate) of potash........................... 1 oz.
Water .... 10 oz.

The first formula works better and quicker, but is a very deadly poison and should be used with extreme care.

To use either formula wrap a piece of rubber cloth about the roll of film which is to be reduced, leaving the end on which you are to work projecting about a foot longer than the fade-out which you intend to make and fasten securely with rubber bands.

To 4 oz. of the cyanide of potash solution add, before using, 3 dr. of tincture of iodine, or, if you use the ferricyanide solution, take 4 oz. of it and add to an equal quantity of plain 1 to 4 hypo solution. Place whichever solution you are about to use in a saucer or shallow dish and have ready a tray in which you have placed an equal quantity of acid hardener solution and water. This acid hardener and water acts as a shortstop in case your reducing solution should act too quickly.

Lay a clean board or a long strip of glass or even the back of a large tray in the sink and place the end of the film down the incline, with the end which is to be darkened at the lowest point. Then, with a swab of absorbent cotton dipped in the reducing solution, commence to swab the lower end of the film with the solution, gradually working upward, so that, as you come to the roll, the reducer has less and less time to work upon the emulsion. If you are not familiar with this procedure, it is well to experiment a few times with waste strips of negative before attempting to produce a chemical fade-out on a valuable negative. If you have carried the process through correctly, the reducer will have dissolved away the picture entirely at the lower end of the film, leaving it perfectly clear, from which will be a succession of faint images gaining in strength up to the point where they join the roll and the fade begins. Immerse this quickly in the fixing solution to stop the action of the reducer, which will otherwise continue for some time, if not checked; although plain water may be used as a check, it does not stop the reducing action at once, and must be applied before the reduction is quite complete.

In case the formula for hardener is not at hand, it may be mixed up according to the following formula:

Water .... 5 oz.
Sodium sulphite (dessicated)..................................... ½ oz.
Acetic acid No. 8.. 3 oz.
Alum, powdered... ½ oz.

The Dissolve: The dissolve is a combination of a fade-out and fade-in, lapped over one another. The effect is that of a scene gradually disintegrating and dissolving to another. This effect is attained by fading out, and then, with the lens covered, turning the film back to the point where the fade-out began and then fading in the succeeding scene, so that the following scene is fully faded in at the expiration of the fade-out. This may be done by any of the methods described under the fade-out, but in the case of a chemical dissolve it becomes necessary to overlap two pieces of film where the fade-out and fade-in occur, which occasions a great deal of trouble in printing, on account of the extra thickness of film, and the trouble caused by rewinding a negative with this overlap, which can only be cemented at one end, because, if it is cemented at both ends, the rolling up of the negative will cause a buckle in the film at the second joint, because whichever film in the dissolve is on the outside of the roll will prove too short to encircle the roll, having to circumscribe a larger diameter.

Where there are a number of prints to be made from a chemical dissolve, it is often advantageous to make a dupe negative of the dissolve portion and cement that into the negative in place of the cumbersome overlap.

Circle-in and Circle-out: Also called circle vignette or round dissolve. As the instrument with which this effect is produced is an iris diaphragm, it is sometimes miscalled "Diaphragm-in" and Diaphragm-out," but this term should not be applied to it, because it confuses it with an entirely different effect caused by diaphragming in and out with the lens diaphragm, which produces a fade-in or fade-out.

The circling-in instrument or outside diaphragm is mounted upon the end of an extensible lens hood and produces the effect of the image disappearing at the corners of the frame, gradually diminishing to a circular form to a round dot, which also disappears in blackness. The sharpness or diffusion of the edges of this circle are determined by the distance between the outside diaphragm and the lens and also by the lens aperture used. The nearer the outside diaphragm is placed to the lens the more out of focus it becomes and, consequently, the softer the graduation of the edge of the circle. This instrument of late has come into extensive use not only for circling in and circling out but also for isolating the expression of any particular character in the close up from the background, in which case after focusing upon a close view of the character at the stop used, the outside diaphragm is gradually closed until everything except the features to be shown are obliterated by the iris blades.

(To be continued.)

Reviews of Current Productions
EXCLUSIVELY BY OUR OWN STAFF

"The Man Without a Country"

Five-Part Thanhouser Picture Founded on Edward Everett Hale's Story Has Strong Patriotic Appeal—Released by Jewell Productions.

Reviewed by Edward Weitzel.

IN adapting Edward Everett Hale's famous story, "The Man Without a Country," for the screen, Lloyd Lonergan, who made the scenario for the Thanhouser Company, recognized the necessity of supplying considerable new material in order to produce a five-part picture. To this end the photoplay presents a story within a story, most of the action taking place at the present time and centering around a young man named Philip Nolan. He fails to respond when the call comes for volunteers for service in France, and is totally indifferent to every patriotic appeal. In a moment of anger he uses the

Scene from "The Man Without a Country" (Jewel).

same words that Edward Everett Hale put into the mouth of the chief character in his tale: "Damn the United States! I never want to hear her mentioned again." A friend of Nolan's hands him a copy of "The Man Without a Country," and begs him to read it. He does so and the force of its lesson is brought home to him. He hurries to a recruiting office and enlists. There is a love interest connected with the picture, but its chief value lies in its call to duty and its impressive lesson on love of country. The visualization of the Hale classic is brought in naturally and effectively, and the artistic shortcomings of the picture, as a whole, are lost sight of in view of its timeliness and the response its story is bound to command. The average spectator will pass over its slowness of movement, and the lack of engaging qualities in its hero, and feel only the fire of its patriotism and the good Americanism it aims to teach.

H. E. Herbert was a wise selection for the character of Philip Nolan, and his mental awakening seemed genuine. Florence LaBadie had the part of a patriotic American girl, and supplied her with the right qualifications. Other well played parts were contributed by J. H. Gilmour, Carey Hastings, Ernest Howard, and Charles Dundan. Ernest C. Warde's direction of the picture is capable, in the main, but his idea of a naval officer's cabin is peculiar.

"The Lost Express"

New Mutual Serial Proves Worthy Successor in First Two Episodes to Former Helen Holmes Pictures.

Reviewed by Margaret I. MacDonald.

IN the new Mutual serial of two-part episodes, entitled "The Lost Express," we encounter, with one or two exceptions, the same faces as in "The Railroad Raiders" and "The Lass of the Lumberlands." Helen Holmes is still playing the fearless heroine, and Thomas Lingham is back in the role of the double-dyed villain; while L. D. Maloney is playing a "man of mystery" sort of part which keeps the spectator guessing. John McKinnon and Edward Hearn are new members of the company who give promise of accellerating interest in the story.

The first episode draws its title from the name of the serial, "The Lost Express," and tells the story of how when Helen Thurston's father is paralyzed by a shot from the hand of a burglar known as Harelip, the express which she charters to move the contents of her father's vault to safekeeping in a bank of a nearby town, disappears from the tracks in a most mysterious way. A formula for the manufacture of granulated gasoline, and which was hidden in the vault, was the prize for which the burglary had been made, and which disappeared with other valuable papers on the express train.

The second episode, entitled "The Destroyed Document," shows how a missing page of the prized document is found by the gang who, in trying to get away with it, are followed by Helen and a detective. Helen creeping along the top of the moving train focuses a powerful glass on the document which at that moment is being examined by Harelip and his associates, and succeeds in burning it. This incident is not very convincing. The serial is full of action, however, and gives promise of being interesting, providing too much of the "far-fetched" material is not inserted in its makeup.

"The Woman Beneath"

Ethel Clayton in Five-Part Peerless Photoplay, Written by Williard Mack, Gives Convincing Characterization.

Reviewed by Edward Weitzel.

IF playwrights are sometimes forced to present conventional aspects of life it is quite as well that they select pleasing phases of existence for the hero and the heroine. In "The Woman Beneath," a five-part Peerless production, directed by Travers Vale, Willliard Mack, the author, has kept this fact in mind, and treated the spectator to a series of diverting, if familiar, situations. Tom Connolly, a Western millionaire, takes a trip to New York and meets Betty Fair, child, a brilliant bud in the social hothouse. Connolly is a man of action, and once he discovers that he is in love with Betty, sets about to make her Mrs. Connolly. A former suitor of his wife's attempts to force his attentions on her, and Tom is led to believe that Betty does not love him. He pretends to be ruined financially, and the true character of his wife is brought to the surface. She takes to life in a Harlem flat without complaining, and when she finds out that Ruppert Crandall, the former suitor, has betrayed her husband's sister, compromises her own good name so that Tom shall not become a murderer. The misunderstandings are all cleared away at the finish, and Tom and Betty are so happy that they

Scene from "The Woman Beneath" (World).

both continue to smile even after Tom takes his wife riding in a flivver and the machine refuses to run.

The playing of Ethel Clayton as Betty Fairchild, and Curtis Cooksey as Tom Connelly goes a long way toward making the picture acceptable. Miss Clayton, especially, has a convincing characterization to her credit. Her perfomance of Betty presents an easily recognized type of well-bred, true-hearted young womanhood that only needs the test to bring out its real nature. Isabelle Berwin, Frank de Vernon, Crauford Kent and Eugenie Woodward are the remaining members of a competent cast. The production is equal to all demands.

"The Spindle of Life."

Five-Reel Butterfly Release Features Ben Wilson and Neva Gerber in Offering of Light, Pleasant Type.

Reviewed by Robert C. M. Elravy.

COMEDY is the prevailing note in this feature number, which has its principal scenes in a seaside resort, and in the New York stock market. Such drama as there is occurs in the city end of the story, but this is of a quiet and more or less restrained sort. The production, as a whole,

Scene from "The Spindle of Life" (Butterfly).

tells a rather slight but brightly pictured and generally engaging story of the romantic type.

Neva Gerber, who recently did some effective work with Ben Wilson in "The Voice on the Wire" serial, is cast here in a lighter, more spontaneous role, which she handles with equal skill. She plays the part of Gladsome, daughter of a widow with social ambitions. Mrs. Harrison, the mother, has selected Vincent Bradshaw as a desirable son-in-law, but the girl does not like him, and proceeds to work out her own destiny in a way that is also agreeable to her mother in the end.

The girl has a very democratic disposition, and shocks her mother and their society friends by wearing oilskins and enjoying herself in the company of some fishermen with whom she has played ever since she was a child. It is on one of these excursions that she meets a young man with whom she falls desperately in love. He is known to her by the name of "Sandman," but later proves to be a wealthy Wall Street man on a vacation. Ben Wilson plays this part acceptably. On the street he is known as "Alphabet" Carter, and the dramatic end of the story shows the way in which he "breaks" Bradshaw and his father. The latter are speculating with Mrs. Harrison's funds.

The photoplay and scenic effects are very pleasing throughout this feature. Others in the cast are Jessie Pratt, Ed Brady, Richard La Reno, Winter Hall and Hayward Mack. The story was adapted by Karl Coolidge from a novel by Sidney Robinson and was produced by George Cochrane.

"For the Freedom of the World."

Eight-Reel Patriotic Production Featuring E. K. Lincoln, With Barbara Castleton and Romaine Fielding.

Reviewed by Margaret I. MacDonald.

A STIRRING eight-part patriotic production which was produced by Ira M. Lowry and F. J. Carrol, of 220 West 42d street, New York City, from the story of Edwin Bower Hesser, will be found an excellent aid in the work of recruiting. "For the Freedom of the World" is the title of the production which features E. K. Lincoln, with Barbara Castleton and Romaine Fielding, with a supporting cast consisting of Neil Moran, Jane Adler and Walter Weems.

The story of the picture follows the fortunes of a member of the American Legion, and presents some intensely interesting scenes which were evidently photographed at the training camps in Canada, showing how these soldiers are trained for the work ahead of them. One of the features of the picture is the night photography which it contains, and which has been very carefully done. The battle scenes photographed in the darkness, with only the light from bursting shells by which to distinguish objects moving on the horizon, are very effective. E. J. Lincoln plays the role of the son of wealthy parents, who suddenly aroused from his profligate habits by a manly young officer of the American Legion, enlists and finally receives a commission. The character of the slacker is well portrayed by Romaine Fielding in a manner to inspire disgust for this type of man. And especially the earlier portion of the production is constituted to inspire patriotism. Rather an extreme instance has been cited in the picture which might be questioned by the uninformed, in which an officer and his wife, who, disobedient to orders, visits her husband at the front, are condemned to death. This, we under-

stand, is in accordance with an order governing such instances issued by General Joffre some months ago. In this case the officer shoots his wife to save her from death by other means. Barbara Castleton does excellent work as the young wife who in trying to reach her husband at the front steals her passage on a transport carrying members of the Red Cross corps to France, and is disguised as a nurse by a sympathetic fellow passenger.

"Barbary Sheep."

Artcraft Romantic Drama of Fine Artistry With Elsie Ferguson in the Leading Role.

Reviewed by Louis Reeves Harrison.

BARBARY SHEEP" is distinguished for superior artistry of presentation, high suspense and some fascinating psychology, the latter especially where it reveals the effect of primitive passions on the refined mentality of a modern society woman. This last-named feature of the story is largely responsible for the suspense, and it is handled with skill by the director, but there is a lack of intensity on the part of Miss Ferguson, notwithstanding her highly intelligent interpretation of the leading part. Her art is subtle and therefore modern so far as the stage is concerned, but in the absence of that most wondrous stimulant to emotion, the human voice, it is safer to err on the side of exaggeration in screen representation. It is quite evident that the author intends to show a tremendous inner struggle of the civilized woman with the fragmentary remains of barbarous instinct still lingering in her soul, and this is very well done in a ladylike way, perhaps in a consistent manner from some points of view, but it is not strongly enough addressed to the average mixed audience.

Taken as a whole, "Barbary Sheep" is a story which will hold attention, and it is replete with convincing "atmosphere," particularly in the difficult Algerian scenes. The environment helps greatly to enhance the illusion and preserve the charm of reality. It is far from an easy story to make plausible in the matter of surrounding influences, hence the director, Maurice Tournier, deserves high commendation for his work. It is to be deplored, however, that he could not attain something with more zip in it for the last scene rather than the conventional ending. The play is strong enough throughout to deserve something more effective at its conclusion. As a piece of pure artistry it should win.

"Under False Colors."

Pathe-Thanhouser Five-Reel Production Features Frederick Warde and Jeanne Eagels In Russian Revolution Story.

Reviewed by Robert C. McElravy.

INTENSELY modern in every inch is this five-real production, written by Lloyd Lonergan and directed by Emile Chautard. It tells a lively and stirring tale of present times, with the recent Russian revolution as a background.

Frederick Warde gives dignity and sympathy to the part of the American millionaire, John Colton. Mr. Warde plays with the grace and finish that have been his through long years of histrionic fame. Jeanne Eagels is remarkably attractive as the Countess Olga, a young girl of the Russian nobility, who comes to this country to procure funds for the revolution. Her features are expressive and well adapted to the screen, and she had just the right touch of naive eagerness and wonderment to give strength to certain scenes.

The story is quite complicated and entertaining so far as

Scene from "Under False Colors" (Pathe).

the plot is concerned, and the presentation is adequate throughout, though not particularly lavish in settings. It is carried chiefly by the good acting in evidence through its course.

The Countess Olga is befriended in Russia by Jack Colton, son of the American millionaire who gives her money and a passport to bring her to this country. On the trip over she meets Vera Ladislaus, a friend of the Coltons. The ship is torpedoed and Vera dies. Olga then takes her place and goes to the home of John Colton, who takes her in, believing her of course to be Vera. There is a scene of unusual dramatic strength where Vera's father comes and Olga does not recognize him. A little more suspense in certain of the latter scenes would have helped, but the story interest is so strong that its absence is not greatly felt.

Others in the cast are Robert Vaughn, Anne Gregory and Carey Hastings.

"For France."
Five-Part Vitagraph Photoplay of the Great Conflict, Written by Cyrus Townsend Brady, Is Interesting from Start to Finish.
Reviewed by Edward Weitzel.

A YOUNG West Pointer, who goes to France to study aviation and joins the French army at the outbreak of the war, is the hero of "For France," a five-part Vitagraph Blue Ribbon Feature, written by Cyrus Townsend Brady, and directed by Wesley Ruggles. The picture interests. None of the material is new, nor is there anything remarkable in the way it is handled by the director. The entire production maintains a fairly impressive level of merit, however, and the story has enough romance, vital action, and the clash of battle to hold the attention of the average spectator.

Gerald Ackland, the West Pointer, falls in love with the daughter of a celebrated French artist. The girl and her father are living at a farmhouse near Mons, when a party of German soldiers stumble upon the place, and the arrival of Ackland is all that saves his sweetheart from becoming the victim of the officer in command. The picture terminates with a well arranged battle, in which a body of British hold off the Germans until a detachment of French cavalry rides up and force the enemy to retreat. A machine gun, operated by Ackland and the artist's daughter, also has a voice in the matter. The American is dangerously wounded, but is nursed back to health by his sweetheart, who becomes a Red Cross nurse.

The acting is entirely satisfactory. Edward Earle is natural and animated, and always commands respect for the character of Gerald, and Betty Howe represents the French heroine with the same result. Arthur Donaldson, Mary Maurice and Frank Anderson are valuable members of the cast.

"The Hostage."
Wallace Reid the Star in Absorbing Five-Reel Lasky-Paramount Drama Writen by Beulah Marie Dix— Directed by Robert Thornby.
Reviewed by Ben H. Grimm.

F EW photoplays attain the degree of sustained interest that is found in "The Hostage," a five-reel Paramount picture in which Wallace Reid is the star. Suspense—a suspense that holds the spectator's interest tightly captive—is contained

Scene from "The Hostage" (Lasky).

in every foot of the five reels. Even in commonplace action the story is always just a little bit ahead of the viewer. And Mr. Reid and his supporting cast make important even the smallest incidents, all of which have bearing on the story. Beulah Marie Dix has written a war story with a purpose, but the purpose is so cleverly veiled under the cloak of entertainment that one who has seen the picture does not get it until after analyzation. The purpose is not exactly a pacifist argument, but is more an arraignment by either belligerent of the other.

For her story the author has put at sword's points the Highlanders and the Lowlanders. Mr. Reid is seen as the son of the commander of the Lowlanders. He is given the Highlanders by the Lowlanders as hostage—as a guarantee that the Lowlanders will keep their pact with the Highlanders. The lieutenant is billeted at a Highland home where he comes under the scorching heat of the house's occupants. His stoicism, his gentility and honor soon win the compassion and later the love of the daughter of the house. The lieutenant is accused of treachery when his uncle attacks the Highland stronghold.

He is tortured in an endeavor to make him tell the Lowlanders' plans, but is released when it is learned that he forfeited his right to live in defending a Highland girl. He is about to be shot when peace is declared.

Mr. Thornby's direction shows a skill that is evident in every place where directorial skill is most needed. Lightings and photography are fully up to Paramount standard.

Gertrude Short has the leading female role. She acquits herself admirably, as also do Dorothea Abril, C. H. Geldert, Guy Oliver, Camille Ankewich, Noah Beery, George I. Spaulding, Lillian Leighton and Lucien Littlefield.

"One Hour."
Zena Keefe and Alan Hale Featured in Six-Reel Drama— Released Through Hoffman-Foursquare Exchanges— Produced by Harry Rapf.
Reviewed by Ben. H. Grimm.

T HE latest Hoffman-Foursquare picture, "One Hour," is a satisfactory offering. Zena Keefe and Alan Hale are the featured players in a six-reel screen drama that holds the interest throughout. The story is of the type that always has

Scene from "One Hour" (Hoffman).

been popular and the tale has been screened in a manner that adds to its attractiveness. The story centers around the lives of a man and youth and their love. In the early reels there are seen many beautiful exteriors. There is much attractive "snow stuff," and several very effectively lighted night scenes in the forest. Also the film has been edited in a manner that aids it considerably. While the picture is one that will make its biggest appeal to adults, there is nothing shown on the screen that is offensive.

Miss Keefe is seen as a young woman around whom much mystery centers. She lives with her aunt and uncle in a bungalow in the Adirondacks. Near her lives a youth called Stanley (Mr. Hale). The youth rescues the girl when she falls through the ice and brings her to his cabin. As time passes they fall in love. Their happiness is broken by the arrival of a foreign Baron, who tells the girl that she is the princess of a small European kingdom, and that she must marry the profligate king of a neighboring kingdom to save her people from war. In desperation the girl goes to her lover. She is torn from him and brought to Europe, followed by the youth. It develops that the youth is the nephew of the king to whom the princess must be married. Intoxicated, the king endeavors to embrace the princess in her chambers. He is set upon by Prince Stanisi. The excitement kills the king, and the prince succeeds to the throne.

The work of Miss Keefe, Mr. Hale, and the other members of the cast is thoroughly satisfactory. On the screen with the leads are seen D. J. Flanigan, Ina Brooks, Warren Cook, H. W. Pemberton, William Marion, Franklyn Hanna and Herbert Dancey.

The scenario was written by Paul McAllister, who, with Edwin Hollywood, also directed. The direction leaves nothing to be desired. The picture was produced by Harry Rapf.

"Behind the Mask."
Catherine Calvert Featured in Five-Reel Drama Produced by U. S. Amusement Corporation for Release by Art Dramas.
Reviewed by Ben H. Grimm.

I N "Behind the Mask," a five-reel drama produced by the U. S. Amusement Corporation for release on the Art Dramas program, we have a photoplay of medium grade. The story is moderately interesting and its screen presentation fairly well made. Catherine Calvert is seen in the featured role, with Richard Tucker playing the male lead. The story was written by Charles T. Dazey. The production was directed by Mme. Alice Blache. Much of the plot is bridged by titles, some of which are rather long. If the spectator is willing to take much for granted he will get a fair amount of amusement from a view of "Behind the Mask."

The story tells of the revenge of a girl whose father is ruined by a capitalist. She becomes his daughter's social secretary, and in that capacity meets Lord Strathmore, to whom the daughter is affianced. Lost in the woods, the Lord and the girl are forced to spend the night in a lonesome cabin. The Lord is in love with the secretary. The next morning he marries her, the secretary thus being revenged on the daughter of the man who ruined her father. But after marriage hate for her husband springs into the heart of the girl. She leaves him. A baby is born. The mother is made blind through an illness.

Two years later the lord finds his wife. He comes to her as an old friend of her father. He engages a physician who restores her sight. She still hates the man she knew as her husband, but loves the man she knows as the friend of her father. To prevent "them" taking her baby away, as she believes will be done, the mother flees into the woods. When confronted by her husband she is about to fling herself and her baby over the cliff, but when she learns that her husband is the man whom she knew as a friend of her father, she relents.

Both Miss Calvert and Mr. Tucker are capable. Other important parts are in the hands of Kirke Brown, Charles Dungan, Flora Nason and Charles Halton.

"The Conqueror"

Eight-Part Fox Photodrama of the Life of General Sam Houston, William Farnum Starred, Has Historic Value—Directed by R. A. Walsh.

Reviewed by Edward Weitzel.

IN WRITING "The Conqueror," an eight-part photodrama produced by William Fox, with William Farnum in the leading role, the author, Henry Christeen Warnack, has evidently intended to give a fairly truthful picture of the life and times of General Sam Houston, the American pioneer who was so closely identified with the settlement and development of Texas. The page of American history devoted to the romantic figure of this famous son of Tennessee is a fascinating one, and the author of "The Conqueror" has succeeded in transferring a number of its most striking incidents to the screen. William Farnum has the physique and personality that makes him fill the eye in the role of Houston, and director R. A. Walsh has endeavored, with satisfactory results, to give the production a bigness of treatment that would mark the picture as much above the average.

The story of Houston's life is full of diversity and color, and this condition has been used to advantage. His friendship with the Indians permitted the director to bring a large number of redmen into several scenes of the picture, and to use them in the battle at the end. Director Walsh has not lost any of his old cunning, and the ensembles are handled with the effectiveness of which he is a master. Some of the comedy relief might well be spared, so far as the judicious are concerned, but it will bring joy to the rest of the spectators. They will find in Jumbo and his live stock a welcome spring of laughter.

The love interest hangs upon Houston's love for a Nashville, Tennessee, belle, and his struggle upward, socially and politically, until he makes her his wife. They afterward become estranged, and the scene shifts to Texas, where Houston defeats a band of Mexican outlaws and rescues his wife, after the manner made and approved of for men of his character.

Scene from "The Conqueror" (Fox).

William Farnum does all that is demanded of him in the way of acting, with ease and finish, and shows that he suits the part and the part suits him. Jewel Carmen as Eliza Allen is first a "haughty beauty" and then the loving woman who is glad to acknowledge Houston as her husband, and presents both phases of the character convincingly. Charles Clary, J. A. Marcus, Carrie Clark Ward, William Chisholm, Robert Dunbar, Owen Jones and the Indian chiefs, William Eagle Shirt, Chief Birdhead and Little Bear are members of the cast.

"When False Tongues Speak"

Melodrama with Plenty of Old-Time, Sure-Fire Stunts— Some Fine Human Climaxes—Weak Continuity— Went Well at East Side Star Theater.

Reviewed by Hanford C. Judson.

THERE is plenty to trouble a reviewer in the recent Fox five-reel picture, "When False Tongues Speak," and there are plenty of scenes that will be a delight to the most critical. The comic relief—as the drunken man who plays

Scene from "When False Tongues Speak" (Fox).

upon the bars of his prison as on a heavenly harp—is so often ably done that one will have to laugh, even though he laughed at the same thing years ago. There are climaxes, as when the big heroine of the plot meets the little heroine of the counterfoil in the Pullman car, that pulls the heart, even though the picture drops again to a much inferior level. Taken as a whole, the plot is weak in continuity. The villain is loosely connected to the tale, and the hero is faintly set forth and not very convincing. Virginia Pearson, the heroine, is often altogether charming, and Claire Whitney, in the role of the deceived woman, also acts with precision. Carl Harbough as the drunken husband shows his marked ability to make a character convince, and Hardee Kirkland as the villain is all that anyone could be in the role. Many of the lesser characters are commendable.

The picture has many of the earmarks of the old play—it is by George Scarborough—that hasn't been quite remade into a real picture. Take, for instance, that little struggle before the blackboard at the mission school. Personality on the stage might have made it convincingly, because the voice can connote what in film must be told plainly. In the picture, it seems silly for a society woman to get so intimate with a mere reporter on the second short meeting. Yet the director, Carl Harbough, shows marked ability again and again as a picture man by his ease in handling some of the scenes, by his interesting by-play and by the beauty of his close-ups.

I saw the picture at the Fox Star theater, at 107th street and Lexington avenue, New York, with a cheap audience. It was followed closely, and was given a very ample appreciation. The Star is on the East Side in a poor neighborhood.

A Couple of Christie Comedies

"Crazy by Proxy," and "Green Eyes and Bullets" Entertaining One-Reel Comedies.

Reviewed by Margaret I. MacDonald.

THE two pictures under review at the present writing represent a marked improvement in their class of comedy. "Crazy by Proxy" and "Green Eyes and Bullets" were made by the Christie Film Company. They lean to the farce order of comedy without being extreme, are free from vulgarity, and will be found entertaining to the average audience.

The first-named, "Crazy by Proxy," introduces us to a young man who is about to marry; in fact, he enters the picture at the dawn of his wedding morn. The bride-to-be, pretty Betty Compson, is also presented; but while she eagerly pursues preparations for the wedding, the bridegroom is kidnapped by a jealous cousin who is envious of his position as heir of a fortune. An amusing chase, and final escape from a sanitarium where he has been taken brings the picture to a close in a pretty wedding scene.

"Green Eyes and Bullets" tells the story of a young couple, newly married, who have made frequent changes in their place of abode. At last taking quarters at a hotel they feel that they are peaceably settled when a shadow again crosses their sky. This time it is the foolish jealousy of the husband, who goes out one morning taking the key of their door with him, leaving his pretty wife, attired in negligee clothing, in the corridor. Unable to get into her own apartment the young wife accepts the kindly offer of the man across the hall to step into his apartment for shelter while he hunts the janitor for her.

In the meantime the husband returns with the key and discovers his wife in another man's room. This situation, while much hackneyed, has been in the present instance handled in an amusing and unsuggestive manner, which proves harmlessly entertaining.

Conquest Program No. 8

Fine Group of Subjects, Including "T. Haviland Hicks, Freshman," a Stirring College Tale, and R. H. Davis' Story, "Gallegher."

Reviewed by Margaret I. MacDonald.

THE quality of pictures on the Edison Conquest programs still holds good, and program No. 8 has not a dull moment. The first number on the program is a three-reel version of a story by J. Raymond Elderdice, entitled "T. Haviland Hicks, Freshman," which, as the title would suggest, is a story of college life. Raymond McKee gives a lively portrayal of the character of T. Haviland Hicks, a rich young freshman, and fond of adventure. His clever dodging of his fellow students' attempts at hazing him are very amusing and well staged. Others of the cast are Albert Macklin, James Turbell and William Sherwood.

The second number is a two-reel filmization of the Richard Harding Davis story "Gallegher," in which Andy Clark plays the role of the precocious office boy in a newspaper office, who turns detective on his own account and succeeds not only in bringing in the biggest scoop of the season, but in causing the arrest of a murderer. The picture is well made and Andy Clark in the title role does an excellent bit of work. Jack Willard plays effectively the role of Stephen Hade, the murderer, William Wadsworth that of the sporting editor of the "Press," and Lou Stearn that of Detective Hefflefinger.

The educational numbers, "Turning Out Silver Bullets," which was photographed at the Philadelphia Mint; "Young Salts," a review of work and play at the Culver Military Academy, and "The Holy Land," are all well illustrated and interesting, especially the first mentioned, which are unusually good.

New "Ham" Comedies

Kalem Presents "Ham" and "Bud" in a Pair of New Laugh Producers, Directed by Al Santell.

Reviewed by Robert C. McElravy.

IT IS human nature to laugh at certain forms of trickery, and this is perhaps a good thing, for there is always a great deal of it in evidence. "Ham" and "Bud," two laughable individuals who live upon their wits, appear again in two comedy subjects, which will find favor with their former friends. Lloyd V. Hamilton and A. E. Duncan play the leading parts and are supported by a cast which includes Henry Murdoch, John Steppling and Edytha Sterling.

In the number entitled "The Boot and the Loot" Ham begins operations by borrowing the uniform of a street car conductor. He then approaches the Italian proprietor of a bootblack stand and offers to trade him a street car for his stand. The trade is made, and the Italian tries to make off with the car. This starts a number of entertaining developments of a rapid-fire, burlesque sort. Ham and Bud also in the course of the story take up the trail of a badly wanted thief, whom they follow to the home of a millionaire. Here they learn that the man is not a thief at all, but the millionaire's butler. At this moment

Scene from "A Whirlwind of Whiskers" (Kalem).

the Italian again shows up, and all hands indulge in a wild chase.

"A Whirlwind of Whiskers" is a similar type of comedy, in which Ham and Bud visit a detective bureau. They are mistaken for sleuths and are sent out upon the trail of a counterfeiter. They spot a man with a long white beard and follow him to a barber shop, where numerous amusing scenes occur. While they are still looking for the counterfeiter a real detective comes along and chases them over roof tops. Ham and Bud succeed in evading the detective and other pursuers and go on their way, looking for new adventures.

"The Mysterious Mr. Tiller"

Five-Reel Bluebird Features Rupert Julian and Ruth Clifford in Excellent Story of Mystery and Suspense.

Reviewed by Robert C. McElravy.

EVERY foot of this five-reel subject plunges the observer further and further into absorbing complications of plot, which are baffling and thrilling at one and the same time. From the moment Rupert Julian appears as a cravenated, silk-hatted gentleman strolling down Lester street until the close

Scene from "The Mysterious Mr. Tiller" (Bluebird).

of the story there is nothing wanting in the way of dark doings and interesting adventures to hold the attention.

Mr. Julian appears as Prentice Tiller, an individual of whom little is known, but whose movements instantly arouse speculation. He meets, or rather follows, a girl who runs out of a house in which an explosion has occurred. They collide with one another at the end of a blind alley, and the girl asks him to escort her home in safety. He walks with her a certain distance, and she then asks him to leave her. He does so, but watches her further movements with interest.

From this point the story moves on to innumerable adventures. Tiller attends a reception at the Hawthorne residence and recognizes in Clara Hawthorne the girl of his brief acquaintance. During the evening two valuable necklaces are stolen. An arch criminal named Mordant is suspected, but it turns out that Tiller has a hand in the operations. In the course of the tale Mr. Julian also assumes a second part, by means of certain facial distortions which he has successfully employed before. This brings up a situation toward the close which is both interesting and surprising. In the end the theft of the necklaces is cleared up, and the criminal, Mordant, and his accomplices are brought to justice. The production is a strong one of the mystery type.

Ruth Clifford is attractive in the part of Clara Hawthorne, and Frank Brownlee does good work as Mordant. Others in the cast are Wedgewood Nowell, Harry Rattenberry and E. A. Warren. Elliott J. Clawson is the author of the interesting story.

Triangle Releases

"The Bond of Fear," Five-Part Photoplay Featuring Belle Bennett and Roy Stewart, and "Mountain Dew," a Drama of the Cumberlands, Starring Margery Wilson.

Reviewed by Edward Weitzel.

"The Bond of Fear."

THE opening incident of "The Bond of Fear, a five-part photoplay written by Edith Kennedy for Triangle and directed by Jack Conway, gives the picture an excellent start. Judge Camden McClure of Philadelphia is shown in court, giving a convicted man the full extent of the law. That same day the Judge has a quarrel with his brother and strikes him with a decanter in self-defense. Believing he has killed the young man, the cowardly nature of the Judge asserts itself and he becomes a fugitive. He flees to the western desert, meets a woman who nurses him through a fever, and then exhibits a yellow streak, in his treatment of her, that is quite beyond belief. Fortunately, the woman is loved by a real man and she accepts him as the last scene fades out.

Putting aside the overdrawing of the character of the Judge, the dramatic value of the picture is considerable. The production is always in keeping with the subject, and Director Conway has brought out the strong points of the story with skill. The desert scenes, which include a sand storm, are impressive, and the work of the cast is never at fault. Belle Bennett, as Mary Jackson, makes the character womanly and fine, and Roy Stewart is just the sort of man that Cal Nelson is supposed to be. Malborne McDowell, George Webb and John Lince had important allotments.

"Mountain Dew."

Moonshine whiskey, a young novelist, and a mountain maiden who can neither read nor write, are the springs of action in "Mountain Dew," a five-part picture by Julian Josephsen and Monte M. Katterjohn. The part of the Kentucky girl is played by Margery Wilson, the character of the novelist having been intrusted to Charles Gunn. Thomas Heffron directed the pro-

Scene from "Mountain Dew" (Triangle).

duction. Everyone connected with the making of the photoplay have labored earnestly and well. The story is quite as good as any of the numerous ones on the same subject that have preceded it, and many of its scenes have pronounced pictorial charm. Comedy relief is supplied by the colored valet of the novelist. Humor of the brand that was once found in the popular price dramas of the spoken stage is the specialty of Roosevelt Washington. Al. W. Filson, Jack Richardson, Aaron Edwards and Mary Borland contribute well-defined impersonations.

"The Awakening of Ruth."

Five-Part Perfection Picture Released by George Kleine System Features Shirley Mason, and Is Well Produced.

Reviewed by Edward Weitzel.

THE first release of the Perfection make of pictures, distributed by the George Kleine System, is entitled "The Awakening of Ruth," and was produced by Edison. It is a five-part story of the Florida Keys and was written by Lucien Hubbard, the director being E. H. Griffith. The plot is pleasantly entertaining, although not all dramatic, and the author has made no attempt to have his heroine smack of the soil. Ruth Hoagland has been reared upon one of the islands of the Florida Keys, but she talks as correctly as a Boston schoolma'am and exhibits no trace of the peculiarities of character that are looked for in natives of a certain locality. No explanation of her early life is given, and the spectator is at liberty to imagine for himself how Ruth came to be living on the island with her father, a half-witted fisherman, who spends most of his time hunting for buried treasure.

Robert Winthrop, a wealthy young fellow from the North, comes to the island, and he and Ruth fall in love with each other. After Winthrop's return to New York he forgets the little wood girl and becomes interested in a musical comedy star. Ruth finds that she has a voice and goes north to seek her fortune, a doctor from the mainland, who loves her, helping her at great personal sacrifice. Her adventures in New York bring her in contact with Winthrop and his actress friend, and this experience makes her glad to go back to Florida and marry the doctor.

The production of the picture has been made with care, and many of the scenes are attractive, although lacking the southern atmosphere. Speeding up the movement of the story would improve it greatly. Most of the time it merely drifts along. Shirley Mason is a pathetic little figure as the island girl and swims, dives and fills the acting requirements of the part with much skill. Her support is satisfactory, and consists of Donald MacClennan, Joseph Byrke, William Hayes, Donald Hall, Sally Crute, Jessie Stevens, and Edward Elkas.

"Rasputin, the Black Monk."

Eight-Part Brady-Made Production on Russian Conditions Preceding the Revolution Features Montagu Love in Title Role.

Reviewed by Margaret I. MacDonald.

NO PERIOD of history is more fraught with dramatic events for any of the nations of the earth than was that period preceding the Russian revolution. And the fact that two of the most pretentious of present-day moving picture pro-

ductions have been based on the unhappy conditions of that period speaks well for the producer's choice of a subject suited to inspire interest in the mind of the public.

The first of these productions to be given a public screening is that presented by William A. Brady and ably directed by Arthur Ashley. The picture opened for a run of ten days at the Park theater, New York City, on Wednesday, September 12, and was greeted with loud enthusiasm by an audience among whom were many of Russian nationality. It is well and carefully made and covers in a general way the history of events which finally engulfed the royal family of Russia, and in the weave of which Rasputin, the Black Monk, was the chief artist. Lack of knowledge of actual incidents in this chain of events which led the way for the crafty peasant from the ranks of the lowly to the palace of royalty prevents us from passing judgment on the production, except in the general outline, which we believe is true to the history of Russia for the past eighteen to twenty years. It follows in a dramatic way the career of Rasputin, touches delicately the domestic life of the royal family of Russia, with its weak-kneed Czar, and finally, after the splendidly staged assassination of Rasputin, leads from the gloom of cruel conspiracy to the sunshine of liberty and the forced abdication of the Czar. In the role of the latter Hubert Wilkie is highly deserving of praise, and while in feature Mr. Wilkie is not an altogether satisfactory double for the Czar, it must be admitted that he carries out the idea of dignified royalty to the very last letter.

Montagu Love plays the role of Rasputin in a marvelous manner. June Elvidge in the role of Raff's wife is beautiful, and so also is Lillian Cook as her daughter. Others of the cast equally effective in the roles which they portrayed are Irving Cummings, Julia Dean, Henry Hull and Arthur Ashley.

"A Man's Man."

Seven-Part Photo-Melodrama Starring J. Warren Kerrigan Is Full of Action and Humor—A Paralta Release.

Reviewed by Edward Weitzel.

MODERN romantic drama of the quality shown in "A Man's Man," a seven-part photoplay, released by Paralta, with J. Warren Kerrigan as the hero, will entertain any human being with red blood in his veins. No matter if it isn't life and the needs of the handsome young American who wins the heroine were never enacted outside of this Richard Harding Davis sort of tale! More's the pity! We have all wished we could stroll about, rescuing beauty in distress and pulling the nose of the villain every time he pokes it where it doesn't belong. Peter B. Kyne has followed an excellent model in writing this story, and started off with an enter-hero-knock-down-villain scene that gets the spectator in the first five minutes. Events of either a thrilling or an amusing nature follow rapidly, after this, the action skipping from California to South America and involving one of those familiar Latin-American revolutions, without which no story of that region is complete. And he has enlivened his tale with an obvious but beguiling humor, that heads off threatening bits of sentimentality before they can do any serious harm.

To Thomas G. Geraghty, who made the scenario, and to Oscar Apfel, who directed the production, go also a substantial share of the credit for the picture's success. Every detail is handled with skill, and a refreshing disregard of how the other fellow did it. The South American atmosphere, the battle scenes and

Scene from "A Man's Man" (Paralta).

the various features of the production, bear the stamp of authenticity, however.

The acting comes in for some meed of praise. J. Warren Kerrigan fits the character of John Stuart Webster in all its dimensions. He has the beauty, brains and brawn demanded, and never fails to register the humorous touches that fall to his share. Then there is Lois Wilson. This young woman is a real find. Blessed with good looks, a winning personality, and high grade acting ability, she is one of the pleasant surprises disclosed on the screen for some little time. Any male being worthy the name of man would feel just as John Stuart Webster did about her—if he were in J. S. Webster's place. The list of exceptionally good impersonations by the rest of the cast includes Ida Lewis as Mother Jenks, Kenneth Harlan as Billy Geary, Ed. Coxen as John Cafferty, Harry Von Meter as Ricardo Ruey, and Eugene Pallete as Captain Benevido.

Universal Serials

"The Gray Ghost" Now Reaching an Interesting Conclusion —To Be Followed Shortly by "The Red Ace."

Reviewed by Robert C. McElravy.

THE Universal serial known as "The Gray Ghost" is now approaching the final instalments. This has provided a generous combination of mystery and thrills, and the story interest has held up in a gratifying manner throughout its entire course.

"The Gray Ghost" is an adaptation of a story by Arthur Somers Roche, published in the "Saturday Evening Post" under the title of "Loot." Harry Carter is featured in the name part, playing the master criminal in a very satisfying manner. He is supported by a pleasing cast, which includes Eddie Polo, Priscilla Dean, Emory Johnson and others.

The "big" incident of this serial occurs in the early instalments, where "The Gray Ghost", and his followers plan and carry out the wholesale looting of a jewelry house in broad daylight. This operation carries over into two numbers and is staged on an elaborate scale, making a criminal exploit so gigantic in scope that it takes the observer's breath away. The further developments, in which the master criminal and his followers are rounded up, continue the interent well. There is perhaps a little spinning out of certain situations to make the required sixteen instalments, but the love story and various side plot features justify this course. The serial as a whole is one of strong interest.

Immediately following this the Universal will release a new serial, entitled "The Red Ace." This features Marie Walcamp, who had the leading feminine role in "Liberty." The first nine episodes of "The Red Ace" have been seen by the reviewer, and it may be safely promised that admirers of "Liberty" will find this a worthy successor. This, also, is an adventure story, the scenes occurring in a wild and rugged mining country. The heroine, through the death of her father, who was murdered by foreign spies, falls heir to a hidden platinum mine. She visits this region and is immediately set upon by the spies, who seek to gain possession of the key to a cache of platinum left by her father.

This serial, written and directed by Jacques Jaccard, has a sustained story interest and contains many thrills. Larry Peyton, Yvette Mitchell, and many real and "make believe" Indians are in the supporting cast.

Kalem Favorites in "Ham" Comedies

Director Al Santell Recruited Versatile Players from Kalem Dramatic Companies to Support His Stars.

IN ANNOUNCING release of new "Ham" comedies, featuring Ham and Bud, the Kalem Company calls attention to the strong company of funmakers assembled to support the comedians.

Following "Politics at Pumpkin Center," announced last week, Kalem will issue two ludicrous one-reel skits, "The Boot and the Loot" and "A Whirlwind of Whiskers," directed by Al Santell. In "The Boot and the Loot" Edythe Sterling, leading woman in the "Stingaree" series, displays her versatility as a comedienne, and the company also include John Steppling and Henry Murdock. Marin Sais, star of "The American Girl," "The Girl from Frisco" and other Kalem series, is the comedienne in "A Whirlwind of Whiskers," recalling to her many admirers the days in which she made laughs in comedies. R. E. Bradbury and Edward Clisbee, who created many splendid character roles in Kalem series, are also in the cast.

Director Santell went in for spectacular burlesque melodrama in these new issues. A wild street-car that raises havoc and a torrent raging in a sewer figure in "The Boot and the Loot," and "A Whirlwind of Whiskers" presents a sensational chase over the tops of skyscrapers, Ham and Bud precipitating their pursuers through a skylight.

After Mallards on the Carolina Coast.

The eighty-sixth release of Paramount-Bray Pictograph, the "magazine-on-the-screen," is of special interest to every lover of the great outdoors. E. F. Warner, of Field and Stream Magazine, one of America's greatest sportsmen, furnishes the material for an exciting day among the great marshes on the coast of Carolina, where myriads of ducks stop over on their way south for the winter. Here is a hunter's paradise, indeed.

In order to get this picture it was necessary to construct a great blind in which to hide the cameramen, for the birds are easily frightened and would take flight at the slightest provocation. The blind was built on a pile of logs in order to get near enough to the scene of action, and, as logs have a tendency to roll over in water, the cameraman got several wettings before the day was over. Fortunately, however, he managed to keep the camera from sharing his misfortunes, so that none of the film was injured,

Lou Marks Starred in "Three Comedies"

Commonwealth Comedy Company Stars Keystone Player for General Film Releases.

HAILED as a new luminary in the comedy world, Lou Marks, a former Keystone comedian, has been placed under contract by a recently organized company. Releases of his weekly one-reel eccentric comedy subjects begin September 28 through General Film Company. The brand will be known as "Three C Comedies," from the name of the producing organization, the Commonwealth Comedy Co., Inc., of 1545 Broadway, New York City.

Production of "Three C Comedies" has begun at the Thanhouser studio at New Rochelle, where accommodations have been secured under a long lease. Frank P. Donovan is directing Lou Marks, Pearl Shephard, Oom Paul and a large stock company in a series of one-reel pictures which will feature the laugh-inspiring personality of Marks, the piquant beauty of Miss Shephard and the excruciating facial contortions of Paul. Three releases are ready—"His Watery Waterloo," "His Winning Ways" and another subject not yet named. The first-named picture is the first of the series.

Lou Marks.

Pearl Shephard is no stranger to the motion picture world. She is a 20-year-old girl of bewitching attractiveness and the winner in three beauty contests. The first was at a motion picture exhibitors' convention at Madison Square Garden, followed by an engagement with the Thanhouser company. She has played the feminine lead in Pokes & Jabs comedies and later in the Wizard and Vim comedies.

Jos. S. Klein, a New York attorney, is president of the Commonwealth Comedy Co., Inc., and is remembered as prominent in urging the passage of the new act raising municipal courts of New York to courts of record. He is high in lodge circles and in Democratic politics, and made a speech nominating Mr. Wilson for President at the St. Louis convention. Arnold A. Kline, a building magnate of Newark, N. J., is vice president, and Charles W. Reiser, a public school executive of New York City, is secretary.

Clara Kimball Young on New Picture.

Clara Kimball Young, who has just completed her production of "Magda," the first release by her new organization, which she owns and controls, under the management of Harry I. Garson, has started filming "Shirley Kaye" at the Thannhouser studio in New Rochelle.

Joseph Kaufman, who directed "Broadway Jones," "The Traveling Salesman," and many other notable successes, will direct Miss Young in this, her second production, which will be released some time in October.

"Shirley Kaye" will be followed by "The Marionettes," Miss Young having finally established her right to that play, which was contested some time ago by the Charles Frohman interests.

"Magda," "Shirley Kaye," and "The Marionettes" will be the only three pictures Miss Young will do in the East, as she contemplates a de luxe production of "The Savage Woman" as her fourth release. Immediately after the holidays Miss Young will take her entire company to Porto Rico and other islands in the West Indies to film what, in her estimation, is to be her masterpiece.

After "The Savage Woman" is completed, Miss Young will proceed to California, and it may be that a new and strictly modern up-to-date studio will be ready for her new occupancy by that time, as Mr. Garson is already considering several advantageous locations.

The "Magda" release date will be announced in a few days.

New Lloyd Comedy.

"By the Sad Sea Waves" is the title of the Harold Lloyd comedy which Pathe will release on September 30. It is described as a girl show, with Harold Lloyd, Harry Pollard and Bebe Daniels as the Beachhound, Snub, and the Doll, respectively, and it is said to be one of a thousand feet of laughs, girls and prize-winning bathing suits.

The extremely speedy action for the most part revolves around the Sousehem Bathhouse and deals with the very funny and finally successful attempts of the Beachhound to save a man, only to find out that he is the wrong one. He is appointed official lifesaver and gets more joy out of the job than one would think possible. This comedy maintains the high standard set by the long list of those in which Harold Lloyd has scored so heavily.

Comments on the Films

EXCLUSIVELY BY OUR OWN STAFF

General Film Company.

WORLD LIBRARY NO. 18 (Selig), Sept.—The subjects covered in this issue of the World Library are "Harvesting Lima Beans in California," "Famous Zoo at Sidney, Australia," "Oyster Harvest in Chesapeake Bay," and "Famous Mausoleums of Chinese Mings."

WHAT TRANSPIRED AFTER THE WINDUP (Essanay).—One of the George Ade fables, and an entertaining comedy subject. The principles of the fable are Ferdie, a male vampire, and Adele, a graduate of a high-class reform school. The fable follows in the most amusing manner the love story of the pair, and excels as a film production by reason of clever staging.

THE BOOT AND THE LOOT (Kalem).—A comedy number, featuring Lloyd V. Hamilton and A. E. Duncan in the familiar characters of "Ham" and "Bud." Ham poses as a street car conductor and trades a street car to an Italian for his bootblack stand. This results in a number of burlesque comedy situations, which are quite laughable throughout. Later they get into further difficulties by trailing the wrong individual as a criminal suspect.

THE VICTOR OF THE PLOT (Selig).—A two-part military story, the scene of which is laid in India. The picture is a reissue and is slightly out of date in more ways than one, but is not altogether lacking in interest. It contains plenty of action, but has a slender stock which is rather hard to analyze.

BLINDMAN'S HOLIDAY (Broadway Star Feature).—A picturized O. Henry story in four parts, directed by Martin Justice, this photoplay is not one of its famous author's best plots. He has forced the use of coincidence beyond the limit. The story is an appealing one, however, and is fairly well acted. It shows how far a woman will go in sacrificing herself for those she loves.

THE VOICE THAT LED HIM (Selig).—This is a reissue of a one-reel drama in which Kathleen Williams appeared some time ago. It contains some interesting animal scenes, and Miss Williams does a remarkable scuffle with a tiger cub. The picture has, of course the stamp of the period in which it was produced. The story tells of a naturalist who went with his wife to Africa, and while there his wife, through carelessness, breaks a valuable negative belonging to her husband. He leaves the bungalow in a rage, refusing to speak a word of forgiveness. In his absence his wife is killed by a tiger, and the remainder of his life is spent in following the voice of his wife, which is always calling him.

A WHIRLWIND OF WHISKERS (Kalem).—A "Ham" comedy, featuring Lloyd V. Hamilton and A. E. Duncan as Ham and Bud. They are mistaken for detectives and set upon the trail of a counterfeiter. Numerous scenes occur in a barber shop, and at the close there is a chase over roof tops. This is a characteristic number and will bring numerous laughs.

Artcraft Pictures Corporation.

BARBARY SHEEP (Sept. 10).—A romantic drama of exceptionally fine craftsmanship, strong in suspense and in the self-struggle of a refined woman with primitive desire, Elsie Ferguson in the leading role.

Art Dramas, Inc.

BEHIND THE MASK (U. S. Amusement Corporation), Sept. 3.—A five-reel drama, in which Catherine Calvert is featured. The story tells of a woman who marries a man to strike at the daughter of the man who ruined her father. After marriage she hates her husband, becomes blind, and is finally won over by him. A longer review can be found in the review columns.

Bluebird Photoplays, Inc.

THE MYSTERIOUS MR. TILLER, Sept. 17.—An absorbing five-reel mystery number, featuring Rupert Julian and Ruth Clifford. Mr. Julian plays a double role, not by the ordinary means of double exposure, but by clever facial distortions. The plot is complicated and thrilling. Reviewed at length elsewhere.

Butterfly Pictures.

THE SPINDLE OF LIFE, Sept. 17.—A five-reel number of a light, generally engaging type, featuring Ben Wilson and Neva Gerber. The story, adapted from a novel by Sidney Robinson, has its principal scenes at a seaside resort and in the New York stock market. The number is a pleasing one of its kind. Reviewed at length elsewhere.

Christie Film Company.

CRAZY BY PROXY.—An amusing comedy of the farce order in which a bridegroom almost misses his wedding appointment because of being kidnapped. A review of the picture will be found elsewhere.

GREEN EYES AND BULLETS.—A farce comedy in which a young husband causes his bride much distress, carelessness and jealousy. The situation is an amusing one which is explained in a full review of the picture is to be found elsewhere.

Fox Film Corporation.

THE CONQUERORS (Standard Picture).—The life of General Sam Houston is the subject of this eight-part picture, William Farnum having the role. R. A. Walsh had charge of the production. The work is important. A longer review is printed on another page of this issue.

WHEN FALSE TONGUES SPEAK (Fox), Sept. 9.—A five-reel melodrama with Virginia Pearson and, as a whole, a very able cast. It is not an artistic production and a good deal of it is crude. Some of its climaxes are sure to please greatly, and one or two of its subtitles are perfect, though most of its subtitles are weak. It has many pretty scenes. This reviewer saw it with a cheap audience and there it went pretty well. It is not a sure picture for a critical audience.

Greater Vitagraph.

AN ALABASTER BOX (Sept. 10).—Mary E. Wilkins Freeman is the author of this five-part New England romance, in which Alice Joyce and Marc McDermott are featured. The story is interesting and the production does it justice. Reviewed at length on page 1850, issue of Sept. 22.

FOR FRANCE (Sept. 17).—The present war furnishes the background for this five-part Blue Ribbon written by Cyrus Townsend Brady. The picture has a good plot and is well produced. A battle at the finish introduces British, French and German soldiers and an American hero. A longer review will be found on another page of this issue.

RISKS AND ROUGHNECKS (Vitagraph).—Some amazing acrobatic stunts are the principal features of this one-reel knockabout farce, invented by Lawrence Semon and Graham Baker. Everything and everybody moves so fast that the plot is soon left behind, but the supply of broad humor keeps pace with the action.

PLANS AND PAJAMAS (Vitagraph).—Another Semon-Baker one-reel knock-about farce; it shows the interior of a female boarding school and a lively chase by the inmates after a burglar. Up to the average of this brand of pictures.

M. H. Hoffman, Inc,

ONE HOUR.—A satisfactory six-reel drama, featuring Zena Keefe and Alan Hale. There are many beautiful snow exteriors, and the story holds interest throughout the six reels. The tale centers around the lives of two young people who, at first in the Adirondacks, later go to Europe, where each, it develops, is the member of a royal family of small kingdoms. The story at all times interests. A longer review may be found in the review columns.

Jewel Productions, Inc.

THE MAN WITHOUT A COUNTRY (Jewel).—A five-part screen version of Edward Everett Hale's famous story, the patriotic appeal of this picture is timely. A longer review is printed on another page of this issue.

Kleine-Edison-Selig-Essanay.

CONQUEST PROGRAM NO. 8 (Edison), Sept.—The general quality of this program is unusually good. The subjects which it contains, and which have been reviewed at length elsewhere, are a three-part story of college life, entitled, "T. Haviland Hicks, Freshman," the Richard Harding Davis story, "Gallegher," in two parts, and three educationals, "Turning Out Silver Bullets," containing scenes photographed at the Philadelphia Mint; "Young Salts," consisting of some splendidly photographed scenes with the students at the Culver Military Academy, and "The Holy Land."

A CONTENTED WOMAN (Selig).—One of the Charles Hoyt comedies, produced in two parts. This comedy is not high-class, but is amusing. We could not recommend it, however, for a refined motion picture program. As the story runs, a wife who is taken up with the woman suffrage question leaves her husband and son at home to get the dinner while she attends a meeting. The men try to do the cooking, and succeed in making some disgusting exhibitions. They then turn the matter over to a caterer, and go to the theater. Here they are taken up with some dancing girls, one of whom accompanies them home, and is found there by the wife on her return.

Metro Pictures Corporation.

UNDER HANDICAP (Yorke), Sept. 3.—The story of a rich man's son and how he made good in spite of his financial handicap, this eight-part photoplay offers Harold Lockwood a congenial role, and has been carefully produced. A longer review was printed on page 1858 of the issue of Sept. 22.

Mutual Film Corporation.

MUTUAL WEEKLY NO. 141 (Gaumont), Sept. 12.—Interesting items of this issue are scenes in revolutionary Russia, a German aeroplane which took fire and fell behind the French lines, Ruth Law with her aeroplane at the Ohio State University, a hurried erection of barracks at Camp Gordon, Ga., President Wilson leading the parade of the National Army in Washington, and the "Jackies" on the old exposition ground at San Diego. This last presents a beautiful picture.

THE RAINBOW GIRL (American), Sept. 17.—A five-part production featuring pretty Juliette Day, with George Fisher playing opposite her. The production is crude, and what interest the story might succeed in inspiring is partially destroyed by the quality and arrangement of subtitles. The picture treats of the love story of a young woman who meets her Prince Charming through renting one of the rooms in her father's home. The young man who has come to the city for the purpose of selling his own musical compositions finally makes good and tells the girl of his love for her.

THE LOST EXPRESS (Signal), Sept. 17.—The initial release of the new Mutual serial promises that the story of the picture, which is by Frederick B. Bennett, will be an interesting one. Plenty of action marks this serial in which Helen Holmes is again featured, but, as usual with serials of this class, inconsistencies crop out. A full review will be found elsewhere.

THE LOST EXPRESS (Signal), Sept. 24.—The second episode of "The Lost Express" is entitled "The Destroyed Document" and shows how after the mysterious disappearance of the express train on which the contents of the Thurston vault, which included a valuable formula for granulated gasoline, were being conveyed, a missing sheet of this document is found. The thieves trying to make a getaway are traced by Helen and a detective, and Helen, creeping along the top of the train in which they are traveling, succeeds in destroying the document. A full review of the picture will be found elsewhere.

Paramount Pictures Corporation.

SEEING THINGS (Klever), Sept. 3.—A Victor Moore comedy in which the comedian returns from a sanitarium only to find that he is far from being cured. Among the optical illusions which haunt him is in the form of a man whom he calls Gloomy Gus. The picture is not of the highest type of comedy and the optical illusions referred to are really delirium tremens, the man having been sent to the sanitarium to take a drink cure.

THE HOSTAGE (Lasky), Sept. 10.—Wallace Reid is featured in an absorbing five-reel drama written by Beulah Marie Dix. Few photoplays attain the degree of sustained interest found in this one. There is suspense in every foot. Love interest is there, too. The story is a war story, but there are no battle scenes. A longer review is printed in the review columns.

Pathe Exchange, Inc.

IN THE WAKE OF THE HUNS (Pathe), Sept. 23.—Three reels of official French pictures, taken in the battle region after Von Hindenburg's "victorious retreat." The ruin and desolation in the Somme the Oise and on the Aisne are pictured in all their appalling tragedy. Shattered villages, blown up bridges, devastated orchards and every imaginable form of vandalism that may be inflicted upon mere property are shown. Occasional peasants are seen among the ruins and this gives a human touch to the views. Armies on the march and big guns in action are also shown. A strong subject of the kind.

THE DESPERATE CHANCE (Pathe), Sept. 23.—Episode No. 12 of "The Fatal Ring." Numerous events of stirring interest occur in this instalment. Pearl struggles with Carslake on top of a swiftly moving passenger train, which both leave in a daring manner. Tom Carlton proposes to her after some pleasing comedy scenes. In the final reel "The Spider" and his gang join Pearl in pursuit of Carslake and some thrilling roof-top scenes take place.

UNDER FALSE COLORS (Thanhouser-Pathe), Sept. 23.—An "up-to-the-minute" five-reel subject, by Lloyd Lonergan, featuring Frederick Warde and Jeanne Eagles. The story concerns the recent Russian revolution and the scenes are laid in Petrograd and America. This has a good, dramatic plot and is presented by a strong cast. Reviewed at length elsewhere.

PINCHED (Pathe), Sept. 23.—A knockabout comic, featuring Harold Lloyd, Harry Pollard and Bebe Daniels. This is full of amusing small business, which brings numerous laughs. The chief scenes occur in a park and later in a jail, where the leading character finds himself a prisoner. A good light subject.

EMBROIDERY MAKING (Pathe), Sept. 23.—An instructive industrial subject, demonstrating the way in which embroideries are made by machine processes. This is gone into thoroughly and watching it is as good as a trip to the factory itself. A good half reel subject.

THE TANK (Pathe), Sept. 23.—An amusing half reel comic, by F. Opper. This picture in animated drawings the adventures of "Happy Hooligan" with a fearful and wonderful new invention, for making war, though the action is not sanguinary. On same reel with above; very amusing.

Peter Pan Film Corporation.

PUSS IN BOOTS (Moy-Toy).—An amusing film version of the well-known fairy tale in which the actors are toys. Puss does all the things that he's supposed to do, including the shedding of wonderful cat tears. This number will be enjoyed by old and young and is really a delightful addition to any program.

Selznick Pictures.

THE FALL OF THE ROMANOFFS (Brenon).—Herbert Brenon has made a fine production of this eight-part historical subject, which he calls a picture novel. Rasputin, the false prophet who helped to cause

the downfall of the Emperor of Russia, is the leading character. The cast contains a long list of prominent names. The picture is reviewed at length on page 1850 of the issue of Sept. 22.

Triangle Film Corporation.

MOUNTAIN DEW, Sept. 9.—A story of the Kentucky Cumberlands, this five-part photoplay, featuring Margery Wilson, is acted and produced with credit to all concerned. A longer review is printed on another page of this issue.

POLLY ANN, Sept. 9.—Bessie Love has the same part in this five-reel comedy-drama, the scenes of which are laid in a New England village. The star is as engaging as ever and plays a little orphan who comes out on top at the finish. Reviewed at length on page 1857 of the issue of Sept. 22.

FLYING COLORS, Sept. 23.—Five-part photoplay with William Desmond as the star, the story is optimistic and tells how a Yale athlete turns detective and captures a gentleman crook and a sweetheart'. Well acted and produced. Reviewed at length on page 1857 of the issue of Sept. 22.

THE BOND OF FEAR.—Belle Bennett and Roy Stewart are the principal actors in this five-part drama which has a number of its scenes laid in the western desert. The story is an unusual one and is given worthy treatment by the director and his associates. A longer review is printed on another page of this issue.

A MAN'S MAN (Paralta).—Seven-part melodrama made from a story by Peter B. Kyne and starring J. Warren Kerrigan, this picture is full of entertainment. A longer review is printed on another page of this issue.

Universal Film Mfg. Company.

ANIMATED WEEKLY, NO. 88 (Universal Special), Sept. 5.—Sinking of Italian boat, the "Sea Wolf," Annette Kellermann performing at Bar Harbor, women trap shooters winning honors in Chicago, war episodes, and cartoons by Hy Mayer are included in this entertaining number.

CURRENT EVENTS, No. 18 (Universal), Sept. 15.—Contains the usual interesting compilation of scenes, including a Missouri girl wearing a million dollars' worth of diamonds, Lucy Freeman firing for swimming championship, and numerous war episodes.

THE TIGHTENING SNARE (Universal Special), Sept. 17.—No. 13 of "The Gray Ghost" serial. In this number the Gray Ghost captures Hildreth and Morn Light on the eve of their wedding, by passing himself off as their chauffeur. He conveys them to an island, where friends pursue them and give battle to the master criminal and his band. The installment is well constructed and very interesting throughout.

THE FOUNTAIN OF TROUBLE (Joker), Rel. Week of Sept. 24.—A comic number, by A. F. Statler, featuring William Franey, Milburne Moranti and Ida Tenbrook. Franey picks up a small white elephant on the beach and wears it on his coat. A gang of pickpockets, thinking he is one of them, pass their booty over to him. This leads to some amusing knockabout situations. A typical number of the kind.

TAKING THEIR MEDICINE (Nestor), Rel. Week of Sept. 24.—This is a one-reel Western comedy with Edith Roberts, Eddie Lyons, Lee Moran and Fred Gamble. When the girl visits the ranch, all the cowboys pretend to be sick so that they may be nursed by her. Her father fixes up a combination of castor oil and worm medicine for her to administer. This is a very funny comedy.

MARBLE HEADS (Joker), Rel. Week of Sept. 24.—A comic number, by Tom Gibson, featuring Gale Henry, William Franey, Milton Sims and Milburne Moranti. This number is very amusing. Gale appears as a lady art collector who buys a statue for her garden fete. Franey and Moranti pose after the statue has been broken. A familiar idea worked up in a new and enjoyable way.

YOUR BOY AND MINE (Victor), Rel. Week of Sept. 4.—A one-reel get all four parents scrapping. But in the end all make up. The number is a fairly interesting one. Several well-known rural types are burlesqued. The cast includes Lincoln Stedman, Elwood Bredell, Hal Wilson and William Dyer.

THE MASTER SPY (Gold Seal), Rel. Week of Sept. 24.—An episode of the "Perils of the Secret Service" series, by George Bronson Howard. An excellent adventure subject, with the present war as a background. Kingsley Benedict gives a stirring performance as the bearer of a secret message, trying to escape to England. The events pictured are exceptionally vivid and exciting. One of the best of the series.

A ROMANY ROSE (Star Featurette), Rel. Week of Sept. 24.—This is the story of a gypsy girl, played by little Lena Baskette, who shows herself to be an excellent child actress. The girl is sold by her father to an old bachelor. He takes good care of her. But the gypsy father being short of money, attempts to steal his daughter back to put her on the vaudeville stage. This is a good picture for children.

THE DYNAMITE SPECIAL (Bison). Rel. Week of Sept. 24.—A two-reel railroad yarn of an absorbing type, by T. Shelley Sutton. Helen Gibson is seen at her best in this, catching a wild engine by means of a motorcycle. She halts the engine and avoids a collision. The suspense is excellent. The story interest is also good. Others in the cast are Mark Fenton, Al Harris, Millard K. Wilson and Val Paul.

AT BAY (Universal Special), Sept. 24.—No. 14 of 'The Gray Ghost" series. This opens with a continuation of the fight on the island house between friends of Hildreth and Morn Light and the members of the Gray Ghost band. Jean rescues the captives from the burning house. The number contains various thrilling episodes, and as the serial draws to a close the net can be seen tightening about the criminals.

World Film Corporation

BETSY ROSS (Peerless), Sept. 17.—Alice Brady has the title role in this five-part drama, which is built around the making of the first American flag. The story is melodramatic and several historical characters appear in it. A longer review is printed on page 1850 of the issue of Sept. 22.

THE WOMAN BENEATH (Peerless), Sept. 24.—Ethel Clayton and Curtis Coxey have the leading roles in this five-part photoplay, which tells a conventional but interesting story, and is well acted and produced. A longer review is printed on another page of this issue.

RASPUTIN, THE BLACK MONK (Brady), September.—An eight-part production based on events in the history of Russia previous to the revolution, and with which Rasputin was associated. The picture is well made and as a whole be expected is fraught with the tensest sort of drama. A full review of the production will be found elsewhere.

Russian War Films For State Rights

Overland Film Company Distributing Revolution Films for New Russian Pictures Corporation.

THE New Russian Pictures Corporation has bought the films of the Russian revolution and war, which were imported last month by the Skobeloff committee, and the receipts of which have gone toward the relief of Russian soldiers and prisoners of war. These pictures are said to be the sole record of one of the greatest events in the history of the human race, the living memorial of a great people, for centuries under the yoke of tyranny, at last rising to the realization of their power, and overthrowing the most autocratic government in the world. They show the Russian people at war, first under the rule of the Romanoffs, with the country honeycombed with Teutonic intrigue and later genuinely fighting for their Fatherland under a cleansed and popular administration. They are the only official pictures of these great events.

They are not merely a record of historical events, but the human, flesh-and-blood story of the struggle of the Russian people; pictures which will enable the people of this country to better understand the tremendous forces at work in the Russian mind, the inspired courage and devotion to duty in the hearts of these soldiers of the people. Millions of people swarm the streets of Petrograd, wild with joy in their new-found liberty, and hundreds of thousands follow in stately procession the bodies of their comrades who gave their lives that the New Russia might live.

Samuel Rothapfel, director of the Rialto theater, New York, dropped the regular program in favor of the pictures, which made up the bill for an entire week. The Eighty-first Street theater, New York, has been quick to follow his example, and last week gave over their entire program to the showing of these pictures.

The Overland Film Company is distributing them for the New Russian organization, and Samuel Krellberg, president of the former company, states that there already has been a large demand for territorial rights. The pictures are being sold on the state rights market. Mr. Krellberg said that he was having several new prints made to fill the present demand, and that one would shortly be presented to the government and also to one of the country's great historical societies, to be preserved as a permanent record of these stupendous events.

Harry Berg, sales manager of the Overland Company, has started on a trip across the continent, covering the various film centers in the interests of the pictures.

ROBARDS EAST WITH "MOTHERS OF MEN."

Willis Robards, actor-director and manager of the Robards Players, has come East with what is said to be one of the most remarkable pictures yet produced. The story and scenario of the picture, which is entitled "Mothers of Men," was written by Hal Reid, one of the ablest of the present day photoplay writers. It is on the order of suffrage propaganda, based on the election of a woman to the governorship of a Western state and of her finding herself in the position of having to pass judgment upon her husband, accused of murder. A series of complications develops and in their unraveling a story has been constructed.

The cast includes such notables as Dorothy Davenport, Katherine Griffith, Willis Robards, Mr. and Mrs. Hal Reid and others. It is a six-reel picture of the very highest grade in respect to acting, directing and photography.

Willis Robards, the director, is most enthusiastic about his future, for it has been particularly well received at several private showings. Mr. Robards feels confident that it will be a brilliant success.

BOBBY BUMPS STARTS FOR SCHOOL.

In the eighty-fifth release of Paramount-Bray Pictograph, the "magazine-on-the-screen," an adventure which goes down in the life of every youngster, is the saddest in his career, the first day at school, furnishes the material for another of the famous Bobby Bumps series of animated cartoons, and this promises to be the funniest that Earl Hurd, artist and humorist, has contributed.

Two Directors For Bushman and Bayne

Stars Not to Lose Time Between Pictures—Brabin and Carewe the Directors.

FRANCIS X. BUSHMAN, Metro star, will begin immediately on a double director system, whereby he will not lose a moment's time between productions. First under one director and then under another, he and his co-star, Beverly Bayne, will keep constantly busy. Under the new system, to be inaugurated at once by Maxwell Karger, general manager of the Metro studio, one of Metro's directing staff will complete the direction of one Super-Feature and another will begin at once on the direction of the next production. The first director will retire into the inner chambers of the studio to cut and assemble his picture, watch it as shown in the projection room, O. K. the finished proof, and make arrangements for his next picture.

In illustration of this plan Mr. Bushman and Miss Bayne are at present completing work under the direction of Charles Brabin on the production of "God's Outlaw," a screen version of Max Brand's story to appear simultaneously with its release in the All-Story Weekly. Immediately thereafter the two stars will begin work under the direction of Edwin Carewe on a new feature production to be called "The Voice of Conscience." It has been written by Finis Fox, author of "The Jury of Fate," a recent Metro wonderplay starring Mabel Taliaferro. Mr. Fox is a brother of Edwin Carewe, the director, and will be associated with him in this production as co-director. "The Voice of Conscience" is a Southern story, part of the scene being on a cotton plantation. In it Mr. Bushman plays a dual role of an entirely new type.

Gladys Hulette Heads Pathe Program

She Appears in "A Crooked Romance," a Five-Reel Feature—Serials and Single Reels Complete the List for Week of September.

GLADYS HULETTE will again appear as the feature player of Pathe's program for the week of September 30, and the other box office stars on the same program are Mollie King, Pearl White and Harold Lloyd. Miss Hulette is seen in a five-reel feature produced by the Astra Film Corporation under direction of William Parke, and entitled "A Crook of Romance." It is stated that this will probably be even more popular than any Gladys Hulette pictures yet because it has every element that appeals to the public, and because it has in the splendid supporting cast Paul Clerget, one of the most famous actors of France, who recently came to this country and made a hit in "Pierrot the Prodigal," which was produced by Winthrop Ames, and was one of the big successes of last season. There is also J. H. Gilmour and William Parke, Jr., in addition to a number of other well-known players in lesser roles. "A Crooked Romance" is comedy-drama, with a touch of "fantasy" that would do credit to J. M. Barrie.

Mollie King is starred in the third episode of the "Seven Pearls" serial entitled "The Air Peril." She is supported by Creighton Hale and Leon Bary.

This chapter has one of the biggest thrills ever seen on the screen. Mollie King is tied to a balloon by a rope, which is being slowly eaten away by acid. Creighton Hale attempts to rescue her in an aeroplane, and his efforts are combatted by the villain in another machine.

"A Dash for Arabia" is the title of the thirteenth episode of "The Fatal Ring," in which Pearl White stars.

In this chapter, Pearl and Carslake are discovered struggling on a beam between two roofs in midair. In a thrilling manner Pearl escapes. Carslake starts for Arabia, where he expects to use the power given him by the Violet Diamond. He is followed by Pearl, Tom Carleton and the Spider. Pearl is shanghaied, but jumps overboard. Sailors bribed by Carslake pursue her. Tom Carleton and the Spider race to her rescue in a motorboat. The steering gear breaks after they have succeeded in getting Pearl into the boat. They find themselves in the path of a swiftly approaching ferry boat, and Pearl is taken up in the paddle wheel to what looks like certain death as the picture fades out.

"By the Sad Sea Waves" is a one-reel Girl Show, with Harold Lloyd, Harry Pollard, and Bebe Daniels. It is one thousand feet of laughs, girls and prize winning bathing suits.

"The American Switzerland" (Glacier National Park) is a scenic release produced by Ralph Earle, and showing the most beautiful spots in the "Alps of the U. S. A."

An International Cartoon and Scenic split reel subject and Hearst-Pathe News No. 80 and 81 complete this program.

DAVID STERN COMPANY IN NEW HOME.

David Stern Company, dealers in cameras and accessories, formerly at 1047 West Madison street, Chicago, Ill., have recently moved to a new four-story building at 1027-1029 Madison street. The new building has 10,000 square feet of floor space, with a dark room on every floor and a testing room with lens charts on the second floor. The firm's stock of cameras, lenses, plates, paper and other accessories is complete, and mail orders are handled without delay.

State Rights Department

Conducted by BEN H. GRIMM

Independent Producers Organize

Form Producers' Protective Association—Headed by William L. Sherrill—Purpose Is Regulation of State Rights Field.

FOURTEEN independent state rights producers on Wednesday, September 12, met and formed the Producers' Protective Association, an organization whose avowed purpose is to "regulate the state rights field." The meeting was held at the offices of William L. Sherrill, president of the Frohman Amusement Corporation. The certificate of incorporation was presented and accepted, as also were the by-laws under which the organization will operate.

The following were elected directors for the first year: William L. Sherrill, Leopold Wharton, Harry Rapf, Jesse J. Goldburg and I. N. Chadwick. It is expected that one of the directors will withdraw from that position at the next meeting and that M. A. Schlesinger, of the Mayfair Film Corporation, will take his place on the board. It is also understood that one of the officers will withdraw as such in favor of Mr. Schlesinger. The officers elected Wednesday night were William L. Sherrill, president; Leopold Wharton, vice president, and Jesse J. Goldburg, secretary and treasurer.

The objects of the new organization are radical and far-reaching. They tend toward the complete systematization of state rights producing and distributing.

The organization was conceived by Mr. Sherrill and was prompted by the unsettled state of business and the doubtful aspect with which banking institutions doing business with state rights producers view the present manner of conducting and regulating the sales market of independent attractions.

The business affairs of the organization will be in the hands of a board of directors of five headed by the president of the association. The by-laws contain, among others, the following provisions, as objects of the association:

"To regulate the medium of advertising, the members agreeing not to patronize any publication, lithographer, printer, slide manufacturer, engraver or any other concern unless such publication or concern has been listed with the association as one worthy of the patronage of the members of the association.

"To pass upon all grievances of members against any person, concern or corporation, and in the event of the complaint being sustained, the members of the association agree not to employ or do business with such person, firm or corporation. This applies to commercial institutions, trade publications, actors, directors, as well as state rights buyers." (The by-laws do not provide for any hearing to the person or firm against whom a complaint is lodged.)

"The employment of outside brokers for the sale or leasing of the productions of members is prohibited.

"A complete record of all transactions with state rights buyers on the part of members of the association is to be kept to the end that a commercial rating may be had, and the failure of any exchange to live up to its obligation will prevent it from doing business with any other member in the future.

"A central sales exchange is to be established. All productions of the members must be listed on the floor of the association, with territory open and price asked. All productions will be sold by the association for the benefit of its members. A print of each production, with a complete line of advertising matters, must be deposited with the manager of the association, who will have charge of the sales. A percentage of the gross receipts on all productions of a member is payable to the association."

Mr. Sherrill made the following statement as to the future intended operations of the association:

"We have aimed primarily to systematize our business. At present the disposition of state rights production is without a head or tail. We intend encouraging the state rights buyer to assist him in the operation of a legitimate business, but where any given territory is without any buyer with whom we can deal we intend ultimately to open our own producers' exchange in that territory. We are fortifying ourselves against every contingency by the accumulation of a treasury that can meet every new circumstance as it may arise. You can compute the amount in back of this association when I tell you that the average number of productions of the present membership of fourteen is a minimum of five a year, and the minimum average receipts on each production is $50,000. This makes a gross return on the productions of the members of $700,000 annually, and the percentage due the association will amount to a minimum of $35,000, a sum sufficient not alone to establish exchanges but to meet every contingency.

"And, of course, as we live we expect to grow. Other state rights producers will join us. But for the present we have sufficient to know we are a going institution to be reckoned with, and one that will cure, I hope, many of the evils of the motion picture business. We are not in opposition to any other organization but rather in the spirit of good and welfare do we desire to co-operate with them in their legitimate endeavors."

Mr. Sherrill also stated that the organization was going to obtain the services of the ablest man possible, who will become manager of the central exchange. In this exchange will be offices for out-of-town buyers, a projection room, and other conveniences—factors that will make it possible for the buyer to look over virtually every picture produced which is available for his territory.

Another object of the organization will be the active and hearty discouragement of "illegitimate" pictures—pictures that are freaks and which are produced sometimes by unscrupulous persons who hope to clean up quick and get away. In fact, the chief objective of the producers is the stabilization of the state rights field.

Those concerns which are listed as members in the new organization are: The Frohman Amusement Corporation, Wharton, Inc., Mayfair Film Corporation, A. H. Jacobs Photoplays, Inc., Harry Rapf, Edward Warren Productions, W. R. Rothacker, Arrow Film Corporation, Cosmopterfilm, Ivan Film Productions, Inc., Duplex Film Corporation, Crystal Film Corporation, Ogden Pictures Corporation and Author's Film Corporation.

Kopfstein Made Foreign Buyers' Head.

Elected Managing Director of Recently Formed Foreign Film Buyers' Association.

AT a meeting held at the Hotel Astor, New York, on Thursday, September 13, at which a majority of the members of the Foreign Film Buyers' Association were present, it was unanimously decided that Jacques Kopfstein be empowered to transact all business for the association in connection with the screening and purchasing of films for the foreign market. The official title voted upon Mr. Kopfstein was that of managing director.

The representatives of the foreign buyers' association present expressed gratification at the manner in which the association was being rounded into shape, and cables from the firms which they represent were read-at-the-meeting, the tenor of which expressed great satisfaction in the forming of the new body.

The question of the embargo on foreign shipments of American films was discussed, and Mr. Kopfstein was empowered to appoint a committee to cope with this problem. L. R. Thomas was delegated by the association to take the matter up in Washington with the proper individuals, and immediately left for that city.

The question of arranging proper banking connections to facilitate the transfers of credits was also brought up, and Mr. Kopfstein reported that he had taken this matter up with various banks and that they thought favorably of the plan and only awaited more specific details before going further into the matter. Several new buyers made application for membership in the body.

KING-BEE TO THE COAST.

The demand for the King-Bee brand of comedies featuring Billy West is so great that the studio at Bayonne will be vacated next month and the entire organization will be taken to the King-Bee studios in Los Angeles, where they will work night and day to supply the demand for these popular two-reelers.

President Burstein will accompany the company, which will, have a special pullman and baggage car. In the roster are Babe Hardy, Lew White, Bud Ross, Ethel Gibson, Harry Cooper, Martha Dean, Jackie Jackson, Sam LeRose and Ellen Burford. Arvid Gillstrom, director of these comedies, will leave a week earlier.

While on the coast the King-Bee will make in conjunction with their two-reel comedies a special five-reel feature entitled "King Soloman," with the inimitable Billy West in the title role.

LESSER BUYS "MAD LOVER" AND "TODAY."

All Star Features Distributors, Inc., of which Sol. Lesser is the head, has obtained from Pathe the rights to "The Mad Lover" and "Today" for California, Nevada and Arizona. Mr. Lesser states that these two Pathe pictures should break all records in his states. He ranks these pictures very high from every commercial standpoint.

"Grain of Dust" Next Ogden Picture

Lillian Walker to Star in Screen Version of David Graham Phillips' Best Novel.

A CONTRACT was signed by the Ogden Pictures Corporation with the estate of David Graham Phillips, James K. Hackett and the American Play Company, through their representative, Edgar Selden, whereby the Ogden Pictures Corporation receives the world's motion picture rights to David Graham Phillips' most popular novel, "The Grain of Dust."

Lillian Walker, the star of the Ogden Pictures Corporation, will portray the title role.

"The Grain of Dust" is considered the high-water mark of the late David Graham Phillips' novelistic achievement, and the circulation of that novel has exceeded any other published in the past ten years. The story ran serially in the Saturday Evening Post.

"In purchasing the screen rights to 'The Grain of Dust,'" said Albert Scowcroft, president of the Ogden Pictures Corporation, "we are merely carrying out our announced policy of doing the biggest things in the biggest possible way. We are striving to visualize those works of literature which have met the popular approval of men and women the world over and we feel that in acquiring the rights to 'The Grain of Dust' we are adhering to our announced purpose. In these days of extraordinary photoplay attractions where the release of one seems to top the unusual production of the day before, producers are hard put to it to keep pace with the rapid strides of other ambitious producers, to say nothing of excelling them, but we pride ourselves in being able to announce the coming screening of such a wonderful novel as David Graham Phillips' masterpiece, 'The Grain of Dust.'"

SUPREME GETS THREE BIG FILMS.

With the acquisition of three stellar productions—Evelyn Nesbit and her son, Russell Thaw, in "Redemption," William S. Hart in "The Cold Deck," and H. B. Warner in "God's Man," the Supreme Photo-Play Productions of Pittsburgh, Pa., now rank as not only one of the largest individual feature productions exchange in Pennsylvania, but one of the biggest in the United States.

Much credit is due Harry F. Grelle, the general manager, for the phenomenal growth of this concern. Starting in humble quarters on Fourth avenue several years ago, the growth of this company was rapid until today the exchange occupies the fourth floor of the Seltzer building and is the mecca for visiting exhibitors from all over western Pennsylvania and West Virginia.

The Pittsburgh exchange, in addition to looking out for the entire western Pennsylvania territory, also books West Virginia. Among the big productions controlled by this company are the following: "The Masque of Life," "Idle Wives," "The Dumb Girl of Portici," "The Unwritten Law," "The Ne'er Do Well," "The Spoilers," "The Cold Deck," "God's Man" and "Redemption."

"OVER THERE" COMPLETED BY RICHMAN.

The Charles Richman Pictures Corporation has just completed its first picture, entitled "Over There." The title is used through the courtesy of George M. Cohan and is the same as his internationally popular song.

James Kirkwood, formerly director for Mary Pickford, directed the picture, and the cast includes, besides Mr. Richman, Anna Q. Nilsson, Walter McGrail, Gertrude Berkeley, Walter Hiers, Veta Searl and James A. Purey.

The trench and battle scenes were supervised by Lieut. W. A. O'Hara, of the 24th Battalion, Canadian Expeditionary Force, who spent several months in the trenches in France and actively participated in the famous battles of Somme, Ypres and Vimy. It is said that the battle scenes are unusually realistic and thrilling.

MORE "SOULS REDEEMED" TERRITORY SOLD.

Edward Warren reports the sale of the following territories for "Souls Redeemed" (The Warfare of the Flesh) Louisiana, to Pearce & Son, of New Orleans; Eastern Pennsylvania and Southern New Jersey, to The Ideal Film Exchange of Philadelphia; Texas, Oklahoma and Arkansas, to Southwestern Art Dramas, Inc., of Dallas; Michigan and Ohio, to Tri-State Film Exchange, of Detroit; Greater New York, to Elk Photoplays, New York, and Up-State New York to Veribest Pictures, Inc., of 47 West Swan street, Buffalo.

The foreign rights have been taken over by The Piedmont Pictures Corporation, so that practically the entire world rights have been disposed of.

DALLAS FIRM GETS "BABBLING TONGUES."

True T. Thompson and David Reed, of the True Film Company, 1911½ Commerce street, Dallas, Tex., have contracted with Ivan Film Productions, Inc., to distribute "Babbling Tongues" in Oklahoma, Arkansas and Louisiana. Mr. Thompson and Mr. Reed express confidence that the production will be welcomed heartily by exhibitors in the territory.

"Warrior" Now in Seven Reels

Big Spectacular Subject Improved by Cutting—Will Be Released on State Rights Plan.

THE General Enterprises, Inc., gave a second showing of "The Warrior" on Wednesday noon, Sept. 12, in New York, exclusively to the press. The picture originally was shown in nine reels. Since then it has been re-edited and trimmed to seven reels, making a great improvement, condensing the action to complete and continuous picturization of a good story, magnificent Alpine scenery and thrilling situations. Maciste does deeds of daring and strength that were thought impossible. In short, "The Warrior" is a human appeal to emotions and faculties that need exercising to make us feel we are alive.

After the showing the audience was invited to a luncheon at Rector's as the guests of Messrs. Sawyer and Lubin. Those who attended were: Lawrence Reid, New York Review; Charles Condon, Motography; T. O. Eltonhead, Exhibitors' Trade Review; Charles Geigerich, New York Clipper; Sam Spedon, Moving Picture World; Fritz Tidden, Dramatic Mirror; Miss Laura Hostetter, The Billboard; Milton Lowenthal, Theatre Magazine; Mr. Gold, New York Star; James Beecroft, Exhibitors' Herald; George Worts, Motion Picture News; Jake Gerhardt, Dramatic Mirror; Aileen St. John Brenon, Morning Telegraph; Harold Rendall, New York Review; Joshua Lowe, Variety; Bert Ennis, press agent for "The Warrior."

JULES BURNSTEIN LAUNCHES "SHAME."

With the Jimmy Dale serial well on its way to prosperity through the Mutual exchanges, Jules Burnstein is rapidly greasing the ways for the launching of the recently completed John W. Noble picture, "Shame," which will be distributed on the state rights basis.

Mr. Burnstein, whose record as a motion picture distributing expert includes long terms as manager of the Mutual and Pathe exchanges, respectively, has been devoting his time exclusively to the E. K. Lincoln Grey Seal Serial since the starting of the popular set of pictures early last spring.

Few men have made a deeper study of the exchange end of the motion picture business than Mr. Burnstein. Equipped with a valuable business training and blessed with a strong and winning personality, he took his place among the leaders when the art was still young and has kept in intimate touch with the many problems of film distribution during the constantly changing conditions of the industry ever since. As the manager of two of the largest exchanges his wide acquaintance includes active motion picture men in every city of the country, and his frequent trips to the large film centres are always signals for impromptu reunions.

The news that Mr. Burnstein is arranging for the launching of the special state rights picture "Shame," added to the fact that it is a seven-reel John W. Noble feature, speaks volumes for its importance as a production.

GLUCKSMANN OPENS OFFICE IN NEW YORK.

Max Glucksmann, of Buenos Aires, one of the largest film buyers of South America, has established a permanent New York office under the supervision of his brother, Jacobo, at 110 West Fortieth street, New York. The house of Max Glucksmann is one of the largest exchanges operating in Argentine, Uruguay, Paraguay and Chile. It controls the exclusive rights in this territory for the Pathe, American, Signal, Selznick, Kalem and Essanay pictures, of American make, and also a number of French and Italian brands.

On opening his New York office Mr. Glucksmann said: "We have long been represented in the United States by one of the best buyers and judges of film in the country, but we realize the strong demand for American pictures in our territory and believe it best to locate here permanently. I have just closed a big deal with the Speer Carbon Company for the exclusive rights on their product in Argentine, Uruguay, Paraguay and Chile, and invite offers from producers and manufacturers at my new office."

"WEAVERS OF LIFE" NEXT WARREN PICTURE.

Edward Warren has decided on "Weavers of Life" as the title for his forthcoming feature. The title is characteristic of the play itself, being justified by an allegorical reference delicately interspersed in the picture.

The art direction, like in the "Warfare of the Flesh," is under the able direction of Mrs. Warren.

Besides the star, Helen Hayes, whom Mr. Warren considers a real find, the cast contains Howard Hall, Kenneth Hunter, Barney Gilmore, Earl Schenck, Edna Hibbard and others, all especially selected to portray their individual parts.

TURNER & DAHNKEN BUY "LUST OF THE AGES."

Turner & Dahnken, of San Francisco, through Bruce Johnson, secretary and general manager of that firm, have purchased the rights for California, Arizona and Nevada, and the Hawaiian Islands from the Ogden Film Corporation "The Lust of the Ages."

Patch Decries Broadway Runs

Distributor of "The Italian Battlefront," Declares Forced and Inflated Runs Are Absolute Misrepresentation.

A BROADWAY showing continued beyond the period of the natural drawing powers of a production in order to impress the trade is neither good business judgment nor good ethics, in the opinion of William Moore Patch. Mr. Patch, who recently entered the New York field as the distributor of the Italian War pictures, "The Italian Battlefront," which are being presented in important cities throughout the country, is also president and general manager of the Fort Pitt Theater Company, of Pittsburgh.

"It scarcely would be becoming of me, as a distributor, to criticise the policies of contemporary distributors," said Mr. Patch. "As a moving picture theater owner, however, striving to maintain a standard for my house that will compete with the prices and appeal of theaters showing legitimate attractions, naturally I am affected by any inflated or fictitious values.

"Perhaps that last phrase is too strong to apply to productions that are put on Broadway at enormous cost and kept there long after they cease to pay expenses simply to create an impression; but it seems to me that that is as deliberate a misrepresentation as for a merchant to advertise cotton as wool, or for a grocer to short-weight a customer.

"Despite the fact that exaggeration has become such an obsession with us that no one credits anyone's claims, when our turn comes we insist upon deluding ourselves that we can 'get away with it.' This condition has become so general that a real statement of facts, if at all unusual, is given no credence.

"It is a serious condition where business men cannot accept, with reasonable and rational assurance, the statements of other business men as to the value of a given product—serious, not only to the man who is 'taken in' by unfounded claims, but equally as serious to the man, who, because of unfortunate previous experiences, is skeptical even of that which is not overrated, and, therefore, loses the money which he might have made if he had been able to distinguish between the real and the false.

"And now on top of this costly chaos, we have the very marked tendency to add further confustion to the difficulty which already exists by forced and inflated runs along Broadway. For the life of me I cannot see either the commercial justice nor the business advantage to either distributors or exhibitors or promoters deliberately accepting a loss of thousands of dollars in the forlorn hope that the fact that their picture occupied a theater on Broadway for a given number of weeks will induce exhibitors to book that picture.

"It is, it seems to me at least, the most foolish of practices—one that deceives no one except the poor promoters themselves —for bad news travels quicker in the moving picture industry than it can by wireless, and everyone in the country who keeps his fingers on the pulse of things at all knows instantly the real status of the run—whether it is 'starving-to-death,' 'breaking even,' or 'making money.' And yet the idea that it can be 'put over' prevails.

"Years ago, in the legitimate field, a real Broadway run was worth a fortune in prestige and profits. Not so today. The canny legitimate manager plays his offering on Broadway as l-ng as it makes money—and no longer. There are a few who still defy all the laws of economics, in the hope that they will get it back on the road, but these are fast becoming rarities.

'Broadway no longer possesses the magic spell for the rest cf the country that it once did, particularly in the case of moving picture audiences and moving picture theater owners."

"WARRIOR" SHOWN FOR RED CROSS.

Through the courtesy of A. H. Sawyer and Herbert Lubin, of General Enterprises, Inc, the cause of the Red Cross was aided materially on Wednesday, September 4, by a showing of "The Warrior," the film spectacle starring Maciste, giant hero of Gabriele D'Annunzio's "Cabiria." The occasion was a special entertainment of the Nassau County Red Cross Society, an important branch of the official parent body, held at Oyster Bay Reformed Church, Oyster Bay, Long Island.

The Reverend William H. Jackson, a prominent clergyman of the city, and member of the staff of the Moving Picture World, was in charge of the affair, and selected "The Warrior" as a particularly fitting film for exhibition at the Red Cross gathering. It may be remarked in passing that one-third of the expenses incurred through the making of bandages, etc., for the American expeditionary force by the Oyster Bay branch of the society have been earned through the exhibition of motion pictures. Mr. Jackson commented upon the readiness with which all his requests for pictures have been met by the various film producers and distributors.

AUSTRALASIAN BUYS "BOUGHT AND PAID FOR."

Hiller & Wilk, Inc., have arranged for the sale of "Bought and Paid For" for Australia and New Zealand, to the Australasian Films, Ltd. "Bought and Paid For" was a big hit in Australia when produced as a stage play, creating a record of ten-weeks at Sydney.

Hall Sells Circuit Franchise

L. S. Card Booking Corporation the Purchaser—Will Distribute First National Circuit's Pictures in Jersey.

WITH the forming of the L. S. Card Booking Corporation to distribute the Chaplin pictures in New Jersey comes to light the fact that Frank Hall, the prominent New Jersey exhibitor who last spring closed deals for Edgar Lewis' first special feature, "The Bar Sinister," and Edwin Carewe's Jane Grey production, "Her Fighting Chance," sold his franchise in the First National Exhibitors Circuit, Inc., for $32,000. Less than two months before Mr. Hall disposed of the New Jersey franchise he paid exactly $1,750 for it.

The New Jersey franchise for the First National Exhibitors' Circuit, Inc., was purchased by the L. S. Card Booking Corporation, formed for the express purpose of distributing the Chaplin comedies and other productions purchased by the First National. L. S. Card, whose name the new company bears, has been associated with Frank Hall for the past year as manager of his Civilization Film Corporation, booking "Joan the Woman," "Civilization," "The Whip" and other special features in New Jersey from its headquarters in Newark. Mr. Card is well known in motion picture circles, especially in New Jersey, where he served the Mutual Film Corporation as manager of their Newark exchange for several years.

Closely associated with Mr. Card in the new company will be Edward Church, also of the Civilization Film Corporation, and associated with Mr. Hall in an executive capacity for the past year. Mr. Church, who was prominent in the New York office of the General Film Company from the early days of the motion picture industry until he resigned from that organization two years ago, is one of the most widely experienced exchange men in the business and is co-operating with Mr. Card in working out a plan for Chaplin distribution in New Jersey which he believes will make the L. S. Card Booking Corporation one of the most popular exchanges in the state.

HOFFMAN BUYS "GREAT WHITE TRAIL."

"The Great White Trail" has been acquired from Wharton, Inc., by M. H. Hoffman, Inc. Contracts were signed which transfer the entire American rights to this feature—exclusive of Canada.

M. H. Hoffman is jubilant over his latest acquisition. "It is a picture which is truly 'Foursquare,'" he said. "Artistically it will exert a widespread appeal because the story is as clean and straightforward as the snow in the wonderful scenes depicted in Wharton's 'locations.'

BRENON'S ILIODOR PICTURE READY.

Following close on the heels of its initial presentation to a big invitation audience at the Ritz-Carlton Hotel, New York, Herbert Brenon's gigantic historical panorama, "The Fall of the Romanoffs," depicting the collapse of the Russian autocracy, and all of the developments since the abdication of the Czar, is now offered for sale on a territorial rights basis. Buyers of motion pictures who invariably and properly judge pictures by their possibilities for immediate profits are vitally interested in this, by all odds the biggest of Herbert Brenon productions.

CUMMINS MAKES SEVERAL SALES.

Samuel Cummins, film broker, of 1476 Broadway, has been actively engaged recently in closing several film deals for film productions which have been pending. He closed a deal for John Cort on "The Whirl of Life" to Mr. Carlton, for Scandinavia. He also closed a deal for Trans-Oceanic Film Company of a negative to the Phax Pictures Company, and another negative for the Coronet Film Company. Mr. Cummins also has purchased for one of his clients the exclusive rights to "Enlighten Thy Daughter" for Delaware, Maryland, District of Columbia and Virginia.

SAVINI HANDLING MANY FEATURES.

R. M. Savini, of Atlanta, is making rapid strides at the present time handling the following features: "The Land Just Yonder," six parts; "Warning," six parts; "Her Condoned Sin," six parts; "Woman and the Beast," five parts; "Mother Goose," five parts; "Where Cowboy Is King," four parts; "America Is Ready," four parts, and "Lottery Man," five parts. He intends to purchase four or five more features before the fall of the year and he reports business as being exceptionally good and holds great prospects for winter business in the South.

FLAHERTY CHICAGO "FOURSQUARE" MANAGER.

Frank J. Flaherty, for years one of the most successful managers of motion pictures in the west and recently of the Universal, has been engaged to take charge of the Hoffman-Foursquare Exchange in Chicago. His assistant is to be Miss Deborah Finnan, who has long held that position with the Universal Chicago branch.

Manufacturers' Advance Notes

"Aladdin and the Wonderful Lamp"

Famous Arabian Nights Tale to Be Fox Film's Next "Kiddie" Production.

AN AMAZINGLY beautiful film production of "Aladdin and the Wonderful Lamp," the most fascinating perhaps of all the world-classic Arabian Nights' Tales, is announced in a detailed statement from William Fox. The picture is another of the Kiddies Features series which Mr. Fox has

Scene from "Aladdin and the Wonderful Lamp" (Fox).

sponsored, and will begin a run on Broadway soon at the Globe theater.

Francis Carpenter and Virginia Lee Corbin, of "Jack and the Beanstalk" fame, appear in the leading roles of the new cinema—Francis as the son of Mustapha, the tailor, and Virginia as the captivating princess. The production is spectacular in the extreme, and required the services of hundreds of kiddies and the making of countless costumes.

C. M. and S. A. Franklin, who filmed "Jack and the Beanstalk," staged "Aladdin and the Wonderful Lamp." Besides receiving a share of the credit for the children's brilliant dramatic achievements in the new masterpiece, the Franklins have devised a score of ingenious effects in the picture.

The memorable part of the story in which Aladdin rubs the magic lamp and commands the genie who appears to build him a magnificent palace is faithfully reproduced in the photoplay version. A miracle of the screen results in the gradual appearance of a gorgeous structure on the burning sands.

All of the desert scenes are notable because of the splendid photographic record which has been made of them.

From beginning to end the filmed "Aladdin" has a distinct charm. At the very outset the picturegoers are introduced into the wonderful city of old Bagdad. The evening is falling on the Oriental splendor of the ancient mart of the East, and Mohammedans kneel everywhere in prayer.

The Arabs on the heated desert, without the gates, the devout in the Mosques, the powerful in the palaces, and the workers in the bazaars all turn toward Mecca with reverence. Then attention is concentrated on Aladdin.

The genie in "Aladdin" has something of the element of the giant in "Jack and the Beanstalk," and carries out perfectly the impression of being able to do whatever he cares to.

BLACKTON POSTPONES HIS FIRST PARAMOUNT RELEASE.

Rather than be hastened in his productions for Paramount and run the risk of impairing the artistic merit of his photoplays, J. Stuart Blackton has determined to postpone his advent upon the screen as a producer for Paramount. Accordingly, there will be no Blackton production among the Paramount October releases, contrary to a former announcement, and the first Blackton photoplay will not appear until November. Mr. Blackton thereby gains a margin of a full month, which will enable him to conserve to the utmost degree every detail of artistic production in preparing his adaptations of the famous Sir Gilbert Parker novels for the screen.

INDUSTRIAL CONCERNS INSTALLING SIMPLEX.

The National Cash Register Co., Dayton, Ohio, have just added two more Simplex Projectors to their projection equipment, making six Simplex machines now being used by this company.

The selection of Simplex by such well known concerns as the National Cash Register Co., General Chemical Co., Du Pont Powder Co., Larkin Soap Co., Curtis Publishing Co., and others attests to the high esteem in which the Simplex is held by mechanical experts.

The New York State Hospital for the Treatment of Tuberculosis, Ray Brook, N. Y., founded in 1900, for the purpose of giving those having tuberculosis in its early stages an opportunity to recover, have installed a Simplex Projector for the amusement of its guests.

FIRST PARAMOUNT-MACK SENNETT COMEDY FINISHED.

A wire received by Hiram Abrams, president of Paramount Pictures Corporation, from Mack Sennett, in California, imparts the information that the first Paramount-Mack Sennett comedy, "A Bedroom Blunder," is finished, and that he has completed the assembling of the picture.

"I am very happy to state," night-letters Sennett, "that it is a real knockout—a screaming comedy from start to finish, and you can quote me as saying this."

The assembled print was run off before an audience at the studio, and elicited screams of laughter from even those who were more or less impervious to screen humor through long association with pictures of that sort in the making.

"Roping Her Romeo," the next release, is also virtually finished, and will be followed at regular intervals by others of the same type. As each of these comedies will be produced under the personal supervision of Mr. Sennett himself, their excellence is assured, for there is no one in the entire industry better fitted to turn out farcical films than Mack Sennett, who expresses himself as delighted with his new associations,

Scene from "A Bedroom Blunder" (Paramount).

and declares that everything is running with clocklike precision at the studios.

There is no doubt whatever that the Paramount-Mack Sennett comedies will excel anything that has been previously produced of this character—they will be, in brief, the best comedies ever made. The very cream of the companies over which Mack Sennett has held sway has been skimmed for these new productions—every cast is an all-star cast, and every bit of funny "business," every gag, is the result of carefully thought out plan by a director who has made the production of genuinely funny comedies a life study.

The release date and full particulars of "A Bedroom Blunder," first of the new Paramount-Mack Sennett Comedies, will be made public shortly.

U. List for September 24

Headed by New Secret Service Story by Bronson Howard—Five Comedy Novelties and Bison Thriller Completes the Schedule.

THE Master Spy," an episode in the career of Yorke Norroy, secret service agent, written by George Bronson Howard, and directed by Jack Wells, heads Universal's regular schedule of release for the week of September 24th. Kingsley Benedict and Mignon Anderson are the featured players of this stirring Gold Seal drama of life on the border of Russia and Saxonia during the early days of the war.

Yorke Norroy, played by Kingsley Benedict, has secured passports to himself and his fellow agent of the U. S. State Department after considerable difficulty, and is about to leave for home when he is met by John Gaunt, the British agent, with a request to deliver a set of plans of the Saxonia fortresses to Gaunt's superiors in London. Gaunt is in such poor health that he mistrusts his own ability to make the journey, and he tells Norroy that if the documents do not reach their destination he will never be able to collect the two thousand pounds that have been promised him, and his family will be left penniless. Norroy finally agrees to undertake the dangerous mission. The story of the adventures that befall him as a result of his generous impulse provide many blood-stirring scenes to a screen play in which action and vivid characterization are happily blended.

Eddie Lyons and Lee Moran are featured in "Taking Their Medicine," the Nestor comedy to be released Tuesday, September 25th. A burlesque on life as it is lived on the typical cattle ranch of story book and screen is well worked out, with Eddie and Lee the center of the merriment. Edith Roberts, as the belle of the plains, just returned from school, in the cast, also provides her full quota of the entertainment. Fred Palmer prepared the scenario, while Roy Clements is credited with the production.

"Soapsuds and Sirens," a two-reel L-Ko comedy, will be released Wednesday, September 26th, with Gladys Varden, Harry Lorraine, Walter Stephens and Bert Roach in the principal parts. Noel Smith and L. G. Blyston, who are responsible for this merry dissertation upon the craze for classic dancing, have secured several unusual effects in their latest diaphragm-expander. The 31st issue of the Animated Weekly will be released on the same date, containing pictures of the latest and most interesting news events.

Lena Baskette is the star of the dramatic feature scheduled for Thursday, September 27th. "A Romany Rose" is the title of Lena's vehicle, which was written and directed by Myrtle and Marshall Stedman. A number of prominent players appear in support of the little dancing heroine, including Claire McDowell, Charles Hill Mailes, Fred Montague and Nigel Debruiller. The story has to do with a little gypsy girl whose inherent genius as a dancer is exploited by her father without regard for the child's welfare, until fate steps in and changes the course of events.

Widely different in theme is "Marble Heads," the Joker comedy, which will feature Gale Henry and William Franey on the same day. These sure-fire laugh-producers will be shown in a tale which pictures the efforts of an impecunious sculptor to fill the order of a rich patroness who desires two statues for her garden party by whitewashing his two assistants and setting them up on pedestals in place of the real marble gods that were ordered. Tom Gibson and Allen Curtis have done well with script and production, respectively.

Friday, September 28th, will be signalized by the release of an especially good Victor comedy entitled "Your Boy and Mine," in which Lincoln Stedman and Elwood Bredel have the featured roles. The 38th issue of the Universal Screen Magazine will be released on the same date.

Helen Gibson is the star of "The Dynamite Special," the Bison railroad drama, which will be released Saturday, September 29th. The story, which offers Miss Gibson in a strong part, was written by T. Shelley Sutton and George Hively, and produced by J. D. Davis. William Franey will be seen on the same date in a Joker comedy known as "The Fountain of Trouble," written by Arthur F. Statter, and directed by W. W. Beaudine. The 20th issue of Universal Current Events will complete the week's list of releases.

"THE LAST OF THE TROUBADOURS" (General Film).

Handling a tragic climax with such delicate touch as to leave uppermost the humorous atmosphere of unconventional American frontier life, O. Henry wrote in "The Last of the Troubadours" one of his greatest stories. This is the current week's two-reel O. Henry production released through General Film Company as a Broadway Star Feature.

Humorous as is this story is, there exists a pathetic trend throughout it that builds up a mountain of sympathy for the one negative character, Ellison. He is a sheep rancher of the type oppressed by cattle barons, gentle, plodding, patient, peaceful. His fortunes and misfortunes provide the background for the dramatic crises. Nolan Leary has been cast as the Troubadour. Jack Abraham plays Ellison, and S. E. Jennings has the "heavy" role as King James. Dan Duffy is also cast. The production was under the supervision of Dave Smith, who employed actual western atmosphere throughout to make it correct and effective.

JACK PICKFORD AND LOUISE HUFF IN "THE GHOST HOUSE."

Once again that clever and universally approved "kid" duo, Jack Pickford and Louise Huff, will appear in a Paramount picture as co-stars of "The Ghost House," by Beulah Marie Dix. This will be an October release and was directed by William C. DeMille. The story is one wherein the two talented young people find ample opportunity to display their prowess in acting and considering their past performances for Paramount there

Scene from "The Ghost House" (Paramount).

is little doubt that they will achieve another triumph of characterization.

In "The Ghost House" Jack Pickford is a college boy, while Louise Huff is the younger of two great-nieces of an old gardner who inhabits a so-called haunted house, which is left to the girls when the old man dies.

In the supporting cast are many players who are familiar to Paramount audiences through their appearance in numerous plays which have found popular favor. Among them are noted Olga Grey, James Neill, Eugene Pallette, Mrs. Lewis McCord, Horace B. Carpenter, Edythe Chapman, Lillian Leighton and Billy Elmer.

CHAPLIN IN "THE ADVENTURER."

Charlie Chaplin's new picture, "The Adventurer," soon to be released by Mutual, is according to the comedian himself, the picture he has long been trying to achieve. It is an indoor and outdoor story, displaying Mr. Chaplin in the role of a mountain climber as well as in numerous other novel activities.

The motive of "The Adventurer" has to do with the efforts of an unfortunate youth with a sense of humor to escape a horde of pursuers who seem to think it is a part of their business to chase a funny man off the earth. Edna Purviance, who supports Mr. Chaplin in most of his comedies, has plenty to do in luring the inimitable Charles into tight places and in rescuing him after he has become so involved that escape seems impossible.

Talk about fun, Chaplin and his tender feet perambulating the sands of the seashore with unnumerable police and coastguard men on the trail furnish all the fun that can be fixed on a film. The inimitable Charles escapes capture by the narrowest margin dozens of times and eventually emerges from his difficulties, as he always succeeds in doing, right side up with care.

"The Adventurer" is now practically complete, the finishing touches having been added during the last week. More than 20,000 feet of film have been taken in the course of the play's construction. The release date is September 24.

WHERE IS MR. PRICE?

A gentleman representing himself as Roy W. Price, president and treasurer of Park Theater Co., Newton, N. J., succeeded in having two $25 checks cashed by an assistant exchange manager in New York City about ten days ago.

Mr. Price also signed a contract for pictures with this assistant manager, to be played in a new theater. Mr. Price claimed his company was opening up in Hackensack, N. J., and gave as deposit a $40 check, drawn on a Branchville, N. J., bank. This check, together with the two $25 checks, were returned by the bank as forgery.

Mr. Price is about twenty-five years of age, brown hair, blue eyes, heighth 5 ft. 8 in., small scar on right cheek. He claims to have been manager of the Strand theater, Easton, Pa. salesman for Pathe Exchange in Kansas City, Mo., and Detroit, Mich., and Boston salesman for the Metro Exchange.

His whereabouts is desired by the assistant manager of the exchange in question, and if located, kindly communicate with the New York City F. I. L. M. Club, 1482 Broadway.

M. M. MORGAN, Secretary.

New Power's Releases.

The Incandescent Lamp Equipment's Merits Win Recognition at the Safety and Sanitation Exposition.

AT THE Fourth National Safety and Sanitation exposition, held during the week of September 10th, at the Grand Central Palace, New York, one of the drawing features was the program of moving pictures, given twice daily, illustrating safe and unsafe industrial methods and practices.

These pictures were projected by a Power's 6 B equipped with the new incandescent lamp equipment and the excellence of the projection, the ease with which the machine was operated and its extreme portability demonstrated the suitability of the new outfit for church, school and industrial use.

In the Power's booth in the exposition hall a duplicate machine with transformer and switchboard was set up in conjunction with an atmospheric screen, to show the illumination of the incandescent system of lighting.

The 110 volt 7 ampere current at the supply line was transformed to 25 volts 30 amperes, giving 750 watts consumption at the lamp. The switchboard was equipped with an ammeter showing current consumption and permitting the interested observer to see how the outfit was drawing on the supply when the proper illumination was registered on the screen.

The Power Company advises the use of the new system for a throw of from 75 to 80 feet and a picture of from 14 to 15 feet in width and the advantages and capabilities of the outfit as shown evoked much serious interest from visiting manufacturers who are contemplating installing projecting outfits in their plants as an adjunct to their educational systems.

BLUEBIRD FINALLY LIGHTS.

"Anything Once" has been definitely decided upon as the title for the Bluebird in which Franklyn Farnum will appear, Oct. 8, then making his lone-star bow as a stellar Bluebird. When Joseph De Grasse was producing this feature, "The Maverick" was its working title, but for general distribution it was decided that the title would not be illuminating outside of the cattle country. It was changed to "A Fool for Luck," and then the discovery was made that a similar title had been previously copyrighted. Thus for the third and last time, "Anything Once" was selected as the new and permanent title. Isola Forrester and Mann Page wrote "Anything Once," as the second comedy film story of Western life that they have done together. "The Quitter," serving Lionel Barrymore among Metros, was their first collaboration for the screen. Joseph De Grasse who has previously directed Dorothy Phillips produced the feature and Claire Du Brey replaced Brownie Vernon as Mr. Farnum's leading lady. Lon Chaney, who has been one of Miss Phillips' chief supporters, will be featured in "Anything Once" and the other players will include Sam De Grasse, Marjory Lawrence and D. C. Appling.

"SUNDAY IN LAST CHANCE VALLEY" (L-Ko's).

Vin Moore has been directing Myrtle Sterling in L-Ko's for a long time, using all sorts of tricks to surprise laughs from audiences, and has centered in "Sunday in Last Chance Valley" what he declares to be his best efforts. The L-Ko for Oct. 31 is a satire on the methods of a certain evangelist who is now

Scene from "Sunday in Last Chance Valley" (L-Ko).

operating in Los Angeles, giving Director Moore a chance to observe his peculiar methods at close hand.

Al Forbes, Russ Powell and Blance Rose will be the principal's seconds in Myrtle Sterling's leads for laughs. "Sunday in Last Chance Valley" will be pure satire without going into any offensive reflections on the "trail hitters" or their leader. J. G. Blystone, general director of L-Ko's, who supervises all the scenarios and productions, has seen to it that nothing further than comedy reflections on the methods of the evangelist have found reflection upon the screen.

JULIA SANDERSON IN "THE RUNAWAY."

Miss Julia Sanderson, one of the best known stars of the American stage, who was a big hit in "The Siren," as Lolette, at the Knickerbocker theater, New York, and as Dora Dale in "The Sunshine Girl," at the same theater, makes her screen bow as Alice Avery in "The Runaway," Empire All Star productions, scheduled for release September 24th, by the Mutual Film Corporation.

"The Runaway" is a comedy adapted for the American stage by Michael Morton. It had a successful run at the Lyceum

Scene from "The Runaway" (Mutual).

theater, New York, and is considered one of the best of the Charles Frohman offerings under a Mutual-Frohman contract, which provides for the presentation of Charles Frohman plays in photodrama with a majority of the original casts.

Miss Sanderson is the daughter of Albert Sackett, a well known American actor. She made her debut on the Philadelphia stage and later scored success as Mrs. Pineapple in "A Chinese Honeymoon" and as Matay with DeWolf Hopper in "Wang." Her most recent speaking stage successes were as Kitty Gray in "The Arcadians" and "The Siren" in the Sunshine Girl.

Miss Sanderson as Alice is given a part that suits her admirably and one that permits her to display her widely recognized versatility. There is a splendid cast, including performers as well known as Ada St. Claire, Dora Plowden, Jennie Ellison, Norman Trevor, Re McDougall and Edward Fielding.

"UNTO THE END" (Horsley).

"Unto the End," a David Horsley production starring Crane Wilbur, is scheduled to be the next release on the Art Drama program, following "Behind the Mash," a U. S. Amusement Corporation picture, with Catherine Calvert as its star.

"Unto the End" tells an absorbing story of a great love that endures until the very end. Crane Wilbur plays the part of Jim O'Neill, for whom nothing seemed to go right, from the day of his birth. Possibly, he could have blamed the hoodoo, which seemed to cling to him, because of the fact that he was born on Friday, the thirteenth. As he grew to manhood, Jim was continually getting into difficulties, but they were not of a serious nature, and though Jim's aristocratic parents were often deeply mortified by his behavior, they had no occasion to cross his path with an iron hand until Jim met Goldie Gray, a chorus girl. Jim's father then commanded that he give her up.

In a strong scene, Jim comes upon his best friend and Goldie, and believing that she is merely playing with him, gives her up and goes to Hawaii. Here he again meets Goldie, who becomes very ill, and is pronounced a leper. Everyone deserts her but Jim. He follows her to a leper colony, where she dies. Jim, believing that life for him is valueless, carries her to the water and they both disappear beneath the white capped waves.

This is said to be the strongest picture yet produced by Horsley. Crane Wilbur excels himself in the part of Jim, and the supporting cast is admirably suited to the demands of the story.

NEW "HAM COMEDIES."

General Film will have for release in October five new subjects in its series of Ham Comedies from the Kalem Company. These ever popular comedies feature Bud Duncan and Lloyd V. Hamilton. The new one-reelers which will be added to General's list of former Ham Comedies comprise these titles: Oct. 3, "Politics in Pumpkin Center"; Oct. 10. "The Boot and the Loot"; Oct. 17, "A Whirlwind of Whiskers"; Oct. 24, "The Onion Magnate's Revenge"; and Oct. 31, "The Bath Tub Bandit."

Julia Sanderson Makes Debut.

First Appearance on Screen in "The Runaway" on Mutual Program for Week of September 24.

JULIA SANDERSON, the Broadway star, makes her screen debut September 24, when Mutual releases "The Runaway," a five-reel drama produced by the Empire All Star Corporation. On the same date Mutual will release "Sands of Sacrifice," a five-reel drama, starring William Russell.

"The Runaway" was directed for the screen as well as for the stage by Dell Henderson, and the cast which supported Miss Sanderson in the dramatic production was selected to appear with her in the screen version of the play. The result has been as perfect a screen production of the dramatic success as was humanly and photographically possible.

"The Runaway" is part of the series of Charles Frohman's stage successes in motion pictures in which Miss Sanderson, Ann Murdock and Olive Tell will appear. "The Beautiful Adventure" with Miss Murdock as the lead will be the next from the Empire studios released on the Mutual schedule.

"Sands of Sacrifice" gives William Russell a new and interesting hero role. He has plenty of opportunities to fight and there are several fistic encounters in the course of the five reels which show the athletic picture star to the best of advantage. The scenes are laid in the mountains of the east and in the great American desert. The stage settings are up to the standards of the American Film Company, which has gradually established a world-wide reputation for beautiful and realistic sets and locations.

Russell and George Periolat stage a battle in the last scene which is as realistic as any of the fights which Russell has produced for the screen.

"Sands of Sacrifice" is the first of a new series of Russell productions under Mutual's schedule of two a week. It was directed, as were the pictures in the recent series of Russell successes, by Edward S. Sloman. Sloman and Russell have proved to be a most efficient picture producing team and the Russell productions have proved to be box office offerings of first magnitude. Reports reaching Mutual branch offices reveal an exceptionally high batting average for the Russell productions.

The second chapter of "The Lost Express," Mutual-Signal's sensational mystery serial, will be released Monday, September 24. The second chapter bears the title, "The Destroyed Documents." It takes the story into new mysteries following the disappearance of the express train in Chapter I. Miss Holmes plays a conspicuous part in the chaper. First run bookings on "The Lost Express" have been heavy, particularly so with exhibitors who have shown Miss Holmes' previous photo dramas.

The cub comedy released September 27 is "Jerry's Big Deal," one reel in which George Ovey impersonates the new minister in a small village. Jerry makes love to the spinster sisters of the congregation and plays poker with the deacons, much to their financial and moral embarrassment. He is finally routed by the real parson, whose outfit Jerry has had thrust upon him.

Mutual Weekly No. 143, released September 26, will carry scenes from the camp of the American expeditionary force in France, together with news pictures of the preparations for war in this country. "Reel Life" No. 74, the one-reel weekly magazine, shows the interesting method by which clocks are corrected in all part of the country from the naval observatory. It pictures the portable bakeries which have been designed for the American army, shows the progress which has been made in the processes for manufacturing eye glasses and contains an animated drawing from Life.

The Week's Work in the Fox Studios.

Some New Subjects Recently Turned Out by Fox Players East and West.

GEORGE WALSH, "The Smile-a-Minute Man," is the hero of William Fox's mid-September release, "The Yankee Way," a bright comedy of international romance which has its beginning in a Chicago cabaret, and concludes with a wedding ring in the ever-boiling Balkans. The picture presents the breezy and genial George with abundant opportunity to display his physical prowess. The film starts, in fact, with a fight.

In the supporting cast are Enid Markey, Joe Dowling, Charles Elder, James O'Shea, Ed. Sedgwick, Count Hardenberg, Edward Cecil and Tom Wilson. Richard Stanton, who made "The Spy," the sensational unveiling of German secret service methods now being presented at the Globe theater, in New York city, was the director of "The Yankee Way," so a splendid production is assured.

"Smiling George" has begun work on a new special feature under the direction of his brother, R. A. Walsh. James A. Marcus and Ralph Lewis who have had important roles in many William Fox productions, have been selected by Director Walsh to appear prominently in George's forthcoming screen drama. The only film in which "Jim Marcus" has been seen which R. A. Walsh did not direct was "The Mediator," and in that George Walsh was starred. Marcus will be remembered particularly for his admirable characterization of the Governor in "The Honor System."

June Caprice, William Fox's "Sunshine Maid," has also started work on another production for the silent stage. Harry Millarde, who directed Miss Caprice in "Every Girl's Dream," her most recent release, is again in charge of the

direction. A title has been determined upon by William Fox for the picture, which Gladys Brockwell now has in the making. This will be called "Conscience." The story is being interpreted by a wonderful cast and is being filmed under the supervision of Bertram Bracken.

After the release of "The Yankee Way," on September 16, will come "North of Fifty Three." The latter will be followed in turn by "A Rich Man's Plaything," a subject of strong dramatic action. This production was screened in the Fox studios in the East, at Fort Lee, N. J.

COMPLETING "WHO IS 'NUMBER ONE?'"

So rapidly is Paramount progressing in its work of polishing "Who is 'Number One?'" its first serial, written by Anna Katharine Green and starring Kathleen Clifford, that the entire fifteen episodes will be complete and in the exchanges several weeks before the release date of the first episode.

Miss Clifford is cutting short a vaudeville tour to return to make new scenes and new thrills which will be completed and edited within the next few weeks. A corps of artists has nearly finished the work of lettering the new titles and will soon set to work on the novel trailers that are to be added to each episode. These trailers, a unique idea in motion pictures, are especially devised to pile up added interest so that every theater patron who sees an episode of "Who Is 'Number One?'" will be eagerly watching for a chance to see the next one. Every episode of "Who Is 'Number One?'" is being edited and re-edited and no print will be released until it is in every detail up to the Paramount standard.

ANOTHER POPULAR BOOK STORY FOR ELSIE FERGUSON.

Following the sensational success of Elsie Ferguson's initial photoplay characterization in "Barbary Sheep," at the Rialto theater, New York, and throughout the country, under the auspices of Adolph Zukor for Artcraft pictures, the next screen subject for the popular stage star was announced last week by Walter E. Greene, President of Artcraft. The new film vehicle for Miss Ferguson is an adaptation from the popular book, "The Rise of Jennie Cushing," by Mary S. Watts, author of "Nathan Burke," "Van Cleve" and many other well known works. Work on this production is now well under way at the famous Players-Lasky studios in Fort Lee, under the personal direction of Mr. Tourneur. An exceptional cast has been selected, including Elliott Dexter, Fania Marinoff, Frank Goldsmith, Callie Delatorre, Mae Bates, Edith McAlpin, Isabel Vernon, Blanche Craig, James Cogan and Marie Burk.

"BONDAGE" (Bluebird).

Dorothy Phillips will make her regular monthly appearance among Bluebirds on Oct. 17, presenting her third Ida May Park production. "Bondage" is the title and the story was suggested by Edna Kenton. Miss Park took the idea Miss Kenton advanced, made the scenario and then directed Miss Phillips in the production.

William Stowell, who has always led Miss Phillips' support, will be her leading man in "Bondage," with J. B. McLaughlin, Gretchen Lederer and Gertrude Astor also prominent in the cast. This Bluebird is a straight dramatic offering, the type of

Scene from "Bondage" (Bluebird).

story in which Miss Phillips is seen to best advantage. Its basis is life in New York's "bohemia" with the atmosphere in and around Washington Square predominating.

Ida May Park, having taken over the exclusive screen direction of Miss Phillips, has prepared "Bondage" as her third offering in a series that will continue throughout the coming year. Miss Park has of late, alternated with her husband, Joseph De Grasse, in directing Miss Phillips but the feminine combination worked out so well that Miss Park was given exclusive control of all subsequent Dorothy Phillips Bluebird.

Second O' Henry Four-Reeler

Jean Paige and Carlton King Featured in Drama with Happy Ending, "Blind Man's Holiday."

A NEW featured lead in the O. Henry productions is introduced in the second of the four-reel releases of the new series through General Film Company, the story being "Blind Man's Holiday." Jean Paige as Norah Greenway, the heroine of this fascinating story, makes her debut as a headliner, opposite Carlton King, who plays Lorison, the hero.

Scene from "Blind Man's Holiday" (General Film).

Miss Paige has made a tremendous and brilliant stride in pictures. She is only 20, and was last seen in another Broadway Star Feature in the supporting cast of "Discounters of Money."

An O. Henry two-reel production. She was chosen to play the lead in "Blind Man's Holiday" after Director Martin Justice found her work greatly adapted for the role.

"Blind Man's Holiday" finds the man, Lorison, a victim of his own shifting perspective. Haunted by an accusation of crime, he sees himself at times "an outcast from society," a shady skulker on the ragged edge of respectability." At other times he bores himself "with the serene grandeur akin to greatness." The story is the epic of his moods during a swift, romantic love adventure with a girl he meets casually on the streets.

How, in his more depressed mood he tells her he is unworthy to wed her, and how he becomes elated when she deprecates her own worth by a circumstantial tale of wrongdoing is brought out in many vivid scenes. Then, having married her only to have her depart mysteriously, how he is tortured by mental pictures of his folly that nearly drive him frantic forms another lively series of suspense incidents. At this point a third principal comes vitally into the story. Father Rogan, played by John Costello. To punish and cure Lorison of his morbid state of mind he takes him on a round of certain significant locations, at the end of which, in one of O. Henry's famous "situations" he clears up the mystery, proves the man's doubts to have been unworthy and reunites a remorseful hero with a triumphant heroine.

An excellent production has been given this photoplay, well up to the standard of those O. Henry pictures that have gone before.

"THE LITTLE PRINCESS" NEXT MARY PICKFORD SUBJECT.

Simultaneous with the country-wide success of the latest Mary Pickford picture, "Rebecca of Sunnybrook Farm," Artcraft announces "The Little Princess" as the next vehicle for "Our Mary." This subject has appeared with wide success both in book form and on the stage. The original book which became popular throughout the country is "Sara Crewe," from the pen of Frances Hodgson Burnett. In 1903 Miss Burnett dramatized the book and at the Criterion Theater the story was staged under the management of Charles B. Dillingham.

The story presents a typical Mary Pickford subject on the order of "A Poor Little Rich Girl" and "Rebecca of Sunnybrook Farm," and discloses "Little Mary" in a type of characterisation in which she is most popular, namely, the little girl in short dresses. Both the book and the play are well known and that the subject should prove another triumph for Mary Pickford is readily appreciated by the many thousands who are familiar with it. Work has already been commenced on this new picture at the Lasky Studio in California, under the direction of Marshall Neilan.

The World Film Corporation has presented several of its photoplays to the United States Battleship Missouri, for the entertainment of the sailors and marines.

PERSONALITIES IN THE PUBLIC EYE.

Many interesting personalities figure in the 18th issue of Universal Current Events just released. Among those who might be mentioned are: Donald B. McMillan, the recently returned Arctic explorer; Sir William White, chief of the British recruiting service in America; Miss Lucy Freeman, the 19-year-old girl who holds the national long-distance swimming record; Andre Tardieu, French High Commissioner to the United States, and Rear Admiral Usher, commanding officer in charge of the Brooklyn Navy Yard.

One of the unique features of the issue is the series of pictures showing the pretty Missouri girl who wore an even $1,000,000 worth of diamonds at the National Jewelers' Convention held in St. Louis a few days ago.

The memorial exercises in honor of Lafayette's birth, which were held in New York about the same time, will probably appeal to an equally large number of spectators, although contrasting widely in subject matter.

Some spectacular military scenes, showing one of our military units going into cantonments at Fort Ethan Allen, Vermont, and incidents that occurred during the journey of the Third New York Field Hospital from Manhattan to Spartanburg, S. C., are also well above the average in interest.

A new title has been designed for Current Events which displays the letters of both words as though they were composed of live electric wires.

VOLA VALE IN FALCON FEATURES.

Another bright particular star is presented as the lead in the current Falcon Feature from General Film Company. With Philo McCullough, Miss Vale is strongly featured in "The Secret of Black Mountain," a most dramatic story by Jackson Gregory. This is the sixth release of the Falcon Features, which are issued one every week, and which have been notable for their variety of strong film favorites in specially selected roles.

"The Secret of Black Mountain" is an adventure of the West. The plot of the story concerns the thrilling encounters of a young girl who undertakes to recover the fortune lost by her grandfather in the gold fields of California when he fell among bandits. The production is supervised by H. M. and E. D. Horkheimer, and carries a large and capable cast. Mignon LeBrun, Chas. Dudley, George Austin, Henry Crawford, Jack McLaughlin, T. H. Gibson Gowland, H. C. Russell, James Warner, and Lewis King are in the support to Vola Vale and Philo McCullough.

"A CONTENTED WOMAN" (Selig).

"A Contented Woman" is the title of the Selig comedy released Monday, September 17, in K. E. S. E. service. This comedy is considered one of the cleverest written by Charles Hoyt, the famous American playwright. J. A. Richmond, responsible for the other Selig comedies so successful in K. E. S. E., directed the comedy of "A Contented Woman."

The cast included Wm. Fables as "Uncle Todie," James Harris as "Benton Holme" and Amy Dennis as "Helena Wrangle," the stage beauty. There is promised a wealth of comedy situations and clear-cut photography. The plot, in brief, concerns Uncle Todie and his wife, Aunt Jim. An argument ensues whether man is or is not superior to woman. It results in the men folks remaining at home to prepare the evening meal. They fail of course and engage a caterer. At the theater Uncle Todie

Scene from "A Contented Woman" (Selig).

and Benton Holme discover Helena Wrangle, leading lady. When four irate landlords from four small towns arrive and threaten to tie up the show, Uncle Todie proves an easy victim, and, with Helena Wrangel, hurries to rob his penny bank. But Aunt Jim arrives and there is a terrible time trying to stall her and get Helena out by disguising her as a chair. When success comes and Uncle Todie is giving Aunt Jim the lecture of her life about the superiority of man, the caterer comes in with the dinner and spoils the situation.

Fox October Releases

Great Variety of Subjects Scheduled Among Next Month's Offerings.

WHAT is probably the most varied list of releases William Fox has ever made is announced for October. The pictures star Gladys Brockwell, Virginia Pearson, June Caprice, George Walsh, and Dustin Farnum. Technically, Miss Brockwell's play is a September issue, as it will be released on the last day of the month; but inasmuch as it has been substituted for another production through a change in schedule, it comes practically unheralded. This will be the order of the photoplays:

September 30, Gladys Brockwell in "Conscience."
October 7, Virginia Pearson in "Thou Shalt Not Steal."
October 14, June Caprice in "Miss U. S. A."
October 21, George Walsh in "This is the Life."
October 28, Dustin Farnum in "The Scarlet Pimpernel."

"Conscience," Miss Brockwell's new starring vehicle, is an unusually vivid drama, with an allegorical motif. The central theme has been deftly treated by Bertram Bracken, the director, who returns to the William Fox forces with this picture. Miss Brockwell had the assistance of one of the most distinguished companies that has appeared in any feature production this year in interpreting the story for the screen. The chief roles were taken by Majorie Daw, Eve Southern, Genevieve Blinn, Bertram Grassby, Eugenie Forde, Edward Cecil, Douglas Gerrard, Harry Lonsdale, and Colin Chase. Mr. Grassby has the part opposite Miss Brockwell. Director Bracken screened several films for William Fox in the East.

Miss Pearson's forthcoming subject, "Thou Shalt Not Steal," also required an extraordinarily large supporting cast, prominent in which are Claire Whitney, Eric Mayne, Dan Mason, Mathilde Brundage, John Goldsworthy, Robert Elliott, Martin Faust, Lem Kennedy, Danny Sullivan, and Victor DeLinkey. William Nigh, veteran film-maker, was in charge of the direction.

"Miss U. S. A.," as the title indicates, gives June Caprice a story infused with patriotic spirit. The picture is the most dramatic Miss Caprice has ever had, and shows also many spectacular military scenes. The dainty little Fox star is working under the supervision of Harry Millarde on this film. Mr. Millarde joined the Fox directorial staff recently. His initial production was "Every Girl's Dream," in which Miss Caprice had stellar honors.

On October 21st the public will first have the opportunity of seeing a photoplay made by one brother and starring another. R. A. Walsh is in charge of screening "This Is the Life," and George is doing valiant work in showing just what that life is. The picture is of the light comedy type for which "Smiling George" has become famous. With R. A. Walsh, the man who staged "The Honor System," attending to the production, a remarkable attraction should result. Wanda Petit, who was seen in "The Broadway Sport" and "The Derelict," William Fox features, was sent across the continent to play opposite George Walsh. James A. Marcus and Ralph Lewis have been assigned important parts.

"The Scarlet Pimpernel," the final release of the month, is rich in adventure, and brims with swiftest action, as anyone who has read Baroness Orczy's splendid novel well knows. The stage version has been counted as one of the biggest "hits" of the British theater, and with Dustin Farnum in the starred part, the cinema drama will probably duplicate the success of the play.

The pimpernel is a tiny wayside flower which has been adopted as the emblem of a band of Englishmen engaged in rescuing condemned aristocrats during the French Revolution.

In the cast are Winifred Kingston, William Burress, Bert Hadley and Howard Gaye. Richard Stanton, who made "The Spy," staged the production.

Goldwyn to Distribute "The Manxman"

George Loane Tucker's Film Version of Hall Caine's Famous Story Now Ready for Shipment.

PRINTS for trade showings of George Loane Tucker's picturization of Hall Caine's most famous story, "The Manxman," which has just completed a successful run of four weeks at the Criterion theater, New York City, are ready for shipment throughout North America by the Goldwyn Distributing Corporation. Under an agreement made shortly before his death in an automobile accident, Goldwyn is to distribute "The Manxman" for Henry J. Brock, its owner.

Mr. Brock was killed last week when his automobile, in which he was on his way to his home in Buffalo, overturned in the Adirondacks, near Kingston, N. Y. Two persons who were with him escaped with slight injuries.

Mr. Brock's death, mourned by many friends in the motion picture industry throughout the country, will not upset Goldwyn's plans for systematic distribution and wide exploitation, both by publicity and advertising of his big property.

Attracted by the success of the producton in New York, where it was shown to crowded houses night and day in one of the most popular theaters usually devoted to the spoken drama, exhibitors already are inquiring about first run rights to it.

"The Manxman" will be seen first in the larger cities, where Goldwyn knows it will prove a strong attraction for an extended run in the bigger houses.

Mr. Tucker, who produced "The Manxman," has to his credit half a dozen productions that have proved highly profitable to exhibitors. He is now attached to the directorial staff of Goldwyn, and is making the picturization of the Broadway stage success, "The Cinderella Man."

Elizabeth Risdon, called "The English Mary Pickford," is featured in the production with Henry Ainley.

THE PERFECT FLYING MACHINE MOTOR.

The Secretary of War has confirmed the announcement that Yankee ingenuity has at last perfected an engine for airplanes which is far superior to any aero-motor which has been invented prior to this time. This engine meets all requirements at any altitude. Under the direction of the Aircraft Production Board, the greatest engineers of this country, working together since war was declared, have pooled their trade secrets and developed a motor which is not only the fastest and most reliable known, but is of such a type that the different parts can be manufactured in various factories throughout the country and assembled when the entire flying machine is put together. Secretary Baker proclaims this as probably the greatest achievement of the war. The Gaumont Company was fortunate in being able to photograph the testing of this wonderful engine on Pike's Peak, nearly three miles above sea-level; and these pictures will appear first in Gaumont-Mutual Weekly No. 142 when it is released September 19.

TO REISSUE TALMADGE AND KEENAN TRIANGLES.

Prompted by the success of the Hart-Fairbanks reissues, the Triangle Distributing Corporation has arranged two star series of Triangle plays in which Norma Talmadge and Frank Keenan are featured. These will be reissued on the same plan as the Hart-Fairbanks subjects, and may be booked for independently of one another.

The Keenan plays will be released at intervals of four weeks, commencing with "The Sin Ye Do," on October 7. The pictures starring Norma Talmadge also will appear every four weeks, commencing October 21, with "The Devil's Needle."

"THE EDGE OF THE LAW" (Butterfly).

Ruth Stonehouse is the star of "The Edge of the Law," the Butterfly feature to be released Monday, September 24th.

Arranged for the screen by Harvey Gates, from "A Gentle Ill Wind," a novel by Maude Pettus which appeared recently in the All-Story Magazine, the story deals with the career of Nancy Glenn, better known as "Spider," a modern Oliver Twist of the feminine gender.

Dressed in boy's clothes from her earliest years, Nancy has been known to the police of the big city for some time as one of the cleverest "dips" in the business. But despite their best efforts, none of the limbs of the law—not even Spike Sullivan, the most persistent of Nancy's pursuers—has ever been able to catch her with the goods.

The plot of the tale hinges upon the one occasion when Spike believes he has discovered his quarry in the act of stealing a purse from the seat of an auto occupied by Ralph Harding, a wealthy young Westerner, and some of his friends.

Scene from "The Edge of the Law" (Butterfly).

Harding's party intercedes, however, and Nancy makes her escape—only to run into an even more serious complication when she returns to her quarters at rop Hoagland's, a notorious "fence," who has taught her most of the tricks of her nefarious trade. Hoagland and Pliny Drew, one of his lieutenants, decide that Nancy could be more useful as a young lady, filling the role of a "come-on" for a swindling deal that they have in mind. This leads to a series of rapidly moving events that give novelty and punch to the story in the most unexpected places. Louis Chaudet directed the production.

Arbuckle in "Oh Doctor!" (Paramount)

But Fortunately This Happens Only in His Next Paramount Comedy, "Oh Doctor!" Soon to Be Released.

Paramount's weightiest comedian, Roscoe "Fatty" Arbuckle, has been caught in the toils of a beautiful but unscrupulous vampire, accomplice of a crook. But luckily, this only occurs in "Oh Doctor," a Paramount-Arbuckle comedy which will be released following "His Wedding Night."

The susceptible individual is Dr. I. O. Dine, otherwise Mr. Arbuckle, and the character gives "Fatty" one of the greatest laugh-getting parts he has been called upon to play in some time.

The lenslight first reveals the Doctor, in the person of the rotund Mr. Arbuckle, at the races with his wife and her brother. The trio sits in front of the clubhouse, "Fatty" enlivening his idle moments by a surreptitious flirtation with an extremely pretty girl, who for the purposes of the plot is designated the Vampire. This charming person has as a pal a notorious crook (Al St. John), with whom she is devising ways and means of making easy money, as both are nearly broke.

Doctor I. O. Dine, overhearing a tip given to the crook on the winner of the next race, stakes his every dollar on the horse, which comes in last. All that is saved is Mrs. I. O. Dine's neck-

Scene from "Oh Doctor" (Paramount).

lace, which she had refused to stake. The Vampire and the crook are ruined by the false tip also and the crestfallen losers leave the track together.

OCTOBER L-KO'S.

J. G. Blystone, general director of L-Ko's, has prepared five subjects for October that promise to maintain the standard of fun these pictures have created in winning laughs from audiences. Five releases will be made during the month with all the L-Ko funmakers in evidence.

Phil Dunham directed the release for Oct. 3, entitled "Counting Out the Count." This is Mr. Dunham's second picture since he gave up acting in L-Ko's to stand by the camera. Lucille Hutton, Billy Bevan and a large company of assistants will figure in the fun.

"The Nurse of An Aching Heart," directed by Archie Mayo, L-Ko's newest producer, will be the Oct. 10 release. Eva Novak will be the woman star and Eddie Barry and Bob McKenzie the leading comedians. Scenes in a comedy hospital will be featured.

Eva Novak will also feature in the Oct. 17 comic, "Vamping Reuben's Millions," with Katheryn Young doing an extensive line of comedy vampire work. Eddie Barry and Bob McKenzie will lead the supporting comedians in laughable scenes from rural life.

On Oct. 24 Myrtle Sterling will be the star in "Fat and Furious." Babe Emerson will be featured as an L-Ko beauty and Al Forbes and Russ Powell will handle the comedy. The same company will participate in the release for Oct. 31, both comics having been produced by Vin Moore.

A NEW LUBRICANT ON THE MARKET.

L. A. Reuss, electrician of Nicholas Power Company, claims superiority for a grease manufactured by Messrs. Reuss & Wetter, 212 Broadway, New York City. The product is known as Leonard's Motor Grease and has been subjected to exhaustive tests, and the claims for its excellence have been found to be fully justified. Among the many dealers of motion picture accessories throughout the country who have adopted this grease the most prominent is the United Theater Equipment Corporation, and the chief operator of the Marcus Loew's circuit of motion picture houses has also adopted this grease for use in their houses. The price of the new grease is a trifle higher than most of the other products now offered to the

trade, but the price is reasonable when it is considered that the grease will save wear on bearings and shafts. It is a non-fluid oil, and will not flow over the motor.

TWO WESTERNS ON TRIANGLE PROGRAM.

Roy Stewart as a New Type of Bad Man in "Devil Dodger" —Also Appears with Belle Bennett in "Bond of Fear" for Week of September 23.

DRAMAS of early Western life will be featured on the Triangle program for September 23, and will present Belle Bennett and Roy Stewart as stars. "Bond of Fear," the first release of the week, is the story of two fugitives from the law, a man and a woman, who meet on the desert plains of Arizona. One of the most spectacular effects of the play is a furious sandstorm which engulfs the party in their flight across the alkali parched land. Roy Stewart has the role of Cal Nelson, the ever-devoted friend to Mary, played by Belle Bennett. Melbourne McDowell is said to be admirably cast as the grim letter-of-the-law judge. George Webb, who acted as leading man for Louise Glaum in "Idolators," is also of the cast. Jack Conway directed the play, which was written by Edith Kennedy.

Roy Stewart makes his advent to the screen as a gunfighter of new methods in "The Devil Dodger," by J. G. Hawkes. Jack Gilbert, a Triangle player, whose work has been noteworthy in previous productions, appears as the minister who calls himself "The Devil Dodger." In his attempts to inculcate moral understanding in Fluffy, a dance hall protege of "Silent Scott," he is compelled to assume militant tactics. He meets violent opposition from the gunfighter, Scott, who swears to drive him from the community. Fluffy, however, makes a bargain with her master to settle the dispute by a game of cards. She wins, and the parson is saved. Later, "The Devil Dodger" not only saves the soul of Fluffy, but, at the sacrifice of his life, preserves her happiness.

The Triangle comedies of the week are "His Unconscious Conscience" and "Her Fickle Fortune." Lillian Biron, one of the blonde favorites of the Keystone squad, has the leading feminine role in "Her Fickle Fortune" and Phyllis Haver is the featured lady of "His Unconscious Conscience."

THE DOGS OF WAR IN GAUMONT'S "REEL LIFE."

"Let loose the dogs of war," bids fair to become more than a mere poetic phrase. The newspapers convey the information that the United States is seriously considering the sending of ten thousand dogs to France. While many of these dogs will be used for detecting gas when we capture the German trenches, others will be trained to carry dispatches and aid in the rescue of the wounded. In "Dogs of War," which is featured in the Gaumont-Mutual screen magazine, "Reel Life" No. 75, released October 4, will be shown many unusual scenes illustrating the work of these trained canines which the Red Cross will use on the battlefields of Europe.

The slogan of the Springfield armory, which has been making rifles since the days of President Washington, is: "Get behind our boys in France! Springfield never failed!" With official consent, the Gaumont Company presents another unusual subject, "Making Army Rifles," in this issue of "Reel Life," with scenes taken in this historic arsenal.

Another subject in this release of an entirely different nature

Scene from "Making Springfield Rifles" (Gaumont).

shows how the Japanese, past masters in the floral art, retard the growth of trees and shrubs so they can be made in gardens or conservatories. In "Japanese Dwarf Plants" are pictured pines and cedars more than a century old which are little more than a foot in height.

"The Sign of a City," a huge electric globe which advertises Toledo, Ohio, and two animated drawings from "Life," the leading weekly of humor and satire, complete the reel.

DOROTHY DALTON IN "THE PRICE MARK."

More than ordinary interest attached to the announcement that Dorothy Dalton, the beautiful, talented and youthful star of Thomas H. Ince, would appear in Paramount pictures. It will be of added interest to know that for her Paramount debut a story of remarkable strength, with a wide diversity of locale, and great dramatic appeal, has been chosen, the title of which is "The Price Mark." The picture will be in charge of Roy Neill, who is one of Mr. Ince's most experienced directors, but the latter will supervise all of the situations and devote much time and thought to making this production an outstanding one. "The Price Mark" will be released in October.

Miss Dalton will be surrounded by players of proven worth. She has expressed herself as delighted with the chosen cast, which includes William Conklin, a versatile actor of juvenile leads, who has had wide stage and screen experience; Thurston Hall, who has been a leading man in stock, in various productions for the legitimate stage, and for pictures; Adele Farrington, a character actress and comedienne of much ability; Edwin Wallock, Dorcas Matthews and Clio Ayres, all well known players.

Picture Theaters Projected

WILCOX, ARIZ.—Pastime theater is now under the management of H. O. Parks and W. H. Stevenson.

BAKERSFIELD, CAL.—Rex theater has been reconstructed at an expenditure of $6,500.

CULVER CITY, CAL.—Culver City theater has been reopened by Paul Eagler.

MANTECA, CAL.—Mission theater, an open-air structure, will be torn down to make room for a new moving picture house. Mr. Fox, manager of the Mission theater, will lease the building.

SAN FRANCISCO, CAL.—California theater is being erected at the corner of Market and Fourth streets and will cost $1,700,000. It will be controlled by the proprietors of the Portola theater and conducted under the management of Eugene H. Roth.

STOCKTON, CAL.—Strang theater located on Sutter street, between Main and Weber streets, will be reopened under the name of the Hippodrome.

JACKSONVILLE, FLA.—Imperial theater has been repainted, redecorated and reopened to the public. The interior has been finished in gray with lavender, presenting a harmonious contrast. H. B. Hearn, formerly in charge of the Arcade theater, is manager.

ST. PETERSBURG, FLA.—Moving picture theater will be erected on Central avenue, between Fourth and Fifth streets, by A. C. Pheil. It will have seating capacity for 600 persons.

ALBANY, GA.—Rawlins theater, which was recently destroyed by fire is to be rebuilt. Will have seating capacity for 1,400 people.

MONESSEN, PA.—Peter Sotus has purchased the Olympia theater on Donner avenue.

PHILADELPHIA, PA.—Edward Margolies has the contract to erect a seven-story steel, concrete and brick office building, including one-story rear theater structure, 80 by 200.5 feet, at the northwest corner of Broad and Manning streets, for Publicker & Ward, to cost $280,000.

PHILADELPHIA, PA.—William F. Bovgan has taken title from the Tioga Theater Holding Company to the Tioga theater at 3540-42 N. 17th street, for a nominal consideration, subject to a mortgage of $65,000. Transaction includes a two-story brick theater building and a two-story brick store building on a lot 42.6 by 197.10 feet. The assessed valuation is $550,000.

PHILADELPHIA, PA.—George & Bolst have the contract for making interior alterations and repairs to the Chestnut street opera house, Chestnut street, above Tenth.

PHILADELPHIA, PA.—Moving picture theater at 628 South Broad street, owned by John Farmakis, is to be remodeled.

PHILADELPHIA, PA.—Moving picture theater at 2716-18 W. Girard avenue, will be remodeled. G. Hardy is the owner.

PITTSBURGH, PA.—S. Pollock and I. H. Fleishman, 2550 Center avenue, are having plans prepared for a one-story moving picture theater and store building, 60 by 44 feet, to cost $8,000.

PITTSBURGH, PA.—Burry-Erskine Amusement Company has been incorporated with a capital of $100,000 by A. A. Alles, H. W. Erskine and George Burry. The purpose of the new company is to conduct places of amusement of all kinds.

GREENVILLE, S. C.—Owners of Colonial Auditorium have plans by F. H. and J. G. Cunningham, and have let contract to W. M. Jordan to supervise remodeling of and for Colonial theater. Plans include construction of entrance to street with

stairway 25 feet wide; ornamented with electric lights of 5,000 candle power; remodel interior; auditorium to seat 1,600 persons.

SPARTANBURG, S. C.—W. F. Neil, manager of Strand and Bijou theaters, is considering erecting theater at Camp Wadsworth.

JUST ISSUED

Our second list of EDUCATIONAL and SELECTED FILMS covering releases from January 1st to June 30th, 1917. A handy reference list for managers and others in selecting programs for children's matinees. A few of the first list containing film releases of last six months of 1916 still on hand. Twenty cents for each list, postage paid.

MOVING PICTURE WORLD
17 Madison Avenue :: :: :: New York

Trade News of the Week

Flood Tide of Business in New England

Season Opens with Full Houses and Many Splendid Picture Offerings — New Theaters and Reopenings — Notes of the Trade.

By Richard Davis Howe, No. 80 Summer St., Boston, Mass.

BOSTON, Mass.—Cold weather has set ahead the regular fall season of the moving picture theaters of New England by several weeks, and today finds theaters enjoying crowded houses. It has put new life into the entire industry, and salesmen touring the New England territory find exhibitors eager to grasp at the best pictures offered.

No season has opened so auspiciously so far as the film offerings are concerned. Here is a good idea of the real gilt-edge productions that are being shown in Boston:

Modern theater—Mary Pickford in "Rebecca of Sunnybrook Farm," and George Beban in "Lost in Transit."

Park theater—Ethel Barrymore in "The Lifted Veil."

Boston theater—Mae Marsh in "Polly of the Circus."

Exeter theater and Gordon's Olympia—Billy Burke in "The Mysterious Miss Terry."

Majestic theater—"The Honor System."

Thus it is seen that some of the foremost stars of the country are represented in first-run production in Boston theaters as a fitting opening of the season, and S. R. O. signs have been hung out where Mary Pickford is being shown and at a number of the other houses.

"The Honor System," the second of the big Fox features to be shown at the Majestic, one of Boston's leading legitimate theaters, is drawing well, and bookings have been made for "The Spy" at the same house next week.

J. B. Hart to Conduct Theater at Bennington, Vt.

Bennington, Vt.—J. B. Hart has taken over the opera house in Bennington, Vt., for number of years under the control of the C. A. Wood Company. Mr. Hart recently married a daughter of Mr. Wood, and comes to Bennington to operate the house.

George Crocker Takes Warwick Theater.

Marblehead, Mass.—George Crocker, formerly house manager for the Drown circuit of moving picture theaters in Greater Boston, has leased the Warwick theater at Marblehead. The Warwick has been completely renovated and is an up-to-date house. The Drown circuit now consists of the Day street Olympia theater, Somerville; Olympia theater, Cambridge; and the Union Square theater, Somerville. They are under Mr. Drown's personal supervision.

Many Film Men Are at Camp.

Ayer, Mass.—There is quite a contingent of moving picture men now training as members of the new National Army at the Ayer, Mass., camp. They include: Walter Young, manager of the Olympia theater at Farmington, N. H.; Nathan Yamins, owner of the Plaza theater in Fall River; Putnam Smith, manager of the Bradley and Empire theaters in Putnam, Conn.; and A. N. Sanborn, who controlled the opera house at Sanbornville.

Selznick Office at 69 Church Street.

Boston, Mass.—Manager Samuel J. Steinfeldt has moved the headquarters of the Lewis J. Selznick Enterprises, Inc., to a larger and more convenient office at No. 69 Church street. His corps of salesmen now touring New England report some good results.

James Orkney Covering Maine.

Boston, Mass.—R. A. Magee, who has been working the Maine territory of the Greater Vitagraph interests, has been succeeded by James Orkney, a well-known New England salesman. Mr. Orkney was with Vitagraph once before, but more recently has been with the K. L. S. E.

Owl Theater Closes for Winter.

Sunapee, N. H.—S. E. Osborne, an employee of the New England Telephone and Telegraph Company, who, during the summer months, run the Owl theater at Sunapee, N. H., has closed the house for the season. He reports a record business for the house.

New Stoneham Theater Nearly Ready.

Stoneham, Mass.—A theater building has been added to the town of Stoneham, Mass., a great Boston residential suburb. The house is being completed for occupancy in November by J. E. Locatelli, Inc. The theater building is the property of Joseph Deffarari, a local business man. The theater has a seating capacity of 1,800, with two balconies.

The building is one of the finest in the town and is centrally located. Every modern appliance and comfort has been installed in the theater. The entrance to the building will be in the center of the block with stores on each side. It is stated that Nathan Gordon, who controls the long chain of Olympia theaters in Massachusetts, has offered to lease the house for a yearly rental of $5,000.

"Honor System" Makes Impression.

Boston, Mass.—"The Honor System" was the second big Fox Feature film to be run at the Majestic theater in Boston under the new policy of showing one big production a week. The production attracted excellent notices in all the Boston papers.

L. A. McDuffee Joins General Film.

Boston, Mass.—The General Film has taken on L. A. McDuffee, former owner of the Scenic theater at Rochester, N. H., as their southern Maine representative. Mr. McDuffee recently sold the Scenic theater to Frederick Couture, brother of Alfred Couture, who controls the Crown theater at Manchester, N. H.

Goldstein Bros. Buy Two Theaters.

Springfield, Mass.—The Town Hall theater at Exeter, N. H., and the Colonial theater at Pittsfield, Mass., have been sold by the Goldstein Brothers, of Springfield. They have instituted a new policy at the Broadway, featuring vaudeville as well as pictures.

Manager Sorerio Books Noted Singer.

Boston, Mass.—Miss Mary Desmond, the noted English opera singer and a member of the Manhattan Opera Company of New York, is a feature attraction which Manager Sorerio, of the Park theater, of Boston, has booked for his musical program the week of Sept. 17. The noted Park theater orchestra is back on the job after a summer recess.

Interesting New England Notes.

Boston, Mass.—General Manager Carl H. Pierce, of the Paramount Exhibitors' Service department, has returned to New York after a tour of New England territory. He made a call upon Manager Harry Asher, of the Boston office, and left later to see Manager Henry T. Sculley, of the New Haven branch.

New Bedford, Mass.—The management of the New Bedford theater at New Bedford, Mass., has been taken over by William Murphy, formerly manager of the Colonial theater in Nashua, N. H. The house runs pictures and vaudeville and is making a fine showing.

Bridgetown, Me.—Bert Avery, of the Riverside theater in Bridgeton, Me., has taken over the Olympia theater at Farmington, N. H.

Thompsonville, Conn.—After having been through the bankruptcy courts, the old Ten Eyke theater in Thompsonville, Conn., has been reopened under the management of a Mr. Franklin.

Providence, R. I.—The Strand, Fay's and the Modern theaters in Providence, R. I., have increased their price of admission and have inaugurated an extra charge over the admission fee for reserved seats. No special reason was announced for the change.

Dorchester, Mass.—The Franklin Park theater has reopened, after being closed for a few months during the warm weather. The house has been thoroughly renovated and repaired and now is one of the finest moving picture theaters in Dorchester.

Boston, Mass.—Jacob Louri has booked "The Seven Pearls," the new Pathe serial picture, for the Beacon theater in this city, as has Victor Morris for the St. James theater.

Boston, Mass.—Miss Molly Sullivan, the attractive young telephone operator in the Boston office of Pathe, has been lost to her many friends in the film world. She was married Sunday evening to Dirk Hanson of Philadelphia. The Pathe Boston office force presented Miss Sullivan with a beautiful chest of silver as a wedding gift.

Business Notes From Baltimore.

E. R. Price, who for about two months has managed the Buffalo exchange for Triangle, visited Baltimore last week for a few days and called on many of his friends. As Mr. Price is very popular among the Baltimore boys we presume it took him some time to get around. He has just been promoted to the position of General Sales Manager for the Triangle, to cover the Eastern district.

Miss Sophia K. Lavine, the cashier at the Mutual Baltimore exchange, is again back at her desk this week with a good deal of tan on her cheeks. Her vacation was quite a success, she states.

Charles E. Ford, manager of Ford's opera house, has booked the eight-part historical feature, "Christus," and it began its run at this house on Monday, September 10. Wm. Fox's "The Spy" played to capacity houses at this theater during the week of September 3.

Col. Jacob W. Hook, vice-president of the Southern Amusement Company, returned from a motor trip to Atlantic City, Asbury Park and Shelter Islands last week.

Harry Lewy, co-proprietor of the Great Wizard theater, 30 West Lexington street, has made a number of slides in the form of appeals for contributions to the Army Girls' Transport Tobacco Fund. These slides are being thrown on the screens at many of the theaters in this city.

Edward C. Hartman, who at one time acted as treasurer for the Colonial theater in this city and then as assistant treasurer of the Auditorium, has now been appointed assistant manager and treasurer of the Lexington theater in New York City.

Baltimore, Md.—Manager Harry A. Henkel, of the Academy of Music, announces that this playhouse will be reopened to the public very shortly. He has his shirt sleeves rolled up, and is busily making big changes in the interior.

Salisbury, Md.—Last week Miss Helen Ullman, of this city, who now attends to the booking of pictures for the Ullman opera house, visited Baltimore while on her way home from Ocean View, Va., where she attended the convention of the West Virginia Exhibitor's League. Miss Ullman stopped in to see her friends at the exchanges.

Havre-de-Grace, Md.—L. H. Thompson, manager of the Bijou theater, took a run down to Baltimore last week. He states that he has now started the Mutual service.

Annapolis, Md.—P. Miller, who manages the Republic theater in this city, was observed along exchange row in Baltimore last week.

Frostburg, Md.—On Tuesday night, Sept. 4, R. L. G. Hitchens, manager of the opera house in this city, arranged for the rousing meeting of the 241 selected soldiers for Allegheny county, outside of Cumberland, and the members of Company G, First Maryland Regiment.

Cambridge, Md.—When it comes to live wire methods of pulling people, J. W. Brown, manager of the Grand Opera House in this city, is there. When the Dorchester County Fair was held, Harry F. Daley, of Baltimore, filmed a moving picture and called it "The Newly Weds at the County Fair." And many people of local importance in this city were in the cast. So as soon as the picture was ready to be booked, Manager Brown signed up for it, and it was screened at his theater on Monday, Sept. 10.

Baltimore, Md.—Through the courtesy of Charles E. Thropp, manager of the Nixon-Victoria theater, 415 East Baltimore street, this pretty playhouse was used on Sunday afternoon to commemorate the twentieth anniversary of the organization of the Zionist movement, by Theodore Herzl.

Baltimore's Strand Reopens Much Prettier

Parkway Theater Company's House on North Howard Street Opens with Second Run Paramount—Some of Its New Decorations.

By J. M. Shellman, 1902 Mt. Royal Terrace, Baltimore, Maryland.

BALTIMORE, MD.—The Strand theater, 404-6 North Howard street, under the management of the Parkway Theater Company, reopened to the public on Monday, Sept. 10. It has been remodeled and renovated. The ticket office, which formerly occupied the center, is now inside the wall on the right. This section of the house has a wainscoting of Maine marble with upper walls of Caenstone, while the ceiling is done in soft gray. The general color scheme of the interior is old ivory, soft gray and gold trimmings with wall panels of old rose silk. The hangings are of old rose velour and the carpets are of a darker shade of rose.

In the auditorium the lighting is by the cove system, the wiring for which has been changed so that it can be controlled from either the operating room or the basement. An exquisite effect by this system is gained on the heavy, ornamental beamed ceiling and plaster tops, which are trimmed in gold leaf. Metal hoods have been placed over all the radiators. Second run weekly stands will be shown here of the big Paramount features.

Prices Go Up at the Parkway.

Baltimore, Md.—Beginning Monday, September 3, the prices at the Parkway theater, 2-9 West North avenues, were raised, but according to the crowds observed around the entrance of the theater during that week, while George M. Cohan was shown in "Seven Keys to Baldpate," the clientele has taken it very calmly. Bernard Depkin, Jr., in speaking of the matter, said: "I am glad to announce that the Parkway has obtained a franchise for all the Paramount and Artcraft pictures."

Weekly runs are now being made at the Parkway of the biggest plays on the Paramount program and the prices are: Entire first floor, 35 cents; box seats (reserved), 50 cents; balcony (first six rows), 25 cents, and the remainder of the balcony 15 cents for the night performances. During the matinees the prices are: Entire first floor, 15 cents; entire balcony, 10 cents; box seats, 25 cents.

A. B. Price Returns From Trip.

Baltimore, Md.—A. B. Price, the progressive manager of the Rialto theater, North avenue, at Linden, and representative of the Triangle Company in the Baltimore territory, returned from a trip on the eastern shore of Maryland, booking the Triangle output. Mr. Price stated that his trip was very successful but that he had to do some tall hustling in the six days.

George Leibold Again With Mutual.

Baltimore, Md.—George Leibold, who has been in the film business for about five years and is well known among the fraternity both here and in Washington, has again returned to Baltimore and is acting in the capacity of booker at the Mutual exchange. Mr. Leibold says he started his career in the film game in that company's office, then he was engaged by J. C. Cremen to manage the Carey theater for some time and later went to Washington, where he was associated with J. H. Buttner in the Triangle exchange in that city. He resigned from the last to accept his present position.

Miss E. Schwab Leaves Mutual.

Baltimore, Md.—When we entered the Mutual exchange last week we missed the glad and welcoming smile of Miss E. Schwab, who for some years has been acting as booker in this office. She has now associated herself with the Parkway Theater Company as secretary to Bernard Depkin, Jr. When interviewed at the office of this company on North Charles street, Miss Schwab still had the same jolly smile, and while she had very little to say regarding her new position, it could be seen that she is very happy.

George C. Brown Is Victoria Treasurer.

Baltimore, Md.—George C. Brown will take over the treasurership of the Nixon-Victoria theater, 415 East Baltimore street, which has just been made vacant by A. M. Seligman having been promoted to a new position at the Nixon theater in Pittsburgh. Mr. Brown has for many years been associated with Charles E. Thropp, the manager of this playhouse, and together they operated the Colonial theater in Philadelphia. Mr. Brown states that another cashier will be taken on.

Auditorium Aids Tobacco Fund.

Baltimore, Md.—While "Jack and the Beanstalk" was the attraction at the Auditorium during the week of September 3, Manager Leonard B. McLaughlin very courteously arranged that part of the receipts of all the performances should be given to the Trasport Tobacco Fund, the idea being to supply our departing soldiers plentifully with tobacco. An eleven o'clock a. m. matinee was arranged on Monday especially for the children and the orphans from St. Mary's Asylum were the guests of the management on this day.

W. G. Pond at Helm of Arcade.

Salisbury, Md.—The Arcade theater, of this city, which has a seating capacity of 1,100, is now under the management of W. G. Pond. Mr. Pond has taken hold of things in a live wire method and is using exceptionally fine attractions in his house. He has had charge now about six weeks.

Camp Meade Theater a Reality.

Odenton, Md.—The Camp Meade Mercantile and Amusement Company is the name of a new corporation which has just been formed with stock-capitalized at $100,000. It is the purpose of the newly formed company to build a theater at Odenton, which is very near to Camp Meade. The incorporators are: Edward M. Lloyd, Clayton E. Husan and Edward J. Norton.

Another Tobacco Fund Benefit.

Baltimore, Md.—Through the courtesy of Charles E. and John T. Ford, co-proprietors of Ford's opera house, a benefit performance was arranged for the Army Girls' Transport Tobacco Fund on Wednesday night, Sept. 12. "Christus" was the attraction, and a generous portion of the box receipts was donated.

J. W. Hawkins Again at His Old Post.

Baltimore, Md.—J. W. Hawkins, president of the Maryland Movie Club, a social organization whose members are employed at the moving picture theaters in the capacities of ushers and cashiers, has again returned to his old post in the Mutual exchange as night film clerk.

Baltimore, Md.—On Monday, Sept. 3, the Frederick theatre, 3435 Frederick avenue, which is now under the control of J. G. Hartman, was reopened to the public.

"Polly" and Her Creator at the Stanley

Many Celebrities Meet Margaret Mayo in Philadelphia at the Premiere of "Polly of the Circus"—Comes as Guest of Stanley Mastbaum.

By F. V. Armato, 144 N. Salford Street, Philadelphia, Pa.

PHILADELPHIA, PA.—Margaret Mayo's "Polly of the Circus," presented last week at the Stanley theater, went even beyond expectations. It was charming, and the presence of the author herself added to the gayety of the evening.

Miss Mayo's brief address was overwhelmed with cheers from the audience. Every spectator was presented with a rose or some other souvenir. The management was obliged to turn away several hundred applicants for tickets.

The box office was converted into an imitation circus ticket booth, and the theater itself represented a circus tent. All the girl ushers were dressed in black and white satin clown attire.

Those who responded to Mr. Mastbaum's invitation to welcome the playwright were Edgar Selwyn, Samuel Goldfish, Hiram Abrams, William Smith, one of the directors of Paramount pictures; John Clark, local manager for Paramount; George Meeker, World Film Corporation; George Ames and his assistant, Oscar Bowers, of the local Goldwyn headquarters; Morey Boney; Albert R. Boyd, managing director of the Arcadia and Family theaters; Mrs. Stanley V. Mastbaum; Abe L. Einstein, publicity manager of the Stanley company; Pierie Garde, city editor, and Harry Knapp, dramatic editor, "Inquirer"; Herman Dieck, "Record"; Richard Beamish, managing director, and H. Lewis, city editor, "Press"; H. Bonte, dramatic editor, and D. Smiley, managing editor, "Public Ledger"; J. Eckels, managing editor, and H. Quicksall, dramatic editor, "North American"; Arthur Tubbs, dramatic editor, "Bulletin"; E. Whitney, city editor, and F. V. Armato, motion picture editor, "Telegraph" and correspondent of the Motion Picture World; H. Eaton, managing editor, H. T. Crane, dramatic editor, and A. Plough, motion picture editor, "Evening Ledger"; Arthur Coombs, "New York Telegraph"; William Connor, "Associated Press"; Clem Congdon, editor, "Transcript"; and Wid Gunning, of New York.

K-E-S-E Office Reports 200 Per Cent. Increase.

Philadelphia, Pa.—A. G. Buck, of the K-E-S-E Company, is receiving numerous inquiries regarding the new Perfection Pictures program, the first release of which will be Shirley Mason in "The Awakening of Ruth." There has been an increase in business of 200 per cent. at this exchange during the past month.

Raymond A. Stewart May Be Magistrate.

Philadelphia, Pa.—Raymond A. Stewart, the popular manager of the Dreamland theater, Thirty-seventh and Haverford avenues, is spending his vacation fishing in the numerous streams around Clarks Mills, Pa. Upon his return he announces that he will become a candidate for magistrate, having fully developed his political aspirations on this point. He will undoubtedly receive the support of a great many men of the motion picture industry, and his numerous friends have promised him their support.

Fairmont Feature Announces Jewel and Century Films.

Philadelphia, Pa.—V. R. Carrick announces that the Jewel productions and the Century comedies will be released exclusively through the Fairmount Feature Film exchange for this territory.

After viewing these pictures, Mr. May, manager of the Fairmount, predicts a huge increase for this season's business. The first Jewel feature to be offered will be "Come Through," to be followed by "Pay, Me," "The Man Without a Country,"

and the "Sirens of the Sea." The latter is at present playing at the Broadway theater in New York. Alice Howell, the well-known and celebrated comedienne, will make her first appearance on the Century program in "The Lunatic."

Adjustment Committee Appointed.

Philadelphia, Pa.—Charles H. Goodwin, secretary of the exhibitors' league of Philadelphia, is sponsor for a new movement which resulted in the appointment of an adjustment committee. The duty of this new body will be to smooth over all difficulties arising between the exchange men and exhibitors or between the exhibitors themselves, in order to pave a smooth path for the future.

The following exhibitors who were appointed for this committee are Columbus Stamper, of the Ford Nirdlinger interests; J. Boyd, of the Jumbo; E. A. Jefferies, of the Roxborough; J. Conway, of the Duray; Sam Blatt, of the Owl; H. Green, of the Aurora & Susquehanna; and J. S. Evans, of the West Allegheny.

Mutual Seeks to Restrain Censors.

Philadelphia, Pa.—B. R. Tolmas, of the Mutual, filed an appeal in court through John H. K. Scott, attorney, last week to restrain the Board of Censors from withholding the release of "The Outcast." This feature at a private review was proclaimed as a most noteworthy production, and for no possible reason could anyone imagine why the censors should refuse to pass the film. Although the Belmont, which is showing the first run Mutual star program, had it booked, it was prevented from being shown.

Permit for New Theater Granted.

Philadelphia, Pa.—The Bureau of Building Inspection granted a permit for a theater and seven-story office building to be erected on the site of Horticultural hall, Broad street, below Locust street, for Berg & Publicker, by Edward Margolies, of New York. The structure will be of brick, 80 by 200 feet, and cost $280,000 to build.

Premiere of New Patriotic Film.

Philadelphia, Pa.—Before several hundred invited guests, including motion picture exhibitors and newspapermen, the patriotic photoplay "For Freedom of the World," the first production of the new S. and M. Film Company, composed of local theatrical men, was shown Monday, September 10, in the Liberty theater, Columbia avenue above Broad street. This film drama proposes to carry a message to the lukewarm citizen of either sex in these stirring war times.

Not Satisfied With Express Service.

Philadelphia, Pa.—Several complaints have been entered against the Adams Express on account of the poor service and late deliveries. The express company claims that this condition has been brought about through the scarcity of office each day to make rapid return deliveries from the station.

B. R. Tolmas, of the Mutual, and Allen May, of the Bluebird, have shown a disposition to co-operate with other exchange men as soon as they are ready.

"Red Ace" Gets Many Contracts.

Philadelphia, Pa.—The Interstate Films Corporation have secured, several high-class vaudeville houses for the first pre-

sentation of their latest serial "The Red Ace," which stars Marie Walcamp, who secured a tremendous following with her last serial, "Liberty."

Victor Theater Opened Labor Day.

Fleetwood, Pa.—Labor Day marked the opening of the regular season of the Victor. This theater, which has been recently purchased by Cook and Hartford, opened with "The Battle Cry of Peace" and packed 'em to the doors. John H. Cook, who is in partnership with Mr. Hartford, was formerly general manager of Carr and Shad's enterprises in Reading and vicinity for the past twelve years.

Philadelphia Trade Notes.

Philadelphia, Pa.—The Bluebird exchange will shortly inaugurate an intensive publicity campaign with 24 sheet posters and a big newspaper advertising campaign starting October 1. Exhibitors displaying Bluebird photoplays will receive some excellent co-operation.

Philadelphia, Pa.—J. M. Graver returned from his vacation last week and is now preparing an eventful season for the Liberty theater. Contracts for several of the leading feature productions have been given, including also Artcraft and Paramount.

Philadelphia, Pa.—Audiences which filled two popular photoplay houses, the Arcadia and the Palace, were captivated by the initial presentation in each instance of Mary Pickford at her very best in "Rebecca of Sunnybrook Farm."

Philadelphia, Pa.—George M. Cohan, in the film version of "Seven Keys to Baldpate," was the feature picture offered last week at the Nixon in West Philadelphia and at the Strand.

Philadelphia, Pa.—Charles H. Goodwin has booked "Twenty Thousand Leagues Under the Sea" for the Eureka for September 19. He had a sea diver doing various interesting things under water.

Philadelphia, Pa.—Edward J. O'Keefe, of the City Square and Cort theaters, paid a visit to the Triangle offices last week and stated that he had done big business with the "Master of His Home" at the Cort. He contemplates extensive improvements at the Cort.

Newark News Letter.

By Jacob J. Kalter, 25 Branford place, Newark, N. J.

Messer & Springer Filed Trade Name.

NEWARK, N. J.—Alonzo N. Messer, 286 North Grove street, East Orange, and J. Harwood Springer, 193 Peshine avenue, Newark, have filed as the trade name of their film rental concern the Classay Feature Film Company. Offices have been opened up in the Proctor theater building, suite 55. Mr. Messer controls the New Jersey state rights for the "Fighting Chance" and also for "Common Sense Brackett." Mr. Springer is the New Jersey distributor for the Ivan features. The combined firm will book these features as well as several other big films, whose purchases are now under consideration.

Newark Theater Shows Departure of Soldiers.

Newark, N. J.—Pictures showing the departure of the first troops were shown last week at the new Newark theater, 196 Market street. The films were taken at the special instance of the management and were shown on the same day. John B. McNally is the resident manager.

"Silent Witness" and "Conqueror" Seen.

Newark, N. J.—During the week of September 16 "The Silent Witness" will be the attraction at Fox's Terminal theater,

Park place. William Farnum in the "Conqueror" is booked for the week of September 23. These pictures will be shown first locally at the Terminal, which is under the house management of Moe Kridell.

Evelyn Nesbit Appears Personally.

Newark, N. J.—Evelyn Nesbit, star of "Redemption" and other features, appeared in person September 14, 15, 16 at Proctor's Palace theater, 116 Market street.

United Cinema Appoints Agent.

Hackensack, N. J.—The United Cinema Theaters, Inc., a Delaware corporation, have appointed as their New Jersey agent Marinus Contant, with offices in the Union Banking building.

The Eliot Files Name.

Newark, N. J.—The Eliot Theater Company is the trade name filed in the county clerk's office for the company controlling the Eliot theater, 244 Washington avenue. Those who filed the trade name are Raymond D. Moffett, of Basking Ridge; Katherine Hoppe, of Bernardsville; and Harriet P. Cook, of East Orange.

Classay Film Company Formed.

Newark, N. J.—The Classay Features Film Company has been formed here to buy features on the state rights plan. The concern has opened offices at suite 55, Proctor theater building, 116 Market street. A. N. Measure, formerly owner and manager of the Ampere theater, East Orange, and J. H. Springer, distributor of Ivan Films, have formed the partnership. The firm controls all of the Ivan productions and "The Fighting Chance," "Common Sense Brackett" and several other high-class productions.

Loew's Theater Reopens.

Newark, N. J.—Loew's theater, 99 Springfield avenue, reopened for the season September 3. The photoplay feature for the first half of the week was Rupert Julian in "Mother 'o Mine." The feature the latter part of the week was Evelyn Nesbit in "Redemption." Eugene Meyers will remain as resident manager of the theater.

"The Spy" at Terminal.

Newark, N. J.—During the week of September 9 Dustin Farnum in the "Spy" was the attraction at Fox's Terminal theater, Park place. Moe Kridell is the manager of the theater.

New Camden Incorporation.

Camden, N. J.—The F. N. F. Amusement Company, with registered offices at 419 Market street, has filed articles of incorporation September 1 at Trenton. The New Jersey Corporation Guarantee and Trading Company, of the above address, is named as registered agent. The concern is capitalized at $10,000, and is authorized to operate and control theaters. The incorporators are F. R. Hansel, J. A. MacPeak, and I. C. Clow.

Stray Michigan Notes.

Abe Steinberg, secretary of the National Poster Co., Chicago, was a recent Detroit visitor. He came here to buy some five and two-reel features.

The new Colonial theater, Detroit, will open for business about Sept. 25 with vaudeville and pictures.

New Goldwyn contracts in Michigan are Rialto and Majestic theaters in Muskegon; Vaudette, Mt. Pleasant; Arcade, Ann Arbor; Globe, Detroit; Lyric, Lapeer, and Majestic, in Wyandotte.

The first Goldwyn picture in Michigan, "Polly of the Circus," has its premier this week (Sept. 9) at the Madison theater, Detroit.

What Theater Taxes Netted Last Year

Uncle Sam Collected $1,027,927 from Amusement Licenses in 1916-17—Amount Is More Than Previous Year and Cost Less to Collect.

By Clarence L. Linz, 622 Riggs Building, Washington, D. C.

WASHINGTON, D. C.—Uncle Sam was made the richer during the fiscal year ending June 30, 1917, by $1,027,927.63, this being the amount of money he exacted from the motion picture, the legitimate theaters, the museums and concert halls of the United States.

A comparison of the taxes paid by the amusement places of the country as provided under the war emergency revenue laws to be placed upon them according to their seating capacities, is contained in the preliminary report of Commission of Internal Revenue W. H. Osborn, which has been sent to Secretary of the Treasury McAdoo. The revenue obtained from this source during the twelve months ending with June 30, 1916, amounted to $1,014,911.28, the fiscal year 1917 exceeding this by $13,016.35.

The receipts for the fiscal year 1917 exceeded those of any other years since the establishment of the Internal Revenue Bureau. The total amount collected was $809,393,640.44, an increase of $296,670,352.67 over the fiscal year 1916 when the Bureau took in $512,723,287.77, and Commissioner Osborn thought the limit had been reached.

The cost of collecting this huge sum was also much lower than ever before. For every $1,000 taken in, Uncle Sam's representatives paid out $9.53 in the work, this being .95 per cent. In the fiscal year 1916 the cost per $1,000 of collections was $14.04, or 1.4 per cent. The average cost of collection since the establishment of the bureau is $22.21, or 2.22 per cent.

Permits Granted for Two New Theaters.

Washington, D. C.—The Rialto Theater Company, of which Tom Moore is at the head, has been granted a permit to erect the Rialto theater at 713 to 717 Ninth street and 712 to 720 Eighth street, Northwest, at a cost estimated at $250,000. Blank & Zink are the architects of the structure, and M. A. Weller, the building contractor. The structures formerly on the site of the new house have been demolished and the way clear for the builder to go ahead with his work.

Arthur L. Robb Goes Over to Crandall.

Washington, D. C.—Quite a surprise was sprung in film circles here last week when it was announced that Arthur L. Robb had severed his connection with the Moore string of houses and had joined the Crandall string. He is to become the manager of the Knickerbocker theater, which is rapidly nearing completion at Eighteenth street and Columbia road, and which is scheduled for opening late this month. However, when the Metropolitan on F street is completed he is to be transferred to that house.

Mr. Robb was identified with the Tom Moore enterprises for about five years. Before coming to Washington he had been connected with various theatrical enterprises in the east for about ten years. Prior to entering the theatrical business he was connected with newspaper work, and is accredited with being the pioneer publicity agent in this territory in connection with moving pictures, for he early instituted a regular press department in connection with the Garden and Strand theaters.

George Schneider Succeeds Robb.

Mr. Robb has been succeeded as manager of the Garden and Strand theaters by George Schneider, who comes to Washington from Baltimore, where he has been in the theatrical profession for a number of years. He has been manager of the Garden theater in Baltimore for about three years, previous to which time he was manager of the New theater for about

four years. Both of these are vaudeville houses and he was slated to take up similar work in connection with the combined moving picture and vaudeville theater which Mr. Moore has in prospect.

Paramount-Artcraft Takes New Space.

Washington, D. C.—The Paramount Artcraft exchange is being enlarged by addition of space on the first floor of the building at 525 Thirteenth street, Northwest. This new room will be utilized by the paper department which will permit the doubling of the office space on the floor above.

Since taking over the management of the exchange, Manager Barron has found himself badly cramped because of the combination of Paramount with Artcraft. This move, according to Manager Barron, will enable the enlargement also of the service department under the new scheme of handling business in this territory.

Mr. Barron has the distinction of now furnishing service to every city and town in this territory having a population of 5,000 or more.

J. H. Butner Pleased in Atlanta.

Washington, D. C.—James H. Butner, ex-president of the Washington Exchange Managers' Association and former manager of the local Triangle exchange, has assumed charge of the Atlanta, Ga., exchange of the First National Exhibitors' Circuit. Mr. Butner is to look after the distribution in North and South Carolina, Georgia, Florida, Alabama and Tennessee of the big subjects that the organization plans to buy, and also of the Chaplin pictures, which it already controls. At present his office is located in the Lyric Theater Building, but, according to a letter just received at the Washington office of the Moving Picture World, he will soon become established in the film district. Mr. Butner declares himself to be "in the land of the blest, where censors do not rule, and where regulations hold not their sway."

Theatrical Waste of Food Deprecated.

Washington, D. C.—The actor folk have just been told of another way in which they can help Uncle Sam in the war—they have just been appealed to by the United States Food Administration to substitute imitation banquets for the real thing in those productions requiring the use of food. Better still, however, to the Food Administration's way of thinking, would be the total elimination of all scenes depicting feasts.

"The Food Administration desires to stop not merely the actual waste of this food material that is used in the production of motion picture films and on the stage," a statement from the Administration declares, "but to prevent the unconscious bad effect on audience at this time when every effort is being made to drive home the need of the elimination of every possible food waste as a means of helping to win the war. The amount of food unprofitably used in theatrical performances throughout the country amounts to a much larger bulk than is ordinarily realized. The Administration is of the opinion that in meals on the stage and in the making of films, imitations can be used in most cases, and believes that where this is not possible the scenes showing the use of food can be omitted."

Pittsburgh Film Men Give a Corn Roast

Have Outing to Raise Funds to Help in Campaigns Against Freak Legislation, All Go Out to Groveton, Pa., for a Pleasant Time.

From Pittsburgh News Service, 6104 Jenk ins' Arcade, Pittsburgh, Pa.

PITTSBURGH, PA.—The allied moving picture interests of Pittsburgh and vicinity were to assemble at Gazaza Camp, Groveton, Pa., on Sunday, September 16, for an elaborate family gathering and cornroast—the first event of its kind to be put on by the local film folk. From all indications it will prove a largely attended and successful affair. Members of the F. I. L. M. club, exchangemen and exhibitors were heartily co-operating with the various committees, so that nothing will be left undone which will contribute to the enjoyment of the guests.

The following circular has been issued: 'The object of this gathering is to create a fund to be used for any and all cases of adverse legislation to the film industry. Different organizations have at various times in years past been compelled to solicit funds for this purpose, and always the same few people have paid the bills. In asking your support to make this gathering a success we are simply asking you to DO YOUR BIT, for every dollar received will be used for beneficial purposes of the motion picture interests.'

The hard-working committees in charge are as follows: On arrangements—Al. W. Cross, chairman; H. P. Greele, C. F. Campbell. Sports—F. C. Burhans, Walter Kinson, C. F. Schwerin. Film to be made on the grounds—C. F. Miller. Publicity—M. J. C. Kornblum, William Mayer, P. A. Mansfield, C. B. Frost, R. Warren.

Edgar Wolberg Goes to Missouri and Kansas.

Pittsburgh, Pa.—Edgar H. Wolberg, formerly manager of the Harris P. Wolfberg attractions, Lyceum building, Pittsburgh, is leaving the local office of that concern to take charge of the distribution of "The Deemster" in Missouri and Kansas, which has recently been added to the Eastern states already controlled by the Wolfberg Exchange.

"Efficiency" Edgar, as E. H. Wolfberg's friends in the Pittsburgh territory have nicknamed him, is versatile. During the past six months he has played an important part in staging "The Crisis" in Western Pennsylvania, Ohio and West Virginia. His sensational success in this city was the talk of moving picture circles. Newspapermen estimate that he was accorded the largest amount of publicity ever secured by any photoplay.

Previous to his connection with the Harris P. Wolfberg attractions, he was assistant manager of the General Film office in St. Louis. It was during these days that he created "The Film General," a house-organ that received the approbation of all the photoplay journals.

New Exchange to Handle Big Subjects.

Pittsburgh, Pa.—The Fort Pitt Theater exchange, the latest film concern to enter the field in Pittsburgh, has completed plans for elaborate and prominently located headquarters to be occupied in the near future. The exchange will take over a portion of the Pitt Theater building, at the corner of Penn avenue and Seventh street. Alterations are now going forward and the company expects to do business in its new quarters within the next week or ten days.

The Fort Pitt theater exchange handles only big subjects, especially those which have had a long run at the Pitt theater. William Moore Patch is president of the company; L. Newman, representative; Norman S. Carroll, publicity manager; Harry Marcus, office manager.

H. C. Allen Now Heads Triangle Branch.

Pittsburgh, Pa.—H. C. Allen has succeeded J. C. Greer as manager of the Pittsburgh branch of the Triangle. Mr. Allen was formerly assistant manager of the Triangle exchange at Dallas, Tex., and is an able and experienced film man. The announcement of his appointment is received with much approval by the local trade.

G. R. Ainsworth on Road for Supreme.

Pittsburgh, Pa.—Guy R. Ainsworth, until recently manager of the local office of the Fox Film, has joined the road force of the Supreme Photoplay Productions, Seltzer Film building, Pittsburgh. Mr. Ainsworth is specializing with excellent results on the new acquisitions of the Supreme exchange, "Redemption," "God's Man" and "The Cold Deck."

G. H. Garfunkle Building Theater.

Farrell, Pa.—A large new theater is to be erected soon at Farrell, Pa., by G. H. Garfunkle, a prominent manufacturer of that place. The house will occupy the site of the present Rex theater, operated by Stahl Brothers. Work will be started about January 1, at the expiration of the lease held by that firm on the Rex. The projected theater will have a seating capacity of 1,500 and will be modern in every respect. It will be erected at a cost of about $75,000.

H. E. Stahler Promoted.

Pittsburgh, Pa.—The many friends of H. E. Stahler will be glad to hear of his promotion to the position of manager of the Pittsburgh offices of the Harris P. Wolfberg attractions, Lyceum building. Mr. Stahler formerly was in charge of the publicity department of the Wolfberg Exchange. Previous to that he represented the V. L. S. E. in St. Louis, and later the Essanay.

In connection with Mr. Stahler's promotion, Mr. Wolfberg made the following statement: "It was Mr. Stahler's fine work with 'The Crisis' and 'The Deemster' that has hurried his promotion. His method of exhibitor co-operation, which is the outstanding feature of the distribution of these pictures, is largely responsible for his success.

"The States Rights men of the future," continued Mr. Wolfberg, "must recognise the importance of exhibitor co-operation. In the field of merchandising, dealer co-operation is developed to a fine point, and the manufacturer does not stop when the goods are on the dealer's shelf. He helps him sell, and by helping the dealer he helps himself. There is no reason why the same intensive co-operation should not exist in the photoplay business."

Park Theater Taken by T. A. Kinney.

Franklin, Pa.—The Park theater, Franklin, Pa., has been taken over by T. A. Kinney, who is now sole owner of this attractive picture house. Mr. Kinney announces that his future policy will probably be big feature productions. The Park was formerly operated by the Park Theater Amusement company.

J. F. Young Now With Goldwyn.

J. F. Young, for the past year travelling representative out of the Pittsburgh office of the General has joined the road staff of the local Goldwyn exchange.

Trade Notes for Western Pennsylvania.

A largely attended trade showing of the first three episodes of the new Pathe serial, "The Seven Pearls," featuring Mollie King, was given on Thursday, September 13, at the Majestic theater, Erie, Pa. The showing was in charge of Manager Fuller, of the Pittsburgh office of Pathe. He reports excellent advance bookings on "The Seven Pearls," which will be released September 17.

Claysville, Pa.—The handsome new Rex theater, Claysville, Pa., will be formally opened within the next few days. The Rex is a fine addition to the list of up-to-date theaters in its locality. Exclusively high-class feature pictures will be shown. This house has been erected by a company of Washington, Pa., business men.

Pittsburgh, Pa.—George See, auditor of the Pittsburgh Paramount exchange, left September 5 for the United States Army training camp at Petersburg, Va. Mr. See was one of the first members of the local film industry to be drafted. A lively send-off was accorded him by the Paramount organization.

Punxsutawney, Pa.—The Jefferson theater, Punxsutawney, Pa., has been closed for remodeling and redecorating, and the management plans to make it one of the most attractive houses in that section. A formal reopening will be held in about three weeks. The Jefferson's well-known policy of high-class feature productions will be resumed.

Maritime News Letter.

By Alice Fairweather, The Standard, St. John, N. B.

A. K. Mundee Opens St. John Triangle.

ST. JOHN, N. B.—A new film office has opened in St. John, The Triangle, with A. K. Mundee as local manager. Mr. Mundee is a theatrical man of many years' experience, and will no doubt be very successful. He prepared for the convention a splendid advertising button, a white button bearing the name of the delegate in black letters, the trade mark of the Triangle showing on the background of the button. New offices have been taken in the Robinson building, Market square, and large space was given in the papers to the announcement of the opening.

Pathe Manager Returns from Western Trip.

St. John, N. B.—L. Ernest Ouimet, who was in St. John for the convention has lately done much work in the filming of "Progress and Prosperity Films" for the Canadian provinces. Included in this series are splendid views of new Brunswick. Mr. Ouimet, who is general manager for the Specialty Film Import, Canadian distributors of Pathe, has also taken several interesting pictures showing the work done by returned soldiers for the Canadian Military Hospitals Commission, paying particular attention to the vocational training going on at those institutions. He has recently completed 2,000 feet of film showing the Royal Flying Corps at Camp Borden with Canadian aviators in the making.

"Polly" Much Appreciated in St. John.

St. John, N. B.—Charles Berman, through the courtesy of the Imperial theater management, gave a trade showing of the first Goldwyn release in this territory Wednesday morning, Aug. 8. A number of exhibitors and invited guests were present, and all expressed themselves as greatly pleased with the production, especially the horse race, which excited even the most blase of the exhibitors. Music was furnished by members of the Imperial orchestra, with M. C. Ewing at the piano, and this added greatly to the enjoyment of the audience. The picture made a very good impression upon those present.

G. B. Abbineau's Theater Now Larger.

G. B. Abbineau, of the Palace theater at Chatham, has brought his house downstairs, increasing the capacity of his theater from 550 to 1,000 seats. He now has a fine picture house.

Convention Notes of the Trade.

St. John, N. B.—The Pathe Company (Specialty Film Import) had a window on one of the principal streets filled with pictures and cards illustrative of the Pathe films, and with the familiar Rooster in the centre.

The Triangle Company displayed a banner with "Welcome" near the Imperial theater. Their new manager, A. K. Mundee, is a wideawake advertiser, and his company will profit by his ingenuity.

"The Flame of the Yukon" (Triangle) was screened at the Imperial theater, as was also "Within the Law" (Vitagraph) and "The Seven Pearls" (Pathe). Many screenings were held at the exchanges.

F. G. Spencer Gets Nova Scotia Film Theater.

Wolfville, N. S.—F. G. Spencer, of St. John, has taken over the opera house at Wolfville, N. S., and the moving picture theater at Hantsport, N. S. The opera house is managed by Archer W. Mason, formerly of St. John. The theater at Woodstock recently leased by F. G. Spencer opened on Monday, Sept. 10, under his new management.

The Gem theater at Fredericton, N. B. controlled by F. G. Spencer, also will reopen Thursday, Sept. 20. The theater has been renovated, many improvements installed and the seating capacity increased. The opening will be held in collaboration with the Red Cross Society of Fredericton, of which Countess of Ashburnham is the president.

A Daughter to the O'Rourkes.

Fairville, N. B.—Mr. and Mrs. Edward O'Rourke, of Fairvale, are rejoicing over the arrival of a daughter at their home on Sunday, Sept. 9. Mr. O'Rourke is the proprietor and manager of the Galety theater, Fairville.

Notes from Maritime Provinces.

St. John, N. B.—A. B. Farmer, of the Star theater, upon the finish of "Patria" will start next week. "The Double Cross Mystery," and later the Pathe serial "The Neglected Wife." This will give the Star patrons a serial at the beginning and end of the week. It takes Pathe for serials, says Mr. Farmer, and accordingly he has booked these two from R. G. March of the Specialty Film Import, at St. John.

St. John, N. B.—The Fox production, "A Tale of Two Cities" had very heavy bookings throughout this territory and repeat bookings were asked for in several instances.

St. John, N. B.—About the villages of Newcastle, Bathurst and Chatham road, shows are playing to fairly good business. The French people in that section of the country cry out for stage productions, but are gradually being educated to the motion picture, and the houses in these towns do good business as a general thing.

St. John, N. B.—Special Labor Day programmes were provided. At the Imperial, which did splendidly with Robert Warwick in "The Silent Master," and at the Opera House showing vaudeville with "Gloria's Romance." The Unique theater started "The Fatal Ring" with the popular Pearl White, on Monday, September 10. The same day marked the return of the Arlington orchestra to the Unique, where their tuneful music will be enjoyed for a long engagement.

Campbellton Man Starts Traveling Show.

Campbellton, N. B.—S. W. Dimmock, of the opera house at Campbellton, has a novel idea. He is now on a tour of the Gaspe coast with several pictures which he will show to the people up that way who do not have many opportunities of seeing motion pictures. Dimmock goes in his car, carrying his own equipment on his trusty auto.

General Trade Conditions in Canada Good

New Theater Being Built on St. Clair Avenue, Toronto—Opening of the New Allen Theater Soon—Jewel Productions Opens Exchange.

By W. M. Gladish, 1263 Gerrard street East, Toronto.

TORONTO, ONTARIO.—The fall boom in moving picture circles of Ontario is on in earnest. Everywhere there are signs of structural development and improvement, the many good releases are attracting great crowds and, according to statements of big men in the Canadian industry, general conditions throughout this territory were never so healthy as at present.

One of several substantial film houses which are being built in Toronto and vicinity is the theatre on St. Clair avenue, one of the finest thoroughfares in the northern section of the city. This theatre is being erected by James Crang, a prominent local contractor. The completed structure will cost about $75,000 and its features will be up-to-date in every particular. The seating capacity will be 1,400 with all seats on the one floor. Mr. Crang's address is 96 St. Clair avenue West.

The Allen theater, a fine new structure in the downtown section, is practically finished and the official announcement regarding the opening is being awaited with interest by most everybody in the film business. Manager Ben Cronk, formerly of Calgary, is busy with preparations.

Another modern picture theater, with a seating capacity of 900, has been opened in Guelph, while the Windsor theater, Windsor, which was destroyed by fire last summer, has been rebuilt and is again in operation.

The Colonial theater, City Hall square, Toronto, has also been given a new front. The alterations were made without closing the theatre.

Class to Teach Soldiers How to Operate.

Toronto, Ont.—Announcement has been made by the Military Hospitals Commission that a class for moving picture operators has been started at the Central Technical School, Toronto, in connection with the vocational training of returned convalescent soldiers. The class has attracted much interest among returned men as a step toward new means of livelihood.

Sam Glazer Wins Promotion.

Toronto, Ont.—Sam Glazer has become Toronto branch manager of the Famous Players. This is some promotion for

Glazer who has been with the F. P. for many months.

The Monarch Film, which is closely allied with the Famous Players service, has acquired the Canadian rights to a number of big attractions, including "The Garden of Allah," "The Public Be Damned," "Joan, the Woman," and "Beware of Strangers." The Monarch also controls Canadian releases of Selznick productions.

J. A. Morrison Now in Oregon.

Toronto, Ont.—J. A. Morrison, formerly proprietor of the Star theater, Meaford, Ontario, is now in business in Eugene, Oregon, where he is running the Eugene theater, according to word received from him at the Canadian headquarters of the Universal. Morrison is forever a Universal booster.

Local Universal News Items.

Toronto, Ont.—Clair Hague, general manager of the Canadian Universal, was the Toronto representative at the convention of Motion Picture Exhibitors' League of the Maritime Provinces at St. John, N. B. Mr. Hague also inspected the Montreal and St. John branches of the Universal on his Eastern trip.

The Bluebird, "Mother o'Mine," which was first released in Canada at Shea's Hippodrome, Toronto, during the week of September 3, is booked solid in Ontario until Christmas, according to Manager McKenney of the Bluebird offices here.

Shea's Hippodrome has also booked "Come Through" as the film attraction for the week of September 24.

D. G. Walkley, Calgary, Western Canadian manager of the Universal, has returned to his Alberta headquarters after an official visit at the Toronto headquarters of the Universal which he made to arrange business details for the coming twelve months. He is tickled beyond measure with film prospects all over the Dominion.

J. Belmont has been appointed Western Canadian representative for the state rights feature department of the Canadian Universal. G. A. Margetts, manager of the "U" office in St. John, will look after this business in the Maritime Provinces while H. Fischer will handle the State Rights in Ontario, according to a statement handed out from the Canadian Universal headquarters here.

Montreal's St. Denis Theater Reopens

Roland Roberts Starts Beautiful Picture Theater Again with "Polly"—Has 3,000 Seats at Ten Cents to Twenty-five Cents.

MONTREAL, QUEBEC.—The St. Denis theater, Montreal, the largest and one of the most elaborate amusement houses in the whole of Canada, was reopened on Saturday, September 8, under the management of Roland Roberts, manager of the Regent theater, Toronto. The managing director of the new company which will operate the St. Denis is N. L. Nathanson, who is also general manager of the Regal Films, Limited, distributors in Canada of Goldwyn, World, and other pictures.

The feature at the St. Denis for the re-opening performance was the first Goldwyn release, "Polly of the Circus," and the scale of admission prices was from 25c to 10c. The house now has a symphony orchestra of sixteen pieces under the direction of Mr. J. J. Goulet, late of the Montreal Symphony Orchestra, and under the supervision of Leon Kofman. The Hope Jones organ will again be used. Frank Oldfield, the New York baritone, was also one of the attractions for the opening week.

The St. Denis was closed last spring after it had passed into the hands of receivers and had been sold at public auction. The seating capacity is roughly

3,000, and the many structural appointments are the finest obtainable.

Independent Will Distribute War Films.

Montreal, Que.—Announcement has also been made in Montreal that the Independent Film and Theater Supply Company has acquired the distribution rights for official British War Office film releases in Canada. The company will take four prints of the big war specials, it is declared. The company has branches in Montreal, Winnipeg, Toronto and St. John. One of the first releases will show the arrival of the American fleet in British waters and the arrival of American troops somewhere across the pond. The "Battle of Arras" will also be a coming feature.

Regal Will Distribute Rex Beach Films.

Toronto, Ont.—All Rex Beach features, with the exception of "The Barrier," will be distributed in Canada by Regal Films, Limited. Regal has also contracted to handle "The Great White Trail" in the Dominion for John C. Green of Galt, Ontario.

Cleveland Operators Demand New Scale

Higher Wages Again Asked for—New Scale Calls for $40 a Week for Matinee and Night Shows—Special Rate for Screenings.

From M. A. Malaney, 218 Columbia Building, Cleveland, Ohio.

CLEVELAND, OHIO.—Increases of from eight to ten dollars a week are indicated in the new wage scale drawn up by the Cleveland operators union and sent the theaters which run all day or afternoons and evenings.

For several years there has been a steady increase in wage scales of operators each fall. Other years the Exhibitors' League has fought them, but usually without success, except that some theater owners discharged their operators and did their own operating.

The new scale goes into effect October 1, but at this writing the exhibitors have not indicated that they would fight it.

The new scale calls for a wage, of $40 per week for operators who work matinees and nights; operators who work in double-shift theaters ask $25 per week where the theaters are running but ten hours a day; $35 per week where they run 14 hours a day and $40 per week where they run 16 hours per day. The hours indicated, of course, are divided up so that the two operators on double shifts work each half of the time.

For overtime, the new scale calls for $1 per hour or fraction thereof and for screenings, etc., $1.50 per hour or fraction thereof.

At this rate, screenings will cost film exchanges $3 unless a five-reel feature can be run in an hour.

This is the second raise in wages of theater employes in Cleveland lately, the musicians, especially organists, having se-cured an increase, in some cases amounting to $10 a week.

Exhibitors Tackle the Pass Nuisance.

Cleveland, O.—Cleveland theater managers are up in arms at the practice of abusing season passes. Here are some of the charges gathered from the managers:

Such passes are used usually on Saturdays or Sundays, when the theaters need their seats the most.

Some parties loan their passes—one pass came in four times in a week, a total of eighteen persons gaining admission.

A great many people who have season passes consider themselves privileged after entering the theater. They sit in box seats and complain when the ushers ask them to move.

Many with passes who have to stand in the rear or in the lobbies complain or make sarcastic remarks.

One of the city's leading moving picture theaters has called in all season passes and will issue new ones only to the press, while another has taken up the pass at the door and is issuing new ones marked "not good Sundays or Holidays."

Nearly all of the theaters now keep track of all passes, which are numbered, and are refusing to honor them a second time during the engagement of any picture.

"Persons with passes should remember that they are getting something for nothing, which others pay for, and act accordingly," said one manager.

Cleveland Screen Club Plans Benefit

Screens Hope to Keep Young Son of Burt Garrett in School—Deceased Left Son and Daughter—Appeal to His Old Friends for Help.

CLEVELAND, O.—The Cleveland Screen Club is about to attempt something never before tried by a like organization—a benefit for the children of a deceased member.

The children are those of Burton Garrett, who was found dead in his apartments in Indianapolis a few weeks ago.

They are Carlos, nine years old, and Marion, four. The boy is now in an English military college in Havana, Cuba, and it is for the principal purpose of enabling the youngster to complete his education that the benefit will be held.

A committee was appointed at the last meeting of the club to make arrangements for the benefit. M. A. Malaney is chairman and he has appointed the following members of this committee for these various duties:

Dave Adler, in charge of theater arrangements; G. W. Erdmann and George Cole, to obtain vaudeville acts; Joseph Grossman, in charge of distribution of tickets, and Tom Colby, treasurer of committee.

Burt Garrett had a legion of friends among the film men of Ohio, Indiana and New York City. The committee makes an appeal to them to help this worthy cause along. The tickets for the benefit which will be in the nature of a vaudeville show at 11 p. m. some evening in September or the fore part of October, date to be announced later, are $1 each, and may be purchased from M. A. Malaney, 218 Columbia Building, or Joseph Grossman, Standard theater, Cleveland.

Elyria Opera House Burns.

Elyria, O.—The Elyria opera house, which was bought about a week ago by Melton Phelos and others, was destroyed by fire last Tuesday, after Labor Day.

The theater was to be remodeled for pictures. The fire started about 2 a. m. and in two hours the playhouse was ruined. At times it was thought that the blaze would spread to other buildings, among them a theater. The loss was estimated at $60,000.

Newspaper's Film Edition Claims Success.

Cleveland, O.—After several months of experimenting, the Cleveland Plain Dealer officials believe their weekly magazine is a sure success. They base this upon the large number of inquiries from newspaper subscribers and the increase in bookings by Cleveland theaters.

Fox's Features Doing Well in Ohio.

Cleveland, O.—The big Fox productions are well on their way in Ohio, "The Honor System" having opened at the Ceramic theater, East Liverpool, for four days, and "The Spy" at the Park, Youngstown, for four days. These and other Fox super productions will be shown for one and two week runs in the Standard theater, Cleveland, and for week runs in the Temple theater, Toledo.

Cleveland, O.—Walter W. Irwin, general manager of Vitagraph, was in Cleveland last week and inspected the local branch. He also conferred with Manager Johnson about the prospects for this season's business.

Dayton News Letter

By Paul J. Gray, Alhambra Theater Bldg., Dayton, Oo.

Division of Paramount and Artcraft Pictures in Dayton.

DAYTON, OHIO.—Until further announcement the Columbia theater in Dayton will run the attractions in which appear William S. Hart, Mary Pickford, Dorothy Dalton, George Beban, all the Ince productions and also all the Petrova pictures.

The Columbia will also run Charles Ray and all the other stars not mentioned for the Strand, which is the other house to run Paramount and Artcraft pictures.

The Strand will have Marguerite Clark,

Douglas Fairbanks, Billie Burke, Ann Pennington, Pickford and Huff, Vivian Martin, Julian Eltinge, and the rest of the regular Paramount stars.

Business Good at All Dayton Theaters.

Dayton, O.—With the closing of B. F. Keith's summer vaudeville here at ten and twenty-cent admission prices, the picture business should pick up considerably. Most of the houses have been doing good all summer and the hot weather did not interfere with business. The Majestic, which has been closed for some time owing to receivers' proceedings, is expected to open within the next few months and will then make Dayton's picture houses complete in their quota, with the exception of a few neighborhood houses which never will open again.

Buffalo News Letter

By Joseph A. McGuire, 183 North Elmwood St., Buffalo, N. Y.

N. I. Filkins Becomes Pathe Manager.

BUFFALO, N. Y.—N. I. Filkins has been appointed manager of the Pathe exchange, Buffalo. He succeeds J. W. Fuller, who has become assistant manager of the company's St. Louis office. Mr. Filkins was formerly city salesman for the Pathe in Buffalo for three years. On the day he assumed his new position several exhibitors sent him a large bouquet in honor of the occasion. With the flowers was a card bearing these words: "Hon. Filkins, the man that showed the Path.E in Buffalo." The recipient is a pioneer in the film business, having opened the first Pathe office in this city. A. Teschemacher, former Pathe booker, has succeeded Mr. Filkins as city salesman.

Mr. Filkins takes particular pride in his reorganized staff, which he says shows made several promotions and appointments, which will be announced next week.

H. L. Taylor, Rochester representative of the Pathe, was a Buffalo caller. Mr. Taylor is learning to write down film orders with his left hand. The reason is that while cranking his machine in front of the Lyndhurst theater, Rochester, recently he had the misfortune to break his right arm in two places.

George Hickey Has Handsome Office.

Buffalo, N. Y.—George A. Hickey, Goldwyn representative, Buffalo, has returned from a business tour of New York State. He is delighted with the demand for these pictures. The Goldwyn office has new green plush carpets, mahogany furniture and partitions of the same material. "A model exchange" is the way Edgar Weill of the Strand theater, Syracuse, has described this branch.

John Sitterly Walks in Fear of a Certain Printer.

Buffalo, N. Y.—John Sitterly of the Popular exchange, Buffalo, has in his possession a theatrical handbill. It came from a village in New York near Buffalo that boasts of its "electric lights, paved streets, mammoth cheese factory" and other city improvements. The purpose of the dodger was to advertise the versatility of a comedian at the local opera house. It had large wood cut, which had outlived its usefulness right after the Civil War. The drawing showed a grinning creature wearing a hat of ante-bellum style. Under the cut were the words: "One of our townsmen laughing at our shows." The theatrical manager responsible for the handbill probably didn't intend to use "laughing at," but he did just the same.

"The opera house in question enforces the 'hats off' rule among its women patrons," Mr. Sitterly assured me, but the cut shows that this rule doesn't apply to the men. The handbill looks like a stage souvenir of fifty years ago. The general make-up of the sheet made it seem as if it had been produced in the village cheese factory.

"Believe me," said he, "if I play 'The Daughter of the Gods' at this opera house, I will closely censor every bit of advertising used. I hate to think of what kind of an old-fashioned wood cut the village printer might dig up to represent Miss Kellerman in her diving costume."

Exhibitor Dillon Visits Buffalo.

Ithaca, N. Y.—Will Dillon, former vaudevillian and song writer, recently visited Mr. Hickey. Before pictures were the vogue these two played stock together. Mr. Dillon is now owner of the Strand theater, Ithaca. He has opened his autumn season with Goldwyn productions.

Jottings Caught in Passing.

Buffalo, N. Y.—G. A. Woodard, Goldwyn road representative, is now at his home in Luzerne, N. Y.

"Polly of the Circus," a film production, has played successfully at Shea's Hippodrome, Buffalo; Strand, Syracuse; Alhambra, Utica, and Picadilly, Rochester.

Recent visitors in Buffalo included Fred B. Murphy, vice-president of the Unicorn Film; Harris Lumberg, of the Lumberg theater, Niagara Falls; Mr. Landers, an exhibitor and postmaster of Fredonia; Mr. Pierce, of the Temple theater, Geneva, and Mr. Petersen, of the Winter Garden theater, Jamestown.

Street Cars Try to Put One Over.

Buffalo, N. Y.—Exhibitors and other business men along Broadway, Buffalo, have protested to Mayor Fuhrmann against the line of the International Railway Co. The plan is to have the cars stop at alternate corners to save time. The objectors claim that the cars are too often crowded and that more cars are needed.

Buffalo Theaters Start in on Their Coal.

Buffalo, N. Y.—A sudden drop in temperature has driven home nearly the last contingent of summer colonists from Buffalo's lake and river resorts and has helped the business of the local exhibitors. The theatrical managers have discarded all summer advertising about their cool, wind-swept houses and have started their fires. Firing a theater these days requires as much courage as firing a manager, on account of the scarcity and high price of coal.

The exhibitors have learned that anthracite in Buffalo, despite the government's price fixing, costs seventy-five cents a ton more now than it did any time last winter. It is said that this city's soft coal industry is also thoroughly demoralized. Last winter the cold weather and the coal shortage gave some of the local theaters a barn-like temperature.

Michigan Notes of the Trade.

Battle Creek, Mich.—Ray Branch, of the United Theater Equipment Corporation, has installed two Powers 6A machines in the Majestic theater, Battle Creek, and has taken an order for two Powers 6B machines from the Crescent theater, Adrian.

Detroit, Mich.—The Columbia Booking Exchange has moved from 34 Farmer street, Detroit, to the fifth floor of the new Madison theater building.

Detroit, Mich.—The Dawn Film exchange is reported as having purchased "Redemption" for Michigan. This firm recently established offices at 202 Owen building.

Pontiac, Mich.—Mrs. A. J. Kleist, Jr., Pontiac, is handling the affairs of the Howland and New Eagle theaters, while her husband is in training at Camp Custer, having been taken on the first selective draft.

Detroit, Mich.—"The Bar Sinister" the first Fourquare picture released in Michigan, played the week of Sept. 9th at the Washington theater, Detroit.

What Should a Seat Cost?--Let Us Know

The Price of Every Other Thing Is Up, Should Exhibitors Still Be Content? Tell Us Whether You Are Satisfied with Prices You Get.

By Jacob Smith, 718 Free Press Building, Detroit, Mich.

DETROIT, MICH.—The question of whether to increase prices—and whether higher prices would "kill the goose" is puzzling many exhibitors. Can they get more? That is the question. If they do as much business at increased prices, it certainly would help a lot towards helping to pay part of the increased film rental and the general increased cost of operation.

The exhibitor today is paying more for film—more for his help—invariably more for his rent of theater or property—more taxes and more everything—as compared to previous years. Yet it's a fact that he isn't able to do much more business for the reason that competition is a whole lot keener and he is unable to increase the size of his theater. The big house downtown opens at noon and runs continuously until 11 p. m.—it is very easy for such a house to materially increase the receipts one week over another. But the neighborhood house has only a limited population to cater to and proprietor or manager of such a house is fighting problems that do not confront the downtown theatre. The number of transients downtown is so great that the more theatres the merrier—but not so in the residential sections, where it is impossible for the exhibitor to give the same value for the money as the downtown theaters give.

Many exhibitors in the small towns and in the residential theaters have asked The World correspondent if he thought it advisable to raise prices. One thing is certain—there is no excuse for any theater charging five cents—ten cents should be the minimum admission price, because it is just as easy to get ten as five. For the neighborhood house, 10, 15 and 20 cents, with 25 cents for the boxes seems to be a good average scale. In some sections 10 and 15 strikes a better average. The fact must not be overlooked that most people in the residential sections go from one to four times a week, and they usually take the children along. If the admission price is too high, they won't want to take the children along so they simply stay home, and instead of going maybe three times they go but once. There are some sections and some theaters that could easily raise their prices from 5 to 10, from 10 to 15 and 15 to 20. One thing is certain—we have yet to run across a single theater that had to come down on its prices, showing that thus far exhibitors have used very good judgment in arranging their prices.

Another point about prices that is troubling exhibitors right now—and more than ever before—is whether to charge higher prices for special productions. Some argue that it's a bad policy to raise your prices for any special pictures—that it is a whole lot better to establish a regular schedule of prices and stick to them regardless of what the attraction is. There is some logic to this from the exhibitor's standpoint. Take the legitimate amusement business—if shows are playing the K. & E. attractions, a scale of $2 top is established throughout the entire season, year in and year out—the same thing applies to the Shubert houses—the same thing to the burlesque houses—and the vaudeville houses. People know week in and week out what the prices are, whereas they would kick very strenuously if the prices were advanced whenever a special good attraction was announced.

On the other hand, the exhibitors ought to realize that they cannot possibly give their patrons a big feature costing $300,-000 for the same price of one costing only $25,000. The producer who puts big money into a picture cannot get it back unless he can get a better rental price than the regular so-called feature, and if the exhibitor pays considerably more for such a big feature he cannot make money unless he asks more from his patrons.

There are good arguments pro and con

on this subject, and it would be mighty interesting to have exhibitors express themselves on this important topic. Michigan exhibitors should send all communications to our Detroit correspondent, Jacob Smith, 718 Free Press Building.

Features Shown Week of Sept. 9.

Detroit, Mich.—Here is a list of the full week first-run attractions in leading Detroit theaters for the week of September 9th—remember all of these attractions are shown a full week, there being eight theaters now showing pictures seven days each:

Madison; "Polly of the Circus," Goldwyn.

Majestic; "Efficiency Edgar's Courtship," K. E. S. E.

Broadway-Strand, "Rebecca of Sunnybrook Farm," Artcraft.

Liberty, "Down to Earth," Artcraft, second run.

Drury Lane, "The Christian," second run.

Regent, "The Battle of the Tanks." Pathe.

Orpheum, "Wooden Shoes." Triangle.

Washington, "The Bar Sinister," Foursquare, and George Ade Fable, General.

Standard Buys New Features.

Detroit, Mich.—J. C. Fishman, manager of the Standard Film Exchange, Detroit, says his company has purchased a new feature called "Captivating Mary Carstairs" with Norma Talmadge; also Vaughn Glaser in "The House of Shadows." The Standard isn't releasing Art Dramas on Sept. 16th. It is already releasing the New Billy West comedies and the Christie comedies.

Harry Charnas, president of the company, was a recent Detroit visitor.

Notes at K. E. S. E. Exchange.

Detroit, Mich.—A. J. Reed, manager of the K. E. S. E. exchange has appointed Harry A. Trask, as city salesman in Detroit, and E. J. Taylor has been sent to the northern peninsula. W. S. Faber has been appointed bookkeeper and Jos. A. Parthum, bookkeeper.

The next K. E. S. E. picture which the Majestic theater, Detroit will show a full week, first run, is "Pants" with Little Mary McAlister.

Exchanges in the New Film Building.

Detroit, Mich.—The Mutual has already moved to the new film building, John R and Elizabeth streets, Detroit. The K. E. S. E. exchange will move about Sept. 15. The Fox exchange will move about Sept. 27. Others will move about the first of October and most of the film companies will be doing business there by Oct. 15. Twenty film exchanges have already leased space in the film building.

C. H. Townsend Covering Michigan for Metro.

Detroit, Mich.—Four prints of "The Slacker" are working in the state of Michigan. The week of Sept. 5th was the biggest in the history of the Michigan Metro exchange. "Under Handicap" with Harold Lockwood, is booked for the Madison theater the week of Sept. 23. "Their Compact" with Bushman and Bayne, goes into the Madison the week of Sept. 30. C. H. Townsend formerly with K. E. S. E. is now covering Michigan for Metro.

J. T. Haggerty New General Salesman.

Detroit, Mich.—J. T. Haggerty, formerly Vitagraph salesman in Kansas City, is now with the sales department of the General at Detroit, under Dave Prince whom he worked for when the latter was at Dallas.

Memphis Mayor Orders Sunday Closing

Newly Elected City Official Begins With a Rush—Takes Warning from Past and Has Police Close Everything Lest He Too Fall.

J. L. Ray, 1014 Stahlman Building, Nashville, Tenn.

MEMPHIS, TENN.—Mayor Harry H. Litty, recently elected to office following ouster proceedings instituted against former Mayor Thos. C. Ashcroft, has set about the business of Sunday closing and enforcement of the antiquated "blue laws" with a rush. Statements were issued to the effect that all laws governing the operation of theaters and moving picture shows on Sunday would be enforced to the letter, "not because they are right in my opinion, but because they are on the books," according to Mayor Litty. "Personally, I am going fishing Sunday. I fail to see the harm in it, and there is no law against it. Regarding Memphis, I have no other choice open to me. It is not a question of what I think, but what the state laws say," said the mayor. The whole action is a result of a political turmoil of city affairs in Memphis, in which the mayor and several city officials were ousted from office, and the new mayor, evidently fearing a like fate, is playing on the safe side.

Police Inspector Hayes immediately issued orders to the police force, advising them of the mayor's order. The inspector was positive in his statement preceding the effective date of the order that the amusement houses would be closed. He declared that his men would arrest the proprietors and require them to pay a forfeit, but that unlike other times when they have been arrested the theater men will not be permitted to return to their houses after making bond, but that after posting the forfeit the police would see to it that the houses stayed closed for the balance of the day. Complaints made to the city government that the laboring men would have no place of amusement to carry their families on Sunday other than the parks, etc., were answered by stating that former Mayor Ashcroft, so far as possible, had permitted the theaters to remain open, and had been ousted, and that every law on the statute books would be enforced to the letter to prevent a recurrence.

Under a ruling of City Attorney Henry J. Livingston, so long as the profits were to charity they are within the law in remaining open on Sunday. It was hinted that the theater men and officials of the Associated Charities, which have benefited from the admission receipts, would join hands and test the validity of the order.

Sunday Injunction Prevents Closing.

At a late hour Saturday an injunction was granted the theater managers, restraining city or county officials from closing the moving picture and vaudeville shows, and as a result Sunday, September 2, found the town "wide open" insofar as the theaters were concerned. Managers of two combination vaudeville and picture houses had complaints to make. The business of both these houses was hurt through the public's anticipation of a tight Sunday, which was brought about through the lack of publicity given issuance of the injunction, and the Sunday crowds were small in comparison to normal business, picking up, however, with each performance, as the news spread. It was the last day of the first week at the Orpheum, and only about one-third of the seats were filled at the opening performance. The local Loew house had opened the season the day before, and suffered along the same lines as the Orpheum. The straight moving picture houses did not suffer to such a material extent. Followers of the screen productions, in their wanderings up and down Main street and in the neighborhood picture show localities, soon found their way to the bright lights over the film houses, and a thriving business resulted.

Providing the injunction assumes a permanent aspect, the picture men have little to worry about. If, however, a

vigorous fight is made against them, it will mean a revival of the strife arising some months ago when the Protestant Pastors' Association raised its several hands skyward to voice its earnest disapproval of Sunday opening. The Memphis managers are as hard a bunch of nuts to crack as one will find anywhere over the country, and when they set their heads on remaining open Sundays, they intend to remain open, regardless. The outcome of the fight will be watched with interest.

Pictures a Success at Monteagle.

Monteagle, Tenn.—The success attained through the exhibition of moving pictures for the season at this popular summer report has surpassed that of any former season since the custom has been established. A feature of this year's exhibition has been the presentation of high class subjects, in keeping with the highly educational atmosphere surrounding the chautauqua, which includes such pictures as Dickens' "Great Expectations," and other famous works. The pictures have been furnished for several years by a Nashville amusement company, and have always been one of the most pleasant and popular attractions at Monteagle.

The Advantage of Seat Covers.

Nashville, Tenn.—As time goes on, moving picture managers begin to see more and more each day the many advantages of placing washable seat covers over the backs of the seats in the auditoriums of their houses. During the warm days, especially, the women can be found wending their way to the houses where this convenience is thoughtfully provided by the management, and many are the praises which come from the ladies who witness a show in comfort, with the aid of these covers, particularly after they have been in a theater where the seats are bare. The first cost is not so great that any house will have to take the bankrupt law, while the laundry bill is of minor consequence in comparison with the shekels they bring into the coffers.

"The Slacker" Good in Alabama.

Birmingham, Ala.—Packed houses daily greeted each performance of "The Slacker" at the Rialto theater, where the picture was booked for a solid week, having created quite a sensation here. Local officials of the press, clergy, army and navy have been loud in their praise of the film.

Cincinnati News Letter

By Kenneth C. Crain, 307 First National Bank, Cincinnati.

Cincinnati Theater Offers Prize for Name.

CINCINNATI, O.—A contest is on in which the name of the new McMahan & Jackson theater at Sixth and Vine streets will be selected, together with a slogan to be used with the name in the theater's advertising. A local paper is offering a prize of $55 for the best name and slogan, and competition is keen for the honor of naming the new house, and incidentally winning the money. Work on the building is going on rapidly, and it is evident that by pushing things the house will be completed early in the fall, which is the object of the firm. The contest for the best name and slogan will be kept open until the house is practically ready for opening, in order to secure as many suggestions as possible.

Exhibitor Has to Appear Before Court.

Cincinnati, O.—Edward Linch, manager of a house on Central avenue, was before

the juvenile court last week on a charge of permitting a juvenile under fourteen years to perform in his theater, and was given a suspended sentence when it developed that he had been deceived as to the boy's age. Then Mr. Linch was called before the municipal court on a charge of promoting a game of chance, this being based on the "country store" idea which was tried at the theater recently. As it was held by the court not long ago in a similar case that a "country store" is not a gambling device, Mr. Linch was again dismissed, and his legal troubles are probably over for the time being, at least.

F. H. Richardson Designs Lighting System.

Youngstown, O.—The Federal Holding Co., which is erecting the Liberty theater, at Federal and Hazel streets, intends to omit no step which will make the theater all that could be desired in efficiency, as far as the projection of pictures is concerned, and to that end has secured the services of F. H. Richardson, the well-known projection expert of the Moving Picture World, to arrange this detail. Mr. Richardson has designed the entire lighting system of the house with a view to securing the most agreeable light for the audience, and the best for the pictures, and has so arranged the lights that the screen and the walls will be in shadow, while the audience itself will be in the light, making an ideal arrangement. The house is making rapid progress, and will be completed on schedule.

Mae Marsh Picture Shown to Trade.

Cincinnati, O.—Manager C. C. Hite, of the Goldwyn Cincinnati office, held a highly successful private showing of "Polly of the Circus," the film version of the popular play of that name, at his offices not long ago. He was especially pleased at the presence of Alfred Weiss, vice-president of the company, who came all the way from New York to be at the exhibition, while many exhibitors from the territory handled out of the Cincinnati office, including Kentucky and Indiana, as well as Ohio, were also on hand. Bookings have been liberal, and the picture bids fair to be as great a success as the play, Mr. Hite declares.

Mayor of Hamilton Enforces Blue Laws.

Hamilton, O.—Enforcement of the Ohio blue laws has been ordered by Mayor John A. Holzberger, of Hamilton, due to troubles arising out of the several big strikes which have been going on in the city, and also on account of political reasons, he declares. The mayor specifically directed the police to see that all moving-picture houses, cigar stores, news stands, ice-cream parlors and drug stores be closed. Several moving-picture exhibitors have announced their intention of defying the mayor's orders and taking whatever consequences may come, and the outcome of the matter bids fair to afford some interesting developments. Several years ago the blue laws were rigidly enforced in Hamilton, and proved highly unpopular, as they are today.

Akron Theater Will Give Prize for Name.

Akron, O.—Horace Parks, manager of the new theater on West Market street in Akron, which is to cost $150,000, and which will be one of the most roomy and modern houses in Ohio, is offering a series of prizes for the best suggestions for a name for the theater. A jury of three Akron newspaper men will select the names of the prize-winners, the first of which will receive $25 in cash, the second a pass to the theater for six months, and on down to the next fifty best, each of which will be awarded a pass. The conditions of the contest are that the name must be appropriate to the times, location and class of the house, and that it must not be similar to that of any other theater now in use in Akron; and no person connected directly or indirectly with the owners or with the management of the house, or any persons who are interested in the building of the theater, or in furnishing supplies or equipment to it, will be eligible.

Trade Notes from Ohio.

Piqua, O.—The Bijou theater has opened for the regular winter season, after a summer of pictures, followed by remodeling and redecorating, and is doing nicely with its joint offerings of vaudeville and pictures.

Springfield, O.—Gus Sun was the host to forty children from the Ohio Masonic Home at a performance of "Skinner's Baby" at the Fairbanks theater recently.

Midwest News Letter

By Frank H. Madison, 62 S. Washington Ave., Chicago, Ill.

New Amusement Company in Taylorville.

TAYLORVILLE, ILL.—The Empress Amusement company has been formed here by Joseph McCarthy and J. A. Humphreys who will operate both the Empress and the Grand theaters. McCarthy who has been operating the Empress has taken over the three-year lease of Charles Vance on the Grand. His new house will run road shows and occasionally big pictures of "The Birth of a Nation" class.

New Theaters and Showmanship Notes.

Little York, Ill.—The erection of an opera house here is contemplated.

Manteno, Ill.—The moving picture theater here has been closed and the equipment has been moved to Aroma Park.

Kewanee, Ill.—Dreamland theater which was closed for remodeling has been reopened.

Lincoln, Ill.—Business at the Star theater was boosted by showing "surprise pictures" of Lincoln residents.

Galesburg, Ill.—The West theater has installed a new organ.

Farmington, Ill.—The Women's Relief corps needed more yarn to knit for the local soldier boys. The Strand theater gave a benefit show and got it.

Among Michigan Exhibitors.

Adrian, Mich.—Vincent J. Williams has become associated with his father-in-law, W. O. Kenan, in the management of the Crescent theater. They have taken a twenty-year lease on the building and closed the house for four weeks to make improvements and alterations which will cost about $10,000.

Adrian, Mich.—The Croswell theater is now under the control of the Garden theater company with E. M. Simons as acting manager. Road shows will be booked as well as feature pictures, the policy including Sunday afternoon and evening photoplay shows.

Saginaw, Mich.—The Franklin theater will take over some of the theatrical bookings which would have been filled in the Academy of Music, now burned. This will interfere with the moving picture policy only on those dates.

Jackson, Mich.—R. J. Clifford, formerly manager of the Strand and Colonial theaters at South Bend, Ind., has been engaged as manager of the Crown theater on West Main street which recently was purchased by Mrs. Mary A. Jacklin. It will be opened as a 10 cent moving picture house.

Among Wisconsin Exhibitors.

Darlington, Wis.—The opera house was destroyed by fire.

New Lisbon, Wis.—Joseph Jax has purchased the moving picture theater from R. W. Sharp who has gone to Alabama.

Milwaukee, Wis.—The Alhambra theater did not close for four days to remodel until it had met an apparent demand for an additional two days booking of "The Little American."

Hayward, Wis.—The Grand theater is now under the management of Henry Ernst.

Co-operate to Buy, Store and Deliver Coal

Louisville Exhibitors and Others Combine to Handle Winter's Coal—Many Theaters Use Much Coal but Have Small Bins.

By Ohio Valley News Service, 1404 Starks Bldg., Louisville, Ky.

LOUISVILLE, KY.—The coal supply situation and heating theaters and moving picture houses is one of great interest to the exhibitor at this time. A number of the local theaters buy their steam, and have been notified of an increased rate on account of the cost of coal. The weather turned so cold, September 10 and 11, that theaters used steam when the low mark of 44 degrees was reached, a record for early September.

Many of the theaters operate their own heating plants and in an effort to buy coal in car lots, and save something on the cost, the Consumers' Fuel & Supplies Co., has been incorporated with a capital of $5,000 by real estate men, theater managers, apartment house owners, etc., this being a co-operative company which will supply its members coal at cost, cost including delivery, etc. Few theaters or apartment houses have storage capacity for a car of coal, and are unable to buy in car lots. The new company will buy and deliver this coal as needed, on a co-operative basis at cost of operation.

This promises to be a big aid to some of the local theater owners who have been up in the air for months over the situation. Very little coal has been purchased as contracts are not to be had, and the situation is such that no one is anxious to place contracts, fearing that the Government will shortly take action and that prices will be much lower. On the other hand there is a strike in Eastern Kentucky of the coal miners, a car shortage that is growing steadily worse, and at the same time the uncertainty concerning price has resulted in practically no deliveries or yard stocks, while there is very little storage coal anywhere. This means that when cold weather and the big demand is here that the coal will go out of sight as regardless of set prices, it will be a question of getting coal at any price.

Mutual and Co-operative Stamp Companies Merge.

Louisville, Ky.—Fred Dolle, manager of the Fourth Ave., Amusement, operators of the Alamo theater, and also connected with the Broadway Amusement Enterprises, has merged his interests known as the Mutual Trading Stamp Co., with the Co-Operative Trading Stamp Co. and along with the announcement of the merger announced that arrangements had been made whereby the trading stamps of the Co-Operative Company would be accepted in payment of admission to the following theaters: Alamo, Highland, Broadway, Ideal, West Broadway, Crown, Rex and Aristo. Making the stamps redeemable at the theaters is expected to result in additional business for both the theaters and trading stamp organization, and as the stamps have a cash surrender value the deal is a good one.

William Wise Takes Charge of the Amusu.

Midway, Ky.—Wm. Wise has taken charge of the Amusu theater, of this city, succeeding W. A. Anderson, who has gone with the Ligget & Muers Tobacco Co.

Makes His Current by Gasoline Engine.

Warsaw, Ky.—After considerable trouble in getting current to operate the Lyric theater, Manager Leonard Bradley, has had a power house erected, and is operating a gasoline engine, dynamo and complete outfit for making light and power. Instead of one show each evening, two shows and a Saturday afternoon matinee will start.

Praise for M. L. Stockley.

Hopkinsville, Ky.—A recent industrial edition of the "Hopkinsville Kentuckian," carried an interesting item of the fine work that M. L. Stockley has done in the

moving picture field of that city. Mr. Stockley for three and a half years has been operating the Princess and Rex theaters, located directly across the street from one another on Ninth street.

Film News Notes in Louisville.

Louisville, Ky.—The Mary Anderson theater did a rattling good business with the film "On Trial," the stage interpretation of which was shown at Macauley's theater a little more than a year ago.

Louisville, Ky.—The Switow Amusement Co., has filed suit through attorney R. A. McDowell against the Metropolitan Realty Co., to recover $235, alleged to have been paid in taxes by the plaintiff on a piece of property in New Albany, Ind.

Lawrenceburg, Ky.—Meisburg, Wiseman and Reed, a firm of Harrodsburg, Ky., has purchased the Lyric theater, of this city, and following a few changes the theater will be placed in operation.

Atlanta News Letter

By A. M. Beatty, 42 Copenhill Ave., Atlanta, Ga.

Louis Hasse Takes Charge of the Atlanta.

ATLANTA, GA.—Louis Hasse, of New York, will succeed Homer George this season as manager of the Atlanta theater, owned and operated by Klaw & Erlanger. Mr. Hasse will arrive within the next few days.

Mr. George, who made the announcement that he has severed his connection with the theatrical business, has been manager of the Atlanta theater since its opening. He expects to divide his time in the future between Atlanta and New York.

Carlyle Blackwell Coming to Loew's Grand.

Atlanta, Ga.—Following the personal appearance of Alice Brady, the charming picture star, at Loew's Grand theater, Tuesday, Sept. 4, announcement was made at the Grand Monday that another film favorite is shortly to appear there.

This time it will be Carlyle Blackwell, who has won thousands of friends and admirers in Atlanta through his acting upon the screen. Just when Mr. Blackwell will come to Atlanta is not yet known, but it is promised that his appearance will be some time in the near future.

Loew Anniston House Opens.

Anniston, Ala.—Marcus Loew added another theater to his Southern circuit of vaudeville houses Monday, Sept. 10, when Loew's Noble theater threw open its doors in Anniston, Ala.

Alice Brady in Atlanta.

Atlanta, Ga.—Alice Brady, famous moving picture star, arrived in Atlanta Tuesday afternoon, Sept. 11, at 5 o'clock for a personal appearance on the stage of Loew's Grand theater Tuesday night. Elaborate preparations had been made for her reception. A big new Packard automobile was engaged for her use while she is in Atlanta. Her personal friends here tendered her a dinner party, and a sort of informal reception for her was held back of the scenes at the theater practically all evening. Miss Brady left Wednesday morning for Birmingham.

L. J. Selznick Guest of Walter Price.

Atlanta, Ga.—Louis J. Selznick will be in Atlanta this week. While here he will be the guest of Walter Price, manager of the Select Pictures Corporation, and Sig Samuels, directing manager of the Criterion theater.

Kansas City Notes and Filmdom Happenings

Strike in Two Express Companies Hinders Shipments from Exchanges—New Jewel Exchanges Opened—Local Personals.

By Kansas City News Service, 205 Corn Belt Building, Kansas City, Mo.

KANSAS CITY, MO.—The Kansas City moving picture exchanges have been severely crippled in the general strike of the Adams and Wells Fargo Express Company offices in which clerks, teamsters and freight handlers have walked out following demands which the companies declare are uncommon to other companies.

The strike began September 7 and after two days the film companies had resigned themselves to getting all of their films out by the American Express or by parcels post. The trouble has come in getting the films out to the exhibitor as the companies must either rely on the one company or else get their films to the post office in any manner possible. The lesser inconvenience is the bringing back of films to the exchange that have been returned to the city by the exhibitor. This is handled by having a special express man call for the film with a wagon or truck. The effect of the strike has been the tieing up of shipments to such an extent that all the offices are receiving many wires inquiring for the pictures. There have been only a few cancellations so far.

J. Erwin Dodson Will Visit Many Exhibitors.

Kansas City, Mo.—J. Erwin Dodson, assistant to D. O. Reese, manager of the Universal Film and Supply Company, will soon make a trip through the territory in behalf of the company and the Universal exhibitors. He will endeavor on this trip to assist the exhibitors in every way possible to bring the company and the exhibitors in a closer relationship.

J. H. Skirbold Covering Missouri for Metro.

Kansas City, Mo.—Jack H. Skirbold, formerly a salesman out of the Chicago office of the Metro Company, is now working out of the Kansas City office of the company. He will travel a Missouri territory.

"Junk" Picture Replevined by General Film.

Kansas City, Mo.—The General Film Company recently showed a local exhibitor the error of his ways when a picture he was showing was replevined by the company. It seems as if the exhibitor had bought the picture from a "junk dealer" in Birmingham, Alabama, not knowing from whom the picture had come, and that the Alabama man had undoubtedly gotten the picture by foul means. P. J. Swift, manager of the Kansas City office, heard of the running of the picture, and replevined it, and in so doing saved the exhibitor from future embarrassment and secured the return of the picture to its proper owners.

Theater Notes from Kansas and the Southwest.

Junction City, Kans.—The New Columbian theater is nearing completion.

Solomon, Kans.—The Cozy theater has been sold to W. W. Brown by H. C. Collins. It will be managed by Mrs. W. W. Brown.

Arkansas City, Kans.—J. R. Burford is now the sole owner of the Rex theater here, as he has bought the interest of his partner, William Voiles, of Wellington, Kansas. This theater will be soon put in first class condition, and will have a seating capacity of between 800 and 900.

Ottawa, Kans.—A new modern theater will be built soon by Lee Cohn.

El Paso, Texas.—A new theater for G. W. Bush is being erected here by Braun-

ton and Leibert. It will be completed in two weeks. The theater will have a seating capacity of about 2,000 and will cost $15,000.

La Grange, Texas.—The Cozy theater has been bought by Gerhard von Minden and Frank Bacs.

Dallas, Texas.—The Opera House here will be managed by Miss Mamie Greenwall.

Lockney, Texas.—The Olympic theater here has been sold to S. S. Williams and F. C. Scott of Plainview by J. R. Scott.

Casey, Iowa.—L. C. Plummer is the new manager of the Opera House.

Spencer, Iowa.—The Fraser moving picture theater here has been sold to Messrs. Stow and Gray of Fort Dodge, Iowa, by Mr. and Mrs. William Fraser.

Rock Rapids, Iowa.—A new moving picture theater here has been opened by R. W. Steen.

Storm Lake, Iowa.—The Princess theater here has been opened with moving pictures. It will be managed by Edward Roberts, a new manager for the theater.

Gallaway, Nebr.—The Star theater here is now owned by R. R. Barnard.

Earle, Ark.—A stock company has been organized in Earle to build a moving picture theater with a seating capacity of 800. The new theater will be called the Princess.

Santa Rosa, N. M.—The new theater here will soon be finished. It will be called the Electric.

Coal Hill, Ark.—W. Pendergrass has opened a new moving picture theater here.

El Reno, Oklahoma.—The grand opening of the El Reno theater was held August 30 by the new management.

Hoxie, Kan.—The new theater here was opened August 22. The new house seats 250 people.

Santa Fe, Kan.—The new theater here has been opened to the public. It was completed by Frank Hutchison.

Fort Worth, Texas.—Phil W. Greenwall and Albert Weiss have leased the Savoy theater, which they have leased for the season.

Deming, Texas.—The new theater of Raymond Teal is fast nearing completion.

Fort Scott, Kan.—The Pictureland theater here has been reopened.

Creston, Iowa.—The Willard theater here has been sold by W. H. Hoffman to William Weldon.

Toledo, Ia.—The Grand theater has been sold to W. B. Pearsons of Wall Lake by C. E. Olson.

Conway, Ark.—J. H. Lincoln, manager of the Grand theater, is improving the house in many ways, one of which is to increase the seating capacity of his house to accommodate 200 people.

Sioux Falls, N. D.—H. J. Updegraff has bought a half interest in the Princess theater.

Indianola, Miss.—The James Chapman theater here was damaged to the extent of $1,500, $1,000 of which was covered by insurance. The fire was caused by an explosion of a gasoline engine in a nearby basement.

Jewel Productions Exchange Opens.

Kansas City, Mo.—A new film exchange has entered Kansas City in the Jewell Productions, Incorporated, handling states rights pictures. This concern has opened a branch office at 1025-27 Main street, on the fourth floor. The branch will be managed by M. B. Ward, who although a young man, has had considerable experi-

ence in the film business. He was with the local Paramount office here for one year, with the General Film for two years, and with the Central Motion Picture for two years. He was manager at the last mentioned office. There will be about six traveling salesmen working out of the Kansas City office. The prints of the first release, "Come Through," featuring Herbert Rawlinson, have already been received. The second release will be "Pay Me." This will be followed by "The Sirens of the Sea," and "The Man Without a Country." None of the force has been selected as yet.

General Film Loans Films for Benefit.

Kansas City, Mo.—The General Film Company loaned two pictures for the benefit of a local artillery company that is soon to leave for a concentration camp in the near future. The benefit was held at Convention Hall, September 5, at which an entertainment consisting of moving pictures, vaudeville, and drills by the soldiers was given.

Many Exhibitors See "Polly."

The local Goldwin office has been conducting trade showings for the last week on "Polly of the Circus," featuring Mae Marsh, which have been well attended by out-of-town exhibitors. Several of the Kansas City exhibitors became wildly enthusiastic over the race horse scene in the picture, saying that it was the most thrilling bit of picture that they have seen for a long time.

Business Jottings in Kansas City.

Kansas City, Mo.—The Universal Film and Supply Company has secured a continuous run of ten days on the serial, "The Red Ace," in four houses, the Globe, Saphire, The World in Motion, and the Palace. The company is soon to start an advertising campaign for the run of the picture at the Globe. This will be done by the placing of large announcements on the fronts of 250 street cars, also by newspaper space, by novelty advertising, and by bill-boards.

Richard Robertson, manager of the Kansas City Goldwyn office, says that his salesmen are booking towns of less than 3,000 population for two days' run. Several examples of this occur in such places as Falls City, Nebraska; Ridgeway, Missouri, with 800 people; Eldorado, Kansas; Bethany, Missouri; Plattsburg, Missouri.

The General Film gave a private showing of one of the new Falcon, "The Stolen Play," and one of the new George Ade's, "The Fable of the Twelve-Cylinder Speed of the Leisure Class," at the Columbia theater on September 7.

Personal Notes from Local Exchanges.

C. A. (Red-Sunshine) Jones, Missouri representative of the Universal, was in the office September 8 after a two-weeks trip on his territory.

D. R. Patterson, southwestern Missouri traveler for the Southern Triangle, was in Kansas City for several days following a trip to Webb City, Carthage, and Joplin, Missouri.

J. D. Thatcher, Jr., Kansas representative of the Southern Triangle, was in Kansas City this week. He says that every town of over 10,000 population in the state of Kansas is showing the pictures he sells.

E. R. Reynolds, assistant branch manager of the Southern Triangle at Kansas City, spent a day in Marshall, Missouri, arranging with exhibitors in that place for the Triangle re-issues.

G. E. Akers, special representative for the Kansas City Feature Film, has returned to the Kansas City office after a trip through southern Kansas and northern Oklahoma. He motored to Kansas City from St. Louis, Missouri. He reports an unusually good business and that the Sennett Comedies are very popular in the places he visited.

IN THE TWIN CITIES.

"Joan" at Regular Prices.

Minneapolis, Minn.—Perhaps the greatest bargain week bill ever offered by a local playhouse was scheduled for the local Strand theater the week of Sept. 16 when Manager Charles G. Branham offered Geraldine Farrar in "Joan the Woman" at regular admission prices. Mr. Branham has launched a big advertising campaign on the feature and has arranged special music. "On Trial," "Within the Law" and "To the Death," are expected to make their appearance at the Strand shortly.

Other Features at Mill City Theater.

Minneapolis, Minn.—Manager Lowell V. Calvert extended his run of Mary Pickford's "Rebecca of Sunnybrook Farm" three days and his capacity business continued. Julius Johnson, Mr. Calvert's organist rendered some exceptional music in accompanying the production and a country band placed on the stage furnished real music for the dancing scenes in the fifth reel.

"Polly of the Circus" drew big crowds to the New Garrick the first half of the week of Sept. 9, while "Rebecca" continued playing to a big business at the New Garrick in St. Paul.

"The Slacker" following a good week's run at The Strand, Minneapolis, opened a good week's business at the Blue Mouse, St. Paul, Sept. 9.

Dan Esslin opened the University theatre, 14th and University here Sept. 1 with a Bluebird feature to a good business.

Manager George Granstrom of the New Franklin, Minneapolis, has installed a "jazz band" in his theater.

Changes Along Mill City's Film Row

J. E. Keough Comes Back as Manager of New Lyric—Vitagraph Manager Goes to Chicago and E. S. Holmes Takes His Place—Other Notes.

By John L. Johnston 704 Film Exchange Building, Minneapolis, Minn.

MINNEAPOLIS, MINN.—The unexpected is always happening in Minneapolis. After an unusually quiet week, August 26 to Sept 2, things picked up and film talk began sparking on all twelve cylinders and also backfiring during the days that have followed.

J. E. Keough Managing New Lyric.

James E. Keough, former manager of the Minneapolis Strand returned last week from Chicago and is now managing The New Lyric theater, recently taken over by Ruben & Finkelstein. What the future plans of former manager Hugh C. Andress are to be have not been officially announced to date but our high powered monacle shows Mr. Andress's smile and cheerful countenance intact.

W. H. Strauss Enters State Rights Field.

But hold—Mr. Keough's reappearance is not the only surprise of the week. While applications have been pouring in on Harry Cohen and he has been besieged with inquiries as to who is to be the new Metro manager here, Walter H. Strauss, manager pro tem has resigned. Mr. Strauss was formerly assistant manager to W. K. Howard at the Vitagraph and Metro exchanges here, practiced law one year and served a time on the copy desk of the Cincinnati Enquirer. He will enter the local state rights field and plans on

opening offices in the Produce Exchange building.

E. S. Holmes Comes as Vitagraph Manager.

Manager H. C. Bayley of the Greater Vitagraph exchange is leaving. He has been appointed manager of the Chicago Vitagraph offices and assumes his new duties at once. He is succeeded at his Minneapolis Post by E. S. Holmes, former manager of the Vitagraph's New Orleans' exchange. Mr. Holmes comes to Minneapolis with a good record and a hearty grip for all exhibitors in the territory. He has appointed A. L. Picker and H. D. Ection to his sales force and asserts the "Welcome" and "Satisfaction Guaranteed" signs will hang side by side at the Greater Vitagraph offices as long as he remains here. Mr. Bayley has not been in Minneapolis long enough to get well acquainted with exhibitors, but he makes some good friends among those who have been fortunate enough to meet him.

Manager Edward A. Westcott of the Fox exchange spent two days in Chicago last week in conference with W. R. Sheehan, general manager of the Fox forces and in listening to battle plans in the "Spy" war-Fox vs. Major Funkhouser.

Lee A. Horn Goes to Supreme Feature.

Minneapolis, Minn.—Lee A. Horn has resigned as manager of the Longacre exchange to accept a position as manager of the Supreme Feature exchange branch at Fargo, N. D. Lee was formerly Dakota salesman for Jas. V. Bryson, Fargo manager for the Universal-Laemmle exchange, manager of the Minneapolis Selznick exchange and roadman for the same firm. His successor at the Longacre exchange has not been named.

Supreme Will Open Two New Branches.

Minneapolis, Minn.—Manager Myron Conhaim of the Supreme has announced that branch offices will be opened at Des Moines, Iowa, and Fargo, N. D., within the next ten days.

Notes of the Trade in Minneapolis.

Manager Harry Rathner of the Selznick exchange has been informed that Lewis J. Selznick is coming to Minneapolis shortly to meet exhibitors. Mr. Rathner is making preparations to properly entertain Mr. Selznick and exhibitors of the territory when the former arrives.

Manager Ralph Bradford of the Goldwyn exchange, Minneapolis, is preparing to entertain Roi Cooper Megrue, novelist, when the author of several Goldwyn plays arrives here next week.

Manager E. C. Davies of the Saxe Feature, Minneapolis exchange is in Chicago planning a campaign to boost "On Trial" and National Exhibitors Circuit Chaplin releases. He will spend several days at the Milwaukee branch exchange before turning to Minneapolis.

John Bachman of the Saxe exchange has returned from a six weeks' road trip through Northern Minnesota and the Dakotas.

Ira Manteke, Mutual roadman has gone out on a tour of Eastern Dakotas and Western Minnesota in the interests of the new Helen Holmes serial and Star productions.

C. L. Booth, Metro roadman has been offered a position as Omaha exchange manager for the Jewel Film Co. He will confer with officers of the firm at Omaha this week. A. J. Mentz, formerly of the Minneapolis Vitagraph exchange is Cleveland exchange manager for the Jewel Co.

Mayor Bauer of Lafayette, Plans Theater

New House Will Cost $150,000—Site is Seventh and Main Streets—Seeks Ten Business Men to Aid in Financing Project.

By Indiana Trade News Service, 816 State Life Bldg., Indianapolis.

LAFAYETTE, IND.—Plans are being prepared for a new $150,000 theater in this city, to be erected on the old Shearman property at Seventh and Main streets. Thomas Bauer, mayor of the city, is at the head of the movement, and his plan is for ten business men to subscribe $10,000 to a fund, thus making $100,000, which, it is believed, would be ample to start the erection of the building.

Leopold Dryfus, who owned the Dreyfus theater, which was destroyed by fire two years ago, has said he will contribute the first $10,000. The new house will be devoted to high class legitimate productions as well as motion picture feature films. Lafayette has had no legitimate show-house since the destruction of the Dreyfus. The new theater will be fireproof in its construction and here will be office rooms in the front part of the building.

Luna Will Be Brighter Still.

Lafayette, Ind.—Extensive improvements are to be made in the Luna Theater, Lafayette's popular photoplay house, in the near future, according to a recent announcement. About $55,000, including ground leases, etc., will be expended on the building in the hope of making it one of the finest in this section of the state. Work will be started about the latter part of September.

The extensions and underground work will be carried on with the theater in operation, but its doors will be closed for about six weeks to allow the finishing touches to the interior. When finished it will be large enough to accommodate the largest pictures on the road as well as occasional vaudeville performances. A new ventilating system is to be one of the additional features.

The room adjoining the theater on the east, now occupied by Roth the florist, has been leased and additional space in the rear of the building also has been contracted for. The present lobby will be enlarged to take in the Roth flower shop and the main stairway will be widened to serve as an exit for the bal-

cony, that is to be added to the theater. The first floor will have a seating capacity of 700 and the balcony will seat 300 persons, in addition to the loges which will seat fifty people. The ceiling will be raised fifteen feet for the installation of the balcony and to provide height for the immense organ to be installed and additional stage equipment.

The interior decorations will be in the hands of a Chicago artist and the lighting system will be the latest improved indirect. A battery of the latest model motion picture machines will be installed in a fireproof and soundproof room on the first floor. The acoustics will be as nearly perfect as possible, and the new theater will be furnished throughout with the most improved seating ideas.

Colonial Theater Adds Vaudeville.

Indianapolis, Ind.—Bingham, Crose and Cohen, managers of the Colonial theater, have made a change in the policy, taking effect Sunday, Sept. 2. In addition to the feature photoplays which they have been offering to the public heretofore, a vaudeville bill will be given and the entertainment will be operated continuously, as now, from 12 noon until 11 p. m.

Irwin Moss Will Conduct the Princess.

Frankfort, Ind.—The active management of the Princess theater, which is now being operated by the Bon Ton Amusement Company, has been taken over by Irwin Moss, formerly a resident of Culver, Ind. Charles Spray, a member of the concern, will now manage the Blinn theater.

George G. Ball Dies After Brief Illness.

Lafayette, Ind.—George G. Ball, who established Lafayette's first motion picture theater, died at his home here last week as a result of a brief illness. He was graduated from Purdue University in 1888 and for several years prior to entering the motion picture business he operated a plumbing supply house. He was fifty-one years old.

Sunday Theaters Expected at Fort Worth

Need of Pictures at Camp Bowie Told by Former Correspondent of Moving Picture World—Some Items Gathered in the City.

By Kent Watson, Battery D, 1st Texas F. A., Former Correspondent of Moving Picture World.

FORT WORTH, TEXAS.—Picture theaters will be running wide open in Fort Worth on Sundays within the very near future. That is not prediction, indication or presumption. The facts are stated unreservedly in the first sentence. And the rabid ranters who found so valiantly six months ago to close those picture shows will be allowed to sit back, without more than a whimper, and watch their strenuous labors go to naught. The master has willed that picture shows are a good thing for the soldier boys camped at Fort Worth and so it is that the darkened doors are to re-invite a more enlightened enlightenment to the city of Forth Worth.

With 40,000 Texas and Oklahoma troops in training at Camp Bowie, three miles from the city, it was deemed necessary by military authorities that legitimate Sunday amusement should be furnished the soldiers. And with a stack of unpaid fines aggregating possibly $15,000, chucked off into the pigeon-hole of his desk, the City Attorney of Fort Worth has made no claim for a legal fight.

"They jest gotta have the movies," is what the C. O. would say if interviewed, I think, because he's that sort of a fellow. He's rubbed the rugged rocks of soldiering and his sympathies are formed into sentiments that perhaps would be unethical for him to make public for political reasons.

I am among the soldiers who came happily on to training camp and I'll admit that I was somewhat shocked at seeing picture shows dark in this city on Sunday. I interviewed some of the theater exhibitors.

They advised that the only way to get the shows opened was to take it up through the military authorities.

"When a soldier hollers," stated Manager Levy of the Hippodrome and Strand theaters, "He'll get what he wants. We exhibitors dare not take an open hand in this game, but you can bet your necks that we're with you until the cows come home."

Within an hour after that statement two hundred and eleven men had signed a petition requesting their commander to urge the camp commander to wield his influence in favor of Sunday picture shows in Fort Worth. Petitions from other military units followed the first and the officers of the camp realized that the soldiers were "hollering for what they want."

Diplomacy Plays the Cards.

The agitation has been of the diplomatic sort. It has not been of the bitter sort that preceded the former fight when the exhibitors and their adherents lost the case of Sunday opening in Texas courts. No demonstrations have been made and will not be made. Little publicity has been given to the crusade.

While no statement has been officially authorized to this effect it is known that the city officials feel that the officers at Camp Bowie had a right to-make the demand, which later will be properly presented and it is known authoritatively that no concerted legal action will be taken against the move which was so quietly instituted and successfully waged.

"We want the amusement places of Fort Worth open on Sundays," is the authorized statement of Colonel O. C. Guessaa, commanding the First Texas Infantry. "At present Sunday is the only day that the soldiers at Camp Bowie have off and yet at the same time it is the only day that there is no legitimate amusement in Fort Worth for them. They go down town and wander about the streets seeking something to do, but are severely criticized if they get into mischief.

"The amusement places can easily be regulated by boards of censorship so that they will provide the cleanest of entertainment. What could be more instructive than pictures of the war or the activities of the Red Cross? The boys at Camp Bowie are red-blooded men and singing parties will not appeal to all of them. THE OPENING OF PICTURE SHOWS IN FORT WORTH ON SUNDAY IS THE ONLY SOLUTION."

The city attorney of Fort Worth has stated that the picture shows will be opened within the very near future.

Every Uniform Is a Ticket.

Fort Worth, Texas.—"If you have on a uniform bust right in—no ticket is needed —our treat." That's the sign that greeted men passing soldiers in Fort Worth Sunday—the first time a picture show has been known to dare intimate the possibility of opening for more than eight months. The sign was hanging in front of the popular Alps theater and soldiers flocked in by the hundreds. The show was open from 1 p. m. until 7 p. m. and none except soldiers were allowed within. 'Twas just a free show to the khaki-clad youths of Uncle Sam, many of whom felt more at home for the pictures than for the cordiality and condolence of the manager who will never cease to be a life-long friend of every man who went into the Alps theater. He made the soldiers glad and advertised his house just as good as if he'd read Epes Winthrop Sargent's little book.

Pershing Theater Now Open.

Fort Worth, Texas.—The Pershing theater, recently completed, is now opened to the public with motion pictures and vaudeville as the attraction. The new theater is one of the most attractive in the city.

Prairie State's News Letter

By Frank H. Madison, 623 S. Wabash Ave., Chicago, Ill.

Two New Theaters in Omaha.

OMAHA, NEB.—The Creighton block property at the northwest corner of Fifteenth and Douglas streets has been leased for ninety-nine years by the World Realty company which will erect thereon a theater and store building. The theater which will be on the ground floor will have a seating capacity of 2,500. The World company owns and was the builder of the Sun theater.

The Blank Realty company, of which A. H. Blank, the Des Moines exhibitor, is the head, has taken a ninety-nine year lease on the site of the old Continental block at the Northeast corner of Fifteenth and Douglas streets. It will erect a four-story building to cost $300,000, the lower floor of which will be occupied by a moving picture theater to be known as the Rialto. Contracts have already been let for the construction. It will seat 2,500, will be 132 feet square and will have walls of polychrome terra cotta with white and ivory as a base.

One of the features of the house will be a separate projection room forty feet long which will be used for the trying out of pictures, the booking of which is contemplated. The ladies' parlor and rest room will be commodious, 36x20. A nurse will be in attendance upon the children's play room. Besides an echo organ, the house will maintain an orchestra. The contract calls for the completion of the building by February 1, 1918.

What Nebraska Exhibitors Are Doing.

Antioch, Neb.—A moving picture show has been opened here by the Antioch Amusement company.

Peru, Neb.—D. Emerett Donovan has taken over the Crystal theater which has been under the management of A. M. McCommons.

Callaway, Neb.—Change of ownership of the Star theater will result in the lease of that house to C. W. Wright, who at one time had an interest in it, it is reported. The Star was sold by W. E. Reeder to R. R. Barnard who resold it to Mrs. C. Ahrendt.

Alliance, Neb.—George J. Burke has reopened his moving picture theater here.

Stanton, Neb.—Manager Fullner has sold Empress theater to William Alderman.

New Theaters and Changes in the Dakotas.

Dickinson, N. D.—The contract has been let for the construction of the Davis-Grand theater. It will be 149x25 feet and will cost $10,000. The contract calls for completion within sixty days.

Lake Preston, S. D.—Richard Linstrom has sold the Princess theater to Oscar E. Jordet.

Church's Ferry, N. D.—The Star theater is again under the-management of George Steig.

Garrettson, S. D.—The moving picture theater here has been sold to Albert Peterson.

Hillsboro, N. D.—Gunder Howard has opened a moving picture show in the opera house.

Iowa News Letter

By Dorothy Day, Register-Tribune, Des Moines, Ia.

Arrival of Army at Camp Dodge Boosts Pictures.

DES MOINES, IA.—With the arrival of the first contingent of the conscript army at Camp Dodge, twelve miles from Des Moines, the picture people of Des Moines are beginning their plans for the entertainment of the boys in khaki. The Majestic theater is the first to make a big bid for their patronage by the opening of the series of seven two-reel Pathe pictures of "The Battle of the Somme." On Friday, September 7, the management of the Majestic in conjunction with the Evening Tribune, entertained all of the men in uniform and civilians who could show their credentials between the hours of eleven and six, with the first of the two-reel episodes. The house was jammed from eleven all through the afternoon and evening with soldiers and civilians attracted by the big publicity given the series by the Tribune. The war pictures will be shown every Friday.

Des Moines Visitors and Happenings.

Des Moines, Ia.—C. B. Owens, of the Pastime in Bagley, and W. C. Treloar, of the Treloar opera house in Ogden, were callers at the Pathe office this week.

The Mutual exchange reported O. D. Benjamin of the Electric in Ruthven and J. A. Price of the Empress in Indianola, visiting last week.

Film Jottings Over Iowa.

Somers, Ia.—R. S. Skiver has purchased the opera house in Somers from Allen Miller. Mr. Miller is a farmer and has been operating the opera house and running his farm at the same time, now he is going to devote all of-his time to the latter.

Olwein, Ia.—E. N. Ney has re-opened the Orpheum in Oelwein. The Orpheum was changed some time ago to the Plaza.

Ballantyne Enthusiastic Over Mutual New System.

Des Moines, Ia.—Manager Ballantyne of the local Mutual exchange is most enthusiastic over contracts on the Mutual All-stars program. He reports long-time contracts with A. J. Deibold of the Palace in Cedar Rapids and W. V. Silvers of the Strand in Ottumwa. He is exceptionally proud of his landing'the big Royal contract, with two Mutual releases a week. The Royal is one of Des Moines large down-town houses, recently remodeled and enlarged.

Selznick Office to Distribute "Public Be Damned."

Des Moines, Ia.—The Garden theater office of the Mid West are announcing to its territory that it will have the new Selznick acquisition, "Public Be Damned," for release in a few days.

ON PACIFIC COAST.

San Francisco Briefs.

George Chamberlain, proprietor of the Independent Film exchange, San Francisco, has moved his residence from Alameda to this city to avoid the loss of time incident with the daily trip across the bay.

Arents, the sign man, who does much work for moving picture houses, has moved to 124 Golden Gate avenue, San Francisco, in the heart of Film Row.

Hugh Hoffman, who is connected with the Universal, was in San Francisco recently from Universal City.

M. M. Morris, of the Western Poster Company, is making a trip to the southern part of California, going by the Valley route and planning to return along the Coast.

Recent visitors have included Charles Rohrer, of the Nippon theater, Sacramento; Frank Atkins, of the Marysville theater, Marysville; W. S. Webster, of the Strand theater, Woodland; C. C. Kaufman, of Colusa; "Candy" Howard, of Oroville, and Joe Cohen, of Honolulu.

Northern California Notes.

San Rafael, Cal.—Charles Martin, formerly of Salinas, has taken over the Star theater and will open it as Martin's theater.

Fresno, Cal.—Delays have been encountered by James Beatty and associates in the construction of the new Liberty theater and White's theater has been secured for the presentation of some of the big features that have been booked. It will be opened with "The Barrier" and will be maintained until the new house is ready.

San Jose, Cal.—The State Normal School has installed moving picture equipment, including an Atlas projector, purchased through Walter Preddey of San Francisco.

California Office Being Remodeled.

San Francisco, Cal.—The offices of the California Film exchange on Golden Gate avenue are being remodeled and changes made in their arrangement. The bookkeeping department has been moved to the opposite side of the building and the offices of manager, M. L. Markowitz, have been moved to the front. Mr. Markowitz recently returned from a trip to Los Angeles, where he conferred with Carl Laemmle, and may make another visit to that city again within a few days.

Rialto Has Stellar Attraction.

San Francisco, Cal.—"Jack and the Bean Stalk" is enjoying a heavy run at the Rialto and will be held for an indefinite period, probably for three or four weeks. Some very effective advertising is being done and use is even being made of the department store windows, a fine display of cut-outs being shown at Hale Bros.

Australian Buys Films

San Francisco, Cal.—N. Crown, who recently arrived here from Australia to purchase the Australian rights to large film productions, has closed several deals, including one for the rights to the Ivan picture, "Babbling Tongues." He recently made a trip in the interior of the state looking at moving picture houses with the idea of purchasing one for his brother.

San Francisco Operators Give Movie Ball

Financial Success Follows Fifth Annual Ball of Local 162—Provides a Death and Sick Fund—General Committee in Charge.

By T. A. Church, 1507 North St., Berkeley, Cal.

SAN FRANCISCO, CAL.—The fifth annual Movie Ball, tendered by the San Francisco Moving Picture Operators' Union No. 162 for the benefit of the sick and death fund, was held in the Exposition Auditorium in the Civic Center on September 1st, and was a very successful event. This organization has the exclusive right to hold a "Movie Ball" here, having taken the precaution to register the term for its protection.

The recent event drew a larger attendance that was thought possible, considering the circumstances, a street car strike being in progress at the time. However, municipal cars were operated to the Civic Center and automobiles brought large numbers so that the transportation strike did not seriously interfere with its success. Several local vaudeville houses furnished acts and there were many novelties in the line of electrical effects.

The affair was handled by a general committee consisting of Peter Boyle, chairman; Anthony L. Noreiga, secretary; L. G. Dolliver, financial secretary; C. E. Jones, treasurer; A. F. Howell and M. Goodman. The various committees that assisted the general committee, with their chairmen, were as follows: Reception, A. F. Howell; floor, E. P. Jones; entertainment, W. de Latimer; Publicity, Anthony L. Noreiga, and finance, M. Goodman. The officials of the local union are Peter Boyle, president; M. Fairbanks, vice-president; Anthony L. Noreiga, secretary; C. E. Jones, treasurer; E. Ahern, sergeant-at-arms, and L. G. Dolliver, business agent.

Express Ruling Causes Trouble.

San Francisco, Cal.—The three express companies doing business here, Wells Fargo, Adams and the American Express, have notified the trade that it will make deliveries of nothing received later than three o'clock each day and that no pickups will be made after five o'clock. This will not affect ordinary mercantile lines to any marked extent, but will prove a serious matter for film exchange interests. It will necessitate the maintainance of a special delivery service on the part of some of the large exchanges, especially during the winter months, when train service is apt to be delayed. The Motion Picture Industries of Northern California has taken the matter up with the different express companies, but without securing any promise of relief.

Sunset Theater Sold to A. R. Oberle.

San Francisco, Cal.—The Sunset theater on Haight street, conducted for several years by Oppenheimer, Karski & Levy, has been sold to A. R. Oberle, who conducts the Bay Station theater at Alameda. The former owners of the Sunset are now devoting their attention to the management of the Royal theater on Polk street, but at the same time are investigating other locations with the idea of erecting another house with a seating capacity of not less than 2,000.

Garrick Again a Picture House.

San Francisco, Cal.—Following a short run of musical comedy the New Garrick theater, Fillmore and Ellis streets, has gone back to moving pictures, planning to present big features only. Two changes of program will be made each week and the prices of admission will be ten cents for adults and five cents for children. The first film offering under the change in policy was "The Fires of Rebellion," featuring Dorothy Phillips.

Mutual Manager Enthusiastic.

San Francisco, Cal.—Newton Levy, manager of the local Mutual branch, returned recently from a trip to Northern California and Nevada and reports that exhibitors in the territory he covered are

doing a fine business and are preparing for a great fall season. He had a very successful trip and is delighted with the showing that is being made by this office with the new two-a-week releases, business having shown a great gain since this policy was inaugurated.

Portola Books "Les Miserables."

San Francisco, Cal.—"Les Miserables" has been booked for a week's run at the Portola theater

H. Solmson, a Peerless Hustler.

San Francisco, Cal.—H. Solmson, manager of the local office of the Peerless Film Service, Inc., is one of the youngest exchange managers on the Coast, but this does not prevent him from keeping pace with many of the veterans in the busi-

Left to right: B. Schwartz, George George, manager of Palm Theater; H. Solmson, manager Peerless Film Exchange.

ness. In the accompanying picture he is seen on the right, and his assistant, B. Schwartz is on the left, while between them is George George, manager of the Palm theater of this city, who has just signed up for Christie comedies for a full year.

For the past two years Mr. Solmson has been with E. H. Emmick, of the Peerless Film Service, most of the time as manager of this office, and before coming here handled several pictures on his own account in Missouri. His duties have been added to of late as the Peerless Film Service has taken over all of the features formerly handled by the De Luxe Film-Lasky Corp. in Northern California and Nevada. He states that a big business is being done in the southern territory on the "Bar Sinister," which is being handled by the Peerless for Nat A. Magner.

W. E. Matthews Made Branch Manager.

San Francisco, Cal.—W. E. Matthews, who has made an enviable record for himself at the local office of the General Film, has been made manager of the new branch office established this month at Portland, Ore. The San Francisco branch is making a steady gain in business, the new four-reel productions attracting much attention and the Essanay reissue of "The Champion" bringing in a flood of bookings.

Calendar of Daily Program Releases

Releases for Weeks Ending September 29 and October 6

For Extended Table of Current Releases See Pages 2055, 2056, 2057, 2058.)

Universal Film Mfg. Company

RELEASES FOR WEEK OF SEPTEMBER 24.

GOLD SEAL—The Master Spy (An Episode of The Perils of The Secret Service) (Three Parts—Drama)	
NESTOR—Taking Their Medicine (Comedy)	02693
L-KO—Soapsuds and Sirens (Two-Reel Comedy)	02694
	02695
UNIVERSAL ANIMATED WEEKLY—Weekly No. 91 (Topical)	02696
STAR FEATURETTE—A Romany Rose (Two-Reel Drama)	02697
JOKER—Marble Heads (Comedy)	02698
VICTOR—Your Boy and Mine (Comedy)	02699
UNIVERSAL SCREEN MAGAZINE—Issue No. 38 (Topical)	02701
UNIVERSAL CURRENT EVENTS—Issue No. 20 (Education)	02700
JOKER—The Fountain of Trouble (Comedy)	02702
BISON—The Dynamite Special (Two Parts—Dr.)	02703
UNIVERSAL SPECIAL—"The Gray Ghost" (Episode No. 13)—"The Tightening Snare" (Two Parts—Drama)	02704

RELEASES FOR WEEK OF OCTOBER 1.

GOLD SEAL—The Storm Woman (Three Parts—Drama)	02706
NESTOR—Pete The Prowler (Comedy)	02707
L-KO—Counting Out the Count (Comedy)	02708
UNIVERSAL ANIMATED WEEKLY—Weekly No. 92 (Topical)	02709
STAR FEATURETTE—A Prairie Romeo (Two Parts—Comedy-Drama)	02710
JOKER—Her Naughty Choice (Comedy)	02711
VICTOR—Kicked in the Kitchen (Comedy)	02712
UNIVERSAL SCREEN MAGAZINE—Issue No. 39 (Educational)	02713
UNIVERSAL CURRENT EVENTS—Issue No. 21 (Topical)	02714
JOKER—The Masked Marvels (Comedy)	02715
BISON—The Lion's Lair (Two Parts—Drama)	02716
UNIVERSAL SPECIAL—The Gray Ghost (Episode No. 14, At Bay) (Two Parts—Drama)	02717

Mutual Film Corporation

MONDAY, SEPTEMBER 24, 1917.

MUTUAL STAR PRODUCTION—The Runaway (Frohman—Six Parts—Drama)	05770-71-72-73-74-75
MUTUAL STAR PRODUCTION—Sands of Sacrifice (American—Five Parts—Drama)	05776-77-78-79-80

WEDNESDAY, SEPTEMBER 26, 1917.

MUTUAL—Mutual Weekly No. 143 (Topical)	05781

THURSDAY, SEPTEMBER 27, 1917.

CUB—Jerry's Big Deal (Comedy)	05782
GAUMONT—Reel Life No. 74 (Subjects on Reel: The Soldiers' Staff of Life; The Correct Time—as Determined by the U. S. Naval Observatory; Beans and Lady Bugs; The Lamprey—A Blood-Sucking Fish; Making Eyeglasses—So Easy (An Animated Drawing from "Life").	

MONDAY, OCTOBER 1, 1917.

MUTUAL STAR PRODUCTION—Her Country's Call (American—Five Parts—Drama)	05788-89-90-91-92
MUTUAL STAR PRODUCTION—Queen X (Goodrich —Five Parts—Drama)	05793-94-95-96-97

WEDNESDAY, OCTOBER 3, 1917.

MUTUAL—Mutual Weekly No. 144 (Topical)	05798

THURSDAY, OCTOBER 4, 1917.

CUB—Jerry in Yodel Land (Comedy)	05799
GAUMONT—Reel Life No. 75 (Subjects on Reel: Dogs of War; The Sign of a City; Making Army Rifles; Japanese Dwarf Plants; Animated Drawings from "Life"—Who Hesitates Is Lost; The Chorus Girl).	
MUTUAL SERIAL—The Lost Express (Episode No. 3—"The Wreck at the Crossing"—Two Parts—Drama)	05801-02

Can You Blame Us
for Printing the Following

In the July 5th issue of our well known British contemporary, of London, England, "The Kinematograph and Lantern Weekly," there is an article on "The Making of a Model Trade Paper," by A. E. Newbould (Chairman of the Cinematograph Exhibitors' Association), from which we quote the following:

"I would like to put on record my opinion that the Trade Press has been going ahead lately by leaps and bounds. There has been a definite effect toward freer criticism, more up-to-date methods and constructive assistance.

"But we have still a long way to go, and I am in cordial agreement with Mr. Montagu when he points to the MOVING PICTURE WORLD as a model Trade Paper. It is dignified, judicial, undeniably independent and very capably edited. It is in the best sense of the word a trade organ to which a wealthy industry can point with pride."

The above is all the more gratifying as Mr. Newbould is unknown to us except as we have noted his name from time to time in the British trade press in connection with his activities on behalf of the exhibitors of Great Britain.

Stories of the Films

General Film Company, Inc.

SPARKLE COMEDY.

HEARTS AND HARPOONS (One Reel).—In a fishing hamlet Captain Peters and Captain Hankins, retired sea captains, are old cronies. Mrs. Scribbier, a widow and writer of sea stories, comes to the town to get atmosphere. On her arrival both old captains fall in love with her and a strong rivalry springs up between them. Captain Hankins proposes, a sail down the bay and the widow accepts. Captain Peters bribes Clarence, a hoodlum, to bore a hole in the boat. He then makes a daring rescue of the widow from the sinking yawl, to the discomfiture of his rival.

Captain Hankins learns that Captain Peters is responsible for the leaky yawl and determines to get even. Learning that Captain Peters is to take the widow out driving he fixes it with the liveryman to give them a balky horse and later relieves Captain Peters of his prize and turns the tables. That night a duel is proposed, the choice of weapons being harpoons at twenty paces. Just before the signal to begin is given the widow and Jack Mertia, who has been trying to induce the lady to marry him, rush in and matters are explained. The two captains make up and Jack leads his widow away.

MIXED NUTS (One Reel).—The cast: A. Wall Nut (Alfred Swenson); Hazel Nut (Marguerite Chafee); Belle Bun (Lottie Palmer); Mr. Winslow (Edward Lawrence); His Wife (Ione Bright).

A. Wall Nut and his wife, Hazel, are a happy young people, but the spectre of gray hair threatens to mar their happiness. The young husband is sent to Europe by his firm and cautions his wife not to dye her hair in his absence or he will divorce her. But the sight of fresh gray hairs is too much for her and she goes to the hairdresser to have her locks retouched. Falling asleep, she is frantic to find on awakening that her hair has been dyed a deep and lasting black, and decides to go to California with her sister until the dye wears off.

A Wall Nut is recalled by his firm and wires his wife that he is returning. The Swedish servant receives the message and answers it, cutting down the cable until it reads: "Your wife died. It was terrible. Her sister has taken her to California." Wall Nut receives the message and is overcome. He writes a letter enclosing some money and gives it to a loiterer in the hotel lobby to mail. The latter is a thief and is run down while making off with the letter and money and mistaken for A. Wall Nut.

Word is sent to Hazel that her husband has been killed. On the way home Nut tells Mrs. Winslow, a friend, of his wife's death. In the meantime Hazel, waiting at the dock to receive her husband's body, meets Mr. Winslow. Through glasses they see Nut and Mrs. Winslow apparently in close embrace. The boat docks, mutual explanations follow and the reunited Nuts wend their way home.

FALCON FEATURES.

THE CLIMBER (Four Parts—The cast: William Beerdheim Van Broon (Henry King); Bruce Crosby (Jack McLaughlin); Buck Stringer (T. H. Gibson Gowland); Grafton (Bert Ensminger); Tom Tarney (Chas. Blaisdell); Sweeney (James Kerr); Slats O'Keefe (Bruce Smith); "Happy" (Frank Erlanger); Eva Crosby (Lucille Pietz); Ethel Crosby (Leah Gibbs); Madelyn Rosseau (Arma Carlton); Mrs. Crosby (Mollie McConnell); Mrs. Tarney (Ruth Lackaye). From story by George Foxhall. Directed by Henry King.

William Beerdheim Van Broon, of a very old family, has come down until now he is a marker in Tom Tarney's bowling alleys. Tarney, seeing him deal a fellow a knockout blow, puts him in training, seeing great pugilistic possibilities in the boy.

Buck Stringer, the local champion, has a brother and sister, both employed in the house of Bruce Crosby, whom they are plotting to blackmail. One day while Bruce and his sister, Eva, are motoring through the slum district they have a blowout and Buck and his gang happen along and insult him. William appears and finishes Buck for the day. Eva invites him home and he meets Madelyn and Grafton, Buck's brother and sister, whom he faintly remembers seeing before.

Tarney signs William with Buck under the name of William Brown, and William wins in the first round. Bruce is present, and while Eva is not pleased at discovering that William is a prize fighter, Bruce is enraged. Although on the culmination of the plot against him Bruce is saved by William, he accuses William of being responsible for the whole affair. Eva's faith, however, remains unshaken and she goes to William's home to tell him so. About this time William is discovered by family attorneys through the publicity gained in winning the championship and comes into an inheritance of several million dollars.

THE SECRET OF BLACK MOUNTAIN (Four Parts).—The cast: Miriam Vale (Vola Vale); Blake Stanley (Philo McCullough); Ed Stanley (Chas. Dudley); George Cooper (George Austin); Barton (Henry Crawford); Sarah Stanley (Miguon LeBrun); Henry Scanley (James Warner); Jake DeWitt (Lewis King); Jim Vale (Jack McLaughlin); Jack Rance (T. H. Gibson Gowland); "Old Bill" (H. C. Russell). Story by Jackson Gregory. Directed by Otto Hoffman.

In search of information about her grandfather, a gold prospector, Miriam Vale comes to California and teaches school to defray her expenses. She learns that years ago Jim Vale came to Boulder with a chest of gold, buried some dust, but was beset by road agents and robbed. Suspicion was directed against Henry Stanley, a renegade, but nothing could be proven.

Miriam has decided to return to Vermont, when out of Black Mountain rides a horseman who commands Miriam to return with him, saying, "There's a woman in pretty deep trouble." When Miriam fears to go, he proceeds to use force. They ride away. The man meanwhile tells her his name is Stanley. Inside a cabin Miriam finds a dying woman and a dead man. When Stanley leaves the room, the woman tells Miriam she has been killed by her husband. Ed Stanley, and begs her to look under a certain stone near the fireplace. She fearfully awaits the return of the man, but when he appears Miriam learns that he is not the murderer, Stanley, but a cousin, Blake Stanley.

Ed Stanley and Cooper, his partner, arrive and order Blake to leave. A sharp fight follows, in which Cooper is badly wounded. Blake fetches him into the cabin and tells Miriam the whole story. He goes back to the death of old Henry Stanley and tells of the rifling of a safe deposit box containing the secret of his treasure, the elopement of Sarah Stanley with a bank cashier,

Barton, the dead man. Miriam gives Blake a slip of paper found under the fireplace.—Its message means success to their adventure, and incidentally a friendship auguring a fine romance is ratified.

JAXON COMEDY.

WILD INJUNS (One Reel).—Mrs. Gotrox, an enthusiast over the civilization of the Indian, has contributed liberally toward their education, and after the graduation exercises at the agency the commissioner decides to send two chiefs, "Rolling Thunder" and "Tossing Ball," to thank her in person. Mrs. Gotrox plans a novel reception for them. All the decorations are to be Indian, and the guests are to wear Indian costumes.

Pokes and Jabs are seated on a freight car enjoying their scant morning repast, when the Indians arrive and ask to be directed to the Gotrox mansion. Pokes and Jabs, mistaking their actions for threats, take to their heels, followed by the two Indians. Finally they find two coupling pins, and when the Indians come up they quickly overpower them. Finding the introductions to Mrs. Gotrox, they decide to become Indians. At least long enough to satisfy the cravings of the inner man. The reception is in full blast when Pokes and Jabs arrive. As a bit of realism, Jabs proceeds to scalp the colored butler. Pokes, not to be outdone, drains the punch bowl and chases the guests and ends by scalping his hostess, exposing her bald head to the company. The two chiefs, hearing the women scream, rush in. A wild fight follows, and Pokes and Jabs flee, followed by the trusty arrows of the Indians.

SPEED DEMONS (One Reel).—Jabs, who is suffering from an attack of speeditis, is hustled off to Dr. Dippy's sanitarium, while Pokes, another auto enthusiast, wanders at large without a car. On the day of the world's championship auto race between Oldfield and DePalma, Jabs escapes and follows the crowds to the race. Pokes goes also and invites himself to ride in Lotta Wealth's speedster, but is ejected. Just then Jabs happens along and with aid of Pokes gains admittance to the race track, but Jabs is left outside. Seeing the guards on his trail he beats it back to the sanitarium. The race takes place and after many incidents Oldfield wins. Lotta Wealth remarks that she could beat Oldfield's record. Pokes double it, so off they went, through fences, over hills, through valleys and over bridges, until they finally run through an open draw. As they are swimming for shore Pokes remarks to Lotta, "I knew when we started you couldn't do it," but her reply is lost in the noise of the waves.

THE COLLECTORS (One Reel).—Jabs runs a female gymnasium and his motto is, "Get all the trust you can and pay me one." His landlord notifies him that if he does not pay the back rent it will be collected by force. Numerous collectors try but all fail. Pokes finally gets the job and starts out to collect. Whether it is his winning ways, his dogged persistence, or his bullet-proof armor that caused the success is unknown, but the landlord is telephoned for, and when he arrives at the gymnasium he finds Pokes calmly sitting on Jabs' chest, with Jabs' sweetheart on his lap counting the roll to see if it will cover the amount owed.

BROADWAY STAR FEATURE.

BLIND MAN'S HOLIDAY (One of the O. Henry Series—4 Parts).—The cast: Norah Greenway (Jean Paige); John Lorison (Carleton King); Father Rogan (John Costello); Norah's Little Brother (Alda Horton). Directed by Martin Justice.

John Lorison, self-exiled in New Orleans, meets a girl night after night in a cheap little restaurant. After dinner they take a little walk, but invariably she leaves him at 8 o'clock at a certain corner. One evening Lorison realizes that he is no longer willing to be left on the corner of his plans. With dread of her verdict, he tells her that he loves her but his past is marred with a charge of theft, and that he dare not ask an untarnished woman to marry him. Norah eases his mind by disclosing her own "past." She had been an actress, had stolen diamonds from her very wicked, but was never repentant. Lorison proposes, and they are married by Father Rogan that night. But she leaves him at 8 o'clock as usual, at the same corner, promising to go with him after tonight. Lorison consents to this, but gradually becomes torn with suspicion. Wandering about, he runs into a crowd gathered about a woman in a white satin stage costume, in charge of two policemen, who explain that she is wanted for stealing diamonds. The coincidence makes Lorison feel that his marriage to another diamond thief is a terrible mistake. He hunts out Father Rogan and begs him to undo the hasty marriage of a few hours before.

The priest says he will show him into what a predicament his hasty marriage has led him. He takes Lorison to Norah's house, where a woman tells them that Norah is out again, with a beautiful white satin dress. Upstairs her little brother tells them that Norah cried tonight and promised never to go out at night any more. Next the priest takes Lorison to a tall building. They climb to the third floor. Looking through a glass door, he sees among a score of others toiling at sewing machines over beautiful satins and laces the tired, happy face of his wife. The priest now tells him he has known Norah since the day she was born, and that for love of Lorison she had told a "desperate, beautiful lie."

THE LAST OF THE TROUBADOURS (One of the O. Henry Series—Two Parts).—The cast: King James (S. E. Jennings); His Catellite (Dan Duffy); Sam Galloway (Nolan Leary); Ellison (Jake Abraham). Directed by David Smith.

Sam Galloway, a surviving representative of the medieval troubadours, toils not—save with his fingers on guitar; neither does he save yarns. But he is the one apostle of Art in southwestern Texas and is welcome—implored—to stay as long as he likes at any ranch between San Antonio and Brownsville.

He is visiting Old Man Ellison, one of the few remaining sheep ranchers, when the old man is given a week to vacate his ranch by the local cattle king. As this is the only available grass left in Texas it is a death blow. He has no redress in law and he is sixty-five, weighs ninety-eight and loves a quiet life. The old man is forced to tell his lazy guest, Galloway, the reason for his sadness. Next day Ellison, on his way to Frio City for supplies, meets the cattle king, who, having learned that Ellison is from his home county and a relative, tells the old man that he will give him his ranch, help him financially and set him on his feet. Old Man Ellison's future changes from black to a rosy pink. He drives lazily home, contemplating blissfully his prospects. At the ranch he learns that Galloway has left for some place unknown—to return in the evening. And the old man sits down and dreams until his return.

But there is in Galloway's eyes and bearing, when he does arrive, an unaccustomed look. The soft, lazy expression of the artist has given place to that of the man of action.

"Ben," says Sam, "I couldn't let you be put on like that. I borrowed your revolver, rode into town this afternoon—you'd just gone when I got there—and filled Mr. King James full of lead. I reckon he won't bother you any more."

Old man Ellison makes no direct reply. He scratches his sparse whiskers and meditates forlornly a moment. Then: "Sam," eh say, "would you mind getting the guitar and playing that little piece I like once or twice? It's kind of soothing and comforting when a man's tired or fagged out."

THE DUPLICITY OF HARGRAVES (One of the O. Henry Series—Four Parts).—The cast: Major Talbot of Mobile (Charles Kent); Henry Hopkins Hargraves (J. Frank Glendon); Miss Lydia (Myrtis Coney); Mrs. Vardeman (Mrs. Fisher). Directed by Thomas R. Mills.

When Major Pendleton Talbot, of Mobile, and his daughter, Lydia, came to Washington, of course they selected an old-fashioned boarding house. Major Talbot was of the old, old South. He was a relic and dressed like one, in a ceremonial coat, and the young government clerks dubbed him a Father Hubbard. But he was courtly and dignified, and his daughter believed in him, and she scrimped and saved to keep up the family's appearance. For the Talbots were needy.

Among the boarders was Henry Hopkins Hargraves, a quiet sort of chap who was tolerated in spite of being a vaudeville actor. Hargraves cultivated the Major and his prim daughter, and used never to tire of the old man's stories and peculiar characteristics. One night in a fit of princely extravagance, the Major bought tickets to the opening of a new play. He and his daughter found on the stage Hargraves performing in the character of a typical Southern grandee—making a tremendous hit. The Major recognized it, however, as a caricature, and next morning when Hargraves came to boast of his success, bitterly upraided him. Hargraves would excuse himself for using the Major as "copy," and would even reimburse him handsomely, but the aid is refused though the old man is practically starving. Abashed, Hargraves disappears, causing a pang in the heart of Lydia.

Some time later the Major is in dire straits, when he is approached by an old colored man, also a relic of the South, who has prospered, and who presses a goodly sum on the Major in repayment of a debt owed the family. The Major accepts it ,though he remembers nothing about its origin. It is the beginning of his rise, and soon, with new courage, he is up in the world again. He never learns the secret of his windfall. But Lydia does—in a letter from Hargraves. He, masquerading, was the old colored man.

KALEM.

A CHAMPION OF THE LAW (An Episode of The Further Adventures of Stingaree—Two Parts).—The cast: Stingaree (True Boardman); Howie (Paul C. Hurst); Ethel Porter (Marin Sais); Tom Deane (Chris Lynton); Edna Deane (Edythe Sterling); Richard Falkland (Edward Hearn); Caspar Urie (R. S. Bradbury); Bill Savage (Hart Hoxie); The Governor (Frank Jonasson); His Secretary (Edward Clisbee).

Richard Falkland, an officer of the ship "Sydney," and Caspar Urie, an overseas trader of questionable character, are rivals for the hand of Edna Deane. She chooses Falkland. Arriving in Australia, Urie persuades Falkland to abandon his ship and accompany him to the gold diggings. Losing their way, they encounter Stingaree, the gentleman bushranger, who tells them the way to the Deane cattle run. Urie recognizes Stingaree and proposes to Falkland that they turn him over to the police and obtain the reward offered for his capture. Stingaree overhears Falkland refuse to betray a man who has just saved their lives. In gratitude he gives Falkland a slip of paper, saying: "That will tell you where to find me. If you ever need a friend, come to me."

After a raid by Ben Savage and his band of outlaws, the governor offers a reward of a thousand pounds for the capture of the bandits. When Ethel Porter, Stingaree's sweetheart from London, appeals to the governor for a pardon for the bushranger, he refuses. Riding out into the bush country, Ethel comes upon the camp of Stingaree while he is out. She is recognized by Howie, Stingaree's partner, and waits for his return.

When Urie and Falkland arrive at the Deane cattle run, Edna's father is enraged that his daughter should wish to marry a man who would desert his ship. He orders Falkland from the house.

Hearing of the reward offered for their capture, Ben Savage's band of outlaws set out to hold up the stage in which the governor is traveling. They shoot the driver from his seat, and the horses run away. The runaway is seen by Ethel, who, upon Stingaree's failure to return to his camp, has set out in search of him. She effects a rescue, but as the bandits are still in pursuit, the governor, his secretary and Ethel take refuge in the Deane home, which is nearby. The bandits attack the house. Falkland sees the attack from the distance and realizes the danger of the occupants. He remembers Stingaree and the note he had given him. He rides to the bushranger's camp to obtain his help.

After a grueling battle, the bandits break into the Deane house. Savage rides through a window on horseback and carries the governor off with him. Stingaree, Howie, and Falkland, riding to the rescue, arrive just in time to save the governor from the outlaws.

In appreciation, the governor grants Stingaree a pardon and Deane gives his consent to Falkland's marriage with his daughter. After a touching good-bye to his old pal, Howie, Stingaree sails for London with Ethel Porter, there to abandon the role of bushranger for that of an English gentleman.

SELIG.

SELIG WORLD LIBRARY NO. 18.

Harvesting Lima Beans in California.—"Capt'n Jenks of the Horse Marines," it will be recalled, "fed his horse good corn an' beans"—particularly beans. Here we see beans harvested in California.

Famous Zoo at Sydney, Australia.—The crane is considered sacred in sections of Irdia and Japan. Ah, the cassowary, five feet high and full o' pep! Wild kiwies! The Kangaroo, direct to you! Australian emu.

The Oyster Harvest in Chesapeake Bay.—The oyster comes into his own with the beginning of the "R" months. The oyster schooner. Schucking oysters. Canning oysters. M-m-m-m! On th' half shell!

Mausoleums of the Ming Emperors of China.—There are many magnificent ruins of the great Ming dynasty at Peking. Memorial archways. The immense stone figures of camels and elephants are tombs of the Ming emperors.

Coal Production of the U. S. A.—Uncle Sam and John Bull supply two-thirds of the world's demands. First mine worked in the United States was opened at Richmond, Va., in 1750. Electric dumping device.

THE VICTOR OF THE PLOT (Two Parts.—The cast: John Morris (Wheeler Oakman); Major Goe (Gordon Sackville); Colonel Warren (Frank Clark); Ayoob (Jack F. McDonald); Leukman (William Elmer); Viceroy (Al. W. Filson); Nourmalie (Bessie Eyton). Directed by Colin Campbell.

Nourmalie, only daughter of Colonel Warren, loses her heart to John Morris and thus Morris wins the enmity of Major Goe, who is infatuated with Warren's daughter. The regiment is quartered in a distant land, and Goe becomes the more infuriated when Nourmalie continues to treat his courtship with disdain.

In a fight with the savages Morris saves Major Goe's life, which but increases Goe's bitterness. Goe plots with natives, who capture young Morris and plan to put him to the torture. Goe brags to the girl who had spurned him of the fact that Morris is to meet death at the hands of the savages. He is unwise to divulge this information, for the girl through her resourcefulness liberates Morris and brings about the punishment of the villainous major.

THE VOICE THAT LED HIM (One Reel).—The cast: Will Everyman (Charles Clary); Hindu Guide (L. F. McKee); Daisy, Everyman's wife (Kathlyn Williams); May Skillman, Daisy's double (Kathlyn Williams); Mrs. Everyman (Emma Bell); Mrs. Skillman (Lillian Leighton). Written by Gilson Willets. Directed by F. J. Grandon.

In the jungles of Africa a naturalist photographs a wild beast in its native state. Later his wife accidentally breaks the negative just as it is to be developed. The naturalist upbraids his wife and despite her pleadings he leaves the house in a rage. In his absence a wild beast attacks the wife and takes her life.

The naturalist returns to his home in another land. However, his conscience will not permit him to rest. Always he is thinking of and having visions of the faithful wife whose life ended in the jungles. Later he falls in love with the counterpart of his dead wife. However, the marriage is never performed, for his conscience will not permit him to wed the girl. He finally resolves to live only for his mother, and then the terrible burden on his mind is lifted.

Universal Film Mfg. Co

GOLD SEAL.

THE MASTER SPY (An Episode of "The Perils of the Secret Service") (Three Parts—Rel. Week of Sept. 24).—The cast: Yorke Norroy (Kingsley Benedict); Carson Huntley (Jay Belasco); John Gaunt (Al. MacQuarrie); Von Linden (Baron Von Ritzau); Irma Malloff (Mignon Anderson); Boris Von Haden (Frank Lanning). Written by George Bronson Howard. Produced by Jack Wells and Kingsley Benedict.

The two agents of the U. S. State Department, Yorke Norroy and Carson Huntley, are about to leave the town of Eukrain, on the border of Russia and Saxonia, a neighborhood which is becoming unhealthy for those in government service. Just as they are about to leave their apartment John Gaunt, well known to them as a representative of the British Secret Service, but traveling as a tourist, appears. Gaunt is in a miserable state of health. He tells Norroy and Huntley that he has received the plans of the forts and that he is to get two thousand pounds for bringing them to headquarters in England, but if he dies without doing it, his wife and children will be penniless. He implores Norroy to take the plans to England, and get the money for his family. Norroy agrees.

Norroy persuades Huntley to cross the border before him. Huntley is stopped by officers who search him and his baggage. Norroy, too, is examined, but he slips the plans into his driver's pocket and is allowed to go. When Norroy attempts to remove the plans from the pocket the coachman sets up a howl to call the soldiers. Norroy knocks him unconscious and, unhitching the horse, starts down the road at a swift pace on its back, the soldiers pursuing him.

Arrived at an inn, Norroy is delighted to see Georgio, a man whom he had seen kill another in Budapest. Threatening to report the incident if Georgio does not hide him from the authorities, Norroy is led to a secret room. There is a door behind a big picture of the Virgin, and Norroy goes through this door.

Meanwhile the Countess Irma Malloff has left her guardian's roof to join Prince Darien across the border. Captain Boris Von Haden, son of the guardian, is following the Countess. There is only one place where she can take a train, and that is near the inn of Georgio. The Countess arrives, and bribes Georgio to conceal her until the train comes. He shows her into the room with the picture. When Georgio refuses to open it for Captain Boris, the latter climbs through the window and confronts Irma. She cries for help. Norroy cannot resist her calls, and, springing the panel, soon overpowers the captain.

Norroy escapes with the Countess in her car, rushing toward the frontier. Passing through a village, he has the luck to find one of his men waiting for him. He tells him to take the Countess to the Three Pigeon Inn. He then makes his way through the hills by a short cut, and manages to pass the border patrol. But they catch sight of him and pursue. He swims his horse through a lake and escapes. After crossing the frontier, he meets a band of Russian mountaineers.

"Soldiers of Saxonia on Russian soil!" he cries to them. "What is your answer?"

The peasants attack the patrol, and Norroy escapes and joins the Countess, who has met the Prince, her sweetheart.

BISON.

THE DYNAMITE SPECIAL (Two Parts—Rel. Week of Sept. 24).—The cast: David Carleton (George Williams); Ralph Carleton (M. K. Wilson; Bill Manville (Marc Fenton); Ruth Manville (Helen Gibson); Joe Brooks (Val Paul); Jimmy Thurman (Al. Harris). Scenario by George Hively. Produced by J. D. Davis.

Jimmy Thurman, the fireman on Bill Manville's engine, is in love with Ruth, Bill's daughter. He believes that she doesn't care for him any more since Ralph Carleton, the son of the district superintendent, has become agent at Wellville. Joe Brooks, the dispatcher, is another who is interested in Bill's daughter, Ruth. So much so that he determines to get Ralph out of the running. When Ralph's father comes to see how his son is getting on, Joe tells him that Ruth is keeping the young fellow from his work. His plan succeeds, for Mr. Carleton sends his son to another station. Carleton, meantime, has discharged Joe for drinking, and the man vows vengeance.

A dynamite special is to go west the next day and Bill and Jimmy are to pull her over. Ruth pleads with Jimmy to tell her where Ralph is, and he says that Ralph is at Crestmore. That night, Ruth, in overalls and cap, hides in an empty car of the Dynamite Special, and while concealed, overhears Brooks and his companion planning to blow up the superintendent's special, which the dynamite special is to meet at Crestmore.

Brooks and Leeds make their way to the dynamite car and steal a box marked "Nitro-Glycerine." Ruth watches them. The men uncouple the engine and drive away, while Ruth rushes to the station to warn her father. Ralph thinks of his father's special. Brooks and Leeds jump from the engine, thus allowing it to speed ahead by itself.

Ruth jumps on a motor-cycle and rides after the runaway. The special is coming from the other direction. Ralph is unable to help, as the special has already left Hilidale, the nearest station. Gaining on the engine, Ruth jumps from the motor-cycle to the cab, shuts off the throttle, and reverses the engine. She runs ahead with a flag and hails the approaching special. Before she can tell Carleton the trouble, she faints away. Carleton leaves Ralph with Ruth, going to Bill, with whom he shakes hands. Brooks and Leeds are captured.

NESTOR.

TAKING THEIR MEDICINE (One Reel—Rel. Week of Sept. 21).—The cast: Nifty Nat (Eddie Lyons); Double Draw Dan (Lee Moran); Helen Hilliard (Edith Roberts); Dick Parks (Fred Gamble). Scenario by Fred Palmer. Produced by Roy Clements.

When Helen Hilliard arrived at the Circle W ranch every one of the cowboys made plans to stay around the place as much as possible, though the old man was determined that the [illegible] should go on. Nifty Nat had the [illegible] swell idea. When daylight came, he awoke groaning and clutching his stomach. He said that he was deathly sick, though. Double Draw Dan had his suspicions. However, Nat's plan worked. He stayed behind, and Helen came in and nursed him. Nat got away with it because Uncle had driven to town.

The boys were out on the range, but it was queer how many things, absolutely essential to their work, had been forgotten that morning. Double Draw was the first to discover that there was no hammer to nail up the wire of the broken fences. Back he went full speed to fetch it—Dan was always so helpful!

Helen immediately found herself with another patient on her hands. But she was equal to the emergency, and took care of each suffering ranch hand as he appeared, smoothing his hair, and holding as many hands as she could manage.

The boys were having the time of their lives, when Uncle suddenly reappeared. One look was enough for him. Off he went to the harness room where he concocted a mixture of harness oil, soft soap, and other ingredients. He then entered the sick chamber, and told Helen that he had a sovereign remedy, and that he would repeat the dose every fifteen minutes till the boys were recovered. One spoonful was forced down the reluctant throat of each. And certainly the remedy was a wonder, for the boys were cured as if by magic.

VICTOR.

YOUR BOY AND MINE (One Reel—Rel. Week of Sept. 24.—The cast: Tub (Lincoln Stedman); Skinny (Elwood Bredell); Tub's Mother (Lydia Yeamans Titus); Skinny's Mother (Grace Marvin); Tub's Male Parent (Hal Wilson); Skinny's Mother's Husband (William Dyer); The Village News (Harry Mann). Written by Roy Clements. Produced by Roy Clements.

Tub's mother turned abruptly from her doughnut frying, and the big wooden spoon found its way to Tubs' head. Over on Skinny's back porch almost the same scene was in progress. The two fathers made their appearance on their way to work, and Tub's mother took a plate of hot doughnuts over to Skinny's house. As soon as her back was turned, Tub deserted the churn, crammed his pockets, his shirt, and his mouth with doughnuts, and climbed out of the kitchen window.

Skinny and Tub had plenty of time to meet behind the barn, and commence to dig worms, while the two mothers were discussing the weather over the back fence. Skinny was on his knees digging hard, when Tub pulled a doughnut out of his pocket and started to eat it right before Skinny. That started a fight.

"The Village News," the worst gossip in the county, was on his way to town, when he heard the rumpus. He rushed to their mothers with the news. The two ladies ran to the rescue of their sons. The women became involved in the fray, and the "News" rushed to get the two fathers. Very soon there were three fights raging—the boys', the mothers' and the fathers'. The "News" then went for the militia.

"Let's quit," said Tub suddenly to Skinny.

"All right," said Skinny, signing peace terms on the spot. And when the "News" arrived with the sheriff, he found two boys eating the same doughnut, two fathers smoking in perfect amity, and two mothers crying on each other's shoulders.

STAR FEATURETTE.

A ROMANY ROSE (Two parts—Rel. Week of Sept. 24).—The cast: Rozeska (Lena Baskette); Her Mother (Claire McDowell); Her Father (Charles Hill Mailes); Richard Lorraine (Fred Montague); His Housekeeper (Martha Mattox); Dancing Master (Nigel Debrullier). Scenario and production by Marshall Stedman.

Rozeska's father tore her away from her mother's arms, thrust her tambourine into her hand, and sent her out to entertain the auto party, halted on account of tire trouble, beside the road.

"See the pretty little girl! What charming movements! A natural dancer!" cried the tourists, among whom was Carter Hargrave, the head of the vaudeville circuit. The child's father was all smiles when he gave him his card, and said that the girl would be a success in vaudeville.

In the outskirts of the village near the gypsies' camp, lived Richard Lorraine, who, bereft of his wife and child, lives in a world of memories. He notices the gypsies' camp and wanders over to it. There he sees little Rozeska teaching her doll to dance. The next morning he calls at the camp and pays the father a large sum to allow him to adopt the child, to take the place of his own. The mother is grieved at the parting, but realizes it is for the best.

Following the legal adoption, Rozeska is given everything she wishes. The father soon spends the money, and then, remembering the vaudeville manager, calls on him. Hargrave offers him seventy-five dollars a week for the child to dance. The father agrees to bring her, and that day breaks camp without telling the mother of his plans. In the night they arrive in the neighborhood of the Lorraine house. The father sets out for the house, but arouses the mother's suspicions. She questions him, and he tells her of the offer, and that he is going after Rozeska. She struggles to prevent him. He binds and gags her, but she succeeds in releasing herself and follows. The father is about to make away with Rozeska, when the mother arrives and raises the alarm. In an effort to escape, the father falls from the window and is killed. Rozeska clings to her mother, and Lorraine, seeing the affection between the two, offers the gypsy a home with her child.

L-KO.

SOAPSUDS AND SIRENS (Two Parts—Rel. Week of Sept. 26).—The cast: Prof. Thinem (Harry Lorrane); the Janitor (Walter Stephens); Mr. Printum (Bert Roach); Mrs. Printum (Gladys Varden). Directed by Noel Smith. Supervised by J. G. Blystone.

The janitor lost his last pail of water. The faucet was out of order so it was impossible to get water. Prof. Thinem, one of the most successful failures in the dancing profession, was crying profusely. The janitor took his pail and held it under the professor's eyes, and secured enough water for cleaning purposes. At that moment in came a large, stout lady, and the dancing master conducted her to the studio. He warned her that the floor would sustain only fifty pounds to the square inch. After a high kick the floor buckled under the strain, and landed the fat lady in the plunge below. But the janitor was on the job, he rescued her, and then he sawed a hole in her purse, as the professor was reviving her, and recovered all her money. The professor, having obtained a little coin, sent the janitor to Mr. Printum to have a hand-bill advertisement printed for him.

Mrs. Printum was a devotee of dancing. She would dance right over her husband's head, as she lived above the print shop. She, too, fell through the weakened floor, and right into the press, where the announcement of the prof's studio was imprinted upon the back of her dress. Hubby was furious, and chased her down the street, but the ad did its work. In her flight, many ladies, tall and short, fat and thin, saw the ad, and made a bee-line for the dancing academy.

A bevy of lovely pupils arrived at the academy. Some of them disported themselves in the plunge and all of them were robed in imitation of the Goddess Diana. The prof wished to show them all out in the park. Mr. Printum had struggled out of the barrel of printer's ink into which he had fallen, and was still pursuing his wife. She decided to change clothes with the janitor to save herself. Then the lovely dancers were very nice to the disguised janitor, and shoved Mrs. Printum—in his overalls—out into the cold. Mr. Printum chased the party to the park, and began to beat up the supposed janitor. She managed to get hold of the real janitor and changed her clothes again. Then Mr. Printum did not know what to think. The chase was on again, and they all ended their troubles in the park lake.

JOKER.

MARBLE HEADS (One Reel—Rel. Week of Sept. 24).—The cast: Julep Jasbo (Milton Sims); Claribell Lotsadough (Gale Henry); Jake (William Franey); Joe (Milburn Moranti). Written by Tom Gibson. Produced by Allen Curtis.

"Send up the statue this afternoon, so I can have it in the garden for my party," said Mrs. Claribell Lotsadough as she pressed a roll of bills into the outstretched hand of Julep Jasbo, the sculptor.

Jasbo hadn't made a sale in months, and he rushed downstairs as hard as he could go, and called the expressmen to the job. It certainly was hard luck for Jasbo that Jake and Joe should have been within hearing, for after boxing up his work of art, and carrying it safely down six or seven stories, they dropped the whole thing down the last flight of stairs.

Panic-stricken, Jasbo forced the two expressmen to don the garb of ancient Roman warriors, while he prepared a whitewash bath for them. Then he jammed them into the box, and sent them off to the garden party.

Claribell was awaiting her work of art. Jasbo had to lure her away while the two gladiators clambered out of the box and set themselves up on the pedestal at the head of the refreshment table. Jake and Joe made beautiful statues until the eats were passed. Then they could not resist trying for their share of the spoils. They are discovered, and Claribell's guests, thinking that she has been making game of them, all leave in a huff. When she returns to wreak vengeance on the statues, they are not to be seen. Before she reappears, Jasbo has arrived and set up the real statue in their places; he meanwhile having repaired them. She doesn't know what to think, while down in the corner of the garden the pseudo-gladiators are feasting on chicken and champagne.

THE FOUNTAIN OF TROUBLE (One Reel—Rel. Week of Sept. 24).—The cast: Mr. Cramp (William Franey); Mrs. Cramp (Ida Tenbrook); Pickpocket Chief (Milburn Moranti); Josie Jones (Nellie Allen). Written by Arthur F. Slater. Produced by W. W. Beaudine.

Mrs. Cramp sends her husband to the foot of a hill to get her a glass of water. As he nears the fountain a woman's handbag is stuffed into his hand, and the giver disappears. Mr. Cramp gets the water, and as he is bringing it to his wife, he trips over a lady's foot. It is Josie Jones, sitting under her beach parasol.

"Oh! my bag! Have you seen it?" cries Josie.

"Is this it?" says Mr. Cramp. It is, and Josie's beaming eyes reward him. He has spilled the water, however, so he goes back to the fountain.

Again a man approaches and slips a bag into his hand. It is the same bag! Josie sees him returning to his wife, and snatches the bag from him, accusing him of stealing it. He apologizes, but the water is spilled again, so back he goes to the fountain.

The next man who approaches warns him to look out for the cops, and dashes away. Cramp follows, and is led into the pickpocket's den. One of the crooks rushes in and says he has lost his elephant. Cramp had found a little elephant stick-pin, and he innocently hands it to the man. The next minute he is out of the door with the band after him. The police get the crooks, but Cramp just manages to get back to his wife.

"Where's my drink of water? Heavens! what a time you've been!" says Mrs. Cramp. And back he goes to the fountain.

ANIMATED WEEKLY.

ISSUE NO. 89 (Sept. 12).

Famous Stallion Smashes Record in Grand Circuit Races.—"St. Frisco," with veteran "Pop" Geers holding the "ribbons," sets new mark for his class—Poughkeepsie, N. Y. Subtitles: The famous Knickerbocker attracted a great field. In the final heat "Busy's Lassie" beats "Brescia." "St. Frisco," "Pop" Geers driving, time 2.01¾. Popular "Tom" Murphy honored by friends.

If All War Camps Are Like This, Prisoners Are Lucky.—German crew of Kron Prinz Wilhelm live, work and play under model conditions—Near Ft. McPherson, Ga. Subtitles: Erecting a new Y. M. C. A. building. Cobble! Cobble! Cobble! Money for tobacco is earned by selling prison-made toys. Sports are permitted and encouraged.

Girl Scouts Will Substitute for Farmhands Called to War.—Society buds on Nicoll Estate make khaki the favored "gown" as they work in the open—Ossining, N. Y. Subtitles: "Always and forever—Our Flag!" Primitive—but wholesome! Canning is mastered.

West Coast Comes Thru With Early Football.—University of California freshmen and sophomores open season with lively game—Berkeley, Cal.

Civilian Speed Boys Set Records in Building Cantonment for Uncle Sam.—At Camp Gordon 8,000 workmen handle half-million feet of lumber daily.—Atlanta, Ga. Subtitles: In eight hours 200 carpenters, using 75,000 ft. of lumber, 2,500 lbs. of nails and 8,000 ft. of roofing, build a barracks 140-42 ft., 2 stories high, with kitchen, mess-hall and sleeping quarters for 200 men! How our speed looks to the enemy.

Roosevelt for Woman Suffrage Where Duty is Done.—Tells National League of Women Suffragists right to vote should be reward for loyalty—Oyster Bay, L. I. Subtitles: "Teddy" to Mrs. Ogden Mills, Mrs. Norman Whitehouse and Mrs. James L. Laidlaw: "I would put the mother ahead of every other human being!" "The Lord knows I despise Pacificists!" "When the right appeal is made, the mothers, wives and daughters of America will stand just a trifle *ahead* of their sons, husbands and fathers in sacrificing *everything!*"

Maybe Ponce De Leon Sought This?—"Fountain of Youth" of famous explorer located by Universal cameraman at Galveston, Texas. Subtitles: Mere maids—or mermaids?

Cartoons by Hy. Mayer.

UNIVERSAL CURRENT EVENTS.

ISSUE NO. 18 (Sept. 15).

British Recruiting Chief Visits Great Southwest.—Sir William White, distinguished Briton, honored in pretty West Coast City—Los Angeles, Cal. Subtitles: General White and his staff of recruiting officers who have done fine work in America. Mayor Woodman welcomes General White.

Uncle Sam's Jack Tars Enjoy Work and Nature.—Beautiful Balboa Park scene of activity while boys await orders to fight—San Diego, Cal. Subtitle: No hotel boasts a more wonderful dining-room.

Let's Clean 'Em Out.—Device shows mild treatment which should be given traitors who live here, eat here and do their dirty work here — Unfortunately - too - many-places-in-America. Subtitle: "Freedom of speech will be respected, but in Illinois will not be permitted as a cloak of treason. The time has come in Illinois and elsewhere to find out who are for the government and who are against it." Governor Frank O. Lowden of Illinois.

Says Far North Will Be Explored by Aeros on Future Expeditions.—Donald B. McMillan, head of Crocker Land expedition, who put 1,000 more miles on map, says dog sleds are thru—New York City. Subtitle: Explorer McMillan and his chief assistant, W. E. Ekbraw.

Girl National Long-Distance Champion in Fifteen-Mile Swim.—Miss Lucy Freeman, 19 years old, braves tides and current over hazardous course—New York Harbor, N. Y. Subtitle: She finishes smiling.

Medical Needs of Our Boys Will Be Properly Cared for.—3,000 in one unit are about ready to join Pershing and his fighters—Fort Ethan Allen, Vt.

Miss Columbia Bo Peep Will Raise More Sheep.—And we'll know where to find 'em—the wool to France in shirts and pants—so that Sammies, warm clad, will make Wilhelm dance!—Chicago, Ill. Subtitle: There's a moral in the fact that even sheep give up for our soldiers!

"Old Sol" Blinked When He Saw This.—Missouri girl wears $1,000,000 in diamonds for the National Jewelers Convention—St. Louis, Mo. Subtitles: Necklace and lavalliere, $150,000! Hands and arms, $100,000! Anklets and shoe-buckles, $25,000! Gart——(Censored).

"Fighting Dozen" Guests of National League Teams.—12th New York witnesses exciting game between Giants and Dodgers at Ebbets Field—Brooklyn, N. Y. Subtitle: Ready for two national games—baseball and "Kanning the Kaiser."

Did You Know That Mexico Raises Seals?—One of the largest rookeries on the American continent is only forty miles from famous Coronado Beach, Coronado Islands, Mexico. Subtitle: The trainer has a "pull" with his pets.

UNIVERSAL SCREEN MAGAZINE.

ISSUE NO. 38 (Released Sept. 28).

The first number of this issue gives views of the revival of the ancient art of spinning and weaving, as it is practised on the estate of Mrs. George W. Vanderbilt, at the school which she has started on her estate at Biltmore, North Carolina. All the processes from carding the wool to weaving on handlooms is shown.

"What We Eat" is the second number, showing the "Evolution of the Squab"—the edible kind, not the Broadway variety. From the pigeon's eggs in the nest to the roast birds on the table, we trace the squab's progress.

A new invention is illustrated in the bicycle speedometer, which allows a rider to race his head off, and yet never move out of his own back yard. A movable device of rollers keeps the wheel revolving fact in one place, while the speed is registered on a clock-like dial, in full view of the rider.

Physical exercises for women, arranged by Bernarr Macfadden and posed by Helen Tyler, is a subject which is of wide interest. Movements for health and beauty are clearly demonstrated and if persisted in for fifteen minutes each day are sure to bring fine results.

The apricot industry makes a good subject. School girls are aiding Uncle Sam in vacation time by picking, cutting and pitting the fruit in Pomona, California. The halved apricots are laid in shallow trays, and exposed to the sun, which dries them by natural process.

A Miracle in Mud, called "Two Nuts and a Chocolate Drop," by Willie Hopkins, the Screen Magazines' wizard sculptor, completes the reel.

UNIVERSAL SPECIAL FEATURE.

THE GRAY GHOST (Episode 13, "The Tightening Snare"—Two Parts—Rel. Week of Sept. 17).—The cast: Morn Light (Priscilla Dean); Hildreth (Emory Johnson); Marco (Eddie Polo); the Gray Ghost (Harry Carter); Arabin (Howard Crampton); the Commissioner (Sidney Dean); Tryon (Lou Short); Cecelia (Gypsy Hart).

"And that is all right," said The Ghost as he arranged four aces on the table, and took the necklace out of the drawer where the commissioner had hidden it. The two police officers with Arabin, entered to find the necklace also gone.

Marco, rushing to save Morn Light from the poisoned ring which Hildreth was just about to place on her finger, manages to elude Cecelia, and enters the room just in time. The Ghost follows, and hears their plan for a speedy marriage. He goes out, and when the taxi which Hildreth orders, drives up, he overpowers the chauffeur and takes his place. He has instructed Cecelia to summon the gang to the island. Hildreth and the girl come out and get into the car. Marco, leaving them, looks back, and sees the chauffeur struggling out of the shrubbery. He calls a motor cop and they follow the taxi. The Ghost drives to the waterfront and forces the two to enter a boat to go to the island. Marco sends the cop back to report ,and starts to swim across. The Ghost fires and when Marco dives, thinks that he has killed him, but Marco makes the swim and arrives at the island.

The crooks on the island fight Marco, while The Ghost locks Hildreth and Morn Light in a secret room, having shown them the necklace. The motor-cycle cop has summoned the commissioner and his men, who also arrive at the island. They fight the crooks and get the best of it. Cecelia, determined to put an end once and for all to Morn Light, her rival, touches the button which lowers the secret room to the basement of the house. She tells the commissioner that they have escaped. The commissioner plans to blow up the house, but first searches it thoroughly for Hildreth and Morn Light. Then a quantity of dynamite is placed under the house.

"They are down on the beach now, I tell you!" says Cecelia to Marco, who rushes off to hunt. He returns and tells the commissioner that there is no trace of the two. Cecelia laughs. At that moment the house goes up in a cloud of smoke and debris.

"They were in the secret room of the house all the time," cries Cecelia, and the police, with Marco and the commissioner, make a rush for the ruins. Fire has broken out, and the situation of Hildreth and the girl is desperate, if indeed, they are still alive.

Mutual Film Corp.

SIGNAL.

THE LOST EXPRESS (Chapter 3—"The Wreck at the Crossing"—Two Parts—Oct. 1).—Helen is seized with a brilliant idea. Taking a sun glass from her wrist bag, she clambers down the rocking car roof and focuses the sun on the blue print as it lies on the table.

Suddenly the paper catches fire. It is destroyed. Helen is discovered and pursued. Chased over the sloping roofs of the passenger train by "The Baron" and "The Leach," Helen makes a desperate flight. She escapes by jumping and catching a bridge guard. Hand over hand along the wires she makes her way to earth. She is near a village. From the drug store she telephones the railway offices. A motor car is sent to take her to the Thurston home.

To save the only existing duplicates of the Thurston invention—the shop plans—Helen sends young Bonner to fetch them. He is intercepted by Pitts, the secretary, who possesses himself of the combustion chamber plans. "The Baron" and his gang undertake to steal them from Pitts, not recognizing him as "Harelip." Homer, determined to get the plans from Pitts, fights him for them. While the fight is on "The Baron" steals the paper. He escapes in an automobile. Helen and Bonner, with "Harelip" pretending to be aiding, in his character of Pitts, pursue. Helen's machine is wrecked in a terrific smashup at the crossing when it is hit by a fast express. Helen is unconscious and taken to the Valquez oil works.

CUB.

JERRY'S BIG DEAL (Sept. 27).—The cast: Jerry (George Ovey); Rev. J. H. Long (George George); Deacon Jones (Gordon MacGregor); Sara (Sadie Gordon); Girl (Beulah Booker). Written and produced by Milton H. Fahrney.

A minister who is about to leave the city for a small country town where he is to have charge of a pastorate makes the unforgiveable mistake of asking Jerry to watch his grip while he buys a ticket. Coincidently a squad of police seize the minister and drag him off to jail. Jerry, not caring to enter into conversation with policemen, appropriates the grip, examines its contents and finds therein a minister's paraphernalia.

Jerry conceals himself in a box car, which is soon made up into a train and starts on its journey. When Jerry arrives in the little town he finds a welcoming delegation headed by

Deacon Jones and Sarn, an old maid. He is conducted to his abode, which happens to be a rooming house also housing the deacon and a motley array of his flock. Jerry flirts with a young girl, is discovered by stars and policy demands that he pay her a certain degree of attention.

Surprises come to a head when Jerry, dressed as the minister, breaks in upon the deacon playing a friendly game of poker with a gathering of old cronies. Their fear is dissipated when Jerry agrees to take a hand with them. Jerry proves to be a wizard with the cards and soon has relieved them of their money and most of their personal belongings, such as watches, rings, etc.

Meanwhile the imprisoned minister has proven his innocence and makes his way to his congregation. He arrives upon the scene just as Jerry makes his getaway. The vision of a holy card hanging behind the table at which he has made his winning streak, "The Lord Loves a Cheerful Giver," causes Jerry to make a substantial donation to a winsome Red Cross nurse.

MUTUAL WEEKLY.

ISSUE NO. 142 (Sept. 19).
Honolulu, Hawaii. A Rare Occasion. Millions of fish blacken the waters of the harbor. The natives get out the old hook and line and enjoy the sport. Subtitles: Amazing mackerel run on the Pacific Coast draws 10,000 fishermen to the Redondo Beach Pier, where it is estimated 100,000 fish were caught in a few hours.
Philadelphia, Pa. Lafayette Day Celebrated. M. Jules Jusserand, French Ambassador, delivers oration in Independence Square. Subtitles: In New York, Mr. André Tardieu, High Commissioner of France and head of the French War Missions, is the guest of honor.
Charleston, Mass. Submarines for Chili Start on Long Homeward Journey. Passing through Cape Cod Canal.
New York City. Famous "7th" Departs to Win New Laurels. City's millions bid farewell as Crack Regiment leaves for camp.
A Western Port. Sailor Boys Off for Final Training. A few weeks more instruction and then off to European waters.
Washington, D. C. Human Fly, High in Air, Thrills Throng in Street. "Daredevil" Johnny Reynolds proves to aviation corps that he is qualified to fly over Europe and drop bombs on the Germans. Subtitle: Another Daredevil. With Special Message for War Department, Joe Dawson races the Royal Blue Express from Baltimore to Washington at the rate of 80 miles an hour.
Polo Grounds, N. Y. C. Fun, Beauty and Sport Harvest Shekels for N. Y. Sun Tobacco Fund. Ziegfeld's "Follies" and Hitchcock's "Hitchy-Koo" companies raise money to provide smokes for our soldiers in France. Subtitles: Ned Wayburn, Czar of all the chorus girls, warms up. Benny Kauff buys a score card at $3 per. Raymond Hitchcock, Billy Sunday's pal, comes across. The oldest and the youngest Follies' rooters. Will Rogers, King of the Cowboys. Beauties from the Follies, Frolic and Century. Part of the contribution.
New York City. Latest Styles in Early Fall Coats. Courtesy of Garment Specialty Co., New York City.

MUTUAL STAR PRODUCTION.

SANDS OF SACRIFICE (American—Five Parts—Sept. 24).—The cast: "Big Bill" Darcey (William Russell); Nora Farnes (Francelia Billington); Enoch Foyle (George Periolat); "Sammy" Goode (John Gough); Sophier (Joe King). Directed by Edward B. Sloman.
"Big Bill" Darcey has no ambition on earth except his own pleasure until he meets Nora Farnes. Nora's mother's fortune has been taken by Enoch Foyle, an unscrupulous promoter, and Nora, going to his country place to force him to make an accounting, runs into a group of his friends, of which Darcey is one. Darcey protects the girl from the crowd and is alone in the lodge with her when Foyle arrives.
In a struggle in which Foyle is attempting to get into the room where Nora is hiding, he is shot and Darcey and Nora flee. Darcey keeps Nora at his own lodge all night and so protects her name by refusing to marry him. They are about to start on their wedding trip when Darcey learns that Foyle has fleeced him of his fortune. He goes to Foyle's office and finds Nora there. His faith in her is wrecked, and

Fill Up Our Soldiers' Pipes

America's fighting men need tobacco to make trench life a little more comfortable. Here's a chance to treat the boys at the front.

"Our Boys in France Tobacco Fund" has been organized to furnish "smokes" for the American soldiers and sailors in active service.

All labor and administrative expenses are contributed, so that every cent you give goes to pay for tobacco which is purchased in large quantities at a low price.

One dollar buys four packages of tobacco and sends them to France. Each package, costing twenty-five cents, has a retail value of forty-five cents, and keeps a man in "smokes" for a week. Every dollar sent to "Our Boys in France Tobacco Fund" buys a bundle of tobacco that would cost $1.80 at your cigar store.

In every package is a postcard addressed to a contributor to the tobacco fund. In accepting the package the soldier or sailor agrees to send on the card a message to his benefactor in the United States. According to the plan, every person who gives a quarter gets his receipt from a fighting man in France.

The work of this fund is approved by the Secretary of War and the Secretary of the Navy.

Send as many dollars as you can spare. Write your name and address clearly.

**"Our Boys in France Tobacco Fund"
19 West 44th Street
New York City**

after turning over what money he has left to her account, he leaves her for the desert with Sammy Goode, a consumptive.
Sammy dies in a battle for health after making Darcey promise to return to Nora and listen to an explanation. Nora determines to wreck Foyle. She uses a woman's weapon, and on the night she has set for the trap she secretes detectives in her apartment and wins a confession from the broker. In the midst of the scene Darcey enters the apartment, and staggered by what he sees, starts away. He recalls his promise and enters. The presence of detectives is explained and Foyle is led away to prison, while Darcey and Nora finish the dinner which had been prepared.

EMPIRE ALL STAR CORP.

THE RUNAWAY (Five Parts—Sept. 24).— The cast: Alice Avery (Julia Sanderson); Aunt Jane (Ada St. Claire); Nancy Arnold (Dore Plowden); Sarah (Jennie Ellison); Clarence's Mother (Josephine Morse); Richard Danforth (Norman Trevor); Saunders (Rex McDougall); Foster (Edward Fielding); Uncle Ezra (James C. Malaide); Peter Burton (Stanhope Wheatcroft); Jim (Sheridan Tansey); Eddie (Robert Tansey); Jim (Sheridan Tansey); Minister (Edward Broadley). Directed by Dell Henderson.

Alice Avery was an orphan who lived with her pious aunt and uncle. Her mother had been a stage singer, and her aunt's great dread was that she would follow in her footsteps. Richard Danforth, an artist, in search of mental and physical health, comes to board at her house. When he returns to his studio in New York he promises that if she comes to the city he will care for her. She runs away from the country village and arrives at his studio. He is at a loss to know what to do with the innocent little girl. He introduces her as a distant relative and sends for Sarah, the child's maid, and only friend. Alice meets Nancy Arnold, a model, is in love with Danforth and quarrels over the presence of Alice in the studio. In anger she turns on the girl, and Alice, stunned, takes the faithful Sarah and disappears. She gets a place in a chorus and works and works until she is finally chosen for the lead. Her success is instant, and she is recognized by friends who have spent endless hours in search of her. Danforth claims her for his wife and she gives up her stage career for life in his studio.

Miscellaneous Subjects

PATHE EXCHANGE, INC.

THE STREETS OF ILLUSION (Gold Rooster —Five Parts—Aug. 12).—The cast: Beam (Gladys Hulette); Her Father (J. H. Gilmour); Her Brother (William Parks, Jr.); Donald Morton (Richard Barthelmess); Col. Thompson (William Dudley).
Beam only saw the silver lining of the dark clouds, for she lived in the streets of illusion. She wove a small chain around the room from which hung a gold medal with the inscription of "I3." This was her winning charm. Her fondest pleasure was caring for her blind father and she would read him false stories regarding her brother who was fighting in Mexico. On the other hand, Robert was fighting a bigger battle than that of war. Reduced in circumstances, Beam was forced to rent the vacant rooms in the old house which at one time was the social center in New York.
Donald Morton, a wealthy young man, was in love with Beam. He spoke to his father about her but he received little encouragement as his father was not interested in anything, as he imagined he was always ill. Wishing to end it all, he rents a room in an out of the way place. Fortunately, it was Beam's home in which he engaged the room. Beam was reading to her father, when suddenly her attention was attracted to the door. Astounded she sees Robert. He had deserted. Stealing away from her father, she brings Robert upstairs and is tenderly embracing him, when Donald came out into the hall. Seeing Donald, Beam quickly conceals Robert in her room. Donald insists on an explanation. To save her brother, Beam tells him that the man was a new boarder. She appointed. Donald leaves. A few minutes later, Robert heard Beam pleading with someone on the stairs. Leaving the room, he discovers Beam in the arms of one of the boarders. For the first time he felt the spirit to fight. With a quick dash, he overpowers the man. Hearing the voice of his son, his father comes out and proclaims him a hero. Just then the phone rang. Col. Thompson, of Robert's regiment, notified him to report back to camp as he had it so clear that it was believed he was on a furlough.

IRIS (Gold Rooster—Five Parts—Aug. 26).— The cast: Iris Bellamy (Alma Taylor); Fred Maldonado (Henry Ainley); Lawrence Trenwith (Stuart Rome).
According to the last will of her husband, Iris, a wealthy widow, was unable to remarry unless she sacrificed her wealth. All a reception given in her home she accepts a proposal from Fred Maldonado, a rich clubman, who has

persistently loved her for some time. Iris was not overjoyed, as she loved Lawrence Trenwith, a struggling engineer. Downcast at her actions, he calls to see her after everyone departed. Listening to his profession of love, Iris writes Maldonado a note, telling him that it is impossible for her to keep her promise. She consents to marry Trenwith after he becomes successful in Canada.

Angry at Iris's refusal, Maldonado plans to have revenge. It occurs that Iris loses her money and finds herself in deplorable circumstances. Maldonado offers her a check book as a loan and she accepts. A short while later the account is overdrawn and no way possible to return the money. Iris leaves the city. As a last resort she attempts to secure work, but to no avail. Maldonado again traces Iris and offers her assistance. Giving her a key to a lavishly furnished apartment, he tells her it is hers.

The inevitable thought of starvation causes Iris to accept. Not hearing from Iris, Trenwith returns to the city. Meeting a former friend, he has him arrange a meeting. Unknown to Iris, Maldonado overhears her making an appointment for nine that evening. Nine that evening finds Trenwith punctual. Overjoyed, they embrace. Looking around the apartment, Trenwith admires it greatly, but to his sorrow he learns the bitter truth of the whole thing. Disgusted he casts Iris to the floor and leaves. Maldonado enters. Having heard the conversation, he orders Iris to leave. With no earthly friend, Iris decides to end it all. Seeking diversion, Trenwith walks along the bank of the river. Suddenly he sees Iris about to leap into the water.

HEARST-PATHE NEWS NO. 73 (Sept. 8).
Somewhere in England.—The American troops, who recently arrived in England, on their way to the firing line, are reviewed by King George. Subtitles: The column then flies past his Majesty. Three cheers for the Allies.
Framingham, Mass.—Impressive scenes are witnessed as Cardinal O'Connell bids farewell and Godspeed to departing New England troops. Subtitles: The soldier boys receiving communion. Cardinal O'Connell between the State and American flags.
Redondo, Cal.—The biggest run of mackerel ever known on the Pacific leads many to try their luck at Izaak Walton's noble art. Subtitles: At last—a place where there is no waiting for a "bite." A "fish-eye" view of the wharf.
The Flanders Advance.—A devastated, shell-plowed field is mute evidence of the terrific artillery duel that preceded the Flanders battle. Subtitles: Pictures taken by the Cinematograph division of the French Army. But behind the firing line all is hustle and bustle. There the auxiliary railways are built, which are then sent to the front in sections. King Albert, of Belgium, hero of his army in the great advance.
Mineola, L. I.—Col. Theodore Roosevelt visits the members of the Rainbow Division who are already training at Camp Mills. Subtitles: Proud of those who are fortunate enough to be able to serve the nation. These men will be the first of the National Guardsmen to leave for the firing line.
San Francisco, Cal.—All kinds of vehicles are pressed into service; the strike of street railway employees paralyzes car lines. Subtitles: The cars in use are armored because of the damage done to some of them. The city operates a "municipal special" for the workers at the big government shipyards.
New York City.—Sixth Avenue is transformed into a Venetian street when the twenty-inch main of the new aqueduct system bursts. Subtitles: The water soon finds it way into the subway excavations.
Spartanburg, S. C.—The first contingent of National Guardsmen reach their cantonments, and the task of building the new army begins. Subtitles: Approved by Committee on Public Information. The bike to camp. The Commissary is soon established and the grounds cleared of stumps. The end of the first day finds all in jolly spirit. They have the "Kaiser's goat."
Washington, D. C.—America's mobilization behind her leader is fittingly symbolized as the President leads a parade of drafted men. Subtitles: Cabinet officers, Congressmen—the entire country joins in the tribute to the National Army. No flashing bayonets, no imposing military display—just a plain citizenry of America, about to defend the nation. Victory, liberty and democracy.

St. Louis, Mo. (Local)—Thousands of men of the city's quota to the National Army march to Washington University for a farewell gathering. Subtitle: They are informed of their new duties by army officers.
Chicago, Ill. (Local)—A new national society is organized to encourage sheep raising to supply the wool for Uncle Sam's big army. Subtitles: Sheep herded in Grant Park, and some of the fair shepherdesses. A demonstration of how the wool for the soldiers' clothes is gathered.
Columbus, Ohio (Local)—Citizens of this city invite the members of the National Guard, stationed here, to their homes for dinner.
Newark, N. J. (Local)—The city bids Godspeed to the First New Jersey Regiment of Infantry which entrains for Camp McClellan in Alabama. Subtitles: Large crowds of friends and relatives gather at the railroad station. Last moments of farewell.

HEARST-PATHE NEWS NO. 74 (Sept. 12).
Philadelphia, Pa.—The nation pays fitting tribute to General Lafayette, who helped her realize her ideals of Liberty and Democracy. Subtitles: Ambassador Jusserand extends France's grateful thanks for America's reciprocity in 1917. Unfurling a replica of this country's first standard, the flag of Betsy Ross.
Berkeley, Cal.—King Football rules again and Freshmen of the University of California meet Sophomores in the first game of the season. Subtitles: This is the way our boys will push through the German lines. The Sophs drub the lowly Freshies with the score of 10-6.
San Francisco, Cal.—Chinese residents of this city operate their own telephone exchange, which is the only one of its kind in the U. S. Subtitles: The Chinese "Hello" girls at work. Here's your bill.
Buenos Aires, Argentina.—South America's sympathy with this Nation's cause is shown by the great reception given visiting U. S. warships. Subtitles: The Argentine men-of-war salute the American ships. Immense crowds fill the wharf to bid welcome to Uncle Sam's warriors. The American Admiral arriving at the U. S. Embassy.
Paris, France.—Major-General Pershing attends a garden party given by American Red Cross workers in aid of the wounded soldiers. Subtitles: Alsatian girls, recently liberated from German yoke, dance the dance of freedom and joy. Mrs. Hamilton Shields, of Virginia, and her daughter, who organized the relief benefit.
Ossining, N. Y.—Old or young, man or woman—all can serve America now in some special way. The little Girl Scouts gladly do their bit. Subtitles: Still in their 'teens, but already they are promising cooks. The youth of the Nation pledges allegiance to the flag.
San Francisco, Cal.—The great need for bottoms leads the owners of the SS. Del Norte, wrecked some time ago, to try to salvage the ship. Subtitles: But when the vessel is righted it is found to be a total loss. Pumping out the water to get the brass and iron that may be saved.
Oyster Bay, L. I.—Woman's right to vote is ardently championed by Colonel Roosevelt at a rally of N. Y. suffrage workers at his home. Subtitles: 'In this terrible war the woman force has been squarely behind the man force in every country. The suffrage leaders who hope to win New York to their cause this year.
Sagamore, Mass.—Three of the submarines built here for the Chilean government start on their air-thousand-mile journey for home. Subtitles: The undersea crafts are of the latest type and very fast. A race with a train. Fall Styles for Men.—(Cartoon.)

THE SEVEN PEARLS (Episode Three—"The Air Peril'—Two Parts—Sept. 30).—Ilma had just recovered two of the pearls from the burglar when they were taken away from her. She joins Harry and tells him of her loss. They are accosted by an old woman, who is strangely disappointed when she finds they did not recover the pearls. Harry escorts Ilma to her apartment after trying in vain to console her. The next morning Ilma is puzzling out a note of sympathy she has received from some one who signs himself 'Nemesis,' when the Sultan's executioner drops an envelope into the mail slot in her door. Ilma opens the envelope and finds in it the two pearls and a note which reads: "Here are your pearls. Nemesis is not a woman, but a dangerous man. Don't trust him. Nemesis."
Ilma 'phones Harry, telling him she has the

two pearls. While she is talking Stayne, a member of the Grady gang, is announced by Harry's butler. Harry tells Ilma of Stayne's coming and imparts the information that this member of the gang had two of the pearls. Ilma says she will visit him at once to help him recover the pearls from Stayne. Stayne tells Harry that the night before he attempted to rob the Mason home, but was caught by Perry Mason and his brother. He was searched and the pearls found on him. Perry kept one and gave the other back to Stayne and after taking his finger prints released him. In the morning papers was a story that Perry's brother had been murdered and Stayne was accused of the crime.

Ilma arrives and learns of Stayne's predicament, who offers them the pearl he has if they will clear him of the charge of murder. Harry and Ilma, pretending to be reporters, call on Perry Mason and are recognized by him. He tells his story and shows them the pearl. As they are leaving the Mason home Ilma secures a key to the front door. Later she tries to persuade Harry to return to the Mason home, but when he refused, she goes alone. In the Mason home she hears a conversation between Perry Mason and his servant which convinces her that the man killed his brother and that the servant helped him.

When Perry and the servant leave the room Ilma recovers the pearl from a vase in which Perry placed it, and is about to depart when Perry returns and captures her. Perry is about to call the police when Ilma warns him that if he does she will tell he murdered his brother. Perry decides to get her out of the way, and with the aid of her servant he ties Ilma with a rope which is attached to a ring at the bottom of a balloon. The room in which Ilma has been captured has a sliding roof and when this is shoved to one side the balloon is inflated. Before it is released a tube filled with acid is fixed so that by degrees it will eat away the rope with which Ilma is attached to the balloon while it is in midair. Perry cuts the rope and the balloon rises, carrying the struggling body of Ilma up toward the unknown.

KING BEE FILMS CORP.

THE FLY COP (Two parts—Sept. 15).—The cast: The Fly Cop (Billy West); Proprietor (Babe Hardy); Handy Man (Budd Ross); Mayor (Leo White); Foreladr (Ellen Burford); Chief of Police (Charles Slattery); A Chicken (Ethlyn Gibson). Directed by Arvid E. Gillstrom.

Disguised as a beauty parlor and a modiste shop, a high-class ladies gambling parlor is flourishing in the city. The Mayor hears of it and warns the Chief of Police that he must either close it up or lose his job. The Chief counts on the gambling parlor for a large part of his revenue and is loath to close it up, but he realizes he must do something to pacify the Mayor. He engages Billy, the most harmless "boob" he can find on the force, makes a detective of him and sends him up to the "beauty parlor" to get a job, and then spy upon the gambling room. He phones the manager of the place that to pacify the Mayor, he is sending up a harmless spy and asks the manager to furnish a job for him.

Under these conditions it is easy for Billy to get a job and he goes to work at once as general handy man around the place. He scrubs floors, shines shoes, gives massages, sells underwear, flirts with the customers, fights with the assistants and gets on the manager's nerves until he is nearly crazy. In all this time, Billy never gets a suspicion that there is a gambling parlor about, and the Chief, when he calls, compliments Billy on his good work.

Finally a bad loser among the women gamblers comes out of the gambling room and, running into Billy, complains that she was trimmed by the crooked game in the next room. This is a revelation to Billy. He rushes back to make the raid single-handed. He charges into the outer shop, but one of the attendants sees him and gives the warning. In a flash the card tables are turned into pews, the cashier's desk into an organ and the faro table into a pulpit. The manager, with a quick change, becomes a minister, and when Billy bursts into the room he finds a revival meeting in full swing. He is given a hymn book and joins in the singing. Presently he gets a burst of religion and comes forward, converted.

About this time the Mayor decides to take matters into his own hands. He gets a bunch of regular "cops" together and raids the place,

only to find Billy, in uniform, leading the singing. When the pulpit accidentally turns over and discloses a faro table, Billy is dumfounded. The manager accuses Billy of running the place and, while the "cops" chase Billy around the shop, the manager packs up all the coin and tries for a get-away. Billy eludes all the "cops" and, seeing the manager about to escape, he wallops him with a mallet and captures him single-handed. The Mayor is delighted and promptly makes Billy the new Chief of Police.

K-E-S-E.

MEN OF THE DESERT (Essanay—Four Parts —Sept. 24).—The cast: Jack (Jack Gardner); May (Ruth King); Mason (Carl Stockdale).

Some of the most sanguinary feuds in America have been fought out, not in the mountains of the South, but on the deserts of the great West, where cattlemen and sheepmen often dealt out death to each other with the aid of their old friends, Winchester and Colt. Such a feud is in progress between the men of the desert when Jack, a nomadic cowboy, wanders into the scene. He is outspoken against the outlawry, and the sheriff, in jest, hands him his badge and asks him if he can do any better. Jack accepts the challenge and arrests one of the most recent slayers. The latter's companions immediately storm the jail and rescue him. In the fight Jack is desperately wounded. May, a girl of the ranch, finds the cowboy half dead and hides him in an isolated hut while she nurses him back to health. The feudists discover Jack's hiding place and attack him. He and the girl escape, and while Jack holds a narrow canyon against his pursuers the girl dashes across the desert in search of aid. Jack's life seems as good as lost when May returns with the opposing feudists, who save him. The wedding between Jack and the girl on the battleground reconciles the feudists and restores order on the desert.

PARAMOUNT PICTURES CORP.

SEEING THINGS (Klever Comedy—Sept. 3). —Vic has been in a sanitarium for some time for the "cure," he having had "too many horrors after the night before." He is almost well and his doctor is about to discharge him, hoping that the change will also cure him of a delusion that he has. It seems Vic has a delusion that a certain "Gloomy Gus" looking creature is always following him wherever he goes and this annoys to get him into no end of trouble. The doctor wires this fact to Vic's wife and prepares to start Vic on his way. Vic, after bidding good-bye to the other inmates, goes, only to be, so he thinks, followed by his friend "Gloomy Gus." He feels that he is with him all the way home and he certainly has his troubles with him.

Vic arrives home much to the delight of his wife, but much to the disgust of his mother-in-law. It is not long after his arrival home that the "optical illusion" again starts working and poor Vic gets himself into lots of difficulties and at the finish gives it up as a bad job.

CAMPING (Klever Komedy—Sept. 10).—Vic is a lover of fresh air and decides that the best way to get it is to go "camping." He manages to induce his wife to go along with him and take the kids. He also takes his nephew and two nieces. After equipping them with camping outfits, and also buying his Ford up with the necessary camping things, they make a start. The car looks like a moving circus, and the kids have the time of their young lives. Vic encounters many troubles en route to the camping place, the last one being the climbing of a mountain, which is very exciting and funny. He eventually arrives at a spot he thinks will do. The tent is put up and camping life is on in full blast. Everything would have been ideal if it was not for a "wood be" Indian who tries to scalp Vic.

He nearly scares the daylight out of Vic, and only the arrival of an old hermit and the kids save him. They knock the spots out of the Indian and the hermit takes him off in his custody. By this time the nightfall is coming on and Vic and the family get in the sleeping bag to get into the arms of Morpheus. It had to pick out that night to rain, and rain it does as it never did before. Vic unfortunately built the trench around the tent the wrong way, and consequently the water runs in the tent instead of out. Added to this comes a gale which blows the tent away and they are all left standing in their "nighties." Vic makes them all get under the Ford, which he says is like a rich uncle—it always comes in handy.

IN BED—IN BAD (Klever Komedy—Sept. 24).—Vic is a "busy bee" at his office, and he is working so hard that his office stall becomes alarmed for fear he may overwork. They all impress this strongly upon him. Needless to say he laughs at them, for he never was sick a day in his life.

On his arrival home, his wife greets him with great concern over the way he looks and insists upon sending for the doctor. She 'phones him, and he tells her to put Vic to bed at once, that he will be over with a nurse. She does.

The fact that Vic has been put to bed sick becomes the talk of the neighborhood and each neighbor comes over to do their "bit." Each one suggests a different doctor, and "Mrs. Vic" has them all. One doctor says it's his heart, the other his chest, and another says it's his throat. However, after a final consultation, they all decide that he should be operated on for appendicitis. Vic is alarmed and wants to know what caused this, and the doctors tell him he does not get enough exercise. Vic announces that he will get some right away, and he ends up by "walloping" the life out of all the doctors.

PARAMOUNT PICTURES CORP.

THE HOSTAGE (Lasky—Five Parts—Sept. 10).—The cast: Lieutenant Ivo Kemper (Wallace Reid); Nathalia (Dorothea Abril); Sophie, her sister (Gertrude Short); Kemper (C. H. Geldert); Vanvoyd (Guy Oliver); Eunice (Camille Ankewich); Boyadi (Noah Beery); Ragnor (George L. Spaulding); Marieuka (Lillian Leighton); Paul (Lucien Littlefield). Directed by Robert Thornby.

Brigadier Kemper, at the head of a division of Lowlanders, has invaded the peaceful country of the Mountaineers. Caught in a bad position, he is forced to give his only son, Lieutenant Ivo Kemper, as hostage for the good conduct of the invaders on their retreat. The brigadier means to violate the truce, so he persuades his son to carry a dirk concealed in his person and warns him to be prepared, on a given night, to make good his escape from the Mountaineers.

Turned over to the custody of Boyadi, one of the Mountaineer leaders, Lieutenant Kemper is prepared for mistreatment at the hands of those whom he looks upon as savages. Instead of that, however, he finds Boyadi all that is considerate and kind, and after some preliminary skirmishing he becomes much interested in Boyadi's daughter, the beautiful Nathalia. The night appointed for his escape comes speedily, but Lieutenant Kemper realizes, to his horror, that he can escape only by killing Boyadi.

This he cannot bring himself to do, so he finds himself the next morning a prisoner at the hands of the outraged mountaineers, who are furious at the treachery of his people. Moreover, he himself is in disgrace, for the dirk has been discovered in his possession. At this seeming proof of his treachery, even Nathalia turns away from him.

In the effort to make him reveal his father's plans—of which he is entirely ignorant, by the way, the mountaineers put the young Lieutenant Kemper through a pretty rough sort of "third degree." He is saved at last only by the interference and protest of Boyadi and the fact that he behaved himself with credit while he was with the army of invaders.

On these grounds he is reprieved for twelve hours before his execution, and allowed to take a farewell of Nathalia, who had come to look more kindly upon this young man who had proven himself so courageous under the terrific torture he had undergone.

Brought out for execution at the appointed time at dawn the next morning, and stood against the firing wall. The men are about to shoot when a messenger brings word that the lowlanders and the mountaineers have declared peace in order to fight together against a common enemy.

Lieutenant Kemper is not only freed by this peace movement, but becomes a kind of hero to the very people who had been about to spill his blood. He returns in triumph to the waiting Nathalia, to whom each moment since his departure had been agonies of torture, and the two are made happy at last.

TRIANGLE FILM CORP.

POLLY ANN (Five Parts—Sept. 9).—The cast: Polly Ann (Bessie Love); Howard Straightlane (Rowland Lee); Jacob Straightline (Walt Whitman); Jud Simpkins (John Lockney); Squire Bacon (William Ellingford); Hubert de Courcey (David Foss); Jushie Trewalker (Alfred Hollingsworth); Mrs. Porter (Josephine Headley). Directed by Charles F. Miller.

Polly Ann was an orphan in the poor farm home until Jud Simpkins takes her to his tavern to work as slavey. There she meets a company of fly-by-night players and decides to become an actress. The opportune arrival of Howard Straightlane, who has come to teach the village school, save Polly from the obnoxious attentions of Robert de Courcey, one of the actors. Polly is attracted to the new teacher, and on one occasion takes him a bottle of Jud Simpkins' "bitters," which in reality is whiskey. Young Straightlane feels again the craving for drink that had caused a breach between him and his wealthy uncle. This same uncle was also a distant relative of Polly's, and later he sent for her. Discovering that the teacher, to whom she is still devoted, is a cast-off heir, Polly brings about a reconciliation between the old gentleman and his nephew.

MOUNTAIN DEW (Five Parts—Sept. 10).— J. Hamilton Vance (Margery Wilson); J. Hamilton Vance (Charles Gunn); Roosevelt Washington (Thomas Washington); Squire Bradley (Al. W. Filson); Milt Sears (Jack Richardson); Lafe Grider (Aaron Edwards); Lily Bud Raines (Mary Borland). Directed by Thomas Heffron.

J. Hamilton Vance, a magazine writer from the north, while gypsying through the Kentucky Cumberlands, enters Trigger Creek, a hill settlement in Breathitt County. Milt Sears, feudist, ex-convict and school teacher, recognizes in Vance a possible competitor for the "teaching job" and orders him to leave. To protect his manuscripts Vance agrees, while Sears shreds his hat with bullets to demonstrate his marksmanship.

While leaving the valley Vance meets a girl astride a bullock, returning from the grist mill. He is attracted and determines to stay. A notice announcing a "new boss of the teachin' job" is desired results in his going to the store of Squire Eli Bradley to apply. There he finds the Squire has been defeated at checkers. Vance challenges and beats the champion to the house, and there Vance learns the girl on the bullock is the Squire's daughter, Roxie. Lafe Grider, the Squire's farm manager and suitor for Roxie's hand, suspects Vance of being a federal agent hunting moonshiners. He attempts to incite the neighborhood against Vance. Further complications come when Vance learns Roxie does not know how to read or write. She agrees to attend school. Milt Sears attempts to assassinate Vance in the schoolroom. Roxie is injured. When taken home her attendance at school is exposed. Her father is angered and denounces Vance. The latter determines he shall instruct the girl, and has his negro servant hold the Squire a captive with a gun at his head, while he instructs Roxie in reading.

The Squire again turns a champion of Vance to change again when Lily Bud Raines, a poor relation, reads a paragraph in one of Vance's fiction stories mentioning moonshining in the hills. That is taken as a confession he is a federal agent. The mountaineers prepare to bushwack him, but Roxie goes to warn him. He avoids the posse, marries the girl and then salutes the posse as a moonshiner himself, for he is one of the family.

THE HAUNTED HOUSE (Five Parts—Sept. 10).—The cast: Anne (Winifred Allen); Jimmy (Dick Rosson); Pete Parks (Albert Parker); Anne's Uncle (Albert Day); the Sheriff (Mac Barnes); Anne's Spirit Mother (Mabel Wright); the Vegg (Eddie Kelly). Directed by Albert Parker.

Anne is permitted none of the pleasures of the modern girl. She is quaint and somewhat "queer," according to the superstitious villagers. She spends much of her time in the woods, where she hears fairies and spirits whispering to her from the stirring leaves.

There is an old mansion near the village that has a reputation for being haunted by a ghost. No one dares live in it, and those who have had the courage to approach it at night have been frightened away by a ghost. When Jimmy, a young crook, robs the village bank, he seeks to escape his pursuers by taking refuge in the "haunted house." The ghost

comes out to meet him, but, finding him wounded, takes pity and conducts him inside.
When outsiders dare to penetrate the fearful domain of "the haunted house," the little ghost uses wit and force to protect the boy. Strange and picturesque scenes are revealed within the old walls, for the ghost seems very human and welcomes the spirit of romance that has entered.

FLYING COLORS (Five Parts—Sept. 23).— The cast: Brent Brewster (William Desmond); Ann (Golda Madden); Capt. Drake (Jack Livingston); Ruth Lansing (Laura Sears); Craig Lansing (J. Barney Sherry); Jimmy McMahon (Geo. W. Chase); Brewster, Sr. (John Lockney); the Cockney (Bert Offerd); Stenographer (Mary McIvor); Manager's Son (Ray Jackson). Directed by Frank Borzage.
Brent Brewster, famous Yale athlete, turns detective, after failing at several other professions when cast out by his wealthy relative. His first case is at the home of Mrs. Lansing, who has been robbed of valuable jewels during the course of a house party. Brewster rather forgets his Sherlock Holmes role in his admiration for Mrs. Lansing's sister, but when that young woman states that she could get along nicely on $40,000 a year, Brewster decides he had better attend to business. He apprehends the thief and, calling into service some practical stunts he learned on the college cinder track, makes a capture. An inheritance permits him to win the girl with the $40,000 idea.

GREATER VITAGRAPH.

FOR FRANCE (Five Parts—Sept. 17).— The cast: Gerald Ackland (Edward Earle); Martha Landeau (Betty Howe); Rudolph Von Glemm (Arthur Donaldson); Mere Loubette (Mary Maurice); Monsieur Landeau (Frank Anderson). Author—Cyrus Townsend Brady. Director—Wesley Ruggles.
Gerald Ackland, a West Pointer and former Lieutenant in the U. S. Field Artillery, goes to Paris two years before the outbreak of the European war to learn aviation. At a garden party given by the American ambassador, he is introduced to Mlle. Landeau, a beautiful girl, the daughter of a famous painter. She is the possessor of a splendid voice, and on the occasion of the garden party captures the heart of Ackland by her singing of the immortal "La Marseillaise."
Mlle. Landeau, however, mingled little in society, helping her aged father in his art classes. Ackland, driven to desperation by his inability to meet her and press his suit, finally joined the class, although he realized he would make a sorry pupil. It early appeared he had a rival in Rudolph Von Glahm, who made no secret of his infatuation for the young woman, much to her embarrassment and Ackland's disgust. There was no love lost between the two men, but no open break until one afternoon when the German, under the influence of liquor, made an insulting reference to Mlle. Landeau, when at his easel. The American knocked him down and a duel was averted only by the arrest of Von Glahm on a charge of espionage and ordered deported.
War soon was declared and Ackland joined the French army as an aviator, while Mlle. Landeau and her father retired to a farmhouse near the Mons. Fate directed the American's scouting war plane to this farm in time to enable him to rescue his sweetheart from brutal German prisoners. He, himself, was captured but freed by British cavalry.
Their's developed into a real war romance when a decisive battle was fought about the farm, in which Ackland held off the Germans by manning the last British gun, assisted by Mlle. Landeau. French cavalry arrived in the nick of time, and the young American, dangerously wounded, was taken to Paris, where the girl, wearing the Red Cross, nursed him back to health.

BLUEBIRD PHOTOPLAYS, INC.

A STORMY KNIGHT (Five Parts—Sept. 10).— The cast: John Winton (Franklyn Farnum); Dr. Fraser (Jean Hersholt); Mary Weller (Brownie Vernon); Richard Weller (Hayward Mack); Mr. Weller (Frank McQuarrie). Scenario written by Waldemar Young. Produced by Elmer Clifton.
John Winton was an easy going young man. He managed his father's branch office, and because of his careless methods was constantly reprimanded by the elder Winton.
During the worst storm he had ever experienced, John was alone in his bungalow late one night when he was attracted by the cries of distress. John hurried to his door and was astounded to find a girl, soaked to the skin,

who begged of him to hurry with her into the swamp nearby.
She guided him to a prostrate man. John carried the man into his cabin and hurried for a doctor. Upon returning the bungalow was empty and the only memento of the occasion John was able to discover was a white glove, containing a written message that served rather to deepen the mystery than to clear things up.
When John was talking with his father at the office next morning the old man discovered on his son's desk a white glove which, on inquiry, John found had just been delivered by a pretty girl who left no name when she made her hasty exit.
John did not long hesitate before attempting to follow the girl who had so mysteriously made this second attempt to attract him. He hurried to the street, saw his girl of the storm in a limousine and had barely time to start his own motor and follow her as she sped away. The automobile rushed with the girl through side streets at top speed, John following at a little distance, until a stop was made before an apparently empty house.
When John arrived the girl had disappeared and the young man hurried to investigate the premises. Through a window he saw the object of his chase being roughly handled by a man. When John broke through the window in his attempted rescue, four men appeared from an adjoining room and overpowered him. John was effectually disposed of, and then the girl hurried away with his assailants.
Upon going to his club that day for lunch, John was surprised to hear the recital of an adventure one of his clubmates encountered the night before, when, upon returning home, he found a masked woman searching his effects. The clubman explained how the girl managed to escape and exhibited, as a memento of the affair, a white glove—that matched the two that had already come into John's possession under such baffling circumstances. When John, next day, received a fourth glove through the mail, and had read the note it contained, he decided to take measures to dispose of the problem.
The girl, in her third note, made an appointment to meet John at his bungalow, with the promise to fully explain her conduct. Believing that she would again be attended by confederates, John equipped himself accordingly, securing his revolver and filling a few of his pockets with handcuffs. When the girl approached the bungalow with her associates, John met them at a little distance down the road, halting their automobile by placing his own motor in their path.
John then, at the point of his gun, lined up and handcuffed the men. With another pair of "bracelets" he attached the girl to her own limousine, and then hurried away with his prisoners. His destination was the local jail, and when his captives were behind the bars John hastened to a justice of the peace. This official he loaded into his motor and then drove back to the girl he had left safely under guard of his own chauffeur.
"Young lady," said John, when he had reached the girl by the roadside, "we shall now be married." And it was not until the ceremony was then and there performed that John's "storm girl" confessed that her father and the elder Winton, friends since boyhood, had arranged the trick that had united their children in marriage and promised to turn John into a staid and dependable business man.

FOX FILMS CORP.

THE YANKEE WAY (Five Parts—Sept. 15).— The cast: Dick Mason (George Walsh); Princess Alexia (Enid Markey); Colonel Mason (Joe Dowling); "Coyote" Jones (Charles Elder); James O'Malley (James O'Shea); Robert Gillette (Ed. Sedgwick); Baron Marsvitch (Count Hardenberg); Count Vortsky (Edward Cecil); George Washington Brown (Tom Wilson). Story by Ed. Sedgwick and Ralph H. Spence. Directed by Richard Stanton.
Dick Mason stops a young ruffian who is annoying a girl in a big restaurant. Dick has to break his opponent's nose, several dishes and a couple of fingers of his own to do it. The result is that Mason has to spend a night in jail for his flasco exhibition. Dick's father rewards his adventurous son by exiling him to the little Balkan kingdom of Lithunia, where Mr. Mason, Sr., has just purchased a share in a cattle concession.
Dick manifests little interest in his trip until he discovers on shipboard the girl for whom he had come battle (and one day behind bars). At first she shows no more regard for Mason than she did for the man who Dick knocked down, but on the last night out Dick is overjoyed to receive this unsigned note : "Thanks

for your interest in me, both in Chicago and
aboard the ship,—you most wonderful boy!"

When Dick arrives in far-off Lithuania, he
goes immediately to see Count Vortsky, the
Minister of Finance, who has been carrying on
a plot with the Bulgarian Ambassador. Vortsky
only awaits word from Col. Mason's representative—his son—that he will sell. Dick agrees
to give his final decision in the council room
next day in the presence of the Princess Alexia,
ruler of Lithuania.

Dick discovers that the Princess is no other
than the girl of the cabaret and when she sig-
nifies that she does not wish him to dispose of
his holdings, he changes his decision and announces he will keep the concession.

Vortsky, to whom the Princess is engaged,
stirs up a revolution, but Dick and a few able
Chicago assistants, commence a counter movement which wins the day—and the Princess—
for himself.

WORLD PICTURES.

THE WOMAN BENEATH (Five Parts—Sept.
24).—The cast: Betty Fairchild (Ethel Clayton); Tom Connolly (Curtie Cooksey); Mrs.
Fairchild (Isabelle Berwin); Mr. Fairchild
(Frank de Vernon); Rupert Crandall (Craw-
furd Kent); Mrs. Connolly (Eugenie Woodward). Directed by Travers Vale.

Betty Fairchild is sought after by Rupert
Brantley. Mr. and Mrs. Fairchild favor his
suit. Tom Connolly, who within three years
rose from a miser to one of the wealthiest men
in Colorado, comes East, where he meets and
falls in love with Betty. Three years have
passed since Ellen, Tom's sister, disappeared
from a New York boarding school. A human
wreck, Ellen returns to her mother, pleading
for forgiveness. Tom arrives in response to his
mother's summons, but Ellen refuses to tell the
name of her betrayer. After her death, Tom
returns East. Mrs. Connolly remains at her
western home.

Tom and Betty are married. Tom notices
Brantley's attentions and resents them. When
Tom asks Betty why the men hang around her
now that she is married, she says she believes
they are trying to keep her from being too
bored with matrimony. When he says she cannot love him much, she asserts she does not
love him at all, but had followed the social law
of her class and made what the world calls "a
good match." Tom is stunned.

Tom reads that a former millionaire had committed suicide when deserted by his wife because his fortune collapsed. He decides that as
Betty married him for his money, if she thought
he had suddenly lost everything she would leave
him. He plunges into a wild stock market and
purposely suffers a financial loss. Tom tells
Betty he is ruined, having gambled away everything except the home, which is in her name.
He suggests that she dispose of the house. When
she attempts to sympathize with him, he begs
her not to lie again, he can never again believe
she loves him. She makes arrangements with
real estate agents to have the house sold.

Unknown to Tom, Betty sells her jewels and
rents and furnishes an apartment in Harlem.
Tom is very enthusiastic and can't understand
why she has gone to all that trouble, unless she
is scheming to put something over on him. She
is hurt by his attitude. Mrs. Fairchild is indignant at Betty's reduced circumstances. Tom
tells Mrs. Fairchild he would rather have Betty
return home with her, but Betty says Tom will
want her when she has become worthy of him.

In Colorado Tom's mother comes across some
old letters in the traveling bag which Ellen
had brought with her. They are from Rupert
Brantley. There is also a photo, autographed
"From your sweetheart now, your husband to
be." Ellen's mother decides to have her daughter's betrayer punished. Betty receives a packet
addressed to Tom. She opens the envelope. It
contains the letters and photo of Brantley,
indicating his villainy toward Ellen, and a letter from Tom's mother urging him not to allow
Ellen's betrayer to escape unpunished.

She does not show these to Tom, realizing he
will kill Brantley. After dinner, eager to get
Tom out of the house, she arouses his suspi-

---

cions. She sets out for Brantley's apartment
to warn him and give him time to leave and
Tom follows. Betty tells Brantley that Tom
will kill him if he finds this out, saying she has
come to give him time to get out of the country,
not that she cares about Brantley, but she
wishes to save Tom from the electric chair.

There is a knock on the door and Tom enters.
When Tom attacks Brantley, Betty comes forward, saying she had hoped Tom would never
find out. Misunderstanding, Tom asks her
whether she is Brantley's sweetheart. Betty,
to save Tom from being a murderer, falsely
admits the relation. Brantley snatches the letters and photograph from Betty and burns them.
He says she may tell Tom what she pleases,
he will not believe her. Ellen is dead and her
proof is gone.

Betty returns to her room. Tom tells her that
after he has whipped Brantley he is going
where she will never see him again. Realizing
he is working under a false impression of her
relations with Brantley, Betty persuades him
to return with her to Brantley's apartment.
Without explaining, she tells him to say to
Brantley: "My wife has told me everything and
I will tell you if I ever lay eyes on you again."
Then she says if he ever loved her he will allow
it now—she promises to prove her innocence.

They return to Brantley's apartment, where
Tom repeats what Betty directed him to say.
Brantley becomes weak in the knees, and after
the Connollys go he prepares to leave the country. At their apartment Betty shows Tom the
envelope and his mother's letter. She explains
she did not tell him the truth before because
she feared he would kill Brantley, and though
he deserved it, Tom would not have been justified in sacrificing her, who loved him. Assured
of her love, Tom forgives Betty, confessing the
ruse regarding his lost fortune. When he suggests that they return to their Riverside Drive
home she urges him to remain where they are
for another year, all to themselves. He agrees.

M. H. HOFFMAN, INC.

ONE HOUR (Sept.—Six Parts).—The cast:
Ivan Treut (U. J. Flannigan); His Wife (Ina
Brooks); Their Niece, Opal (Zena Keefe);
O. D. Stanley (Alan Hale); Karpoff (Warren
Cook); Jaeger (H. W. Pemberton); Butler
(William Marion); King Ruthevan (Franklyn
Hanna); Prime Minister (Herbert Dansey).
Scenario by Paul McAllister and Edwin L. Hollywood.

The story opens in the Adirondacks where a
young woman, Opal, and a young man, Stanley,
are the principal characters. Opal, wandering
through the snow, takes refuge from a pack of
wolves and is rescued by Stanley. During a
hand to hand fight which he has with one of
the brute Opal falls through an air hole into
icy water. Rescued by Stanley a second time,
she is borne to his cabin, where only his prompt
aid in removing the drenched garments saves
her life.

During the ensuing months the two young
people and themselves in love—then a shadow
crosses their happiness. From a small European kingdom comes a trusted diplomat to take
the princess (Opal) back to her native land. of
which she has so far known nothing. Seeking
to escape, she flees to Stanley and is followed
by her uncle, aunt, the diplomat and others of
the household, and in the fight which follows
Stanley is left unconscious upon the floor of his
cabin and Opal borne away.

Arriving in the palace, where she is to marry
the king of a neighboring monarchy—a marriage with a beast which is entered into to save
her own people from conquest by war—she
awaits a future filled with misgivings.

Here, too, comes Stanley, who, it develops, is
the nephew of the brutal monarch who is about
to marry the woman Stanley loves, the woman
whose whereabouts and identity he now learns
for the first time. Attempting to enter Princess
Opal's apartments at night while in a state of
intoxication, the king is attacked by Stanley,
who hears Opal's cries for help and arrives at
the opportune moment. In the struggle between
the king and Stanley—the former dies of his
exertion and Stanley—now believing—finds the barrier between him and Opal raised.

SITUATIONS WANTED.

TOM BRET—Title and scenario. Rm. 616, 220 West 42d St., N. Y. City. Phone Bryant 8419.

CAMERAMAN—Seven years' practical experience on educational, scenic and industrial pictures, desires connection. Will go anywhere. Have my own outfit. Married, steady, conscientious. Address F. R. E., 56 Grove Hill, New Britain, Conn.

BUSINESS OPPORTUNITIES.

FOR SALE—Theater and store building, store rents for one hundred twenty-five per month. Address J. Rantschler, Harlem, Mont.

PRIVILEGE using exceptionally fine detached corner mansion for movies. Call or write, 355 Riverside Drive (108th St.). Moderate.

THEATERS WANTED.

WANTED—To lease or buy, theater in city of 20,000 population or larger, with large seating capacity. Must be up-to-date house. Send full particulars first letter. Fischer, 514 S. Carroll St., Madison, Wis.

THEATERS FOR SALE OR RENT.

THEATER TO RENT IN WORCESTER, MASSACHUSETTS (THE CITY OF PROSPERITY). CITY OF 175,000 PEOPLE. CENTRALLY LOCATED. SEATING 1,300. APPLY F. W. TAYLOR, 438 MAIN ST.

EQUIPMENT WANTED.

WANTED—300 18-inch opera chairs in sections of 6 chairs. State price, kind, make, finish, condition. What pitch floor can they be used. H. M. Marsh, Box 22, Vero, Fla.

EQUIPMENT FOR SALE.

FOR SALE—Asbestos curtain, 24x20 feet, new, never been used, rigging and everything complete, also seven regulation exit signs. Must be seen to be appreciated. G. W. Muller, 2904 3d Ave. opposite 154th St., N. Y. City.

300 BEAUTIFUL upholstered chairs in excellent condition, must be disposed of at once. Will let go for 95c each to quick buyer. Atlas Seating Co., 10 East 43d St., N. Y. City.

FOR SALE—Electric sign reading "Regent." Very attractive, spectacular design of diving girls. The best ever erected on any theater. Very cheap to quick buyer for the reason of tearing down. P. Magaro, 410 Market St., Harrisburg, Pa.

GUARANTEED MACHINES—Slightly used type S-101T model, Simplex motor drive, factory guarantee, at reasonable prices. Room 206, 1482 Broadway, N. Y. City.

FOR SALE—A full moving picture house equipment, 300 opera chairs, machines, operating booths, fans, and miscellaneous equipment. Reasonable price to quick buyer. Must vacate at once. Address Box 23 Norwalk, Conn.

USED opera and folding chairs, large quantities in stock; also upholstered; all in excellent condition. Bargains. Atlas Seating Co., 10 East 43d St., N. Y. City.

3,000 OPERA CHAIRS, steel and cast frames. 60c. up. All serviceable goods, cut prices on new chairs. Six standard asbestos booths. Send for weekly list of close outs and save half. J. P. Redington, Scranton, Pa.

FOR SALE at your own figure, one Wotton transverter. 110 volts, 60 cycles, in good running order; also switchboard for same, and electric baseball game board for stage. If taken at once, fifty dollars takes the whole outfit. F. O. B. Salamanca. Address Strand Theater, Salamanca, N. Y.

CAMERAS, ETC., FOR SALE.

DAVID STERN COMPANY, INCORPORATED. "EVERYTHING IN CAMERAS." PIONEERS IN THE MOVING PICTURE FIELD. SPECIAL——400 ft. Pathe, outside magazines, 2-inch Carl Zeiss Tessar F 3.5, $275.00. EXCLUSIVE DISTRIBUTORS FOR THE DAV&CO. AGENTS FOR THE UNIVERSAL. WRITE OR WIRE FOR OUR SPECIAL PROPOSITION. DAVID STERN COMPANY—"Everything in Cameras." In business since 1885. 1027-29 R Madison St., Chicago, Ill.

BASS CAMERA COMPANY ANNOUNCES THAT THEY HAVE SECURED THE SOLE SALES DISTRIBUTION FOR THE FAMOUS K. B. COMBINED MOTION PICTURE CAMERA AND PROJECTOR. THE MOTION CAMERA SENSATION. WONDERFULLY PRACTICAL, EVERY ONE CAN OPERATE THIS MARVELOUS OUTFIT. TAKES 200 FT. OF STANDARD FILM IN ONE LOADING. DIRECT FOCUS DEVICE, REGULAR AND TRICK CRANK, WEIGHT, COMPLETE, 7½ LBS. PRICE COMPLETE, FITTED WITH B. & L. TESSAR SERIES IC F 3.5 LENS, $117.50. HEAVY TRIPOD, $5.00; PANORAM AND TILTING TOP TRIPOD, $22.50; PROJECTOR ATTACHMENT, $37.50. DETAILS AND FREE BOOKLET SENT ON REQUEST. IMMEDIATE DELIVERY. WRITE TODAY TO AMERICA'S CAMERA HEADQUARTERS. BASS CAMERA COMPANY, CHARLES BASS, PRES., 109 N. DEARBORN ST., CHICAGO, ILL. M. P. CAMERA DEPT.

FILMS, ETC., WANTED.

WANTED—Motion picture negative pertaining to outdoor and athletic sports of all descriptions. No current events. Magazine subjects. Pathe frame line. Physical Culture Photo Plays, Flatiron Bld., New York City.

WANTED—One and two reelers, no paper required. Must be in first class condition. Federal Film Co., 145 West 45th St., N. Y. City.

MUSICAL INSTRUMENTS FOR SALE.

NEW SEEBURG photo player with $150.00 worth of music rolls, $450.00 cash. Pitts Pipe Organ Co., Omaha, Neb.

MISCELLANEOUS.

PATENTS—Free search through Patent Office records and report as to patentability. Send sketch and description of your invention. Prompt and personal service. Attorney fee returned if application not allowed. Frank M. Stephen, Riggs Bldg., Washington, D. C.

SCENARIOS WANTED—Strong two-reel Western stories for male lead. Mail to Great Western Film Corporation, 520 Van Nuys Bldg., Los Angeles, Cal.

■ INDEX ■

In Answering Advertisements, Please Mention THE MOVING PICTURE WORLD

List of Current Film Release Dates

ON GENERAL FILM, PATHE AND PARAMOUNT PROGRAMS

(For Daily Calendar of Program Releases See Page 2040.)

General Film Company, Inc.

(Note—Pictures given below are listed in the order of their release. Additions are made from week to week in the order of release.)

BROADWAY STAR FEATURES.

Discounters of Money (One of the O. Henry Series—Two parts—Comedy-Drama).
The Furnished Room (One of the O. Henry Series—Two parts—Drama).
The Defeat of the City (One of the O. Henry Series—Four parts—Drama).
John Tom Little Bear (One of the O. Henry Series—Two parts—Drama).
Blind Man's Holiday (One of the O. Henry Series—Four parts—Drama).
The Last of the Troubadours (One of the O. Henry Series—two parts—Drama).
The Duplicity of the Hargraves (One of the O. Henry Series—two parts—Drama).
The Lonesome Road (One of the O. Henry Series—Two parts—Drama).

ESSANAY.

Vernon, the Bountiful (Black Cat Feature—Two Parts—Comedy-Drama).
The Long-Green Trail (Black Cat Feature—Two parts—Comedy-Drama).
Don't Lose Your Cost (Black Cat Feature—Two parts—Comedy).
Star Dust—Black Cat Feature—Two parts—Comedy-Drama).
Twelve Cylinder Speed of the Leisure Class (George Ade Fables—Two parts—Comedy).
The Wandering Boy and the Wayward Parents (George Ade Fables—Two parts—Comedy).
What Transpires After the Wind-Up (George Ade Fable—Two parts—Comedy).
What the Best People Are Not Doing (George Ade Fable—Two parts—Comedy).

FALCON FEATURES.

The Mainspring (Four parts—Drama).
The Martinache Marriage (Four parts—Dr.).
The Stolen Play (Four parts—Drama).
The Phantom Shotgun (Four parts—Drama).
His Unpolished Self (Four parts—Drama).
A Man of His Word (Four parts—Drama).
The Secret of Black Mountain (Four parts—Drama).
The Climber (Four Parts—Drama).

KALEM.

Through Fire and Water (Episode of the Further Adventures of Stingaree—Two parts—Drama).
A Bushranger's Strategy (Episode of the Further Adventures of Stingaree—Two parts—Drama).
The Stranger at Dunraffel (Episode of "The Further Adventures of Stingaree"—Two parts—Drama).
A Champion of the Law (Episode of "The Further Adventures of Stingaree"—Two parts—Drama).
Politics in Pumpkin Center (Ham Comedy).
A Boot and the Loot (Ham Comedy).
A Whirlwind of Whiskers (Ham Comedy).
The Onion Magnate's Revenge (Ham Comedy).
The Bath Tub Bandit (Ham Comedy).

JAXON COMEDIES.

(Third Series.)

Speed Demons.
The Collectors.
Jolly Tars.
Wild Injuns.
Deviled Crabs.
The Triple Cross.

SELIG.

The Smoldering Spark (Two parts—Drama).
The Love of Madge O'Hara (Drama).
Selig World Library No. 13 (Educational).
A Man, a Girl and a Lion (Two parts—Drama).
Her Perilous Ride (One part—Drama).

Selig World Library No. 14 (Educational).
The Sole Survivor (Two parts—Drama).
Her Heart's Desire (One parts—Drama).
Selig World Library No. 15 (Educational).
Between Man and Beast (Two parts—Drama).
Her Salvation (One part—Drama).
Selig World Library No. 16 (Educational).
Pioneer Days (Two parts—Drama).
In After Years (One part—Drama).
The House of Mystery (Two parts—Drama).
Selig World Library No. 17 (Educational).
The Convert of the North (One part—Drama).
The Victor of the Plot (Two parts—Drama).
The Voice That Led Him (One part—Drama).
Selig World Library No. 18 (Educational).
The Law North of 65 (Two Parts—Drama).
Vengeance vs. Mercy (One Part—Drama).
Training Our Khaki-Clad Heroes (Two Parts—Military).
Selig-World Library No. 19 (Edu.).
The Angel of Poverty Row (One Part—Drama).

RAY COMEDIES.

A Peaceful Flat
Cheating His Wife.
A Bathtub Marriage.

SPARKLE COMEDIES.

(Second Series.)

Those Terrible Telegrams.
The Stag Party.
Bragg's Little Poker Party.
Mixed Nuts.
Hearts and Harpoons.
Toodles.
Bangs Renigs.
Triple Entente.
Whose Hooley.
Wrong Wrights.

Pathe Exchange, Inc.

RELEASES FOR WEEK OF SEPT. 2.

Tears and Smiles. (Lasslide—Five parts—Drama).
The Fatal Ring (Episode No. 9, "The Dice of Death") (Two parts—Drama—Astra).
Lonesome Luke's Wild Women (Two parts—Comedy—Rolin).
Know America No. 21, "Central Colorado" (Scenic-Combitone).
Scenic and Cartoon (International Split Reel) Title not reported).
Hearst-Pathe News No. 72 (Topical).
Hearst-Pathe News No. 73 (Topical).
Happy Gets the Razoo (Happy Hooligan Cartoon Comedy) and "Making a Marine Officer" (Educational) (International Split Reel).

RELEASED FOR WEEK OF SEPT. 9.

War and the Woman (Thanhouser—Five parts—Drama).
The Fatal Ring Episode No. 10, "The Perilous Plunge"—Two parts—Drama—Astra).
Know America No. 22, "Colorado's Scenic Wonders" (Scenic-Combitone).
Over the Fence (Comedy—Rolin).
Happy Hooligan in the Zoo (Cartoon Comedy); and "From Rookie to Regular" (Educational) (International Split Reel).
Hearst-Pathe News No. 74 (Topical).
Hearst-Pathe News No. 75 (Topical).
Les Miserables (Special—Eight parts—Drama).

RELEASES FOR WEEK OF SEPT. 16.

The Angel Factory (Astra—Five parts—Drama).
The Fatal Ring (Episode No. 11, "The Short Circuit"—two parts—Drama).
The Seven Pearls (Episode No. 1, "The Sultan's Necklace"—Astra—Three parts—Drama).
Triple Divide Mountains (Glacier Park) (Scenic Half Reel) and Japan the Floral (reeled) (Pathe-Educational) (Pathe split reel).
Lonesome Luke Loses Patients (Rolin—Two parts—Comedy).
Hearst-Pathe News No. 76 (Topical).
Hearst-Pathe News No. 77 (Topical).

Happy Hooligan—"The Tanks" (Cartoon Comedy —Half Reel), and Embroidery Making (Educational) (International Split Reel).

RELEASES FOR WEEK OF SEPT. 23.

Under False Colors (Thanhouser—Five Parts—Drama).
The Fatal Ring (Episode No. 12, "The Desperate Chance"—Two parts—Drama—Astra).
The Seven Pearls (Episode No. 2, "The Bowstring"—Two parts—Drama—Astra).
Pinched One-Reel Rolin Comedy).
In the Wake of the Huns (War Film—Three parts—Pathe).
Hearst-Pathe News No. 78 (Topical).
Hearst-Pathe News No. 79 (Topical).

Paramount Pictures Corp.

BLACK DIAMOND COMEDY.

Aug. 6—Susie the Sleepwalker.
July 9—Wits and Fits.
July 23—The Rejuvenator.
Aug. 6—Susie the Sleepwalker.
Sept. 17—Susie's Scheme.

KLEVER KOMEDY.

July 30—Motor Boating.
Aug. 14—Summer Boarding (Comedy).
Aug. 20—Egged On.
Aug. 27—The Cinderella Husband.
Sept. 3—Seeing Things.
Sept. 10—Camping.
Sept. 24—In Bed—In Bad.

PARAMOUNT-ARBUCKLE COMEDY.

June 25—The Rough House (Two parts)
Aug. 20—His Wedding Night (Two parts).
Sept. 30—Oh, Doctor! (Two parts).

PARAMOUNT FEATURES.

Aug. 13—The Mysterious Miss Terry (Five parts—Drama).
Aug. 16—Hashimura Toro (Five parts—Dr.).
Aug. 23—Close to Nature (Five parts—Drama).
Aug. 26—Little Miss Optimist (Five parts—Drama).
Sept. 3—Lost in Transit (Five parts—Drama).
Sept. 10—The Hostage (Five parts—Drama).
Sept. 10—On the Level (Five parts—Drama).
Sept. 17—Her Double Cross (Five parts—Dr.).
Sept. 17—Exile (Five parts—Drama).
Sept. 17—The Sunset Trail (Five parts—Dr.).
Sept. 24—The Countess Charming (Five parts—Drama).
Sept. 24—Bab's Diary (Five parts—Drama.

PARAMOUNT-BURTON HOLMES.

Aug. 20—Tropical Nassau (Scenic).
Aug. 27—Madrid to Madeira (Scenic).
Sept. 3—Norway (Scenic).
Sept. 10—Hong Kong and the Pearl River (Scenic).
Sept. 17—Canton and Shanghai (Scenic).
Sept. 24—Picturesque Peking (Scenic).

PARAMOUNT-BRAY PICTOGRAPHS.

Aug. 13—No. 80—Subjects on Reel: Otto Luck's Flivvered Romance; Rough Sports in Southern California; Helping the Deaf to Hear.
Aug. 20—No. 81—Subjects on Reel: Uncle Sam's Dinner Party; Tea Industry in Japan; Land and Water Submarine; Speedy Day at Coney Island.
Aug. 27—No. 82—Subjects on Reel: Bobby Bumps Surf Rider; A Day at Deephaven; Efficiency via Express.
Sept. 3—No. 83—Subjects on Reel: Goodrich Dirt Among the Beach Nuts; Goal Ranching in America; Art in Bookbinding.
Sept. 10—No. 84—Subjects on Reel: Quacky Doodles Signs the Pledge; A Quail Hunt in Old Virginny; How the Cowboy Makes His Lariat; A Scenic Gem from South America.

Producers—Kindly Furnish Titles and Dates of All New Releases Before Saturday.

List of Current Film Release Dates

ON UNIVERSAL, METRO AND TRIANGLE PROGRAMS

(For Daily Calendar of Program Releases See Page 2040.)

Universal Film Mfg. Co.

ANIMATED WEEKLY.

Aug. 2—Number 83 (Topical).
Aug. 9—Number 84 (Topical).
Aug. 16—Number 85 (Topical).
Aug. 23—Number 86 (Topical).
Aug. 30—Number 87 (Topical).
Sept. 6—Number 88 (Topical).
Sept. 13—Number 89 (Topical).
Sept. 20—Number 90 (Topical).
Sept. 27—Number 91 (Topical).
Oct. 4—Number 92—(Topical).

BISON.

Aug. 27—Jungle Treachery (Two parts—Dr.).
Sept. 3—The Lure of the Circus (Two parts—Comedy—Drama), and Sierra Winter Sports (Scenic).
Sept. 10.—The Texas Sphinx (Two parts—Western Drama).
Sept. 17—The Last of the Night Riders (Two parts—Drama).
Sept. 24—The Dynamite Special (Two parts—Drama).
Oct. 1.—The Lion's Liar (Two parts—Drama).

GOLD SEAL.

July 30—Right of Way Casey (Three parts—Drama).
Aug. 13—A Wife's Suspicion (Three parts—Drama).
Aug. 27—The Winning Pair (Three parts—Dr.).
Sept. 3.—The Empty Gun (Three parts—Dr.).
Sept. 10.—The Perilous Leap (Three parts—Railroad Drama).
Sept. 17—The Pullman Mystery (Three parts—Drama).
Sept. 24—The Master Spy (An episode of "The Perils of the Secret Service"—Three parts—Drama).
Oct. 1—The Storm Woman (Three parts—Drama).

JOKER.

Aug. 20—Behind the Map (Comedy).
Aug. 20—Mrs. Madam Manager (Comedy).
Aug. 27—Why They Left Home (Comedy).
Aug. 27—Bustling Into Society (Comedy).
Sept. 3—Officer, Call a Cop (Comedy).
Sept. 3—A Gale of Verse (Comedy).
Sept. 10.—Short Skirts and Deep Water (Comedy).
Sept. 10.—Nearly a Queen (Comedy).
Sept. 17—Hawaiian Nuts (Comedy).
Sept. 17—Circus Sarah (Comedy).
Sept. 24—Marble Heads (Comedy).
Sept. 24—The Fountain of Trouble (Comedy).
Oct. 1—Her Naughty Choice (Comedy).
Oct. 1—The Masked Marvels (Comedy).

L-KO.

Aug. 6—The Little Fat Rascal (Two parts—Comedy).
Aug. 13—Rough Stuff (Two parts—Comedy).
Aug. 20—Street Cars and Carbunkles (Two parts —Comedy).
Aug. 27—Props, Drops and Flops (Two parts—Comedy).
Sept. 3—Backward Sons and Forward Daughters (Two parts—Comedy).
Sept. 10.—From Cactus to Kale (Two parts—Comedy).
Sept. 17—A Prairie Chicken (Two parts—Com.).
Sept. 24—Soapsuds and Sirens.
Oct. 1—Counting Out the Count (Comedy).

NESTOR.

Aug. 6—The Love Slacker (Comedy).
Aug. 13—The Rushin' Dancers (Comedy).
Aug. 20—Move Over (Comedy).
Aug. 27—The Night Cap (Comedy).
Sept. 3—Looking 'Em Over (Comedy).
Sept. 10.—The Boulevard Speed Hounds (Comedy).
Sept. 17—Welcome Home (Comedy).
Sept. 24—Taking Their Medicine (Comedy).
Oct. 1—Pete the Prowler (Comedy).
Oct. 1—A Prairie Romeo (Two parts—Drama).

POWERS.

Aug. 6—Seeing Ceylon with Hy Mayer (Travelaugh).
Aug. 13—Doing His bit (Cartoon Comedy), and Algieria, Old and New) (Scenic) (Split reel).
Aug. 20—Colonel Pepper's Mobilized Farm (Cartoon Comedy), and "The Home Life of the Spider (Ditmar's Edu.) (Split Reel.)

STAR FEATURETTE.

July 30—The Woman Who Would Not Pay (Two parts—Society—Drama).
Aug. 6—The Untamed (Two parts—Drama).
Aug. 13—Cheyenne's Pal (Two parts—Drama).
Aug. 20—The Golden Heart (Two parts—Dr.).
Aug. 27—Hands in the Dark (Two parts—Dr.), and Old French Towns (Short Scenic on Same Reel).
Sept. 3—A Dream of Egypt (Two parts—Dr.).
Sept. 10.—To the Highest Bidder (Two parts—Society Drama).
Sept. 17—The Right Man (Two parts—Drama).
Sept. 24—A Romney Rose (Two parts—Drama).

VICTOR.

July 16—One Bride Too Many (Two parts—Comedy-Drama).
July 30—Where Are My Trousers? (Two parts —Comedy).
Aug. 6—Like Babes in the Wood (Two parts—Juvenile Comedy).
Aug. 13—The Brass Girl (Two parts—Comedy-Drama).
Aug. 20—A Five Foot Ruler (Two parts—Comedy-Drama).
Aug. 27—Scandal Everywhere (Comedy).
Sept. 3—The Curse of a Flirting Heart (Com.).
Sept. 10.—In the Clutches of Milk (Comedy).
Sept. 17—Marathon Maniacs (Comedy).
Sept. 24—Your Boy and Mine (Comedy).
Oct. 1—Kicked in the Kitchen (Comedy).

UNIVERSAL SCREEN MAGAZINE.

July 30—Issue No. 30 (Educational).
Aug. 6—Issue No. 31 (Topical).
Aug. 13—Issue No. 32 (Topical).
Aug. 20—Issue No. 33 (Educational).
Aug. 27—Issue No. 34 (Educational).
Sept. 3—Issue No. 35 (Educational).
Sept. 10.—Issue No. 36 (Educational).
Sept. 17—Issue No. 37 (Educational).
Sept. 24—Issue No. 38 (Educational).
Oct. 1—Issued No. 39 (Educational).

UNIVERSAL SPECIAL FEATURE.

July 22—The Gray Ghost (Episode No. 4—"The Night"—Two parts—Drama).
July 29—The Gray Ghost (Episode No. 5—"Plunder"—Two parts—Drama).
Aug. 6—The Gray Ghost (Episode No. 6, "The House of Mystery"—Two parts—Comedy).
Aug. 13—The Gray Ghost (Episode No. 7) (The Double Floor) (Two parts—Drama).
Aug. 20—The Gray Ghost (Episode No. 8, "The Pearl Necklace"—Two parts—Dr.).
Aug. 27—The Gray Ghost (Episode No. 9—Title Not Reported—Two parts—Drama).
Sept. 3—The Gray Ghost (Episode No. 10—Shadows—Two parts—Drama).
Sept. 10.—The Gray Ghost (Episode No. 11— "The Flaming Meteor"—Two parts—Drama).
Sept. 17—The Gray Ghost (Episode No. 12—The Poisoned Ring—Two parts—Drama).
Sept. 24—The Gray Ghost (Episode No. 13—The Tightening Snare."—Two parts—Dr.).
Oct. 1—The Gray Ghost (Episode No. 14, "At Bay"—Two parts—Drama).

UNIVERSAL CURRENT EVENTS.

July 28—Issue No. 11 (Topical).
Aug. 4—Issue No. 12 (Topical).
Aug. 10—Issue No. 13 (Topical).
Aug. 17—Issue No. 14 (Topical).
Aug. 24—Issue No. 15 (Topical).
Aug. 31—Issue No. 16 (Topical).
Sept. 7—Issue No. 17 (Topical).
Sept. 14—Issue No. 18 (Topical).
Sept. 21—Issue No. 19 (Topical).

Metro Pictures Corporation.

METRO PICTURES CORP.

July 9—Peggy, the Will o' the Wisp (Five parts—Drama).
July 30—Miss Robinson Crusoe (Five parts—Drama).
Special—The Slacker (Seven parts—Drama).
Aug. 6—The Jury of Fate (Rolfe—Five parts—Drama).
Aug. 13—The Girl Without a Soul (Five parts—Drama).
Aug. 27—To the Death (Five parts—Drama).
Sept. 10—The Lifted Veil (Five parts—Drama).
Sept. 17—Their Compact (Seven parts—Drama).
Sept. 24—Idle Curiosity (Drew).

YORKE FILM CORP.

July 16—The Hidden Spring (Five parts—Dr.).
Sept. 3—Under Handicap (Seven parts—Drama).

METRO COMEDIES.

July 23—Mr. Parker—Hero (Drew).
July 30—Henry's Ancestors (Drew).
Aug. 6—His Ear for Music (Drew).
Aug. 13—Her Economic Independence (Drew).
Aug. 20—Her First Game (Drew).
Aug. 27—The Patriot (Drew).
Sept. 3—Music Hath Charms (Drew).
Sept. 10—Rubbing It In (Drew).
Sept. 17—Henry's Ancestors (Drew).
Sept. 24—The Silent Sellers (Five parts—Dr.).

Triangle Film Corporation.

TRIANGLE PRODUCTIONS.

Aug. 12—Golden Rule Kate (Five parts—Dr.).
Aug. 19—Wee Lady Betty (Five parts—Drama).
Aug. 19—They're Off (Five parts—Drama).
Aug. 26—Grafters (Five parts—Drama).
Sept. 2.—Ten of Diamonds (Five parts —Drama).
Sept. 2.—The Man Hater (Five parts—Drama).
Sept. 9—Idolators (Five parts—Drama).
Sept. 9—Polly Ann (Five parts—Drama).
Sept. 16—Mountain Dew (Five parts—Drama).
Sept. 16—The Haunted House (Five parts—Dr.).
Sept. 23—Flying Colors (Five parts—Drama).
Sept. 23—Devil Dodger (Five parts—Drama).
Sept. 30—Broadway, Arizona (Five parts—Drama).
Sept. 30—The Tar-Heel Warrior (Five parts—Drama).

TRIANGLE KOMEDY.

Aug. 19—A Love Chase.
Aug. 19—His Hidden Talent.
Aug. 26—Their Domestic Deception.
Aug. 26—Wooden Shoes (Five parts—Drama).
Sept. 2—A Fallen Star.
Sept. 2.—His Foot-Hill Folly.
Sept. 9—A Dark Room Secret.
Sept. 9—A Warm Reception.
Sept. 16—His Baby Doll.
Sept. 16—His Unconscious Conscience.
Sept. 23—His Taking Ways.
Sept. 23—Her Fickle Fortune.
Sept. 30—His Saving Grace.
Sept. 30—Caught In the End.

KEYSTONE.

July 29—Thirst (Two parts).
Aug. 5—His Uncle Dudley (Two parts).
Aug. 12—Lost—A Cook (Two parts).
Aug. 19—The Pawnbroker's Heart (Two parts).
Aug. 26—Two Crooks (Two parts).
Sept. 2.—A Sheephead Jonah (Two parts Comedy).
Sept. 9—His Precious Life (Two parts—Com.).
Sept. 16—Hula Hula Land (Two parts—Com.).
Sept. 23—The Late Lamented (Two parts—Comedy).
Sept. 30—The Sultan's Wife (Two parts—Comedy).

PARALTA.

Rose O' Paradise.
A Man's Man.

Producers.—Kindly Furnish Titles and Dates of All New Releases Before Saturday.

List of Current Film Release Dates
MUTUAL PROGRAM AND MISCELLANEOUS FEATURES

(For Daily Calendar of Program Releases See Page 2040.)

Mutual Film Corp.

CUB.

Aug. 9—Jerry on the Railroad (Comedy).
Aug. 16—Beach Nuts (Comedy).
Aug. 23—Jerry on the Farm (Comedy).
Aug. 30—Jerry's Eugenic Marriage (Comedy).
Sept. 6—Jerry Tries Again (Comedy).
Sept. 13—Jerry's Whirlwind Finish (Comedy).
Sept. 20—Officer Jerry (Comedy).
Sept. 27—Jerry's Big Deal (Comedy).

GAUMONT.

Sept. 6.—Reel Life No. 71. Subjects on reel:
   A Watering System for a Small
   Farm; Pets Which Will Never Be
   Popular; Handling the Mail; The
   Five Senses; Drawing from "Life."
Sept. 13—Reel Life No. 72; Subjects on Reel:
   An Unusual Colt; Hunting Turtle
   Eggs; Testing an Auto Tube; Tree
   Planting in the National Forests;
   The Midnight Sun.
Sept. 20—Reel Life No. 73 (Subjects on Reel:
   Weaving the President's Portrait;
   Running an Aeroplane Without
   Danger; The Principle of the Gyro-
   scope; When a Big Car Goes By
   (Animated Drawing from "Life").
Sept. 27—Reel Life No. 74 (Subjects on reel:
   The Soldier's Staff of Life; The
   Correct Time—as Determined by
   the U. S. Naval Observatory;
   Beans and Lady Bugs; The Lam-
   prey—a Blood-Sucking Fish; Mak-
   ing Eyeglasses; So Easy (An Ani-
   mated Drawing from "Life").

MUTUAL WEEKLY.

Aug. 8—Number 136 (Topical).
Aug. 15—Number 137 (Topical).
Aug. 22—Number 138 (Topical).
Aug. 29—Number 139 (Topical).
Sept. 5.—Number 140 (Topical).
Sept. 12—Number 141 (Topical).
Sept. 19—Number 142 (Topical).
Sept. 26—Number 143 (Topical) .

MUTUAL STAR PRODUCTIONS.

Sept. 3.—Reputation (Goodrich—Five parts—
   Drama).
Sept. 3.—Charity Castle (American—Five parts
   Drama).
Sept. 10—Outcast (Empire—Six parts—Drama).
Sept. 10—The Bride's Silence (American—Five
   parts—Drama).
Sept. 17—The Rainbow Girl (Five parts—Dr.).
Sept. 17—The Girl Who Couldn't Grow Up
   (Five parts—Drama).
Sept. 24—Sands of Sacrifice (Five parts—Dr.).
Sept. 24—The Runaway (Five parts—Drama).

SIGNAL.

Sept. 17—The Lost Express (Episode No. 1, "The
   Lost Express"—Two parts—Dr.).
Sept. 24—The Lost Express (Episode No. 2,
   "The Destroyed Documents"—Two
   parts—Drama).
Oct. 1—The Lost Express (Episode No. 3,
   "The Wreck at the Crossing"—
   Two parts—Drama).

Feature Releases

ARTCRAFT PICTURES CORPORATION.

Aug. 12—Down to Earth (Five parts—Comedy-
   Drama).
Aug. 26—Seven Keys to Baldpate (Five parts—
   Drama).
Sept. 3—Rebecca of Sunnybrook Farm (Five
   parts—Drama).
Sept. 10—Barbary Sheep (Five parts—Drama).

ART DRAMAS, INC.

Aug. 27.—The Little Samaritan (Erbograph
   —Five parts—Drama).
Sept. 3.—Behind the Mask (U. S. Amusement
   Co.—Five parts—Drama).
Sept. 10—Blood of His Fathers (Horsley—Five
   parts—Drama).
Sept. 17—Peg o' the Sea (Van Dyke—Five parts
   —Drama).

BLUEBIRD PHOTOPLAYS, INC.

Sept. 3—Triumph (Five parts—Comedy-Dr.).
Sept. 3—Mother O' Mine (Five Parts—Drama
   —Special).
Sept. 10—A Stormy Knight (Five parts—Com-
   edy-Drama).
Sept. 17—The Mysterious Mr. Tiller (Five parts
   —Drama).
Sept. 24—Flirting With Death (Five parts—Dr.).

BUTTERFLY PICTURES.

Sept. 3—Who Was the Other Man? (Five parts·
   —Drama).
Sept. 10.—The Little Pirate (Five parts—
   Drama).
Sept. 17—The Spindle of Life (Five parts—Dr.).
Sept. 24—The Edge of the Law (Five parts.—
   Drama).
Oct. 1—The Secret Man (Five parts—Drama).

CINEMA WAR NEWS SYNDICATE.

Sept. 8—American War News Weekly No. 19
   (Topical).
Sept. 15—American War News Weekly No. 20
   (Topical).
Sept. 22—American War News Weekly No. 21
   (Topical).
Sept. 29—American War News Weekly No. 22
   (Topical).

EDUCATIONAL FILMS CORP.

Sept. 3—Living Book of Nature, "Kangaroos
   and Their Allies" (Ditmars).
Sept. 5—Land That Does Not Wiggle Much
   (Scenic and Educational).
Sept. 10—The Animals of Australia (Living
   Book of Nature).
Sept. 12—Tinklebottom Passes Through (Scenic
   and Educational).
Sept. 17—The Smaller Monkeys (Ditmars' Liv-
   ing Book of Nature).
Sept. 19—Fading of Local Color (Scenic and
   Educational).
Sept. 24—Enemies of the Garden (Ditmars' Liv-
   ing Book of Nature).
Sept. 26—Tinklebottom's Finish (Scenic and
   Educational).

FOX FILM CORPORATION.

Aug. 26—Every Girl's Dream (Five parts—Dr.).
Sept. 2—Betrayed (Five parts—Drama).
Sept. 9—When False Tongue Speak (Five
   parts—Drama).
Sept. 16—The Yankee Way (Five parts—Dr.).
Sept. 23—North of Fifty-Three (Five parts—
   Drama).
Sept. 30—Conscience (Five parts—Drama).

FOXFILM COMEDIES.

July 23—A Soft Tenderfoot (Two parts).
Aug. 6—A Domestic Hound (Two parts).

GOLDWYN PICTURES CORP.

Sept. 9—Polly of the Circus (Eight parts—
   Drama).
Sept. 23—Baby Mine (Six parts—Drama).

GREATER VITAGRAPH (V-L-S-E).

Sept. 10.—An Alabaster Box (Five parts—
   Drama).
Sept. 17—For France (Five parts—Drama).
Sept. 17—Favorite Film Features; "Winning the
   Stepchildren" (One Reel Drama);
   "Goodness Gracious" (Two Reel
   Comedy).
Sept. 24—The Bandit's Double (Five parts—
   Drama).
Sept. 24—Favorite Film Features, "The Rein-
   carnation of Karma" (Two parts—
   Drama) and "A Lesson in Jeal-
   ousy" (One Reel Comedy).

KLEINE-EDISON-SELIG-ESSANAY.

Sept. 1—Conquest Program No. 8 (Edison-Per-
   fection Pictures). Subjects: The
   Princess' Necklace (Four parts—
   Drama); The Puzzling Bill-Board,
   and in Old England (Split Reel);
   The Brook, and Woodcraft for
   Boys; Shipping Live Fish (Split
   Reel); The Blind Fiddler (One
   Reel).
Sept. 3—Efficiency Edgar's Courtship (Five
   parts — Drama — Essanay-Perfec-
   tion Pictures).
Sept. 3—A Midnight Bell (Hoyt Comedy—Two
   parts).
Sept. 8—Conquest Program No. 9 (Edison-Per-
   fection Pictures). Subjects:
   "Quaint Provincetown, Cape Cod,
   Mass. (Scenic), 500 feet ; "Little
   Red Riding Hood" (Animated Sil-
   houette), 500 feet; "Kidnapped"
   (Drama), 4,650 feet; "Microscopic
   "Pond Life" (Scientific), 350 feet;
   "Friends, Romans, and Leo" (Com-
   edy), 1,000 feet.
Sept. 10—Pants (Five parts—Drama—Essanay-
   Perfection Pictures).
Sept. 15—Conquest Program No. 10 (Edison-
   Perfection Pictures). Subjects:
   "The Pied Piper of Hamelin" (Le-
   gend), 1,000 feet; "Angling for
   Trout" (Sport), 500 feet; "America's
   Greatest Wonder" (Scenic), 500
   feet; "Your Obedient Servant"
   (Drama), 2,658 feet; "Raising Os-
   triches in South Africa" (Indus-
   trial), 350 feet; "A Duke for a
   Day" (Comedy), 2,000 feet.
Sept. 17—The Awakening of Ruth (Five parts—
   D r a m a—Edison-Perfection Pic-
   tures).
Sept. 17—A Contented Woman (Hoyt Comedy—
   Two parts—Drama).
Sept. 22—Conquest Program No. 11 (Edison-
   Perfection Pictures). Subjects:
   "Man's Triumph Over the Mighty
   Forest" (Industrial), 1,000 feet;
   "Getting Acquainted With Bees"
   (Nature Studies), 800 feet; "An
   Ocean Recluse" (Nature)—The Her-
   mit Crab, New York Aquarium, 200
   feet; "The Story that the Keg Told
   Me" (Drama), 3,000 feet; "Curious
   Scenes in Far-Off India" (Scenic),
   400 feet; "Wild Arnika" (Comedy),
   1,000 feet.
Sept. 24—Men of the Desert (Five parts—
   D r a m a—Essanay-Perfection Pic-
   tures).

SELECT PICTURES CORP.

Magda (C. K. Y. Corp.).

SELZNICK PICTURES.

The Lash of Jealousy (Drama).
The Lesson (Drama).
The Moth (Drama).
The Wild Girl.

STANDARD PICTURES.

Aug. 19—The Spy (Ten parts).
Aug. 26—The Honor System (Ten parts).
Sept. 2—Jack and the Beanstalk (Ten parts).
Sept. 16—The Conqueror (Ten parts).
Sept. 30—Camille.

WHOLESOME FILMS CORPORATION.

Sept. 3—The Penny Philanthropist (Five parts
   —Drama).
Sept. 3—Cinderella and the Magic Slipper
   (Four parts—Drama).

WORLD PICTURES.

Sept. 3—Tides of Fate (Five parts—Drama).
Sept. 10—The Marriage Market (Five parts
   —Drama).
Sept. 17—Betsy Ross (Five parts—Drama).
Sept. 24—The Woman Beneath (Five parts—
   Drama).

Producers.—Kindly Furnish Titles and Dates of All New Releases Before Saturday.

List of State Rights Pictures

(For Daily Calendar of Program Releases See Page 2040.)

Note—For further information regarding pictures listed on this page, address State Rights Department, Moving Picture World, and same will be gladly furnished.

ARIZONA FILM CO.
May—Should She Obey (Drama).

BERNSTEIN FILM PRODUCTION.
Humility (First of "Seven Cardinal Virtues"—Drama).
June—Who Knows? (Six parts—Drama).

J. FRANK BROCKLISS, INC.
U. S. Navy (Five parts).
Terry Human Interest Reels (900 Feet Every Other Week).
Russian Revolution (Three parts).
Land of the Rising Sun (10,000 feet—issued complete or in series of 2,000 feet or 8,000 feet).

BUD FISHER FILMS CORP.
Mutt and Jeff Animated Cartoons.

CAMERAGRAPH FILM MFG. CO.
June—What of You Boy? (Three parts—Patriotic).
June—The Automobile Owner Gets Acquainted With His Automobile (Educational).

CARONA CINEMA CO.
May—The Curse of Eve (Seven parts—Dr.).

CENTURY COMEDIES.
Sept. 1—Balloonatics (Two parts—Comedy).

BENJAMIN CHAPIN PRODUCTIONS.
(The Lincoln Cycle Pictures.)
My Mother (Two parts).
My Father (Two parts).
Myself (Two parts).
The Call to Arms (Two parts).

CHRISTIE FILM CO.
July 9—The Fourteenth Man (Comedy).
July 16—Down By the Sea (Comedy).
July 23—Skirts (Comedy).
July 30—Won in a Cabaret (Comedy).
Aug. 7—His Merry Mix-Up (Comedy).
Aug. 14—A Smokey Love Affair (Comedy).

CINEMA DISTRIBUTING CORP.
June—The 13th Labor of Hercules (Twelve single parts).

CORONET FILM CORP.
Living Studies in Natural History.
Animal World—Issue No. 1.
Animal World—Issue No. 2.
Birdland Studies.
Horticultural Phenomena.

COSMOFOTOFILM, INC.
June—I Believe (Seven parts—Drama).

E. I. S. MOTION PICTURES CORP.
Trooper 44 (Five parts—Drama).

EXPORT AND IMPORT FILM CO.
June—Robespierre.
June—Ivan the Terrible.

FAIRMOUNT FILM CORP.
June—Hate (Seven parts—Drama).

FLORA FINCH FILM CO.
"War Brides" (Two parts—Comedy).

FORT PITT CORPORATION.
The Italian Battlefront.

FRATERNITY FILMS, INC.
May—Devil's Playground (Nine parts—Drama).

FRIEDMAN ENTERPRISES.
A Mormon Maid (Six parts—Drama).

FRIEDER FILM CORP.
June—A Bit o' Heaven (Five parts—Drama).

FROHMAN AMUSEMENT CORP.
April—God's Man (Nine parts—Drama).
August—The Italian Battlefront.

GENERAL ENTERPRISES, INC.
The Warrior (Seven parts—Comedy-Drama).

GOLDIN FEATURES.
A Bit of Life (One Reel Comedy-Drama).

F. G. HALL PRODUCTIONS, INC.
May—Her Fighting Chance (Seven parts—Dr.). (Mr. Hall has world rights to this picture.)
May—The Bar Sinister (Drama). (Mr. Hall has world rights to this picture.)

HISTORIC FEATURES.
June—Christus (Eight parts—Drama).

M. H. HOFFMAN.
September—Silent Witness (Seven parts—Drama).
One Hour (Six parts—Drama).

ILIODR PICTURES CORP.
June—The Fall of the Romanoffs (Drama).

IVAN FILM PRODUCTIONS.
Apr. —One Law or Both (8 parts—Drama).
August—Babbling Tongues (Six parts—Dr.).

JEWEL PRODUCTIONS, INC.
Pay Me (Drama).
Sirens of the Sea.
The Man Without a Country (Drama).

KING BEE FILMS CORP.
July 1—Cupid's Rival (Two parts—Comedy).
July 15—The Villain (Two parts—Comedy).
Aug. 1—The Millionaire (Two parts—Com.).
Aug. 15—The Goat (Two parts—Comedy).
Sept. 1—The Fly Cop (Two parts—Comedy).
Sept. 15—The Star Boarder (Two parts—Com.).

A KAY CO.
Some Barrier (Terry Cartoon Burlesque).
His Trial (Terry Cartoon Burlesque).
Terry Human Interest Reel No. 1 (Character As Revealed in the Face).
Terry Human Interest Reel No. 2 (Character As Revealed in the Eyes).

KLOTZ & STREIMER.
June—Whither Thou Goest (Five parts—Drama).
June—The Secret Trap (Five parts—Drama).

MANX-MAN COMPANY.
The Manx-Man (Eight parts—Drama).

MARINE FILM CORP.
August—Lorelei of the Sea (Drama).

MAYFAIR FILM CORP.
Persuasive Peggy (Drama).

MOE STREIMER.
June—A Daughter of the Don (Ten parts—Drama).

B. S. MOSS MOTION PICTURE CORP.
April—Birth Control (Five parts—Drama).

NEVADA MOTION PICTURE CORP.
June—The Planter (Drama).

NEWFIELDS PRODUCING CORP.
Alma, Where Do You Live? (Six parts—Dr.).

OGDEN PICTURES CORP.
August—The Lust of the Ages (Drama).

PARAGON FILMS, INC.
The Whip (Eight parts—Drama).

PETER PAN FILM CORP.
Mo-Toy Troupe (Release No. 7—"Dinkling of the Circus").
Mo-Toy Troupe (Release No. 8—"A Trip to the Moon").
Mo-Toy Troupe (Release No. 9, "Golden Locks and the Three Bears").
Mo-Toy Troupe (Release No. 10, "Dolly Doings").
Mo-Toy Troupe (Release No. 11 "School Days").
Moy-toy Troupe (Release No. 12, "Little Red Riding Hood").
Moy-toy Troupe (Release No. 13, "Puss in Boots").
Mo-Toy Troupe (Release No. 14—"Jimmie the Soldier Boy").
Mo-Toy Troupe (Release No. 15—"Jimmie and Jam").
Mo-Toy Troupe (Release No. 16—"In Japoland").

PURKALL FILM CO.
July—The Liar (Six parts—Drama).

RENOWNED PICTURES CORP.
June—In Treason's Grasp (Five parts—Drama)

REX BEACH PICTURES CO.
March—The Barrier (Nine parts—Drama).

SELECT PHOTOPLAY CO.
May—Humanity (Six parts—Drama).

SELECT PICTURES CORP.
The Public Be Damned.

WILLIAM N. SELIG.
April—The Garden of Allah
May—Beware of Strangers (Eight parts—Dr.).

FRANK J. SENG.
May—Parentage (Drama).

SHERMAN PICTURE CORP.
July—Corruption (Six parts—Drama).
August—I Believe.

SKOBELOFF COMMITTEE.
The Great Russian Revolution.
Behind the Battle Line in Russia.

JULIUS STEGER.
May—Redemption (Six parts—Drama).

SUPREME FEATURE FILMS, INC.
May—Trip Through China (Ten parts).

ULTRA FILMS, INC.
A Day at West Point (Educational).
West is West.
Rustlers' Frame-Up at Big Horn.

UNIVERSAL (STATE RIGHTS).
May—The Hand that Rocks the Cradle (Six parts—Drama).
June—The Cross-Eyed Submarine (Three parts—Comedy).
June—Come Through (Seven parts—Drama).

E. WARREN PRODUCTION,
April—The Warfare of the Flesh (Drama).

WHARTON, INC.
June—The Great White Trail (Seven parts—Drama).

WILLIAMSON BROS.
April—The Submarine Eye (Drama).

Producers.—Kindly Furnish Titles and Dates of All New Releases Before Saturday.

Lightning Source UK Ltd.
Milton Keynes UK
UKHW042044050119
334993UK00017BA/348/P